HARRAP'S SCHOOL

DICTIONARY and FRENCH GRAMMAR

English-French

French-English

HARRAP'S SCHOOL

DICTIONARY and FRENCH GRAMMAR

English-French

French-English

Editor
Michael Janes

Consultant Editors
Fabrice Antoine
Isabelle Elkaim

HARRAP

First published in Great Britain 1991
by Harrap Books Ltd
43–45 Annandale Street, Edinburgh EH7 4AZ, UK

ISBN 0 245 60569 X

Dictionary typeset by Hewer Text Composition Services
Grammar typeset by Roger King Graphic Studios
Printed in Great Britain by Mackays of Chatham plc

Contents

Trademarks

Words considered to be trademarks have been designated in this dictionary by the symbol ®. However, no judgment is implied concerning the legal status of any trademark by virtue of the presence or absence of such a symbol.

Preface

This is the second edition of Harrap's *French School Dictionary*. Many new words and phrases have been added, and entries have been presented in an even clearer and more attractive form. Our aim is for the dictionary to continue to be an up-to-date, practical and reliable work of reference, providing translations of the most useful words and expressions of French and English. A new and important feature of this edition is the integration of the French grammar into the main body of the dictionary text. The grammar itself has been completely revised and updated, and its scope has been widened to include many more examples of usage covering useful points of grammar.

The dictionary

Entries in the dictionary consist of headwords followed by pronunciation and part of speech. When there is more than one translation, context words in brackets are supplied to help the user make the correct choice. Further guidance in the understanding of translations is provided by the use of labels to indicate the level of style (eg *Fam* for 'familiar' or colloquial) or to define a particular usage or field (eg *Am* for 'American' or *Mus* for 'music'). Context words and labels are also given when considered helpful for the understanding of single translations (eg **article** *n* (*object, in newspaper*) & *Gram* article *m*, or **putty** *n* mastic *m* (*pour vitres*)). The user is also helped by having context indicators and labels in French in the French section and in English in the English section of the dictionary.

Style and field labels follow bracketed indicators (eg **corner** *vt* (*market*) *Com* monopoliser, or **bidule** *nm* (*chose*) *Fam* whatsit). In the event of more than one translation within a grammatical category being qualified by the same style or field label, the label may then precede (see **trucker** where *Am* covers both senses given).

The user will find in the text important abbreviated words in English (eg BA, HIV) and in French (eg SVP, OVNI), useful geographical information such as names of countries, and a wide coverage of American words and usage (eg diaper, pinkie). The vocabulary includes French and English colloquialisms and slang, and important technical jargon.

In order to save space, some derived words are included within the entry of a headword. All such words are highlighted by means of the symbol •. Derivatives may be written in full or abbreviated, as is usually the case for important derived forms (such as English **-ly** or French **-ment**).

An oblique stroke in bold is used to mark the stem of a headword at which point the derived ending is added. A bold dash stands for the headword or the portion of the headword to the left of the oblique stroke (eg **awkward** *a* . . . **●–ly** *adv* . . .; **boulevers/er** *vt* . . . **●–ant** *a* . . . **●–ement** *nm*).

An oblique stroke within an entry is a useful space-saving device to separate non-interchangeable parts of a phrase or expression matched exactly in French and English (eg **to be able to swim/drive** savoir nager/conduire is to be understood as: **to be able to swim** savoir nager and **to be able to drive** savoir conduire).

In common with other Harrap dictionaries, when a headword appears in an example in the same form, it is represented by its initial letter (eg **at h.** stands for **at home** in headword **home**). This applies whether the headword starts a new line or appears within an entry (eg **● household** *a* . . . **h. name** . . .).

The pronunciation of both French and English is shown using the latest symbols of the International Phonetic Alphabet. Pronunciation is given for headwords at the start of an entry, and, as an additional help to the user, for those words within the entry where the correct pronunciation may be difficult to derive (eg **● aristocratie** [-asi] not [-ati]; **● rabid** ['ræbɪd] not ['reɪbɪd]).

Stress in English is indicated for headwords and for derived words in which stress differs from that of a headword (eg **miracle** ['mɪrək(ə)l] and **● mi'raculous**). American English pronunciation is listed wherever it is considered to show a marked difference from that of British English (eg **tomato** [tə'mɑːtəʊ, *Am* tə'meɪtəʊ]). American spelling is also supplied if sufficiently different from British (eg **tire** and **tyre**, **plow** and **plough**).

An original feature of this dictionary is its semantic approach to the order and arrangement of entries: the meaning of words determines the structure of entries. Important semantic categories have been indicated by bold Arabic numerals within an entry (eg **1**, **2**, **3**, **4**) (see **bolt**, **tail**, **général**) or have been entered as separate headwords (see **bug**[1] and **bug**[2], **draw**[1] and **draw**[2], **start**[1] and **start**[2]). The different grammatical divisions of separate headwords are easily identified by means of the symbol ▌. The symbol ▌ is used in lists of English phrasal verbs (eg **▌ to move along** or **▌ to move away**) to mark the start of each new phrasal.

Words are usually entered under the headword from which they are considered to derive (eg **● astronomer** follows **astronomy**, and **● planétaire** follows **planète**). Present and past participles are, in most cases, entered, usually in abbreviated form, within an entry immediately after the infinitive, any other derived words there may be following in alphabetical order (eg **exagér/er** *vt* ... **●–é** *a* ... **● exagération** *nf*; **accommodat/e** *vt* ... **●–ing** *a* ... **● accommo'dation** *n*.

In the French section of the dictionary a single asterisk is used to mark those irregular verbs whose partial conjugations are listed in section 7 L 2 of the French grammar. A double asterisk in the dictionary serves to pinpoint the most common of these irregular verbs, carefully selected to have their conjugations displayed in full in section 7 L 1 of the grammar.

Preface

The grammar

The French grammar has been written to meet the demands of language teaching in schools and colleges. The essential rules of the French language have been set out in terms that are as accessible as possible to all users. Where technical terms have been used then full explanations of these terms have been supplied. There is also a full glossary of grammatical terminology in the opening pages.

The grammar, with its wealth of lively and typical illustrations of usage taken from the present-day language, is the ideal study tool for all levels – from the beginner who is starting to come to grips with the French language through to the advanced user who requires a comprehensive and readily accessible work of reference.

The integration of the grammar into the main body of the dictionary text has been achieved thanks to a carefully worked out system of cross-references from specially selected individual dictionary headwords to the appropriate page(s) and sections of the grammar where those headwords are discussed at greater length. Over 250 words ranging from such important items as **le**, **de**, **pour** and **faire** to less frequent words such as **douteux**, **suffire** and **guère** have been cross-referred to the grammar where explanations and translations will be found clearly set out. Each cross-reference stands on a new line in the entry, and is indicated by the symbol ❶. The symbol is followed by the relevant page(s) to be consulted in the grammar, with grammar pages being distinguished from the dictionary text by the prefix G (eg **G1**, **G2**, **G3**). For even greater clarity, the cross-reference also contains the subject covered and its section number in the grammar. See, for example, headword **pour** (p183) which contains a cross-reference at the end of the entry. While most cross-references occur at the end of the entry, they do sometimes occur within the body of an entry, at the point which is considered most helpful to the user (see, for example, the headword **le, la, les** (pp139–140).

The author wishes to express his gratitude to Stuart Fortey and Hazel Curties for their substantial contributions to the first edition of this dictionary, and to his wife, Susan, for her help with Americanisms. He would also like to acknowledge the contribution of Lexus who with Raymond Perrez, Noël Peacock and Sabine Citron compiled the original text of the French grammar.

M. Janes
London 1995

Abbreviations		Abréviations
adjective	*a*	adjectif
abbreviation	*abbr, abrév*	abréviation
adverb	*adv*	adverbe
agriculture	*Agr*	agriculture
American	*Am*	américain
anatomy	*Anat*	anatomie
architecture	*Archit*	architecture
slang	*Arg*	argot
article	*art*	article
cars, motoring	*Aut*	automobile
auxiliary	*aux*	auxiliaire
aviation, aircraft	*Av*	aviation
biology	*Biol*	biologie
botany	*Bot*	botanique
British	*Br*	britannique
Canadian	*Can*	canadien
carpentry	*Carp*	menuiserie
chemistry	*Ch*	chimie
cinema	*Cin*	cinéma
commerce	*Com*	commerce
computing	*Comptr*	informatique
conjunction	*conj*	conjonction
cookery	*Culin*	cuisine
definite	*def, déf*	défini
demonstrative	*dem, dém*	démonstratif
economics	*Econ, Écon*	économie
electricity	*El, Él*	électricité
et cetera	*etc*	et cetera
feminine	*f*	féminin
familiar	*Fam*	familier
football	*Fb*	football
figurative	*Fig*	figuré
finance	*Fin*	finance
feminine plural	*fpl*	féminin pluriel
French	*Fr*	français
geography	*Geog, Géog*	géographie
geology	*Geol, Géol*	géologie
geometry	*Geom, Géom*	géométrie
grammar	*Gram*	grammaire
history	*Hist*	histoire
humorous	*Hum*	humoristique
indefinite	*indef, indéf*	indéfini
indicative	*indic*	indicatif
infinitive	*inf*	infinitif
interjection	*int*	interjection

Abbreviations		Abréviations
invariable	*inv*	invariable
ironic	*Iron*	ironique
legal, law	*Jur*	juridique
linguistics	*Ling*	linguistique
literary	*Lit, Litt*	littéraire
literature	*Liter, Littér*	littérature
masculine	*m*	masculin
mathematics	*Math*	mathématiques
medicine	*Med, Méd*	médecine
carpentry	*Menuis*	menuiserie
meteorology	*Met, Mét*	météorologie
military	*Mil*	militaire
masculine plural	*mpl*	masculin pluriel
music	*Mus*	musique
noun	*n*	nom
nautical	*Nau*	nautique
noun feminine	*nf*	nom féminin
noun masculine	*nm*	nom masculin
noun masculine and feminine	*nmf*	nom masculin et féminin
computing	*Ordinat*	informatique
pejorative	*Pej, Péj*	péjoratif
philosophy	*Phil*	philosophie
photography	*Phot*	photographie
physics	*Phys*	physique
plural	*pl*	pluriel
politics	*Pol*	politique
possessive	*poss*	possessif
past participle	*pp*	participe passé
prefix	*pref, préf*	préfixe
preposition	*prep, prép*	préposition
present participle	*pres p, p prés*	participe présent
present tense	*pres t*	temps présent
pronoun	*pron*	pronom
psychology	*Psy*	psychologie
past tense	*pt*	prétérit
	qch	quelque chose
	qn	quelqu'un
registered trademark	®	marque déposée
radio	*Rad*	radio
railway, *Am* railroad	*Rail*	chemin de fer
relative	*rel*	relatif
religion	*Rel*	religion
school	*Sch, Scol*	école
singular	*sing*	singulier
slang	*Sl*	argot
someone	*s.o.*	

Abbreviations		Abréviations
sport	*Sp*	sport
something	*sth*	
subjunctive	*sub*	subjonctif
suffix	*suff*	suffixe
technical	*Tech*	technique
telephone	*Tel, Tél*	téléphone
textiles	*Tex*	industrie textile
theatre	*Th*	théâtre
television	*TV*	télévision
typography, printing	*Typ*	typographie
university	*Univ*	université
United States	*US*	États-Unis
auxiliary verb	*v aux*	verbe auxiliaire
intransitive verb	*vi*	verbe intransitif
impersonal verb	*v imp*	verbe impersonnel
pronominal verb	*vpr*	verbe pronominal
transitive verb	*vt*	verbe transitif
transitive and intransitive verb	*vti*	verbe transitif et intransitif
vulgar	*Vulg*	vulgaire

Pronunciation of French

Table of Phonetic Symbols

Vowels

[i]	vite, cygne, sortie	[y]	cru, sûr, rue
[e]	été, donner	[ϕ]	feu, meule, nœud
[ɛ]	elle, mais, père	[œ]	œuf, jeune
[a]	chat, fameux	[ə]	le, refaire, entre
[ɑ]	pas, âgé	[ɛ̃]	vin, plein, faim, saint
[ɔ]	donne, fort, album	[ɑ̃]	enfant, temps, paon
[o]	dos, chaud, peau	[ɔ̃]	mon, nombre
[u]	tout, cour, roue	[œ̃]	lundi, humble

Consonants

[p]	pain, absolu, frapper	[n]	né, canne
[b]	beau, abbé	[ɲ]	campagne
[t]	table, nette	[ŋ]	jogging
[d]	donner, sud	[']	This symbol is placed before the phonetics of a word beginning with **h** to show that there is no elision or liaison: the preceding word must not be abbreviated (eg la hache and not l'hache), and the final consonant of the preceding word must not be pronounced (eg les haches: [leaʃ] and not [lezaʃ]).
[k]	camp, képi, qui		
[g]	garde, guerre, second		
[f]	feu, phrase		
[v]	voir, wagon		
[s]	sou, cire, nation		
[z]	cousin, zéro		
[ʃ]	chose, schéma		
[ʒ]	gilet, jeter		
[l]	lait, facile, elle		
[r]	rare, rhume, barreau		
[m]	mon, flamme		

Semi-consonants

[j]	piano, voyage, fille
[w]	ouest, noir, tramway
[ɥ]	muet, lui

ENGLISH – FRENCH

A

A, a [eɪ] *n* A, a *m*; **5A** (*number*) 5 bis; **A1** (*dinner etc*) *Fam* super, superbe.

a [ə, *stressed* eɪ] (*before vowel or mute h*) **an** [ən, *stressed* æn] *indef art* **1** un, une; **a man** un homme; **an apple** une pomme.

2 (= *def art in Fr*) **sixty pence a kilo** soixante pence le kilo; **50 km an hour** 50 km à l'heure; **I have a broken arm** j'ai le bras cassé.

3 (*art omitted in Fr*) **he's a doctor** il est médecin; **Caen, a town in Normandy** Caen, ville de Normandie; **what a man!** quel homme!

4 (*a certain*) **a Mr Smith** un certain M. Smith.

5 (*time*) **twice a month** deux fois par mois.

6 (*some*) **to make a noise/a fuss** faire du bruit/des histoires.

aback [ə'bæk] *adv* **taken a.** déconcerté.

abandon [ə'bændən] **1** *vt* abandonner. **2** *n* (*freedom of manner*) laisser-aller *m*.

abashed [ə'bæʃt] *a* confus, gêné.

abate [ə'beɪt] *vi* (*of storm, pain*) se calmer.

abbey ['æbɪ] *n* abbaye *f*.

abbot ['æbət] *n* abbé *m*.

abbreviate [ə'briːvɪeɪt] *vt* abréger. ● **abbreviation** [-'eɪʃ(ə)n] *n* abréviation *f*.

abdicate ['æbdɪkeɪt] *vti* abdiquer.

abdomen ['æbdəmən] *n* abdomen *m*.

abduct [æb'dʌkt] *vt* (*kidnap*) enlever. ● **abduction** [əb'dʌkʃ(ə)n] *n* enlèvement *m*, rapt *m*.

abet [ə'bet] *vt* (**-tt-**) **to aid and a. s.o.** *Jur* être le complice de qn.

abide [ə'baɪd] **1** *vi* **to a. by** (*promise etc*) rester fidèle à. **2** *vt* supporter; **I can't a. him** je ne peux pas le supporter.

ability [ə'bɪlətɪ] *n* capacité *f* (**to do** pour faire), aptitude *f* (**to do** à faire); **to the best of my a.** de mon mieux.

abject ['æbdʒekt] *a* abject; **a. poverty** la misère.

ablaze [ə'bleɪz] *a* en feu; **a. with** (*light*) resplendissant de.

able ['eɪb(ə)l] *a* (**-er, -est**) capable, compétent; **to be a. to do** être capable de faire, pouvoir faire; **to be a. to swim/drive** savoir nager/conduire. ● **a.-'bodied** *a* robuste. ● **ably** *adv* habilement.

abnormal [æb'nɔːm(ə)l] *a* anormal. ● **abnor'mality** *n* anomalie *f*; (*of body*) difformité *f*. ● **abnormally** *adv Fig* exceptionnellement.

aboard [ə'bɔːd] *adv Nau* à bord; **all a.** *Rail* en voiture ‖ *prep* **a. the ship** à bord du navire; **a. the train** dans le train.

abolish [ə'bɒlɪʃ] *vt* supprimer, abolir. ● **abolition** [æbə'lɪʃ(ə)n] *n* suppression *f*, abolition *f*.

aboriginal [æbə'rɪdʒən(ə)l] *n* aborigène *m*.

abort [ə'bɔːt] *vt* (*space flight, computer program*) abandonner. ● **abortion** [-ʃ(ə)n] *n Med* avortement *m*; **to have an a.** se faire avorter. ● **abortive** *a* (*plan etc*) manqué, avorté.

abound [ə'baʊnd] *vi* abonder (**in** en).

about [ə'baʊt] *adv* **1** (*approximately*) à peu près, environ; **(at) a. two o'clock** vers deux heures.

2 (*here and there*) çà et là, ici et là; (*ideas, flu*) *Fig* dans l'air; (*rumour*) qui circule; **to look a.** regarder autour de soi; **to follow a.** suivre partout; **to bustle a.** s'affairer; **there are lots a.** il en a beaucoup; **(out and) a.** (*after illness*) sur pied, guéri; **(up and) a.** (*out of bed*) levé, debout; **a. turn, a. face** *Mil* demi-tour *m*; *Fig* volte-face *f inv*.

‖ *prep* **1** (*around*) **a. the garden** autour du jardin; **a. the streets** par *or* dans les rues.

2 (*near to*) **a. here** par ici.

3 (*concerning*) au sujet de; **to talk a.** parler de; **a book a.** un livre sur; **what's it (all) a.?** de quoi s'agit-il?; **what** *or* **how a. me?** et moi alors?; **what** *or* **how a. a drink?** que dirais-tu de prendre un verre?

4 (+ *inf*) **a. to do** sur le point de faire.

above [ə'bʌv] *adv* au-dessus; (*in book*) ci-dessus; **from a.** d'en haut; **floor a.** étage *m* supérieur *or* du dessus ‖ *prep* au-dessus de; **a. all** par-dessus tout, surtout; **he's a. me** (*in rank*) c'est mon supérieur; **a. lying** incapable de mentir; **a. asking** trop fier pour demander. ● **a.-'mentioned** *a* susmentionné. ● **aboveboard** *a* ouvert, honnête ‖ *adv* sans tricherie, cartes sur table.

abrasive [ə'breɪsɪv] *a* (*substance*) abrasif; (*rough*) *Fig* rude, dur; (*irritating*) agaçant.

abreast [ə'brest] *adv* côte à côte, de front; **four a.** par rangs de quatre; **to keep a. of** *or* **with** se tenir au courant de.

abridge [ə'brɪdʒ] *vt* (*book etc*) abréger.

abroad [ə'brɔːd] *adv* (*in or to a foreign*

country) à l'étranger; **from a.** de l'étranger.

abrupt [ə'brʌpt] *a* (*sudden*) brusque; (*person*) brusque, abrupt; (*slope, style*) abrupt. ● **—ly** *adv* (*suddenly*) brusquement; (*rudely*) avec brusquerie.

abscess ['æbses] *n* abcès *m*.

abscond [əb'skɒnd] *vi Jur* s'enfuir.

absence ['æbsəns] *n* absence *f*; **in the a. of sth** à défaut de qch, faute de qch; **a. of mind** distraction *f*.

absent ['æbsənt] *a* absent (**from** de); (*look*) distrait. ● **a.-'minded** *a* distrait. ● **a.-'mindedness** *n* distraction *f*. ● **absen'tee** *n* absent, -ente *mf*.

absolute ['æbsəlu:t] *a* absolu; (*proof etc*) indiscutable; (*coward etc*) parfait, véritable. ● **—ly** *adv* absolument; (*forbidden*) formellement.

absolve [əb'zɒlv] *vt Rel Jur* absoudre; **to a. from** (*vow*) libérer de.

absorb [əb'zɔ:b] *vt* (*liquid etc*) absorber; (*shock*) amortir; **to become absorbed in** (*work*) s'absorber dans. ● **—ing** *a* (*work*) absorbant; (*book, film*) prenant. ● **absorbent** *a* absorbant; **a. cotton** *Am* coton *m* hydrophile *f*, ouate *f*. ● **absorber** *n* **shock a.** *Aut* amortisseur *m*.

abstain [əb'steɪn] *vi* s'abstenir (**from** de). ● **abstention** [-enʃ(ə)n] *n* abstention *f*.

abstract ['æbstrækt] **1** *a* & *n* abstrait (*m*). **2** *n* (*summary*) résumé *m*.

absurd [əb'sɜ:d] *a* absurde, ridicule. ● **absurdity** *n* absurdité *f*.

abundant [ə'bʌndənt] *a* abondant. ● **abundance** *n* abondance *f*. ● **abundantly** *adv* **a. clear** tout à fait clair.

abuse [ə'bju:s] *n* (*abusing*) abus *m* (**of** de); (*of child*) mauvais traitements *mpl*; (*curses*) injures *fpl* ‖ [ə'bju:z] *vt* (*misuse*) abuser de; (*ill-treat*) maltraiter; (*speak ill of*) dire du mal de; (*insult*) injurier. ● **abusive** [ə'bju:sɪv] *a* (*person*) grossier; (*words*) injurieux.

abysmal [ə'bɪzm(ə)l] *a* (*bad*) *Fam* désastreux, exécrable.

abyss [ə'bɪs] *n* abîme *m*.

academic [ækə'demɪk] *a* (*year etc*) universitaire; (*scholarly*) érudit, intellectuel; (*issue etc*) *Pej* théorique ‖ *n* (*teacher*) universitaire *mf*.

academy [ə'kædəmɪ] *n* (*society*) académie *f*; *Mil* école *f*; *Mus* conservatoire *m*.

accede [ək'si:d] *vi* **to a. to** (*request, throne, position*) accéder à.

accelerate [ək'seləreɪt] *vt* accélérer ‖ *vi* s'accélérer; *Aut* accélérer. ● **acceleration** [-'reɪʃ(ə)n] *n* accélération *f*. ● **accelerator** *n Aut* accélérateur *m*.

accent ['æksənt] *n* accent *m*. ● **accentuate** [æk'sentʃʊeɪt] *vt* accentuer.

accept [ək'sept] *vt* accepter. ● **—ed** *a* (*opinion*) reçu; (*fact*) reconnu. ● **acceptable** *a* (*worth accepting, tolerable*) acceptable. ● **acceptance** *n* acceptation *f*; (*approval, favour*) accueil *m* favorable.

access ['ækses] *n* accès *m* (**to sth** à qch, **to s.o.** auprès de qn). ● **ac'cessible** *a* accessible.

accessories [ək'sesərɪz] *npl* (*objects*) accessoires *mpl*.

accident ['æksɪdənt] *n* accident *m*; **by a.** (*by chance*) par accident; (*unintentionally*) accidentellement, sans le vouloir. ● **a.-prone** *a* qui attire les accidents. ● **acci'dental** *a* accidentel, fortuit. ● **acci'dentally** *adv* accidentellement, par mégarde; (*by chance*) par accident.

acclaim [ə'kleɪm] *vt* (*cheer*) acclamer; (*praise*) faire l'éloge de ‖ *n* **(critical) a.** éloges *mpl* (de la critique).

acclimate ['æklɪmeɪt] *vti Am* = **acclimatize.** ● **ac'climatize** *vt* acclimater ‖ *vi* s'acclimater.

accommodat/e [ə'kɒmədeɪt] *vt* (*of house*) loger, recevoir; (*have room for*) avoir de la place pour (mettre); (*oblige*) rendre service à. ● **—ing** *a* accommodant, obligeant. ● **accommodation** [-'deɪʃ(ə)n] *n* (*lodging*) logement *m*; (*rented room or rooms*) chambre(s) *f(pl)*; *pl* (*in hotel*) *Am* chambre(s) *f(pl)*.

accompany [ə'kʌmpənɪ] *vt* accompagner. ● **accompaniment** *n* accompagnement *m*. ● **accompanist** *n Mus* accompagnateur, -trice *mf*.

accomplice [ə'kʌmplɪs] *n* complice *mf*.

accomplish [ə'kʌmplɪʃ] *vt* (*task, duty*) accomplir; (*aim*) atteindre. ● **—ed** *a* accompli. ● **—ment** *n* accomplissement *m*; (*thing achieved*) réalisation *f*; *pl* (*skills*) talents *mpl*.

accord [ə'kɔ:d] **1** *n* accord *m*; **of my own a.** volontairement, de mon plein gré. **2** *vt* (*grant*) accorder. ● **accordance** *n* **in a. with** conformément à.

according to [ə'kɔ:dɪŋtu:] *prep* selon, d'après, suivant. ● **accordingly** *adv* en conséquence.

accordion [ə'kɔ:dɪən] *n* accordéon *m*.

accost [ə'kɒst] *vt* accoster, aborder.

account [ə'kaʊnt] **1** *n Com* compte *m*; **accounts department** comptabilité *f*. **2** *n* (*report*) compte rendu *m*, récit *m*; (*explanation*) explication *f*; **by all accounts**

au dire de tous; **to give a good a. of oneself** s'en tirer à son avantage ▮ *vi* **to a. for** (*explain*) expliquer; (*give reckoning of*) rendre compte de; (*represent*) représenter. **3** (*expressions*) **on a. of** à cause de; **on no a.** en aucun cas; **of some a.** d'une certaine importance; **to take into a.** tenir compte de. ● **accountable** *a* responsable (**for** de, **to** devant).

accountant [ə'kaʊntənt] *n* comptable *mf.* ● **accountancy** *n* comptabilité *f.*

accumulate [ə'kju:mjʊleɪt] *vt* accumuler, amasser ▮ *vi* s'accumuler. ● **accumulation** [-'leɪʃ(ə)n] *n* accumulation *f*; (*mass*) amas *m.*

accurate ['ækjʊrət] *a* exact, précis. ● **accuracy** *n* exactitude *f*, précision *f.* ● **accurately** *adv* avec précision.

accus/e [ə'kju:z] *vt* accuser (**of** de). ● **—ed** *n* **the a.** *Jur* l'inculpé, -ée *mf*, l'accusé, -ée *mf.* ● **accusation** [ækjʊ'zeɪʃ(ə)n] *n* accusation *f.*

accustom [ə'kʌstəm] *vt* habituer, accoutumer. ● **—ed** *a* habitué (**to sth** à qch, **to doing** à faire); **to get a. to** s'habituer à, s'accoutumer à.

ace [eɪs] *n* (*card, person*) as *m.*

ache [eɪk] *n* douleur *f*, mal *m*; **to have an a. in one's arm** avoir mal au bras ▮ *vi* faire mal; **my head aches** la tête me fait mal; **I'm aching all over** j'ai mal partout; **to be aching to do** brûler de faire. ● **aching** *a* douloureux.

achieve [ə'tʃi:v] *vt* (*success, result*) obtenir; (*aim*) atteindre; (*ambition*) réaliser; (*victory*) remporter; **he can never a. anything** il n'arrive jamais à faire quoi que ce soit. ● **—ment** *n* (*success*) réussite *f*; (*of ambition*) réalisation *f.*

acid ['æsɪd] *a* & *n* acide (*m*).

acknowledge [ək'nɒlɪdʒ] *vt* reconnaître (**as** pour); (*greeting*) répondre à; **to a. (receipt of)** accuser réception de. ● **acknowledg(e)ment** *n* reconnaissance *f*; (*of letter*) accusé *m* de réception; (*receipt*) reçu *m*; (*confession*) aveu *m* (**of** de).

acne ['æknɪ] *n* acné *f.*

acorn ['eɪkɔ:n] *n* *Bot* gland *m.*

acoustics [ə'ku:stɪks] *npl* acoustique *f.*

acquaint [ə'kweɪnt] *vt* **to a. s.o. with sth** informer qn de qch; **to be acquainted with** (*person*) connaître; (*fact*) savoir; **we are acquainted** on se connaît. ● **acquaintance** *n* connaissance *f.*

acquire [ə'kwaɪər] *vt* acquérir; (*taste*) prendre (**for** à); (*friends*) se faire; **acquired taste** goût *m* qui s'acquiert.

acquit [ə'kwɪt] *vt* (**-tt-**) **to a. s.o. (of a crime)** acquitter qn. ● **acquittal** *n* acquittement *m.*

acre ['eɪkər] *n* acre *f* (*= 0,4 hectare*).

acrimonious [ækrɪ'məʊnɪəs] *a* acerbe.

acrobat ['ækrəbæt] *n* acrobate *mf.* ● **acro'batic** *a* acrobatique. ● **acro'batics** *npl* acrobaties *fpl.*

across [ə'krɒs] *adv* & *prep* (*from side to side* (*of*)) d'un côté à l'autre (de); (*on the other side* (*of*)) de l'autre côté (de); (*crossways*) en travers (de); **to be a kilometre**/*etc* **a.** (*wide*) avoir un kilomètre/*etc* de large; **to walk** *or* **go a.** (*street etc*) traverser; **to run a.** (*street*) traverser en courant.

acrylic [ə'krɪlɪk] *n* acrylique *m*; **a. socks**/*etc* chaussettes *fpl*/*etc* en acrylique.

act [ækt] **1** *n* (*deed*) acte *m*; **a. (of parliament)** loi *f*; **caught in the a.** pris sur le fait; **a. of walking** action *f* de marcher.
2 *n* (*of play*) *Th* acte *m*; (*in circus, cabaret*) numéro *m*; **to put on an a.** *Fam* jouer la comédie ▮ *vt* (*part in play or film*) jouer ▮ *vi* *Th Cin* jouer; (*pretend*) jouer la comédie.
3 *vi* (*do sth, behave*) agir; **to a. as** (*secretary etc*) faire office de; (*of object*) servir de; **to a. (up)on** (*affect*) agir sur; (*advice*) suivre; **to a. on behalf of** représenter. ● **acting 1** *a* (*manager etc*) intérimaire. **2** *n* (*actor's art*) jeu *m*; (*career*) théâtre *m.*

action ['ækʃ(ə)n] *n* action *f*; *Mil* combat *m*; *Jur* procès *m*, action *f*; **to take a.** prendre des mesures; **to put into a.** (*plan*) exécuter; **out of a.** hors d'usage, hors (de) service; (*person*) hors (de) combat.

active ['æktɪv] *a* actif; (*interest, dislike*) vif; (*volcano*) en activité ▮ *n* *Gram* actif *m.* ● **activate** *vt* (*mechanism*) actionner. ● **ac'tivity** *n* activité *f*; (*in street*) animation *f.*

actor ['æktər] *n* acteur *m.* ● **actress** *n* actrice *f.*

actual ['æktʃʊəl] *a* réel, véritable; (*example*) concret; **the a. book** le livre même. ● **—ly** *adv* (*truly*) réellement; (*in fact*) en réalité, en fait.

acupuncture ['ækjʊpʌŋktʃər] *n* acupuncture *f.*

acute [ə'kju:t] *a* aigu (*f* -uë); (*emotion*) vif, profond; (*shortage*) grave. ● **—ly** *adv* (*to suffer, feel*) vivement, profondément. ● **—ness** *n* acuité *f.*

ad [æd] *n* *Fam* pub *f*; (*private, in newspaper*) annonce *f*; **small ad**, *Am* **want ad** petite annonce.

AD [eɪ'di:] *abbr* (*anno Domini*) après Jésus-Christ.

adamant ['ædəmənt] *a* inflexible; **to be a. that** maintenir que.

adapt [ə'dæpt] *vt* adapter (**to** à); **to a. (oneself)** s'adapter. ● **adaptable** *a* (*person*) souple, capable de s'adapter. ● **adaptor** *n* (*plug*) prise *f* multiple.

add [æd] *vt* ajouter (**to** à, **that** que); **to a. (up** *or* **together)** (*numbers*) additionner; **to a. in** inclure ‖ *vi* **to a. to** (*increase*) augmenter; **to a. up to** (*total*) s'élever à; (*mean*) signifier; (*represent*) constituer; **it all adds up** *Fam* ça s'explique. ● **adding machine** *n* machine *f* à calculer. ● **addition** [ə'dɪʃ(ə)n] *n* addition *f*; **in a.** de plus; **in a. to** en plus de. ● **a'dditional** *a* supplémentaire.

adder ['ædər] *n* vipère *f*.

addict ['ædɪkt] *n* (*drugs etc*) intoxiqué, -ée *mf*; *Fig* **jazz/***etc* **a.** fana(tique) *mf* du jazz/*etc*; **drug a.** drogué, -ée *mf*. ● **a'ddicted** *a* **to be a. to** (*music, sport*) se passionner pour; (*have the habit of*) avoir la manie de; **a. to drink** alcoolique; **a. to cigarettes** accroché à la cigarette. ● **addiction** [ə'dɪkʃ(ə)n] *n* (*habit*) manie *f*; (*dependency*) dépendance *f*; **drug a.** toxicomanie *f*. ● **a'ddictive** *a* qui crée une dépendance.

additive ['ædɪtɪv] *n* additif *m*.

address [ə'dres, *Am* 'ædres] *n* (*on letter etc*) adresse *f*; (*speech*) allocution *f* ‖ [ə'dres] *vt* (*person*) s'adresser à; (*audience*) parler devant; (*words*) adresser (**to** à); (*letter*) mettre l'adresse sur.

adenoids ['ædɪnɔɪdz] *npl* végétations *fpl* (adénoïdes).

adept [ə'dept] *a* expert (**in, at** à).

adequate ['ædɪkwət] *a* (*quantity etc*) suffisant; (*acceptable*) convenable; (*person*) compétent; (*performance*) acceptable. ● **adequately** *adv* suffisamment; convenablement.

adhere [əd'hɪər] *vi* **to a. to** adhérer à; (*decision, rule*) s'en tenir à. ● **adhesive** *a* & *n* adhésif (*m*).

adjective ['ædʒɪktɪv] *n* adjectif *m*.

adjoining [ə'dʒɔɪnɪŋ] *a* voisin.

adjourn [ə'dʒɜːn] *vt* (*postpone*) ajourner; (*session*) lever, suspendre ‖ *vi* lever la séance; **to a. to** (*go*) passer à.

adjust [ə'dʒʌst] *vt* (*machine*) régler, ajuster; (*prices, salaries*) ajuster; (*arrange*) arranger; **to a. (oneself) to** s'adapter à. ● **—able** *a* (*seat*) réglable. ● **—ment** *n Tech* réglage *m*; (*of person*) adaptation *f*.

ad-lib [æd'lɪb] *vi* (**-bb-**) improviser ‖ *a* (*joke etc*) improvisé.

administer [əd'mɪnɪstər] *vt* (*manage, dispense*) administrer (**to** à). ● **administration** [-'streɪʃ(ə)n] *n* administration *f*; (*government*) gouvernement *m*. ● **administrative** *a* administratif.

admiral ['ædmərəl] *n* amiral *m*.

admir/e [əd'maɪər] *vt* admirer (**for** pour, **for doing** de faire). ● **—ing** *a* admiratif. ● **—er** *n* admirateur, -trice *mf*. ● **'admirable** *a* admirable. ● **admiration** [ædmə'reɪʃ(ə)n] *n* admiration *f*.

admit [əd'mɪt] *vt* (**-tt-**) (*let in*) laisser entrer, admettre; (*acknowledge*) reconnaître, admettre (**that** que) ‖ *vi* **to a. to sth** (*confess*) avouer qch. ● **admission** *n* (*entry to theatre etc*) entrée *f* (**to** à, de); (*to club, school*) admission *f*; (*acknowledgment*) aveu *m*; **a. (charge)** (prix *m* d')entrée *f*. ● **admittance** *n* entrée *f*; **'no a.'** 'entrée interdite'. ● **admittedly** [-ɪdlɪ] *adv* c'est vrai (que).

ado [ə'duː] *n* **without further a.** sans (faire) plus de façons.

adolescent [ædə'lesənt] *n* adolescent, -ente *mf*. ● **adolescence** *n* adolescence *f*.

adopt [ə'dɒpt] *vt* (*child, method, attitude etc*) adopter. ● **—ed** *a* (*child*) adoptif; (*country*) d'adoption. ● **adoption** [-ʃ(ə)n] *n* adoption *f*.

adore [ə'dɔːr] *vt* adorer (**doing** faire); **he adores being flattered** il adore qu'on le flatte. ● **adorable** *a* adorable.

adorn [ə'dɔːn] *vt* (*room, book*) orner; (*person, dress*) parer.

Adriatic [eɪdrɪ'ætɪk] *n* **the A.** l'Adriatique *f*.

adrift [ə'drɪft] *a* & *adv Nau* à la dérive.

adult ['ædʌlt, ə'dʌlt] *n* adulte *mf* ‖ *a* (*animal etc*) adulte; **a. class/film/***etc* classe *f*/film *m*/*etc* pour adultes. ● **adulthood** *n* âge *m* adulte.

adultery [ə'dʌltərɪ] *n* adultère *m*.

advance [əd'vɑːns] *n* (*movement, money*) avance *f*; (*of science*) progrès *mpl*; *pl* (*of love, friendship*) avances *fpl*; **in a.** à l'avance, d'avance; (*to arrive*) en avance; **in a. of s.o.** avant qn.

‖ *a* (*payment*) anticipé; **a. booking** réservation *f*.

‖ *vt* (*put forward, lend*) avancer; (*science, one's work*) faire avancer.

‖ *vi* (*go forward, progress*) avancer; **to a. towards s.o.** (s')avancer vers qn. ● **advanced** *a* avancé; (*studies*) supérieur; (*course*) de niveau supérieur.

advantage [əd'vɑːntɪdʒ] *n* avantage *m* (**over** sur); **to take a. of** (*situation*) profiter de; (*person*) tromper, exploiter.

advent ['ædvent] *n* arrivée *f*, avènement *m*; **A.** *Rel* l'Avent *m*.

adventure [əd'ventʃər] *n* aventure *f* ‖ *a* (*film etc*) d'aventures. ● **adventurer** *n* aventurier, -ière *mf*.

adverb ['ædvɜːb] *n* adverbe *m*.
adverse ['ædvɜːs] *a* hostile, défavorable.
advert ['ædvɜːt] *n Fam* pub *f*; (*private, in newspaper*) annonce *f*.
advertis/e ['ædvətaɪz] *vt* (*commercially*) faire de la publicité pour; (*privately*) passer une annonce pour vendre; (*make known*) annoncer ‖ *vi* faire de la publicité; (*privately*) passer une annonce (**for** pour trouver). ●**—ing** *n* publicité *f*. ●**advertiser** *n* annonceur *m*.
advertisement [əd'vɜːtɪsmənt, *Am* ædvə'taɪzmənt] *n* publicité *f*; (*private, in newspaper*) annonce *f*; (*poster*) affiche *f*; **classified a.** petite annonce; **the advertisements** *TV* la publicité.
advice [əd'vaɪs] *n* conseil(s) *m(pl)*; *Com* avis *m*; **a piece of a.** un conseil.
advis/e [əd'vaɪz] *vt* conseiller; (*recommend*) recommander; (*notify*) informer; **to a. s.o. to do** conseiller à qn de faire; **to a. against** déconseiller. ●**—able** *a* (*wise*) prudent (**to do** de faire); (*action*) à conseiller. ●**adviser** *or* **advisor** *n* conseiller, -ère *mf*.
advocate 1 ['ædvəkət] *n* (*of cause*) défenseur *m*, avocat, -ate *mf*. **2** ['ædvəkeɪt] *vt* préconiser, recommander.
aerial ['eərɪəl] *n* antenne *f*.
aerobics [eə'rəʊbɪks] *npl* aérobic *f*.
aerodrome ['eərədrəʊm] *n* aérodrome *m*.
aeroplane ['eərəpleɪn] *n* avion *m*.
aerosol ['eərəsɒl] *n* aérosol *m*.
afar [ə'fɑːr] *adv* **from a.** de loin.
affable ['æfəb(ə)l] *a* affable, aimable.
affair [ə'feər] *n* (*matter, concern*) affaire *f*; **(love) a.** liaison *f*; **state of affairs** situation *f*.
affect [ə'fekt] *vt* (*concern, move*) toucher, affecter; (*harm*) nuire à; (*influence*) influer sur. ●**—ed** *a* (*manner*) affecté; (*by disease*) atteint.
affection [ə'fekʃ(ə)n] *n* affection *f* (**for** pour). ●**affectionate** *a* affectueux.
affix [ə'fɪks] *vt* apposer.
afflict [ə'flɪkt] *vt* affliger (**with** de).
affluent ['æflʊənt] *a* riche; **a. society** société *f* d'abondance. ●**affluence** *n* richesse *f*.
afford [ə'fɔːd] *vt* (*pay for*) avoir les moyens d'acheter, pouvoir se payer; **he can't a. the time (to read it)** il n'a pas le temps (de le lire); **I can a. to wait** je peux me permettre d'attendre. ●**—able** *a* (*price etc*) abordable.
Afghanistan [æf'gænɪstɑːn] *n* Afghanistan *m*. ●**Afghan** *a* & *n* afghan, -ane (*mf*).
afield [ə'fiːld] *adv* **further a.** plus loin; **too far a.** trop loin.
afloat [ə'fləʊt] *adv* (*ship, swimmer, business*) à flot; **life a.** la vie sur l'eau.
afoot [ə'fʊt] *adv* **there's something a.** il se trame quelque chose; **there's a plan a. to . . .** on prépare un projet pour. . . .
afraid [ə'freɪd] *a* **to be a.** avoir peur (**of, to** de); **to make s.o. afraid** faire peur à qn; **he's a. (that) she may be ill** il a peur qu'elle (ne) soit malade; **I'm a. he's out** (*I regret to say*) je regrette, il est sorti.
afresh [ə'freʃ] *adv* de nouveau.
Africa ['æfrɪkə] *n* Afrique *f*. ●**African** *a* & *n* africain, -aine (*mf*).
after ['ɑːftər] *adv* après; **the month a.** le mois suivant, le mois d'après ‖ *prep* après; **a. all** après tout; **a. eating** après avoir mangé; **day a. day** jour après jour; **time a. time** bien des fois; **a. you!** je vous en prie!; **ten a. four** *Am* quatre heures dix; **to be a. sth/s.o.** (*seek*) chercher qch/qn ‖ *conj* après que; **a. he saw you** après qu'il t'a vu.
aftereffects ['ɑːftərɪfekts] *npl* suites *fpl*, séquelles *fpl*. ●**aftermath** [-mɑːθ] *n* suites *fpl*. ●**after'noon** *n* après-midi *m or f inv*; **in the a.** l'après-midi; **good a.!** (*hello*) bonjour!; (*goodbye*) au revoir! ●**after'noons** *adv Am* l'après-midi. ●**aftersales service** *n* service *m* après-vente. ●**aftershave (lotion)** *n* lotion *f* après-rasage. ●**afterthought** *n* réflexion *f* après coup; **as an a.** après coup. ●**afterward(s)** *adv* après, plus tard.
afters ['ɑːftəz] *npl Fam* dessert *m*.
again [ə'gen, ə'geɪn] *adv* de nouveau, encore une fois; **to go down/up a.** redescendre/remonter; **he won't do it a.** il ne le fera plus; **never a.** plus jamais; **a. and a., time and (time) a.** bien des fois; **what's his name a.?** comment s'appelle-t-il déjà?
against [ə'genst, ə'geɪnst] *prep* contre; **to go** *or* **be a.** s'opposer à; **a. the law** illégal; **a law a. drinking** une loi qui interdit de boire; **a. the light** à contre-jour.
age [eɪdʒ] *n* âge *m*; **(old) a.** vieillesse *f*; **five years of a.** âgé de cinq ans; **to be of a.** être majeur; **under a.** trop jeune, mineur; **to wait (for) ages** *Fam* attendre une éternité; **a. group** tranche *f* d'âge; **a. limit** limite *f* d'âge ‖ *vti* (*pres p* **ag(e)ing**) vieillir. ●**aged** *a* [eɪdʒd] **a. ten** âgé de dix ans; ['eɪdʒɪd] vieux, âgé; **the a.** les personnes *fpl* âgées.
agenda [ə'dʒendə] *n* ordre *m* du jour.
agent ['eɪdʒənt] *n* agent *m*; (*dealer for cars etc*) concessionnaire *mf*. ●**agency** *n* (*office*) agence *f*.
aggravate ['ægrəveɪt] *vt* (*make worse*) aggraver; **to a. s.o.** *Fam* exaspérer qn.

● **aggravation** [-'veɪʃ(ə)n] *n* (*bother*) *Fam* ennui(s) *m*(*pl*).

aggression [ə'greʃ(ə)n] *n* agression *f*. ● **aggressive** *a* agressif. ● **agressor** *n* agresseur *m*.

agile ['ædʒaɪl, *Am* 'ædʒ(ə)l] *a* agile.

agitate ['ædʒɪteɪt] *vt* (*worry*) agiter; **to be agitated** être agité.

ago [ə'gəʊ] *adv* **a year a.** il y a un an; **how long a.?** il y a combien de temps (de cela)?; **as long a. as 1800** (déjà) en 1800.

agog [ə'gɒg] *a* (*excited*) en émoi.

agony ['ægənɪ] *n* (*pain*) douleur *f* atroce; (*anguish*) angoisse *f*; **to be in a.** souffrir horriblement. ● **agonize** *vi* se faire beaucoup de souci.

agree [ə'griː] *vi* (*come to an agreement*) se mettre d'accord; (*be in agreement*) être d'accord (**with** avec); (*of facts, dates etc*) concorder; *Grammar* s'accorder; **to a. (up)on** (*decide*) convenir de; **to a. to sth/to doing** consentir à qch/à faire; **it doesn't a. with me** (*food, climate*) ça ne me réussit pas. ‖ *vt* **to a. to do** accepter de faire; **to a. that** (*admit*) admettre que. ● **agreed** *a* (*time, place*) convenu; **we are a.** nous sommes d'accord; **a.!** entendu!

agreeable [ə'griːəb(əl] *a* **1** (*pleasant*) agréable. **2 to be a.** (*agree*) être d'accord. ● **agreement** *n* accord *m* (**with** avec); **in a. with/on** d'accord avec/sur.

agriculture ['ægrɪkʌltʃər] *n* agriculture *f*. ● **agri'cultural** *a* agricole.

aground [ə'graʊnd] *adv* **to run a.** (*of ship*) (s')échouer.

ah! [ɑː] *int* ah!

ahead [ə'hed] *adv* (*in space*) en avant; (*leading*) en tête; (*in the future*) dans l'avenir; **a. (of time)** en avance (sur l'horaire); **one hour**/*etc* **a.** une heure/*etc* d'avance (**of** sur); **a. of** (*space*) devant; (*time, progress*) en avance sur; **to get a.** prendre de l'avance; (*succeed*) réussir; **to think a.** penser à l'avenir; **straight a.** (*to walk*) tout droit; (*to look*) droit devant soi.

aid [eɪd] *n* (*help*) aide *f*; (*device*) accessoire *m*; (*visual*) moyen *m*, support *m*; **with the a. of** (*a stick etc*) à l'aide de; **in a. of** (*charity etc*) au profit de ‖ *vt* aider (**s.o. to do** qn à faire).

AIDS [eɪdz] *n Med* SIDA *m*; **A. virus** virus *m* du SIDA.

ailing ['eəlɪŋ] *a* souffrant; (*company*) en difficulté. ● **ailment** *n* ennui *m* de santé.

aim [eɪm] *n* but *m*; **to take a.** viser; **with the a. of** dans le but de ‖ *vt* (*gun*) braquer, diriger (**at** sur); (*stone*) lancer (**at** à, vers); **aimed at children**/*etc* (*product*) destiné aux enfants/*etc* ‖ *vi* viser; **to a. at s.o.** viser qn; **to a. to do** *or* **at doing** avoir l'intention de faire. ● **—less** *a*, ● **—lessly** *adv* sans but.

air [eər] **1** *n* air *m*; **in the open a.** en plein air; **by a.** (*to travel*) en *or* par avion; (*letter, goods*) par avion; **to go on the a.** (*person*) passer à l'antenne; (*programme*) être diffusé; **to throw (up) in(to) the a.** jeter en l'air ‖ *a* (*raid, base etc*) aérien; **a. fare** prix *m* du billet d'avion; **a. force/hostess** armée *f*/hôtesse *f* de l'air; **a. terminal** aérogare *f* ‖ *vt* (*room*) aérer; **airing cupboard** armoire *f* sèche-linge.

2 *n* (*appearance, tune*) air *m*.

airborne ['eəbɔːn] *a* en (cours de) vol; **to become a.** (*of aircraft*) décoller. ● **air-conditioned** *a* climatisé. ● **air-conditioning** *n* climatisation *f*. ● **aircraft** *n inv* avion(s) *m*(*pl*); **a. carrier** porte-avions *m inv*. ● **airfield** *n* terrain *m* d'aviation. ● **airgun** *n* carabine *f* à air comprimé. ● **airletter** *n* aérogramme *m*. ● **airline** *n* ligne *f* aérienne; **a. ticket** billet *m* d'avion. ● **airliner** *n* avion *m* de ligne. ● **airmail** *n* poste *f* aérienne; **by a.** par avion. ● **airman** *n* (*pl* **-men**) aviateur *m*. ● **airplane** *n Am* avion *m*. ● **airpocket** *n* trou *m* d'air. ● **airport** *n* aéroport *m*. ● **airship** *n* dirigeable *m*. ● **airsickness** *n* mal *m* de l'air. ● **airstrip** *n* terrain *m* d'atterrissage. ● **airtight** *a* hermétique. ● **air traffic controller** *n* contrôleur *m* aérien, aiguilleur *m* du ciel.

airy ['eərɪ] *a* (**-ier, -iest**) (*room*) bien aéré.

aisle [aɪl] *n* (*in plane, supermarket, cinema etc*) allée *f*; (*in church*) allée *f* centrale.

ajar [ə'dʒɑːr] *a* & *adv* (*door*) entrouvert.

akin [ə'kɪn] *a* **a. (to)** apparenté (à).

à la mode [ælæ'məʊd] *a Culin Am* avec de la crème glacée.

alarm [ə'lɑːm] *n* (*warning, fear, device in house or car*) alarme *f*; (*mechanism*) sonnerie *f* (d'alarme); **false a.** fausse alerte *f*; **a. (clock)** réveil *m* ‖ *vt* (*frighten*) alarmer; (*worry*) inquiéter; **to be alarmed** s'inquiéter (**at** de).

alas! [ə'læs] *int* hélas!

album ['ælbəm] *n* (*book, record*) album *m*.

alcohol ['ælkəhɒl] *n* alcool *m*. ● **alco'holic** *a* (*person*) alcoolique; **a. drink** boisson *f* alcoolisée ‖ *n* (*person*) alcoolique *mf*. ● **alcoholism** *n* alcoolisme *m*.

alcove ['ælkəʊv] *n* alcôve *f*.

ale [eɪl] *n* bière *f*.

alert [ə'lɜːt] *a* (*paying attention*) vigilant; (*mind, baby*) éveillé ‖ *n* alerte *f*; **on the a.** sur le qui-vive ‖ *vt* alerter.

A level ['eɪlev(ə)l] *n* (*exam*) *Br* = épreuve *f* de bac.

algebra ['ældʒɪbrə] *n* algèbre *f*.

Algeria [æl'dʒɪərɪə] *n* Algérie *f*. ● **Algerian** *a* & *n* algérien, -ienne (*mf*).

alias ['eɪlɪəs] *adv* alias ‖ *n* nom *m* d'emprunt.

alibi ['ælɪbaɪ] *n* alibi *m*.

alien ['eɪlɪən] *n* étranger, -ère *mf*. ● **alienate** *vt* **to a. s.o.** (*make unfriendly*) se mettre qn à dos.

alight [ə'laɪt] **1** *a* (*fire*) allumé; (*building*) en feu; **to set a.** mettre le feu à. **2** *vi* descendre (**from** de).

align [ə'laɪn] *vt* **to a. oneself with** *Pol* s'aligner sur.

alike [ə'laɪk] **1** *a* (*people, things*) semblables, pareils; **to look** *or* **be a.** se ressembler. **2** *adv* de la même manière.

alimony ['ælɪmənɪ, *Am* 'ælɪməʊnɪ] *n Jur* pension *f* alimentaire.

alive [ə'laɪv] *a* vivant, en vie; **a. with** (*insects etc*) grouillant de; **to keep a.** (*custom, memory*) entretenir, perpétuer; **a. and kicking** *Fam* plein de vie.

all [ɔːl] *a* tout, toute, *pl* tous, toutes; **a. day** toute la journée; **a. (the) men** tous les hommes; **for a. his wealth** malgré toute sa fortune.

‖ *pron* tous *mpl*, toutes *fpl*; (*everything*) tout; **a. will die** tous mourront; **my sisters are a. here** toutes mes sœurs sont ici; **he ate it a., he ate a. of it** il a tout mangé; **take a. of it** prends (le) tout; **a. (that) he has** tout ce qu'il a; **a. of us** nous tous; **a. in a.** à tout prendre; **in a., a. told** en tout; **a. but impossible**/*etc* presque impossible/*etc*; **anything at a.** quoi que ce soit; **if he comes at a.** s'il vient effectivement; **if there's any wind at a.** s'il y a le moindre vent; **nothing at a.** rien du tout; **not at a.** pas du tout; (*after 'thank you'*) il n'y a pas de quoi.

‖ *adv* tout; **a. alone** tout seul; **a. bad** entièrement mauvais; **a. over** (*everywhere*) partout; (*finished*) fini; **six a.** *Fb* six buts partout; **a. in** *Fam* épuisé. ● **a.-night** *a* (*party*) qui dure toute la nuit. ● **a.-out** *a* (*effort*) énergique. ● **a.-purpose** *a* (*tool*) universel. ● **a.-round** *a* (*knowledge*) approfondi; (*athlete*) complet. ● **a.-time** *a* (*record*) jamais atteint; **to reach an a.-time low/high** arriver au point le plus bas/le plus haut.

allegation [ælɪ'geɪʃ(ə)n] *n* accusation *f*.

alleg/e [ə'ledʒ] *vt* prétendre (**that** que). ● **—ed** *a* (*author, culprit*) présumé; **he is a. to be** on prétend qu'il est.

allegiance [ə'liːdʒəns] *n* fidélité *f* (**to** à).

allegory ['ælɪgərɪ, *Am* 'æləgɔːrɪ] *n* allégorie *f*.

allergy ['ælədʒɪ] *n* allergie *f*. ● **allergic** [ə'lɜːɪk] *a* allergique (**to** à).

alleviate [ə'liːvɪeɪt] *vt* (*pain etc*) soulager; (*burden etc*) alléger.

alley ['ælɪ] *n* ruelle *f*; **blind a.** impasse *f*. ● **alleyway** *n* ruelle *f*.

alliance [ə'laɪəns] *n* alliance *f*.

allied ['ælaɪd] *a* (*country*) allié.

alligator ['ælɪgeɪtər] *n* alligator *m*.

allocate ['æləkeɪt] *vt* (*assign*) attribuer, allouer (**to** à); (*distribute*) répartir.

allot [ə'lɒt] *vt* (**-tt-**) (*assign*) attribuer; (*distribute*) répartir. ● **—ment** *n* (*land*) lopin *m* de terre (*loué pour la culture*).

allow [ə'laʊ] **1** *vt* permettre; (*give*) accorder (**s.o. sth** qch à qn); (*a request*) accéder à; **to a. a discount** accorder une réduction; **to a. s.o. to do** permettre à qn de faire; **to a. an hour/a metre** (*estimated period or quantity*) prévoir une heure/un mètre; **a. me!** permettez(-moi)!; **it's not allowed** c'est interdit; **you're not allowed to go** on vous interdit de partir. **2** *vi* **to a. for sth** tenir compte de qch.

allowance [ə'laʊəns] *n* allocation *f*; (*for travel, housing, food*) indemnité *f*; (*for duty-free goods*) tolérance *f*; **to make allowances for** (*person*) être indulgent envers; (*thing*) tenir compte de.

alloy ['ælɔɪ] *n* alliage *m*.

all right [ɔːl'raɪt] *a* (*satisfactory*) bien *inv*; (*unharmed*) sain et sauf; (*undamaged*) intact; (*without worries*) tranquille; **it's all r.** ça va; **I'm all r.** (*healthy*) je vais bien ‖ *adv* (*well*) bien; **all r.!** (*agreement*) d'accord!; **I received your letter all r.** (*emphatic*) j'ai bien reçu votre lettre.

ally ['ælaɪ] *n* allié, -ée *mf*.

almanac ['ɔːlmənæk] *n* almanach *m*.

almighty [ɔːl'maɪtɪ] *a* tout-puissant; (*enormous*) *Fam* terrible.

almond ['ɑːmənd] *n* amande *f*.

almost ['ɔːlməʊst] *adv* presque; **he a. fell/***etc* il a failli tomber/*etc*.

alone [ə'ləʊn] *a* & *adv* seul; **an expert a. can . . .** seul un expert peut . . .; **to leave a.** (*person*) laisser tranquille; (*thing*) ne pas toucher à.

along [ə'lɒŋ] *prep* **(all) a.** (tout) le long de; **to go** *or* **walk a.** (*street*) passer par; **a. here** par ici; **a. with** avec ‖ *adv* **all a.** (*all the time*) dès le début; (*all the way*) d'un bout à l'autre; **to move a.** avancer; **he'll be** *or* **come a.** il viendra.

alongside [əlɒŋ'saɪd] *prep* & *adv* à côté (de); **a. the kerb** le long du trottoir.
aloof [ə'lu:f] *a* distant ‖ *adv* à distance; **to keep a.** garder ses distances (**from** par rapport à).
aloud [ə'laʊd] *adv* à haute voix.
alphabet ['ælfəbet] *n* alphabet *m*. ●**alpha'betical** *a* alphabétique.
Alps [ælps] *npl* **the A.** les Alpes *fpl*. ●**alpine** *a* (*club*, *range etc*) alpin; (*scenery*) alpestre.
already [ɔ:l'redɪ] *adv* déjà.
alright [ɔ:l'raɪt] *adv Fam* = **all right.**
Alsatian [æl'seɪʃ(ə)n] *n* (*dog*) berger *m* allemand, chien-loup *m*.
also ['ɔ:lsəʊ] *adv* aussi, également.
altar ['ɔ:ltər] *n* autel *m*.
alter ['ɔ:ltər] *vt* changer; (*clothing*) retoucher ‖ *vi* changer. ●**alteration** [-'reɪʃ(ə)n] *n* changement *m*; retouche *f*; *pl* (*to building*) travaux *mpl*.
alternate [ɔ:l'tɜ:nət] *a* alterné; **on a. days** tous les deux jours ‖ ['ɔ:ltəneɪt] *vi* alterner (**with** avec) ‖ *vt* faire alterner. ●**—ly** *adv* alternativement.
alternative [ɔ:l'tɜ:nətɪv] *a* (*other*) **an a. way**/*etc* une autre façon/*etc*; **a. answers**/*etc* d'autres réponses/*etc* (différentes) ‖ *n* (*choice*) alternative *f*. ●**—ly** *adv* **(or) a.** (*or else*) ou alors, ou bien.
although [ɔ:l'ðəʊ] *adv* bien que (+ *sub*).
altitude ['æltɪtju:d] *n* altitude *f*.
altogether [ɔ:ltə'geðər] *adv* (*completely*) tout à fait; (*on the whole*) somme toute; **how much a.?** combien en tout?
aluminium [æljʊ'mɪnjəm] (*Am* **aluminum** [ə'lu:mɪnəm]) *n* aluminium *m*.
always ['ɔ:lweɪz] *adv* toujours.
am [æm, *unstressed* əm] *see* **be.**
a.m. [eɪ'em] *adv* du matin.
amalgamate [ə'mælgəmeɪt] *vi* (*of organizations*) fusionner.
amass [ə'mæs] *vt* (*riches*) amasser.
amateur ['æmətər] *n* amateur *m*; **a. painter**/*etc* peintre/*etc* amateur ‖ *a* (*interest*, *sports*) d'amateur.
amaz/e [ə'meɪz] *vt* stupéfier, étonner. ●**—ed** *a* stupéfait (**at sth** de qch), étonné (**at sth** par *or* de qch); (*filled with wonder*) émerveillé; **a. at seeing**/*etc* stupéfait *or* étonné de voir/*etc*. ●**—ing** *a* stupéfiant; (*incredible*) extraordinaire. ●**amazement** *n* stupéfaction *f*.
ambassador [æm'bæsədər] *n* ambassadeur *m*; (*woman*) ambassadrice *f*.
amber ['æmbər] *n* ambre *m*; **a. (light)** (*of traffic signal*) *Aut* (feu *m*) orange *m*.
ambiguous [æm'bɪgjʊəs] *a* ambigu (*f* -uë).
ambition [æm'bɪʃ(ə)n] *n* ambition *f*. ●**ambitious** *a* ambitieux.
amble ['æmb(ə)l] *vi* marcher d'un pas tranquille.
ambulance ['æmbjʊləns] *n* ambulance *f*; **a. driver** ambulancier, -ière *mf*.
ambush ['æmbʊʃ] *n* embuscade *f* ‖ *vt* prendre en embuscade; **to be ambushed** tomber dans une embuscade.
amend [ə'mend] *vt* (*text*) modifier; *Pol* (*law etc*) amender. ●**—ment** *n Pol* amendement *m*.
amends [ə'mendz] *npl* **to make a. for** réparer; **to make a.** réparer son erreur.
amenities [ə'mi:nɪtɪz, *Am* ə'menɪtɪz] *npl* (*of sports club etc*) équipement *m*; (*of town*) aménagements *mpl*.
America [ə'merɪkə] *n* Amérique *f*; **North/South A.** Amérique du Nord/du Sud. ●**American** *a* & *n* américain, -aine (*mf*).
amicab/le ['æmɪkəb(ə)l] *a* amical. ●**—ly** *adv* amicalement; *Jur* à l'amiable.
amid(st) [ə'mɪd(st)] *prep* au milieu de, parmi.
amiss [ə'mɪs] *adv* & *a* mal (à propos); **sth is a.** (*wrong*) qch ne va pas.
ammonia [ə'məʊnjə] *n* (*gas*) ammoniac *m*; (*liquid*) ammoniaque *f*.
ammunition [æmjʊ'nɪʃ(ə)n] *n* munitions *fpl*.
amnesty ['æmnəstɪ] *n* amnistie *f*.
amok [ə'mɒk] *adv* **to run a.** (*of crowd*) se déchaîner; (*of person*) devenir fou furieux.
among(st) [ə'mʌŋ(st)] *prep* (*amidst*) parmi; (*between*) entre; **a. the crowd/books** parmi la foule/les livres; **a. themselves/friends** entre eux/amis; **a. the French**/*etc* (*group*) chez les Français/*etc*.
amorous ['æmərəs] *a* (*look*) polisson; (*person*) d'humeur polissonne.
amount [ə'maʊnt] **1** *n* quantité *f*; (*sum of money*) somme *f*; (*total of bill*, *Am check etc*) montant *m*; (*scope*, *size*) importance *f*. **2** *vi* **to a. to** s'élever à; (*mean*) *Fig* signifier; (*represent*) représenter.
amp [æmp] *n El* ampère *m*.
ample ['æmp(ə)l] *a* (*enough*) largement assez de; (*roomy*) ample; (*reasons*, *means*) solides; **you have a. time** tu as largement le temps; **that's a.** c'est largement suffisant. ●**amply** *adv* amplement.
amplify ['æmplɪfaɪ] *vt* (*sound etc*) amplifier. ●**amplifier** *n El* amplificateur *m*.
amputate ['æmpjʊteɪt] *vt* amputer. ●**amputation** [-'teɪʃ(ə)n] *n* amputation *f*.
amus/e [ə'mju:z] *vt* amuser; **to keep s.o. amused** amuser qn. ●**—ing** *a* amusant. ●**—ement** *n* amusement *m*; (*pastime*) distraction *f*; *pl* (*at fairground*) attractions *fpl*;

(*gambling machines*) machines *fpl* à sous; **a. arcade** salle *f* de jeux; **a. park** parc *m* d'attractions.

an [æn, *unstressed* ən] *see* **a.**

an(a)emic [ə'niːmɪk] *a* anémique.

an(a)esthetic [ænɪs'θetɪk] *n* anesthésie *f*; (*substance*) anesthésique *m*; **general/local a.** anesthésie *f* générale/locale.

analogy [ə'nælədʒɪ] *n* analogie *f*.

analyse ['ænəlaɪz] *vt* analyser. • **analysis,** *pl* **-yses** [ə'næləsɪs, -ɪsiːz] *n* analyse *f*. • **analyst** *n* analyste *mf*. • **ana'lytical** *a* analytique.

anarchy ['ænəkɪ] *n* anarchie *f*. • **anarchist** *n* anarchiste *mf*.

anathema [ə'næθəmə] *n* **it is (an) a. to me** j'ai une sainte horreur de cela.

anatomy [ə'nætəmɪ] *n* anatomie *f*.

ancestor ['ænsestər] *n* ancêtre *m*.

anchor ['æŋkər] *n* ancre *f*; **to weigh a.** lever l'ancre ▌*vt* (*ship*) mettre à l'ancre ▌*vi* jeter l'ancre. • **—ed** *a* ancré.

anchovy ['æntʃəvɪ, *Am* æn'tʃəʊvɪ] *n* anchois *m*.

ancient ['eɪnʃənt] *a* ancien; (*pre-medieval*) antique; (*person*) d'un grand âge.

and [ænd, *unstressed* ən(d)] *conj* et; **a knife a. fork** un couteau et une fourchette; **two hundred a. two** deux cent deux; **better a. better** de mieux en mieux; **go a. see** va voir.

anecdote ['ænɪkdəʊt] *n* anecdote *f*.

angel ['eɪndʒəl] *n* ange *m*. • **an'gelic** *a* angélique.

anger ['æŋgər] *n* colère *f*; **in a., out of a.** sous le coup de la colère ▌*vt* mettre en colère, fâcher.

angle ['æŋg(ə)l] *n* angle *m*; **at an a.** en biais.

angler ['æŋglər] *n* pêcheur, -euse *mf* à la ligne. • **angling** *n* pêche *f* à la ligne.

Anglican ['æŋglɪkən] *a* & *n* anglican, -ane (*mf*).

anglo- ['æŋgləʊ] *pref* anglo-. • **Anglo-'Saxon** *a* & *n* anglo-saxon, -onne (*mf*).

angora [æŋ'gɔːrə] *n* (*wool*) angora *m*.

angry ['æŋgrɪ] *a* (**-ier, -iest**) (*person*) en colère, fâché; (*look*) fâché; (*letter*, *words*) indigné; **to get a.** se fâcher, se mettre en colère (**with** contre). • **angrily** *adv* en colère; (*to speak*) avec colère.

anguish ['æŋgwɪʃ] *n* angoisse *f*.

angular ['æŋgjʊlər] *a* (*face*) anguleux.

animal ['ænɪməl] *a* (*kingdom*, *fat etc*) animal ▌*n* animal *m*, bête *f*.

animate ['ænɪmət] *a* (*alive*) animé. • **animated** *a* animé; **to become a.** s'animer. • **animation** [-'meɪʃ(ə)n] *n* animation *f*.

aniseed ['ænɪsiːd] *n Culin* anis *m*.

ankle ['æŋk(ə)l] *n* cheville *f*; **a. sock** socquette *f*.

annex [ə'neks] *vt* annexer.

annex(e) ['æneks] *n* (*building*) annexe *f*.

annihilate [ə'naɪəleɪt] *vt* anéantir.

anniversary [ænɪ'vɜːsərɪ] *n* (*of event*) anniversaire *m*.

announc/e [ə'naʊns] *vt* annoncer; (*birth*, *marriage*) faire part de. • **—ement** *n* (*statement*) annonce *f*; (*of birth*, *marriage*, *death*) avis *m*. • **—er** *n TV* speaker *m*, speakerine *f*.

annoy [ə'nɔɪ] *vt* (*inconvenience*) ennuyer, gêner; (*irritate*) agacer, contrarier. • **—ed** *a* fâché, contrarié; **to get a.** se fâcher (**with** contre). • **—ing** *a* ennuyeux, contrariant. • **annoyance** *n* ennui *m*, contrariété *f*.

annual ['ænjʊəl] *a* annuel ▌*n* (*children's book*) album *m*.

anomaly [ə'nɒməlɪ] *n* anomalie *f*.

anon [ə'nɒn] *adv Hum* tout à l'heure.

anonymous [ə'nɒnɪməs] *a* anonyme; **to remain a.** garder l'anonymat.

anorak ['ænəræk] *n* anorak *m*.

anorexia [ænə'reksɪə] *n* anorexie *f*. • **anorexic** *a* & *n* anorexique (*mf*).

another [ə'nʌðər] *a* & *pron* un(e) autre; **a. man** (*different*) un autre homme; **a. month** (*additional*) encore un mois, un autre mois; **a. ten** encore dix; **one a.** l'un(e) l'autre, *pl* les un(e)s les autres; **they love one a.** ils s'aiment (l'un l'autre).

answer ['ɑːnsər] *n* réponse *f*; (*to problem*) solution (**to** de); **in a. to** en réponse à. ▌*vt* (*person*, *question*, *letter*, *phone*) répondre à; (*prayer*, *wish*) exaucer; **he answered 'yes'** il a répondu 'oui'; **to a. the bell** *or* **the door** ouvrir la porte. ▌*vi* répondre; **to a. back** (*rudely*) répondre; **to a. for s.o./sth** répondre de qn/qch; **answering machine** répondeur *m*. • **answerable** *a* responsable (**for sth** de qch, **to s.o.** devant qn).

ant [ænt] *n* fourmi *f*.

antagonize [æn'tægənaɪz] *vt* provoquer (l'hostilité de).

Antarctic [æn'tɑːktɪk] *n* **the A.** l'Antarctique *m*.

antelope ['æntɪləʊp] *n* antilope *f*.

antenatal [æntɪ'neɪt(ə)l] *a* prénatal (*mpl* -als) ▌*n* examen *m* prénatal.

antenna[1], *pl* **-ae** [æn'tenə, -iː] *n* (*of insect etc*) antenne *f*.

antenna[2] [æn'tenə] *n* (*pl* **-as**) (*for TV*, *radio*) *Am* antenne *f*.

anthem ['ænθəm] *n* **national a.** hymne *m* national.

anthology [æn'θɒlədʒɪ] *n* recueil *m*.

anti- ['æntɪ, *Am* 'æntaɪ] *pref* anti-. ●**antibi'otic** *n* antibiotique *m*. ●**antibody** *n* anticorps *m*. ●**anti'climax** *n* chute *f* dans l'ordinaire; (*letdown*) déception *f*. ●**anti'clockwise** *adv* dans le sens inverse des aiguilles d'une montre. ●**antifreeze** *n Aut* antigel *m*. ●**anti'histamine** *n Med* antihistaminique *m*. ●**anti-Se'mitic** *a* antisémite. ●**anti-'Semitism** *n* antisémitisme *m*. ●**anti'septic** *a* & *n* antiseptique (*m*). ●**anti'social** *a* (*misfit*) asocial; (*unsociable*) peu sociable.

anticipate [æn'tɪsɪpeɪt] *vt* (*foresee*) prévoir; (*expect*) s'attendre à. ●**anticipation** [-'peɪʃ(ə)n] *n* attente *f*; **in a. of** en prévision de, dans l'attente de.

antics ['æntɪks] *npl* singeries *fpl*.

antiquated ['æntɪkweɪtɪd] *a* (*phrase, custom*) vieilli; (*person*) vieux jeu *inv*; (*machine etc*) antédiluvien.

antique [æn'ti:k] *a* (*furniture etc*) ancien; (*of Greek or Roman period*) antique; **a. dealer** antiquaire *mf*; **a. shop** magasin *m* d'antiquités ‖ *n* antiquité *f*, objet *m* ancien.

antlers ['æntləz] *n* (*of deer*) *npl* bois *mpl*.

Antwerp ['æntwɜ:p] *n* Anvers *m or f*.

anus ['eɪnəs] *n* anus *m*.

anvil ['ænvɪl] *n* enclume *f*.

anxiety [æŋ'zaɪətɪ] *n* (*worry*) inquiétude *f* (**about** au sujet de); (*fear*) anxiété *f*.

anxious ['æŋkʃəs] *a* (*worried*) inquiet (**about** de, pour); (*troubled*) anxieux; (*eager*) impatient (**to do** de faire); **I'm a. (that) he should leave** je tiens beaucoup à ce qu'il parte. ●**—ly** *adv* (*to wait*) impatiemment.

any ['enɪ] *a* **1** (*in questions*) du, de la, des; **have you a. milk/tickets?** avez-vous du lait/des billets?; **is there a. man (at all) who . . . ?** y a-t-il un homme (quelconque) qui . . . ?
2 (*negative*) de; (*not the slightest*) aucun; **he hasn't got a. milk/tickets** il n'a pas de lait/de billets; **there isn't a. proof/doubt** il n'y a aucune preuve/aucun doute.
3 (*no matter which*) n'importe quel; **a. time** n'importe quand.
4 (*every*) tout; **at a. moment** à tout moment; **in a. case, at a. rate** de toute façon.
‖ *pron* **1** (*no matter which one*) n'importe lequel; (*somebody*) quelqu'un; **if a. of you** si l'un d'entre vous.
2 (*quantity*) en; **have you got a.?** en as-tu?; **I don't see a.** je n'en vois pas.
‖ *adv* **not a. further/happier/***etc* pas plus loin/plus heureux/*etc*; **I don't see him a. more** je ne le vois plus; **a. more tea?** encore du thé?, encore un peu de thé?; **a. better?** (un peu) mieux?

anybody ['enɪbɒdɪ] *pron* **1** (*somebody*) quelqu'un; **do you see a.?** vois-tu quelqu'un?; **more than a.** plus que tout autre. **2** (*negative*) personne; **he doesn't know a.** il ne connaît personne. **3** (*no matter who*) n'importe qui; **a. would think that . . .** on croirait que . . .; **come along with a. you wish** venez avec qui vous voulez.

anyhow ['enɪhaʊ] *adv* (*at any rate*) de toute façon; (*badly*) n'importe comment; (*in confusion*) sens dessus dessous.

anyone ['enɪwʌn] *pron* = **anybody.**

anyplace ['enɪpleɪs] *adv Am* = **anywhere.**

anything ['enɪθɪŋ] *pron* **1** (*something*) quelque chose; **can you see a.?** voyez-vous quelque chose? **2** (*negative*) rien; **he doesn't do a.** il ne fait rien; **without a.** sans rien. **3** (*everything*) tout; **a. you like** (tout) ce que tu veux; **like a.** (*to work, run etc*) *Fam* comme un fou. **4** (*no matter what*) **a. (at all)** n'importe quoi.

anyway ['enɪweɪ] *adv* (*at any rate*) de toute façon.

anywhere ['enɪweər] *adv* **1** (*no matter where*) n'importe où. **2** (*everywhere*) partout; **a. you go** où que vous alliez, partout où vous allez; **a. you like** (là) où tu veux. **3** (*somewhere*) quelque part; **is he going a.?** va-t-il quelque part? **4** (*negative*) nulle part; **he doesn't go a.** il ne va nulle part; **without a. to put it** sans un endroit où le mettre.

apart [ə'pɑ:t] *adv* **1** (*separated*) **we kept them a.** nous les tenions séparés; **with legs (wide) a.** les jambes écartées; **they are a metre a.** ils se trouvent à un mètre l'un de l'autre; **to come a.** (*of two objects*) se séparer; (*of knot etc*) se défaire; **to tell two things/people a.** distinguer deux choses/personnes.
2 (*to pieces*) **to tear a.** mettre en pièces; **to take a.** démonter.
3 a. from (*except for*) à part.

apartment [ə'pɑ:tmənt] *n* (*flat*) *Am* appartement *m*; **a. house** *Am* immeuble *m* (*d'habitation*).

apathy ['æpəθɪ] *n* apathie *f*. ●**apa'thetic** *a* apathique.

ape [eɪp] *n* singe *m* ‖ *vt* (*imitate*) singer.

aperitif [ə'perəti:f] *n* apéritif *m*.

aperture ['æpətʃʊər] *n* ouverture *f*.

apiece [ə'pi:s] *adv* chacun; **a pound a.** une livre (la) pièce *or* chacun.

apologetic [əpɒlə'dʒetɪk] *a* (*letter*) plein d'excuses; **to be a. (about)** s'excuser (de). ●**apologetically** *adv* en s'excusant.

apology [ə'pɒlədʒɪ] *n* excuses *fpl*. ●**apologize** *vi* s'excuser (**for** de); **to a. to s.o.** faire ses excuses à qn (**for** pour).

apostle [ə'pɒs(ə)l] *n* apôtre *m*.
apostrophe [ə'pɒstrəfɪ] *n* apostrophe *f*.
appal [ə'pɔːl] (*Am* **appall**) *vt* (**-ll-**) consterner; **to be appalled (at)** être horrifié (de). ● **appalling** *a* épouvantable.
apparatus [æpə'reɪtəs, *Am* -'rætəs] *n* (*equipment*, *organization*) appareil *m*; (*in gym*) agrès *mpl*.
apparent [ə'pærənt] *a* (*obvious*, *seeming*) apparent; **it's a. that** il est évident que. ● **—ly** *adv* apparemment.
appeal [ə'piːl] *n* (*charm*) attrait *m*; (*interest*) intérêt *m*; (*call*) & *Jur* appel *m*.
▮ *vt* **to a. to** (*s.o.*, *s.o.'s kindness*) faire appel à; **to a. to s.o.** (*attract*) plaire à qn; (*interest*) intéresser qn; **to a. to s.o. for sth** demander qch à qn; **to a. to s.o. to do** supplier qn de faire.
▮ *vi Jur* faire appel. ● **appealing** *a* (*attractive*) séduisant.
appear [ə'pɪər] *vi* (*become visible*) apparaître; (*present oneself*) se présenter; (*seem*, *be published*) paraître; (*on stage*, *in film*) jouer; (*in court*) comparaître; **it appears that** (*it seems*) il semble que (+ *sub or indic*); (*it is rumoured*) il paraîtrait que (+ *indic*). ● **appearance** *n* (*act*) apparition *f*; (*look*) apparence *f*; **to put in an a.** faire acte de présence.
appease [ə'piːz] *vt* (*soothe*) apaiser.
appendix, *pl* **-ixes** *or* **-ices** [ə'pendɪks, -ɪksɪz, -ɪsiːz] *n* (*in book*) & *Anat* appendice *m*. ● **appendicitis** [əpendɪ'saɪtɪs] *n* appendicite *f*.
appetite ['æpɪtaɪt] *n* appétit *m*. ● **appetizer** *n* (*drink*) apéritif *m*; (*food*) amuse-gueule *m inv*. ● **appetizing** *a* appétissant.
applaud [ə'plɔːd] *vt* (*clap*) applaudir; (*approve of*) approuver ▮ *vi* applaudir. ● **applause** *n* applaudissements *mpl*.
apple ['æp(ə)l] *n* pomme *f*; **stewed apples**, *Am* **a. sauce** compote *f* de pommes; **cooking a.** pomme *f* à cuire; **a. pie** tarte *f* aux pommes; **a. tree** pommier *m*.
appliance [ə'plaɪəns] *n* appareil *m*.
applicant ['æplɪkənt] *n* candidat, -ate *mf* (**for** à). ● **application** [-'keɪʃ(ə)n] *n* (*for job*) candidature *f*; (*for membership*) demande *f* d'adhésion; (*request*) demande *f* (**for** de); **a. (form)** (*job*) formulaire *m* de candidature.
apply [ə'plaɪ] **1** *vt* (*put on*, *carry out*) appliquer; (*brake*) *Aut* appuyer sur; **to a. oneself to** s'appliquer à. **2** *vi* (*be relevant*) s'appliquer (**to** à); **to a. for** (*job*) poser sa candidature à; **to a. to s.o.** (*ask*) s'adresser à qn (**for** pour). ● **applied** *a Math Ling etc* appliqué.
appoint [ə'pɔɪnt] *vt* (*person*) nommer (**to sth** à qch); (*director etc*) nommer; (*secretary etc*) engager; (*time*, *place*) fixer; **at the appointed time** à l'heure dite. ● **—ment** *n* nomination *f*; (*meeting*) rendez-vous *m inv*; (*post*) situation *f*.
appraisal [ə'preɪz(ə)l] *n* évaluation *f*.
appreciate [ə'priːʃɪeɪt] **1** *vt* (*enjoy*, *value*) apprécier; (*understand*) comprendre; (*be grateful for*) être reconnaissant de. **2** *vi* prendre de la valeur. ● **appreci'ation** *n* **1** (*gratitude*) reconnaissance *f*; (*judgment*) appréciation *f*. **2** (*rise in value*) augmentation *f* (de la valeur). ● **appreciative** *a* (*grateful*) reconnaissant (**of** de); (*favourable*) élogieux.
apprehensive [æprɪ'hensɪv] *a* inquiet (**about** de, au sujet de).
apprentice [ə'prentɪs] *n* apprenti, -ie *mf*. ● **apprenticeship** *n* apprentissage *m*.
approach [ə'prəʊtʃ] *vt* (*person*, *door etc*) s'approcher de; (*age*, *result*, *town*) approcher de; (*subject*) aborder; (*accost*) aborder (*qn*) ▮ *vi* (*of person*, *vehicle*) s'approcher; (*of date etc*) approcher ▮ *n* (*method*) façon *f* de s'y prendre; (*path*, *route*) (voie *f* d')accès *m*; **at the a. of** à l'approche de.
appropriate [ə'prəʊprɪət] *a* (*place*, *clothes*, *remark*, *means etc*) qui convient (**to** *or* **for sth** à qch). ● **—ly** *adv* convenablement.
approve [ə'pruːv] *vt* approuver; **to a. of sth** approuver qch; **I don't a. of him** il ne me plaît pas; **I a. of his going** je trouve bon qu'il y aille. ● **approval** *n* approbation *f*; **on a.** (*goods*) à l'essai.
approximate [ə'prɒksɪmət] *a* approximatif. ● **—ly** *adv* à peu près, approximativement. ● **approximation** [-'meɪʃ(ə)n] *n* approximation *f*.
apricot ['eɪprɪkɒt] *n* abricot *m*.
April ['eɪprəl] *n* avril *m*; **to make an A. fool of s.o.** faire un poisson d'avril à qn.
apron ['eɪprən] *n* (*garment*) tablier *m*.
apt [æpt] *a* (*remark*, *reply*, *time etc*) qui convient; (*word*, *name*) bien choisi; (*student*) doué; **it's a. to fall** (*likely*) (*in general*) ça a tendance à tomber; (*on particular occasion*) ça pourrait bien tomber. ● **aptitude** *n* aptitude *f* (**for** à, pour); (*of student*) don *m* (**for** pour).
aqualung ['ækwəlʌŋ] *n* scaphandre *m* autonome.
aquarium [ə'kweərɪəm] *n* aquarium *m*.
Aquarius [ə'kweərɪəs] *n* (*sign*) le Verseau.
aquatic [ə'kwætɪk] *a* (*plant etc*) aquatique; (*sport*) nautique.
aqueduct ['ækwɪdʌkt] *n* aqueduc *m*.

Arab ['ærəb] *a* & *n* arabe (*mf*). ● **Arabian** [ə'reɪbɪən] *a* arabe. ● **Arabic** *a* & *n* (*language*) arabe (*m*); **A. numerals** chiffres *mpl* arabes.
arbiter ['ɑ:bɪtər] *n* arbitre *m*. ● **arbitrate** *vti* arbitrer.
arbitrary ['ɑ:bɪtrərɪ] *a* (*decision etc*) arbitraire.
arc [ɑ:k] *n* (*of circle*) arc *m*.
arcade [ɑ:'keɪd] *n* (*for shops*) (*small*) passage *m* couvert; (*large*) galerie *f* marchande.
arch [ɑ:tʃ] *n* (*of bridge*) arche *f*; (*of building*) voûte *f*; (*of foot*) cambrure *f* ‖ *vt* (*one's back etc*) arquer, courber. ● **archway** *n* passage *m* voûté, voûte *f*.
arch(a)eology [ɑ:kɪ'ɒlədʒɪ] *n* archéologie *f*. ● **arch(a)eologist** *n* archéologue *mf*.
archaic [ɑ:'keɪɪk] *a* archaïque.
archbishop [ɑ:tʃ'bɪʃəp] *n* archevêque *m*.
arch-enemy [ɑ:tʃ'enəmɪ] *n* ennemi *m* numéro un.
archer ['ɑ:tʃər] *n* archer *m*. ● **archery** *n* tir *m* à l'arc.
archipelago [ɑ:kɪ'peləgəʊ] *n* (*pl* **-oes** *or* **-os**) archipel *m*.
architect ['ɑ:kɪtekt] *n* architecte *mf*. ● **architecture** *n* architecture *f*.
archives ['ɑ:kaɪvz] *npl* archives *fpl*. ● **archivist** ['ɑ:kɪvɪst] *n* archiviste *mf*.
arctic ['ɑ:ktɪk] *a* arctique; (*weather*) polaire, glacial ‖ *n* **the A.** l'Arctique *m*.
ardent ['ɑ:dənt] *a* (*supporter*) ardent.
arduous ['ɑ:djʊəs] *a* pénible, ardu.
are [ɑ:*r*] *see* **be.**
area ['eərɪə] *n Geog* région *f*; *Geom* superficie *f*; (*of town*) quartier *m*; *Mil* zone *f*; (*domain*) *Fig* domaine *m*, secteur *m*; **parking a.** aire *f* de stationnement; **dining/kitchen a.** coin-repas *m*/coin-cuisine *m*; **a. code** (*phone number*) *Am* indicatif *m*.
arena [ə'ri:nə] *n* (*for sports etc*) & *Fig* arène *f*.
aren't [ɑ:nt] = **are not.**
Argentina [ɑ:dʒən'ti:nə] *n* Argentine *f*. ● **Argentinian** *a* & *n* argentin, -ine (*mf*).
arguab/le ['ɑ:gʊəb(ə)l] *a* discutable. ● **—ly** *adv* on pourrait soutenir que.
argue ['ɑ:gju:] *vi* (*quarrel*) se disputer (**with** avec, **about** au sujet de); (*reason*) raisonner (**with** avec, **about** sur) ‖ *vt* (*matter*) discuter; **to a. that** (*maintain*) soutenir que.
argument ['ɑ:gjʊmənt] *n* (*quarrel*) dispute *f*; (*reasoning*) argument *m*; (*debate*) discussion *f*; **to have an a.** se disputer. ● **argu'mentative** *a* querelleur.
arid ['ærɪd] *a* aride.

Aries ['eəri:z] *n* (*sign*) le Bélier.
arise [ə'raɪz] *vi* (*pt* **arose,** *pp* **arisen**) (*of problem opportunity etc*) se présenter; (*result*) résulter (**from** de).
aristocracy [ærɪ'stɒkrəsɪ] *n* aristocratie *f*. ● **aristocrat** ['ærɪstəkræt, *Am* ə'rɪstəkræt] *n* aristocrate *mf*. ● **aristo'cratic** *a* aristocratique.
arithmetic [ə'rɪθmətɪk] *n* arithmétique *f*.
ark [ɑ:k] *n* **Noah's a.** l'arche *f* de Noé.
arm [ɑ:m] **1** *n* bras *m*; **with open arms** à bras ouverts. **2** *vt* (*with weapon*) armer (**with** de). ● **armband** *n* brassard *m*; (*for swimming*) manchon *m*. ● **armchair** *n* fauteuil *m*. ● **armpit** *n* aisselle *f*. ● **armrest** *n* accoudoir *m*.
armistice ['ɑ:mɪstɪs] *n* armistice *m*.
armour ['ɑ:mər] *n* (*of knight etc*) armure *f*; (*of tank etc*) blindage *m*. ● **armoured** *or* **armour-plated** *a* (*car etc*) blindé.
arms [ɑ:mz] *npl* (*weapons*) armes *fpl*.
army ['ɑ:mɪ] *n* armée *f*; **to join the a.** s'engager ‖ *a* (*uniform etc*) militaire.
aroma [ə'rəʊmə] *n* arôme *m*.
arose [ə'rəʊz] *pt of* **arise.**
around [ə'raʊnd] *prep* autour de; (*approximately*) environ, autour de ‖ *adv* autour; **all a.** tout autour; **to follow s.o. a.** suivre qn partout; **to rush a.** courir çà et là; **a. here** par ici; **he's still a.** il est encore là; **there's a lot of flu a.** il y a pas mal de grippe en ce moment; **up and a.** (*after illness*) *Am* sur pied.
arouse [ə'raʊz] *vt* (*suspicion etc*) éveiller, susciter; (*sexually*) exciter (*qn*).
arrange [ə'reɪndʒ] *vt* arranger; (*time, meeting*) fixer; **it was arranged that** il était convenu que; **to a. to do** s'arranger pour faire. ● **—ment** *n* (*layout, agreement*) arrangement *m*; *pl* préparatifs *mpl*; (*plans*) projets *mpl*; **to make arrangements to** s'arranger pour.
array [ə'reɪ] *n* (*display*) étalage *m*.
arrears [ə'rɪəz] *npl* (*payment*) arriéré *m*; **to be in a.** avoir du retard dans ses paiements.
arrest [ə'rest] *vt* (*criminal*) arrêter ‖ *n* arrestation *f*; **under a.** en état d'arrestation.
arrive [ə'raɪv] *vi* arriver (**at** à). ● **arrival** *n* arrivée *f*; **new a.** nouveau venu *m*, nouvelle venue *f*; (*baby*) nouveau-né, -ée *mf*.
arrogant ['ærəgənt] *a* arrogant. ● **arrogance** *n* arrogance *f*.
arrow ['ærəʊ] *n* flèche *f*.
arsenal ['ɑ:sən(ə)l] *n* arsenal *m*.
arson ['ɑ:s(ə)n] *n* incendie *m* volontaire. ● **arsonist** *n* incendiaire *mf*.
art [ɑ:t] *n* art *m*; **work of a.** œuvre *f* d'art;

faculty of arts faculté *f* des lettres; **a. school** école *f* des beaux-arts.
artery ['ɑːtərɪ] *n Anat Aut* artère *f.*
artful ['ɑːtfəl] *a* rusé, astucieux.
arthritis [ɑː'θraɪtɪs] *n* arthrite *f.*
artichoke ['ɑːtɪtʃəʊk] *n* **(globe) a.** artichaut *m*; **Jerusalem a.** topinambour *m.*
article ['ɑːtɪk(ə)l] *n* (*object, in newspaper*) & *Gram* article *m*; **a. of clothing** vêtement *m*; **articles of value** objets *mpl* de valeur.
articulate [ɑː'tɪkjʊlət] *a* (*person*) qui s'exprime clairement ‖ [ɑː'tɪkjʊleɪt] *vti* (*speak*) articuler; **articulated lorry** semi-remorque *m.*
artificial [ɑːtɪ'fɪʃ(ə)l] *a* artificiel. ● **artificially** *adv* artificiellement.
artillery [ɑː'tɪlərɪ] *n* artillerie *f.*
artist ['ɑːtɪst] *n* (*painter, actor etc*) artiste *mf.* ● **artiste** [ɑː'tiːst] *n* (*singer, dancer*) artiste *m.* ● **ar'tistic** *a* (*pattern etc*) artistique; (*person*) artiste.
artless ['ɑːtləs] *a* naturel, naïf.
as [æz, *unstressed* əz] *adv* & *conj* **1** (*manner etc*) comme; **as you like** comme tu veux; **such as** comme, tel que; **dressed up as a clown** déguisé en clown; **as much** *or* **as hard as I can** (au)tant que je peux; **as it is** (*to leave sth*) comme ça, tel quel; **as if, as though** comme si.
2 (*comparison*) **as tall as you** aussi grand que vous; **is he as tall as you?** est-il aussi *or* si grand que vous?; **as white as a sheet** blanc comme un linge; **as much** *or* **as hard as you** autant que vous; **the same as** le même que; **twice as big as** deux fois plus grand que.
3 (*though*) **(as) clever as he is** si *or* aussi intelligent qu'il soit.
4 (*capacity*) **as a teacher** comme professeur, en tant que professeur; **to act as a father** agir en père.
5 (*reason*) puisque, comme; **as it's late** puisqu'il est tard, comme il est tard.
6 (*time*) **as I was leaving** comme je partais; **as one grows older** à mesure que l'on vieillit; **as he slept** pendant qu'il dormait; **as from, as of** (*time*) à partir de.
7 (*concerning*) **as for that, as to that** quant à cela.
8 (+ *inf*) **so as to** de manière à; **so stupid as to** assez bête pour.
asap [eɪeseɪ'piː] *abbr* (*as soon as possible*) le plus tôt possible.
asbestos [æs'bestəs] *n* amiante *f.*
ascend [ə'send] *vt* (*throne*) monter sur; (*mountain*) faire l'ascension de. ● **ascent** *n* ascension *f* **(of** de); (*slope*) côte *f.*
ascertain [æsə'teɪn] *vt* établir; (*truth*) découvrir; **to a. that** s'assurer que.
ash [æʃ] *n* **1** (*of cigarette etc*) cendre *f*; **A. Wednesday** mercredi *m* des Cendres. **2** (*tree*) frêne *m.* ● **ashtray** *n* cendrier *m.*
ashamed [ə'ʃeɪmd] *a* **to be** *or* **feel a.** avoir honte **(of s.o./sth** de qn/qch); **to be a. of oneself** avoir honte.
ashen ['æʃən] *a* (*face*) pâle.
ashore [ə'ʃɔːr] *adv* **to go a.** débarquer; **to put s.o. a.** débarquer qn.
Asia ['eɪʃə, 'eɪʒə] *n* Asie *f.* ● **Asian** *a* asiatique ‖ *n* Asiatique *mf.*
aside [ə'saɪd] *adv* de côté; **to take** *or* **draw s.o. a.** prendre qn à part; **to step a.** s'écarter; **a. from** *Am* en dehors de.
ask [ɑːsk] *vt* demander; (*invite*) inviter **(to** à); **to a. (s.o.) a question** poser une question (à qn); **to a. s.o. (for) sth** demander qch à qn; **to a. s.o. to do** demander à qn de faire; **to a. to do** demander à faire.
‖ *vi* demander; **to a. for sth/s.o.** demander qch/qn; **to a. for sth back** redemander qch; **to a. about sth** se renseigner sur qch; **to a. after** *or* **about s.o.** demander des nouvelles de qn; **to a. s.o. about sth/s.o.** interroger qn sur qch/qn; **asking price** prix *m* demandé.
askance [ə'skɑːns] *adv* **to look a. at** regarder avec méfiance.
askew [ə'skjuː] *adv* de biais, de travers.
asleep [ə'sliːp] *a* endormi; **to be a.** dormir; **to fall a.** s'endormir.
asparagus [ə'spærəgəs] *n* (*shoots for cooking*) asperges *fpl.*
aspect ['æspekt] *n* aspect *m*; (*of house*) orientation *f.*
asphyxiate [əs'fɪksɪeɪt] *vt* asphyxier.
aspire [ə'spaɪər] *vi* **to a. to** aspirer à. ● **aspiration** [æspə'reɪʃ(ə)n] *n* aspiration *f.*
aspirin ['æsprɪn] *n* aspirine *f.*
ass [æs] *n* (*animal*) âne *m*; (*person*) *Fam* imbécile *mf*, âne *m.*
assailant [ə'seɪlənt] *n* agresseur *m.*
assassin [ə'sæsɪn] *n Pol* assassin *m.* ● **assassinate** *vt* assassiner. ● **assassination** [-'neɪʃ(ə)n] *n* assassinat *m.*
assault [ə'sɔːlt] *n Mil* assaut *m*; (*crime*) agression *f* ‖ *vt* (*attack*) agresser; (*woman*) violenter.
assemble [ə'semb(ə)l] *vt* (*objects, ideas*) assembler; (*people*) rassembler; (*machine*) monter ‖ *vi* se rassembler. ● **assembly** *n* (*meeting*) assemblée *f*; *Sch* rassemblement *m*; **a. line** (*in factory*) chaîne *f* de montage.
assert [ə'sɜːt] *vt* affirmer **(that** que); (*rights*) revendiquer. ● **assertion** [-ʃ(ə)n] *n* (*statement*) affirmation *f.*

assess [ə'ses] *vt* (*estimate*) évaluer; (*decide amount of*) fixer le montant de. ●**—ment** *n* évaluation *f*.

asset ['æset] *n* (*advantage*) atout *m*; *pl* (*of business*) biens *mpl*.

assign [ə'saɪn] *vt* (*give*) attribuer; (*day etc*) fixer; (*appoint*) nommer. ●**—ment** *n* (*task*) mission *f*; *Sch* devoir *m*.

assimilate [ə'sɪmɪleɪt] *vt* assimiler ‖ *vi* s'assimiler.

assist [ə'sɪst] *vti* aider (**in doing, to do** à faire). ●**assistance** *n* aide *f*; **to be of a. to s.o.** aider qn. ●**assistant** *n* assistant, -ante *mf*; (*in shop*) vendeur, -euse *mf* ‖ *a* adjoint.

associate [ə'səʊʃɪeɪt] *vt* associer (**with sth** à *or* avec qch, **with s.o.** à qn) ‖ *vi* **to a. with s.o.** (*mix socially*) fréquenter qn; (*in business venture*) s'associer à *or* avec qn ‖ [ə'səʊʃɪət] *n* & *a* associé, -ée (*mf*). ●**association** [-'eɪʃ(ə)n] *n* association *f*.

assorted [ə'sɔːtɪd] *a* (*different*) variés; (*foods*) assortis. ●**assortment** *n* assortiment *m*.

assume [ə'sjuːm] *vt* **1** (*suppose*) supposer, présumer (**that** que). **2** (*take on*) prendre; (*responsibility, role*) assumer; (*attitude, name*) adopter; **assumed name** nom *m* d'emprunt. ●**assumption** [ə'sʌmpʃ(ə)n] *n* supposition *f*.

assure [ə'ʃʊər] *vt* assurer (**s.o. that** à qn que, **s.o. of** qn de). ●**assurance** *n* assurance *f*.

asterisk ['æstərɪsk] *n* astérisque *m*.

asthma ['æsmə] *n* asthme *m*. ●**asth'matic** *a* & *n* asthmatique (*mf*).

astonish [ə'stɒnɪʃ] *vt* étonner; **to be astonished** s'étonner (**at sth** de qch). ●**—ing** *a* étonnant. ●**astonishment** *n* étonnement *m*.

astound [ə'staʊnd] *vt* stupéfier, étonner. ●**—ing** *a* stupéfiant.

astray [ə'streɪ] *adv* **to go a.** s'égarer; **to lead a.** égarer.

astride [ə'straɪd] *adv* à califourchon ‖ *prep* à cheval sur.

astrology [ə'strɒlədʒɪ] *n* astrologie *f*. ●**astrologer** *n* astrologue *mf*.

astronaut ['æstrənɔːt] *n* astronaute *mf*.

astronomy [ə'strɒnəmɪ] *n* astronomie *f*. ●**astronomer** *n* astronome *mf*.

astute [ə'stjuːt] *a* (*crafty*) rusé; (*clever*) astucieux.

asylum [ə'saɪləm] *n* asile *m*.

at [æt, *unstressed* ət] *prep* **1** à; **at the end** à la fin; **at work** au travail; **at six (o'clock)** à six heures; **at Easter** à Pâques.
2 chez; **at the doctor's** chez le médecin; **at home** chez soi, à la maison.
3 en; **at sea** en mer; **at war** en guerre; **good at** (*geography etc*) fort en.
4 contre; **angry at** fâché contre.
5 sur; **to shoot at** tirer sur; **at my request** sur ma demande.
6 de; **to laugh at** rire de; **surprised at** surpris de.
7 (au)près de; **at the window** (au)près de la fenêtre.
8 par; **to come in at the door** entrer par la porte; **six at a time** six par six.
9 (*phrases*) **at night** la nuit; **to look at** regarder; **to be (hard) at it** travailler dur; **he's always (on) at me** *Fam* il est toujours après moi.

ate [et, *Am* eɪt] *pt of* **eat**.

atheist ['eɪθɪɪst] *n* athée *mf*.

Athens ['æθɪnz] *n* Athènes *m or f*.

athlete ['æθliːt] *n* athlète *mf*. ●**ath'letic** *a* athlétique; **a. meeting** réunion *f* sportive. ●**ath'letics** *npl* athlétisme *m*.

Atlantic [ət'læntɪk] *a* (*coast*) atlantique ‖ *n* **the A.** l'Atlantique *m*.

atlas ['ætləs] *n* atlas *m*.

atmosphere ['ætməsfɪər] *n* atmosphère *f*.

atom ['ætəm] *n* atome *m*; **a. bomb** bombe *f* atomique. ●**a'tomic** *a* (*bomb etc*) atomique.

atone [ə'təʊn] *vi* **to a. for** expier.

atrocious [ə'trəʊʃəs] *a* atroce. ●**atrocity** *n* atrocité *f*.

attach [ə'tætʃ] *vt* attacher (**to** à); (*document*) joindre (**to** à); **attached to** (*fond of*) attaché à. ●**—ment** *n* (*tool*) accessoire *m*; (*affection*) attachement *m* (**to s.o.** à qn).

attaché case [ə'tæʃeɪkeɪs] *n* attaché-case *m*, mallette *f*.

attack [ə'tæk] *n* attaque *f*; (*of illness*) crise *f*; **heart a.** crise *f* cardiaque ‖ *vti* attaquer. ●**—er** *n* agresseur *m*.

attain [ə'teɪn] *vt* (*aim, rank*) parvenir à; (*ambition*) réaliser.

attempt [ə'tempt] *n* tentative *f*; **to make an a. to do** tenter de faire; **a. on s.o.'s life** attentat *m* contre qn ‖ *vt* tenter; (*task*) entreprendre; **to a. to do** tenter de faire; **attempted murder** tentative *f* de meurtre.

attend [ə'tend] *vt* (*meeting etc*) assister à; (*course*) suivre; (*school, church*) aller à; (*patient*) soigner; **well-attended** (*course*) très suivi; (*meeting*) où il y a du monde ‖ *vi* assister; **to a. to** (*take care of*) s'occuper de (*travail, client etc*).

attendance [ə'tendəns] *n* présence *f* (**at** à); **(school) a.** scolarité *f*; **in a.** de service. ●**attendant** *n* employé, -ée *mf*; (*in service station*) pompiste *mf*; (*in museum*) gardien, -ienne *mf*.

attention [ə'tenʃ(ə)n] *n* attention *f*; **to pay a.** faire attention (**to** à); **a.!** *Mil* garde-à-vous!; **a. to detail** minutie *f*. ● **attentive** *a* (*heedful*) attentif (**to** à); (*thoughtful*) attentionné (**to** pour).
attic ['ætɪk] *n* grenier *m*.
attitude ['ætɪtju:d] *n* attitude *f*.
attorney [ə'tɜ:nɪ] *n* (*lawyer*) *Am* avocat *m*; **district a.** *Am* = procureur *m* (de la République).
attract [ə'trækt] *vt* attirer. ● **attraction** [-ʃ(ə)n] *n* (*charm, appeal*) attrait *m*; (*person, place etc*) attraction *f*; (*between people*) attirance *f*.
attractive [ə'træktɪv] *a* (*house, car etc*) beau (*f* belle); (*price, offer etc*) intéressant; **a. girl** belle fille *f*; **a. boy** beau garçon *m*.
attribute 1 ['ætrɪbju:t] *n* (*quality*) attribut *m*. **2** [ə'trɪbju:t] *vt* (*ascribe*) attribuer (**to** à).
aubergine ['əʊbəʒi:n] *n* aubergine *f*.
auburn ['ɔ:bən] *a* (*hair*) châtain roux.
auction ['ɔ:kʃən] *n* vente *f* (aux enchères) ‖ *vt* **to a. (off)** vendre (aux enchères). ● **auctio'neer** *n* commissaire-priseur *m*.
audacity [ɔ:'dæsətɪ] *n* audace *f*.
audible ['ɔ:dɪb(ə)l] *a* perceptible.
audience ['ɔ:dɪəns] *n* (*of speaker, musician*) auditoire *m*, public *m*; *Th Cin* spectateurs *mpl*, public *m*; *Rad* auditeurs *mpl*; (*interview*) audience *f*; **TV a.** téléspectateurs *mpl*.
audio ['ɔ:dɪəʊ] *a* (*cassette etc*) audio *inv*. ● **audiotypist** *n* dactylo *f* au magnétophone, audiotypiste *mf*. ● **audio-'visual** *a* audiovisuel.
audit ['ɔ:dɪt] *vt* (*accounts*) vérifier. ● **auditor** *n* commissaire *m* aux comptes.
audition [ɔ:'dɪʃ(ə)n] *n* audition *f* ‖ *vti* auditionner.
augur ['ɔ:gər] *vi* **to a. well** être de bon augure.
August ['ɔ:gəst] *n* août *m*.
aunt [ɑ:nt] *n* tante *f*. ● **auntie** *or* **aunty** *n Fam* tata *f*.
au pair [əʊ'peər] *adv* au pair ‖ *n* **au p. (girl)** jeune fille *f* au pair.
aura ['ɔ:rə] *n* (*of place*) atmosphère *f*; (*of person*) aura *f*.
austere [ɔ:'stɪər] *a* austère. ● **austerity** *n* austérité *f*.
Australia [ɒ'streɪlɪə] *n* Australie *f*. ● **Australian** *a* & *n* australien, -ienne (*mf*).
Austria ['ɒstrɪə] *n* Autriche *f*. ● **Austrian** *a* & *n* autrichien, -ienne (*mf*).
authentic [ɔ:'θentɪk] *a* authentique. ● **authenticate** *vt* authentifier.
author ['ɔ:θər] *n* auteur *m*.
authority [ɔ:'θɒrɪtɪ] *n* autorité *f*; (*permission*) autorisation *f* (**to do** de faire); **to be in a.** (*in charge*) être responsable. ● **authori'tarian** *a* & *n* autoritaire (*mf*). ● **authoritative** *a* (*report, book*) qui fait autorité; (*tone, person*) autoritaire.
authorize ['ɔ:θəraɪz] *vt* autoriser (**to do** à faire). ● **authorization** [-'zeɪʃ(ə)n] *n* autorisation *f* (**to do** de faire).
autistic [ɔ:'tɪstɪk] *a* autiste.
autobiography [ɔ:təʊbaɪ'ɒgrəfɪ] *n* autobiographie *f*.
autocratic [ɔ:tə'krætɪk] *a* autocratique.
autograph ['ɔ:təgrɑ:f] *n* autographe *m* ‖ *vt* dédicacer (**for** à).
automatic [ɔ:tə'mætɪk] *a* automatique. ● **automatically** *adv* automatiquement.
automation [ɔ:tə'meɪʃ(ə)n] *n* automatisation *f*.
automobile ['ɔ:təməbi:l] *n Am* auto(mobile) *f*.
autonomous [ɔ:'tɒnəməs] *a* autonome. ● **autonomy** *n* autonomie *f*.
autopsy ['ɔ:tɒpsɪ] *n* autopsie *f*.
autumn ['ɔ:təm] *n* automne *m*; **in (the) a.** en automne.
auxiliary [ɔ:g'zɪljərɪ] *a* & *n* auxiliaire (*mf*); **a. (verb)** (verbe *m*) auxiliaire *m*.
avail [ə'veɪl] **1** *vt* **to a. oneself of** tirer avantage de. **2** *n* **to no a.** en vain.
available [ə'veɪləb(ə)l] *a* (*thing, person*) disponible; **a. to all** (*education etc*) accessible à tous. ● **availa'bility** *n* disponibilité *f*.
avalanche ['ævəlɑ:nʃ] *n* avalanche *f*.
Ave *abbr* = **avenue**.
avenge [ə'vendʒ] *vt* venger; **to a. oneself** se venger (**on** de).
avenue ['ævənju:] *n* avenue *f*; (*way to a result*) *Fig* voie *f*.
average ['ævərɪdʒ] *n* moyenne *f*; **on a.** en moyenne ‖ *a* moyen ‖ *vt* (*do*) faire en moyenne; (*reach*) atteindre la moyenne de.
averse [ə'vɜ:s] *a* **to be a. to doing** répugner à faire.
avert [ə'vɜ:t] *vt* (*prevent*) éviter.
aviary ['eɪvɪərɪ] *n* volière *f*.
aviation [eɪvɪ'eɪʃ(ə)n] *n* aviation *f*.
avid ['ævɪd] *a* avide (**for** de).
avocado [ævə'kɑ:dəʊ] *n* (*pl* **-os**) **a. (pear)** avocat *m*.
avoid [ə'vɔɪd] *vt* éviter; **to a. doing** éviter de faire. ● **—able** *a* évitable.
await [ə'weɪt] *vt* attendre.
awake [ə'weɪk] *vi* (*pt* **awoke**, *pp* **awoken**) se réveiller ‖ *vt* réveiller ‖ *a* **(wide-)a.** éveillé; **to keep s.o. a.** empêcher qn de dormir; **he's (still) a.** il ne dort pas (encore). ● **awaken 1** *vti* = **awake**. **2** *vt* **to a. s.o. to sth** faire

prendre conscience de qch à qn. ● **awakening** *n* réveil *m*.

award [ə'wɔːd] *vt* (*money*, *prize*) attribuer; (*damages*) accorder ‖ *n* (*prize*) prix *m*, récompense *f*; (*scholarship*) bourse *f*.

aware [ə'weər] *a* **a. of** (*conscious*) conscient de; (*informed*) au courant de; **to become a. of** se rendre compte de, prendre conscience de; **to be** *or* **become a. that** (*realize*) se rendre compte que. ● **—ness** *n* conscience *f*.

awash [ə'wɒʃ] *a* inondé (**with** de).

away [ə'weɪ] *adv* **1** (*distant*) loin; **far a.** au loin, très loin; **5 km a.** à 5 km (de distance).
2 (*in time*) **ten days a.** dans dix jours.
3 (*absent*, *gone*) parti, absent; **a. with you!** va-t-en!; **to drive a.** partir (en voiture); **to fade a.** disparaître complètement.
4 (*continuously*) **to work/talk/***etc* **a.** travailler/parler/*etc* sans arrêt.
5 to play a. *Sp* jouer à l'extérieur.

awe [ɔː] *n* crainte *f* (*mêlée de respect*). ● **awesome** *a* (*impressive*) imposant; (*frightening*) effrayant; (*marvellous*) *Fam* super.

awful ['ɔːfəl] *a* affreux; (*terrifying*) épouvantable; (*ill*) malade; **an a. lot of** *Fam* un nombre incroyable de; **I feel a. (about it)** j'ai vraiment honte. ● **—ly** *adv* (*very*) (*good*, *pretty etc*) extrêmement; (*bad*, *late etc*) affreusement.

awhile [ə'waɪl] *adv* (*to stay*, *wait*) un peu.

awkward ['ɔːkwəd] *a* **1** (*clumsy*) maladroit. **2** (*difficult*) difficile; (*cumbersome*) gênant; (*tool*) peu commode; (*time*) mal choisi; (*silence*) gêné. ● **—ly** *adv* maladroitement; (*placed*) à un endroit peu pratique.

awning ['ɔːnɪŋ] *n* (*over shop*, *window*) store *m*; (*of hotel*) marquise *f*.

awoke, awoken [ə'wəʊk, ə'wəʊk(ə)n] *pt & pp of* **awake**.

axe [æks] (*Am* **ax**) *n* hache *f*; (*reduction*) *Fig* coupe *f* sombre ‖ *vt* réduire; (*job etc*) supprimer.

axis, *pl* **axes** ['æksɪs, 'æksiːz] *n* axe *m*.

axle ['æks(ə)l] *n* essieu *m*.

B

B, b [biː] *n* B, b *m*; **2B** (*number*) 2 ter.
BA *abbr* = **Bachelor of Arts.**
babble ['bæb(ə)l] *vi* (*mumble*) bredouiller ▮ *n inv* (*of voices*) rumeur *f*.
baboon [bə'buːn] *n* babouin *m*.
baby ['beɪbɪ] *n* bébé *m*; **b. boy** petit garçon *m*; **b. girl** petite fille *f*; **b. tiger**/*etc* bébé-tigre/*etc m*; **b. clothes/ toys**/*etc* vêtements *mpl*/jouets *mpl*/*etc* de bébé; **b. carriage** *Am* voiture *f* d'enfant. ● **b.-minder** *n* gardien, -ienne *mf* d'enfants. ● **b.-sit** *vi* (*pt & pp* **-sat,** *pres p* **-sitting**) garder les enfants, faire du baby-sitting. ● **b.-sitter** *n* baby-sitter *mf*. ● **b.-walker** *n* trotteur *m*, youpala® *m*.
babyish ['beɪbɪɪʃ] *a Pej* de bébé; (*puerile*) enfantin.
bachelor ['bætʃələr] *n* **1** célibataire *m*. **2 B. of Arts/of Science** licencié, -ée *mf* ès lettres/ès sciences.
back[1] [bæk] *n* (*of person, animal*) dos *m*; (*of chair*) dossier *m*; (*of hand*) revers *m*; (*of house*) arrière *m*, derrière *m*; (*of vehicle, head*) arrière *m*; (*of room*) fond *m*; (*of page*) verso *m*; (*of fabric*) envers *m*; *Fb* arrière *m*; **at the b. of** (*book*) à la fin de; **in the b. of** (*vehicle*) à l'arrière de; **b. to front** devant derrière, à l'envers; **to get s.o.'s b. up** *Fam* irriter qn; **in b. of** *Am* derrière.
back[2] [bæk] *a* (*wheel, seat*) arrière *inv*; **b. door** porte *f* de derrière; **b. room** pièce *f* du fond; **b. number** (*of magazine etc*) vieux numéro *m*; **b. pay** rappel *m* de salaire; **b. street** rue *f* écartée; **b. tooth** molaire *f*.
back[3] [bæk] *adv* (*behind*) en arrière; **far b., a long way b.** loin derrière; **a month b.** il y a un mois; **to stand b.** (*of house*) être en retrait (**from** par rapport à); **to go b. and forth** aller et venir; **to come b.** revenir; **he's b.** il est de retour, il est revenu; **the trip there and b.** le voyage aller et retour.
back[4] [bæk] *vt* (*with money*) financer; (*horse etc*) parier sur, jouer; (*vehicle*) faire reculer; **to b. s.o (up)** (*support*) appuyer qn; **to b. up** *Comptr* sauvegarder.
▮ *vi* **to b. down** se dégonfler; **to b. out** (*withdraw*) se retirer; (*of vehicle*) sortir en marche arrière; **to b. up** (*of vehicle*) faire marche arrière.
backache ['bækeɪk] *n* mal *m* de dos. ● **back'bencher** *n Pol* membre *m* sans portefeuille. ● **backcloth** *n* toile *f* de fond. ● **back'date** *vt* (*cheque, Am check*) antidater. ● **back'handed** *a* (*compliment*) équivoque. ● **backhander** *n* (*bribe*) *Fam* pot-de-vin *m*. ● **backpack** *n* sac *m* à dos. ● **backrest** *n* dossier *m*. ● **backside** *n* (*buttocks*) *Fam* derrière *m*. ● **back'stage** *adv* dans les coulisses. ● **backstroke** *n Sp* dos *m* crawlé. ● **backup** *n* (*support*) appui *m*; (*tailback*) *Am* embouteillage *m*; *Comptr* sauvegarde *f*; **b. lights** *Aut Am* feux *mpl* de recul. ● **backwater** *n* (*place*) trou *m* perdu. ● **back'yard** *n* arrière-cour *f*; *Am* jardin *m* (*à l'arrière d'une maison*).
backbone ['bækbəʊn] *n* colonne *f* vertébrale; (*main support*) pivot *m*.
backer ['bækər] *n* (*supporter*) partisan *m*; *Sp* parieur, -euse *mf*; *Fin* bailleur *m* de fonds.
backfire [bæk'faɪər] *vi* **1** *Aut* pétarader. **2** (*of plot etc*) échouer.
backgammon ['bækgæmən] *n* trictrac *m*.
background ['bækgraʊnd] *n* fond *m*; (*events*) *Fig* antécédents *mpl*; (*education*) formation *f*; (*environment*) milieu *m*; (*social, political etc conditions*) contexte *m*; **b. music** musique *f* de fond.
backing ['bækɪŋ] *n* (*aid*) soutien *m*; (*material*) support *m*, renfort *m*.
backlash ['bæklæʃ] *n* retour *m* de flamme.
backlog ['bæklɒg] *n* **b. of work** travail *m* en retard.
backward ['bækwəd] *a* (*person, country etc*) arriéré; (*glance etc*) en arrière ▮ *adv* = **backwards.** ● **—ness** *n* (*of country etc*) retard *m*. ● **backwards** *adv* en arrière; (*to walk*) à reculons; (*to fall*) à la renverse; **to go** *or* **move b.** reculer; **to go b. and forwards** aller et venir.
bacon ['beɪkən] *n* lard *m*; (*in rashers*) bacon *m*; **b. and eggs** œufs *mpl* au bacon.
bacteria [bæk'tɪərɪə] *npl* bactéries *fpl*.
bad [bæd] *a* (**worse, worst**) mauvais; (*wicked*) méchant; (*accident, wound etc*) grave; (*tooth*) carié; (*arm, leg*) malade; (*pain*) violent; **to feel b.** (*ill*) se sentir mal; **things are b.** ça va mal; **not b.!** pas mal!; **to go b.** (*of fruit, meat*) se gâter; (*of milk*) tourner; **too b.!** tant pis! ● **b.-'mannered** *a* mal élevé. ● **b.-'tempered** *a* grincheux.
badge [bædʒ] *n* (*of plastic*) badge *m*; (*of*

metal, bearing logo) pin's *m*; (*of postman, policeman*) plaque *f*; (*on school uniform*) insigne *m*.

badger ['bædʒər] *n* (*animal*) blaireau *m*.

badly ['bædlɪ] *adv* mal; (*hurt*) grièvement; **b. affected** très touché; **to be b. mistaken** se tromper lourdement; **b. off** dans la gêne; **to want b.** avoir grande envie de.

badminton ['bædmɪntən] *n* badminton *m*.

baffle ['bæf(ə)l] *vt* (*person*) déconcerter.

bag [bæg] **1** *n* sac *m*; *pl* (*luggage*) valises *fpl*, bagages *mpl*; (*under the eyes*) poches *fpl*; **bags of** *Fam* (*lots of*) beaucoup de; **an old b.** une vieille taupe. **2** *vt* (**-gg-**) (*take, steal*) *Fam* piquer.

baggage ['bægɪdʒ] *n* bagages *mpl*; **b. car** *Am* fourgon *m*; **b. handler** bagagiste *m*; **b. room** *Am* consigne *f*.

baggy ['bægɪ] *a* (**-ier, -iest**) (*trousers, Am pants*) faisant des poches.

bagpipes ['bægpaɪps] *npl* cornemuse *f*.

Bahamas [bə'hɑːməz] *npl* **the B.** les Bahamas *fpl*.

bail [beɪl] **1** *n Jur* caution *f*; **on b.** en liberté provisoire ‖ *vt* **to b. (out)** fournir une caution pour; **to b. out** (*person, company*) venir en aide à. **2** *vi* **to b. out** *Av* sauter (en parachute).

bailiff ['beɪlɪf] *n Jur* huissier *m*.

bait [beɪt] **1** *n* amorce *f*, appât *m*. **2** *vt* (*annoy*) asticoter, tourmenter.

bak/e [beɪk] *vt* (faire) cuire (au four) ‖ *vi* (*of cook*) faire de la pâtisserie *or* du pain; (*of cake etc*) cuire (au four); **it's baking (hot)** *Fam* on cuit. • **—ed** *a* (*potatoes, apples*) au four; **b. beans** haricots *mpl* blancs (à la tomate). • **—ing** *n* cuisson *f*.

baker ['beɪkər] *n* boulanger, -ère *mf*. • **bakery** *n* boulangerie *f*.

balaclava [bælə'klɑːvə] *n* **b. (helmet)** passe-montagne *m*.

balance ['bæləns] *n* équilibre *m*; (*of account*) solde *m*; (*remainder*) reste *m*; *Econ Pol* balance *f*; **to lose one's b.** perdre l'équilibre; **to strike a b.** trouver le juste milieu; **in the b.** incertain; **b. sheet** bilan *m* ‖ *vt* tenir en équilibre (**on** sur); (*budget, account*) équilibrer; (*compensate for*) compenser ‖ *vi* (*of person*) se tenir en équilibre, s'équilibrer; (*of accounts*) être en équilibre; **to b. out** (*even out*) s'équilibrer.

balcony ['bælkənɪ] *n* balcon *m*.

bald [bɔːld] *a* (**-er, -est**) chauve; (*tyre, Am tire*) lisse; **b. patch** tonsure *f*. • **b.-'headed** *a* chauve. • **baldness** *n* calvitie *f*.

bale [beɪl] **1** *n* (*of cotton etc*) balle *f*. **2** *vi* **to b. out** *Av* sauter (en parachute).

balk [bɔːk] *vi* reculer (**at** devant).

ball[1] [bɔːl] *n* balle *f*; (*inflated*) *Fb Rugby etc* ballon *m*; *Billiards* bille *f*; (*of string, wool*) pelote *f*; (*sphere*) boule *f*; (*of meat or fish*) boulette *f*; **on the b.** (*alert*) *Fam* éveillé; **he's on the b.** (*efficient, knowledgeable*) *Fam* il connaît son affaire, il est au point; **it's a whole new b. game** *Am* c'est une tout autre affaire.

ball[2] [bɔːl] *n* (*dance*) bal *m* (*pl* bals).

ballad ['bæləd] *n* (*poem*) ballade *f*.

ballast ['bæləst] *n* lest *m*.

ballet ['bæleɪ] *n* ballet *m*. • **balle'rina** *n* ballerine *f*.

balloon [bə'luːn] *n* (*toy*) & *Av* ballon *m*.

ballot ['bælət] *n* (*voting*) scrutin *m*.

ballpoint ['bɔːlpɔɪnt] *n* **b. (pen)** stylo *m* à bille.

ballroom ['bɔːlruːm] *n* salle *f* de danse.

balmy ['bɑːmɪ] *a* (**-ier, -iest**) (*crazy*) *Fam* dingue, timbré.

Baltic ['bɔːltɪk] *n* **the B.** la Baltique.

bamboo [bæm'buː] *n* bambou *m*.

ban [bæn] *n* interdiction *f* ‖ *vt* (**-nn-**) interdire; **to ban s.o. from doing** interdire à qn de faire; **to b. from** (*club etc*) exclure de.

banal [bə'nɑːl, *Am* 'beɪn(ə)l] *a* banal (*mpl* -als).

banana [bə'nɑːnə] *n* banane *f*.

band [bænd] **1** *n* (*strip*) bande *f*; **rubber** *or* **elastic b.** élastique *m*. **2** *n* (*group of people*) bande *f*; *Mus* (petit) orchestre *m*; (*pop group*) groupe *m*; **(brass) b.** fanfare *f* ‖ *vi* **to b. together** se grouper.

bandage ['bændɪdʒ] *n* (*strip*) bande *f*; (*dressing*) bandage *m* ‖ *vt* **to b. (up)** (*arm, leg*) bander; (*wound*) mettre un bandage sur.

Band-Aid® ['bændeɪd] *n* pansement *m* adhésif.

bandit ['bændɪt] *n* bandit *m*.

bandwagon ['bændwægən] *n* **to jump on the b.** *Fig* suivre le mouvement.

bandy[1] ['bændɪ] *a* (**-ier, -iest**) (*person*) bancal (*mpl* -als); (*legs*) arqué. • **b.-'legged** *a* bancal (*mpl* -als).

bandy[2] ['bændɪ] *vt* **to b. about** (*story etc*) faire circuler.

bang[1] [bæŋ] *n* (*noise*) coup *m* (violent); (*of gun*) détonation *f*; (*of door*) claquement *m* ‖ *vt* cogner, frapper; (*door*) (faire) claquer; **to b. one's head** se cogner la tête; **to b. down** (*lid*) rabattre (violemment) ‖ *vi* cogner, frapper; (*of door*) claquer; **to b. into sth/s.o.** heurter qch/qn ‖ *int* vlan!, pan!; **to go (off) b.** éclater.

bang[2] [bæŋ] *adv Fam* (*exactly*) exactement;

b. in the middle en plein milieu; **b. on six** à six heures tapantes.

banger ['bæŋər] *n* **1** *Culin Fam* saucisse *f*. **2** **old b.** (*car*) *Fam* tacot *m*.

bangle ['bæŋg(ə)l] *n* bracelet *m* (rigide).

bangs [bæŋz] *npl* (*of hair*) *Am* frange *f*.

banish ['bænɪʃ] *vt* bannir.

banister ['bænɪstər] *n* **banister(s)** rampe *f* (d'escalier).

banjo ['bændʒəʊ] *n* (*pl* **-os** *or* **-oes**) banjo *m*.

bank [bæŋk] **1** *n* (*of river*) bord *m*; (*raised*) berge *f*; **the Left B.** (*in Paris*) la Rive gauche.

2 *n Com* banque *f*; **b. account** compte *m* en banque; **b. card** carte *f* d'identité bancaire; **b. holiday** jour *m* férié; **b. note** billet *m* de banque; **b. rate** taux *m* d'escompte ‖ *vt* (*money*) mettre en banque ‖ *vi* avoir un compte en banque (**with** à).

3 *vi* (*of aircraft*) virer.

4 *vi* **to b. on s.o./sth** (*rely on*) compter sur qn/qch. •**—ing** *a* bancaire ‖ *n* (*activity*) la banque. •**banker** *n* banquier *m*.

bankrupt ['bæŋkrʌpt] *a* **to go b.** faire faillite ‖ *vt* mettre en faillite. •**bankruptcy** *n* faillite *f*.

banner ['bænər] *n* (*at rallies, on two poles*) banderole *f*; (*flag*) bannière *f*.

banns [bænz] *npl* bans *mpl*.

banquet ['bæŋkwɪt] *n* banquet *m*.

banter ['bæntər] *vti* plaisanter ‖ *n* plaisanterie *f*.

baptism ['bæptɪzəm] *n* baptême *m*. •**bap'tize** *vt* baptiser.

bar [bɑːr] **1** *n* barre *f*; (*of gold*) lingot *m*; (*of chocolate*) tablette *f*; (*on window*) barreau *m*; **b. of soap** savonnette *f*; **behind bars** (*criminal*) sous les verrous; **the B.** *Jur* le barreau.

2 *n* (*pub, counter*) bar *m*.

3 *n* (*group of notes*) *Mus* mesure *f*.

4 *vt* (**-rr-**) **to b. s.o.'s way** bloquer le passage à qn.

5 *vt* (*prohibit*) interdire (**s.o. from doing** à qn de faire); (*exclude*) exclure (**from** à). •**barmaid** *n* serveuse *f* de bar. •**barman** *or* **bartender** *n* barman *m*.

Barbados [bɑː'beɪdɒs] *n* Barbade *f*.

barbarian [bɑː'beərɪən] *n* barbare *mf*. •**barbaric** *a* barbare.

barbecue ['bɑːbɪkjuː] *n* barbecue *m* ‖ *vt* griller (au barbecue).

barbed wire[bɑːbd'waɪər] *n* fil *m* de fer barbelé; (*fence*) barbelés *mpl*.

barber ['bɑːbər] *n* coiffeur *m* (*pour hommes*).

bare [beər] *a* (**-er, -est**) nu; (*tree etc*) dénudé; (*cupboard, Am closet*) vide; **the b. necessities** le strict nécessaire; **with his b. hands** à mains nues. •**barefoot** *adv* nu-pieds ‖ *a* aux pieds nus. •**bare'headed** *a* & *adv* nu-tête *inv*.

barely ['beəlɪ] *adv* (*scarcely*) à peine.

bargain ['bɑːgɪn] *n* (*deal*) marché *m*, affaire *f*; **a b.** (*cheap buy*) une occasion, une bonne affaire; **to make a b.** faire un marché (**with** avec); **into the b.** par-dessus le marché; **b. price** prix *m* exceptionnel; **b. counter** rayon *m* des soldes ‖ *vi* (*negotiate*) négocier; (*haggle*) marchander; **to b. for sth** (*expect*) s'attendre à qch.

barge [bɑːdʒ] **1** *n* chaland *m*, péniche *f*. **2** *vi* **to b. in** (*enter a room*) faire irruption; (*interrupt s.o.*) interrompre; **to b. into** (*hit*) se cogner contre.

bark [bɑːk] **1** *n* (*of tree*) écorce *f*. **2** *vi* (*of dog*) aboyer ‖ *n* aboiement *m*. •**—ing** *n* aboiements *mpl*.

barley ['bɑːlɪ] *n* orge *f*.

barmy [bɑːmɪ] *a* (**-ier, -iest**) (*crazy*) *Fam* dingue, timbré.

barn [bɑːn] *n* (*for crops etc*) grange *f*; •**barnyard** *n* basse-cour *f*.

barometer [bə'rɒmɪtər] *n* baromètre *m*.

baron ['bærən] *n* baron *m*; **press/oil b.** magnat *m* de la presse/du pétrole. •**baroness** *n* baronne *f*.

barracks ['bærəks] *npl* caserne *f*.

barrage ['bærɑːʒ, *Am* bə'rɑːʒ] *n* (*across river*) barrage *m*; **a b. of** (*questions etc*) un feu roulant de.

barrel ['bærəl] *n* **1** (*cask*) tonneau *m*; (*of oil*) baril *m*. **2** (*of gun*) canon *m*.

barren ['bærən] *a* stérile; (*style*) *Fig* aride.

barrette [bə'ret] *n* (*hair slide*) *Am* barrette *f*.

barricade ['bærɪkeɪd] *n* barricade *f* ‖ *vt* barricader; **to b. oneself (in)** se barricader.

barrier ['bærɪər] *n* barrière *f*; *Fig* obstacle *m*, barrière *f*; **(ticket) b.** *Rail* portillon *m*.

barring ['bɑːrɪŋ] *prep* sauf, excepté.

barrister ['bærɪstər] *n* avocat *m*.

barrow ['bærəʊ] *n* (*wheelbarrow*) brouette *f*; (*cart*) charrette *f* à bras.

barter ['bɑːtər] *vt* troquer, échanger (**for** contre) ‖ *n* troc *m*, échange *m*.

base [beɪs] **1** *n* (*bottom*) base *f*; (*of tree, lamp*) pied *m*. **2** *n Mil* base *f*. **3** *vt* baser, fonder (**on** sur); **based in London** basé à Londres. •**baseboard** *n Am* plinthe *f*.

baseball ['beɪsbɔːl] *n* base-ball *m*.

basement ['beɪsmənt] *n* sous-sol *m*.

bash [bæʃ] *n* (*bang*) coup *m*; **to have a b.** (*try*) *Fam* essayer un coup ‖ *vt* (*hit*) cogner; (*ill-treat*) malmener; **to b. s.o. up** tabasser qn; **to b. down** (*door*) défoncer. ●**—ing** *n* (*thrashing*) *Fam* raclée *f*.

bashful ['bæʃfəl] *a* timide.

basic ['beɪsɪk] *a* essentiel, de base; (*elementary*) élémentaire; (*pay, food*) de base; (*room, house*) tout simple ‖ *n* **the basics** *Fam* l'essentiel *m*. ●**basically** [-klɪ] *adv* au fond.

basil ['bæz(ə)l] *n* basilic *m*.

basin ['beɪs(ə)n] *n* bassine *f*; (*for soup, food*) (grand) bol *m*; (*of river*) bassin *m*; (*sink*) lavabo *m*.

basis, *pl* **-ses** ['beɪsɪs, -siːz] *n* (*of agreement etc*) bases *fpl*; **on the b. of** d'après; **on that b.** dans ces conditions; **on a weekly b.** chaque semaine.

bask [bɑːsk] *vi* se chauffer.

basket ['bɑːskɪt] *n* panier *m*; (*for bread, laundry, litter*) corbeille *f*. ●**basketball** *n* basket(-ball) *m*.

Basque [bæsk] *a* & *n* basque (*mf*).

bass [beɪs] *n Mus* basse *f*.

bastard ['bɑːstəd] **1** *n* & *a* (*child*) bâtard, -arde (*mf*). **2** *n Pej Sl* salaud *m*, salope *f*.

bat [bæt] **1** *n* (*animal*) chauve-souris *f*. **2** *n Cricket Baseball* batte *f*; *Table Tennis* raquette *f*; **off my own b.** de ma propre initiative ‖ *vt* (**-tt-**) (*ball*) frapper. **3** *vt* **she didn't b. an eyelid** elle n'a pas sourcillé.

batch [bætʃ] *n* (*of people*) groupe *m*; (*of letters*) paquet *m*; (*of loaves*) fournée *f*; (*of papers*) liasse *f*.

bated ['beɪtɪd] *a* **with b. breath** en retenant son souffle.

bath [bɑːθ] *n* (*pl* **-s** [bɑːðz]) bain *m*; (*tub*) baignoire *f*; **to have** *or* **take a b.** prendre un bain; **b. towel** serviette *f* de bain; **swimming baths** piscine *f* ‖ *vt* baigner. ●**bathrobe** *n* peignoir *m* (de bain); *Am* robe *f* de chambre. ●**bathroom** *n* salle *f* de bain(s); (*toilet*) *Am* toilettes *fpl*. ●**bathtub** *n* baignoire *f*.

bath/e [beɪð] *vt* baigner; (*wound*) laver ‖ *vi* se baigner; *Am* prendre un bain ‖ *n* **to go for a b.** se baigner. ●**—ing** *n* baignade(s) *f*(*pl*); **b. costume** *or* **suit** maillot *m* de bain.

baton ['bætən, *Am* bə'tɒn] *n* (*of conductor*) baguette *f*; (*of policeman*) matraque *f*.

battalion [bə'tæljən] *n* bataillon *m*.

batter ['bætər] **1** *n* pâte *f* à frire. **2** *vt* (*peson*) rouer de coups; (*object*) frapper (à coups redoublés); (*baby*) martyriser. ●**—ed** *a* (*car*) cabossé; **b. wife** femme *f* battue. ●**—ing** *n* **to take a b.** souffrir beaucoup.

battery ['bætərɪ] *n Aut Mil* batterie *f*; (*in radio, appliance etc*) pile *f*.

battle ['bæt(ə)l] *n* bataille *f*; (*struggle*) lutte *f*; **b. dress** tenue *f* de campagne ‖ *vi* se battre, lutter. ●**battlefield** *n* champ *m* de bataille. ●**battleship** *n* cuirassé *m*.

baulk [bɔːk] *vi* reculer (**at** devant).

bawdy ['bɔːdɪ] *a* (**-ier, -iest**) grossier.

bawl [bɔːl] *vti* **to b. (out)** beugler, brailler; **to b. s.o. out** *Am Sl* engueuler qn.

bay [beɪ] *n* **1** (*of coastline*) baie *f*. **2** (*for loading etc*) aire *f*. **3** (*in room*) renfoncement *m*; **b. window** bow-window *m*. **4 to keep** *or* **hold at b.** (*enemy, dog etc*) tenir en respect.

bayonet ['beɪənɪt] *n* baïonnette *f*.

bazaar [bə'zɑːr] *n* (*market, shop*) bazar *m*; (*charity sale*) vente *f* de charité.

BC [biː'siː] *abbr* (*before Christ*) avant Jésus-Christ.

be [biː] *vi* (*pres t* **am, are, is;** *pt* **was, were;** *pp* **been;** *pres p* **being**) **1** être; **it is green/small** c'est vert/petit; **he's a doctor** il est médecin; **he's an Englishman** c'est un Anglais; **it's him** c'est lui; **it's 3 (o'clock)** il est trois heures; **it's the sixth of May**, *Am* **it's May sixth** c'est *or* nous sommes le six mai.

2 avoir; **to be hot/right/lucky** avoir chaud/raison/de la chance; **my feet are cold** j'ai froid aux pieds; **he's 20** (*age*) il a 20 ans; **to be 2 metres high** avoir 2 mètres de haut; **to be 6 feet tall** mesurer 1,80 m.

3 (*health*) aller; **how are you?** comment vas-tu?; **I'm well** je vais bien.

4 (*exist*) être; **the best painter there is** le meilleur peintre qui soit; **leave me be** laissez-moi (tranquille); **that may be** cela se peut.

5 (*go, come*) **I've been to see her** je suis allé *or* j'ai été la voir; **he's (already) been** il est (déjà) venu.

6 (*weather, calculations*) faire; **it's fine** il fait beau; **it's foggy** il y a du brouillard; **2 and 2 are 4** 2 et 2 font 4.

7 (*cost*) coûter, faire; **it's 20 pence** ça coûte 20 pence; **how much is it?** ça fait combien?, c'est combien?

8 (*auxiliary*) **I am/was doing** je fais/faisais; **I'll be staying** je resterai, je vais rester; **I'm listening to the radio** (*in the process of*) je suis en train d'écouter la radio; **he was killed** il a été tué, on l'a tué; **I've been waiting (for) two hours** j'attends depuis deux heures; **it is said** on dit; **to be pitied** à plaindre.

9 (*in questions and answers*) **isn't it?, aren't you?** *etc* n'est-ce pas?, non?; **I am!, he is!** *etc* oui!

10 (+ *inf*) **he is to come at once** (*must*) il doit venir tout de suite; **he's shortly to go** (*intends to*) il va bientôt partir.

11 there is *or* **are** il y a; (*pointing*) voilà; **here is** *or* **are** voici; **there she is** la voilà; **here they are** les voici.
beach [biːtʃ] *n* plage *f*.
beacon ['biːkən] *n Nau Av* balise *f*; (*lighthouse*) phare *m*.
bead [biːd] *n* perle *f*; (*of rosary*) grain *m*; (*of sweat*) goutte *f*; **(string of) beads** collier *m*.
beak [biːk] *n* bec *m*.
beaker ['biːkər] *n* gobelet *m*.
beam [biːm] **1** *n* (*of wood*) poutre *f*. **2** *n* (*of sunlight*) rayon *m*; (*of headlight, flashlight*) faisceau *m* ▮ *vi* (*of light*) rayonner; (*of person*) rayonner (de joie); (*smile*) sourire largement. ●**beaming** *a* (*radiant*) radieux.
bean [biːn] *n* haricot *m*; (*of coffee*) grain *m*; **(broad) b.** fève *f*. ●**beanshoots** *or* **beansprouts** *npl* germes *mpl* de soja.
bear[1] [beər] *n* (*animal*) ours *m*.
bear[2] [beər] *vt* (*pt* **bore,** *pp* **borne**) (*carry, show*) porter; (*endure*) supporter; (*resemblance*) offrir; (*responsibility*) assumer; **to b. in mind** tenir compte de; **to b. out** corroborer.
▮ *vi* **to b. left/right** (*turn*) tourner à gauche/droite; **to b. north**/*etc* (*go*) aller en direction du nord/*etc*; **to b. (up)on** (*relate to*) se rapporter à; **to b. with s.o.** être patient avec qn; **to b. up** ne pas se décourager; **b. up!** du courage!
bearable ['beərəb(ə)l] *a* supportable.
beard [bɪəd] *n* barbe *f*; **to have a b.** porter la barbe. ●**bearded** *a* barbu.
bearing ['beərɪŋ] *n* (*relevance*) relation *f* (**on** avec); (*posture, conduct*) maintien *m*; **to get one's bearings** s'orienter.
beast [biːst] *n* bête *f*, animal *m*; (*cruel person*) brute *f*. ●**beastly** *a Fam* (*bad*) vilain; (*spiteful*) méchant.
beat [biːt] *n* (*of heart, drum*) battement *m*; (*of policeman*) ronde *f*; *Mus* mesure *f*, rythme *m*.
▮ *vt* (*pt* **beat,** *pp* **beaten**) battre; (*defeat*) vaincre, battre; **to b. a drum** battre du tambour; **b. it!** *Fam* fichez le camp!; **to b. back** *or* **off** repousser; **to b. in** *or* **down** (*door*) défoncer; **to b. s.o. up** tabasser qn.
▮ *vi* battre; (*at door*) frapper (**at** à); **to b. about** *or* **around the bush** *Fam* tourner autour du pot; **to b. down** (*of rain*) tomber à verse; (*of sun*) taper. ●**beating** *n* (*blows, defeat*) raclée *f*; (*of heart, drums*) battement *m*; **to take a b.** souffrir beaucoup. ●**beater** *n* (*for eggs*) batteur *m*.
beautiful ['bjuːtɪf(ə)l] *a* (très) beau (*f* belle); (*superb*) merveilleux. ●**beautifully** *adv* (*after verb*) à merveille; (*before adjective*) merveilleusement.
beauty ['bjuːtɪ] *n* (*quality, woman*) beauté *f*; **it's a b.!** (*car etc*) c'est une merveille!; **b. parlour** institut *m* de beauté; **b. spot** (*on skin*) grain *m* de beauté; (*in countryside*) endroit *m* pittoresque.
beaver ['biːvər] *n* castor *m* ▮ *vi* **to b. away** travailler dur (**at sth** à qch).
because [bɪ'kɒz] *conj* parce que; **b. of** à cause de.
beck [bek] *n* **at s.o.'s b. and call** aux ordres de qn.
beckon ['bekən] *vti* **to b. (to) s.o.** faire signe à qn (**to do** de faire).
become [bɪ'kʌm] *vi* (*pt* **became,** *pp* **become**) devenir; **to b. a painter** devenir peintre; **to b. worried** commencer à s'inquiéter; **what has b. of her?** qu'est-elle devenue?
becoming [bɪ'kʌmɪŋ] *a* (*clothes*) seyant; (*modesty*) bienséant.
bed [bed] *n* lit *m*; (*of sea*) fond *m*; (*flower bed*) parterre *m*; **to go to b.** (aller) se coucher; **in b.** couché; **to get out of b.** se lever; **b. and breakfast** (*in hotel etc*) chambre *f* avec petit déjeuner; **air b.** matelas *m* pneumatique. ●**bedclothes** *npl* couvertures *fpl* et draps *mpl*. ●**bedding** *n* literie *f*. ●**bedridden** *a* alité. ●**bedroom** *n* chambre *f* à coucher. ●**bedside** *n* chevet *m* ▮ *a* (*lamp, book, table*) de chevet. ●**bed'sitter** *or* **bedsit** *n* chambre *f* meublée. ●**bedspread** *n* dessus-de-lit *m. inv*. ●**bedtime** *n* heure *f* du coucher.
bedlam ['bedləm] *n* (*noise*) *Fam* chahut *m*.
bedraggled [bɪ'dræg(ə)ld] *a* (*clothes, person*) débraillé.
bee [biː] *n* abeille *f*. ●**beehive** *n* ruche *f*. ●**beekeeping** *n* apiculture *f*.
beech [biːtʃ] *n* (*tree, wood*) hêtre *m*.
beef [biːf] *n* bœuf *m*. ●**beefburger** *n* hamburger *m*. ●**beefy** *a* (**-ier, -iest**) *Fam* musclé, costaud.
been [biːn] *pp of* **be**.
beer [bɪər] *n* bière *f*; **b. glass** chope *f*.
beet [biːt] *n Am* = **beetroot.** ●**beetroot** *n* betterave *f* (potagère).
beetle ['biːt(ə)l] **1** *n* scarabée *m*; (*any beetle-shaped insect*) bestiole *f*. **2** *vi* **to b. off** *Fam* se sauver.
befit [bɪ'fɪt] *vt* (**-tt-**) convenir à.
before [bɪ'fɔːr] *adv* avant; (*already*) déjà; (*in front*) devant; **the month b.** le mois d'avant; **the day b.** la veille; **I've never done it b.** je ne l'ai (encore) jamais fait.
▮ *prep* (*time*) avant; (*place*) devant; **the year b. last** il y a deux ans.
▮ *conj* avant que (+ ne + *sub*), avant de

(+ *inf*); **b. he goes** avant qu'il (ne) parte; **b. going** avant de partir. ● **beforehand** *adv* à l'avance, avant.

befriend [bɪ'frend] *vt* offrir son amitié à, aider.

beg [beg] *vt* (**-gg-**) **to b. (for)** solliciter, demander; (*bread, money*) mendier; **to b. s.o. to do** supplier qn de faire; **to b. the question** esquiver la question ‖ *vi* (*in street etc*) mendier; **to go begging** (*of food, articles*) ne pas trouver d'amateurs.

beggar ['begər] *n* mendiant, -ante *mf*; **lucky b.** *Fam* veinard, -arde *mf*.

begin [bɪ'gɪn] *vt* (*pt* **began,** *pp* **begun,** *pres p* **beginning**) commencer; (*campaign*) lancer; (*conversation*) engager; **to b. doing** *or* **to do** commencer *or* se mettre à faire ‖ *vi* commencer (**with** par, **by doing** par faire); **to b. with** (*first*) d'abord. ● **—ning** *n* commencement *m*, début *m*. ● **beginner** *n* débutant, -ante *mf*.

begrudge [bɪ'grʌdʒ] *vt* (*envy*) envier (**s.o. sth** qch à qn); (*give unwillingly*) donner à contrecœur; **to b. doing sth** faire qch à contrecœur.

behalf [bɪ'hɑːf] *n* **on b. of** pour, au nom de; (*in the interests of*) en faveur de.

behave [bɪ'heɪv] *vi* se conduire; (*of machine*) fonctionner; **to b. (oneself)** se tenir bien; (*of child*) être sage. ● **behaviour** (*Am* **behavior**) *n* conduite *f*, comportement *m*.

behead [bɪ'hed] *vt* décapiter.

behind [bɪ'haɪnd] **1** *prep* derrière; (*in progress*) en retard sur ‖ *adv* derrière; (*late*) en retard (**with** *or* **in one's work**/*etc* dans son travail/*etc*). **2** *n* (*buttocks*) *Fam* derrière *m*.

beholden [bɪ'həʊldən] *a* redevable (**to** à, **for** de).

beige [beɪʒ] *a* & *n* beige (*m*).

Beijing [beɪ'dʒɪŋ] *n* Beijing *m or f*.

being ['biːɪŋ] *n* (*person, soul*) être *m*; **to come into b.** naître, être créé.

belated [bɪ'leɪtɪd] *a* tardif.

belch [beltʃ] **1** *vi* (*of person*) faire un renvoi ‖ *n* renvoi *m*. **2** *vt* **to b. (out)** (*smoke*) vomir.

Belgium ['beldʒəm] *n* Belgique *f*. ● **Belgian** ['beldʒən] *a* & *n* belge (*mf*).

belie [bɪ'laɪ] *vt* démentir.

belief [bɪ'liːf] *n* croyance *f* (**in s.o./sth** en qn/qch); (*trust*) confiance *f*, foi *f*; (*opinion*) opinion *f*.

believ/e [bɪ'liːv] *vti* croire (**in sth** à qch, **in God** en Dieu); **I b. so** je crois que oui; **to b. in doing** croire qu'il faut faire; **he doesn't b. in smoking** il désapprouve que l'on fume. ● **—able** *a* croyable. ● **—er** *n Rel* croyant, -ante *mf*; **to be a b. in** = **believe in**.

belittle [bɪ'lɪt(ə)l] *vt* dénigrer.

bell [bel] *n* (*of church etc*) cloche *f*; (*small*) clochette *f*; (*in phone, mechanism*) sonnerie *f*; (*on door, bicycle*) sonnette *f*. ● **bellboy** *n Am* groom *m*.

belligerent [bɪ'lɪdʒərənt] *a* belligérant.

bellow ['beləʊ] *vi* beugler, mugir.

bellows ['beləʊz] *npl* soufflet *m*.

belly ['belɪ] *n* ventre *m*; **b. button** *Fam* nombril *m*. ● **bellyache** *n Fam* mal *m* au ventre. ● **bellyful** *n* **to have had a b.** *Sl* en avoir plein le dos.

belong [bɪ'lɒŋ] *vi* appartenir (**to** à); **to b. to** (*club*) être membre de; **the cup belongs here** la tasse se range ici. ● **—ings** *npl* affaires *fpl*.

beloved [bɪ'lʌvɪd] *a* & *n* bien-aimé, -ée (*mf*).

below [bɪ'ləʊ] *prep* au-dessous de ‖ *adv* en dessous; **see b.** (*in book*) voir ci-dessous.

belt [belt] **1** *n* ceinture *f*; (*in machine*) courroie *f* ‖ *vi* **to b. up** attacher sa ceinture. **2** *vt* (*hit*) *Sl* rosser. **3** *vi* **to b. (along)** (*rush*) *Sl* filer à toute allure; **b. up!** (*shut up*) *Sl* boucle-la!

bemused [bɪ'mjuːzd] *a* perplexe.

bench [bentʃ] *n* (*seat*) banc *m*; (*work table*) établi *m*; **the B.** *Jur* la magistrature (assise); (*court*) le tribunal.

bend [bend] *n* courbe *f*; (*in river, pipe*) coude *m*; (*in road*) virage *m*; (*of arm, knee*) pli *m*; **round the b.** (*mad*) *Fam* cinglé ‖ *vt* (*pt* & *pp* **bent**) courber; (*leg, arm*) plier; (*head*) baisser ‖ *vi* (*of branch*) plier; (*of road*) tourner; **to b. (down)** (*stoop*) se baisser; **to b. (over** *or* **forward)** se pencher.

beneath [bɪ'niːθ] *prep* au-dessous de, sous ‖ *adv* (au-)dessous.

benefactor ['benɪfæktər] *n* bienfaiteur *m*.

beneficial [benɪ'fɪʃəl] *a* bénéfique.

benefit ['benɪfɪt] *n* avantage *m*; (*money*) allocation *f*; *pl* (*of education etc*) bienfaits *mpl*; **child b.** allocations *fpl* familiales; **for your (own) b.** pour vous, pour votre bien; **to be of b.** faire du bien (**to** à); **to give s.o. the b. of the doubt** accorder à qn le bénéfice du doute. ‖ *vt* faire du bien à; (*be useful to*) profiter à.
‖ *vi* **you'll b. from it** ça vous fera du bien; **to b. from doing** gagner à faire.

benevolent [bɪ'nevələnt] *a* bienveillant.

benign [bɪ'naɪn] *a* (*kind*) bienveillant; **b. tumour** *Med* tumeur *f* bénigne.

bent [bent] **1** *pt* & *pp of* **bend** ‖ *a* (*nail*) tordu; (*dishonest*) *Fam* corrompu; **b. on doing** résolu à faire. **2** *n* (*talent*) aptitude *f* (**for** pour); (*inclination*) penchant *m* (**for** pour).

bequeath [bɪ'kwiːð] *vt* léguer (**to** à). ● **bequest** *n* legs *m*.

bereaved [bɪ'riːvd] *a* endeuillé ▮ *n* **the b.** la famille (*or* la femme *etc*) du défunt *or* de la défunte. ● **bereavement** *n* deuil *m*.

beret ['bereɪ, *Am* bə'reɪ] *n* béret *m*.

berk [bɜːk] *n Sl* imbécile *mf*.

Bermuda [bə'mjuːdə] *n* Bermudes *fpl*.

berry ['berɪ] *n* baie *f*.

berserk [bə'zɜːk] *a* **to go b.** devenir fou.

berth [bɜːθ] *n* **1** (*in ship, train*) couchette *f*. **2** (*anchorage*) mouillage *m* ▮ *vi* (*of ship*) mouiller.

beset [bɪ'set] *vt* (*pt & pp* **beset,** *pres p* **besetting**) assaillir (*qn*); **b. with obstacles**/*etc* semé *or* hérissé d'obstacles/*etc*.

beside [bɪ'saɪd] *prep* à côté de; **that's b. the point** ça n'a rien à voir.

besides [bɪ'saɪdz] *prep* (*in addition to*) en plus de; (*except*) excepté; **there are ten of us b. Paul** nous sommes dix sans compter Paul ▮ *adv* de plus; (*moreover*) d'ailleurs.

besiege [bɪ'siːdʒ] *vt* (*of soldiers, crowd*) assiéger.

bespectacled [bɪ'spektɪk(ə)ld] *a* à lunettes.

best [best] *a* meilleur (**in** de); **the b. part of** (*most*) la plus grande partie de; **the b. thing** le mieux; **b. man** (*at wedding*) témoin *m*.
▮ *n* **the b. (one)** le meilleur, la meilleure; **it's for the b.** c'est pour le mieux; **at b.** au mieux; **to do one's b.** faire de son mieux; **to the b. of my knowledge** autant que je sache; **to make the b. of** s'accommoder de (*situation etc*); **in one's Sunday b.** endimanché; **all the b.!** portez-vous bien!; (*in letter*) amicalement.
▮ *adv* **(the) b.** (*to play etc*) le mieux; (*to like, love*) le plus; **the b. loved** le plus aimé. ● **b.-'seller** *n* (*book*) best-seller *m*.

bestow [bɪ'stəʊ] *vt* accorder (**on** à).

bet [bet] *n* pari *m* ▮ *vti* (*pt & pp* **bet** *or* **betted,** *pres p* **betting**) parier (**on** sur, **that** que); **you b.!** *Fam* (*of course*) tu parles! ● **betting** *n* pari(s) *m(pl)*; **b. shop** *or* **office** bureau *m* du pari mutuel.

betray [bɪ'treɪ] *vt* trahir; **to b. to s.o.** (*give away to*) livrer à qn. ● **betrayal** *n* (*disloyalty*) trahison *f*.

better ['betər] *a* meilleur (**than** que); **she's (much) b.** (*in health*) elle va (bien) mieux; **he's b. than** (*at sports*) il joue mieux que; (*at French etc*) il est plus fort que; **that's b.** c'est mieux; **to get b.** (*recover*) se remettre; (*improve*) s'améliorer; **it's b. to go** il vaut mieux partir.
▮ *adv* mieux (**than** que); **I had b. go** il vaut mieux que je parte; **all the b.** tant mieux (**for** pour).
▮ *n* **to get the b. of s.o.** l'emporter sur qn; **change for the b.** amélioration *f*.
▮ *vt* (*improve*) améliorer; **to b. oneself** améliorer sa condition.

between [bɪ'twiːn] *prep* entre; **b. you and me** entre nous; **in b. sth and sth/two things** entre qch et qch/deux choses.
▮ *adv* **in b.** (*space*) au milieu; (*time*) dans l'intervalle.

beverage ['bevərɪdʒ] *n* boisson *f*.

beware [bɪ'weər] *vi* **to b. of** (*s.o., sth*) se méfier de; **b.!** méfiez-vous!; **'b. of the trains'** 'attention aux trains'.

bewilder [bɪ'wɪldər] *vt* dérouter.

beyond [bɪ'jɒnd] *prep* (*further than*) au-delà de; (*reach, doubt*) hors de; **b. belief** incroyable; **b. my means** au-dessus de mes moyens; **it's b. me** ça me dépasse ▮ *adv* au-delà.

bias ['baɪəs] *n* penchant *m* (**towards** pour); (*prejudice*) préjugé *m*, parti pris *m*. ● **bias(s)ed** *a* partial; **to be b. against** avoir des préjugés contre.

bib [bɪb] *n* (*baby's*) bavoir *m*.

bible ['baɪb(ə)l] *n* bible *f*; **the B.** la Bible. ● **biblical** ['bɪblɪk(ə)l] *a* biblique.

bibliography [bɪblɪ'ɒgrəfɪ] *n* bibliographie *f*.

biceps ['baɪseps] *n Anat* biceps *m*.

bicker ['bɪkər] *vi* se chamailler.

bicycle ['baɪsɪk(ə)l] *n* bicyclette *f*.

bid[1] [bɪd] *vt* (*pt & pp* **bid,** *pres p* **bidding**) (*sum of money*) offrir, faire une offre de ▮ *vi* faire une offre (**for** pour) ▮ *n* (*at auction*) offre *f*, enchère *f*; (*for doing a job*) soumission *f*; (*attempt*) tentative *f*. ● **bidder** *n* **to the highest b.** au plus offrant.

bid[2] [bɪd] *vt* (*pt* **bade** [bæd], *pp* **bidden** *or* **bid,** *pres p* **bidding**) (*command*) commander (**s.o. to do** à qn de faire); (*say, wish*) dire, souhaiter.

bide [baɪd] *vt* **to b. one's time** attendre le bon moment.

big [bɪg] *a* (**bigger, biggest**) grand, gros (*f* grosse); (*in age, generous*) grand; (*in bulk, amount*) gros; **b. deal!** *Fam* (bon) et alors!; **b. toe** gros orteil *m* ▮ *adv* **to talk b.** fanfaronner. ● **bighead** *n or* **big'headed** *a Fam* (*conceited*) prétentieux, -euse (*mf*); (*boasting*) vantard, -arde (*mf*). ● **bigshot** *or* **bigwig** *n Fam* gros bonnet *m*.

bigot ['bɪgət] *n* sectaire *mf*. ● **bigoted** *a* sectaire.

bike [baɪk] *n Fam* vélo *m*.

bikini [bɪ'kiːnɪ] *n* deux-pièces *m inv*; **b. briefs** mini-slip *m*.

bile [baɪl] *n* bile *f*.
bilingual [baɪ'lɪŋgwəl] *a* bilingue.
bill[1] [bɪl] **1** *n* (*invoice*) facture *f*, note *f*; (*in restaurant*) addition *f*; (*in hotel*) note *f*; (*banknote*) *Am* billet *m* ‖ *vt* **to b. s.o.** envoyer la facture à qn. **2** *n* (*proposed law*) projet *m* de loi; **b. of rights** déclaration *f* des droits. **3** *n* (*poster*) *Th* affiche *f* ‖ *vt Th* mettre à l'affiche. ●**billboard** *n Am* panneau *m* d'affichage. ●**billfold** *n Am* portefeuille *m*.
bill[2] *n* (*of bird*) bec *m*.
billiard ['bɪljəd] *a* (*table etc*) de billard. ●**billiards** *n* (jeu *m* de) billard *m*.
billion ['bɪljən] *n* milliard *m*. ●**billio'naire** milliardaire *mf*.
bin [bɪn] *n* boîte *f*; (*for bread*) huche *f*, boîte *f*; (*for litter*) poubelle *f*.
bind [baɪnd] **1** *vt* (*pt* & *pp* **bound**) (*fasten*) attacher, lier; (*book*) relier; (*unite*) lier; **to b. s.o. to do** obliger qn à faire. **2** *n* (*bore*) *Fam* plaie *f*. ●**—ing 1** *n* (*of book*) reliure *f*. **2** *a* (*contract*) irrévocable; **to be b. on s.o.** (*legally*) lier qn.
binge [bɪndʒ] *n* **to go on a b.** *Fam* faire la bringue.
bingo ['bɪŋgəʊ] *n* loto *m*.
binoculars [bɪ'nɒkjʊləz] *npl* jumelles *fpl*.
biochemistry [baɪəʊ'kemɪstrɪ] *n* biochimie *f*.
biodegradable [baɪəʊdɪ'greɪdəb(ə)l] *a* biodégradable.
biography [baɪ'ɒgrəfɪ] *n* biographie *f*.
biology [baɪ'ɒlədʒɪ] *n* biologie *f*. ●**bio'logical** *a* biologique.
birch [bɜːtʃ] *n* **(silver) b.** (*tree*) bouleau *m*.
bird [bɜːd] *n* oiseau *m*; (*fowl*) volaille *f*; **b.'s-eye view** vue *f* d'ensemble. ●**birdseed** *n* grains *mpl* de millet.
biro® ['baɪərəʊ] *n* (*pl* **-os**) stylo *m* à bille, bic® *m*.
birth [bɜːθ] *n* naissance *f*; **to give b. to** donner naissance à; **b. certificate** acte *m* de naissance; **b. control** limitation *f* des naissances. ●**birthday** *n* anniversaire *m*; **happy b.!** bon anniversaire!; **b. party** fête *f* d'anniversaire. ●**birthmark** *n* tache *f* de vin. ●**birthrate** *n* (taux *m* de) natalité *f*.
biscuit ['bɪskɪt] *n* biscuit *m*, gâteau *m* sec; *Am* petit pain *m* au lait.
bishop ['bɪʃəp] *n* évêque *m*; (*in chess*) fou *m*.
bit[1] [bɪt] *n* **1** morceau *m*; (*of string, time*) bout *m*; **a b.** (*a little*) un peu; **a tiny b.** un tout petit peu; **quite a b.** (*very*) très; (*a lot*) beaucoup; **not a b.** pas du tout; **a b. of luck** une chance; **b. by b.** petit à petit; **in bits** en morceaux; **to come to bits** se démonter.
2 (*coin*) pièce *f*.
3 (*of horse*) mors *m*.
4 (*computer information*) bit *m*.
bit[2] [bɪt] *pt of* **bite.**
bitch [bɪtʃ] **1** *n* chienne *f*; (*woman*) *Pej Fam* garce *f*.
bite [baɪt] *n* (*wound*) morsure *f*; (*from insect*) piqûre *f*; (*mouthful*) bouchée *f*; **a b. to eat** un morceau à manger ‖ *vti* (*pt* **bit,** *pp* **bitten**) mordre; (*of insect*) piquer, mordre; **to b. one's nails** se ronger les ongles; **to b. sth off** arracher qch d'un coup de dent(s).
bitter ['bɪtər] **1** *a* (*person, taste etc*) amer; (*cold, wind*) glacial; (*criticism*) acerbe; (*conflict*) violent; **to feel b.** être plein d'amertume (**about** à cause de). **2** *n* bière *f* (pression). ● **—ly** *adv* (*to cry, regret*) amèrement; **it's b. cold** il fait un froid glacial. ●**—ness** *n* amertume *f*; violence *f*.
bizarre [bɪ'zɑːr] *a* bizarre.
blab [blæb] *vi* (**-bb-**) jaser. ●**blabber** *vi* jaser. ●**blabbermouth** *n* jaseur, -euse *mf*.
black [blæk] *a* (**-er, -est**) noir; **b. eye** œil *m* poché; **to give s.o. a b. eye** pocher l'œil à qn; **b. and blue** (*bruised*) couvert de bleus; **b. sheep** *Fig* brebis *f* galeuse; **b. ice** verglas *m*; **b. pudding** boudin *m* ‖ *n* (*colour*) noir *m*; (*person*) Noir, -e *mf* ‖ *vi* **to b. out** (*faint*) s'évanouir. ●**blacken** *vt* noircir. ●**blackish** *a* noirâtre.
blackberry ['blækbərɪ, *Am* -berɪ] *n* mûre *f*. ●**blackbird** *n* merle *m*. ●**blackboard** *n* tableau *m* (noir); **on the b.** au tableau. ●**black'currant** *n* cassis *m*. ●**blackleg** *n* (*strike breaker*) jaune *m*. ●**blacklist** *n* liste *f* noire ‖ *vt* mettre sur la liste noire. ●**blackmail** *n* chantage *m* ‖ *vt* faire chanter. ●**blackmailer** *n* maître chanteur *m*. ●**blackout** *n* panne *f* d'électricité; (*fainting fit*) syncope *f*; **(news) b.** black-out *m*. ●**blacksmith** *n* forgeron *m*.
blackguard ['blægɑːd, -gəd] *n* canaille *f*.
bladder ['blædər] *n* vessie *f*.
blade [bleɪd] *n* lame *f*; (*of grass*) brin *m*.
blame [bleɪm] *vt* accuser; **to b. s.o. for sth** rejeter la responsabilité de qch sur qn; (*reproach*) reprocher qch à qn; **you're to b.** c'est ta faute ‖ *n* faute *f*. ●**—less** *a* irréprochable.
bland [blænd] *a* (**-er, -est**) (*food*) (*mild*) sans saveur particulière; (*insipid*) fade.
blank [blæŋk] *a* (*paper, page*) blanc (*f* blanche), vierge; (*cheque, Am check*) en blanc; (*look*) vide; (*refusal*) absolu; **b. tape** cassette *f* vierge ‖ *a* & *n* **b. (space)** blanc *m*;

b. (cartridge) cartouche *f* à blanc.

blanket ['blæŋkɪt] **1** *n* couverture *f*; (*of snow*) couche *f* ‖ *vt* (*cover*) *Fig* recouvrir. **2** *a* (*term etc*) général.

blare [bleər] *vi* **to b. (out)** (*of radio*) beugler; (*of music*) retentir.

blasphemy ['blæsfəmɪ] *n* blasphème *m*.

blast [blɑːst] **1** *n* explosion *f*; (*air from explosion*) souffle *m*; (*of wind*) rafale *f*; **(at) full b.** (*loud*) à plein volume ‖ *vt* (*blow up*) faire sauter; **to b. s.o.** *Fam* réprimander qn. **2** *int Fam* zut!, merde! ●**—ed** *a Fam* fichu. ●**blast-off** *n* (*of spacecraft*) mise *f* à feu.

blaz/e [bleɪz] **1** *n* (*flame*) flamme *f*; (*fire*) feu *m*; (*large*) incendie *m*; **b. of light** torrent *m* de lumière ‖ *vi* (*of fire*) flamber; (*of sun*) flamboyer. **2** *vt* **to b. a trail** marquer la voie. ●**—ing** *a* (*burning*) en feu; (*sun*) brûlant.

blazer ['bleɪzər] *n* blazer *m*.

bleach [bliːtʃ] *n* (*household*) eau *f* de Javel; (*for hair*) décolorant *m* ‖ *vt* (*hair*) décolorer; (*linen*) blanchir.

bleak [bliːk] *a* **(-er, -est)** (*appearance*) morne; (*future, situation*) sombre; (*countryside*) désolé.

bleary ['blɪərɪ] *a* (*eyes*) troubles, voilés.

bleat [bliːt] *vi* bêler.

bleed [bliːd] *vti* (*pt & pp* **bled**) saigner; **to b. to death** perdre tout son sang. ●**—ing** *a* (*wound*) saignant.

bleep [bliːp] *n* bip *m* ‖ *vt* appeler au bip-(bip). ●**bleeper** *n* bip(-bip) *m*.

blemish ['blemɪʃ] *n* (*fault*) défaut *m*; (*on fruit, reputation*) tache *f*.

blend [blend] *n* mélange *m* ‖ *vt* mélanger (**with** à) ‖ *vi* se mélanger; (*go together*) se marier (**with** avec). ●**—er** *n* (*for food*) mixer *m*.

bless [bles] *vt* bénir; **b. you!** (*sneezing*) à vos souhaits! ●**—ed** [-ɪd] *a* **1** saint, béni; **2** (*blasted*) *Fam* fichu, sacré. ●**—ing** *n* bénédiction *f*; (*benefit*) bienfait *m*; **what a b. that . . .** quelle chance que. . . .

blew [bluː] *pt of* **blow**².

blight [blaɪt] *n* (*scourge*) fléau *m*; **to be a b. on** avoir une influence néfaste sur; **urban b.** (*area*) quartier *m* délabré; (*condition*) délabrement *m* (de quartier).

blimey! ['blaɪmɪ] *int Fam* zut!, mince!

blind [blaɪnd] **1** *a* aveugle; **b. person** aveugle *mf*; **he's b. to** (*fault*) il ne voit pas; **b. alley** impasse *f* ‖ *n* **the b.** les aveugles *mpl* ‖ *vt* (*of light etc*) aveugler (*qn*). **2** *n* (*on window*) store *m*. ●**—ly** *adv* aveuglément. ●**—ness** *n* cécité *f*.

blinders ['blaɪndəz] *npl* (*of horse*) *Am* œillères *fpl*.

blindfold ['blaɪndfəʊld] *n* bandeau *m* ‖ *vt* bander les yeux à ‖ *adv* les yeux bandés.

blink [blɪŋk] *vi* (*of person*) cligner des yeux; (*of eyes*) cligner; (*of light*) clignoter ‖ *vt* **to b. one's eyes** cligner des yeux ‖ *n* clignement *m*. ●**—ing** *a* (*bloody*) *Fam* sacré.

blinkers ['blɪŋkəz] *npl* (*of horse*) œillères *fpl*; (*indicators*) *Aut* clignotants *mpl*.

bliss [blɪs] *n* félicité *f*. ●**blissful** *a* (*wonderful*) merveilleux. ●**blissfully** *adv* (*happy*) parfaitement.

blister ['blɪstər] *n* (*on skin*) ampoule *f*.

blitz [blɪts] *n* (*onslaught*) *Fam* offensive *f*.

blizzard ['blɪzəd] *n* tempête *f* de neige.

bloated ['bləʊtɪd] *a* gonflé.

blob [blɒb] *n* (*of water*) (grosse) goutte *f*; (*of ink*) tache *f*.

block [blɒk] **1** *n* (*of stone etc*) bloc *m*; (*of buildings*) pâté *m* (de maisons); **b. of flats** immeuble *m*; **a b. away** *Am* une rue plus loin; **b. capitals** *or* **letters** majuscules *fpl*. **2** *vt* (*obstruct*) bloquer; (*pipe*) boucher; (*s.o.'s view*) boucher; **to b. off** (*road*) barrer; (*light*) intercepter; **to b. up** (*pipe, hole*) bloquer. ●**blo'ckade** *n* blocus *m* ‖ *vt* bloquer. ●**blockage** *n* obstruction *f*. ●**blockbuster** *n Cin* film *m* à grand spectacle. ●**blockhead** *n Fam* imbécile *mf*.

bloke [bləʊk] *n Fam* type *m*.

blond [blɒnd] *a & n* blond (*m*). ●**blonde** *a & n* blonde (*f*).

blood [blʌd] *n* sang *m* ‖ *a* (*group, cell*) sanguin; (*poisoning, bank*) du sang; **b. donor/bath** donneur, -euse *mf*/bain *m* de sang; **b. pressure** tension *f* (artérielle); **to have high b. pressure** avoir de la tension; **b. test** analyse *f* de sang. ●**bloodhound** *n* (*dog, detective*) limier *m*. ●**bloodshed** *n* effusion *f* de sang. ●**bloodshot** *a* (*eye*) injecté de sang. ●**bloodstained** *a* taché de sang. ●**bloodthirsty** *a* sanguinaire.

bloody ['blʌdɪ] **1** *a* **(-ier, -iest)** sanglant. **2** *a* (*weather, liar etc*) *Fam* sale ‖ *adv* (*very, completely*) *Fam* vachement. ●**b.-'minded** *a* hargneux.

bloom [bluːm] *n* fleur *f*; **in b.** en fleur(s) ‖ *vi* fleurir. ●**—ing** *a* **1** (*in bloom*) en fleur(s). **2** (*bloody*) *Fam* sacré, fichu.

blossom ['blɒsəm] *n* fleur(s) *f(pl)* ‖ *vi* fleurir; **to b. (out)** (*of person*) s'épanouir.

blot [blɒt] *n* tache *f* ‖ *vt* **(-tt-)** (*stain*) tacher; **to b. out** (*obliterate*) effacer. ●**blotting paper** *n* (papier *m*) buvard *m*.

blotch [blɒtʃ] *n* tache *f*. ●**blotchy** *a* **(-ier, -iest)** couvert de taches; (*face*) marbré.

blouse [blaʊz, *Am* blaʊs] *n* chemisier *m*.
blow[1] [bləʊ] *n* (*with fist etc*) coup *m*; **to come to blows** en venir aux mains.
blow[2] [bləʊ] *vt* (*pt* **blew,** *pp* **blown**) (*of wind*) pousser (*un navire etc*), chasser (*la pluie etc*); (*smoke*) souffler; (*bubbles*) faire; (*trumpet*) souffler dans; **to b. a fuse** faire sauter un plomb; **to b. one's nose** se moucher; **to b. a whistle** siffler ‖ *vi* (*of wind, person*) souffler; (*of fuse*) sauter; (*of papers etc*) (*in wind*) s'éparpiller.
blow away *vt* (*of wind*) emporter (*qch*) ‖ *vi* (*of hat etc*) s'envoler **to blow down** *vt* (*chimney etc*) faire tomber ‖ *vi* tomber **to blow off** *vt* (*hat etc*) emporter ‖ *vi* s'envoler **to blow out** *vt* (*candle*) souffler ‖ *vi* (*of light*) s'éteindre. ●**blowout** *n* (*of tyre, Am tire*) éclatement *m*. **to blow over 1** *vti* = **blow down. 2** *vi* (*of quarrel etc*) passer **to blow up** *vt* (*building etc*) faire sauter; (*pump up*) gonfler; (*photo*) agrandir ‖ *vi* (*explode*) exploser. ●**blow-up** *n* (*of photo*) agrandissement *m*.
blow-dry ['bləʊdraɪ] *n* brushing *m*.
blowlamp ['bləʊlæmp] *n* chalumeau *m*.
blowtorch ['bləʊtɔ:ʃ] *n Am* chalumeau *m*.
blowy ['bləʊɪ] *a* **it's b.** *Fam* il y a du vent.
bludgeon ['blʌdʒən] *n* gourdin *m* ‖ *vt* matraquer.
blue [blu:] *a* (**bluer, bluest**) bleu (*mpl* bleus); **b. film** *Fam* film *m* porno ‖ *n* bleu *m* (*pl* bleus); **the blues** (*depression*) *Fam* le cafard. ●**bluebell** *n* jacinthe *f* des bois. ●**blueberry** *n* airelle *f*. ●**blueprint** *n Fig* plan *m* (de travail).
bluff [blʌf] *vti* bluffer ‖ *n* bluff *m*.
blunder ['blʌndər] *n* (*mistake*) gaffe *f* ‖ *vi* faire une gaffe.
blunt [blʌnt] *a* (**-er, -est**) (*edge*) émoussé; (*pencil*) mal taillé; (*person, speech*) franc (*f* franche), brusque. ●**—ly** *adv* carrément.
blur [blɜ:r] *n* tache *f* floue ‖ *vt* (**-rr-**) rendre flou. ●**blurred** *a* (*image*) flou.
blurb [blɜ:b] *n Fam* résumé *m* publicitaire, laïus *m*.
blurt [blɜ:t] *vt* **to b. (out)** (*secret*) laisser échapper; (*excuse*) bredouiller.
blush [blʌʃ] *vi* rougir (**with** de).
blustery ['blʌstərɪ]*a* (*weather*) de grand vent.
boar [bɔ:r] *n* (**wild**) **b.** sanglier *m*.
board[1] [bɔ:d] **1** *n* (*piece of wood*) planche *f*; (*for notices*) tableau *m*; (*for games*) plateau *m*; (*cardboard*) carton *m*; (*committee*) conseil *m*, commission *f*; (*of examiners*) *Sch* jury *m* (*pl* jurys); **b. (of directors)** conseil *m* d'administration; **on b.** (*ship, aircraft*) à bord (de).
2 *vt* (*ship, aircraft*) monter à bord de; (*bus, train*) monter dans; **to b. up** (*door*) boucher. ●**boarding** *n* (*of passengers*) embarquement *m*; **b. pass** carte *f* d'embarquement. ●**boardwalk** *n Am* promenade *f*.
board[2] [bɔ:d] *n* (*food*) pension *f*; **b. and lodging** (chambre *f* avec) pension *f* ‖ *vi* (*lodge*) être en pension (**with** chez); **boarding house** pension *f* (de famille); **boarding school** pensionnat *m*. ●**boarder** *n* pensionnaire *mf*.
boast [bəʊst] *vi* se vanter (**about, of** de) ‖ *vt* se glorifier de; **to b. that one can do sth** se vanter de (pouvoir) faire qch ‖ *n* vantardise *f*. ●**—ing** *n* vantardise *f*. ●**boastful** *a* vantard.
boat [bəʊt] *n* bateau *m*; (*small*) barque *f*, canot *m*; (*liner*) paquebot *m*; **in the same b.** *Fig* logé à la même enseigne. ●**—ing** *n* canotage *m*.
bob [bɒb] *vi* (**-bb-**) **to b. (up and down)** (*on water*) danser sur l'eau.
bobby ['bɒbɪ] *n* **1** (*policeman*) *Fam* flic *m*, agent *m*. **2 b. pin** *Am* pince *f* à cheveux.
bode [bəʊd] *vi* **to b. well/ill** être de bon/mauvais augure.
body ['bɒdɪ] *n* corps *m*; (*institution*) organisme *m*; **b. building** culturisme *m*; **b. warmer** gilet *m* matelassé. ●**bodily** *a* (*need*) physique. ●**bodyguard** *n* garde *m* du corps, *Fam* gorille *m*. ●**bodywork** *n* carrosserie *f*.
bog [bɒg] *n* marécage *m* ‖ *vt* **to get bogged down** s'enliser. ●**boggy** *a* (**-ier, -iest**) marécageux.
boggle ['bɒg(ə)l] *vi* **the mind boggles** cela confond l'imagination.
bogus ['bəʊgəs] *a* faux (*f* fausse).
boil[1] [bɔɪl] *n* (*pimple*) furoncle *m*.
boil[2] [bɔɪl] *vi* bouillir; **to b. down to** *Fig* se ramener à; **to b. over** (*of milk etc*) déborder ‖ *vt* **to b. (up)** faire bouillir ‖ *n* **to come to the b.** bouillir; **to bring to the b.** amener à ébullition. ●**—ed** *a* (*beef*) bouilli; (*potato*) à l'anglaise; **b. egg** œuf *m* à la coque. ●**—ing** *a* **to be at b. point** (*of liquid*) bouillir; **b. (hot)** bouillant; **it's b. (hot)** (*weather*) il fait une chaleur infernale.
boiler ['bɔɪlər] *n* chaudière *f*; **b. suit** bleus *mpl* (de travail).
boisterous ['bɔɪstərəs] *a* (*noisy*) tapageur; (*child*) turbulent.
bold [bəʊld] *a* (**-er, -est**) hardi; **in b. type** en (caractères) gras. ●**—ness** *n* hardiesse *f*.
bollard ['bɒləd, 'bɒlɑ:d] *n Aut* borne *f*.
bolster ['bəʊlstər] **1** *n* (*pillow*) traversin *m*,

polochon *m*. **2** *vt* **to b. (up)** (*support*) soutenir.

bolt [bəʊlt] **1** *n* (*on door etc*) verrou *m*; (*for nut*) boulon *m* ‖ *vt* (*door*) fermer au verrou. **2** *vi* (*dash*) se précipiter; (*run away*) détaler; (*of horse*) s'emballer. **3** *n* **b. (of lightning)** éclair *m*. **4** *vt* (*food*) engloutir.

bomb [bɒm] *n* bombe *f*; **letter b.** lettre *f* piégée ‖ *vt* (*from the air*) bombarder; (*of terrorist*) faire sauter une bombe dans *or* à. ●**—ing** *n* bombardement *m*; (*by terrorist*) attentat *m* à la bombe. ●**bomber** *n* (*aircraft*) bombardier *m*; (*terrorist*) plastiqueur *m*. ●**bombshell** *n* **to come as a b.** tomber comme une bombe.

bombard [bɒm'bɑːd] *vt* bombarder (**with** de). ●**—ment** *n* bombardement *m*.

bona fide [bəʊnə'faɪdɪ, *Am* -'faɪd] *a* sérieux.

bond [bɒnd] *n* (*link*) lien *m*; (*investment certificate*) bon *m*, obligation *f*; (*promise*) engagement *m*; (*adhesion*) adhérence *f*.

bone [bəʊn] **1** *n* os *m*; (*of fish*) arête *f*; **b. china** porcelaine *f* tendre ‖ *vt* (*meat*) désosser. **2** *vi* **to b. up on** (*subject*) *Am Fam* bûcher.

bone-dry [bəʊn'draɪ] *a* tout à fait sec. ●**b.-idle** *a* paresseux comme une couleuvre.

bonfire ['bɒnfaɪər] *n* (*for celebration*) feu *m* de joie; (*for dead leaves*) feu *m* (de jardin).

bonkers ['bɒŋkəz] *a* (*crazy*) *Fam* dingue.

bonnet ['bɒnɪt] *n* (*hat*) bonnet *m*; (*of vehicle*) capot *m*.

bonus ['bəʊnəs] *n* prime *f*; **no claims b.** *Aut* bonus *m*.

bony ['bəʊnɪ] *a* (**-ier, -iest**) (*thin*) osseux; (*fish*) plein d'arêtes.

boo [buː] *vti* siffler ‖ *npl* sifflets *mpl*.

boob [buːb] *n* (*mistake*) *Fam* gaffe *f* ‖ *vi Sl* gaffer.

booby-trap ['buːbɪtræp] *n* engin *m* piégé ‖ *vt* (**-pp-**) piéger.

book[1] [bʊk] *n* livre *m*; (*of tickets*) carnet *m*; (*record*) registre *m*; *pl* (*accounts*) comptes *mpl*; **(exercise) b.** cahier *m*; **(bank) b.** livret *m* (de banque).

book[2] [bʊk] *vt* **to b. (up)** (*seat etc*) réserver; **to b. s.o.** *Jur* donner un procès-verbal à qn; **to b. (down)** (*write down*) inscrire; **(fully) booked (up)** (*hotel, concert*) complet ‖ *vi* **to b. (up)** réserver des places; **to b. in** (*in hotel*) prendre une chambre; (*sign register*) signer le registre. ●**booking** *n* réservation *f*; **b. office** bureau *m* de location, guichet *m*.

bookcase ['bʊkkeɪs] *n* bibliothèque *f*. ●**bookends** *npl* serre-livres *m inv*. ●**bookkeeper** *n* comptable *mf*. ●**bookkeeping** *n* comptabilité *f*. ●**booklet** *n* brochure *f*. ●**bookmaker** *n* bookmaker *m*. ●**bookmark** *n* marque *f*, marque-page *m*. ●**bookseller** *n* libraire *mf*. ●**bookshelf** *n* rayon *m*. ●**bookshop** *or Am* **bookstore** *n* librairie *f*. ●**bookstall** *n* kiosque *m* (à journaux).

boom [buːm] **1** *vi* (*of thunder, gun etc*) gronder ‖ *n* grondement *m*. **2** *n Econ* expansion *f*, boom *m*.

boon [buːn] *n* avantage *m*.

boost [buːst] *vt* (*increase*) augmenter; (*product*) faire de la réclame pour; (*economy*) stimuler; (*morale*) remonter ‖ *n* **to give a b. to** = **to boost.** ●**—er** *n* (*injection*) (piqûre *f* de) rappel *m*.

boot [buːt] **1** *n* (*shoe*) botte *f*; **(ankle) b.** bottillon *m*; **to get the b.** *Fam* être mis à la porte; **b. polish** cirage *m* ‖ *vt* (*kick*) donner un coup *or* des coups de pied à; **to b. out** mettre à la porte. **2** *n Aut* coffre *m*. **3** *n* **to b.** en plus.

booth [buːð, buːθ] *n* (*for phone*) cabine *f*; (*at fair*) baraque *f*; (*voting*) isoloir *m*.

booty ['buːtɪ] *n* (*stolen goods*) butin *m*.

booz/e [buːz] *n Fam* alcool *m*, boisson(s) *f(pl)* ‖ *vi Fam* boire (beaucoup). ●**—er** *n Fam* (*person*) buveur, -euse *mf*.

border ['bɔːdər] *n* (*of country*) frontière *f*; (*edge*) bord *m*; (*of garden*) bordure *f* ‖ *vt* **to b. (on)** (*country*) toucher à; **to b. (up)on** (*verge on*) être voisin de. ●**borderline** *n* frontière *f*; **b. case** cas *m* limite.

bor/e[1] [bɔːr] **1** *vt* (*weary*) ennuyer; **to be bored** s'ennuyer; **I'm bored with that** ça m'ennuie ‖ *n* (*person*) raseur, -euse *mf*; **it's a b.** c'est ennuyeux. **2** *vt* (*hole*) percer. **3** *n* (*of gun*) calibre *m*. ●**—ing** *a* ennuyeux. ●**boredom** *n* ennui *m*.

bore[2] [bɔːr] *pt of* **bear**[2].

born [bɔːn] *a* né; **to be b.** naître; **he was b.** il est né.

borne [bɔːn] *pp of* **bear**[2].

borough ['bʌrə] *n* (*town*) municipalité *f*; (*part of town*) arrondissement *m*.

borrow ['bɒrəʊ] *vt* emprunter (**from** à). ●**—ing** *n* emprunt *m*.

Bosnia ['bɒznɪə] *n* Bosnie *f*.

bosom ['bʊzəm] *n* (*chest*) poitrine *f*, seins *mpl*; (*breast*) & *Fig* sein *m*; **b. friend** ami, -ie *mf* intime.

boss [bɒs] *n Fam* patron, -onne *mf*, chef *m* ‖ *vt* **to b. s.o. around** *or* **about** *Fam* commander qn. ●**bossy** *a* (**-ier, -iest**) *Fam* autoritaire.

boss-eyed [bɒ'saɪd] *a* **to be b.-eyed** loucher.

bosun ['bəʊs(ə)n] *n* maître *m* d'équipage.

botany ['bɒtənɪ] *n* botanique *f*. ●**bo'tanical** *a* botanique.

botch [bɒtʃ] *vt* **to b. (up)** (*spoil*) bâcler.

both [bəʊθ] *a* les deux ‖ *pron* tous *or* toutes (les) deux; **b. (of) the boys** les deux garçons; **b. of us** nous deux ‖ *adv* (*at the same time*) à la fois; **b. you and I** vous et moi.

bother ['bɒðər] *vt* (*annoy, worry*) ennuyer; (*disturb*) déranger; (*pester*) importuner; (*hurt etc*) (*of foot etc*) gêner; **to b. doing** *or* **to do** se donner la peine de faire; **I can't be bothered!** je n'en ai pas envie! ‖ *vi* **to b. about** (*worry about*) se préoccuper de; (*deal with*) s'occuper de ‖ *n* (*trouble*) ennui *m*; (*effort*) peine *f*; (*inconvenience*) dérangement *m*; **(oh) b.!** zut alors!

bottle ['bɒt(ə)l] *n* bouteille *f*; (*small*) flacon *m*; (*for baby*) biberon *m*; **(hot-water) b.** bouillotte *f*; **b. opener** ouvre-bouteilles *m inv*; **b. bank** conteneur *m* pour verre usagé ‖ *vt* mettre en bouteilles; **to b. up** (*feeling*) contenir. ●**bottlefeed** *vt* (*pt & pp* **-fed**) nourrir au biberon. ●**bottleneck** *n* (*in road*) goulot *m* d'étranglement; (*traffic holdup*) bouchon *m*.

bottom ['bɒtəm] *n* (*of sea, box*) fond *m*; (*of page, hill*) bas *m*; (*buttocks*) *Fam* derrière *m*; (*of table*) bout *m*; **to be at the b. of the class** être le dernier de la classe ‖ *a* (*shelf*) inférieur, du bas; **b. floor** rez-de-chaussée *m*; **b. part** partie *f* inférieure.

bought [bɔːt] *pt & pp of* **buy**.

boulder ['bəʊldər] *n* rocher *m*.

boulevard ['buːləvɑːd] *n* boulevard *m*.

bounce [baʊns] **1** *vi* (*of ball*) rebondir; (*of person*) faire des bonds ‖ *vt* faire rebondir ‖ *n* (re)bond *m*. **2** *vi* (*of cheque, Am check*) *Fam* être sans provision.

bound[1] [baʊnd] *pt & pp of* **bind**. **1** *a* **b. to do** (*obliged*) obligé de faire; (*certain*) sûr de faire; **it's b. to happen/snow/***etc* ça arrivera/il neigera/*etc sûrement;* **b. for** (*of person, ship*) en route pour; (*of train, plane*) à destination de. **2** *a* **b. up with** (*connected*) lié à.

bound[2] [baʊnd] *n* (*leap*) bond *m* ‖ *vi* bondir.

boundary ['baʊnd(ə)rɪ] *n* limite *f*.

bounds [baʊndz] *npl* **out of b.** (*place*) interdit.

bouquet [bəʊ'keɪ, buː-] *n* (*of flowers, wine*) bouquet *m*.

bout [baʊt] *n* (*of fever, coughing etc*) accès *m*; (*of asthma etc*) crise *f*; *Boxing* combat *m*; (*session*) séance *f*; **a b. of flu** une grippe.

boutique [buː'tiːk] *n* boutique *f* (de mode).

bow[1] [bəʊ] *n* (*weapon*) arc *m*; *Mus* archet *m*; (*knot*) nœud *m*; **b. tie** nœud *m* papillon. ●**b.-'legged** *a* aux jambes arquées.

bow[2] [baʊ] **1** *n* (*with knees bent*) révérence *f*; (*nod*) salut *m* ‖ *vt* (*one's head*) incliner ‖ *vi* s'incliner (**to** devant); (*nod*) incliner la tête (**to** devant). **2** *n Nau* proue *f*.

bowels ['baʊəlz] *npl* intestins *mpl*.

bowl [bəʊl] **1** *n* (*for food*) bol *m*; (*basin*) cuvette *f*; (*for sugar*) sucrier *m*; (*for salad*) saladier *m*; (*for fruit*) (*of glass, plastic*) coupe *f*. **2** *vi Cricket* lancer la balle. **3** *vt* **to b. s.o. over** (*astound*) bouleverser qn. ●**—ing** *n* **(tenpin) b.** bowling *m*; **b. alley** bowling *m*.

bowler ['bəʊlər] *n* **b. (hat)** (chapeau *m*) melon *m*.

bowls [bəʊlz] *npl* (*game*) boules *fpl*.

box [bɒks] **1** *n* boîte *f*; (*large*) caisse *f*; (*of cardboard*) carton *m*; *Th* loge *f*; *TV Fam* télé *f*; **b. office** bureau *m* de location; **b. room** (*lumber room*) débarras *m*; (*bedroom*) petite chambre *f* (carrée) ‖ *vt* **to b. (up)** mettre en boîte; **to b. in** (*enclose*) enfermer. **2** *vi Boxing* boxer. ●**—ing** *n* **1** boxe *f*; **b. ring** ring *m*. **2 B. Day** le lendemain de Noël. ●**boxer** *n* boxeur *m*.

boy [bɔɪ] *n* garçon *m*; **English b.** jeune Anglais *m*; **old b.** *Sch* ancien élève *m*; **oh b.!** mon Dieu!

boycott ['bɔɪkɒt] *vt* boycotter ‖ *n* boycottage *m*.

boyfriend ['bɔɪfrend] *n* (petit) ami *m*.

bra [brɑː] *n* soutien-gorge *m*.

brace [breɪs] **1** *n* (*dental*) appareil *m*; *pl* (*trouser straps*) bretelles *fpl*. **2** *vt* **to b. oneself for** (*news, shock*) se préparer à.

bracelet ['breɪslɪt] *n* bracelet *m*.

bracket ['brækɪt] *n* (*for shelf etc*) équerre *f*; (*round sign*) *Typ* parenthèse *f*; (*square sign*) *Typ* crochet *m*; *Fig* groupe *m*, tranche *f* ‖ *vt* mettre entre parenthèses *or* crochets.

brag [bræg] *vi* **(-gg-)** se vanter (**about, of** de). ●**bragging** *n* vantardise *f*.

braid [breɪd] *vt* (*hair*) *Am* tresser ‖ *n Am* tresse *f*.

Braille [breɪl] *n* braille *m*.

brain [breɪn] **1** *n* cerveau *m*; (*of animal, bird*) cervelle *f*; **to have brains** (*sense*) avoir de l'intelligence; **b. drain** fuite *f* des cerveaux. **2** *vt* (*hit*) *Fam* assommer. ●**brainstorm** *n Am* idée *f* géniale. ●**brainwash** *vt* faire un lavage de cerveau à. ●**brainwave** *n* idée *f* géniale.

brainy ['breɪnɪ] *a* **(-ier, -iest)** *Fam* intelligent.

brak/e [breɪk] *n* frein *m*; **b. light** *Aut* stop *m* ‖ *vi* freiner. ●**—ing** *n* freinage *m*.

bramble ['bræmb(ə)l] *n* (*bush*) ronce *f*.

bran [bræn] *n* (*of wheat*) son *m*.

branch [brɑːntʃ] *n* branche *f*; (*of road*) embranchement *m*; (*of store*, *office*) succursale *f* ‖ *vi* **to b. off** (*of road*) bifurquer; **to b. out** (*of firm*, *person*) étendre ses activités (**into** à).
brand [brænd] **1** *n* (*trademark*) marque *f*; (*variety*) type *m*. **2** *vt* **to be branded as** avoir une réputation de.
brandish ['brændɪʃ] *vt* brandir.
brand-new [brænd'njuː] *a* tout neuf (*f* toute neuve), flambant neuf (*f* flambant neuve).
brandy ['brændɪ] *n* cognac *m*; (*made with pears etc*) eau-de-vie *f*.
brash [bræʃ] *a* effronté.
brass [brɑːs] *n* cuivre *m*; **the top b.** (*officers*, *executives*) *Fam* les huiles *fpl*; **b. band** fanfare *f*.
brassiere ['bræzɪər, *Am* brə'zɪər] *n* soutien-gorge *m*.
brat [bræt] *n* (*badly behaved*) sale gosse *mf*.
brave [breɪv] *a* (**-er, -est**) courageux, brave ‖ *vt* (*danger etc*) braver. • **bravery** *n* courage *m*.
brawl [brɔːl] *n* (*fight*) bagarre *f* ‖ *vi* se bagarrer.
brawn [brɔːn] *n* muscles *mpl*. • **brawny** *a* (**-ier, -iest**) musclé.
bray [breɪ] *vi* (*of ass*) braire.
brazen ['breɪz(ə)n] *a* (*shameless*) effronté.
Brazil [brə'zɪl] *n* Brésil *m*. • **Brazilian** *a* & *n* brésilien, -ienne (*mf*).
breach [briːtʃ] **1** *n* violation *f*; (*of contract*) rupture *f* ‖ *vt* (*code*) violer. **2** *n* (*gap*) brèche *f* ‖ *vt* (*wall*) ouvrir une brèche dans.
bread [bred] *n inv* pain *m*; **loaf of b.** pain *m*; **(slice** *or* **piece of) b. and butter** tartine *f*. • **breadbin** *or Am* **breadbox** *n* boîte *f* à pain. • **breadboard** *n* planche *f* à pain. • **breadcrumb** *n* miette *f* (de pain); *pl Culin* chapelure *f*. • **breadline** *n* **on the b.** indigent. • **breadwinner** *n* soutien *m* de famille.
breadth [bretθ] *n* largeur *f*.
break [breɪk] *vt* (*pt* **broke,** *pp* **broken**) casser; (*into pieces*) briser; (*silence*, *spell*) rompre; (*strike*, *heart*, *ice*) briser; (*record*) *Sp* battre; (*law*) violer; (*one's promise*) manquer à; (*journey*) interrompre; (*news*) annoncer (**to** à); (*habit*) se débarrasser de; **to b. open** (*safe*) percer; **to b. new ground** innover.
‖ *vi* (se) casser; se briser; se rompre; (*of voice*) s'altérer; (*of boy's voice*) muer; (*of weather*) se gâter; (*of news*) éclater; (*of day*) se lever; (*stop work*) faire la pause; **to b. loose** s'échapper; **to b. with s.o.** rompre avec qn.
‖ *n* cassure *f*; (*in bone*) fracture *f*; (*with person*, *group*) rupture *f*; (*in journey*) interruption *f*; (*rest*) repos *m*; (*in activity*, *for tea*) pause *f*; *Sch* récréation *f*; (*in weather*) changement *m*; **a lucky b.** *Fam* une chance. • **breaking point** *n* **at b. point** (*person*) sur le point de craquer.
breakable ['breɪkəb(ə)l] *a* fragile.
break away *vi* se détacher ‖ *vt* détacher **to break down** *vt* (*door*) enfoncer; (*analyse*) analyser ‖ *vi* (*of vehicle*, *machine*) tomber en panne; (*of talks*) échouer; (*collapse*) (*of person*) s'effondrer. • **breakdown** *n* panne *f*; analyse *f*; (*in talks*) rupture *f*; (*nervous*) dépression *f*; **b. lorry** dépanneuse *f*. **to break in** *vi* (*of burglar*) entrer par effraction ‖ *vt* (*door*) enfoncer; (*horse*) dresser; (*vehicle*) *Am* roder. • **break-in** *n* cambriolage *m*. **to break into** *vt* (*safe*) forcer **to break off** *vt* détacher; (*relations*) rompre ‖ *vi* se détacher; (*stop*) s'arrêter; **to break off with s.o.** rompre avec qn **to break out** *vi* (*of war*, *fire*) éclater; (*escape*) s'échapper **to break through** *vi* (*of sun*) percer ‖ *vt* (*defences*) percer. • **breakthrough** *n* (*discovery*) percée *f*, découverte *f*. **to break up** *vt* mettre en morceaux; (*marriage*) briser; (*fight*) mettre fin à ‖ *vi* (*of group*) se disperser; (*of marriage*) se briser; (*from school*) partir en vacances. • **breakup** *n* fin *f*; (*in marriage*) rupture *f*.
breakfast ['brekfəst] *n* petit déjeuner *m*.
breast [brest] *n* sein *m*; (*of chicken*) blanc *m*. • **breastfeed** *vt* (*pt* & *pp* **-fed**) allaiter. • **breaststroke** *n* brasse *f*.
breath [breθ] *n* haleine *f*, souffle *m*; **out of b.** (tout) essoufflé; **to get a b. of air** prendre l'air; **to take a deep b.** respirer profondément; **under one's b.** tout bas. • **breathalyser**® *n* alcootest® *m*. • **breathtaking** *a* sensationnel.
breath/e [briːð] *vti* respirer; **to b. in** aspirer; **to b. out** expirer; **to b. air into sth** souffler dans qch. • **—ing** *n* respiration *f*; **b. space** moment *m* de repos. • **breather** *n Fam* moment *m* de repos.
bred [bred] *pt* & *pp of* **breed 1** ‖ *a* **well-b.** bien élevé.
breeches ['brɪtʃɪz] *npl* culotte *f*.
breed [briːd] **1** *vt* (*pt* & *pp* **bred**) (*animals*) élever ‖ *vi* (*of animals*) se reproduire. **2** *n* race *f*, espèce *f*. • **—ing** *n* élevage *m*; reproduction *f*. • **breeder** *n* éleveur, -euse *mf*.
breeze [briːz] *n* brise *f*. • **breezy** *a* (**-ier, -iest**) (*weather*, *day*) frais (*f* fraîche).
brevity ['brevɪtɪ] *n* brièveté *f*.
brew [bruː] *vt* (*beer*) brasser; (*plot*) pré-

parer; **to b. tea** préparer du thé; (*infuse*) (faire) infuser du thé ‖ *vi* (*of storm*) se préparer; (*of tea*) infuser; **something is brewing** il se prépare quelque chose ‖ *n* (*drink*) breuvage *m*; (*of tea*) infusion *f*. ●**brewery** *n* brasserie *f*.

bribe [braɪb] *n* pot-de-vin *m* ‖ *vt* acheter (*qn*). ●**bribery** *n* corruption *f*.

brick [brɪk] *n* brique *f*; (*child's*) cube *m* ‖ *vt* **to b. up** (*gap*, *door*) murer. ●**bricklayer** *n* maçon *m*. ●**brickwork** *n* (*bricks*) briques *fpl*.

bride [braɪd] *n* mariée *f*; **the b. and groom** les mariés *mpl*. ●**bridegroom** *n* marié *m*. ●**bridesmaid** *n* demoiselle *f* d'honneur.

bridge [brɪdʒ] **1** *n* pont *m*; (*on ship*) passerelle *f* ‖ *vt* **to b. a gap** combler une lacune. **2** *n Cards* bridge *m*.

bridle ['braɪd(ə)l] *n* (*for horse*) bride *f*; **b. path** allée *f* cavalière.

brief[1] [bri:f] *a* (**-er, -est**) bref (*f* brève); **in b.** en résumé. ●**—ly** *adv* (*quickly*) en vitesse.

brief[2] [bri:f] (*instructions*) *Mil Pol etc* instructions *fpl* ‖ *vt* donner des instructions à; (*inform*) mettre au courant (**on** de). ●**—ing** *n Mil Pol* instructions *fpl*.

briefcase ['bri:fkeɪs] *n* serviette *f*.

briefs [bri:fs] *npl* (*underpants*) slip *m*.

brigade [brɪ'geɪd] *n* brigade *f*.

bright [braɪt] *a* (**-er, -est**) (*star, eyes, situation, future*) brillant; (*colour, light*) vif; (*weather, room*) clair; (*clever*) intelligent; (*happy*) joyeux; (*idea*) génial; **b. interval** *Met* éclaircie *f* ‖ *adv* **b. and early** de bonne heure. ●**—ly** *adv* avec éclat. ●**—ness** *n* éclat *m*.

brighten ['braɪtən] *vt* **to b. (up)** (*room*) égayer ‖ *vi* **to b. (up)** (*of weather*) s'éclaircir; (*of face*) s'éclairer.

brilliant ['brɪljənt] *a* (*light*) éclatant; (*clever*) brillant; (*fantastic*) *Fam* super. ●**brilliance** *n* éclat *m*; (*of person*) grande intelligence *f*.

brim [brɪm] *n* bord *m* ‖ *vi* (**-mm-**) **to b. over** déborder (**with** de).

bring [brɪŋ] *vt* (*pt & pp* **brought**) (*person, vehicle*) amener; (*object*) apporter; (*to cause*) amener; **to b. sth to** (*perfection, a peak etc*) porter qch à; **to b. to an end** mettre fin à; **to b. to mind** rappeler.

bring about *vt* provoquer **to bring along** *vt* (*object*) apporter; (*person*) amener **to bring back** *vt* (*person*) ramener; (*object*) rapporter; (*memories*) rappeler **to bring down** *vt* (*object*) descendre; (*overthrow*) faire tomber; (*reduce*) réduire **to bring forward** *vt* (*in time or space*) avancer **to bring in** *vt* (*object*) rentrer; (*person*) faire entrer; (*introduce*) introduire; (*income*) rapporter **to bring off** *vt* (*task*) mener à bien; (*object*) sortir **to bring out** *vt* (*object*) sortir; (*person*) faire sortir; (*meaning*) faire ressortir; (*book*) publier; (*product*) lancer **to bring round** *vt Med* ranimer (*qn*); (*convert*) convertir (*qn*) (**to** à) **to bring to** *Med vt* ranimer (*qn*) **to bring together** *vt* (*friends etc*) réunir; (*reconcile*) réconcilier **to bring up** *vt* (*object*) monter; (*child etc*) élever; (*subject*) mentionner; (*food*) vomir.

brink [brɪŋk] *n* bord *m*.

brisk [brɪsk] *a* (**-er, -est**) vif; **at a b. pace** vite. ●**—ly** *adv* (*to walk*) vite.

bristle ['brɪs(ə)l] *n* poil *m* ‖ *vi* se hérisser.

Britain ['brɪt(ə)n] *n* Grande-Bretagne *f*. ●**British** *a* britannique; **the B. Isles** les îles *fpl* Britanniques ‖ *n* **the B.** les Britanniques *mpl*. ●**Briton** *n* Britannique *mf*.

Brittany ['brɪtənɪ] *n* Bretagne *f*.

brittle ['brɪt(ə)l] *a* fragile.

broach [brəʊtʃ] *vt* (*topic*) entamer.

broad [brɔ:d] *a* (**-er, -est**) (*wide*) large; (*outline*) général; (*accent*) prononcé; **in b. daylight** en plein jour; **b. bean** fève *f*; **b. jump** *Sp Am* saut *m* en longueur. ●**b.-'minded** *a* à l'esprit large. ●**b.-'shouldered** *a* large d'épaules. ●**broaden** *vt* élargir ‖ *vi* s'élargir. ●**broadly** *adv* **b. (speaking)** en gros.

broadcast ['brɔ:dkɑ:st] *vt* (*pt & pp* **broadcast**) diffuser, retransmettre ‖ *vi* (*of station*) émettre; (*person*) parler à la radio *or* à la télévision ‖ *n* émission *f*.

broccoli ['brɒkəlɪ] *n inv* brocolis *mpl*.

brochure ['brəʊʃər] *n* brochure *f*, dépliant *m*.

broil [brɔɪl] *vti* griller.

broke [brəʊk] **1** *pt of* **break. 2** *a* (*penniless*) fauché. ●**broken** *pp of* **break** ‖ *a* (*man, voice, line*) brisé; **in b. English** en mauvais anglais; **b. home** foyer *m* brisé. ●**broken-'down** *a* (*machine*) (tout) déglingué.

broker [brəʊkər] *n* courtier, -ière *mf*.

brolly ['brɒlɪ] *n* (*umbrella*) *Fam* pépin *m*.

bronchitis [brɒŋ'kaɪtɪs] *n* bronchite *f*.

bronze [brɒnz] *n* bronze *m* ‖ *a* (*statue etc*) en bronze.

brooch [brəʊtʃ] *n* (*ornament*) broche *f*.

brood [bru:d] **1** *n* couvée *f*, nichée *f*. **2** *vi* méditer tristement (**over** sur); **to b. over** (*a plan*) ruminer. ●**broody** *a* (**-ier, -iest**) (*person*) maussade.

brook [brʊk] *n* ruisseau *m*.

broom [bru:m] *n* balai *m*. ●**broomstick** *n* manche *m* à balai.

Bros *abbr* (*Brothers*) Frères *mpl*.

broth [brɒθ] *n* bouillon *m*.

brothel ['brɒθ(ə)l] *n* maison *f* close.
brother ['brʌðər] *n* frère *m*. ● **b.-in-law** *n* (*pl* **brothers-in-law**) beau-frère *m*. ● **brotherly** *a* fraternel.
brought [brɔːt] *pt & pp of* **bring**.
brow [braʊ] *n* **1** (*forehead*) front *m*. **2** (*of hill*) sommet *m*.
brown [braʊn] *a* (**-er, -est**) brun; (*reddish*) marron; (*hair*) châtain; (*tanned*) bronzé ‖ *n* brun *m*; marron *m* ‖ *vt* (*of sun*) bronzer (*la peau*); *Culin* faire dorer; **to be browned off** *Fam* en avoir marre.
Brownie ['braʊnɪ] *n* (*girl scout*) jeannette *f*.
browse [braʊz] *vi* (*in bookshop*) feuilleter des livres; (*in shop*) regarder; **to b. through** (*book*) feuilleter.
bruis/e [bruːz] *vt* **to b. one's knee**/*etc* se faire un bleu au genou/*etc* ‖ *n* bleu *m*, contusion *f*. ● **—ed** *a* couvert de bleus.
brunch [brʌntʃ] *n* brunch *m*.
brunette [bruː'net] *n* brunette *f*.
brunt [brʌnt] *n* **to bear the b. of** (*attack etc*) subir le plus gros de.
brush [brʌʃ] *n* brosse *f*; (*for shaving*) blaireau *m*; (*for sweeping*) balayette *f*; (*action*) coup *m* de brosse ‖ *vt* (*teeth, hair*) brosser; (*clothes*) donner un coup de brosse à; **to b. aside** écarter; **to b. away** *or* **off** enlever; **to b. up (on)** (*language*) se remettre à ‖ *vi* **to b. against** effleurer. ● **brushwood** *n* broussailles *fpl*.
Brussels ['brʌs(ə)lz] *n* Bruxelles *m or f*; **B. sprouts** choux *mpl* de Bruxelles.
brutal ['bruːt(ə)l] *a* brutal. ● **bru'tality** *n* brutalité *f*.
brute [bruːt] *n* (*animal, person*) brute *f*.
BSc, *Am* **BS** *abbr* = **Bachelor of Science.**
bubble ['bʌb(ə)l] *n* (*of air, soap, in boiling liquid*) bulle *f*; **b. bath** bain *m* moussant; **b. gum** bubble-gum *m* ‖ *vi* bouillonner; **to b. over** déborder (**with** de).
buck [bʌk] **1** *n Am Fam* dollar *m*. **2** *n* (*animal*) mâle *m*. **3** *vt* **to b. up** remonter le moral à (*qn*) ‖ *vi* **to b. up** (*become livelier*) reprendre du poil de la bête; (*hurry*) se grouiller.
bucket ['bʌkɪt] *n* seau *m*.
buckle ['bʌk(ə)l] **1** *n* boucle *f* ‖ *vt* boucler. **2** *vti* (*warp*) voiler. **3** *vi* **to b. down to** (*task*) s'atteler à.
bud [bʌd] *n* (*of tree*) bourgeon *m*; (*of flower*) bouton *m* ‖ *vi* (**-dd-**) bourgeonner; pousser des boutons. ● **budding** *a* (*talent*) naissant; (*doctor etc*) en herbe.
Buddhist ['bʊdɪst] *a & n* bouddhiste (*mf*).
buddy ['bʌdɪ] *n Am Fam* copain *m*, pote *m*.
budge [bʌdʒ] *vi* bouger ‖ *vt* faire bouger.
budgerigar ['bʌdʒərɪgɑːr] *n* perruche *f*.
budget ['bʌdʒɪt] *n* budget *m* ‖ *vi* **to b. for** inscrire au budget.
budgie ['bʌdʒɪ] *n Fam* perruche *f*.
buff [bʌf] **1** *a* **b.(-coloured)** chamois *inv*. **2** *n* **jazz**/*etc* **b.** *Fam* fana(tique) *mf* de jazz/*etc*.
buffalo ['bʌfələʊ] *n* (*pl* **-oes** *or* **-o**) buffle *m*; **(American) b.** bison *m*.
buffer ['bʌfər] *n* (*on train*) tampon *m*; (*at end of track*) butoir *m*.
buffet[1] ['bʊfeɪ] *n* (*table, meal, café*) buffet *m*; **cold b.** viandes *fpl* froides; **b. car** (*on train*) voiture-bar *f*.
buffet[2] ['bʊfɪt] *vt* (*of waves*) battre (*navire etc*).
bug[1] [bʌg] **1** *n* punaise *f*; (*any insect*) bestiole *f*; (*germ*) *Fam* microbe *m*, virus *m*. **2** *n Fam* (*in machine*) défaut *m*; (*in computer program*) erreur *f*. **3** *n* (*listening device*) micro *m* (clandestin) ‖ *vt* (**-gg-**) (*room*) installer des micros dans.
bug[2] [bʌg] *vt* (**-gg-**) (*annoy*) *Fam* embêter.
buggy ['bʌgɪ] *n* **(baby) b.** poussette *f*; (*folding pushchair*) poussette-canne *f*; (*pram*) *Am* landau *m* (*pl* -aus).
bugle ['bjuːg(ə)l] *n* clairon *m*.
build [bɪld] **1** *n* (*of person*) carrure *f*. **2** *vt* (*pt & pp* **built**) construire; (*house, town*) construire, bâtir ‖ *vi* bâtir, construire. **3 to b. up** *vt* (*increase*) augmenter; (*collection*) constituer; (*business*) monter; (*speed*) prendre; (*reputation*) bâtir ‖ *vi* (*of tension, pressure*) augmenter, monter; (*of dust*) s'accumuler.
builder ['bɪldər] *n* (*of houses etc*) (*workman*) maçon *m*; (*contractor*) entrepreneur *m*.
building ['bɪldɪŋ] *n* bâtiment *m*; (*flats, offices*) immeuble *m*; (*action*) construction *f*; **b. society** = société *f* de crédit immobilier.
built-in [bɪlt'ɪn] *a* (*cupboard, Am closet*) encastré; (*part of machine*) incorporé.
built-up [bɪlt'ʌp] *a* urbanisé; **b.-up area** agglomération *f*.
bulb [bʌlb] *n* (*of plant*) oignon *m*; (*of lamp*) ampoule *f*.
Bulgaria [bʌl'geərɪə] *n* Bulgarie *f*. ● **Bulgarian** *a & n* bulgare (*mf*).
bulg/e [bʌldʒ] *vi* **to b. (out)** se renfler, bomber ‖ *n* renflement *m*. ● **—ing** *a* renflé, bombé; **to be b.** (*of bag etc*) être plein à craquer (**with** de).
bulk [bʌlk] *n inv* (*of building etc*) volume *m*; (*of person*) grosseur *f*; **the b. of** (*most*) la majeure partie de; **in b.** (*to buy, sell*) en gros. ● **bulky** *a* (**-ier, -iest**) gros (*f* grosse).
bull [bʊl] *n* taureau *m*.

bulldog ['bʊldɒg] *n* bouledogue *m*.
bulldozer ['bʊldəʊzər] *n* bulldozer *m*.
bullet ['bʊlɪt] *n* balle *f* (*de revolver etc*). ● **bulletproof** *a* (*jacket*, *Am vest*) pare-balles *inv*; (*car*) blindé.
bulletin ['bʊlətɪn] *n* bulletin *m*; **b. board** *Am* tableau *m* d'affichage.
bullfight ['bʊlfaɪt] *n* corrida *f*. ● **bullring** *n* arène *f*.
bull's-eye ['bʊlzaɪ] *n* (*of target*) centre *m*; **to hit the b.-eye** faire mouche.
bully ['bʊlɪ] *n* (grosse) brute *f* ▮ *vt* brutaliser; **to b. into doing** forcer à faire.
bum [bʌm] **1** *n Fam* (*loafer*) clochard, -arde *mf*; (*good-for-nothing*) propre *mf* à rien ▮ *vi* (**-mm-**) **to b. (around)** se balader. **2** *n* (*buttocks*) *Fam* derrière *m*; **b. bag** banane *f*.
bumblebee ['bʌmb(ə)lbiː] *n* bourdon *m*.
bump [bʌmp] *vt* (*of car etc*) heurter; **to b. one's head/knee** se cogner la tête/le genou; **to b. into** se cogner contre; (*of car*) rentrer dans; (*meet*) tomber sur ▮ *vi* **to b. along** (*on rough road*) (*in car etc*) cahoter.
▮ *n* (*impact*) choc *m*; (*jerk*) cahot *m*; (*on road, body*) bosse *f*. ● **bumper** *n* (*of car etc*) pare-chocs *m inv* ▮ *a* (*crop etc*) exceptionnel; **b. cars** autos *fpl* tamponneuses. ● **bumpy** *a* (**-ier, -iest**) (*road, ride*) cahoteux.
bun [bʌn] *n* (*cake*) petit pain *m* au lait.
bunch [bʌntʃ] *n* (*of flowers*) bouquet *m*; (*of keys*) trousseau *m*; (*of bananas*) régime *m*; (*of people*) bande *f*; **b. of grapes** grappe *f* de raisin; **a b. of** (*mass*) *Fam* un tas de.
bundle ['bʌnd(ə)l] **1** *n* paquet *m*; (*of papers*) liasse *f*; (*of firewood*) fagot *m*. **2** *vt* (*put*) fourrer; (*push*) pousser (**into** dans). **3** *vti* **to b. (oneself) up** se couvrir (bien).
bung [bʌŋ] **1** *vt* **to b. up** (*stop up*) boucher. **2** *vt* (*toss*) *Fam* balancer.
bungalow ['bʌŋgələʊ] *n* bungalow *m*.
bungle ['bʌŋg(ə)l] *vt* gâcher.
bunion ['bʌnjən] *n* (*on toe*) oignon *m*.
bunk [bʌŋk] *n Rail Nau* couchette *f*; **b. beds** lits *mpl* superposés.
bunker ['bʌŋkər] *n Mil Golf* bunker *m*.
bunny ['bʌnɪ] *n* **b. (rabbit)** *Fam* Jeannot *m* lapin.
buoy [bɔɪ] *n* bouée *f*.
buoyant ['bɔɪənt] *a* (*cheerful*) gai, optimiste.
burden ['bɜːd(ə)n] *n* fardeau *m*; (*of tax*) poids *m* ▮ *vt* accabler (**with** de).
bureau, *pl* **-eaux** *or* **-eaus** ['bjʊərəʊ, -əʊz] *n* (*office*) bureau *m*; (*desk*) secrétaire *m*; (*chest of drawers*) *Am* commode *f*.
bureaucracy [bjʊə'rɒkrəsɪ] *n* bureaucratie *f*. ● **bureaucrat** ['bjʊərəkræt] *n* bureaucrate *mf*.
burger ['bɜːgər] *n Fam* hamburger *m*.
burglar ['bɜːglər] *n* cambrioleur, -euse *mf*; **b. alarm** alarme *f* antivol. ● **burglarize** *vt Am* cambrioler. ● **burglary** *n* cambriolage *m*. ● **burgle** *vt* cambrioler.
burial ['berɪəl] *n* enterrement *m*.
burly ['bɜːlɪ] *a* (**-ier, -iest**) costaud.
Burma ['bɜːmə] *n* Birmanie *f*. ● **Bur'mese** *a* & *n* birman, -ane (*mf*).
burn [bɜːn] *n* brûlure *f*.
▮ *vt* (*pt* & *pp* **burned** *or* **burnt**) brûler; **burnt alive** brûlé vif; **to b. down** (*house*) détruire par le feu.
▮ *vi* brûler; **to b. down** (*of house*) brûler (complètement), être réduit en cendres; **to b. out** (*of fire*) s'éteindre; (*of fuse*) sauter.
● **—ing** *a* en feu; (*fire, light*) allumé; (*topic etc*) *Fig* brûlant ▮ *n* **smell of b.** odeur *f* de brûlé. ● **burner** *n* (*of stove*) brûleur *m*.
burp [bɜːp] *n Fam* rot *m* ▮ *vi Fam* roter.
burrow ['bʌrəʊ] *n* (*hole*) terrier *m* ▮ *vti* creuser.
burst [bɜːst] *n* (*of laughter*) éclat *m*; (*of applause*) salve *f*; (*of thunder*) coup *m*; (*explosion*) éclatement *m*; (*surge*) élan *m*; (*fit*) accès *m*.
▮ *vi* (*pt* & *pp* **burst**) (*with force*) éclater; (*of bubble, balloon, boil, tyre, cloud*) crever; **to b. into** (*room*) faire irruption dans; **to b. into tears** fondre en larmes; **to b. into flames** prendre feu; **to b. out laughing** éclater de rire.
▮ *vt* (*bubble, balloon etc*) crever. ● **bursting** *a* (*full*) plein à craquer (**with** de).
bury ['berɪ] *vt* (*dead person*) enterrer; (*hide*) enfouir; (*plunge*) plonger; **buried in one's work**/*etc* plongé dans son travail/*etc*.
bus [bʌs] *n* (auto)bus *m*; (*long-distance*) (auto)car *m* ▮ *a* (*driver, ticket etc*) d'autobus; d'autocar; **b. shelter** Abribus® *m*; **b. station** gare *f* routière; **b. stop** arrêt *m* d'autobus.
bush [bʊʃ] *n* buisson *m*; **the b.** (*land*) la brousse. ● **bushy** *a* (**-ier, -iest**) (*hair, tail etc*) broussailleux.
bushed [bʊʃt] *a* (*tired*) *Fam* crevé.
business ['bɪznɪs] *n* affaires *fpl*, commerce *m*; (*shop*) commerce *m*; (*task, concern, matter*) affaire *f*; **big b.** les grosses entreprises *fpl* commerciales; **on b.** (*to travel*) pour affaires; **it's your b. to . . .** c'est à vous de . . . ; **that's none of your b.!, mind you own b.!** ça ne vous regarde pas!
▮ *a* commercial; (*meeting, trip*) d'affaires; **b. hours** (*office*) heures *fpl* de travail; (*shop*) heures *fpl* d'ouverture; **b. card** carte *f* de

visite. • **businesslike** *a* sérieux, pratique. • **businessman** *n* (*pl* **-men**) homme *m* d'affaires. • **businesswoman** *n* (*pl* **-women**) femme *f* d'affaires.

busker ['bʌskər] *n* musicien, -ienne *mf* des rues.

bust [bʌst] **1** *n* (*sculpture*) buste *m*; (*woman's breasts*) poitrine *f*. **2** *a* (*broken*) *Fam* fichu; **to go b.** (*bankrupt*) faire faillite.

bustl/e ['bʌs(ə)l] *vi* s'affairer ‖ *n* activité *f*. • **—ing** *a* (*street*) bruyant.

busy ['bɪzɪ] *a* (**-ier, -iest**) occupé (**doing** à faire); (*active*) actif; (*day*) chargé; (*street*) animé; (*phone*) *Am* occupé; **to be b. doing** être en train de faire; **b. signal** *Am* sonnerie *f* 'occupé' ‖ *vt* **to b. oneself** s'occuper (**with sth** à qch, **doing** à faire). • **busybody** *n* **to be a b.** faire la mouche du coche.

but [bʌt, *unstressed* bət] **1** *conj* mais. **2** *prep* (*except*) sauf; **b. for that** sans cela; **b. for him** sans lui; **no one b. you** personne d'autre que toi. **3** *adv* (*only*) ne . . . que, seulement; **he's b. a boy** ce n'est qu'un garçon.

butane ['bjuːteɪn] *n* (*gas*) butane *m*.

butcher ['bʊtʃər] *n* boucher *m*; **b.'s shop** boucherie *f* ‖ *vt* (*people*) massacrer; (*animal*) abattre.

butler ['bʌtlər] *n* maître *m* d'hôtel.

butt [bʌt] **1** *n* (*of cigarette*) mégot *m*; (*of gun*) crosse *f*; (*buttocks*) *Am Fam* derrière *m*; **b. for ridicule** objet *m* de risée. **2** *vi* **to b. in** interrompre.

butter ['bʌtər] *n* beurre *m*; **b. dish** beurrier *m* ‖ *vt* beurrer. • **buttercup** *n* bouton-d'or *m*. • **buttermilk** *n* lait *m* de beurre.

butterfly ['bʌtəflaɪ] *n* papillon *m*; **to have butterflies** *Fam* avoir le trac; **b. stroke** brasse *f* papillon.

buttock ['bʌtək] *n* fesse *f*.

button ['bʌtən] *n* bouton *m*; (*of phone*) touche *f*; (*badge*) *Am* badge *m* ‖ *vt* **to b. (up)** boutonner ‖ *vi* **to b. (up)** (*of garment*) se boutonner. • **buttonhole** *n* boutonnière *f*; (*flower*) fleur *f*.

buy [baɪ] *vt* (*pt* & *pp* **bought**) acheter (**from s.o.** à qn, **for s.o.** à *or* pour qn); (*story etc*) *Am Fam* croire, avaler; **to b. back** racheter; **to b. up** acheter en bloc ‖ *n* **a good b.** une bonne affaire. • **—er** *n* acheteur, -euse *mf*.

buzz [bʌz] **1** *vi* bourdonner; **to b. off** *Fam* décamper ‖ *n* bourdonnement *m*. **2** *n* (*phone call*) **to give s.o. a b.** passer un coup de fil à qn. • **—er** *n* interphone *m*; (*of bell, clock*) sonnerie *f*.

by [baɪ] *prep* **1** (*agent*) par; de; **hit/chosen/***etc* **by** frappé/choisi/*etc* par; **surrounded/followed/***etc* **by** entouré/suivi/*etc* de; **a book by** . . . un livre de . . . .

2 (*manner, means*) **by sea** par mer; **by mistake** par erreur; **by car** en voiture; **by bicycle** à bicyclette; **by doing** en faisant; **one by one** un à un; **day by day** de jour en jour; **by sight/day/far** de vue/jour/loin; **by the door** (*through*) par la porte; **(all) by oneself** tout seul.

3 (*next to*) à côté de; (*near*) près de; **by the lake/sea** au bord du lac/de la mer; **to go** *or* **pass by the bank** passer devant la banque.

4 (*before in time*) avant; **by Monday** avant lundi; **by now** à cette heure-ci; **by yesterday** (dès) hier.

5 (*amount, measurement*) à; **by the kilo** au kilo; **paid by the hour** payé à l'heure; **taller by a metre** plus grand d'un mètre.

6 (*according to*) à, d'après; **by my watch** à *or* d'après ma montre; **it's fine** *or* **all right by me** si vous voulez.

‖ *adv* **close by** tout près; **to go by, pass by** passer; **to put by** mettre de côté; **by and large** en gros. • **by-election** *n* élection *f* partielle. • **by-law** *n* arrêté (municipal) *m*. • **by-product** *n* sous-produit *m*.

bye(-bye)! [baɪ('baɪ)] *int Fam* salut!, au revoir!

bypass ['baɪpɑːs] *n* déviation *f* (routière) ‖ *vt* (*town*) contourner; (*ignore*) *Fig* éviter de passer par.

bystander ['baɪstændər] *n* spectateur, -trice *mf*.

C

C, c [siː] *n* C, c *m*.
c *abbr* = **cent.**
cab [kæb] *n* taxi *m*; (*of train driver etc*) cabine *f*.
cabaret ['kæbəreɪ] *n* (*show*) spectacle *m*.
cabbage ['kæbɪdʒ] *n* chou *m* (*pl* choux).
cabin ['kæbɪn] *n* (*on ship, aircraft*) cabine *f*; (*hut*) cabane *f*; **c. crew** *Av* équipage *m*.
cabinet ['kæbɪnɪt] **1** *n* (*cupboard, Am closet*) armoire *f*; (*for display*) vitrine *f*; **(filing) c.** classeur *m* (de bureau). **2** *n* (*government ministers*) gouvernement *m*; **c. meeting** conseil *m* des ministres; **c. minister** ministre *m*. ● **c.-maker** *n* ébéniste *m*.
cable ['keɪb(ə)l] *n* câble *m*; **c. car** téléphérique *m*; (*on tracks*) funiculaire *m*; **c. television** la télévision par câble; **to have c.** *Fam* avoir le câble ‖ *vt* (*message etc*) câbler (**to** à).
caboose [kə'buːs] *n Rail Am* fourgon *m* (de queue).
cache [kæʃ] *n* **an arms' c.** une cache d'armes.
cackle ['kæk(ə)l] *vi* (*of hen*) caqueter ‖ *n* caquet *m*.
cactus, *pl* **-ti** *or* **-tuses** ['kæktəs, -taɪ, -təsɪz] *n* cactus *m*.
caddie ['kædɪ] *n Golf* caddie *m*.
cadet [kə'det] *n Mil* élève *m* officier.
cadge [kædʒ] *vt* (*meal*) se faire payer (**off s.o.** par qn); **to c. money off s.o.** taper qn.
Caesarean [sɪ'zeərɪən] *n Med* césarienne *f*.
café ['kæfeɪ] *n* café(-restaurant) *m*. ● **cafeteria** [kæfɪ'tɪərɪə] *n* cafétéria *f*.
caffeine ['kæfiːn] *n* caféine *f*.
cage [keɪdʒ] *n* cage *f*.
Cairo ['kaɪərəʊ] *n* Le Caire.
cajole [kə'dʒəʊl] *vt* amadouer, enjôler.
cake [keɪk] *n* gâteau *m*; (*small*) pâtisserie *f*; **c. shop** pâtisserie *f*.
caked [keɪkt] *a* **c. mud/blood** boue *f*/sang *m* séché(e).
calamine ['kæləmaɪn] *n* **c. (lotion)** lotion *f* apaisante (à la calamine).
calamity [kə'læmɪtɪ] *n* calamité *f*.
calcium ['kælsɪəm] *n* calcium *m*.
calculat/e ['kælkjʊleɪt] *vti* calculer; **to c. that** *Fam* supposer que; **calculated risk** risque *m* calculé. ● **—ing** *a* (*shrewd*) calculateur. ● **calculation** [-'leɪʃ(ə)n] *n* calcul *m*. ● **calculator** *n* **(pocket) c.** calculatrice *f* (de poche).
calculus ['kælkjʊləs] *n Math* calcul *m*.
calendar ['kælɪndər] *n* calendrier *m*; (*diary*) *Am* agenda *m*.
calf [kɑːf] *n* (*pl* **calves**) **1** (*animal*) veau *m*. **2** *Anat* mollet *m*.
calibre ['kælɪbər] (*Am* **caliber**) *n* calibre *m*.
call [kɔːl] *n* appel *m*; (*shout*) cri *m*; (*visit*) visite *f*; **(telephone) c.** communication *f*, appel *m* téléphonique; **to make a c.** *Tel* téléphoner (**to** à); **on c.** de garde; **c. box** cabine *f* (téléphonique).
‖ *vt* appeler; (*shout*) crier; (*wake up*) réveiller; (*person to meeting*) convoquer (**to** à); (*attention*) attirer (**to** sur); (*truce*) demander; **he's called David** il s'appelle David; **to c. a meeting** convoquer une assemblée; **to c. s.o. a liar**/*etc* traiter qn de menteur/*etc*; **to c. into question** mettre en question.
‖ *vi* appeler; (*cry out*) crier; (*visit*) passer.
call back *vti* rappeler ‖ **to call by** *vi* (*visit*) passer ‖ **to call for** *vt* (*require*) demander; (*summon*) appeler; (*collect*) passer prendre ‖ **to call in** *vt* (*into room etc*) faire venir *or* entrer; (*police*) appeler ‖ *vi* **to c. in (on s.o.)** (*visit*) passer (chez qn); **c.-in programme** *Rad* émission *f* à ligne ouverte ‖ **to call off** *vt* (*cancel*) annuler; (*dog*) rappeler ‖ **to call on** *vt* (*visit*) passer voir, passer chez; **to call on s.o. to do** inviter qn à faire; (*urge*) sommer qn de faire ‖ **to call out** *vt* (*shout*) crier; (*doctor*) appeler ‖ *vi* (*shout*) crier; **to call out for** demander à haute voix ‖ **to call round** *vi* (*visit*) passer ‖ **to call up** *vt Tel* appeler; (*recruits*) *Mil* appeler, mobiliser. ● **call-up** *n Mil* appel *m*, mobilisation *f*.
caller ['kɔːlər] *n* visiteur, -euse *mf*; *Tel* correspondant, -ante *mf*.
calling ['kɔːlɪŋ] *n* vocation *f*; **c. card** *Am* carte *f* de visite.
callous ['kæləs] *a* cruel, insensible.
callus ['kæləs] *n* durillon *m*, cal *m*.
calm [kɑːm] *a* (**-er, -est**) calme, tranquille; **keep c.!** (*don't panic*) du calme! ‖ *n* calme *m* ‖ *vt* **to c. (down)** calmer ‖ *vi* **to c. down** se calmer. ● **—ly** *adv* calmement.
Calor gas ['kæləgæs] *n* butagaz® *m*.
calorie ['kælərɪ] *n* calorie *f*.
camcorder [kæm'kɔːdər] *n* caméscope *m*.
came [keɪm] *pt of* **come.**

camel ['kæməl] *n* chameau *m*.
camellia [kə'mi:lıə] *n Bot* camélia *m*.
camera ['kæmrə] *n* appareil (photo) *m*; (**TV** *or* **film**) **c.** caméra *f*. ● **cameraman** *n* (*pl* **-men**) cameraman *m*.
camouflage ['kæməflɑ:ʒ] *n* camouflage *m* ‖ *vt* camoufler.
camp[1] [kæmp] *n* camp *m*; **c. bed** lit *m* de camp ‖ *vi* **to c. (out)** camper. ● **—ing** *n Sp* camping *m*; **c. site** (terrain *m* de) camping *m*. ● **camper** *n* (*person*) campeur, -euse *mf*; (*vehicle*) camping-car *m*. ● **campfire** *n* feu *m* de camp. ● **campsite** *n* camping *m*.
camp[2] [kæmp] *a* (*affected*) affecté (et risible).
campaign [kæm'peın] *n Pol Mil etc* campagne *f* ‖ *vi* faire campagne. ● **—er** *n* militant, -ante *mf* (**for** pour).
campus ['kæmpəs] *n Univ* campus *m*.
can[1] [kæn, *unstressed* kən] *v aux* (*pres t* **can**; *pt* **could**) (*be able to*) pouvoir; (*know how to*) savoir; **he couldn't help me** il ne pouvait pas m'aider; **if I c.** si je peux; **she c. swim** elle sait nager; **if I could swim** si je savais nager; **he could do it tomorrow** il pourrait le faire demain; **he could have done it** il aurait pu le faire; **you could be wrong** (*possibility*) tu as peut-être tort; **he can't be dead** (*probability*) il ne peut pas être mort; **c. I come in?** puis-je entrer?; **I c. see** je vois.
can[2] [kæn] *n* (*for water etc*) bidon *m*; (*for food, beer*) boîte *f* ‖ *vt* (**-nn-**) mettre en boîte. ● **canned** *a* en boîte, en conserve; **c. food** conserves *fpl*. ● **can-opener** *n* ouvre-boîtes *m inv*.
Canada ['kænədə] *n* Canada *m*. ● **Canadian** [kə'neıdıən] *a* & *n* canadien, -ienne (*mf*).
canal [kə'næl] *n* canal *m*.
canary [kə'neərı] *n* canari *m*, serin *m*.
cancel ['kænsəl] *vt* (**-ll-**, *Am* **-l-**) (*flight, appointment etc*) annuler; (*goods, taxi etc*) décommander; (*train*) supprimer; (*stamp*) oblitérer; **to c. a ticket** (*punch*) (*with date*) composter un billet; (*with hole*) poinçonner un billet; **to c. each other out** s'annuler. ● **cancellation** [-'leıʃ(ə)n] *n* annulation *f*; suppression *f*; oblitération *f*.
cancer ['kænsə*r*] *n* cancer *m*; **C.** (*sign*) le Cancer; **c. patient** cancéreux, -euse *mf*. ● **cancerous** *a* cancéreux.
candid ['kændıd] *a* franc (*f* franche). ● **candour** (*Am* **candor**) *n* franchise *f*.
candidate ['kændıdeıt] *n* candidat, -ate *mf*.
candle ['kænd(ə)l] *n* bougie *f*; (*in church*) cierge *m*. ● **candlelight** *n* **by c.** à la (lueur d'une) bougie; **to have dinner by c.** dîner aux chandelles. ● **candlestick** *n* bougeoir *m*; (*tall*) chandelier *m*.
candy ['kændı] *n Am* bonbon(s) *m*(*pl*); **c. store** *Am* confiserie *f*. ● **candyfloss** *n* barbe *f* à papa.
cane [keın] *n* (*stick*) canne *f*; (*for punishing*) rotin *m*; *Sch* baguette *f* ‖ *vt* (*punish*) fouetter.
canister ['kænıstə*r*] *n* boîte *f* (*en métal*).
cannabis ['kænəbıs] *n* (*drug*) haschisch *m*.
cannibal ['kænıbəl] *n* cannibale *mf*.
cannon ['kænən] *n* (*pl* **-s** *or inv*) canon *m*.
cannot ['kænɒt] = **can not.**
canny ['kænı] *a* (**-ier, -iest**) rusé, malin.
canoe [kə'nu:] *n* canoë *m*, kayak *m*; ● **—ing** *n* **to go c.** *Sp* faire du canoë-kayak. ● **canoeist** *n* canoéiste *mf*.
canopy ['kænəpı] *n* (*hood of pram or Am baby carriage*) capote *f*; (*small roof*) auvent *m*; (*over bed, altar etc*) dais *m*.
can't [kɑ:nt] = **can not.**
cantaloup(e) ['kæntəlu:p, *Am* -ləʊp] *n* (*melon*) cantaloup *m*.
cantankerous [kæn'tæŋkərəs] *a* grincheux, acariâtre.
canteen [kæn'ti:n] *n* (*in school, factory etc*) cantine *f*; (*flask*) gourde *f*; **c. of cutlery** ménagère *f*.
canvas ['kænvəs] *n* (grosse) toile *f*; (*for embroidery*) canevas *m*.
canvass ['kænvəs] *vt* (*an area*) faire du démarchage dans; **to c. s.o.** *Pol* solliciter des voix de qn; *Com* solliciter des commandes de qn. ● **—ing** *n Com Pol* démarchage *m*. ● **—er** *n Pol* agent *m* électoral; *Com* démarcheur, -euse *mf*.
canyon ['kænjən] *n* cañon *m*, canyon *m*.
cap[1] [kæp] *n* **1** (*hat*) casquette *f*; (*for shower, of sailor*) bonnet *m*; (*of soldier*) képi *m*. **2** (*of bottle, tube*) bouchon *m*; (*of milk or beer bottle*) capsule *f*; (*of pen*) capuchon *m*. **3** (*of child's gun*) amorce *f*.
cap[2] [kæp] *vt* (**-pp-**) (*outdo*) surpasser; **to c. it all** pour comble; **capped with** (*crowned*) surmonté de.
capable ['keıpəb(ə)l] *a* (*person*) capable (**of sth** de qch, **of doing** de faire); **c. of** (*situation etc*) susceptible de. ● **capa'bility** *n* capacité *f*.
capacity [kə'pæsətı] *n* (*of container*) capacité *f*; (*ability*) aptitude *f*, capacité *f* (**for sth** pour qch, **for doing** à faire); **in my c. as** en ma qualité de; **in an advisory/***etc* **c.** à titre consultatif/*etc*; **filled to c.** absolument plein, comble.
cape [keıp] *n* **1** (*cloak*) cape *f*; (*of cyclist*) pèlerine *f*. **2** *Geog* cap *m*; **C. Town** Le Cap.
caper ['keıpə*r*] **1** *n* (*activity*) *Sl* affaire *f*;

(*prank*) *Fam* farce *f*. **2** *n Bot Culin* câpre *f*.

capital ['kæpɪtəl] **1** *a* (*punishment, importance*) capital ‖ *n* **c. (city)** capitale *f*; **c. (letter)** majuscule *f*, capitale *f*. **2** *n* (*money*) capital *m*. ● **capitalist** *a* & *n* capitaliste (*mf*).

capitalize ['kæpɪtəlaɪz] *vi* **to c. on** tirer parti de.

capricious [kə'prɪʃəs] *a* capricieux.

Capricorn ['kæprɪkɔːn] *n* (*sign*) le Capricorne.

capsize [kæp'saɪz] *vi* (*of boat*) chavirer ‖ *vt* (faire) chavirer.

capsule ['kæpsəl, 'kæpsjuːl] *n* (*medicine, of spaceship etc*) capsule *f*.

captain ['kæptɪn] *n* capitaine *m* ‖ *vt* (*team*) être le capitaine de.

caption ['kæpʃ(ə)n] *n* (*under illustration*) légende *f*.

captivating ['kæptɪveɪtɪŋ] *a* captivant.

captive ['kæptɪv] *n* prisonnier, -ière *mf*. ● **cap'tivity** *n* captivité *f*.

capture ['kæptʃər] *vt* (*person, animal*) prendre, capturer; (*town*) prendre; (*attention*) capter; (*represent on film etc*) rendre ‖ *n* capture *f*.

car [kɑːr] *n* voiture *f*, auto *f*; *Rail* wagon *m*, voiture *f*; **c. boot sale** (*sorte de*) braderie *f*; **c. ferry** ferry-boat *m*; **c. hire** location *f* de voitures; **c. park** parking *m*; **c. phone** téléphone *m* de voiture; **c. radio** autoradio *m*; **c. rental** *Am* = **c. hire**; **c. wash** (*machine*) lave-auto *m*. ● **carfare** *n Am* frais *mpl* de voyage. ● **carport** *n* auvent *m* (pour voiture). ● **carsick** *a* **to be c.** être malade en voiture.

carafe [kə'ræf] *n* carafe *f*.

caramel ['kærəməl] *n* caramel *m*.

carat ['kærət] *n* carat *m*.

caravan ['kærəvæn] *n Aut* caravane *f*; (*horse-drawn*) roulotte *f*; **c. site** camping *m* pour caravanes.

carbohydrates [kɑːbəʊ'haɪdreɪts] *npl* (*in diet*) féculents *mpl*.

carbon ['kɑːbən] *n* carbone *m*; **c. copy** double *m* (au carbone); **c. paper** (papier *m*) carbone *m*.

carburettor [kɑːbjʊ'retər] (*Am* **carburetor** ['kɑːbəreɪtər]) *n* carburateur *m*.

carcinogenic [kɑːsɪnə'dʒenɪk] *a* cancérigène.

card [kɑːd] *n* carte *f*; (*cardboard*) carton *m*; **(index) c.** fiche *f*; **c. index** fichier *m*; **c. game** jeu *m* de cartes; (*game of cards*) partie *f* de cartes; **c. table** table *f* de jeu; **to play cards** jouer aux cartes; **on** *or Am* **in the cards** *Fam* très vraisemblable. ● **cardboard** *n* carton *m*. ● **cardphone** *n* téléphone *m* à carte.

cardiac ['kɑːdɪæk] *a* cardiaque.

cardigan ['kɑːdɪgən] *n* gilet *m*.

cardinal ['kɑːdɪn(ə)l] **1** *a* (*number, point*) cardinal. **2** *n* (*priest*) cardinal *m*.

care [keər] **1** *vi* **to c. about** (*feel concern about*) se soucier de, s'intéresser à; **I don't c.** ça m'est égal; **I couldn't c. less** *Fam* je m'en fiche; **who cares?** qu'est-ce que ça fait?

2 *vi* (*like*) aimer, vouloir; **would you c. to try?** voulez-vous essayer?, aimeriez-vous essayer?; **to c. for** (*a drink, a change etc*) avoir envie de; **to c. about** *or* **for s.o.** (*be fond of*) avoir de la sympathie pour qn; **to c. for s.o.** (*look after*) s'occuper de qn; (*sick person*) soigner qn.

3 *n* (*attention*) soin(s) *m*(*pl*); (*protection*) garde *f*, soin *m*; (*anxiety*) souci *m*; **to take c. not to do** faire attention à ne pas faire; **to take c. to do** veiller à faire; **to take c. of** s'occuper de (*qch, qn*); (*sick person*) prendre soin de; **to take c. of oneself** (*manage*) se débrouiller; (*keep healthy*) faire bien attention à soi.

career [kə'rɪər] *n* carrière *f*.

carefree ['keəfriː] *a* insouciant.

careful ['keəf(ə)l] *a* (*exact, thorough*) soigneux (**about** de); (*work*) soigné; (*cautious*) prudent; **to be c. of** *or* **with** faire attention à; **to be c. not to do** faire attention à ne pas faire. ● **—ly** *adv* avec soin; prudemment.

careless ['keələs] *a* négligent; (*absent-minded*) étourdi; (*work*) peu soigné; **c. about** peu soigneux de.

caress [kə'res] *n* caresse *f* ‖ *vt* (*stroke*) caresser; (*kiss*) embrasser.

caretaker ['keəteɪkər] *n* gardien, -ienne *mf*, concierge *mf*.

cargo ['kɑːgəʊ] *n* (*pl* **-oes,** *Am* **-os**) cargaison *f*; **c. boat** cargo *m*.

Caribbean [kærɪ'biːən, *Am* kə'rɪbɪən] *a* caraïbe ‖ *n* **the C. (Islands)** les Antilles *fpl*.

caricature ['kærɪkətʃʊər] *n* caricature *f*.

caring ['keərɪŋ] *a* (*loving*) aimant; (*understanding*) très humain.

carnation [kɑː'neɪʃən] *n* œillet *m*.

carnival ['kɑːnɪvəl] *n* carnaval *m* (*pl* -als).

carol ['kærəl] *n* chant *m* (de Noël).

carp [kɑːp] *n* (*fish*) carpe *f*.

carpenter ['kɑːpɪntər] *n* (*for house building*) charpentier *m*; (*for light woodwork*) menuisier *m*. ● **carpentry** *n* charpenterie *f*; menuiserie *f*.

carpet ['kɑːpɪt] *n* tapis *m*; (*wall-to-wall*) moquette *f*; **c. sweeper** balai *m* mécanique

| *vt* recouvrir d'un tapis *or* d'une moquette. **•—ing** *n* (*carpets*) tapis *mpl*; **(wall-to-wall) c.** moquette *f*.
carriage ['kærɪdʒ] *n* (*of train, horse-drawn*) voiture *f*; *Com* transport *m*; **c. paid** port payé. **•carriageway** *n* (*of road*) chaussée *f*.
carrier ['kærɪər] *n Med* porteur, -euse *mf*; *Com* entreprise *f* de transports; **c. (bag)** sac *m* (en plastique).
carrot ['kærət] *n* carotte *f*.
carry ['kærɪ] *vt* porter; (*goods*) transporter; (*by wind*) emporter; (*sound*) conduire; (*motion*) *Pol* faire passer, voter; (*sell*) stocker; (*in calculation*) *Math* retenir; **to c. sth too far** pousser qch trop loin **|** *vi* (*of sound*) porter.
carry away *vt* emporter; **to be** *or* **get carried away** (*excited*) s'emballer **| to carry back** *vt* (*thing*) rapporter; (*person*) ramener **| to carry off** *vt* emporter; (*kidnap*) enlever; (*prize*) remporter; **to c. it off** réussir **| to carry on** *vt* continuer (**doing** à faire); (*conduct*) diriger, mener; (*sustain*) soutenir **|** *vi* continuer; (*behave*) *Pej* se conduire (mal); (*complain*) se plaindre; **to c. on with sth** continuer qch **| to carry out** *vt* (*plan, order, promise*) exécuter, réaliser; (*repair, reform*) effectuer; (*duty*) accomplir; (*meal*) *Am* emporter **| to carry through** *vt* (*plan etc*) mener à bonne fin.
carryall ['kærɪɔːl] *n Am* fourre-tout *m inv*. **•carrycot** *n* (nacelle *f*) porte-bébé *m*.
cart [kɑːt] **1** *n* (*horse-drawn*) charrette *f*; (*in supermarket*) *Am* caddie[1] *m*; **(serving) c.** *Am* table *f* roulante. **2** *vt* (*goods, people*) transporter; **to c. (around)** *Fam* trimbal(l)er; **to c. away** emporter.
carton ['kɑːtən] *n* (*box*) carton *m*; (*of milk, fruit juice etc*) brique *f*; (*of cigarettes*) cartouche *f*; (*of cream*) pot *m*.
cartoon [kɑː'tuːn] *n* (*in newspaper*) dessin *m* (humoristique); (*film*) dessin *m* animé; **(strip) c.** bande *f* dessinée. **•cartoonist** *n* dessinateur, -trice *mf* (humoristique).
cartridge ['kɑːtrɪdʒ] *n* (*of firearm, pen, camera, tape deck*) cartouche *f*; (*of record player*) cellule *f*.
carv/e [kɑːv] *vt* (*cut*) tailler (**out of** dans); (*initials etc*) graver; (*sculpt*) sculpter; **to c. (up)** (*meat*) découper; **to c. up** (*country*) dépecer, morceler. **•—ing** *n* **wood c.** sculpture *f* sur bois.
cascade [kæs'keɪd] *vi* (*fall*) tomber; (*hang*) pendre.
case [keɪs] *n* **1** (*instance, in hospital*) cas *m*; *Jur* affaire *f*; *Phil* arguments *mpl*; **in any c.** en tout cas; **in c. it rains** pour le cas où il pleuvrait; **in c. of** en cas de; **(just) in c.** à tout hasard. **2** (*bag*) valise *f*; (*crate*) caisse *f*; (*for pen, glasses, camera, violin, cigarettes*) étui *m*; (*for jewels*) coffret *m*.
cash [kæʃ] *n* argent *m*; **to pay (in) c.** payer en espèces *or* en liquide; **to pay c. (down)** (*not on credit*) payer comptant; **c. price** prix *m* (au) comptant; **c. desk** caisse *f*; **c. machine** distributeur *m* de billets; **c. register** caisse *f* enregistreuse.
| *vt* **to c. a cheque** *or Am* **check** (*of person*) encaisser un chèque; (*of bank*) payer un chèque; **to c. in on** *Fam* profiter de.
cashier ['kæʃɪər] *n* caissier, -ière *mf*.
cashew ['kæʃuː] *n* noix *f* de cajou *m*.
cashmere ['kæʃmɪər] *n* cachemire *m*.
casino [kə'siːnəʊ] *n* (*pl* **-os**) casino *m*.
casket ['kɑːskɪt] *n* (*box*) coffret *m*; (*coffin*) cercueil *m*.
casserole ['kæsərəʊl] *n* (*covered dish*) cocotte *f*; (*stew*) ragoût *m* en cocotte.
cassette [kə'set] *n* (*audio, video*) cassette *f*; *Phot* cartouche *f*; **c. player** lecteur *m* de cassettes; **c. recorder** magnétophone *m* à cassettes.
cast [kɑːst] **1** *n* (*actors*) acteurs *mpl*; (*list of actors*) distribution *f*; (*mould*) moulage *m*; (*for broken bone*) plâtre *m*.
2 *vt* (*pt & pp* **cast**) (*throw*) jeter; (*light, shadow*) projeter; (*glance*) jeter (**at** à); (*metal*) couler; (*role*) *Th* distribuer; **to c. doubt/a spell on** jeter le doute/un sort sur; **to c. one's mind back** se reporter en arrière; **to c. a vote** voter; **to c. aside** rejeter; **to c. off** (*chains etc*) se libérer de; **to c. off its skin** (*of animal*) muer.
3 *vi* **to c. off** (*of ship*) appareiller.
4 *n* **c. iron** fonte *f*. **•c.-'iron** *a* (*pan etc*) en fonte; (*will*) *Fig* de fer; (*alibi*) *Fig* en béton.
castaway ['kɑːstəweɪ] *n* naufragé, -ée *mf*.
caster ['kɑːstər] *n* (*wheel*) roulette *f*; **c. sugar** sucre *m* en poudre.
castle ['kɑːs(ə)l] *n* château *m*; *Chess* tour *f*.
castoffs ['kɑːstɒfs] *npl* vieux vêtements *mpl*.
castor ['kɑːstər] *n* (*wheel*) roulette *f*; **c. oil** huile *f* de ricin; **c. sugar** sucre *m* en poudre.
castrate [kæ'streɪt] *vt* châtrer.
casual ['kæʒjʊəl] *a* (*remark*) fait en passant; (*stroll*) sans but; (*meeting*) fortuit; (*offhand*) désinvolte; (*worker*) temporaire; (*work*) irrégulier; **c. clothes** vêtements *mpl* sport; **a c. acquaintance** quelqu'un que l'on connaît un peu. **•casually** *adv* (*informally*) avec désinvolture; (*to remark*) en passant.
casualty ['kæʒjʊəltɪ] *n* (*dead*) mort *m*, morte *f*; (*wounded*) blessé, -ée *mf*; (*acci-*

dent victim) accidenté, -ée *mf*; **casualties** morts et blessés *mpl*; **c. (department)** (*in hospital*) (service *m* des) urgences *fpl*.
cat [kæt] *n* chat *m*; (*female*) chatte *f*; **c. food** pâteé *f*.
catalogue ['kætəlɒg] (*Am* **catalog**) *n* catalogue *m* ‖ *vt* cataloguer.
catalyst ['kætəlɪst] *n Ch* & *Fig* catalyseur *m*.
catalytic [kætə'lɪtɪk] *a* **c. converter** *Aut* pot *m* catalytique.
catapult ['kætəpʌlt] *n* (*toy*) lance-pierres *m inv*.
cataract ['kætərækt] *n* (*eye condition*) cataracte *f*.
catarrh [kə'tɑːr] *n* gros rhume *m*.
catastrophe [kə'tæstrəfɪ] *n* catastrophe *f*. ●**cata'strophic** *a* catastrophique.
catch [kætʃ] *vt* (*pt* & *pp* **caught**) (*ball, thief, illness, train etc*) attraper; (*grab*) prendre, saisir; (*surprise*) (sur)prendre; (*understand*) saisir; (*attention*) attirer; (*on nail etc*) accrocher (**on** à); (*finger etc*) se prendre (**in** dans); **to c. sight of** apercevoir; **to c. fire** prendre feu; **to c. one's breath** (*rest*) reprendre haleine; **I didn't c. the train**/*etc* j'ai manqué le train/*etc*; **to c. s.o. doing** (sur)prendre qn à faire; **to c. s.o. out** prendre qn en défaut; **to c. s.o. up** rattraper qn.
‖ *vi* (*of fire*) prendre; **her skirt (got) caught in the door** sa jupe s'est prise *or* coincée dans la porte; **to c. on** (*became popular*) prendre; (*understand*) saisir; **to c. up** se rattraper; **to c. up with s.o.** rattraper qn.
‖ *n* (*captured animal*) capture *f*, prise *f*; (*haul of fish*) pêche *f*; (*trick, snare*) piège *m*; (*on door*) loquet *m*. ●**catching** *a* contagieux.
catchy ['kætʃɪ] *a* (**-ier, -iest**) (*tune*) *Fam* facile à retenir.
category ['kætɪgərɪ] *n* catégorie *f*. ●**cate'gorical** *a* catégorique.
cater ['keɪtər] *vi* **to c. for** *or* **to** (*need, taste*) satisfaire; (*of book etc*) s'adresser à (*enfants, étudiants etc*). ●**—er** *n* traiteur *m*.
caterpillar ['kætəpɪlər] *n* chenille *f*.
cathedral [kə'θiːdrəl] *n* cathédrale *f*.
Catholic ['kæθlɪk] *a* & *n* catholique (*mf*). ●**Ca'tholicism** *n* catholicisme *m*.
cattle ['kæt(ə)l] *npl* bétail *m*, bestiaux *mpl*.
caucus ['kɔːkəs] *n Pol Am* comité *m* électoral.
caught [kɔːt] *pt* & *pp of* **catch.**
cauldron ['kɔːldrən] *n* chaudron *m*.
cauliflower ['kɒlɪflaʊər] *n* chou-fleur *m*.
cause [kɔːz] *n* (*origin, reason, ideal etc*) & *Jur* cause *f* ‖ *vt* causer; **to c. sth/s.o. to fall**/*etc* faire tomber/*etc* qch/qn.
caution ['kɔːʃ(ə)n] *n* (*care*) prudence *f*; (*warning*) avertissement *m* ‖ *vt* (*warn*) avertir; **to c. s.o. against sth** mettre qn en garde contre qch. ●**cautious** *a* prudent. ●**cautiously** *adv* prudemment.
cavalier [kævə'lɪər] *a* (*selfish*) cavalier.
cavalry ['kævəlrɪ] *n* cavalerie *f*.
cave [keɪv] **1** *n* caverne *f*, grotte *f*. **2** *vi* **to c. in** (*fall in*) s'effondrer. ●**caveman** *n* (*pl* **-men**) homme *m* des cavernes.
cavern ['kævən] *n* caverne *f*.
caviar(e) ['kævɪɑːr] *n* caviar *m*.
cavity ['kævɪtɪ] *n* cavité *f*.
CD [siː'diː] *n abbr* (*compact disc or Am disk*) CD *m*.
cease [siːs] *vti* cesser (**doing** de faire). ●**c.-fire** *n* cessez-le-feu *m inv*. ●**ceaseless** *a* incessant.
cedar ['siːdər] *n* (*tree, wood*) cèdre *m*.
ceiling ['siːlɪŋ] *n* (*of room, Fig on wages etc*) plafond *m*.
celebrat/e ['selɪbreɪt] *vt* (*event*) fêter; (*mass*) célébrer ‖ *vi* faire la fête; **we should c. (that)!** il faut fêter ça! ●**—ed** *a* célèbre. ●**celebration** [-'breɪʃ(ə)n] *n* (*event*) fête *f*; **the celebrations** les festivités *fpl*.
celebrity [sə'lebrətɪ] *n* (*person*) célébrité *f*.
celery ['selərɪ] *n* céleri *m*.
cell [sel] *n* cellule *f*; *El* élément *m*.
cellar ['selər] *n* cave *f*.
cello ['tʃeləʊ] *n* (*pl* **-os**) violoncelle *m*. ●**cellist** *n* violoncelliste *mf*.
cellophane® ['seləfeɪn] *n* cellophane® *f*.
cellular ['seljʊlər] *a* **c. blanket** couverture *f* en cellular; **c. phone** téléphone *m* cellulaire.
Celsius ['selsɪəs] *a* Celsius *inv*.
Celt [kelt] *n* Celte *mf*. ●**Celtic** *a* celtique, celte.
cement [sɪ'ment] *n* ciment *m*; **c. mixer** bétonnière *f* ‖ *vt* cimenter.
cemetery ['semətrɪ, *Am* 'seməterɪ] *n* cimetière *m*.
censor ['sensər] *vt* (*film etc*) censurer. ●**censorship** *n* censure *f*.
cent [sent] *n* (*coin*) cent *m*.
centenary [sen'tiːnərɪ, *Am* sen'tenərɪ] *n* centenaire *m*.
centigrade ['sentɪgreɪd] *a* centigrade.
centimetre ['sentɪmiːtər] *n* centimètre *m*.
centipede ['sentɪpiːd] *n* mille-pattes *m inv*.
centre ['sentər] (*Am* **center**) *n* centre *m*; **c. forward** *Fb* avant-centre *m* ‖ *vt* centrer; *Phot* cadrer ‖ *vi* **to c. on** (*of question*) tourner autour de. ●**central** *a* central. ●**centralize** *vt* centraliser.
century ['sentʃərɪ] *n* siècle *m*.

ceramic [sə'ræmɪk] *a* (*tile etc*) de céramique.
cereal ['sɪərɪəl] *n* céréale *f*; (**breakfast**) **c.** céréales *fpl* (pour petit déjeuner).
ceremony ['serɪmənɪ] *n* (*event*) cérémonie *f*; **to stand on c.** faire des cérémonies *or* des façons.
certain ['sɜːtən] *a* (*sure, particular*) certain; **c. people** certaines personnes *fpl*; **she's c. to come** c'est certain qu'elle viendra; **I'm not c. what to do** je ne sais pas très bien ce qu'il faut faire; **to be c. of sth/that** être certain de qch/que; **for c.** (*to say, know*) avec certitude; **to make c. of** (*fact*) s'assurer de; (*seat etc*) s'assurer. ●**—ly** *adv* certainement; (*yes*) bien sûr; (*without fail*) sans faute. ●**certainty** *n* certitude *f*.
certificate [sə'tɪfɪkɪt] *n* certificat *m*; *Univ* diplôme *m*.
certify ['sɜːtɪfaɪ] *vt* (*document etc*) certifier; **certified public accountant** *Am* expert-comptable *m*.
chaffinch ['tʃæfɪntʃ] *n* (*bird*) pinson *m*.
chain [tʃeɪn] *n* (*of rings, mountains*) chaîne *f*; (*of ideas, events*) enchaînement *m*, suite *f*; (*of lavatory*) chasse *f* d'eau; **c. reaction** réaction *f* en chaîne; **to be a c.-smoker** fumer cigarette sur cigarette; **c. saw** tronçonneuse *f*; **c. store** magasin *m* à succursales multiples ▮ *vt* **to c. (down)** enchaîner; **to c. (up)** (*dog*) mettre à l'attache.
chair [tʃeər] *n* chaise *f*; (*armchair*) fauteuil *m*; *Univ* chaire *f*; **c. lift** télésiège *m* ▮ *vt* (*meeting*) présider. ●**chairman** *n* (*pl* **-men**) président, -ente *mf*. ●**chairmanship** *n* présidence *f*.
chalet ['ʃæleɪ] *n* chalet *m*.
chalk [tʃɔːk] *n* craie *f* ▮ *vt* écrire à la craie; **to c. up** (*success*) *Fig* remporter. ●**chalky** *a* (**-ier, -iest**) crayeux.
challeng/e ['tʃælɪndʒ] *n* défi *m*; (*task*) challenge *m*, gageure *f* ▮ *vt* défier (**s.o. to do** qn de faire); (*dispute*) contester; **to c. s.o. to a game** inviter qn à jouer. ●**—ing** *a* (*job*) exigeant; (*book*) stimulant. ●**challenger** *n Sp* challenger *m*.
chamber ['tʃeɪmbər] *n* (*room, of gun etc*) chambre *f*; **c. of commerce** chambre *f* de commerce ▮ *a* (*music, orchestra*) de chambre; **c. pot** pot *m* de chambre. ●**chambermaid** *n* femme *f* de chambre.
chamois ['ʃæmɪ] *n* **c. (leather)** peau *f* de chamois.
champagne [ʃæm'peɪn] *n* champagne *m*.
champion ['tʃæmpɪən] *n* champion, -onne *mf*; **c. skier** champion, -onne de ski ▮ *vt* (*support*) se faire le champion de. ●**championship** *n* championnat *m*.
chance [tʃɑːns] *n* (*luck*) hasard *m*; (*possibility*) chances *fpl*; (*opportunity*) occasion *f*; (*risk*) risque *m*; **by c.** par hasard; **by any c.** (*possibly*) par hasard; **to take a c.** tenter le coup.
▮ *a* (*remark*) fait au hasard; (*meeting*) fortuit; (*occurrence*) accidentel.
▮ *vt* **to c. doing** prendre le risque de faire; **to c. it** risquer le coup.
chancellor ['tʃɑːnsələr] *n Pol etc* chancelier *m*.
chandelier [ʃændə'lɪər] *n* lustre *m*.
change [tʃeɪndʒ] *n* changement *m*; (*money*) monnaie *f*; **for a c.** pour changer; **it makes a c. from** ça change de; **a c. of clothes** des vêtements de rechange.
▮ *vt* (*modify*) changer; (*exchange*) échanger (**for** contre); (*money, wheel*) changer; (*transform*) changer, transformer (*qn, qch*) (**into** en); **to c. trains/one's skirt**/*etc* changer de train/de jupe/*etc*; **to c. gear/the subject** changer de vitesse/de sujet.
▮ *vi* (*alter*) changer; (*change clothes*) se changer; **to c. into** se changer en; **to c. over** passer (**from** de, **to** à); **changing room** vestiaire *m*. ●**changeable** *a* (*weather, mood etc*) changeant. ●**change-over** *n* passage *m* (**from** de, **to** à).
channel ['tʃæn(ə)l] *n TV* chaîne *f*, canal *m*; (*for irrigation*) rigole *f*; (*for boats*) chenal *m*; (*groove*) rainure *f*; (*of inquiry etc*) voie *f*; **to go through the usual channels** passer par la voie normale; **the C.** *Geog* la Manche; **the C. Islands** les îles anglo-normandes ▮ *vt* (**-ll-**, *Am* **-l-**) (*energies, crowd etc*) canaliser (**into** vers).
chant [tʃɑːnt] *vt* (*slogan*) scander ▮ *vi* (*of demonstrators*) scander des slogans.
chaos ['keɪɒs] *n* chaos *m*. ●**cha'otic** *a* (*room*) sens dessus dessous; (*situation*) chaotique.
chap [tʃæp] **1** *n* (*fellow*) *Fam* type *m*; **old c.!** mon vieux! **2** *n* (*on skin*) gerçure *f*.
chapel ['tʃæp(ə)l] *n* chapelle *f*.
chaperon(e) ['ʃæpərəʊn] *n* chaperon *m*.
chaplain ['tʃæplɪn] *n* aumônier *m*.
chapped [tʃæpt] *a* (*hand, lip etc*) gercé.
chapter ['tʃæptər] *n* chapitre *m*.
char [tʃɑːr] **1** *vt* (**-rr-**) carboniser; (*scorch*) brûler légèrement. **2** *n* (*cleaning woman*) *Fam* femme *f* de ménage.
character ['kærɪktər] *n* (*of person, place etc*) & *Typ* caractère *m*; (*in book, film*) personnage *m*; (*strange person*) numéro *m*. ●**characte'ristic** *a* & *n* caractéristique (*f*).
charade [ʃə'rɑːd, *Am* ʃə'reɪd] *n* (*game*)

charade *f* (mimée); (*travesty*) parodie *f*, comédie *f*.

charcoal ['tʃɑːkəʊl] *n* charbon *m* (de bois); (*crayon*) fusain *m*, charbon *m*.

charge[1] [tʃɑːdʒ] *n* (*cost*) prix *m*; *pl* (*expenses*) frais *mpl*; **there's a c. (for it)** c'est payant; **to make a c. for sth** faire payer qch; **free of c.** gratuit; **extra c.** supplément *m* ‖ *vt* (*amount*) demander (**for** pour); **to c. s.o.** *Com* faire payer qn; **to c. sth to s.o.** mettre qch sur le compte de qn.

charge[2] [tʃɑːdʒ] *n* (*in battle*) charge *f*; *Jur* accusation *f*; (*responsibility*) charge *f*; (*care*) garde *f*; **to take c. of** prendre en charge; **to be in c. of** (*child*) avoir la garde de; (*office*) être responsable de; **the person in c.** le *or* la responsable; **who's in c. here?** qui commande ici? ‖ *vt* (*battery*, *soldiers*) charger; *Jur* accuser (**with** de) ‖ *vi* (*rush*) se précipiter; **c.!** *Mil* chargez! • **charger** *n* (*for battery*) chargeur *m*.

chariot ['tʃærɪət] *n* (*Roman etc*) char *m*.

charity ['tʃærɪtɪ] *n* (*kindness*, *alms*) charité *f*; (*society*) œuvre *f* charitable; **to give to c.** faire la charité.

charm [tʃɑːm] *n* (*attractiveness*, *spell*) charme *m*; (*trinket*) breloque *f* ‖ *vt* charmer. • **—ing** *a* charmant.

chart [tʃɑːt] *n* (*map*) carte *f*; (*table*) tableau *m*; **(pop) charts** hit-parade *m* ‖ *vt* (*route*) porter sur la carte.

charter ['tʃɑːtər] *n* (*aircraft*) charter *m*; **c. flight** (vol *m*) charter *m* ‖ *vt* (*aircraft etc*) affréter. • **chartered accountant** *n* expert-comptable *m*.

charwoman ['tʃɑːwʊmən] *n* (*pl* **-women**) femme *f* de ménage.

chase [tʃeɪs] *n* poursuite *f*, chasse *f* ‖ *vt* poursuivre; **to c. s.o. away** *or* **off** chasser qn ‖ *vi* **to c. after s.o./sth** courir après qn/qch.

chasm ['kæzəm] *n* abîme *m*, gouffre *m*.

chassis ['ʃæsɪ, *Am* 'tʃæsɪ] *n* *Aut* châssis *m*.

chaste [tʃeɪst] *a* chaste.

chat [tʃæt] *n* petite conversation *f*; **to have a c.** bavarder ‖ *vi* (**-tt-**) causer, bavarder (**with** avec) ‖ *vt* **to c. s.o. up** *Fam* baratiner qn.

chatty ['tʃætɪ] *a* (**-ier, -iest**) (*person*) bavard; (*style*) familier.

chatter ['tʃætər] *vi* bavarder; (*of birds*) jacasser; **his teeth are chattering** il claque des dents ‖ *n* bavardage *m*; jacassement *m*. • **chatterbox** *n* bavard, -arde *mf*.

chauffeur ['ʃəʊfər] *n* chauffeur *m* (de maître).

chauvinist ['ʃəʊvɪnɪst] *n* **(male) c.** *Pej* macho *m*, phallocrate *m*.

cheap [tʃiːp] *a* (**-er, -est**) bon marché *inv*, pas cher; (*rate*, *fare*) réduit; (*worthless*) sans valeur; (*mean*, *petty*) mesquin; **cheaper** moins cher, meilleur marché ‖ *adv* (*to buy*) (à) bon marché. • **cheaply** *adv* (à) bon marché.

cheat [tʃiːt] *vt* (*deceive*) tromper; (*defraud*) frauder; **to c. s.o. out of sth** escroquer qch à qn ‖ *vi* (*at games etc*) tricher ‖ *n* tricheur, -euse *mf*; (*crook*) escroc *m*. • **—ing** *n* (*at games etc*) tricherie *f*. • **cheater** *n* *Am* = **cheat.**

check[1] [tʃek] *a* (*dress etc*) à carreaux ‖ *n* (*pattern*) carreaux *mpl*. • **checked** *a* à carreaux.

check[2] [tʃek] *vt* (*examine*) vérifier; (*inspect*) contrôler; (*mark off*, *tick*) cocher, pointer; (*stop*) arrêter, enrayer; (*restrain*) contenir, maîtriser; (*baggage*) *Am* mettre à la consigne.

‖ *vi* vérifier; **to c. on sth** vérifier qch.

‖ *n* vérification *f*; (*inspection*) contrôle *m*; (*halt*) arrêt *m*; *Chess* échec *m*; (*curb*) frein *m*; (*tick*) *Am* = croix *f*; (*receipt*) *Am* reçu *m*; (*bill in restaurant etc*) *Am* addition *f*; (*cheque*) *Am* chèque *m*; **to keep a c. on** contrôler; **to put a c. on** mettre un frein à. • **checkbook** *Am* *n* carnet *m* de chèques. • **checking account** *n* *Am* compte *m* courant. • **checkmate** *n* *Chess* échec et mat *m*. • **checkroom** *n* *Am* vestiaire *m*; (*left-luggage office*) *Am* consigne *f*.

checkered ['tʃekəd] *a* *Am* = **chequered.**

checkers ['tʃekəz] *npl* *Am* jeu *m* de dames. • **checkerboard** *n* *Am* damier *m*.

check in *vt* (*luggage*) enregistrer ‖ *vi* (*at hotel*) signer le registre; (*arrive*) arriver; (*at airport*) se présenter (à l'enregistrement. • **check-in** *n* (*at airport*) enregistrement *m* (des bagages) ‖ **to check off** *vt* (*names on list etc*) cocher ‖ **to check out** *vt* (*confirm*) confirmer ‖ *vi* (*at hotel*) régler sa note. • **checkout** *n* (*in supermarket*) caisse *f*. ‖ **to check up** *vi* vérifier. • **checkup** *n* *Med* bilan *m* de santé.

cheddar ['tʃedər] *n* (*cheese*) cheddar *m*.

cheek [tʃiːk] *n* joue *f*; (*impudence*) *Fig* culot *m*. • **cheeky** *a* (**-ier, -iest**) (*person*, *reply etc*) insolent.

cheep [tʃiːp] *vi* (*of bird*) piauler.

cheer [tʃɪər] *n* **cheers** (*shouts*) acclamations *fpl*; **cheers!** *Fam* à votre santé! ‖ *vt* (*applaud*) acclamer; **to c. up** donner du courage à; (*amuse*) égayer ‖ *vi* applaudir; **to c. up** prendre courage; s'égayer; **c. up!** (du) courage! • **—ing** *n* (*shouts*) acclamations *fpl*.

cheerful ['tʃɪəfəl] *a* gai.
cheerio! [tʃɪərɪ'əʊ] *int* salut!, au revoir!
cheese [tʃi:z] *n* fromage *m*. ●**cheeseburger** *n* cheeseburger *m*. ●**cheesecake** *n* tarte *f* au fromage blanc.
cheetah ['tʃi:tə] *n* guépard *m*.
chef [ʃef] *n* (*cook*) chef *m*.
chemical ['kemɪkəl] *a* chimique ▮ *n* produit *m* chimique.
chemist ['kemɪst] *n* (*pharmacist*) pharmacien, -ienne *mf*; (*scientist*) chimiste *mf*; **c.'s shop** pharmacie *f*. ●**chemistry** *n* chimie *f*.
cheque [tʃek] *n* chèque *m*. ●**chequebook** *n* carnet *m* de chèques.
chequered ['tʃekəd] *a* (*pattern*) à carreaux.
cherish ['tʃerɪʃ] *vt* (*hope*) nourrir; (*person*) chérir.
cherry ['tʃerɪ] *n* cerise *f*; **c. brandy** cherry *m*.
chess [tʃes] *n* échecs *mpl*. ●**chessboard** *n* échiquier *m*.
chest [tʃest] *n* **1** *Anat* poitrine *f*. **2** (*box*) coffre *m*; **c. of drawers** commode *f*.
chestnut ['tʃestnʌt] *n* châtaigne *f* ▮ *a* (*hair*) châtain; **c. tree** châtaignier *m*.
chew [tʃu:] *vt* **to c. (up)** mâcher ▮ *vi* mastiquer; **chewing gum** chewing-gum *m*.
chick [tʃɪk] *n* poussin *m*. ●**chicken 1** *n* poulet *m*. **2** *a* (*cowardly*) *Fam* froussard ▮ *vi* **to c. out** *Fam* se dégonfler. ●**chickenpox** *n* varicelle *f*.
chickpea ['tʃɪkpi:] *n* pois *m* chiche.
chicory ['tʃɪkərɪ] *n* (*for salad*) endive *f*; (*in coffee etc*) chicorée *f*.
chide [tʃaɪd] *vt* gronder.
chief [tʃi:f] *n* chef *m*; **in c.** (*commander, editor*) en chef ▮ *a* (*main, highest in rank*) principal. ●**—ly** *adv* principalement, surtout.
chilblain ['tʃɪlbleɪn] *n* engelure *f*.
child, *pl* **children** [tʃaɪld, 'tʃɪldrən] *n* enfant *mf*; **c. care** (*for working parents*) crèches *fpl* et garderies *fpl*; **c. minder** nourrice *f*, assistante *f* maternelle. ●**childbearing** *n* (*act*) accouchement *m*. ●**childbirth** *n* accouchement *m*. ●**childhood** *n* enfance *f*. ●**childish** *a* puéril, enfantin. ●**childlike** *a* naïf, innocent.
Chile ['tʃɪlɪ] *n* Chili *m*.
chill [tʃɪl] *n* froid *m*; (*coldness in feelings*) froideur *f*; (*illness*) refroidissement *m*; **to catch a c.** prendre froid ▮ *vt* (*wine, melon*) faire rafraîchir; (*meat*) réfrigérer; **to c. s.o.** (*with cold etc*) faire frissonner qn (**with** de); **to be chilled to the bone** être transi; **chilled wine** vin *m* frais. ●**chilly** *a* (**-ier, -iest**) froid; **it's c.** il fait (un peu) froid.
chilli ['tʃɪlɪ] *n* (*pl* **-ies**) piment *m* (de Cayenne).
chime [tʃaɪm] *vi* (*of bell*) carillonner; (*of clock*) sonner ▮ *n* carillon *m*; sonnerie *f*.
chimney ['tʃɪmnɪ] *n* cheminée *f*. ●**chimneypot** *n* tuyau *m* de cheminée. ●**chimneysweep** *n* ramoneur *m*.
chimpanzee [tʃɪmpæn'zi:] *n* chimpanzé *m*.
chin [tʃɪn] *n* menton *m*.
china ['tʃaɪnə] *n inv* porcelaine *f* ▮ *a* en porcelaine.
China ['tʃaɪnə] *n* Chine *f*. ●**Chi'nese** *a* chinois ▮ *n inv* (*person*) Chinois, -oise *mf*; (*language*) chinois *m*; (*meal*) *Fam* repas *m* chinois.
chink [tʃɪŋk] *n* (*slit*) fente *f*.
chip [tʃɪp] *vt* (**-pp-**) (*cup, blade*) ébrécher; (*paint*) écailler ▮ *vi* **to c. in** *Fam* contribuer ▮ *n* (*splinter*) éclat *m*; (*break*) ébréchure *f*; (*microchip*) puce *f*; (*counter*) jeton *m*; *pl* (*French fries*) frites *fpl*; (*crisps*) *Am* chips *fpl*. ●**chipboard** *n* (bois *m*) aggloméré *m*.
chiropodist [kɪ'rɒpədɪst] *n* pédicure *mf*.
chirp [tʃɜ:p] *vi* (*of bird*) pépier.
chirpy ['tʃɜ:pɪ] *a* (**-ier, -iest**) gai, plein d'entrain.
chisel ['tʃɪz(ə)l] *n* ciseau *m* ▮ *vt* (**-ll-**, *Am* **-l-**) ciseler.
chitchat ['tʃɪttʃæt] *n* bavardage *m*.
chivalrous ['ʃɪvəlrəs] *a* (*man*) galant.
chives [tʃaɪvz] *npl* ciboulette *f*.
chlorine ['klɔ:ri:n] *n* chlore *m*. ●**chlorinated** *a* **c. water** eau *f* chlorée.
choc-ice ['tʃɒkaɪs] *n* (*ice cream*) esquimau *m*.
chock-a-block [tʃɒkə'blɒk] *or* **chock-'full** *a* *Fam* archiplein.
chocolate ['tʃɒklɪt] *n* chocolat *m*; **milk c.** chocolat au lait; **plain** *or Am* **bittersweet c.** chocolat à croquer ▮ *a* (*cake*) au chocolat; (*egg*) en chocolat; (*colour*) chocolat *inv*.
choice [tʃɔɪs] *n* choix *m*; **from c.** de son propre choix ▮ *a* (*goods*) de choix.
choir ['kwaɪər] *n* chœur *m*, chorale *f*. ●**choirboy** *n* jeune choriste *m*.
choke [tʃəʊk] **1** *vt* (*person*) étrangler, étouffer; (*clog*) boucher (*tuyau*); **to c. back** (*sobs etc*) étouffer ▮ *vi* s'étrangler, étouffer; **to c. on** (*fish bone etc*) s'étrangler avec. **2** *n* *Aut* starter *m*.
cholera ['kɒlərə] *n* choléra *m*.
cholesterol [kə'lestərɒl] *n* cholestérol *m*.
choose [tʃu:z] *vt* (*pt* **chose,** *pp* **chosen**) choisir; **to c. to do** (*make a firm choice*) choisir de faire; (*decide*) juger bon de faire ▮ *vi* choisir; **as I/you c.** comme il me/vous plaît. ●**choos(e)y** *a* (**-sier, -siest**) difficile (**about** sur).

chop [tʃɒp] **1** *n* (*of lamb, pork*) côtelette *f*; **to get the c.** *Sl* être flanqué à la porte. **2** *vt* (**-pp-**) couper (à la hache); (*food*) hacher; **to c. down** (*tree*) abattre; **to c. off** (*branch, finger*) couper; **to c. up** couper en morceaux. ●**chopper** *n* hachoir *m*; (*helicopter*) *Sl* hélico *m*.

choppy ['tʃɒpɪ] *a* (*sea*) agité.

chopsticks ['tʃɒpstɪks] *npl Culin* baguettes *fpl* (*pour manger*).

chord [kɔːd] *n Mus* accord *m*.

chore [tʃɔːr] *n* travail *m* (routinier); (*unpleasant*) corvée *f*; *pl* (*household*) (travaux *mpl* du) ménage *m*.

choreographer [kɒrɪ'ɒgrəfər] *n* chorégraphe *mf*.

chorus ['kɔːrəs] *n* (*of song*) refrain *m*; (*singers*) chœur *m*.

chose, chosen [tʃəʊz, 'tʃəʊz(ə)n] *pt & pp of* **choose.**

Christ [kraɪst] *n* Christ *m*. ●**Christian** ['krɪstʃən] *a & n* chrétien, -ienne (*mf*); **C. name** prénom *m*.

christen ['krɪs(ə)n] *vt* (*person, ship*) baptiser. ●**—ing** *n* baptême *m*.

Christmas ['krɪsməs] *n* Noël *m*; **at C. (time)** à (la) Noël; **Merry** *or* **Happy C.** Joyeux Noël; **Father C.** le père Noël ▮ *a* (*tree, card, day, party etc*) de Noël; **C. box** étrennes *fpl;* **C. Eve** la veille de Noël.

chrome [krəʊm] *or* **chromium** *n* chrome *m*.

chronic ['krɒnɪk] *a* (*disease, state etc*) chronique.

chronicle ['krɒnɪk(ə)l] *n* chronique *f*.

chronological [krɒnə'lɒdʒɪk(ə)l] *a* chronologique.

chrysanthemum [krɪ'sænθəməm] *n* chrysanthème *m*.

chubby ['tʃʌbɪ] *a* (**-ier, -iest**) (*person, hands*) potelé; (*cheeks*) rebondi.

chuck [tʃʌk] *vt* (*throw*) *Fam* jeter, lancer; **to c. away** (*old clothes etc*) *Fam* balancer; **to c. out** (*old clothes, person etc*) *Fam* balancer; **to c. in** *or* **up** (*job*) *Fam* laisser tomber.

chuckle ['tʃʌk(ə)l] *vi* glousser, rire ▮ *n* gloussement *m*.

chug [tʃʌg] *vi* (**-gg-**) **to c. along** (*of vehicle*) avancer lentement (*en faisant teuf-teuf*).

chum [tʃʌm] *n Fam* copain *m*. ●**chummy** *a* (**-ier, -iest**) *Fam* amical; **c. with** copain avec.

chunk [tʃʌŋk] *n* (gros) morceau *m*.

church [tʃɜːtʃ] *n* église *f*; **in c.** à l'église. ●**churchgoer** *n* pratiquant, -ante *mf*. ●**churchyard** *n* cimetière *m*.

churlish ['tʃɜːlɪʃ] *a* (*rude*) grossier; (*bad-tempered*) hargneux.

chute [ʃuːt] *n* (*in pool, playground*) toboggan *m*; (*for rubbish, Am garbage*) vide-ordures *m inv*.

chutney ['tʃʌtnɪ] *n* condiment *m* épicé (*à base de fruits*).

CID [siːaɪ'diː] *abbr* (*Criminal Investigation Department*) *Br* = PJ *f*.

cider ['saɪdər] *n* cidre *m*.

cigar [sɪ'gɑːr] *n* cigare *m*.

cigarette [sɪgə'ret] *n* cigarette *f*; **c. end** mégot *m*; **c. lighter** briquet *m*.

cinch [sɪntʃ] *n* **it's a c.** *Fam* (*easy*) c'est facile; (*sure*) c'est (sûr et) certain.

Cinderella [sɪndə'relə] *n* Cendrillon *f*.

cine-camera ['sɪnɪkæmrə] *n* caméra *f*.

cinema ['sɪnəmə] *n* cinéma *m*. ●**cinemagoer** *n* cinéphile *mf*.

cinnamon ['sɪnəmən] *n Bot Culin* cannelle *f*.

circle ['sɜːk(ə)l] *n* (*shape, group, range etc*) cercle *m*; (*around eyes*) cerne *m*; *Th* balcon *m*; *pl* (*political etc*) milieux *mpl* ▮ *vt* (*move round*) faire le tour de; (*word*) encadrer ▮ *vi* (*of aircraft, bird*) décrire des cercles.

circuit ['sɜːkɪt] *n* (*electrical path, in sport etc*) circuit *m*; **c. breaker** *El* disjoncteur *m*.

circular ['sɜːkjʊlər] *a* circulaire ▮ *n* (*letter*) circulaire *f*; (*advertisement*) prospectus *m*.

circulate ['sɜːkjʊleɪt] *vi* circuler ▮ *vt* faire circuler. ●**circulation** [-'leɪʃ(ə)n] *n* circulation *f*; (*of newspaper etc*) tirage *m*.

circumcised ['sɜːkəmsaɪzd] *a* circoncis.

circumference [sɜː'kʌmfərəns] *n* circonférence *f*.

circumstance ['sɜːkəmstæns] *n* circonstance *f*; *pl Com* situation *f* financière; **in** *or* **under no circumstances** en aucun cas.

circus ['sɜːkəs] *n* cirque *m*.

CIS *abbr* (*Commonwealth of Independent States*) CEI *f*.

cistern ['sɪstən] *n* (*for lavatory*) réservoir *m* (de la chasse d'eau).

citadel ['sɪtəd(ə)l] *n* citadelle *f*.

citizen ['sɪtɪz(ə)n] *n* citoyen, -enne *mf*; (*of town*) habitant, -ante *mf*; **Citizens' Band (Radio)** la CB. ●**citizenship** *n* citoyenneté *f*.

citrus ['sɪtrəs] *a* **c. fruit(s)** agrumes *mpl*.

city ['sɪtɪ] *n* (grande) ville *f*, cité *f*; **c. centre** centre-ville *m*; **c. hall** *Am* hôtel *m* de ville.

civic ['sɪvɪk] *a* (*duty*) civique; (*centre*) administratif; (*authorities*) municipal.

civil ['sɪv(ə)l] *a* **1** (*rights, war, marriage etc*) civil; **c. servant** fonctionnaire *mf*; **c. service** fonction *f* publique. **2** (*polite*) civil.

civilian [sɪ'vɪljən] *a & n* civil, -ile (*mf*).

civilize ['sɪvɪlaɪz] *vt* civiliser. ●**civilization** [-'zeɪʃ(ə)n] *n* civilisation *f*.

claim [kleɪm] *vt* (*one's due etc*) réclamer, revendiquer; (*benefit, payment etc*) demander à bénéficier de; **to c. that** (*assert*) prétendre que ▮ *n* (*demand*) revendication *f*; (*statement*) affirmation *f*; (*complaint*) réclamation *f*; (*right*) droit *m* (**to** à); **(insurance) c.** demande *f* d'indemnité. ● **claimant** *n* demandeur, -euse *mf*.

clam [klæm] *n* (*shellfish*) palourde *f*.

clamber ['klæmbər] *vi* grimper; **to c. up the stairs** grimper l'escalier.

clamour ['klæmər] (*Am* **clamor**) *n* clameur *f* ▮ *vi* **to c. for** demander à grands cris.

clamp [klæmp] *n* (*clip-like*) pince *f*; (*large, iron*) crampon *m*; **(wheel) c.** *Aut* sabot *m* (de Denver) ▮ *vt* serrer; (*car*) mettre un sabot à ▮ *vi* **to c. down** sévir (**on** contre). ● **clampdown** *n* coup *m* d'arrêt, restriction *f* (**on** à).

clan [klæn] *n* clan *m*.

clang [klæŋ] *n* son *m* métallique. ● **clanger** *n* *Sl* gaffe *f*; **to drop a c.** faire une gaffe.

clap [klæp] **1** *vti* (**-pp-**) (*applaud*) applaudir; **to c. (one's hands)** battre des mains. **2** *vt* (**-pp-**) (*put*) *Fam* fourrer. ● **clapped-'out** *a* (*car, person*) *Fam* HS. ● **clapping** *n* applaudissements *mpl*.

claret ['klærət] *n* (*wine*) bordeaux *m* rouge.

clarify ['klærɪfaɪ] *vt* clarifier. ● **clarification** [-'ɪkeɪʃ(ə)n] *n* clarification *f*.

clarinet [klærɪ'net] *n* clarinette *f*.

clarity ['klærətɪ] *n* (*of expression etc*) clarté *f*; (*of sound*) pureté *f*

clash [klæʃ] *vi* (*of plates, pans*) s'entrechoquer; (*of interests, armies*) se heurter; (*of colours*) jurer (**with** avec); (*of people*) se bagarrer; (*coincide*) tomber en même temps (**with** que) ▮ *n* (*noise*) choc *m*, heurt *m*; (*of interests*) conflit *m*.

clasp [klɑːsp] *vt* (*hold*) serrer; **to c. one's hands** joindre les mains ▮ *n* (*fastener*) fermoir *m*; (*of belt*) boucle *f*.

class [klɑːs] *n* classe *f*; (*lesson*) cours *m*; (*university grade*) mention *f*; **the c. of 1993** *Am* la promotion de 1993 ▮ *vt* classer. ● **classmate** *n* camarade *mf* de classe. ● **classroom** *n* (salle *f* de) classe *f*.

classic ['klæsɪk] *a* classique ▮ *n* (*writer, work etc*) classique *m*; **to study classics** étudier les humanités *fpl*. ● **classical** *a* classique.

classify ['klæsɪfaɪ] *vt* classer, classifier. ● **classification** [-'keɪʃ(ə)n] *n* classification *f*.

classy ['klɑːsɪ] *a* (**-ier, -iest**) *Fam* chic *inv*.

clatter ['klætər] *n* bruit *m*, fracas *m*.

clause [klɔːz] *n* (*in sentence*) proposition *f*; (*in document*) *Jur* clause *f*.

claw [klɔː] *n* (*of lobster*) pince *f*; (*of cat, sparrow etc*) griffe *f*; (*of eagle*) serre *f* ▮ *vt* (*scratch*) griffer.

clay [kleɪ] *n* argile *f*.

clean [kliːn] *a* (**-er, -est**) propre; (*clear-cut*) net (*f* nette); (*joke*) pour toutes les oreilles; **c. living** vie *f* saine.

▮ *adv* (*utterly*) complètement, carrément; (*to break, cut*) net.

▮ *n* **to give sth a c.** nettoyer qch.

▮ *vt* nettoyer; (*wash*) laver; (*wipe*) essuyer; **to c. one's teeth** se brosser *or* se laver les dents; **to c. out** (*room etc*) nettoyer; (*empty*) vider; **to c. up** (*room etc*) nettoyer; (*reform*) *Fig* épurer.

▮ *vi* **to c. (up)** faire le nettoyage. ● **cleaning** *n* nettoyage *m*; (*housework*) ménage *m*; **c. woman** femme *f* de ménage. ● **cleaner** *n* femme *f* de ménage; **(dry) c.** teinturier, -ière *mf*. ● **cleanly** *adv* (*to break, cut*) net.

clean-cut [kliːn'kʌt] *a* net (*f* nette). ● **clean-'shaven** *a* (*with no beard etc*) glabre. ● **clean-up** *n* *Fig* purge *f*, coup *m* de balai.

cleanliness ['klenlɪnɪs] *n* propreté *f*.

cleans/e [klenz] *vt* nettoyer; *Fig* purifier; **cleansing cream** crème *f* démaquillante. ● **—er** *n* (*for skin*) démaquillant *m*.

clear [klɪər] *a* (**-er, -est**) (*sky, water, sound, thought etc*) clair; (*glass*) transparent; (*outline, photo*) net (*f* nette), clair; (*profit, majority*) net (*f* nette); (*mind*) lucide; (*road*) libre, dégagé; (*obvious*) évident, clair (**that** que); (*certain*) certain; (*complete*) entier; **to be c. of** (*free of*) être libre de; (*out of*) être hors de; **to make oneself c.** se faire comprendre; **c. conscience** conscience *f* nette.

▮ *adv* **to keep** *or* **steer c. of** se tenir à l'écart de; **to get c. of** (*away from*) s'éloigner de.

▮ *vt* (*path, table*) débarrasser, dégager; (*land*) défricher; (*fence*) franchir; (*obstacle*) éviter; (*person*) *Jur* disculper; (*cheque, Am check*) faire passer (sur un compte); (*debts*) liquider; (*through customs*) dédouaner; (*for security*) autoriser; **to c. one's throat** s'éclaircir la gorge.

▮ *vi* **to c. (up)** (*of weather*) s'éclaircir; (*of fog*) se dissiper. ● **clearing** *n* (*in woods*) clairière *f*. ● **clearly** *adv* clairement; (*obviously*) évidemment.

clearance ['klɪərəns] *n* (*sale*) soldes *mpl*; (*space*) dégagement *m*; (*permission*) autorisation *f*.

clear away *vt* (*remove*) enlever ▮ *vi* (*of fog*) se dissiper ▮ **to c. off** *vi* (*leave*) *Fam* filer ▮ *vt* (*table*) débarrasser ▮ **to c. out** *vt* (*empty*) vider; (*clean*) nettoyer; (*remove*) enlever ▮**to c. up** *vt* (*mystery etc*) éclaircir ▮ *vti* (*tidy*) ranger.

clear-cut [klɪə'kʌt] *a* net (*f* nette). ●**clear-'headed** *a* lucide.

clearway ['klɪəweɪ] *n* route *f* à stationnement interdit.

clement ['klemənt] *a* clément.

clementine ['kleməntaɪn] *n* clémentine *f*.

clench [klentʃ] *vt* (*fist*, *teeth*) serrer.

clergyman ['klɜːdʒɪmən] *n* (*pl* **-men**) ecclésiastique *m*.

clerical ['klerɪk(ə)l] *a* (*job*) d'employé; (*work*) de bureau; (*error*) d'écriture.

clerk [klɑːk, *Am* klɜːk] *n* employé, -ée *mf* (de bureau); (*in store*) *Am* vendeur, -euse *mf*; **solicitor's c.** *Br* clerc *m* de notaire.

clever ['klevər] *a* (**-er, -est**) intelligent; (*smart*, *shrewd*) astucieux; (*skilful*) habile (**at sth** à qch, **at doing** à faire); (*ingenious*) (*machine*, *plan*) ingénieux; (*gifted*) doué; **c. at** (*English etc*) fort en; **c. with one's hands** habile de ses mains.

cliché ['kliːʃeɪ] *n* (*idea*) cliché *m*.

click [klɪk] *n* déclic *m*, bruit *m* sec ▮ *vi* (*of machine etc*) faire un déclic; *Comptr* cliquer (**on** sur); **it suddenly clicked** (*I realized*) *Fam* j'ai compris tout à coup.

client ['klaɪənt] *n* client, -ente *mf*. ●**clientele** [kliːən'tel] *n* clientèle *f*.

cliff [klɪf] *n* falaise *f*.

climate ['klaɪmɪt] *n Met & Fig* climat *m*.

climax ['klaɪmæks] *n* point *m* culminant; (*sexual*) orgasme *m*.

climb [klaɪm] *vt* **to c. (up)** (*steps*) monter; (*hill*, *mountain*) gravir, faire l'ascension de; (*tree*, *ladder*) monter à; **to c. (over)** (*wall*) escalader; **to c. down (from)** (*wall*, *tree*, *hill*) descendre de.

▮ *vi* (*of plant*) grimper; **to c. (up)** (*up steps etc*) monter; (*up hill etc*) gravir; **to c. down** descendre.

▮*n* montée *f*. ●**—ing** *n* **(mountain) c.** alpinisme *m*. ●**climber** *n* (*mountaineer*) alpiniste *mf*.

clinch [klɪntʃ] *vt* (*deal*) conclure.

cling [klɪŋ] *vi* (*pt & pp* **clung**) se cramponner (**to** à); (*stick*) adhérer (**to** à). ●**clingfilm** *n* film *m* plastique.

clinic ['klɪnɪk] *n* (*private*) clinique *f*; (*health centre*) centre *m* médical.

clink [klɪŋk] *vi* tinter ▮ *vt* faire tinter ▮ *n* tintement *m*.

clip [klɪp] **1** *vt* (**-pp-**) (*cut*) couper; (*hedge*) tailler; (*ticket*) poinçonner. **2** *n* (*for paper*) trombone *m*; (*fastener*) attache *f*; (*of brooch*, *of cyclist*, *for hair*) pince *f* ▮ *vt* (**-pp-**) **to c. (on)** (*attach*) attacher. **3** *n* (*of film*) extrait *m*. ●**clipping** *n* (*from newspaper*) *Am* coupure *f*. ●**clippers** *npl* (*for hair*) tondeuse *f*; (*for finger nails*) coupe-ongles *m inv*.

cloak [kləʊk] *n* (grande) cape *f*. ●**cloakroom** *n* vestiaire *m*; (*lavatory*) toilettes *fpl*.

clobber ['klɒbər] *vt* (*hit*) *Sl* tabasser.

clock [klɒk] *n* (*large*) horloge *f*; (*small*) pendule *f*; *Aut* compteur *m*; **(alarm) c.** réveil *m*; **a race against the c.** une course contre la montre; **round the c.** vingt-quatre heures sur vingt-quatre; **c. tower** clocher *m*.

▮ *vt Sp* chronométrer; **to c. up** (*miles*) (*in car*) *Fam* faire.

▮ *vi* **to c. in** *or* **out** (*of worker*) pointer. ●**clockwise** *adv* dans le sens des aiguilles d'une montre. ●**clockwork** *a* mécanique ▮ *n* **to go like c.** aller *or* marcher comme sur des roulettes.

clog [klɒg] **1** *n* (*shoe*) sabot *m*. **2** *vt* (**-gg-**) **to c. (up)** (*obstruct*) boucher.

cloister ['klɔɪstər] *n* cloître *m*.

close[1] [kləʊs] *a* (**-er, -est**) (*place*, *relative etc*) proche; (*collaboration*, *resemblance*, *connection*) étroit; (*friend*) intime; (*contest*) serré; (*atmosphere*) *Met* lourd; **to have a c. shave** *or* **call** l'échapper belle.

▮ *adv* **c. (by), c. at hand** (tout) près; **c. to** près de; **c. behind** juste derrière; **c. on** (*almost*) *Fam* pas loin de; **we stood c. together** nous étions debout serrés les uns contre les autres; **to follow c.** suivre de près. ●**c.-'cropped** *a* (*hair*) (coupé) ras. ●**c.-'knit** (*group etc*) *a* très uni. ●**c.-up** *n* gros plan *m*.

close[2] [kləʊz] *n* (*end*) fin *f*; **to bring sth to a c.** mettre fin a qch; **to draw to a c.** tirer à sa fin.

▮ *vt* (*door*, *shop etc*) fermer; (*discussion*) clore; (*opening*) boucher; (*road*) barrer; (*gap*) réduire; (*deal*) conclure; **to c. the meeting** lever la séance.

▮ *vi* se fermer; (*end*) (se) terminer; (*of shop*) fermer. ●**closing** *n* fermeture *f*; **c. date** date *f* limite; **c. time** heure *f* de fermeture.

close down *vti* (*for good*) fermer (définitivement) ▮ **close in** *vt* (*enclose*) enfermer ▮ *vi* (*approach*) approcher ▮**to close up** *vi* (*of shopkeeper*) fermer; (*of line of people*) se resserrer.

closely ['kləʊslɪ] *adv* (*to follow*, *guard*) de près; (*to listen*) attentivement; **c. linked** étroitement lié (**to** à); **to hold s.o. c.** tenir qn contre soi.

closet ['klɒzɪt] *n Am* (*cupboard*) placard *m*; (*wardrobe*) penderie *f*.

closure ['kləʊʒər] *n* fermeture *f*.
clot [klɒt] **1** *n* (*of blood*) caillot *m* ‖ *vi* (*of blood*) se coaguler. **2** *n* (*person*) *Fam* imbécile *mf*.
cloth [klɒθ] *n* tissu *m*, étoffe *f*; (*for dishes*) torchon *m*; (*tablecloth*) nappe *f*.
cloth/e [kləʊð] *vt* habiller, vêtir (**in** de). ●**—ing** *n* (*clothes*) vêtements *mpl*; **an article of c.** un vêtement.
clothes [kləʊðz] *npl* vêtements *mpl*; **to put one's c. on** s'habiller; **c. shop** magasin *m* d'habillement; **c. brush** brosse *f* à habits; **c. peg,** *Am* **c. pin** pince *f* à linge; **c. line** corde *f* à linge.
cloud [klaʊd] *n* nuage *m* ‖ *vi* **to c. over** (*of sky*) se couvrir. ●**cloudburst** *n* averse *f*. ●**cloudy** *a* (**-ier, -iest**) (*weather, sky*) couvert, nuageux; **it's c.** le temps est couvert, il y a des nuages.
clout [klaʊt] **1** *n* (*blow*) *Fam* taloche *f* ‖ *vt Fam* flanquer une taloche à. **2** *n Pol Fam* influence *f*, pouvoir *m*.
clove [kləʊv] *n* clou *m* de girofle; **c. of garlic** gousse *f* d'ail.
clover ['kləʊvər] *n* trèfle *m*.
clown [klaʊn] *n* clown *m* ‖ *vi* **to c. (around)** faire le clown.
club [klʌb] **1** *n* (*weapon*) matraque *f*; **(golf) c.** (*stick*) club *m* ‖ *vt* (**-bb-**) matraquer. **2** *n* (*society*) club *m*. **3** *n* **club(s)** *Cards* trèfle *m*. ●**club soda** *n Am* eau *f* gazeuse.
cluck [klʌk] *vi* (*of hen*) glousser.
clue [klu:] *n* indice *m*; (*of crossword*) définition *f*; (*to mystery*) clef *f*; **I don't have a c.** *Fam* je n'en ai pas la moindre idée. ●**clueless** *a Fam* stupide, nul (*f* nulle).
clump [klʌmp] *n* (*of flowers, trees*) massif *m*.
clumsy ['klʌmzɪ] *a* (**-ier, -iest**) maladroit; (*shape*) lourd; (*tool*) peu commode.
clung [klʌŋ] *pt & pp of* **cling.**
cluster ['klʌstər] *n* groupe *m*; (*of flowers*) grappe *f* ‖ *vi* se grouper.
clutch [klʌtʃ] **1** *vt* (*hold tight*) serrer; (*cling to*) se cramponner à; (*grasp*) saisir ‖ *vi* **to c. at** essayer de saisir. **2** *n Aut* embrayage *m*; (*pedal*) pédale *f* d'embrayage.
clutter ['klʌtər] *n* (*objects*) fouillis *m* ‖ *vt* **to c. (up)** (*room etc*) encombrer (**with** de).
cm *abbr* (*centimetre*) cm.
co- [kəʊ] *pref* co-.
Co *abbr* (*company*) Cie.
coach [kəʊtʃ] **1** *n* (*of train*) voiture *f*, wagon *m*; (*bus*) autocar *m*; (*horse-drawn*) carrosse *m*. **2** *n* (*person*) *Sp* entraîneur, -euse *mf* ‖ *vt* (*pupil*) donner des leçons (particulières) à; (*sportsman etc*) entraîner; **to c. s.o. for** (*exam*) préparer qn à.
coal [kəʊl] *n* charbon *m* ‖ *a* (*merchant*) de charbon; (*cellar, bucket, shovel*) à charbon; **c. fire** feu *m* de cheminée. ●**coalfield** *n* bassin *m* houiller. ●**coalmine** *n* mine *f* de charbon.
coarse [kɔ:s] *a* (**-er, -est**) (*person, manners*) grossier, vulgaire; (*surface*) rude; (*fabric*) grossier.
coast [kəʊst] *n* côte *f*. ●**coastal** *a* côtier. ●**coastguard** *n* (*person*) garde *m* maritime, garde-côte *m*. ●**coastline** *n* littoral *m*.
coaster ['kəʊstər] *n* (*for glass etc*) dessous *m* de verre.
coat [kəʊt] *n* manteau *m*; (*jacket*) veste *f*; (*of animal*) pelage *m*; (*of paint*) couche *f*; **c. of arms** armoiries *fpl* ‖ *vt* couvrir (**with** de); (*with chocolate*) enrober (**with** de); **coated tongue** langue *f* chargée. ●**—ing** *n* couche *f*.
coathanger ['kəʊthæŋər] *n* cintre *m*.
coax [kəʊks] *vt* amadouer; **to c. s.o. into doing** amadouer qn pour qu'il fasse.
cob [kɒb] *n* **corn on the c.** épi *m* de maïs.
cobbled ['kɒb(ə)ld] *a* pavé. ●**cobblestone** *n* pavé *m*.
cobbler ['kɒblər] *n* cordonnier *m*.
cobweb ['kɒbweb] *n* toile *f* d'araignée.
cocaine [kəʊ'keɪn] *n* cocaïne *f*.
cock [kɒk] **1** *n* (*rooster*) coq *m*; (*male bird*) (oiseau *m*) mâle *m*. **2** *vt* (*gun*) armer. ●**c.-a-doodle-'doo** *n & int* cocorico (*m*). ●**c.-and-'bull story** *n* histoire *f* à dormir debout.
cocker ['kɒkər] *n* **c. (spaniel)** cocker *m*.
cockerel ['kɒk(ə)rəl] *n* coquelet *m*.
cock-eyed [kɒk'aɪd] *a Fam* **1** (*cross-eyed*) bigleux. **2** (*crooked*) de travers. **3** (*crazy*) absurde, stupide.
cockle ['kɒk(ə)l] *n* (*shellfish*) coque *f*.
cockney ['kɒknɪ] *a & n* cockney (*mf*) (*natif des quartiers est de Londres*).
cockpit ['kɒkpɪt] *n Av* poste *m* de pilotage.
cockroach ['kɒkrəʊtʃ] *n* cafard *m*.
cocktail ['kɒkteɪl] *n* (*drink*) cocktail *m*; **(fruit) c.** macédoine *f* (de fruits); **c. party** cocktail *m*; **prawn c.** crevettes *fpl* à la mayonnaise.
cocky ['kɒkɪ] *a* (**-ier, -iest**) *Fam* trop sûr de soi, arrogant.
cocoa ['kəʊkəʊ] *n* cacao *m*.
coconut ['kəʊkənʌt] *n* noix *f* de coco; **c. palm** cocotier *m*.
cocoon [kə'ku:n] *n* cocon *m*.
cod [kɒd] *n* morue *f*; (*bought fresh*) cabillaud *m*. ●**c.-liver 'oil** *n* huile *f* de foie de morue.
COD [si:əʊ'di:] *abbr* (*cash on delivery*)

contre remboursement.

code [kəʊd] *n* code *m* ‖ *vt* coder.

co-educational [kəʊedjʊ'keɪʃən(ə)l] *a* (*school, teaching*) mixte.

coerce [kəʊ'ɜːs] *vt* contraindre (**s.o. into doing** qn à faire). ● **coercion** [-ʃ(ə)n] *n* contrainte *f*.

coexist [kəʊɪg'zɪst] *vi* coexister. ● **coexistence** *n* coexistence *f*.

coffee ['kɒfɪ] *n* café *m*; **white c.**, *Am* **c. with milk** café *m* au lait; (*in restaurant etc*) (café *m*) crème *m*; **black c.** café *m* noir; **c. bar** café *m*; **c. break** pause-café *f*; **c. table** table *f* basse. ● **coffeepot** *n* cafetière *f*.

coffers ['kɒfəz] *npl* (*funds*) coffres *mpl*.

coffin ['kɒfɪn] *n* cercueil *m*.

cog [kɒg] *n* (*tooth of wheel*) dent *f*; (*person*) *Fig* rouage *m*.

cognac ['kɒnjæk] *n* cognac *m*.

cohabit [kəʊ'hæbɪt] *vi* (*of unmarried people*) vivre en concubinage.

coherent [kəʊ'hɪərənt] *a* (*idea etc*) cohérent; (*way of speaking*) compréhensible.

coil [kɔɪl] *n* (*of wire, rope etc*) rouleau *m*; (*of snake*) anneau *m*; *El* bobine *f*; (*contraceptive*) stérilet *m* ‖ *vt* (*rope*) enrouler.

coin [kɔɪn] *n* pièce *f* (de monnaie); **c. bank** *Am* tirelire *f* ‖ *vt* (*word*) *Fig* forger; **to c. a phrase** pour ainsi dire. ● **c.-operated** *a* automatique.

coincide [kəʊɪn'saɪd] *vi* coïncider (**with** avec). ● **co'incidence** *n* coïncidence *f*.

coke [kəʊk] *n* **1** (*fuel*) coke *m*. **2** (*Coca-Cola*®) coca *m*.

colander ['kʌləndər, 'kɒl-] *n* (*for vegetables etc*) passoire *f*.

cold [kəʊld] *n* froid *m*; *Med* rhume *m*; **to catch c.** prendre froid; **to get a c.** s'enrhumer.

‖ *a* (**-er, -est**) froid; **to be** *or* **feel c.** (*of person*) avoir froid; **my hands are c.** j'ai froid aux mains; **it's c.** (*of weather*) il fait froid; **to get c.** (*of weather*) se refroidir; (*of food*) refroidir; **in c. blood** de sang-froid; **c. cream** crème *f* de beauté; **c. meats,** *Am* **c. cuts** assiette *f* anglaise. ● **c.-'blooded** *a* (*person*) cruel; (*murder*) de sang-froid. ● **coldness** *n* froideur *f*.

coleslaw ['kəʊlslɔː] *n* salade *f* de chou cru.

colic ['kɒlɪk] *n* *Med* coliques *fpl*.

collaborate [kə'læbəreɪt] *vi* collaborer (**on** à). ● **collaboration** [-'reɪʃ(ə)n] *n* collaboration *f*.

collage ['kɒlɑːʒ] *n* (*picture*) collage *m*.

collapse [kə'læps] *vi* (*of person, building*) s'effondrer; (*of government*) tomber; (*faint*) se trouver mal ‖ *n* effondrement *m*; (*of government*) chute *f*.

collar ['kɒlər] *n* (*on garment*) col *m*; (*of dog*) collier *m* ‖ *vt* (*seize*) *Fam* saisir (*qn*) au collet; (*buttonhole*) retenir (*qn*). ● **collarbone** *n* clavicule *f*.

colleague ['kɒliːg] *n* collègue *mf*.

collect [kə'lekt] *vt* (*pick up*) ramasser; (*gather*) rassembler, recueillir; (*taxes*) percevoir; (*rent*) encaisser; (*stamps etc as hobby*) collectionner; (*call for*) (passer) prendre; **to c. money** (*in street, church*) quêter (**for** pour) ‖ *vi* (*of dust*) s'accumuler; (*in street, church*) quêter (**for** pour) ‖ *adv* **to call c.** *Am* téléphoner en PCV.

collection [kə'lekʃ(ə)n] *n* (*of objects*) collection *f*; (*of poems etc*) recueil *m*; (*of money in church etc*) quête *f*; (*of mail*) levée *f*; (*of taxes*) perception *f*.

collector [kə'lektər] *n* (*of stamps etc*) collectionneur, -euse *mf*.

college ['kɒlɪdʒ] *n* université *f*; (*within university*) collège *m*; *Pol Rel* collège *m*; *Mus* conservatoire *m*; **art c.** école *f* des beaux-arts.

collide [kə'laɪd] *vi* entrer en collision (**with** avec). ● **collision** *n* collision *f*.

colliery ['kɒlɪərɪ] *n* houillère *f*.

colloquial [kə'ləʊkwɪəl] *a* (*word etc*) familier.

collusion [kə'luːʒ(ə)n] *n* collusion *f*.

cologne [kə'ləʊn] *n* eau *f* de Cologne.

colon ['kəʊlən] *n* **1** (*punctuation mark*) deux-points *m inv*. **2** *Anat* côlon *m*.

colonel ['kɜːn(ə)l] *n* colonel *m*.

colony ['kɒlənɪ] *n* colonie *f*.

colonial [kə'ləʊnɪəl] *a* colonial. ● **'colonize** *vt* coloniser.

colossal [kə'lɒs(ə)l] *a* colossal.

colour ['kʌlər] (*Am* **color**) *n* couleur *f*.

‖ *a* (*photo, TV set*) en couleurs; (*problem*) racial; **c. supplement** (*of newspaper*) supplément *m* illustré; **off c.** (*not well*) mal fichu.

‖ *vt* colorer; **to c. (in)** (*drawing*) colorier. ● **—ed** *a* (*person, pencil*) de couleur; (*glass, water*) coloré. ● **—ing** *n* (*in food*) colorant *m*; (*complexion*) teint *m*; (*with crayons*) coloriage *m*; (*shade, effect*) coloris *m*; **c. book** album *m* de coloriages. ● **colour-blind** *a* daltonien. ● **colourful** *a* (*crowd*) coloré; (*person*) pittoresque.

colt [kəʊlt] *n* (*horse*) poulain *m*.

column ['kɒləm] *n* colonne *f*; (*newspaper feature*) chronique *f*. ● **columnist** *n* chroniqueur *m*; **gossip c.** échotier, -ière *mf*.

coma ['kəʊmə] *n* coma *m*; **in a c.** dans le coma.

comb [kəʊm] *n* peigne *m* ‖ *vt* (*hair*) peigner;

(*search*) *Fig* ratisser; **to c. one's hair** se peigner.

combat ['kɒmbæt] *n* combat *m*.

combine[1] [kəm'baɪn] *vt* (*activities*, *qualities*, *elements*) combiner; (*efforts*) joindre; **our combined efforts produced a result** en joignant nos efforts nous avons obtenu un résultat ‖ *vi* s'unir; (*of elements*) se combiner. ●**combination** [-'neɪʃ(ə)n] *n* combinaison *f*; (*of qualities*) réunion *f*; (*of events*) concours *m*.

combine[2] ['kɒmbaɪn] *n* **1** *Com* association *f*; (*cartel*) cartel *m*. **2 c. harvester** *Agr* moissonneuse-batteuse *f*.

combustion [kəm'bʌstʃ(ə)n] *n* combustion *f*.

come [kʌm] *vi* (*pt* **came,** *pp* **come**) venir (**from** de, **to** à); **to c. first** (*in race*) arriver premier; (*in exam*) être le premier; **c. and see me** viens me voir; **I've just c. from** j'arrive de; **to c. home** rentrer; **coming!** j'arrive!; **to c. as a surprise (to)** surprendre; **to c. close to doing** faillir faire; **nothing came of it** ça n'a abouti à rien; **to c. true** se réaliser; **c. May**/*etc* *Fam* en mai/*etc*; **how c. that ...?** *Fam* comment se fait-il que...?

come about *vi* (*happen*) se faire, arriver ‖ **to c. across** *vi* (*of speech*) faire de l'effet; (*of feelings*) se montrer ‖ *vt* (*person*, *reference*) tomber sur; (*lost object*) trouver (par hasard) ‖ **to come along** *vi* venir (**with** avec); (*progress*) (*of work etc*) avancer; **c. along!** allons! ‖ **to come apart** *vi* (*of two objects*) se séparer ‖ **to c. away** *vi* (*leave*, *come off*) partir ‖ **to come back** *vi* revenir; (*return home*) rentrer. ●**comeback** *n* (*of actor*, *politician etc*) retour *m*. ‖ **to come by** *vt* (*obtain*) obtenir; (*find*) trouver ‖ **to come down** *vi* descendre; (*of rain*, *price*) tomber; (*of building*) être démoli ‖ *vt* (*stairs*, *hill etc*) descendre; **to c. down with** (*illness*) attraper. ●**comedown** *n* *Fam* humiliation *f*. ‖ **to come for** *vt* venir chercher (*qch*, *qn*) ‖ **to come forward** *vi* (*volunteer*) se présenter; **to c. forward with sth** offrir qch ‖ **to come in** *vi* entrer; (*of tide*) monter; (*of train*) arriver; *Pol* arriver au pouvoir; (*of money*) rentrer; **to c. in for** (*criticism*) essuyer ‖ **to come into** *vt* (*room etc*) entrer dans; (*money*) hériter de ‖ **to come off** *vi* (*of button etc*) se détacher, partir; (*succeed*) réussir; (*happen*) avoir lieu ‖ *vt* (*fall from*) tomber de; (*get down from*) descendre de ‖ **to come on** *vi* (*progress*) (*of work etc*) avancer; (*start*) commencer; (*of play*) être joué; **c. on!** allez! ‖ **to come out** *vi* sortir; (*of sun*, *book*) paraître; (*of stain*) partir; (*of photo*) réussir; **to c. out (on strike)** se mettre en grève ‖ **to come over** *vi* (*visit*) venir, passer (**to** chez); **to c. over to** (*approach*) s'approcher de; **to c. over funny** se trouver mal ‖ *vt* (*take hold of*) (*of feeling*) saisir (*qn*) ‖ **to come round** *vi* (*visit*) venir, passer (**to** chez); (*of date*) revenir; (*regain consciousness*) revenir à soi ‖ **to come through** *vi* (*survive*) s'en tirer ‖ *vt* (*crisis etc*) se tirer indemne de ‖ **to come to** *vi* (*regain consciousness*) revenir à soi ‖ *vt* (*amount to*) *Com* revenir à; (*a decision*) parvenir à; **to c. to an end** toucher à sa fin; **to c. to understand**/*etc* en venir à comprendre/*etc* ‖ **to come under** *vt* (*heading*) être classé sous; (*s.o.'s influence*) tomber sous ‖ **to come up** *vi* (*rise*) monter; (*of plant*) sortir; (*of question*, *job*) se présenter ‖ *vt* (*stairs etc*) monter ‖ **to come up against** *vt* (*wall*, *problem*) se heurter à ‖ **to come up to** *vt* (*reach*) arriver jusqu'à; (*approach*) s'approcher de ‖ **to come up with** *vt* (*idea*, *money*) trouver ‖ **to come upon** *vt* (*book*, *reference*) tomber sur.

comedy ['kɒmɪdɪ] *n* comédie *f*. ●**co'median** *n* (acteur *m*) comique *m*, actrice *f* comique.

comet ['kɒmɪt] *n* comète *f*.

comeuppance [kʌm'ʌpəns] *n* **he got his c.** *Pej Fam* il n'a eu que ce qu'il mérite.

comfort ['kʌmfət] *n* confort *m*; (*consolation*) réconfort *m*, consolation *f*; **to like one's comforts** aimer ses aises *fpl* ‖ *vt* consoler; (*cheer*) réconforter. ●**—er** *n* (*quilt*) *Am* édredon *m*.

comfortable ['kʌmfətəb(ə)l] *a* (*chair*, *house etc*) confortable; (*rich*) aisé; **he's c.** (*in chair etc*) il est à l'aise, il est bien; **make yourself c.** mets-toi à l'aise. ●**comfortably** *adv* (*to sit*) confortablement; **to live c.** vivre à l'aise.

comic ['kɒmɪk] *a* comique ‖ *n* (*actor*) comique *m*; (*actress*) actrice *f* comique; (*magazine*) illustré *m*; **c. strip** bande *f* dessinée. ●**comical** *a* comique, drôle.

coming ['kʌmɪŋ] *a* (*future*) à venir ‖ *n* **comings and goings** allées *fpl* et venues.

comma ['kɒmə] *n* *Gram* virgule *f*.

command [kə'mɑːnd] *vt* (*order*) commander (**s.o. to do** à qn de faire); (*control*) commander (*régiment*, *navire etc*) ‖ *vi* commander ‖ *n* (*order*) ordre *m*; (*authority*) commandement *m*; (*mastery*) maîtrise *f* (**of** de); *Comptr* commande *f*; **at one's c.** (*disposal*) à sa disposition; **to be in c. (of)** (*ship*, *army etc*) commander; (*situation*) être maître (de); **commanding officer** com-

mandant *m*. •**commander** *n Mil* commandant *m*.
commandment [kə'mɑːndmənt] *n Rel* commandement *m*.
commandeer [kɒmən'dɪər] *vt* réquisitionner.
commando [kə'mɑːndəʊ] *n* (*pl* **-os** *or* **-oes**) *Mil* commando *m*.
commemorate [kə'meməreɪt] *vt* commémorer.
commence [kə'mens] *vti* commencer (**doing** à faire).
commend [kə'mend] *vt* (*praise*) louer; (*recommend*) recommander. •**—able** *a* louable.
comment ['kɒment] *n* commentaire *m*, remarque *f*; **'no c.!'** 'rien à dire' ‖ *vi* faire des commentaires *or* des remarques (**on** sur); **to c. on** (*text*, *event*) commenter ‖ *vt* **to c. that** remarquer que. •**commentary** *n* commentaire *m*; **(live) c.** *TV Rad* reportage *m*. •**commentator** *n TV Rad* commentateur, -trice *mf*.
commerce ['kɒmɜːs] *n* commerce *m*. •**co'mmercial 1** *a* commercial; **c. traveller** voyageur *m* de commerce. **2** *n* (*advertisement*) *TV* publicité *f*; **the commercials** *TV* la publicité.
commiserate [kə'mɪzəreɪt] *vi* **to c. with s.o.** s'apitoyer sur (le sort de) qn.
commission [kə'mɪʃ(ə)n] *n* (*fee*, *group*) commission *f*; (*order for work*) commande *f* ‖ *vt* (*artist*) passer une commande à; (*book*) commander.
commissionaire [kəmɪʃə'neər] *n* (*in hotel etc*) commissionnaire *m*. •**commissioner** *n* **(police) c.** préfet *m* (de police).
commit [kə'mɪt] *vt* (**-tt-**) (*crime*) commettre; (*bind*) engager (*qn*); (*devote*) consacrer (*efforts etc*) (**to** à); **to c. suicide** se suicider; **to c. to memory** apprendre par cœur; **to c. to prison** incarcérer; **to c. oneself** (*make a promise*) s'engager (**to** à). •**—ment** *n* (*duty*, *responsibility*) obligation *f*; (*promise*) engagement *m*; (*devotion*) dévouement *m*.
committee [kə'mɪtɪ] *n* comité *m*.
commodity [kə'mɒdɪtɪ] *n* produit *m*.
common ['kɒmən] **1** *a* (**-er, -est**) (*shared*, *vulgar*) commun; (*frequent*) courant, commun; **in c.** (*shared*) en commun (**with** avec); **to have nothing in c.** n'avoir rien de commun (**with** avec); **in c. with** (*like*) comme; **C. Market** Marché *m* commun; **c. room** (*for students*) salle *f* commune; (*for teachers*) salle *f* des professeurs; **c. or garden** ordinaire. **2** *n* (*land*) terrain *m* communal; **House of Commons** *Pol* Chambre *f* des Communes; **the Commons** les Communes *fpl*. •**commony** *adv* (*generally*) en général; (*vulgarly*) d'une façon commune.
commonplace [kɒmənpleɪs] *a* banal (*mpl* -als).
commonsense [kɒmən'sens] *n* sens *m* commun, bon sens *m*.
Commonwealth ['kɒmənwelθ] *n* **the C.** le Commonwealth.
commotion [kə'məʊʃ(ə)n] *n* agitation *f*.
communal [kə'mjuːn(ə)l] *a* (*shared*) (*bathroom etc*) commun; (*of the community*) communautaire.
commune 1 ['kɒmjuːn] *n* (*district*) commune *f*; (*group*) communauté *f*. **2** [kə'mjuːn] *vi* **to c. with nature/God** être en communion avec la nature/Dieu. •**co'mmunion** *n* communion *f* (**with** avec).
communicate [kə'mjuːnɪkeɪt] *vt* communiquer; (*illness*) transmettre ‖ *vi* (*of person*, *rooms etc*) communiquer. •**communication** [-'keɪʃ(ə)n] *n* communication *f*; **c. cord** *Rail* signal *m* d'alarme.
communiqué [kə'muːnɪkeɪ] *n Pol etc* communiqué *m*.
communism ['kɒmjʊnɪz(ə)m] *n* communisme *m*. •**communist** *a* & *n* communiste (*mf*).
community [kə'mjuːnɪtɪ] *n* communauté *f*; **the student c.** les étudiants *mpl*; **c. centre** centre *m* socio-culturel; **c. worker** animateur, -trice *mf* socio-culturel(le).
commut/e [kə'mjuːt] *vi* (*travel*) faire la navette (**to work** pour se rendre à son travail). •**—ing** *n* trajets *mpl* journaliers. •**commuter** *n* banlieusard, -arde *mf*; **c. train** train *m* de banlieue.
compact[1] [kəm'pækt] *a* (*car*, *substance*) compact; **c. disc** *or Am* **disk** ['kɒmpækt] disque *m* compact.
compact[2] ['kɒmpækt] *n* (*for face powder*) poudrier *m*.
companion [kəm'pænjən] *n* (*person*) compagnon *m*, compagne *f*. •**companionship** *n* camaraderie *f*.
company ['kʌmpənɪ] *n* (*companionship*, *business*) compagnie *f*; (*guests*) invités, -ées *mfpl*; (*people present*) assemblée *f*; **to keep s.o. c.** tenir compagnie à qn; **to keep good c.** avoir de bonnes fréquentations; **he's good c.** c'est un bon compagnon; **c. car** voiture *f* de société.
compare [kəm'peər] *vt* comparer (**with, to** à); **compared to** *or* **with** en comparaison de ‖ *vi* être comparable, se comparer (**with** à).

• **comparable** ['kɒmpərəb(ə)l] *a* comparable (**with, to** à).
comparative [kəm'pærətɪv] *a* (*relative*) relatif; (*method etc*) comparatif; (*law etc*) comparé. • **comparatively** *adv* relativement. • **comparison** *n* comparaison *f* (**with** avec).
compartment [kəm'pɑːtmənt] *n* compartiment *m*.
compass ['kʌmpəs] *n* **1** (*for direction*) boussole *f*; (*on ship*) compas *m*. **2** (*for drawing etc*) *Am* compas *m*; **(pair of) compasses** compas *m*.
compassion [kəm'pæʃ(ə)n] *n* compassion *f*.
compatible [kəm'pætɪb(ə)l] *a* compatible.
compatriot [kəm'pætrɪət, kəm'peɪtrɪət] *n* compatriote *mf*.
compel [kəm'pel] *vt* (**-ll-**) forcer, contraindre (**to do** à faire); **compelled to do** forcé *or* contraint de faire. • **compelling** *a* irrésistible.
compensate ['kɒmpənseɪt] *vt* **to c. s.o.** dédommager qn (**for** de) ▮ *vi* compenser; **to c. for sth** (*make up for*) compenser qch. • **compensation** [-'seɪʃ(ə)n] *n* (*financial*) dédommagement *m*; **in c. for** en compensation de.
compère ['kɒmpeər] *n TV Rad* animateur, -trice *mf* ▮ *vt* (*a show*) animer.
compete [kəm'piːt] *vi* (*in race etc*) concourir; **to c. (with s.o.)** rivaliser (avec qn); *Com* faire concurrence (à qn); **to c. for sth** se disputer qch; **to c. in a race** courir dans une course.
competent ['kɒmpɪtənt] *a* compétent (**to do** pour faire); (*sufficient*) (*knowledge etc*) suffisant. • **—ly** *adv* avec compétence. • **competence** *n* compétence *f*.
competition [kɒmpə'tɪʃ(ə)n] *n* (*rivalry*) compétition *f*, concurrence *f*; **a c.** (*contest*) un concours; *Sp* une compétition. • **com'petitive** *a* (*price, market*) compétitif; (*person*) aimant la compétition; **c. examination** concours *m*. • **com'petitor** *n* concurrent, -ente *mf*.
compile [kəm'paɪl] *vt* (*dictionary*) rédiger; (*list*) dresser.
complacent [kəm'pleɪsənt] *a* content de soi. • **complacence** *or* **complacency** *n* autosatisfaction *f*.
complain [kəm'pleɪn] *vi* se plaindre (**to** à; **of, about** de; **that** que). • **complaint** *n* plainte *f*; (*in shop etc*) réclamation *f*; *Med* maladie *f*; **(cause for) c.** sujet *m* de plainte.
complement ['kɒmplɪmənt] *n* complément *m* ▮ ['kɒmplɪment] *vt* compléter. • **comple'mentary** *a* complémentaire.
complete [kəm'pliːt] *a* (*total*) complet; (*finished*) achevé; **a c. idiot** un parfait imbécile ▮ *vt* (*add sth missing to*) compléter; (*finish*) achever; (*a form*) remplir. • **—ly** *adv* complètement. • **completion** [-ʃ(ə)n] *n* achèvement *m*.
complex ['kɒmpleks] **1** *a* complexe. **2** *n* (*feeling, buildings*) complexe *m*; **housing c.** grand ensemble *m*. • **com'plexity** *n* complexité *f*.
complexion [kəm'plekʃ(ə)n] *n* (*of the face*) teint *m*.
complicat/e ['kɒmplɪkeɪt] *vt* compliquer. • **—ed** *a* compliqué. • **complication** [-'keɪʃ(ə)n] *n* complication *f*.
complicity [kəm'plɪsɪtɪ] *n* complicité *f*.
compliment ['kɒmplɪmənt] *n* compliment *m*; **compliments of the season** meilleurs vœux pour Noël et la nouvelle année ▮ ['kɒmplɪment] *vt* complimenter. • **compli'mentary** *a* **1** (*flattering*) flatteur. **2** (*free*) (offert) à titre gracieux; (*ticket*) de faveur.
comply [kəm'plaɪ] *vi* obéir (**with** à).
component [kəm'pəʊnənt] *n* (*of structure, self-assembly furniture etc*) élément *m*; (*of machine*) pièce *f*; (*chemical*) composant *m*.
compos/e [kəm'pəʊz] *vt* composer; **to c. oneself** se calmer. • **—ed** *a* calme. • **—er** *n* *Mus* compositeur, -trice *mf*. • **composition** [kɒmpə'zɪʃ(ə)n] *n Mus Liter Ch* composition *f*; (*school essay*) rédaction *f*.
compost ['kɒmpɒst, *Am* 'kɒmpəʊst] *n* compost *m*.
composure [kəm'pəʊʒər] *n* calme *m*, sang-froid *m*.
compound ['kɒmpaʊnd] *n* (*substance, word*) composé *m*; (*area*) enclos *m* ▮ *a* (*substance, word*) composé; (*sentence, number*) complexe.
comprehend [kɒmprɪ'hend] *vt* comprendre. • **comprehension** [-ʃ(ə)n] *n* compréhension *f*. • **comprehensive** *a* complet; (*view, measure*) d'ensemble; (*insurance*) tous risques *inv* ▮ *a* & *n* **c. (school)** = collège *m* d'enseignement secondaire.
compress [kəm'pres] *vt* (*gas, air*) comprimer.
comprise [kəm'praɪz] *vt* (*consist of*) comprendre; (*make up*) constituer.
compromise ['kɒmprəmaɪz] *vt* compromettre ▮ *vi* accepter un compromis ▮ *n* compromis *m*.
compulsion [kəm'pʌlʃ(ə)n] *n* contrainte *f*. • **compulsive** *a* (*smoker, gambler, liar*) invétéré.

compulsory [kəm'pʌlsərɪ] *a* obligatoire.
computer [kəm'pju:tər] *n* ordinateur *m*; **c. game** jeu *m* électronique; **c. operator** opérateur, -trice *mf* sur ordinateur; **c. program** programme *m* informatique; **c. science** informatique *f*; **c. scientist** informaticien, -ienne *mf*. ●**computerized** *a* informatisé. ●**computing** *n* informatique *f*.
comrade ['kɒmreɪd] *n* camarade *mf*.
con [kɒn] *vt* (**-nn-**) (*deceive*) *Sl* rouler, escroquer ‖ *n Sl* escroquerie *f*; **c. man** escroc *m*.
concave ['kɒnkeɪv] *a* concave.
conceal [kən'si:l] *vt* (*hide*) dissimuler, cacher (*objet, sentiment*) (**from s.o.** à qn).
concede [kən'si:d] *vt* concéder (**to** à, **that** que) ‖ *vi* céder.
conceit [kən'si:t] *n* vanité *f*. ●**conceited** *a* vaniteux.
conceiv/e [kən'si:v] *vt* (*idea, child etc*) concevoir; (*believe*) voir ‖ *vi* (*of woman*) concevoir; **to c. of** concevoir. ●**—able** *a* concevable, envisageable (**that** que + *sub*).
concentrate ['kɒnsəntreɪt] *vt* concentrer ‖ *vi* (*mentally & converge*) se concentrer (**on** sur); **to c. on doing** s'appliquer à faire; **to c. on one's exams**/*etc* se consacrer particulièrement à ses examens/*etc*. ●**concentration** [-'treɪʃ(ə)n] *n* concentration *f*; **c. camp** camp *m* de concentration.
concept ['kɒnsept] *n* concept *m*. ●**conception** [kən'sepʃ(ə)n] *n* (*idea*) & *Med* conception *f*.
concern [kən'sɜ:n] *vt* concerner; **to be concerned** (*anxious*) être inquiet; **to be concerned with/about** s'occuper de/s'inquiéter de; **the main person concerned** le principal intéressé ‖ *n* (*matter*) affaire *f*; (*anxiety*) inquiétude *f*; **his c. for** son souci de; **(business) c.** entreprise *f*. ●**—ing** *prep* en ce qui concerne.
concert ['kɒnsət] *n* concert *m*; **c. hall** salle *f* de concert. ●**c.-goer** *n* habitué, -ée *mf* des concerts.
concerted [kənsɜ:tɪd] *a* (*effort*) concerté.
concertina [kɒnsə'ti:nə] *n* concertina *m*.
concession [kən'seʃ(ə)n] *n* concession *f* (**to** à).
conciliation [kənsɪlɪ'eɪʃ(ə)n] *n* conciliation *f*.
concise [kən'saɪs] *a* concis. ●**—ly** *adv* avec concision. ●**concision** [-ʒ(ə)n] *n* concision *f*.
conclude [kən'klu:d] *vt* (*end, settle*) conclure; **to c. that** (*infer*) conclure que ‖ *vi* (*of event*) se terminer (**with** par); (*of speaker*) conclure. ●**conclusion** [-ʒ(ə)n] *n* conclusion *f*; **in c.** pour conclure. ●**conclusive** *a* concluant.
concoct [kən'kɒkt] *vt* (*dish*) *Pej* concocter; (*scheme*) combiner. ●**concoction** [-ʃ(ə)n] *n* (*substance*) *Pej* mixture *f*.
concourse ['kɒŋkɔ:s] *n* (*hall*) hall *m*.
concrete ['kɒŋkri:t] **1** *n* béton *m* ‖ *a* en béton. **2** *a* (*real, positive*) concret.
concurrently [kən'kʌrəntlɪ] *adv* simultanément.
concussion [kən'kʌʃ(ə)n] *n Med* commotion *f* (cérébrale).
condemn [kən'dem] *vt* condamner (*qn*) (**to** à); (*building*) déclarer inhabitable.
condense [kən'dens] *vt* condenser. ●**condensation** [kɒndən'seɪʃ(ə)n] *n* (*mist*) buée *f*.
condescend [kɒndɪ'send] *vi* condescendre (**to do** à faire).
condiment ['kɒndɪmənt] *n* condiment *m*.
condition [kən'dɪʃ(ə)n] **1** *n* (*stipulation, circumstance, state etc*) condition *f*; **on c. that one does** à condition de faire, à condition que l'on fasse; **in good c.** en bon état; **out of c.** en mauvaise forme. **2** *vt* (*action, person*) conditionner. ●**conditional** *a* conditionnel; **to be c. upon** dépendre de.
conditioner [kən'dɪʃənər] *n* **(hair) c.** après-shampooing *m*.
condo ['kɒndəʊ] *n abbr* (*pl* **-os**) *Am* = **condominium.**
condolences [kən'dəʊlənsɪz] *npl* condoléances *fpl*.
condom ['kɒndəm, -dɒm] *n* préservatif *m*, capote *f* (anglaise).
condominium [kɒndə'mɪnɪəm] *n Am* (*building*) copropriété *f*; (*apartment*) appartement *m* dans une copropriété.
condone [kən'dəʊn] *vt* (*overlook*) fermer les yeux sur; (*forgive*) excuser.
conducive [kən'dju:sɪv] *a* **c. to** favorable à.
conduct ['kɒndʌkt] *n* (*behaviour*) conduite *f* ‖ [kən'dʌkt] *vt* (*lead*) conduire, mener (*touristes, enquête etc*); (*orchestra*) diriger; (*electricity, heat*) conduire; **to c. oneself** se conduire. ●**—ed** *a* (*visit*) guidé; **c. tour** excursion *f* accompagnée; (*of building etc*) visite *f* guidée.
conductor [kən'dʌktər] *n Mus* chef *m* d'orchestre; (*on bus*) receveur *m*; (*on train*) *Am* chef *m* de train. ●**conductress** *n* (*on bus*) receveuse *f*.
cone [kəʊn] *n* cône *m*; (*of ice cream*) cornet *m*; **traffic c.** cône *m* de chantier.
confectioner [kən'fekʃənər] *n* (*of sweets, Am candies*) confiseur, -euse *mf*. ●**confectionery** *n* confiserie *f*.
confederation [kənfedə'reɪʃ(ə)n] *n* confédération *f*.

confer [kən'fɜːr] **1** *vt* (**-rr-**) (*grant*) conférer (**on** à); **to c. a degree on** remettre un diplôme à. **2** *vi* (**-rr-**) (*talk together*) se consulter; **to c. with s.o.** consulter qn.

conference ['kɒnfərəns] *n* conférence *f*; (*scientific etc*) congrès *m*.

confess [kən'fes] **1** *vt* avouer (**that** que, **to s.o.** à qn) ‖ *vi* avouer; **to c. to** (*crime etc*) avouer. **2** *vt Rel* confesser ‖ *vi* se confesser. ●**confession** [-ʃ(ə)n] *n* aveu(x) *m(pl)*; *Rel* confession *f*.

confetti [kən'fetɪ] *n* confettis *mpl*.

confide [kən'faɪd] *vt* confier (**to** à, **that** que) ‖ *vi* **to c. in** (*talk to*) se confier à.

confidence ['kɒnfɪdəns] *n* (*trust*) confiance *f*; (**self-)c.** confiance *f* en soi; **in c.** en confidence; **motion of no c.** *Pol* motion *f* de censure; **c. trick** escroquerie *f*. ●**confident** *a* sûr; (**self-)c.** sûr de soi. ●**confidently** *adv* avec confiance.

confidential [kɒnfɪ'denʃəl] *a* confidentiel. ●**—ly** *adv* en confidence.

confin/e [kən'faɪn] *vt* **1** (*limit*) limiter (**to** à); **to c. oneself to doing** se limiter à faire. **2** (*keep prisoner*) enfermer (*qn*) (**to, in** dans). ●**—ed** *a* (*space*) réduit; **c. to bed** cloué au lit.

confirm [kən'fɜːm] *vt* confirmer (**that** que); (*strengthen*) raffermir. ●**—ed** *a* (*bachelor*) endurci; (*smoker*) invétéré. ●**confirmation** [kɒnfə'meɪʃ(ə)n] *n* confirmation *f*.

confiscate ['kɒnfɪskeɪt] *vt* confisquer (**from s.o.** à qn).

conflict ['kɒnflɪkt] *n* conflit *m* ‖ [kən'flɪkt] *vi* être en contradiction (**with** avec); (*of dates, events, TV programmes*) tomber en même temps (**with** que). ●**—ing** *a* (*views etc*) contradictoires; (*dates*) incompatibles.

conform [kən'fɔːm] *vi* (*of person*) se conformer (**to** à); (*of ideas etc*) être en conformité. ●**conformist** *a* & *n* conformiste (*mf*).

confound [kən'faʊnd] *vt* (*surprise, puzzle*) confondre.

confront [kən'frʌnt] *vt* (*danger, problems*) faire face à; **to c. s.o.** (*be face to face with*) se trouver en face de qn; (*oppose*) s'opposer à qn. ●**confrontation** [kɒnfrən'teɪʃ(ə)n] *n* confrontation *f*.

confus/e [kən'fjuːz] *vt* (*make unsure*) embrouiller (*qn*); **to c. with** (*mistake for*) confondre avec. ●**—ed** *a* (*situation, noises etc*) confus; **to be c.** (*of person*) s'y perdre; **to get c.** s'embrouiller. ●**—ing** *a* déroutant. ●**confusion** [-ʒ(ə)n] *n* confusion *f*; **in c.** en désordre.

congealed [kən'dʒiːld] *a* **c. blood** sang *m* coagulé.

congenial [kən'dʒiːnɪəl] *a* sympathique.

congenital [kən'dʒenɪtəl] *a* congénital.

congested [kən'dʒestɪd] *a* (*street*) encombré; (*district*) surpeuplé; (*nose*) bouché; (*lungs*) congestionné. ●**congestion** [-tʃ(ə)n] *n* encombrement *m*; (*traffic*) encombrement(s) *m(pl)*; *Med* congestion *f*.

Congo ['kɒŋgəʊ] *n* Congo *m*.

congratulate [kən'grætʃʊleɪt] *vt* féliciter (**s.o. on sth** qn de qch, **s.o. on doing sth** qn d'avoir fait qch). ●**congratulations** [-'leɪʃ(ə)nz] *npl* félicitations *fpl* (**on** pour).

congregate ['kɒŋgrɪgeɪt] *vi* se rassembler. ●**congregation** [-'geɪʃ(ə)n] *n* (*worshippers*) fidèles *mfpl*.

congress ['kɒŋgres] *n* congrès *m*; **C.** *Pol Am* le Congrès. ●**Congressman** *n* (*pl* **-men**) *Am* membre *m* du Congrès. ●**Con'gressional** *a Am* du Congrès.

conical ['kɒnɪk(ə)l] *a* conique.

conifer ['kɒnɪfər] *n* (*tree*) conifère *m*.

conjugal ['kɒndʒʊgəl] *a* conjugal.

conjugate ['kɒndʒʊgeɪt] *vt* (*verb*) conjuguer. ●**conjugation** [-'geɪʃ(ə)n] *n* conjugaison *f*.

conjunction [kən'dʒʌŋkʃ(ə)n] *n Gram* conjonction *f*; **in c. with** conjointement avec.

conjunctivitis [kəndʒʌŋktɪ'vaɪtɪs] *n* conjonctivite *f*.

conjur/e ['kʌndʒər] *vt* **to c. (up)** (*by magic*) faire apparaître; **to c. up** (*memories etc*) *Fig* évoquer; **conjuring trick** tour *m* de prestidigitation. ●**—er** *n* prestidigitateur, -trice *mf*.

conk [kɒŋk] *vi* **to c. out** (*break down*) *Fam* tomber en panne.

connect [kə'nekt] *vt* relier (**with, to** à); (*telephone, washing machine etc*) brancher; **to c. with** *Tel* mettre (*qn*) en communication avec; (*in memory*) associer (*qch, qn*) avec.
‖ *vi* (*be connected*) être relié; **to c. with** (*of train, bus*) assurer la correspondance avec. ●**—ed** *a* (*facts etc*) liés; **to be c. with** (*have dealings with, relate to*) être lié à.

connection [kə'nekʃ(ə)n] *n* (*link*) rapport *m*, relation *f* (**with** avec); (*train, bus etc*) correspondance *f*; (*phone call*) communication; *pl* (*contacts*) relations *fpl*; **in c. with** à propos de.

connive [kə'naɪv] *vi* **to c. at** fermer les yeux sur; **to c. together** agir en complicité.

connotation [kɒnə'teɪʃ(ə)n] *n* connotation *f*.

conquer ['kɒŋkər] *vt* (*country, freedom etc*) conquérir; (*enemy, habit*) vaincre. ●**—ing** *a* victorieux. ●**conqueror** *n* conquérant,

-ante *mf*. • **conquest** *n* conquête *f*.

cons [kɒnz] *npl* **the pros and (the) c.** le pour et le contre.

conscience ['kɒnʃəns] *n* conscience *f*.

conscientious [kɒnʃɪ'enʃəs] *a* consciencieux. • **—ness** *n* application *f*, sérieux *m*.

conscious ['kɒnʃəs] *a* (*awake*) conscient; (*intentional*) délibéré; **c. of sth** (*aware*) conscient de qch; **to be c. of doing** avoir conscience de faire. • **—ly** *adv* (*knowingly*) consciemment. • **—ness** *n* **to lose/regain c.** perdre/reprendre connaissance.

conscript ['kɒnskrɪpt] *n Mil* conscrit *m* ‖ [kən'skrɪpt] *vt* enrôler (par conscription). • **conscription** [kən'skrɪpʃ(ə)n] *n* conscription *f*.

consecutive [kən'sekjʊtɪv] *a* consécutif. • **—ly** *adv* consécutivement.

consensus [kən'sensəs] *n* consensus *m*.

consent [kən'sent] *vi* consentir (**to** à) ‖ *n* consentement *m*; **by common c.** de l'aveu de tous; **by mutual c.** d'un commun accord.

consequence ['kɒnsɪkwəns] *n* (*result*) conséquence *f*; (*importance*) importance *f*. • **consequently** *adv* par conséquent.

conservative [kən'sɜːvətɪv] **1** *a* (*view*) traditionnel; (*estimate*) modeste. **2** *a* & *n* **C.** *Br Pol* conservateur, -trice (*mf*).

conservatory [kən'sɜːvətrɪ] *n* (*room*) véranda *f*.

conserve [kən'sɜːv] *vt* (*energy, water etc*) économiser, faire des économies de; (*preserve*) préserver (*privilèges, faune etc*); **to c. one's strength** économiser ses forces. • **conservation** [kɒnsə'veɪʃ(ə)n] *n* (*energy-saving*) économies *fpl* d'énergie; (*of nature*) protection *f* de l'environnement; **c. area** zone *f* naturelle protégée.

consider [kən'sɪdər] *vt* considérer (**that** que); (*take into account*) tenir compte de; **I'll c. it** j'y réfléchirai; **to c. doing** envisager de faire; **all things considered** tout compte fait. • **consideration** [-'reɪʃ(ə)n] *n* (*thought, thoughtfulness, reason*) considération *f*; **under c.** à l'étude; **to take into c.** prendre en considération.

considerable [kən'sɪdərəb(ə)l] *a* (*large*) considérable; (*much*) beaucoup de. • **considerably** *adv* beaucoup, considérablement.

considerate [kən'sɪdərət] *a* plein d'égards (**to** pour), attentionné (**to** à l'égard de).

considering [kən'sɪdərɪŋ] *prep* compte tenu de; **c. that** étant donné que.

consign [kən'saɪn] *vt* (*send*) expédier (*marchandises*) (**to** à). • **—ment** *n* (*goods*) arrivage *m*.

consist [kən'sɪst] *vi* consister (**of** en, **in** dans, **in doing** à faire).

consistent [kən'sɪstənt] *a* (*unchanging*) constant; (*coherent*) (*ideas etc*) cohérent, logique; **to be c. with** concorder avec. • **—ly** *adv* (*always*) constamment. • **consistency** *n* **1** (*of liquid etc*) consistance *f*. **2** (*of ideas etc*) cohérence *f*.

console[1] [kən'səʊl] *vt* consoler. • **consolation** [kɒnsə'leɪʃ(ə)n] *n* consolation *f*; **c. prize** lot *m* de consolation.

console[2] ['kɒnsəʊl] *n* (*control desk*), console *f*.

consolidate [kən'sɒlɪdeɪt] *vt* consolider.

consonant ['kɒnsənənt] *n* consonne *f*.

conspicuous [kən'spɪkjʊəs] *a* (*noticeable*) visible, en évidence; (*striking*) remarquable; (*showy*) voyant; **to make oneself c.** se faire remarquer.

conspire [kən'spaɪər] *vi* (*plot*) conspirer (**against** contre); **to c. to do** comploter de faire. • **conspiracy** [-'spɪrəsɪ] *n* conspiration *f*.

constable ['kɒnstəb(ə)l] *n* **(police) c.** agent *m* (de police); **chief c.** = préfet *m* de police.

constant ['kɒnstənt] *a* (*frequent*) incessant; (*unchanging*) constant. • **constantly** *adv* constamment, sans cesse.

constellation [kɒnstə'leɪʃ(ə)n] *n* constellation *f*.

constipated ['kɒnstɪpeɪtɪd] *a* constipé. • **constipation** [-'peɪʃ(ə)n] *n* constipation *f*.

constituent [kən'stɪtjʊənt] *n Pol* électeur, -trice *mf*. • **constituency** *n* circonscription *f* électorale; (*voters*) électeurs *mpl*.

constitute ['kɒnstɪtjuːt] *vt* constituer. • **constitution** [-'tjuːʃ(ə)n] *n* (*of person*) & *Pol* constitution *f*. • **consti'tutional** *a Pol* constitutionnel.

constraint [kən'streɪnt] *n* contrainte *f*.

constrict [kən'strɪkt] *vt* (*tighten, narrow*) resserrer; (*movement*) gêner.

construct [kən'strʌkt] *vt* construire. • **construction** [-ʃ(ə)n] *n* construction *f*; **under c.** en construction. • **constructive** *a* constructif.

consul ['kɒnsəl] *n* consul *m*. • **consular** *a* consulaire. • **consulate** *n* consulat *m*.

consult [kən'sʌlt] *vt* consulter ‖ *vi* **to c. with** discuter avec; **consulting room** (*of doctor*) cabinet *m* de consultation. • **consultation** [kɒnsəl'teɪʃ(ə)n] *n* consultation *f*.

consultancy [kən'sʌltənsɪ] *n* **c. (firm)** cabinet *m* d'experts-conseils; **c. fee** honoraires *mpl* de conseils. • **consultant** *n* (*doctor*) spécialiste *mf*; (*financial, legal*) expert-conseil *m*.

consum/e [kən'sju:m] *vt* (*food, supplies etc*) consommer; (*of grief, hate etc*) dévorer (*qn*); **to be consumed by** (*grief etc*) être dévoré de. ●**—er** *n* consommateur, -trice *mf*; **gas/electricity c.** abonné, -ée *mf* au gaz/à l'électricité; **c. goods/society** biens *mpl*/société *f* de consommation. ●**consumption** [-'sʌmpʃ(ə)n] *n* consommation *f* (**of** de).

contact ['kɒntækt] *n* contact *m*; (*person*) contact *m*, relation *f*; **in c. with** en contact avec; **c. lenses** lentilles *fpl or* verres *mpl* de contact ▮ *vt* contacter, se mettre en contact avec.

contagious [kən'teɪdʒəs] *a* contagieux.

contain [kən'teɪn] *vt* (*enclose, hold back*) contenir. ●**—er** *n* récipient *m*; (*for transporting goods*) conteneur *m*.

contaminate [kən'tæmɪneɪt] *vt* contaminer.

contemplate ['kɒntəmpleɪt] *vt* (*look at*) contempler; (*consider*) envisager (**doing** de faire).

contemporary [kən'tempərərɪ] *a* contemporain (**with** de); (*pattern, style etc*) moderne ▮ *n* (*person*) contemporain, -aine *mf*.

contempt [kən'tempt] *n* mépris *m*; **to hold in c.** mépriser. ●**contemptible** *a* méprisable. ●**contemptuous** *a* dédaigneux (**of** de).

contend [kən'tend] *vi* **to c. with** (*problem etc*) faire face à; **to c. with s.o.** (*deal with*) avoir affaire à qn; (*compete*) rivaliser avec qn. ●**—er** *n* concurrent, -ente *mf*.

content[1] [kən'tent] *a* satisfait (**with** de); **he's c. to do** il ne demande pas mieux que de faire. ●**—ed** *a* satisfait.

content[2] ['kɒntent] *n* (*of text etc*) (*subject matter*) contenu *m*; *pl* (*of container, letter etc*) (*total within*) contenu *m*; **(table of) contents** (*of book*) table *f* des matières; **alcoholic c.** teneur *f* en alcool.

contentious [kən'tenʃəs] *a* (*issue*) litigieux.

contest [kən'test] *vt* (*dispute*) contester; (*fight for*) disputer ▮ ['kɒntest] *n* (*competition*) concours *m*; (*fight*) lutte *f*. ●**con'testant** *n* concurrent, -ente *mf*; (*in fight*) adversaire *mf*.

context ['kɒntekst] *n* contexte *m*.

continent ['kɒntɪnənt] *n* continent *m*; **the C.** l'Europe *f* (continentale). ●**conti'nental** *a* européen; *Geog* continental; **c. breakfast** petit déjeuner *m* à la française.

contingent [kən'tɪndʒənt] **1** *a* **to be c. upon** dépendre de. **2** *nm* (*group*) contingent *m*. ●**contingency** *n* éventualité *f*; **c. plan** plan *m* d'urgence.

continual [kən'tɪnjʊəl] *a* continuel. ●**continually** *adv* continuellement.

continue [kən'tɪnju:] *vt* continuer (**to do** *or* **doing** à *or* de faire); **to c. (with)** (*work etc*) poursuivre, continuer; (*resume*) reprendre; **to be continued** (*of story*) à suivre ▮ *vi* continuer; (*resume*) reprendre. ●**continuation** [-'eɪʃ(ə)n] *n* continuation *f*; (*resumption*) reprise *f*; (*new episode*) suite *f*.

continuous [kən'tɪnjʊəs] *a* continu; **c. film programme** cinéma *m* permanent. ●**continuously** *adv* sans interruption.

contort [kən'tɔ:t] *vt* (*twist*) tordre; **to c. oneself** se contorsionner.

contour ['kɒntʊər] *n* contour *m*.

contraception [kɒntrə'sepʃ(ə)n] *n* contraception *f*. ●**contraceptive** *a* & *n* contraceptif (*m*).

contract[1] ['kɒntrækt] *n* contrat *m*; **c. work** travail *m* en sous-traitance. ●**con'tractor** *n* entrepreneur *m*.

contract[2] [kən'trækt] *vt* (*illness, debt, muscle etc*) contracter ▮ *vi* (*of heart*) se contracter. ●**contraction** [-ʃ(ə)n] *n* (*of muscle, word*) contraction *f*.

contradict [kɒntrə'dɪkt] *vt* contredire. ●**contradiction** [-ʃ(ə)n] *n* contradiction *f*. ●**contradictory** *a* contradictoire.

contralto [kən'træltəʊ] *n* (*pl* **-os**) contralto *m*.

contraption [kən'træpʃ(ə)n] *n Fam* engin *m*, machin *m*.

contrary ['kɒntrərɪ] *a* contraire (**to** à) ▮ *adv* **c. to** contrairement à ▮ *n* contraire *m*; **on the c.** au contraire; **unless you, I** *etc* **hear to the c.** sauf avis contraire.

contrast 1 ['kɒntrɑ:st] *n* contraste *m*; **in c. to** par opposition à. **2** [kən'trɑ:st] *vi* contraster (**with** avec) ▮ *vt* mettre en contraste. ●**—ing** *a* (*colours, opinions etc*) opposés.

contravene [kɒntrə'vi:n] *vt* (*law*) enfreindre.

contribute [kən'trɪbju:t] *vt* donner (**to** à); (*article*) écrire (**to** pour); **to c. money to** contribuer à ▮ *vi* **to c. to** contribuer à; (*publication*) collaborer à. ●**contribution** [kɒntrɪ'bju:ʃ(ə)n] *n* contribution *f*; (*to fund etc*) cotisation(s) *f(pl)*; (*newspaper article*) article *m*. ●**contributor** *n* (*to newspaper*) collaborateur, -trice *mf*; (*of money*) donateur, -trice *mf*.

contrive [kən'traɪv] *vt* **to c. to do** trouver moyen de faire.

contrived [kən'traɪvd] *a* artificiel.

control [kən'trəʊl] *vt* (**-ll-**) (*business, organization*) diriger; (*traffic*) régler; (*prices, quality, situation, emotion*) contrôler; (*child, animal*) tenir; **to c. oneself** se contrôler.

▮ *n* (*authority*) autorité *f* (**over** sur); (*over*

prices, quality) contrôle *m*; (*over one's emotions*) maîtrise *f*; **the controls** (*of train etc*) les commandes *fpl*; (*knobs*) *TV Rad* les boutons *mpl*; **(self-)c.** le contrôle de soi-même, la maîtrise (de soi); **to keep s.o. under c.** tenir qn; **to bring under c.** (*fire, inflation*) maîtriser; **everything is under c.** tout est en ordre; **in c. of** (*situation, vehicle*) maître de; **I'm in c.** (*of situation*) j'ai la situation en main; **to lose c. of** (*situation, vehicle*) perdre le contrôle de; **out of c.** (*situation, crowd*) difficilement maîtrisable; **c. tower** *Av* tour *f* de contrôle. ● **controller** *n* **air traffic c.** contrôleur *m* aérien, aiguilleur *m* du ciel.

controversy ['kɒntrəvɜːsɪ] *n* controverse *f*. ● **contro'versial** *a* (*book, author*) contesté, controversé; (*doubtful*) discutable.

convalesce [kɒnvə'les] *vi* (*rest*) être en convalescence. ● **convalescence** *n* convalescence *f*. ● **convalescent home** *n* maison *f* de convalescence.

convector [kən'vektər] *n* **c. (heater)** convecteur *m*.

convenience [kən'viːnɪəns] *n* commodité *f*; (*advantage*) avantage *m*; **at your c.** quand vous voudrez; **(public) conveniences** toilettes *fpl*; **c. food(s)** plats *mpl* tout préparés; **c. store** magasin *m* de proximité.

convenient [kən'viːnɪənt] *a* commode, pratique; (*well-situated*) bien situé (**for the shops**/*etc* par rapport aux magasins/*etc*); (*moment*) convenable, opportun; **to be c. (for)** (*suit*) convenir (à). ● **—ly** *adv* **c. situated** bien situé.

convent ['kɒnvənt] *n* couvent *m*.

convention [kən'venʃ(ə)n] *n* (*custom*) usage *m*, convention *f*; (*meeting*) assemblée *f*; (*agreement*) convention *f*. ● **conventional** *a* conventionnel.

converg/e [kən'vɜːdʒ] *vi* converger. ● **—ing** *a* convergent.

conversant [kən'vɜːsənt] *a* **to be c. with** (*custom, author etc*) connaître; (*fact*) savoir.

conversation [kɒnvə'seɪʃ(ə)n] *n* conversation *f*. ● **conversational** *a* (*tone*) de la conversation.

converse **1** [kən'vɜːs] *vi* s'entretenir (**with** avec). **2** ['kɒnvɜːs] *a* & *n* inverse (*m*). ● **con'versely** *adv* inversement.

convert [kən'vɜːt] *vt* (*change*) convertir (**into** en); (*building*) aménager (**into** en); **to c. s.o.** *Rel* convertir qn (**to** à) ‖ ['kɒnvɜːt] *n* converti, -ie *mf*.

convertible [kən'vɜːtəb(ə)l] *n* (*car*) (voiture *f*) décapotable *f* ‖ *a* (*sofa*) convertible.

convex ['kɒnveks] *a* convexe.

convey [kən'veɪ] *vt* (*goods, people*) transporter; (*sound, message, order*) transmettre; (*idea*) communiquer (**to** à); (*evoke*) évoquer; (*water etc through pipes*) amener. ● **conveyor belt** *n* tapis *m* roulant.

convict ['kɒnvɪkt] *n* forçat *m* ‖ [kən'vɪkt] *vt* reconnaître *or* déclarer coupable (**of** de). ● **conviction** [-ʃ(ə)n] *n Jur* condamnation *f*; (*belief*) conviction *f*.

convinc/e [kən'vɪns] *vt* convaincre, persuader (**of** de). ● **—ing** *a* convaincant.

convoluted [kɒnvə'luːtɪd] *a* (*argument, style*) compliqué, tarabiscoté.

convoy ['kɒnvɔɪ] *n* (*ships, cars*) convoi *m*.

convulsion [kən'vʌlʃ(ə)n] *n* convulsion *f*.

coo [kuː] *vi* (*of dove*) roucouler.

cook [kʊk] *vt* (*food*) (faire) cuire; **to c. up** *Fam* inventer ‖ *vi* (*of food*) cuire; (*of person*) faire la cuisine; **what's cooking?** *Fam* qu'est-ce qui se passe? ‖ *n* (*person*) cuisinier, -ière *mf*. ● **—ing** *n* cuisine *f*; **c. apple** pomme *f* à cuire. ● **cooker** *n* (*stove*) cuisinière *f*.

cookbook ['kʊkbʊk] *n* livre *m* de cuisine. ● **cookery** *n* cuisine *f*; **c. book** livre *m* de cuisine.

cookie ['kʊkɪ] *n Am* biscuit *m*, gâteau *m* sec.

cool [kuːl] *a* (**-er, -est**) (*weather, place, drink etc*) frais (*f* fraîche); (*having cooled down*) (*tea etc*) qui n'est plus très chaud; (*calm*) (*manner, person*) calme; (*unfriendly*) (*reception etc*) froid; **I feel c.** (*cold*) j'ai (un peu) froid; (*no longer hot*) j'ai moins chaud; **to keep sth c.** tenir qch au frais. ‖ *n* (*of evening*) fraîcheur *f*; **to keep/lose one's c.** garder/perdre son sang-froid. ‖ *vt* **to c. (down)** refroidir, rafraîchir. ‖ *vi* **to c. (down** *or* **off)** (*of hot liquid*) refroidir; (*of enthusiasm*) se refroidir; (*of anger, angry person*) se calmer; **to c. off** (*refresh oneself by drinking, swimming etc*) se rafraîchir. ● **cooler** *n* (*for food*) glacière *f*. ● **coolly** *adv* calmement; (*to welcome*) froidement. ● **coolness** *n* fraîcheur *f*; (*unfriendliness*) froideur *f*.

cool-headed [kuːl'hedɪd] *a* calme.

coop [kuːp] **1** *n* (*for chickens*) poulailler *m*. **2** *vt* **to c. s.o. up** enfermer qn.

co-op ['kəʊɒp] *n Am* appartement *m* en copropriété.

co-operate [kəʊ'ɒpəreɪt] *vi* coopérer (**in** à, **with** avec). ● **co-operation** [-'reɪʃ(ə)n] *n* coopération *f*.

co-operative [kəʊ'ɒpərətɪv] *a* coopératif ‖ *n* coopérative *f*.

co-ordinate [kəʊ'ɔːdɪneɪt] *vt* coordonner.
cop [kɒp] *n* (*policeman*) *Fam* flic *m*.
cope [kəʊp] *vi* **to c. with** s'occuper de; (*problem*) faire face à; **(to be able) to c.** (savoir) se débrouiller.
co-pilot ['kəʊpaɪlət] *n* copilote *m*.
copper ['kɒpər] *n* (*metal*) cuivre *m*; *pl* (*coins*) petite monnaie *f*.
copy ['kɒpɪ] *n* copie *f*; (*of book, magazine etc*) exemplaire *m* ‖ *vti* copier ‖ *vt* **to c. out** *or* **down** (*text, letter etc*) (re)copier. ●**copyright** *n* copyright *m*.
coral ['kɒrəl] *n* corail *m*; **c. reef** récif *m* de corail.
cord [kɔːd] **1** *n* (*heavy string*) corde *f*; (*of curtain etc*) cordon *m*; *El* cordon *m* électrique; **vocal cords** cordes *fpl* vocales. **2** *npl* (*trousers, Am pants*) *Fam* velours *m*.
cordial ['kɔːdɪəl] **1** *a* (*friendly*) cordial. **2** *n* **(fruit) c.** sirop *m*.
cordon ['kɔːdən] *n* cordon *m* ‖ *vt* **to c. off** (*of police*) interdire l'accès de (*lieu*).
corduroy ['kɔːdərɔɪ] *n* (*fabric*) velours *m* côtelé; *pl* (*trousers, Am pants*) pantalon *m* en velours (côtelé).
core [kɔːr] *n* (*of apple etc*) trognon *m*; (*of problem*) cœur *m*; (*group of people*) noyau *m* ‖ *vt* (*apple*) vider.
cork [kɔːk] *n* liège *m*; (*for bottle*) bouchon *m* ‖ *vt* **to c. (up)** (*bottle*) boucher. ●**corkscrew** *n* tire-bouchon *m*.
corn [kɔːn] *n* **1** (*wheat*) blé *m*; (*maize*) *Am* maïs *m*; **c. on the cob** épi *m* de maïs. **2** (*hard skin on foot*) cor *m*. ●**corned beef** *n* corned-beef *m*. ●**cornflakes** *npl* céréales *fpl*. ●**cornflour** (*Am* **cornstarch**) *n* farine *f* de maïs, maïzena® *f*.
corner ['kɔːnər] **1** *n* coin *m*; (*bend in road*) virage *m*; *Fb* corner *m*; **in a (tight) c.** dans une situation difficile; **around the c.** (*shops etc*) à deux pas. **2** *vt* (*person in corridor etc*) coincer; (*animal*) acculer; (*market*) *Com* monopoliser ‖ *vi Aut* prendre un virage.
cornet ['kɔːnɪt] *n* (*of ice cream*) cornet *m*.
Cornwall ['kɔːnwəl] *n* Cornouailles *f*. ●**Cornish** *a* de Cornouailles.
corny ['kɔːnɪ] *a* (**-ier, -iest**) (*joke*) rebattu.
coronary ['kɒrənərɪ] *n Med* infarctus *m*.
coronation [kɒrə'neɪʃ(ə)n] *n* couronnement *m*, sacre *m*.
coroner ['kɒrənər] *n* coroner *m* (*officier de police judiciaire qui enquête en cas de mort suspecte*).
corporal ['kɔːpərəl] **1** *n Mil* caporal(-chef) *m*. **2** *a* **c. punishment** châtiment *m* corporel.
corporation [kɔːpə'reɪʃ(ə)n] *n* (*business*) société *f* commerciale.
corporate ['kɔːpərət] *a* (*decision etc*) collectif.
corps [kɔːr, *pl* kɔːz] *n Mil Pol* corps *m*.
corpse [kɔːps] *n* cadavre *m*.
corpulent ['kɔːpjʊlənt] *a* corpulent.
correct [kə'rekt] *a* (*right, accurate*) (*answer etc*) exact, correct; (*proper*) correct; **he's c.** il a raison ‖ *vt* corriger. ●**—ly** *adv* correctement. ●**correction** [-ʃ(ə)n] *n* correction *f*.
correspond [kɒrɪ'spɒnd] *vi* **1** (*agree, be similar*) correspondre (**to, with** à). **2** (*by letter*) correspondre (**with** avec). ●**—ing** *a* (*matching*) correspondant. ●**correspondence** *n* correspondance *f*; **c. course** cours *m* par correspondance. ●**correspondent** *n* (*journalist*) envoyé, -ée *mf*.
corridor ['kɒrɪdɔːr] *n* couloir *m*.
corrode [kə'rəʊd] *vt* ronger, corroder ‖ *vi* se corroder; (*rust*) rouiller.
corrugated ['kɒrəgeɪtɪd] *a* **c. iron** tôle *f* ondulée; **c. cardboard** carton *m*.
corrupt [kə'rʌpt] *vt* corrompre ‖ *a* corrompu. ●**corruption** [-ʃ(ə)n] *n* corruption *f*.
corset ['kɔːsɪt] *n* (*boned*) corset *m*; (*elasticated*) gaine *f*.
Corsica ['kɔːsɪkə] *n* Corse *f*.
cos [kɒs] *n* **c. (lettuce)** (laitue *f*) romaine *f*.
cosh [kɒʃ] *n* matraque *f* ‖ *vt* matraquer.
cosmetic [kɒz'metɪk] *n* produit *m* de beauté ‖ *a* (*surgery*) esthétique; *Fig* superficiel.
cosmic ['kɒzmɪk] *a* cosmique. ●**cosmonaut** *n* cosmonaute *mf*.
cosset ['kɒsɪt] *vt* choyer.
cost [kɒst] *vti* (*pt & pp* **cost**) coûter; **how much does it c.?** ça coûte *or* ça vaut combien?; **to c. a lot** coûter cher; **to c. the earth** *Fam* coûter les yeux de la tête ‖ *n* prix *m*; **to my c.** à mes dépens; **at all costs** à tout prix; **the c. of living** le coût de la vie. ●**c.-effective** *a* rentable. ●**costly** *a* (**-ier, -iest**) (*expensive*) coûteux; (*valuable*) de valeur.
co-star ['kəʊstɑːr] *n Cin Th* partenaire *mf*.
costume ['kɒstjuːm] *n* costume *m*; (*woman's suit*) tailleur *m*; **(swimming) c.** maillot *m* (de bain); **c. jewellery** *or Am* **jewelry** bijoux *mpl* de fantaisie.
cosy ['kəʊzɪ] **1** *a* (**-ier, -iest**) (*house etc*) douillet (*f* -ette); **make yourself c.** mets-toi à l'aise; **we're c.** on est bien ici. **2** *n* **(tea) c.** couvre-théière *m*.
cot [kɒt] *n* (*for baby*) lit *m* d'enfant; (*camp bed*) *Am* lit *m* de camp.
cottage ['kɒtɪdʒ] *n* petite maison *f* de campagne; **(thatched) c.** chaumière *f*; **c. cheese** fromage *m* blanc (maigre).

cotton ['kɒtən] *n* coton *m*; (*yarn*) fil *m* (de coton); **c. wool**, *Am* **absorbent c.** coton *m* hydrophile, ouate *f*; **c. candy** *Am* barbe *f* à papa ▌*a* (*shirt etc*) de *or* en coton.
couch [kaʊtʃ] *n* canapé *m*.
couchette [kuː'ʃet] *n* (*on train*) couchette *f*.
cough [kɒf] **1** *n* toux *f*; **c. syrup** *or* **mixture** sirop *m* contre la toux ▌*vi* tousser ▌*vt* **to c. up** (*blood*) cracher. **2** *vti* **to c. up** (*pay*) *Sl* casquer.
could [kʊd, *unstressed* kəd] *see* **can**[1].
couldn't ['kʊd(ə)nt] = **could not.**
council ['kaʊns(ə)l] *n* conseil *m*; (**town** *or* **city**) **c.** conseil *m* municipal; **c. flat/house** appartement *m*/maison *f* loué(e) à la municipalité, =HLM *m or f*. ●**councillor** *n* (**town**) **c.** conseiller *m* municipal.
counsel ['kaʊnsəl] *n inv* (*advice*) conseil *m* ▌*vt* (**-ll-**, *Am* **-l-**) conseiller (**s.o. to do** à qn de faire). ●**counsellor** (*Am* **counselor**) *n* conseiller, -ère *mf*.
count[1] [kaʊnt] *vt* compter; **not counting Paul** sans compter Paul; **to c. in** (*include*) inclure; **to c. out** (*exclude*) exclure; (*money*) compter.
▌*vi* (*calculate, be important*) compter; **to c. on s.o./sth** (*rely on*) compter sur qn/qch; **to c. on doing** compter faire.
▌*n* **he's lost c. of** *or* **he can't keep c. of the books he has** il ne sait plus combien il a de livres. ●**countdown** *n* compte *m* à rebours.
count[2] [kaʊnt] *n* (*title*) comte *m*.
countenance ['kaʊntɪnəns] *n* (*face*) *Lit* mine *f*, expression *f*.
counter ['kaʊntər] **1** *n* (*in shop, bar etc*) comptoir *m*; (*in bank etc*) guichet *m*. **2** *n* (*in games*) jeton *m*. **3** *adv* **c. to** à l'encontre de. **4** *vt* (*threat*) répondre à; (*decision*) s'opposer à; (*effect*) neutraliser; (*blow*) parer ▌*vi* riposter (**with** par).
counter- ['kaʊntər] *pref* contre-.
counteract [kaʊntə'rækt] *vt* (*influence etc*) neutraliser.
counterattack ['kaʊntərətæk] *n* contre-attaque *f* ▌*vti* contre-attaquer.
counterclockwise [kaʊntə'klɒkwaɪz] *a* & *adv Am* dans le sens inverse des aiguilles d'une montre.
counterfeit ['kaʊntəfɪt] *a* faux (*f* fausse) ▌*n* contrefaçon *f*, faux *m* ▌*vt* contrefaire.
counterfoil ['kaʊntəfɔɪl] *n* souche *f*.
counterpart ['kaʊntəpɑːt] *n* (*thing*) équivalent *m*; (*person*) homologue *mf*.
counterproductive [kaʊntəprə'dʌktɪv] *a* (*action*) inefficace, qui produit l'effet contraire.
countess ['kaʊntes] *n* comtesse *f*.
countless ['kaʊntləs] *a* innombrable.
country ['kʌntrɪ] *n* pays *m*; (*regarded with affection*) patrie *f*; (*opposed to town*) campagne *f* ▌*a* (*house etc*) de campagne; **c. dancing** la danse folklorique. ●**countryside** *n* campagne *f*.
county ['kaʊntɪ] *n* comté *m*.
coup [kuː, *pl* kuːz] *n Pol* coup *m* d'État.
couple ['kʌp(ə)l] *n* (*of people*) couple *m*; **a c. of** deux ou trois; (*a few*) quelques.
coupon ['kuːpɒn] *n* (*voucher for gift, meal etc*) bon *m*.
courage ['kʌrɪdʒ] *n* courage *m*. ●**courageous** [kə'reɪdʒəs] *a* courageux.
courgette [kʊə'ʒet] *n* courgette *f*.
courier ['kʊrɪər] *n* (*for tourists*) guide *m*; (*messenger*) messager *m*; **c. service** service *m* de messagerie.
course [kɔːs] **1** *n* (*duration, movement*) cours *m*; (*of ship*) route *f*; (*way*) *Fig* route *f*, chemin *m*; **c.** (**of action**) ligne *f* de conduite; (*option*) parti *m*; **in the c. of** au cours de; **in due c.** en temps utile.
2 *n* (*lessons*) *Sch Univ* cours *m*; **c. of lectures** série *f* de conférences.
3 **c.** (**of treatment**) *Med* traitement *m*.
4 *n* (*of meal*) plat *m*; **first c.** entrée *f*.
5 *n* (*racecourse*) champ *m* de courses; (**golf**) **c.** terrain *m* (de golf).
6 *adv* **of c.!** bien sûr!, mais oui!; **of c. not!** bien sûr que non!
court [kɔːt] **1** *n* (*of king etc*) cour *f*; *Jur* cour *f*, tribunal *m*; (**tennis**) **c.** court *m* (de tennis); **high c.** cour *f* suprême; **to take s.o to c.** poursuivre qn en justice; **c. shoe** escarpin *m*.
2 *vt* (*woman*) faire la cour à; (*danger*) aller au-devant de. ●**courthouse** *n* palais *m* de justice. ●**courtroom** *n* salle *f* du tribunal. ●**courtyard** *n* cour *f*.
courteous ['kɜːtɪəs] *a* poli, courtois. ●**courtesy** *n* politesse *f*, courtoisie *f*.
courtier ['kɔːtɪər] *n Hist* courtisan *m*.
court-martial [kɔːt'mɑːʃəl] *n* conseil *m* de guerre, tribunal *m* militaire ▌*vt* (**-ll-**, *Am* **-l-**) faire passer en conseil de guerre.
cousin ['kʌz(ə)n] *n* cousin, -ine *mf*.
Coventry ['kɒvəntrɪ] *n* **to send s.o. to C.** (*punish*) mettre qn en quarantaine.
cover ['kʌvər] *n* (*lid*) couvercle *m*; (*of book*) couverture *f*; (*for furniture, typewriter*) housse *f*; **the covers** (*on bed*) les couvertures *fpl* et les draps *mpl*; **to take c.** se mettre à l'abri; **c. charge** (*in restaurant*) couvert *m*; **c. note** certificat *m* provisoire d'assurance.
▌*vt* couvrir (**with** de); (*protect*) protéger,

couvrir; (*distance*) parcourir, couvrir; (*insure*) assurer; **to c. over** (*floor etc*) recouvrir; **to c. up** recouvrir; (*truth, tracks*) dissimuler; (*scandal*) étouffer.
▮ *vi* **to c. (oneself) up** (*wrap up*) se couvrir; **to c. up for s.o.** couvrir qn. ●**cover-up** *n* tentative *f* pour camoufler une affaire.

coverage ['kʌvərɪdʒ] *n TV etc* reportage *m* (**of** sur).

coveralls ['kʌvərɔːlz] *npl Am* bleu *m* de travail.

covering ['kʌvərɪŋ] *n* (*wrapping*) enveloppe *f*; (*layer*) couche *f*; **c. letter** lettre *f* jointe (*à un document*).

covet ['kʌvɪt] *vt* convoiter.

cow [kaʊ] **1** *n* vache *f*; (*nasty woman*) *Fam* chameau *m*. **2** *vt* **to be cowed** (*afraid*) être intimidé. ●**cowboy** *n* cow-boy *m*. ●**cowshed** *n* étable *f*.

coward ['kaʊəd] *n* lâche *mf*. ●**cowardly** *a* lâche. ●**cowardice** *n* lâcheté *f*.

cower ['kaʊər] *vi* (*with fear*) trembler.

coy [kɔɪ] *a* (**-er, -est**) qui fait son *or* sa timide.

coyote [kaɪ'əʊtɪ] *n* (*wolf*) *Am* coyote *m*.

cozy ['kəʊzɪ] *a Am* = **cosy.**

crab [kræb] **1** *n* crabe *m*. **2** *vi* (**-bb-**) (*complain*) *Fam* rouspéter. ●**crabby** *a* (**-ier, -iest**) (*person*) grincheux.

crack[1] [kræk] *n* fente *f*; (*in glass, china, bone*) fêlure *f*; (*in skin*) crevasse *f*; (*noise*) craquement *m*; (*of whip*) claquement *m*; (*joke*) *Fam* plaisanterie *f* (**at** aux dépens de); **at the c. of dawn** au point du jour.
▮ *vt* (*glass, ice*) fêler; (*nut*) casser; (*skin*) crevasser; (*whip*) faire claquer; (*joke*) lancer; (*code*) déchiffrer; (*safe*) percer.
▮ *vi* se fêler; se crevasser; (*of branch, wood*) craquer; **to get cracking** (*get to work*) *Fam* s'y mettre; **to c. down on** sévir contre; **to c. up** (*mentally*) *Fam* craquer. ●**cracker** *n* **1** (*biscuit*) biscuit *m* (salé). **2** (*firework*) pétard *m*; **Christmas c.** diablotin *m*. ●**crackers** *a* (*mad*) *Sl* cinglé. ●**crackpot** *n Fam* cinglé, -ée *mf*.

crack[2] [kræk] *a* (*first-rate*) de premier ordre; **c. shot** tireur *m* d'élite.

crackle ['kræk(ə)l] *vi* (*of fire*) crépiter; (*of sth frying*) grésiller ▮ *n* crépitement *m*; grésillement *m*.

cradle ['kreɪd(ə)l] *n* berceau *m* ▮ *vt* bercer.

craft [krɑːft] **1** *n* (*skill*) art *m*; (*job*) métier *m* (artisanal). **2** *n inv* (*boat*) bateau *m*. ●**craftsman** *n* (*pl* **-men**) artisan *m*. ●**craftsmanship** *n* (*skill*) art *m*

crafty ['krɑːftɪ] *a* (**-ier, -iest**) astucieux; *Pej* rusé.

crag [kræg] *n* rocher *m* à pic.

cram [kræm] *vt* (**-mm-**) **to c. sth into** (*force*) fourrer qch dans; **to c. with** (*fill*) bourrer de ▮ *vi* **to c. into** (*of people*) s'entasser dans; **to c. (for an exam)** bachoter.

cramp [kræmp] *n Med* crampe *f* (**in** à).

cramped [kræmpt] *a* (*in a room or one's clothes*) à l'étroit; **in c. conditions** à l'étroit.

cranberry ['krænbərɪ] *n* canneberge *f*.

crane [kreɪn] *n* (*machine, bird*) grue *f*.

crank [kræŋk] **1** *n* (*person*) *Fam* excentrique *mf*; (*fanatic*) fanatique *mf*. **2** *n* (*handle*) *Tech* manivelle *f*. ●**cranky** *a* (**-ier, -iest**) excentrique; (*bad-tempered*) *Am* grincheux.

crannies ['krænɪz] *npl* **nooks and c.** coins et recoins *mpl*.

crash [kræʃ] *n* accident *m*; (*of firm*) faillite *f*; (*noise*) fracas *m*; (*of thunder*) coup *m*; **c. course/diet** cours *m*/régime *m* intensif; **c. barrier** glissière *f* de sécurité; **c. helmet** casque *m* (anti-choc); **c. landing** atterrissage *m* en catastrophe.
▮ *int* (*of fallen object*) patatras!
▮ *vt* (*car*) avoir un accident avec; **to c. one's car into** faire rentrer sa voiture dans.
▮ *vi* (*of car, plane*) s'écraser; **to c. into** rentrer dans; **the cars crashed into each other** les voitures se sont percutées; **to c. (down)** (*fall*) tomber; (*break*) se casser. ●**crash-land** *vi* atterrir en catastrophe.

crate [kreɪt] *n* (*large*) caisse *f*; (*small*) cageot *m*; (*for bottles*) casier *m*.

crater ['kreɪtər] *n* cratère *m*.

cravat [krə'væt] *n* foulard *m* (*autour du cou*).

craving ['kreɪvɪŋ] *n* désir *m*, grand besoin *m* (**for** de).

crawl [krɔːl] *vi* ramper; (*of child*) marcher à quatre pattes; (*of vehicle*) avancer au pas; **to be crawling with** grouiller de ▮ *n Swimming* crawl *m*; **to move at a c.** *Aut* avancer au pas.

crayfish ['kreɪfɪʃ] *n inv* (*freshwater*) écrevisse *f*.

crayon ['kreɪən] *n* crayon *m* de couleur (*en cire*).

craze [kreɪz] *n* manie *f* (**for** de). ●**crazed** *a* affolé.

crazy ['kreɪzɪ] *a* (**-ier, -iest**) fou (*f* folle); **c. about sth** fana de qch; **c. about s.o.** fou de qn.

creak [kriːk] *vi* (*of hinge*) grincer; (*floorboards*) craquer. ●**creaky** *a* grinçant; qui craque.

cream [kriːm] *n* crème *f*; **c. cake** gâteau *m* à la crème; **c.(-coloured)** crème *inv*; **c. cheese**

fromage *m* blanc ▮ *vt* **to c. off** *Fig* écrémer. ●**creamy** *a* (**-ier, -iest**) crémeux.

crease [kri:s] *vt* froisser ▮ *vi* se froisser ▮ *n* pli *m*. ●**c.-resistant** *a* infroissable.

create [kri:'eɪt] *vt* créer; (*impression, noise*) faire. ●**creation** [-ʃ(ə)n] *n* création *f*. ●**creative** *a* (*person, activity*) créatif. ●**creator** *n* créateur, -trice *mf*.

creature ['kri:tʃər] *n* animal *m*, bête *f*; (*person*) créature *f*.

crèche [kreʃ] *n* (*nursery*) crèche *f*.

credentials [krɪ'denʃəlz] *npl* références *fpl*; (*identity*) pièces *fpl* d'identité; (*of diplomat*) lettres *fpl* de créance.

credible ['kredɪb(ə)l] *a* croyable; (*politician, information*) crédible. ●**credi'bility** *n* crédibilité *f*.

credit ['kredɪt] *n* (*financial*) crédit *m*; (*merit*) mérite *m*; *Univ* unité *f* de valeur; *pl* (*of film*) générique *m*; **to give c. to** (*person*) *Fig* reconnaître le mérite de; (*statement*) ajouter foi à; **to be a c. to** faire honneur à; **on c.** à crédit; **in c.** (*account*) créditeur; **to one's c.** *Fig* à son actif; **c. balance** solde *m* créditeur; **c. card** carte *f* de crédit; **c. facilities** facilités *fpl* de paiement.
▮ *vt* (*of bank*) créditer (**s.o. with sth** qn de qch). ●**creditor** *n* créancier, -ière *mf*. ●**creditworthy** *a* solvable.

creed [kri:d] *n* credo *m*.

creek [kri:k] *n* (*stream*) *Am* ruisseau *m*; (*bay*) crique *f*.

creep [kri:p] **1** *vi* (*pt & pp* **crept**) ramper; (*silently*) se glisser (furtivement); (*slowly*) avancer lentement. **2** *n* (*person*) *Sl* salaud *m*; **it gives me the creeps** *Fam* ça me fait froid dans le dos. ●**creepy** *a* (**-ier, -iest**) *Fam* terrifiant; (*nasty*) vilain. ●**creepy-'crawly** *or Am* **creepy-'crawler** *n Fam* bestiole *f*.

cremate [krɪ'meɪt] *vt* incinérer. ●**cremation** [-ʃ(ə)n] *n* crémation *f*. ●**crema'torium** *n* crématorium *m*. ●**crematory** ['kri:mətɔ:rɪ] *n Am* crématorium *m*.

crêpe [kreɪp] *n* (*fabric, rubber*) crêpe *m*; **c. paper** papier *m* crêpon.

crept [krept] *pt & pp of* **creep 1.**

crescent ['kres(ə)nt] *n* croissant *m*; (*street*) *Fig* rue *f* (en demi-lune).

cress [kres] *n* cresson *m*.

crest [krest] *n* (*of wave, mountain*) crête *f*; (*of hill*) sommet *m*.

Crete [kri:t] *n* Crète *f*.

cretin ['kretɪn, *Am* 'kri:t(ə)n] *n* crétin, -ine *mf*

crevice ['krevɪs] *n* (*crack*) crevasse *f*, fente *f*.

crew [kru:] *n* (*of ship, plane*) équipage *m*; (*gang*) équipe *f*; **c. cut** (coupe *f* en) brosse *f*. ●**c.-neck(ed)** *a* à col ras.

crib [krɪb] **1** *n* (*cot*) *Am* lit *m* d'enfant; (*cradle*) berceau *m*; *Rel* crèche *f*. **2** *n* (*list of answers*) *Sch* pompe *f*, antisèche *f* ▮ *vti* (**-bb-**) copier.

crick [krɪk] *n* **c. in the neck** torticolis *m*.

cricket ['krɪkɪt] *n* **1** (*game*) cricket *m*. **2** (*insect*) grillon *m*.

crime [kraɪm] *n* crime *m*; (*not serious*) délit *m*; (*criminal practice*) criminalité *f*. ●**criminal** *a & n* criminel, -elle (*mf*); **c. record** casier *m* judiciaire.

crimson ['krɪmz(ə)n] *a & n* cramoisi (*m*).

cringe [krɪndʒ] *vi* reculer (**from** devant).

crinkle ['krɪŋk(ə)l] *vt* froisser ▮ *vi* se froisser.

crippl/e ['krɪpəl] *n* (*disabled*) infirme *mf* ▮ *vt* rendre infirme, estropier; (*nation etc*) *Fig* paralyser. ●**—ed** *a* infirme; **c. with** (*rheumatism, pains*) perclus de.

crisis, *pl* **-ses** ['kraɪsɪs, -si:z] *n* crise *f*.

crisp [krɪsp] **1** *a* (**-er, -est**) (*biscuit*) croustillant; (*apple*) croquant; (*snow*) craquant; (*air*) vif. **2** *npl* **(potato) crisps** (pommes *fpl*) chips *fpl*; **packet of crisps** sachet *m* de chips. ●**crispbread** *n* pain *m* suédois.

criss-cross ['krɪskrɒs] *a* (*lines*) entrecroisés ▮ *vi* s'entrecroiser ▮ *vt* sillonner (en tous sens).

criterion, *pl* **-ia** [kraɪ'tɪərɪən, -ɪə] *n* critère *m*.

critic ['krɪtɪk] *n* critique *m*. ●**critical** *a* critique. ●**critically** *adv* (*to examine*) en critique; **c. ill** gravement, malade. ●**criticism** *n* critique *f*. ●**criticize** *vti* critiquer.

croak [krəʊk] *vi* (*of frog*) croasser ▮ *n* croassement *m*.

Croatia [krəʊ'eɪʃə] *n* Croatie *f*.

crochet ['krəʊʃeɪ] *vt* faire au crochet ▮ *vi* faire du crochet ▮ *n* (travail *m* au) crochet *m*.

crockery ['krɒkərɪ] *n* (*cups etc*) vaisselle *f*.

crocodile ['krɒkədaɪl] *n* crocodile *m*.

crocus ['krəʊkəs] *n* crocus *m*.

crony ['krəʊnɪ] *n Pej Fam* copain *m*, copine *f*.

crook [krʊk] *n* **1** (*thief*) escroc *m*. **2** (*shepherd's stick*) houlette *f*.

crooked ['krʊkɪd] *a* (*stick*) courbé; (*path*) tortueux; (*hat, picture*) de travers; (*deal, person*) malhonnête ▮ *adv* de travers.

crop [krɒp] **1** *n* (*harvest*) récolte *f*; (*produce*) culture *f*. **2** *vt* (**-pp-**) (*hair*) couper (ras) ▮ *n* **c. of hair** chevelure *f*. **3** *vi* (**-pp-**) **to c. up** se présenter, survenir. ●**cropper** *n* **to come a c.** *Sl* (*fall*) ramasser une pelle; (*fail*) échouer.

croquet ['krəʊkeɪ] *n* (*game*) croquet *m*.

cross[1] [krɒs] **1** *n* croix *f*; **a c. between** (*animal*) un croisement entre *or* de; *Fig* un compromis entre.
2 *vt* (*street*, *room etc*) traverser; (*barrier*) franchir; (*legs*) croiser; (*cheque*, *Am check*) barrer; **to c. off** *or* **out** (*word*, *name etc*) rayer; **to c. over** (*road etc*) traverser; **it never crossed my mind that...** il ne m'est pas venu à l'esprit que... ▮ *vi* (*of paths*) se croiser; **to c. over** traverser. ●**c.-country 'race** *n* cross(-country) *m*. ●**c.-examination** [-'neɪʃ(ə)n] *n* contre-interrogatoire *m*. ●**c.-e'xamine** *vt* interroger. ●**c.-'eyed** *a* qui louche. ●**c.-'reference** *n* renvoi *m*. ●**c.-section** [-ʃ(ə)n] *n* coupe *f* transversale; (*sample*) échantillon *m*.
cross[2] [krɒs] *a* (*angry*) fâché (**with** contre).
crossfire ['krɒsfaɪər] *n* feux *mpl* croisés.
crossing ['krɒsɪŋ] *n* (*by ship*) traversée *f*; **(pedestrian) c.** passage *m* protégé.
crossroads ['krɒsrəʊdz] *n* carrefour *m*.
crosswalk ['krɒswɔːk] *n Am* passage *m* protégé.
crossword ['krɒswɜːd] *n* **c. (puzzle)** mots *mpl* croisés.
crotch [krɒtʃ] *n* (*of garment*, *person*) entrejambe *m*.
crotchety ['krɒtʃɪtɪ] *a* grincheux.
crouch [kraʊtʃ] *vi* **to c. (down)** s'accroupir. ●**—ing** *a* accroupi.
croupier ['kruːpɪər] *n* (*in casino*) croupier *m*.
crow [krəʊ] **1** *n* corbeau *m*; **as the c. flies** à vol d'oiseau. **2** *vi* (*of cock*) chanter. ●**crowbar** *n* levier *m*.
crowd [kraʊd] *n* foule *f*; (*particular group*) bande *f*; **quite a c.** beaucoup de monde.
▮ *vi* **to c. into** (*of people*) s'entasser dans; **to c. round s.o./sth** se presser autour de qn/qch; **to c. together** se serrer.
▮ *vt* (*fill*) remplir; **to c. sth into** (*press*) entasser qch dans. ●**crowded** *a* plein (**with** de); **it's very c.!** il y a beaucoup de monde!
crown [kraʊn] *n* (*of king etc*) couronne *f*; **C. jewels** joyaux *mpl* de la Couronne ▮ *vt* couronner.
crucial ['kruːʃəl] *a* crucial.
crucifix ['kruːsɪfɪks] *n* crucifix *m*.
crude [kruːd] *a* **(-er, -est)** (*manners*, *person*, *language*) grossier; (*painting*, *work*) rudimentaire; **c. oil** pétrole *m* brut.
cruel [krʊəl] *a* **(crueller, cruellest)** cruel. ●**cruelty** *n* cruauté *f*; **an act of c.** une cruauté.
cruet ['kruːɪt] *n* **c. (stand)** salière *f*, poivrière *f* et huilier *m*.
cruis/e [kruːz] *n* croisière *f* ▮ *vi* (*of ship*) croiser; (*of car*) rouler; (*of plane*) voler; (*of tourists*) faire une croisière; **cruising speed** *Nau Av* vitesse *f* de croisière. ●**—er** *n* (*ship*) croiseur *m*.
crumb [krʌm] *n* miette *f*.
crumble ['krʌmb(ə)l] *vt* (*bread*) émietter ▮ *vi* (*in small pieces*) s'effriter; (*of bread*) s'émietter; (*become ruined*) tomber en ruine. ●**crumbly** *a* (*pastry etc*) friable.
crummy ['krʌmɪ] *a* **(-ier, -iest)** *Fam* moche.
crumpet ['krʌmpɪt] *n* petite crêpe *f* grillée (*servie beurrée*).
crumple ['krʌmp(ə)l] *vt* froisser ▮ *vi* se froisser.
crunch [krʌntʃ] *vt* (*food*) croquer. ●**crunchy** *a* **(-ier, -iest)** (*apple etc*) croquant; (*bread*, *biscuit*, *Am cookie*) croustillant.
crusade [kruː'seɪd] *n* croisade *f*.
crush [krʌʃ] **1** *n* (*crowd*) cohue *f*; (*rush*) bousculade *f*; **to have a c. on s.o.** *Fam* en pincer pour qn. **2** *vt* écraser; (*hope*) détruire; (*clothes*) froisser; (*cram*) entasser (**into** dans). ●**—ing** *a* (*defeat*) écrasant.
crust [krʌst] *n* croûte *f*. ●**crusty** *a* **(-ier, -iest)** (*bread*) croustillant.
crutch [krʌtʃ] *n* **1** *Med* béquille *f*. **2** (*crotch*) entrejambe *m*.
crux [krʌks] *n* **the c. of the matter** le nœud de l'affaire.
cry [kraɪ] *n* (*shout*) cri *m*; **to have a c.** *Fam* pleurer.
▮ *vi* (*weep*) pleurer; **to c. (out)** pousser un cri, crier; (*exclaim*) s'écrier; **to c. (out) for** (*of person*) demander (à grands cris); **to be crying out for** (*of thing*) avoir grand besoin de; **to c. off (sth)** se désintéresser (de qch); **to c. over sth/s.o.** pleurer (sur) qch/qn.
▮ *vt* **to c. (out)** (*shout*) crier. ●**crying** *n* cris *mpl*; (*weeping*) pleurs *mpl*.
crypt [krɪpt] *n* crypte *f*.
crystal ['krɪst(ə)l] *n* cristal *m*. ●**c.-'clear** *a* (*water*, *sound*) cristallin; *Fig* clair comme le jour.
cub [kʌb] *n* **1** (*of animal*) petit *m*, petite *f*. **2** (*scout*) louveteau *m*.
Cuba ['kjuːbə] *n* Cuba *m*. ●**Cuban** *a* & *n* cubain, -aine (*mf*).
cubbyhole ['kʌbɪhəʊl] *n* cagibi *m*.
cube [kjuːb] *n* cube *m*; (*of meat etc*) dé *m*. ●**cubic** *a* (*metre etc*) cube; **c. capacity** volume *m*; *Aut* cylindrée *f*.
cubicle ['kjuːbɪk(ə)l] *n* (*for changing clothes*) cabine *f*; (*in hospital*) box *m*.
cuckoo ['kʊkuː, *Am* 'kuːkuː] *n* (*bird*) coucou *m*; **c. clock** coucou *m*.
cucumber ['kjuːkʌmbər] *n* concombre *m*.

cuddle ['kʌd(ə)l] *vt* (*hug*) serrer (dans ses bras); (*caress*) câliner ‖ *vi* (*of lovers*) se serrer; **to (kiss and) c.** s'embrasser; **to c. up to s.o.** (*huddle*) se serrer contre qn ‖ *n* caresse *f*. ●**cuddly** *a* (**-ier, -iest**) *a* câlin, caressant; (*toy*) doux (*f* douce).

cudgel ['kʌdʒəl] *n* trique *f*, gourdin *m*.

cue [kjuː] *n* **1** *Th* réplique *f*; (*signal*) signal *m*. **2 (billiard) c.** queue *f* (de billard).

cuff [kʌf] *n* (*of shirt etc*) poignet *m*; (*of trousers*) *Am* revers *m*; **off the c.** impromptu; **c. link** bouton *m* de manchette.

cul-de-sac ['kʌldəsæk] *n* impasse *f*.

culminate ['kʌlmɪneɪt] *vi* **to c. in** finir par.

culprit ['kʌlprɪt] *n* coupable *mf*.

cult [kʌlt] *n* culte *m*.

cultivat/e ['kʌltɪveɪt] *vt* (*land, mind etc*) cultiver. ●**—ed** *a* cultivé. ●**cultivation** [-'veɪʃ(ə)n] *n* culture *f*; **fields under c.** cultures *fpl*.

culture ['kʌltʃər] *n* culture *f*. ●**cultural** *a* culturel. ●**cultured** *a* cultivé.

cumbersome ['kʌmbəsəm] *a* encombrant.

cunning ['kʌnɪŋ] *a* astucieux; *Pej* rusé ‖ *n* astuce *f*; *Pej* ruse *f*.

cup [kʌp] *n* tasse *f*; (*goblet, prize*) coupe *f*; **c. final** *Fb* finale *f* de la coupe. ●**cupful** *n* tasse *f*.

cupboard ['kʌbəd] *n* armoire *f*; (*built into wall*) placard *m*.

cuppa ['kʌpə] *n Fam* tasse *f* de thé.

curable ['kjʊərəb(ə)l] *a* guérissable.

curate ['kjʊərɪt] *n* vicaire *m*.

curator [kjʊə'reɪtər] *n* (*of museum*) conservateur *m*.

curb [kɜːb] **1** *n* (*kerb*) *Am* bord *m* du trottoir. **2** *vt* (*feelings*) refréner; (*ambitions*) modérer; (*expenses*) limiter ‖ *n* frein *m*; **to put a c. on** mettre un frein à.

curd cheese ['kɜːdtʃiːz] *n* fromage *m* blanc (maigre).

curdle ['kɜːd(ə)l] *vi* se cailler.

cure [kjʊər] *vt* (*illness, person*) guérir (**of** de) ‖ *n* remède *m* (**for** contre); (*recovery*) guérison *f*; **rest c.** cure *f* de repos.

curfew ['kɜːfjuː] *n* couvre-feu *m*.

curio ['kjʊərɪəʊ] *n* (*pl* **-os**) bibelot *m*.

curious ['kjʊərɪəs] *a* (*odd*) curieux; (*inquisitive*) curieux (**about** de); **c. to know** curieux de savoir. ●**curi'osity** *n* curiosité *f*.

curl [kɜːl] **1** *vti* (*hair*) boucler, friser ‖ *n* boucle *f*. **2** *vi* **to c. up** (*shrivel*) se racornir; **to c. (oneself) up** (*into a ball*) se pelotonner. ●**—er** *n* bigoudi *m*. ●**curly** *a* (**-ier, -iest**) bouclé; (*with tight curls*) frisé.

currant ['kʌrənt] *n* (*dried grape*) raisin *m* de Corinthe; (*fruit*) groseille *f*.

currency ['kʌrənsɪ] *n* (*money*) monnaie *f*; **(foreign) c.** devises *fpl* (étrangères).

current ['kʌrənt] **1** *a* (*fashion etc*) actuel; (*opinion, use, phrase*) courant; (*year, month*) en cours; **c. affairs** questions *fpl* d'actualité; **c. events** actualité *f*; **the c. issue** (*of magazine etc*) le dernier numéro. **2** *n* (*of river*) & *El* courant *m*. ●**—ly** *adv* actuellement, à présent.

curriculum, *pl* **-la** [kə'rɪkjʊləm, -lə] *n* programme *m* (scolaire); **c. vitæ** curriculum vitae *m inv*.

curry ['kʌrɪ] *n* curry *m*, cari *m*.

curse [kɜːs] *n* malédiction *f*; (*swearword*) juron *m*; (*scourge*) fléau *m* ‖ *vt* maudire ‖ *vi* (*swear*) jurer.

cursor ['kɜːsər] *n* (*on computer screen*) curseur *m*.

cursory ['kɜːsərɪ] *a* (trop) rapide, superficiel.

curt [kɜːt] *a* brusque. ●**—ly** *adv* d'un ton brusque.

curtail [kɜː'teɪl] *vt* (*visit etc*) écourter; (*expenses*) réduire.

curtain ['kɜːt(ə)n] *n* rideau *m*.

curts(e)y ['kɜːtsɪ] *n* révérence *f* ‖ *vi* faire une révérence.

curve [kɜːv] *n* courbe *f*; (*in road*) virage *m* ‖ *vt* courber ‖ *vi* se courber; (*of road*) tourner.

cushion ['kʊʃən] *n* coussin *m* ‖ *vt* (*shock*) amortir. ●**cushioned** *a* (*seat*) rembourré; **c. against** *Fig* protégé contre.

cushy ['kʊʃɪ] *a* (**-ier, -iest**) (*job, life*) *Fam* pépère, facile.

custard ['kʌstəd] *n* crème *f* anglaise; (*when set*) crème *f* renversée.

custody ['kʌstədɪ] *n* (*care*) garde *f*; **to take s.o. into c.** *Jur* mettre qn en détention préventive.

custom ['kʌstəm] *n* coutume *f*; (*customers*) clientèle *f*. ●**customary** *a* habituel; **it is c. to** il est d'usage de. ●**custom-built** *or* **customized** *a* (*car etc*) (fait) sur commande. ●**custom-made** *a* (*shirt etc*) (fait) sur mesure.

customer ['kʌstəmər] *n* client, -ente *mf*.

customs ['kʌstəmz] *n(pl)* **(the) c.** la douane; **c. (duties)** droits *mpl* de douane; **c. officer** douanier *m*.

cut [kʌt] *n* (*mark*) coupure *f*; (*stroke*) coup *m*; (*of clothes, hair*) coupe *f*; (*in salary, prices etc*) réduction *f*; (*of meat*) morceau *m* ‖ *vt* (*pt* & *pp* **cut,** *pres p* **cutting**) couper; (*meat*) découper; (*glass, tree*) tailler; (*salary, price etc*) réduire; (*tooth*) percer; **to c. open** ouvrir (*au couteau etc*); **to c. short**

(*visit*) abréger ▮ *vi* (*of person, scissors*) couper.

cut away *vt* (*remove*) enlever ▮ **to cut back (on)** *vti* réduire. ● **cutback** *n* réduction *f* ▮ **to cut down** *vt* (*tree*) abattre, couper ▮ **to cut down (on)** *vti* réduire ▮ **to cut in** *vi* (*interrupt*) interrompre ▮ **to cut into** *vt* (*cake etc*) entamer ▮ **to cut off** *vt* couper; (*isolate*) isoler ▮ **to cut out** *vi* (*of car engine*) caler ▮ *vt* (*article*) découper; (*garment*) tailler; (*remove*) enlever; (*eliminate*) supprimer; **to c. out drinking** (*stop*) s'arrêter de boire; **c. it out!** *Fam* ça suffit!; **c. out to be a doctor**/*etc* fait pour être médecin/*etc*. ● **cutout** *n* (*picture*) découpage *m*; *El* coupe-circuit *m inv*. ▮ **to cut up** *vt* couper (en morceaux); **c. up about** démoralisé par.

cute [kju:t] *a* (**-er, -est**) (*pretty*) *Fam* mignon (*f* mignonne).

cutlery ['kʌtlərɪ] *n* couverts *mpl*.

cutlet ['kʌtlɪt] *n* (*of veal etc*) côtelette *f*.

cut-price [kʌt'praɪs] *a* à prix réduit.

cutting ['kʌtɪŋ] *n* coupe *f*; (*newspaper article*) coupure *f*; (*plant*) bouture *f*; **c. edge** tranchant *m*.

CV [si:'vi:] *n abbr* curriculum (vitae) *m inv*.

cwt *abbr* = **hundredweight**.

cyanide ['saɪənaɪd] *n* cyanure *m*.

cycle ['saɪk(ə)l] **1** *n* bicyclette *f*, vélo *m*; **c. path** *or* **track** piste *f* cyclable; **c. race** course *f* cycliste ▮ *vi* aller à bicyclette (**to** à); *Sp* faire de la bicyclette. **2** *n* (*series, period*) cycle *m*. ● **cycling** *n* cyclisme *m*. ● **cyclist** *n* cycliste *mf*.

cyclone ['saɪkləʊn] *n* cyclone *m*.

cylinder ['sɪlɪndər] *n* cylindre *m*.

cymbal ['sɪmb(ə)l] *n* cymbale *f*.

cynic ['sɪnɪk] *n* cynique *mf*. ● **cynical** *a* cynique.

Cyprus ['saɪprəs] *n* Chypre *f*. ● **Cypriot** ['sɪprɪət] *a* & *n* cypriote (*mf*).

cyst [sɪst] *n Med* kyste *m*

Czech [tʃek] *a* & *n* tchèque (*mf*). ● **Czecho'slovak** *a* & *n* tchécoslovaque (*mf*). ● **Czechoslo'vakia** *n* Tchécoslovaquie *f*. ● **Czechoslo'vakian** *a* & *n* tchécoslovaque (*mf*).

D

D, d [diː] *n* D, d *m*. ● **D.-day** *n* le jour J.

dab [dæb] *vt* (**-bb-**) (*wound etc*) tamponner; **to d. sth on sth** appliquer qch (à petits coups) sur qch.

dabble ['dæb(ə)l] *vi* **to d. in** s'occuper *or* se mêler un peu de.

Dacron® ['dækrɒn] *n Am* tergal® *m*.

dad [dæd] *n Fam* papa *m*. ● **daddy** *n Fam* papa *m*; **d. longlegs** (*cranefly*) tipule *f*; (*spider*) *Am* faucheur *m*.

daffodil ['dæfədɪl] *n* jonquille *f*.

daft [dɑːft] *a* (**-er, -est**) *Fam* idiot, bête.

dagger ['dægər] *n* poignard *m*.

dahlia ['deɪljə, *Am* 'dæljə] *n* dahlia *m*.

daily ['deɪlɪ] *a* quotidien, journalier ‖ *adv* chaque jour ‖ *n* **d. (paper)** quotidien *m*; **d. (help)** (*cleaning woman*) femme *f* de ménage.

dainty ['deɪntɪ] *a* (**-ier, -iest**) délicat; (*pretty*) mignon (*f* -onne).

dairy ['deərɪ] *n* (*on farm*) laiterie *f*; (*shop*) crémerie *f*; **d. product/produce** produit *m*/produits *mpl* laitier(s) ‖ *a* laitier.

daisy ['deɪzɪ] *n* pâquerette *f*.

dale [deɪl] *n Lit* vallée *f*.

dam [dæm] *n* (*wall*) barrage *m* ‖ *vt* (**-mm-**) (*river*) barrer.

damag/e ['dæmɪdʒ] *n* dégâts *mpl*; (*harm*) préjudice *m*; *pl Jur* dommages-intérêts *mpl* ‖ *vt* (*object*) endommager, abîmer; (*eyesight, health*) abîmer; (*plans, reputation etc*) *Fig* compromettre. ● **—ing** *a* (*harmful*) préjudiciable (**to** à).

damn [dæm] *vt* (*condemn*) condamner; *Rel* damner; **d. him!** *Fam* qu'il aille se faire voir! ‖ *int* **d. (it)!** *Fam* merde! ‖ *n* **he doesn't care a d.** *Fam* il s'en fiche pas mal ‖ *a* (*awful*) *Fam* fichu, sacré ‖ *adv* (*very*) *Fam* vachement. ● **—ed** *a Fam* = **damn** *a* & *adv*.

damp [dæmp] *a* (**-er, -est**) humide ‖ *n* humidité *f*. ● **damp(en)** *vt* humecter; **to d. (down)** (*enthusiasm*) refroidir. ● **dampness** *n* humidité *f*.

danc/e [dɑːns] *n* danse *f*; (*social event*) bal *m* (*pl* bals); **d. hall** salle *f* de danse ‖ *vi* danser ‖ *vt* (*waltz etc*) danser. ● **—ing** *n* danse *f*. ● **dancer** *n* danseur, -euse *mf*.

dandelion ['dændɪlaɪən] *n* pissenlit *m*.

dandruff ['dændrʌf] *n* pellicules *fpl*.

Dane [deɪn] *n* Danois, -oise *mf*.

danger ['deɪndʒər] *n* danger *m* (**to** pour); **in d.** en danger; **in d. of** (*threatened by*) menacé de; **to be in d. of falling**/*etc* risquer de tomber/*etc*; **d. zone** zone *f* dangereuse. ● **dangerous** *a* (*place, illness, person etc*) dangereux (**to** pour). ● **dangerously** *adv* **d. ill** gravement malade.

dangle ['dæŋg(ə)l] *vt* balancer ‖ *vi* (*hang*) pendre; (*swing*) se balancer.

Danish ['deɪnɪʃ] *a* danois ‖ *n* (*language*) danois *m*.

dar/e [deər] *vt* oser (**do** faire); **she d. not come** elle n'ose pas venir; **he doesn't d. (to) go** il n'ose pas y aller; **I d. say he tried** il a sans doute essayé; **to d. s.o. to do** défier qn de faire. ● **—ing** *a* audacieux. ● **daredevil** *n* casse-cou *m inv*.

dark [dɑːk] *a* (**-er, -est**) obscur, noir, sombre; (*colour*) foncé, sombre; (*skin, hair*) brun, foncé; (*eyes*) foncé; (*gloomy*) sombre; **it's d.** il fait nuit *or* noir; **d. glasses** lunettes *fpl* noires.
‖ *n* noir *m*, obscurité *f*; **after d.** après la tombée de la nuit. ● **d.-'haired** *a* aux cheveux bruns. ● **d.-'skinned** *a* brun. ● **darken** *vt* assombrir, obscurcir ‖ *vi* s'assombrir. ● **darkness** *n* obscurité *f*, noir *m*.

darkroom ['dɑːkruːm] *n Phot* chambre *f* noire.

darling ['dɑːlɪŋ] *n* (*favourite*) chouchou, -oute *mf*; **(my) d.** (mon) chéri, (ma) chérie; **he's a d.** c'est un amour; **be a d.!** sois un ange! ‖ *a* chéri.

darn [dɑːn] **1** *vt* (*socks*) repriser. **2** *int* **d. it!** bon sang!

dart [dɑːt] **1** *vi* (*dash*) se précipiter (**for** vers). **2** *n Sp* fléchette *f*; *pl* (*game*) fléchettes *fpl*. ● **dartboard** *n* cible *f*.

dash [dæʃ] **1** *n* (*run, rush*) ruée *f*; **to make a d.** se précipiter (**for** vers) ‖ *vi* se précipiter; **to d. off** *or* **away** partir *or* filer en vitesse ‖ *vt* jeter (avec force); (*hopes*) *Fig* briser; **to d. off** (*letter*) faire en vitesse. **2** *n* **a d. of** un (petit) peu de. **3** *n* (*handwritten stroke*) trait *m*; *Typ* tiret *m*.

dashboard ['dæʃbɔːd] *n Aut* tableau *m* de bord.

data ['deɪtə] *npl* données *fpl*; **d. base** base *f* de données; **d. processing** informatique *f*.

date[1] [deɪt] *n* (*time*) date *f*; (*meeting*) *Fam* rendez-vous *m inv*; (*person*) *Fam* copain, -ine *mf* (*avec qui on a un rendez-vous*); **up to**

d. moderne; (*information*) à jour; (*well-informed*) au courant (**on** de); **out of d.** (*old-fashioned*) démodé; (*expired*) périmé; **d. stamp** (tampon *m*) dateur *m*; (*mark*) cachet *m*.

▮ *vt* (*letter etc*) dater; (*girl, boy*) *Fam* sortir avec.

▮ *vi* (*become out of date*) dater; **to d. back to** dater de. • **dated** *a* démodé.

date[2] [deɪt] *n* (*fruit*) datte *f*.

datebook ['deɪtbʊk] *n Am* agenda *m*.

daub [dɔ:b] *vt* barbouiller (**with** de).

daughter ['dɔ:tər] *n* fille *f*. • **d.-in-law** *n* (*pl* **daughters-in-law**) belle-fille *f*.

daunt [dɔ:nt] *vt* décourager, rebuter. • **—less** *a* intrépide.

dawdl/e ['dɔ:d(ə)l] *vi* traîner. • **—er** *n* traînard, -arde *mf*.

dawn [dɔ:n] *n* aube *f*, aurore *f* ▮ *vi* (*of day*) se lever; (*of new era*) naître; **it dawned upon him that...** il lui est venu à l'esprit que....

day [deɪ] *n* jour *m*; (*whole day long*) journée *f*; *pl* (*period*) époque *f*, temps *mpl*; **all d. (long)** toute la journée; **the following** *or* **next d.** le lendemain; **the d. before** la veille; **the d. before yesterday** *or* **before last** avant-hier; **the d. after tomorrow** après-demain; **d. boarder** demi-pensionnaire *mf*; **d. nursery** crèche *f*; **d. return** *Rail* aller et retour *m* (*pour une journée*); **d. tripper** excursionniste *mf*. • **d.-to-'day** *a* quotidien, journalier; **on a d.-to-day basis** (*every day*) journellement.

daybreak ['deɪbreɪk] *n* point *m* du jour. • **daycare** *n* (*for children*) service *m* de garderie. • **daydream** *n* rêverie *f* ▮ *vi* rêvasser. • **daylight** *n* (lumière *f* du) jour *m*; **it's d.** il fait jour. • **daytime** *n* journée *f*, jour *m*.

daze [deɪz] *vt* (*by blow*) étourdir ▮ *n* **in a d.** étourdi; (*because of drugs*) hébété.

dazzle ['dæz(ə)l] *vt* éblouir.

dead [ded] *a* mort; (*numb*) (*arm etc*) engourdi; (*telephone*) sans tonalité; **in d. centre** au beau milieu; **to be a d. loss** (*of person*) *Fam* n'être bon à rien; **it's a d. loss** *Fam* ça ne vaut rien; **d. silence** un silence de mort; **a d. stop** un arrêt complet; **d. end** (*street*) impasse *f*; **a d.-end job** un travail sans avenir.

▮ *adv* (*completely*) absolument; (*very*) très; **d. beat** *Fam* éreinté; **d. drunk** *Fam* ivre mort; **to stop d.** s'arrêter net.

▮ *n* **the d.** les morts *mpl*. • **deadline** *n* date *f* limite; (*hour*) heure *f* limite.

deaden ['ded(ə)n] *vt* (*shock*) amortir; (*pain*) calmer; (*feeling*) émousser.

deadly ['dedlɪ] *a* (**-ier, -iest**) (*enemy, silence*) mortel; (*weapon*) meurtrier; **d. sins** péchés *mpl* capitaux.

deaf [def] *a* sourd; **d. and dumb** sourd-muet ▮ *n* **the d.** les sourds *mpl*. • **deafen** *vt* assourdir. • **deafness** *n* surdité *f*.

deal[1] [di:l] *n* **a good** *or* **great d.** (*a lot*) beaucoup (**of** de).

deal[2] [di:l] *n* **1** *Com* marché *m*, affaire *f*; **to give s.o. a fair d.** traiter qn équitablement; **it's a d.** d'accord; **big d.!** *Iron* la belle affaire!

2 *vt* (*pt & pp* **dealt** [delt]) (*blow*) porter (**to** à); **to d. (out)** (*cards*) donner.

3 *vi* (*trade*) traiter (**with s.o.** avec qn); **to d. in** faire le commerce de; **to d. with** (*take care of*) s'occuper de; (*concern*) (*of book etc*) traiter de. • **dealings** *npl* relations *fpl* (**with** avec); *Com* transactions *fpl*.

dealer ['di:lər] *n* marchand, -ande *mf* (**in** de); (*agent*) dépositaire *mf*; (*for cars*) concessionnaire *mf*; (*in drugs*) revendeur, -euse *mf* (de drogues).

dean [di:n] *n Rel Univ* doyen *m*.

dear [dɪər] *a* (**-er, -est**) (*loved, expensive*) cher; (*price*) élevé; **D. Sir** (*in letter*) Monsieur; **D. Uncle** (mon) cher oncle; **oh d.!** oh là là!, oh mon Dieu! ▮ *n* **(my) d.** (*darling*) (mon) chéri, (ma) chérie; (*friend*) mon cher, ma chère; **she's a d.** c'est un amour; **be a d.!** sois un ange! • **dearly** *adv* (*to love*) tendrement; (*very much*) beaucoup; **to pay d. for sth** payer qch cher.

dearth [dɜ:θ] *n* manque *m*, pénurie *f*.

death [deθ] *n* mort *f*; **to put to d.** mettre à mort; **to be bored to d.** s'ennuyer à mourir; **to be sick to d.** en avoir vraiment marre; **many deaths** (*people killed*) de nombreux morts *mpl*; **d. certificate** acte *m* de décès; **d. duty** *or* **duties,** *Am* **d. taxes** droits *mpl* de succession; **d. penalty** peine *f* de mort; **d. rate** mortalité *f*; **d. sentence** condamnation *f* à mort; **it's a d. trap** il y a danger de mort. • **deathbed** *n* lit *m* de mort. • **deathly** *a* (*silence*) de mort ▮ *adv* **d. pale** d'une pâleur mortelle.

debat/e [dɪ'beɪt] *vti* discuter; **to d. whether to leave**/*etc* se demander si on doit partir/*etc* ▮ *n* débat *m*, discussion *f*. • **—able** *a* discutable; **its d. whether...** il est difficile de dire si....

debit ['debɪt] *n* débit *m*; **in d.** (*account*) débiteur; **d. balance** solde *m* débiteur ▮ *vt* débiter (**s.o. with sth** qn de qch).

debris ['debri:] *n* débris *mpl*.

debt [det] *n* dette *f*; **to be in d.** avoir des dettes; **to be 50 dollars in d.** devoir 50 dollars; **to run** *or* **get into d.** faire des dettes. ●**debtor** *n* débiteur, -trice *mf*.

debut ['debju:] *n Th* début *m*.

decade ['dekeɪd] *n* décennie *f*.

decadent ['dekədənt] *a* décadent. ●**decadence** *n* décadence *f*.

decaffeinated [di:'kæfɪneɪtɪd] *a* décaféiné.

decal ['di:kæl] *n Am* décalcomanie *f*.

decant [dɪ'kænt] *vt* (*wine*) décanter. ●**—er** *n* carafe *f*.

decapitate [dɪ'kæpɪteɪt] *vt* décapiter.

decathlon [dɪ'kæθlɒn] *n Sp* décathlon *m*.

decay [dɪ'keɪ] *vi* (*go bad*) se gâter; (*rot*) pourrir; (*of tooth*) se carier; (*of building*) tomber en ruine ‖ *n* pourriture *f*; (*of building*) délabrement *m*; (*of tooth*) carie(s) *f*(*pl*). ●**—ing** *a* (*meat, fruit etc*) pourrissant.

deceased [dɪ'si:st] *a* décédé, défunt ‖ *n* **the d.** le défunt, la défunte; *pl* les défunt(e)s.

deceit [dɪ'si:t] *n* tromperie *f*. ●**deceitful** *a* trompeur.

deceive [dɪ'si:v] *vti* tromper; **to d. oneself** se faire des illusions.

December [dɪ'sembər] *n* décembre *m*.

decent ['di:sənt] *a* (*respectable*) convenable, décent; (*good*) bon (*f* bonne); (*kind*) gentil (*f* -ille). ●**decency** *n* décence *f*; (*kindness*) gentillesse *f*.

deception [dɪ'sepʃ(ə)n] *n* tromperie *f*. ●**deceptive** *a* trompeur.

decide [dɪ'saɪd] *vt* (*question etc*) décider, régler; (*s.o.'s career, fate etc*) décider de; **to d. to do** décider de faire; **to d. that** décider que; **to d. s.o. to do** décider qn à faire. ‖ *vi* (*make decisions*) décider; (*make up one's mind*) se décider (**on doing** à faire); **to d. on sth** décider de qch; (*choose*) se décider pour qch; **the deciding factor** le facteur décisif. ●**decided** *a* (*firm*) décidé (*clear*) net (*f* nette).

decimal ['desɪməl] *a* décimal; **d. point** virgule *f* ‖ *n* décimale *f*.

decimate ['desɪmeɪt] *vt* décimer.

decipher [dɪ'saɪfər] *vt* déchiffrer.

decision [dɪ'sɪʒ(ə)n] *n* décision *f*.

decisive [dɪ'saɪsɪv] *a* (*defeat, tone etc*) décisif; (*victory*) net (*f* nette).

deck [dek] **1** *n Nau* pont *m*; **top d.** (*of bus*) impériale *f*. **2** *n* **d. of cards** jeu *m* de cartes. **3** *n* (*of record player*) platine *f*. ●**deckchair** *n* chaise *f* longue.

declare [dɪ'kleər] *vt* déclarer (**that** que); (*verdict, result*) proclamer. ●**declaration** [deklə'reɪʃ(ə)n] *n* déclaration *f*; proclamation *f*.

decline [dɪ'klaɪn] **1** *vi* (*become less*) (*of popularity etc*) être en baisse; (*deteriorate*) (*of health etc*) décliner; **to d. in importance** perdre de l'importance ‖ *n* déclin *m*; (*fall*) baisse *f*. **2** *vt* (*offer etc*) refuser, décliner; **to d. to do** refuser de faire.

decod/e [di:'kəʊd] *vt* (*message*) décoder. ●**—er** *n Comptr TV* décodeur *m*.

decompose [di:kəm'pəʊz] *vi* (*rot*) se décomposer.

decor ['deɪkɔ:r] *n* décor *m*.

decorate ['dekəreɪt] *vt* (*cake, house, soldier*) décorer (**with** de); (*hat, skirt etc*) orner (**with** de); (*paint etc*) peindre (et tapisser) (*pièce, maison*). ●**decoration** [-'reɪʃ(ə)n] *n* décoration *f*. ●**decorative** *a* décoratif. ●**decorator** *n* (*house painter etc*) peintre *m* décorateur; **(interior) d.** décorateur, -trice *mf*.

decreas/e [dɪ'kri:s] *vti* diminuer ‖ ['di:kri:s] *n* diminution *f* (**in** de). ●**—ing** *a* (*number etc*) décroissant.

decree [dɪ'kri:] *n Pol Rel* décret *m*; *Jur* jugement *m*; (*municipal*) arrêté *m* ‖ *vt* (*pt & pp* **decreed**) décréter (**that** que).

decrepit [dɪ'krepɪt] *a* (*building*) en ruine.

dedicat/e ['dedɪkeɪt] *vt* (*devote*) consacrer (**to** à); (*book*) dédier (**to** à). ●**—ed** *a* (*teacher etc*) consciencieux. ●**dedication** [-'keɪʃ(ə)n] *n* (*in book*) dédicace *f*; (*devotion*) dévouement *m*.

deduce [dɪ'dju:s] *vt* (*conclude*) déduire (**from** de, **that** que).

deduct [dɪ'dʌkt] *vt* (*subtract*) déduire (**from** de); (*from wage, account*) prélever (**from** sur). ●**deduction** [-ʃ(ə)n] *n* déduction *f*.

deed [di:d] *n* action *f*, acte *m*; (*feat*) exploit *m*; *Jur* acte *m* (notarié).

deep [di:p] *a* (**-er, -est**) profond; (*snow*) épais (*f* épaisse); (*voice*) grave; (*note*) *Mus* bas (*f* basse); **to be six metres/***etc* **d.** avoir six mètres/*etc* de profondeur; **d. in thought** absorbé dans ses pensées; **the d. end** (*in swimming pool*) le grand bain; **d. red** rouge foncé. ●**—ly** *adv* (*grateful, to breathe, regret etc*) profondément. ●**deep-'freeze** *vt* surgeler ‖ *n* congélateur *m*. ●**d.-'rooted** *or* **d.-'seated** *a* bien ancré, profond.

deepen ['di:pən] *vt* approfondir; (*increase*) augmenter ‖ *vi* devenir plus profond.

deer [dɪər] *n inv* cerf *m*.

deface [dɪ'feɪs] *vt* (*damage*) dégrader; (*daub*) barbouiller.

default [dɪ'fɔ:lt] *n* **by d.** *Comptr Jur* par défaut; **to win by d.** gagner par forfait.

defeat [dɪ'fi:t] *vt* (*opponent etc*) battre,

vaincre ▮ *n* défaite *f*.
defect[1] ['di:fekt] *n* défaut *m*. ● **de'fective** *a* défectueux.
defect[2] [dɪ'fekt] *vi Pol* déserter; **to d. to** (*the enemy etc*) passer à.
defence [dɪ'fens] (*Am* **defense**) *n* défense *f*; **the body's defences** la défense de l'organisme (**against** contre); **in his d.** *Jur* à sa décharge. ● **defenceless** *a* sans défense. ● **defensive** *a* défensif ▮ *n* **on the d.** sur la défensive.
defend [dɪ'fend] *vt* défendre. ● **defendant** *n* (*accused*) *Jur* prévenu, -ue *mf*. ● **defender** *n* (*of title*) *Sp* détenteur, -trice *mf*.
defense [dɪ'fens] *n Am* = **defence**.
defer [dɪ'fɜ:r] *vt* (**-rr-**) (*postpone*) différer.
defiant [dɪ'faɪənt] *a* (*tone, attitude etc*) de défi; (*person*) rebelle. ● **defiance** *n* (*resistance*) défi *m* (**of** à); **in d. of** (*contempt*) au mépris de.
deficient [dɪ'fɪʃənt] *a* (*not adequate*) insuffisant; (*faulty*) défectueux; **to be d. in** manquer de. ● **deficiency** *n* manque *m*; (*of vitamins etc*) carence *f*; (*flaw*) défaut *m*.
deficit ['defɪsɪt] *n* déficit *m*.
define [dɪ'faɪn] *vt* définir.
definite ['defɪnɪt] *a* (*date, plan*) précis, déterminé; (*reply, improvement*) net (*f* nette); (*order, offer*) ferme; (*certain, sure*) certain; **d. article** *Gram* article *m* défini. ● **—ly** *adv* certainement; (*considerably*) nettement; (*to say*) catégoriquement.
definition [defɪ'nɪʃ(ə)n] *n* définition *f*.
deflect [dɪ'flekt] *vt* (*bullet etc*) faire dévier; **to d. s.o. from sth** détourner qn de qch.
deformed [dɪ'fɔ:md] *a* (*body*) difforme. ● **deformity** *n* difformité *f*.
defraud [dɪ'frɔ:d] *vt* (*customs etc*) frauder; **to d. s.o. of sth** escroquer qch à qn.
defrost [di:'frɒst] *vt* (*fridge*) dégivrer; (*food*) décongeler.
defuse [di:'fju:z] *vt* (*bomb, conflict*) désamorcer.
defy [dɪ'faɪ] *vt* (*person, death etc*) défier; (*efforts*) résister à; **to d. s.o. to do** défier qn de faire.
degenerate [dɪ'dʒenəreɪt] *vi* dégénérer (**into** en).
degrade [dɪ'greɪd] *vt* dégrader.
degree [dɪ'gri:] *n* **1** (*angle, temperature etc*) degré *m*; **it's 20 degrees** il fait 20 degrés; **not in the slightest d.** pas du tout; **to such a d.** à tel point (**that** que). **2** *Univ* diplôme *m*; (*Bachelor's*) licence *f*; (*Master's*) maîtrise *f*; (*PhD*) doctorat *m*.
dehydrated [di:haɪ'dreɪtɪd] *a* déshydraté; **to get d.** se déshydrater.
de-ice [di:'aɪs] *vt* (*car window etc*) dégivrer.
dejected [dɪ'dʒektɪd] *a* abattu, découragé. ● **dejection** *n* abattement *m*.
delay [dɪ'leɪ] *vt* retarder; (*payment*) différer ▮ *vi* (*be slow*) tarder (**doing, in doing** à faire); (*linger*) s'attarder ▮ *n* (*lateness*) retard *m*; (*waiting period*) délai *m*; **without d.** sans tarder.
delectable [dɪ'lektəb(ə)l] *a* délectable.
delegate **1** ['delɪgeɪt] *vt* déléguer (**to** à). **2** ['delɪgət] *n* délégué, -ée *mf*. ● **delegation** [-'geɪʃ(ə)n] *n* délégation *f*.
delete [dɪ'li:t] *vt* rayer, supprimer. ● **deletion** [-ʃ(ə)n] *n* (*thing deleted*) rature *f*.
deliberate[1] [dɪ'lɪbərət] *a* (*intentional*) intentionnel, délibéré; (*slow*) mesuré. ● **—ly** *adv* (*intentionally*) exprès; (*to walk*) avec mesure.
deliberate[2] [dɪ'lɪbəreɪt] *vi* délibérer ▮ *vt* délibérer sur.
delicate ['delɪkət] *a* délicat. ● **delicacy** *n* délicatesse *f*; (*food*) mets *m* délicat.
delicatessen [delɪkə'tesən] *n* traiteur *m* et épicerie *f* fine.
delicious [dɪ'lɪʃəs] *a* délicieux.
delight [dɪ'laɪt] *n* (*pleasure*) délice *m*, (grand) plaisir *m*, joie *f*; (*delicious food etc*) délice *m*; *pl* (*pleasures, things*) délices *fpl*; **to take d. in sth/in doing** se délecter de qch/à faire ▮ *vt* réjouir ▮ *vi* **to d. in doing** se délecter à faire. ● **—ed** *a* ravi, enchanté (**with sth** de qch, **to do** de faire, **that** que).
delightful [dɪ'laɪtfəl] *a* charmant; (*meal, perfume*) délicieux.
delinquent [dɪ'lɪŋkwənt] *a* & *n* délinquant, -ante (*mf*).
delirious [dɪ'lɪərɪəs] *a* délirant; **to be d.** avoir le délire, délirer.
deliver [dɪ'lɪvər] *vt* **1** (*goods, milk etc*) livrer; (*letters*) distribuer; (*hand over*) remettre (**to** à). **2** (*rescue*) délivrer (**from** de). **3** (*give birth to*) mettre au monde. **4** (*speech*) prononcer; (*warning*) lancer; (*blow*) porter. ● **delivery** *n* **1** livraison *f*; (*of letters*) distribution *f*; (*handing over*) remise *f*. **2** (*birth*) accouchement *m*. ● **deliveryman** *n* (*pl* **-men**) livreur *m*.
delude [dɪ'lu:d] *vt* tromper; **to d. oneself** se faire des illusions. ● **delusion** [-ʒ(ə)n] *n* illusion *f*.
deluge ['delju:dʒ] *n* (*of water, questions etc*) déluge *m*.
de luxe [dɪ'lʌks] *a* de luxe.
delve [delv] *vi* **to d. into** (*question, past*) fouiller; (*books*) fouiller dans.
demand [dɪ'mɑ:nd] *vt* exiger (**sth from s.o.** qch de qn); (*rights, more pay*) revendiquer;

to **d. that** exiger que; **to d. to know** insister pour savoir ‖ *n* exigence *f*; (*claim*) revendication *f*; (*for goods*) demande *f*; **in great d.** très demandé; **to make demands on s.o.** exiger beaucoup de qn. ●**demanding** *a* exigeant.
demean [dɪ'miːn] *vt* **to d. oneself** s'abaisser. ●**—ing** *a* dégradant.
demeanour [dɪ'miːnər] (*Am* **demeanor**) *n* (*behaviour*) comportement *m*.
demerara [demə'reərə] *n* **d. (sugar)** sucre *m* roux.
demister [diː'mɪstər] *n Aut* dispositif *m* de désembuage.
demo ['deməʊ] *n* (*pl* **-os**) (*demonstration*) *Fam* manif *f*.
demobilize [diː'məʊbɪlaɪz] *vt* démobiliser.
democracy [dɪ'mɒkrəsɪ] *n* démocratie *f*. ●**democrat** ['deməkræt] *n* démocrate *mf*. ●**demo'cratic** *a* démocratique; (*person*) démocrate.
demolish [dɪ'mɒlɪʃ] *vt* démolir. ●**demolition** [demə'lɪʃ(ə)n] *n* démolition *f*.
demon ['diːmən] *n* démon *m*.
demonstrate ['demənstreɪt] *vt* démontrer; (*machine*) faire une démonstration de; **to d. how to do** montrer comment faire ‖ *vi* (*protest*) manifester. ●**demonstration** [-'streɪʃ(ə)n] *n* démonstration *f*; (*protest*) manifestation *f*. ●**demonstrator** *n* (*protester*) manifestant, -ante *mf*.
demonstrative [dɪ'mɒnstrətɪv] *a* & *n Gram* démonstratif (*m*).
demoralize [dɪ'mɒrəlaɪz] *vt* démoraliser.
demote [dɪ'məʊt] *vt* rétrograder.
den [den] *n* tanière *f*.
denial [dɪ'naɪəl] *n* (*of rumour*) démenti *m*; (*of truth etc*) dénégation *f*; **to issue a d.** publier un démenti.
denim ['denɪm] *n* (toile *f* de) coton *m*; *pl* (*jeans*) (blue-)jean *m*.
Denmark ['denmɑːk] *n* Danemark *m*.
denomination [dɪnɒmɪ'neɪʃ(ə)n] *n Rel* confession *f*, religion *f*; (*of coin, banknote*) valeur *f*.
denote [dɪ'nəʊt] *vt* dénoter.
denounce [dɪ'naʊns] *vt* (*person, injustice etc*) dénoncer (**to** à); **to d. s.o. as a spy**/*etc* accuser qn publiquement d'être un espion/*etc*.
dense [dens] *a* (**-er, -est**) dense; (*stupid*) *Fam* lourd, bête. ●**—ly** *adv* **d. populated**/*etc* très peuplé/*etc*. ●**density** *n* densité *f*.
dent [dent] *n* (*in car, metal etc*) bosse *f*; **full of dents** (*car etc*) cabossé ‖ *vt* cabosser.
dental ['dent(ə)l] *a* dentaire; **d. surgeon** chirurgien *m* dentiste. ●**dentist** *n* dentiste *mf*. ●**dentistry** *n* médecine *f* dentaire. ●**dentures** *npl* dentier *m*.
deny [dɪ'naɪ] *vt* nier (**doing** avoir fait, **that** que); (*rumour*) démentir; (*authority*) rejeter; **to d. s.o. sth** refuser qch à qn.
deodorant [diː'əʊdərənt] *n* déodorant *m*.
depart [dɪ'pɑːt] *vi* partir; (*deviate*) s'écarter (**from** de). ●**—ed** *n* **the d.** le défunt, la défunte, *pl* les défunt(e)s.
department [dɪ'pɑːtmənt] *n* département *m*; (*in office*) service *m*; (*in shop*) rayon *m*; *Univ* section *f*, département *m*; **that's your d.** (*sphere*) c'est ton rayon; **d. store** grand magasin *m*.
departure [dɪ'pɑːtʃər] *n* départ *m*; **a d. from** (*custom, rule*) un écart par rapport à; **to be a new d. for** constituer une nouvelle voie pour; **d. lounge** (*in airport*) salle *f* de départ.
depend [dɪ'pend] *vi* dépendre (**on, upon** de); **to d. (up)on** (*rely on*) compter sur (**for sth** pour qch). ●**—able** *a* (*person, information, machine etc*) sûr. ●**dependant** *n* personne *f* à charge.
dependent [dɪ'pendənt] *a* dépendant (**on, upon** de); (*relative*) à charge; **to be d. (up)on** dépendre de.
depict [dɪ'pɪkt] *vt* (*describe*) dépeindre; (*in pictures*) représenter.
deplete [dɪ'pliːt] *vt* (*use up*) épuiser; (*reduce*) réduire.
deplor/e [dɪ'plɔːr] *vt* déplorer. ●**—able** *a* déplorable.
deploy [dɪ'plɔɪ] *vt* (*troops etc*) déployer.
deport [dɪ'pɔːt] *vt* (*foreigner etc*) expulser.
deposit [dɪ'pɒzɪt] **1** *vt* (*object, money etc*) déposer ‖ *n* (*in bank*) dépôt *m*; (*part payment*) acompte *m*; (*against damage*) caution *f*; (*on bottle*) consigne *f*; **d. account** compte *m* d'épargne. **2** *n* (*sediment*) dépôt *m*; (*of gold, oil etc*) gisement *m*. ●**depositor** *n* déposant, -ante *mf*.
depot ['depəʊ, *Am* 'diːpəʊ] *n* dépôt *m*; (*railroad station*) *Am* gare *f*; **(bus) d.** *Am* gare *f* routière.
depraved [dɪ'preɪvd] *a* dépravé.
depreciate [dɪ'priːʃɪeɪt] *vi* (*in value*) se déprécier. ●**depreciation** [-'eɪʃ(ə)n] *n* dépréciation *f*.
depress [dɪ'pres] *vt* (*discourage*) déprimer; (*push down*) appuyer sur. ●**—ed** *a* (*person*) déprimé; (*industry*) (*in decline*) en déclin; (*in crisis*) en crise; **to get d.** se décourager. ●**depression** [-ʃ(ə)n] *n* dépression *f*.
depriv/e [dɪ'praɪv] *vt* priver (**of** de). ●**—ed** *a* (*child etc*) déshérité.
depth [depθ] *n* profondeur *f*; (*of snow*)

épaisseur *f*; **in the depths of** (*forest, despair*) au plus profond de; (*winter*) au cœur de; **in d.** en profondeur.

deputize ['depjʊtaɪz] *vi* assurer l'intérim (**for s.o.** de qn).

deputy ['depjʊtɪ] *n* (*replacement*) remplaçant, -ante *mf*; (*assistant*) adjoint, -ointe *mf*; **d. (sheriff)** *Am* shérif *m* adjoint; **d. chairman** vice-président, -ente *mf*.

derailed [dɪ'reɪld] *a* **to be d.** (*of train*) dérailler. ● **derailment** *n* déraillement *m*.

derby ['dɜːbɪ] *n* (*hat*) *Am* (chapeau *m*) melon *m*.

derelict ['derɪlɪkt] *a* (*building etc*) abandonné.

deride [dɪ'raɪd] *vt* tourner en dérision. ● **derisory** *a* (*amount etc*) dérisoire.

derive [dɪ'raɪv] *vt* **to d. from sth** (*pleasure etc*) tirer de qch; **to be derived from** (*of word etc*) dériver de. ● **derivation** [derɪ'veɪʃ(ə)n] *n Ling* dérivation *f*.

dermatologist [dɜːmə'tɒlədʒɪst] *n* dermatologue *mf*.

derogatory [dɪ'rɒgət(ə)rɪ] *a* (*word*) péjoratif; (*remark*) désobligeant (**to** pour).

derrick ['derɪk] *n* (*over oil well*) derrick *m*.

derv [dɜːv] *n* gazole *m*, gas-oil *m*.

descend [dɪ'send] *vi* descendre (**from** de); **to d. upon** (*of tourists*) envahir; (*attack*) faire une descente sur; **in descending order** en ordre décroissant ‖ *vt* (*stairs*) descendre; **to be descended from** descendre de. ● **descendant** *n* descendant, -ante *mf*. ● **descent** *n* **1** (*of aircraft etc*) descente *f*. **2** (*ancestry*) origine *f*.

describe [dɪ'skraɪb] *vt* décrire. ● **description** [-ʃ(ə)n] *n* description *f*; (*on passport*) signalement *m*; **of every d.** de toutes sortes. ● **descriptive** *a* descriptif.

desecrate ['desɪkreɪt] *vt* profaner.

desert[1] ['dezət] *n* désert *m*; **d. animal** animal *m* du désert; **d. island** île *f* déserte.

desert[2] [dɪ'zɜːt] *vt* abandonner, déserter; **to d. s.o.** (*of luck etc*) abandonner qn ‖ *vi Mil* déserter. ● **—ed** *a* (*place*) désert. ● **—er** *n Mil* déserteur *m*.

deserv/e [dɪ'zɜːv] *vt* mériter (**to do** de faire). ● **—ing** *a* (*person*) méritant; (*cause*) louable; **d. of** digne de.

desiccated ['desɪkeɪtɪd] *a* (des)séché.

design [dɪ'zaɪn] **1** *vt* (*car, dress, furniture etc*) dessiner; (*devise*) concevoir (*projet etc*); **designed to do/for s.o.** conçu pour faire/pour qn; **well designed** bien conçu. ‖ *n* (*pattern*) motif *m*, dessin *m*; (*sketch*) plan *m*, dessin *m*; (*type of dress or car*) modèle *m*; (*planning*) conception *f*, création *f*; **industrial d.** dessin *m* industriel; **to study d.** étudier le design.
2 *n* (*aim*) dessein *m*; **by d.** intentionnellement. ● **designer** *n* (*artistic, industrial*) dessinateur, -trice *mf*; (*of clothes*) styliste *mf*; (*well-known*) couturier *m*; **d. clothes** vêtements *mpl* griffés.

designate ['dezɪgneɪt] *vt* désigner.

desir/e [dɪ'zaɪər] *n* désir *m*; **I've got no d. to** je n'ai aucune envie de ‖ *vt* désirer (**to do** faire). ● **—able** *a* désirable.

desk [desk] *n* (*in school*) table *f*; (*in office*) bureau *m*; (*in shop*) caisse *f*; **(reception) d.** (*in hotel etc*) réception *f*; **d. clerk** (*in hotel*) *Am* réceptionniste *mf*.

desolate ['desələt] *a* (*deserted*) désolé; (*dreary, bleak*) triste; (*person*) affligé.

despair [dɪ'speər] *n* désespoir *m*; **to be in d.** être au désespoir ‖ *vi* désespérer (**of s.o.** de qn, **of doing** de faire).

despatch [dɪ'spætʃ] *vt* & *n* = **dispatch.**

desperate ['despərət] *a* désespéré; (*criminal*) capable de tout; **to be d. for** (*money, love etc*) avoir désespérément besoin de; (*a cigarette, baby etc*) mourir d'envie d'avoir. ● **desperation** [-'reɪʃ(ə)n] *n* désespoir *m*; **in d.** (*as a last resort*) en désespoir de cause.

despicable [dɪ'spɪkəb(ə)l] *a* méprisable.

despise [dɪ'spaɪz] *vt* mépriser.

despite [dɪ'spaɪt] *prep* malgré.

despondent [dɪ'spɒndənt] *a* découragé.

despot ['despɒt] *n* despote *m*.

dessert [dɪ'zɜːt] *n* dessert *m*. ● **dessertspoon** *n* cuillère *f* à dessert.

destination [destɪ'neɪʃ(ə)n] *n* destination *f*.

destine ['destɪn] *vt* destiner (**for** à, **to do** à faire); **it was destined to happen** ça devait arriver.

destiny ['destɪnɪ] *n* destin *m*; (*fate of individual*) destinée *f*.

destitute ['destɪtjuːt] *a* (*poor*) indigent.

destroy [dɪ'strɔɪ] *vt* détruire; (*horse*) abattre; (*cat, dog*) faire piquer.

destruction [dɪ'strʌkʃ(ə)n] *n* destruction *f*. ● **destructive** *a* (*person, war*) destructeur; (*child*) qui casse tout.

detach [dɪ'tætʃ] *vt* détacher (**from** de). ● **—ed** *a* (*indifferent*) détaché; **d. house** maison *f* individuelle.

detachable [dɪ'tætʃəb(ə)l] *a* (*lining*) amovible.

detachment [dɪ'tætʃmənt] *n* (*attitude*) & *Mil* détachement *m*.

detail ['diːteɪl, *Am* dɪ'teɪl] *n* détail *m*; **in d.** en détail ‖ *vt* raconter en détail. ● **—ed** *a* (*account etc*) détaillé.

detain [dɪ'teɪn] *vt* retenir; (*prisoner*) détenir;

(*in hospital*) garder, hospitaliser. ●**detention** [dɪ'tenʃ(ə)n] *n* (*school punishment*) retenue *f*; (*in prison*) détention *f*.

detect [dɪ'tekt] *vt* (*find*) découvrir; (*see, hear*) distinguer; (*mine*) détecter; (*illness*) dépister.

detective [dɪ'tektɪv] *n* inspecteur *m* de police, policier *m* (en civil); (*private*) détective *m* (privé); **d. film/novel** film *m*/roman *m* policier.

detector [dɪ'tektər] *n* détecteur *m*; **smoke d.** détecteur *m* de fumée.

deter [dɪ'tɜːr] *vt* (**-rr-**) **to d. s.o.** dissuader *or* décourager qn (**from doing** de faire, **from sth** de qch).

detergent [dɪ'tɜːdʒənt] *n* détergent *m*.

deteriorate [dɪ'tɪərɪəreɪt] *vi* se détériorer. ●**deterioration** [-'reɪʃ(ə)n] *n* détérioration *f*.

determin/e [dɪ'tɜːmɪn] *vt* déterminer; (*price*) fixer; **to d. to do** se déterminer à faire. ●**—ed** *a* (*look, person*) déterminé; **d. to do** décidé à faire; **I'm d. she'll succeed** je suis bien décidé à ce qu'elle réussisse.

deterrent [dɪ'terənt, *Am* dɪ'tɜːrənt] *n Mil* force *f* de dissuasion; **to be a d.** *Fig* être dissuasif.

detest [dɪ'test] *vt* détester (**doing** faire). ●**—able** *a* détestable.

detonate ['detəneɪt] *vt* faire exploser. ●**detonator** *n* détonateur *m*.

detour ['diːtʊər] *n* détour *m*.

detract [dɪ'trækt] *vi* **to d. from** (*make less*) diminuer.

detriment ['detrɪmənt] *n* **to the d. of** au détriment de. ●**detri'mental** *a* préjudiciable (**to** à).

devalue [diː'væljuː] *vt* (*money*) & *Fig* dévaluer. ●**devaluation** [-'eɪʃ(ə)n] *n* dévaluation *f*.

devastat/e ['devəsteɪt] *vt* (*lay waste*) dévaster; (*upset, shock*) *Fig* foudroyer (*qn*). ●**—ing** *a* (*storm etc*) dévastateur; (*overwhelming*) (*news etc*) accablant; (*shock*) terrible.

develop [dɪ'veləp] *vt* développer; (*area, land*) mettre en valeur; (*habit, illness*) contracter; (*talent*) manifester; *Phot* développer; **to d. a liking for** prendre goût à. ‖*vi* se développer; (*of event, crisis*) se produire; (*of talent, illness*) se manifester; **to d. into** devenir; **developing country** pays *m* en voie de développement. ●**—er** *n* **(property) d.** promoteur *m* (de construction). ●**—ment** *n* développement *m*; **(housing) d.** lotissement *m*; (*large*) grand ensemble *m*; **a (new) d.** (*in situation*) un fait nouveau.

deviate ['diːvɪeɪt] *vi* dévier (**from** de); **to d. from the norm** s'écarter de la norme.

device [dɪ'vaɪs] *n* dispositif *m*; (*scheme*) procédé *m*; **left to one's own devices** livré à soi-même.

devil ['dev(ə)l] *n* diable *m*; **a** *or* **the d. of a problem** *Fam* un problème épouvantable; **I had a** *or* **the d. of a job** *Fam* j'ai eu un mal fou (**doing, to do** à faire); **what/where/why the d.?** *Fam* que/où/pourquoi diable? ●**devilish** *a* diabolique.

devious ['diːvɪəs] *a* (*mind, behaviour*) tortueux; **he's d.** il a l'esprit tortueux.

devise [dɪ'vaɪz] *vt* (*a plan*) combiner; (*a plot*) tramer; (*invent*) inventer.

devoid [dɪ'vɔɪd] *a* **d. of** dénué de.

devolution [diːvə'luːʃ(ə)n] *n Pol* décentralisation *f*.

devot/e [dɪ'vəʊt] *vt* consacrer (**to** à). ●**—ed** *a* dévoué; (*admirer*) fervent. ●**devo'tee** *n Sp Mus* passionné, -ée *mf*. ●**devotion** [-ʃ(ə)n] *n* dévouement *m* (**to s.o.** à qn).

devour [dɪ'vaʊər] *vt* dévorer.

devout [dɪ'vaʊt] *a* dévot; (*supporter*) fervent.

dew [djuː] *n* rosée *f*. ●**dewdrop** *n* goutte *f* de rosée.

diabetes [daɪə'biːtiːz] *n Med* diabète *m*. ●**diabetic** [-'betɪk] *n* diabétique *mf* ‖*a* diabétique; **d. jam**/*etc* confiture *f*/*etc* pour diabétiques.

diabolical [daɪə'bɒlɪk(ə)l] *a* (*bad*) épouvantable.

diagnose ['daɪəgnəʊz, *Am* -'nəʊs] *vt* diagnostiquer. ●**diagnosis,** *pl* **-oses** [daɪəg'nəʊsɪs, -əʊsiːz] *n* diagnostic *m*.

diagonal [daɪ'ægən(ə)l] *a* diagonal ‖*n* **d. (line)** diagonale *f*. ●**—ly** *adv* en diagonale.

diagram ['daɪəgræm] *n* schéma *m*, diagramme *m*; *Geom* figure *f*.

dial ['daɪəl] *n* cadran *m* ‖*vt* (**-ll-**, *Am* **-l-**) (*phone number*) faire, composer; (*person*) appeler; **d. tone** *Am* tonalité *f*. ●**dialling** *a* **d. code** indicatif *m*; **d. tone** tonalité *f*.

dialect ['daɪəlekt] *n* (*regional*) dialecte *m*; (*rural*) patois *m*.

dialogue ['daɪəlɒg] (*Am* **dialog**) *n* dialogue *m*.

dialysis, *pl* **-yses** [daɪ'ælɪsɪs, -ɪsiːz] *n Med* dialyse *f*.

diameter [daɪ'æmɪtər] *n* diamètre *m*. ●**dia'metrically** *adv* (*opposed*) diamétralement.

diamond ['daɪəmənd] **1** *n* (*stone*) diamant *m*; (*shape*) losange *m*; **(baseball) d.** *Am* terrain *m* (de baseball); **d. necklace**/*etc* rivière *f*/*etc* de diamants. **2** *n* & *npl Cards* carreau *m*.

diaper ['daɪəpər] *n* (*for baby*) *Am* couche *f*.

diaphragm ['daɪəfræm] *n* diaphragme *m*.

diarrh(o)ea [daɪə'riːə] *n* diarrhée *f*.

diary ['daɪərɪ] *n* (*calendar*) agenda *m*; (*private*) journal *m* (intime).

dice [daɪs] *n inv* dé *m* (à jouer) ‖ *vt* (*food*) couper en dés.

dictaphone® ['dɪktəfəʊn] *n* dictaphone® *m*.

dictate [dɪk'teɪt] *vt* dicter (**to** à) ‖ *vi* dicter; **to d. to s.o.** (*order around*) faire la loi à qn. ● **dictation** [-ʃ(ə)n] *n* dictée *f*.

dictator [dɪk'teɪtər] *n* dictateur *m*. ● **dictatorship** *n* dictature *f*.

diction ['dɪkʃ(ə)n] *n* langage *m*; (*way of speaking*) diction *f*.

dictionary ['dɪkʃənərɪ] *n* dictionnaire *m*; **English d.** dictionnaire *m* d'anglais.

did [dɪd] *pt of* **do**.

die [daɪ] **1** *vi* (*pt & pp* **died**, *pres p* **dying**) mourir (**of, from** de); **to be dying to do** mourir d'envie de faire; **to be dying for sth** avoir une envie folle de qch; **to d. away** (*of noise*) mourir; **to d. down** (*of fire*) mourir; (*of storm*) se calmer; **to d. off** mourir (les uns après les autres); **to d. out** (*of custom*) mourir.
2 *n* (*in engraving*) coin *m*; **the d. is cast** *Fig* les dés sont jetés.

diehard ['daɪhɑːd] *n* réactionnaire *mf*.

diesel ['diːzəl] *a & n* **d. (engine)** (moteur *m*) diesel *m*; **d. (oil)** gazole *m*.

diet ['daɪət] *n* (*for losing weight*) régime *m*; (*usual food*) alimentation *f*; **to go on a d.** faire un régime ‖ *vi* suivre un régime. ● **dietary** *a* diététique; **d. fibre** fibre(s) *f(pl)* alimentaire(s). ● **die'tician** *n* diététicien, -ienne *mf*.

differ ['dɪfər] *vi* différer (**from** de); (*disagree*) ne pas être d'accord (**from** avec).

difference ['dɪf(ə)rəns] *n* différence *f* (**in** de); **d. (of opinion)** différend *m*; **it makes no d.** ça n'a pas d'importance; **it makes no d. to me** ça m'est égal. ● **different** *a* différent (**from, to** de); (*another*) autre; (*various*) divers, différents. ● **differently** *adv* autrement (**from, to** que).

differentiate [dɪfə'renʃɪeɪt] *vt* différencier (**from** de) ‖ *vti* **to d. (between)** faire la différence entre.

difficult ['dɪfɪkəlt] *a* difficile (**to do** à faire); **it's d. for us to...** il nous est difficile de.... ● **difficulty** *n* difficulté *f*; **to have d. doing** avoir du mal à faire; **to be in d.** avoir des difficultés; **to have d. with** avoir des ennuis avec.

diffident ['dɪfɪdənt] *a* (*person*) qui manque d'assurance.

diffuse [dɪ'fjuːz] *vt* (*spread*) diffuser.

dig [dɪg] *vt* (*pt & pp* **dug**, *pres p* **digging**) (*ground, garden*) bêcher; (*hole, grave etc*) creuser; **to d. sth into** (*push*) planter qch dans; **to d. out** (*from ground*) déterrer; (*accident victim*) dégager; (*find*) *Fam* dénicher; **to d. up** (*from ground*) déterrer; (*weed*) arracher; (*earth*) retourner; (*street*) piocher.
‖ *vi* (*dig a hole*) creuser; **to d. in** (*eat*) *Fam* manger; **to d. into** (*s.o.'s past*) fouiller dans; (*one's savings*) puiser dans; (*meal*) *Fam* attaquer.
‖ *n* (*with spade*) coup *m* de bêche; (*with elbow*) coup *m* de coude; (*remark*) *Fam* coup *m* de griffe.

digest [daɪ'dʒest] *vti* digérer ● **digestion** [-tʃ(ə)n] *n* digestion *f*. ● **digestive** *a* digestif.

digger ['dɪgər] *n* (*machine*) pelleteuse *f*.

digit ['dɪdʒɪt] *n* (*number*) chiffre *m*. ● **digital** *a* (*watch*) numérique.

dignified ['dɪgnɪfaɪd] *a* digne. ● **dignify** *vt* donner de la dignité à. ● **dignity** *n* dignité *f*.

digress [daɪ'gres] *vi* faire une digression; **to d. from** s'écarter de.

digs [dɪgz] *npl Fam* chambre *f* (meublée).

dilapidated [dɪ'læpɪdeɪtɪd] *a* (*house*) délabré.

dilemma [daɪ'lemə] *n* dilemme *m*.

diligent ['dɪlɪdʒənt] *a* assidu, appliqué; **to be d. in doing sth** faire qch avec zèle. ● **diligence** *n* zèle *m*, assiduité *f*.

dilute [daɪ'luːt] *vt* diluer ‖ *a* dilué.

dim [dɪm] *a* (**dimmer, dimmest**) (*light*) faible; (*colour*) terne; (*room*) sombre; (*memory, outline*) vague; (*person*) stupide ‖ *vt* (**-mm-**) (*light*) baisser; (*memory*) estomper; **to d. one's headlights** *Am* se mettre en code. ● **dimly** *adv* (*to shine*) faiblement; (*vaguely*) vaguement.

dime [daɪm] *n US Can* (pièce *f* de) dix cents *mpl*; **a d. store** = un Prisunic®, un Monoprix®.

dimension [daɪ'menʃ(ə)n] *n* dimension *f*; (*extent*) *Fig* étendue *f*. ● **dimensional** *a* **two-d.** à deux dimensions.

diminish [dɪ'mɪnɪʃ] *vti* diminuer.

diminutive [dɪ'mɪnjʊtɪv] **1** *a* (*tiny*) minuscule. **2** *a & n Gram* diminutif (*m*).

dimmers ['dɪməz] *npl* (*low beams*) *Am Aut* phares *mpl* code *inv*, codes *mpl*.

dimple ['dɪmp(ə)l] *n* fossette *f*.

dimwit ['dɪmwɪt] *n* idiot, -ote *mf*. ● **dim'witted** *a* idiot.

din [dɪn] **1** *n* (*noise*) vacarme *m*. **2** *vt* (**-nn-**) **to**

d. into s.o. that rabâcher à qn que.

din/e [daɪn] *vi* dîner (**on** de); **to d. out** dîner en ville; **dining car** *Rail* wagon-restaurant *m*; **dining room** salle *f* à manger. ●**—er** *n* dîneur, -euse *mf*; *Rail* wagon-restaurant *m*; (*short-order restaurant*) *Am* petit restaurant *m*.

dinghy ['dɪŋgɪ] *n* petit canot *m*; **(rubber) d.** canot *m* pneumatique.

dingy ['dɪndʒɪ] *a* (**-ier, -iest**) (*room etc*) minable; (*colour*) terne.

dinner ['dɪnər] *n* (*evening meal*) dîner *m*; (*lunch*) déjeuner *m*; **to have d.** dîner; **to have s.o. to d.** avoir qn à dîner; **d. jacket** smoking *m*; **d. party** dîner *m* (à la maison); **d. plate** grande assiette *f*; **d. service, d. set** service *m* de table.

dinosaur ['daɪnəsɔːr] *n* dinosaure *m*.

dip [dɪp] *vt* (**-pp-**) plonger; **to d. one's headlights** se mettre en code ‖ *vi* (*of road*) plonger; **to d. into** (*pocket, savings*) puiser dans; (*book*) feuilleter ‖ *n* (*in road*) petit creux *m*; **to go for a d.** (*swim*) faire trempette.

diphtheria [dɪp'θɪərɪə] *n* diphtérie *f*.

diphthong ['dɪfθɒŋ] *n* diphtongue *f*.

diploma [dɪ'pləʊmə] *n* diplôme *m*.

diplomacy [dɪ'pləʊməsɪ] *n* (*tact*) & *Pol* diplomatie *f*. ●**'diplomat** *n* diplomate *mf*. ●**diplo'matic** *a* diplomatique; **to be d.** (*tactful*) être diplomate.

dipper ['dɪpər] *n* **the big d.** (*at fairground*) les montagnes *fpl* russes.

dire ['daɪər] *a* affreux; (*poverty, need*) extrême.

direct [daɪ'rekt] **1** *a* (*result, flight, person etc*) direct; (*danger*) immédiat ‖ *adv* directement.

2 *vt* (*work, one's attention*) diriger; (*letter, remark*) adresser (**to** à); (*efforts*) orienter (**to, towards** vers); (*film*) réaliser; (*play*) mettre en scène; **to d. s.o. to** (*place*) indiquer à qn le chemin de; **to d. s.o. to do** charger qn de faire. ●**directly** *adv* (*without detour*) directement; (*at once*) tout de suite; (*to speak*) franchement; **d. behind**/*etc* juste derrière/*etc* ‖ *conj Fam* aussitôt que (+ *indic*).

direction [daɪ'rekʃ(ə)n] *n* direction *f*, sens *m*; (*management*) direction *f*; *pl* (*orders*) indications *fpl*; **directions (for use)** mode *m* d'emploi; **in the opposite d.** en sens inverse.

director [daɪ'rektər] *n* directeur, -trice *mf*; (*of film*) réalisateur, -trice *mf*; (*of play*) metteur *m* en scène; (*board member in firm*) administrateur, -trice *mf*.

directory [daɪ'rektərɪ] *n* (*phone book*) annuaire *m* (du téléphone); (*of streets*) guide *m*; *Comptr* répertoire *m*; **d. inquiries** *Tel* renseignements *mpl*.

dirt [dɜːt] *n* saleté *f*; (*earth*) terre *f*; **d. cheap** *Fam* très bon marché; **d. road** chemin *m* de terre; **d. track** *Sp* cendrée *f*.

dirty ['dɜːtɪ] *a* (**-ier, -iest**) sale; (*job*) salissant; (*obscene, unpleasant*) sale; (*word*) grossier; **to get d.** se salir; **to get sth d.** salir qch; **a d. joke** une histoire cochonne; **a d. trick** un sale tour ‖ *vt* salir ‖ *vi* se salir.

dis- [dɪs] *pref* dé-, dés-.

disabled [dɪs'eɪb(ə)ld] *a* handicapé ‖ *n* **the d.** les handicapés *mpl*. ●**disa'bility** *n* infirmité *f*.

disadvantage [dɪsəd'vɑːntɪdʒ] *n* désavantage *m*.

disagree [dɪsə'griː] *vi* ne pas être d'accord (**with** avec); (*of figures*) ne pas concorder; **to d. with s.o.** (*of food etc*) ne pas réussir à qn. ●**—able** *a* désagréable. ●**—ment** *n* désaccord *m*; (*quarrel*) différend *m*.

disappear [dɪsə'pɪər] *vi* disparaître. ●**disappearance** *n* disparition *f*.

disappoint [dɪsə'pɔɪnt] *vt* décevoir; **I'm disappointed with it** ça m'a déçu. ●**—ing** *a* décevant. ●**—ment** *n* déception *f*.

disapprov/e [dɪsə'pruːv] *vi* **to d. of s.o./sth** désapprouver qn/qch; **I d.** je suis contre. ●**—ing** *a* (*look etc*) désapprobateur. ●**disapproval** *n* désapprobation *f*.

disarm [dɪs'ɑːm] *vti* désarmer. ●**disarmament** *n* désarmement *m*.

disarray [dɪsə'reɪ] *n* **in d.** (*army, party*) en plein désarroi; (*clothes*) en désordre.

disaster [dɪ'zɑːstər] *n* désastre *m*; **d. area** région *f* sinistrée. ●**disastrous** *a* désastreux.

disband [dɪs'bænd] *vt* disperser ‖ *vi* se disperser.

disbelief [dɪsbə'liːf] *n* incrédulité *f*.

disc [dɪsk] (*Am* **disk**) *n* disque *m*; **identity d.** plaque *f* d'identité; **d. jockey** disc-jockey *m*.

discard [dɪs'kɑːd] *vt* (*get rid of*) se débarrasser de; (*plan, hope etc*) *Fig* abandonner.

discern [dɪ'sɜːn] *vt* discerner. ●**—ing** *a* (*person*) averti, sagace. ●**—ment** *n* discernement *m*.

discharge [dɪs'tʃɑːdʒ] *vt* (*patient, employee*) renvoyer; (*soldier*) libérer; (*gun, accused person*) décharger; (*liquid*) déverser ‖ *vi* (*of wound*) suppurer ‖ ['dɪstʃɑːdʒ] *n* (*of gun, electrical*) décharge *f*; (*of liquid, pus*) écoulement *m*; (*dismissal*) renvoi *m*; (*freeing*) libération *f*.

disciple [dɪ'saɪp(ə)l] *n* disciple *m*.

discipline ['dɪsɪplɪn] *n* (*behaviour, subject*) discipline *f* ‖ *vt* (*control*) discipliner; (*punish*) punir. ●**discipli'narian** *n* **to be a (strict) d.** être très à cheval sur la discipline.
disclaim [dɪs'kleɪm] *vt* (*responsibility*) (dé)nier.
disclose [dɪs'kləʊz] *vt* révéler. ●**disclosure** *n* révélation *f*.
disco ['dɪskəʊ] *n* (*pl* **-os**) *Fam* discothèque *f*.
discolour [dɪs'kʌlər] (*Am* **discolor**) *vt* décolorer; (*teeth*) jaunir.
discomfort [dɪs'kʌmfət] *n* (*physical*) douleur *f*; (*mental*) malaise *m*; **I get d. from my wrist** mon poignet me gêne.
disconcert [dɪskən'sɜːt] *vt* déconcerter.
disconnect [dɪskə'nekt] *vt* (*unfasten etc*) détacher; (*unplug*) débrancher; (*wires*) déconnecter; (*gas, telephone*) couper.
discontent [dɪskən'tent] *n* mécontentement *m*. ●**discontented** *a* mécontent.
discontinu/e [dɪskən'tɪnjuː] *vt* cesser, interrompre. ●**—ed** *a* (*article*) *Com* qui ne se fait plus.
discord ['dɪskɔːd] *n* (*disagreement*) discorde *f*.
discotheque ['dɪskətek] *n* (*club*) discothèque *f*.
discount 1 ['dɪskaʊnt] *n* (*on article*) remise *f*, réduction *f*; **at a d.** (*to buy, sell*) à prix réduit; **d. store** solderie *f*. **2** [dɪs'kaʊnt] *vt* (*story etc*) ne pas tenir compte de.
discourage [dɪs'kʌrɪdʒ] *vt* décourager (**s.o. from doing** qn de faire); **to get discouraged** se décourager. ●**—ment** *n* découragement *m*.
discourteous [dɪs'kɜːtɪəs] *a* discourtois.
discover [dɪs'kʌvər] *vt* découvrir (**that** que). ●**discovery** *n* découverte *f*.
discredit [dɪs'kredɪt] *vt* (*cast slur on*) discréditer ‖ *n* discrédit *m*.
discreet [dɪ'skriːt] *a* (*unassuming, reserved etc*) discret. ●**discretion** [dɪs'kreʃ(ə)n] *n* discrétion *f*; **I'll use my own d.** je ferai comme bon me semblera.
discrepancy [dɪ'skrepənsɪ] *n* divergence *f*, contradiction *f* (**between** entre).
discriminat/e [dɪ'skrɪmɪneɪt] *vi* **to d. against** faire de la discrimination contre. ●**—ing** *a* (*person*) averti, sagace; (*ear*) fin. ●**discrimination** [-'neɪʃ(ə)n] *n* (*against s.o.*) discrimination *f*; (*judgment*) discernement *m*; (*distinction*) distinction *f*.
discus ['dɪskəs] *n Sp* disque *m*.
discuss [dɪ'skʌs] *vt* (*talk about*) discuter de (*politique etc*); (*examine in detail*) discuter (*projet, question, prix*). ●**discussion** [-ʃ(ə)n] *n* discussion *f*; **under d.** (*matter etc*) en question.
disdain [dɪs'deɪn] *n* dédain *m*.
disease [dɪ'ziːz] *n* maladie *f*. ●**diseased** *a* malade.
disembark [dɪsɪm'bɑːk] *vti* débarquer.
disenchant [dɪsɪn'tʃɑːnt] *vt* désenchanter. ●**—ment** *n* désenchantement *m*.
disentangle [dɪsɪn'tæŋg(ə)l] *vt* (*string etc*) démêler; **to d. oneself from** se dégager de.
disfavour ['dɪsfeɪvər] (*Am* **disfavor**) *n* défaveur *f*.
disfigure [dɪs'fɪgər] *vt* défigurer.
disgrac/e [dɪs'greɪs] *n* (*shame*) honte *f* (**to** à); (*disfavour*) disgrâce *f* ‖ *vt* déshonorer. ●**—ed** *a* (*politician etc*) disgracié.
disgraceful [dɪs'greɪsfəl] *a* honteux (**of s.o.** de la part de qn). ●**disgracefully** *adv* honteusement.
disgruntled [dɪs'grʌnt(ə)ld] *a* mécontent.
disguise [dɪs'gaɪz] *vt* déguiser (**as** en) ‖ *n* déguisement *m*; **in d.** déguisé.
disgust [dɪs'gʌst] *n* dégoût *m* (**for, at, with** de); **in d.** dégoûté ‖ *vt* dégoûter. ●**—ed** *a* dégoûté (**at, by, with** de); **to be d. with s.o.** (*annoyed*) être fâché contre qn. ●**—ing** *a* dégoûtant.
dish [dɪʃ] **1** *n* (*container, food*) plat *m*; **the dishes** la vaisselle. **2** *vt* **to d. out** *Fam* distribuer; **to d. out** *or* **up** (*food*) servir.
dishcloth ['dɪʃklɒθ] *n* (*for washing*) lavette *f*; (*for drying*) torchon *m*.
dishearten [dɪs'hɑːt(ə)n] *vt* décourager.
dishevelled [dɪ'ʃevəld] (*Am* **disheveled**) *a* (*person, hair*) hirsute, ébouriffé.
dishonest [dɪs'ɒnɪst] *a* malhonnête. ●**dishonesty** *n* malhonnêteté *f*.
dishonour [dɪs'ɒnər] (*Am* **dishonor**) *n* déshonneur *m* ‖ *vt* déshonorer. ●**—able** *a* peu honorable.
dishtowel ['dɪʃtaʊəl] *n* torchon *m*.
dishwasher ['dɪʃwɒʃər] *n* lave-vaisselle *m inv*.
dishy ['dɪʃɪ] *a* (**-ier, -iest**) (*woman, man*) *Fam* sexy, qui a du chien.
disillusion [dɪsɪ'luːʒ(ə)n] *vt* décevoir; **to be disillusioned (with)** être déçu (de).
disincentive [dɪsɪn'sentɪv] *n* mesure *f* dissuasive; **to be a d. to s.o.** décourager qn.
disinclined [dɪsɪŋ'klaɪnd] *a* peu disposé (**to** à).
disinfect [dɪsɪn'fekt] *vt* désinfecter. ●**disinfectant** *a* & *n* désinfectant (*m*).
disintegrate [dɪs'ɪntɪgreɪt] *vi* se désintégrer.
disinterested [dɪs'ɪntrɪstɪd] *a* (*impartial*) désintéressé; (*uninterested*) *Fam* indifférent (**in** à).
disk [dɪsk] *n* **1** *Am* = **disc. 2** (*of computer*)

disque *m*; **hard d.** disque *m* dur; **d. drive** lecteur *m* de disquettes *or* de disques. ●**diskette** [dɪs'ket] *n* disquette *f*.

dislike [dɪs'laɪk] *vt* ne pas aimer (**doing** faire); **he doesn't d. it** ça ne lui déplaît pas ‖ *n* aversion *f* (**for, of** pour); **to take a d. to s.o./sth** prendre qn/qch en grippe.

dislocate ['dɪsləkeɪt] *vt* (*limb*) démettre; **to d. one's shoulder** se démettre l'épaule.

dislodge [dɪs'lɒdʒ] *vt* faire bouger, déplacer; (*enemy*) déloger.

disloyal [dɪs'lɔɪəl] *a* déloyal.

dismal ['dɪzməl] *a* morne, triste. ●**—ly** *adv* (*to fail, behave*) lamentablement.

dismantle [dɪs'mænt(ə)l] *vt* (*machine*) démonter.

dismay [dɪs'meɪ] *vt* consterner ‖ *n* consternation *f*.

dismiss [dɪs'mɪs] *vt* (*from job*) renvoyer (**from** de); (*official*) destituer; (*appeal*) *Jur* rejeter; (*thought, suggestion etc*) *Fig* écarter; **d.!** *Mil* rompez! ●**dismissal** *n* renvoi *m*; destitution *f*.

dismount [dɪs'maʊnt] *vi* descendre (**from** de).

disobey [dɪsə'beɪ] *vt* désobéir à ‖ *vi* désobéir. ●**disobedience** *n* désobéissance *f*. ●**disobedient** *a* désobéissant.

disorder [dɪs'ɔːdər] *n* (*confusion*) désordre *m*; (*illness*) troubles *mpl*; (*riots*) désordres *mpl*. ●**disorderly** *a* (*behaviour, room*) désordonné; (*meeting*) houleux.

disorganized [dɪs'ɔːgənaɪzd] *a* désorganisé.

disorientate [dɪs'ɔːrɪənteɪt] (*Am* **disorient** [dɪs'ɔːrɪənt]) *vt* désorienter.

disown [dɪs'əʊn] *vt* désavouer, renier.

disparaging [dɪs'pærɪdʒɪŋ] *a* peu flatteur, désobligeant.

disparity [dɪs'pærətɪ] *n* écart *m*, disparité *f* (**between** entre).

dispatch [dɪs'pætʃ] *vt* (*send*) expédier (*lettre etc*); (*troops, messenger*) envoyer; (*finish*) expédier (*travail etc*) ‖ *n* (*sending*) expédition *f* (**of** de); (*report*) dépêche *f*.

dispel [dɪs'pel] *vt* (**-ll-**) dissiper.

dispensary [dɪs'pensərɪ] *n* (*in hospital*) pharmacie *f*; (*in chemist's shop*) officine *f*.

dispense [dɪs'pens] **1** *vt* (*give out*) distribuer; (*medicine*) préparer. **2** *vi* **to d. with** (*do without*) se passer de. ●**dispenser** *n* (*device*) distributeur *m*; **cash d.** distributeur *m* de billets.

disperse [dɪ'spɜːs] *vt* disperser ‖ *vi* se disperser. ●**dispersal** *n* dispersion *f*.

dispirited [dɪ'spɪrɪtɪd] *a* découragé.

displace [dɪs'pleɪs] *vt* (*refugees, furniture*) déplacer; (*replace*) supplanter.

display [dɪ'spleɪ] *vt* montrer; (*notice, electronic data*) afficher; (*painting, goods*) exposer; (*courage etc*) faire preuve de ‖ *n* (*in shop*) étalage *m*; (*of electronic data*) affichage *m*; (*of force*) déploiement *m*; (*of anger*) manifestation *f*; (*of paintings*) exposition *f*; **d. (unit)** (*of computer*) moniteur *m*; **on d.** exposé.

displeas/e [dɪs'pliːz] *vt* déplaire à. ●**—ed** *a* mécontent (**with** de). ●**displeasure** *n* mécontentement *m*.

disposal [dɪ'spəʊzəl] *n* (*sale*) vente *f*; (*of waste*) évacuation *f*; **at the d. of** à la disposition de.

dispos/e[1] [dɪ'spəʊz] *vi* **to d. of** (*get rid of*) se débarrasser de; (*throw away*) jeter (*papier etc*); (*one's time, money*) disposer de; (*sell*) vendre. ●**—able** *a* (*plate etc*) à jeter, jetable; (*income*) disponible.

dispose[2] [dɪ'spəʊz] *vt* **to d. s.o. to do** disposer qn à faire; **disposed to do** disposé à faire; **well-disposed towards** bien disposé envers.

disposition [dɪspə'zɪʃ(ə)n] *n* (*character*) naturel *m*; (*readiness*) inclination *f*.

disproportionate [dɪsprə'pɔːʃ(ə)nət] *a* disproportionné.

disprove [dɪs'pruːv] *vt* réfuter.

dispute [dɪ'spjuːt] *n* (*quarrel*) dispute *f*; *Pol* conflit *m*; *Jur* litige *m*; **beyond d.** incontestable; **in d.** (*matter*) débattu; (*facts, territory*) contesté; (*competence*) en question ‖ *vt* (*claim etc*) contester.

disqualify [dɪs'kwɒlɪfaɪ] *vt* (*make unfit*) rendre inapte (**from** à); *Sp* disqualifier; **to d. s.o. from driving** retirer son permis à qn.

disregard [dɪsrɪ'gɑːd] *vt* ne tenir aucun compte de ‖ *n* indifférence *f* (**for** à); (*for the law*) désobéissance *f* (**for** à).

disrepair [dɪsrɪ'peər] *n* **in (a state of) d.** en mauvais état.

disrepute [dɪsrɪ'pjuːt] *n* **to bring into d.** jeter le discrédit sur.

disrespect [dɪsrɪ'spekt] *n* manque *m* de respect. ●**disrespectful** *a* irrespectueux (**to** envers).

disrupt [dɪs'rʌpt] *vt* (*traffic, class etc*) perturber; (*communications*) interrompre; (*plan, s.o.'s books etc*) déranger. ●**disruption** [-ʃ(ə)n] *n* perturbation *f*; (*of plan etc*) dérangement *m*. ●**disruptive** *a* (*child*) turbulent.

dissatisfied [dɪ'sætɪsfaɪd] *a* mécontent (**with** de). ●**dissatisfaction** [-'fækʃ(ə)n] *n* mécontentement *m* (**with** devant).

dissect [daɪ'sekt] *vt* disséquer.

dissent [dɪ'sent] *n* dissentiment *m*.
dissertation [dɪsə'teɪʃ(ə)n] *n Univ* mémoire *m*.
dissident ['dɪsɪdənt] *a* & *n* dissident, -ente (*mf*).
dissimilar [dɪ'sɪmɪlər] *a* différent (**to** de).
dissipate ['dɪsɪpeɪt] *vt* (*clouds*, *fears etc*) dissiper; (*energy*) gaspiller.
dissociate [dɪ'səʊʃieɪt] *vt* dissocier (**from** de).
dissolve [dɪ'zɒlv] *vt* dissoudre ‖ *vi* se dissoudre.
dissuade [dɪ'sweɪd] *vt* dissuader (**from doing** de faire); **to d. s.o. from sth** détourner qn de qch.
distance ['dɪstəns] *n* distance *f*; **in the d.** au loin; **from a d.** de loin; **at a d.** à quelque distance; **it's within walking d.** on peut y aller à pied; **to keep one's d.** garder ses distances.
distant ['dɪstənt] *a* éloigné, lointain; (*relative*) éloigné; (*reserved*) distant.
distaste [dɪs'teɪst] *n* aversion *f* (**for** pour). ● **distasteful** *a* désagréable.
distil [dɪ'stɪl] *vt* (**-ll-**) distiller; **distilled water** (*for car*, *iron*) eau *f* déminéralisée.
distinct [dɪ'stɪŋkt] *a* **1** (*clear*) (*voice*, *light etc*) distinct; (*difference*, *improvement*) net (*f* nette), marqué. **2** (*different*) distinct (**from** de).
distinction [dɪ'stɪŋkʃ(ə)n] *n* distinction *f*; *Univ* mention *f* très bien.
distinctive [dɪ'stɪŋktɪv] *a* distinctif. ● **—ly** *adv* distinctement; (*to forbid*) formellement; (*definitely*) sensiblement; **d. possible** tout à fait possible.
distinguish [dɪ'stɪŋgwɪʃ] *vti* distinguer (**from** de, **between** entre); **distinguishing mark** signe *m* particulier. ● **—ed** *a* distingué.
distort [dɪ'stɔːt] *vt* déformer. ● **—ed** *a* (*false*) faux (*f* fausse).
distract [dɪ'strækt] *vt* distraire (**from** de). ● **—ed** *a* (*troubled*) préoccupé; (*with worry*) éperdu. ● **—ing** *a* (*noise*) gênant.
distraction [dɪ'strækʃ(ə)n] *n* (*lack of attention*, *amusement*) distraction *f*.
distraught [dɪ'strɔːt] *a* éperdu, affolé.
distress [dɪ'stres] *n* (*pain*) douleur *f*; (*anguish*, *misfortune*) détresse *f*; **in d.** (*ship*) en détresse; (*poverty*) dans la détresse ‖ *vt* affliger. ● **—ing** *a* affligeant.
distribute [dɪ'strɪbjuːt] *vt* distribuer; (*spread evenly*) répartir. ● **distribution** [-'bjuːʃ(ə)n] *n* distribution *f*. ● **distributor** *n Aut Cin etc* distributeur *m*; (*commercial dealer*) concessionnaire *mf*.
district ['dɪstrɪkt] *n* région *f*; (*of town*) quartier *m*; (*administrative*) district *m*; **postal d.** division *f* postale; **d. attorney** *Am* = procureur *m* (de la République); **d. nurse** infirmière *f* visiteuse.
distrust [dɪs'trʌst] *vt* se méfier de ‖ *n* méfiance *f* (**of** de). ● **distrustful** *a* méfiant; **to be d. of** se méfier de.
disturb [dɪ'stɜːb] *vt* (*sleep*, *water*) troubler; (*papers*, *belongings*) déranger; **to d. s.o.** (*bother*) déranger qn; (*worry*) troubler qn. ● **—ed** *a* (*person*) (*mentally*) perturbé. ● **—ing** *a* (*worrying*) inquiétant.
disturbance [dɪ'stɜːbəns] *n* (*noise*) tapage *m*; *pl* (*riots*) troubles *mpl*.
disuse [dɪs'juːs] *n* **to fall into d.** tomber en désuétude. ● **disused** [-'juːzd] *a* désaffecté.
ditch [dɪtʃ] **1** *n* fossé *m*. **2** *vt* (*dump*) *Fam* se débarrasser de.
dither ['dɪðər] *vi Fam* hésiter, tergiverser.
ditto ['dɪtəʊ] *adv* idem.
divan [dɪ'væn] *n* divan *m*.
div/e [daɪv] *vi* (*pt* **dived,** *Am* **dove** [dəʊv]) plonger; (*rush*) se précipiter, se jeter ‖ *n* (*of swimmer*, *goalkeeper*) plongeon *m*; (*of submarine*) plongée *f*; (*of aircraft*) piqué *m*. ● **—ing** *n* (*underwater*) plongée *f* sous-marine; **d. board** plongeoir *m*. ● **diver** *n* plongeur, -euse *mf*.
diverge [daɪ'vɜːdʒ] *vi* diverger (**from** de). ● **divergent** *a* divergent.
diverse [daɪ'vɜːs] *a* divers. ● **diversity** *n* diversité *f*.
divert [daɪ'vɜːt] *vt* (*attention*, *person etc*) détourner (**from** de); (*traffic*) dévier; (*aircraft*) dérouter; (*amuse*) divertir. ● **diversion** [-ʃ(ə)n, *Am* -ʒ(ə)n] *n Aut* déviation *f*; (*distraction*) & *Mil* diversion *f*.
divide [dɪ'vaɪd] *vt* diviser (**into** en); **to d. sth (off)** séparer qch (**from sth** de qch); **to d. sth up** (*share out*) partager qch; **to d. one's time between** partager son temps entre ‖ *vi* (*of group*, *road*) se diviser. ● **divided** *a* (*family etc*) divisé; (*opinions*) partagés.
dividend ['dɪvɪdənd] *n Fin* dividende *m*.
divine [dɪ'vaɪn] *a* divin.
division [dɪ'vɪʒ(ə)n] *n* division *f*; (*dividing object*) séparation *f*. ● **divisible** *a* divisible. ● **divisive** [-'vaɪsɪv] *a* qui cause des dissensions.
divorc/e [dɪ'vɔːs] *n* divorce *m* ‖ *vt* (*husband*, *wife*) divorcer d'avec ‖ *vi* divorcer. ● **—ed** *a* divorcé (**from** d'avec); **to get d.** divorcer. ● **divorcee** [dɪvɔː'siː, *Am* dɪvɔː'seɪ] *n* divorcé, -ée *mf*.
divulge [dɪ'vʌldʒ] *vt* divulguer.
DIY [diːaɪ'waɪ] *n abbr* (*do-it-yourself*) bricolage *m*.

dizzy ['dɪzɪ] *a* (**-ier, -iest**) **to be** *or* **feel d.** avoir le vertige; **to make s.o. (feel) d.** donner le vertige à qn. •**dizziness** *n* vertige *m*.

DJ [diː'dʒeɪ] *n abbr* = **disc jockey.**

do [duː] **1** *v aux* (*3rd person sing pres t* **does;** *pt* **did;** *pp* **done;** *pres p* **doing**) **do you know?** savez-vous?, est-ce que vous savez?; **I do not** *or* **don't see** je ne vois pas; **he** *did* **say so** (*emphasis*) il l'a bien dit; **do stay** reste donc; **you know him, don't you?** tu le connais, n'est-ce pas?; **neither do I** moi non plus; **so do I** moi aussi; **oh, does he?** (*surprise*) ah oui?; **don't!** non!
2 *vt* faire; **to do nothing but sleep** ne faire que dormir; **what does she do?** (*in general*), **what is she doing?** (*now*) qu'est-ce qu'elle fait?, que fait-elle?; **what have you done (with)...?** qu'as-tu fait (de)...?; **well done** (*congratulations*) bravo!; (*steak etc*) bien cuit; **that'll do me** (*suit*) ça fera mon affaire; **I've been done** (*cheated*) *Fam* je me suis fait avoir; **to do s.o. out of sth** escroquer qch à qn; **I'm done (in)** (*tired*) *Sl* je suis claqué; **he's done for** *Fam* il est fichu; **to do in** (*kill*) *Sl* supprimer; **to do out** (*clean*) nettoyer; **to do over** (*redecorate*) refaire; **to do up** (*coat, button*) boutonner; (*zip, Am zipper*) fermer; (*house*) refaire; (*goods*) emballer; **do yourself up (well)!** (*wrap up*) couvre-toi (bien)!
3 *vi* (*get along*) aller, marcher; (*suit*) faire l'affaire, convenir; (*be enough*) suffire; (*finish*) finir; **how do you do?** (*introduction*) enchanté; (*greeting*) bonjour; **he did well** *or* **right to leave** il a bien fait de partir; **do as I do** fais comme moi; **to make do** se débrouiller; **to do away with sth/s.o.** supprimer qch/qn; **I could do with a coffee**/*etc* (*need, want*) j'aimerais bien (prendre) un café/*etc*; **to do without sth/s.o.** se passer de qch/qn; **to have to do with** (*relate to*) avoir à voir avec; (*concern*) concerner.
4 *n* (*pl* **dos** *or* **do's**) (*party*) *Fam* soirée *f*, fête *f*; **the do's and don'ts** ce qu'il faut faire ou ne pas faire.

docile ['dəʊsaɪl] *a* docile.

dock [dɒk] **1** *n* (*for ship*) dock *m* ‖ *vi* (*at quayside*) se mettre à quai; (*of spacecraft*) s'arrimer. **2** *n Jur* banc *m* des accusés. •**—er** *n* docker *m*. •**dockyard** *n* chantier *m* naval.

doctor ['dɒktər] **1** *n Med* médecin *m*, docteur *m*; *Univ* docteur *m*. **2** *vt* (*text, food*) altérer. •**doctorate** ['dɒktərət] *n* doctorat *m* (**in** ès, en).

doctrine ['dɒktrɪn] *n* doctrine *f*.

document ['dɒkjʊmənt] *n* document *m*. •**docu'mentary** *n* (*film*) documentaire *m*.

dodge [dɒdʒ] *vt* (*question, acquaintance etc*) esquiver; (*pursuer*) échapper à; (*tax*) éviter de payer ‖ *vi* (*to one side*) faire un saut (de côté); **to d. through** (*crowd*) se faufiler dans ‖ *n* mouvement *m* de côté; (*trick*) *Fig* truc *m*.

dodgems ['dɒdʒəmz] *npl* autos *fpl* tamponneuses.

dodgy ['dɒdʒɪ] *a* (**-ier, -iest**) *Fam* (*tricky*) délicat; (*dubious*) douteux; (*unreliable*) peu sûr.

doe [dəʊ] *n* (*deer*) biche *f*.

does [dʌz] *see* **do.** •**doesn't** ['dʌz(ə)nt] = **does not.**

dog[1] [dɒg] *n* chien *m*; (*female*) chienne *f*; **d. biscuit** biscuit *m* pour chien; **d. food** pâtée *f*; **d. collar** *Fam* col *m* de pasteur. •**d.-eared** *a* (*page etc*) écorné. •**d.-'tired** *a Fam* claqué.

dog[2] [dɒg] *vt* (**-gg-**) (*follow*) poursuivre.

dogged ['dɒgɪd] *a* obstiné. •**—ly** *adv* obstinément.

doggy ['dɒgɪ] *n Fam* toutou *m*; **d. bag** (*in restaurant*) petit sac *m* pour emporter les restes.

doghouse ['dɒghaʊs] *n Am* niche *f*.

dogmatic [dɒg'mætɪk] *a* dogmatique.

dogsbody ['dɒgzbɒdɪ] *n Pej* factotum *m*, sous-fifre *m*.

doing ['duːɪŋ] *n* **that's your d.** c'est toi qui as fait ça; **doings** *Fam* activités *fpl*.

do-it-yourself [duːɪtjə'self] *n* bricolage *m* ‖ *a* (*store, book*) de bricolage.

doldrums ['dɒldrəmz] *npl* **to be in the d.** (*of person*) avoir le cafard; (*of business*) être en plein marasme.

dole [dəʊl] **1** *n* **d. (money)** allocation *f* de chômage; **to go on the d.** s'inscrire au chômage. **2** *vt* **to d. out** distribuer au compte-gouttes.

doll [dɒl] *n* poupée *f*; **doll's house,** *Am* **dollhouse** maison *f* de poupée.

dollar ['dɒlər] *n* dollar *m*.

dollop ['dɒləp] *n* (*of food*) gros morceau *m*.

dolphin ['dɒlfɪn] *n* (*sea animal*) dauphin *m*.

domain [dəʊ'meɪn] *n* (*land, sphere*) domaine *m*.

dome [dəʊm] *n* dôme *m*, coupole *f*.

domestic [də'mestɪk] *a* familial, domestique; (*animal*) domestique; (*trade, flight*) intérieur; **d. science** arts *mpl* ménagers.

dominant ['dɒmɪnənt] *a* dominant; (*person*) dominateur.

dominate ['dɒmɪneɪt] *vti* dominer.

domineering [dɒmɪ'nɪərɪŋ] *a* dominateur.

dominion [də'mɪnjən] *n* domination *f*;

(*land*) territoire *m*.

domino ['dɒmɪnəʊ] *n* (*pl* **-oes**) domino *m*; *pl* (*game*) dominos *mpl*.

don [dɒn] *n Univ* professeur *m*.

donate [dəʊ'neɪt] *vt* faire don de; (*blood*) donner ▮ *vi* donner. ●**donation** [-ʃ(ə)n] *n* don *m*.

done [dʌn] *pp of* **do.**

donkey ['dɒŋkɪ] *n* âne *m*; **for d.'s years** *Fam* depuis belle lurette.

donor ['dəʊnər] *n* (*of blood, organ*) donneur, -euse *mf*.

don't [dəʊnt] = **do not.**

doom [du:m] *n* ruine *f*; (*fate*) destin *m*; (*gloom*) *Fam* tristesse *f* ▮ *vt* condamner (**to** à); **to be doomed (to failure)** être voué à l'échec.

door [dɔ:r] *n* porte *f*; (*of vehicle*) portière *f*, porte *f*; **out of doors** dehors; **d.-to-door salesman** démarcheur *m*. ●**doorbell** *n* sonnette *f*. ●**doorknob** *n* bouton *m or* poignée *f* de porte. ●**doorknocker** *n* marteau *m*. ●**doorman** *n* (*pl* **-men**) (*of hotel etc*) portier *m*, concierge *m*. ●**doormat** *n* paillasson *m*. ●**doorstep** *n* seuil *m*. ●**doorstop(per)** *n* butoir *m* (de porte). ●**doorway** *n* **in the d.** dans l'encadrement de la porte.

dope [dəʊp] **1** *n* (*drugs*) *Fam* drogue *f*; (*for horse, athlete*) dopant *m* ▮ *vt* doper. **2** *n* (*idiot*) *Fam* imbécile *mf*. ●**dopey** *a* (**-ier, -iest**) *Fam* (*stupid*) abruti; (*sleepy*) endormi.

dormant ['dɔ:mənt] *a* (*volcano, matter*) en sommeil.

dormer ['dɔ:mər] *n* **d. (window)** lucarne *f*.

dormitory ['dɔ:mɪtrɪ, *Am* 'dɔ:mɪtɔ:rɪ] *n* dortoir *m*; *Am* résidence *f* (universitaire).

dormouse, *pl* **-mice** ['dɔ:maʊs, -maɪs] *n* loir *m*.

dose [dəʊs] *n* dose *f*; (*of hard work*) *Fig* période *f* ▮ *vt* **to d. oneself (up)** se bourrer de médicaments. ●**dosage** *n* (*amount*) dose *f*.

dosshouse ['dɒshaʊs] *n Sl* asile *m* (de nuit).

dossier ['dɒsɪeɪ] *n* (*papers*) dossier *m*.

dot [dɒt] *n* point *m*; **polka d.** pois *m*; **on the d.** *Fam* à l'heure pile ▮ *vt* (**-tt-**) (*an i*) mettre un point sur; **dotted with** parsemé de; **dotted line** pointillé *m*. ●**dot matrix printer** *n Comptr* imprimante *f* matricielle.

dot/e [dəʊt] *vt* **to d. on** être gaga de. ●**—ing** *a* affectueux; **her d. husband** son mari qui lui passe tout.

dotty ['dɒtɪ] *a* (**-ier, -iest**) *Fam* cinglé.

double ['dʌb(ə)l] *a* double; **a d. bed** un grand lit; **a d. room** une chambre pour deux personnes; **d. 's'** deux 's'; **d. three four two** (*phone number*) trente-trois quarante-deux.
▮ *adv* (*twice*) deux fois, le double; (*to fold*) en deux; **he earns d. what I earn** il gagne le double de moi *or* deux fois plus que moi.
▮ *n* double *m*; (*person*) double *m*, sosie *m*; (*stand-in*) *Cin* doublure *f*; **on the d.** au pas de course.
▮ *vt* doubler; **to d. over** (*fold*) replier; **doubled over in pain** plié (en deux) de douleur.
▮ *vi* doubler; **to d. back** (*of person*) revenir en arrière; **to d. up** (*with pain, laughter*) être plié (en deux).

double-bass [dʌb(ə)l'beɪs] *n Mus* contrebasse *f*. ●**d.-'breasted** *a* (*jacket*) croisé. ●**d.-'cross** *vt* tromper. ●**d.-'decker (bus)** *n* autobus *m* à impériale. ●**d.-'glazing** *n* (*window*) double vitrage *m*. ●**d.-'parking** *n* stationnement *m* en double file. ●**d.-'quick** *adv* en vitesse.

doubly ['dʌblɪ] *adv* doublement.

doubt [daʊt] *n* doute *m*; **to be in d. about** avoir des doutes sur; **no d.** (*probably*) sans doute; **in d.** (*result, career etc*) dans la balance ▮ *vt* douter de; **to d. whether** *or* **that** *or* **if** douter que (+*sub*).

doubtful ['daʊtfəl] *a* (*person, future etc*) incertain; (*dubious*) douteux; **to be d. (about sth)** avoir des doutes (sur qch); **it's d. whether** *or* **that** *or* **if** ce n'est pas certain que (+*sub*). ●**doubtless** *adv* sans doute.

dough [dəʊ] *n* pâte *f*; (*money*) *Fam* fric *m*, blé *m*.

doughnut ['dəʊnʌt] *n* beignet *m* (rond).

dove[1] [dʌv] *n* colombe *f*.

dove[2] [dəʊv] *Am pt of* **dive.**

Dover ['dəʊvər] *n* Douvres *m or f*.

dowdy ['daʊdɪ] *a* (**-ier, -iest**) peu élégant, sans chic.

down[1] [daʊn] *adv* en bas; (*to the ground*) par terre; (*from upstairs*) descendu; (*of sun*) couché; (*of curtain, temperature*) baissé; (*of tyre, Am tire*) dégonflé; **d. (in writing)** inscrit; **(lie) d.!** (*to dog*) couché!; **to come** *or* **go d.** descendre; **to come d. from** (*place*) arriver de; **to fall d.** tomber (par terre); **d. there** *or* **here** en bas; **d. with traitors/***etc*! à bas les traîtres/*etc*!; **d. with (the) flu** grippé; **to feel d.** (*depressed*) *Fam* avoir le cafard; **d. to** (*in numbers, dates etc*) jusqu'à; **d. payment** acompte *m*; **d. under** aux antipodes, en Australie.
▮ *prep* (*at bottom of*) en bas de; (*from top to bottom of*) du haut en bas de; (*along*) le

long de; **to go d.** (*hill*, *street*, *stairs*) descendre; **to live d. the street** habiter plus loin dans la rue.

▮ *vt* **to d. a drink** vider un verre.

down² [daʊn] *n* (*on bird*, *person etc*) duvet *m*.

down-and-out ['daʊnənaʊt] *a* sur le pavé ▮ *n* clochard, -arde *mf*. ●**downbeat** *a* (*gloomy*) *Fam* pessimiste. ●**downcast** *a* découragé. ●**downfall** *n* chute *f*. ●**down'hearted** *a* découragé, déprimé. ●**down'hill** *adv* en pente; **to go d.** descendre; (*of sick person*, *business*) aller de plus en plus mal. ●**downmarket** *a Com* bas de gamme; (*neighbourhood etc*) populaire; (*person*) ordinaire. ●**downpour** *n* averse *f*, pluie *f* torrentielle. ●**downright** *a* (*rogue*) véritable; (*refusal*) catégorique ▮ *adv* (*rude etc*) franchement. ●**downscale** *a Am* = **downmarket.** ●**downstairs** ['daʊnsteəz] *a* (*room*, *neighbours*) d'en bas ▮ [daʊn'steəz] *adv* (*to live etc*) en bas; **to come** *or* **go d.** descendre l'escalier. ●**down'stream** *adv* en aval. ●**down-to-'earth** *a* terre-à-terre *inv*. ●**down'town** *adv* en ville; **d. Chicago**/*etc* le centre de Chicago/*etc*. ●**downward** *a* vers le bas; (*path*) qui descend. ●**downward(s)** *adv* vers le bas.

Down's [daʊnz] *a* **D. syndrome** mongolisme *m*.

dowry ['daʊərɪ] *n* dot *f*.

doze [dəʊz] *n* petit somme *m* ▮ *vi* sommeiller; **to d. off** s'assoupir. ●**dozy** *a* (**-ier, -iest**) somnolent; (*silly*) *Fam* gourde.

dozen ['dʌz(ə)n] *n* douzaine *f*; **a d.** (*eggs*, *books etc*) une douzaine de; **dozens of** *Fig* des dizaines de.

Dr *abbr* (*Doctor*) Docteur.

drab [dræb] *a* terne; (*weather*) gris.

draft [drɑːft] **1** *n* (*outline*) ébauche *f*; (*of letter*) brouillon *m* ▮ *vt* **to d. (out)** (*sketch out*) faire le brouillon de; (*write out*) rédiger. **2** *n Mil Am* conscription *f* ▮ *vt* (*conscript*) appeler (sous les drapeaux). **3** *n Am* = **draught.**

draftsman ['drɑːftsmən] *n* (*pl* **-men**) *Am* = **draughtsman.**

drafty ['drɑːftɪ] *a Am* = **draughty**.

drag [dræg] *vt* (**-gg-**) traîner; (*river*) draguer; **to d. s.o./sth along** (en)traîner qn/qch; **to d. s.o. away from** arracher qn à; **to d. s.o. into** entraîner qn dans ▮ *vi* traîner; **to d. on** *or* **out** (*last a long time*) se prolonger ▮ *n Fam* (*boring task*) corvée *f*; (*person*) raseur, -euse *mf*; **in d.** (*clothing*) en travesti.

dragon ['drægən] *n* dragon *m*. ●**dragonfly** *n* libellule *f*.

drain [dreɪn] *n* (*sewer*) égout *m*; (*outside house*) puisard *m*; (*in street*) bouche *f* d'égout; **it's down the d.** (*wasted*) *Fam* c'est fichu; **to be a d. on** (*resources*, *patience*) épuiser.

▮ *vt* (*tank*, *glass*) vider; (*vegetables*) égoutter; (*land*) drainer; (*resources*) épuiser; **to d. (off)** (*liquid*) faire écouler.

▮ *vi* **to d. (off)** (*of liquid*) s'écouler; **draining board** paillasse *f*. ●**drainage** *n* (*sewers*) système *m* d'égouts. ●**drainer** *n* (*board*) paillasse *f*; (*rack*, *basket*) égouttoir *m*.

drainboard ['dreɪnbɔːd] *n Am* paillasse *f*. ●**drainpipe** *n* tuyau *m* d'évacuation.

drake [dreɪk] *n* canard *m* (mâle).

drama ['drɑːmə] *n* (*event*) drame *m*; (*dramatic art*) théâtre *m*; **d. critic** critique *m* dramatique.

dramatic [drə'mætɪk] *a* dramatique; (*very great*, *striking*) spectaculaire. ●**dramatically** *adv* (*to change*, *drop etc*) de façon spectaculaire.

dramatist ['dræmətɪst] *n* dramaturge *m*. ●**dramatize** *vt* (*exaggerate*) dramatiser; (*novel etc*) adapter (pour la scène *or* l'écran).

drank [dræŋk] *pt of* **drink.**

drape [dreɪp] *vt* (*person*, *shoulder*) draper (**with** de) ▮ *n* **drapes** (*heavy curtains*) *Am* rideaux *mpl*.

drastic ['dræstɪk] *a* radical; **d. reductions** (*in shop*) soldes *mpl* monstres. ●**drastically** *adv* radicalement.

draught [drɑːft] (*Am* **draft**) **1** *n* (*wind*) courant *m* d'air; **d. excluder** bourrelet *m* (*de porte*, *de fenêtre*). **2** *npl* (*game*) dames *fpl*. ●**draught beer** *n* bière *f* pression. ●**draughtboard** *n* damier *m*.

draughtsman ['drɑːftsmən] *n* (*pl* **-men**) dessinateur, -trice *mf* (industriel(le) *or* technique).

draughty ['drɑːftɪ] *a* (**-ier, -iest**) (*room*) plein de courants d'air.

draw¹ [drɔː] *n Sp* match *m* nul; (*of lottery*) tirage *m* au sort; (*attraction*) attraction *f*.

▮ *vt* (*pt* **drew,** *pp* **drawn**) (*pull*) tirer; (*pass*, *move*) passer (**over** sur, **into** dans); (*prize*) gagner; (*money from bank*) retirer (**from** de); (*salary*) toucher; (*attract*) attirer; (*comfort*) puiser (**from** dans); **to d. sth to a close** mettre fin à qch; **to d. a match** *Sp* faire match nul; **to d. out** (*money*) retirer; **to d. up** (*chair*) approcher; (*contract*, *list*, *plan*) dresser; **to d. (up)on** (*savings*) puiser dans.

▮ *vi Sp* faire match nul; **to d. near (to)** s'approcher (de); (*of time*) approcher (de); **to d. to a close** tirer à sa fin; **to d. back** (*go backwards*) reculer; **to d. in** (*of days*) diminuer; (*of train*) arriver (en gare); **to d. up** (*of vehicle*) s'arrêter.

draw[2] [drɔː] *vt* (*pt* **drew,** *pp* **drawn**) (*picture*) dessiner; (*circle*) tracer; (*distinction*) *Fig* faire (**between** entre) ▮ *vi* (*as artist*) dessiner.

drawback ['drɔːbæk] *n* inconvénient *m.*

drawbridge ['drɔːbrɪdʒ] *n* pont-levis *m.*

drawer [drɔːr] *n* (*in furniture*) tiroir *m.*

drawing ['drɔːɪŋ] *n* dessin *m*; **d. board** planche *f* à dessin; **d. pin** punaise *f*; **d. room** salon *m.*

drawl [drɔːl] *vi* parler d'une voix traînante ▮ *n* voix *f* traînante.

drawn [drɔːn] *pp of* **draw**[1,2] ▮ *a* (*face*) tiré; **d. match** *or* **game** match *m* nul.

dread [dred] *vt* (*exam etc*) appréhender; **to d. doing** appréhender de faire ▮ *n* crainte *f.*

dreadful ['dredfəl] *a* épouvantable; (*child*) insupportable; (*ill*) malade; **I feel d. about it** j'ai vraiment honte. ●**—ly** *adv* terriblement; **to be d. sorry** regretter infiniment.

dream [driːm] *vi* (*pt* & *pp* **dreamed** *or* **dreamt** [dremt]) rêver (**of, about** de, **of** *or* **about doing** de faire); **I wouldn't d. of it!** pas question! ▮ *vt* rêver (**that** que); **to d. sth up** imaginer qch ▮ *n* rêve *m*; **to have a d.** faire un rêve (**about** de); **to have dreams of** rêver de; **a d. house**/*etc* une maison/*etc* de rêve. ●**dreamer** *n* rêveur, -euse *mf.* ●**dreamy** *a* (**-ier, -iest**) rêveur.

dreary ['drɪərɪ] *a* (**-ier, -iest**) (*gloomy*) morne; (*monotonous*) monotone; (*boring*) ennuyeux.

dredge [dredʒ] *vt* (*river*) draguer.

dregs [dregz] *npl* **the d.** (*in liquid, of society*) la lie.

drench [drentʃ] *vt* tremper; **to get drenched** se faire tremper (jusqu'aux os).

dress [dres] **1** *n* (*woman's garment*) robe *f*; (*style of dressing*) tenue *f*; **d. circle** *Th* (premier) balcon *m*; **d. rehearsal** *Th* (répétition *f*) générale *f.*
2 *vt* (*person*) habiller; (*wound*) panser; (*salad*) assaisonner; **to get dressed** s'habiller; **dressed for tennis** en tenue de tennis. ▮ *vi* s'habiller; **to d. up** (*smartly*) bien s'habiller; (*in disguise*) se déguiser (**as** en). ●**dressmaker** *n* couturière *f.* ●**dressmaking** *n* couture *f.*

dresser ['dresər] **1** (*furniture*) vaisselier *m*; *Am* coiffeuse *f.* **2 she's a good d.** elle s'habille toujours bien.

dressing ['dresɪŋ] *n* *Med* pansement *m*; (*seasoning*) assaisonnement *m*; **d. gown** robe *f* de chambre; **d. room** *Th* loge *f*; **d. table** coiffeuse *f.*

dressy ['dresɪ] *a* (**-ier, -iest**) (*smart*) chic *inv*; **(too) d.** trop habillé.

drew [druː] *pt of* **draw**[1,2].

dribble ['drɪb(ə)l] **1** *vi* (*of baby*) baver; (*of liquid*) tomber goutte à goutte. ▮**2** *vi* *Fb* dribbler ▮ *vt* (*ball*) dribbler.

dribs [drɪbz] *npl* **in d. and drabs** par petites quantités; (*to arrive*) par petits groupes.

dried [draɪd] *a* (*fruit*) sec (*f* sèche); (*milk*) en poudre; (*flowers*) séché.

drier ['draɪər] *n* = **dryer.**

drift [drɪft] *vi* être emporté par le vent *or* le courant; (*of ship*) dériver; (*of snow*) s'amonceler; **to d. about (aimlessly)** se promener sans but; **to d. apart** (*of husband and wife*) devenir des étrangers l'un pour l'autre; **to d. into crime**/*etc* sombrer dans le crime/*etc.*
▮ *n* mouvement *m*; (*direction*) sens *m*; (*of snow*) congère *f*; (*meaning*) sens *m* général. ●**driftwood** *n* bois *m* flotté.

drill [drɪl] **1** *n* (*tool*) perceuse *f*; (*bit*) mèche *f*; (*pneumatic*) marteau *m* piqueur; (*dentist's*) roulette *f* ▮ *vt* percer; (*tooth*) fraiser; (*oil well*) forer ▮ *vi* **to d. for oil** faire de la recherche pétrolière. **2** *n* (*exercise*) *Mil Sch* exercice(s) *m*(*pl*) ▮ *vi* faire l'exercice.

drink [drɪŋk] *n* boisson *f*; (*alcoholic*) verre *m*; **to give s.o. a d.** donner (quelque chose) à boire à qn; **to have a d.** boire quelque chose; (*alcoholic drink*) prendre un verre.
▮ *vt* (*pt* **drank,** *pp* **drunk**) boire; **to d. sth down** *or* **up** boire qch.
▮ *vi* boire (**out of** dans); **to d. up** finir son verre; **to d. to s.o.** boire à la santé de qn; **drinking bout** beuverie *f*; **drinking chocolate** chocolat *m* en poudre; **drinking water** eau *f* potable. ●**drinkable** *a* (*fit for drinking*) potable; (*not unpleasant*) buvable. ●**drinker** *n* buveur, -euse *mf.*

drip [drɪp] *vi* (**-pp-**) dégouliner; (*of washing, vegetables*) s'égoutter; (*of tap, Am faucet*) goutter ▮ *vt* (*paint etc*) laisser couler ▮ *n* (*drop*) goutte *f*; (*sound*) bruit *m* de goutte; *Med* goutte-à-goutte *m inv*; (*fool*) *Fam* nouille *f.* ●**d.-dry** *a* (*shirt etc*) sans repassage. ●**dripping** *a* & *adv* **d. (wet)** dégoulinant.

drive [draɪv] *n* promenade *f* en voiture; (*energy*) énergie *f*; (*campaign*) campagne *f*; (*road to house*) allée *f*; **an hour's d.** une heure de voiture; **left-hand d.** (véhicule *m* à) conduite *f* à gauche; **disk d.** *Comptr* lecteur *m* de disquettes.
▮ *vt* (*pt* **drove,** *pp* **driven**) (*vehicle, train,*

passenger) conduire (**to** à); (*machine*) actionner; (*chase away*) chasser; **to d. s.o. to do** pousser qn à faire; **to d. s.o. to despair** réduire qn au désespoir; **to d. s.o. mad** *or* **crazy** rendre qn fou; **to d. the rain against** (*of wind*) rabattre la pluie contre; **he drives a Ford** il a une Ford.
▌*vi* (*drive a car*) conduire; (*go by car*) rouler; **to d. on the left** rouler à gauche; **to d. to Paris**/*etc* aller (en voiture) à Paris/*etc*; **what are you driving at?** *Fig* où veux-tu en venir?

drive along *vi* (*in car*) rouler ▌**to drive away** *vt* (*chase*) chasser ▌*vi* partir (en voiture) ▌**to drive back** *vt* (*passenger*) ramener (en voiture); (*enemy*) repousser ▌*vi* revenir (en voiture) ▌**to drive in** *vt* (*nail etc*) enfoncer ▌**to drive off** *vi* (*in car*) partir en voiture ▌**to drive on** *vi* (*in car*) continuer ▌**to drive out** *vt* (*chase away*) chasser (*qn, qch*) ▌**to drive up** *vi* arriver (en voiture).

drive-in [draɪvɪn] *n* (*movie theater*) *Am* drive-in *m*.

drivel ['drɪv(ə)l] *n* (*nonsense*) idioties *fpl*.

driver ['draɪvər] *n* (*of car etc*) conducteur, -trice *mf*; **(train** *or* **engine) d.** mécanicien *m*; **she's a good d.** elle conduit bien; **driver's license** *Am* permis *m* de conduire.

driveway ['draɪvweɪ] *n* (*to house*) allée *f*.

driving ['draɪvɪŋ] **1** *n Aut* conduite *f*; **d. lesson** leçon *f* de conduite; **d. licence** permis *m* de conduire; **d. school** auto-école *f*. **2** *a* **d. force** force *f* agissante.

drizzle ['drɪz(ə)l] *n* bruine *f* ▌*vi* bruiner. •**drizzly** *a* **it's d.** il bruine.

dromedary ['drɒmədərɪ, *Am* 'drɒmɪderɪ] *n* dromadaire *m*.

drone [drəʊn] *n* (*hum*) bourdonnement *m*; (*purr*) ronronnement *m* ▌*vi* (*of engine*) ronronner.

drool [druːl] *vi* (*slaver*) baver; **to d. over** *Fig* s'extasier devant.

droop [druːp] *vi* (*of flower*) se faner; (*of head*) pencher; (*of eyelid*) tomber.

drop [drɒp] **1** *n* (*of liquid*) goutte *f*.
2 *n* (*fall*) baisse *f*, chute *f* (**in** de); (*distance of fall*) hauteur *f* (de chute); (*jump*) *Av* saut *m*.
▌*vt* (**-pp-**) laisser tomber; (*price, voice*) baisser; (*bomb*) larguer; (*passenger, goods from vehicle*) déposer; (*put*) mettre; (*leave out*) faire sauter; (*get rid of*) supprimer; (*team member*) écarter; **to d. s.o. off** (*from vehicle*) déposer qn; **to d. a line** écrire un petit mot (**to** à); **to d. a hint** faire une allusion; **to d. a hint that** laisser entendre que; **to d. a word in s.o.'s ear** glisser un mot à l'oreille de qn.
▌*vi* (*fall*) tomber; (*of price*) baisser; **he's ready to d.** *Fam* il tombe de fatigue; **to d. back** *or* **behind** rester en arrière; **to d. by** *or* **in** (*visit s.o.*) passer (chez qn); **to d. off** (*fall asleep*) s'endormir; (*fall off*) tomber; (*of interest, sales*) diminuer; **to d. out** (*fall out*) tomber; (*withdraw*) se retirer; (*of student*) laisser tomber ses études. •**drop-out** *n* (*student*) étudiant, -ante *mf* qui abandonne ses études. •**dropper** *n Med* compte-gouttes *m inv*. •**droppings** *npl* (*of animal*) crottes *fpl*; (*of bird*) fiente *f*.

drought [draʊt] *n* sécheresse *f*.

drove [drəʊv] *pt of* **drive.**

droves [drəʊvz] *npl* **in d.** en foule.

drown [draʊn] *vi* se noyer ▌*vt* noyer; **to d. oneself, be drowned** se noyer. •**—ing** *a* (*man etc*) qui se noie ▌*n* (*death*) noyade *f*.

drowse [draʊz] *vi* somnoler. •**drowsy** *a* (**-ier, -iest**) somnolent; **to feel** *or* **be d.** avoir sommeil; **to make s.o. d.** assoupir qn.

drudge [drʌdʒ] *n* homme *m or* femme *f* de peine. •**drudgery** *n* corvée(s) *f(pl)*.

drug [drʌg] *n Med* médicament *m*, drogue *f*; (*narcotic*) stupéfiant *m*, drogue *f*; *Fig* drogue *f*; **drugs** (*narcotics in general*) la drogue; **to be on drugs, take drugs** se droguer; **d. addict** drogué, -ée *mf*; **d. taking** usage *m* de la drogue ▌*vt* (**-gg-**) droguer (*qn*); (*drink*) mêler un somnifère à. •**druggist** *n Am* pharmacien, -ienne *mf*. •**drugstore** *n Am* drugstore *m*.

drum [drʌm] *n Mus* tambour *m*; (*for oil*) bidon *m*; **the drums** (*of orchestra etc*) la batterie ▌*vi* (**-mm-**) *Mus* battre du tambour ▌*vt* **I tried to d. it into him** j'ai essayé de le lui faire rentrer dans le crâne; **to d. up business** attirer les clients. •**drummer** *n* (joueur, -euse *mf* de) tambour *m*; (*in pop group*) batteur *m*. •**drumstick** *n Mus* baguette *f* (de tambour); (*of chicken*) pilon *m*.

drunk [drʌŋk] *pp of* **drink** ▌*a* ivre; **to get d.** s'enivrer ▌*n* ivrogne *mf*. •**drunkard** *n* ivrogne *mf*. •**drunken** *a* (*person*) (*regularly*) ivrogne; (*driver*) ivre; **d. driving** conduite *f* en état d'ivresse.

dry [draɪ] *a* (**drier, driest**) sec (*f* sèche); (*well, river*) à sec; (*day*) sans pluie; (*wit*) caustique; (*subject, book*) aride; **to keep sth d.** tenir qch au sec; **to wipe sth d.** essuyer qch; **to run d.** se tarir; **to feel** *or* **be d.** (*thirsty*) avoir soif.
▌*vt* sécher; (*clothes in tumble drier*) faire sécher; (*by wiping*) essuyer; **to d. sth off** *or*

up sécher qch.
▮ *vi* sécher; **to d. off** sécher; **to d. up** sécher; (*dry the dishes*) essuyer la vaisselle; (*run dry*) (*of stream*) se tarir. ● **dryer** *n* (*for hair, clothes*) séchoir *m*; (*helmet-style for hair*) casque *m*. ● **dryness** *n* sécheresse *f*.
dry-clean [draɪ'kliːn] *vt* nettoyer à sec. ● **—er** *n* teinturier, -ière *mf*; **the d.-cleaner's** (*shop*) le pressing.
dual ['djuːəl] *a* double; **d. carriageway** route *f* à deux voies (séparées).
dub [dʌb] *vt* (**-bb-**) (*film*) doubler.
dubious ['djuːbɪəs] *a* (*offer, person etc*) douteux; **I'm d. about going** je me demande si je dois y aller; **to be d. about sth** douter de qch.
duchess ['dʌtʃɪs] *n* duchesse *f*.
duck [dʌk] **1** *n* canard *m*. **2** *vi* se baisser (vivement) ▮ *vt* (*head*) baisser. ● **duckling** *n* caneton *m*.
dud [dʌd] *a Fam* (*coin*) faux (*f* fausse); (*cheque, Am check*) en bois; (*watch etc*) qui ne marche pas.
due[1] [djuː] *a* (*money, sum*) dû (**to** à); (*rent, bill*) à payer; (*respect*) qu'on doit (**to** à); (*proper*) qui convient; **to fall d.** échoir; **she's d. for** (*salary increase etc*) elle doit *or* devrait recevoir; **he's d. (to arrive)** (*is awaited*) il doit arriver; **I'm d. there** je dois être là-bas; **in d. course** (*at proper time*) en temps utile; (*finally*) à la longue; **d. to** (*caused by*) dû à; (*because of*) à cause de. ▮ *n* dû *m*; *pl* (*of club*) cotisation *f*; (*official charges*) droits *mpl*.
due[2] [djuː] *adv* **d. north/south/***etc* plein nord/sud/*etc*.
duel ['djuːəl] *n* duel *m*.
duet [djuː'et] *n* duo *m*.
duffel, duffle ['dʌf(ə)l] *a* **d. bag** sac *m* de marin; **d. coat** duffel-coat *m*.
dug [dʌg] *pt & pp of* **dig**.
duke [djuːk] *n* duc *m*.
dull [dʌl] *a* (**-er, -est**) (*boring*) ennuyeux; (*colour, character*) terne; (*weather*) maussade; (*sound, ache*) sourd; (*mind*) lourd; (*edge*) émoussé ▮ *vt* (*sound, pain*) amortir; (*senses*) émousser; (*mind*) engourdir. ● **—ness** *n* (*of life, town*) monotonie *f*; (*of colour*) manque *m* d'éclat.
duly ['djuːlɪ] *adv* (*properly*) comme il convient; (*in fact*) en effet; (*in due time*) en temps utile.
dumb [dʌm] *a* (**-er, -est**) muet (*f* muette); (*stupid*) idiot, bête *f*.
dumbfound [dʌm'faʊnd] *vt* sidérer, ahurir.
dummy [dʌmɪ] **1** *n* (*of baby*) sucette *f*; (*for clothes*) mannequin *m*; (*of ventriloquist*) pantin *m*; (*fool*) *Fam* idiot, -ote *mf*. **2** *a* factice, faux (*f* fausse).
dump [dʌmp] *vt* (*rubbish, Am garbage*) déposer; **to d. (down)** (*put down*) déposer; **to d. s.o.** (*ditch*) *Fam* plaquer qn ▮ *n* (*for ammunition*) *Mil* dépôt *m*; (*dull town*) *Fam* trou *m*; (*house*) *Fam* baraque *f*; **(rubbish** *or Am* **garbage) d.** tas *m* d'ordures; (*place*) dépôt *m* d'ordures; (*untidy room*) dépotoir *m*; **to be (down) in the dumps** *Fam* avoir le cafard; **d. truck** camion *m* à benne basculante.
dumpling ['dʌmplɪŋ] *n Culin* boulette *f* (de pâte).
dumpy ['dʌmpɪ] *a* (**-ier, -iest**) (*person*) boulot, gros et court.
dunce [dʌns] *n* cancre *m*, âne *m*.
dune [djuːn] *n* **(sand) d.** dune *f*.
dung [dʌŋ] *n* (*of horse*) crotte *f*; (*of cattle*) bouse *f*; (*manure*) fumier *m*.
dungarees [dʌŋgə'riːz] *npl* (*of child, workman*) salopette *f*; (*jeans*) *Am* jean *m*.
dungeon ['dʌndʒən] *n* cachot *m*.
dunk [dʌŋk] *vt* (*bread etc*) tremper.
dupe [djuːp] *vt* duper.
duplex ['duːpleks] *n* (*apartment*) *Am* duplex *m*.
duplicate ['djuːplɪkeɪt] *vt* (*key etc*) faire un double de; (*on machine*) polycopier ▮ ['djuːplɪkət] *n* double *m*; **in d.** en deux exemplaires; **a d. copy** une copie en double; **a d. key** un double de la clef.
durable ['djʊərəb(ə)l] *a* (*material*) résistant; (*friendship*) durable.
duration [djʊə'reɪʃ(ə)n] *n* durée *f*.
duress [djʊ'res] *n* **under d.** sous la contrainte.
during ['djʊərɪŋ] *prep* pendant.
dusk [dʌsk] *n* (*twilight*) crépuscule *m*.
dust [dʌst] **1** *n* poussière *f*; **d. cloth** *Am* chiffon *m*; **d. cover** (*for furniture*) housse *f*; (*for book*) jaquette *f* ▮ *vt* (*furniture etc*) essuyer (la poussière de) ▮ *vi* faire la poussière. **2** *vt* (*sprinkle*) saupoudrer (**with** de). ● **dustbin** *n* poubelle *f*. ● **dustcart** *n* camion-benne *m*. ● **dustman** *n* (*pl* **-men**) éboueur *m*. ● **dustpan** *n* petite pelle *f* (à poussière).
duster ['dʌstər] *n* chiffon *m*.
dusty ['dʌstɪ] *a* (**-ier, -iest**) poussiéreux.
Dutch [dʌtʃ] *a* hollandais, néerlandais ▮ *n* (*language*) hollandais *m*; **the D.** (*people*) les Hollandais *mpl*. ● **Dutchman** *n* (*pl* **-men**) Hollandais *m*. ● **Dutchwoman** *n* (*pl* **-women**) Hollandaise *f*.
dutiful ['djuːtɪfəl] *a* (*son, child*) respectueux, obéissant.

duty ['dju:tɪ] *n* devoir *m*; (*tax*) droit *m*; *pl* (*responsibilities*) fonctions *fpl*; **on d.** (*policeman, teacher*) de service; (*doctor*) de garde; **off d.** libre. ● **d.-'free** *a* (*goods, shop*) hors-taxe *inv*.

duvet [du:'veɪ] *n* couette *f*.

dwarf [dwɔ:f] *n* (*pl* **dwarfs** *or* **dwarves**) nain *m*, naine *f*.

dwell [dwel] *vi* (*pt* & *pp* **dwelt** *or* **dwelled**) demeurer; **to d. on** penser sans cesse à; (*speak about*) parler sans cesse de. ● **—ing** *n* habitation *f*.

dwindl/e ['dwɪnd(ə)l] *vt* diminuer (peu à peu). ● **—ing** *a* (*interest etc*) décroissant.

dye [daɪ] *n* teinture *f* ‖ *vt* teindre; **to d. green**/*etc* teindre en vert/*etc*.

dying ['daɪɪŋ] *pres p of* **die 1** ‖ *a* (*person*) mourant; (*custom*) qui se perd; (*words*) dernier.

dyke [daɪk] *n* (*wall*) digue *f*.

dynamic [daɪ'næmɪk] *a* dynamique.

dynamite ['daɪnəmaɪt] *n* dynamite *f* ‖ *vt* dynamiter.

dynamo ['daɪnəməʊ] *n* (*pl* **-os**) dynamo *f*.

dysentery ['dɪsəntrɪ] *n Med* dysenterie *f*.

dyslexic [dɪs'leksɪk] *a* & *n* dyslexique (*mf*).

E

E, e [iː] *n* E, e *m*.

each [iːtʃ] *a* chaque ▮ *pron* **e. (one)** chacun, -une; **e. other** l'un(e) l'autre, *pl* les un(e)s les autres; **to see e. other** se voir (l'un(e) l'autre); **e. of us** chacun, -une d'entre nous.

eager ['iːgər] *a* impatient (**to do** de faire); (*enthusiastic*) plein d'enthousiasme; **to be e. for** désirer vivement; **to be e. to do** (*want*) tenir (beaucoup) à faire. ●**—ly** *adv* (*to work etc*) avec enthousiasme; (*to await*) avec impatience. ●**—ness** *n* impatience *f* (**to do** de faire); (*zeal*) enthousiasme *m* (**for sth** pour qch).

eagle ['iːg(ə)l] *n* aigle *m*.

ear[1] [ɪər] *n* oreille *f*; **all ears** *Fam* tout ouïe; **to play it by e.** *Fam* agir selon la situation. ●**earache** *n* mal *m* d'oreille. ●**eardrum** *n* tympan *m*.

ear[2] [ɪər] *n* (*of corn*) épi *m*.

earl [ɜːl] *n* comte *m*.

early ['ɜːlɪ] *a* (**-ier, -iest**) (*first*) premier; (*death*) prématuré; (*age*) jeune; (*painting, work*) de jeunesse; (*reply*) rapide; (*retirement*) anticipé; (*ancient*) ancien; **it's e.** (*on clock*) il est tôt; (*referring to meeting etc*) c'est tôt; **it's too e. to get up** il est trop tôt pour se lever; **to be e.** (*ahead of time*) être en avance; (*in getting up*) être matinal; **to have an e. meal/night** manger/se coucher de bonne heure; **in e. summer** au début de l'été.

▮ *adv* tôt, de bonne heure; (*ahead of time*) en avance; (*to book*) à l'avance; (*to die*) prématurément; **as e. as possible** le plus tôt possible; **earlier (on)** plus tôt; **at the earliest** au plus tôt.

earmark ['ɪəmɑːk] *vt* (*funds*) assigner (**for** à).

earmuffs ['ɪəmʌfs] *npl* protège-oreilles *m inv*.

earn [ɜːn] *vt* gagner; (*interest*) *Fin* rapporter. ●**—ings** *npl* (*wages*) rémunérations *fpl*; (*profits*) bénéfices *mpl*.

earnest ['ɜːnɪst] *a* sérieux; (*sincere*) sincère ▮ *n* **in e.** sérieusement; **it's raining in e.** il pleut pour de bon; **he's in e.** il est sérieux.

earphones ['ɪəfəʊnz] *npl* casque *m*. ●**earplug** *n* boule *f* Quiès®. ●**earring** *n* boucle *f* d'oreille. ●**earshot** *n* **within e.** à portée de voix.

earth [ɜːθ] *n* (*world, ground*) terre *f*; *El* terre *f*, masse *f*; **nothing/nobody on e.** rien/personne au monde; **where/what on e.?** où/que diable?

earthenware ['ɜːθənweər] *n* faïence *f* ▮ *a* en faïence.

earthly ['ɜːθlɪ] *a* (*possessions*) terrestre; **for no e. reason** *Fam* sans la moindre raison.

earthquake ['ɜːθkweɪk] *n* tremblement *m* de terre.

earwig ['ɪəwɪg] *n* (*insect*) perce-oreille *m*.

ease [iːz] **1** *n* (*facility*) facilité *f*; (*physical*) bien-être *m*; (*mental*) tranquillité *f*; **with e.** facilement; **(ill) at e.** (mal) à l'aise; **at e.** (*of mind*) tranquille.

2 *vt* (*pain*) soulager; (*mind*) calmer; (*tension*) diminuer; **to e. sth off/along** enlever/déplacer qch doucement; **to e. oneself through** se glisser par.

▮ *vi* **to e. (off** *or* **up)** (*become less*) (*of pressure*) diminuer; (*of demand*) baisser; (*of pain*) se calmer; (*not work so hard*) se relâcher.

easel ['iːz(ə)l] *n* chevalet *m*.

easily ['iːzɪlɪ] *adv* facilement; **e. the best**/*etc* de loin le meilleur/*etc*.

east [iːst] *n* est *m*; **(to the) e. of** à l'est de; **the E.** (*Eastern Europe*) l'Est *m*; (*Orient*) l'Orient *m*.

▮ *a* (*coast*) est *inv*; (*wind*) d'est; **E. Africa** Afrique *f* orientale.

▮ *adv* à l'est, vers l'est. ●**eastbound** *a* (*traffic*) en direction de l'est. ●**easterly** *a* (*point*) est *inv*; (*direction*) de l'est; (*wind*) d'est. ●**eastern** *a* (*coast*) est *inv*; **E. France** l'Est *m* de la France; **E. Europe** Europe *f* de l'Est. ●**eastward(s)** *a* & *adv* vers l'est.

Easter ['iːstər] *n* Pâques *m sing or fpl*; **Happy E.!** joyeuses Pâques!; **E. egg** œuf *m* de Pâques.

easy ['iːzɪ] *a* (**-ier, -iest**) facile; (*life*) tranquille; (*pace*) modéré; **it's e. to do** c'est facile à faire; **e. chair** fauteuil *m* (rembourré).

▮ *adv* doucement; **go e. on** (*sugar etc*) vas-y doucement avec; (*person*) ne sois pas trop dur avec; **take it e.** (*rest*) repose-toi; (*work less*) ne te fatigue pas; (*calm down*) calme-toi; (*go slow*) ne te presse pas. ●**easy'going** *a* (*carefree*) insouciant; (*easy to get along with*) facile à vivre.

eat [iːt] *vt* (*pt* **ate** [et, *Am* eɪt], *pp* **eaten** ['iːt(ə)n]) manger; (*meal*) prendre; **to e. sth**

up (*finish*) finir qch ‖ *vi* manger; **to e. into sth** (*of acid*) ronger qch; **to e. out** manger dehors; **eating place** restaurant *m*. • **eater** *n* **big e.** gros mangeur *m*, grosse mangeuse *f*.

eau de Cologne [əʊdəkə'ləʊn] *n* eau *f* de Cologne.

eaves [i:vz] *npl* avant-toit *m*. • **eavesdrop** *vti* (**-pp-**) **to e. (on)** écouter (de façon indiscrète).

ebb [eb] *n* reflux *m*; **e. and flow** le flux et le reflux; **at a low e.** (*patient, spirits*) *Fig* très bas ‖ *vi* refluer; **to e. (away)** (*of strength*) *Fig* décliner.

ebony ['ebənɪ] *n* (*wood*) ébène *f*.

EC [i:'si:] *n abbr* (*European Community*) CEE *f*.

eccentric [ɪk'sentrɪk] *a* & *n* excentrique (*mf*).

echo ['ekəʊ] *n* (*pl* **-oes**) écho *m* ‖ *vt* (*sound*) répercuter; (*repeat*) *Fig* répéter ‖ *vi* **the explosion/***etc* **echoed** l'écho de l'explosion/*etc* se répercuta; **the room/***etc* **echoes** la pièce/*etc* est sonore.

éclair [eɪ'kleər] *n* (*cake*) éclair *m*.

eclipse [ɪ'klɪps] *n* (*of sun etc*) éclipse *f*.

ecology [ɪ'kɒlədʒɪ] *n* écologie *f*.

economic [i:kə'nɒmɪk] *a* économique; (*profitable*) rentable. • **economical** *a* économique; (*thrifty*) économe. • **economics** *n* science *f* économique; (*of a business etc*) aspect *m* financier.

economy [ɪ'kɒnəmɪ] *n* économie *f*; **e. class** (*on aircraft*) classe *f* touriste. • **economist** *n* économiste *mf*. • **economize** *vti* économiser (**on** sur).

ecstasy ['ekstəsɪ] *n* extase *f*. • **ec'static** *a* extasié; **to be e. about** s'extasier sur.

ECU [eɪ'kju:] *n abbr* (*European Currency Unit*) ECU *m inv*.

eczema ['eksɪmə] *n Med* eczéma *m*.

edge [edʒ] *n* bord *m*; (*of forest*) lisière *f*; (*of town*) abords *mpl*; (*of page*) marge *f*; (*of knife*) tranchant *m*; **on e.** (*person*) énervé; (*nerves*) tendu ‖ *vt* (*clothing etc*) border (**with** de) ‖ *vti* **to e. (oneself) into** (*move*) se glisser dans; **to e. (oneself) forward** avancer doucement. • **edging** *n* (*border*) bordure *f*.

edgeways [e'dʒweɪz] (*Am* **edgewise**) *adv* **to get a word in e.** *Fam* placer un mot.

edgy ['edʒɪ] *a* (**-ier, -iest**) énervé.

edible ['edɪb(ə)l] *a* (*mushroom etc*) comestible; (*not unpleasant*) mangeable.

edifice ['edɪfɪs] *n* (*building*) édifice *m*.

Edinburgh ['edɪnb(ə)rə] *n* Édimbourg *m or f*.

edit ['edɪt] *vt* (*newspaper*) diriger; (*article*) mettre au point; (*film*) monter; (*text*) éditer; (*compile*) rédiger (*dictionnaire etc*); (*cut out*) couper.

editor ['edɪtər] *n* (*of newspaper*) rédacteur, -trice *mf* en chef; (*of review*) directeur, -trice *mf*; (*compiler of dictionary, newspaper column*) rédacteur, -trice *mf*; (*of text*) éditeur, -trice *mf*; (*proofreader*) correcteur, -trice *mf*; *TV Rad* réalisateur, -trice *mf*; **the e. in chief** (*of newspaper*) le rédacteur *or* la rédactrice en chef. • **edi'torial** *a* de la rédaction; **e. staff** rédaction *f* ‖ *n* éditorial *m*.

edition [ɪ'dɪʃ(ə)n] *n* édition *f*.

educate ['edjʊkeɪt] *vt* (*family, children*) éduquer; (*in school*) instruire; (*pupil, mind*) former, éduquer; **to be educated at** faire ses études à; **(well-)educated** (*person*) instruit. • **education** [-'keɪʃ(ə)n] *n* éducation *f*; (*teaching*) instruction *f*, enseignement *m*; (*training*) formation *f*. • **edu'cational** *a* (*establishment*) d'enseignement; (*method, theory*) pédagogique; (*game, film*) éducatif; (*experience*) instructif.

EEC [i:i:'si:] *n abbr* (*European Economic Community*) CEE *f*.

eel [i:l] *n* anguille *f*.

eerie ['ɪərɪ] *a* (**-ier, -iest**) sinistre, étrange.

efface [ɪ'feɪs] *vt* effacer.

effect [ɪ'fekt] **1** *n* (*result, impression*) effet *m* (**on** sur); **in e.** en fait; **to put into e.** mettre en application; **to come into e., take e.** (*of law*) entrer en vigueur; **to take e.** (*of drug*) agir; **to have an e.** (*of medicine*) faire de l'effet; **to have no e.** rester sans effet. **2** *vt* (*carry out*) effectuer.

effective [ɪ'fektɪv] *a* (*efficient*) efficace; (*striking*) frappant; (*actual*) effectif; **to become e.** (*of law*) prendre effet. • **—ly** *adv* efficacement; (*in fact*) effectivement.

effeminate [ɪ'femɪnɪt] *a* efféminé.

efficient [ɪ'fɪʃ(ə)nt] *a* (*method, organization*) efficace; (*person*) compétent, efficace; (*machine*) performant. • **efficiency** *n* efficacité *f*; (*of machine*) performances *fpl*. • **efficiently** *adv* efficacement; **to work e.** (*of machine*) bien fonctionner.

effigy ['efɪdʒɪ] *n* effigie *f*.

effort ['efət] *n* effort *m*; **to make an e.** faire un effort (**to** pour); **it isn't worth the e.** ça ne *or* n'en vaut pas la peine. • **effortlessly** *adv* facilement, sans effort.

effusive [ɪ'fju:sɪv] *a* (*person*) expansif; (*thanks, excuses*) sans fin.

e.g. [i:'dʒi:] *abbr* (*exempli gratia*) par exemple.

egg[1] [eg] *n* œuf *m*; **e. timer** sablier *m*;

• **eggcup** *n* coquetier *m*. • **eggplant** *n Am* aubergine *f*. • **eggshell** *n* coquille *f* (d'œuf).
egg² [eg] *vt* **to e. on** (*encourage*) inciter (**to do** à faire).
ego ['iːgəʊ] *n* (*pl* **-os**) **the e.** l'ego *m*; **one's e.** (*self-image*) son image *f* de soi; (*self-esteem*) son amour-propre *m*. • **egoist** ['egəʊɪst] *n* égoïste *mf*.
Egypt ['iːdʒɪpt] *n* Égypte *f*. • **Egyptian** [ɪ'dʒɪpʃən] *a* & *n* égyptien, -ienne (*mf*).
eh? [eɪ] *int Fam* hein?
eiderdown ['aɪdədaʊn] *n* édredon *m*.
eight [eɪt] *a* & *n* huit (*m*). • **eigh'teen** *a* & *n* dix-huit (*m*). • **eighth** *a* & *n* huitième (*mf*). • **eightieth** *a* & *n* quatre-vingtième (*mf*). • **eighty** *a* & *n* quatre-vingts (*m*); **e.-one** quatre-vingt-un.
Eire ['eərə] *n* Eire *f*, République *f* d'Irlande.
either ['aɪðər] **1** *a* & *pron* (*one or other*) l'un(e) ou l'autre; (*with negative*) ni l'un(e) ni l'autre; (*each*) chaque; **on e. side** de chaque côté. **2** *adv* **she can't swim e.** elle ne sait pas nager non plus; **I don't e.** (ni) moi non plus. **3** *conj* **e. ... or** ou (bien) ... ou (bien), soit ... soit; (*with negative*) ni ... ni.
eject [ɪ'dʒekt] *vt* (*from hall etc*) expulser (*qn*) (**from** de) ▮ *vi* (*of pilot*) s'éjecter.
eke [iːk] *vt* **to e. out** (*income*) faire durer; **to e. out a living** gagner (difficilement) sa vie.
elaborate [ɪ'læbərət] *a* compliqué; (*preparation*) minutieux; (*meal*) raffiné ▮ [ɪ'læbəreɪt] *vt* (*theory*) élaborer ▮ *vi* entrer dans les détails (**on** de).
elapse [ɪ'læps] *vi* s'écouler.
elastic [ɪ'læstɪk] *a* élastique; **e. band** élastique *m* ▮ *n* (*fabric*) élastique *m*.
elated [ɪ'leɪtɪd] *a* transporté de joie.
elbow ['elbəʊ] *n* coude *m* ▮ *vt* **to e. one's way** se frayer un chemin (à coups de coude) (**through** à travers).
elder¹ ['eldər] *a* & *n* (*of two people*) aîné, -ée (*mf*).
elder² ['eldər] *n* (*tree*) sureau *m*.
elderly ['eldəlɪ] *a* assez âgé ▮ *n* **the e.** les personnes *fpl* âgées. • **eldest** *a* & *n* aîné, -ée (*mf*); **his** *or* **her e. brother** l'aîné de ses frères.
elect [ɪ'lekt] *vt* (*by voting*) élire (*qn*) (**to** à); **to e. to do** choisir de faire ▮ *a* **the president e.** le président désigné. • **election** [ɪ'lekʃ(ə)n] *n* élection *f*; **general e.** élections *fpl* législatives ▮ *a* (*campaign*) électoral; (*day*, *results*) du scrutin.
electoral [ɪ'lektər(ə)l] *a* électoral. • **electorate** [ɪ'lektərət] *n* électorat *m*.
electric [ɪ'lektrɪk] *a* électrique; **e. blanket** couverture *f* chauffante; **e. shock** décharge *f* électrique. • **electrical** *a* électrique. • **electrician** [-'trɪʃən] *n* électricien *m*. • **elec'tricity** *n* électricité *f*.
electrify [ɪ'lektrɪfaɪ] *vt Rail* électrifier; (*excite*) *Fig* électriser.
electrocute [ɪ'lektrəkjuːt] *vt* électrocuter.
electronic [ɪlektrɒnɪk] *a* électronique. • **electronics** *n* électronique *f*.
elegant ['elɪgənt] *a* élégant. • **elegance** *n* élégance *f*. • **elegantly** *adv* avec élégance.
element ['eləmənt] *n* (*component*, *chemical etc*) élément *m*; (*of heater*, *kettle*) résistance *f*; **an e. of truth** un grain de vérité; **the human e.** le facteur humain; **in one's e.** dans son élément.
elementary [elɪ'ment(ə)rɪ] *a* élémentaire; (*school*) *Am* primaire.
elephant ['elɪfənt] *n* éléphant *m*.
elevate ['elɪveɪt] *vt* élever (**to** à). • **elevation** [-'veɪʃ(ə)n] *n* élévation *f* (**of** de); (*height*) altitude *f*.
elevator ['elɪveɪtər] *n Am* ascenseur *m*.
eleven [ɪ'lev(ə)n] *a* & *n* onze (*m*). • **elevenses** [ɪ'lev(ə)nzɪz] *n Fam* pause-café *f* (*vers onze heures du matin*). • **eleventh** *a* & *n* onzième (*mf*).
elf [elf] *n* (*pl* **elves**) lutin *m*.
elicit [ɪ'lɪsɪt] *vt* tirer, obtenir (**from** de).
elision [ɪ'lɪʒ(ə)n] *n* (*of vowel*) élision *f*.
eligible ['elɪdʒəb(ə)l] *a* (*for post etc*) admissible (**for** à); **to be e. for sth** (*entitled to*) avoir droit à qch; **an e. young man** (*suitable as husband*) un beau parti.
eliminate [ɪ'lɪmɪneɪt] *vt* supprimer (**from** de); (*applicant*, *possibility*) éliminer.
elite [eɪ'liːt] *n* élite *f* (**of** de).
elk [elk] *n* (*animal*) élan *m*.
elm [elm] *n* (*tree*, *wood*) orme *m*.
elocution [elə'kjuːʃ(ə)n] *n* élocution *f*.
elongated ['iːlɒŋgeɪtɪd] *a* allongé.
elope [ɪ'ləʊp] *vi* s'enfuir (**with** avec).
eloquent ['eləkwənt] *a* éloquent.
else [els] *adv* d'autre; **someone e.** quelqu'un d'autre; **everybody e.** tous les autres; **nobody/nothing e.** personne/rien d'autre; **something e.** autre chose; **anything e.?** (*in shop etc*) autre chose?; **anything e. to add?** encore quelque chose à ajouter?; **somewhere e.** ailleurs, autre part; **nowhere e.** nulle part ailleurs; **who e.?** qui d'autre?; **how e.?** de quelle autre façon?; **or e.** ou bien, sinon. • **elsewhere** *adv* ailleurs.
elude [ɪ'luːd] *vt* (*of word*, *name*) échapper à (*qn*); (*question*) éluder; (*blow*) esquiver. • **elusive** *a* (*enemy*, *aims*) insaisissable; (*reply*) évasif.

emaciated [ɪ'meɪsɪeɪtɪd] *a* émacié.
embankment [ɪm'bæŋkmənt] *n* (*of path etc*) talus *m*; (*of river*) berge *f*.
embargo [ɪm'bɑːgəʊ] *n* (*pl* **-oes**) embargo *m*.
embark [ɪm'bɑːk] *vi* (s')embarquer; **to e. on** (*start*) commencer; (*launch into*) se lancer dans. ●**embarkation** [embɑː'keɪʃ(ə)n] *n* embarquement *m*.
embarrass [ɪm'bærəs] *vt* embarrasser, gêner. ●**—ing** *a* (*question etc*) embarrassant. ●**—ment** *n* embarras *m*, gêne *f*.
embassy ['embəsɪ] *n* ambassade *f*.
embedded [ɪm'bedɪd] *a* (*stick, bullet etc*) enfoncé (**in** dans).
embellish [ɪm'belɪʃ] *vt* embellir.
embers ['embəz] *npl* braise(s) *f(pl)*.
embezzl/e [ɪm'bez(ə)l] *vt* (*money*) détourner. ●**—er** *n* escroc *m*, voleur *m*.
embittered [ɪm'bɪtəd] *a* (*person*) aigri.
emblem ['embləm] *n* emblème *m*.
embody [ɪm'bɒdɪ] *vt* (*express*) exprimer; (*represent*) incarner; (*include*) réunir.
embossed [ɪm'bɒst] *a* (*pattern, characters*) en relief; (*paper*) gaufré.
embrace [ɪm'breɪs] *vt* prendre dans ses bras, étreindre; (*include, adopt*) embrasser ▮ *vi* s'étreindre, s'embrasser ▮ *n* étreinte *f*.
embroider [ɪm'brɔɪdər] *vt* (*cloth*) broder. ●**embroidery** *n* broderie *f*.
embryo ['embrɪəʊ] *n* (*pl* **-os**) embryon *m*.
emcee [em'siː] *n Am* présentateur, -trice *mf*.
emerald ['emərəld] *n* émeraude *f*.
emerge [ɪ'mɜːdʒ] *vi* apparaître (**from** de); (*from hole*) sortir; (*of truth, from water*) émerger; **it emerges that** il apparaît que.
emergency [ɪ'mɜːdʒənsɪ] *n* urgence *f*; **in an e.** en cas d'urgence ▮ *a* (*measure etc*) d'urgence; (*exit, brake*) de secours; **e. ward** *or Am* **room** salle *f* des urgences; **e. landing** atterrissage *m* forcé.
emery ['emərɪ] *a* **e. board** lime *f* à ongles en carton.
emigrant ['emɪgrənt] *n* émigrant, -ante *mf*. ●**emigrate** *vi* émigrer.
eminent ['emɪnənt] *a* éminent.
emission [ɪ'mɪʃ(ə)n] *n* (*of pollutant*) émission *f*.
emotion [ɪ'məʊʃ(ə)n] *n* (*strength of feeling*) émotion *f*; (*joy, love etc*) sentiment *m*. ●**emotional** *a* (*person, reaction*) émotif; (*story, speech*) émouvant; (*moment*) d'intense émotion. ●**emotive** *a* (*word*) affectif; **an e. issue** une question sensible.
emperor ['empərər] *n* empereur *m*.
emphasize ['emfəsaɪz] *vt* souligner (**that** que); (*word, fact, syllable*) appuyer sur.
emphasis ['emfəsɪs] *n* (*in word or phrase*) accent *m*; (*insistence*) insistance *f*; **to lay** *or* **put e. on** mettre l'accent sur.
emphatic [em'fætɪk] *a* (*refusal etc*) (*clear*) catégorique; (*forceful*) énergique; **to be e. about** insister sur; **she was e.** elle a été catégorique. ●**emphatically** *adv* (*to refuse etc*) catégoriquement; énergiquement.
empire ['empaɪər] *n* empire *m*.
employ [ɪm'plɔɪ] *vt* (*person, means*) employer. ●**employee** [ɪm'plɔɪiː] *n* employé, -ée *mf*. ●**employer** *n* patron, -onne *mf*. ●**employment** *n* emploi *m*; **place of e.** lieu *m* de travail; **e. agency** bureau *m* de placement.
empress ['emprɪs] *n* impératrice *f*.
empty ['emptɪ] *a* (**-ier, -iest**) vide; (*threat, promise etc*) vain; **on an e. stomach** à jeun; **to return e.-handed** revenir les mains vides.
▮ *n* **empties** (*bottles*) bouteilles *fpl* vides.
▮ *vt* **to e. (out)** (*box, liquid etc*) vider; (*vehicle*) décharger; (*objects in box etc*) sortir (**from** de).
▮ *vi* (*of building, tank etc*) se vider. ●**emptiness** *n* vide *m*.
emulsion [ɪ'mʌlʃ(ə)n] *n* (*paint*) peinture *f* acrylique (mate).
enable [ɪ'neɪb(ə)l] *vt* **to e. s.o. to do** permettre à qn de faire.
enamel [ɪ'næm(ə)l] *n* émail *m* (*pl* émaux) ▮ *a* en émail.
enamoured [ɪn'æməd] *a* **e. of** (*thing*) séduit par; (*person*) amoureux de.
encase [ɪn'keɪs] *vt* (*cover*) recouvrir (**in** de).
enchanting [ɪn'tʃɑːntɪŋ] *a* enchanteur.
encircle [ɪn'sɜːk(ə)l] *vt* entourer; *Mil* encercler.
enclos/e [ɪn'kləʊz] *vt* (*send with letter*) joindre (**in, with** à); (*fence off*) clôturer; **to e. sth with** (*a wall etc*) entourer qch de. ●**—ed** *a* (*space*) clos; (*receipt etc*) ci-joint; (*market*) couvert.
enclosure [ɪn'kləʊʒər] *n* (*in letter*) pièce *f* jointe; (*place*) enceinte *f*.
encompass [ɪn'kʌmpəs] *vt* (*include*) inclure.
encore ['ɒŋkɔːr] *int* & *n* bis (*m*).
encounter [ɪn'kaʊntər] *vt* rencontrer ▮ *n* rencontre *f*.
encourage [ɪn'kʌrɪdʒ] *vt* encourager (**to do** à faire). ●**—ment** *n* encouragement *m*.
encroach [ɪn'krəʊtʃ] *vi* empiéter (**on, upon** sur).
encyclop(a)edia [ɪnsaɪklə'piːdɪə] *n* encyclopédie *f*.
end [end] *n* (*of street, box etc*) bout *m*; (*of

meeting, month, book etc) fin *f*; (*purpose*) fin *f*, but *m*; **at an e.** (*discussion etc*) fini; (*patience*) à bout; **in the e.** à la fin; **to come to an e.** prendre fin; **to put an e. to, bring to an e.** mettre fin à; **there's no e. to it** ça n'en finit plus; **no e. of** *Fam* beaucoup de; **six days on e.** six jours d'affilée; **for days on e.** pendant des jours et des jours; **to stand a box on e.** mettre une boîte debout.
▮ *a* (*row, house*) dernier; **e. product** *Com* produit *m* fini; *Fig* résultat *m*.
▮ *vt* finir, terminer (**with** par); (*rumour*) mettre fin à.
▮ *vi* finir, se terminer; **to e. in failure** se solder par un échec; **to e. up doing** finir par faire; **to e. up in** (*London etc*) se retrouver à; **he ended up in prison/a doctor** il a fini en prison/médecin.

endanger [ɪn'deɪndʒər] *vt* mettre en danger; **endangered species** espèce *f* menacée.

endearing [ɪn'dɪərɪŋ] *a* (*person*) sympathique.

endeavour [ɪn'devər] (*Am* **endeavor**) *vi* s'efforcer (**to do** de faire) ▮ *n* effort *m* (**to do** pour faire).

ending ['endɪŋ] *n* fin *f*; (*of word*) terminaison *f*.

endive ['endɪv, *Am* 'endaɪv] *n* (*curly*) chicorée *f*; (*smooth*) endive *f*.

endless ['endləs] *a* (*speech, series etc*) interminable; (*countless*) innombrable. ●**—ly** *adv* interminablement.

endorse [ɪn'dɔːs] *vt* (*cheque, Am check*) endosser; (*action, plan*) approuver. ●**—ment** *n* (*on driving licence*) = point(s) enlevé(s) sur le permis de conduire.

endow [ɪn'daʊ] *vt* (*institution*) doter (**with** de); **endowed with** (*person*) *Fig* doté de.

endure [ɪn'djʊər] **1** *vt* (*bear*) supporter (**doing** de faire). **2** *vi* (*last*) durer. ●**endurance** *n* endurance *f*, résistance *f*.

enemy ['enəmɪ] *n* ennemi, -ie *mf*; **the e.** *Mil* l'ennemi *m* ▮ *a* (*tank etc*) ennemi.

energy ['enədʒɪ] *n* énergie *f* ▮ *a* (*crisis, resources etc*) énergétique. ●**ener'getic** *a* énergique; **to feel e.** se sentir en pleine forme.

enforce [ɪn'fɔːs] *vt* (*law*) faire respecter; (*discipline*) imposer (**on** à).

engag/e [ɪn'geɪdʒ] *vt* (*take on*) engager, prendre ▮ *vi* **to e. in** (*launch into*) se lancer dans; (*be involved in*) être mêlé à. ●**—ed** *a* **1** (*person, toilet, phone*) occupé; **e. in doing** occupé à faire; **to be e. in business/***etc* être dans les affaires/*etc*. **2 e. (to be married)** fiancé; **to get e.** se fiancer.

engaging [ɪn'geɪdʒɪŋ] *a* (*smile*) engageant.

engagement [ɪn'geɪdʒmənt] *n* (*to marry*) fiançailles *fpl*; (*meeting*) rendez-vous *m inv*; (*undertaking*) engagement *m*; **e. ring** bague *f* de fiançailles.

engine ['endʒɪn] *n* *Aut* moteur *m*; *Rail* locomotive *f*; *Nau* machine *f*; **e. driver** mécanicien *m*.

engineer [endʒɪ'nɪər] *n* ingénieur *m*; (*repairer*) dépanneur, -euse *mf*; (*train driver*) *Am* mécanicien *m*; **civil e.** ingénieur *m* des travaux publics. ●**—ing** *n* ingénierie *f*; **(civil) e.** génie *m* civil; **(mechanical) e.** mécanique *f*.

England ['ɪŋglənd] *n* Angleterre *f*.

English ['ɪŋglɪʃ] *a* anglais; **the E. Channel** la Manche ▮ *n* (*language*) anglais *m*; **the E.** (*people*) les Anglais *mpl*. ●**Englishman** *n* (*pl* **-men**) Anglais *m*. ●**English-speaking** *a* anglophone. ●**Englishwoman** *n* (*pl* **-women**) Anglaise *f*.

engrav/e [ɪn'greɪv] *vt* graver. ●**—ing** *n* gravure *f*. ●**engraver** *n* graveur *m*.

engrossed [ɪn'grəʊst] *a* **e. in one's work/book** absorbé par son travail/dans sa lecture.

engulf [ɪn'gʌlf] *vt* engloutir.

enhance [ɪn'hɑːns] *vt* (*beauty etc*) rehausser; (*value*) augmenter.

enigma [ɪ'nɪgmə] *n* énigme *f*.

enjoy [ɪn'dʒɔɪ] *vt* aimer (**doing** faire); (*meal*) apprécier; (*good health etc*) jouir de; **to e. the evening** passer une bonne soirée; **to e. oneself** s'amuser; **to e. being in London/***etc* se plaire à Londres/*etc*. ●**—able** *a* agréable; (*meal*) excellent. ●**—ment** *n* plaisir *m*.

enlarge [ɪn'lɑːdʒ] *vt* agrandir ▮ *vi* s'agrandir. ●**—ment** *n* *Phot* agrandissement *m*.

enlighten [ɪn'laɪt(ə)n] *vt* éclairer (**s.o. on** *or* **about sth** qn sur qch). ●**—ing** *a* instructif.

enlist [ɪn'lɪst] *vi* (*in the army etc*) s'engager ▮ *vt* (*recruit*) engager; (*supporter*) recruter; (*support*) obtenir.

enliven [ɪn'laɪv(ə)n] *vt* (*meeting etc*) animer.

enormous [ɪ'nɔːməs] *a* énorme; (*explosion, blow*) terrible; (*success, patience*) immense. ●**—ly** *adv* (*very much*) énormément; (*very*) extrêmement.

enough [ɪ'nʌf] *a* & *n* assez (de); **e. time/cups/***etc* assez de temps/de tasses/*etc*; **to have e. to live on** avoir de quoi vivre; **to have e. to drink** avoir assez à boire; **to have had e. of** en avoir assez de; **that's e.** ça suffit, c'est assez ▮ *adv* (*to work etc*) assez; **big/good/***etc* **e.** assez grand/bon/*etc* (**to** pour); **strangely e., he left** chose curieuse, il est parti.

enquire [ɪn'kwaɪər] *vi* = **inquire.**
enquiry [ɪn'kwaɪərɪ] *n* = **inquiry.**
enrage [ɪn'reɪdʒ] *vt* mettre en rage.
enrich [ɪn'rɪtʃ] *vt* enrichir; (*soil*) fertiliser.
enrol [ɪn'rəʊl] (*Am* **enroll**) *vi* (**-ll-**) s'inscrire (**in, for** à) ‖ *vt* inscrire. ●**—ment** (*Am* **enrollment**) *n* inscription *f*.
ensemble [ɒn'sɒmb(ə)l] *n* (*clothes*) & *Mus* ensemble *m*.
ensu/e [ɪn'sjuː] *vi* s'ensuivre. ●**—ing** *a* (*day, year etc*) suivant; (*event*) qui s'ensuit.
ensure [ɪn'ʃʊər] *vt* assurer; **to e. that** (*make sure*) s'assurer que.
entail [ɪn'teɪl] *vt* (*imply, involve*) supposer.
entangle [ɪn'tæŋg(ə)l] *vt* emmêler, enchevêtrer; **to get entangled** s'empêtrer (**in** dans).
enter ['entər] *vt* (*room, vehicle, army etc*) entrer dans; (*road*) s'engager dans; (*university*) s'inscrire à; (*write down*) inscrire (**in** dans, **on** sur); (*introduce*) *Comptr* entrer, introduire (*données etc*); **to e. s.o. for** (*exam*) présenter qn à; **to e. a painting/** *etc* **in** (*competition*) présenter un tableau/*etc* à; **it didn't e. my head** *or* **mind** ça ne m'est pas venu à l'esprit (**that** que).
‖ *vi* entrer; **to e. for** (*race, exam*) s'inscrire pour; **to e. into** (*conversation, relations*) entrer en; (*career*) entrer dans; (*negotiations, explanation*) entamer; (*agreement*) conclure.
enterpris/e ['entəpraɪz] *n* (*undertaking, firm*) entreprise *f*; (*spirit*) initiative *f*. ●**—ing** *a* (*person*) plein d'initiative.
entertain [entə'teɪn] *vt* amuser, distraire; (*guest*) recevoir; (*idea, possibility*) envisager; (*hope*) nourrir ‖ *vi* (*receive guests*) recevoir. ●**—ing** *a* amusant. ●**entertainer** *n* artiste *mf*. ●**entertainment** *n* amusement *m*, distraction *f*; (*show*) spectacle *m*.
enthral(l) [ɪn'θrɔːl] *vt* (**-ll-**) (*delight*) captiver.
enthuse [ɪn'θjuːz] *vi* **to e. over** *Fam* s'emballer pour.
enthusiasm [ɪn'θjuːzɪæz(ə)m] *n* enthousiasme *m*. ●**enthusiast** *n* enthousiaste *mf*; **jazz/***etc* **e.** passionné, -ée *mf* de jazz/*etc*.
enthusiastic [ɪnθuːzɪ'æstɪk] *a* enthousiaste; (*golfer etc*) passionné; **to be e. about** (*hobby*) être passionné de; (*gift etc*) être emballé par; **to get e.** s'emballer (**about** pour). ●**enthusiastically** *adv* avec enthousiasme.
entic/e [ɪn'taɪs] *vt* attirer (par la ruse) (**into** dans); **to e. s.o. to do** entraîner qn (par la ruse) à faire. ●**—ing** *a* séduisant.
entire [ɪn'taɪər] *a* entier. ●**—ly** *adv* tout à fait, entièrement. ●**entirety** [ɪn'taɪərətɪ] *n* **in its e.** en entier.
entitl/e [ɪn'taɪt(ə)l] *vt* **to e. s.o. to do** donner à qn le droit de faire; **to e. s.o. to sth** donner à qn (le) droit à qch. ●**—ed** *a* (*book*) intitulé; **to be e. to do** avoir le droit de faire; **to be e. to sth** avoir droit à qch.
entity ['entɪtɪ] *n* entité *f*.
entrance ['entrəns] *n* entrée *f* (**to** de); (*to university*) admission *f* (**to** à); **e. examination** examen *m* d'entrée.
entrant ['entrənt] *n* (*in race*) concurrent, -ente *mf*; (*for exam*) candidat, -ate *mf*.
entreat [ɪn'triːt] *vt* supplier (**to do** de faire).
entrée ['ɒntreɪ] *n* (*main dish*) *Am* plat *m* principal.
entrench [ɪn'trentʃ] *vt* **to e. oneself** *Mil* & *Fig* se retrancher.
entrust [ɪn'trʌst] *vt* confier (**to** à); **to e. s.o. with sth** confier qch à qn.
entry ['entrɪ] *n* (*way in, action*) entrée *f*; (*bookkeeping item*) écriture *f*; (*term in dictionary or logbook*) entrée *f*; (*thing to be judged in competition*) objet *m* (*or* œuvre *f or* projet *m*) soumis au jury; **e. form** feuille *f* d'inscription; **'no e.'** (*on door etc*) 'entrée interdite'; (*road sign*) 'sens interdit'.
enumerate [ɪ'njuːməreɪt] *vt* énumérer.
enunciate [ɪ'nʌnsɪeɪt] *vt* (*word*) articuler.
envelop [ɪn'veləp] *vt* envelopper (**in mystery/***etc* de mystère/*etc*).
envelope ['envələʊp] *n* enveloppe *f*.
envious ['envɪəs] *a* envieux (**of sth** de qch); **e. of s.o.** jaloux de qn. ●**enviable** *a* enviable.
environment [ɪn'vaɪərənmənt] *n* milieu *m*; **the e.** (*natural*) l'environnement *m*; **e.-friendly** (*product*) qui ne nuit pas à l'environnement. ●**environ'mental** *a* du milieu; de l'environnement, écologique.
envisage [ɪn'vɪzɪdʒ] *vt* (*imagine*) envisager (**doing** de faire); (*foresee*) prévoir.
envision [ɪn'vɪʒ(ə)n] *vt Am* = **envisage.**
envoy ['envɔɪ] *n* (*messenger*) envoyé, -ée *mf*.
envy ['envɪ] *n* envie *f* ‖ *vt* envier (**s.o. sth** qch à qn).
epic ['epɪk] *a* épique ‖ *n* épopée *f*; **(screen) e.** film *m* à grand spectacle.
epidemic [epɪ'demɪk] *n* épidémie *f*.
epidural [epɪ'djʊərəl] *n Med* (anesthésie *f*) péridurale *f*.
epilepsy ['epɪlepsɪ] *n* épilepsie *f*. ●**epi'leptic** *a* & *n* épileptique (*mf*).
episode ['epɪsəʊd] *n* épisode *m*.
epitaph ['epɪtɑːf] *n* épitaphe *f*.
epithet ['epɪθet] *n* épithète *f*.

epitome [ɪ'pɪtəmɪ] *n* **the e. of** l'exemple même de. ● **epitomize** *vt* incarner.
epoch ['iːpɒk] *n* époque *f*. ● **e.-making** *a* (*event*) qui fait date.
equal ['iːkwəl] *a* égal (**to** à); **with e. hostility** avec la même hostilité; **on an e. footing** sur un pied d'égalité (**with** avec); **to be e. to** (*in quantity*, *number*) égaler; **e. to** (*task*) *Fig* à la hauteur de.
▮ *n* (*person*) égal, -ale *mf*; **to treat s.o. as an e.** traiter qn en égal *or* d'égal à égal.
▮ *vt* (**-ll-**, *Am* **-l-**) égaler (**in beauty**/*etc* en beauté/*etc*); **equals sign** *Math* signe *m* d'égalité. ● **equally** *adv* (*to an equal degree*, *also*) également; (*to divide*) en parts égales; **he's e. stupid** (*just as*) il est tout aussi bête.
equality [ɪ'kwɒlɪtɪ] *n* égalité *f*.
equalize ['iːkwəlaɪz] *vi* (*score*) *Sp* égaliser.
equate [ɪ'kweɪt] *vt* mettre sur le même pied (**with** que), assimiler (**with** à).
equation [ɪ'kweɪʒ(ə)n] *n Math* équation *f*.
equator [ɪ'kweɪtər] *n* équateur *m*; **at** *or* **on the e.** sous l'équateur.
equilibrium [iːkwɪ'lɪbrɪəm] *n* équilibre *m*.
equinox ['ɪːkwɪnɒks] *n* équinoxe *m*.
equip [ɪ'kwɪp] *vt* (**-pp-**) équiper (**with** de); **(well-)equipped with** pourvu de; **(well-)equipped to do** compétent pour faire. ● **—ment** *n* équipement *m*, matériel *m*.
equities ['ekwɪtɪz] *npl* (*shares*) *Com* actions *fpl* (ordinaires).
equivalent [ɪ'kwɪvələnt] *a* & *n* équivalent (*m*). ● **equivalence** *n* équivalence *f*.
era ['ɪərə, *Am* 'erə] *n* époque *f*; (*historical*, *geological*) ère *f*.
eradicate [ɪ'rædɪkeɪt] *vt* supprimer; (*evil*, *prejudice*) extirper.
erase [ɪ'reɪz, *Am* ɪ'reɪs] *vt* effacer. ● **eraser** *n* (*rubber for pencil marks*) gomme *f*.
erect [ɪ'rekt] **1** *a* (*upright*) (bien) droit. **2** *vt* (*build*) construire; (*statue*, *monument*) ériger; (*scaffolding*, *tent*) monter.
erode [ɪ'rəʊd] *vt* éroder; (*confidence etc*) *Fig* miner, ronger.
erotic [ɪ'rɒtɪk] *a* érotique.
err [ɜːr] *vi* (*be wrong*) se tromper.
errand ['erənd] *n* commission *f*, course *f*.
erratic [ɪ'rætɪk] *a* (*service*, *machine etc*) capricieux, fantaisiste; (*person*, *behaviour*) lunatique; (*results etc*) irrégulier.
error ['erər] *n* (*mistake*) erreur *f*; **to do sth in e.** faire qch par erreur.
erupt [ɪ'rʌpt] *vi* (*of volcano*) entrer en éruption; (*of war*, *violence*) éclater. ● **eruption** [-ʃ(ə)n] *n* (*of volcano*) éruption *f* (**of** de); (*of violence*) flambée *f*.
escalate ['eskəleɪt] *vi* (*of war*, *violence*) s'intensifier; (*of prices*) monter en flèche.
escalator ['eskəleɪtər] *n* escalier *m* roulant.
escapade ['eskəpeɪd] *n* (*prank*) frasque *f*.
escape [ɪ'skeɪp] *vi* (*of gas*, *animal*, *prisoner etc*) s'échapper; **to e. from** (*person*) échapper à; (*place*) s'échapper de; **escaped prisoner** évadé, -ée *mf*.
▮ *vt* (*death*) échapper à; (*punishment*) éviter; **that name escapes me** ce nom m'échappe.
▮ *n* (*of gas*) fuite *f*; (*of person*) évasion *f*, fuite *f*; **to have a lucky** *or* **narrow e.** l'échapper belle.
escort ['eskɔːt] *n Mil Nau* escorte *f*; (*of woman*) cavalier *m* ▮ [ɪ'skɔːt] *vt* escorter.
Eskimo ['eskɪməʊ] *n* (*pl* **-os**) Esquimau, -aude *mf* ▮ *a* esquimau (*inv or f* -aude).
esoteric [esəʊ'terɪk] *a* obscur, ésotérique.
especially [ɪ'speʃəlɪ] *adv* (tout) spécialement; (*particularly*) particulièrement; **e. as** d'autant plus que.
espionage ['espɪənɑːʒ] *n* espionnage *m*.
esplanade ['esplənеɪd] *n* esplanade *f*.
espresso [e'spresəʊ] *n* (*pl* **-os**) (café *m*) express *m*.
Esq [ɪ'skwaɪər] *abbr* (*esquire*) **J. Smith Esq** (*on envelope*) Monsieur J. Smith.
essay ['eseɪ] *n Sch* rédaction *f*; *Univ* dissertation *f*; (*literary*) essai *m* (**on** sur).
essence ['esəns] *n* essence *f*; *Culin* extrait *m*; (*main point*) essentiel *m* (**of** de); **in e.** essentiellement.
essential [ɪ'senʃ(ə)l] *a* (*principal*, *necessary*) essentiel; **it's e. that** il est indispensable que (+ *sub*) ▮ *npl* **the essentials** l'essentiel *m* (**of** de); (*of grammar*) les éléments *mpl*. ● **—ly** *adv* essentiellement.
establish [ɪ'stæblɪʃ] *vt* établir; (*state*, *society*) fonder; **(well-)established** (*business company*) solide; (*fact*) reconnu; **she's (well-)established** elle a une réputation établie. ● **—ment** *n* (*institution*, *business company*) établissement *m*; **the E.** les classes *fpl* dirigeantes.
estate [ɪ'steɪt] *n* (*land*) terre(s) *f(pl)*, propriété *f*; (*property after death*) *Jur* succession *f*; **housing e.** lotissement *m*; (*workers'*) cité *f* (ouvrière); **industrial e.** zone *f* industrielle; **e. agency** agence *f* immobilière; **e. agent** agent *m* immobilier; **e. car** break *m*.
esteem [ɪ'stiːm] *vt* estimer; **highly esteemed** très estimé ▮ *n* estime *f*.
esthetic [es'θetɪk] *a Am* esthétique.
estimate ['estɪmeɪt] *vt* (*value*, *consider*) estimer (**that** que) ▮ ['estɪmət] *n* (*assess-*

ment, *judgment*) évaluation *f*; (*price for work to be done*) devis *m*; **rough e.** chiffre *m* approximatif.

estuary ['estjʊərɪ] *n* estuaire *m*.

etc [et'setərə] *adv* etc.

etch [etʃ] *vti* graver à l'eau forte. ● **—ing** *n* (*picture*) eau-forte *f*.

eternal [ɪ'tɜːn(ə)l] *a* éternel. ● **eternity** *n* éternité *f*.

ethical ['eθɪk(ə)l] *a* moral, éthique.

Ethiopia [iːθɪ'əʊpɪə] *n* Éthiopie *f*. ● **Ethiopian** *a* & *n* éthiopien, -ienne (*mf*).

ethnic ['eθnɪk] *a* (*minority etc*) ethnique; **e. music**/*etc* musique *f*/*etc* traditionnelle (*d'Afrique etc*).

etiquette ['etɪket] *n* (*rules*) bienséances *fpl*; **(diplomatic) e.** protocole *m*.

etymology [etɪ'mɒlədʒɪ] *n* étymologie *f*.

eucalyptus [juːkə'lɪptəs] *n* (*tree*) eucalyptus *m*.

euphemism ['juːfəmɪz(ə)m] *n* euphémisme *m*.

euphoria [juː'fɔːrɪə] *n* euphorie *f*.

Euro- ['jʊərəʊ] *pref* euro-; **Euro-MP** membre *m* du parlement européen.

Europe ['jʊərəp] *n* Europe *f*. ● **European** [jʊərə'piːən] *a* & *n* européen, -éenne (*mf*).

evacuate [ɪ'vækjʊeɪt] *vt* évacuer.

evade [ɪ'veɪd] *vt* éviter; (*pursuer*, *tax*) échapper à; (*law*, *question*) éluder.

evaluate [ɪ'væljʊeɪt] *vt* évaluer (**at** à).

evaporate [ɪ'væpəreɪt] *vi* (*of liquid*) s'évaporer; **evaporated milk** lait *m* concentré.

evasion [ɪ'veɪʒ(ə)n] *n* **e. of** (*pursuer*) fuite *f* devant; **tax e.** évasion *f* fiscale.

evasive [ɪ'veɪsɪv] *a* évasif.

eve [iːv] *n* **on the e. of** à la veille de.

even ['iːv(ə)n] **1** *a* (*flat*) uni, égal; (*equal*) égal; (*regular*) régulier; (*number*) pair; **to get e. with s.o.** se venger de qn; **we're e.** (*quits*) nous sommes quittes; (*in score*) nous sommes à égalité; **to break e.** (*financially*) s'y retrouver ‖ *vt* **to e. sth (out** *or* **up)** égaliser qch.
2 *adv* même; **e. better/more** encore mieux/plus; **e. if** *or* **though** même si; **e. so** quand même. ● **evenly** *adv* de manière égale; (*regularly*) régulièrement.

evening ['iːvnɪŋ] *n* soir *m*; (*whole evening*, *event*) soirée *f*; **in the e.** le soir; **at seven in the e.** à sept heures du soir; **every Tuesday e.** tous les mardis soir; **all e. (long)** toute la soirée ‖ *a* (*newspaper*, *meal etc*) du soir; **e. performance** *Th* soirée *f*; **e. dress** (*of man*) tenue *f* de soirée; (*of woman*) robe *f* du soir.

event [ɪ'vent] *n* événement *m*; *Sp* épreuve *f*; **in the e. of death** en cas de décès; **in any e.** en tout cas. ● **eventful** *a* (*journey etc*) mouvementé; (*occasion*) mémorable.

eventual [ɪ'ventʃʊəl] *a* final. ● **eventu'ality** *n* éventualité *f*. ● **eventually** *adv* finalement, à la fin; (*some day or other*) un jour ou l'autre.

ever ['evər] *adv* jamais; **has he e. seen it?** l'a-t-il jamais vu?; **more than e.** plus que jamais; **nothing e.** jamais rien; **hardly e.** presque jamais; **the first e.** le tout premier; **e. since** (*that event etc*) depuis; **e. since then** depuis lors, dès lors; **for e.** (*for always*) pour toujours; (*continually*) sans cesse; **the best son e.** le meilleur fils du monde; **e. so sorry/happy/***etc* vraiment désolé/heureux/*etc*; **thank you e. so much** merci mille fois; **it's e. such a pity** c'est vraiment dommage; **why e. not?** mais pourquoi pas?

evergreen ['evəgriːn] *n* arbre *m* à feuilles persistantes. ● **ever'lasting** *a* éternel. ● **ever'more** *adv* **for e.** à (tout) jamais.

every ['evrɪ] *a* chaque; **e. child** chaque enfant, tous les enfants; **e. one** chacun; **e. single one** tous (sans exception); **e. second** *or* **other day** tous les deux jours; **her e. gesture** ses moindres gestes; **e. bit as big** tout aussi grand (**as** que); **e. so often, e. now and then** de temps en temps.

everybody ['evrɪbɒdɪ] *pron* tout le monde; **e. in turn** chacun à son tour. ● **everyday** *a* (*happening*), de tous les jours; (*ordinary*) banal (*mpl* -als); **in e. use** d'usage courant. ● **everyone** *pron* = **everybody.** ● **everyplace** *adv Am* = **everywhere.** ● **everything** *pron* tout; **e. I have** tout ce que j'ai. ● **everywhere** *adv* partout; **e. she goes** où qu'elle aille, partout où elle va.

evict [ɪ'vɪkt] *vt* expulser (**from** de). ● **eviction** [-ʃ(ə)n] *n* expulsion *f*.

evidence ['evɪdəns] *n* (*proof*) preuve(s) *f*(*pl*); (*given by witness*) témoignage *m*; **to give e.** témoigner (**against** contre); **e. of** (*wear etc*) des signes *mpl* de; **in e.** (*noticeable*) (bien) en vue.

evident ['evɪdənt] *a* évident (**that** que); **it is e. from...** il apparaît de... (**that** que). ● **—ly** *adv* (*obviously*) évidemment; (*apparently*) apparemment.

evil ['iːv(ə)l] *a* (*influence*, *person etc*) malfaisant; (*deed*, *advice*, *system*) mauvais ‖ *n* mal *m*; **to speak e.** dire du mal (**about, of** de).

evoke [ɪ'vəʊk] *vt* (*recall*, *conjure up*) évoquer. ● **evocative** [ɪ'vɒkətɪv] *a* évocateur.

evolution [iːvə'luːʃ(ə)n] *n* évolution *f*.

evolve [ɪ'vɒlv] *vi* (*of society*, *idea etc*) évoluer ‖ *vt* (*system etc*) développer.

ewe [juː] *n* brebis *f*.

ex- [eks] *pref* ex-; **ex-wife** ex-femme *f*.

exact [ɪg'zækt] **1** *a* (*accurate, precise*) exact; **to be e. about sth** préciser qch. **2** *vt* (*demand*) exiger (**from** de); (*money*) extorquer (**from** à). ● **—ing** *a* exigeant. ● **—ly** *adv* exactement.

exaggerate [ɪg'zædʒəreɪt] *vti* exagérer. ● **exaggeration** [-'reɪʃ(ə)n] *n* exagération *f*.

exam [ɪg'zæm] *n abbr* (*examination*) examen *m*.

examine [ɪg'zæmɪn] *vt* examiner; (*accounts, luggage*) vérifier; (*passport*) contrôler; (*question*) interroger (*élève, témoin*). ● **examination** [-'neɪʃ(ə)n] *n Sch Univ* examen *m*; (*inspection*) examen *m*; (*of passport*) contrôle *m*; **class e.** devoir *m* surveillé *or* sur table. ● **examiner** *n Sch* examinateur, -trice *mf*.

example [ɪg'zɑːmp(ə)l] *n* exemple *m*; **for e.** par exemple; **to set an e.** *or* **a good e.** donner l'exemple *or* le bon exemple (**to** à); **to set a bad e.** donner le mauvais exemple.

exasperate [ɪg'zɑːspəreɪt] *vt* exaspérer.

excavate ['ekskəveɪt] *vt* (*dig*) creuser; (*for relics etc*) fouiller; (*uncover*) déterrer.

exceed [ɪk'siːd] *vt* dépasser. ● **—ingly** *adv* extrêmement.

excel [ɪk'sel] *vi* (**-ll-**) **to e. in** *or* **at sth** être excellent en qch.

excellent ['eksələnt] *a* excellent. ● **excellence** *n* excellence *f*.

except [ɪk'sept] *prep* sauf, excepté; **e. for** à part; **e. that** sauf que; **e. if** sauf si; **to do nothing e. wait** ne rien faire sinon attendre ‖ *vt* excepter.

exception [ɪk'sepʃ(ə)n] *n* exception *f*; **with the e. of** à l'exception de; **to take e. to** (*object to*) désapprouver; (*be hurt by*) s'offenser de. ● **exceptional** *a* exceptionnel. ● **exceptionally** *adv* exceptionnellement.

excerpt ['eksɜːpt] *n* (*from film etc*) extrait *m*.

excess ['ekses] *n* excès *m*; (*surplus*) *Com* excédent *m*; **to e.** à l'excès; **e. calories**/*etc* des calories *fpl*/*etc* en trop; **e. fare** supplément *m* (de billet); **e. luggage** *or* **baggage** excédent *m* de bagages; **e. weight** kilos *mpl* en trop.

excessive [ɪk'sesɪv] *a* excessif. ● **excessively** *adv* (*too, too much*) excessivement; (*very*) extrêmement.

exchange [ɪks'tʃeɪndʒ] *vt* échanger (**for** contre) ‖ *n* échange *m*; (*of foreign currencies*) change *m*; **(telephone) e.** central *m* (téléphonique); **in e.** en échange (**for** de).

Exchequer [ɪks'tʃekər] *n* **Chancellor of the E.** = ministre *m* des Finances.

excitable [ɪk'saɪtəb(ə)l] *a* excitable.

excit/e [ɪk'saɪt] *vt* (*enthuse*) passionner; (*agitate, provoke, stimulate*) exciter. ● **—ed** *a* (*happy*) surexcité; (*nervous*) énervé; **to get e.** (*nervous, enthusiastic*) s'exciter; **to be e. about** (*new car etc*) se réjouir de. ● **—ing** *a* (*book, adventure etc*) passionnant. ● **excitement** *n* agitation *f*, excitation *f*; (*emotion*) vive émotion *f*.

exclaim [ɪk'skleɪm] *vti* s'exclamer (**that** que). ● **exclamation** [ekskləˈmeɪʃ(ə)n] *n* exclamation *f*; **e. mark** *or Am* **point** point *m* d'exclamation.

exclude [ɪks'kluːd] *vt* exclure (**from** de). ● **exclusion** [-ʒ(ə)n] *n* exclusion *f*.

exclusive [ɪk'skluːsɪv] *a* exclusif; (*club, group*) fermé; (*interview, news item*) en exclusivité; **e. of wine**/*etc* vin/*etc* non compris.

excruciating [ɪk'skruːʃɪeɪtɪŋ] *a* insupportable, atroce.

excursion [ɪk'skɜːʃ(ə)n] *n* excursion *f*.

excuse [ɪk'skjuːz] *vt* (*forgive*) excuser (**s.o. for doing** qn d'avoir fait, qn de faire); (*exempt*) dispenser (**from** de); **e. me for asking** permettez-moi de demander; **e. me!** excusez-moi!, pardon! ‖ [ɪk'skjuːs] *n* excuse *f*; **to make an e.** se trouver une excuse; **it was an e. for** cela a servi de prétexte à.

ex-directory [eksdaɪ'rektərɪ] *a* (*telephone number*) sur la liste rouge.

execute ['eksɪkjuːt] *vt* (*criminal, order etc*) exécuter. ● **execution** [-'kjuːʃ(ə)n] *n* exécution *f*. ● **exe'cutioner** *n* bourreau *m*.

executive [ɪg'zekjʊtɪv] *a* (*job*) de cadre; (*car, plane*) de direction; (*power*) exécutif ‖ *n* (*person*) cadre *m*; (*board, committee*) bureau *m*; **the e.** *Pol* l'exécutif *m*; **(senior) e.** cadre *m* supérieur; **junior e.** jeune cadre *m*; **sales e.** cadre *m* commercial.

exemplify [ɪg'zemplɪfaɪ] *vt* (*show*) illustrer; (*serve as example of*) servir d'exemple de.

exempt [ɪg'zempt] *a* dispensé (**from** de) ‖ *vt* dispenser (**from** de). ● **exemption** [-ʃ(ə)n] *n* dispense *f*.

exercise ['eksəsaɪz] *n Sch Sp Mil* exercice *m*; **e. book** cahier *m* ‖ *vt (muscles, rights etc*) exercer; (*dog, horse etc*) promener; (*tact, judgment etc*) faire preuve de ‖ *vi* (*take exercise*) faire de l'exercice.

exert [ɪg'zɜːt] *vt* exercer; (*force*) employer; **to e. oneself** (*physically*) se dépenser; **don't e. yourself** ne te fatigue pas. ● **exertion** [-ʃ(ə)n] *n* effort *m*.

exhaust [ɪg'zɔːst] **1** *vt* (*use up, tire*) épuiser; **to become exhausted** s'épuiser. **2** *n* **e. (pipe)** *Aut* tuyau *m* d'échappement; **e. (fumes)** gaz *mpl* d'échappement. ● **—ing** *a* épuisant. ● **exhaustion** [[-stʃ(ə)n] *n* épuisement *m*.

exhaustive [ɪg'zɔːstɪv] *a* (*study etc*) complet, exhaustif.

exhibit [ɪg'zɪbɪt] *vt* (*put on display*) exposer; (*courage etc*) montrer ▮ *n* objet *m* exposé; *Jur* pièce *f* à conviction.

exhibition [egzɪ'bɪʃ(ə)n] *n* exposition *f*; **an e. of** (*skill, arrogance etc*) une démonstration de. ● **exhibitionist** *n* exhibitionniste *mf*.

exhibitor [ɪg'zɪbɪtər] *n* exposant, -ante *mf*.

exhilarating [ɪg'zɪləreɪtɪŋ] *a* (*experience etc*) grisant; (*air*) vivifiant. ● **exhilaration** [-'reɪʃ(ə)n] *n* joie *f*.

exile ['egzaɪl] *vt* exiler ▮ *n* (*absence*) exil *m*; (*person*) exilé, -ée *mf*.

exist [ɪg'zɪst] *vi* exister; (*live*) vivre (**on** de). ● **—ing** *a* (*situation*) actuel; (*law*) existant. ● **existence** *n* existence *f*; **to come into e.** être créé; **to be in e.** exister.

exit ['eksɪt, 'egzɪt] *n* (*action, door, window*) sortie *f*.

exodus ['eksədəs] *n inv* exode *m*.

exonerate [ɪg'zɒnəreɪt] *vt* (*from blame*) disculper (**from** de).

exorbitant [ɪg'zɔːbɪtənt] *a* exorbitant.

exotic [ɪg'zɒtɪk] *a* exotique.

expand [ɪk'spænd] *vt* (*knowledge, influence etc*) étendre; (*trade, idea*) développer; (*production*) augmenter; (*gas, metal*) dilater ▮ *vi* s'étendre; se développer; augmenter; se dilater; **to e. on** développer ses idées sur; **expanding sector** *Com* secteur *m* en (pleine) expansion.

expanse [ɪk'spæns] *n* étendue *f*.

expansion [ɪk'spænʃ(ə)n] *n* (*of economy, gas, metal etc*) expansion *f*; (*of trade etc*) développement *m*.

expatriate [eks'pætrɪət, *Am* eks'peɪtrɪət] *a* & *n* expatrié, -ée (*mf*).

expect [ɪk'spekt] *vt* (*anticipate*) s'attendre à; (*think*) penser (**that** que); (*suppose*) supposer (**that** que); (*await*) attendre (*qn*); **to e. sth from s.o./sth** attendre qch de qn/qch; **to e. to do** compter faire; **to e. that** s'attendre à ce que (+ *sub*); **I e. you to come** (*want*) je compte que vous viendrez; **it was expected** c'était prévu (**that** que); **she's expecting (a baby)** elle attend un bébé.

expectancy [ɪk'spektənsɪ] *n* **life e.** espérance *f* de vie. ● **expectant** *a* **e. mother** future mère *f*.

expectation [ekspek'teɪʃ(ə)n] *n* attente *f*; **to come up to s.o.'s expectations** répondre à l'attente de qn.

expedient [ɪks'piːdɪənt] *a* avantageux; (*suitable*) opportun ▮ *n* expédient *m*.

expedition [ekspɪ'dɪʃ(ə)n] *n* expédition *f*.

expel [ɪk'spel] *vt* (**-ll-**) (*from school*) renvoyer; (*foreigner, demonstrator etc*) expulser (**from** de).

expenditure [ɪk'spendɪtʃər] *n* (*money*) dépenses *fpl*.

expense [ɪk'spens] *n* frais *mpl*; **business/travelling expenses** frais *mpl* généraux/de déplacement; **at the e. of s.o./sth** (*causing harm*) aux dépens de qn/qch; **one's e. account** sa note de frais (professionnels).

expensive [ɪk'spensɪv] *a* (*goods, hotel etc*) cher; (*tastes*) de luxe; **to be e.** coûter *or* être cher. ● **—ly** *adv* (*dressed etc*) luxueusement.

experienc/e [ɪk'spɪərɪəns] *n* (*knowledge, event*) expérience *f*; **from** *or* **by e.** par expérience; **he has had e. of this work** il a déjà fait ce travail; **I've had e. of driving** j'ai déjà conduit; **practical e.** pratique *f* ▮ *vt* (*undergo*) connaître; (*difficulty*) éprouver. ● **—ed** *a* (*person*) expérimenté; (*eye, ear*) exercé; **to be e. in** s'y connaître en.

experiment [ɪk'sperɪmənt] *n* expérience *f* ▮ [ɪk'sperɪment] *vi* faire une expérience *or* des expériences; **to e. with sth** (*in science*) expérimenter qch. ● **experi'mental** *a* expérimental.

expert ['ekspɜːt] *n* expert *m* (**on, in** en) ▮ *a* expert (**in sth** en qch, **in** *or* **at doing** à faire); **e. advice** le conseil d'un expert; **e. touch** grande habileté *f*. ● **expertise** [-'tiːz] *n* compétence *f* (**in** en).

expir/e [ɪk'spaɪər] *vi* expirer. ● **—ed** *a* (*ticket, passport etc*) périmé.

expiry [ɪk'spaɪərɪ] (*Am* **expiration** [ekspə'reɪʃ(ə)n]) *n* expiration *f*; **e. date** (*on ticket*) date *f* d'expiration; (*on product*) date *f* limite d'utilisation.

explain [ɪk'spleɪn] *vt* expliquer (**to** à, **that** que); (*reasons*) exposer; **to e. sth away** justifier qch. ● **explanation** [eksplə'neɪʃ(ə)n] *n* explication *f*.

explanatory [ɪk'splænət(ə)rɪ] *a* explicatif.

expletive [ɪk'spliːtɪv, *Am* 'eksplətɪv] *n* juron *m*.

explicit [ɪk'splɪsɪt] *a* explicite. ● **—ly** *adv* explicitement.

explode [ɪk'spləʊd] *vi* exploser ▮ *vt* faire exploser.

exploit **1** [ɪk'splɔɪt] *vt* (*person, land etc*) exploiter. **2** ['eksplɔɪt] *n* (*feat*) exploit *m*. ● **exploitation** [-'teɪʃ(ə)n] *n* exploitation *f*.

explore [ɪk'splɔːr] *vt* explorer; (*causes etc*)

examiner. • **exploration** [ekspləˈreɪʃ(ə)n] *n* exploration *f*.

exploratory [ɪkˈsplɒrət(ə)rɪ] *a* (*talks etc*) préliminaire, exploratoire; **e. operation** *Med* sondage *m*.

explorer [ɪkˈsplɔːrər] *n* explorateur, -trice *mf*.

explosion [ɪkˈspləʊʒ(ə)n] *n* explosion *f*.

explosive [ɪkˈspləʊsɪv] *a* (*weapon, situation*) explosif; **e. device** engin *m* explosif ▮ *n* explosif *m*.

export [ˈekspɔːt] *n* exportation *f* ▮ [ɪkˈspɔːt] *vt* exporter (**to** vers, **from** de). • **exˈporter** *n* exportateur, -trice *mf*; (*country*) pays *m* exportateur.

expose [ɪkˈspəʊz] *vt* (*leave uncovered*) & *Phot* exposer; (*plot, scandal etc*) révéler; (*crook etc*) démasquer; **to e. s.o. to** (*subject to*) exposer qn à.

exposure [ɪkˈspəʊʒər] *n* exposition *f* (**to** à); *Phot* pose *f*; **to die of e.** mourir de froid.

express [ɪkˈspres] **1** *vt* exprimer; **to e. oneself** s'exprimer. **2** *a* (*letter, delivery*) exprès *inv*; (*train*) rapide, express *inv*; (*order*) exprès; (*intention*) explicite; **with the e. purpose of** dans le seul but de ▮ *adv* (*to send*) par exprès ▮ *n* (*train*) rapide *m*, express *m inv*. • **expression** [-ʃ(ə)n] *n* (*phrase, look*) expression *f*; **an e. of** (*gratitude etc*) un témoignage de. • **expressly** *adv* expressément.

expressive [ɪkˈspresɪv] *a* expressif.

expressway [ɪkˈspresweɪ] *n Am* autoroute *f*.

exquisite [ɪkˈskwɪzɪt] *a* exquis. • **—ly** *adv* d'une façon exquise.

ex-serviceman [eksˈsɜːvɪsmən] *n* (*pl* **-men**) ancien combattant *m*.

extend [ɪkˈstend] *vt* (*arm, business*) étendre; (*line, visit, meeting*) prolonger (**by** de); (*hand*) tendre (**to s.o.** à qn); (*house*) agrandir; (*time limit*) reculer; (*help, thanks*) offrir (**to** à) ▮ *vi* (*of wall, plain etc*) s'étendre (**to** jusqu'à); (*in time*) se prolonger.

extension [ɪkˈstenʃ(ə)n] *n* (*in time*) prolongation *f*; (*of meaning*) extension *f*; (*for table*) rallonge *f*; (*to building*) agrandissement(s) *m*(*pl*); (*of phone*) appareil *m* supplémentaire; (*of office phone*) poste *m*; **e. (cable** *or* **lead)** rallonge *f*.

extensive [ɪkˈstensɪv] *a* étendu, vaste; (*repairs, damage*) important. • **extensively** *adv* (*very much*) énormément, considérablement; **to be e. damaged** subir des dégâts importants.

extent [ɪkˈstent] *n* (*scope*) étendue *f*; (*size*) importance *f*; **to a large/certain e.** dans une large/certaine mesure; **to such an e. that** à tel point que.

extenuating [ɪkˈstenjʊeɪtɪŋ] *a* **e. circumstances** circonstances *fpl* atténuantes.

exterior [ɪksˈtɪərɪər] *a* & *n* extérieur (*m*).

exterminate [ɪkˈstɜːmɪneɪt] *vt* (*people, animals*) exterminer.

external [ekˈstɜːn(ə)l] *a* extérieur; **for e. use** (*medicine*) à usage externe.

extinct [ɪkˈstɪŋkt] *a* (*volcano*) éteint; (*species, animal*) disparu.

extinguish [ɪkˈstɪŋgwɪʃ] *vt* éteindre. • **—er** *n* **(fire) e.** extincteur *m*.

extort [ɪkˈstɔːt] *vt* (*money*) extorquer (**from** à). • **extortion** *n Jur* extorsion *f* de fonds. • **extortionate** *a* (*price etc*) exorbitant.

extra [ˈekstrə] *a* (*additional*) supplémentaire; **one e. glass** un verre de *or* en plus; **(any) e. bread?** encore du pain?; **to be e.** (*spare*) être en trop; (*cost more*) être en supplément; **e. charge** *or* **portion** supplément *m*; **e. time** *Fb* prolongation *f*.
▮ *adv* **to pay e.** payer un supplément; **wine costs** *or* **is 3 francs e.** il y a un supplément de 3F pour le vin; **e. big** plus grand que d'habitude.
▮ *n* (*perk*) à-côté *m*; *Cin Th* figurant, -ante *mf*; *pl* (*expenses*) frais *mpl* supplémentaires.

extra- [ˈekstrə] *pref* extra-. • **e.-ˈdry** *a* (*champagne*) brut. • **e.-ˈstrong** *a* extra-fort.

extract [ɪkˈstrækt] *vt* extraire (**from** de); (*tooth, promise*) arracher; (*money*) soutirer (**from** à) ▮ [ˈekstrækt] *n* (*of book etc, food substance*) extrait *m*.

extra-curricular [ekstrəkəˈrɪkjʊlər, *Am* -erɪ] *a* (*activities*) extrascolaire.

extradite [ˈekstrədaɪt] *vt* extrader. • **extradition** [-ˈdɪʃ(ə)n] *n* extradition *f*.

extraordinary [ɪkˈstrɔːdən(ə)rɪ, *Am* -erɪ] *a* extraordinaire.

extra-special [ekstrəˈspeʃəl] *a* (*occasion*) très spécial; (*care*) tout particulier.

extravagant [ɪkˈstrævəgənt] *a* (*behaviour, idea etc*) extravagant; (*wasteful with money*) dépensier. • **extravagance** *n* (*wastefulness*) prodigalité *f*; (*thing bought*) folle dépense *f*; (*wasteful expenses*) prodigalités *fpl*.

extreme [ɪkˈstriːm] *a* (*exceptional, furthest*) extrême; (*danger, poverty, importance*) très grand ▮ *n* (*furthest degree*) extrême *m*; **to carry** *or* **take sth to extremes** pousser qch à l'extrême; **extremes of temperature** températures *fpl* extrêmes. • **extremely** *adv* extrêmement.

extremist [ɪk'striːmɪst] *a* & *n* extrémiste (*mf*).
extremity [ɪk'stremɪtɪ] *n* extrémité *f*.
extricate ['ekstrɪkeɪt] *vt* (*free*) dégager (*qn*, *qch*) (**from** de).
extrovert ['ekstrəvɜːt] *n* extraverti, -ie *mf*.
exuberant [ɪg'z(j)uːbərənt] *a* exubérant.
eye[1] [aɪ] *n* œil *m* (*pl* yeux); **before my very eyes** sous mes yeux; **as far as the e. can see** à perte de vue; **to have one's e. on** (*house*, *car*) avoir en vue; **to keep an e. on** surveiller; **to lay** *or* **set eyes on** voir; **to take one's eyes off s.o./sth** quitter qn/qch des yeux; **to catch s.o.'s e.** attirer l'attention de qn; **keep your eyes open!** ouvre l'œil!; **we don't see e. to e.** nous ne voyons pas les choses du même œil; **to be an e.-opener for s.o.** *Fam* être une révélation pour qn.
eye[2] [aɪ] *vt* regarder; (*with envy*) dévorer des yeux; (*with lust*) reluquer.
eyeball ['aɪbɔːl] *n* globe *m* oculaire. • **eyebrow** *n* sourcil *m*. • **eyeglasses** *npl* (*spectacles*) *Am* lunettes *fpl*. • **eyelash** *n* cil *m*. • **eyelid** *n* paupière *f*. • **eyeliner** *n* eye-liner *m*. • **eye shadow** *n* ombre *f* à paupières. • **eyesight** *n* vue *f*. • **eyesore** *n* (*building etc*) horreur *f*. • **eyestrain** *n* **to have e.** avoir les yeux qui tirent. • **eyewitness** *n* témoin *m* oculaire.

F

F, f [ef] *n* F, f *m*.
fable ['feɪb(ə)l] *n* fable *f*.
fabric ['fæbrɪk] *n* (*cloth*) tissu *m*, étoffe *f*;
fabricate ['fæbrɪkeɪt] *vt* (*invent, make*) fabriquer.
fabulous ['fæbjʊləs] *a* (*wonderful*) *Fam* formidable; (*incredible, legendary*) fabuleux.
façade [fə'sɑːd] *n* (*of building*) & *Fig* façade *f*.
face [feɪs] *n* (*of person*) visage *m*, figure *f*; (*of clock*) cadran *m*; (*of cube, mountain*) face *f*; (*of cliff*) paroi *f*; **f. down** (*person*) face contre terre; (*thing*) tourné à l'envers; **f. to f.** face à face; **in the f. of** devant; (*despite*) en dépit de; **to save/lose f.** sauver/perdre la face; **to make** *or* **pull faces** faire des grimaces; **f. powder** poudre *f*; **f. value** (*of stamp etc*) valeur *f*.
▮ *vt* (*danger, enemy, problem etc*) faire face à; (*accept*) accepter; (*look in the face*) regarder (*qn*) bien en face; **to f., be facing** (*be opposite*) être en face de; (*of window, room etc*) donner sur (*le jardin etc*); **faced with** (*problem*) confronté à; (*defeat*) menacé par; (*bill*) contraint à payer; **he can't f. leaving** il n'a pas le courage de partir.
▮ *vi* (*of house*) être orienté (**north**/*etc* au nord/*etc*); (*of person*) se tourner; (*be turned*) être tourné (**towards** vers); **to f. up to** (*danger, problem*) faire face à; (*fact*) accepter; **about f.!** *Am Mil* demi-tour!
facecloth ['feɪsklɒθ] *n* gant *m* de toilette.
facelift ['feɪslɪft] *n Med* lifting *m*; (*of building*) ravalement *m*.
faceless ['feɪsləs] *a* anonyme.
facetious [fə'siːʃəs] *a* (*person*) facétieux; (*remark*) plaisant.
facial ['feɪʃ(ə)l] *a* du visage ▮ *n* soin *m* du visage.
facile ['fæsaɪl, *Am* 'fæs(ə)l] *a* facile, superficiel.
facilitate [fə'sɪlɪteɪt] *vt* faciliter.
facilities [fə'sɪlɪtɪz] *npl* (*for sports, cooking etc*) équipements *mpl*; (*in harbour, airport*) installations *fpl*; (*possibilities*) facilités *fpl*; (*means*) moyens *mpl*; **special f.** (*conditions*) conditions *fpl* spéciales (**for** pour); **credit f.** facilités *fpl* de paiement.
fact [fækt] *n* fait *m*; **as a matter of f., in f.** en fait; **the facts of life** les choses *fpl* de la vie.
faction ['fækʃ(ə)n] *n* (*group*) faction *f*.
factor ['fæktər] *n* (*element*) facteur *m*.
factory ['fækt(ə)rɪ] *n* usine *f*; **arms f.** manufacture *f* d'armes.
factual ['fæktʃʊəl] *a* objectif, basé sur les faits; (*error*) de fait.
faculty ['fækəltɪ] *n* (*aptitude*) & *Univ* faculté *f*.
fad [fæd] *n* (*fashion*) folie *f*, mode *f* (**for** de).
fade [feɪd] *vi* (*of flower*) se faner; (*of light*) baisser; (*of colour*) passer; (*of fabric*) se décolorer; **to f. (away)** (*of sound*) s'affaiblir; (*of memory etc*) s'effacer.
fag [fæg] *n* **1** (*cigarette*) *Fam* clope *m or f*; **f. end** mégot *m*. **2** (*homosexual*) *Am Sl Pej* pédé *m*.
fail [feɪl] *vi* (*of person, plan etc*) échouer; (*of business*) faire faillite; (*of health, sight, light*) baisser; (*of memory, strength*) défaillir; (*of brakes*) *Aut* lâcher; (*of engine*) tomber en panne; **to f. in an exam** échouer à un examen; **to f. in one's duty** manquer à son devoir.
▮ *vt* (*exam*) rater, échouer à; (*candidate*) refuser, recaler; **to f. s.o.** (*let down*) laisser tomber qn; (*of words*) manquer à qn; **to f. to do** (*forget*) manquer de faire; (*not be able*) ne pas arriver à faire.
▮ *n* **without f.** à coup sûr. ●**failed** *a* (*attempt, poet*) manqué. ●**failing** *n* (*fault*) défaut *m* ▮ *prep* à défaut de; **f. that** à défaut.
failure ['feɪljər] *n* échec *m*; (*of business*) faillite *f*; (*of engine, machine*) panne *f*; (*person*) raté, -ée *mf*; **f. to do** incapacité *f* de faire; **her f. to leave** le fait qu'elle n'est pas partie; **to end in f.** se solder par un échec; **heart f.** arrêt *m* du cœur.
faint [feɪnt] **1** *a* (**-er, -est**) (*weak*); (*voice, trace, hope etc*) faible; (*colour*) pâle; **I haven't got the faintest idea** je n'en ai pas la moindre idée. **2** *a* **to feel f.** se trouver mal ▮ *vi* s'évanouir. ●**—ly** *adv* (*weakly*) faiblement; (*slightly*) légèrement.
fair[1] [feər] *n* foire *f*; (*for charity*) fête *f*; (*funfair*) fête *f* foraine. ●**fairground** *n* champ *m* de foire.
fair[2] [feər] **1** *a* (**-er, -est**) (*just*) juste; (*game, fight*) loyal; **she is/that is f. to him** elle est juste envers lui/c'est juste pour lui; **f. (and square)** honnête(ment); **f. play** fair-play *m*

inv; **that's not f. play!** ce n'est pas du jeu!; **f. enough!** très bien! ▮ *adv* (*to play, fight*) loyalement.

2 *a* (*rather good*) passable, assez bon; (*price, warning*) raisonnable; **a f. amount (of)** pas mal (de); **f. copy** copie *f* au propre. **3** *a* (*wind*) favorable; (*weather*) beau. ●**fairly** *adv* **1** (*to treat*) équitablement; (*to play, fight, get*) loyalement. **2** (*rather*) assez, plutôt; **f. sure** presque sûr. ●**fairness** *n* justice *f*; (*of person*) impartialité *f*. ●**fair-'sized** *a* assez grand.

fair[3] [feər] *a* (*hair, person*) blond; (*complexion, skin*) clair. ●**fair-'haired** *a* blond. ●**fair-'skinned** *a* à la peau claire.

fairy ['feərɪ] *n* fée *f*; **f. tale** *or* **story** conte *m* de fées.

faith [feɪθ] *n* foi *f*; **to have f. in s.o.** avoir confiance en qn; **to put one's f. in** (*justice etc*) se fier à; **in good f.** de bonne foi. ●**faithful** *a* fidèle (**to** à). ●**faithfully** *adv* fidèlement; **yours f.** (*in letter*) veuillez agréer l'expression de mes salutations distinguées.

fake [feɪk] *n* (*document etc*) faux *m*; (*person*) imposteur *m* ▮ *vt* (*document, signature etc*) falsifier; (*election*) truquer ▮ *vi* (*pretend*) faire semblant ▮ *a* faux (*f* fausse); (*elections*) truqué.

falcon ['fɔːlkən] *n* faucon *m*.

fall [fɔːl] *n* chute *f*; (*in price, demand etc*) baisse *f* (**in** de); **the f.** (*season*) *Am* l'automne *m*; **in the f.** en automne.

▮ *vi* (*pt* **fell**, *pp* **fallen**) tomber; **to f. into** (*hole, trap*) tomber dans; **to f. off** *or* **down sth, f. out of sth** tomber de qch; **to f. on a Monday**/*etc* (*of event*) tomber un lundi/*etc*; **to f. over sth** (*chair etc*) tomber en butant contre qch; (*balcony etc*) tomber de qch; **to f. victim** devenir victime (**to** de); **to f. asleep** s'endormir; **to f. ill** tomber malade; **to f. due** échoir.

fall apart *vi* (*of machine*) tomber en morceaux; (*of group*) se désagréger ▮ **to fall away** (*come off*) se détacher, tomber ▮ **to fall back on** *vt* (*as last resort*) se rabattre sur ▮ **to fall behind** *vi* rester en arrière; (*in work, payment*) prendre du retard ▮ **to fall down** *vi* tomber; (*of building*) s'effondrer ▮ **to fall for** *vt* (*person*) tomber amoureux de; (*trick*) se laisser prendre à ▮ **to fall in** *vi* (*collapse*) s'écrouler ▮ **to fall off** *vi* (*come off*) se détacher, tomber; (*of numbers*) diminuer ▮ **to fall out** *vi* (*quarrel*) se brouiller (**with** avec) ▮ **to fall over** *vi* tomber; (*of table, vase*) se renverser ▮ **to fall through** *vi* (*of plan*) tomber à l'eau.

fallacy ['fæləsɪ] *n* erreur *f*; *Phil* faux raisonnement *m*.

fallout ['fɔːlaʊt] *n* (*radioactive*) retombées *fpl*.

fallow ['fæləʊ] *a* (*land*) en jachère.

false [fɔːls] *a* faux (*f* fausse); **f. teeth** fausses dents *fpl* ●**falsehood** *n* mensonge *m*.

falsify ['fɔːlsɪfaɪ] *vt* falsifier.

falter ['fɔːltər] *vi* (*of step*) chanceler; (*of voice*) hésiter.

fame [feɪm] *n* renommée *f*.

familiar [fə'mɪljər] *a* (*task, person, atmosphere etc*) familier (**to** à); (*event*) habituel; **f. with s.o.** (*too friendly*) familier avec qn; **to be f. with** (*know*) connaître; **to make oneself f. with** se familiariser avec; **he looks f. (to me)** je l'ai déjà vu (quelque part). ●**famili'arity** *n* familiarité *f* (**with** avec); (*of event, sight etc*) caractère *m* familier.

familiarize [fə'mɪljəraɪz] *vt* **to f. oneself with** se familiariser avec.

family ['fæmɪlɪ] *n* famille *f* ▮ *a* (*name, doctor etc*) de famille; (*problems*) familial; **f. man** père *m* de famille.

famine ['fæmɪn] *n* famine *f*.

famished ['fæmɪʃt] *a* affamé.

famous ['feɪməs] *a* célèbre (**for** pour).

fan[1] [fæn] *n* (*held in hand*) éventail *m*; (*mechanical*) ventilateur *m*; **f. heater** radiateur *m* soufflant ▮ *vt* (**-nn-**) (*person etc*) éventer; (*fire*) attiser.

fan[2] [fæn] *n* (*of person*) fan *mf*; *Sp* supporter *m*; **to be a jazz/sports f.** être passionné de jazz/de sport.

fanatic [fə'nætɪk] *n* fanatique *mf*. ●**fanatical** *a* fanatique.

fanciful ['fænsɪfəl] *a* fantaisiste.

fancy ['fænsɪ] **1** *n* (*whim*) fantaisie *f*; (*liking*) goût *m*; **to take a f. to s.o.** se prendre d'affection pour qn; **I took a f. to it, it took my f.** j'en ai eu envie ▮ *a* (*hat, button etc*) fantaisie *inv*; (*car*) de luxe; (*house, restaurant*) chic; **f. dress** travesti *m*; **f.-dress ball** bal *m* masqué. **2** *vt* (*want*) avoir envie de; **to f. that** (*think*) croire que; **f. that!** tiens (donc)!; **he fancies her** *Fam* elle lui plaît.

fanfare ['fænfeər] *n* *Mus* fanfare *f*.

fang [fæŋ] *n* (*of dog, wolf*) croc *m*; (*of snake*) crochet *m*.

fanny ['fænɪ] *n* (*buttocks*) *Am Fam* derrière *m*; **f. pack** banane *f*.

fantastic [fæn'tæstɪk] *a* fantastique.

fantasy ['fæntəsɪ] *n* (*imagination*) fantaisie *f*; (*dream*) rêve *m*; (*fanciful, sexual*) fantasme *m*. ●**fantasize** *vi* fantasmer (**about** sur).

far [fɑːr] *adv* (**farther** *or* **further, farthest** *or*

furthest) (*distance*) loin; **f. bigger/more expensive/***etc* beaucoup plus grand/plus cher/*etc* (**than** que); **f. advanced** très avancé; **how f. is it to...?** combien y a-t-il d'ici à...?; **is it f. to...?** sommes-nous, suis-je *etc* loin de...?; **how f. are you going?** jusqu'où vas-tu?; **how f. has he got with?** (*plans, work etc*) où en est-il de?; **so f.** (*time*) jusqu'ici; (*place*) jusque-là; **as f. as** (*place*) jusqu'à; **as f. as I know** autant que je sache; **as f. as I'm concerned** en ce qui me concerne; **f. from doing** loin de faire; **f. away** *or* **off** au loin; **to be f. away** être loin (**from** de); **by f.** de loin.
▮ *a* (*other*) (*side, end*) autre; **it's a f. cry from** on est loin de; **the F. East** l'Extrême-Orient *m*.

faraway [fɑːrə'weɪ] *a* (*country*) lointain; (*look*) distrait. ●**far-'fetched** *a* tiré par les cheveux. ●**far-'off** *a* lointain. ●**far-'reaching** *a* de grande portée.

farce [fɑːs] *n* farce *f*. ●**farcical** *a* grotesque.

fare [feər] **1** *n* (*price of journey*) (*in bus etc*) prix *m* du billet; (*in taxi*) prix *m* de la course. **2** *n* (*food*) nourriture *f*. **3** *vi* (*manage*) se débrouiller; **how did she f.?** comment ça s'est passé (pour elle)?

farewell [feə'wel] *n* & *int* adieu (*m*).

farm [fɑːm] *n* ferme *f*; **on a f.** dans une ferme ▮ *a* (*worker, produce*) agricole; **f. land** terres *fpl* cultivées ▮ *vt* cultiver. ●**—ing** *n* agriculture *f*; (*breeding*) élevage *m*; **dairy f.** industrie *f* laitière. ●**farmer** *n* fermier, -ière *mf*.

farmhand ['fɑːmhænd] *n* ouvrier, -ière *mf* agricole. ●**farmhouse** *n* ferme *f*. ●**farmyard** *n* basse-cour *f*.

farther ['fɑːðər] *adv* plus loin; **f. forward** plus avancé; **to get f. away** s'éloigner. ●**farthest** *a* le plus éloigné ▮ *adv* le plus loin.

fascinate ['fæsɪneɪt] *vt* fasciner. ●**fascination** [-'neɪʃ(ə)n] *n* fascination *f*.

fascist ['fæʃɪst] *a* & *n* fasciste (*mf*).

fashion ['fæʃ(ə)n] **1** *n* (*style in clothes etc*) mode *f*; **in f.** à la mode; **out of f.** démodé; **f. designer** (grand) couturier *m*; **f. show** présentation *f* de collections. **2** *n* (*manner*) façon *f*; (*custom*) habitude *f*. **3** *vt* (*make*) façonner. ●**fashionable** *a* à la mode; (*place*) chic *inv*; **it's f. to do that** il est de bon ton de faire cela.

fast [fɑːst] **1** *a* (**-er, -est**) rapide; **to be f.** (*of clock*) avancer (**by** de); **f. colour** couleur *f* grand teint *inv*; **f. food** restauration *f* rapide; **f. food restaurant** fast-food *m* ▮ *adv* (*quickly*) vite; **how f.?** à quelle vitesse?; **f. asleep** profondément endormi. **2** *vi* (*go without food*) jeûner ▮ *n* jeûne *m*.

fasten ['fɑːs(ə)n] *vt* attacher (**to** à); (*door, window*) fermer (bien); **to f. sth down** *or* **up** attacher qch ▮ *vi* (*of dress etc*) s'attacher; (*of door, window*) se fermer. ●**fastener** *or* **fastening** *n* (*clip*) attache *f*; (*of garment*) fermeture *f*; (*of bag*) fermoir *m*; (*hook*) agrafe *f*.

fastidious [fə'stɪdɪəs] *a* difficile (à contenter), exigeant.

fat [fæt] **1** *n* graisse *f*; (*on meat*) gras *m*; **vegetable f.** huile *f* végétale. **2** *a* (**fatter, fattest**) gras (*f* grasse); (*cheeks, salary*) gros (*f* grosse); **to get f.** grossir.

fatal ['feɪt(ə)l] *a* mortel; (*mistake, blow etc*) *Fig* fatal (*mpl* fatals). ●**—ly** *adv* (*wounded*) mortellement.

fatality [fə'tælɪtɪ] *n* **1** (*person killed*) victime *f*. **2** (*of event*) fatalité *f*.

fate [feɪt] *n* destin *m*, sort *m*; (*of person*) sort *m*. ●**fated** *a* **our meeting/***etc* **was f.** notre rencontre/*etc* devait arriver. ●**fateful** *a* (*important*) fatal; (*prophetic*) fatidique; (*disastrous*) néfaste.

father ['fɑːðər] *n* père *m*. ●**f.-in-law** *n* (*pl* **fathers-in-law**) beau-père *m*. ●**fatherhood** *n* paternité *f*. ●**fatherly** *a* paternel.

fathom ['fæðəm] **1** *n* *Nau* brasse *f* (= *1,8 m*). **2** *vt* **to f. (out)** (*understand*) comprendre.

fatigue [fə'tiːg] *n* fatigue *f*.

fatten ['fæt(ə)n] *vt* engraisser. ●**—ing** *a* (*food*) qui fait grossir.

fatty ['fætɪ] *a* (**-ier, -iest**) (*food*) gras (*f* grasse) ▮ *n* (*person*) *Fam* gros lard *m*.

faucet ['fɔːsɪt] *n* (*tap*) *Am* robinet *m*.

fault [fɔːlt] *n* (*blame*) faute *f*; (*defect*) défaut *m*; (*mistake*) erreur *f*; *Geol* faille *f*; **it's your f.** c'est ta faute; **to find f. (with)** critiquer ▮ *vt* **to f. s.o./sth** trouver des défauts chez qn/à qch. ●**faultless** *a* irréprochable. ●**faulty** *a* (**-ier, -iest**) défectueux.

favour ['feɪvər] (*Am* **favor**) *n* (*act of kindness*) service *m*; (*approval*) faveur *f*; **to do s.o. a f.** rendre service à qn; **in f.** (*fashion*) en vogue; **in f. of** (*for the sake of*) au profit de; **to be in f. of** (*support*) être pour; (*prefer*) préférer ▮ *vt* (*encourage*) favoriser; (*prefer*) préférer; (*support*) être partisan de. ●**favourable** *a* favorable (**to** à).

favourite ['feɪv(ə)rɪt] (*Am* **favorite**) *a* favori, préféré ▮ *n* favori, -ite *mf*. ●**favouritism** *n* favoritisme *m*.

fawn [fɔːn] *n* (*deer*) faon *m* ▮ *a* & *n* (*colour*) fauve (*m*).

fax [fæks] *n* (*machine*) télécopieur *m*, fax *m*;

(*message*) télécopie *f*, fax *m* ‖ *vt* (*message*) faxer; **to f. s.o.** envoyer une télécopie *or* un fax à qn.

fear [fɪər] *n* crainte *f*, peur *f*; **for f. of doing** de peur de faire; **for f. that** de peur que (+ ne + *sub*); **there are fears he might leave** on craint qu'il (ne) parte ‖ *vt* craindre; **I f. he might leave** je crains qu'il (ne) parte. •**fearful** *a* (*timid*) peureux; (*awful*) (*noise etc*) affreux. •**fearless** *a* intrépide. •**fearsome** *a* redoutable.

feasible ['fiːzəb(ə)l] *a* (*practicable*) faisable; (*theory etc*) plausible.

feast [fiːst] *n* festin *m*; *Rel* fête *f* ‖ *vi* banqueter; **to f. on** (*cakes etc*) se régaler de.

feat [fiːt] *n* exploit *m*; **f. of skill** tour *m* d'adresse.

feather ['feðər] *n* plume *f*; **f. duster** plumeau *m*.

feature ['fiːtʃər] **1** *n* (*of face, person*) trait *m*; (*of thing, place, machine*) caractéristique *f*; **f. (article)** article *m* de fond; **f. (film)** grand film *m*. **2** *vt* (*of newspaper, film etc*) (*present*) présenter; (*portray*) représenter; **a film featuring Chaplin** un film avec Charlot en vedette ‖ *vi* (*appear*) figurer (**in** dans).

February ['februərɪ, *Am* -erɪ] *n* février *m*.

fed [fed] *pt* & *pp of* **feed** ‖ **to be f. up** *Fam* en avoir marre *or* ras le bol (**with** de).

federal ['fedərəl] *a* fédéral. •**federation** [-'reɪʃ(ə)n] *n* fédération *f*.

fee [fiː] *n* (*price*) prix *m*; **fee(s)** (*professional*) honoraires *mpl*; (*for registration, examination*) droits *mpl*; **to charge a f. (for a job)** se faire payer (pour un travail); **school** *or* **tuition fees** frais *mpl* de scolarité; **entrance f.** droit *m or* prix *m* d'entrée; **membership fee(s)** cotisation *f*.

feeble ['fiːb(ə)l] *a* (**-er, -est**) faible; (*excuse*) pauvre; (*joke, attempt*) pitoyable.

feed [fiːd] *n* (*for animal*) aliments *mpl*; (*baby's breast feed*) tétée *f*; (*baby's bottle feed*) biberon *m* ‖ *vt* (*pt* & *pp* **fed**) donner à manger à, nourrir; (*breastfeed*) allaiter (*un bébé*); (*bottlefeed*) donner le biberon à (*un bébé*); **to f. s.o. sth** faire manger qch à qn; **to f. sth into** (*machine*) introduire qch dans; (*computer*) entrer qch dans.
‖ *vi* (*eat*) manger; **to f. on** se nourrir de.

feedback ['fiːdbæk] *n* réaction(s) *f(pl)*.

feel [fiːl] *n* (*touch*) toucher *m*; (*feeling*) sensation *f*.
‖ *vt* (*pt* & *pp* **felt**) (*be aware of*) sentir; (*experience*) éprouver; (*touch*) tâter; **to f. that** avoir l'impression que; **to f. one's way** avancer à tâtons.
‖ *vi* (*tired, old etc*) se sentir; **to f. (about)** (*grope*) tâtonner; (*in pocket etc*) fouiller (**for sth** pour trouver qch); **it feels hard** c'est dur (au toucher); **I f. hot/sleepy/hungry/***etc* j'ai chaud/sommeil/faim/*etc*; **she feels better** elle va mieux; **to f. like sth** (*want*) avoir envie de qch; **it feels like cotton** on dirait du coton; **to f. as if** avoir l'impression que; **what do you f. about...?** que pensez-vous de...?; **I f. bad about it** ça m'ennuie; **to f. up to doing** être (assez) en forme pour faire.

feeler ['fiːlər] *n* (*of snail*) antenne *f*; **to put out a f.** *Fig* lancer un ballon d'essai.

feeling ['fiːlɪŋ] *n* (*emotion, impression*) sentiment *m*; (*physical*) sensation *f*; **a f. for s.o.** de la sympathie pour qn.

feet [fiːt] *see* **foot**[1].

feline ['fiːlaɪn] *a* félin.

fell [fel] **1** *pt of* **fall. 2** *vt* (*tree*) abattre.

fellow ['feləʊ] *n* **1** (*man, boy*) type *m*; **an old f.** un vieux; **poor f.!** pauvre malheureux! **2** (*companion*) **f. being** semblable *m*; **f. countryman, f. countrywoman** compatriote *mf*; **f. passenger** compagnon *m* de voyage, compagne *f* de voyage. **3** (*of society*) membre *m*.

fellowship ['feləʊʃɪp] *n* camaraderie *f*; (*group*) association *f*; (*scholarship*) bourse *f* universitaire.

felony ['felənɪ] *n* crime *m*.

felt[1] [felt] *pt* & *pp of* **feel.**

felt[2] [felt] *n* feutre *m*; **f.-tip (pen)** crayon *m* feutre.

female ['fiːmeɪl] *a* (*name, voice etc*) féminin; (*animal*) femelle; **f. student** étudiante *f* ‖ *n* (*woman*) femme *f*; (*girl*) fille *f*; (*animal*) femelle *f*.

feminine ['femɪnɪn] *a* féminin. •**feminist** *a* & *n* féministe (*mf*).

fenc/e [fens] **1** *n* barrière *f*, clôture *f*; (*in race*) obstacle *m* ‖ *vt* **to f. (in)** (*land*) clôturer. **2** *vi* (*with sword*) faire de l'escrime. •**—ing** *n Sp* escrime *f*.

fend [fend] **1** *vi* **to f. for oneself** se débrouiller. **2** *vt* **to f. off** (*blow*) parer.

fender ['fendər] *n* (*of car*) *Am* aile *f*.

ferment ['fɜːment] *n* ferment *m*; (*excitement*) *Fig* effervescence *f* ‖ [fə'ment] *vi* fermenter.

fern [fɜːn] *n* fougère *f*.

ferocious [fə'rəʊʃəs] *a* féroce. •**ferocity** [fə'rɒsətɪ] *n* férocité *f*.

ferret ['ferɪt] *n* (*animal*) furet *m* ‖ *vt* **to f. out** dénicher.

Ferris wheel ['ferɪswiːl] *n* grande roue *f*.

ferry ['ferɪ] *n* ferry-boat *m*; (*small, for river*) bac *m* ‖ *vt* transporter.

fertile ['fɜːtaɪl, *Am* 'fɜːt(ə)l] *a* (*land, imagination*) fertile; (*person, animal*) fécond. ● **fertilize** *vt* (*land*) fertiliser; (*egg*) féconder. ● **fertilizer** *n* engrais *m*.

fervent ['fɜːv(ə)nt] *a* fervent.

fester ['festər] *vi* (*of wound*) suppurer.

festival ['festɪv(ə)l] *n Mus Cin* festival *m* (*pl* -als); *Rel* fête *f*.

festive ['festɪv] *a* (*atmosphere etc*) de fête; (*mood*) joyeux; **f. season** période *f* des fêtes. ● **fe'stivities** *npl* festivités *fpl*.

fetch [fetʃ] *vt* **1** (*bring*) amener (*qn*); (*object*) apporter; **to (go and) f.** aller chercher; **to f. sth in** rentrer qch; **to f. sth out** sortir qch. **2** (*be sold for*) rapporter (**ten pounds**/*etc* dix livres/*etc*).

fête [feɪt] *n* fête *f*.

fetish ['fetɪʃ] *n* (*obsession*) manie *f*; **to make a f. of** être obsédé par.

fetus ['fiːtəs] *n Am* fœtus *m*.

feud [fjuːd] *n* querelle *f*, dissension *f*.

feudal ['fjuːd(ə)l] *a* féodal.

fever ['fiːvər] *n* fièvre *f*; **to have a f.** (*temperature*) avoir de la fièvre; **a high f.** une forte fièvre. ● **feverish** *a* (*person, activity*) fiévreux.

few [fjuː] *a* & *pron* peu (de); **f. towns**/*etc* peu de villes/*etc*; **a f. towns**/*etc* quelques villes/*etc*; **f. of them** peu d'entre eux; **a f.** quelques-un(e)s (**of** de); **a f. of us** quelques-uns d'entre nous; **one of the f. books** l'un des rares livres; **quite a f., a good f.** bon nombre (de); **a f. more books**/*etc* encore quelques livres/*etc*; **f. and far between** rares (et espacés); **f. came** peu sont venus; **every f. days** tous les trois ou quatre jours.

fewer ['fjuːər] *a* & *pron* moins (de) (**than** que); **f. houses (than)** moins de maisons (que); **no f. than** pas moins de. ● **fewest** ['fjuːɪst] *a* & *pron* le moins (de).

fiancé(e) [fɪ'ɒnseɪ] *n* fiancé, -ée *mf*.

fiasco [fɪ'æskəʊ] *n* (*pl* **-os,** *Am* **-oes**) fiasco *m*.

fib [fib] *n Fam* blague *f*, bobard *m* ▮ *vi* (**-bb-**) *Fam* raconter des blagues.

fibre ['faɪbər] (*Am* **fiber**) *n* fibre *f*; (*in diet*) fibre(s) *f*(*pl*). ● **fibreglass** *n* fibre *f* de verre.

fickle ['fɪk(ə)l] *a* inconstant.

fiction ['fɪkʃ(ə)n] *n* (*imagination*) fiction *f*; **(works of) f.** romans *mpl*; **that's pure f.** ce sont des histoires. ● **fictional** *or* **fictitious** [-'tɪʃəs] *a* fictif.

fiddle ['fɪd(ə)l] **1** *n* (*violin*) *Fam* violon *m*. **2** *vi Fam* **to f. about** (*waste time*) traînailler; **to f. (about) with** (*watch, pen etc*) tripoter; (*cars*) bricoler. **3** *n* (*dishonest act*) *Fam* combine *f* ▮ *vt* (*accounts etc*) *Fam* falsifier. ● **fiddler** *n* **1** *Fam* joueur, -euse *mf* de violon. **2** (*swindler*) *Fam* combinard, -arde *mf*.

fiddly ['fɪdlɪ] *a* (**-ier, -iest**) (*task*) délicat.

fidget ['fɪdʒɪt] *vi* **to f. (about)** gigoter; **to f. (about) with** tripoter ▮ *n* personne *f* qui ne tient pas en place. ● **fidgety** *a* agité, remuant.

field [fiːld] *n* champ *m*; *Sp* terrain *m*; (*sphere*) domaine *m*; **f. glasses** jumelles *fpl*; **f. marshal** maréchal *m*.

fiend [fiːnd] *n* démon *m*; **(sex) f.** *Fam* satyre *m*. ● **fiendish** *a* (*cruel*) diabolique; (*awful*) abominable.

fierce [fɪəs] *a* (**-er, -est**) féroce; (*attack, wind*) furieux.

fiery ['faɪərɪ] *a* (**-ier, -iest**) (*person, speech*) fougueux.

fiesta [fɪ'estə] *n* fiesta *f*.

fifteen [fɪf'tiːn] *a* & *n* quinze (*m*). ● **fifteenth** *a* & *n* quinzième (*mf*).

fifth [fɪfθ] *a* & *n* cinquième (*mf*); **a f.** un cinquième.

fifty ['fɪftɪ] *a* & *n* cinquante (*m*); **a f.-fifty chance** une chance sur deux. ● **fiftieth** *a* & *n* cinquantième (*mf*).

fig [fɪg] *n* figue *f*; **f. tree** figuier *m*.

fight [faɪt] *n* bagarre *f*; *Mil Boxing* combat *m*; (*struggle*) lutte *f*; (*quarrel*) dispute *f*; **to put up a f.** bien se défendre.

▮ *vi* (*pt* & *pp* **fought**) se battre (**against** contre); (*struggle*) lutter (**for** pour, **against** contre); (*quarrel*) se disputer; **to f. back** se défendre; **to f. over sth** se disputer qch.

▮ *vt* se battre avec (*qn*); (*evil*) lutter contre; **to f. a battle** livrer bataille; **to f. an election** se présenter à une élection; **to f. back** (*tears*) refouler; **to f. off** (*attacker*) repousser; **to f. it out** se bagarrer. ● **fighting** *n Mil* combat(s) *m*(*pl*); (*brawling*) bagarres *fpl*; **f. troops** troupes *fpl* de combat. ● **fighter** *n* (*determined person*) battant, -ante *mf*; (*in brawl*) combattant, -ante *mf*; *Boxing* boxeur *m*; (*aircraft*) chasseur *m*.

figment ['fɪgmənt] *n* **a f. of one's imagination** une création de son esprit.

figurative ['fɪgjʊrətɪv] *a* (*meaning*) figuré. ● **—ly** *adv* au figuré.

figure[1] ['fɪgər, *Am* 'fɪgjər] *n* **1** (*numeral*) chiffre *m*; (*price*) prix *m*; *pl* (*arithmetic*) calcul *m*. **2** (*shape*) forme *f*; (*outline*) silhouette *f*; (*of woman*) ligne *f*; **she has a nice f.** elle est bien faite. **3** (*diagram*) & *Liter* figure *f*; **a f. of speech** (*figurative usage*) une façon de parler; **f. skating** patinage *m* artistique. **4** (*important person*) figure *f*.

figure² ['fɪgər, *Am* 'fɪgjər] *vt* **to f. that** (*guess*) penser que; **to f. out** arriver à comprendre; (*problem*) résoudre; (*answer*) trouver; (*price*) calculer ▮ *vi* (*make sense*) s'expliquer; **to f. on doing** compter faire.

figurehead ['fɪgəhed] *n* (*of organization*) potiche *f*.

filch [fɪltʃ] *vt* (*steal*) voler (**from** à).

file [faɪl] **1** *n* (*tool*) lime *f* ▮ *vt* **to f. (down)** limer.

2 *n* (*folder, information*) dossier *m*; (*loose-leaf*) classeur *m*; (*for card index, computer data*) fichier *m*; **to be on f.** figurer au dossier ▮ *vt* (*application, complaint*) déposer; **to f. (away)** (*document*) classer.

3 *n* **in single f.** en file ▮ *vi* **to f. in/out** entrer/sortir à la queue leu leu; **to f. past** (*general, coffin*) défiler devant. ●**filing cabinet** *n* classeur *m*.

fill [fɪl] *vt* remplir (**with** de); (*tooth*) plomber; (*need*) répondre à; **to f. in** (*form, hole*) remplir; **to f. s.o. in on sth** mettre qn au courant de qch; **to f. out** (*form*) remplir; **to f. up** (*container, form*) remplir.

▮ *vi* **to f. (up)** se remplir; **to f. out** (*get fatter*) grossir; **to f. up** *Aut* faire le plein. ▮ *n* **to eat one's f.** manger à sa faim; **to have had one's f. of s.o./sth** en avoir assez de qn/qch. ●**filling** *a* (*meal*) nourrissant ▮ *n* (*in tooth*) plombage *m*; *Culin* garniture *f*; **f. station** poste *m* d'essence.

fillet ['fɪlɪt, *Am* fɪ'leɪ] *n Culin* filet *m* ▮ *vt* (*pt & pp Am* [fɪ'leɪd]) (*fish*) découper en filets.

filly ['fɪlɪ] *n* (*horse*) pouliche *f*.

film [fɪlm] *n* film *m*; (*layer*) & *Phot* pellicule *f* ▮ *a* (*festival*) du film; (*studio, critic*) de cinéma; **f. fan** *or* **buff** cinéphile *mf*; **f. maker** cinéaste *m*; **f. star** vedette *f* (de cinéma) ▮ *vt* filmer ▮ *vi* (*of film maker, actor*) tourner.

Filofax® ['faɪləʊfæks] *n* (agenda *m*) organiseur *m*.

filter ['fɪltər] *n* filtre *m*; **f. tip** (bout *m*) filtre *m*; **f.-tipped cigarette** cigarette *f* (à bout) filtre ▮ *vt* filtrer ▮ *vi* filtrer (**through sth** à travers qch).

filth [fɪlθ] *n* saleté *f*; (*obscenities*) *Fig* saletés *fpl*. ●**filthy** *a* (**-ier, -iest**) (*hands, shoes etc*) sale; (*language*) obscène.

fin [fɪn] *n* (*of fish, seal*) nageoire *f*.

final ['faɪn(ə)l] *a* (*last*) dernier; (*decision*) définitif ▮ *n Sp* finale *f*; *pl Univ* examens *mpl* de dernière année. ●**finalist** *n Sp* finaliste *mf*. ●**finalize** *vt* (*plan*) mettre au point; (*date*) fixer. ●**finally** *adv* (*lastly, eventually*) enfin; (*once and for all*) définitivement.

finale [fɪ'nɑːlɪ] *n Mus* finale *m*.

finance ['faɪnæns] *n* finance *f*; *pl* (*of person*) finances *fpl*; (*of company*) situation *f* financière ▮ *vt* financer.

financial [faɪ'nænʃəl] *a* financier; **f. year** année *f* budgétaire. ●**—ly** *adv* financièrement.

find [faɪnd] *n* (*discovery*) trouvaille *f* ▮ *vt* (*pt & pp* **found**) trouver; (*sth or s.o. lost*) retrouver; **to f. difficulty doing** éprouver de la difficulté à faire; **I f. that** je trouve que; **to f. s.o. guilty** *Jur* déclarer qn coupable.

find out *vt* (*secret etc*) découvrir; (*person*) démasquer ▮ *vi* (*inquire*) se renseigner (**about** sur); **to f. out about sth** (*discover*) découvrir qch.

findings ['faɪndɪŋz] *npl* conclusions *fpl*.

fine¹ [faɪn] *n* (*money*) amende *f*; (*for driving offence*) contravention *f* ▮ *vt* **to f. s.o. (£10/***etc*) infliger une amende (de dix livres/*etc*) à qn.

fine² [faɪn] **1** *a* (**-er, -est**) (*thin, not coarse*) fin; (*distinction*) subtil ▮ *adv* (*to cut, write*) menu. **2** *a* (**-er, -est**) (*very good*) excellent; (*weather, statue*) beau (*f* belle); **it's f.** (*weather*) il fait beau; **he's f.** (*healthy*) il va bien ▮ *adv* (*well*) très bien.

finery ['faɪnərɪ] *n* (*clothes*) parure *f*.

finger ['fɪŋgər] *n* doigt *m*; **little f.** petit doigt *m*; **middle f.** majeur *m*; **f. mark** trace *f* de doigt ▮ *vt* toucher (des doigts). ●**fingernail** *n* ongle *m*. ●**fingerprint** *n* empreinte *f* (digitale). ●**fingertip** *n* bout *m* du doigt.

finicky ['fɪnɪkɪ] *a* (*precise*) méticuleux; (*difficult*) difficile (**about** sur).

finish ['fɪnɪʃ] *n* (*end*) fin *f*; (*of race*) arrivée *f*; (*of article, car etc*) finition *f*; **paint with a matt f.** peinture *f* mate.

▮ *vt* **to f. (off** *or* **up)** finir, terminer; **to f. doing** finir de faire; **to f. s.o. off** (*kill*) achever qn.

▮ *vi* (*of meeting etc*) finir, se terminer; (*of person*) finir, terminer; **to have finished with** (*object*) ne plus avoir besoin de; (*situation, person*) en avoir fini avec; **to f. off** *or* **up** (*of person*) finir, terminer; **to f. up in** (*end up in*) se retrouver à; **to f. up doing** finir par faire; **to put the finishing touch to sth** mettre la dernière main à qch. ●**finished** *a* (*ended, ruined etc*) fini.

finite ['faɪnaɪt] *a* fini.

Finland ['fɪnlənd] *n* Finlande *f*. ●**Finn** *n* Finlandais, -aise *mf*. ●**Finnish** *a* finlandais ▮ *n* (*language*) finnois *m*.

fir [fɜːr] *n* (*tree, wood*) sapin *m*.

fire¹ ['faɪər] *n* feu *m*; (*accidental*) incendie

m; (*electric heater*) radiateur *m*; **to light** *or* **make a f.** faire du feu; **to set f. to** mettre le feu à; **to catch f.** prendre feu; **on f.** en feu; **(there's a) f.!** au feu!; **f.!** *Mil* feu!; **f. alarm** alarme *f* d'incendie; **f. brigade,** *Am* **f. department** pompiers *mpl*; **f. engine** (*vehicle*) voiture *f* de pompiers; **f. escape** escalier *m* de secours; **f. station** caserne *f* de pompiers.

fire[2] ['faɪər] *vt* (*cannon*) tirer; **to f. a gun** tirer un coup de fusil *or* de pistolet; **to f. questions at s.o.** bombarder qn de questions; **to f. s.o.** (*dismiss*) renvoyer qn ‖ *vi* tirer (**at** sur); **firing squad** peloton *m* d'exécution.

firearm ['faɪərɑːm] *n* arme *f* à feu. ● **firecracker** *n Am* pétard *m*. ● **fireguard** *n* garde-feu *m inv*. ● **fireman** *n* (*pl* **-men**) (sapeur-)pompier *m*. ● **fireplace** *n* cheminée *f*. ● **fireproof** *a* (*door*) ignifugé. ● **fireside** *n* coin *m* du feu. ● **firewood** *n* bois *m* de chauffage. ● **firework** *n* fusée *f*; (*firecracker*) pétard *m*; **a f. display, fireworks** feu *m* d'artifice.

firm [fɜːm] **1** *n Com* entreprise *f*, maison *f*. **2** *a* (**-er, -est**) (*earth, decision etc*) ferme; **f. with s.o.** (*strict*) ferme avec qn ‖ *adv* **to stand f.** tenir bon. ● **—ly** *adv* fermement; (*to speak*) d'une voix ferme.

first [fɜːst] *a* premier; **f. cousin** cousin, -ine *mf* germain(e).

‖ *adv* (*firstly*) d'abord, premièrement; (*for the first time*) pour la première fois; **f. of all** tout d'abord; **at f.** d'abord; **to come f.** (*in race*) arriver premier; (*in exam*) être premier.

‖ *n* premier, -ière *mf*; **from the f.** dès le début; **f. aid** premiers secours *mpl*; **f. (gear)** *Aut* première *f*.

first-class [fɜːst'klɑːs] *a* excellent; (*ticket, seat*) de première (classe); (*mail*) ordinaire ‖ *adv* (*to travel*) en première. ● **f.-'hand** *a* **to have (had) f.-hand experience of** avoir fait l'expérience personnelle de. ● **f.-'rate** *a* excellent.

firstly ['fɜːstlɪ] *adv* premièrement.

fish [fɪʃ] *n inv* poisson *m*; **f. market** marché *m* aux poissons; **f. bone** arête *f*; **f. fingers,** *Am* **f. sticks** *Culin* bâtonnets *mpl* de poisson; **f. shop** poissonnerie *f*; **f.-and-chip shop** boutique *f* de fritures.

‖ *vi* pêcher; **to f. for** (*salmon etc*) pêcher.

‖ *vt* **to f. out** (*from water*) repêcher; (*from pocket etc*) sortir. ● **—ing** *n* pêche *f*; **to go f.** aller à la pêche; **f. boat**/*etc* bateau *m*/*etc* de pêche; **f. net** (*of fisherman*) filet *m* (de pêche); (*of angler*) épuisette *f*; **f. rod** canne *f* à pêche. ● **fisherman** *n* (*pl* **-men**) pêcheur *m*. ● **fishmonger** *n* poissonnier, -ière *mf*.

fishy ['fɪʃɪ] *a* (**-ier, -iest**) (*story etc*) louche.

fist [fɪst] *n* poing *m*. ● **fistful** *n* poignée *f*.

fit[1] [fɪt] **1** *a* (**fitter, fittest**) (*healthy*) en bonne santé; (*in good shape*) en forme; (*suitable*) propre (**for** à, **to do** à faire); (*worthy*) digne (**for** de, **to do** de faire); (*able*) apte (**for** à, **to do** à faire); **f. to eat** bon à manger; **to see f. to do** juger à propos de faire; **to keep f.** se maintenir en forme.

2 *vt* (*pt & pp* **fitted**, *Am* **fit**) (*of clothes*) aller (bien) à (*qn*); (*match*) répondre à, correspondre à; (*put in*) poser (*fenêtre, moquette etc*); **to f. sth (on) to sth** (*put*) poser qch sur qch; (*fix*) fixer qch à qch; **to f. (out** *or* **up) with sth** (*house, ship etc*) équiper de qch; **to f. in** (*insert*) faire entrer qch; **to f. s.o. in** (*find time to see*) prendre qn; **to f. (in) sth** (*go in*) aller dans qch; **to f. (on) sth** (*go on*) aller sur qch.

‖ *vi* (*of clothes*) aller (bien) (*à qn*); **this shirt fits** (*fits me*) cette chemise me va (bien); **to f. (in)** (*go in*) entrer, aller; (*of facts, plans*) s'accorder (**with** avec); **he doesn't f. in** il ne peut pas s'intégrer.

‖ *n* **a good f.** (*clothes*) à la bonne taille; **a close** *or* **tight f.** ajusté. ● **fitted** *a* (*cupboard*) encastré; (*garment*) ajusté; **f. carpet** moquette *f*; **f. kitchen** cuisine aménagée. ● **fitting 1** *a* (*suitable*) convenable. **2** *n* (*of clothes*) essayage *m*; **f. room** (*booth*) cabine *f* d'essayage. **3** *npl* (*in house etc*) installations *fpl*.

fit[2] [fɪt] *n* (*attack*) *Med & Fig* accès *m*, crise *f*; **a f. of crying** une crise de larmes; **in fits and starts** par à-coups.

fitment ['fɪtmənt] *n* (*furniture*) meuble *m* encastré.

fitness ['fɪtnɪs] *n* (*health*) santé *f*; (*for job*) aptitudes *fpl* (**for** pour).

fitter ['fɪtər] *n Tech* monteur, -euse *mf*.

five [faɪv] *a & n* cinq (*m*). ● **fiver** *n Br Fam* billet *m* de cinq livres; *Am Fam* billet *m* de cinq dollars.

fix [fɪks] **1** *vt* (*make firm, decide*) fixer; (*tie with rope*) attacher; (*mend*) réparer; (*deal with*) arranger; (*prepare, cook*) préparer, faire; (*rig*) *Fam* truquer; (*bribe*) *Fam* acheter; (*put*) mettre (*ses espoirs etc*) (**on** en); **to f. (on)** (*lid etc*) mettre en place; **to f. up** (*trip etc*) arranger; **to f. s.o. up with a job**/*etc* procurer un travail/*etc* à qn.

2 *n* **in a f.** *Fam* dans le pétrin. ● **fixed** *a* (*idea, price etc*) fixe; **how's he f. for...?** *Fam* (*cash*) a-t-il assez de...?; (*tomorrow*) qu'est-ce qu'il fait pour...?

fixture ['fɪkstʃər] **1** *n Sp* rencontre *f* (prévue). **2** *npl* **fixtures** (*in house*) installations *fpl*.
fizz [fɪz] *vi* (*of champagne*) pétiller. ● **fizzy** *a* (**-ier, -iest**) pétillant.
fizzle ['fɪz(ə)l] *vi* **to f. out** (*of firework*) rater; (*of plan*) *Fig* tomber à l'eau.
flabbergasted ['flæbəgɑːstɪd] *a Fam* sidéré.
flabby ['flæbɪ] *a* (**-ier, -iest**) (*skin, person*) mou (*f* molle), flasque.
flag [flæg] **1** *n* drapeau *m*; *Nau* pavillon *m*; (*for charity*) insigne *m*; **f. stop** *Am* arrêt *m* facultatif ‖ *vt* (**-gg-**) **to f. down** (*taxi*) faire signe à. **2** *vi* (**-gg-**) (*of conversation*) languir; (*of worker*) fléchir. ● **flagpole** *n* mât *m*.
flagrant ['fleɪgrənt] *a* flagrant.
flair [fleər] *n* (*intuition*) flair *m*; **to have a f. for** (*talent*) avoir un don pour.
flake [fleɪk] *n* (*of snow etc*) flocon *m*; (*of soap, metal*) paillette *f* ‖ *vi* **to f. (off)** (*of paint*) s'écailler. ● **flaky** *a* **f. pastry** pâte *f* feuilletée.
flamboyant [flæm'bɔɪənt] *a* (*person, manner*) extravagant.
flame [fleɪm] *n* flamme *f*; **to burst into flame(s), go up in flames** prendre feu.
flaming ['fleɪmɪŋ] *a* (*damn*) *Fam* fichu.
flamingo [flə'mɪŋgəʊ] *n* (*pl* **-os** *or* **-oes**) (*bird*) flamant *m*.
flammable ['flæməb(ə)l] *a* inflammable.
flan [flæn] *n* tarte *f*.
flank [flæŋk] *n* flanc *m* ‖ *vt* flanquer; **flanked by** flanqué de.
flannel ['flænəl] *n* (*cloth*) flanelle *f*; **(face) f.** gant *m* de toilette.
flap [flæp] **1** *vi* (**-pp-**) (*of wings, sail etc*) battre ‖ *vt* **to f. its wings** (*of bird*) battre des ailes. **2** *n* (*of pocket, envelope*) rabat *m*; (*of table*) abattant *m*.
flare [fleər] *n Mil* fusée *f* éclairante; (*for runway*) balise *f* ‖ *vi* (*blaze*) flamber; **to f. up** (*of fire*) prendre; (*of violence, war*) éclater; (*get angry*) s'emporter. ● **f.-up** *n* (*of violence, fire*) flambée *f*.
flared [fleəd] *a* (*skirt*) évasé; (*trousers, Am pants*) (à) pattes d'éléphant.
flash [flæʃ] *n* (*of light*) éclat *m*; (*of genius*) éclair *m*; *Phot* flash *m*; **f. of lightning** éclair *m*; **news f.** flash *m*; **in a f.** en un clin d'œil. ‖ *vi* (*shine*) briller; (*on and off*) clignoter. ‖ *vt* (*a light*) projeter; (*aim*) diriger (**on, at** sur); **to f. one's (head)lights** faire un appel de phares. ● **flashback** *n* retour *m* en arrière. ● **flashlight** *n* (*torch*) lampe *f* de poche; *Phot* flash *m*.
flashy ['flæʃɪ] *a* (**-ier, -iest**) *a* voyant, tape-à-l'œil *inv*.
flask [flɑːsk] *n* thermos® *m or f inv*; (*for brandy, medicine etc*) flacon *m*.
flat[1] [flæt] *a* (**flatter, flattest**) plat; (*tyre or Am tire, battery*) à plat; (*nose*) aplati; (*beer*) éventé; (*refusal*) net (*f* nette); (*rate, fare*) fixe; **f. fee** prix *m* unique; **to put sth (down) f.** mettre qch à plat; **to be f.-footed** avoir les pieds plats.
‖ *adv* **to sing f.** chanter trop bas; **to fall f. on one's face** tomber à plat ventre; **in two minutes f.** en deux minutes pile; **f. out** (*to work*) d'arrache-pied; (*to run*) à toute vitesse.
‖ *n* (*puncture*) *Aut* crevaison *f*; (*of hand*) plat *m*; *Mus* bémol *m*. ● **flatly** *adv* (*to deny, refuse etc*) catégoriquement.
flat[2] [flæt] *n* (*rooms*) appartement *m*.
flatten ['flætən] *vt* (*crops*) coucher; (*town*) raser; **to f. (out)** (*metal etc*) aplatir.
flatter ['flætər] *vt* flatter. ● **—ing** *a* (*remark etc*) flatteur; **it's a f. hat** ce chapeau vous avantage. ● **flattery** *n* flatterie *f*.
flaunt [flɔːnt] *vt* (*show off*) faire étalage de; (*defy*) *Am* narguer, défier.
flautist ['flɔːtɪst] *n* flûtiste *mf*.
flavour ['fleɪvər] (*Am* **flavor**) *n* (*taste*) goût *m*, saveur *f*; (*of ice cream etc*) parfum *m* ‖ *vt* (*food*) (*with seasoning*) assaisonner; (*ice cream etc*) parfumer (**with** à); **lemon-flavoured** (parfumé) au citron. ● **—ing** *n* assaisonnement *m*; (*in cake, ice cream etc*) parfum *m*.
flaw [flɔː] *n* défaut *m*. ● **flawless** *a* parfait.
flax [flæks] *n* lin *m*.
flea [fliː] *n* puce *f*; **f. market** marché *m* aux puces. ● **fleapit** *n Fam* cinéma *m* miteux.
fleck [flek] *n* (*mark*) petite tache *f*.
flee [fliː] *vi* (*pt & pp* **fled**) s'enfuir, fuir ‖ *vt* (*place*) s'enfuir de; (*danger etc*) fuir.
fleece [fliːs] **1** *n* (*sheep's coat*) toison *f*. **2** *vt* (*rob*) *Fam* voler (*qn*).
fleet [fliːt] *n* (*of ships*) flotte *f*; **a f. of buses/***etc* (*of company*) un parc d'autobus/*etc*; (*shuttle service*) une noria d'autobus/*etc*.
fleeting ['fliːtɪŋ] *a* (*visit, moment*) bref (*f* brève).
Flemish ['flemɪʃ] *a* flamand ‖ *n* (*language*) flamand *m*.
flesh [fleʃ] *n* chair *f*; **in the f.** en chair et en os; **he's your f. and blood** (*child*) c'est la chair de ta chair; (*brother etc*) il est de ton sang. ● **fleshy** *a* (**-ier, -iest**) charnu.
flew [fluː] *pt of* **fly**[2].
flex [fleks] **1** *vt* (*limb*) fléchir; (*muscle*) faire jouer. **2** *n* (*wire*) fil *m* (souple); (*for telephone*) cordon *m*.

flexible ['fleksɪb(ə)l] *a* (*person, wire etc*) souple.

flick [flɪk] *vt* donner un petit coup à; **to f. sth off** (*remove*) enlever qch (d'une chiquenaude); **to f. a switch** pousser un bouton ‖ *vi* **to f. through** (*pages*) feuilleter ‖ *n* (*with finger*) chiquenaude *f*; (*with whip etc*) petit coup *m*; **f. knife** couteau *m* à cran d'arrêt.

flicker ['flɪkər] *vi* (*of flame, light*) vaciller; (*of needle*) osciller.

flier ['flaɪər] *n* **1** (*leaflet*) *Am* prospectus *m*. **2 high f.** (*ambitious person*) jeune loup *m*.

flies [flaɪz] *npl* (*on trousers, Am pants*) braguette *f*.

flight [flaɪt] *n* **1** (*of bird, aircraft etc*) vol *m*; **f. to/from** vol *m* à destination de/en provenance de; **to have a good f.** faire bon voyage; **f. attendant** steward *m or* hôtesse *f* de l'air; **f. deck** cabine *f* de pilotage. **2** (*floor, storey, Am story*) étage *m*; **f. of stairs** escalier *m*. **3** (*escape*) fuite *f* (**from** de); **to take f.** prendre la fuite.

flimsy ['flɪmzɪ] *a* (**-ier, -iest**) (*cloth etc*) (*light*) (trop) léger; (*thin*) (trop) mince; (*excuse*) mince.

flinch [flɪntʃ] *vi* (*with pain*) tressaillir; **to f. from** (*duty*) se dérober à; **without flinching** (*complaining*) sans broncher.

fling [flɪŋ] *vt* (*pt & pp* **flung**) lancer; **to f. open** (*door*) ouvrir brutalement.

flint [flɪnt] *n* silex *m*; (*for cigarette lighter*) pierre *f*.

flip [flɪp] *vt* (**-pp-**) (*with finger*) donner une chiquenaude à ‖ *vi* **to f. through** (*book*) feuilleter.

flip-flops ['flɪpflɒps] *npl* tongs *fpl*.

flippant ['flɪpənt] *a* irrévérencieux; (*offhand*) désinvolte.

flipper ['flɪpər] *n* (*of swimmer*) palme *f*; (*of seal*) nageoire *f*.

flirt [flɜːt] *vi* flirter (**with** avec) ‖ *n* flirteur, -euse *mf*.

flit [flɪt] *vi* (**-tt-**) (*fly*) voltiger.

float [fləʊt] *n Fishing* flotteur *m*; (*in parade*) char *m* ‖ *vi* flotter (**on** sur); **to f. down the river** descendre la rivière. ●**—ing** *a* (*wood etc*) flottant; **f. voters** électeurs *mpl* indécis.

flock [flɒk] *n* (*of sheep*) troupeau *m*; (*of birds*) volée *f*; (*of tourists etc*) foule *f* ‖ *vi* venir en foule.

flog [flɒg] *vt* (**-gg-**) **1** (*beat*) flageller. **2** (*sell*) *Sl* bazarder.

flood [flʌd] *n* inondation *f*; (*of letters, tears etc*) *Fig* flot *m*, déluge *m* ‖ *vt* (*field, house etc*) inonder (**with** de) ‖ *vi* (*of river*) déborder; (*of building*) être inondé; **to f. in** (*of money*) affluer; **to f. into** (*of tourists etc*) envahir (*un pays etc*). ●**—ing** *n* inondation *f*; (*floods*) inondations *fpl*.

floodlight ['flʌdlaɪt] *n* projecteur *m* ‖ *vt* (*pt & pp* **floodlit**) illuminer; **floodlit match** *Sp* (match *m* en) nocturne *f*.

floor [flɔːr] **1** *n* (*ground*) sol *m*; (*wooden etc in building*) plancher *m*; (*storey, Am story*) étage *m*; **(dance) f.** piste *f* (de danse); **on the f.** par terre; **on the first f.** au premier étage; (*ground floor*) *Am* au rez-de-chaussée; **f. show** spectacle *m* (de cabaret). **2** *vt* (*knock down*) terrasser; (*puzzle*) stupéfier. ●**floorboard** *n* planche *f*.

flop [flɒp] **1** *vi* (**-pp-**) **to f. down** (*collapse*) s'effondrer. **2** *vi* (**-pp-**) *Fam* (*fail*) échouer; (*of play, film etc*) faire un four ‖ *n Fam* échec *m*; *Th Cin* four *m*.

floppy ['flɒpɪ] *a* (**-ier, -iest**) (*soft*) mou (*f* molle); (*clothes*) (trop) large; **f. disk** (*of computer*) disquette *f*.

floral ['flɔːrəl] *a* floral; (*material, pattern*) à fleurs.

florist ['flɒrɪst] *n* fleuriste *mf*.

floss [flɒs] *n* **(dental) f.** fil *m* (de soie) dentaire.

flotilla [flə'tɪlə] *n Nau* flottille *f*.

flounce [flaʊns] *n* (*on dress etc*) volant *m*.

flounder ['flaʊndər] **1** *vi* (*in water, speech etc*) patauger. **2** *n* (*fish*) carrelet *m*.

flour ['flaʊər] *n* farine *f*.

flourish ['flʌrɪʃ] **1** *vi* (*of person, business, plant*) prospérer; (*of the arts*) fleurir. **2** *vt* (*wave*) brandir (*bâton etc*). **3** *n* (*decoration*) fioriture *f*; *Mus* fanfare *f*. ●**—ing** *a* prospère.

flout [flaʊt] *vt* narguer, braver.

flow [fləʊ] *vi* couler; (*of electric current*) circuler; (*of hair*) flotter; (*of traffic*) s'écouler; **to f. in** (*of people, money*) affluer; **to f. into the sea** (*of river*) se jeter dans la mer ‖ *n* (*of river*) courant *m*; (*of tide*) flux *m*; (*of current, information, blood*) circulation *f*; (*of traffic, liquid*) écoulement *m*; (*of visitors, insults*) flot *m*; **f. chart** organigramme *m*. ●**flowing** *a* (*movement*) gracieux; (*style*) coulant.

flower ['flaʊər] *n* fleur *f*; **in f.** en fleur(s); **f. bed** parterre *m*; **f. pot** pot *m* de fleurs; **f. shop** (boutique *f* de) fleuriste *mf* ‖ *vi* fleurir. ●**—ed** *a* (*dress*) à fleurs. ●**—ing** *a* (*in bloom*) en fleurs; (*with flowers*) (*shrub etc*) à fleurs. ●**flowery** *a* (*material*) à fleurs.

flown [fləʊn] *pp of* **fly**[2].

flu [fluː] *n* (*influenza*) *Fam* grippe *f*.

fluctuate ['flʌktʃʊeɪt] *vi* varier. ●**fluctuation(s)** [-'eɪʃ(ə)n(z)] *n(pl)* (*in prices etc*) fluctuations *fpl* (**in** de).

fluent ['flu:ənt] *a* **he's f. in Russian, his Russian is f.** il parle couramment le russe; **to be f., be a f. speaker** s'exprimer avec facilité. ●**—ly** *adv* (*to speak a language*) couramment.

fluff [flʌf] *n* (*of material*) peluche(s) *f(pl)*; (*on floor*) moutons *mpl*. ●**fluffy** *a* (**-ier, -iest**) (*bird*) duveteux; (*material*) pelucheux; (*toy*) en peluche; **light and f.** (*cake*) très léger.

fluid ['flu:ɪd] *a* fluide; (*plans*) flexible ‖ *n* fluide *m*.

fluke [flu:k] *n Fam* coup *m* de chance; **by a f.** par raccroc.

flung [flʌŋ] *pt* & *pp of* **fling.**

flunk [flʌŋk] *vi* (*in exam*) *Am Fam* être collé ‖ *vt Am Fam* (*exam*) être collé à; (*pupil*) coller.

fluorescent [flʊə'res(ə)nt] *a* fluorescent.

fluoride ['flʊəraɪd] *n* fluor *m*; **f. toothpaste** dentifrice *m* au fluor.

flurry ['flʌrɪ] *n* **1** (*of activity*) poussée *f*. **2** (*of snow*) rafale *f*.

flush [flʌʃ] **1** *n* (*blush*) rougeur *f*; (*of youth, beauty*) éclat *m* ‖ *vi* (*blush*) rougir. **2** *vt* **to f. sth (out)** (*clean*) nettoyer qch à grande eau; **to f. the pan** *or* **toilet** tirer la chasse d'eau; **to f. s.o. out** (*chase away*) faire sortir qn (**from** de). **3** *a* (*level*) de niveau (**with** de). ●**flushed** *a* (*cheeks etc*) rouge; **f. with** (*success*) ivre de.

fluster ['flʌstər] *vt* énerver; **to get flustered** s'énerver.

flute [flu:t] *n* flûte *f*. ●**flutist** *n Am* flûtiste *mf*.

flutter ['flʌtər] *vi* (*of bird*) voltiger; (*of wing*) battre; (*of flag*) flotter (mollement) ‖ *vt* **to f. its wings** battre des ailes.

fly[1] [flaɪ] *n* (*insect*) mouche *f*.

fly[2] [flaɪ] *vi* (*pt* **flew,** *pp* **flown**) (*of bird, aircraft etc*) voler; (*of passenger*) aller en avion; (*of time*) passer vite; (*of flag*) flotter; **to f. away** *or* **off** s'envoler; **to f. out** (*of passenger*) partir en avion; (*from room*) sortir à toute vitesse; **I must f.!** il faut que je file!; **to f. at s.o.** (*attack*) sauter sur qn. ‖ *vt* (*aircraft*) piloter; (*passengers*) transporter (par avion); (*airline*) voyager par; (*flag*) arborer; (*kite*) faire voler; **to f. the French flag** battre pavillon français; **to f. across** *or* **over** (*country etc*) survoler. ●**flying** *n* (*flight*) vol *m*; (*air travel*) (*as passenger*) l'avion *m*; ‖ *a* (*doctor, personnel*) volant; **with f. colours** (*to succeed*) haut la main; **f. saucer** soucoupe *f* volante; **f. visit** visite *f* éclair *inv*; **f. time** (*length*) *Av* durée *f* du vol; **ten hours'/***etc* **f. time** dix heures/*etc* de vol.

fly[3] [flaɪ] *n* (*on trousers*) braguette *f*.

flyby ['flaɪbaɪ] *n Av Am* défilé *m* aérien. ●**fly-by-night** *a* (*firm*) véreux. ●**flyover** *n* (*bridge*) toboggan *m*. ●**flypast** *n Av* défilé *m* aérien.

foal [fəʊl] *n* poulain *m*.

foam [fəʊm] *n* (*on sea, in mouth*) écume *f*; (*on beer*) mousse *f*; **f. rubber** caoutchouc *m* mousse; **f. mattress/***etc* matelas *m*/*etc* mousse ‖ *vi* (*of sea, mouth*) écumer; (*of beer, soap*) mousser.

fob [fɒb] *vt* (**-bb-**) **to f. s.o. off with sth** se débarrasser de qn en lui donnant *or* lui racontant qch.

focus ['fəʊkəs] *n* (*of attention, interest*) centre *m*; *Geom etc* foyer *m*; **in f.** (*photo etc*) net (*f* nette); **out of f.** flou ‖ *vt* (*image, camera*) mettre au point; (*efforts*) concentrer (**on** sur) ‖ *vti* **to f. (one's attention) on** se tourner vers; **to f. (one's eyes) on** fixer les yeux sur.

fodder ['fɒdər] *n* fourrage *m*.

foe [fəʊ] *n* ennemi, -ie *mf*.

foetus ['fi:təs] *n* fœtus *m*.

fog [fɒg] *n* brouillard *m*. ●**fogbound** *a* bloqué par le brouillard. ●**foglamp** *or* **foglight** *n Aut* (phare *m*) anti-brouillard *m*.

fogey ['fəʊgɪ] *n* **old f.** vieille baderne *f*.

foggy ['fɒgɪ] *a* (**-ier, -iest**); **it's f.** il y a du brouillard; **f. weather** brouillard *m*; **on a f. day** par un jour de brouillard; **she hasn't the foggiest idea** *Fam* elle n'en a pas la moindre idée.

foil [fɔɪl] **1** *n* (*for cooking*) papier *m* alu(minium). **2** *n* (*contrasting person*) repoussoir *m*. **3** *vt* (*plans etc*) déjouer.

fold[1] [fəʊld] *n* (*in paper etc*) pli *m* ‖ *vt* plier; (*wrap*) envelopper (**in** dans); **to f. away** *or* **down** *or* **up** (*chair etc*) plier; **to f. back** *or* **over** (*blanket etc*) replier; **to f. one's arms** (se) croiser les bras ‖ *vi* (*of chair etc*) se plier; **to f. away** *or* **down** *or* **up** (*of chair etc*) se plier; **to f. back** *or* **over** (*of blanket etc*) se replier. ●**—ing** *a* (*chair etc*) pliant. ●**folder** *n* (*file holder*) chemise *f*; (*pamphlet*) dépliant *m*.

fold[2] [fəʊld] *n* (*for sheep*) parc *m* à moutons.

-fold [fəʊld] *suff* **tenfold** *a* par dix ‖ *adv* dix fois.

foliage ['fəʊlɪɪdʒ] *n* feuillage *m*.

folk [fəʊk] **1** *npl* (*Am* **folks**) gens *mpl or fpl*; **my folks** (*parents*) *Fam* mes parents *mpl*; **old f.** les vieux *mpl*. **2** *a* (*dance etc*) folklorique; **f. music** (*contemporary*) (musique *f*) folk *m*.

folklore ['fəʊklɔ:r] *n* folklore *m*.

follow ['fɒləʊ] *vt* suivre; (*career*) poursuivre; **followed by** suivi de; **to f. s.o. around** suivre qn partout; **to f. through** (*plan, idea etc*) poursuivre jusqu'au bout; **to f. up** (*idea, story*) creuser; (*clue, suggestion*) suivre; (*letter*) donner suite à.
▮ *vi* (*of person, event etc*) suivre; **it follows that** il s'ensuit que; **to f. on** (*come after*) suivre. ●**following 1** *a* suivant ▮*prep* à la suite de. **2** *n* (*supporters*) partisans *mpl*; **to have a large f.** (*of TV programme, fashion*) être très suivi.
follower ['fɒləʊər] *n* (*supporter*) partisan *m*.
folly ['fɒlɪ] *n* folie *f*; **an act of f.** une folie.
fond [fɒnd] *a* (**-er, -est**) (*loving*) tendre; (*doting*) indulgent; **to be (very) f. of** aimer beaucoup. ●**—ness** *n* prédilection *f* (**for sth** pour qch); (*for people*) affection *f* (**for** pour).
fondle ['fɒnd(ə)l] *vt* caresser.
food [fuːd] *n* nourriture *f*; (*particular substance*) aliment *m*; (*cooking*) cuisine *f*; (*for cats, dogs etc*) pâtée *f*; *pl* (*foodstuffs*) aliments *mpl* ▮ *a* (*needs etc*) alimentaire; **f. poisoning** intoxication *f* alimentaire. ●**foodstuffs** *npl* denrées *fpl* alimentaires.
fool [fuːl] *n* imbécile *mf*; **(you) silly f.!** espèce d'imbécile!; **to make a f. of s.o.** (*ridicule*) ridiculiser qn; **to play the f.** faire l'imbécile ▮ *vt* (*trick*) rouler ▮ *vi* **to f. (about** *or* **around)** faire l'imbécile; (*waste time*) perdre son temps.
foolhardy ['fuːlhɑːdɪ] *a* téméraire.
foolish ['fuːlɪʃ] *a* bête. ●**—ly** bêtement. ●**—ness** *n* bêtise *f*.
foolproof ['fuːlpruːf] *a* (*scheme etc*) infaillible.
foot[1], *pl* **feet** [fʊt, fiːt] *n* pied *m*; (*of animal*) patte *f*; (*measure*) pied *m* (= *30,48 cm*); **at the f. of** (*page, stairs*) au bas de; (*table*) au bout de; **on f.** à pied; **on one's feet** (*standing*) debout; **f. brake** *Aut* frein *m* au plancher.
foot[2] [fʊt] *vt* (*bill*) payer.
football ['fʊtbɔːl] *n* (*game*) football *m*; (*ball*) ballon *m*. ●**footballer** *n* joueur, -euse *mf* de football. ●**footbridge** *n* passerelle *f*. ●**foothills** *npl* contreforts *mpl*. ●**foothold** *n* prise *f* (de pied); *Fig* position *f*; **to gain a f.** prendre pied. ●**footlights** *npl Th* rampe *f*. ●**footmark** *n* empreinte *f* (de pied). ●**footnote** *n* note *f* au bas de la page; *Fig* post-scriptum *m*. ●**footpath** *n* sentier *m*; (*at roadside*) chemin *m* (piétonnier). ●**footprint** *n* empreinte *f* (de pied *or* de pas). ●**footstep** *n* pas *m*; **to follow in s.o.'s footsteps** suivre les traces de qn. ●**footwear** *n* chaussures *fpl*.
footing ['fʊtɪŋ] *n* prise *f* (de pied); *Fig* position *f*; **on an equal f.** sur un pied d'égalité.
for [fɒr, *unstressed* fər] **1** *prep* pour; (*for a distance or period of*) pendant; (*in spite of*) malgré; **f. you/me/***etc* pour toi/moi/*etc*; **what's it f.?** ça sert à quoi?; **f. love** par amour; **to swim f.** (*towards*) nager vers; **a train f.** un train à destination de, un train pour; **the road f. London** la route (en direction) de Londres; **to come f. dinner** venir dîner; **it's time f. breakfast** c'est l'heure du petit déjeuner; **to sell sth f. seven dollars** vendre qch sept dollars; **what's the Russian f. 'book'?** comment dit-on 'livre' en russe?; **she walked f. a kilometre** elle a marché pendant un kilomètre; **he was away f. a month** (*throughout*) il a été absent pendant un mois; **he won't be back f. a month** il ne sera pas de retour avant un mois; **he's been here f. a month** (*he's still here*) il est ici depuis un mois; **I haven't seen him f. ten years** voilà dix ans que je ne l'ai vu, je ne l'ai pas vu depuis dix ans; **it's easy/possible f. her to do it** il lui est facile/possible de le faire; **it's f. you to say** c'est à toi de dire; **f. that to be done** pour que ça soit fait.
2 *conj* (*because*) car.
forbid [fə'bɪd] *vt* (*pt* **forbad(e),** *pp* **forbidden,** *pres p* **forbidding**) interdire, défendre (**s.o. to do** à qn de faire); **to f. s.o. sth** interdire *or* défendre qch à qn. ●**forbidden** *a* (*fruit etc*) défendu; **she is f. to leave** il lui est interdit de partir.
force [fɔːs] *n* force *f*; **the (armed) forces** *Mil* les forces armées; **by (sheer) f.** de force; **in f.** (*rule*) en vigueur; (*in great numbers*) en grand nombre.
▮ *vt* forcer (*qn*) (**to do** à faire); (*impose*) imposer (**on** à); (*door, lock*) forcer; (*confession*) arracher (**from** à); **to f. one's way into** entrer de force dans; **to f. back** (*enemy*) faire reculer; **to f. down** (*aircraft*) forcer à atterrir; **to f. sth into sth** faire entrer qch de force dans qch; **to f. sth out** faire sortir qch de force. ●**forced** *a* **f. to do** obligé *or* forcé de faire; **a f. smile** un sourire forcé.
forceful ['fɔːsfəl] *a* énergique.
forceps ['fɔːseps] *n* forceps *m*.
forcibly ['fɔːsəblɪ] *adv* (*by force*) de force.
ford [fɔːd] *n* gué *m*.
fore [fɔːr] *n* **to come to the f.** passer au premier plan.
forearm ['fɔːrɑːm] *n* avant-bras *m inv*.
foreboding [fɔː'bəʊdɪŋ] *n* (*feeling*) pressentiment *m*.

forecast ['fɔːkɑːst] *vt* (*pt* & *pp* **forecast**) prévoir ‖ *n* prévision *f*; (*of weather*) prévisions *fpl*; *Sp* pronostic *m*.
forecourt ['fɔːkɔːt] *n* (*of hotel etc*) avant-cour *f*; (*of petrol or Am gas station*) aire *f* (de service), devant *m*.
forefinger ['fɔːfɪŋgər] *n* index *m*.
forefront ['fɔːfrʌnt] *n* **in the f. of** au premier rang de.
forego [fɔː'gəʊ] *vt* (*pp* **foregone**) renoncer à.
foreground ['fɔːgraʊnd] *n* premier plan *m*.
forehead ['fɒrɪd, 'fɔːhed] *n* (*brow*) front *m*.
foreign ['fɒrən] *a* étranger; (*trade*) extérieur; (*travel, correspondent*) à l'étranger; (*produce*) de l'étranger; **F. Minister,** *Br* **F. Secretary** ministre *m* des Affaires étrangères. ● **foreigner** *n* étranger, -ère *mf*.
foreman ['fɔːmən] *n* (*pl* **-men**) (*worker*) contremaître *m*.
foremost ['fɔːməʊst] **1** *a* principal. **2** *adv* **first and f.** tout d'abord.
forensic [fə'rensɪk] *a* (*laboratory, evidence*) médico-légal; **f. medicine** médecine *f* légale.
forerunner ['fɔːrʌnər] *n* précurseur *m*.
foresee [fɔː'siː] *vt* (*pt* **foresaw,** *pp* **foreseen**) prévoir. ● **—able** *a* prévisible.
foreshadow [fɔː'ʃædəʊ] *vt* présager.
foresight ['fɔːsaɪt] *n* prévoyance *f*.
forest ['fɒrɪst] *n* forêt *f*.
forestall [fɔː'stɔːl] *vt* devancer.
foretaste ['fɔːteɪst] *n* avant-goût *m* (**of** de).
foretell [fɔː'tel] *vt* (*pt* & *pp* **foretold**) prédire.
forever [fə'revər] *adv* (*for always*) pour toujours; (*continually*) sans cesse.
forewarn [fɔː'wɔːn] *vt* avertir.
foreword ['fɔːwɜːd] *n* avant-propos *m inv*.
forfeit ['fɔːfɪt] *vt* (*lose*) perdre ‖ *n* (*penalty*) peine *f*; (*in game*) gage *m*.
forg/e [fɔːdʒ] **1** *vt* (*signature, money*) contrefaire; (*document*) falsifier. **2** *vi* **to f. ahead** (*progress*) aller de l'avant. **3** *vt* (*metal*) forger ‖ *n* forge *f*. ● **—ed** *a* (*passport etc*) faux (*f* fausse); **f. money** fausse monnaie *f*. ● **—er** *n* (*of documents etc*) faussaire *m*.
forgery ['fɔːdʒərɪ] *n* faux *m*.
forget [fə'get] *vt* (*pt* **forgot,** *pp* **forgotten,** *pres p* **forgetting**) oublier (**to do** de faire); **f. it!** *Fam* (*it doesn't matter*) peu importe!; **to f. oneself** s'oublier ‖ *vi* oublier; **to f. about** oublier.
forgetful [fə'getfəl] *a* **he's f.** il n'a pas de mémoire.
forgiv/e [fə'gɪv] *vt* (*pt* **forgave,** *pp* **forgiven**) pardonner (**s.o. sth** qch à qn). ● **—ing** *a* indulgent. ● **forgiveness** *n* pardon *m*.
forgo [fɔː'gəʊ] *vt* (*pp* **forgone**) renoncer à.
fork [fɔːk] **1** *n* (*for eating*) fourchette *f*; (*for garden*) fourche *f*. **2** *vi* (*of road*) bifurquer; **to f. left** (*in vehicle*) prendre à gauche ‖ *n* (*in road*) bifurcation *f*. **3** *vt* **to f. out** (*money*) *Fam* allonger. ● **—ed** *a* fourchu. ● **forklift truck** *n* chariot *m* élévateur.
forlorn [fə'lɔːn] *a* (*forsaken*) abandonné; (*unhappy*) triste.
form [fɔːm] *n* (*shape, type, style*) forme *f*; (*document*) formulaire *m*; *Sch* classe *f*; **in the f. of** en forme de; **on f., in good f.** en (pleine) forme ‖ *vt* (*group, basis, character*) former; (*habit*) contracter; (*an opinion*) se former; (*constitute*) constituer, former; **to f. part of** faire partie de ‖ *vi* (*appear*) se former. ● **formation** [-'meɪʃ(ə)n] *n* formation *f*.
formal ['fɔːm(ə)l] *a* (*person, tone etc*) cérémonieux; (*stuffy*) compassé; (*official*) (*announcement etc*) officiel; (*denial, structure, logic*) formel; **f. dress** tenue *f* de cérémonie; **f. education** éducation *f* scolaire. ● **for'mality** *n* (*requirement*) formalité *f*. ● **formally** *adv* (*to declare etc*) officiellement; **f. dressed** en tenue de cérémonie.
format ['fɔːmæt] *n* (*layout*) présentation *f*; (*size*) format *m* ‖ *vt Comptr* formater.
formative ['fɔːmətɪv] *a* formateur.
former ['fɔːmər] **1** *a* (*previous*) (*teacher, job, house etc*) ancien; (*situation, life*) antérieur; **my f. colleague** mon ancien collègue; **in f. days** autrefois. **2** *a* (*of two*) premier ‖ *pron* **the f.** celui-là, celle-là, le premier, la première. ● **—ly** *adv* (*in the past*) autrefois; (*before*) avant.
formidable ['fɔːmɪdəb(ə)l] *a* effroyable.
formula ['fɔːmjʊlə] *n* **1** (*pl* **-as** *or* **-ae** [-iː]) formule *f*. **2** (*pl* **-as**) (*baby food*) lait *m* maternisé (en poudre).
forsake [fə'seɪk] *vt* (*pt* **forsook,** *pp* **forsaken**) abandonner.
fort [fɔːt] *n Mil* fort *m*.
forte ['fɔːteɪ, *Am* fɔːt] *n* (*strong point*) fort *m*.
forth [fɔːθ] *adv* en avant; **and so f.** et ainsi de suite; **to go back and f.** aller et venir.
forthcoming [fɔːθ'kʌmɪŋ] *a* **1** (*event*) à venir; (*book, film*) qui va sortir; **my f. book** mon prochain livre. **2** (*available*) disponible. **3** (*open*) (*person*) communicatif.
forthright ['fɔːθraɪt] *a* direct, franc (*f* franche).
forthwith [fɔːθ'wɪð] *adv* sur-le-champ.
fortieth ['fɔːtɪəθ] *a* & *n* quarantième (*mf*).
fortify ['fɔːtɪfaɪ] *vt* (*strengthen*) fortifier; **to f. s.o.** (*of food, drink*) réconforter qn. ● **fortification** [-'keɪʃ(ə)n] *n* fortification *f*.
fortnight ['fɔːtnaɪt] *n* quinze jours *mpl*.

●—**ly** *a* bimensuel ‖ *adv* tous les quinze jours.

'ortress ['fɔːtrɪs] *n* forteresse *f*.

'ortunate ['fɔːtʃənɪt] *a* (*choice*, *event etc*) heureux; **to be f.** (*of person*) avoir de la chance; **it's f. that** c'est heureux que (+ *sub*). ●—**ly** *adv* heureusement.

'ortune ['fɔːtʃuːn] *n* (*wealth*) fortune *f*; (*luck*) chance *f*; (*chance*) sort *m*; **to have the good f. to do** avoir la chance de faire; **to tell s.o.'s f.** dire la bonne aventure à qn; **to make one's f.** faire fortune. ●**f.-teller** *n* diseur, -euse *mf* de bonne aventure.

orty ['fɔːtɪ] *a* & *n* quarante (*m*).

orum ['fɔːrəm] *n* forum *m*.

orward ['fɔːwəd] *adv* **forward(s)** en avant; **to go f.** avancer; **from this time f.** désormais ‖ *a* (*movement*) en avant; (*child*) *Fig* précoce; (*impudent*) effronté ‖ *n* *Fb* avant *m* ‖ *vt* (*letter*) faire suivre; (*goods*) expédier.

'ossil ['fɒs(ə)l] *n* fossile *m*.

oster ['fɒstər] **1** *vt* (*music*, *art etc*) encourager. **2** *vt* (*child*) élever en famille d'accueil ‖ *a* (*child*, *parents*) adoptif; **f. home** *or* **family** famille *f* d'accueil.

ought [fɔːt] *pt* & *pp of* **fight.**

oul [faʊl] **1** *a* (**-er, -est**) (*smell*, *taste*, *weather etc*) infect; (*language*) grossier; **to be f.-mouthed** avoir un langage grossier. **2** *n* *Sp* coup *m* irrégulier; *Fb* faute *f* ‖ *a* **f. play** *Sp* jeu *m* irrégulier; *Jur* acte *m* criminel. **3** *vt* **to f. (up)** salir; (*pipe*, *drain*) encrasser; **to f. up** (*plans*) *Fam* gâcher.

ound[1] [faʊnd] *pt* & *pp of* **find.**

ound[2] [faʊnd] *vt* (*town etc*) fonder; (*opinion etc*) fonder, baser (**on** sur). ●—**er**[1] *n* fondateur, -trice *mf*.

oundation [faʊn'deɪʃ(ə)n] *n* (*basis of agreement etc*) bases *fpl*; **the foundations** (*of building*) les fondations *fpl*; **without f.** sans fondement.

'ounder[2] ['faʊndər] *vi* (*of ship*) sombrer.

oundry ['faʊndrɪ] *n* fonderie *f*.

'ountain ['faʊntɪn] *n* fontaine *f*; **f. pen** stylo(-plume) *m*.

our [fɔːr] *a* & *n* quatre (*m*); **on all fours** à quatre pattes; **f.-letter word** = mot *m* de cinq lettres. ●**fourfold** *a* quadruple ‖ *adv* au quadruple. ●**foursome** *n* (*two couples*) deux couples *mpl*. ●**four'teen** *a* & *n* quatorze (*m*). ●**fourth** *a* & *n* quatrième (*mf*).

'owl [faʊl] *n* (*hens etc*) la volaille; **a f.** une volaille.

'ox [fɒks] **1** *n* renard *m*. **2** *vt* (*puzzle*) mystifier; (*trick*) tromper.

'oxglove ['fɒksglʌv] *n* *Bot* digitale *f*.

'oyer ['fɔɪeɪ, *Am* 'fɔɪər] *n* *Th* foyer *m*; (*in hotel*) hall *m*.

fraction ['frækʃ(ə)n] *n* fraction *f*.

fracture ['fræktʃər] *n* fracture *f* ‖ *vt* fracturer; **to f. one's leg**/*etc* se fracturer la jambe/*etc* ‖ *vi* se fracturer.

fragile ['frædʒaɪl, *Am* 'frædʒ(ə)l] *a* fragile.

fragment ['frægmənt] *n* fragment *m*.

fragrant ['freɪgrənt] *a* parfumé. ●**fragrance** *n* parfum *m*.

frail [freɪl] *a* (**-er, -est**) (*person*, *health etc*) fragile.

frame [freɪm] **1** *n* (*of building*, *person*) charpente *f*; (*of picture*, *bicycle*) cadre *m*; (*of window*) châssis *m*; (*of spectacles*) monture *f*; **f. of mind** humeur *f* ‖ *vt* (*picture*) encadrer; (*proposals*, *ideas*) *Fig* formuler. **2** *vt* **to f. s.o.** *Fam* monter un coup contre qn. ●**framework** *n* structure *f*; **in the f. of** (*context*) dans le cadre de.

franc [fræŋk] *n* franc *m*.

France [frɑːns] *n* France *f*.

franchise ['fræntʃaɪz] *n* **1** *Pol* droit *m* de vote. **2** (*right to sell product*) franchise *f*.

Franco- ['fræŋkəʊ] *pref* franco-.

frank [fræŋk] **1** *a* (**-er, -est**) (*honest*) franc (*f* franche). **2** *vt* (*letter*) affranchir. ●—**ly** *adv* franchement. ●—**ness** *n* franchise *f*.

frankfurter ['fræŋkfɜːtər] *n* saucisse *f* de Francfort.

frantic ['fræntɪk] *a* (*activity*, *shouts*) frénétique; (*rush*, *efforts*) effréné; (*person*) hors de soi; **f. with joy** fou de joie. ●**frantically** *adv* (*to run etc*) comme un fou.

fraternity [frə'tɜːnətɪ] *n* *Univ* *Am* association *f* de camarades de classe; **the publishing**/*etc* **f.** la grande famille de l'édition/*etc*. ●**fraternize** ['frætənaɪz] *vi* fraterniser (**with** avec).

fraud [frɔːd] *n* **1** (*crime*) fraude *f*. **2** (*person*) imposteur *m*. ●**fraudulent** *a* frauduleux.

fraught [frɔːt] *a* **f. with** plein de; **to be f.** (*of situation*, *person*) être tendu.

fray [freɪ] **1** *vi* (*of garment*) s'effilocher; (*of rope*) s'user. **2** *n* (*fight*) rixe *f*. ●—**ed** *a* **my nerves are f.** j'ai les nerfs à vif.

freak [friːk] *n* (*person*) phénomène *m*, monstre *m*; **a jazz**/*etc* **f.** *Fam* un(e) fana de jazz/*etc* ‖ *a* (*result*, *weather etc*) anormal.

freckle ['frek(ə)l] *n* tache *f* de rousseur. ●**freckled** *a* couvert de taches de rousseur.

free [friː] *a* (**freer, freest**) (*at liberty*, *not occupied*) libre; (*without cost*) gratuit; (*lavish*) généreux (**with** de); **to get f.** se libérer; **f. to do** libre de faire; **f. of charge** gratuit; **f. of** (*pain*, *person etc*) débarrassé de; **f. and easy** décontracté; **f. gift** prime *f*; **f. kick** *Fb* coup *m* franc; **f.-range egg** œuf *m* de ferme; **f. speech** liberté *f* d'expression; **f. trade** libre-échange *m*.

▮ *adv* **f. (of charge)** gratuitement.

▮ *vt* (*pt* & *pp* **freed**) (*prisoner, country etc*) libérer; (*trapped person*) dégager; (*untie*) détacher.

freedom ['fri:dəm] *n* liberté *f*; **f. from** (*worry, responsibility*) absence *f* de.

Freefone® ['fri:fəʊn] *Tel* = numéro *m* vert. ●**free-for-'all** *n* mêlée *f* générale. ●**freehold** *n* propriété *f* foncière libre. ●**freelance** *a* indépendant ▮ *n* collaborateur, -trice *mf* indépendant(e). ●**freeloader** *n* (*sponger*) parasite *m*. ●**Freemason** *n* franc-maçon *m*. ●**freeway** *n Am* autoroute *f*.

freely ['fri:lı] *adv* (*to speak, circulate etc*) librement; (*to give*) libéralement.

freez/e [fri:z] *vi* (*pt* **froze**, *pp* **frozen**) geler; **to f. to death** mourir de froid; **f.!** *Am* ne bougez plus!; **to f. up** *or* **over** geler; (*of window*) se givrer.

▮ *vt* (*food*) congeler; (*credits, river*) geler; (*prices, wages*) bloquer; **frozen food** surgelés *mpl*.

▮ *n* (*freezing weather*) gel *m*; (*of prices etc*) blocage *m*. ●**—ing** *a* (*weather*) glacial; (*hands, person*) gelé; **it's f.** on gèle; **I'm f. cold** j'ai très froid ▮ *n* **below f.** au-dessous de zéro. ●**freezer** *n* (*deep-freeze*) congélateur *m*; (*in fridge*) freezer *m*.

freight [freıt] *n* (*goods, price for transport*) fret *m*; (*transport*) transport *m*; **f. train** *Am* train *m* de marchandises. ●**—er** *n* (*ship*) cargo *m*.

French [frentʃ] *a* français; (*teacher*) de français; (*embassy*) de France; **F. fries** *Am* frites *fpl* ▮ *n* (*language*) français *m*; **the F.** (*people*) les Français *mpl*. ●**Frenchman** *n* (*pl* **-men**) Français *m*. ●**French-speaking** *a* francophone. ●**Frenchwoman** *n* (*pl* **-women**) Française *f*.

frenzy ['frenzı] *n* frénésie *f*. ●**frenzied** *a* (*shouts*) frénétique; (*attack*) violent.

frequent ['fri:kwənt] *a* fréquent; **f. visitor** habitué, -ée *mf* (**to** de) ▮ [frı'kwent] *vt* fréquenter. ●**frequency** *n* fréquence *f*. ●**frequently** *adv* fréquemment.

fresh [freʃ] **1** *a* (**-er, -est**) frais (*f* fraîche); (*new*) nouveau (*f* nouvelle); (*impudent*) *Fam* culotté; **to get some f. air** prendre l'air. **2** *adv* **to be f. from** arriver tout juste de; (*university*) sortir tout juste de. ●**—ly** *adv* (*arrived, picked etc*) fraîchement. ●**—ness** *n* fraîcheur *f*.

freshen ['freʃən] *vi* **to f. up** (*have a wash*) faire un brin de toilette ▮ *vt* **to f. up** (*house*) retaper; **to f. s.o. up** (*of bath*) rafraîchir qn. ●**—er** *n* **air f.** désodorisant *m*.

fret [fret] *vi* (**-tt-**) (*worry*) se faire du souci; (*of baby*) pleurer. ●**fretful** *a* (*baby etc*) grognon (*f* -onne).

friction ['frıkʃ(ə)n] *n* friction *f*.

Friday ['fraıdı, *Am* -deı] *n* vendredi *m*; **Good F.** Vendredi Saint.

fridge [frıdʒ] *n* frigo *m*.

fried [fraıd] *pt* & *pp of* **fry 1** ▮ *a* (*fish etc*) frit; **f. egg** œuf *m* sur le plat.

friend [frend] *n* ami, -ie *mf*; (*from school, work*) camarade *mf*; **to be friends with s.o.** être ami avec qn; **to make friends** se lier (**with** avec). ●**friendly** *a* (**-ier, -iest**) aimable, gentil (**to** avec); (*child, animal*) gentil; (*attitude, smile*) amical; **some f. advice** un conseil d'ami; **to be f. with s.o., be on f. terms with s.o.** être en bons termes avec qn. ●**friendship** *n* amitié *f*.

frieze [fri:z] *n Archit* frise *f*.

frigate ['frıgət] *n* (*ship*) frégate *f*.

fright [fraıt] *n* peur *f*; **to have a f.** avoir peur; **to give s.o. a f.** faire peur à qn. ●**frighten** *vt* effrayer; **to f. away** *or* **off** (*animal, person*) faire fuir. ●**frightened** *a* effrayé; **to be f.** avoir peur (**of** de). ●**frightening** *a* effrayant.

frightful ['fraıtfəl] *a* affreux.

frigid ['frıdʒıd] *a* (*greeting etc*) froid; (*woman*) frigide.

frill [frıl] *n* **1** (*on dress etc*) volant *m*. **2 frills** (*useless embellishments*) fioritures *fpl*; **no frills** (*machine, Br holiday, Am vacation*) sans rien de superflu.

fringe [frındʒ] **1** *n* (*of hair, on clothes etc*) frange *f*. **2** *n* (*of forest*) lisière *f*; **on the f. of society** en marge de la société ▮ *a* (*group*) marginal; **f. benefits** avantages *mpl* divers.

Frisbee® ['frızbi:] *n* Frisbee® *m*.

frisk [frısk] **1** *vt* (*search*) fouiller (au corps). **2** *vi* **to f. (about)** gambader.

fritter ['frıtər] **1** *vt* **to f. away** (*waste*) gaspiller. **2** *n Culin* beignet *m*.

frivolous ['frıvələs] *a* frivole.

frizzy ['frızı] *a* (*hair*) crépu.

fro [frəʊ] *adv* **to go to and f.** aller et venir.

frock [frɒk] *n* (*dress*) robe *f*; (*of monk*) froc *m*.

frog [frɒg] *n* grenouille *f*. ●**frogman** *n* (*pl* **-men**) homme-grenouille *m*.

frolic ['frɒlık] *vi* (*pt* & *pp* **frolicked**) **to f. (about)** gambader.

from [frɒm, *unstressed* frəm] *prep* **1** de; **a letter f.** une lettre de; **to suffer f.** souffrir de; **where are you f.?** d'où êtes-vous?; **a train f.** un train en provenance de; **to be ten metres (away) f. the house** être à dix mètres de la maison.

2 (*time onwards*) à partir de, dès, depuis; **f. today (on), as f. today** à partir d'aujourd'hui, dès aujourd'hui; **f. her childhood** dès *or* depuis son enfance.
3 (*numbers, prices, onwards*) à partir de; **f. five francs** à partir de cinq francs.
4 (*away from*) à; **to take/hide/borrow f.** prendre/cacher/emprunter à.
5 (*out of*) dans; sur; **to take f.** (*box*) prendre dans; (*table*) prendre sur; **to drink f. a cup** boire dans une tasse; **to drink (straight) f. the bottle** boire à la bouteille.
6 (*according to*) d'après; **f. what I saw** d'après ce que j'ai vu.
7 (*cause*) par; **f. habit**/*etc* par habitude/*etc.*
8 (*on behalf of*) de la part de; **tell her f. me** dis-lui de ma part.

front [frʌnt] *n* (*of garment, building*) devant *m*; (*of boat, car*) avant *m*; (*of crowd*) premier rang *m*; (*of book*) début *m*; *Mil Pol Met* front *m*; (*beach*) front *m* de mer; **in f. (of)** devant; **in f.** (*ahead*) en avant; (*in race*) en tête; **in the f.** (*in vehicle*) à l'avant; (*of house*) devant.
▮ *a* (*tooth etc*) de devant; (*part, wheel, car seat*) avant *inv*; (*row, page*) premier; **f. door** porte *f* d'entrée; **f. line** *Mil* front *m*; **f. room** (*lounge*) salon *m*; **f. runner** *Fig* favori, -ite *mf*; **f.-wheel drive** (*on vehicle*) traction *f* avant.

frontier ['frʌntɪər] *n* frontière *f*.

frost [frɒst] *n* gel *m*, gelée *f*; (*frozen drops on window, grass etc*) givre *m* ▮ *vi* **to f. up** (*of window etc*) se givrer. ●**frostbite** *n* gelure *f*. ●**frostbitten** *a* gelé.

frosted ['frɒstɪd] *a* (*glass*) dépoli.

frosting ['frɒstɪŋ] *n* (*icing*) *Am Culin* glaçage *m*.

frosty ['frɒstɪ] *a* (**-ier, -iest**) (*air, night etc*) glacial; (*window*) givré; **it's f.** il gèle.

froth [frɒθ] *n* mousse *f* ▮ *vi* mousser.

frown [fraʊn] *n* froncement *m* de sourcils ▮ *vi* froncer les sourcils; **to f. (up)on** *Fig* désapprouver.

froze, frozen [frəʊz, 'frəʊz(ə)n] *pt & pp of* **freeze.**

frugal ['fruːg(ə)l] *a* (*meal, life, person*) frugal.

fruit [fruːt] *n* fruit *m*; **(some) f.** (*one item*) un fruit; (*more than one*) des fruits; **to like f.** aimer les fruits; **f. basket** corbeille *f* à fruits; **f. drink** boisson *f* aux fruits; **f. juice** jus *m* de fruit; **f. salad** salade *f* de fruits; **f. tree** arbre *m* fruitier; **f. machine** *Fig* machine *f* à sous. ●**fruitcake** *n* cake *m*. ●**fruitful** *a* (*meeting*) fructueux. ●**fruitless** *a* stérile.

frustrat/e [frʌ'streɪt] *vt* (*person*) frustrer; (*plans*) faire échouer; (*ambitions*) décevoir. ●**—ed** *a* (*mentally, sexually*) frustré. ●**—ing** *a* irritant. ●**frustration** [-'streɪʃ(ə)n] *n* frustration *f*.

fry [fraɪ] **1** *vt* faire frire ▮ *vi* frire. **2** *n* **small f.** (*people*) menu fretin *m*. ●**—ing** *n* friture *f*; **f. pan** poêle *f* (à frire).

ft *abbr* (*measure*) = **foot, feet.**

fuddy-duddy ['fʌdɪdʌdɪ] *n* **he's an old f.-duddy** *Fam* c'est un vieux schnoque.

fudge [fʌdʒ] **1** *n* (*sweet, Am candy*) caramel *m* mou. **2** *vt* **to f. the issue** refuser d'aborder le problème.

fuel [fjʊəl] *n* combustible *m*; *Aut* carburant *m*; **f. (oil)** mazout *m*; **f. tank** *Aut* réservoir *m*.

fugitive ['fjuːdʒɪtɪv] *n* fugitif, -ive *mf*.

fulfil, *Am* **fulfill** [fʊl'fɪl] *vt* (**-ll-**) (*ambition, dream*) réaliser; (*condition, duty, promise*) remplir; (*desire*) satisfaire; **to f. oneself** s'épanouir. ●**fulfilling** *a* satisfaisant. ●**fulfilment** *or Am* **fulfillment** *n* (*feeling*) satisfaction *f*.

full [fʊl] *a* (**-er, -est**) plein (**of** de); (*bus, theatre etc*) complet; (*life, day*) rempli; (*skirt*) ample; **the f. price** le prix fort; **to pay f. fare** payer plein tarif; **a f. member** un membre à part entière; **a f. hour** une heure entière; **to be f. (up)** (*of person*) n'avoir plus faim; (*of hotel*) être complet; **at f. speed** à toute vitesse; **f. name** (*on form*) nom et prénom; **f. stop** *Gram* point *m*.
▮ *adv* **to know f. well** savoir fort bien.
▮ *n* **in f.** (*to read sth, publish sth*) en entier; (*to write one's name*) en toutes lettres; **to pay in f.** tout payer; **to the f.** (*completely*) tout à fait.

full-back ['fʊlbæk] *n Fb* arrière *m*. ●**f.-'length** *a* (*film*) de long métrage; (*portrait*) en pied; (*dress*) long. ●**f.-'scale** *a* (*model etc*) grandeur nature *inv*; (*operation, attack etc*) de grande envergure. ●**f.-'sized** *a* (*model*) grandeur nature *inv*. ●**f.-'time** *a & adv* à plein temps.

fully ['fʊlɪ] *adv* entièrement; (*thoroughly*) à fond; (*at least*) au moins.

fully-fledged, *Am* **full-fledged** [fʊl(ɪ)'fledʒd] *a* (*engineer etc*) diplômé; (*member*) à part entière.

fumble ['fʌmb(ə)l] *vi* **to f. (about)** (*grope*) tâtonner; (*search*) fouiller (**for** pour trouver); **to f. (about) with** tripoter.

fume [fjuːm] **1** *vi* (*of person*) rager. **2** *npl* **fumes** vapeurs *fpl*; (*from car exhaust*) gaz *mpl*.

fumigate ['fjuːmɪgeɪt] *vt* désinfecter (par fumigation).

fun [fʌn] *n* amusement *m*; **to be (good) f.** être très amusant; **to have (some) f.** s'amuser; **to make f. of, poke f. at** se moquer de; **for f.** pour le plaisir.

function ['fʌŋkʃ(ə)n] **1** *n* (*role, duty*) & *Math* fonction *f*; (*party*) réception *f*; (*ceremony*) cérémonie *f* (publique). **2** *vi* (*work*) fonctionner. ●**functional** *a* fonctionnel.

fund [fʌnd] *n* (*for pension etc*) caisse *f*, fonds *m*; (*of knowledge*) *Fig* fond *m*; *pl* (*money resources*) fonds *mpl*; (*for special purpose*) crédits *mpl* ‖ *vt* (*with money*) fournir des fonds *or* des crédits à.

fundamental [fʌndə'ment(ə)l] *a* fondamental.

funeral ['fju:nərəl] *n* enterrement *m* ‖ *a* (*service, march*) funèbre.

funfair ['fʌnfeər] *n* fête *f* foraine; (*larger*) parc *m* d'attractions.

fungus, *pl* **-gi** ['fʌŋgəs, -gaɪ] *n Bot* champignon *m*; (*mould, Am mold*) moisissure *f*.

funnel ['fʌn(ə)l] *n* **1** (*of ship*) cheminée *f*. **2** (*for pouring*) entonnoir *m*.

funny ['fʌnɪ] *a* **(-ier, -iest)** (*amusing*) drôle; (*strange*) bizarre; **a f. idea** une drôle d'idée; **to feel f.** ne pas se sentir très bien.

fur [fɜ:r] **1** *n* (*of animal, for wearing*) fourrure *f*; (*of dog, cat*) pelage *m*, poil *m*. **2** *n* (*in kettle*) dépôt *m* (de tartre) ‖ *vi* **(-rr-) to f. (up)** s'entartrer.

furious ['fjʊərɪəs] *a* (*violent, angry*) furieux (**with, at** contre); (*efforts*) acharné.

furnace ['fɜ:nɪs] *n* (*forge*) fourneau *m*.

furnish ['fɜ:nɪʃ] *vt* **1** (*room*) meubler. **2** (*supply*) fournir (**s.o. with sth** qch à qn). ●**—ings** *npl* ameublement *m*.

furniture ['fɜ:nɪtʃər] *n* meubles *mpl*; **a piece of f.** un meuble.

furrow ['fʌrəʊ] *n* (*on brow*) & *Agr* sillon *m*.

furry ['fɜ:rɪ] *a* (*animal*) à poil; (*toy*) en peluche.

further ['fɜ:ðər] **1** *adv* & *a* = **farther. 2** *adv* (*more*) davantage, plus; (*besides*) en outre ‖ *a* (*additional*) supplémentaire; **f. details** de plus amples détails; **a f. case**/*etc* (*another*) un autre cas/*etc*; **without f. delay** sans plus attendre; **f. education** enseignement *m* post-scolaire. **3** *vt* (*cause, research*) promouvoir. ●**furthermore** *adv* en outre. ●**furthest** *a* & *adv* = **farthest**.

furtive ['fɜ:tɪv] *a* (*smile etc*) furtif; (*person*) sournois.

fury ['fjʊərɪ] *n* (*violence, anger*) fureur *f*.

fuse [fju:z] **1** *vt* **to f. the lights** *etc* faire sauter les plombs ‖ *vi* **the lights** *etc* **have fused** les plombs ont sauté ‖ *n* (*wire*) fusible *m*. **2** *n* (*of bomb*) amorce *f*. **3** *vt* (*metal*) fondre; (*join together*) réunir par fusion. ●**fused** *a* (*electric plug*) avec fusible incorporé.

fuselage ['fju:zəlɑ:ʒ] *n Av* fuselage *m*.

fusion ['fju:ʒ(ə)n] *n Phys Biol* fusion *f*.

fuss [fʌs] *n* chichis *mpl*, façons *fpl*; (*noise*) agitation *f*; **what a f.!** quelle histoire!; **to kick up** *or* **make a f.** faire des histoires; **to make a f. of** être aux petits soins pour. ‖ *vi* faire des chichis; (*worry*) se tracasser (**about** pour); (*rush about*) s'agiter; **to f. over s.o.** être aux petits soins pour qn. ●**fusspot** *or Am* **fussbudget** *n Fam* enquiquineur, -euse *mf*. ●**fussy** *a* **(-ier, -iest)** tatillon; (*difficult*) difficile (**about** sur).

futile ['fju:taɪl, *Am* 'fju:t(ə)l] *a* futile, vain.

future ['fju:tʃər] *n* avenir *m*; *Gram* futur *m*; **in f.** (*from now on*) à l'avenir; **in the f.** (*one day*) un jour (futur) ‖ *a* futur.

fuze [fju:z] *n, vt* & *vi Am* = **fuse 1** & **2**.

fuzz [fʌz] *n Am* (*of material*) peluche(s) *f(pl)*; (*on floor*) moutons *mpl*.

fuzzy ['fʌzɪ] *a* **(-ier, -iest)** (*picture, idea*) flou; **f. hair** cheveux *mpl* crépus.

G

G, g [dʒiː] *n* G, g *m*. ● **G.-string** *n* (*cloth*) cache-sexe *m inv*.

gabble [ˈgæb(ə)l] *vi* (*chatter*) jacasser; (*indistinctly*) bredouiller ‖ *n* baragouin *m*.

gad [gæd] *vi* (**-dd-**) **to g. about** vadrouiller.

gadget [ˈgædʒɪt] *n* gadget *m*.

Gaelic [ˈgeɪlɪk, ˈgælɪk] *a* & *n* gaélique (*m*).

gag [gæg] **1** *n* (*over mouth*) bâillon *m* ‖ *vt* (**-gg-**) (*victim etc*) bâillonner. **2** *n* (*joke*) plaisanterie *f*; *Cin Th* gag *m*. **3** *vi* (**-gg-**) (*choke*) s'étouffer (**on** avec).

gaiety [ˈgeɪɪtɪ] *n* gaieté *f*. ● **gaily** *adv* gaiement.

gain [geɪn] *vt* (*obtain, win*) gagner; (*experience, reputation*) acquérir; **to g. speed/weight** prendre de la vitesse/du poids; **to g. popularity** gagner en popularité ‖ *vi* (*of watch*) avancer; **to g. in strength** gagner en force; **to g. on** (*catch up with*) rattraper ‖ *n* (*increase*) augmentation *f* (**in** de); (*profit*) bénéfice *m*.

gait [geɪt] *n* (*walk*) démarche *f*.

gala [ˈgɑːlə, *Am* ˈgeɪlə] *n* gala *m*; **swimming g.** concours *m* de natation.

galaxy [ˈgæləksɪ] *n* galaxie *f*.

gale [geɪl] *n* grand vent *m*, rafale *f* (de vent).

gall [gɔːl] *n* **1** (*impudence*) *Fam* effronterie *f*; **g. bladder** vésicule *f* biliaire. **2** *vt* (*vex*) blesser, froisser.

gallant [ˈgælənt] *a* (*chivalrous*) galant; (*brave*) courageux.

galleon [ˈgælɪən] *n* (*ship*) *Hist* galion *m*.

gallery [ˈgælərɪ] *n* (*room*) galerie *f*; (*for public, press*) tribune *f*; **art g.** (*private*) galerie *f* d'art; (*public*) musée *m* d'art.

Gallic [ˈgælɪk] *a* (*French*) français.

gallivant [ˈgælɪvænt] *vi* **to g. (about)** *Fam* vadrouiller.

gallon [ˈgælən] *n* gallon *m* (*Br* = *4,5 litres, Am* = *3,8 litres*).

gallop [ˈgæləp] *n* galop *m* ‖ *vi* galoper; **galloping inflation** l'inflation *f* galopante.

gallows [ˈgæləʊz] *npl* potence *f*.

gallstone [ˈgɔːlstəʊn] *n Med* calcul *m* biliaire.

galore [gəˈlɔːr] *adv* à gogo, en abondance.

galoshes [gəˈlɒʃɪz] *npl* (*shoes*) caoutchoucs *mpl*.

gambl/e [ˈgæmb(ə)l] *vi* jouer (**on** sur, **with** avec) ‖ *vt* (*bet*) parier, jouer (**ten dollars**/*etc* dix dollars/*etc*); **to g. (away)** (*lose*) perdre (au jeu) ‖ *n* (*risk*) coup *m* risqué. ● **—ing** *n* jeu *m*. ● **gambler** *n* joueur, -euse *mf*.

game [geɪm] **1** *n* jeu *m*; (*of football, cricket etc*) match *m*; (*of tennis, chess, cards*) partie *f*; **to have a g. of** jouer un match de; faire une partie de; **games** *Sch* le sport. **2** *n* (*animals, birds*) gibier *m*. **3** *a* (*brave*) courageux; **g. for sth** (*willing to do*) prêt à qch; **I'm g.** je suis partant. **4** *a* **to have a g. leg** être boiteux. ● **gamekeeper** *n* garde-chasse *m*.

gammon [ˈgæmən] *n* (*ham*) jambon *m* fumé.

gammy [ˈgæmɪ] *a Fam* = **game 4.**

gang [gæŋ] *n* (*of children, friends etc*) bande *f*; (*of workers*) équipe *f*; (*of criminals*) gang *m* ‖ *vi* **to g. up on** *or* **against** se mettre à plusieurs contre. ● **gangster** *n* gangster *m*.

gangrene [ˈgæŋgriːn] *n* gangrène *f*.

gangway [ˈgæŋweɪ] *n* passage *m*; (*in train*) couloir *m*; (*in bus, theatre etc*) allée *f*; (*footbridge*) *Av Nau* passerelle *f*.

gaol [dʒeɪl] *n* & *vt* = **jail.**

gap [gæp] *n* (*empty space*) trou *m*; (*in time*) intervalle *m*; (*in knowledge*) lacune *f*; **the g. between** (*difference*) l'écart *m* entre.

gap/e [geɪp] *vi* (*stare*) rester bouche bée; **to g. at** regarder bouche bée. ● **—ing** *a* (*hole, wound*) béant.

garage [ˈgærɑː(d)ʒ, *Am* gəˈrɑːʒ] *n* garage *m* ‖ *vt* mettre au garage.

garbage [ˈgɑːbɪdʒ] *n Am* ordures *fpl*; **g. can** poubelle *f*; **g. man** éboueur *m*; **g. truck** camion-benne *m*.

garden [ˈgɑːd(ə)n] *n* jardin *m*; **the gardens** (*park*) le parc; **g. centre** (*store*) jardinerie *f*; **g. party** garden-party *f* ‖ *vi* jardiner. ● **—ing** *n* jardinage *m*. ● **gardener** *n* jardinier, -ière *mf*.

gargle [ˈgɑːg(ə)l] *vi* se gargariser.

garish [ˈgeərɪʃ, *Am* ˈgærɪʃ] *a* (*clothes*) voyant, criard; (*light*) cru.

garland [ˈgɑːlənd] *n* guirlande *f*.

garlic [ˈgɑːlɪk] *n* ail *m*; **g. sausage** saucisson *m* à l'ail.

garment [ˈgɑːmənt] *n* vêtement *m*.

garret [ˈgærət] *n* (*room*) mansarde *f*.

garrison [ˈgærɪsən] *n Mil* garnison *f*.

garter [ˈgɑːtər] *n* (*round leg*) jarretière *f*;

(*attached to belt*) *Am* jarretelle *f*.

gas [gæs] *n* gaz *m inv*; (*gasoline*) *Am* essence *f*; **g. cooker/mask/meter/***etc* cuisinière *f*/masque *m*/compteur *m*/*etc* à gaz; **g. fire** *or* **heater** appareil *m* de chauffage à gaz; **g. heating** chauffage *m* au gaz; **g. pipe** tuyau *m* de gaz; **g. station** *Am* station-service *f*; **g. stove** cuisinière *f* à gaz; (*portable*) réchaud *m* à gaz ‖ *vt* (**-ss-**) (*poison*) asphyxier (*qn*).

gash [gæʃ] *n* entaille *f* ‖ *vt* (*skin*) entailler; **to g. one's knee** se faire une blessure profonde au genou.

gasket ['gæskɪt] *n Aut* joint *m* de culasse.

gasman ['gæsmæn] *n* (*pl* **-men**) employé *m* du gaz.

gasoline ['gæsəliːn] *n Am* essence *f*.

gasp [gɑːsp] **1** *vi* **to g. (for breath)** haleter ‖ *n* halètement *m*. **2** *vi* **to g. in surprise/***etc* avoir le souffle coupé de surprise/*etc*.

gassy ['gæsɪ] *a* (**-ier, -iest**) (*drink*) gazeux.

gastric ['gæstrɪk] *a* (*ulcer etc*) gastrique.

gasworks ['gæswɜːks] *n* usine *f* à gaz.

gate [geɪt] *n* (*at level crossing, field etc*) barrière *f*; (*metal, of garden*) grille *f*; (*of castle, in airport etc*) porte *f*; (*at stadium*) entrée *f*. ● **gateway** *n* **the g. to success** le chemin du succès.

gâteau, *pl* **-eaux** ['gætəʊ, -əʊz] *n* gros gâteau *m* à la crème.

gatecrash ['geɪtkræʃ] *vti* **to g. (a party)** s'inviter de force (à une réception).

gather ['gæðər] *vt* (*people, objects*) rassembler; (*pick up*) ramasser; (*flowers*) cueillir; (*information*) recueillir; (*fabric*) froncer; **I g. that...** je crois comprendre que...; **to g. speed** prendre de la vitesse; **to g. in** (*crops*) rentrer; (*exam papers*) ramasser; **to g. (up) one's strength** rassembler ses forces. ‖ *vi* (*of people*) se rassembler; (*of clouds*) se former; (*of dust*) s'accumuler; **to g. round** (*come closer*) s'approcher; **to g. round s.o.** entourer qn. ● **gathering** *n* (*group*) rassemblement *m*.

gaudy ['gɔːdɪ] *a* (**-ier, -iest**) voyant, criard.

gauge [geɪdʒ] *n* (*instrument*) jauge *f*, indicateur *m* ‖ *vt* (*estimate*) évaluer, jauger; (*measure*) mesurer.

gaunt [gɔːnt] *a* (*thin*) décharné.

gauze [gɔːz] *n* (*fabric*) gaze *f*.

gave [geɪv] *pt of* **give.**

gawk [gɔːk] *vi* **to g. (at)** regarder bouche bée.

gawp [gɔːp] *vi* = **gawk.**

gay [geɪ] *a* (**-er, -est**) **1** *a* & *n* homosexuel (*m*), homo (*m inv*). **2** (*cheerful*) gai; (*colour*) vif, gai.

gaze [geɪz] *n* regard *m* (fixe) ‖ *vi* regarder; **to g. at** regarder (fixement).

gazelle [gə'zel] *n* (*animal*) gazelle *f*.

GB [dʒiː'biː] *abbr* (*Great Britain*) Grande-Bretagne *f*.

GCE [dʒiːsiː'iː] *abbr Br* (*General Certificate of Education*) = épreuve *f* de bac.

GCSE [dʒiːsiːes'iː] *abbr Br* (*General Certificate of Secondary Education*) = épreuve *f* de brevet.

gear [gɪər] **1** *n* équipement *m*, matériel *m*; (*belongings*) affaires *fpl*; (*clothes*) *Fam* vêtements; (*speed*) *Aut* vitesse *f*; **in g.** *Aut* en prise; **not in g.** *Aut* au point mort; **g. lever,** *Am* **g. shift** levier *m* de (changement de) vitesse. **2** *vt* (*adapt*) adapter (**to** à); **geared up to do** prêt à faire; **to g. oneself up for** se préparer pour. ● **gearbox** *n* boîte *f* de vitesses.

gee! [dʒiː] *int Am Fam* ça alors!

geese [giːs] *see* **goose.**

Geiger counter ['gaɪgəkaʊntər] *n* compteur *m* Geiger.

gel [dʒel] *n* (*substance*) gel *m*.

gelignite ['dʒelɪgnaɪt] *n* dynamite *f* (au nitrate de soude).

gem [dʒem] *n* pierre *f* précieuse; (*person of value*) *Fig* perle *f*; (*thing of value*) bijou *m* (*pl* -oux).

Gemini ['dʒemɪnaɪ] *n* (*sign*) les Gémeaux *mpl*.

gen [dʒen] *n* (*information*) *Fam* tuyaux *mpl*.

gender ['dʒendər] *n Gram* genre *m*; (*of person*) sexe *m*.

gene [dʒiːn] *n* (*of cell*) gène *m*.

general ['dʒenərəl] **1** *a* général; **in g.** en général; **the g. public** le (grand) public; **for g. use** à l'usage du public; **g. delivery** *Am* poste *f* restante; **to be g.** (*widespread*) être très répandu. **2** *n* (*officer*) *Mil* général *m*.

generalize ['dʒen(ə)rəlaɪz] *vti* généraliser. ● **generalization** [-'zeɪʃ(ə)n] *n* généralisation *f*.

generally ['dʒen(ə)rəlɪ] *adv* généralement; **g. speaking** en général.

generate ['dʒenəreɪt] *vt* (*heat*) produire; (*fear, hope etc*) engendrer.

generation [dʒenə'reɪʃ(ə)n] *n* génération *f*; **g. gap** conflit *m* des générations.

generator ['dʒenəreɪtər] *n El* groupe *m* électrogène.

generous ['dʒenərəs] *a* généreux (**with** de); (*helping, meal*) copieux. ● **gene'rosity** *n* générosité *f*. ● **generously** *adv* généreusement.

genetic [dʒɪ'netɪk] *a* génétique; **g. engineering** génie *m* génétique. ● **genetics** *n* génétique *f*.

Geneva [dʒɪ'ni:və] *n* Genève *m or f*.
genial ['dʒi:nɪəl] *a* (*kind*) affable; (*cheerful*) jovial.
genie ['dʒi:nɪ] *n* (*goblin*) génie *m*.
genital ['dʒenɪt(ə)l] *a* génital ▌ *npl* **genitals** organes *mpl* génitaux.
genius ['dʒi:nɪəs] *n* (*ability*, *person*) génie *m*; **to have a g. for doing/sth** avoir le génie pour faire/de qch.
gent [dʒent] *n* **gents' shoes** *Com* chaussures *fpl* pour hommes; **the gents** les toilettes *fpl* pour hommes.
gentle ['dʒent(ə)l] *a* (**-er**, **-est**) (*person*, *sound*, *slope etc*) doux (*f* douce); (*hint*, *reminder*) discret; (*touch*, *breeze*) léger; (*exercise*, *speed*) modéré; **to be g. with s.o.** traiter qn avec douceur. ●**gentleman** *n* (*pl* **-men**) monsieur *m*; (*well-bred*) gentleman *m*. ●**gentleness** *n* douceur *f*. ●**gently** *adv* doucement; (*smoothly*) (*to land in aircraft etc*) en douceur.
genuine ['dʒenjʊɪn] *a* (*leather etc*) véritable; (*signature etc*) authentique; (*sincere*) sincère. ●**—ly** *adv* (*surprised etc*) véritablement; (*to think etc*) sincèrement.
geography [dʒɪ'ɒgrəfɪ] *n* géographie *f*. ●**geo'graphical** *a* géographique.
geology [dʒɪ'ɒlədʒɪ] *n* géologie *f*. ●**geo'logical** *a* géologique.
geometry [dʒɪ'ɒmɪtrɪ] *n* géométrie *f*. ●**geo'metric(al)** *a* géométrique.
geranium [dʒɪ'reɪnɪəm] *n* géranium *m*.
geriatric [dʒerɪ'ætrɪk] *a* (*hospital*) gériatrique; **g. ward** service *m* de gériatrie.
germ [dʒɜ:m] *n Med* microbe *m*; (*seed*) *Biol & Fig* germe *m*.
German ['dʒɜ:mən] *a* allemand; **G. measles** *Med* rubéole *f*; **G. shepherd** (*dog*) *Am* berger *m* allemand ▌ *n* (*person*) Allemand, -ande *mf*; (*language*) allemand *m*.
Germany ['dʒɜ:mənɪ] *n* Allemagne *f*.
gesticulate [dʒes'tɪkjʊleɪt) *vi* gesticuler.
gesture ['dʒestʃər] *n* geste *m* ▌ *vi* **to g. to s.o. to do** faire signe à qn de faire.
get [get] **1** *vt* (*pt & pp* **got**, *pp Am* **gotten**, *pres p* **getting**) (*obtain*) obtenir, avoir; (*find*) trouver; (*buy*) acheter; (*receive*) recevoir, avoir; (*catch*) attraper; (*bus*, *train*) prendre; (*seize*) prendre, saisir; (*fetch*) aller chercher (*qn*, *qch*); (*put*) mettre; (*derive*) tirer (**from** de); (*understand*) comprendre, saisir; (*prepare*) préparer; (*lead*) mener; (*hit with fist*, *stick etc*) atteindre; (*reputation*) se faire; **I have got**, *Am* **I have gotten** j'ai; **to g. s.o. to do sth** faire faire qch à qn; **to g. sth built**/*etc* faire construire/*etc* qch; **to g. things going** *or* **started** faire démarrer les choses; **to g. sth to s.o.** (*send*) faire parvenir qch à qn; **to g. s.o. to sth** (*bring*) amener qn à qch.
2 *vi* (*go*) aller (**to** à); (*arrive*) arriver (**to** à); (*become*) devenir; **to g. caught/run over**/*etc* se faire prendre/écraser/*etc*; **to g. dressed/washed** s'habiller/se laver; **to g. paid** être payé; **where have you got** *or Am* **gotten to?** où en es-tu?; **you've got to stay** (*must*) tu dois rester; **to g. to do** (*succeed in doing*) parvenir à faire; **I'm getting to understand** (*starting*) je commence à comprendre; **to g. working** (*start*) se mettre à travailler.
get about *or* **(a)round** *vi* se déplacer; (*of news*) circuler ▌ **to get across** *vt* (*road*) traverser; (*message*) communiquer; **to g. s.o. across** faire traverser qn ▌ *vi* traverser; **to g. across to s.o. that** faire comprendre à qn que **to get along** *vi* (*manage*) se débrouiller; (*progress*) avancer; (*be on good terms*) s'entendre (**with** avec) **to get at** *vt* (*reach*) parvenir à, atteindre; **what is he getting at?** où veut-il en venir? **to get away** *vi* (*leave*) partir, s'en aller; (*escape*) s'échapper; **to g. away with a fine** s'en tirer avec une amende. ●**getaway** *n* (*escape*) fuite *f*. **to get back** *vt* (*recover*) récupérer; (*replace*) remettre ▌ *vi* (*return*) revenir, retourner; (*move back*) reculer **to get by** *vi* (*pass*) passer; (*manage*) se débrouiller **to get down** *vi* (*go down*) descendre (**from** de); **to g. down to** (*task*, *work*) se mettre à ▌ *vt* (*bring down*) descendre (**from** de); **to g. s.o. down** (*depress*) *Fam* déprimer qn **to get in** *vt* (*bicycle*, *washing etc*) rentrer; (*buy*) acheter; **to g. s.o. in** (*call for*) faire venir qn; **to g. in a car**/*etc* monter dans une voiture/*etc* ▌ *vi* (*enter*) entrer; (*come home*) rentrer; (*enter vehicle or train*) monter; (*of plane*, *train*) arriver; (*of candidate*) *Pol* être élu **to get into** *vt* entrer dans; (*vehicle*, *train*) monter dans; (*habit*) prendre; **to g. into bed/a rage** se mettre au lit/en colère **to get off** *vi* (*leave*) partir; (*from vehicle or train*) descendre (**from** de); (*finish work*) sortir; (*be acquitted*) *Jur* être acquitté ▌ *vt* (*remove*) enlever; (*send*) expédier; **to g. off a chair** se lever d'une chaise; **to g. off a bus** descendre d'un bus **to get on** *vt* (*shoes*, *clothes*) mettre; (*bus*, *train*) monter dans ▌ *vi* (*progress*) marcher, avancer; (*manage*) se débrouiller; (*succeed*) réussir; (*enter bus or train*) monter; (*be on good terms*) s'entendre (**with** avec); **how are you getting on?** comment ça va?; **to g. on to s.o.** (*on phone*) contacter qn; **to g. on with** (*task*)

continuer **to get out** *vi* sortir; (*from vehicle or train*) descendre (**of** de); **to g. out of** (*obligation*) échapper à; (*danger*) se tirer de; (*habit*) perdre ‖ *vt* (*remove*) enlever; (*bring out*) sortir (*qch*), faire sortir (*qn*) **to get over** *vt* (*road*) traverser; (*obstacle*) surmonter; (*fence*) franchir; (*illness*) se remettre de; (*surprise*) revenir de; (*ideas*) communiquer ‖ *vi* (*cross*) traverser; (*visit*) passer **to get round** *vt* (*obstacle*) contourner ‖ *vi* (*visit*) passer; **to g. round to doing** en venir à faire **to get through** *vi* (*pass*) passer; (*finish*) finir; (*pass exam*) être reçu; **to g. through to s.o.** (*on the phone*) contacter qn ‖ *vt* (*hole etc*) passer par; (*task, meal*) venir à bout de; (*exam*) être reçu à **to get together** *vi* (*of people*) se rassembler. ● **get-together** *n* réunion *f*. **to get up** *vi* (*rise*) se lever (**from** de); **to g. up to** (*in book*) en arriver à; **to g. up to something** *or* **to mischief** faire des bêtises ‖ *vt* (*ladder, stairs etc*) monter; **to g. sth up** (*bring up*) monter qch. ● **get-up** *n* (*clothes*) *Fam* accoutrement *m*.

geyser ['gi:zər] *n* **1** (*water heater*) chauffe-eau *m inv* (à gaz). **2** *Geol* geyser *m*.

Ghana ['gɑ:nə] *n* Ghana *m*.

ghastly ['gɑ:stlɪ] *a* (**-ier, -iest**) (*horrible*) affreux; (*pale*) blême, pâle.

gherkin ['gɜ:kɪn] *n* cornichon *m*.

ghetto ['getəʊ] *n* (*pl* **-os**) ghetto *m*; **g. blaster** *Fam* mini-stéréo *f* portable.

ghost [gəʊst] *n* fantôme *m*; **g. story** histoire *f* de fantômes; **g. town** ville *f* fantôme.

giant ['dʒaɪənt] *n* géant *m* ‖ *a* (*tree, packet etc*) géant, gigantesque; (*steps*) de géant.

gibberish ['dʒɪbərɪʃ] *n* baragouin *m*.

gibe [dʒaɪb] *vi* railler; **to g. at** railler ‖ *n* raillerie *f*.

giblets ['dʒɪblɪts] *npl* (*of fowl*) abats *mpl*.

giddy ['gɪdɪ] *a* (**-ier, -iest**) **to be** *or* **feel g.** (*at height*) avoir le vertige; (*in room*) avoir un *or* des vertige(s); **to make s.o. g.** donner le vertige à qn. ● **giddiness** *n* vertige *m*.

gift [gɪft] *n* cadeau *m*; (*talent, donation*) don *m*; **g. voucher** *or* **token** chèque-cadeau *m*. ● **gifted** *a* doué (**with** de, **for** pour). ● **gift-wrapped** *a* en paquet-cadeau.

gig [gɪg] *n Mus Fam* engagement *m*.

gigantic [dʒaɪ'gæntɪk] *a* gigantesque.

giggle ['gɪg(ə)l] *vi* rire (bêtement) ‖ *n* petit rire *m* bête; **to have the giggles** avoir le fou rire.

gills [gɪlz] *npl* (*of fish*) ouïes *fpl*.

gimmick ['gɪmɪk] *n* (*trick, object*) truc *m*.

gin [dʒɪn] *n* (*drink*) gin *m*.

ginger ['dʒɪndʒər] **1** *a* (*hair*) roux (*f* rousse). **2** *n Bot Culin* gingembre *m*; **g. beer** boisson *f* gazeuse au gingembre. ● **gingerbread** *n* pain *m* d'épice.

gipsy ['dʒɪpsɪ] *n* bohémien, -ienne *mf*; (*Central European*) Tsigane *mf*.

giraffe [dʒɪ'ræf, dʒɪ'rɑ:f] *n* girafe *f*.

girder ['gɜ:dər] *n* (*metal beam*) poutre *f*.

girdle ['gɜ:d(ə)l] *n* (*belt*) ceinture *f*; (*corset*) gaine *f*.

girl [gɜ:l] *n* (petite) fille *f*, fillette *f*; (*young woman*) jeune fille *f*; (*daughter*) fille *f*; **English g.** jeune Anglaise *f*; **g. guide** éclaireuse *f*. ● **girlfriend** *n* amie *f*; (*of boy*) petite amie *f*.

giro ['dʒaɪrəʊ] *n* (*welfare payment*) chèque *m* de paiement d'indemnités (maladie *or* chômage); **bank g.** virement *m* bancaire; **g. account** compte *m* courant postal.

gist [dʒɪst] *n* **to get the g. of** comprendre l'essentiel de.

give [gɪv] *vt* (*pt* **gave,** *pp* **given**) donner (**to** à); (*support*) apporter; (*a smile, gesture*) faire; (*a sigh*) pousser; (*a look*) jeter; (*a blow*) porter; **g. me York 234** (*phone number*) passez-moi le 234 à York; **to g. way** (*of branch, person etc*) céder (**to** à); (*collapse*) (*of roof etc*) s'effondrer; *Aut* céder la priorité (**to** à) ‖ *n* (*in fabric*) élasticité *f*.

give away *vt* (*free of charge*) donner; (*prize*) distribuer; (*secret*) révéler; (*betray*) trahir (*qn*) **to give back** *vt* (*return*) rendre **to give in** *vi* (*surrender*) céder (**to** à) ‖ *vt* (*hand in*) remettre **to give off** *vt* (*smell, heat*) dégager **to give out** *vt* (*hand out*) distribuer; (*news*) annoncer ‖ *vi* (*of patience*) s'épuiser **to give over** *vt* (*devote*) consacrer (**to** à) ‖ *vi* **g. over!** (*stop*) *Fam* arrête! **to give up** *vi* abandonner, renoncer ‖ *vt* abandonner, renoncer à; (*seat*) céder (**to** à); (*prisoner*) livrer (**to** à); **to g. up smoking** cesser de fumer.

given ['gɪv(ə)n] *a* (*fixed*) donné; **to be g. to doing** (*prone to do*) avoir l'habitude de faire; **g. your age** (*in view of*) étant donné votre âge.

glacier ['glæsɪər, *Am* 'gleɪʃər] *n* glacier *m*.

glad [glæd] *a* (*person*) content (**of, about** de; **that** que + *sub*); **I'm g. to know that...** je suis content de savoir que.... ● **gladly** *adv* (*willingly*) volontiers.

glamour ['glæmər] *n* (*charm*) enchantement *m*; (*splendour*) éclat *m*; (*of job*) prestige *m*. ● **glamorous** *a* (*person, dress etc*) séduisant; (*job*) prestigieux.

glance [glɑ:ns] *n* coup *m* d'œil ‖ *vi* jeter un coup d'œil (**at** à, sur).

gland [glænd] *n* glande *f*.
glar/e [gleər] **1** *vi* **to g. at s.o.** foudroyer qn (du regard) ‖ *n* regard *m* furieux. **2** *vi* (*of sun*) briller d'un éclat aveuglant ‖ *n* éclat *m* aveuglant. •**—ing** *a* (*light*) éblouissant; (*sun*) aveuglant; (*injustice*) flagrant; **a g. mistake** une faute grossière.
glass [glɑːs] *n* verre *m*; (*mirror*) miroir *m*, glace *f*; **a pane of g.** une vitre, un carreau; **g. door** porte *f* vitrée. •**glasses** *npl* (*spectacles*) lunettes *fpl*. •**glassful** *n* (plein) verre *m*.
glaze [gleɪz] *vt* (*door*) vitrer; (*pottery*) vernisser ‖ *n* (*on pottery*) vernis *m*.
gleam [gliːm] *n* lueur *f* ‖ *vi* (re)luire.
glean [gliːn] *vt* (*information*) glaner.
glee [gliː] *n* joie *f*. •**gleeful** *a* joyeux.
glen [glen] *n* vallon *m*.
glib [glɪb] *a* (*person*) qui a la parole facile; (*speech*) peu sincère.
glid/e [glaɪd] *vi* glisser; (*of aircraft*, *bird*) planer. •**—ing** *n Av Sp* vol *m* à voile. •**glider** *n Av* planeur *m*.
glimmer ['glɪmər] *vi* luire (faiblement) ‖ *n* (*light*, *of hope etc*) lueur *f*.
glimpse [glɪmps] *n* aperçu *m*; **to catch** *or* **get a g. of** entrevoir.
glisten ['glɪs(ə)n] *vi* (*of wet surface*) briller; (*of water*) miroiter.
glitter ['glɪtər] *vi* scintiller, briller.
gloat [gləʊt] *vi* jubiler (**over** à l'idée de).
globe [gləʊb] *n* globe *m*. •**global** *a* (*universal*) mondial; (*comprehensive*) global.
gloom [gluːm] *n* (*sadness*) tristesse *f*; (*darkness*) obscurité *f*. •**gloomy** *a* (**-ier, -iest**) (*sad*) triste; (*pessimistic*) pessimiste; (*dark*) sombre.
glorified ['glɔːrɪfaɪd] *a* **it's a g. barn/***etc* ce n'est guère plus qu'une grange/*etc*.
glorious ['glɔːrɪəs] *a* (*splendid*) magnifique; (*full of glory*) glorieux.
glory ['glɔːrɪ] *n* gloire *f*; (*great beauty*) splendeur *f*.
gloss [glɒs] *n* (*shine*) brillant *m*; **g. paint** peinture *f* brillante; **g. finish** brillant *m*. •**glossy** *a* (**-ier, -iest**) brillant; (*photo*) glacé; (*magazine*) de luxe.
glossary ['glɒsərɪ] *n* glossaire *m*.
glove [glʌv] *n* gant *m*; **g. compartment** *Aut* (*shelf*) vide-poches *m inv*; (*enclosed*) boîte *f* à gants.
glow [gləʊ] *vi* (*of sky*, *fire*) rougeoyer; (*of lamp*) luire; (*of eyes*, *person*) *Fig* rayonner (**with** de) ‖ *n* rougeoiement *m*; (*of lamp*) lueur *f*. •**—ing** *a* (*account*, *terms etc*) très favorable.
glucose ['gluːkəʊs] *n* glucose *m*.
glue [gluː] *n* colle *f* ‖ *vt* coller (**to, on** à); **with one's eyes glued to** *Fam* les yeux fixés sur; **glued to the television** *Fam* cloué devant la télévision.
glum [glʌm] *a* (**glummer, glummest**) triste.
glut [glʌt] *n* (*of goods*, *oil etc*) surplus *m* (**of** de).
glutton ['glʌt(ə)n] *n* glouton, -onne *mf*; **g. for work** bourreau *m* de travail; **g. for punishment** masochiste *mf*. •**gluttony** *n* gloutonnerie *f*.
GMT [dʒiːem'tiː] *abbr* (*Greenwich Mean Time*) GMT.
gnarled [nɑːld] *a* noueux.
gnash [næʃ] *vt* **to g. one's teeth** grincer des dents.
gnat [næt] *n* (petit) moustique *m*.
gnaw [nɔː] *vti* ronger.
go [gəʊ] **1** *vi* (*3rd person sing pres t* **goes;** *pt* **went;** *pp* **gone;** *pres p* **going**) aller (**to** à, **from** de); (*depart*) partir, s'en aller; (*disappear*) disparaître, partir; (*be sold*) se vendre; (*function*) marcher; (*progress*) aller, marcher; (*become*) devenir; (*of time*) passer; (*of hearing*, *strength*) baisser; (*of fuse*) sauter; (*of bulb*) griller; (*of material*) s'user; **to go well/badly** (*of event*) se passer bien/mal; **she's going to do** (*is about to*, *intends to*) elle va faire; **it's all gone** (*finished*) il n'y en a plus; **to go and get** (*fetch*) aller chercher; **to go and see** aller voir; **to go riding/on a trip/***etc* faire du cheval/un voyage/*etc*; **to let go of** lâcher; **to go to a doctor/***etc* aller voir un médecin/*etc*; **to get things going** faire démarrer les choses; **is there any beer going?** (*available*) y a-t-il de la bière?; **two hours/***etc* **to go** (*still left*) encore deux heures/*etc*.
2 *n* (*pl* **goes**) (*attempt*) coup *m*; (*energy*) dynamisme *m*; **to have a go at (doing) sth** essayer (de faire) qch; **at one go** d'un seul coup; **on the go** actif; **to make a go of sth** (*make a success of*) réussir qch.
go about *or* **(a)round** *vi* se déplacer; (*of news*, *rumour*) circuler **to go about** *vt* (*one's duties etc*) s'occuper de; **to know how to go about it** savoir s'y prendre **to go across** *vt* traverser ‖ *vi* (*cross*) traverser; (*go*) aller (**to** à) **to go after** *vt* (*chase*) poursuivre; (*seek*) (re)chercher; (*job*) essayer d'obtenir **to go against** *vt* (*of result*) être défavorable à; (*s.o.'s wishes*) aller contre **to go ahead** *vi* avancer; (*continue*) continuer; (*start*) commencer; **go ahead!** allez-y!; **to go ahead with** (*plan etc*) poursuivre. •**go-ahead** *a* dynamique

‖ *n* **to get the go-ahead** avoir le feu vert **to go along** *vi* aller; (*move forward, progress*) avancer; **to go along with** (*agree*) être d'accord avec **to go away** *vi* partir, s'en aller **to go back** *vi* retourner; (*in time*) remonter; (*step back*) reculer; **to go back on** (*promise*) revenir sur **to go by** *vi* passer ‖ *vt* (*judge from*) juger d'après; (*instruction*) suivre **to go down** *vi* descendre; (*fall down*) tomber; (*of ship*) couler; (*of sun*) se coucher; (*of storm*) s'apaiser; (*of temperature, price*) baisser; (*of tyre, Am tire*) se dégonfler; **to go down well** (*of speech*) être bien reçu; **to go down with** (*illness*) attraper ‖ *vt* **to go down the stairs/street** descendre l'escalier/la rue **to go for** *vt* (*fetch*) aller chercher; (*attack*) attaquer; (*like*) *Fam* aimer beaucoup **to go forward(s)** *vi* avancer **to go in** *vi* (r)entrer; (*of sun*) se cacher; **to go in for** (*exam*) se présenter à; (*hobby, sport*) faire ‖ *vt* **to go in a room/***etc* entrer dans une pièce/*etc* **to go into** *vt* (*room etc*) entrer dans; (*question*) examiner **to go off** *vi* (*leave*) partir; (*go bad*) se gâter; (*of alarm*) se déclencher; (*of gun*) partir; (*of event*) se passer ‖ *vt* (*one's food*) perdre le goût de **to go on** *vi* continuer (**doing** à faire); (*travel*) poursuivre sa route; (*happen*) se passer; (*last*) durer; (*of time*) passer; **to go on at** (*nag*) *Fam* s'en prendre à **to go out** *vi* sortir; (*of light, fire*) s'éteindre; (*of newspaper, product*) être distribué (**to** à); **to go out to work** travailler (au dehors) **to go over** *vi* (*go*) aller (**to** à); (*cross over*) traverser; (*to enemy*) passer (**to** à); **to go over to s.o.('s)** faire un saut chez qn ‖ *vt* examiner; (*in one's mind*) repasser; (*speech*) revoir; (*touch up*) retoucher **to go round** *vi* (*turn*) tourner; (*make a detour*) faire le tour; (*be sufficient*) suffire; **to go round to s.o.('s)** faire un saut chez qn; **enough to go round** assez pour tout le monde ‖ *vt* (*corner*) tourner; (*world*) faire le tour de **to go through** *vi* passer ‖ *vt* (*suffer*) subir; (*examine*) examiner; (*search*) fouiller; (*spend*) dépenser; (*wear out*) user; (*perform*) accomplir; **to go through with** (*carry out*) aller jusqu'au bout de **to go under** *vi* (*of ship, person, firm*) couler **to go up** *vi* monter; (*explode*) sauter ‖ *vt* **to go up the stairs/street** monter l'escalier/la rue **to go without** *vi* se passer de.

goad [gəʊd] *vt* **to g. s.o. (on)** aiguillonner qn.

go-ahead ['gəʊəhed] *a* dynamique ‖ *n* **to get the g.** avoir le feu vert.

goal [gəʊl] *n* but *m*. ●**goalkeeper** *n Fb* gardien *m* de but, goal *m*. ●**goalpost** *n Fb* poteau *m* de but.

goat [gəʊt] *n* chèvre *f*.

gobble ['gɒb(ə)l] *vt* **to g. (up)** engloutir.

go-between ['gəʊbɪtwiːn] *n* intermédiaire *mf*.

goblin ['gɒblɪn] *n* (*evil spirit*) lutin *m*.

god [gɒd] *n* dieu *m*; **G.** Dieu *m*; **the gods** *Th Fam* le poulailler. ●**g.-forsaken** *a* (*place*) perdu.

godchild ['gɒdtʃaɪld] *n* (*pl* **-children**) filleul, -eule *mf*. ●**goddaughter** *n* filleule *f*. ●**godfather** *n* parrain *m*. ●**godmother** *n* marraine *f*. ●**godson** *n* filleul *m*.

goddam(n) ['gɒdæm] *a Am Fam* foutu.

goddess ['gɒdɪs] *n* déesse *f*.

godsend ['gɒdsend] *n* **to be a g.** (*of thing, person*) être un don du ciel.

goes [gəʊz] *see* **go 1**.

gofer ['gəʊfər] *n Am Sl* bonniche *f*.

goggles ['gɒg(ə)lz] *npl* (*spectacles*) lunettes *fpl* (*de protection, de plongée*).

going ['gəʊɪŋ] **1** *n* (*conditions*) conditions *fpl*; **it's hard** *or* **heavy g.** c'est difficile. **2** *a* **the g. price** le prix pratiqué (**for** pour); **the g. rate** le tarif en vigueur; **a g. concern** une entreprise qui marche bien. ●**goings-'on** *npl Pej* activités *fpl*.

go-kart ['gəʊkɑːt] *n Sp* kart *m*.

gold [gəʊld] *n* or *m* ‖ *a* (*watch etc*) en or; (*coin, dust*) d'or; **g. medal** *Sp* médaille *f* d'or. ●**golden** *a* (*in colour*) doré; (*rule*) d'or; **a g. opportunity** une occasion en or. ●**goldmine** *n* mine *f* d'or. ●**gold-'plated** *a* plaqué or. ●**goldsmith** *n* orfèvre *m*.

goldfish ['gəʊldfɪʃ] *n* poisson *m* rouge.

golf [gɒlf] *n* golf *m*. ●**golfer** *n* golfeur, -euse *mf*.

gondola ['gɒndələ] *n* (*boat*) gondole *f*.

gone [gɒn] *pp of* **go 1** ‖ *a* **it's g. two** *Fam* il est plus de deux heures.

gong [gɒŋ] *n* gong *m*.

goo [guː] *n Fam* truc *m* collant *or* visqueux.

good [gʊd] *a* (**better, best**) bon (*f* bonne); (*kind*) gentil; (*weather*) beau; (*well-behaved*) sage; **my g. friend** mon cher ami; **a g. fellow** *or* **guy** un brave type; **a g. (long) walk** une bonne promenade; **very g.!** (*all right*) très bien!; **that's g. of you** c'est gentil de ta part; **to feel g.** se sentir bien; **that isn't g. enough** (*bad*) ça ne va pas; (*not sufficient*) ça ne suffit pas; **it's g. for us** ça nous fait du bien; **g. at French/***etc* (*at school*) bon *or* fort en français/*etc*; **to be g. with** (*children*) savoir s'y prendre avec; **it's a g. thing (that)...** heureusement que...; **a g. many,**

a **g. deal (of)** beaucoup (de); **as g. as** (*almost*) pratiquement; **g. afternoon, g. morning** bonjour; (*on leaving*) au revoir; **g. evening** bonsoir; **g. night** bonsoir; (*before going to bed*) bonne nuit.
▮ *n* (*advantage, virtue*) bien *m*; **for her own g.** pour son bien; **for the g. of** (*one's family etc*) pour; **it will do you g.** ça te fera du bien; **it's no g. crying/shouting/***etc* ça ne sert à rien de pleurer/crier/*etc*; **that's no g.** (*worthless*) ça ne vaut rien; (*not all right, bad*) ça ne va pas; **what's the g. of crying/** *etc*? à quoi bon pleurer/*etc*?; **for g.** (*to leave etc*) pour de bon. ●**g.-for-nothing** *a* & *n* propre à rien (*mf*). ●**g.-'looking** *a* beau (*f* belle).

goodbye! [gʊd'baɪ] *int* au revoir!

goodness ['gʊdnɪs] *n* bonté *f*; **my g.!** mon Dieu!

goods [gʊdz] *npl* marchandises *fpl*; (*articles for sale*) articles *mpl*; **g. train** train *m* de marchandises.

goodwill [gʊd'wɪl] *n* bonne volonté *f*; (*zeal*) zèle *m*.

gooey ['guːɪ] *a Fam* gluant, poisseux.

goof [guːf] *vi* **to g. (up)** (*blunder*) *Am* faire une gaffe.

goose, *pl* **geese** [guːs, giːs] *n* oie *f*; **g. pimples** *or* **bumps** chair *f* de poule. ●**gooseflesh** *n* chair *f* de poule.

gooseberry ['gʊzbərɪ, *Am* 'guːsberɪ] *n* groseille *f* à maquereau.

gorge [gɔːdʒ] **1** *n* (*ravine*) gorge *f*. **2** *vt* **to g. oneself** se gaver (**on** de).

gorgeous ['gɔːdʒəs] *a* magnifique.

gorilla [gə'rɪlə] *n* gorille *m*.

gormless ['gɔːmləs] *a Fam* stupide.

gorse [gɔːs] *n inv* ajonc(s) *m*(*pl*).

gory ['gɔːrɪ] *a* (**-ier, -iest**) (*bloody*) sanglant; (*details*) *Fig* horrible.

gosh! [gɒʃ] *int Fam* mince (alors)!

go-slow [gəʊ'sləʊ] *n* (*strike*) grève *f* perlée.

gospel ['gɒspəl] *n* évangile *m*.

gossip ['gɒsɪp] *n* (*talk*) bavardage(s) *m*(*pl*); (*malicious*) cancan(s) *m*(*pl*); (*person*) commère *f* ▮ *vi* bavarder; (*maliciously*) cancaner.

got [gɒt] *pt* & *Br pp of* **get**.

Gothic ['gɒθɪk] *a* gothique.

gotten ['gɒt(ə)n] *Am pp of* **get**.

gourmet ['gʊəmeɪ] *n* gourmet *m*; **g. restaurant** restaurant *m* gastronomique.

gout [gaʊt] *n Med* goutte *f*.

govern ['gʌvən] *vt* (*rule*) gouverner; (*city, province*) administrer; (*emotion*) maîtriser; (*influence*) déterminer ▮ *vi Pol* gouverner; **governing body** conseil *m* d'administration. ●**governess** *n* gouvernante *f*.

government ['gʌvənmənt] *n* gouvernement *m*; (*local*) administration *f*.

governor ['gʌvənər] *n* gouverneur *m*; (*of school*) administrateur, -trice *mf*.

gown [gaʊn] *n* (*of woman*) robe *f*; (*of judge, lecturer*) toge *f*.

GP [dʒiː'piː] *n abbr* (*general practitioner*) (médecin *m*) généraliste *m*.

grab [græb] *vt* (**-bb-**) **to g. (hold of)** saisir; **to g. sth from s.o.** arracher qch à qn.

grace [greɪs] **1** *n* (*charm, goodwill etc*) & *Rel* grâce *f*; (*extension of time*) délai *m* de grâce; **10 days' g.** 10 jours de grâce. **2** *vt* (*adorn*) orner; (*honour*) honorer (**with** de). ●**graceful** *a* gracieux. ●**gracefully** *adv* (*to dance etc*) avec grâce.

gracious ['greɪʃəs] *a* (*kind*) aimable (**to** envers).

grade [greɪd] *n* catégorie *f*; *Mil* grade *m*; (*of product*) qualité *f*; (*level*) niveau *m*; (*in exam etc*) note *f*; (*class in school*) *Am* classe *f*; **g. school** *Am* école *f* primaire; **g. crossing** *Am* passage *m* à niveau ▮ *vt* (*classify*) classer; (*colours etc*) graduer; (*school paper*) noter.

gradient ['greɪdɪənt] *n* (*slope*) inclinaison *f*.

gradual ['grædʒʊəl] *a* progressif; (*slope*) doux (*f* douce). ●**—ly** *adv* progressivement, peu à peu.

graduate ['grædʒʊeɪt] *vi Univ* obtenir son diplôme; *Am Sch* obtenir son baccalauréat; **to g. from** sortir de ▮ ['grædʒʊət] *n* diplômé, -ée *mf*, licencié, -ée *mf*. ●**graduation** [-'eɪʃ(ə)n] *n Univ* remise *f* des diplômes.

graduated ['grædʒʊeɪtɪd] *a* (*tube etc*) gradué.

graffiti [grə'fiːtɪ] *npl* graffiti *mpl*.

graft [grɑːft] *n Med Bot* greffe *f* ▮ *vt* greffer (**on to** à).

grain [greɪn] *n* (*seed*) grain *m*; (*cereals*) céréales *fpl*; (*in wood*) fibre *f*; (*in leather, paper*) grain *m*.

gram(me) [græm] *n* gramme *m*.

grammar ['græmər] *n* grammaire *f*; **g. school** *Br* lycée *m*. ●**gra'mmatical** *a* grammatical.

grand [grænd] **1** *a* (**-er, -est**) (*splendid*) magnifique; (*style*) grandiose; (*gesture*) majestueux; **g. piano** piano *m* à queue; **the g. tour** (*of town etc*) la visite complète. **2** *n inv Am Sl* mille dollars *mpl*; *Br Sl* mille livres *fpl*.

grandchild ['græntʃaɪld] *n* (*pl* **-children**) petit(e)-enfant *mf*. ●**grand(d)ad** *n Fam* papi *m*. ●**granddaughter** *n* petite-fille *f*.

● **grandfather** *n* grand-père *m*. ● **grandma** [-mɑː] *n Fam* mamie *f*. ● **grandmother** *n* grand-mère *f*. ● **grandpa** [-pɑː] *n Fam* papi *m*. ● **grandparents** *npl* grands-parents *mpl*. ● **grandson** *n* petit-fils *m*.
grandstand ['grændstænd] *n Sp* tribune *f*.
granite ['grænɪt] *n* granit(e) *m*.
granny ['grænɪ] *n Fam* mamie *f*.
grant [grɑːnt] **1** *vt* accorder (**to** à); (*request*) accéder à; (*prayer, wish*) exaucer; (*admit*) admettre (**that** que); **to take sth for granted** considérer qch comme acquis; **I take it for granted that...** je présume que.... **2** *n* subvention *f*; (*for study*) *Univ* bourse *f*.
granulated ['grænjʊleɪtɪd] *a* **g. sugar** sucre *m* cristallisé.
grape [greɪp] *n* grain *m* de raisin; *pl* le raisin, les raisins *mpl*; **to eat (some) grapes** manger du raisin *or* des raisins.
grapefruit ['greɪpfruːt] *n* pamplemousse *m*.
graph [græf, grɑːf] *n* courbe *f*; **g. paper** papier *m* millimétré.
graphic ['græfɪk] *a* (*description*) explicite, vivant; (*art*) graphique; **g. design** arts *mpl* graphiques. ● **graphics** *npl Comptr* graphiques *mpl*.
grapple ['græp(ə)l] *vi* **to g. with** (*person, problem*) se colleter avec.
grasp [grɑːsp] *vt* (*seize, understand*) saisir ‖ *n* (*firm hold*) prise *f*; (*understanding*) compréhension *f*; (*knowledge*) connaissance *f*; **within s.o.'s g.** (*reach*) à la portée de qn.
grass [grɑːs] *n* herbe *f*; (*lawn*) gazon *m*; **the g. roots** *Pol* la base. ● **grasshopper** *n* sauterelle *f*. ● **grassland** *n* prairie *f*.
grat/e [greɪt] **1** *n* (*for fireplace*) grille *f* de foyer. **2** *vt* (*cheese etc*) râper. **3** *vi* (*of sound*) grincer (**on sth** sur qch); **to g. on the ears** écorcher les oreilles. ● **—ing 1** *a* (*sound*) grinçant. **2** *n* (*bars*) grille *f*. ● **grater** *n Culin* râpe *f*.
grateful ['greɪtfəl] *a* reconnaissant (**to** à, **for** de); (*words, letter*) de remerciement; (*attitude*) plein de reconnaissance; **I'm g. (to you) for your help** je vous suis reconnaissant de votre aide; **g. thanks** mes sincères remerciements.
gratified ['grætɪfaɪd] *a* (*pleased*) très content (**by sth** de qch, **to do** de faire). ● **gratifying** *a* très satisfaisant *or* agréable.
gratis ['grætɪs] *adv* gratis.
gratitude ['grætɪtjuːd] *n* reconnaissance *f*, gratitude *f* (**for** de).
gratuity [grə'tjuːɪtɪ] *n* (*tip*) pourboire *m*.
grave[1] [greɪv] *n* tombe *f*; **g. digger** fossoyeur *m*. ● **gravestone** *n* pierre *f* tombale. ● **graveyard** *n* cimetière *m*; **auto g.** *Am Fam* cimetière *m* de voitures.
grave[2] [greɪv] *a* (**-er, -est**) (*serious*) grave.
gravel ['græv(ə)l] *n* gravier *m*.
gravitate ['grævɪteɪt] *vi* **to g. towards** (*be drawn towards*) être attiré vers; (*move towards*) se diriger vers.
gravity ['grævɪtɪ] *n* **1** *Phys* pesanteur *f*. **2** (*seriousness*) gravité *f*.
gravy ['greɪvɪ] *n* jus *m* de viande.
gray [greɪ] *a* & *vi Am* = **grey.**
graze [greɪz] **1** *vt* (*scrape*) écorcher; (*touch lightly*) frôler ‖ *n* (*wound*) écorchure *f*. **2** *vi* (*of cattle*) paître.
grease [griːs] *n* graisse *f* ‖ *vt* graisser. ● **greaseproof (paper)** *a* & *n* papier *m* sulfurisé. ● **greasy** *a* (**-ier, -iest**) plein de graisse; (*hair*) gras.
great [greɪt] *a* (**-er, -est**) grand; (*excellent*) *Fam* magnifique; **a g. deal** *or* **number (of), a g. many** beaucoup (de); **a very g. age** un âge très avancé; **the greatest team**/*etc* (*best*) la meilleure équipe/*etc*; **Greater London** le grand Londres. ● **g.-'grandfather** *n* arrière-grand-père *m*. ● **g.-'grandmother** *n* arrière-grand-mère *f*.
Great Britain [greɪt'brɪt(ə)n] *n* Grande-Bretagne *f*.
greatly ['greɪtlɪ] *adv* (*much*) beaucoup; (*very*) très; **I g. prefer** je préfère de beaucoup.
Greece [griːs] *n* Grèce *f*.
greed [griːd] *n* avidité *f* (**for** de); (*for food*) gourmandise *f*. ● **greedy** *a* (**-ier, -iest**) avide (**for** de); (*for food*) glouton (*f* -onne), gourmand.
Greek [griːk] *a* grec (*f* grecque) ‖ *n* Grec *m*, Grecque *f*; (*language*) grec *m*.
green [griːn] *a* (**-er, -est**) vert; (*immature*) *Fig* inexpérimenté; *Pol* vert, écologiste; **to turn** *or* **go g.** devenir vert; (*of garden etc*) verdir; **to get the g. light** avoir le (feu) vert; **g. with envy** *Fig* vert de jalousie; **g. card** *US* permis *m* de travail.
‖ *n* (*colour*) vert *m*; (*lawn*) pelouse *f*; (*village square*) place *f* gazonnée; *pl* (*vegetables*) légumes *mpl* verts; **the Greens** *Pol* les Verts. ● **greenery** *n* (*plants, leaves*) verdure *f*. ● **greenfly** *n* puceron *m* (des plantes). ● **greengrocer** *n* marchand, -ande *mf* de légumes. ● **greenhouse** *n* serre *f*; **the g. effect** l'effet *m* de serre.
Greenland ['griːnlənd] *n* Groenland *m*.
greet [griːt] *vt* (*with a nod etc*) saluer (*qn*); (*welcome, receive*) accueillir; **to g. s.o.** (*of sight*) s'offrir aux regards de qn. ● **—ing** *n*

salutation *f*; (*welcome*) accueil *m*; *pl* (*for birthday, festival*) vœux *mpl*; **greetings card** carte *f* de vœux.

grenade [grə'neɪd] *n* (*bomb*) grenade *f*.

grew [gruː] *pt of* **grow.**

grey [greɪ] *a* (**-er, -est**) gris; (*pale*) (*complexion*) blême; **to be going g.** grisonner ‖ *vi* **to be greying** être grisonnant. • **g.-'haired** *a* aux cheveux gris. • **greyhound** *n* lévrier *m*.

grid [grɪd] *n* (*grating, on map*) grille *f*.

griddle ['grɪd(ə)l] *n* (*on stove*) plaque *f* à griller.

grief [griːf] *n* chagrin *m*, douleur *f*; **to come to g.** (*of driver, pilot etc*) avoir un accident; (*of plan*) échouer.

grieve [griːv] *vi* s'affliger (**over sth** de qch); **to g. for s.o.** pleurer qn ‖ *vt* peiner, affliger. • **grievance** *n* grief *m*; *pl* (*complaints*) doléances *fpl*; **to have a g. against s.o.** avoir à se plaindre de qn.

grill [grɪl] *n* (*utensil*) gril *m*; (*dish*) grillade *f* ‖ *vti* griller.

grille [grɪl] *n* (*metal bars*) grille *f*.

grim [grɪm] *a* (**grimmer, grimmest**) (*face, future*) sombre; (*horrifying*) sinistre; (*bad*) *Fam* affreux; **a g. determination** une volonté inflexible.

grimace ['grɪməs] *n* grimace *f* ‖ *vi* grimacer.

grime [graɪm] *n* crasse *f*. • **grimy** *a* (**-ier, -iest**) crasseux.

grin [grɪn] *vi* (**-nn-**) avoir un large sourire ‖ *n* large sourire *m*.

grind [graɪnd] **1** *vt* (*pt & pp* **ground**) (*coffee, pepper etc*) moudre; (*meat*) *Am* hacher; (*blade, tool*) aiguiser; **to g. one's teeth** grincer des dents ‖ *vi* **to g. to a halt** s'arrêter (progressivement). **2** *n* (*work, routine*) *Fam* corvée *f*. • **grinder** *n* **coffee g.** moulin *m* à café.

grip [grɪp] *vt* (**-pp-**) (*seize*) saisir; (*hold*) tenir serré; (*of story*) *Fig* empoigner (*qn*) ‖ *n* (*hold*) prise *f*; (*with hand*) poigne *f*; (*on situation*) contrôle *m*; (*handle*) poignée *f*; **to get to grips with** (*problem*) s'attaquer à; **in the g. of** (*despair etc*) en proie à. • **gripping** *a* (*film etc*) passionnant.

grisly ['grɪzlɪ] *a* (*gruesome*) horrible.

gristle ['grɪs(ə)l] *n Culin* cartilage *m*.

grit [grɪt] **1** *n* (*sand*) sable *m*; (*gravel*) gravillon *m* ‖ *vt* (**-tt-**) (*road*) sabler. **2** *n* (*courage*) *Fam* cran *m*. **3** *vt* (**-tt-**) **to g. one's teeth** serrer les dents.

groan [grəʊn] *vi* (*with pain, as a complaint*) gémir ‖ *n* gémissement *m*.

grocer ['grəʊsər] *n* épicier, -ière *mf*; **g.'s shop** épicerie *f*. • **grocery** *n* (*shop*) *Am* épicerie *f*; *pl* (*food*) provisions *fpl*.

groggy ['grɒgɪ] *a* (**-ier, -iest**); (*shaky*) pas solide sur les jambes; (*from a blow*) groggy.

groin [grɔɪn] *n Anat* aine *f*; (*genitals*) bas-ventre *m*.

groom [gruːm] **1** *n* (*bridegroom*) marié *m*. **2** *n* (*for horses*) lad *m* ‖ *vt* (*horse*) panser; **well groomed** (*person*) très soigné.

groove [gruːv] *n* (*slot for sliding door etc*) rainure *f*.

grope [grəʊp] *vi* **to g. (about)** tâtonner; **to g. for** chercher à tâtons.

gross [grəʊs] *a* **1** (*total*) (*weight, income*) brut; **g. national product** *Econ* produit *m* national brut. **2** (**-er, -est**) (*coarse*) grossier; (*injustice*) flagrant. • **—ly** *adv* (*very*) extrêmement.

grotesque [grəʊ'tesk] *a* (*ludicrous*) grotesque; (*frightening*) monstrueux.

grotto ['grɒtəʊ] *n* (*pl* **-oes** *or* **-os**) grotte *f*.

grotty ['grɒtɪ] *a* (**-ier, -iest**) *Fam* (*ugly*) moche; (*of poor quality*) nul.

ground[1] [graʊnd] **1** *n* terre *f*, sol *m*; (*for camping, football etc*) terrain *m*; (*electrical wire*) *Am* terre *f*; *pl* (*reasons*) raisons *fpl*, motifs *mpl*; (*gardens*) parc *m*; **on the g.** (*lying, sitting*) par terre; **to lose g.** perdre du terrain; **g. crew** (*at airport*) personnel *m* au sol; **g. floor** rez-de-chaussée *m inv*; **g. frost** gelée *f* blanche.

2 *vt* (*aircraft*) bloquer *or* retenir au sol. • **grounding** *n* connaissances *fpl* (de fond) (**in** en). • **groundnut** *n* arachide *f*. • **groundsheet** *n* tapis *m* de sol. • **groundwork** *n* préparation *f*.

ground[2] [graʊnd] *pt & pp of* **grind** ‖ *a* (*coffee*) moulu; **g. meat** viande *f* hachée ‖ *npl* **(coffee) grounds** marc *m* (de café).

group [gruːp] *n* groupe *m* ‖ *vt* **to g. (together)** grouper ‖ *vi* se grouper. • **—ing** *n* (*group*) groupe *m*.

grove [grəʊv] *n* bocage *m*.

grovel ['grɒv(ə)l] *vi* (**-ll-**, *Am* **-l-**) *Pej* ramper, s'aplatir (**to s.o.** devant qn).

grow [grəʊ] *vi* (*pt* **grew**, *pp* **grown**) (*of person*) grandir; (*of plant, hair*) pousser; (*increase*) augmenter, grandir; (*of firm, town*) se développer; **to g. fat(ter)** grossir; **to g. to like** finir par aimer; **to g. into** devenir; **to g. out of** (*one's clothes*) devenir trop grand pour; (*a habit*) perdre; **to g. up** devenir adulte; **when I g. up** quand je serai grand.

‖ *vt* (*plant, crops*) cultiver; (*beard, hair*) laisser pousser. • **growing** *a* (*child*) qui grandit; (*number, discontent*) grandissant.

● **grown** *a* (*man, woman*) adulte. ● **grown-up** *n* grande personne *f*, adulte *mf*.

growl [graʊl] *vi* grogner (**at** contre) ‖ *n* grognement *m*.

growth [grəʊθ] *n* croissance *f*; (*increase*) augmentation *f* (**in** de); (*lump*) *Med* tumeur *f* (**on** à).

grub [grʌb] *n* (*food*) *Fam* bouffe *f*.

grubby ['grʌbɪ] *a* (**-ier, -iest**) sale.

grudg/e [grʌdʒ] **1** *n* rancune *f*; **to have a g. against s.o.** garder rancune à qn. **2** *vt* (*give*) donner à contrecœur; (*reproach*) reprocher (**s.o. sth** qch à qn); **to g. doing sth** faire qch à contrecœur. ● **—ingly** *adv* (*to give etc*) à contrecœur.

gruelling, *Am* **grueling** ['grʊəlɪŋ] *a* (*day, detail etc*) éprouvant, atroce.

gruesome ['gru:səm] *a* horrible.

gruff [grʌf] *a* (**-er, -est**) (*voice, person*) bourru.

grumble ['grʌmb(ə)l] *vi* (*complain*) râler, grogner (**about, at** contre).

grumpy ['grʌmpɪ] *a* (**-ier, -iest**) grincheux.

grunt [grʌnt] *vti* grogner ‖ *n* grognement *m*.

guarantee [gærən'ti:] *n* garantie *f* ‖ *vt* garantir (**against** contre); **to g. s.o. that** garantir à qn que. ● **guarantor** *n* garant, -ante *mf*.

guard [gɑ:d] *n* (*vigilance, soldiers etc*) garde *f*; (*individual person*) garde *m*; *Rail* chef *m* de train; **to keep a g. on** surveiller; **under g.** sous surveillance; **on one's g.** sur ses gardes; **to catch s.o. off his g.** prendre qn au dépourvu; **on g. (duty)** de garde; **to stand g.** monter la garde.
‖ *vt* (*protect*) protéger (**against** contre); (*watch over*) surveiller, garder.
‖ *vi* **to g. against** (*protect oneself*) se prémunir contre; (*prevent*) empêcher. ● **guardian** *n* (*of child*) *Jur* tuteur, -trice *mf*; (*protector*) gardien, -ienne *mf*.

guerrilla [gə'rɪlə] *n* (*person*) guérillero *m*; **g. warfare** guérilla *f*.

guess [ges] *n* conjecture *f*; (*intuition*) intuition *f*; (*estimate*) estimation *f*; **to make a g.** (essayer de) deviner; **at a g.** à vue de nez ‖ *vt* deviner (**that** que); (*length, number etc*) estimer; (*suppose*) *Am* supposer (**that** que); (*think*) *Am* croire (**that** que) ‖ *vi* deviner; **I g. (so)** *Am* je suppose; je crois. ● **guesswork** *n* hypothèse *f*; **by g.** à vue de nez.

guest [gest] *n* invité, -ée *mf*; (*in hotel*) client, -ente *mf*; (*at meal*) convive *mf*; **our g. speaker**/*etc* le conférencier/*etc* qui est notre invité. ● **guesthouse** *n* pension *f* de famille. ● **guestroom** *n* chambre *f* d'ami.

guffaw [gə'fɔ:] *vi* rire bruyamment.

guidance ['gaɪdəns] *n* (*advice*) conseils *mpl*.

guid/e [gaɪd] *n* (*person*) guide *m*; (*indication*) indication *f*; **g. (book)** guide *m*; **(girl) g.** éclaireuse *f*; **g. dog** chien *m* d'aveugle ‖ *vt* (*lead*) guider. ● **—ed** *a* (*missile*) guidé; **g. tour** visite *f* guidée. ● **guidelines** *npl* indications *fpl* (à suivre).

guild [gɪld] *n* association *f*.

guillotine ['gɪləti:n] *n* (*for execution*) guillotine *f*.

guilt [gɪlt] *n* culpabilité *f*. ● **guilty** *a* (**-ier, -iest**) coupable; **g. person** coupable *mf*; **to find s.o. g./not g.** déclarer qn coupable/non coupable.

guinea pig ['gɪnɪpɪg] *n* (*animal*) & *Fig* cobaye *m*.

guise [gaɪz] *n* **under the g. of** sous l'apparence de.

guitar [gɪ'tɑ:*r*] *n* guitare *f*. ● **guitarist** *n* guitariste *mf*.

gulf [gʌlf] *n* (*in sea*) golfe *m*; (*chasm*) gouffre *m*; **a g. between** *Fig* un abîme entre.

gull [gʌl] *n* (*bird*) mouette *f*.

gullible ['gʌlɪb(ə)l] *a* crédule.

gulp [gʌlp] **1** *vt* **to g. (down)** avaler (vite) ‖ *n* (*of drink*) gorgée *f*. **2** *vi* (*with emotion*) avoir la gorge serrée.

gum[1] [gʌm] *n* *Anat* gencive *f*.

gum[2] [gʌm] **1** *n* (*glue*) colle *f* ‖ *vt* (**-mm-**) coller. **2** *n* (*for chewing*) chewing-gum *m*.

gun [gʌn] *n* pistolet *m*, revolver *m*; (*rifle*) fusil *m*; (*firing shells*) canon *m* ‖ *vt* (**-nn-**) **to g. down** abattre. ● **gunfight** *n* échange *m* de coups de feu. ● **gunfire** *n* coups *mpl* de feu; *Mil* tir *m* d'artillerie. ● **gunman** *n* (*pl* **-men**) bandit *m* armé. ● **gunpoint** *n* **at g.** sous la menace d'une arme. ● **gunpowder** *n* poudre *f* à canon. ● **gunshot** *n* coup *m* de feu; **g. wound** blessure *f* par balle.

gunge [gʌndʒ] *n* *Fam* magma *m*.

gurgle ['gɜ:g(ə)l] *vi* (*of water*) glouglouter; (*of baby*) gazouiller.

gush [gʌʃ] *vi* **to g. (out)** jaillir (**of** de).

gust [gʌst] *n* **g. (of wind)** rafale *f* (de vent). ● **gusty** *a* (**-ier, -iest**) (*weather*) venteux; (*day*) de vent.

gusto ['gʌstəʊ] *n* **with g.** avec entrain.

gut [gʌt] **1** *n* *Anat* intestin *m*; *pl* *Fam* (*insides*) ventre *m*; (*courage*) cran *m*. **2** *vt* (**-tt-**) (*of fire*) ne laisser que les quatre murs de (*maison etc*).

gutter ['gʌtər] *n* (*on roof*) gouttière *f*; (*in street*) caniveau *m*.

guy [gaɪ] *n* (*fellow*) *Fam* type *m*.

guzzle ['gʌz(ə)l] *vi* (*eat*) bâfrer ‖ *vt* (*eat*) engloutir (*qch*); (*drink*) siffler (*qch*).

gym [dʒɪm] *n* gym(nastique) *f*; (*gymnasium*) gymnase *m*; **g. shoes** tennis *fpl or mpl*. ● **gymnasium** [-'neɪzɪəm] *n* gymnase *m*. ● **gymnast** *n* gymnaste *mf*. ● **gym'nastics** *n* gymnastique *f*.

gynaecologist, *Am* **gynecologist** [gaɪnɪ'kɒlədʒɪst] *n* gynécologue *mf*.

gypsy ['dʒɪpsɪ] *n* = **gipsy**.

H

H, h [eɪtʃ] *n* H, h *m*; **H bomb** bombe *f* H.

haberdasher ['hæbədæʃər] *n* mercier, -ière *mf*; (*men's outfitter*) *Am* chemisier *m*.

habit ['hæbɪt] *n* **1** habitude *f*; **to be in/get into the h. of doing** avoir/prendre l'habitude de faire. **2** (*addiction*) *Med* accoutumance *f*; **a h.-forming drug** une drogue qui crée une accoutumance. **3** (*of monk*, *nun*) habit *m*.

habitual [hə'bɪtʃʊəl] *a* habituel; (*smoker etc*) invétéré.

habitat ['hæbɪtæt] *n* (*of animal*, *plant*) habitat *m*.

hack [hæk] **1** *vt* (*cut*) tailler. **2** *n* **h. (writer)** *Pej* écrivaillon *m*.

hacker ['hækər] *n Comptr* pirate *m* (informatique).

hackneyed ['hæknɪd] *a* (*saying*) rebattu.

had [hæd] *pt* & *pp of* **have**.

haddock ['hædək] *n* (*fish*) aiglefin *m*; **smoked h.** haddock *m*.

haemorrhage ['hemərɪdʒ] *n Med* hémorragie *f*.

haemorrhoids ['hemərɔɪdz] *npl* hémorroïdes *fpl*.

hag [hæg] *n* **(old) h.** (vieille) sorcière *f*.

haggard ['hægəd] *a* (*person*, *face*) hâve, émacié.

haggl/e ['hæg(ə)l] *vi* marchander; **to h. over** (*article*) marchander; (*price*) discuter. ●**—ing** *n* marchandage *m*.

Hague (The) [ðə'heɪg] *n* La Haye.

ha-ha! [hɑː'hɑː] *int* (*laughter*) ha, ha!

hail[1] [heɪl] *n Met* & *Fig* grêle *f* ‖ *vi Met* grêler; **it's hailing** il grêle. ●**hailstone** *n* grêlon *m*.

hail[2] [heɪl] **1** *vt* (*greet*) saluer; (*taxi*) héler. **2** *vi* **to h. from** (*of person*) être originaire de.

hair [heər] *n* (*on head*) cheveux *mpl*; (*on body*, *of animal*) poils *mpl*; **a h.** (*on head*) un cheveu; (*on body*, *of animal*) un poil; **h. cream** brillantine *f*; **h. dryer** sèche-cheveux *m inv*; **h. spray** (bombe *f* de) laque *f*.

hairbrush ['heəbrʌʃ] *n* brosse *f* à cheveux. ●**haircut** *n* coupe *f* de cheveux; **to have a h.** se faire couper les cheveux. ●**hairdo** *n* (*pl* **-dos**) *Fam* coiffure *f*. ●**hairdresser** *n* coiffeur, -euse *mf*. ●**hairnet** *n* résille *f*. ●**hairpin** *n* épingle *f* à cheveux; **h. bend** *Aut* virage *m* en épingle à cheveux. ●**hair-raising** *a* effrayant. ●**hairslide** *n* barrette *f*. ●**hairstyle** *n* coiffure *f*.

-haired [heəd] *suff* **long-/red-/*etc* haired** aux cheveux longs/roux/*etc*.

hairy ['heərɪ] *a* (**-ier, -iest**) (*person*, *animal*, *body*) poilu; (*frightening*) *Fam* effrayant.

hake [heɪk] *n* (*fish*) colin *m*.

half [hɑːf] *n* (*pl* **halves**) moitié *f*, demi, -ie *mf*; (*of match*) *Sp* mi-temps *f*; **h. (of) the apple/*etc*** la moitié de la pomme/*etc*; **ten and a h.** dix et demi; **ten and a h. weeks** dix semaines et demie; **to cut in h.** couper en deux.

‖ *a* demi; **h. a day, a h.-day** une demi-journée; **h. a dozen, a h.-dozen** une demi-douzaine; **at h. price** à moitié prix; **h. man h. beast** mi-homme mi-bête ‖ *adv* (*dressed*, *full etc*) à moitié, à demi; (*almost*) presque; **h. asleep** à moitié endormi; **h. past one** une heure et demie; **he isn't h. lazy/*etc*** *Fam* il est drôlement paresseux/*etc*; **h. as much as** moitié moins que.

half-back ['hɑːfbæk] *n Fb* demi *m*. ●**h.-'baked** *a* (*idea*) *Fam* à la manque. ●**h.-caste** *n* métis, -isse *mf*. ●**h.-'dozen** *n* demi-douzaine *f*. ●**h.-'hearted** *a* (*person*, *manner*) peu enthousiaste. ●**h.-'hour** *n* demi-heure *f*. ●**h.-'mast** *n* **at h.-mast** (*flag*) en berne. ●**h.-'open** *a* entrouvert. ●**h.-'price** *a* & *adv* à moitié prix. ●**h.-'term** *n* (*in British school*) petites vacances *fpl*. ●**h.-'time** *n Sp* mi-temps *f*. ●**half'way** *adv* à mi-chemin (**between** entre); **to fill/*etc* h.** remplir/*etc* à moitié; **h. through** (*book*) à la moitié de. ●**h.-wit** *n* imbécile *mf*.

halibut ['hælɪbət] *n* (*fish*) flétan *m*.

hall [hɔːl] *n* (*room*) salle *f*; (*house entrance*) entrée *f*; (*of hotel*) hall *m*; (*mansion*) manoir *m*; **h. of residence** *Univ* résidence *f* universitaire; **halls of residence** cité *f* universitaire; **lecture h.** *Univ* amphithéâtre *m*.

hallmark ['hɔːlmɑːk] *n* (*on silver or gold*) poinçon *m*.

hallo! [hə'ləʊ] *int* = **hello**.

Hallowe'en [hæləʊ'iːn] *n* la veille de la Toussaint.

hallstand ['hɔːlstænd] *n* portemanteau *m*.

hallucination [həluːsɪ'neɪʃ(ə)n] *n* hallucination *f*.

hallway ['hɔːlweɪ] *n* entrée *f*.

halo ['heɪləʊ] *n* (*pl* **-oes** *or* **-os**) auréole *f*.

halt [hɔːlt] *n* halte *f*; **to call a h. to** mettre fin à ‖ *vi* (*of soldiers etc*) faire halte; (*of production etc*) s'arrêter ‖ *vt* arrêter ‖ *int Mil* halte!

halve [hɑːv] *vt* (*time, expense*) réduire de moitié; (*number*) diviser en deux.

ham [hæm] *n* jambon *m*; **h. and eggs** œufs *mpl* au jambon.

hamburger ['hæmbɜːgər] *n* hamburger *m*.

hammer ['hæmər] *n* marteau *m* ‖ *vt* (*nail*) enfoncer (**into** dans); (*metal*) marteler; (*defeat*) *Fam* battre à plate(s) couture(s); **to h. out** (*agreement*) mettre au point ‖ *vi* frapper (au marteau). ●**—ing** *n* (*defeat*) *Fam* raclée *f*.

hammock ['hæmək] *n* hamac *m*.

hamper ['hæmpər] **1** *vt* gêner. **2** *n* (*basket*) panier *m* (*à provisions*); (*laundry basket*) *Am* panier *m* à linge.

hamster ['hæmstər] *n* hamster *m*.

hand[1] [hænd] **1** *n* main *f*; **to hold in one's h.** tenir à la main; **by h.** (*to make, sew etc*) à la main; **at** *or* **to h.** (*within reach*) sous la main; **(close) at h.** (*person*) tout près; (*day etc*) proche; **in h.** (*situation*) bien en main; **the matter in h.** l'affaire *f* en question; **on h.** (*ready for use*) disponible; **on the one h....** d'un côté, d'une part...; **on the other h....** d'un autre côté, d'autre part...; **hands up!** (*in attack*) haut les mains!; (*to schoolchildren*) levez la main!; **hands off!** pas touche!; **to give s.o. a (helping) h.** donner un coup de main à qn; **out of h.** (*child*) impossible; (*situation*) incontrôlable; **h. in h.** la main dans la main; **h. in h. with** (*together with*) *Fig* de pair avec; **at first h.** de première main; **h. luggage** bagages *mpl* à main. **2** *n* (*worker*) ouvrier, -ière *mf*; (*of clock*) aiguille *f*; *Cards* jeu *m*.

hand[2] [hænd] *vt* (*give*) donner (**to** à); **to h. down** (*bring down*) descendre; (*knowledge*) transmettre (**to** à); **to h. in** remettre; **to h. out** distribuer; **to h. over** remettre; (*power*) transmettre; **to h. round** (*cakes*) passer.

handbag ['hændbæg] *n* sac *m* à main. ●**handbook** *n* (*manual*) manuel *m*; (*guide*) guide *m*. ●**handbrake** *n* frein *m* à main. ●**handbrush** *n* balayette *f*. ●**handcuff** *vt* passer les menottes à; **to be handcuffed** avoir les menottes aux poignets. ●**handcuffs** *npl* menottes *fpl*. ●**hand'made** *a* fait à la main. ●**hand'picked** *a* (*team member etc*) trié sur le volet. ●**handrail** *n* (*on stairs*) rampe *f*. ●**handshake** *n* poignée *f* de main. ●**hands-on** *a* (*experience*) pratique. ●**handwriting** *n* écriture *f*. ●**hand'written** *a* écrit à la main.

handful ['hændfʊl] *n* (*bunch*) poignée *f*; **she's (quite) a h.** elle est difficile.

handicap ['hændɪkæp] *n* (*disadvantage*) & *Sp* handicap *m* ‖ *vt* (**-pp-**) handicaper; **to be handicapped** (*after accident*) rester handicapé. ●**handicapped** *a* (*disabled*) handicapé.

handicraft ['hændɪkrɑːft] *n* artisanat *m* d'art. ●**handiwork** *n* (*action*) ouvrage *m*.

handkerchief ['hæŋkətʃɪf] *n* (*pl* **-fs**) mouchoir *m*.

handle ['hænd(ə)l] **1** *n* (*of door*) poignée *f*; (*of knife*) manche *m*; (*of bucket*) anse *f*; (*of saucepan*) queue *f*; (*of pump*) bras *m*. **2** *vt* (*manipulate*) manier; (*touch*) toucher à; (*vehicle, ship*) manœuvrer; (*deal with*) s'occuper de.

handlebars ['hænd(ə)lbɑːz] *npl* guidon *m*.

handout ['hændaʊt] *n* (*leaflet*) prospectus *m*; (*money*) aumône *f*.

handsome ['hænsəm] *a* (*person, building etc*) beau (*f* belle); (*profit*) considérable; (*gift*) généreux.

handy ['hændɪ] *a* (**-ier, -iest**) (*convenient, practical*) commode, pratique; (*skilful*) habile (**at doing** à faire); (*within reach*) sous la main; (*place*) accessible; **to come in h.** se révéler utile. ●**handyman** *n* (*pl* **-men**) (*DIY enthusiast*) bricoleur *m*; (*workman*) homme *m* à tout faire.

hang[1] [hæŋ] **1** *vt* (*pt & pp* **hung**) suspendre (**on, from** à); (*on hook*) accrocher (**on, from** à), suspendre; (*wallpaper*) poser; (*let dangle*) laisser pendre (**from, out of** de) ‖ *vi* (*dangle*) pendre; (*of fog, smoke*) flotter. **2** *n* **to get the h. of sth** *Fam* arriver à comprendre qch; **to get the h. of doing** *Fam* trouver le truc pour faire. ●**—ing**[1] *a* suspendu (**from** à); **h. on** (*wall*) accroché à.

hang[2] [hæŋ] *vt* (*pt & pp* **hanged**) (*criminal*) pendre (**for** pour) ‖ *vi* (*of criminal*) être pendu. ●**—ing**[2] *n Jur* pendaison *f*. ●**hangman** *n* (*pl* **-men**) bourreau *m*.

hang about *vi* (*loiter*) traîner; (*wait*) *Fam* attendre **to hang down** *vi* (*dangle*) pendre; (*of hair*) tomber **to hang on** *vi* (*hold out*) résister; (*wait*) *Fam* attendre; **to h. on to** (*cling to*) ne pas lâcher; (*keep*) garder **to hang out** *vt* (*washing*) étendre; (*flag*) arborer ‖ *vi* (*of shirt, tongue*) pendre **to hang up** *vt* (*picture etc*) accrocher ‖ *vi* (*on phone*) raccrocher.

hangar ['hæŋər] *n Av* hangar *m*.

hanger ['hæŋər] *n* **(coat) h.** cintre *m*. ●**hanger-'on** *n* (*pl* **hangers-on**) (*person*) *Pej* parasite *m*.

hang-glider [hæŋ'glaɪdər] *n* delta-plane® *m.* ● **hang-gliding** *n* vol *m* libre. ● **hangover** *n Fam* gueule *f* de bois. ● **hangup** *n Fam* complexe *m.*

hanker ['hæŋkər] *vi* **to h. after** avoir envie de. ● **—ing** *n* (forte) envie *f.*

hankie, hanky ['hæŋkɪ] *n Fam* mouchoir *m.*

hanky-panky [hæŋkɪ'pæŋkɪ] *n inv Fam* (*sexual behaviour*) galipettes *fpl.*

haphazard [hæp'hæzəd] *a* au hasard, au petit bonheur.

happen ['hæpən] *vi* arriver, se passer; **to h. to s.o./sth** arriver à qn/qch; **I h. to know** il se trouve que je sais; **do you h. to have...?** est-ce que par hasard vous avez...?; **whatever happens** quoi qu'il arrive. ● **—ing** *n* événement *m.*

happy ['hæpɪ] *a* (**-ier, -iest**) heureux (**to do** de faire, **about sth** de qch); **I'm not (too** *or* **very) h. about it** ça ne me plaît pas beaucoup; **H. New Year!** bonne année!; **H. Christmas!** Joyeux Noël! ● **h.-go-'lucky** *a* insouciant. ● **happily** *adv* joyeusement; (*contentedly*) tranquillement; (*fortunately*) heureusement. ● **happiness** *n* bonheur *m.*

harass ['hærəs, *Am* hə'ræs] *vt* harceler.

harbour ['hɑːbər] (*Am* **harbor**) **1** *n* port *m.* **2** *vt* (*criminal*) cacher; (*fear, secret*) nourrir.

hard [hɑːd] *a* (**-er, -est**) (*not soft, severe, difficult*) dur; (*fact*) brut; (*water*) calcaire; **to be h. on** *or* **to s.o.** être dur avec qn; **to find it h. to sleep** avoir du mal à dormir; **no h. feelings!** sans rancune!; **h. of hearing** dur d'oreille; **h. core** (*group*) noyau *m*; **h. disk** *Comptr* disque *m* dur; **h. evidence** preuves *fpl* tangibles; **a h. frost** une forte gelée; **h. labour** *Jur* travaux *mpl* forcés; **h. worker** gros travailleur *m*; **h. up** (*broke*) *Fam* fauché; **to be h. up for** manquer de.
▮ *adv* (**-er, -est**) (*to work, hit, freeze*) dur; (*to pull*) fort; (*to rain*) à verse; (*badly*) mal; **to think h.** réfléchir bien; **h. at work** en plein travail; **h. done by** traité injustement.

hard-and-fast [hɑːdən(d)'fɑːst] *a* (*rule*) strict. ● **'hardboard** *n* Isorel® *m.* ● **hard-'boiled** *a* (*egg*) dur. ● **hard'headed** *a* réaliste. ● **hard'wearing** *a* résistant. ● **hard-'working** *a* travailleur.

harden ['hɑːd(ə)n] *vti* durcir; **to become hardened to** s'endurcir à. ● **—ed** *a* (*criminal*) endurci.

hardly ['hɑːdlɪ] *adv* à peine; **h. anyone/ever** presque personne/jamais.

hardness ['hɑːdnɪs] *n* dureté *f.*

hardship ['hɑːdʃɪp] *n* (*ordeal*) épreuve(s) *f(pl)*; (*deprivation*) privation(s) *f(pl).*

hardware ['hɑːdweər] *n inv* quincaillerie *f*; (*of computer*) & *Mil* matériel *m.*

hardy ['hɑːdɪ] *a* (**-ier, -iest**) (*person, plant*) résistant.

hare [heər] *n* lièvre *m.*

harm [hɑːm] *n* (*hurt*) mal *m*; (*wrong*) tort *m*; **she'll come to no h.** il ne lui arrivera rien ▮ *vt* (*physically*) faire du mal à (*qn*); (*health, interests etc*) nuire à; (*object*) endommager. ● **harmful** *a* nuisible. ● **harmless** *a* (*person, treatment, fumes*) inoffensif; (*hobby, act*) innocent.

harmonica [hɑː'mɒnɪkə] *n* harmonica *m.*

harmonious [hɑː'məʊnɪəs] *a* harmonieux.

harmonize ['hɑːmənaɪz] *vt* harmoniser ▮ *vi* s'harmoniser.

harmony ['hɑːmənɪ] *n* harmonie *f.*

harness ['hɑːnɪs] *n* (*for horse, baby*) harnais *m* ▮ *vt* (*horse*) harnacher; (*energy*) *Fig* exploiter.

harp [hɑːp] **1** *n Mus* harpe *f.* **2** *vt* **to h. on about sth** *Fam* ne pas s'arrêter de parler de qch.

harpoon [hɑː'puːn] *n* harpon *m.*

harrowing ['hærəʊɪŋ] *a* (*story, memory*) poignant; (*experience*) très éprouvant; (*cry, sight*) déchirant.

harsh [hɑːʃ] *a* (**-er, -est**) (*severe*) dur, sévère; (*winter, climate*) rude; (*sound*) discordant; (*voice*) rauque; (*taste*) âpre; (*surface*) rugueux; **h. light** lumière *f* crue. ● **—ly** *adv* durement, sévèrement. ● **—ness** *n* (*severity*) dureté *f.*

harvest ['hɑːvɪst] *n* moisson *f*; (*of fruit*) récolte *f* ▮ *vt* moissonner; (*fruit*) récolter.

has [hæz] *see* **have.** ● **has-been** *n Fam* personne *f* finie.

hash [hæʃ] **1** *n Culin* hachis *m.* **2** *n* (*mess*) *Fam* gâchis *m.* **3** *n* (*hashish*) *Fam* hasch *m*, H *m.*

hashish ['hæʃiːʃ] *n* haschisch *m.*

hassle ['hæs(ə)l] *n Fam* (*trouble*) histoires *fpl*; (*bother*) mal *m*, peine *f.*

haste [heɪst] *n* hâte *f*; **in h.** à la hâte; **to make h.** se hâter. ● **hasten** ['heɪs(ə)n] *vi* se hâter (**to do** de faire) ▮ *vt* hâter.

hasty ['heɪstɪ] *a* (**-ier, -iest**) (*sudden*) précipité; (*visit*) rapide; (*decision*) hâtif. ● **hastily** *adv* (*quickly*) à la hâte.

hat [hæt] *n* chapeau *m*; (*of child*) bonnet *m*; (*cap*) casquette *f*; **that's old h.** *Fam* (*old-fashioned*) c'est vieux jeu; (*stale*) c'est vieux comme les rues.

hatch [hætʃ] **1** *vi* (*of chick, egg*) éclore ▮ *vt* faire éclore; (*plot*) *Fig* tramer. **2** *n* (*in kitchen wall*) passe-plats *m inv.*

hatchback ['hætʃbæk] *n* (*car*) trois-portes *f*

inv, cinq-portes *f inv*.

hatchet ['hætʃɪt] *n* hachette *f*.

hate [heɪt] *vt* détester, haïr; **to h. doing** *or* **to do** détester faire ‖ *n* haine *f*; **pet h.** *Fam* bête *f* noire. • **hateful** *a* haïssable. • **hatred** *n* haine *f*.

hatstand ['hætstænd] *n* portemanteau *m*.

haughty ['hɔːtɪ] *a* (**-ier, -iest**) hautain.

haul [hɔːl] **1** *vt* (*pull*) tirer; (*goods*) camionner. **2** *n* (*fish caught*) prise *f*; (*of thief*) butin *m*; **a long h.** un long voyage. • **haulier** *or Am* **hauler** *n* transporteur *m* routier.

haunt [hɔːnt] **1** *vt* hanter. **2** *n* endroit *m* favori; (*of criminal*) repaire *m*.

have [hæv] **1** (*3rd person sing pres t* **has;** *pt & pp* **had;** *pres p* **having**) *vt* avoir; (*meal, shower etc*) prendre; **he has got, he has** il a; **to h. a walk/dream** faire une promenade/ un rêve; **to h. a drink** prendre un verre; **to h. a wash** se laver; **to h. a pleasant holiday** *or Am* **vacation** (*spend*) passer d'agréables vacances; **will you h....?** (*a cake, some tea etc*) est-ce que tu veux...?; **to let s.o. h. sth** donner qch à qn; **I won't h. this** (*allow*) je ne tolérerai pas ça; **you've had it!** *Fam* tu es fichu!; **to h. on** (*clothes*) porter; **to have something on** (*be busy*) être pris; **to h. s.o. over** *or* **round** inviter qn chez soi.

2 *v aux* avoir; (*with monter, sortir etc & pronominal verbs*) être; **to h. decided** avoir décidé; **to h. gone** être allé; **to h. cut oneself** s'être coupé; **she has been punished** elle a été punie; **I've just done it** je viens de le faire; **to h. to do** (*must*) devoir faire; **I've got to go, I h. to go** je dois partir, je suis obligé de partir, il faut que je parte; **I don't h. to go** je ne suis pas obligé de partir; **to h. sth done** faire faire qch; **he's had his suitcase brought up** il a fait monter sa valise; **she's had her hair cut** elle s'est fait couper les cheveux; **I've had my car stolen** on m'a volé mon auto; **I've been doing it for months** je le fais depuis des mois; **haven't I?, hasn't she?** *etc* n'est-ce pas?; **no I haven't!** non!; **yes I h.!** si!; **after he had eaten, he left** après avoir mangé, il partit.

3 *npl* **the haves and have-nots** les riches *mpl* et les pauvres *mpl*.

haven ['heɪv(ə)n] *n* refuge *m*.

haven't ['hævənt] = **have not**.

haversack ['hævəsæk] *n* (*shoulder bag*) musette *f*.

havoc ['hævək] *n* ravages *mpl*.

hawk [hɔːk] *n* (*bird*) & *Pol* faucon *m*.

hawthorn ['hɔːθɔːn] *n* aubépine *f*.

hay [heɪ] *n* foin *m*; **h. fever** rhume *m* des foins. • **haystack** *n* meule *f* de foin.

haywire ['heɪwaɪər] *a* **to go h.** (*of machine*) se détraquer; (*of plan*) mal tourner.

hazard ['hæzəd] *n* risque *m*; **health h.** risque *m* pour la santé; **h. (warning) light** *Aut* feux *mpl* de détresse ‖ *vt* (*guess, remark*) hasarder. • **hazardous** *a* hasardeux.

haze [heɪz] *n* brume *f*. • **hazy** *a* (**-ier, -iest**) (*weather*) brumeux; (*sun*) voilé; (*photo, idea*) flou; **I'm h. about my plans** je ne suis pas sûr de mes projets.

hazel ['heɪz(ə)l] *n* (*bush*) noisetier *m* ‖ *a* (*eyes*) noisette *inv*. • **hazelnut** *n* noisette *f*.

he [hiː] *pron* il; (*stressed*) lui; **he wants** il veut; **he's a happy man** c'est un homme heureux; **he and I** lui et moi ‖ *n Fam* mâle *m*; **it's a he** (*baby*) c'est un garçon.

head [hed] **1** *n* (*of person, hammer etc*) tête *f*; (*leader*) chef *m*; (*headmaster*) directeur *m*; (*headmistress*) directrice *f*; **h. of hair** chevelure *f*; **h. first** la tête la première; **it didn't enter my h.** ça ne m'est pas venu à l'esprit; **to take it into one's h. to do** se mettre en tête de faire; **to shout one's h. off** *Fam* crier à tue-tête; **at the h. of** (*in charge of*) à la tête de; **at the h. of the list** en tête de liste; **at the h. of the page** en haut de (la) page; **it's above my h.** ça me dépasse; **to keep one's h.** garder son sang-froid; **it's coming to a h.** (*of situation*) ça devient critique; **heads or tails?** pile ou face?; **per h., a h.** (*each*) par personne; **h. cold** rhume *m* de cerveau.

2 *a* principal; (*gardener*) en chef; **h. waiter** maître *m* d'hôtel; **a h. start** une grosse avance.

3 *vt* (*group, firm*) être à la tête de; (*list*) être en tête de; (*vehicle*) diriger (**towards** vers); **to h. the ball** *Fb* faire une tête; **to h. off** (*person*) détourner de son chemin; (*prevent*) empêcher; **to be headed for** *Am* = **to h. for**.

4 *vi* **to h. for, be heading for** (*place*) se diriger vers; (*ruin*) *Fig* aller à. • **heading** *n* (*of chapter, page*) titre *m*; (*of subject*) rubrique *f*; (*on letter etc*) en-tête *m*.

headache ['hedeɪk] *n* mal *m* de tête; (*difficulty, person*) *Fig* problème *m*; **to have a h.** avoir mal à la tête. • **headlamp** *or* **headlight** *n Aut* phare *m*. • **headline** *n* (*of newspaper*) manchette *f*; *pl* (gros) titres *mpl*; *Rad TV* (grands) titres *mpl*. • **headlong** *adv* (*to fall*) la tête la première; (*to rush*) tête baissée. • **head'master** *n* (*of school*) directeur *m*. • **head'mistress** *n* (*of school*) directrice *f*. • **head-'on** *adv & a* (*to collide, collision*) de plein fouet. • **headphones** *npl* casque *m* (à écouteurs).

• **headquarters** *npl Com Pol* siège *m* (central); *Mil* quartier *m* général. • **headrest** *n* appuie-tête *m inv*. • **headscarf** *n* (*pl* **-scarves**) foulard *m*. • **headstrong** *a* têtu. • **headway** *n* progrès *mpl*.

heady ['hedɪ] *a* (**-ier, -iest**) (*wine*) capiteux; (*speech*) impétueux.

heal [hiːl] *vi* (*of wound*) se cicatriser; (*of bruise*) disparaître; (*of bone*) se ressouder ‖ *vt* (*wound*) cicatriser; (*bruise*) faire disparaître; (*bone*) ressouder; (*person*) guérir.

health [helθ] *n* santé *f*; **h. food** aliment *m* naturel; **h. food shop** *or Am* **store** magasin *m* de produits diététiques; **h. food restaurant** restaurant *m* diététique; **h. resort** station *f* climatique; **the (National) H. Service** = la Sécurité Sociale. • **healthy** *a* (**-ier, -iest**) (*person*) en bonne santé, sain; (*food, attitude*) sain; (*appetite*) robuste.

heap [hiːp] *n* tas *m*; **heaps of** (*money, people*) *Fam* des tas de; **to have heaps of time** *Fam* avoir largement le temps ‖ *vt* entasser; **to h. on s.o.** (*praise*) couvrir qn de; (*insults*) accabler qn de.

hear [hɪər] *vt* (*pt & pp* **heard** [hɜːd]) entendre; (*listen to*) écouter; (*learn*) apprendre (**that** que); **I heard him come** *or* **coming** je l'ai entendu venir; **have you heard the news?** connais-tu la nouvelle?; **h., h.!** bravo!

‖ *vi* entendre; (*get news*) recevoir des nouvelles (**from** de); **I've heard of** *or* **about him** j'ai entendu parler de lui; **she wouldn't h. of it** elle ne veut pas en entendre parler; **I wouldn't h. of it!** pas question! • **hearing 1** *n* (*sense*) ouïe *f*; **h. aid** appareil *m* auditif. **2** (*of committee*) séance *f*; **to get a (fair) h.** avoir la possibilité de s'exprimer. • **hearsay** *n* **by h.** par ouï-dire; **it's h.** ce ne sont que des bruits qui courent.

hearse [hɜːs] *n* corbillard *m*.

heart [hɑːt] *n* cœur *m*; **heart(s)** *Cards* cœur *m*; **(off) by h.** par cœur; **to lose h.** perdre courage; **at h.** au fond; **his h. is set on it** il le veut à tout prix, il y tient; **h. attack** crise *f* cardiaque; **h. disease** maladie *f* de cœur.

heartache ['hɑːteɪk] *n* chagrin *m*. • **heartbeat** *n* battement *m* de cœur. • **heartbreaking** *a* navrant, déchirant. • **heartbroken** *a* inconsolable. • **heartburn** *n Med* brûlures *fpl* d'estomac.

hearten ['hɑːt(ə)n] *vt* encourager. • **—ing** *a* encourageant.

hearth [hɑːθ] *n* foyer *m*.

hearty ['hɑːtɪ] *a* (**-ier, -iest**) (*appetite, meal*) gros (*f* grosse).

heat [hiːt] **1** *n* chaleur *f*; (*heating*) chauffage *m*; **in the h. of the argument** dans le feu de la discussion; **at low h.** *Culin* à feu doux; **h. wave** vague *f* de chaleur ‖ *vti* **to h. (up)** chauffer.

2 *n* (*in race, competition*) éliminatoire *f*; **it was a dead h.** ils sont arrivés ex aequo. • **—ed** *a* (*swimming pool*) chauffé; (*argument*) passionné. • **—ing** *n* chauffage *m*; **central h.** chauffage *m* central. • **heater** *n* appareil *m* de chauffage; **water h.** chauffe-eau *m inv*.

heath [hiːθ] *n* (*land*) lande *f*.

heather ['heðər] *n* (*plant*) bruyère *f*.

heave [hiːv] *vt* (*lift*) soulever; (*pull*) tirer; (*drag*) traîner; (*throw*) *Fam* lancer; (*a sigh*) pousser ‖ *vi* (*of stomach, chest*) se soulever; (*feel sick*) *Fam* avoir des haut-le-cœur.

heaven ['hev(ə)n] *n* ciel *m*, paradis *m*; **h. knows when** *Fam* Dieu sait quand; **good heavens!** *Fam* mon Dieu! • **—ly** *a* céleste; (*pleasing*) *Fam* divin.

heavy ['hevɪ] *a* (**-ier, -iest**) lourd; (*work, cold*) gros (*f* grosse); (*blow*) violent; (*rain*) fort; (*traffic*) dense; (*smoker, drinker*) grand; **a h. day** (*busy*) une journée chargée; **h. casualties** de nombreuses victimes; **h. snow** d'abondantes chutes de neige; **it's h. going** c'est difficile. • **heavily** *adv* (*to walk, tax*) lourdement; (*to breathe*) péniblement; (*to smoke, drink, snow*) beaucoup; **h. in debt** lourdement endetté; **to rain h.** pleuvoir à verse. • **heavyweight** *n Boxing* poids *m* lourd.

Hebrew ['hiːbruː] *n* (*language*) hébreu *m*.

heck [hek] *int Fam* zut! ‖ *n* = **hell** *in expressions*.

heckl/e ['hek(ə)l] *vt* interpeller. • **—ing** *n* interpellations *fpl*.

hectic ['hektɪk] *a* (*activity*) fiévreux; (*period*) très agité; (*trip*) mouvementé; **h. life** vie *f* trépidante.

he'd [hiːd] = **he had & he would.**

hedge [hedʒ] **1** *n* (*bushes*) haie *f*. **2** *vi* (*answer evasively*) ne pas se mouiller.

hedgehog ['hedʒhɒg] *n* (*animal*) hérisson *m*.

heed [hiːd] *vt* faire attention à.

heel [hiːl] *n* talon *m*; **down at h.**, *Am* **down at the heels** (*shabby*) miteux; **h. bar** cordonnerie *f* express; (*on sign*) 'talon minute'.

hefty ['heftɪ] *a* (**-ier, -iest**) (*large, heavy*) gros (*f* grosse).

height [haɪt] *n* hauteur *f*; (*of person*) taille *f*; (*of mountain, aircraft*) altitude *f*; **the h. of** (*success, fame*) le sommet de; (*folly*) le comble de; **at the h. of** (*summer, storm*) au cœur de. • **heighten** *vt* (*tension, interest*)

augmenter.
heir [eər] *n* héritier *m*. ● **heiress** *n* héritière *f*.
held [held] *pt* & *pp of* **hold.**
helicopter ['helɪkɒptər] *n* hélicoptère *m*. ● **heliport** *n* héliport *m*.
hell [hel] *n* enfer *m*; **a h. of a lot (of)** *Fam* énormément (de); **what the h. are you doing?** *Fam* qu'est-ce que tu fous?; **to h. with him** *Fam* qu'il aille se faire voir; **h.!** *Fam* zut!; **h.-bent on doing**, *Am* **h.-bent to do** *Fam* acharné à faire.
he'll [hi:l] = **he will.**
hello! [hə'ləʊ] *int* bonjour!; (*answering phone*) allô!; (*surprise*) tiens!
helm [helm] *n Nau* barre *f*.
helmet ['helmɪt] *n* casque *m*.
help [help] *n* aide *f*, secours *m*; (*cleaning woman*) femme *f* de ménage; (*office or shop workers*) employés, -ées *mfpl*; **with the h. of** (*stick etc*) à l'aide de; **h.!** au secours!
▮ *vt* aider (**s.o. do** *or* **to do** qn à faire); **to h. s.o. to soup**/*etc* (*serve*) servir du potage/*etc* à qn; **h. yourself** servez-vous (**to** de); **to h. s.o. out** aider qn; (*of trouble*) dépanner qn; **to h. s.o. up** aider qn à monter; **I can't h. laughing** je ne peux (pas) m'empêcher de rire; **he can't h. being blind** ce n'est pas sa faute s'il est aveugle.
▮ *vi* **to h. (out)** aider. ● **helping** *n* (*serving*) portion *f*. ● **helper** *n* assistant, -ante *mf*.
helpful ['helpfəl] *a* (*useful*) utile; (*person*) serviable.
helpless ['helpləs] *a* (*powerless*) impuissant; (*disabled*) impotent.
helter-skelter [heltə'skeltər] *n* (*slide*) toboggan *m*.
hem [hem] *n* ourlet *m* ▮ *vt* (**-mm-**) (*garment*) ourler; **to be hemmed in** (*surrounded*) être cerné (**by** de); (*unable to move*) être coincé.
hemorrhage ['hemərɪdʒ] *n Med* hémorragie *f*.
hemorrhoids ['hemərɔɪdz] *npl* hémorroïdes *fpl*.
hen [hen] *n* poule *f*. ● **henpecked** *a* (*husband*) dominé par sa femme.
hence [hens] *adv* **1** (*therefore*) d'où. **2** (*from now*) **ten years h.** d'ici dix ans. ● **henceforth** *adv* désormais.
henchman ['hentʃmən] *n* (*pl* **-men**) *Pej* acolyte *m*.
hepatitis [hepə'taɪtɪs] *n* hépatite *f*.
her [hɜ:r] **1** *pron* la, l'; (*after prep, 'than', 'it is'*) elle; **(to) h.** lui; **I see h.** je la vois; **I saw h.** je l'ai vue; **I give (to) h.** je lui donne; **with h.** avec elle. **2** *poss a* son, sa, *pl* ses.
herald ['herəld] *vt* annoncer.
herb [hɜ:b, *Am* ɜ:b] *n* herbe *f*; *pl Culin* fines herbes *fpl*. ● **herbal** *a* **h. tea** infusion *f* (d'herbes).
herd [hɜ:d] *n* troupeau *m*.
here [hɪər] **1** *adv* ici; **h. is, h. are** voici; **h. she is** la voici; **summer is h.** l'été est là; **h. and there** çà et là; **h. you are!** (*take this*) tenez! **2** *int* **h.!** (*calling s.o.'s attention*) holà!; (*giving s.o. sth*) tenez! ● **herea'bouts** *adv* par ici. ● **here'by** *adv* (*to declare etc*) par le présent acte. ● **here'with** *adv* (*with letter*) *Com* ci-joint.
hereditary [hɪ'redɪtərɪ] *a* héréditaire.
heritage ['herɪtɪdʒ] *n* héritage *m*.
hermit ['hɜ:mɪt] *n* solitaire *mf*, ermite *m*.
hernia ['hɜ:nɪə] *n* hernie *f*.
hero ['hɪərəʊ] *n* (*pl* **-oes**) héros *m*. ● **he'roic** *a* héroïque. ● **heroine** ['herəʊɪn] *n* héroïne *f*. ● **heroism** ['herəʊɪz(ə)m] *n* héroïsme *m*.
heroin ['herəʊɪn] *n* (*drug*) héroïne *f*.
heron ['herən] *n* (*bird*) héron *m*.
herring ['herɪŋ] *n* hareng *m*.
hers [hɜ:z] *poss pron* le sien, la sienne, *pl* les sien(ne)s; **this hat is h.** ce chapeau est à elle *or* est le sien; **a friend of h.** une amie à elle.
herself [hɜ:'self] *pron* elle-même; (*reflexive*) se, s'; (*after prep*) elle; **she cut h.** elle s'est coupée; **she thinks of h.** elle pense à elle.
hesitant ['hezɪtənt] *a* hésitant.
hesitate ['hezɪteɪt] *vi* hésiter (**over, about** sur) ▮ *vt* **to h. to do** hésiter à faire. ● **hesitation** [-'teɪʃ(ə)n] *n* hésitation *f*.
het up [het'ʌp] *a Fam* énervé.
hew [hju:] *vt* (*pp* **hewn** *or* **hewed**) tailler.
hexagon ['heksəgən] *n* hexagone *m*. ● **hex'agonal** *a* hexagonal.
hey! [heɪ] *int* (*calling s.o.*) hé!; (*surprise, annoyance*) ho!
heyday ['heɪdeɪ] *n* **in its h.** à son âge d'or; **in my h.** à l'apogée de ma vie *or* de ma carrière.
hi! [haɪ] *int Fam* salut!
hibernate ['haɪbəneɪt] *vi* hiberner.
hiccup ['hɪkʌp] *n* hoquet *m*; *Fig* (petit) problème *m*; **to have (the) hiccups** avoir le hoquet ▮ *vi* hoqueter.
hide[1] [haɪd] *vt* (*pt* **hid**, *pp* **hidden**) cacher (**from** à) ▮ *vi* se cacher (**from** de). ● **h.-and-'seek** *n* cache-cache *m inv*. ● **hideout** *n* cachette *f*. ● **hiding** *n* **1 to go into h.** se cacher; **h. place** cachette *f*. **2 a good h.** (*thrashing*) *Fam* une bonne raclée.
hide[2] [haɪd] *n* (*skin*) peau *f*.
hideous ['hɪdɪəs] *a* (*person, sight, weather etc*) horrible. ● **—ly** *adv* (*badly, very*) horriblement.
hi-fi ['haɪfaɪ] *n* (*system*) chaîne *f* hi-fi ▮ *a* hi-fi *inv*.

high [haɪ] *a* (**-er, -est**) haut; (*speed*) grand; (*price, number*) élevé; (*on drugs*) *Fam* défoncé; **to be five metres h.** avoir *or* faire cinq mètres de haut; **it is h. time that** il est grand temps que (+ *sub*); **h. fever** forte *or* grosse fièvre *f*; **h. jump** *Sp* saut *m* en hauteur; **h. noon** plein midi *m*; **h. school** = lycée *m*; **h. spirits** entrain *m*; **h. spot** (*of visit*) point *m* culminant; (*of show*) clou *m*; **h. street** grand-rue *f*; **h. table** table *f* d'honneur; **h. voice** voix *f* aiguë.
▮ *adv* **h. (up)** (*to fly, throw etc*) haut; **to aim h.** viser haut.
▮ *n* **a new h., an all-time h.** (*peak*) un nouveau record.

highbrow ['haɪbraʊ] *a* & *n* intellectuel, -elle (*mf*).

high-chair ['haɪtʃeər] *n* chaise *f* haute. ● **h.-'class** *a* (*service*) de premier ordre; (*building*) de luxe. ● **h.-'handed** *a* tyrannique. ● **h.-'pitched** *a* (*sound*) aigu (*f* -uë). ● **h.-'powered** *a* (*person*) très dynamique. ● **h.-rise** *a* **h.-rise flats** tour *f*. ● **h.-'speed** *a* ultra-rapide; **h.-speed train** train *m* à grande vitesse. ● **h.-'strung** *a Am* nerveux. ● **h.-'up** *a* (*person*) *Fam* haut placé.

higher ['haɪər] *a* (*number, speed etc*) supérieur (**to** à); **h. education** enseignement *m* supérieur ▮ *adv* (*to fly etc*) plus haut (**than** que).

highlands ['haɪləndz] *npl* régions *fpl* montagneuses.

highlight ['haɪlaɪt] *n* (*of visit, day*) point *m* culminant; (*of show*) clou *m*; (*in hair*) reflet *m* ▮ *vt* souligner; (*with marker*) surligner. ● **highlighter** *n* (*coloured marker*) surligneur *m*.

highly ['haɪlɪ] *adv* (*very*) (*interesting, amusing etc*) très; (*to recommend*) chaudement; **h. paid** très bien payé; **to speak h. of** dire beaucoup de bien de; **h. strung** nerveux.

Highness ['haɪnɪs] *n* (*title*) Altesse f.

highroad ['haɪrəʊd] *n* grand-route *f*.

highway ['haɪweɪ] *n Am* autoroute *f*; **public h.** voie *f* publique; **H. Code** Code *m* de la route.

hijack ['haɪdʒæk] *vt* (*aircraft, vehicle*) détourner ▮ *n* détournement *m*. ● **—ing** *n* (*air piracy*) piraterie *f* aérienne; (*hijack*) détournement *m*. ● **hijacker** *n* pirate *m* de l'air.

hik/e [haɪk] **1** *n* excursion *f* à pied ▮ *vi* marcher à pied. **2** *n* (*increase*) *Fam* hausse *f*. ● **—er** *n* excursionniste *mf*.

hilarious [hɪ'leərɪəs] *a* (*funny*) désopilant.

hill [hɪl] *n* colline *f*; (*small*) coteau *m*; (*slope*) pente *f*. ● **hillside** *n* **on the h.** à flanc de colline *or* de coteau. ● **hilly** *a* (**-ier, -iest**) accidenté.

hilt [hɪlt] *n* (*of sword*) poignée *f*; **to the h.** *Fig* au maximum.

him [hɪm] *pron* le, l'; (*after prep, 'than', 'it is'*) lui; **(to) h.** lui; **I see h.** je le vois; **I saw h.** je l'ai vu; **I give (to) h.** je lui donne; **with h.** avec lui.

himself [hɪm'self] *pron* lui-même; (*reflexive*) se, s'; (*after prep*) lui; **he cut h.** il s'est coupé; **he thinks of h.** il pense à lui.

hind [haɪnd] *a* **h. legs** pattes *fpl* de derrière.

hinder ['hɪndər] *vt* (*obstruct*) gêner; (*prevent*) empêcher (**from doing** de faire). ● **hindrance** *n* gêne *f*.

hindsight ['haɪndsaɪt] *n* **with h.** rétrospectivement.

Hindu ['hɪndu:] *a* & *n* hindou, -oue (*mf*).

hinge [hɪndʒ] **1** *n* charnière *f*. **2** *vi* **to h. on** dépendre de.

hint [hɪnt] *n* (*insinuation*) allusion *f*; (*sign*) indication *f*; (*trace*) trace *f*; *pl* (*advice*) conseils *mpl* ▮ *vt* laisser entendre (**that** que) ▮ *vi* **to h. at** faire allusion à.

hip [hɪp] *n* hanche *f*.

hippie ['hɪpɪ] *n* hippie *mf*.

hippopotamus [hɪpə'pɒtəməs] *n* hippopotame *m*.

hire ['haɪər] *vt* (*vehicle etc*) louer; (*worker*) engager; **to h. out** donner en location, louer ▮ *n* location *f*; **for h.** à louer; **h. purchase** vente *f* *or* achat *m* à crédit; **on h. purchase** à crédit.

his [hɪz] **1** *poss a* son, sa, *pl* ses. **2** *poss pron* le sien, la sienne, *pl* les sien(ne)s; **this hat is h.** ce chapeau est à lui *or* est le sien; **a friend of h.** un ami à lui.

Hispanic [hɪs'pænɪk] *a* & *n Am* hispano-américain, -aine (*mf*).

hiss [hɪs] *vti* siffler ▮ *n* sifflement *m*.

history ['hɪstərɪ] *n* (*study, events*) histoire *f*; **your medical h.** vos antécédents médicaux. ● **hi'storian** *n* historien, -ienne *mf*. ● **hi'storic(al)** *a* historique.

hit [hɪt] *vt* (*pt & pp* **hit**, *pres p* **hitting**) (*beat etc*) frapper; (*bump into*) heurter; (*reach*) atteindre; (*affect*) toucher; (*find*) rencontrer (*problème*); **to h. it off** *Fam* s'entendre bien (**with s.o.** avec qn).
▮ *vi* frapper; **to h. back** rendre coup pour coup; (*answer criticism etc*) riposter; **to h. out (at)** *Fam* attaquer; **to h. (up)on** (*find*) tomber sur.
▮ *n* (*blow*) coup *m*; (*play, film, book*) succès *m*; **h. (song)** chanson *f* à succès; **to make a h. with** *Fam* avoir un succès avec. ● **hit-and-run driver** *n* chauffard *m* (*qui prend la fuite*).

• **hit-or-'miss** *a* (*chancy*) aléatoire.

hitch [hɪtʃ] **1** *n* (*snag*) problème *m*. **2** *vt* (*fasten*) accrocher (**to** à). **3** *vti* **to h.** (**a lift** *or* **a ride**) *Fam* faire du stop (**to** jusqu'à).

hitchhik/e ['hɪtʃhaɪk] *vi* faire de l'auto-stop (**to** jusqu'à). •**—ing** *n* auto-stop *m*. • **hitchhiker** *n* auto-stoppeur, -euse *mf*.

hi-tech [haɪ'tek] *a* (*industry*) de pointe.

HIV [eɪtʃaɪ'viː] *n* **HIV positive/negative** *Med* séropositif/séronégatif.

hive [haɪv] *n* ruche *f*.

hoard [hɔːd] *n* réserve *f*; (*of money*) trésor *m* ‖ *vt* amasser.

hoarding ['hɔːdɪŋ] *n* panneau *m* d'affichage.

hoarse [hɔːs] *a* (**-er, -est**) (*person, voice*) enroué.

hoax [həʊks] *n* canular *m* ‖ *vt* faire un canular à.

hob [hɒb] *n* (*on stove*) plaque *f* chauffante.

hobble ['hɒb(ə)l] *vi* (*walk*) boitiller.

hobby ['hɒbɪ] *n* passe-temps *m inv*; **my h.** mon passe-temps favori. • **hobbyhorse** *n* (*favourite subject*) dada *m*.

hobnob ['hɒbnɒb] *vi* (**-bb-**) **to h. with** frayer avec.

hobo ['həʊbəʊ] *n* (*pl* **-oes** *or* **-os**) *Am* vagabond, -onde *mf*.

hockey ['hɒkɪ] *n* hockey *m*; **ice h.** hockey sur glace.

hodgepodge ['hɒdʒpɒdʒ] *n* fatras *m*.

hoe [həʊ] *n* binette *f* ‖ *vt* biner.

hog [hɒg] **1** *n* (*pig*) cochon *m*, porc *m*. **2** *n* **to go the whole h.** *Fam* aller jusqu'au bout. **3** *vt* (**-gg-**) *Fam* monopoliser.

hoist [hɔɪst] *vt* hisser ‖ *n* (*machine*) palan *m*.

hold [həʊld] *n* (*grip*) prise *f*; (*of ship*) cale *f*; (*of aircraft*) soute *f*; **to get h. of** (*grab*) saisir; (*contact*) joindre; (*find*) trouver.

‖ *vt* (*pt & pp* **held**) tenir; (*breath, interest, heat, attention*) retenir; (*a post*) occuper; (*a record*) détenir; (*weight*) supporter; (*party, bazaar etc*) organiser; (*ceremony, mass*) célébrer; (*possess*) posséder; (*contain*) contenir; (*keep*) garder; **to h. hands** se tenir par la main; **to h. one's own** se débrouiller; (*of sick person*) se maintenir; **h. the line!** *Tel* ne quittez pas!; **h. it!** (*stay still*) ne bouge pas!; **to be held** (*of event*) avoir lieu.

‖ *vi* (*of nail, rope*) tenir; (*of weather*) se maintenir; **to h. good** (*of argument*) valoir (**for** pour). • **holdall** *n* (*bag*) fourre-tout *m inv*.

hold back *vt* (*crowd, tears*) contenir; (*hide*) cacher (**from** à) **to hold down** *vt* (*price*) maintenir bas; (*keep*) garder (*un emploi*); (*person on ground*) maintenir au sol **to hold off** *vt* (*enemy*) tenir à distance ‖ *vi* **if the rain holds off** s'il ne pleut pas **to hold on** *vi* (*wait*) attendre; (*stand firm*) tenir bon; **h. on!** *Tel* ne quittez pas!; **h. on (tight)!** tenez bon! **to hold onto** *vt* (*cling to*) tenir bien; (*keep*) garder **to hold out** *vt* (*offer*) offrir; (*arm*) étendre ‖ *vi* (*resist*) résister; (*last*) durer **to hold over** *vt* (*postpone*) remettre **to hold up** *vt* (*raise*) lever; (*support*) soutenir; (*delay*) retarder; (*bank*) attaquer (à main armée).

holder ['həʊldər] *n* (*of passport, post*) titulaire *mf*; (*of record*) détenteur, -trice *mf*; (*container*) support *m*.

holdings ['həʊldɪŋz] *npl Fin* possessions *fpl*.

holdup ['həʊldʌp] *n* (*attack*) hold-up *m inv*; (*traffic jam*) bouchon *m*; (*delay*) retard *m*.

hole [həʊl] *n* trou *m* ‖ *vi* **to h. up** (*hide*) *Fam* se terrer.

holiday ['hɒlɪdeɪ] *n* **holiday(s)** (*from work, school etc*) vacances *fpl*; **a h.** (*day off*) un congé; *Rel* une fête; **a (public** *or* **bank) h.,** *Am* **a legal h.** un jour férié; **on h.** en vacances; **holidays with pay** congés *mpl* payés ‖ *a* (*camp, clothes etc*) de vacances. • **holidaymaker** *n* vacancier, -ière *mf*.

Holland ['hɒlənd] *n* Hollande *f*.

hollow ['hɒləʊ] *a* creux ‖ *n* creux *m* ‖ *vt* **to h. out** creuser.

holly ['hɒlɪ] *n* houx *m*.

holster ['həʊlstər] *n* étui *m* de revolver.

holy ['həʊlɪ] *a* (**-ier, -iest**) saint; (*bread, water*) bénit; (*ground*) sacré.

homage ['hɒmɪdʒ] *n* hommage *m*; **to pay h. to** rendre hommage à.

home [həʊm] *n* maison *f*; (*country*) pays *m* (natal); **(old people's) h.** maison *f* de retraite; **at h.** à la maison, chez soi; **to make oneself at h.** se mettre à l'aise; **to play at h.** *Fb* jouer à domicile; **a broken h.** un foyer désuni; **a good h.** une bonne famille; **to make one's h. in** s'installer à *or* en.

‖ *adv* à la maison, chez soi; **to go** *or* **come (back) h.** rentrer; **to be h.** être rentré; **to drive h.** ramener (*qn*) (en voiture); (*nail*) enfoncer.

‖ *a* (*life, cooking etc*) de famille, familial; *Pol* national; (*visit, match*) à domicile; **h. computer** ordinateur *m* domestique; **h. help** aide *f* ménagère; **H. Office** = ministère *m* de l'Intérieur; **h. rule** *Pol* autonomie *f*; **H. Secretary** = ministre *m* de l'Intérieur; **h. town** (*birth place*) ville *f* natale.

homecoming ['həʊmkʌmɪŋ] *n* retour *m* au foyer. • **homeland** *n* patrie *f*. • **homeloving** *a* casanier. • **home'made** *a* (fait à la) maison *inv*.

homeless ['həʊmləs] *a* sans abri ▮ *n* **the h.** les sans-abri *m inv*.

homely ['həʊmlɪ] *a* (**-ier, -iest**) (*simple*) simple; (*ugly*) *Am* laid.

homesick ['həʊmsɪk] *a* **to be h.** avoir envie de rentrer chez soi.

homeward ['həʊmwəd] *a* (*trip*) de retour ▮ *adv* **h. bound** sur le chemin de retour.

homework ['həʊmwɜːk] *n Sch* devoir(s) *m(pl)*.

homey ['həʊmɪ] *a* (**-ier, -iest**) *Am Fam* accueillant.

homicide ['hɒmɪsaɪd] *n* (*murder*) homicide *m;* **two homicides** *Am* deux meurtres *mpl*.

homosexual [həʊmə'sekʃʊəl] *a* & *n* homosexuel, -elle (*mf*).

honest ['ɒnɪst] *a* honnête; (*frank*) franc (*f* franche) (**with** avec); **the h. truth** la pure vérité; **to be (quite) h....** pour être franc.... ● **honesty** *n* honnêteté *f*; franchise *f*.

honey ['hʌnɪ] *n* miel *m*; (*person*) *Fam* chéri, -ie *mf*. ● **honeycomb** *n* rayon *m* de miel. ● **honeymoon** *n* lune *f* de miel; **to be on one's h.** être en voyage de noces. ● **honeysuckle** *n Bot* chèvrefeuille *f*.

honk [hɒŋk] *vi Aut* klaxonner ▮ *n* coup *m* de klaxon®.

honour ['ɒnər] (*Am* **honor**) *n* honneur *m*; **in h. of** en l'honneur de; **honours degree** *Univ* = licence *f* ▮ *vt* honorer (**with** de). ● **honorary** *a* (*member*) honoraire; (*title*) honorifique. ● **honourable** *a* honorable.

hood [hʊd] *n* capuchon *m*; (*mask of robber*) cagoule *f*; (*soft car roof, roof of pram or Am baby carriage*) capote *f*; (*car bonnet*) capot *m*; (*above stove*) hotte *f*. ● **hooded** *a* (*person*) encapuchonné; (*coat*) à capuchon.

hoodlum ['huːdləm] *n* (*gangster*) *Fam* gangster *m*.

hoof, *pl* **-fs** *or* **-ves** [huːf, -fs, -vz] (*Am* [hʊf, -fs, huːvz]) *n* sabot *m*.

hook [hʊk] *n* crochet *m*; (*on clothes*) agrafe *f*; *Fishing* hameçon *m*; **off the h.** (*phone*) décroché; **to let** *or* **get s.o. off the h.** tirer qn d'affaire ▮ *vt* **to h. (on** *or* **up)** accrocher (**to** à). ● **—ed** *a* (*nose, end, object*) recourbé; **h. on chess/***etc Fam* enragé d'échecs/*etc*, accro des échecs/*etc*; **to be h. on drugs** *Fam* être accro. ● **hooker** *n Fam* prostituée *f*.

hook(e)y ['hʊkɪ] *n* **to play h.** *Am Fam* sécher (la classe).

hooligan ['huːlɪgən] *n* vandale *m*, voyou *m;* **football** *ou* **soccer h.** hooligan *m*.

hoop [huːp] *n* cerceau *m*.

hoot [huːt] *vi Aut* klaxonner; (*of train*) siffler; (*of owl*) hululer ▮ *n Aut* coup *m* de klaxon®. ● **—er** *n Aut* klaxon® *m*; (*of factory*) sirène *f*.

hoover® ['huːvər] *n* aspirateur *m* ▮ *vt* (*room*) passer l'aspirateur dans; (*carpet*) passer l'aspirateur sur.

hop [hɒp] *vi* (**-pp-**) (*of person*) sauter (à cloche-pied); (*of kangaroo etc*) sauter; (*of bird*) sautiller; **h. in!** (*in car*) montez!; **to h. on a bus** monter dans un autobus ▮ *vt* **h. it!** *Fam* fiche le camp! ▮ *n* (*leap*) saut *m*.

hope [həʊp] *n* espoir *m* ▮ *vi* espérer; **to h. for** (*wish for*) espérer; (*expect*) attendre; **I h. so/not** j'espère que oui/non ▮ *vt* espérer (**to do** faire, **that** que).

hopeful ['həʊpfəl] *a* (*person*) optimiste; (*promising*) prometteur; **to be h. that** avoir bon espoir que. ● **—ly** *adv* avec optimisme; (*one hopes*) on espère (que).

hopeless ['həʊpləs] *a* désespéré, sans espoir; (*useless, bad*) nul. ● **—ly** *adv* (*extremely*) (*lost*) complètement; (*in love*) éperdument.

hops [hɒps] *npl* (*for beer*) houblon *m*.

hopscotch ['hɒpskɒtʃ] *n* (*game*) marelle *f*.

horde [hɔːd] *n* horde *f*, foule *f*.

horizon [hə'raɪz(ə)n] *n* horizon *m*; **on the h.** à l'horizon.

horizontal [hɒrɪ'zɒnt(ə)l] *a* horizontal.

hormone ['hɔːməʊn] *n* hormone *f*.

horn [hɔːn] **1** *n* (*of animal*) corne *f*; *Aut* klaxon® *m*; *Mus* cor *m*. **2** *vi* **to h. in** *Am Fam* mêler son grain de sel.

hornet ['hɔːnɪt] *n* (*insect*) frelon *m*.

horny ['hɔːnɪ] *a* (**-ier, -iest**) (*aroused*) *Fam* excité.

horoscope ['hɒrəskəʊp] *n* horoscope *m*.

horrendous [hə'rendəs] *a* horrible.

horrible ['hɒrəb(ə)l] *a* horrible, affreux. ● **horribly** *adv* horriblement.

horrid ['hɒrɪd] *a* horrible; (*child*) épouvantable.

horrific [hə'rɪfɪk] *a* horrible, horrifiant.

horrify ['hɒrɪfaɪ] *vt* horrifier.

horror ['hɒrər] *n* horreur *f*; **(little) h.** (*child*) *Fam* petit monstre *m*; **h. film** film *f* d'épouvante.

hors-d'œuvre [ɔː'dɜːv] *n* hors-d'œuvre *m inv*.

horse [hɔːs] *n* **1** cheval *m*; **to go h. riding** faire du cheval. **2 h. chestnut** marron *m* (d'Inde).

horseback ['hɔːsbæk] *n* **on h.** à cheval; **to go h. riding** *Am* faire du cheval. ● **horseplay** *n* jeux *mpl* brutaux. ● **horsepower** *n* cheval *m* (vapeur). ●**horseracing** *n* courses *fpl.* ●**horseradish** *n* radis *m* noir, raifort *m.* ●**horseshoe** *n* fer *m* à cheval.

hose [həʊz] *n* (*tube*) tuyau *m*; **garden h.** tuyau *m* d'arrosage. ●**hosepipe** *n* = **hose.**

hospice ['hɒspɪs] *n* (*for dying people*) hospice *m.*

hospitable [hɒ'spɪtəb(ə)l] *a* accueillant. ●**hospi'tality** *n* hospitalité *f.*

hospital ['hɒspɪt(ə)l] *n* hôpital *m*; **in h.**, *Am* **in the h.** à l'hôpital ▮ *a* (*bed, food*) d'hôpital; (*staff*) hospitalier. ●**hospitalize** *vt* hospitaliser.

host [həʊst] *n* **1** (*man who receives guests*) hôte *m*; *TV Rad* présentateur, -trice *mf.* **2 a h. of** (*many*) une foule de. ●**hostess** *n* (*in house, aircraft, nightclub*) hôtesse *f.*

hostage ['hɒstɪdʒ] *n* otage *m*; **to take/hold s.o. h.** prendre/retenir qn en otage.

hostel ['hɒst(ə)l] *n* foyer *m*; **youth h.** auberge *f* de jeunesse.

hostile ['hɒstaɪl, *Am* 'hɒst(ə)l] *a* hostile (**to, towards** à). ●**ho'stility** *n* hostilité *f* (**to, towards** envers); *pl Mil* hostilités *fpl.*

hot[1] [hɒt] *a* (**hotter, hottest**) chaud; (*spice*) fort; **to be** *or* **feel h.** avoir chaud; **it's h.** il fait chaud; **not so h. at** (*good at*) *Fam* pas très calé en; **h. dog** (*sausage*) hot-dog *m.* ●**hotbed** *n Pej* foyer *m* (**of** de). ●**hothead** *n* tête *f* brûlée. ●**hot'headed** *a* impétueux. ●**hotplate** *n* chauffe-plats *m inv*; (*on stove*) plaque *f* chauffante. ●**hot-'tempered** *a* emporté. ●**hot-'water bottle** *n* bouillotte *f.*

hot[2] [hɒt] *vi* (**-tt-**) **to h. up** (*increase*) s'intensifier; (*become dangerous or excited*) chauffer.

hotchpotch ['hɒtʃpɒtʃ] *n* fatras *m.*

hotel [həʊ'tel] *n* hôtel *m*; **h. room**/*etc* chambre *f*/*etc* d'hôtel; **h. prices** le prix des hôtels.

hotly ['hɒtlɪ] *adv* passionnément.

hound [haʊnd] **1** *vt* (*pursue*) traquer; (*bother*) harceler. **2** *n* (*dog*) chien *m* courant.

hour ['aʊər] *n* heure *f*; **half an h., a half-h.** une demi-heure; **a quarter of an h.** un quart d'heure; **paid fifty francs an h.** payé cinquante francs (de) l'heure; **ten miles an h.** dix miles à l'heure; **h. hand** (*of watch, clock*) petite aiguille *f.* ●**—ly** *a* (*pay*) horaire; **an h. bus**/*etc* un bus/*etc* toutes les heures ▮ *adv* toutes les heures; **h. paid** payé à l'heure.

house[1], *pl* **-ses** [haʊs, -zɪz] *n* maison *f*; (*audience*) *Th* salle *f*; (*performance*) *Th* séance *f*; **the H.** *Pol* la Chambre; **at** *or* **to my h.** chez moi; **on the h.** (*free of charge*) aux frais de la maison; **h. prices** prix *mpl* immobiliers.

hous/e[2] [haʊz] *vt* loger; (*of building*) abriter; **it is housed in** (*kept*) on le garde dans. ●**—ing** *n* logement *m*; (*houses*) logements *mpl.*

housebound ['haʊsbaʊnd] *a* confiné chez soi. ●**housebreaking** *n Jur* cambriolage *m.* ●**housebroken** *a* (*dog etc*) *Am* propre. ●**household** *n* famille *f*; **h. duties** soins *mpl* du ménage; **a h. name** un nom très connu. ●**householder** *n* (*owner*) propriétaire *mf.* ●**housekeeper** *n* (*employee*) gouvernante *f.* ●**housekeeping** *n* ménage *m* (*entretien*). ●**houseproud** *a* qui s'occupe méticuleusement de sa maison. ●**house-trained** *a* (*dog etc*) propre. ●**house-warming** *n* & *a* **to have a h.-warming (party)** pendre la crémaillère. ●**housewife** *n* (*pl* **-wives**) ménagère *f.* ●**housework** *n* (travaux *mpl* de) ménage *m.*

hovel ['hɒv(ə)l] *n* (*slum*) taudis *m.*

hover ['hɒvər] *vi* (*of bird, aircraft, Fig danger*) planer. ●**hovercraft** *n* aéroglisseur *m.*

how [haʊ] *adv* comment; **h. come?** *Fam* comment ça?; **h. kind!** comme c'est gentil!; **h. do you do?** bonjour; **h. long/high is...?** quelle est la longueur/hauteur de...?; **h. much?, h. many?** combien?; **h. much time**/*etc*? combien de temps/*etc*?; **h. many apples**/*etc*? combien de pommes/*etc*?; **h. about some coffee?** (si on prenait) du café?; **h. about me?** et moi?

however [haʊ'evər] **1** *adv* **h. big he may be** si *or* quelque grand qu'il soit; **h. she may do it** de quelque manière qu'elle le fasse; **h. that may be** quoi qu'il en soit. **2** *conj* cependant.

howl [haʊl] *vi* hurler; (*of wind*) mugir ▮ *n* hurlement *m*; mugissement *m*; (*of laughter*) éclat *m.*

howler ['haʊlər] *n* (*mistake*) *Fam* gaffe *f.*

HP [eɪtʃ'piː] *abbr* = **hire purchase.**

hp *abbr* (*horsepower*) CV.

HQ [eɪtʃ'kjuː] *abbr* = **headquarters.**

hub [hʌb] *n* (*of wheel*) moyeu *m*; *Fig* centre *m.* ●**hubcap** *n Aut* enjoliveur *m.*

huddle ['hʌd(ə)l] *vi* **to h. (together)** se blottir (les uns contre les autres).

hue [hjuː] *n* teinte *f*, couleur *f.*

huff [hʌf] *n* **in a h.** (*offended*) *Fam* fâché.

hug [hʌg] *vt* (**-gg-**) (*person*) serrer (dans ses bras); **to h. the kerb/coast** serrer le trottoir/la côte ▮ *n* **to give s.o. a h.** serrer qn (dans ses bras).

huge [hjuːdʒ] *a* énorme.

hull [hʌl] *n* (*of ship*) coque *f.*

hullo! [hʌ'ləʊ] *int* = **hello.**
hum [hʌm] *vi* (**-mm-**) (*of insect*) bourdonner; (*of person*) fredonner; (*of top*) ronfler; (*of engine*) vrombir ▮ *vt* (*tune*) fredonner ▮ *n* (*of insect*) bourdonnement *m*.
human ['hju:mən] *a* humain; **h. being** être *m* humain ▮ *npl* humains *mpl*.
humane [hju:'meɪn] *a* (*kind*) humain.
humanity [hju:'mænətɪ] *n* (*human beings, kindness*) humanité *f*.
humble ['hʌmb(ə)l] *a* humble ▮ *vt* humilier.
humbug ['hʌmbʌg] *n* (*talk*) fumisterie *f*; (*person*) fumiste *mf*.
humdrum ['hʌmdrʌm] *a* monotone.
humid ['hju:mɪd] *a* humide. ●**hu'midity** *n* humidité *f*.
humiliate [hju:'mɪlɪeɪt] *vt* humilier. ●**humiliation** [-'eɪʃ(ə)n] *n* humiliation *f*.
humour ['hju:mər] (*Am* **humor**) **1** *n* (*fun*) humour *m*; (*temper*) humeur *f*; **to have a sense of h.** avoir le sens de l'humour. **2** *vt* **to h. s.o.** faire plaisir à qn. ●**humorous** *a* (*book etc*) humoristique; (*person*) plein d'humour.
hump [hʌmp] *n* **1** (*lump, mound*) bosse *f*. **2 to have the h.** (*depression*) *Fam* avoir le cafard. ●**humpback bridge** *n Aut* pont *m* en dos d'âne.
hunch [hʌntʃ] **1** *n* (*idea*) *Fam* intuition *f*. **2** *vt* (*one's shoulders*) voûter. ●**hunchback** *n* bossu, -ue *mf*.
hundred ['hʌndrəd] *a* & *n* cent (*m*); **a h. pages** cent pages; **two h. pages** deux cents pages; **hundreds of** des centaines de. ●**hundredth** *a* & *n* centième (*mf*). ●**hundredweight** *n* 112 livres (= *50,8 kg*); *Am* 100 livres (= *45,3 kg*).
hung [hʌŋ] *pt* & *pp of* **hang**[1].
Hungary ['hʌŋgərɪ] *n* Hongrie *f*. ●**Hungarian** [hʌŋ'geərɪən] *a* & *n* hongrois, -oise (*mf*) ▮ *n* (*language*) hongrois *m*.
hunger ['hʌŋgər] *n* faim *f*. ●**hungry** *a* (**-ier, -iest**) **to be** *or* **feel h.** avoir faim; **to go h.** souffrir de la faim; **to make s.o. h.** donner faim à qn.
hunk [hʌŋk] *n* (gros) morceau *m*.
hunt [hʌnt] *n* (*search*) recherche *f* (**for** de); (*for animals*) chasse *f* ▮ *vt* (*animals*) chasser; (*pursue*) poursuivre; (*seek*) chercher; **to h. down** (*fugitive etc*) traquer ▮ *vi* (*kill animals*) chasser; **to h. for sth** (re)chercher qch. ●**—ing** *n* chasse *f*. ●**hunter** *n* chasseur *m*.
hurdle ['hɜ:d(ə)l] *n* (*fence*) *Sp* haie *f*; (*problem*) *Fig* obstacle *m*.
hurl [hɜ:l] *vt* (*stone, abuse etc*) lancer (**at** à); **to h. oneself at s.o.** se ruer sur qn.
hurray! [hʊ'reɪ] *int* hourra!
hurricane ['hʌrɪkən, *Am* 'hʌrɪkeɪn] *n* ouragan *m*.
hurried ['hʌrɪd] *a* (*steps, decision*) précipité; (*work*) fait à la hâte; **to be h.** être pressé.
hurry ['hʌrɪ] *n* hâte *f*; **in a h.** à la hâte; **to be in a h.** être pressé; **to be in a h. to do** avoir hâte de faire; **there's no h.** rien ne presse ▮ *vi* se dépêcher (**to do** de faire); **to h. out** sortir à la hâte; **to h. towards** se précipiter vers; **to h. up** se dépêcher ▮ *vt* (*person*) bousculer; **to h. one's meal** manger à toute vitesse; **to h. one's work** se précipiter dans son travail; **to h. s.o. out** faire sortir qn à la hâte.
hurt [hɜ:t] *vt* (*pt* & *pp* **hurt**) (*physically*) faire du mal à; (*emotionally*) faire de la peine à; (*offend*) blesser; (*damage*) nuire à (*réputation etc*); **to h. s.o.'s feelings** blesser qn ▮ *vi* faire mal ▮ *n* mal *m*. ●**hurtful** *a* (*remark*) blessant.
hurtle ['hɜ:t(ə)l] *vi* **to h. along** aller à toute vitesse; **to h. down** dégringoler.
husband ['hʌzbənd] *n* mari *m*.
hush [hʌʃ] *n* silence *m* ▮ *int* chut! ▮ *vt* **to h. up** (*scandal*) étouffer. ●**hush-hush** *a Fam* ultra-secret.
husk [hʌsk] *n* (*of rice, grain*) enveloppe *f*.
husky ['hʌskɪ] *a* (**-ier, -iest**) (*voice*) enroué.
hustle ['hʌs(ə)l] **1** *vt* (*shove*) bousculer (*qn*). **2** *n* **h. and bustle** tourbillon *m*.
hut [hʌt] *n* cabane *f*, hutte *f*.
hutch [hʌtʃ] *n* (*for rabbit*) clapier *m*.
hyacinth ['haɪəsɪnθ] *n* jacinthe *f*.
hybrid ['haɪbrɪd] *a* & *n* hybride (*m*).
hydrangea [haɪ'dreɪndʒə] *n* (*shrub*) hortensia *m*.
hydrant ['haɪdrənt] *n* **(fire) h.** bouche *f* d'incendie.
hydrofoil ['haɪdrəfɔɪl] *n* hydrofoil *m*.
hydrogen ['haɪdrədʒən] *n* hydrogène *m*.
hyena [haɪ'i:nə] *n* (*animal*) hyène *f*.
hygiene ['haɪdʒi:n] *n* hygiène *f*. ●**hy'gienic** *a* hygiénique.
hymn [hɪm] *n Rel* cantique *m*.
hype [haɪp] *n Fam* grand battage *m* publicitaire.
hyper- ['haɪpər] *pref* hyper-.
hypermarket ['haɪpəmɑ:kɪt] *n* hypermarché *m*.
hyphen ['haɪf(ə)n] *n* trait *m* d'union. ●**hyphenated** *a* (*word*) à trait d'union.
hypnotism ['hɪpnətɪz(ə)m] *n* hypnotisme *m*. ●**hypnotize** *vt* hypnotiser.
hypoallergenic [haɪpəʊælə'dʒenɪk] *a* hypoallergénique.
hypocrisy [hɪ'pɒkrɪsɪ] *n* hypocrisie *f*. ●**hypocrite** ['hɪpəkrɪt] *n* hypocrite *mf*.

● **hypo'critical** *a* hypocrite.

hypothesis, *pl* **-eses** [haɪ'pɒθɪsɪs, -ɪsiːz] *n* hypothèse *f*. ● **hypothetical** [-'θetɪk(ə)l] *a* hypothétique

hysterical [hɪ'sterɪk(ə)l] *a* (*very upset*) qui a une crise de nerfs; (*funny*) *Fam* désopilant. ● **hysterically** *adv* (*to cry*) sans pouvoir s'arrêter; **to laugh h.** rire aux larmes. ● **hysterics** *npl* (*tears etc*) crise *f* de nerfs; (*laughter*) crise *f* de rire.

I

I, i [aɪ] *n* I, i *m*.
I [aɪ] *pron* je, j'; (*stressed*) moi; **I want** je veux; **he and I** lui et moi.
ice¹ [aɪs] *n* glace *f*; (*on road*) verglas *m*; **i. cream** glace *f*; **i. cube** glaçon *m* ‖ *vi* **to i. (over** *or* **up)** (*of lake*) geler; (*of window*) se givrer.
ice² [aɪs] *vt* (*cake*) glacer. ● **icing** *n* (*on cake etc*) glaçage *m*.
iceberg ['aɪsbɜːg] *n* iceberg *m*. ● **icebox** *n Am* réfrigérateur *m*. ● **ice-'cold** *a* glacial; (*drink*) glacé. ● **ice-skating** *n* patinage *m* (sur glace).
Iceland ['aɪslənd] *n* Islande *f*. ● **Ice'landic** *a* islandais.
icicle ['aɪsɪk(ə)l] *n* glaçon *m* (*naturel*).
icy ['aɪsɪ] *a* (**-ier, -iest**) (*water, hands, room*) glacé; (*weather*) glacial; (*road*) verglacé.
ID [aɪdiː] *n* pièce *f* d'identité.
I'd [aɪd] = **I had & I would.**
idea [aɪ'dɪə] *n* idée *f*; **I have an i. that...** j'ai l'impression que...; **that's the i.!** *Fam* c'est ça!; **not the slightest** *or* **foggiest i.** pas la moindre idée.
ideal [aɪ'dɪəl] *a* idéal (*mpl* -aux *or* -als) ‖ *n* idéal *m* (*pl* -aux *or* -als). ● **idealist** *n* idéaliste *mf*. ● **ideally** *adv* idéalement; **i. we should stay** l'idéal, ce serait de rester *or* que nous restions.
identical [aɪ'dentɪk(ə)l] *a* identique (**to, with** à).
identify [aɪ'dentɪfaɪ] *vt* identifier; **to i. (oneself) with** s'identifier avec. ● **identifi-cation** [-'keɪʃ(ə)n] *n* identification *f*; (*document*) pièce *f* d'identité.
identikit [aɪ'dentɪkɪt] *n* portrait-robot *m*.
identity [aɪ'dentɪtɪ] *n* identité *f*; **i. card** carte *f* d'identité.
idiom ['ɪdɪəm] *n* expression *f* idiomatique. ● **idio'matic** *a* idiomatique.
idiosyncrasy [ɪdɪə'sɪŋkrəsɪ] *n* particularité *f*.
idiot ['ɪdɪət] *n* idiot, -ote *mf*. ● **idi'otic** *a* idiot, bête.
idle ['aɪd(ə)l] *a* (*unoccupied*) inactif; (*lazy*) paresseux; (*unemployed*) au chômage; (*machine*) au repos; (*promise, pleasure*) vain; (*rumour*) sans fondement; **an i. moment** un moment de loisir ‖ *vi* (*of engine*) tourner au ralenti ‖ *vt* **to i. away** (*time*) gaspiller. ● **idler** *n* paresseux, -euse *mf*.
idol ['aɪd(ə)l] *n* idole *f*. ● **idolize** *vt* (*adore*) traiter comme une idole.
i.e. [aɪ'iː] *abbr* (*id est*) c'est-à-dire.
if [ɪf] *conj* si; **if he comes** s'il vient; **even if** même si; **if so** dans ce cas; **if not** sinon; **if only I were rich** si seulement j'étais riche; **if only to look** ne serait-ce que pour regarder; **as if** comme si; **if necessary** s'il le faut.
igloo ['ɪgluː] *n* igloo *m*.
ignite [ɪg'naɪt] *vt* mettre le feu à ‖ *vi* prendre feu. ● **ignition** [ɪg'nɪʃ(ə)n] *n Aut* allumage *m*; **to switch on/off the i.** mettre/couper le contact.
ignorance ['ɪgnərəns] *n* ignorance *f* (**of** de). ● **ignorant** *a* ignorant (**of** de).
ignore [ɪg'nɔːr] *vt* ne prêter aucune attention à, ne tenir aucun compte de (*qch*); (*pretend not to recognize*) faire semblant de ne pas reconnaître (*qn*).
ill [ɪl] *a* (*sick*) malade; (*bad*) mauvais; **i. will** malveillance *f* ‖ *npl* **ills** (*misfortunes*) maux *mpl* ‖ *adv* mal; **to speak i. of** dire du mal de.
I'll [aɪl] = **I will** *or* **I shall.**
ill-advised [ɪləd'vaɪzd] *a* peu judicieux. ● **ill-'fated** *a* malheureux. ● **ill-in'formed** *a* mal renseigné. ● **ill-'mannered** *a* mal élevé. ● **ill-'natured** *a* (*mean, unkind*) désagréable. ● **ill-'timed** *a* inopportun. ● **ill-'treat** *vt* maltraiter.
illegal [ɪ'liːg(ə)l] *a* illégal.
illegible [ɪ'ledʒəb(ə)l] *a* illisible.
illegitimate [ɪlɪ'dʒɪtɪmət] *a* illégitime.
illicit [ɪ'lɪsɪt] *a* illicite.
illiterate [ɪ'lɪtərət] *a & n* illettré, -ée (*mf*). ● **illiteracy** *n* analphabétisme *m*.
illness ['ɪlnɪs] *n* maladie *f*.
illuminate [ɪ'luːmɪneɪt] *vt* (*street etc*) éclairer; (*monument etc for special occasion*) illuminer. ● **illuminations** [-'neɪʃ(ə)nz] *npl* (*decorative lights*) illuminations *fpl*.
illusion [ɪ'luːʒ(ə)n] *n* illusion *f* (**about** sur); **to be under the i. that** avoir l'illusion que.
illustrate ['ɪləstreɪt] *vt* (*with pictures, examples*) illustrer (**with** de). ● **illustration** [-'streɪʃ(ə)n] *n* illustration *f*.
image ['ɪmɪdʒ] *n* image *f*; **(public) i.** (*of company*) image *f* de marque; **he's the i. of his brother** c'est tout le portrait de son frère.
imaginary [ɪ'mædʒɪn(ə)rɪ] *a* imaginaire.
imagination [ɪmædʒɪ'neɪʃ(ə)n] *n* imagination *f*.

imaginative [ɪ'mædʒɪnətɪv] *a* (*plan*, *person etc*) plein d'imagination.

imagin/e [ɪ'mædʒɪn] *vt* (*picture to oneself*) (s')imaginer (**that** que); (*suppose*) imaginer (**that** que); **you're imagining (things)!** tu te fais des illusions! ●**—able** *a* imaginable; **the worst thing i.** le pire que l'on puisse imaginer.

imbecile ['ɪmbəsiːl, *Am* 'ɪmbəs(ə)l] *a* & *n* imbécile (*mf*).

imbued [ɪm'bjuːd] *a* **i. with** (*ideas*) imprégné de.

imitate ['ɪmɪteɪt] *vt* imiter. ●**imitation** [-'teɪʃ(ə)n] *n* imitation *f*; **i. jewellery** *or Am* **jewelry** bijoux *mpl* fantaisie; **i. leather** similicuir *m*.

immaculate [ɪ'mækjʊlət] *a* (*person*, *shirt etc*) impeccable.

immaterial [ɪmə'tɪərɪəl] *a* peu important.

immature [ɪmə'tʃʊər] *a* (*person*) qui manque de maturité; (*animal*) jeune.

immediate [ɪ'miːdɪət] *a* immédiat. ●**immediately** *adv* (*at once*) tout de suite, immédiatement; **i. above/below** juste au-dessus/en dessous ▮ *conj* (*as soon as*) dès que.

immense [ɪ'mens] *a* immense. ●**immensely** *adv* extraordinairement.

immerse [ɪ'mɜːs] *vt* (*in liquid*) plonger; **immersed in work** plongé dans le travail. ●**immersion** [-ʃ(ə)n] *n* **i. heater** chauffe-eau *m inv* électrique.

immigrate ['ɪmɪgreɪt] *vi* immigrer. ●**immigrant** *n* immigré, -ée *mf* ▮ *a* immigré. ●**immigration** [-'greɪʃ(ə)n] *n* immigration *f*.

imminent ['ɪmɪnənt] *a* imminent.

immobile [ɪ'məʊbaɪl, *Am* ɪ'məʊb(ə)l] *a* immobile. ●**immobilize** *vt* immobiliser.

immoral [ɪ'mɒrəl] *a* immoral.

immortal [ɪ'mɔːt(ə)l] *a* immortel. ●**immortalize** *vt* immortaliser.

immune [ɪ'mjuːn] *a* (*naturally*) immunisé (**to** contre); (*vaccinated*) vacciné; **i. to** *Fig* à l'abri de. ●**'immunize** *vt* vacciner (**against** contre).

imp [ɪmp] *n* diablotin *m*, lutin *m*.

impact ['ɪmpækt] *n* (*shock*) impact; (*effect*) effet *m* (**on** sur).

impair [ɪm'peər] *vt* détériorer; (*hearing*, *health*) abîmer.

impale [ɪm'peɪl] *vt* empaler.

impart [ɪm'pɑːt] *vt* communiquer (**to** à).

impartial [ɪm'pɑːʃ(ə)l] *a* impartial.

impassable [ɪm'pɑːsəb(ə)l] *a* (*road*) impraticable; (*river*) infranchissable.

impassive [ɪm'pæsɪv] *a* impassible.

impatient [ɪm'peɪʃ(ə)nt] *a* impatient (**to do** de faire); **i. with s.o.** intolérant à l'égard de qn. ●**impatience** *n* impatience *f*. ●**impatiently** *adv* avec impatience.

impeccable [ɪm'pekəb(ə)l] *a* (*manners*, *person*) impeccable.

impecunious [ɪmpɪ'kjuːnɪəs] *a* sans le sou.

impede [ɪm'piːd] *vt* (*hamper*) gêner; **to i. s.o. from doing** (*prevent*) empêcher qn de faire.

impediment [ɪm'pedɪmənt] *n* **(speech) i.** défaut *m* d'élocution.

impending [ɪm'pendɪŋ] *a* imminent.

imperative [ɪm'perətɪv] *a* (*necessary*) indispensable; **it is i. that** il est indispensable que (+ *sub*) ▮ *n Gram* impératif *m*.

imperfect [ɪm'pɜːfɪkt] **1** *a* imparfait; (*goods*) défectueux. **2** *a* & *n* **i. (tense)** *Gram* imparfait *m*. ●**imperfection** [ɪmpə'fekʃ(ə)n] *n* imperfection *f*.

imperial [ɪm'pɪərɪəl] *a* impérial; **i. measure** *Br* mesure *f* légale (anglo-saxonne).

impersonal [ɪm'pɜːsən(ə)l] *a* impersonnel.

impersonate [ɪm'pɜːsəneɪt] *vt* (*pretend to be*) se faire passer pour; (*on TV etc*) imiter. ●**impersonation** [-'neɪʃ(ə)n] *n* imitation *f*. ●**impersonator** *n* (*on TV etc*) imitateur, -trice *mf*.

impertinent [ɪm'pɜːtɪnənt] *a* impertinent (**to** envers). ●**impertinence** *n* impertinence *f*.

impervious [ɪm'pɜːvɪəs] *a* imperméable (**to** à).

impetuous [ɪm'petjʊəs] *a* impétueux.

impetus ['ɪmpɪtəs] *n* impulsion *f*.

impinge [ɪm'pɪndʒ] *vi* **to i. on** (*affect*) affecter; (*encroach on*) empiéter sur.

impish ['ɪmpɪʃ] *a* (*naughty*) espiègle.

implant [ɪm'plɑːnt] *vt* (*surgically*) implanter (**in** dans); (*ideas*) inculquer (**in** à).

implement[1] ['ɪmplɪmənt] *n* (*tool*) instrument *m*; (*utensil*) ustensile *m*.

implement[2] ['ɪmplɪment] *vt* (*carry out*) mettre en œuvre, exécuter.

implicate ['ɪmplɪkeɪt] *vt* impliquer (**in** dans). ●**implication** [-'keɪʃ(ə)n] *n* (*consequence*) conséquence *f*; (*involvement*) implication *f*; (*impact*) portée *f*; **by i.** implicitement.

implicit [ɪm'plɪsɪt] *a* (*implied*) implicite; (*obedience etc*) absolu. ●**—ly** *adv* implicitement.

implore [ɪm'plɔːr] *vt* implorer (**s.o. to do** qn de faire).

imply [ɪm'plaɪ] *vt* (*suggest*) laisser entendre (**that** que); (*assume*) impliquer (**that** que); (*insinuate*) insinuer (**that** que). ●**implied** *a* implicite.

impolite [ɪmpə'laɪt] *a* impoli.

import [ɪm'pɔːt] *vt* (*goods etc*) importer

(**from** de) ‖ ['ɪmpɔːt] *n* (*imported product*) importation *f*. ● **im'porter** *n* importateur, -trice *mf*.
importance [ɪm'pɔːtəns] *n* importance *f*; **to be of i.** avoir de l'importance; **of no i.** sans importance.
important [ɪm'pɔːtənt] *a* important (**that** que (+ *sub*)).
impose [ɪm'pəʊz] *vt* imposer (**on** à); (*fine, punishment*) infliger (**on** à) ‖ *vi* (*cause trouble*) déranger; **to i. on s.o.** déranger qn. ● **imposition** [-pə'zɪʃ(ə)n] *n* (*inconvenience*) dérangement *m*.
imposing [ɪmɪ'pəʊzɪŋ] *a* (*building*) impressionnant.
impossible [ɪm'pɒsəb(ə)l] *a* impossible (**to do** à faire); **it is i. (for us) to do** il (nous) est impossible de faire; **it is i. that** il est impossible que (+ *sub*) ‖ *n* **to do the i.** faire l'impossible. ● **impossi'bility** *n* impossibilité *f*.
impostor [ɪm'pɒstər] *n* imposteur *m*.
impotent ['ɪmpətənt] *a Med* impuissant.
impound [ɪm'paʊnd] *vt* (*of police*) saisir, confisquer.
impoverished [ɪm'pɒvərɪʃt] *a* appauvri.
impracticable [ɪm'præktɪkəb(ə)l] *a* impraticable.
impractical [ɪm'præktɪk(ə)l] *a* peu réaliste.
imprecise [ɪmprɪ'saɪs] *a* imprécis.
impregnable [ɪm'pregnəb(ə)l] *a* (*fortress etc*) imprenable.
impresario [ɪmprɪ'sɑːrɪəʊ] *n* (*pl* **-os**) impresario *m*.
impress [ɪm'pres] *vt* impressionner (*qn*); **to i. sth on s.o.** faire comprendre qch à qn.
impression [ɪm'preʃ(ə)n] *n* impression *f*; **to be under** *or* **have the i. that** avoir l'impression que. ● **impressionable** *a* (*person*) impressionnable.
impressionist [ɪm'preʃənɪst] *n* (*entertainer*) imitateur, -trice *mf*.
impressive [ɪm'presɪv] *a* impressionnant.
imprint [ɪm'prɪnt] *vt* imprimer ‖ ['ɪmprɪnt] *n* empreinte *f*.
imprison [ɪm'prɪz(ə)n] *vt* emprisonner. ● **—ment** *n* emprisonnement *m*; **life i.** la prison à vie.
improbable [ɪm'prɒbəb(ə)l] *a* peu probable; (*story, excuse*) invraisemblable. ● **improba'bility** *n* improbabilité *f*.
improper [ɪm'prɒpər] *a* (*indecent*) indécent; (*wrong*) (*use etc*) incorrect.
improve [ɪm'pruːv] *vt* améliorer; (*mind*) cultiver; **to i. oneself** se cultiver ‖ *vi* s'améliorer; (*of business*) reprendre; **to i. on** (*do better than*) faire mieux que. ● **—ment** *n* amélioration *f* (**in** de); (*progress*) progrès *m(pl)*; **to be an i. on sth** être supérieur à qch.
improvise ['ɪmprəvaɪz] *vti* improviser. ● **improvisation** [-'zeɪʃ(ə)n] *n* improvisation *f*.
impudent ['ɪmpjʊdənt] *a* impudent.
impulse ['ɪmpʌls] *n* impulsion *f*; **on i.** sur un coup de tête. ● **im'pulsive** *a* (*person, act*) impulsif, irréfléchi.
impunity [ɪm'pjuːnɪtɪ] *n* **with i.** impunément.
impurity [ɪm'pjʊərɪtɪ] *n* impureté *f*.
in [ɪn] *prep* **1** dans; **in the box/the school/***etc* dans la boîte/l'école/*etc*; **in an hour('s time)** dans une heure; **in luxury** dans le luxe; **in so far as** dans la mesure où.
2 à; **in school** à l'école; **in the sun** au soleil; **in Paris** à Paris; **in the USA** aux USA; **in Portugal** au Portugal; **in fashion** à la mode; **in ink** à l'encre; **in spring** au printemps.
3 en; **in summer/May/French** en été/mai/français; **in Spain** en Espagne; **in secret** en secret; **in an hour** (*during that period*) en une heure; **in doing** en faisant; **dressed in black** habillé en noir; **in all** en tout.
4 de; **in a soft voice** d'une voix douce; **the best in the class** le meilleur de la classe; **an increase in** une augmentation de; **at six in the evening** à six heures du soir.
5 chez; **in children/animals** chez les enfants/les animaux; **in Shakespeare** chez Shakespeare.
6 in the rain sous la pluie; **in the morning** le matin; **he hasn't done it in years** ça fait des années qu'il ne l'a pas fait; **in an hour** (*at the end of that period*) au bout d'une heure; **one in ten** un sur dix; **in tens** dix par dix; **in thousands** par milliers; **in here** ici; **in there** là-dedans.
‖ *adv* **to be in** (*home*) être là, être à la maison; (*of train*) être arrivé; (*in fashion*) être à la mode; (*in season*) être de saison; (*in power*) *Pol* être au pouvoir; **day in day out** jour après jour; **we're in for some rain/trouble** on va avoir de la pluie/des ennuis; **it's the in thing** *Fam* c'est dans le vent.
‖ *npl* **the ins and outs of** les moindres détails de.
in- [ɪn] *pref* in-.
inability [ɪnə'bɪlɪtɪ] *n* incapacité *f* (**to do** de faire).
inaccessible [ɪnək'sesəb(ə)l] *a* inaccessible.
inaccurate [ɪn'ækjʊrət] *a* inexact. ● **inaccuracy** *n* (*error*) inexactitude *f*.
inaction [ɪn'ækʃ(ə)n] *n* inaction *f*.
inactive [ɪn'æktɪv] *a* inactif; (*mind*) inerte.
inadequate [ɪn'ædɪkwət] *a* (*quantity*) in-

suffisant; (*person*) pas à la hauteur; (*work*) médiocre. ● **inadequacy** *n* insuffisance *f*.

inadvertently [ɪnəd'vɜːtəntlɪ] *adv* par inadvertance.

inadvisable [ɪnəd'vaɪzəb(ə)l] *a* (*action*) à déconseiller; **it is i. to ...** il est déconseillé de....

inanimate [ɪn'ænɪmət] *a* inanimé.

inappropriate [ɪnə'prəʊprɪət] *a* (*unsuitable*) (*place, remark etc*) qui ne convient pas.

inarticulate [ɪnɑː'tɪkjʊlət] *a* (*person*) incapable de s'exprimer; (*sound*) inarticulé.

inasmuch as [ɪnəz'mʌtʃəz] *adv* (*because*) vu que; (*to the extent that*) en ce sens que.

inattentive [ɪnə'tentɪv] *a* inattentif (**to** à).

inaugural [ɪ'nɔːgjʊrəl] *a* inaugural. ● **inaugurate** *vt* (*building*) inaugurer. ● **inauguration** [-'reɪʃ(ə)n] *n* inauguration *f*.

inborn [ɪn'bɔːn] *a* inné.

Inc *abbr* (*Incorporated*) *Am Com* SA, SARL.

incalculable [ɪn'kælkjʊləb(ə)l] *a* incalculable.

incapable [ɪn'keɪpəb(ə)l] *a* incapable (**of doing** de faire); **i. of** (*pity etc*) inaccessible à.

incapacitate [ɪnkə'pæsɪteɪt] *vt* (*for work*) rendre incapable (*de travailler*).

incendiary [ɪn'sendɪərɪ] *a* (*bomb*) incendiaire.

incense 1 [ɪn'sens] *vt* mettre en colère. **2** ['ɪnsens] *n* (*substance*) encens *m*.

incentive [ɪn'sentɪv] *n* encouragement *m*, motivation *f*; **to give s.o. an i. to work** encourager qn à travailler.

incessant [ɪn'ses(ə)nt] *a* incessant. ● **—ly** *adv* sans cesse.

incest ['ɪnsest] *n* inceste *m*.

inch [ɪntʃ] *n* pouce *m* (*= 2,54 cm*); **within an i. of** (*success*) à deux doigts de; **i. by i.** petit à petit ‖ *vi* **to i. forward** avancer petit à petit.

incident ['ɪnsɪdənt] *n* incident *m*; (*in book, film etc*) épisode *m*.

incidental [ɪnsɪ'dent(ə)l] *a* (*additional*) accessoire, secondaire. ● **—ly** *adv* (*by the way*) à propos.

incinerator [ɪn'sɪnəreɪtər] *n* incinérateur *m*.

incision [ɪn'sɪʒ(ə)n] *n* incision *f*.

incite [ɪn'saɪt] *vt* inciter (**to do** à faire). ● **—ment** *n* incitation *f* (**to do** à faire).

incline 1 [ɪn'klaɪn] *vt* (*bend*) incliner; **to be inclined to do** (*feel a wish to*) avoir bien envie de faire; (*tend to*) avoir tendance à faire. **2** ['ɪnklaɪn] *n* (*slope*) inclinaison *f*. ● **inclination** [-'neɪʃ(ə)n] *n* (*tendency*) inclination *f*; (*desire*) envie *f* (**to do** de faire).

includ/e [ɪn'kluːd] *vt* (*contain*) comprendre; **my invitation includes you** mon invitation s'adresse aussi à vous; **to be included** être compris; (*on list*) être inclus. ● **—ing** *prep* y compris; **i. service** service *m* compris; **up to and including Monday** jusqu'à lundi inclus.

inclusion [ɪn'kluːʒ(ə)n] *n* inclusion *f*.

inclusive [ɪn'kluːsɪv] *a* inclus; **from the fourth to the tenth of May i.** du quatre jusqu'au dix mai inclus; **to be i. of** comprendre; **i. charge** prix *m* global.

incoherent [ɪnkəʊ'hɪərənt] *a* incohérent.

income ['ɪŋkʌm] *n* revenu *m* (**from** de); **private i.** rentes *fpl*; **i. tax** impôt *m* sur le revenu.

incoming ['ɪnkʌmɪŋ] *a* (*president etc*) nouveau (*f* nouvelle); **i. tide** marée *f* montante; **i. calls** *Tel* appels *mpl* de l'extérieur.

incompatible [ɪnkəm'pætəb(ə)l] *a* incompatible (**with** avec).

incompetent [ɪn'kɒmpɪtənt] *a* incompétent.

incomplete [ɪnkəm'pliːt] *a* incomplet.

incomprehensible [ɪnkɒmprɪ'hensəb(ə)l] *a* incompréhensible.

inconceivable [ɪnkən'siːvəb(ə)l] *a* inconcevable.

inconclusive [ɪnkən'kluːsɪv] *a* peu concluant.

incongruous [ɪn'kɒŋgrʊəs] *a* (*building, colours*) qui jure(nt) (**with** avec); (*remark*) incongru; (*absurd*) absurde.

inconsiderate [ɪnkən'sɪdərət] *a* (*action, remark*) irréfléchi; (*person*) pas très gentil (**towards** avec).

inconsistent [ɪnkən'sɪstənt] *a* (*reports etc*) en contradiction (**with** avec); (*person*) inconséquent, incohérent. ● **inconsistency** *n* incohérence *f*.

inconspicuous [ɪnkən'spɪkjʊəs] *a* peu en évidence.

inconvenient [ɪnkən'viːnɪənt] *a* (*moment, situation etc*) gênant; (*house, school*) mal situé; **it's i. (for me) to...** ça me dérange de.... ● **inconvenience** *n* (*bother*) dérangement *m*; (*disadvantage*) inconvénient *m* ‖ *vt* déranger, gêner.

incorporate [ɪn'kɔːpəreɪt] *vt* (*contain*) contenir; (*introduce*) incorporer (**into** dans); **incorporated society** *Am* société *f* anonyme, société *f* à responsabilité limitée.

incorrect [ɪnkə'rekt] *a* inexact; **you're i.** vous avez tort.

increas/e [ɪn'kriːs] *vi* augmenter; (*of effort, noise*) s'intensifier; **to i. in weight** prendre du poids ‖ *vt* augmenter; in-tensifier ‖ ['ɪnkriːs] *n* augmentation *f* (**in, of** de); intensification *f* (**in, of** de); **on the i.** en hausse. ● —**ing** *a* (*amount etc*) croissant. ● —**ingly** *adv* de plus en plus.

incredible [ɪn'kredəb(ə)l] *a* incroyable. ● **incredibly** *adv* incroyablement.

incredulous [ɪn'kredjʊləs] *a* incrédule.

increment ['ɪŋkrəmənt] *n* augmentation *f*.

incriminat/e [ɪn'krɪmɪneɪt] *vt* incriminer. ● —**ing** *a* compromettant.

incubate ['ɪŋkjʊbeɪt] *vt* (*eggs*) couver. ● **incubator** *n* (*for baby, eggs*) couveuse *f*.

incur [ɪn'kɜːr] *vt* (**-rr-**) (*expenses*) faire; (*loss*) subir; (*debt*) contracter; (*criticism*) s'attirer.

incurable [ɪn'kjʊərəb(ə)l] *a* incurable.

indebted [ɪn'detɪd] *a* **i. to s.o. for sth/for doing sth** redevable à qn de qch/d'avoir fait qch.

indecent [ɪn'diːs(ə)nt] *a* (*obscene*) indécent. ● **indecency** *n* (*crime*) outrage *m* à la pudeur.

indecisive [ɪndɪ'saɪsɪv] *a* (*person, answer*) indécis.

indeed [ɪn'diːd] *adv* en effet; **very good**/*etc* **i.** vraiment très bon/*etc*; **yes i.!** bien sûr!; **thank you very much i.!** merci infiniment!

indefinite [ɪn'defɪnət] *a* (*feeling, duration*) indéfini; (*plan*) mal déterminé. ● —**ly** *adv* indéfiniment.

indelible [ɪn'deləb(ə)l] *a* (*ink, memory*) indélébile; **i. pen** stylo *m* à encre indélébile.

indemnify [ɪn'demnɪfaɪ] *vt* indemniser (**for** de). ● **indemnity** *n* (*compensation*) indemnité *f*.

indented [ɪn'dentɪd] *a* (*edge*) dentelé.

independent [ɪndɪ'pendənt] *a* indépendant (**of** de); (*reports*) de sources différentes. ● **independence** *n* indépendance *f*. ● **independently** *adv* de façon indépendante; **i. of** indépendamment de.

indestructible [ɪndɪ'strʌktəb(ə)l] *a* indestructible.

index ['ɪndeks] *n* (*in book*) index *m*; (*in library*) catalogue *m*; (*number, sign*) indice *m*; **i. card** fiche *f*; **i. finger** index *m* ‖ *vt* (*classify*) classer. ● **i.-'linked** *a* (*wages etc*) indexé (**to** sur).

India ['ɪndɪə] *n* Inde *f*. ● **Indian** *a* & *n* indien, -ienne (*mf*).

indicate ['ɪndɪkeɪt] *vt* indiquer (**that** que); **I was indicating right** *Aut* j'avais mis mon clignotant droit. ● **indication** [-'keɪʃ(ə)n] *n* (*sign*) indice *m*, indication *f*; (*idea*) idée *f*.

indicative [ɪn'dɪkətɪv] *a* **i. of** (*symptomatic*) symptomatique de ‖ *n* (*mood*) *Gram* indicatif *m*.

indicator ['ɪndɪkeɪtər] *n* (*instrument*) indicateur *m*; (*sign*) indication *f* (**of** de); *Aut* clignotant *m*.

indict [ɪn'daɪt] *vt* inculper (**for** de).

Indies ['ɪndɪz] *npl* **the West I.** les Antilles *fpl*.

indifferent [ɪn'dɪf(ə)rənt] *a* indifférent (**to** à); (*mediocre*) médiocre. ● **indifference** *n* indifférence *f* (**to** à).

indigestion [ɪndɪ'dʒestʃ(ə)n] *n* problèmes *mpl* de digestion; **(an attack of) i.** une indigestion.

indignant [ɪn'dɪgnənt] *a* indigné (**at** de); **to become i.** s'indigner. ● —**ly** *adv* avec indignation. ● **indignation** [-'neɪʃ(ə)n] *n* indignation *f*.

indigo ['ɪndɪgəʊ] *n* & *a* (*colour*) indigo *m* & *a inv*.

indirect [ɪndaɪ'rekt] *a* indirect. ● —**ly** *adv* indirectement.

indiscreet [ɪndɪ'skriːt] *a* indiscret.

indiscriminate [ɪndɪ'skrɪmɪnət] *a* (*random*) fait, donné *etc* au hasard; (*person*) qui manque de discernement. ● —**ly** *adv* (*at random*) au hasard.

indispensable [ɪndɪ'spensəb(ə)l] *a* indispensable (**to** à).

indisposed [ɪndɪ'spəʊzd] *a* (*unwell*) indisposé.

indisputable [ɪndɪ'spjuːtəb(ə)l] *a* incontestable.

indistinct [ɪndɪ'stɪŋkt] *a* indistinct.

indistinguishable [ɪndɪ'stɪŋgwɪʃəb(ə)l] *a* indifférenciable (**from** de).

individual [ɪndɪ'vɪdʒʊəl] *a* (*separate, personal*) individuel; (*specific*) particulier ‖ *n* (*person*) individu *m*. ● **individualist** *n* individualiste *mf*. ● **individually** *adv* (*separately*) individuellement; (*unusually*) de façon (très) personnelle.

indivisible [ɪndɪ'vɪzəb(ə)l] *a* indivisible.

Indo-China [ɪndəʊ'tʃaɪnə] *n* Indochine *f*.

indoctrinate [ɪn'dɒktrɪneɪt] *vt* endoctriner. ● **indoctrination** [-'neɪʃ(ə)n] *n* endoctrinement *m*.

Indonesia [ɪndəʊ'niːʒə] *n* Indonésie *f*.

indoor ['ɪndɔːr] *a* (*games, shoes etc*) d'intérieur; (*swimming pool etc*) couvert. ● **in'doors** *adv* à l'intérieur; **to go** *or* **come i.** rentrer.

induce [ɪn'djuːs] *vt* (*persuade*) persuader (*qn*) (**to do** de faire); (*cause*) provoquer.

indulge [ɪn'dʌldʒ] *vt* (*s.o.'s wishes*) satisfaire; (*child etc*) gâter; **to i. oneself** se gâter ‖ *vi* **to i. in** (*ice cream etc*) se permettre; (*vice etc*) s'adonner à. ● **indulgence** *n* indulgence *f*. ● **indulgent** *a* indulgent (**to** envers).

industrial [ɪn'dʌstrɪəl] *a* industriel; (*con-

flict) du travail; **to take i. action** se mettre en grève; **i. estate**, *Am* **i. park** zone *f* industrielle. ● **industrialist** *n* industriel *m*. ● **industrialized** *a* industrialisé.

industrious [ɪn'dʌstrɪəs] *a* travailleur.

industry ['ɪndəstrɪ] *n* industrie *f*; (*hard work*) application *f*.

inedible [ɪn'edəb(ə)l] *a* immangeable.

ineffective [ɪnɪ'fektɪv] *a* (*measure etc*) inefficace; (*person*) incapable.

ineffectual [ɪnɪ'fektʃʊəl] *a* = **ineffective.**

inefficient [ɪnɪ'fɪʃ(ə)nt] *a* (*person, measure etc*) inefficace; (*machine*) peu performant. ● **inefficiency** *n* inefficacité *f*.

inept [ɪ'nept] *a* (*unskilled*) peu habile (**at sth** à qch); (*incompetent*) incapable.

inequality [ɪnɪ'kwɒlətɪ] *n* inégalité *f*.

inert [ɪ'nɜːt] *a* inerte.

inescapable [ɪnɪ'skeɪpəb(ə)l] *a* inéluctable.

inevitable [ɪn'evɪtəb(ə)l] *a* inévitable. ● **inevitably** *adv* inévitablement.

inexcusable [ɪnɪk'skjuːzəb(ə)l] *a* inexcusable.

inexorable [ɪn'eksərəb(ə)l] *a* inexorable.

inexpensive [ɪnɪk'spensɪv] *a* bon marché *inv*.

inexperience [ɪnɪk'spɪərɪəns] *n* inexpérience *f*. ● **inexperienced** *a* inexpérimenté.

inexplicable [ɪnɪk'splɪkəb(ə)l] *a* inexplicable.

infallible [ɪn'fæləb(ə)l] *a* infaillible.

infamous ['ɪnfəməs] *a* (*evil*) infâme. ● **infamy** *n* infamie *f*.

infancy ['ɪnfənsɪ] *n* petite enfance *f*; **to be in its i.** (*of technique etc*) en être à ses premiers balbutiements.

infant ['ɪnfənt] *n* (*child*) petit(e) enfant *mf*; (*baby*) nourrisson *m*; **i. school** classes *fpl* préparatoires. ● **infantile** [-aɪl] *a* (*illness, reaction*) infantile.

infantry ['ɪnfəntrɪ] *n* infanterie *f*.

infatuated [ɪn'fætʃʊeɪtɪd] *a* amoureux (**with s.o.** de qn). ● **infatuation** [-'eɪʃ(ə)n] *n* engouement *m* (**for, with** pour).

infect [ɪn'fekt] *vt* infecter; **to become** *or* **get infected** s'infecter. ● **infection** [-ʃ(ə)n] *n* infection *f*. ● **infectious** [-ʃəs] *a* (*disease, person*) contagieux.

infer [ɪn'fɜːr] *vt* (**-rr-**) déduire (**from** de, **that** que).

inferior [ɪn'fɪərɪər] *a* inférieur (**to** à); (*goods, work*) de qualité inférieure ‖ *n* (*person*) inférieur, -eure *mf*. ● **inferi'ority** *n* infériorité *f*.

infernal [ɪn'fɜːn(ə)l] *a* infernal.

inferno [ɪn'fɜːnəʊ] *n* (*pl* **-os**) (*blaze*) brasier *m*; (*hell*) enfer *m*.

infertile [ɪn'fɜːtaɪl, *Am* ɪn'fɜːt(ə)l] *a* (*person, land*) stérile.

infest [ɪn'fest] *vt* infester (**with** de).

infidelity [ɪnfɪ'delɪtɪ] *n* infidélité *f*.

infighting ['ɪnfaɪtɪŋ] *n* (*within group*) luttes *fpl* intestines.

infiltrate ['ɪnfɪltreɪt] *vi* s'infiltrer (**into** dans) ‖ *vt* (*group etc*) s'infiltrer dans.

infinite ['ɪnfɪnɪt] *a* & *n* infini (*m*). ● **—ly** *adv* infiniment. ● **in'finity** *n Math Phot* infini *m*.

infinitive [ɪn'fɪnɪtɪv] *n Gram* infinitif *m*.

infirm [ɪn'fɜːm] *a* infirme. ● **infirmary** *n* (*hospital*) hôpital *m*.

inflam/e [ɪn'fleɪm] *vt* enflammer. ● **—ed** *a* (*throat etc*) enflammé. ● **inflammable** *a* inflammable. ● **inflammation** [ɪnflə'meɪʃ(ə)n] *n Med* inflammation *f*.

inflate [ɪn'fleɪt] *vt* (*balloon, prices etc*) gonfler. ● **inflatable** *a* gonflable. ● **inflation** [-ʃ(ə)n] *n Econ* inflation *f*. ● **inflationary** *a Econ* inflationniste.

inflection [ɪn'flekʃ(ə)n] *n Gram* flexion *f*.

inflexible [ɪn'fleksəb(ə)l] *a* inflexible.

inflict [ɪn'flɪkt] *vt* (*wound*) occasionner (**on** à); (*punishment*) infliger (**on** à); **to i. pain on s.o.** faire souffrir qn.

influence ['ɪnflʊəns] *n* influence *f*; **under the i. of** (*drugs*) sous l'effet de; **under the i. (of drink)** *Jur* en état d'ébriété ‖ *vt* influencer. ● **influential** [-'enʃəl] *a* **to be i.** avoir une grande influence.

influenza [ɪnflʊ'enzə] *n Med* grippe *f*.

influx ['ɪnflʌks] *n* afflux *m* (**of** de).

info ['ɪnfəʊ] *n Fam* tuyaux *mpl*, renseignements *mpl* (**on** sur).

inform [ɪn'fɔːm] *vt* informer (**of** de, **that** que); **to keep s.o. informed of** tenir qn au courant de ‖ *vi* **to i. on s.o.** dénoncer qn.

informal [ɪn'fɔːm(ə)l] *a* (*manner, person etc*) simple, décontracté; (*tone, expression*) familier; (*announcement*) officieux; (*meeting*) non-officiel. ● **informally** *adv* sans cérémonie; (*to dress*) simplement; (*to discuss*) à titre non-officiel; (*to meet*) officieusement.

informant [ɪn'fɔːmənt] *n* informateur, -trice *mf*.

information [ɪnfə'meɪʃ(ə)n] *n* (*facts*) renseignements *mpl* (**about, on** sur); (*knowledge*) & *Comptr* information *f*; **a piece of i.** un renseignement; **to get some i.** se renseigner.

informative [ɪn'fɔːmətɪv] *a* instructif.

informer [ɪn'fɔːmər] *n* (**police**) **i.** indicateur, -trice *mf*.

infrequent [ɪn'friːkwənt] *a* peu fréquent. ● **—ly** *adv* rarement.

infringe [ɪn'frɪndʒ] *vt* (*rule*) contrevenir à ‖ *vi* **to i. upon** (*encroach on*) empiéter sur.

infuriat/e [ɪn'fjʊərɪeɪt] *vt* exaspérer. ● **—ing** *a* exaspérant.

ingenious [ɪn'dʒiːnɪəs] *a* ingénieux. ● **ingenuity** [ɪndʒɪ'njuːɪtɪ] *n* ingéniosité *f*.

ingrained [ɪn'greɪnd] *a* (*prejudice*) enraciné; **i. dirt** crasse *f*.

ingratiate [ɪn'greɪʃɪeɪt] *vt* **to i. oneself with** s'insinuer dans les bonnes grâces de.

ingredient [ɪn'griːdɪənt] *n* ingrédient *m*.

inhabit [ɪn'hæbɪt] *vt* habiter. ● **—able** *a* habitable. ● **inhabitant** *n* habitant, -ante *mf*.

inhale [ɪn'heɪl] *vt* (*smell etc*) aspirer; (*fumes etc*) respirer; **to i. the smoke** (*of smoker*) avaler la fumée.

inherent [ɪn'hɪərənt] *a* inhérent (**in** à).

inherit [ɪn'herɪt] *vt* hériter (de). ● **inheritance** *n* héritage *m*.

inhibit [ɪn'hɪbɪt] *vt* (*hinder*) gêner; (*prevent*) empêcher (**from doing** de faire); **to be inhibited** avoir des inhibitions. ● **inhibition** [-'bɪʃ(ə)n] *n* inhibition *f*.

inhospitable [ɪnhɒ'spɪtəb(ə)l] *a* peu accueillant, inhospitalier.

inhuman [ɪn'hjuːmən] *a* (*not human, cruel*) inhumain. ● **inhu'mane** *a* (*not kind*) inhumain.

initial [ɪ'nɪʃ(ə)l] *a* premier, initial ‖ *npl* **initials** (*letters*) initiales *fpl*; (*signature*) paraphe *m* ‖ *vt* (**-ll-**, *Am* **-l-**) parapher. ● **—ly** *adv* au début.

initiate [ɪ'nɪʃɪeɪt] *vt* (*reform*) amorcer; (*attack, fashion*) lancer; (*policy*) inaugurer; **to i. s.o. into** initier qn à.

initiative [ɪ'nɪʃətɪv] *n* initiative *f*.

inject [ɪn'dʒekt] *vt* injecter (**into sth** dans qch); **to i. sth into s.o.** faire une piqûre de qch à qn. ● **injection** [-ʃ(ə)n] *n* injection *f*, piqûre *f*.

injur/e ['ɪndʒər] *vt* (*physically*) blesser, faire du mal à; **to i. one's foot**/*etc* se blesser au pied/*etc*. ● **—ed** *a* blessé ‖ *n* **the i.** les blessés *mpl*. ● **injury** *n* (*to flesh*) blessure *f*; (*fracture*) fracture *f*; (*sprain*) foulure *f*; (*bruise*) contusion *f*.

injustice [ɪn'dʒʌstɪs] *n* injustice *f*.

ink [ɪŋk] *n* encre *f*; **Indian i.** encre *f* de Chine. ● **inkwell** *n* encrier *m*.

inkling ['ɪŋklɪŋ] *n* (petite) idée *f*.

inlaid [ɪn'leɪd] *a* (*marble*) incrusté (**with** de); (*wood*) marqueté.

inland ['ɪnlənd] *a* intérieur; **the I. Revenue** *Br* le fisc ‖ [ɪn'lænd] *adv* à l'intérieur (*des terres*).

in-laws ['ɪnlɔːz] *npl* belle-famille *f*.

inlet ['ɪnlet] *n* (*of sea*) crique *f*.

inmate ['ɪnmeɪt] *n* (*of prison*) détenu, -ue *mf*; (*of asylum*) interné, -ée *mf*.

inn [ɪn] *n* auberge *f*.

innards ['ɪnədz] *npl Fam* entrailles *fpl*.

innate [ɪ'neɪt] *a* inné.

inner ['ɪnər] *a* intérieur; (*feelings*) intime; **an i. circle** (*group of people*) un cercle restreint; **the i. city** les quartiers du centre-ville; **i. tube** (*of tyre, Am tire*) chambre *f* à air. ● **innermost** *a* le plus profond.

inning ['ɪnɪŋ] *n Baseball* tour *m* de batte. ● **innings** *n inv Cricket* tour *m* de batte.

innkeeper ['ɪnkiːpər] *n* aubergiste *mf*.

innocent ['ɪnəs(ə)nt] *a* innocent. ● **innocence** *n* innocence *f*.

innovate ['ɪnəveɪt] *vi* innover. ● **innovation** [-'veɪʃ(ə)n] *n* innovation *f*.

innuendo [ɪnjʊ'endəʊ] *n* (*pl* **-oes** *or* **-os**) insinuation *f*.

innumerable [ɪ'njuːmərəb(ə)l] *a* innombrable.

inoculate [ɪ'nɒkjʊleɪt] *vt* vacciner (**against** contre). ● **inoculation** [-'leɪʃ(ə)n] *n* vaccination *f*.

inoffensive [ɪnə'fensɪv] *a* inoffensif.

inopportune [ɪn'ɒpətjuːn] *a* inopportun.

inordinate [ɪ'nɔːdɪnət] *a* excessif. ● **—ly** *adv* excessivement.

in-patient ['ɪnpeɪʃ(ə)nt] *n* malade *mf* hospitalisé(e).

input ['ɪnpʊt] *n* (*computer operation*) entrée *f*; (*data*) données *fpl*; (*resources*) ressources *fpl*.

inquest ['ɪnkwest] *n* enquête *f*.

inquire [ɪn'kwaɪər] *vi* se renseigner (**about** sur); **to i. after s.o.** demander des nouvelles de qn; **to i. into** faire une enquête sur ‖ *vt* demander; **to i. how to get to** demander le chemin de.

inquiry [ɪn'kwaɪərɪ] *n* demande *f* de renseignements; (*investigation*) enquête *f*; **to make inquiries** demander des renseignements; (*of police*) enquêter.

inquisitive [ɪn'kwɪzɪtɪv] *a* curieux. ● **inquisitively** *adv* avec curiosité.

inroads ['ɪnrəʊdz] *npl* (*attacks*) incursions *fpl* (**into** dans); **to make i. into** (*start on*) entamer.

insane [ɪn'seɪn] *a* fou (*f* folle). ● **insanity** *n* folie *f*.

insatiable [ɪn'seɪʃəb(ə)l] *a* insatiable.

inscribe [ɪn'skraɪb] *vt* inscrire; (*book*) dédicacer (**to** à). ● **inscription** [-'skrɪpʃ(ə)n] *n* inscription *f*; dédicace *f*.

insect ['ɪnsekt] *n* insecte *m*; **i. repellent** crème *f* anti-insecte. ● **in'secticide** *n* insecticide *m*.

insecure [ɪnsɪ'kjʊər] *a* (*not securely fixed*) mal fixé; (*furniture*, *ladder*) branlant; (*uncertain*) incertain; (*person*) qui manque d'assurance.
insemination [ɪnsemɪ'neɪʃ(ə)n] *n* **artificial i.** *Med* insémination *f* artificielle.
insensitive [ɪn'sensɪtɪv] *a* insensible (**to** à). • **insensi'tivity** *n* insensibilité *f*.
inseparable [ɪn'sep(ə)rəb(ə)l] *a* inséparable (**from** de).
insert [ɪn'sɜːt] *vt* insérer (**in, into** dans). • **insertion** [-ʃ(ə)n] *n* insertion *f*.
inshore ['ɪnʃɔːr] *a* côtier ▮ *adv* près de la côte.
inside [ɪn'saɪd] *adv* dedans, à l'intérieur; **come i.!** entrez! ▮ *prep* à l'intérieur de; (*time*) en moins de ▮ *n* dedans *m*, intérieur *m*; *pl* (*stomach*) *Fam* ventre *m*; **on the i.** à l'intérieur (**of** de); **i. out** (*socks etc*) à l'envers; (*to know etc*) à fond.
▮ ['ɪnsaɪd] *a* intérieur; (*information*) obtenu à la source; **the i. lane** *Aut* la voie de gauche, *Am* la voie de droite.
insider [ɪn'saɪdər] *n* initié, -ée *mf*; **i. trading** *ou* **dealing** (*on Stock Exchange*) délit *m* d'initié.
insidious [ɪn'sɪdɪəs] *a* insidieux.
insight ['ɪnsaɪt] *n* perspicacité *f*; (*into question etc*) aperçu *m* (**into** de).
insignificant [ɪnsɪg'nɪfɪkənt] *a* insignifiant. • **insignificance** *n* insignifiance *f*.
insincere [ɪnsɪn'sɪər] *a* peu sincère. • **insincerity** *n* manque *m* de sincérité.
insinuate [ɪn'sɪnjʊeɪt] *vt Pej* insinuer (**that** que).
insipid [ɪn'sɪpɪd] *a* insipide.
insist [ɪn'sɪst] *vi* insister (**on doing** pour faire); **to i. on sth** (*demand*) exiger qch; (*assert*) affirmer qch ▮ *vt* (*order*) insister (**that** pour que + *sub*); (*declare*) affirmer (**that** que).
insistence [ɪn'sɪstəns] *n* insistance *f*; **her i. on seeing me** l'insistance qu'elle met à vouloir me voir. • **insistent** *a* insistant; **to be i. (that)** insister (pour que + *sub*). • **insistently** *adv* avec insistance.
insolent ['ɪnsələnt] *a* insolent. • **insolence** *n* insolence *f*.
insoluble [ɪn'sɒljʊb(ə)l] *a* insoluble.
insolvent [ɪn'sɒlvənt] *a* insolvable.
insomnia [ɪn'sɒmnɪə] *n* insomnie *f*.
insomuch as [ɪnsəʊ'mʌtʃəz] *adv* = **inasmuch as.**
inspect [ɪn'spekt] *vt* inspecter; (*tickets*) contrôler. • **inspection** [-ʃ(ə)n] *n* inspection *f*; (*of tickets*) contrôle *m*. • **inspector** *n* inspecteur, -trice *mf*; (*on train*) contrôleur, -euse *mf*.
inspire [ɪn'spaɪər] *vt* inspirer (**s.o. with sth** qch à qn); **to be inspired to do** avoir l'inspiration de faire. • **inspiration** [-spə'reɪʃ(ə)n] *n* inspiration *f*; (*person*) source *f* d'inspiration.
instability [ɪnstə'bɪlɪtɪ] *n* instabilité *f*.
install [ɪn'stɔːl] (*Am* **instal**) *vt* installer. • **installation** [-stə'leɪʃ(ə)n] *n* installation *f*.
instalment [ɪn'stɔːlmənt] (*Am* **installment**) *n* (*of money*) acompte *m*; (*of serial*, *story*) épisode *m*; (*of publication*) fascicule *m*; **to buy on the i. plan** *Am* acheter à crédit.
instance ['ɪnstəns] *n* (*example*) exemple *m*; (*case*) cas *m*; **for i.** par exemple; **in the first i.** en premier lieu.
instant ['ɪnstənt] *a* immédiat; **i. coffee** café instantané *or* soluble; **of the 3rd i.** (*in letter*) *Com* du 3 courant ▮ *n* (*moment*) instant *m*; **this (very) i.** (*at once*) à l'instant. • **instantly** *adv* immédiatement.
instead [ɪn'sted] *adv* plutôt, au lieu de cela; **i. of (doing) sth** au lieu de (faire) qch; **i. of s.o.** à la place de qn; **i. (of him** *or* **her)** à sa place.
instep ['ɪnstep] *n* (*of foot*) cou-de-pied *m*; (*of shoe*) cambrure *f*.
instigate ['ɪnstɪgeɪt] *vt* provoquer. • **instigator** *n* instigateur, -trice *mf*.
instil [ɪn'stɪl] *vt* (**-ll-**) (*idea*) inculquer (**into** à); (*courage*) insuffler (**into** à).
instinct ['ɪnstɪŋkt] *n* instinct *m*; **by i.** d'instinct. • **in'stinctive** *a* instinctif. • **in'stinctively** *adv* instinctivement.
institute ['ɪnstɪtjuːt] **1** *n* institut *m*. **2** *vt* (*rule*) instituer; (*inquiry*, *proceedings*) *Jur* entamer.
institution [ɪnstɪ'tjuːʃ(ə)n] *n* (*organization*, *custom etc*) institution *f*; **educational/financial i.** établissement *m* scolaire/financier.
instruct [ɪn'strʌkt] *vt* (*teach*) enseigner (**s.o. in sth** qch à qn); **to i. s.o. about sth** (*inform*) instruire qn de qch; **to i. s.o. to do** (*order*) charger qn de faire. • **instruction** [-ʃ(ə)n] *n* (*teaching*) instruction *f*; *pl* (*for use*) mode *m* d'emploi; (*orders*) instructions *fpl*. • **instructive** *a* instructif. • **instructor** *n* professeur *m*; (*for skiing*) moniteur, -trice *mf*; **driving i.** moniteur, -trice *mf* d'auto-école.
instrument ['ɪnstrʊmənt] *n* instrument *m*. • **instru'mental** *a Mus* instrumental; **to be i. in sth/in doing sth** contribuer à qch/à faire qch.
insubordinate [ɪnsə'bɔːdɪnət] *a* indiscipliné.
insufferable [ɪn'sʌfərəb(ə)l] *a* intolérable.
insufficient [ɪnsə'fɪʃənt] *a* insuffisant.

● **—ly** *adv* insuffisamment.

insular ['ɪnsjʊlər] *a* (*climate*) insulaire; (*views*) étroit.

insulate ['ɪnsjʊleɪt] *vt* (*against cold and electrically*) isoler; (*against sound*) insonoriser; **to i. s.o. from** protéger qn de; **insulating tape** chatterton *m*. ● **insulation** [-'leɪʃ(ə)n] *n* isolation *f*; insonorisation *f*; (*material*) isolant *m*.

insulin ['ɪnsjʊlɪn] *n* insuline *f*.

insult [ɪn'sʌlt] *vt* insulter ‖ ['ɪnsʌlt] *n* insulte *f* (**to** à).

insure [ɪn'ʃʊər] *vt* **1** (*car, goods etc*) assurer (**against** contre). **2** *Am* = **ensure.** ● **insurance** *n* assurance *f*; **i. company** compagnie *f* d'assurances; **i. policy** police *f* d'assurance.

insurmountable [ɪnsə'maʊntəb(ə)l] *a* insurmontable.

intact [ɪn'tækt] *a* intact.

intake ['ɪnteɪk] *n* (*of food*) consommation *f*; (*of students, schoolchildren*) admissions *fpl*.

intangible [ɪn'tændʒəb(ə)l] *a* intangible.

integral ['ɪntɪgrəl] *a* intégral; **to be an i. part of** faire partie intégrante de.

integrate ['ɪntɪgreɪt] *vt* intégrer (**into** dans); **integrated school** école *f* où se pratique la déségrégation raciale ‖ *vi* s'intégrer (**into** dans). ● **integration** [-'greɪʃ(ə)n] *n* intégration *f*; (*racial*) déségrégation *f* raciale.

integrity [ɪn'tegrɪtɪ] *n* intégrité *f*.

intellect ['ɪntɪlekt] *n* (*cleverness, faculty*) intelligence *f*. ● **inte'llectual** *a* & *n* intellectuel, -elle (*mf*).

intelligence [ɪn'telɪdʒəns] *n* intelligence *f*. ● **intelligent** *a* intelligent.

intelligible [ɪn'telɪdʒəb(ə)l] *a* compréhensible.

intend [ɪn'tend] *vt* (*gift, remark etc*) destiner (**for** à); **to be intended to do/for s.o.** être destiné à faire/à qn; **to i. to do** avoir l'intention de faire. ● **—ed** *a* (*deliberate*) voulu.

intention [ɪn'tenʃ(ə)n] *n* intention *f* (**of doing** de faire).

intentional [ɪn'tenʃ(ə)n(ə)l] *a* voulu; **it wasn't i.** ce n'était pas fait exprès. ● **—ly** *adv* exprès.

intense [ɪn'tens] *a* intense; (*interest*) vif. ● **—ly** *adv* intensément; *Fig* extrêmement.

intensify [ɪn'tensɪfaɪ] *vt* intensifier ‖ *vi* s'intensifier.

intensity [ɪn'tensətɪ] *n* intensité *f*.

intensive [ɪn'tensɪv] *a* intensif; **in i. care** *Med* en réanimation.

intent [ɪn'tent] **1** *a* (*look*) attentif; **i. on doing** résolu à faire; **i. on** (*task*) absorbé par. **2** *n* intention *f*; **to all intents and purposes** en fait.

inter [ɪn'tɜːr] *vt* (**-rr-**) enterrer.

inter- ['ɪntə(r)] *pref* inter-.

interact [ɪntə'rækt] *vi* (*of people*) agir conjointement; *Ch* interagir. ● **interaction** [-ʃ(ə)n] *n* interaction *f*. ● **inter-active** *a* *Comptr* interactif.

intercept [ɪntə'sept] *vt* intercepter.

interchange ['ɪntətʃeɪndʒ] *n* (*on road*) échangeur *m*. ● **inter'changeable** *a* interchangeable.

inter-city [ɪntə'sɪtɪ] *a* **i.-city train** train *m* de grandes lignes.

intercom ['ɪntəkɒm] *n* interphone *m*.

interconnect/ed [ɪntəkə'nektɪd] *a* (*facts etc*) liés. ● **—ing** *a* **i. rooms** pièces *fpl* communicantes.

intercourse ['ɪntəkɔːs] *n* (*sexual*) rapports *mpl*.

interdependent [ɪntədɪ'pendənt] *a* interdépendant; (*parts of machine*) solidaire.

interest ['ɪnt(ə)rɪst] *n* intérêt *m*; (*money*) intérêts *mpl*; **his** *or* **her i. is** (*hobby etc*) ce qui l'intéresse c'est; **to take an i. in sth/s.o.** s'intéresser à qch/qn; **to lose i. in** se désintéresser de; **to be of i. to s.o.** intéresser qn.
‖ *vt* intéresser. ● **interested** *a* (*motive, person*) intéressé; **to be i. in sth/s.o.** s'intéresser à qch/qn; **I'm i. in doing** ça m'intéresse de faire; **are you i.?** ça vous intéresse? ● **interesting** *a* intéressant.

interface ['ɪntəfeɪs] *n* *Comptr* & *Fig* interface *f*.

interfer/e [ɪntə'fɪər] *vi* se mêler des affaires des autres; **to i. in** s'ingérer dans; **to i. with** (*upset*) déranger; (*touch*) toucher (à). ● **—ing** *a* (*person*) qui se mêle de tout. ● **interference** *n* ingérence *f*; *Rad* parasites *mpl*.

interim ['ɪntərɪm] *n* **in the i.** entre-temps ‖ *a* (*measure etc*) provisoire.

interior [ɪn'tɪərɪər] *a* intérieur ‖ *n* intérieur *m*; **Department of the I.** *Am* ministère *m* de l'Intérieur.

interjection [ɪntə'dʒekʃ(ə)n] *n* *Gram* interjection *f*.

interlock [ɪntə'lɒk] *vi* *Tech* s'emboîter.

interloper ['ɪntələʊpər] *n* intrus, -use *mf*.

interlude ['ɪntəluːd] *n* *TV* interlude *m*; *Th* entracte *m*.

intermediary [ɪntə'miːdɪərɪ] *a* & *n* intermédiaire (*mf*).

intermediate [ɪntə'miːdɪət] *a* intermédiaire; (*course*) de niveau moyen.

intermission [ɪntə'mɪʃ(ə)n] *n* *Cin Th* entracte *m*.

intermittent [ɪntə'mɪtənt] *a* intermittent. ●**—ly** *adv* par intermittence.
intern 1 [ɪn'tɜːn] *vt Pol* interner. **2** ['ɪntɜːn] *n* (*doctor*) *Am* interne *mf* (des hôpitaux).
internal [ɪn'tɜːn(ə)l] *a* interne; (*flight*, *policy*) intérieur; **the I. Revenue Service** *Am* le service des impôts, le fisc.
international [ɪntə'næʃ(ə)nəl] *a* international ‖ *n* (*match*) rencontre *f* internationale; (*player*) international *m*.
interplanetary [ɪntə'plænɪt(ə)rɪ] *a* interplanétaire.
interplay ['ɪntəpleɪ] *n* interaction *f*.
interpret [ɪn'tɜːprɪt] *vt* interpréter ‖ *vi* faire l'interprète. ●**interpreter** *n* interprète *mf*.
interrelated [ɪntərɪ'leɪtɪd] *a* en corrélation.
interrogate [ɪn'terəgeɪt] *vt* interroger. ●**interrogation** [-'geɪʃ(ə)n] *n* interrogation *f*; (*by police*) interrogatoire *m*.
interrogative [ɪntə'rɒgətɪv] *a* & *n Gram* interrogatif (*m*).
interrupt [ɪntə'rʌpt] *vt* interrompre. ●**interruption** [-ʃ(ə)n] *n* interruption *f*.
intersect [ɪntə'sekt] *vt* couper ‖ *vi* se couper, s'entrecouper. ●**intersection** [-ʃ(ə)n] *n* (*crossroads*) croisement *m*, intersection *f*; (*of lines*) intersection *f*.
interval ['ɪntəv(ə)l] *n* intervalle *m*; *Th Cin* entracte *m*; **at intervals** (*time*) de temps à autre; (*space*) par intervalles; **bright intervals** éclaircies *fpl*.
intervene [ɪntə'viːn] *vi* (*of person*) intervenir; (*of event*) survenir; **ten years intervened** dix années s'écoulèrent. ●**intervention** [-'venʃ(ə)n] *n* intervention *f*.
interview ['ɪntəvjuː] *n* entrevue *f*, entretien *m* (**with** avec); *TV etc* interview *f*; **to call s.o. for an i.** convoquer qn ‖ *vt* avoir une entrevue avec; *TV etc* interviewer. ●**—er** *n TV etc* interviewer *m*.
intestine [ɪn'testɪn] *n* intestin *m*.
intimate[1] ['ɪntɪmət] *a* intime; (*friendship*) profond; (*knowledge*) approfondi. ●**intimacy** *n* intimité *f*.
intimate[2] ['ɪntɪmeɪt] *vt* (*hint*) suggérer (**that** que).
intimidate [ɪn'tɪmɪdeɪt] *vt* intimider. ●**intimidation** [-'deɪʃ(ə)n] *n* intimidation *f*.
into ['ɪntuː, *unstressed* 'ɪntə] *prep* **1** dans; **to put i.** mettre dans; **to go i.** (*room*, *detail*) entrer dans. **2** en; **to translate i.** traduire en; **to change s.o. i.** transformer *or* changer qn en; **to go i. town** aller en ville; **i. pieces** (*to break*) en morceaux. **3 to be i. yoga**/*etc Fam* être à fond dans le yoga/*etc*.
intolerable [ɪn'tɒlərəb(ə)l] *a* intolérable (**that** que + *sub*).
intolerant [ɪn'tɒlərənt] *a* intolérant (**of** de). ●**intolerance** *n* intolérance *f*.
intonation [ɪntə'neɪʃ(ə)n] *n Ling* intonation *f*.
intoxicate [ɪn'tɒksɪkeɪt] *vt* enivrer. ●**intoxicated** *a* ivre.
intra- ['ɪntrə] *pref* intra-.
intransigent [ɪn'trænsɪdʒənt] *a* intransigeant.
intransitive [ɪn'trænsɪtɪv] *a Gram* intransitif.
intravenous [ɪntrə'viːnəs] *a Med* intraveineux.
intrepid [ɪn'trepɪd] *a* intrépide.
intricate ['ɪntrɪkət] *a* complexe, compliqué. ●**intricacy** *n* complexité *f*.
intrigu/e 1 [ɪn'triːg] *vt* (*interest*) intriguer; **I'm intrigued to know...** je suis curieux de savoir.... **2** ['ɪntriːg] *n* (*plot*) intrigue *f*. ●**—ing** *a* (*news etc*) curieux.
intrinsic [ɪn'trɪnsɪk] *a* intrinsèque.
introduce [ɪntrə'djuːs] *vt* (*bring in*, *insert*) introduire (**into** dans); (*programme*, *subject*) présenter; **to i. s.o. to s.o.** présenter qn à qn; **to i. s.o. to Dickens**/*etc* faire découvrir Dickens/*etc* à qn.
introduction [ɪntrə'dʌkʃ(ə)n] *n* introduction *f*; (*of person to person*) présentation *f*; **her i. to** (*life abroad etc*) son premier contact avec. ●**introductory** *a* (*words*) d'introduction; (*speech*) de présentation; (*course*) d'initiation.
introspective [ɪntrə'spektɪv] *a* introspectif.
introvert ['ɪntrəvɜːt] *n* introverti, -ie *mf*.
intrude [ɪn'truːd] *vi* (*of person*) déranger (**on s.o.** qn). ●**intruder** *n* intrus, -use *mf*. ●**intrusion** [-ʒ(ə)n] *n* (*bother*) dérangement *m*; (*interference*) intrusion *f* (**into** dans); **forgive my i.** pardonnez-moi de vous avoir dérangé.
intuition [ɪntjuː'ɪʃ(ə)n] *n* intuition *f*. ●**in'tuitive** *a* intuitif.
inundate ['ɪnʌndeɪt] *vt* inonder (**with** de); **inundated with work/letters**/*etc* submergé de travail/lettres/*etc*.
invad/e [ɪn'veɪd] *vt* envahir; **to i. s.o.'s privacy** violer la vie privée de qn. ●**—er** *n* envahisseur, -euse *mf*.
invalid[1] ['ɪnvəlɪd] *a* & *n* malade (*mf*); (*through injury*) infirme (*mf*); **i. car** voiture *f* d'infirme.
invalid[2] [ɪn'vælɪd] *a* (*ticket etc*) non valable.
invaluable [ɪn'væljʊəb(ə)l] *a* (*help etc*) inestimable.
invariable [ɪn'veərɪəb(ə)l] *a* invariable. ●**invariably** *adv* (*always*) toujours.

invasion [ɪn'veɪʒ(ə)n] *n* invasion *f*; **i. of s.o.'s privacy** atteinte *f* à la vie privée de qn.
invent [ɪn'vent] *vt* inventer. ● **invention** [-ʃ(ə)n] *n* invention *f*. ● **inventive** *a* inventif. ● **inventor** *n* inventeur, -trice *mf*.
inventory ['ɪnvənt(ə)rɪ] *n* inventaire *m*.
invert [ɪn'vɜːt] *vt* (*order etc*) intervertir; (*object*) retourner; **inverted commas** guillemets *mpl*.
invest [ɪn'vest] *vt* (*money*) placer, investir (**in** dans); (*time*, *effort*) consacrer (**in** à) ‖ *vi* **to i. in** (*project*) placer son argent dans; (*company*) investir dans; (*new radio etc*) *Fig* se payer. ● **investment** *n* investissement *m*, placement *m*. ● **investor** *n* (*in shares*) actionnaire *mf*; (*saver*) épargnant, -ante *mf*.
investigate [ɪn'vestɪgeɪt] *vt* examiner, étudier; (*crime*) enquêter sur. ● **investigation** [-'geɪʃ(ə)n] *n* examen *m*, étude *f*; (*inquiry by journalist*, *police etc*) enquête *f* (**of, into** sur). ● **investigator** *n* (*detective*) enquêteur, -euse *mf*; (*private*) détective *m*.
invigilate [ɪn'vɪdʒɪleɪt] *vi* être de surveillance (*à un examen*). ● **invigilator** *n* surveillant, -ante *mf*.
invigorating [ɪn'vɪgəreɪtɪŋ] *a* stimulant.
invincible [ɪn'vɪnsəb(ə)l] *a* invincible.
invisible [ɪn'vɪzəb(ə)l] *a* invisible; **i. ink** encre *f* sympathique.
invit/e [ɪn'vaɪt] *vt* inviter (**to do** à faire); (*ask for*) demander; (*give occasion for*) provoquer, appeler; **to i. s.o. out** inviter qn (à sortir); **to i. s.o. over** inviter qn (à venir) ‖ ['ɪnvaɪt] *n Fam* invitation *f*. ● **—ing** *a* engageant; (*food*) appétissant. ● **invitation** [-'teɪʃ(ə)n] *n* invitation *f*.
invoice ['ɪnvɔɪs] *n* facture *f* ‖ *vt* facturer.
invoke [ɪn'vəʊk] *vt* invoquer.
involuntary [ɪn'vɒləntərɪ] *a* involontaire.
involve [ɪn'vɒlv] *vt* (*include*) mêler (*qn*) (**in** à); (*associate*) associer (*qn*) (**in** à); (*entail*) entraîner; **to get involved** (*commit oneself*) s'engager (**in** dans); **the job involves going abroad** le poste nécessite des déplacements à l'étranger. ● **involved** *a* (*concerned*) concerné; (*committed*) engagé (**in** dans); (*complicated*) compliqué; **the factors**/*etc* **i.** (*at stake*) les facteurs/*etc* en jeu; **the person i.** la personne en question; **i. with s.o.** mêlé aux affaires de qn; (*emotionally*) amoureux de qn.
involvement [ɪn'vɒlvmənt] *n* participation *f* (**in** à); (*commitment*) engagement *m* (**in** dans); (*emotional*) liaison *f*.
invulnerable [ɪn'vʌln(ə)rəb(ə)l] *a* invulnérable.
inward ['ɪnwəd] *a* & *adv* (*movement*, *to move*) vers l'intérieur ‖ *a* (*inner*) intérieur; (*thoughts*) intime. ● **inwardly** *adv* (*to laugh*, *curse etc*) intérieurement. ● **inwards** [-wədz] *adv* vers l'intérieur.
iodine ['aɪədiːn, *Am* 'aɪədaɪn] *n* (*antiseptic*) teinture *f* d'iode.
IOU [aɪəʊ'juː] *n abbr* (*I owe you*) reconnaissance *f* de dette.
IQ [aɪ'kjuː] *n abbr* (*intelligence quotient*) QI *m inv*.
Iran [ɪ'rɑːn, ɪ'ræn] *n* Iran *m*. ● **Iranian** [ɪ'reɪnɪən] *a* & *n* iranien, -ienne (*mf*).
Iraq [ɪ'rɑːk] *n* Irak *m*. ● **Iraqi** *a* & *n* irakien, -ienne (*mf*).
irascible [ɪ'ræsəb(ə)l] *a* irascible.
irate [aɪ'reɪt] *a* furieux.
Ireland ['aɪələnd] *n* Irlande *f*. ● **Irish** *a* irlandais ‖ *n* (*language*) irlandais *m*; **the I.** (*people*) les Irlandais *mpl*. ● **Irishman** *n* (*pl* **-men**) Irlandais *m*. ● **Irishwoman** *n* (*pl* **-women**) Irlandaise *f*.
iris ['aɪərɪs] *n Anat Bot* iris *m*.
irk [ɜːk] *vt* ennuyer. ● **irksome** [-səm] *a* ennuyeux.
iron ['aɪən] *n* fer *m*; (*for clothes*) fer *m* (à repasser); **old i., scrap i.** ferraille *f* ‖ *vt* (*clothes*) repasser; **to i. out** (*difficulties*) aplanir. ● **—ing** *n* repassage *m*; **i. board** planche *f* à repasser.
ironmonger ['aɪənmʌŋgər] *n* quincaillier, -ière *mf*.
irony ['aɪərənɪ] *n* ironie *f*. ● **i'ronic(al)** *a* ironique.
irradiate [ɪ'reɪdɪeɪt] *vt* irradier; **irradiated food** aliments *mpl* irradiés.
irrational [ɪ'ræʃən(ə)l] *a* (*person*) peu rationnel; (*act*) irrationnel; (*fear*) irraisonné.
irrefutable [ɪrɪ'fjuːtəb(ə)l] *a* irréfutable.
irregular [ɪ'regjʊlər] *a* irrégulier. ● **irregu'larity** *n* irrégularité *f*.
irrelevant [ɪ'reləvənt] *a* sans rapport (**to** avec); (*activity*) peu utile; **that's i.** ça n'a rien à voir. ● **irrelevance** *n* manque *m* de rapport.
irreparable [ɪ'rep(ə)rəb(ə)l] *a* (*harm*, *loss*) irréparable.
irreplaceable [ɪrɪ'pleɪsəb(ə)l] *a* irremplaçable.
irrepressible [ɪrɪ'presəb(ə)l] *a* (*laughter etc*) irrépressible.
irresistible [ɪrɪ'zɪstəb(ə)l] *a* (*person*, *charm etc*) irrésistible.
irrespective of [ɪrɪ'spektɪvəv] *prep* sans tenir compte de.
irresponsible [ɪrɪ'spɒnsəb(ə)l] *a* (*act*) irréfléchi; (*person*) irresponsable.

irretrievable [ɪrɪ'triːvəb(ə)l] *a* irréparable.
irreversible [ɪrɪ'vɜːsəb(ə)l] *a* (*process*) irréversible; (*decision*) irrévocable.
irrevocable [ɪ'revəkəb(ə)l] *a* irrévocable.
irrigate ['ɪrɪgeɪt] *vt* irriguer. ● **irrigation** [-'geɪʃ(ə)n] *n* irrigation *f*.
irritat/e ['ɪrɪteɪt] *vt* (*annoy, inflame*) irriter. ● **—ing** *a* irritant. ● **irritable** *a* (*easily annoyed*) irritable. ● **irritation** [-'teɪʃ(ə)n] *n* (*anger, inflammation*) irritation *f*.
is [ɪz] *see* **be.**
Islam ['ɪzlɑːm] *n* islam *m*. ● **Islamic** [ɪz'læmɪk] *a* islamique.
island ['aɪlənd] *n* île *f*. ● **isle** [aɪl] *n* île *f*; **the British Isles** les îles Britanniques.
isn't ['ɪz(ə)nt] = **is not.**
isolate ['aɪsəleɪt] *vt* isoler (**from** de). ● **isolated** *a* (*remote, unique*) isolé. ● **isolation** [-'leɪʃ(ə)n] *n* isolement *m*; **in i.** isolément.
Israel ['ɪzreɪl] *n* Israël *m*. ● **Is'raeli** *a* & *n* israélien, -ienne (*mf*).
issue ['ɪʃuː] *vt* (*book etc*) publier; (*tickets*) distribuer; (*passport*) délivrer; (*an order*) donner; (*warning*) lancer; (*supply*) fournir (**with** de, **to** à)
▮ *vi* **to i. from** (*of smell*) se dégager de
▮ *n* (*of newspaper, magazine*) numéro *m*; (*matter*) question *f*; (*outcome*) résultat *m*; (*of stamps etc*) émission *f*; **at i.** (*at stake*) en cause; **to make an i. of** faire toute une affaire de.
isthmus ['ɪsməs] *n Geog* isthme *m*.
it [ɪt] *pron* **1** (*subject*) il, elle; (*object*) le, la, l'; **(to) it** (*indirect object*) lui; **it bites** il mord; **I've done it** je l'ai fait.
2 (*impersonal*) il; **it's snowing** il neige; **it's hot** il fait chaud.
3 (*non specific*) ce, cela, ça; **it's good** c'est bon; **who is it?** qui est-ce?; **that's it!** (*I agree*) c'est ça!; (*it's done*) ça y est!; **to consider it wise to do** juger prudent de faire; **it was Paul who...** c'est Paul qui...; **to have it in for s.o.** *Fam* en vouloir à qn.
4 of it, from it, about it en; **in it, to it, at it** y; **on it** dessus; **under it** dessous.
italics [ɪ'tælɪks] *npl* italique *m*.
Italy ['ɪtəlɪ] *n* Italie *f*. ● **I'talian** *a* & *n* italien, -ienne (*mf*) ▮ *n* (*language*) italien *m*.
itch [ɪtʃ] *n* démangeaison(s) *f(pl)* ▮ *vi* démanger; (*of person*) avoir des démangeaisons; **his arm itches** son bras le démange; **I'm itching to do** *Fig* ça me démange de faire. ● **—ing** *n* démangeaison(s) *f(pl)*. ● **itchy** *a* **I have an i. hand** j'ai une main qui me démange; **I'm i.** j'ai des démangeaisons.
item ['aɪtəm] *n* (*object for sale in newspaper etc*) article *m*; (*matter*) question *f*; **news i.** information *f*. ● **itemize** *vt* (*invoice etc*) détailler.
itinerant [aɪ'tɪnərənt] *a* (*musician*) ambulant; (*judge*) itinérant.
itinerary [aɪ'tɪnərərɪ] *n* itinéraire *m*.
its [ɪts] *poss a* son, sa, *pl* ses.
itself [ɪt'self] *pron* lui-même, elle-même; (*reflexive*) se, s'; **goodness i.** la bonté même; **by i.** tout seul.
IUD [aɪjuː'diː] *n abbr* (*intrauterine device*) stérilet *m*.
ivory ['aɪvərɪ] *n* ivoire *m*.
ivy ['aɪvɪ] *n* lierre *m*.

J

J, j [dʒeɪ] *n* J, j *m*.

jab [dʒæb] *vt* (**-bb-**) (*knife etc*) enfoncer (**into** dans); (*prick*) piquer (*qn*) (**with sth** du bout de qch) ▮ *n* coup *m* (sec); (*injection*) *Fam* piqûre *f*.

jabber ['dʒæbər] *vi* bavarder.

jack [dʒæk] **1** *n Aut* cric *m* ▮ *vt* **to j. up** (*vehicle*) soulever (*avec un cric*); (*price*) *Fig* augmenter. **2** *n Cards* valet *m*. **3** *n* **j. of all trades** homme *m* à tout faire. ● **j.-in-the-box** *n* diable *m* (à ressort).

jackal ['dʒæk(ə)l] *n* (*animal*) chacal *m*.

jackass ['dʒækæs] *n* (*fool*) idiot, -ote *mf*.

jackdaw ['dʒækdɔː] *n* (*bird*) choucas *m*.

jacket ['dʒækɪt] *n* (*short coat*) veste *f*; (*of man's suit*) veston *m*; (*bulletproof*) gilet *m*; **(dust) j.** (*of book*) jaquette *f*; **j. potato** pomme *f* de terre en robe des champs.

jack-knife ['dʒæknaɪf] **1** *n* couteau *m* de poche. **2** *vi* (*of lorry, truck*) se mettre en travers de la route.

jackpot ['dʒækpɒt] *n* gros lot *m*.

jacuzzi [dʒə'kuːzɪ] *n* (*bath, pool*) jacuzzi *m*.

jaded ['dʒeɪdɪd] *a* blasé.

jagged ['dʒægɪd] *a* déchiqueté.

jaguar ['dʒægjʊər, *Am* -wɑːr] *n* (*animal*) jaguar *m*.

jail [dʒeɪl] *n* prison *f* ▮ *vt* emprisonner (**for theft**/*etc* pour vol/*etc*); **to j. s.o. for ten years** condamner qn à dix ans de prison.

jam[1] [dʒæm] *n* (*preserve*) confiture *f*. ● **jam-jar** *n* pot *m* à confiture.

jam[2] [dʒæm] **1** *n* **(traffic) j.** embouteillage *m*; **in a j.** (*trouble*) *Fam* dans le pétrin.
2 *vt* (**-mm-**) (*squeeze, make stuck*) coincer, bloquer; (*street etc*) encombrer; *Rad* brouiller; **to j. sth into** (*cram*) (en)tasser qch dans; **to j. on** (*brakes*) bloquer.
▮ *vi* (*get stuck*) se coincer, se bloquer; **to j. into** (*of crowd*) s'entasser dans. ● **jammed** *a* (*machine etc*) coincé, bloqué; (*street etc*) encombré. ● **jam-'packed** *a* (*hall etc*) bourré de monde.

Jamaica [dʒə'meɪkə] *n* Jamaïque *f*.

jangle ['dʒæŋg(ə)l] *vi* cliqueter.

janitor ['dʒænɪtər] *n Am* concierge *m*.

January ['dʒænjʊərɪ, *Am* -erɪ] *n* janvier *m*.

Japan [dʒə'pæn] *n* Japon *m*. ● **Japa'nese** *a* & *n inv* japonais, -aise (*mf*) ▮ *n* (*language*) japonais *m*.

jar [dʒɑːr] **1** *n* (*container*) pot *m*; (*large, glass*) bocal *m*. **2** *n* (*jolt*) choc *m* ▮ *vt* (**-rr-**) (*shake*) ébranler. **3** *vi* (**-rr-**) (*of noise*) grincer; (*of note*) *Mus* détonner; (*of colours*) jurer (**with** avec). ● **jarring** *a* (*noise*) discordant.

jargon ['dʒɑːgən] *n* jargon *m*.

jaundice ['dʒɔːndɪs] *n Med* jaunisse *f*. ● **jaundiced** *a* (*bitter*) aigri; **to take a j. view of** voir d'un mauvais œil.

jaunt [dʒɔːnt] *n* (*journey*) balade *f*.

jaunty ['dʒɔːntɪ] *a* (**-ier, -iest**) (*carefree*) insouciant; (*cheerful*) allègre.

javelin ['dʒævlɪn] *n* javelot *m*.

jaw [dʒɔː] *n* mâchoire *f*.

jaywalker ['dʒeɪwɔːkər] *n* piéton *m* imprudent.

jazz [dʒæz] *n* jazz *m* ▮ *vt* **to j. up** *Fam* (*enliven*) animer; (*room*) égayer.

jealous ['dʒeləs] *a* jaloux (*f* -ouse) (**of** de). ● **jealousy** *n* jalousie *f*.

jeans [dʒiːnz] *npl* **(pair of) j.** jean *m*.

jeep® [dʒiːp] *n* jeep® *f*.

jeer [dʒɪər] *vti* **to j. (at)** (*mock*) railler; (*boo*) huer ▮ *npl* **jeers** (*boos*) huées *fpl* ● **—ing** *n* (*of crowd*) huées *fpl*.

jell [dʒel] *vi* (*of ideas etc*) *Fam* prendre tournure.

jello® ['dʒeləʊ] *n inv* (*dessert*) *Am* gelée *f*. ● **jelly** *n* (*preserve, dessert*) gelée *f*. ● **jellyfish** *n* méduse *f*.

jeopardy ['dʒepədɪ] *n* danger *m*. ● **jeopardize** *vt* mettre en danger.

jerk [dʒɜːk] **1** *vt* donner une secousse à ▮ *n* secousse *f*. **2** *n* (*person*) **(stupid) j.** *Fam* crétin, -ine *mf*. ● **jerky** *a* (**-ier, -iest**) (*movement etc*) saccadé.

jersey ['dʒɜːzɪ] *n* (*garment*) tricot *m* (de laine); *Fb* maillot *m*; (*cloth*) jersey *m*.

Jersey ['dʒɜːzɪ] *n* Jersey *f*.

jest [dʒest] *n* plaisanterie *f*; **in j.** pour rire.

Jesus ['dʒiːzəs] *n* Jésus *m*.

jet [dʒet] **1** *n* (*plane*) avion *m* à réaction ▮ *a* (*engine*) à réaction; **j. lag** fatigue *f* (due au décalage horaire). **2** *n* (*of steam etc*) jet *m*. ● **jet-lagged** *a Fam* qui souffre du décalage horaire.

jet-black [dʒet'blæk] *a* (noir) de jais.

jettison ['dʒetɪs(ə)n] *vt* (*cargo*) *Nau* jeter à la mer; (*fuel*) *Av* larguer.

jetty ['dʒetɪ] *n* jetée *f*; (*landing-place*) embarcadère *m*.

Jew [dʒuː] *n* (*man*) Juif *m*; (*woman*) Juive *f*. ●**Jewish** *a* juif.

jewel ['dʒuːəl] *n* bijou *m* (*pl* -oux); (*in watch*) rubis *m*. ●**jeweller** *or Am* **jeweler** *n* bijoutier, -ière *mf*. ●**jewellery** *or Am* **jewelry** *n* bijoux *mpl*.

jibe [dʒaɪb] *vi* & *n* = **gibe.**

jiffy ['dʒɪfɪ] *n Fam* instant *m*.

Jiffy bag® ['dʒɪfɪbæg] *n* enveloppe *f* matelassée.

jigsaw ['dʒɪgsɔː] *n* **j. (puzzle)** puzzle *m*.

jilt [dʒɪlt] *vt* (*lover*) laisser tomber.

jingle ['dʒɪŋg(ə)l] *vi* (*of keys, bell etc*) tinter ‖ *vt* faire tinter ‖ *n* tintement *m*.

jinx [dʒɪŋks] *n* (*person, object*) porte-malheur *m inv*.

jitters ['dʒɪtəz] *npl* **to have the j.** *Fam* avoir la frousse. ●**jittery** *a* **to be j.** *Fam* avoir la frousse.

job [dʒɒb] *n* (*task, work*) travail *m*; (*post*) poste *m*, emploi *m*, situation *f*; **to have a (hard) j. doing** *or* **to do** *Fam* avoir du mal à faire; **to have the j. of doing** (*unpleasant task*) être obligé de faire; (*for a living etc*) être chargé de faire; **it's a good j. (that)** *Fam* heureusement que (+ *indic*); **out of a j.** au chômage. ●**jobcentre** *n* agence *f* nationale pour l'emploi. ●**jobless** *a* au chômage.

jockey ['dʒɒkɪ] *n* jockey *m*.

jocular ['dʒɒkjʊlər] *a* jovial, amusant.

jog [dʒɒg] **1** *n* (*shake*) secousse *f*; (*nudge*) coup *m* de coude ‖ *vt* **(-gg-)** (*shake*) secouer; (*push*) pousser; (*memory*) *Fig* rafraîchir. **2** *vi* **(-gg-) to j. along** (*of vehicle*) cahoter; (*of work*) aller tant bien que mal. **3** *vi* **(-gg-)** *Sp* faire du jogging. ●**jogging** *n Sp* jogging *m*.

john [dʒɒn] *n* **the j.** (*lavatory*) *Am Fam* le petit coin.

join [dʒɔɪn] **1** *vt* (*put together*) joindre; (*wires, pipes*) raccorder; (*words, towns*) relier; **to j. s.o.** (*catch up with, meet*) rejoindre qn; (*go with*) se joindre à qn (**in doing** pour faire); **to j. hands** se donner la main; **to j. together** *or* **up** (*objects*) joindre.
‖ *vi* (*of roads, rivers etc*) se rejoindre; **to j. (together** *or* **up)** (*of objects*) se joindre (**with** à); **to j. in** prendre part; **to j. in a game**/*etc* prendre part à un jeu/*etc*.
‖ *n* raccord *m*, joint *m*.
2 *vt* (*become a member of*) s'inscrire à (*club, parti*); (*army, police, company*) entrer dans; **to j. the queue** *or Am* **line** prendre la queue.
‖ *vi* (*become a member*) devenir membre; **to j. up** *Mil* s'engager.

joiner ['dʒɔɪnər] *n* menuisier *m*.

joint [dʒɔɪnt] **1** *n Anat* articulation *f*; *Culin* rôti *m*; *Tech* joint *m*. **2** *n* (*nightclub*) *Fam* boîte *f*. **3** (*cigarette*) *Fam* joint *m*. **4** *a* (*decision etc*) commun; **j. account** compte *m* joint; **j. efforts** efforts *mpl* conjugués.

jok/e [dʒəʊk] *n* plaisanterie *f*; (*trick*) tour *m* ‖ *vi* plaisanter (**about** sur). ●**—er** *n* plaisantin *m*; *Cards* joker *m*. ●**—ingly** *adv* en plaisantant.

jolly ['dʒɒlɪ] **1** *a* **(-ier, -iest)** (*happy*) gai; (*drunk*) *Fam* éméché. **2** *adv* (*very*) *Fam* rudement; **j. good!** très bien!

jolt [dʒəʊt] *vt* (*shake*) secouer; **to j. s.o.** (*of vehicle*) cahoter qn; (*shock*) secouer qn ‖ *n* cahot *m*, secousse *f*; (*shock*) secousse *f*.

Jordan ['dʒɔːd(ə)n] *n* Jordanie *f*.

jostle ['dʒɒs(ə)l] *vti* (*push*) bousculer ‖ *vi* (*push each other*) se bousculer (**for sth** pour obtenir qch).

jot [dʒɒt] *vt* **(-tt-) to j. down** noter. ●**jotter** *n* (*notepad*) bloc-notes *m*.

journal ['dʒɜːn(ə)l] *n* (*periodical*) revue *f*. ●**journalism** *n* journalisme *m*. ●**journalist** *n* journaliste *mf*.

journey ['dʒɜːnɪ] *n* (*trip*) voyage *m*; (*distance*) trajet *m*; **to go on a j.** partir en voyage.

jovial ['dʒəʊvɪəl] *a* jovial.

joy [dʒɔɪ] *n* joie *f*; **the joys of** (*motherhood etc*) les plaisirs *mpl* de. ●**joyful** *a* joyeux. ●**joyride** *n* équipée *f* en voiture volée, rodéo *m*.

joystick ['dʒɔɪstɪk] *n* (*of aircraft, computer*) manche *m* à balai.

JP [dʒeɪ'piː] *abbr* = **Justice of the Peace.**

jubilant ['dʒuːbɪlənt] *a* **to be j.** jubiler.

judder ['dʒʌdər] *vi* (*shake*) vibrer ‖ *n* vibration *f*.

judg/e [dʒʌdʒ] *n* juge *m* ‖ *vti* juger; **judging by** à en juger par. ●**—(e)ment** *n* jugement *m*.

judicial [dʒuː'dɪʃ(ə)l] *a* judiciaire. ●**judiciary** *n* magistrature *f*.

judo ['dʒuːdəʊ] *n* judo *m*.

jug [dʒʌg] *n* cruche *f*; (*for milk*) pot *m*.

juggernaut ['dʒʌgənɔːt] *n* (*truck*) poids *m* lourd, mastodonte *m*.

juggl/e ['dʒʌg(ə)l] *vi* jongler ‖ *vt* jongler avec. ●**—er** *n* jongleur, -euse *mf*.

juice [dʒuːs] *n* jus *m*; (*in stomach*) suc *m*. ●**juicy** *a* **(-ier, -iest)** (*fruit*) juteux; (*story*) *Fig* savoureux.

jukebox ['dʒuːkbɒks] *n* juke-box *m*.

July [dʒuː'laɪ] *n* juillet *m*.

jumble ['dʒʌmb(ə)l] *vt* **to j. (up)** (*objects, facts etc*) mélanger ‖ *n* (*disorder*) fouillis *m*;

j. sale vente *f* de charité; (*for school etc*) vente *f* (*au profit de l'école etc*).

jumbo ['dʒʌmbəʊ] *a* géant; **j. jet** gros-porteur *m*.

jump [dʒʌmp] *n* (*leap*) saut *m*, bond *m*; (*start*) sursaut *m*; (*increase*) hausse *f*; **j. rope** *Am* corde *f* à sauter.
▮ *vi* sauter (**at** sur); (*start*) sursauter; **to j. to conclusions** tirer des conclusions hâtives; **to j. in** *or* **on** (*train*, *vehicle*) monter *or* sauter dans; **to j. off** *or* **out** sauter; (*from bus etc*) descendre; **to j. off sth, j. out of sth** sauter de qch; **to j. out of the window** sauter par la fenêtre; **to j. up** se lever d'un bond.
▮ *vt* (*ditch*) sauter; **to j. the lights** *Aut* griller un feu rouge; **to j. the rails** (*of train*) dérailler; **to j. the queue** passer avant son tour; **to j. rope** *Am* sauter à la corde.

jumper ['dʒʌmpər] *n* pull(-over) *m*; (*dress*) *Am* robe *f* chasuble.

jumpy ['dʒʌmpɪ] *a* (**-ier, -iest**) nerveux.

junction ['dʒʌŋkʃ(ə)n] *n* (*crossroads*) carrefour *m*; **j. 23** (*exit on motorway*) la sortie 23.

June [dʒuːn] *n* juin *m*.

jungle ['dʒʌŋg(ə)l] *n* jungle *f*.

junior ['dʒuːnɪər] *a* (*younger*) plus jeune; (*in rank etc*) subalterne; (*teacher*, *doctor*) jeune; **to be s.o.'s j.** être plus jeune que qn; (*in rank*, *status*) être au-dessous de qn; **Smith j.** Smith fils; **j. school** école *f* primaire; **j. high school** *Am* = collège *m* d'enseignement secondaire ▮ *n* cadet, -ette *mf*; *Sch* petit, -ite *mf*; *Sp* junior *mf*.

junk [dʒʌŋk] **1** *n* (*objects*) bric-à-brac *m inv*; (*metal*) ferraille *f*; (*inferior*, *goods*) camelote *f*; (*waste*) ordures *fpl*; **j. food** aliment *m* peu nutritif; **j. shop** (boutique *f* de) brocanteur *m*. **2** *vt* (*get rid of*) *Am Fam* balancer.

junkie ['dʒʌŋkɪ] *n Fam* drogué, -ée *mf*.

junta ['dʒʌntə, *Am* 'hʊntə] *n Pol* junte *f*.

jury ['dʒʊərɪ] *n* (*in competition*) & *Jur* jury *m*.

just [dʒʌst] **1** *adv* (*exactly*, *only*) juste; **she has/had j. left** elle vient/venait de partir; **I've j. come from** j'arrive de; **I'm j. coming!** j'arrive!; **he'll (only) j. catch the bus** il aura son bus de justesse; **he j. missed it** il l'a manqué de peu; **j. as big/***etc* tout aussi grand/*etc* (**as** que); **j. listen!** écoute donc!; **j. a moment!** un instant!; **j. over ten** un peu plus de dix; **j. one** un(e) seul(e) (**of** de); **j. about** (*approximately*) à peu près; (*almost*) presque; **j. about to do** sur le point de faire. **2** *a* (*fair*) juste (**to** envers).

justice ['dʒʌstɪs] *n* justice *f*; **to do j. to** (*meal*) faire honneur à; **J. of the Peace** juge *m* de paix.

justify ['dʒʌstɪfaɪ] *vt* justifier; **to be justified in doing** être fondé à faire. ●**justi'fiable** *a* justifiable. ●**justification** [-'keɪʃ(ə)n] *n* justification *f*.

jut [dʒʌt] *vi* (**-tt-**) **to j. out** faire saillie; **to j. out over sth** surplomber qch.

juvenile ['dʒuːvənaɪl] *n* adolescent, -ente *mf* ▮ *a* (*court*, *book etc*) pour enfants; (*delinquent*) jeune; (*behaviour*) puéril.

K

K, k [keɪ] *n* K, k *m*.
kaleidoscope [kə'laɪdəskəʊp] *n* kaléidoscope *m*.
kangaroo [kæŋgə'ruː] *n* (*pl* **-oos**) kangourou *m*.
karate [kə'rɑːtɪ] *n Sp* karaté *m*.
kebab [kə'bæb] *n* brochette *f*.
keel [kiːl] *n Nau* quille *f* ‖ *vi* **to k. over** (*of boat*) chavirer.
keen [kiːn] *a* (*eager*) plein d'enthousiasme; (*edge*) aiguisé; (*interest*) vif; (*mind*) pénétrant; (*wind*) coupant; **k. eyesight** vue *f* perçante; **a k. sportsman** un passionné de sport; **to be k. to do** *or* **on doing** (*want*) tenir (beaucoup) à faire; **to be k. on doing** (*like*) aimer (beaucoup) faire; **to be k. on** (*music, sport etc*) être passionné de; **he is k. on her/the idea** elle/l'idée lui plaît beaucoup.
keep[1] [kiːp] *vt* (*pt* & *pp* **kept**) garder; (*shop, car*) avoir; (*diary, promise*) tenir; (*family*) entretenir; (*rule*) respecter; (*feast day*) célébrer; (*delay*) retenir; **to k. doing** (*continue*) continuer à faire; **to k. sth clean** tenir *or* garder qch propre; **to k. sth from s.o.** (*hide*) cacher qch à qn; **to k. s.o. from doing** (*prevent*) empêcher qn de faire; **to k. s.o. waiting/working** faire attendre/travailler qn; **to k. sth going** (*engine*) laisser qch en marche; **to k. an appointment** se rendre à un rendez-vous.
‖ *vi* (*remain*) rester; (*continue*) continuer; (*of food*) se garder; **how is he keeping?** comment va-t-il?; **to k. still** rester tranquille; **to k. left** tenir sa gauche; **to k. from doing** (*refrain*) s'abstenir de faire; **to k. going** (*continue*) continuer; **to k. at it** continuer à le faire.
‖ *n* (*food*) nourriture *f*, subsistance *f*; **to have one's k.** être logé et nourri; **for keeps** *Fam* pour toujours.
keep[2] [kiːp] *n* (*tower*) *Hist* donjon *m*.
keep away *vt* (*person*) éloigner (**from** de) ‖ *vi* ne pas s'approcher (**from** de) ‖ **to keep back** *vt* (*crowd*) contenir; (*delay*) retenir; (*hide*) cacher (**from** à) ‖ *vi* ne pas s'approcher (**from** de) ‖ **to keep down** *vt* (*restrict*) limiter; (*price, costs*) maintenir bas ‖ **to keep in** *vt* empêcher (*qn*) de sortir; (*as punishment*) *Sch* consigner (*élève*) ‖ **to keep off** *vt* (*person*) éloigner; **'k. off the grass'** 'ne pas marcher sur les pelouses' ‖ *vi* (*not go near*) ne pas s'approcher; **if the rain keeps off** s'il ne pleut pas ‖ **to keep on** *vt* (*hat, employee*) garder; **to k. on doing** continuer à faire ‖ **to keep out** *vt* empêcher (*qn*) d'entrer ‖ *vi* rester en dehors (**of** de) ‖ **to keep to** *vt* (*subject, path*) ne pas s'écarter de; (*room*) garder; **to k. to the left** tenir la gauche ‖ **to keep up** *vt* (*continue*) continuer (**doing sth** à faire qch); (*road, building*) entretenir ‖ *vi* (*continue*) continuer; (*follow*) suivre; **to k. up with s.o** (*follow*) suivre qn.
keeper ['kiːpər] *n* (*in park, zoo*) gardien, -ienne *mf*.
keeping ['kiːpɪŋ] *n* **in k. with** en rapport avec.
keepsake ['kiːpseɪk] *n* souvenir *m*.
keg [keg] *n* tonnelet *m*.
kennel ['ken(ə)l] *n* niche *f*; (*for boarding dogs*) *Am* chenil *m*; **kennels** chenil *m*.
Kenya ['kiːnjə, 'kenjə] *n* Kenya *m*.
kept [kept] *pt* & *pp of* **keep**[1] ‖ *a* **well k.** (*house etc*) bien tenu.
kerb [kɜːb] *n* bord *m* du trottoir.
kernel ['kɜːn(ə)l] *n* (*of nut*) amande *f*.
kerosene ['kerəsiːn] *n* (*paraffin*) *Am* pétrole *m* (lampant).
ketchup ['ketʃəp] *n* ketchup *m*.
kettle ['ket(ə)l] *n* bouilloire *f*; **the k. is boiling** l'eau bout.
key [kiː] *n* clef *f*, clé *f*; (*of piano, typewriter, computer*) touche *f* ‖ *a* (*industry, post etc*) clef (*f inv*), clé (*f inv*); **k. person** pivot *m*; **k. ring** porte-clefs *m inv* ‖ *vt Comptr* **to k. in** (*data*) saisir. ●**keyboard** *n* clavier *m*. ●**keyhole** *n* trou *m* de (la) serrure. ●**keynote** *n* (*of speech*) note *f* dominante.
keyed [kiːd] *a* **to be k. up** avoir les nerfs tendus.
khaki ['kɑːkɪ] *a* kaki *a inv*.
kick [kɪk] *n* coup *m* de pied; (*of horse*) ruade *f*; **for kicks** *Fam* pour le plaisir ‖ *vt* donner un coup de pied à; (*of horse*) lancer une ruade à; **to k. down** *or* **in** (*door etc*) démolir à coups de pied; **to k. out** (*throw out*) *Fam* flanquer dehors ‖ *vi* donner des coups de pied; (*of horse*) ruer; **to k. off** *Fb* donner le coup d'envoi; (*start*) démarrer. ●**k.-off** *n Fb* coup *m* d'envoi.
kid [kɪd] **1** *n* (*child*) *Fam* gosse *mf*; **my k. brother** *Am Fam* mon petit frère. **2** *n* (*goat*)

chevreau *m.* **3** *vti* (**-dd-**) (*joke, tease*) *Fam* blaguer.

kidnap ['kɪdnæp] *vt* (**-pp-**) kidnapper. ● **kidnapper** *n* ravisseur, -euse *mf.*

kidney ['kɪdnɪ] *n Anat* rein *m*; *Culin* rognon *m*; **on a k. machine** sous rein artificiel.

kill [kɪl] *vt* tuer; **my feet are killing me** *Fam* je ne sens plus mes pieds; **to k. off** détruire ‖ *vi* tuer ‖ *n* mise *f* à mort; (*prey*) animaux *mpl* tués. ● **—ing** *n* (*of person*) meurtre *m*; (*of group*) massacre *m*; (*of animal*) mise *f* à mort; **to make a k.** *Fin* réussir un beau coup. ● **killer** *n* tueur, -euse *mf.*

killjoy ['kɪldʒɔɪ] *n* rabat-joie *m inv.*

kiln [kɪln] *n* (*for pottery*) four *m.*

kilo ['kiːləʊ] *n* (*pl* **-os**) kilo *m.* ● **kilogram(me)** ['kɪləʊgræm] *n* kilogramme *m.*

kilometre [kɪ'lɒmɪtər] *n* (*Am* **kilometer**) kilomètre *m.*

kilowatt ['kɪləʊwɒt] *n* kilowatt *m.*

kilt [kɪlt] *n* kilt *m.*

kin [kɪn] *n* **one's next of k.** son plus proche parent.

kind[1] [kaɪnd] *n* (*sort*) sorte *f*, genre *m*, espèce *f* (**of** de); **all kinds of** toutes sortes de; **what k. of drink/***etc* **is it?** qu'est-ce que c'est comme boisson/*etc*?; **nothing of the k.!** absolument pas!; **k. of worried/sad/***etc* plutôt inquiet/triste/*etc*; **it's the only one of its k.** c'est unique en son genre; **we are two of a k.** nous nous ressemblons.

kind[2] [kaɪnd] *a* (**-er, -est**) (*helpful, pleasant*) gentil (**to** avec, pour); **that's k. of you** c'est gentil *or* aimable à vous. ● **k.-'hearted** *a* qui a bon cœur.

kindergarten ['kɪndəgɑːt(ə)n] *n* jardin *m* d'enfants.

kindle ['kɪnd(ə)l] *vt* allumer.

kindly ['kaɪndlɪ] *adv* avec bonté; **k. wait/***etc* ayez la bonté d'attendre/*etc* ‖ *a* (*person*) bienveillant.

kindness ['kaɪndnɪs] *n* gentillesse *f.*

king [kɪŋ] *n* roi *m.* ● **k.-size(d)** *a* géant; (*cigarette*) long. ● **kingdom** *n* royaume *m*; **animal/plant k.** règne *m* animal/végétal.

kingfisher ['kɪŋfɪʃər] *n* martin-pêcheur *m.*

kinky ['kɪŋkɪ] *a* (**-ier, -iest**) (*person*) qui a des goûts bizarres; (*clothes*) bizarre.

kinship ['kɪnʃɪp] *n* parenté *f.*

kiosk ['kiːɒsk] *n* kiosque *m*; **(telephone) k.** cabine *f* (téléphonique).

kipper ['kɪpər] *n* (*herring*) kipper *m.*

kiss [kɪs] *n* baiser *m*; **the k. of life** *Med* le bouche-à-bouche ‖ *vt* (*person*) embrasser; **to k. s.o.'s hand** baiser la main de qn ‖ *vi* s'embrasser.

kit [kɪt] *n* équipement *m*, matériel *m*; (*set of articles*) trousse *f*; (*belongings*) affaires *fpl*; **(do-it-yourself) k.** kit *m*; **first-aid k.** trousse *f* de pharmacie; **tool k.** trousse *f* à outils; **k. bag** sac *m* (*de soldat etc*) ‖ *vt* (**-tt-**) **to k. s.o. out** équiper qn (**with** de).

kitchen ['kɪtʃɪn] *n* cuisine *f*; **k. cabinet** buffet *m* de cuisine; **k. garden** jardin *m* potager; **k. sink** évier *m*; **k. units** éléments *mpl* de cuisine. ● **kitche'nette** *n* coin-cuisine *m.*

kite [kaɪt] *n* (*toy*) cerf-volant *m.*

kitten ['kɪt(ə)n] *n* chaton *m.*

kitty ['kɪtɪ] *n* (*fund*) cagnotte *f.*

kiwi ['kiːwiː] *n* (*bird, fruit*) kiwi *m.*

km *abbr* (*kilometre*) km.

knack [næk] *n* (*skill*) coup *m* (de main) (**of doing** pour faire); **to have a** *or* **the k. of doing** (*tendency*) avoir le don de faire.

knapsack ['næpsæk] *n* sac *m* à dos.

knead [niːd] *vt* (*dough*) pétrir.

knee [niː] *n* genou *m*; **to go down on one's knees** se mettre à genoux; **k. pad** *Sp* genouillère *f.* ● **kneecap** *n Anat* rotule *f.*

kneel [niːl] *vi* (*pt & pp* **knelt** *or* **kneeled**) **to k. (down)** s'agenouiller; **to be kneeling (down)** être à genoux.

knew [njuː] *pt of* **know.**

knickers ['nɪkəz] *npl* (*woman's undergarment*) slip *m*; (*longer*) culotte *f.*

knife [naɪf] *n* (*pl* **knives**) couteau *m*; (*penknife*) canif *m* ‖ *vt* poignarder.

knight [naɪt] *n* chevalier *m*; *Chess* cavalier *m* ‖ *vt* **to be knighted** *Br* être fait chevalier. ● **knighthood** *n Br* titre *m* de chevalier.

knit [nɪt] *vt* (**-tt-**) tricoter; **to k. one's brow** froncer les sourcils ‖ *vi* tricoter; **to k. together** (*of bones*) se souder. ● **knitting** *n* (*activity, material*) tricot *m*; **k. needle** aiguille *f* à tricoter. ● **knitwear** *n* tricots *mpl.*

knob [nɒb] *n* (*on door etc*) bouton *m*; (*of butter*) noix *f.*

knock [nɒk] *vt* (*strike*) frapper; (*collide with*) heurter; (*criticize*) *Fam* critiquer; **to k. one's head on sth** se cogner la tête contre qch; **to k. to the ground** jeter à terre ‖ *vi* (*strike*) frapper; **to k. against** *or* **into** (*bump into*) heurter ‖ *n* (*blow*) coup *m*; (*collision*) heurt *m*; **there's a k. at the door** quelqu'un frappe; **I heard a k.** j'ai entendu frapper.

knock about *vt* (*ill-treat*) malmener ‖ **to knock back** *vt* (*drink, glass etc*) *Fam* s'envoyer (derrière la cravate) ‖ **to knock down** *vt* (*vase, pedestrian etc*) renverser; (*house, wall etc*) abattre; (*price*) baisser ‖ **to knock in** *vt* (*nail*) enfoncer ‖ **to knock off** *vt* (*person, object*) faire tomber (**from** de); (*steal*) *Fam* piquer; **to knock £5 off the price** baisser le prix de cinq livres ‖ *vi* (*stop* *work*) *Fam* s'arrêter de travailler ‖ **to knock out** *vt* (*make unconscious*) assommer; *Boxing* mettre k.-o.; (*beat in competition*) éliminer; **to k. oneself out** (*tire*) *Fam* s'esquinter (**doing** à faire). ●**knock-out** *n* *Boxing* knock-out *m*. ‖ **to knock over** *vt* (*pedestrian, vase etc*) renverser ‖ **to knock up** *vt* (*meal*) *Fam* préparer à la hâte.

knocker ['nɒkər] *n* (*for door*) marteau *m*.

knot [nɒt] **1** *n* (*in rope etc*) nœud *m* ‖ *vt* (**-tt-**) nouer. **2** *n* (*unit of speed*) *Nau* nœud *m*.

know [nəʊ] *vt* (*pt* **knew,** *pp* **known**) (*facts, language etc*) savoir; (*person, place etc*) connaître; (*recognize*) reconnaître (**by** à); **to k. that** savoir que; **to k. how to do** savoir faire; **for all I k.** (autant) que je sache; **I'll let you k.** je vous le ferai savoir; **I'll have you k. that**... sachez que...; **to k. (a lot) about** (*person, event*) en savoir long sur; (*cars, sewing etc*) s'y connaître en; **to get to k. (about) sth** apprendre qch; **to get to k. s.o.** (*meet*) faire la connaissance de qn.
‖ *vi* savoir; **I k.** je (le) sais; **I wouldn't k.** je n'en sais rien; **I k. about that** je suis au courant; **do you k. of a good dentist**/*etc*? connais-tu un bon dentiste/*etc*?; **you should k. better than to do that** tu es trop intelligent pour faire ça; **you should have known better** tu aurais dû réfléchir.
‖ *n* **in the k.** *Fam* au courant. ●**knowingly** *adv* (*consciously*) sciemment. ●**known** *a* connu; **a k. expert** un expert reconnu; **well k.** (bien) connu (**that** que); **she is k. to be...** on sait qu'elle est....

know-all ['nəʊɔːl] *or Am* **know-it-all** *n Pej* je-sais-tout *mf inv*. ●**know-how** *n* (*skill*) savoir-faire *m inv*.

knowledge ['nɒlɪdʒ] *n* connaissance *f* (**of** de); (*learning*) connaissances *fpl*, savoir *m*; **to (the best of) my k.** à ma connaissance; **general k.** culture *f* générale. ●**knowledgeable** *a* bien informé (**about** sur).

knuckle ['nʌk(ə)l] **1** *n* articulation *f* (du doigt). **2** *vi* **to k. down to** (*task*) *Fam* s'atteler à.

Koran [kə'rɑːn] *n* **the K.** le Coran.

Korea [kə'rɪə] *n* Corée *f*.

kosher ['kəʊʃər] *a* (*food*) kascher *inv*.

Kuwait [kjuː'weɪt] *n* Koweït *m*.

L

L, l [el] L, l *m*.
lab [læb] *n Fam* labo *m*. ●**laboratory** [lə'bɒrət(ə)rɪ, *Am* 'læbrətɔːrɪ] *n* laboratoire *m*; **language l.** laboratoire *m* de langues.
label ['leɪb(ə)l] *n* étiquette *f* ‖ *vt* (**-ll-**, *Am* **-l-**) (*with price*) étiqueter; (*for identification*) mettre une étiquette sur.
laborious [lə'bɔːrɪəs] *a* laborieux.
labour ['leɪbər] (*Am* **labor**) *n* (*work*) travail *m*; (*workers*) main-d'œuvre *f*; **L.** *Br Pol* les travaillistes *mpl*; **in l.** (*woman*) en train d'accoucher ‖ *a* (*market*, *situation*) du travail; **l. dispute** conflit *m* ouvrier; **l. force** main-d'œuvre *f*; **l. union** *Am* syndicat *m* ‖ *vi* (*toil*) peiner. ●**labourer** *n* (*on roads etc*) manœuvre *m*; (*on farm*) ouvrier *m* agricole.
labyrinth ['læbɪrɪnθ] *n* labyrinthe *m*.
lace [leɪs] **1** *n* (*cloth*) dentelle *f*. **2** *n* (*of shoe etc*) lacet *m* ‖ *vt* **to l. (up)** (*shoe etc*) lacer.
lack [læk] *n* manque *m*; **for l. of** à défaut de ‖ *vt* manquer de ‖ *vi* **to be lacking** manquer (**in** de).
lacquer ['lækər] *n* (*for wood*, *hair*) laque *f*.
lad [læd] *n* gamin *m*, garçon *m*.
ladder ['lædər] *n* échelle *f*; (*in stocking*) maille *f* filée ‖ *vti* (*stocking*) filer.
laden ['leɪd(ə)n] *a* chargé (**with** de).
ladle ['leɪd(ə)l] *n* louche *f*.
lady ['leɪdɪ] *n* dame *f*; **a young l.** une jeune fille; (*married*) une jeune femme; **Ladies and Gentlemen!** Mesdames, Mesdemoiselles, Messieurs!; **l. doctor** femme *f* médecin; **l. friend** amie *f*; **the ladies' room, the ladies** les toilettes *fpl* pour dames. ●**ladybird** *or Am* **ladybug** *n* coccinelle *f*. ●**ladylike** *a* (*manner*) distingué; **she's (very) l.** elle est très grande dame.
lag [læg] **1** *vi* (**-gg-**) **to l. behind** (*in progress*) avoir du retard; (*dawdle*) traîner; **to l. behind s.o.** avoir du retard sur qn. **2** *vt* (**-gg-**) (*pipe*) calorifuger.
lager ['lɑːgər] *n* bière *f* blonde.
lagoon [lə'guːn] *n* lagune *f*; (*small*, *coral*) lagon *m*.
laid [leɪd] *pt* & *pp of* **lay**[2]. ●**l.-'back** *a Fam* relax.
lain [leɪn] *pp of* **lie**[1].
lair [leər] *n* tanière *f*.
lake [leɪk] *n* lac *m*.
lamb [læm] *n* agneau *m*. ●**lambswool** *n* laine *f* d'agneau, lambswool *m*.
lame [leɪm] *a* (**-er, -est**) (*person*, *argument*) boiteux; (*excuse*) piètre; **to be l.** boiter.
lament [lə'ment] *n* lamentation *f* ‖ *vt* **to l. (over)** se lamenter sur.
laminated ['læmɪneɪtɪd] *a* (*glass*) feuilleté.
lamp [læmp] *n* lampe *f*; (*on vehicle*) feu *m*. ●**lamppost** *n* lampadaire *m* (*de rue*). ●**lampshade** *n* abat-jour *m inv*.
lanai [lə'naɪ] *n Am* véranda *f*.
lance [lɑːns] **1** *n* (*weapon*) lance *f*. **2** *vt* inciser.
land[1] [lænd] *n* terre *f*; (*country*) pays *m*; **(plot of) l.** terrain *m* ‖ *a* (*transport etc*) terrestre; (*reform*) agraire; (*tax*) foncier.
land[2] [lænd] *vi* (*of aircraft*) atterrir, se poser; (*of ship*) mouiller; (*of passengers*) débarquer; (*of bomb*) tomber; **to l. up** (*end up*) se retrouver.
‖ *vt* (*aircraft*) poser; (*passengers*, *cargo*) débarquer; (*job*, *prize*) *Fam* décrocher; **to l. s.o. in trouble** *Fam* mettre qn dans le pétrin; **to be landed with** *Fam* (*person*) avoir sur les bras; (*fine*) ramasser. ●**landing** *n* **1** *Av* atterrissage *m*; *Nau* débarquement *m*; **forced l.** atterrissage *m* forcé; **l. stage** débarcadère *m*. **2** *n* (*at top of stairs*) palier *m*.
landlady ['lændleɪdɪ] *n* propriétaire *f*; (*of pub*) patronne *f*. ●**landlord** *n* propriétaire *m*; (*of pub*) patron *m*. ●**landmark** *n* point *m* de repère. ●**landslide** *n* éboulement *m*; *Pol* raz-de-marée *m inv* électoral.
landscape ['lændskeɪp] *n* paysage *m*.
lane [leɪn] *n* (*in country*) chemin *m*; (*in town*) ruelle *f*; (*division of road*) voie *f*; (*line of traffic*) file *f*; *Av Nau Sp* couloir *m*.
language ['læŋgwɪdʒ] *n* (*English etc*) langue *f*; (*faculty*, *style*) langage *m*; **computer l.** langage *m* machine ‖ *a* (*laboratory*) de langues; (*teacher*, *studies*) de langue(s).
languish ['læŋgwɪʃ] *vi* languir (**for, after** après).
lanky ['læŋkɪ] *a* (**-ier, -iest**) dégingandé.
lantern ['læntən] *n* lanterne *f*.
lap [læp] **1** *n* (*of person*) genoux *mpl*; **in the l. of luxury** dans le plus grand luxe. **2** *n Sp* tour *m* (de piste). **3** *vt* (**-pp-**) **to l. up** (*drink*) laper. **4** *vi* (**-pp-**) **to l. over** (*overlap*) se chevaucher.
lapel [lə'pel] *n* (*of jacket etc*) revers *m*.
lapse [læps] **1** *n* (*fault*) faute *f*; (*weakness*)

défaillance *f*; **a l. of memory** un trou de mémoire ▮ *vi* commettre une faute; **to l. into** retomber dans. **2** *n* (*interval*) intervalle *m*; **a l. of time** un intervalle (**between** entre). **3** *vi* (*expire*) (*of ticket etc*) se périmer; (*of subscription*) prendre fin; (*of insurance policy*) cesser d'être valable.

laptop ['læptɒp] *a* **l. computer** ordinateur *m* portable.

lard [lɑːd] *n* saindoux *m*.

larder ['lɑːdər] *n* (*cupboard*) garde-manger *m inv*.

large [lɑːdʒ] *a* (**-er, -est**) (*in size or extent*) grand; (*in volume, bulkiness*) gros (*f* grosse); **to grow** *or* **get l.** grossir, grandir; **at l.** (*of prisoner, animal*) en liberté; (*as a whole*) en général; **by and l.** dans l'ensemble. ●**l.-scale** *a* (*operation etc*) de grande envergure. ●**largely** *adv* (*to a great extent*) en grande mesure.

lark [lɑːk] **1** *n* (*bird*) alouette *f*. **2** *n* (*joke*) *Fam* rigolade *f*, blague *f* ▮ *vi* **to l. about** *Fam* s'amuser.

larva, *pl* **-vae** ['lɑːvə, -viː] *n* (*of insect*) larve *f*.

laryngitis [lærɪn'dʒaɪtəs] *n* laryngite *f*.

lasagna [lə'zænjə] *n* lasagne *f*.

laser ['leɪzər] *n* laser *m*; **l. beam** rayon *m* laser.

lash[1] [læʃ] *n* (*with whip*) coup *m* de fouet ▮ *vt* (*strike*) fouetter; (*tie*) attacher (**to** à) ▮ *vi* **to l. out** (*spend wildly*) *Fam* claquer son argent; **to l. out at** envoyer des coups à; (*criticize*) *Fig* fustiger.

lash[2] [læʃ] *n* (*eyelash*) cil *m*.

lashings ['læʃɪŋz] *npl* **l. of** (*jam etc*) *Fam* une montagne de.

lass [læs] *n* jeune fille *f*.

lasso [læ'suː, *Am* 'læsəʊ] *n* (*pl* **-os**) lasso *m* ▮ *vt* attraper au lasso.

last[1] [lɑːst] *a* dernier; **the l. ten lines** les dix dernières lignes; **l. but one** avant-dernier; **l. night** (*evening*) hier soir; (*night*) la nuit dernière.
▮ *adv* (*lastly*) en dernier lieu, enfin; (*on the last occasion*) (pour) la dernière fois; **to leave l.** sortir en dernier.
▮ *n* (*person, object*) dernier, -ière *mf*; (*end*) fin *f*; **the l. of the beer**/*etc* le reste de la bière/*etc*; **at (long) l.** enfin. ●**l.-ditch** *a* (*attempt*) désespéré. ●**l.-minute** *a* de dernière minute. ●**lastly** *adv* en dernier lieu, enfin.

last[2] [lɑːst] *vi* durer; **to l. (out)** (*endure*) tenir; (*of money, supplies*) durer. ●**—ing** *a* durable.

latch [lætʃ] **1** *n* loquet *m*; **the door is on the l.** la porte n'est pas fermée à clef. **2** *vi* **to l. on to** (*idea etc*) *Fam* adopter.

late[1] [leɪt] *a* (**-er, -est**) (*not on time*) en retard (**for** à); (*meal, season, hour*) tardif; (*stage*) avancé; (*edition*) dernier; **he's an hour l.** il a une heure de retard; **to make s.o. l.** mettre qn en retard; **it's l.** il est tard; **Easter**/*etc* **is l.** Pâques/*etc* est tard; **in l. June**/*etc* fin juin/*etc*; **a later edition**/*etc* une édition/*etc* plus récente; **the latest edition**/*etc* la dernière édition/*etc;* **to take a later train** prendre un train plus tard; **at a later date** à une date ultérieure; **the latest date** la date limite; **at the latest** au plus tard; **of l.** dernièrement. ▮ *adv* (*in the day, season etc*) tard; (*not on time*) en retard; **it's getting l.** il se fait tard; **later (on)** plus tard; **no later than** pas plus tard que.

late[2] [leɪt] *a* **the l. Mr Smith**/*etc* (*deceased*) feu Monsieur Smith/*etc*.

latecomer ['leɪtkʌmər] *n* retardataire *mf*. ●**lately** *adv* dernièrement. ●**lateness** *n* (*of person, train etc*) retard *m*; **constant l.** des retards continuels.

latent ['leɪtənt] *a* latent.

lateral ['lætərəl] *a* latéral.

lathe [leɪð] *n Tech* tour *m*.

lather ['lɑːðər] *n* mousse *f* (de savon) ▮ *vt* savonner.

Latin ['lætɪn] *a* latin; **L. America** Amérique *f* latine ▮ *n* (*language*) latin *m*. ●**Latin American** *a* d'Amérique latine ▮ *n* Latino-Américain, -aine *mf*.

latitude ['lætɪtjuːd] *n Geog & Fig* latitude *f*.

latter ['lætər] *a* (*later, last-named*) dernier; (*second*) deuxième ▮ *n* dernier, -ière *mf*; second, -onde *mf*. ●**—ly** *adv* récemment, dernièrement.

laudable ['lɔːdəb(ə)l] *a* louable.

laugh [lɑːf] *n* rire *m*; **to have a l.** rire ▮ *vi* rire (**at, about** de) ▮ *vt* **to l. off** tourner en plaisanterie. ●**—ing** *a* riant; **it's no l. matter** il n'y a pas de quoi rire; **to be the l. stock of** être la risée de. ●**laughable** *a* ridicule. ●**laughter** *n* rire(s) *m*(*pl*); **to roar with l.** rire aux éclats.

launch [lɔːntʃ] **1** *n* (*motor boat*) vedette *f* **2** *vt* (*rocket, boat, fashion etc*) lancer ▮ *vi* **to l. (out) into** (*begin*) se lancer dans ▮ *n* lancement *m*.

launder ['lɔːndər] *vt* (*clothes*) blanchir; (*money from drugs*) *Fig* blanchir.

launderette [lɔːndə'ret] *or Am* **Laundromat®** *n* laverie *f* automatique.

laundry ['lɔːndrɪ] *n* (*place*) blanchisserie *f*; (*clothes*) linge *m*.

lava ['lɑːvə] *n Geol* lave *f*.

lavatory ['lævətrɪ] *n* cabinets *mpl*.
lavender ['lævɪndər] *n* lavande *f*.
lavish ['lævɪʃ] *a* prodigue (**with** de); (*helping, meal*) généreux; (*house*) somptueux ▮ *vt* prodiguer (**on s.o.** à qn).
law [lɔː] *n* (*rule, rules*) loi *f*; (*study, profession*) droit *m*; **court of l., l. court** cour *f* de justice; **l. and order** l'ordre public; **l. student** étudiant, -ante *mf* en droit. ●**lawful** *a* (*action, age etc*) légal. ●**lawless** *a* (*country*) anarchique.
lawn [lɔːn] *n* pelouse *f*, gazon *m*; **l. mower** tondeuse *f* (à gazon); **l. tennis** tennis *m* (sur gazon).
lawsuit ['lɔːsuːt] *n* procès *m*.
lawyer ['lɔːjər] *n* (*in court*) avocat *m*; (*for wills, sales*) notaire *m*; (*legal expert*) juriste *m*.
lax [læks] *a* (*person*) négligent; (*discipline*) relâché; **to be l. in doing sth** négliger de faire qch.
laxative ['læksətɪv] *n* laxatif *m*.
lay[1] [leɪ] *a* (*non-religious*) laïque; **l. person** profane *mf*. ●**layman** *n* (*pl* **-men**) (*non-specialist*) profane *mf*.
lay[2] [leɪ] (*pt & pp* **laid**) **1** *vt* (*put down*) poser; (*blanket*) étendre (**over** sur); (*trap*) tendre; (*money*) miser (**on** sur); (*accusation*) porter; **to l. the table** mettre la table; **to l. bare** mettre à nu; **to l. waste** ravager; **to l. s.o. open to** exposer qn à; **to l. one's hands on** mettre la main sur.
2 *vt* (*egg*) pondre.
lay[3] [leɪ] *pt of* **lie**[1].
layabout ['leɪəbaʊt] *n Fam* fainéant, -ante *mf*. ●**lay-by** *n* (*pl* **-bys**) *Aut* aire *f* de stationnement *or* de repos. ●**layout** *n* disposition *f*; *Typ* mise *f* en pages.
lay down *vt* (*put down*) poser; (*arms*) déposer; (*condition*) (im)poser; **to l. down the law** faire la loi (**to** à) **to lay into** *vt Fam* attaquer **to lay off** *vt* (*worker*) licencier ▮ *vi* (*stop*) *Fam* arrêter; **l. off!** (*don't touch*) *Fam* pas touche! **to lay on** *vt* (*install*) installer; (*supply*) fournir **to l. out** *vt* (*garden*) dessiner; (*house*) concevoir; (*prepare*) préparer; (*display*) disposer; (*money*) *Fam* mettre (**on** dans); **to be laid up** (*in bed*) être alité.
layer ['leɪər] *n* couche *f*.
layman ['leɪmən] *n see* **lay**[1].
laze [leɪz] *vi* **to l. (about** *or* **around)** paresser.
lazy ['leɪzɪ] *a* (**-ier, -iest**) (*person etc*) paresseux. ●**lazybones** *n Fam* paresseux, -euse *mf*.
lb *abbr* (*libra*) = **pound** (*weight*).
lead[1] [liːd] *vt* (*pt & pp* **led**) (*guide, take*) mener, conduire (**to** à); (*team, government etc*) diriger; (*life*) mener; **to l. s.o. in/out**/*etc* faire entrer/sortir/*etc* qn; **to l. s.o. to do** (*cause*) amener qn à faire; **to l. the way** montrer le chemin; **easily led** influençable; **to l. s.o. away** *or* **off** emmener (qn); **to l. s.o. back** ramener qn.
▮ *vi* (*of street, door etc*) mener, conduire (**to** à); (*in race*) être en tête; (*in match*) mener; (*go ahead*) aller devant; **to l. to** (*result in*) aboutir à; (*cause*) causer, amener; **to l. up to** (*of street etc*) conduire à, mener à; (*precede*) précéder.
▮ *n* (*distance or time ahead*) avance *f* (**over** sur); (*example*) exemple *m*; (*clue*) piste *f*; (*star part*) *Cin Th* rôle *m* principal; (*for dog*) laisse *f*; (*wire*) *El* fil *m*; **to take the l.** prendre la tête; **to be in the l.** (*in race*) être en tête; (*in match*) mener.
lead[2] [led] *n* (*metal*) plomb *m*; (*of pencil*) mine *f*; **l. pencil** crayon *m* à mine de plomb. ●**leaded** *a* (*petrol, Am gas*) au plomb. ●**lead-free** *a* (*petrol, Am gas*) sans plomb.
leader ['liːdər] *n* chef *m*; *Pol* dirigeant, -ante *mf*; (*of strike*) meneur, -euse *mf*; (*guide*) guide *m*. ●**leadership** *n* direction *f*; (*qualities*) qualités *fpl* de chef; (*leaders*) *Pol* dirigeants *mpl*.
leading ['liːdɪŋ] *a* (*main*) principal; (*important*) important; (*front*) (*runner, car etc*) de tête; **a l. figure** un personnage marquant; **the l. lady** *Cin* la vedette féminine; **l. article** (*in newspaper*) éditorial *m*.
leaf [liːf] **1** *n* (*pl* **leaves**) *Bot* feuille *f*; (*of book*) feuillet *m*; (*of table*) rallonge *f*. **2** *vi* **to l. through** (*book*) feuilleter.
leaflet ['liːflɪt] *n* prospectus *m*; (*containing instructions*) notice *f*.
league [liːg] *n* (*alliance*) ligue *f*; *Sp* championnat *m*; **in l. with** *Pej* de connivence avec.
leak [liːk] *n* (*of gas etc*) fuite *f*; (*in boat*) voie *f* d'eau ▮ *vi* (*of liquid, pipe, tap etc*) fuir; (*of ship*) faire eau ▮ *vt* (*liquid*) répandre; (*information*) *Fig* divulguer. ●**—age** *n* fuite *f*; (*amount lost*) perte *f*.
lean[1] [liːn] *a* (**-er, -est**) (*thin*) maigre; (*year*) difficile.
lean[2] [liːn] *vi* (*pt & pp* **leaned** *or* **leant** [lent]) (*of object*) pencher; (*of person*) se pencher; **to l. against/on sth** (*of person*) s'appuyer contre/sur qch; **to l. back against** s'adosser à; **to l. forward** (*of person*) se pencher (en avant); **to l. over** (*of person*) se pencher; (*of object*) pencher ▮ *vt* appuyer (*qch*) (**against** contre); **to l. one's head on/out of sth** pencher la tête sur/par qch. ●**leaning 1** *a*

penché; **l. against** appuyé contre. **2** *npl* tendances *fpl* (**towards** à). ● **lean-to** *n* (*pl* **-tos**) (*building*) appentis *m*.

leap [li:p] *n* (*jump*) bond *m*, saut *m*; (*increase*) *Fig* bond *m*; **l. year** année *f* bissextile ‖ *vi* (*pt* & *pp* **leaped** *or* **leapt** [lept]) bondir; (*of flames*) jaillir; (*of profits*) faire un bond. ● **leapfrog** *n* saute-mouton *m inv*.

learn [lɜ:n] *vt* (*pt* & *pp* **learned** *or* **learnt**) apprendre (**that** que); **to l. (how) to do** apprendre à faire ‖ *vi* apprendre; **to l. about** (*study*) étudier; (*hear about*) apprendre. ● **—ed** [-ɪd] *a* savant. ● **—ing** *n* (*of language*) apprentissage *m* (**of** de); (*knowledge*) érudition *f*. ● **learner** *n* débutant, -ante *mf*.

lease [li:s] *n* bail *m* ‖ *vt* (*house etc*) louer à bail.

leash [li:ʃ] *n* laisse *f*; **on a l.** en laisse.

least [li:st] *a* **the l.** (*smallest amount of*) le moins de; (*slightest*) le *or* la moindre; **he has the l. talent** il a le moins de talent (**of all** de tous); **the l. effort**/*etc* le moindre effort/*etc*.

‖ *n* **the l.** le moins; **at l.** du moins; (*with quantity*) au moins; **not in the l.** pas du tout.

‖ *adv* (*to work, eat etc*) le moins; (*with adjective*) le *or* la moins; **l. of all** surtout pas.

leather ['leðər] *n* cuir *m*; **(wash) l.** peau *f* de chamois.

leave [li:v] **1** *n* (*holiday, Am vacation*) congé *m*; (*consent*) & *Mil* permission *f*; **l. of absence** congé *m* exceptionnel.

2 *vt* (*pt* & *pp* **left**) (*allow to remain, forget*) laisser; (*go away from*) quitter; **to l. the table** sortir de table; **to l. s.o. in charge of s.o./sth** laisser à qn la garde de qn/qch; **to l. sth with s.o.** (*entrust*) laisser qch à qn; **to be left (over)** rester; **there's no bread**/*etc* **left** il ne reste plus de pain/*etc*; **I'll l. it to you** je m'en remets à toi; **to l. go (of)** (*release*) lâcher; **to l. behind** (*not take*) laisser; (*in race, at school*) distancer; **to l. off** (*lid*) ne pas mettre; **to l. on** (*hat, gloves*) garder; **to l. out** (*forget to put*) oublier (de mettre) (*accent etc*); (*word, line*) sauter; (*exclude*) exclure.

‖ *vi* (*go away*) partir (**from** de, **for** pour); **to l. off** (*stop*) *Fam* s'arrêter. ● **leavings** *npl* restes *mpl*.

Lebanon ['lebənən] *n* Liban *m*. ● **Leba'nese** *a* & *n* libanais, -aise (*mf*).

lecture ['lektʃər] **1** *n* (*public speech*) conférence *f*; (*as part of series*) *Univ* cours *m* (magistral) ‖ *vi* faire une conférence *or* un cours. **2** *vt* (*scold*) faire la morale à ‖ *n* (*scolding*) sermon *m*. ● **lecturer** *n* conférencier, -ière *mf*; *Univ* professeur *m*.

led [led] *pt* & *pp of* **lead**[1].

ledge [ledʒ] *n* (*on wall, window*) rebord *m*.

ledger ['ledʒər] *n Com* grand livre *m*.

leek [li:k] *n* poireau *m*.

leer [lɪər] *vi* **to l. (at)** lorgner ‖ *n* regard *m* sournois.

leeway ['li:weɪ] *n* (*freedom*) liberté *f* d'action; (*safety margin*) marge *f* de sécurité.

left[1] [left] *pt* & *pp of* **leave 2** ‖ *a* **l. luggage office** consigne *f*. ● **leftovers** *npl* restes *mpl*.

left[2] [left] *a* (*side, hand etc*) gauche ‖ *adv* à gauche ‖ *n* gauche *f*; **on** *or* **to the l.** à gauche (**of** de). ● **l.-hand** *a* à *or* de gauche; **on the l.-hand side** à gauche (**of** de). ● **l.-'handed** *a* (*person*) gaucher. ● **l.-wing** *a Pol* de gauche.

leg [leg] *n* jambe *f*; (*of dog, bird etc*) patte *f*; (*of table*) pied *m*; (*of journey*) étape *f*; **l. (of chicken)** cuisse *f* de poulet; **l. of lamb** gigot *m* d'agneau; **to pull s.o.'s l.** (*make fun of*) mettre qn en boîte. ● **l.-room** *n* place *f* pour les jambes.

legacy ['legəsɪ] *n Jur* & *Fig* legs *m*.

legal ['li:g(ə)l] *a* (*lawful*) légal; (*affairs, adviser*) juridique; **l. aid** assistance *f* judiciaire; **l. expert** juriste *m*; **l. proceedings** procès *m*. ● **legalize** *vt* légaliser. ● **legally** *adv* légalement.

legend ['ledʒənd] *n* (*story, inscription*) légende *f*. ● **legendary** *a* légendaire.

leggings ['legɪŋz] *npl* jambières *fpl*.

legible ['ledʒəb(ə)l] *a* lisible. ● **legibly** *adv* lisiblement.

legion ['li:dʒən] *n Mil* & *Fig* légion *f*.

legislation [ledʒɪs'leɪʃ(ə)n] *n* (*laws*) législation *f*; **(piece of) l.** loi *f*. ● **legislative** ['ledʒɪslətɪv] *a* législatif.

legitimate [lɪ'dʒɪtɪmət] *a* (*reason, child etc*) légitime.

legless ['legləs] *a* (*drunk*) *Fam* (complètement) bourré.

leg-room ['legru:m] *n see* **leg**.

leisure ['leʒər, *Am* 'li:ʒər] *n* **l. (time)** loisirs *mpl*; **l. activities** loisirs *mpl*; **l. centre** centre *m* de loisirs; **at (one's) l.** à tête reposée. ● **—ly** *a* (*walk, occupation*) peu fatigant; (*meal, life*) calme; **at a l. pace** sans se presser.

lemon ['lemən] *n* citron *m*; **l. drink, l. squash** citronnade *f*; **l. tea** thé *m* au citron. ● **lemo'nade** *n* (*fizzy*) limonade *f*; (*still*) *Am* citronnade *f*.

lend [lend] *vt* (*pt* & *pp* **lent**) prêter (**to** à); (*charm, colour etc*) *Fig* donner (**to** à). ● **—er** *n* prêteur, -euse *mf*.

length [leŋθ] *n* longueur *f*; (*section of rope, pipe etc*) morceau *m*; (*of road*) tronçon *m*; (*of cloth*) métrage *m*; (*duration*) durée *f*; **l. of time** temps *m*; **at l.** (*at last*) enfin; (*in detail*) dans le détail. ●**lengthen** *vt* allonger; (*in time*) prolonger. ●**lengthy** *a* (**-ier, -iest**) long.

lenient ['li:nɪənt] *a* indulgent (**to** envers). ●**leniently** *adv* avec indulgence.

lens [lenz] *n* lentille *f*; (*in spectacles*) verre *m*; (*of camera*) objectif *m*.

Lent [lent] *n Rel* Carême *m*.

lentil ['lent(ə)l] *n Bot Culin* lentille *f*.

Leo ['li:əʊ] *n* (*sign*) le Lion.

leopard ['lepəd] *n* léopard *m*.

leotard ['li:ətɑ:d] *n* collant *m* (*de danse*).

leper ['lepər] *n* lépreux, -euse *mf*. ●**leprosy** *n* lèpre *f*.

lesbian ['lezbɪən] *n* lesbienne *f*.

less [les] *a* & *n* moins (de) (**than** que); **l. time/***etc* moins de temps/*etc*; **she has l. (than you)** elle en a moins (que toi); **l. than a kilo/ten/***etc* (*with quantity, number*) moins d'un kilo/de dix/*etc*.
▮*adv* (*to sleep, know etc*) moins (**than** que); **l. (often)** moins souvent; **l. and l.** de moins en moins; **one l.** un(e) de moins.
▮*prep* moins; **l. six francs** moins six francs.

-less [ləs] *suff* sans; **childless** sans enfants.

lessen ['les(ə)n] *vti* diminuer.

lesser ['lesər] *a* moindre ▮*n* **the l. of** le *or* la moindre de.

lesson ['les(ə)n] *n* leçon *f*; **an English l.** une leçon *or* un cours d'anglais.

lest [lest] *conj Lit* de peur que (+ ne + *sub*).

let[1] [let] **1** *vt* (*pt* & *pp* **let**, *pres p* **letting**) (*allow*) laisser (**s.o. do** qn faire); **to l. s.o. have sth** donner qch à qn. **2** *v aux* **l. us eat/go/***etc*, **l.'s eat/go/***etc* mangeons/partons/*etc*; **l.'s go for a stroll** allons nous promener; **l. him come** qu'il vienne.

let[2] [let] *vt* (*pt* & *pp* **let**, *pres p* **letting**) **to l. (out)** (*house, room etc*) louer.

let down *vt* (*lower*) baisser; (*hair*) dénouer; (*dress*) rallonger; (*tyre, Am tire*) dégonfler; **to l. s.o. down** décevoir qn; **the car l. me down** la voiture est tombée en panne. **to let in** *vt* (*person, dog*) faire entrer; (*noise, light*) laisser entrer; **to l. s.o. in on sth** mettre qn au courant de qch; **to l. oneself in for trouble** s'attirer des ennuis **to let off** *vt* (*firework, gun*) faire partir; **to l. s.o. off** laisser partir qn; (*not punish*) ne pas punir qn; (*clear of crime*) disculper qn; **to l. s.o. off doing** dispenser qn de faire **to let on** *vi* **not to l. on** *Fam* ne rien dire; **to l. on that** *Fam* (*admit*) avouer que **to let out** *vt* faire *or* laisser sortir; (*prisoner*) relâcher; (*cry, secret*) laisser échapper; (*skirt*) élargir; **to l. s.o. out (of the house)** ouvrir la porte à qn **to let up** *vi* (*of rain etc*) s'arrêter.

letdown ['letdaʊn] *n* déception *f*.

lethal ['li:θ(ə)l] *a* (*blow etc*) mortel; (*weapon*) meurtrier.

lethargic [lə'θɑ:dʒɪk] *a* léthargique.

letter ['letər] *n* (*message, part of word*) lettre *f*; **l. bomb** lettre *f* piégée; **l. writer** correspondant, -ante *mf*. ●**letterbox** *n* boîte *f* aux *or* à lettres. ●**lettering** *n* (*letters*) lettres *fpl*.

lettuce ['letɪs] *n* laitue *f*, salade *f*.

letup ['letʌp] *n* arrêt *m*, répit *m*.

leuk(a)emia [lu:'ki:mɪə] *n* leucémie *f*.

level ['lev(ə)l] **1** *n* niveau *m*; (*rate*) taux *m* ▮*a* (*surface*) plat; (*object on surface*) d'aplomb; (*equal in score*) à égalité (**with** avec); (*in height*) au même niveau (**with** que); **l. crossing** *Rail* passage *m* à niveau ▮*vt* (**-ll-**, *Am* **-l-**) (*surface, differences*) aplanir, niveler; (*building*) raser; (*gun*) braquer (**at** sur); (*accusation*) lancer (**at** contre) ▮*vi* **to l. off** *or* **out** (*stabilize*) se stabiliser.
2 *n* **on the l.** *Fam* (*honest*) honnête; (*frankly*) honnêtement ▮*vi* (**-ll-**, *Am* **-l-**) **to l. with s.o.** *Fam* être franc avec qn. ●**level-headed** *a* équilibré.

lever ['li:vər, *Am* 'levər] *n* levier *m*.

levy ['levɪ] *vt* (*tax*) lever ▮*n* (*tax*) impôt *m*.

lewd [lu:d] *a* (**-er, -est**) obscène.

liable ['laɪəb(ə)l] *a* **l. to** (*dizziness etc*) sujet à; (*fine, tax*) passible de; **l. to do** susceptible de faire; **l. for** responsable de. ●**lia'bility** *n* responsabilité *f* (**for** de); (*disadvantage*) handicap *m*; *pl* (*debts*) dettes *fpl*.

liaise [lɪ'eɪz] *vi* travailler en liaison (**with** avec). ●**liaison** *n* (*contact*) & *Mil* liaison *f*.

liar ['laɪər] *n* menteur, -euse *mf*.

libel ['laɪb(ə)l] *vt* (**-ll-**, *Am* **-l-**) diffamer (par écrit) ▮*n* diffamation *f*.

liberal ['lɪbərəl] *a* (*open-minded*) & *Pol* libéral; (*generous*) généreux (**with** de) ▮*n* *Pol* libéral, -ale *mf*.

liberate ['lɪbəreɪt] *vt* libérer. ●**liberation** [-'reɪʃ(ə)n] *n* libération *f*.

liberty ['lɪbətɪ] *n* liberté *f*; **at l. to do** libre de faire; **what a l.!** *Fam* quel culot!; **to take liberties with s.o.** se permettre des familiarités avec qn.

Libra ['li:brə] *n* (*sign*) la Balance.

library ['laɪbrərɪ] *n* bibliothèque *f*. ●**li'brarian** *n* bibliothécaire *mf*.

libretto [lɪ'bretəʊ] *n* (*pl* **-os**) *Mus* livret *m*.

Libya ['lɪbjə] *n* Libye *f*. ● **Libyan** *a* & *n* libyen, -enne (*mf*).
lice [laɪs] *see* **louse.**
licence, *Am* **license** ['laɪsəns] *n* (*document*) permis *m*, autorisation *f*; (*for driving*) permis *m*; *Com* licence *f*; **pilot's l.** brevet *m* de pilote; **l. fee** *Rad TV* redevance *f*; **l. plate/number** *Aut* plaque *f*/numéro *m* d'immatriculation.
license ['laɪsəns] *vt* accorder un permis *or* une licence à, autoriser; **licensed premises** établissement *m* qui a une licence de débit de boissons.
lick [lɪk] *vt* lécher; (*defeat*) *Fam* écraser; **to be licked** (*by problem*) *Fam* être dépassé. ● **—ing** *n* (*defeat*) *Fam* déculottée *f*.
licorice ['lɪkərɪʃ, -rɪs] *n Am* réglisse *f*.
lid [lɪd] *n* **1** (*of box etc*) couvercle *m*. **2** (*of eye*) paupière *f*.
lie[1] [laɪ] *vi* (*pt* **lay,** *pp* **lain,** *pres p* **lying**) (*in flat position*) s'allonger, s'étendre; (*remain*) rester; (*be*) être; (*in grave*) reposer; **to be lying** (*on the grass etc*) être allongé *or* étendu; **he lay asleep** il dormait; **here lies** (*on tomb*) ci-gît; **the problem lies in** le problème réside dans.
lie[2] [laɪ] *vi* (*pt* & *pp* **lied,** *pres p* **lying**) (*tell lies*) mentir ▮ *n* mensonge *m*; **to give the l. to sth** (*show as untrue*) démentir qch.
lie about *or* **around** *vi* (*of objects, person*) traîner **to lie down** *vi* s'allonger, se coucher; **lying down** allongé, couché **to lie in** *vi Fam* faire la grasse matinée. ● **lie-down** *n* **to have a l.-down = lie down.** ● **lie-in** *n* **to have a l.-in = lie in.**
lieutenant [lef'tenənt, *Am* luː'tenənt] *n* lieutenant *m*.
life [laɪf] *n* (*pl* **lives**) vie *f*; (*of battery*) durée *f* (de vie); **to come to l.** (*of party etc*) s'animer; **loss of l.** perte *f* en vies humaines; **l. insurance** assurance-vie *f*; **l. jacket** gilet *m* de sauvetage; **l. peer** pair *m* à vie; **l. preserver** *Am* ceinture *f* de sauvetage; **l. span** durée *f* de vie; **l. style** style *m* de vie.
lifebelt ['laɪfbelt] *n* ceinture *f* de sauvetage. ● **lifeboat** *n* canot *m* de sauvetage. ● **lifebuoy** *n* bouée *f* de sauvetage. ● **lifeguard** *n* maître nageur *m* (sauveteur). ● **lifeless** *a* sans vie. ● **lifelike** *a* qui semble vivant. ● **lifelong** *a* de toute sa vie; (*friend*) de toujours. ● **lifesize(d)** *a* grandeur nature *inv*. ● **lifetime** *n* vie *f*; *Fig* éternité *f*; **in my l.** de mon vivant; **a once-in-a-l. experience** l'expérience de votre vie.
lift [lɪft] *vt* lever; (*ban, siege*) *Fig* lever; (*idea etc*) *Fig* voler (**from** à); **to l. down** *or* **off** (*take down*) descendre (**from** de); **to l. out** (*take out*) sortir; **to l. up** (*arm, object*) lever.
▮ *vi* (*of fog*) se lever; **to l. off** (*of space vehicle*) décoller.
▮ *n* (*elevator*) ascenseur *m*; **to give s.o. a l.** emmener qn (en voiture) (**to** à). ● **lift-off** *n* (*of space vehicle*) décollage *m*.
ligament ['lɪgəmənt] *n* ligament *m*.
light[1] [laɪt] *n* lumière *f*; (*on vehicle*) feu *m*; (*vehicle headlight*) phare *m*; **by the l. of** à la lumière de; **in the l. of** (*considering*) à la lumière de; **against the l.** à contre-jour; **to bring to l.** mettre en lumière; **to throw l. on** (*matter*) éclaircir; **do you have a l.?** (*for cigarette*) est-ce que vous avez du feu?; **to set l. to** mettre le feu à; **l. bulb** ampoule *f* (électrique).
▮ *vt* (*pt* & *pp* **lit** *or* **lighted**) (*match, fire, gas*) allumer; **to l. (up)** (*room*) éclairer; (*cigarette*) allumer
▮ *vi* **to l. up** (*of face, sky*) s'illuminer. ● **lighting** *n* (*lights*) éclairage *m*.
light[2] [laɪt] *a* (*bright, not dark*) clair; **a l. green jacket** une veste vert clair.
light[3] [laɪt] *a* (*in weight, strength etc*) léger; **l. rain** pluie *f* fine; **to travel l.** voyager avec peu de bagages. ● **l.-'headed** *a* (*giddy, foolish*) étourdi. ● **l.-'hearted** *a* gai.
lighten ['laɪt(ə)n] *vt* **to l. a weight** *or* **a load** diminuer un poids.
lighter ['laɪtər] *n* (*for cigarettes etc*) briquet *m*; (*for cooker, Am stove*) allume-gaz *m inv*.
lighthouse ['laɪthaʊs] *n* phare *m*.
lightly ['laɪtlɪ] *adv* légèrement. ● **lightness** *n* légèreté *f*.
lightning ['laɪtnɪŋ] *n* (*flashes*) éclairs *mpl*; (*charge*) la foudre; **(flash of) l.** éclair *m*; **l. conductor** *or Am* **rod** paratonnerre *m*.
lightweight ['laɪtweɪt] *a* (*cloth, shoes etc*) léger.
like[1] [laɪk] *prep* comme; **l. this** comme ça; **what's he l.?** comment est-il?; **to be** *or* **look l.** ressembler à; **what was the book l.?** comment as-tu trouvé le livre?; **what does it smell l.?** cela sent quoi?; **I have one l. it** j'en ai un pareil.
▮ *adv* **nothing l. as big**/*etc* loin d'être aussi grand/*etc*.
▮ *conj* (*as*) *Fam* comme; **do l. I do** fais comme moi.
▮ *n* **... and the l.** ... et ainsi de suite; **the likes of you** des gens de ton acabit.
▮ *a* (*alike*) semblable, pareil.
like[2] [laɪk] *vt* aimer (bien) (**to do, doing** faire); **I l. him** je l'aime bien, il me plaît; **she likes it here** elle se plaît ici; **to l. sth/s.o. best** aimer mieux qch/qn, aimer qch/qn le plus; **I'd l. to come** je voudrais (bien) *or* j'aimer-

ais (bien) venir; **I'd l. a kilo of apples** je voudrais un kilo de pommes; **would you l. an apple?** voulez-vous une pomme?; **if you l.** si vous voulez. • **liking** *n* **a l. for** (*person*) de la sympathie pour; (*thing*) du goût pour; **to my l.** à mon goût.

likeable ['laɪkəb(ə)l] *a* sympathique.

likely ['laɪklɪ] *a* (**-ier, -iest**) (*result etc*) probable; (*excuse*) vraisemblable; **a l. excuse!** *Iron* belle excuse!; **it's l. (that) she'll come, she's l. to come** il est probable qu'elle viendra; **he's not l. to come** il ne risque pas de venir.

▌*adv* **very l.** très probablement; **not l.!** pas question! • **likelihood** *n* probabilité *f*; **there isn't much l. that** il y a peu de chances que (+ *sub*).

liken ['laɪkən] *vt* comparer (**to** à).

likeness ['laɪknɪs] *n* ressemblance *f*; **a family l.** un air de famille.

likewise ['laɪkwaɪz] *adv* (*similarly*) de même, pareillement.

lilac ['laɪlək] *n* lilas *m* ▌*a* (*colour*) lilas *inv*.

Lilo® ['laɪləʊ] *n* (*pl* **-os**) matelas *m* pneumatique.

lily ['lɪlɪ] *n* lis *m*, lys *m*; **l. of the valley** muguet *m*.

limb [lɪm] *n* (*of body*) membre *m*.

limber ['lɪmbər] *vi* **to l. up** faire des exercices d'assouplissement.

lime [laɪm] *n* **1** (*fruit*) citron *m* vert. **2** (*tree*) tilleul *m*. **3** (*substance*) chaux *f*.

limelight ['laɪmlaɪt] *n* **in the l.** (*glare of publicity*) en vedette.

limit ['lɪmɪt] *n* limite *f*; **that's the l.!** *Fam* c'est le comble!; **within limits** dans une certaine limite ▌*vt* limiter (**to** à); **to l. oneself to doing** se borner à faire. • **—ed** *a* (*restricted*) limité; **l. company** *Com* société *f* à responsabilité limitée; **(public) l. company** (*with shareholders*) société *f* anonyme; **to a l. degree** jusqu'à un certain point. • **limitation** [-'teɪʃ(ə)n] *n* limitation *f*.

limousine [lɪmə'ziːn] *n* (*airport etc shuttle*) *Am* voiture-navette *f*; (*car*) limousine *f*.

limp [lɪmp] **1** *vi* (*of person*) boiter ▌*n* **to have a l.** boiter. **2** *a* (**-er, -est**) (*soft*) mou (*f* molle); (*flabby*) flasque.

linchpin ['lɪntʃpɪn] *n* (*person*) pivot *m*.

linctus ['lɪŋktəs] *n* *Med* sirop *m* (contre la toux).

line[1] [laɪn] *n* ligne *f*; (*of poem*) vers *m*; (*wrinkle*) ride *f*; (*track*) voie *f*; (*rope*) corde *f*; (*row*) rangée *f*, ligne *f*; (*of vehicles, people*) file *f*; (*business*) métier *m*; **one's lines** (*of actor*) son texte *m*; **on the l.** (*phone*) au bout du fil; (*at risk*) (*job etc*) menacé; **hold the l.!** *Tel* ne quittez pas!; **the hot l.** *Tel* le téléphone rouge; **to stand in l.** *Am* faire la queue; **to step** *or* **get out of l.** (*misbehave*) faire une incartade; **in l. with** conforme à; **he's in l. for** (*promotion etc*) il doit recevoir; **to drop a l.** (*send a letter*) *Fam* envoyer un mot (**to** à); **where do we draw the l.?** où fixer les limites?

▌*vt* **to l. the street** (*of trees*) border la rue; (*of people*) faire la haie le long de la rue; **to l. up** (*children, objects*) aligner; (*arrange*) organiser; (*get ready*) préparer; **to have sth lined up** (*in mind*) avoir qch en vue; **lined face** visage *m* ridé; **lined paper** papier *m* réglé.

▌*vi* **to l. up** s'aligner; (*queue up*) *Am* faire la queue. • **line-up** *n* (*row*) file *f*; (*of TV programmes*) programme(s) *m(pl)*; (*of TV guests*) invités *mpl*.

line[2] [laɪn] *vt* (*clothes*) doubler; **to l. one's pockets** *Fig* se remplir les poches. • **lining** *n* (*of clothes*) doublure *f*.

linen ['lɪnɪn] *n* (*sheets etc*) linge *m*; (*material*) (toile *f* de) lin *m*; **l. basket** panier *m* à linge.

liner ['laɪnər] *n* **1 (ocean) l.** paquebot *m*. **2 (dust)bin l.**, *Am* **garbage can l.** sac *m* poubelle.

linesman ['laɪnzmən] *n* (*pl* **-men**) *Fb etc* juge *m* de touche.

linger ['lɪŋgər] *vi* **to l. (on)** (*of person*) s'attarder; (*of smell, memory*) persister; (*of doubt*) subsister.

lingo ['lɪŋgəʊ] *n* (*pl* **-oes**) *Hum Fam* jargon *m*.

linguist ['lɪŋgwɪst] *n* linguiste *mf*; **to be a good l.** être doué pour les langues. • **lin'guistic** *a* linguistique. • **lin'guis-tics** *n* linguistique *f*.

link [lɪŋk] *vt* (*connect*) relier (**to** à); (*relate, associate*) lier (**to** à); **to l. up** relier ▌*vi* **to l. up** (*of companies, countries etc*) s'associer; (*of computers*) se connecter; (*of roads*) se rejoindre ▌*n* (*connection*) lien *m*; (*of chain*) maillon *m*; (*by road, rail*) liaison *f*.

lino ['laɪnəʊ] *n* (*pl* **-os**) lino *m*.

lint [lɪnt] *n* *Med* tissu *m* ouaté; (*fluff*) peluche(s) *f(pl)*.

lion ['laɪən] *n* lion *m*; **l. cub** lionceau *m*; **l. tamer** dompteur, -euse *mf* de lions. • **lioness** *n* lionne *f*.

lip [lɪp] *n* lèvre *f*; (*rim*) bord *m*. • **l.-read** *vi* (*pt & pp* **-read** [red]) lire sur les lèvres. • **lipstick** *n* bâton *m* de rouge; (*substance*) rouge *m* à lèvres.

liqueur [lɪ'kjʊər, *Am* lɪ'kɜːr] *n* liqueur *f*.

liquid ['lɪkwɪd] *n* & *a* liquide (*m*).

liquidate ['lɪkwɪdeɪt] *vt* (*debt*, *Fam person*) liquider.

liquidizer ['lɪkwɪdaɪzər] *n* mixer *m*. ● **liquidize** *vt* passer au mixer.

liquor ['lɪkər] *n* alcool *m*; **l. store** *Am* magasin *m* de vins et de spiritueux.

liquorice ['lɪkərɪʃ, -rɪs] *n* réglisse *f*.

lira, *pl* **lire** ['lɪərə, 'lɪəreɪ] *n* (*currency*) lire *f*.

lisp [lɪsp] *vi* zézayer ▌ *n* **to have a l.** zézayer.

list [lɪst] *n* liste *f* ▌ *vt* (*one's possessions etc*) faire la liste de; (*names*) mettre sur la liste; (*name one by one*) énumérer; **listed building** monument *m* classé.

listen ['lɪsən] *vi* écouter; **to l. to** écouter; **to l. (out) for** guetter (le bruit *or* les cris *etc* de). ● **—er** *n* (*to radio*) auditeur, -trice *mf*; **to be a good l.** savoir écouter.

listless ['lɪstləs] *a* apathique.

lit [lɪt] *pt* & *pp of* **light**[1].

litany ['lɪtənɪ] *n Rel* litanies *fpl*.

liter ['liːtər] *n Am* litre *m*.

literal ['lɪtərəl] *a* littéral; (*not exaggerated*) réel. ● **—ly** *adv* littéralement; (*really*) réellement; **he took it l.** il l'a pris au pied de la lettre.

literate ['lɪtərət] *a* qui sait lire et écrire. ● **literacy** *n* capacité *f* de lire et d'écrire; (*of country*) degré *m* d'alphabétisation.

literature ['lɪt(ə)rɪtʃər] *n* littérature *f*; (*pamphlets etc*) documentation *f*. ● **literary** *a* littéraire.

lithe [laɪð] *a* agile, souple.

litigation [lɪtɪ'geɪʃ(ə)n] *n Jur* litige *m*.

litre ['liːtər] (*Am* **liter**) *n* litre *m*.

litter ['lɪtər] **1** *n* (*rubbish*, *Am garbage*) détritus *m*; (*papers*) papiers *mpl*; **l. basket** *or* **bin** boîte *f* à ordures ▌ *vt* **to l. (with papers)** (*street etc*) laisser traîner des papiers dans; **a street littered with** une rue jonchée de. **2** *n* (*young animals*) portée *f*.

little[1] ['lɪt(ə)l] **1** *a* (*small*) petit; **the l. ones** les petits; **a l. bit** un (petit) peu.

little[2] ['lɪt(ə)l] **1** *a* & *n* (*not much*) peu (de); **l. time/money/***etc* peu de temps/d'argent/*etc*; **I've l. left** il m'en reste peu; **she eats l.** elle mange peu; **to have l. to say** avoir peu de chose à dire; **as l. as possible** le moins possible.

2 *a* & *n* **a l.** (*some*) un peu (de); **a l. money/time/***etc* un peu d'argent/de temps/*etc*; **I have a l.** j'en ai un peu; **the l. that I have** le peu que j'ai.

▌ *adv* (*somewhat, rather*) peu; **a l. heavy/***etc* un peu lourd/*etc*; **to work/***etc* **a l.** travailler/*etc* un peu; **l. by l.** peu à peu.

live[1] [lɪv] *vi* vivre; (*reside*) habiter, vivre; **where do you l.?** où habitez-vous? ▌ *vt* (*life*) mener, vivre; **to l. it up** *Fam* mener la grande vie.

live[2] [laɪv] **1** *a* (*electric wire*) sous tension; (*switch*) mal isolé; (*plugged in*) (*appliance*) branché; (*alive*) (*animal etc*) vivant; (*ammunition*) réel; **a real l. king** un roi en chair et en os. **2** *a* & *adv Rad TV* en direct; **a l. broadcast** une émission en direct; **a l. audience** le *or* un public.

live down *vt* faire oublier (avec le temps) **to live off** *or* **on** *vt* (*eat*) vivre de; (*sponge on*) vivre aux crochets de (*qn*) **to live on** *vi* (*of memory etc*) survivre **to live through** *vt* (*experience*) vivre; (*survive*) survivre à **to live up to** *vt* (*s.o.'s expectations*) se montrer à la hauteur de .

livelihood ['laɪvlɪhʊd] *n* **my l.** mon gagne-pain; **to earn one's l.** gagner sa vie.

lively ['laɪvlɪ] *a* (**-ier, -iest**) (*person*, *style*) vif, vivant; (*street*) vivant; (*interest*, *mind*) vif; (*day*) mouvementé; (*discussion*) animé.

liven ['laɪv(ə)n] *vt* **to l. up** (*person*) égayer; (*party*) animer ▌ *vi* **to l. up** (*of person, party*) s'animer.

liver ['lɪvər] *n* foie *m*.

livestock ['laɪvstɒk] *n* bétail *m*.

livid ['lɪvɪd] *a* (*angry*) furieux; (*blue-grey*) (*complexion*) livide.

living ['lɪvɪŋ] **1** *a* (*alive*) vivant; **not a l. soul** (*nobody*) personne; **within l. memory** de mémoire d'homme; **the l.** les vivants *mpl*. **2** *n* (*livelihood*) vie *f*; **to make** *or* **earn a** *or* **one's l.** gagner sa vie; **to work for a l.** travailler pour vivre; **the cost of l.** le coût de la vie; **l. conditions** conditions *fpl* de vie. ● **living room** *n* salle *f* de séjour.

lizard ['lɪzəd] *n* lézard *m*.

llama ['lɑːmə] *n* (*animal*) lama *m*.

load [ləʊd] *n* (*object carried*, *burden*) charge *f*; (*strain*, *weight*) poids *m*; **a l. of, loads of** (*people*, *money etc*) *Fam* un tas de, énormément de.

▌ *vt* (*truck*, *gun etc*) charger (**with** de); **to l. s.o. down with** charger qn de; **to l. up** (*car*, *ship etc*) charger (**with** de).

▌ *vi* **to l. (up)** charger la voiture, le navire *etc*. ● **loaded** *a* (*gun*, *vehicle etc*) chargé; (*rich*) *Fam* plein aux as; **l. (down) with** (*debts*) accablé de.

loaf [ləʊf] **1** *n* (*pl* **loaves**) pain *m*; **French l.** baguette *f*. **2** *vi* **to l. (about)** fainéanter. ● **—er** *n* fainéant, -ante *mf*.

loan [ləʊn] *n* (*money lent*) prêt *m*; (*money borrowed*) emprunt *m*; **to get a l.** faire un emprunt; **on l. from** prêté par; **(out) on l.** (*book*) sorti ▌ *vt* (*lend*) prêter (**to** à).

loath [ləʊθ] *a* **l. to do** *Lit* peu disposé à faire.

loathe [ləʊð] *vt* détester (**doing** faire).
lobby ['lɒbɪ] **1** *n* (*of hotel*) vestibule *m*, hall *m*; *Th* foyer *m*. **2** *n Pol* groupe *m* de pression, lobby *m* ‖ *vt* faire pression sur.
lobe [ləʊb] *n* (*of ear*) lobe *m*.
lobster ['lɒbstər] *n* homard *m*; (*spiny*) langouste *f*.
local ['ləʊk(ə)l] *a* local; (*regional*) régional; (*of the neighbourhood*) du *or* de quartier; (*of the region*) de la région; **are you l.?** êtes-vous du coin *or* d'ici?; **a l. phone call** (*within town*) une communication urbaine ‖ *n* (*pub*) *Fam* bistrot *m* du coin, pub *m*; **she's a l.** elle est du coin; **the locals** les gens du coin.
locality [ləʊ'kælətɪ] *n* (*neighbourhood*) environs *mpl*; (*region*) région *f*; (*place*) lieu *m*.
locally ['ləʊkəlɪ] *adv* dans le coin; (*around here*) par ici.
locate [ləʊ'keɪt] *vt* (*find*) trouver, repérer; (*pain, noise, leak*) localiser; **to be located** (*situated*) être situé. ●**location** [-ʃ(ə)n] *n* (*site*) emplacement *m*; **on l.** *Cin* en extérieur.
lock [lɒk] **1** *vt* (*door, car etc*) fermer à clef ‖ *vi* fermer à clef ‖ *n* (*on door etc*) serrure *f*; **(anti-theft) l.** *Aut* antivol *m*; **under l. and key** sous clef. **2** *n* (*on canal*) écluse *f*. **3** *n* (*of hair*) mèche *f*.
lock away *vt* (*prisoner, jewels etc*) enfermer **to lock in** *vt* (*person*) enfermer; **to lock s.o. in sth** enfermer qn dans qch **to l. out** *vt* (*person*) (*accidentally*) enfermer dehors **to lock up** *vt* (*house, car etc*) fermer à clef; (*prisoner, jewels etc*) enfermer ‖ *vi* fermer à clef.
locker ['lɒkər] *n* casier *m*; (*for luggage*) casier *m* de consigne automatique; (*for clothes*) vestiaire *m* (métallique); **l. room** *Sp Am* vestiaire *m*.
locket ['lɒkɪt] *n* (*jewel*) médaillon *m*.
locksmith ['lɒksmɪθ] *n* serrurier *m*.
loco ['ləʊkəʊ] *a Sl* cinglé, fou (*f* folle).
locomotion [ləʊkə'məʊʃ(ə)n] *n* locomotion *f*. ●**locomotive** *n* locomotive *f*.
locum ['ləʊkəm] *n* (*doctor*) remplaçant, -ante *mf*.
locust ['ləʊkəst] *n* criquet *m*, sauterelle *f*.
lodge [lɒdʒ] **1** *vt* (*person*) loger; **to l. a complaint** porter plainte ‖ *vi* (*of bullet*) se loger (**in** dans); **to be lodging** (*accommodated*) être logé (**with** chez). **2** *n* (*house*) pavillon *m* de gardien; (*of porter*) loge *f*.
lodger ['lɒdʒər] *n* (*room and meals*) pensionnaire *mf*; (*room only*) locataire *mf*.
lodgings ['lɒdʒɪŋz] *npl* (*flat, Am apartment*) logement *m*; (*room*) chambre *f*; **in l.** en meublé.
loft [lɒft] *n* (*attic*) grenier *m*.
lofty ['lɒftɪ] *a* (**-ier, -iest**) (*high, noble*) élevé; (*proud, superior*) hautain.
log [lɒg] **1** *n* (*tree trunk*) tronc *m* d'arbre; (*for fire*) bûche *f*; **l. fire** feu *m* de bois. **2** *vt* (**-gg-**) (*facts*) noter. ●**logbook** *n Nau* journal *m* de bord; *Av* carnet *m* de vol.
loggerheads (at) [æt'lɒgəhedz] *adv* en désaccord (**with** avec).
logic ['lɒdʒɪk] *n* logique *f*. ●**logical** *a* logique. ●**logically** *adv* logiquement.
logistics [lə'dʒɪstɪks] *n* logistique *f*.
logo ['ləʊgəʊ] *n* (*pl* **-os**) logo *m*.
loin [lɔɪn] *n* (*meat*) filet *m*.
loiter ['lɔɪtər] *vi* traîner.
loll [lɒl] *vi* (*in armchair etc*) se prélasser.
lollipop ['lɒlɪpɒp] *n* (*sweet, Am candy*) sucette *f*; (*ice*) esquimau *m*. ●**lolly** *n Fam* sucette *f*; **(ice) l.** esquimau *m*.
London ['lʌndən] *n* Londres *m or f* ‖ *a* (*taxi etc*) londonien. ●**Londoner** *n* Londonien, -ienne *mf*.
lone [ləʊn] *a* solitaire. ●**loneliness** *n* solitude *f*. ●**lonely** *a* (**-ier, -iest**) (*road, life etc*) solitaire; (*person*) seul, solitaire. ●**loner** *n* solitaire *mf*.
long[1] [lɒŋ] **1** *a* (**-er, -est**) long (*f* longue); **to be ten metres l.** avoir dix mètres de long; **to be six weeks l.** durer six semaines; **how l. is...?** quelle est la longueur de...?; (*time*) quelle est la durée de...?; **a l. time** longtemps; **in the l. run** à la longue; **l. jump** *Sp* saut *m* en longueur.
2 *adv* (*a long time*) longtemps; **l. before** longtemps avant; **has he been here l.?** il y a longtemps qu'il est ici?; **how l. ago?** il y a combien de temps?; **not l. ago** il y a peu de temps; **before l.** sous peu; **no longer** ne plus; **she no longer swims** elle ne nage plus; **a bit longer** (*to wait etc*) encore un peu; **I won't be l.** je n'en ai pas pour longtemps; **don't be l.** dépêche-toi; **all summer l.** tout l'été; **l. live the queen** vive la reine; **as l. as, so l. as** (*provided that*) pourvu que (+ *sub*); **as l. as I live** tant que je vivrai.
long[2] [lɒŋ] *vi* **to l. for sth** avoir très envie de qch; **to l. to do** avoir très envie de faire. ●**—ing** *n* désir *m*, envie *f*.
long-distance [lɒŋ'dɪstəns] *a* (*race*) de fond; (*phone call*) interurbain; (*flight*) long-courrier. ●**long'haired** *a* aux cheveux longs. ●**'long-life** *a* (*battery*) longue durée *inv*; (*milk*) longue conservation. ●**long-'playing** *a* **l.-playing record** 33 tours *m inv*. ●**'long-range** *a* (*forecast*) à long terme. ●**long'sighted** *a Med* presbyte. ●**long-'term**

a à long terme. • **long'winded** *a* (*speech*, *speaker*) verbeux.

longways ['lɒŋweɪz] *adv* en longueur.

loo [lu:] *n* **the l.** (*toilet*) *Fam* le petit coin.

look [lʊk] *n* regard *m*; (*appearance*) air *m*; **(good) looks** un beau physique; **to have a l. (at)** jeter un coup d'œil (à), regarder; **to have a l. (for)** chercher; **to have a l. (a)round** regarder; (*walk*) faire un tour; **let me have a l.** fais voir; **I like the l. of him** il me fait bonne impression.
‖ *vti* regarder; **to l. s.o. in the face** regarder qn dans les yeux; **to l. tired/happy/***etc* sembler *or* avoir l'air fatigué/heureux/*etc*; **to l. pretty/ugly** être joli/laid; **to l. one's age** faire son âge; **you l. like** *or* **as if you're tired** on dirait que tu es fatigué; **it looks like it!** c'est probable; **to l. like a child** avoir l'air d'un enfant; **to l. like an apple** avoir l'air d'être une pomme; **you l. like my brother** tu ressembles à mon frère; **it looks like rain (to me)** il me semble qu'il va pleuvoir; **what does he l. like?** comment est-il?; **to l. well** *or* **good** (*of person*) avoir bonne mine; **you l. good in that hat/***etc* ce chapeau/*etc* te va très bien; **that looks bad** (*action etc*) ça fait mauvais effet.

look after *vt* (*deal with*) s'occuper de (*qch*, *qn*); (*sick person*, *hair*) soigner; (*keep safely*) garder (**for s.o.** pour qn); **to l. after oneself** (*in health*) faire bien attention à soi; (*manage*) se débrouiller **to look around** *vt* visiter ‖ *vi* (*have a look*) regarder; (*walk round*) faire un tour **to look at** *vt* regarder; (*consider*) considérer **to look away** *vi* détourner les yeux **to look back** *vi* regarder derrière soi **to look down** *vi* baisser les yeux; (*from a height*) regarder en bas; **to l. down on** (*scornfully*) mépriser **to look for** *vt* chercher **to look forward to** *vt* (*event*) attendre avec impatience; **to l. forward to doing** avoir hâte de faire **to look in** *vi* regarder (à l'intérieur); **to l. in on s.o.** passer voir qn **to look into** *vt* examiner; (*find out about*) se renseigner sur **to look on** *vi* (*watch*) regarder ‖ *vt* (*consider*) considérer **to look out** *vi* (*be careful*) faire attention (**for** à); **to l. out for** (*seek*) chercher; **to look (out) on to** (*of window*, *house etc*) donner sur **to look over** *vt* examiner, regarder de près; (*briefly*) parcourir; (*region*, *town*) parcourir, visiter **to look round** *vt* visiter ‖ *vi* regarder; (*walk round*) faire un tour; (*look back*) se retourner **to look through** *vt* = **look over to look up** *vi* (*of person*) lever les yeux; (*into the air*) regarder en l'air; (*improve*) s'améliorer; **to l. up to s.o.** *Fig* respecter qn ‖ *vt* (*word*) chercher; **to l. s.o. up** (*visit*) passer voir qn.

-looking ['lʊkɪŋ] *suff* **pleasant-/tired-/***etc* **l.** à l'air agréable/fatigué/*etc*.

lookout ['lʊkaʊt] *n* (*high place*) observatoire *m*; (*soldier*) guetteur *m*; **l. (post)** poste *m* de guet; (*on ship*) vigie *f*; **to be on the l.** faire le guet; **to be on the l. for** guetter.

loom [lu:m] **1** *vi* **to l. (up)** (*of mountain etc*) apparaître indistinctement; (*of event etc*) paraître imminent. **2** *n Tex* métier *m* à tisser.

loony ['lu:nɪ] *n* & *a Sl* imbécile (*mf*).

loop [lu:p] *n* (*in river etc*) & *Av* boucle *f*.

loophole ['lu:phəʊl] *n* (*in rules*) point *m* faible, lacune *f*; (*way out*) échappatoire *f*.

loose [lu:s] *a* (**-er, -est**) (*screw*, *belt*, *knot*) desserré; (*tooth*) branlant; (*page*) détaché; (*clothes*) flottant; (*hair*) dénoué; (*wording*, *translation*) approximatif; (*link*) vague; (*discipline*) relâché; (*articles*) *Com* en vrac; (*cheese*, *tea etc*) *Com* au poids; (*having escaped*) (*animal*) échappé; (*prisoner*) évadé; **l. change** petite monnaie *f*; **l. covers** housses *fpl*; **l. living** vie *f* dissolue; **to come** *or* **get l.** (*of knot*, *screw*) se desserrer; (*of page*) se détacher; **to get l.** (*of dog*) se détacher; **to set** *or* **turn l.** (*dog etc*) lâcher. ‖ *n* **on the l.** (*prisoner*) évadé; (*animal*) échappé.

loosely ['lu:slɪ] *adv* (*to hang*) lâchement; (*to hold*, *tie*) sans serrer; (*to translate*) librement; (*to link*) vaguement.

loosen ['lu:s(ə)n] *vt* (*knot*, *belt*, *screw*) desserrer; (*rope*) détendre; (*grip*) relâcher.

loot [lu:t] *n* butin *m*; (*money*) *Sl* fric *m* ‖ *vt* piller. • **—ing** *n* pillage *m*. • **looter** *n* pillard, -arde *mf*.

lop [lɒp] *vt* (**-pp-**) **to l. (off)** couper.

lop-sided [lɒp'saɪdɪd] *a* (*crooked*) de travers; **to walk l.-sided** se déhancher.

lord [lɔ:d] *n* seigneur *m*; (*British title*) lord *m*; **the L.** (*God*) le Seigneur; **L. knows if...** Dieu sait si...; **oh L.!** *Fam* mince!; **the House of Lords** *Pol* la Chambre des Lords. • **lordship** *n* **Your L.** (*to judge*) Monsieur le juge.

lorry ['lɒrɪ] *n* camion *m*; (*heavy*) poids *m* lourd; **l. driver** camionneur *m*; **long-distance l. driver** routier *m*.

los/e [lu:z] *vt* (*pt* & *pp* **lost**) perdre; **to get lost** (*of person*) se perdre; **the ticket/***etc* **got lost** on a perdu le billet/*etc*; **I've lost my bearings** je suis désorienté; **the clock loses six minutes a day** la pendule retarde de six minutes par jour; **to l. one's life** trouver la mort (**in** dans).

▮ *vi* perdre; **to l. out** être perdant; **to l. to s.o.** *Sp* être battu par qn. ● **—ing** *a* (*number, team*) perdant; **a l. battle** une bataille perdue d'avance. ● **loser** *n* (*in contest etc*) perdant, -ante *mf*; (*failure in life*) *Fam* paumé, -ée *mf*.

loss [lɒs] *n* perte *f*; **to sell at a l.** vendre à perte; **at a l. to do sth** (*unable*) incapable de faire qch.

lost [lɒst] *pt & pp of* **lose** ▮ *a* perdu; **l. property,** *Am* **l. and found** objets *mpl* trouvés.

lot[1] [lɒt] *n* (*destiny*) sort *m*; (*batch, plot of land*) lot *m*; **to draw lots** tirer au sort.

lot[2] [lɒt] **the l.** (*everything*) (le) tout; **the l. of you** vous tous; **a l. of, lots of** beaucoup de; **a l.** beaucoup; **quite a l.** pas mal (**of** de); **such a l.** tellement (**of** de); **what a l. of flowers/water/***etc***!** regarde toutes ces fleurs/toute cette eau/*etc*!; **what a l.!** quelle quantité!; **what a l. of flowers/***etc* **you have!** (ce) que vous avez (beaucoup) de fleurs/*etc*!

lotion ['ləʊʃ(ə)n] *n* lotion *f*.

lottery ['lɒtərɪ] *n* loterie *f*.

lotto ['lɒtəʊ] *n* (*game*) loto *m*.

loud [laʊd] *a* (**-er, -est**) (*voice, music*) fort; (*noise, cry*) grand; (*gaudy*) voyant ▮ *adv* (*to shout etc*) fort; **out l.** tout haut. ● **—ly** *adv* (*to speak, shout etc*) fort. ● **loud'hailer** *n* mégaphone *m*. ● **loud'speaker** *n* haut-parleur *m*; (*for speaking to crowd*) porte-voix *m inv*.

lounge [laʊndʒ] **1** *n* salon *m*; **departure l.** (*in airport*) salle *f* d'embarquement; **l. suit** complet *m* veston. **2** *vi* (*in armchair etc*) se prélasser; **to l. about** (*idle*) paresser; (*stroll*) flâner.

louse, *pl* **lice** [laʊs, laɪs] **1** *n* (*insect*) pou *m*. **2** *n inv* (*person*) *Pej Sl* salaud *m*.

lousy ['laʊzɪ] *a* (**-ier, -iest**) (*food, weather etc*) *Fam* infect.

lout [laʊt] *n* rustre *m*.

lovable ['lʌvəb(ə)l] *a* adorable.

love [lʌv] *n* amour *m*; **in l.** amoureux (**with** de); **they're in l.** ils s'aiment; **yes, my l.** oui, mon amour; **give him** *or* **her my l.** (*greeting*) dis-lui bien des choses de ma part; **l. affair** liaison *f* (amoureuse); **15 l.** *Tennis* 15 à rien.

▮ *vt* aimer; (*like very much*) aimer (beaucoup) (**to do, doing** faire). ● **loving** *a* affectueux.

lovely ['lʌvlɪ] *a* (**-ier, -iest**) (*pleasing*) agréable; (*excellent*) excellent; (*pretty*) joli; (*charming*) charmant; (*kind*) gentil; **l. to see you!** je suis ravi de te voir; **l. and warm/***etc* bien chaud/*etc*.

lover ['lʌvər] *n* (*man*) amant *m*; (*woman*) maîtresse *f*; **a l. of** (*music, art etc*) un amateur de; **a nature l.** un amoureux de la nature.

low[1] [ləʊ] *a* (**-er, -est**) bas (*f* basse); (*speed, income, intelligence*) faible; (*opinion, quality*) mauvais; **she's l. on** (*money etc*) elle n'a plus beaucoup de; **to feel l.** être déprimé; **in a l. voice** à voix basse; **lower** inférieur.

▮ *adv* (**-er, -est**) bas; **to turn (down) l.** mettre plus bas; **to run l.** (*of supplies*) s'épuiser.

▮ *n* **to reach an all-time l.** (*of prices etc*) atteindre leur niveau le plus bas.

low[2] [ləʊ] *vi* (*of cattle*) meugler.

low beams [ləʊ'bi:mz] *npl Aut Am* codes *mpl*. ● **low-'calorie** *a* (*diet*) (à) basses calories. ● **'low-cut** *a* décolleté. ● **'low-down** *a Fam* méprisable. ● **'lowdown** *n* (*facts*) *Fam* tuyaux *mpl*. ● **low-'fat** *a* (*milk*) écrémé; (*cheese*) allégé. ● **low-'key** *a* (*discreet*) discret. ● **'lowland(s)** *n* plaine *f*. ● **low-'salt** *a* (*food*) à faible teneur en sel.

lower ['ləʊər] *vt* baisser; (*by rope*) descendre; **to l. oneself** *Fig* s'abaisser. ● **—ing** *n* (*drop*) baisse *f*.

lowly ['ləʊlɪ] *a* (**-ier, -iest**) humble.

lox [lɒks] *n Am* saumon *m* fumé.

loyal ['lɔɪəl] *a* fidèle (**to** à), loyal (**to** envers). ● **loyalty** *n* fidélité *f*, loyauté *f*.

lozenge ['lɒzɪndʒ] *n* (*tablet*) pastille *f*; (*shape*) losange *m*.

LP [el'pi:] *n abbr* (*long-playing record*) 33 tours *m inv*.

L-plates ['elpleɪts] *npl Aut* plaques *fpl* d'apprenti conducteur.

Ltd *abbr* (*Limited*) *Com* SARL.

lubricate ['lu:brɪkeɪt] *vt* lubrifier; *Aut* graisser. ● **lubrication** [-'keɪʃ(ə)n] *n Aut* graissage *m*.

lucid ['lu:sɪd] *a* lucide.

luck [lʌk] *n* (*chance, good fortune*) chance *f*; (*fate*) hasard *m*, fortune *f*; **bad l.** malchance *f*, malheur *m*; **hard l.!** pas de chance!; **to be in l.** avoir de la chance.

lucky ['lʌkɪ] *a* (**-ier, -iest**) (*person*) chanceux, heureux; (*guess, event*) heureux; **to be l.** avoir de la chance (**to do** de faire); **it's l. that** c'est une chance que (+ *sub*); **I've had a l. day** j'ai eu de la chance aujourd'hui; **l. charm** porte-bonheur *m inv*; **l. number/***etc* chiffre *m*/*etc* porte-bonheur. ● **luckily** *adv* heureusement.

lucrative ['lu:krətɪv] *a* lucratif.

ludicrous ['lu:dɪkrəs] *a* ridicule.

ludo ['lu:dəʊ] *n* jeu *m* des petits chevaux.

lug [lʌg] *vt* (**-gg-**) (*pull*) traîner; **to l. sth around** trimbaler qch.
luggage ['lʌgɪdʒ] *n* bagages *mpl*; **a piece of l.** un bagage; **hand l.** bagages *mpl* à main; **l. compartment** compartiment *m* à bagages.
lukewarm ['lu:kwɔ:m] *a* tiède.
lull [lʌl] **1** *n* arrêt *m*; (*in storm*) accalmie *f*. **2** *vt* (**-ll-**) **to l. s.o. to sleep** endormir qn.
lullaby ['lʌləbaɪ] *n* berceuse *f*.
lumber[1] ['lʌmbər] *n* (*timber*) bois *m* de charpente; (*junk*) bric-à-brac *m inv*. ● **lumberjack** *n Am Can* bûcheron *m*. ● **lumberjacket** *n* blouson *m*.
lumber[2] ['lʌmbər] *vt* **to l. s.o. with sth/s.o.** *Fam* coller qch/qn à qn; **he got lumbered with the chore** il s'est appuyé la corvée.
luminous ['lu:mɪnəs] *a* (*colour, paper etc*) fluo *inv*; (*dial, clock*) lumineux.
lump [lʌmp] *n* morceau *m*; (*bump*) bosse *f*; (*swelling*) grosseur *f*; **l. sum** somme *f* forfaitaire ‖ *vt* **to l. together** réunir; *Fig Pej* mettre dans le même sac. ● **lumpy** *a* (**-ier, -iest**) (*soup*) grumeleux; (*surface*) bosselé.
lunacy ['lu:nəsɪ] *n* folie *f*.
lunar ['lu:nər] *a* lunaire.
lunatic ['lu:nətɪk] *n* fou *m*, folle *f*.
lunch [lʌntʃ] *n* déjeuner *m*; **to have l.** déjeuner; **l. break, l. hour, l. time** heure *f* du déjeuner ‖ *vi* déjeuner (**on, off** de). ● **lunchbox** *n* boîte *f* à sandwichs.
luncheon ['lʌntʃ(ə)n] *n* déjeuner *m*; **l. meat** pâté *m* de viande, = mortadelle *f*; **l. voucher** chèque-déjeuner *m*.
lung [lʌŋ] *n* poumon *m*; **l. cancer** cancer *m* du poumon.
lunge [lʌndʒ] *vi* **to l. at s.o.** se ruer sur qn.
lurch [lɜ:tʃ] **1** *vi* (*of person*) tituber. **2** *n* **to leave s.o. in the l.** *Fam* laisser qn en plan.
lure [lʊər] *vt* attirer (par la ruse) (**into** dans) ‖ *n* (*attraction*) attrait *m*.
lurid ['lʊərɪd] *a* (*horrifying*) horrible; (*sensational*) à sensation; (*gaudy*) voyant.
lurk [lɜ:k] *vi* (*hide*) se cacher (**in** dans); (*prowl*) rôder; (*of suspicion etc*) persister.
luscious ['lʌʃəs] *a* (*food*) appétissant.
lush [lʌʃ] *a* (*vegetation*) luxuriant; (*surroundings etc*) opulent.
lust [lʌst] *n* (*for person, object*) convoitise *f* (**for** de); (*for power, knowledge*) soif *f* (**for** de) ‖ *vi* **to l. after** convoiter; (*power etc*) avoir soif de.
lustre ['lʌstər] (*Am* **luster**) *n* (*gloss*) lustre *m*.
Luxembourg ['lʌksəmbɜ:g] *n* Luxembourg *m*.
luxury ['lʌkʃərɪ] *n* luxe *m* ‖ *a* (*goods, car etc*) de luxe. ● **luxurious** [lʌg'ʒʊərɪəs] *a* luxueux.
lying ['laɪɪŋ] *pres p of* **lie**[1] & [2] ‖ *n* le mensonge ‖ *a* (*journalist etc*) menteur.
lynch [lɪntʃ] *vt* lyncher.
lyric ['lɪrɪk] *a* lyrique ‖ *npl* **lyrics** (*of song*) paroles *fpl*. ● **lyrical** *a* (*enthusiastic etc*) lyrique.

M

M, m [em] *n* M, m *m.*
m *abbr* **1** (*metre*) mètre *m.* **2** (*mile*) mile *m.*
MA [em'eɪ] *abbr* = **Master of Arts.**
mac [mæk] *n* (*raincoat*) *Fam* imper *m.*
macaroni [mækə'rəʊnɪ] *n* macaroni(s) *m*(*pl*); **m. cheese** macaroni(s) au gratin.
machine [mə'ʃiːn] *n* machine *f*; **change/cash m.** distributeur *m* de monnaie/billets. ●**machinegun** *n* (*heavy*) mitrailleuse *f*; (*portable*) mitraillette *f.* ●**machinery** *n* machines *fpl*; (*works*) mécanisme *m*; *Fig* rouages *mpl.* ●**machinist** *n* (*on sewing machine*) piqueur, -euse *mf.*
macho ['mætʃəʊ] *n* (*pl* **-os**) macho *m* ‖ *a* (*attitude etc*) macho (*f inv*).
mackerel ['mækrəl] *n inv* (*fish*) maquereau *m.*
mackintosh ['mækɪntɒʃ] *n* imperméable *m.*
mad [mæd] *a* (**madder, maddest**) fou (*f* folle); **m. dog** chien *m* enragé; **m. (at)** (*angry*) furieux (contre); **m. about** (*person*) fou de; (*films etc*) passionné de; **to drive s.o. m.** rendre qn fou; (*irritate*) énerver qn; **to run/***etc* **like m.** courir/*etc* comme un fou *or* une folle.
Madagascar [mædə'gæskər] *n* Madagascar *f.*
madam ['mædəm] *n* (*married*) madame *f*; (*unmarried*) mademoiselle *f.*
maddening ['mæd(ə)nɪŋ] *a* exaspérant.
made [meɪd] *pt & pp of* **make.**
Madeira [mə'dɪərə] *n* (*island*) Madère *f*; (*wine*) madère *m.*
madhouse ['mædhaʊs] *n Fam* maison *f* de fous. ●**madly** *adv* (*in love etc*) follement; (*desperately*) désespérément. ●**madman** *n* (*pl* **-men**) fou *m.* ●**madness** *n* folie *f.*
Mafia ['mæfɪə] *n* maf(f)ia *f.*
magazine [mægə'ziːn] *n* (*periodical*) magazine *m*, revue *f*; (*broadcast*) *TV Rad* magazine *m.*
maggot ['mægət] *n* ver *m*, asticot *m.*
magic ['mædʒɪk] *n* magie *f* ‖ *a* (*wand etc*) magique. ●**magical** *a* magique. ●**magician** [mə'dʒɪʃən] *n* magicien, -ienne *mf.*
magistrate ['mædʒɪstreɪt] *n* magistrat *m.*
magnet ['mægnɪt] *n* aimant *m.* ●**mag'netic** *a* magnétique. ●**magnetism** *n* magnétisme *m.*
magnificent [mæg'nɪfɪsənt] *a* magnifique.
magnify ['mægnɪfaɪ] *vt* (*image*) grossir; (*sound*) amplifier; **magnifying glass** loupe *f.*
magnolia [mæg'nəʊlɪə] *n* (*tree*) magnolia *m.*
magpie ['mægpaɪ] *n* (*bird*) pie *f.*
mahogany [mə'hɒgənɪ] *n* acajou *m.*
maid [meɪd] *n* (*servant*) bonne *f*; **old m.** *Pej* vieille fille *f.*
maiden ['meɪd(ə)n] *n Old-fashioned* jeune fille *f* ‖ *a* (*speech, flight*) inaugural; **m. name** nom *m* de jeune fille.
mail [meɪl] *n* (*system*) poste *f*; (*letters*) courrier *m* ‖ *a* (*bag etc*) postal; **m. order** vente *f* par correspondance; **m. van** (*vehicle*) camion *m* des postes ‖ *vt* (*letter*) poster; **mailing list** liste *f* d'adresses. ●**mailbox** *n Am* boîte *f* aux *or* à lettres. ●**mailman** *n* (*pl* **-men**) *Am* facteur *m.*
maim [meɪm] *vt* mutiler, estropier.
main [meɪn] **1** *a* principal; **the m. thing is to...** l'essentiel est de...; **m. line** *Rail* grande ligne *f*; **m. road** grand-route *f.* **2** *n* **water/gas m.** conduite *f* d'eau/de gaz; **the mains** *El* le secteur; **a mains radio** une radio secteur. ●**—ly** *adv* surtout.
mainland ['meɪnlænd] *n* continent *m.* ●**mainstay** *n* (*of family etc*) soutien *m*; (*of policy*) pilier *m.* ●**mainstream** *n* tendance *f* dominante.
maintain [meɪn'teɪn] *vt* (*continue*) maintenir (*tradition etc*); (*vehicle, family etc*) entretenir; **to m. law and order** faire respecter l'ordre public; **to m. that** affirmer *or* maintenir que. ●**maintenance** *n* (*of vehicle, road etc*) entretien *m*; (*alimony*) pension *f* alimentaire.
maisonette [meɪzə'net] *n* duplex *m.*
maître d' [meɪtrə'diː] *n* (*in restaurant*) *Am* maître *m* d'hôtel.
maize [meɪz] *n* (*cereal*) maïs *m.*
majesty ['mædʒəstɪ] *n* majesté *f*; **Your M.** Votre Majesté. ●**ma'jestic** *a* majestueux.
major ['meɪdʒər] **1** *a* (*main, great*) & *Mus* majeur; **a m. road** une grande route. **2** *n Mil* commandant *m.* **3** *n* (*subject*) *Univ Am* dominante *f* ‖ *vi* **to m. in** se spécialiser en.
Majorca [mə'jɔːkə] *n* Majorque *f.*
majorette [meɪdʒə'ret] *n* majorette *f.*
majority [mə'dʒɒrɪtɪ] *n* majorité *f* (**of** de); **in the m.** en majorité; **the m. of people** la plupart des gens ‖ *a* (*vote etc*) majoritaire.
make [meɪk] *vt* (*pt & pp* **made**) faire; (*tool,*

vehicle etc) fabriquer; (*decision*) prendre; (*friends*, *salary*) se faire; (*destination*) arriver à; **to m. s.o. happy/tired/***etc* rendre qn heureux/fatigué/*etc*; **she made the train** (*did not miss*) elle a eu le train; **to m. s.o. do sth** faire faire qch à qn; **to m. oneself heard** se faire entendre; **to m. oneself at home** se mettre à l'aise; **to m. sth ready** préparer qch; **to m. do** (*manage*) se débrouiller (**with** avec); **to m. do with** (*be satisfied with*) se contenter de; **to m. it** arriver; (*succeed*) réussir; **I m. it five o'clock** j'ai cinq heures; **what do you m. of it?** qu'en penses-tu?; **you're made (for life)** ton avenir est assuré; **to m. believe** (*pretend*) faire semblant (**that one is** d'être); **to m. good** (*loss*) compenser; (*damage*) réparer; **to m. light of sth** prendre qch à la légère.

▮ *n* (*brand*) marque *f*; **of French/***etc* **m.** de fabrication française/*etc*.

make-believe ['meɪkbəli:v] *n* **it's m.-believe** (*story etc*) c'est (de la) pure invention.

make for *vi* (*go towards*) aller vers ▮ **to make off** *vi* (*run away*) se sauver ▮ **to make out** *vt* (*see*) distinguer; (*understand*) comprendre; (*write*) faire (*chèque*, *liste*); (*claim*) prétendre (**that** que) ▮ *vi* (*manage*) *Fam* se débrouiller ▮ **to make up** *vt* (*story*) inventer; (*put together*) faire (*collection*, *liste*, *lit etc*); (*prepare*) préparer; (*form*) former; (*loss*) compenser; (*quantity*) compléter; (*quarrel*) régler; (*one's face*) maquiller ▮ *vti* **to m. (it) up** (*of friends*) se réconcilier; **to m. up for** (*loss*, *damage*) compenser; (*lost time*, *mistake*) rattraper. ● **make-up** *n* (*for face*) maquillage *m*; (*of object etc*) constitution *f*; **to wear m.-up** se maquiller.

maker ['meɪkər] *n* (*of product*) fabricant, -ante *mf*.

makeshift ['meɪkʃɪft] *n* expédient *m* ▮ *a* (*arrangement etc*) de fortune.

makings ['meɪkɪŋz] *npl* **the m. of** les éléments *mpl* (essentiels) de; **to have the m. of a pianist/***etc* avoir l'étoffe d'un pianiste/*etc*.

malaise [mæ'leɪz] *n* malaise *m*.

malaria [mə'leərɪə] *n* malaria *f*.

Malaysia [mə'leɪzɪə] *n* Malaisie *f*.

male [meɪl] *a Biol Bot etc* mâle; (*clothes*, *sex*) masculin ▮ *n* mâle *m*.

malevolent [mə'levələnt] *a* malveillant.

malfunction [mæl'fʌŋkʃ(ə)n] *n* mauvais fonctionnement *m* ▮ *vi* fonctionner mal.

malice ['mælɪs] *n* méchanceté *f*; **to bear s.o. m.** vouloir du mal à qn. ● **malicious** [mə'lɪʃəs] *a* malveillant.

malignant [mə'lɪgnənt] *a* **m. tumour** *Med* tumeur *f* maligne.

mall [mɔ:l] *n* **(shopping) m.** (*covered*) galerie *f* marchande; *Am* centre *m* commercial.

mallet ['mælɪt] *n* (*tool*) maillet *m*.

malnutrition [mælnju:'trɪʃ(ə)n] *n* malnutrition *f*, sous-alimentation *f*.

malt [mɔ:lt] *n* malt *m*.

Malta ['mɔ:ltə] *n* Malte *f*. ● **Mal'tese** *a* & *n* maltais, -aise (*mf*).

mammal ['mæm(ə)l] *n* mammifère *m*.

mammoth ['mæməθ] *a* (*large*) monstre ▮ *n* (*extinct animal*) mammouth *m*.

man [mæn] *n* (*pl* **men** [men]) homme *m*; (*player*) *Sp* joueur *m*; (*chess piece*) pièce *f*; **to be m. and wife** être mari et femme; **my old m.** *Fam* (*father*) mon père; (*husband*) mon homme; **yes old m.!** *Fam* oui mon vieux!

▮ *vt* (**-nn-**) (*be on duty at*) être de service à; (*ship*) pourvoir d'un équipage; (*guns*) servir; **manned spacecraft** engin *m* spatial habité. ● **manhood** *n* (*period*) âge *m* d'homme. ● **manhunt** *n* chasse *f* à l'homme. ● **man'kind** *n* le genre humain. ● **manly** *a* (**-ier, -iest**) viril. ● **man-'made** *a* artificiel; (*fibre*) synthétique.

manage ['mænɪdʒ] *vt* (*run*) diriger; (*handle*) manier; (*take*) *Fam* prendre; (*eat*) *Fam* manger; (*contribute*) *Fam* donner; **to m. to do** (*succeed*) réussir à faire; (*by being smart*) se débrouiller pour faire; **I'll m. it** j'y arriverai.

▮ *vi* (*succeed*) y arriver; (*make do*) se débrouiller (**with** avec); **to m. without sth** se passer de qch; **the managing director** le PDG. ● **manageable** *a* (*parcel*, *person*, *car etc*) maniable (*feasible*) (*task etc*) faisable. ● **management** *n* (*running*, *managers*) direction *f*; (*of property*) gestion *f*; (*executive staff*) cadres *mpl*.

manager ['mænɪdʒər] *n* directeur *m*; (*of shop*, *café*) gérant *m*; **(business) m.** (*of boxer etc*) manager *m*. ● **manage'ress** *n* directrice *f*; gérante *f*. ● **managerial** [mænə'dʒɪərɪəl] *a* **m. job** *m* poste de direction; **the m. staff** les cadres *mpl*.

mandarin ['mændərɪn] **1** *a* & *n* **m. (orange)** mandarine *f*. **2** *n* (*high-ranking official*) haut fonctionnaire *m*.

mandate ['mændeɪt] *n Pol* mandat *m*.

mandatory ['mændətərɪ] *a* obligatoire.

mane [meɪn] *n* crinière *f*.

maneuver [mə'nu:vər] *n* & *vti Am* = **manoeuvre.**

mangle ['mæŋg(ə)l] *vt* (*damage*) mutiler.

mango ['mæŋgəʊ] *n* (*pl* **-oes** *or* **-os**) (*fruit*) mangue *f*.

manhandle [mæn'hænd(ə)l] *vt* maltraiter.
manhole ['mænhəʊl] *n* trou *m* d'homme; **m. cover** plaque *f* d'égout.
mania ['meɪnɪə] *n* manie *f*. ● **maniac** *n* fou *m*, folle *f*; **sex m.** obsédé *m* sexuel.
manicure ['mænɪkjʊər] *n* soin *m* des mains ▮ *vt* (*person*) manucurer; (*s.o.'s nails*) faire.
manifest ['mænɪfest] **1** *a* (*plain*) manifeste. **2** *vt* (*show*) manifester.
manifesto [mænɪ'festəʊ] *n* (*pl* **-os** *or* **-oes**) *Pol* manifeste *m*.
manifold ['mænɪfəʊld] *a* multiple.
manipulate [mə'nɪpjʊleɪt] *vt* manœuvrer; (*facts, electors*) *Pej* manipuler.
manner ['mænər] *n* (*way*) manière *f*; (*behaviour*) attitude *f*; *pl* (*social habits*) manières *fpl*; **to have no manners** être mal élevé; **in this m.** de cette manière; **all m. of** toutes sortes de. ● **mannered** *a* **well-/bad-m.** bien/mal élevé.
mannerism ['mænərɪz(ə)m] *n* *Pej* tic *m*.
manoeuvre [mə'nu:vər] (*Am* **maneuver**) *n* manœuvre *f* ▮ *vti* manœuvrer.
manor ['mænər] *n* **m. (house)** manoir *m*.
manpower ['mænpaʊər] *n* (*labour*) main-d'œuvre *f*; *Mil* effectifs *mpl*.
mansion ['mænʃ(ə)n] *n* hôtel *m* particulier; (*in country*) manoir *m*.
manslaughter ['mænslɔ:tər] *n* *Jur* homicide *m* involontaire.
mantelpiece ['mænt(ə)lpi:s] *n* (*shelf*) cheminée *f*.
manual ['mænjʊəl] **1** *a* (*work etc*) manuel. **2** *n* (*book*) manuel *m*.
manufactur/e [mænjʊ'fæktʃər] *vt* fabriquer ▮ *n* fabrication *f*. ● **—er** *n* fabricant, -ante *mf*.
manure [mə'njʊər] *n* fumier *m*.
manuscript ['mænjʊskrɪpt] *n* manuscrit *m*.
many ['menɪ] *a* & *n* beaucoup (de); **m. things** beaucoup de choses; **m. came** beaucoup sont venus; **very m., a good** *or* **great m.** un très grand nombre (de); **m. of** un grand nombre de; **m. of them** un grand nombre d'entre eux; **m. times** bien des fois; **m. kinds** toutes sortes (**of** de); **how m.?** combien (de)?; **too m.** trop (de); **one too m.** un de trop; **there are too m. of them** ils sont trop nombreux; **so m.** tant (de); **as m. books/***etc* **as** autant de livres/*etc* que; **as m. as** (*up to*) jusqu'à.
map [mæp] *n* (*of country, region*) carte *f*; (*of town, bus network etc*) plan *m* ▮ *vt* (**-pp-**) **to m. out** (*road*) faire le tracé de; (*one's day etc*) *Fig* organiser.
maple ['meɪp(ə)l] *n* (*tree, wood*) érable *m*.
mar [mɑ:r] *vt* (**-rr-**) gâter.
marathon ['mærəθən] *n* marathon *m*.
marble ['mɑ:b(ə)l] *n* (*substance*) marbre *m*; (*toy ball*) bille *f*.
march [mɑ:tʃ] *n* *Mil* marche *f* ▮ *vi* (*of soldiers etc*) défiler; (*walk in step*) marcher (au pas); **to m. in/out** *Fig* entrer/sortir d'un pas décidé; **to m. past** défiler; **to m. past s.o.** défiler devant qn. ● **m.-past** *n* défilé *m*.
March [mɑ:tʃ] *n* mars *m*.
mare [meər] *n* jument *f*.
margarine [mɑ:dʒə'ri:n] *n* margarine *f*.
marge [mɑ:dʒ] *n* *Fam* margarine *f*.
margin ['mɑ:dʒɪn] *n* (*of page etc*) marge *f*; ● **marginal** *a* (*unimportant*) négligeable; **m. seat** *Pol* siège *m* disputé. ● **marginally** *adv* très légèrement.
marigold ['mærɪgəʊld] *n* (*flower*) souci *m*.
marijuana [mærɪ'wɑ:nə] *n* marijuana *f*.
marina [mə'ri:nə] *n* marina *f*.
marine [mə'ri:n] **1** *a* (*life etc*) marin. **2** *n* (*soldier*) fusilier *m* marin, *Am* marine *m*.
marionette [mærɪə'net] *n* marionnette *f*.
marital ['mærɪt(ə)l] *a* matrimonial; (*relations*) conjugal; **m. status** situation *f* de famille.
maritime ['mærɪtaɪm] *a* (*climate etc*) maritime.
mark[1] [mɑ:k] *n* (*symbol*) marque *f*; (*stain, trace*) trace *f*, tache *f*; (*token, sign*) signe *m*; (*for school exercise etc*) note *f*; (*target*) but *m*; (*model of machine etc*) série *f*; **up to the m.** (*person, work*) à la hauteur.
▮ *vt* marquer; (*exam etc*) corriger, noter; **to m. time** *Mil* marquer le pas; *Fig* piétiner; **to m. down** (*price*) baisser; **to m. off** séparer; (*on list*) cocher; (*area*) délimiter; **to m. up** (*price*) augmenter. ● **marked** *a* (*noticeable*) marqué. ● **markedly** [-ɪdlɪ] *adv* visiblement. ● **markings** (*pl*) (*on animal etc*) marques *fpl*; (*on road*) signalisation *f* horizontale.
mark[2] [mɑ:k] *n* (*currency*) mark *m*.
marker ['mɑ:kər] *n* (*pen*) marqueur *m*; (*bookmark*) signet *m*.
market ['mɑ:kɪt] *n* marché *m*; **on the black m.** au marché noir; **the Common M.** le Marché commun; **m. value** valeur *f* marchande; **m. price** prix *m* courant; **m. gardener** maraîcher, -ère *mf* ▮ *vt* (*sell*) vendre; (*launch*) commercialiser. ● **—ing** *n* marketing *m*.
marksman ['mɑ:ksmən] *n* (*pl* **-men**) tireur *m* d'élite.
marmalade ['mɑ:məleɪd] *n* confiture *f* d'oranges.
maroon [mə'ru:n] *a* (*colour*) bordeaux *inv*.
marooned [mə'ru:nd] *a* abandonné; (*in snowstorm etc*) bloqué (**by** par).

marquee [mɑː'kiː] *n* (*for concerts etc*) chapiteau *m*; (*awning*) *Am* marquise *f*.

marquis ['mɑːkwɪs] *n* marquis *m*.

marriage ['mærɪdʒ] *n* mariage *m*; **m. bureau** agence *f* matrimoniale; **m. certificate** extrait *m* d'acte de mariage.

marrow ['mærəʊ] *n* **1** (*of bone*) moelle *f*. **2** (*vegetable*) courge *f*.

marr/y ['mærɪ] *vt* épouser, se marier avec; (*of priest etc*) marier ‖ *vi* se marier. ●**—ied** *a* marié; (*life*) conjugal; **m. name** nom *m* de femme mariée; **to get m.** se marier.

marsh [mɑːʃ] *n* marais *m*, marécage *m*. ●**marshland** *n* marécages *mpl*. ●**marsh'mallow** *n Culin* (pâte *f* de) guimauve *f*.

marshal ['mɑːʃ(ə)l] **1** *n* (*in army*) maréchal *m*; (*in airforce*) général *m*; (*at public event*) membre *m* du service d'ordre; *Jur Am* shérif *m*. **2** *vt* (**-ll-**, *Am* **-l-**) (*gather*) rassembler.

martial ['mɑːʃ(ə)l] *a* martial; **m. law** loi *f* martiale.

Martian ['mɑːʃ(ə)n] *n* & *a* martien, -ienne (*mf*).

martyr ['mɑːtər] *n* martyr, -yre *mf*. ●**martyrdom** *n* martyre *m*.

marvel ['mɑːv(ə)l] *n* (*wonder*) merveille *f* ‖ *vi* (**-ll-**, *Am* **-l-**) s'émerveiller (**at** de).

marvellous ['mɑːv(ə)ləs] (*Am* **marvelous**) *a* merveilleux.

Marxist ['mɑːksɪst] *a* & *n* marxiste (*mf*).

marzipan ['mɑːzɪpæn] *n* pâte *f* d'amandes.

mascara [mæ'skɑːrə] *n* mascara *m*.

mascot ['mæskɒt] *n* mascotte *f*.

masculine ['mæskjʊlɪn] *a* masculin.

mash [mæʃ] *n* (*potatoes*) purée *f* ‖ *vt* **to m. (up)** (*crush*) écraser (en purée); **mashed potatoes** purée *f* (de pommes de terre).

mask [mɑːsk] *n* masque *m* ‖ *vt* (*cover*, *hide*) masquer (**from** à).

masochist ['mæsəkɪst] *n* masochiste *mf*.

mason ['meɪs(ə)n] *n* maçon *m*. ●**masonry** *n* maçonnerie *f*.

masquerade [mɑːskə'reɪd] *vi* **to m. as** se faire passer pour.

mass[1] [mæs] **1** *n* (*quantity*) masse *f*; **a m. of** (*many*) une multitude de; (*pile*) un tas de, une masse de; **masses of** des masses de; **the masses** (*people*) les masses *fpl*.
‖ *a* (*education*) des masses; (*demonstration*) de masse; (*protests*, *departure*) en masse; (*unemployment*) massif; (*hysteria*) collectif; **m. media** mass media *mpl*; **m. production** production *f* en série.
2 *vi* (*of troops*) se masser. ●**mass-pro'duce** *vt* fabriquer en série.

mass[2] [mæs] *n Rel* messe *f*.

massacre ['mæsəkər] *n* massacre *m* ‖ *vt* massacrer.

massage ['mæsɑːʒ] *n* massage *m* ‖ *vt* masser. ●**ma'sseur** *n* masseur *m*. ●**ma'sseuse** *n* masseuse *f*.

massive ['mæsɪv] *a* (*huge*) énorme; (*solid*) (*building etc*) massif. ●**—ly** *adv* énormément.

mast [mɑːst] *n Nau* mât *m*; *Rad TV* pylône *m*.

master ['mɑːstər] *n* maître *m*; (*in secondary school*) professeur *m*; **a m.'s degree** une maîtrise (**in** de); **M. of Arts/Science** (*person*) Maître *m* ès lettres/sciences; **m. of ceremonies** (*presenter*) *Am* animateur, -trice *mf*; **m. key** passe-partout *m inv*; **m. plan** plan *m or* stratégie d'ensemble; **old m.** (*painting*) tableau *m* de maître.
‖ *vt* (*control*) maîtriser; (*subject*, *situation*) dominer; **she has mastered Latin** elle possède le latin. ●**masterly** *a* magistral. ●**mastery** *n* maîtrise *f* (**of** de).

mastermind ['mɑːstəmaɪnd] *n* (*person*) cerveau *m* (**behind** derrière) ‖ *vt* organiser.

masterpiece ['mɑːstəpiːs] *n* chef-d'œuvre *m*.

mastic ['mæstɪk] *n* mastic *m* (silicone).

masturbate ['mæstəbeɪt] *vi* se masturber.

mat[1] [mæt] *n* tapis *m*; (*of straw*) natte *f*; (*at door*) paillasson *m*; (*for table*) (*of fabric*) napperon *m*; (*hard*) dessous-de-plat *m inv*; **(place) m.** set *m* (de table).

mat[2] [mæt] *a* (*paint*) mat (*f* mate).

match[1] [mætʃ] *n* (*stick*) allumette *f*; **book of matches** pochette *f* d'allumettes. ●**matchbox** *n* boîte *f* d'allumettes. ●**matchstick** *n* allumette *f*.

match[2] [mætʃ] *n* (*game*) match *m*; (*equal*) égal, -ale *mf*; (*marriage*) mariage *m*; **to be a good m.** (*of colours*, *people etc*) être bien assortis.
‖ *vt* (*of clothes*, *colour etc*) aller (bien) avec; **to m. (up)** (*plates etc*) assortir; **to m. (up to)** (*equal*) égaler; (*s.o.'s hopes or expectations*) répondre à; **to be well-matched** (*of colours*, *people etc*) être (bien) assortis.
‖ *vi* (*go with each other*) être assortis. ●**matching** *a* (*dress etc*) assorti.

mate [meɪt] **1** *n* (*friend*) camarade *mf*; (*of animal*) mâle *m*, femelle *f*; **builder's/electrician's/***etc* **m.** aide-maçon/-électricien/*etc m*. **2** *vi* (*of animals*) s'accoupler (**with** avec). **3** *n Chess* mat *m*.

material [mə'tɪərɪəl] **1** *a* (*need etc*) matériel; (*important*) important. **2** *n* (*substance*) matière *f*; (*cloth*) tissu *m*; **material(s)**

(*equipment*) matériel *m*; **building materials** matériaux *mpl* de construction.

materialist [mə'tɪərɪəlɪst] *n* matérialiste *mf*. ● **materia'listic** *a* matérialiste.

materialize [mə'tɪərɪəlaɪz] *vi* se matérialiser.

maternal [mə'tɜːn(ə)l] *a* maternel. ● **maternity** *n* maternité *f* ‖ *a* (*clothes*) de grossesse; (*allowance, leave*) de maternité; **m. hospital** maternité *f*.

mathematical [mæθə'mætɪk(ə)l] *a* mathématique. ● **mathematician** [-mə'tɪʃ(ə)n] *n* mathématicien, -ienne *mf*. ● **mathematics** *n* mathématiques *fpl*. ● **maths** *or Am* **math** *n Fam* maths *fpl*.

matinée ['mætɪneɪ] *n Th Cin* matinée *f*.

matrimony ['mætrɪmənɪ] *n* mariage *m*. ● **matri'monial** *a* matrimonial.

matrix, *pl* **-ices** ['meɪtrɪks, -ɪsiːz] *n Math* matrice *f*.

matron ['meɪtrən] *n* (*nurse*) infirmière *f* (en) chef; *Lit* mère *f* de famille, dame *f* âgée. ● **matronly** *a* (*air*) de mère de famille; (*stout*) corpulent.

matt [mæt] *a* (*paint, paper*) mat (*f* mate).

matter[1] ['mætər] *n* matière *f*; (*subject, affair*) affaire *f*, question *f*; **no m.!** peu importe!; **no m. what she does** quoi qu'elle fasse; **no m. where you go** où que tu ailles; **no m. who you are** qui que vous soyez; **what's the m.?** qu'est-ce qu'il y a?; **what's the m. with you?** qu'est-ce que tu as?; **there's something the m.** il y a quelque chose qui ne va pas; **there's something the m. with my leg** j'ai quelque chose à la jambe; **there's nothing the m. with him** il n'a rien.
‖ *vi* (*be important*) importer (**to** à); **it doesn't m. if/who/***etc* peu importe si/qui/*etc*; **it doesn't m.!** ça ne fait rien!, peu importe! ● **matter-of-'fact** *a* (*person, manner*) terre à terre.

matter[2] ['mætər] *n* (*pus*) *Med* pus *m*.

matting ['mætɪŋ] *n* **a piece of m., some m.** une natte.

mattress ['mætrəs] *n* matelas *m*.

mature [mə'tʃʊər] *a* mûr; (*cheese*) fait ‖ *vi* mûrir; (*of cheese*) se faire. ● **maturity** *n* maturité *f*.

maul [mɔːl] *vt* (*of animal*) mutiler.

mausoleum [mɔːsə'lɪəm] *n* mausolée *m*.

mauve [məʊv] *a* & *n* (*colour*) mauve (*m*).

maximum ['mæksɪməm] *n* (*pl* **-ima** [-ɪmə] *or* **-imums**) maximum *m* ‖ *a* maximum (*f inv*). ● **maximize** [-maɪz] *vt* porter au maximum.

may [meɪ] *v aux* (*pt* **might**) **1** (*possibility*) **he m. come** il peut arriver; **he might come** il pourrait arriver; **I m.** *or* **might be wrong** il se peut que je me trompe; **you m.** *or* **might have** tu aurais pu; **I m.** *or* **might have forgotten it** je l'ai peut-être oublié; **we m.** *or* **might as well go** nous ferions aussi bien de partir; **she's afraid I m.** *or* **might get lost** elle a peur que je ne me perde.
2 (*permission*) **m. I stay?** puis-je rester?; **m. I?** vous permettez?; **you m. go** tu peux partir.
3 (*wish*) **m. you be happy** (que tu) sois heureux.

May [meɪ] *n* mai *m*.

maybe ['meɪbiː] *adv* peut-être.

mayonnaise [meɪə'neɪz] *n* mayonnaise *f*.

mayor [meər] *n* (*man, woman*) maire *m*.

maze [meɪz] *n* labyrinthe *m*.

MC [em'siː] *abbr* = **master of ceremonies.**

me [miː] *pron* me, m'; (*after prep, 'than', 'it is' etc*) moi; **(to) me** me, m'; **she knows me** elle me connaît; **he helps me** il m'aide; **he gives (to) me** il me donne; **with me** avec moi.

meadow ['medəʊ] *n* pré *m*, prairie *f*.

meagre ['miːgər] (*Am* **meager**) *a* maigre.

meal [miːl] *n* (*food*) repas *m*.

mean[1] [miːn] *vt* (*pt* & *pp* **meant** [ment]) (*signify*) vouloir dire, signifier; (*intend*) destiner (**for** à); (*result in*) entraîner; (*represent*) représenter; (*refer to*) faire allusion à; **to m. to do** (*intend*) avoir l'intention de faire; **I m. it** je suis sérieux; **to m. something to s.o.** (*matter*) avoir de l'importance pour qn; **I didn't m. to!** je ne l'ai pas fait exprès!; **you were meant to come** vous étiez censé venir.

mean[2] [miːn] *a* (**-er, -est**) (*with money etc*) avare; (*petty*) mesquin; (*nasty*) méchant; (*inferior*) misérable. ● **—ness** *n* (*greed*) avarice *f*; (*nastiness*) méchanceté *f*.

mean[3] [miːn] *a* (*average*) (*distance etc*) moyen ‖ *n* (*middle position*) milieu *m*; (*average*) *Math* moyenne *f*.

meander [mɪ'ændər] *vi* (*of river*) faire des méandres.

meaning ['miːnɪŋ] *n* sens *m*, signification *f*. ● **meaningful** *a* significatif. ● **meaningless** *a* qui n'a pas de sens.

means [miːnz] *n*(*pl*) (*method*) moyen(s) *m*(*pl*) (**to do, of doing** de faire); (*wealth*) moyens *mpl*; **by m. of** (*stick etc*) au moyen de; (*work etc*) à force de; **by all m.!** très certainement!; **by no m.** nullement; **private m.** fortune *f* personnelle.

meant [ment] *pt* & *pp of* **mean**[1].

meantime ['miːntaɪm] *adv* & *n* **(in the) m.** entre-temps. ● **meanwhile** *adv* entre-temps.

measles ['mi:z(ə)lz] *n* rougeole *f*.
measly ['mi:zlɪ] *a* (*contemptible*) *Fam* minable.
measure ['meʒər] *n* (*action*, *amount*) mesure *f*; (*ruler*) règle *f*; **made to m.** fait sur mesure ▮ *vt* mesurer; (*adjust*) adapter (**to** à); **to m. up** (*plank etc*) mesurer ▮ *vi* **to m. up to** (*task etc*) être à la hauteur de.
measurement ['meʒəmənt] *n* (*of chest*, *waist etc*) tour *m*; *pl* (*dimensions*) mesures *fpl*; **your hip**/*etc* **measurement(s)** votre tour de hanches/*etc*.
meat [mi:t] *n* viande *f*; (*of crab*, *lobster etc*) chair *f*; **m. diet** régime *m* carné. ● **meatball** *n* boulette *f* (de viande).
Mecca ['mekə] *n* la Mecque.
mechanic [mɪ'kænɪk] *n* mécanicien, -ienne *mf*. ● **mechanical** *a* mécanique. ● **mechanics** *n* (*science*) mécanique *f*; *pl* (*working parts*) mécanisme *m*.
mechanism ['mekənɪz(ə)m] *n* mécanisme *m*.
medal ['med(ə)l] *n* médaille *f*. ● **me'dallion** *n* médaillon *m*. ● **medallist** (*Am* **medalist**) *n* médaillé, -ée *mf*; **to be a gold/silver m.** *Sp* être médaille d'or/d'argent.
meddle ['med(ə)l] *vi* (*interfere*) se mêler (**in** de); (*tamper*) toucher (**with** à).
media ['mi:dɪə] *npl* **1 the (mass) m.** les médias *mpl*. **2** *see* **medium 2**.
mediaeval [medɪ'i:v(ə)l] *a* médiéval.
median ['mi:dɪən] *a* & *n* **m. (strip)** *Aut Am* bande *f* médiane.
mediate ['mi:dɪeɪt] *vi* servir d'intermédiaire (**between** entre). ● **mediator** *n* médiateur, -trice *mf*.
Medicaid ['medɪkeɪd] *n Am* = assistance *f* médicale aux défavorisés.
medical ['medɪk(ə)l] *a* médical; (*school*, *studies*) de médecine; (*student*) en médecine; **m. insurance** assurance *f* maladie ▮ *n* (*in school*, *army*) visite *f* médicale.
Medicare ['medɪkeər] *n Am* = assistance *f* médicale aux personnes âgées.
medication [medɪ'keɪʃ(ə)n] *n* médicaments *mpl*.
medicine ['medəsən] *n* médicament *m*; (*science*) médecine *f*; **m. cabinet, m. chest** (armoire *f* à) pharmacie *f*.
medieval [medɪ'i:v(ə)l] *a* médiéval.
mediocre [mi:dɪ'əʊkər] *a* médiocre.
meditate ['medɪteɪt] *vi* méditer (**on** sur).
Mediterranean [medɪtə'reɪnɪən] *a* méditerranéen ▮ *n* **the M.** la Méditerranée.
medium ['mi:dɪəm] **1** *a* (*average*, *middle*) moyen. **2** *n* (*pl* **media** ['mi:dɪə]) *Phys* véhicule *m*; *Biol* milieu *m*; (*for conveying data*) support *m*; **through the m. of** par l'intermédiaire de; **happy m.** juste milieu *m*. **3** *n* (*person*) médium *m*. ● **m.-sized** *a* moyen, de taille moyenne.
medley ['medlɪ] *n* mélange *m*; *Mus* pot-pourri *m*.
meek [mi:k] *a* (**-er, -est**) doux (*f* douce).
meet [mi:t] *vt* (*pt* & *pp* **met**) (*person*, *team etc*) rencontrer; (*person by arrangement*) retrouver; (*pass in street*, *road etc*) croiser; (*fetch*) (aller *or* venir) chercher; (*wait for*) attendre; (*debt*, *danger*) faire face à; (*need*) combler; (*be introduced to*) faire la connaissance de; **to arrange to m. s.o.** donner rendez-vous à qn.
▮ *vi* (*of people*, *teams*, *rivers*) se rencontrer; (*of people by arrangement*) se retrouver; (*be introduced*) se connaître; (*of club etc*) se réunir; (*of trains*, *vehicles*) se croiser.
▮ *n* **to make a m. with s.o.** *Fam* donner rendez-vous à qn.
meeting ['mi:tɪŋ] *n* réunion *f*; (*large*) assemblée *f*; (*between two people*) (*by chance*) rencontre *f*; (*arranged*) rendez-vous *m inv*; **in a m.** en conférence.
meet up *vi* (*of people*) se rencontrer; (*by arrangement*) se retrouver; **to m. up with s.o.** rencontrer qn; retrouver qn ▮ **to meet with** *vt* (*accident*, *problem*) avoir; (*refusal*) essuyer; (*difficulty*) rencontrer; **to m. with s.o.** *Am* rencontrer qn; (*by arrangement*) retrouver qn.
mega- ['megə] *pref* méga-.
megaphone ['megəfəʊn] *n* porte-voix *m inv*.
melancholy ['melənkəlɪ] *n* mélancolie *f*.
mellow ['meləʊ] *a* (**-er, -est**) (*fruit*) mûr; (*voice*, *wine*) moelleux; (*character*) mûri par l'expérience ▮ *vi* (*of person*) s'adoucir.
melodrama ['melədrɑ:mə] *n* mélodrame *m*.
melody ['melədɪ] *n* mélodie *f*.
melon ['melən] *n* melon *m*.
melt [melt] *vi* fondre; **to m. into** (*merge*) *Fig* se fondre dans ▮ *vt* (faire) fondre; **to m. down** (*metal object*) fondre; **melting point** point *m* de fusion; **melting pot** *Fig* creuset *m*.
member ['membər] *n* membre *m*; **M. of Parliament** député *m*. ● **membership** *n* adhésion *f* (**of** à); (*members*) membres *mpl*; **m. (fee)** cotisation *f*.
memento [mə'mentəʊ] *n* (*pl* **-os** *or* **-oes**) (*object*) souvenir *m*.
memo ['meməʊ] *n* (*pl* **-os**) note *f*.
memoirs ['memwɑ:z] *npl* (*essays*) mémoires *mpl*.
memorable ['memərəb(ə)l] *a* mémorable.

memorial [mə'mɔːrɪəl] *a* (*plaque*) commémoratif ‖ *n* mémorial *m*.

memory ['memərɪ] *n* mémoire *f*; (*recollection*) souvenir *m*; **in m. of** à la mémoire de. ●**memorize** *vt* apprendre par cœur.

men [men] *see* **man; the men's room** les toilettes *fpl* pour hommes.

menace ['menɪs] *n* danger *m*; (*threat*) menace *f*; (*nuisance*) *Fam* plaie *f* ‖ *vt* menacer.

mend [mend] *vt* (*repair*) réparer; (*clothes*) raccommoder; **to m. one's ways** se corriger ‖ *n* **to be on the m.** (*after illness*) aller mieux.

menial ['miːnɪəl] *a* inférieur.

meningitis [menɪn'dʒaɪtɪs] *n Med* méningite *f*.

menopause ['menəpɔːz] *n* ménopause *f*.

menstruation [menstrʊ'eɪʃ(ə)n] *n* menstruation *f*.

mental ['ment(ə)l] *a* mental; (*hospital*) psychiatrique; **m. block** blocage *m*; **m. strain** tension *f* nerveuse. ●**—ly** *adv* **he's m. handicapped** c'est un handicapé mental; **she's m. ill** c'est une malade mentale.

mentality [men'tælətɪ] *n* mentalité *f*.

mention ['menʃ(ə)n] *vt* mentionner, faire mention de; **not to m....** sans parler de...; **don't m. it!** il n'y a pas de quoi! ‖ *n* mention *f*.

menu ['menjuː] *n* (*in restaurant*) & *Comptr* menu *m*; **on the m.** au menu.

MEP [emiː'piː] *n abbr* (*Member of the European Parliament*) membre *m* du Parlement européen.

mercenary ['mɜːsɪnərɪ] *n* mercenaire *m*.

merchandise ['mɜːtʃəndaɪz] *n* (*articles*) marchandises *fpl*; (*total stock*) marchandise *f*.

merchant ['mɜːtʃ(ə)nt] *n* (*trader*) négociant, -ante *mf*; (*shopkeeper*, *Am storekeeper*) commerçant *m*, -ante *mf*; **m. bank** banque *f* de commerce; **m. navy** *or Am* **marine** marine *f* marchande.

mercury ['mɜːkjʊrɪ] *n* mercure *m*.

mercy ['mɜːsɪ] *n* pitié *f*; *Rel* miséricorde *f*; **to beg for m.** demander grâce; **at the m. of** à la merci de. ●**merciful** *a* miséricordieux (**to** pour). ●**merciless** *a* impitoyable.

mere [mɪər] *a* simple; (*only*) ne... que; **she's a m. child** ce n'est qu'une enfant; **it's a m. kilometre** ça ne fait qu'un kilomètre; **by m. chance** par pur hasard. ●**—ly** *adv* (tout) simplement.

merg/e [mɜːdʒ] *vi* (*blend*) se mêler (**with** à); (*of roads*) se (re)joindre; (*of companies*) fusionner ‖ *vt* (*companies*) & *Comptr* fusionner. ●**—er** *n Com* fusion *f*.

meringue [mə'ræŋ] *n* (*cake*) meringue *f*.

merit ['merɪt] *n* mérite *m* ‖ *vt* mériter.

mermaid ['mɜːmeɪd] *n* (*woman*) sirène *f*.

merry ['merɪ] *a* (**-ier, -iest**) gai; (*drunk*) éméché; **M. Christmas** Joyeux Noël. ●**m.-go-round** *n* (*at funfair etc*) manège *m*. ●**m.-making** *n* réjouissances *fpl*.

mesh [meʃ] *n* (*of net*) maille *f*; (*fabric*) tissu *m* à mailles; **wire m.** grillage *m*.

mesmerize ['mezməraɪz] *vt* hypnotiser.

mess[1] [mes] **1** *n* (*confusion*) désordre *m*, pagaïe *f*; (*muddle*) gâchis *m*; (*dirt*) saleté *f*; **in a m.** sens dessus dessous; (*trouble*) dans le pétrin; (*sorry state*) dans un triste état; **to make a m. of** gâcher.

2 *vt* **to m. s.o. about** (*bother*) *Fam* déranger qn; **to m. up** (*spoil*) gâcher; (*dirty*) salir; (*room*) mettre sens dessous.

‖ *vi* **to m. about** (*have fun*) s'amuser; (*play the fool*) faire l'idiot; **to m. about with sth** (*fiddle with*) s'amuser avec qch. ●**messy** *a* (**-ier, -iest**) (*untidy*) en désordre; (*dirty*) sale.

mess[2] [mes] *n Mil* mess *m inv*.

message ['mesɪdʒ] *n* message *m*.

messenger ['mesɪndʒər] *n* messager, -ère *mf*; (*in office, hotel*) coursier, -ière *mf*.

Messiah [mɪ'saɪə] *n* Messie *m*.

Messrs ['mesəz] *npl* **M. Brown** Messieurs *or* MM Brown.

messy ['mesɪ] *a see* **mess**[1].

met [met] *pt* & *pp of* **meet.**

metal ['met(ə)l] *n* métal *m*; **m. ladder**/*etc* échelle *f*/*etc* métallique. ●**me'tallic** *a* (*sound*) métallique; (*paint*) métallisé. ●**metalwork** *n* (*craft*) travail *m* des métaux.

metaphor ['metəfər] *n* métaphore *f*. ●**meta'phorical** *a* métaphorique.

mete [miːt] *vt* **to m. out** (*punishment*) infliger (**to** à).

meteor ['miːtɪər] *n* météore *m*.

meteorology [miːtɪə'rɒlədʒɪ] *n* météorologie *f*.

meter[1] ['miːtər] *n* (*device*) compteur *m*; **(parking) m.** parcmètre *m*; **m. maid** *Aut Fam* & *Am* contractuelle *f*.

meter[2] ['miːtər] *n* (*measurement*) *Am* mètre *m*.

method ['meθəd] *n* méthode *f*. ●**me'thodical** *a* méthodique.

Methodist ['meθədɪst] *a* & *n Rel* méthodiste (*mf*).

methylated ['meθɪleɪtɪd] *a* **m. spirit(s)** alcool *m* à brûler. ●**meths** *n Fam* = **methylated spirits.**

meticulous [mɪ'tɪkjʊləs] *a* méticuleux.

netre ['mi:tər] (*Am* **meter**) *n* mètre *m*. ● **metric** ['metrɪk] *a* métrique.

netropolitan [metrə'pɒlɪtən] *a* métropolitain.

new [mju:] *vi* (*of cat*) miauler.

news [mju:z] *n* (*street*) ruelle *f*; **m. flat** appartement *m* chic (*aménagé dans une ancienne écurie*).

Mexico ['meksɪkəʊ] *n* Mexique *m*. ● **Mexican** *a* & *n* mexicain, -aine (*mf*).

niaow [mi:'aʊ] *vi* (*of cat*) miauler ‖ *n* miaulement *m* ‖ *int* miaou.

nice [maɪs] *see* **mouse.**

nickey ['mɪkɪ] *n* **to take the m. out of s.o.** *Fam* charrier qn.

nicro- ['maɪkrəʊ] *pref* micro-.

nicrobe ['maɪkrəʊb] *n* microbe *m*.

nicrochip ['maɪkrəʊtʃɪp] *n Comptr* puce *f*.

nicrofilm ['maɪkrəʊfɪlm] *n* microfilm *m*.

nicrolight ['maɪkrəʊlaɪt] *n Av* ULM *m*.

nicrophone ['maɪkrəfəʊn] *n* micro *m*.

nicroprocessor [maɪkrəʊ'prəʊsesər] *n* microprocesseur *m*.

nicroscope ['maɪkrəskəʊp] *n* microscope *m*.

nicrowave ['maɪkrəʊweɪv] *n* **m. (oven)** four *m* à micro-ondes.

nid [mɪd] *a* **(in) m.-June** (à) la mi-juin; **(in) m. morning** au milieu de la matinée; **in m. air** en plein ciel.

nidday [mɪd'deɪ] *n* midi *m* ‖ *a* (*sun etc*) de midi.

niddle ['mɪd(ə)l] *n* milieu *m*; (*waist*) *Fam* taille *f*; **(right) in the m. of** au (beau) milieu de; **in the m. of saying/working/***etc* en train de dire/travailler/*etc*.
‖ *a* (*central*) du milieu; (*class*, *quality*) moyen; (*name*) deuxième; **the M. Ages** le moyen âge; **in m. age** vers la cinquantaine; **the M. East** le Moyen-Orient. ● **m.-'aged** *a* d'un certain âge. ● **m.-'class** *a* bourgeois.

niddling ['mɪdlɪŋ] *a* moyen, passable.

nidge [mɪdʒ] *n* (*fly*) moucheron *m*.

nidget ['mɪdʒɪt] *n* nain *m*, naine *f*.

Aidlands ['mɪdləndz] *npl* **the M.** les comtés *mpl* du centre de l'Angleterre.

nidnight ['mɪdnaɪt] *n* minuit *m*.

nidst [mɪdst] *n* **in the m. of** au milieu de; **in our/their m.** parmi nous/eux.

nidsummer [mɪd'sʌmər] *n* milieu *m* de l'été.

nidway [mɪd'weɪ] *a* & *adv* à mi-chemin.

nidweek [mɪd'wi:k] *n* milieu *m* de la semaine.

nidwife ['mɪdwaɪf] *n* (*pl* **-wives**) sage-femme *f*.

nidwinter [mɪd'wɪntər] *n* milieu *m* de l'hiver.

niffed [mɪft] *a Fam* vexé (**by** de).

might [maɪt] **1** *see* **may. 2** *n* (*strength*) force *f*. ● **mighty** *a* (**-ier, -iest**) puissant; (*very great*) *Fam* sacré ‖ *adv* (*very*) *Am Fam* rudement.

migraine ['mi:greɪn, 'maɪgreɪn] *n* migraine *f*.

migrate [maɪ'greɪt] *vi* (*of people*) émigrer; (*of birds*) migrer. ● **'migrant** *a* & *n* **m. (worker)** migrant, -ante (*mf*).

mike [maɪk] *n Fam* micro *m*.

mild [maɪld] *a* (**-er, -est**) (*weather*, *taste etc*) doux (*f* douce); (*beer*, *punishment*) léger; (*medicine*, *illness*) bénin (*f* bénigne); (*exercise*) modéré. ● **—ly** *adv* doucement; (*slightly*) légèrement; **to put it m.** pour ne pas dire plus. ● **—ness** *n* (*of weather*) douceur *f*.

mildew ['mɪldju:] *n* (*on cheese etc*) moisissure *f*.

mile [maɪl] *n* mile *m* (= *1,6 km*); **to walk for miles** marcher pendant des kilomètres; **miles better** *Fam* bien mieux. ● **mileage** *n* = kilométrage *m*; (*per gallon*) = consommation *f* aux cent kilomètres. ● **mileometer** *n* = **milometer**. ● **milestone** *n* = borne *f* kilométrique; *Fig* jalon *m*.

militant ['mɪlɪtənt] *a* & *n* militant, -ante (*mf*).

military ['mɪlɪt(ə)rɪ] *a* militaire.

militate ['mɪlɪteɪt] *vi* (*of arguments etc*) militer (**against** contre).

milk [mɪlk] *n* lait *m* ‖ *a* (*chocolate*) au lait; (*bottle*) à lait; (*diet*) lacté; (*produce*) laitier; **m. float** voiture *f* de laitier; **m. shake** milk-shake *m* ‖ *vt* (*cow*) traire; (*exploit*) *Fig* exploiter. ● **milkman** *n* (*pl* **-men**) laitier *m*. ● **milky** *a* (**-ier, -iest**) (*diet*) lacté; (*coffee*, *tea*) au lait; **the M. Way** la Voie lactée.

mill [mɪl] **1** *n* moulin *m*; (*factory*) usine *f*; **cotton m.** filature *f* de coton; **paper m.** papeterie *f*. **2** *vi* **to m. around** (*of crowd*) grouiller. ● **miller** *n* meunier, -ière *mf*. ● **millstone** *n* (*burden*) boulet *m* **(round one's neck** qu'on traîne).

millet ['mɪlɪt] *n Bot* millet *m*.

milli- [mɪlɪ] *pref* milli-.

millimetre ['mɪlɪmi:tər] (*Am* **millimeter**) *n* millimètre *m*.

million ['mɪljən] *n* million *m*; **a m. men/***etc* un million d'hommes/*etc*; **two m.** deux millions. ● **millio'naire** *n* millionnaire *mf*.

milometer [maɪ'lɒmətər] *n* = compteur *m* (kilométrique).

mime [maɪm] *n* (*actor*) mime *mf*; (*art*) mime *m* ‖ *vti* mimer.

mimic ['mɪmɪk] *vt* (**-ck-**) imiter ‖ *n* imitateur, -trice *mf*.

minaret [mɪnə'ret] *n* (*of mosque*) minaret *m*.
mince [mɪns] *n* (*meat*) viande *f* hachée, hachis *m*; (*fruit*) *Am* = **mincemeat** ‖ *vt* hacher. ● **mincemeat** *n* (*dried fruit*) mélange *m* de fruits secs; (*meat*) = **mince.** ● **mincer** *n* hachoir *m*.
mind[1] [maɪnd] *n* esprit *m*; (*sanity*) raison *f*; (*memory*) mémoire *f*; (*head*) tête *f*; **to change one's m.** changer d'avis; **to my m.** à mon avis; **in two minds** (*undecided*) irrésolu; **to make up one's m.** se décider; **to be on s.o.'s m.** préoccuper qn; **out of one's m.** (*mad*) fou; **to bring to m.** (*recall*) rappeler; **to bear in m.** (*remember*) se souvenir de; **to have in m.** (*person, plan*) avoir en vue; **to have a good m. to do sth** avoir bien envie de faire qch.
mind[2] [maɪnd] *vti* (*pay attention to*) faire attention à; (*look after*) garder; (*noise, dirt etc*) être gêné par; **m. you don't fall** prends garde de ne pas tomber; **m. you do it** n'oublie pas de le faire; **do you m. if?** (*I smoke etc*) ça vous gêne si?; (*I leave etc*) ça ne vous fait rien si?; **I don't m.** ça m'est égal; **I wouldn't m. a cup of tea** j'aimerais bien une tasse de thé; **I m. that...** ça me gêne que...; **never m.!** ça ne fait rien!; (*don't worry*) ne vous en faites pas!; **m. (out)!** (*watch out*) attention!; **m. you...** remarquez, . . .; **m. your own business!** ça ne vous regarde pas!
mind-boggling ['maɪndbɒglɪŋ] *a* stupéfiant.
minder ['maɪndər] *n* (*for children*) nourrice *f*; (*bodyguard*) *Fam* gorille *m*; **child m.** nourrice *f*.
mindless ['maɪndləs] *a* stupide.
mine[1] [maɪn] *poss pron* le mien, la mienne, *pl* les mien(ne)s; **this hat is m.** ce chapeau est à moi *or* est le mien; **a friend of m.** un ami à moi.
min/e[2] [maɪn] **1** *n* (*for coal, gold etc*) & *Fig* mine *f* ‖ *vt* (*coal etc*) extraire. **2** *n* (*explosive*) mine *f* ‖ *vt* (*bridge etc*) miner. ● **—ing** *n* exploitation *f* minière. ● **miner** *n* mineur *m*.
mineral ['mɪnərəl] *a* & *n* minéral (*m*); **m. water** eau *f* minérale.
mingle ['mɪŋg(ə)l] *vi* se mêler (**with** à); **to m. with** (*socially*) fréquenter.
mingy ['mɪndʒɪ] *a* (**-ier, -iest**) (*mean*) *Fam* radin.
mini ['mɪnɪ] *pref* mini-.
miniature ['mɪnɪtʃər] *a* (*train etc*) miniature *inv* ‖ *n* miniature *f*; **in m.** en miniature.
minibus ['mɪnɪbʌs] *n* minibus *m*. ● **minicab** *n* (radio-)taxi *m*.
minim ['mɪnɪm] *n Mus* blanche *f*.
minimum ['mɪnɪməm] *n* (*pl* **-ima** [-ɪmə] *or* **-imums**) minimum *m* ‖ *a* minimum (*f inv*). ● **minimal** *a* minimal. ● **minimize** [-maɪz] *vt* minimiser.
mining ['maɪnɪŋ] *n see* **mine**[2].
minister ['mɪnɪstər] *n Pol* ministre *m*; *Rel* pasteur *m*. ● **mini'sterial** *a Pol* ministériel. ● **ministry** *n Pol* ministère *m*.
mink [mɪŋk] *n* (*animal, fur*) vison *m*.
minor ['maɪnər] *a* (*detail, operation etc*) petit; *Mus Rel etc* mineur ‖ *n Jur* mineur, -eure *mf*.
Minorca [mɪ'nɔːkə] *n* Minorque *f*.
minority [maɪ'nɒrɪtɪ] *n* minorité *f*; **in the** *or* **a m.** en minorité ‖ *a* minoritaire.
mint [mɪnt] **1** *n* (*place*) Hôtel *m* de la Monnaie; **a m. (of money)** *Fig* une petite fortune ‖ *vt* (*money*) frapper ‖ *a* (*stamp*) neuf. **2** *n* (*herb*) menthe *f*; (*sweet, Am candy*) bonbon *m* à la menthe; **m. tea**/*etc* thé *m*/*etc* à la menthe.
minus ['maɪnəs] *prep* moins; (*without*) *Fam* sans; **it's m. ten (degrees)** il fait moins dix (degrés) ‖ *n* **m. (sign)** (signe *m*) moins *m*.
minute[1] ['mɪnɪt] **1** *n* minute *f*; **any m. (now)** d'une minute à l'autre; **m. hand** (*of clock*) grande aiguille *f*. **2** *npl* **minutes** (*of meeting*) procès-verbal *m*.
minute[2] [maɪ'njuːt] *a* (*tiny*) minuscule; (*careful*) minutieux.
miracle ['mɪrək(ə)l] *n* miracle *m*. ● **mi'raculous** *a* miraculeux.
mirage ['mɪrɑːʒ] *n* mirage *m*.
mirror ['mɪrər] *n* miroir *m*, glace *f*; *Aut* rétroviseur *m* ‖ *vt* refléter.
mirth [mɜːθ] *n Lit* gaieté *f*, hilarité *f*.
misapprehension [mɪsæprɪ'henʃ(ə)n] *n* malentendu *m*.
misbehave [mɪsbɪ'heɪv] *vi* se conduire mal.
miscalculate [mɪs'kælkjʊleɪt] *vt* mal calculer ‖ *vi Fig* se tromper. ● **miscalculation** [-'leɪʃ(ə)n] *n* erreur *f* de calcul.
miscarriage [mɪs'kærɪdʒ] *n* **to have a m.** *Med* faire une fausse couche; **m. of justice** erreur *f* judiciaire. ● **miscarry** *vi Med* faire une fausse couche.
miscellaneous [mɪsɪ'leɪnɪəs] *a* divers.
mischief ['mɪstʃɪf] *n* espièglerie *f*; (*malice*) méchanceté *f*; **to get into m.** faire des bêtises; **to make m. for s.o.** créer des ennuis à qn; **to do s.o. a m.** faire mal à qn. ● **mischievous** *a* (*naughty*) espiègle; (*malicious*) méchant.
misconception [mɪskən'sepʃ(ə)n] *n* idée *f* fausse.
misconduct [mɪs'kɒndʌkt] *n* mauvaise conduite *f*.

misdeed [mɪs'diːd] *n* méfait *m*.
misdemeanor [mɪsdɪ'miːnər] *n Am Jur* délit *m*.
misdirect [mɪsdɪ'rekt] *vt* (*letter*) mal adresser; (*person*) mal renseigner.
miser ['maɪzər] *n* avare *mf*. ● **—ly** *a* avare.
miserable ['mɪzərəb(ə)l] *a* (*wretched*) misérable; (*unhappy*) malheureux; (*awful*) affreux; (*salary*) dérisoire.
misery ['mɪzərɪ] *n* (*suffering*) souffrances *fpl*; (*sadness*) tristesse *f*; (*person*) *Fam* grincheux, -euse *mf*; *pl* (*misfortunes*) misères *fpl*.
misfire [mɪs'faɪər] *vi* (*of plan*) rater.
misfit ['mɪsfɪt] *n Pej* inadapté, -ée *mf*.
misfortune [mɪs'fɔːtʃuːn] *n* malheur *m*.
misgivings [mɪs'gɪvɪŋz] *npl* (*doubts*) doutes *mpl* (**about** sur); (*fears*) craintes *fpl*.
misguided [mɪs'gaɪdɪd] *a* (*action etc*) imprudent; **to be m.** (*of person*) se tromper.
mishandle [mɪs'hænd(ə)l] *vt* (*affair, situation*) traiter avec maladresse.
mishap ['mɪshæp] *n* (*hitch*) contretemps *m*; (*accident*) mésaventure *f*.
misinform [mɪsɪn'fɔːm] *vt* mal renseigner.
misinterpret [mɪsɪn'tɜːprɪt] *vt* mal interpréter.
mislay [mɪs'leɪ] *vt* (*pt & pp* **mislaid**) égarer.
mislead [mɪs'liːd] *vt* (*pt & pp* **misled**) tromper. ● **—ing** *a* trompeur.
mismanage [mɪs'mænɪdʒ] *vt* mal administrer.
misnomer [mɪs'nəʊmər] *n* nom *m or* terme *m* impropre.
misplace [mɪs'pleɪs] *vt* (*lose*) égarer.
misprint ['mɪsprɪnt] *n* faute *f* d'impression.
mispronounce [mɪsprə'naʊns] *vt* mal prononcer.
misrepresent [mɪsreprɪ'zent] *vt* présenter sous un faux jour.
miss[1] [mɪs] *vt* (*train, target, opportunity etc*) manquer, rater; (*not see*) ne pas voir; (*not understand*) ne pas comprendre; (*deceased person etc*) regretter; (*sth just lost*) remarquer l'absence de; **he misses Paris/her** Paris/elle lui manque; **I m. you** tu me manques; **we'll be missed** on remarquera notre absence; **don't m. seeing this play** ne manque pas de voir cette pièce; **to m. sth out** (*leave out*) sauter qch.
▮ *vi* manquer, rater; **to m. out** (*lose a chance*) rater l'occasion; **to m. out on** (*opportunity*) rater.
▮ *n* coup *m* manqué; **we had a near m.** on l'a échappé belle; **I'll give it a m.** *Fam* (*not go*) je n'y irai pas. ● **missing** *a* absent; (*in war, after disaster*) disparu; (*object*) manquant; **there are two cups/students m.** il manque deux tasses/deux étudiants; **to go m.** disparaître.
miss[2] [mɪs] *n* (*woman*) mademoiselle *f*; **Miss Brown** Mademoiselle *or* Mlle Brown.
misshapen [mɪs'ʃeɪp(ə)n] *a* difforme.
missile ['mɪsaɪl, *Am* 'mɪs(ə)l] *n* (*rocket*) missile *m*; (*object thrown*) projectile *m*.
mission ['mɪʃ(ə)n] *n* mission *f*. ● **missionary** *n* missionnaire *m*.
missive ['mɪsɪv] *n* (*letter*) missive *f*.
misspell [mɪs'spel] *vt* (*pt & pp* **-ed** *or* **misspelt**) mal écrire.
mist [mɪst] *n* (*fog*) brume *f*; (*on glass*) buée *f* ▮ *vi* **to m. over** *or* **up** s'embuer.
mistake [mɪ'steɪk] *n* erreur *f*, faute *f*; **to make a m.** se tromper, faire (une) erreur; **by m.** par erreur.
▮ *vt* (*pt* **mistook,** *pp* **mistaken**) (*meaning, intention etc*) se tromper sur; **to m. the date/***etc* se tromper de date/*etc*; **you can't m. it** (*face, car etc*) il est impossible de ne pas le reconnaître; **to m. s.o./sth for** prendre qn/qch pour. ● **mistaken** *a* (*idea etc*) erroné; **to be m.** (*of person*) se tromper. ● **mistakenly** *adv* par erreur.
mister ['mɪstər] *n Fam* monsieur *m*.
mistletoe ['mɪs(ə)ltəʊ] *n Bot* gui *m*.
mistreat [mɪs'triːt] *vt* maltraiter.
mistress ['mɪstrɪs] *n* maîtresse *f*; (*in secondary school*) professeur *m*; (*in primary school*) institutrice *f*.
mistrust [mɪs'trʌst] *n* méfiance *f* ▮ *vt* se méfier de.
misty ['mɪstɪ] *a* (**-ier, -iest**) (*foggy*) brumeux; (*glass*) embué.
misunderstand [mɪsʌndə'stænd] *vti* (*pt & pp* **-stood**) mal comprendre. ● **misunderstanding** *n* malentendu *m*.
misuse [mɪs'juːz] *vt* (*word, tool*) mal employer; (*power etc*) abuser de ▮ [mɪs'juːs] *n* (*of word*) emploi *m* abusif; (*of tool*) usage *m* abusif; (*of power etc*) abus *m*.
mite [maɪt] *n* **1** (*insect*) mite *f*. **2 (poor) m.** (*child*) (pauvre) petit, -ite *mf*.
mitigate ['mɪtɪgeɪt] *vt* atténuer.
mitt(en) [mɪt, 'mɪt(ə)n] *n* (*glove*) moufle *f*.
mix [mɪks] *vt* mélanger, mêler; (*cement, cake*) préparer; (*salad*) remuer; **to m. up** (*drinks, papers etc*) mélanger; (*make confused*) embrouiller (*qn*); (*mistake*) confondre (**with** avec); **to be mixed up with s.o.** être mêlé aux affaires de qn.
▮ *vi* se mêler; (*of colours*) s'allier; **to m. with s.o.** (*socially*) fréquenter qn; **she doesn't m.** elle n'est pas sociable.
▮ *n* (*mixture*) mélange *m*. ● **mixed** *a* (*school,*

marriage) mixte; (*feelings*) mitigés; (*chocolates etc*) assortis; **m. grill** assortiment *m* de grillades; **to be m. up** (*of person*) être désorienté; (*of facts etc*) être embrouillé. ● **mixer** *n* (*electric, for food*) mixe(u)r *m*; **to be a good m.** (*of person*) être sociable. ● **mixture** *n* mélange *m*; (*for cough*) sirop *m*. ● **mix-up** *n* confusion *f*.

mm *abbr* (*millimetre*) mm.

moan [məʊn] *vi* (*groan*) gémir; (*complain*) se plaindre (**to** à, **about** de, **that** que) ‖ *n* gémissement *m*; plainte *f*.

moat [məʊt] *n* douve(s) *f(pl)*.

mob [mɒb] *n* (*crowd*) foule *f*, cohue *f*; (*gang*) bande *f* ‖ *vt* (**-bb-**) (*person, store etc*) assiéger.

mobile ['məʊbaɪl, *Am* 'məʊb(ə)l] *a* mobile; (*having a car*) *Fam* motorisé; **m. home** mobil-home *m*; **m. library** bibliobus *m*; **m. phone** téléphone *m* portatif ‖ *n* (*Am* ['məʊbi:l]) (*ornament*) mobile *m*. ● **mo'bility** *n* mobilité *f*.

mobilize ['məʊbɪlaɪz] *vti* mobiliser.

moccasin ['mɒkəsɪn] *n* (*shoe*) mocassin *m*.

mocha ['məʊkə] *n* (*coffee*) moka *m*.

mock [mɒk] **1** *vt* se moquer de; (*mimic*) singer ‖ *vi* se moquer (**at** de). **2** *a* (*false*) simulé; **m. exam** examen *m* blanc. ● **—ing** *a* moqueur. ● **mockery** *n* (*act*) moquerie *f*; (*parody*) parodie *f*; **to make a m. of sth** tourner qch en ridicule.

mock-up ['mɒkʌp] *n* (*model*) maquette *f*.

mod cons [mɒd'kɒnz] *npl abbr* (*modern conveniences*) tout le confort moderne.

mode [məʊd] *n* (*manner*) & *Comptr* mode *m*.

model ['mɒd(ə)l] *n* (*example, person posing for artist etc*) modèle *m*; **(fashion) m.** mannequin *m*; **(scale) m.** modèle *m* (réduit).

‖ *a* (*behaviour, student etc*) modèle; (*car, plane etc*) modèle réduit *inv*; **m. railway** train *n* miniature.

‖ *vt* (*clay etc*) modeler (*hats etc*) présenter (les modèles de); **to m. sth/s.o. on** modeler qch/qn sur.

‖ *vi* (*for fashion*) être mannequin; (*pose for artist*) poser.

modem ['maʊdəm] *n Comptr* modem *m*.

moderate[1] ['mɒdərət] *a* modéré; (*in speech*) mesuré ‖ *n Pol* modéré, -ée *mf*. ● **—ly** *adv* modérément; (*averagely*) moyennement.

moderate[2] ['mɒdəreɪt] *vt* (*tone down*) modérer. ● **moderation** [-'reɪʃ(ə)n] *n* modération *f*; **in m.** avec modération.

modern ['mɒd(ə)n] *a* moderne; **m. languages** langues *fpl* vivantes.

modernize ['mɒdənaɪz] *vt* moderniser ‖ *vi* se moderniser.

modest ['mɒdɪst] *a* modeste. ● **modesty** *n* (*quality*) modestie *f*.

modify ['mɒdɪfaɪ] *vt* (*alter*) modifier; (*tone down*) modérer. ● **modification** [-'keɪʃ(ə)n] *n* modification *f*.

mohair ['məʊheər] *n* mohair *m*.

moist [mɔɪst] *a* (**-er, -est**) humide; (*sticky*) moite. ● **moisten** ['mɔɪs(ə)n] *vt* humecter.

moisture ['mɔɪstʃər] *n* humidité *f*; (*on glass*) buée *f*. ● **moisturizer** *n* (*for skin*) crème *f* hydratante.

molar ['məʊlər] *n* (*tooth*) molaire *f*.

molasses [mə'læsɪz] *n* (*treacle*) *Am* mélasse *f*.

mold [məʊld] *Am* = **mould.**

mole [məʊl] *n* **1** (*on skin*) grain *m* de beauté. **2** (*animal, spy*) taupe *f*.

molecule ['mɒlɪkju:l] *n* molécule *f*.

molest [mə'lest] *vt* (*annoy*) importuner; (*child, woman*) *Jur* attenter à la pudeur de.

molt [məʊlt] *Am* = **moult.**

molten ['məʊlt(ə)n] *a* (*metal*) en fusion.

mom [mɒm] *n Am Fam* maman *f*.

moment ['məʊmənt] *n* moment *m*; **this (very) m.** (*now*) à l'instant; **the m. she leaves** dès qu'elle partira; **any m. (now)** d'un moment à l'autre.

momentary ['məʊməntərɪ, *Am* -erɪ] *a* momentané. ● **momentarily** (*Am* [məʊmən'terɪlɪ]) *adv* (*temporarily*) momentanément; (*soon*) *Am* tout à l'heure.

momentum [məʊ'mentəm] *n* (*speed*) élan *m*; **to gather m.** (*of ideas etc*) gagner du terrain.

mommy ['mɒmɪ] *n Am Fam* maman *f*.

Monaco ['mɒnəkəʊ] *n* Monaco *f*.

monarch ['mɒnək] *n* monarque *m*. ● **monarchy** *n* monarchie *f*.

monastery ['mɒnəst(ə)rɪ] *n* monastère *m*.

Monday ['mʌndɪ, *Am* -deɪ] *n* lundi *m*.

monetary ['mʌnɪt(ə)rɪ] *a* monétaire.

money ['mʌnɪ] *n* argent *m*; **to get one's m.'s worth** en avoir pour son argent; **m. order** mandat *m*. ● **moneybox** *n* tirelire *f*. ● **moneychanger** *n* changeur *m*. ● **moneylender** *n* prêteur, -euse *mf* sur gages. ● **moneymaking** *a* lucratif. ● **money-spinner** *n Fam* mine *f* d'or.

mongrel ['mʌŋgrəl] *n* (*dog*) bâtard *m*.

monitor ['mɒnɪtər] **1** *n* (*screen, device*) *Comptr TV etc* moniteur *m*. **2** *vt* (*radio broadcast*) écouter; (*check*) contrôler.

monk [mʌŋk] *n* moine *m*, religieux *m*.

monkey ['mʌŋkɪ] *n* singe *m*; **m. wrench** clef *f* anglaise.

mono ['mɒnəʊ] *a* (*record etc*) mono *inv.* ▮ *n* **in m.** en monophonie.
mono- ['mɒnəʊ] *pref* mono-.
monologue ['mɒnəlɒg] *n* monologue *m.*
monopoly [mə'nɒpəlɪ] *n* monopole *m.* ● **monopolize** *vt* monopoliser.
monotony [mə'nɒtənɪ] *n* monotonie *f.* ● **monotonous** *a* monotone.
monsoon [mɒn'su:n] *n* (*wind, rain*) mousson *f.*
monster ['mɒnstər] *n* monstre *m.* ● **mon'strosity** *n* monstruosité *f.* ● **monstrous** *a* (*terrible, enormous*) monstrueux.
month [mʌnθ] *n* mois *m.* ● **monthly** *a* mensuel ▮ *n* (*periodical*) mensuel *m* ▮ *adv* (*every month*) mensuellement.
Montreal [mɒntrɪ'ɔ:l] *n* Montréal *m or f.*
monument ['mɒnjʊmənt] *n* monument *m.*
moo [mu:] *vi* meugler ▮ *n* meuglement *m.*
mooch [mu:tʃ] *vi* **to m. around** *Fam* flâner.
mood [mu:d] *n* (*of person*) humeur *f*; (*of country*) état *m* d'esprit; *Gram* mode *m*; **in a good/bad m.** de bonne/mauvaise humeur; **to be in the m. to do** être d'humeur à faire. ● **moody** *a* (**-ier, -iest**) (*bad-tempered*) de mauvaise humeur; (*changeable*) d'humeur changeante.
moon [mu:n] *n* lune *f*; **full m.** pleine lune; **over the m.** (*delighted*) *Fam* ravi (**about** de). ● **moonlight** *n* clair *m* de lune; **by m.** au clair de lune.
moor [mʊər] **1** *vt Nau* amarrer ▮ *vi* mouiller. **2** *n* (*open land*) lande *f.*
moose [mu:s] *n inv* (*animal*) élan *m.*
mop [mɒp] *n* balai *m* (à laver); **dish m.** lavette *f*; **m. of hair** tignasse *f* ▮ *vt* (**-pp-**) **to m. (up)** (*floor etc*) essuyer; **to m. up** (*liquid*) éponger.
mope [məʊp] *vi* **to m. about** errer comme une âme en peine.
moped ['məʊped] *n* mobylette® *f.*
moral ['mɒrəl] *a* moral ▮ *n* (*of story*) morale *f*; *pl* (*standards*) moralité *f.* ● **morale** [mə'rɑ:l, *Am* mə'ræl] *n* moral *m.* ● **mo'rality** *n* (*morals*) moralité *f.*
morbid ['mɔ:bɪd] *a* morbide.
more [mɔ:r] *a* & *n* plus (de) (**than** que); (*other*) d'autres; **m. cars/***etc* plus de voitures/*etc*; **he has m. (than you)** il en a plus (que toi); **a few m. months** encore quelques mois; **(some) m. tea/***etc* encore du thé/*etc*; **(some) m. details** d'autres détails; **m. than a kilo/ten** (*with quantity, number*) plus d'un kilo/de dix.
▮ *adv* (*tired, rapidly etc*) plus (**than** que); **m. and m.** de plus en plus; **m. or less** plus ou moins; **the m. he shouts the m. hoarse he gets** plus il crie plus il s'enroue; **she doesn't have any m.** elle n'en a plus.
moreover [mɔ:'rəʊvər] *adv* de plus.
morgue [mɔ:g] *n* (*mortuary*) morgue *f.*
morning ['mɔ:nɪŋ] *n* matin *m*; (*duration of morning*) matinée *f*; **in the m.** le matin; (*tomorrow*) demain matin; **at seven in the m.** à sept heures du matin; **every Tuesday m.** tous les mardis matin ▮ *a* du matin. ● **mornings** *adv Am* le matin.
Morocco [mə'rɒkəʊ] *n* Maroc *m.* ● **Moroccan** *a* & *n* marocain, -aine (*mf*).
moron ['mɔ:rɒn] *n* crétin, -ine *mf.*
morphine ['mɔ:fi:n] *n* morphine *f.*
Morse [mɔ:s] *n* & *a* **M. (code)** morse *m.*
mortal ['mɔ:t(ə)l] *a* & *n* mortel, -elle (*mf*).
mortar ['mɔ:tər] *n* mortier *m.*
mortgage ['mɔ:gɪdʒ] *n* prêt-logement *m.*
mortician [mɔ:'tɪʃ(ə)n] *n Am* entrepreneur *m* de pompes funèbres.
mortuary ['mɔ:tʃʊərɪ] *n* morgue *f.*
mosaic [məʊ'zeɪɪk] *n* mosaïque *f.*
Moscow ['mɒskəʊ, *Am* 'mɒskaʊ] *n* Moscou *m or f.*
Moses ['məʊzɪz] *a* **M. basket** couffin *m.*
Moslem ['mɒzlɪm] *a* & *n* musulman, -ane (*mf*).
mosque [mɒsk] *n* mosquée *f.*
mosquito [mɒ'ski:təʊ] *n* (*pl* **-oes**) moustique *m*; **m. net** moustiquaire *f.*
moss [mɒs] *n* mousse *f* (*plante*).
most [məʊst] *a* & *n* **the m.** (*greatest in amount etc*) le plus (de); **I have (the) m. books** j'ai le plus de livres; **I have (the) m.** j'en ai le plus; **m. (of the) books/***etc* la plupart des livres/*etc*; **m. of the cake/***etc* la plus grande partie du gâteau/*etc*; **m. of them** la plupart d'entre eux; **m. of it** la plus grande partie; **at (the very) m.** tout au plus; **to make the m. of sth** profiter (au maximum) de qch.
▮ *adv* (le) plus; (*very*) très; **the m. beautiful** le plus beau, la plus belle (**in, of** de); **to talk (the) m.** parler le plus; **m. of all** surtout. ● **mostly** *adv* surtout.
MOT [eməʊ'ti:] *n abbr* (*Ministry of Transport*) = contrôle *m* obligatoire des véhicules de plus de trois ans.
motel [məʊ'tel] *n* motel *m.*
moth [mɒθ] *n* papillon *m* de nuit; (*in clothes*) mite *f.* ● **m.-eaten** *a* mité. ● **mothball** *n* boule *f* de naphtaline.
mother ['mʌðər] *n* mère *f*; **M.'s Day** la fête des Mères; **m. tongue** langue *f* maternelle. ● **motherhood** *n* maternité *f.* ● **motherly** *a* maternel.
mother-in-law ['mʌðərɪnlɔ:] *n* (*pl* **mothers-**

in-law) belle-mère *f*. ● **m.-of-pearl** *n* (*substance*) nacre *f*. ● **m.-to-'be** *n* (*pl* **mothers-to-be**) future mère *f*.

motion ['məʊʃ(ə)n] *n* (*of arm etc*) mouvement *m*; *Pol* motion *f*; **to set in m.** mettre en mouvement; **m. picture** film *m* ‖ *vti* **to m. (to) s.o. to do** faire signe à qn de faire. ● **—less** *a* immobile.

motive ['məʊtɪv] *n* motif *m* (**for** de).

motivate ['məʊtɪveɪt] *vt* (*person*, *decision*) motiver. ● **motivation** [-'veɪʃ(ə)n] *n* motivation *f*; (*incentive*) encouragement *m*.

motley ['mɒtlɪ] *a* (*collection*) hétéroclite.

motor ['məʊtər] *n* (*engine*) moteur *m*; (*car*) *Fam* auto *f* ‖ *a* (*industry etc*) automobile; (*accident*) d'auto; **m. boat** canot *m* automobile ‖ *vi* (*drive*) rouler en auto. ● **—ing** *n Sp* automobilisme *m*; **school of m.** auto-école *f*.

motorbike ['məʊtəbaɪk] *n Fam* moto *f*. ● **motorcar** *n* automobile *f*. ● **motorcycle** *n* moto *f*. ● **motorcyclist** *n* motocycliste *mf*. ● **motorist** *n* automobiliste *mf*. ● **motorway** *n* autoroute *f*.

motto ['mɒtəʊ] *n* (*pl* **-oes** *or* **-os**) devise *f*.

mould [məʊld] (*Am* **mold**) **1** *n* (*shape*) moule *m* ‖ *vt* (*clay etc*) mouler; (*character*) modeler. **2** *n* (*growth*) moisissure *f*. ● **mouldy** (*Am* **moldy**) *a* (**-ier, -iest**) moisi; **to go m.** moisir.

moult [məʊlt] (*Am* **molt**) *vi* muer. ● **—ing** *n* mue *f*.

mound [maʊnd] *n* (*of earth*) tertre *m*; (*untidy pile*) *Fig* monceau *m*.

mount [maʊnt] **1** *n* (*frame for photo or slide*) cadre *m*; (*horse*) monture *f* ‖ *vt* (*horse*, *jewel*, *photo etc*) monter; (*ladder etc*) monter sur ‖ *vi* **to m. (up)** (*on horse*) se mettre en selle. **2** *vi* (*increase*, *rise*) monter; **to m. up** (*add up*) chiffrer (**to** à); (*accumulate*) s'accumuler.

Mount [maʊnt] *n* (*in place names*) mont *m*.

mountain ['maʊntɪn] *n* montagne *f*; **m. bike** VTT *m inv*. ● **mountai'neer** *n* alpiniste *mf*. ● **mountai'neering** *n* alpinisme *m*. ● **mountainous** *a* montagneux.

mourn [mɔːn] *vti* **to m. (for) s.o., m. the loss of s.o.** pleurer (la perte de) qn; **she's mourning** elle est en deuil. ● **—ing** *n* deuil *m*; **in m.** en deuil. ● **mourner** *n* parent, -ente *mf or* ami, -ie *mf* du défunt *or* de la défunte.

mouse, *pl* **mice** [maʊs, maɪs] *n* (*animal*) & *Comptr* souris *f*. ● **mousetrap** *n* souricière *f*.

mousse [muːs] *n* mousse *f* (*dessert*).

moustache [mə'stɑːʃ, *Am* 'mʌstæʃ] *n* moustache *f*.

mouth [maʊθ] *n* (*pl* **-s** [maʊðz]) bouche *f*; (*of dog*, *lion etc*) gueule *f*; (*of river*) embouchure *f*; (*of cave*) entrée *f*. ● **mouthful** *n* (*of food*) bouchée *f*; ● **mouthorgan** *n* harmonica *m*. ● **mouthpiece** *n Mus* embouchure *f*; (*spokesperson*) porte-parole *m inv*. ● **mouthwash** *n* bain *m* de bouche. ● **mouth-watering** *a* appétissant.

movable ['muːvəb(ə)l] *a* mobile.

move [muːv] *n* mouvement *m*; (*change of house*) déménagement *m*; (*change of job*) changement *m* d'emploi; (*in game*) coup *m*, (*one's turn*) tour *m*; (*act*) démarche *f*; (*attempt*) tentative *f*; **to make a m.** (*leave*) se préparer à partir; (*act*) passer à l'action; **to get a m. on** *Fam* se dépêcher; **on the m.** en marche.
‖ *vt* déplacer, remuer, bouger; (*arm*, *leg*) remuer; (*put*) mettre; (*transport*) transporter; (*piece in game*) jouer; **to m. s.o.** (*emotionally*) émouvoir qn; (*transfer in job*) muter qn; **to m. house** déménager.
‖ *vi* bouger, remuer; (*go*) aller (**to** à); (*pass*) passer (**to** à); (*change seats*) changer de place; (*progress*) avancer; (*act*) agir; (*play*) jouer; (*out of house*) déménager; **to m. to a new house**/*etc* aller habiter une nouvelle maison/*etc*; **to m. into a house** emménager dans une maison.

move about *or* **around** *vi* se déplacer; (*fidget*) remuer ‖ **to move along** *vi* avancer ‖ **to move away** *vi* (*go away*) s'éloigner; (*move house*) déménager ‖ **to move back** *vt* (*chair etc*) reculer; (*to its position*) remettre ‖ *vi* reculer; (*return*) retourner ‖ **to move down** *vt* descendre (*qch*) ‖ **to move forward** *vti* avancer ‖ **to move in** *vi* (*into house*) emménager ‖ **to move off** *vi* (*go away*) s'éloigner; (*of vehicle*) démarrer ‖ **to move on** *vi* avancer; **m. on!** circulez! ‖ **to move out** *vi* (*out of house*) déménager ‖ **to move over** *vt* pousser ‖ *vi* (*make room*) se pousser ‖ **to move up** *vi* (*on seats etc*) se pousser.

moveable ['muːvəb(ə)l] *a* mobile.

movement ['muːvmənt] *n* (*action*, *group etc*) & *Mus* mouvement *m*.

movie ['muːvɪ] *n Fam* film *m*; **the movies** (*cinema*) le cinéma; **m. camera** caméra *f*; **m. theater** *Am* cinéma *m*.

moving ['muːvɪŋ] *a* en mouvement; (*touching*) émouvant; **m. stairs** escalier *m* mécanique.

mow [məʊ] *vt* (*pp* **mown** *or* **mowed**) (*field*) faucher; **to m. the lawn** tondre le gazon; **to m. down** (*kill*) *Fig* faucher. ● **—er** *n* **(lawn) m.** tondeuse *f* (à gazon).

MP [em'piː] *n abbr* (*Member of Parliament*) député *m*.

Mr ['mɪstər] *n* **Mr Brown** Monsieur *or* M. Brown.

Mrs ['mɪsɪz] *n* (*married woman*) **Mrs Brown** Madame *or* Mme Brown.

Ms [mɪz] *n* (*married or unmarried woman*) **Ms Brown** Madame *or* Mme Brown.

MSc [emes'si:], *Am* **MS** *abbr* = **Master of Science.**

much [mʌtʃ] *a* & *n* beaucoup (de); **not m. time/money/***etc* pas beaucoup de temps/d'argent/*etc*; **not m.** pas beaucoup; **m. of sth** (*a good deal of*) une bonne partie de qch; **as m. as** autant que; **as m. wine/***etc* **as** autant de vin/*etc* que; **as m. as you like** autant que tu veux; **twice as m.** deux fois plus (de); **how m.?** combien (de)?; **too m.** trop (de); **so m.** tant (de); **I know this m.** je sais ceci (du moins); **it's not m. of a garden** ce n'est pas merveilleux comme jardin.
▮ *adv* **very m.** beaucoup; **not (very) m.** pas beaucoup.

muck [mʌk] **1** *n* (*manure*) fumier *m*; (*filth*) *Fig* saleté *f*.
2 *vi* **to m. about** *Fam* (*have fun*) s'amuser; (*play the fool*) faire l'idiot; **to m. about with sth** (*fiddle with*) *Fam* s'amuser avec qch; **to m. in** *Fam* participer, contribuer.
▮ *vt* **to m. s.o. about** *Fam* embêter qn; **to m. sth up** *Fam* gâcher qch ● **m.-up** *n Fam* gâchis *m*. ● **mucky** *a* (**-ier, -iest**) sale.

mud [mʌd] *n* boue *f*. ● **muddy** *a* (**-ier, -iest**) (*water, road*) boueux; (*hands etc*) couvert de boue. ● **mudguard** *n* garde-boue *m inv*.

muddle ['mʌd(ə)l] *n* (*mix-up*) confusion *f*; (*mess*) désordre *m*; **in a m.** (*person*) désorienté; (*mind, ideas*) embrouillé ▮ *vt* (*person, facts etc*) embrouiller; (*papers*) mélanger ▮ *vi* **to m. through** *Fam* se débrouiller.

muesli ['mju:zlɪ] *n* muesli *m*.

muffin ['mʌfɪn] *n* (*cake*) *sorte de petite brioche*.

muffl/e ['mʌf(ə)l] *vt* (*noise*) assourdir. ● **—ed** *a* (*noise*) sourd. ● **—er** *n Aut Am* silencieux *m*.

mug [mʌg] **1** *n* grande tasse *f*; **(beer) m.** chope *f*. **2** *n* (*face*) *Fam* gueule *f*. **3** *n* (*fool*) *Fam* niais, -aise *mf*. **4** *vt* (**-gg-**) (*in street*) agresser, attaquer. ● **mugger** *n* agresseur *m*. ● **mugging** *n* agression *f*.

muggy ['mʌgɪ] *a* (**-ier, -iest**) (*weather*) lourd.

mule [mju:l] *n* (*male*) mulet *m*; (*female*) mule *f*.

multi- ['mʌltɪ] *pref* multi-.

multicoloured ['mʌltɪkʌləd] (*Am* **multicolored**) *a* multicolore.

multimillionaire [mʌltɪmɪljə'neər] *n* milliardaire *mf*.

multiple ['mʌltɪp(ə)l] *a* multiple ▮ *n Math* multiple *m*.

multiply ['mʌltɪplaɪ] *vt* multiplier ▮ *vi* (*of animals, insects*) se multiplier. ● **multiplication** [-'keɪʃ(ə)n] *n* multiplication *f*.

multistorey [mʌltɪ'stɔ:rɪ] (*Am* **multistoried**) *a* à étages.

multitude ['mʌltɪtju:d] *n* multitude *f*.

mum [mʌm] *n Fam* maman *f*.

mumble ['mʌmb(ə)l] *vti* marmotter.

mummy ['mʌmɪ] *n* **1** (*mother*) *Fam* maman *f*. **2** (*body*) momie *f*.

mumps [mʌmps] *n* oreillons *mpl*.

munch [mʌntʃ] *vti* (*chew*) mastiquer; (*eat*) *Fam* manger à belles dents.

mundane [mʌn'deɪn] *a* banal (*mpl* -als).

municipal [mju:'nɪsɪp(ə)l] *a* municipal.

mural ['mjʊərəl] *n* fresque *f*, peinture *f* murale.

murder ['mɜ:dər] *n* meurtre *m*, assassinat *m*; **it's m.** (*dreadful*) *Fam* c'est affreux ▮ *vt* (*kill*) assassiner. ● **—er** *n* meurtrier, -ière *mf*, assassin *m*.

murky ['mɜ:kɪ] *a* (**-ier, -iest**) obscur; (*water, business, past*) trouble.

murmur ['mɜ:mər] *n* murmure *m* ▮ *vti* murmurer.

muscle ['mʌs(ə)l] *n* muscle *m*. ● **muscular** *a* (*arm etc*) musclé.

museum [mju:'zɪəm] *n* musée *m*.

mush [mʌʃ] *n* (*soft mass*) bouillie *f*. ● **mushy** *a* (**-ier, -iest**) (*food etc*) en bouillie.

mushroom ['mʌʃrʊm] *n* champignon *m*.

music ['mju:zɪk] *n* musique *f*; **m. centre** chaîne *f* stéréo compacte; **m. hall** music-hall *m*; **m. lover** mélomane *mf*; **canned** *or* **piped m.** musique *f* (de fond) enregistrée. ● **musical** *a* musical; (*instrument*) de musique; **to be m.** être musicien ▮ *n* (*film, play*) comédie *f* musicale. ● **musician** [-'zɪʃ(ə)n] *n* musicien, -ienne *mf*.

Muslim ['mʊzlɪm] *a* & *n* musulman, -ane (*mf*).

muslin ['mʌzlɪn] *n* (*cotton*) mousseline *f*.

mussel ['mʌs(ə)l] *n* (*shellfish*) moule *f*.

must [mʌst] *v aux* **1** (*necessity*) **you m. obey** tu dois obéir, il faut que tu obéisses. **2** (*certainty*) **she m. be clever** elle doit être intelligente; **I m. have seen it** j'ai dû le voir ▮ *n* **this is a m.** ceci est indispensable.

mustache ['mʌstæʃ] *n Am* moustache *f*.

mustard ['mʌstəd] *n* moutarde *f*.

muster ['mʌstər] *vt* (*gather*) rassembler (*troupes, courage etc*).

mustn't ['mʌs(ə)nt] = **must not.**
musty ['mʌstɪ] *a* **(-ier, -iest)** (*smell*) de moisi; **it smells m., it's m.** ça sent le moisi.
mute [mjuːt] *a* (*silent*) & *Ling* muet (*f* muette).
muted ['mjuːtɪd] *a* (*criticism*) voilé.
mutilate ['mjuːtɪleɪt] *vt* mutiler.
mutiny ['mjuːtɪnɪ] *n* mutinerie *f* ‖ *vi* se mutiner.
mutter ['mʌtər] *vti* marmonner.
mutton ['mʌt(ə)n] *n* (*meat*) mouton *m*.
mutual ['mjuːtʃʊəl] *a* (*help etc*) mutuel; (*friend etc*) commun; **m. fund** *Fin Am* fonds *m* commun de placement. ●**—ly** *adv* mutuellement.
muzzle ['mʌz(ə)l] *n* (*for animal*) muselière *f*; (*snout*) museau *m* ‖ *vt* museler.
my [maɪ] *poss a* mon, ma, *pl* mes.
myself [maɪ'self] *pron* moi-même; (*reflexive*) me, m'; (*after prep*) moi; **I wash m.** je me lave; **I think of m.** je pense à moi.
mystery ['mɪstərɪ] *n* mystère *m*. ●**my'sterious** *a* mystérieux.
mystical ['mɪstɪk(ə)l] *a* mystique.
mystify ['mɪstɪfaɪ] *vt* (*bewilder*) laisser perplexe; (*fool*) mystifier.
myth [mɪθ] *n* mythe *m*. ●**my'thology** *n* mythologie *f*.

N

N, n [en] *n* N, n *m*.
nab [næb] *vt* (**-bb-**) (*catch*) *Fam* épingler.
naff [næf] *a Fam* (*stupid*) bête; (*unfashionable*) ringard.
nag [næg] *vt* (**-gg-**) **to n. s.o.** (*pester*) embêter qn (**to do** pour qu'il fasse); (*find fault with*) critiquer qn. ● **nagging** *a* (*doubt*, *headache*) qui subsiste.
nail [neɪl] **1** *n* (*of finger*, *toe*) ongle *m*; **n. file/polish** lime *f*/vernis *m à* ongles. **2** *n* (*metal*) clou *m* ▮ *vt* **to n. (down)** (*lid etc*) clouer.
naïve [naɪ'iːv] *a* naïf.
naked ['neɪkɪd] *a* (*person*) (tout) nu; (*flame*) nu; **to see with the n. eye** voir à l'œil nu.
name [neɪm] *n* nom *m*; (*reputation*) réputation *f*; **my n. is...** je m'appelle...; **in the n. of** au nom de; **to put one's n. down for** (*school*, *course*) s'inscrire à; **to call s.o. names** injurier qn; **first n.** prénom *m*; **last n.** nom *m* de famille; **n. plate** plaque *f*. ▮ *vt* nommer; (*ship*, *street*) baptiser; (*date*, *price*) fixer; **he was named after** *or Am* **for...** il a reçu le nom de....
namely ['neɪmlɪ] *adv* (*that is*) à savoir.
namesake ['neɪmseɪk] *n* (*person*) homonyme *m*.
nanny ['nænɪ] *n* nurse *f*; (*grandmother*) *Fam* mamie *f*.
nap [næp] *n* (*sleep*) petit somme *m*; **to have** *or* **take a n.** faire un petit somme; (*after lunch*) faire la sieste ▮ *vi* (**-pp-**) sommeiller.
nape [neɪp] *n* **n. (of the neck)** nuque *f*.
napkin ['næpkɪn] *n* (*at table*) serviette *f*. ● **nappy** *n* (*for baby*) couche *f*. ● **nappy-liner** *n* protège-couche *m*.
narcotic [nɑː'kɒtɪk] *a* & *n* narcotique (*m*).
narrate [nə'reɪt] *vt* raconter. ● **narrative** ['nærətɪv] *n* (*story*) récit *m*. ● **narrator** *n* narrateur, -trice *mf*.
narrow ['nærəʊ] *a* (**-er, -est**) étroit ▮ *vi* (*of path*) se rétrécir ▮ *vt* **to n. (down)** (*choice*, *meaning etc*) limiter. ● **—ly** *adv* (*to miss etc*) de justesse; **he n. escaped** *or* **missed being killed**/*etc* il a failli être tué/*etc*.
narrow-minded [nærəʊ'maɪndɪd] *a* borné.
nasty ['nɑːstɪ] *a* (**-ier, -iest**) (*bad*) mauvais, vilain; (*spiteful*) méchant (**to, towards** avec). ● **nastily** *adv* (*to behave*) méchamment; (*to rain*) horriblement.
nation ['neɪʃ(ə)n] *n* nation *f*. ● **national** ['næʃən(ə)l] *a* national; **n. anthem** hymne *m* national; **N. Health Service** = Sécurité *f* Sociale; **n. insurance** = assurances *fpl* sociales ▮ *n* (*citizen*) ressortissant, -ante *mf*. ● **nationalist** *n* nationaliste *mf*. ● **natio'nality** *n* nationalité *f*. ● **nationalize** *vt* nationaliser. ● **nationally** *adv* (*to travel etc*) dans le pays (tout) entier.
nationwide ['neɪʃənwaɪd] *a* & *adv* dans le pays (tout) entier.
native ['neɪtɪv] *a* (*country*) natal (*mpl* -als); (*habits*, *costume*) du pays; (*tribe*) indigène; **n. language** langue *f* maternelle; **to be an English n. speaker** parler l'anglais comme langue maternelle ▮ *n* (*formerly*, *non-European in colony*) indigène *mf*; **to be a n. of** être originaire de.
NATO ['neɪtəʊ] *n abbr* (*North Atlantic Treaty Organization*) OTAN *f*.
natter ['nætər] *vi Fam* bavarder.
natural ['nætʃ(ə)rəl] *a* naturel; (*actor*, *gardener etc*) né. ● **naturally** *adv* (*as normal*, *of course*) naturellement; (*by nature*) de nature; (*to behave etc*) avec naturel.
naturalized ['nætʃ(ə)rəlaɪzd] *a* **to become n.** se faire naturaliser.
nature ['neɪtʃər] *n* (*natural world*, *character*) nature *f*; **by n.** de nature; **n. study** sciences *fpl* naturelles.
naught [nɔːt] *n Math* zéro *m*.
naught/y ['nɔːtɪ] *a* (**-ier, -iest**) (*child*) vilain, malicieux; (*joke*, *story*) osé. ● **—iness** *n* mauvaise conduite *f*.
nausea ['nɔːzɪə] *n* nausée *f*. ● **nauseate** *vt* écœurer. ● **nauseous** ['nɔːʃəs] *a* **to feel n.** (*sick*) *Am* avoir envie de vomir.
nautical ['nɔːtɪk(ə)l] *a* nautique.
naval ['neɪv(ə)l] *a* naval (*mpl* -als); (*hospital*) maritime; (*officer*) de marine.
nave [neɪv] *n* (*of church*) nef *f*.
navel ['neɪv(ə)l] *n* nombril *m*.
navigate ['nævɪgeɪt] *vi* naviguer ▮ *vt* (*boat*) diriger; (*river*) naviguer sur. ● **navigation** [-'geɪʃ(ə)n] *n* navigation *f*. ● **navigator** *n Av Nau* navigateur *m*.
navy ['neɪvɪ] *n* marine *f* ▮ *a* **n. (blue)** bleu marine *inv*.
Nazi ['nɑːtsɪ] *a* & *n Pol Hist* nazi, -ie (*mf*).
near [nɪər] *adv* (**-er, -est**) près; **quite n.** tout près; **to draw n.** (s')approcher (**to** de); (*of date*) approcher; **n. to** près de; **to come n. to being killed**/*etc* faillir être tué/*etc*; **n. en-**

ough (*more or less*) plus ou moins.
▮*prep* (**-er, -est**) **n. (to)** près de; **n. the bed** près du lit; **n. (to) the end** vers la fin; **to come n. s.o.** s'approcher de qn.
▮*a* (**-er, -est**) proche; **the nearest hospital** l'hôpital le plus proche; **the nearest way** la route la plus directe; **in the n. future** dans un avenir proche; **to the nearest franc** (*to calculate*) à un franc près; **n. side** *Aut* côté *m* gauche, *Am* côté *m* droit.
▮*vt* (*approach*) approcher de; **nearing completion** près d'être achevé. ●**near'by** *adv* tout près ▮['nɪəbaɪ] *a* proche.

nearly ['nɪəlɪ] *adv* presque; **she (very) n. fell** elle a failli tomber; **not n. as clever/***etc* **as** loin d'être aussi intelligent/*etc* que.

neat [ni:t] *a* (**-er, -est**) (*clothes, work*) soigné, propre; (*room*) bien rangé; (*style*) élégant; (*pleasant*) *Fam* agréable; (*good*) *Fam* super; **to drink one's whisky n.** prendre son whisky sec. ●**—ly** *adv* avec soin; (*skilfully*) habilement.

necessary ['nesɪs(ə)rɪ] *a* nécessaire; **it's n. to do** il est nécessaire de faire; **to make it n. for s.o. to do** mettre qn dans la nécessité de faire; **to do what's n.** faire le nécessaire (**for** pour). ●**nece'ssarily** *adv* **not n.** pas forcément.

necessity [nɪ'sesɪtɪ] *n* (*obligation, need*) nécessité *f*; **there's no n. for you to do that** tu n'es pas obligé de faire cela; **to be a n.** être indispensable; **the (bare) necessities** le (strict) nécessaire. ●**necessitate** *vt* nécessiter.

neck[1] [nek] *n* cou *m*; (*of dress, horse*) encolure *f*; (*of bottle*) col *m*; **low n.** (*of dress*) décolleté *m*; **n. and n.** *Sp* à égalité. ●**necklace** *n* collier *m*. ●**neckline** *n* encolure *f*. ●**necktie** *n* cravate *f*.

neck[2] [nek] *vi* (*kiss etc*) *Fam* se peloter.

nectarine ['nektəri:n] *n* (*fruit*) nectarine *f*.

need [ni:d] **1** *n* (*necessity, want, poverty*) besoin *m*; **in n.** dans le besoin; **to be in n. of** avoir besoin de; **there's no n. (for you) to do that** tu n'as pas besoin de faire cela; **if n. be** si besoin est.
▮*vt* avoir besoin de; **you n. it** tu en as besoin; **it needs an army** *or* **an army is needed to do that** il faut une armée pour faire cela; **this sport needs patience** ce sport demande de la patience; **to n. to do** avoir besoin de faire; (*obligation*) être obligé de faire; **her hair needs cutting** il faut qu'elle se fasse couper les cheveux.
2 *v aux* **n. he wait?** est-il obligé d'attendre?; **I needn't have rushed** ce n'était pas la peine de me presser. ●**needlessly** *adv* inutilement. ●**needy** *a* (**-ier, -iest**) *a* nécessiteux.

needle ['ni:d(ə)l] **1** *n* aiguille *f*; (*of record player*) saphir *m*. **2** *vt* (*irritate*) *Fam* agacer. ●**needlework** *n* couture *f*; (*object*) ouvrage *m*.

negative ['negətɪv] *a* négatif ▮*n Phot* négatif *m*; (*word*) *Gram* négation *f*; (*form*) *Gram* forme *f* négative; **to answer in the n.** répondre par la négative.

neglect [nɪ'glekt] *vt* (*person, health, work, duty etc*) négliger; (*garden, car*) ne pas s'occuper de; **to n. to do** négliger de faire
▮*n* (*of person*) manque *m* de soins (**of** envers); (*carelessness*) négligence *f*; **in a state of n.** (*garden, house*) mal tenu. ●**neglected** *a* (*appearance*) négligé; (*garden, house*) mal tenu; **to feel n.** sentir qu'on vous néglige.

negligent ['neglɪdʒənt] *a* négligent. ●**negligence** *n* négligence *f*.

negligible ['neglɪdʒəb(ə)l] *a* négligeable.

negotiate [nɪ'gəʊʃɪeɪt] **1** *vti* (*discuss*) négocier. **2** *vt* (*fence, obstacle*) franchir; (*bend*) *Aut* négocier. ●**negotiation** [-'eɪʃ(ə)n] *n* négociation *f*; **in n. with** en pourparlers avec.

Negro ['ni:grəʊ] *n* (*pl* **-oes**) *often Pej* (*man*) Noir *m*; (*woman*) Noire *f*.

neigh [neɪ] *vi* (*of horse*) hennir.

neighbour ['neɪbər] (*Am* **neighbor**) *n* voisin, -ine *mf*. ●**neighbourhood** *n* (*district*) quartier *m*; (*neighbours*) voisinage *m*; **in the n. of ten pounds** dans les dix livres. ●**neighbouring** *a* voisin. ●**neighbourly** *a* (*feeling etc*) amical; **they're n. (people)** ils sont bons voisins.

neither ['naɪðər, *Am* 'ni:ðər] *adv* **n. . . . nor** ni . . . ni; **n. you nor me** ni toi ni moi; **he n. sings nor dances** il ne chante ni ne danse.
▮*conj* (*not either*) (ne). . .non plus; **n. will I go** je n'y irai pas non plus; **n. do I, n. can I** *etc* (ni) moi non plus.
▮*a* **n. boy (came)** aucun des deux garçons (n'est venu); **on n. side** ni d'un côté ni de l'autre.
▮*pron* **n. (of them)** ni l'un(e) ni l'autre, aucun(e) (des deux).

neon ['ni:ɒn] *a* (*lighting etc*) au néon; **n. sign** enseigne *f* au néon.

nephew ['nevju:, 'nefju:] *n* neveu *m*.

nerve [nɜ:v] *n* nerf *m*; (*courage*) courage *m* (**to do** de faire); (*confidence*) assurance *f*; (*calm*) sang-froid *m*; (*impudence*) *Fam* culot *m* (**to do** de faire); **you get on my nerves** *Fam* tu me tapes sur les nerfs; **to have an attack of nerves** (*anxiety*) avoir le trac; **a bundle of nerves** (*person*) *Fam* un paquet de nerfs; **to have bad nerves** être nerveux; **n. centre** centre *m* nerveux. • **n.-racking** *a* éprouvant pour les nerfs.

nervous ['nɜːvəs] *a* (*tense*) nerveux; (*worried*) inquiet (**about** de); (*uneasy*) mal à l'aise; **to be** *or* **feel n.** (*before exam etc*) avoir le trac. • **—ly** *adv* nerveusement; (*worriedly*) avec inquiétude.

nest [nest] *n* nid *m*; **n. egg** (*money saved*) pécule *m* ‖ *vi* (*of bird*) (se) nicher.

nestle ['nes(ə)l] *vi* se pelotonner (**up to** contre).

net [net] **1** *n* filet *m*; **n. curtain** voilage *m*. **2** *a* (*profit, weight etc*) net (*f* nette) ‖ *vt* (**-tt-**) (*of person etc*) gagner net; **this venture netted them...** cette entreprise leur a rapporté.... • **netting** *n* (*nets*) filets *mpl*; (*mesh*) mailles *fpl*; **(wire) n.** grillage *m*.

Netherlands (the) [ðə'neðələndz] *npl* les Pays-Bas *mpl*.

nettle ['net(ə)l] *n* ortie *f*.

network ['netwɜːk] *n* réseau *m*.

neurotic [njʊ'rɒtɪk] *a* & *n* névrosé, -ée (*mf*).

neuter ['njuːtər] **1** *a* & *n Gram* neutre (*m*). **2** *vt* (*cat*) châtrer.

neutral ['njuːtrəl] *a* neutre; (*policy*) de neutralité ‖ *n* **in n. (gear)** *Aut* au point mort. • **neutralize** *vt* neutraliser.

never ['nevər] *adv* **1** (*not ever*) (ne...) jamais; **she n. lies** elle ne ment jamais; **n. in my life** jamais de ma vie; **n. again** plus jamais. **2** (*not*) *Fam* **I n. did it** je ne l'ai pas fait. • **n.-'ending** *a* interminable.

nevertheless [nevəðə'les] *adv* néanmoins.

new [njuː] *a* (**-er, -est**) nouveau (*f* nouvelle); (*brand-new*) neuf (*f* neuve); **a n. glass/pen/** *etc* (*different*) un autre verre/stylo/*etc*; **a n. boy** (*in school*) un nouveau; **what's n.?** *Fam* quoi de neuf?; **n. look** (*of person*) nouveau look *m*; **a n.-born baby** un nouveau-né, une nouveau-née. • **newcomer** *n* nouveau-venu *m*, nouvelle-venue *f*. • **new'fangled** *a* (trop) moderne. • **newly** *adv* (*recently*) nouvellement; **the n.-weds** les nouveaux mariés.

news [njuːz] *n* nouvelle(s) *f(pl)*; (*in the media*) informations *fpl*, actualités *fpl*; **sports/***etc* **n.** (*newspaper column*) chronique *f* sportive/*etc*; **a piece of n., some n.** une nouvelle; (*in the media*) une information; **n. flash** flash *m*.

newsagent ['njuːzeɪdʒənt] *n* marchand, -ande *mf* de journaux. • **newscaster** *n* présentateur, -trice *mf*. • **newsdealer** *n Am* = **newsagent**. • **newsletter** *n* (*of club etc*) bulletin *m*. • **newspaper** *n* journal *m*. • **newsprint** *n* papier *m* (de) journal. • **newsreader** *n* présentateur, -trice *mf*. • **newsy** *a* (**-ier, -iest**) (*letter etc*) *Fam* plein de nouvelles.

newt [njuːt] *n* (*animal*) triton *m*.

New Zealand [njuː'ziːlənd] *n* Nouvelle-Zélande *f* ‖ *a* néo-zélandais. • **New Zealander** *n* Néo-Zélandais, -aise *mf*.

next [nekst] *a* prochain; (*room, house*) d'à-côté; (*following*) suivant; **n. month** (*in the future*) le mois prochain; **he returned the n. month** (*in the past*) il revint le mois suivant; **the n. day** le lendemain; **the n. morning** le lendemain matin; **within the n. ten days** d'ici (à) dix jours; **(by) this time n. week** d'ici (à) la semaine prochaine; **from one year to the n.** d'une année à l'autre; **you're n.** c'est ton tour; **n. (please)!** (au) suivant!; **the n. size** la taille au-dessus; **to live/***etc* **n. door** habiter/*etc* à côté (**to** de); **n.-door neighbour** voisin *m* d'à-côté.
‖ *n* (*in series etc*) suivant, -ante *mf*.
‖ *adv* (*afterwards*) ensuite, après; (*now*) maintenant; **when you come n.** la prochaine fois que tu viendras.
‖ *prep* **n. to** (*beside*) à côté de; **n. to nothing** presque rien.

NHS [enetʃ'es] *n abbr* (*National Health Service*) = Sécurité *f* Sociale.

nib [nɪb] *n* (*of pen*) plume *f*, bec *m*.

nibble ['nɪb(ə)l] *vti* (*eat*) grignoter; (*bite*) mordiller.

nice [naɪs] *a* (**-er, -est**) (*pleasant*) agréable; (*charming*) charmant; (*good*) bon (*f* bonne); (*fine*) beau (*f* belle); (*pretty*) joli; (*kind*) gentil (**to** avec); (*respectable*) bien *inv*; **it's n. here** c'est bien ici; **n. and easy/***etc* (*very*) bien facile/*etc*. • **n.-'looking** *a* beau (*f* belle). • **nicely** *adv* agréablement; (*kindly*) gentiment; (*well*) bien.

niceties ['naɪsətɪz] *npl* (*subtleties*) subtilités *fpl*.

niche [niːʃ, nɪtʃ] *n* **1** (*recess*) niche *f*. **2** (*job*) **to make a n. for oneself** faire son trou.

nick [nɪk] **1** *n* (*on wood*) entaille *f*; (*in blade*) brèche *f*. **2** *n* (*prison*) *Sl* taule *f* ‖ *vt* (*steal, arrest*) *Sl* piquer. **3** *n* **in the n. of time** juste à temps.

nickel ['nɪk(ə)l] *n* (*metal*) nickel *m*; (*coin*) *Am* pièce *f* de cinq cents.

nickname ['nɪkneɪm] *n* surnom *m*; (*short form*) diminutif *m* ‖ *vt* surnommer.

nicotine ['nɪkətiːn] *n* nicotine *f*.

niece [niːs] *n* nièce *f*.

Nigeria [naɪ'dʒɪərɪə] *n* Nigéria *m*. • **Nigerian** *a* & *n* nigérian, -ane (*mf*).

niggling ['nɪglɪŋ] *a* (*trifling*) insignifiant; (*doubt*) persistant.

night [naɪt] *n* nuit *f*; (*evening*) soir *m*; **at n.** la nuit; **last n.** (*evening*) hier soir; (*night*) cette nuit, la nuit dernière; **to have an early/late n.** se coucher tôt/tard; **to have a good night('s sleep)** bien dormir; **first n.** *Th* première *f* ▮ *a* (*work etc*) de nuit; (*life*) nocturne; **n. school** cours *mpl* du soir; **n. watchman** veilleur *m* de nuit.

nightcap ['naɪtkæp] *n* boisson *f* (*prise avant de se coucher*). ●**nightclub** *n* boîte *f* de nuit. ●**nightdress** *or* **nightgown** *or Fam* **nightie** *n* (*woman's*) chemise *f* de nuit. ●**nightfall** *n* **at n.** à la tombée de la nuit. ●**nightlight** *n* veilleuse *f*. ●**nightmare** *n* cauchemar *m*. ●**nighttime** *n* nuit *f*.

nightingale ['naɪtɪŋgeɪl] *n* rossignol *m*.

nightly ['naɪtlɪ] *adv* chaque nuit *or* soir ▮ *a* de chaque nuit *or* soir.

nil [nɪl] *n* (*nothing*) & *Sp* zéro *m*; **the risk is n.** le risque est nul.

Nile [naɪl] *n* **the N.** le Nil.

nimble ['nɪmb(ə)l] *a* (**-er, -est**) agile.

nine [naɪn] *a* & *n* neuf (*m*). ●**nine'teen** *a* & *n* dix-neuf (*m*). ●**ninetieth** *a* & *n* quatre-vingt-dixième (*mf*). ●**ninety** *a* & *n* quatre-vingt-dix (*m*). ●**ninth** *a* & *n* neuvième (*mf*); **a n.** un neuvième.

nip [nɪp] **1** *vt* (**-pp-**) (*pinch, bite*) pincer ▮ *n* pinçon *m*; **there's a n. in the air** ça pince. **2** *vi* (**-pp-**) **to n. round to s.o.** *Fam* faire un saut chez qn; **to n. in/out** (*dash*) *Fam* entrer/sortir un instant.

nipple ['nɪp(ə)l] *n* bout *m* de sein; (*on baby's bottle*) *Am* tétine *f*.

nippy ['nɪpɪ] *a* (**-ier, -iest**) **it's n.** (*weather*) *Fam* ça pince.

nitwit ['nɪtwɪt] *n* (*fool*) *Fam* idiot, -ote *mf*.

nitrogen ['naɪtrədʒən] *n* azote *m*.

no [nəʊ] *adv* & *n* non (*m inv*); **no!** non!; **no more than ten/a kilo**/*etc* pas plus de dix/d'un kilo/*etc*; **no less than ten**/*etc* pas moins de dix/*etc*; **no more time**/*etc* plus de temps/*etc*; **no more/less than you** pas plus/moins que vous.
▮ *a* aucun(e); pas de; **I have no idea** je n'ai aucune idée; **no child came** aucun enfant n'est venu; **I have no money/time**/*etc* je n'ai pas d'argent/de temps/*etc*; **of no importance**/*etc* sans importance/*etc*; **with no gloves**/*etc* **on** sans gants/*etc*; **'no smoking'** 'défense de fumer'; **no way!** *Fam* pas question!; **no one** = **nobody.**

noble ['nəʊb(ə)l] *a* (**-er, -est**) noble. ●**no'bility** *n* noblesse *f*. ●**nobleman** *n* (*pl* **-men**) noble *m*.

nobody ['nəʊbɒdɪ] *pron* (ne. . .) personne; **n. came** personne n'est venu; **he knows n.** il ne connaît personne; **n.!** personne!

nod [nɒd] **1** *vti* (**-dd-**) **to n. (one's head)** faire un signe de tête ▮ *n* signe *m* de tête. **2** *vi* (**-dd-**) **to n. off** (*go to sleep*) s'assoupir.

noise [nɔɪz] *n* bruit *m*; (*of bell, drum*) son *m*; **to make a n.** faire du bruit.

noisy ['nɔɪzɪ] *a* (**-ier, -iest**) bruyant. ●**noisily** *adv* bruyamment.

nominal ['nɒmɪn(ə)l] *a* (*value*) nominal; (*rent, salary*) symbolique.

nominate ['nɒmɪneɪt] *vt* (*appoint*) nommer; (*as candidate*) proposer (**for** comme candidat à). ●**nomi'nation** [-'neɪʃ(ə)n] *n* nomination *f*; (*as candidate*) proposition *f* de candidat.

non- [nɒn] *pref* non-.

non-committal [nɒnkə'mɪt(ə)l] *a* (*answer, person*) évasif.

nondescript ['nɒndɪskrɪpt] *a* quelconque, très ordinaire.

none [nʌn] *pron* aucun(e) *mf*; (*in filling out a form*) néant; **n. of them** aucun d'eux; **she has n. (at all)** elle n'en a pas (du tout); **n. (at all) came** pas un(e) seul(e) n'est venu(e); **n. of the cake**/*etc* pas une seule partie du gâteau/*etc*; **n. of the trees**/*etc* aucun des arbres/*etc*; **n. of it** *or* **this** rien (de ceci).
▮ *adv* **n. too hot**/*etc* pas tellement chaud/*etc*; **he's n. the happier**/*etc* il n'est pas plus heureux/*etc*; **n. the better/worse** pas mieux/pas plus mal. ●**nonethe'less** *adv* néanmoins.

nonentity [nɒ'nentɪtɪ] *n* (*person*) nullité *f*.

non-existent [nɒnɪg'zɪstənt] *a* inexistant.

non-fiction [nɒn'fɪkʃ(ə)n] *n* littérature *f* non-romanesque; (*in library*) ouvrages *mpl* généraux.

nonplus [nɒn'plʌs] *vt* (**-ss-**) dérouter.

nonsense ['nɒnsəns] *n* absurdités *fpl*; **that's n.** c'est absurde.

non-smoker [nɒn'sməʊkər] *n* (*person*) non-fumeur, -euse *mf*; (*train compartment*) compartiment *m* non-fumeurs.

non-stick [nɒn'stɪk] *a* (*pan*) anti-adhésif.

non-stop [nɒn'stɒp] *a* sans arrêt; (*train, flight*) direct ▮ *adv* (*to work*) sans arrêt; (*to fly*) sans escale.

noodles ['nuːd(ə)lz] *npl* nouilles *fpl*; (*in soup*) vermicelle(s) *m*(*pl*).

nook [nʊk] *n* coin *m*; **in every n. and cranny** dans tous les coins (et recoins).

noon [nuːn] *n* midi *m*; **at n.** à midi ▮ *a* (*sun etc*) de midi.

no-one ['nəʊwʌn] *pron* = **nobody**.

noose [nuːs] *n* (*loop*) nœud *m* coulant; (*of hangman*) corde *f*.

nor [nɔːr] *conj* ni; **neither you n. me** ni toi ni moi; **she neither drinks n. smokes** elle ne fume ni ne boit; **n. do I, n. can I** *etc* (ni) moi non plus; **n. will I (go)** je n'y irai pas non plus.

norm [nɔːm] *n* norme *f*.

normal ['nɔːm(ə)l] *a* normal ▮ *n* **above/below n.** au-dessus/au-dessous de la normale. • **normally** *adv* normalement.

Normandy ['nɔːməndɪ] *n* Normandie *f*.

north [nɔːθ] *n* nord *m*; **(to the) n. of** au nord de.

▮ *a* (*coast*) nord *inv*; (*wind*) du nord; **N. America/Africa** Amérique *f*/Afrique *f* du Nord; **N. American** (*a* & *n*) nord-américain, -aine (*mf*).

▮ *adv* au nord, vers le nord. • **northbound** *a* (*traffic*) en direction du nord. • **north-'east** *n* & *a* nord-est *m* & *a inv*. • **northerly** ['nɔːðəlɪ] *a* (*point*) nord *inv*; (*direction*, *wind*) du nord. • **northern** ['nɔːðən] *a* (*coast*) nord *inv*; (*town*) du nord; **N. France** le Nord de la France; **N. Europe** Europe *f* du Nord; **N. Ireland** Irlande *f* du Nord. • **northerner** *n* habitant, -ante *mf* du Nord. • **northward(s)** *a* & *adv* vers le nord. • **north-'west** *n* & *a* nord-ouest *m* & *a inv*.

Norway ['nɔːweɪ] *n* Norvège *f*. • **Nor'wegian** [-'wiːdʒən] *a* & *n* norvégien, -ienne (*mf*) ▮ *n* (*language*) norvégien *m*.

nose [nəʊz] *n* nez *m*; **her n. is bleeding** elle saigne du nez; **to turn one's n. up** *Fig* faire le dégoûté (**at** devant). • **nosebleed** *n* saignement *m* de nez. • **nosedive** *n Av* piqué *m*.

nosey ['nəʊzɪ] *a* (**-ier, -iest**) indiscret; **n. parker** fouineur, -euse *mf*.

nosh [nɒʃ] *n Fam* (*light meal*) (petit) en-cas *m*; (*food*) bouffe *f*.

nostalgic [nɒ'stældʒɪk] *a* nostalgique.

nostril ['nɒstr(ə)l] *n* (*of person*) narine *f*; (*of horse*) naseau *m*.

nosy ['nəʊzɪ] *a* = **nosey**.

not [nɒt] *adv* **1** (ne...) pas; **he's n. there, he isn't there** il n'est pas là; **n. yet** pas encore; **why n.?** pourquoi pas?; **n. one reply/***etc* pas une seule réponse/*etc*; **n. at all** pas du tout; (*after 'thank you'*) je vous en prie. **2** non; **I think/hope n.** je pense/j'espère que non; **isn't she?, don't you?** *etc* non?

notable ['nəʊtəb(ə)l] *a* (*remarkable*) notable. • **notably** *adv* (*noticeably*) notablement; (*particularly*) notamment.

notch [nɒtʃ] **1** *n* (*in wood*) encoche *f*, entaille *f*; (*in belt*, *wheel*) cran *m*. **2** *vt* **to n. up** (*a score*) marquer.

note [nəʊt] *n* (*comment*, *tone etc*) & *Mus* note *f*; (*banknote*) billet *m*; (*piano key*) touche *f*; (*message*, *letter*) petit mot *m*; **to take n. of, make a n. of** prendre note de.

▮ *vt* (*take note of*, *notice*) noter; **to n. down** (*word etc*) noter. • **notebook** *n* carnet *m*; *Sch* cahier *m*. • **notepad** *n* bloc-notes *m*. • **notepaper** *n* papier *m* à lettres.

noted ['nəʊtɪd] *a* **to be n. for** être connu pour.

nothing ['nʌθɪŋ] *pron* (ne...) rien; **he knows n.** il ne sait rien; **n. to do/eat/***etc* rien à faire/manger/*etc*; **n. big/***etc* rien de grand/*etc*; **n. much** pas grand-chose; **n. but** (*problems etc*) rien que; **I've got n. to do with it** je n'y suis pour rien; **I can do n. (about it)** je n'y peux rien; **to come to n.** (*of efforts etc*) ne rien donner; **for n.** (*in vain*, *free of charge*) pour rien; **to have n. on** être tout nu.

▮ *adv* **n. like as large/***etc* loin d'être aussi grand/*etc*.

notice ['nəʊtɪs] *n* (*notification*) avis *m*; (*in newspaper*) annonce *f*; (*sign*) pancarte *f*; (*poster*) affiche *f*; (*review of film etc*) critique *f*; (*attention*) attention *f*; **n. (of dismissal)** congé *m*; **to give (in) one's n.** (*resignation*) donner sa démission; **to give s.o. (advance) n.** (*inform*) avertir qn (**of** de); **to take n.** faire attention (**of** à); **to bring sth to s.o.'s n.** porter qch à la connaissance de qn; **until further n.** jusqu'à nouvel ordre; **at short n.** au dernier moment; **n. board** tableau *m* d'affichage.

▮ *vt* (*person*, *fact*, *danger etc*) remarquer; **I n. that** je m'aperçois que, je remarque que. • **noticeable** *a* visible; **that's n.** ça se voit; **she's n.** elle se fait remarquer.

notify ['nəʊtɪfaɪ] *vt* (*inform*) avertir (**s.o. of sth** qn de qch); (*announce*) notifier (**to** à). • **notification** [-'keɪʃ(ə)n] *n* avis *m*.

notion ['nəʊʃ(ə)n] *n* (*thought*) idée *f*; (*awareness*) notion *f*; **some n. of** (*knowledge*) quelques notions de.

notorious [nəʊ'tɔːrɪəs] *a* (*event*, *person*) tristement célèbre; (*stupidity*, *criminal*) notoire.

notwithstanding [nɒtwɪð'stændɪŋ] *prep* malgré ▮ *adv* tout de même.

nougat ['nuːgɑː, 'nʌgət] *n* nougat *m*.

nought [nɔːt] *n Math* zéro *m*.

noun [naʊn] *n Gram* nom *m*.

nourish ['nʌrɪʃ] *vt* nourrir. • **—ing** *a* nourrissant. • **—ment** *n* nourriture *f*.

novel ['nɒv(ə)l] **1** *n* roman *m*. **2** *a* (*new*) nouveau (*f* nouvelle). • **novelist** *n* romancier, -ière *mf*. • **novelty** *n* (*object*, *idea*) nouveauté *f*.

November [nəʊ'vembər] *n* novembre *m*.

novice ['nɒvɪs] *n* novice *mf* (**at** en).

now [naʊ] *adv* maintenant; **just n., right n.**

en ce moment; **I saw her just n.** je l'ai vue à l'instant; **for n.** pour le moment; **from n. on** désormais; **before n.** avant; **n. and then** de temps à autre; **n. hot, n. cold** tantôt chaud, tantôt froid; **n. (then)!** bon!; (*telling s.o. off*) allons!; **n. it happened that...** or il advint que...
▮ *conj* **n. (that)** maintenant que. ● **nowadays** *adv* aujourd'hui, de nos jours.
noway ['nəʊweɪ] *adv Am* nullement.
nowhere ['nəʊweər] *adv* nulle part; **n. else** nulle part ailleurs; **n. near the house** loin de la maison; **n. near enough** loin d'être assez.
nozzle ['nɒz(ə)l] *n* (*of hose*) jet *m*; (*of tube*) embout *m*.
nuance ['nju:ɑ:ns] *n* nuance *f*.
nuclear ['nju:klɪər] *a* nucléaire; **n. scientist** spécialiste *mf* du nucléaire.
nucleus, *pl* **-clei** ['nju:klɪəs, -klɪaɪ] *n* noyau *m*.
nude [nju:d] *a* nu ▮ *n* (*figure*) nu *m*; **in the n.** (tout) nu. ● **nudist** *n* nudiste *mf* ▮ *a* (*camp*) de nudistes.
nudge [nʌdʒ] *vt* pousser du coude ▮ *n* coup *m* de coude.
nuisance ['nju:s(ə)ns] *n* embêtement *m*; (*person*) peste *f*; **that's a n.** c'est embêtant; **he's being a n.** il nous embête, il m'embête *etc*.
null [nʌl] *a* **n. (and void)** nul (et non avenu).
numb [nʌm] *a* (*hand etc*) engourdi; **n. with cold** engourdi par le froid ▮ *vt* engourdir.
number ['nʌmbər] *n* nombre *m*; (*of page, house, telephone etc*) numéro *m*; **a dance n.** un numéro de danse; **a n. of** un certain nombre de; **n. plate** (*of vehicle*) plaque *f* d'immatriculation ▮ *vt* (*page etc*) numéroter; (*include, count, amount to*) compter.
numeral ['nju:m(ə)rəl] *n* chiffre *m*.
numerical [nju:'merɪk(ə)l] *a* numérique.
numerous ['nju:mərəs] *a* nombreux.
nun [nʌn] *n* religieuse *f*.
nurs/e [nɜ:s] **1** *n* infirmière *f*; **(male) n.** infirmier *m*. **2** *vt* (*look after*) soigner; (*suckle*) nourrir, allaiter; (*a grudge*) *Fig* nourrir. ● **—ing** *a* (*mother*) qui allaite; **the n. staff** le personnel infirmier ▮ *n* (*care*) soins *mpl*; (*job*) profession *f* d'infirmière *or* d'infirmier; **n. home** clinique *f*.
nursery ['nɜ:sərɪ] *n* chambre *f* d'enfants; (*for plants, trees*) pépinière *f*; **(day) n.** (*school*) crèche *f*; **n. rhyme** chanson *f* enfantine; **n. school** école *f* maternelle.
nut[1] [nʌt] *n* fruit *m* à coque; (*walnut*) noix *f*; (*hazelnut*) noisette *f*; (*peanut*) cacah(o)uète *f*; **Brazil/cashew n.** noix *f* du Brésil/de cajou. ● **nutcracker(s)** *n*(*pl*) casse-noix *m inv*. ● **nutshell** *n* **in a n.** *Fig* en un mot.
nut[2] [nʌt] *n* **1** (*for bolt*) écrou *m*. **2** (*person*) *Sl* cinglé, -ée *mf*. ● **nutcase** *n Sl* cinglé, -ée *mf*. ● **nuts** *a Sl* cinglé (**about** de).
nutmeg ['nʌtmeg] *n* muscade *f*.
nutritious [nju:'trɪʃəs] *a* nutritif. ● **nutrition** [-ʃ(ə)n] *n* nutrition *f*.
nylon ['naɪlɒn] *n* nylon *m*; *pl* (*stockings*) bas *mpl* nylon ▮ *a* (*shirt etc*) en nylon.

O

O, o [əʊ] *n* O, o *m*.

oaf [əʊf] *n* balourd, -ourde *mf*.

oak [əʊk] *n* chêne *m*.

OAP [əʊeɪ'piː] *n abbr* (*old age pensioner*) retraité, -ée *mf*.

oar [ɔːr] *n* aviron *m*, rame *f*.

oasis, *pl* **oases** [əʊ'eɪsɪs, əʊ'eɪsiːz] *n* oasis *f*.

oath [əʊθ] *n* (*pl* **-s** [əʊðz]) (*promise*) serment *m*; (*profanity*) juron *m*; **to take an o. to do** faire le serment de faire.

oats [əʊts] *npl* avoine *f*; **(porridge) o.** flocons *mpl* d'avoine.

obedient [ə'biːdɪənt] *a* obéissant. ● **obedience** *n* obéissance *f* (**to** à).

obese [əʊ'biːs] *a* obèse.

obey [ə'beɪ] *vt* (*person*, *order etc*) obéir à; **to be obeyed** être obéi ▮ *vi* obéir.

obituary [ə'bɪtʃʊərɪ] *n* nécrologie *f*.

object[1] ['ɒbdʒɪkt] *n* (*thing*) objet *m*; (*aim*) but *m*, objet *m*; *Gram* complément *m* (d'objet); **that's no o.** (*no problem*) ça ne pose pas de problème.

object[2] [əb'dʒekt] *vi* **to o. to sth/s.o.** désapprouver qch/qn; **I o. to you(r) doing that** ça me gêne que tu fasses ça; **I o.!** je proteste!

objection [əb'dʒekʃ(ə)n] *n* objection *f*; **I've got no o.** ça ne me gêne pas, je n'y vois pas d'objection. ● **objectionable** *a* très désagréable.

objective [əb'dʒektɪv] **1** *n* (*aim*, *target*) objectif *m*. **2** *a* (*opinion etc*) objectif. ● **objectively** *adv* objectivement.

obligation [ɒblɪ'geɪʃ(ə)n] *n* obligation *f*; **under an o. to do** dans l'obligation de faire.

obligatory [ə'blɪgət(ə)rɪ] *a* (*compulsory*) obligatoire; (*imposed by custom*) de rigueur.

oblig/e [ə'blaɪdʒ] *vt* **1** (*compel*) contraindre (**s.o. to do** qn à faire); **obliged to do** contraint à faire. **2** (*help*) rendre service à (*qn*); **obliged to s.o.** reconnaissant à qn (**for** de); **much obliged!** merci infiniment! ● **—ing** *a* (*kind*) serviable.

oblique [ə'bliːk] *a* (*line etc*) oblique; (*reference*) indirect.

obliterate [ə'blɪtəreɪt] *vt* effacer.

oblivion [ə'blɪvɪən] *n* oubli *m*. ● **oblivious** *a* inconscient (**to, of** de).

oblong ['ɒblɒŋ] *a* (*elongated*) oblong (*f* oblongue); (*rectangular*) rectangulaire ▮ *n* rectangle *m*.

obnoxious [əb'nɒkʃəs] *a* odieux.

oboe ['əʊbəʊ] *n Mus* hautbois *m*.

obscene [əb'siːn] *a* obscène. ● **obscenity** *n* obscénité *f*.

obscure [əb'skjʊər] *a* (*word*, *actor etc*) obscur ▮ *vt* (*hide*) cacher; (*confuse*) embrouiller.

observatory [əb'zɜːvət(ə)rɪ] *n* observatoire *m*.

observe [əb'zɜːv] *vt* (*notice*, *respect*) observer; (*say*) (faire) remarquer (**that** que); **to o. the speed limit** respecter la limitation de vitesse. ● **observant** *a* observateur. ● **observation** [ɒbzə'veɪʃ(ə)n] *n* (*observing*, *remark*) observation *f*; (*by police*) surveillance *f*; **under o.** (*hospital patient*) en observation. ● **observer** *n* observateur, -trice *mf*.

obsess [əb'ses] *vt* obséder. ● **obsession** [-ʃ(ə)n] *n* obsession *f*; **to have an o. with** *or* **about sth** avoir l'obsession de qch. ● **obsessive** *a* (*memory*, *idea*) obsédant; (*fear*) obsessif; (*neurotic*) obsessionnel; **to be o. about sth** avoir l'obsession de qch.

obsolete ['ɒbsəliːt] *a* (*out of date*) dépassé; (*ticket*) périmé; (*machinery*) archaïque.

obstacle ['ɒbstək(ə)l] *n* obstacle *m*.

obstinate ['ɒbstɪnət] *a* (*person*, *resistance etc*) obstiné, opiniâtre; (*pain*) rebelle.

obstruct [əb'strʌkt] *vt* (*block*) boucher; (*hinder*) gêner. ● **obstruction** [-ʃ(ə)n] *n* (*act*, *state*) & *Med Pol Sp* obstruction *f*; (*obstacle*) obstacle *m*; (*in pipe*) bouchon *m*. ● **obstructive** *a* **to be o.** faire de l'obstruction.

obtain [əb'teɪn] *vt* obtenir. ● **—able** *a* (*available*) disponible.

obvious ['ɒbvɪəs] *a* évident (**that** que); **he's the o. man to see** c'est évidemment l'homme qu'il faut voir. ● **—ly** *adv* (*evidently*, *of course*) évidemment.

occasion [ə'keɪʒ(ə)n] *n* (*time*, *opportunity*) occasion *f*; (*event*, *ceremony*) événement *m*; **on the o. of** à l'occasion de; **on o.** à l'occasion.

occasional [ə'keɪʒənəl] *a* (*infrequent*) qu'on fait, voit *etc* de temps en temps; (*rain*, *showers*) intermittent; **she drinks the o. whisky** elle boit un whisky de temps en temps. ● **occasionally** *adv* de temps en temps.

occupy ['ɒkjʊpaɪ] *vt* (*house, time, space, post etc*) occuper; **to keep oneself occupied** s'occuper (**doing** à faire). ● **occupant** *n* (*inhabitant*) occupant, -ante *mf*. ● **occupation** [-'peɪʃ(ə)n] *n* (*activity*) occupation *f*; (*job*) emploi *m*; (*trade*) métier *m*; (*profession*) profession *f*; **the o. of** (*country etc*) l'occupation *f* de. ● **occu'pational** *a* **o. hazard** risque *m* du métier. ● **occupier** *n* (*of house*) occupant, -ante *mf*; *Mil* occupant *m*.

occur [ə'kɜːr] *vt* (**-rr-**) (*happen*) avoir lieu; (*be found*) se rencontrer; (*arise*) se présenter; **it occurs to me that...** il me vient à l'esprit que.... ● **occurrence** [ə'kʌrəns] *n* (*event*) événement *m*; (*existence*) existence *f*.

ocean ['əʊʃ(ə)n] *n* océan *m*.

o'clock [ə'klɒk] *adv* **(it's) three o'c.**/*etc* (il est) trois heures/*etc*.

octagon ['ɒktəgən] *n* octogone *m*.

October [ɒk'təʊbər] *n* octobre *m*.

octopus ['ɒktəpəs] *n* pieuvre *f*.

OD [əʊ'diː] *vi* **to OD on heroin**/*etc* prendre une overdose d'héroïne/*etc*.

odd [ɒd] *a* **1** (*strange*) bizarre, curieux; **an o. size** une taille peu courante.
2 (*number*) impair.
3 (*left over*) **I have an o. penny** il me reste un penny; **a few o. stamps** quelques timbres (qui restent); **the o. man out** l'exception *f*; **sixty o.** soixante et quelques; **an o. glove**/*etc* un gant/*etc* dépareillé.
4 (*occasional*) qu'on fait, voit *etc* de temps en temps; **to find the o. mistake** trouver de temps en temps une erreur; **o. jobs** (*around house*) menus travaux *mpl*; **o. job man** homme *m* à tout faire. ● **oddity** *n* (*person*) personne *f* bizarre; (*object*) curiosité *f*. ● **oddly** *adv* bizarrement; **o. enough, he was...** chose curieuse, il était.... ● **oddment** *n Com* fin *f* de série.

odds [ɒdz] *npl* **1** (*in betting*) cote *f*; (*chances*) chances *fpl*. **2 it makes no o.** (*no difference*) *Fam* ça ne fait rien. **3 at o.** (*in disagreement*) en désaccord (**with** avec). **4 o. and ends** des petites choses.

odious ['əʊdɪəs] *a* détestable, odieux.

odometer [əʊ'dɒmɪtər] *n Am* compteur *m* (kilométrique).

odour ['əʊdər] (*Am* **odor**) *n* odeur *f*.

of [əv, *stressed* ɒv] *prep* de, d' (de + le = du, de + les = des); **of the table** de la table; **of the boy** du garçon; **of the boys** des garçons; **of a book** d'un livre; **of wood**/*etc* de *or* en bois/*etc*; **of it, of them** en; **she has a lot of it** *or* **of them** elle en a beaucoup; **a friend of his** un ami à lui, un de ses amis; **there are ten of us** nous sommes dix; **that's nice of you** c'est gentil de ta part; **of no value**/*etc* sans valeur/*etc*; **a man of fifty** un homme de cinquante ans; **the fifth of June** le cinq juin.

off [ɒf] **1** *adv* (*gone away*) parti; (*light, gas, radio etc*) éteint, fermé; (*tap, Am faucet*) fermé; (*switched off at mains*) coupé; (*detached*) détaché; (*removed*) enlevé; (*cancelled*) annulé; (*not fit to eat or drink*) mauvais; (*milk, meat*) tourné; **2 km o.** à 2 km (d'ici *or* de là); **to be** *ou* **go o.** (*leave*) partir; **where are you o. to?** où vas-tu?; **he has his hat o.** il a enlevé son chapeau; **with his, my** *etc* **gloves o.** sans gants; **a day o.** un jour de congé; **time o.** du temps libre; **I'm o. today** j'ai congé aujourd'hui; **5% o.** une réduction de 5%; **hands o.!** pas touche!; **on and o.** (*sometimes*) de temps à autre; **to be better o.** (*wealthier, in a better position*) être mieux.
2 *prep* (*from*) de; (*distant*) éloigné de; **to get o. the bus**/*etc* descendre du bus/*etc*; **to take sth o. the table**/*etc* prendre qch sur la table/*etc*; **to eat o. a plate** manger dans une assiette; **to keep o. the grass** ne pas marcher sur les pelouses; **she's o. her food** elle ne mange plus rien; **o. Dover**/*etc Nau* au large de Douvres/*etc*; **o. limits** interdit; **the o. side** *Aut* le côté droit, *Am* le côté gauche.

offal ['ɒf(ə)l] *n Culin* abats *mpl*.

off-colour [ɒf'kʌlər] *a* (*ill*) patraque; (*indecent*) scabreux. ● **off'hand** *a* (*abrupt*) brusque, impoli ‖ *adv* (*to say, know etc*) comme ça. ● **off-licence** *n* magasin *m* de vins et de spiritueux. ● **off-line** *a* (*computer*) autonome. ● **off-'load** *vt* **to o.-load sth onto s.o.** (*task etc*) se décharger de qch sur qn. ● **off-'peak** *a* (*traffic*) aux heures creuses; (*rate, price*) heures creuses *inv*. ● **off-putting** *a Fam* rebutant. ● **off'side** *a* **to be o.** *Fb* être hors jeu. ● **off'stage** *a* & *adv* dans les coulisses. ● **off-the-peg** (*Am* **off-the-rack**) *a* (*clothes*) de confection. ● **off-the-'wall** *a* (*crazy*) *Am* dément.

offence [ə'fens] (*Am* **offense**) *n* (*crime*) délit *m*; **to take o.** s'offenser (**at** de); **to give o. (to s.o.)** offenser (qn).

offend [ə'fend] *vt* froisser, offenser (*qn*); **to be offended (at)** se froisser (de), s'offenser (de). ● **offender** *n* (*criminal*) délinquant, -ante *mf*; (*habitual*) récidiviste *mf*.

offensive [ə'fensɪv] **1** *a* (*unpleasant*) choquant; (*words etc*) insultant (**to s.o.** pour qn); (*weapon*) offensif; **o. to s.o.** (*of person*) insultant avec qn. **2** *n Mil* & *Fig* offensive *f*.

offer ['ɒfər] *n* offre *f*; **on (special) o.** *Com* en promotion ▮ *vt* offrir; (*opinion, remark*) proposer; **to o. to do** offrir *or* proposer de faire. ● **—ing** *n* (*gift*) offrande *f*.

office ['ɒfɪs] *n* **1** (*room*) bureau *m*; (*of doctor*) *Am* cabinet *m*; **head o.** siège *m* central; **o. block** *or* **building** immeuble *m* de bureaux. **2** (*post*) fonction *f*; (*duty*) fonctions *fpl*; **to be in o.** (*of political party*) être au pouvoir.

officer ['ɒfɪsər] *n* (*in the army, navy etc*) officier *m*; (*in company*) responsable *mf*, directeur, -trice *mf*; **(police) o.** agent *m* (de police).

official [ə'fɪʃ(ə)l] **1** *a* officiel. **2** *n* (*person of authority*) responsable *mf*, officiel *m*; (*civil servant*) fonctionnaire *mf*; (*employee*) employé, -ée *mf*. ● **officially** *adv* officiellement.

officiate [ə'fɪʃɪeɪt] *vi* (*preside*) présider; *Rel* officier.

offing ['ɒfɪŋ] *n* **in the o.** en perspective.

offset ['ɒfset, ɒf'set] *vt* (*pt & pp* **offset,** *pres p* **offsetting**) (*compensate for*) compenser; (*s.o.'s beauty etc by contrast*) faire ressortir.

offshoot ['ɒfʃuːt] *n* (*of organization, group etc*) ramification *f*.

offspring ['ɒfsprɪŋ] *n* progéniture *f*.

often ['ɒf(t)ən] *adv* souvent; **how o.?** combien de fois?; **how o. do they run?** (*trains, buses etc*) il y en a tous les combien?; **once too o.** une fois de trop; **every so o.** de temps en temps.

ogre ['əʊgər] *n* ogre *m*.

oh! [əʊ] *int* oh!, ah!; (*pain*) aïe!; **oh yes!** mais oui!; **oh yes?** ah oui?, ah bon?

oil [ɔɪl] *n* huile *f*; (*extracted from ground*) pétrole *m*; (*fuel*) mazout *m* ▮ *a* (*industry, product*) pétrolier; (*painting, paints*) à l'huile; **o. lamp** lampe *f* à pétrole; **o. change** *Aut* vidange *f* ▮ *vt* (*machine*) graisser, huiler.

oilcan ['ɔɪlkæn] *n* burette *f*. ● **oilfield** *n* gisement *m* de pétrole. ● **oilskin(s)** *n(pl)* (*garment*) ciré *m*. ● **oily** *a* (**-ier, -iest**) (*substance, skin*) huileux; (*hands*) graisseux; (*food*) gras (*f* grasse).

ointment ['ɔɪntmənt] *n* pommade *f*.

OK, okay [əʊ'keɪ] *a & adv see* **all right** ▮ *vt* (*pt & pp* **OKed, okayed,** *pres p* **OKing, okaying**) approuver.

old [əʊld] *a* (**-er, -est**) vieux (*f* vieille); (*former*) ancien; **how o. is he?** quel âge a-t-il?; **he's ten years o.** il a dix ans, il est âgé de dix ans; **he's older than me** il est plus âgé que moi; **an older son** un fils aîné; **the oldest son** le fils aîné; **o. enough to do** assez grand pour faire; **o. enough to marry** en âge de se marier; **o. age** vieillesse *f*; **o. man** vieillard *m*; **o. woman** vieille femme *f*; **to get** *or* **grow old(er)** vieillir ▮ *n* **the o.** (*people*) les vieux *mpl*.

older & oldest **G53** La Comparaison: L'Emploi 4 4g) iv)

olden ['əʊld(ə)n] *a* **in o. days** jadis.

old-fashioned [əʊld'fæʃənd] *a* (*out-of-date*) démodé; (*person*) rétro *inv*.

olive ['ɒlɪv] *n* olive *f* ▮ *a* **o. (green)** (vert) olive *inv*; **o. oil** huile *f* d'olive.

Olympic [ə'lɪmpɪk] *a* (*games etc*) olympique.

ombudsman ['ɒmbʊdzmən] *n* (*pl* **-men**) médiateur *m*.

omelet(te) ['ɒmlɪt] *n* omelette *f*; **cheese/***etc* **o.** omelette au fromage/*etc*.

omen ['əʊmən] *n* augure *m*. ● **ominous** *a* de mauvais augure; (*tone*) menaçant.

omit [əʊ'mɪt] *vt* (**-tt-**) omettre (**to do** de faire). ● **omission** [-ʃ(ə)n] *n* omission *f*.

on [ɒn] *prep* **1** (*position*) sur; **on the chair** sur la chaise; **to put on (to)** mettre sur.

2 (*concerning, about*) sur; **an article on** un article sur; **to speak on Dickens/***etc* parler sur Dickens/*etc*.

3 (*manner, means*) **on foot** à pied; **on the blackboard** au tableau; **on the radio** à la radio; **on the train/***etc* dans le train/*etc*; **on holiday,** *Am* **on vacation** en vacances; **to be on** (*course*) suivre; (*project*) travailler à; (*salary*) toucher; (*team, committee*) être membre de; **to keep** *or* **stay on** (*path etc*) suivre; **it's on me!** (*I'll pay*) *Fam* c'est moi qui paie!

4 (*time*) **on Monday** lundi; **on Mondays** le lundi; **on May 3rd** le 3 mai; **on the evening of May 3rd** le 3 mai au soir; **on my arrival** à mon arrivée.

5 (+ *present participle*) en; **on seeing this** en voyant ceci.

▮ *adv* (*ahead*) en avant; (*in progress*) en cours; (*lid, brake*) mis; (*light, radio*) allumé; (*gas, tap, Am faucet*) ouvert; (*machine*) en marche; **on (and on)** sans cesse; **to play/***etc* **on** continuer à jouer/*etc*; **she has her hat on** elle a mis *or* elle porte son chapeau; **he has something/nothing on** il est habillé/tout nu; **the strike is on** la grève aura lieu; **what's on?** *TV* qu'y a-t-il à la télé?; *Cin Th* qu'est-ce qu'on joue?; **there's a film on** on passe un film; **I've been on to him** (*on phone*) je l'ai eu au bout du fil; **from then on** à partir de là. ● **on-coming** *a* (*vehicle*) qui vient en sens inverse. ● **on-**

going *a* (*project*) en cours. ● **on-line** *a* (*computer*) en ligne.

once [wʌns] *adv* (*on one occasion*) une fois; (*formerly*) autrefois; **o. a month**/*etc* une fois par mois/*etc*; **o. again, o. more** encore une fois; **at o.** tout de suite; **all at o.** (*suddenly*) tout à coup; (*at the same time*) à la fois; **o. and for all** une fois pour toutes ▮ *conj* une fois que.

one [wʌn] *a* **1** un, une; **o. man** un homme; **o. woman** une femme; **page o.** la page un; **twenty-o.** vingt-et-un.

2 (*only*) seul; **my o. (and only) aim** mon seul (et unique) but.

3 (*same*) même; **in the o. bus** dans le même bus.

▮ *pron* **1** un, une; **do you want o.?** en veux-tu (un)?; **he's o. of us** il est des nôtres; **o. of them** l'un d'eux, l'une d'elles; **a big/small/** *etc* **o.** un grand/petit/*etc*; **she's o.** (*a teacher, gardener etc*) elle l'est; **this o.** celui-ci, celle-ci; **that o.** celui-là, celle-là; **the o. who** *or* **which** celui *or* celle qui; **it's Paul's o.** *Fam* c'est celui de Paul; **it's my o.** *Fam* c'est à moi; **another o.** un(e) autre.

2 (*impersonal*) on; **o. knows** on sait; **it helps o.** ça nous *or* vous aide; **one's family** sa famille.

one-'armed [wʌn'a:md] *a* (*person*) manchot. ● **one-'eyed** *a* borgne. ● **one-legged** [-legɪd] *a* **o.-legged man** *or* **woman** unijambiste *mf*. ● **one-'off** *or* *Am* **one-of-a-'kind** *a* *Fam* unique, exceptionnel. ● **one-parent family** *n* famille *f* monoparentale. ● **one-'sided** *a* (*judgment etc*) partial; (*contest*) inégal; (*decision*) unilatéral. ● **one-time** *a* (*former*) ancien. ● **one-'way** *a* (*street*) à sens unique; (*traffic*) en sens unique; (*ticket*) simple.

oneself [wʌn'self] *pron* soi-même; (*reflexive*) se, s'; **to cut o.** se couper.

onion ['ʌnjən] *n* oignon *m*.

onlooker ['ɒnlʊkər] *n* spectateur, -trice *mf*.

only ['əʊnlɪ] *a* seul; **the o. house**/*etc* la seule maison/*etc*; **the o. one** le seul, la seule; **an o. son** un fils unique.

▮ *adv* seulement, ne... que; **I o. have ten** je n'en ai que dix, j'en ai dix seulement; **if o.** si seulement; **not o.** non seulement; **I have o. just seen it** je viens tout juste de le voir; **o. he knows** lui seul le sait.

▮ *conj* (*but*) *Fam* seulement; **o. I can't** seulement je ne peux pas.

onset ['ɒnset] *n* (*of disease etc*) début *m*; (*of old age*) approche *f*.

onslaught ['ɒnslɔ:t] *n* attaque *f*.

onto ['ɒntu:, *unstressed* 'ɒntə] *prep* = **on to.**

onus ['əʊnəs] *n inv* **the o. is on you** c'est votre responsabilité (**to do** de faire).

onward(s) ['ɒnwəd(z)] *adv* en avant; **from that time o.** à partir de là.

ooze [u:z] *vi* **to o. (out)** suinter.

opaque [əʊ'peɪk] *a* opaque.

open ['əʊpən] *a* ouvert; (*view, road*) dégagé; (*car*) décapoté; (*meeting*) public (*f* -ique); (*post, job*) vacant; (*attempt, envy*) manifeste; (*airline ticket*) open *inv*; **wide o.** grand ouvert; **in the o. air** en plein air; **the o. spaces** les grands espaces; **it's o. to doubt** c'est douteux; **o. to** (*criticism, attack*) exposé à; (*ideas, suggestions*) ouvert à; **I've got an o. mind on it** je n'ai pas d'opinion arrêtée là-dessus; **to leave o.** (*date*) ne pas préciser.

▮ *n* **(out) in the o.** (*outside*) en plein air; **to sleep (out) in the o.** dormir à la belle étoile; **to bring (out) into the o.** (*reveal*) divulguer.

▮ *vt* ouvrir; (*legs*) écarter; **to o. out** *or* **up** ouvrir.

▮ *vi* (*of flower, door, eyes etc*) s'ouvrir; (*of shop, office, person*) ouvrir; (*of play*) débuter; (*of film*) sortir; **the door opens** (*is opened by s.o.*) la porte s'ouvre; (*can open*) la porte ouvre; **to o. on to** (*of window*) donner sur; **to o. out** *or* **up** s'ouvrir; **to o. out** (*widen*) s'élargir; **to o. up** (*open a or the door*) ouvrir.

open-air [əʊpən'eər] *a* (*pool, market etc*) en plein air. ● **o.-'necked** *a* (*shirt*) sans cravate. ● **o.-'plan** *a* (*office etc*) sans cloisons.

opening ['əʊpənɪŋ] *n* ouverture *f*; (*career prospect, trade outlet*) débouché *m*; **late o.** nocturne *f* ▮ *a* (*time, speech*) d'ouverture; **o. night** *Th* première *f*.

openly ['əʊpənlɪ] *adv* (*not secretly, frankly*) ouvertement; (*publicly*) publiquement. ● **openness** *n* (*frankness*) franchise *f*.

opera ['ɒprə] *n* opéra *m*; **o. glasses** jumelles *fpl* de théâtre. ● **ope'ratic** *a* d'opéra.

operat/e ['ɒpəreɪt] **1** *vi* (*of surgeon*) opérer (**on s.o.** qn, **for** de). **2** *vi* (*of machine etc*) fonctionner; (*proceed*) opérer ▮ *vt* faire fonctionner; (*business*) gérer. ● **—ing** *a* **o. theatre,** *Am* **o. room** salle *f* d'opération; **o. wing** *Med* bloc *m* opératoire. ● **operation** [-'reɪʃ(ə)n] *n Med Mil Math etc* opération *f*; (*working*) fonctionnement *m*; **in o.** (*machine*) en service; **to have an o.** se faire opérer.

operative ['ɒpərətɪv] *a* (*scheme, measure etc*) en vigueur.

operator ['ɒpəreɪtər] *n* (*on phone*) standardiste *mf*; (*on machine*) opérateur, -trice *mf*; **tour o.** organisateur, -trice *mf* de voyages.

opinion [ə'pɪnjən] *n* opinion *f*, avis *m*; **in my o.** à mon avis.
opium ['əʊpɪəm] *n* opium *m*.
opponent [ə'pəʊnənt] *n* adversaire *mf*.
opportune ['ɒpətju:n] *a* opportun.
opportunity [ɒpə'tju:nɪtɪ] *n* occasion *f* (**to do, of doing** de faire); *pl* (*prospects*) perspectives *fpl*; **equal opportunities** des chances *fpl* égales.
oppos/e [ə'pəʊz] *vt* (*person, measure etc*) s'opposer à; (*motion*) *Pol* faire opposition à. ●**—ed** *a* opposé (**to** à); **as o. to** par opposition à. ●**—ing** *a* (*team, interests*) opposé. ●**opposition** [ɒpə'zɪʃ(ə)n] *n* opposition *f* (**to** à); **the o.** (*rival camp*) l'adversaire *m*; (*in business*) la concurrence; **he put up no o.** il n'a opposé aucune résistance.
opposite ['ɒpəzɪt] *a* (*side etc*) opposé; (*house*) d'en face; **one's o. number** son homologue *mf* ‖ *adv* (*to sit etc*) en face ‖ *prep* **o. (to)** en face de ‖ *n* **the o.** le contraire.
oppress [ə'pres] *vt* (*treat cruelly*) opprimer; (*of heat, anguish*) oppresser. ●**oppression** [-ʃ(ə)n] *n* oppression *f*. ●**oppressive** *a* (*heat, weather*) étouffant; (*régime*) oppressif; (*ruler*) tyrannique.
opt [ɒpt] *vi* **to o. for sth** décider pour qch; **to o. to do** choisir de faire; **to o. out** refuser de participer (**of** à). ●**option** [-ʃ(ə)n] *n* (*choice*) choix *m*; *Sch* matière *f* à option; **she has no o.** elle n'a pas le choix. ●**optional** *a* facultatif; **o. extra** (*on car*) accessoire *m* en option.
optical ['ɒptɪk(ə)l] *a* (*instrument etc*) d'optique; (*lens, fibre etc*) optique.
optician [ɒp'tɪʃ(ə)n] *n* opticien, -ienne *mf*.
optimism ['ɒptɪmɪz(ə)m] *n* optimisme *m*. ●**optimist** *n* optimiste *mf*. ●**opti'mistic** *a* optimiste.
optimum ['ɒptɪməm] *a* optimum; **the o. temperature** la température optimum.
opulent ['ɒpjʊlənt] *a* opulent.
or [ɔ:r] *conj* ou; **one or two** un ou deux; **he doesn't drink or smoke** il ne boit ni ne fume; **ten or so** environ dix.
oral ['ɔ:rəl] *a* oral ‖ *n* (*exam*) oral *m*.
orange ['ɒrɪndʒ] **1** *n* (*fruit*) orange *f*; **o. juice** jus *m* d'orange *m*. **2** *a* & *n* (*colour*) orange *a* & *m inv*. ●**orangeade** *n* orangeade *f*.
orator ['ɒrətər] *n* orateur *m*.
orbit ['ɔ:bɪt] *n* (*of planet etc*) orbite *f* ‖ *vt* (*sun etc*) graviter autour de.
orchard ['ɔ:tʃəd] *n* verger *m*.
orchestra ['ɔ:kɪstrə] *n* orchestre *m*; **the o.** (*seats in theater*) *Am* l'orchestre *m*.
orchid ['ɔ:kɪd] *n* orchidée *f*.
ordain [ɔ:'deɪn] *vt* (*priest*) ordonner.
ordeal [ɔ:'di:l] *n* épreuve *f*.
order ['ɔ:dər] *n* (*command*) ordre *m*; (*purchase*) commande *f*; **in o.** (*passport etc*) en règle; (*drawer etc*) en ordre; **in (numerical) o.** dans l'ordre numérique; **in working o.** en état de marche; **in o. to do** pour faire; **in o. that** pour que (+ *sub*); **it's in o. to smoke/** *etc* (*allowed*) il est permis de fumer/*etc*; **out of o.** (*machine*) en panne; (*telephone*) en dérangement; **to make an o.** (*purchase*) passer une commande.
‖ *vt* (*command*) ordonner (**s.o. to do** à qn de faire); (*meal, goods etc*) commander; (*taxi*) appeler; **to o. s.o. around** commander qn.
‖ *vi* (*in café etc*) commander.
orderly ['ɔ:dəlɪ] **1** *a* (*tidy*) ordonné; (*mind*) méthodique; (*crowd*) discipliné. **2** *n* *Mil* planton *m*; (*in hospital*) garçon *m* de salle.
ordinal ['ɔ:dɪnəl] *a* (*number*) ordinal.
ordinary ['ɔ:d(ə)nrɪ] *a* (*usual, commonplace*) ordinaire; (*average*) moyen; **an o. individual** un simple particulier; **in o. use** d'usage courant; **in the o. way** normalement; **it's out of the o.** ça sort de l'ordinaire.
ore [ɔ:r] *n* minerai *m*.
organ ['ɔ:gən] *n* **1** *Anat* & *Fig* organe *m*. **2** *Mus* orgue *m*, orgues *fpl*; **barrel o.** orgue *m* de Barbarie.
organic [ɔ:'gænɪk] *a* organique; (*vegetables etc*) biologique.
organization [ɔ:gənaɪ'zeɪʃ(ə)n] *n* (*arrangement, association*) organisation *f*.
organiz/e ['ɔ:gənaɪz] *vt* organiser. ●**—er** *n* organisateur, -trice *mf*; **(personal) o.** (agenda *m*) organiseur *m*.
orgasm ['ɔ:gæz(ə)m] *n* orgasme *m*.
orgy ['ɔ:dʒɪ] *n* orgie *f*.
orient ['ɔ:rɪənt] *vt* *Am* = **orientate.** ●**orientate** *vt* orienter.
Orient ['ɔ:rɪənt] *n* **the O.** l'Orient *m*. ●**ori'ental** *a* oriental.
orifice ['ɒrɪfɪs] *n* orifice *m*.
origin ['ɒrɪdʒɪn] *n* origine *f*.
original [ə'rɪdʒɪn(ə)l] *a* (*idea, artist etc*) original; (*first*) premier; (*copy, version*) original ‖ *n* (*document etc*) original *m*. ●**origi'nality** *n* originalité *f*. ●**originally** *adv* (*at first*) au départ; **she comes o. from** elle est originaire de.
originate [ə'rɪdʒɪneɪt] *vi* (*begin*) prendre naissance (**in** dans); **to o. from** (*of idea etc*) émaner de ‖ *vt* être l'auteur de.
ornament ['ɔ:nəmənt] *n* (*on dress etc*) ornement *m*; (*vase etc*) bibelot *m*. ●**orna'mental** *a* décoratif, ornemental.

orphan ['ɔ:f(ə)n] *n* orphelin, -ine *mf*. • **orphaned** *a* orphelin; **he was o. by the accident** l'accident l'a rendu orphelin. • **orphanage** *n* orphelinat *m*.
orthodox ['ɔ:θədɒks] *a* orthodoxe.
orthop(a)edic [ɔ:θə'pi:dɪk] *a* orthopédique *f*.
Oscar ['ɒskər] *n Cin* oscar *m*.
ostensibly [ɒ'stensɪblɪ] *adv* apparemment.
ostentatious [ɒsten'teɪʃ(ə)s] *a* prétentieux.
ostrich ['ɒstrɪtʃ] *n* autruche *f*.
other ['ʌðər] *a* autre; **o. doctors** d'autres médecins; **o. people** d'autres; **the o. one** l'autre *mf*; **I have no o. gloves than these** je n'ai pas d'autres gants que ceux-ci. ‖ *pron* **the o.** l'autre *mf*; **(some) others** d'autres; **some do, others don't** les uns le font, les autres ne le font pas; **none o. than** nul autre que.
‖ *adv* **o. than** autrement que. • **otherwise** *adv & conj* autrement ‖ *a* (*different*) (tout) autre.
OTT [əʊti:'ti:] *a abbr* (*over the top*) *Fam* outrancier.
otter ['ɒtər] *n* loutre *f*.
ouch! [aʊtʃ] *int* aïe!, ouille!
ought [ɔ:t] *v aux* **1** (*obligation, desirability*) **you o. to leave** tu devrais partir; **I o. to have done it** j'aurais dû le faire; **he said he o. to stay** il a dit qu'il devait rester. **2** (*probability*) **it o. to be ready** ça devrait être prêt.
ounce [aʊns] *n* once *f* (= *28,35 g*).
our [aʊər] *poss a* notre, *pl* nos. • **ours** *pron* le nôtre, la nôtre, *pl* les nôtres; **this book is o.** ce livre est à nous *or* est le nôtre; **a friend of o.** un ami à nous. • **our'selves** *pron* nous-mêmes; (*reflexive & after prep*) nous; **we wash o.** nous nous lavons.
oust [aʊst] *vt* évincer (**from** de).
out [aʊt] *adv* (*outside*) dehors; (*not at home etc*) sorti; (*light, fire*) éteint; (*news, secret*) connu; (*flower*) ouvert; (*book*) publié; (*eliminated from game*) éliminé; **to be** *or* **go o. a lot** sortir beaucoup; **he's o. in Italy** il est (parti) en Italie; **to have a day o.** sortir pour la journée; **5 km o.** *Nau* à 5 km du rivage; **the sun's o.** il fait (du) soleil; **the tide's o.** la marée est basse; **the trip** *or* **journey o.** l'aller *m*; **o. there** là-bas.
‖ *prep* **o. of** (*outside*) en dehors de; (*danger, reach, water*) hors de; (*without*) sans; **o. of the window** par la fenêtre; **o. of pity/love/***etc* par pitié/amour/*etc*; **to drink/take/copy o. of sth** boire/prendre/copier dans qch; **made o. of** (*wood etc*) fait en; **to make sth o. of a box/***etc* faire qch avec une boîte/*etc*; **she's o. of town** elle n'est pas en ville; **four o. of five** quatre sur cinq; **o. of the blue** de manière inattendue; **to feel o. of place** ne pas se sentir intégré.
out-and-out ['aʊtənaʊt] *a* (*cheat, liar etc*) achevé. • **o.-of-'date** *a* (*expired*) périmé; (*old-fashioned*) démodé. • **o.-of-'doors** *adv* dehors. • **o.-of-the-'way** *a* (*place*) écarté.
outbid [aʊt'bɪd] *vt* (*pt & pp* **outbid,** *pres p* **outbidding**) **to o. s.o.** (sur)enchérir sur qn.
outboard ['aʊtbɔ:d] *a* **o. motor** (*of boat*) moteur *m* hors-bord *inv*.
outbreak ['aʊtbreɪk] *n* (*of war, epidemic*) début *m*; (*of violence*) éruption *f*; (*of fever*) accès *m*; (*of hostilities*) ouverture *f*.
outburst ['aʊtbɜ:st] *n* (*of anger, joy*) explosion *f*; (*of violence*) flambée *f*.
outcast ['aʊtkɑ:st] *n* **(social) o.** paria *m*.
outcome ['aʊtkʌm] *n* résultat *m*, issue *f*.
outcry ['aʊtkraɪ] *n* tollé *m*.
outdated [aʊt'deɪtɪd] *a* démodé.
outdo [aʊt'du:] *vt* (*pt* **outdid,** *pp* **outdone**) surpasser (**in** en).
outdoor ['aʊtdɔ:r] *a* (*pool, market, life*) en plein air; (*game*) de plein air; **o. clothes** tenue *f* pour sortir. • **out'doors** *adv* dehors.
outer ['aʊtər] *a* extérieur; **o. space** l'espace *m* (cosmique).
outfit ['aʊtfɪt] *n* (*clothes*) costume *m*; (*for woman*) toilette *f*; (*toy*) panoplie *f* (*de cowboy etc*); (*kit*) trousse *f*; (*group, gang*) *Fam* bande *f*; **sports/ski o.** tenue *f* de sport/de ski.
outgoing ['aʊtgəʊɪŋ] **1** *a* (*minister etc*) sortant; (*mail*) en partance; **o. calls** *Tel* appels *mpl* vers l'extérieur. **2** *a* (*sociable*) liant. **3** *npl* **outgoings** (*expenses*) dépenses *fpl*.
outgrow [aʊt'grəʊ] *vt* (*pt* **outgrew,** *pp* **outgrown**) (*clothes*) devenir trop grand pour; (*habit*) perdre (en grandissant).
outhouse ['aʊthaʊs] *n* (*of mansion, farm*) dépendance *f*; (*lavatory*) *Am* cabinets *mpl* extérieurs.
outing ['aʊtɪŋ] *n* sortie *f*, excursion *f*.
outlandish [aʊt'lændɪʃ] *a* (*weird*) bizarre.
outlast [aʊt'lɑ:st] *vt* durer plus longtemps que; (*survive*) survivre à.
outlaw ['aʊtlɔ:] *n* hors-la-loi *m inv* ‖ *vt* (*ban*) proscrire.
outlay ['aʊtleɪ] *n* (*expense*) dépense(s) *f(pl)*.
outlet ['aʊtlet] *n* (*market for goods*) débouché *m*; (*for liquid*) sortie *f*; *El* prise *f* de courant; (*for feelings, energy*) exutoire *m*; **retail o.** point *m* de vente; **factory o.** magasin *m* d'usine.
outline ['aʊtlaɪn] *n* (*shape*) contour *m*; **(rough) o.** (*of article, plan etc*) esquisse *f*; **the broad** *or* **general outline(s)** les grandes

lignes ‖ *vt* (*plan, situation*) esquisser; (*book, speech*) résumer; **to be outlined against** (*of tree etc*) se profiler sur.
outlive [aʊt'lɪv] *vt* survivre à.
outlook ['aʊtlʊk] *n inv* (*for future*) perspective(s) *f*(*pl*); (*point of view*) perspective *f* (**on** sur); (*weather forecast*) prévisions *fpl*.
outlying ['aʊtlaɪɪŋ] *a* (*remote*) isolé.
outmoded [aʊt'məʊdɪd] *a* démodé.
outnumber [aʊt'nʌmbər] *vt* être plus nombreux que.
outpatient ['aʊtpeɪʃ(ə)nt] *n* malade *mf* en consultation externe.
outpost ['aʊtpəʊst] *n* avant-poste *m*.
output ['aʊtpʊt] *n* rendement *m*, production *f*; (*computer data*) données *fpl* de sortie; (*computer process*) sortie *f*.
outrage ['aʊtreɪdʒ] *n* (*scandal*) scandale *m*; (*anger*) indignation *f*; (*crime*) atrocité *f*; **bomb o.** attentat *m* à la bombe ‖ *vt* (*morals*) outrager; **outraged by sth** indigné de qch.
outrageous [aʊt'reɪdʒəs] *a* (*shocking*) scandaleux; (*hat etc*) grotesque; (*atrocious*) atroce.
outright [aʊt'raɪt] *adv* (*to say, tell*) franchement; (*completely*) complètement; (*to be killed*) sur le coup ‖ ['aʊtraɪt] *a* (*complete*) complet; (*lie*) pur; (*refusal*) catégorique; (*winner*) incontesté.
outset ['aʊtset] *n* **at the o.** au début; **from the o.** dès le départ.
outside [aʊt'saɪd] *adv* (au) dehors, à l'extérieur; **to go o.** sortir.
‖ *prep* à l'extérieur de, en dehors de; (*beyond*) *Fig* en dehors de; **o. my room** à la porte de ma chambre.
‖ *n* extérieur *m*, dehors *m*.
‖ ['aʊtsaɪd] *a* extérieur; **the o. lane** *Aut* la voie de droite *or Am* de gauche; **an o. chance** une faible chance. ● **out'sider** *n* (*stranger*) étranger, -ère *mf*; *Sp* outsider *m*.
outsize ['aʊtsaɪz] *a* (*clothes*) grande taille *inv*.
outskirts ['aʊtskɜːts] *npl* banlieue *f*.
outsmart [aʊt'smɑːt] *vt* être plus malin que.
outspoken [aʊt'spəʊk(ə)n] *a* (*frank*) franc (*f* franche).
outstanding [aʊt'stændɪŋ] *a* remarquable; (*problem, business*) non réglé; (*debt*) impayé; **work o.** travail *m* à faire.
outstay [aʊt'steɪ] *vt* **to o. one's welcome** abuser de l'hospitalité de son hôte.
outstretched [aʊt'stretʃt] *a* (*arm*) tendu.
outstrip [aʊt'strɪp] *vt* (**-pp-**) devancer.
outward ['aʊtwəd] *a* (*sign, appearance*) extérieur; (*movement*) vers l'extérieur; **o. journey** *or* **trip** aller *m*. ● **outward(s)** *adv* vers l'extérieur.
outweigh [aʊt'weɪ] *vt* (*be more important than*) l'emporter sur.
outwit [aʊt'wɪt] *vt* (**-tt-**) être plus malin que.
oval ['əʊv(ə)l] *a* & *n* ovale (*m*).
ovary ['əʊvərɪ] *n Anat* ovaire *m*.
oven ['ʌv(ə)n] *n* four *m*; **o. glove** gant *m* isolant.
over ['əʊvər] *prep* (*on*) sur; (*above*) au-dessus de; (*on the other side of*) de l'autre côté de; **bridge o. the river** pont *m* sur le fleuve; **to jump/look/***etc* **o. sth** sauter/regarder/*etc* par-dessus qch; **to fall o. the balcony** tomber du balcon; **she fell o. it** elle en est tombée; **o. it** (*on*) dessus; (*above*) au-dessus; (*to jump etc*) par-dessus; **to criticize/***etc* **o. sth** (*about*) critiquer/*etc* à propos de qch; **o. the phone** au téléphone; **o. the holidays** pendant les vacances; **o. ten days** (*more than*) plus de dix jours; **men o. sixty** les hommes de plus de soixante ans; **o. and above** en plus de; **he's o. his flu** il est remis de sa grippe; **all o. Spain** dans toute l'Espagne; **all o. the carpet** partout sur le tapis.
‖ *adv* (*above*) (par-)dessus; (*finished*) fini; (*danger*) passé; (*again*) encore; (*too*) trop; **jump o.!** sautez par-dessus!; **o. here** ici; **o. there** là-bas; **to come** *or* **go o.** (*visit*) passer; **to ask s.o. o.** inviter qn (à venir); **he's o. in Italy** il est (parti) en Italie; **she's o. from Paris** elle est venue de Paris; **all o.** (*everywhere*) partout; **it's all o.!** (*finished*) c'est fini!; **a kilo or o.** un kilo ou plus; **I have ten o.** il m'en reste dix; **there's some bread o.** il reste du pain; **o. and o. (again)** à plusieurs reprises; **to start all o. (again)** recommencer à zéro; **o. pleased/***etc* trop content/*etc*.
over-abundant [əʊvərə'bʌndənt] *a* surabondant. ● **o.-de'veloped** *a* trop développé. ● **o.-fa'miliar** *a* trop familier. ● **o.-in'dulge** *vt* (*one's desires*) céder trop facilement à; (*person*) trop gâter.
overall 1 [əʊvər'ɔːl] *a* (*length etc*) total; (*result etc*) global ‖ *adv* globalement. 2 ['əʊvərɔːl] *n* blouse *f* (de travail); *pl* (*of workman*) bleu *m* de travail.
overbearing [əʊvə'beərɪŋ] *a* autoritaire.
overboard ['əʊvəbɔːd] *adv* à la mer.
overbook [əʊvə'bʊk] *vt* (*flight, hotel*) surréserver.
overcast [əʊvə'kɑːst] *a* (*sky*) couvert.
overcharge [əʊvə'tʃɑːdʒ] *vt* **to o. s.o. for sth** faire payer qch trop cher à qn.
overcoat ['əʊvəkəʊt] *n* pardessus *m*.
overcome [əʊvə'kʌm] *vt* (*pt* **overcame**, *pp*

overcome) (*problem*) surmonter; (*shyness etc*) vaincre; **to be o. by** (*fatigue, grief*) être accablé par; (*fumes, temptation*) succomber à.

overcook [əʊvə'kʊk] *vt* faire cuire trop.

overcrowded [əʊvə'kraʊdɪd] *a* (*house, country*) surpeuplé; (*bus, train*) bondé.

overdo [əʊvə'du:] *vt* (*pt* **overdid,** *pp* **overdone**) exagérer; *Culin* faire cuire trop; **to o. it** ne pas y aller doucement; **don't o. it!** vas-y doucement!

overdose ['əʊvədəʊs] *n* overdose *f*.

overdraft ['əʊvədrɑ:ft] *n Fin* découvert *m*. ● **over'drawn** *a* (*account*) à découvert.

overdue [əʊvə'dju:] *a* (*train etc*) en retard; (*debt*) arriéré.

overeat [əʊvər'i:t] *vi* manger trop.

overestimate [əʊvər'estɪmeɪt] *vt* surestimer.

overexcited [əʊvərɪk'saɪtɪd] *a* surexcité.

overflow 1 [əʊvə'fləʊ] *vi* (*of river, bath etc*) déborder; **to be overflowing with** (*of town, house etc*) regorger de (*visiteurs etc*). **2** ['əʊvəfləʊ] *n* (*outlet*) trop-plein *m*.

overgrown [əʊvə'grəʊn] *a* envahi par la végétation; **o. with** (*weeds etc*) envahi par.

overhaul [əʊvə'hɔ:l] *vt* (*vehicle, schedule etc*) réviser ▮ ['əʊvəhɔ:l] *n* révision *f*.

overhead [əʊvə'hed] *adv* au-dessus; ▮ ['əʊvəhed] **1** *a* (*cable etc*) aérien. **2** *npl* (*expenses*) frais *mpl* généraux.

overhear [əʊvə'hɪər] *vt* (*pt* & *pp* **overheard**) surprendre, entendre.

overheat [əʊvə'hi:t] *vt* surchauffer ▮ *vi* (*of engine*) chauffer.

overjoyed [əʊvə'dʒɔɪd] *a* fou (*f* folle) de joie.

overland ['əʊvəlænd] *a* & *adv* par voie de terre.

overlap [əʊvə'læp] *vi* (**-pp-**) se chevaucher ▮ *vt* chevaucher.

overleaf [əʊvə'li:f] *adv* au verso.

overload [əʊvə'ləʊd] *vt* surcharger.

overlook [əʊvə'lʊk] *vt* **1** (*not notice*) ne pas remarquer; (*forget*) oublier; (*ignore*) passer sur. **2** (*of window etc*) donner sur; (*of tower, fort*) dominer.

overly ['əʊvəlɪ] *adv* excessivement.

overnight [əʊvə'naɪt] *adv* (pendant) la nuit; (*suddenly*) *Fig* du jour au lendemain; **to stay o.** passer la nuit ▮ ['əʊvənaɪt] *a* (*train, flight*) de nuit; (*stay*) d'une nuit; **o. stop** arrêt *m* pour la nuit.

overpass ['əʊvəpæs] *n* (*bridge*) *Am* toboggan *m*.

overpopulated [əʊvə'pɒpjʊleɪtɪd] *a* surpeuplé.

overpower [əʊvə'paʊər] *vt* (*physically*) maîtriser; (*defeat*) vaincre; *Fig* accabler. ● **—ing** *a* (*heat etc*) accablant.

overpriced [əʊvə'praɪst] *a* trop cher.

overrated [əʊvə'reɪtɪd] *a* surfait.

overreact [əʊvərɪ'ækt] *vi* réagir excessivement.

overrid/e [əʊvə'raɪd] *vt* (*pt* **overrode,** *pp* **overridden**) (*invalidate*) annuler; (*take no notice of*) passer outre à; (*be more important than*) l'emporter sur. ● **—ing** *a* (*importance*) primordial; **my o. consideration** ma priorité.

overrule [əʊvə'ru:l] *vt* (*decision*) annuler; (*objection*) repousser.

overrun [əʊvə'rʌn] *vt* (*pt* **overran,** *pp* **overrun,** *pres p* **overrunning**) **1** (*invade*) envahir. **2** (*go beyond*) aller au-delà de.

overseas [əʊvə'si:z] *adv* (*Africa etc*) outre-mer; (*abroad*) à l'étranger ▮ ['əʊvəsi:z] *a* (*visitor etc*) d'outre-mer; étranger; (*trade*) extérieur.

oversee [əʊvə'si:] *vt* (*pt* **oversaw,** *pp* **overseen**) (*work*) superviser.

overshadow [əʊvə'ʃædəʊ] *vt* (*make less important*) éclipser; (*make gloomy*) assombrir.

oversight ['əʊvəsaɪt] *n* oubli *m*, omission *f*; (*mistake*) erreur *f*.

oversimplify [əʊvə'sɪmplɪfaɪ] *vti* trop simplifier.

oversleep [əʊvə'sli:p] *vi* (*pt* & *pp* **overslept**) dormir trop longtemps.

overspend [əʊvə'spend] *vi* dépenser trop.

overstaffed [əʊvə'stɑ:ft] *a* au personnel pléthorique.

overstay [əʊvə'steɪ] *vt* **to o. one's welcome** abuser de l'hospitalité de son hôte.

overstep [əʊvə'step] *vt* (**-pp-**) (*limit*) dépasser; **to o. the mark** dépasser les bornes.

overt ['əʊvɜ:t] *a* manifeste.

overtake [əʊvə'teɪk] *vt* (*pt* **overtook,** *pp* **overtaken**) dépasser; (*vehicle*) doubler, dépasser ▮ *vi* (*in vehicle*) doubler, dépasser.

overthrow [əʊvə'θrəʊ] *vt* (*pt* **overthrew,** *pp* **overthrown**) (*dictator etc*) renverser.

overtime ['əʊvətaɪm] *n* heures *fpl* supplémentaires ▮ *adv* **to work o.** faire des heures supplémentaires.

overtones ['əʊvətəʊnz] *npl* (*traces*) note *f*, nuance *f* (**of** de).

overture ['əʊvətjʊər] *n Mus* & *Fig* ouverture *f*.

overturn [əʊvə'tɜ:n] *vi* (*of car, boat*) se retourner ▮ *vt* (*chair etc*) renverser; (*car, boat*) retourner.

overweight [əʊvə'weɪt] *a* **to be o.** (*of person*) avoir des kilos en trop.

overwhelm [əʊvə'welm] *vt* (*of feelings, heat etc*) accabler; (*defeat*) écraser; (*amaze*) bouleverser. ● **—ed** *a* (*overjoyed*) ravi (**by, with** de); **o. with** (*work, offers*) submergé de; **o. by** (*gift etc*) vivement touché par. ● **—ing** *a* (*heat etc*) accablant; (*majority, defeat*) écrasant; (*desire*) irrésistible; (*impression*) dominant. ● **—ingly** *adv* (*to vote*) en masse.

overwork [əʊvə'wɜːk] *n* surmenage *m* ‖ *vi* se surmener.

overwrought [əʊvə'rɔːt] *a* (*tense*) tendu.

owe [əʊ] *vt* (*money, respect etc*) devoir (**to** à); **to o. it to oneself to do** se devoir de faire. ● **owing 1** *a* (*money*) dû. **2** *prep* **o. to** à cause de.

owl [aʊl] *n* hibou *m* (*pl* hiboux).

own [əʊn] **1** *a* propre; **my o. house** ma propre maison ‖ *pron* **it's my (very) o.** c'est à moi (tout seul); **a house of his o.** sa propre maison; **(all) on one's o.** (*alone*) tout seul; **to get one's o. back** se venger (**on s.o.** de qn, **for sth** de qch); **to come into one's o.** (*fulfil oneself*) s'épanouir.
2 *vt* (*possess*) posséder; **who owns this ball/etc?** à qui appartient cette balle/*etc*?
3 *vi* **to o. up** (*confess*) avouer (**to sth** qch). ● **owner** *n* propriétaire *mf*. ● **ownership** *n* possession *f*; **home o.** accession *f* à la propriété.

ox, *pl* **oxen** [ɒks, 'ɒks(ə)n] *n* bœuf *m*.

oxygen ['ɒksɪdʒ(ə)n] *n* oxygène *m* ‖ *a* (*mask, tent*) à oxygène.

oyster ['ɔɪstər] *n* huître *f*.

oz *abbr* (*ounce*) once *f*.

ozone ['əʊzəʊn] *n* ozone *m*; **o. layer** couche *f* d'ozone. ● **o.-friendly** *a* (*product*) qui préserve la couche d'ozone.

P

P, p [piː] *n* P, p *m*.

p [piː] *abbr* = **penny, pence.**

pa [pɑː] *n Fam* papa *m*.

pace [peɪs] *n* (*speed, step*) pas *m*; **to keep p. with** (*follow*) suivre; (*in work, progress*) se maintenir à la hauteur de ▮ *vi* **to p. up and down** faire les cent pas. ●**pacemaker** *n* (*for heart*) stimulateur *m* cardiaque.

Pacific [pə'sɪfɪk] *a* (*coast etc*) pacifique ▮ *n* **the P.** le Pacifique.

pacify ['pæsɪfaɪ] *vt* (*country*) pacifier; (*crowd, angry person*) calmer; (*nervous person*) apaiser. ●**pacifier** *n* (*of baby*) *Am* sucette *f*. ●**pacifist** *n* pacifiste *mf*.

pack¹ [pæk] *n* (*bundle, packet*) paquet *m*; (*rucksack*) sac *m* (à dos); (*of animal*) charge *f*; (*of hounds, wolves*) meute *f*; (*of runners*) *Sp* peloton *m*; (*of thieves*) bande *f*; (*of cards*) jeu *m*; (*of lies*) tissu *m*.

pack² [pæk] *vt* (*fill*) remplir (**with** de); (*suitcase*) faire; (*object into box etc*) emballer; (*object into suitcase*) mettre dans sa valise; (*crush*) tasser ▮ *vi* (*fill one's bags*) faire ses valises. ●**packed** *a* (*bus, room etc*) bourré; **p. lunch** panier-repas *m*. ●**packing** *n* (*material, action*) emballage *m*; **p. case** caisse *f* d'emballage.

pack away *vt* (*tidy away*) ranger **to pack down** *vt* (*crush*) tasser **to pack in** *vt* (*give up*) laisser tomber; (*stop*) arrêter; **p. it in!** laisse tomber! **to pack into** *vt* (*cram*) entasser dans; (*put*) mettre dans ▮ *vi* (*crowd into*) s'entasser dans **to pack up** *vt* (*put into box*) emballer; (*give up*) *Fam* laisser tomber ▮ *vi Fam* (*stop*) s'arrêter; (*of machine, vehicle*) tomber en rade.

packag/e ['pækɪdʒ] *n* paquet *m*; (*computer programs*) progiciel *m*; **p. tour** voyage *m* organisé ▮ *vt* emballer. ●**—ing** *n* (*material*) emballage *m*.

packet ['pækɪt] *n* paquet *m*; **to make/cost a p.** *Fam* faire/coûter beaucoup d'argent.

pact [pækt] *n* pacte *m*.

pad [pæd] *n* (*of cloth etc*) tampon *m*; (*for writing*) bloc *m*; (*on knee*) *Sp* genouillère *f*; (*room*) *Sl* piaule *f*; **launch(ing) p.** aire *f* de lancement ▮ *vt* (**-dd-**) (*armchair etc*) rembourrer; (*jacket etc*) matelasser; **to p. out** (*text*) délayer. ●**padding** *n* rembourrage *m*.

paddle ['pæd(ə)l] **1** *vi* (*dip one's feet*) se mouiller les pieds; **paddling pool** (*inflatable*) piscine *f* gonflable; (*purpose-built*) pataugeoire *f* ▮ *n* **to have a (little) p.** se mouiller les pieds. **2** *n* (*pole*) pagaie *f*; **p. boat** bateau *m* à roues ▮ *vt* **to p. a canoe** pagayer.

paddock ['pædək] *n* enclos *m*; (*at racecourse*) paddock *m*.

padlock ['pædlɒk] *n* (*on door etc*) cadenas *m*; (*on bicycle, moped*) antivol *m* ▮ *vt* (*door etc*) cadenasser.

p(a)ediatrician [piːdɪə'trɪʃ(ə)n] *n* (*doctor*) pédiatre *mf*.

pagan ['peɪgən] *a* & *n* païen, -enne (*mf*).

page [peɪdʒ] **1** *n* (*of book etc*) page *f*. **2** *n* **p. (boy)** (*in hotel etc*) groom *m*; (*at court*) *Hist* page *m*; (*at wedding*) garçon *m* d'honneur ▮ *vt* **to p. s.o.** faire appeler qn. ●**pager** *n* récepteur *m* d'appel.

pageant ['pædʒənt] *n* grand spectacle *m* historique.

pagoda [pə'gəʊdə] *n* pagode *f*.

paid [peɪd] *pt* & *pp of* **pay** ▮ *a* (*assassin etc*) à gages; **to put p. to** (*hopes, plans*) anéantir.

pail [peɪl] *n* seau *m*.

pain [peɪn] *n* (*physical*) douleur *f*; (*grief*) peine *f*; *pl* (*efforts*) efforts *mpl*; **to have a p. in one's arm** avoir mal *or* une douleur au bras; **to be in p.** souffrir; **to take (great) pains to do** se donner du mal à faire; **to take (great) pains not to do** prendre bien soin de ne pas faire; **to be a p. (in the neck)** (*of person*) *Fam* être casse-pieds. ●**painkiller** *n* calmant *m*; **on painkillers** sous calmants.

painful ['peɪnfəl] *a* (*illness, arm, sight etc*) douloureux; (*difficult*) pénible. ●**painless** *a* sans douleur; (*operation*) indolore; (*easy*) *Fam* facile.

painstaking ['peɪnzteɪkɪŋ] *a* (*person*) soigneux; (*work*) soigné.

paint [peɪnt] *n* peinture *f*; *pl* (*in box, tube*) couleurs *fpl*; **p. stripper** décapant ▮ *vti* peindre; **to p. sth blue**/*etc* peindre qch en bleu/*etc*. ●**—ing** *n* (*activity*) peinture *f*; (*picture*) tableau *m*, peinture *f*. ●**painter** *n* peintre *m*.

paintbrush ['peɪntbrʌʃ] *n* pinceau *m*.

pair [peər] *n* (*two*) paire *f*; (*man and woman*) couple *m*; **a p. of shorts** un short.

pajamas [pə'dʒɑːməz] *npl Am* = **pyjamas.**

Pakistan [pɑːkɪ'stɑːn] *n* Pakistan *m*. ●**Pakistani** *a* & *n* pakistanais, -aise (*mf*).

pal [pæl] *n Fam* copain *m*, copine *f* ‖ *vi* (**-ll-**) **to p. up** devenir copains; **to p. up with s.o.** devenir copain avec qn.

palace ['pælɪs] *n* palais *m*. ●**palatial** [pə'leɪʃ(ə)l] *a* comme un palais.

palatable ['pælətəb(ə)l] *a* (*food*) agréable; (*idea etc*) acceptable.

palate ['pælɪt] *n Anat* palais *m*.

pale [peɪl] *a* (**-er, -est**) (*face, colour etc*) pâle; **p. ale** bière *f* blonde ‖ *vi* pâlir.

Palestine ['pæləstaɪn] *n* Palestine *f*. ●**Pale'stinian** *a* & *n* palestinien, -ienne (*mf*).

palette ['pælɪt] *n* (*of artist*) palette *f*.

pall [pɔːl] **1** *vi* devenir insipide *or* ennuyeux (**on** pour). **2** *n* (*of smoke*) voile *m*.

pallid ['pælɪd] *a* pâle. ●**pallor** *n* pâleur *f*.

pally ['pælɪ] *a* (**-ier, -iest**) *Fam* copain *am*, copine *af* (**with** avec).

palm [pɑːm] **1** *n* (*of hand*) paume *f*. **2** *n* **p. (tree)** palmier *m*; **p. (leaf)** palme *f*; **P. Sunday** les Rameaux *mpl*. **3** *vt Fam* **to p. sth off** refiler qch (**on s.o.** à qn); **to p. s.o. off on s.o.** coller qn à qn.

palmist ['pɑːmɪst] *n* chiromancien, -ienne *mf*.

palpitation [pælpɪ'teɪʃ(ə)n] *n* palpitation *f*.

paltry ['pɔːltrɪ] *a* (**-ier, -iest**) (*sum etc*) dérisoire; **a p. excuse** une piètre excuse.

pamper ['pæmpər] *vt* dorloter.

pamphlet ['pæmflɪt] *n* brochure *f*.

pan [pæn] **1** *n* casserole *f*; (*for frying*) poêle *f* (à frire); (*of lavatory*) cuvette *f*. **2** *vi* (**-nn-**) **to p. out** (*succeed*) aboutir.

pancake ['pænkeɪk] *n* crêpe *f*.

panda ['pændə] *n* (*animal*) panda *m*; **P. car** = voiture *f* pie *inv* (de la police).

pandemonium [pændɪ'məʊnɪəm] *n* (*chaos*) chaos *m*; (*uproar*) tumulte *m*.

pander ['pændər] *vi* **to p. to** (*tastes, fashion etc*) sacrifier à; **to p. to s.o.** se plier aux désirs de qn.

pane [peɪn] *n* vitre *f*, carreau *m*.

panel ['pæn(ə)l] *n* **1** (*of door etc*) panneau *m*; **(control) p.** *Tech El* console *f*; **(instrument) p.** *Av Aut* tableau *m* de bord. **2** (*of judges*) jury *m*; (*of experts*) groupe *m*; **a p. of guests** des invités; **a p. game** *TV Rad* un jeu par équipes. ●**panelled** (*Am* **paneled**) *a* (*room etc*) lambrissé. ●**panelling** (*Am* **paneling**) *n* lambris *m*.

pangs [pæŋz] *npl* **p. of conscience** remords *mpl* (de conscience); **p. of hunger** tiraillements *mpl* d'estomac.

panic ['pænɪk] *n* panique *f*; **to get into a p.** paniquer ‖ *vi* (**-ck-**) s'affoler, paniquer. ●**p.-stricken** *a* affolé. ●**panicky** (*person*) *a Fam* qui s'affole facilement.

panorama [pænə'rɑːmə] *n* panorama *m*.

pansy ['pænzɪ] *n Bot* pensée *f*.

pant [pænt] *vi* (*gasp*) haleter.

panther ['pænθər] *n* panthère *f*.

panties ['pæntɪz] *npl* (*female underwear*) slip *m*; (*longer*) culotte *f*.

pantomime ['pæntəmaɪm] *n* spectacle *m* de Noël.

pantry ['pæntrɪ] *n* (*larder*) garde-manger *m inv*.

pants [pænts] *npl* (*male underwear*) slip *m*; (*long*) caleçon *m*; (*trousers*) *Am* pantalon *m*.

pantyhose ['pæntɪhəʊz] *n* (*tights*) *Am* collant(s) *m*(*pl*).

paper ['peɪpər] *n* papier *m*; (*newspaper*) journal *m*; (*wallpaper*) papier *m* peint; (*exam*) épreuve *f* (écrite); (*student's exercise*) copie *f*; (*learned article*) exposé *m*, communication *f*; **brown p.** papier *m* d'emballage; **to put sth down on p.** mettre qch par écrit.
‖ *a* (*bag etc*) en papier; (*cup, plate*) en carton; **p. clip** trombone *m*; **p. knife** coupe-papier *m inv*; **p. shop** marchand *m* de journaux.
‖ *vt* (*room, wall*) tapisser.

paperback ['peɪpəbæk] *n* (*book*) livre *m* de poche. ●**paperboy** *n* livreur *m* de journaux. ●**paperweight** *n* presse-papiers *m inv*. ●**paperwork** *n Com* écritures *fpl*; (*red tape*) paperasserie *f*.

paprika ['pæprɪkə] *n* paprika *m*.

par [pɑːr] *n* **on a p.** au même niveau (**with** que); **below p.** (*unwell*) *Fam* pas en forme.

parable ['pærəb(ə)l] *n* (*story*) parabole *f*.

paracetamol [pærə'siːtəmɒl] *n* paracétamol *m*; (*tablet*) comprimé *m* de paracétamol.

parachute ['pærəʃuːt] *n* parachute *m*; **to drop by p.** (*men, supplies*) parachuter.

parade [pə'reɪd] **1** *n* (*procession*) défilé *m*; (*ceremony*) *Mil* parade *f*; **fashion p.** défilé *m* de mode ‖ *vi Mil etc* défiler; **to p. about** (*walk about*) se balader ‖ *vt* faire étalage de. **2** *n* (*street*) avenue *f*.

paradise ['pærədaɪs] *n* paradis *m*.

paradox ['pærədɒks] *n* paradoxe *m*. ●**para'doxically** *adv* paradoxalement.

paraffin ['pærəfɪn] *n* pétrole *m* (lampant); (*wax*) *Am* paraffine *f*; **p. lamp** lampe *f* à pétrole.

paragraph ['pærəgrɑːf] *n* paragraphe *m*; **'new p.'** 'à la ligne'.

parakeet ['pærəkiːt] *n* perruche *f*.

parallel ['pærəlel] *a* (*comparable*) & *Math*

parallèle (**with, to** à); **to run p. to** *or* **with** être parallèle à ▮ *n* (*comparison*) & *Geog* parallèle *m*; (*line*) *Math* parallèle *f*.

paralysis [pə'ræləsɪs] *n* paralysie *f*.

paralyse ['pærəlaɪz] (*Am* **-lyze**) *vt* paralyser.

paramount ['pærəmaʊnt] *a* **of p. importance** de la plus haute importance.

paranoia [pærə'nɔɪə] *n* paranoïa *f*. ● **'paranoid** *a* paranoïaque.

parapet ['pærəpɪt] *n* parapet *m*.

paraphernalia [pærəfə'neɪlɪə] *n* attirail *m*.

paraphrase ['pærəfreɪz] *n* paraphrase *f* ▮ *vt* paraphraser.

parasite ['pærəsaɪt] *n* (*person, animal*) parasite *m*.

parasol ['pærəsɒl] *n* (*over table, on beach*) parasol *m*; (*lady's*) ombrelle *f*.

paratroops [pærətruːps] *npl Mil* parachutistes *mpl*.

parcel ['pɑːs(ə)l] **1** *n* colis *m*, paquet *m*; **to be part and p. of** faire partie intégrante de. **2** *vt* (**-ll-**, *Am* **-l-**) **to p. sth up** faire un paquet de qch.

parched [pɑːtʃt] *a* **to be parched** (*thirsty*) être assoiffé.

parchment ['pɑːtʃmənt] *n* parchemin *m*.

pardon ['pɑːd(ə)n] *n* (*by king, president etc*) grâce *f*; (*forgiveness*) pardon *m*; *Jur* grâce *f*; **general p.** amnistie *f*; **I beg your p.** (*apologize*) je vous prie de m'excuser; (*not hearing*) vous dites?; **p.?** (*not hearing*) comment?; **p. (me)!** (*sorry*) pardon! ▮ *vt* pardonner (**s.o. for sth** qch à qn); **to p. s.o.** (*of king etc*) gracier qn.

parent ['peərənt] *n* père *m*, mère *f*; **one's parents** ses parents *mpl*; **p. company** maison *f* mère. ● **parental** [pə'rent(ə)l] *a* (*responsibility etc*) des parents.

Paris ['pærɪs] *n* Paris *m or f*. ● **Parisian** [pə'rɪzɪən, *Am* pə'riːʒən] *a* & *n* parisien, -ienne (*mf*).

parish ['pærɪʃ] *n Rel* paroisse *f*; (*civil*) commune *f* ▮ *a* (*church, register*) paroissial; **p. council** conseil *m* municipal.

park [pɑːk] **1** *n* (*garden*) parc *m*. **2** *vt* (*vehicle*) garer ▮ *vi Aut* se garer; (*remain parked*) stationner. ● **parking** *n* stationnement *m*; **'no p.'** 'défense de stationner'; **p. light** veilleuse *f*; **p. lot** *Am* parking *m*; **p. meter** parcmètre *m*; **p. place** *or* **space** place *f* de parking; **p. ticket** contravention *f*.

parkway ['pɑːkweɪ] *n Am* avenue *f*.

parliament ['pɑːləmənt] *n* parlement *m*. ● **parlia'mentary** *a* parlementaire.

parlour ['pɑːlər] (*Am* **parlor**) *n* (*in mansion*) (petit) salon *m*; **ice-cream p.** *Am* salon de glaces.

parochial [pə'rəʊkɪəl] *a* (*mentality*) *Pej* de clocher; (*person*) *Pej* provincial; **p. school** *Am* école *f* catholique.

parody ['pærədɪ] *n* parodie *f* ▮ *vt* parodier.

parole [pə'rəʊl] *n* **on p.** *Jur* en liberté conditionnelle.

parquet ['pɑːkeɪ] *n* **p. (floor)** parquet *m*.

parrot ['pærət] *n* perroquet *m*.

parry ['pærɪ] *vt* (*blow*) parer; (*question*) éluder.

parsimonious [pɑːsɪ'məʊnɪəs] *a* parcimonieux.

parsley ['pɑːslɪ] *n* persil *m*.

parsnip ['pɑːsnɪp] *n* panais *m*.

parson ['pɑːs(ə)n] *n* (*Protestant priest*) pasteur *m*.

part[1] [pɑːt] *n* partie *f*; (*of machine*) pièce *f*; (*of periodical*) fascicule *m*; (*of serial*) épisode *m*; (*role in play etc*) rôle *m*; (*in hair*) *Am* raie *f*; **to take p.** participer (**in** à); **to take s.o.'s p.** prendre parti pour qn; **in p.** en partie; **for the most p.** dans l'ensemble; **to be a p. of** faire partie de; **on the p. of** (*on behalf of*) de la part de; **for my p.** pour ma part; **in these parts** dans ces parages; **p. exchange** reprise *f*; **to take in p. exchange** reprendre; **p. payment** paiement *m* partiel. ▮ *adv* (*partly*) en partie.

part[2] [pɑːt] *vt* (*separate*) séparer; **to p. company with s.o.** quitter qn ▮ *vi* (*of friends etc*) se quitter; (*of married couple*) se séparer; **to p. with sth** (*get rid of*) se séparer de qch.

partake [pɑː'teɪk] *vi* (*pt* **partook**, *pp* **partaken**) **to p. in** participer à.

partial ['pɑːʃəl] *a* (*not total*) partiel; (*biased*) partial (**towards** envers); **to be p. to sth** (*fond of*) *Fam* avoir un faible pour qch.

participate [pɑː'tɪsɪpeɪt] *vi* participer (**in** à). ● **participant** *n* participant, -ante *mf*. ● **partici'pation** *n* participation *f*.

participle [pɑː'tɪsɪp(ə)l] *n Gram* participe *m*.

particle ['pɑːtɪk(ə)l] *n* (*of atom, dust*) particule *f*; (*of truth*) grain *m*.

particular [pə'tɪkjʊlər] **1** *a* (*specific, special*) particulier; (*fussy*) difficile (**about** sur); (*showing care*) méticuleux; **this p. book** ce livre-ci en particulier; **in p.** en particulier. **2** *npl* **particulars** détails *mpl*, renseignements *mpl*; (*address etc*) coordonnées *fpl*. ● **—ly** *adv* particulièrement.

parting ['pɑːtɪŋ] **1** *n* (*in hair*) raie *f*. **2** *n* (*separation*) séparation *f* ▮ *a* (*gift, words*) d'adieu.

partition [pɑːˈtɪʃ(ə)n] **1** *n* (*in room*) cloison *f* ▮ *vt* **to p. off** cloisonner. **2** *n* (*of country*) partition *f* ▮ *vt* (*country*) partager.
partly [ˈpɑːtlɪ] *adv* en partie; **p. English p. French** moitié anglais moitié français.
partner [ˈpɑːtnər] *n* (*in business*) associé, -ée *mf*; (*lover*, *spouse*) & *Sp Pol* partenaire *mf*; **(dancing) p.** cavalier, -ière *mf*. ● **partnership** *n* association *f*; **in p. with** en association avec.
partridge [ˈpɑːtrɪdʒ] *n* perdix *f*.
part-time [pɑːtˈtaɪm] *a* & *adv* à temps partiel.
party [ˈpɑːtɪ] *n* **1** (*gathering*) (*formal*) réception *f*; (*with friends*) soirée *f*; (*for birthday*) fête *f*. **2** (*group*) groupe *m*; *Pol* parti *m*; (*in contract*, *lawsuit*) partie *f*; **rescue p.** équipe *f* de secours; **innocent p.** innocent, -ente *mf*; **p. line** *Tel* ligne *f* partagée; *Pol* ligne *f* du parti; **p. ticket** billet *m* collectif.
pass[1] [pɑːs] *n* (*entry permit*) laissez-passer *m inv*; (*free ticket*) *Th etc* billet *m* de faveur; (*over mountains*) col *m*; *Fb etc* passe *f*; **to get a p.** (*in exam*) être reçu **(in French**/*etc* en français/*etc*); **to make a p. at s.o.** faire des avances à qn; **p. mark** (*in exam*) moyenne *f*.
pass[2] [pɑːs] *vi* (*go*, *come*, *disappear*) passer (**to** à, **through** par); (*overtake in vehicle*) dépasser; (*in exam*) être reçu **(in French**/*etc* en français/*etc*); **he can p. for thirty** on lui donnerait trente ans.
▮ *vt* (*move*, *spend*, *give etc*) passer (**to** à); (*go past*) passer devant (*immeuble etc*); (*vehicle*) dépasser; (*exam*) être reçu à; (*candidate*) recevoir; (*opinion*) prononcer (**on** sur); (*remark*) faire; (*allow*) autoriser; (*bill*, *law*) (*of parliament*) voter; **to p. s.o.** (*in street*) croiser qn.
passable [ˈpɑːsəb(ə)l] *a* (*not bad*) passable; (*road*) praticable; (*river*) franchisssable.
passage [ˈpæsɪdʒ] *n* (*of text*, *act of passing etc*) passage *m*; (*of time*) écoulement *m*; (*corridor*) couloir *m*; (*by boat*) traversée *f*. ● **passageway** *n* (*corridor*) couloir *m*; (*alleyway*) passage *m*.
pass along *vi* passer **to pass away** *vi* (*die*) mourir **to pass by** *vi* passer (à côté) ▮ *vt* (*building etc*) passer devant; **to p. by s.o.** (*in street*) croiser qn **to pass off** *vi* (*happen*) se passer ▮ *vt* **to p. oneself off as** se faire passer pour; **to p. sth off on s.o.** refiler qch à qn **to pass on** *vt* (*message*, *illness etc*) transmettre (**to** à) **to pass out** *vi* (*faint*) s'évanouir ▮ *vt* (*hand out*) distribuer **to pass over** *vt* (*ignore*) passer sur (*qch*) **to pass round** *vt* (*cakes*, *document etc*) faire passer; (*hand out*) distribuer (*tracts etc*) **to pass through** *vi* passer **to pass up** *vt* (*chance etc*) laisser passer.
passbook [ˈpɑːsbʊk] *n* livret *m* de caisse d'épargne.
passenger [ˈpæsɪndʒər] *n* passager, -ère *mf*; *Rail* voyageur, -euse *mf*.
passer-by [pɑːsəˈbaɪ] *n* (*pl* **passers-by**) passant, -ante *mf*.
passing [ˈpɑːsɪŋ] *a* (*vehicle etc*) qui passe; (*beauty*) passager ▮ *n* (*of vehicle etc*) passage *m*; (*of time*) écoulement *m*; **in p.** en passant.
passion [ˈpæʃ(ə)n] *n* passion *f*; **to have a p. for** (*cars etc*) avoir la passion de. ● **passionate** *a* passionné.
passive [ˈpæsɪv] *a* (*not active*) & *Gram* passif ▮ *n Gram* passif *m*; **in the p.** au passif.
Passover [ˈpɑːsəʊvər] *n Rel* Pâque *f*.
passport [ˈpɑːspɔːt] *n* passeport *m*; **p. control** le contrôle des passeports.
password [ˈpɑːswɜːd] *n* mot *m* de passe.
past [pɑːst] **1** *n* (*time*, *history*) passé *m*; **in the p.** (*formerly*) dans le temps.
▮ *a* (*gone by*) passé; (*former*) ancien; **these p. months** ces derniers mois; **in the p. tense** *Gram* au passé.
2 *prep* (*in front of*) devant; (*after*) après; (*further than*) plus loin que; (*too old for*) trop vieux pour; **p. four o'clock** quatre heures passées; **to be p. fifty** avoir cinquante ans passés.
▮ *adv* devant; **to go p.** passer (devant); **to run p.** passer en courant.
pasta [ˈpæstə] *n Culin* pâtes *fpl*.
paste [peɪst] **1** *n* (*mixture*) pâte *f*; (*of meat*) pâté *m*; (*of fish*) beurre *m*. **2** *n* (*glue*) colle *f* (blanche) ▮ *vt* coller; **to p. up** (*notice etc*) coller.
pastel [ˈpæstəl, *Am* pæˈstel] *n* pastel *m*.
pasteurized [ˈpæstəraɪzd] *a* (*milk*) pasteurisé.
pastille [ˈpæstɪl, *Am* pæˈstiːl] *n* pastille *f*.
pastime [ˈpɑːstaɪm] *n* passe-temps *m inv*.
pastor [ˈpɑːstər] *n Rel* pasteur m.
pastry [ˈpeɪstrɪ] *n* (*dough*) pâte *f*; (*cake*) pâtisserie *f*.
pasture [ˈpɑːstʃər] *n* pâturage *m*.
pasty [ˈpæstɪ] *n Culin* petit pâté *m* (en croûte).
pat [pæt] *vt* **(-tt-)** (*cheek etc*) tapoter; (*animal*) caresser ▮ *n* petite tape; caresse *f*.
patch [pætʃ] *n* (*for clothes*) pièce *f*; (*over eye*) bandeau *m*; (*of colour*) tache *f*; (*of fog*) nappe *f*; (*of ice*) plaque *f*; **a cabbage p.** un carré de choux; **bad p.** *Fig* mauvaise période *f* ▮ *vt* **to p. (up)** (*clothing*) rapié-

cer; **to p. up** (*quarrel*) régler. ●**patchwork** *n* patchwork *m*. ●**patchy** *a* (**-ier, -iest**) inégal.
patent ['peɪtənt] **1** *a* **p. leather** cuir *m* verni. **2** *n* brevet *m* (d'invention) ‖ *vt* (faire) breveter. ●**—ly** *adv* manifestement; **p. obvious** absolument évident.
paternal [pə'tɜːn(ə)l] *a* paternel.
path [pɑːθ] *n* (*pl* **-s** [pɑːðz]) sentier *m*, chemin *m*; (*in park*) allée *f*; (*of river*) cours *m*; (*of bullet*) trajectoire *f*. ●**pathway** *n* sentier *m*, chemin *m*.
pathetic [pə'θetɪk] *a* (*results etc*) lamentable.
pathology [pə'θɒlədʒɪ] *n* pathologie *f*.
patient ['peɪʃ(ə)nt] **1** *a* patient. **2** *n* (*in hospital*) malade *mf*, patient, -ente *mf*; (*on doctor's or dentist's list*) patient, -ente *mf*. ●**patience** *n* patience *f*; **to have p.** prendre patience; **to lose p.** perdre patience (**with s.o.** avec qn); **to play p.** (*card game*) faire des réussites. ●**patiently** *adv* patiemment.
patio ['pætɪəʊ] *n* (*pl* **-os**) terrasse *f*; **p. doors** porte-fenêtre *f*.
patriot ['peɪtrɪət] *n* patriote *mf*. ●**patri'otic** *a* patriotique; (*person*) patriote. ●**patriotism** *n* patriotisme *m*.
patrol [pə'trəʊl] *n* patrouille *f*; **police p. car** voiture *f* de police ‖ *vi* (**-ll-**) patrouiller ‖ *vt* patrouiller dans. ●**patrolman** *n* (*pl* **-men**) *Am* agent *m* de police.
patron ['peɪtrən] *n* (*of artist*) protecteur, -trice *mf*; (*customer*) client, -ente *mf*; (*of theatre etc*) habitué, -ée *mf*.
patroniz/e ['pætrənaɪz, *Am* 'peɪtrənaɪz] *vt* *Pej* traiter (*qn*) avec condescendance. ●**—ing** *a* condescendant.
patter ['pætər] **1** *n* (*of footsteps*) petit bruit *m*; (*of rain*) crépitement *m* ‖ *vi* (*of rain*) crépiter. **2** *n* (*talk*) baratin *m*.
pattern ['pæt(ə)n] *n* dessin *m*, motif *m*; (*paper model for garment*) patron *m*; *Fig* modèle *m*; (*plan*) plan *m*; (*tendency*) tendance *f*; (*of a crime*) scénario *m*. ●**patterned** *a* (*dress, cloth*) à motifs.
paunch [pɔːntʃ] *n* panse *f*, bedon *m*.
pauper ['pɔːpər] *n* pauvre *mf*.
pause [pɔːz] *n* pause *f*; (*in conversation*) silence *m* ‖ *vi* (*stop*) faire une pause; (*hesitate*) hésiter.
pav/e [peɪv] *vt* paver; **to p. the way for** *Fig* ouvrir la voie à. ●**—ing** *n* (*surface*) pavage *m*; **p. stone** pavé *m*.
pavement ['peɪvmənt] *n* trottoir *m*; (*roadway*) *Am* chaussée *f*.
pavilion [pə'vɪljən] *n* (*building*) pavillon *m*.
paw [pɔː] *n* patte *f* ‖ *vt* (*of animal*) donner des coups de patte à.
pawn [pɔːn] **1** *n Chess* pion *m*. **2** *vt* mettre en gage. ●**pawnbroker** *n* prêteur, -euse *mf* sur gages. ●**pawnshop** *n* bureau *m* de prêteur sur gages.
pay [peɪ] *n* salaire *m*; (*of workman*) paie *f*; (*of soldier*) solde *f*; **p. day** jour *m* de paie; **p. slip** *or Am* **stub** bulletin *m* de paie.
‖ *vt* (*pt & pp* **paid**) (*person, sum*) payer; (*deposit*) verser; (*of investment*) rapporter; (*compliment, visit*) faire (**to** à); **to p. s.o. to do** *or* **for doing** payer qn pour faire; **to p. s.o. for sth** payer qch à qn; **to p. money into one's account** *or* **the bank** verser de l'argent sur son compte; **to p. homage** *or* **tribute to** rendre hommage à.
‖ *vi* payer; **to p. a lot** payer cher; **it pays to be cautious** on a intérêt à être prudent. ●**paying** *a* (*guest*) payant; (*profitable*) (*scheme etc*) rentable.
payable ['peɪəb(ə)l] *a* (*due*) payable; **a cheque** *or Am* **check p. to** un chèque à l'ordre de.
pay back *vt* (*person, loan*) rembourser; **I'll p. you back for this!** je te revaudrai ça! **to pay for** *vt* payer (*qch*) **to pay in** *vt* (*cheque, Am check*) verser (**to one's account** sur son compte) **to pay off** *vt* (*debt, person*) rembourser; (*in instalments*) rembourser par acomptes; **to p. off an old score** *Fig* régler un vieux compte ‖ *vi* (*be successful*) être payant **to pay out** *vt* (*spend*) dépenser **to pay up** *vti* payer.
paycheck ['peɪtʃek] *n Am* chèque *m* de règlement de salaire. ●**payoff** *n Fam* (*reward*) récompense *f*. ●**payphone** *n* téléphone *m* public. ●**payroll** *n* **to be on the p. of** (*factory etc*) être employé par.
payment ['peɪmənt] *n* paiement *m*; (*of deposit*) versement *m*; **on p. of 20 francs** moyennant 20 francs.
PC [piː'siː] *n abbr* = **personal computer**.
PE [piː'iː] *n abbr* (*physical education*) EPS *f*.
pea [piː] *n* pois *m*; **garden** *or* **green peas** petits pois *mpl*; **p. soup** soupe *f* aux pois.
peace [piːs] *n* paix *f*; **p. of mind** tranquillité *f* d'esprit; **in p.** en paix; **at p.** en paix (**with** avec); **to have (some) p. and quiet** avoir la paix; **to disturb the p.** troubler l'ordre public. ●**p.-loving** *a* pacifique.
peaceful ['piːsfəl] *a* paisible, calme; (*demonstration, coexistence*) pacifique.
peach [piːtʃ] *n* (*fruit*) pêche *f* ‖ *a* (*colour*) pêche *inv*.
peacock ['piːkɒk] *n* paon *m*.
peak [piːk] *n* (*mountain top*) sommet *m*; (*mountain*) pic *m*; (*of cap*) visière *f*; (*of fame etc*) *Fig* sommet *m*; **the traffic is at its p.** la

circulation est à son maximum ▮ *a* (*hours, period*) de pointe; (*production*) maximum. • **peaked cap** *n* casquette *f*.

peaky ['piːkɪ] *a* (**-ier, -iest**) *Fam* (*ill*) patraque; (*pale*) pâlot.

peal [piːl] *n* (*of laughter*) éclat *m*; (*of thunder*) roulement *m*; **p. of bells** carillon *m* ▮ *vi* (*of bells*) carillonner.

peanut ['piːnʌt] *n* cacah(o)uète *f*; **p. butter** beurre *m* de cacah(o)uètes.

pear [peər] *n* poire *f*; **p. tree** poirier *m*.

pearl [pɜːl] *n* perle *f*; **p. necklace** collier *m* de perles.

peasant ['pezənt] *n* paysan, -anne *mf*.

peashooter ['piːʃuːtər] *n* sarbacane *f*.

peat [piːt] *n* tourbe *f*.

pebble ['peb(ə)l] *n* (*stone*) caillou *m* (*pl* -oux) (*on beach*) galet *m*. • **pebbly** *a* (*beach*) (couvert) de galets.

pecan ['piːkæn] *n* (*nut*) *Am* noix *f* de pécan.

peck [pek] *vti* **to p. (at)** (*of bird*) picorer (*du pain etc*); donner un coup de bec à (*qn*) ▮ *n* coup *m* de bec; (*kiss*) *Fam* bécot *m*.

peckish ['pekɪʃ] *a* **to be p.** (*hungry*) *Fam* avoir un petit creux.

peculiar [pɪ'kjuːlɪər] *a* (*strange*) bizarre; (*special*) particulier (**to** à). • **peculi'arity** *n* (*feature*) particularité *f*.

pedal ['ped(ə)l] *n* pédale *f*; **p. boat** pédalo *m* ▮ *vi* (**-ll-**, *Am* **-l-**) pédaler ▮ *vt* **to p. a bicycle** faire marcher un vélo; (*ride*) rouler en vélo. • **pedalbin** *n* poubelle *f* à pédale.

pedantic [pə'dæntɪk] *a* pédant.

peddl/e ['ped(ə)l] *vt* colporter; (*drugs*) faire le trafic de. • **—er** *n* (*door-to-door*) colporteur, -euse *mf*; (*in street*) camelot *m*; **drug p.** revendeur, -euse *mf* de drogues.

pedestal ['pedɪst(ə)l] *n Archit & Fig* piédestal *m*.

pedestrian [pə'destrɪən] *n* piéton *m*; **p. crossing** passage *m* pour piétons. • **pedestrianized** *a* **p. street** rue *f* piétonne *or* piétonnière.

pediatrician [piːdɪə'trɪʃ(ə)n] *n* (*doctor*) pédiatre *mf*.

pedigree ['pedɪgriː] *n* (*of dog etc*) pedigree *m*; (*of person*) ascendance *f* ▮ *a* (*dog etc*) de race.

pedlar ['pedlər] *n* (*door-to-door*) colporteur, -euse *mf*; (*in street*) camelot *m*.

pee [piː] *n* **to go for a p.** *Fam* faire pipi.

peek [piːk] *n* **to have a p.** = **to peek** ▮ *vi* jeter un petit coup d'œil (**at** à).

peel [piːl] *n* (*of vegetable, fruit*) épluchure(s) *f*(*pl*); **a piece of p., some p.** une épluchure ▮ *vt* (*apple, potato etc*) éplucher; **to p. off** (*label etc*) décoller ▮ *vi* (*of sunburnt skin*) peler; (*of paint*) s'écailler. • **—ings** *npl* épluchures *fpl*. • **peeler** *n* **(potato) p.** éplucheur *m*.

peep [piːp] **1** *n* **to have a p.** = **to peep** ▮ *vi* jeter un petit coup *m* d'œil; **to p. out** se montrer; **peeping Tom** voyeur, -euse *mf*. **2** *vi* (*of bird*) pépier. • **peephole** *n* judas *m*.

peer [pɪər] **1** *n* (*equal*) pair *m*, égal, -ale *mf*; (*noble*) pair *m*. **2** *vi* **to p. (at)** regarder attentivement (*comme pour mieux voir*). • **peerage** *n* (*rank*) pairie *f*.

peeved [piːvd] *a Fam* irrité.

peevish ['piːvɪʃ] *a* grincheux, irritable.

peg [peg] *n* (*for coat, hat*) patère *f*; (*for clothes*) pince *f* (à linge); (*for tent*) piquet *m*; (*wooden*) cheville *f*; **to buy sth off the p.** acheter qch en prêt-à-porter.

pejorative [pɪ'dʒɒrətɪv] *a* péjoratif.

Peking [piː'kɪŋ] *n* Pékin *m or f*.

pelican ['pelɪk(ə)n] *n* (*bird*) pélican *m*; **p. crossing** passage *m* pour piétons (*avec feux à déclenchement manuel*).

pellet ['pelɪt] *n* (*of paper*) boulette *f*; (*for gun*) (grain *m* de) plomb *m*.

pelt [pelt] **1** *vi* **it's pelting (down)** (*raining*) il pleut à verse. **2** *vt* **to p. s.o. with** (*stones etc*) bombarder qn de. **3** *n* (*skin*) peau *f*.

pelvis [pelvɪs] *n Anat* bassin *m*.

pen [pen] **1** *n* (*fountain pen*) stylo *m* (à plume); (*ballpoint*) stylo *m* (à bille); (*dipped in ink*) porte-plume *m inv*; **p. friend, p. pal** correspondant, -ante *mf*; **p. name** pseudonyme *m*; **p. nib** (bec *m* de) plume *f* ▮ *vt* (**-nn-**) (*write*) écrire. **2** *n* (*enclosure for baby, sheep or cattle*) parc *m*.

penal ['piːn(ə)l] *a* (*code etc*) pénal; (*colony*) pénitentiaire. • **penalize** *vt* (*punish*) *Sp* pénaliser (**for** pour); (*handicap*) désavantager.

penalty ['pen(ə)ltɪ] *n* (*prison sentence*) peine *f*; (*fine*) amende *f*; *Sp* pénalisation *f*; *Fb* penalty *m*; *Rugby* pénalité *f*.

pence [pens] *npl see* **penny.**

pencil ['pens(ə)l] *n* crayon *m*; **in p.** au crayon; **p. case** trousse *f*; **p. sharpener** taille-crayon(s) *m inv* ▮ *vt* (**-ll-**, *Am* **-l-**) **to p. in** (*note down*) noter provisoirement.

pendant ['pendənt] *n* (*around neck*) pendentif *m*.

pending ['pendɪŋ] **1** *a* (*matter*) en suspens. **2** *prep* (*until*) en attendant.

pendulum ['pendjʊləm] *n* (*of clock*) balancier *m*.

penetrat/e ['penɪtreɪt] *vt* (*substance*) pénétrer; (*secret*) découvrir; (*forest, group*) pénétrer dans. • **—ing** *a* (*mind etc*) pénétrant.

penguin ['peŋgwɪn] *n* manchot *m*.
penicillin [penɪ'sɪlɪn] *n* pénicilline *f*.
peninsula [pə'nɪnsjʊlə] *n* presqu'île *f*, péninsule *f*.
penis ['piːnɪs] *n* pénis *m*.
penitent ['penɪtənt] *a* repentant.
penitentiary [penɪ'tenʃərɪ] *n Am* prison *f* (centrale).
penknife ['pennaɪf] *n* (*pl* **-knives**) canif *m*.
pennant ['penənt] *n* (*flag*) fanion *m*.
penny ['penɪ] *n* **1** (*pl* **pennies**) (*coin*) penny *m*; *Am Can* cent *m*; **I don't have a p.** *Fig* je n'ai pas le *or* un sou. **2** (*pl* **pence** [pens]) (*value, currency*) penny *m*. ●**penniless** *a* sans le sou.
pension ['penʃ(ə)n] *n* pension *f*; **(retirement) p.** retraite *f*; **to retire on a p.** toucher une retraite; **p. scheme** régime *m* de retraite ‖ *vt* **to p. s.o. off** mettre qn à la retraite. ●**—er** *n* pensionné, -ée *mf*; (*on retirement pension*) retraité, -ée *mf*; **old age p.** retraité, -ée *mf*.
Pentagon ['pentəgən] *n* **the P.** *Am Pol* le Pentagone.
Pentecost ['pentɪkɒst] *n* (*Whitsun*) *Am* Pentecôte *f*.
penthouse ['penthaʊs] *n* appartement *m* de luxe (*construit sur le toit d'un immeuble*).
pent-up [pent'ʌp] *a* (*feelings*) refoulé.
penultimate [pɪ'nʌltɪmət] *a* avant-dernier.
people ['piːp(ə)l] *npl* (*in general*) gens *mpl or fpl*; (*specific persons*) personnes *fpl*; **the p.** (*citizens*) le peuple; **old p.** les personnes *fpl* âgées; **old people's home** hospice *m* de vieillards; (*private*) maison *f* de retraite; **two p.** deux personnes; **English p.** les Anglais *mpl*; **p. think that...** on pense que... ‖ *n* (*nation*) peuple *m*.
pep [pep] *n Fam* dynamisme; **p. talk** petit laïus d'encouragement ‖ *vt* (**-pp-**) **to p. s.o. up** (*perk up*) ragaillardir qn.
pepper ['pepər] *n* poivre *m*; (*vegetable*) poivron *m* ‖ *vt* poivrer. ●**pepperpot** *n* poivrière *f*.
peppermint ['pepəmɪnt] *n* (*flavour*) menthe *f*; (*sweet, Am candy*) bonbon *m* à la menthe.
per [pɜːr] *prep* par; **p. annum** par an; **p. head, p. person** par personne; **p. cent** pour cent; **50 pence p. kilo** 50 pence le kilo; **40 km p. hour** 40 km à l'heure. ●**per'centage** *n* pourcentage *m*.
perceive [pə'siːv] *vt* (*see, hear*) percevoir; (*notice*) remarquer (**that** que). ●**perception** [-ʃ(ə)n] *n* perception *f* (**of** de); (*intuition*) intuition *f*. ●**perceptive** *a* (*person*) perspicace; (*study, remark*) pénétrant.
perch [pɜːtʃ] **1** *n* (*for bird*) perchoir *m* ‖ *vi* (*of bird*) se percher (**on** sur); (*of person*) *Fig* se percher ‖ *vt* (*put*) percher. **2** *n* (*fish*) perche *f*.
percolator ['pɜːkəleɪtər] *n* cafetière *f*; (*in café or restaurant*) percolateur *m*.
perennial [pə'renɪəl] **1** *a* (*complaint etc*) perpétuel. **2** *a* (*plant*) vivace ‖ *n* plante *f* vivace.
perfect ['pɜːfɪkt] *a* parfait ‖ *a* & *n* **p. (tense)** *Gram* parfait *m* ‖ [pə'fekt] *vt* (*piece of work*) parachever; (*technique*) mettre au point; (*one's French etc*) parfaire ses connaissances en. ●**'perfectly** *adv* parfaitement.
perfection [pə'fekʃ(ə)n] *n* perfection *f*; **to p.** à la perfection. ●**perfectionist** *n* perfectionniste *mf*.
perforate ['pɜːfəreɪt] *vt* perforer. ●**perforation** [-'reɪʃ(ə)n] *n* perforation *f*.
perform [pə'fɔːm] *vt* (*task, miracle*) accomplir; (*one's duty, a function*) remplir; (*surgical operation*) pratiquer (**on** sur); (*a play, piece of music*) jouer ‖ *vi* (*act, play*) jouer; (*sing*) chanter; (*dance*) danser; (*of circus animal*) faire un numéro; (*of machine, vehicle*) fonctionner; (*in one's job*) réussir.
performance [pə'fɔːməns] *n* **1** (*show*) (*in theatre*) représentation *f*, séance *f*; (*in concert hall, cinema, Am movie theater*) séance *f*. **2** (*of actor, musician etc*) interprétation *f*; (*of athlete, machine etc*) performance *f*; (*in job, of company*) performances *fpl*; (*fuss*) *Fam* histoire(s) *f*(*pl*).
performer [pə'fɔːmər] *n* (*entertainer*) artiste *mf*.
perfume ['pɜːfjuːm] *n* parfum *m*.
perhaps [pə'hæps] *adv* peut-être; **p. not** peut-être que non.
peril ['perɪl] *n* péril *m*; **at your p.** à vos risques et péril. ●**perilous** *a* périlleux.
period ['pɪərɪəd] **1** *n* période *f*; (*historical*) époque *f*; (*time limit*) délai *m*; (*lesson*) *Sch* leçon *f*; (*full stop*) *Am Gram* point *m*; **in the p. of a month** en l'espace d'un mois; **I refuse, p.!** *Am* je refuse, un point c'est tout! ‖ *a* (*furniture*) d'époque; (*costume*) de l'époque. **2** *n* **(monthly) period(s)** (*of woman*) règles *fpl*.
periodic [pɪərɪ'ɒdɪk] *a* périodique. ●**periodical** *n* (*magazine*) périodique *m*.
peripheral [pə'rɪfər(ə)l] *a* (*question*) sans rapport direct (**to** avec); (*region etc*) & *Comptr* périphérique ‖ *npl* **peripherals** *Comptr* périphériques *mpl*.

periscope ['perɪskəʊp] *n* périscope *m*.

perish ['perɪʃ] *vi* (*die*) périr; (*of food, substance*) se détériorer. ●**—ing** *a* (*cold, weather*) *Fam* glacial. ●**perishable** *a* (*food*) périssable ▮*npl* **perishables** denrées *fpl* périssables.

perjury ['pɜːdʒərɪɪ] *n* **to commit p.** faire un faux témoignage.

perk [pɜːk] **1** *vi* **to p. up** (*become livelier*) reprendre du poil de la bête ▮ *vt* **to p. s.o. up** remonter qn. **2** *n* (*in job*) avantage *m* en nature. ●**perky** *a* (**-ier, -iest**) (*cheerful*) guilleret.

perm [pɜːm] *n* (*of hair*) permanente *f* ▮ *vt* **to have one's hair permed** se faire faire une permanente.

permanent ['pɜːmənənt] *a* permanent; (*address*) fixe. ●**—ly** *adv* à titre permanent.

permeate ['pɜːmɪeɪt] *vt* **to p. (through) sth** (*of liquid etc*) pénétrer qch.

permissible [pə'mɪsəb(ə)l] *a* permis.

permission [pə'mɪʃ(ə)n] *n* permission *f* (**to do** de faire); **to ask/give p.** demander/donner la permission.

permissive [pə'mɪsɪv] *a* (trop) tolérant, laxiste.

permit [pə'mɪt] *vt* (**-tt-**) permettre (**s.o. to do** à qn de faire); **weather permitting** si le temps le permet ▮ ['pɜːmɪt] *n* permis *m*; (*entrance pass*) laissez-passer *m inv*.

perpendicular [pɜːpən'dɪkjʊlər] *a* & *n* perpendiculaire (*f*).

perpetrate ['pɜːpɪtreɪt] *vt* (*crime*) commettre, perpétrer. ●**perpetrator** *n* auteur *m*.

perpetual [pə'petʃʊəl] *a* perpétuel. ●**perpetuate** *vt* perpétuer.

perplex [pə'pleks] *vt* rendre perplexe, dérouter. ●**—ed** *a* perplexe. ●**—ing** *a* déroutant.

persecute ['pɜːsɪkjuːt] *vt* persécuter. ●**persecution** [-'kjuːʃ(ə)n] *n* persécution *f*.

persever/e [pɜːsɪ'vɪər] *vi* persévérer (**in** dans). ●**—ing** *a* (*persistent*) persévérant. ●**perseverance** *n* persévérance *f*.

Persian ['pɜːʃ(ə)n, 'pɜːʒ(ə)n] *a* (*language, cat etc*) persan; **the P. Gulf** le golfe Persique ▮ *n* (*language*) persan *m*.

persist [pə'sɪst] *vi* persister (**in doing** à faire, **in sth** dans qch). ●**persistence** *n* persistance *f*. ●**persistent** *a* (*person*) obstiné; (*fever etc*) persistant; (*noise etc*) continuel.

person ['pɜːs(ə)n] *n* personne *f*; **in p.** en personne.

personal ['pɜːsən(ə)l] *a* personnel; (*application*) en personne; (*friend, hygiene*) intime; (*life*) privé; (*indiscreet*) indiscret; **p. assistant** secrétaire *m* particulier, secrétaire *f* particulière; **p. computer** ordinateur *m* personnel; **p. stereo** baladeur *m*. ●**—ly** *adv* personnellement; (*in person*) en personne.

personality [pɜːsə'nælətɪ] *n* (*character, famous person*) personnalité *f*; **a television p.** une vedette de la télévision.

personify [pə'sɒnɪfaɪ] *vt* personnifier.

personnel [pɜːsə'nel] *n* (*staff*) personnel *m*.

perspective [pə'spektɪv] *n* (*artistic & viewpoint*) perspective *f*; **in p.** *Fig* sous son vrai jour.

Perspex ['pɜːspeks] *n* Plexiglas® *m*.

perspire [pə'spaɪər] *vi* transpirer. ●**perspiration** [pɜːspə'reɪʃ(ə)n] *n* transpiration *f*.

persuade [pə'sweɪd] *vt* persuader (**s.o. to do** qn de faire). ●**persuasion** [-ʒ(ə)n] *n* persuasion *f*; (*creed*) religion *f*. ●**persuasive** *a* (*person, argument etc*) persuasif.

pert [pɜːt] *a* (*impertinent*) impertinent; (*lively*) plein d'entrain.

pertain [pə'teɪn] *vi* **to p. to** (*relate*) se rapporter à; (*belong*) appartenir à.

pertinent ['pɜːtɪnənt] *a* pertinent.

perturb [pə'tɜːb] *vt* troubler, perturber.

Peru [pə'ruː] *n* Pérou *m*. ●**Peruvian** *a* & *n* péruvien, -ienne (*mf*).

peruse [pə'ruːz] *vt* lire (attentivement); (*skim through*) parcourir.

pervade [pə'veɪd] *vt* se répandre dans. ●**pervasive** *a* qui se répand partout.

perverse [pə'vɜːs] *a* (*awkward*) contrariant; (*obstinate*) entêté; (*wicked*) pervers. ●**perversion** *n* [-ʃ(ə)n, *Am* -ʒ(ə)n] perversion *f*.

pervert [pə'vɜːt] *vt* pervertir; (*mind*) corrompre; (*truth*) travestir ▮ ['pɜːvɜːt] *n* **(sexual) p.** détraqué, -ée *mf*, pervers, -erse *mf*.

pesky ['peskɪ] *a* (**-ier, -est**) *Am Fam* embêtant.

pessimism ['pesɪmɪz(ə)m] *n* pessimisme *m*. ●**pessimist** *n* pessimiste *mf*. ●**pessi'mistic** *a* pessimiste.

pest [pest] *n* animal *m or* insecte *m* nuisible; (*person*) casse-pieds *mf inv*, peste *f*.

pester ['pestər] *vt* harceler (**with questions** de questions); **to p. s.o. to do sth/for sth** harceler qn pour qu'il fasse qch/jusqu'à ce qu'il donne qch.

pesticide ['pestɪsaɪd] *n* pesticide *m*.

pet [pet] **1** *n* animal *m* (domestique); (*favourite person*) chouchou, -oute *mf*; **yes p.** *Fam* oui mon chou; **to have** *or* **keep a p.** avoir un animal chez soi ▮ *a* (*dog, cat etc*) domestique; (*favourite*) favori; **p. shop** magasin *m* d'animaux; **p. hate** bête *f* noire. **2** *vt* (**-tt-**) (*fondle*) caresser; (*sexually*) *Fam* peloter ‖ *vi Fam* se peloter.

petal ['pet(ə)l] *n* pétale *m.*

peter ['piːtər] *vi* **to p. out** (*dry up*) tarir; (*die out*) mourir; (*disappear*) disparaître.

petite [pə'tiːt] *a* (*woman*) menue.

petition [pə'tɪʃ(ə)n] *n* (*signatures*) pétition *f*; (*request*) *Jur* requête *f.*

petrified ['petrɪfaɪd] *a* (*frightened*) pétrifié de terreur.

petrol ['petrəl] *n* essence *f*; **p. can** bidon *m* à essence; **p. station** station-service *f*; **p. tank** réservoir *m* (d'essence).

petroleum [pə'trəʊlɪəm] *n* pétrole *m.*

petticoat ['petɪkəʊt] *n* jupon *m.*

petty ['petɪ] *a* (**-ier, -iest**) (*minor*) petit; (*trivial*) insignifiant; (*mean*) mesquin; **p. cash** *Com* petite caisse *f*, menue monnaie *f.*

petulant ['petjʊlənt] *a* irritable.

pew [pjuː] *n* banc *m* d'église; **take a p.!** *Hum* assieds-toi!

pewter ['pjuːtər] *n* étain *m.*

phallic ['fælɪk] *a* phallique.

phantom ['fæntəm] *n* fantôme *m.*

pharmacy ['fɑːməsɪ] *n* pharmacie *f.* ● **pharmacist** *n* pharmacien, -ienne *mf.*

pharyngitis [færɪn'dʒaɪtəs] *n Med* pharyngite *f.*

phase [feɪz] *n* (*stage*) phase *f* ‖ *vt* **to p. sth in/out** introduire/supprimer qch progressivement.

PhD [piːeɪtʃ'diː] *n abbr* (*Doctor of Philosophy*) (*university degree*) doctorat *m.*

pheasant ['fezənt] *n* (*bird*) faisan *m.*

phenomenon, *pl* **-ena** [fɪ'nɒmɪnən, -ɪnə] *n* phénomène *m.* ● **phenomenal** *a* phénoménal.

philanthropist [fɪ'lænθrəpɪst] *n* philanthrope *mf.*

philately [fɪ'lætəlɪ] *n* philatélie. ● **philatelist** *n* philatéliste *mf.*

Philippines ['fɪlɪpiːnz] *npl* **the P.** les Philippines *fpl.*

philistine ['fɪlɪstaɪn] *n* béotien, -ienne *mf.*

philosophy [fɪ'lɒsəfɪ] *n* philosophie *f.* ● **philosopher** *n* philosophe *mf.* ● **philo'sophical** *a* philosophique; (*resigned*) *Fig* philosophe.

phlegm [flem] *n* (*in throat*) glaires *fpl.*

phobia ['fəʊbɪə] *n* phobie *f.*

phone [fəʊn] *n* téléphone *m*; **on the p.** (*speaking here*) au téléphone; (*at other end*) au bout du fil; **to be on the p.** (*as subscriber*) avoir le téléphone; **p. call** coup *m* de fil *or* de téléphone; **to make a p. call** téléphoner (**to** à); **p. book** annuaire *m*; **p. booth, p. box** cabine *f* téléphonique; **p. number** numéro *m* de téléphone.

‖ *vt* **to p. s.o. (up)** téléphoner à qn; **to p. s.o. back** rappeler qn.

‖ *vi* **to p. (up)** téléphoner; **to p. back** rappeler. ● **phonecard** *n* télécarte ® *f.*

phonetic [fə'netɪk] *a* phonétique.

phoney ['fəʊnɪ] *a* (**-ier, -iest**) *Fam* (*jewels, writer etc*) faux (*f* fausse); (*company, excuse*) bidon *inv* ‖ *n Fam* (*impostor*) imposteur *m*; (*insincere person*) faux-jeton *m.*

phonograph ['fəʊnəgræf] *n Am* électrophone *m.*

photo ['fəʊtəʊ] *n* (*pl* **-os**) photo *f*; **to take a p. of** prendre une photo de; **to have one's p. taken** se faire prendre en photo.

photocopy ['fəʊtəʊkɒpɪ] *n* photocopie *f* ‖ *vt* photocopier. ● **photocopier** *n* (*machine*) photocopieuse *f.*

photogenic [fəʊtəʊ'dʒenɪk] *a* photogénique.

photograph ['fəʊtəʊgræf] *n* photographie *f* ‖ *vt* photographier. ● **photographer** [fə'tɒgrəfər] *n* photographe *mf.* ● **photo'graphic** *a* photographique. ● **photography** [fə'tɒgrəfɪ] *n* (*activity*) photographie *f.*

photostat® ['fəʊtəʊstæt] *n* = **photocopy.**

phrase [freɪz] *n* (*saying*) expression *f*; (*idiom*) & *Gram* locution *f* ‖ *vt* (*express*) exprimer. ● **phrasebook** *n* (*for tourists*) manuel *m* de conversation.

Phys Ed [fɪz'ed] *n abbr* (*physical education*) *Am* EPS *f.*

physical ['fɪzɪk(ə)l] *a* physique; (*object, world*) matériel; **p. examination** examen *m* médical; **p. education** éducation *f* physique. ● **physically** *adv* physiquement; **p. impossible** matériellement impossible.

physician [fɪ'zɪʃ(ə)n] *n* médecin *m.*

physics ['fɪzɪks] *n* (*science*) physique *f.* ● **physicist** *n* physicien, -ienne *mf.*

physiology [fɪzɪ'ɒlədʒɪ] *n* physiologie *f.*

physiotherapy [fɪzɪəʊ'θerəpɪ] *n* kinésithérapie *f.* ● **physiotherapist** *n* kinésithérapeute *mf.*

physique [fɪ'ziːk] *n* (*appearance*) physique *m*; (*constitution*) constitution *f.*

piano [pɪ'ænəʊ] *n* (*pl* **-os**) piano *m.* ● **pianist** ['pɪənɪst] *n* pianiste *mf.*

pick [pɪk] *n* (*choice*) choix *m*; **to take one's p.** faire son choix, choisir; **the p. of** (*best*) le meilleur de.

‖ *vt* (*choose*) choisir; (*flower, fruit etc*) cueillir; (*hole*) faire (**in** dans); (*pimple etc*) gratter; (*lock*) crocheter; **to p. one's nose** se mettre les doigts dans le nez; **to p. a fight** chercher la bagarre (**with** avec); **to p. holes in** *Fig* relever les défauts de.

pick at *vt* **to p. at one's food** picorer **to pick off** *vt* (*remove*) enlever; (*shoot*) abattre un à un **to pick on** *vt* (*nag, blame*) s'en prendre à (*qn*) **to pick out** *vt* (*choose*) choisir; (*identify*) reconnaître **to pick up** *vt* (*sth dropped*) ramasser; (*fallen person or chair*) relever; (*person into air, weight*) soulever; (*a cold*) attraper; (*habit, accent, speed*) prendre; (*fetch, collect*) (passer) prendre; (*find*) trouver; (*programme*) *Rad* capter; (*survivor*) recueillir; (*arrest*) arrêter; (*learn*) apprendre ‖ *vi* (*improve*) s'améliorer; (*of business, trade*) reprendre; (*of patient*) aller mieux; (*resume*) continuer.

pick(axe) (*Am* (**-ax**)) ['pɪk(æks)] *n* (*tool*) pioche *f*; **ice pick** pic *m* à glace.

picket ['pɪkɪt] *n* (*striker*) gréviste *mf*; **p. (line)** piquet *m* (de grève) ‖ *vt* (*factory*) installer des piquets de grève aux portes de.

pickle ['pɪk(ə)l] **1** *npl* **pickles** (*vegetables*) pickles *mpl*; *Am* concombres *mpl*, cornichons *mpl* ‖ *vt* mariner; **pickled onion**/*etc* oignon *m*/*etc* au vinaigre. **2** *n* **in a p.** (*trouble*) *Fam* dans le pétrin.

pick-me-up ['pɪkmi:ʌp] *n* (*drink*) *Fam* remontant *m*.

pickpocket ['pɪkpɒkɪt] *n* pickpocket *m*.

pick-up ['pɪkʌp] *n* **1 p.-up (truck)** pick-up *m*. **2 p.-up point** (*for bus passengers*) point *m* de ramassage.

picky ['pɪkɪ] *a* (**-ier, -iest**) (*choosey*) *Am* difficile.

picnic ['pɪknɪk] *n* pique-nique *m*; **p. basket** *or* **hamper** panier *m* à pique-nique ‖ *vi* (**-ck-**) pique-niquer.

picture ['pɪktʃər] **1** *n* image *f*; (*painting*) tableau *m*, peinture *f*; (*drawing*) dessin *m*; (*photo*) photo *f*; (*film*) film *m*; **the pictures** *Fam* le cinéma; **to put s.o. in the p.** *Fig* mettre qn au courant; **p. frame** cadre *m*. **2** *vt* (*imagine*) s'imaginer (**that** que).

picturesque [pɪktʃə'resk] *a* pittoresque.

pie [paɪ] *n* (*open*) tarte *f*; (*with pastry on top*) tourte *f*; **meat p.** pâté *m* en croûte; **cottage p.** hachis *m* Parmentier.

piece [pi:s] *n* morceau *m*; (*of fabric, machine, in game*) pièce *f*; (*coin*) pièce *f*; **bits and pieces** des petites choses; **in pieces** en morceaux; **to smash to pieces** briser en morceaux; **to take to pieces** (*machine*) démonter; **to come to pieces** se démonter; **a p. of news/advice**/*etc* une nouvelle/un conseil/*etc*; **in one p.** (*object*) intact; (*person*) indemne. ‖ *vt* **to p. together** (*facts*) reconstituer. • **piecemeal** *adv* petit à petit ‖ *a* (*unsystematic*) peu méthodique.

pier [pɪər] *n* (*for walking, with entertainments*) jetée *f*.

pierc/e [pɪəs] *vt* percer (*qch*); (*of cold, bullet*) transpercer (*qn*). • **—ing** *a* (*voice etc*) perçant; (*wind etc*) glacial.

pig [pɪg] *n* cochon *m*, porc *m*; (*glutton*) goinfre *m*. • **piggy** *a* (*greedy*) *Fam* goinfre.

pigeon ['pɪdʒɪn] *n* pigeon *m*. • **pigeonhole** *n* casier *m* ‖ *vt* classer.

piggyback ['pɪgɪbæk] *n* **to give s.o. a p.** porter qn sur le dos.

piggybank ['pɪgɪbæŋk] *n* tirelire *f* (*en forme de cochon*).

pigheaded [pɪg'hedɪd] *a* obstiné.

pigment ['pɪgmənt] *n* pigment *m*.

pigsty ['pɪgstaɪ] *n* porcherie *f*.

pigtail ['pɪgteɪl] *n* (*hair*) natte *f*.

pike [paɪk] *n* (*fish*) brochet *m*.

pilchard ['pɪltʃəd] *n* pilchard *m* (*grosse sardine*).

pile[1] [paɪl] *n* tas *m*; (*neatly arranged*) pile *f*; (*fortune*) *Fam* fortune *f*; **piles of** *Fam* beaucoup de ‖ *vt* **to p. (up)** entasser; (*neatly*) empiler ‖ *vi* **to p. into** (*crowd into*) s'entasser dans; **to p. up** (*accumulate*) s'accumuler. • **p.-up** *n Aut* carambolage *m*.

pile[2] [paɪl] *n* (*of carpet*) poils *mpl*.

piles [paɪlz] *npl Med* hémorroïdes *fpl*.

pilfer ['pɪlfər] *vt* (*steal*) chaparder (**from s.o.** à qn). • **—ing** *n* chapardage *m*.

pilgrim ['pɪlgrɪm] *n* pèlerin *m*. • **pilgrimage** *n* pèlerinage *m*.

pill [pɪl] *n* pilule *f*; **to be on the p.** prendre la pilule; **to go on/off the p.** se mettre à/arrêter la pilule.

pillage ['pɪlɪdʒ] *vti* piller ‖ *n* pillage *m*.

pillar ['pɪlər] *n* pilier *m*. • **p.-box** *n* boîte *f* aux *or* à lettres (*située sur le trottoir*).

pillion ['pɪljən] *adv* **to ride p.** (*on motorbike*) monter derrière.

pillow ['pɪləʊ] *n* oreiller *m*. • **pillowcase** *n* taie *f* d'oreiller.

pilot ['paɪlət] **1** *n* (*of aircraft*) pilote *m* ‖ *vt* piloter ‖ *a* **p. light** (*on appliance*) voyant *m*. **2** *a* (*experimental*) (-)pilote; **p. scheme** projet(-)pilote *m*.

pimento [pɪ'mentəʊ] *n* (*pl* **-os**) piment *m*.

pimple ['pɪmp(ə)l] *n* bouton *m*.

pin [pɪn] *n* épingle *f*; (*drawing pin*) punaise *f*; *Tech* goupille *f*; **to have pins and needles** *Fam* avoir des fourmis (**in** dans); **p. money** argent *m* de poche.
‖ *vt* (**-nn-**) **to p. (on)** (*attach*) épingler (**to** sur, à); (*to wall*) punaiser (**to, on** à); **to p. one's hopes on** mettre tous ses espoirs dans;

to p. on (to) s.o. (*crime*) accuser qn de; **to p. sth down** immobiliser qch; (*fix*) fixer qch; **to p. s.o. down** *Fig* forcer qn à préciser ses idées; **to p. up** (*notice*) punaiser, afficher.

PIN [pɪn] *n abbr* (*personal identification number*) **PIN number** code *m* confidentiel.

pinafore ['pɪnəfɔːr] *n* (*apron*) tablier *m*; (*dress*) robe *f* chasuble.

pinball ['pɪnbɔːl] *n* flipper *m*; **p. machine** flipper *m*.

pincers ['pɪnsəz] *npl* (*tool*) tenailles *fpl*.

pinch [pɪntʃ] **1** *n* (*mark*) pinçon *m*; (*of salt*) pincée *f*; **to give s.o. a p.** pincer qn; **at a p.,** *Am* **in a p.** (*if necessary*) au besoin ▮ *vt* pincer. **2** *vt* (*steal*) *Fam* piquer (**from** à); (*arrest*) pincer.

pincushion ['pɪnkʊʃ(ə)n] *n* pelote *f* (à épingles).

pine [paɪn] **1** *n* (*tree, wood*) pin *m*; **p. forest** pinède *f*. **2** *vi* **to p. for** désirer vivement (retrouver).

pineapple ['paɪnæp(ə)l] *n* ananas *m*.

ping-pong ['pɪŋpɒŋ] *n* ping-pong *m*.

pink [pɪŋk] *a & n* (*colour*) rose (*m*).

pinkie ['pɪŋkɪ] *n Am* petit doigt *m*.

pinnacle ['pɪnək(ə)l] *n Fig* apogée *m*.

pinpoint ['pɪnpɔɪnt] *vt* (*locate*) repérer; (*define*) définir.

pinstripe ['pɪnstraɪp] *a* (*suit*) rayé.

pint [paɪnt] *n* pinte *f* (*Br = 0,57 litre, Am = 0,47 litre*); **a p. of beer** = un demi.

pinup ['pɪnʌp] *n* (*girl*) pin-up *f inv*.

pioneer [paɪə'nɪər] *n* pionnier, -ière *mf*.

pious ['paɪəs] *a* (*person, deed*) pieux.

pip [pɪp] **1** *n* (*of fruit*) pépin *m*. **2** *npl* **the pips** (*sound*) *Rad etc* le top.

pipe [paɪp] **1** *n* tuyau *m*; (*of smoker*) pipe *f*; *Mus* pipeau *m*; **the pipes** (*bagpipes*) la cornemuse; **to smoke a p.** fumer la pipe; **p. cleaner** cure-pipe *m*; **p. dream** chimère *f*. **2** *vi* **to p. down** (*shut up*) *Fam* la boucler. ● **piping** *n* (*pipes*) tuyaux *mpl*; **length of p.** tuyau *m* ▮ *adv* **it's p. hot** (*soup etc*) c'est très chaud.

pipeline ['paɪplaɪn] *n* pipeline *m*; **it's in the p.** *Fig* c'est en route.

pirate ['paɪərət] *n* pirate *m* ▮ *a* (*radio, ship*) pirate. ● **piracy** *n* piraterie *f*. ● **pirated** *a* (*book, CD etc*) pirate.

Pisces ['paɪsiːz] *npl* (*sign*) les Poissons *mpl*.

pistachio [pɪ'stæʃɪəʊ] *n* (*pl* **-os**) (*fruit, flavour*) pistache *f*.

pistol ['pɪstəl] *n* pistolet *m*.

piston ['pɪst(ə)n] *n Aut* piston *m*.

pit [pɪt] **1** *n* (*hole*) trou *m*; (*coalmine*) mine *f*; (*quarry*) carrière *f*; (*of stomach*) creux *m*; *Th* orchestre. **2** *vt* (**-tt-**) **to p. one's wits against** se mesurer à. **3** *n* (*stone of fruit*) *Am* noyau *m*; (*smaller*) pépin *m*.

pitch[1] [pɪtʃ] **1** *n Fb etc* terrain *m*. **2** *n* (*degree*) degré *m*; (*of voice*) hauteur *f*; *Mus* ton *m*. **3** *vt* (*tent*) dresser; (*camp*) établir; (*ball*) lancer; **a pitched battle** *Mil* une bataille rangée; *Fig* une belle bagarre. **4** *vi* (*of ship*) tanguer. **5** *vi* **to p. in** (*cooperate*) *Fam* se mettre de la partie.

pitch[2] [pɪtʃ] *n* (*tar*) poix *f*. ● **p.-'black** *or* **p.-'dark** *a* noir comme dans un four.

pitcher ['pɪtʃər] *n* cruche *f*.

pitchfork ['pɪtʃfɔːk] *n* fourche *f* (à foin).

pitfall ['pɪtfɔːl] *n* (*trap*) piège *m*.

pith [pɪθ] *n* (*of orange*) peau *f* blanche.

pitiful ['pɪtɪfəl] *a* pitoyable. ● **pitiless** *a* impitoyable.

pitta ['piːtə] *adj* **p. bread** pitta *m*.

pittance ['pɪtəns] *n* (*income*) revenu *m or* salaire *m* misérable.

pitted ['pɪtɪd] *a* (*face*) grêlé.

pitter-patter ['pɪtəpætər] *n* = **patter 1.**

pity [pɪtɪ] *n* pitié *f*; **(what) a p.!** (quel) dommage!; **it's a p.** c'est *or* il est dommage (**that** que (+ *sub*), **to do** de faire); **to take p. on s.o.** avoir pitié de qn ▮ *vt* plaindre.

pivot ['pɪvət] *n* pivot *m* ▮ *vi* pivoter.

pizza ['piːtsə] *n* pizza *f*.

placard ['plækɑːd] *n* (*notice*) affiche *f*.

placate [plə'keɪt, *Am* 'pleɪkeɪt] *vt* calmer.

place [pleɪs] *n* endroit *m*, lieu *m*; (*house*) maison *f*; (*seat, position, rank*) place *f*; **in the first p.** en premier lieu; **to take p.** avoir lieu; **p. of work** lieu *m* de travail; **market p.** place *f* du marché; *Fin* marché *m*; **at my p., to my p.** (*house*) chez moi; **some p.** (*somewhere*) *Am* quelque part; **no p.** (*nowhere*) *Am* nulle part; **all over the p.** partout; **to lose one's p.** perdre sa place; (*in book*) perdre sa page; **p. setting** couvert *m*; **to set** *or* **lay three places** mettre trois couverts; **to take the p. of** remplacer; **in p. of** à la place de; **out of p.** (*remark*) déplacé; (*object*) pas à sa place; **p. mat** set *m* (de table).
▮ *vt* (*put, invest*) & *Sp* placer; (*an order*) passer (**with s.o.** à qn); **to p. s.o.** (*identify*) remettre qn.

placid ['plæsɪd] *a* placide.

plague [pleɪg] **1** *n* (*disease*) peste *f*; (*nuisance*) *Fam* plaie *f*. **2** *vt* (*pester*) harceler (**with** de).

plaice [pleɪs] *n* (*fish*) carrelet *m*.

plaid [plæd] *n* (*fabric*) tissu *m* écossais.

plain[1] [pleɪn] *a* (**-er, -est**) (*clear, obvious*) clair; (*simple*) simple; (*madness*) pur; (*without a pattern*) uni; (*woman, man*) sans beauté; (*sheer*) pur; **in p. clothes** en civil; **to make it p. to s.o. that** faire comprendre à qn que ▮ *adv* (*tired etc*) tout bonnement. ●**—ly** *adv* clairement; (*frankly*) franchement.

plain² [pleɪn] *n Geog* plaine *f*.

plaintiff ['pleɪntɪf] *n Jur* plaignant, -ante *mf*.

plait [plæt] *n* tresse *f* ▮ *vt* tresser.

plan [plæn] *n* projet *m*; (*elaborate*) plan *m*; (*economic, of house, book etc*) plan *m*; **the best p. would be to...** le mieux serait de...; **according to p.** comme prévu; **to have no plans** (*be free*) n'avoir rien de prévu; **master p.** stratégie *f or* plan *m* d'ensemble.
▮ *vt* (**-nn-**) (*foresee*) prévoir, projeter; (*organize*) organiser; (*prepare*) préparer; (*design*) concevoir; **to p. to do** *or* **on doing** avoir l'intention de faire; **as planned** comme prévu.
▮ *vi* faire des projets; **to p. for** (*rain, disaster*) prévoir.

plane [pleɪn] **1** *n* (*aircraft*) avion *m*. **2** *n* (*tool*) rabot *m* ▮ *vt* raboter. **3** *n* **p. (tree)** platane *m*. **4** *n* (*level*) & *Fig* plan *m*.

planet ['plænɪt] *n* planète *f*. ●**planetary** *a* planétaire.

plank [plæŋk] *n* planche *f*.

planner ['plænər] *n* **(town) p.** urbaniste *mf*.

planning ['plænɪŋ] *n* (*economic, industrial, commercial*) planification *f*; **family p.** planning *m* familial.

plant [plɑːnt] **1** *n* plante *f*; **house p.** plante *f* verte ▮ *vt* (*flower, field*) planter (**with** en, de); (*bomb*) *Fig* poser; **to p. sth on s.o.** cacher qch sur qn. **2** *n* (*factory*) usine *f*; (*machinery*) matériel *m*. ●**plantation** [-'teɪʃ(ə)n] *n* (*trees etc*) plantation *f*.

plaque [plæk] *n* (*commemorative plate*) plaque *f*.

plaster ['plɑːstər] *n* plâtre *m*; **(sticking) p.** sparadrap *m*; **p. of Paris** plâtre *m* à mouler; **in p.** (*arm etc*) dans le plâtre; **p. cast** *Med* plâtre *m* ▮ *vt* plâtrer; **to p. down** (*hair*) plaquer; **to p. with** (*cover*) couvrir de. ●**—ed** *a* (*drunk*) *Fam* bourré.

plastic ['plæstɪk] *a* (*object*) en plastique; (*substance*) plastique; **p. surgery** chirurgie *f* esthétique ▮ *n* plastique *m*.

plasticine® ['plæstɪsiːn] *n* pâte *f* à modeler.

plate [pleɪt] *n* (*dish*) assiette *f*; (*metal sheet on door etc*) plaque *f*; (*book illustration*) gravure *f*; **to have a lot on one's p.** (*work*) avoir du pain sur la planche; **p. glass** verre *m* à vitre. ●**plateful** *n* assiettée *f*.

plateau ['plætəʊ] *n* (*pl* **-s** *or* **-x**) *Geog* plateau *m*.

platform ['plætfɔːm] *n* (*at train station*) quai *m*; (*on bus etc*) plate-forme *f*; (*for speaker etc*) estrade *f*.

platinum ['plætɪnəm] *n* (*metal*) platine *m* ▮ *a* **p.** *or* **p.-blond(e) hair** cheveux *mpl* platinés.

platonic [plə'tɒnɪk] *a* (*love etc*) platonique.

platoon [plə'tuːn] *n Mil* section *f*.

plausible ['plɔːzəb(ə)l] *a* (*argument etc*) plausible.

play [pleɪ] *n Th* pièce *f* (de théâtre); (*amusement, looseness*) jeu *m*; **a p. on words** un jeu de mots; **to come into p.** entrer en jeu.
▮ *vt* (*part, tune etc*) jouer; (*game*) jouer à; (*instrument*) jouer de; (*match*) disputer (**with** avec); (*team, opponent*) jouer contre; (*record, compact disc*) passer; (*radio*) faire marcher; **to p. the fool** faire l'idiot; **to p. a part in doing/in sth** contribuer à faire/à qch; **to p. it cool** *Fam* garder son sang-froid.
▮ *vi* jouer (**with** avec, **at** à); (*of tape recorder etc*) marcher; **what are you playing at?** *Fam* qu'est-ce que tu fais?

play about *or* **around** *vi* jouer, s'amuser **to play back** *vt* (*tape*) réécouter **to play down** *vt* (*reduce importance of*) minimiser **to play out** *vt* (*scene etc*) jouer; **to be played out** (*of idea etc*) *Fam* être périmé **to play up** *vi* (*of child, machine etc*) *Fam* faire des siennes ▮ *vt Fam* (*of child etc*) faire enrager (*qn*); (*of bad back etc*) tracasser (*qn*).

play-act ['pleɪækt] *vi* jouer la comédie. ●**playboy** *n* playboy *m*. ●**playground** *n Sch* cour *f* de récréation; (*with swings etc*) terrain *m* de jeux. ●**playgroup** *n* = **playschool.** ●**playmate** *n* camarade *mf*. ●**playpen** *n* parc *m* (pour enfants). ●**playroom** *n* (*in house*) salle *f* de jeux. ●**playschool** *n* garderie *f* (d'enfants). ●**playtime** *n Sch* récréation *f*. ●**playwright** *n* dramaturge *mf*.

player ['pleɪər] *n* (*in game, of instrument*) joueur, -euse *mf*; *Th* acteur *m*, actrice *f*; **clarinet/***etc* **p.** joueur, -euse *mf* de clarinette/*etc*; **cassette/CD p.** lecteur *m* de cassettes/de CD.

playful ['pleɪfəl] *a* enjoué; (*child*) joueur.

playing ['pleɪɪŋ] *n* jeu *m*; **p. card** carte *f* à jouer; **p. field** terrain *m* de jeu(x).

plc [piːel'siː] *abbr* (*public limited company*) SA.

plea [pliː] *n* (*request*) appel *m*; **to make a p. of guilty** plaider coupable. ●**plead** *vi* (*pt & pp* **pleaded**, *Am* **pled**) Jur plaider; **to p. with s.o. to do** implorer qn de faire; **to p. for** (*help etc*) implorer ▮ *vt Jur* plaider; (*as excuse*) alléguer.

pleasant ['plezənt] *a* agréable (**to** avec). ●**—ly** *adv* agréablement.
pleasantries ['plezəntrɪz] *npl* (*polite remarks*) civilités *fpl*.
please [pli:z] *adv* s'il vous plaît, s'il te plaît; **p. do!** bien sûr!, je vous en prie!; **'no smoking p.'** 'prière de ne pas fumer'. ▮ *vt* **to p. s.o.** plaire à qn; (*satisfy*) contenter qn; **hard to p.** difficile (à contenter), exigeant; **p. yourself!** comme tu veux! ▮ *vi* plaire; **do as you p.** fais comme tu veux; **as much** *or* **as many as you p.** autant qu'il vous plaira. ●**pleased** *a* content (**with** de, **that** que (+ *sub*), **to do** de faire); **p. to meet you!** enchanté! ●**pleasing** *a* agréable.
pleasure ['pleʒər] *n* plaisir *m*; **p. boat** bateau *m* de plaisance. ●**pleasurable** *a* très agréable.
pleat [pli:t] *n* (*in skirt*) pli *m*. ●**pleated** *a* plissé.
pledge [pledʒ] *n* (*promise*) promesse *f* (**to do** de faire) ▮ *vt* promettre (**to do** de faire).
plenty ['plentɪ] *n* abondance *f*; **in p.** en abondance; **p. of** beaucoup de; **that's p.** c'est assez. ●**plentiful** *a* abondant.
pliable ['plaɪəb(ə)l] *a* souple.
pliers ['plaɪəz] *npl* (*tool*) pince(s) *f(pl)*.
plight [plaɪt] *n* situation *f* critique; **(sorry) p.** triste situation *f*.
plimsoll ['plɪmsəʊl] *n* (chaussure *f* de) tennis *m*.
plinth [plɪnθ] *n* socle *m*.
plod [plɒd] *vi* (**-dd-**) **to p. (along)** avancer *or* travailler laborieusement; **to p. through** (*book*) lire laborieusement. ●**plodding** *a* (*slow*) lent; (*step*) pesant.
plonk [plɒŋk] **1** *vt* **to p. sth (down)** (*drop*) *Fam* poser qch (bruyamment). **2** *n* (*wine*) *Sl* pinard *m*.
plot [plɒt] **1** *n* complot *m* (**against** contre); (*story*) intrigue *f* ▮ *vti* (**-tt-**) comploter (**to do** de faire). **2** *n* **p. (of land)** terrain *m*; (*patch in garden*) carré *m* de terre; **building p.** terrain *m* à bâtir. **3** *vt* (**-tt-**) **to p. (out)** (*route*) déterminer; (*diagram*) tracer.
plough [plaʊ] (*Am* **plow**) *n* charrue *f* ▮ *vt* (*field*) labourer; **to p. money into** mettre beaucoup d'argent dans ▮ *vi* labourer; **to p. into** (*crash into*) percuter; **to p. through** (*snow*) avancer péniblement dans; (*fence, wall*) défoncer. ●**ploughman** *n* (*pl* **-men**) **p.'s lunch** *Culin* assiette *f* composée (*de crudités et fromage*).
plow [plaʊ] *Am* = **plough.**
ploy [plɔɪ] *n* stratagème *m*.
pluck [plʌk] **1** *vt* (*fowl*) plumer; (*flower*) cueillir; (*eyebrows*) épiler; (*string*) *Mus* pincer. **2** *n* courage *m* ▮ *vt* **to p. up courage** s'armer de courage.
plug [plʌg] **1** *n* (*of cotton wool*, *Am absorbent cotton etc*) tampon *m*; (*for sink, bath*) bonde *f*; **(wall) p.** (*for screw*) cheville *f* ▮ *vt* (**-gg-**) **to p. (up)** (*stop up*) boucher. **2** *n El* fiche *f*, prise *f* (mâle); (*socket*) prise *f* de courant ▮ *vt* (**-gg-**) **to p. in** brancher. **3** *n Aut* bougie *f*. **4** *vt* (**-gg-**) (*book etc*) *Fam* faire du battage publicitaire pour. ●**plughole** *n* trou *m* (du lavabo *etc*).
plum [plʌm] *n* prune *f*; **a p. job** *Fam* un travail en or.
plumb [plʌm] **1** *vt* **to p. in** (*washing machine*) raccorder. **2** *adv* (*crazy etc*) *Am Fam* complètement.
plumber ['plʌmər] *n* plombier *m*. ●**plumbing** *n* plomberie *f*.
plume [plu:m] *n* (*feather*) plume *f*; (*on hat etc*) plumet *m*.
plummet ['plʌmɪt] *vi* (*of prices*) dégringoler; (*of aircraft etc*) plonger.
plump [plʌmp] **1** *a* (**-er, -est**) (*person, arm etc*) potelé; (*cheek*) rebondi. **2** *vi* **to p. for** (*choose*) se décider pour, choisir.
plunder ['plʌndər] *vt* piller ▮ *n* (*act*) pillage *m*; (*goods*) butin *m*.
plung/e [plʌndʒ] *vt* plonger (*qch*) (**into** dans) ▮ *vi* (*dive*) plonger (**into** dans); (*fall*) tomber (**from** de); (*rush*) se lancer; **plunging neckline** décolleté *m* plongeant ▮ *n* (*dive*) plongeon *m*; (*fall*) chute *f*; **to take the p.** *Fig* sauter le pas. ●**—er** *n* ventouse *f* (*pour déboucher un tuyau*).
plural ['plʊərəl] *a* (*form*) pluriel; (*noun*) au pluriel ▮ *n* pluriel *m*; **in the p.** au pluriel.
plus [plʌs] *prep* plus; (*as well as*) en plus de; **two p. two** deux plus deux ▮ *a* (*factor*) & *El* positif; **twenty p.** vingt et quelques ▮ *n* **p. (sign)** *Math* (signe *m*) plus *m*; **that's a p.** c'est un plus.
plush [plʌʃ] *a* (**-er, -est**) somptueux.
ply [plaɪ] **1** *vt* (*a trade*) exercer. **2** *vi* **to p. between** (*travel*) faire la navette entre. **3** *vt* **to p. s.o. with** (*whisky etc*) faire boire continuellement à qn; (*questions*) bombarder qn de.
plywood ['plaɪwʊd] *n* contre-plaqué *m*.
p.m. [pi:'em] *adv* (*afternoon*) de l'après-midi; (*evening*) du soir.
PM [pi:'em] *n abbr* (*Prime Minister*) Premier ministre *m*.
pneumatic [nju:'mætɪk] *a* **p. drill** marteau piqueur *m*.
pneumonia [nju:'məʊnɪə] *n* pneumonie *f*.
poach [pəʊtʃ] **1** *vt* (*egg*) pocher. **2** *vi* (*hunt, steal*) braconner ▮ *vt* (*employee from rival*

company) débaucher. ●**—ing** *n* braconnage *m*. ●**poacher** *n* **1** (*person*) braconnier *m*. **2** **(egg) p.** pocheuse *f*.

PO Box [piːəʊ'bɒks] *abbr* (*Post Office Box*) boîte *f* postale, BP *f*.

pocket ['pɒkɪt] *n* poche *f*; (*small area*) *Fig* petite zone *f*; (*of resistance*) poche *f*; **I'm 50 francs out of p.** j'ai perdu 50 francs ▮ *a* (*money, handkerchief etc*) de poche ▮ *vt* (*gain*) empocher. ●**pocketbook** *n* (*notebook*) carnet *m*; (*handbag*) *Am* sac *m* à main. ●**pocketful** *n* **a p. of** une pleine poche de.

pockmarked ['pɒkmɑːkt] *a* (*face*) grêlé.

pod [pɒd] *n* cosse *f*.

podgy ['pɒdʒɪ] *a* (**-ier, -iest**) (*person*) rondelet (*f* -ette); (*arm etc*) dodu.

podiatrist [pə'daɪətrɪst] *n Am* pédicure *mf*.

podium ['pəʊdɪəm] *n* podium *m*.

poem ['pəʊɪm] *n* poème *m*. ●**poet** *n* poète *m*. ●**po'etic** *a* poétique. ●**poetry** *n* poésie *f*.

point [pɔɪnt] **1** *n* (*of knife etc*) pointe *f*; *pl Rail* aiguillage *m*; **(power) p.** *El* prise *f* (de courant).

2 *n* (*dot, position, score, degree etc*) point *m*; (*decimal*) virgule *f*; (*meaning*) sens *m*; (*importance*) intérêt *m*; (*remark*) remarque *f*; **p. of view** point *m* de vue; **at this p. (in time)** en ce moment; **on the p. of doing** sur le point de faire; **what's the p.?** à quoi bon? **(of waiting/***etc* attendre/*etc*); **there's no p. (in) staying/***etc* ça ne sert à rien de rester/*etc*; **that's not the p.** il ne s'agit pas de ça; **that's beside the p.** c'est à côté de la question; **to the p.** pertinent; **his good points** ses qualités *fpl*; **his bad points** ses défauts *mpl*.

3 *vt* (*aim*) pointer (**at** sur); (*vehicle*) tourner (**towards** vers); **to p. the way** indiquer le chemin (**to** à); **to p. one's finger at** montrer du doigt; **to p. out** (*show*) indiquer; (*mention*) signaler (**to** à, **that** que).

▮ *vi* montrer du doigt; **to p. at** *or* **to s.o./sth** (*with finger*) montrer qn/qch; **to p. to** (*indicate*) indiquer; **to p. east** indiquer l'est; **to be pointing at** (*of gun*) être braqué sur.

point-blank [pɔɪnt'blæŋk] *adv & a* (*to shoot, a shot*) à bout portant; (*to refuse, a refusal*) *Fig* (tout) net.

pointed ['pɔɪntɪd] *a* pointu; (*remark, criticism*) *Fig* pertinent; (*incisive*) mordant.

pointer ['pɔɪntər] *n* (*on dial etc*) index *m*; (*advice*) conseil *m*; (*clue*) indice *m*.

pointless ['pɔɪntləs] *a* inutile. ●**—ly** *adv* inutilement.

poise [pɔɪz] *n* (*confidence*) assurance *f*; (*composure*) calme *m*; (*grace*) grâce *f*. ●**poised** *a* (*composed*) calme; (*hanging*) suspendu; **p. to attack/***etc* prêt à attaquer/*etc*.

poison ['pɔɪz(ə)n] *n* poison *m*; (*of snake*) venin *m* ▮ *vt* empoisonner; **to p. s.o.'s mind** corrompre qn. ●**poisoning** *n* empoisonnement *m*. ●**poisonous** *a* (*substance*) toxique; (*snake*) venimeux; (*plant*) vénéneux.

poke [pəʊk] *vt* pousser (*du doigt, avec un bâton etc*); (*fire*) tisonner; **to p. sth into sth** fourrer *or* enfoncer qch dans qch; **to p. one's finger at s.o.** pointer son doigt vers qn; **to p. one's nose into** fourrer le nez dans; **to p. one's head out of the window** passer la tête par la fenêtre; **to p. out s.o.'s eye** crever un œil à qn.

▮ *vi* pousser; **to p. about** *or* **around in** (*drawer etc*) fouiner dans.

▮ *n* (*jab*) (petit) coup *m*; (*shove*) poussée *f*. ●**poker** *n* **1** (*for fire*) tisonnier *m*. **2** *Cards* poker *m*.

poky ['pəʊkɪ] *a* (**-ier, -iest**) (*small*) exigu (*f* -guë) et misérable; (*slow*) *Am* lent.

Poland ['pəʊlənd] *n* Pologne *f*. ●**Pole** *n* Polonais, -aise *mf*.

pole [pəʊl] *n* **1** (*rod*) perche *f*; (*fixed*) poteau *m*; (*for flag*) mât *m*. **2** *Geog* pôle *m*; **North/South P.** pôle Nord/Sud. ●**polar** *a* polaire; **p. bear** ours *m* blanc.

police [pə'liːs] *n* police *f*; **extra p.** des renforts *mpl* de police ▮ *a* (*inquiry, dog, State etc*) policier; **p. car** voiture *f* de police; **p. force** police *f*; **p. station** commissariat *m* de police.

▮ *vt* (*city etc*) maintenir l'ordre dans; (*frontier*) contrôler. ●**policeman** *n* (*pl* **-men**) agent *m* de police. ●**policewoman** *n* (*pl* **-women**) femme-agent *f*.

policy ['pɒlɪsɪ] *n* **1** *Pol Econ etc* politique *f*; (*individual course of action*) règle *f*. **2** **(insurance) p.** police *f* (d'assurance); **p. holder** assuré, -ée *mf*.

polio ['pəʊlɪəʊ] *n* polio *f*; **p. victim** polio *mf*.

polish ['pɒlɪʃ] *vt* (*floor, shoes etc*) cirer; (*metal*) astiquer; (*rough surface, Fig style*) polir; **to p. off** (*food, work etc*) *Fam* liquider; **to p. up** (*one's French etc*) travailler ▮ *n* (*for shoes*) cirage *m*; (*for floor, furniture*) cire *f*; (*shine*) vernis *m*; **to give sth a p.** faire briller qch. ●**polished** *a* (*manners*) raffiné.

Polish ['pəʊlɪʃ] *a* polonais ▮ *n* (*language*) polonais *m*.

polite [pə'laɪt] *a* (**-er, -est**) poli (**to, with** avec). ●**—ly** *adv* poliment. ●**—ness** *n* politesse *f*.

political [pə'lıtık(ə)l] *a* politique. ● **politician** [pɒlı'tıʃ(ə)n] *n* homme *m or* femme *f* politique. ● **politics** ['pɒlıtıks] *n* politique *f.*

polka ['pɒlkə, *Am* 'pəʊlkə] *n* (*dance*) polka *f*; **p. dot** pois *m.*

poll [pəʊl] *n* (*voting*) scrutin *m*, élection *f*; (*vote*) vote *m*; **to go to the polls** aller aux urnes; **(opinion) p.** sondage *m* (d'opinion) ▮ *vt* (*votes*) obtenir. ● **—ing** *n* élections *fpl*; **p. booth** isoloir *m*; **p. station**, *Am* **p. place** bureau *m* de vote.

pollen ['pɒlən] *n* pollen *m.*

pollute [pə'lu:t] *vt* polluer. ● **pollutant** *n* polluant *m.* ● **pollution** [-ʃ(ə)n] *n* pollution *f.*

polo ['pəʊləʊ] *n Sp* polo *m*; **p. neck** (*sweater*) col *m* roulé.

polyester [pɒlı'estər] *n* polyester *m* ▮ *a* (*shirt etc*) en polyester.

polytechnic [pɒlı'teknık] *n* institut *m* universitaire de technologie, IUT *m.*

polythene ['pɒlıθi:n] *n* polyéthylène *m*; **p. bag** sac *m* en plastique.

pomegranate ['pɒmıgrænıt] *n* (*fruit*) grenade *f.*

pomp [pɒmp] *n* pompe *f.*

pompous ['pɒmpəs] *a* pompeux.

pond [pɒnd] *n* étang *m*; (*artificial*) bassin *m.*

ponder ['pɒndər] *vt* **to p. (over) sth** réfléchir à qch ▮ *vi* réfléchir.

pong [pɒŋ] *n Sl* mauvaise odeur *f.*

pony ['pəʊnı] *n* poney *m.* ● **ponytail** *n* (*hair*) queue *f* de cheval.

poodle ['pu:d(ə)l] *n* caniche *m.*

pooh! [pu:] *int* bah!; (*bad smell*) ça pue!

pool [pu:l] **1** *n* (*puddle*) flaque *f*; (*of blood*) mare *f*; (*for swimming*) piscine *f.* **2** *n* (*of experience, talent*) réservoir *m*; (*of advisers*) équipe *f*; (*of typists*) pool *m*; **(football) pools** pronostics *mpl* (*sur les matchs de football*) ▮ *vt* (*share*) mettre en commun; (*combine*) unir. **3** *n* (*billiards*) billard *m* américain.

pooped [pu:pt] *a* (*exhausted*) *Am Fam* vanné, crevé.

poor [pʊər] *a* (**-er, -est**) (*not rich, deserving pity*) pauvre; (*bad*) mauvais; (*weak*) faible; **p. thing!** le *or* la pauvre! ▮ *n* **the p.** les pauvres *mpl.* ● **—ly 1** *adv* (*badly*) mal; (*clothed*) pauvrement. **2** *a* (*ill*) malade.

pop[1] [pɒp] **1** *n* (*noise*) bruit *m* sec; **to go p.** faire pan; (*of champagne bottle*) faire pop ▮ *vt* (**-pp-**) (*balloon etc*) crever ▮ *vi* (*burst*) crever; (*of ears*) se déboucher.
2 *vt* (*put*) *Fam* mettre ▮ *vi Fam* (*go*) **to p. in** entrer (un instant); **to p. off** (*leave*) partir; **to p. out** sortir (un instant); **to p. over** *or* **round** faire un saut (**to** chez); **to p. up** (*of person, question etc*) surgir.

pop[2] [pɒp] **1** *n* (*music*) pop *m* ▮ *a* (*concert, singer etc*) pop *inv.* **2** *n* (*father*) *Am Fam* papa *m.* **3** *n* **(soda) p.** (*drink*) *Am* soda *m.*

popcorn ['pɒpkɔ:n] *n* pop-corn *m.*

pope [pəʊp] *n* pape *m.*

poplar ['pɒplər] *n* (*tree*) peuplier *m.*

popper ['pɒpər] *n* (*on clothes etc*) pression *f.*

poppy ['pɒpı] *n* (*wild*) coquelicot *m*; (*cultivated*) pavot *m.*

popsicle® ['pɒpsık(ə)l] *n* (*ice lolly*) *Am* = esquimau *m.*

popular ['pɒpjʊlər] *a* (*person, song etc*) populaire; (*fashionable*) à la mode; **to be p. with** plaire beaucoup à. ● **popu'larity** *n* popularité *f* (**with** auprès de).

populated ['popjʊleıtıd] *a* **highly/sparsely/** *etc* **p.** très/peu/*etc* peuplé; **p. by** peuplé de.

population [pɒpjʊ'leıʃ(ə)n] *n* population *f.*

porcelain ['pɔ:səlın] *n* porcelaine *f.*

porch [pɔ:tʃ] *n* porche *m*; (*veranda*) *Am* véranda *f.*

porcupine ['pɔ:kjʊpaın] *n* porc-épic *m.*

pore [pɔ:r] **1** *n* (*of skin*) pore *m.* **2** *vi* **to p. over** (*book etc*) étudier de près.

pork [pɔ:k] *n* (*meat*) porc *m*; **p. pie** pâté *m* (de porc) en croûte.

pornography [pɔ:'nɒgrəfı] *n* (*Fam* **porn**) pornographie *f.* ● **porno'graphic** *a* pornographique.

porpoise ['pɔ:pəs] *n* (*sea animal*) marsouin *m.*

porridge ['pɒrıdʒ] *n* porridge *m* (*bouillie de flocons d'avoine*).

port [pɔ:t] **1** *n* (*harbour*) port *m*; **p. of call** escale *f* ▮ *a* (*authorities etc*) portuaire. **2** *n* **p. (side)** (*left*) *Nau Av* bâbord *m.* **3** *n* (*wine*) porto *m.*

portable ['pɔ:təb(ə)l] *a* portable, portatif.

porter ['pɔ:tər] *n* (*for luggage*) porteur *m*; (*doorman at hotel*) portier *m.*

portfolio [pɔ:t'fəʊlıəʊ] *n* (*pl* **-os**) (*for documents*) serviette *f*; *Pol Fin* portefeuille *m.*

porthole ['pɔ:thəʊl] *n Nau Av* hublot *m.*

portion ['pɔ:ʃ(ə)n] *n* (*share, helping*) portion *f*; (*of train, book etc*) partie *f.*

portly ['pɔ:tlı] *a* (**-ier, -iest**) corpulent.

portrait ['pɔ:treıt] *n* portrait *m.*

portray [pɔ:'treı] *vt* (*describe*) représenter. ● **portrayal** *n* représentation *f.*

Portugal ['pɔ:tjʊg(ə)l] *n* Portugal. ● **Portu'guese** *a* & *n inv* portugais, -aise (*mf*) ▮ *n* (*language*) portugais *m.*

pose [pəʊz] **1** *n* (*of model etc*) pose *f* ▮ *vi* (*of model etc*) poser (**for** pour); **to p. as a lawyer/***etc* se faire passer pour un avocat/

etc. **2** *vt* (*question*) poser.

posh [pɒʃ] *a Fam* (*smart*) chic *inv*; (*snobbish*) snob (*f inv*).

position [pəˈzɪʃ(ə)n] *n* (*place, opinion etc*) position *f*; (*job, circumstances*) situation *f*; (*customer window in bank etc*) guichet *m*; **in a p. to do** en mesure de faire; **in a good p. to do** bien placé pour faire; **in p.** en place, en position ▮ *vt* (*camera etc*) mettre en position; (*put*) placer.

positive [ˈpɒzɪtɪv] *a* positif; (*progress, change*) réel; (*sure*) certain (**of** de, **that** que); **p. reply** (*yes*) réponse *f* affirmative; **a p. genius** *Fam* un vrai génie. ●**—ly** *adv* (*for certain*) positivement; (*completely*) complètement; (*categorically*) catégoriquement; (*to reply*) par l'affirmative.

possess [pəˈzes] *vt* posséder. ●**possession** [-ʃ(ə)n] *n* possession *f*; *pl* (*belongings*) biens *mpl*; **in p. of** en possession de. ●**possessive** *a* (*person, adjective etc*) possessif ▮ *n Gram* possessif *m*.

possible [ˈpɒsəb(ə)l] *a* possible; **it is p. (for us) to do it** il (nous) est possible de le faire; **it is p. that** il est possible que (+ *sub*); **as far as p.** autant que possible; **if p.** si possible; **as much** *or* **as many as p.** le plus possible.

possibility [pɒsɪˈbɪlɪtɪ] *n* possibilité *f*; **there's some p. that** il est (tout juste) possible que (+ *sub*); **she has possibilities** elle promet; **it's a distinct p.** c'est bien possible.

possibly *adv* **1** (*perhaps*) peut-être. **2** (*with can, could etc*) **if you p. can** si cela t'est possible; **to do all one p. can** faire tout son possible; **he cannot p. stay** il ne peut absolument pas rester.

post[1] [pəʊst] *n* (*system*) poste *f*; (*letters*) courrier *m*; **by p.** par la poste; **to catch/miss the p.** avoir/manquer la levée; **p. office** (bureau *m* de) poste *f*; **the P. Office** (*administration*) les postes *fpl* ▮ *vt* (*put in postbox*) poster, mettre à la poste; (*send*) envoyer; **to keep s.o. posted** *Fig* tenir qn au courant.

post[2] [pəʊst] *n* (*job, place*) & *Mil* poste *m* ▮ *vt* (*sentry, guard*) poster; (*employee*) affecter (**to** à). ●**—ing** *n* (*appointment*) affectation *f*.

post[3] [pəʊst] *n* (*pole*) poteau *m*; (*of door*) montant *m*; **winning p.** *Sp* poteau *m* d'arrivée ▮ *vt* **to p. (up)** (*notice etc*) afficher, coller.

post- [pəʊst] *pref* post-; **p.-1800** après 1800.

postage [ˈpəʊstɪdʒ] *n* tarif *m* (postal), tarifs *mpl* (postaux) (**to** pour); **p. stamp** timbre-poste *m*.

postal [ˈpəʊstəl] *a* (*services, district etc*) postal; **p. order** mandat *m* postal.

postbag [ˈpəʊstbæg] *n* sac *m* postal. ●**postbox** *n* boîte *f* aux *or* à lettres. ●**postcard** *n* carte *f* postale. ●**postcode** *n* code *m* postal. ●**post-ˈfree** *adv* franco.

postdate [pəʊstˈdeɪt] *vt* postdater.

poster [ˈpəʊstər] *n* affiche *f*; (*for decoration*) poster *m*.

postgraduate [pəʊstˈgrædʒʊət] *n* étudiant, -ante *mf* de troisième cycle.

postman [ˈpəʊstmən] *n* (*pl* **-men**) facteur *m*. ●**postmark** *n* cachet *m* de la poste. ●**postmaster** *n* receveur *m* (des postes).

post-mortem [pəʊstˈmɔːtəm] *n* **p.-mortem (examination)** autopsie *f* (**on** de).

postpone [pəʊˈspəʊn] *vt* remettre (**for** de, **until** à). ●**—ment** *n* remise *f*.

posture [ˈpɒstʃər] *n* (*of body*) posture *f*; *Fig* attitude *f*.

postwar [ˈpəʊstwɔːr] *a* d'après-guerre.

posy [ˈpəʊzɪ] *n* petit bouquet *m* (de fleurs).

pot [pɒt] **1** *n* pot *m*; (*for cooking*) marmite *f*; **pots and pans** casseroles *fpl*; **jam p.** pot *m* à confiture; **to take p. luck** (*with food*) manger à la fortune du pot; **to go to p.** *Fam* aller à la ruine; **gone to p.** (*person, plans etc*) *Fam* fichu. **2** *n* (*drug*) *Fam* hasch *m*.

potato [pəˈteɪtəʊ] *n* (*pl* **-oes**) pomme *f* de terre; **p. crisps,** *Am* **p. chips** pommes *fpl* chips.

potbelly [ˈpɒtbelɪ] *n* bedaine *f*. ●**potbellied** *a* ventru.

potent [ˈpəʊtənt] *a* (*drug, remedy etc*) puissant; (*drink*) fort.

potential [pəˈtenʃ(ə)l] *a* (*client, sales*) éventuel; (*danger, resources*) potentiel; (*leader etc*) en puissance ▮ *n* potentiel *m*; *Fig* (perspectives *fpl* d')avenir *m*; **to have p.** (*of person, company etc*) avoir de l'avenir. ●**—ly** *adv* potentiellement.

pothole [ˈpɒthəʊl] *n* (*in road*) nid *m* de poules; (*cave*) caverne *f*. ●**potholing** *n* spéléologie *f*.

potion [ˈpəʊʃ(ə)n] *n* breuvage *m* magique; *Med* potion *f*.

potshot [ˈpɒtʃɒt] *n* **to take a p.** faire un carton (**at** sur).

potted [ˈpɒtɪd] *a* **1** (*plant*) en pot. **2** (*version etc*) abrégé, condensé.

potter [ˈpɒtər] **1** *n* (*person*) potier *m*. **2** *vi* **to p. (about)** bricoler. ●**pottery** *n* (*art*) poterie *f*; (*objects*) poteries *fpl*; **a piece of p.** une poterie.

potty [ˈpɒtɪ] **1** *n* pot *m* (de bébé). **2** *a* (**-ier, -iest**) (*mad*) *Fam* toqué.

pouch [paʊtʃ] *n* petit sac *m*; (*of kangaroo*) poche *f*; (*for tobacco*) blague *f*.
pouf(fe) [puːf] *n* (*seat*) pouf *m*.
poultry ['pəʊltrɪ] *n* volaille *f*.
pounce [paʊns] *vi* (*leap*) sauter, bondir (**on** sur) ‖ *n* bond *m*.
pound [paʊnd] **1** *n* (*weight*) livre *f* (= *453,6 grammes*); (*money*) livre *f* (sterling). **2** *n* (*for cars, dogs*) fourrière *f*. **3** *vt* (*spices etc*) piler; (*meat*) attendrir; (*bombard*) *Mil* pilonner (*ville*); (*thump*) tambouriner sur, marteler (*table etc*); (*of sea*) battre (*bateau etc*) ‖ *vi* (*of heart*) battre à tout rompre.
pour [pɔːr] *vt* (*liquid*) verser; **to p. money into sth** investir beaucoup d'argent dans qch ‖ *vi* **it's pouring (down)** il pleut à verse; **pouring rain** pluie *f* torrentielle.
pour away *vt* (*liquid*) vider **to pour in** *vt* (*liquid*) verser ‖ *vi* (*of water, rain, sunshine*) entrer à flots; (*of people, money*) affluer **to pour off** *vt* (*liquid*) vider **to pour out** *vt* (*liquid*) verser; (*cup etc*) vider ‖ *vi* (*of liquid*) couler à flots; (*of people*) sortir en masse; (*of smoke*) s'échapper (**from** de).
pout [paʊt] *vti* **to p. (one's lips)** faire la moue ‖ *n* moue *f*.
poverty ['pɒvətɪ] *n* pauvreté *f*; **(extreme) p.** la misère *f*. ●**p.-stricken** *a* (*person*) indigent.
powder ['paʊdər] *n* poudre *f*; **p. puff** houppette *f*; **p. room** toilettes *fpl* (*pour dames*) ‖ *vt* (*body, skin*) poudrer; **to p. one's face** *or* **nose** se poudrer. ●**—ed** *a* (*milk, eggs*) en poudre.
power ['paʊər] *n* (*ability, authority*) pouvoir *m*; (*strength, nation*) & *Math Tech* puissance *f*; (*energy*) énergie *f*; (*current*) *El* courant *m*; **in p.** *Pol* au pouvoir; **in one's p.** en son pouvoir; **p. cut** coupure *f* de courant; **p. station,** *Am* **p. plant** centrale *f* (électrique) ‖ *vt* **to be powered by** être actionné par; (*gas, oil etc*) fonctionner à. ●**powerful** *a* puissant. ●**powerless** *a* impuissant (**to do** à faire).
PR [piː'ɑːr] *n abbr* = **public relations.**
practical ['præktɪk(ə)l] *a* (*tool, knowledge, person etc*) pratique; **p. joke** farce *f*. ●**practi'calities** *npl* (*of scheme, situation etc*) aspect *m* pratique.
practically ['præktɪk(ə)lɪ] *adv* (*almost*) pratiquement.
practice ['præktɪs] *n* (*exercise, way of proceeding*) pratique *f*; (*habit*) habitude *f*; (*training*) entraînement *m*; (*rehearsal*) répétition *f*; (*clients*) clientèle *f*; **to be out of p.** manquer d'entraînement; **to put into p.** mettre en pratique; **to be in p.** (*of doctor, lawyer*) exercer.
practis/e ['præktɪs] (*Am* **practice**) *vt* (*sport, art etc*) pratiquer; (*medicine, law etc*) exercer; (*flute, piano etc*) s'exercer à; (*language*) (s'exercer à) parler (**on** avec); (*work at*) travailler (*ses maths etc*) ‖ *vi Mus Sp* s'exercer; (*of doctor, lawyer*) exercer. ●**—ed** *a* (*experienced*) chevronné; (*ear, eye*) exercé. ●**—ing** *a* (*Catholic etc*) pratiquant.
practitioner [præk'tɪʃ(ə)nər] *n* **general p.** (médecin *m*) généraliste *m*.
pragmatic [præg'mætɪk] *a* pragmatique.
prairie(s) ['preərɪ(z)] *n(pl)* (*in North America*) Prairies *fpl*.
praise [preɪz] *vt* louer (*qn*) (**for sth** de qch); **to p. s.o. for doing** louer qn d'avoir fait ‖ *n* louange(s) *f(pl)*, éloge(s) *m(pl)*; **in p. of** à la louange de. ●**praiseworthy** *a* digne d'éloges.
pram [præm] *n* landau *m* (*pl* -aus).
prance [prɑːns] *vi* **to p. about** (*of dancer*) caracoler; (*strut*) se pavaner; (*go about*) *Fam* se balader.
prank [præŋk] *n* (*trick*) farce *f*.
prawn [prɔːn] *n* crevette *f* (rose).
pray [preɪ] *vi* prier; **to p. for good weather/a miracle** prier pour avoir du beau temps/pour un miracle ‖ *vt* **to p. that** prier pour que (+ *sub*).
prayer [preər] *n* prière *f*.
pre- [priː] *pref* **p.-1800** avant 1800.
preach [priːtʃ] *vti* prêcher; **to p. to s.o.** *Rel* & *Fig* prêcher qn; **to p. a sermon** faire un sermon.
prearrange [priːə'reɪndʒ] *vt* arranger à l'avance.
precarious [prɪ'keərɪəs] *a* précaire.
precaution [prɪ'kɔːʃ(ə)n] *n* précaution *f* (**of doing** de faire); **as a p.** par précaution.
preced/e [prɪ'siːd] *vti* précéder; **to p. sth by sth** faire précéder qch de qch. ●**—ing** *a* précédent.
precedence ['presɪdəns] *n* **to take p. over** (*priority*) avoir la priorité sur. ●**precedent** *n* précédent *m*.
precinct ['priːsɪŋkt] *n* (*of convent etc*) enceinte *f*; (*electoral district*) *Am* circonscription *f*; (*police district*) *Am* secteur *m*; (*for shopping*) zone *f* piétonnière *or* piétonne.
precious ['preʃəs] **1** *a* précieux. **2** *adv* **p. few, p. little** *Fam* très peu (de).
precipice ['presɪpɪs] *n* (*sheer face*) *Geog* à-pic *m inv*; (*chasm*) *Fig* précipice *m*.
precipitate [prɪ'sɪpɪteɪt] *vt* (*hasten, throw*) & *Ch* précipiter; (*reaction etc*) provoquer.
precise [prɪ'saɪs] *a* précis; (*person*) minutieux. ●**—ly** *adv* (*accurately, exactly*)

précisément; **at 3 o'clock p.** à 3 heures précises. ●**precision** [-ʒ(ə)n] *n* précision *f*.
preclude [prɪ'klu:d] *vt* (*prevent*) empêcher (**from doing** de faire); (*possibility*) exclure.
precocious [prɪ'kəʊʃəs] *a* (*child*) précoce.
preconception [pri:kən'sepʃ(ə)n] *n* préconception *f*.
precondition [pri:kən'dɪʃ(ə)n] *n* préalable *m*.
predate [pri:'deɪt] *vt* (*precede*) précéder; (*document*) antidater.
predator ['predətər] *n* (*animal*) prédateur *m*.
predecessor ['pri:dɪsesər] *n* prédécesseur *m*.
predicament [prɪ'dɪkəmənt] *n* situation *f* fâcheuse.
predict [prɪ'dɪkt] *vt* prédire. ●**predictable** *a* prévisible. ●**prediction** [-ʃ(ə)n] *n* prédiction *f*.
predispose [pri:dɪ'spəʊz] *vt* prédisposer (**to do** à faire).
predominant [prɪ'dɒmɪnənt] *a* prédominant. ●**—ly** *adv* (*almost all*) pour la plupart. ●**predominate** *vi* prédominer (**over** sur).
pre-empt [pri:'empt] *vt* (*decision etc*) devancer.
preen [pri:n] *vt* (*feathers*) lisser; **she's preening herself** *Fig* elle se bichonne.
prefab ['pri:fæb] *n Fam* maison *f* préfabriquée.
preface ['prefɪs] *n* préface *f*.
prefect ['pri:fekt] *n Sch* élève *mf* chargé(e) de la discipline; (*French official*) préfet *m*.
prefer [prɪ'fɜ:r] *vt* (**-rr-**) préférer (**to** à), aimer mieux (**to** que); **to p. to do** préférer faire, aimer mieux faire.
preferable ['prefərəb(ə)l] *a* préférable (**to** à). ●**preferably** *adv* de préférence.
preference ['prefərəns] *n* préférence *f* (**for** pour); **in p. to** de préférence à. ●**prefe'rential** *a* (*treatment*) de faveur; (*terms etc*) préférentiel.
prefix ['pri:fɪks] *n* préfixe *m*.
pregnant ['pregnənt] *a* (*woman*) enceinte; (*animal*) pleine; **five months p.** enceinte de cinq mois. ●**pregnancy** *n* (*of woman*) grossesse *f*.
prehistoric [pri:hɪ'stɒrɪk] *a* préhistorique.
prejudic/e ['predʒədɪs] *n* préjugé *m*; (*people's attitude*) préjugés *mpl*; *Jur* préjudice *m*; **to be full of p.** être plein de préjugés ‖ *vt* (*person*) prévenir (**against** contre); (*success etc*) porter préjudice à. ●**—ed** *a* (*idea*) partial; **she's p.** elle a des préjugés *or* un préjugé (**against** contre).
preliminary [prɪ'lɪmɪnərɪ] *a* (*speech, inquiry, exam etc*) préliminaire ‖ *npl* **preliminaries** préliminaires *mpl*.
prelude ['prelju:d] *n* prélude *m* (**to** à).
premarital [pri:'mærɪt(ə)l] *a* avant le mariage.
premature ['premətʃʊər, *Am* pri:mə'tʊər] *a* prématuré.
premeditate [pri:'medɪteɪt] *vt* préméditer.
premier ['premɪər, *Am* prɪ'mɪər] *n* Premier ministre *m*.
première ['premɪeər, *Am* prɪ'mjeər] *n Th Cin* première *f*.
premises ['premɪsɪz] *npl* locaux *mpl*; **on the p.** sur les lieux; **off the p.** hors des lieux.
premium ['pri:mɪəm] *n Fin* prime *f*; **(insurance) p.** prime *f* (d'assurance); **p. bond** bon *m* à lots.
premonition [premə'nɪʃ(ə)n, *Am* pri:mə'nɪʃ(ə)n] *n* pressentiment *m*.
prenatal [pri:'neɪt(ə)l] *a Am* prénatal (*mpl* -als).
preoccupy [pri:'ɒkjʊpaɪ] *vt* (*worry*) préoccuper; **to be preoccupied** être préoccupé (**with** de).
prepaid [pri:'peɪd] *a* (*reply*) payé.
preparatory [prə'pærət(ə)rɪ] *a* préparatoire; **p. school** = **prep school.**
prepar/e [prɪ'peər] *vt* préparer (**sth for** qch pour, **s.o. for** qn à); **to p. to do** se préparer à faire ‖ *vi* **to p. for** (*journey, occasion*) faire des préparatifs pour; (*exam*) préparer. ●**—ed** *a* (*ready*) prêt, disposé (**to do** à faire); **to be p. for sth** (*expect*) s'attendre à qch. ●**preparation** [prepə'reɪʃ(ə)n] *n* préparation *f*; *pl* préparatifs *mpl* (**for** de).
preposition [prepə'zɪʃ(ə)n] *n Gram* préposition *f*.
preposterous [prɪ'pɒstərəs] *a* absurde.
prep school ['prepsku:l] *n* école *f* primaire privée; *Am* école *f* secondaire privée.
prerecorded [pri:rɪ'kɔ:dɪd] *a* (*message etc*) enregistré à l'avance; **p. broadcast** *Rad TV* émission *f* en différé.
prerequisite [pri:'rekwɪzɪt] *n* (condition *f*) préalable *m*.
prerogative [prɪ'rɒgətɪv] *n* prérogative *f*.
preschool ['pri:sku:l] *a* (*age etc*) préscolaire.
prescrib/e [prɪ'skraɪb] *vt* (*of doctor*) prescrire. ●**—ed** *a* (*textbook*) (inscrit) au programme. ●**prescription** [-ʃ(ə)n] *n* (*for medicine*) ordonnance *f*; **on p.** sur ordonnance.
presence ['prezəns] *n* présence *f*; **in the p. of** en présence de; **p. of mind** présence *f* d'esprit.

present[1] ['prezənt] **1** *a* (*not absent*) présent (**at** à, **in** dans). **2** *a* (*year, state etc*) actuel, présent; (*job, house etc*) actuel; **the p. tense** le présent ‖ *n* **the p.** (*time, tense*) le présent *m*; **for the p.** pour le moment; **at p.** à présent. **3** *n* (*gift*) cadeau *m*. ●**—ly** *adv* (*soon*) tout à l'heure; (*now*) à présent.

present[2] [prɪ'zent] *vt* (*show, introduce etc*) présenter (**to** à); (*concert etc*) donner; **to p. s.o. with** (*gift*) offrir à qn; (*prize*) remettre à qn. ●**—able** *a* présentable. ●**—er** *n* présentateur, -trice *mf*. ●**presentation** [prezən'teɪʃ(ə)n] *n* présentation *f*; (*of prize*) remise *f*.

preserve [prɪ'zɜːv] **1** *vt* (*keep*) conserver; (*fruit etc*) mettre en conserve. **2** *n* **preserve(s)** (*jam*) confiture *f*. **3** *n* (*sphere*) domaine *m*. ●**preservation** [prezə'veɪʃ(ə)n] *n* conservation *f*. ●**preservative** *n* (*in food*) agent *m* de conservation. ●**preserver** *n* **life p.** *Am* gilet *m* de sauvetage.

preside [prɪ'zaɪd] *vi* présider; **to p. over a meeting** présider une réunion.

president ['prezɪdənt] *n* président, -ente *mf*. ●**presidency** *n* présidence *f*. ●**presi'dential** *a* présidentiel.

press[1] [pres] **1** *n* (*newspapers*) presse *f*; (**printing**) **p.** presse *f* ‖ *a* (*conference etc*) de presse. **2** *n* (*machine for pressing trousers etc*) presse *f*; (*for making wine*) pressoir *m*.

press[2] [pres] *vt* (*button, doorbell etc*) appuyer sur; (*tube, lemon*) presser; (*hand*) serrer; (*clothes*) repasser; (*insist on*) insister sur; **to p. s.o. to do** (*urge*) presser qn de faire; **to p. charges** *Jur* engager des poursuites (**against** contre) ‖ *vi* (*with finger*) appuyer (**on** sur); (*of weight*) faire pression (**on sur**) ‖ *n* **to give sth a p.** (*trousers, Am pants etc*) repasser qch.

press down *vt* (*button etc*) appuyer sur **to press for** *vt* (*demand*) insister pour obtenir (*qch*) **to press on** *vi* (*carry on*) continuer (**with sth** qch).

pressed [prest] *a* (**hard**) **p.** (*busy*) débordé; **to be hard p.** (*in difficulties*) être en difficultés; **to be p. for** (*time, money*) être à court de.

pressing ['presɪŋ] *a* (*urgent*) pressant.

press-stud ['presstʌd] *n* bouton-pression *m*.

press-up ['presʌp] *n* (*exercise*) pompe *f*.

pressure ['preʃər] *n* pression *f*; **the p. of work** le surmenage; **p. cooker** cocotte-minute *f*; **p. group** groupe *m* de pression; **under p.** (*worker, to work*) sous pression ‖ *vt* **to p. s.o.** faire pression sur qn (**into doing** pour qu'il fasse). ●**pressurize** *vt Av* pressuriser; **to p. s.o.** faire pression sur qn (**into doing** pour qu'il fasse).

prestige [pre'stiːʒ] *n* prestige *m*.

presume [prɪ'zjuːm] *vt* (*suppose*) présumer (**that** que). ●**presumably** *adv* (*you'll come etc*) je présume que. ●**presumption** [-'zʌmpʃ(ə)n] *n* (*supposition*) présomption *f*.

pretence [prɪ'tens] (*Am* **pretense**) *n* (*sham*) feinte *f*; (*claim, affectation*) prétention *f*; **to make a p. of doing sth** feindre de faire qch; **under false pretences** sous des prétextes fallacieux.

pretend [prɪ'tend] *vt* (*make believe*) faire semblant (**to do** de faire, **that** que); (*maintain*) prétendre (**to do** faire, **that** que) ‖ *vi* faire semblant.

pretentious [prɪ'tenʃəs] *a* prétentieux.

pretext ['priːtekst] *n* prétexte *m*; **on the p. of/that** sous prétexte de/que.

pretty ['prɪtɪ] **1** *a* (**-ier, -iest**) joli. **2** *adv Fam* (*rather, quite*) assez; **p. well, p. much** (*almost*) pratiquement.

prevail [prɪ'veɪl] *vi* (*be prevalent*) prédominer; (*win*) prévaloir (**against** contre); **to p. (up)on s.o.** persuader qn (**to do** de faire). ●**—ing** *a* (*most common*) courant; (*situation*) actuel; (*wind*) dominant.

prevalent ['prevələnt] *a* courant, répandu. ●**prevalence** *n* fréquence *f*; (*predominance*) prédominance *f*.

prevent [prɪ'vent] *vt* empêcher (**from doing** de faire). ●**preventable** *a* évitable. ●**prevention** [-ʃ(ə)n] *n* prévention *f*.

preview ['priːvjuː] *n* (*of film, painting*) avant-première *f*.

previous ['priːvɪəs] *a* précédent; (*experience*) préalable; **she's had a p. job** elle a déjà eu un emploi ‖ *adv* **p. to** avant. ●**—ly** *adv* avant.

prewar ['priːwɔːr] *a* d'avant-guerre.

prey [preɪ] *n* proie *f*; **to be (a) p. to** être en proie à; **bird of p.** rapace *m* ‖ *vi* **to p. on** (*of animal*) faire sa proie de; (*of person*) abuser de; **to p. on s.o.'s mind** tracasser qn.

price [praɪs] *n* (*of object, success etc*) prix *m*; **to pay a high p. for sth** payer cher qch; *Fig* payer chèrement qch ‖ *a* (*control, war, rise etc*) des prix; **p. list** tarif *m* ‖ *vt* **it's priced at £5** ça coûte cinq livres. ●**priceless** *a* (*jewel etc*) inestimable. ●**pricey** *a* (**-ier, -iest**) *Fam* cher.

prick [prɪk] *vt* (*jab*) piquer (**with** avec); (*burst*) crever; **to p. up one's ears** dresser l'oreille ‖ *n* piqûre *f*.

prickle ['prɪk(ə)l] *n* (*of animal, plant*) piquant *m*. ●**prickly** *a* (**-ier, -iest**) (*plant, beard*) piquant; (*animal*) hérissé.

pride [praɪd] *n* (*satisfaction*) fierté *f*; (*exaggerated*) orgueil *m*; (*self-respect*) amour-propre *m*; **to take p. in** (*person, work etc*) être fier de; (*look after*) prendre soin de; **to take p. in doing sth** mettre (toute) sa fierté à faire qch ▮ *vt* **to p. oneself on sth/on doing** s'enorgueillir de qch/de faire.

priest [priːst] *n* prêtre *m*.

priggish ['prɪgɪʃ] *a* suffisant.

prim [prɪm] *a* (**primmer, primmest**) **p. (and proper)** (*affected*) bégueule; (*neat*) impeccable.

primary ['praɪmərɪ] *a* (*main, basic*) principal; *Sch Pol Geol etc* primaire; **of p. importance** de première importance; **p. school** école *f* primaire ▮ *n* (*election*) *Am* primaire *f*. ●**primarily** [*Am* praɪ'merɪlɪ] *adv* essentiellement.

prime [praɪm] **1** *a* (*reason etc*) principal; (*quality*) premier; (*example, condition*) excellent, parfait; **of p. importance** de première importance; **P. Minister** Premier ministre *m*; **p. number** nombre *m* premier. **2** *n* **in the p. of life** dans la force de l'âge. **3** *vt* (*gun*) amorcer; (*surface*) apprêter. ●**primer** *n* **1** (*book*) premier livre *m*. **2** (*paint*) apprêt *m*.

primitive ['prɪmɪtɪv] *a* (*society, conditions etc*) primitif.

primrose ['prɪmrəʊz] *n* *Bot* primevère *f* (jaune).

prince [prɪns] *n* prince *m*. ●**prin'cess** *n* princesse *f*.

principal ['prɪnsɪp(ə)l] **1** *a* (*main*) principal. **2** *n* (*of school*) directeur, -trice *mf*; (*of university*) président, -ente *mf*. ●**—ly** *adv* principalement.

principality [prɪnsɪ'pælətɪ] *n* principauté *f*.

principle ['prɪnsɪp(ə)l] *n* principe *m*; **in p.** en principe; **on p.** par principe.

print [prɪnt] *n* (*of finger, foot etc*) empreinte *f*; (*letters*) caractères *mpl*; (*engraving*) gravure *f*; (*fabric, textile design*) imprimé *m*; (*photo*) épreuve *f*; **in p.** (*book*) disponible; **out of p.** (*book*) épuisé.
▮ *vt* (*book etc*) imprimer; (*photo*) tirer; (*write*) écrire en caractères d'imprimerie; **to p. out** (*of computer*) imprimer. ●**printed** *a* imprimé; **p. matter** imprimés *mpl*. ●**printing** *n* (*action*) *Typ* impression *f*; (*technique, art*) imprimerie *f*; **p. press** *Typ* presse *f*.

printer ['prɪntər] *n* (*of computer*) imprimante *f*; (*person*) imprimeur *m*. ●**print-out** *n* (*of computer*) sortie *f* sur imprimante.

prior ['praɪər] *a* précédent, antérieur; (*experience*) préalable ▮ *adv* **p. to sth/to doing** avant qch/de faire.

priority [praɪ'ɒrɪtɪ] *n* priorité *f* (**over** sur).

prise [praɪz] *vt* **to p. open/off** (*box, lid*) ouvrir/enlever (en faisant levier).

prison ['prɪz(ə)n] *n* prison *f*; **in p.** en prison ▮ *a* (*life etc*) pénitentiaire; (*camp*) de prisonniers; **p. officer** gardien, -ienne *mf* de prison. ●**prisoner** *n* prisonnier, -ière *mf*; **to take s.o. p.** faire qn prisonnier.

pristine ['prɪstiːn] *a* (*condition*) parfait; (*primitive*) primitif.

privacy ['praɪvəsɪ] *n* intimité *f*; (*quiet place*) coin *m* retiré; **to give s.o. some p.** laisser qn seul.

private ['praɪvɪt] **1** *a* privé; (*lesson, car etc*) particulier; (*report, letter*) confidentiel; (*personal*) personnel; (*dinner etc*) intime; **a p. citizen** un simple particulier; **p. detective, p. investigator,** *Fam* **p. eye** détective *m* privé; **p. parts** parties *fpl* génitales; **p. place** coin *m* retiré; **p. secretary** secrétaire *m* particulier, secrétaire *f* particulière; **p. tutor** professeur *m* particulier.
▮ *n* **in p.** en privé; (*to have dinner etc*) dans l'intimité.
2 *n* *Mil* (simple) soldat *m*. ●**privately** *adv* en privé; (*personally*) à titre personnel; (*to have dinner etc*) dans l'intimité; **p. owned** appartenant à un particulier.

privatize ['praɪvətaɪz] *vt* privatiser.

privet ['prɪvɪt] *n* (*bush*) troène *m*.

privilege ['prɪvɪlɪdʒ] *n* privilège *m*. ●**privileged** *a* privilégié; **to be p. to do sth** avoir le privilège de faire qch.

prize[1] [praɪz] *n* prix *m*; (*in lottery*) lot *m*; **the first p.** (*in lottery*) le gros lot ▮ *a* (*essay etc*) primé; **a p. fool**/*etc Hum* un parfait idiot/*etc*. ●**p.-giving** *n* distribution *f* des prix. ●**p.-winner** *n* lauréat, -ate *mf*; (*in lottery*) gagnant, -ante *mf*.

prize[2] [praɪz] *vt* = **prise**.

pro [prəʊ] *n* (*professional*) *Fam* pro *mf*.

pro- [prəʊ] *pref* pro-.

probable ['prɒbəb(ə)l] *a* probable (**that** que); (*convincing*) vraisemblable. ●**pro-ba'bility** *n* probabilité *f*; **in all p.** selon toute probabilité. ●**probably** *adv* probablement.

probation [prə'beɪʃ(ə)n] *n* **on p.** *Jur* en liberté surveillée; **p. officer** responsable *mf* des délinquants mis en liberté surveillée.

probe [prəʊb] *n* (*inquiry*) enquête *f* (**into** dans) ▮ *vt* (*investigate*) & *Med* sonder; (*examine*) examiner (*situation etc*) ▮ *vi* (*investigate*) faire des recherches; **to p. into** (*origins etc*) sonder.

problem ['prɒbləm] *n* problème *m*; **he's got**

a drug/a drink p. c'est un drogué/un alcoolique; **no p.!** *Fam* pas de problème!; **to have a p. doing** avoir du mal à faire. ● **proble'matic** *a* problématique; **it's p. whether** il est douteux que (+ *sub*).

procedure [prə'si:dʒər] *n* procédure *f*.

proceed [prə'si:d] *vi* (*go*) avancer, aller; (*act*) procéder; (*continue*) continuer; **to p. to** (*next question etc*) passer à; **to p. with** (*task etc*) continuer; **to p. to do sth** se mettre à faire qch.

proceedings [prə'si:dɪŋz] *npl* (*events*) événements *mpl*; (*meeting*) séance *f*; (*discussions*) débats *mpl*; **to take (legal) proceedings** intenter un procès (**against** contre).

proceeds ['prəʊsi:dz] *npl* (*profits from sale etc*) produit *m*.

process ['prəʊses] **1** *n* (*method*) procédé *m* (**for doing** pour faire); (*chemical, economic etc*) processus *m*; **in the p. of doing** en train de faire. **2** *vt* (*food, data etc*) traiter; (*examine*) examiner; (*photo*) développer; **processed cheese** fromage *m* fondu. ● **processor** *n* **food p.** robot *m* (ménager); **word p.** machine *f* à *or* de traitement de texte.

procession [prə'seʃ(ə)n] *n* cortège *m*, défilé *m*.

proclaim [prə'kleɪm] *vt* proclamer (**that** que); **to p. s.o. king** proclamer qn roi.

procrastinate [prə'kræstɪneɪt] *vi* tergiverser.

procure [prə'kjʊər] *vt* obtenir; **to p. sth for s.o.** procurer qch à qn.

prod [prɒd] *vti* (**-dd-**) **to p. (at)** pousser (*du coude etc*); **to p. s.o. into doing** *Fig* pousser qn à faire ‖ *n* (petit) coup *m*.

prodigal ['prɒdɪg(ə)l] *a* (*son etc*) prodigue.

prodigy ['prɒdɪdʒɪ] *n* prodige *m*; **child p.** enfant *mf* prodige.

produce[1] [prə'dju:s] *vt* (*manufacture, yield etc*) produire; (*bring out*) sortir (*pistolet, mouchoir etc*); (*passport, proof*) présenter; (*profit*) rapporter; (*cause*) provoquer, produire; (*publish*) publier; (*film*) produire; **oil-producing country** pays *m* producteur de pétrole. ● **pro'ducer** *n* (*of goods, film*) producteur, -trice *mf*.

produce[2] ['prɒdju:s] *n* (*agricultural etc*) produits *mpl*.

product ['prɒdʌkt] *n Com Math etc & Fig* produit *m*.

production [prə'dʌkʃ(ə)n] *n* production *f*; (*of play*) mise *f* en scène; **to work on the p. line** travailler à la chaîne.

productive [prə'dʌktɪv] *a* (*land, meeting etc*) productif. ● **produc'tivity** *n* productivité *f*.

profane [prə'feɪn] *a* (*sacrilegious*) sacrilège. ● **profanities** *npl* (*swear words*) grossièretés *fpl*.

profess [prə'fes] *vt* professer; **to p. to be** prétendre être.

profession [prə'feʃ(ə)n] *n* profession *f*. ● **professional** *a* professionnel; (*man, woman*) qui exerce une profession libérale; (*army*) de métier; (*diplomat*) de carrière; (*piece of work*) de professionnel ‖ *n* professionnel, -elle *mf*; (*doctor, lawyer etc*) membre *m* des professions libérales. ● **professionally** *adv* professionnellement; (*to meet s.o.*) dans le cadre de son travail.

professor [prə'fesər] *n* professeur *m* (d'université); *Am* enseignant, -ante *mf* d'université.

proficient [prə'fɪʃ(ə)nt] *a* compétent (**in** en). ● **proficiency** *n* compétence *f*.

profile ['prəʊfaɪl] *n* profil *m*; **in p.** de profil.

profit ['prɒfɪt] *n* profit *m*, bénéfice *m*; **to sell at a p.** vendre à profit; **p. motive** recherche *f* du profit ‖ *vi* **to p. by** *or* **from sth** tirer profit de qch. ● **p.-making** *a* à but lucratif; **non p.-making** sans but lucratif.

profitable ['prɒfɪtəb(ə)l] *a Com & Fig* rentable. ● **profitably** *adv* avec profit.

profound [prə'faʊnd] *a* (*silence, remark etc*) profond. ● **—ly** *adv* profondément.

profusely [prə'fju:slɪ] *adv* (*to bleed*) abondamment; (*to thank*) avec effusion; **to apologize p.** se répandre en excuses.

program[1] ['prəʊgræm] *n* (*of computer*) programme *m*; **computer p.** programme *m* informatique ‖ *vt* (**-mm-**) (*computer*) programmer. ● **programmer** *n* **(computer) p.** programmeur, -euse *mf*.

programme, *Am* **program**[2] ['prəʊgræm] *n* programme *m*; (*broadcast*) émission *f* ‖ *vt* (*machine, VCR etc*) programmer.

progress ['prəʊgres] *n* progrès *m*(*pl*); **to make p.** faire des progrès; (*when driving etc*) bien avancer; **in p.** en cours ‖ [prə'gres] *vi* progresser; (*of story, meeting*) se dérouler. ● **progression** [prə'greʃ(ə)n] *n* progression *f*.

progressive [prə'gresɪv] *a* (*gradual*) progressif; (*company, ideas*) progressiste.

prohibit [prə'hɪbɪt] *vt* interdire (**s.o. from doing** à qn de faire); **we're prohibited from leaving**/*etc* il nous est interdit de partir/*etc*. ● **prohibitive** *a* (*price etc*) prohibitif.

project **1** ['prɒdʒekt] *n* (*plan*) projet *m* (**for sth** pour qch, **to do** pour faire); (*undertaking*) entreprise *f*; (*at school*) étude *f*; **(housing) p.** *Am* cité *f* (ouvrière). **2**

[prəˈdʒekt] *vt* (*throw, show etc*) projeter ‖ *vi* (*jut out*) faire saillie. ●**projection** [prəˈdʒekʃ(ə)n] *n* projection *f*; (*projecting object*) saillie *f*. ●**proˈjector** *n* (*for films or slides*) projecteur *m*.

proliferate [prəˈlɪfəreɪt] *vi* proliférer.

prolific [prəˈlɪfɪk] *a* prolifique.

prolong [prəˈlɒŋ] *vt* prolonger.

promenade [prɒməˈnɑːd] *n* (*at seaside*) promenade *f*.

prominent [ˈprɒmɪnənt] *a* (*person*) important; (*nose*) proéminent; (*chin, tooth*) saillant; (*striking*) frappant; (*conspicuous*) (bien) en vue. ●**—ly** *adv* (*displayed*) bien en vue.

promiscuous [prəˈmɪskjʊəs] *a* (*person*) qui mène une vie très libre; (*behaviour*) immoral.

promis/e [ˈprɒmɪs] *n* promesse *f*; **to show p., be full of p.** être prometteur ‖ *vt* promettre (**s.o. sth, sth to s.o.** qch à qn; **to do** de faire; **that** que) ‖ *vi* **I p.!** je te le promets!; **p.?** promis? ●**—ing** *a* (*situation*) prometteur (*f* -euse); (*person*) qui promet.

promote [prəˈməʊt] *vt* (*product, research*) promouvoir; (*good health, awareness*) favoriser; **to p. s.o.** (*in job*) donner de l'avancement à qn; **promoted (to) manager**/*etc* promu directeur/*etc*. ●**promotion** [-ʃ(ə)n] *n* (*of person*) avancement *m*, promotion *f*; (*of research etc*) promotion *f*.

prompt [prɒmpt] **1** *a* (*speedy*) rapide; (*punctual*) à l'heure; **p. to act** prompt à agir ‖ *adv* **at 8 o'clock p.** à 8 heures pile. **2** *vt* (*urge*) inciter (*qn*) (**to do** à faire); (*cause*) provoquer. **3** *vt* (*actor*) souffler (son rôle) à. ●**—ness** *n* rapidité *f*.

prone [prəʊn] *a* **1 p. to** (*illnesses, accidents etc*) prédisposé à; **to be p. to do sth** avoir tendance à faire qch. **2** (*lying flat*) sur le ventre.

prong [prɒŋ] *n* (*of fork*) dent *f*.

pronoun [ˈprəʊnaʊn] *n Gram* pronom *m*.

pronounce [prəˈnaʊns] *vt* (*say, declare*) prononcer ‖ *vi* (*articulate*) prononcer. ●**pronunciation** [prənʌnsɪˈeɪʃ(ə)n] *n* prononciation *f*.

proof [pruːf] **1** *n* (*evidence*) preuve(s) *fpl*; (*of book, photo*) épreuve *f*. **2** *a* **p. against** (*material*) à l'épreuve de (*feu, acide etc*). ●**proofreader** *n Typ* correcteur, -trice *mf*.

prop [prɒp] **1** *n* (*for wall etc*) étai *m* ‖ *vt* (**-pp-**) **to p. up** (*ladder etc*) appuyer (**against** contre); (*one's head*) caler; (*wall*) étayer. **2** *n* **prop(s)** *Th* accessoire(s) *m(pl)*.

propaganda [prɒpəˈgændə] *n* propagande *f*.

propel [prəˈpel] *vt* (**-ll-**) (*drive, hurl*) propulser. ●**propeller** *n Av Nau* hélice *f*.

proper [ˈprɒpər] *a* (*suitable, respectable*) convenable; (*right*) bon (*f* bonne); (*downright*) véritable; (*noun, meaning*) propre; **the p. address/method**/*etc* (*right*) la bonne adresse/méthode/*etc*; **the village**/*etc* **p.** le village/*etc* proprement dit. ●**—ly** *adv* comme il faut, convenablement; **very p.** (*quite rightly*) à juste titre.

property [ˈprɒpətɪ] **1** *n* (*building*) propriété *f*; (*possessions*) biens *mpl*, propriété *f* ‖ *a* (*market, company etc*) immobilier; (*tax*) foncier; **p. owner** propriétaire *m* foncier. **2** *n* (*of substance etc*) propriété *f*.

prophecy [ˈprɒfɪsɪ] *n* prophétie *f*. ●**prophesy** [-ɪsaɪ] *vti* prophétiser; **to p. that** prédire que.

prophet [ˈprɒfɪt] *n* prophète *m*. ●**proˈphetic** *a* prophétique.

proportion [prəˈpɔːʃ(ə)n] *n* (*ratio*) proportion *f*; (*portion*) partie *f*; *pl* (*size*) dimensions *fpl*, proportions *fpl*; **in p.** en proportion (**to** de); **out of p.** hors de proportion (**to** avec) ‖ *vt* **well proportioned** bien proportionné. ●**proportional** *or* **proportionate** *a* proportionnel (**to** à).

propose [prəˈpəʊz] *vt* (*suggest*) proposer (**to** à, **that** que (+ *sub*)); **to p. to do, p. doing** se proposer de faire ‖ *vi* faire une demande (en mariage) (**to** à). ●**proposal** *n* proposition *f*; (*of marriage*) demande *f* (en mariage). ●**proposition** [prɒpəˈzɪʃ(ə)n] *n* proposition *f*; (*matter*) *Fig* affaire *f*.

proprietor [prəˈpraɪətər] *n* propriétaire *mf*.

pros [prəʊz] *npl* **the p. and cons** le pour et le contre.

prosaic [prəʊˈzeɪɪk] *a* prosaïque.

prose [prəʊz] *n* prose *f*; (*translation*) thème *m*.

prosecute [ˈprɒsɪkjuːt] *vt* poursuivre (en justice) (**for stealing**/*etc* pour vol/*etc*). ●**prosecution** [-ˈkjuːʃ(ə)n] *n Jur* poursuites *fpl*; **the p.** (*lawyers*) = le ministère public.

prospect[1] [ˈprɒspekt] *n* (*outlook, possibility*) perspective *f* (**of doing** de faire, **of sth** de qch); **(future) prospects** perspectives *fpl* d'avenir; **it has prospects** c'est prometteur; **she has prospects** elle a de l'avenir. ●**proˈspective** *a* (*possible*) éventuel; (*future*) futur.

prospect[2] [prəˈspekt] *vi* **to p. for** (*gold etc*) chercher. ●**prospector** *n* prospecteur, -trice *mf*.

prospectus [prəˈspektəs] *n* (*leaflet*) prospectus *m*; *Univ* guide *m* (de l'étudiant).

prosper [ˈprɒspər] *vi* prospérer.

• **pro'sperity** *n* prospérité *f*. • **prosperous** *a* (*wealthy*) riche, prospère; (*thriving*) prospère.
prostitute ['prɒstɪtjuːt] *n* prostituée *f*. • **prostitution** [-'tjuːʃ(ə)n] *n* prostitution *f*.
prostrate ['prɒstreɪt] *a* (*prone*) sur le ventre; (*worshipper*, *servant*) prosterné ‖ [prɒ'streɪt] *vt* **to p. oneself** se prosterner (**before** devant).
protagonist [prəʊ'tægənɪst] *n* protagoniste *mf*.
protect [prə'tekt] *vt* protéger (**from** de, **against** contre); (*interests*) sauvegarder. • **protection** [-ʃ(ə)n] *n* protection *f*. • **protective** *a* (*clothes*, *screen etc*) de protection; (*person*, *attitude etc*) protecteur (*f* -trice).
protein ['prəʊtiːn] *n* protéine *f*.
protest ['prəʊtest] *n* protestation *f* (**against** contre); **in p.** en signe de protestation ‖ [prə'test] *vt* protester (**that** que); (*one's innocence*) protester de ‖ *vi* protester (**against** contre); (*of students etc*) contester. • **—er** *n* (*student etc*) contestataire *mf*.
Protestant ['prɒtɪstənt] *a* & *n* protestant, -ante (*mf*).
protocol ['prəʊtəkɒl] *n* protocole *m*.
protracted [prə'træktɪd] *a* prolongé.
protractor [prə'træktər] *n* (*for measuring*) rapporteur *m*.
protrud/e [prə'truːd] *vi* dépasser; (*of tooth*) avancer. • **—ing** *a* (*tooth*) qui avance.
proud [praʊd] *a* (**-er, -est**) fier (**of** de, **to do** de faire); (*superior to others*) orgueilleux. • **—ly** *adv* fièrement; orgueilleusement.
prove [pruːv] *vt* prouver (**that** que); **to p. oneself** faire ses preuves ‖ *vi* **to p. difficult/***etc* s'avérer difficile/*etc*.
proverb ['prɒvɜːb] *n* proverbe *m*. • **pro'verbial** *a* proverbial.
provide [prə'vaɪd] *vt* (*supply*) fournir (**s.o. with sth** qch à qn); **to p. s.o. with sth** (*equip*) pourvoir qn de qch ‖ *vi* **to p. for s.o.** pourvoir aux besoins de qn; (*s.o.'s future*) assurer l'avenir de qn; **to p. for sth** (*make allowance for*) prévoir qch. • **provided** *or* **providing** *conj* **p. (that)** pourvu que (+ *sub*).
province ['prɒvɪns] *n* province *f*; (*field of knowledge*) *Fig* domaine *m*; **the provinces** la province; **in the provinces** en province. • **pro'vincial** *a* & *n* provincial, -ale (*mf*).
provision [prə'vɪʒ(ə)n] *n* (*supply*) provision *f*; (*clause*) disposition *f*; **to make p. for** = **to provide for.**
provisional [prə'vɪʒən(ə)l] *a* provisoire. • **—ly** *adv* provisoirement.
provocation [prɒvə'keɪʃ(ə)n] *n* provocation *f*.
provocative [prə'vɒkətɪv] *a* (*person*, *remark etc*) provocant.
provoke [prə'vəʊk] *vt* (*annoy*) agacer; (*rouse*) provoquer (*qn*) (**to do, into doing** à faire); (*cause*) provoquer (*réaction etc*).
prow [praʊ] *n Nau* proue *f*.
prowess ['praʊes] *n* (*bravery*) courage *m*; (*skill*) talent *m*.
prowl [praʊl] *vi* **to p. (around)** rôder ‖ *n* **to be on the p.** rôder. • **—er** *n* rôdeur, -euse *mf*.
proxy ['prɒksɪ] *n* **by p.** par procuration.
prude [pruːd] *n* prude *f*. • **prudish** *a* prude.
prudent ['pruːdənt] *a* prudent. • **—ly** *adv* prudemment.
prune [pruːn] **1** *n* (*dried plum*) pruneau *m*. **2** *vt* (*tree*, *bush*) tailler, élaguer.
pry [praɪ] **1** *vi* être indiscret; **to p. into** se mêler de; (*s.o.'s reasons etc*) chercher à découvrir. **2** *vt* **to p. open** *Am* forcer (en faisant levier). • **—ing** *a* indiscret.
PS [piː'es] *abbr* (*postscript*) P.-S.
psalm [sɑːm] *n* psaume *m*.
pseudo- ['sjuːdəʊ] *pref* pseudo-.
pseudonym ['sjuːdənɪm] *n* pseudonyme *m*.
psychiatry [saɪ'kaɪətrɪ] *n* psychiatrie *f*. • **psychi'atric** *a* psychiatrique. • **psychiatrist** *n* psychiatre *mf*.
psychic ['saɪkɪk] *a* (méta)psychique; **I'm not p.** *Fam* je ne suis pas devin.
psycho- ['saɪkəʊ] *pref* psycho-. • **psycho'analyst** *n* psychanalyste *mf*.
psychology [saɪ'kɒlədʒɪ] *n* psychologie *f*. • **psycho'logical** *a* psychologique. • **psychologist** *n* psychologue *mf*.
psychopath ['saɪkəʊpæθ] *n* psychopathe *mf*.
PTO *abbr* (*please turn over*) TSVP.
pub [pʌb] *n* pub *m*.
puberty ['pjuːbətɪ] *n* puberté *f*.
public ['pʌblɪk] *a* public (*f* -ique); (*library*, *swimming pool*) municipal; **in the p. eye** très en vue; **p. company** société *f* par actions; **p. figure** personnalité *f* connue; **p. house** pub *m*; **p. life** la vie publique; **p. relations** relations *fpl* publiques.
‖ *n* public *m*; **in p.** en public; **a member of the p.** un simple particulier. • **—ly** *adv* publiquement; **p. owned company** entreprise *f* nationalisée.
publican ['pʌblɪk(ə)n] *n* patron, -onne *mf* d'un pub.
publication [pʌblɪ'keɪʃ(ə)n] *n* (*book etc*) publication *f*.
publicity [pʌb'lɪsɪtɪ] *n* publicité *f*. • **'publicize** *vt* rendre public; (*advertise*) faire de la publicité pour.
public-spirited [pʌblɪk'spɪrɪtɪd] *a* **to be**

p.-spirited avoir le sens civique.
publish ['pʌblɪʃ] *vt* publier; (*book*, *author*) éditer, publier; **'published weekly'** 'paraît toutes les semaines'. ● **—ing** *n* (*profession*) édition *f*. ● **publisher** *n* éditeur, -trice *mf*.
pucker ['pʌkər] *vt* **to p. (up)** (*brow*, *lips*) plisser ‖ *vi* **to p. (up)** se plisser.
pudding ['pʊdɪŋ] *n* pudding *m*; **Christmas p.** pudding *m*; **rice p.** riz *m* au lait.
puddle ['pʌd(ə)l] *n* flaque *f* (d'eau).
pudgy ['pʌdʒɪ] *a* (**-ier, -iest**) = **podgy.**
puerile ['pjʊəraɪl] *a* puérile.
puff [pʌf] *n* (*of smoke*, *wind*, *air*) bouffée *f* ‖ *vi* (*blow*, *pant*) souffler; **to p. at** (*cigar*) tirer sur ‖ *vt* (*smoke*) souffler (**into** dans); **to p. out** (*cheeks*) gonfler. ● **puffy** *a* (**-ier, -iest**) (*swollen*) gonflé.
puke [pju:k] *vi* (*vomit*) *Sl* dégueuler.
pull [pʊl] *n* (*attraction*) attraction *f*; **to give sth a p.** tirer qch ‖ *vt* (*draw*, *tug*) tirer; (*tooth*) arracher; (*trigger*) appuyer sur; (*muscle*) se claquer; **to p. sth apart** *or* **to bits** mettre qch en pièces; **to p. a face** faire la moue ‖ *vi* (*tug*) tirer (**at, on** sur); (*go*, *move*) aller; **to p. at** *or* **on** tirer (sur).
pull along *vt* (*drag*) traîner (**to** jusqu'à) **to pull away** *vt* (*move*) éloigner; (*snatch*) arracher (**from** à) ‖ *vi Aut* démarrer; **to p. away from** s'éloigner de **to pull back** *vi* (*withdraw*) *Mil etc* se retirer ‖ *vt* retirer; (*curtains*) ouvrir **to pull down** *vt* (*lower*) baisser; (*knock down*) faire tomber; (*demolish*) démolir **to pull in** *vt* (*drag into room etc*) faire entrer (de force); (*stomach*) rentrer; (*crowd*) attirer ‖ *vi* (*arrive*) arriver; (*stop*) *Aut* se garer; **to p. into the station** (*of train*) entrer en gare **to pull off** *vt* enlever; (*plan*, *deal*) *Fig* mener à bien **to pull on** *vt* (*boots etc*) mettre **to pull out** *vt* (*tooth*, *hair*) arracher; (*cork*, *pin*) enlever (**from** de); (*from pocket etc*) tirer, sortir (**from** de); (*troops*) retirer ‖ *vi* (*to overtake*) *Aut* déboîter; (*leave*) partir; (*withdraw*) se retirer **to pull over** *vt* (*drag*) traîner (**to** jusqu'à); (*knock down*) faire tomber ‖ *vi Aut* se ranger (sur le côté) **to pull through** *vi* s'en tirer **to pull oneself together** *vt* se ressaisir **to pull up** *vt* (*socks*, *blind*, *Am shade etc*) remonter; (*plant*, *tree*) arracher ‖ *vi Aut* s'arrêter.
pulley ['pʊlɪ] *n* poulie *f*.
pullout ['pʊlaʊt] *n* (*in newspaper etc*) supplément *m* détachable.
pullover ['pʊləʊvər] *n* pull(-over) *m*.
pulp [pʌlp] *n* (*of fruit*) pulpe *f*; **in a p.** *Fig* en bouillie.
pulpit ['pʊlpɪt] *n* (*in church*) chaire *f*.
pulse [pʌls] *n* **1** *Med* pouls *m*. **2 pulses** (*plant seeds*) graines *fpl* de légumineuse.
pulverize ['pʌlvəraɪz] *vt* (*grind*, *defeat*) pulvériser.
pumice ['pʌmɪs] *n* **p. (stone)** pierre *f* ponce.
pump [pʌmp] **1** *n* pompe *f*; **petrol p.**, *Am* **gas p.** pompe *f* à essence; **(petrol) p. attendant** pompiste *mf* ‖ *vt* pomper; (*blood*, *round body*) faire circuler; (*money*) *Fig* injecter (**into** dans); **to p. s.o. (for information)** tirer les vers du nez à qn; **to p. air into, p. up** (*mattress etc*) gonfler. **2** *n* (*shoe*) (*for sports*) tennis *m*; (*for dancing*) escarpin *m*.
pumpkin ['pʌmpkɪn] *n* potiron *m*.
pun [pʌn] *n* calembour *m*.
punch[1] [pʌntʃ] *n* (*blow*) coup *m* de poing; (*force*) *Fig* punch *m*; **p. line** (*of joke*) astuce *f* finale ‖ *vt* (*person*) donner un coup de poing à (**on the chin** au menton). ● **p.-up** *n Fam* bagarre *f*.
punch[2] [pʌntʃ] **1** *n* (*for paper*) perforeuse *f*; (*for tickets*) poinçonneuse *f* ‖ *vt* (*ticket*) poinçonner, (*with date*) composter; (*paper*) perforer; **to p. a hole in sth** faire un trou dans qch. **2** *n* (*drink*) punch *m*.
punctual ['pʌŋktʃʊəl] *a* (*on time*) à l'heure; (*regularly*) ponctuel. ● **—ly** *adv* à l'heure; (*regularly*) ponctuellement.
punctuate ['pʌŋktʃʊeɪt] *vt* ponctuer (**with** de). ● **punctuation** [-'eɪʃ(ə)n] *n* ponctuation *f*; **p. mark** signe *m* de ponctuation.
puncture ['pʌŋktʃər] *n* (*in tyre*, *Am tire*) crevaison *f*; **to have a p.** crever ‖ *vti* (*burst*) crever.
pungent ['pʌndʒənt] *a* âcre, piquant.
punish ['pʌnɪʃ] *vt* punir (**for sth** de qch, **for doing** pour avoir fait). ● **—ing** *a* (*tiring*) éreintant. ● **—ment** *n* punition *f*, châtiment *m*; **capital p.** peine *f* capitale; **to take a lot of p.** (*damage*) *Fig* en encaisser.
punitive ['pju:nɪtɪv] *a* (*measure etc*) punitif.
punk [pʌŋk] *n* **p. (rock)** (*music*) le punk (rock); **p. (rocker)** (*fan*) punk *mf* ‖ *a* punk *inv*.
punnet ['pʌnɪt] *n* (*of strawberries*) barquette *f*.
punt [pʌnt] *n* barque *f* (à fond plat). ● **—ing** *n* canotage *m*. ● **punter** *n* **1** (*gambler*) parieur, -euse *mf*. **2** (*customer*) *Fam* client, -ente *mf*.
puny ['pju:nɪ] *a* (**-ier, -iest**) (*sickly*) chétif; (*small*) petit; (*effort*) faible.
pup ['pʌp] *n* (*dog*) chiot *m*.
pupil ['pju:p(ə)l] *n* **1** (*in school*) élève *mf*. **2** (*of eye*) pupille *f*.
puppet ['pʌpɪt] *n* marionnette *f*; **p. show**

spectacle *m* de marionnettes.

puppy ['pʌpɪ] *n* (*dog*) chiot *m*.

purchas/e ['pɜːtʃɪs] *n* (*article, buying*) achat *m* ‖ *vt* acheter (**from s.o.** à qn, **for s.o.** à *or* pour qn). ●**—er** *n* acheteur, -euse *mf*.

pure [pjʊər] *a* (**-er, -est**) pur.

purée ['pjʊəreɪ] *n* purée *f*.

purely ['pjʊəlɪ] *adv* (*only*) strictement.

purge [pɜːdʒ] *n Pol* purge *f* ‖ *vt* (*rid*) purger (**of** de); (*group*) *Pol* épurer.

purify ['pjʊərɪfaɪ] *vt* purifier.

puritanical [pjʊərɪ'tænɪk(ə)l] *a* puritain.

purple ['pɜːp(ə)l] *a* violet (*f* -ette); **to go p.** (*with anger*) devenir pourpre ‖ *n* violet *n*.

purpose ['pɜːpəs] *n* **1** (*aim*) but *m*; **for this p.** dans ce but; **on p.** exprès; **to serve no p.** ne servir à rien; **for the purposes of** pour les besoins de. **2** (*determination*) résolution *f*; **to have a sense of p.** être résolu. ●**p.-'built** *a* construit spécialement. ●**purposely** *adv* exprès.

purr [pɜːr] *vi* ronronner ‖ *n* ronron(nement) *m*.

purse [pɜːs] **1** *n* (*for coins*) porte-monnaie *m inv*; (*handbag*) *Am* sac *m* à main. **2** *vt* **to p. one's lips** pincer les lèvres.

purser ['pɜːsər] *n Nau* commissaire *m* du bord.

pursue [pə'sjuː] *vt* (*chase, seek, continue*) poursuivre; (*fame, pleasure*) rechercher; (*course of action*) suivre. ●**pursuit** *n* poursuite *f*; (*activity, pastime*) occupation *f*.

pus [pʌs] *n* pus *m*.

push [pʊʃ] *n* (*shove*) poussée *f*; **to give s.o./sth a p.** pousser qn/qch; **to give s.o. the p.** *Fam* flanquer qn à la porte.

‖ *vt* pousser (**to, as far as** jusqu'à); (*button*) appuyer sur; (*lever*) abaisser; (*drugs*) *Fam* revendre; **to p. sth into/between** enfoncer *or* fourrer qch dans/entre; **to p. s.o. into doing** pousser qn à faire; **to p. sth off the table** faire tomber qch de la table (en le poussant); **to p. s.o. off a cliff** pousser qn du haut d'une falaise; **to be pushing forty**/*etc* *Fam* friser la quarantaine/*etc*.

‖ *vi* pousser; (*on button etc*) appuyer (**on** sur).

push about *or* **around** *vt* (*bully*) *Fam* marcher sur les pieds à (*qn*) **to push aside** *vt* (*person, objection*) écarter **to push away** *or* **back** *vt* repousser **to push down** *vt* (*button*) appuyer sur; (*lever*) abaisser **to push for** *vt* faire pression pour obtenir (*qch*) **to push in** *vi* (*in queue, Am line*) *Fam* resquiller **to push off** *vi* (*leave*) *Fam* filer; **p. off!** *Fam* fiche le camp! **to push on** *vi* continuer (**with sth** qch); (*in journey*) poursuivre sa route **to push over** *vt* renverser **to push through** *vt* (*law*) faire adopter ‖ *vti* **to push (one's way) through** se frayer un chemin (**a crowd** à travers une foule) **to push up** *vt* (*lever, sleeve, collar*) relever; (*increase*) augmenter.

pushbike ['pʊʃbaɪk] *n Fam* vélo *m*. ●**push-button** *n* bouton *m*; (*of phone*) touche *f*; **p.-button phone** téléphone *m* à touches. ●**pushchair** *n* poussette *f*. ●**pushover** *n* **to be a p.** *Fam* être facile. ●**push-up** *n* (*exercise*) *Am* pompe *f*.

pushed [pʊʃt] *a* **to be p. (for time)** être très bousculé.

pusher ['pʊʃər] *n* (*of drugs*) revendeur, -euse *mf* (de drogue).

pushy ['pʊʃɪ] *a* (**-ier, -iest**) *Pej* arrogant; (*in job*) arriviste.

puss(y) ['pʊs(ɪ)] *n* (*cat*) minou *m*.

put [pʊt] *vt* (*pt* & *pp* **put,** *pres p* **putting**) mettre; (*money, savings*) placer (**into** dans); (*problem, argument*) présenter (**to** à); (*question*) poser (**to** à); (*say*) dire; (*estimate*) évaluer (**at** à); **to p. pressure on sth/s.o.** faire pression sur qch/qn; **to p. it bluntly** pour parler franc.

put across *vt* (*message etc*) communiquer (**to** à) **to put aside** *vt* (*money, object*) mettre de côté **to put away** *vt* (*in its place*) ranger (*livre, voiture etc*); (*criminal*) mettre en prison; (*insane person*) enfermer **to put back** *vt* (*replace, postpone*) remettre; (*receiver*) *Tel* raccrocher; (*progress, clock*) retarder **to put by** *vt* (*money*) mettre de côté **to put down** *vt* (*on floor etc*) poser; (*passenger*) déposer; (*a deposit*) *Fin* verser; (*write down*) inscrire; (*attribute*) attribuer (**to** à); (*kill*) faire piquer (*chien etc*) **to put forward** *vt* (*clock, meeting, argument*) avancer; (*opinion*) exprimer; (*candidate*) proposer (**for** à) **to put in** *vt* (*sth into box etc*) mettre dedans; (*insert*) introduire; (*add*) ajouter; (*install*) installer; (*application, request*) faire; (*enrol*) inscrire (*qn*) (**for** à); (*spend*) passer (*une heure etc*) (**doing** à faire) **to put off** *vt* (*postpone*) renvoyer (à plus tard); (*passenger*) déposer; (*gas, radio*) fermer; (*dismay*) déconcerter; **to p. s.o. off** dissuader qn (**doing** de faire); (*disgust*) dégoûter qn (**sth** de qch); **to p. s.o. off doing** (*disgust*) ôter à qn l'envie de faire **to put on** *vt* (*clothes etc*) mettre; (*weight*) prendre; (*film, play*) jouer; (*gas, radio*) mettre, allumer; (*record, cassette*) passer; (*clock*) avancer; **to p. s.o. on** (*tease*) *Am* faire marcher qn; **she p. me on to you** elle m'a donné votre adresse **to put out** *vt* (*take outside*) sortir; (*arm*, *leg*) étendre; (*hand*) tendre; (*tongue*) tirer; (*gas*, *light*) éteindre, fermer; (*inconvenience*) déranger; (*upset*) déconcerter **to p. through** *vt Tel* passer (*qn*) (**to** à) **to put together** *vt* mettre ensemble; (*assemble*) assembler; (*compose*) composer; (*prepare*) préparer **to put up** *vi* (*stay*) descendre (**at a hotel** à un hôtel) ‖ *vt* (*lift*) lever; (*window*) remonter; (*tent*, *statue*, *ladder*) dresser; (*flag*) hisser; (*building*) construire; (*umbrella*) ouvrir; (*picture*, *poster*) mettre; (*price*, *numbers*) augmenter; (*resistance*) offrir; (*candidate*) proposer (**for** à); (*guest*) loger **to put up with** *vt* (*tolerate*) supporter (*qch*, *qn*).

putt [pʌt] *n Golf* putt *m*. ● **putting** *n Golf* putting *m*; **p. green** green *m*.

putter ['pʌtər] *vi* **to p. around** *Am* bricoler.

putty ['pʌtɪ] *n* mastic *m* (*pour vitres*).

put-you-up ['pʊtjuːʌp] *n* canapé-lit *m*.

puzzl/e ['pʌz(ə)l] *n* mystère *m*; (*jigsaw*) puzzle *m* ‖ *vt* laisser perplexe ‖ *vi* **to p. over** (*problem etc*) se creuser la tête sur. ● **—ed** *a* perplexe. ● **—ing** *a* curieux.

PVC [piːviːˈsiː] *n* (*plastic*) PVC *m*.

pyjama [pɪ'dʒɑːmə] *a* (*jacket etc*) de pyjama. ● **pyjamas** *npl* pyjama *m*; **a pair of p.** un pyjama; **to be in p.** être en pyjama.

pylon ['paɪlən] *n* pylône *m*.

pyramid ['pɪrəmɪd] *n* pyramide *f*.

Pyrenees [pɪrə'niːz] *npl* **the P.** les Pyrénées *fpl*.

Q

Q, q [kjuː] *n* Q, q *m*.

quack [kwæk] *n* **1** (*of duck*) coin-coin *m inv*. **2** (*doctor*) charlatan *m*.

quad(rangle) ['kwɒd(ræŋg(ə)l)] *n* (*of college, school*) cour *f*.

quadruple [kwɒ'druːp(ə)l] *vti* quadrupler.

quadruplets [kwɒ'druːplɪts] (*Fam* **quads** [kwɒdz]) *npl* quadruplés, -ées *mfpl*.

quail [kweɪl] *n* (*bird*) caille *f*.

quaint [kweɪnt] *a* (**-er, -est**) pittoresque; (*old-fashioned*) vieillot (*f* -otte); (*odd*) bizarre.

quake [kweɪk] *n Fam* tremblement *m* de terre.

Quaker ['kweɪkər] *n* quaker, -eresse *mf*.

qualification [kwɒlɪfɪ'keɪʃ(ə)n] *n* **1** (*diploma*) diplôme *m*; (*competence*) compétence *f*; *pl* (*skills*) qualités *fpl* nécessaires (**for** pour, **to do** pour faire). **2** (*reservation*) réserve *f*.

qualify ['kwɒlɪfaɪ] **1** *vt* (*make competent*) & *Sp* qualifier (*qn*) (**for sth** pour qch, **to do** pour faire) ▮ *vi* obtenir son diplôme (**as a doctor**/*etc* de médecin/*etc*); *Sp* se qualifier (**for** pour); **to q. for** (*post*) remplir les conditions requises pour. **2** *vt* (*opinion, statement*) nuancer; *Gram* qualifier. ●**qualified** *a* (*able*) qualifié (**to do** pour faire); (*teacher etc*) diplômé; (*success*) limité; (*opinion*) nuancé; (*support*) conditionnel.

quality ['kwɒlɪtɪ] *n* qualité *f*.

qualms [kwɑːmz] *npl* (*scruples*) scrupules *mpl*.

quandary ['kwɒndrɪ] *n* **in a q.** bien embarrassé.

quantity ['kwɒntɪtɪ] *n* quantité *f*; **in q.** (*to purchase etc*) en grande(s) quantité(s). ●**quantify** *vt* quantifier.

quarantine ['kwɒrəntiːn] *n Med* quarantaine *f* ▮ *vt* mettre en quarantaine.

quarrel ['kwɒrəl] *n* dispute *f*; **to pick a q.** chercher des histoires (**with s.o.** à qn) ▮ *vi* (**-ll-**, *Am* **-l-**) se disputer (**with s.o.** avec qn). ●**quarrelling** *or Am* **quarreling** *n* (*quarrels*) disputes *fpl*. ●**quarrelsome** *a* querelleur.

quarry ['kwɒrɪ] *n* (*to extract stone etc*) carrière *f*.

quart [kwɔːt] *n* litre *m* (*mesure approximative*) (*Br = 1,14 litres, Am = 0,95 litre*).

quarter ['kwɔːtər] **1** *n* quart *m*; (*money*) *Am Can* quart *m* de dollar; (*of fruit, moon*) quartier *m*; **to divide sth into quarters** diviser qch en quatre; **q. (of a) pound** quart *m* de livre; **a q. past nine,** *Am* **a q. after nine** neuf heures et *or* un quart; **a q. to nine** neuf heures moins le quart; **from all quarters** de toutes parts. **2** *n* (*district*) quartier *m*; **(living) quarters** logement(s) *m(pl)*; (*of soldier*) quartier(s) *m(pl)*.

quarterly ['kwɔːtəlɪ] *a* (*magazine etc*) trimestriel ▮ *adv* trimestriellement ▮ *n* publication *f* trimestrielle.

quartet(te) [kwɔː'tet] *n Mus* quatuor *m*; **(jazz) q.** quartette *m*.

quartz [kwɔːts] *n* quartz *m* ▮ *a* (*watch etc*) à quartz.

quash [kwɒʃ] *vt* (*rebellion*) réprimer; (*verdict*) *Jur* casser.

quaver ['kweɪvər] **1** *n Mus* croche *f*. **2** *vi* chevroter.

quay [kiː] *n Nau* quai *m*. ●**quayside** *n* **on the q.** sur les quais.

queasy ['kwiːzɪ] *a* (**-ier, -iest**) **to feel** *or* **be q.** avoir mal au cœur.

Quebec [kwɪ'bek] *n* le Québec.

queen [kwiːn] *n* reine *f*; *Chess Cards* dame *f*; **the q. mother** la reine mère.

queer ['kwɪər] *a* (**-er, -est**) (*odd*) bizarre; (*ill*) *Fam* patraque.

quell [kwel] *vt* (*revolt etc*) réprimer.

quench [kwentʃ] *vt* **to q. one's thirst** se désaltérer.

query ['kwɪərɪ] *n* question *f* ▮ *vt* poser des questions sur.

quest [kwest] *n* quête *f* (**for** de); **in q. of** en quête de.

question ['kwestʃ(ə)n] *n* question *f*; **there's no q. of it, it's out of the q.** c'est hors de question; **without q.** incontestable(ment); **in q.** en question; **q. mark** point *m* d'interrogation.
▮ *vt* interroger (*qn*) (**about** sur); (*doubt*) mettre (*qch*) en question; **to q. whether** douter que (+ *sub*). ●**questionable** *a* douteux. ●**questio'nnaire** *n* questionnaire *m*.

queue [kjuː] *n* (*of people*) queue *f*; (*of cars*) file *f*; **to form a q.** faire la queue ▮ *vi* **to q. (up)** faire la queue (**for** pour).

quibble ['kwɪb(ə)l] *vi* ergoter, discuter (**over** sur).

quiche [kiːʃ] *n* (*tart*) quiche *f*.
quick [kwɪk] **1** *a* (**-er, -est**) rapide; **q. to react** prompt à réagir; **be q.!** fais vite!; **to have a q. shower/meal/***etc* se doucher/manger/*etc* en vitesse ‖ *adv* (**-er, -est**) vite. **2** *n* **to cut s.o. to the q.** blesser qn au vif. ●**q.-'tempered** *a* irascible. ●**q.-'witted** *a* à l'esprit vif.
quicken ['kwɪk(ə)n] *vt* accélérer ‖ *vi* s'accélérer.
quickly ['kwɪklɪ] *adv* vite.
quicksands ['kwɪksændz] *npl* sables *mpl* mouvants.
quid [kwɪd] *n inv Fam* livre *f* (sterling).
quiet [kwaɪət] *a* (**-er, -est**) (*silent*, *peaceful*) tranquille, calme; (*machine*, *vehicle*) silencieux; (*voice*, *sound*) doux (*f* douce); (*private*) intime; **to be** *or* **keep q.** (*shut up*) se taire; (*make no noise*) ne pas faire de bruit; **q.!** silence!; **to keep q. about sth** ne pas parler de qch; **on the q.** (*secretly*) *Fam* en cachette.
quieten ['kwaɪət(ə)n] *vti* **to q. (down)** (se) calmer.
quietly ['kwaɪətlɪ] *adv* tranquillement; (*not loudly*) doucement; (*silently*) silencieusement; (*secretly*) en cachette.
quilt [kwɪlt] *n* édredon *m*; **(continental) q.** (*duvet*) couette *f* ‖ *vt* (*pad*) matelasser; **quilted jacket** veste *f* matelassée.
quintet(te) [kwɪn'tet] *n* quintette *m*.
quintuplets [kwɪn'tjuːplɪts, *Am* -'tʌplɪts] (*Fam* **quins** [kwɪnz], *Am* **quints** [kwɪnts]) *npl* quintuplés, -ées *mfpl*.
quip [kwɪp] *n* (*remark*) boutade *f*.
quirk [kwɜːk] *n* bizarrerie *f*; (*of fate*) caprice *m*.
quit [kwɪt] *vt* (*pt* & *pp* **quit** *or* **quitted,** *pres p* **quitting**) (*leave*) quitter; **to q. doing** arrêter de faire ‖ *vi* (*give up*) abandonner; (*resign*) démissionner.
quite [kwaɪt] *adv* (*entirely*) tout à fait; (*really*) vraiment; (*rather*) assez; **q. a genius** un véritable génie; **q. (so)!** exactement!; **q. a lot** pas mal **(of** de); **q. a (long) time ago** il y a pas mal de temps.
quits [kwɪts] *a* quitte (**with** envers); **to call it q.** en rester là.
quiver ['kwɪvər] *vi* (*of person*) frémir (**with** de); (*of voice*) trembler.
quiz [kwɪz] *n* (*pl* **quizzes**) (*test*) test *m*; **q. (programme)** *TV Rad* jeu(-concours) *m* ‖ *vt* (**-zz-**) questionner.
quota ['kwəʊtə] *n* quota *m*.
quote [kwəʊt] *vt* citer; (*reference number*) *Com* rappeler; (*price*) indiquer ‖ *vi* **to q. from** (*book*) citer ‖ *n* = **quotation; in quotes** entre guillemets. ●**quotation** [-'teɪʃ(ə)n] *n* citation *f*; (*estimate*) *Com* devis *m*; **q. marks** guillemets *mpl*; **in q. marks** entre guillemets.

R

R, r [ɑːr] *n* R, r *m*.

rabbi ['ræbaɪ] *n* rabbin *m*.

rabbit ['ræbɪt] *n* lapin *m*.

rabble ['ræb(ə)l] *n* **the r.** *Pej* la populace.

rabies ['reɪbiːz] *n Med* rage *f*. ● **rabid** ['ræbɪd] *a* (*dog*) enragé.

raccoon [rə'kuːn] *n* (*animal*) raton *m* laveur.

rac/e[1] [reɪs] *n* (*contest*) course *f* ‖ *vt* (*horse*) faire courir; (*engine*) emballer; **to r. (against** *or* **with) s.o.** faire une course avec qn ‖ *vi* (*run*) courir; (*of engine*) s'emballer. ● **—ing** *n* courses *fpl*; **r. car** voiture *f* de course; **r. driver** coureur *m* automobile. ● **racecourse** *n* champ *m* de courses. ● **racehorse** *n* cheval *m* de course. ● **racetrack** *n* (*for horses*) *Am* champ *m* de courses; (*for cars etc*) piste *f*.

race[2] [reɪs] *n* (*group*) race *f*; **r. relations** rapports *mpl* entre les races.

racial ['reɪʃəl] *a* racial. ● **racialism** *n* racisme *m*. ● **racism** ['reɪsɪz(ə)m] *n* racisme *m*. ● **racist** *a* & *n* raciste (*mf*).

rack [ræk] **1** *n* (*for bottles, letters etc*) casier *m*; (*for drying dishes*) égouttoir *m*; **(luggage) r.** (*on bus, train*) filet *m* à bagages; (*on bicycle*) porte-bagages *m inv*; **(roof) r.** (*of car*) galerie *f*. **2** *vt* **to r. one's brains** se creuser la cervelle. **3** *n* **to go to r. and ruin** (*of building*) tomber en ruine.

racket ['rækɪt] *n* **1** (*for tennis*) raquette *f*. **2** (*din*) vacarme *m*. **3** (*crime*) racket *m*; (*scheme*) combine *f*; **the drugs r.** le trafic de (la) drogue.

racoon [rə'kuːn] *n* (*animal*) raton *m* laveur.

racy ['reɪsɪ] *a* **(-ier, -iest)** (*description etc*) piquant; (*suggestive*) osé.

radar ['reɪdɑːr] *n* radar *m* ‖ *a* (*control, trap etc*) radar *inv*.

radiant ['reɪdɪənt] *a* (*person*) rayonnant (**with** de), radieux.

radiate ['reɪdɪeɪt] *vt* (*heat*) dégager; (*joy*) *Fig* rayonner de ‖ *vi* (*of heat, lines*) rayonner (**from** de). ● **radiation** [-'eɪʃ(ə)n] *n* (*of heat*) rayonnement *m* (**of** de); (*radioactivity*) radiation *f*.

radiator ['reɪdɪeɪtər] *n* (*of central heating, vehicle*) radiateur *m*.

radical ['rædɪk(ə)l] *a* radical ‖ *n* (*person*) *Pol* radical, -ale *mf*.

radio ['reɪdɪəʊ] *n* (*pl* **-os**) radio *f*; **on** *or* **over the r.** à la radio; **car r.** autoradio *m*; **r. set** poste *m* de radio; **r. operator** radio *m* ‖ *vt* **to r. s.o.** appeler qn par radio. ● **r.-con'trolled** *a* radioguidé.

radioactive [reɪdɪəʊ'æktɪv] *a* radioactif. ● **radioac'tivity** *n* radioactivité *f*.

radiographer [reɪdɪ'ɒgrəfər] *n* (*technician*) radiologue *mf*. ● **radiologist** *n* (*doctor*) radiologue *mf*.

radish ['rædɪʃ] *n* radis *m*.

radius, *pl* **-dii** ['reɪdɪəs, -dɪaɪ] *n* (*of circle*) rayon *m*; **within a r. of 10 km** dans un rayon de 10 km.

RAF [ɑːreɪ'ef] *n abbr* (*Royal Air Force*) armée *f* de l'air (britannique).

raffle ['ræf(ə)l] *n* tombola *f*.

raft [rɑːft] *n* (*boat*) radeau *m*.

rag [ræg] *n* **1** (*old clothing*) haillon *m*; (*for dusting etc*) chiffon *m*; **in rags** (*clothes*) en loques; (*person*) en haillons. **2** (*newspaper*) torchon *m*. **3** (*procession*) carnaval *m* d'étudiants (*au profit d'œuvres de charité*).

ragamuffin ['rægəmʌfɪn] *n* va-nu-pieds *m inv*.

rag/e [reɪdʒ] *n* (*anger*) rage *f*; **to fly into a r.** se mettre en rage; **to be all the r.** (*of fashion*) faire fureur ‖ *vi* (*be angry*) rager; (*of storm, battle*) faire rage. ● **—ing** *a* (*storm, fever*) violent.

ragged ['rægɪd] *a* (*clothes*) en loques; (*person*) en haillons.

raid [reɪd] *n Mil* raid *m*; (*by police*) descente *f*; (*by thieves*) hold-up *m inv*; **air r.** raid *m* aérien ‖ *vt* faire un raid *or* une descente *or* un hold-up dans; *Av* attaquer; (*fridge etc*) *Fam* dévaliser. ● **raider** *n* (*criminal*) malfaiteur *m*.

rail [reɪl] **1** *n* (*for train*) rail *m*; **by r.** (*to travel*) par le train; (*to send*) par chemin de fer; **to go off the rails** (*of train*) dérailler ‖ *a* (*ticket*) de chemin de fer; (*strike*) des cheminots. **2** *n* (*rod on balcony*) balustrade *f*; (*on stairs*) rampe *f*; (*curtain rod*) tringle *f*; **(towel) r.** porte-serviettes *m inv*. ● **railing** *n* (*of balcony*) balustrade *f*; *pl* (*fence*) grille *f*.

railcard ['reɪlkɑːd] *n* carte *f* de chemin de fer. ● **railroad** *n Am* = **railway; r. track** voie *f* ferrée. ● **railway** *n* (*system*) chemin *m* de fer; (*track*) voie *f* ferrée ‖ *a* (*ticket*) de chemin de fer; (*timetable*) des chemins de fer; **r. line** (*route*) ligne *f* de chemin de fer;

(*track*) voie *f* ferrée; **r. station** gare *f*.

rain [reɪn] *n* pluie *f*; **in the r.** sous la pluie; **I'll give you a r. check** *Am Fam* j'accepterai volontiers à une date ultérieure ‖ *vi* pleuvoir; **to r. (down)** (*of blows, bullets*) pleuvoir; **it's raining** il pleut. ●**rainbow** *n* arc-en-ciel *m*. ●**raincoat** *n* imper(méable) *m*. ●**raindrop** *n* goutte *f* de pluie. ●**rainfall** *n* (*amount*) précipitations *fpl*. ●**rainforest** *n* forêt *f* tropicale (humide). ●**rainwater** *n* eau *f* de pluie. ●**rainy** *a* (**-ier, -iest**) pluvieux; **the r. season** la saison des pluies.

raise [reɪz] *vt* (*lift*) lever; (*child, family, animal, voice*) élever; (*crops*) cultiver; (*salary, price*) augmenter; (*temperature*) faire monter; (*question*) soulever; (*taxes*) lever; **to r. s.o.'s hopes** faire naître les espérances de qn; **to r. money** réunir des fonds ‖ *n* (*pay rise*) *Am* augmentation *f* (de salaire).

raisin ['reɪz(ə)n] *n* raisin *m* sec.

rake [reɪk] *n* râteau *m* ‖ *vt* (*garden*) ratisser; **to r. (up)** (*leaves*) ratisser; **to r. in** (*money*) *Fam* ramasser à la pelle.

rally ['rælɪ] *vt* (*unite, win over*) rallier (**to** à); **to r. support** rallier des partisans (**for** autour de) ‖ *vi* se rallier (**to** à); (*recover*) reprendre ses forces; **to r. round (s.o.)** (*help*) venir en aide (à qn) ‖ *n Pol* rassemblement *m*; *Aut* rallye *m*.

ram [ræm] **1** *n* (*animal*) bélier *m*. **2** *vt* (**-mm-**) (*vehicle*) emboutir; **to r. sth into sth** enfoncer qch dans qch.

RAM [ræm] *n abbr* = **random access memory**.

rambl/e ['ræmb(ə)l] **1** *n* (*hike*) randonnée *f* ‖ *vi* faire une randonnée *or* des randonnées. **2** *vi* **to r. on** (*talk*) *Pej* discourir. ●**—er** *n* promeneur, -euse *mf*.

rambling ['ræmblɪŋ] **1** *a* (*house*) construit sans plan; (*spread out*) vaste. **2** *a* (*speech*) décousu.

ramp [ræmp] *n* (*slope for wheelchair etc*) rampe *f* (d'accès); (*in garage*) pont *m* (de graissage); **'r.'** *Aut* 'dénivellation'.

rampage ['ræmpeɪdʒ] *n* **to go on the r.** (*of crowd*) se déchaîner; (*loot*) se livrer au pillage.

rampant ['ræmpənt] *a* **to be r.** (*of crime, disease*) sévir.

rampart ['ræmpɑːt] *n* rempart *m*.

ramshackle ['ræmʃæk(ə)l] *a* délabré.

ran [ræn] *pt of* **run**.

ranch [ræntʃ] *n Am* ranch *m*; **r. house** maison *f* genre bungalow (sur sous-sol).

rancid ['rænsɪd] *a* rance.

random ['rændəm] *n* **at r.** au hasard ‖ *a* (*choice*) (fait) au hasard; (*sample*) prélevé au hasard; **r. check** (*by police*) contrôle-surprise *m*; **r. access memory** *Comptr* mémoire *f* vive.

randy ['rændɪ] *a* (**-ier, -iest**) *Fam* excité.

rang [ræŋ] *pt of* **ring**[2].

range [reɪndʒ] **1** *n* (*of gun, voice etc*) portée *f*; (*of singer's voice*) étendue *f*; (*of aircraft, ship*) rayon *m* d'action; (*of colours, prices, products*) gamme *f*; (*of sizes*) choix *m*; (*of temperature*) variations *fpl* ‖ *vi* (*vary*) varier (**from** de, **to** à); (*extend*) s'étendre. **2** *n* (*of mountains*) chaîne *f*; (*grassland*) *Am* prairie *f*. **3** *n* (*stove*) *Am* cuisinière *f*. **4** *n* **(shooting** *or* **rifle) r.** (*at funfair*) stand *m* de tir; (*outdoors*) champ *m* de tir.

ranger ['reɪndʒər] *n* garde *m* forestier.

rank [ræŋk] **1** *n* (*position, class*) rang *m*; (*grade*) *Mil* grade *m*; **the r. and file** (*workers etc*) la base; **taxi r.** station *f* de taxi ‖ *vti* **to r. among** compter parmi. **2** *a* (**-er, -est**) (*smell*) fétide.

ransack ['rænsæk] *vt* (*search*) fouiller; (*plunder*) saccager.

ransom ['ræns(ə)m] *n* (*money*) rançon *f*; **to hold s.o. to r.** rançonner qn.

rant [rænt] *vi* **to r. (and rave)** tempêter (**at** contre).

rap [ræp] **1** *n* petit coup *m* sec ‖ *vi* (**-pp-**) frapper (**at** à). **2** *n* (*music*) rap *m*.

rape [reɪp] *vt* violer ‖ *n* viol *m*. ●**rapist** *n* violeur *m*.

rapid ['ræpɪd] **1** *a* rapide. **2** *npl* **rapids** (*of river*) rapides *mpl*. ●**rapidly** *adv* rapidement.

rapture ['ræptʃər] *n* **to go into raptures** s'extasier (**about** sur). ●**rapturous** *a* (*welcome, applause*) enthousiaste.

rare [reər] *a* (**-er, -est**) rare; (*meat*) bleu; **(medium) r.** (*meat*) saignant; **it's r. for her to do it** il est rare qu'elle le fasse. ●**—ly** *adv* rarement. ●**rarity** *n* (*quality, object*) rareté *f*.

rarefied ['reərɪfaɪd] *a* raréfié.

raring ['reərɪŋ] *a* **r. to start**/*etc* impatient de commencer/*etc*.

rascal ['rɑːsk(ə)l] *n* coquin, -ine *mf*.

rash [ræʃ] **1** *n* (*on skin*) (*patches*) rougeurs *fpl*; (*spots*) (éruption *f* de) boutons *mpl*. **2** *a* (**-er, -est**) irréfléchi. ●**—ly** *adv* sans réfléchir.

rasher ['ræʃər] *n* tranche *f* de lard.

raspberry ['rɑːzbərɪ, *Am* -berɪ] *n* (*fruit*) framboise *f*.

rasping ['rɑːspɪŋ] *a* (*voice*) âpre.

rat [ræt] **1** *n* rat *m*; **the r. race** *Fig* la course au bifteck, la jungle. **2** *vi* (**-tt-**) **to r. on** *Fam* (*denounce*) cafarder sur; (*promise*) manquer à.

rate [reɪt] **1** *n* (*level, percentage*) taux *m*; (*speed*) vitesse *f*; (*price*) tarif *m*; **exchange/interest r.** taux *m* de change/d'intérêt; **insurance rates** primes *fpl* d'assurance; **postage r.** tarif *m* postal; **r. of flow** débit *m*; **at the r. of** à une vitesse de; (*amount*) à raison de; **at this r.** (*slow speed*) à ce train-là; **at any r.** en tout cas; **the success r.** (*chances*) les chances *fpl* de succès.
2 *vt* (*evaluate*) évaluer; (*regard*) considérer (**as** comme); (*deserve*) mériter; **to be highly rated** être très apprécié.

rather ['rɑːðər] *adv* (*preferably, quite*) plutôt; **I'd r. stay** j'aimerais mieux *or* je préférerais rester (**than** que); **I'd r. you came** j'aimerais mieux *or* je préférerais que vous veniez; **r. than leave**/*etc* plutôt que de partir/*etc*; **r. more tired**/*etc* un peu plus fatigué/*etc* (**than** que).

ratify ['rætɪfaɪ] *vt* ratifier.

rating ['reɪtɪŋ] *n* classement *m*; (*wage level*) indice *m*; **credit r.** *Fin* degré *m* de solvabilité; **the ratings** *TV* l'indice *m* d'écoute.

ratio ['reɪʃɪəʊ] *n* (*pl* **-os**) proportion *f*.

ration ['ræʃ(ə)n, *Am* 'reɪʃ(ə)n] *n* ration *f*; *pl* (*food*) vivres *mpl* ‖ *vt* rationner. ●**—ing** *n* rationnement *m*.

rational ['ræʃən(ə)l] *a* (*thought etc*) rationnel; (*person*) raisonnable. ●**rationalize** *vt* (*organize*) rationaliser; (*explain*) justifier. ●**rationally** *adv* raisonnablement.

rattle ['ræt(ə)l] **1** *n* (*baby's toy*) hochet *m*; (*of sports fan*) crécelle *f*. **2** *vi* faire du bruit; (*of window*) trembler ‖ *vt* (*shake*) secouer; (*window*) faire trembler; (*keys*) faire cliqueter. **3** *vt* **to r. s.o.** (*make nervous*) *Fam* ébranler qn; **to r. off** (*poem etc*) *Fam* débiter (à toute vitesse). ●**rattlesnake** *n* serpent *m* à sonnette.

ratty ['rætɪ] *a* (**-ier, -iest**) **1** (*shabby*) *Am Fam* minable. **2 to get r.** (*annoyed*) *Fam* prendre la mouche.

raucous ['rɔːkəs] *a* (*noisy*) bruyant.

ravage ['rævɪdʒ] *vt* ravager.

rav/e [reɪv] *vi* (*talk nonsense*) divaguer; (*rage*) tempêter (**at** contre); **to r. about** (*enthuse*) ne pas tarir d'éloges sur. ●**—ing** *a* **to be r. mad** être fou furieux.

raven ['reɪv(ə)n] *n* corbeau *m*.

ravenous ['rævənəs] *a* (*appetite*) vorace; **I'm r.** j'ai une faim de loup.

ravine [rə'viːn] *n* ravin *m*.

ravioli [rævɪ'əʊlɪ] *n* ravioli *mpl*.

ravishing ['rævɪʃɪŋ] *a* (*beautiful*) ravissant.

raw [rɔː] *a* (**-er, -est**) (*vegetable etc*) cru; (*sugar, data*) brut; (*skin*) écorché; (*immature*) inexpérimenté; (*weather*) rigoureux; **r. material** matière *f* première.

Rawlplug® ['rɔːlplʌg] *n* cheville *f*.

ray [reɪ] *n* (*of light, sun etc*) rayon *m*; (*of hope*) *Fig* lueur *f*.

rayon ['reɪɒn] *n* rayonne *f* ‖ *a* en rayonne.

razor ['reɪzər] *n* rasoir *m*; **r. blade** lame *f* de rasoir.

Rd *abbr* = **road.**

re- [riː, rɪ] *pref* ré-, re-, r-.

reach [riːtʃ] *vt* (*place, distant object, aim*) atteindre; (*gain access to*) accéder à; (*of letter*) parvenir à (*qn*); (*contact*) joindre (*qn*); (*conclusion*) arriver à; **to r. s.o. (over) sth** (*hand over*) passer qch à qn.
‖ *vi* (*extend*) s'étendre (**to** à); **to r. (out)** (*with arm*) (é)tendre le bras (**for** pour prendre).
‖ *n* portée *f*; **within r. of** à portée de; (*near*) à proximité de; **within (easy) r.** (*object*) à portée de main; (*shops*) facilement accessible.

react [rɪ'ækt] *vi* réagir (**against** contre, **to** à). ●**reaction** [-ʃ(ə)n] *n* réaction *f*. ●**reactionary** *a* & *n* réactionnaire (*mf*).

reactor [rɪ'æktər] *n* réacteur *m* (*nucléaire*).

read [riːd] *vt* (*pt* & *pp* **read** [red]) lire; (*meter*) relever; (*of instrument*) indiquer; **to r. French**/*etc Br Univ* faire des études de français/*etc* ‖ *vi* lire; **to r. to s.o.** faire la lecture à qn ‖ *n* **to have a r.** *Fam* faire un peu de lecture. ●**—able** *a* lisible. ●**—er** *n* lecteur, -trice *mf*; (*book*) livre *m* de lecture.

read about *vt* lire quelque chose sur (*qn, qch*) **to read back** *vt* relire **to read out** *vt* lire (*qch*) (à haute voix) **to read over** *vt* relire **to read through** *vt* (*skim*) parcourir **to read up (on)** *vt* (*study*) étudier.

readdress [riːə'dres] *vt* (*letter*) faire suivre.

readily ['redɪlɪ] *adv* (*willingly*) volontiers; (*easily*) facilement. ●**readiness** *n* **in r. for** prêt pour.

reading ['riːdɪŋ] *n* lecture *f*; (*of meter*) relevé *m*; (*by instrument*) indication *f*; (*variant*) variante *f* ‖ *a* (*room, book*) de lecture; **r. matter** choses *fpl* à lire; **r. lamp** (*desk*) lampe *f* de bureau; (*bedside*) lampe *f* de chevet.

readjust [riːə'dʒʌst] *vt* (*instrument*) régler; (*salary*) réajuster ‖ *vi* se réadapter (**to** à).

read-only [riːd'əʊnlɪ] *a* **r.-only memory** *Comptr* mémoire *f* morte.

ready ['redɪ] *a* (**-ier, -iest**) prêt (**to do** à faire, **for sth** à *or* pour qch); (*quick*) *Fig* prompt (**to do** à faire); **to get sth/s.o. r.** préparer qch/qn; **to get r.** se préparer (**for sth** à *or* pour qch, **to do** à faire); **r. cash** argent *m* liquide.

● **r.-'cooked** *a* tout cuit. ● **r.-'made** *a* tout fait; **r.-made clothes** le prêt-à-porter *m*.
real [rɪəl] *a* vrai, véritable; (*world, fact etc*) réel; **in r. life** dans la réalité; **r. estate** *Am* immobilier *m* ‖ *adv Fam* vraiment; **r. stupid** vraiment bête.
realist ['rɪəlɪst] *n* réaliste *mf*. ● **rea'listic** *a* réaliste.
reality [rɪ'ælətɪ] *n* réalité *f*; **in r.** en réalité.
realize ['rɪəlaɪz] *vt* **1** (*know*) se rendre compte de; (*understand*) comprendre (**that** que); **to r. that** (*know*) se rendre compte que. **2** (*carry out*) réaliser. ● **realization** [-'zeɪʃ(ə)n] *n* (*awareness*) (prise *f* de) conscience *f*.
really ['rɪəlɪ] *adv* vraiment; **is it r. true?** est-ce bien vrai?
realm [relm] *n* (*kingdom*) royaume *m*; (*of science etc*) *Fig* domaine *m*.
realtor ['rɪəltər] *n Am* agent *m* immobilier.
ream [ri:m] *n* (*of paper*) rame *f*.
reap [ri:p] *vt* (*field, crop*) moissonner.
reappear [ri:ə'pɪər] *vi* réapparaître.
rear [rɪər] **1** *n* (*back part*) arrière *m*; **in** *or* **at the r.** à l'arrière (**of** de); **from the r.** par derrière ‖ *a* arrière *inv*, de derrière; **r.-view mirror** *Aut* rétroviseur *m*. **2** *vt* (*family, animals*) élever; (*one's head*) relever. **3** *vi* **to r. (up)** (*of horse*) se cabrer.
rearrange [ri:ə'reɪndʒ] *vt* (*hair, room*) réarranger; (*plans*) changer.
reason ['ri:z(ə)n] *n* (*cause, sense*) raison *f*; **the r. for/why...** la raison de/pour laquelle...; **for no r.** sans raison; **that stands to r.** c'est logique; **within r.** avec modération; **to have every r. to believe**/*etc* avoir tout lieu de croire/*etc*. ‖ *vi* raisonner; **to r. with s.o.** raisonner qn. ● **reasoning** *n* raisonnement *m*.
reasonable ['ri:zənəb(ə)l] *a* raisonnable. ● **reasonably** *adv* raisonnablement; (*fairly, rather*) assez.
reassur/e [ri:ə'ʃʊər] *vt* rassurer. ● **—ing** *a* rassurant. ● **reassurance** *n* réconfort *m*.
rebate ['ri:beɪt] *n* (*discount on purchase*) ristourne *f*; (*refund*) remboursement *m* (partiel).
rebel ['reb(ə)l] *n* rebelle *mf*; (*against parents etc*) révolté, -ée *mf* ‖ [rɪ'bel] *vi* (**-ll-**) se révolter (**against** contre). ● **re'bellion** *n* révolte *f*. ● **re'bellious** *a* (*child etc*) rebelle.
rebound [rɪ'baʊnd] *vi* (*of ball*) rebondir; (*of stone*) ricocher; (*of lies etc*) *Fig* retomber (**on** sur) ‖ ['ri:baʊnd] *n* rebond *m*; ricochet *m*.
rebuff [rɪ'bʌf] *vt* repousser ‖ *n* rebuffade *f*.
rebuild [ri:'bɪld] *vt* (*pt & pp* **rebuilt**) reconstruire.
rebuke [rɪ'bju:k] *vt* réprimander ‖ *n* réprimande *f*.
recall [rɪ'kɔ:l] *vt* (*remember*) se rappeler (**that** que, **doing** avoir fait); (*call back*) rappeler; **to r. sth to s.o.** rappeler qch à qn ‖ *n* rappel *m*.
recap ['ri:kæp] *vti* (**-pp-**) récapituler ‖ *n* récapitulation *f*. ● **reca'pitulate** *vti* récapituler.
recapture [ri:'kæptʃər] *vt* (*prisoner etc*) reprendre; (*rediscover*) retrouver; (*recreate*) recréer.
reced/e [rɪ'si:d] *vi* s'éloigner; (*of floods*) baisser. ● **—ing** *a* (*forehead*) fuyant; **his hair(line) is r.** son front se dégarnit.
receipt [rɪ'si:t] *n* (*for payment, object left etc*) reçu *m* (**for** de); (*for letter, parcel*) accusé *m* de réception; *pl* (*money taken*) recettes *fpl*; **to acknowledge r.** accuser réception (**of** de); **on r. of** dès réception de.
receiv/e [rɪ'si:v] *vt* recevoir; (*stolen goods*) receler. ● **—er** *n* (*of phone*) combiné *m*; *Rad* récepteur *m*; (*of stolen goods*) receleur, -euse *mf*; (*in bankruptcy*) administrateur *m* judiciaire; **to pick up the r.** (*of phone*) décrocher.
recent ['ri:sənt] *a* récent; **in r. months** ces mois-ci. ● **—ly** *adv* récemment.
receptacle [rɪ'septək(ə)l] *n* récipient *m*.
reception [rɪ'sepʃ(ə)n] *n* (*party, welcome etc*) & *Rad* réception *f*; **r. (desk)** réception *f*. ● **receptionist** *n* secrétaire *mf*, réceptionniste *mf*.
receptive [rɪ'septɪv] *a* réceptif (**to an idea/** *etc* à une idée/*etc*).
recess [rɪ'ses, *Am* 'ri:ses] *n* **1** (*holiday*, *Am vacation*) vacances *fpl*; *Sch Am* récréation *f*. **2** (*alcove*) renfoncement *m*; (*nook*) & *Fig* recoin *m*.
recession [rɪ'seʃ(ə)n] *n Econ* récession *f*.
recharge [ri:'tʃɑ:dʒ] *vt* (*battery*) recharger. ● **—able** *a* (*battery*) rechargeable.
recipe ['resɪpɪ] *n Culin* & *Fig* recette *f* (**for** de, **for doing** pour faire).
recipient [rɪ'sɪpɪənt] *n* (*of award, honour*) récipiendaire *m*.
reciprocal [rɪ'sɪprək(ə)l] *a* réciproque. ● **reciprocate** *vt* (*compliment*) retourner ‖ *vi* (*do the same*) en faire autant.
recital [rɪ'saɪt(ə)l] *n Mus* récital *m*.
recite [rɪ'saɪt] *vt* (*poem etc*) réciter; (*list*) énumérer.
reckless ['rekləs] *a* (*rash*) imprudent. ● **—ly** *adv* imprudemment.
reckon ['rek(ə)n] *vt* (*calculate*) calculer; (*count*) compter; (*think*) penser (**that** que) ‖ *vi* **to r. with s.o./sth** (*take into*

account) compter avec qch/qn; **to r. on sth/ s.o.** (*rely on*) compter sur qch/qn; **to r. on doing** compter faire. ●**—ing** *n* calcul(s) *m(pl)*.

reclaim [rɪ'kleɪm] *vt* **1** (*ask for back*) réclamer; (*luggage at airport*) récupérer. **2** (*land*) mettre en valeur.

recline [rɪ'klaɪn] *vi* (*of person*) être allongé; **reclining seat** siège *m* à dossier inclinable.

recluse [rɪ'klu:s] *n* reclus, -use *mf*.

recognize ['rekəgnaɪz] *vt* reconnaître (**by** à, **that** que). ●**recognition** [-'nɪʃ(ə)n] *n* reconnaissance *f*; **to change beyond r.** devenir méconnaissable; **to gain r.** être reconnu.

recoil [rɪ'kɔɪl] *vi* reculer (**from doing** à l'idée de faire, **from sth** à la vue de qch).

recollect [rekə'lekt] *vt* se souvenir de; **to r. that** se souvenir que. ●**recollection** [-'lekʃ(ə)n] *n* souvenir *m*.

recommend [rekə'mend] *vt* recommander (**to** à, **for** pour); **to r. s.o. to do** recommander à qn de faire. ●**recommendation** [-'deɪʃ(ə)n] *n* recommandation *f*.

reconcile ['rekənsaɪl] *vt* (*person*) réconcilier (**with, to** avec); (*opinions etc*) concilier; **to r. oneself to sth** se résigner à qch.

reconditioned [ri:kən'dɪʃ(ə)nd] *a* (*engine etc*) refait (à neuf).

reconsider [ri:kən'sɪdər] *vt* reconsidérer ‖ *vi* revenir sur sa décision.

record 1 ['rekɔ:d] *n* (*disc*) disque *m*; **r. library** discothèque *f*; **r. player** électrophone *m*.

2 *n* (*best performance*) *Sp etc* record *m* ‖ *a* (*number etc*) record *inv*; **in r. time** en un temps record.

3 *n* (*report*) rapport *m*; (*register*) registre *m*; (*mention*) mention *f*; (*note*) note *f*; (*background*) antécédents *mpl*; (*case history*) dossier *m*; **(police) r.** casier *m* judiciaire; **(public) records** archives *fpl*; **to keep a r. of** noter; **off the r.** à titre confidentiel; **their safety r.** leurs résultats *mpl* en matière de sécurité.

4 [rɪ'kɔ:d] *vt* (*on tape etc, in register etc*) enregistrer; (*in diary*) noter ‖ *vi* (*on tape etc*) enregistrer. ●**recorded** *a* enregistré; (*prerecorded*) (*TV programme*) en différé; (*fact*) attesté; **letter sent (by) r. delivery** = lettre *f* avec avis de réception. ●**recording** *n* enregistrement *m*.

recorder [rɪkɔ:dər] *n Mus* flûte *f* à bec; **(tape) r.** magnétophone *m*.

recount [rɪ'kaʊnt] *vt* (*relate*) raconter.

recoup [rɪ'ku:p] *vt* (*loss*) récupérer.

recourse ['ri:kɔ:s] *n* **to have r. to** avoir recours à.

recover [rɪ'kʌvər] **1** *vt* (*get back*) retrouver. **2** *vi* (*from illness, shock etc*) se remettre (**from** de); (*of economy*) se redresser. ●**recovery** *n* **1** (*from illness*) guérison *f*; *Econ* redressement *m*. **2 the r. of sth** la récupération de qch.

recreate [ri:krɪ'eɪt] *vt* reçréer.

recreation [rekrɪ'eɪʃ(ə)n] *n* récréation *f*. ●**recreational** *a* (*activity etc*) de loisir.

recruit [rɪ'kru:t] *n* recrue *f* ‖ *vt* recruter; **to r. s.o. to do** (*persuade*) embaucher qn pour faire.

rectangle ['rektæŋg(ə)l] *n* rectangle *m*. ●**rec'tangular** *a* rectangulaire.

rectify ['rektɪfaɪ] *vt* rectifier.

rector ['rektər] *n* (*priest*) pasteur *m* (anglican).

recuperate [rɪ'ku:pəreɪt] *vi* récupérer (ses forces).

recur [rɪ'kɜ:r] *vi* (**-rr-**) (*of event*) se reproduire; (*of illness*) réapparaître; (*of theme*) revenir. ●**recurrence** [rɪ'kʌrəns] *n* (*of illness*) réapparition *f*.

recycle [ri:'saɪk(ə)l] *vt* (*material*) recycler.

red [red] *a* (**redder, reddest**) rouge; (*hair*) roux (*f* rousse); **to turn** *or* **go r.** rougir; **R. Cross** Croix-Rouge *f*; **R. Indian** Peau-Rouge *mf*; **r. light** (*traffic light*) feu *m* rouge; **the r.-light district** le quartier des prostituées; **r. tape** *Fig* paperasserie *f* (administrative).

‖ *n* (*colour*) rouge *m*; **in the r.** (*company, account, person*) dans le rouge. ●**r.-'handed** *adv* **caught r.-handed** pris en flagrant délit. ●**r.-'hot** *a* brûlant.

redecorate [ri:'dekəreɪt] *vt* (*room etc*) refaire ‖ *vi* refaire la peinture et les papiers.

redeem [rɪ'di:m] *vt* (*restore to favour, buy back*) racheter; (*debt*) rembourser; (*convert into cash*) réaliser; **redeeming feature** bon point *m*.

redhead ['redhed] *n* roux *m*, rousse *f*.

redirect [ri:daɪ'rekt] *vt* (*mail*) faire suivre.

redo [ri:'du:] *vt* (*pt* **redid,** *pp* **redone**) (*exercise, house etc*) refaire.

reduce [rɪ'dju:s] *vt* réduire (**to** à, **by** de); (*temperature*) faire baisser; **at a reduced price** (*ticket*, goods) à prix réduit. ●**reduction** [rɪ'dʌkʃ(ə)n] *n* réduction *f* (**in** de); (*of temperature*) baisse *f*.

redundant [rɪ'dʌndənt] *a* (*not needed*) de trop; **to make r.** (*worker*) mettre au chômage, licencier. ●**redundancy** *n* (*of worker*) licenciement *m*; **r. pay** indemnité *f* de licenciement.

reed [ri:d] *n* **1** *Bot* roseau *m*. **2** *Mus* anche *f*.

reef [ri:f] *n* récif *m*, écueil *m*.

reek [riːk] *vi* puer; **to r. of sth** (*smell*) & *Fig* puer qch.

reel [riːl] **1** *n* (*of thread, film*) bobine *f*; (*film itself*) bande *f*; (*for fishing line*) moulinet *m*. **2** *vi* (*stagger*) chanceler; (*of mind*) chavirer. **3** *vt* **to r. off** (*from memory*) débiter (à toute vitesse).

re-entry [riː'entrɪ] *n* (*of spacecraft*) rentrée *f*.

re-establish [riːɪ'stæblɪʃ] *vt* rétablir.

ref [ref] *n abbr* (*referee*) *Sp Fam* arbitre *m*.

refectory [rɪ'fektərɪ] *n* réfectoire *m*.

refer [rɪ'fɜːr] *vi* (**-rr-**) **to r. to** (*mention*) faire allusion à; (*speak of*) parler de; (*apply to*) s'appliquer à; (*consult*) se reporter à ‖ *vt* **to r. sth to s.o.** soumettre qch à qn; **to r. s.o. to** (*article etc*) renvoyer qn à.

referee [refə'riː] *n Fb Boxing etc* arbitre *m*; (*for job*) répondant, -ante *mf* ‖ *vt Sp* arbitrer.

reference ['refərəns] *n* (*in book, for job etc*) référence *f*; (*indirect*) allusion *f* (**to** à); (*mention*) mention *f* (**to** de); **with r. to** concernant; *Com* suite à; **r. book** ouvrage *m* de référence.

referendum [refə'rendəm] *n* référendum *m*.

refill [riː'fɪl] *vt* remplir (à nouveau); (*lighter, pen etc*) recharger ‖ ['riːfɪl] *n* recharge *f*; **a r.** (*drink*) un autre verre.

refine [rɪ'faɪn] *vt* (*oil, sugar, manners*) raffiner; (*metal*) affiner; (*technique, machine*) perfectionner. •**refinement** *n* (*of person*) raffinement *m*; *pl* (*improvements*) améliorations *fpl*. •**refinery** *n* raffinerie *f*.

reflect [rɪ'flekt] **1** *vt* (*light, image etc*) refléter, réfléchir; *Fig* refléter; **to be reflected** (*of light etc*) se refléter ‖ *vi* **to r. on s.o.** (*of prestige etc*) rejaillir sur qn; **to r. badly on s.o.** nuire à l'image de qn. **2** *vi* (*think*) réfléchir (**on** à). •**reflection** [-ʃ(ə)n] *n* **1** (*image*) & *Fig* reflet *m*; (*reflecting*) réflexion *f* (**of** de). **2** (*thought*) réflexion (**on** sur); **on r.** tout bien réfléchi.

reflector [rɪ'flektər] *n* réflecteur *m*.

reflex ['riːfleks] *n* & *a* réflexe (*m*); **r. action** réflexe *m*.

reflexive [rɪ'fleksɪv] *a* (*verb*) réfléchi.

reform [rɪ'fɔːm] *n* réforme *f* ‖ *vt* réformer; (*person, conduct*) corriger ‖ *vi* (*of person*) se réformer.

refrain [rɪ'freɪn] **1** *vi* s'abstenir (**from doing** de faire). **2** *n Mus* refrain *m*.

refresh [rɪ'freʃ] *vt* (*of bath, drink*) rafraîchir; (*of sleep, rest*) délasser; **to r. one's memory** se rafraîchir la mémoire. •**—ing** *a* (*drink etc*) rafraîchissant; (*sleep*) réparateur; (*pleasant*) agréable. •**refresher course** *n* cours *m* de recyclage. •**refreshments** *npl* (*drinks*) rafraîchissements *mpl*; (*snacks*) petites choses *fpl* à grignoter.

refrigerate [rɪ'frɪdʒəreɪt] *vt* (*food*) conserver au frais. •**refrigerator** *n* réfrigérateur *m*.

refuel [riː'fjʊəl] *vi* (**-ll-**, *Am* **-l-**) *Av* se ravitailler ‖ *vt Av* ravitailler.

refuge ['refjuːdʒ] *n* refuge *m*; **to take r.** se réfugier.

refugee [refjʊ'dʒiː] *n* réfugié, -ée *mf*.

refund [rɪ'fʌnd] *vt* rembourser (**s.o. sth** qn de qch) ‖ ['riːfʌnd] *n* remboursement *m*.

refuse[1] [rɪ'fjuːz] *vt* refuser (**s.o. sth** qch à qn, **to do** de faire) ‖ *vi* refuser. •**refusal** *n* refus *m*.

refuse[2] ['refjuːs] *n* (*rubbish*) ordures *fpl*; **r. collector** éboueur *m*; **r. dump** dépôt *m* d'ordures.

refute [rɪ'fjuːt] *vt* réfuter.

regain [rɪ'geɪn] *vt* (*lost ground, favour*) regagner; (*health, sight*) retrouver; **to r. one's strength** retrouver ses forces; **to r. consciousness** reprendre connaissance.

regard [rɪ'gɑːd] *vt* (*consider*) considérer, regarder; (*concern*) regarder, concerner; **as regards** en ce qui concerne ‖ *n* considération *f* (**for** pour); **to have (a) high r. for s.o.** estimer qn; **with r. to** en ce qui concerne; **to give one's regards to s.o.**transmettre son meilleur souvenir à qn. •**—ing** *prep* en ce qui concerne.

regardless [rɪ'gɑːdləs] *a* **r. of** sans tenir compte de ‖ *adv* (*all the same*) quand même.

regatta [rɪ'gætə] *n* régates *fpl*.

reggae ['regeɪ] *n* (*music*) reggae *m*.

régime [reɪ'ʒiːm] *n Pol* régime *m*.

regiment ['redʒɪmənt] *n* régiment *m*.

region ['riːdʒ(ə)n] *n* région *f*; **in the r. of £50**/*etc* (*about*) dans les 50 livres/*etc*, environ 50 livres/*etc*. •**regional** *a* régional.

register ['redʒɪstər] *n* registre *m*; *Sch* cahier *m* d'appel; (*electoral*) liste *f* électorale; **to take the r.** *Sch* faire l'appel.
‖ *vt* (*birth, death*) déclarer; (*record, note*) enregistrer; (*express*) exprimer; (*indicate*) indiquer.
‖ *vi* (*enrol*) s'inscrire (**for a course** à un cours); (*in hotel*) signer le registre; **it hasn't registered (with me)** *Fam* je n'ai pas encore réalisé ça. •**registered** *a* (*member*) inscrit; (*letter, package*) recommandé; **to send by r. post** envoyer en recommandé.

registration [redʒɪ'streɪʃ(ə)n] *n* (*enrolment*) inscription *f*; **r. (number)** *Aut* numéro *m* d'immatriculation; **r. document** *Aut* = carte *f* grise.

registry ['redʒɪstrɪ] *a* **r. office** bureau *m* de l'état civil.

regret [rɪ'gret] *vt* (**-tt-**) regretter (**doing, to do** de faire; **that** que (+ *sub*)); **I r. to hear that...** je suis désolé d'apprendre que.... ‖ *n* regret *m*. ● **regretfully** *adv* **r., I...** à mon grand regret, je.... ● **regrettable** *a* regrettable (**that** que (+ *sub*)).

regroup [riː'gruːp] *vi* se regrouper.

regular ['regjʊlər] *a* (*steady, even*) régulier; (*surface*) uni; (*usual*) habituel; (*price, size*) normal; (*listener*) fidèle; (*staff*) permanent; **a r. guy** *Am Fam* un chic type ‖ *n* (*in bar etc*) habitué, -ée *mf*. ● **regularly** *adv* régulièrement.

regulate ['regjʊleɪt] *vt* régler.

regulation [regjʊ'leɪʃ(ə)n] *n* **regulations** (*rules*) règlement *m* ‖ *a* (*uniform etc*) réglementaire.

rehabilitate [riːhə'bɪlɪteɪt] *vt* (*in public esteem*) réhabiliter; (*drug addict*) désintoxiquer; (*wounded soldier*) réadapter.

rehearse [rɪ'hɜːs] *vt* (*a play, piece of music etc*) répéter; (*prepare*) *Fig* préparer ‖ *vi* répéter. ● **rehearsal** *n Th etc* répétition *f*.

reign [reɪn] *n* règne *m*; **in the r. of** sous le règne de ‖ *vi* régner (**over** sur).

reimburse [riːɪm'bɜːs] *vt* rembourser (**for** de).

rein [reɪn] *n see* **reins.**

reindeer ['reɪndɪər] *n inv* renne *m*.

reinforce [riːɪn'fɔːs] *vt* renforcer (**with** de); **reinforced concrete** béton *m* armé. ● **—ments** *npl* (*troops*) renforts *mpl*.

reins [reɪnz] *npl* (*for horse*) rênes *fpl*; (*for baby*) bretelles *fpl* de sécurité (avec laisse).

reinstate [riːɪn'steɪt] *vt* réintégrer.

reiterate [riː'ɪtəreɪt] *vt* (*say again*) réitérer.

reject [rɪ'dʒekt] *vt* rejeter, refuser ‖ ['riːdʒekt] *n Com* article *m* de rebut ‖ *a* (*article*) de deuxième choix; **r. shop** solderie *f*. ● **rejection** [rɪ'dʒekʃ(ə)n] *n* rejet *m*; (*of candidate etc*) refus *m*.

rejoic/e [rɪ'dʒɔɪs] *vi* (*celebrate*) faire la fête; (*be delighted*) se réjouir (**over** *or* **at sth** de qch). ● **—ing(s)** *n*(*pl*) réjouissance(s) *f*(*pl*).

rejoin [rɪ'dʒɔɪn] *vt* (*join up with*) rejoindre.

rejuvenate [rɪ'dʒuːvəneɪt] *vt* rajeunir.

relapse [rɪ'læps] *n Med* rechute *f* ‖ *vi Med* rechuter.

relat/e [rɪ'leɪt] **1** *vt* (*narrate*) raconter (**that** que). **2** *vt* (*connect*) établir un rapport entre (*faits etc*); **to r. sth to** (*link*) rattacher qch à ‖ *vi* **to r. to** (*apply to*) se rapporter à; (*get along with*) s'entendre avec. ● **—ed** *a* (*linked*) lié (**to** à); (*languages*) apparentés; **to be r. to s.o.** (*by family*) être parent de qn.

relation [rɪ'leɪʃ(ə)n] *n* (*relative*) parent, -ente *mf*; (*relationship*) rapport *m*, relation *f* (**between** entre); **what r. are you to him?** quel est ton lien de parenté avec lui?; **international relations** relations *fpl* internationales. ● **relationship** *n* (*in family*) lien(s) *m*(*pl*) de parenté; (*relations*) relations *fpl*; (*connection*) rapport *m*.

relative ['relətɪv] **1** *n* (*person*) parent, -ente *mf*. **2** *a* relatif (**to** à); (*qualities etc of two or more people*) respectif; **r. to** (*compared to*) relativement à. ● **—ly** *adv* relativement.

relax [rɪ'læks] **1** *vt* (*person, mind*) détendre ‖ *vi* se détendre; **r.!** (*calm down*) du calme! **2** *vt* (*grip, pressure etc*) relâcher; (*restrictions, control*) assouplir. ● **—ed** *a* (*person, atmosphere*) décontracté. ● **—ing** *a* (*bath etc*) délassant. ● **relaxation** [riːlæk'seɪʃ(ə)n] *n* (*rest*) détente *f*.

relay ['riːleɪ] *n* relais *m*; **r. race** course *f* de relais ‖ *vt* (*message etc*) *Rad* retransmettre, *Fig* transmettre (**to** à).

release [rɪ'liːs] *vt* (*free*) libérer (**from** de); (*bomb, s.o.'s hand*) lâcher; (*spring*) déclencher; (*brake*) desserrer; (*film, record*) sortir; (*news*) publier; (*trapped person*) dégager; (*tension*) éliminer.
‖ *n* (*of prisoner etc*) libération *f*; (*of film etc*) sortie *f* (**of** de); (*film*) nouveau film *m*; **a happy r.** (*s.o.'s death*) une délivrance; **press r.** communiqué *m* de presse; **to be on general r.** (*of film*) passer dans toutes les salles.

relent [rɪ'lent] *vi* (*change one's mind*) revenir sur sa décision. ● **—less** *a* implacable.

relevant ['reləvənt] *a* pertinent (**to** à); (*useful*) utile; **that's not r.** ça n'a rien à voir. ● **relevance** *n* pertinence *f* (**to** à); (*connection*) rapport *m* (**to** avec).

reliable [rɪ'laɪəb(ə)l] *a* (*person, information etc*) fiable, sérieux; (*machine*) fiable. ● **relia'bility** *n* fiabilité *f*; (*of person*) sérieux *m*, fiabilité *f*.

reliance [rɪ'laɪəns] *n* (*dependence*) dépendance *f* (**on** de); (*trust*) confiance *f* (**on** en).

relic ['relɪk] *n* relique *f*; *pl* (*of the past*) vestiges *mpl*.

relief [rɪ'liːf] *n* (*from pain etc*) soulagement *m* (**from** à); (*help, supplies*) secours *m*; (*in art*) & *Geog* relief *m*; **tax r.** dégrèvement *m*; **to be on r.** *Am* recevoir l'aide sociale ‖ *a* (*train, bus*) supplémentaire; **r. road** route *f* de délestage.

relieve [rɪ'liːv] *vt* (*pain etc*) soulager; (*boredom*) dissiper; (*take over from*) re-

layer (*qn*); (*help*) secourir; **to r. s.o. of sth** (*rid*) débarrasser qn de qch; **to r. congestion in** (*street*) décongestionner.
religion [rɪ'lɪdʒ(ə)n] *n* religion *f*. ●**religious** *a* religieux.
relinquish [rɪ'lɪŋkwɪʃ] *vt* (*give up*) abandonner; (*let go*) lâcher.
relish ['relɪʃ] *n* (*seasoning*) assaisonnement *m*; (*liking*) goût *m* (**for** pour); **to eat with r.** manger de bon appétit ‖ *vt* (*food etc*) savourer; (*like*) aimer (**doing** faire).
reload [rɪ'ləʊd] *vt* (*gun, camera*) recharger.
relocate [riːləʊ'keɪt, *Am* riː'ləʊkeɪt] *vi* (*to new place*) déménager; **to r. in** *or* **to** s'installer à.
reluctant [rɪ'lʌktənt] *a* peu enthousiaste (**to do** pour faire); **a r. teacher/***etc* un professeur/*etc* malgré lui. ●**reluctance** *n* manque *m* d'enthousiasme (**to do** à faire). ●**reluctantly** *adv* sans enthousiasme.
rely [rɪ'laɪ] *vi* **to r. (up)on** (*count on*) compter sur; (*be dependent on*) dépendre de.
remain [rɪ'meɪn] **1** *vi* rester. **2** *npl* **remains** restes *mpl*. ●**—ing** *a* qui reste(nt). ●**remainder** *n* reste *m*; **the r.** (*remaining people*) les autres *mfpl*.
remand [rɪ'mɑːnd] *vt* **to r. (in custody)** *Jur* placer en détention préventive.
remark [rɪ'mɑːk] *n* remarque *f* ‖ *vt* (faire) remarquer (**that** que) ‖ *vi* **to r. on sth** faire des remarques sur qch. ●**—able** *a* remarquable (**for** par). ●**—ably** *adv* remarquablement.
remarry [riː'mærɪ] *vi* se remarier.
remedial [rɪ'miːdɪəl] *a* **r. class** cours *m* de rattrapage; **r. exercises** gymnastique *f* corrective.
remedy ['remɪdɪ] *vt* remédier à ‖ *n* remède *m* (**for** contre, à).
remember [rɪ'membər] *vt* se souvenir de, se rappeler; **to r. that/doing** se rappeler que/avoir fait, se souvenir que/d'avoir fait; **to r. to do** (*not forget to do*) penser à faire; **r. me to him** *or* **her!** rappelle-moi à son bon souvenir! ‖ *vi* se souvenir, se rappeler. ●**remembrance** *n* **in r. of** en souvenir de.
remind [rɪ'maɪnd] *vt* rappeler (**s.o. of sth** qch à qn, **s.o. that** à qn que); **to r. s.o. to do** faire penser à qn à faire. ●**—er** *n* (*of event & letter*) rappel *m*; (*note to do sth*) pense-bête *m*; **to give s.o. a r. to do sth** faire penser à qn à faire qch.
reminisce [remɪ'nɪs] *vi* raconter *or* se rappeler ses souvenirs (**about** de). ●**reminiscent** *a* **r. of** qui rappelle.
remiss [rɪ'mɪs] *a* négligent.
remittance [rɪ'mɪtəns] *n* (*sum*) paiement *m*.
remnant ['remnənt] *n* (*remaining part*) reste *m*; (*of fabric*) coupon *m*; (*oddment*) fin *f* de série.
remodel [riː'mɒd(ə)l] *vt* (**-ll-**, *Am* **-l-**) remodeler.
remorse [rɪ'mɔːs] *n* remords *m*(*pl*) (**for** pour). ●**—less** *a* implacable.
remote [rɪ'məʊt] *a* (**-er, -est**) **1** (*far-off*) lointain, éloigné; (*isolated*) isolé; (*aloof*) distant; **r. from** loin de; **r. control** télécommande *f*. **2** (*slight*) petit; **not the remotest idea** pas la moindre idée. ●**—ly** *adv* (*slightly*) un peu; **not r. aware/***etc* nullement conscient/*etc*.
remould ['riːməʊld] *n* pneu *m* rechapé.
remove [rɪ'muːv] *vt* (*clothes, stain etc*) enlever (**from s.o.** à qn, **from sth** de qch); (*withdraw*) retirer; (*lead away*) emmener (**to** à); (*obstacle, threat, word*) supprimer; (*fear, doubt*) dissiper. ●**removable** *a* (*lining etc*) amovible. ●**removal** *n* enlèvement *m*; suppression *f*; **r. man** déménageur *m*; **r. van** camion *m* de déménagement. ●**remover** *n* (*for make-up*) démaquillant *m*; (*for nail polish*) dissolvant *m*; (*for stains*) détachant *m*.
remunerate [rɪ'mjuːnəreɪt] *vt* rémunérer.
rename [riː'neɪm] *vt* (*street*) rebaptiser; **to r. a file** *Comptr* renommer un fichier.
render ['rendər] *vt* (*give, make*) rendre; *Mus* interpréter. ●**—ing** *n Mus* interprétation *f*; (*translation*) traduction *f*.
rendez-vous ['rɒndɪvuː, *pl* -vuːz] *n inv* rendez-vous *m inv*.
reneg(u)e [rɪ'niːg, rɪ'neɪg]] *vi* **to r. on** (*promise*) revenir sur.
renew [rɪ'njuː] *vt* renouveler; (*resume*) reprendre; (*library book*) renouveler le prêt de. ●**—ed** *a* (*efforts*) renouvelés; (*attempt*) nouveau (*f* nouvelle). ●**renewal** *n* renouvellement *m*; (*resumption*) reprise *f*.
renounce [rɪ'naʊns] *vt* (*give up*) renoncer à; (*disown*) renier.
renovate ['renəveɪt] *vt* (*house*) rénover; (*painting*) restaurer.
renown [rɪ'naʊn] *n* renommée *f*. ●**renowned** *a* renommé (**for** pour).
rent [rent] *n* (*for house etc*) loyer *m*; **r. collector** encaisseur *m* de loyers ‖ *vt* louer; **to r. out** louer; **rented car** voiture *f* de location. ●**r.-'free** *adv* sans payer de loyer ‖ *a* gratuit. ●**rental** *n* (*of television, car*) (prix *m* de) location *f*; (*of telephone*) abonnement *m*.
reopen [riː'əʊpən] *vti* rouvrir.
reorganize [riː'ɔːgənaɪz] *vt* (*company etc*) réorganiser.

rep [rep] *n Fam* représentant, -ante *mf* de commerce.
repair [rɪ'peər] *vt* réparer ‖ *n* réparation *f*; **beyond r.** irréparable; **in good/bad r.** en bon/mauvais état; **'road under r.'** *Aut* 'travaux'; **r. man** réparateur *m*.
repatriate [riː'pætrɪeɪt] *vt* rapatrier.
repay [riː'peɪ] *vt* (*pt & pp* **repaid**) (*pay back*) rembourser; (*kindness*) payer de retour; (*reward*) récompenser (**for** de). ●**—ment** *n* remboursement *m*; récompense *f*.
repeal [rɪ'piːl] *vt* (*law*) abroger ‖ *n* abrogation *f*.
repeat [rɪ'piːt] *vt* répéter (**that** que); (*promise, threat*) réitérer; (*class*) *Sch* redoubler; **to r. oneself** se répéter ‖ *vi* répéter; **to r. on s.o.** (*of food*) *Fam* revenir à qn ‖ *n TV Rad* rediffusion *f*. ●**—ed** *a* (*attempts etc*) répétés; (*efforts*) renouvelés. ●**—edly** *adv* de nombreuses fois.
repel [rɪ'pel] *vt* (**-ll-**) repousser. ●**repellent** *a* repoussant.
repent [rɪ'pent] *vi* se repentir (**of** de). ●**repentance** *n* repentir *m*. ●**repentant** *a* repentant.
repercussions [riːpə'kʌʃ(ə)nz] *npl* répercussions *fpl*.
repertory ['repət(ə)rɪ] *n Th & Fig* répertoire *m*; **r. (theatre)** théâtre *m* de répertoire.
repetition [repɪ'tɪʃ(ə)n] *n* répétition *f*. ●**repetitious** *or* **re'petitive** *a* répétitif.
replace [rɪ'pleɪs] *vt* (*take the place of*) remplacer (**by, with** par); (*put back*) remettre; **to r. the receiver** *Tel* raccrocher. ●**—ment** *n* remplacement *m* (**of** de); (*person*) remplaçant, -ante *mf*; (*machine part*) pièce *f* de rechange.
replay ['riːpleɪ] *n Sp* match *m* rejoué; **(instant) r.** *TV* répétition *f* immédiate (au ralenti) ‖ [riː'pleɪ] *vt* (*on tape recorder etc*) repasser.
replica ['replɪkə] *n* copie *f* exacte.
reply [rɪ'plaɪ] *vti* répondre (**to** à, **that** que) ‖ *n* réponse *f*; **in r.** en réponse (**to** à).
report [rɪ'pɔːt] *n* (*account*) rapport *m*; (*of meeting*) compte rendu *m*; (*in media*) reportage *m*; *Sch* bulletin *m*; (*rumour*) rumeur *f*; **r. card** *Am* bulletin *m* (scolaire). ‖ *vt* (*give account of*) rapporter, rendre compte de; (*announce*) annoncer (**that** que); (*notify*) signaler (**to** à); (*inform on*) dénoncer (**to** à); (*in newspaper*) faire un reportage sur.
‖ *vi* faire un rapport; (*of journalist*) faire un reportage (**on** sur); (*go*) se présenter (**to** à, **to s.o.** chez qn). ●**reported** *a* (*speech*) *Gram* indirect; **it is r. that** on dit que; **r. missing** porté disparu. ●**reporter** *n* reporter *m*.
repossess [riːpə'zes] *vt Jur* reprendre possession de.
represent [reprɪ'zent] *vt* représenter. ●**representation** [-'teɪʃ(ə)n] *n* représentation *f*. ●**representative** *a* représentatif (**of** de) ‖ *n* représentant, -ante *mf*; *Pol Am* député *m*.
repress [rɪ'pres] *vt* (*feeling, tears*) réprimer, refouler; (*uprising*) réprimer. ●**—ed** *a Psy* refoulé.
reprieve [rɪ'priːv] *n Jur* commutation *f*; (*temporary*) sursis *m* ‖ *vt* accorder une commutation *or* un sursis à.
reprimand ['reprɪmɑːnd] *n* réprimande *f* ‖ *vt* réprimander.
reprisal [rɪ'praɪz(ə)l] *n* **reprisals** représailles *fpl*; **as a r. for** en représailles de.
reproach [rɪ'prəʊtʃ] *n* (*blame*) reproche *m*; **beyond r.** sans reproche ‖ *vt* reprocher (**s.o. for sth** qch à qn). ●**reproachfully** *adv* d'un ton *or* d'un air réprobateur.
reproduce [riːprə'djuːs] *vt* reproduire ‖ *vi Biol Bot* se reproduire. ●**reproduction** [-'dʌkʃ(ə)n] *n* (*of sound etc*) & *Biol Bot* reproduction *f*.
reptile ['reptaɪl] *n* reptile *m*.
republic [rɪ'pʌblɪk] *n* république *f*. ●**republican** *a* & *n* républicain, -aine (*mf*).
repudiate [rɪ'pjuːdɪeɪt] *vt* (*behaviour, violence etc*) condamner; (*accusation*) rejeter; (*idea*) répudier.
repugnant [rɪ'pʌgnənt] *a* répugnant; **he's r. to me** il me répugne.
repulse [rɪ'pʌls] *vt* repousser. ●**repulsive** *a* repoussant.
reputable ['repjʊtəb(ə)l] *a* de bonne réputation. ●**repute** [rɪ'pjuːt] *n* **of r.** de bonne réputation. ●**re'puted** *a* réputé (**to be** pour être).
reputation [repjʊ'teɪʃ(ə)n] *n* réputation *f*; **to have a r. for being** avoir la réputation d'être.
request [rɪ'kwest] *n* demande *f* (**for** de); **on r.** sur demande; **at s.o.'s r.** à la demande de qn; **r. stop** (*for bus*) arrêt *m* facultatif ‖ *vt* demander (**sth from s.o.** qch à qn, **s.o. to do** à qn de faire).
require [rɪ'kwaɪər] *vt* (*of thing*) (*necessitate*) demander; (*demand*) exiger; (*of person*) avoir besoin de (*qch, qn*); (*staff*) rechercher; **to r. s.o. to do** (*order*) exiger de qn qu'il fasse; **if required** s'il le faut; **the required qualities/***etc* les qualités/*etc* qu'il faut; **required condition** condition *f* requise. ●**—ment** *n* (*need*) exigence *f*; (*condition*) condition *f* (requise).
requisite ['rekwɪzɪt] *n* (*for travel etc*) article

m; **toilet requisites** articles *mpl* de toilette.

requisition [rekwɪ'zɪʃ(ə)n] *vt* réquisitionner ‖ *n* réquisition *f*.

reroute [riː'ruːt] *vt* (*aircraft etc*) dérouter.

rerun ['riːrʌn] *n Cin* reprise *f*; *TV* rediffusion *f*.

reschedule [riː'ʃedjuːl, *Am* riːskedjuːl] *vt* (*meeting*) déplacer.

rescu/e ['reskjuː] *vt* (*save*) sauver; (*set free*) délivrer (**from** de) ‖ *n* (*action*) sauvetage *m* (**of** de); (*help, troops*) secours *mpl*; **to go to s.o.'s r.** aller au secours de qn; **to the r.** à la rescousse ‖ *a* (*team, operation*) de sauvetage. ●**—er** *n* sauveteur *m*.

research [rɪ'sɜːtʃ] *n* recherches *fpl* (**on, into** sur); **some r.** des recherches, de la recherche; **a piece of r.** un travail de recherche ‖ *vi* faire des recherches. ●**—er** *n* chercheur, -euse *mf*.

resemble [rɪ'zemb(ə)l] *vt* ressembler à. ●**resemblance** *n* ressemblance *f* (**to** avec).

resent [rɪ'zent] *vt* (*be angry about*) s'indigner de; (*be bitter about*) éprouver de l'amertume à l'égard de; **I r. that** ça m'indigne. ●**resentful** *a* **to be r.** éprouver de l'amertume. ●**resentment** *n* amertume *f*.

reservation [rezə'veɪʃ(ə)n] *n* **1** (*booking*) réservation *f*; (*doubt*) réserve *f*; **to make a r.** réserver. **2** (*land*) *Am* réserve *f*; **central r.** (*on road*) terre-plein *m*.

reserve [rɪ'zɜːv] **1** *vt* (*room, decision etc*) réserver; (*right*) se réserver ‖ *n* (*reticence*) réserve *f*.
2 *n* (*land, stock*) réserve *f*; **r. (player)** *Sp* remplaçant, -ante *mf*; **the reserves** (*troops*) les réserves *fpl*; **nature r.** réserve *f* naturelle; **in r.** en réserve; **r. tank** *Av Aut* réservoir *m* de secours. ●**reserved** *a* (*person, room*) réservé.

reservoir ['rezəvwɑːr] *n* (*of water etc*) & *Fig* réservoir *m*.

reshape [riː'ʃeɪp] *vt* (*industry etc*) réorganiser.

reshuffle [riː'ʃʌf(ə)l] *n* **(cabinet) r.** remaniement *m* (ministériel).

reside [rɪ'zaɪd] *vi* résider.

residence ['rezɪdəns] *n* (*home*) résidence *f*; (*of students*) foyer *m*; **in r.** (*doctor*) sur place; **r. permit** permis *m* de séjour. ●**'resident** *n* habitant, -ante *mf*; (*of hotel*) pensionnaire *mf*; (*foreigner*) résident, -ente *mf* ‖ *a* **to be r. in London** résider à Londres. ●**resi'dential** *a* (*neighbourhood etc*) résidentiel.

resign [rɪ'zaɪn] *vt* (*one's post*) démissionner de; **to r. oneself to sth/to doing** se résigner à qch/à faire ‖ *vi* démissionner (**from** de); **to r. from one's job** démissionner. ●**—ed** *a* résigné. ●**resignation** [rezɪg'neɪʃ(ə)n] *n* (*from job*) démission *f*; (*attitude*) résignation *f*.

resilient [rɪ'zɪlɪənt] *a* élastique; (*person*) *Fig* résistant.

resin ['rezɪn] *n* résine *f*.

resist [rɪ'zɪst] *vt* (*attack etc*) résister à; **to r. doing sth** se retenir de faire qch; **she can't r. cakes** elle ne peut pas résister devant des gâteaux; **he can't r. her** (*indulgence*) il ne peut rien lui refuser; (*charm*) il ne peut pas résister à son charme ‖ *vi* résister. ●**resistance** *n* résistance *f* (**to** à). ●**resistant** *a* résistant (**to** à).

resit [riː'sɪt] *vt* (*pt* & *pp* **resat**, *pres p* **resitting**) (*exam*) repasser.

resolute ['rezəluːt] *a* résolu. ●**resolution** [-'luːʃ(ə)n] *n* résolution *f*.

resolv/e [rɪ'zɒlv] *vt* résoudre (**to do** de faire, **that** que) ‖ *n* résolution *f*. ●**—ed** *a* résolu (**to do** à faire).

resort [rɪ'zɔːt] **1** *vi* **to r. to sth** (*turn to*) avoir recours à qch; **to r. to doing** en venir à faire ‖ *n* **as a last r.** en dernier ressort. **2** *n* **(holiday** *or Am* **vacation) r.** station *f* de vacances; **seaside** *or Am* **beach r.** station *f* balnéaire; **ski r.** station de ski.

resounding [rɪ'zaʊndɪŋ] *a* (*success*) retentissant.

resources [rɪ'sɔːsɪz, rɪ'zɔːsɪz] *npl* (*wealth, means*) ressources *fpl* ●**resourceful** *a* (*person, scheme*) ingénieux.

respect [rɪ'spekt] *n* respect *m* (**for** pour, de); (*aspect*) égard *m*; **with r. to** en ce qui concerne; **with all due r.** sans vouloir vous vexer ‖ *vt* respecter.

respectable [rɪ'spektəb(ə)l] *a* (*honourable, quite good*) respectable; (*satisfying*) (*results, score etc*) honnête; (*clothes, behaviour*) convenable.

respectful [rɪ'spektfəl] *a* respectueux (**to** envers, **of** de).

respective [rɪ'spektɪv] *a* respectif. ●**—ly** *adv* respectivement.

respond [rɪ'spɒnd] *vi* répondre (**to** à); **to r. to treatment** bien réagir au traitement. ●**response** *n* réponse *f*; **in r. to** en réponse à.

responsible [rɪ'spɒnsəb(ə)l] *a* responsable (**for** de, **to s.o.** devant qn); (*job*) à responsabilités. ●**responsi'bility** *n* responsabilité *f*. ●**responsibly** *adv* de façon responsable.

responsive [rɪ'spɒnsɪv] *a* (*reacting*) qui réagit bien; (*alert*) éveillé; (*attentive*) qui fait attention; **r. to** (*kindness*) sensible à; (*suggestion*) réceptif à.

rest[1] [rest] *n* (*relaxation*) repos *m*; (*support*) support *m*; **to have** *or* **take a r.** se reposer; **to put s.o.'s mind at r.** tranquilliser qn; **r. home** maison *f* de repos; **r. room** *Am* toilettes *fpl*.
▮ *vi* (*relax*) se reposer; **to r. on** (*of argument*) reposer sur; **I won't r. till** je n'aurai de repos que (+ *sub*); **to be resting on sth** (*of hand etc*) être posé sur qch; **a resting place** un lieu de repos.
▮ *vt* (*lean*) appuyer (**on** sur); (*base*) fonder; (*eyes etc*) reposer; (*horse etc*) laisser reposer.
rest[2] [rest] *n* (*remainder*) reste *m* (**of** de); **the r.** (*others*) les autres *mfpl*; **the r. of the men/***etc* les autres hommes/*etc* ▮ *vi* (*remain*) **r. assured** soyez assuré (**that** que).
restaurant ['restərɒnt] *n* restaurant *m*; **r. car** *Rail* wagon-restaurant *m*.
restful ['restfəl] *a* reposant.
restless ['restləs] *a* agité. ●**—ness** *n* agitation *f*.
restore [rɪ'stɔːr] *vt* (*give back*) rendre (**to** à); (*order*, *peace*) rétablir; (*building*, *painting*) restaurer.
restrain [rɪ'streɪn] *vt* (*person*) retenir, maîtriser; (*crowd*, *anger*, *inflation*) contenir; **to r. s.o. from doing** retenir qn de faire; **to r. oneself** se retenir, se maîtriser. ●**restraint** *n* (*moderation*) retenue *f*; (*restriction*) contrainte *f*.
restrict [rɪ'strɪkt] *vt* restreindre (**to** à). ●**—ed** *a* (*space*, *use*) restreint. ●**restriction** [-ʃ(ə)n] *n* restriction *f*.
result [rɪ'zʌlt] *n* résultat *m*; **as a r.** en conséquence; **as a r. of** par suite de ▮ *vi* résulter (**from** de); **to r. in** aboutir à.
resume [rɪ'zjuːm] *vti* (*begin or take again*) reprendre; **to r. doing** se remettre à faire. ●**resumption** [rɪ'zʌmpʃ(ə)n] *n* reprise *f*.
résumé ['rezjʊmeɪ] *n Am* curriculum vitae *m inv*.
resurface [riː'sɜːfɪs] *vt* (*road*) refaire le revêtement de.
resurgence [rɪ'sɜːdʒəns] *n* réapparition *f*.
resurrect [rezə'rekt] *vt* (*custom etc*) ressusciter.
retail ['riːteɪl] *n* (vente *f* au) détail *m* ▮ *a* (*price*, *shop*) de détail ▮ *vi* se vendre (au détail) (**at** à) ▮ *adv* (*to sell*) au détail. ●**—er** *n* détaillant, -ante *mf*.
retain [rɪ'teɪn] *vt* (*freshness*, *heat etc*) conserver; (*hold back*, *remember*) retenir. ●**retainer** *n* (*fee*) acompte *m*. ●**retention** [rɪ'tenʃ(ə)n] *n* (*memory*) mémoire *f*.
retaliate [rɪ'tælɪeɪt] *vi* riposter (**against s.o.** contre qn, **against an attack** à une attaque).
retarded [rɪ'tɑːdɪd] *a* (**mentally**) **r.** arriéré.
retch [retʃ] *vi* avoir un *or* des haut-le-cœur.
rethink [riː'θɪŋk] *vt* (*pt* & *pp* **rethought**) repenser.
reticent ['retɪsənt] *a* réticent.
retir/e [rɪ'taɪər] **1** *vi* (*from work*) prendre sa retraite; **retiring age** l'âge *m* de la retraite. **2** *vi* (*withdraw*) se retirer (**from** de, **to** à); (*go to bed*) aller se coucher. ●**—ed** *a* (*no longer working*) retraité. ●**retirement** *n* retraite *f*; **on my r.** dès mon départ à la retraite; **r. age** l'âge *m* de la retraite.
retort [rɪ'tɔːt] *vt* rétorquer.
retrace [riː'treɪs] *vt* (*past event*) se remémorer; **to r. one's steps** revenir sur ses pas.
retract [rɪ'trækt] *vt* (*statement etc*) rétracter ▮ *vi* (*of person*) se rétracter.
retrain [riː'treɪn] *vi* se recycler ▮ *vt* recycler.
retread ['riːtred] *n* pneu *m* rechapé.
retreat [rɪ'triːt] *n* (*withdrawal*) retraite *f*; (*place*) refuge *m* ▮ *vi* se retirer (**from** de); (*of troops*) battre en retraite.
retrieve [rɪ'triːv] *vt* (*recover*) récupérer; (*rescue*) sauver (**from** de); (*loss*, *error*) réparer; (*data*) *Comptr* récupérer. ●**retrieval** *n* **information r.** recherche *f* documentaire; *Comptr* recherche *f* de données.
retroactive [retrəʊ'æktɪv] *a* (*pay increase etc*) avec effet rétroactif.
retrospect ['retrəspekt] *n* **in r.** rétrospectivement. ●**retro'spective 1** *a* (*law*, *effect*) rétroactif. **2** *n* (*of film director etc*) rétrospective *f*.
return [rɪ'tɜːn] *vi* (*come back*) revenir; (*go back*) retourner; (*go back home*) rentrer; **to r. to** (*subject*) revenir à.
▮ *vt* (*give back*) rendre; (*put back*) remettre; (*bring back*) rapporter; (*send back*) renvoyer; (*candidate*) *Pol* élire.
▮ *n* retour *m*; (*on investment*) rendement *m*; *pl* (*profits*) bénéfices *mpl*; **r. (ticket)** (billet *m* d')aller et retour *m*; **tax r.** déclaration *f* de revenus; **many happy returns (of the day)!** bon anniversaire!; **in r.** en échange (**for** de).
▮ *a* (*trip*, *flight etc*) (de) retour; **r. match** *or* **game** match *m* retour. ●**returnable** *a* (*bottle*) consigné.
reunion [riː'juːnɪən] *n* réunion *f*. ●**reu'nite** *vt* réunir; **to be reunited with s.o.** retrouver qn.
rev [rev] *n Aut Fam* tour *m* ▮ *vt* (**-vv-**) **to r. (up)** (*engine*) *Fam* faire ronfler.
revamp [riː'væmp] *vt* (*method etc*) *Fam* remanier.

reveal [rɪ'viːl] *vt* (*make known*) révéler (**that** que); (*make visible*) laisser voir. ●**—ing** *a* (*sign etc*) révélateur.

revel ['rev(ə)l] *vi* (**-ll-**, *Am* **-l-**) faire la fête; **to r. in sth** se délecter de qch. ● **reveller** (*Am* **reveler**) *n* noceur, -euse *mf*.

revelation [revə'leɪʃ(ə)n] révélation *f*.

revenge [rɪ'vendʒ] *n* vengeance *f*; **to get** *or* **have one's r.** se venger (**on s.o.** de qn, **on s.o. for sth** de qch sur qn); **in r.** pour se venger.

revenue ['revənjuː] *n* revenu *m*.

reverence ['revərəns] *n* révérence *f*.

reverend ['rev(ə)rənd] *n* **R. Smith** (*Anglican*) le révérend Smith; (*Catholic*) l'abbé *m* Smith; (*Jewish*) le rabbin Smith.

reversal [rɪ'vɜːsəl] *n* (*of situation*) renversement *m*; (*of policy, opinion*) revirement *m*; (*of fortune*) revers *m*.

reverse [rɪ'vɜːs] *a* (*order, image etc*) inverse; **r. side** (*of coin etc*) revers *m*; (*of paper*) verso *m*.

▮ *n* contraire *m*; (*of coin, fabric etc*) revers *m*; (*of paper*) verso *m*; **in r. (gear)** *Aut* en marche arrière.

▮ *vt* (*situation*) renverser; (*order, policy*) inverser; (*decision*) annuler; **to r. the charges** *Tel* téléphoner en PCV.

▮ *vti* **to r. (the car)** faire marche arrière; **to r. in/out** rentrer/sortir en marche arrière; **reversing lights** feux *mpl* de recul.

revert [rɪ'vɜːt] *vi* **to r. to** revenir à.

review [rɪ'vjuː] **1** *vt* (*book etc*) faire la critique de; (*troops*) passer en revue; (*situation*) réexaminer; (*salary*) réviser ▮ *n* (*of book etc*) critique *f*. **2** *n* (*magazine*) revue *f*. ●**—er** *n* critique *m*.

revise [rɪ'vaɪz] *vt* (*opinion, notes, text*) réviser ▮ *vi* (*for exam*) réviser (**for** pour). ● **revision** [rɪ'vɪʒ(ə)n] *n* révision *f*.

revitalize [riː'vaɪt(ə)laɪz] *vt* revitaliser.

revival [rɪ'vaɪvəl] *n* (*of custom, business, play*) reprise *f*; (*of faith, fashion*) renouveau *m*.

revive [rɪ'vaɪv] *vt* (*unconscious person, memory*) ranimer; (*dying person*) réanimer; (*custom, fashion*) ressusciter; (*hope, interest*) faire renaître ▮ *vi* (*of unconscious person*) reprendre connaissance; (*of hope, interest*) renaître.

revoke [rɪ'vəʊk] *vt* (*decision*) annuler; (*contract*) révoquer.

revolt [rɪ'vəʊlt] **1** *n* révolte *f* ▮ *vi* (*rebel*) se révolter (**against** contre). **2** *vt* (*disgust*) révolter. ●**—ing** *a* dégoûtant.

revolution [revə'luːʃ(ə)n] *n* révolution *f*. ● **revolutionary** *a* & *n* révolutionnaire (*mf*).

revolve [rɪ'vɒlv] *vi* tourner (**around** autour de); **revolving door(s)** (porte *f* à) tambour *m*.

revolver [rɪ'vɒlvər] *n* revolver *m*.

revulsion [rɪ'vʌlʃ(ə)n] *n* (*disgust*) dégoût *m*.

reward [rɪ'wɔːd] *n* récompense *f* (**for** de) ▮ *vt* récompenser (**s.o. for sth** qn de *or* pour qch). ●**—ing** *a* qui vaut la peine; (*satisfying*) satisfaisant; (*financially*) rémunérateur.

rewind [riː'waɪnd] *vt* (*pt* & *pp* **rewound**) (*tape*) rembobiner ▮ *vi* se rembobiner.

rewire [riː'waɪər] *vt* (*house*) refaire l'installation électrique de.

rewrite [riː'raɪt] *vt* (*pt* **rewrote,** *pp* **rewritten**) récrire; (*edit*) réécrire.

rhetoric ['retərɪk] *n* rhétorique *f*.

rheumatism ['ruːmətɪz(ə)m] *n Med* rhumatisme *m*; **to have r.** avoir des rhumatismes.

rhinoceros [raɪ'nɒsərəs] *n* rhinocéros *m*.

rhubarb ['ruːbɑːb] *n* rhubarbe *f*.

rhyme [raɪm] *n* rime *f*; (*poem*) vers *mpl* ▮ *vi* rimer (**with** avec).

rhythm ['rɪð(ə)m] *n* rythme *m*. ● **rhythmic(al)** *a* rythmique.

rib [rɪb] *n Anat* côte *f*.

ribbon ['rɪbən] *n* ruban *m*; **to tear to ribbons** mettre en lambeaux.

rice [raɪs] *n* riz *m*. ● **ricefield** *n* rizière *f*.

rich [rɪtʃ] *a* (**-er, -est**) (*person, food etc*) riche; **r. in** riche en ▮ *n* **the r.** les riches *mpl*. ● **riches** *npl* richesses *fpl*. ● **richly** *adv* (*illustrated etc*) richement.

rick [rɪk] *vt* **to r. one's back** se tordre le dos.

rickety ['rɪkɪtɪ] *a* (*furniture*) branlant.

rid [rɪd] *vt* (*pt* & *pp* **rid,** *pres p* **ridding**) débarrasser (**of** de); **to get r. of, r. oneself of** se débarrasser de. ● **riddance** *n* **good r.!** *Fam* bon débarras!

ridden ['rɪd(ə)n] *pp of* **ride.**

-ridden ['rɪd(ə)n] *suff* **debt-r.** criblé de dettes; **disease-r.** en proie à la maladie.

riddle ['rɪd(ə)l] **1** *n* (*puzzle*) énigme *f*. **2** *vt* **riddled with** (*bullets, holes, mistakes*) criblé de; (*corruption*) en proie à.

ride [raɪd] *n* (*on bicycle, by car etc*) promenade *f*; (*distance*) trajet *m*; (*in taxi*) course *f*; **to go for a (car) r.** faire une promenade (en voiture); **to give s.o. a r.** (*in car*) emmener qn en voiture; **to take s.o. for a r.** (*deceive*) *Fam* mener qn en bateau.

▮ *vi* (*pt* **rode,** *pp* **ridden**) aller (à bicyclette, à moto, à cheval *etc*) (**to** à); **to r., go riding** (*on horse*) monter (à cheval); **to be riding in a car** être en voiture.

▮ *vt* (*a particular horse*) monter; (*distance*) faire (à cheval *etc*); **to r. a horse** *or* **horses** monter à cheval; **I was riding (on) a bicycle/donkey** j'étais à bicyclette/à dos d'âne; **to know how to r. a bicycle** savoir faire de la bicyclette; **to r. a bicycle to** aller à bicylette à.

rider ['raɪdər] *n* (*on horse*) cavalier, -ière *mf*; (*cyclist*) cycliste *mf*.

ridge [rɪdʒ] *n* (*of roof, mountain*) arête *f*, crête *f*.

ridicule ['rɪdɪkjuːl] *n* ridicule *m*; **to hold up to r.** tourner en ridicule; **object of r.** objet *m* de risée ▮ *vt* tourner en ridicule, ridiculiser. ● **ri'diculous** *a* ridicule.

riding ['raɪdɪŋ] *n* **(horse) r.** équitation *f*; **r. boots** bottes *fpl* de cheval.

rife [raɪf] *a* (*widespread*) répandu.

riffraff ['rɪfræf] *n* racaille *f*.

rifle ['raɪf(ə)l] *n* fusil *m*.

rift [rɪft] *n* (*in political party*) scission *f*; (*disagreement*) désaccord *m*; (*crack*) fissure *f*.

rig [rɪg] **1** *n* **(oil) r.** derrick *m*; (*at sea*) plate-forme *f* pétrolière. **2** *vt* **(-gg-)** (*result, election*) *Pej* truquer; **to r. up** (*equipment*) installer. **3** *vt* **(-gg-) to r. out** (*dress*) *Fam* habiller.

right[1] [raɪt] **1** *a* (*correct*) bon (*f* bonne), exact; (*fair*) juste; (*angle*) *Math* droit; **to be r.** (*of person*) avoir raison (**to do** de faire); **it's the r. road** c'est la bonne route; **the r. choice/time** le bon choix/moment; **it's the r. time** (*accurate*) c'est l'heure exacte; **the clock is r.** la pendule est à l'heure; **he's the r. man** c'est l'homme qu'il faut; **the r. thing to do** la meilleure chose à faire; **it's not r. to steal** ce n'est pas bien de voler; **it doesn't look r.** il y a quelque chose qui ne va pas; **to put r.** (*error*) corriger; (*fix*) arranger; **to put s.o. r.** (*inform*) éclairer qn; **r.!** bien!; **that's r.** c'est ça, c'est exact.

▮ *adv* (*straight*) (tout) droit; (*completely*) tout à fait; (*correctly*) juste; (*well*) bien; **she did r.** elle a bien fait; **r. round** tout autour (**sth** de qch); **r. behind** juste derrière; **r. here** ici même; **r. away, r. now** tout de suite.

▮ *n* **to be in the r.** avoir raison; **r. and wrong** le bien et le mal.

2 all r. *see* **all right.**

right[2] [raɪt] *a* (*not left*) (*hand, side etc*) droit ▮ *adv* à droite ▮ *n* droite *f*; **on** *or* **to the r.** à droite (**of** de). ● **r.-hand** *a* à *or* de droite; **on the r.-hand side** à droite (**of** de); **r.-hand man** bras *m* droit. ● **r.-'handed** *a* (*person*) droitier. ● **r.-wing** *a Pol* de droite.

right[3] [raɪt] *n* (*entitlement*) droit *m* (**to do** de faire); **to have a r. to sth** avoir droit à qch; **r. of way** *Aut* priorité *f*; **human rights** les droits de l'homme.

righteous ['raɪtʃəs] *a* (*person*) vertueux; (*cause, indignation*) juste.

rightful ['raɪtfəl] *a* légitime. ● **—ly** *adv* légitimement.

rightly ['raɪtlɪ] *adv* bien, correctement; (*justifiably*) à juste titre; **r. or wrongly** à tort ou à raison.

rigid ['rɪdʒɪd] *a* rigide. *f*.

rigmarole ['rɪgmərəʊl] *n* (*process*) procédure *f* compliquée.

rigour ['rɪgər] (*Am* **rigor**) *n* rigueur *f*. ● **rigorous** *a* rigoureux.

rim [rɪm] *n* (*of cup etc*) bord *m*; (*of wheel*) jante *f*.

rind [raɪnd] *n* (*of cheese*) croûte *f*; (*of bacon*) couenne *f*.

ring[1] [rɪŋ] *n* (*for finger, curtain etc*) anneau *m*; (*for finger with jewel*) bague *f*; (*of people, chairs*) cercle *m*; (*of smoke*) rond *m*; (*gang*) bande *f*; (*at circus*) piste *f*; *Boxing* ring *m*; (*burner on stove*) brûleur *m*; **diamond r.** bague *f* de diamants; **to have rings under one's eyes** avoir les yeux cernés; **r. road** route *f* de ceinture; (*motorway*) périphérique *m*.

▮ *vt* **to r. (round)** entourer (**with** de); (*item on list etc*) encadrer. ● **ringleader** *n Pej* (*of gang*) chef *m* de bande; (*of rebellion*) meneur, -euse *mf*.

ring[2] [rɪŋ] *n* (*sound*) sonnerie *f*; **there's a r.** on sonne; **to give s.o. a r.** (*phone call*) passer un coup de fil à qn.

▮ *vi* (*pt* **rang,** *pp* **rung**) (*of bell, phone, person etc*) sonner; (*of sound, words*) retentir; (*of ears*) bourdonner; (*on phone*) téléphoner.

▮ *vt* sonner; **to r. s.o.** (*on phone*) téléphoner à qn; **to r. the (door)bell** sonner (à la porte); **that rings a bell** *Fam* ça me rappelle quelque chose. ● **ringing tone** *n* (*on phone*) sonnerie *f*.

ring back *vi* (*phone*) rappeler ▮ *vt* **to r. s.o. back** rappeler qn **to ring off** *vi* (*after phoning*) raccrocher **to ring out** *vi* (*of bell*) sonner; (*of sound*) retentir **to ring up** *vi* (*phone*) téléphoner ▮ *vt* **to r. s.o. up** téléphoner à qn.

rink [rɪŋk] *n* (*ice-skating*) patinoire *f*.

rinse [rɪns] *vt* rincer; **to r. one's hands** (*remove soap*) se rincer les mains; **to r. out** rincer ▮ *n* (*hair colouring*) shampooing *m* colorant; **to give sth a r.** rincer qch.

riot ['raɪət] *n* (*uprising*) émeute *f*; (*fighting*) bagarres *fpl*; **a r. of colour** *Fig* une orgie de couleurs; **to run r.** (*of crowd*) se déchaîner; **the r. police** = les CRS *mpl* ▮ *vi* (*rise up*) faire une émeute; (*fight*) se bagarrer. ● **—er**

n émeutier, -ière *mf*; (*vandal*) casseur *m*. ● **riotous** *a* (*crowd etc*) tapageur.

rip [rɪp] *vt* (**-pp-**) déchirer; **to r. off** (*button etc*) arracher; **to r. s.o. off** (*deceive*) *Fam* rouler qn; **to r. out** (*telephone etc*) arracher (**from** de); **to r. sth up** déchirer qch ‖ *vi* (*of fabric*) se déchirer ‖ *n* déchirure *f*; **it's a r.-off** *Fam* c'est du vol organisé.

ripe [raɪp] *a* (**-er, -est**) mûr; (*cheese*) fait. ● **ripen** *vti* mûrir.

ripple ['rɪp(ə)l] *n* (*on water*) ride *f*; (*of laughter*) *Fig* cascade *f* ‖ *vi* (*of water*) se rider.

rise [raɪz] *vi* (*pt* **rose**, *pp* **risen**) (*of temperature, balloon, price etc*) monter, s'élever; (*of hope*) grandir; (*of sun, curtain*) se lever; (*of dough*) lever; (*get up from chair or bed*) se lever; **to r. in price** augmenter de prix; **to r. to the surface** remonter à la surface; **to r. (up)** (*rebel*) se soulever (**against** contre); **to r. to power** accéder au pouvoir.
‖ *n* (*in price etc*) hausse *f* (**in** de); (*in river*) crue *f*; (*of leader*) *Fig* ascension *f*; (*of technology*) essor *m*; (*to power*) accession *f*; (*slope in ground*) montée *f*; **(pay) r.** augmentation *f* (de salaire); **to give r. to sth** donner lieu à qch. ● **rising** *n* (*of curtain*) lever *m*; (*revolt*) soulèvement *m* ‖ *a* (*sun*) levant; (*number*) croissant; **r. prices** la hausse des prix.

riser ['raɪzər] *n* **early r.** lève-tôt *mf inv*; **late r.** lève-tard *mf inv*.

risk [rɪsk] *n* risque *m* (**of doing** de faire, **in doing** à faire); **at r.** (*person*) en danger; (*job*) menacé; **at your own r.** à tes risques et périls ‖ *vt* (*one's life etc*) risquer; **she won't r. leaving** elle ne se risquera pas à partir; **let's r. it** risquons le coup. ● **risky** *a* (**-ier, -iest**) (*full of risks*) risqué.

rite [raɪt] *n* rite *m*; **the last rites** *Rel* les derniers sacrements *mpl*. ● **ritual** *a* & *n* rituel (*m*).

rival ['raɪv(ə)l] *a* (*company etc*) rival; (*forces, claim*) opposé ‖ *n* rival, -ale *mf* ‖ *vt* (**-ll-**, *Am* **-l-**) (*compete with*) rivaliser avec (**in** de); (*equal*) égaler (**in** en). ● **rivalry** *n* rivalité *f* (**between** entre).

river ['rɪvər] *n* (*small*) rivière *f*; (*flowing into sea*) fleuve *m*; **the R. Thames** la Tamise ‖ *a* (*port etc*) fluvial; **r. bank** rive *f*. ● **riverside** *a* & *n* **(by the) r.** au bord de l'eau.

riveting ['rɪvɪtɪŋ] *a* (*story etc*) fascinant.

Riviera [rɪvɪ'eərə] *n* **the (French) R.** la Côte d'Azur.

roach [rəʊtʃ] *n* (*cockroach*) *Am* cafard *m*.

road [rəʊd] *n* route *f* (**to** qui va à); (*small*) chemin *m*; (*in town*) rue *f*; (*roadway*) chaussée *f*; (*path*) *Fig* voie *f*, chemin *m*, route *f* (**to** de); **the Paris r.** la route de Paris; **across** *or* **over the r.** (*building etc*) en face; **by r.** par la route.
‖ *a* (*map, safety*) routier; (*accident*) de la route; **r. hog** *Fam* chauffard *m*; **to have r. sense** (*of child*) avoir conscience des dangers de la rue; **r. sign** panneau *m* (routier); **r. works** travaux *mpl*. ● **roadblock** *n* barrage *m* routier. ● **roadside** *a* & *n* **(by the) r.** au bord de la route. ● **roadway** *n* chaussée *f*. ● **roadworthy** *a* (*vehicle*) en état de marche.

roam [rəʊm] *vt* parcourir ‖ *vi* errer; **to r. (about) the streets** (*of child, dog*) traîner dans les rues.

roar [rɔːr] *vi* (*of lion, wind, engine*) rugir; (*of person*) hurler; (*of thunder*) gronder; **to r. with laughter** éclater de rire ‖ *vt* **to r. (out)** (*threat etc*) hurler ‖ *n* rugissement *m*; hurlement *m*; grondement *m*. ● **—ing** *a* **a r. fire** une belle flambée; **to do a r. trade** vendre beaucoup (**in** de).

roast [rəʊst] *vt* rôtir; (*coffee*) griller ‖ *vi* (*of meat*) rôtir ‖ *n* (*meat*) rôti *m* ‖ *a* (*chicken etc*) rôti; **r. beef** rosbif *m*.

rob [rɒb] *vt* (**-bb-**) (*person*) voler; (*bank*) attaquer; (*shop, house etc*) (*by breaking in*) cambrioler; **to r. s.o. of sth** voler qch à qn; (*deprive*) priver qn de qch. ● **robber** *n* voleur, -euse *mf*. ● **robbery** *n* vol *m*; **it's daylight r.!** c'est du vol organisé; **armed r.** vol *m* à main armée.

robe [rəʊb] *n* (*dressing gown*) robe *f* de chambre; (*of priest, judge*) robe *f*.

robin ['rɒbɪn] *n* (*bird*) rouge-gorge *m*.

robot ['rəʊbɒt] *n* robot *m*.

robust [rəʊ'bʌst] *a* robuste.

rock[1] [rɒk] **1** *vt* (*baby, boat*) bercer, balancer; (*branch*) balancer; (*violently*) secouer ‖ *vi* (*sway*) se balancer; (*of building*) trembler. **2** *n* *Mus* rock *m*. ● **—ing** *a* **r. chair/horse** fauteuil *m*/cheval *m* à bascule.

rock[2] [rɒk] *n* (*substance*) roche *f*; (*boulder, rock face*) rocher *m*; (*stone*) *Am* pierre *f*; **a stick of r.** (*sweet*) un bâton de sucre d'orge; **r. face** paroi *f* rocheuse; **on the rocks** (*whisky*) avec des glaçons; (*marriage*) en pleine débâcle. ● **r.-'bottom** *a* (*prices*) les plus bas. ● **r.-climbing** *n* varappe *f*.

rockery ['rɒkərɪ] *n* (*in garden*) rocaille *f*.

rocket ['rɒkɪt] *n* fusée *f* ‖ *vi* (*of prices*) *Fig* monter en flèche.

rocky ['rɒkɪ] *a* (**-ier, -iest**) (*road*) rocailleux.

rod [rɒd] *n* (*wooden*) baguette *f*; (*metal*) tige *f*; (*of curtain*) tringle *f*; (*for fishing*) canne *f* (à pêche).

rode [rəʊd] *pt of* **ride.**
rodent ['rəʊdənt] *n* (*animal*) rongeur *m*.
rodeo ['rəʊdɪəʊ, *Am* rəʊ'deɪəʊ] *n* (*pl* **-os**) *Am* rodéo *m*.
roe [rəʊ] *n* (*eggs*) œufs *mpl* de poisson.
rogue [rəʊg] *n* (*dishonest*) crapule *f*; (*mischievous*) coquin, -ine *mf*.
role [rəʊl] *n* rôle *m*.
roll [rəʊl] *n* (*of paper etc*) rouleau *m*; (*small bread loaf*) petit pain *m*; (*of fat*) bourrelet *m*; (*of drum, thunder*) roulement *m*; (*list*) liste *f*; **to have a r. call** faire l'appel.
▌*vi* (*of ball etc*) rouler; (*of person, animal*) se rouler; **to r. into a ball** (*of animal*) se rouler en boule; **r. on tonight!** *Fam* vivement ce soir!.
▌*vt* rouler (*qch, qn*).
roll down *vt* (*car window etc*) baisser; (*slope*) descendre (en roulant) **to roll in** *vi* (*flow in*) *Fam* affluer **to roll out** *vt* (*dough*) étaler **to roll over** *vi* (*many times*) se rouler; (*once*) se retourner ▌*vt* retourner **to roll up** *vt* (*map, cloth*) rouler; (*sleeve, trousers, Am pants*) retrousser ▌*vi* (*arrive*) *Fam* s'amener.
roller ['rəʊlər] *n* (*for hair, painting etc*) rouleau *m*; **r. coaster** (*at funfair*) montagnes *fpl* russes. •**roller-skate** *n* patin *m* à roulettes ▌*vi* faire du patin à roulettes.
rolling pin ['rəʊlɪŋpɪn] *n* rouleau *m* à pâtisserie.
ROM [rɒm] *n abbr* = **read-only memory.**
Roman ['rəʊmən] **1** *a* & *n* romain, -aine (*mf*). **2 R. Catholic** *a* & *n* catholique (*mf*).
romance [rəʊ'mæns] *n* (*love*) amour *m*; (*affair*) aventure *f* amoureuse; (*story*) histoire *f* d'amour; (*charm*) poésie *f*. •**romantic** *a* (*of love, tenderness etc*) romantique ▌*n* (*person*) romantique *mf*.
Romania [rəʊ'meɪnɪə] *n* Roumanie *f*. •**Romanian** *a* & *n* roumain, -aine *mf* ▌*n* (*language*) roumain *m*.
romp [rɒmp] *vi* s'ébattre (bruyamment); **to r. through an exam** avoir un examen les doigts dans le nez.
rompers ['rɒmpəz] *npl* (*for baby*) barboteuse *f*.
roof [ru:f] *n* toit *m*; (*of tunnel, cave*) plafond *m*; **r. of the mouth** voûte *f* du palais; **r. rack** (*of car*) galerie *f*. •**rooftop** *n* toit *m*.
rook [rʊk] *n* **1** (*bird*) corneille *f*. **2** *Chess* tour *f*.
room [ru:m, rʊm] *n* **1** (*in house etc*) pièce *f*; (*bedroom*) chambre *f*; (*large, public*) salle *f*; **men's r., ladies' r.** *Am* toilettes *fpl*. **2** (*space*) place *f* (**for** pour); **(some) r.** de la place. •**roommate** *n* camarade *mf* de chambre. •**roomy** *a* (**-ier, -iest**) spacieux; (*clothes*) ample.
roost [ru:st] *vi* (*of bird*) se percher.
rooster ['ru:stər] *n* coq *m*.
root [ru:t] **1** *n* (*of plant etc*) & *Math* racine *f*; (*origin*) *Fig* origine *f*; **to take r.** (*of plant, person*) prendre racine; **to put down (new) roots** *Fig* s'enraciner; **r. cause** cause *f* première ▌*vt* **to r. out** (*destroy*) extirper. **2** *vi* **to r. for** (*cheer, support*) *Fam* encourager. •**rooted** *a* **deeply r.** bien enraciné (**in** dans).
rope [rəʊp] *n* corde *f*; *Nau* cordage *m*; **to know the ropes** *Fam* être au courant ▌*vt* **to r. s.o. in** *Fam* embrigader qn (**to do** pour faire); **to r. off** (*of police etc*) interdire l'accès de.
rop(e)y ['rəʊpɪ] *a* (**-ier, -iest**) *Fam* (*thing*) minable; (*person*) patraque.
rosary ['rəʊzərɪ] *n Rel* chapelet *m*.
rose[1] [rəʊz] *n* (*flower*) rose *f*; (*colour*) rose *m*; **r. bush** rosier *m*.
rose[2] [rəʊz] *pt of* **rise.**
rosé ['rəʊzeɪ] *n* (*wine*) rosé *m*.
rosemary ['rəʊzmərɪ] *n Bot Culin* romarin *m*.
roster ['rɒstər] *n* **(duty) r.** liste *f* (de service).
rostrum ['rɒstrəm] *n* tribune *f*; *Sp* podium *m*.
rosy ['rəʊzɪ] *a* (**-ier, -iest**) (*pink*) rose; (*future*) *Fig* tout en rose.
rot [rɒt] *n* pourriture *f*; (*nonsense*) *Fam* inepties *fpl* ▌*vti* (**-tt-**) **to r. (away)** pourrir.
rota ['rəʊtə] *n* liste *f* (de service).
rotary ['rəʊtərɪ] *a* rotatif ▌*n* (*for traffic*) *Am* sens *m* giratoire.
rotate [rəʊ'teɪt] *vi* tourner ▌*vt* faire tourner.
rote [rəʊt] *n* **by r.** machinalement.
rotten ['rɒt(ə)n] *a* (*fruit, weather etc*) pourri; (*bad*) *Fam* moche; (*corrupt*) pourri; **to feel r.** (*ill*) être mal fichu. •**rotting** *a* (*meat, fruit etc*) qui pourrit.
rough[1] [rʌf] *a* (**-er, -est**) (*surface*) rugueux, rude; (*plank, bark*) rugueux; (*ground*) inégal, (*manners, voice, task*) rude; (*coarse*) grossier; (*brutal*) brutal; (*neighbourhood*) mauvais; (*sea*) agité; **a r. child** (*unruly*) un enfant dur; **to feel r.** (*ill*) *Fam* être mal fichu; **r. and ready** (*conditions etc*) grossier (mais adéquat).
▌*adv* (*to sleep, live*) à la dure; (*to play*) brutalement.
▌*vi* **to r. up** (*hair*) ébouriffer; (*person*) *Fam* malmener. •**roughen** *vt* rendre rude. •**roughly**[1] *adv* (*not gently*) rudement; (*coarsely*) grossièrement; (*brutally*) brutalement.
rough[2] [rʌf] *a* (**-er, -est**) (*calculation, figure*

etc) approximatif; **r. guess,** approximation *f*; **r. book** cahier *m* de brouillon; **r. copy, r. draft** brouillon *m*; **r. paper** du papier brouillon ▮ *vt* **to r. out** (*plan*) ébaucher. •**—ly²** *adv* (*approximately*) à peu (de choses) près.

roughage ['rʌfɪdʒ] *n* (*in food*) fibres *fpl* (alimentaires).

roulette [ruː'let] *n* roulette *f*.

round [raʊnd] **1** *adv* autour; **all r., right r.** tout autour; **to go r. to s.o.'s** passer chez qn; **to ask r.** inviter chez soi; **r. here** par ici; **the long way r.** le chemin le plus long. ▮ *prep* autour de; **r. about** (*approximately*) environ; **r. (about) midday** vers midi; **to go r. a corner** tourner un coin.
2 *a* (**-er, -est**) rond; **r. trip** *Am* aller (et) retour *m*.
3 *n* (*slice*) tranche *f*; (*sandwich*) sandwich *m*; *Sp Pol* manche *f*; (*of golf*) partie *f*; *Boxing* round *m*; (*of talks*) série *f*; (*of drinks*) tournée *f*; **to be on one's round(s)** (*of milkman*) faire sa tournée; (*of doctor*) faire ses visites; (*of policeman*) faire sa ronde; **delivery r.** livraisons *fpl*, tournée *f*; **r. of applause** salve *f* d'applaudissements. ▮ *vt* **to r. off** (*meal, speech etc*) terminer (**with** par); **to r. up** (*gather*) rassembler; (*price*) arrondir au chiffre supérieur. • **r.-'shouldered** *a* voûté. • **rounded** *a* arrondi.

roundabout ['raʊndəbaʊt] **1** *a* indirect, détourné. **2** *n* (*at funfair*) manège *m*; (*road junction*) rond-point *m* (à sens giratoire).

rounders ['raʊndəz] *npl Sp sorte de baseball.*

roundup ['raʊndʌp] *n* (*of criminals*) rafle *f*.

rous/e [raʊz] *vt* éveiller; **roused (to anger)** en colère; **to r. to action** inciter à agir. •**—ing** *a* (*welcome*) enthousiaste.

rout [raʊt] *n* (*defeat*) déroute *f* ▮ *vt* mettre en déroute.

route 1 [ruːt] *n* itinéraire *m*; (*of ship, aircraft*) route *f*; **bus r.** ligne *f* d'autobus. **2** [raʊt] *n* (*delivery round*) *Am* tournée *f*.

routine [ruː'tiːn] **1** *n* routine *f*; **one's daily r.** (*in office*) son travail journalier; **the daily r.** (*monotony*) le train-train quotidien ▮ *a* (*inquiry, work etc*) de routine. **2** *n* (*on stage*) numéro *m*.

rove [rəʊv] *vi* errer ▮ *vt* parcourir.

row¹ [rəʊ] **1** *n* (*line*) rang *m*, rangée *f*; (*one behind another*) file *f*; **two days in a r.** deux jours de suite. **2** *vi* (*in boat*) ramer ▮ *vt* (*boat*) faire aller à la rame; **r. boat** *Am* bateau *m* à rames. •**—ing** *n* canotage *m*; *Sp* aviron *m*; **r. boat** bateau *m* à rames.

row² [raʊ] *n Fam* (*noise*) vacarme *m*; (*quarrel*) dispute *f* ▮ *vi Fam* se disputer (**with** avec).

rowdy ['raʊdɪ] *a* (**-ier, -iest**) chahuteur (et brutal).

royal ['rɔɪəl] *a* royal; **Royal Air Force** armée *f* de l'air (britannique) ▮ *npl* **the royals** *Fam* la famille royale. • **royalty 1** *n* (*persons*) personnages *mpl* royaux. **2** *npl* (*from book*) droits *mpl* d'auteur; (*from invention*) royalties *fpl*.

rpm [ɑːpiː'em] *abbr* (*revolutions per minute*) *Aut* tours/minute *mpl*.

rub [rʌb] *vt* (**-bb-**) frotter; (*person*) frictionner; **to r. shoulders with** *Fig* côtoyer ▮ *vi* frotter ▮ *n* (*massage*) friction *f*; **to give sth a r.** frotter qch. • **rubbing alcohol** *n Am* alcool *m* à 90°.

rub away *vt* (*mark*) effacer **to rub down** *vt* (*person*) frictionner; (*with sandpaper*) poncer (*qch*) **to rub in** *vt* (*cream*) faire pénétrer (en massant); **to r. it in** *Pej Fam* retourner le couteau dans la plaie **to rub off** *vt* (*mask*) effacer ▮ *vi* (*of mark*) partir; (*of manners*) *Fig* déteindre (**on s.o.** sur qn) **to rub out** *vt* (*mark*) effacer.

rubber ['rʌbər] *n* caoutchouc *m*; (*eraser*) gomme *f*; (*for blackboard*) brosse *f*; (*contraceptive*) *Am Sl* capote *f*; **r. stamp** tampon *m*.

rubbish ['rʌbɪʃ] **1** *n* (*waste*) ordures *fpl*; (*junk*) saletés *fpl*; (*nonsense*) *Fig* idioties *fpl*; **that's r.** (*absurd*) c'est absurde; (*worthless*) ça ne vaut rien; **r. bin** poubelle *f*; **r. dump** décharge *f* (publique); (*untidy place*) dépotoir *m*. **2** *vt* **to r. s.o./sth** (*criticize*) *Fam* dénigrer qn/qch. • **rubbishy** *a* (*book, film etc*) nul; (*goods*) de mauvaise qualité.

rubble ['rʌb(ə)l] *n* décombres *mpl*.

ruby ['ruːbɪ] *n* (*gem*) rubis *m*.

rucksack ['rʌksæk] *n* sac *m* à dos.

rudder ['rʌdər] *n* gouvernail *m*.

ruddy [rʌdɪ] *a* (**-ier, -iest**) **1** (*complexion*) coloré. **2** (*bloody*) *Sl* fichu.

rude [ruːd] *a* (**-er, -est**) (*impolite*) impoli (**to** envers); (*coarse, insolent*) grossier (**to** envers); (*indecent*) obscène. •**—ness** *n* impolitesse *f*; grossièreté *f*.

rudiments ['ruːdɪmənts] *npl* rudiments *mpl*.

ruffian ['rʌfɪən] *n* voyou *m*.

ruffle ['rʌf(ə)l] *vt* (*hair*) ébouriffer; **to r. s.o.** (*offend*) froisser qn.

rug [rʌg] *n* carpette *f*; (*over knees*) plaid *m*; **(bedside) r.** descente *f* de lit.

rugby ['rʌgbɪ] *n* **r. (football)** rugby *m*.

rugged ['rʌgɪd] *a* (*surface*) rugueux, rude; (*terrain*) accidenté; (*person, features*) rude.

ruin ['ru:ɪn] *n* (*destruction, building etc*) ruine *f*; **in ruins** (*building*) en ruine ‖ *vt* (*health, country, person*) ruiner; (*clothes*) abîmer; (*effect, meal, party*) gâter. • **ruinous** *a* ruineux.

rule [ru:l] **1** *n* (*principle*) règle *f*; (*regulation*) règlement *m*; (*custom*) coutume *f*; (*authority*) autorité *f*; *Pol* gouvernement *m*; **against the rules** *or Am* **rule** contraire au règlement; **as a r.** en règle générale.
‖ *vt* (*country*) gouverner; (*decide*) *Jur Sp* décider (**that** que); **to r. s.o.** (*dominate*) mener qn; **to r. out** (*exclude*) exclure.
‖ *vi* (*of king etc*) régner (**over** sur); (*of judge*) statuer (**on** sur).
2 *n* (*for measuring*) règle *f*. • **ruling** *a* (*class*) dirigeant; (*party*) *Pol* au pouvoir ‖ *n Jur Sp* décision *f*.

ruler ['ru:lər] *n* **1** (*for measuring*) règle *f*. **2** (*king, queen etc*) souverain, -aine *mf*; *Pol* dirigeant, -ante *mf*.

rum [rʌm] *n* rhum *m*.

Rumania [ru:'meɪnɪə] *see* **Romania.**

rumble ['rʌmb(ə)l] *vi* (*of train, thunder*) gronder; (*of stomach*) gargouiller.

rummage ['rʌmɪdʒ] *vi* **to r. (about)** farfouiller; **r. sale** (*used clothes etc*) *Am* vente *f* de charité.

rumour ['ru:mər] (*Am* **rumor**) *n* bruit *m*, rumeur *f*. • **rumoured** *a* **it is r. that** on dit que.

rump [rʌmp] *n* (*of horse*) croupe *f*; **r. steak** rumsteck *m*.

rumple ['rʌmp(ə)l] *vt* (*clothes*) chiffonner.

run [rʌn] *n* (*series*) série *f*; (*period*) période *f*; (*running*) course *f*; (*outing*) tour *m*; (*journey*) parcours *m*; (*rush*) ruée *f* (**on** sur); (*for skiing*) piste *f*; (*in cricket, baseball*) point *m*; (*in stocking*) maille *f* filée; **to go for a r.** (aller) faire une course à pied; (*in vehicle*) (aller) faire un tour; **on the r.** (*prisoner*) en fuite; **to have the r. of** (*house etc*) avoir à sa disposition; **in the long r.** à la longue.
‖ *vi* (*pt* **ran**, *pp* **run**, *pres p* **running**) courir; (*of river, nose, pen, tap or Am faucet*) couler; (*of colour in washing*) déteindre; (*of ink*) baver; (*of play, film*) se jouer; (*of contract*) être valide; (*last*) durer; (*pass*) passer; (*function*) marcher; (*idle*) *Aut* tourner; (*of stocking*) filer; **to r. down/in/***etc* descendre/entrer/*etc* en courant; **to r. for president** être candidat à la présidence; **to r. between** (*of bus*) faire le service entre; **to go running** *Sp* faire du jogging; **it runs into a hundred pounds** ça va chercher dans les cent livres; **it runs in the family** ça tient de famille.
‖ *vt* (*risk*) courir; (*marathon etc*) courir, prendre part à; (*temperature, errand*) faire; (*machine*) faire fonctionner; (*engine*) *Aut* faire tourner; (*drive*) *Aut* conduire; (*goods*) transporter (**to** à); (*business, country*) diriger; (*courses, events*) organiser; (*house*) tenir; (*computer program*) exécuter; (*article*) publier (**on** sur); (*bath*) faire couler; **to r. one's hand over** passer la main sur; **to r. its course** (*of illness etc*) suivre son cours; **to r. 5 km** *Sp* faire 5 km de course à pied; **to r. a car** avoir une voiture.

run about *or* **around** *vi* courir çà et là **to run across** *vt* (*meet*) tomber sur (qn) **to run along** *vi* **r. along!** filez! **to run away** *vi* s'enfuir, se sauver (**from** de) **to run down** *vt* (*pedestrian*) renverser; (*belittle*) *Fig* dénigrer; (*restrict*) limiter peu à peu. • **run-'down** *a* (*weak, tired*) à plat; (*district*) délabré **to run in** *vt* (*vehicle*) roder **to run into** *vt* (*meet*) tomber sur; (*crash into*) *Aut* percuter; **to r. into debt** s'endetter **to run off** *vi* (*flee*) s'enfuir (**with** avec) **to run out** *vi* (*of stocks*) s'épuiser; (*of lease*) expirer; (*of time*) manquer; **to r. out of** (*time, money*) manquer de; **we've r. out of coffee** on n'a plus de café ‖ *vt* **to r. s.o. out of** chasser qn de **to run over** *vi* (*of liquid*) déborder ‖ *vt* (*kill pedestrian*) écraser; (*knock down pedestrian*) renverser; (*notes, text*) revoir **to run round** *vt* (*surround*) entourer **to run through** *vt* (*recap*) revoir **to run up** *vt* (*debts, bill*) laisser s'accumuler.

runaway ['rʌnəweɪ] *n* fugitif, -ive *mf* ‖ *a* (*car, horse*) emballé; (*lorry, Am truck*) fou (*f* folle) (*inflation*) galopant.

rung[1] [rʌŋ] *n* (*of ladder*) barreau *m*.

rung[2] [rʌŋ] *pp of* **ring**[2].

runner ['rʌnər] *n Sp etc* coureur *m*; **r. bean** haricot *m* (grimpant). • **runner-'up** *n Sp* second, -onde *mf*.

running ['rʌnɪŋ] *n* (*on foot*) course *f*; (*of machine*) fonctionnement *m*; (*of business, country*) direction *f*; **to be out of the r.** ne plus être dans la course ‖ *a* (*commentary*) simultané; **r. water** eau *f* courante; **six days/***etc* **r.** six jours/*etc* de suite.

runny ['rʌnɪ] *a* (**-ier, -iest**) (*cream etc*) liquide; (*nose*) qui coule.

run-of-the-mill [rʌnəvðə'mɪl] *a* ordinaire.

runway ['rʌnweɪ] *n Av* piste *f* (d'envol).

rupture ['rʌptʃər] *n Med* hernie *f* ‖ *vt* rompre.

rural ['rʊərəl] *a* rural.

rush [rʌʃ] *vi* (*move fast*) se précipiter, se ruer (**at** sur, **towards** vers); (*of blood*) affluer (**to** à); (*hurry*) se dépêcher (**to do** de faire); **to r. out** partir en vitesse.
▮ *vt* **to r. s.o.** (*hurry*) bousculer qn; **to r. s.o. to hospital** *or Am* **to the hospital** transporter qn d'urgence à l'hôpital; **to r. (through) sth** (*job, meal etc*) faire, manger *etc* qch en vitesse; **to be rushed into** (*decision, answer etc*) être forcé à prendre, donner *etc*.
▮ *n* ruée *f* (**for** vers); (*confusion*) bousculade *f*; (*hurry*) hâte *f*; (*of orders*) avalanche *f*; **in a r.** pressé (**to do** de faire); **to leave in a r.** partir en vitesse; **the r. hour** l'heure *f* d'affluence; **a r. job** un travail d'urgence.

rushes ['rʌʃɪz] *npl* (*plants*) joncs *mpl*.

rusk [rʌsk] *n* biscotte *f*.

russet ['rʌsɪt] *a* brun roux *inv*.

Russia ['rʌʃə] *n* Russie *f*. ● **Russian** *a* & *n* russe (*mf*) ▮ *n* (*language*) russe *m*.

rust [rʌst] *n* rouille *f* ▮ *vi* (se) rouiller. ● **rustproof** *a* inoxydable. ● **rusty** *a* (**-ier, -iest**) (*metal, Fig memory etc*) rouillé.

rustic ['rʌstɪk] *a* rustique.

rustle ['rʌs(ə)l] **1** *vi* (*of leaves*) bruire. **2** *vt* **to r. up** *Fam* (*prepare*) préparer (*repas etc*).

rut [rʌt] *n* ornière *f*; **to be in a r.** *Fig* être encroûté.

ruthless ['ru:θləs] *a* (*attack, person etc*) impitoyable; (*in taking decisions*) très ferme. ● **—ly** *adv* (*mercilessly*) impitoyablement.

rye [raɪ] *n* seigle *m*; **r. bread** pain *m* de seigle.

S

S, s [es] *n* S, s *m*.
Sabbath ['sæbəθ] *n* (*Jewish*) sabbat *m*; (*Christian*) dimanche *m*.
sabotage ['sæbətɑːʒ] *n* sabotage *m* ▌*vt* saboter. ●**saboteur** [-'tɜːr] *n* saboteur, -euse *mf*.
saccharin ['sækərɪn] *n* saccharine *f*.
sachet ['sæʃeɪ] *n* (*of lavender etc*) sachet *m*; (*of shampoo*) dosette *f*.
sack [sæk] **1** *n* (*bag*) sac *m*. **2** *vt* (*dismiss*) *Fam* virer ▌*n Fam* **to get the s.** se faire virer; **to give s.o. the s.** virer qn. **3** *vt* (*town etc*) mettre à sac. ●**—ing** *n* **1** (*cloth*) toile *f* à sac. **2** (*dismissal*) *Fam* renvoi *m*.
sacrament ['sækrəmənt] *n Rel* sacrement *m*.
sacred ['seɪkrɪd] *a* (*holy*) sacré.
sacrifice ['sækrɪfaɪs] *n* sacrifice *m* ▌*vt* sacrifier (**to** à, pour).
sad [sæd] *a* (**sadder, saddest**) triste. ●**sadden** *vt* attrister. ●**sadly** *adv* tristement; (*unfortunately*) malheureusement; (*very*) (*inadequate etc*) très. ●**sadness** *n* tristesse *f*.
saddle ['sæd(ə)l] *n* selle *f* ▌*vt* (*horse*) seller; **to s. s.o. with sth/s.o.** (*debt, relative etc*) *Fam* coller qch/qn à qn. ●**saddlebag** *n* sacoche *f*.
sadistic [sə'dɪstɪk] *a* sadique.
sae [eseɪ'iː] *abbr* = **stamped addressed envelope.**
safari [sə'fɑːrɪ] *n* safari *m*; **to be** *or* **go on s.** faire un safari.
safe[1] [seɪf] *a* (**-er, -est**) (*person*) en sécurité; (*equipment, toy, animal*) sans danger; (*place, investment, method*) sûr; (*bridge, ladder*) solide; (*prudent*) prudent; **s. (and sound)** sain et sauf; **it's s. to go out** on peut sortir sans danger; **the safest thing is...** le plus sûr est de...; **s. from** à l'abri de; **to be on the s. side** pour plus de sûreté; **in s. hands** en mains sûres; **s. journey!** bon voyage! ●**safe'keeping** *n* **for s.** à garder en sécurité. ●**safely** *adv* (*without accident*) sans accident; (*without risk*) sans risque; (*in a safe place*) en lieu sûr.
safe[2] [seɪf] *n* (*for money etc*) coffre-fort *m*.
safeguard ['seɪfgɑːd] *n* sauvegarde *f* (**against** contre) ▌*vt* sauvegarder.
safety [seɪftɪ] *n* sécurité *f*; (*solidity*) solidité *f* ▌*a* (*belt, device, screen, margin*) de sécurité; (*pin, razor, chain, valve*) de sûreté; **s. precaution** mesure *f* de sécurité.
sag [sæg] *vi* (**-gg-**) (*of roof, ground*) s'affaisser; (*of breasts*) tomber; (*of cheeks*) pendre. ●**sagging** *a* (*roof, ground*) affaissé; (*breasts*) tombant.
saga ['sɑːgə] *n Liter* saga *f*; (*bad sequence of events*) *Fig* feuilleton *m*.
sage [seɪdʒ] *n* **1** *Bot Culin* sauge *f*. **2** (*wise man*) sage *m*.
Sagittarius [sædʒɪ'teərɪəs] *n* (*sign*) le Sagittaire.
Sahara [sə'hɑːrə] *n* **the S. (desert)** le Sahara.
said [sed] *pt & pp of* **say.**
sail [seɪl] *vi* (*navigate*) naviguer; (*leave*) partir; *Sp* faire de la voile; **to s. into port** entrer au port; **to s. round the world/an island** faire le tour du monde/d'une île en bateau; **to s. through** (*exam*) *Fig* passer haut la main.
▌*vt* (*boat*) piloter; (*seas*) parcourir.
▌*n* voile *f*; **to set s.** (*of boat*) partir (**for** à destination de). ●**—ing** *n* navigation *f*; *Sp* voile *f*; (*departure*) départ *m*; (*crossing*) traversée *f*; **s. boat** voilier *m*. ●**sailboard** *n* planche *f* (à voile). ●**sailboat** *n Am* voilier *m*.
sailor ['seɪlər] *n* marin *m*, matelot *m*.
saint [seɪnt] *n* saint *m*, sainte *f*.
sake [seɪk] *n* **for my/your/his/***etc* **s.** pour moi/toi/lui/*etc*; **(just) for the s. of eating/***etc* simplement pour manger/*etc*; **for heaven's** *or* **God's s.** pour l'amour de Dieu.
salad ['sæləd] *n* (*vegetables, fruit etc*) salade *f*; **s. bowl** saladier *m*; **s. cream** mayonnaise *f*; **s. dressing** sauce *f* de salade.
salami [sə'lɑːmɪ] *n* salami *m*.
salary ['sælərɪ] *n* (*professional*) traitement *m*; (*wage*) salaire *m*.
sale [seɪl] *n* vente *f*; **sale(s)** (*at reduced prices*) *Com* soldes *mpl*; **in a** *or* **the s.,** *Am* **on s.** (*cheaply*) en solde; **on s.** (*available*) en vente; **(up) for s.** à vendre; **to put up for s.** mettre en vente; **s. price** *Com* prix *m* de solde; ●**salesclerk** *n Am* vendeur, -euse *mf*. ●**salesman** *n* (*pl* **-men**) (*in shop*) vendeur *m*; **(travelling) s.,** *Am* **(traveling) s.** représentant *m* (de commerce). ●**saleswoman** *n* (*pl* **-women**) vendeuse *f*; (*who travels*) représentante *f* (de commerce).
saliva [sə'laɪvə] *n* salive *f*.

sallow ['sæləʊ] *a* (**-er, -est**) jaunâtre.
salmon ['sæmən] *n* saumon *m*.
salmonella [sælmə'nelə] *n* (*poisoning*) salmonellose *f*.
salon ['sælɒn] *n* **beauty/hairdressing s.** salon *m* de beauté/de coiffure.
saloon [sə'lu:n] *n* (*car*) berline *f*; (*on ship*) salon *m*; (*bar*) *Am* bar *m*; **s. bar** (*of pub*) salle *f* chic.
salt [sɔ:lt] *n* sel *m*; **bath salts** sels *mpl* de bain; **s. free** sans sel; **s. water** eau *f* salée ‖ *vt* saler. ● **saltcellar** *or Am* **saltshaker** *n* salière *f*. ● **salty** *a* (**-ier, -iest**) *a* salé.
salute [sə'lu:t] *n Mil* salut *m*; (*of guns*) salve *f* ‖ *vt* (*greet*) *Mil* saluer ‖ *vi Mil* faire un salut.
salvage ['sælvɪdʒ] *vt* (*save*) sauver (**from** de); (*iron etc to be used again*) récupérer ‖ *n* (*saved goods*) objets *mpl* sauvés (*d'un naufrage etc*); **s. operation/***etc* opération *f*/*etc* de sauvetage.
salvation [sæl'veɪʃ(ə)n] *n* salut *m*; **the S. Army** l'armeé *f* du Salut.
same [seɪm] *a* même; **the (very) s. house as** (exactement) la même maison que ‖ *pron* **the s.** le même, la même, *pl* les mêmes; **it's all the s. to me** ça m'est égal; **all** *or* **just the s.** tout de même; **to do the s.** en faire autant.
sample ['sɑ:mp(ə)l] *n* échantillon *m*; (*of blood*) prélèvement *m* ‖ *vt* (*wine, cheese etc*) goûter; (*product*) essayer; (*army life etc*) goûter de.
sanctify ['sæŋktɪfaɪ] *vt* sanctifier.
sanctimonious [sæŋktɪ'məʊnɪəs] *a* (*person, manner*) tartuffe.
sanction ['sæŋkʃ(ə)n] *n* (*approval, punishment*) sanction *f* ‖ *vt* (*approve*) sanctionner.
sanctuary ['sæŋktʃʊərɪ, *Am* -erɪ] *n Rel* sanctuaire *m*; (*refuge*) & *Pol* asile *m*; (*for animals*) réserve *f*.
sand [sænd] *n* sable *m* ‖ *vt* (*road*) sabler; **to s. (down)** (*wood etc*) poncer. ● **sandbag** *n* sac *m* de sable. ● **sandcastle** *n* château *m* de sable. ● **sandpaper** *n* papier *m* de verre ‖ *vt* (*wood*) poncer. ● **sandstone** *n* (*rock*) grès *m*.
sandal ['sænd(ə)l] *n* sandale *f*.
sandwich ['sænwɪdʒ] **1** *n* sandwich *m*; **cheese/***etc* **s.** sandwich au fromage/*etc*; **hero** *or* **submarine s.** *Am* gros sandwich *m* coupé dans une baguette; **s. bar** snack-bar *m* (*qui ne vend que des sandwichs*). **2** *vt* **to s. (in)** (*fit in*) intercaler; **sandwiched in between** (*caught*) coincé entre.
sandy ['sændɪ] *a* **1** (**-ier, -iest**) (*beach*) de sable; (*road, ground*) sablonneux. **2** (*hair*) blond roux *inv*.

sane [seɪn] *a* (**-er, -est**) (*person*) sain (d'esprit); (*idea, attitude*) raisonnable.
sang [sæŋ] *pt of* **sing**.
sanitary ['sænɪtərɪ, *Am* -erɪ] *a* (*fittings*) sanitaire; (*clean*) hygiénique; **s. towel** *or Am* **napkin** serviette *f* hygiénique. ● **sanitation** [-'teɪʃ(ə)n] *n* hygiène *f* (publique); (*plumbing*) installations *fpl* sanitaires.
sanity ['sænɪtɪ] *n* (*of person*) santé *f* mentale; (*reason*) raison *f*.
sank [sæŋk] *pt of* **sink²**.
Santa Claus ['sæntəklɔ:z] *n* le père Noël.
sap [sæp] **1** *n Bot* sève *f*. **2** *vt* (**-pp-**) (*weaken*) miner (*énergie etc*).
sapphire ['sæfaɪər] *n* (*jewel*) saphir *m*.
sarcastic [sɑ:'kæstɪk] *a* sarcastique.
sardine [sɑ:'di:n] *n* sardine *f*.
Sardinia [sɑ:'dɪnɪə] *n* Sardaigne *f*.
sash [sæʃ] *n* (*on dress*) ceinture *f*; (*of mayor etc*) écharpe *f*.
sat [sæt] *pt* & *pp of* **sit**.
Satan ['seɪt(ə)n] *n* Satan *m*.
satchel ['sætʃ(ə)l] *n* cartable *m*.
satellite ['sætəlaɪt] *n* satellite *m*; **s. (country)** pays *m* satellite; **s. dish** antenne *f* parabolique *or* satellite; **s. TV** télévision *f* par satellite.
satin ['sætɪn] *n* satin *m*.
satire ['sætaɪər] *n* satire *f* (**on** contre). ● **sa'tirical** *a* satirique. ● **satirize** *vt* faire la satire de.
satisfaction [sætɪs'fækʃ(ə)n] *n* satisfaction *f*. ● **satisfactory** *a* satisfaisant.
satisfy ['sætɪsfaɪ] *vt* satisfaire (*qn*); (*convince*) persuader (*qn*) (**that** que); (*demand, condition*) satisfaire à; **to s. oneself that** s'assurer que; **satisfied (with)** satisfait (de). ● **—ing** *a* satisfaisant; (*meal*) substantiel.
satsuma [sæt'su:mə] *n* (*fruit*) satsuma *f*.
saturate ['sætʃəreɪt] *vt* (*soak*) tremper; (*fill*) saturer (**with** de).
Saturday ['sætədɪ, -deɪ] *n* samedi *m*.
sauce [sɔ:s] *n* **1** sauce *f*; **tomato s.** sauce tomate. **2** (*impudence*) *Fam* toupet *m*. ● **saucy** *a* (**-ier, -iest**) (*impudent*) impertinent.
saucepan ['sɔ:spən] *n* casserole *f*.
saucer ['sɔ:sər] *n* soucoupe *f*.
Saudi Arabia [saʊdɪə'reɪbɪə, *Am* sɔ:dɪə'reɪbɪə] *n* Arabie *f* Séoudite.
sauna ['sɔ:nə] *n* sauna *m*.
sausage ['sɒsɪdʒ] *n* (*cooked, for cooking*) saucisse *f*; (*dried, for slicing*) saucisson *m*.
savage ['sævɪdʒ] *a* (*fierce*) féroce; (*brutal, cruel*) brutal, sauvage ‖ *n* (*brute*) sauvage *mf* ‖ *vt* (*of animal, critic etc*) attaquer (férocement).

save[1] [seɪv] *vt* (*rescue*) sauver (**from** de); (*keep*) garder; (*money, time*) économiser; *Comptr* sauvegarder; (*stamps*) collectionner; (*problems*) éviter; **to s. s.o. from doing** (*prevent*) empêcher qn de faire; **that will s. him** *or* **her (the bother of) going** ça lui évitera d'y aller; **to s. up** (*money*) économiser.

‖ *vi* **to s. (up)** faire des économies (**for sth, to buy sth** pour acheter qch).

‖ *n Fb* arrêt *m.* • **saving** *n* (*of time, money*) économie *f* (**of** de); (*thrifty habit*) l'épargne *f*; *pl* (*money*) économies *fpl*; **savings account** compte *m* d'épargne; **savings bank** caisse *f* d'épargne.

save[2] [seɪv] *prep* (*except*) sauf.

saveloy ['sævəlɔɪ] *n* cervelas *m.*

saviour ['seɪvjər] (*Am* **savior**) *n* sauveur *m.*

savour ['seɪvər] (*Am* **savor**) *vt* savourer. • **savoury** (*Am* **savory**) *a* (*not sweet*) *Culin* salé.

saw[1] [sɔː] *n* scie *f* ‖ *vt* (*pt* **sawed,** *pp* **sawn** *or* **sawed**) scier; **to s. off** scier; **a sawn-off** *or Am* **sawed-off shotgun** un fusil à canon scié. • **sawdust** *n* sciure *f.*

saw[2] [sɔː] *pt of* **see.**

saxophone ['sæksəfəʊn] *n* saxophone *m.*

say [seɪ] *vt* (*pt & pp* **said** [sed]) dire (**to** à, **that** que); (*of dial etc*) marquer; **to s. again** répéter; **what do you s. to a walk?** que dirais-tu d'une promenade?; **(let's) s. tomorrow** disons demain; **to s. nothing of...** sans parler de...; **that's to s.** c'est-à-dire.

‖ *vi* dire; **you don't s.!** *Fam* sans blague!; **s.!** *Am Fam* dis donc!; **that goes without saying** ça va sans dire.

‖ *n* **to have one's s.** dire ce que l'on a à dire; **to have no s.** ne pas avoir voix au chapitre (**in** pour). • **saying** *n* dicton *m*, proverbe *m.*

scab [skæb] *n* (*of wound*) croûte *f.*

scaffold ['skæfəld] *n* échafaudage *m*; (*gallows*) échafaud *m.* •**—ing** *n* échafaudage *m.*

scald [skɔːld] *vt* (*burn, cleanse*) ébouillanter ‖ *n* brûlure *f.*

scale [skeɪl] **1** *n* (*of map, wages etc*) échelle *f*; (*of numbers*) série *f*; *Mus* gamme *f*; **on a small/large s.** sur une petite/grande échelle; **s. model** modèle *m* réduit ‖ *vt* **to s. down** réduire (proportionnellement). **2** *n* (*on fish*) écaille *f* ‖ *vt* (*teeth*) détartrer. **3** *vt* (*wall*) escalader.

scales [skeɪlz] *npl* (*for weighing*) balance *f*; **(bathroom) s.** pèse-personne *m*; **(baby) s.** pèse-bébé *m.*

scallion ['skæljən] *n Am* oignon *m* vert.

scallop ['skɒləp] *n* coquille *f* Saint-Jacques.

scalp [skælp] *n Med* cuir *m* chevelu.

scalpel ['skælp(ə)l] *n* scalpel *m.*

scalper ['skælpər] n *Am* revendeur, -euse *mf* de billets.

scam [skæm] *n* (*swindle*) *Am Fam* escroquerie *f.*

scamper ['skæmpər] *vi* **to s. off** détaler.

scampi ['skæmpɪ] *npl* scampi *mpl.*

scan [skæn] **1** *vt* (**-nn-**) (*look at briefly*) parcourir (des yeux); (*scrutinize*) scruter; (*of radar*) balayer. **2** *n* **to have a s.** (*of pregnant woman*) passer une échographie.

scandal ['skænd(ə)l] *n* (*disgrace*) scandale *m*; (*gossip*) médisances *fpl*; **to cause a s.** (*of book etc*) causer un scandale; (*of conduct etc*) faire scandale. • **scandalize** *vt* scandaliser. • **scandalous** *a* scandaleux.

Scandinavia [skændɪ'neɪvɪə] *n* Scandinavie *f.* • **Scandinavian** *a & n* scandinave (*mf*).

scanner ['skænər] *n Med Comptr* scanner *m.*

scant [skænt] *a* (*meal, amount*) insuffisant; **s. attention/regard** peu d'attention/de cas. • **scanty** *a* (**-ier, -iest**) insuffisant; (*bikini etc*) minuscule.

scapegoat ['skeɪpgəʊt] *n* bouc *m* émissaire.

scar [skɑːr] *n* cicatrice *f* ‖ *vt* (**-rr-**) marquer d'une cicatrice; *Fig* marquer.

scarce [skeəs] *a* (**-er, -est**) (*food, book etc*) rare; • **scarcely** *adv* à peine. • **scarcity** *n* (*shortage*) pénurie *f.*

scare [skeər] *n* **to give s.o. a s.** faire peur à qn; **bomb s.** alerte *f* à la bombe ‖ *vt* faire peur à; **to s. off** (*person*) faire fuir; (*animal*) effaroucher. • **scared** *a* (*look, people*) effrayé; **to be s. (stiff)** avoir (très) peur. • **scarecrow** *n* épouvantail *m.*

scarf [skɑːf] *n* (*pl* **scarves** *or* **scarfs**) (*long*) écharpe *f*; (*square, for women*) foulard *m.*

scarlet ['skɑːlət] *a* écarlate; **s. fever** scarlatine *f.*

scary ['skeərɪ] *a* (**-ier, -iest**) **it's s.** *Fam* ça fait peur.

scathing ['skeɪðɪŋ] *a* (*remark*) acerbe; **to be s. about** critiquer de façon acerbe.

scatter ['skætər] *vt* (*disperse*) disperser (*foule, nuages etc*); (*throw or dot about*) éparpiller (*papiers etc*); (*spread*) répandre ‖ *vi* (*of crowd*) se disperser. •**—ing** *n* **a s. of houses/***etc* quelques maisons/*etc* dispersées. • **scatterbrain** *n* écervelé, -ée *mf.*

scaveng/e ['skævɪndʒ] *vi* fouiller dans les ordures (**for** pour trouver). •**—er** *n* clochard, -arde *mf* (qui fait les poubelles).

scenario [sɪ'nɑːrɪəʊ] *n* (*pl* **-os**) *Cin & Fig* scénario *m.*

scene [siːn] *n* (*setting, fuss*) & *Th* scène *f*;

(*of crime, accident*) lieu *m*; (*incident*) incident *m*; (*view*) vue *f*; **behind the scenes** *Th* dans les coulisses; **on the s.** sur les lieux; **to make a s.** faire une scène (à qn). ● **scenery** *n* paysage *m*; *Th* décor(s) *m(pl)*. ● **scenic** *a* (*beauty*) pittoresque; (*route*) touristique.

scent [sent] *n* (*fragrance, perfume*) parfum *m*; (*animal's track*) piste *f* ▮ *vt* parfumer (**with** de); (*smell*) flairer.

sceptical [skeptɪk(ə)l] (*Am* **skeptical**) *a* sceptique.

schedule ['ʃedju:l, *Am* 'skedjʊl] *n* (*of work etc*) programme *m*; (*timetable*) horaire *m*; (*list*) liste *f*; **on s.** (*on time*) à l'heure; (*up to date*) à jour; **ahead of s.** en avance; **to be behind s.** avoir du retard; **according to s.** comme prévu.

▮ *vt* (*to plan*) prévoir; (*event*) fixer le programme de. ● **scheduled** *a* (*planned*) prévu; (*service, flight, train etc*) régulier; **she's s. to leave at 8** elle doit partir à 8 h.

schem/e [ski:m] *n* (*plan*) plan *m* (**to do** pour faire); (*dishonest trick*) combine *f*; (*arrangement*) arrangement *m*. ● **—ing** *a* intrigant ▮ *n Pej* machinations *fpl*. ● **schemer** *n* intrigant, -ante *mf*.

scholar ['skɒlər] *n* érudit, -ite *mf*; (*specialist*) spécialiste *mf*; (*grant holder*) boursier, -ière *mf*. ● **scholarly** *a* érudit. ● **scholarship** *n* érudition *f*; (*grant*) bourse *f* (d'études).

school [sku:l] *n* école *f*; (*teaching, lessons*) classe *f*; (*college*) *Am Fam* université *f*; (*within university*) institut *m*, département *m*; **in** *or* **at s.** à l'école; **secondary s.,** *Am* **high s.** collège *m*, lycée *m*; **public s.** école *f* privée; *Am* école publique; **s. of motoring** auto-école *f*; **summer s.** cours *mpl* d'été *or* de vacances.

▮ *a* (*year, book, equipment etc*) scolaire; (*hours*) de classe; **s. fees** frais *mpl* de scolarité; **s. yard** *Am* cour *f* (de récréation). ● **schooling** *n* (*learning*) instruction *f*; (*attendance*) scolarité *f*.

schoolboy ['sku:lbɔɪ] *n* écolier *m*. ● **schoolchildren** *npl* écoliers *mpl*. ● **schoolgirl** *n* écolière *f*. ● **school'leaver** *n* jeune *mf* qui a terminé ses études secondaires. ● **schoolmaster** *n* (*primary*) instituteur *m*; (*secondary*) professeur *m*. ● **schoolmate** *n* camarade *mf* de classe. ● **schoolmistress** *n* institutrice *f*; professeur *m*. ● **schoolteacher** *n* (*primary*) instituteur, -trice *mf*; (*secondary*) professeur *m*.

science ['saɪəns] *n* science *f*; **to study s.** étudier les sciences ▮ *a* (*subject*) scientifique; (*teacher*) de sciences; **s. fiction** science-fiction *f*. ● **scien'tific** *a* scientifique. ● **scientist** *n* scientifique *mf*.

scissors ['sɪzəz] *npl* ciseaux *mpl*; **a pair of s.** une paire de ciseaux.

sclerosis [sklɪ'rəʊsɪs] *n* **multiple s.** sclérose *f* en plaques.

scoff [skɒf] **1** *vi* **to s. at** (*scorn*) se moquer de. **2** *vti* (*eat*) *Fam* bouffer.

scold [skəʊld] *vt* gronder (**for doing** pour avoir fait).

scone [skəʊn, skɒn] *n* petit pain *m* au lait.

scoop [sku:p] *n* (*shovel*) pelle *f* (à main); *Culin* cuillère *f*; (*in newspaper*) exclusivité *f* ▮ *vt* (*prizes*) rafler; **to s. out** (*hollow out*) évider; **to s. up** ramasser (avec une pelle *or* une cuillère).

scoot [sku:t] *vi* (*rush, leave*) *Fam* filer.

scooter ['sku:tər] *n* (*child's*) trottinette *f*; (*motorcycle*) scooter *m*.

scope [skəʊp] *n* (*range*) étendue *f*; (*competence*) compétence(s) *f(pl)*; (*limits*) limites *fpl*; **s. for sth/for doing** (*opportunity*) des possibilités *fpl* de qch/de faire.

scorch [skɔ:tʃ] *vt* (*linen, grass etc*) roussir ▮ *n* **s. (mark)** brûlure *f* légère. ● **—ing** *a* (*day*) torride; (*sun, sand*) brûlant.

score¹ [skɔ:r] *n Sp* score *m*; *Cards* marque *f*; *Mus* partition *f*; (*of film*) musique *f*; **a s. to settle** *Fig* un compte à régler; **on that s.** à cet égard ▮ *vt* (*point, goal*) marquer; (*exam mark*) avoir; (*success*) remporter ▮ *vi* marquer un point *or* un but; (*count points*) marquer les points. ● **scoreboard** *n Sp* tableau *m* d'affichage.

score² [skɔ:r] *n* **a s. (of)** (*twenty*) une vingtaine (de); **scores of** *Fig* un grand nombre de.

scorn [skɔ:n] *vt* mépriser ▮ *n* mépris *m*. ● **scornful** *a* méprisant; **to be s. of** mépriser. ● **scornfully** *adv* avec mépris.

Scorpio ['skɔ:pɪəʊ] *n* (*sign*) le Scorpion.

scorpion ['skɔ:pɪən] *n* scorpion *m*.

Scot [skɒt] *n* Écossais, -aise *mf*. ● **Scotland** *n* Écosse *f*. ● **Scotsman** *n* (*pl* **-men**) Écossais *m*. ● **Scotswoman** *n* (*pl* **-women**) Écossaise *f*. ● **Scottish** *a* écossais.

scotch [skɒtʃ] **1** *a* **s. tape**® *Am* scotch® *m*. **2** *vt* (*rumour*) étouffer; (*attempt*) faire échouer.

Scotch [skɒtʃ] *n* (*whisky*) scotch *m*.

scot-free [skɒt'fri:] *adv* sans être puni.

scoundrel ['skaʊndr(ə)l] *n* vaurien *m*.

scour ['skaʊər] *vt* (*pan*) récurer; (*streets*) *Fig* parcourir (**for** à la recherche de). ● **—er** *n* tampon *m* à récurer.

scourge [skɜ:dʒ] *n* fléau *m*.

scout [skaʊt] **1** *n* (*soldier*) éclaireur *m*; **(boy)**

s. scout *m*; **girl s.** *Am* éclaireuse *f*; **s. camp** camp *m* scout. **2** *vi* **to s. round for** chercher.
scowl [skaʊl] *vi* se renfrogner; **to s. at s.o.** regarder qn d'un air mauvais.
scraggy ['skrægɪ] *a* (**-ier, -iest**) (*bony*) maigrichon (*f* -onne).
scram [skræm] *vi* (**-mm-**) *Fam* filer.
scramble ['skræmb(ə)l] **1** *vi* **to s. for** se ruer vers; **to s. up** (*climb*) grimper; **to s. through** traverser avec difficulté. **2** *vt* (*egg*) brouiller.
scrap [skræp] **1** *n* (*piece*) petit morceau *m* (of de); (*of information, news*) fragment *m*; *pl* (*food*) restes *mpl*; **s. paper** (papier *m*) brouillon *m*.
2 *n* (*metal*) ferraille *f*; **to sell for s.** vendre à la casse ‖ *a* (*yard, heap*) de ferraille; **s. dealer** marchand *m* de ferraille; **s. metal** ferraille *f*; **on the s. heap** *Fig* au rebut ‖ *vt* (**-pp-**) se débarrasser de; (*vehicle*) mettre à la ferraille; (*plan, idea*) *Fig* abandonner.
3 *n* (*fight*) *Fam* bagarre *f*. • **scrapbook** *n* album *m* (*pour collages etc*).
scrap/e [skreɪp] **1** *vt* racler, gratter; (*skin, knee etc*) érafler ‖ *vi* **to s. against** frotter contre ‖ *n* (*on skin*) éraflure *f*. **2** *n* **to get into a s.** *Fam* s'attirer des ennuis. • **—er** *n* racloir *m*.
scrape away *or* **off** *vt* (*mud etc*) racler **to scrape through** *vi* (*in exam*) réussir de justesse **to scrape together** *vt* (*money, people*) réunir (difficilement).
scratch [skrætʃ] *n* (*mark, injury*) éraflure *f*; (*on glass*) rayure *f*; **to start from s.** (re)partir de zéro; **it isn't up to s.** ce n'est pas au niveau.
‖ *vt* (*arm etc that itches*) gratter; (*skin, furniture etc*) érafler; (*glass*) rayer; (*with claw*) griffer; (*one's name*) graver (**on** sur).
‖ *vi* (*relieve an itch*) se gratter; (*of cat etc*) griffer; (*of pen*) gratter.
scrawl [skrɔːl] *vt* gribouiller ‖ *n* gribouillis *m*.
scrawny ['skrɔːnɪ] *a* (**-ier, -iest**) (*bony*) maigrichon (*f* -onne).
scream [skriːm] *vti* crier, hurler; **to s. at s.o.** crier après qn; **to s. with pain** hurler de douleur ‖ *n* cri *m* (perçant).
screech [skriːtʃ] *vi* crier, hurler; (*of tyres, Am tires*) crisser; (*of brakes*) hurler.
screen [skriːn] **1** *n* écran *m*; **(folding) s.** paravent *m*. **2** *vt* (*hide*) cacher (**from s.o.** à qn); (*protect*) protéger (**from** de); (*a film*) projeter; (*visitors, documents*) filtrer; (*for cancer etc*) faire subir un test de dépistage à (*qn*) (**for** pour). • **—ing** *n* (*of film*) projection *f*; (*selection*) tri *m*; *Med* (test *m* de) dépistage *m*. • **screenplay** *n* *Cin* scénario *m*.
screw [skruː] *n* vis *f* ‖ *vt* visser (**to** à); **to s. down** *or* **on** visser; **to s. off** dévisser; **to s. up** (*paper*) chiffonner; (*eyes*) plisser; (*mess up*) *Sl* gâcher. • **screwdriver** *n* tournevis *m*. • **screwy** *a* (**-ier, -iest**) (*idea, person*) farfelu.
scribble ['skrɪb(ə)l] *vti* griffonner ‖ *n* griffonnage *m*.
scrimmage ['skrɪmɪdʒ] *n* *Fb* *Am* mêlée *f*.
script [skrɪpt] *n* (*of film*) scénario *m*; (*of play*) texte *m*; (*in exam*) copie *f*; (*system of writing*) écriture *f*; (*handwriting*) script *m*.
Scripture(s) ['skrɪptʃə(z)] *n*(*pl*) Rel Écriture *f* (sainte), (Saintes) Écritures *fpl*.
scroll [skrəʊl] *n* rouleau *m* (de parchemin) ‖ *vi* *Comptr* défiler.
scroung/e [skraʊndʒ] *vt* (*meal*) se faire payer (**off s.o.** par qn); **to s. money off s.o.** taper qn ‖ *vi* vivre en parasite; **to s. around for** *Pej* chercher. • **—er** *n* parasite *m*.
scrub [skrʌb] **1** *vt* (**-bb-**) (*surface*) nettoyer (à la brosse); (*pan*) récurer; (*washing*) frotter; **scrubbing brush** brosse *f* dure ‖ *n* **to give sth a s.** = **to scrub sth**; **s. brush** *Am* brosse *f* dure. **2** *n* (*land*) broussailles *fpl*.
scruff [skrʌf] *n* **by the s. of the neck** par la peau du cou.
scruffy ['skrʌfɪ] *a* (**-ier, -iest**) (*untidy*) négligé; (*dirty*) malpropre.
scrum [skrʌm] *n* *Rugby* mêlée *f*.
scruple ['skruːp(ə)l] *n* scrupule *m*. • **scrupulous** *a* scrupuleux. • **scrupulously** *adv* (*completely*) (*clean, honest*) absolument.
scrutinize ['skruːtɪnaɪz] *vt* scruter. • **scrutiny** *n* examen *m* minutieux.
scuba diving ['skuːbədaɪvɪŋ] *n* la plongée sous-marine.
scuff [skʌf] *vt* **to s. (up)** (*scrape*) érafler.
scuffle ['skʌf(ə)l] *n* bagarre *f*.
sculpt [skʌlpt] *vti* sculpter. • **sculptor** *n* sculpteur *m*. • **sculpture** *n* (*art, object*) sculpture *f* ‖ *vti* sculpter.
scum [skʌm] *n* **1** (*on liquid*) écume *f*. **2** *Pej* (*people*) racaille *f*; **the s. of** (*society*) la lie de.
scurry ['skʌrɪ] *vi* (*rush*) se précipiter; **to s. off** décamper.
scuttle ['skʌt(ə)l] **1** *vt* (*ship*) saborder. **2** *vi* **to s. off** filer.
scythe [saɪð] *n* faux *f*.
sea [siː] *n* mer *f*; **(out) at s.** en mer; **by s.** par mer; **by** *or* **beside the s.** au bord de la mer; **to be all at s.** *Fig* nager complètement ‖ *a* (*level, breeze*) de la mer; (*water, fish*) de mer; (*air, salt*) marin; (*battle, power*) naval;

(*route*) maritime; **s. bed** fond *m* de la mer; **s. lion** otarie *f*.
seaboard ['si:bɔ:d] *n* littoral *m*. ●**seafood** *n* fruits *mpl* de mer. ●**seafront** *n* front *m* de mer. ●**seagull** *n* mouette *f*. ●**seaman** *n* (*pl* **-men**) marin *m*. ●**seaplane** *n* hydravion *m*. ●**seaport** *n* port *m* de mer. ●**seashell** *n* coquillage *m*. ●**seashore** *n* bord *m* de la mer. ●**seasick** *a* **to be s.** avoir le mal de mer. ●**seasickness** *n* mal *m* de mer. ●**seaside** *n* bord *m* de la mer. ●**seaweed** *n* algue(s) *f*(*pl*). ●**seaworthy** *a* (*ship*) en état de naviguer.
seal [si:l] **1** *n* (*animal*) phoque *m*. **2** *n* (*mark, design*) sceau *m*; (*of wax on document etc*) cachet *m* (de cire) ▮ *vt* (*document, container*) sceller; (*stick down*) cacheter (*enveloppe etc*); (*with putty*) boucher; **to s. off** (*of police, troops*) interdire l'accès de (*quartier, lieu*).
seam [si:m] *n* (*in cloth*) couture *f*; (*of coal etc*) veine *f*.
search [sɜ:tʃ] *n* recherche *f* (**for** de); (*of person, place*) fouille *f*; **in s. of** à la recherche de; **to do a s. for sth** *Comptr* rechercher qch; **s. party** équipe *f* de secours ▮ *vt* (*person, place*) fouiller (**for** pour trouver); **to s. (through) one's papers/***etc* **for sth** chercher qch dans ses papiers/*etc* ▮ *vi* chercher; **to s. for sth** chercher qch.
searchlight ['sɜ:tʃlaɪt] *n* projecteur *m*.
season ['si:z(ə)n] **1** *n* saison *f*; **the festive s.** la période des fêtes; **in (the) high s.** en pleine saison; **in the low s.** en basse saison; **a Truffaut s.** *Cin* un cycle Truffaut; **s. ticket** carte *f* d'abonnement. **2** *vt* (*food*) assaisonner; **highly seasoned** (*dish*) relevé. ●**—ing** *n* *Culin* assaisonnement *m*.
seasonal ['si:zən(ə)l] *a* saisonnier.
seasoned ['si:zənd] *a* (*worker etc*) expérimenté.
seat [si:t] *n* (*for sitting, centre*) & *Pol* siège *m*; (*on train, bus*) banquette *f*; *Cin Th* fauteuil *m*; (*place*) place *f*; (*of trousers, Am pants*) fond *m*; **to take** *or* **have a s.** s'asseoir; **s. belt** ceinture *f* de sécurité.
▮ *vt* (*at table*) placer (*qn*); (*on one's lap*) asseoir (*qn*); **the room seats 50** la salle a 50 places (assises); **be seated!** asseyez-vous! ●**seated** *a* (*sitting*) assis. ●**seating** *n* (*seats*) places *fpl* assises; **s. capacity** nombre *m* de places assises.
secluded [sɪ'klu:dɪd] *a* (*remote*) isolé. ●**seclusion** [-ʒ(ə)n] *n* solitude *f*.
second[1] ['sekənd] *a* deuxième, second; **every s. week** une semaine sur deux; **in s. (gear)** *Aut* en seconde; **to be s. in command** commander en second.
▮ *adv* **to come s.** *Sp* se classer deuxième; **the s. biggest** le deuxième en ordre de grandeur; **the s. richest country** le deuxième pays le plus riche.
▮ *n* (*person, object*) deuxième *mf*, second, -onde *mf*; *pl* (*goods*) articles *mpl* de second choix; **Louis the S.** Louis Deux.
▮ *vt* (*motion*) appuyer. ●**s.-'class** *a* (*ticket on train etc*) de seconde (classe); (*mail*) non urgent. ●**s.-'rate** *a* médiocre.
second[2] ['sekənd] *n* (*part of minute*) seconde *f*; **s. hand** (*of clock, watch*) trotteuse *f*.
second[3] [sɪ'kɒnd] *vt* (*employee*) détacher (**to** à).
secondary ['sekəndərɪ] *a* secondaire.
secondhand [sekənd'hænd] **1** *a* & *adv* (*not new*) d'occasion. **2** *a* (*report, news*) de seconde main.
secondly ['sekəndlɪ] *adv* deuxièmement.
secret ['si:krɪt] *a* secret ▮ *n* secret *m*; **in s.** en secret. ●**secrecy** *n* (*discretion, silence*) secret *m*; **in s.** en secret.
secretary ['sekrət(ə)rɪ] *n* secrétaire *mf*; **Foreign S.**, *Am* **S. of State** = ministre *m* des Affaires étrangères. ●**secre'tarial** *a* (*work, post*) de secrétaire; (*school*) de secrétariat.
secretive ['si:krətɪv] *a* (*person*) cachottier; (*organization*) qui a le goût du secret; **to be s. about** être très discret sur.
sect [sekt] *n* secte *f*.
section ['sekʃ(ə)n] *n* (*of town, country, book etc*) partie *f*; (*of road, wood etc*) section *f*; (*of machine, furniture*) élément *m*; (*department*) section *f*; (*in store*) rayon *m*; **the sports/***etc* **s.** (*of newspaper*) la page des sports/*etc* ▮ *vt* **to s. off** (*separate*) séparer.
sector ['sektər] *n* secteur *m*.
secular ['sekjʊlər] *a* (*teaching etc*) laïque; (*music, art*) profane.
secure [sɪ'kjʊər] **1** *a* (*person, valuables*) en sûreté, en sécurité; (*place*) sûr; (*solid, firm*) solide; (*door, window*) bien fermé; (*certain*) assuré; **s. from** à l'abri de; **(emotionally) s.** sécurisé ▮ *vt* (*fasten*) attacher; (*window etc*) bien fermer; (*success etc*) *Fig* assurer.
2 *vt* (*obtain*) procurer (**sth for s.o.** qch à qn); **to s. sth (for oneself)** se procurer qch. ●**securely** *adv* (*firmly*) solidement; (*safely*) en sûreté.
security [sɪ'kjʊərətɪ] *n* sécurité *f*; (*for loan, bail*) caution *f*; **s. guard** agent *m* de sécurité; (*transferring money*) convoyeur *m* de fonds.
sedan [sɪ'dæn] *n* (*saloon*) *Aut Am* berline *f*.
sedate [sɪ'deɪt] **1** *a* calme. **2** *vt* mettre sous

calmants. ● **sedation** [-ʃ(ə)n] *n* **under s.** sous calmants.

sedative ['sedətɪv] *n* calmant *m*.

sedentary ['sedəntərɪ] *a* sédentaire.

sediment ['sedɪmənt] *n* sédiment *m*.

sedition [sə'dɪʃ(ə)n] *n* sédition *f*.

seduce [sɪ'dju:s] *vt* séduire. ● **seduction** [sɪ'dʌkʃ(ə)n] *n* séduction *f*. ● **seductive** *a* (*person, offer*) séduisant.

see [si:] *vti* (*pt* **saw,** *pp* **seen**) voir; **we'll s.** on verra (bien); **I s.!** je vois!; **I saw him run(ning)** je l'ai vu courir; **to s. reason** entendre raison; **s. who it is** va voir qui c'est; **s. you (later)!** à tout à l'heure!; **s. you (soon)!** à bientôt!; **to s. that** (*take care that*) = **to s. to it that.**

see about *vt* (*deal with*) s'occuper de; (*consider*) songer à **to see off** *vt* accompagner (*qn*) (*à la gare etc*) **to see out** *vt* raccompagner (*qn*) **to see through** *vt* (*task*) mener à bonne fin; **to s. s.o. through** (*be enough for*) suffire à qn **to see to** *vt* (*deal with*) s'occuper de (*qch, qn*); (*mend*) réparer (*qch*); **to s. to it that** veiller à ce que (+ *sub*); (*check*) s'assurer que; **to s. s.o. to** (*accompany*) raccompagner qn à.

seed [si:d] *n* graine *f*; (*in grape*) pépin *m*; (*source*) *Fig* germe; **to go to s.** (*of lettuce etc*) monter en graine. ● **seedling** *n* (*plant*) semis *m*.

seedy ['si:dɪ] *a* (**-ier, -iest**) miteux.

seeing ['si:ɪŋ] *conj* **s. (that)** vu que.

seek [si:k] *vt* (*pt* & *pp* **sought**) chercher (**to do** à faire); (*ask for*) demander (**from** à); **to s. (after)** rechercher; **to s. out** aller trouver.

seem [si:m] *vi* sembler (**to do** faire); **it seems that...** (*impression*) il semble que... (+ *sub or indic*); (*rumour*) il paraît que...; **it seems to me that...** il me semble que...; **we s. to know each other** il me semble qu'on se connaît; **I can't s. to do it** je n'arrive pas à le faire. ● **—ingly** *adv* apparemment.

seemly ['si:mlɪ] *a* convenable.

seen [si:n] *pp of* **see.**

seep [si:p] *vi* (*ooze*) suinter; **to s. into** s'infiltrer dans.

seesaw ['si:sɔ:] *n* (jeu *m* de) bascule *f*.

seethe [si:ð] *vi* **to s. with anger** bouillir de colère; **to s. with people** (*swarm*) grouiller de monde.

see-through ['si:θru:] *a* (*dress etc*) transparent.

segment ['segmənt] *n* segment *m*; (*of orange*) quartier *m*.

segregate ['segrɪgeɪt] *vt* séparer; **(racially) segregated** (*school*) où se pratique la ségrégation raciale. ● **segregation** [-'geɪʃ(ə)n] *n* ségrégation *f*.

seize [si:z] **1** *vt* saisir; (*power, land*) s'emparer de ‖ *vi* **to s. (up)on** (*offer etc*) saisir. **2** *vi* **to s. up** (*of engine*) (se) gripper.

seizure ['si:ʒər] *n Med* crise *f*; **s. of power** prise *f* de pouvoir.

seldom ['seldəm] *adv* rarement.

select [sɪ'lekt] *vt* choisir (**from** parmi); (*candidates, players etc*) sélectionner ‖ *a* (*chosen*) choisi; (*exclusive*) sélect, chic *inv*. ● **selection** [-ʃ(ə)n] *n* sélection *f*. ● **selective** *a* (*memory etc*) sélectif; **to be s.** (*of person*) opérer un choix; (*choosey*) être difficile (**about sth** sur qch).

self [self] *n* (*pl* **selves**) **he's back to his old s.** *Fam* il est redevenu lui-même. ● **s.-a'ssurance** *n* assurance *f*. ● **s.-a'ssured** *a* sûr de soi. ● **s.-'catering** *a* où l'on fait la cuisine soi-même. ● **s.-con'fessed** *a* (*liar etc*) de son propre aveu. ● **s.-'confidence** *n* assurance *f*. ● **s.-'confident** *a* sûr de soi. ● **s.-'conscious** *a* gêné. ● **s.-con'tained** *a* (*flat, Am apartment*) indépendant. ● **s.-con'trol** *n* maîtrise *f* de soi. ● **s.-de'fence** (*Am* **-defense**) *n Jur* légitime défense *f*. ● **s.-'discipline** *n* autodiscipline *f*. ● **s.-em'ployed** *a* qui travaille à son compte. ● **s.-es'teem** *n* amour-propre *m*. ● **s.-'evident** *a* évident, qui va de soi. ● **s.-ex'planatory** *a* qui tombe sous le sens. ● **s.-'governing** *a* autonome. ● **s.-im'portant** *a* suffisant. ● **s.-in'dulgent** *a* qui ne se refuse rien. ● **s.-'interest** *n* intérêt *m* (personnel). ● **s.-'pity** *n* **to feel s.-pity** s'apitoyer sur son propre sort. ● **s.-'portrait** *n* autoportrait *m*. ● **s.-re'liant** *a* indépendant. ● **s.-re'spect** *n* amour-propre *m*. ● **s.-'righteous** *a* trop content de soi. ● **s.-'sacrifice** *n* abnégation *f*. ● **s.-'satisfied** *a* content de soi. ● **s.-'service** *n* & *a* libre-service (*m inv*). ● **s.-su'fficient** *a* indépendant. ● **s.-su'pporting** *a* financièrement indépendant.

selfish ['selfɪʃ] *a* égoïste; (*motive*) intéressé. ● **selfishness** *n* égoïsme *m*.

sell [sel] *vt* (*pt* & *pp* **sold**) vendre; (*idea etc*) *Fig* faire accepter; **she sold it to me for twenty pounds** elle me l'a vendu vingt livres; **to s. back** revendre; **to s. off** liquider; **to have** *or* **be sold out of sth** n'avoir plus de qch; **this book is sold out** ce livre est épuisé.

‖ *vi* (*of product*) se vendre; (*of idea etc*) *Fig* être accepté; **to s. up** vendre sa maison; *Com* vendre son affaire; **selling price** prix *m* de vente. ● **sell-by date** *n* (*on product*) date *f* limité de vente. ● **seller** *n* vendeur, -euse

mf. ● **sellout** *n* **it was a s.** *Th Cin* tous les billets ont été vendus.
sellotape® ['seləteɪp] *n* scotch® *m* ▮ *vt* scotcher.
semblance ['sembləns] *n* semblant *m.*
semen ['siːmən] *n* sperme *m.*
semester [sɪ'mestər] *n Univ* semestre *m.*
semi- ['semɪ] *pref* semi-, demi-. ● **semibreve** [-briːv] *n Mus* ronde *f.* ● **semicircle** *n* demi-cercle *m.* ● **semi'circular** *a* semi-circulaire. ● **semi'colon** *n* point-virgule *m.* ● **semi-de'tached** *a* **s. house** maison *f* jumelle. ● **semi'final** *n Sp* demi-finale *f.* ● **semi(trailer)** *n Am* semi-remorque *m.*
seminar ['semɪnɑːr] *n Univ* séminaire *m.*
semolina [semə'liːnə] *n* semoule *f.*
senate ['senɪt] *n Pol* sénat *m.* ● **senator** *n Pol* sénateur *m.*
send [send] *vt* (*pt* & *pp* **sent**) envoyer (**to** à); **to s. s.o. for sth/s.o.** envoyer qn chercher qch/qn; **to s. s.o. mad** rendre qn fou; **to s. s.o. packing** *Fam* envoyer promener qn. ● **—er** *n* expéditeur, -trice *mf*; **'return to s.'** 'retour à l'expéditeur'.
send away *vt* envoyer (**to** à); (*dismiss*) renvoyer ▮ *vi* **to s. away for sth** commander qch (par courrier) **to send back** *vt* renvoyer **to send for** *vt* (*doctor etc*) faire venir; (*by mail*) commander (par courrier) **to send in** *vt* (*form*) envoyer; (*person*) faire entrer **to send off** *vt* (*letter etc*) envoyer (**to** à) ▮ *vi* = **send away to send on** *vt* (*letter, luggage*) faire suivre **to send out** *vt* (*invitation etc*) envoyer; (*from room etc*) faire sortir (*qn*); **to s. out for** (*meal etc*) envoyer chercher **to send up** *vt* (*luggage etc*) faire monter; (*rocket, balloon*) lancer.
send-off ['sendɒf] *n* **to give s.o. a s.-off** *Fam* faire des adieux chaleureux à qn.
send-up ['sendʌp] *n Fam* parodie *f.*
senile ['siːnaɪl] *a* gâteux, sénile.
senior ['siːnɪər] *a* (*older*) plus âgé; (*position, rank, executive*) supérieur; (*teacher, partner*) principal; **to be s.o.'s s.** être plus âgé que qn; (*in rank, status*) être au-dessus de qn; **Brown s.** Brown père; **s. citizen** personne *f* âgée; **s. year** *Sch Univ Am* dernière année *f.*
▮ *n* aîné, -ée *mf*; *Sch* grand, grande *mf*; *Sch Univ Am* étudiant, -ante *mf* de dernière année; *Sp* senior *mf.* ● **seni'ority** *n* (*in service*) ancienneté *f*; (*in rank*) supériorité *f.*
sensation [sen'seɪʃ(ə)n] *n* sensation *f.* ● **sensational** *a* (*event*) qui fait sensation; (*terrific*) *Fam* sensationnel.
sense [sens] *n* (*faculty, awareness, meaning*) sens *m*; **s. of smell** odorat *m*; **a s. of** (*shame etc*) un sentiment de; **a s. of warmth/pleasure** une sensation de chaleur/plaisir; **a s. of direction** le sens de l'orientation; **to have a s. of humour** avoir de l'humour; **to have (good) s.** avoir du bon sens; **to have the s. to do** avoir l'intelligence de faire; **to make s.** (*of story etc*) avoir un sens, tenir debout; **to make s. of** comprendre.
▮ *vt* sentir (intuitivement) (**that** que).
senseless ['sensləs] *a* (*stupid, meaningless*) insensé.
sensibility [sensɪ'bɪlətɪ] *n* sensibilité *f*; *pl* (*touchiness*) susceptibilité *f.*
sensible ['sensəb(ə)l] *a* (*wise*) raisonnable; (*clothes, shoes*) pratique.
sensitive ['sensɪtɪv] *a* (*responsive, painful*) sensible; (*delicate*) (*skin, question*) délicat; (*touchy*) susceptible (**about** à propos de); **s. to** (*the cold etc*) sensible à. ● **sensi'tivity** *n* sensibilité *f*; (*touchiness*) susceptibilité *f.*
sensual ['senʃʊəl] *a* (*bodily, sexual*) sensuel. ● **sensuous** *a* (*pleasing, refined*) sensuel.
sent [sent] *pt* & *pp of* **send.**
sentence ['sentəns] **1** *n Gram* phrase *f.* **2** *n* (*punishment, in prison*) peine *f*; (*conviction*) condamnation *f*; **to pass s.** prononcer une condamnation (**on s.o.** contre qn) ▮ *vt* **to s. s.o. to 3 years** condamner qn à 3 ans de prison.
sentiment ['sentɪmənt] *n* sentiment *m.* ● **senti'mental** *a* sentimental.
sentry ['sentrɪ] *n* sentinelle *f.*
separate ['sepərət] *a* (*distinct*) séparé; (*independent*) indépendant; (*different*) différent ▮ ['sepəreɪt] *vt* séparer (**from** de) ▮ *vi* se séparer (**from** de). ● **'separately** *adv* séparément. ● **separation** [sepə'reɪʃ(ə)n] *n* séparation *f.*
September [sep'tembər] *n* septembre *m.*
septic ['septɪk] *a* (*wound*) infecté; **to turn s.** s'infecter.
sequel ['siːkw(ə)l] *n* suite *f.*
sequence ['siːkwəns] *n* (*order*) ordre *m*; (*series*) succession *f*; *Mus Cards* séquence *f*; **film s.** séquence de film; **in s.** dans l'ordre.
sequin ['siːkwɪn] *n* paillette *f.*
Serbia ['sɜːbɪə] *n* Serbie *f.*
serene [sə'riːn] *a* serein.
sergeant ['sɑːdʒənt] *n Mil* sergent *m*; (*in police force*) brigadier *m.*
serial ['sɪərɪəl] *n* (*story, film*) feuilleton *m*; **s. number** (*on appliance etc*) numéro de série.
series ['sɪəriːz] *n inv* série *f*; (*book collection*) collection *f.*

serious ['sɪərɪəs] *a* sérieux; (*illness, mistake, tone*) grave, sérieux; (*damage*) important. ●**—ly** *adv* sérieusement; (*ill*) gravement; **to take s.** prendre au sérieux. ●**—ness** *n* sérieux *m*; (*of illness, situation etc*) gravité *f*.

sermon ['sɜːmən] *n* sermon *m*.

serpent ['sɜːpənt] *n* serpent *m*.

serrated [sə'reɪtɪd] *a* (*knife*) à dents (de scie).

servant ['sɜːvənt] *n* (*in house etc*) domestique *mf*; (*person who serves*) *Fig* serviteur *m*; **public s.** fonctionnaire *mf*.

serve [sɜːv] *vt* (*master, cause etc*) servir; (*at table, in shop etc*) servir (**to s.o.** à qn, **s.o. with sth** qch à qn); (*of train, bus etc*) desservir (*un village, quartier etc*); (*supply with electricity etc*) alimenter; (*apprenticeship*) faire; **to s. a sentence** (*in prison*) purger une peine; **it serves its purpose** ça fait l'affaire; **(it) serves you right!** *Fam* ça t'apprendra!; **to s. up** *or* **out** (*meal etc*) servir.
▮ *vi* servir (**as** de); **to s. on** (*committee*) être membre de; **to s. to show**/*etc* servir à montrer/*etc*.
▮ *n Tennis* service *m*.

service ['sɜːvɪs] *n* (*serving, help, dishes etc*) & *Mil Rel Tennis* service *m*; (*machine or vehicle repair*) révision *f*; **to be of s. to** être utile à; **the (armed) services** les forces *fpl* armées; **s. (charge)** (*in restaurant*) service *m*; **s. area** (*on motorway*) aire *f* de service; **s. station** station-service *f*.
▮ *vt* (*machine, vehicle*) réviser. ●**servicing** *n Aut* révision *f*.

serviceable ['sɜːvɪsəb(ə)l] *a* (*usable*) utilisable; (*useful*) commode.

serviceman ['sɜːvɪsmən] *n* (*pl* **-men**) *n* militaire *m*.

serviette [sɜːvɪ'et] *n* serviette *f* (de table).

serving ['sɜːvɪŋ] *n* (*of food*) portion *f*.

session ['seʃ(ə)n] *n* séance *f*; *Univ Am* semestre *m* universitaire.

set [set] **1** *n* (*of keys, needles, tools etc*) jeu *m*; (*of stamps, numbers*) série *f*; (*of people*) groupe *m*; *Math* ensemble *m*; (*of books*) collection *f*; (*of dishes*) service *m*; (*scenery*) *Th Cin* décor *m*; (*stage*) *Th Cin* plateau *m*; (*hairstyle*) mise *f* en plis; *Tennis* set *m*; **television** *or* **TV s.** téléviseur *m*; **chess s.** (*box*) jeu *m* d'échecs; **the skiing s.** le monde du ski.
2 *a* (*time, price etc*) fixe; (*lunch*) à prix fixe; (*school book etc*) au programme; (*speech*) préparé à l'avance; (*in one's habits*) régulier; (*situated*) situé; **s. phrase** expression *f* consacrée; **the s. menu** le plat du jour; **dead s. against** absolument opposé à; **s. on doing** résolu à faire; **to be s. on sth** vouloir qch à tout prix; **all s.** (*ready*) prêt (**to do** pour faire).
3 *vt* (*pt* & *pp* **set**, *pres p.* **setting**) (*put*) mettre, poser; (*date, limit etc*) fixer; (*record*) *Sp* établir; (*mechanism, clock*) régler; (*alarm clock*) mettre (**for** pour); (*arm etc in plaster*) plâtrer; (*task*) donner (**for s.o.** à qn); (*trap*) tendre; (*problem*) poser; (*diamond*) monter; (*precedent*) créer; **to have one's hair s.** se faire faire une mise en plis; **to s. loose** (*dog*) lâcher (**on** contre).
▮ *vi* (*of sun*) se coucher; (*of jelly, Am jello®*) prendre; (*of bone*) se ressouder.

set about *vt* (*begin*) se mettre à (*qch*); **to s. about doing sth** se mettre à faire qch **to set back** *vt* (*in time*) retarder (*qn*); (*cost*) *Fam* coûter (*à qn*) **to set down** *vt* (*object*) déposer **to set in** *vi* (*start*) commencer **to set off** *vt* (*bomb*) faire exploser; (*mechanism*) déclencher; (*beauty*) *Fig* rehausser; **to s. s.o. off crying**/*etc* faire pleurer/*etc* qn ▮ *vi* (*leave*) partir **to set out** *vt* (*display, explain*) exposer (**to** à); (*arrange*) disposer ▮ *vi* (*leave*) partir; **to s. out to do** entreprendre de faire **to set up** *vt* (*tent, statue*) dresser; (*table*) installer; (*business*) créer, monter; (*meeting*) organiser; (*government*) établir; (*inquiry*) ouvrir ▮ *vi* **to s. up in business** monter une affaire.

setback ['setbæk] *n* (*hitch*) revers *m*; *Med* rechute *f*.

setsquare ['setskweər] *n Math* équerre *f*.

settee [se'tiː] *n* canapé *m*.

setting ['setɪŋ] *n* (*surroundings*) cadre *m*; (*of sun*) coucher *m*.

settle ['set(ə)l] *vt* (*decide, arrange, pay*) régler; (*date*) fixer; (*place in position*) placer; (*person*) installer (*dans son lit etc*); (*nerves*) calmer; (*land*) coloniser; **let's s. things** arrangeons les choses; **that's (all) settled** c'est décidé *or* réglé.
▮ *vi* (*live*) s'installer; (*of dust*) se déposer; (*of bird*) se poser; (*of snow*) tenir; **to s. (down) into** (*armchair*) s'installer dans; (*job*) s'habituer à; **to s. (up) with s.o.** (*pay*) régler qn; **to s. down** (*in chair or house*) s'installer; (*calm down*) se calmer; (*in one's lifestyle*) se ranger; **to s. down to** (*get used to*) s'habituer à; (*work*) se mettre à; **to s. for** accepter; **to s. in** s'installer. ●**settled** *a* (*weather*) stable. ●**settlement** *n* (*agreement*) accord *m*; (*payment*) règlement *m*; (*colony*) colonie *f*. ●**settler** *n* colon *m*.

setup ['setʌp] *n Fam* situation *f*.

seven ['sev(ə)n] *a* & *n* sept (*m*). ●**se-ven'teen** *a* & *n* dix-sept (*m*). ●**seventh** *a* & *n* septième (*mf*). ●**seventieth** *a* & *n* soixante-dixième (*mf*). ●**seventy** *a* & *n* soixante-dix (*m*); **s.-one** soixante et onze.

sever ['sevər] *vt* sectionner, couper; (*relations*) *Fig* rompre.

several ['sev(ə)rəl] *a* & *pron* plusieurs (**of** d'entre).

severe [sə'vɪər] *a* (*tone, judge etc*) sévère; (*winter*) rigoureux; (*test*) dur; (*injury*) grave; (*blow, pain*) violent; (*cold, frost*) intense; **a s. cold** *Med* un gros rhume; **s. with s.o.** sévère envers qn. ●**severely** *adv* (*to punish*) sévèrement; (*damaged*) gravement; **to be s. handicapped** souffrir d'un handicap sévère.

sew [səʊ] *vti* (*pt* **sewed,** *pp* **sewn** [səʊn] *or* **sewed**) coudre; **to s. on** (*button*) (re)coudre; **to s. up** (*tear*) (re)coudre. ●**—ing** *n* couture *f*; **s. machine** machine *f* à coudre.

sewage ['suːɪdʒ] *n* eaux *fpl* d'égout. ●**sewer** ['suːər] *n* égout *m*.

sewn [səʊn] *pp of* **sew.**

sex [seks] *n* (*gender*) sexe *m*; (*activity*) relations *fpl* sexuelles; **the opposite s.** l'autre sexe; **to have s. with** coucher avec ‖ *a* (*education, life etc*) sexuel; **s. maniac** obsédé, -ée *mf* sexuel(le). ●**sexist** *a* & *n* sexiste (*mf*). ●**sexual** *a* sexuel. ●**sexy** *a* (**-ier, -iest**) (*book, clothes, person*) sexy *inv*; (*aroused*) qui a envie (de faire l'amour).

sextet [sek'stet] *n* sextuor *m*.

sh! [ʃ] *int* chut! [ʃyt].

shabby ['ʃæbɪ] *a* (**-ier, -iest**) (*room etc*) minable; (*person*) pauvrement vêtu; (*mean*) *Fig* mesquin.

shack [ʃæk] *n* cabane *f*.

shackles ['ʃæk(ə)lz] *npl* chaînes *fpl*.

shade [ʃeɪd] *n* ombre *f*; (*of colour*) ton *m*; (*of opinion, meaning*) nuance *f*; (*of lamp*) abat-jour *m inv*; **(window) s.** *Am* store *m*; **in the s.** à l'ombre; **a s. taller**/*etc* (*slightly*) un rien plus grand/*etc* ‖ *vt* (*of tree*) ombrager; **to s. in** (*drawing*) ombrer. ●**shady** *a* (**-ier, -iest**) (*place*) ombragé; (*person etc*) *Fig* louche.

shadow ['ʃædəʊ] **1** *n* ombre *f*. **2** *a* **s. cabinet** *Br Pol* cabinet *m* fantôme. **3** *vt* **to s. s.o.** (*follow*) filer qn. ●**shadowy** *a* (**-ier, -iest**) (*form etc*) obscur, vague.

shaft [ʃɑːft] *n* **1** (*of tool*) manche *m*; (*in machine*) arbre *m*; **s. of light** trait *m* de lumière. **2** (*of mine*) puits *m*; (*of lift, Am elevator*) cage *f*.

shaggy ['ʃægɪ] *a* (**-ier, -iest**) (*hair, beard*) broussailleux; (*dog*) à longs poils.

shake [ʃeɪk] *vt* (*pt* **shook,** *pp* **shaken**) secouer; (*bottle, fist*) agiter; (*belief etc*) *Fig* ébranler; (*upset*) bouleverser; **to s. the windows** (*of shock*) ébranler les vitres; **to s. one's head** (*say no*) secouer la tête; **to s. hands with** serrer la main à; **we shook hands** nous nous sommes serré la main; **to s. off** (*dust etc*) secouer; (*cough, pursuer*) *Fig* se débarrasser de; **to s. up** (*organization*) réorganiser; **to s. s.o. up** (*disturb, rouse to action*) secouer qn; **s. yourself out of it!** secoue-toi!
‖ *vi* trembler (**with** de).
‖ *n* secousse *f*; **to give sth a s.** secouer qch.
●**shake-up** *n Fig* (grande) réorganisation *f*.

shaky [ʃeɪkɪ] *a* (**-ier, -iest**) tremblant; (*ladder*) branlant; (*memory, health*) chancelant; (*on one's legs, in a language*) mal assuré.

shall [ʃæl, *unstressed* ʃəl] *v aux* **1** (*future*) **I s. come, I'll come** je viendrai; **we s. not come, we shan't come** nous ne viendrons pas. **2** (*question*) **s. I leave?** veux-tu que je parte?; **s. we leave?** on part? **3** (*order*) **he s. do it if I order it** il devra le faire si je l'ordonne.

shallow ['ʃæləʊ] *a* (**-er, -est**) (*water, river etc*) peu profond; *Fig Pej* superficiel.

sham [ʃæm] *n* (*pretence*) comédie *f*; (*person*) imposteur *m*; **it's a s.** c'est du bidon! ‖ *a* (*false*) faux (*f* fausse); (*emotion*) feint ‖ *vt* (**-mm-**) feindre.

shambles ['ʃæmb(ə)lz] *n* désordre *m*, pagaille *f*; **to be a s.** être en pagaille; **to make a s. of** (*room etc*) mettre en pagaille.

shame [ʃeɪm] *n* (*feeling, disgrace*) honte *f*; **it's a s.** c'est dommage (**to do** de faire); **it's a s. (that)** c'est dommage que (+ *sub*); **what a s.!** (quel) dommage!; **to put s.o. to s.** faire honte à qn ‖ *vt* (*disgrace*) faire honte à. ●**shameful** *a* honteux. ●**shameless** *a* (*brazen*) effronté; (*indecent*) impudique.

shammy ['ʃæmɪ] *n Fam* peau *f* de chamois.

shampoo [ʃæm'puː] *n* shampooing *m* ‖ *vt* (*carpet*) shampooiner; **to s. s.o.'s hair** faire un shampooing à qn.

shandy ['ʃændɪ] *n* (*beer*) panaché *m*.

shan't [ʃɑːnt] = **shall not.**

shanty[1] ['ʃæntɪ] *n* (*hut*) baraque *f*. ●**shantytown** *n* bidonville *f*.

shanty[2] ['ʃæntɪ] *n* **sea s.** chanson *f* de marins.

shape [ʃeɪp] *n* forme *f*; **in (good) s.** (*fit*) en (pleine) forme; **to be in good/bad s.** (*of vehicle, house etc*) être en bon/mauvais état; (*of business*) marcher bien/mal; **to take s.** (*of plan, book etc*) prendre forme;

(*progress well*) avancer; **in the s. of** en forme de.
▮ *vt* (*fashion*) façonner (**into** en); (*one's life*) *Fig* déterminer.
▮ *vi* **to s. up** (*of plans*) prendre (bonne) tournure; (*of pupil, wrongdoer*) s'y mettre. ● **-shaped** *suff* **pear-s.**/*etc* en forme de poire/*etc*. ● **shapeless** *a* informe. ● **shapely** *a* (**-ier, -iest**) (*woman, legs*) bien tourné.

share [ʃeər] *n* part *f* (**of, in** de); (*in company*) *Fin* action *f*; **to do one's (fair) s.** fournir sa part d'efforts; **stocks and shares** *Fin* valeurs *fpl* (boursières) ▮ *vt* (*meal, opinion etc*) partager (**with** avec); (*characteristic*) avoir en commun; **to s. sth out** partager *or* répartir qch (**among** entre) ▮ *vi* **to s. in sth** avoir sa part de qch. ● **shareholder** *n Fin* actionnaire *mf*.

shark [ʃɑːk] *n* (*fish*) requin *m*.

sharp [ʃɑːp] **1** *a* (**-er, -est**) (*knife, blade etc*) tranchant; (*pointed*) pointu; (*point, pain, voice*) aigu (*f* -uë); (*mind*) vif; (*bend*) brusque; (*taste*) piquant; (*words, wind, tone*) âpre; (*eyesight*) perçant; (*outline*) net (*f* nette); (*lawyer etc*) *Pej* peu scrupuleux; **s. practice** *Pej* procédé(s) *m(pl)* malhonnête(s).
▮ *adv* (*to stop*) net; **five o'clock**/*etc* **s.** cinq heures/*etc* pile; **s. right/left** tout de suite à droite/à gauche.
2 *n Mus* dièse *m*.

sharpen ['ʃɑːp(ə)n] *vt* (*knife*) aiguiser; (*pencil*) tailler. ● **—er** *n* (*for pencils*) taille-crayon(s) *m inv*.

sharply ['ʃɑːplɪ] *adv* (*suddenly*) brusquement; (*harshly*) vivement; (*clearly*) nettement.

shatter ['ʃætər] *vt* (*door, arm etc*) fracasser; (*glass*) faire voler en éclats; (*career, health*) briser; (*person, hopes*) anéantir ▮ *vi* (*smash*) se fracasser; (*of glass*) voler en éclats. ● **—ed** *a* (*exhausted*) anéanti. ● **—ing** *a* (*defeat*) accablant; (*experience*) bouleversant.

shav/e [ʃeɪv] *vt* (*person, head*) raser; **to s. off one's beard** se raser la barbe ▮ *vi* se raser ▮ *n* **to have a s.** se raser; **to have a close s.** *Fig* l'échapper belle. ● **—ing** *n* (*strip of wood*) copeau *m*; **s. brush** blaireau *m*; **s. cream, s. foam** crème *f* à raser. ● **shaver** *n* rasoir *m* électrique.

shawl [ʃɔːl] *n* châle *m*.

she [ʃiː] *pron* elle; **s. wants** elle veut; **she's a happy woman** c'est une femme heureuse ▮ *n Fam* femelle *f*; **it's a s.** (*baby*) c'est une fille.

sheaf [ʃiːf] *n* (*pl* **sheaves**) (*of corn*) gerbe *f*.

shear [ʃɪər] *vt* tondre ▮ *npl* **shears** cisaille(s) *f(pl)*; **pruning shears** sécateur *m*.

sheath [ʃiːθ] *n* (*pl* **-s** [shiːðz]) (*container*) fourreau *m*; (*contraceptive*) préservatif *m*.

shed [ʃed] **1** *n* (*in garden*) abri *m* (de jardin); (*for goods or machines*) hangar *m*. **2** *vt* (*pt* & *pp* **shed,** *pres p* **shedding**) (*lose*) perdre; (*tears, warmth*) répandre; (*get rid of*) se défaire de; **to s. light on** *Fig* éclairer.

she'd [ʃiːd] = **she had** & **she would**.

sheep [ʃiːp] *n inv* mouton *m*. ● **sheepdog** *n* chien *m* de berger. ● **sheepskin** *n* peau *f* de mouton.

sheepish ['ʃiːpɪʃ] *a* penaud. ● **—ly** *adv* d'un air penaud.

sheer [ʃɪər] **1** *a* (*luck, madness*) pur; (*impossibility*) absolu; **it's s. hard work** ça demande du travail; **by s. hard work** à force de travail. **2** *a* (*cliff*) à pic ▮ *adv* (*to rise*) à pic. **3** *a* (*fabric*) très fin.

sheet [ʃiːt] *n* (*on bed*) drap *m*; (*of paper etc*) feuille *f*; (*of glass, ice*) plaque *f*; (*dust cover*) housse *f*; (*canvas*) bâche *f*; **s. metal** tôle *f*.

sheikh [ʃeɪk] *n* scheik *m*, cheik *m*.

shelf [ʃelf] *n* (*pl* **shelves**) étagère *f*; (*in shop*) rayon *m*.

shell [ʃel] **1** *n* (*of egg etc*) coquille *f*; (*of tortoise*) carapace *f*; (*seashell*) coquillage *m*; (*of building*) carcasse *f* ▮ *vt* (*peas*) écosser; (*nut, shrimp*) décortiquer. **2** *n* (*explosive*) obus *m* ▮ *vt* (*town etc*) *Mil* bombarder. ● **shellfish** *npl* (*oysters etc*) fruits *mpl* de mer. ● **shell suit** *n* survêtement *m*.

she'll [ʃiːl] = **she will**.

shelter ['ʃeltər] *n* (*place, protection*) abri *m*; **to take s.** se mettre à l'abri (**from** de) ▮ *vt* abriter (**from** de); (*criminal*) protéger ▮ *vi* s'abriter. ● **—ed** *a* (*place*) abrité; (*life*) très protégé.

shelve [ʃelv] *vt* (*postpone*) laisser en suspens.

shelving ['ʃelvɪŋ] *n* (*shelves*) rayonnage(s) *m(pl)*; **s. unit** (*set of shelves*) étagère *f*.

shepherd ['ʃepəd] **1** *n* berger *m*; **s.'s pie** hachis *m* Parmentier. **2** *vt* **to s. s.o. around** piloter qn. ● **shepherdess** *n* bergère *f*.

sherbet ['ʃɜːbət] *n* (*powder*) poudre *f* acidulée; (*water ice*) *Am* sorbet *m*.

sheriff ['ʃerɪf] *n Am* shérif *m*.

sherry ['ʃerɪ] *n* sherry *m*.

shield [ʃiːld] *n* bouclier *m*; (*on coat of arms*) écu *m*; (*screen*) *Tech* écran *m* ▮ *vt* protéger (**from** de).

shift [ʃɪft] *n* (*change*) changement *m* (**of, in** de); (*period of work*) poste *m*; (*workers*) équipe *f*; **gear s.** *Aut Am* levier *m* de vitesse; **s. work** travail *m* en équipe.

▮ *vt* (*move*) bouger; (*employee*) muter (**to** à); (*blame*) rejeter (**on to** sur); **to s. places** changer de place; **to s. gear(s)** *Aut Am* changer de vitesse.

▮ *vi* bouger; (*of views*) changer; (*pass*) passer (**to** à); (*go*) aller (**to** à); **to s. over** *or* **up** se pousser.

shiftless ['ʃɪftləs] *a* (*apathetic*) mou (*f* molle); (*lazy*) paresseux.

shifty ['ʃɪftɪ] *a* (**-ier, -iest**) (*sly*) sournois; (*dubious*) louche.

shimmer ['ʃɪmər] *vi* chatoyer, miroiter.

shin [ʃɪn] *n* tibia *m*; **s. pad** *n Sp* jambière *f*.

shin/e [ʃaɪn] *vi* (*pt & pp* **shone** [ʃɒn, *Am* ʃəʊn]) briller ▮ *vt* (*polish*) faire briller; **to s. a light** *or* **a torch on sth** éclairer qch ▮ *n* (*on shoes, cloth*) brillant *m*; (*on metal etc*) éclat *m*. ● **—ing** *a* (*bright, polished*) brillant.

shingle ['ʃɪŋg(ə)l] *n* (*on beach*) galets *mpl*.

shingles ['ʃɪŋg(ə)lz] *n Med* zona *m*.

shiny ['ʃaɪnɪ] *a* (**-ier, -iest**) (*bright, polished*) brillant; (*clothes, through wear*) lustré.

ship [ʃɪp] *n* navire *m*, bateau *m*; **by s.** en bateau ▮ *vt* (**-pp-**) (*send*) expédier (par mer); (*transport*) transporter (par mer). ● **shipping** *n* (*traffic*) navigation *f*; (*ships*) navires *mpl*; **s. line** compagnie *f* de navigation.

shipbuilding ['ʃɪpbɪldɪŋ] *n* construction *f* navale. ● **shipment** *n* (*goods*) cargaison *f*. ● **shipowner** *n* armateur *m*. ● **shipshape** *a* & *adv* en ordre. ● **shipwreck** *n* naufrage *m*. ● **shipwrecked** *a* naufragé; **to be s.** faire naufrage. ● **shipyard** *n* chantier *m* naval.

shirk [ʃɜːk] *vt* (*duty*) se dérober à; (*work*) éviter de faire ▮ *vi* tirer au flanc.

shirt [ʃɜːt] *n* chemise *f*; (*of woman*) chemisier *m*; (*of sportsman*) maillot *m*. ● **shirtsleeves** *npl* **in (one's) s.** en bras de chemise.

shiver ['ʃɪvər] *vi* frissonner (**with** de) ▮ *n* frisson *m*.

shoal [ʃəʊl] *n* (*of fish*) banc *m*.

shock [ʃɒk] *n* (*emotional, physical*) choc *m*; (*impact*) & *Med* choc *m*; (*of explosion*) secousse *f*; **(electric) s.** décharge *f* (électrique) (**from sth** en touchant qch); **suffering from s.** en état de choc; **to come as a s. to s.o.** stupéfier qn.

▮ *a* (*tactics, wave*) de choc; (*effect, image*) -choc *inv*; **s. absorber** *Aut* amortisseur *m*.

▮ *vt* (*offend*) choquer; (*surprise*) stupéfier. ● **shocking** *a* affreux; (*outrageous*) scandaleux; (*indecent*) choquant. ● **shockproof** *a* résistant au choc.

shoddy ['ʃɒdɪ] *a* (**-ier, -iest**) (*goods*) de mauvaise qualité.

shoe [ʃuː] *n* chaussure *f*, soulier *m*; (*for horse*) fer *m*; **(brake) s.** *Aut* sabot *m* (de frein); **in your shoes** *Fig* à ta place; **s. polish** cirage *m* ▮ *vt* (*pt & pp* **shod**) (*horse*) ferrer. ● **shoehorn** *n* chausse-pied *m*. ● **shoelace** *n* lacet *m*. ● **shoeshop** *n* magasin *m* de chaussures. ● **shoestring** *n* **on a s.** *Fig* avec peu d'argent (en poche).

shone [ʃɒn, *Am* ʃəʊn] *pt & pp of* **shine.**

shoo [ʃuː] *vt* **to s. (away)** chasser ▮ *int* ouste!

shook [ʃʊk] *pt of* **shake.**

shoot[1] [ʃuːt] *vt* (*pt & pp* **shot**) (*kill*) tuer (d'un coup de feu), abattre; (*wound*) blesser (d'un coup de feu); (*execute*) fusiller; (*hunt*) chasser; (*gun*) tirer un coup de; (*missile, Fig glance*) lancer (**at** à); (*film*) tourner; **to s. down** (*aircraft*) abattre.

▮ *vi* (*with gun etc*) tirer (**at** sur); *Fb etc* shooter; **to s. ahead/off** (*rush*) avancer/partir à toute vitesse; **to s. up** (*of price*) monter en flèche; (*grow*) pousser vite; (*spurt*) jaillir. ● **shooting** *n* (*shots*) coups *mpl* de feu; (*murder*) meurtre *m*; (*execution*) fusillade *f*; (*hunting*) chasse *f*. ● **shootout** *n Fam* fusillade *f*.

shoot[2] [ʃuːt] *n* (*on plant*) pousse *f*.

shop [ʃɒp] *n* magasin *m*; (*small*) boutique *f*; (*workshop*) atelier *m*; **at the baker's s.** à la boulangerie, chez le boulanger; **s. assistant** vendeur, -euse *mf*; **s. front** devanture *f*; **s. steward** délégué, -ée *mf* syndical(e); **s. window** vitrine *f*.

▮ *vi* (**-pp-**) faire ses courses (**at** chez); **to s. around** comparer les prix. ● **shopping** *n* (*goods*) achats *mpl*; **to go s.** faire des courses; **to do one's s.** faire ses courses; **s. bag** sac *m* à provisions; **s. centre** centre *m* commercial. ● **shopper** *n* (*customer*) client, -ente *mf*; **lots of shoppers** beaucoup de gens qui font leurs courses.

shopkeeper ['ʃɒpkiːpər] *n* commerçant, -ante *mf*. ● **shoplifter** *n* voleur, -euse *mf* à l'étalage. ● **shoplifting** *n* vol *m* à l'étalage. ● **shopsoiled** *or Am* **shopworn** *a* abîmé.

shore [ʃɔːr] **1** *n* (*of sea, lake*) rivage *m*; (*coast*) côte *f*, bord *m* de (la) mer; (*beach*) plage *f*; **on s.** (*passenger*) à terre. **2** *vt* **to s. up** (*prop up*) étayer.

short [ʃɔːt] *a* (**-er, -est**) court; (*person, distance*) petit; (*syllable*) bref; (*impatient*) brusque; **a s. time** *or* **while (ago)** (il y a) peu de temps; **to be s. of money/time** être à court d'argent/de temps; **we're s. of ten men** il nous manque dix hommes; **money/time is s.** l'argent/le temps manque; **s. of** (*except*) sauf; (*before*) avant; **not far s. of** pas loin de; **s. of a miracle** à moins d'un miracle; **to be s. for** (*of name*) être l'abréviation de; **in s.** bref; **s. circuit** *El* court-

circuit *m*; **s. cut** raccourci *m*; **s. list** liste *f* de candidats retenus.
‖ *adv* **to cut s.** (*hair*) couper court; (*visit etc*) raccourcir; (*person*) couper la parole à; **to get** *or* **run s.** manquer (**of** de); **to stop s.** s'arrêter net.

shortage ['ʃɔːtɪdʒ] *n* manque *m*.

shortbread ['ʃɔːtbred] *n* sablé *m*. ●**short-'change** *vt* (*buyer*) ne pas rendre juste à. ●**short-'circuit** *vt El & Fig* court-circuiter. ●**shortcoming** *n* défaut *m*. ●**shorthand** *n* sténo *f*; **s. typist** sténodactylo *f*. ●**short-'lived** *a* de courte durée. ●**short'sighted** *a Med & Fig* myope. ●**short-'sleeved** *a* à manches courtes. ●**short-'staffed** *a* à court de personnel. ●**short-'term** *a* à court terme.

shorten ['ʃɔːt(ə)n] *vt* (*dress, text etc*) raccourcir.

shortening ['ʃɔːt(ə)nɪŋ] *n Culin* matière *f* grasse.

shortly ['ʃɔːtlɪ] *adv* (*soon*) bientôt; **s. after** peu après.

shorts [ʃɔːts] *npl* **(a pair of) s.** un short; **(boxer) s.** caleçon *m*.

shot [ʃɒt] *pt of* **shoot**[1] ‖ *n* (*from gun*) coup *m*; (*bullet*) balle *f*; *Cin Phot* prise *f* de vues; (*injection*) *Med* piqûre *f*; **a good s.** (*person*) un bon tireur; **to have a s. at (doing) sth** essayer de faire qch; **like a s.** (*at once*) tout de suite; **to be s. of** *Fam* être débarrassé de. ●**shotgun** *n* fusil *m* (de chasse).

should [ʃʊd, *unstressed* ʃəd] *v aux* **1** (= *ought to*) **you s. do it** vous devriez le faire; **I s. have stayed** j'aurais dû rester; **that s. be Paul** ça doit être Paul. **2** (= *would*) **I s. like to** j'aimerais bien; **it's strange she s. say no** il est étrange qu'elle dise non. **3** (*possibility*) **if he s. come** s'il vient; **s. I be free** si je suis libre.

shoulder ['ʃəʊldər] **1** *n* épaule *f*; **(hard) s.** (*of motorway*) bas-côté *m*; **s. bag** sac *m* à bandoulière; **s. blade** omoplate *f*; **s. pad** (*of jacket*) épaulette *f*. **2** *vt* (*responsibility*) endosser.

shout [ʃaʊt] *n* cri *m*; **to give s.o. a s.** appeler qn ‖ *vi* **to s. (out)** crier; **to s. to s.o. to do** crier à qn de faire; **to s. at s.o.** (*scold*) crier après qn ‖ *vt* **to s. (out)** (*insult etc*) crier. ●**—ing** *n* (*shouts*) cris *mpl*.

shove [ʃʌv] *n* poussée *f*; **to give a s. (to)** pousser ‖ *vt* pousser; (*put*) *Fam* fourrer **(into** dans) ‖ *vi* pousser; **to s. off** (*leave*) *Fam* ficher le camp; **to s. over** (*move over*) *Fam* se pousser.

shovel ['ʃʌv(ə)l] *n* pelle *f* ‖ *vt* (**-ll-**, *Am* **-l-**) **to s. (up)** (*snow*) enlever à la pelle; (*leaves etc*) ramasser à la pelle; **to s. sth into** *Fam* fourrer qch dans.

show [ʃəʊ] *n Th TV* spectacle *m*; *Cin* séance *f*; (*exhibition*) exposition *f*; (*of force*) démonstration *f* (**of** de); (*semblance*) semblant *m* (**of** de); (*ostentation*) parade *f*; **the Motor S.** le Salon de l'Automobile; **(just) for s.** pour l'effet; **on s.** (*painting etc*) exposé; **s. business** le monde du spectacle. ‖ *vt* (*pt* **showed,** *pp* **shown** *or* **showed**) montrer (**to** à, **that** que); (*in exhibition*) exposer; (*film*) passer; (*indicate*) indiquer, montrer; **to s. s.o. to the door** reconduire qn; **I'll s. him!** *Fam* je vais lui apprendre! ‖ *vi* (*be visible*) se voir; (*of film*) passer.

show around *vt* faire visiter; **she was shown around the house** on lui a fait visiter la maison **to show in** *vt* (*visitor*) faire entrer **to show off** *vt* (*display*) *Pej* étaler; (*highlight*) faire valoir ‖ *vi Pej* crâner. ●**show-off** *n Pej* crâneur, -euse *mf*. **to show out** *vt* (*visitor*) reconduire **to show round** *vt* = **show around to show up** *vt* (*embarrass*) mettre (*qn*) dans l'embarras; (*fault*) faire ressortir ‖ *vi* ressortir (**against** sur); (*of person*) *Fam* arriver.

showcase ['ʃəʊkeɪs] *n* vitrine *f*. ●**showdown** *n* confrontation *f*. ●**showjumping** *n Sp* jumping *m*. ●**showpiece** *n* modèle *m* du genre. ●**showroom** *n* (*for cars*) salle *f* d'exposition.

shower ['ʃaʊər] *n* (*bath*) douche *f*; (*of rain*) averse *f*; (*of blows*) déluge *m*; **to have** *or* **take a s.** prendre une douche ‖ *vt* **to s. s.o. with** (*gifts, abuse*) couvrir qn de. ●**showery** *a* pluvieux.

showing ['ʃəʊɪŋ] *n* (*performance*) *Cin* séance *f*; (*of film*) projection *f* (**of** de); (*of team, player*) performance *f*.

shown [ʃəʊn] *pp of* **show.**

showy ['ʃəʊɪ] *a* (**-ier, -iest**) (*colour, hat*) voyant; (*person*) prétentieux.

shrank [ʃræŋk] *pt of* **shrink 1.**

shrapnel ['ʃræpn(ə)l] *n* éclats *mpl* d'obus.

shred [ʃred] *n* lambeau *m*; **not a s. of evidence** pas la moindre preuve ‖ *vt* (**-dd-**) mettre en lambeaux; (*cabbage, carrots*) râper. ●**shredder** *n Culin* râpe *f*; (*in office*) destructeur *m* de documents.

shrew [ʃruː] *n* (*woman*) *Pej* mégère *f*.

shrewd [ʃruːd] *a* (**-er, -est**) (*person, plan*) astucieux.

shriek [ʃriːk] *n* cri *m* (aigu) ‖ *vi* crier; **to s. with laughter** hurler de rire.

shrill [ʃrɪl] *a* (**-er, -est**) aigu (*f* -uë), strident.

shrimp [ʃrɪmp] *n* crevette *f* (*grise*).

shrine [ʃraɪn] *n* lieu *m* saint; (*tomb*) chasse *f*.

shrink [ʃrɪŋk] **1** *vi* (*pt* **shrank** *or* **shrunk**, *pp* **shrunk** *or* **shrunken**) (*of clothes*) rétrécir; (*of audience, amount etc*) diminuer; **to s. from** reculer devant (**doing** l'idée de faire) ‖ *vt* rétrécir. **2** *n* (*person*) *Am Hum* psy(chiatre) *m*. • **s.-wrapped** *a* emballé sous pellicule plastique.

shrivel ['ʃrɪv(ə)l] *vi* (**-ll-**, *Am* **-l-**) **to s. (up)** se ratatiner ‖ *vt* **to s. (up)** ratatiner.

shroud [ʃraʊd] *n* linceul *m* ‖ *vt* **shrouded in mist** enseveli sous la brume; **shrouded in mystery** enveloppé de mystère.

Shrove Tuesday [ʃrəʊv'tju:zdɪ] *n* Mardi *m* gras.

shrub [ʃrʌb] *n* arbuste *m*.

shrug [ʃrʌg] *vt* (**-gg-**) **to s. one's shoulders** hausser les épaules; **to s. off** (*dismiss*) écarter (dédaigneusement).

shrunk(en) ['ʃrʌŋk(ən)] *pp of* **shrink 1**.

shudder ['ʃʌdər] *vi* frémir (**with** de); (*of machine*) vibrer.

shuffle ['ʃʌf(ə)l] **1** *vt* (*cards*) battre. **2** *vti* **to s. (one's feet)** traîner les pieds.

shun [ʃʌn] *vt* (**-nn-**) fuir, éviter.

shunt [ʃʌnt] *vt* (*train*) aiguiller (**on to** sur); **we were shunted (to and fro)** *Fam* on nous a baladés (**from office to office**/*etc* de bureau en bureau/*etc*).

shush! [ʃʊʃ] *int* chut! [ʃyt].

shut [ʃʌt] *vt* (*pt* & *pp* **shut**, *pp* **shutting**) fermer; **to s. one's finger in** (*door etc*) se prendre le doigt dans ‖ *vi* (*of door etc*) se fermer; (*of shop, museum etc*) fermer; **the door doesn't s.** la porte ne ferme pas.

shut away *vt* (*lock away*) enfermer **to shut down** *vt* fermer ‖ *vi* (*of shop etc*) fermer (définitivement) **to shut in** *vt* (*lock in*) enfermer **to shut off** *vt* (*gas etc*) fermer; (*engine*) arrêter; (*isolate*) isoler **to shut out** *vt* (*light*) empêcher d'entrer; (*view*) boucher; **to s. s.o. out** (*accidentally*) enfermer qn dehors **to shut up** *vt* (*house etc*) fermer; (*lock up*) enfermer (*personne, objet précieux*); (*silence*) *Fam* faire taire (*qn*) ‖ *vi* (*be quiet*) *Fam* se taire.

shutter ['ʃʌtər] *n* (*on window*) volet *m*; (*of shop*) rideau *m* (métallique); (*of camera*) obturateur *m*.

shuttle ['ʃʌt(ə)l] *n* **s. (service)** navette *f*; **space s.** navette spatiale ‖ *vi* faire la navette.

shy [ʃaɪ] *a* (**-er, -est**) timide ‖ *vi* **to s. away** reculer (**from s.o.** devant qn, **from doing** à l'idée de faire). • **—ness** *n* timidité *f*.

sibling ['sɪblɪŋ] *n* frère *m*, sœur *f*.

Sicily ['sɪsɪlɪ] *n* Sicile *f*.

sick [sɪk] *a* (**-er, -est**) (*ill*) malade; (*mind*) malsain; (*humour*) noir; **to be s.** (*vomit*) vomir; **off s., on s. leave** en congé de maladie; **to feel s.** avoir mal au cœur; **to be s. (and tired) of sth/s.o.** *Fam* en avoir marre de qch/qn; **he makes me s.** *Fam* il m'écœure ‖ *n* **the s.** les malades *mpl* ‖ *vti* **to s. up** (*vomit*) *Fam* vomir. • **sickbay** *n* infirmerie *f*. • **sickbed** *n* lit *m* de malade.

sicken ['sɪkən] **1** *vt* écœurer. **2** *vi* **to be sickening for** (*illness*) couver. • **—ing** *a* écœurant.

sickly ['sɪklɪ] *a* (**-ier, -iest**) maladif; (*pale*) pâle; (*taste*) écœurant.

sickness ['sɪknɪs] *n* (*illness*) maladie *f*.

side [saɪd] *n* côté *m*; (*of hill, animal*) flanc *m*; (*of road, river*) bord *m*; (*of question, character*) aspect *m*; *Sp* équipe *f*; **the right s.** (*of fabric*) l'endroit *m*; **the wrong s.** (*of fabric*) l'envers *m*; **at** *or* **by the s. of** (*nearby*) à côté de; **at** *or* **by my s.** à côté de moi, à mes côtés; **s. by s.** l'un à côté de l'autre; **to move to one s.** s'écarter; **on this s.** de ce côté; **on the other s.** de l'autre côté; **to take sides with s.o.** se ranger du côté de qn; **on our s.** de notre côté.

‖ *a* (*lateral*) latéral; (*view*) de côté; (*street*) transversal.

‖ *vi* **to s. with s.o.** se ranger du côté de qn.

• **-sided** *suff* **ten-s.** à dix côtés.

sideboard ['saɪdbɔ:d] *n* **1** buffet *m*. **2 sideboards** (*hair*) pattes *fpl*. • **sideburns** *npl* (*hair*) *Am* pattes *fpl*. • **sidelight** *n* *Aut* veilleuse *f*. • **sideline** *n* (*activity*) activité *f* secondaire. • **sidesaddle** *adv* (*to ride*) en amazone. • **sidestep** *vt* (**-pp-**) éviter. • **sidetrack** *vt* **to get sidetracked** s'écarter du sujet. • **sidewalk** *n* *Am* trottoir *m*. • **sideways** *adv* & *a* de côté.

siding ['saɪdɪŋ] *n* *Rail* voie *f* de garage.

siege [si:dʒ] *n* *Mil* siège *m*.

siesta [sɪ'estə] *n* sieste *f*; **to take a s.** faire la sieste.

sieve [sɪv] *n* tamis *m*; (*for liquids*) passoire *f*. • **sift** *vt* (*flour etc*) tamiser ‖ *vi* **to s. through** (*papers*) examiner (à la loupe).

sigh [saɪ] *n* soupir *m* ‖ *vti* soupirer.

sight [saɪt] *n* vue *f*; (*thing seen*) spectacle *m*; (*on gun*) mire *f*; **to lose s. of** perdre de vue; **to catch s. of** apercevoir; **to come into s.** apparaître; **at first s.** à première vue; **by s.** de vue; **in s.** (*target, end etc*) en vue; **out of s.** (*hidden*) caché; (*no longer visible*) disparu; **the (tourist) sights** les attractions *fpl* touristiques; **to set one's sights on** (*job etc*) viser. • **sightseer** *n* touriste *mf*. • **sightseeing** *n* **to go s.** faire du tourisme.

sign [saɪn] **1** *n* signe *m*; (*notice*) panneau *m*;

(*over shop, inn*) enseigne *f*; **no s. of** aucune trace de; **to use s. language** parler par signes.
2 *vt* (*put signature to*) signer; **to s. sth over** céder qch (**to** à) ‖ *vi* signer; **to s. for** (*letter*) signer le reçu de; **to s. in** (*in hotel etc*) signer le registre; **to s. on** (*on the dole*) s'inscrire au chômage; **to s. on** *or* **up** (*of soldier, worker*) s'engager; (*for course*) s'inscrire.
signal ['sɪgnəl] *n* signal *m*; **busy s.** *Tel Am* sonnerie *f* 'occupé'; **traffic signals** feux *mpl* de circulation; **s. box,** *Am* **s. tower** *Rail* poste *m* d'aiguillage ‖ *vt* (**-ll-,** *Am* **-l-**) (*be a sign of*) indiquer; (*arrival etc*) signaler (**to** à) ‖ *vi* faire des signaux; (*with indicator*) *Aut* mettre son clignotant; **to s. (to) s.o. to do** faire signe à qn de faire. ● **signalman** *n* (*pl* **-men**) *Rail* aiguilleur *m*.
signature ['sɪgnətʃər] *n* signature *f*; **s. tune** indicatif *m* (musical).
signet ring ['sɪgnɪtrɪŋ] *n* chevalière *f*.
significant [sɪg'nɪfɪkənt] *a* (*important, large*) important. ● **significance** *n* (*meaning*) signification *f*; (*importance*) importance *f*. ● **significantly** *adv* (*appreciably*) sensiblement.
signify ['sɪgnɪfaɪ] *vt* (*mean, make known*) signifier (**that** que).
signpost ['saɪnpəʊst] *n* poteau *m* indicateur ‖ *vt* flécher.
silence ['saɪləns] *n* silence *m*; **in s.** en silence ‖ *vt* faire taire. ● **silencer** *n* (*on gun*) silencieux *m*. ● **silent** *a* silencieux; (*film, anger*) muet (*f* muette); **to keep s.** garder le silence (**about** sur). ● **silently** *adv* silencieusement.
silhouette [sɪlu:'et] *n* silhouette *f*.
silicon ['sɪlɪkən] *n* silicium *m*; **s. chip** puce *f* de silicium.
silk [sɪlk] *n* soie *f*. ● **silky** *a* (**-ier, -iest**) soyeux.
sill [sɪl] *n* (*of window*) rebord *m*.
silly ['sɪlɪ] *a* (**-ier, -iest**) bête; **to do something s.** faire une bêtise.
silver ['sɪlvər] *n* argent *m*; (*plates etc*) argenterie *f* ‖ *a* (*spoon etc*) en argent, (*hair, colour*) argenté; **s. paper** papier *m* d'argent. ● **s.-'plated** *a* plaqué argent. ● **silversmith** *n* orfèvre *m*. ● **silverware** *n* argenterie *f*. ● **silvery** *a* (*colour*) argenté.
similar ['sɪmɪlər] *a* semblable (**to** à). ● **simi'larity** *n* ressemblance *f* (**to** avec). ● **similarly** *adv* de la même façon; (*likewise*) de même.
simile ['sɪmɪlɪ] *n Liter* comparaison *f*.
simmer ['sɪmər] *vi Culin* mijoter; (*of water*) frémir; (*of revolt etc*) couver; **to s. down** (*calm down*) *Fam* se calmer.
simple ['sɪmp(ə)l] *a* (**-er, -est**) (*basic, easy etc*) simple. ● **s.-'minded** *a* simple d'esprit. ● **simpleton** *n* nigaud, -aude *mf*. ● **sim'plicity** *n* simplicité *f*. ● **simplification** [-'keɪʃ(ə)n] *n* simplification *f*. ● **simplify** *vt* simplifier. ● **simply** *adv* (*plainly, merely*) simplement; (*absolutely*) absolument.
simultaneous [sɪməl'teɪnɪəs, *Am* saɪməl'teɪnɪəs] *a* simultané. ● **—ly** *adv* simultanément.
sin [sɪn] *n* péché *m* ‖ *vi* (**-nn-**) pécher.
since [sɪns] **1** *prep* (*in time*) depuis ‖ *conj* depuis que; **s. she's been here** depuis qu'elle est ici; **it's a year s. I saw him** ça fait un an que je ne l'ai pas vu ‖ *adv* **(ever) s.** depuis. **2** *conj* (*because*) puisque.
sincere [sɪn'sɪər] *a* sincère. ● **sincerely** *adv* sincèrement; **yours s.** (*in letter*) veuillez croire à mes sentiments dévoués. ● **sin'cerity** *n* sincérité *f*.
sinew ['sɪnju:] *n Anat* tendon *m*.
sinful ['sɪnfəl] *a* (*act etc*) coupable; **he's s.** c'est un pécheur; **that's s.** c'est un péché.
sing [sɪŋ] *vti* (*pt* **sang,** *pp* **sung**) chanter. ● **—ing** *n* (*of bird & musical technique*) chant *m* ‖ *a* (*lesson etc*) de chant. ● **singer** *n* chanteur, -euse *mf*.
singe [sɪndʒ] *vt* (*cloth*) roussir; (*hair*) brûler.
single ['sɪŋg(ə)l] *a* seul; (*room, bed*) pour une personne; (*unmarried*) célibataire; **not a s. book/***etc* pas un seul livre/*etc*; **every s. day** tous les jours sans exception; **s. ticket** billet *m*; simple; **s. parent** père *m or* mère *f* célibataire; **s.-parent family** famille *f* monoparentale; **s. European market** marché *m* unique européen.
‖ *n* (*ticket*) aller *m* (simple); (*record*) 45 tours *m inv*; *pl Tennis* simples *mpl*; **singles bar** bar *m* pour célibataires.
‖ *vt* **to s. out** (*choose*) choisir. ● **s.-'breasted** *a* (*jacket*) droit. ● **s.-'decker** *n* (*bus*) autobus *m* sans impériale. ● **s.-'handed** *a* sans aide. ● **s.-'minded** *a* (*person*) résolu.
singly ['sɪŋglɪ] *adv* (*one by on*) un à un.
singsong ['sɪŋsɒŋ] *n* **to get together for a s.** se réunir pour chanter.
singular ['sɪŋgjʊlər] *a Gram* (*form*) singulier; (*noun*) au singulier ‖ *n Gram* singulier *m*; **in the s.** au singulier.
sinister ['sɪnɪstər] *a* sinistre.
sink[1] [sɪŋk] *n* (*in kitchen*) évier *m*; (*washbasin*) lavabo *m*.
sink[2] [sɪŋk] *vi* (*pt* **sank,** *pp* **sunk**) (*of ship, person etc*) couler; (*of water level*) baisser; (*collapse, subside*) s'affaisser; **to s. (down) into** (*mud*) s'enfoncer dans; (*armchair*)

s'affaler dans; **to s. in** (*of fact etc*) *Fam* rentrer (dans le crâne); **has that sunk in?** *Fam* as-tu compris ça?
‖ *vt* (*ship*) couler; **to s. into** (*knife etc*) enfoncer dans; (*money*) investir dans.

sinner ['sɪnər] *n* pécheur *m*, pécheresse *f*.

sinus ['saɪnəs] *n Anat* sinus *m inv*. • **sinu'sitis** *n* sinusite *f*.

sip [sɪp] *vt* (**-pp-**) boire à petites gorgées ‖ *n* (*mouthful*) petite gorgée *f*; (*drop*) goutte *f*.

siphon ['saɪfən] *n* siphon *m* ‖ *vt* **to s. off** (*money*) détourner.

sir [sɜːr] *n* monsieur *m*; **S.** (*title*) sir.

siren ['saɪərən] *n* (*of factory etc*) sirène *f*.

sirloin ['sɜːlɔɪn] *n* aloyau *m*.

sissy ['sɪsɪ] *n* (*boy, man*) *Fam* femmelette *f*.

sister ['sɪstər] *n* sœur *f*; (*nurse*) infirmière *f* en chef. • **s.-in-law** *n* (*pl* **sisters-in-law**) belle-sœur *f*.

sit [sɪt] *vi* (*pp & pp* **sat**, *pres p* **sitting**) s'asseoir; (*for artist*) poser (**for** pour); (*of assembly etc*) siéger; **to be sitting** être assis; **she was sitting reading** elle était assise à lire ‖ *vt* (*child on chair etc*) asseoir; (*exam*) se présenter à.

sit around *vi* traîner; (*do nothing*) ne rien faire **to sit back** *vi* (*in chair*) se caler; (*rest*) se reposer; (*do nothing*) ne rien faire **to sit down** *vi* s'asseoir; **to be sitting down** être assis ‖ *vt* asseoir (*qn*) **to sit for** *vt* (*exam*) se présenter à **to sit in on** *vt* (*lecture*) assister à **to sit on** (*jury*) être membre de **to sit through** *vt* (*film*) rester jusqu'au bout de **to sit up** *vi* **to s. up (straight)** s'asseoir (bien droit); **to s. up waiting for s.o.** ne pas se coucher en attendant qn.

site [saɪt] *n* (*position*) emplacement *m*; **(building) s.** chantier *m*; **launching s.** aire *f* de lancement.

sit-in ['sɪtɪn] *n Pol* sit-in *m inv*.

sitting ['sɪtɪŋ] *n* séance *f*; (*for one's portrait*) séance *f* de pose; (*in restaurant*) service *m*. • **sitting room** *n* salon *m*.

situate ['sɪtʃʊeɪt] *vt* situer; **to be situated** être situé, se situer. • **situation** [-'eɪʃ(ə)n] *n* situation *f*.

six [sɪks] *a & n* six (*m*). • **six'teen** *a & n* seize (*m*). • **sixth** *a & n* sixième (*mf*); **(lower) s. form** *Sch* = classe *f* de première; **(upper) s. form** *Sch* = classe *f* terminale. • **sixtieth** *a & n* soixantième (*mf*). • **sixty** *a & n* soixante (*m*).

size [saɪz] **1** *n* (*of person, clothes, packet etc*) taille *f*; (*measurements*) dimensions *fpl*; (*of town, sum, damage*) importance *f*; (*of shoes, gloves*) pointure *f*; (*of shirt*) encolure *f*; **hip/chest s.** tour *m* de hanches/de poitrine. **2** *vt* **to s. up** (*person*) jauger; (*situation*) évaluer. • **sizeable** *a* assez grand *or* gros.

sizzle ['sɪz(ə)l] *vi* grésiller.

skat/e[1] [skeɪt] *n* patin *m* ‖ *vi* patiner. • **—ing** *n* patinage *m*; **to go s.** faire du patinage; **s. rink** (*ice-skating*) patinoire *f*. • **skateboard** *n* planche *f* à roulettes. • **skater** *n* patineur, -euse *mf*.

skate[2] [skeɪt] *n* (*fish*) raie *f*.

skeleton ['skelɪt(ə)n] *n* squelette *m* ‖ *a* (*crew, staff*) (réduit au) minimum.

skeptical ['skeptɪk(ə)l] *Am* = **sceptical.**

sketch [sketʃ] *n* (*drawing*) croquis *m*; (*comic play*) sketch *m*; **a rough s. of** (*plan*) une esquisse de ‖ *vt* **to s. (out)** (*idea etc*) esquisser ‖ *vi* faire un *or* des croquis. • **sketchy** *a* (**-ier, -iest**) incomplet.

skewer ['skjʊər] *n* (*for meat etc*) broche *f*; (*for kebab*) brochette *f*.

ski [skiː] *n* (*pl* **skis**) ski *m*; **s. lift** remonte-pente *m*; **s. mask** *Am* cagoule *f*, passe-montagne *m*; **s. pants** fuseau *m*; **s. run** piste *f* de ski ‖ *vi* (*pt* **skied** [skiːd], *pres p* **skiing**) faire du ski. • **—ing** *n Sp* ski *m* ‖ *a* (*school, clothes etc*) de ski. • **skier** *n* skieur, -euse *mf*.

skid [skɪd] *vi* (**-dd-**) *Aut* déraper; **to s. into sth** déraper et heurter qch ‖ *n* dérapage *m*.

skill [skɪl] *n* habileté *f*, adresse *f* (**at** à); (*technique*) technique *f*; **one's skills** (*aptitudes*) ses compétences *fpl*. • **skilful** *or Am* **skillful** *a* habile (**at doing** à faire, **at sth** en qch). • **skilled** *a* habile; (*worker*) qualifié; (*work*) de spécialiste.

skim [skɪm] **1** *vt* (**-mm-**) (*milk*) écrémer; (*soup*) écumer; **skimmed milk** lait *m* écrémé. **2** *vti* (**-mm-**) **to s. (over)** (*surface*) effleurer; **to s. through** (*book*) parcourir.

skimp [skɪmp] *vi* (*on food etc*) lésiner (**on** sur). • **skimpy** *a* (**-ier, -iest**) (*clothes*) étriqué; (*meal*) insuffisant.

skin [skɪn] *n* peau *f*; **s. diving** plongée *f* sous-marine; **s. test** cuti(-réaction) *f* ‖ *vt* (**-nn-**) (*fruit*) peler. • **s.-'deep** *a* superficiel. • **s.-'tight** *a* moulant.

skinhead ['skɪnhed] *n* skinhead *m*.

skinny ['skɪnɪ] *a* (**-ier, -iest**) maigre.

skint [skɪnt] *a* (*penniless*) *Fam* fauché.

skip[1] [skɪp] **1** *vi* (**-pp-**) (*hop about*) sautiller; (*with rope*) sauter à la corde; **skipping rope** corde *f* à sauter. **2** *vt* (**-pp-**) (*miss*) sauter (*repas, classe etc*); **to s. classes** (*miss school*) sécher les cours.

skip[2] [skɪp] *n* (*container for rubbish*) benne *f*.

skipper ['skɪpər] *n Nau Sp* capitaine *m*.

skirmish ['skɜːmɪʃ] *n* accrochage *m*.
skirt [skɜːt] **1** *n* jupe *f*. **2** *vt* **to s. round** contourner; **skirting board** (*on wall*) plinthe *f*.
skittle ['skɪt(ə)l] *n* quille *f*; **to play skittles** jouer aux quilles.
skiv/e [skaɪv] *vi* (*shirk*) *Fam* tirer au flanc; **to s. off** *Fam* se défiler. ●**—er** *n Fam* tire-au-flanc *m inv*.
skulk [skʌlk] *vi* rôder (furtivement).
skull [skʌl] *n* crâne *m*.
skunk [skʌŋk] *n* (*animal*) mouffette *f*.
sky [skaɪ] *n* ciel *m*. ●**skydiving** *n* parachutisme *m* (en chute libre). ●**skylight** *n* lucarne *f*. ●**skyline** *n* (*outline of buildings*) ligne *f* d'horizon. ●**skyscraper** *n* gratte-ciel *m inv*.
slab [slæb] *n* (*of concrete etc*) bloc *m*; (*thin, flat*) plaque *f*; (*of chocolate*) tablette *f*; (*of meat*) tranche *f* épaisse; (*paving stone*) dalle *f*.
slack [slæk] *a* (**-er, -est**) (*knot, spring*) lâche; (*discipline, security*) relâché; (*trade*) faible; (*lax, careless*) négligent; (*worker, student*) peu sérieux; **s. periods** périodes *fpl* creuses; (*hours*) heures *fpl* creuses; **to be s.** (*of rope*) avoir du mou; (*in office etc*) être calme. ●**slacken** *vi* **to s. (off)** (*in effort*) se relâcher; (*of production, speed*) diminuer ▮ *vt* **to s. (off)** (*rope*) relâcher; (*pace, effort*) ralentir. ●**slackness** *n* (*of person*) négligence *f*; (*of rope*) mou *m*.
slacks [slæks] *npl* pantalon *m*.
slalom ['slɑːləm] *n* (*ski race*) slalom *m*.
slam [slæm] **1** *vt* (**-mm-**) (*door, lid*) claquer; (*hit*) frapper violemment; (*put down*) poser violemment; **to s. on the brakes** écraser le frein ▮ *vi* (*of door*) claquer ▮ *n* claquement *m*. **2** *vt* (**-mm-**) (*criticize*) *Fam* critiquer (avec virulence).
slander ['slɑːndər] *n* diffamation *f*, calomnie *f* ▮ *vt* diffamer.
slang [slæŋ] *n* argot *m* ▮ *a* (*word etc*) d'argot, argotique. ●**slanging match** *n Fam* engueulade *f*.
slant [slɑːnt] *n* inclinaison *f*; (*point of view*) *Fig* angle *m* (**on** sur) ▮ *vi* (*of roof*) être en pente; (*of writing*) pencher. ●**—ed** *or* ●**—ing** *a* penché; (*roof*) en pente.
slap [slæp] **1** *n* tape *f*; (*on face*) gifle *f* ▮ *vt* (**-pp-**) (*person*) donner une tape à; **to s. s.o.'s face** gifler qn; **to s. s.o.'s bottom** donner une fessée à qn.
2 *vt* (**-pp-**) (*put*) mettre; **to s. on** (*apply*) appliquer à la va-vite.
3 *adv* **s. in the middle** *Fam* en plein milieu. ●**slapdash** *a* (*person*) négligent; (*task*) fait à la va-vite ▮ *adv* à la va-vite. ●**slaphappy** *a Fam* je-m'en-fichiste. ●**slap-up 'meal** *n Fam* gueuleton *m*.
slash [slæʃ] **1** *vt* (*with blade etc*) taillader; (*sever*) trancher ▮ *n* entaille *f*. **2** *vt* (*reduce*) réduire radicalement; (*prices*) écraser.
slat [slæt] *n* (*in blind, Am shade*) lame *f*.
slate [sleɪt] *n* ardoise *f*.
slaughter ['slɔːtər] *vt* (*people*) massacrer; (*animal*) abattre ▮ *n* massacre *m*; abattage *m*. ●**slaughterhouse** *n* abattoir *m*.
slave [sleɪv] *n* esclave *mf* ▮ *vi* **to s. (away)** se crever (au travail). ●**slavery** *n* esclavage *m*. ●**slavish** *a* servile.
slay [sleɪ] *vt* (*pt* **slew**, *pp* **slain**) *Lit* tuer.
sleazy ['sliːzɪ] *a* (**-ier, -iest**) *Fam* sordide.
sledge [sledʒ] (*Am* **sled** [sled]) *n* luge *f*; (*horse-drawn*) traîneau *m*.
sledgehammer ['sledʒhæmər] *n* masse *f*.
sleek [sliːk] *a* (**-er, -est**) (*smooth*) lisse; (*manner*) *Pej* onctueux.
sleep [sliːp] *n* sommeil *m*; **to have a s., get some s.** dormir ▮ *vi* (*pt & pp* **slept**) dormir; (*spend the night*) coucher; **to go** *or* **get to s.** s'endormir; **to send s.o. to s.** endormir qn ▮ *vt* **to s. it off** *Fam*, **s. off a hangover** cuver son vin. ●**—ing** *a* (*asleep*) endormi; **s. bag** sac *m* de couchage; **s. car** wagon-lit *m*; **s. pill** somnifère *m*; **s. quarters** chambre(s) *f(pl)*. ●**sleeper** *n* **1 to be a light s.** avoir le sommeil léger. **2** (*bed in train*) couchette *f*; (*train*) train *m* couchettes. ●**sleepless** *a* (*night*) d'insomnie. ●**sleepwalker** *n* somnambule *mf*. ●**sleepy** *a* (**-ier, -iest**) (*town*) endormi; **to be s.** (*of person*) avoir sommeil.
sleet [sliːt] *n* neige *f* fondue ▮ *vi* **it's sleeting** il tombe de la neige fondue.
sleeve [sliːv] *n* (*of shirt etc*) manche *f*; (*of record*) pochette *f*; **long-/short-sleeved** à manches longues/courtes.
sleigh [sleɪ] *n* traîneau *m*.
slender ['slendər] *a* (*person*) mince; (*neck, hand*) fin; (*small*) *Fig* faible.
slept [slept] *pt & pp of* **sleep.**
slice [slaɪs] *n* tranche *f*; (*portion*) *Fig* partie *f* ▮ *vt* **to s. (up)** couper (en tranches); **to s. off** (*cut off*) couper.
slick [slɪk] **1** *a* (**-er, -est**) (*glib*) qui a la parole facile; (*manner*) mielleux; (*film, book*) bien fait mais superficiel. **2** *n* **oil s.** nappe *f* de pétrole; (*large*) marée *f* noire.
slid/e [slaɪd] *n* (*in playground*) toboggan *m*; (*on ice*) glissoire *f*; (*for hair*) barrette *f*; *Phot* diapositive *f*; (*in value etc*) (légère) baisse *f* ▮ *vi* (*pt & pp* **slid**) glisser ▮ *vt* (*letter etc*) glisser (**into** dans); (*table, chair etc*)

faire glisser. ●**—ing** *a* (*door*, *panel*) coulissant; **s. roof** toit *m* ouvrant; **s. scale** *Com* échelle *f* mobile
slight [slaɪt] **1** *a* (**-er, -est**) (*noise, mistake etc*) léger, petit; (*chance*) faible; (*person, figure*) (*slim*) mince; (*frail*) frêle; **the slightest thing** la moindre chose; **not in the slightest** pas le moins du monde. **2** *vt* (*offend*) offenser; (*ignore*) bouder. ●**—ly** *adv* légèrement.
slim [slɪm] *a* (**slimmer, slimmest**) mince ‖ *vi* (**-mm-**) maigrir. ●**slimming** *a* (*diet*) amaigrissant.
slime [slaɪm] *n* boue *f* (visqueuse); (*of snail*) bave *f*. ●**slimy** *a* (**-ier, -iest**) boueux; (*sticky, Fig smarmy*) visqueux.
sling [slɪŋ] **1** *n* (*weapon*) fronde *f*; (*toy*) lance-pierres *m inv*; (*for arm*) écharpe *f*; **in a s.** en écharpe. **2** *vt* (*pt* & *pp* **slung**) (*throw*) jeter; **to s. out** *Fam* balancer. ●**slingshot** *n Am* lance-pierres *m inv*.
slip [slɪp] **1** *n* (*mistake*) erreur *f*; (*woman's undergarment*) combinaison *f*; **a s. of paper** (*bit*) un bout de papier; (*for filing*) une fiche de papier; **a s. of the tongue** un lapsus; **to give s.o. the s.** fausser compagnie à qn; **s. road** *Aut* bretelle *f* (d'accès *or* de sortie). **2** *vi* (**-pp-**) glisser ‖ *vt* (*slide*) glisser (*qch*) (**to** à, **into** dans); **it slipped his mind** ça lui est sorti de l'esprit.
slip away *vi* (*escape*) s'esquiver **to slip in** *vi* (*enter*) entrer furtivement **to slip into** *vt* (*room etc*) se glisser dans; (*bathrobe etc*) mettre, passer **to slip off** *vt* (*coat etc*) enlever **to slip on** *vt* (*coat etc*) mettre **to slip out** *vi* sortir furtivement; (*for a moment*) sortir (un instant). **to slip past** *vt* (*guard*) passer sans être vu de **to slip up** *vi* (*make a mistake*) gaffer.
slipcover ['slɪpkʌvər] *n Am* housse *f*.
slipper ['slɪpər] *n* pantoufle *f*.
slippery ['slɪpərɪ] *a* glissant.
slipshod ['slɪpʃɒd] *a* (*negligent*) négligent; (*slovenly*) négligé.
slip-up ['slɪpʌp] *n Fam* gaffe *f*.
slit [slɪt] *n* (*opening*) fente *f*; (*cut*) coupure *f* ‖ *vt* (*pt* & *pp* **slit,** *pres p* **slitting**) (*cut*) couper; **to s. open** (*sack*) éventrer.
slither ['slɪðər] *vi* glisser; (*of snake*) se couler.
sliver ['slɪvər] *n* (*of wood*) éclat *m*; (*of cheese etc*) fine tranche *f*.
slobber ['slɒbər] *vi* (*of dog etc*) baver (**over** sur).
slog [slɒg] *n* **a (hard) s.** (*effort*) un gros effort; (*work*) un travail dur ‖ *vi* (**-gg-**) **to s. (away)** bosser.
slogan ['sləʊgən] *n* slogan *m*.
slop [slɒp] *vi* (**-pp-**) **to s. (over)** (*spill*) se répandre ‖ *vt* répandre.
slop/e [sləʊp] *n* pente *f*; (*of mountain*) versant *m*; (*for skiing*) piste *f* ‖ *vi* (*of ground, roof etc*) être en pente. ●**—ing** *a* en pente; (*handwriting*) penché.
sloppy [slɒpɪ] *a* (**-ier, -iest**) (*work, appearance*) négligé; (*person*) négligent; (*sentimental*) sentimental.
slot [slɒt] *n* (*slit*) fente *f*; (*groove*) rainure *f*; (*in programme*) *Rad TV* créneau *m*; **s. machine** distributeur *m* automatique; (*for gambling*) machine *f* à sous ‖ *vt* (**-tt-**) (*insert*) insérer (**into** dans) ‖ *vi* s'insérer (**into** dans).
slouch [slaʊtʃ] *vi* ne pas se tenir droit; (*have stoop*) avoir le dos voûté; (*in chair*) se vautrer (**in** dans); **slouching over** (*desk*) penché sur ‖ *n* mauvaise tenue *f*.
slovenly ['slʌvənlɪ] *a* négligé.
slow [sləʊ] *a* (**-er, -est**) lent; (*business*) calme; **at a s. speed** à vitesse réduite; **to be a s. walker** marcher lentement; **to be s.** (*of clock, watch*) retarder; **to be five minutes s.** retarder de cinq minutes; **in s. motion** au ralenti ‖ *adv* lentement ‖ *vti* **to s. down** *or* **up** ralentir. ●**—ly** *adv* lentement; (*bit by bit*) peu à peu.
slowcoach ['sləʊkəʊtʃ] *n Fam* tortue *f*. ●**slow-down (strike)** *n Am* grève *f* perlée. ●**slowpoke** *n Am Fam* tortue *f*.
sludge [slʌdʒ] *n* gadoue *f*.
slug [slʌg] **1** *n* (*mollusc*) limace *f*. **2** *n* (*bullet*) *Am Sl* pruneau *m*. **3** *vt* (**-gg-**) (*hit*) *Am Fam* frapper.
sluggish ['slʌgɪʃ] *a* (*person*) amorphe; (*machine*) peu nerveux; (*business*) peu actif.
slum [slʌm] *n* (*house*) taudis *m*; **the slums** les quartiers *mpl* pauvres ‖ *a* (*district*) pauvre ‖ *vt* (**-mm-**) **to s. it** *Fam* (*have lean times*) manger de la vache enragée; (*mix with bad company*) s'encanailler.
slumber ['slʌmbər] *n Lit* sommeil *m*.
slump [slʌmp] **1** *n* baisse *f* soudaine (**in** de); (*in prices*) effrondement *m*; *Econ* crise *f* ‖ *vi* baisser; (*of prices*) s'effondrer. **2** *vi* **to s. into** (*armchair*) s'affaisser dans.
slung [slʌŋ] *pt* & *pp of* **sling 2.**
slur [slɜːr] **1** *vt* (**-rr-**) prononcer indistinctement. **2** *n* **to cast a s. on** (*reputation*) porter atteinte à. ●**slurred** *a* (*speech*) indistinct.
slush [slʌʃ] *n* (*snow*) neige *f* fondue.
slut [slʌt] *n Pej* (*immoral*) salope *f*; (*untidy*) souillon *f*.

sly [slaɪ] *a* (**-er, -est**) (*cunning*) rusé ‖ *n* **on the s.** en cachette.

smack [smæk] **1** *n* claque *f*; gifle *f*; fessée *f* ‖ *vt* (*person*) donner une claque à; **to s. s.o.'s face** gifler qn; **to s. s.o.('s bottom)** donner une fessée à qn. **2** *adv* **s. in the middle** *Fam* en plein milieu. **3** *vi* **to s. of** avoir des relents de.

small [smɑːl] *a* (**-er, -est**) petit; **s. change** petite monnaie *f*; **s. talk** menus propos *mpl* ‖ *adv* (*to cut, chop*) menu ‖ *n* **the s. of the back** le creux *m* des reins. ●**smallholding** *n* petite ferme *f*. ●**small-scale** *a Fig* peu important.

smallpox ['smɔːlpɒks] *n* petite vérole *f*.

smarmy ['smɑːmɪ] *a* (**-ier, -iest**) *Pej Fam* visqueux.

smart[1] [smɑːt] *a* (**-er, -est**) (*in appearance*) élégant; (*clever*) intelligent; (*astute*) astucieux; (*quick*) rapide; **s. aleck** *Fam* je-sais-tout *mf inv*; **s. card** carte *f* à puce *or* à mémoire. ●**smarten** *vt* **to s. up** (*room etc*) embellir ‖ *vti* **to s. (oneself) up** se faire beau. ●**smartly** *adv* (*dressed*) avec élégance.

smart[2] [smɑːt] *vi* (*sting*) brûler, faire mal.

smash [smæʃ] *vt* (*break*) briser; (*shatter*) fracasser; (*record*) pulvériser; **to s. s.o.'s face** *Fam* casser la gueule à qn ‖ *vi* se briser ‖ *n* (*accident*) collision *f*; **s. hit** *Fam* succès *m* fou. ●**s.-up** *n* collision *f*.

smash down *or* **in** *vt* (*door*) enfoncer **to smash into** *vt* (*of vehicle*) (r)entrer dans (*lampadaire etc*) **to smash up** *vt* (*vehicle*) esquinter; (*room*) démolir.

smashing ['smæʃɪŋ] *a Fam* formidable.

smattering ['smætərɪŋ] *n* **a s. of** (*French etc*) quelques notions *fpl* de.

smear [smɪər] *vt* (*coat*) enduire (**with** de); (*stain*) tacher (**with** de); (*smudge*) laisser une trace sur ‖ *n* (*mark*) trace *f*; **s. campaign** campagne *f* de diffamation.

smell [smel] *n* odeur *f*; **(sense of) s.** odorat *m* ‖ *vt* (*pt & pp* **smelled** *or* **smelt**) sentir; (*of animal*) flairer ‖ *vi* (*stink*) sentir (mauvais); (*have a smell*) avoir une odeur; **to s. of smoke**/*etc* sentir la fumée/*etc*. ●**smelly** *a* (**-ier, -iest**) **to be s.** sentir (mauvais).

smelt[1] [smelt] *pt & pp of* **smell**.

smelt[2] [smelt] *vt* (*ore*) fondre; **smelting works** fonderie *f*.

smil/e [smaɪl] *n* sourire *m* ‖ *vi* sourire (**at s.o.** à qn). ●**—ing** *a* souriant.

smirk [smɜːk] *n* (*smug*) sourire *m* suffisant; (*scornful*) sourire *m* goguenard.

smock [smɒk] *n* blouse *f*.

smog [smɒg] *n* brouillard *m* épais.

smoke [smәʊk] *n* fumée *f*; **to have a s.** fumer une cigarette *etc*; **s. detector** *or* **alarm** détecteur *m* de fumée. ‖ *vt* (*cigarette etc*) fumer; **smoked salmon/***etc* saumon *m*/*etc* fumé. ‖ *vi* fumer; **'no smoking'** 'défense de fumer'; **smoking compartment** *Rail* compartiment *m* fumeurs. ●**smoker** *n* fumeur, -euse *mf*; *Rail* compartiment *m* fumeurs. ●**smokestack** *n* cheminée *f* (d'usine). ●**smoky** *a* (**-ier, -iest**) (*air*) enfumé; **it's s. here** il y a de la fumée ici.

smooth [smuːð] *a* (**-er, -est**) (*surface, skin etc*) lisse; (*movement*) régulier; (*flight*) agréable; (*cream*) onctueux; (*sea*) calme; (*person, manners*) *Pej* doucereux; **the s. running** la bonne marche (**of** de) ‖ *vt* **to s. down** *or* **out** (*dress, hair etc*) lisser; **to s. over** (*problems*) *Fig* aplanir. ●**—ly** *adv* (*to land*) en douceur.

smother ['smʌðər] *vt* (*stifle*) étouffer; **to s. with** (*kisses etc*) *Fig* couvrir de.

smoulder ['smәʊldər] (*Am* **smolder**) *vi* (*of fire, Fig passion etc*) couver.

smudge [smʌdʒ] *n* tache *f*, bavure ‖ *vt* (*paper etc*) faire des taches sur.

smug [smʌg] *a* (*smile etc*) béat; (*person*) content de soi. ●**—ly** *adv* avec suffisance.

smuggl/e ['smʌg(ә)l] *vt* passer (en fraude); **smuggled goods** contrebande *f*. ●**—ing** *n* contrebande *f*. ●**smuggler** *n* contrebandier, -ière *mf*.

smut [smʌt] *n inv* (*obscenity*) cochonneries *fpl*.

snack [snæk] *n* (*meal*) casse-croûte *m inv*; *pl* (*things to eat*) petites choses *fpl* à grignoter; (*sweets, Am candies*) friandises *fpl*; **to eat a s.** *or* **snacks** grignoter; **s. bar** snack(-bar) *m*.

snag [snæg] *n* (*hitch*) inconvénient *m*, problème *m*.

snail [sneɪl] *n* escargot *m*.

snake [sneɪk] *n* serpent *m*.

snap [snæp] **1** *vt* (**-pp-**) (*break*) casser (avec un bruit sec); (*fingers*) faire claquer; **to s. up a bargain** sauter sur une occasion ‖ *vi* se casser net; (*of person*) *Fig* parler sèchement (**at** à); **to s. off** (*break off*) se casser; **s. out of it!** *Fam* secoue-toi! ‖ *n* bruit *m* sec; *Phot* photo *f*; **s. (fastener)** pression *f*; **cold s.** *Met* coup *m* de froid.
2 *a* **to make a s. decision** décider sans réfléchir. ●**snapshot** *n* photo *f*.

snappy ['snæpɪ] *a* **make it s.!** *Fam* dépêche-toi!

snare [sneәr] *n* piège *m*.

snarl [snɑːl] *vi* gronder (en montrant les dents). ●**s.-up** *n Aut Fam* embouteillage *m*.

snatch [snætʃ] *vt* saisir (*d'un geste vif*); (*some rest etc*) *Fig* (réussir à) prendre; **to s. sth from s.o.** arracher qch à qn.

sneak [sni:k] **1** *vi* (*pt & pp Am* **sneaked** *or* **snuck**) **to s. in/out** entrer/sortir furtivement; **to s. off** s'esquiver. **2** *n* (*telltale*) *Fam* rapporteur, -euse *mf* ‖ *vi* **to s. on s.o.** (*of child*) *Fam* rapporter sur qn. • **sneaky** *a* (**-ier, -iest**) (*sly*) *Fam* sournois.

sneaker ['sni:kər] *n* (chaussure *f* de) tennis *m*.

sneer [snɪər] *vi* ricaner; **to s. at** se moquer de ‖ *n* ricanement *m*.

sneeze [sni:z] *n* éternuement *m* ‖ *vi* éternuer.

snicker ['snɪkər] *vi Am* = **snigger.**

snide [snaɪd] *a* (*remark etc*) sarcastique.

sniff [snɪf] *vt* renifler; **to s. glue** sniffer de la colle; **to s. out** (*bargain*) *Fig* renifler ‖ *vi* **to s. (at)** renifler. • **sniffle** *n* **a s., the sniffles** *Fam* un petit rhume.

snigger ['snɪgər] *vi* ricaner.

snip [snɪp] *n* (*bargain*) *Fam* bonne affaire *f*; **to make a s.** couper ‖ *vt* (**-pp-**) **to s. (off)** couper.

sniper ['snaɪpər] *n Mil* tireur *m* embusqué.

snivel ['snɪv(ə)l] *vi* (**-ll-**, *Am* **-l-**) pleurnicher.

snob [snɒb] *n* snob *mf*. • **snobbery** *n* snobisme *m*. • **snobbish** *a* snob *inv*.

snooker ['snu:kər] *n* snooker *m* (*sorte de jeu de billard*).

snoop [snu:p] *vi* fourrer son nez partout; **to s. on s.o.** espionner qn.

snooze [snu:z] *n* petit somme *m*.

snor/e [snɔ:r] *vi* ronfler. • **—ing** *n* ronflements *mpl*.

snorkel ['snɔ:k(ə)l] *n Sp Nau* tuba *m*.

snort [snɔ:t] *vi* (*grunt*) grogner; (*sniff*) renifler; (*of horse*) renâcler.

snotty ['snɒtɪ] *a* (**-ier, -iest**) *Fam* (*nose*) qui coule; (*handkerchief*) plein de morve.

snout [snaʊt] *n* museau *m*.

snow [snəʊ] *n* neige *f* ‖ *vi* neiger; **it is snowing** il neige ‖ *vt* **to be snowed in** être bloqué par la neige; **to be s. under with** (*work*) être submergé de. • **snowball** *n* boule *f* de neige. • **snowbound** *a* bloqué par la neige. • **snowdrift** *n* congère *f*. • **snowfall** *n* chute *f* de neige. • **snowflake** *n* flocon *m* de neige. • **snowman** *n* (*pl* **-men**) bonhomme *m* de neige. • **snowplough** *or Am* **snowplow** *n* chasseneige *m inv*. • **snowstorm** *n* tempête *f* de neige. • **snowy** *a* (**-ier, -iest**) (*weather etc*) neigeux.

snub [snʌb] *n* rebuffade *f* ‖ *vt* (**-bb-**) (*offer etc*) rejeter; **to s. s.o.** snober qn.

snuff [snʌf] *vt* **to s. (out)** (*candle*) moucher.

snug [snʌg] *a* (*house etc*) douillet; (*garment*) bien ajusté; **we're s.** (*in chair etc*) on est bien; **s. in bed** bien au chaud dans son lit.

snuggle ['snʌg(ə)l] *vi* **to s. up to s.o.** se pelotonner contre qn.

so [səʊ] **1** *adv* (*to such a degree*) si, tellement (**that** que); (*thus*) ainsi; **so that** (*purpose*) pour que (+ *sub*); (*result*) si bien que; **so as to do** pour faire; **I think so** je le pense; **do so!** faites-le!; **if so** si oui; **is that so?** c'est vrai?; **so am I, so do I** *etc* moi aussi; **so much** (*to work etc*) tant, tellement (**that** que); **so much courage/***etc* tant *or* tellement de courage/*etc* (**that** que); **so many** tant, tellement; **so many books/***etc* tant *or* tellement de livres/*etc* (**that** que); **ten or so** environ dix; **and so on** et ainsi de suite; **so long!** *Fam* au revoir! **2** *conj* (*therefore*) donc; (*in that case*) alors; **so what?** et alors? • **So-and-so** *n* **Mr So-and-so** Monsieur Un tel. • **so-'called** *a* prétendu, soi-disant *inv*. • **so-so** *a Fam* comme ci comme ça.

soak [səʊk] *vt* (*drench*) tremper (*qn*); (*washing, food*) faire tremper; **soaked through** trempé jusqu'aux os; **to s. up** absorber ‖ *vi* (*of washing etc*) tremper; **to s. in** (*of liquid*) s'infiltrer. • **—ing** *a & adv* **s. (wet)** trempé.

soap [səʊp] *n* savon *m*; **s. opera** feuilleton *m* (télé) à l'eau de rose; **s. powder** lessive *f*. • **soapflakes** *npl* savon *m* en paillettes. • **soapsuds** *npl* mousse *f* de savon. • **soapy** *a* (**-ier, -iest**) *a* savonneux.

soar [sɔ:r] *vi* (*of bird etc*) s'élever; (*of price*) monter (en flèche).

sob [sɒb] *n* sanglot *m* ‖ *vi* (**-bb-**) sangloter.

sober ['səʊbər] **1** *a* **he's s.** (*not drunk*) il n'est pas ivre ‖ *vti* **to s. up** dessoûler. **2** *a* (*serious*) sérieux; (*style*) sobre.

soccer ['sɒkər] *n* football *m*.

sociable ['səʊʃəb(ə)l] *a* (*person*) sociable.

social ['səʊʃəl] *a* social; **s. club** club *m*; **s. evening** soirée *f*; **to have a good s. life** sortir beaucoup; **s. security** (*aid*) aide *f* sociale; (*pension*) *Am* pension *f* de retraite; **s. services, S. Security** = Sécurité *f* sociale; **s. worker** assistant, -ante *mf* social(e). • **socialize** *vi* (*mix*) se mêler aux autres. • **socially** *adv* (*to meet s.o.*) en société.

socialist ['səʊʃəlɪst] *a & n* socialiste (*mf*).

society [sə'saɪətɪ] *n* (*community, club etc*) société *f*.

sociology [səʊsɪ'ɒlədʒɪ] *n* sociologie *f*.

sock [sɒk] *n* chaussette *f*.

socket ['sɒkɪt] *n* (*for electric plug*) prise *f* de courant; (*of lamp*) douille *f*; (*of eye*) orbite *f*.

sod [sɒd] *n* (*turf*) *Am* gazon *m*.

soda ['səʊdə] *n* **1** *Ch* soude *f*. **2 s. (water)** eau *f* gazeuse; **s. (pop)** *Am* soda *m*.

sofa ['səʊfə] *n* canapé *m*; **s. bed** canapé-lit *m*.

soft [sɒft] *a* (**-er, -est**) (*gentle, not stiff*) doux (*f* douce); (*butter, ground, paste*) mou (*f* molle); (*colour*) tendre; (*indulgent*) indulgent; (*cowardly*) *Fam* poltron; **it's too s.** (*radio etc*) ce n'est pas assez fort; **s. drink** boisson *f* non alcoolisée; **s. drugs** drogues *fpl* douces. ●**s.-'boiled** *a* (*egg*) à la coque. ●**soften** ['sɒf(ə)n] *vt* (*object*) ramollir; (*colour, light*) adoucir ‖ *vi* **to s. up** se ramollir. ●**softly** *adv* doucement. ●**softness** *n* douceur *f*.

software ['sɒftweər] *n inv* (*of computer*) logiciel *m*; **s. package** progiciel *m*.

soggy ['sɒgɪ] *a* (**-ier, -iest**) (*ground*) détrempé; (*biscuit, bread*) ramolli.

soil [sɔɪl] **1** *n* (*earth*) sol *m*, terre *f*. **2** *vt* (*dirty*) salir.

solar ['səʊlər] *a* solaire; **s. power** énergie *f* solaire.

sold [səʊld] *pt & pp of* **sell.**

solder ['sɒldər, *Am* 'sɒdər] *vt* souder ‖ *n* soudure *f*.

soldier ['səʊldʒər] **1** *n* soldat *m*, militaire *m*. **2** *vi* **to s. on** persévérer.

sole [səʊl] **1** *n* (*of shoe*) semelle *f*; (*of foot*) plante *f*. **2** *a* (*only*) seul, unique; (*rights*) *Com* exclusif. **3** *n* (*fish*) sole *f*. ●**—ly** *adv* uniquement.

solemn ['sɒləm] *a* (*formal*) solennel; (*serious*) grave.

solicit [sə'lɪsɪt] *vt* (*seek*) solliciter ‖ *vi* (*of prostitute*) racoler. ●**solicitor** *n* (*for wills etc*) notaire *m*.

solid ['sɒlɪd] *a* (*car, meal, state etc*) solide; (*wall, ball*) plein; (*gold, rock*) massif; (*crowd, mass*) compact; **s. line** ligne *f* continue; **frozen s.** entièrement gelé ‖ *n Ch* solide *m*; *pl* (*foods*) aliments *mpl* solides. ●**solidly** *adv* (*built etc*) solidement.

solidarity [sɒlɪ'dærətɪ] *n* solidarité *f* (**with** avec).

solitary ['sɒlɪtərɪ] *a* (*lonely, alone*) solitaire; (*only*) seul; **s. confinement** *Jur* isolement *m* (cellulaire). ●**solitude** *n* solitude *f*.

solo ['səʊləʊ] *n* (*pl* **-os**) *Mus* solo *m* ‖ *a* solo *inv* ‖ *adv Mus* en solo; (*to fly*) en solitaire. ●**soloist** *n Mus* soliste *mf*.

soluble ['sɒljʊb(ə)l] *a* soluble.

solution [sə'luːʃ(ə)n] *n* (*to problem etc*) & *Ch* solution *f* (**to** de).

solve [sɒlv] *vt* (*problem etc*) résoudre.

solvent ['sɒlvənt] **1** *a* (*financially*) solvable. **2** *n Ch* (dis)solvant *m*; **s. abuse** usage *m* de solvants hallucinogènes.

sombre ['sɒmbər] *a* sombre, triste.

some [sʌm] *a* **1** (*amount, number*) du, de la, des; **s. wine** du vin; **s. water** de l'eau; **s. dogs** des chiens; **s. pretty flowers** de jolies fleurs. **2** (*unspecified*) un, une; **s. man (or other)** un homme (quelconque); **s. charm** (*a certain amount of*) un certain charme; **s. other way** un autre moyen.
3 (*a few*) quelques, certains; (*a little*) un peu de.
‖ *pron* **1** (*number*) quelques-un(e)s, certain(e)s (**of** de).
2 (*a certain quantity*) en; **I want s.** j'en veux; **do you have s.?** en as-tu?; **s. of it is over** il en reste un peu.
‖ *adv* (*about*) environ, quelque; **s. ten years** environ *or* quelque dix ans.

somebody ['sʌmbɒdɪ] *pron* = **someone.** ●**someday** *adv* un jour. ●**somehow** *adv* (*in some way*) d'une manière ou d'une autre; (*for some reason*) on ne sait pourquoi. ●**someone** *pron* quelqu'un; **at s.'s house** chez qn; **s. small/***etc* quelqu'un de petit/*etc*. ●**someplace** *adv Am* quelque part. ●**something** *pron* quelque chose; **s. awful/***etc* quelque chose d'affreux/*etc*; **s. of a liar/***etc* un peu menteur/*etc* ‖ *adv* **she plays s. like...** elle joue un peu comme.... ●**sometime** *adv* un jour; **s. before his departure** avant son départ. ●**sometimes** *adv* quelquefois, parfois. ●**somewhat** *adv* quelque peu. ●**somewhere** *adv* quelque part; **s. about fifteen** environ quinze.

somersault ['sʌməsɔːlt] *n* (*on ground*) culbute *f* ‖ *vi* faire la culbute.

son [sʌn] *n* fils *m*. ●**s.-in-law** *n* (*pl* **sons-in-law**) gendre *m*.

song [sɒŋ] *n* chanson *f*. ●**songbook** *n* recueil *m* de chansons.

sonic ['sɒnɪk] *a* **s. boom** bang *m* (supersonique).

soon [suːn] *adv* (**-er, -est**) (*in a short time*) bientôt; (*quickly*) vite; (*early*) tôt; **s. after** peu après; **as s. as she leaves** aussitôt qu'elle partira; **no sooner had he spoken than** à peine avait-il parlé que; **I'd sooner leave** je préférerais partir; **I'd just as s. leave** j'aimerais autant partir; **sooner or later** tôt ou tard.

soot [sʊt] *n* suie *f*.

soothe [suːð] *vt* (*pain, nerves*) calmer.

sophisticated [sə'fɪstɪkeɪtɪd] *a* (*person, taste*) raffiné; (*machine, method*) sophistiqué.
sophomore ['sɒfəmɔːr] *n Am* étudiant, -ante *mf* de seconde année.
sopping ['sɒpɪŋ] *a & adv* **s. (wet)** trempé.
soppy ['sɒpɪ] *a* (**-ier, -iest**) *Fam* (*silly*) idiot, bête; (*sentimental*) sentimental.
soprano [sə'prɑːnəʊ] *n* (*pl* **-os**) *Mus* (*singer*) soprano *mf.*
sorbet ['sɔːbeɪ] *n* (*water ice*) sorbet *m.*
sorcerer ['sɔːsərər] *n* sorcier *m.*
sordid ['sɔːdɪd] *a* (*act, street etc*) sordide.
sore [sɔːr] *a* (**-er, -est**) (*painful*) douloureux; (*angry*) *Am* fâché (**at** contre); **she has a s. throat** elle a mal à la gorge; **he's still s.** *Med* il a encore mal ▮ *n Med* plaie *f.* ●**—ness** *n* (*pain*) douleur *f.*
sorrow ['sɒrəʊ] *n* chagrin *m,* peine *f.*
sorry ['sɒrɪ] *a* (**-ier, -iest**) (*sight etc*) triste; **to be s.** (*regret*) être désolé, regretter (**to do** de faire); **I'm s. she can't come** je regrette qu'elle ne puisse pas venir; **I'm s. about the delay** excusez-moi de ce retard; **s.!** pardon!; **to say s.** demander pardon (**to** à); **to feel** *or* **be s. for s.o.** plaindre qn.
sort[1] [sɔːt] *n* espèce *f,* sorte *f* (**of** de); **all sorts of** toutes sortes de; **what s. of drink/***etc* **is it?** qu'est-ce que c'est comme boisson/*etc*?; **s. of sad/***etc* plutôt triste/*etc.*
sort[2] [sɔːt] *vt* (*papers etc*) trier; **to s. out** (*classify, select*) trier; (*separate*) séparer (**from** de); (*arrange*) arranger; (*tidy*) ranger; (*problem*) régler ▮ *vi* **to s. through** (*letters etc*) trier; **sorting office** centre *m* de tri.
SOS [esəʊ'es] *n* SOS *m.*
sought [sɔːt] *pt & pp of* **seek.**
soul [səʊl] *n* âme *f;* **not a living s.** (*nobody*) personne, pas âme qui vive.
sound[1] [saʊnd] *n* son *m;* (*noise*) bruit *m;* **I don't like the s. of it** ça ne me plaît pas du tout; **s. barrier** mur *m* du son; **s. effects** bruitage *m.*
▮ *vt* (*bell, alarm etc*) sonner; (*bugle, horn*) sonner de; (*letter*) *Gram* prononcer; **to s. one's horn** *Aut* klaxonner.
▮ *vi* (*of bell etc*) sonner; (*seem*) sembler; **to s. like** sembler être; (*resemble*) ressembler à; **it sounds like** *or* **as if** il semble que (+ *sub or indic*). ●**soundproof** *a* insonorisé ▮ *vt* insonoriser. ●**soundtrack** *n* (*of film*) bande *f* sonore.
sound[2] [saʊnd] *a* (**-er, -est**) (*healthy*) sain; (*good, reliable*) solide ▮ *adv* **s. asleep** profondément endormi. ●**—ly** *adv* (*asleep, to sleep*) profondément.
sound[3] [saʊnd] *vt* (*test, measure*) sonder; **to s. s.o. out** sonder qn (**about** sur).
soup [suːp] *n* soupe *f,* potage *m;* **s. dish** *or* **plate** assiette *f* creuse.
sour ['saʊər] *a* (**-er, -est**) aigre; (*milk*) tourné; **to turn s.** (*of wine*) s'aigrir; (*of milk*) tourner; (*of friendship*) se détériorer.
source [sɔːs] *n* (*origin*) source *f.*
south [saʊθ] *n* sud *m;* **(to the) s. of** au sud de.
▮ *a* (*coast*) sud *inv;* (*wind*) du sud; **S. America/Africa** Amérique *f*/Afrique *f* du Sud; **S. American** (*a & n*) sud-américain, -aine (*mf*); **S. African** (*a & n*) sud-africain, -aine (*mf*).
▮ *adv* au sud, vers le sud. ●**southbound** *a* (*traffic*) en direction du sud. ●**south-'east** *n & a* sud-est *m & a inv.* ●**southerly** ['sʌðəlɪ] *a* (*point*) sud *inv;* (*direction, wind*) du sud. ●**southern** ['sʌðən] *a* (*town*) du sud; (*coast*) sud *inv;* **S. Italy** le Sud de l'Italie; **S. Africa** Afrique *f* australe. ●**southerner** ['sʌðənər] *n* habitant, -ante *mf* du Sud. ●**southward(s)** *a & adv* vers le sud. ●**south-'west** *n & a* sud-ouest *m & a inv.*
souvenir [suːvə'nɪər] *n* (*object*) souvenir *m.*
sovereign ['sɒvrɪn] *n* souverain, -aine *mf* ▮ *a* (*State, authority*) souverain.
sow[1] [səʊ] *vt* (*pt* **sowed,** *pp* **sowed** *or* **sown**) (*seeds, doubt etc*) semer.
sow[2] [saʊ] *n* (*pig*) truie *f.*
soya ['sɔɪə] *n* **s. (bean)** graine *f* de soja. ●**soybean** *n Am* graine *f* de soja.
spa [spɑː] *n* (*town*) station *f* thermale; (*spring*) source *f* minérale.
space [speɪs] *n* (*gap, emptiness, atmosphere*) espace *m;* (*period*) période *f;* (*for parking*) place *f;* **blank s.** espace *m,* blanc *m;* **to take up s.** (*room*) prendre de la place; **in the s. of** en l'espace de ▮ *a* (*voyage etc*) spatial ▮ *vt* **to s. out** espacer. ●**spacing** *n* **in double/single spacing** (*to type*) à double/simple interligne. ●**spaceman** *n* (*pl* **-men**) astronaute *m.* ●**spaceship** *n* engin *m* spatial. ●**spacesuit** *n* combinaison *f* spatiale. ●**spacewoman** *n* (*pl* **-women**) astronaute *f.*
spacious ['speɪʃəs] *a* spacieux, grand.
spade [speɪd] *n* **1** (*for garden*) bêche *f;* (*of child*) pelle *f.* **2 spade(s)** *Cards* pique *m.*
spaghetti [spə'getɪ] *n* spaghetti(s) *mpl.*
Spain [speɪn] *n* Espagne *f.*
span [spæn] *n* (*of arch*) portée *f;* (*of wings*) envergure *f;* (*of life*) *Fig* durée *f* ▮ *vt* (**-nn-**) (*of bridge etc*) enjamber (*rivière etc*); *Fig* couvrir.
Spaniard ['spænjəd] *n* Espagnol, -ole *mf.*

• **Spanish** *a* espagnol ▮ *n* (*language*) espagnol *m*. • **Spanish-A'merican** *a* hispano-américain.
spaniel ['spænjəl] *n* épagneul *m*.
spank [spæŋk] *vt* donner une fessée à. • **—ing** *n* fessée *f*.
spanner ['spænər] *n* (*tool*) clef *f* (à écrous); **adjustable s.** clef *f* à molette.
spare[1] [speər] **1** *a* (*extra*) de *or* en trop; (*clothes, tyre, Am tire*) de rechange; (*wheel*) de secours; (*available*) disponible; (*bed, room*) d'ami; **s. time** loisirs *mpl* ▮ *n* **s. (part)** *Tech Aut* pièce *f* détachée.
2 *vt* (*do without*) se passer de (*qn, qch*); (*efforts*) ménager; **to s. s.o.** (*not kill*) épargner qn; (*details etc*) épargner à qn; (*time*) accorder à qn; (*money*) donner à qn; **I can't s. the time** je n'ai pas le temps. • **sparing** *a* **to be s. with** (*butter etc*) ménager. • **sparingly** *adv* avec modération.
spare[2] [speər] *a* (*lean*) maigre.
spark [spɑːk] **1** *n* étincelle *f*. **2** *vt* **to s. off** (*cause*) provoquer. • **spark(ing) plug** *n Aut* bougie *f*.
sparkl/e ['spɑːk(ə)l] *vi* (*of diamond, star*) étinceler ▮ *n* éclat *m*. • **—ing** *a* (*wine, water*) pétillant.
sparrow ['spærəʊ] *n* moineau *m*.
sparse [spɑːs] *a* clairsemé.
spartan ['spɑːtən] *a* spartiate, austère.
spasm ['spæzəm] *n* (*of muscle*) spasme *m*; (*of coughing etc*) *Fig* accès *m*.
spastic ['spæstɪk] *n* handicapé, -ée *mf* moteur.
spat [spæt] *pt & pp of* **spit 1.**
spate [speɪt] *n* **a s. of** (*orders etc*) une avalanche de.
spatter ['spætər] *vt* (*clothes, person etc*) éclabousser (**with** de).
spawn [spɔːn] *n* (*of fish etc*) frai *m* ▮ *vi* frayer ▮ *vt Fig* engendrer.
speak [spiːk] *vi* (*pt* **spoke,** *pp* **spoken**) parler (**about, of** de); (*in assembly*) prendre la parole; **so to s.** pour ainsi dire; **to s. well of s.o./sth** dire du bien de qn/qch; **Bob speaking!** *Tel* Bob à l'appareil!; **that's spoken for** c'est pris; **to s. up** (*more loudly*) parler plus fort; (*boldly*) parler (franchement).
▮ *vt* (*language*) parler; (*say*) dire; **to s. one's mind** dire ce que l'on pense. • **speaking** *a* **to be on s. terms with s.o.** parler à qn; **English-/French-speaking** qui parle anglais/français.
speaker ['spiːkər] *n* (*public*) orateur *m*; (*in dialogue*) interlocuteur, -trice *mf*; (*loudspeaker*) *El* haut-parleur *m*; (*of stereo system*) enceinte *f*; **to be a Spanish/***etc* **s.** parler espagnol/*etc*.
spear [spɪər] *n* lance *f*.
spearmint ['spɪəmɪnt] *a* (*sweet, Am candy*) à la menthe; (*flavour*) de menthe; (*chewing-gum*) mentholé.
special ['speʃ(ə)l] *a* spécial; (*care, attention*) (tout) particulier; (*favourite*) préféré ▮ *n* **today's s.** (*in restaurant*) le plat du jour. • **specialist** *n* spécialiste *mf* (**in** de). • **speci'ality** *n* spécialité *f*. • **specialize** *vi* se spécialiser (**in** dans). • **specialized** *a* spécialisé. • **specially** *adv* spécialement; (*particularly*) particulièrement. • **specialty** *n Am* spécialité *f*.
species ['spiːʃiːz] *n inv* espèce *f*.
specific [spə'sɪfɪk] *a* précis, explicite. • **specifically** *adv* (*purposely*) expressément; (*exactly*) précisément; (*particularly*) spécifiquement.
specify ['spesɪfaɪ] *vt* spécifier (**that** que). • **specification** [-'keɪʃ(ə)n] *n* spécification *f*; *pl* (*of machine etc*) caractéristiques *fpl*.
specimen ['spesɪmɪn] *n* (*example, person*) spécimen *m*; (*of blood*) prélèvement *m*; (*of urine*) échantillon *m*.
speck [spek] *n* (*stain*) petite tache *f*; (*of dust*) grain *m*; (*dot*) point *m*.
speckled ['spek(ə)ld] *a* tacheté.
specs [speks] *npl Fam* lunettes *fpl*.
spectacle ['spektək(ə)l] *n* **1** (*sight*) spectacle *m*. **2 spectacles** (*glasses*) lunettes *fpl*. • **spec'tacular** *a* spectaculaire. • **spec'tator** *n Sp etc* spectateur, -trice *mf*.
spectrum, *pl* **-tra** ['spektrəm, -trə] *n Phys* spectre *m*; (*range*) *Fig* gamme *f*.
speculate ['spekjʊleɪt] *vi Fin Phil* spéculer; **to s. about** (*s.o.'s motives etc*) s'interroger sur ▮ *vt* **to s. that** conjecturer que. • **speculation** [-'leɪʃ(ə)n] *n Fin Phil* spéculation *f*; (*guessing*) conjectures *fpl* (**about** sur).
sped [sped] *pt & pp of* **speed 1.**
speech [spiːtʃ] *n* (*talk, lecture*) discours *m* (**on, about** sur); (*power of language*) parole *f*; (*diction*) élocution *f*; (*spoken language*) langage *m*; **freedom of s.** liberté *f* d'expression; **part of s.** catégorie *f* grammaticale. • **—less** *a* muet (*f* muette) (**with** de).
speed [spiːd] **1** *n* (*rate*) vitesse *f*; (*swiftness*) rapidité *f*; **s. limit** *Aut* limitation *f* de vitesse ▮ *vt* (*pt & pp* **sped**) **to s. up** accélérer ▮ *vi* **to s. up** (*of person*) aller plus vite; (*of pace*) s'accélérer; **to s. past** passer à toute vitesse (**sth** devant qch). **2** *vi* (*pt & pp* **speeded**) (*drive too fast*) aller trop vite. • **speeding** *n Aut* excès *m* de vitesse.
speedboat ['spiːdbəʊt] *n* vedette *f*.

• **spee'dometer** *n Aut* compteur *m* (de vitesse). • **speedway** *n Sp* piste *f* de vitesse pour motos; *Sp Aut Am* autodrome *m*.
speedy ['spi:dɪ] *a* (**-ier, -iest**) rapide. • **speedily** *adv* rapidement.
spell[1] [spel] *n* (*magic*) charme *m* (*curse*) sort *m*; **under a s.** envoûté. • **spellbound** *a* (*audience etc*) captivé.
spell[2] [spel] *n* (*period*) (courte) période *f*; (*while*) moment *m*; **cold s.** vague *f* de froid.
spell[3] [spel] *vt* (*pt & pp* **spelled** *or* **spelt**) (*write*) écrire; (*say aloud*) épeler; (*of letters*) former (*mot*); (*mean*) *Fig* signifier; **to be able to s.** savoir l'orthographe; **how is it spelt?** comment cela s'écrit-il?; **to s. out** *Fig* expliquer clairement. • **—ing** *n* orthographe *f*; **s. mistake** faute *f* d'orthographe.
spelunking [spə'lʌŋkɪŋ] *n* spéléologie *f*.
spend [spend] **1** *vt* (*pt & pp* **spent**) (*money*) dépenser (**on** pour) ‖ *vi* dépenser. **2** *vt* (*pt & pp* **spent**) (*time etc*) passer (**on sth** sur qch, **doing** à faire); (*energy*) consacrer (**on sth** à qch). • **—ing** *a* **s. money** argent *m*. • **spendthrift** *n* **to be a s.** être dépensier.
spent [spent] *pt & pp of* **spend**.
sperm [spɜ:m] *n* (*pl* **sperm** *or* **sperms**) sperme *m*.
spew [spju:] *vt* vomir.
sphere [sfɪər] *n* (*of influence etc*) & *Geom Pol* sphère *f*; (*of music etc*) domaine *m*.
sphinx [sfɪŋks] *n* sphinx *m*.
spice [spaɪs] *n* épice *f*; (*interest etc*) *Fig* piment *m* ‖ *vt* épicer. • **spicy** *a* (**-ier, -iest**) (*food*) épicé; (*story*) *Fig* pimenté.
spick-and-span [spɪkən'spæn] *a* (*clean*) impeccable.
spider ['spaɪdər] *n* araignée *f*; **s.'s web** toile *f* d'araignée.
spike [spaɪk] *n* (*of metal*) pointe *f*.
spill [spɪl] *vt* (*pt & pp* **spilled** *or* **spilt**) (*liquid*) répandre, renverser (**on, over** sur) ‖ *vi* se répandre, se renverser.
spill out *vt* (*empty*) vider (*café, verre etc*) ‖ *vi* (*of coffee etc*) se renverser (**on, over** sur) **to spill over** *vi* (*of liquid*) déborder.
spin [spɪn] *n* (*motion*) tour *m*; (*car ride*) petit tour *m*; (*on washing machine*) essorage *m* ‖ *vt* (*pt & pp* **spun,** *pres p* **spinning**) (*wheel, top*) faire tourner; (*web, wool etc*) filer; (*washing*) essorer; **to s. out** (*speech*) faire durer. ‖ *vi* (*of spinner, spider*) filer; **to s. (round)** (*of dancer, wheel etc*) tourner; (*of head*) *Fig* tourner; (*of vehicle*) faire un tête-à-queue. • **spinning** *a* **s. top** toupie *f*; **s. wheel** rouet *m*.
spinach ['spɪnɪdʒ, *Am* -ɪtʃ] *n* (*food*) épinards *mpl*.
spin-dry ['spɪndraɪ] *vt* essorer. • **spin dryer** *n* essoreuse *f*.
spine [spaɪn] *n Anat* colonne *f* vertébrale; (*spike of animal or plant*) épine *f*. • **spinal** *a* (*injury*) à la colonne vertébrale.
spinster ['spɪnstər] *n* célibataire *f*; *Pej* vieille fille *f*.
spiral ['spaɪərəl] **1** *n* spirale *f* ‖ *a* en spirale; (*staircase*) en colimaçon. **2** *vi* (**-ll-**, *Am* **-l-**) (*of prices*) monter en flèche.
spire ['spaɪər] *n* (*of church*) flèche *f*.
spirit ['spɪrɪt] *n* (*soul etc*) esprit *m*; (*courage*) *Fig* courage *m*; *pl* (*drink*) alcool *m*, spiritueux *mpl*; **spirit(s)** (*morale*) moral *m*; *Ch* alcool *m*; **in good spirits** de bonne humeur ‖ *a* (*lamp*) à alcool. • **spirited** *a* (*campaign, attack etc*) vigoureux.
spiritual ['spɪrɪtʃʊəl] *a* (*life etc*) & *Rel* spirituel.
spit [spɪt] **1** *n* crachat *m*; (*in mouth*) salive *f* ‖ *vi* (*pt & pp* **spat** *or* **spit,** *pres p* **spitting**) cracher ‖ *vt* cracher; **to s. out** (re)cracher; **the spitting image of s.o.** le portrait (tout craché) de qn. **2** *n* (*for meat*) broche *f*.
spite [spaɪt] **1** *n* **in s. of** malgré; **in s. of the fact that** bien que (+ *sub*). **2** *n* (*dislike*) rancune *f* ‖ *vt* (*annoy*) contrarier. • **spiteful** *a* méchant.
spittle ['spɪt(ə)l] *n* crachat *m*; (*in mouth*) salive *f*.
splash [splæʃ] *vt* éclabousser (**with** de, **over** sur); (*spill*) répandre ‖ *vi* (*of mud etc*) faire des éclaboussures; (*of waves*) clapoter; **to s. over sth/s.o.** éclabousser qch/qn; **to s. (about)** (*in river, mud*) patauger; (*in bath*) barboter ‖ *n* (*mark*) éclaboussure *f*; (*of colour*) *Fig* tache *f*; **s.!** plouf!
splendid ['splendɪd] *a* (*wonderful, rich etc*) splendide.
splint [splɪnt] *n Med* attelle *f*.
splinter ['splɪntər] *n* (*of wood etc*) éclat *m*; (*in finger*) écharde *f*.
split [splɪt] *n* fente *f*; (*tear*) déchirure *f*; *Pol* scission *f*; **one's s.** (*share*) *Fam* sa part.
‖ *vt* (*pt & pp* **split,** *pres p* **splitting**) (*break apart*) fendre; (*tear*) déchirer; **to s. (up)** (*group*) diviser; (*money, work*) partager (**between** entre); **to s. one's sides (laughing)** se tordre (de rire).
‖ *vi* se fendre; (*tear*) se déchirer; **to s. (up)** (*of group*) se diviser (**into** en); **to s. up** (*of couple, friends etc*) se séparer; (*of lovers*) rompre; (*of crowd*) se disperser. • **split-up** *n* (*of couple*) séparation *f*, rupture *f*.
‖ *a* **a s. second** une fraction de seconde; **s.-level apartment** duplex *m*.
splutter ['splʌtər] *vi* (*spit*) (*of person*) cra-

choter; (*of sparks, fat*) crépiter.

spoil [spɔɪl] *vt* (*pt* & *pp* **spoilt** *or* **spoiled**) (*make unpleasant*) gâter; (*damage, ruin*) abîmer; (*child, dog etc*) gâter. ● **spoilsport** *n* rabat-joie *m inv*.

spoils [spɔɪlz] *npl* (*rewards*) butin *m*.

spoke[1] [spəʊk] *n* (*of wheel*) rayon *m*.

spoke[2] [spəʊk] *pt of* **speak.** ● **spoken** *pp of* **speak** ‖ *a* (*language etc*) parlé. ● **spokesman** *n* (*pl* **-men**) *or* **spokeswoman** *n* (*pl* **-women**) porte-parole *m inv* (**for, of** de).

sponge [spʌndʒ] **1** *n* éponge *f*; **s. bag** trousse *f* de toilette; **s. cake** gâteau *m* de Savoie ‖ *vt* **to s. down/off** laver/enlever à l'éponge. **2** *vi* **to s. off** *or* **on s.o.** *Fam* vivre aux crochets de qn. ● **sponger** *n Fam* parasite *m*.

sponsor ['spɒnsər] *n* (*of appeal, advertiser etc*) personne *f* assurant le patronage (**of** de); (*for membership*) parrain *m*, marraine *f*; *Jur* garant, -ante *mf*; *Sp* sponsor *m* ‖ *vt* (*appeal etc*) patronner; (*member, company*) parrainer; *Sp* sponsoriser. ● **sponsorship** *n* patronage *m*; parrainage *m*; sponsoring *m*.

spontaneous [spɒn'teɪnɪəs] *a* spontané. ● **—ly** *adv* spontanément.

spooky ['spuːkɪ] *a* (**-ier, -iest**) *Fam* qui donne le frisson.

spool [spuːl] *n* bobine *f*.

spoon [spuːn] *n* cuillère *f*. ● **spoonfeed** *vt* (*pt* & *pp* **spoonfed**) (*help*) *Fig* mâcher le travail à. ● **spoonful** *n* cuillerée *f*.

sporadic [spə'rædɪk] *a* sporadique; **s. fighting** échauffourées *fpl*.

sport [spɔːt] **1** *n* sport *m*; **to play s.** *or Am* **sports** faire du sport; **sports club** club *m* sportif; **sports car/jacket/ground** voiture *f*/ veste *f*/terrain *m* de sport; **sports results** résultats *mpl* sportifs. **2** *vt* (*wear*) arborer. ● **—ing** *a* (*attitude, person etc*) sportif; **that's s. of you** *Fig* c'est chic de ta part.

sportsman ['spɔːtsmən] *n* (*pl* **-men**) sportif *m*. ● **sportswear** *n* vêtements *mpl* de sport. ● **sportswoman** *n* (*pl* **-women**) sportive *f*. ● **sporty** *a* (**-ier, -iest**) sportif.

spot[1] [spɒt] *n* (*stain, mark*) tache *f*; (*dot*) point *m*; (*pimple*) bouton *m*; (*place*) endroit *m*, (*act*) *Th* numéro *m*; (*drop*) goutte *f*; **a s. of** *Fam* un peu de; **a soft s. for** un faible pour; **on the s.** sur place; **(accident) black s.** *Aut* point *m* noir; **s. check** contrôle *m* au hasard. ● **spotless** *a* (*clean*) impeccable. ● **spotlight** *n Th* projecteur *m*; (*for photography*) spot *m*. ● **spotted** *a* (*fur*) tacheté; (*dress*) à pois. ● **spotty** *a* (**-ier, -iest**) **1** (*face etc*) boutonneux. **2** (*patchy*) *Am* inégal.

spot[2] [spɒt] *vt* (**-tt-**) (*notice*) apercevoir.

spouse [spaʊs, spaʊz] *n* époux *m*, épouse *f*.

spout [spaʊt] **1** *n* (*of teapot etc*) bec *m*. **2** *vi* **to s. (out)** jaillir.

sprain [spreɪn] *n* foulure *f*; **to s. one's ankle/wrist** se fouler la cheville/le poignet.

sprang [spræŋ] *pt of* **spring**[1].

sprawl [sprɔːl] *vi* (*of town, person*) s'étaler; **to be sprawling** être étalé ‖ *n* **the urban s.** les banlieues *fpl* tentaculaires.

spray [spreɪ] **1** *n* (*can*) bombe *f*; (*water drops*) gouttelettes *fpl*; (*from sea*) embruns *mpl*; **hair s.** laque *f* à cheveux ‖ *vt* (*liquid, surface*) vaporiser; (*plant, crops*) arroser, traiter; (*car*) peindre à la bombe. **2** *n* (*of flowers*) petit bouquet *m*.

spread [spred] *vt* (*pt* & *pp* **spread**) (*stretch, open out*) étendre; (*legs, fingers*) écarter; (*distribute*) répandre (**over** sur); (*paint, payment, visits*) étaler; (*news, germs*) propager; **to s. out** étendre; écarter; étaler.
‖ *vi* (*of fire, town, fog*) s'étendre; (*of news, epidemic*) se propager; **to s. out** (*of people*) se disperser.
‖ *n* (*of fire, germs, ideas*) propagation *f*; (*paste*) *Culin* pâte *f* (à tartiner); (*meal*) festin *m*; **cheese s.** fromage *m* à tartiner. ● **s.-'eagled** *a* bras et jambes écartés. ● **spreadsheet** *n Comptr* tableur *m*.

spree [spriː] *n* **to go on a spending s.** faire des achats extravagants.

sprightly ['spraɪtlɪ] *a* (**-ier, -iest**) alerte.

spring[1] [sprɪŋ] *n* (*metal device*) ressort *m*; (*leap*) bond *m* ‖ *vi* (*pt* **sprang,** *pp* **sprung**) (*leap*) bondir; **to s. to mind** venir à l'esprit; **to s. from** provenir de; **to s. up** surgir ‖ *vt* (*news*) annoncer brusquement (**on** à); **to s. a leak** (*of boat*) commencer à faire eau. ● **springboard** *n* tremplin *m*.

spring[2] [sprɪŋ] *n* (*season*) printemps *m*; **in (the) s.** au printemps; **s. onion** oignon *m* vert. ● **s.-'cleaning** *n* nettoyage *m* de printemps. ● **springlike** *a* printanier. ● **springtime** *n* printemps *m*.

spring[3] [sprɪŋ] *n* (*of water*) source *f*; **s. water** eau *f* de source.

sprinkl/e ['sprɪŋk(ə)l] *vt* (*sand etc*) répandre (**on, over** sur); **to s. with water, s. water on** asperger d'eau; **to s. with** (*sugar, salt, flour*) saupoudrer de. ● **—er** *n* (*in garden*) arroseur *m*.

sprint [sprɪnt] *n Sp* sprint *m* ‖ *vi* sprinter. ● **—er** *n* sprinter *m*, sprinteuse *f*.

sprout [spraʊt] **1** *vi* (*of seed etc*) germer, pousser; **to s. up** pousser vite; (*appear*) surgir ‖ *vt* (*leaves*) pousser. **2** *n* **(Brussels) s.** chou *m* de Bruxelles.

spruce [spruːs] *a* (**-er, -est**) (*neat*) pimpant ‖ *vt* **to s. oneself up** se faire beau.

sprung [sprʌŋ] *pp of* **spring**[1].

spry [spraɪ] *a* (**spryer, spryest**) (*old person*) alerte.

spud [spʌd] *n* (*potato*) *Fam* patate *f*.

spun [spʌn] *pt & pp of* **spin**.

spur [spɜːr] *n* (*of horse rider*) éperon *m*; (*stimulus*) *Fig* aiguillon *m*; **on the s. of the moment** sur un coup de tête ‖ *vt* (**-rr-**) **to s. s.o. on** (*urge on*) aiguillonner qn.

spurn [spɜːn] *vt* rejeter (avec mépris).

spurt [spɜːt] *vi* **to s. (out)** (*of liquid*) jaillir ‖ *n* (*of energy*) sursaut *m*; **to put on a s.** (*rush*) foncer.

spy [spaɪ] *n* espion, -onne *mf*; **s. hole** judas *m*; **s. ring** réseau *m* d'espionnage ‖ *vi* **to s. on s.o.** espionner qn. ●**—ing** *n* espionnage *m*.

squabble ['skwɒb(ə)l] *vi* se chamailler (**over** à propos de) ‖ *n* chamaillerie *f*.

squad [skwɒd] *n* (*group*) & *Mil* escouade *f*; (*team*) *Sp* équipe *f*.

squadron ['skwɒdrən] *n Mil* escadron *m*; *Nau Av* escadrille *f*.

squalid ['skwɒlɪd] *a* sordide. ●**squalor** *n* conditions *fpl* sordides.

squall [skwɔːl] *n* (*of wind*) rafale *f*.

squander ['skwɒndər] *vt* (*money, time*) gaspiller (**on** en).

square ['skweər] *n* carré *m*; (*on chessboard, graph paper*) case *f*; (*in town*) place *f* ‖ *a* carré; (*in order, settled*) *Fig* en ordre; (*meal*) solide; **(all) s.** (*quits*) quitte (**with** envers) ‖ *vt* (*settle*) mettre en ordre, régler; (*arrange*) arranger; *Math* mettre au carré ‖ *vi* (*tally*) cadrer (**with** avec). ●**squarely** *adv* (*honestly*) honnêtement.

squash [skwɒʃ] **1** *vt* (*crush*) écraser; (*squeeze*) serrer ‖ *n* **lemon/orange s.** sirop *m* de citron/d'orange; (*diluted*) citronnade *f*/orangeade *f*. **2** *n* (*game*) squash *m*. **3** *n* (*vegetable*) *Am* courge *f*.

squat [skwɒt] **1** *vi* (**-tt-**) **to s. (down)** s'accroupir; **squatting (down)** accroupi. ●**squatter** *n* squatter *m*. **2** *a* (*short and thick*) trapu.

squeak [skwiːk] *vi* (*of door*) grincer; (*of shoe*) craquer; (*of mouse*) faire couic.

squeal [skwiːl] *vi* pousser des cris aigus ‖ *n* cri *m* aigu. **2** *vi* **to s. on s.o.** (*inform on*) *Fam* balancer qn.

squeamish ['skwiːmɪʃ] *a* facilement dégoûté.

squeeze [skwiːz] *vt* (*press*) presser; (*hand, arm*) serrer; **to s. sth into sth** faire rentrer qch dans qch; **to s. (out)** (*juice etc*) faire sortir (**from** de).
‖ *vi* **to s. through/into/***etc* (*force oneself*) se glisser par/dans/*etc*; **to s. in** trouver un peu de place; **to s. up** se serrer (**against** contre). ‖ *n* **to give sth a s.** presser qch; **it's a tight s.** il y a peu de place. ●**squeezer** *n* **lemon s.** presse-citron *m*.

squelch [skweltʃ] *vi* patauger (*en faisant floc-floc*).

squid [skwɪd] *n* (*mollusc*) calmar *m*.

squiggle ['skwɪg(ə)l] *n* gribouillis *m*; (*line*) ligne *f* onduleuse.

squint [skwɪnt] *n* **to have a s.** loucher ‖ *vi* loucher; (*in the sunlight etc*) plisser les yeux.

squirm [skwɜːm] *vi* (*wriggle*) se tortiller.

squirrel ['skwɪrəl, *Am* 'skwɜːrəl] *n* écureuil *m*.

squirt [skwɜːt] *vt* (*liquid*) faire gicler ‖ *vi* gicler ‖ *n* giclée *f*, jet *m*.

stab [stæb] *vt* (**-bb-**) (*with knife etc*) poignarder ‖ *n* **s. (wound)** coup *m* (de couteau).

stable[1] ['steɪb(ə)l] *a* (**-er, -est**) stable; **mentally s.** bien équilibré. ●**sta'bility** *n* stabilité *f*. ●**stabilize** *vt* stabiliser ‖ *vi* se stabiliser.

stable[2] ['steɪb(ə)l] *n* écurie *f*.

stack [stæk] *n* (*heap*) tas *m*; **stacks of** *Fam* un *or* des tas de ‖ *vt* **to s. (up)** entasser.

stadium ['steɪdɪəm] *n Sp* stade *m*.

staff [stɑːf] *n* personnel *m*; (*of school*) professeurs *mpl*; (*of army*) état-major *m*; **a member of s.** (*in office*) un(e) employé, -ée; **s. meeting** *Sch* conseil *m* des professeurs; **s. room** *Sch* salle *f* des professeurs.

stag [stæg] *n* cerf *m*.

stage[1] [steɪdʒ] *n* (*platform*) *Th* scène *f*; **the s.** (*profession*) le théâtre; **s. door** entrée *f* des artistes ‖ *vt* (*play*) monter; *Fig* organiser. ●**s.-hand** *n* machiniste *m*. ●**s.-manager** *n* régisseur *m*.

stage[2] [steɪdʒ] *n* (*phase*) stade *m*, étape *f*; (*of journey*) étape *f*; **in (easy) stages** par étapes; **at an early s.** au début.

stagecoach ['steɪdʒkəʊtʃ] *n Hist* diligence *f*.

stagger ['stægər] **1** *vi* chanceler. **2** *vt* (*holidays, Am vacation etc*) étaler. **3** *vt* **to s. s.o.** stupéfier qn. ●**—ing** *a* stupéfiant.

stagnant ['stægnənt] *a* stagnant. ●**stag'nate** *vi* stagner.

staid [steɪd] *a* posé, sérieux.

stain [steɪn] **1** *vt* (*to mark*) tacher (**with** de) ‖ *n* tache *f*; **s. remover** détachant *m*. **2** *vt* (*colour*) teinter (*du bois*); **stained glass window** vitrail *m* (*pl* vitraux). ●**stainless steel** *n* inox *m*; **s.-steel knife/***etc* couteau *m*/*etc* en inox.

stair [steər] *n* **a s.** (*step*) une marche; **the**

stairs (*staircase*) l'escalier *m.* ● **staircase** *or* **stairway** *n* escalier *m.*
stake [steɪk] **1** *n* (*post*) pieu *m*; (*for plant*) tuteur *m* ▮ *vt* **to s. one's claim to** revendiquer. **2** *n* (*betting*) enjeu *m*; (*investment*) investissement *m*; **at s.** en jeu ▮ *vt* (*bet*) jouer (**on** sur).
stale [steɪl] *a* (**-er, -est**) (*bread*) rassis (*f* rassie); (*food*) pas frais (*f* fraîche); (*air*) vicié; (*smell*) de renfermé; (*news*) *Fig* vieux (*f* vieille).
stalemate ['steɪlmeɪt] *n Chess* pat *m*; *Fig* impasse *f*.
stalk [stɔːk] **1** *n* (*of plant*) tige *f*; (*of fruit*) queue *f*. **2** *vt* (*animal*) traquer.
stall [stɔːl] **1** *n* (*in market*) étal *m*; (*for newspapers, flowers*) kiosque *m*; (*in stable*) stalle *f*; **the stalls** *Cin* l'orchestre *m.* **2** *vti Aut* caler. **3** *vi* **to s. (for time)** chercher à gagner du temps.
stallion ['stæljən] *n* (*horse*) étalon *m.*
stamina ['stæmɪnə] *n* vigueur *f*, résistance *f*.
stammer ['stæmər] *vi* bégayer ▮ *n* bégaiement *m*; **to have a s.** être bègue.
stamp [stæmp] **1** *n* (*for postage, instrument*) timbre *m*; (*mark*) cachet *m*; **the s. of** *Fig* la marque de; **s. collecting** philatélie *f* ▮ *vt* (*document*) tamponner; (*letter*) timbrer; (*metal*) estamper; **to s. out** (*rebellion*) écraser; (*disease*) supprimer; **stamped addressed envelope**, *Am* **stamped self-addressed envelope** enveloppe *f* timbrée à votre adresse.
2 *vti* **to s. (one's feet)** taper des pieds.
stampede [stæm'piːd] *n* fuite *f* précipitée; (*rush*) ruée *f*.
stance [stɑːns] *n* position *f*.
stand [stænd] *n* (*position*) position *f*; (*support*) support *m*; (*at exhibition*) stand *m*; (*for spectators*) *Sp* tribune *f*; **(witness) s.** *Am* barre *f*; **news/flower s.** kiosque *m* à journaux/à fleurs.
▮ *vt* (*pt & pp* **stood**) (*pain, person etc*) supporter; (*put straight*) mettre (debout); **to s. a chance** avoir une chance.
▮ *vi* être *or* se tenir (debout); (*get up*) se lever; (*remain*) rester (debout); (*be situated*) se trouver.
stand about *or* **around** *vi* (*in street etc*) traîner **to stand aside** *vi* s'écarter **to stand back** *vi* reculer **to stand by** *vi* (*do nothing*) rester là (sans rien faire); (*be ready*) être prêt (à intervenir *etc*) ▮ *vt* (*friend*) rester fidèle à **to stand down** *vi* (*withdraw*) se désister **to stand for** *vt* (*mean*) signifier, représenter; *Pol* être candidat à; (*put up with*) supporter **to stand in for** *vt* (*replace*) remplacer **to stand out** *vi* (*be conspicuous*) ressortir (**against** sur) **to stand over** *vt* (*watch*) surveiller (*qn*) **to stand up** *vt* mettre debout ▮ *vi* (*get up*) se lever **to stand up for** *vt* défendre **to stand up to** *vt* (*resist*) résister à; (*defend onself*) tenir tête à (*qn*).
standard ['stændəd] **1** *n* (*norm*) norme *f*; (*level*) niveau *m*; (*of weight, gold*) étalon *m*; **standards (of behaviour)** principes *mpl*; **s. of living, living standards** niveau *m* de vie; **up to s.** (*work etc*) au niveau; (*person*) à la hauteur ▮ *a* (*average*) ordinaire; (*model, size*) standard *inv*; (*dictionary*) classique; **s. lamp** lampadaire *m.* **2** *n* (*flag*) étendard *m.* ● **standardize** *vt* standardiser.
standby ['stændbaɪ] *n* (*pl* **-bys**) **on s.** prêt à partir *or* à intervenir ▮ *a* (*battery etc*) de réserve; (*ticket*) *Av* sans garantie.
stand-in ['stædɪn] *n Th* doublure *f* (**for** de).
standing ['stændɪŋ] *a* debout *inv*; (*committee, offer*) permanent; **s. order** (*in bank*) virement *m* automatique ▮ *n* réputation *f*; (*social, professional*) rang *m*; (*financial*) situation *f*.
stand-offish [stænd'ɒfɪʃ] *a* (*person*) distant, froid.
standpoint ['stændpɔɪnt] *n* point *m* de vue.
standstill ['stændstɪl] *n* **to bring to a s.** immobiliser; **to come to a s.** s'immobiliser; **at a s.** immobile; (*negotiations*) paralysé.
stank [stæŋk] *pt of* **stink.**
stapl/e ['steɪp(ə)l] **1** *a* **s. food** *or* **diet** nourriture *f* de base. **2** *n* (*for paper etc*) agrafe *f* ▮ *vt* agrafer. ● **—er** *n* agrafeuse *f*.
star [stɑːr] *n* étoile *f*; (*person*) vedette *f*; **shooting s.** étoile *f* filante; **s. part** rôle *m* principal; **the Stars and Stripes, the S.-Spangled Banner** *Am* la bannière étoilée; **four-s. (petrol)** du super ▮ *vi* (**-rr-**) (*of actor*) être la vedette (**in** de) ▮ *vt* (*of film*) avoir pour vedette. ● **stardom** *n* célébrité *f*. ● **starfish** *n* étoile *f* de mer.
starboard ['stɑːbəd] *n Nau Av* tribord *m.*
starch [stɑːtʃ] *n* (*for stiffening*) amidon *m*; (*in food*) fécule *f*. ● **starchy** *a* (**-ier, -iest**) **s. food(s)** féculents *mpl.*
stare [steər] *n* regard *m* (fixe) ▮ *vi* **to s. at s.o./sth** fixer qn/qch (du regard).
stark [stɑːk] *a* (**-er, -est**) (*place*) désolé; (*austere*) austère; (*fact, reality*) brutal; **to be in s. contrast to** contraster nettement avec ▮ *adv* **s. naked** complètement nu.
starling ['stɑːlɪŋ] *n* étourneau *m.*
start[1] [stɑːt] *n* commencement *m*, début *m*; (*of race*) départ *m*; (*lead*) *Sp & Fig* avance *f*

(**on** sur); **to make a s.** commencer; **for a s.** pour commencer; **from the s.** dès le début. ▮ *vt* commencer; (*fashion*) lancer; (*engine, vehicle*) mettre en marche; (*business*) fonder; **to s. a war/fire** (*cause*) provoquer une guerre/un incendie; **to s. doing** *or* **to do** commencer à faire.

▮ *vi* commencer (**with sth** par qch, **by doing** par faire); (*of vehicle*) démarrer; (*leave*) partir (**for** pour); **to s. with** (*firstly*) pour commencer. ● **starting** *a* (*point, line*) de départ; **s. post** *Sp* ligne *f* de départ; **s. from** à partir de. ● **starter** *n* (*in vehicle*) démarreur *m*; (*course of meal*) hors-d'œuvre *m inv*, entrée *f*; (*soup*) potage *m*; (*runner*) partant *m*.

start[2] [stɑ:t] *vi* (*be startled, jump*) sursauter ▮ *n* sursaut *m*.

start back *vi* (*return*) repartir **to start off** *vi* (*leave*) partir (**for** pour) **to start on** *vt* commencer (*qch*); **to s. s.o. on** (*career*) lancer qn dans **to start out** *vi* = **start off to start up** *vt* (*engine, vehicle*) mettre en marche; (*business*) fonder ▮ *vi* (*of engine, vehicle*) démarrer.

startle ['stɑ:t(ə)l] *vt* (*make jump*) faire sursauter; (*alarm*) *Fig* alarmer.

starve [stɑ:v] *vi* souffrir de la faim; (*die*) mourir de faim; **I'm starving!** (*hungry*) je meurs de faim! ▮ *vt* (*make suffer*) faire souffrir de la faim; (*deprive*) *Fig* priver (**of** de). ● **starvation** [-'veɪʃ(ə)n] *n* faim *f*; **on a s. diet** à la diète.

stash [stæʃ] *vt* **to s. away** (*hide*) *Fam* cacher.

state[1] [steɪt] **1** *n* (*condition*) état *m*; **in no (fit) s. to** hors d'état de; **in a s.** (*bad shape*) dans un drôle d'état.

2 *n* **S.** (*nation etc*) État *m*; **the States** *Fam* les États-Unis *mpl* ▮ *a* (*secret*) d'État; (*control*) de l'État; (*school, education*) public; **s. visit** voyage *m* officiel. ● **s.-of-the-'art** *a* (*technology etc*) de pointe; (*up-to-date*) dernier cri. ● **state-'owned** *a* étatisé. ● **statesman** *n* (*pl* **-men**) homme *m* d'État.

state[2] [steɪt] *vt* déclarer (**that** que); (*problem*) exposer; (*time, date*) fixer. ● **statement** *n* déclaration *f*; *Jur* déposition *f*; **(bank) s.** relevé *m* de compte.

stately ['steɪtlɪ] *a* (**-ier, -iest**) majestueux; **s. home** château *m*.

static ['stætɪk] *a* statique.

station ['steɪʃ(ə)n] *n* (*for trains*) gare *f*; (*underground*) station *f*; (*social*) rang *m*; **(police) s.** commissariat *m* (de police); **bus** *or* **coach s.** gare *f* routière; **radio/space s.** station *f* de radio/spatiale; **service** *or* **petrol** *or Am* **gas s.** station-service *f*; **s. wagon** *Aut Am* break *m* ▮ *vt* (*troops*) poster. ● **stationmaster** *n Rail* chef *m* de gare.

stationary ['steɪʃən(ə)rɪ] *a* (*vehicle*) à l'arrêt.

stationer ['steɪʃ(ə)nər] *n* papetier, -ière *mf*; **s.'s (shop)** papeterie *f*. ● **stationery** *n* articles *mpl* de bureau.

statistic [stə'tɪstɪk] *n* (*fact*) statistique *f*; **statistics** (*science*) la statistique.

statue ['stætʃu:] *n* statue *f*.

stature ['stætʃər] *n* stature *f*.

status ['steɪtəs] *n* (*position*) situation *f*; (*legal, official*) statut *m*; (*prestige*) standing *m*; **s. symbol** marque *f* de standing.

statute ['stætʃu:t] *n* (*law*) loi *f*; *pl* (*of institution*) statuts *mpl*.

staunch [stɔ:ntʃ] *a* (**-er, -est**) loyal, fidèle.

stave [steɪv] *vt* **to s. off** (*disaster*) conjurer; (*hunger*) tromper.

stay [steɪ] *n* (*visit*) séjour *m* ▮ *vi* (*remain*) rester; (*reside*) loger; (*visit*) séjourner; **to s. put** ne pas bouger. ● **s.-at-home** *n Pej* casanier, -ière *mf*.

stay away *vi* ne pas s'approcher (**from** de); **to s. away from** (*school*) ne pas aller à **to stay in** *vi* (*at home*) rester à la maison; (*of nail, screw etc*) tenir **to stay out** *vi* (*outside*) rester dehors; (*not come home*) ne pas rentrer; **to s. out of sth** (*not interfere in*) ne pas se mêler de qch; (*avoid*) éviter qch ▮ **to stay up** *vi* (*at night*) ne pas se coucher; (*of fence etc*) tenir; **to s. up late** se coucher tard.

stead [sted] *n* **to stand s.o. in good s.** être bien utile à qn; **in s.o.'s s.** à la place de qn.

steadfast ['stedfɑ:st] *a* (*intention etc*) ferme.

steady ['stedɪ] *a* (**-ier, -iest**) stable; (*hand*) sûr; (*progress, speed, demand*) régulier; (*nerves*) solide; **a s. boyfriend** un petit ami; **s. (on one's feet)** solide sur ses jambes ▮ *vt* (*chair etc*) maintenir (en place); (*nerves*) calmer. ● **steadily** *adv* (*to walk*) d'un pas assuré; (*gradually*) progressivement; (*regularly*) régulièrement; (*continuously*) sans arrêt.

steak [steɪk] *n* steak *m*, bifteck *m*. ● **steakhouse** *n* grill(-room) *m*.

steal[1] [sti:l] *vti* (*pt* **stole**, *pp* **stolen**) voler (**from s.o.** à qn).

steal[2] [sti:l] *vi* (*pt* **stole**, *pp* **stolen**) **to s. in/out** entrer/sortir furtivement. ● **stealthy** ['stelθɪ] *a* (**-ier, -iest**) furtif.

steam [sti:m] *n* vapeur *f*; (*on glass*) buée *f*; **to let off s.** *Fam* décompresser; **s. engine** locomotive *f* à vapeur ▮ *vt* (*food*) cuire à la vapeur; **to get steamed up** (*of glass*) se couvrir de buée ‖ *vi* (*of kettle*) fumer. ● **steamer** *or* **steamship** *n* (bateau *m* à) vapeur *m*; (*liner*) paquebot *m*. ● **steamroller** *n* rouleau *m* compresseur. ● **steamy** *a* (**-ier, -iest**) humide; (*window*) embué.

steel [sti:l] **1** *n* acier *m*; **s. industry** sidérurgie *f*. **2** *vt* **to s. oneself** s'armer de courage.

steep [sti:p] **1** *a* (**-er, -est**) (*stairs, slope etc*) raide; (*hill, path*) escarpé; (*price*) *Fig* excessif. **2** *vt* (*soak*) tremper (**in** dans). ● **—ly** *adv* (*to rise*) en pente raide, (*of prices*) *Fig* excessivement.

steeple ['sti:p(ə)l] *n* clocher *m*.

steer [stɪər] *vt* (*vehicle, ship, person*) diriger (**towards** vers) ‖ *vi Nau* tenir le gouvernail; **to s. towards** faire route vers; **to s. clear of** éviter. ● **—ing** *n Aut* direction *f*; **s. wheel** volant *m*.

stem [stem] **1** *n* (*of plant*) tige *f*. **2** *vt* (**-mm-**) **to s. (the flow of)** (*stop*) arrêter. **3** *vi* (**-mm-**) **to s. from** provenir de.

stench [stentʃ] *n* puanteur *f*.

stencil ['stens(ə)l] *n* (*metal, plastic*) pochoir *m*; (*paper, for typing*) stencil *m*.

stenographer [stə'nɒgrəfər] *n Am* sténodactylo *f*.

step [step] *n* pas *m*; (*of stairs*) marche *f*; (*on train, bus*) marchepied *m*; (*doorstep*) pas *m* de la porte; (*action*) *Fig* mesure *f*; **(flight of) steps** escalier *m*; (*outdoors*) perron *m*; **(pair of) steps** (*ladder*) escabeau *m*; **s. by s.** pas à pas; **in s. with** *Fig* en accord avec ‖ *vi* (**-pp-**) (*walk*) marcher (**on** sur). ● **stepladder** *n* escabeau *m*. ● **stepping-stone** *n Fig* tremplin *m* (**to** pour arriver à).

step aside *vi* s'écarter **to step back** *vi* reculer **to step down** *vi* descendre (**from** de); (*withdraw*) *Fig* se retirer **to step forward** *vi* faire un pas en avant **to step in** *vi* (*intervene*) intervenir **to step into** *vt* (*car etc*) monter dans **to step out** *vi* (*of car etc*) descendre (**of** de) **to step over** *vt* (*obstacle*) enjamber **to step up** *vt* (*increase*) augmenter; (*speed up*) activer.

stepbrother ['stepbrʌðər] *n* demi-frère *m*. ● **stepdaughter** *n* belle-fille *f*. ● **stepfather** *n* beau-père *m*. ● **stepmother** *n* belle-mère *f*. ● **stepsister** *n* demi-sœur *f*. ● **stepson** *n* beau-fils *m*.

stereo ['sterɪəʊ] *n* (*pl* **-os**) (*record player etc*) chaîne *f* (stéréo *inv*); **in s.** en stéréo; **(personal) s.** baladeur *m* ‖ *a* (*record etc*) stéréo *inv*; (*broadcast*) en stéréo.

stereotype ['sterɪətaɪp] *n* stéréotype *m*.

sterile ['steraɪl, *Am* 'sterəl] *a* stérile. ● **sterilize** *vt* stériliser.

sterling ['stɜ:lɪŋ] *n* (*currency*) livre(s) *f(pl)* sterling *inv*; **the pound s.** la livre sterling *inv*.

steroid ['stɪərɔɪd] *n* stéroïde *m*.

stern [stɜ:n] **1** *a* (**-er, -est**) sévère. **2** *n* (*of ship*) arrière *m*.

stethoscope ['steθəskəʊp] *n* stéthoscope *m*.

stew [stju:] *n* ragoût *m*; **s. pot** cocotte *f* ‖ *vt* (*meat*) faire en ragoût; (*fruit*) faire cuire; **stewed fruit** compote *f* ‖ *vi* cuire.

steward ['stju:əd] *n* (*on plane, ship*) steward *m*; **shop s.** délégué, -ée *mf* syndical(e). ● **stewar'dess** *n* (*on plane*) hôtesse *f*.

stick[1] [stɪk] *n* (*of wood, chalk etc*) bâton *m*; (*for walking*) canne *f*; **in the sticks** *Pej Fam* à la cambrousse.

stick[2] [stɪk] *vt* (*pt & pp* **stuck**) (*glue*) coller; (*put*) *Fam* mettre, fourrer; (*tolerate*) *Fam* supporter; **to s. sth into sth** fourrer qch dans qch ‖ *vi* coller (**to** à); (*of food in pan*) attacher (**to** dans); (*of drawer etc*) se coincer, être coincé; (*remain*) *Fam* rester; **sticking plaster** sparadrap *m*.

stick around *vi Fam* rester dans les parages **to stick by** *vt* rester fidèle à (*qn*) **to stick down** *vt* (*envelope*) coller; (*put down*) *Fam* poser **to stick on** *vt* (*stamp*) coller; (*hat etc*) mettre **to stick out** *vt* (*tongue*) tirer; (*head*) sortir; **to s. it out** *Fam* tenir le coup ‖ *vi* (*of petticoat, balcony etc*) dépasser **to stick up** *vt* (*notice*) coller, afficher; (*hand*) *Fam* lever **to stick up for** *vt* défendre.

sticker ['stɪkər] *n* (*label*) autocollant *m*.

stick-up ['stɪkʌp] *n Fam* hold-up *m inv*.

sticky ['stɪkɪ] *a* (**-ier, -iest**) collant; (*label*) adhésif; (*problem*) *Fig* difficile.

stiff [stɪf] *a* (**-er, -est**) raide; (*leg etc*) ankylosé; (*brush*) dur; (*person*) *Fig* guindé; (*price*) élevé; **to have a s. neck** avoir le torticolis; **to feel s.** être courbatu(ré); **to be bored s.** *Fam* s'ennuyer à mourir; **frozen s.** *Fam* complètement gelé. ● **stiffen** *vt* raidir ‖ *vi* se raidir. ● **stiffness** *n* raideur *f*.

stifle ['staɪf(ə)l] *vt* étouffer ‖ *vi* **it's stifling** on étouffe.

stigma ['stɪgmə] *n* (*moral stain*) flétrissure *f*; **there's no s. attached to...** il n'y a aucune honte à....

stiletto [stɪ'letəʊ] *a* **s. heel** talon *m* aiguille.

still[1] [stɪl] *adv* encore, toujours; (*even*) encore; (*nevertheless*) tout de même.

still[2] [stɪl] *a* (**-er, -est**) (*not moving*) immobile; (*calm*) calme, tranquille; (*drink*) non gazeux; **to keep** *or* **stand s.** rester tranquille; **s. life** nature *f* morte. ● **stillborn** *a* mort-né.

stilt [stɪlt] *n* (*pole*) échasse *f*.
stilted ['stɪltɪd] *a* (*speech, person*) guindé.
stimulate ['stɪmjʊleɪt] *vt* stimuler. ● **stimulus,** *pl* **-li** [-laɪ] *n* (*encouragement*) stimulant *m*.
sting [stɪŋ] *vti* (*pt* & *pp* **stung**) (*of insect, ointment etc*) piquer ▮ *n* piqûre *f*; (*insect's organ*) dard *m*.
stingy ['stɪndʒɪ] *a* (**-ier, -iest**) avare, mesquin; **s. with** (*money, praise*) avare de; (*food*) mesquin sur.
stink [stɪŋk] *n* puanteur *f* ▮ *vi* (*pt* **stank** *or* **stunk,** *pp* **stunk**) puer; (*of book, film etc*) *Fam* être infect; **to s. of smoke/***etc* empester la fumée/*etc* ▮ *vt* **to s. out** (*room*) empester. ● **—ing** *a Fam* infect.
stint [stɪnt] **1** *n* (*period*) période *f* de travail; (*share*) part *f* de travail. **2** *vi* **to s. on** lésiner sur.
stipulate ['stɪpjʊleɪt] *vt* stipuler (**that** que).
stir [stɜːr] *n* **to give sth a s.** remuer qch; **to cause** *or* **create a s.** *Fig* faire du bruit ▮ *vt* (**-rr-**) (*coffee, leaves etc*) remuer; (*excite*) *Fig* exciter; (*incite*) inciter (**to do** à faire); **to s. up** (*trouble*) provoquer ▮ *vi* remuer. ● **stirring** *a* (*speech*) émouvant.
stirrup ['stɪrəp] *n* étrier *m*.
stitch [stɪtʃ] *n* point *m*; (*in knitting*) maille *f*; (*in wound*) point *m* de suture; **a s.** (*pain*) un point de côté; **to be in stitches** *Fam* se tordre (de rire) ▮ *vt* **to s. (up)** (*sew up*) coudre; (*repair*) recoudre; *Med* suturer.
stock [stɒk] *n* (*supply*) provision *f*, stock *m*; (*of knowledge, jokes*) fonds *m*, mine *f*; (*family*) souche *f*; (*soup*) bouillon *m*; **stocks and shares** *Fin* valeurs *fpl* (boursières); **in s.** (*goods*) en magasin, en stock; **out of s.** épuisé; **to take s.** *Fig* faire le point (**of** de); **s. phrase** expression *f* toute faite; **the S. Exchange** *or* **Market** la Bourse.
▮ *vt* (*sell*) vendre; (*keep in store*) stocker; **to s. (up)** (*shop, larder*) approvisionner; **well-stocked** bien approvisionné.
▮ *vi* **to s. up** s'approvisionner (**with** de, en).
stockbroker ['stɒkbrəʊkər] *n* agent *m* de change. ● **stockist** *n* dépositaire *mf*. ● **stockpile** *vt* stocker, amasser. ● **stocktaking** *n Com* inventaire *m*.
stocking ['stɒkɪŋ] *n* (*garment*) bas *m*.
stocky ['stɒkɪ] *a* (**-ier, -iest**) trapu.
stodgy ['stɒdʒɪ] *a* (**-ier, -iest**) (*food*) *Fam* lourd, indigeste.
stoke [stəʊk] *vt* (*fire*) entretenir; (*furnace*) alimenter.
stole[1] [stəʊl] *n* (*shawl*) étole *f*.
stole[2], **stolen** [stəʊl, 'stəʊl(ə)n] *pt* & *pp of* **steal**[1,2].
stomach ['stʌmək] **1** *n* (*for digestion*) estomac *m*; (*front of body*) ventre *m*. **2** *vt* (*put up with*) supporter. ● **stomach-ache** *n* mal *m* de ventre; **to have a s.-ache** avoir mal au ventre.
stone [stəʊn] *n* pierre *f*; (*pebble*) caillou *m* (*pl* -oux); (*in fruit*) noyau *m*; (*in kidney*) calcul *m*; (*weight*) = 6,348 kg; **a stone's throw away** *Fig* à deux pas d'ici ▮ *vt* lancer des pierres sur.
stone- [stəʊn] *pref* complètement. ● **s.-'broke** *a Am Sl* fauché. ● **s.-'deaf** *a* sourd comme un pot.
stoned [stəʊnd] *a* (*on drugs*) *Fam* camé.
stony ['stəʊnɪ] *a* **1** (**-ier, -iest**) (*path etc*) caillouteux. **2 s. broke** *Sl* fauché.
stood [stʊd] *pt* & *pp of* **stand.**
stool [stuːl] *n* tabouret *m*.
stoop [stuːp] **1** *n* **to have a s.** être voûté ▮ *vi* se baisser; **to s. to doing** *Fig* s'abaisser à faire. **2** *n* (*in front of house*) *Am* perron *m*.
stop [stɒp] *n* (*place, halt*) arrêt *m*, halte *f*; (*for plane, ship*) escale *f*; *Gram* point *m*; **bus s.** arrêt *m* d'autobus; **to put a s. to sth** mettre fin à qch; **to come to a s.** s'arrêter; **s. light** (*on vehicle*) stop *m*; **s. sign** (*on road*) stop *m*.
▮ *vt* (**-pp-**) arrêter; (*end*) mettre fin à; (*prevent*) empêcher (**from doing** de faire).
▮ *vi* s'arrêter; (*of pain, conversation etc*) cesser; (*stay*) rester; **to s. eating/***etc* s'arrêter de manger/*etc*; **to s. snowing/***etc* cesser de neiger/*etc*.
stop by *vi* passer (**s.o.'s** chez qn) **to stop off** *or* **over** *vi* (*on journey*) s'arrêter **to stop up** *vt* (*sink, pipe etc*) boucher.
stopgap ['stɒpgæp] *n* bouche-trou *m*.
stoppage ['stɒpɪdʒ] *n* (*in work*) arrêt *m* de travail; (*strike*) débrayage *m*; (*in pay*) retenue *f*.
stopper ['stɒpər] *n* bouchon *m*. ● **stopoff** *or* **stopover** *n* halte *f*. ● **stopwatch** *n* chronomètre *m*.
store [stɔːr] *n* (*supply*) provision *f*; (*of information etc*) mine *f*; (*warehouse*) entrepôt *m*; (*shop*) *Am* magasin *m*; (*computer memory*) mémoire *f*; **(department) s.** grand magasin *m*; **to have sth in s. for s.o.** (*surprise*) réserver qch à qn.
▮ *vt* (*in warehouse etc*) stocker; *Comptr* mettre en mémoire; **to s. (up)** (*for future use*) mettre en réserve; **to s. (away)** (*furniture*) entreposer. ● **storage** *n* **s. space** *or* **room** espace *m* de rangement; **s. capacity**

Comptr capacité *f* de mémoire. ● **storekeeper** *n* (*shopkeeper*) *Am* commerçant, -ante *mf*. ● **storeroom** *n* (*in house*) débarras *m*; (*in office, shop*) réserve *f*.
storey ['stɔːrɪ] *n* étage *m*.
stork [stɔːk] *n* cigogne *f*.
storm [stɔːm] **1** *n* tempête *f*; (*thunderstorm*) orage *m*. **2** *vt* (*attack*) *Mil* prendre d'assaut. **3** *vi* **to s. out** (*angrily*) sortir comme une furie. ● **stormy** *a* (**-ier, -iest**) (*weather, Fig meeting*) orageux.
story ['stɔːrɪ] *n* **1** histoire *f*; (*newspaper article*) article *m*; **s. (line)** (*plot*) intrigue *f*; **short s.** *Liter* nouvelle *f*; **fairy s.** conte *m* de fées. **2** (*of building*) *Am* étage *m*. ● **storybook** *n* livre *m* d'histoires. ● **storyteller** *n* conteur, -euse *mf*.
stout [staʊt] **1** *a* (**-er, -est**) (*person*) corpulent; (*volume*) épais (*f* épaisse). **2** *n* (*beer*) bière *f* brune.
stove [stəʊv] *n* (*for cooking*) cuisinière *f*; (*solid fuel*) fourneau *m*; (*portable*) réchaud *m*; (*for heating*) poêle *m*.
stow [stəʊ] **1** *vt* **to s. away** (*put away*) ranger. **2** *vi* **to s. away** *Nau* voyager clandestinement. ● **stowaway** *n Nau* passager, -ère *mf* clandestin(e).
straddle ['stræd(ə)l] *vt* (*chair, fence*) se mettre *or* être à califourchon sur; (*line in road*) chevaucher.
straggl/e ['stræg(ə)l] *vi* (*trail*) traîner (en désordre). ● **—er** *n* traînard, -arde *mf*.
straight [streɪt] *a* (**-er, -est**) droit; (*hair*) raide; (*route*) direct; (*tidy*) en ordre; (*frank*) franc (*f* franche); (*refusal*) net (*f* nette); **let's get this s.** comprenons-nous bien; **to keep a s. face** garder son sérieux; **to put s.** (*tidy*) ranger.
▌*adv* (*to walk etc*) droit; (*directly*) tout droit; (*to drink whisky etc*) sec; **s. away** tout de suite; **s. opposite** juste en face; **s. ahead** *or* **on** tout droit; **to look s. ahead** regarder droit devant soi. ● **straighten** *vt* **to s. (up)** (*tie, hair, room*) arranger; **to s. things out** arranger les choses. ● **straight'forward** *a* (*easy, clear*) simple.
strain [streɪn] **1** *n* tension *f*; (*tiredness*) fatigue *f*; (*mental*) tension *f* nerveuse; (*effort*) effort *m* ▌*vt* (*muscle*) se froisser; (*ankle, wrist*) se fouler; (*eyes*) fatiguer; (*voice*) forcer; *Fig* mettre à l'épreuve; **to s. one's ears** tendre l'oreille; **to s. ones back** se faire mal au dos ▌*vi* fournir un effort (**to do** pour faire).
2 *vt* (*soup etc*) passer; (*vegetables*) égoutter.
3 *n* (*breed*) lignée *f*; (*of virus*) souche *f*. ● **strained** *a* (*relations*) tendu; (*muscle*) froissé; (*ankle, wrist*) foulé. ● **strainer** *n* passoire *f*.
strait [streɪt] *n* **1 strait(s)** *Geog* détroit *m*. **2 in financial straits** dans l'embarras. ● **straitjacket** *n* camisole *f* de force.
strand [strænd] *n* (*of wool*) brin *m*; (*of hair*) mèche *f*; (*of story*) *Fig* fil *m*.
stranded ['strændɪd] *a* en rade.
strange [streɪndʒ] *a* (**-er, est**) (*odd*) étrange; (*unknown*) inconnu. ● **strangely** *adv* étrangement; **s. (enough) she...** chose étrange elle.... ● **stranger** *n* (*unknown*) inconnu, -ue *mf*; (*outsider*) étranger, -ère *mf*; **he's a s. here** il n'est pas d'ici.
strangle ['stræŋg(ə)l] *vt* étrangler. ● **strangler** *n* étrangleur, -euse *mf*.
strap [stræp] *n* sangle *f*, courroie *f*; (*on dress*) bretelle *f*; (*on watch*) bracelet *m*; (*on sandal*) lanière *f* ▌*vt* (**-pp-**) **to s. (down** *or* **in)** attacher (avec une sangle).
strapping ['stræpɪŋ] *a* (*well-built*) robuste.
strategy ['strætədʒɪ] *n* stratégie *f*. ● **strategic** [strə'tiːdʒɪk] *a* stratégique.
straw [strɔː] *n* paille *f*; **(drinking) s.** paille *f*; **that's the last s.!** c'est le comble!
strawberry ['strɔːbərɪ, *Am* -berɪ] *n* fraise *f* ▌*a* (*flavour, ice cream*) à la fraise; (*jam*) de fraises; (*tart*) aux fraises.
stray [streɪ] *a* (*animal*) perdu; **a few s. cars/** *etc* quelques rares voitures/*etc* ▌*n* animal *m* perdu ▌*vi* s'égarer; **to s. from** (*subject, path*) s'écarter de; **don't s. too far** ne t'éloigne pas.
streak [striːk] *n* (*line*) raie *f*; (*of light*) filet *m*; (*of colour*) strie *f*; (*of paint*) traînée *f*; (*trace*) *Fig* trace *f*; **grey/***etc* **streaks** (*in hair*) mèches *fpl* grises/*etc*. ● **streaked** *a* strié, zébré; (*stained*) taché (**with** de).
stream [striːm] *n* (*brook*) ruisseau *m*; (*flow*) flot *m*; *Sch* classe *f* (de niveau) ▌*vi* ruisseler (**with** de); **to s. in** (*of sunlight, people*) entrer à flots.
streamer ['striːmər] *n* (*paper*) serpentin *m*; (*banner*) banderole *f*.
streamlin/e ['striːmlaɪn] *vt* (*work etc*) rationaliser. ● **—ed** *a* (*shape*) aérodynamique.
street [striːt] *n* rue *f*; **s. door** porte *f* d'entrée; **s. lamp, s. light** lampadaire *m*; **s. map, s. plan** plan *m* des rues; ● **streetcar** *n* (*tram*) *Am* tramway *m*.
strength [streŋθ] *n* force *f*; (*health, energy*) forces *fpl*; (*of wood etc*) solidité *f*; **on the s. of** *Fig* en vertu de. ● **strengthen** *vt* (*building, position*) renforcer; (*body, limb*) fortifier.
strenuous ['strenjʊəs] *a* (*effort etc*) vigoureux, énergique; (*work*) ardu.

strep [strep] *a* **s. throat** *Am* forte angine *f.*

stress [stres] *n* (*pressure*) pression *f*; (*mental*) stress *m*; (*emphasis*) & *Gram* accent *m*; *Tech* tension *f*; **under s.** stressé ▮ *vt* insister sur; (*word*) accentuer; **to s. that** souligner que. ● **stressful** *a* stressant.

stretch [stretʃ] *vt* (*rope, neck*) tendre; (*shoe, rubber*) étirer; **to s. (out)** (*arm, leg*) étendre, allonger; **to s. (out) one's arm** (*reach out*) tendre le bras (**to take** pour prendre); **to s. one's legs** se dégourdir les jambes; **to s. out** (*visit*) prolonger.
▮ *vi* (*of person, elastic*) s'étirer; (*of influence*) s'étendre; **to s. (out)** (*of plain etc*) s'étendre.
▮ *n* (*area, duration*) étendue *f*; (*of road*) tronçon *m*; (*route, trip*) trajet *m*; **ten/***etc* **hours at a s.** dix/*etc* heures d'affilée.

stretcher ['stretʃər] *n* brancard *m.*

strew [struː] *vt* (*pt* **strewed,** *pp* **strewed** *or* **strewn**) répandre; **strewn with** jonché de.

stricken ['strɪk(ə)n] *a* (*town, region etc*) sinistré; **s. with** (*illness*) atteint de.

strict [strɪkt] *a* (**-er, -est**) (*severe, absolute*) strict. ●**—ly** *adv* strictement; **s. forbidden** formellement interdit. ●**—ness** *n* sévérité *f.*

stride [straɪd] *n* (grand) pas *m*, enjambée *f*; **to make great strides** *Fig* faire de grands progrès ▮ *vi* (*pt* **strode**) **to s. across** *or* **over** enjamber; **to s. along/out/***etc* avancer/sortir/*etc* à grands pas.

strife [straɪf] *n inv* conflit(s) *m(pl)*.

strike [straɪk] **1** *n* (*attack*) *Mil* raid *m* (aérien).
▮ *vt* (*pt* & *pp* **struck**) (*hit, impress*) frapper; (*collide with*) heurter; (*a blow*) donner; (*a match*) frotter; (*gold*) trouver; (*of clock*) sonner (*l'heure*); **to s. a bargain** conclure un accord; **it strikes me that** il me semble que (+ *indic*); **how did it s. you?** quelle impression ça t'a fait?; **to s. s.o. down** (*of illness etc*) terrasser qn; **to s. s.o. off** (*from list*) rayer qn (**from** de); **to s. up a friendship** lier amitié (**with** avec).
▮ *vi* (*attack*) attaquer; **to s. back** (*retaliate*) riposter.
2 *n* (*of workers*) grève *f*; **to go (out) on s.** se mettre en grève (**for** pour obtenir, **against** pour protester contre) ▮ *vi* (*pt* & *pp* **struck**) (*of workers*) faire grève. ● **striking** *a* (*impressive*) frappant. ● **striker** *n* (*worker*) gréviste *mf*; *Fb* buteur *m.*

string [strɪŋ] *n* ficelle *f*; (*of anorak, apron*) cordon *m*; (*of violin, racket etc*) corde *f*; (*of pearls*) collier *m*; (*of insults*) chapelet *m*; (*of vehicles*) file *f*; (*of questions*) série *f*; **to pull strings** *Fig* faire jouer ses relations; **to pull strings for s.o.** pistonner qn.
▮ *a* (*instrument*) *Mus* à cordes; **s. bean** haricot *m* vert.
▮ *vt* (*pt* & *pp* **strung**) **to s. up** (*hang up*) suspendre. ● **stringed** *a* (*instrument*) *Mus* à cordes.

stringent ['strɪndʒ(ə)nt] *a* rigoureux.

strip [strɪp] **1** *n* (*piece*) bande *f*; **(thin) s.** (*of metal etc*) lamelle *f*; **landing s.** piste *f* d'atterrissage; **s. cartoon, comic s.** bande *f* dessinée.
2 *vt* (**-pp-**) (*undress*) déshabiller; (*bed*) défaire; (*machine*) démonter; **to s. off** (*remove*) enlever ▮ *vi* **to s. (off)** (*undress*) se déshabiller. ● **stripper** *n* (*woman*) strip-teaseuse *f*; **(paint) s.** décapant *m.*

stripe [straɪp] *n* rayure *f*; *Mil* galon *m.* ● **striped** *a* rayé (**with** de).

strive [straɪv] *vi* (*pt* **strove,** *pp* **striven**) s'efforcer (**to do** de faire, **for** d'obtenir).

strode [strəʊd] *pt of* **stride.**

stroke [strəʊk] *n* (*movement*) coup *m*; (*of pen, genius*) trait *m*; (*of brush*) touche *f*; (*caress*) caresse *f*; *Med* coup *m* de sang, attaque *f*; **(swimming) s.** nage *f*; **at a s.** d'un coup; **a s. of luck** un coup de chance ▮ *vt* (*beard, cat etc*) caresser.

stroll [strəʊl] *n* promenade *f* ▮ *vi* se promener, flâner; **to s. in/***etc* entrer/*etc* sans se presser.

stroller ['strəʊlər] *n* (*for baby*) *Am* poussette *f.*

strong [strɒŋ] *a* (**-er, -est**) fort; (*shoes, chair, nerves etc*) solide; (*interest*) vif; (*measures*) énergique; **sixty s.** au nombre de soixante ▮ *adv* **to be going s.** aller toujours bien. ●**—ly** *adv* (*to protest, defend*) énergiquement; (*to advise*) fortement; (*to feel*) profondément. ● **strongbox** *n* coffre-fort *m.* ● **stronghold** *n* bastion *m.*

strove [strəʊv] *pt of* **strive.**

struck [strʌk] *pt* & *pp of* **strike 1 & 2.**

structure ['strʌktʃər] *n* structure *f*; (*building*) construction *f.* ● **structural** *a* structural; (*building defect*) de construction; **s. damage** (*to building*) dommage *m* au gros œuvre.

struggle ['strʌg(ə)l] *n* (*fight*) lutte *f* (**to do** pour faire); (*effort*) effort *m*; **to put up a s.** résister; **to have a s. doing** *or* **to do** avoir du mal à faire ▮ *vi* (*fight*) lutter, se battre (**with** avec); (*move about wildly*) se débattre; **to be struggling** (*financially*) avoir du mal; **to s. to do** s'efforcer de faire.

strum [strʌm] *vt* (**-mm-**) (*guitar*) gratter de.

strung [strʌŋ] *pt* & *pp of* **string** ▮ *a* **s. out** (*things*) espacés; (*washing*) étendu.

strut [strʌt] **1** *vi* (**-tt-**) **to s. (about** *or* **around)** se pavaner. **2** *n* (*support*) *Tech* étai *m*.

stub [stʌb] **1** *n* (*of pencil, cigarette etc*) bout *m*; (*of ticket, cheque, Am check*) talon *m* ‖ *vt* (**-bb-**) **to s. out** (*cigarette*) écraser. **2** *vt* (**-bb-**) **to s. one's toe** se cogner le doigt de pied (**on** contre).

stubble ['stʌb(ə)l] *n* barbe *f* de plusieurs jours.

stubborn ['stʌbən] *a* (*person*) entêté; (*cough, manner etc*) opiniâtre. ●**—ness** *n* entêtement *m*.

stuck [stʌk] *pt* & *pp of* **stick**[2] ‖ *a* (*caught, jammed*) coincé; **s. indoors** cloué chez soi; **I'm s.** (*unable to carry on*) je ne sais par quoi faire *or* dire *etc*; **to be s. with sth/s.o.** se farcir qch/qn. ●**s.-'up** *a Fam* prétentieux.

stud [stʌd] *n* **1** (*on football boot*) crampon *m*; (*earring*) clou *m* d'oreille; **(collar) s.** bouton *m* de col. **2** (*farm*) haras *m*; (*horses*) écurie *f*; (*stallion*) étalon *m*. ●**studded** *a* **s. with** (*covered*) constellé de.

student ['stju:dənt] *n Univ* étudiant, -ante *mf*; *Sch* élève *mf*; **music**/*etc* **s.** étudiant, -ante en musique/*etc* ‖ *a* (*life, protest*) étudiant; (*restaurant, residence, grant*) universitaire.

studio ['stju:dɪəʊ] *n* (*pl* **-os**) (*of painter etc*) & *Cin TV Phot* studio *m*; **s. flat** *or Am* **apartment** studio *m*.

studious ['stju:dɪəs] *a* (*person*) studieux.

study ['stʌdɪ] *n* étude *f*; (*office*) bureau *m* ‖ *vt* (*learn, observe*) étudier ‖ *vi* étudier; **to s. to be a doctor**/*etc* faire des études pour devenir médecin/*etc*; **to s. for** (*exam*) préparer.

stuff [stʌf] **1** *n* (*thing*) truc *m*; (*substance*) substance *f*; (*things*) trucs *mpl*; (*possessions*) affaires *fpl*; **it's good s.** c'est bon (ça). **2** *vt* (*fill*) bourrer (**with** de); (*cushion, armchair etc*) rembourrer (**with** avec); (*animal*) empailler; (*put*) fourrer (**into** dans); (*chicken etc*) farcir; **my nose is stuffed (up)** j'ai le nez bouché. ●**—ing** *n* (*padding*) bourre *f*; *Culin* farce *f*.

stuffy ['stʌfɪ] *a* (**-ier, -iest**) (*room etc*) mal aéré; (*old-fashioned*) vieux jeu *inv*; **it smells s.** ça sent le renfermé.

stumble ['stʌmb(ə)l] *vi* trébucher (**over** sur); **to s. across** *or* **on** (*find*) tomber sur; **stumbling block** pierre *f* d'achoppement.

stump [stʌmp] *n* (*of tree*) souche *f*; (*of limb*) moignon *m*.

stun [stʌn] *vt* (**-nn-**) (*with punch etc*) étourdir; (*amaze*) *Fig* stupéfier. ●**stunned** *a* (*amazed*) stupéfait (**by** par). ●**stunning** *a* (*news*) stupéfiant; (*terrific*) *Fam* sensationnel.

stung [stʌŋ] *pt* & *pp of* **sting.**

stunk [stʌŋk] *pt* & *pp of* **stink.**

stunt [stʌnt] **1** *n* tour *m* (de force); *Cin* cascade *f*; (*trick*) truc *m*; **publicity s.** coup *m* de pub; **s. man** *Cin* cascadeur *m*; **s. woman** cascadeuse *f*. **2** *vt* (*growth*) retarder. ●**—ed** *a* (*person*) rabougri.

stupendous [stju:'pendəs] *a* prodigieux.

stupid ['stju:pɪd] *a* stupide, bête; **a s. thing** une stupidité; **s. fool** idiot, -ote *mf*. ●**stu'pidity** *n* stupidité *f*.

sturdy ['stɜ:dɪ] *a* (**-ier, -iest**) robuste.

stutter ['stʌtər] *vi* bégayer ‖ *n* bégaiement *m*; **to have a s.** être bègue.

sty [staɪ] *n* (*for pigs*) porcherie *f*.

sty(e) [staɪ] *n* (*on eye*) orgelet *m*.

style [staɪl] *n* style *m*; (*fashion*) mode *f*; (*design of dress etc*) modèle *m*; (*of hair*) coiffure *f*; **to have s.** avoir de la classe; **in s.** (*to live, travel*) dans le luxe ‖ *vt* (*design*) créer; **to s. s.o.'s hair** coiffer qn. ●**stylish** *a* chic *inv*, élégant. ●**stylist** *n* **(hair) s.** coiffeur, -euse *mf*.

sub- [sʌb] *pref* sous-, sub-.

subconscious [sʌb'kɒnʃəs] *a* & *n* subconscient (*m*).

subcontract [sʌbkən'trækt] *vt* sous-traiter. ●**subcontractor** *n* sous-traitant *m*.

subdivide [sʌbdɪ'vaɪd] *vt* subdiviser.

subdu/e [səb'dju:] *vt* (*country*) asservir; (*feelings*) maîtriser. ●**—ed** *a* (*light*) atténué; (*voice, tone*) bas (*f* basse); (*person*) qui manque d'entrain.

subject[1] ['sʌbdʒɪkt] *n* **1** (*matter*) & *Gram* sujet *m*; *Sch Univ* matière *f*; **s. matter** (*topic*) sujet *m*; (*content*) contenu *m*. **2** (*citizen*) ressortissant, -ante *mf*; (*of monarch*) sujet, -ette *mf*; (*in experiment*) sujet *m*.

subject[2] ['sʌbdʒekt] *a* **s. to** (*prone to*) sujet à (*maladie etc*); (*ruled by*) soumis à (*loi etc*); (*conditional upon*) sous réserve de; **prices are s. to change** les prix peuvent être modifiés ‖ [səb'dʒekt] *vt* soumettre (**to** à); (*expose*) exposer (**to** à).

subjective [səb'dʒektɪv] *a* subjectif. ●**—ly** *adv* subjectivement.

subjunctive [səb'dʒʌŋktɪv] *n Gram* subjonctif *m*.

sublet [sʌb'let] *vt* (*pt* & *pp* **sublet,** *pres p* **subletting**) sous-louer.

sublime [sə'blaɪm] *a* sublime; (*indifference*) suprême.

submarine ['sʌbməri:n] *n* sous-marin *m*.

submerge [səb'mɜ:dʒ] *vt* (*flood, over-

whelm) submerger; (*immerse*) immerger (**in** dans).

submit [səb'mɪt] *vt* (**-tt-**) soumettre (**to** à) ▮ *vi* se soumettre (**to** à). ● **submission** [-ʃ(ə)n] *n* soumission *f*.

subordinate [sə'bɔːdɪnət] *a* subalterne; *Gram* subordonné ▮ *n* subordonné, -ée *mf* ▮ [sə'bɔːdɪneɪt] *vt* subordonner (**to** à).

subpoena [səb'piːnə] *vt Jur* citer ▮ *n Jur* citation *f*.

subscribe [səb'skraɪb] *vi* (*pay money*) cotiser (**to** a); **to s. to** (*take out subscription*) s'abonner à (*journal etc*); (*be a subscriber*) être abonné à (*journal etc*); (*fund, idea*) souscrire à. ● **subscriber** *n* (*to newspaper etc*) & *Tel* abonné, -ée *mf*. ● **subscription** [-'skrɪpʃ(ə)n] *n* abonnement *m*; (*to fund etc*) souscription *f*; (*to club*) cotisation *f*.

subsequent ['sʌbsɪkwənt] *a* postérieur (**to** à); **our s. problems** les problèmes que nous avons eus par la suite. ● **—ly** *adv* par la suite.

subside [səb'saɪd] *vi* (*of ground, building*) s'affaisser; (*of wind*) baisser. ● **'subsidence** *n* affaissement *m*.

subsidiary [səb'sɪdɪərɪ, *Am* -erɪ] *a* accessoire ▮ *n* (*company*) filiale *f*.

subsidize ['sʌbsɪdaɪz] *vt* subventionner. ● **subsidy** *n* subvention *f*.

substance ['sʌbstəns] *n* substance *f*; (*firmness*) solidité *f*. ● **substantial** [səb'stænʃ(ə)l] *a* important; (*meal*) copieux. ● **sub'stantially** *adv* considérablement; **s. true/***etc* en grande partie vrai/*etc*; **s. different** très différent.

substandard [sʌb'stændəd] *a* de qualité inférieure.

substitute ['sʌbstɪtjuːt] *n* produit *m* de remplacement; (*person*) remplaçant, -ante *mf* (**for** de); **there's no s. for…** rien ne peut remplacer… ▮ *vt* **to s. sth/s.o. for** substituer qch/qn à, remplacer qch/qn par ▮ *vi* **to s. for s.o.** remplacer qn.

subtitle ['sʌbtaɪt(ə)l] *n* sous-titre *m* ▮ *vt* sous-titrer.

subtle ['sʌt(ə)l] *a* (**-er, -est**) subtil.

subtotal [sʌb'təʊt(ə)l] *n* sous-total *m*.

subtract [səb'trækt] *vt* soustraire (**from** de). ● **subtraction** [-ʃ(ə)n] *n* soustraction *f*.

suburb ['sʌbɜːb] *n* banlieue *f*; **the suburbs** la banlieue; **in the suburbs** en banlieue. ● **su'burban** *a* (*train etc*) de banlieue. ● **su'burbia** *n* la banlieue.

subversive [səb'vɜːsɪv] *a* subversif.

subway ['sʌbweɪ] *n* passage *m* souterrain; *Rail Am* métro *m*.

succeed [sək'siːd] **1** *vi* réussir (**in doing** à faire, **in sth** dans qch). **2** *vt* **to s. s.o.** (*follow*) succéder à qn. ● **—ing** *a* (*in past*) suivant; (*in future*) futur; (*consecutive*) consécutif.

success [sək'ses] *n* succès *m*, réussite *f*; **to make a s. of sth** réussir qch; **he was a s.** il a eu du succès; **it was a s.** c'était réussi; **her s. in the exam** sa réussite à l'examen. ● **successful** *a* (*effort etc*) couronné de succès, réussi; (*outcome*) heureux; (*company*) prospère; (*candidate in exam*) admis, reçu; (*writer, film etc*) à succès; **to be s.** réussir (**in** dans, **in an exam** à un examen, **in doing** à faire). ● **successfully** *adv* avec succès.

succession [sək'seʃ(ə)n] *n* succession *f*; **ten days in s.** dix jours consécutifs; **in rapid s.** coup sur coup. ● **successive** *a* (*governments etc*) successif; **ten s. days** dix jours consécutifs. ● **successor** *n* successeur *m* (**of, to** de).

succulent ['sʌkjʊlənt] *a* succulent.

succumb [sə'kʌm] *vi* succomber (**to** à).

such [sʌtʃ] *a* (*of this or that kind*) tel, telle; **s. a car/***etc* une telle voiture/*etc*; **s. happiness/s. noise/***etc* (*so much*) tant *or* tellement de bonheur/de bruit/*etc*; **s. as** comme, tel que; **s. and s.** tel ou tel.
▮ *adv* (*so very*) si; (*in comparisons*) aussi; **s. long trips** de si longs voyages; **s. a large helping** une si grosse portion; **s. a kind woman as you** une femme aussi gentille que vous.
▮ *pron* **happiness/***etc* **as s.** le bonheur/*etc* en tant que tel.

suck [sʌk] *vt* sucer; (*of baby*) téter (*lait, biberon etc*); **to s. (up)** (*with straw, pump*) aspirer ▮ *vi* (*of baby*) téter. ● **—er** *n* (*rubber pad*) ventouse *f*.

suckle ['sʌk(ə)l] *vt* (*of woman*) allaiter ▮ *vi* (*of baby*) téter.

suction ['sʌkʃ(ə)n] *n* succion *f*; **s. pad** ventouse *f*.

Sudan [suː'dɑːn] *n* Soudan *m*.

sudden ['sʌd(ə)n] *a* soudain; **all of a s.** tout à coup. ● **—ly** *adv* subitement.

suds [sʌdz] *npl* mousse *f* de savon.

sue [suː] *vt* poursuivre (en justice) ▮ *vi* engager des poursuites (judiciaires).

suede [sweɪd] *n* daim *m* ▮ *a* de daim.

suffer ['sʌfər] *vi* souffrir (**from** de); **to s. from pimples** avoir des boutons; **your work/***etc* **will s.** ton travail/*etc* s'en ressentira ▮ *vt* (*loss etc*) subir; (*pain*) ressentir. ● **—ing** *n* souffrance(s) *f(pl)*. ● **sufferer** *n* (*from misfortune*) victime *f*; **AIDS s.** malade *mf* du SIDA; **asthma s.** asthmatique *mf*.

suffice [sə'faɪs] *vi* suffire.
sufficient [sə'fɪʃ(ə)nt] *a* (*quantity*) suffisant; **s. money/***etc* suffisamment d'argent/*etc*. ● **—ly** *adv* suffisamment.
suffix ['sʌfɪks] *n Gram* suffixe *m*.
suffocate ['sʌfəkeɪt] *vti* suffoquer.
sugar ['ʃʊgər] *n* sucre *m*; **lump s.** sucre en morceaux; **brown s.** sucre *m* brun; **s. bowl** sucrier *m*; **s. cane/tongs** canne *f*/pince *f* à sucre ‖ *vt* sucrer. ● **sugary** *a* (*taste*) sucré.
suggest [sə'dʒest] *vt* (*propose*) suggérer, proposer (**to** à, **doing** de faire, **that** que (+ *sub*)); (*evoke, imply*) suggérer. ● **suggestion** [-tʃ(ə)n] *n* suggestion. ● **suggestive** *a* suggestif; **to be s. of** suggérer.
suicide ['su:ɪsaɪd] *n* suicide *m*. ● **sui'cidal** *a* suicidaire.
suit[1] [su:t] **1** *n* (*man's*) costume *m*; (*woman's*) tailleur *m*; **flying/diving/ski s.** combinaison *f* de vol/plongée/ski. **2** *n* (*lawsuit*) procès *m*. **3** *n Cards* couleur *f*.
suit[2] [su:t] *vt* (*please, be acceptable to*) convenir à; (*of dress, colour etc*) aller (bien) à; (*adapt*) adapter (**to** à); **it suits me to stay** ça m'arrange de rester; **suited to** (*job, activity*) fait pour; **well suited** (*couple etc*) bien assorti.
suitable ['su:təb(ə)l] *a* qui convient (**for** à), convenable (**for** pour); (*dress, colour*) qui va (bien). ● **suitably** *adv* convenablement; **s. impressed** très impressionné.
suitcase ['su:tkeɪs] *n* valise *f*.
suite [swi:t] *n* (*rooms*) suite *f*; (*furniture*) mobilier *m*; **bedroom s.** (*furniture*) chambre *f* à coucher.
sulfur ['sʌlfər] *n Am* soufre *m*.
sulk [sʌlk] *vi* bouder. ● **sulky** *a* (**-ier, -iest**) boudeur.
sullen ['sʌlən] *a* maussade. ● **—ly** *adv* d'un air maussade.
sulphur ['sʌlfər] *n* soufre *m*.
sultan ['sʌltən] *n* sultan *m*.
sultana [sʌl'tɑ:nə] *n* raisin *m* (de Smyrne).
sultry ['sʌltrɪ] *a* (**-ier, -iest**) (*heat*) étouffant.
sum [sʌm] **1** *n* (*amount of money, total*) somme *f*; (*calculation*) calcul *m*; *pl* (*arithmetic*) le calcul. **2** *vt* (**-mm-**) **to s. up** (*facts etc*) récapituler, résumer; (*situation*) évaluer; (*person*) jauger ‖ *vi* **to s. up** récapituler.
summarize ['sʌməraɪz] *vt* résumer ‖ *vi* récapituler. ● **summary** *n* résumé *m*.
summer ['sʌmər] *n* été *m*; **in (the) s.** en été ‖ *a* d'été; **s. camp** *Am* colonie *f* de vacances; **s. holidays** *or Am* **vacation** grandes vacances *fpl*. ● **summertime** *n* été *m*; **in (the) s.** en été.
summit ['sʌmɪt] *n* (*of mountain, power etc*) sommet *m*; **s. (conference)** *Pol* conférence *f* au sommet.
summon ['sʌmən] *vt* appeler; (*meeting, s.o. to meeting*) convoquer (**to** à); **to s.o. to do** sommer qn de faire; **to s. up** (*courage*) rassembler.
summons ['sʌmənz] *n Jur* assignation *f* ‖ *vt Jur* assigner.
sumptuous ['sʌmptʃʊəs] *a* somptueux.
sun [sʌn] *n* soleil *m*; **in the s.** au soleil; **the sun is shining** il fait (du) soleil; **s. lotion/***etc* crème *f*/*etc* solaire ‖ *vt* (**-nn-**) **to s. oneself** se chauffer au soleil.
sunbathe ['sʌnbeɪð] *vi* prendre un bain de soleil. ● **sunbed** *n* lit *m* à ultraviolets. ● **sunblock** *n* écran *m* total. ● **sunburn** *n Med* coup *m* de soleil; (*tan*) bronzage *m*. ● **sunburnt** *a* (*tanned*) bronzé; *Med* brûlé par le soleil. ● **sundial** *n* cadran *m* solaire. ● **sundown** *n* coucher *m* du soleil. ● **sunflower** *n* tournesol *m*. ● **sunglasses** *npl* lunettes *fpl* de soleil. ● **sunlamp** *n* lampe *f* à bronzer. ● **sunlight** *n* (lumière *f* du) soleil *m*. ● **sun lounge** *n* (*in house*) véranda *f*. ● **sunrise** *n* lever *m* du soleil. ● **sunroof** *n Aut* toit *m* ouvrant. ● **sunset** *n* coucher *m* du soleil. ● **sunshade** *n* (*on table*) parasol *m*. ● **sunshine** *n* soleil *m*. ● **sunstroke** *n* insolation *f*. ● **suntan** *n* bronzage *m*; **s. lotion/oil** crème *f*/huile *f* solaire. ● **suntanned** *a* bronzé.
sundae ['sʌndeɪ] *n* glace *f* aux fruits.
Sunday ['sʌndɪ, -deɪ] *n* dimanche *m*; **S. school** *Rel* = catéchisme *m*.
sundry ['sʌndrɪ] *a* divers ‖ *n* **all and s.** tout le monde.
sung [sʌŋ] *pp of* **sing**.
sunk [sʌŋk] *pp of* **sink**[2]. ● **sunken** *a* (*treasure etc*) submergé; (*eyes*) cave.
sunny ['sʌnɪ] *a* (**-ier, -iest**) (*day etc*) ensoleillé; **it's s.** il fait (du) soleil; **s. periods** *or* **intervals** éclaircies *fpl*.
super ['su:pər] *a Fam* super, sensationnel.
super- ['su:pər] *pref* super-.
superb [su:'pɜ:b] *a* superbe.
superficial [su:pə'fɪʃ(ə)l] *a* superficiel.
superfluous [su:'pɜ:flʊəs] *a* superflu.
superglue ['su:pəglu:] *n* colle *f* extra-forte.
superhuman [su:pə'hju:mən] *a* surhumain.
superintendent [su:pərɪn'tendənt] *n* (**police**) **s.** commissaire *m* (de police).
superior [su'pɪərɪər] *a* supérieur (**to** à); (*goods*) de qualité supérieure ‖ *n* (*person*) supérieur, -eure *mf*. ● **superi'ority** *n* supériorité *f*.

superlative [su:'pɜ:lətɪv] *a* sans pareil ▮ *a* & *n Gram* superlatif (*m*).
supermarket ['su:pəmɑ:kɪt] *n* supermarché *m*.
supernatural [su:pə'nætʃ(ə)rəl] *a* & *n* surnaturel (*m*).
superpower ['su:pəpaʊər] *n Pol* superpuissance *f*.
supersede [su:pə'si:d] *vt* supplanter.
supersonic [su:pə'sɒnɪk] *a* supersonique.
superstar ['supəstɑ:r] *n Cin* superstar *f*.
superstition [su:pə'stɪʃ(ə)n] *n* superstition *f*. ● **superstitious** *a* superstitieux.
supertanker ['su:pətæŋkər] *n* pétrolier *m* géant.
supervise ['su:pəvaɪz] *vt* (*person*, *work*) surveiller; (*office*, *research*) diriger. ● **supervision** [-'vɪʒ(ə)n] *n* surveillance *f*; direction *f*. ● **supervisor** *n* surveillant, -ante *mf*; (*in office*) chef *m* de service; (*in store*) chef *m* de rayon.
supper ['sʌpər] *n* dîner *m*, souper *m*; (*late-night*) souper *m*; **to have s.** dîner, souper.
supple ['sʌp(ə)l] *a* souple.
supplement ['sʌplɪmənt] *n* supplément *m* (**to** à) ▮ ['sʌplɪment] *vt* compléter. ● **supple'mentary** *a* supplémentaire.
supply [sə'plaɪ] *vt* (*provide*) fournir; (*with electricity, gas, water*) alimenter (**with** en); (*equip*) équiper (**with** de); **to s. s.o. with sth, s. sth to s.o.** fournir qch à qn.
▮ *n* (*stock*) réserve *f*; *pl* (*equipment*) matériel *m*; **(food) supplies** vivres *mpl*; **(office) supplies** fournitures *fpl* (de bureau); **s. and demand** l'offre *f* et la demande; **to be in short s.** manquer; **s. ship**/*etc* navire *m*/*etc* ravitailleur. ● **supplier** *n Com* fournisseur *m*.
support [sə'pɔ:t] *vt* (*bear weight of*) supporter; (*help*, *encourage*) soutenir, appuyer; (*be in favour of*) être en faveur de; (*family etc*) subvenir aux besoins de; (*endure*) supporter.
▮ *n* (*help*) soutien *m*, appui *m*; (*object*) support *m*; **means of s.** moyens *mpl* de subsistance; **income s.** *Br* allocation *f* d'aide sociale; **in s. of s.o.** en faveur de qn. ● **supporter** *n* partisan *m*; *Sp* supporter *m*. ● **supportive** *a* **to be s. of s.o.** soutenir qn.
suppos/e [sə'pəʊz] *vti* supposer (**that** que); **I'm supposed to work** *or* **be working** (*ought*) je suis censé travailler; **he's s. to be rich** on le dit riche; **I s. (so)** je pense; **you're tired, I s.** vous êtes fatigué, je suppose; **s.** *or* **supposing we go** (*suggestion*) si nous partions; **s.** *or* **supposing you're right** supposons que tu aies raison.
suppress [sə'pres] *vt* (*abuse etc*) supprimer; (*feelings*) réprimer; (*scandal*, *yawn*, *revolt*, *information*) étouffer.
supreme [su:'pri:m] *a* suprême.
surcharge ['sɜ:tʃɑ:dʒ] *n* (*extra charge*) supplément *m*.
sure [ʃʊər] *a* (**-er, -est**) sûr (**of** de, **that** que); **she's s. to accept** c'est sûr qu'elle acceptera; **it's s. to snow** il va sûrement neiger; **to make s. of sth** s'assurer de qch; **for s.** à coup sûr, pour sûr; **s.!** bien sûr!; **be s. to do it!** ne manquez pas de le faire! ● **surely** *adv* sûrement; **s. he didn't refuse?** (*I hope*) il n'a tout de même pas refusé?
surf [sɜ:f] *n* (*foam*) ressac *m*. ● **surfboard** *n* planche *f* (de surf). ● **surfing** *n Sp* surf *m*; **to go s.** faire du surf.
surface ['sɜ:fɪs] *n* surface *f*; **s. area** superficie *f*; **s. mail** courrier *m* par voie(s) de surface ▮ *vi* (*of swimmer etc*) remonter à la surface; (*of person, thing*) *Fam* réapparaître.
surge ['sɜ:dʒ] *n* (*of enthusiasm etc*) vague *f*; (*in prices etc*) montée *f* ▮ *vi* (*of crowd*, *hatred*) déferler; (*of prices etc*) monter (soudainement); **to s. forward** se lancer en avant.
surgeon ['sɜ:dʒ(ə)n] *n* chirurgien *m*. ● **surgery** *n* (*doctor's office*) cabinet *m*; (*period*) consultation *f*; (*science*) chirurgie *f*; **to have s.** avoir une opération (**for** pour). ● **surgical** *a* chirurgical; (*appliance*) orthopédique; **s. spirit** alcool *m* à 90°.
surly ['sɜ:lɪ] *a* (**-ier, -iest**) bourru.
surname ['sɜ:neɪm] *n* nom *m* de famille.
surpass [sə'pɑ:s] *vt* surpasser (**in** en).
surplus ['sɜ:pləs] *n* surplus *m* ▮ *a* (*goods*) en surplus; **some s. material**/*etc* un surplus de tissu/*etc*.
surpris/e [sə'praɪz] *n* surprise *f*; **to give s.o. a s.** faire une surprise à qn; **to take s.o. by s.** prendre qn au dépourvu ▮ *a* (*visit etc*) inattendu ▮ *vt* (*astonish*) étonner, surprendre; (*come upon*) surprendre. ● **—ed** *a* surpris (**that** que (+ *sub*), **at sth** de qch); **I'm s. at his stupidity** sa bêtise m'étonne; **I'm s. to see you** je suis surpris de te voir. ● **—ing** *a* surprenant. ● **—ingly** *adv* étonnamment.
surrender [sə'rendər] **1** *vi* se rendre (**to** à) ▮ *n Mil* capitulation *f*. **2** *vt* (*hand over*) remettre (**to** à); (*right*, *claim*) renoncer à.
surrogate ['sʌrəgət] *n* substitut *m*; **s. mother** mère *f* porteuse.
surround [sə'raʊnd] *vt* entourer (**with** de); (*of army*, *police*) encercler; **surrounded by**

entouré de. ● **—ing** *a* environnant. ● **—ings** *npl* environs *mpl*; (*setting*) cadre *m*.
surveillance [sɜː'veɪləns] *n* (*of prisoner etc*) surveillance *f*.
survey [sə'veɪ] *vt* (*look at*) regarder; (*house*) inspecter; (*land*) arpenter ▮ ['sɜːveɪ] *n* enquête *f*; (*of opinion*) sondage *m*; (*of house*) inspection *f*. ● **sur'veyor** *n* (*of land*) géomètre *m*; (*of house*) expert *m*.
survive [sə'vaɪv] *vi* survivre ▮ *vt* survivre à (*qn, qch*). ● **survival** *n* (*act*) survie *f*; (*relic*) vestige *m*. ● **survivor** *n* survivant, -ante *mf*.
susceptible [sə'septəb(ə)l] *a* sensible (**to** à); **s. to colds**/*etc* prédisposé aux rhumes/*etc*.
suspect ['sʌspekt] *n* & *a* suspect, -ecte (*mf*) ▮ [sə'spekt] *vt* soupçonner (**of sth** de qch, **of doing** d'avoir fait, **that** que); (*question, doubt*) suspecter (*l'honnêteté de qn etc*).
suspend [sə'spend] *vt* **1** (*stop, postpone, dismiss*) suspendre; (*pupil*) renvoyer; (*passport*) retirer; **suspended sentence** *Jur* condamnation *f* avec sursis. **2** (*hang*) suspendre (**from** à). ● **suspender** *n* (*for stocking*) jarretelle *f*; *pl* (*for trousers, Am pants*) *Am* bretelles *fpl*. ● **suspension** [-ʃ(ə)n] *n* (*of vehicle*) suspension *f*; **s. bridge** pont *m* suspendu.
suspense [sə'spens] *n* attente *f* (angoissée); (*in film, book etc*) suspense *m*.
suspicion [sə'spɪʃ(ə)n] *n* soupçon *m*; **to arouse s.** éveiller les soupçons; **with s.** avec méfiance; **under s.** considéré comme suspect. ● **suspicious** *a* (*person*) soupçonneux, méfiant; (*behaviour*) suspect; **s.(-looking)** suspect; **to be s. of** *or* **about** se méfier de.
sustain [sə'steɪn] *vt* (*effort, theory*) soutenir; (*weight*) supporter; (*with food*) nourrir; (*damage, loss*) subir; (*injury*) recevoir. ● **—able** *a* (*growth rate etc*) qui peut être maintenu. ● **'sustenance** *n* (*food*) nourriture *f*; (*quality*) valeur *f* nutritive.
swab [swɒb] *n Med* (*pad*) tampon *m*; (*specimen*) prélèvement *m*.
swagger ['swægər] *vi* (*walk*) parader.
swallow ['swɒləʊ] **1** *vt* avaler; **to s. down** avaler; **to s. up** (*savings etc*) *Fig* engloutir ▮ *vi* avaler. **2** *n* (*bird*) hirondelle *f*.
swam [swæm] *pt of* **swim.**
swamp [swɒmp] *n* marécage *m*, marais *m* ▮ *vt* (*flood, Fig overwhelm*) submerger (**with** de). ● **swampy** *a* (**-ier, -iest**) marécageux.
swan [swɒn] *n* cygne *m*.
swap [swɒp] *n* échange *m*; *pl* (*stamps etc*) doubles *mpl* ▮ *vt* (**-pp-**) échanger (**for** contre); **to s. seats** changer de place ▮ *vi* échanger.
swarm [swɔːm] *n* (*of bees etc*) essaim *m* ▮ *vi* (*of streets, insects, people etc*) fourmiller (**with** de).
swat [swɒt] *vt* (**-tt-**) (*fly etc*) écraser.
sway [sweɪ] *vi* se balancer ▮ *vt* balancer; *Fig* influencer.
swear ['sweər] *vt* (*pt* **swore,** *pp* **sworn**) (*promise*) jurer (**to do** de faire, **that** que); **to s. an oath** prêter serment; **to s. s.o. to secrecy** faire jurer le silence à qn ▮ *vi* (*curse*) jurer, pester (**at** contre); **she swears by this lotion** elle ne jure que par cette lotion. ● **swearword** *n* gros mot *m*, juron *m*.
sweat [swet] *n* sueur *f*; **s. shirt** sweat-shirt *m* ▮ *vi* (*of person*) transpirer, suer; **I'm sweating** je suis en sueur ▮ *vt* **to s. out** (*a cold*) se débarrasser de (*en transpirant*). ● **sweater** *n* (*garment*) pull *m*. ● **sweaty** *a* (**-ier, -iest**) (*shirt etc*) plein de sueur; (*hand*) moite; (*person*) (tout) en sueur.
Swede [swiːd] *n* Suédois, -oise *mf*. ● **Sweden** *n* Suède *f*. ● **Swedish** *a* suédois ▮ *n* (*language*) suédois *m*.
sweep [swiːp] *n* (*with broom*) coup *m* de balai ▮ *vt* (*pt* & *pp* **swept**) (*with broom*) balayer; (*chimney*) ramoner; (*river*) draguer ▮ *vi* balayer. ● **—ing** *a* (*gesture*) large; (*change*) radical; (*statement*) trop général.
sweep aside *vt* (*dismiss*) écarter **to sweep away** *vt* (*leaves*) balayer; (*carry off*) emporter **to sweep out** *vt* (*room etc*) balayer **to sweep through** *vt* (*of fear*) saisir (*groupe*); (*of disease*) ravager (*pays*) **to sweep up** *vt* (*dust, floor etc*) balayer.
sweet [swiːt] *a* (**-er, -est**) (*not sour*) doux (*f* douce); (*tea, coffee, cake*) sucré; (*child, house, cat*) mignon (*f* mignonne); (*sound, smile*) doux; (*pleasant*) agréable; (*kind*) aimable; **to have a s. tooth** aimer les sucreries; **s. potato** patate *f* douce; **s. shop** confiserie *f*.
▮ *n* (*candy*) bonbon *m*; (*dessert*) dessert *m*. ● **sweeten** *vt* (*tea etc*) sucrer; *Fig* adoucir. ● **sweetener** *n* (*for tea etc*) édulcorant *m*. ● **sweetly** *adv* (*kindly*) aimablement; (*agreeably*) agréablement. ● **sweetness** *n* douceur *f*; (*taste*) goût *m* sucré.
sweetheart ['swiːthɑːt] *n* petit ami *m*, petite amie *f*.
swell[1] [swel] *vi* (*pt* **swelled,** *pp* **swollen** *or* **swelled**) (*of hand, leg etc*) enfler; (*of wood, dough*) gonfler; (*of river, numbers*) grossir; **to s. up** (*of hand etc*) enfler ▮ *vt* (*river, numbers*) grossir. ● **—ing** *n Med* enflure *f*.
swell[2] [swel] **1** *n* (*of sea*) houle *f*. **2** *a* (*very good*) *Am Fam* formidable.
swelter ['sweltər] *vi* étouffer. ● **—ing** *a*

étouffant; **it's s.** on étouffe.
swept [swept] *pp of* **sweep.**
swerve [swɜːv] *vi* (*of vehicle*) faire une embardée; (*while running*) faire un écart.
swift [swɪft] **1** *a* (**-er, -est**) rapide. **2** *n* (*bird*) martinet *m*. ●**—ly** *adv* rapidement.
swill [swɪl] *vt* (*beer etc*) *Fam* boire, siffler; **to s. sth (out)** laver qch (à grande eau).
swim [swɪm] *n* **to go for a s.** se baigner.
‖ *vi* (*pt* **swam,** *pp* **swum,** *pres p* **swimming**) nager; *Sp* faire de la natation; **to go swimming** aller nager; **to s. away** se sauver (à la nage).
‖ *vt* (*river*) traverser à la nage; (*length, crawl etc*) nager. ●**swimming** *n* natation *f*; **s. costume** maillot *m* de bain; **s. pool** piscine *f*; **s. trunks** slip *m* de bain. ●**swimmer** *n* nageur, -euse *mf*. ●**swimsuit** *n* maillot *m* de bain.
swindl/e ['swɪnd(ə)l] *n* escroquerie *f* ‖ *vt* escroquer. ●**—er** *n* escroc *m*.
swine [swaɪn] *n inv* (*person*) *Pej* salaud *m*.
swing [swɪŋ] *n* (*in playground etc*) balançoire *f*; (*of pendulum*) oscillation *f*; (*in opinion*) revirement *m*; (*rhythm*) rythme *m*; **to be in full s.** battre son plein; **s. door** porte *f* de saloon.
‖ *vi* (*pt & pp* **swung**) (*sway*) se balancer; (*of pendulum*) osciller; (*turn*) virer; **to s. round** (*suddenly*) virer, tourner; (*of person*) se retourner (vivement); **to s. into action** passer à l'action.
‖ *vt* (*arms etc*) balancer; (*axe*) brandir. ●**—ing** *a Fam* (*trendy*) dans le vent; (*lively*) plein de vie; (*music*) entraînant.
swipe [swaɪp] **1** *vti* **to s. (at)** (*hit*) (essayer de) frapper (*qn, qch*). **2** *vt* **to s. sth** (*steal*) *Fam* piquer qch (**from s.o.** à qn).
swirl [swɜːl] *vi* tourbillonner.
swish [swɪʃ] **1** *a* (*posh*) *Fam* rupin, chic. **2** *vi* (*of whip etc*) siffler; (*of fabric*) froufrouter.
Swiss [swɪs] *a* suisse ‖ *n inv* Suisse *m*, Suissesse *f*; **the S.** les Suisses *mpl*.
switch [swɪtʃ] *n El* bouton *m* (électrique), interrupteur *m*; (*change*) changement *m*; (*reversal*) revirement *m* (**in** de).
‖ *vt* (*money, employee*) transférer (**to** à); (*support*) reporter (**to** sur, **from** de); (*exchange*) échanger (**for** contre); **to s. places** *or* **seats** changer de place.
‖ *vi* **to s. to** (*change*) passer à. ●**switchblade** *n Am* couteau *m* à cran d'arrêt. ●**switchboard** *n Tel* standard *m*; **s. operator** standardiste *mf*.
switch off *vt* (*lamp, gas, radio etc*) éteindre; (*engine*) arrêter; (*electricity*) couper **to switch on** *vt* (*lamp, gas, radio etc*) mettre, allumer; (*engine*) mettre en marche **to switch over** *vi* (*change TV channels*) changer de chaîne.
Switzerland ['swɪtsələnd] *n* Suisse *f*.
swivel ['swɪv(ə)l] *vi* (**-ll-,** *Am* **-l-**) **to s. (round)** (*of chair*) pivoter ‖ *a* **s. chair** fauteuil *m* pivotant.
swollen ['swəʊl(ə)n] *pp of* **swell**[1] ‖ *a* (*leg etc*) enflé; (*stomach*) gonflé.
swoon [swuːn] *vi Lit* se pâmer.
swoop [swuːp] **1** *vi* **to s. (down) on** (*of bird*) fondre sur. **2** *n* (*of police*) descente *f* ‖ *vi* faire une descente (**on** dans).
swop [swɒp] *n, vt & vi* = **swap.**
sword [sɔːd] *n* épée *f*. ●**swordfish** *n* espadon *m*.
swore, sworn [swɔːr, swɔːn] *pt & pp of* **swear.**
swot [swɒt] *vti* (**-tt-**) **to s. (up)** (*study*) *Fam* potasser; **to s. (up) for** (*exam*) *Fam* potasser.
swum [swʌm] *pp of* **swim.**
swung [swʌŋ] *pt & pp of* **swing.**
sycamore ['sɪkəmɔːr] *n* (*maple tree*) sycomore *m*; (*plane tree*) *Am* platane *m*.
syllable ['sɪləb(ə)l] *n* syllabe *f*.
syllabus ['sɪləbəs] *n* programme *m* (scolaire).
symbol ['sɪmb(ə)l] *n* symbole *m*. ●**sym'bolic** *a* symbolique. ●**symbolize** *vt* symboliser.
sympathy ['sɪmpəθɪ] *n* (*pity*) compassion *f*; (*understanding*) compréhension *f*; (*when s.o. dies*) condoléances *fpl*; (*solidarity*) solidarité *f* (**for** avec); **(political) sympathies** tendances *fpl* (politiques); **he's in s. with, he has sympathies with** (*workers in dispute*) il est du côté de. ●**sympa'thetic** *a* (*showing pity*) compatissant; (*understanding*) compréhensif; **s. to** bien disposé à l'égard de. ●**sympathize** *vi* **I s. (with you)** (*pity*) je suis désolé (pour vous); (*understanding*) je vous comprends. ●**sympathizer** *n Pol* sympathisant, -ante *mf*.
symphony ['sɪmfənɪ] *n* symphonie *f* ‖ *a* (*orchestra, concert*) symphonique.
symptom ['sɪmptəm] *n* symptôme *m*.
synagogue ['sɪnəgɒg] *n* synagogue *f*.
synchronize ['sɪŋkrənaɪz] *vt* synchroniser.
syndicate ['sɪndɪkət] *n* (*of businessmen*) syndicat *m*.
syndrome ['sɪndrəʊm] *n Med & Fig* syndrome *m*.
synonym ['sɪnənɪm] *n* synonyme *m*. ●**sy'nonymous** *a* synonyme (**with** de).
synopsis, *pl* **-opses** [sɪ'nɒpsɪs, -ɒpsiːz] *n* résumé *m*.

synthetic [sɪn'θetɪk] *a* synthétique.
Syria ['sɪrɪə] *n* Syrie *f*. • **Syrian** *a* & *n* syrien, -ienne (*mf*).
syringe [sɪ'rɪndʒ] *n* seringue *f*.
syrup ['sɪrəp] *n* sirop *m*; **(golden) s.** (*treacle*) mélasse *f* (raffinée).
system ['sɪstəm] *n* (*structure etc*) & *Anat Comptr etc* système *m*; (*human body*) organisme *m*; (*order*) méthode *f*; **the immune s.** le système immunitaire; **operating s.** *Comptr* système *m* d'exploitation; **systems analyst** analyste-programmeur, -euse *mf*. • **syste'matic** *a* systématique.

T

T, t [tiː] *n* T, t *m*. •**T-shirt** *n* tee-shirt *m*.

ta! [tɑː] *int Sl* merci!

tab [tæb] *n* (*cloth etc flap*) patte *f*; (*label*) étiquette *f*; (*on can of drink*) languette *f*; (*bill*) *Am* addition *f*; **to keep tabs on** *Fam* surveiller (de près).

table[1] ['teɪb(ə)l] *n* **1** (*furniture*) table *f*; **bedside/card/operating t.** table de nuit/de jeu/d'opération; **to lay** *or* **set/clear the t.** mettre/débarrasser la table; **(sitting) at the t.** à table; **t. wine** vin *m* de table. **2** (*list*) table *f*; **t. of contents** table des matières. •**tablecloth** *n* nappe *f*. •**tablemat** *n* (*of cloth*) napperon *m*; (*hard*) dessous-de-plat *m inv*. •**tablespoon** *n* = cuillère *f* à soupe. •**tablespoonful** *n* = cuillerée *f* à soupe.

table[2] ['teɪb(ə)l] *vt* (*motion*) *Pol* présenter; (*postpone*) *Am* ajourner.

tablet ['tæblɪt] *n* **1** (*pill*) comprimé *m*. **2** (*inscribed stone*) plaque *f*.

tabloid ['tæblɔɪd] *n* (*newspaper*) quotidien *m* populaire.

taboo [tə'buː] *a* & *n* tabou (*m*).

tacit ['tæsɪt] *a* tacite.

tack [tæk] **1** *n* (*nail*) petit clou *m*; (*thumbtack*) *Am* punaise *f* ‖ *vt* **to t. (down)** clouer. **2** *n* (*stitch*) point *m* de bâti ‖ *vt* **to t. (down)** bâtir; **to t. on** (*add*) *Fig* (r)ajouter. **3** *n* (*course of action*) *Fig* voie *f*.

tackle ['tæk(ə)l] **1** *n* (*gear*) matériel *m*. **2** *vt* (*problem etc*) s'attaquer à; (*thief*) saisir (à bras-le-corps); *Rugby* plaquer; *Fb* tacler.

tacky ['tækɪ] *a* **(-ier, -iest) 1** (*wet*) pas sec (*f* sèche). **2** *Fam* (*in appearance*) moche; (*remark etc*) de mauvais goût.

tact [tækt] *n* tact *m*. •**tactful** *a* (*remark etc*) plein de tact; **to be t.** (*of person*) avoir du tact. •**tactfully** *adv* avec tact. •**tactless** *a* qui manque de tact.

tactic ['tæktɪk] *n* **a t.** une tactique; **tactics** la tactique. •**tactical** *a* tactique.

tadpole ['tædpəʊl] *n* têtard *m*.

taffy ['tæfɪ] *n* (*toffee*) *Am* caramel *m* (*dur*).

tag [tæg] **1** *n* (*label*) étiquette *f*. **2** *vi* **(-gg-) to t. along** (*follow*) suivre.

Tahiti [tɑː'hiːtɪ] *n* Tahiti *m*.

tail [teɪl] **1** *n* (*of animal etc*) queue *f*; (*of shirt*) pan *m*; *pl* (*outfit*) queue-de-pie *f*; **t. end** fin *f*, bout *m*; **heads or tails?** pile ou face? **2** *vt* (*follow*) suivre, filer. **3** *vi* **to t. off** (*lessen*) diminuer. •**tailback** *n* (*of traffic*) bouchon *m*. •**tailgate** *n Aut* hayon *m*. •**taillight** *n Aut Am* feu *m* arrière *inv*.

tailor ['teɪlər] *n* (*person*) tailleur *m* ‖ *vt* (*adjust*) *Fig* adapter (**to, to suit** à). •**t.-'made** *a* fait sur mesure; **t.-made for** (*specially designed*) conçu pour.

tainted ['teɪntɪd] *a* (*air*) pollué; (*food*) gâté.

take [teɪk] *vt* (*pt* **took,** *pp* **taken**) prendre; (*prize*) remporter; (*exam*) passer; (*choice*) faire; (*contain*) contenir; *Math* soustraire (**from** de); (*tolerate*) supporter; (*bring*) amener (*qn*) (**to** à); (*by car*) conduire (*qn*) (**to** à); (*escort*) accompagner (*qn*) (**to** à); (*lead away*) emmener (*qn*) (**to** à); (*of road*) mener (*qn*) (**to** à); **to t. s.o. to** (*theatre etc*) emmener qn à; **to t. sth to s.o.** (ap)porter qch à qn; **to t. sth with one** emporter qch; **to t. s.o. home** (*on foot, by car*) ramener qn; **it takes an army/courage/** *etc* il faut une armée/du courage/*etc* (**to do** pour faire); **I took an hour to do it** j'ai mis une heure à le faire.

take after *vt* **to t. after s.o.** ressembler à qn **to take along** *vt* (*object*) emporter; (*person*) emmener **to take apart** *vt* (*machine*) démonter **to take away** *vt* (*thing*) emporter; (*person*) emmener; (*remove*) enlever (**from** à); *Math* soustraire (**from** de) **to take back** *vt* reprendre; (*return*) rapporter; (*accompany*) ramener (*qn*) (**to** à) **to take down** *vt* (*object*) descendre; (*notes*) prendre **to take in** *vt* (*chair, car etc*) rentrer; (*orphan*) recueillir; (*skirt*) reprendre; (*include*) inclure; (*understand*) comprendre; (*deceive*) *Fam* rouler **to take off** *vt* (*remove*) enlever; (*lead away*) emmener; (*mimic*) imiter; *Math* déduire (**from** de) ‖ *vi* (*of aircraft*) décoller **to take on** *vt* (*work, staff, passenger, shape*) prendre **to take out** *vt* (*from pocket etc*) sortir; (*stain*) enlever; (*tooth*) arracher; (*insurance*) prendre; **to t. s.o. out to** (*theatre etc*) emmener qn à **to take over** *vt* (*company etc*) prendre la direction de; (*overrun*) envahir; (*buy out*) racheter (*compagnie*); **to t. over s.o.'s job** remplacer qn ‖ *vi* prendre la relève (**from** de); (*permanently*) prendre la succession (**from** de) **to take round** *vt* (*bring*) apporter (*qch*) (**to** à); amener (*qn*) (**to** à); (*distribute*) distribuer; (*visitor*) faire visiter **to take to** *vt* **to t. to doing** se mettre à faire; **I didn't t. to him/**

it il/ça ne m'a pas plu **to take up** *vt* (*carry up*) monter; (*continue*) reprendre; (*space, time*) prendre; (*offer*) accepter; (*hobby*) se mettre à.

take-away ['teɪkəweɪ] *a* (*meal*) à emporter ‖ *n* (*shop*) restaurant *m* qui fait des plats à emporter; (*meal*) plat *m* à emporter. ●**takeoff** *n* (*of aircraft*) décollage *m*. ●**take-out** *a* & *n Am* = **take-away.** ●**take-over** *Com* rachat *m*.

taken ['teɪk(ə)n] *a* (*seat*) pris; **to be t. ill** tomber malade.

takings ['teɪkɪŋz] *npl* (*money*) recette *f*.

talcum ['tælkəm] *a* **t. powder** talc *m*.

tale [teɪl] *n* (*story*) conte *m*; (*account*) récit *m*; (*lie*) histoire *f*; **to tell tales** rapporter (**on** sur).

talent ['tælənt] *n* talent *m*; (*talented people*) talents *mpl*; **to have a t. for** avoir du talent pour. ●**talented** *a* doué.

talk [tɔːk] *n* (*words*) propos *mpl*; (*gossip*) bavardage(s) *m(pl)*; (*conversation*) conversation *f*; (*lecture*) exposé *m* (**on** sur); (*informal*) causerie *f* (**on** sur); (*interview*) entretien *m*; *pl* (*negotiations*) pourparlers *mpl*; **to have a t. with s.o.** parler avec qn; **there's t. of** on parle de.

‖ *vi* parler (**to** à; **with** avec; **about, of** de); (*chat*) bavarder.

‖ *vt* (*nonsense*) dire; **to t. politics** parler politique; **to t. s.o. into doing/out of doing** persuader qn de faire/de ne pas faire; **to t. sth over** discuter (de) qch. ●**talking-to** *n* **to give s.o. a t.-to** *Fam* passer un savon à qn.

talkative ['tɔːkətɪv] *a* bavard.

tall [tɔːl] *a* (**-er, -est**) (*person*) grand; (*tree, house, wall etc*) haut; **how t. are you?** combien mesures-tu?; **a t. story** *Fig* une histoire invraisemblable.

tally ['tælɪ] *vi* correspondre (**with** à).

tambourine [tæmbə'riːn] *n* tambourin *m*.

tame [teɪm] *a* (**-er, -est**) (*animal*) apprivoisé; (*person*) *Fig* docile; (*book*) fade ‖ *vt* apprivoiser; (*lion*) dompter.

tamper ['tæmpər] *vi* **to t. with** (*lock, car etc*) (essayer de) forcer; (*machine, etc*) toucher à; (*text*) altérer. ●**t.-proof** *a* (*seal*) de sécurité; (*lock*) inviolable; (*jar*) à fermeture de sécurité.

tampon ['tæmpɒn] *n* tampon *m* (périodique).

tan [tæn] **1** *n* (*suntan*) bronzage *m* ‖ *vti* (**-nn-**) bronzer. **2** *a* (*colour*) marron clair *inv*.

tandem ['tændəm] *n* **1** (*bicycle*) tandem *m*. **2 in t.** (*to work*) en tandem.

tang [tæŋ] *n* (*taste*) saveur *f* piquante; (*smell*) odeur *f* piquante. ●**tangy** *a* (**-ier, -iest**) piquant.

tangerine [tændʒə'riːn] *n* mandarine *f*.

tangle ['tæŋg(ə)l] *n* **to get into a t.** (*of rope*) s'enchevêtrer; (*of hair*) s'emmêler. ●**tangled** *a* enchevêtré; (*hair*) emmêlé; **to get t.** = **to get into a tangle.**

tank [tæŋk] *n* **1** (*for storing liquid or gas*) réservoir *m*; (*vat*) cuve *f*; **(fish) t.** aquarium *m*. **2** (*vehicle*) *Mil* char *m*. **3** *vi* **to t. up on** (*snacks etc*) *Fam* se remplir le ventre de.

tanker ['tæŋkər] *n* (*truck*) *Aut* camion-citerne *m*; **(oil) t.** (*ship*) pétrolier *m*.

Tannoy® ['tænɔɪ] *n* **over the T.** au(x) haut-parleur(s).

tantalizing ['tæntəlaɪzɪŋ] *a* (irrésistiblement) tentant.

tantamount ['tæntəmaʊnt] *a* **it's t. to** cela équivaut à.

tantrum ['tæntrəm] *n* colère *f*; **to have a t.** (*of child*) faire une colère.

tap [tæp] **1** *n* (*for water*) robinet *m*; **on t.** *Fig* disponible. **2** *vti* (**-pp-**) (*hit*) frapper légèrement, tapoter ‖ *n* petit coup *m*; **t. dancing** claquettes *fpl*. **3** *vt* (**-pp-**) (*phone*) placer sur table d'écoute. **4** *vt* (**-pp-**) (*resources*) exploiter.

tape [teɪp] **1** *n* ruban *m*; **(sticky** *or* **adhesive) t.** ruban adhésif; **t. measure** mètre *m* (à) ruban ‖ *vt* (*stick*) coller (*avec du ruban adhésif*). **2** *n* (*for sound or video recording*) bande *f* (magnétique *or* vidéo); **t. recorder** magnétophone *m*; **t. deck** platine *f* cassette ‖ *vt* (*a film, music, voice etc*) enregistrer; (*event*) faire une cassette de ‖ *vi* enregistrer.

taper ['teɪpər] **1** *vi* (*of fingers etc*) s'effiler; **to t. off** *Fig* diminuer. **2** *n* (*candle*) *Rel* cierge *m*. ●**—ed** *a* (*trousers, Am pants*) à bas étroits. ●**—ing** *a* (*fingers*) fuselé.

tapestry ['tæpəstrɪ] *n* tapisserie *f*.

tar [tɑːr] *n* goudron *m* ‖ *vt* (**-rr-**) goudronner.

target ['tɑːgɪt] *n* cible *f*; (*objective*) objectif *m* ‖ *vt* (*campaign, product etc*) destiner (**at** à); (*age group etc*) viser.

tariff ['tærɪf] *n* (*tax*) tarif *m* douanier; (*price list*) tarif *m*.

tarmac ['tɑːmæk] *n* macadam *m* (goudronné); (*runway*) piste *f*.

tarnish ['tɑːnɪʃ] *vt* ternir.

tarpaulin [tɑː'pɔːlɪn] *n* bâche *f* (goudronnée).

tart [tɑːt] **1** *n* (*pie*) (*open*) tarte *f*; (*with pastry on top*) tourte *f*. **2** *a* (**-er, -est**) (*taste*) aigre.

tartan ['tɑːt(ə)n] *n* tartan *m* ‖ *a* (*skirt etc*) écossais.

tartar ['tɑːtər] *a* **t. sauce** sauce *f* tartare.

task [tɑːsk] *n* travail *m*, tâche *f*; **t. force** *Mil* détachement *m* spécial; *Pol* commission *f* spéciale.

tassel ['tas(ə)l] *n* (*on clothes etc*) gland *m*.

taste [teɪst] *n* goût *m*; (*general idea*) *Fig* idée *f*, aperçu *m*; **in good/bad t.** de bon/mauvais goût; **to have a t. of** goûter; (*try*) goûter à ‖ *vt* (*eat, drink*) goûter; (*try*) goûter à; (*make out the taste of*) sentir (le goût de) ‖ *vi* **to t. of** *or* **like** avoir un goût de; **to t. delicious/***etc* avoir un goût délicieux/*etc*.

tasteful ['teɪstfəl] *a* de bon goût. ●**tastefully** *adv* avec goût. ●**tasteless** *a* (*food etc*) sans goût; (*joke etc*) *Fig* de mauvais goût. ●**tasty** *a* (**-ier, -iest**) savoureux.

tattered ['tætəd] *a* (*clothes*) en lambeaux. ●**tatters** *npl* **in t.** en lambeaux.

tattoo [tæ'tuː] **1** *n* (*pl* **-oos**) (*on body*) tatouage *m* ‖ *vt* tatouer. **2** *n* (*pl* **-oos**) *Mil* spectacle *m* militaire.

tatty ['tætɪ] *a* (**-ier, -iest**) (*clothes etc*) *Fam* miteux.

taught [tɔːt] *pt & pp of* **teach.**

taunt [tɔːnt] *vt* railler ‖ *n* raillerie *f*.

Taurus ['tɔːrəs] *n* (*sign*) le Taureau.

taut [tɔːt] *a* (*rope etc*) tendu.

tavern ['tævən] *n* taverne *f*.

tax[1] [tæks] *n* (*on goods*) taxe *f*, impôt *m*; (*on income*) impôts *mpl* ‖ *a* fiscal; **t. collector** percepteur *m*; **t. relief** dégrèvement *m* (d'impôt); **(road) t. disc** vignette *f* (automobile) ‖ *vt* (*person*) imposer; (*goods*) taxer. ●**taxable** *a* imposable. ●**taxation** [-'eɪʃ(ə)n] *n* (*taxes*) impôts *mpl*; **the burden of t.** le poids de l'impôt. ●**tax-free** *a* exempt d'impôts. ●**taxman** *n* (*pl* **-men**) *Fam* percepteur *m*. ●**taxpayer** *n* contribuable *mf*.

tax[2] [tæks] *vt* (*patience*) mettre à l'épreuve; (*tire*) fatiguer.

taxi ['tæksɪ] **1** *n* taxi *m*; **t. cab** taxi *m*; **t. rank,** *Am* **t. stand** station *f* de taxis. **2** *vi* (*of aircraft*) rouler au sol.

TB [tiː'biː] *n* tuberculose *f*.

tea [tiː] *n* thé *m*; (*snack*) goûter *m*; **high t.** goûter *m* (dînatoire); **to have t.** prendre le thé; (*afternoon snack*) goûter; **t. break** pause-thé *f*; **t. cloth** (*for drying dishes*) torchon *m*; **t. party** thé *m*; **t. set** service *m* à thé; **t. towel** torchon *m*. ●**teabag** *n* sachet *m* de thé. ●**teacup** *n* tasse *f* à thé. ●**teapot** *n* théière *f*. ●**tearoom** *n* salon *m* de thé. ●**teaspoon** *n* petite cuillère *f*. ●**teaspoonful** *n* cuillerée *f* à café. ●**teatime** *n* l'heure *f* du thé.

teach [tiːtʃ] *vt* (*pt & pp* **taught**) apprendre (**s.o. sth** qch à qn, **that** que); (*in school etc*) enseigner (**s.o. sth** qch à qn); **to t. s.o. (how) to do** apprendre à qn à faire ‖ *vi* enseigner. ●**—ing** *n* enseignement *m* ‖ *a* (*method, material*) pédagogique; **the t. profession** l'enseignement *m*; (*teachers*) le corps enseignant; **t. staff** personnel *m* enseignant.

teacher ['tiːtʃər] *n* professeur *m*; (*in primary school*) instituteur, -trice *mf*.

team [tiːm] *n* *Sp* équipe *f*; (*of horses*) attelage *m*; **t. mate** coéquipier, -ière *mf* ‖ *vi* **to t. up** faire équipe (**with** avec). ●**teamster** *n* *Am* routier *m*. ●**teamwork** *n* collaboration *f*.

tear[1] [teər] **1** *n* déchirure *f* ‖ *vt* (*pt* **tore,** *pp* **torn**) (*rip*) déchirer; (*snatch*) arracher (**from s.o.** à qn); **torn between** *Fig* tiraillé entre; **to t. down** (*house*) démolir; **to t. off** *or* **out** (*remove with force*) arracher; (*receipt, stamp etc*) détacher; **to t. up** déchirer ‖ *vi* (*of cloth etc*) se déchirer. **2** *vi* (*pt* **tore,** *pp* **torn**) **to t. along/off** (*rush*) aller/partir à toute vitesse.

tear[2] [tɪər] *n* larme *f*; **in tears** en larmes; **close to tears** au bord des larmes. ●**tearful** *a* (*eyes, voice*) larmoyant; (*person*) en larmes. ●**teargas** *n* gaz *m* lacrymogène.

tearaway ['teərəweɪ] *n* *Fam* casse-cou *m*.

tease [tiːz] *vt* taquiner; (*harshly*) tourmenter.

teat [tiːt] *n* (*of bottle, animal*) tétine *f*.

technical ['teknɪk(ə)l] *a* technique. ●**techni'cality** *n* (*detail*) détail *m* technique. ●**technically** *adv* techniquement; *Fig* théoriquement. ●**tech'nician** *n* technicien, -ienne *mf*. ●**tech'nique** *n* technique *f*. ●**technocrat** *n* technocrate *m*. ●**techno'logical** *a* technologique. ●**tech'nology** *n* technologie *f*.

teddy ['tedɪ] *n* **t. (bear)** ours *m* (en peluche).

tedious ['tiːdɪəs] *a* fastidieux.

teem [tiːm] *vi* **1** (*swarm*) grouiller (**with** de). **2 to t. (with rain)** pleuvoir à torrents.

teenage ['tiːneɪdʒ] *a* (*boy, girl*) adolescent; (*fashion*) pour adolescents. ●**teenager** *n* adolescent, -ente *mf*. ●**teens** *npl* **in one's t.** adolescent.

teeny (weeny) ['tiːnɪ('wiːnɪ)] *a* *Fam* minuscule.

tee-shirt ['tiːʃɜːt] *n* tee-shirt *m*.

teeth [tiːθ] *see* **tooth.**

teeth/e [tiːð] *vi* faire ses dents. ●**—ing** *n* dentition *f*; **t. ring** anneau *m* de dentition; **t. troubles** *Fig* difficultés *fpl* de mise en route.

teetotaller [tiː'təʊt(ə)lər] *n* personne *f* qui ne boit pas d'alcool.

tele- ['telɪ] *pref* télé-.

telecommunications [telɪkəmjuːnɪ'keɪʃ(ə)nz] *npl* télécommunications *fpl*.

telegram ['telıgræm] *n* télégramme *m*.
telegraph ['telıgrɑːf] *a* **t. pole/wire** poteau *m*/fil *m* télégraphique.
Telemessage® ['telımesıdʒ] *n* (*in UK*) = télégramme *m*.
telephone ['telıfəʊn] *n* téléphone *m*; **on the t.** (*speaking*) au téléphone ‖ *a* (*call, line, message*) téléphonique; **t. booth, t. box** cabine *f* téléphonique; **t. directory** annuaire *m* du téléphone; **t. number** numéro *m* de téléphone ‖ *vi* téléphoner ‖ *vt* (*message*) téléphoner (**to** à); **to t. s.o.** téléphoner à qn. ●**te'lephonist** *n* standardiste *mf*.
telephoto ['telıfəʊtəʊ] *a* **t. lens** téléobjectif *m*.
teleprinter ['telıprıntər] *n* téléscripteur *m*.
telescope ['telıskəʊp] *n* télescope *m*. ●**tele'scopic** *a* (*umbrella etc*) télescopique.
teletypewriter [telı'taıpraıtər] *n Am* téléscripteur *m*.
televise ['telıvaız] *vt* retransmettre à la télévision. ●**tele'vision** *n* télévision *f*; **on (the) t.** à la télévision; **t. set** téléviseur *m* ‖ *a* (*programme, screen etc*) de télévision; (*interview etc*) télévisé.
telex ['teleks] *n* (*service, message*) télex *m* ‖ *vt* envoyer par télex.
tell [tel] *vt* (*pt & pp* **told**) dire (**s.o. sth** qch à qn, **that** que); (*story*) raconter; (*distinguish*) distinguer (**from** de); (*know*) savoir; **to t. s.o. to do** dire à qn de faire; **to know how to t. the time** savoir lire l'heure; **to t. the difference** voir la différence; **to t. s.o. off** *Fam* disputer qn.
‖ *vi* dire; (*have an effect*) avoir un effet; (*know*) savoir; **to t. of** *or* **about sth/s.o.** parler de qch/qn; **to t. on s.o.** *Fam* rapporter sur qn. ●**telltale** *n Fam* rapporteur, -euse *mf*.
teller ['telər] *n* **(bank) t.** guichetier, -ière *mf* (*de banque*).
telly ['telı] *n Fam* télé *f*.
temp [temp] *n* (*secretary*) *Fam* intérimaire *mf*.
temper ['tempər] **1** *n* (*mood, nature*) humeur *f*; **to lose one's t.** se mettre en colère; **in a bad t.** de mauvaise humeur; **to have a (bad) t.** avoir un caractère de cochon. **2** *vt* (*moderate*) tempérer.
temperament ['temp(ə)rəmənt] *n* tempérament *m*. ●**tempera'mental** *a* (*person, machine*) capricieux.
temperate ['tempərət] *a* (*climate*) tempéré.
temperature ['temp(ə)rətʃər] *n* température *f*; **to have a t.** *Med* avoir de la température *or* de la fièvre.
template ['templət] *n* (*of plastic, metal etc*) patron *m*.
temple ['temp(ə)l] *n* **1** (*building*) *Rel* temple *m*. **2** *Anat* tempe *f*.
tempo ['tempəʊ] *n* (*pl* **-os**) (*of life etc*) rythme *m*.
temporary ['temp(ə)rərı, *Am* -erı] *a* provisoire; (*job*) temporaire; (*secretary*) intérimaire.
tempt [tempt] *vt* tenter; **tempted to do** tenté de faire; **to t. s.o. to do** persuader qn de faire. ●**—ing** *a* tentant. ●**temptation** [-'teıʃ(ə)n] *n* tentation *f*.
ten [ten] *a & n* dix (*m*). ●**tenfold** *a* **t. increase** augmentation *f* par dix ‖ *adv* **to increase t.** (se) multiplier par dix.
tenacious [tə'neıʃəs] *a* tenace.
tenant ['tenənt] *n* locataire *nmf*. ●**tenancy** *n* (*lease*) location *f*; (*period*) occupation *f*.
tend [tend] **1** *vi* **to t. to do** avoir tendance à faire; **to t. towards** incliner vers. **2** *vt* (*look after*) s'occuper de. ●**tendency** *n* tendance *f* (**to do** à faire).
tender[1] ['tendər] *a* (*soft, loving*) tendre; (*painful*) sensible. ●**—ness** *n* tendresse *f*; (*pain*) (petite) douleur *f*.
tender[2] ['tendər] **1** *vt* (*offer*) offrir; **to t. one's resignation** donner sa démission. **2** *n* **to be legal t.** (*of money*) avoir cours. **3** *n* (*for services etc*) soumission *f* (**for** pour).
tenement ['tenəmənt] *n* immeuble *m* (de rapport).
tenner ['tenər] *n Fam* billet *m* de dix livres.
tennis ['tenıs] *n* tennis *m*; **table t.** tennis de table; **t. court** court *m* (de tennis).
tenor ['tenər] *n Mus* ténor *m*.
tenpin ['tenpın] *a* **t. bowling** bowling *m*. ●**tenpins** *n Am* bowling *m*.
tense [tens] **1** *a* (**-er, -est**) (*person, muscle, situation*) tendu ‖ *vt* tendre, crisper. **2** *n Gram* temps *m*.
tension ['tenʃ(ə)n] *n* tension *f*.
tent [tent] *n* tente *f*; **t. peg** piquet *m* de tente.
tentacle ['tentək(ə)l] *n* tentacule *m*.
tentative ['tentətıv] *a* (*not definite*) provisoire; (*hesitant*) timide. ●**—ly** *adv* provisoirement.
tenterhooks ['tentəhʊks] *npl* **on t.** (*anxious*) sur des charbons ardents.
tenth [tenθ] *a & n* dixième (*mf*); **a t.** un dixième.
tenuous ['tenjʊəs] *a* (*link*) ténu.
tepid ['tepıd] *a* (*liquid*) & *Fig* tiède.
term [tɜːm] *n* (*word*) terme *m*; (*period*) période *f*; (*of school year*) trimestre *m*; (*semester*) *Am* semestre *m*; *pl* (*conditions*) conditions *fpl*; (*prices*) prix *mpl*; **t. (of office)** *Pol* mandat *m*; **easy terms** *Fin*

facilités *fpl* de paiement; **on good/bad terms** en bons/mauvais termes (**with s.o.** avec qn); **on close terms** intime (**with** avec); **in terms of** (*speaking of*) sur le plan de; **to come to terms with** (*situation*) faire face à; **in the long/short t.** à long/court terme ▮ *vt* (*name, call*) appeler.

terminal ['tɜːmɪn(ə)l] **1** *n* **(air) t.** aérogare *f*; **(computer) t.** terminal *m* (d'ordinateur); **(oil) t.** terminal *m* (pétrolier). **2** *a* (*patient, illness*) incurable; **in its t. stage** (*illness*) en phase terminale. ●**—ly** *adv* **t. ill** (*patient*) incurable.

terminate ['tɜːmɪneɪt] *vt* mettre fin à; (*contract*) résilier; (*pregnancy*) interrompre.

terminus ['tɜːmɪnəs] *n* terminus *m*.

termite ['tɜːmaɪt] *n* (*insect*) termite *m*.

terrace ['terɪs] *n* terrasse *f*; (*houses*) maisons *fpl* en bande; **the terraces** *Sp* les gradins *mpl*. ●**terraced house** *n* maison *f* attenante aux maisons voisines.

terrain [tə'reɪn] *n Mil Geol* terrain *m*.

terrible ['terəb(ə)l] *a* affreux, terrible. ●**terribly** *adv* (*badly, very*) affreusement.

terrier ['terɪər] *n* (*dog*) terrier *m*.

terrific [tə'rɪfɪk] *a* (*excellent, very great*) *Fam* formidable, terrible. ●**terrifically** *adv Fam* (*extremely*) terriblement; (*extremely well*) terriblement bien.

terrify ['terɪfaɪ] *vt* terrifier; **to be terrified of** avoir très peur de. ●**—ing** *a* terrifiant.

territory ['terɪtərɪ] *n* territoire *m*.

terror ['terər] *n* terreur *f*; (*child*) *Fam* polisson, -onne *mf*. ●**terrorism** *n* terrorisme *m*. ●**terrorist** *n* & *a* terroriste (*mf*). ●**terrorize** *vt* terroriser.

terry(cloth) ['terɪ(klɒθ)] *n* tissu-éponge *m*.

terse [tɜːs] *a* laconique.

Terylene® ['terəliːn] *n* tergal® *m*.

test [test] *vt* (*try*) essayer; (*product, machine*) tester; (*pupil*) interroger; (*of doctor*) examiner (*les yeux etc*); (*analyse*) analyser (*le sang etc*); (*courage*) *Fig* éprouver.

▮*n* (*trial*) essai *m*; (*of product*) test *m*; *Sch* interrogation *f*, test *m*; (*by doctor*) examen *m*; (*of blood etc*) analyse *f*; **driving t.** (examen *m* du) permis *m* de conduire; **eye t.** examen *m* de la vue.

▮*a* (*pilot, flight*) d'essai; **t. match** *Sp* match *m* international; **t. tube** éprouvette *f*; **t. tube baby** bébé *m* éprouvette.

testament ['testəmənt] *n* testament *m*; **Old/New T.** *Rel* Ancien/Nouveau Testament.

testicle ['testɪk(ə)l] *n Anat* testicule *m*.

testify ['testɪfaɪ] *vi Jur* témoigner (**against** contre); **to t. to sth** témoigner de qch ▮ *vt* **to t. that** *Jur* témoigner que. ●**testi'monial** *n* références *fpl*.

tetanus ['tetənəs] *n Med* tétanos *m*.

tether ['teðər] *n* **at the end of one's t.** à bout (de nerfs).

text [tekst] *n* texte *m*. ●**textbook** *n* manuel *m* (scolaire).

textile ['tekstaɪl] *a* & *n* textile (*m*).

texture ['tekstʃər] *n* (*of fabric etc*) texture *f*; (*of paper, wood*) grain *m*.

Thames [temz] *n* **the T.** la Tamise.

than [ðən, *stressed* ðæn] *conj* **1** que; **happier t.** plus heureux que; **he has more t. you** il en a plus que toi; **fewer oranges t. plums** moins d'oranges que de prunes. **2** (*with numbers*) de; **more t. six** plus de six.

thank [θæŋk] *vt* remercier (**for sth** de qch, **for doing** d'avoir fait); **t. you** merci (**for sth** pour *or* de qch, **for doing** d'avoir fait); **no, t. you** (non) merci; **t. God, t. heavens** Dieu merci.

▮*npl* remerciements *mpl*; **(many) thanks!** merci (beaucoup)!; **thanks to** (*because of*) grâce à. ●**thankful** *a* reconnaissant (**for** de); **t. that** bien heureux que (+ *sub*). ●**thankless** *a* ingrat. ●**Thanks'giving (day)** *n Am* jour *m* d'action de grâce(s).

that [ðət, *stressed* ðæt] **1** *conj* que; **to say t.** dire que.

2 *rel pron* (*subject*) qui; (*object*) que; (*with prep*) lequel, laquelle, *pl* lesquel(le)s; **the boy t. left** le garçon qui est parti; **the book t. I read** le livre que j'ai lu; **the carpet t. I put it on** le tapis sur lequel je l'ai mis; **the house t. she told me about** la maison dont elle m'a parlé; **the day/morning t. she arrived** le jour/matin où elle est arrivée.

3 *dem a* (*pl see* **those**) ce, cet (*before vowel or mute h*), cette; (*opposed to 'this'*) ... + -là; **t. day** ce jour; ce jour-là; **t. girl** cette fille; cette fille-là.

4 *dem pron* (*pl see* **those**) ça, cela; ce; **t. (one)** celui-là *m*, celle-là *f*; **give me t.** donne-moi ça *or* cela; **I prefer t. (one)** je préfère celui-là; **before t.** avant ça *or* cela; **t.'s right** c'est juste; **who's t.?** qui est-ce?; **t.'s the house** c'est la maison; (*pointing*) voilà la maison; **t. is (to say)...** c'est-à-dire....

5 *adv* (*so*) *Fam* si; **not t. good** pas si bon; **t. high** (*pointing*) haut comme ça; **t. much** (*to cost etc*) (au)tant que ça.

thatched [θætʃt] *a* (*roof*) de chaume; **t. cottage** chaumière *f*.

thaw [θɔː] *n* dégel *m* ▮ *vi* dégeler; (*of snow, ice*) fondre; (*of food*) décongeler; **it's thawing** ça dégèle ▮ *vt* (*snow etc*) faire fondre; **to t. (out)** (*food*) (faire) décongeler.

the [ðə, *before vowel* ðɪ, *stressed* ðiː] *def art* le, l', la, *pl* les; **t. roof** le toit; **t. man** l'homme; **t. moon** la lune; **t. orange** l'orange; **t. boxes** les boîtes; **the smallest** le plus petit; **of t., from t.** du, de l', de la, *pl* des; **to t., at t.** au, à l', à la, *pl* aux; **Elizabeth t. Second** Élisabeth Deux.

theatre ['θɪətər] (*Am* **theater**) *n* (*place*, *art*) théâtre *m*. ●**theatregoer** *n* amateur *m* de théâtre. ●**the'atrical** *a* théâtral; **t. company** troupe *f* de théâtre.

theft [θeft] *n* vol *m*.

their [ðeər] *poss a* leur, *pl* leurs; **t. house** leur maison *f*. ●**theirs** [ðeəz] *poss pron* le leur, la leur, *pl* les leurs; **this book is t.** ce livre est à eux *or* est le leur; **a friend of t.** un ami à eux.

them [ðəm, *stressed* ðem] *pron* les; (*after prep, 'than', 'it is'*) eux *mpl*, elles *fpl*; **(to) t.** leur; **I see t.** je les vois; **I give (to) t.** je leur donne; **with t.** avec eux, avec elles; **ten of t.** dix d'entre eux *or* elles; **all of t. came** tous sont venus, toutes sont venues; **I like all of t.** je les aime tous *or* toutes.

theme [θiːm] *n* thème *m*; **t. music** musique *f* (de film); **t. song** chanson *f* (de film); **t. park** parc *m* (de loisirs) à thème.

themselves [ðem'selvz] *pron* eux-mêmes *mpl*, elles-mêmes *fpl*; (*reflexive*) se, s'; (*after prep etc*) eux *mpl*, elles *fpl*; **they wash t.** ils *or* elles se lavent; **they think of t.** ils pensent à eux, elles pensent à elles.

then [ðen] **1** *adv* (*at that time*) à cette époque-là; (*just a moment ago*) à ce moment-là; (*next*) ensuite, puis; **from t. on** dès lors; **before t.** avant cela; **until t.** jusque-là ‖ *a* **the t. mayor/***etc* le maire/*etc* de l'époque. **2** *conj* (*therefore*) donc, alors.

theology [θɪ'ɒlədʒɪ] *n* théologie *f*.

theory ['θɪərɪ] *n* théorie *f*; **in t.** en théorie. ●**theo'retical** *a* théorique.

therapy ['θerəpɪ] *n* thérapeutique *f*. ●**thera'peutic** *a* thérapeutique.

there [ðeər] *adv* là; **(down** *or* **over) t.** là-bas; **on t.** là-dessus; **t. is, t. are** il y a; (*pointing*) voilà; **t. he is** le voilà; **t. they are** les voilà; **that man t.** cet homme-là; **t. (you are)!** (*take this*) tenez!; **t., don't cry!** allons, ne pleure pas! ●**therea'bout(s)** *adv* par là; (*in amount*) à peu près. ●**there'after** *adv* après cela. ●**thereby** *adv* de ce fait. ●**therefore** *adv* donc. ●**thereu'pon** *adv* sur ce.

thermal ['θɜːm(ə)l] *a* (*underwear*) en thermolactyl®; **t. springs** eaux *fpl* thermales.

thermometer [θə'mɒmɪtər] *n* thermomètre *m*.

Thermos® ['θɜːməs] *n* (*pl* **-es**) **T. (flask** *or* *Am* **bottle)** thermos® *m or f inv*.

thermostat ['θɜːməstæt] *n* thermostat *m*.

thesaurus [θɪ'sɔːrəs] *n* dictionnaire *m* de synonymes.

these [ðiːz] **1** *dem a* (*sing see* **this**) ces; (*opposed to 'those'*) ... + -ci; **t. men** ces hommes; ces hommes-ci. **2** *dem pron* (*sing see* **this**) **t. (ones)** ceux-ci *mpl*, celles-ci *fpl*; **t. are my friends** ce sont mes amis.

thesis, *pl* **theses** ['θiːsɪs, 'θiːsiːz] *n* thèse *f*.

they [ðeɪ] *pron* **1** ils *mpl*, elles *fpl*; (*stressed*) eux *mpl*, elles *fpl*; **t. go** ils vont, elles vont; **t. are doctors** ce sont des médecins. **2** (*people in general*) on; **t. say** on dit. ●**they'd** = **they had** & **they would**. ●**they'll** = **they will**.

thick [θɪk] *a* (**-er, -est**) épais (*f* épaisse); (*stupid*) *Fam* lourd ‖ *adv* (*to spread*) en couche épaisse; (*to grow*) dru ‖ *n* **in the t. of** (*battle etc*) au cœur de. ●**—ly** *adv* (*to spread*) en couche épaisse; (*to grow*) dru; (*populated*) très. ●**—ness** *n* épaisseur *f*.

thicken ['θɪk(ə)n] *vt* épaissir ‖ *vi* (*of fog etc*) s'épaissir; (*of cream etc*) épaissir.

thickset [θɪk'set] *a* (*person*) trapu. ●**thick-skinned** *a* (*person*) peu sensible.

thief [θiːf] *n* (*pl* **thieves**) voleur, -euse *mf*. ●**thieving** *a* voleur ‖ *n* vol *m*.

thigh [θaɪ] *n* cuisse *f*.

thimble ['θɪmb(ə)l] *n* dé *m* (à coudre).

thin [θɪn] *a* (**thinner, thinnest**) (*slice*, *paper etc*) mince; (*person*, *leg*) maigre, mince; (*soup*) peu épais (*f* épaisse); (*crowd*) clairsemé; (*powder*) fin ‖ *adv* (*to spread*) en couche mince; (*to cut*) en tranches minces ‖ *vt* (**-nn-**) **to t. (down)** (*paint etc*) diluer. ●**—ly** *adv* en couche mince; en tranches minces; (*disguised*) à peine.

thing [θɪŋ] *n* chose *f*; **one's things** (*belongings*) ses affaires *fpl*; **poor little t.!** pauvre petit!; **how are things?** comment ça va?; **I'll think things over** j'y réfléchirai; **for one t...., and for another t.** d'abord... et ensuite. ●**thingummy** *n Fam* truc *m*, machin *m*.

think [θɪŋk] *vi* (*pt* & *pp* **thought**) penser (**about, of** à); **to t. (carefully)** réfléchir (**about, of** à); **to t. of doing** penser à faire; **to t. a lot of** penser beaucoup de bien de; **she doesn't t. much of it** ça ne lui dit pas grand-chose; **I can't t. of it** je n'arrive pas à m'en souvenir.

‖ *vt* penser (**that** que); **I t. so** je pense *or* crois que oui; **what do you t. of him?** que penses-tu de lui?; **I thought it difficult** je l'ai trouvé difficile; **to t. sth over** réfléchir à qch; **to t. sth up** inventer qch. ●**thinker** *n* penseur, -euse *mf*.

third [θɜːd] *a* troisième; **t. person** *or* **party** tiers *m*; **t.-party insurance** assurance *f* au tiers; **T. World** Tiers-Monde *m* ‖ *n* troisième *mf*; **a t.** (*fraction*) un tiers ‖ *adv* **to come t.** se classer troisième. ●**—ly** *adv* troisièmement.

third-class [θɜːd'klɑːs] *a* de troisième classe. ●**t.-rate** *a* (très) inférieur.

thirst [θɜːst] *n* soif *f* (**for** de). ●**thirsty** *a* (**-ier, -iest**) **to be** *or* **feel t.** avoir soif; **to make s.o. t.** donner soif à qn.

thirteen [θɜː'tiːn] *a* & *n* treize (*m*). ●**thirteenth** *a* & *n* treizième (*mf*). ●**'thirtieth** *a* & *n* trentième (*mf*). ●**'thirty** *a* & *n* trente (*m*).

this [ðɪs] **1** *dem a* (*pl see* **these**) ce, cet (*before vowel or mute h*), cette; (*opposed to 'that'*) ... + -ci; **t. book** ce livre; ce livre-ci; **t. photo** cette photo; cette photo-ci. **2** *dem pron* (*pl see* **these**) ceci; ce; **t. (one)** celui-ci *m*, celle-ci *f*; **give me t.** donne-moi ceci; **I prefer t. (one)** je préfère celui-ci; **before t.** avant ceci; **who's t.?** qui est-ce?; **t. is Paul** c'est Paul; (*pointing*) voici Paul. **3** *adv* (*so*) **t. high** (*pointing*) haut comme ceci; **t. far** (*until now*) jusqu'ici.

thistle ['θɪs(ə)l] *n* chardon *m*.

thorn [θɔːn] *n* épine *f*. ●**thorny** *a* (**-ier, -iest**) (*bush etc*) épineux.

thorough ['θʌrə] *a* (*careful*) minutieux; (*knowledge, examination*) approfondi; (*liar*) parfait; (*disaster*) complet; **to give sth a t. washing**/*etc* laver/*etc* qch à fond. ●**—ly** *adv* (*completely*) tout à fait; (*carefully*) avec minutie; (*to know, clean etc*) à fond.

thoroughbred ['θʌrəbred] *n* (*horse*) pur-sang *m inv*.

thoroughfare ['θʌrəfeər] *n* artère *f*, rue *f*; **'no t.'** 'passage interdit'.

those [ðəʊz] **1** *dem a* (*sing see* **that**) ces; (*opposed to 'these'*) ... + -là; **t. men** ces hommes; ces hommes-là. **2** *dem pron* (*sing see* **that**) **t. (ones)** ceux-là *mpl*, celles-là *fpl*; **t. are my friends** ce sont mes amis.

though [ðəʊ] **1** *conj* **(even) t.** bien que (+ *sub*); **as t.** comme si. **2** *adv* (*however*) pourtant.

thought [θɔːt] *pt* & *pp of* **think** ‖ *n* pensée *f*; **(careful) t.** réflexion *f*; **to have second thoughts** changer d'avis.

thoughtful ['θɔːtfəl] *a* (*considerate*) gentil, attentionné; (*pensive*) pensif. ●**thoughtfully** *adv* (*considerately*) gentiment. ●**thoughtless** *a* (*towards others*) pas très gentil; (*absent-minded*) étourdi. ●**thoughtlessly** *adv* (*inconsiderately*) pas très gentiment.

thousand ['θaʊzənd] *a* & *n* mille *a* & *m inv*; **a t. pages** mille pages; **two t. pages** deux mille pages; **thousands of** des milliers de.

thrash [θræʃ] **1** *vt* **to t. s.o.** donner une correction à qn; (*defeat*) écraser qn; **to t. out** (*plan*) élaborer (à force de discussions). **2** *vi* **to t. around** (*struggle*) se débattre. ●**—ing** *n* (*beating*) correction *f*.

thread [θred] *n* (*yarn*) & *Fig* fil *m*; (*of screw*) pas *m* ‖ *vt* (*needle, beads*) enfiler; **to t. one's way** se faufiler. ●**threadbare** *a* élimé, râpé.

threat [θret] *n* menace *f*. ●**threaten** *vi* menacer ‖ *vt* menacer (**to do** de faire, **with sth** de qch). ●**threatening** *a* menaçant.

three [θriː] *a* & *n* trois (*m*); **t.-piece suite** canapé *m* et deux fauteuils. ●**threefold** *a* triple ‖ *adv* **to increase t.** tripler.

thresh [θreʃ] *vt Agr* battre.

threshold ['θreʃhəʊld] *n* seuil *m*.

threw [θruː] *pt of* **throw**.

thrifty ['θrɪftɪ] *a* (**-ier, -iest**) économe.

thrill [θrɪl] *n* frisson *m*; **to get a t. out of doing** prendre plaisir à faire ‖ *vt* (*delight*) réjouir; (*excite*) faire frissonner. ●**—ed** *a* ravi (**with sth** de qch, **to do** de faire). ●**—ing** *a* passionnant. ●**thriller** *n* film *m or* roman *m* à suspense.

thriv/e [θraɪv] *vi* (*of business, plant etc*) prospérer; **she thrives on hard work** le travail lui profite. ●**—ing** *a* prospère.

throat [θrəʊt] *n* gorge *f*.

throb [θrɒb] *vi* (**-bb-**) (*of heart*) palpiter; (*of engine*) vrombir; (*vibrate*) vibrer; **my finger is throbbing** mon doigt me fait des élancements.

throes [θrəʊz] *npl* **in the t. of** au milieu de; (*illness, crisis*) en proie à; **in the t. of doing** en train de faire.

throne [θrəʊn] *n* trône *m*.

throng [θrɒŋ] *Lit n* foule *f* ‖ *vi* (*rush*) affluer ‖ *vt* (*station etc*) se presser dans.

throttle ['θrɒt(ə)l] **1** *n Aut* accélérateur *m*. **2** *vt* (*strangle*) étrangler.

through [θruː] *prep* (*place*) à travers; (*window, door*) par; (*time*) pendant; (*means*) par; (*thanks to*) grâce à; **to go** *or* **get t.** (*forest etc*) traverser; (*hole etc*) passer par; (*wall etc*) passer à travers; **Tuesday t. Saturday** *Am* de mardi à samedi.
‖ *adv* à travers; **to go t.** (*cross*) traverser; (*pass*) passer; **to let t.** laisser passer; **to be t.** (*finished*) *Am* avoir fini; **we're t.** *Am* c'est fini entre nous; **I'm t. with the book** *Am* je n'ai plus besoin du livre; **all** *or* **right t.** (*to the end*) jusqu'au bout; **t. to** *or* **till** jusqu'à; **I'll put you t. (to him)** *Tel* je vous le passe. ‖ *a* (*train, traffic*) direct; **'no t. road'** 'voie sans issue'.

throughout [θru:'aʊt] *prep* **t. the neighbourhood**/*etc* dans tout le quartier/*etc*; **t. the day**/*etc* pendant toute la journée/*etc* ‖ *adv* (*everywhere*) partout; (*all the time*) tout le temps.

throughway ['θru:weɪ] *n Am* autoroute *f*.

throw [θrəʊ] *n* (*of stone etc*) jet *m*; *Sp* lancer *m*; (*of dice*) coup *m* ‖ *vt* (*pt* **threw,** *pp* **thrown**) jeter (**to, at** à); (*stone, ball*) lancer, jeter; (*hurl*) projeter; (*of horse*) désarçonner (*qn*); (*party*) donner.

throw away *vt* (*unwanted object*) jeter; (*waste*) *Fig* gâcher **to throw back** *vt* (*ball*) renvoyer (**to** à) **to throw in** *vt* (*as extra*) *Fam* donner en prime **to throw out** *vt* (*unwanted object*) jeter; (*suggestion*) repousser; (*expel*) mettre (*qn*) à la porte **to throw up** *vt Fam* (*job*) laisser tomber; (*food*) rendre ‖ *vi* (*vomit*) *Fam* rendre.

throwaway ['θrəʊəweɪ] *a* (*disposable*) jetable.

thrush [θrʌʃ] *n* (*bird*) grive *f*.

thrust [θrʌst] *n* (*push, lunge etc*) coup *m* ‖ *vt* (*pt* & *pp* **thrust**) (*push*) pousser; (*put*) mettre; **to t. sth into sth** (*stick, knife etc*) enfoncer qch dans qch.

thud [θʌd] *n* bruit *m* sourd.

thug [θʌg] *n* voyou *m*.

thumb [θʌm] *n* pouce *m* ‖ *vt* **to t. (through)** (*book*) feuilleter; **to t. a lift** *or* **a ride** *Fam* faire du stop. ●**thumbtack** *n Am* punaise *f*.

thump [θʌmp] *vt* (*person*) frapper, cogner sur; (*table*) taper sur; **to t. one's head** se cogner la tête (**on** contre) ‖ *vi* frapper, cogner (**on** sur); (*of heart*) battre à grands coups ‖ *n* (grand) coup *m*; (*noise*) bruit *m* sourd.

thunder ['θʌndər] *n* tonnerre *m* ‖ *vi* (*of guns etc*) tonner; **it's thundering** il tonne; **to t. past** passer dans un bruit de tonnerre. ●**thunderbolt** *n* coup *m* de foudre; (*event*) *Fig* coup *m* de tonnerre. ●**thunderclap** *n* coup *m* de tonnerre. ●**thunderstorm** *n* orage *m*.

Thursday ['θɜ:zdɪ, -deɪ] *n* jeudi *m*.

thus [ðʌs] *adv* ainsi.

thwart [θwɔ:t] *vt* (*plan, person*) contrecarrer.

thyme [taɪm] *n Bot Culin* thym *m*.

tiara [tɪ'ɑ:rə] *n* (*of woman*) diadème *m*.

tick [tɪk] **1** *n* (*of clock*) tic-tac *m* ‖ *vi* faire tic-tac; **to t. over** (*of engine, business*) tourner au ralenti. **2** *n* (*mark*) = croix *f* ‖ *vt* **to t. (off)** (*on list etc*) cocher; **to t. s.o. off** *Fam* passer un savon à qn. **3** *n* (*insect*) tique *f*. ●**—ing** *n* (*of clock*) tic-tac *m*; **to give s.o. a t.-off** *Fam* passer un savon à qn.

ticket ['tɪkɪt] *n* billet *m*; (*for bus, underground, cloakroom*) ticket *m*; (*for library*) carte *f*; (*fine*) *Aut Fam* contravention *f*; *Pol Am* liste *f*; **(price) t.** étiquette *f*; **t. collector** contrôleur, -euse *mf*; **t. office** guichet *m*.

tickle ['tɪk(ə)l] *vt* chatouiller ‖ *n* chatouillement *m*. ●**ticklish** *a* (*person*) chatouilleux; (*garment*) qui chatouille.

tidbit ['tɪdbɪt] *n* (*food*) *Am* bon morceau *m*.

tide [taɪd] **1** *n* marée *f*; **against the t.** *Nau* & *Fig* à contre-courant. **2** *vt* **to t. s.o. over** (*help out*) dépanner qn. ●**tidal** *a* (*river*) qui a une marée; **t. wave** raz-de-marée *m inv*; (*in public opinion etc*) *Fig* vague *f* de fond.

tidings ['taɪdɪŋz] *npl Lit* nouvelles *fpl*.

tidy ['taɪdɪ] *a* (**-ier, -iest**) (*place, toys etc*) bien rangé; (*clothes, hair*) soigné; (*person*) (*methodical*) ordonné; (*in appearance*) soigné; (*sum*) *Fam* joli; **to make t.** ranger ‖ *vt* **to t. sth (up** *or* **away)** ranger qch; **to t. out** (*drawer etc*) vider; **to t. oneself up** s'arranger ‖ *vi* **to t. up** ranger. ●**tidily** *adv* (*to put away etc*) soigneusement.

tie [taɪ] *n* (*around neck*) cravate *f*; (*string, strap etc*) & *Fig* lien *m*, attache *f*; *Sp* égalité *f* de points; (*drawn match*) match *m* nul ‖ *vt* (*fasten*) attacher, lier (**to** à); (*a knot*) faire (**in** à); (*shoe*) lacer; (*link*) lier (**to** à) ‖ *vi Sp* finir à égalité de points; *Fb* faire match nul; (*in race*) être ex aequo.

tie down *vt* attacher; **to t. s.o. down to** (*date etc*) obliger qn à accepter **to tie in** *vi* (*be linked*) être lié; **to t. in with** se rapporter à **to tie up** *vt* attacher (*qn*) (**to** à); (*person*) ligoter; **tied up** (*linked*) lié (**with** avec); (*busy*) *Fam* occupé.

tier [tɪər] *n* (*seats*) gradin *m*; (*of cake*) étage *m*.

tiff [tɪf] *n* petite querelle *f*.

tiger ['taɪgər] *n* tigre *m*.

tight [taɪt] *a* (**-er, -est**) (*clothes fitting too closely*) (trop) étroit, (trop) serré; (*skin-tight*) ajusté, collant; (*drawer, lid*) dur; (*knot, screw*) serré; (*rope, wire*) raide; (*control*) strict; (*schedule*) serré; **a t. spot** *Fam* une situation difficile; **it's a t. squeeze** il y a juste la place ‖ *adv* (*to hold, shut*) bien; (*to squeeze*) fort. ●**tighten** *vt* **to t. (up)** (*bolt etc*) (res)serrer; (*rope*) tendre; (*security*) *Fig* renforcer ‖ *vi* **to t. up on** se montrer plus strict à l'égard de. ●**tightly** *adv* (*to hold*) bien; (*to squeeze*) fort.

tight-fitting [taɪt'fɪtɪŋ] *a* (*garment*) ajusté. ●**tightfisted** *a* avare. ●**'tightrope** *n* corde *f* raide. ●**'tightwad** *n Am Fam* grippe-sou *m*.

tights [taɪts] *npl* collant(s) *m*(*pl*).

til/e [taɪl] *n* (*on roof*) tuile *f*; (*on wall or floor*)

carreau *m* ‖ *vt* (*wall, floor*) carreler. ●**—ed** *a* (*roof*) de tuiles; (*wall, floor*) carrelé.
till [tɪl] **1** *prep & conj* = **until. 2** *n* (*for money*) caisse *f* (enregistreuse). **3** *vt* (*land*) cultiver.
tilt [tɪlt] *vti* pencher ‖ *n* inclinaison *f*.
timber ['tɪmbər] *n* bois *m* (de construction); (*trees*) arbres *mpl*.
time [taɪm] *n* temps *m*; (*point in time*) moment *m*; (*period in history*) époque *f*; (*on clock*) heure *f*; (*occasion*) fois *f*; *Mus* mesure *f*; **in (the course of) t.** avec le temps; **it's t. (to do)** il est temps (de faire); **some/most of the t.** une partie/la plupart du temps; **all of the t.** tout le temps; **in a year's t.** dans un an; **a long t.** longtemps; **a short t.** peu de temps; **to have a good t.** s'amuser (bien); **to have a hard t. doing** avoir du mal à faire; **t. off** du temps libre; **in no t. (at all)** en un rien de temps; **(just) in t.** (*to arrive*) à temps (**for sth** pour qch, **to do** pour faire); **from t. to t.** de temps en temps; **what t. is it?** quelle heure est-il?; **the right t.** l'heure *f* exacte; **on t.** à l'heure; **at the same t.** en même temps (**as** que); (*simultaneously*) à la fois; **for the t. being** pour le moment; **at the present t.** à l'heure actuelle; **at times** parfois; **(the) next t. you come** la prochaine fois que tu viendras; **one at a t.** un à un; **ten times ten** dix fois dix; **t. bomb** bombe *f* à retardement; **t. lag** décalage *m*; **t. limit** délai *m*; **t switch** = **timer**; **t. zone** fuseau *m* horaire.
‖ *vt* (*sportsman etc*) chronométrer; (*activity*) minuter; (*choose the time of*) choisir le moment de; (*to plan*) prévoir. ●**time-consuming** *a* qui prend du temps.
timeless ['taɪmləs] *a* éternel.
timely ['taɪmlɪ] *a* à propos.
timer ['taɪmər] *n* (*device*) minuteur *m*, compte-minutes *m inv*; (*built into appliance*) programmateur *m*; (*plugged into socket*) prise *f* programmable.
timetable ['taɪmteɪb(ə)l] *n* horaire *m*; (*in school*) emploi *m* du temps.
timid ['tɪmɪd] *a* (*afraid*) craintif; (*shy*) timide.
timing ['taɪmɪŋ] *n* (*judgment of artist etc*) rythme *m*; **the t. of** (*time*) le moment choisi pour; **what good t.!** quelle synchronisation!
tin [tɪn] *n* (*metal*) étain *m*; (*coated steel or iron*) fer-blanc *m*; (*can*) boîte *f*; **cake t.** moule *m* à gâteaux; **t. opener** ouvre-boîtes *m inv*. ●**tinfoil** *n* papier *m* (d')alu(minium). ●**tinned** *a* en boîte.
tinge [tɪndʒ] *n* teinte *f*. ●**tinged** *a* **t. with** (*pink etc*) teinté de; (*jealousy etc*) *Fig* empreint de.
tingle ['tɪŋg(ə)l] *vi* picoter; **it's tingling** ça me picote.
tinker ['tɪŋkər] *vi* **to t. (about) with** bricoler.
tinkle ['tɪŋk(ə)l] *vi* tinter.
tinsel ['tɪns(ə)l] *n* guirlandes *fpl* de Noël.
tint [tɪnt] *n* teinte *f*; (*for hair*) shampooing *m* colorant. ●**tinted** *a* (*paper, glass*) teinté; **t. glasses** verres *mpl* teintés.
tiny ['taɪnɪ] *a* (**-ier, -iest**) tout petit.
tip[1] [tɪp] **1** *n* (*end*) bout *m*; (*pointed*) pointe *f*. **2** *n* (*money*) pourboire *m* ‖ *vt* (**-pp-**) (*waiter etc*) donner un pourboire à. **3** *n* (*advice*) conseil *m*; (*information*) & *Sp* tuyau *m*; **to get a t.-off** se faire tuyauter ‖ *vt* **to t. off** (*police*) prévenir. **4** *n* (*for rubbish, Am garbage*) décharge *f*.
tip[2] [tɪp] *vt* (**-pp-**) **to t. (up** *or* **over)** (*tilt*) pencher; (*overturn*) faire basculer; **to t. (out)** (*liquid, load*) déverser (**into** dans) ‖ *vi* **to t. (up** *or* **over)** (*tilt*) pencher; (*overturn*) basculer.
tipped [tɪpt] *a* **t. cigarette** cigarette *f* (à bout) filtre.
tipsy ['tɪpsɪ] *a* (**-ier, -iest**) (*drunk*) éméché.
tiptoe ['tɪptəʊ] *n* **on t.** sur la pointe des pieds ‖ *vi* marcher sur la pointe des pieds.
tiptop ['tɪptɒp] *a Fam* excellent.
tir/e[1] ['taɪər] *vt* fatiguer; **to t. s.o. out** épuiser qn ‖ *vi* se fatiguer. ●**—ed** *a* fatigué; **to be t. of sth/s.o./doing** en avoir assez de qch/de qn/de faire; **to get t. of doing** se lasser de faire. ●**—ing** *a* fatigant. ●**tiredness** *n* fatigue *f*. ●**tireless** *a* infatigable. ●**tiresome** *a* ennuyeux.
tire[2] ['taɪər] *n Am* pneu *m* (*pl* pneus).
tissue ['tɪʃuː] *n* (*handkerchief*) mouchoir *m* en papier; *Biol* tissu *m*; **t. paper** papier *m* de soie.
tit [tɪt] *n* **to give t. for tat** rendre coup pour coup.
titbit ['tɪtbɪt] *n* (*food*) bon morceau *m*.
titillate ['tɪtɪleɪt] *vt* exciter.
title ['taɪt(ə)l] *n* (*name, claim*) & *Sp* titre *m*; **t. deed** titre *m* de propriété; **t. role** *Th Cin* rôle *m* principal.
to [tə, *stressed* tuː] *prep* **1** à; (*towards*) vers; (*of attitude, feelings*) envers; (*right up to*) jusqu'à; **give it to him** *or* **her** donne-le-lui; **to France** en France; **to Portugal** au Portugal; **to the butcher('s)**/*etc* chez le boucher/*etc*; **the road to London** la route de Londres; **the train to Paris** le train pour Paris; **kind/cruel**/*etc* **to s.o.** gentil/cruel/*etc* pour *or* envers qn; **it's ten (minutes) to one** il est une heure moins dix; **ten to one** (*proportion*) dix contre un; **one person to a room** une personne par chambre.

2 (*with infinitive*) **to say/do/***etc* dire/faire/*etc*; **(in order) to** pour; **she tried to** elle a essayé.
3 (*with adjective*) de; à; **happy/***etc* **to do** heureux/*etc* de faire; **it's easy/difficult/***etc* **to do** c'est facile/difficile/*etc* à faire.
▮ *adv* **to push to** (*door*) fermer.

toad [təʊd] *n* crapaud *m*.

toadstool ['təʊdstuːl] *n* champignon *m* (vénéneux).

toast [təʊst] **1** *n* pain *m* grillé; **piece** *or* **slice of t.** tranche *f* de pain grillé, toast *m* ▮ *vt* (*bread*) (faire) griller. **2** *n* (*drink*) toast *m* ▮ *vt* (*person*) porter un toast à; (*success, event*) arroser. ● **toaster** *n* grille-pain *m inv*.

tobacco [tə'bækəʊ] *n* (*pl* **-os**) tabac *m*; **t. store** *Am* (bureau *m* de) tabac *m*. ● **tobacconist** *n* buraliste *mf*; **t.'s (shop)** (bureau *m* de) tabac *m*.

toboggan [tə'bɒgən] *n* luge *f*.

today [tə'deɪ] *adv* & *n* aujourd'hui (*m*).

toddler ['tɒdlər] *n* petit(e) enfant *mf* (en bas âge).

to-do [tə'duː] *n* (*fuss*) *Fam* histoire *f*.

toe [təʊ] **1** *n* orteil *m*; **on one's toes** *Fig* vigilant. **2** *vt* **to t. the line** (*respect the rules*) se soumettre. ● **toenail** *n* ongle *m* du pied.

toffee ['tɒfɪ] *n* caramel *m* (*dur*); **t. apple** pomme *f* d'amour.

together [tə'geðər] *adv* ensemble; (*at the same time*) en même temps; **t. with** avec.

toil [tɔɪl] *n* labeur *m* ▮ *vi* travailler dur.

toilet ['tɔɪlɪt] *n* (*room*) toilettes *fpl*; (*bowl, seat*) cuvette *f or* siège *m* des toilettes; **to go to the t.** aller aux toilettes ▮ *a* (*articles*) de toilette; **t. flush** chasse *f* d'eau; **t. paper** papier *m* hygiénique; **t. roll** rouleau *m* de papier hygiénique; **t. water** (*perfume*) eau *f* de toilette. ● **toiletries** *npl* articles *mpl* de toilette.

token ['təʊkən] *n* (*disc, Am disk*) jeton *m*; (*voucher*) bon *m*; (*sign*) témoignage *m*; **gift t.** chèque-cadeau *m*; **book t.** chèque-livre *m*; **record t.** chèque-disque *m*.

told [təʊld] *pt* & *pp of* **tell** ▮ *adv* **all t.** en tout.

tolerable ['tɒlərəb(ə)l] *a* (*bearable*) tolérable; (*fairly good*) passable.

tolerant ['tɒlərənt] *a* tolérant (**of** à l'égard de). ● **tolerance** *n* tolérance *f*.

tolerate ['tɒləreɪt] *vt* tolérer.

toll [təʊl] **1** *n* (*fee*) péage *m* ▮ *a* (*road, bridge*) à péage. **2** *n* **the death t.** le nombre de morts. **3** *vi* (*of bell*) sonner. ● **tollfree number** *n Tel Am* = numéro *m* vert.

tomato [tə'mɑːtəʊ, *Am* tə'meɪtəʊ] *n* (*pl* **-oes**) tomate *f*.

tomb [tuːm] *n* tombeau *m*. ● **tombstone** *n* pierre *f* tombale.

tomboy ['tɒmbɔɪ] *n* (*girl*) garçon *m* manqué.

tomcat ['tɒmkæt] *n* matou *m*.

tomorrow [tə'mɒrəʊ] *adv* & *n* demain (*m*); **t. morning/evening** demain matin/soir; **the day after t.** après-demain.

ton [tʌn] *n* tonne *f* (*Br* = *1016 kg*, *Am* = *907 kg*); **metric t.** tonne *f* (= *1000 kg*); **tons of** (*lots of*) *Fam* des tonnes de.

tone [təʊn] *n* ton *m*; (*of telephone, radio*) tonalité *f*; **engaged t.** *Tel* sonnerie *f* 'occupé'; **in that t.** sur ce ton; **she's t.-deaf** elle n'a pas d'oreille ▮ *vt* **to t. down** atténuer; **to t. up** (*muscles*) tonifier.

tongs [tɒŋz] *npl* **sugar t.** pince *f* à sucre.

tongue [tʌŋ] *n* langue *f*; **t. in cheek** ironique(ment).

tonic ['tɒnɪk] *n Med* fortifiant *m*; **t. (water)** eau *f* gazeuse (tonique); **gin and t.** gin-tonic *m*.

tonight [tə'naɪt] *adv* & *n* (*this evening*) ce soir (*m*); (*during the night*) cette nuit (*f*).

tonne [tʌn] *n* (*metric*) tonne *f*.

tonsil ['tɒns(ə)l] *n* amygdale *f*. ● **tonsillitis** [tɒnsə'laɪtəs] *n* **to have t.** avoir une angine.

too [tuː] *adv* **1** trop; **t. tired to play** trop fatigué pour jouer; **t. hard to solve** trop difficile à résoudre; **t. much, t. many** trop; **t. much salt/***etc* trop de sel/*etc*; **t. many people/***etc* trop de gens/*etc*; **one t. many** un de trop. **2** (*also*) aussi; (*moreover*) en plus.

took [tʊk] *pt of* **take.**

tool [tuːl] *n* outil *m*; **t. bag, t. kit** trousse *f* à outils.

tooth, *pl* **teeth** [tuːθ, tiːθ] *n* dent *f*; **milk/wisdom t.** dent de lait/de sagesse; **t. decay** carie *f* dentaire; **to have a sweet t.** aimer les sucreries.

toothache ['tuːθeɪk] *n* mal *m* de dents; **to have a t.** avoir mal aux dents. ● **toothbrush** *n* brosse *f* à dents. ● **toothpaste** *n* dentifrice *m*. ● **toothpick** *n* cure-dent *m*.

top[1] [tɒp] *n* (*of mountain, tower, tree*) sommet *m*; (*of wall, ladder, page*) haut *m*; (*of table, surface*) dessus *m*; (*of list*) tête *f*; (*of car*) toit *m*; (*of bottle, tube*) bouchon *m*; (*bottle cap*) capsule *f*; (*of saucepan*) couvercle *m*; (*of pen*) capuchon *m*; **pyjama t.** haut *m or* veste *f* de pyjama; **(at the) t. of the class** le premier de la classe; **on t. of** sur; (*in addition to*) *Fig* en plus de; **on t.** (*in bus etc*) en haut; **from t. to bottom** de fond en comble; **the big t.** (*circus*) le chapiteau.
▮ *a* (*drawer, shelf*) du haut; (*step, layer*) dernier; (*upper*) supérieur; (*in rank, exam*)

premier; (*chief*) principal; (*best*) meilleur; (*distinguished*) éminent; (*maximum*) maximum; **on the t. floor** au dernier étage; **in t. gear** *Aut* en quatrième vitesse; **at t. speed** à toute vitesse; **t. copy** original *m*; **t. hat** (chapeau *m*) haut-de-forme *m*. ●**top-level** *a* (*talks*) au sommet. ●**t.-'notch** *a Fam* excellent. ●**t.-'ranking** *a* (*official*) haut placé. ●**t.-'secret** *a* ultra-secret.

top² [tɒp] *vt* (**-pp-**) (*exceed*) dépasser; **to t. up** (*glass*) remplir (de nouveau); (*coffee, tea*) remettre; **topped with** *Culin* nappé de.

top³ [tɒp] *n* **(spinning) t.** toupie *f*.

topic ['tɒpɪk] *n* sujet *m*. ●**topical** *a* d'actualité.

topless ['tɒpləs] *a* (*woman*) aux seins nus.

topple ['tɒp(ə)l] *vi* **to t. (over)** tomber ‖ *vt* **to t. (over)** faire tomber.

topsy-turvy [tɒpsɪ'tɜːvɪ] *a & adv* sens dessus dessous [sɑ̃dsydsu].

torch [tɔːtʃ] *n* (*electric*) lampe *f* électrique; (*flame*) torche *f*.

tore [tɔːr] *pt of* **tear¹**.

torment [tɔː'ment] *vt* (*annoy*) agacer; (*make suffer*) tourmenter ‖ ['tɔːment] *n* tourment *m*.

tornado [tɔː'neɪdəʊ] *n* (*pl* **-oes**) tornade *f*.

torpedo [tɔː'piːdəʊ] *n* (*pl* **-oes**) torpille *f*.

torrent ['tɒrənt] *n* torrent *m*. ●**torrential** [tə'renʃ(ə)l] *a* torrentiel.

tortoise ['tɔːtəs] *n* tortue *f*. ●**tortoiseshell** *a* (*comb etc*) en écaille; (*spectacles*) à monture d'écaille.

torture ['tɔːtʃər] *n* torture *f* ‖ *vt* torturer.

Tory ['tɔːrɪ] *Pol n* tory *m* ‖ *a* tory *inv*.

toss [tɒs] *vt* (*throw*) jeter, lancer (**to** à); **to t. s.o. (about)** (*of boat, vehicle*) ballotter qn; **to t. a coin** jouer à pile ou face ‖ *vi* **to t. (about), t. and turn** (*in one's sleep*) se tourner et se retourner; **let's t. up, let's t. (up) for it** jouons-le à pile ou face.

tot [tɒt] *n* **(tiny) t.** petit(e) enfant *mf*.

total ['təʊt(ə)l] *a* total; **the t. sales** le total des ventes ‖ *n* total *m* ‖ *vt* (**-ll-**, *Am* **-l-**) (*of debt, invoice*) s'élever à; **to t. (up)** (*find the total of*) totaliser; **that totals $9** ça fait neuf dollars en tout. ●**—ly** *adv* totalement.

totter ['tɒtər] *vi* chanceler.

touch [tʌtʃ] *n* (*contact*) contact *m*; (*sense*) toucher *m*; (*of painter*) *& Fb Rugby* touche *f*; **a t. of** (*small amount*) un petit peu de; **to put the finishing touches to** mettre la dernière touche à; **in t. with s.o.** en contact avec qn; **to be out of t. with** ne plus être en contact avec; (*situation*) ne plus être au courant de; **to get in t.** se mettre en contact (**with** avec); **we lost t.** on s'est perdu de vue.
‖ *vt* toucher; (*interfere with, eat*) toucher à; (*move emotionally*) toucher; (*equal*) *Fig* égaler.
‖ *vi* (*of lines, hands etc*) se toucher; **don't t.!** n'y *or* ne touche pas! ●**touching** *a* (*story etc*) touchant.

touch down *vi* (*of aircraft*) atterrir **to touch on** *vt* (*subject*) aborder **to touch up** *vt* (*photo etc*) retoucher.

touchdown ['tʌtʃdaʊn] *n Av* atterrissage *m*; *Rugby Am Fb* essai *m*. ●**touchline** *n Fb Rugby* (ligne *f* de) touche *f*.

touchy ['tʌtʃɪ] *a* (**-ier, -iest**) susceptible (**about** à propos de).

tough [tʌf] *a* (**-er, -est**) (*hard*) (*meat etc*) dur; (*sturdy*) solide; (*strong*) fort; (*difficult, harsh*) dur; (*businessman*) dur en affaires; **t. guy** dur *m*. ●**toughen** *vt* (*body, person*) endurcir; (*reinforce*) renforcer.

toupee ['tuːpeɪ] *n* postiche *m*.

tour [tʊər] *n* (*journey*) voyage *m*; (*visit*) visite *f*; (*by artist, team etc*) tournée *f*; **(package) t.** voyage *m* organisé; **on t.** en voyage; en tournée ‖ *vt* visiter; (*of artist etc*) être en tournée en *or* dans. ●**—ing** *n* tourisme *m*; **to go t.** faire du tourisme.

tourism ['tʊərɪz(ə)m] *n* tourisme *m*. ●**tourist** *n* touriste *mf* ‖ *a* (*region etc*) touristique; **t. office** syndicat *m* d'initiative.

tournament ['tʊənəmənt] *n Sp & Hist* tournoi *m*.

tout [taʊt] *vi* **to t. for** (*customers*) racoler ‖ *n* racoleur, -euse *mf*; **ticket t.** revendeur, -euse *mf* (en fraude) de billets.

tow [təʊ] *vt* (*car, boat*) remorquer; (*caravan, trailer*) tracter; **to t. away** (*vehicle*) emmener à la fourrière ‖ *n* **'on t.'**, *Am* **'in t.'** 'en remorque'; **t. truck** *Am* dépanneuse *f*. ●**towrope** *n* (câble *m* de) remorque *f*.

toward(s) [tə'wɔːd(z), *Am* tɔːd(z)] *prep* vers; (*of feelings*) envers; **cruel/***etc* **t. s.o.** cruel/*etc* envers qn; **money t.** de l'argent pour (acheter).

towel ['taʊəl] *n* serviette *f* (de toilette); (*for dishes*) torchon *m*; **t. rail,** *Am* **t. rack** porte-serviettes *m inv*. ●**towelling** *or Am* **toweling** *n* tissu-éponge *m*; **(kitchen) t.** *Am* essuie-tout *m inv*.

tower ['taʊər] *n* tour *f*; **t. block** tour *f*, immeuble *m* ‖ *vi* **to t. above** *or* **over** dominer. ●**—ing** *a* très haut.

town [taʊn] *n* ville *f*; **in t., (in)to t.** en ville; **out of t.** en province; **t. centre** centre-ville *m*; **t. council** conseil *m* municipal; **t. hall** mairie *f*; **t. planning** urbanisme *m*. ●**township** *n* (*in South Africa*) commune *f* (noire).

toxic ['tɒksɪk] *a* toxique.

toy [tɔɪ] *n* jouet *m*; **soft t.** (jouet *m* en) peluche *f* ‖ *a* (*gun*) d'enfant; (*house*, *car*) miniature *inv* ‖ *vi* **to t. with** (*idea etc*) caresses. ● **toyshop** *n* magasin *m* de jouets.

trace [treɪs] *n* trace *f* (**of** de); **to vanish without t.** disparaître sans laisser de traces ‖ *vt* (*draw*) tracer; (*with tracing paper*) (dé)calquer; (*find*) retrouver (la trace de); (*follow*) suivre (la piste de) (**to** à). ● **tracing** *n* (*drawing*) calque *m*; **t. paper** papier-calque *m inv*.

track [træk] *n* (*of animal, suspect, sports stadium etc*) piste *f*; *Rail* voie *f*; (*path*) chemin *m*; (*of rocket*) trajectoire *f*; (*race-track*) *Am* champ *m* de courses; **the tracks** (*of wheels*) les traces *fpl*; **to keep t. of** suivre; **to lose t. of** (*friend*) perdre de vue; **on the right t.** sur la bonne voie; **t. event** *Sp* épreuve *f* sur piste; **t. record** *Fig* antécédents *mpl*.
‖ *vt* **to t. (down)** (*locate*) retrouver; (*pursue*) traquer. ● **track shoes** *npl Am* baskets *mpl*, tennis *mpl*. ● **tracksuit** *n Sp* survêtement *m*.

tract [trækt] *n* (*land*) étendue *f*.

tractor ['træktər] *n* tracteur *m*.

trade [treɪd] *n* commerce *m*; (*job*) métier *m*; (*exchange*) échange *m* ‖ *a* (*fair*, *secret*) commercial; (*barrier*) douanier; **t. union** syndicat *m*; **t. unionist** syndicaliste *mf* ‖ *vi* faire du commerce (**with** avec); **to t. in** faire le commerce de ‖ *vt* échanger (**for** contre); **to t. sth in** (*old article*) faire reprendre qch. ● **trade-in** *n Com* reprise *f*.

trademark ['treɪdmɑːk] *n* marque *f* de fabrique; **(registered) t.** marque déposée.

trader ['treɪdər] *n* (*shopkeeper*) commerçant, -ante *mf*. ● **tradesman** *n* (*pl* **-men**) commerçant *m*.

trading ['treɪdɪŋ] *n* commerce *m* ‖ *a* (*port*, *debts etc*) commercial; (*nation*) commerçant.

tradition [trə'dɪʃ(ə)n] *n* tradition *f*. ● **tra'ditional** *a* traditionnel.

traffic ['træfɪk] **1** *n* (*on road*) circulation *f*; *Av Nau Rail* trafic *m*; **heavy t.** beaucoup de circulation; **t. circle** *Am* rond-point *m*; **t. cone** cône *m* de chantier; **t. island** refuge *m* (*pour piétons*); **t. jam** embouteillage *m*; **t. lights** feux *mpl* (de signalisation); (*when red*) feu *m* rouge; **t. sign** panneau *m* de signalisation.
2 *n* (*trade*) *Pej* trafic *m* (**in** de) ‖ *vi* (**-ck-**) trafiquer (**in** de). ● **trafficker** *n Pej* trafiquant, -ante *mf*.

tragedy ['trædʒədɪ] *n* tragédie *f*. ● **tragic** *a* tragique.

trail [treɪl] *n* (*of smoke, blood etc*) traînée *f*; (*track*) piste *f*, trace *f*; (*path*) sentier *m*; **in its t.** (*wake*) dans son sillage ‖ *vt* (*drag*) traîner; (*follow*) suivre (la piste de) ‖ *vi* (*on the ground etc*) traîner; **to t. (behind)** (*lag behind*) traîner. ● **—er** *n* **1** (*for car*) remorque *f*; *Am* caravane *f*; (*camper*) *Am* camping-car *m*; **t. truck** *Am* semi-remorque *m*. **2** *Cin* bande *f* annonce.

train [treɪn] **1** *n* train *m*; (*underground*) rame *f*; **to go** *or* **come by t.** prendre le train; **t. set** (*toy*) petit train *m*.
2 *n* (*procession*) file *f*; (*of events*) suite *f*; **my t. of thought** le fil de ma pensée.
3 *vt* (*teach*) former (**to do** à faire); *Sp* entraîner; (*animal*, *child*) dresser (**to do** à faire); (*ear*) exercer ‖ *vi* recevoir une formation (**as a doctor**/*etc* de médecin/*etc*); *Sp* s'entraîner. ● **trained** *a* (*skilled*) qualifié; (*nurse, engineer etc*) diplômé; (*ear*) exercé. ● **training** *n* formation *f*; *Sp* entraînement *m*; **to be in t.** *Sp* s'entraîner; **(teachers') t. college** école *f* normale.

trainee [treɪ'niː] *n* & *a* stagiaire (*mf*).

trainer ['treɪnər] *n* (*of athlete*, *racehorse*) entraîneur *m*; (*of dog etc*) dresseur *m*; **trainers** (*shoes*) baskets *mpl*, tennis *mpl*.

traipse [treɪps] *vi* **to t. around** *Fam* (*tiredly*) traîner les pieds; (*wander*) se balader.

traitor ['treɪtər] *n* traître *m*.

tram [træm] *n* tramway *m*.

tramp [træmp] **1** *n* (*vagrant*) clochard, -arde *mf*; (*woman*) *Pej* traînée *f*. **2** *vi* (*walk*) marcher d'un pas lourd.

trample ['træmp(ə)l] *vti* **to t. sth (underfoot), t. on sth** piétiner qch.

trampoline [træmpə'liːn] *n* trampoline *m*.

trance [trɑːns] *n* **in a t.** en transe.

tranquil ['træŋkwɪl] *a* tranquille. ● **tranquillizer** *n Med* tranquillisant *m*.

trans- [træns, trænz] *pref* trans-.

transaction [trænz'ækʃ(ə)n] *n* (*in bank*) opération *f*; (*on Stock Market*) transaction *f*.

transatlantic [trænzət'læntɪk] *a* transatlantique.

transfer [træns'fɜːr] *vt* (**-rr-**) (*person*, *goods etc*) transférer (**to** à); (*power*) *Pol* faire passer (**to** à); **to t. the charges** téléphoner en PCV ‖ ['trænsfɜːr] *n* transfert *m* (**to** à); (*of power*) *Pol* passation *f*; (*image*) décalcomanie *f*; **bank** *or* **credit t.** virement *m* (bancaire).

transform [træns'fɔːm] *vt* transformer (**into** en). ● **transformation** [-fə'meɪʃ(ə)n] *n* transformation *f*. ● **transformer** *n El* transformateur *m*.

transfusion [træns'fjuːʒ(ə)n] *n* **(blood) t.**

transfusion *f* (sanguine).
transistor [træn'zɪstər] *n* **t. (radio)** transistor *m*.
transit ['trænzɪt] *n* **in t.** en transit; **t. lounge** *Av* salle *f* de transit.
transition [træn'zɪʃ(ə)n] *n* transition *f*. ●**transitional** *a* (*government etc*) de transition.
transitive ['trænsɪtɪv] *a Gram* transitif.
translate [træns'leɪt] *vt* traduire (**from** de, **into** en). ●**translation** *n* traduction *f*. ●**translator** *n* traducteur, -trice *mf*.
transmit [trænz'mɪt] *vt* (**-tt-**) (*send, pass*) transmettre ‖ *vti* (*broadcast*) émettre. ●**transmission** [-ʃ(ə)n] *n* transmission *f*; (*broadcast*) émission *f*. ●**transmitter** *n* *Rad TV* émetteur *m*.
transparent [træns'pærənt] *a* transparent. ●**transparency** *n* transparence *f*; (*slide*) *Phot* diapositive *f*.
transpire [træn'spaɪər] *vi* (*happen*) *Fam* arriver; **it transpired that...** il s'est avéré que....
transplant [træns'plɑːnt] *vt* (*plant*) transplanter; (*organ*) *Med* greffer ‖ ['trænsplɑːnt] *n* *Med* greffe *f*.
transport [træn'spɔːt] *vt* transporter ‖ ['trænspɔːt] *n* transport *m* (**of** de); **(means of) t.** moyen *m* de transport; **public t.** les transports en commun; **t. café** routier *m*. ●**transportation** [-'teɪʃ(ə)n] *n* transport *m*; (*means*) moyen *m* de transport.
transvestite [trænz'vestaɪt] *n* travesti *m*.
trap [træp] *n* piège *m*; **t. door** trappe *f* ‖ *vt* (**-pp-**) (*animal*) prendre (au piège); (*jam*) coincer; (*cut off by snow etc*) bloquer (**by** par).
trapeze [trə'piːz] *n* (*in circus*) trapèze *m*; **t. artist** trapéziste *mf*.
trappings ['træpɪŋz] *npl* signes *mpl* extérieurs.
trash [træʃ] *n* (*nonsense*) sottises *fpl*; (*junk*) bric-à-brac *m inv*; (*waste*) *Am* ordures *fpl*; (*riffraff*) *Am* racaille *f*. ●**trashcan** *n Am* poubelle *f*. ●**trashy** *a* (**-ier, -iest**) (*book etc*) qui ne vaut rien; (*goods*) de camelote.
trauma ['trɔːmə, 'traʊmə] *n* (*shock*) traumatisme *m*. ●**trau'matic** *a* traumatisant.
travel ['træv(ə)l] *vi* (**-ll-**, *Am* **-l-**) (*on journey*) voyager; (*move, go*) aller, se déplacer ‖ *vt* (*country, distance*) parcourir ‖ *n* **travel(s)** voyages *mpl*; **on one's travels** en voyage ‖ *a* (*agency, book*) de voyages; **t. brochure** dépliant *m* touristique. ●**travelled** *a* **to be well t.** avoir beaucoup voyagé. ●**travelling** *n* voyages *mpl* ‖ *a* (*bag etc*) de voyage; (*expenses*) de déplacement; (*musician*) ambulant.
traveller ['trævələr] (*Am* **traveler**) *n* voyageur, -euse *mf*; **traveller's cheque,** *Am* **traveler's check** chèque *m* de voyage.
travelsickness ['trævəlsɪknɪs] *n* (*in car*) mal *m* de la route; (*in aircraft*) mal *m* de l'air.
travesty ['trævəstɪ] *n* parodie *f*.
trawler ['trɔːlər] *n* (*ship*) chalutier *m*.
tray [treɪ] *n* plateau *m*; (*for office correspondence*) corbeille *f*.
treacherous ['tretʃ(ə)rəs] *a* (*road, conditions*) très dangereux; (*person, action*) traître. ●**treachery** *n* traîtrise *f*.
treacle ['triːk(ə)l] *n* mélasse *f*.
tread [tred] *vi* (*pt* **trod,** *pp* **trodden**) (*walk*) marcher (**on** sur); (*proceed*) *Fig* avancer ‖ *vt* **to t. sth into a carpet** étaler qch (avec les pieds) sur un tapis ‖ *n* (*step of stairs*) marche *f*; (*of tyre, Am tire*) bande *f* de roulement.
treason ['triːz(ə)n] *n* trahison *f*.
treasure ['treʒər] *n* trésor *m*; **t. hunt** chasse *f* au trésor ‖ *vt* (*value*) tenir à; (*keep*) conserver (précieusement). ●**treasurer** *n* trésorier, -ière *mf*. ●**Treasury** *n* **the T.** *Pol* = le ministère des Finances.
treat [triːt] **1** *vt* (*person, product etc*) & *Med* traiter; (*consider*) considérer (**as** comme); **to t. s.o. to sth** offrir qch à qn. **2** *n* **(special) t.** petit extra *m*, gâterie *f*; (*meal*) régal *m*; **to give s.o. a (special) t.** donner une surprise à qn; **it was a t. (for me) to do it** ça m'a fait plaisir de le faire.
treatment ['triːtmənt] *n* (*behaviour*) & *Med* traitement *m*; **rough t.** mauvais traitements *mpl*.
treaty ['triːtɪ] *n Pol* traité *m*.
treble ['treb(ə)l] *a* triple ‖ *vti* tripler ‖ *n* le triple; **it's t. the price** c'est le triple du prix.
tree [triː] *n* arbre *m*; **Christmas t.** arbre *m or* sapin *m* de Noël; **family t.** arbre *m* généalogique. ●**t.-lined** *a* bordé d'arbres. ●**t.-top** *n* cime *f* (d'un arbre). ●**t.-trunk** *n* tronc *m* d'arbre.
trek [trek] *vi* (**-kk-**) cheminer (péniblement) ‖ *n* voyage *m* (pénible); (*distance*) *Fam* tirée *f*.
tremble ['tremb(ə)l] *vi* trembler (**with** de). ●**tremor** *n* tremblement *m*; **(earth) t.** secousse *f* (sismique).
tremendous [trə'mendəs] *a* (*huge*) énorme; (*dreadful*) terrible; (*wonderful*) formidable.
trench [trentʃ] *n* tranchée *f*.
trend [trend] *n* tendance *f* (**towards** à); (*fashion*) mode *f*. ●**trendy** *a* (**-ier, -iest**)

(*person, clothes etc*) *Fam* à la mode.

trepidation [trepɪ'deɪʃ(ə)n] *n* inquiétude *f*.

trespass ['trespəs] *vi* s'introduire sans autorisation (**on, upon** dans); **'no trespassing'** 'entrée interdite'.

trestle ['tres(ə)l] *n* tréteau *m*.

trial ['traɪəl] *n Jur* procès *m*; (*test*) essai *m*; (*ordeal*) épreuve *f*; **to go** *or* **be on t.**, être jugé, passer en jugement; **to put s.o. on t.** juger qn; **by t. and error** par tâtonnements ‖ *a* (*period, flight*) d'essai.

triangle ['traɪæŋg(ə)l] *n* triangle *m*; (*setsquare*) *Am* équerre *f*. ●**tri'angular** *a* triangulaire.

tribe [traɪb] *n* tribu *f*. ●**tribal** *a* tribal.

tribunal [traɪ'bjuːn(ə)l] *n* commission *f*; *Mil* tribunal *m*.

tributary ['trɪbjʊtərɪ] *n* affluent *m*.

tribute ['trɪbjuːt] *n* hommage *m*; **to pay t. to** rendre hommage à.

trick [trɪk] *n* (*joke, of conjurer etc*) tour *m*; (*clever method*) astuce *f*; **to play a t. on s.o.** jouer un tour à qn; **card t.** tour *m* de cartes; **that will do the t.** *Fam* ça fera l'affaire ‖ *vt* (*deceive*) tromper, attraper; **to t. s.o. into doing sth** amener qn à faire qch par la ruse. ●**trickery** *n* ruse *f*.

trickle ['trɪk(ə)l] *n* (*of liquid*) filet *m*; **a t. of** (*letters*) *Fig* un petit nombre de ‖ *vi* (*flow*) couler (lentement); **to t. in** (*of letters etc*) *Fig* arriver en petit nombre.

tricky ['trɪkɪ] *a* (**-ier, -iest**) (*problem etc*) difficile.

tricycle ['traɪsɪk(ə)l] *n* tricycle *m*.

trifl/e ['traɪf(ə)l] *n* (*insignificant thing, money*) bagatelle *f*; (*dessert*) diplomate *m* ‖ *adv* **a t. small/***etc* un tantinet petit/*etc* ‖ *vi* **to t. with** (*s.o.'s feelings*) jouer avec. ●**—ing** *a* insignifiant.

trigger ['trɪgər] *n* (*of gun*) gâchette *f* ‖ *vt* **to t. (off)** (*start*) déclencher.

trim [trɪm] **1** *a* (**trimmer, trimmest**) (*neat*) soigné; (*slim*) svelte. **2** *n* (*cut*) légère coupe *f*; **to have a t.** (*haircut*) se faire rafraîchir les cheveux ‖ *vt* (**-mm-**) couper (un peu); (*finger nail, edge*) rogner; (*hair*) rafraîchir. **3** *n* (*on garment*) garniture *f*; (*on car*) garnitures *fpl* ‖ *vt* (**-mm-**) **to t. with** orner de. ●**trimmings** *npl* garniture(s) *f(pl)*; (*extras*) *Fig* accessoires *mpl*.

trinket ['trɪŋkɪt] *n* colifichet *m*.

trio ['trɪəʊ] *n* (*pl* **-os**) (*group*) & *Mus* trio *m*.

trip [trɪp] **1** *n* (*journey*) voyage *m*; (*outing*) excursion *f*; **to take a t. to** (*shops etc*) aller à. **2** *vi* (**-pp-**) **to t. (over** *or* **up)** (*stumble*) trébucher; **to t. over sth** trébucher contre qch ‖ *vt* **to t. s.o. up** faire trébucher qn.

tripe [traɪp] *n Culin* tripes *fpl*; (*nonsense*) *Fam* bêtises *fpl*.

triple ['trɪp(ə)l] *a* triple ‖ *vti* tripler. ●**triplets** *npl* (*children*) triplés, -ées *mfpl*.

triplicate ['trɪplɪkət] *n* **in t.** en trois exemplaires.

tripod ['traɪpɒd] *n* trépied *m*.

tripper ['trɪpər] *n* **day t.** excursionniste *mf*.

trite [traɪt] *a* banal (*mpl* -als).

triumph ['traɪʌmf] *n* triomphe *m* (**over** sur) ‖ *vi* triompher (**over** de). ●**tri'umphant** *a* (*team, army*) triomphant; (*success, welcome, return*) triomphal.

trivial ['trɪvɪəl] *a* (*unimportant*) insignifiant; (*trite*) banal (*mpl* -als).

trod, trodden [trɒd, 'trɒd(ə)n] *pt* & *pp of* **tread.**

trolley ['trɒlɪ] *n* (*for luggage*) chariot *m*; (*in supermarket*) caddie® *m*; (*for shopping*) poussette *f* (de marché); **(tea) t.** table *f* roulante; **t. (car)** *Am* tramway *m*. ●**trolleybus** *n* trolley(bus) *m*.

trombone [trɒm'bəʊn] *n Mus* trombone *m*.

troop [truːp] *n* bande *f*; *Mil* troupe *f*; **the troops** (*soldiers*) les troupes *fpl* ‖ *vi* **to t. in/out/***etc* entrer/sortir/*etc* en masse. ●**—er** *n* **(state) t.** *Am* membre *m* de la police montée.

trophy ['trəʊfɪ] *n* coupe *f*, trophée *m*.

tropics ['trɒpɪks] *npl* **the t.** les tropiques *mpl*. ●**tropical** *a* tropical.

trot [trɒt] *n* (*of horse*) trot *m*; **on the t.** *Fam* de suite ‖ *vi* (**-tt-**) trotter; **to t. off** *Hum Fam* se sauver ‖ *vt* **to t. out** (*say*) *Fam* débiter.

trouble ['trʌb(ə)l] *n* (*difficulty*) ennui(s) *m(pl)*; (*effort*) peine *f* (*inconvenience*) dérangement *m*; **trouble(s)** (*social unrest, illness*) troubles *mpl*; **to be in t.** avoir des ennuis; **to get into t.** s'attirer des ennuis (**with** avec); **to go to the t. of doing, take the t. to do** se donner la peine de faire; **I didn't put her to any t.** je ne l'ai pas dérangée; **to find the t.** trouver le problème.
‖ *vt* (*inconvenience*) déranger; (*worry, annoy*) ennuyer; (*grieve*) peiner; ●**troubled** *a* (*worried*) inquiet; (*period*) agité. ●**trouble-free** *a* (*machine*) qui ne tombe jamais en panne. ●**troublemaker** *n Scol* élément *m* perturbateur; *Pol* fauteur *m* de troubles.

troublesome ['trʌb(ə)ls(ə)m] *a* ennuyeux; (*leg etc*) qui fait mal.

trough [trɒf] *n* (*for drinking*) abreuvoir *m*; (*for feeding*) auge *f*; **t. of low pressure** *Met* dépression *f*.

trousers ['traʊzəz] *npl* pantalon *m*; **a pair of t., some t.** un pantalon; **(short) t.** culottes *fpl* courtes.

trout [traʊt] *n* truite *f*.
truant ['tru:ənt] *n* (*pupil*) absentéiste *mf*; **to play t.** sécher (la classe), faire l'école buissonnière.
truce [tru:s] *n Mil* trêve *f*.
truck [trʌk] *n* **1** (*lorry*) camion *m*; *Rail* wagon *m* plat; **t. driver** camionneur *m*; (*long-distance*) routier *m*; **t. stop** (*restaurant*) *Am* routier *m*. **2 t. farmer** *Am* maraîcher, -ère *mf*. ●**trucker** *n Am* (*for goods*) transporteur *m* routier; (*driver*) camionneur *m*, routier *m*.
trudge [trʌdʒ] *vi* marcher d'un pas pesant.
true [tru:] *a* (**-er, -est**) vrai; (*accurate*) exact; **t. to** (*promise etc*) fidèle à; **to come t.** se réaliser; **to hold t.** (*of argument*) valoir (**for** pour). ●**truly** *adv* vraiment; (*faithfully*) fidèlement; **well and t.** bel et bien.
truffle ['trʌf(ə)l] *n* (*mushroom*) truffe *f*.
trump [trʌmp] *n Cards* atout *m*; **t. card** (*advantage*) *Fig* atout *m*.
trumpet ['trʌmpɪt] *n* trompette *f*.
truncheon ['trʌntʃ(ə)n] *n* (*weapon*) matraque *f*.
trundle ['trʌnd(ə)l] *vti* **to t. along** rouler bruyamment.
trunk [trʌŋk] *n* (*of tree, body*) tronc *m*; (*of elephant*) trompe *f*; (*case*) malle *f*; (*of vehicle*) *Am* coffre *m*; *pl* (*for swimming*) slip *m* de bain; (*shorts*) caleçon *m* de bain; **t. road** route *f* nationale.
truss [trʌs] *vt* **to t. (up)** (*prisoner*) ligoter.
trust [trʌst] *n* (*faith*) confiance *f* (**in** en); (*group*) *Fin* trust *m*; *Jur* fidéicommis *m* ‖ *vt* (*person, judgment*) avoir confiance en, se fier à; (*instinct*) se fier à; **to t. s.o. with sth, t. sth to s.o.** confier qch à qn; **I t. that** j'espère que ‖ *vi* **to t. in s.o.** avoir confiance en qn, se fier à qn. ●**trusted** *a* (*friend, method etc*) éprouvé. ●**trusting** *a* confiant. ●**trustworthy** *a* digne de confiance.
truth [tru:θ] *n* (*pl* **-s** [tru:ðz]) vérité *f*; **there's some t. in...** il y a du vrai dans.... ●**truthful** *a* (*statement*) véridique; (*person*) sincère.
try [traɪ] **1** *vt* (*attempt, sample, use*) essayer; (*s.o.'s patience*) mettre à l'épreuve; **to t. doing** *or* **to do** essayer de faire; **to t. one's hand at** s'essayer à; **to t. one's luck** tenter sa chance ‖ *vi* essayer (**for sth** d'obtenir qch); **to t. hard** faire un gros effort; **t. and come!** essaie de venir! ‖ *n* (*attempt*) & *Rugby* essai *m*; **to have a t.** essayer; **at first t.** du premier coup.
2 *vt* (*person*) *Jur* juger (**for theft**/*etc* pour vol/*etc*). ●**trying** *a* éprouvant.
try on *vt* (*clothes, shoes*) essayer **to try out** *vt* (*car, method etc*) essayer; (*person*) mettre à l'essai.
T-shirt ['ti:ʃɜ:t] *n* tee-shirt *m*.
tub [tʌb] *n* (*basin*) baquet *m*; (*bath*) baignoire *f*; (*for ice cream*) pot *m*.
tuba ['tju:bə] *n Mus* tuba *m*.
tubby ['tʌbɪ] *a* (**-ier, -iest**) *Fam* dodu.
tube [tju:b] *n* tube *m*; (*underground railway*) *Fam* métro *m*; (*of tyre, Am tire*) chambre *f* à air.
tuberculosis [tju:bɜ:kjʊ'ləʊsɪs] *n* tuberculose *f*.
TUC [ti:ju:'si:] *n abbr* (*Trades Union Congress*) = confédération *f* des syndicats britanniques.
tuck [tʌk] **1** *vt* (*put*) mettre; **to t. away** ranger; (*hide*) cacher; **to t. in** (*shirt, blanket*) rentrer; (*person in bed*) border; **to t. up** (*sleeves*) remonter. **2** *vi* **to t. in** (*eat*) *Fam* manger; **to t. into** (*meal*) *Fam* attaquer ‖ *n* **t. shop** *Sch* boutique *f* à provisions.
Tuesday ['tju:zdɪ, -deɪ] *n* mardi *m*.
tuft [tʌft] *n* (*of hair, grass*) touffe *f*.
tug [tʌg] **1** *vt* (**-gg-**) (*pull*) tirer ‖ *vi* tirer (**at** sur) ‖ *n* **to give sth a t.** tirer (sur) qch. **2** *n* **tug(boat)** remorqueur *m*.
tuition [tju:'ɪʃ(ə)n] *n* enseignement *m*; (*lessons*) leçons *fpl*; (*fee*) frais *mpl* de scolarité.
tulip ['tju:lɪp] *n* tulipe *f*.
tumble ['tʌmb(ə)l] *vi* **to t. (down** *or* **over)** (*fall*) dégringoler ‖ *n* dégringolade *f*; **t. dryer** *or* **drier** sèche-linge *m inv*.
tumbledown ['tʌmb(ə)ldaʊn] *a* délabré.
tumbler ['tʌmblər] *n* (*glass*) gobelet *m*.
tummy ['tʌmɪ] *n Fam* ventre *m*.
tumour ['tju:mər] (*Am* **tumor**) *n* tumeur *f*.
tuna ['tju:nə] *n* **t. (fish)** thon *m*.
tune [tju:n] *n* (*melody*) air *m*; **in t.** (*instrument*) accordé; **out of t.** désaccordé; **to sing in t./out of t.** chanter juste/faux; **in t. with** *Fig* en accord avec ‖ *vt* **to t. (up)** (*instrument*) accorder; (*engine*) régler ‖ *vi* **to t. in (to)** *Rad TV* se mettre à l'écoute (de). ●**tuning** *n Aut* réglage *m*; **t. fork** *Mus* diapason *m*.
tunic ['tju:nɪk] *n* tunique *f*.
Tunisia [tju:'nɪzɪə] *n* Tunisie *f*.
tunnel ['tʌn(ə)l] *n* tunnel *m*; **the Channel T.** le tunnel sous la Manche ‖ *vi* (**-ll-**, *Am* **-l-**) percer un tunnel (**into** dans).
turban ['tɜ:bən] *n* turban *m*.
turbine ['tɜ:baɪn, *Am* 'tɜ:bɪn] *n* turbine *f*.
turbulence ['tɜ:bjʊləns] *n Av etc* turbulences *fpl*.
turf [tɜ:f] **1** *n* (*grass*) gazon *m*; **piece of t.** motte *f* de gazon. **2** *vt* **to t. s.o. out** *Fam* jeter qn dehors.

turkey ['tɜːkɪ] *n* dindon *m*, dinde *f*; (*as food*) dinde *f*.

Turkey ['tɜːkɪ] *n* Turquie *f*. ●**Turk** *n* Turc *m*, Turque *f*. ●**Turkish** *a* turc (*f* turque); **T. delight** loukoum *m* ▮ *n* (*language*) turc *m*.

turmoil ['tɜːmɔɪl] *n* confusion *f*; **in t.** en ébullition.

turn [tɜːn] *n* (*movement, in game etc*) tour *m*; (*in road*) tournant *m*; (*of events*) tournure *f*; *Med* crise *f*; **t. of phrase** tour *m or* tournure *f* (de phrase); **to take turns** se relayer; **in t.** à tour de rôle; **it's your t. (to play)** c'est à toi *or* (à) ton tour (de jouer); **to do s.o. a good t.** rendre service à qn; **the t. of the century** le début *or* la fin du siècle. ▮ *vt* tourner; (*mattress, pancake*) retourner; **to turn s.o./sth into** (*change*) changer *or* transformer qn/qch en; **to t. sth red/***etc* rougir/*etc* qch; **she has turned twenty** elle a vingt ans passés; **it turns my stomach** cela me soulève le cœur. ▮ *vi* (*of wheel, driver etc*) tourner; (*turn head or body*) se (re)tourner (**towards** vers); (*become*) devenir; **to t. red/***etc* rougir/*etc*; **to t. to** (*question, adviser*) se tourner vers; **to t. into** (*change*) se changer *or* se transformer en.

turn against *vt* se retourner contre (*qn*) **to turn around** *vi* (*of person*) se retourner **to turn away** *vt* (*eyes*) détourner (**from** de); (*person*) renvoyer ▮ *vi* se détourner **to turn back** *vt* (*bed sheet etc*) replier; (*person*) renvoyer; (*clock*) reculer (**to** jusqu'à) ▮ *vi* retourner (sur ses pas) **to turn down** *vt* (*gas, radio etc*) baisser; (*fold down*) rabattre; (*refuse*) refuser (*qn, offre etc*) **to turn in** *vt* (*prisoner*) *Fam* livrer (à la police) ▮ *vi* (*go to bed*) *Fam* se coucher **to turn off** *vt* (*light, radio etc*) éteindre; (*tap, Am faucet*) fermer; (*machine*) arrêter **to turn on** *vt* (*light, radio etc*) mettre, allumer; (*tap, Am faucet*) ouvrir; (*machine*) mettre en marche; **to t. s.o. on** (*sexually*) *Fam* exciter qn **to turn out** *vt* (*light*) éteindre; (*contents of box*) vider (**from** de); (*produce*) produire ▮ *vi* (*of crowds*) venir; (*happen*) se passer; **she turned out to be...** elle s'est révélée être... **to turn over** *vt* (*page*) tourner ▮ *vi* (*of vehicle, person*) se retourner **to turn round** *vt* (*head, object*) tourner; (*vehicle*) faire faire demi-tour à ▮ *vi* (*of person*) se retourner **to turn up** *vt* (*radio, light etc*) mettre plus fort; (*collar*) remonter ▮ *vi* (*arrive*) arriver; (*be found*) être retrouvé.

turning ['tɜːnɪŋ] *n* (*street*) petite rue *f*; (*bend in road*) tournant *m*; **t. point** (*in time*) tournant *m*.

turnip ['tɜːnɪp] *n* navet *m*.

turn-off ['tɜːnɒf] *n* (*in road*) embranchement *m*. ●**turnout** *n* (*people*) assistance *f*; (*at polls*) participation *f*. ●**turnover** *n* (*sales*) *Com* chiffre *m* d'affaires; (*of stock, staff*) rotation *f*; **apple t.** chausson *m* (aux pommes). ●**turn-up** *n* (*on trousers*) revers *m*.

turnpike ['tɜːnpaɪk] *n Am* autoroute *f* à péage.

turnstile ['tɜːnstaɪl] *n* (*gate*) tourniquet *m*.

turntable ['tɜːnteɪb(ə)l] *n* (*of record player*) platine *f*.

turpentine ['tɜːpəntaɪn] (*Fam* **turps** [tɜːps]) *n* térébenthine *f*.

turquoise ['tɜːkwɔɪz] *a* turquoise *inv*.

turret ['tʌrɪt] *n* tourelle *f*.

turtle ['tɜːt(ə)l] *n* tortue *f* de mer; *Am* tortue *f*. ●**turtleneck** *a* (*sweater*) à col roulé ▮ *n* col *m* roulé.

tusk [tʌsk] *n* (*of elephant*) défense *f*.

tussle ['tʌs(ə)l] *n* bagarre *f*.

tutor ['tjuːtər] *n* professeur *m* particulier; (*in British university*) directeur, -trice *mf* d'études ▮ *vt* donner des cours particuliers à. ●**tu'torial** *n Univ* = travaux *mpl* dirigés.

tuxedo [tʌk'siːdəʊ] *n* (*pl* **-os**) *Am* smoking *m*.

TV [tiː'viː] *n* télé *f*.

twang [twæŋ] *n* **(nasal) t.** nasillement *m*.

tweed [twiːd] *n* tweed *m*; **t. jacket/***etc* veste *f/etc* en tweed.

tweezers ['twiːzəz] *npl* pince *f* à épiler.

twelve [twelv] *a* & *n* douze (*m*). ●**twelfth** *a* & *n* douzième (*mf*).

twenty ['twentɪ] *a* & *n* vingt (*m*). ●**twentieth** *a* & *n* vingtième (*mf*).

twice [twaɪs] *adv* deux fois; **t. as heavy/***etc* deux fois plus lourd/*etc*.

twiddle ['twɪd(ə)l] *vti* **to t. (with) sth** (*knob etc*) tripoter qch; **to t. one's thumbs** se tourner les pouces.

twig [twɪg] *n* (*of branch*) brindille *f*.

twilight ['twaɪlaɪt] *n* crépuscule *m*.

twin [twɪn] *n* jumeau *m*, jumelle *f*; **identical t.** vrai jumeau, vraie jumelle; **t. brother** frère *m* jumeau; **t. sister** sœur *f* jumelle; **t. beds** lits *mpl* jumeaux ▮ *vt* (**-nn-**) (*town*) jumeler. ●**twinning** *n* jumelage *m*.

twine [twaɪn] *n* (*string*) ficelle *f*.

twinge [twɪndʒ] *n* **a t. (of pain)** un élancement; **a t. of remorse** un pincement de remords.

twinkle ['twɪŋk(ə)l] *vi* (*of star*) scintiller; (*of eye*) pétiller.

twirl [twɜːl] *vi* tournoyer ▮ *vt* faire tournoyer.

twist [twɪst] *vt* (*wire, arm etc*) tordre; (*roll*)

enrouler (**round** autour de); (*knob*) tourner; **to t. one's ankle** se tordre la cheville; **to t. off** (*lid*) dévisser ‖ *vi* (*wind*) s'entortiller (**round sth** autour de qch); (*of road, river*) serpenter ‖ *n* (*turn*) tour *m*; (*in road*) zigzag *m*; (*in rope*) entortillement *m*; (*in story*) coup *m* de théâtre. ●**twisted** *a* (*ankle, wire, mind*) tordu. ●**twister** *n* **tongue t.** mot *m or* expression *f* imprononçable.

twit [twɪt] *n Fam* idiot, -ote *mf*.

twitch [twɪtʃ] **1** *n* (*nervous*) tic *m* ‖ *vi* (*of person*) avoir un tic. **2** *n* (*jerk*) secousse *f*.

twitter ['twɪtər] *vi* (*of bird*) pépier.

two [tuː] *a* & *n* deux (*m*). ●**t.-'faced** *a Fig* hypocrite. ●**t.-piece** *n* (*woman's suit*) tailleur *m*; (*swimsuit*) deux-pièces *m inv*. ●**t.-'seater** *n Aut* voiture *f* à deux places. ●**t.-way** *a* **t.-way traffic** circulation *f* dans les deux sens; **t.-way radio** émetteur-récepteur *m*.

twofold ['tuːfəʊld] *a* double ‖ *adv* **to increase t.** doubler.

twosome ['tuːsəm] *n* couple *m*.

tycoon [taɪ'kuːn] *n* magnat *m*.

type[1] [taɪp] *n* **1** (*sort*) genre *m*, type *m*; (*example*) type *m*; **blood t.** groupe *m* sanguin. **2** (*print*) caractères *mpl*; **in large t.** en gros caractères.

typ/e[2] [taɪp] *vti* (*write*) taper (à la machine). ●**—ing** *n* dactylo *f*; **a page of t.** une page dactylographiée; **t. error** faute *f* de frappe. ●**typewriter** *n* machine *f* à écrire. ●**typewritten** *a* dactylographié. ●**typist** *n* dactylo *f*.

typhoid ['taɪfɔɪd] *n Med* typhoïde *f*.

typhoon [taɪ'fuːn] *n Met* typhon *m*.

typical ['tɪpɪk(ə)l] *a* typique (**of** de); (*customary*) habituel; **that's t. (of him)!** c'est bien lui!

tyranny ['tɪrənɪ] *n* tyrannie *f*. ●**tyrant** ['taɪərənt] *n* tyran *m*.

tyre ['taɪər] *n* pneu *m* (*pl* pneus).

U

U, u [juː] *n* U, u *m*. • **U-turn** *n Aut* demi-tour *m*; *Fig* volte-face *f inv*.
udder [ˈʌdər] *n* (*of cow etc*) pis *m*.
UFO [juːefˈəʊ] *n abbr* (*unidentified flying object*) OVNI *m*.
ugh! [ɜː(h)] *int* pouah!
ugly [ˈʌglɪ] *a* (**-ier, -iest**) laid. • **ugliness** *n* laideur *f*.
UK [juːˈkeɪ] *abbr* = **United Kingdom.**
Ukraine [juːˈkreɪn] *n* **the U.** l'Ukraine *f*.
ulcer [ˈʌlsər] *n* ulcère *m*.
ulterior [ʌlˈtɪərɪər] *a* **u. motive** arrière-pensée *f*.
ultimate [ˈʌltɪmət] *a* (*final, last*) ultime; (*basic*) fondamental; (*authority*) suprême. • **—ly** *adv* (*finally*) à la fin; (*fundamentally*) en fin de compte.
ultimatum [ʌltɪˈmeɪtəm] *n* ultimatum *m*.
ultramodern [ʌltrəˈmɒdən] *a* ultramoderne.
ultrasound [ˈʌltrəsaʊnd] *n* (*scan, technique*) échographie *f*.
ultraviolet [ʌltrəˈvaɪələt] *a* ultraviolet.
umbrella [ʌmˈbrelə] *n* parapluie *m*; (*for sun*) parasol *m*.
umpire [ˈʌmpaɪər] *n Sp* arbitre *m*.
umpteen [ʌmpˈtiːn] *a* **u. times**/*etc Fam* je ne sais combien de fois/*etc*. • **umpteenth** *a Fam* énième.
un- [ʌn] *pref* in-, peu, non, sans.
UN [juːˈen] *abbr* = **United Nations.**
unabated [ʌnəˈbeɪtɪd] *adv* **to continue u.** se poursuivre avec la même intensité.
unable [ʌnˈeɪb(ə)l] *a* **to be u. to do** être incapable de faire; **he's u. to swim** il ne sait pas nager.
unabridged [ʌnəˈbrɪdʒd] *a* intégral.
unacceptable [ʌnəkˈseptəb(ə)l] *a* inacceptable.
unaccompanied [ʌnəˈkʌmpənɪd] *a* (*person*) non accompagné.
unaccountable [ʌnəˈkaʊntəb(ə)l] *a* inexplicable.
unaccounted [ʌnəˈkaʊntɪd] *a* **to be (still) u. for** rester introuvable.
unaccustomed [ʌnəˈkʌstəmd] *a* inaccoutumé; **to be u. to sth/to doing** ne pas être habitué à qch/à faire.
unaided [ʌnˈeɪdɪd] *adv* sans aide.
unanimous [juːˈnænɪməs] *a* unanime. • **—ly** *adv* à l'unanimité.
unappetizing [ʌnˈæpɪtaɪzɪŋ] *a* peu appétissant.
unarmed [ʌnˈɑːmd] *a* non armé; **u. combat** combat *m* à mains nues.
unashamedly [ʌnəˈʃeɪmɪdlɪ] *adv* sans aucune honte.
unassailable [ʌnəˈseɪləb(ə)l] *a* inattaquable.
unassuming [ʌnəˈsjuːmɪŋ] *a* modeste.
unattached [ʌnəˈtætʃt] *a* (*independent, not married*) libre.
unattainable [ʌnəˈteɪnəb(ə)l] *a* (*aim*) inaccessible.
unattractive [ʌnəˈtræktɪv] *a* (*idea, appearance etc*) peu attrayant; (*ugly*) laid.
unauthorized [ʌnˈɔːθəraɪzd] *a* non autorisé.
unavailable [ʌnəˈveɪləb(ə)l] *a* (*person*) qui n'est pas disponible; (*article*) épuisé.
unavoidab/le [ʌnəˈvɔɪdəb(ə)l] *a* inévitable. • **—ly** *adv* inévitablement; (*delayed*) pour une raison indépendante de sa volonté.
unaware [ʌnəˈweər] *a* **to be u. of sth** ignorer qch; **to be u. that** ignorer que. • **unawares** *adv* **to catch s.o. u.** prendre qn au dépourvu.
unbalanced [ʌnˈbælənst] *a* (*mind, person*) déséquilibré.
unbearable [ʌnˈbeərəb(ə)l] *a* insupportable.
unbeatable [ʌnˈbiːtəb(ə)l] *a* imbattable. • **unbeaten** *a* (*player*) invaincu; (*record*) non battu.
unbeknown(st) [ʌnbɪˈnəʊn(st)] *a* **u. to s.o.** à l'insu de qn.
unbelievable [ʌnbɪˈliːvəb(ə)l] *a* incroyable.
unbias(s)ed [ʌnˈbaɪəst] *a* impartial.
unblock [ʌnˈblɒk] *vt* (*sink etc*) déboucher.
unborn [ʌnˈbɔːn] *a* (*child*) à naître.
unbreakable [ʌnˈbreɪkəb(ə)l] *a* incassable. • **unbroken** *a* intact; (*continuous*) continu; (*record*) non battu.
unbutton [ʌnˈbʌt(ə)n] *vt* déboutonner.
uncalled-for [ʌnˈkɔːldfɔːr] *a* déplacé.
uncanny [ʌnˈkænɪ] *a* (**-ier, -iest**) étrange, mystérieux.
unceasing [ʌnˈsiːsɪŋ] *a* incessant.
unceremoniously [ʌnserɪˈməʊnɪəslɪ] *adv* (*to treat*) sans ménagement.
uncertain [ʌnˈsɜːt(ə)n] *a* incertain (**about,**

of de); **it's u. whether** *or* **that** il n'est pas certain que (+ *sub*); **I'm u. whether to stay** je ne sais pas très bien si je dois rester. • **uncertainty** *n* incertitude *f*.

unchanged [ʌn'tʃeɪndʒd] *a* inchangé. • **unchanging** *a* immuable.

unchecked [ʌn'tʃekt] *adv* (*to spread etc*) sans que rien ne soit fait.

uncivilized [ʌn'sɪvɪlaɪzd] *a* barbare.

uncle ['ʌŋk(ə)l] *n* oncle *m*.

unclear [ʌn'klɪər] *a* (*meaning*) qui n'est pas clair; (*result*) incertain; **it's u. whether...** on ne sait pas très bien si....

uncomfortable [ʌn'kʌmftəb(ə)l] *a* (*chair etc*) inconfortable; (*heat*) désagréable; **she feels u.** (*uneasy*) elle est mal à l'aise.

uncommon [ʌn'kɒmən] *a* rare.

uncomplicated [ʌn'kɒmplɪkeɪtɪd] *a* simple.

uncompromising [ʌn'kɒmprəmaɪzɪŋ] *a* intransigeant.

unconcerned [ʌnkən'sɜːnd] *a* (*indifferent*) indifférent (**by, with** à).

unconditional [ʌnkən'dɪʃ(ə)nəl] *a* (*offer*) inconditionnel; (*surrender*) sans condition.

unconfirmed [ʌnkən'fɜːmd] *a* non confirmé.

unconnected [ʌnkə'nektɪd] *a* (*facts, events etc*) sans rapport (**with** avec).

unconscious [ʌn'kɒnʃəs] *a* (*person*) sans connaissance; (*desire*) inconscient; **u. of** inconscient de ‖ *n* *Psy* inconscient *m*. • **—ly** *adv* inconsciemment.

uncontrollable [ʌnkən'trəʊləb(ə)l] *a* (*emotion, laughter*) irrépressible.

unconventional [ʌnkən'venʃ(ə)nəl] *a* peu conventionnel; (*person*) anticonformiste.

unconvinced [ʌnkən'vɪnst] *a* **to be** *or* **remain u.** ne pas être convaincu (**of** de). • **unconvincing** *a* peu convaincant.

uncooked ['ʌnkʊkt] *a* cru.

uncooperative [ʌnkəʊ'ɒp(ə)rətɪv] *a* peu coopératif.

uncork [ʌn'kɔːk] *vt* (*bottle*) déboucher.

uncouth [ʌn'kuːθ] *a* grossier.

uncover [ʌn'kʌvər] *vt* (*conspiracy etc*) découvrir.

undamaged [ʌn'dæmɪdʒd] *a* (*goods*) en bon état.

undaunted [ʌn'dɔːntɪd] *a* nullement découragé.

undecided [ʌndɪ'saɪdɪd] *a* (*person*) indécis (**about** sur); **I'm u. whether to do it or not** je n'ai pas décidé si je le ferai ou non.

undeniable [ʌndɪ'naɪəb(ə)l] *a* incontestable.

under ['ʌndər] *prep* sous; (*less than*) moins de; (*according to*) selon; **children u. nine** les enfants de moins de neuf ans; **u. the circumstances** dans les circonstances; **u. there** là-dessous; **u. it** dessous; **u. (the command of) s.o.** sous les ordres de qn; **u. repair** en réparation; **u. way** (*in progress*) en cours; (*on the way*) en route; **to get u. way** (*of campaign etc*) démarrer ‖ *adv* au-dessous.

under- ['ʌndər] *pref* sous-.

undercarriage ['ʌndəkærɪdʒ] *n* (*of aircraft*) train *m* d'atterrissage.

undercharge [ʌndə'tʃɑːdʒ] *vt* **I undercharged him (for it)** je ne (le) lui ai pas fait payer assez.

underclothes ['ʌndəkləʊðz] *npl* sous-vêtements *mpl*.

undercoat ['ʌndəkəʊt] *n* (*of paint*) couche *f* de fond.

undercooked [ʌndə'kʊkt] *a* pas assez cuit.

undercover [ʌndə'kʌvər] *a* (*agent, operation*) secret.

undercut [ʌndə'kʌt] *vt* (*pt* & *pp* **undercut,** *pres p* **undercutting**) *Com* vendre moins cher que.

underdeveloped [ʌndədɪ'veləpt] *a* (*country*) sous-développé.

underdog ['ʌndədɒg] *n* (*politically, socially*) opprimé, -ée *mf*.

underdone [ʌndə'dʌn] *a* pas assez cuit; (*steak*) saignant.

underestimate [ʌndər'estɪmeɪt] *vt* sous-estimer.

underfed [ʌndə'fed] *a* sous-alimenté.

underfoot [ʌndə'fʊt] *adv* sous les pieds.

undergo [ʌndə'gəʊ] *vt* (*pt* **underwent,** *pp* **undergone**) subir.

undergraduate [ʌndə'grædʒʊət] *n* étudiant, -ante *mf* (de licence).

underground ['ʌndəgraʊnd] *a* souterrain; (*secret*) *Fig* clandestin ‖ *n* *Rail* métro *m*; (*organization*) *Pol* résistance *f* ‖ [ʌndə'graʊnd] *adv* sous terre.

undergrowth ['ʌndəgrəʊθ] *n* sous-bois *m inv*.

underhand [ʌndə'hænd] *a* (*dishonest*) sournois.

underlying [ʌndə'laɪɪŋ] *a* (*basic*) fondamental; (*hidden*) profond.

underline [ʌndə'laɪn] *vt* (*word etc*) souligner.

undermine [ʌndə'maɪn] *vt* (*society, building, strength*) miner, saper.

underneath [ʌndə'niːθ] *prep* sous ‖ *adv* (en) dessous; **the book u.** le livre d'en dessous ‖ *n* dessous *m*.

underpaid [ʌndə'peɪd] *a* sous-payé.

underpants ['ʌndəpænts] *npl* slip *m*; (*loose,*

long) caleçon *m*.
underpass ['ʌndəpɑːs] *n* (*for pedestrians*) passage *m* souterrain; (*for vehicles*) passage *m* inférieur.
underpriced [ʌndə'praɪst] *a* **it's u.** le prix est trop bas, c'est bradé.
underprivileged [ʌndə'prɪvɪlɪdʒd] *a* défavorisé.
underrate [ʌndə'reɪt] *vt* sous-estimer.
undershirt ['ʌndəʃɜːt] *n Am* tricot *m* de corps.
underside ['ʌndəsaɪd] *n* dessous *m*.
undersized [ʌndə'saɪzd] *a* trop petit.
underskirt ['ʌndəskɜːt] *n* jupon *m*.
understaffed [ʌndə'stɑːft] *a* à court de personnel.
understand [ʌndə'stænd] *vti* (*pt* & *pp* **understood**) comprendre; **I've been given to u. that** on m'a fait comprendre que. ●**—ing** *n* compréhension *f*; (*agreement*) accord *m*; (*sympathy*) entente *f*; **on the u. that** à condition que (+ *sub*) ‖ *a* (*person*) compréhensif. ●**understood** *a* (*agreed*) entendu; (*implied*) sous-entendu.
understandab/le [ʌndə'stændəb(ə)l] *a* compréhensible. ●**—ly** *adv* naturellement.
understatement ['ʌndəsteɪtmənt] *n* euphémisme *m*.
understudy ['ʌndəstʌdɪ] *n Th* doublure *f*.
undertak/e [ʌndə'teɪk] *vt* (*pt* **undertook,** *pp* **undertaken**) (*task etc*) entreprendre; (*responsibility*) assumer; **to u. to do** entreprendre de faire. ●**—ing** *n* (*task*) entreprise *f*; (*promise*) promesse *f*; **to give an u.** promettre (**that** que).
undertaker ['ʌndəteɪkər] *n* entrepreneur *m* de pompes funèbres.
undertone ['ʌndətəʊn] *n* **in an u.** à mi-voix.
underwater [ʌndə'wɔːtər] *a* sous-marin ‖ *adv* sous l'eau.
underwear ['ʌndəweər] *n* sous-vêtements *mpl*.
underweight [ʌndə'weɪt] *a* (*person*) qui ne pèse pas assez.
underworld ['ʌndəwɜːld] *n* **the u.** (*criminals*) le milieu, la pègre.
undesirable [ʌndɪ'zaɪərəb(ə)l] *a* peu souhaitable (**that** que (+ *sub*)); (*person*) indésirable.
undetected [ʌndɪ'tektɪd] *a* **to go u.** passer inaperçu.
undies ['ʌndɪz] *npl* (*female underwear*) *Fam* dessous *mpl*.
undignified [ʌn'dɪgnɪfaɪd] *a* qui manque de dignité.
undisciplined [ʌn'dɪsɪplɪnd] *a* indiscipliné.
undisputed [ʌndɪ'spjuːtɪd] *a* incontesté.
undistinguished [ʌndɪ'stɪŋgwɪʃt] *a* médiocre.
undivided [ʌndɪ'vaɪdɪd] *a* **my u. attention** toute mon attention.
undo [ʌn'duː] *vt* (*pt* **undid,** *pp* **undone**) défaire; (*bound person, hands*) détacher. ●**—ing** *n* (*downfall*) perte *f*. ●**undone** *a* **to come u.** (*of knot etc*) se défaire.
undoubtedly [ʌn'daʊtɪdlɪ] *adv* sans aucun doute.
undreamt-of [ʌn'dremtɒv] *a* insoupçonné.
undress [ʌn'dres] *vi* se déshabiller ‖ *vt* déshabiller; **to get undressed** se déshabiller.
undrinkable [ʌn'drɪŋkəb(ə)l] *a* imbuvable.
undue [ʌn'djuː] *a* excessif. ●**unduly** *adv* excessivement.
unearned [ʌn'ɜːnd] *a* **u. income** rentes *fpl*.
unearth [ʌn'ɜːθ] *vt* (*from ground*) déterrer; (*discover*) *Fig* dénicher, déterrer.
unearthly [ʌn'ɜːθlɪ] *a* **at an u. hour** *Fam* à une heure impossible.
uneasy [ʌn'iːzɪ] *a* (*ill at ease*) mal à l'aise; (*worried*) inquiet; (*peace*) précaire; (*silence*) gêné.
uneconomic(al) [ʌniːkə'nɒmɪk((ə)l)] *a* peu économique.
uneducated [ʌn'edʒʊkeɪtɪd] *a* (*person*) inculte; (*accent*) populaire.
unemployed [ʌnɪm'plɔɪd] *a* au chômage ‖ *n* **the u.** les chômeurs *mpl*. ●**unemployment** *n* chômage *m*; **u. benefit** allocation *f* de chômage.
unending [ʌn'endɪŋ] *a* interminable.
unenthusiastic [ʌnɪnθjuːzɪ'æstɪk] *a* peu enthousiaste.
unenviable [ʌn'envɪəb(ə)l] *a* peu enviable.
unequal [ʌn'iːkwəl] *a* inégal.
unequivocal [ʌnɪ'kwɪvək(ə)l] *a* sans équivoque.
uneven [ʌn'iːv(ə)n] *a* inégal.
uneventful [ʌnɪ'ventfəl] *a* (*trip, life etc*) sans histoires.
unexpected [ʌnɪk'spektɪd] *a* inattendu. ●**—ly** *adv* à l'improviste; (*suddenly*) subitement; (*unusually*) exceptionnellement.
unexplained [ʌnɪk'spleɪnd] *a* inexpliqué.
unfailing [ʌn'feɪlɪŋ] *a* (*optimism etc*) inébranlable.
unfair [ʌn'feər] *a* injuste (**to s.o.** envers qn); (*competition*) déloyal. ●**—ly** *adv* injustement. ●**—ness** *n* injustice *f*.
unfaithful [ʌn'feɪθfəl] *a* infidèle (**to** à).
unfamiliar [ʌnfə'mɪlɪər] *a* inconnu; **to be u. with sth** ne pas connaître qch.
unfashionable [ʌn'fæʃ(ə)nəb(ə)l] *a* (*subject etc*) démodé; (*restaurant etc*) peu chic

inv, ringard; **it's u. to do** il n'est pas de bon ton de faire.

unfasten [ʌn'fɑːs(ə)n] *vt* défaire.

unfavourable [ʌn'feɪv(ə)rəb(ə)l] (*Am* **unfavorable**) *a* défavorable.

unfeeling [ʌn'fiːlɪŋ] *a* insensible.

unfinished [ʌn'fɪnɪʃt] *a* inachevé.

unfit [ʌn'fɪt] *a* en mauvaise santé; (*in bad shape*) pas en forme; (*unsuitable*) impropre (**for sth** à qch, **to do** à faire); (*unworthy*) indigne (**for sth** de qch, **to do** de faire); (*incapable*) inapte (**for sth** à qch, **to do** à faire).

unflinching [ʌn'flɪntʃɪŋ] *a* (*fearless*) intrépide.

unfold [ʌn'fəʊld] *vt* déplier; (*wings*) déployer ‖ *vi* (*of story*) se dérouler.

unforeseeable [ʌnfɔː'siːəb(ə)l] *a* imprévisible. ● **unforeseen** *a* imprévu.

unforgettable [ʌnfə'getəb(ə)l] *a* inoubliable.

unforgivable [ʌnfə'gɪvəb(ə)l] *a* impardonnable.

unfortunate [ʌn'fɔːtʃ(ə)nət] *a* malheureux; (*event*) fâcheux; **you were u.** tu n'as pas eu de chance. ● **—ly** *adv* malheureusement.

unfounded [ʌn'faʊndɪd] *a* (*rumour*) sans fondement.

unfriendly [ʌn'frendlɪ] *a* froid, peu aimable (**to** avec).

unfulfilled [ʌnfʊl'fɪld] *a* (*desire*) insatisfait.

unfurnished [ʌn'fɜːnɪʃt] *a* non meublé.

ungainly [ʌn'geɪnlɪ] *a* (*clumsy*) gauche.

ungodly [ʌn'gɒdlɪ] *a* **at an u. hour** *Fam* à une heure impossible.

ungrateful [ʌn'greɪtfəl] *a* ingrat.

unhappy [ʌn'hæpɪ] *a* (**-ier, -iest**) (*sad*) malheureux; **u. with** *or* **about sth** (*not pleased*) mécontent de qch; **he's u. about doing it** ça le dérange de le faire. ● **unhappiness** *n* tristesse *f*.

unharmed [ʌn'hɑːmd] *a* (*person*) indemne.

unhealthy [ʌn'helθɪ] *a* (**-ier, -iest**) (*climate etc*) malsain; (*person*) en mauvaise santé; (*lungs*) malade.

unheard-of [ʌn'hɜːdɒv] *a* (*unprecedented*) inouï.

unheeded [ʌn'hiːdɪd] *a* **it went u.** on n'en a pas tenu compte.

unhelpful [ʌn'helpfəl] *a* (*person*) peu serviable; (*advice*) peu utile.

unhook [ʌn'hʊk] *vt* (*picture, curtain*) décrocher; (*dress*) dégrafer.

unhurt [ʌn'hɜːt] *a* indemne.

unhygienic [ʌnhaɪ'dʒiːnɪk] *a* pas très hygiénique.

uniform ['juːnɪfɔːm] **1** *n* uniforme *m*. **2** *a* (*regular*) uniforme; (*temperature*) constant.

unify ['juːnɪfaɪ] *vt* unifier.

unimaginable [ʌnɪ'mædʒɪnəb(ə)l] *a* inimaginable. ● **unimaginative** *a* (*person, plan etc*) qui manque d'imagination.

unimpaired [ʌnɪm'peəd] *a* intact.

unimportant [ʌnɪm'pɔːtənt] *a* peu important.

uninhabitable [ʌnɪn'hæbɪtəb(ə)l] *a* inhabitable. ● **uninhabited** *a* inhabité.

uninhibited [ʌnɪn'hɪbɪtɪd] *a* (*person*) sans complexes.

uninjured [ʌn'ɪndʒəd] *a* indemne.

uninspiring [ʌnɪn'spaɪərɪŋ] *a* (*subject etc*) pas très inspirant.

unintelligible [ʌnɪn'telɪdʒəb(ə)l] *a* inintelligible.

unintentional [ʌnɪn'tenʃ(ə)nəl] *a* involontaire.

uninterested [ʌn'ɪntrɪstɪd] *a* indifférent (**in** à). ● **uninteresting** *a* (*book etc*) peu intéressant; (*person*) fastidieux.

uninterrupted [ʌnɪntə'rʌptɪd] *a* ininterrompu.

uninvited [ʌnɪn'vaɪtɪd] *adv* (*to arrive*) sans invitation. ● **uninviting** *a* peu attrayant.

union ['juːnɪən] *n* union *f*; (*trade or Am labor union*) syndicat *m* ‖ *a* syndical; **u. member** syndiqué, -ée *mf*; **the U. Jack** le drapeau britannique.

unique [juː'niːk] *a* unique. ● **—ly** *adv* exceptionnellement.

unisex ['juːnɪseks] *a* (*clothes etc*) unisexe.

unison ['juːnɪs(ə)n] *n* **in u.** à l'unisson (**with** de).

unit ['juːnɪt] *n* unité *f*; (*of furniture etc*) élément *m*; (*group, team*) groupe *m*; **psychiatric u.** service *m* de psychiatrie; **research u.** centre *m* de recherche; **u. trust** *Fin* fonds *m* commun de placement.

unite [juː'naɪt] *vt* unir; (*country, party*) unifier; **United Kingdom** Royaume-Uni *m*; **United Nations** (Organisation *f* des) Nations unies *fpl*; **United States (of America)** États-Unis *mpl* (d'Amérique) ‖ *vi* (*of students etc*) s'unir.

unity ['juːnətɪ] *n* unité *f*.

universal [juːnɪ'vɜːs(ə)l] *a* universel.

universe ['juːnɪvɜːs] *n* univers *m*.

university [juːnɪ'vɜːsɪtɪ] *n* université *f*; **at u.** à l'université ‖ *a* (*teaching, town etc*) universitaire; (*student, teacher*) d'université.

unjust [ʌn'dʒʌst] *a* injuste.

unjustified [ʌn'dʒʌstɪfaɪd] *a* injustifié.

unkempt [ʌn'kempt] *a* (*appearance*) négligé; (*hair*) mal peigné.

unkind [ʌn'kaɪnd] *a* peu gentil (**to s.o.** avec qn); (*nasty*) méchant (**to s.o.** avec qn).
unknowingly [ʌn'nəʊɪŋlɪ] *adv* inconsciemment.
unknown [ʌn'nəʊn] *a* inconnu ‖ *n* (*person*) inconnu, -ue *mf*; **the u.** *Phil* l'inconnu *m*; **u. (quantity)** *Math & Fig* inconnue *f*.
unlawful [ʌn'lɔːfəl] *a* illégal.
unleaded [ʌn'ledɪd] *a* (*petrol, Am gasoline*) sans plomb.
unleash [ʌn'liːʃ] *vt* (*force etc*) déchaîner.
unless [ʌn'les] *conj* à moins que (+ *sub*); **u. she comes** à moins qu'elle (ne) vienne; **u. you work harder, you'll fail** à moins de travailler plus dur, vous échouerez.
unlike [ʌn'laɪk] *a* différent ‖ *prep* **u. me, she...** à la différence de moi, elle...; **he's u. his father** il n'est pas comme son père; **that's u. him** ça ne lui ressemble pas.
unlikely [ʌn'laɪklɪ] *a* peu probable; (*unbelievable*) incroyable; **she's u. to win** il est peu probable qu'elle gagne.
unlimited [ʌn'lɪmɪtɪd] *a* illimité.
unlisted [ʌn'lɪstɪd] *a* (*phone number*) *Am* sur la liste rouge.
unload [ʌn'ləʊd] *vt* décharger.
unlock [ʌn'lɒk] *vt* ouvrir (*avec une clef*).
unlucky [ʌn'lʌkɪ] *a* (**-ier, -iest**) (*person*) malchanceux; (*number etc*) qui porte malheur; **you're u.** tu n'as pas de chance. ● **unluckily** *adv* malheureusement.
unmade [ʌn'meɪd] *a* (*bed*) défait.
unmanageable [ʌn'mænɪdʒəb(ə)l] *a* (*child*) difficile; (*hair*) difficile à coiffer.
unmanned [ʌn'mænd] *a* (*spacecraft*) inhabité.
unmarried [ʌn'mærɪd] *a* célibataire.
unmask [ʌn'mɑːsk] *vt* démasquer.
unmentionable [ʌn'menʃ(ə)nəb(ə)l] *a* dont il ne faut pas parler.
unmistakable [ʌnmɪ'steɪkəb(ə)l] *a* (*obvious*) indubitable; (*face, voice*) facilement reconnaissable.
unmitigated [ʌn'mɪtɪgeɪtɪd] *a* (*disaster*) absolu; (*folly*) pur.
unmoved [ʌn'muːvd] *a* impassible (**by** devant); (*unconcerned*) indifférent (**by** à).
unnatural [ʌn'nætʃ(ə)rəl] *a* (*not normal*) pas naturel; (*affected*) qui manque de naturel.
unnecessary [ʌn'nesəs(ə)rɪ] *a* inutile.
unnerve [ʌn'nɜːv] *vt* déconcerter.
unnoticed [ʌn'nəʊtɪst] *a* **to go u.** passer inaperçu.
unobstructed [ʌnəb'strʌktɪd] *a* (*view*) dégagé.
unobtainable [ʌnəb'teɪnəb(ə)l] *a* impossible à obtenir.
unobtrusive [ʌnəb'truːsɪv] *a* discret.
unoccupied [ʌn'ɒkjʊpaɪd] *a* (*house*) inoccupé; (*seat*) libre.
unofficial [ʌnə'fɪʃ(ə)l] *a* officieux; (*visit*) privé; (*strike*) sauvage.
unorthodox [ʌn'ɔːθədɒks] *a* peu orthodoxe.
unpack [ʌn'pæk] *vt* (*suitcase*) défaire; (*goods, belongings*) déballer; **to u. a comb/***etc* **from** sortir un peigne/*etc* de ‖ *vi* défaire sa valise; (*take out goods*) déballer.
unpaid [ʌn'peɪd] *a* (*bill, sum*) impayé; (*work, worker*) bénévole; (*leave*) non payé.
unpalatable [ʌn'pælətəb(ə)l] *a* désagréable.
unparalleled [ʌn'pærəleld] *a* sans égal.
unplanned [ʌn'plænd] *a* (*visit, baby*) imprévu.
unpleasant [ʌn'plezənt] *a* désagréable (**to s.o.** avec qn).
unplug [ʌn'plʌg] *vt* (**-gg-**) (*appliance*) débrancher.
unpopular [ʌn'pɒpjʊlər] *a* peu populaire; **to be u. with s.o.** ne pas plaire à qn.
unprecedented [ʌn'presɪdentɪd] *a* sans précédent.
unpredictable [ʌnprɪ'dɪktəb(ə)l] *a* imprévisible; (*weather*) indécis.
unprepared [ʌnprɪ'peəd] *a* **to be u. for sth** (*not expect*) ne pas s'attendre à qch.
unpretentious [ʌnprɪ'tenʃəs] *a* sans prétention.
unprofessional [ʌnprə'feʃ(ə)nəl] *a* (*person, behaviour*) pas très professionnel.
unpublished [ʌn'pʌblɪʃt] *a* inédit.
unpunished [ʌn'pʌnɪʃt] *a* **to go u.** rester impuni.
unqualified [ʌn'kwɒlɪfaɪd] *a* **1** (*teacher etc*) non diplômé; **he's u. to do** il n'est pas qualifié pour faire. **2** (*support*) sans réserve; (*success*) parfait.
unquestionable [ʌn'kwestʃ(ə)nəb(ə)l] *a* incontestable.
unravel [ʌn'ræv(ə)l] *vt* (**-ll-**, *Am* **-l-**) (*threads etc*) démêler; (*mystery*) *Fig* éclaircir.
unreal [ʌn'rɪəl] *a* irréel. ● **unrea'listic** *a* peu réaliste.
unreasonable [ʌn'riːz(ə)nəb(ə)l] *a* qui n'est pas raisonnable; (*price*) excessif.
unrecognizable [ʌnrekəg'naɪzəb(ə)l] *a* méconnaissable.
unrelated [ʌnrɪ'leɪtɪd] *a* (*facts etc*) sans rapport (**to** avec).
unrelenting [ʌnrɪ'lentɪŋ] *a* (*person*) implacable; (*effort*) acharné.

unreliable [ʌnrɪ'laɪəb(ə)l] *a* (*person*) peu sûr; (*machine*) peu fiable.
unrepentant [ʌnrɪ'pentənt] *a* impénitent.
unreservedly [ʌnrɪ'zɜːvɪdlɪ] *adv* sans réserve.
unrest [ʌn'rest] *n* agitation *f*.
unrestricted [ʌnrɪ'strɪktɪd] *a* illimité; (*access*) libre.
unripe [ʌn'raɪp] *a* (*fruit*) vert, pas mûr.
unroll [ʌn'rəʊl] *vt* dérouler ‖ *vi* se dérouler.
unruffled [ʌn'rʌf(ə)ld] *a* (*person*) calme.
unruly [ʌn'ruːlɪ] *a* (**-ier, -iest**) indiscipliné.
unsafe [ʌn'seɪf] *a* (*place, machine etc*) dangereux; (*person*) en danger.
unsaid [ʌn'sed] *a* **to leave sth u.** passer qch sous silence.
unsatisfactory [ʌnsætɪs'fækt(ə)rɪ] *a* peu satisfaisant. ● **un'satisfied** *a* insatisfait; **u. with** peu satisfait de.
unsavoury [ʌn'seɪv(ə)rɪ] (*Am* **unsavory**) *a* (*person, place*) répugnant.
unscathed [ʌn'skeɪðd] *a* indemne.
unscrew [ʌn'skruː] *vt* dévisser.
unscrupulous [ʌn'skruːpjʊləs] *a* peu scrupuleux.
unseemly [ʌn'siːmlɪ] *a* inconvenant.
unseen [ʌn'siːn] *n* (*translation*) version *f*.
unselfish [ʌn'selfɪʃ] *a* désintéressé.
unsettled [ʌn'set(ə)ld] *a* (*weather*) instable.
unshakeable [ʌn'ʃeɪkəb(ə)l] *a* inébranlable.
unshaven [ʌn'ʃeɪv(ə)n] *a* pas rasé.
unsightly [ʌn'saɪtlɪ] *a* laid, disgracieux.
unskilled [ʌn'skɪld] *a* **u. worker** ouvrier, -ière *mf* non qualifié(e).
unsociable [ʌn'səʊʃəb(ə)l] *a* peu sociable.
unsolved [ʌn'sɒlvd] *a* (*problem*) non résolu; (*mystery*) inexpliqué; (*crime*) dont l'auteur n'est pas connu.
unsound [ʌn'saʊnd] *a* (*construction*) peu solide; (*method*) peu sûr; (*decision*) peu judicieux.
unspeakable [ʌn'spiːkəb(ə)l] *a* (*horrible*) innommable.
unspecified [ʌn'spesɪfaɪd] *a* indéterminé.
unstable [ʌn'steɪb(ə)l] *a* instable.
unsteady [ʌn'stedɪ] *a* (*hand, voice, step etc*) mal assuré; (*table, ladder etc*) instable. ● **unsteadily** *adv* (*to walk*) d'un pas mal assuré.
unstuck [ʌn'stʌk] *a* **to come u.** (*of stamp etc*) se décoller; (*fail*) (*of person*) *Fam* se planter.
unsuccessful [ʌnsək'sesfəl] *a* (*attempt etc*) vain, infructueux; (*outcome, candidate*) malheureux; (*application*) non retenu; **to be u.** ne pas réussir (**in doing** à faire); (*of book, artist*) ne pas avoir de succès. ● **—ly** *adv* en vain.
unsuitable [ʌn'suːtəb(ə)l] *a* qui ne convient pas (**for** à); (*manners, clothes*) peu convenable. ● **unsuited** *a* **u. to** (*job, activity*) peu fait pour; **they're u.** ils ne sont pas compatibles.
unsupervised [ʌn'suːpəvaɪzd] *adv* (*to play etc*) sans surveillance.
unsure [ʌn'ʃʊər] *a* incertain (**of, about** de).
unsuspecting [ʌnsə'spektɪŋ] *a* qui ne se doute de rien.
unsympathetic [ʌnsɪmpə'θetɪk] *a* incompréhensif; **u. to** indifférent à.
untangle [ʌn'tæŋg(ə)l] *vt* (*rope, hair etc*) démêler.
untenable [ʌn'tenəb(ə)l] *a* (*position*) intenable.
unthinkable [ʌn'θɪŋkəb(ə)l] *a* impensable.
untidy [ʌn'taɪdɪ] *a* (**-ier, -iest**) (*clothes, hair*) peu soigné; (*room*) en désordre; (*person*) désordonné; (*in appearance*) peu soigné.
untie [ʌn'taɪ] *vt* (*person, hands*) détacher; (*knot, parcel*) défaire.
until [ʌn'tɪl] *prep* jusqu'à; **u. then** jusque-là; **I didn't come u. yesterday** je ne suis venu qu'hier; **not u. tomorrow** pas avant demain ‖ *conj* jusqu'à ce que (+ *sub*); **u. she comes** jusqu'à ce qu'elle vienne; **do nothing u. I come** ne fais rien avant que j'arrive.
untimely [ʌn'taɪmlɪ] *a* inopportun; (*death*) prématuré.
untiring [ʌn'taɪ(ə)rɪŋ] *a* infatigable.
untold [ʌn'təʊld] *a* (*wealth*) incalculable.
untoward [ʌntə'wɔːd] *a* fâcheux.
untranslatable [ʌntræns'leɪtəb(ə)l] *a* intraduisible.
untrue [ʌn'truː] *a* faux (*f* fausse).
unusable [ʌn'juːzəb(ə)l] *a* inutilisable.
unused 1 [ʌn'juːzd] *a* (*new*) neuf (*f* neuve); (*not in use*) inutilisé. **2** [ʌn'juːst] *a* **u. to sth/to doing** peu habitué à qch/à faire.
unusual [ʌn'juːʒʊəl] *a* exceptionnel; (*strange*) étrange. ● **—ly** *adv* exceptionnellement.
unveil [ʌn'veɪl] *vt* dévoiler.
unwanted [ʌn'wɒntɪd] *a* (*useless*) dont on n'a pas besoin; (*child*) non désiré.
unwelcome [ʌn'welkəm] *a* (*news, fact*) fâcheux; (*gift, visit*) inopportun; (*person*) importun.
unwell [ʌn'wel] *a* indisposé.
unwieldy [ʌn'wiːldɪ] *a* (*package etc*) encombrant.
unwilling [ʌn'wɪlɪŋ] *a* **he's u. to do** il ne veut pas faire. ● **—ly** *adv* à contrecœur.
unwind [ʌn'waɪnd] **1** *vt* (*thread etc*

dérouler ▮ *vi* se dérouler. **2** *vi* (*relax*) *Fam* décompresser.

unwise [ʌn'waɪz] *a* imprudent.

unwittingly [ʌn'wɪtɪŋlɪ] *adv* involontairement.

unworkable [ʌn'wɜːkəb(ə)l] *a* (*idea etc*) impraticable.

unworthy [ʌn'wɜːðɪ] *a* indigne (**of** de).

unwrap [ʌn'ræp] *vt* (**-pp-**) ouvrir, défaire.

unwritten [ʌn'rɪt(ə)n] *a* (*agreement*) tacite.

unzip [ʌn'zɪp] *vt* (**-pp-**) ouvrir (la fermeture éclair® de).

up [ʌp] *adv* en haut; (*in the air*) en l'air; (*of sun*) levé; (*out of bed*) levé, debout; (*finished*) fini; **to come** *or* **go up** monter; **prices are up** les prix ont augmenté; **up there** là-haut; **up above** au-dessus; **up on the roof** sur le toit; **further** *or* **higher up** plus haut; **up to** (*as far as*) jusqu'à; (*task*) *Fig* à la hauteur de; **to be up to doing** (*capable*) être de taille à faire; **it's up to you to do it** c'est à toi de le faire; **that's up to you** ça dépend de toi; **where are you up to?** (*in book etc*) où en es-tu?; **what are you up to?** que fais-tu?; **what's up?** (*what's the matter?*) *Fam* qu'est-ce qu'il y a?; **time's up** c'est l'heure; **to walk up and down** marcher de long en large; **to be up against** (*confront*) être confronté à.
▮ *prep* (*a hill*) en haut de; (*a tree*) dans; (*a ladder*) sur; **to go up** (*hill, stairs*) monter.
▮ *npl* **to have ups and downs** avoir des hauts et des bas.

up-and-coming [ʌpənd'kʌmɪŋ] *a* plein d'avenir. ● **upbeat** *a* (*cheerful*) *Am Fam* optimiste. ● **upbringing** *n* éducation *f*. ● **upcoming** *a Am* imminent. ● **up'date** *vt* mettre à jour. ● **up'grade** *vt* (*job*) revaloriser; (*person*) promouvoir. ● **up'hill 1** *adv* **to go u.** monter. **2** ['ʌphɪl] *a* (*struggle, task*) pénible. ● **up'hold** *vt* (*pt & pp* **upheld**) maintenir. ● **upkeep** *n* entretien *m*. ● **upmarket** *a Com* haut de gamme. ● **upright 1** *a & adv* (*straight*) droit. **2** *a* (*honest*) droit. ● **uprising** *n* insurrection *f*. ● **up'root** *vt* (*plant, person*) déraciner. ● **upside 'down** *adv* à l'envers; **to turn u. down** (*plans etc*) *Fig* chambouler. ● **up'stairs** *adv* en haut; **to go u.** monter (l'escalier); ▮ ['ʌpsteəz] *a* (*room*) du dessus. ● **up'stream** *adv* en amont. ● **up'tight** *a Fam* (*tense*) crispé; (*angry*) en colère. ● **up-to-'date** *a* moderne; (*information*) à jour; (*well-informed*) au courant (**on** de). ● **upturn** *n* (*improvement*) amélioration *f* (**in** de). ● **upward** *a* (*movement*) ascendant; (*path*) qui monte; (*trend*) à la hausse. ● **upwards** *adv* vers le haut; **from five francs u.** à partir de cinq francs.

upheaval [ʌp'hiːv(ə)l] *n* bouleversement *m*.

upholster [ʌp'həʊlstər] *vt* (*pad*) rembourrer; (*cover*) recouvrir. ● **upholstery** *n* (*padding*) rembourrage *m*; (*covering*) revêtement *m*; (*in car*) garniture *f*.

upon [ə'pɒn] *prep* sur.

upper ['ʌpər] **1** *a* supérieur; **u. class** aristocratie *f*; **to have the u. hand** avoir le dessus. **2** *n* (*of shoe*) dessus *m*. ● **u.-'class** *a* aristocratique. ● **uppermost** *a* le plus haut; (*on top*) en dessus; (*in importance*) de la plus haute importance.

uproar ['ʌprɔːr] *n* vacarme *m*, tapage *m*.

upset [ʌp'set] *vt* (*pt & pp* **upset**, *pres p* **upsetting**) (*knock over, spill*) renverser; (*plans, stomach, routine etc*) déranger; **to u. s.o.** (*make sad*) faire de la peine à qn; (*offend*) vexer qn; (*aggravate*) exaspérer qn ▮ *a* peiné; vexé; exaspéré; (*stomach*) dérangé ▮ ['ʌpset] *n* (*in plans etc*) dérangement *m* (**in** de); (*grief*) peine *f*; **to have a stomach u.** avoir l'estomac dérangé.

upshot ['ʌpʃɒt] *n* résultat *m*.

urban ['ɜːbən] *a* urbain.

urchin ['ɜːtʃɪn] *n* polisson, -onne *mf*.

urge [ɜːdʒ] *vt* **to u. s.o. to do** conseiller vivement à qn de faire; **to u. on** (*person, team*) encourager ▮ *n* forte envie *f*.

urgency ['ɜːdʒənsɪ] *n* urgence *f*; (*of tone, request*) insistance *f*. ● **urgent** *a* urgent; (*tone*) insistant. ● **urgently** *adv* d'urgence.

urinal [jʊ'raɪn(ə)l] *n* urinoir *m*.

urine ['jʊ(ə)rɪn] *n* urine *f*. ● **urinate** *vi* uriner.

urn [ɜːn] *n* urne *f*; (*for coffee or tea*) fontaine *f*.

us [əs, *stressed* ʌs] *pron* nous; **(to) us** nous; **she sees us** elle nous voit; **he gives (to) us** il nous donne; **with us** avec nous; **all of us** nous tous; **let's** *or* **let us eat!** mangeons!

US [juː'es] *abbr* = **United States.**

USA [juːes'eɪ] *abbr* = **United States of America.**

usage ['juːsɪdʒ] *n* (*custom*) & *Ling* usage *m*.

use [juːs] *n* emploi *m*, usage *m*; (*usefulness*) utilité *f*; **to have the u. of** avoir l'usage de; **to make u. of** se servir de; **not in u.** hors d'usage; **ready for u.** prêt à l'emploi; **to be of u.** être utile; **it's no u. crying/***etc* ça ne sert à rien de pleurer/*etc*; **what's the u. of worrying/***etc*? à quoi bon s'inquiéter/*etc*?, à quoi ça sert de s'inquiéter/*etc*?; **he's no u.** il est nul.
▮ [juːz] *vt* se servir de, utiliser, employer (**as** comme; **to do, for doing** pour faire); **it's**

used to do *or* **for doing** ça sert à faire; **it's used as** ça sert de; **to u. (up)** (*fuel*) consommer; (*supplies*) épuiser; (*money*) dépenser.

used [ju:zd] **1** *a* (*second-hand*) d'occasion. **2** [ju:st] *v aux* **I u. to sing/***etc* avant, je chantais/*etc* ▌*a* **u. to sth/to doing** habitué à qch/à faire; **to get u. to** s'habituer à.

useful ['ju:sfəl] *a* utile (**to** à); **to come in u.** être utile; **to make oneself u.** se rendre utile. ● **usefulness** *n* utilité *f*. ● **useless** *a* inutile; (*person*) nul.

user ['ju:zər] *n* (*of road etc*) usager *m*; (*of machine, computer, dictionary*) utilisateur, -trice *mf*. ● **u.-friendly** *a Comptr* convivial.

usher ['ʌʃər] *n* (*in church or theatre*) placeur *m* ▌*vt* **to u. in** faire entrer (*qn*); (*period etc*) *Fig* inaugurer. ● **ushe'rette** *n Cin* ouvreuse *f*.

usual ['ju:ʒʊəl] *a* habituel, normal; **as u.** comme d'habitude ▌*n* **the u.** (*food, excuse etc*) *Fam* la même chose que d'habitude. ● **—ly** *adv* d'habitude.

usurp [ju:'zɜ:p] *vt* usurper.

utensil [ju:'tens(ə)l] *n* ustensile *m*.

utility [ju:'tɪlətɪ] *n* **(public) u.** service *m* public.

utilize ['ju:tɪlaɪz] *vt* utiliser.

utmost ['ʌtməʊst] *a* **the u. ease/***etc* la plus grande facilité/*etc*; **the u. danger/limit/***etc* un danger/une limite/*etc* extrême ▌*n* **to do one's u.** faire tout son possible (**to do** pour faire).

utter ['ʌtər] **1** *a* complet, total; (*folly*) pur; (*idiot*) parfait; **it's u. nonsense** c'est complètement absurde. **2** *vt* (*a cry, sigh*) pousser; (*a word*) dire; (*a threat*) proférer. ● **utterly** *adv* complètement.

U-turn ['ju:tɜ:n] *n Aut* demi-tour *m*; *Fig* volte-face *f inv*.

V

V, v [viː] *n* V, v *m*. ●**V.-neck** *n* (*sweater etc*) col *m* en V.
vacant ['veɪkənt] *a* (*room, seat*) libre; (*post*) vacant; (*look*) vague. ●**vacancy** *n* (*post*) poste *m* vacant; (*room*) chambre *f* libre; **'no vacancies'** (*in hotel*) 'complet'.
vacate [və'keɪt, *Am* 'veɪkeɪt] *vt* quitter.
vacation [veɪ'keɪʃ(ə)n] *n Am* vacances *fpl*; **on v.** en vacances. ●**—er** *n Am* vacancier, -ière *mf*.
vaccinate ['væksɪneɪt] *vt* vacciner. ●**vaccination** [-'neɪʃ(ə)n] *n* vaccination *f*. ●**vaccine** [-iːn] *n* vaccin *m*.
vacuum ['vækjʊ(ə)m] *n* vide *m*; **v. cleaner** aspirateur *m*; **v. flask** thermos® *m or f inv* ‖ *vt* (*room*) passer l'aspirateur dans; (*carpet*) passer l'aspirateur sur. ●**v.-packed** *a* emballé sous vide.
vagabond ['vægəbɒnd] *n* vagabond, -onde *mf*.
vagina [və'dʒaɪnə] *n* vagin *m*.
vagrant ['veɪgrənt] *n Jur* vagabond, -onde *mf*.
vague [veɪg] *a* (**-er, -est**) vague; (*outline, memory*) flou; **he was v. (about it)** il est resté vague. ●**—ly** *adv* vaguement.
vain [veɪn] *a* (**-er, -est**) **1** (*attempt, hope*) vain; **in v.** en vain; **her efforts were in v.** ses efforts ont été inutiles. **2** (*conceited*) vaniteux. ●**—ly** *adv* (*in vain*) vainement.
valentine ['væləntaɪn] *n* (*card*) carte *f* de la Saint-Valentin.
valiant ['væljənt] *a* courageux. ●**valour** (*Am* **valor**) *n* bravoure *f*.
valid ['vælɪd] *a* (*ticket, excuse etc*) valable. ●**validate** *vt* valider. ●**va'lidity** *n* validité *f*.
valley ['vælɪ] *n* vallée *f*.
valuable ['væljʊəb(ə)l] *a* (*object*) de (grande) valeur; (*help, time etc*) précieux ‖ *npl* **valuables** objets *mpl* de valeur.
value ['væljuː] *n* valeur *f*; **it's good v. (for money)** ça a un bon rapport qualité/prix; **v. added tax** taxe *f* à la valeur ajoutée ‖ *vt* (*appreciate*) attacher de la valeur à; (*assess*) évaluer. ●**valuation** [-'eɪʃ(ə)n] *n* (*by expert*) expertise *f*.
valve [vælv] *n* (*of machine*) soupape *f*; (*in radio*) lampe *f*; (*of tyre, Am tire*) valve *f*; (*of heart*) valvule *f*.
vampire ['væmpaɪər] *n* vampire *m*.
van [væn] *n* (*small*) camionnette *f*, fourgonnette *f*; (*large*) camion *m*; *Rail* fourgon *m*.
vandal ['vænd(ə)l] *n* vandale *mf*. ●**vandalism** *n* vandalisme *m*. ●**vandalize** *vt* saccager.
vanguard ['vængɑːd] *n* **in the v. of** (*progress etc*) à l'avant-garde de.
vanilla [və'nɪlə] *n* vanille *f* ‖ *a* (*ice cream*) à la vanille.
vanish ['vænɪʃ] *vi* disparaître.
vanity ['vænɪtɪ] *n* vanité *f*.
vantage point ['vɑːntɪdʒpɔɪnt] *n* (*place, point of view*) (bon) point *m* de vue.
vapour ['veɪpər] (*Am* **vapor**) *n* vapeur *f*; (*on glass*) buée *f*.
variable ['veərɪəb(ə)l] *a* variable. ●**variation** [-'eɪʃ(ə)n] *n* variation *f*.
varicose ['værɪkəʊs] *a* **v. veins** varices *fpl*.
variety [və'raɪətɪ] *n* **1** (*diversity*) variété *f*; **a v. of reasons/***etc* (*many*) diverses raisons/*etc*; **a v. of** (*articles*) *Com* toute une gamme de. **2 v. show** *Th* spectacle *m* de variétés.
various ['veərɪəs] *a* divers. ●**—ly** *adv* diversement.
varnish ['vɑːnɪʃ] *vt* vernir ‖ *n* vernis *m*.
vary ['veərɪ] *vti* varier (**from** de). ●**varied** *a* varié.
vase [vɑːz, *Am* veɪs] *n* vase *m*.
Vaseline® ['væsəliːn] *n* vaseline *f*.
vast [vɑːst] *a* vaste. ●**—ly** *adv* (*very*) infiniment.
vat [væt] *n* cuve *f*.
VAT [viːeɪ'tiː, væt] *n abbr* (*value added tax*) TVA *f*.
Vatican ['vætɪkən] *n* **the V.** le Vatican.
vault [vɔːlt] **1** *n* (*in bank*) salle *f* des coffres; (*tomb*) caveau *m*; (*roof*) voûte *f*. **2** *vti* (*jump*) sauter.
VCR [viːsiː'ɑːr] *n abbr* (*video cassette recorder*) magnétoscope *m*.
VD [viː'diː] *n abbr* (*venereal disease*) MST *f*.
VDU [viːdiː'juː] *n abbr* (*visual display unit*) moniteur *m*.
veal [viːl] *n* (*meat*) veau *m*.
veer [vɪər] *vi* (*of car*) virer; (*of wind*) tourner; **to v. off the road** quitter la route.
vegetable ['vedʒtəb(ə)l] *n* légume *m*; **v. garden** (jardin *m*) potager *m*; **v. oil** huile *f* végétale. ●**vege'tarian** *a* & *n* végétarien, -ienne (*mf*). ●**vegetation** [-'teɪʃ(ə)n] *n* végétation *f*.

vehicle ['viːɪk(ə)l] *n* véhicule *m*; **heavy goods v.** poids *m* lourd; **off-road v.** véhicule *m* tout terrain.
veil [veɪl] *n* (*covering*) & *Fig* voile *m*. ●**veiled** *a* (*criticism, woman etc*) voilé.
vein [veɪn] *n* (*in body or rock*) veine *f*; (*in leaf*) nervure *f*; (*mood*) *Fig* esprit *m*.
Velcro® [velkrəʊ] *n* Velcro® *m*.
velvet ['velvɪt] *n* velours *m* ‖ *a* de velours.
vending machine ['vendɪŋməʃiːn] *n* distributeur *m* automatique.
vendor ['vendər] *n* vendeur, -euse *mf*.
veneer [və'nɪər] *n* (*wood*) placage *m*; (*appearance*) *Fig* vernis *m*.
venerable ['ven(ə)rəb(ə)l] *a* vénérable.
venetian [və'niːʃ(ə)n] *a* **v. blind** store *m* vénitien.
vengeance ['vendʒəns] *n* vengeance *f*; **with a v.** (*to work, study etc*) furieusement; (*to rain, catch up etc*) pour de bon.
venison ['venɪs(ə)n] *n* venaison *f*.
venom ['venəm] *n* (*poison*) venin *m*.
vent [vent] **1** *n* (*hole*) orifice *m*; (*for air*) bouche *f* d'aération. **2** *n* **to give v. to** (*feeling*) donner libre cours à ‖ *vt* (*one's anger*) décharger (**on** sur).
ventilate ['ventɪleɪt] *vt* ventiler. ●**ventilation** [-'leɪʃ(ə)n] *n* (*in room*) aération *f*. ●**ventilator** *n* (*in wall etc*) ventilateur *m*.
ventriloquist [ven'trɪləkwɪst] *n* ventriloque *mf*.
venture ['ventʃər] *n* entreprise *f* (risquée); **my v. into** mon incursion *f* dans ‖ *vt* (*opinion*) hasarder; **to v. to do** oser faire ‖ *vi* s'aventurer, se risquer (**into** dans).
venue ['venjuː] *n* lieu *m* de rencontre.
veranda(h) [və'rændə] *n* véranda *f*.
verb [vɜːb] *n* verbe *m*. ●**verbal** *a* (*skill etc*) verbal.
verdict ['vɜːdɪkt] *n* verdict *m*.
verge [vɜːdʒ] *n* (*of road*) accotement *m*; **on the v. of** *Fig* (*ruin, tears*) au bord de; **on the v. of doing** sur le point de faire ‖ *vi* **to v. on** friser; (*of colour*) tirer sur.
verify ['verɪfaɪ] *vt* vérifier; (*passport etc*) contrôler.
vermin ['vɜːmɪn] *n* (*animals*) animaux *mpl* nuisibles; (*insects, people*) vermine *f*.
versatile ['vɜːsətaɪl, *Am* 'vɜːsət(ə)l] *a* (*mind*) souple; (*tool, computer*) polyvalent; **he's v.** il est polyvalent.
verse [vɜːs] *n* (*part of song*) couplet *m*; (*poetry*) poésie *f*; (*of Bible*) verset *m*; **in v.** en vers.
versed [vɜːst] *a* **(well) v. in** versé dans.
version ['vɜːʃ(ə)n, *Am* 'vɜːʒ(ə)n] *n* version *f*.
versus ['vɜːsəs] *prep* contre.
vertical ['vɜːtɪk(ə)l] *a* vertical.
very ['verɪ] **1** *adv* très; **I'm v. hot** j'ai très chaud; **v. much** beaucoup; **the v. first** le tout premier; **at the v. least** tout au moins; **at the v. latest** au plus tard. **2** *a* (*actual*) même; **his v. brother** son frère même; **to the v. end** jusqu'au bout.
vessel ['ves(ə)l] *n* *Nau Anat Bot* vaisseau *m*; (*receptacle*) récipient *m*.
vest [vest] *n* tricot *m* de corps; (*woman's*) chemise *f* (américaine); (*waistcoat*) *Am* gilet *m*.
vested ['vestɪd] *a* **v. interests** *Pol etc* intérêt(s) *m(pl)*; **she's got a v. interest in** *Fig* elle est directement intéressée dans.
vestige ['vestɪdʒ] *n* vestige *m*; **not a v. of truth** pas un grain de vérité.
vet [vet] **1** *n* vétérinaire *mf*. **2** *vt* (**-tt-**) (*document*) examiner de près; (*candidate*) se renseigner à fond sur. ●**veteri'narian** *n* *Am* vétérinaire *mf*. ●**veterinary** *a* **v. surgeon** vétérinaire *mf*.
veteran ['vet(ə)rən] *n* vétéran *m*; **(war) v.** ancien combattant *m*.
veto ['viːtəʊ] *n* (*pl* **-oes**) (*refusal*) veto *m inv*; (*power*) droit *m* de veto ‖ *vt* mettre son veto à.
vex [veks] *vt* contrarier; **vexed question** question *f* controversée.
VHF [viːeɪtʃ'ef] *n abbr* (*very high frequency*) **on VHF** sur modulation de fréquence.
via ['vaɪə, *Am* 'vɪə] *prep* par, via.
viable ['vaɪəb(ə)l] *a* (*plan etc*) viable.
viaduct ['vaɪədʌkt] *n* viaduc *m*.
vibrate [vaɪ'breɪt] *vi* vibrer. ●**vibration** [-'breɪʃ(ə)n] *n* vibration *f*.
vicar ['vɪkər] *n* (*in Church of England*) pasteur *m*. ●**vicarage** *n* presbytère *m*.
vicarious [vɪ'keərɪəs] *a* (*emotion*) ressenti indirectement.
vice [vaɪs] *n* **1** (*depravity, fault*) vice *m*; **v. squad** brigade *f* des mœurs. **2** (*tool*) étau *m*.
vice- [vaɪs] *pref* vice-.
vice versa [vaɪs(ɪ)'vɜːsə] *adv* vice versa.
vicinity [və'sɪnɪtɪ] *n* environs *mpl*; **in the v. of** (*place, amount*) aux environs de.
vicious ['vɪʃəs] *a* (*spiteful*) méchant; (*violent*) brutal; **v. circle** cercle *m* vicieux. ●**—ly** *adv* méchamment; brutalement.
victim ['vɪktɪm] *n* victime *f*; **to be the v. of** être victime de. ●**victimize** *vt* persécuter.
Victorian [vɪk'tɔːrɪən] *a* victorien.
victory ['vɪktərɪ] *n* victoire *f*. ●**victor** *n* vainqueur *m*. ●**vic'torious** *a* victorieux.
video ['vɪdɪəʊ] *n* (*cassette*) cassette *f*; **v. cassette** vidéocassette *f*; **v. (recorder)** mag-

nétoscope *m*; **on v.** sur cassette; **to make a v. of** faire une cassette de ‖ *a* (*game, camera etc*) vidéo *inv* ‖ *vt* (*event*) faire une (vidéo)cassette de. ● **videotape** *n* bande *f* vidéo.

vie [vaɪ] *vi* (*pres p* **vying**) rivaliser (**with** avec).

Vienna [vɪ'enə] *n* Vienne *m or f*.

Vietnam [vjet'næm, *Am* -'nɑːm] *n* Viêt Nam *m*. ● **Vietna'mese** *a* & *n* vietnamien, -ienne (*mf*).

view [vjuː] *n* vue *f*; (*opinion*) opinion *f*, avis *m*; **to come into v.** apparaître; **in my v.** à mon avis; **on v.** (*exhibit*) exposé; **in v. of** compte tenu de; **with a v. to doing** afin de faire ‖ *vt* (*regard*) considérer; (*house*) visiter. ● **—er** *n* **1** *TV* téléspectateur, -trice *mf*. **2** (*for slides*) visionneuse *f*. ● **viewpoint** *n* point *m* de vue.

vigilant ['vɪdʒɪlənt] *a* vigilant. ● **vigilance** *n* vigilance *f*.

vigour ['vɪgər] (*Am* **vigor**) *n* vigueur *f*. ● **vigorous** *a* (*person, speech etc*) vigoureux.

vile [vaɪl] *a* (**-er, -est**) (*base*) infâme; (*unpleasant*) abominable.

villa ['vɪlə] *n* grande maison *f*; (*holiday or Am vacation home*) maison *f* de vacances.

village ['vɪlɪdʒ] *n* village *m*. ● **villager** *n* villageois, -oise *mf*.

villain ['vɪlən] *n* canaille *f*; (*in story or play*) méchant *m*.

vindicate ['vɪndɪkeɪt] *vt* justifier.

vindictive [vɪn'dɪktɪv] *a* vindicatif, rancunier.

vine [vaɪn] *n* (*grapevine*) vigne *f*; **v. grower** viticulteur *m*. ● **vineyard** ['vɪnjəd] *n* vignoble *m*.

vinegar ['vɪnɪgər] *n* vinaigre *m*.

vintage ['vɪntɪdʒ] **1** *n* (*year*) année *f*. **2** *a* (*wine*) de grand cru; (*car*) d'époque; (*film*) classique; (*good*) *Fig* bon.

vinyl ['vaɪn(ə)l] *n* vinyle *m*.

violate ['vaɪəleɪt] *vt* violer.

violence ['vaɪələns] *n* violence *f*. ● **violent** *a* violent; **a v. dislike** une aversion vive (**of** pour). ● **violently** *adv* violemment.

violet ['vaɪələt] **1** *a* & *n* (*colour*) violet (*m*). **2** *n* (*plant*) violette *f*.

violin [vaɪə'lɪn] *n* violon *m*. ● **violinist** *n* violoniste *mf*.

VIP [viːaɪ'piː] *n abbr* (*very important person*) personnage *m* de marque.

viper ['vaɪpər] *n* vipère *f*.

virgin ['vɜːdʒɪn] *n* vierge *f*; **to be a v.** (*of woman, man*) être vierge.

Virgo ['vɜːgəʊ] *n* (*sign*) la Vierge.

virile ['vɪraɪl, *Am* 'vɪrəl] *a* viril.

virtual ['vɜːtʃʊəl] *a* **1 it was a v. failure/***etc* ce fut en fait un échec/*etc*. **2** *Phys Comptr* virtuel. ● **—ly** *adv* (*in fact*) en fait; (*almost*) pratiquement.

virtue ['vɜːtʃuː] *n* **1** (*goodness*) vertu *f*; (*advantage*) mérite *m*. **2 by v. of** en raison de. ● **virtuous** *a* vertueux.

virtuoso, *pl* **-si** [vɜːtʃʊ'əʊsəʊ, -siː] *n* virtuose *mf*.

virulent ['vɪrʊlənt] *a* virulent.

virus ['vaɪ(ə)rəs] *n Med Comptr* virus *m*.

visa ['viːzə] *n* visa *m*.

Visa® ['viːzə] *n* **V. (card)** carte *f* Visa®.

viscount ['vaɪkaʊnt] *n* vicomte *m*. ● **viscountess** *n* vicomtesse *f*.

vise [vaɪs] *n* (*tool*) *Am* étau *m*.

visible ['vɪzəb(ə)l] *a* visible. ● **visi'bility** *n* visibilité *f*.

vision ['vɪʒ(ə)n] *n* (*eyesight, foresight etc*) vision *f*; **a woman of v.** *Fig* une femme qui voit loin.

visit ['vɪzɪt] *n* visite *f*; (*stay*) séjour *m* ‖ *vt* (*place*) visiter; **to visit s.o.** rendre visite à qn; (*stay with*) faire un séjour chez qn ‖ *vi* être en visite (*Am* **with** chez). ● **—ing** *a* (*card, hours*) de visite. ● **visitor** *n* visiteur, -euse *mf*; (*guest*) invité, -ée *mf*; (*in hotel*) client, -ente *mf*.

visor ['vaɪzər] *n* (*of helmet*) visière *f*.

vista ['vɪstə] *n* (*view of place*) vue *f*.

visual ['vɪʒʊəl] *a* visuel; **v. aid** (*in teaching*) support *m* visuel. ● **visualize** *vt* (*imagine*) se représenter.

vital ['vaɪt(ə)l] *a* essentiel; **it's v. that** il est essentiel que (+ *sub*); **of v. importance** d'importance capitale; **v. statistics** (*of woman*) mensurations *fpl*. ● **—ly** *adv* (*important*) extrêmement.

vitality [vaɪ'tælɪtɪ] *n* vitalité *f*.

vitamin ['vɪtəmɪn, *Am* 'vaɪtəmɪn] *n* vitamine *f*.

vivacious [vɪ'veɪʃəs] *a* plein d'entrain.

vivid ['vɪvɪd] *a* (*imagination*) vif; (*description*) vivant. ● **—ly** *adv* (*to describe*) de façon vivante; **to remember sth v.** avoir un vif souvenir de qch.

V-neck [viː'nek] *n* (*sweater etc*) col *m* en V.

vocabulary [və'kæbjʊlərɪ, *Am* -erɪ] *n* vocabulaire *m*.

vocal ['vəʊk(ə)l] *a* (*cords, music*) vocal; (*outspoken, noisy*) qui se fait entendre.

vocation [vəʊ'keɪʃ(ə)n] *n* vocation *f*. ● **vocational** *a* professionnel.

vociferous [və'sɪf(ə)rəs] *a* bruyant.

vodka ['vɒdkə] *n* vodka *f*.

vogue [vəʊg] *n* vogue *f*; **in v.** en vogue.

voice [vɔɪs] *n* voix *f*; **at the top of one's v.** à

tue-tête ▮ *vt* (*opinion etc*) formuler.

void [vɔɪd] **1** *n* vide *m*. **2** *a* (*not valid*) *Jur* nul.

volatile ['vɒlətaɪl, *Am* 'vɒlət(ə)l] *a* (*person*) versatile; (*situation*) explosif.

volcano [vɒl'keɪnəʊ] *n* (*pl* **-oes**) volcan *m*.

volition [və'lɪʃ(ə)n] *n* **of one's own v.** de son propre gré.

volley ['vɒlɪ] *n* (*gunfire*) salve *f*; (*of insults*) bordée *f*; *Tennis* volée *f*. ● **volleyball** *n Sp* volley(-ball) *m*.

volt [vəʊlt] *n El* volt *m*. ● **voltage** *n* voltage *m*.

volume ['vɒlju:m] *n* (*book, capacity, loudness*) volume *m*.

voluntary ['vɒlənt(ə)rɪ, *Am* -'terɪ] *a* volontaire; (*unpaid*) bénévole. ● **voluntarily** *adv* volontairement; bénévolement.

volunteer [vɒlən'tɪər] *n* volontaire *mf* ▮ *vi* se proposer (**for sth** pour qch, **to do** pour faire) ▮ *vt* (*information*) offrir (spontanément).

vomit ['vɒmɪt] *vti* vomir ▮ *n* (*matter*) vomi *m*.

voracious [və'reɪʃəs] *a* (*appetite, reader etc*) vorace.

vot/e [vəʊt] *n* vote *m*; (*right to vote*) droit *m* de vote; **to win votes** gagner des voix; **v. of no confidence** *Pol* motion *f* de censure; **v. of thanks** discours *m* de remerciement ▮ *vt* (*funds etc*) voter; **to be voted president** (*elected*) être élu président ▮ *vi* voter; **to v. Labour** voter travailliste. ● **—ing** *n* (*polling*) scrutin *m*. ● **voter** *n Pol* électeur, -trice *mf*.

vouch [vaʊtʃ] *vi* **to v. for** répondre de.

voucher ['vaʊtʃər] *n* (*for meals, gift etc*) chèque *m*; (*for price reduction*) bon *m* de réduction.

vow [vaʊ] *n* vœu *m* ▮ *vt* (*obedience etc*) jurer (**to** à); **to v. to do** jurer de faire.

vowel ['vaʊəl] *n* voyelle *f*.

voyage ['vɔɪɪdʒ] *n* voyage *m* (par mer).

vulgar ['vʌlgər] *a* vulgaire.

vulnerable ['vʌln(ə)rəb(ə)l] *a* vulnérable.

vulture ['vʌltʃər] *n* vautour *m*.

W

W, w ['dʌb(ə)ljuː] *n* W, w *m*.

wacky ['wækɪ] *a* **(-ier, -iest)** *Am Fam* farfelu.

wad [wɒd] *n* (*of banknotes, papers*) liasse *f*; (*of cotton wool, Am absorbent cotton*) tampon *m*.

waddle ['wɒd(ə)l] *vi* se dandiner.

wade [weɪd] *vi* **to w. through** (*mud, water etc*) patauger dans; (*book etc*) *Fig* avancer péniblement dans; **wading pool** *Am* (*inflatable*) piscine *f* gonflable; (*purpose-built*) pataugeoire *f*.

wafer ['weɪfər] *n* (*biscuit*) gaufrette *f*.

waffle ['wɒf(ə)l] **1** *n* (*talk*) *Fam* blabla *m* ▮ *vi Fam* parler pour ne rien dire, blablater. **2** *n* (*cake*) gaufre *f*.

wag [wæg] *vt* **(-gg-)** (*tail, finger*) remuer ▮ *vi* (*of tail*) remuer.

wage [weɪdʒ] **1** *n* **wage(s)** salaire *m*, paie *f*; **w. claim** revendication *f* salariale; **w. earner** salarié, -ée *mf*; (*breadwinner*) soutien *m* de famille; **w. freeze** blocage *m* des salaires; **w. increase** augmentation *f* de salaire. **2** *vt* (*campaign*) mener; **to w. war** faire la guerre **(on** à).

wager ['weɪdʒər] *n* pari *m*.

waggle ['wæg(ə)l] *vti* remuer.

wag(g)on ['wægən] *n Rail* wagon *m* (de marchandises); (*horse-drawn*) chariot *m*.

wail [weɪl] *vi* (*cry out, complain*) gémir; (*of siren*) hurler.

waist [weɪst] *n* taille *f*; **stripped to the w.** torse nu. ● **waistcoat** ['weɪskəʊt] *n* gilet *m*. ● **waistline** *n* taille *f*.

wait [weɪt] **1** *n* attente *f*; **to lie in w. (for)** guetter ▮ *vi* attendre; **to w. for s.o./sth** attendre qn/qch; **w. until I've gone, w. for me to go** attends que je sois parti; **to keep s.o. waiting** faire attendre qn; **I can't w. to do it** j'ai hâte de le faire.
2 *vi* (*serve*) **to w. at table** servir à table; **to w. on s.o.** servir qn. ● **waiting** *n* attente *f*; **'no w.'** (*street sign*) 'arrêt interdit' ▮ *a* **w. list/room** liste *f*/salle *f* d'attente.

wait around *vi* attendre **to wait behind** *vi* rester **to wait up** *vi* veiller; **to w. up for s.o.** attendre le retour de qn avant de se coucher.

waiter ['weɪtər] *n* garçon *m* (de café), serveur *m*; **w.!** garçon! ● **waitress** *n* serveuse *f*; **w.!** mademoiselle!

waive [weɪv] *vt* renoncer à; **to w. a requirement (for s.o.)** dispenser qn d'une condition requise.

wake[1] [weɪk] *vi* (*pt* **woke,** *pp* **woken) to w. (up)** se réveiller; **to w. up to** (*fact etc*) prendre conscience de ▮ *vt* **to w. (up)** réveiller. ● **waken** *vt Lit* éveiller ▮ *vi Lit* s'éveiller.

wake[2] [weɪk] *n* (*of ship*) & *Fig* sillage *m*; **in the w. of** *Fig* dans le sillage de.

Wales [weɪlz] *n* pays *m* de Galles; **the Prince of W.** le prince de Galles.

walk [wɔːk] *n* promenade *f*; (*shorter*) (petit) tour *m*; (*way of walking*) démarche *f*; (*path*) allée *f*, chemin *m*; **to go for a w., take a w.** faire une promenade; (*shorter*) faire un (petit) tour; **to take for a w.** (*child*) emmener se promener; (*baby, dog*) promener; **five minutes' w. (away)** à cinq minutes à pied; **from all walks of life** *Fig* de toutes conditions sociales.
▮ *vi* marcher; (*stroll*) se promener; (*go on foot*) aller à pied; **w.!** (*don't run*) ne cours pas!
▮ *vt* (*distance*) faire à pied; (*streets*) (par)courir; (*take for a walk*) promener (*bébé, chien*); **to w. s.o. to** (*station etc*) accompagner qn à.

walk away *vi* s'éloigner **(from** de); **to w. away with** (*steal*) *Fam* faucher **to walk in** *vi* entrer; **to w. into** (*tree etc*) rentrer dans **to walk off** *vi* = **walk away to walk out** *vi* (*leave*) partir; **to w. out on s.o.** abandonner qn **to walk over** *vi* **to w. over to** (*go up to*) s'approcher de.

walker ['wɔːkər] *n* marcheur, -euse *mf*; (*for pleasure*) promeneur, -euse *mf*. ● **walking stick** *n* canne *f*. ● **walkout** *n* (*strike*) grève *f* surprise. ● **walkover** *n* (*in contest etc*) victoire *f* facile. ● **walkway** *n* **moving w.** trottoir *m* roulant.

walkie-talkie [wɔːkɪ'tɔːkɪ] *n* talkie-walkie *m*.

Walkman® ['wɔːkmən] *n* (*pl* **Walkmans**) baladeur *m*.

wall [wɔːl] *n* mur *m*; (*of cabin, tunnel, stomach*) paroi *f* ▮ *a* (*map etc*) mural. ● **walled** *a* **w. city** ville *f* fortifiée. ● **wallflower** *n Bot* giroflée *f*. ● **wallpaper** *n* papier *m* peint ▮ *vt* tapisser. ● **wall-to-wall 'carpet(ing)** *n* moquette *f*.

wallet ['wɒlɪt] *n* portefeuille *m*.
wallop ['wɒləp] *vt* (*hit*) *Fam* taper sur ‖ *n Fam* grand coup *m*.
wallow ['wɒləʊ] *vi* **to w. in** (*mud, vice etc*) se vautrer dans.
wally ['wɒlɪ] *n* (*idiot*) *Fam* andouille *f*.
walnut ['wɔːlnʌt] *n* (*nut*) noix *f*; (*tree, wood*) noyer *m*.
walrus ['wɔːlrəs] *n* (*animal*) morse *m*.
waltz [wɔːls, *Am* wɒlts] *n* valse *f* ‖ *vi* valser.
wand [wɒnd] *n* baguette *f* (magique).
wander ['wɒndər] *vi* (*of thoughts*) vagabonder; **to w. (about** *or* **around)** (*roam*) errer; (*stroll*) flâner; **to w. from** (*path, subject*) s'écarter de; **to w. off** s'éloigner ‖ *vt* **to w. the streets** errer dans les rues. •**—ing** *a* (*life, tribe*) vagabond, nomade.
wane [weɪn] *vi* (*of moon, fame etc*) décroître ‖ *n* **to be on the w.** décroître.
wangle ['wæŋg(ə)l] *vt* (*obtain*) *Fam* se débrouiller pour obtenir.
want [wɒnt] *vt* vouloir (**to do** faire); (*ask for*) demander (*qn*); (*need*) avoir besoin de; **I w. him to go** je veux qu'il parte; **you're wanted** on vous demande ‖ *vi* **not to w. for** (*not lack*) ne pas manquer de ‖ *n* (*lack*) manque *m* (**of** de); **for w. of** par manque de; **for w. of money/time** faute d'argent/de temps; **for w. of anything better** faute de mieux. •**wanted** *a* (*criminal*) recherché par la police. •**wanting** *a* (*inadequate*) insuffisant.
wanton ['wɒntən] *a* (*gratuitous*) gratuit; (*immoral*) *Old-fashioned* impudique.
war [wɔːr] *n* guerre *f*; **at w.** en guerre (**with** avec); **to declare w.** déclarer la guerre (**on** à); **w. memorial** monument *m* aux morts.
ward[1] [wɔːd] *n* **1** (*in hospital*) salle *f*. **2** (*child*) *Jur* pupille *mf*. **3** (*electoral division*) circonscription *f* électorale.
ward[2] [wɔːd] *vt* **to w. off** (*blow, anger*) détourner; (*danger*) éviter.
warden ['wɔːd(ə)n] *n* (*of institution, Am of prison*) directeur, -trice *mf*; **(traffic) w.** contractuel, -elle *mf*.
warder ['wɔːdər] *n* gardien *m* (de prison).
wardrobe ['wɔːdrəʊb] *n* (*cupboard, Am closet*) penderie *f*; (*clothes*) garde-robe *f*.
warehouse, *pl* **-ses** ['weəhaʊs, -zɪz] *n* entrepôt *m*.
wares [weəz] *npl* marchandises *fpl*.
warfare ['wɔːfeər] *n* guerre *f*. •**warhead** *n* (*of missile*) ogive *f*.
warily ['weərɪlɪ] *adv* avec précaution.
warm [wɔːm] *a* (**-er, -est**) chaud; (*welcome, thanks etc*) *Fig* chaleureux; **to be** *or* **feel w.** avoir chaud; **it's (nice and) w.** (*of weather*) il fait (agréablement) chaud; **to get w.** (*of person, room*) se réchauffer ‖ *vt* **to w. (up)** (*person, food etc*) réchauffer ‖ *vi* **to w. up** (*of person, room, engine*) se réchauffer; (*of food, water*) chauffer. •**warmly** *adv* (*to wrap up etc*) chaudement; (*to welcome etc*) *Fig* chaleureusement. •**warmth** *n* chaleur *f*.
warn [wɔːn] *vt* avertir, prévenir (**that** que); **to w. s.o. against sth** mettre qn en garde contre qch; **to w. s.o. against doing** conseiller à qn de ne pas faire. •**—ing** *n* avertissement *m*; (*advance notice*) (pré)avis *m*; *Met* avis *m*; (*device*) alarme *f*; **without w.** sans prévenir; **a note** *or* **word of w.** une mise en garde; **w. light** (*on appliance*) voyant *m* lumineux; **(hazard) w. lights** *Aut* feux *mpl* de détresse.
warp [wɔːp] *vt* (*wood etc*) voiler; (*judgment*) *Fig* pervertir; **a warped mind** un esprit tordu ‖ *vi* se voiler.
warpath ['wɔːpɑːθ] *n* **to be on the w.** (*angry*) *Fam* être d'humeur massacrante.
warrant ['wɒrənt] *n Jur* mandat *m*; **a w. for your arrest** un mandat d'arrêt contre vous; **search w.** mandat *m* de perquisition. •**warranty** *n Com* garantie *f*.
warren ['wɒrən] *n* **(rabbit) w.** garenne *f*.
warring ['wɔːrɪŋ] *a* (*countries etc*) en guerre.
warrior ['wɒrɪər] *n* guerrier, -ière *mf*.
warship ['wɔːʃɪp] *n* navire *m* de guerre.
wart [wɔːt] *n* verrue *f*.
wartime ['wɔːtaɪm] *n* **in w.** en temps de guerre.
wary ['weərɪ] *a* (**-ier, -iest**) prudent; **to be w. of s.o./sth** se méfier de qn/qch; **to be w. of doing** hésiter beaucoup à faire.
was [wəz, *stressed* wɒz] *see* **be**.
wash [wɒʃ] *n* (*clothes*) lessive *f*; **to have a w.** se laver; **to give sth a w.** laver qch; **to do the w.** faire la lessive ‖ *vt* laver; **to w. one's hands** se laver les mains (*Fig* **of sth** de qch) ‖ *vi* (*have a wash*) se laver. •**washable** *a* lavable. •**washbasin** *n* lavabo *m*. •**washcloth** *n Am* gant *m* de toilette. •**washout** *n* (*event*) *Fam* fiasco *m*. •**washroom** *n Am* toilettes *fpl*.
wash away *vt* (*stain*) faire partir (en lavant) ‖ *vi* (*of stain*) partir (au lavage) **to wash down** *vt* (*vehicle, deck*) laver à grande eau; (*food*) arroser (**with** de) **to wash off** *vti* = **wash away to wash out** *vt* (*bowl*) laver ‖ *vti* = **wash away to wash up** *vt* (*dishes*) laver ‖ *vi* (*do the dishes*) faire la vaisselle; (*have a wash*) *Am* se laver.
washer ['wɒʃər] *n* (*ring*) rondelle *f*, joint *m*.
washing ['wɒʃɪŋ] *n* (*act*) lavage *m*; (*clothes*)

lessive *f*, linge *m*; **to do the w.** faire la lessive; **w. line** corde *f* à linge; **w. machine** machine *f* à laver; **w. powder** lessive *f*. • **w.-'up** *n* vaisselle *f*; **to do the w.-up** faire la vaisselle; **w.-up liquid** produit *m* pour la vaisselle.

wasp [wɒsp] *n* guêpe *f*.

wastage ['weɪstɪdʒ] *n* gaspillage *m*; (*losses*) pertes *fpl*; **some w.** (*of goods*) du déchet.

waste [weɪst] *n* gaspillage *m*; (*of time*) perte *f*; (*rubbish, Am garbage*) déchets *mpl*; **w. disposal unit** broyeur *m* d'ordures; **w. products** déchets *mpl*; **w. ground** (*in town*) terrain *m* vague; **w. land** terres *fpl* incultes; **w. paper** vieux papiers *mpl*; **w. pipe** tuyau *m* d'évacuation ‖ *vt* (*money*, *food etc*) gaspiller; (*time*, *opportunity*) perdre; **to w. one's life** gâcher sa vie ‖ *vi* **to w. away** dépérir. • **wasted** *a* (*effort*) inutile.

wastebin ['weɪstbɪn] *n* (*in kitchen*) poubelle *f*. • **wastepaper basket** *n* corbeille *f* (à papier).

wasteful ['weɪstfəl] *a* (*person*) gaspilleur; (*process*) peu économique.

watch [wɒtʃ] **1** *n* (*small clock*) montre *f*. **2** *n* (*over suspect*, *baby etc*) surveillance *f*; **to keep (a) w. over** surveiller; **to keep w.** faire le guet ‖ *vt* regarder; (*observe*) observer; (*suspect*, *baby etc*) surveiller; (*be careful of*) faire attention à ‖ *vi* regarder; **to w. (out) for sth/s.o.** (*wait for*) guetter qch/qn; **to w. out** (*take care*) faire attention (**for** à); **w. out!** attention!; **to w. over** surveiller.

watchdog ['wɒtʃdɒg] *n* chien *m* de garde. • **watchmaker** *n* horloger, -ère *mf*. • **watchman** *n* (*pl* **-men**) **night w.** veilleur *m* de nuit. • **watchstrap** *n* bracelet *m* de montre.

watchful ['wɒtʃfəl] *a* vigilant.

water ['wɔːtər] *n* eau *f*; **under w.** (*road etc*) inondé; (*to swim*) sous l'eau; **in hot w.** *Fig* dans le pétrin; **w. cannon** lance *f* à eau; **w. ice** sorbet *m*; **w. lily** nénuphar *m*; **w. pistol** pistolet *m* à eau; **w. polo** *Sp* water-polo *m*; **w. skiing** ski *m* nautique; **w. tank** réservoir *m* d'eau.

‖ *vt* (*plant etc*) arroser; **to w. down** (*wine etc*) couper (d'eau); (*text*) édulcorer.

‖ *vi* (*of eyes*) larmoyer; **it makes his mouth w.** ça lui fait venir l'eau à la bouche. • **watering can** *n* arrosoir *m*.

watercolour ['wɔːtəkʌlər] (*Am* **-color**) *n* (*picture*) aquarelle *f*; (*paint*) couleur *f* pour aquarelle. • **watercress** *n* cresson *m* (de fontaine). • **waterfall** *n* chute *f* d'eau. • **waterlogged** *a* délavé. • **watermark** *n* (*in paper*) filigrane *m*. • **watermelon** *n* pastèque *f*. • **waterproof** *a* (*material*) imperméable. • **watershed** *n* (*turning point*) tournant *m* (décisif). • **watertight** *a* (*container*) étanche. • **waterway** *n* voie *f* navigable. • **waterworks** *n* station *f* hydraulique.

watery ['wɔːtərɪ] *a* (*soup*) trop liquide; **w. tea** *or* **coffee** de la lavasse.

watt [wɒt] *n El* watt *m*.

wave [weɪv] *n* (*of sea*) & *Fig* vague *f*; (*in hair*) ondulation *f*; (*sign*) signe *m* (de la main); **medium/short w.** *Rad* ondes *fpl* moyennes/courtes; **long w.** *Rad* grandes ondes, ondes longues ‖ *vi* (*with hand*) faire signe (de la main); (*of flag*) flotter; **to w. to s.o.** (*greet*) saluer qn de la main ‖ *vt* (*arm*, *flag etc*) agiter; **to w. s.o. on** faire signe à qn d'avancer. • **waveband** *n Rad* bande *f* de fréquence. • **wavelength** *n Rad* & *Fig* longueur *f* d'ondes.

waver ['weɪvər] *vi* (*of person etc*) vaciller.

wavy ['weɪvɪ] *a* (**-ier, -iest**) (*line*) onduleux; (*hair*) ondulé.

wax [wæks] **1** *n* cire *f*; (*for ski*) fart *m* ‖ *vt* cirer; (*ski*) farter; (*car*) lustrer ‖ *a* (*candle etc*) de cire; **w. paper** *Culin Am* papier *m* paraffiné. **2** *vi* (*of moon*) croître. • **waxworks** *npl* musée *m* de cire; (*dummies*) moulages *mpl* de cire.

way[1] [weɪ] *n* (*path*, *road*) chemin *m* (**to** de); (*direction*) sens *m*, direction *f*; (*distance*) distance *f*; **all the w., the whole w.** (*to talk etc*) pendant tout le chemin; **this w.** par ici; **that w.** par là; **which w.?** par où?; **to lose one's w.** se perdre; **I'm on my w.** j'arrive; (*going*) je pars; **to make one's w. towards** se diriger vers; **the w. there** l'aller *m*; **the w. back** le retour; **the w. in** l'entrée *f*; **the w. out** la sortie; **a w. out of** (*problem*) *Fig* une solution à; **the w. is clear** *Fig* la voie est libre; **on the w.** en route (**to** pour); **by w. of** (*via*) par; **out of the w.** (*isolated*) isolé; **by the w.**... *Fig* à propos...; **to be** *or* **stand in s.o.'s w.** être sur le chemin de qn; **to get out of the w.** s'écarter; **a long w. (away** *or* **off)** très loin; **do it the other w. round** fais le contraire ‖ *adv* (*behind etc*) très loin; **w. ahead** très en avance (**of** sur).

way[2] [weɪ] *n* (*manner*) façon *f*; (*means*) moyen *m*; (*habit*) habitude *f*; (*particular*) égard *m*; **one's ways** (*behaviour*) ses manières *fpl*; **to get one's own w.** obtenir ce qu'on veut; **(in) this w.** de cette façon; **in a w.** dans un certain sens; **w. of life** mode *m* de vie; **no w.!** *Fam* pas question!

wayside ['weɪsaɪd] *n* **by the w.** au bord le la route.

wayward ['weɪwəd] *a* rebelle, capricieux.

WC [dʌb(ə)ljuː'siː] *n* w-c *mpl*.

we [wi:] *pron* nous; **we go** nous allons; **we teachers** nous autres professeurs; **we never know** (*indefinite*) on ne sait jamais.

weak [wi:k] *a* (**-er, -est**) faible; (*tea, coffee*) léger; (*health, stomach*) fragile. ● **w.-'willed** *a* faible. ● **weaken** *vt* affaiblir ‖ *vi* faiblir. ● **weakling** *n* (*in body*) mauviette *f*; (*in character*) faible *mf*. ● **weakness** *n* faiblesse *f*; (*fault*) point *m* faible; **a w. for** (*liking*) un faible pour.

wealth [welθ] *n* richesse(s) *f(pl)*; **a w. of** (*abundance*) une profusion de. ● **wealthy** *a* (**-ier, -iest**) riche ‖ *n* **the w.** les riches *mpl*.

wean [wi:n] *vt* (*baby*) sevrer.

weapon ['wepən] *n* arme *f*.

wear [weər] **1** *vt* (*pt* **wore,** *pp* **worn**) (*have on body*) porter; (*put on*) mettre; **to have nothing to w.** n'avoir rien à se mettre ‖ *n* **men's/sports w.** vêtements *mpl* pour hommes/de sport; **evening w.** tenue *f* de soirée.

2 *vt* (*pt* **wore,** *pp* **worn**) (*material, patience etc*) user ‖ *vi* (*last*) faire de l'usage; (*become worn*) s'user ‖ *n* **w. (and tear)** usure *f*. ● **wearing** *a* (*tiring*) épuisant.

wear away *vt* (*clothes etc*) user; (*person*) épuiser ‖ *vi* s'user; (*of colours, ink*) s'effacer **to wear down** *vt* = **wear out to wear off** *vi* (*of colour, pain etc*) disparaître **to wear out** *vt* (*clothes etc*) user; (*person*) épuiser ‖ *vi* (*of clothes etc*) s'user.

weary ['wɪərɪ] *a* (**-ier, -iest**) (*tired*) fatigué (**of doing** de faire); (*tiring*) fatigant; (*look*) las (*f* lasse) ‖ *vi* **to w. of** se lasser de.

weasel ['wi:z(ə)l] *n* belette *f*.

weather ['weðər] *n* temps *m*; **what's the w. like?** quel temps fait-il?; **under the w.** (*ill*) patraque; **w. forecast, w. report** (bulletin *m*) météo *f*; **w. vane** girouette *f* ‖ *vt* (*storm*) essuyer; (*crisis*) *Fig* surmonter. ● **weather-beaten** *a* (*face, person*) tanné. ● **weather-cock** *n* girouette *f*. ● **weatherman** *n* (*pl* **-men**) *TV Rad Fam* présentateur *m* météo.

weav/e [wi:v] *vt* (*pt* **wove,** *pp* **woven**) (*cloth, Fig plot*) tisser; (*basket*) tresser ‖ *vi* **to w. in and out of** (*crowd, cars etc*) se faufiler entre. ● **—er** *n* tisserand, -ande *mf*.

web [web] *n* (*of spider*) toile *f*; (*of lies*) *Fig* tissu *m*.

wed [wed] *vt* (**-dd-**) (*marry*) épouser ‖ *vi* se marier.

we'd [wi:d] = **we had & we would.**

wedding ['wedɪŋ] *n* (*ceremony*) mariage *m*; **golden/silver w.** noces *fpl* d'or/d'ar-gent ‖ *a* (*cake*) de noces; (*anniversary, present*) de mariage; (*dress*) de mariée; **w. ring,** *Am* **w. band** alliance *f*.

wedge [wedʒ] *n* (*under wheel etc*) cale *f* ‖ *vt* (*wheel, table etc*) caler; (*push*) enfoncer (**into** dans); **wedged (in) between** (*caught*) coincé entre.

Wednesday ['wenzdɪ, -deɪ] *n* mercredi *m*.

wee [wi:] *a* (*tiny*) *Fam* tout petit.

weed [wi:d] *n* mauvaise herbe *f*; **w. killer** désherbant *m* ‖ *vti* désherber ‖ *vt* **to w. out** *Fig* éliminer (**from** de). ● **weedy** *a* (**-ier, -iest**) (*person*) *Fam* maigre et chétif.

week [wi:k] *n* semaine *f*; **tomorrow w., a w. tomorrow** demain en huit. ● **weekday** *n* jour *m* de semaine, jour *m* ouvrable. ● **week'end** *n* week-end *m*; **at** *or* **on** *or* **over the w.** ce week-end. ● **weekly** *a* hebdomadaire ‖ *adv* toutes les semaines ‖ *n* (*magazine*) hebdomadaire *m*.

weep [wi:p] *vi* (*pt* & *pp* **wept**) pleurer; (*of wound*) suinter; **to w. for s.o.** pleurer qn; **weeping willow** saule *m* pleureur.

weigh [weɪ] *vt* peser; **to w. sth/s.o. down** (*with load*) surcharger qch/qn (**with** de); **to be weighed down by** (*of branch etc*) plier sous le poids de; **weighed down with** (*worry etc*) *Fig* accablé de; **to w. up** (*goods, chances*) peser ‖ *vi* peser. ● **weigh-ing-machine** *n* balance *f*.

weight [weɪt] *n* poids *m*; **by w.** au poids; **to put on w.** grossir; **to lose w.** maigrir; **to pull one's w.** *Fig* faire sa part du travail; **w. lifter** haltérophile *mf*; **w. lifting** haltérophilie *f* ‖ *vt* **to w. sth (down)** faire tenir qch avec un poids; **to w. sth/s.o. down with** (*overload*) surcharger qch/qn de. ● **weighty** *a* (**-ier, -iest**) (*argument, subject*) *Fig* de poids.

weighting ['weɪtɪŋ] *n* (*on salary*) indemnité *f* de résidence.

weir [wɪər] *n* (*across river*) barrage *m*.

weird [wɪəd] *a* (**-ier, -iest**) (*odd*) bizarre; (*eerie*) mystérieux.

welcome ['welkəm] *a* (*pleasant*) agréable; (*timely*) opportun; **to be w.** (*warmly received, of person*) être bien reçu; **w.!** bienvenue!; **w. back!** bienvenue!; **to make s.o. (feel) w.** faire bon accueil à qn; **you're w.!** (*after 'thank you'*) il n'y a pas de quoi!; **a coffee/a break would be w.** un café/une pause ne ferait pas de mal; **w. to do** (*free*) libre de faire; **you're w. to my bike** mon vélo est à ta disposition.

‖ *n* accueil *m*; **to extend a w. to** (*greet*) souhaiter la bienvenue à.

‖ *vt* accueillir; (*warmly*) faire bon accueil à; **I w. you!** (*say welcome to you*) je vous souhaite la bienvenue! ● **welcoming** *a* (*smile*) accueillant; (*speech*) de bienvenue.

weld [weld] *vt* **to w. (together)** souder;

(*groups*) *Fig* unir. ● **—ing** *n* soudure *f.* ● **welder** *n* soudeur *m.*

welfare ['welfeər] *n* (*material*) bien-être *m*; (*public aid*) aide *f* sociale; **to be on w.** *Am* percevoir des allocations; **the w. state** (*in Great Britain*) l'État-providence *m*; **w. work** assistance *f* sociale.

well[1] [wel] **1** *n* (*for water*) puits *m*; **(oil) w.** puits de pétrole. **2** *vi* **to w. up** (*rise*) monter.

well[2] [wel] *adv* (**better, best**) bien; **to do w.** (*succeed*) réussir; **you'd do w. to refuse** tu ferais bien de refuser; **w. done!** bravo!; **I, you, she** *etc* **might (just) as w. have left** il valait mieux partir; **as w.** (*also*) aussi; **as w. as** aussi bien que; **as w. as two cats, he has...** en plus de deux chats, il a....
▮ *a* **she's w.** (*healthy*) elle va bien; **to get w.** se remettre; **all's w.** tout va bien.
▮ *int* eh bien!; **w., w.!** (*surprise*) tiens, tiens!; **huge, w., quite big** énorme, enfin, assez grand.

we'll [wi:l] = **we will** *or* **we shall.**

well-behaved [welbɪ'heɪvd] *a* sage. ● **w.-'being** *n* bien-être *m.* ● **w.-'built** *a* (*person, car*) solide. ● **w.-'heeled** *a* (*rich*) *Fam* nanti. ● **w.-in'formed** *a* bien informé. ● **w.-'known** *a* (bien) connu. ● **w.-'mannered** *a* bien élevé. ● **w.-'meaning** *a* bien intentionné. ● **w.-'off** *a* riche. ● **w.-'read** *a* instruit. ● **w.-'thought-of** *a* hautement considéré. ● **w.-thought-'out** *a* bien conçu. ● **w.-'timed** *a* opportun. ● **w.-to-'do** *a* riche. ● **w.-'tried** *a* (*method*) éprouvé. ● **w.-wishers** *npl* admirateurs, -trices *mfpl.*

wellington ['welɪŋtən] *n* **w. (boot)** botte *f* de caoutchouc.

Welsh [welʃ] *a* gallois; **W. rabbit** *or* **rarebit** *Culin* toast *m* au fromage ▮ *n* (*language*) gallois *m*; **the W.** (*people*) les Gallois *mpl.* ● **Welshman** *n* (*pl* **-men**) Gallois *m.* ● **Welshwoman** *n* (*pl* **-women**) Galloise *f.*

wend [wend] *vt* **to w. one's way** s'acheminer (**to** vers).

went [went] *pt of* **go 1.**

wept [wept] *pt of* **weep.**

were [wər, *stressed* wɜːr] *see* **be.**

west [west] *n* ouest *m*; **(to the) w. of** à l'ouest de; **the W.** *Pol* l'Occident *m.*
▮ *a* (*coast*) ouest *inv*; (*wind*) d'ouest; **W. Africa** Afrique *f* occidentale; **W. Indian** (*a & n*) antillais, -aise (*mf*); **the W. Indies** les Antilles *fpl.*
▮ *adv* à l'ouest, vers l'ouest. ● **westbound** *a* (*traffic*) en direction de l'ouest. ● **westerly** *a* (*point*) ouest *inv*; (*direction*) de l'ouest; (*wind*) d'ouest. ● **western** *a* (*coast*) ouest *inv*; (*culture etc*) *Pol* occidental; **W. Europe** Europe *f* de l'Ouest ▮ *n* (*film*) western *m.* ● **westward(s)** *a* & *adv* vers l'ouest.

wet [wet] *a* (**wetter, wettest**) mouillé; (*damp, rainy*) humide; (*day, month*) de pluie; **'w. paint'** 'peinture fraîche'; **to get w.** se mouiller; **to make w.** mouiller; **it's w.** (*raining*) il pleut; **w. suit** combinaison *f* de plongée ▮ *n* **the w.** (*rain*) la pluie; (*damp*) l'humidité *f* ▮ *vt* (**-tt-**) mouiller.

we've [wi:v] = **we have.**

whack [wæk] *n* (*blow*) grand coup *m* ▮ *vt* donner un grand coup à. ● **—ed** *a* (*tired*) *Fam* claqué. ● **—ing** *a* (*big*) *Fam* énorme.

whale [weɪl] *n* baleine *f.*

wham! [wæm] *int* vlan!

wharf [wɔ:f] *n* (*pl* **wharfs** *or* **wharves**) (*for ships*) quai *m.*

what [wɒt] **1** *a* quel, quelle, *pl* quel(le)s; **w. book?** quel livre?; **w. a fool/***etc***!** quel idiot/*etc*!; **w. little she has** le peu qu'elle a.
2 *pron* (*in questions*) (*subject*) qu'est-ce qui; (*object*) (qu'est-ce) que; (*after prep*) quoi; **w.'s happening?** qu'est-ce qui se passe?; **w. does he do?** qu'est-ce qu'il fait?, que fait-il?; **w. is it?** qu'est-ce que c'est?; **w.'s that book?** c'est quoi, ce livre?; **w.!** (*surprise*) quoi!, comment!; **w.'s it called?** comment ça s'appelle?; **w. for?** pourquoi?; **w. about me/***etc***?** et moi/*etc*?; **w. about leaving/***etc***?** si on partait/*etc*?
3 *pron* (*indirect, relative*) (*subject*) ce qui; (*object*) ce que; **I know w. will happen/w. she'll do** je sais ce qui arrivera/ce qu'elle fera; **w. happens is...** ce qui arrive c'est que...; **w. I need** ce dont j'ai besoin.

whatever [wɒt'evər] *a* **w. (the) mistake/***etc* quelle que soit l'erreur/*etc*; **of w. size** de n'importe quelle taille; **no chance w.** pas la moindre chance; **nothing w.** rien du tout ▮ *pron* (*no matter what*) quoi que (+ *sub*); **w. you do** quoi que tu fasses; **w. happens** quoi qu'il arrive; **w. is important** fais tout ce qui est important; **do w. you want** fais tout ce que tu veux.

what's-it ['wɒtsɪt] *n* (*thing*) *Fam* machin *m.*

whatsoever [wɒtsəʊ'evər] *a* & *pron* = **whatever.**

wheat [wi:t] *n* blé *m*, froment *m.* ● **wheatgerm** *n* germes *mpl* de blé.

wheedle ['wi:d(ə)l] *vt* **to w. s.o.** enjôler qn (**into doing** pour qu'il fasse); **to w. sth out of s.o.** obtenir qch de qn par la flatterie.

wheel [wi:l] *n* roue *f*; **at the w.** *Aut* au volant; *Nau* au gouvernail ▮ *vt* (*bicycle etc*) pousser. ● **wheelbarrow** *n* brouette *f.* ● **wheelchair** *n* fauteuil *m* roulant.

wheeze [wi:z] *vi* respirer bruyamment.

● **wheezy** *a* (**-ier, -iest**) poussif.

when [wen] *adv* quand ‖ *conj* quand, lorsque; **w. I finish, w. I've finished** quand j'aurai fini; **w. I saw him** *or* **w. I'd seen him, I left** après l'avoir vu, je suis parti; **the day/moment w.** le jour/moment où.

whenever [wen'evər] *conj* (*at whatever time*) quand; (*each time that*) chaque fois que.

where [weər] *adv* où; **w. are you from?** d'où êtes-vous? ‖ *conj* (là) où; **I found it w. she'd left it** je l'ai trouvé là où elle l'avait laissé; **the place/house w.** l'endroit/la maison où; **that's w. you'll find it** c'est là que tu le trouveras. ● **whereabouts** *adv* où (donc) ‖ *n* **his w.** l'endroit *m* où il est. ● **where'as** *conj* alors que. ● **where'by** *adv* par quoi. ● **where'upon** *adv* sur quoi. ● **wher'ever** *conj* **w. you go** (*everywhere*) partout où tu iras, où que tu ailles; **I'll go w. you like** (*anywhere*) j'irai (là) où vous voudrez.

whet [wet] *vt* (**-tt-**) (*appetite*) aiguiser.

whether ['weðər] *conj* si; **I don't know w. to leave** je ne sais pas si je dois partir; **w. she does it or not** qu'elle le fasse ou non; **it's doubtful w.** il est douteux que (+ *sub*).

which [wɪtʃ] **1** *a* (*in questions etc*) quel, quelle, *pl* quel(le)s; **w. hat?** quel chapeau?; **in w. case** auquel cas.

2 *rel pron* (*subject*) qui; (*object*) que; (*after prep*) lequel, laquelle, *pl* lesquel(le)s; (*after clause*) ce qui; (*object*) ce que; **the house w. is old** la maison qui est vieille; **the book w. I like** le livre que j'aime; **the table w. I put it on** la table sur laquelle je l'ai mis; **the film of w....** le film dont *or* duquel...; **she's ill, w. is sad** elle est malade, ce qui est triste; **he lies, w. I don't like** il ment, ce que je n'aime pas; **after w.** (*whereupon*) après quoi.

3 *pron* **w. (one)** (*in questions*) lequel, laquelle, *pl* lesquel(le)s; **w. (one) of us?** lequel *or* laquelle d'entre nous *or* de nous?; **w. (ones) are the best of the books?** quels sont les meilleurs de ces livres?

4 *pron* **w. (one)** (*the one that*) (*subject*) celui qui, celle qui, *pl* ceux qui, celles qui; (*object*) celui *etc* que; **show me w. (one) is red** montrez-moi celui *or* celle qui est rouge; **I know w. (ones) you want** je sais ceux *or* celles que vous désirez.

whichever [wɪtʃ'evər] *a & pron* **w. book/** *etc or* **w. of the books/***etc* **you buy** quel que soit le livre/*etc* que tu achètes; **take w. books** *or* **w. of the books interest you** prenez les livres qui vous intéressent; **take w. (one) you like** prends celui *or* celle que tu veux; **w. (ones) remain** ceux *or* celles qui restent.

whiff [wɪf] *n* (*puff*) bouffée *f*; (*smell*) odeur *f*.

while [waɪl] *conj* (*when*) pendant que; (*although*) bien que (+ *sub*); (*as long as*) tant que; (*whereas*) tandis que; **w. eating/** *etc* en mangeant/*etc* ‖ *n* **a w.** un moment; **all the w.** tout le temps ‖ *vt* **to w. away** (*time*) passer. ● **whilst** [waɪlst] *conj* = **while.**

whim [wɪm] *n* caprice *m*.

whimper ['wɪmpər] *vi* (*of dog, person*) gémir faiblement; (*snivel*) pleurnicher.

whimsical ['wɪmzɪk(ə)l] *a* (*look, idea*) bizarre; (*person*) fantasque, capricieux.

whine [waɪn] *vi* gémir; (*complain*) *Fig* se plaindre.

whip [wɪp] *n* fouet *m* ‖ *vt* (**-pp-**) fouetter; **whipped cream** crème *f* fouettée ‖ *vi* (*rush*) aller à toute vitesse. ● **w.-round** *n Fam* collecte *f*.

whip off *vt* (*take off*) *Fam* enlever brusquement **to whip out** *vt* (*from pocket etc*) *Fam* sortir brusquement (**from** de) **to whip round** *vi Fam* faire un saut (**to s.o.'s** chez qn) **to whip up** *vt* (*interest*) susciter; (*meal*) *Fam* préparer rapidement.

whirl [wɜːl] *vi* **to w. (round)** tourbillonner, tournoyer; (*of spinning top*) tourner ‖ *vt* **to w. (round)** faire tourbillonner; faire tourner. ● **whirlpool** *n* tourbillon *m*; **w. bath** *Am* bain *m* à remous. ● **whirlwind** *n* tourbillon *m* (de vent).

whirr [wɜːr] *vi* (*of engine*) vrombir; (*of spinning top*) ronronner.

whisk [wɪsk] **1** *n Culin* fouet *m* ‖ *vt* fouetter.
2 *vt* **to w. away** *or* **off** enlever rapidement; (*person*) emmener rapidement.

whiskers ['wɪskəz] *npl* (*of cat*) moustaches *fpl*; **(side) w.** favoris *mpl*.

whisky, *Am* **whiskey** ['wɪskɪ] *n* whisky *m*.

whisper ['wɪspər] *vti* chuchoter; **to w. sth to s.o.** chuchoter qch à l'oreille de qn ‖ *n* chuchotement *m*.

whistle ['wɪs(ə)l] *n* sifflement *m*; (*object*) sifflet *m*; **to blow the** *or* **one's w.** siffler ‖ *vti* siffler.

white [waɪt] *a* (**-er, -est**) blanc (*f* blanche); **to go** *or* **turn w.** blanchir; **w. coffee** café *m* au lait; **w. lie** pieux mensonge *m*; **w. man** Blanc *m*; **w. woman** Blanche *f* ‖ *n* (*colour, of egg*) blanc *m*. ● **white-collar 'worker** *n* employé, -ée *mf* de bureau. ● **whiteness** *n* blancheur *f*. ● **whitewash** *vt* (*wall*) badigeonner; (*person*) *Fig* blanchir.

whiting ['waɪtɪŋ] *n inv* (*fish*) merlan *m*.

Whitsun ['wɪts(ə)n] *n* la Pentecôte.
whizz [wɪz] *vi* **to w. past** *or* **by** (*rush*) passer à toute vitesse. **2** *a* **w. kid** *Fam* petit prodige *m*.
who [huː] *pron* qui; **w. did it?** qui (est-ce qui) a fait ça?; **the woman w.** la femme qui; **w. did she see?** qui a-t-elle vu?
whoever [huː'evər] *pron* (*no matter who*) qui que ce soit qui; (*object*) qui que ce soit que; **w. has travelled** (*anyone who*) quiconque a voyagé; **w. you are** qui que vous soyez; **this man, w. he is** cet homme, quel qu'il soit; **w. did that?** qui donc a fait ça?
whodunit [huː'dʌnɪt] *n* (*detective story*) *Fam* polar *m*.
whole [həʊl] *a* entier; (*intact*) intact; **the w. time** tout le temps; **the w. apple** toute la pomme, la pomme (tout) entière; **the w. world** le monde entier; **the w. lot** le tout; **w. food** aliment *m* complet ‖ *n* (*unit*) tout *m*; (*total*) totalité *f*; **the w. of the village** le village (tout) entier, tout le village; **on the w.** dans l'ensemble. ●**whole-'hearted** *a* or **whole-'heartedly** *adv* sans réserve. ●**wholemeal** or *Am* **wholewheat** *a* (*bread*) complet.
wholesale ['həʊlseɪl] *n* **to deal in w.** *Com* faire de la vente en gros ‖ *a* (*price etc*) de gros; (*destruction etc*) *Fig* en masse ‖ *adv* (*to sell, buy*) au prix de gros; (*in bulk*) en gros; (*to destroy etc*) *Fig* en masse. ●**wholesaler** *n* grossiste *mf*.
wholesome ['həʊlsəm] *a* (*food, climate etc*) sain.
wholly ['haʊlɪ] *adv* entièrement.
whom [huːm] *pron* (*object*) que; (*in questions and after prep*) qui; **w. did she see?** qui a-t-elle vu?; **the man w. you know** l'homme que tu connais; **with w.** avec qui.
whooping cough ['huːpɪŋkɒf] *n* coqueluche *f*.
whopping ['wɒpɪŋ] *a* (*big*) *Fam* énorme.
whore [hɔːr] *n* (*prostitute*) putain *f*.
whose [huːz] *poss pron* & *a* à qui, de qui; **w. book is this?** à qui est ce livre?; **w. daughter are you?** de qui es-tu la fille?; **the woman w. book I have** la femme dont *or* de qui j'ai le livre; **the man w. mother I spoke to** l'homme à la mère de qui j'ai parlé.
why [waɪ] **1** *adv* pourquoi; **w. not?** pourquoi pas? ‖ *conj* **the reason w. they...** la raison pour laquelle ils.... **2** *int* (*surprise*) eh bien!, tiens!
wick [wɪk] *n* (*of candle, lighter*) mèche *f*.
wicked ['wɪkɪd] *a* (*evil*) méchant; (*mischievous*) malicieux. ●**—ness** *n* méchanceté *f*.
wicker ['wɪkər] *n* osier *m*; **w. basket** panier *m* d'osier.
wicket ['wɪkɪt] *n* (*cricket stumps*) guichet *m*.
wide [waɪd] *a* (**-er, -est**) large; (*ocean*) vaste; (*choice, variety*) grand; **to be three metres w.** avoir trois mètres de large ‖ *adv* (*to open*) tout grand; (*to fall*) loin du but. ●**wide-'awake** *a* éveillé. ●**widely** *adv* (*to travel*) beaucoup; (*to broadcast*) largement; **w. different** très différent; **it's w. believed that...** on pense généralement que.... ●**widen** *vt* élargir ‖ *vi* s'élargir.
widespread ['waɪdspred] *a* (très) répandu.
widow ['wɪdəʊ] *n* veuve *f*. ●**widowed** *a* **to be w.** (*of man*) devenir veuf; (*of woman*) devenir veuve. ●**widower** *n* veuf *m*.
width [wɪdθ] *n* largeur *f*.
wield [wiːld] *vt* (*brandish*) brandir; (*power*) *Fig* exercer.
wife [waɪf] *n* (*pl* **wives**) femme *f*, épouse *f*.
wig [wɪg] *n* perruque *f*.
wiggle ['wɪg(ə)l] *vt* agiter; **to w. one's hips** tortiller des hanches ‖ *vi* (*of worm etc*) se tortiller; (*of tail*) remuer.
wild [waɪld] *a* (**-er, -est**) (*animal, flower etc*) sauvage; (*idea, life*) fou (*f* folle); (*look*) farouche; (*angry*) furieux (**with** contre); **w. with** (*joy etc*) fou de; **I'm not w. about it** *Fam* ça ne m'emballe pas; **to grow w.** (*of plant*) pousser à l'état sauvage; **to run w.** (*of animals*) courir en liberté; (*of crowd*) se déchaîner; **the W. West** *Am* le Far West ‖ *npl* **the wilds** les régions *fpl* sauvages. ●**wild-'goose chase** *n* fausse piste *f*. ●**wildlife** *n* faune *f*.
wilderness ['wɪldənəs] *n* désert *m*.
wildly ['waɪldlɪ] *adv* (*madly*) follement; (*violently*) violemment.
wile [waɪl] *n* ruse *f*, artifice *m*.
wilful ['wɪlfəl] (*Am* **willful**) *a* (*intentional, obstinate*) volontaire.
will[1] [wɪl] *v aux* **he will come, he'll come** (*future tense*) il viendra (**won't he?** n'est-ce pas?); **you will not come, you won't come** tu ne viendras pas (**will you?** n'est-ce pas?); **w. you have a tea?** veux-tu prendre un thé?; **w. you be quiet!** veux-tu te taire!; **I w.!** (*yes*) oui!; **it won't open** ça ne veut pas s'ouvrir.
will[2] [wɪl] **1** *vt* (*intend*) *Old-fashioned* vouloir (**that** que (+ *sub*)); **to w. oneself to do** faire un effort de volonté pour faire ‖ *n* volonté *f*; **ill w.** mauvaise volonté; **free w.** libre arbitre *m*; **of one's own free w.** de son plein gré; **against one's w.** à contrecœur; **at w.** (*to leave etc*) quand on veut. **2** *n* (*legal document*) testament *m*.

willing ['wɪlɪŋ] *a* (*helper*, *worker*) de bonne volonté; **to be w. to do** être disposé *or* prêt à faire, vouloir bien faire ‖ *n* **to show w.** faire preuve de bonne volonté. ●**—ly** *adv* (*with pleasure*) volontiers; (*voluntarily*) volontairement. ●**—ness** *n* bonne volonté *f*; **her w. to do** son empressement *m* à faire.
willow ['wɪləʊ] *n* (*tree*, *wood*) saule *m*.
willpower ['wɪlpaʊər] *n* volonté *f*.
willy-nilly [wɪlɪ'nɪlɪ] *adv* bon gré mal gré.
wilt [wɪlt] *vi* (*of plant*) dépérir.
wily [waɪlɪ] *a* (**-ier, -iest**) rusé.
wimp [wɪmp] *n Fam* femmelette *f*, mauviette *f*.
win [wɪn] *n* (*victory*) victoire *f* ‖ *vi* (*pt* & *pp* **won,** *pres p* **winning**) gagner ‖ *vt* (*money*, *race etc*) gagner; (*victory*, *prize*) remporter; (*friends*) se faire; **to w. s.o. over** gagner qn (**to** à). ●**winning** *a* (*number*, *horse etc*) gagnant; (*team*) victorieux ‖ *npl* **winnings** gains *mpl*.
wince [wɪns] *vi* faire une grimace (de douleur, dégoût *etc*).
winch [wɪntʃ] *n* treuil *m*.
wind[1] [wɪnd] *n* vent *m*; (*breath*) souffle *m*; **to have w.** (*in stomach*) avoir des gaz; **to get w. of sth** entendre parler de qch; **w. instrument** *Mus* instrument *m* à vent ‖ *vt* **to w. s.o.** (*of blow*) couper le souffle à qn. ●**windcheater** *or Am* **windbreaker** *n* blouson *m*, coupe-vent *m inv*. ●**windfall** *n* (*unexpected money*) aubaine *f*. ●**windmill** *n* moulin *m* à vent. ●**windpipe** *n Anat* trachée *f*. ●**windscreen** *or Am* **windshield** *n Aut* pare-brise *m inv*; **w. wiper** essuie-glace *m inv*. ●**windsurfer** *n* (*person*) véliplanchiste *mf*. ●**windsurfing** *n* **to go w.** faire de la planche à voile. ●**windswept** *a* (*street etc*) balayé par les vents. ●**windy** *a* (**-ier, -iest**) **it's w.** (*of weather*) il y a du vent; **w. day** jour *m* de grand vent.
wind[2] [waɪnd] *vt* (*pt* & *pp* **wound**) (*roll*) enrouler (**round** autour de); (*clock*) remonter ‖ *vi* (*of river*, *road*) serpenter. ●**—ing** *a* (*road etc*) sinueux; (*staircase*) tournant.
wind down *vt* (*car window*) baisser **to wind up** *vt* (*clock*) remonter; (*meeting*, *speech*) terminer ‖ *vi* (*end up*) finir (**doing** par faire); **to w. up with sth** se retrouver avec qch.
window ['wɪndəʊ] *n* fenêtre *f*; (*pane*) vitre *f*, carreau *m*; (*in vehicle or train*) vitre *f*; (*in shop*) vitrine *f*; (*counter*) guichet *m*; **French w.** porte-fenêtre *f*; **w. box** jardinière *f*; **w. cleaner** *or Am* **washer** laveur, -euse *mf* de carreaux; **w. ledge** = **windowsill; to go w. shopping** faire du lèche-vitrines. ●**windowpane** *n* vitre *f*, carreau *m*. ●**windowsill** *n* (*inside*) appui *m* de (la) fenêtre; (*outside*) rebord *m* de (la) fenêtre.
windy ['wɪndɪ] *a see* **wind**[1].
wine [waɪn] *n* vin *m*; **w. bar/bottle** bar *m*/bouteille *f* à vin; **w. cellar** cave *f* (à vin); **w. list** carte *f* des vins; **w. waiter** sommelier *m*. ●**wineglass** *n* verre *m* à vin. ●**wine-growing** *a* viti-cole.
wing [wɪŋ] *n* aile *f*; **the wings** *Th* les coulisses *fpl*. ●**winger** *n Fb* ailier *m*.
wink [wɪŋk] *vi* faire un clin d'œil (**at, to** à) ‖ *n* clin *m* d'œil.
winner ['wɪnər] *n* gagnant, -ante *mf*; (*of argument*, *fight*) vainqueur *m*. ●**winning** *a* & *n see* **win**.
winter ['wɪntər] *n* hiver *m* **in (the) w.** en hiver ‖ *a* d'hiver. ●**wintertime** *n* hiver *m*. ●**wintry** *a* hivernal; **w. day** jour *m* d'hiver.
wipe [waɪp] *vt* essuyer; **to w. one's feet/hands** s'essuyer les pieds/les mains; **to w. away** *or* **off** *or* **up** (*liquid*) essuyer; **to w. out** (*clean*) essuyer; (*destroy*) anéantir; (*erase*) effacer ‖ *vi* **to w. up** (*dry the dishes*) essuyer la vaisselle ‖ *n* **to give sth a w.** donner un coup de torchon *or* d'éponge à qch. ●**wiper** *n Aut* essuie-glace *m inv*.
wir/e ['waɪər] *n* fil *m*; **w. mesh** *or* **netting** grillage *m* ‖ *vt* **to w. sth (up) to sth** (*connect*) *El* relier qch à qch; **to w. a hall for sound** sonoriser une salle. ●**—ing** *n El* installation *f* électrique.
wisdom ['wɪzdəm] *n* sagesse *f*.
wise [waɪz] *a* (**-er, -est**) (*in knowledge*) sage; (*advisable*) prudent. ●**wisecrack** *n Fam* (*joke*) astuce *f*; (*sarcastic remark*) sarcasme *m*. ●**wisely** *adv* prudemment.
-wise [waɪz] *suff* (*with regard to*) **money/***etc*-**wise** question argent/*etc*.
wish [wɪʃ] *vt* souhaiter, vouloir (**to do** faire); **I w. (that) you could help me/could have helped me** je voudrais que/j'aurais voulu que vous m'aidiez; **I w. I hadn't done that** je regrette d'avoir fait ça; **if you w.** si tu veux; **I w. you a happy birthday** je vous souhaite (un) bon anniversaire; **I w. I could** si seulement je pouvais.
‖ *vi* **to w. for sth** souhaiter qch.
‖ *n* (*specific*) souhait *m*, vœu *m*; (*general*) désir *m*; **the w. for sth/to do** le désir de qch/de faire; **best wishes** (*on greeting card*) meilleurs vœux *mpl*; (*in letter*) amitiés *fpl*; **send him my best wishes** fais-lui mes amitiés. ●**wishful** *a* **it's w. thinking (on your part)** tu rêves, tu prends tes désirs pour la réalité.
wisteria [wɪ'stɪərɪə] *n Bot* glycine *f*.
wistful ['wɪstfəl] *a* mélancolique et rêveur.

wit [wɪt] *n* **1** (*humour*) esprit *m*; (*person*) homme *m or* femme *f* d'esprit. **2 wit(s)** (*intelligence*) intelligence *f* (**to do** de faire).
witch [wɪtʃ] *n* sorcière *f*. ● **witchcraft** *n* sorcellerie *f*.
with [wɪð] *prep* **1** avec; **come w. me** viens avec moi; **w. no hat**/*etc* sans chapeau/*etc*; **I'll be right w. you** je suis à vous dans une seconde; **I'm w. you** (*I understand*) *Fam* je te suis; **w. it** (*up-to-date*) *Fam* dans le vent.
2 (*at the house etc of*) chez; **she's staying w. me** elle loge chez moi.
3 (*cause*) de; **to jump w. joy** sauter de joie.
4 (*instrument, means*) avec, de; **to write w. a pen** écrire avec un stylo; **to fill w.** remplir de; **satisfied w.** satisfait de.
5 (*description*) à; **w. blue eyes** aux yeux bleus.
withdraw [wɪð'drɔː] *vt* (*pt* **withdrew**, *pp* **withdrawn**) retirer (**from** de) ‖ *vi* se retirer. ● **withdrawn** *a* (*person*) renfermé. ● **withdrawal** *n* retrait *m*.
wither ['wɪðər] *vi* (*of plant etc*) se flétrir.
withhold [wɪð'həʊld] *vt* (*pt & pp* **withheld**) (*permission etc*) refuser (**from** à); (*decision*) différer; (*money*) retenir (**from** de); (*information*) cacher (**from** à).
within [wɪ'ðɪn] *adv* à l'intérieur ‖ *prep* (*place, box etc*) à l'intérieur de; **w. 10 km (of)** (*less than*) à moins de 10 km (de); (*inside an area of*) dans un rayon de 10 km (de); **w. a month** (*to return etc*) avant un mois; (*to finish sth*) en moins d'un mois; **w. my means** dans mes moyens; **w. sight** en vue.
without [wɪ'ðaʊt] *prep* sans; **w. a tie**/*etc* sans cravate/*etc*; **w. doing** sans faire.
withstand [wɪð'stænd] *vt* (*pt & pp* **withstood**) résister à.
witness ['wɪtnɪs] *n* (*person*) témoin *m*; **to bear w. to** témoigner de ‖ *vt* (*accident etc*) être (le) témoin de; (*document*) signer (pour attester l'authenticité de).
witty ['wɪtɪ] *a* (**-ier, -iest**) spirituel.
wives [waɪvz] *see* **wife.**
wizard ['wɪzəd] *n* magicien *m*; (*genius*) *Fig* génie *m*.
wobble ['wɒb(ə)l] *vi* (*of chair etc*) branler; (*of cyclist, pile*) osciller; (*of jelly, Am jello*®) trembler. ● **wobbly** *a* (*table, tooth*) branlant.
woe [wəʊ] *n* malheur *m*.
woke, woken [wəʊk, 'wəʊkən] *pt & pp of* **wake**[1].
wolf [wʊlf] **1** *n* (*pl* **wolves**) loup *m*. **2** *vt* **to w. (down)** (*food*) engloutir.
woman, *pl* **women** ['wʊmən, 'wɪmɪn] *n* femme *f*; **w. doctor** femme *f* médecin; **women drivers** les femmes *fpl* au volant; **w. friend** amie *f*; **w. teacher** professeur *m* femme; **women's** (*clothes, attitudes etc*) féminin. ● **womanhood** *n* **to reach w.** devenir (une) femme. ● **womanly** *a* féminin.
womb [wuːm] *n* utérus *m*.
women ['wɪmɪn] *see* **woman.**
won [wʌn] *pt & pp of* **win.**
wonder ['wʌndər] **1** *n* (*marvel*) merveille *f*, miracle *m*; (*feeling*) émerveillement *m*; **in w.** (*to watch etc*) émerveillé; **(it's) no w.** ce n'est pas étonnant (**that** que (+ *sub*)) ‖ *vi* (*marvel*) s'étonner (**at** de). **2** *vt* (*ask oneself*) se demander (**if** si, **why** pourquoi) ‖ *vi* (*ask oneself questions*) s'interroger (**about** au sujet de, sur); **I was just wondering** je réfléchissais.
wonderful ['wʌndəfəl] *a* (*excellent, astonishing*) merveilleux.
wonky ['wɒŋkɪ] *a* (**-ier, -iest**) *Fam* (*table etc*) bancal; (*picture*) de travers.
won't [wəʊnt] = **will not.**
woo [wuː] *vt* (*voters etc*) *Fig* chercher à plaire à.
wood [wʊd] *n* (*material, forest*) bois *m*. ● **wooded** *a* (*valley etc*) boisé. ● **wooden** *a* de *or* en bois; (*manner, dancer etc*) *Fig* raide. ● **woodland** *n* région *f* boisée. ● **woodpecker** *n* (*bird*) pic *m*. ● **woodwork** *n* (*school subject*) menuiserie *f*. ● **woodworm** *n* vers *mpl* (du bois); **it has w.** c'est vermoulu.
wool [wʊl] *n* laine *f*. ● **woollen** (*Am* **woolen**) *a* en laine ‖ *npl* **woollens,** *Am* **woolens** lainages *mpl*. ● **woolly** *a* (**-ier, -iest**) laineux; (*unclear*) *Fig* nébuleux ‖ *n* (*garment*) *Fam* lainage *m*.
word [wɜːd] *n* mot *m*; (*spoken*) parole *f*, mot *m*; (*promise*) parole *f*; (*command*) ordre *m*; (*news*) nouvelles *fpl*; *pl* (*of song etc*) paroles *fpl*; **to have a w. with s.o.** parler à qn; (*advise, criticize*) avoir un mot avec qn; **in other words** autrement dit; **w. processing** traitement *m* de texte; **w. processor** machine *f à or* de traitement de texte ‖ *vt* (*express*) formuler. ● **wording** *n* termes *mpl*. ● **wordy** *a* (**-ier, -iest**) verbeux.
wore [wɔːr] *pt of* **wear.**
work [wɜːk] *n* travail *m*; (*product, book etc*) œuvre *f*, ouvrage *m*; (*building or repair work*) travaux *mpl*; **to be at w.** travailler; **farm w.** travaux *mpl* agricoles; **out of w.** au chômage; **a day off w.** un jour de congé; **he's off w.** il n'est pas allé travailler; **the works** (*of clock etc*) le mécanisme; **gas works** usine *f* à gaz; **w. force** main-d'œuvre

f; **w. permit** permis *m* de travail; **w. station** poste *m* de travail.
▮ *vi* travailler; (*of machine etc*) marcher, fonctionner; (*of drug*) agir; **to w. loose** (*of knot, screw*) se desserrer; **to w. towards** (*result, aim*) travailler à.
▮ *vt* (*person*) faire travailler; (*machine*) faire marcher; (*miracle*) faire; (*metal, wood etc*) travailler.

workable ['wɜːkəb(ə)l] *a* (*plan*) praticable.

workaholic [wɜːkə'hɒlɪk] *n Fam* bourreau *m* de travail. ● **'workbench** *n* établi *m*. ● **'workman** *n* (*pl* **-men**) ouvrier *m*. ● **'workmate** *n* camarade *mf* de travail. ● **'workout** *n Sp* séance *f* d'entraînement *m*. ● **'workroom** *n* salle *f* de travail. ● **'workshop** *n* atelier *m*. ● **work-to-'rule** *n* grève *f* du zèle.

work at *vt* (*improve*) travailler (*qch*) **to work off** *vt* (*debt*) payer en travaillant; (*excess fat*) se débarrasser de (par l'exercice) **to work on** *vt* (*book, problem*) travailler à; (*improve*) travailler (*son français etc*) **to work out** *vi* (*succeed*) marcher; (*do exercises*) s'entraîner; **it works out at 50 francs** ça fait 50 francs ▮ *vt* (*calculate*) calculer; (*problem*) résoudre; (*scheme*) préparer; (*understand*) comprendre **to work up** *vt* **to w. up an appetite** s'ouvrir l'appétit; **to get worked up** s'énerver ▮ *vi* **it works up to** (*climax*) ça tend vers; **to w. up to sth** en venir à qch.

worker ['wɜːkər] *n* travailleur, -euse *mf*; (*manual*) ouvrier, -ière *mf*; **(office) w.** employé, -ée *mf* (de bureau).

working ['wɜːkɪŋ] *a* (*day, clothes*) de travail; (*population*) actif; **w. class** classe *f* ouvrière; **in w. order** en état de marche. ● **working-'class** *a* ouvrier.

world [wɜːld] *n* monde *m*; **all over the w.** dans le monde entier; **the richest/*etc* in the world** le *or* la plus riche/*etc* du monde ▮ *a* (*war etc*) mondial; (*champion, cup, record*) du monde. ● **world-'famous** *a* de renommée mondiale. ● **worldly** *a* (*pleasures*) de ce monde; (*person*) qui a l'expérience du monde. ● **world'wide** *a* universel.

worm [wɜːm] **1** *n* ver *m*. **2** *vt* **to w. one's way into** s'insinuer dans.

worn [wɔːn] *pt of* **wear** ▮ *a* (*clothes etc*) usé. ● **worn-'out** *a* (*object*) complètement usé; (*person*) épuisé.

worry ['wʌrɪ] *n* souci *m* ▮ *vi* s'inquiéter (**about sth** de qch, **about s.o.** pour qn) ▮ *vt* inquiéter; **to be worried** être inquiet (**about** au sujet de). ● **—ing** *a* inquiétant. ● **worrier** *n* anxieux, -euse *mf*.

worse [wɜːs] *a* pire, plus mauvais (**than** que); **to get w.** se détériorer; **he's getting w.** (*in health*) il va de plus en plus mal.
▮ *adv* plus mal (**than** que); **I could do w.** je pourrais faire pire; **from bad to w.** de mal en pis; **to be w. off** aller moins bien financièrement.
▮ *n* **there's w. (to come)** il y a pire encore; **a change for the w.** une détérioration. ● **worsen** *vti* empirer.

worship ['wɜːʃɪp] *n* culte *m*; **his W. the Mayor** Monsieur le Maire ▮ *vt* (**-pp-**) (*person, god*) adorer; (*money*) *Pej* avoir le culte de.

worst [wɜːst] *a* pire, plus mauvais ▮ *adv* **(the) w.** le plus mal ▮ *n* **the w. (one)** le *or* la pire, le *or* la plus mauvais(e); **the w. (thing) is that...** le pire c'est que...; **at w.** au pire; **to be at its w.** (*of crisis*) avoir atteint son paroxysme; **to get the w. of it** (*in struggle etc*) avoir le dessous.

worth [wɜːθ] *n* valeur *f*; **to buy 50 pence w. of chocolates** acheter pour cinquante pence de chocolats ▮ *a* **to be w. sth** valoir qch; **how much** *or* **what is it w.?** ça vaut combien?; **the film's w. seeing** le film vaut la peine *or Fam* le coup d'être vu; **it's w. (one's) while** ça (en) vaut la peine *or Fam* le coup; **it's w. (while) waiting** ça vaut la peine d'attendre. ● **worthless** *a* qui ne vaut rien.

worthwhile [wɜːθ'waɪl] *a* (*book, film etc*) qui vaut la peine d'être lu, vu *etc*; (*activity*) qui (en) vaut la peine; (*plan*) valable; (*satisfying*) qui donne des satisfactions.

worthy ['wɜːðɪ] *a* (**-ier, -iest**) (*person*) digne; (*cause, act*) louable; **w. of sth/s.o.** digne de qch/qn.

would [wʊd, *unstressed* wəd] *v aux* **I w. stay, I'd stay** (*conditional tense*) je resterais; **he w. have done it** il l'aurait fait; **w. you help me, please?** voulez-vous m'aider, s'il vous plaît?; **w. you like some tea?** voudriez-vous (prendre) du thé?; **the wound wouldn't heal** la blessure ne voulait pas cicatriser; **I w. see her every day** (*used to*) je la voyais chaque jour.

wound[1] [wuːnd] *vt* (*hurt*) blesser; **the wounded** les blessés *mpl* ▮ *n* blessure *f*.

wound[2] [waʊnd] *pt & pp of* **wind**[2].

wove, woven [wəʊv, 'wəʊv(ə)n] *pt & pp of* **weave.**

wow! [waʊ] *int Fam* oh là là!

wrap [ræp] *vt* (**-pp-**) **to w. (up)** envelopper; (*parcel*) emballer ▮ *vti* **to w. (oneself) up** (*dress warmly*) se couvrir ▮ *n* (*shawl*) châle *m*; **plastic w.** *Am* film *m* plastique. ● **wrapping** *n* (*action, material*) emballage *m*; **w.**

paper papier *m* d'emballage. • **wrapper** *n* (*of sweet, Am candy*) papier *m*.

wrath [rɒθ] *n Lit* courroux *m*.

wreak [ri:k] *vt* **to w. vengeance on** se venger de; **to w. havoc on** ravager.

wreath [ri:θ] *n* (*pl* **-s** [ri:ðz]) (*of flowers*) couronne *f*.

wreck [rek] *n* (*ship*) épave *f*; (*sinking*) naufrage *m*; (*train etc*) train *m etc* accidenté; (*person*) épave *f* (humaine); **to be a nervous w.** être à bout de nerfs ‖ *vt* (*object, Fig hopes etc*) détruire. • **—age** *n* (*of plane etc*) débris *mpl*. • **—er** *n* (*truck*) *Am* dépanneuse *f*.

wren [ren] *n* (*bird*) roitelet *m*.

wrench [rentʃ] **1** *n* (*tool*) clef *f* (à écrous), *Am* clef *f* à molette *f*. **2** *vt* (*tug at*) tirer sur; (*twist*) tordre; **to w. sth from s.o.** arracher qch à qn.

wrestl/e ['res(ə)l] *vi* lutter (**with s.o.** avec qn); **to w. with** (*problem etc*) *Fig* se débattre avec. • **—ing** *n Sp* lutte *f*; **(all-in) w.** catch *m*. • **wrestler** *n* lutteur, -euse *mf*; catcheur, -euse *mf*.

wretch [retʃ] *n* malheureux, -euse *mf*; (*rascal*) misérable *mf*. • **wretched** [-ɪd] *a* (*poor, pitiful*) misérable; (*dreadful*) affreux; (*annoying*) maudit.

wriggle ['rɪg(ə)l] *vi* **to w. (about)** se tortiller; (*of fish*) frétiller.

wring [rɪŋ] *vt* (*pt & pp* **wrung**) **to w. (out)** (*clothes by hand*) tordre.

wrinkle ['rɪŋk(ə)l] *n* (*on skin*) ride *f*; (*in cloth or paper*) pli *m* ‖ *vt* (*skin*) rider; (*cloth, paper*) plisser ‖ *vi* se rider; faire des plis.

wrist [rɪst] *n* poignet *m*. • **wristwatch** *n* montre *f*.

writ [rɪt] *n* acte *m* judiciaire; **to issue a w. against s.o.** assigner qn (en justice).

write [raɪt] *vti* (*pt* **wrote,** *pp* **written**) écrire. • **w.-off** *n* **a (complete) w.-off** (*car*) une véritable épave. • **w.-up** *n* (*report*) compte rendu *m*.

write away for *vt* (*details etc*) écrire pour demander **to write back** *vi* répondre **to write down** *vt* noter **to write off** *vt* (*debt*) passer aux profits et pertes; **to w. off for** = **write away for to write out** *vt* écrire; (*copy*) recopier **to write up** *vt* (*notes*) mettre à jour; **to w. up for** = **write away for**.

writer ['raɪtər] *n* auteur *m* (**of** de); (*literary*) écrivain *m*.

writhe [raɪð] *vi* (*in pain etc*) se tordre.

writing ['raɪtɪŋ] *n* (*handwriting*) écriture *f*; *pl* (*of author*) écrits *mpl*; **to put sth (down) in w.** mettre qch par écrit; **some w.** (*on page*) quelque chose d'écrit; **w. desk** secrétaire *m*; **w. pad** bloc *m* de papier à lettres; (*for notes*) bloc-notes *m*; **w. paper** papier *m* à lettres.

written ['rɪt(ə)n] *pp of* **write.**

wrong [rɒŋ] *a* (*sum, idea etc*) faux (*f* fausse); (*direction, road etc*) mauvais; (*unfair*) injuste; **to be w.** (*of person*) avoir tort (**to do** de faire); (*mistaken*) se tromper; **it's w. to swear**/*etc* c'est mal de jurer/*etc*; **the clock's w.** la pendule n'est pas à l'heure; **something's w.** quelque chose ne va pas; **something's w. with the phone** le téléphone ne marche pas bien; **something's w. with her arm** elle a quelque chose au bras; **nothing's w.** tout va bien; **what's w. with you?** qu'est-ce que tu as?; **the w. way round** *or* **up** à l'envers.

‖ *adv* mal; **to go w.** (*of plan*) mal tourner; (*of machine*) tomber en panne; (*of person*) se tromper.

‖ *n* (*injustice*) injustice *f*; **to be in the w.** être dans son tort; **right and w.** le bien et le mal.

‖ *vt* faire (du) tort à (*qn*). • **wrongful** *a* (*arrest*) arbitraire. • **wrongly** *adv* (*to inform, translate etc*) mal; (*to suspect etc*) à tort.

wrote [rəʊt] *pt of* **write.**

wrought [rɔ:t] *a* **w. iron** fer *m* forgé. • **w.-'iron** *a* en fer forgé.

wrung [rʌŋ] *pt & pp of* **wring.**

wry [raɪ] *a* (**wryer, wryest**) (*comment*) ironique; (*smile*) forcé.

X

X, x [eks] *n* X, x *m*.
xenophobia [zenə'fəʊbɪə, *Am* ziːnəʊ-] *n* xénophobie *f*.
Xerox® ['zɪərɒks] *n* photocopie *f* ‖ *vt* photocopier.
Xmas ['krɪsməs] *n Fam* Noël *m*.
X-ray ['eksreɪ] *n* (*photo*) radio(graphie) *f*; (*beam*) rayon *m* X; **to have an X-ray** passer une radio ‖ *vt* radiographier.
xylophone ['zaɪləfəʊn] *n* xylophone *m*.

Y

Y, y [waɪ] *n* Y, y *m*.
yacht [jɒt] *n* yacht *m*. ●**—ing** *n* yachting *m*.
Yank [jæŋk] *n Fam* Ricain, -aine *mf*.
yap [jæp] *vi* (**-pp-**) (*of dog*) japper.
yard [jɑːd] *n* **1** (*of farm, school etc*) cour *f*; (*for storage*) dépôt *m*, chantier *m*; (*garden*) *Am* jardin *m* (*à l'arrière de la maison*). **2** (*measure*) yard *m* (= *91,44 cm*). ●**yardstick** *n* (*criterion*) critère *m*.
yarn [jɑːn] *n* **1** (*thread*) fil *m*. **2** (*tale*) *Fam* longue histoire *f*.
yawn [jɔːn] *vi* bâiller ‖ *n* bâillement *m*.
year [jɪər] *n* an *m*, année *f*; **school/tax y.** année *f* scolaire/fiscale; **this y.** cette année; **in the y. 1994** en (l'an) 1994; **he's ten years old** il a dix ans; **New Y.** Nouvel An; **New Year's Day** le jour de l'An; **New Year's Eve** la Saint-Sylvestre. ●**yearly** *a* annuel ‖ *adv* annuellement.
yearn [jɜːn] *vi* **to y. for s.o.** languir après qn; **to y. for sth** avoir très envie de qch; **to y. to do** avoir très envie de faire.
yeast [jiːst] *n* levure *f*.
yell [jel] *vti* **to y. (out)** hurler; **to y. at s.o.** (*scold*) crier après qn ‖ *n* hurlement *m*.
yellow ['jeləʊ] *a* & *n* (*colour*) jaune (*m*).
yes [jes] *adv* oui; (*contradicting negative question*) si ‖ *n* oui *m inv*.
yesterday ['jestədɪ] *adv* & *n* hier (*m*); **y. morning/evening** hier matin/soir; **the day before y.** avant-hier.
yet [jet] **1** *adv* encore; (*already*) déjà; **she hasn't come (as) y.** elle n'est pas encore venue; **has he come y.?** est-il déjà arrivé?; **the best y.** le meilleur jusqu'ici. **2** *conj* (*nevertheless*) pourtant.
yew [juː] *n* (*tree, wood*) if *m*.
yield [jiːld] *n* (*of farm etc*) rendement *m*; (*profit*) rapport *m* ‖ *vt* (*produce*) produire; (*profit*) rapporter; (*give up*) céder (**to** à) ‖ *vi* (*surrender, give way*) céder (**to** à); (*of tree etc*) rendre; **'y.'** (*road sign*) *Am* 'cédez le passage'.
yoga ['jəʊgə] *n* yoga *m*.
yog(h)urt ['jɒgət, *Am* 'jəʊgɜːt] *n* yaourt *m*.
yoke [jəʊk] *n* (*for oxen*) & *Fig* joug *m*.
yolk [jəʊk] *n* jaune *m* (d'œuf).
you [juː] *pron* **1** (*polite form singular*) vous; (*familiar form singular*) tu; (*polite and familar form plural*) vous; (*object*) vous; te, t'; *pl* vous; (*after prep, 'than', 'it is'*) vous; toi; *pl* vous; **(to) y.** vous; te, t'; *pl* vous; **y. are** vous êtes; tu es; **I see y.** je vous vois; je te vois; **I give it to y.** je vous le donne; je te le donne; **with y.** avec vous; avec toi; **y. teachers** vous autres professeurs; **y. idiot!** espèce d'imbécile!
2 (*indefinite*) on; (*object*) vous; te, t'; *pl* vous; **y. never know** on ne sait jamais. ●**you'd** = **you had** & **you would**. ●**you'll** = **you will**.
young [jʌŋ] *a* (**-er, -est**) jeune; **my young(er) brother** mon (frère) cadet; **her youngest brother** le cadet de ses frères; **the youngest son** le cadet ‖ *n* (*of animals*) petits *mpl*; **the y.** (*people*) les jeunes *mpl*. ●**youngster** *n* jeune *mf*.
your [jɔːr] *poss a* (*polite form singular, polite and familiar form plural*) votre, *pl* vos; (*familiar form singular*) ton, ta, *pl* tes; (*one's*) son, sa, *pl* ses.
yours [jɔːz] *poss pron* le vôtre, la vôtre, *pl* les vôtres; (*familiar form singular*) le tien, la tienne, *pl* les tien(ne)s; **this book is y.** ce livre est à vous *or* est le vôtre; ce livre est à

toi *or* est le tien; **a friend of y.** un ami à vous; un ami à toi.

yourself [jɔː'self] *pron* (*polite form*) vous-même; (*familiar form*) toi-même; (*reflexive*) vous; te, t'; (*after prep*) vous; toi; **you wash y.** vous vous lavez; tu te laves. ● **your'selves** *pron pl* vous-mêmes; (*reflexive & after prep*) vous.

youth [juːθ] *n* (*pl* **-s** [juːðz]) (*age, young people*) jeunesse *f*; (*young man*) jeune *m*; **y. club** maison *f* des jeunes. ● **youthful** *a* jeune.

yoyo ['jəʊjəʊ] *n* (*pl* **-os**) yo-yo *m inv*.

yucky ['jʌkɪ] *a Fam* dégueulasse.

yummy ['jʌmɪ] *a* (**-ier, -iest**) *Sl* délicieux.

yuppie ['yʌpɪ] *n* jeune cadre *m* dynamique.

Z

Z, z [zed, *Am* ziː] *n* Z, z *m*.

zany ['zeɪnɪ] *a* (**-ier, -iest**) farfelu.

zap [zæp] *vt Comptr* effacer. ● **zapper** *n* (*for TV channels*) télécommande *f*.

zeal [ziːl] *n* zèle *m*. ● **zealous** ['zeləs] *a* zélé.

zebra ['ziːbrə, 'zebrə] *n* zèbre *m*; **z. crossing** passage *m* pour piétons.

zero ['zɪərəʊ] *n* (*pl* **-os**) zéro *m*.

zest [zest] *n* **1** (*enthusiasm*) entrain *m*; **z. for living** appétit *m* de vivre. **2** (*of lemon, orange*) zeste *m*.

zigzag ['zɪgzæg] *n* zigzag *m* ‖ *a & adv* en zigzag.

zinc [zɪŋk] *n* (*metal*) zinc *m*.

zip [zɪp] **1** *n* **z. (fastener)** fermeture *f* éclair® ‖ *vt* (**-pp-**) **to z. (up)** fermer (avec une fermeture éclair®). **2** *vi* (**-pp-**) (*go quickly*) aller comme l'éclair. **3** *a* **z. code** *Am* code *m* postal. ● **zipper** *n Am* fermeture *f* éclair®.

zit [zɪt] *n* (*pimple*) *Am Fam* bouton *m*.

zodiac ['zəʊdɪæk] *n* zodiaque *m*.

zone [zəʊn] *n* zone *f*; (*division of city*) secteur *m*.

zoo [zuː] *n* (*pl* **zoos**) zoo *m*; **z. keeper** gardien, -ienne *mf* de zoo.

zoom [zuːm] **1** *vi* (*rush*) se précipiter; **to z. past** passer comme un éclair. **2** *n* **z. lens** zoom *m*.

zucchini [zuː'kiːnɪ] *n* (*pl* **-ni** *or* **-nis**) *Am* courgette *f*.

FRENCH – ENGLISH

A

A, a [ɑ] *nm* A, a.

a [a] *voir* **avoir.**

à [a] *prép* (**à** + **le** = **au** [o], **à** + **les** = **aux** [o]) **1** (*direction: lieu*) to; (*temps*) till, to; **aller à Paris** to go to Paris; **de 3 à 4 h** from 3 till *ou* to 4 (o'clock).
2 (*position: lieu*) at, in; (*surface*) on; (*temps*) at; **être au bureau/à la ferme/au jardin/à Paris** to be at *ou in* the office/on *ou* at the farm/in the garden/in Paris; **à la maison** at home; **à l'horizon** on the horizon; **à 8 h** at 8 (o'clock); **à mon arrivée** on (my) arrival; **à lundi!** see you (on) Monday!
3 (*description*) **l'homme à la barbe** the man with the beard; **verre à liqueur** liqueur glass.
4 (*attribution*) **donner qch à qn** to give sth to s.o., give s.o. sth.
5 (*devant inf*) **apprendre à lire** to learn to read; **travail à faire** work to do; **maison à vendre** house for sale; **prêt à partir** ready to leave.
6 (*appartenance*) **c'est (son livre) à lui** it's his (book); **c'est à vous de** (*décider, protester etc*) it's up to you to; (*lire, jouer etc*) it's your turn to.
7 (*prix*) for; **pain à 2F** loaf for 2F.
8 (*poids*) by; **vendre au kilo** to sell by the kilo.
9 (*vitesse*) **100 km à l'heure** 100km an *ou* per hour.
10 (*moyen, manière*) **à bicyclette** by bicycle; **à la main** by hand; **à pied** on foot; **au crayon** with a pencil, in pencil; **au galop** at a gallop; **à la française** in the French style *ou* way; **deux à deux** two by two.
ⓘ**G58** Indirect Pronouns 6 D 2c) ii)
ⓘ**G103** The Subjunctive 7 G 2b)
ⓘ**G110** & **111** The Infinitive 7 H 2b) ii) & c)
ⓘ**G165**, **167**, **168** & **169** Verb Constructions 7 M 1b), M 2b) & d), M 3 & 4
ⓘ**G170** Prepositions 8

abaisser [abese] *vt* to lower ▌**s'a.** *vpr* (*barrière*) to lower; (*température*) to drop; **s'a. à faire** to stoop to doing.

abandon [abɑ̃dɔ̃] *nm* abandonment; desertion; *Sp* withdrawal; (*naturel*) abandon; **à l'a.** in a neglected state. ● **abandonner** *vt* (*travail, tentative*) to give up, abandon; (*endroit, animal*) to desert, abandon ▌*vi* to give up; *Sp* to withdraw.

abasourdir [abazurdir] *vt* to stun, astound.

abat-jour [abaʒur] *nm inv* lampshade.

abats [aba] *nmpl* offal; (*de volaille*) giblets.

abattoir [abatwar] *nm* slaughterhouse.

abattre* [abatr] *vt* (*mur*) to knock down; (*arbre*) to cut down; (*personne, gros gibier*) to shoot; (*vache etc*) to slaughter; (*avion*) to shoot down; (*déprimer*) *Fig* to demoralize ▌**s'a.** *vpr* (*tomber*) to collapse; (*oiseau*) to swoop down (**sur** on); **s'a. sur** (*pluie*) to come down on; (*tempête*) to hit.

abattu [abaty] *a* (*triste*) demoralized.

abbaye [abei] *nf* abbey.

abbé [abe] *nm* (*chef d'abbaye*) abbot; (*prêtre*) priest.

abcès [apsɛ] *nm* abscess.

abdomen [abdɔmɛn] *nm* stomach, abdomen. ● **abdominal, -aux** *a* abdominal.

abeille [abɛj] *nf* bee.

aberrant [abɛrɑ̃] *a* (*idée etc*) ludicrous, absurd.

abîme [abim] *nm* abyss, chasm, gulf.

abîmer [abime] *vt* to spoil, damage ▌**s'a.** *vpr* to get spoilt.

abject [abʒɛkt] *a* abject, despicable.

aboiement [abwamɑ̃] *nm voir* **aboyer**.

abois (aux) [ozabwa] *adv* at bay.

abolir [abɔlir] *vt* to abolish. ● **abolition** *nf* abolition.

abominable [abɔminabl] *a* terrible.

abondant [abɔ̃dɑ̃] *a* plentiful, abundant. ● **abondamment** *adv* abundantly. ● **abondance** *nf* abundance (**de** of); **une a. de** plenty of, an abundance of; **en a.** in abundance. ● **abonder** *vi* to abound (**en** in).

abonné, -ée [abɔne] *nmf* (*à un journal, au téléphone*) subscriber; *Rail Sp Th* season ticket holder; (*du gaz etc*) consumer. ● **abonnement** *nm* subscription; (**carte d')a.** *Rail Th* season ticket. ● **s'abonner** *vpr* to subscribe, take out a subscription (**à** to); to buy a season ticket.

abord [abɔr] **1** *nm* (*vue*) **au premier a.** at first sight. **2** *nmpl* (*environs*) surroundings; **aux abords de** around, nearby.

abordable [abɔrdabl] *a* (*prix, marchandises*) affordable; (*personne*) approachable.

abord (d') [dabɔr] *adv* first.

abord/er [abɔrde] *vi* to land ▌*vt* (*personne, lieu*) to approach; (*problème*) to tackle, approach. • **—age** *nm* (*assaut*) *Nau* boarding.

about/ir [abutir] *vi* to succeed; **a. à** to end at, lead to, end up in; **n'a. à rien** to come to nothing. • **—issement** *nm* (*résultat*) outcome.

aboyer [abwaje] *vi* to bark. • **aboiement** *nm* bark; *pl* barking.

abréger [abreʒe] *vt* (*récit*) to shorten; (*mot*) to abbreviate. • **abrégé** *nm* **en a.** (*phrase*) in shortened form; (*mot*) in abbreviated form.

abreuvoir [abrœvwar] *nm* (*lieu*) watering place; (*récipient*) drinking trough.

abréviation [abrevjasjɔ̃] *nf* abbreviation.

abri [abri] *nm* shelter; **a. (de jardin)** (garden) shed; **à l'a. de** (*vent*) sheltered from; (*besoin*) safe from; **sans a.** homeless. • **Abribus®** *nm* bus shelter. • **abriter** *vt* (*protéger*) to shelter; (*loger*) to house ‖ **s'a.** *vpr* to (take) shelter.

abricot [abriko] *nm* apricot. • **abricotier** *nm* apricot tree.

abrupt [abrypt] *a* (*pente etc*) steep, sheer, abrupt; (*personne*) abrupt.

abrut/ir [abrytir] *vt* **a. qn** (*travail, télévision*) to turn s.o. into a vegetable. • **—i, -ie** *nmf* idiot ‖ *a* idiotic.

absence [apsɑ̃s] *nf* absence. • **absent, -ente** *a* (*personne*) absent, away; (*chose*) missing ‖ *nmf* absentee. • **s'absenter** *vpr* to go away.

absolu [apsɔly] *a* absolute. • **—ment** *adv* absolutely.

absorb/er [apsɔrbe] *vt* to absorb; (*manger* to eat. • **—ant** *a* (*papier*) absorbent; (*travail, lecture*) absorbing. • **absorption** *nf* absorption.

abstenir* (s') [sapstənir] *vpr Pol* to abstain; **s'a. de qch/de faire** to refrain from sth/doing. • **abstention** *nf Pol* abstention.

abstrait [apstrɛ] *a* abstract. • **abstraction** *nf* abstraction; **faire a. de** to disregard, leave aside.

absurde [apsyrd] *a* & *nm* absurd. • **absurdité** *nf* absurdity; **dire des absurdités** to talk nonsense.

abus [aby] *nm* abuse, misuse (**de** of); over-indulgence (**de** in); (*injustice*) abuse; **a. d'alcool** alcohol abuse. • **abuser** *vi* to go too far; **a. de** (*situation, personne*) to take unfair advantage of; (*autorité*) to abuse, misuse; (*friandises*) to over-indulge in.

abusif, -ive [abyzif, -iv] *a* excessive; **emploi a.** *Ling* improper use, misuse.

acabit [akabi] *nm* **de cet a.** *Péj* of that ilk.

acacia [akasja] *nm* (*arbre*) acacia.

académie [akademi] *nf* academy; *Univ* = (regional) education authority. • **académique** *a* academic.

acajou [akaʒu] *nm* mahogany; **cheveux a.** auburn hair.

acariâtre [akarjɑtr] *a* cantankerous.

accabl/er [akɑble] *vt* to overwhelm (**de** with); **a. d'injures** to heap insults upon; **accablé de dettes** (over)burdened with debt; **accablé de chaleur** overcome by heat; **chaleur accablante** oppressive heat. • **—ement** *nm* dejection.

accalmie [akalmi] *nf* lull.

accaparer [akapare] *vt* to monopolize; (*personne*) to take up all the time of.

accéder [aksede] *vi* **a. à** (*lieu*) to reach; (*pouvoir, trône, demande*) to accede to.

accélérer [akselere] *vi Aut* to accelerate ‖ *vt* (*travaux etc*) to speed up; (*allure, pas*) to quicken, speed up ‖ **s'a.** *vpr* to speed up. • **accélérateur** *nm Aut* accelerator. • **accélération** *nf* acceleration; speeding up.

accent [aksɑ̃] *nm* accent; (*sur une syllabe*) stress; **mettre l'a. sur** to stress. • **accentuer** *vt* to emphasize, accentuate, stress ‖ **s'a.** *vpr* to become more pronounced.

accepter [aksɛpte] *vt* to accept; **a. de faire** to agree to do. • **acceptable** *a* acceptable. • **acceptation** *nf* acceptance.

accès [aksɛ] *nm* **1** access (**à** to); **'a. interdit'** 'no entry'; **les a. de** (*routes*) the approaches to. **2** (*de folie, colère, toux*) fit; (*de fièvre*) bout. • **accessible** *a* accessible; (*personne*) approachable.

accessoire [akseswar] *a* secondary ‖ *nmpl Th* props; (*de voiture etc*) accessories; **accessoires de toilette** toilet requisites.

accident [aksidɑ̃] *nm* accident; **a. d'avion/de train** plane/train crash; **par a.** by accident, by chance. • **accidenté, -ée** *a* (*terrain*) uneven; (*région*) hilly; (*voiture*) damaged (in an accident). • **accidentel, -elle** *a* accidental. • **accidentellement** *adv* accidentally, unintentionally.

acclamer [aklame] *vt* to cheer, acclaim. • **acclamations** *nfpl* cheers.

acclimater [aklimate] *vt*, **s'a.** *vpr* to acclimatize, *Am* acclimate.

accolade [akɔlad] *nf* (*embrassade*) embrace; *Typ* brace, bracket.

accoler [akɔle] *vt* to place (side by side) (**à** against).

accommod/er [akɔmɔde] *vt* to adapt; *Culin* to prepare; **s'a. à** to adapt (oneself) to. • **—ant** *a* accommodating, easy to please.

accompagner [akɔ̃paɲe] *vt* (*personne*) to

go *ou* come with, accompany, escort; (*chose*) & *Mus* to accompany. • **accompagnateur, -trice** *nmf* (*de touristes*) guide; (*musical*) accompanist. • **accompagnement** *nm* (*musical*) accompaniment.

accompl/ir [akɔ̃plir] *vt* to carry out, fulfil, accomplish. • **—i** *a* accomplished.

accord [akɔr] *nm* agreement; (*harmonie*) harmony; *Mus* chord; **être d'a.** to agree, be in agreement (**avec** with); **d'a.!** all right! • **accorder** *vt* (*donner*) to grant; *Mus* to tune; *Gram* to make agree ‖ **s'a.** *vpr* to agree; (*s'entendre*) to get along.

accordéon [akɔrdeɔ̃] *nm* accordion.

accoster [akɔste] *vt* to accost; *Nau* to come alongside ‖ *vi Nau* to berth.

accotement [akɔtmɑ̃] *nm* roadside, shoulder, verge.

accouch/er [akuʃe] *vi* to give birth (**de** to) ‖ *vt* (*enfant*) to deliver. • **—ement** *nm* delivery.

accouder (s') [sakude] *vpr* **s'a. à** *ou* **sur** to lean on (*with one's elbows*). • **accoudoir** *nm* armrest.

accoupler (s') [sakuple] *vpr* (*animaux*) to mate (**à** with).

accourir* [akurir] *vi* to come running, run over.

accoutumer [akutyme] *vt* to accustom ‖ **s'a.** *vpr* to get accustomed (**à** to); **comme à l'accoutumée** as usual. • **accoutumance** *nf* familiarization (**à** with); *Méd* addiction.

accroc [akro] *nm* (*déchirure*) tear; (*difficulté*) hitch, snag.

accrocher [akrɔʃe] *vt* (*déchirer*) to catch; (*fixer*) to hook; (*suspendre*) to hang up (*on a hook*); (*heurter*) to hit, knock ‖ **s'a.** *vpr* (*ne pas céder*) to persevere; (*se disputer*) *Fam* to clash; **s'a. à** (*se cramponner etc*) to cling to; (*s'écorcher*) to catch oneself on. • **accrochage** *nm Aut* minor collision, knock; (*friction*) *Fam* clash.

accroître* [akrwatr] *vt*, **s'a.** *vpr* to increase. • **accroissement** *nm* increase.

accroupir (s') [sakrupir] *vpr* to squat *ou* crouch (down). • **accroupi** *a* squatting, crouching.

accueil [akœj] *nm* welcome, reception. • **accueillir*** *vt* to receive, welcome, greet. • **accueillant** *a* welcoming.

acculer [akyle] *vt* **a. qn à qch** to drive s.o. to *ou* against sth.

accumuler [akymyle] *vt*, **s'a.** *vpr* to pile up, accumulate. • **accumulation** *nf* accumulation.

accus/er [akyze] *vt* (*dénoncer*) to accuse (**de** of); (*rendre responsable*) to blame (**de** for); (*révéler*) to show; (*faire ressortir*) to bring out; **a. réception** to acknowledge receipt (**de** of); **a. qn de faire** to accuse s.o. of doing; to blame s.o. for doing. • **—é, -ée 1** *nmf* accused; (*cour d'assises*) defendant. **2** *a* prominent. • **accusateur, -trice** *a* (*look*) accusing. • **accusation** *nf* accusation; *Jur* charge.

acéré [asere] *a* sharp.

achalandé [aʃalɑ̃de] *a* **bien a.** (*magasin*) well-stocked.

acharner (s') [saʃarne] *vpr* **s'a. sur** (*attaquer*) to set upon, lay into; **s'a. contre** (*poursuivre*) to pursue (relentlessly); **s'a. à faire** to struggle to do, try desperately to do. • **acharné** *a* (*travail, effort*) relentless. • **acharnement** *nm* (*au travail*) (stubborn) determination.

achat [aʃa] *nm* purchase; *pl* shopping.

achet/er [aʃte] *vti* to buy, purchase; **a. à qn** (*vendeur*) to buy from s.o.; (*pour qn*) to buy for s.o. • **—eur, -euse** *nmf* buyer, purchaser; (*dans un magasin*) shopper.

achever [aʃve] *vt* to finish (off); **a. de faire qch** (*personne*) to finish doing sth; **a. qn** (*tuer*) to finish s.o. off ‖ **s'a.** *vpr* to end, finish.

acide [asid] *a* acid, sour ‖ *nm* acid.

acier [asje] *nm* steel. • **aciérie** *nf* steelworks.

acné [akne] *nf* acne.

acompte [akɔ̃t] *nm* part payment, deposit.

acoustique [akustik] *nf* acoustics.

acquérir* [akerir] *vt* (*obtenir*) to acquire, gain; (*acheter*) to purchase. • **acquéreur** *nm* purchaser. • **acquisition** *nf* purchase; acquisition.

acquiescer [akjese] *vi* to acquiesce (**à** to).

acquit [aki] *nm* receipt; **par a. de conscience** to ease one's conscience. • **acquitter** *vt* (*accusé*) to acquit; (*dette*) to clear, pay; **s'a. de** (*devoir, promesse*) to discharge; **s'a. envers qn** to repay s.o. • **acquittement** *nm* (*d'un accusé*) acquittal.

âcre [ɑkr] *a* bitter, acrid, pungent.

acrobate [akrɔbat] *nmf* acrobat. • **acrobaties** *nfpl* acrobatics. • **acrobatique** *a* acrobatic.

acrylique [akrilik] *a* & *nm* acrylic.

acte [akt] *nm* act, deed, action; *Th* act; **un a. de** an act of; **a. de naissance** birth certificate.

acteur, -trice [aktœr, -tris] *nmf* actor, actress.

actif, -ive [aktif, -iv] *a* active ‖ *nm Gram* active.

action [aksjɔ̃] *nf* action; (*en Bourse*) share. • **actionnaire** *nmf* shareholder. • **actionner**

vt to set in motion, activate, actuate.

activer [aktive] *vt* (*accélérer*) to speed up ▮ **s'a.** *vpr* (*se dépêcher*) *Fam* to get a move on.

activité [aktivite] *nf* activity; **en a.** (*personne*) fully active; (*volcan*) active.

actualité [aktɥalite] *nf* (*événements*) current events; *pl TV* news; **d'a.** topical.

actuel, -elle [aktɥɛl] *a* (*présent*) present; (*contemporain*) topical. • **actuellement** *adv* at present, at the present time.

acupuncture [akypɔ̃ktyr] *nf* acupuncture. • **acupuncteur, -trice** *nmf* acupuncturist.

adapter [adapte] *vt* to adapt; (*ajuster*) to fit (**à** to); **s'a. à** (*s'habituer*) to adapt to, adjust to; (*tuyau etc*) to fit. • **adaptateur, -trice** *nmf* adapter. • **adaptation** *nf* adjustment; (*de roman*) adaptation.

additif [aditif] *nm* additive.

addition [adisjɔ̃] *nf* addition; (*au restaurant*) bill, *Am* check. • **additionner** *vt* to add (**à** to); (*nombres*) to add up.

adhérer [adere] *vi* **a. à** (*coller*) to stick to; (*s'inscrire*) to join; (*pneu*) to grip. • **adhérence** *nf* (*de pneu*) grip. • **adhérent, -ente** *nmf* member.

adhésif, -ive [adezif, -iv] *a* & *nm* adhesive.

adieu, -x [adjø] *int* & *nm* farewell, goodbye.

adjectif [adʒɛktif] *nm* adjective.

adjoint, -ointe [adʒwɛ̃, -wɛ̃t] *nmf* assistant; **a. au maire** deputy mayor.

adjuger [adʒyʒe] *vt* (*accorder*) to award (*prize*).

admettre* [admɛtr] *vt* (*laisser entrer, accueillir, reconnaître*) to admit; (*autoriser, tolérer*) to allow; (*candidat*) to pass; **être admis à** (*examen*) to have passed.

administrer [administre] *vt* (*gérer, donner*) to administer. • **administrateur, -trice** *nmf* administrator. • **administratif, -ive** *a* administrative. • **administration** *nf* administration; **l'A.** (*service public*) government service, the Civil Service.

admirer [admire] *vt* to admire. • **admirable** *a* admirable. • **admirateur, -trice** *nmf* admirer. • **admiratif, -ive** *a* admiring. • **admiration** *nf* admiration.

admissible [admisibl] *a* (*comportement etc*) acceptable. • **admission** *nf* admission.

adolescent, -ente [adɔlesɑ̃, -ɑ̃t] *nmf* adolescent, teenager. • **adolescence** *nf* adolescence, *Fam* teens.

adopter [adɔpte] *vt* to adopt. • **adoptif, -ive** *a* (*fils, patrie*) adopted. • **adoption** *nf* adoption.

adorer [adɔre] *vt Rel* to worship; (*chose, personne*) to love, adore; **a. faire** to love *ou* adore doing. • **adorable** *a* adorable. • **adoration** *nf* worship; **être en a. devant** to love, adore.

adosser [adose] *vt* **a. qch à** to lean sth back against; **s'a. à** to lean back against.

adoucir [adusir] *vt* (*voix, traits etc*) to tone down ▮ **s'a.** *vpr* (*temps*) to turn milder; (*caractère*) to mellow. • **adoucissement** *nm* **a. de la température** milder weather.

adresse [adrɛs] *nf* **1** (*domicile*) address. **2** (*habileté*) skill. • **adresser** *vt* (*lettre*) to send; (*remarque etc*) to address; **a. la parole à** to speak to; **s'a. à** to speak to; (*aller trouver*) to go and see; (*bureau*) to inquire at; (*être destiné à*) to be aimed at.

Adriatique [adriatik] *nf* **l'A.** the Adriatic.

adroit [adrwa] *a* skilful, clever.

adulte [adylt] *a* adult ▮ *nmf* adult, grown-up; **être a.** to be an adult *or* a grown-up.

adverbe [advɛrb] *nm* adverb.

adversaire [advɛrsɛr] *nmf* opponent. • **adverse** *a* opposing.

aérer [aere] *vt* (*chambre, lit*) to air (out) ▮ **s'a.** *vpr Fam* to get some air. • **aéré** *a* airy. • **aération** *nf* ventilation. • **aérien, -ienne** *a* (*attaque, transport etc*) air; (*photo*) aerial; (*câble*) overhead; **ligne aérienne** airline.

aérobic [aerɔbik] *nf* aerobics.

aéro-club [aerɔklœb] *nm* flying club. • **aérodrome** *nm* aerodrome. • **aérogare** *nf* air terminal. • **aéroglisseur** *nm* hovercraft. • **aéromodélisme** *nm* model aircraft building and flying. • **aéronautique** *nf* aeronautics. • **aéroport** *nm* airport. • **aéroporté** *a* airborne. • **aérosol** *nm* aerosol.

affaiblir [afeblir] *vt*, **s'a.** *vpr* to weaken.

affaire [afɛr] *nf* (*question*) matter; (*scandale*) affair; (*procès*) case; *pl Com* business; (*d'intérêt public, personnel*) affairs; (*effets*) belongings, things; **avoir a. à** to have to deal with; **c'est mon a.** that's my business *ou* affair *ou* concern; **faire une bonne a.** to get a good deal, get a bargain; **ça fera l'a.** that will do nicely; **toute une a.** (*histoire*) quite a business.

affairer (s') [safere] *vpr* bustle about. • **affairé** *a* busy.

affaisser (s') [safese] *vpr* (*personne*) to collapse; (*plancher*) to give way; (*sol*) to subside. • **affaissement** *nm* (*du sol*) subsidence.

affaler (s') [safale] *vpr* to flop down.

affamé [afame] *a* starving.

affecter [afɛkte] *vt* (*nommer à un poste*) to post.

affection [afɛksjɔ̃] *nf* (*attachement*) affection; (*maladie*) ailment. ● **affectionner** *vt* to be fond of. ● **affectueux, -euse** *a* affectionate, loving.

affermir [afɛrmir] *vt* (*autorité*) to strengthen.

affiche [afiʃ] *nf* notice; (*publicitaire*) poster; *Th* bill. ● **afficher** *vt* (*avis, affiche*) to put up, stick up; (*concert etc*) to put up a notice about; *Ordinat* to display. ● **affichage** *nm* (bill-)posting; *Ordinat* display; **panneau d'a.** hoarding, *Am* billboard.

affilée (d') [dafile] *adv* (*à la suite*) in a row, at a stretch.

affirmatif, -ive [afirmatif, -iv] *a* (*ton*) assertive, positive; (*proposition*) affirmative; **il a été a.** he was quite positive.

affirmer [afirme] *vt* to assert. ● **affirmation** *nf* assertion.

affliger [afliʒe] *vt* to distress.

affluence [aflyɑ̃s] *nf* crowd; **heure(s) d'a.** rush hour(s).

affluent [aflyɑ̃] *nm* tributary.

affoler [afɔle] *vt* to drive crazy; (*effrayer*) to terrify ‖ **s'a.** *vpr* to panic. ● **affolant** *a* terrifying. ● **affolement** *nm* panic.

affranchir [afrɑ̃ʃir] *vt* (*timbrer*) to stamp (*letter*).

affreux, -euse [afrø, -øz] *a* horrible, dreadful, awful. ● **affreusement** *adv* dreadfully, awfully.

affront [afrɔ̃] *nm* insult, affront; **faire un a. à** to insult.

affront/er [afrɔ̃te] *vt* to confront, face; (*mauvais temps, difficultés etc*) to brave. ● **—ement** *nm* confrontation.

affût [afy] *nm* **à l'a. de** *Fig* on the look-out for.

affûter [afyte] *vt* (*outil*) to sharpen.

Afghanistan [afganistɑ̃] *nm* Afghanistan.

afin [afɛ̃] *prép* **a. de** (+ *inf*) in order to ‖ *conj* **a. que** (+ *sub*) so that.

Afrique [afrik] *nf* Africa. ● **africain, -aine** *a* & *nmf* African.

agac/er [agase] *vt* (*personne*) to irritate, annoy. ● **—ement** *nm* irritation.

âge [ɑʒ] *nm* age; **quel â. as-tu?** how old are you?; **avant l'â.** before one's time; **d'un certain â.** middle-aged; **l'â. adulte** adulthood; **le moyen â.** the Middle Ages. ● **âgé** *a* elderly; **â. de six ans** six years old; **un enfant â. de six ans** a six-year-old child; **plus â. que** older than.

agence [aʒɑ̃s] *nf* agency; (*succursale*) branch office; **a. immobilière** estate agent's office, *Am* real estate office.

agenda [aʒɛ̃da] *nm* diary, *Am* datebook.

agenouiller (s') [saʒnuje] *vpr* to kneel (down); **être agenouillé** to be kneeling (down).

agent [aʒɑ̃] *nm* agent; **a. (de police)** policeman; **a. de change** stockbroker; **a. immobilier** estate agent, *Am* real estate agent.

agglomération [aglɔmerɑsjɔ̃] *nf* (*habitations*) built-up area; (*ville*) town.

aggloméré [aglɔmere] *nm* (*bois*) chipboard, fibreboard.

aggraver [agrave] *vt*, **s'a.** *vpr* to worsen. ● **aggravation** *nf* worsening.

agile [aʒil] *a* agile. ● **agilité** *nf* agility.

agir [aʒir] **1** *vi* to act. **2 s'agir** *v imp* **il s'agit d'argent/***etc* it's a question *ou* matter of money/*etc*, it concerns money/*etc*; **de quoi s'agit-il?** what is it?, what's it about?; **il s'agit de se dépêcher** (*il faut*) we have to hurry.

agiter [aʒite] *vt* (*remuer*) to stir; (*secouer*) to shake; (*brandir*) to wave ‖ **s'a.** *vpr* (*enfant*) to fidget. ● **agité** *a* (*mer*) rough; (*personne*) restless, agitated; (*enfant*) fidgety, restless. ● **agitation** *nf* (*de la mer*) roughness; (*d'une personne*) restlessness; (*nervosité*) agitation; (*de la rue*) bustle; *Pol* unrest.

agneau, -x [aɲo] *nm* lamb.

agonie [agɔni] *nf* death throes. ● **agoniser** *vi* to be dying.

agrafe [agraf] *nf* hook; (*pour papiers*) staple. ● **agrafer** *vt* (*robe etc*) to fasten, do up; (*papiers*) to staple. ● **agrafeuse** *nf* stapler.

agrandir [agrɑ̃dir] *vt* to enlarge; (*grossir*) to magnify ‖ **s'a.** *vpr* to expand, grow. ● **agrandissement** *nm* (*de ville*) expansion; (*de maison*) extension; (*de photo*) enlargement.

agréable [agreabl] *a* pleasant, agreeable, nice. ● **—ment** [-əmɑ̃] *adv* pleasantly.

agréer [agree] *vt* to accept; **veuillez a. mes salutations distinguées** (*dans une lettre*) yours faithfully, *Am* sincerely.

agrès [agrɛ] *nmpl Nau* tackle, rigging; (*de gymnastique*) apparatus, *Am* equipment.

agresser [agrese] *vt* to attack; (*dans la rue, pour voler*) to mug. ● **agresseur** *nm* (*dans la rue*) mugger. ● **agression** *nf* attack; (*dans la rue*) mugging.

agressif, -ive [agrɛsif, -iv] *a* aggressive. ● **agressivité** *nf* aggressiveness.

agricole [agrikɔl] *a* (*ouvrier, machine*) farm; **travaux agricoles** farm work.

agriculteur [agrikyltœr] *nm* farmer. ● **agriculture** *nf* farming, agriculture.

agripper [agripe] *vt* to clutch, grip; **s'a. à** to cling to, clutch, grip.

agrumes [agrym] *nmpl* citrus fruit(s).

aguets (aux) [ozagɛ] *adv* on the look-out.
ah! [ɑ] *int* ah!, oh!
ahuri [ayri] *a* astounded, bewildered.
ai [e] *voir* **avoir.**
aide [ɛd] *nf* help, assistance, aid; **à l'a. de** with the help *ou* aid of ‖ *nmf* (*personne*) assistant. • **a.-mémoire** *nm inv Scol* handbook (*of facts etc*).
aider [ede] *vt* to help, assist, aid (**à faire** to do); **s'a. de** to make use of.
aïe! [aj] *int* ouch!, ow!
aie(s), aient [e] *voir* **avoir.**
aigle [ɛgl] *nm* eagle.
aigre [ɛgr] *a* (*acide*) sour; (*voix*, *vent*) sharp, cutting. • **aigreur** *nf* sourness; (*de ton*) sharpness.
aigri [egri] *a* embittered, bitter.
aigu, -uë [egy] *a* (*douleur*, *crise etc*) acute; (*dents*) sharp, pointed; (*voix*) shrill.
aiguille [egɥij] *nf* (*à coudre*, *de pin*) needle; (*de montre*) hand; (*de balance*) pointer; **a. (rocheuse)** peak.
aiguill/er [egɥije] *vt* (*train*) to shunt, *Am* switch; (*personne*) to steer, direct. • **—age** *nm* (*appareil*) *Rail* points, *Am* switches. • **—eur** *nm Rail* signalman; **a. du ciel** air traffic controller.
aiguiser [eg(ɥ)ize] *vt* (*affiler*) to sharpen; (*appétit*) to whet.
ail [aj] *nm* garlic.
aile [ɛl] *nf* wing; (*de moulin*) sail; *Aut* wing, *Am* fender. • **aileron** *nm* (*de requin*) fin. • **ailier** [elje] *nm Fb* wing(er).
aille(s), aillent [aj] *voir* **aller**[1].
ailleurs [ajœr] *adv* somewhere else, elsewhere; **partout a.** everywhere else; **d'a.** (*du reste*) besides, anyway.
aimable [ɛmabl] *a* (*gentil*) kind; (*sympathique*) likeable, amiable; (*agréable*) pleasant. • **—ment** [-əmɑ̃] *adv* kindly.
aimant [ɛmɑ̃] *nm* magnet. • **aimanter** *vt* to magnetize.
aimer [eme] *vt* to love; **a. (bien)** (*apprécier*) to like, be fond of; **a. faire** to like doing *ou* to do; **j'aimerais qu'il vienne** I would like him to come; **a. mieux** to prefer; **ils s'aiment** they're in love.
ⓘ**G99** The Subjunctive 7 G 1b)
aine [ɛn] *nf* groin.
aîné, -ée [ene] *a* (*de deux frères etc*) elder, older; (*de plus de deux*) eldest, oldest ‖ *nmf* (*enfant*) elder *ou* older (child); eldest *ou* oldest (child); **c'est mon a.** he's my senior.
ainsi [ɛ̃si] *adv* (*comme ça*) (in) this *ou* that way; (*alors*) so; **a. que** as well as; **et a. de suite** and so on; **pour a. dire** so to speak.
air [ɛr] *nm* **1** air; **en plein a.** in the open (air), outdoors; **en l'a.** (*jeter*) (up) in the air; (*paroles*, *menaces*) empty; **ficher** *ou* **flanquer en l'a.** *Fam* (*jeter*) to chuck away; (*gâcher*) to mess up; **dans l'a.** (*grippe*, *idées*) about, around. **2** (*expression*) look, appearance; **avoir l'a.** to look, seem; **avoir l'a. de** to look like. **3** (*mélodie*) tune.
aire [ɛr] *nf* (*de stationnement etc*) & *Géom* area.
aisance [ɛzɑ̃s] *nf* (*facilité*) ease; (*prospérité*) affluence.
aise [ɛz] *nf* **à l'a.** (*dans un vêtement etc*) comfortable; (*dans une situation*) at ease; (*fortuné*) comfortably off; **aimer ses aises** to like one's comforts; **mal à l'a.** uncomfortable, ill at ease. • **aisé** [eze] *a* (*fortuné*) comfortably off; (*facile*) easy. • **aisément** *adv* easily.
aisselle [ɛsɛl] *nf* armpit.
ait [ɛ] *voir* **avoir.**
ajouré [aʒure] *a* (*dentelle etc*) openwork.
ajourner [aʒurne] *vt* to postpone, adjourn.
ajout [aʒu] *nm* addition. • **ajouter** *vti* to add (à to); **s'a. à** to add to.
ajust/er [aʒyste] *vt* (*pièce*, *salaires*) to adjust; **a. à** (*adapter*) to fit to. • **—é** *a* (*serré*) close-fitting.
alaise [alɛz] *nf* (waterproof) undersheet.
alambiqué [alɑ̃bike] *a* convoluted.
alarme [alarm] *nf* (*signal*, *inquiétude*) alarm; **jeter l'a.** to cause alarm; **a. antivol/d'incendie** burglar/fire alarm. • **alarmer** *vt* to alarm; **s'a. de** to become alarmed at.
album [albɔm] *nm* (*de timbres etc*) album; (*de dessins*) sketchbook.
alcool [alkɔl] *nm* alcohol; (*spiritueux*) spirits; **a. à 90%** surgical spirit, *Am* rubbing alcohol; **a. à brûler** methylated spirit(s). • **alcoolique** *a* & *nmf* alcoholic. • **alcoolisée** *af* **boisson a.** alcoholic drink. • **alcoolisme** *nm* alcoholism. • **alcootest**® *nm* breath test; (*appareil*) breathalyzer.
aléas [alea] *nmpl* hazards, risks.
alentours [alɑ̃tur] *nmpl* sourroundings, vicinity; **aux alentours de** in the vicinity of.
alerte [alɛrt] **1** *a* (*leste*) spry; (*éveillé*) alert. **2** *nf* alarm; **en état d'a.** on the alert; **a. aérienne** air-raid warning. • **alerter** *vt* to warn, alert.
algèbre [alʒɛbr] *nf* algebra.
Alger [alʒe] *nm ou f* Algiers.
Algérie [alʒeri] *nf* Algeria. • **algérien, -ienne** *a* & *nmf* Algerian.
algue(s) [alg] *nf*(*pl*) seaweed.
alibi [alibi] *nm* alibi.
aliéné, -ée [aljene] *nmf* insane person; *Péj* lunatic.

aligner [aliɲe] *vt* to line up, align ▮ **s'a.** *vpr* (*personnes*) to fall into line, line up; *Pol* to align oneself (**sur** with). • **alignement** *nm* alignment.

aliment [alimɑ̃] *nm* food. • **alimentaire** *a* (*ration, industrie etc*) food; **produits alimentaires** foods. • **alimentation** *nf* (*action*) feeding; supply(ing); (*régime*) diet, nutrition; (*nourriture*) food; **magasin d'a.** grocer's, grocery store. • **alimenter** *vt* (*nourrir*) to feed; (*fournir*) to supply (**en** with).

alité [alite] *a* bedridden.

allaiter [alete] *vti* to breastfeed (*baby*); (*animal*) to suckle.

allécher [aleʃe] *vt* to tempt.

allée [ale] *nf* (*de parc etc*) path, walk; (*de cinéma, supermarché etc*) aisle; (*devant une maison*) drive(way); **allées et venues** comings and goings.

alléɡ/er [aleʒe] *vt* to make lighter. • **—é** *a* (*fromage etc*) low-fat.

allégresse *nf* gladness, rejoicing.

Allemagne [almaɲ] *nf* Germany. • **allemand, -ande** *a* & *nmf* German ▮ *nm* (*langue*) German.

aller[1]** [ale] **1** *vi* (*aux* **être**) to go; (*montre etc*) to work, go; **a. à** (*convenir à*) to suit; **a. avec** (*vêtement*) to go with, match; **a. bien/mieux** (*personne*) to be well/better; **il va savoir/venir/***etc* he'll know/come/*etc*, he's going to know/come/*etc*; **il va partir** he's about to leave, he's going to leave; **va voir!** go and see!; **comment vas-tu?, (comment) ça va?** how are you?; **ça va!** all right!, fine!; **ça va (comme ça)!** that's enough!; **allez-y** go on, go ahead; **allez! au lit!** come on *ou* go on, (to) bed!; **ça va de soi** that's obvious.

❶**aller G90** Impersonal Verbs 7 E 2g)

❶**aller G108** The Infinitive 7 H 2b) i)

❶**aller G217** To Be 13 B 3b)

2 s'en aller *vpr* to go away; (*tache*) to come out; **je m'en vais** I'm off.

aller[2] *nm* outward journey; **a. (simple)** single (ticket), *Am* one-way (ticket); **a. (et) retour** return (ticket), *Am* round-trip (ticket).

allergie [alɛrʒi] *nf* allergy. • **allergique** *a* allergic (**à** to).

alliage [aljaʒ] *nm* alloy.

alliance [aljɑ̃s] *nf* (*anneau*) wedding ring; *Pol* alliance.

allier [alje] *vt* (*associer*) to combine (**à** with) ▮ **s'a.** *vpr* (*pays*) to become allied (**à** with, to). • **allié, -ée** *nmf* ally.

allô [alo] *int Tél* hello!

allocation [alɔkɑsjɔ̃] *nf* allowance, benefit; **a. (de) chômage** unemployment benefit; **allocations familiales** child benefit.

allocution [alɔkysjɔ̃] *nf* (short) speech.

allonger [alɔ̃ʒe] *vt* (*bras*) to stretch out; (*jupe*) to lengthen ▮ *vi* (*jours*) to get longer ▮ **s'a.** *vpr* to stretch out, lie. • **allongé** *a* lying, stretched out; (*étiré*) elongated.

allumer [alyme] *vt* (*feu, pipe etc*) to light; (*électricité, radio*) to turn *ou* switch on ▮ **s'a.** *vpr* (*lumière*) to come on; (*feu, guerre*) to flare up. • **allumage** *nm* lighting; *Aut* ignition • **allume-gaz** *nm inv* gas lighter.

allumette [alymɛt] *nf* match.

allure [alyr] *nf* (*vitesse*) pace; (*de véhicule*) speed; (*démarche*) walk; (*air*) look.

allusion [alyzjɔ̃] *nf* allusion; (*voilée*) hint; **faire a. à** to refer *ou* allude to; to hint at.

alors [alɔr] *adv* (*en ce cas-là*) so, then; (*en ce temps-là*) then; **a. que** (*tandis que*) whereas; (*lorsque*) when; **et a.?** so what?

alouette [alwɛt] *nf* (sky)lark.

alourdir [alurdir] *vt* to weigh down ▮ **s'a.** *vpr* to become heavy *ou* heavier. • **alourdi** *a* heavy.

alpage [alpaʒ] *nm* mountain pasture. • **Alpes** *nfpl* **les A.** the Alps. • **alpin** *a* alpine. • **alpinisme** *nm* mountaineering. • **alpiniste** *nmf* mountaineer.

alphabet [alfabɛ] *nm* alphabet. • **alphabétique** *a* alphabetical.

altérer [altere] **1** *vt* (*denrée, santé*) to spoil. **2** (*donner soif à*) to make thirsty. **3 s'altérer** *vpr* (*santé, relations*) to deteriorate.

alternative [altɛrnativ] *nf* alternative.

alterner [altɛrne] *vti* to alternate. • **alternance** *nf* alternation.

altesse [altɛs] *nf* (*titre*) Highness.

altitude [altityd] *nf* height, altitude.

aluminium [alyminjɔm] *nm* aluminium, *Am* aluminum; **papier (d')a.**, *Fam* **papier (d')alu** tinfoil.

alunir [alynir] *vi* to land on the moon.

alvéole [alveɔl] *nf* (*de ruche*) cell; (*dentaire*) socket.

amabilité [amabilite] *nf* kindness; **faire des amabilités à** to show kindness to.

amadouer [amadwe] *vt* to coax.

amaigr/ir [amegrir] *vt* to make thin(ner); **régime amaigrissant** *Br* slimming diet, *Am* weight reduction diet. • **—i** *a* thin(ner). • **—issement** *nm* (*volontaire*) *Br* slimming, *Am* dieting.

amande [amɑ̃d] *nf* almond.

amarre [amar] *nf* (mooring) rope; *pl* moorings. • **amarrer** (*bateau*) *vt* to moor.

amas [amɑ] *nm* heap, pile. • **amasser** *vt* to pile up; (*fortune, preuves*) to amass ▮ **s'a.** *vpr* to pile up.

amateur [amatœr] *nm* (*d'art etc*) lover; *Sp*

amateur; (*travail*) *Péj* amateurish; **une équipe a.** an amateur team.
ambassade [ɑ̃basad] *nf* embassy. ●**ambassadeur, -drice** *nmf* ambassador.
ambiance [ɑ̃bjɑ̃s] *nf* atmosphere. ●**ambiant** *a* surrounding.
ambigu, -guë [ɑ̃bigy] *a* ambiguous. ●**ambiguïté** [-gɥite] *nf* ambiguity.
ambitieux, -euse [ɑ̃bisjø, -øz] *a* ambitious. ●**ambition** *nf* ambition.
ambulance [ɑ̃bylɑ̃s] *nf* ambulance. ●**ambulancier, -ière** *nmf* ambulance driver.
ambulant [ɑ̃bylɑ̃] *a* travelling, itinerant.
âme [ɑm] *nf* soul; **â. qui vive** a living soul.
améliorer [ameljɔre] *vt*, **s'a.** *vpr* to improve. ●**amélioration** *nf* improvement.
amen [amɛn] *adv* amen.
aménag/er [amenaʒe] *vt* (*arranger, installer*) to fit out (**en** as); (*transformer*) to convert (**en** into); (*construire*) to set up. ●**—ement** *nm* fitting out; conversion; setting up.
amende [amɑ̃d] *nf* fine; **infliger une a. à** to impose a fine on.
amener [amne] *vt* to bring; (*causer*) to bring about.
amer, -ère [amɛr] *a* bitter. ●**amèrement** *adv* bitterly.
Amérique [amerik] *nf* America; **A. du Nord/du Sud** North/South America. ●**américain, -aine** *a* & *nmf* American.
amertume [amɛrtym] *nf* bitterness.
ameublement [amœbləmɑ̃] *nm* furniture.
ameuter [amøte] *vt* (*voisins*) to bring out.
ami, -e [ami] *nmf* friend; (*de la nature, des livres etc*) lover (**de** of); **petit a.** boyfriend; **petite amie** girlfriend.
amiable (à l') [alamjabl] *a* amicable ‖ *adv* amicably.
amiante [amjɑ̃t] *nm* asbestos.
amical, -aux [amikal, -o] *a* friendly. ●**—ement** *adv* in a friendly manner.
amiral, -aux [amiral, -o] *nm* admiral.
amitié [amitje] *nf* friendship; (*amabilité*) kindness; *pl* kind regards; **prendre qn en a.** to take a liking to s.o.
ammoniac [amɔnjak] *nm* (*gaz*) ammonia. ●**ammoniaque** *nf* (*liquide*) ammonia.
amnésie [amnezi] *nf* amnesia.
amnistie [amnisti] *nf* amnesty.
amoindrir [amwɛ̃drir] *vt*, **s'a.** *vpr* to decrease, diminish.
amonceler (s') [samɔ̃sle] *vpr* to pile up.
amont (en) [ɑ̃namɔ̃] *adv* upstream.
amorce [amɔrs] *nf* (*début*) start; (*de pêcheur*) bait; (*de pistolet d'enfant*) cap. ●**amorcer** *vt*, **s'a.** *vpr* to start.
amort/ir [amɔrtir] *vt* (*coup*) to cushion, (*bruit*) to deaden. ●**—isseur** *nm* shock absorber.
amour [amur] *nm* love; **pour l'a. de** for the sake of; **mon a.** my darling, my love. ●**a.-propre** *nm* self-respect, self-esteem. ●**amoureux, -euse** *nmf* lover ‖ *a* **a. (de qn)** in love (with s.o.).
amovible [amɔvibl] *a* removable, detachable.
amphithéâtre [ɑ̃fiteɑtr] *nm* (*romain*) amphitheatre; *Univ* lecture hall.
ample [ɑ̃pl] *a* (*vêtement*) full, ample, roomy; (*provision*) full. ●**amplement** *adv* amply, fully; **a. suffisant** ample. ●**ampleur** *nf* (*de robe*) fullness; (*importance, étendue*) scale, extent; **prendre de l'a.** to grow.
amplifier [ɑ̃plifje] *vt* (*son, courant*) to amplify; (*exagérer*) to magnify ‖ **s'a.** *vpr* to increase. ●**amplificateur** *nm* *El* amplifier.
ampoule [ɑ̃pul] *nf* (*électrique*) (light) bulb; (*aux pieds etc*) blister; (*de médicament*) phial.
amputer [ɑ̃pyte] *vt* (*membre*) to amputate; **a. qn de la jambe** to amputate s.o.'s leg. ●**amputation** *nf* amputation.
amuser [amyze] *vt* (*divertir*) to amuse, entertain ‖ **s'a.** *vpr* to enjoy oneself, have fun; **s'a. avec** to play with; **s'a. à faire** to amuse oneself doing. ●**amusant** *a* amusing. ●**amusement** *nm* amusement; (*jeu*) game.
amygdales [amidal] *nfpl* tonsils.
an [ɑ̃] *nm* year; **il a dix ans** he's ten (years old); **par a.** (*dix fois etc*) a *ou* per year; **Nouvel A.** New Year.
ⓘ**G199** Dates 11 B 2b) Note ii)
ⓘ**G202** Age 11 C 3
analogue [analɔg] *a* similar.
analyse [analiz] *nf* analysis; *Méd* test; **a. grammaticale** parsing. ●**analyser** *vt* to analyse; (*phrase*) to parse.
ananas [anana(s)] *nm* pineapple.
anarchie [anarʃi] *nf* anarchy. ●**anarchiste** *nmf* anarchist.
anatomie [anatɔmi] *nf* anatomy.
ancêtre [ɑ̃sɛtr] *nm* ancestor.
anche [ɑ̃ʃ] *nf* *Mus* reed.
anchois [ɑ̃ʃwa] *nm* anchovy.
ancien, -ienne [ɑ̃sjɛ̃, -jɛn] *a* (*vieux*) old; (*meuble*) antique; (*qui n'est plus*) former, ex-, old; (*antique*) ancient; (*dans une fonction*) senior; **a. élève** old boy, *Am* alumnus; **a. combattant** ex-serviceman, *Am* veteran.
ⓘ**G32** Position of Adjectives 4 D 3
‖ *nmf* (*par l'âge*) elder; (*dans une fonction*) senior; **les anciens** (*auteurs, peuples*) the

ancients. • **anciennement** *adv* formerly. • **ancienneté** *nf* age; (*dans une fonction*) seniority.
ancre [ɑ̃kr] *nf* anchor; **jeter l'a.** to (cast) anchor; **lever l'a.** to weigh anchor. • **ancrer** *vt* (*navire*) to anchor; (*idée*) *Fig* to root, fix.
andouille [ɑ̃duj] *nf* (*idiot*) *Fam* nitwit; **espèce d'a.!** *Fam* (you) nitwit!
âne [ɑn] *nm* (*animal*) donkey, ass; (*personne*) *Péj* ass.
anéant/ir [aneɑ̃tir] *vt* to annihilate, wipe out. • **—issement** *nm* annihilation.
anecdote [anɛkdɔt] *nf* anecdote.
anémie [anemi] *nf* an(a)emia. • **anémique** *a* an(a)emic. • **s'anémier** *vpr* to become an(a)emic.
anémone [anemɔn] *nf* anemone.
ânerie [ɑnri] *nf* stupidity; (*action etc*) stupid thing. • **ânesse** *nf* she-ass.
anesthésie [anɛstezi] *nf* an(a)esthesia; **a. générale/locale** general/local an(a)esthetic. • **anesthésier** *vt* to an(a)esthetize.
ange [ɑ̃ʒ] *nm* angel; **être aux anges** to be in seventh heaven. • **angélique** *a* angelic.
angine [ɑ̃ʒin] *nf* sore throat.
anglais, -aise [ɑ̃glɛ, -ɛz] *a* English ‖ *nmf* Englishman, Englishwoman; **les A.** the English ‖ *nm* (*langue*) English ‖ *af* **filer à l'anglaise** to take French leave.
angle [ɑ̃gl] *nm* (*point de vue*) & *Géom* angle; (*de rue*) corner.
Angleterre [ɑ̃glətɛr] *nf* England.
anglican, -ane [ɑ̃glikɑ̃, -an] *a* & *nmf* Anglican.
anglo- [ɑ̃glɔ] *préf* Anglo-. • **anglophone** *a* English-speaking ‖ *nmf* English speaker. • **anglo-saxon, -onne** *a* & *nmf* Anglo-Saxon.
angoisse [ɑ̃gwas] *nf* (great) anxiety, anguish. • **angoissant** *a* distressing. • **angoissé** *a* (*personne*) in (a state of) anguish; (*geste, cri*) anguished.
angora [ɑ̃gɔra] *nm* (*laine*) angora.
anguille [ɑ̃gij] *nf* eel.
animal, -aux [animal, -o] *nm* animal ‖ *a* (*règne, graisse etc*) animal.
animer [anime] *vt* (*débat, groupe*) to lead; (*soirée*) to liven up; (*mécanisme*) to drive; **la joie qui animait son regard** the joy which made his face light up; **animé de** (*sentiment*) prompted by.
‖ **s'animer** *vpr* (*rue etc*) to come to life; (*yeux*) to light up. • **animé** *a* (*rue conversation*) lively; (*doué de vie*) animate. • **animateur, -trice** *nmf* *TV* compere, *Am* master of ceremonies, emcee; (*de club*) leader, organizer. • **animation** *nf* (*des rues*) activity; (*de réunion*) liveliness; (*de visage*) brightness.
anis [ani(s)] *nm* (*boisson, parfum*) aniseed.
ankyloser (s') [sɑ̃kiloze] *vpr* to stiffen up. • **ankylosé** *a* stiff.
anneau, -x [ano] *nm* ring; (*de chaîne*) link.
année [ane] *nf* year; **bonne a.!** Happy New Year!
ⓘ**G200** Dates 11 B 3
annexe [anɛks] *nf* (*bâtiment*) annex(e). • **annexer** *vt* (*pays*) to annex. • **annexion** *nf* annexation.
anniversaire [anivɛrsɛr] *nm* (*d'événement*) anniversary; (*de naissance*) birthday.
annonce [anɔ̃s] *nf* (*avis*) announcement; (*publicitaire*) advertisement; **petites annonces** classified advertisements, small ads. • **annoncer** *vt* (*signaler*) to announce, report; (*vente*) to advertise; **a. le printemps** to herald spring; **s'a. pluvieux/difficile/***etc* to look (like being) rainy/difficult/*etc*.
annuaire [anɥɛr] *nm* (*téléphonique*) phone book, directory.
annuel, -elle [anɥɛl] *a* annual, yearly.
annulaire [anylɛr] *nm* ring *ou* third finger.
annuler [anyle] *vt* (*visite etc*) to cancel; (*jugement*) to quash ‖ **s'a.** *vpr* to cancel each other out. • **annulation** *nf* cancellation; quashing.
anodin [anɔdɛ̃] *a* harmless.
anomalie [anɔmali] *nf* (*bizarrerie*) anomaly.
ânon [ɑnɔ̃] *nm* baby donkey.
ânonner [ɑnɔne] *vt* to stumble through (*poem etc*).
anonymat [anɔnima] *nm* anonymity; **garder l'a.** to remain anonymous. • **anonyme** *a* & *nmf* anonymous (person).
anorak [anɔrak] *nm* anorak.
anorexie [anɔrɛksi] *nf* anorexia. • **anorexique** *a* & *nmf* anorexic.
anormal, -aux [anɔrmal, -o] *a* abnormal; (*enfant*) educationally subnormal.
anse [ɑ̃s] *nf* (*de tasse etc*) handle; (*baie*) cove.
Antarctique [ɑ̃tarktik] *a* antarctic ‖ *nm* **l'A.** the Antarctic, Antarctica.
antécédent [ɑ̃tesedɑ̃] *nm* *Gram* antecedent.
antenne [ɑ̃tɛn] *nf* *TV Rad* aerial, *Am* antenna; (*d'insecte*) antenna, feeler; **sur** *ou* **à l'a.** on the air.
antérieur [ɑ̃terjœr] *a* (*précédent*) former, previous, earlier; (*placé devant*) front; **membre a.** forelimb; **a. à** prior to.
anthropophage [ɑ̃trɔpɔfaʒ] *nm* cannibal.
antiatomique [ɑ̃tiatɔmik] *a* **abri a.** fallout shelter.

antibiotique [ɑ̃tibjɔtik] *nm* antibiotic.
antibrouillard [ɑ̃tibrujar] *a* & *nm* **(phare) a.** fog lamp.
antichoc [ɑ̃tiʃɔk] *a inv* shockproof.
anticip/er [ɑ̃tisipe] *vti* **a. (sur)** to anticipate. ●**—é** *a* (*retraite etc*) early; **avec mes remerciements anticipés** thanking you in advance.
anticonstitutionnel, -elle [ɑ̃tikɔ̃stitysjɔnɛl] *a* unconstitutional.
anticorps [ɑ̃tikɔr] *nm* antibody.
anticyclone [ɑ̃tisiklon] *nm* anticyclone.
antidémocratique [ɑ̃tidemɔkratik] *a* undemocratic.
antidérapant [ɑ̃tiderapɑ̃] *a* non-skid.
antidote [ɑ̃tidɔt] *nm* antidote.
antigel [ɑ̃tiʒɛl] *nm* antifreeze.
Antilles [ɑ̃tij] *nfpl* **les A.** the West Indies. ●**antillais, -aise** *a* & *nmf* West Indian.
antilope [ɑ̃tilɔp] *nf* antelope.
antimite [ɑ̃timit] *nm* **de l'a.** moth balls.
antipathique [ɑ̃tipatik] *a* disagreeable.
antipodes [ɑ̃tipɔd] *nmpl* **aux a.** (*partir*) to the antipodes; **aux a. de** (*la vérité etc*) poles apart from.
antique [ɑ̃tik] *a* ancient. ●**antiquaire** *nmf* antique dealer. ●**antiquité** *nf* (*temps, ancienneté*) antiquity; (*objet ancien*) antique.
antisémite [ɑ̃tisemit] *a* anti-Semitic. ●**antisémitisme** *nm* anti-Semitism.
antiseptique [ɑ̃tisɛptik] *a* & *nm* antiseptic.
antivol [ɑ̃tivɔl] *nm* anti-theft lock *ou* device.
antre [ɑ̃tr] *nm* (*de lion etc*) den.
anus [anys] *nm* anus.
Anvers [ɑ̃vɛr(s)] *nm ou f* Antwerp.
anxiété [ɑ̃ksjete] *nf* anxiety. ●**anxieux, -euse** *a* anxious.
août [u(t)] *nm* August. ●**aoûtien, -ienne** [ausjɛ̃, -jɛn] *nmf* August holidaymaker *ou Am* vacationer.
apaiser [apeze] *vt* (*personne*) to calm, pacify; (*faim*) to appease; (*douleur*) to soothe; (*craintes*) to calm ‖ **s'a.** *vpr* (*personne*) to calm down; (*tempête, douleur*) to die down. ●**apaisant** *a* soothing.
aparté [aparte] *nm* **en a.** in private.
apercevoir* [apɛrsəvwar] *vt* to see; (*brièvement*) to catch a glimpse of; **s'a. de** to realize, notice; **s'a. que** to realize *ou* notice that. ●**aperçu** *nm* overall view.
apéritif [aperitif] *nm* aperitif.
apeuré [apœre] *a* frightened, scared.
aphone [afɔn] *a* voiceless, completely hoarse.
aphte [aft] *nm* mouth ulcer.
apiculture [apikyltyr] *nf* beekeeping.
apitoyer [apitwaje] *vt* to move (to pity); **s'a. sur** to pity.
aplanir [aplanir] *vt* (*terrain*) to level; (*difficulté*) to iron out, smooth out.
aplatir [aplatir] *vt* to flatten (out) ‖ **s'a.** *vpr* (*s'étendre*) to lie flat; (*s'humilier*) to grovel; **s'a. contre** to flatten oneself against. ●**aplati** *a* flat.
aplomb [aplɔ̃] *nm* **d'a.** (*meuble etc*) level, straight; (*personnne*) (*sur ses jambes*) steady; (*bien portant*) in good shape.
apocalypse [apɔkalips] *nf* apocalypse; **d'a.** (*vision etc*) apocalyptic.
apogée [apɔʒe] *nm* (*de carrière etc*) peak.
apostrophe [apɔstrɔf] *nf* **1** (*signe*) apostrophe. **2** (*interpellation*) sharp *ou* rude remark. ●**apostropher** *vt* to shout at.
apothéose [apɔteoz] *nf* final triumph.
apôtre [apotr] *nm* apostle.
apparaître* [aparɛtr] *vi* (*se montrer, sembler*) to appear.
appareil [aparɛj] *nm* (*instrument, machine*) apparatus; (*électrique*) appliance; *Tél* telephone; (*avion*) aircraft; *Anat* system; **a. (photo)** camera; **a. (auditif)** hearing aid; **a. (dentaire)** brace; **qui est à l'a.?** *Tél* who's speaking?
appareiller [apareje] *vi Nau* to get under way.
apparence [aparɑ̃s] *nf* appearance; **en a.** outwardly; **sauver les apparences** to keep up appearances. ●**apparemment** [-amɑ̃] *adv* apparently. ●**apparent** *a* apparent; (*très visible*) conspicuous.
apparenté [aparɑ̃te] *a* (*semblable*) similar.
apparition [aparisjɔ̃] *nf* appearance; (*fantôme*) apparition.
appartement [apartəmɑ̃] *nm* flat, *Am* apartment.
appartenir* [apartənir] *vi* to belong (**à** to); **il vous appartient de** it's your responsibility to. ●**appartenance** *nf* membership (**à** of).
appât [apɑ] *nm* (*amorce*) bait. ●**appâter** *vt* (*attirer*) to lure.
appauvrir [apovrir] *vt* to make poorer ‖ **s'a.** *vpr* to become poorer.
appel [apɛl] *nm* (*cri, attrait etc*) call; (*demande pressante*) & *Jur* appeal; *Mil* call-up; **faire l'a.** *Scol* to take the register; *Mil* to have a roll call; **faire a. à** to appeal to, call upon.
appeler [aple] *vt* (*personne, nom etc*) to call; (*en criant*) to call out to; *Mil* to call up; (*nécessiter*) to call for; **a. à l'aide** to call for help; **en a. à** to appeal to; **il est appelé à** (*de hautes fonctions*) he is marked out for; (*témoigner etc*) he is called upon to.

‖ **s'appeler** *vpr* to be called; **il s'appelle Paul** his name is Paul. ● **appelé** *nm Mil* conscript. ● **appellation** *nf* (*nom*) term.
appendice [apɛ̃dis] *nm* (*du corps, de livre*) appendix. ● **appendicite** *nf* appendicitis.
appesantir (s') [sapəzɑ̃tir] *vpr* **s'a. sur** (*sujet*) to dwell upon.
appétit [apeti] *nm* appetite (**de** for); **mettre qn en a.** to whet s.o.'s appetite; **bon a.!** enjoy your meal! ● **appétissant** *a* appetizing.
applaud/ir [aplodir] *vti* to applaud, clap. ● **—issements** *nmpl* applause.
applique [aplik] *nf* wall lamp.
appliqu/er [aplike] *vt* to apply (**à** to); (*loi, décision*) to put into effect; **s'a. à** (*un travail*) to apply oneself to; (*concerner*) to apply to; **s'a. à faire** to take pains to do. ● **—é** *a* (*travailleur*) painstaking. ● **application** *nf* application.
appoint [apwɛ̃] *nm* **faire l'a.** to give the correct money *ou* change.
appontement [apɔ̃tmɑ̃] *nm* landing stage.
apport [apɔr] *nm* contribution.
apporter [apɔrte] *vt* to bring.
apposition [apozisjɔ̃] *nf Gram* apposition.
apprécier [apresje] *vt* (*aimer, percevoir*) to appreciate; (*évaluer*) to assess. ● **appréciable** *a* appreciable. ● **appréciation** *nf* (*de professeur*) comment (**sur** on); (*de distance etc*) assessment.
appréhender [apreɑ̃de] *vt* (*craindre*) to dread (**de faire** doing); (*arrêter*) to arrest, apprehend. ● **appréhension** *nf* anxiety, apprehension.
apprendre* [aprɑ̃dr] *vti* (*étudier*) to learn; (*événement, fait*) to hear of, learn of; (*nouvelle*) to hear; **a. à faire** to learn to do; **a. qch à qn** (*enseigner*) to teach s.o. sth; (*informer*) to tell s.o. sth; **a. à qn à faire** to teach s.o. to do; **a. que** to learn that; (*être informé*) to hear that.
apprenti, -ie [aprɑ̃ti] *nmf* apprentice; (*débutant*) novice. ● **apprentissage** *nm* apprenticeship; (*d'une langue*) learning (**de** of).
apprêter (s') [saprete] *vpr* to get ready (**à faire** to do).
apprivoiser [aprivwaze] *vt* to tame ‖ **s'a.** *vpr* to become tame. ● **apprivoisé** *a* tame.
approbation [aprɔbɑsjɔ̃] *nf* approval.
approche [aprɔʃ] *nf* approach.
approcher [aprɔʃe] *vt* (*chaise etc*) to draw up (**de** to); (*personne*) to come *ou* get close to, approach ‖ *vi* to draw near(er) (**de** to), approach ‖ **s'a.** *vpr* to come *ou* get near(er) (**de** to); **il s'est approché de moi** he came up to me.
approfond/ir [aprɔfɔ̃dir] *vt* (*trou etc*) to dig deeper; (*question*) to go into thoroughly. ● **—i** *a* thorough.
approprié [aprɔprije] *a* appropriate.
approprier (s') [saprɔprije] *vpr* **s'a. qch** to take sth, help oneself to sth.
approuver [apruve] *vt* (*autoriser*) to approve; (*apprécier*) to approve of.
approvisionner [aprɔvizjɔne] *vt* (*ville etc*) to supply (with provisions); (*magasin*) to stock ‖ **s'a.** *vpr* to get one's supplies (**de, en** of).
approximatif, -ive [aprɔksimatif, -iv] *a* approximate. ● **approximativement** *adv* approximately.
appui [apɥi] *nm* support; (*pour coude etc*) rest; (*de fenêtre*) sill. ● **appui-tête** *nm ou* **appuie-tête** *nm inv* headrest.
appuyer [apɥije] *vt* (*soutenir*) to support; **a. qch sur/contre** (*poser*) to rest *ou* lean sth on/against; **s'a. sur** to lean on, rest on; (*compter*) to rely on; **s'a. contre** to lean against ‖ *vi* **a. sur** (*bouton etc*) to press; (*etre posé sur*) to rest on. ● **appuyé** *a* leaning (**contre, sur** against, on).
après [aprɛ] **1** *prép* (*temps*) after; (*espace*) beyond, past; **a. un an** after a year; **a. le pont** beyond *ou* past the bridge; **a. tout** after all; **a. coup** after the event; **a. avoir mangé** after eating; **a. qu'il t'a vu** after he saw you ‖ *adv* after(wards); **l'année d'a.** the following year; **et a.?** and then what? **2** *prép* **d'a.** (*selon*) according to.
après-demain [aprɛdmɛ̃] *adv* the day after tomorrow. ● **a.-midi** *nm ou f inv* afternoon. ● **a.-shampooing** *nm* (hair) conditioner. ● **a.-ski** *nm* ankle boot, snow boot.
apte [apt] *a* suited (**à** to), capable (**à** of). ● **aptitude** *nf* aptitude (**à, pour** for); **avoir des aptitudes pour qch** to have an aptitude for sth.
aquarelle [akwarɛl] *nf* watercolour.
aquarium [akwarjɔm] *nm* aquarium.
aquatique [akwatik] *a* aquatic.
arabe [arab] *a* & *nmf* Arab ‖ *a* & *nm* (*langue*) Arabic; **chiffres arabes** Arabic numerals. ● **Arabie** *nf* **A. Séoudite** Saudi Arabia.
arachide [araʃid] *nf* peanut.
araignée [areɲe] *nf* spider.
arbitraire [arbitrɛr] *a* arbitrary.
arbitre [arbitr] *nm Fb Boxe* referee; *Tennis* umpire; **libre a.** free will. ● **arbitrer** *vt* to referee; to umpire. ● **arbitrage** *nm* refereeing; umpiring.

arborer [arbɔre] *vt* (*insigne, vêtement*) to sport.
arbre [arbr] *nm* tree; *Aut* shaft, axle.
arbuste [arbyst] *nm* (small) shrub, bush.
arc [ark] *nm* (*arme*) bow; (*voûte*) arch; (*de cercle*) arc; **tir à l'a.** archery. • **arcade** *nf* arch(way); *pl* arcade, arches.
arc-en-ciel [arkɑ̃sjɛl] *nm* (*pl* **arcs-en-ciel**) rainbow.
archaïque [arkaik] *a* archaic.
arche [arʃ] *nf* (*voûte*) arch; **l'a. de Noé** Noah's ark.
archéologie [arkeɔlɔʒi] *nf* arch(a)eol-ogy. • **archéologue** *nmf* arch(a)eol-ogist.
archer [arʃe] *nm* archer.
archet [arʃɛ] *nm Mus* bow.
archevêque [arʃəvɛk] *nm* archbishop.
archipel [arʃipɛl] *nm* archipelago.
archiplein [arʃiplɛ̃] *a* chock-a-block.
architecte [arʃitɛkt] *nm* architect. • **architecture** *nf* architecture.
archives [arʃiv] *nfpl* archives, records.
Arctique [arktik] *nm* **l'A.** the Arctic.
ardent [ardɑ̃] *a* (*passionné*) ardent, fervent; (*empressé*) eager; (*soleil*) scorching. • **ardemment** [-amɑ̃] *adv* eagerly, fervently. • **ardeur** *nf* (*énergie*) enthusiasm, fervour.
ardoise [ardwaz] *nf* slate.
are [ar] *nm* = 100 square metres.
arène [arɛn] *nf* (*pour taureaux*) bullring; *pl* bullring; *Hist* amphitheatre.
arête [arɛt] *nf* (*de poisson*) bone; (*de cube etc*) edge, ridge; (*de montagne*) ridge.
argent [arʒɑ̃] *nm* (*métal*) silver; (*monnaie*) money; **a. comptant** *ou* **liquide** cash. • **argenterie** *nf* silverware.
Argentine [arʒɑ̃tin] *nf* Argentina. • **argentin, -ine** *a* & *nmf* Argentinian.
argile [arʒil] *nf* clay.
argot [argo] *nm* slang.
argument [argymɑ̃] *nm* argument. • **argumentation** *nf* arguments.
aride [arid] *a* arid, barren.
aristocrate [aristɔkrat] *nmf* aristocrat. • **aristocratie** [-asi] *nf* aristocracy. • **aristocratique** *a* aristocratic.
arithmétique [aritmetik] *nf* arithmetic.
armateur [armatœr] *nm* shipowner.
armature [armatyr] *nf* (*charpente*) framework; (*de lunettes, tente*) frame.
arme [arm] *nf* weapon; *pl* weapons, arms; **a. à feu** firearm. • **armer** *vt* (*personne etc*) to arm (**de** with); (*fusil*) to cock; (*appareil photo*) to wind on ‖ **s'a.** *vpr* to arm oneself (**de** with). • **armement(s)** *nm(pl)* arms.
armée [arme] *nf* army; **a. de l'air** air force.
armistice [armistis] *nm* armistice.
armoire [armwar] *nf* (*penderie*) wardrobe, *Am* closet; **a. à pharmacie** medicine chest *ou* cabinet.
armure [armyr] *nf* armour.
armurier [armyrje] *nm* gunsmith.
arôme [arom] *nm* (*goût*) flavour; (*odeur*) (pleasant) smell.
arpent/er [arpɑ̃te] *vt* (*terrain*) to survey; (*trottoir etc*) to pace up and down. • **—eur** *nm* (land) surveyor.
arqué [arke] *a* arched, curved; (*jambes*) bandy.
arrache-pied (d') [daraʃpje] *adv* relentlessly.
arrach/er [araʃe] *vt* (*clou, dent, cheveux, page etc*) to pull out; (*plante*) to pull up; **a. qch à qn** to snatch sth from s.o.; (*aveu, argent*) to force sth out of s.o.; **a. qn de son lit** to drag s.o. out of bed. • **—age** *nm* (*de plante*) pulling up.
arranger [arɑ̃ʒe] *vt* (*chambre, visite etc*) to fix up, arrange; (*voiture, texte etc*) to put right; (*différend*) to settle; **ça m'arrange** that suits me ‖ **s'a.** *vpr* (*se mettre d'accord*) to come to an agreement *ou* arrangement; (*finir bien*) to turn out fine; **s'a. pour faire** to arrange to do, manage to do. • **arrangeant** *a* accommodating.
arrestation [arɛstɑsjɔ̃] *nf* arrest.
arrêt [arɛ] *nm* (*halte, endroit*) stop; (*action*) stopping; **temps d'a.** pause; **à l'a.** stationary; **a. de travail** (*grève*) stoppage; (*congé*) sick leave; **sans a.** constantly, non-stop.
arrêté [arete] *nm* order, decision.
arrêter [arete] *vt* to stop; (*appréhender*) to arrest; (*regard, date*) to fix ‖ *vi* to stop; **il n'arrête pas de critiquer/***etc* he's always criticizing/*etc*, he doesn't stop criticizing/*etc* ‖ **s'a.** *vpr* to stop; **s'a. de faire** to stop doing.
arrière [arjɛr] *adv* **en a.** (*marcher etc*) backwards; (*rester*) behind; (*regarder*) back, behind; **en a. de qn/qch** behind s.o./sth ‖ *nm* & *a inv* back, rear; **à l'a.** in *ou* at the back; **faire marche a.** to reverse, back ‖ *nm Fb* (full) back.
arrière-boutique [arjɛrbutik] *nm* back room (*of a shop*). • **a.-goût** *nm* aftertaste. • **a.-grand-mère** *nf* great-grand-mother. • **a.-grand-père** *nm* (*pl* **arrière-grands-pères**) great-grand-father. • **a.-pensée** *nf* ulterior motive. • **a.-plan** *nm* background.
arrimer [arime] *vt* (*fixer*) to secure.
arriv/er [arive] *vi* (*aux* **être**) (*venir*) to arrive, come; (*survenir*) to happen; (*réussir*) to succeed; **a. à** (*atteindre*) to reach; **a.**

à faire to manage to do, succeed in doing; **a. à qn** to happen to s.o. ‖ *v imp* **il m'arrive d'oublier**/*etc* I (sometimes) forget/*etc*. ●**—ée** *nf* arrival; *Sp* (winning) post. ●**arrivage** *nm* consignment.

arrogant [arɔgɑ̃] *a* arrogant.

arrond/ir [arɔ̃dir] *vt chiffre, angle, jupe*) to round off; (*rendre rond*) to make round (*pebble etc*). ●**—i** *a* rounded.

arrondissement [arɔ̃dismɑ̃] *nm* (*d'une ville*) district.

arros/er [aroze] *vt* (*terre*) to water; (*succès*) to drink to. ●**—age** *nm* watering. ●**arrosoir** *nm* watering can.

art [ar] *nm* art; **film/critique d'a.** art film/ critic; **arts ménagers** domestic science.

artère [artɛr] *nf Anat* artery; *Aut* main road.

artichaut [artiʃo] *nm* artichoke.

article [artikl] *nm* (*de presse, de commerce*) & *Gram* article; (*dans un contrat, catalogue*) item; **articles de toilette** toiletries.

articuler [artikyle] *vt* (*mot etc*) to articulate. ●**articulation** *nf Ling* articulation; *Anat* joint; **a. (du doigt)** knuckle.

artifice [artifis] *nm* **feu d'a.** (*spectacle*) firework display, fireworks.

artificiel, -ielle [artifisjɛl] *a* artificial. ●**artificiellement** *adv* artificially.

artillerie [artijri] *nf* artillery. ●**artilleur** *nm* gunner.

artisan [artizɑ̃] *nm* craftsman, artisan. ●**artisanal, -aux** *a* **métier a.** craftsman's trade; **objet a.** object made by craftsmen. ●**artisanat** *nm* (*métier*) craftsman's trade.

artiste [artist] *nmf* artist; *Th Mus Cin* performer, artist. ●**artistique** *a* artistic.

as [ɑs] *nm* (*carte, champion*) ace; **a. du volant** brilliant *ou* crack driver.

ascenseur [asɑ̃sœr] *nm* lift, *Am* elevator.

ascension [asɑ̃sjɔ̃] *nf* ascent; **l'A.** Ascension Day.

Asie [azi] *nf* Asia. ●**asiatique** *a* & *nmf* Asian, Asiatic.

asile [azil] *nm* (*abri*) shelter; *Pol* asylum; **a. (d'aliénés)** *Péj* (lunatic) asylum.

aspect [aspɛ] *nm* (*air*) appearance; (*perspective*) & *Gram* aspect.

asperges [aspɛrʒ] *nfpl* asparagus.

asperger [aspɛrʒe] *vt* (*par jeu ou accident*) to splash (**de** with); (*pour humecter*) to spray, sprinkle (**de** with).

aspérité [asperite] *nf* bump.

asphalte [asfalt] *nm* asphalt.

asphyxie [asfiksi] *nf* suffocation. ●**asphyxier** *vt* to suffocate, asphyxiate.

aspirateur [aspiratœr] *nm* vacuum cleaner, hoover® **passer (à) l'a.** to vacuum, hoover.

aspir/er [aspire] **1** *vt* (*liquide*) to suck up; (*respirer*) to breathe in, inhale. **2** *vi* **a. à qch** to aspire to sth. ●**—é** *a Ling* aspirate(d).

aspirine [aspirin] *nf* aspirin.

assagir (s') [sasaʒir] *vpr* to settle down.

assaill/ir [asajir] *vt* to attack; **a. de** (*questions etc*) to assail with. ●**—ant** *nm* attacker, assailant.

assaisonn/er [asɛzɔne] *vt* to season. ●**—ement** *nm* seasoning.

assassin [asasɛ̃] *nm* murderer. ●**assassinat** *nm* murder. ●**assassiner** *vt* to murder.

assaut [aso] *nm* onslaught, assault; **prendre d'a.** to (take by) storm.

assemblée [asɑ̃ble] *nf* (*personnes réunies*) gathering; (*parlement*) assembly; (*de fidèles*) congregation.

assembler [asɑ̃ble] *vt* to put together, assemble ‖ **s'a.** *vpr* to gather. ●**assemblage** *nm* (*montage*) assembly; (*réunion d'objets*) collection.

asseoir* [aswar] *vt* **a. qn** to sit s.o. (down), seat s.o. (**sur** on) ‖ **s'a.** *vpr* to sit (down).

assez [ase] *adv* enough; **a. de pain/de gens** enough bread/people; **j'en ai a.** I've had enough; **a. grand/intelligent**/*etc* (*suffisamment*) big/clever/*etc* enough (**pour faire** to do); **a. fatigué**/*etc* (*plutôt*) fairly *ou* rather *ou* quite tired/*etc*.

assidu [asidy] *a* (*toujours présent*) regular; (*appliqué*) diligent; **a. auprès de qn** attentive to s.o.

assiéger [asjeʒe] *vt* (*ville*) to besiege; (*magasin, vedette*) to mob, crowd round; (*importuner*) to pester.

assiette [asjɛt] *nf* (*récipient*) plate; **a. anglaise** *Culin* (assorted) cold meats, *Am* cold cuts; **ne pas être dans son a.** *Fig* to be feeling out of sorts. ●**assiettée** *nf* plateful.

assimiler [asimile] *vt* to assimilate.

assis [asi] (*pp de* **asseoir**) *a* sitting (down); **rester a.** to remain seated; **place assise** seat (*on bus etc*).

assises [asiz] *nfpl* **(cour d')a.** court of assizes.

assistance [asistɑ̃s] *nf* **1** (*assemblée*) audience; (*nombre de personnes présentes*) attendance, turnout. **2** (*aide*) assistance; **l'A. (publique)** the child care service; **enfant de l'A.** child in care.

assister [asiste] **1** *vt* (*aider*) to help, assist. **2** *vi* **a. à** (*réunion, cours etc*) to attend, be present at; (*accident*) to witness. ●**assistant, -ante** *nmf* assistant; **les assistants** (*spectateurs*) the members of the audience; (*témoins*) the onlookers; **assis-**

(eg **G1**, **G2**, **G3**) in French **G**rammar, at the end of the dictionary. Also see p. ix.

tant(e) social(e) social worker; **assistante maternelle** child minder, *Am* baby-sitter.
association [asɔsjɑsjɔ̃] *nf* association.
associer [asɔsje] *vt* to associate (**à** with); **a. qn à** (*ses travaux*) to involve s.o. in; (*profits*) to give s.o. a share in ‖ **s'a.** *vpr* to join forces; **s'a. à** (*collaborer*) to associate with, join forces with. ● **associé, -ée** *nmf* partner, associate.
assoiffé [aswafe] *a* thirsty (**de** for).
assombrir [asɔ̃brir] *vt* (*obscurcir*) to darken ‖ **s'a.** *vpr* (*ciel*) to cloud over.
assomm/er [asɔme] *vt* (*personne*) to knock unconscious; (*animal*) to stun, brain; (*ennuyer*) to bore stiff. ● **—ant** *a* (*ennuyeux*) tiresome, boring.
assortir [asɔrtir] *vt*, **s'a.** *vpr* to match. ● **assortis** *apl* (*objets semblables*) matching; (*fromages etc variés*) assorted. ● **assortiment** *nm* assortment.
assoupir (s') [sasupir] *vpr* to doze off. ● **assoupi** *a* (*personne*) drowsy.
assoupl/ir [asuplir] *vt* (*étoffe*, *muscles*) to make supple; (*corps*) to limber up; (*règles*) to ease, relax. ● **—issement** *nm* **exercices d'a.** limbering-up exercises.
assourd/ir [asurdir] *vt* (*personne*) to deafen; (*son*) to muffle. ● **—issant** *a* deafening.
assujettir [asyʒetir] *vt* (*soumettre*) to subject (**à** to); (*peuple*) to subjugate.
assumer [asyme] *vt* (*tâche*, *rôle*) to assume, take on; (*emploi*) to take up, assume.
assurance [asyrɑ̃s] *nf* (*aplomb*) (self-) assurance; (*promesse*) assurance; (*contrat*) insurance; **a. au tiers/tous risques** third-party/comprehensive insurance; **assurances sociales** = national insurance, *Am* = social security.
assurer [asyre] *vt* (*par un contrat*) to insure; (*travail etc*) to carry out; **a. à qn que** to assure s.o. that; **a. qn de qch, a. qch à qn** to assure s.o. of sth.
‖ **s'assurer** *vpr* (*par un contrat*) to insure oneself, get insured (**contre** against); **s'a. que/de** to make sure that/of. ● **assuré, -ée** *a* (*succès*) assured, certain; (*pas*) firm, secure; (*air*) (self-)confident ‖ *nmf* policyholder, insured person. ● **assureur** *nm* insurer.
astérisque [asterisk] *nm* asterisk.
asthme [asm] *nm* asthma. ● **asthmatique** *a* & *nmf* asthmatic.
asticot [astiko] *nm* maggot, *Am* worm.
astiquer [astike] *vt* to polish.
astre [astr] *nm* star.
astrologie [astrɔlɔʒi] *nf* astrology.
astronaute [astrɔnot] *nmf* astronaut. ● **astronautique** *nf* space travel.
astronomie [astrɔnɔmi] *nf* astronomy. ● **astronome** *nmf* astronomer. ● **astronomique** *a* astronomical.
astuce [astys] *nf* (*pour faire qch*) knack, trick; (*invention*) gadget; (*plaisanterie*) clever joke, (*finesse*) astuteness. ● **astucieux, -euse** *a* clever, astute.
atelier [atəlje] *nm* (*d'ouvrier etc*) workshop; (*de peintre*) studio.
athée [ate] *nmf* atheist.
Athènes [atɛn] *nm ou f* Athens.
athlète [atlɛt] *nmf* athlete. ● **athlétique** *a* athletic. ● **athlétisme** *nm* athletics.
atlantique [atlɑ̃tik] *a* Atlantic ‖ *nm* **l'A.** the Atlantic.
atlas [atlɑs] *nm* atlas.
atmosphère [atmɔsfɛr] *nf* atmosphere. ● **atmosphérique** *a* atmospheric.
atome [atom] *nm* atom. ● **atomique** [atɔmik] *a* (*bombe*, *énergie etc*) atomic.
atomiseur [atɔmizœr] *nm* spray.
atout [atu] *nm* trump (card); (*avantage*) *Fig* asset.
âtre [ɑtr] *nm* (*foyer*) hearth.
atroce [atrɔs] *a* atrocious; (*crime*) heinous, atrocious. ● **atrocités** *nfpl* (*horreurs*) atrocities.
attabler (s') [satable] *vpr* to sit down at the table. ● **attablé** *a* (seated) at the table.
attache [ataʃ] *nf* (*objet*) fastening; *pl* (*liens*) links.
attaché-case [ataʃekɛz] *nm* attaché case.
attach/er [ataʃe] *vt* (*lier*) to tie (up), attach (**à** to); (*boucler*, *fixer*) to fasten; **a. de l'importance à qch** to attach great importance to sth; **s'a. à** (*se lier*) to become attached to (*s.o.*); (*se consacrer*) to apply oneself to (*task etc*) ‖ *vi* (*en cuisant*) to stick. ● **—ant** *a* (*enfant etc*) likeable. ● **—ement** *nm* (*affection*) attachment (**à** to).
attaque [atak] *nf* attack; **a. aérienne** air raid. ● **attaquer** *vt*, **s'a. à** to attack; (*difficulté*, *sujet*) to tackle ‖ *vi* to attack. ● **attaquant, -ante** *nmf* attacker.
attarder (s') [satarde] *vpr* (*en chemin*) to dawdle, loiter; **s'a. sur** *ou* **à** (*détails etc*) to linger over.
atteindre* [atɛ̃dr] *vt* (*parvenir à*) to reach; (*cible*) to hit; (*idéal*) to achieve; (*blesser*) to hit, wound; **être atteint de** (*maladie*) to be suffering from.
atteinte [atɛ̃t] *nf* **hors d'a.** (*objet*, *personne*) out of reach.
attel/er [atle] *vt* (*bêtes*) to harness, hitch up; (*remorque*) to hook up. ● **—age** *nm* (*crochet*) hook (*for towing*); (*bêtes*) team.

attendre [atɑ̃dr] *vt* to wait for; (*escompter*) to expect (**de** of, from); **elle attend un bébé** she's expecting a baby; **a. que qn vienne** to wait for s.o. to come, wait until s.o. comes; **a. d'être informé** to wait to be informed. ‖ *vi* to wait; **faire a. qn** to keep s.o. waiting; **se faire a.** (*réponse, personne etc*) to be a long time coming; **attends voir!** *Fam* let me see!; **en attendant** meanwhile; **en attendant que** (+ *sub*) until.
‖ **s'attendre** *vpr* **s'a. à qch/à faire** to expect sth/to do; **s'a. à ce que qn fasse qch** to expect s.o. to do sth. • **attendu** *a* (*avec joie*) eagerly-awaited; (*prévu*) expected.

attendrir [atɑ̃drir] *vt* (*émouvoir*) to move (to compassion) ‖ **s'a.** *vpr* to be moved (**sur** by). • **attendrissant** *a* moving.

attentat [atɑ̃ta] *nm* attempt on s.o.'s life, murder attempt; **a. (à la bombe)** (bomb) attack.

attente [atɑ̃t] *nf* (*temps*) wait(ing); (*espérance*) expectation(s); **salle d'a.** waiting room.

attentif, -ive [atɑ̃tif, -iv] *a* (*personne*) attentive; (*travail, examen*) careful. • **attentivement** *adv* attentively.

attention [atɑ̃sjɔ̃] *nf* attention; *pl* (*égards*) consideration; **faire a. à** (*écouter, remarquer*) to pay attention to; (*prendre garde*) to be careful of; **faire a. (à ce) que** (+ *sub*) to be careful that; **a.!** watch out!, be careful!; **a. à la voiture!** watch out for the car! • **attentionné** *a* considerate.

atténuer [atenɥe] *vt* to mitigate, attenu-ate ‖ **s'a.** *vpr* to subside.

atterré [atere] *a* **être a.** to be dismayed.

atterr/ir [aterir] *vi Av* to land. • **—issage** *nm Av* landing; **a. forcé** crash landing.

attirail [atiraj] *nm* (*équipement*) *Fam* gear, equipment.

attirer [atire] *vt* (*faire venir, plaire à*) to attract; (*attention*) to attract, catch; **a. l'a. de qn sur** to draw s.o.'s attention to; **a. qch à qn** (*ennuis etc*) to bring s.o. sth; **a. dans** (*coin, piège*) to lure into ‖ **s'a.** *vpr* (*ennuis etc*) to bring upon oneself. • **attirant** *a* attractive.

attitude [atityd] *nf* attitude; (*maintien*) bearing.

attraction [atraksjɔ̃] *nf* attraction.

attrait [atrɛ] *nm* attraction.

attrape [atrap] *nf* (*objet*) trick. • **a.-nigaud** (*ruse*) *nm* trick.

attraper [atrape] *vt* (*ballon, maladie, voleur, train etc*) to catch; (*accent, contravention etc*) to pick up; **se laisser a.** (*duper*) to get taken in *ou* tricked; **se faire a.** (*gronder*) *Fam* to get a telling-off.

attrayant [atrɛjɑ̃] *a* attractive.

attribuer [atribɥe] *vt* (*donner*) to assign (**à** to); (*décerner*) to award (*prize*) (**à** to). • **attribution** *nf* assignment; (*de prix*) awarding.

attribut [atriby] *nm Gram* predicate adjective; (*caractéristique*) attribute.

attrister [atriste] *vt* to sadden.

attrouper [atrupe] *vt*, **s'a.** *vpr* to gather. • **attroupement** *nm* (disorderly) crowd.

au [o] *voir* **à.**

aubaine [obɛn] *nf* **(bonne) a.** stroke of good luck, godsend.

aube [ob] *nf* dawn; **à l'a.** at dawn; **dès l'a.** at the crack of dawn.

aubépine [obepin] *nf* hawthorn.

auberge [obɛrʒ] *nf* inn; **a. de jeunesse** youth hostel.

aubergine [obɛrʒin] *nf* aubergine, *Am* eggplant.

aucun, -une [okœ̃, -yn] *a* no, not any; **il n'a a. talent** he has no talent, he doesn't have any talent; **a. professeur n'est venu** no teacher has come ‖ *pron* none, not any; **il n'en a a.** he has none (at all), he doesn't have any (at all); **a. d'entre nous** none of us; **a. des deux** neither of the two.
ⓘ**G50** Indefinite Pronouns 6 B 2
ⓘ**G204, 205 & 206** Negative Expressions 12 B 1, 2 & 3
ⓘ**G102** The Subjunctive 7 G 1i)

audace [odas] *nf* (*courage*) daring, boldness; (*impudence*) audacity. • **audacieux, -euse** *a* daring, bold.

au-dessous [odsu] *prép* **au-d. de** (*arbre etc*) below, under, beneath; (*âge, prix*) under; (*température*) below.

au-dessus [odsy] *adv* above; over; on top; (*à l'étage supérieur*) upstairs ‖ *prép* **au-d. de** above; (*âge, température, prix*) over; (*posé sur*) on top of.

au-devant de [odvɑ̃də] *prép* **aller au-d. de qn** to go to meet s.o.

audience [odjɑ̃s] *nf* (*entretien*) audience; *Jur* hearing.

audio [odjo] *a inv* (*cassette etc*) audio. • **audio-visuel, -elle** *a* audio-visual.

auditeur, -trice [oditœr, -tris] *nmf Rad* listener; **les auditeurs** the audience. • **audition** *nf* (*ouïe*) hearing; (*séance musicale*) recital. • **auditoire** *nm* audience. • **auditorium** *nm* concert hall; *Rad* recording studio (*for recitals*).

auge [oʒ] *nf* (feeding) trough.

augmenter [ɔgmɑ̃te] *vt* to increase (**de** by); (*prix, impôt*) to raise, increase; **a. qn** to give

s.o. a rise *ou Am* raise ‖ *vi* to increase (**de** by); (*prix*) to rise, go up, increase. ● **augmentation** *nf* increase (**de** in, of); **a. de salaire** (pay) rise, *Am* raise; **a. de prix** price rise *ou* increase.
augure [ɔgyr] *nm* **être de bon/mauvais a.** to be a good/bad omen.
aujourd'hui [oʒurdɥi] *adv* today; (*actuellement*) nowadays, today; **a. en quinze** two weeks from today.
aumône [omon] *nf* alms.
aumônier [omonje] *nm* chaplain.
auparavant [oparavɑ̃] *adv* (*avant*) before(hand); (*d'abord*) first.
auprès de [oprɛdə] *prép* (*assis, situé etc*) by, close to, next to; (*en comparaison de*) compared to.
auquel [okɛl] *voir* **lequel**.
aura, aurait [ora, orɛ] *voir* **avoir**.
auréole [ɔreɔl] *nf* (*de saint etc*) halo; (*sur tissu etc*) ring.
auriculaire [ɔrikylɛr] *nm* **l'a.** the little finger.
aurore [ɔrɔr] *nf* dawn, daybreak.
ausculter [ɔskylte] *vt* (*malade*) to examine (*with a stethoscope*); (*cœur*) to listen to.
aussi [osi] *adv* **1** (*comparaison*) as; **a. lourd que** as heavy as. **2** (*également*) too, also, as well; **moi a.** so do, can, am *etc* I; **a. bien que** as well as. **3** (*tellement*) so; **un repas a. délicieux** such a delicious meal, so delicious a meal. **4** *conj* (*donc*) therefore, so.
ⓘ**G188** Conjunctions 9 A 3
ⓘ**G204** Inversion 12 A 7a)
aussitôt [osito] *adv* immediately, at once; **a. que** as soon as; **a. levé, il partit** as soon as he was up, he left; **a. dit, a. fait** no sooner said than done.
ⓘ**aussitôt que G97** Tenses 7 F 11
austral, *mpl* **-als** [ostral] *a* southern.
Australie [ostrali] *nf* Australia. ● **australien, -ienne** *a & nmf* Australian.
autant [otɑ̃] *adv* **1 a. de ... que** (*quantité*) as much ... as; (*nombre*) as many ... as; **il a a. d'argent/de pommes que vous** he has as much money/as many apples as you.
2 a. de (*tant de*) so much; (*nombre*) so many; **je n'ai jamais vu a. d'argent/de pommes** I've never seen so much money/so many apples; **pourquoi manges-tu a.?** why are you eating so much?
3 a. que (*lire etc*) as much as; **il lit a. que vous/que possible** he reads as much as you/as possible; **il n'a jamais souffert a.** he's never suffered as *ou* so much; **a. que je sache** as far as I know; **d'a. (plus) que** all the more (so) since; **a. avouer/***etc* we, you *etc* might as well confess/*etc*; **en faire/dire a.** to do/say the same; **j'aimerais a. aller au musée** I'd just as soon go to the museum.
autel [otɛl] *nm* altar.
auteur [otœr] *nm* (*de livre*) author, writer; (*de chanson*) composer; (*de crime*) perpetrator; **droit d'a.** copyright; **droits d'a.** royalties.
authentique [otɑ̃tik] *a* genuine, authentic.
auto [oto] *nf* car; **autos tamponneuses** bumper cars, dodgems.
auto- [oto] *préf* self-.
autobus [otobys] *nm* bus.
autocar [otokar] *nm* bus, coach.
autocollant [otokɔlɑ̃] *nm* sticker ‖ *a* (*enveloppe etc*) self-seal.
autocuiseur [otokɥizœr] *nm* pressure cooker.
autodéfense [otodefɑ̃s] *nf* self-defence.
auto-école [otoekɔl] *nf* driving school, school of motoring.
autographe [otograf] *nm* autograph.
automate [ɔtɔmat] *nm* automaton. ● **automatisation** *nf* automation. ● **automatiser** *vt* to automate.
automatique [ɔtɔmatik] *a* automatic. ● **—ment** *adv* automatically.
automne [otɔn] *nm* autumn, *Am* fall; **en a.** in (the) autumn, in the fall.
automobile [otɔmɔbil] *nf* car, *Am* automobile. ● **automobiliste** *nmf* motorist, driver.
autonome [otonɔm] *a* (*région etc*) autonomous, self-governing; (*personne*) *Fig* independent; (*ordinateur*) off-line. ● **autonomie** *nf* autonomy.
autopsie [ɔtɔpsi] *nf* autopsy, post-mortem.
autoradio [otoradjo] *nm* car radio.
autorail [otorɑj] *nm* railcar.
autoriser [ɔtɔrize] *vt* (*permettre*) to permit (**à faire** to do). ● **autorisation** *nf* permission, authorization.
autorité [ɔtɔrite] *nf* authority. ● **autoritaire** *a* authoritarian.
autoroute [otorut] *nf* motorway, *Am* highway, freeway.
auto-stop [otostɔp] *nm* hitchhiking; **faire de l'a.** to hitchhike. ● **auto-stoppeur, -euse** *nmf* hitchhiker.
autour [otur] *adv* around; **tout a.** all around ‖ *prép* **a. de** around.
autre [otr] *a & pron* other; **un a. livre** another book; **un a.** another (one); **d'autres** others; **d'autres médecins** other doctors; **as-tu d'autres questions?** have you any other *ou* further questions?; **qn/personne/rien d'a.** s.o./no one/nothing else; **a. chose/part** something/somewhere else; **qui/quoi**

ⓘFor further information on grammar points, turn to the page indicated

d'a.? who/what else?; **l'un l'a., les uns les autres** each other; **l'un et l'a.** both (of them); **l'un ou l'a.** either (of them); **ni l'un ni l'a.** neither (of them); **les uns . . . les autres** some . . . others; **nous/vous autres Anglais** we/you English; **d'un moment à l'a.** any moment (now).

G48 Indefinite Adjectives and Pronouns 6 B

autrement [otrəmɑ̃] *adv* (*différemment*) differently; (*sinon*) otherwise.

autrefois [otrəfwa] *adv* in the past, long ago.

Autriche [otriʃ] *nf* Austria. • **autrichien, -ienne** *a* & *nmf* Austrian.

autruche [otryʃ] *nf* ostrich.

autrui [otrɥi] *pron* others, other people.

auvent [ovɑ̃] *nm* (*de tente, magasin*) awning.

aux [o] *voir* **à**.

auxiliaire [ɔksiljɛr] *a* & *nm Gram* **(verbe) a.** auxiliary (verb) ‖ *nmf* (*aide*) helper.

auxquels, -elles [okɛl] *voir* **lequel.**

av. *abrév* **avenue.**

avachir (s') [savaʃir] *vpr* (*soulier, personne*) to become flabby *ou* limp.

avait [avɛ] *voir* **avoir.**

aval (en) [ɑ̃naval] *adv* downstream **(de** from).

avalanche [avalɑ̃ʃ] *nf* avalanche.

avaler [avale] *vt* to swallow; **a. ses mots** to mumble ‖ *vi* to swallow.

avance [avɑ̃s] *nf* (*marche, acompte*) advance; (*de coureur, chercheur etc*) lead; *pl* (*diplomatiques*) overtures; **à l'a., d'a., par a.** in advance; **en a.** (*arriver, partir*) early; (*avant l'horaire prévu*) ahead (of time); (*dans son développement*) ahead, in advance; (*montre etc*) fast; **en a. sur** (*qn, son époque etc*) ahead of; **avoir une heure d'a.** (*train etc*) to be an hour early.

avancé [avɑ̃se] *a* (*âge, enfant etc*) advanced; (*season*) well advanced.

avancement [avɑ̃smɑ̃] *nm* (*de personne*) promotion; (*de travail*) progress.

avancer [avɑ̃se] *vt* (*date, réunion*) to bring forward; (*main, chaise, pion*) to move forward; (*travail*) to speed up; (*argent*) to advance; (*montre*) to put forward.
‖ *vi* (*personne, véhicule etc*) to move forward, advance; (*travail*) to progress, advance; (*faire saillie*) to jut out **(sur** over); **a. de cinq minutes** (*montre*) to be five minutes fast; **alors, ça avance?** are things progressing?
‖ **s'avancer** *vpr* to move forward, advance.

avant [avɑ̃] *prép* before; **a. de voir** before seeing; **a. qu'il (ne) parte** before he leaves; **a. huit jours** within a week; **a. tout** above all; **a. toute chose** first and foremost; **a. peu** before long ‖ *adv* before; **en a.** (*mouvement*) forward; (*en tête*) ahead; **la nuit d'a.** the night before ‖ *nm* & *a inv* front ‖ *nm* (*joueur*) *Fb* forward.

avantage [avɑ̃taʒ] *nm* advantage; (*bénéfice*) *Fin* benefit; **tirer a. de** to benefit from. • **avantager** *vt* (*favoriser*) to favour. • **avantageux, -euse** *a* (*prix etc*) worthwhile, attractive; **a. pour qn** advantageous to s.o.

avant-bras [avɑ̃bra] *nm inv* forearm. • **a.-centre** *nm Fb* centre-forward. • **a.-dernier, -ière** *a* & *nmf* last but one. • **a.-garde** *nf Mil* advance guard; **d'a.-garde** (*idée, film etc*) avant-garde. • **a.-goût** *nm* foretaste. • **a.-guerre** *nm ou f* pre-war period; **d'a.-guerre** pre-war. • **a.-hier** [avɑ̃tjɛr] *adv* the day before yesterday. • **a.-première** *nf* preview. • **a.-propos** *nm inv* foreword. • **a.-veille** *nf* **l'a.-veille (de)** two days before.

avare [avar] *a* miserly; **a. de** (*compliments etc*) sparing of ‖ *nmf* miser. • **avarice** *nf* avarice.

avarie(s) [avari] *nf(pl)* damage. • **avarié** *a* (*aliment*) rotting, rotten.

avec [avɛk] *prép* with; (*envers*) to(wards); **et a. ça?** (*dans un magasin*) *Fam* anything else? ‖ *adv* **il est venu a.** (*son chapeau etc*) *Fam* he came with it.

avenant [avnɑ̃] *a* pleasing, attractive.

avènement [avɛnmɑ̃] *nm* **l'a. de** the coming *ou* advent of; (*roi*) the accession of.

avenir [avnir] *nm* future; **à l'a.** (*désormais*) in future; **d'a.** (*personne, métier*) with future prospects.

aventure [avɑ̃tyr] *nf* adventure; (*en amour*) affair; **à l'a.** (*marcher etc*) aimlessly. • **aventurer (s')** *vpr* to venture **(sur** on to, **dans** into, **à faire** to do). • **aventureux, -euse** *a* (*personne, vie*) adventurous; (*risqué*) risky. • **aventurier, -ière** *nmf* adventurer.

avenue [avny] *nf* avenue.

avérer (s') [savere] *vpr* (*juste etc*) to prove (to be); **il s'avère que** it turns out that.

averse [avɛrs] *nf* shower, downpour.

aversion [avɛrsjɔ̃] *nf* aversion **(pour** to).

avert/ir [avɛrtir] *vt* (*mettre en garde, menacer*) to warn; (*informer*) to notify, inform. • **—i** *a* informed. • **—issement** *nm* warning. • **—isseur** *nm Aut* horn; **a. d'incendie** fire alarm.

aveu, -x [avø] *nm* confession; **de l'a. de** by the admission of.

aveugle [avœgl] *a* blind ‖ *nmf* blind man, blind woman; **les aveugles** the blind.

• aveuglément [-emɑ̃] *adv* blindly. **• aveugler** *vt* to blind.

aveuglette (à l') [alavœglɛt] *adv* blindly; **chercher qch à l'a.** to grope for sth.

aviateur, -trice [avjatœr, -tris] *nmf* airman, airwoman. **• aviation** *nf* (*industrie, science*) aviation; (*armée de l'air*) air force; (*avions*) aircraft *inv*; **l'a.** *Sp* flying.

avide [avid] *a* (*d'argent*) greedy (**de** for); **a. d'apprendre**/*etc* eager to learn/*etc*. **• —ment** [-əmɑ̃] *adv* greedily. **• avidité** *nf* greed.

avilir [avilir] *vt* to degrade, debase.

avion [avjɔ̃] *nm* aircraft *inv*, (aero)plane, *Am* airplane; **a. à réaction** jet; **a. de ligne** airliner; **par a.** (*lettre*) airmail; **en a., par a.** (*voyager*) by plane, by air.

aviron [avirɔ̃] *nm* oar; **l'a.** *Sp* rowing; **faire de l'a.** to row, practise rowing.

avis [avi] *nm* opinion; *Pol Jur* judgment; (*communiqué*) notice; (*conseil*) & *Fin* advice; **à mon a.** in my opinion; **changer d'a.** to change one's mind.

avis/er [avize] *vt* to advise, inform; **s'a. de qch** to realize sth suddenly; **s'a. de faire** to venture to do. **• —é** *a* prudent, wise; **bien/mal a.** well-/ill-advised.

avocat, -ate [avɔka, -at] **1** *nmf* barrister, *Am* attorney, counselor; (*d'une cause*) *Fig* advocate. **2** *nm* (*fruit*) avocado (pear).

avoine [avwan] *nf* oats; **farine d'a.** oatmeal.

avoir** [avwar] **1** *v aux* to have; **je l'ai/l'avais vu** I've/I'd seen him.

ⓘ**avoir G80, 81 & 83** Auxiliaries and the Formation of Compound Tenses 7 C 1, 2 & 4

2 *vt* (*posséder*) to have; (*obtenir*) to get; (*tromper*) *Fam* to take for a ride; **il a** he has, he's got; **qu'est-ce que tu as?** what's the matter with you?, what's wrong with you?; **j'ai à lui parler** I have to speak to her; **il n'a qu'à essayer** he only has to try; **a. faim/chaud**/*etc* to be *ou* feel hungry/hot/*etc*; **a. cinq ans**/*etc* to be five (years old)/*etc*; **en a. pour longtemps** to be busy for quite a while; **j'en ai pour dix minutes** this will take me ten minutes; (*ne bougez pas*) I'll be with you in ten minutes; **en a. pour son argent** to get *ou* have one's money's worth.

ⓘ**avoir G217** To Be 13 B 3a)

3 *v imp* **il y a** there is, *pl* there are; **il y a six ans** six years ago; **il n'y a pas de quoi!** don't mention it!; **qu'est-ce qu'il y a?** what's the matter?, what's wrong?

ⓘ**il y a G89** Impersonal Verbs 7 E 2b)

ⓘ**il y a G96** Tenses 7 F 9a) Note i)

4 *nm* assets, property.

avoisinant [avwazinɑ̃] *a* neighbouring, nearby.

avort/er [avɔrte] *vi* (*projet etc*) *Fig* to miscarry, fail; **(se faire) a.** (*femme*) to have *ou* get an abortion. **• —ement** *nm* abortion; *Fig* failure.

avou/er [avwe] *vt* to confess, admit (**que** that); (*crime*) to confess to, admit to; **s'a. vaincu** to admit defeat ‖ *vi* (*coupable*) to confess. **• —é** *a* (*ennemi, but*) declared.

avril [avril] *nm* April; **un poisson d'a.** (*farce*) an April fool joke; **faire un poisson d'a. à** to make an April fool of.

axe [aks] *nm Math Astron* axis; (*essieu*) axle; (*d'une politique*) broad direction; **grands axes** (*routes*) main roads.

ayant [ɛjɑ̃] *voir* **avoir**.

azimuts [azimyt] *nmpl* **dans tous les a.** *Fam* here there and everywhere; **tous a.** (*guerre, publicité etc*) all-out.

azote [azot] *nm* nitrogen.

azur [azyr] *nm* azure, (sky) blue; **la Côte d'A.** the (French) Riviera.

B

B, b [be] *nm* B, b.
babill/er [babije] *vi* to babble. ●**—age** *nm* babble.
babines [babin] *nfpl* (*lèvres*) chops.
babiole [babjɔl] *nf* (*objet*) knick-knack.
bâbord [bɑbɔr] *nm Nau Av* port (side).
babouin [babwɛ̃] *nm* baboon.
baby-foot [babifut] *nm inv* table *ou* miniature football.
bac [bak] *nm* **1** (*bateau*) ferry(boat). **2** (*cuve*) tank; **b. à glace** ice tray; **b. à légumes** vegetable compartment. **3** *abrév* = **baccalauréat.**
baccalauréat [bakalɔrea] *nm* school leaving certificate.
bâche [bɑʃ] *nf* (*de toile*) tarpaulin; (*de plastique*) plastic sheet. ●**bâcher** *vt* to cover over (*with a tarpaulin ou plastic sheet*).
bachelier, -ière [baʃəlje, -jɛr] *nmf* holder of the *baccalauréat*.
bacille [basil] *nm* germ.
bâcler [bɑkle] *vt* (*travail*) to dash off carelessly, botch (up).
bactéries [bakteri] *nfpl* bacteria.
badaud, -aude [bado, -od] *nmf* (inquisitive) onlooker, bystander.
badge [badʒ] *nm* badge, *Am* button.
badigeon [badiʒɔ̃] *nm* whitewash. ●**badigeonner** *vt* (*mur*) to whitewash; (*écorchure*) to paint (with antiseptic).
badiner [badine] *vi* to jest, joke; **b. avec** (*prendre à la légère*) to trifle with.
bafouer [bafwe] *vt* to mock *ou* scoff at.
bafouiller [bafuje] *vti* to stammer.
bagage [bagaʒ] *nm* (*valise etc*) piece of luggage *ou* baggage; (*connaissances*) *Fig* (fund of) knowledge; *pl* (*ensemble des valises*) luggage, baggage. ●**bagagiste** *nm* baggage handler.
bagarre [bagar] *nf* fight, brawl; **aimer la b.** to like a fight *ou* a brawl. ●**bagarrer (se)** *vpr* to fight, brawl; (*se disputer*) to fight, quarrel.
bagatelle [bagatɛl] *nf* trifle.
bagne [baɲ] *nm* convict prison; **c'est le b. ici** *Fig* this place is a real sweatshop *ou* workhouse. ●**bagnard** *nm* convict.
bagnole [baɲɔl] *nf Fam* car.
bagou(t) [bagu] *nm Fam* glibness; **avoir du b.** to have the gift of the gab.
bague [bag] *nf* (*anneau*) ring; (*de cigare*) band.
baguette [bagɛt] *nf* (*canne*) stick; (*de chef d'orchestre*) baton; (*pain*) (long thin) loaf, baguette; *pl* (*de tambour*) drumsticks; (*pour manger*) chopsticks; **b. (magique)** (magic) wand; **mener qn à la b.** to rule s.o. with an iron hand.
bahut [bay] *nm* (*meuble*) chest, cabinet; (*lycée*) *Fam* school.
baie [bɛ] *nf* **1** (*de côte*) bay. **2** *Bot* berry. **3** (*fenêtre*) picture window.
baignade [bɛɲad] *nf* swim, bathe; (*activité*) swimming, bathing; (*endroit*) bathing place.
baigner [beɲe] *vt* to bathe; (*enfant*) to bath, *Am* bathe; **baigné de** (*sueur, lumière*) bathed in; (*sang*) soaked in.
▮ *vi* **b. dans** (*tremper*) to be steeped in (*sauce etc*).
▮ **se baigner** *vpr* to go swimming *ou* bathing; (*dans une baignoire*) to have *ou* take a bath. ●**baigneur, -euse 1** *nmf* bather. **2** *nm* (*poupée*) baby doll.
baignoire [bɛɲwar] *nf* bath (tub).
bail, *pl* **baux** [baj, bo] *nm* lease.
bâill/er [bɑje] *vi* to yawn. ●**—ement** *nm* yawn.
bâillon [bɑjɔ̃] *nm* gag. ●**bâillonner** *vt* (*victime, presse etc*) to gag.
bain [bɛ̃] *nm* bath; (*de mer*) swim, bathe; **prendre un b. de soleil** to sunbathe; **salle de bain(s)** bathroom; **être dans le b.** *Fam* to have got *ou Am* gotten into the swing of things; **petit/grand b.** (*piscine*) shallow/deep end; **b. de bouche** mouthwash. ●**b.-marie** *nm* (*pl* **bains-marie**) *Culin* double boiler.
baïonnette [bajɔnɛt] *nf* bayonet.
baiser [beze] *vt* **b. au front/sur la joue** to kiss on the forehead/cheek ▮ *nm* kiss; **bons baisers** (*dans une lettre*) (with) love.
baisse [bɛs] *nf* fall, drop (**de** in); **en b.** (*température*) falling; (*popularité*) declining.
baisser [bese] *vt* (*voix, prix etc*) to lower, drop; (*tête*) to bend; (*radio, chauffage*) to turn down ▮ *vi* (*prix, niveau etc*) to go down, drop; (*soleil*) to go down; (*marée*) to go out; (*santé, popularité*) *Fig* to decline ▮ **se b.** *vpr* to bend down, stoop.

(eg **G1**, **G2**, **G3**) in French **G**rammar, at the end of the dictionary. Also see p. ix.

bajoues [baʒu] *nfpl* (*d'animal, de personne*) chops.
bal, *pl* **bals** [bal] *nm* ball; (*populaire*) dance.
balade [balad] *nf Fam* walk; (*en auto*) drive; (*excursion*) tour. ●**balader (se)** *vpr Fam* (*à pied*) to (go for a) walk; (*excursionner*) to tour (around); **se b. (en voiture)** to go for a drive. ●**baladeur** *nm* Walkman®, (personal) stereo.
balafre [balafr] *nf* (*cicatrice*) scar; (*blessure*) gash, slash. ●**balafré** *a* scarred.
balai [balɛ] *nm* broom; **manche à b.** broomstick; *Av Ordinat* joystick; **donner un coup de b.** to sweep up. ●**b.-brosse** *nm* (*pl* **balais-brosses**) garden brush (*for scrubbing paving stones*).
balance [balɑ̃s] *nf* (*instrument*) (pair of) scales; **la B.** (*signe*) Libra.
balancer [balɑ̃se] *vt* (*hanches, tête, branches*) to sway; (*bras*) to swing; (*lancer*) *Fam* to chuck; (*se débarrasser de*) *Fam* to chuck out.
‖ **se balancer** *vpr* (*personne*) to swing (from side to side); (*arbre, bateau etc*) to sway; **je m'en balance!** I couldn't care less! ●**balancier** *nm* (*d'horloge*) pendulum; (*de montre*) balance wheel. ●**balançoire** *nf* (*suspendue*) swing; (*bascule*) seesaw.
balayer [baleje] *vt* (*chambre*) to sweep (out); (*rue, feuilles*) to sweep (up); (*enlever, chasser*) to sweep away. ●**balayette** *nf* (hand) brush; (*balai*) short-handled broom. ●**balayeur, -euse** *nmf* (*personne*) roadsweeper ‖ *nf* (*véhicule*) roadsweeper.
balbutier [balbysje] *vti* to stammer.
balcon [balkɔ̃] *nm* balcony; *Th* dress circle.
baldaquin [baldakɛ̃] *nm* (*de lit etc*) canopy.
baleine [balɛn] *nf* (*animal*) whale; (*de parapluie*) rib.
balise [baliz] *nf Nau* beacon; *Av* (ground) light; *Aut* road sign. ●**baliser** *vt* to mark with beacons *ou* lights; (*route*) to signpost. ●**balisage** *nm Nau* beacons; *Av* lighting; *Aut* signposting.
ballade [balad] *nf* (*légende, poème long*) ballad; (*poème court*) & *Mus* ballade.
ballant [balɑ̃] *a* (*bras, jambes*) dangling.
ballast [balast] *nm* ballast.
balle [bal] *nf* (*de tennis, golf etc*) ball; (*projectile*) bullet; (*paquet*) bale; *pl* (*francs*) *Fam* francs; **se renvoyer la b.** to pass the buck (to each other).
ballet [balɛ] *nm* ballet. ●**ballerine** *nf* ballerina.
ballon [balɔ̃] *nm* (*jouet d'enfant, dirigeable*) balloon; (*de sport*) ball; **b. de football** football, *Am* soccer ball.
ballonné [balɔne] *am* (*ventre*) bloated.
ballot [balo] *nm* (*paquet*) bundle.
ballottage [balɔtaʒ] *nm* second ballot (*no candidate having achieved the required number of votes*).
ballotter [balɔte] *vti* to shake (about).
balnéaire [balneɛr] *a* **station b.** seaside resort, *Am* beach resort.
balourd, -ourde [balur, -urd] *nmf* (clumsy) oaf.
Baltique [baltik] *nf* **la B.** the Baltic.
balustrade [balystrad] *nf* (hand)rail, railing(s).
bambin [bɑ̃bɛ̃] *nm* tiny tot, toddler.
bambou [bɑ̃bu] *nm* bamboo.
ban [bɑ̃] *nm* (*applaudissements*) round of applause; *pl* (*de mariage*) banns; **mettre qn au b. de** to outlaw s.o. from; **un (triple) b. pour...** three cheers for..., a big hand for....
banal, *mpl* **-als** [banal] *a* (*fait, accident*) commonplace, banal; (*idée, propos*) banal, trite. ●**banalité** *nf* banality; *pl* (*propos*) banalities.
banane [banan] *nf* banana. ●**bananier** *nm* banana tree.
banc [bɑ̃] *nm* (*siège*) bench; (*de poissons*) shoal; **b. des accusés** *Jur* dock; **b. d'église** pew; **b. de sable** sandbank; **b. d'essai** *Fig* testing ground.
bancaire [bɑ̃kɛr] *a* **compte/***etc* **b.** bank account/*etc*; **opération b.** banking operation.
bancal, *mpl* **-als** [bɑ̃kal] *a* (*personne*) bandy, bow-legged; (*meuble*) wobbly; (*idée*) shaky.
bandage [bɑ̃daʒ] *nm* (*pansement*) bandage.
bande [bɑ̃d] *nf* **1** (*de terrain, papier etc*) strip; (*de film*) reel; (*de journal*) wrapper; (*rayure*) stripe; (*pansement*) bandage; (*sur la chaussée*) line; (*de fréquences*) *Rad* band; **b. (magnétique)** tape; **b. vidéo** videotape; **b. sonore** sound track; **une b. dessinée** a comic strip, a strip cartoon; **aimer la b. dessinée** to like comic strips *ou* comics.
2 (*groupe*) gang, band; **b. d'idiots!** you load of idiots!
bandeau, -x [bɑ̃do] *nm* (*sur les yeux*) blindfold; (*pour la tête*) headband; (*pansement*) head bandage.
bander [bɑ̃de] *vt* (*blessure etc*) to bandage; (*yeux*) to blindfold; (*muscle*) to tense.
banderole [bɑ̃drɔl] *nf* (*de manifestants*) banner.
bandit [bɑ̃di] *nm* robber, gangster. ●**banditisme** *nm* crime.
bandoulière [bɑ̃duljɛr] *nf* shoulder strap;

en b. slung across the shoulder.
banjo [bɑ̃dʒo] *nm Mus* banjo.
banlieue [bɑ̃ljø] *nf* **la b.** the suburbs, the outskirts; **une b.** a suburb; **la grande b.** the outer suburbs; **de b.** (*maison etc*) suburban; **train de b.** commuter train. ● **banlieusard, -arde** *nmf* (*habitant*) suburbanite; (*voyageur*) commuter.
bannir [banir] *vt* (*exiler, supprimer*) to banish (**de** from).
banque [bɑ̃k] *nf* bank; (*activité*) banking.
banqueroute [bɑ̃krut] *nf* (fraudulent) bankruptcy.
banquet [bɑ̃kɛ] *nm* banquet.
banquette [bɑ̃kɛt] *nf* (*de véhicule, train*) seat.
banquier [bɑ̃kje] *nm* banker.
banquise [bɑ̃kiz] *nf* ice floe *ou* field.
baptême [batɛm] *nm* christening, baptism; (*de navire*) christening; **b. de l'air** first flight. ● **baptiser** [batize] *vt* (*enfant*) to christen, baptize; (*appeler*) *Fig* to christen (*ship*).
baquet [bakɛ] *nm* tub, basin.
bar [bar] *nm* (*lieu, comptoir*) bar.
baragouiner [baragwine] *vt* (*langue*) to gabble a few words of.
baraque [barak] *nf* hut, shack; (*maison*) *Fam* house; *Péj* hovel; (*de forain*) stall. ● **—ment** *nm* (makeshift) huts.
baratin [baratɛ̃] *nm Fam* sweet talk; *Com* sales talk, patter. ● **baratiner** *vt* (*fille*) to chat up, *Am* sweet-talk.
barbare [barbar] *a* (*manières, crime*) barbaric; (*peuple, invasions*) barbarian ‖ *nmf* barbarian. ● **barbarie** *nf* (*cruauté*) barbarity.
barbe [barb] *nf* beard; **une b. de trois jours** three days' growth of beard; **se faire la b.** to shave; **la b.!** enough!; **quelle b.!** what a drag!; **b. à papa** candyfloss, *Am* cotton candy.
barbecue [barbəkju] *nm* barbecue.
barbelé [barbəle] *am* **fil de fer b.** barbed wire ‖ *nmpl* **barbelés** barbed wire.
barbiche [barbiʃ] *nf* goatee (beard).
barbot/er [barbɔte] *vi* (*s'agiter*) to splash about, paddle. ● **—euse** *nf* (*de bébé*) playsuit, rompers.
barbouill/er [barbuje] *vt* (*salir*) to smear; (*gribouiller*) to scribble; (*peindre*) to daub; **avoir l'estomac barbouillé** *Fam* to feel queasy. ● **—age** *nm* smear; scribble; daub.
barbu [barby] *a* bearded.
bardé [barde] *a* **b. de** (*décorations etc*) covered with.
barder [barde] *v imp* **ça va b.!** *Fam* there'll be fireworks!
barème [barɛm] *nm* (*des tarifs*) table; (*des salaires*) scale.
baril [bari(l)] *nm* barrel; **b. de poudre** powder keg; **b. de lessive** box of laundry detergent.
bariolé [barjɔle] *a* brightly-coloured.
barman, *pl* **-men** *ou* **-mans** [barman, -mɛn] *nm* barman, *Am* bartender.
baromètre [barɔmɛtr] *nm* barometer.
baron, -onne [barɔ̃, -ɔn] *nm* baron ‖ *nf* baroness.
baroque [barɔk] *a & nm Archit Mus etc* baroque.
barque [bark] *nf* (small) boat.
barre [bar] *nf* bar; *Nau* helm; (*trait*) line, stroke; **b. de soustraction** minus sign; **b. fixe** *Sp* horizontal bar. ● **barreau, -x** *nm* (*de fenêtre etc*) & *Jur* bar; (*d'échelle*) rung.
barrer [bare] *vt* (*route etc*) to close (off); (*obstruer*) to block (off); (*porte*) to bar; (*chèque*) to cross; (*phrase*) to cross out; (*bateau*) to steer; **b. la route à qn, b. qn** to bar s.o.'s way; **'rue barrée'** 'road closed'. ● **barrage** *nm* (*sur une route*) roadblock; (*sur un fleuve*) dam.
barrette [barɛt] *nf* (*pince*) (hair)slide, *Am* barrette.
barricade [barikad] *nf* barricade. ● **barricader** *vt* to barricade ‖ **se b.** *vpr* to barricade oneself (**dans** in).
barrière [barjɛr] *nf* (*porte*) gate; (*clôture*) fence; (*obstacle, mur*) barrier.
barrique [barik] *nf* (large) barrel.
bas[1]**, basse** [bɑ, bɑs] *a* (*table, prix etc*) low; (*action*) vile, base, mean; (*partie de ville*) lower; **au b. mot** at the very least; **enfant en b. âge** young child; **avoir la vue basse** to be short-sighted.
‖ *adv* low; (*parler*) in a whisper, softly; **mettre b.** (*animal*) to give birth; **à b. les dictateurs/***etc*! down with dictators/*etc*!
‖ *nm* (*de côte, page, mur etc*) bottom, foot; **tiroir/***etc* **du b.** bottom drawer/*etc*; **en b.** down (below); (*par l'escalier*) downstairs; **en** *ou* **au b. de** at the foot *ou* bottom of; **de haut en b.** from top to bottom.
bas[2] [bɑ] *nm* (*chaussette*) stocking.
basané [bazane] *a* (*visage etc*) tanned.
bas-côté [bɑkote] *nm* (*de route*) roadside, shoulder, verge.
bascule [baskyl] *nf* (*balançoire*) seesaw; **(balance à) b.** weighing machine; **cheval/fauteuil à b.** rocking horse/chair. ● **basculer** *vti* (*personne*) to topple over; (*benne*) to tip up.
base [bɑz] *nf Ch Math Mil Av etc* base;

bases (*d'un argument, accord etc*) basis; **de b.** (*salaire etc*) basic; **produit à b. de lait** milk-based product. • **baser** *vt* to base (**sur** on).
bas-fond [bɑfɔ̃] *nm* (*eau*) shallows.
basilic [bazilik] *nm Bot Culin* basil.
basilique [bazilik] *nf* basilica.
basket(-ball) [baskɛt(bol)] *nm* basketball.
baskets [baskɛt] *nfpl* (*chaussures*) trainers, *Am* track shoes.
basque [bask] *a* & *nmf* Basque.
basse [bɑs] **1** *voir* **bas**[1]. **2** *nf Mus* bass.
basse-cour [bɑskur] *nf* (*pl* **basses-cours**) farmyard.
bassement [bɑsmɑ̃] *adv* basely, meanly. • **bassesse** *nf* baseness, meanness; (*action*) vile *ou* base *ou* mean act.
bassin [basɛ̃] *nm* (*pièce d'eau*) pond; (*de port*) dock; (*de piscine*) pool; (*cuvette*) bowl, basin; *Anat* pelvis; *Géog* basin; **b. houiller** coalfield. • **bassine** *nf* bowl.
basson [bɑsɔ̃] *nm* (*instrument*) bassoon.
bastingage [bastɛ̃gaʒ] *nm* (ship's) rail.
bastion [bastjɔ̃] *nm Fig* bastion, stronghold.
bas-ventre [bɑvɑ̃tr] *nm* lower abdomen; (*sexe*) *Fam* genitals.
bat [ba] *voir* **battre.**
bât [bɑ] *nm* packsaddle.
bataclan [bataklɑ̃] *nm Fam* paraphernalia; **et tout le b.** *Fam* and the whole caboodle.
bataille [batɑj] *nf* battle; *Cartes* beggar-my-neighbour. • **batailler** *vi* to fight, battle. • **batailleur, -euse** *nmf* fighter ‖ *a* fond of fighting. • **bataillon** *nm* batallion.
bâtard, -arde [bɑtar, -ard] *a* & *nmf* bastard; **chien b.** mongrel.
bateau, -x [bato] *nm* boat; (*grand*) ship.
batifoler [batifɔle] *vi Hum* to fool about.
bâtiment [bɑtimɑ̃] *nm* (*édifice*) building; (*navire*) vessel; **le b., l'industrie du b.** the building trade; **ouvrier du b.** building worker. • **bâtir** *vt* (*construire*) to build; (*coudre*) to baste, tack; **terrain à b.** building site. • **bâti** *a* **bien b.** well-built. • **bâtisse** *nf Péj* building.
bâton [bɑtɔ̃] *nm* (*canne*) stick; (*d'agent*) baton; **b. de rouge** lipstick; **donner des coups de b. à qn** to beat s.o. (with a stick); **parler à bâtons rompus** to ramble from one subject to another; **mettre des bâtons dans les roues à qn** to put obstacles in s.o.'s way.
battage [bataʒ] *nm* (*du blé*) threshing; (*publicité*) *Fam* publicity, hype.
battant [batɑ̃] *nm* (*de porte etc*) flap; **porte à deux battants** double door.
battante [batɑ̃t] *af* **pluie b.** driving rain.
battement [batmɑ̃] *nm* **1** (*de tambour*) beat(ing); (*de paupières*) blink(ing); **b. de cœur** heartbeat. **2** (*délai*) interval.
batterie [batri] *nf Mil Aut* battery; **la b.** *Mus* the drums; **b. de cuisine** set of kitchen utensils.
batteur [batœr] *nm* **1** (*musicien*) drummer. **2 b. à œufs** egg beater.
battre* [batr] **1** *vt* (*frapper, vaincre*) to beat; (*blé*) to thresh; (*cartes*) to shuffle (*œufs*) to beat; (*à coups redoublés*) to batter; **b. la mesure** to beat time; **b. à mort** to batter *ou* beat to death.
‖ *vi* to beat; (*porte*) to bang; **b. des mains** to clap (one's hands); **b. des paupières** to blink; **b. des ailes** (*oiseau*) to flap its wings. **2 se battre** *vpr* to fight (**avec** with, **pour** for).
baume [bom] *nm* (*résine, consolation*) balm.
baux [bo] *voir* **bail.**
bavard, -arde [bavar, -ard] *a* (*élève etc*) talkative ‖ *nmf* chatterbox. • **bavarder** *vi* to chat, chatter; (*divulguer des secrets*) to blab. • **bavardage** *nm* chatting, chatter(ing).
bave [bav] *nf* dribble, slobber; foam; (*de limace*) slime. • **baver** *vi* to dribble, slobber; (*chien enragé*) to foam; (*stylo*) to smudge. • **baveux, -euse** *a* (*bouche*) slobbery; (*omelette*) runny. • **bavoir** *nm* bib. • **bavure** *nf* (*tache*) smudge; (*erreur*) blunder; **sans b.** flawless(ly).
bazar [bazar] *nm* (*magasin, marché*) bazaar; (*désordre*) mess, clutter; (*attirail*) *Fam* stuff, gear.
BCBG [besebeʒe] *a inv abrév* (*bon chic bon genre*) stylish, classy.
bd *abrév* **boulevard.**
BD [bede] *nf abrév* **bande dessinée.**
béant [beɑ̃] *a* (*plaie*) gaping; (*gouffre*) yawning.
beau (*or* **bel** *before vowel or mute h*), **belle,** *pl* **beaux, belles** [bo, bɛl] *a* (*femme, fleur, histoire etc*) beautiful; (*homme*) handsome, good-looking; (*voyage, temps*) fine, lovely; (*occasion, talent*) fine; **au b. milieu** right in the middle; **j'ai b. crier**/*etc* it's no use (my) shouting/*etc*; **un b. morceau** a good bit; **de plus belle** (*recommencer etc*) worse than ever.
‖ *nm* **le b.** the beautiful; **faire le b.** (*chien*) to sit up and beg.
‖ *nf Cartes etc* deciding game.
beaucoup [boku] *adv* (*lire etc*) a lot, a great deal; **aimer b.** to like very much *ou* a lot; **s'intéresser b. à** to be very interested in; **b.**

de (*livres etc*) many, a lot *ou* a great deal of; (*courage etc*) a lot *ou* a great deal of, much; **pas b. d'argent**/*etc* not much money/*etc*; **j'en ai b.** (*quantité*) I have a lot; (*nombre*) I have lots; **b. plus** much more, a lot more; many more, a lot more (**que** than); **b. trop** much too much; much too many; **b. trop petit**/*etc* much too small/*etc*; **b. sont...** many are....

beau-fils [bofis] *nm* (*pl* **beaux-fils**) (*d'un précédent mariage*) stepson; (*gendre*) son-in-law. ●**b.-frère** *nm* (*pl* **beaux-frères**) brother-in-law. ●**b.-père** *nm* (*pl* **beaux-pères**) father-in-law; (*second mari de la mère*) stepfather.

beauté [bote] *nf* beauty; **institut** *ou* **salon de b.** beauty salon.

beaux-arts [bozar] *nmpl* fine arts. ●**b.-parents** *nmpl* parents-in-law.

bébé [bebe] *nm* baby; **b.-lion**/*etc* (*pl* **bébés-lions**/*etc*) baby lion/*etc*.

bec [bɛk] *nm* (*d'oiseau*) beak, bill; (*de cruche*) spout; (*bouche*) *Fam* mouth; *Mus* mouthpiece; **coup de b.** peck; **clouer le b. à qn** *Fam* to shut s.o. up.

bécasse [bekas] *nf* (*oiseau*) woodcock; (*personne*) *Fam* simpleton.

bêche [bɛʃ] *nf* spade. ●**bêcher** *vt* (*cultiver*) to dig.

becquée [beke] *nf* beakful; **donner la b. à** (*oiseau*) to feed. ●**becqueter** *vt* (*picorer*) to peck (at).

bedaine [bədɛn] *nf Fam* paunch, potbelly. ●**bedonnant** *a* potbellied, paunchy.

bée [be] *af* **bouche b.** open-mouthed.

beffroi [befrwa] *nm* belfry.

bégayer [begeje] *vi* to stutter. ●**bègue** [bɛg] *nmf* stutterer ‖ *a* **être b.** to stutter.

beige [bɛʒ] *a & nm* beige.

beignet [bɛɲɛ] *nm* (*pâtisserie*) fritter.

Beijing [beidʒiŋ] *nm ou f* Beijing.

bel [bɛl] *voir* **beau.**

bêler [bele] *vi* to bleat.

belette [bəlɛt] *nf* weasel.

Belgique [bɛlʒik] *nf* Belgium. ●**belge** *a & nmf* Belgian.

bélier [belje] *nm* (*animal, machine*) ram; **le B.** (*signe*) Aries.

belle [bɛl] *voir* **beau.**

belle-fille [bɛlfij] *nf* (*pl* **belles-filles**) (*d'un précédent mariage*) stepdaughter; (*épouse d'un fils*) daughter-in-law. ●**b.-mère** *nf* (*pl* **belles-mères**) mother-in-law; (*deuxième femme du père*) stepmother. ●**b.-sœur** *nf* (*pl* **belles-sœurs**) sister-in-law.

belliqueux, -euse [bɛlikø, -øz] *a* (*action, ton*) warlike; (*personne*) aggressive.

belvédère [bɛlvedɛr] *nm* (*sur une route*) viewpoint.

bémol [bemɔl] *nm Mus* flat.

bénédiction [benediksjɔ̃] *nf* blessing.

bénéfice [benefis] *nm* (*financier*) profit; (*avantage*) benefit. ●**bénéficier** *vi* **b. de** to benefit from. ●**bénéfique** *a* beneficial.

Bénélux [benelyks] *nm* Benelux.

bénévole [benevɔl] *a & nmf* voluntary (worker).

bénin, -igne [benɛ̃, -iɲ] *a* (*tumeur*) benign; (*accident*) minor.

bénir [benir] *vt* to bless; (*remercier*) to give thanks to. ●**bénit** *a* (*pain*) consecrated; **eau bénite** holy water. ●**bénitier** [-itje] *nm* (holy-water) stoup.

benjamin, -ine [bɛ̃ʒamɛ̃, -in] *nmf* youngest child; *Sp* young junior.

benne [bɛn] *nf* (*de camion*) (movable) container; (*de grue*) scoop; **camion à b. basculante** dump truck; **b. à ordures** skip, *Am* Dumpster®.

béquille [bekij] *nf* (*canne*) crutch; (*de moto*) stand.

berceau, -x [bɛrso] *nm* cradle.

berc/er [bɛrse] *vt* (*balancer*) to rock; (*apaiser*) to soothe, lull. ●**—euse** *nf* lullaby.

béret [berɛ] *nm* beret.

berge [bɛrʒ] *nm* (*rive*) (raised) bank.

berger, -ère [bɛrʒe, -ɛr] **1** *nm* shepherd; **chien (de) b.** sheepdog ‖ *nf* shepherdess. **2** *nm* **b. allemand** Alsatian (dog), *Am* German shepherd. ●**bergerie** *nf* sheepfold.

berlingot [bɛrlɛ̃go] *nm* (*bonbon*) boiled sweet, *Am* hard candy; (*à la menthe*) mint; (*emballage*) (milk) carton.

berne (en) [ɑ̃bɛrn] *adv* at half-mast.

besogne [bəzɔɲ] *nf* job, task, work *inv*.

besoin [bəzwɛ̃] *nm* need; **avoir b. de qch/de faire** to need sth/to do; **au b.** if necessary, if need be; **dans le b.** in need, needy.

bestial, -aux [bɛstjal, -o] *a* bestial, brutish. ●**bestiaux** *nmpl* livestock; (*bovins*) cattle. ●**bestiole** *nf* (*insecte*) bug.

bétail [betaj] *nm* livestock; (*bovins*) cattle.

bête[1] [bɛt] *nf* animal; (*insecte*) bug, creature; **b. noire** pet hate, pet peeve; **chercher la petite b.** (*critiquer*) to pick holes.

bête[2] [bɛt] *a* stupid, silly. ●**bêtement** *adv* stupidly; **tout b.** quite simply. ●**bêtise** *nf* stupidity; (*action, parole*) stupid *ou* silly thing.

béton [betɔ̃] *nm* concrete; **mur**/*etc* **en b.** concrete wall/*etc*; **b. armé** reinforced concrete. ●**bétonnière** *nf* cement *ou* concrete mixer.

betterave [bɛtrav] *nf* beetroot, *Am* beet; **b. sucrière** *ou* **à sucre** sugar beet.
beugler [bøgle] *vi* (*taureau*) to bellow; (*vache*) to moo; (*radio*) *Fig* to blare (out).
beur [bœr] *nm* = North African born in France of immigrant parents.
beurre [bœr] *nm* butter. ●**beurrer** *vt* to butter. ●**beurrier** *nm* butter dish.
beuverie [bøvri] *nf* drinking session.
bévue [bevy] *nf* blunder, mistake.
biais [bjɛ] *nm* (*moyen détourné*) device, expedient; **regarder de b.** to look at sidelong; **traverser en b.** to cross at an angle.
bibelot [biblo] *nm* (small) ornament, trinket.
biberon [bibrɔ̃] *nm* (feeding) bottle; **nourrir au b.** to bottlefeed.
bible [bibl] *nf* bible; **la B.** the Bible. ●**biblique** *a* biblical.
bibliobus [biblijɔbys] *nm* mobile library.
bibliographie [biblijɔgrafi] *nf* bibliography.
bibliothèque [biblijɔtɛk] *nf* library; (*meuble*) bookcase. ●**bibliothécaire** *nmf* librarian.
bic® [bik] *nm* ballpoint, biro®.
biceps [bisɛps] *nm* (*muscle*) biceps.
biche [biʃ] *nf* doe, hind; **ma b.** *Fig* my pet.
bicolore [bikɔlɔr] *a* two-coloured.
bicoque [bikɔk] *nf Péj* shack, hovel.
bicyclette [bisiklɛt] *nf* bicycle; **la b.** *Sp* cycling; **aller à b.** to cycle.
bidet [bidɛ] *nm* (*cuvette*) bidet.
bidon [bidɔ̃] **1** *nm* (*d'essence*) can; (*pour boissons*) canteen. **2** *nm* **du b.** *Fam* bull, baloney ∥ *a inv* (*simulé*) *Fam* phoney, fake.
bidonville [bidɔ̃vil] *nf* shantytown.
bidule [bidyl] *nm* (*chose*) *Fam* whatsit.
bien [bjɛ̃] *adv* well; **il joue b.** he plays well; **je vais b.** I'm fine *ou* well; **b. fatigué/souvent/***etc* (*très*) very tired/often/*etc*; **merci b.!** thanks very much!; **b.!** fine!, right!; **b. des fois/des gens/***etc* lots of *ou* many times/people/*etc*; **je l'ai b. dit** (*intensif*) I *did* say so; **c'est b. compris?** is that quite understood?; **tu as b. fait** you did right; **c'est b. fait (pour lui)** it serves him right.
∥ *a inv* (*convenable, à l'aise*) all right, fine; (*agréable*) nice, fine; (*compétent, bon*) good, fine; (*beau*) attractive; (*en forme*) well; **une fille b.** (*moralement*) a nice *ou* respectable girl; **ce n'est pas b. de...** it's not nice *ou* right to....
∥ *nm* (*avantage*) good; (*chose*) possession; **ça te fera du b.** it will do you good; **pour ton b.** for your own good; **le b. et le mal** good and evil; **biens de consommation** consumer goods. ●**bien-être** *nm* well-being.
bienfaisance [bjɛ̃fəzɑ̃s] *nf* **œuvre de b.** charity. ●**bienfaisant** *a* beneficial.
bienfait [bjɛ̃fɛ] *nm* (*générosité*) favour; (*d'un remède etc*) beneficial effect. ●**bienfaiteur, -trice** *nmf* benefactor, benefactress.
bienheureux, -euse [bjɛ̃nœrø, -øz] *a* blessed, blissful.
bien que [bjɛ̃k(ə)] *conj* (+*sub*) although, though.
bienséant [bjɛ̃seɑ̃] *a* proper.
bientôt [bjɛ̃to] *adv* soon; **à b.!** see you soon!; **il est b. dix heures/***etc* it's nearly ten o'clock/*etc*.
bienveillant [bjɛ̃vɛjɑ̃] *a* kindly.
bienvenu, -ue [bjɛ̃vny] *a* welcome ∥ *nmf* **soyez le b.!** welcome! ∥ *nf* **souhaiter la bienvenue à qn** to welcome s.o.
bière [bjɛr] *nf* (*boisson*) beer; **b. pression** draught *ou Am* draft beer.
bifteck [biftɛk] *nm* steak.
bifurquer [bifyrke] *vi* (*route etc*) to fork, branch off; (*vehicule*) to turn off, fork. ●**bifurcation** *nf* fork, junction.
bigarré [bigare] *a* (*étoffe etc*) mottled; (*foule, société*) motley.
bigler [bigle] *vi* (*loucher*) *Fam* to squint.
bigorneau, -x [bigɔrno] *nm* (*coquillage*) winkle.
bigot, -ote [bigo, -ɔt] *nmf Péj* churchy person ∥ *a Péj* churchy, over-devout.
bigoudi [bigudi] *nm* (hair) curler *ou* roller.
bigrement [bigrəmɑ̃] *adv Fam* awfully.
bijou, -x [biʒu] *nm* jewel; (*ouvrage élégant*) *Fig* gem. ●**bijouterie** *nf* (*commerce*) jeweller's shop, *Am* jewelry shop; (*bijoux*) jewellery, *Am* jewelry. ●**bijoutier, -ière** *nmf* jeweller, *Am* jeweler.
bikini [bikini] *nm* bikini.
bilan [bilɑ̃] *nm Fin* balance sheet; (*résultat*) outcome; (*d'un accident*) (casualty) toll; **b. de santé** checkup.
bile [bil] *nf* bile; **se faire de la b.** *Fam* to worry.
bilingue [bilɛ̃g] *a* bilingual.
billard [bijar] *nm* (*jeu*) billiards; (*table*) billiard table.
bille [bij] *nf* (*d'enfant*) marble; (*de billard*) billiard ball; **stylo à b.** ballpoint (pen).
billet [bijɛ] *nm* ticket; **b. (de banque)** (bank)note, *Am* bill; **b. aller, b. simple** single ticket, *Am* one-way ticket; **b. (d')aller et retour** return ticket, *Am* round trip ticket.
billot [bijo] *nm* (*de bois*) block.
bimensuel, -elle [bimɑ̃sɥɛl] *a* bimonthly.
biner [bine] *vt* to hoe. ●**binette** *nf* hoe.
biochimie [bjɔʃimi] *nf* biochemistry.

biodégradable [bjɔdegradabl] *a* biodegradable.
biographie [bjɔgrafi] *nf* biography. ● **biographique** *a* biographical.
biologie [bjɔlɔʒi] *nf* biology. ● **biologique** *a* biological; (*légumes etc*) organic.
bip [bip] *nm* bleeper.
bique [bik] *nf Fam* nanny-goat.
bis [bis] *adv* (*cri*) *Th* encore; *Mus* repeat; **4 bis** (*numéro*) 4A ‖ *nm Th* encore.
biscornu [biskɔrny] *a* distorted, misshapen; (*idée*) cranky.
biscotte [biskɔt] *nf* (*pain*) Melba toast.
biscuit [biskɥi] *nm* (*sucré*) biscuit, *Am* cookie; (*salé*) biscuit, *Am* cracker; **b. de Savoie** sponge (cake).
bise [biz] *nf* **1** (*vent*) north wind. **2** (*baiser*) *Fam* kiss.
bison [bizɔ̃] *nm* (American) buffalo, bison.
bisou [bizu] *nm Fam* kiss.
bissextile [bisɛkstil] *af* **année b.** leap year.
bistouri [bisturi] *nm* scalpel, lancet.
bistro(t) [bistro] *nm* bar, café.
bitume [bitym] *nm* (*revêtement*) asphalt.
bivouac [bivwak] *nm* (*campement*) bivouac.
bizarre [bizar] *a* peculiar, odd. ● **—ment** *adv* oddly. ● **bizarrerie** *nf* peculiarity.
blabla(bla) [blabla(bla)] *nm* claptrap.
blafard [blafar] *a* pale, pallid.
blague [blag] *nf* **1** (*plaisanterie, farce*) *Fam* joke; *pl* (*absurdités*) *Fam* nonsense; **sans b.!** you're joking! **2** (*à tabac*) pouch. ● **blaguer** *vi* to be joking ‖ *vt* to tease (*s.o.*). ● **blagueur, -euse** *nmf* joker.
blaireau, -x [blɛro] *nm* **1** (*animal*) badger. **2** (*brosse*) (shaving) brush.
blâme [blɑm] *nm* (*critique*) criticism, blame; (*réprimande*) rebuke. ● **blâmable** *a* blameworthy. ● **blâmer** *vt* to criticize, blame; (*réprimander*) to rebuke.
blanc, blanche [blɑ̃, blɑ̃ʃ] **1** *a* white; (*page etc*) blank; **nuit blanche** sleepless night ‖ *nmf* **Blanc, Blanche** (*personne*) white man *ou* woman ‖ *nm* (*couleur*) white; (*de poulet*) breast; (*espace, interligne*) blank; **b. (d'œuf)** (egg) white; **laisser en b.** to leave blank; **chèque en b.** blank cheque *ou Am* check; **cartouche à b.** blank (cartridge). **2** *nf Mus* minim, *Am* half-note. ● **blanchâtre** *a* whitish. ● **blancheur** *nf* whiteness.
blanchir [blɑ̃ʃir] *vt* (*mur*) to whitewash; (*drap*) to launder; **b. qn** (*disculper*) to clear s.o. ‖ *vi* to turn white. ● **blanchissage** *nm* laundering. ● **blanchisserie** *nf* (*lieu*) laundry. ● **blanchisseur, -euse** *nmf* laundryman, laundrywoman.
blasé [blɑze] *a* blasé.
blason [blazɔ̃] *nm* (*écu*) coat of arms.
blasphème [blasfɛm] *nf* blasphemy. ● **blasphématoire** *a* (*propos*) blasphemous. ● **blasphémer** *vi* to blaspheme.
blazer [blazœr] *nm* blazer.
blé [ble] *nm* wheat.
bled [blɛd] *nm* (*village etc*) *Péj Fam* dump of a place.
blême [blɛm] *a* sickly pale; **b. de colère** livid with anger.
bless/er [blese] *vt* to injure, hurt; (*avec un couteau, d'une balle etc*) to wound; (*offenser*) to hurt, offend; **se b. le** *ou* **au bras/***etc* to hurt one's arm/*etc*. ● **—ant** *a* (*parole, personne*) hurtful. ● **—é, -ée** *nmf* casualty, injured *ou* wounded person. ● **blessure** *nf* injury; wound.
bleu [blø] *a* (*mpl* **bleus**) blue; **b. de colère** blue in the face ‖ *nm* (*pl* **-s**) (*couleur*) blue; (*contusion*) bruise; (*vêtement*) overalls; **bleus de travail** overalls; **se faire un b. au genou/***etc* to bruise one's knee/*etc*.
blindé [blɛ̃de] *a* (*voiture etc*) armoured; **porte blindée** reinforced steel door; **une vitre blindée** bulletproof glass ‖ *nm* armoured vehicle.
bloc [blɔk] *nm* (*de pierre etc*) block; (*de papier*) pad; (*masse compacte*) unit; **en b.** all together; **à b.** (*visser etc*) tight, hard. ● **b.-notes** *nm* (*pl* **blocs-notes**) writing pad.
blocage [blɔkaʒ] *nm* (*des roues*) locking; **b. des prix** price freeze.
blond, -onde [blɔ̃, -ɔ̃d] *a* fair(-haired), blond ‖ *nm* fair-haired man; (*couleur*) blond ‖ *nf* fair-haired woman, blonde; **(bière) blonde** lager, pale *ou* light ale.
bloquer [blɔke] *vt* (*obstruer*) to block; (*coincer*) to jam; (*roue*) to lock; (*freins*) to slam on; (*salaires, prix*) to freeze; **bloqué par la neige** snowbound ‖ **se b.** *vpr* to jam, stick; (*roue*) to lock.
blottir (se) [səblɔtir] *vpr* (*dans un coin etc*) to crouch; (*dans son lit*) to snuggle down; **se b. contre** to snuggle up to.
blouse [bluz] *nf* (*tablier*) smock, overall; (*corsage*) blouse. ● **blouson** *nm* windcheater, *Am* windbreaker.
blue-jean(s) [bludʒin(z)] *nm* jeans, denims.
bluff [blœf] *nm* bluff. ● **bluffer** *vti* to bluff.
boa [bɔa] *nm* (*serpent, tour de cou*) boa.
bobine [bɔbin] *nf* (*de fil, film etc*) reel, spool; (*pour machine à coudre*) bobbin, spool; *Él* coil.
bobo [bobo] *nm* (*langage enfantin*) hurt; **j'ai b., ça fait b.** it hurts.
bocal, -aux [bɔkal, -o] *nm* glass jar; (*à poissons*) bowl.

bœuf, *pl* **-fs** [bœf, bø] *nm* (*animal*) ox (*pl* oxen), bullock; (*viande*) beef.
bof! [bɔf] *int* (*indifférence*) *Fam* don't know and don't care!, big deal!
bohémien, -ienne [bɔemjɛ̃, -jɛn] *a* & *nmf* gipsy.
boire* [bwar] *vt* to drink; (*absorber*) to soak up; (*paroles*) *Fig* to take in; **b. un coup** to have a drink; **offrir à b. à qn** to offer s.o. a drink; **b. à petits coups** to sip ▮ *vi* to drink.
bois[1] [bwa] *voir* **boire.**
bois[2] [bwa] *nm* (*matière, forêt*) wood; (*de construction*) timber; *pl* (*de cerf*) antlers; **en** *ou* **de b.** wooden; **b. de chauffage** firewood; •**boisé** *a* wooded. •**boiserie(s)** *nf(pl)* panelling.
boisson [bwasɔ̃] *nf* drink.
boit [bwa] *voir* **boire.**
boîte [bwat] *nf* box; (*de conserve*) tin, *Am* can; (*de bière*) can; **b. de nuit** nightclub; **mettre qn en b.** *Fam* to pull s.o.'s leg. •**boîtier** *nm* (*de montre etc*) case.
boiter [bwate] *vi* (*personne*) to limp. •**boiteux, -euse** *a* lame; (*projet etc*) *Fig* shaky.
bol [bɔl] *nm* (*récipient*) bowl; **prendre un b. d'air** to get a breath of fresh air.
bolide [bɔlid] *nm* (*véhicule*) racing car.
bombard/er [bɔ̃barde] *vt* (*ville etc*) to bomb; (*avec des obus*) to shell; **b. de** (*questions*) to bombard with; (*objets*) to pelt with. •**—ement** *nm* bombing; shelling. •**bombardier** *nm* (*avion*) bomber.
bombe [bɔ̃b] *nf* (*projectile*) bomb; (*de laque etc*) spray; **faire l'effet d'une b.** *Fig* to be a bombshell, be quite unexpected.
bomb/er [bɔ̃be] *vt* **b. la poitrine** to throw out one's chest. •**—é** *a* (*vitre etc*) rounded; (*route*) cambered.
bon[1], **bonne** [bɔ̃, bɔn] *a* **1** (*satisfaisant etc*) good.
2 (*agréable*) nice, good; **il fait b. se reposer** it's nice *ou* good to rest; **b. anniversaire!** happy birthday!
3 (*charitable*) kind, good (**avec qn** to s.o.).
4 (*qui convient*) right; **le b. choix/moment** the right choice/moment.
5 (*approprié, apte*) fit; **b. à manger** fit to eat; **ce n'est b. à rien** it's useless; **comme b. te semble** as you think fit; **c'est b. à savoir** it's worth knowing.
6 (*prudent*) wise, good; **croire b. de...** to think it wise *ou* good to....
7 (*compétent*) good; **b. en français** good at French.
8 (*valable*) good; **ce billet est encore b.** this ticket is still good.
9 (*intensif*) **un b. moment** a good while.
10 (*locutions*) **à quoi b.?** what's the use *ou* point *ou* good?; **pour de b.** really (and truly); **ah b.?** is that so?
▮ *adv* **sentir b.** to smell good; **il fait b.** it's nice (and warm).
bon[2] [bɔ̃] *nm* (*billet*) coupon, voucher.
bonbon [bɔ̃bɔ̃] *nm* sweet, *Am* candy. •**bonbonnière** *nf* sweet box, *Am* candy box.
bonbonne [bɔ̃bɔn] *nf* (*bouteille*) demijohn.
bond [bɔ̃] *nm* leap, bound; **faire un b.** to leap (into the air); (*prix*) to shoot up.
bonde [bɔ̃d] *nf* (*bouchon*) plug.
bondé [bɔ̃de] *a* packed, crammed.
bondir [bɔ̃dir] *vi* to leap.
bonheur [bɔnœr] *nm* happiness; (*chance*) good luck, good fortune; **par b.** luckily.
bonhomme, *pl* **bonshommes** [bɔnɔm, bɔ̃zɔm] *nm* fellow, guy; **b. de neige** snowman.
boniment(s) [bɔnimɑ̃] *nm(pl)* (*baratin*) patter.
bonjour [bɔ̃ʒur] *nm* & *int* good morning; (*après-midi*) good afternoon; **donner le b. à, dire b. à** to say hello to.
bonne[1] [bɔn] *voir* **bon**[1].
bonne[2] *nf* (*domestique*) maid.
bonnement [bɔnmɑ̃] *adv* **tout b.** simply.
bonnet [bɔnɛ] *nm* (*de ski etc*) cap; (*de femme, d'enfant*) hat, bonnet; (*de soutien-gorge*) cup; **b. d'âne** dunce's cap.
bonsoir [bɔ̃swar] *nm* & *int* (*en rencontrant qn*) good evening; (*en quittant qn*) goodbye; (*au coucher*) good night.
bonté [bɔ̃te] *nf* kindness, goodness.
boom [bum] *nm* *Écon* boom.
bord [bɔr] *nm* (*rebord*) edge; (*rive*) bank; (*de chapeau*) brim; (*de verre*) rim, brim, edge; **au b. de la mer/route** at *ou* by the seaside/roadside; **b. du trottoir** kerb, *Am* curb; **au b. de** (*précipice*) on the brink of; **au b. des larmes** on the verge of tears; **à bord (de)** *Nau Av* on board; **jeter par-dessus b.** to throw overboard.
bordeaux [bɔrdo] *a inv* maroon.
border [bɔrde] *vt* (*lit, personne*) to tuck in; **b. la rue/***etc* (*maisons, arbres etc*) to line the street/*etc.*
bordure [bɔrdyr] *nf* border; **en b. de** bordering on.
borgne [bɔrɲ] *a* (*personne*) one-eyed, blind in one eye.
borne [bɔrn] *nf* (*pierre*) boundary mark; *pl* (*limites*) *Fig* bounds; **b. kilométrique** = milestone; **dépasser les bornes** to go too far.
born/er [bɔrne] *vt* (*limiter*) to confine; **se b.**

à to confine oneself to. • **—é** *a* (*personne*) narrow-minded.
Bosnie [bɔsni] *nf* Bosnia.
bosquet [bɔskɛ] *nm* grove, thicket.
bosse [bɔs] *nf* (*dans le dos*) hump; (*enflure*) bump, lump; (*de terrain*) bump; **avoir la b. de** *Fam* to have a flair for.
bosseler [bɔsle] *vt* (*déformer*) to dent.
bossu, -ue [bɔsy] *a* hunchbacked ‖ *nmf* (*personne*) hunchback.
botanique [bɔtanik] *nf* botany.
botte [bɔt] *nf* **1** (*chaussure*) boot. **2** (*de radis etc*) bunch; (*de paille*) bundle. • **botter** *vt* (*ballon etc*) *Fam* to boot. • **bottillon** *nm ou* **bottine** *nf* (ankle) boot.
Bottin® [bɔtɛ̃] *nm* phone book.
bouc [buk] *nm* billy goat; (*barbe*) goatee.
boucan [bukɑ̃] *nm Fam* din, racket.
bouche [buʃ] *nf* mouth; **faire la fine b.** *Péj* to turn up one's nose; **b. de métro** métro entrance; **b. d'égout** drain opening, manhole; **le b.-à-b.** the kiss of life. • **bouchée** *nf* mouthful.
bouch/er[1] [buʃe] *vt* (*évier, nez etc*) to stop up, block (up); (*bouteille*) to cork; (*vue, rue etc*) to block; **se b. le nez** to hold one's nose.
boucher[2] [buʃe] *nm* butcher. • **boucherie** *nf* butcher's (shop); (*carnage*) butchery.
bouchon [buʃɔ̃] *nm* stopper, top; (*de liège*) cork; (*de tube, bidon*) cap, top; *Pêche* float; (*embouteillage*) *Fig* traffic jam.
boucle [bukl] *nf* **1** (*de ceinture*) buckle; (*de fleuve etc*) & *Av* loop; (*de ruban*) bow; **b. d'oreille** earring. **2 b. (de cheveux)** curl.
boucler [bukle] **1** *vt* (*attacher*) to fasten, buckle; (*travail etc*) to finish off; (*fermer*) *Fam* to lock up; (*encercler*) to surround, cordon off; **boucle-la!** *Fam* shut up! **2** *vt* (*cheveux*) to curl ‖ *vi* to be curly. • **bouclé** *a* (*cheveux*) curly.
bouclier [buklije] *nm* shield.
bouddhiste [budist] *a* & *nmf* Buddhist.
bouder [bude] *vi* to sulk. • **bouderie** *nf* sulkiness. • **boudeur, -euse** *a* sulky.
boudin [budɛ̃] *nm* black pudding, *Am* blood sausage.
boue [bu] *nf* mud. • **boueux, -euse** [bwø, -øz] *a* muddy.
bouée [bwe] *nf* buoy; **b. de sauvetage** lifebuoy; **b. (gonflable)** rubber ring.
bouffe [buf] *nf Fam* food, grub. • **bouffer** *vti* (*manger*) *Fam* to eat.
bouffée [bufe] *nf* (*de fumée*) puff; (*de parfum*) whiff.
bouffi [bufi] *a* puffy, bloated.
bouffon, -onne [bufɔ̃, -ɔn] *nm* buffoon.
bougeoir [buʒwar] *nm* candlestick.
bougeotte [buʒɔt] *nf* **avoir la b.** *Fam* to have the fidgets.
bouger [buʒe] *vi* to move; (*agir*) to stir ‖ *vt* to move.
bougie [buʒi] *nf* candle; *Aut* spark(ing) plug.
bougon, -onne [bugɔ̃, -ɔn] *a Fam* grumpy. • **bougonner** *vi Fam* to grumble.
bouillabaisse [bujabɛs] *nf* fish soup.
bouillie [buji] *nf* porridge; (*pour bébé*) cereal; **en b.** in a mush, mushy.
bouill/ir* [bujir] *vi* to boil; **b. à gros bouillons** to bubble, boil hard; **faire b. qch** to boil sth; **b. de colère** to be seething with anger. • **—ant** *a* boiling. • **bouilloire** *nf* kettle. • **bouillon** *nm* (*aliment*) broth, stock; (*bulles*) bubbles. • **bouillonner** *vi* to bubble. • **bouillotte** *nf* hot water bottle.
boulanger, -ère [bulɑ̃ʒe, -ɛr] *nmf* baker. • **boulangerie** *nf* baker's (shop).
boule [bul] *nf* (*sphère*) ball; *pl* (*jeu*) bowls; **b. de neige** snowball; **se mettre en b.** (*chat etc*) to curl up into a ball; (*en colère*) *Fam* to fly off the handle; **boules Quiès**® earplugs.
bouleau, -x [bulo] *nm* (silver) birch.
bouledogue [buldɔg] *nm* bulldog.
boulet [bulɛ] *nm* (*de forçat*) ball and chain; **b. de canon** cannonball.
boulette [bulɛt] *nf* (*de papier*) ball; (*de viande*) meatball.
boulevard [bulvar] *nm* boulevard.
boulevers/er [bulvɛrse] *vt* (*déranger*) to turn upside down; (*émouvoir*) to upset (greatly), distress; (*vie de qn, pays*) to disrupt. • **—ant** *a* upsetting, distressing. • **—ement** *nm* upheaval.
boulon [bulɔ̃] *nm* bolt.
boulot [bulo] *nm* (*travail*) *Fam* work; (*emploi*) *Fam* job.
boum [bum] **1** *int* & *nm* bang. **2** *nf* (*surprise-partie*) *Fam* party.
bouquet [bukɛ] *nm* (*de fleurs*) bunch, bouquet; (*d'arbres*) clump; (*de vin*) bouquet; **c'est le b.!** that's the last straw!
bouquin [bukɛ̃] *nm Fam* book. • **bouquiniste** *nmf* second-hand bookseller.
bourbeux, -euse [burbø, -øz] *a* muddy. • **bourbier** *nm* (*lieu, situation*) quagmire.
bourdon [burdɔ̃] *nm* (*insecte*) bumblebee. • **bourdonner** *vi* to buzz, hum. • **bourdonnement** *nm* buzzing, humming.
bourg [bur] *nm* (small) market town. • **bourgade** *nf* (large) village.
bourgeois, -oise [burʒwa, -waz] *a* & *nmf* middle-class (person). • **bourgeoisie** *nf* middle class.

bourgeon [burʒɔ̃] *nm* bud. ●**bourgeonner** *vi* to bud.
bourgmestre [burgmɛstr] *nm* (*en Belgique, Suisse*) burgomaster.
bourgogne [burgɔɲ] *nm* (*vin*) Burgundy.
bourrade [burad] *nf* (*du coude etc*) shove.
bourrage [buraʒ] *nm* **b. de crâne** brainwashing.
bourrasque [burask] *nf* squall, gust of wind.
bourratif, -ive [buratif, -iv] *a* (*aliment*) *Fam* filling, stodgy.
bourreau, -x [buro] *nm* executioner; **b. d'enfants** child batterer; **b. de travail** workaholic.
bourrelet [burlɛ] *nm* weather strip; **b. de graisse** roll of fat.
bourrer [bure] *vt* to stuff, cram (**de** with); (*pipe, coussin*) to fill; **b. de coups** to thrash; **b. le crâne à qn** to brainwash s.o.
bourrique [burik] *nf* ass.
bourru [bury] *a* surly, rough.
bourse [burs] *nf* (*sac*) purse; (*d'études*) grant, scholarship; **la B.** the Stock Exchange. ●**boursier, -ière** *nmf Scol Univ* grant holder, scholar.
boursouflé [bursufle] *a* (*visage etc*) puffy.
bousculer [buskyle] *vt* (*heurter, pousser*) to jostle; (*presser*) to rush, push. ●**bousculade** *nf* jostling, rush.
bouse [buz] *nf* **une b. (de vache)** a cowpat; **de la b. (de vache)** cow dung.
bousiller [buzije] *vt Fam* to mess up, wreck.
boussole [busɔl] *nf* compass.
bout [bu] *nm* end; (*de langue, canne, doigt*) tip; (*de papier, pain, ficelle*) bit; **un b. de temps/chemin** a little while/way; **au b. d'un moment** after a while; **jusqu'au b.** (*lire etc*) (right) to the end; **à b. (de forces)** exhausted; **à b. de souffle** out of breath; **à b. de bras** at arm's length; **venir à b. de** (*travail*) to get through; (*adversaire*) to get the better of; **à b. portant** point-blank.
boutade [butad] *nf* (*plaisanterie*) quip, witticism.
boute-en-train [butɑ̃trɛ̃] *nm inv* (*personne*) live wire.
bouteille [butɛj] *nf* bottle; (*de gaz*) cylinder.
boutique [butik] *nf* shop.
bouton [butɔ̃] *nm* (*bourgeon*) bud; (*au visage etc*) pimple, spot; (*de vêtement*) button; (*poussoir*) (push-)button; (*de porte, télévision*) knob; **b. de manchette** cuff link. ●**b.-d'or** *nm* (*pl* **boutons-d'or**) buttercup. ●**boutonner** *vt*, **se b.** *vpr* to button (up). ●**boutonneux, -euse** *a* pimply, spotty. ●**boutonnière** *nf* buttonhole.
bouture [butyr] *nf* (*plante*) cutting.
bovins [bɔvɛ̃] *nmpl* cattle.
bowling [boliŋ] *nm* (tenpin) bowling; (*lieu*) bowling alley.
box, *pl* **boxes** [bɔks] *nm* (*garage*) lockup *ou* individual garage; (*d'écurie*) (loose) box; (*des accusés*) dock.
boxe [bɔks] *nf* boxing. ●**boxer** *vi Sp* to box ‖ *vt Fam* to whack, punch. ●**boxeur** *nm* boxer.
boyau, -x [bwajo] *nm Anat* gut; (*corde*) catgut; (*de bicyclette*) (racing) tyre *ou Am* tire.
boycotter [bɔjkɔte] *vt* to boycott.
BP [bepe] *nf abrév* (*boîte postale*) PO Box.
bracelet [braslɛ] *nm* bracelet, bangle; (*de montre*) strap, *Am* band.
braconner [brakɔne] *vi* to poach. ●**braconnier** *nm* poacher.
brader [brade] *vt* to sell off cheaply.
braguette [bragɛt] *nf* (*de pantalon*) fly, flies.
braille [brɑj] *nm* Braille.
brailler [brɑje] *vti* to bawl.
braire* [brɛr] *vi* (*âne*) to bray.
braise(s) [brɛz] *nf(pl)* embers, live coals.
brancard [brɑ̃kar] *nm* (*civière*) stretcher; (*de charrette*) shaft. ●**brancardier** *nm* stretcher-bearer.
branche [brɑ̃ʃ] *nf* (*d'arbre, d'une science etc*) branch; (*de compas*) leg, arm; (*de lunettes*) side (piece). ●**branchages** *nmpl* (cut *ou* fallen) branches.
branché [brɑ̃ʃe] *a* (*informé*) *Fam* with it.
branch/er [brɑ̃ʃe] *vt* (*lampe etc*) to plug in; (*installer*) to connect. ●**—ement** *nm Él* connection.
brandir [brɑ̃dir] *vt* to brandish, flourish.
branle [brɑ̃l] *nm* **mettre en b.** to set in motion. ●**b.-bas** *nm inv* turmoil. ●**branlant** *a* (*table etc*) wobbly, shaky.
braquer [brake] **1** *vt* (*arme etc*) to point, aim (**sur** at); (*yeux*) to fix. **2** *vi Aut* to turn the steering wheel, steer.
bras [bra] *nm* arm; **en b. de chemise** in one's shirtsleeves; **b. dessus b. dessous** arm in arm; **à b. ouverts** with open arms; **son b. droit** *Fig* his right-hand man; **à tour de b.** with all one's might; **à b.-le-corps** round the waist. ●**brassard** *nm* armband. ●**brassée** *nf* armful.
brasier [brɑzje] *nm* blaze, inferno.
brasse [bras] *nf* (*nage*) breaststroke; (*mesure*) fathom; **b. papillon** butterfly stroke.
brasserie [brasri] *nf* (*usine*) brewery; (*café*) brasserie.
brassière [brasjɛr] *nf* (*de bébé*) vest, *Am* undershirt.

bravade [bravad] *nf* **par b.** out of bravado.
brave [brav] *a* (*hardi*) brave; (*honnête*) good. ▌*nm* brave man; good man. ●**bravement** *adv* bravely. ●**braver** *vt* to defy.
❶brave G32 Position of Adjectives 4 D 3
bravo [bravo] *int* well done ▌*nm* cheer.
bravoure [bravur] *nf* bravery.
break [brɛk] *nm* estate car, *Am* station wagon.
brebis [brəbi] *nf* ewe; **b. galeuse** (*indésirable*) black sheep.
brèche [brɛʃ] *nf* gap, breach.
bredouille [brəduj] *a* **rentrer b.** to come back empty-handed.
bredouiller [brəduje] *vti* to mumble.
bref, brève [brɛf, brɛv] *a* brief, short ▌*adv* **(enfin) b.** in a word.
Brésil [brezil] *nm* Brazil. ●**brésilien, -ienne** *a* & *nmf* Brazilian.
Bretagne [brətaɲ] *nf* Brittany. ●**breton, -onne** *a* & *nmf* Breton.
bretelle [brətɛl] *nf* strap; (*route d'accès*) access road; *pl* (*pour pantalon*) braces, *Am* suspenders.
brève [brɛv] *voir* **bref.**
brevet [brəvɛ] *nm* diploma; **b. (des collèges)** = GCSE (*examination for 16-year-olds*); **b. (d'invention)** patent. ●**breveter** *vt* to patent.
bribes [brib] *nfpl* scraps, bits.
bric-à-brac [brikabrak] *nm inv* bric-à-brac, jumble, junk.
bricole [brikɔl] *nf* (*objet*, *futilité*) trifle.
bricol/er [brikɔle] *vi* to do odd jobs ▌*vt* (*réparer*) to patch up; (*fabriquer*) to put together. ●**—age** *nm* (*passe-temps*) do-it-yourself; (*petits travaux*) odd jobs; **salon/rayon du b.** do-it-yourself exhibition/department. ●**—eur, -euse** *nmf* handyman, handywoman.
bravoure [bravur] *nf* bravery.
bride [brid] *nf* (*de cheval*) bridle. ●**brider** *vt* (*cheval*) to bridle; **avoir les yeux bridés** to have slanting eyes.
bridge [bridʒ] *nm* (*jeu*) bridge.
brièvement [briɛvmɑ̃] *adv* briefly. ●**brièveté** *nf* shortness, brevity.
brigade [brigad] *nf* (*de gendarmerie*) squad; *Mil* brigade. ●**brigadier** *nm* police sergeant; *Mil* corporal.
brigand [brigɑ̃] *nm* robber; (*enfant*) rascal.
brillant [brijɑ̃] *a* (*luisant*) shining; (*astiqué*) shiny; (*couleur*) bright; (*doué, remarquable*) *Fig* brilliant ▌*nm* shine; (*diamant*) diamond. ●**brillamment** *adv* brilliantly.
briller [brije] *vi* to shine; **faire b.** (*meuble*) to polish (up).
brin [brɛ̃] *nm* (*d'herbe*) blade; (*de corde*, *fil*) strand; (*de muguet*) spray; **un b. de** *Fig* a bit of.
brindille [brɛ̃dij] *nf* twig.
bringuebaler [brɛ̃gbale] *vi* to shake about; (*véhicule*) to rattle along.
brio [brijo] *nm* (*virtuosité*) brilliance.
brioche [brijɔʃ] *nf* (*pâtisserie*) brioche (*light sweet bun*).
brique [brik] *nf* brick; (*de lait, jus de fruit*) carton.
briquer [brike] *vt* to polish (up).
briquet [brikɛ] *nm* (cigarette) lighter.
brise [briz] *nf* breeze.
briser [brize] *vt* to break; (*en morceaux*) to smash, break; (*espoir*, *carrière*) to wreck, shatter ▌**se b.** *vpr* to break. ●**brisants** *nmpl* reefs.
britannique [britanik] *a* British ▌*nmpl* **les Britanniques** the British.
broc [bro] *nm* pitcher, jug.
brocanteur, -euse [brɔkɑ̃tœr, -øz] *nmf* secondhand dealer (*in furniture etc*).
broche [brɔʃ] *nf Culin* spit; (*bijou*) brooch; *Méd* pin. ●**brochette** *nf* (*tige*) skewer; (*plat*) kebab.
brochet [brɔʃɛ] *nm* (*poisson*) pike.
brochure [brɔʃyr] *nf* brochure, booklet.
brocolis [brɔkɔli] *nmpl* broccoli.
broder [brɔde] *vt* to embroider (**de** with). ●**broderie** *nf* embroidery.
broncher [brɔ̃ʃe] *vi* (*bouger*) to budge; (*reculer*) to flinch; (*protester*) to balk.
bronches [brɔ̃ʃ] *nfpl* bronchial tubes. ●**bronchite** *nf* bronchitis.
bronze [brɔ̃z] *nm* bronze.
bronz/er [brɔ̃ze] *vt* to tan; **se (faire) b.** to sunbathe, get a (sun)tan ▌*vi* to get (sun)tanned. ●**—age** *nm* (sun)tan, sunburn.
brosse [brɔs] *nf* brush; **b. à dents** toothbrush; **cheveux en b.** crew cut. ●**brosser** *vt* to brush; **se b. les dents/cheveux** to brush one's teeth/hair.
brouette [bruɛt] *nf* wheelbarrow.
brouhaha [bruaa] *nm* hubbub.
brouillard [brujar] *nm* fog; **il y a du b.** it's foggy.
brouille [bruj] *nf* disagreement, quarrel.
brouiller [bruje] **1** *vt* (*idées etc*) to mix up; (*vue*) to blur; (*œufs*) to scramble ▌**se b.** *vpr* (*idées*) to be *ou* get confused; (*temps*) to cloud over; (*vue*) to get blurred. **2** *vt* (*amis*) to cause a split between ▌**se b.** *vpr* to fall out (**avec** with).
brouillon [brujɔ̃] *nm* rough draft.
broussailles [brusɑj] *nfpl* bushes.

brousse [brus] *nf* **la b.** the bush.
brouter [brute] *vti* to graze.
broyer [brwaje] *vt* to grind; (*doigt, bras*) to crush.
bru [bry] *nf* daughter-in-law.
brugnon [bryɲɔ̃] *nm* (*fruit*) nectarine.
bruine [brɥin] *nf* drizzle. ●**bruiner** *v imp* to drizzle.
bruissement [brɥismɑ̃] *nm* (*de feuilles*) rustle, rustling.
bruit [brɥi] *nm* noise, sound; (*nouvelle*) rumour; **faire du b.** to make a noise. ●**bruitage** *nm Cin* sound effects.
brûlant [brylɑ̃] *a* (*objet, soleil*) burning (hot); (*sujet*) *Fig* red-hot.
brûlé [bryle] *nm* **odeur de b.** smell of burning.
brûle-pourpoint (à) [abrylpurpwɛ̃] *adv* point-blank.
brûler [bryle] *vt* to burn; (*consommer*) to use up, burn; **b. un feu (rouge)** to go through *ou* jump the lights ‖ *vi* to burn; **b. (d'envie) de faire** to be dying to do ‖ **se b.** *vpr* to burn oneself.
brûlure [brylyr] *nf* burn; **brûlures d'estomac** heartburn.
brume [brym] *nf* mist, haze. ●**brumeux, -euse** *a* misty, hazy; (*obscur*) *Fig* hazy.
brun, brune [brœ̃, bryn] *a* brown; (*cheveux*) dark, brown; (*personne*) dark-haired ‖ *nm* (*couleur*) brown ‖ *nmf* dark-haired person. ●**brunir** *vt* (*peau*) to tan ‖ *vi* to turn brown; (*cheveux*) to go darker.
brushing [brœʃiŋ] *nm* blow-dry.
brusque [brysk] *a* (*manière, personne etc*) abrupt, blunt; (*subit*) sudden, abrupt. ●**brusquement** *adv* suddenly, abruptly. ●**brusquer** *vt* to rush. ●**brusquerie** *nf* abruptness.
brut [bryt] *a* (*pétrole*) crude; (*sucre*) unrefined; (*soie*) raw; (*poids, revenu*) gross.
brutal, -aux [brytal, -o] *a* (*violent*) savage, brutal; (*enfant*) rough; (*franchise, réponse*) crude, blunt. ●**brutaliser** *vt* to ill-treat. ●**brutalité** *nf* (*violence, acte*) brutality. ●**brute** *nf* brute.
Bruxelles [brysɛl] *nm ou f* Brussels.
bruyant [brɥijɑ̃] *a* noisy. ●**bruyamment** *adv* noisily.
bruyère [bryjɛr] *nf* (*plante*) heather.
bu [by] *pp de* **boire.**
buanderie [bɥɑ̃dri] *nf* (*lieu*) laundry.
bûche [byʃ] *nf* log. ●**bûcher** *nm* (*local*) woodshed; (*supplice*) stake. ●**bûcheron** *nm* lumberjack, woodcutter.
budget [bydʒɛ] *nm* budget. ●**budgétaire** *a* budgetary; (*année*) financial.
buée [bɥe] *nf* mist, condensation.
buffet [byfɛ] *nm* (*armoire*) sideboard; (*table, repas*) buffet.
buffle [byfl] *nm* buffalo.
buis [bɥi] *nm* (*arbre*) box; (*bois*) boxwood.
buisson [bɥisɔ̃] *nm* bush.
buissonnière [bɥisɔnjɛr] *af* **faire l'école b.** to play truant *ou Am* hookey.
bulbe [bylb] *nm* bulb.
Bulgarie [bylgari] *nf* Bulgaria. ●**bulgare** *a & nmf* Bulgarian.
bulldozer [byldozœr] *nm* bulldozer.
bulle [byl] *nf* bubble; (*de bande dessinée*) balloon.
bulletin [byltɛ̃] *nm* (*méteo*) report; (*scolaire*) report, *Am* report card; (*communiqué, revue*) bulletin; **b. de paie** pay slip *ou Am* stub; **b. de vote** ballot paper.
buraliste [byralist] *nmf* (*au tabac*) tobacconist.
bureau, -x [byro] *nm* **1** (*table*) desk. **2** (*lieu*) office; **b. de change** foreign exchange office, bureau de change; **b. de location** *Th Cin* box office; **b. de tabac** tobacconist's (shop), *Am* tobacco store. ●**bureautique** *nf* office automation.
burette [byrɛt] *nf* oilcan; *Culin* cruet.
burlesque [byrlɛsk] *a* (*idée etc*) ludicrous.
bus[1] [bys] *nm* bus.
bus[2] [by] *pt de* **boire.**
buste [byst] *nm* (*torse, sculpture*) bust.
but[1] [by(t)] *nm* (*objectif*) aim, goal; (*cible*) target; *Fb* goal; **aller droit au b.** to go straight to the point; **j'ai pour b. de...** my aim is to....
but[2] [by] *pt de* **boire.**
butane [bytan] *nm* (*gaz*) butane.
buter [byte] **1** *vi* **b. contre** to stumble over; (*difficulté*) *Fig* to come up against. **2 se buter** *vpr* (*s'entêter*) to become *ou* be obstinate. ●**buté** *a* obstinate.
butin [bytɛ̃] *nm* loot, haul, booty.
butiner [bytine] *vi* (*abeille*) to gather pollen and nectar.
butoir [bytwar] *nm* (*pour train*) buffer; (*de porte*) stop(per).
butte [byt] **1** *nf* mound, hillock. **2 en b. à** (*calomnie etc*) exposed to.
buvable [byvabl] *a* drinkable. ●**buveur, -euse** *nmf* drinker.
buvard [byvar] *a & nm* **(papier) b.** blotting paper.
buvette [byvɛt] *nf* refreshment bar.

C

C, c [se] *nm* C, c
c *abrév* centime.
c' [s] *voir* **ce**[1].
ça [sa] *pron dém* (*abrév de* **cela**) (*pour désigner*) that; (*plus près*) this; (*sujet indéfini*) it, that; **ça m'amuse que...** it amuses me that...; **où/quand/comment/***etc* **ça?** where?/when?/how?/*etc*; **ça va (bien)?** how's it going?; **ça va!** fine!, OK!; **ça alors!** (*surprise, indignation*) how about that!; **c'est ça** that's right; **et avec ça?** (*dans un magasin*) anything else?
G47 Ceci, cela, ça 6 A 3
çà [sa] *adv* **çà et là** here and there.
caban [kabɑ̃] *nm* (*veste*) reefer.
cabane [kaban] *nf* hut, cabin; (*à outils*) shed; (*à lapins*) hutch.
cabas [kabɑ] *nm* shopping bag.
cabillaud [kabijo] *nm* (fresh) cod.
cabine [kabin] *nf* (*de bateau*) cabin; *Tél* phone booth, phone box; (*de camion*) cab; (*d'ascenseur*) car; (*à la piscine*) cubicle; **c. (de pilotage)** cockpit; (*d'un grand avion*) flight deck; **c. d'essayage** fitting room.
cabinet [kabinɛ] *nm* (*de médecin*) surgery, *Am* office; (*d'avocat*) office; (*clientèle de médecin ou d'avocat*) practice; (*de ministre*) department; *pl* (*toilettes*) toilet, lavatory; **c. de toilette** (small) bathroom, toilet; **c. de travail** study.
câble [kɑbl] *nm* cable; (*cordage*) rope; **la télévision par c.** cable television; **le c.** *TV* cable. • **câbler** *vt* **être câblé** *TV* to have cable.
cabosser [kabɔse] *vt* to dent.
cabrer (se) [səkabre] *vpr* (*cheval*) to rear (up).
cabri [kabri] *nm* (*chevreau*) kid.
cabrioles [kabriɔl] *nfpl* **faire des c.** (*sauts*) to cavort, caper (about).
cabriolet [kabriɔlɛ] *nm Aut* convertible.
cacah(o)uète [kakawɛt] *nf* peanut.
cacao [kakao] *nm* (*boisson*) cocoa.
cachalot [kaʃalo] *nm* sperm whale.
cache-cache [kaʃkaʃ] *nm inv* hide-and-seek. • **c.-nez** *nm inv* scarf, muffler.
cachemire [kaʃmir] *nm* (*tissu*) cashmere.
cacher [kaʃe] *vt* to hide, conceal (**à** from); **je ne cache pas que...** I don't hide the fact that... ▮ **se c.** *vpr* to hide.
cachet [kaʃɛ] *nm* (*de la poste*) postmark; (*comprimé*) tablet; *Fig* distinctive character. • **cacheter** *vt* to seal.
cachette [kaʃɛt] *nf* hiding place; **en c.** in secret; **en c. de qn** without s.o. knowing.
cachot [kaʃo] *nm* dungeon.
cachotteries [kaʃɔtri] *nfpl* secretiveness; (*petits secrets*) little mysteries. • **cachottier, -ière** *a* & *nmf* secretive (person).
cacophonie [kakɔfɔni] *nf* cacophony.
cactus [kaktys] *nm* cactus.
cadavre [kadɑvr] *nm* corpse. • **cadavérique** *a* (*teint etc*) cadaverous; **rigidité c.** rigor mortis.
caddie® [kadi] *nm* (supermarket) trolley *ou Am* cart.
cadeau, -x [kado] *nm* present, gift.
cadenas [kadnɑ] *nm* padlock. • **cadenasser** *vt* to padlock.
cadence [kadɑ̃s] *nf* rhythm; *Mus* cadence; (*taux, vitesse*) rate; **en c.** in time.
cadet, -ette [kadɛ, -ɛt] *a* (*de deux frères etc*) younger; (*de plus de deux*) youngest ▮ *nmf* (*enfant*) younger (child); youngest (child); *Sp* junior; **c'est mon c.** he's my junior.
cadran [kadrɑ̃] *nm* (*de téléphone etc*) dial; (*de montre*) face; **c. solaire** sundial.
cadre [kɑdr] *nm* **1** (*de photo, vélo etc*) frame; (*décor*) setting; (*sur un imprimé*) box. **2** (*chef*) *Com* executive, manager; *pl* (*personnel*) *Com* management, managers.
cadrer [kɑdre] *vi* to tally (**avec** with).
cafard, -arde [kafar, -ard] *nm* **1** (*insecte*) cockroach. **2 avoir le c.** to be in the dumps; **ça me donne le c.** it depresses me. • **cafardeux, -euse** *a* (*personne*) in the dumps.
café [kafe] *nm* coffee; (*bar*) café; **c. au lait, c. crème** white coffee, coffee with milk; **c. noir, c. nature** black coffee; **c. soluble** *ou* **instantané** instant coffee; **tasse de c.** cup of black coffee. • **cafétéria** *nf* cafeteria. • **cafetière** *nf* coffeepot; (*électrique*) percolator.
cage [kaʒ] *nf* cage; **c. (d'escalier)** (stair)well; **c. des buts** *Fb* goal (area).
cageot [kaʒo] *nm* crate, box.
cagibi [kaʒibi] *nm* (storage) room.
cagnotte [kaɲɔt] *nf* (*tirelire*) kitty.
cagoule [kagul] *nf* (*de bandit, moine*) hood; (*d'enfant*) balaclava, *Am* ski mask.
cahier [kaje] *nm Scol* exercise book; (*carnet*) (note)book; **c. de brouillon** rough book, *Am* = scratch pad; **c. d'appel**

register (*in school*).
cahin-caha [kaɛ̃kaa] *adv* **aller c.-caha** to jog along (with ups and downs).
cahot [kao] *nm* jolt, bump. •**cahoter** *vi* (*véhicule*) to jolt along. •**cahoteux, -euse** *a* bumpy.
caille [kɑj] *nf* (*oiseau*) quail.
cailler [kɑje] *vti*, **se c.** *vpr* (*sang*) to clot, congeal; (*lait*) to curdle; **faire c.** (*lait*) to curdle. •**caillot** *nm* (blood) clot.
caillou, -x [kaju] *nm* stone; (*galet*) pebble. •**caillouteux, -euse** *a* stony.
Caire [kɛr] *nm* **le C.** Cairo.
caisse [kɛs] *nf* (*boîte*) case, box; (*cageot*) crate; (*guichet*) cash desk, pay desk; (*de supermarché*) checkout; (*tambour*) drum; **c. (enregistreuse)** till, cash register; **c. d'épargne** savings bank.
caissier, -ière [kɛsje, -jɛr] *nmf* cashier; (*de supermarché*) checkout assistant.
cajoler [kaʒɔle] *vt* (*câliner*) to pamper, make a fuss of.
cajou [kaʒu] *nm* **noix de c.** cashew nut.
cake [kɛk] *nm* fruit cake.
calamité [kalamite] *nf* calamity.
calandre [kalɑ̃dr] *nf* *Aut* radiator grille.
calcaire [kalkɛr] *a* (*eau*) hard ‖ *nm* *Géol* limestone.
calciné [kalsine] *a* charred, burnt to a cinder.
calcium [kalsjɔm] *nm* calcium.
calcul [kalkyl] *nm* calculation; (*discipline*) arithmetic.
calcul/er [kalkyle] *vt* to calculate. •**—é** *a* (*risque etc*) calculated. •**calculatrice** *nf* (*ordinateur*) calculator. •**calculette** *nf* pocket calculator.
cale [kal] *nf* **1** (*pour maintenir*) wedge. **2** (*de bateau*) hold.
calé [kale] *a* *Fam* (*instruit*) clever (**en qch** at sth).
caleçon [kalsɔ̃] *nm* underpants, boxer shorts; **c. de bain** bathing trunks.
calendrier [kalɑ̃drije] *nm* (*mois et jours*) calendar; (*programme*) timetable.
cale-pied [kalpje] *nm* (*de bicyclette*) toe-clip.
calepin [kalpɛ̃] *nm* (pocket) notebook.
caler [kale] **1** *vt* (*meuble etc*) to wedge; (*appuyer*) to prop (up). **2** *vt* (*moteur*) to stall ‖ *vi* to stall.
calfeutrer [kalføtre] *vt* (*avec du bourrelet*) to draughtproof; **se c. (chez soi)** to shut oneself away *ou* up.
calibre [kalibr] *nm* (*diamètre*) calibre.
calice [kalis] *nm* (*vase*) *Rel* chalice.
califourchon (à) [akalifurʃɔ̃] *adv* astride; **se mettre à c. sur** to straddle.
câlin [kɑlɛ̃] *a* affectionate ‖ *nm* cuddle. •**câliner** *vt* (*caresser*) to cuddle.
calleux, -euse [kalø, -øz] *a* covered in calluses, callous.
calme [kalm] *a* calm; (*journée etc*) quiet, calm ‖ *nm* calm(ness); **du c.!** keep quiet!; (*pas de panique*) keep calm!; **dans le c.** (*travailler, étudier*) in peace and quiet. •**—ment** [-əmɑ̃] *adv* calmly.
calmer [kalme] *vt* (*douleur*) to soothe; (*inquiétude*) to calm; **c. qn** to calm s.o. (down) ‖ **se c.** *vpr* to calm down. •**calmant** *nm* (*pour la nervosité*) sedative; (*la douleur*) painkiller; **sous calmants** under sedation; on painkillers.
calomnie [kalɔmni] *nf* slander; (*par écrit*) libel. •**calomnier** *vt* to slander; to libel. •**calomnieux, -euse** *a* slanderous; libellous.
calorie [kalɔri] *nf* calorie.
calot [kalo] *nm* *Mil* forage cap.
calotte [kalɔt] *nf* *Rel* skull cap; **c. glaciaire** icecap.
calque [kalk] *nm* (*dessin*) tracing; **(papier-)c.** tracing paper. •**calquer** *vt* to trace; (*imiter*) *Fig* to copy.
calvaire [kalvɛr] *nm* *Rel* calvary; *Fig* agony.
camarade [kamarad] *nmf* friend; **c. de jeu** playmate; **c. d'atelier** workmate, *Am* work colleague. •**camaraderie** *nf* friendship, companionship.
cambouis [kɑ̃bwi] *nm* (dirty) oil.
cambrer [kɑ̃bre] *vt* to arch; **c. les reins** *ou* **le buste** to throw out one's chest.
cambriol/er [kɑ̃brijɔle] *vt* to burgle, *Am* burglarize. •**—age** *nm* burglary. •**—eur, -euse** *nmf* burglar.
camélia [kamelja] *nm* *Bot* camellia.
camelot [kamlo] *nm* street hawker. •**camelote** *nf* cheap goods, junk.
camembert [kamɑ̃bɛr] *nm* Camembert (cheese).
caméra [kamera] *nf* (TV *ou* film) camera. •**cameraman** *nm* (*pl* **-mans** *ou* **-men**) cameraman.
caméscope [kamɛskɔp] *nm* camcorder.
camion [kamjɔ̃] *nm* lorry, *Am* truck; **c. de déménagement** removal van, *Am* moving van. •**c.-benne** *nm* (*pl* **camions-bennes**) dustcart, *Am* garbage truck. •**c.-citerne** *nm* (*pl* **camions-citernes**) tanker, *Am* tank truck. •**camionnette** *nf* van. •**camionneur** *nm* (*conducteur*) lorry *ou* *Am* truck driver.
camisole [kamizɔl] *nf* **c. de force** straitjacket.

camomille [kamɔmij] *nf Bot* camomile; (*tisane*) camomile tea.

camoufl/er [kamufle] *vt* to camouflage. ●**—age** *nm* camouflage.

camp [kɑ̃] *nm* camp; **feu de c.** campfire; **lit de c.** camp bed; **c. de concentration** concentration camp; **dans mon c.** (*jeu*) on my side.

campagne [kɑ̃paɲ] *nf* **1** country(side); **à la c.** in the country. **2** (*électorale, militaire etc*) campaign. ●**campagnard, -arde** *a* **style/***etc* **c.** country style/*etc* ‖ *nm* countryman ‖ *nf* countrywoman.

camp/er [kɑ̃pe] *vi* to camp. ●**—ement** *nm* encampment, camp. ●**—eur, -euse** *nmf* camper.

camping [kɑ̃piŋ] *nm* camping; (*terrain*) camp(ing) site. ●**c.-car** *nm* camper.

campus [kɑ̃pys] *nm Univ* campus.

Canada [kanada] *nm* Canada. ●**canadien, -ienne** *a* & *nmf* Canadian ‖ *nf* fur-lined jacket.

canaille [kanɑj] *nf* rogue, scoundrel.

canal, -aux [kanal, -o] *nm* (*artificiel*) canal; *TV* channel. ●**canalisation** *nf* (*de gaz etc*) mains, main pipe. ●**canaliser** *vt* (*rivière etc*) to canalize; (*diriger*) *Fig* to channel.

canapé [kanape] *nm* (*siège*) sofa, couch, settee.

canard [kanar] *nm* **1** duck; (*mâle*) drake. **2** (*journal*) *Péj* rag.

canari [kanari] *nm* canary.

cancans [kɑ̃kɑ̃] *nmpl* (malicious) gossip.

cancer [kɑ̃sɛr] *nm* cancer; **le C.** (*signe*) Cancer. ●**cancéreux, -euse** *a* cancerous ‖ *nmf* cancer patient. ●**cancérigène** *a* carcinogenic.

cancre [kɑ̃kr] *nm* (*élève*) *Péj* dunce.

cancrelat [kɑ̃krəla] *nm* cockroach.

candidat, -ate [kɑ̃dida, -at] *nmf* candidate; (*à un poste*) applicant, candidate; **être** *ou* **se porter c. à** to apply for. ●**candidature** *nf* application; *Pol* candidacy; **poser sa c.** to apply (**à** for).

cane [kan] *nf* (female) duck. ●**caneton** *nm* duckling.

canette [kanɛt] *nf* **1** (*de bière*) (small) bottle. **2** (*bobine*) spool.

canevas [kanva] *nm* (*toile*) canvas; (*ébauche*) framework, outline.

caniche [kaniʃ] *nm* poodle.

canicule [kanikyl] *nf* scorching heat; **la c.** (*période*) the dog days.

canif [kanif] *nm* penknife.

canine [kanin] **1** *af* (*espèce, race*) canine; **exposition c.** dog show. **2** *nf* (*dent*) canine (tooth).

caniveau, -x [kanivo] *nm* gutter (*in street*).

canne [kan] *nf* (walking) stick; (*à sucre, de bambou*) cane; **c. à pêche** fishing rod.

cannelle [kanɛl] *nf Bot Culin* cinnamon.

cannette [kanɛt] *nf* = **canette.**

cannibale [kanibal] *nmf* & *a* cannibal.

canoë [kanɔe] *nm* canoe; *Sp* canoeing.

canon [kanɔ̃] *nm* (big) gun; *Hist* cannon; (*de fusil etc*) barrel.

cañon [kaɲɔ̃] *nm* canyon.

canot [kano] *nm* boat; **c. de sauvetage** lifeboat; **c. pneumatique** rubber dinghy. ●**canoter** *vi* to go boating.

cantatrice [kɑ̃tatris] *nf* opera singer.

cantine [kɑ̃tin] *nf* **1** (*réfectoire*) canteen; **manger à la c.** (*écolier*) to have school dinners *ou Am* school lunch. **2** (*coffre*) tin trunk.

cantique [kɑ̃tik] *nm* hymn.

canton [kɑ̃tɔ̃] *nm* (*en France*) district (*division of arrondissement*); (*en Suisse*) canton.

cantonade (à la) [alakɑ̃tɔnad] *adv* (*parler*) to all and sundry, to everyone in general.

cantonnier [kɑ̃tɔnje] *nm* road mender.

canyon [kaɲɔ̃] *nm* canyon.

caoutchouc [kautʃu] *nm* rubber; (*élastique*) rubber band; *pl* (*chaussures*) galoshes, (rubber) overshoes; **balle/***etc* **en c.** rubber ball/*etc*; **c. mousse**® foam. ●**caoutchouteux, -euse** *a* rubbery.

CAP [seɑpe] *nm abrév* (*certificat d'aptitude professionnelle*) technical and vocational diploma.

cap [kap] *nm Géog* cape, headland; (*direction*) *Nau* course; **mettre le c. sur** to steer a course for; **franchir le c. de** (*difficulté*) to get over the worst of; **franchir le c. de la trentaine/***etc* to turn thirty/*etc*.

capable [kapabl] *a* capable, able; **c. de faire** able to do, capable of doing. ●**capacité** *nf* ability, capacity; (*contenance*) capacity.

cape [kap] *nf* cape; (*grande*) cloak.

capillaire [kapilɛr] *a* **lotion/***etc* **c.** hair lotion/*etc*.

capitaine [kapitɛn] *nm* captain.

capital, -ale, -aux [kapital, -o] **1** *a* major, fundamental; (*peine*) capital; (*péché*) deadly. **2** *a* **lettre capitale** capital letter ‖ *nf* (*lettre, ville*) capital. **3** *nm* & *nmpl* (*argent*) capital. ●**capitaliste** *a* & *nmf* capitalist.

capituler [kapityle] *vi* to surrender. ●**capitulation** *nf* surrender.

caporal, -aux [kapɔral, -o] *nm* corporal.

capot [kapo] *nm Aut* bonnet, *Am* hood.

capote [kapɔt] *nf Aut* hood, *Am* (convertible) top; *Mil* greatcoat; **c. (anglaise)** (*préservatif*) *Fam* condom. •**capoter** *vi Aut Av* to overturn.

câpre [kɑpr] *nf Bot Culin* caper.

caprice [kapris] *nm* (passing) whim. •**capricieux, -euse** *a* temperamental.

Capricorne [kaprikɔrn] *nm* **le C.** (*signe*) Capricorn.

capsule [kapsyl] *nf* (*spatiale*) & *Méd etc* capsule; (*de bouteille, pistolet d'enfant*) cap.

capter [kapte] *vt* (*signal, radio*) to pick up; (*attention*) to capture, win; (*eau*) to draw off.

captif, -ive [kaptif, -iv] *a* & *nmf* captive. •**captiver** *vt* to fascinate, captivate. •**captivité** *nf* captivity.

capture [kaptyr] *nf* catch, capture. •**capturer** *vt* (*animal etc*) to capture.

capuche [kapyʃ] *nf* hood. •**capuchon** *nm* hood; (*de stylo*) cap, top.

capucine [kapysin] *nf* (*plante*) nasturtium.

caqueter [kakte] *vi* (*poule, personne*) to cackle.

car [kar] **1** *conj* because, for. **2** *nm* bus, coach; **c. de police** police van.

carabine [karabin] *nf* rifle; **c. à air comprimé** airgun.

caracoler [karakɔle] *vi* to prance, caper.

caractère[1] [karaktɛr] *nm* (*lettre*) *Typ* character; **petits caractères** small letters; **caractères d'imprimerie** (block) capitals; **caractères gras** bold type *ou* characters.

caractère[2] [karaktɛr] *nm* (*tempérament, nature*) character, nature; **avoir bon c.** to be good-natured. •**caractériel, -ielle** *a* & *nmf* disturbed (child).

caractériser [karakterize] *vt* to characterize; **se c. par** to be characterized by.

caractéristique [karakteristik] *a* & *nf* characteristic.

carafe [karaf] *nf* decanter, carafe.

carambolage [karɑ̃bɔlaʒ] *nm* pileup (*of vehicles*).

caramel [karamɛl] *nm* caramel; (*bonbon dur*) toffee, *Am* taffy.

carapace [karapas] *nf* (*de tortue etc*) & *Fig* shell.

carat [kara] *nm* carat.

caravane [karavan] *nf* (*pour camper*) caravan, *Am* trailer; (*dans le désert*) caravan; **c. publicitaire** publicity convoy. •**caravaning** *n* caravanning.

carbone [karbɔn] *nm* **(papier) c.** carbon (paper).

carboniser [karbɔnize] *vt* to burn (to ashes), char; **mourir carbonisé** to be burned to death.

carburant [karbyrɑ̃] *nm Aut* fuel. •**carburateur** *nm* carburettor, *Am* carburetor.

carcasse [karkas] *nf Anat* carcass; (*d'immeuble etc*) frame, shell.

cardiaque [kardjak] *a* **être c.** to have a weak heart; **crise/problème c.** heart attack/trouble; **arrêt c.** cardiac arrest. •**cardiologue** *nmf* heart specialist.

cardinal, -aux [kardinal, -o] **1** *a* (*nombre, point*) cardinal. **2** *nm Rel* cardinal.

Carême [karɛm] *nm* Lent.

carence [karɑ̃s] *nf Méd* deficiency.

caresse [karɛs] *nf* caress. •**caresser** [karese] *vt* (*animal, enfant etc*) to stroke, pat; (*femme, homme*) to caress; (*espoir*) to cherish.

cargaison [kargɛzɔ̃] *nf* cargo, freight. •**cargo** *nm* cargo boat.

caricature [karikatyr] *nf* caricature. •**caricaturer** *vt* to caricature.

carie [kari] *nf* **la c. (dentaire)** tooth decay; **une c.** a cavity. •**cariée** *af* **dent c.** decayed *ou* bad tooth.

carillon [karijɔ̃] *nm* (*cloches*) chimes; (*horloge*) chiming clock. •**carillonner** *vi* to chime.

carlingue [karlɛ̃g] *nf* (*fuselage*) *Av* cabin.

carnage [karnaʒ] *nm* carnage.

carnassier, -ière [karnasje, -jɛr] *a* carnivorous ‖ *nm* carnivore.

carnaval, *pl* **-als** [karnaval] *nm* carnival.

carnet [karnɛ] *nm* notebook; (*de timbres, chèques, adresses*) book; **c. de notes** school report, *Am* report card.

carnivore [karnivɔr] *a* carnivorous ‖ *nm* carnivore.

carotte [karɔt] *nf* carrot.

carpe [karp] *nf* carp.

carpette [karpɛt] *nf* rug.

carré [kare] *a* square; **mètre c.** square metre ‖ *nm* square; (*de jardin*) patch; **c. de soie** (square) silk scarf.

carreau, -x [karo] *nm* (*vitre*) (window) pane; (*pavé*) tile; (*sol*) tiled floor; (*couleur*) *Cartes* diamonds; **à carreaux** (*nappe etc*) check(ed).

carrel/er [karle] *vt* to tile. •**—age** *nm* (*sol*) tiled floor.

carrefour [karfur] *nm* crossroads.

carrément [karemɑ̃] *adv* (*dire etc*) bluntly; (*complètement*) downright.

carrer (se) [səkare] *vpr* to settle down firmly.

carrière [karjɛr] *nf* **1** (*terrain*) quarry. **2** (*métier*) career.

carrosse [karɔs] *nm Hist* (horse-drawn)

carriage. •**carrossable** *a* suitable for vehicles. •**carrosserie** *nf Aut* body(work).
carrure [karyr] *nf* build, breadth of shoulders.
cartable [kartabl] *nm* (*d'écolier*) satchel.
carte [kart] *nf* card; (*de lecteur*) ticket; *Géog* map; *Nau Mét* chart; (*menu*) menu; **c. (postale)** (post)card; **c. (à jouer)** (playing) card; **jouer aux cartes** to play cards; **c. de crédit** credit card; **c. d'identité bancaire** bank card; **c. de visite** visiting card; (*professionnelle*) business card; **c. des vins** wine list; **c. grise** vehicle registration document; **avoir c. blanche** *Fig* to have a free hand.
cartilage [kartilaʒ] *nm* cartilage.
carton [kartɔ̃] *nm* cardboard; (*boîte*) cardboard box, carton; **c. à dessin** portfolio. •**cartonner** *vt* (*livre*) to case; **livre cartonné** hardback. •**cartonnage** *nm* (*emballage*) cardboard package.
cartouche [kartuʃ] *nf* cartridge; (*de cigarettes*) carton; *Phot* cassette. •**cartouchière** *nf* cartridge belt.
cas [kɑ] *nm* case; **en tout c.** in any case *ou* event; **en aucun c.** on no account; **en c. de besoin** if need be; **en c. d'accident** in the event of an accident; **en c. d'urgence** in an emergency; **au c. où elle tomberait** if she should fall; **pour le c. où il pleuvrait** in case it rains.
casaque [kazak] *nf* (*de jockey*) shirt.
cascade [kaskad] *nf* **1** waterfall; (*série*) *Fig* spate; **en c.** in succession. **2** *Cin* stunt. •**cascadeur, -euse** *nmf Cin* stunt man, stunt woman.
case [kɑz] *nf* **1** pigeonhole; (*de tiroir*) compartment; (*d'échiquier etc*) square; (*de formulaire*) box. **2** (*hutte*) hut, cabin.
caser [kaze] *vt Fam* (*ranger*) to place, stash.
caserne [kazɛrn] *nf Mil* barracks; **c. de pompiers** fire station.
casier [kɑzje] *nm* pigeonhole; (*meuble à tiroirs*) filing cabinet; (*fermant à clef*) locker; **c. à bouteilles/à disques** bottle/record rack; **c. judiciaire** criminal *ou* police record.
casino [kazino] *nm* casino.
casque [kask] *nm* helmet; (*de coiffeur*) (hair) dryer; **c. (à écouteurs)** headphones; **les Casques bleus** the UN peace-keeping force. •**casqué** *a* helmeted.
casquette [kaskɛt] *nf* (*coiffure*) cap.
casse [kɑs] *nf* (*action*) breakage; (*objets*) breakages; **mettre à la c.** to scrap.
casse-cou [kɑsku] *nmf inv* (*personne*) *Fam* daredevil. •**c.-croûte** *nm inv* snack. •**c.-noisettes** *nm inv ou* **c.-noix** *nm inv* nutcracker(s). •**c.-pieds** *nmf inv* (*personne*) *Fam* pain in the neck. •**c.-tête** *nm inv* (*problème*) headache; (*jeu*) puzzle, brain teaser.
casser [kɑse] *vt* to break; (*noix*) to crack; (*annuler*) *Jur* to annul; **elle me casse les pieds** *Fam* she's getting on my nerves; **c. la figure à qn** *Fam* to smash s.o.'s face in ‖ *vi*, **se c.** *vpr* to break; **se c. la tête** *Fam* to rack one's brains; **se c. la figure** (*tomber*) *Fam* to come a cropper, *Am* take a spill. •**cassant** *a* (*fragile*) brittle; (*brusque*) curt.
casserole [kasrɔl] *nf* (sauce)pan.
cassette [kasɛt] *nf* (*audio*) cassette; (*vidéo*) video, cassette; **sur c.** (*film*) on video; **faire une c. de** to make a video of.
cassis **1** [kasis] *nm* (*fruit*) blackcurrant; (*boisson*) blackcurrant liqueur. **2** [kasi] *nm* (*obstacle*) dip (*across road*).
cassoulet [kasulɛ] *nm* stew (*of meat and beans*).
caste [kast] *nf* caste.
castor [kastɔr] *nm* beaver.
castrer [kastre] *vt* to castrate.
cataclysme [kataklism] *nm* cataclysm.
catacombes [katakɔ̃b] *nfpl* catacombs.
catalogue [katalɔg] *nm* catalogue, *Am* catalog. •**cataloguer** *vt* (*livres etc*) to catalogue, *Am* catalog.
catalyseur [katalizœr] *nm Ch & Fig* catalyst.
catalytique [katalitik] *a* **pot c.** *Aut* catalytic converter.
cataplasme [kataplasm] *nm Méd* poultice.
catapulte [katapylt] *nf Hist Av* catapult.
cataracte [katarakt] *nf* **1** *Méd* cataract. **2** (*cascade*) falls.
catastrophe [katastrɔf] *nf* disaster, catastrophe; **atterrir en c.** to make an emergency landing. •**catastrophique** *a* disastrous, catastrophic.
catch [katʃ] *nm* (all-in) wrestling. •**catcheur, -euse** *nmf* wrestler.
catéchisme [kateʃism] *nm* catechism.
catégorie [kategɔri] *nf* category. •**catégorique** *a* categorical.
cathédrale [katedral] *nf* cathedral.
catholicisme [katɔlisism] *nm* Catholicism. •**catholique** *a & nmf* (Roman) Catholic; **pas (très) c.** (*affaire, personne*) *Fig* shady, dubious.
catimini (en) [ɑ̃katimini] *adv* on the sly.
cauchemar [koʃmar] *nm* nightmare.
cause [koz] *nf* cause; *Jur* case; **à c. de** because of, on account of; **pour c. de** on account of; **en connaissance de c.** in full

knowledge of the facts; **mettre en c.** (*la bonne foi de qn etc*) to (call into) question; (*personne*) to implicate.
causer [koze] **1** *vt* (*provoquer*) to cause. **2** *vi* (*bavarder*) to chat (**de** about); (*discourir*) to talk. • **causerie** *nf* talk. • **causette** *nf* **faire la c.** *Fam* to have a little chat.
caustique [kostik] *a* (*substance, esprit*) caustic.
caution [kosjɔ̃] *nf* surety; (*pour libérer qn*) *Jur* bail.
cavalcade [kavalkad] *nf Fam* stampede.
cavaler [kavale] *vi Fam* to run, rush.
cavalerie [kavalri] *nf Mil* cavalry. • **cavalier, -ière 1** *nmf* rider ▮ *nm Mil* trooper; *Échecs* knight. **2** *nmf* (*pour danser*) partner. **3** *a* (*insolent*) offhand.
cave [kav] *nf* cellar. • **caveau, -x** *nm* (burial) vault.
caverne [kavɛrn] *nf* cave; **homme des cavernes** caveman.
caverneux, -euse [kavɛrnø, -øz] *a* (*voix, rire*) hollow, deep-sounding.
caviar [kavjar] *nm* caviar(e).
cavité [kavite] *nf* hollow.
CCP [sesepe] *nm abrév* (*compte chèque postal*) PO Giro account, *Am* Post Office checking account.
ce[1] [s(ə)] (**c'** *before e and é*) *pron dém* **1** it, that; **c'est toi/bon/***etc* it's *ou* that's you/good/*etc*; **c'est un médecin** he's a doctor; **ce sont eux qui...** they are the people *ou* the ones who...; **c'est à elle de jouer** it's her turn to play; **est-ce que tu viens?** are you coming?; **sur ce** at this point, thereupon.
ⓘ**G47** Demonstrative Pronouns 6 A 2b)
ⓘ**G215** It Is 13 B 2b)
2 ce que, ce qui what; (*pour reprendre une proposition*) which; **je sais ce qui est bon/ce que tu veux** I know what is good/what you want; **elle est malade, ce qui est triste/ce que je ne savais pas** she's ill, which is sad/ which I didn't know; **ce que c'est beau!** it's so beautiful!, how beautiful it is!
ⓘ**ce, ce que, ce qui G67** Relative Pronouns 6 F 3
ⓘ**ce que, ce qui G67** Interrogative Pronouns 6 C 3g)
ce[2], **cette,** *pl* **ces** [s(ə), sɛt, se] (**ce** *becomes* **cet** *before a vowel or mute h*) *a dém* this, that, *pl* these, those; (+ *-ci*) this, *pl* these; (+ *-là*) that, *pl* those; **cet homme** this *ou* that man; **cet homme-ci** this man; **cet homme-là** that man.
ⓘ**G45** Demonstrative Adjectives 6 A 1
ceci [səsi] *pron dém* this; **écoutez bien c.** listen to this.
ⓘ**G47** Ceci, cela, ça 6 A 3
céder [sede] *vt* to give up (**à** to) ▮ *vi* (*personne*) to give in, give way (**à** to); (*branche, chaise etc*) to give way.
cédille [sedij] *nf Gram* cedilla.
cèdre [sɛdr] *nm* (*arbre, bois*) cedar.
CEE [seøø] *abrév* (*Communauté économique européenne*) EEC.
CEI [seəi] *nf abrév* (*Communauté des États Indépendants*) CIS.
ceinture [sɛ̃tyr] *nf* belt; (*de robe de chambre*) cord; (*taille*) *Anat* waist; **c. de sécurité** *Aut Av* seatbelt; **c. de sauvetage** lifebelt. • **ceinturer** *vt* to seize round the waist.
cela [s(ə)la] *pron dém* (*pour désigner*) that; (*sujet indéfini*) it, that; **c. m'attriste que...** it saddens me that...; **quand/comment/***etc* **c.?** when?/how?/*etc*; **c'est c.** that is so.
ⓘ**G47** Ceci, cela, ça 6 A 3
célèbre [selɛbr] *a* famous. • **célébrité** *nf* fame; (*personne*) celebrity.
célébrer [selebre] *vt* to celebrate. • **célébration** *nf* celebration (**de** of).
céleri [sɛlri] *nm* (*en branches*) celery.
célibataire [selibatɛr] *a* (*non marié*) single, unmarried ▮ *nm* bachelor ▮ *nf* unmarried woman.
celle *voir* **celui.**
cellier [selje] *nm* storeroom (*for wine etc*).
cellophane® [selɔfan] *nf* cellophane®.
cellule [selyl] *nf* cell.
celui, celle, *pl* **ceux, celles** [səlɥi, sɛl, sø, sɛl] *pron dém* **1** the one, *pl* those, the ones; **c. de Jean** John's (one); **ceux de Jean** John's (ones), those of John. **2** (+ *-ci*) this one, *pl* these (ones); (*dont on vient de parler*) the latter; (+ *-là*) that one, *pl* those (ones); the former; **ceux-ci sont gros** these (ones) are big.
ⓘ**G46** Demonstrative Pronouns 6 A 2a)
cendre [sɑ̃dr] *nf* ash.
cendrier [sɑ̃drije] *nm* ashtray.
Cendrillon [sɑ̃drijɔ̃] *nm* Cinderella.
censé [sɑ̃se] *a* supposed; **il n'est pas c. le savoir** he's not supposed to know.
censeur [sɑ̃sœr] *nm* censor; *Scol* assistant headmaster, *Am* assistant principal. • **censure** *nf* **la c.** (*examen*) censorship; (*comité, service*) the censor. • **censurer** *vt* (*film etc*) to censor.
cent [sɑ̃] ([sɑ̃t] *pl* [sɑ̃z] *before vowel and mute h except* **un** *and* **onze**) *a* & *nm* hundred; **c. pages** a *ou* one hundred pages; **deux cents pages** two hundred pages; **deux c. trois pages** two hundred and three pages; **cinq pour c.** five per cent. • **centaine** *nf* **une c. (de)** about a hundred; **des centaines de** hundreds of. • **centenaire**

a & nmf centenarian ▌*nm* (*anniversaire*) centenary. • **centième** *a & nmf* hundredth; **un c.** a hundredth. • **centigrade** *a* centigrade. • **centime** *nm* centime. • **centimètre** *nm* centimetre; (*ruban*) tape measure.

central, -aux [sɑ̃tral, -o] **1** *a* central. **2** *nm* **c. (téléphonique)** (telephone) exchange. • **centrale** *nf* (*usine*) power station, *Am* power plant. • **centraliser** *vt* to centralize.

centre [sɑ̃tr] *nm* centre; **c. commercial** shopping centre *ou* mall. • **c.-ville** *nm* (*pl* **centres-villes**) city *ou* town centre, *Am* downtown area. • **centrer** *vt* to centre.

centuple [sɑ̃typl] *nm* hundredfold; **au c.** a hundredfold.

cep [sɛp] *nm* vine stock.

cependant [səpɑ̃dɑ̃] *conj* however, yet.

céramique [seramik] *nf* (*matière*) ceramic; (*art*) pottery, ceramics; **de** *ou* **en c.** ceramic.

cerceau, -x [sɛrso] *nm* hoop.

cercle [sɛrkl] *nm* (*forme, groupe*) circle.

cercueil [sɛrkœj] *nm* coffin.

céréale [sereal] *nf* cereal.

cérébral, -aux [serebral, -o] *a* cerebral.

cérémonie [seremɔni] *nf* ceremony; **de c.** (*tenue etc*) ceremonial. • **cérémonieux, -euse** *a* ceremonious.

cerf [sɛr] *nm* deer *inv*; (*mâle*) stag. • **cerf-volant** *nm* (*pl* **cerfs-volants**) (*jouet*) kite.

cerise [s(ə)riz] *nf* cherry. • **cerisier** *nm* cherry tree.

cerne [sɛrn] *nm* (*cercle, marque*) ring. • **cerner** *vt* to surround; **avoir les yeux cernés** to have rings under one's eyes.

certain [sɛrtɛ̃] **1** *a* (*sûr*) certain, sure; (*preuve, décision, avantage*) definite; **il est** *ou* **c'est c. que tu réussiras** you're certain *ou* sure to succeed; **je suis c. de réussir** I'm certain *ou* sure I'll succeed; **être c. de qch** to be certain *ou* sure of sth.
2 *a* (*imprécis, difficile à fixer*) certain; *pl* certain, some; **un c. temps** a certain (amount of) time ▌*pron pl* some (people), certain people. • **certainement** *adv* certainly. • **certes** *adv* indeed, most certainly.

ⓘ**certain G32** Position of Adjectives 4 D 3

ⓘ**certain G48** Indefinite Adjectives and Pronouns 6 B

ⓘ**certain G100** The Subjunctive 7 G 1e)

certificat [sɛrtifika] *nm* certificate.

certifier [sɛrtifje] *vt* to certify; **je vous certifie que** I assure you that.

certitude [sɛrtityd] *nf* certainty; **avoir la c. que** to be certain that.

cerveau, -x [sɛrvo] *nm* (*organe*) brain; (*intelligence*) mind, brain(s); **rhume de c.** head cold.

cervelas [sɛrvəla] *nm* saveloy.

cervelle [sɛrvɛl] *nf* (*substance*) brain; *Culin* brains.

ces *voir* **ce**[2].

CES [seəɛs] *nm abrév* (*collège d'enseignement secondaire*) comprehensive school, *Am* high school.

césarienne [sezarjɛn] *nf Méd* Caesarean.

cesse [sɛs] *nf* **sans c.** constantly.

cesser [sese] *vti* to stop; **faire c.** to put a stop to; **il ne cesse de parler** he doesn't stop talking. • **cessez-le-feu** *nm inv* ceasefire.

c'est-à-dire [setadir] *conj* that is (to say), in other words.

cet, cette *voir* **ce**[2].

ceux *voir* **celui**.

chacun, -une [ʃakœ̃, -yn] *pron* each (one), every one; (*tout le monde*) everyone.

chagrin [ʃagrɛ̃] *nm* grief, sorrow; **avoir du c.** to be very upset. • **chagriner** *vt* to upset, distress.

chahut [ʃay] *nm* (*bruit*) racket. • **chahuter** *vi* to create a racket ▌*vt* (*professeur*) to be rowdy with, play up. • **chahuteur, -euse** *nmf* rowdy.

chaîne [ʃɛn] *nf* chain; *TV* channel, network; (*de montagnes*) chain, range; **c. de montage** assembly line; **travail à la c.** production-line work; **c. hi-fi** hi-fi (system); **collision en c.** *Aut* multiple collision. • **chaînette** *nf* (small) chain. • **chaînon** *nm* (*anneau*) link.

chair [ʃɛr] *nf* flesh; **(couleur) c.** flesh-coloured; **en c. et en os** in the flesh; **la c. de poule** goose pimples *ou* bumps; **bien en c.** plump; **c. à saucisses** sausage meat.

chaise [ʃɛz] *nf* chair; **c. longue** deckchair; **c. d'enfant, c. haute** high-chair.

châle [ʃɑl] *nm* shawl.

chalet [ʃalɛ] *nm* chalet.

chaleur [ʃalœr] *nf* heat; (*douce*) warmth; (*d'un accueil etc*) warmth. • **chaleureux, -euse** *a* warm.

challenge [ʃalɑ̃ʒ] *nm Sp* challenge match.

chaloupe [ʃalup] *nf* (*bateau*) launch.

chalumeau, -x [ʃalymo] *nm* blowlamp, *Am* blowtorch.

chalut [ʃaly] *nm* trawl net. • **chalutier** *nm* (*bateau*) trawler.

chamailler (se) [səʃamɑje] *vpr* to squabble.

chamarré [ʃamare] *a* (*robe etc*) richly coloured.

chambouler [ʃɑ̃bule] *vt Fam* to make topsy-turvy, turn upside down.

chambre [ʃɑ̃br] *nf* (bed)room; *Pol Jur Tech Anat* chamber; **c. à coucher** bedroom;

(*mobilier*) bedroom suite; **c. à air** (*de pneu*) inner tube; **C. des Communes** *Br Pol* House of Commons; **c. d'ami** guest *ou* spare room; **garder la c.** to stay indoors.

chameau, -x [ʃamo] *nm* camel.

chamois [ʃamwa] *nm* (*animal*) chamois; **peau de c.** wash leather, chamois, shammy.

champ [ʃɑ̃] *nm* field; (*domaine*) *Fig* field, scope; **c. de bataille** battlefield; **c. de courses** racecourse, *Am* racetrack; **c. de foire** fairground. ●**champêtre** *a* rural.

champagne [ʃɑ̃paɲ] *nm* champagne; **c. brut** extra-dry champagne.

champignon [ʃɑ̃piɲɔ̃] *nm Bot* mushroom; **c. vénéneux** toadstool, poisonous mushroom.

champion, -onne [ʃɑ̃pjɔ̃, -jɔn] *nmf* champion. ●**championnat** *nm* championship.

chance [ʃɑ̃s] *nf* luck; (*probabilité de réussir, occasion*) chance; **avoir de la c.** to be lucky; **tenter sa c.** to try one's luck; **c'est une c. que...** it's lucky that.... ●**chanceux, -euse** *a* lucky.

chancel/er [ʃɑ̃sle] *vi* to stagger. ●**—ant** *a* (*pas, santé*) faltering, shaky.

chancelier [ʃɑ̃səlje] *nm* chancellor.

chandail [ʃɑ̃daj] *nm* (thick) sweater.

chandelier [ʃɑ̃dəlje] *nm* candlestick.

chandelle [ʃɑ̃dɛl] *nf* candle; **voir trente-six chandelles** *Fig* to see stars; **en c.** (*tir*) straight into the air.

change [ʃɑ̃ʒ] *nm Fin* exchange; **le contrôle des changes** exchange control.

changer [ʃɑ̃ʒe] *vt* (*modifier, remplacer, échanger*) to change; **c. qn en** to change s.o. into; **ça la changera de ne pas travailler** it'll be a change for her not to be working. ‖ *vi* to change; **c. de voiture/d'adresse/***etc* to change one's car/address/*etc*; **c. de train/de place** to change trains/places; **c. de vitesse/de sujet** to change gear/the subject. ‖ **se changer** *vpr* to change (one's clothes). ●**changement** *nm* change; **aimer le c.** to like change.

chanson [ʃɑ̃sɔ̃] *nf* song. ●**chant** *nm* singing; (*chanson*) song; (*hymne*) chant; **c. de Noël** Christmas carol.

chant/er [ʃɑ̃te] *vi* to sing; (*coq*) to crow; **si ça te chante** *Fam* if you feel like it; **faire c. qn** to blackmail s.o. ‖ *vt* to sing. ●**—ant** *a* (*air, voix*) melodious. ●**chantage** *nm* blackmail. ●**chanteur, -euse** *nmf* singer.

chantier [ʃɑ̃tje] *nm* (building) site; (*sur route*) roadworks; **c. naval** shipyard, dockyard.

chantonner [ʃɑ̃tɔne] *vti* to hum.

chanvre [ʃɑ̃vr] *nm* hemp.

chaos [kao] *nm* chaos. ●**chaotique** *a* chaotic.

chaparder [ʃaparde] *vt Fam* to pinch (**à** from).

chapeau, -x [ʃapo] *nm* hat; (*de champignon, roue*) cap; **c.!** well done!

chapelet [ʃaplɛ] *nm* rosary; **un c. de** (*saucisses, injures*) a string of.

chapelle [ʃapɛl] *nf* chapel; **c. ardente** chapel of rest.

chapelure [ʃaplyr] *nf* breadcrumbs.

chapiteau, -x [ʃapito] *nm* (*de cirque*) big top; (*pour expositions etc*) marquee, tent.

chapitre [ʃapitr] *nm* chapter; **sur le c. de** on the subject of.

chaque [ʃak] *a* each, every.

char [ʃar] *nm* (*romain*) chariot; (*de carnaval*) float; *Can Fam* car; **c. (d'assaut)** *Mil* tank.

charabia [ʃarabja] *nm Fam* gibberish.

charade [ʃarad] *nf* (*énigme*) riddle.

charbon [ʃarbɔ̃] *nm* coal; **c. de bois** charcoal; **sur des charbons ardents** on tenterhooks.

charcuterie [ʃarkytri] *nf* pork butcher's shop; (*aliments*) cooked (pork) meats. ●**charcutier, -ière** *nmf* pork butcher.

chardon [ʃardɔ̃] *nm Bot* thistle.

charge [ʃarʒ] *nf* (*poids*) load; (*fardeau*) burden; *Jur Él Mil* charge; (*fonction*) office; *pl* (*dépenses*) expenses; (*de locataire*) (maintenance) charges; **charges sociales** national insurance contributions, *Am* Social Security contributions; **à c.** (*enfant, parent*) dependent; **à la c. de qn** (*personne*) dependent on s.o.; (*frais*) payable by s.o.; **prendre en c.** to take charge of, take responsibility for.

charg/er [ʃarʒe] *vt* to load; (*soldats, batterie*) to charge; **se c. de** (*enfant, tâche etc*) to take charge of; **c. qn de** (*tâche etc*) to entrust s.o. with; (*paquets etc*) to load s.o. with; **se c. de faire** to undertake to do; **c. qn de faire** to instruct s.o. to do. ●**—é, -ée** *a* (*personne, véhicule, arme etc*) loaded; (*journée etc*) busy. ●**—ement** *nm* (*action*) loading; (*objet*) load.

chariot [ʃarjo] *nm* (*à bagages etc*) trolley, *Am* cart; (*de ferme*) waggon; (*de machine à écrire*) carriage.

charité [ʃarite] *nf* (*secours, vertu*) charity; **faire la c.** to give to charity; **faire la c. à** (*mendiant*) to give (money) to. ●**charitable** *a* charitable (**pour, envers** towards).

charivari [ʃarivari] *nm Fam* din, hubbub.

charlatan [ʃarlatɑ̃] *nm* charlatan, quack.

charme [ʃarm] *nm* charm; (*magie*) spell.

charm/er [ʃarme] *vt* to charm; **je suis**

charmé de vous voir I'm delighted to see you. ● **—ant** *a* charming. ● **—eur, -euse** *a* engaging.
charnière [ʃarnjɛr] *nf* hinge.
charogne [ʃarɔɲ] *nf* carrion.
charpente [ʃarpɑ̃t] *nf* frame(work); (*de personne*) build. ● **charpentier** *nm* carpenter.
charpie [ʃarpi] *nf* **mettre en c.** (*déchirer*) to tear to shreds.
charrette [ʃarɛt] *nf* cart. ● **charrier** *vt* (*transporter*) to cart; (*rivière*) to carry along (*sand etc*).
charrue [ʃary] *nf* plough, *Am* plow.
charter [ʃartɛr] *nm* (*vol*) charter (flight).
chas [ʃa] *nm* eye (*of a needle*).
chasse[1] [ʃas] *nf* hunting, hunt; (*poursuite*) chase; **c. sous-marine** underwater (harpoon) fishing; **c. à courre** hunting; **avion/pilote de c.** fighter plane/pilot; **faire la c. à** to hunt for; **c. à l'homme** manhunt.
chasse[2] [ʃas] *nf* **c. d'eau** toilet *ou* lavatory flush; **tirer la c.** to flush the toilet *ou* lavatory.
chass/er [ʃase] *vt* (*animal*) to hunt; (*papillon*) to chase; (*faire partir*) to chase (*s.o.*) away, drive (*s.o.*) out; (*mouche*) to brush away; (*odeur*) to get rid of ▮ *vi* to hunt. ● **—eur, -euse** *nmf* hunter ▮ *nm* (*d'hôtel*) pageboy, bellboy. ● **chasse-neige** *nm inv* snowplough, *Am* snowplow.
châssis [ʃɑsi] *nm* frame; *Aut* chassis.
chaste [ʃast] *a* chaste. ● **chasteté** *nf* chastity.
chat [ʃa] *nm* cat; **un c. dans la gorge** a frog in one's throat; **d'autres chats à fouetter** other fish to fry; **c. perché** (*jeu*) tag.
châtaigne [ʃɑtɛɲ] *nf* chestnut. ● **châtaignier** *nm* chestnut tree. ● **châtain** *a inv* (chestnut) brown.
château, -x [ʃɑto] *nm* (*forteresse*) castle; (*palais*) palace, stately home; **c. fort** fortified castle; **c. d'eau** water tower; **c. de cartes** house of cards. ● **châtelain, -aine** *nmf* lord *ou* lady of the manor.
châtier [ʃɑtje] *vt* (*punir*) *Litt* to chastise.
châtiment [ʃɑtimɑ̃] *nm* punishment.
chaton [ʃatɔ̃] *nm* (*chat*) kitten.
chatouiller [ʃatuje] *vt* to tickle. ● **chatouillis** *nm* tickle; (*action*) tickling. ● **chatouilleux, -euse** *a* ticklish; (*irritable*) touchy.
chatte [ʃat] *nf* (she-)cat; **ma petite c.** *Fam* my darling.
chatterton [ʃatɛrtɔn] *nm* (adhesive) insulating tape.
chaud [ʃo] *a* hot; (*doux*) warm; **pleurer à chaudes larmes** to cry bitterly ▮ *nm* heat, warmth; **avoir c.** to be hot; to be warm; **il fait c.** it's hot; it's warm; **être au c.** to be in the warm. ● **chaudement** *adv* warmly.
chaudière [ʃodjɛr] *nf* boiler.
chauffage [ʃofaʒ] *nm* heating.
chauffard [ʃofar] *nm* road hog, reckless driver.
chauff/er [ʃofe] *vt* to heat up, warm up; (*métal*) to heat ▮ *vi* to heat up, warm up; (*moteur*) to overheat ▮ **se c.** *vpr* to warm oneself up. ● **—ant** *a* (*couverture*) electric; **plaque chauffante** hot plate. ● **—é** *a* (*piscine etc*) heated. ● **chauffe-bain** *nm ou* **chauffe-eau** *nm inv* water heater.
chauffeur [ʃofœr] *nm Aut* driver; (*employé*) chauffeur.
chaume [ʃom] *nm* (*pour toiture*) thatch; **toit de c.** thatched roof. ● **chaumière** *nf* thatched cottage.
chaussée [ʃose] *nf* road(way).
chausser [ʃose] *vt* (*chaussures*) to put on; **c. qn** to put shoes on (to) s.o.; **se c.** to put on one's shoes; **c. du 40** to take a size 40 shoe. ● **chausse-pied** *nm* shoehorn.
chausson [ʃosɔ̃] *nm* slipper; (*de danse*) shoe; **c. (aux pommes)** apple turnover.
chaussure [ʃosyr] *nf* shoe.
chaussette [ʃosɛt] *nf* sock.
chauve [ʃov] *a & nmf* bald (person).
chauve-souris [ʃovsuri] *nf* (*pl* **chauves-souris**) (*animal*) bat.
chauvin, -ine [ʃovɛ̃, -in] *a* chauvinistic ▮ *nmf* chauvinist.
chaux [ʃo] *nf* lime; **blanc de c.** whitewash.
chavirer [ʃavire] *vti Nau* to capsize.
chef [ʃɛf] *nm* leader, head; (*de tribu*) chief; *Culin* chef; **en c.** (*commandant, rédacteur*) in chief; **c. d'atelier** (shop) foreman; **c. d'entreprise** company head; **c. d'équipe** foreman; **c. d'État** head of state; **c. de famille** head of the family; **c. de gare** stationmaster; **c. d'orchestre** conductor. ● **chef-lieu** *nm* (*pl* **chefs-lieux**) chief town (*of a département*).
chef-d'œuvre [ʃɛdœvr] *nm* (*pl* **chefs-d'œuvre**) masterpiece.
chemin [ʃ(ə)mɛ̃] *nm* **1** road, path; (*trajet, direction*) way; **beaucoup de c. à faire** a long way to go; **dix minutes de c.** ten minutes' walk; **se mettre en c.** to set out, start out; **à mi-c.** half-way. **2 c. de fer** railway, *Am* railroad.
cheminot [ʃ(ə)mino] *nm* railway *ou Am* railroad employee.
cheminée [ʃ(ə)mine] *nf* fireplace; (*encadrement*) mantelpiece; (*sur le toit*) chimney; (*de navire*) funnel.

chemise [ʃ(ə)miz] *nf* shirt; (*couverture cartonnée*) folder; **c. de nuit** nightdress. ● **chemisette** *nf* short-sleeved shirt. ● **chemisier** *nm* (*vêtement*) blouse.
chenapan [ʃ(ə)napɑ̃] *nm Hum* rogue.
chêne [ʃɛn] *nm* (*arbre, bois*) oak.
chenet [ʃ(ə)nɛ] *nm* andiron.
chenil [ʃ(ə)ni(l)] *nm* kennels, *Am* kennel.
chenille [ʃ(ə)nij] *nf* caterpillar; (*de char*) *Mil* caterpillar track.
chèque [ʃɛk] *nm* cheque, *Am* check; **c. de voyage** traveller's cheque, *Am* traveler's check. ● **c.-repas** *nm* (*pl* **chèques-repas**) luncheon voucher, *Am* meal ticket. ● **chéquier** *nm* cheque book, *Am* checkbook.
cher, chère [ʃɛr] **1** *a* (*aimé*) dear (**à** to). **2** *a* (*coûteux*) expensive, dear; (*quartier, hôtel etc*) expensive; **payer c.** (*objet*) to pay a lot for; (*erreur etc*) *Fig* to pay dearly for; **coûter c.** to cost a lot.
ⓘ**G32** Position of Adjectives 4 D 3
cherch/er [ʃɛrʃe] *vt* to look for, search for; (*du secours, la paix etc*) to seek; (*dans un dictionnaire*) to look up; **c. ses mots** to fumble for one's words; **aller c.** to (go and) get *ou* fetch; **c. à faire** to attempt to do. ● **—eur, -euse** *nmf* research worker; **c. d'or** gold-digger.
chér/ir [ʃerir] *vt* to cherish. ● **—i, -ie** *a* dearly loved, beloved ‖ *nmf* darling.
chétif, -ive [ʃetif, -iv] *a* puny; (*dérisoire*) wretched.
cheval, -aux [ʃ(ə)val, -o] *nm* horse; **c. (vapeur)** *Aut* horsepower; **à c.** on horseback; **faire du c.** to go horse riding *ou Am* horseback riding; **à c. sur** straddling; **c. à bascule** rocking horse; **chevaux de bois** (*manège*) merry-go-round.
chevaleresque [ʃ(ə)valrɛsk] *a* chivalrous.
chevalet [ʃ(ə)valɛ] *nm* easel; (*de menuisier*) trestle.
chevalier [ʃ(ə)valje] *nm* knight.
chevalière [ʃ(ə)valjɛr] *nf* signet ring.
chevaline [ʃ(ə)valin] *af* **boucherie c.** horse butcher's (shop).
chevauchée [ʃ(ə)voʃe] *nf* (horse) ride.
chevaucher [ʃ(ə)voʃe] *vt* to straddle ‖ *vi*, **se c.** *vpr* to overlap.
chevelu [ʃ(ə)vly] *a* hairy. ● **chevelure** *nf* (head of) hair.
chevet [ʃ(ə)vɛ] *nm* bedhead; **table/livre de c.** bedside table/book; **au c. de** at the bedside of.
cheveu, -x [ʃ(ə)vø] *nm* **un c.** a hair; **cheveux** hair; **avoir les cheveux noirs** to have black hair; **couper les cheveux en quatre** *Fig* to split hairs.
cheville [ʃ(ə)vij] *nf* **1** *Anat* ankle. **2** (*pour vis*) (wall) plug; (*pour joindre*) peg, pin.
chèvre [ʃɛvr] *nf* goat; (*femelle*) nanny-goat. ● **chevreau, -x** *nm* (*petit de la chèvre*) kid.
chèvrefeuille [ʃɛvrəfœj] *nm* honeysuckle.
chevreuil [ʃəvrœj] *nm* roe deer; *Culin* venison.
chevron [ʃəvrɔ̃] *nm* (*poutre*) rafter; **à chevrons** (*tissu, veste etc*) herringbone.
chevronné [ʃəvrɔne] *a* seasoned, experienced.
chez [ʃe] *prép* **c. qn** at s.o.'s house, flat *etc*; **il est c. Jean/c. l'épicier** he's at John's (place)/at the grocer's; **il va c. Jean/c. l'épicier** he's going to John's (place)/to the grocer's; **c. moi, c. nous** at home; **je vais c. moi** I'm going home; **une habitude c. elle** a habit with her; **c. Mme Dupont** (*adresse*) care of *ou* c/o Mme Dupont; **c. les Suisses** among the Swiss; **c. Camus** in (the work of) Camus.
ⓘ**G174** Prepositions 8
chic [ʃik] *a inv* smart, stylish; (*gentil*) *Fam* nice, decent ‖ *int* **c. (alors)!** great! ‖ *nm* style, elegance.
chicanes [ʃikan] *nfpl* (*obstacles*) zigzag barriers.
chiche [ʃiʃ] **1** *a* mean, niggardly; **c. de** sparing of. **2** *int* (*défi*) *Fam* I bet you I do, can *etc*; **c. que je parte sans lui** I bet I leave without him.
chicorée [ʃikɔre] *nf* (*à café*) chicory; (*pour salade*) endive.
chien [ʃjɛ̃] *nm* dog; **un mal de c.** *Fam* an awful lot of trouble; **temps de c.** *Fam* rotten weather. ● **c.-loup** *nm* (*pl* **chiens-loups**) wolfhound. ● **chienne** *nf* dog, bitch.
chiendent [ʃjɛ̃dɑ̃] *nm Bot* couch grass.
chiffon [ʃifɔ̃] *nm* rag; **c. (à poussière)** duster, *Am* dustcloth. ● **chiffonner** *vt* to crumple. ● **chiffonnier** *nm* ragman.
chiffre [ʃifr] *nm* figure, number; (*romain, arabe*) numeral; **c. d'affaires** (sales) turnover. ● **chiffrer** *vt* (*montant*) to assess, work out ‖ **se c.** *vpr* to amount to, work out at.
chignon [ʃiɲɔ̃] *nm* bun, chignon.
Chili [ʃili] *nm* Chile. ● **chilien, -ienne** *a & nmf* Chilean.
chimie [ʃimi] *nf* chemistry. ● **chimique** *a* chemical. ● **chimiste** *nmf* (research) chemist.
chimpanzé [ʃɛ̃pɑ̃ze] *nm* chimpanzee.
Chine [ʃin] *nf* China. ● **chinois, -oise** *a & nmf* Chinese ‖ *nmf* Chinese man *ou* woman, Chinese *inv*; **les C.** the Chinese ‖ *nm* (*langue*) Chinese.

chiot [ʃjo] *nm* pup(py).
chiper [ʃipe] *vt Fam* to pinch (**à** from).
chipie [ʃipi] *nf* **vieille c.** (*femme*) *Péj* old crab.
chipoter [ʃipɔte] *vi* (*discuter*) to quibble.
chips [ʃips] *nfpl* (potato) crisps, *Am* chips.
chiquenaude [ʃiknod] *nf* flick (of the finger).
chirurgie [ʃiryrʒi] *nf* surgery. ●**chirurgical, -aux** *a* surgical. ●**chirurgien** *nm* surgeon.
chlore [klɔr] *nm* chlorine.
choc [ʃɔk] *nm* (*d'objets*) impact, shock; (*émotion*) & *Méd* shock.
chocolat [ʃɔkɔla] *nm* chocolate; **c. à croquer** plain *ou Am* bittersweet chocolate; **c. au lait** milk chocolate; **c. glacé** choc-ice, *Am* chocolate ice-cream bar. ●**chocolaté** *a* chocolate-flavoured.
chœur [kœr] *nm* (*chanteurs, nef*) *Rel* choir; **en c.** (all) together, in chorus.
choir [ʃwar] *vi* **laisser c. qn** *Fam* to turn one's back on s.o.
chois/ir [ʃwazir] *vt* to choose, pick, select. ●**—i** *a* (*œuvres*) selected; (*terme*) well-chosen; (*public*) select. ●**choix** *nm* choice; (*assortiment*) selection; **morceau de c.** choice piece.
choléra [kɔlera] *nm* cholera.
cholestérol [kɔlɛsterɔl] *nm* cholesterol.
chôm/er [ʃome] *vi* (*ouvrier etc*) to be unemployed. ●**—age** *nm* unemployment; **au** *ou* **en c.** unemployed; **mettre en c. technique** to lay off. ●**—eur, -euse** *nmf* unemployed person; **les chômeurs** the unemployed.
chope [ʃɔp] *nf* beer mug; (*contenu*) pint.
choqu/er [ʃɔke] *vt* (*scandaliser*) to shock; (*commotionner*) to shake up. ●**—ant** *a* shocking.
chorale [kɔral] *nf* choir, choral society. ●**choriste** *nmf* chorister.
chorégraphe [kɔregraf] *nmf* choreographer.
chose [ʃoz] *nf* thing; **état de choses** state of affairs; **dis-lui bien des choses de ma part** remember me to him *ou* her; **monsieur C.** Mr What's-his-name.
chou, -x [ʃu] *nm* cabbage; **choux de Bruxelles** Brussels sprouts; **mon c.!** my pet!; **c. à la crème** cream puff. ●**c.-fleur** *nm* (*pl* **choux-fleurs**) cauliflower.
chouchou, -oute [ʃuʃu, -ut] *nmf* (*favori*) *Fam* pet, darling. ●**chouchouter** *vt* to pamper.
choucroute [ʃukrut] *nf* sauerkraut.
chouette [ʃwɛt] **1** *nf* (*oiseau*) owl. **2** *a* (*chic*) *Fam* super, great.
choyer [ʃwaye] *vt* to pamper.
chrétien, -ienne [kretjɛ̃, -jɛn] *a* & *nmf* Christian. ●**Christ** [krist] *nm* Christ. ●**christianisme** *nm* Christianity.
chrome [krom] *nm* chrome, chromium. ●**chromé** *a* chrome- *ou* chromium-plated.
chronique [krɔnik] **1** *a* (*malade, chômage etc*) chronic. **2** *nf* (*à la radio*) report; (*dans le journal*) column. ●**chroniqueur** *nm Journ* reporter, columnist.
chronologie [krɔnɔlɔʒi] *nf* chronology. ●**chronologique** *a* chronological.
chronomètre [krɔnɔmɛtr] *nm* stopwatch. ●**chronométrer** *vt Sp* to time.
chrysanthème [krizɑ̃tɛm] *nm* chrysanthemum.
chuchot/er [ʃyʃɔte] *vti* to whisper. ●**—ement** *nm* whisper(ing).
chut! [ʃyt] *int* sh!, shush!
chute [ʃyt] *nf* fall; (*défaite*) (down)fall; **c. d'eau** waterfall; **c. de neige** snowfall; **c. de pluie** rainfall; **c. des cheveux** hair loss.
Chypre [ʃipr] *nf* Cyprus. ●**chypriote** *a* & *nmf* Cypriot.
ci [si] **1** *adv* **par-ci par-là** here and there. **2** *pron dém* **comme ci comme ça** so so. **3** *voir* **ce²**, **celui.**
ci-après [siaprɛ] *adv* below, hereafter. ●**ci-dessous** *adv* below. ●**ci-dessus** *adv* above. ●**ci-gît** *adv* here lies (*on gravestones*). ●**ci-joint** *a* (*inv before n*) (*dans une lettre*) enclosed (herewith).
cible [sibl] *nf* target.
cicatrice [sikatris] *nf* scar.
cicatriser [sikatrize] *vt*, **se c.** *vpr* to heal (up) (*leaving a scar*). ●**cicatrisation** *nf* healing (up).
cidre [sidr] *nm* cider.
Cie *abrév* (*compagnie*) Co.
ciel [sjɛl] *nm* **1** (*pl* **ciels**) sky; **à c. ouvert** (*piscine etc*) open-air. **2** (*pl* **cieux** [sjø]) *Rel* heaven; **juste c.!** good heavens!
cierge [sjɛrʒ] *nm Rel* candle.
cigale [sigal] *nf* (*insecte*) cicada.
cigare [sigar] *nm* cigar. ●**cigarette** *nf* cigarette.
cigogne [sigɔɲ] *nf* stork.
cil [sil] *nm* (eye)lash.
cime [sim] *nf* (*d'un arbre*) top; (*d'une montagne*) & *Fig* peak.
ciment [simɑ̃] *nm* cement. ●**cimenter** *vt* to cement.
cimetière [simtjɛr] *nm* cemetery, graveyard.
ciné [sine] *nm Fam* = **cinéma.** ●**c.-club** *nm* film society. ●**cinéaste** *nm* film maker. ●**cinéphile** *nmf* film buff.

cinéma [sinema] *nm* (*art*) cinema; (*salle*) cinema, *Am* movie theater; **aller au c.** to go to the movies *ou* the cinema; **acteur de c.** movie *ou* film actor. • **cinématographique** *a* **industrie/***etc* **c.** film industry/*etc*.
cinglé [sɛ̃gle] *a Fam* crazy.
cinq [sɛ̃k] *nm* five ‖ *a* ([sɛ̃] *before consonant*) five. • **cinquième** *a* & *nmf* fifth; **un c.** a fifth.
cinquante [sɛ̃kɑ̃t] *a* & *nm* fifty. • **cinquantaine** *nf* **une c. (de)** about fifty. • **cinquantième** *a* & *nmf* fiftieth.
cintre [sɛ̃tr] *nm* coathanger.
cirage [siraʒ] *nm* (shoe) polish.
circoncis [sirkɔ̃si] *a* circumcised.
circonférence [sirkɔ̃ferɑ̃s] *nf* circumference.
circonflexe [sirkɔ̃flɛks] *a Gram* circumflex.
circonscrire [sirkɔ̃skrir] *vt* to circumscribe. • **circonscription** *nf* division; **c. (électorale)** constituency, *Am* district.
circonspect, -ecte [sirkɔ̃spɛ(kt), -ɛkt] *a* cautious.
circonstance [sirkɔ̃stɑ̃s] *nf* circumstance; **pour/en la c.** for/on this occasion; **de c.** (*habit*, *parole etc*) appropriate. • **circonstancié** *a* detailed. • **circonstanciel, -ielle** *a Gram* adverbial.
circuit [sirkɥi] *nm Sp Él Fin* circuit; (*voyage*) tour, trip.
circulaire [sirkylɛr] *a* circular ‖ *nf* (*lettre*) circular.
circulation [sirkylɑsjɔ̃] *nf* circulation; *Aut* traffic. • **circuler** *vi* to circulate; (*véhicule*, *train*) to travel, go, move; (*passant*) to walk about; (*rumeur*) to go round, circulate; **faire c.** to circulate; (*piétons*) to move on; **circulez!** keep moving!
cire [sir] *nf* wax; (*pour meubles*) polish, wax. • **cirer** *vt* to polish.
ciré [sire] *nm* (*vêtement*) oilskin(s).
cirque [sirk] *nm* circus.
cisaille(s) [sizɑj] *nf(pl)* shears. • **ciseau, -x** *nm* chisel; **(une paire de) ciseaux** (a pair of) scissors.
citadelle [sitadɛl] *nf* citadel.
cité [site] *nf* city; **c. (ouvrière)** housing estate (*for workers*), *Am* housing project; **c. universitaire** (students') halls of residence, *Am* university dormitory complex. • **citadin, -ine** *nmf* city dweller ‖ *a* urban.
citer [site] *vt* to quote; *Jur* to summon. • **citation** *nf* quotation; *Jur* summons.
citerne [sitɛrn] *nf* (*réservoir*) tank.
citoyen, -enne [sitwajɛ̃, -ɛn] *nmf* citizen.
citron [sitrɔ̃] *nm* lemon; **c. pressé** (fresh) lemon juice. • **citronnade** *nf* lemon drink, (still) lemonade.
citrouille [sitruj] *nf* pumpkin.
civet [sivɛ] *nm* stew; **c. de lièvre** jugged hare.
civière [sivjɛr] *nf* stretcher.
civil [sivil] **1** *a* (*guerre*, *mariage etc*) civil; (*non militaire*) civilian; **année civile** calendar year. **2** *nm* civilian; **dans le c.** in civilian life; **en c.** (*policier*) in plain clothes; (*soldat*) in civilian clothes.
civilisation [sivilizɑsjɔ̃] *nf* civilization. • **civiliser** *vt* to civilize ‖ **se c.** *vpr* to become civilized. • **civilisé** *a* civilized.
civique [sivik] *a* civic; **instruction c.** *Scol* civics.
clair [klɛr] *a* (*distinct*, *limpide*, *évident*) clear; (*éclairé*) light; (*pâle*) light(-coloured); **bleu/vert c.** light blue/green; **il fait c.** it's light *ou* bright ‖ *adv* (*voir*) clearly ‖ *nm* **c. de lune** moonlight; **tirer au c.** (*question etc*) to clear up. • **—ement** *adv* clearly.
clairière [klɛrjɛr] *nf* clearing.
clairon [klɛrɔ̃] *nm* bugle. • **claironner** *vt* (*annoncer*) to trumpet forth.
clairsemé [klɛrsəme] *a* sparse.
clairvoyant [klɛrvwajɑ̃] *a* (*perspicace*) clear-sighted.
clam/er [klame] *vt* to cry out. • **—eur** *nf* clamour, outcry.
clan [klɑ̃] *nm* clan, clique, set.
clandestin [klɑ̃dɛstɛ̃] *a* secret, clandestine; (*journal*, *mouvement*) underground; **passager c.** stowaway.
clapier [klapje] *nm* (rabbit) hutch.
claque [klak] *nf* smack, slap. • **claquer** *vt* (*porte*) to slam, bang; (*fouet*) to crack; **se c. un muscle** to pull a muscle; **faire c.** (*doigts*) to snap; (*langue*) to click; (*fouet*) to crack. ‖ *vi* (*porte*) to slam, bang; (*drapeau*) to flap; (*coup de feu*) to ring out; **elle claque des dents** her teeth are chattering. • **claquage** *nm* pulled muscle; **se faire un c.** to pull a muscle. • **claquement** *nm* (*de porte*) slam(ming).
claquettes [klakɛt] *nfpl* tap dancing.
clarifier [klarifje] *vt* to clarify.
clarinette [klarinɛt] *nf* clarinet.
clarté [klarte] *nf* light, brightness; (*précision*) clarity.
classe [klɑs] *nf* class; **aller en c.** to go to school; **c. ouvrière/moyenne** working/middle class; **avoir de la c.** to have class.
class/er [klɑse] *vt* to classify; (*papiers*) to file; (*candidats*) to grade; (*affaire*) to close; **se c. premier** to come first. • **—ement** *nm* classification; filing; grading; (*rang*) place;

Sp placing. ● **—eur** *nm* (*meuble*) filing cabinet; (*portefeuille*) (loose leaf) file *ou* binder.

classique [klasik] *a* classical; (*typique*) classic. ● **classicisme** *nm* classicism.

clause [kloz] *nf* clause.

clavecin [klavsɛ̃] *nm Mus* harpsichord.

clavicule [klavikyl] *nf* collarbone.

clavier [klavje] *nm* keyboard.

clé, clef [kle] *nf* key; (*outil*) spanner, wrench; *Mus* clef; **fermer à c.** to lock; **sous c.** under lock and key; **c. de contact** ignition key; **poste/industrie c.** key post/ industry; **prix clés en main** (*voiture*) on-the-road price.

clément [klemɑ̃] *a* clement.

clémentine [klemɑ̃tin] *nf* clementine.

clerc [klɛr] *nm* (*de notaire*) clerk. ● **clergé** *nm* clergy.

cliché [kliʃe] *nm Phot* negative; (*idée*) cliché.

client, -ente [klijɑ̃, -ɑ̃t] *nmf* (*de magasin etc*) customer; (*d'un avocat etc*) client; (*d'un médecin*) patient; (*d'hôtel*) guest. ● **clientèle** *nf* customers; (*d'un avocat*) practice; (*d'un médecin*) practice, patients.

cligner [kliɲe] *vi* **c. des yeux** (*ouvrir et fermer*) to blink; (*fermer à demi*) to screw up one's eyes; **c. de l'œil** to wink.

clignot/er [kliɲɔte] *vi* to blink; (*lumière*) to flicker; (*étoile*) to twinkle. ● **—ant** *nm Aut* indicator, *Am* directional signal.

climat [klima] *nm Mét & Fig* climate. ● **climatique** *a* climatic.

climatisation [klimatizɑsjɔ̃] *nf* air-conditioning. ● **climatiser** *vt* to air-condition.

clin d'œil [klɛ̃dœj] *nm* wink; **en un c. d'œil** in no time (at all).

clinique [klinik] *nf* (private) clinic.

clip [klip] *nm* (*film*) video (clip).

cliquer [klike] *vi* to click (**sur** on).

cliqueter [klikte] *vi* to clink. ● **cliquetis** *nm* clink(ing).

clochard, -arde [klɔʃar, -ard] *nmf* down-and-out, tramp.

cloche [klɔʃ] *nf* **1** bell; **c. à fromage** cheese cover. **2** (*personne*) *Fam* idiot, oaf. ● **clocher** *nm* bell tower; (*en pointe*) steeple. ● **clochette** *nf* (small) bell.

cloche-pied (à) [aklɔʃpje] *adv* **sauter à c.-pied** to hop on one foot.

cloison [klwazɔ̃] *nf* partition. ● **cloisonner** *vt* to partition.

cloître [klwɑtr] *nm* cloister.

clope [klɔp] *nm ou f* (*cigarette*) *Fam* fag, smoke, *Am* butt.

clopin-clopant [klɔpɛ̃klɔpɑ̃] *adv* **aller c.-clopant** to hobble.

cloque [klɔk] *nf* blister.

clore [klɔr] *vt* (*débat, lettre*) to close. ● **clos, close** *a* (*incident*) closed; (*espace*) enclosed.

clôture [klotyr] *nf* (*barrière*) fence; (*fermeture*) closing. ● **clôturer** *vt* to enclose; (*compte, séance etc*) to close.

clou [klu] *nm* nail; (*furoncle*) boil; **le c. (du spectacle)** *Fam* the star attraction; **les clous** (*passage*) pedestrian crossing. ● **clouer** *vt* to nail; **cloué au lit** confined to bed. ● **clouté** *a* (*pneus*) studded; **passage c.** pedestrian crossing, *Am* crosswalk.

clown [klun] *nm* clown.

club [klœb] *nm* (*association*) club.

cm *abrév* (*centimètre*) cm.

co- [kɔ] *préf* co-.

coaguler [kɔagyle] *vti*, **se c.** *vpr* (*sang*) to clot.

coaliser (se) [səkɔalize] *vpr* to form a coalition, join forces. ● **coalition** *nf* coalition.

coasser [kɔase] *vi* (*grenouille*) to croak.

cobaye [kɔbaj] *nm* (*animal*) & *Fig* guinea pig.

cobra [kɔbra] *nm* (*serpent*) cobra.

coca [kɔka] *nm* (*Coca-Cola*®) coke.

cocaïne [kɔkain] *nf* cocain.

cocarde [kɔkard] *nf* rosette; *Av* roundel.

cocasse [kɔkas] *a* droll, comical.

coccinelle [kɔksinɛl] *nf* ladybird, *Am* ladybug.

cocher¹ [kɔʃe] *vt* to tick (off), *Am* check (off).

cocher² [kɔʃe] *nm* coachman.

cochon, -onne [kɔʃɔ̃, -ɔn] **1** *nm* pig; (*mâle*) hog; **c. d'Inde** guinea pig. **2** *nmf* (*personne sale*) (dirty) pig ‖ *a* (*histoire, film*) dirty. ● **cochonnerie(s)** *nf(pl)* (*obscénité(s)*) filth; (*pacotille*) *Fam* trash, rubbish.

cocktail [kɔktɛl] *nm* (*boisson*) cocktail; (*réunion*) cocktail party.

coco [kɔko] *nm* **noix de c.** coconut. ● **cocotier** *nm* coconut palm.

cocon [kɔkɔ̃] *nm* cocoon.

cocorico [kɔkɔriko] *int & nm* cock-a-doodle-doo.

cocotte [kɔkɔt] *nf* (*marmite*) casserole; **c. minute**® pressure cooker.

code [kɔd] *nm* code; **codes, phares c.** *Aut* dipped headlights, *Am* low beams; **C. de la route** Highway Code, *Am* traffic regulations. ● **coder** *vt* to code.

coéquipier, -ière [kɔekipje, -jɛr] *nmf* team mate.

cœur [kœr] *nm* heart; (*couleur*) *Cartes* hearts; **au c. de** (*ville, hiver etc*) in the heart of; **par c.** (off) by heart; **ça me (sou)lève le c.** that turns my stomach; **à c. ouvert** (*opération*) open-heart; **avoir mal au c.** to feel sick; **avoir le c. gros** to have a heavy heart; **ça me tient à c.** that's important to me; **avoir bon c.** to be kind-hearted; **de bon c.** (*offrir*) willingly; (*rire*) heartily; **si le c. vous en dit** if you so desire.

coffre [kɔfr] *nm* chest; (*de banque*) safe; (*de voiture*) boot, *Am* trunk. ●**c.-fort** *nm* (*pl* **coffres-forts**) safe. ●**coffret** *nm* (*à bijoux etc*) box.

cognac [kɔɲak] *nm* cognac.

cogner [kɔɲe] *vti* to knock, bang; **se c. la tête**/*etc* to knock *ou* bang one's head/*etc*; **se c. à qch** to knock *ou* bang into sth.

cohérent [kɔerɑ̃] *a* coherent.

cohue [kɔy] *nf* crowd, mob.

coiff/er [kwafe] *vt* **c. qn** to do s.o.'s hair; **se c.** to do one's hair; **c. qn d'un chapeau** to put a hat on s.o.; **se c. d'un chapeau** to put on a hat. ●**—eur, -euse**[1] *nmf* (*pour hommes*) barber, hairdresser; (*pour dames*) hairdresser. ●**—euse**[2] *nf* dressing table. ●**coiffure** *nf* hat, headgear; (*arrangement*) hairstyle; (*métier*) hairdressing.

coin [kwɛ̃] *nm* (*angle*) corner; (*endroit*) spot; (*de terre, de ciel*) patch; **du c.** (*magasin, gens etc*) local; **dans le c.** in the (local) area; **au c. du feu** by the fireside.

coincer [kwɛ̃se] *vt* (*mécanisme, tiroir*) to jam ‖ **se c.** *vpr* (*mécanisme etc*) to get stuck *ou* jammed; **se c. le doigt** to get one's finger stuck. ●**coincé** *a* (*tiroir etc*) stuck, jammed.

coïncider [kɔɛ̃side] *vi* to coincide. ●**coïncidence** *nf* coincidence.

coing [kwɛ̃] *nm* (*fruit*) quince.

col [kɔl] *nm* (*de chemise*) collar; (*de bouteille*) & *Anat* neck; (*de montagne*) pass; **c. roulé** polo neck, *Am* turtleneck.

colère [kɔlɛr] *nf* anger; **une c.** (*accès*) a fit of anger; **en c.** angry (**contre** with); **se mettre en c.** to lose one's temper. ●**coléreux, -euse** *a* quick-tempered.

colimaçon (en) [ɑ̃kɔlimasɔ̃] *adv* **escalier en c.** spiral staircase.

colique [kɔlik] *nf* diarrh(o)ea.

colis [kɔli] *nm* parcel, package.

collaborer [kɔlabɔre] *vi* to collaborate (**avec** with, **à** on); **c. à** (*journal*) to contribute to. ●**collaborateur, -trice** *nmf* collaborator; contributor. ●**collaboration** *nf* collaboration; contribution.

collage [kɔlaʒ] *nm* (*œuvre*) collage.

collant [kɔlɑ̃] **1** *a* (*papier*) sticky; (*vêtement*) skin-tight. **2** *nm* (pair of) tights; (*de danse*) leotard.

colle [kɔl] *nf* (*transparente*) glue; (*blanche*) paste; (*question*) *Fam* poser, teaser; (*punition*) *Scol Arg* detention.

collecte [kɔlɛkt] *nf* (*quête*) collection. ●**collecter** *vt* to collect.

collectif, -ive [kɔlɛktif, -iv] *a* collective; (*hystérie, démission*) mass; **billet c.** group ticket. ●**collectivement** *adv* collectively. ●**collectivité** *nf* community.

collection [kɔlɛksjɔ̃] *nf* collection. ●**collectionner** *vt* (*timbres etc*) to collect. ●**collectionneur, -euse** *nmf* collector.

collège [kɔlɛʒ] *nm* (secondary) school, *Am* (high) school; (*électoral*) college. ●**collégien** *nm* schoolboy. ●**collégienne** *nf* schoolgirl.

collègue [kɔlɛg] *nmf* colleague.

coller [kɔle] *vt* (*timbre etc*) to stick; (*à la colle transparente*) to glue; (*à la colle blanche*) to paste; (*affiche*) to stick up; (*papier peint*) to hang; (*mettre*) *Fam* to stick, shove; **c. contre** (*nez, oreille etc*) to press against; **c. qn** (*consigner*) *Scol* to keep s.o. in; **être collé à** (*examen*) *Fam* to fail, flunk ‖ *vi* to stick, cling. ●**colleur, -euse** *nmf* **c. d'affiches** billsticker.

collet [kɔlɛ] *nm* (*piège*) snare; **prendre qn au c.** to grab s.o. by the scruff of the neck.

collier [kɔlje] *nm* (*bijou*) necklace; (*de chien, cheval*) & *Tech* collar.

colline [kɔlin] *nf* hill.

collision [kɔlizjɔ̃] *nf* (*de véhicules*) collision; **entrer en c. avec** to collide with.

colloque [kɔlɔk] *nm* symposium.

colmater [kɔlmate] *vt* (*fuite, fente*) to seal.

colombe [kɔlɔ̃b] *nf* dove.

colon [kɔlɔ̃] *nm* settler, colonist. ●**colonial, -aux** *a* colonial. ●**colonie** *nf* colony; **c. de vacances** (children's) holiday camp *ou Am* vacation camp, *Am* = summer camp.

coloniser [kɔlɔnize] *vt* (*région*) to colonize.

colonel [kɔlɔnɛl] *nm* colonel.

colonne [kɔlɔn] *nf* column; **c. vertébrale** spine.

color/er [kɔlɔre] *vt* to colour; **c. en vert** to colour green. ●**—ant** *a* & *nm* colouring. ●**—é** *a* (*verre etc*) coloured; (*foule*) colourful.

coloriage [kɔlɔrjaʒ] *nm* colouring; (*dessin*) coloured drawing. ●**colorier** *vt* (*dessin etc*) to colour (in). ●**coloris** *nm* (*effet*) colouring; (*nuance*) shade.

colosse [kɔlɔs] *nm* giant. ●**colossal, -aux** *a* colossal.

colporter [kɔlpɔrte] *vt* to peddle, hawk.

coma [kɔma] *nm* coma; **dans le c.** in a coma.

combat [kɔ̃ba] *nm* fight. ●**combatif, -ive** *a* (*personne*) eager to fight; (*esprit*) fighting.

combatt/re* [kɔ̃batr] *vti* to fight. ●**—ant** *nm* (*bagarreur*) *Fam* fighter, brawler.

combien [kɔ̃bjɛ̃] **1** *adv* (*quantité*) how much; (*nombre*) how many; **c. de** (*temps, argent etc*) how much; (*gens, livres etc*) how many.
2 *adv* (*à quel point*) how; **tu verras c. il est bête** you'll see how silly he is.
3 *adv* (*distance*) **c. y a-t-il d'ici à...?** how far is it to...?
4 *nm inv* **le c. sommes-nous?** *Fam* what date is it?; **tous les c.?** *Fam* how often?

combin/er [kɔ̃bine] *vt* (*assembler*) to combine. ●**—é** *nm* (*de téléphone*) receiver. ●**combinaison** *nf* **1** combination; (*manœuvre*) scheme. **2** (*vêtement de femme*) slip; (*de mécanicien*) boiler suit, *Am* overalls; **c. de vol/plongée/ski** flying/diving/ski suit; **c. spatiale** spacesuit.

comble [kɔ̃bl] **1** *nm* **le c. de** (*la joie etc*) the height of; **c'est un** *ou* **le c.!** that's the limit! **2** *nmpl* **sous les combles** beneath the roof, in the loft *ou* attic. **3** *a* (*bondé*) packed.

combler [kɔ̃ble] *vt* (*trou etc*) to fill; (*vœu*) to fulfil; **c. son retard** to make up lost time; **c. qn de** (*joie*) to fill s.o. with; **je suis comblé** I'm completely satisfied.

combustible [kɔ̃bystibl] *nm* fuel ▮ *a* combustible.

comédie [kɔmedi] *nf* comedy; **c. musicale** musical; **jouer la c.** *Fig* to put on an act, pretend; **c'est de la c.** (*faux*) it's a sham. ●**comédien** *nm* actor. ●**comédienne** *nf* actress.

comestible [kɔmɛstibl] *a* edible.

comète [kɔmɛt] *nf* comet.

comique [kɔmik] *a* (*amusant*) *Fig* funny, comical; (*acteur etc*) comic.

comité [kɔmite] *nm* committee.

commande [kɔmɑ̃d] **1** *nf* (*achat*) order; **sur c.** to order. **2** *nfpl* **les commandes** (*d'un avion etc*) the controls.

command/er [kɔmɑ̃de] **1** *vt* (*diriger, exiger, dominer*) to command; (*faire fonctionner*) to control ▮ *vi* **c. à qn de faire** to command s.o. to do. **2** *vt* (*acheter*) to order. ●**—ant** *nm Nau* captain; **c. de bord** *Av* captain. ●**—ement** *nm* (*autorité*) command; *Rel* commandment. ●**commando** *nm Mil* commando.

comme [kɔm] *adv & conj* **1** like; **un peu c.** a bit like; **c. moi** like me; **c. cela** like that.
2 as; **il parle c. il écrit** he speaks as he writes; **blanc c. neige** (as) white as snow; **c. si** as if; **c. pour faire** as if to do; **c. par hasard** as if by chance; **c. ami** (*en tant que*) as a friend; **qu'as-tu c. diplômes?** what do you have in the way of certificates?; **joli c. tout** *Fam* ever so pretty.
▮ *adv* (*exclamatif*) **regarde c. il pleut!** look how it's raining!; **c. c'est petit!** isn't it small!, it's so small!
▮ *conj* (*temps*) as; (*cause*) as, since; **c. elle entrait** (just) as she was coming in; **c. tu es mon ami** as *ou* since you're my friend.

commémoration [kɔmemɔrɑsjɔ̃] *nf* commemoration.

commenc/er [kɔmɑ̃se] *vti* to begin, start (**à faire** to do, doing; **par** with; **par faire** by doing); **pour c.** to begin with. ●**—ement** *nm* beginning, start.

comment [kɔmɑ̃] *adv* how; **c. le sais-tu?** how do you know?; **et c.!** and how!; **c.?** (*répétition*) pardon?, what?; (*surprise*) what?; **c.!** (*indignation*) what!; **c. est-il?** what is he like?; **c. faire?** what's to be done?; **c. t'appelles-tu?** what's your name?; **c. allez-vous?** how are you?
ⓘG208 & **209** Direct and Indirect Questions 12 C 1 & 2

commentaire [kɔmɑ̃tɛr] *nm* (*explications*) commentary; (*remarque*) comment. ●**commenter** *vt* to comment (up)on.

commerçant, -ante [kɔmɛrsɑ̃, -ɑ̃t] *nmf* shopkeeper ▮ *a* **quartier**/*etc* **c.** shopping district/*etc*.

commerce [kɔmɛrs] *nm* trade, commerce; (*magasin*) shop, business; **de c.** (*voyageur, maison, tribunal*) commercial; **chambre de c.** chamber of commerce; **faire du c.** to trade (**avec** with); **dans le c.** (*objet*) (on sale) in the shops *ou Am* stores. ●**commercial, -aux** *a* commercial.

commettre* [kɔmɛtr] *vt* (*délit etc*) to commit; (*erreur*) to make.

commissaire [kɔmisɛr] *nm* **c. (de police)** police superintendent *ou Am* chief. ●**c.-priseur** *nm* (*pl* **commissaires-priseurs**) auctioneer. ●**commissariat** *nm* **c. (de police)** (central) police station.

commission [kɔmisjɔ̃] *nf* (*course*) errand; (*message*) message; (*pourcentage*) commission (**sur** on); **faire les commissions** to do the shopping.

commode [kɔmɔd] **1** *a* (*pratique*) handy; (*simple*) easy; **il n'est pas c.** (*pas aimable*) he's unpleasant. **2** *nf* chest of drawers, *Am* dresser.

commun [kɔmœ̃] *a* (*collectif, habituel*) common; (*frais, cuisine etc*) shared; (*action, démarche etc*) joint; **ami c.** mutual friend; **peu c.** uncommon; **en c.** in common; **transports en c.** public transport; **avoir** *ou* **mettre en c.** to share. ● **—ément** [kɔmynemɑ̃] *adv* commonly.

communauté [kɔmynote] *nf* community.

commune [kɔmyn] *nf* (*municipalité française*) commune; **les Communes** *Br Pol* the Commons. ● **communal, -aux** *a* local, municipal.

communication [kɔmynikɑsjɔ̃] *nf* communication; **c. (téléphonique)** (telephone) call; **mauvaise c.** *Tél* bad line.

communi/er [kɔmynje] *vi* to receive Holy Communion. ● **—ant, -ante** *nmf Rel* communicant. ● **communion** *nf* communion; *Rel* (Holy) Communion.

communiqu/er [kɔmynike] *vt* to communicate, pass on; **se c. à** (*feu*, *rire*) to spread to ‖ *vi* (*personne*, *pièces etc*) to communicate. ● **—é** *nm* (*avis*) (official) statement; **c. de presse** press release.

communisme [kɔmynism] *nm* communism. ● **communiste** *a* & *nmf* communist.

commutateur [kɔmytatœr] *nm* (*bouton*) *Él* switch.

compact [kɔ̃pakt] *a* (*foule*, *matière*) dense; (*appareil*, *véhicule*) compact.

compagne [kɔ̃paɲ] *nf* (*camarade*) friend; (*épouse*) companion.

compagnie [kɔ̃paɲi] *nf* (*présence*, *société*) company; **tenir c. à qn** to keep s.o. company.

compagnon [kɔ̃paɲɔ̃] *nm* companion; (*ouvrier*) workman; **c. de route** travelling companion, fellow traveller; **c. de jeu** playmate; **c. de travail** fellow worker, workmate.

comparaître* [kɔ̃parɛtr] *vi Jur* to appear (in court) (**devant** before).

comparer [kɔ̃pare] *vt* to compare (**à** to, with) ‖ **se c.** *vpr* to be compared (**à** to, with). ● **comparable** *a* comparable. ● **comparaison** *nf* comparison (**avec** with); *Littér* simile. ● **comparatif** *nm Gram* comparative.

compartiment [kɔ̃partimɑ̃] *nm* compartment.

compas [kɔ̃pa] *nm* **1** (*pour mesurer etc*) (pair of) compasses, *Am* compass. **2** (*boussole*) *Nau* compass.

compassion [kɔ̃pɑsjɔ̃] *nf* compassion.

compatible [kɔ̃patibl] *a* compatible (**avec** with).

compatir [kɔ̃patir] *vi* to sympathize; **c. à** (*la douleur etc de qn*) to share in.

compatriote [kɔ̃patrijɔt] *nmf* compatriot.

compenser [kɔ̃pɑ̃se] *vt* to make up for, compensate for ‖ *vi* to compensate. ● **compensation** *nf* compensation; **en c. de** in compensation for.

compétent [kɔ̃petɑ̃] *a* competent. ● **compétence** *nf* competence.

compétition [kɔ̃petisjɔ̃] *nf* competition; (*épreuve*) *Sp* event; **de c.** (*esprit*, *sport*) competitive. ● **compétitif, -ive** *a* competitive.

complaisant [kɔ̃plɛzɑ̃] *a* kind, obliging. ● **complaisance** *nf* kindness.

complément [kɔ̃plemɑ̃] *nm* complement; **le c.** (*le reste*) the rest. ● **complémentaire** *a* complementary; (*détails*) additional.

complet, -ète [kɔ̃plɛ, -ɛt] **1** *a* complete; (*train*, *hôtel etc*) full; (*aliment*) whole. **2** *nm* (*costume*) suit. ● **complètement** *adv* completely.

compléter [kɔ̃plete] *vt* to complete; (*ajouter à*) to complement; (*somme*) to make up ‖ **se c.** *vpr* (*caractères*) to complement each other.

complexe [kɔ̃plɛks] **1** *a* complex. **2** *nm* (*sentiment*, *construction*) complex; **avoir des complexes** to be hung up, have hang-ups.

complication [kɔ̃plikɑsjɔ̃] *nf* complication.

complice [kɔ̃plis] *nm* accomplice ‖ *a* (*regard*) knowing; (*attitude*) conniving. ● **complicité** *nf* complicity.

compliment [kɔ̃plimɑ̃] *nm* compliment; *pl* (*éloges*) compliments; (*félicitations*) congratulations.

compliquer [kɔ̃plike] *vt* to complicate ‖ **se c.** *vpr* (*situation*) to get complicated. ● **compliqué** *a* (*mécanisme*, *histoire etc*) complicated.

complot [kɔ̃plo] *nm* plot (**contre** against). ● **comploter** [kɔ̃plɔte] *vti* to plot (**de faire** to do).

comporter [kɔ̃pɔrte] **1** *vt* to contain. **2 se comporter** *vpr* to behave; (*joueur*, *voiture*) to perform. ● **comportement** *nm* behaviour; (*de joueur etc*) performance.

compos/er [kɔ̃poze] *vt* (*former*, *constituer*) to make up, compose; (*musique*) to compose; (*numéro*) *Tél* to dial; **se c. de, être composé de** to be composed of. ● **—ant** *nm* (*chimique*, *électronique*) component. ● **—é** *a* (*mot etc*) & *Ch* compound; **temps c.** compound tense; **passé c.** perfect (tense) ‖ *nm* compound.

compositeur, -trice [kɔ̃pozitœr, -tris] *nmf Mus* composer.

composition [kɔ̃pozisjɔ̃] *nf Mus Littér Ch* composition; *Scol* test, class exam; **c. française** *Scol* French essay.

composter [kɔ̃pɔste] *vt* (*billet*) to punch.

compote [kɔ̃pɔt] *nf* stewed fruit, *Am* sauce;

c. de pommes stewed apples, *Am* applesauce.

compréhensible [kɔ̃preɑ̃sibl] *a* understandable, comprehensible. • **compréhensif, -ive** *a* (*personne*) understanding. • **compréhension** *nf* understanding.

comprendre* [kɔ̃prɑ̃dr] *vt* to understand; (*comporter*) to include, comprise; **je n'y comprends rien** I don't understand anything about it; **ça se comprend** that's understandable. • **compris** *a* (*inclus*) included (**dans** in); **tout c.** (all) inclusive; **y c.** including.

compresse [kɔ̃prɛs] *nf Méd* compress.

comprim/er [kɔ̃prime] *vt* to compress. • **—é** *nm Méd* tablet.

compromettre* [kɔ̃prɔmɛtr] *vt* to compromise. • **compromis** *nm* compromise.

comptable [kɔ̃tabl] *a nmf* bookkeeper; (*expert*) accountant. • **comptabilité** *nf* (*comptes*) accounts; (*service*) accounts department.

comptant [kɔ̃tɑ̃] *a* **argent c.** (hard) cash ‖ *adv* **payer c.** to pay (in) cash; **(au) c.** (*acheter*, *vendre*) for cash.

compte [kɔ̃t] *nm* (*comptabilité*) account; (*calcul*) count; (*nombre*) (right) number; **avoir un c. en banque** to have a bank account; **c. chèque** cheque account, *Am* checking account; **tenir c. de** to take into account; **c. tenu de** considering; **se rendre c. de** to realize; **rendre c. de** (*exposer*) to report on; (*justifier*) to account for; **à son c.** (*travailler*) for oneself; (*s'installer*) on one's own; **pour le c. de** on behalf of; **en fin de c.** all things considered; **avoir un c. à régler avec qn** to have a score to settle with s.o.; **c. à rebours** countdown. • **compte-gouttes** *nm inv Méd* dropper; **au c.-gouttes** very sparingly.

compter [kɔ̃te] *vt* (*calculer*) to count; (*prévoir*) to allow, reckon; **c. faire** to expect to do; (*avoir l'intention de*) to intend to do; **c. qch à qn** (*facturer*) to charge s.o. for sth.
‖ *vi* (*calculer*, *avoir de l'importance*) to count; **c. sur** to rely on; **c. avec** to reckon with; **c. parmi** to be (numbered) among. • **compteur** *nm Él* meter; **c. (de vitesse)** *Aut* speedometer; **c. (kilométrique)** milometer, clock, *Am* odometer.

compte rendu [kɔ̃trɑ̃dy] *nm* report; (*de livre*, *film*) review.

comptoir [kɔ̃twar] *nm* (*de magasin*) counter; (*de café*) bar; (*de bureau*) (reception) desk.

comte [kɔ̃t] *nm* (*noble*) count; *Br* earl. • **comtesse** *nf* countess.

con, conne [kɔ̃, kɔn] *a* (*idiot*) *Fam* (damn) stupid ‖ *nmf Fam* (damn) stupid fool.

concave [kɔ̃kav] *a* concave.

concentrer [kɔ̃sɑ̃tre] *vt* to concentrate; (*attention etc*) to focus, concentrate ‖ **se c.** *vpr* (*réfléchir*) to concentrate. • **concentré** *a* (*lait*) condensed; (*attentif*) concentrating (hard) ‖ *nm* **c. de tomates** tomato purée. • **concentration** *nf* concentration.

concentrique [kɔ̃sɑ̃trik] *a* concentric.

concerner [kɔ̃sɛrne] *vt* to concern; **en ce qui me concerne** as far as I'm concerned.

concert [kɔ̃sɛr] *nm Mus* concert; (*de louanges*) chorus; **de c.** (*agir*) together.

concerter (se) [səkɔ̃sɛrte] *vpr* to consult (together).

concession [kɔ̃sesjɔ̃] *nf* concession (**à** to). • **concessionnaire** *nmf Com* (authorized) dealer, agent.

concev/oir* [kɔ̃səvwar] *vt* (*imaginer*, *éprouver*, *engendrer*) to conceive; (*comprendre*) to understand. • **—able** *a* conceivable.

concierge [kɔ̃sjɛrʒ] *nmf* caretaker, *Am* janitor.

concili/er [kɔ̃silje] *vt* (*choses*) to reconcile. • **—ant** *a* conciliatory.

concis [kɔ̃si] *a* concise, terse.

concitoyen, -enne [kɔ̃sitwajɛ̃, -ɛn] *nmf* fellow citizen.

conclu/re* [kɔ̃klyr] *vt* (*terminer*, *régler*) to conclude; **c. que** (*déduire*) to conclude that; **c. un marché** to make a deal ‖ *vi* (*orateur etc*) to conclude. • **—ant** *a* conclusive. • **conclusion** *nf* conclusion.

concombre [kɔ̃kɔ̃br] *nm* cucumber.

concorde [kɔ̃kɔrd] *nf* concord, harmony.

concord/er [kɔ̃kɔrde] *vi* (*faits etc*) to agree; **c. avec** to match. • **—ant** *a* in agreement.

concourir* [kɔ̃kurir] *vi* (*candidat*) to compete (**pour** for); **c. à** (*un but*) to contribute to.

concours [kɔ̃kur] *nm Scol Univ* competitive examination; (*jeu*) competition; (*aide*) assistance; (*de circonstances*) combination; **c. hippique** horse show, show-jumping event.

concret, -ète [kɔ̃krɛ, -ɛt] *a* concrete. • **concrétiser** *vt* to give concrete form to ‖ **se c.** *vpr* to materialize.

conçu [kɔ̃sy] *pp de* **concevoir** ‖ *a* **c. pour faire/pour qn** designed to do/for s.o.; **bien c.** (*maison etc*) well designed.

concurrent, -ente [kɔ̃kyrɑ̃, -ɑ̃t] *nmf* competitor. • **concurrence** *nf* competition; **faire c. à** to compete with. • **concurrencer** *vt* to compete with.

condamn/er [kɔ̃dane] *vt* to condemn; (*accusé*) to sentence (**à** to); (*porte*) to block up; (*pièce*) to keep locked; **c. qn à une amende** to fine s.o. ●**—é, -ée** *nmf Jur* condemned man *ou* woman; **être c.** (*malade*) to be a hopeless case, be terminally ill. ●**condamnation** *nf Jur* sentence; (*censure*) condemnation.
condenser [kɔ̃dɑ̃se] *vt*, **se c.** *vpr* to condense.
condescendant [kɔ̃desɑ̃dɑ̃] *a* condescending.
condiment [kɔ̃dimɑ̃] *nm* condiment.
condition [kɔ̃disjɔ̃] *nf* (*état, stipulation, rang*) condition; *pl* (*clauses, tarifs*) *Com* terms; **à c. de faire, à c. que l'on fasse** providing *ou* provided (that) one does. ●**conditionnel** *nm Gram* conditional.
conditionn/er [kɔ̃disjɔne] *vt* (*influencer*) to condition. ●**—é** *a* (*réflexe*) conditioned; **à air c.** (*pièce etc*) air-conditioned.
condoléances [kɔ̃dɔleɑ̃s] *nfpl* sympathy, condolences.
conducteur, -trice [kɔ̃dyktœr, -tris] *nmf Aut Rail* driver.
conduire** [kɔ̃dɥir] **1** *vt* to lead; *Aut* to drive; (*eau*) to carry; (*affaire etc*) & *Él* to conduct; **c. qn à** (*accompagner*) to take s.o. to. **2 se conduire** *vpr* to behave.
conduite [kɔ̃dɥit] *nf* conduct, behaviour; *Aut* driving (**de** of); (*d'eau, de gaz*) main; (*d'entreprise etc*) conduct; **c. à gauche** (*volant*) left-hand drive.
cône [kon] *nm* cone.
confection [kɔ̃fɛksjɔ̃] *nf* making (**de** of); **vêtements de c.** ready-to-wear clothes; **magasin de c.** clothes shop, *Am* clothing store. ●**confectionner** *vt* (*gâteau, robe*) to make.
confédération [kɔ̃federɑsjɔ̃] *nf* confederation.
conférence [kɔ̃ferɑ̃s] *nf* conference; (*exposé*) lecture; **en c.** in a meeting. ●**conférencier, -ière** *nmf* lecturer.
confesser [kɔ̃fese] *vt* to confess ‖ **se c.** *vpr Rel* to confess (**à** to). ●**confession** *nf* confession. ●**confessionnal, -aux** *nm Rel* confessional.
confettis [kɔ̃feti] *nmpl* confetti.
confiance [kɔ̃fjɑ̃s] *nf* trust, confidence; **faire c. à qn, avoir c. en qn** to trust s.o.; **c. en soi** (self-)confidence; **poste/abus de c.** position/breach of trust; **homme de c.** reliable man; **en toute c.** (*acheter*) quite confidently. ●**confiant** *a* trusting; (*sûr de soi*) confident; **être c. en** *ou* **dans** to have confidence in.
confidence [kɔ̃fidɑ̃s] *nf* (*secret*) confidence; **en c.** in confidence; **faire une c. à qn** to confide in s.o. ●**confident** *nm* confidant. ●**confidente** *nf* confidante. ●**confidentiel, -ielle** *a* confidential.
confier [kɔ̃fje] *vt* **c. à qn** (*enfant, objet*) to give s.o. to look after, entrust s.o. with; **c. un secret**/*etc* **à qn** to confide a secret/*etc* to s.o.; **se c. à qn** to confide in s.o.
confirmer [kɔ̃firme] *vt* to confirm (**que** that). ●**confirmation** *nf* confirmation.
confiserie [kɔ̃fizri] *nf* (*magasin*) sweet shop, *Am* candy store; *pl* (*produits*) confectionery, sweets, *Am* candy. ●**confiseur, -euse** *nmf* confectioner.
confisquer [kɔ̃fiske] *vt* to confiscate (**à qn** from s.o.).
confit [kɔ̃fi] *a* **fruits confits** crystallized *ou* candied fruit. ●**confiture** *nf* jam, preserves.
conflit [kɔ̃fli] *nm* conflict.
confondre [kɔ̃fɔ̃dr] *vt* (*choses, personnes*) to mix up, confuse; (*consterner, étonner*) to confound; **c. qch/qn avec** to mistake sth/s.o. for ‖ **se c.** *vpr* (*s'unir*) to merge; **se c. en excuses** to be very apologetic.
conforme [kɔ̃fɔrm] *a* **c. à** in accordance with, in keeping with; (*modèle*) true to; **copie c. à l'original** true copy, copy true to the original. ●**conformément** *adv* **c. à** in accordance with.
conformer (se) [səkɔ̃fɔrme] *vpr* to conform (**à** to).
conformiste [kɔ̃fɔrmist] *a* & *nmf* conformist. ●**conformité** *nf* conformity.
confort [kɔ̃fɔr] *nm* comfort. ●**confortable** *a* comfortable.
confrère [kɔ̃frɛr] *nm* colleague.
confronter [kɔ̃frɔ̃te] *vt Jur etc* to confront (**avec** with); **confronté à** confronted with. ●**confrontation** *nf* confrontation.
confus [kɔ̃fy] *a* (*esprit, situation, idée, bruit etc*) confused; (*gêné*) embarrassed; **je suis c.!** (*désolé*) I'm terribly sorry! ●**confusément** *adv* indistinctly, vaguely. ●**confusion** *nf* confusion; (*gêne, honte*) embarrassment.
congé [kɔ̃ʒe] *nm* leave (of absence); (*vacances*) holiday, *Am* vacation; (*avis pour locataire*) notice (to quit); (*pour salarié*) notice (of dismissal); **c. de maladie** sick leave; **congés payés** paid holidays *ou Am* vacation; **donner son c. à** (*employé, locataire*) to give notice to; **prendre c. de** to take leave of.
congédier [kɔ̃ʒedje] *vt* (*domestique etc*) to dismiss.
congeler [kɔ̃ʒle] *vt* to freeze. ●**congélateur**

nm freezer, deep-freeze. ● **congélation** *nf* freezing.
congère [kɔ̃ʒɛr] *nf* snowdrift.
congestion [kɔ̃ʒɛstjɔ̃] *nf* **c. cérébrale** *Méd* stroke.
Congo [kɔ̃go] *nm* Congo. ● **congolais, -aise** *a & nmf* Congolese.
congratuler [kɔ̃gratyle] *vt Iron* to congratulate.
congrès [kɔ̃grɛ] *nm* congress.
conifère [kɔnifɛr] *nm* conifer.
conique [kɔnik] *a* conic(al), cone-shaped.
conjecture [kɔ̃ʒɛktyr] *nf* conjecture.
conjoint [kɔ̃ʒwɛ̃] *nm* spouse; *pl* husband and wife.
conjonction [kɔ̃ʒɔ̃ksjɔ̃] *nf Gram* conjunction.
conjoncture [kɔ̃ʒɔ̃ktyr] *nf* circumstances; *Écon* economic situation.
conjugal, -aux [kɔ̃ʒygal, -o] *a* conjugal.
conjuguer [kɔ̃ʒyge] *vt* (*verbe*) to conjugate; (*efforts*) to combine ‖ **se c.** *vpr* (*verbe*) to be conjugated. ● **conjugaison** *nf Gram* conjugation.
conjur/er [kɔ̃ʒyre] *vt* (*danger*) to avert; (*mauvais sort*) to ward off; **c. qn** to beg s.o., implore s.o. (**de faire** to do).
connaissance [kɔnɛsɑ̃s] *nf* knowledge; (*personne*) acquaintance; *pl* (*science*) knowledge (**en** of); **faire la c. de qn, faire c. avec qn** (*inconnu*) to meet s.o., make s.o.'s acquaintance; (*ami, époux etc*) to get to know s.o.; **à ma c.** as far as I know; **avoir c. de** to be aware of; **perdre c.** to lose consciousness, faint; **sans c.** unconscious. ● **connaisseur** *nm* connoisseur.
connaître** [kɔnɛtr] *vt* to know; (*rencontrer*) to meet; (*un succès*) to have; (*un malheur*) to experience; **faire c.** to make known ‖ **se c.** *vpr* (*amis etc*) to get to know each other; **nous nous connaissons déjà** we've met before; **s'y c. à** *ou* **en qch** to know (all) about sth.
connerie [kɔnri] *nf Fam* (*bêtise*) (damn) stupidity; (*action*) (damn) stupid thing; *pl* (*paroles*) (damn) stupid nonsense.
connivence [kɔnivɑ̃s] *nf* connivance.
connu *pp de* **connaître** ‖ *a* (*célèbre*) well-known.
conquér/ir* [kɔ̃kerir] *vt* (*pays, marché etc*) to conquer. ● **—ant, -ante** *nmf* conqueror. ● **conquête** *nf* conquest; **faire la c. de** (*pays, marché etc*) to conquer.
consacrer [kɔ̃sakre] *vt* (*temps, vie etc*) to devote (**à** to); **se c. à** to devote oneself to.
consciemment [kɔ̃sjamɑ̃] *adv* consciously.
conscience [kɔ̃sjɑ̃s] *nf* **1** (*psychologique*) consciousness; **la c. de qch** the awareness of sth; **avoir/prendre c. de** to be/become aware *ou* conscious of. **2** (*morale*) conscience; **avoir mauvaise c.** to have a guilty conscience; **c. professionnelle** conscientiousness. ● **consciencieux, -euse** *a* conscientious. ● **conscient** *a* conscious; **c. de** aware *ou* conscious of.
conscrit [kɔ̃skri] *nm Mil* conscript.
consécutif, -ive [kɔ̃sekytif, -iv] *a* consecutive; **c. à** following upon.
conseil[1] [kɔ̃sɛj] *nm* **un c.** a piece of advice, some advice; **des conseils** advice.
conseil[2] [kɔ̃sɛj] *nm* (*assemblée*) council, committee; **c. d'administration** board of directors; **c. des ministres** (*réunion*) *Pol* cabinet meeting.
conseiller[1] [kɔ̃seje] *vt* (*guider, recommander*) to advise; **c. qch à qn** to recommend sth to s.o.; **c. à qn de faire** to advise s.o. to do. ● **conseiller**[2], **-ère** *nmf* (*expert*) consultant, adviser; (*d'un conseil*) councillor, *Am* councilor; **c. municipal** town councillor, *Am* councilman.
consent/ir* [kɔ̃sɑ̃tir] *vi* **c. à** to consent to. ● **—ement** *nm* consent.
conséquence [kɔ̃sekɑ̃s] *nf* consequence; (*conclusion*) conclusion; **en c.** accordingly; **sans c.** (*importance*) of no importance.
conséquent (par) [parkɔ̃sekɑ̃] *adv* consequently.
conservateur, -trice [kɔ̃sɛrvatœr, -tris] **1** *a & nmf Pol* Conservative. **2** *nm* (*de musée*) curator.
conservatoire [kɔ̃sɛrvatwar] *nm* school (*of music, drama*).
conserve [kɔ̃sɛrv] *nf* **conserves** canned *ou* tinned food; **de** *ou* **en c.** canned, tinned; **mettre en c.** to can, tin.
conserver [kɔ̃sɛrve] *vt* (*ne pas perdre*) to keep, retain; (*fruits, tradition etc*) to preserve ‖ **se c.** *vpr* (*aliment*) to keep. ● **conservation** *nf* preservation.
considérable [kɔ̃siderabl] *a* considerable.
considérer [kɔ̃sidere] *vt* to consider (**que** that, **comme** to be); **tout bien considéré** all things considered. ● **considération** *nf* (*respect*) regard, esteem; **prendre en c.** to take into consideration.
consigne [kɔ̃siɲ] *nf* (*instruction*) orders; (*de gare*) left-luggage office, *Am* baggage checkroom; *Scol* detention; (*somme*) deposit; **c. automatique** (*de gare*) luggage lockers, *Am* baggage lockers. ● **consigner** *vt* (*bouteille etc*) to charge a deposit on; (*élève*) *Scol* to keep in.

consistant [kɔ̃sistɑ̃] *a* (*sauce, bouillie*) thick; (*repas*) solid. ●**consistance** *nf* (*de liquide*) consistency.

consister [kɔ̃siste] *vi* **c. en/dans** to consist of/in; **c. à faire** to consist in doing.

console [kɔ̃sɔl] *nf Tech Él* console.

consoler [kɔ̃sɔle] *vt* to comfort, console; **se c. de** (*la mort de qn etc*) to get over. ●**consolation** *nf* comfort, consolation.

consolider [kɔ̃sɔlide] *vt* to strengthen.

consommer [kɔ̃sɔme] *vt* (*aliment, carburant etc*) to consume ‖ *vi* (*au café*) to drink; **c. beaucoup/peu** (*véhicule*) to be heavy/light on petrol *ou Am* gas. ●**consommateur, -trice** *nmf Com* consumer; (*au café*) customer. ●**consommation** *nf* consumption; (*boisson*) drink; **biens/société de c.** consumer goods/society.

consonne [kɔ̃sɔn] *nf* consonant.

conspirer [kɔ̃spire] *vi* to plot, conspire (**contre** against). ●**conspirateur, -trice** *nmf* plotter. ●**conspiration** *nf* plot, conspiracy.

constant [kɔ̃stɑ̃] *a* constant. ●**constamment** *adv* constantly. ●**constance** *nf* constancy.

constat [kɔ̃sta] *nm* (official) report; **dresser un c. d'échec** to acknowledge one's failure.

constater [kɔ̃state] *vt* to note, observe (**que** that); (*vérifier*) to establish; (*enregistrer*) to record; **je ne fais que c.** I'm merely stating a fact. ●**constatation** *nf* (*remarque*) observation.

constellation [kɔ̃stelɑsjɔ̃] *nf* constellation. ●**constellé** *a* **c. de** (*étoiles, joyaux*) studded with.

consterner [kɔ̃stɛrne] *vt* to distress, dismay. ●**consternation** *nf* distress, dismay.

constipé [kɔ̃stipe] *a* constipated. ●**constipation** *nf* constipation.

constituer [kɔ̃stitɥe] *vt* (*composer*) to make up; (*représenter*) to represent; (*organiser*) to form; **constitué de** made up of; **se c. prisonnier** to give oneself up. ●**constitution** *nf* (*santé*) & *Pol* constitution; (*composition*) composition. ●**constitutionnel, -elle** *a* constitutional.

constructeur [kɔ̃stryktœr] *nm* builder; (*fabricant*) maker (**de** of). ●**constructif, -ive** *a* constructive. ●**construction** *nf* (*de pont etc*) building, construction (**de** of); (*édifice*) building; (*de théorie etc*) & *Gram* construction; **matériaux/jeu de c.** building materials/set.

construire* [kɔ̃strɥir] *vt* (*maison, route etc*) to build, construct; (*phrase, théorie etc*) to construct.

consul [kɔ̃syl] *nm* consul. ●**consulat** *nm* consulate.

consulter [kɔ̃sylte] **1** *vt* to consult ‖ **se c.** *vpr* to consult (each other), confer. **2** *vi* (*médecin*) to hold surgery, *Am* hold office hours. ●**consultation** *nf* consultation; **cabinet de c.** *Méd* surgery, *Am* (doctor's) office; **heures de c.** *Méd* surgery hours, *Am* office hours.

consumer [kɔ̃syme] *vt* (*détruire, miner*) to consume.

contact [kɔ̃takt] *nm* contact; (*toucher*) touch; *Aut* ignition; **être en c. avec** to be in touch *ou* contact with; **prendre c.** to get in touch (**avec** with); **entrer en c. avec** to come into contact with; **prise de c.** first meeting; **mettre/couper le c.** *Aut* to switch on/off the ignition; **lentilles** *ou* **verres de c.** contact lenses. ●**contacter** *vt* to contact.

contagieux, -euse [kɔ̃taʒjø, -øz] *a* (*maladie, rire*) contagious, infectious; **c'est c.** it's catching *ou* contagious. ●**contagion** *nf Méd* infection.

contaminer [kɔ̃tamine] *vt* to contaminate.

conte [kɔ̃t] *nm* tale; **c. de fée** fairy tale.

contempler [kɔ̃tɑ̃ple] *vt* to gaze at. ●**contemplation** *nf* contemplation.

contemporain, -aine [kɔ̃tɑ̃pɔrɛ̃, -ɛn] *a* & *nmf* contemporary.

contenance [kɔ̃tnɑ̃s] *nf* **1** (*d'un récipient*) capacity. **2 perdre c.** (*allure*) to lose one's composure.

contenir* [kɔ̃tnir] *vt* (*renfermer*) to contain; (*avoir comme capacité*) to hold; (*contrôler*) to hold back, contain ‖ **se c.** *vpr* to contain oneself. ●**conteneur** *nm* (freight) container.

content [kɔ̃tɑ̃] *a* pleased, happy, glad (**de faire** to do); **c. de qn/qch** pleased *ou* happy with s.o./sth; **c. de soi** self-satisfied; **non c. d'avoir fait** not content with having done.

ⓘ**G98** The Subjunctive 7 G 1a)

content/er [kɔ̃tɑ̃te] *vt* to satisfy, please; **se c. de qch/de faire** to be content *ou* happy with sth/content *ou* happy doing, make do with sth/with doing. ●**—ement** *nm* contentment, satisfaction.

contenu [kɔ̃tny] *nm* (*de récipient*) contents; (*de texte, film etc*) content.

cont/er [kɔ̃te] *vt* (*histoire etc*) to tell (**à** to). ●**—eur, -euse** *nmf* storyteller.

contestable [kɔ̃tɛstabl] *a* debatable.

contestataire [kɔ̃tɛstatɛr] *a* **étudiant/ouvrier c.** student/worker protester ‖ *nmf* protester. ●**contestation** *nf* (*discussion*) dispute; **faire de la c.** to protest (against the Establishment).

conteste (sans) [sɑ̃kɔ̃tɛst] *adv* unquestionably.

contester [kɔ̃tɛste] **1** *vi* (*étudiants etc*) to

protest ‖ *vt* to protest against. **2** *vt* (*fait etc*) to dispute, contest.

contexte [kɔ̃tɛkst] *nm* context.

contigu, -uë [kɔ̃tigy] *a* **c. (à)** (*maisons etc*) adjoining.

continent [kɔ̃tinɑ̃] *nm* continent; (*opposé à une île*) mainland. ● **continental, -aux** *a* continental.

continu [kɔ̃tiny] *a* continuous. ● **continuel, -elle** *a* continual. ● **continuellement** *adv* continually.

continuer [kɔ̃tinɥe] *vt* to continue, carry on (**à** *ou* **de faire** doing); (*prolonger*) to continue ‖ *vi* to continue, go on.

contorsion [kɔ̃tɔrsjɔ̃] *nf* contortion. ● **se contorsionner** *vpr* to contort oneself.

contour [kɔ̃tur] *nm* outline, contour; *pl* (*de route, rivière*) twists, bends.

contourner [kɔ̃turne] *vt* (*colline etc*) to go round, skirt; (*difficulté, loi*) to get round.

contraception [kɔ̃trasɛpsjɔ̃] *nf* contraception. ● **contraceptif, -ive** *a* & *nm* contraceptive.

contracter [kɔ̃trakte] *vt* (*muscle, habitude, dette etc*) to contract ‖ **se c.** *vpr* (*cœur etc*) to contract.

contractuel, -elle [kɔ̃traktɥɛl] *nmf* traffic warden, *Am* meter man *ou* maid.

contradiction [kɔ̃tradiksjɔ̃] *nf* contradiction. ● **contradictoire** *a* (*propos etc*) contradictory; (*rapports, théories*) conflicting.

contraindre* [kɔ̃trɛ̃dr] *vt* to compel, force (**à faire** to do). ● **contraignant** *a* constraining, restricting. ● **contrainte** *nf* constraint.

contraire [kɔ̃trɛr] *a* opposite; (*défavorable*) contrary; **c. à** contrary to ‖ *nm* opposite; **(bien) au c.** on the contrary. ● **—ment** *adv* **c. à** contrary to.

contrari/er [kɔ̃trarje] *vt* (*projet, action*) to spoil, thwart; (*personne*) to annoy. ● **—ant** *a* (*action etc*) annoying; (*personne*) difficult, perverse. ● **contrariété** *nf* annoyance.

contraste [kɔ̃trast] *nm* contrast. ● **contraster** *vi* to contrast (**avec** with).

contrat [kɔ̃tra] *nm* contract.

contravention [kɔ̃travɑ̃sjɔ̃] *nf* (*pour stationnement interdit*) (parking) ticket; (*amende*) *Aut* fine.

contre [kɔ̃tr] *prép* & *adv* against; (*en échange de*) (in exchange) for; **échanger c.** to exchange for; **fâché c.** angry with; **six voix c. deux** six votes to two; **Nîmes c. Arras** (*match*) Nîmes versus *ou* against Arras; **un médicament c.** (*toux etc*) a medicine for; **par c.** on the other hand; **tout c. qch/qn** close to sth/s.o.

contre- [kɔ̃tr] *préf* counter-.

contre-attaque [kɔ̃tratak] *nf* counterattack. ● **contre-attaquer** *vt* to counterattack.

contrebalancer [kɔ̃trəbalɑ̃se] *vt* to counterbalance; (*compenser*) *Fig* to offset.

contrebande [kɔ̃trəbɑ̃d] *nf* (*fraude*) smuggling; (*marchandises*) smuggled goods; **de c.** (*tabac etc*) smuggled; **faire de la c.** to smuggle; **passer qch en c.** to smuggle sth. ● **contrebandier, -ière** *nmf* smuggler.

contrebas (en) [ɑ̃kɔ̃trəbɑ] *adv* & *prép* **en c. (de)** down below.

contrebasse [kɔ̃trəbɑs] *nf Mus* double-bass.

contrecarrer [kɔ̃trəkare] *vt* to thwart, frustrate.

contrecœur (à) [akɔ̃trəkœr] *adv* reluctantly.

contrecoup [kɔ̃trəku] *nm* (indirect) effect *ou* consequence.

contredire* [kɔ̃trədir] *vt* to contradict ‖ **se c.** *vpr* to contradict oneself.

contrée [kɔ̃tre] *nf* region, land.

contrefaçon [kɔ̃trəfasɔ̃] *nf* counterfeiting, forgery; (*objet imité*) counterfeit, forgery.

contre-indiqué [kɔ̃trɛ̃dike] *a* (*médicament*) dangerous, not recommended.

contre-jour (à) [akɔ̃trəʒur] *adv* against the (sun)light.

contremaître [kɔ̃trəmɛtr] *nm* foreman.

contrepartie [kɔ̃trəparti] *nf* **en c.** in exchange.

contre-pied [kɔ̃trəpje] *nm* **le c.-pied d'une opinion/attitude** the (exact) opposite view/attitude.

contre-plaqué [kɔ̃trəplake] *nm* plywood.

contrepoids [kɔ̃trəpwa] *nm* **faire c. (à)** to counterbalance.

contresens [kɔ̃trəsɑ̃s] *nm* misinterpretation; (*en traduisant*) mistranslation; **à c.** the wrong way.

contretemps [kɔ̃trətɑ̃] *nm* hitch, mishap; **à c.** (*arriver etc*) at the wrong moment.

contribu/er [kɔ̃tribɥe] *vi* to contribute (**à** to). ● **—able** *nmf* taxpayer. ● **contribution** *nf* contribution; (*impôt*) tax; **mettre qn à c.** to use s.o.'s services.

contrit [kɔ̃tri] *a* (*air etc*) contrite.

contrôle [kɔ̃trol] *nm* inspection, check(ing) (**de** of); (*des prix, de la qualité*) control; (*maîtrise*) control; **un c.** (*examen*) a check (**sur** on); **le c. de soi(-même)** self-control; **le c. des naissances** birth control; **un c. d'identité** an identity check.

contrôler [kɔ̃trole] *vt* (*examiner*) to inspect, check; (*maîtriser, surveiller*) to control ‖ **se c.** *vpr* (*se maîtriser*) to control oneself. ● **contrôleur, -euse** *nmf* (*de train*) (ticket)

inspector; (*au quai*) ticket collector; (*de bus*) conductor, conductress; **c. de la navigation aérienne** air-traffic controller.
contrordre [kɔ̃trɔrdr] *nm* change of orders.
controverse [kɔ̃trɔvɛrs] *nf* controversy.
contumace (par) [parkɔ̃tymas] *adv Jur* in one's absence.
contusion [kɔ̃tyzjɔ̃] *nf* bruise.
convainc/re* [kɔ̃vɛ̃kr] *vt* to convince (**de** of); **c. qn de faire** to persuade s.o. to do. ●**—ant** *a* convincing. ●**—u** *a* (*certain*) convinced (**de** of).
convalescent, -ente [kɔ̃valesɑ̃, -ɑ̃t] *nmf* convalescent ‖ *a* **être c.** to convalesce. ●**convalescence** *nf* convalescence; **être en c.** to convalesce.
convenable [kɔ̃vnabl] *a* (*acceptable*) (*réponse etc*) suitable; (*correct*) (*tenue etc*) decent. ●**—ment** [-əmɑ̃] *adv* suitably; decently.
convenance [kɔ̃vnɑ̃s] *nf* **convenances** (*usages*) convention(s), proprieties; **à sa c.** to one's satisfaction *ou* taste.
conven/ir* [kɔ̃vnir] *vi* **1 c. à** (*être fait pour*) to be suitable for; (*plaire à, aller à*) to suit; **ça convient** (*date etc*) that's suitable; **il convient de faire** it's advisable to do. **2 c. de** (*lieu etc*) to agree upon; (*erreur*) to admit. ●**—u** *a* (*prix etc*) agreed.
convention [kɔ̃vɑ̃sjɔ̃] *nf* (*accord*) agreement, convention.
conventionné [kɔ̃vɑ̃sjɔne] *a* **médecin c.** = National Health Service doctor (*bound by agreement with the State*).
conversation [kɔ̃vɛrsɑsjɔ̃] *nf* conversation.
conversion [kɔ̃vɛrsjɔ̃] *nf* conversion. ●**convertir** *vt* to convert (**à** to, **en** into) ‖ **se c.** *vpr* to be converted, convert. ●**convertible** *nm* **(canapé) c.** bed settee.
convexe [kɔ̃vɛks] *a* convex.
conviction [kɔ̃viksjɔ̃] *nf* (*certitude, croyance*) conviction; **pièce à c.** *Jur* exhibit.
convier [kɔ̃vje] *vt* to invite (**à une soirée**/*etc* to a party/*etc*).
convive [kɔ̃viv] *nmf* guest (*at table*).
convoi [kɔ̃vwa] *nm* (*véhicules, personnes etc*) convoy; *Rail* train; **c. (funèbre)** funeral procession.
convoyeur [kɔ̃vwajœr] *nm* **c. de fonds** security guard (*transferring money*).
convoquer [kɔ̃vɔke] *vt* (*candidats, membres etc*) to summon *ou* invite (to attend); (*assemblée*) to convene, summon; **c. qn à** to summon *ou* invite s.o. to. ●**convocation** *nf* (*lettre*) (written) notice to attend.
convulsion [kɔ̃vylsjɔ̃] *nf* convulsion.
coopérer [kɔɔpere] *vi* to co-operate (**à** in, avec with). ●**coopération** *nf* co-operation.
coordonnées *nfpl* [kɔɔrdɔne] (*adresse, téléphone*) *Fam* contact address and phone number, particulars.
coordonner [kɔɔrdɔne] *vt* to co-ordinate.
copain [kɔpɛ̃] *nm Fam* (*camarade*) pal; (*petit ami*) boyfriend; **être c. avec** to be pals with.
copeau, -x [kɔpo] *nm* (*de bois*) shaving.
copie [kɔpi] *nf* copy; (*devoir, examen*) paper. ●**copier** *vti* to copy; *Scol* to copy, crib (**sur** from). ●**copieur, -euse** *nmf* (*élève etc*) copycat.
copieux, -euse [kɔpjø, -øz] *a* plentiful, copious.
copine [kɔpin] *nf Fam* (*camarade*) pal; (*petite amie*) girlfriend; **être c. avec** to be pals with.
copropriété [kɔprɔprijete] *nf* joint ownership; **(immeuble en) c.** block of flats in joint ownership, *Am* condominium.
coq [kɔk] *nm* rooster, cock; **passer du c. à l'âne** to jump from one subject to another.
coque [kɔk] *nf* **1** (*de noix*) shell; (*fruit de mer*) cockle; **œuf à la c.** boiled egg. **2** (*de navire*) hull.
coquelicot [kɔkliko] *nm* poppy.
coqueluche [kɔklyʃ] *nf Méd* whooping cough.
coquet, -ette [kɔkɛ, -ɛt] *a* (*chic*) smart; (*joli*) pretty; (*somme*) *Fam* tidy. ●**coquetterie** *nf* smartness; (*goût de la toilette*) dress sense.
coquetier [kɔktje] *nm* egg cup.
coquille [kɔkij] *nf* shell; **c. Saint-Jacques** scallop. ●**coquillage** *nm* shellfish *inv*; (*coquille*) shell.
coquin, -ine [kɔkɛ̃, -in] *nmf* rascal ‖ *a* mischievous; (*histoire*) naughty.
cor [kɔr] *nm Mus* horn; **c. (au pied)** corn; **réclamer** *ou* **demander à c. et à cri** to clamour for.
corail, -aux [kɔraj, -o] *nm* coral.
Coran [kɔrɑ̃] *nm* **le C.** the Koran.
corbeau, -x [kɔrbo] *nm* crow; **(grand) c.** raven.
corbeille [kɔrbɛj] *nf* basket; **c. à papier** waste paper basket.
corbillard [kɔrbijar] *nm* hearse.
cordage [kɔrdaʒ] *nm Nau* rope.
corde [kɔrd] *nf* rope; (*plus mince*) cord; (*de raquette, violon etc*) string; **instrument à cordes** *Mus* string(ed) instrument; **c. à linge** (washing- *ou* clothes-) line; **c. à sauter** skipping rope, *Am* jump rope; **usé jusqu'à la c.** threadbare; **cordes vocales** vocal cords; **pas dans mes cordes** *Fam* not my

line. • **cordée** *nf* roped (climbing) party. • **cordelette** *nf* (fine) cord.

cordial, -aux [kɔrdjal, -o] *a* warm. • **cordialité** *nf* warmth.

cordon [kɔrdɔ̃] *nm* (*de tablier, sac etc*) string; (*de rideau*) cord, rope; (*de soulier*) lace; (*d'agents de police*) cordon; (*ombilical*) cord. • **c.-bleu** *nm* (*pl* **cordons-bleus**) first-class cook.

cordonnier [kɔrdɔnje] *nm* shoe repairer. • **cordonnerie** *nf* shoe repair *ou* repairer's shop.

Corée [kɔre] *nf* Korea. • **coréen, -enne** *a* & *nmf* Korean.

coriace [kɔrjas] *a* (*aliment, personne*) tough.

corne [kɔrn] *nf* (*de chèvre etc*) horn; (*de cerf*) antler; (*matière, instrument*) horn; (*angle, pli*) corner.

cornée [kɔrne] *nf Anat* cornea.

corneille [kɔrnɛj] *nf* crow.

cornemuse [kɔrnəmyz] *nf* bagpipes.

corner [kɔrne] **1** *vt* (*page*) to turn down the corner of, dog-ear. **2** [kɔrnɛr] *nm Fb* corner.

cornet [kɔrnɛ] *nm* (*de glace*) cornet, cone; **c. (de papier)** (paper) cone.

corniche [kɔrniʃ] *nf* (*route*) cliff road; *Archit* cornice.

cornichon [kɔrniʃɔ̃] *nm* **1** (*concombre*) gherkin. **2** (*niais*) *Fam* clot, twit.

corps [kɔr] *nm* body; *Mil Pol* corps; **c. électoral** electorate; **c. enseignant** teaching profession; **garde du c.** bodyguard; **un c. de bâtiment** a main building; **c. et âme** body and soul; **lutter c. à c.** to fight hand-to-hand; **à son c. défendant** under protest; **prendre c.** (*projet*) to take shape; **faire c. avec** to form a part of, belong with. • **corporel, -elle** *a* bodily; (*châtiment*) corporal.

corpulent [kɔrpylɑ̃] *a* stout, corpulent. • **corpulence** *nf* stoutness, corpulence.

correct [kɔrɛkt] *a* (*exact*) correct; (*bienséant, honnête*) proper, correct; (*passable*) adequate. • **—ement** [-əmɑ̃] *adv* correctly; properly; adequately. • **correcteur, -trice 1** *a* **verres correcteurs** corrective lenses. **2** *nmf Scol* examiner.

correction [kɔrɛksjɔ̃] *nf* correction; (*punition*) thrashing; (*exactitude, bienséance*) correctness; **la c. de** (*devoirs, examen*) the marking of. • **correctionnel** *am* **tribunal c.** magistrates' court, *Am* police court.

correspondance [kɔrɛspɔ̃dɑ̃s] *nf* correspondence; (*de train, d'autocar*) connection, *Am* transfer.

correspond/re [kɔrɛspɔ̃dr] **1** *vi* (*s'accorder*) to correspond (**à** to, with). **2** *vi* (*écrire*) to correspond (**avec** with). • **—ant, -ante** *a* corresponding ▮ *nmf* correspondent; (*d'un élève etc*) pen friend, *Am* pen pal; *Tél* caller.

corrida [kɔrida] *nf* bullfight.

corridor [kɔridɔr] *nm* corridor.

corrig/er [kɔriʒe] *vt* (*texte, injustice etc*) to correct; (*devoir*) to mark, correct; (*châtier*) to beat, punish; **c. qn de** (*défaut*) to cure s.o. of; **se c. de** to cure oneself of. • **—é** *nm Scol* model (answer), correct version.

corromp/re* [kɔrɔ̃pr] *vt* to corrupt; (*soudoyer*) to bribe. • **—u** *a* corrupt. • **corruption** *nf* (*de juge etc*) bribery; (*vice*) corruption.

corsage [kɔrsaʒ] *nm* (*chemisier*) blouse; (*de robe*) bodice.

Corse [kɔrs] *nf* Corsica. • **corse** *a* & *nmf* Corsican.

corser (se) [səkɔrse] *vpr* **l'affaire se corse** things are hotting up. • **corsé** *a* (*café*) strong; (*sauce, histoire*) spicy.

cortège [kɔrtɛʒ] *nm* (*défilé*) procession; (*suite*) retinue; **c. officiel** (*automobiles*) motorcade.

corvée [kɔrve] *nf* chore, drudgery.

cosmos [kɔsmɔs] *nm* (*univers*) cosmos; (*espace*) outer space. • **cosmonaute** *nmf* cosmonaut.

cosse [kɔs] *nf* (*de pois etc*) pod.

cossu [kɔsy] *a* (*maison etc*) opulent.

costaud [kɔsto] *a Fam* brawny ▮ *nm Fam* strong man.

costume [kɔstym] *nm* (*déguisement*) costume; (*complet*) suit. • **se costumer** *vpr* **se c. en** to dress up as; **bal costumé** fancy-dress ball, costume ball.

cote [kɔt] *nf* (*évaluation, popularité*) rating; (*des valeurs boursières*) quotation; **c. d'alerte** danger level.

côte [kot] *nf* **1** *Anat* rib; (*de mouton*) chop; (*de veau*) cutlet; **c. à c.** side by side. **2** (*montée*) hill; (*versant*) hillside. **3** (*littoral*) coast.

côté [kote] *nm* side; (*direction*) way; **de l'autre c.** on the other side (**de** of); (*direction*) the other way; **de ce c.** (*passer*) this way; **du c. de** (*vers, près de*) towards; **de c.** (*se jeter, regarder, mettre de l'argent etc*) to one side; **à c.** nearby; (*pièce*) in the other room; (*maison*) next door; **la maison (d')à c.** the house next door; **à c. de** next to, beside; (*comparaison*) compared to; **venir de tous côtés** to come from all directions; **d'un c., . . . d'un autre**

c. on the one hand, . . . on the other hand; **de mon c.** for my part; **à mes côtés** by my side; **laisser de c.** (*travail*) to neglect; **le bon c.** (*d'une affaire*) the bright side (**de** of).

coteau, -x [kɔto] *nm* (small) hill; (*versant*) hillside.

côtelé [kotle] *am* **velours c.** cord(uroy).

côtelette [kotlɛt] *nf* (*d'agneau, de porc*) chop; (*de veau*) cutlet.

côtier, -ière [kotje, -jɛr] *a* coastal.

cotiser [kɔtize] *vi* to contribute (**à** to, **pour** towards); **c. (à)** (*club*) to subscribe (to) ‖ **se c.** *vpr* to club together (**pour acheter** to buy). •**cotisation** *nf* (*de club*) dues, subscription; (*de retraite etc*) contribution(s).

coton [kɔtɔ̃] *nm* cotton; **c. (hydrophile)** cotton wool, *Am* (absorbent) cotton.

côtoyer [kotwaje] *vt* **c. qn** (*fréquenter*) to rub shoulders with s.o.

cou [ku] *nm* neck; **sauter au c. de qn** to throw one's arms around s.o.; **jusqu'au c.** *Fig* up to one's eyes *ou* ears.

couchage [kuʃaʒ] *nm* **sac de c.** sleeping bag.

couche [kuʃ] *nf* **1** (*épaisseur*) layer; (*de peinture*) coat; **couches sociales** social strata. **2** (*pour bébé*) nappy, *Am* diaper. **3 faire une fausse c.** *Méd* to have a miscarriage.

coucher [kuʃe] *vt* to put to bed; (*héberger*) to put up; (*allonger*) to lay (down *ou* out) ‖ *vi* to sleep (**avec** with) ‖ **se c.** *vpr* to go to bed; (*s'allonger*) to lie flat *ou* down; (*soleil*) to set, go down ‖ *nm* **c. de soleil** sunset. •**couchant** *a* (*soleil*) setting. •**couché** *a* **être c.** to be in bed; (*étendu*) to be lying (down).

couchette [kuʃɛt] *nf* (*de train*) sleeper, sleeping berth; (*de bateau*) bunk.

coucou [kuku] *nm* (*oiseau*) cuckoo; (*pendule*) cuckoo clock; (*fleur*) cowslip.

coude [kud] *nm* elbow; (*de chemin, rivière*) bend; **se serrer les coudes** to help one another, stick together; **c. à c.** side by side; **coup de c.** nudge; **pousser du c.** to nudge.

coudre* [kudr] *vti* to sew.

couenne [kwan] *nf* (pork) crackling.

couette [kwɛt] *nf* (*édredon*) duvet, continental quilt.

couffin [kufɛ̃] *nm* (*de bébé*) Moses basket, *Am* bassinet.

coul/er[1] [kule] *vi* (*eau etc*) to flow; (*robinet, nez, sueur*) to run; (*fuir*) to leak. •**—ée** *nf* **c. de lave** lava flow.

couler[2] [kule] *vi* (*bateau, nageur*) to sink; **c. à pic** to sink to the bottom ‖ *vt* to sink.

couleur [kulœr] *nf* colour; (*colorant*) paint; *Cartes* suit; *pl* (*teint*) colour; **c. chair** flesh-coloured; **de c.** (*homme, habit etc*) coloured; **photo/***etc* **en couleurs** colour photo/*etc*; **téléviseur c.** colour TV set.

couleuvre [kulœvr] *nf* (grass) snake.

coulisses [kulis] *nfpl* **dans les c.** *Th* in the wings, backstage.

coulissant [kulisɑ̃] *a* (*porte etc*) sliding.

couloir [kulwar] *nm* corridor; (*de circulation, d'une piste*) lane; (*dans un bus*) gangway.

coup [ku] *nm* blow, knock; (*léger*) tap, touch; (*choc moral*) blow; (*de fusil etc*) shot; (*de crayon, d'horloge*) & *Sp* stroke; (*aux échecs etc*) move; (*fois*) *Fam* time; **donner des coups à** to hit; **c. de brosse** brush(-up); **c. de chiffon** wipe (with a rag); **c. de sonnette** ring (on a bell); **c. de dents** bite; **c. de chance** stroke of luck; **c. d'État** coup; **c. dur** *Fam* nasty blow; **mauvais c.** piece of mischief; **c. franc** *Fb* free kick; **tenter le c.** *Fam* to have a go; **réussir son c.** to bring it off; **faire les quatre cents coups** to get into all kinds of mischief; **tenir le c.** to hold out; **avoir/attraper le c.** to have/get the knack; **sous le c. de** (*émotion etc*) under the influence of; **il est dans le c.** *Fam* he's in the know; **après c.** afterwards, after the event; **sur le c. de midi** on the stroke of twelve; **tué sur le c.** killed outright; **à c. sûr** for sure; **c. sur c.** (*à la suite*) one after the other; **tout à c., tout d'un c.** suddenly; **d'un seul c.** in one go; **du premier c.** *Fam* (at the) first go; **du c.** (*de ce fait*) as a result; **pour le c.** this time.

coupable [kupabl] *a* guilty (**de** of); **déclarer c.** *Jur* to convict, find guilty ‖ *nmf* guilty person, culprit.

coupe [kup] *nf* **1** (*trophée*) cup; (*à fruits*) dish; (*à boire*) goblet, glass. **2** (*de vêtement etc*) cut; **c. de cheveux** haircut.

coupe-ongles [kupɔ̃gl] *nm inv* (nail) clippers. •**c.-papier** *nm inv* paper knife. •**c.-vent** *nm* windcheater, *Am* windbreaker.

couper [kupe] *vt* to cut; (*arbre*) to cut down; (*téléphone, vivres etc*) to cut off; (*courant*) to switch off; (*faim, souffle etc*) to take away; (*vin*) to water down; (*morceler*) to cut up; (*croiser*) to cut across; **c. la parole à qn** to cut s.o. short.
‖ *vi* to cut; **ne coupez pas!** *Tél* hold the line!
‖ **se couper** *vpr* (*routes*) to intersect; **se c. au doigt** to cut one's finger. •**coupant** *a* sharp.

couple [kupl] *nm* couple.

couplet [kuplɛ] *nm* verse.

coupole [kupɔl] *nf* dome.

coupon [kupɔ̃] *nm* (*tissu*) remnant, odd-

ment; (*ticket*, *titre*) coupon; **c. réponse** reply coupon.
coupure [kupyr] *nf* cut; (*de journal*) cutting, *Am* clipping; (*billet*) banknote, *Am* bill; **c. d'électricité** blackout, power cut.
cour [kur] *nf* **1** court(yard); **c. (de récréation)** *Scol* playground, *Am* school yard. **2** (*de roi*) & *Jur* court. **3** (*de femme*, *d'homme*) courtship; **faire la c. à qn** to court s.o.
courage [kuraʒ] *nm* courage; **perdre c.** to lose heart *ou* courage; **s'armer de c.** to pluck up courage; **bon c.!** good luck! •**courageux, -euse** *a* courageous.
couramment [kuramɑ̃] *adv* (*parler*) fluently; (*souvent*) frequently.
courant [kurɑ̃] **1** *a* (*fréquent*) common; (*modèle*, *taille*) standard; (*compte*, *langage*) current; (*affaires*) routine; **eau courante** running water. **2** *nm* (*de l'eau*, *électrique*) current; **c. d'air** draught, *Am* draft; **dans le c. de** (*mois etc*) during the course of; **être/mettre au c.** to know/tell (**de** about).
courbature [kurbatyr] *nf* (muscular) ache. •**courbaturé** *a* aching (all over).
courbe [kurb] *a* curved ‖ *nf* curve. •**courber** *vti* to bend ‖ **se c.** *vpr* to bend (over).
courgette [kurʒɛt] *nf* courgette, *Am* zucchini.
courir* [kurir] *vi* to run; (*se hâter*) to rush; (*à bicyclette*, *en auto*) to race; **en courant** (*vite*) in a rush; **le bruit court que...** there's a rumour going around that...; **faire c.** (*nouvelle*) to spread.
‖ *vt* (*risque*) to run; (*épreuve sportive*) to run (in); (*danger*) to face; (*magasins*, *cafés*) to go round; (*filles*) to run after. •**coureur** *nm* *Sp etc* runner; (*cycliste*) cyclist; (*automobile*) racing driver.
couronne [kurɔn] *nf* (*de roi*, *dent*) crown; (*pour enterrement*) wreath. •**couronner** (*roi etc*) *vt* to crown. •**couronnement** *nm* (*de roi etc*) coronation.
courrier [kurje] *nm* post, mail; **par retour du c.** by return of post, *Am* by return mail.
courroie [kurwa] *nf* (*attache*) strap; (*de transmission*) *Tech* belt.
cours [kur] *nm* **1** (*de maladie*, *rivière*, *astre*, *pensées etc*) course; (*d'une monnaie etc*) rate; **c. d'eau** river, stream; **suivre son c.** (*déroulement*) to follow its course; **en c.** (*travail*) in progress; (*année*) current; (*affaires*) outstanding; **en c. de route** on the way; **au c. de** during.
2 (*leçon*) class; (*série de leçons*) course; (*conférence*) lecture; **c. magistral** lecture; **faire c.** (*professeur*) to teach.
course[1] [kurs] *nf* (*action*) run(ning); (*épreuve de vitesse*) & *Fig* race; *pl* (*de chevaux*) races; **cheval de c.** racehorse; **voiture de c.** racing car.
course[2] [kurs] *nf* (*commission*) errand; *pl* (*achats*) shopping; **faire une c.** to run an errand; **faire les courses** to do the shopping.
coursier, -ière [kursje, -jɛr] *nmf* messenger.
court [kur] **1** *a* short ‖ *adv* (*couper*, *s'arrêter*) short; **tout c.** quite simply; **à c. de** (*argent etc*) short of; **pris de c.** caught unawares. **2** *nm* *Tennis* court. •**c.-circuit** *nm* (*pl* **courts-circuits**) *Él* short circuit. •**c.-circuiter** *vt* to short-circuit.
courtois [kurtwa] *a* courteous. •**courtoisie** *nf* courtesy.
couru [kury] *a* **c'est c. (d'avance)** *Fam* it's a sure thing.
couscous [kuskus] *nm* *Culin* couscous.
cousin, -ine [kuzɛ̃, -in] *nmf* cousin.
coussin [kusɛ̃] *nm* cushion.
cousu [kuzy] *a* sewn; **c. main** handsewn.
coût [ku] *nm* cost. •**coûter** *vti* to cost; **ça coûte combien?** how much is it?, how much does it cost?; **coûte que coûte** at all costs; **c. les yeux de la tête** to cost the earth. •**coûtant** *am* **prix c.** cost price.
coûteux, -euse [kutø, -øz] *a* costly, expensive.
couteau, -x [kuto] *nm* knife; **coup de c.** stab; **retourner le c. dans la plaie** *Fig* to rub it in.
coutume [kutym] *nf* custom; **avoir c. de faire** to be accustomed to doing; **comme de c.** as usual.
couture [kutyr] *nf* sewing, needlework; (*métier*) dressmaking; (*raccord*) seam; **maison de c.** fashion house. •**couturier** *nm* fashion designer. •**couturière** *nf* dressmaker.
couvent [kuvɑ̃] *nm* (*pour religieuses*) convent; (*pour moines*) monastery.
couv/er [kuve] *vt* (*œufs*) to sit on, hatch; (*rhume etc*) to be getting; **c. des yeux** to look at enviously ‖ *vi* (*poule*) to brood; (*feu*) to smoulder; (*mal*, *complot*) to be brewing. •**—ée** *nf* (*oiseaux*) brood. •**couveuse** *nf* (*pour nouveaux-nés*, *œufs*) incubator.
couvercle [kuvɛrkl] *nm* lid, cover.
couvert [kuvɛr] **1** *nm* (*cuillère*, *fourchette*, *couteau*) (set of) cutlery; **mettre le c.** to set *ou* lay the table; **table de cinq couverts** table set *ou* laid for five. **2** *nm* **se mettre à c.** to take cover. **3** *a* covered (**de** with, in); (*ciel*) overcast.

couverture [kuvɛrtyr] *nf* (*de lit*) blanket; (*de livre etc*) cover; **c. chauffante** electric blanket.
couvre-feu [kuvrəfø] *nm* (*pl* **-x**) curfew. ●**c.-lit** *nm* bedspread. ●**c.-pied** *nm* quilt.
couvrir* [kuvrir] *vt* to cover (**de** with); (*voix*) to drown ‖ **se c.** *vpr* (*s'habiller*) to wrap up, cover up; (*se coiffer*) to cover one's head; (*ciel*) to cloud over. ●**couvreur** *nm* roofer.
cow-boy [kɔbɔj] *nm* cowboy.
crabe [krab] *nm* crab.
cracher [kraʃe] *vi* to spit ‖ *vt* to spit (out). ●**crachat** *nm* spit, spittle.
crack [krak] *nm Fam* ace, wizard, real champ.
craie [krɛ] *nf* chalk.
craindre* [krɛ̃dr] *vt* (*personne, mort, douleur etc*) to be afraid of, fear; (*chaleur, froid etc*) to be sensitive to; **c. de faire** to be afraid of doing *ou* to do; **je crains qu'elle (ne) vienne** I'm afraid *ou* I fear (that) she might come; **c. pour qch** to fear for sth; **ne craignez rien** don't be afraid, have no fear.
crainte [krɛ̃t] *nf* fear; **de c. de faire** for fear of doing; **de c. que (... ne)** (+ *sub*) for fear that. ●**craintif, -ive** *a* timid.
cramoisi [kramwazi] *a* crimson.
crampe [krɑ̃p] *nf Méd* cramp.
cramponner (se) [səkrɑ̃pɔne] *vpr* **se c. à** to hold on to, cling to.
crampons [krɑ̃pɔ̃] *nmpl* (*de chaussures*) studs.
cran [krɑ̃] *nm* **1** (*entaille*) notch; (*de ceinture*) hole; **c. d'arrêt** catch; **couteau à c. d'arrêt** flick-knife, *Am* switchblade; **c. de sûreté** safety catch. **2** (*audace*) *Fam* pluck, guts.
crâne [krɑn] *nm* skull; (*tête*) *Fam* head. ●**crânienne** *af* **boîte c.** skull, cranium.
crapaud [krapo] *nm* toad.
crapule [krapyl] *nf* villain, scoundrel.
craqueler [krakle] *vt*, **se c.** *vpr* to crack.
craqu/er [krake] *vi* (*branche*) to snap; (*bois sec*) to crack; (*sous la dent*) to crunch; (*se déchirer*) to split, rip; (*personne*) to break down, reach breaking point. ●**—ement** *nm* snapping *ou* cracking (sound).
crasse [kras] *nf* filth. ●**crasseux, -euse** *a* filthy.
cratère [kratɛr] *nm* crater.
cravache [kravaʃ] *nf* horsewhip, riding crop.
cravate [kravat] *nf* (*autour du cou*) tie.
crawl [krol] *nm* (*nage*) crawl.
crayon [krɛjɔ̃] *nm* (*en bois*) pencil; **c. de couleur** coloured pencil; (*en cire*) crayon; **c. à bille** ballpoint (pen). ●**crayonner** *vt* to pencil.
créateur, -trice [kreatœr, -tris] *nmf* creator. ●**créatif, -ive** *a* creative. ●**création** *nf* creation. ●**créativité** *nf* creativity.
créature [kreatyr] *nf* (*être*) creature.
crèche [krɛʃ] *nf* (*de Noël*) manger, crib; (*pour bébé*) (day) nursery, crèche.
crédit [kredi] *nm* (*influence*) & *Fin* credit; *pl* (*sommes*) funds; **à c.** (*acheter*) on credit, on hire purchase; **faire c.** (*prêter*) to give credit (**à** to). ●**créditeur, -euse** *a* **compte c.** account in credit; **solde c.** credit balance.
créer [kree] *vt* to create.
crémaillère [kremajɛr] *nf* **pendre la c.** to have a house-warming (party).
crématorium [krematɔrjɔm] *nm* crematorium, *Am* crematory.
crème [krɛm] *nf* cream; (*dessert*) cream dessert; **café c.** white coffee, coffee with cream *ou* milk; **c. Chantilly** whipped cream; **c. glacée** ice cream; **c. à raser** shaving cream; **c. anglaise** custard ‖ *a inv* cream(-coloured). ●**crémerie** *nf* (*magasin*) dairy (shop). ●**crémeux, -euse** *a* creamy. ●**crémier, -ière** *nmf* dairyman, dairywoman.
créneau, -x [kreno] *nm Hist* crenellation; *Com* gap; *TV Rad* slot; **faire un c.** *Aut* to park between two vehicles.
créole [kreɔl] *nmf* Creole ‖ *nm Ling* Creole.
crêpe [krɛp] **1** *nf Culin* pancake. **2** *nm* (*tissu*) crepe; (*caoutchouc*) crepe (rubber). ●**crêperie** *nf* pancake bar.
crépiter [krepite] *vi* to crackle.
crépu [krepy] *a* (*cheveux, personne*) frizzy.
crépuscule [krepyskyl] *nm* twilight, dusk.
cresson [kresɔ̃] *nm* (water)cress.
crête [krɛt] *nf* (*de montagne, d'oiseau*) crest; **c. de coq** cockscomb.
Crète [krɛt] *nf* Crete.
crétin, -ine [kretɛ̃, -in] *nmf* cretin, idiot.
creuser [krøze] **1** *vt* (*terre, sol*) to dig (a hole *ou* holes in); (*trou, puits*) to dig; (*évider*) to hollow (out); **c. l'estomac** to whet the appetite. **2 se creuser** *vpr* (*joues etc*) to become hollow; **se c. la tête** *ou* **la cervelle** to rack one's brains.
creux, -euse [krø, -øz] *a* (*tube, joues, paroles etc*) hollow; (*estomac*) empty; (*sans activité*) slack; **assiette creuse** soup plate ‖ *nm* hollow; (*de l'estomac*) pit; (*moment*) slack period.
crevaison [krəvɛzɔ̃] *nf* (*de pneu*) puncture, flat.
crevasse [krəvas] *nf* (*trou*) crevice, crack; (*de glacier*) crevasse.

crever [krəve] *vi* (*bulle, pneu etc*) to burst; (*mourir*) *Fam* to die; **c. de faim** *Fam* to be starving ▮ *vt* to burst; (*œil*) to put *ou* knock out; **c. qn** *Fam* to wear s.o. out; **ça (vous) crève les yeux** *Fam* it's staring you in the face. ●**crevant** *a* (*fatigant*) *Fam* exhausting. ●**crevé** *a* (*fatigué*) *Fam* worn out; (*mort*) *Fam* dead.

crevette [krəvɛt] *nf* (*grise*) shrimp; (*rose*) prawn.

cri [kri] *nm* (*de joie, surprise*) cry, shout; (*de peur*) scream; (*de douleur, d'alarme*) cry; (*appel*) call, cry.

criard [krijar] *a* (*son*) screeching; (*couleur*) gaudy, showy.

criblé [krible] *a* **c. de** (*balles, dettes etc*) riddled with.

cric [krik] *nm Aut* jack.

crier [krije] *vi* to shout (out), cry (out); (*de peur*) to scream; (*oiseau*) to chirp; **c. après qn** *Fam* to shout at s.o. ▮ *vt* (*injure, ordre*) to shout (out); (*son innocence etc*) to proclaim.

G204 Word Order: Inversion 12 A 7b)

crime [krim] *nm* crime; (*assassinat*) murder. ●**criminalité** *nf* crime (in general). ●**criminel, -elle** *a* criminal ▮ *nmf* criminal; (*assassin*) murderer.

crinière [krinjɛr] *nf* mane.

crique [krik] *nf* creek, cove.

criquet [krikɛ] *nm* locust.

crise [kriz] *nf* crisis; (*accès*) attack; (*de colère etc*) fit; (*pénurie*) shortage; **c. de conscience** (moral) dilemma.

crisp/er [krispe] *vt* (*visage*) to make tense; (*poing*) to clench; (*muscle*) to tense; **c. qn** *Fam* to aggravate s.o. ●**—ant** *a* aggravating. ●**—é** *a* (*personne*) tense.

crisser [krise] *vi* (*pneu, roue*) to screech; (*neige*) to crunch.

cristal, -aux [kristal, -o] *nm* crystal; *pl* (*objets*) crystal(ware).

critère [kritɛr] *nm* criterion.

critiquable [kritikabl] *a* open to criticism.

critique [kritik] *a* critical ▮ *nf* (*reproche*) criticism; (*analyse de film, livre etc*) review; (*de texte*) critique; **faire la c. de** (*film etc*) to review ▮ *nm* critic. ●**critiquer** *vt* to criticize.

croasser [krɔase] *vi* (*corbeau*) to caw.

Croatie [krɔasi] *nf* Croatia.

croc [kro] *nm* (*dent*) fang.

croc-en-jambe [krɔkɑ̃ʒɑ̃b] *nm* (*pl* **crocs-en-jambe**) = **croche-pied**.

croche-pied [krɔʃpje] *nm* **faire un c.-pied à qn** to trip s.o. up.

crochet [krɔʃɛ] *nm* (*pour accrocher*) & *Boxe* hook; (*aiguille*) crochet hook; (*travail*) crochet; *Typ* (square) bracket; **faire qch au c.** to crochet sth; **faire un c.** (*personne*) to make a detour *ou* side trip.

crochu [krɔʃy] *a* (*nez*) hooked.

crocodile [krɔkɔdil] *nm* crocodile.

crocus [krɔkys] *nm Bot* crocus.

croire** [krwar] *vt* to believe; (*estimer*) to think, believe (**que** that); **j'ai cru la voir** I thought I saw her; **je crois que oui** I think *ou* believe so; **je n'en crois pas mes yeux** I can't believe my eyes; **il se croit malin/quelque chose** he thinks he's smart/quite something ▮ *vi* to believe (**à, en** in).

G100 The Subjunctive 7 G 1e)

croiser [krwaze] *vt* (*jambes, ligne etc*) to cross; (*bras*) to fold, cross; **c. qn** to pass *ou* meet s.o.

▮ **se croiser** *vpr* (*voitures etc*) to pass *ou* meet (each other); (*routes*) to cross, intersect; (*lettres*) to cross in the post *ou* mail. ●**croisé** *a* (*bras*) folded, crossed; (*veston*) double-breasted; **mots croisés** crossword. ●**croisement** *nm* (*de routes*) crossroads, intersection; (*action*) crossing; (*de véhicules*) passing.

croisière [krwazjɛr] *nf* cruise.

croître* [krwatr] *vi* (*plante etc*) to grow; (*augmenter*) to grow, increase. ●**croissant** **1** *nm* crescent; (*pâtisserie*) croissant. **2** *a* (*nombre etc*) growing. ●**croissance** *nf* growth.

croix [krwa] *nf* cross.

croque-monsieur [krɔkməsjø] *nm inv* toasted cheese and ham sandwich. ●**c.-mort** *nm Fam* undertaker's assistant.

croqu/er [krɔke] *vt* (*manger*) to crunch ▮ *vi* (*fruit etc*) to be crunchy. ●**—ant** *a* (*biscuit etc*) crunchy. ●**croquette** *nf Culin* croquette.

croquis [krɔki] *nm* sketch.

crosse [krɔs] *nf* (*de fusil*) butt; (*de hockey*) stick; (*d'évêque*) crook.

crotte [krɔt] *nf* (*de lapin etc*) droppings, mess. ●**crottin** *nm* (horse) dung.

crouler [krule] *vi* **c. sous une charge** (*porteur*) to totter beneath a burden.

croupe [krup] *nf* (*de cheval*) rump. ●**croupion** *nm* (*de poulet*) parson's nose, *Am* pope's nose.

croupier [krupje] *nm* (*au casino*) croupier.

croupir [krupir] *vi* (*eau*) to stagnate, become foul.

croustill/er [krustije] *vi* to be crusty; to be crunchy. ●**—ant** *a* (*pain*) crusty; (*biscuit*) crunchy.

croûte [krut] *nf* (*de pain etc*) crust; (*de*

fromage) rind; (*de plaie*) scab; **casser la c.** *Fam* to have a snack. •**croûton** *nm* crust (*at end of loaf*); *pl* (*avec soupe*) croûtons.
croyable [krwajabl] *a* credible, believable. •**croyance** *nf* belief (**à, en** in). •**croyant, -ante** *a* **être c.** to be a believer ‖ *nmf* believer.
CRS [seɛrɛs] *nmpl abrév* (*Compagnies républicaines de sécurité*) riot police, State security police.
cru[1] [kry] *pp de* **croire.**
cru[2] [kry] **1** *a* (*aliment etc*) raw; (*propos*) crude. **2** *nm* (*vignoble*) vineyard; **un grand c.** (*vin*) a vintage wine.
cruauté [kryote] *nf* cruelty (**envers** to).
cruche [kryʃ] *nf* pitcher, jug.
crucial, -aux [krysjal, -o] *a* crucial.
crucifier [krysifje] *vt* to crucify. •**crucifix** [krysifi] *nm* crucifix. •**crucifixion** *nf* crucifixion.
crudités [krydite] *nfpl Culin* assorted raw vegetables.
crue [kry] *nf* (*de cours d'eau*) swelling, flood; **en c.** in spate.
cruel, -elle [kryɛl] *a* cruel (**envers, avec** to).
crustacés [krystase] *nmpl* shellfish.
crypte [kript] *nf* crypt.
Cuba [kyba] *nm* Cuba. •**cubain, -aine** *a* & *nmf* Cuban.
cube [kyb] *nm* cube; *pl* (*jeu*) building blocks ‖ *a* (*mètre etc*) cubic.
cueillir* [kœjir] *vt* to pick, gather. •**cueillette** *nf* picking, gathering; (*fruits cueillis*) harvest.
cuiller, cuillère [kɥijɛr] *nf* spoon; **petite c., c. à café** teaspoon; **c. à soupe** soup spoon, tablespoon. •**cuillerée** *nf* spoonful; **c. à café** teaspoonful; **c. à soupe** tablespoonful.
cuir [kɥir] *nm* leather; (*peau épaisse d'un animal vivant*) hide; **c. chevelu** scalp.
cuire* [kɥir] *vt* to cook; (*à l'eau*) to boil; **c. (au four)** to bake; (*viande*) to roast ‖ *vi* to cook; to boil; to bake; to roast; **faire c.** to cook.
cuisant [kɥizɑ̃] *a* (*affront, blessure etc*) stinging.
cuisine [kɥizin] *nf* (*pièce*) kitchen; (*art*) cookery, cooking; (*aliments, préparation*) cooking; **faire la c.** to cook, do the cooking; **livre de c.** cook(ery) book; **haute c.** high-class cooking. •**cuisiner** *vti* to cook. •**cuisinier, -ière** *nmf* cook. •**cuisinière** (*appareil*) cooker, stove, *Am* range.
cuisse [kɥis] *nf* thigh; (*de poulet, mouton*) leg.
cuisson [kɥisɔ̃] *nm* cooking.
cuit [kɥi] *pp de* **cuire** ‖ *a* cooked; **bien c.** well done *ou* cooked.
cuivre [kɥivr] *nm* (*rouge*) copper; (*jaune*) brass.
cul [ky] *nm* (*derrière*) *Fam* backside; (*de bouteille etc*) bottom. •**c.-de-sac** *nm* (*pl* **culs-de-sac**) dead end, cul-de-sac.
culbute [kylbyt] *nf* (*saut*) sommersault; (*chute*) (backward) tumble; **faire une c.** to sommersault; to tumble. •**culbuter** *vt* (*personne, chaise*) to knock over.
culminant [kylminɑ̃] *a* **point c.** (*de réussite, montagne etc*) peak.
culot [kylo] *nm* (*aplomb*) *Fam* nerve, cheek. •**culotté** *a* **être c.** *Fam* to have plenty of nerve *ou* cheek.
culotte [kylɔt] *nf Sp* (pair of) shorts; (*de femme*) (pair of) knickers *ou Am* panties; **culottes (courtes)** (*de jeune garçon*) short trousers *ou Am* pants; **c. de cheval** riding breeches.
culpabilité [kylpabilite] *nf* guilt.
culte [kylt] *nm* (*de dieu*) worship; (*religion*) form of worship, religion; (*service protestant*) service; (*admiration*) *Fig* cult.
cultiver [kyltive] *vt* (*terre*) to farm, cultivate; (*plantes*) to grow ‖ **se c.** *vpr* to improve one's mind. •**cultivé** *a* (*esprit, personne*) cultured, cultivated. •**cultivateur, -trice** *nmf* farmer.
culture [kyltyr] *nf* **1** (*action, agriculture*) farming; (*de légumes*) growing; *pl* (*terres*) fields (under cultivation); (*plantes*) crops. **2** (*éducation, civilisation*) culture; **c. générale** general knowledge. •**culturel, -elle** *a* cultural.
cumuler [kymyle] *vt* **c. deux fonctions** to hold two offices (at the same time).
cupide [kypid] *a* avaricious. •**cupidité** *nf* avarice.
curable [kyrabl] *a* curable.
cure [kyr] *nf* **1** (course of) treatment, cure. **2** (*résidence*) presbytery. •**curé** *nm* (parish) priest.
curer [kyre] *vt* to clean out; **se c. le nez/les dents** to pick one's nose/teeth. •**cure-dent** *nm* toothpick. •**cure-ongles** *nm inv* nail cleaner. •**cure-pipe** *nm* pipe cleaner.
curieux, -euse [kyrjø, -øz] *a* (*bizarre*) curious; (*indiscret*) inquisitive, curious (**de** about); **c. de savoir** curious to know ‖ *nmf* inquisitive person; (*badaud*) onlooker. •**curiosité** *nf* (*de personne, forme etc*) curiosity; (*chose*) curiosity; (*spectacle*) unusual sight.
curriculum (vitæ) [kyrikylɔm(vite)] *nm inv*

curriculum (vitae), *Am* résumé.

curseur [kyrsœr] *nm* (*d'un ordinateur*) cursor.

cuve [kyv] *nf* vat; (*réservoir*) & *Phot* tank. • **cuvée** *nf* (*récolte de vin*) vintage. • **cuvette** *nf* (*récipient*) & *Géog* basin, bowl; (*des toilettes*) bowl, pan.

CV [seve] *nm abrév* (*curriculum vitae*) CV, *Am* résumé.

cyanure [sjanyr] *nm* cyanide.

cycle [sikl] *nm* **1** (*série, révolution*) cycle. **2** (*bicyclette*) cycle. • **cyclable** *a* **piste c.** cycle path *ou* track. • **cyclique** *a* cyclic(al).

cyclisme [siklism] *nm Sp* cycling. • **cycliste** *nmf* cyclist ‖ *a* **course c.** cycle *ou* bicycle race; **champion c.** cycling champion; **coureur c.** racing cyclist.

cyclomoteur [siklɔmɔtœr] *nm* moped.

cyclone [siklon] *nm* cyclone.

cygne [siɲ] *nm* swan.

cylindre [silɛ̃dr] *nm* cylinder. • **cylindrée** *nf Aut* (engine) capacity. • **cylindrique** *a* cylindrical.

cymbale [sɛ̃bal] *nf* cymbal.

cynique [sinik] *a* cynical. • **cynisme** *nm* cynicism.

cyprès [siprɛ] *nm* (*arbre*) cypress.

D

D, d [de] *nm* D, d.

d' [d] *voir* **de**[1,2].

d'abord [dabɔr] *adv* (*en premier lieu, au début*) first.

dactylo [daktilo] *nf* (*personne*) typist; (*action*) typing. ●**dactylographie** *nf* typing. ●**dactylographier** *vt* to type.

dada [dada] *nm* (*manie*) hobby horse, pet subject.

dahlia [dalja] *nm* dahlia.

daigner [deɲe] *vt* **d. faire** to condescend to do.

daim [dɛ̃] *nm* fallow deer; (*mâle*) buck; (*cuir*) suede.

dalle [dal] *nf* paving stone; (*funèbre*) (flat) gravestone. ●**dallé** *a* (*pièce, cour etc*) paved.

daltonien, -ienne [daltɔnjɛ̃, -jɛn] *a & n* colour-blind (person).

dame [dam] *nf* **1** lady; (*mariée*) married lady. **2** *Échecs Cartes* queen; (*au jeu de dames*) king; **(jeu de) dames** draughts, *Am* checkers. ●**damier** *nm* draughtboard, *Am* checkerboard.

damner [dane] *vt* to damn; **faire d.** *Fam* to torment, drive mad.

dandiner (se) [sədɑ̃dine] *vpr* to waddle.

Danemark [danmark] *nm* Denmark. ●**danois, -oise** *a* Danish ‖ *nmf* Dane ‖ *nm* (*langue*) Danish.

danger [dɑ̃ʒe] *nm* danger; **en d.** in danger; **mettre en d.** to endanger; **en cas de d.** in an emergency; **en d. de mort** in mortal danger; **'d. de mort'** (*panneau*) 'danger'; **être sans d.** to be safe; **pas de d.!** *Fam* no way! ●**dangereux, -euse** *a* dangerous (**pour** to). ●**dangereusement** *adv* dangerously.

dans [dɑ̃] *prép* **1** in; (*changement de lieu*) into; (*à l'intérieur de*) inside; **d. le jardin** in the garden; **d. la boîte** in *ou* inside the box; **mettre d.** to put in(to); **entrer d.** to go in(to); **d. Paris** in Paris (itself); **d. un rayon de** within (a radius of); **marcher d. les rues** to walk through *ou* about the streets.

2 (*provenance*) from, out of; **boire/prendre/***etc* **d.** to drink/take/*etc* from *ou* out of.

3 (*temps futur*) in; **d. deux jours/***etc* in two days/*etc*, in two days'/*etc* time.

4 (*quantité approximative*) about; **d. les dix francs/***etc* (*quantité*) about ten francs/*etc*.

danse [dɑ̃s] *nf* dance; (*art*) dancing. ●**danser** *vti* to dance. ●**danseur, -euse** *nmf* dancer.

dard [dar] *nm* (*d'insecte*) sting.

date [dat] *nf* date; **de longue d.** (*amitié etc*) of long-standing; **en d. du...** dated the...; **d. d'expiration** expiry *or Am* expiration date; **d. limite** deadline; **d. limite de vente** sell-by date; **d. de naissance** date of birth.

dater [date] *vt* (*lettre etc*) to date ‖ *vi* (*être dépassé*) to date, be dated; **d. de** to date back to, date from; **à d. de** as from.

datte [dat] *nf* (*fruit*) date. ●**dattier** *nm* date palm.

dauphin [dofɛ̃] *nm* dolphin.

davantage [davɑ̃taʒ] *adv* (*quantité*) more; (*temps*) longer; **d. de temps/***etc* more time/*etc*; **d. que** more than; longer than.

de[1] [d(ə)] (**d'** *before a vowel or mute h*; **de + le = du, de + les = des**) *prép* **1** (*complément d'un nom*) of; **les rayons du soleil** the rays of the sun, the sun's rays; **le livre de Paul** Paul's book; **la ville de Paris** the city of Paris; **un pont de fer** an iron bridge; **une augmentation/diminution de salaire/***etc* an increase/decrease in salary/*etc*.

2 (*complément d'un adjectif*) **digne de** worthy of; **heureux de partir** happy to leave; **content de qch/qn** pleased with sth/s.o.

3 (*complément d'un verbe*) **parler de** to speak of *ou* about; **se souvenir de** to remember; **décider de faire** to decide to do; **traiter qn de lâche** to call s.o. a coward.

4 (*provenance: lieu & temps*) from; **venir/dater de** to come/date from; **mes amis du village** my friends from the village, my village friends.

5 (*agent*) **accompagné de** accompanied by.

6 (*moyen*) **armé de** armed with; **se nourrir de** to live on.

7 (*manière*) **d'une voix douce** in *ou* with a gentle voice.

8 (*cause*) **mourir de faim** to die of hunger; **sauter de joie** to jump for joy.

9 (*temps*) **travailler de nuit** to work by night; **six heures du matin** six o'clock in the morning.

10 (*mesure*) **avoir** *ou* **faire six mètres de haut, être haut de six mètres** to be six metres high; **homme de trente ans** thirty-year-old man; **gagner cent francs de l'heure** to earn a hundred francs an hour.

ⓘ**G103** The Subjunctive 7 G 2a)

ⓘ**G110** & **111** The Infinitive 7 H 2b) iii) & c)
ⓘ**G119** The Passive 7 J 1
ⓘ**G165**, **167**, **168** & **169** Verb Constructions 7 M 1c), 2c) & d) and 4
ⓘ**G175** Prepositions 8
ⓘ**G194** Expressions of Quantity 10 F
ⓘ**G220** Noun Phrases 13 B 7

de[2] [d(ə)] *art partitif* some; **elle boit du vin** she drinks (some) wine; **il ne boit pas de vin** (*négation*) he doesn't drink (any) wine; **il y en a six de tués** (*avec un nombre*) there are six killed.
ⓘ**G15** The Partitive Article 2 C

de[3] [d(ə)] *art indéf pl* **de, des** some; **des fleurs** (some) flowers; **de jolies fleurs** (some) pretty flowers; **d'agréables soirées** (some) pleasant evenings.
ⓘ**G14** The Indefinite Article 2 B

dé [de] *nm* (*à jouer*) dice; (*à coudre*) thimble; **jouer aux dés** to play dice.

déambuler [deɑ̃byle] *vi* to stroll.

débâcle [debɑkl] *nf Mil* rout; (*ruine*) downfall.

déball/er [debale] *vt* to unpack; (*étaler*) to display. ●**—age** *nm* unpacking; display.

débandade [debɑ̃dad] *nf* (mad) rush, stampede.

débarbouiller (se) [sədebarbuje] to wash one's face.

débarcadère [debarkadɛr] *nm* quay, wharf.

débardeur [debardœr] *nm* (*vêtement*) slipover, *Am* (sweater) vest.

débarqu/er [debarke] *vt* (*passagers*) to land; (*marchandises*) to unload ‖ *vi* (*passagers*) to land, disembark; (*être naïf*) *Fam* not to be quite with it; **d. chez qn** *Fam* to turn up suddenly at s.o.'s place. ●**—ement** *nm* landing; (*de marchandises*) unloading; *Mil* landing.

débarras [debara] *nm* lumber room, *Am* storeroom; **bon d.!** *Fam* good riddance! ●**débarrasser** *vt* (*chambre, table etc*) to clear (**de** of); **d. qn de** (*ennemi, soucis etc*) to rid s.o. of; (*manteau etc*) to relieve s.o. of; **se d. de** to get rid of.

débat [deba] *nm* discussion, debate. ●**débattre*** **1** *vt* to discuss; **d. (d')une question** to discuss *ou* debate a question; **prix à d.** price by arrangement. **2 se débattre** *vpr* to struggle *ou* fight (to get free).

débauche [deboʃ] *nf* debauchery. ●**débauché** *a* (*libertin*) debauched.

débaucher [deboʃe] *vt* **d. qn** (*licencier*) to lay s.o. off; (*détourner*) *Fam* to entice s.o. away from his work.

débile [debil] *a* (*esprit, enfant etc*) weak, feeble; *Péj Fam* idiotic.

débit [debi] *nm* **1** (*vente*) turnover, sales; (*de fleuve*) (rate of) flow; (*d'un orateur*) delivery; **d. de boissons** bar, café; **d. de tabac** tobacconist's shop, *Am* tobacco store. **2** (*compte*) debit.

débiter [debite] *vt* **1** (*découper*) to cut up, slice up (**en** into); (*dire*) *Péj* to utter, spout. **2** (*compte*) to debit. ●**débiteur, -trice** *nmf* debtor ‖ *a* **solde d.** debit balance; **son compte est d.** his account is in debit.

déblayer [debleje] *vt* (*terrain, décombres*) to clear.

débloquer [deblɔke] **1** *vt* (*mécanisme*) to unjam; (*freins*) to release; (*compte, prix, crédits*) to unfreeze. **2** *vi* (*divaguer*) *Fam* to talk nonsense.

déboires [debwar] *nmpl* disappointments.

déboiser [debwaze] *vt* (*terrain*) to clear (of trees).

déboît/er [debwate] **1** *vt* **se d. l'épaule**/*etc* to dislocate one's shoulder/*etc*. **2** *vi Aut* to pull out, change lanes. ●**—ement** *nm Méd* dislocation.

débonnaire [debɔnɛr] *a* good-natured.

déborder [debɔrde] *vi* (*fleuve, liquide*) to overflow; (*en bouillant*) to boil over; **l'eau déborde du vase** the water is running over the top of the vase *ou* is overflowing the vase; **d. de** (*vie, joie etc*) *Fig* to be bubbling over with.
‖ *vt* (*dépasser*) to go *ou* extend beyond; **débordé de travail/visites** snowed under with work/visits. ●**débordement** *nm* overflowing; (*de joie, activité*) outburst.

débouché [debuʃe] *nm* (*carrière*) (career) opening *ou* prospect; (*marché pour produit*) outlet.

déboucher [debuʃe] **1** *vt* (*bouteille*) to open, uncork; (*lavabo, tuyau*) to clear, unblock. **2** *vi* (*surgir*) to emerge, come out (**de** from); **d. sur** (*rue*) to lead out onto, lead into.

débourser [deburse] *vt* to pay out.

debout [d(ə)bu] *adv* standing (up); **mettre d.** (*planche etc*) to stand up, put upright; **se mettre d.** to stand *ou* get up; **se tenir** *ou* **rester d.** (*personne*) to stand (up), remain standing (up); **être d.** (*levé*) to be up (and about); **d.!** get up!; **ça ne tient pas d.** (*théorie etc*) that doesn't hold water.

déboutonner [debutɔne] *vt* to unbutton, undo.

débraillé [debrɑje] *a* (*tenue etc*) slovenly.

débrancher [debrɑ̃ʃe] *vt Él* to unplug, disconnect ‖ *vi* (*se détendre*) *Fam* to unwind, take a break.

débrayer [debreje] *vi* **1** *Aut* to press the clutch. **2** (*se mettre en grève*) to stop work.

débris [debri] *nmpl* fragments, scraps; (*restes*) remains; (*détritus*) rubbish, *Am* garbage.
débrouiller [debruje] **1** *vt* (*écheveau etc*) to unravel; (*affaire*) to sort out. **2 se débrouiller** *vpr Fam* to manage, get by; **se d. pour faire** to manage to do. • **débrouillard** *a* smart, resourceful.
débroussailler [debrusɑje] *vt* (*chemin*) to clear (of brushwood).
débusquer [debyske] *vt* (*gibier, personne*) to drive out, dislodge.
début [deby] *nm* beginning, start; **au d.** at the beginning; **faire ses débuts** (*sur la scène etc*) to make one's debut. • **débuter** *vi* to start, begin; (*dans une carrière*) to start out in life; (*sur la scène etc*) to make one's debut. • **debutant, -ante** *nmf* beginner.
déca [deka] *nm Fam* decaffeinated coffee.
décacheter [dekaʃte] *vt* (*lettre etc*) to open, unseal.
décadence [dekadɑ̃s] *nf* decadence, decay.
décaféiné [dekafeine] *a* decaffeinated.
décalcomanie [dekalkɔmani] *nf* (*image*) transfer, *Am* decal.
décal/er [dekale] *vt* **1** (*dans le temps*) to change the time of (*departure etc*); (*dans l'espace*) to shift *ou* move (slightly) (*chair etc*). **2** (*ôter les cales de*) to unwedge. • **—age** *nm* (*écart*) gap, discrepancy; **d. horaire** time difference; **souffrir du d. horaire** to suffer from jet lag.
décalquer [dekalke] *vt* (*dessin*) to trace.
décamper [dekɑ̃pe] *vi* to clear off.
décap/er [dekape] *vt* (*métal*) to clean, scrape down; (*surface peinte*) to strip. • **—ant** *nm* cleaning agent; (*pour enlever la peinture*) paint remover *ou* stripper.
décapiter [dekapite] *vt* to behead, decapitate.
décapotable [dekapɔtabl] *a & nf* (*voiture*) convertible.
décapsul/er [dekapsyle] *vt* **d. une bouteille** to take the top *ou* cap off a bottle. • **—eur** *nm* bottle-opener.
décarcasser (se) [sədekarkase] *vpr Fam* to flog oneself to death (**pour faire** doing).
décéd/er [desede] *vi* to die. • **—é** *a* deceased.
déceler [desle] *vt* (*trouver*) to detect.
décembre [desɑ̃br] *nm* December.
décennie [deseni] *nf* decade.
décent [desɑ̃] *a* (*bienséant, acceptable*) decent. • **décemment** [-amɑ̃] *adv* decently. • **décence** *nf* decency.
déception [desɛpsjɔ̃] *nf* disappointment. • **décevoir*** *vt* to disappoint. • **décevant** *a* disappointing.
décerner [desɛrne] *vt* (*prix etc*) to award.
décès [desɛ] *nm* death.
déchaîner [deʃene] *vt* (*colère, violence*) to unleash; **d. l'enthousiasme** to set off wild enthusiasm.
‖ **se déchaîner** *vpr* (*tempête, rires*) to break out; (*foule*) to run riot; (*personne*) to fly into a rage. • **déchaîné** *a* (*foule, flots*) wild, raging. • **déchaînement** [-ɛnmɑ̃] *nm* (*de rires, de haine etc*) outburst; (*de violence*) outbreak; **le d. de la tempête** the raging of the storm.
déchanter [deʃɑ̃te] *vi Fam* to become disillusioned.
décharge [deʃarʒ] *nf* **d. (publique)** (rubbish) dump *ou* tip, *Am* (garbage) dump; **d. (électrique)** (electric) shock; **recevoir une d. (électrique)** to get a shock.
décharger [deʃarʒe] *vt* to unload; (*batterie*) *Él* to discharge; **d. qn de** (*travail etc*) to relieve s.o. of ‖ **se d.** *vpr* (*batterie*) to go flat. • **déchargement** *nm* unloading.
déchausser (se) [sədeʃose] *vpr* to take one's shoes off; (*dent*) to get loose.
dèche [dɛʃ] *nf* **être dans la d.** *Fam* to be flat broke.
déchéance [deʃeɑ̃s] *nf* (*déclin*) decay, decline.
déchet [deʃɛ] *nm* **déchets** (*restes*) (*de viande etc*) scraps; (*industriels etc*) waste (products); (*ordures*) rubbish, *Am* garbage; **il y a du d.** there's some waste.
déchiffrer [deʃifre] *vt* (*message, mauvaise écriture*) to decipher.
déchiqueter [deʃikte] *vt* to tear to shreds.
déchirer [deʃire] *vt* (*page etc*) to tear (up), rip (up); (*vêtement*) to tear, rip; (*ouvrir*) to tear *ou* rip open; **d. l'air** (*bruit*) to pierce the air; **ce bruit me déchire les oreilles** this noise is ear- splitting.
‖ **se déchirer** *vpr* (*robe etc*) to tear, rip; **se d. un muscle** to tear a muscle. • **déchirant** *a* (*douloureux*) heart-breaking. • **déchirement** *nm* (*souffrance*) heartbreak. • **déchirure** *nf* tear, rip; **d. musculaire** torn muscle.
décider [deside] *vt* (*envoi, opération*) to decide on; **d. que** to decide that; **d. de faire** to decide to do; **d. qn (à faire)** to persuade s.o. (to do) ‖ *vi* **d. de** (*destin de qn*) to decide; (*voyage etc*) to decide on ‖ **se d.** *vpr* (*question*) to be decided; **se d. (à faire)** to make up one's mind (to do); **se d. pour qch** to decide on sth *ou* in favour of sth. • **décidé** *a* (*air, ton*) determined, decided; **c'est d.** it's settled; **être d. à faire** to be determined to do. • **décidément** *adv* undoubtedly.

décilitre [desilitr] *nm* decilitre.
décimal, -aux [desimal, -o] *a* decimal. ● **décimale** *nf* decimal.
décimètre [desimɛtr] *nm* decimetre; **double d.** ruler.
décisif, -ive [desizif, -iv] *a* decisive. ● **décision** *nf* decision (**de faire** to do); (*fermeté*) determination; **prendre une d.** to make a decision; **avec d.** decisively.
déclarer [deklare] *vt* to declare (**que** that); (*vol, décès etc*) to notify; **d. qn coupable** to convict s.o., find s.o. guilty; **d. la guerre** to declare war (**à** on) ‖ **se d.** *vpr* (*incendie, maladie*) to break out; (*s'expliquer*) to declare one's views; **se d. contre** to come out against. ● **déclaration** *nf* declaration; (*de vol etc*) notification; (*commentaire*) statement, comment; **d. d'impôts** tax return.
déclasser [deklɑse] *vt* (*livres etc*) to put out of order; (*hôtel etc*) to downgrade; **d. qn** *Sp* to relegate s.o. (in the placing).
déclencher [deklɑ̃ʃe] *vt* (*mécanisme*) to set *ou* trigger off, start (off); (*attaque*) to launch; (*provoquer*) *Fig* to trigger off (*crisis, reaction*) ‖ **se d.** *vpr* (*alarme etc*) to go off; (*attaque, grève*) to start. ● **déclenchement** *nm* (*d'un appareil*) release.
déclic [deklik] *nm* (*bruit*) click; (*mécanisme*) catch, trigger.
déclin [deklɛ̃] *nm* decline. ● **décliner 1** *vi* (*forces etc*) to decline, wane; (*jour*) to draw to a close. **2** *vt* (*refuser*) to decline.
décod/er [dekɔde] *vt* (*message*) to decode. ● **—eur** *nm* decoder.
décoiffer [dekwafe] *vt* **d. qn** to mess up s.o.'s hair; **se d.** to mess up one's hair.
décoincer [dekwɛ̃se] *vt* to unjam.
décoller [dekɔle] **1** *vi* (*avion etc*) to take off. **2** *vt* (*timbre etc*) to unstick ‖ **se d.** *vpr* to come unstuck. ● **décollage** *nm* (*d'avion*) takeoff.
décolleté [dekɔlte] *a* (*robe*) low-cut ‖ *nm* (*de robe*) low neckline.
décolorer [dekɔlɔre] *vt* (*tissu*) to fade, discolour; (*cheveux*) to bleach ‖ **se d.** *vpr* (*tissu*) to fade. ● **décoloration** *nf* discolo(u)ration; bleaching.
décombres [dekɔ̃br] *nmpl* rubble, ruins.
décommander [dekɔmɑ̃de] *vt* (*marchandises, invitation*) to cancel; (*invités*) to put off ‖ **se d.** *vpr* to cancel (one's appointment).
décomposer [dekɔ̃poze] *vt* to decompose ‖ **se d.** *vpr* (*pourrir*) to decompose; (*visage*) to become distorted.
décompresser [dekɔ̃prese] *vi Psy Fam* to unwind.
décompte [dekɔ̃t] *nm* deduction; (*détail*) breakdown. ● **décompter** *vt* to deduct.
déconcerter [dekɔ̃sɛrte] *vt* to disconcert.
déconfit [dekɔ̃fi] *a* downcast. ● **déconfiture** *nf* (state of) collapse *ou* defeat.
décongeler [dekɔ̃ʒle] *vt* **(faire) d.** (*aliment*) to thaw, defrost ‖ *vi* **mettre qch à d.** to thaw *ou* defrost sth.
déconnecter [dekɔnɛkte] *vt Él & Fig* to disconnect.
déconner [dekɔne] *vi* (*divaguer*) *Arg* to talk a lot of nonsense.
déconseiller [dekɔ̃seje] *vt* **d. qch à qn** to advise s.o. against sth; **d. à qn de faire** to advise s.o. against doing; **c'est déconseillé** it is not advisable.
déconsidérer [dekɔ̃sidere] *vt* to discredit.
décontenancer [dekɔ̃tnɑ̃se] *vt* to disconcert ‖ **se d.** *vpr* to lose one's composure.
décontracter [dekɔ̃trakte] *vt* (*muscle*) to relax ‖ **se d.** *vpr* to relax.
décor [dekɔr] *nm Th Cin etc* scenery, decor; (*paysage*) scenery; (*d'intérieur*) decoration; (*cadre, ambiance*) setting; **les décors** *Th etc* the scenery; **un d.** *Th etc* a set.
décorer [dekɔre] *vt* (*maison, soldat etc*) to decorate (**de** with). ● **décorateur, -trice** *nmf* (interior) decorator; *Th* stage designer. ● **décoratif, -ive** *a* decorative. ● **décoration** *nf* decoration.
décortiquer [dekɔrtike] *vt* (*graine*) to husk; (*homard etc*) to shell.
découdre [dekudr] *vt* to unstitch ‖ *vi* **en d. (avec qn)** *Fam* to fight it out (with s.o.) ‖ **se d.** *vpr* to come unstitched.
découp/er [dekupe] *vt* (*viande*) to carve; (*article de journal etc*) to cut out; **se d. sur** to stand out against. ● **—é** *a* (*côte*) jagged. ● **découpage** *nm* carving; cutting out; (*image*) cutout.
décourager [dekuraʒe] *vt* (*dissuader, démoraliser*) to discourage (**de faire** from doing) ‖ **se d.** *vpr* to get discouraged. ● **découragement** *nm* discouragement.
décousu [dekuzy] *a* unstitched; (*propos, idées*) *Fig* disconnected.
découverte [dekuvɛrt] *nf* discovery; **partir à la d.** to explore; **partir** *ou* **aller à la d. de qch** to go in search of sth.
découvrir* [dekuvrir] *vt* (*trésor, terre etc*) to discover; (*secret, vérité etc*) to find out, discover; (*casserole etc*) to take the lid off; (*dénuder*) to uncover, expose; (*voir*) to perceive; **d. que** to discover *ou* find out that ‖ **se d.** *vpr* (*dans son lit*) to push the bedclothes off; (*enlever son chapeau*) to take one's hat off; (*ciel*) to clear (up). ● **découvert 1** *a* (*terrain*) open; (*tête etc*) bare; **à d.**

exposed, unprotected; **agir à d.** to act openly. **2** *nm* (*d'un compte*) overdraft.

décrasser [dekrase] *vt* (*nettoyer*) to clean.

décrépit [dekrepi] *a* (*vieillard*) decrepit.

décret [dekrɛ] *nm* decree.

décrier [dekrije] *vt* to run down, disparage.

décrire* [dekrir] *vt* to describe.

décrocher[1] [dekrɔʃe] *vt* (*détacher*) to unhook; (*tableau*) to take down; (*obtenir*) *Fam* to get, land; **d. (le téléphone)** to pick up the phone ‖ **se d.** *vpr* (*tableau*) to fall down. • **décroché** *a* (*téléphone*) off the hook.

décrocher[2] [dekrɔʃe] *vi Fam* (*abandonner*) to give up; (*perdre le fil*) to be unable to follow, lose track.

décroître* [dekrwatr] *vi* to decrease, decline; (*eaux*) to subside; (*jours*) to draw in.

décrypter [dekripte] *vt* to decipher, decode.

déçu [desy] *pp de* **décevoir** ‖ *a* disappointed.

ⓘ**G98** The Subjunctive 7 ⓘ**G 1a)**

décupler [dekyple] *vti* to increase tenfold.

dédaigner [dedeɲe] *vt* (*personne, richesse etc*) to scorn, despise; (*repas*) to turn up one's nose at; (*ne pas tenir compte de*) to disregard. • **dédaigneux, -euse** *a* scornful (**de** of).

dédain [dedɛ̃] *nm* scorn, disdain (**pour, de** for).

dédale [dedal] *nm* maze, labyrinth.

dedans [d(ə)dɑ̃] *adv* inside; **de d.** from (the) inside; **en d.** on the inside; **au-d. (de), au d. (de)** inside; **tomber d.** (*trou*) to fall in (it); **mettre d.** (*tromper*) *Fam* to take in; **je me suis fait rentrer d.** (*accident de voiture*) *Fam* someone went into me ‖ *nm* **le d.** the inside.

dédicace [dedikas] *nf* dedication, inscription. • **dédicacer** *vt* (*livre etc*) to inscribe, dedicate (**à** to).

dédier [dedje] *vt* to dedicate.

dédire (se) [sədedir] *vpr* to go back on one's word.

dédommag/er [dedɔmaʒe] *vt* to compensate (**de** for). • **—ement** *nm* compensation.

dédouaner [dedwane] *vt* (*marchandises*) to clear through customs.

dédoubler [deduble] *vt* (*classe etc*) to split into two; **d. un train** to run an extra train ‖ **se d.** *vpr* to be in two places at once.

déduire* [dedɥir] *vt* (*retirer*) to deduct (**de** from); (*conclure*) to deduce (**de** from). • **déductible** *a* (*frais*) deductible. • **déduction** *nf* (*raisonnement*) & *Com* deduction.

déesse [deɛs] *nf* goddess.

défaillir* [defajir] *vi* (*s'évanouir*) to faint; (*forces, mémoire*) to fail; **sans d.** without flinching. • **défaillance** *nf* (*évanouissement*) fainting fit; (*faiblesse*) weakness; (*panne*) fault; **une d. cardiaque** heart failure.

défaire* [defɛr] *vt* (*nœud etc*) to undo, untie; (*valises*) to unpack; (*installation*) to take down; (*coiffure*) to mess up ‖ **se d.** *vpr* (*nœud etc*) to come undone *ou* untied; **se d. de** to get rid of. • **défait** *a* (*lit*) unmade; (*cheveux*) dishevelled, untidy; (*visage*) drawn.

défaite [defɛt] *nf* defeat.

défaut [defo] *nm* (*faiblesse de caractère*) fault, shortcoming; (*de fabrication*) defect; (*de diamant*) flaw; (*désavantage*) drawback; **le d. de la cuirasse** the chink in the armour; **faire d.** to be lacking; **le temps me fait d.** I lack time; **à d. de** for want of; **prendre qn en d.** to catch s.o. out; **ou, à d....** or, failing that....

défavorable [defavɔrabl] *a* unfavourable (**à** to). • **défavoriser** *vt* to put at a disadvantage, be unfair to.

défection [defɛksjɔ̃] *nf* defection, desertion; **faire d.** to desert; (*ne pas venir*) to fail to turn up.

défectueux, -euse [defɛktɥø, -øz] *a* faulty, defective.

défendre [defɑ̃dr] **1** *vt* (*protéger*) to defend (**contre** against) ‖ **se d.** *vpr* to defend oneself; **se d. de** (*pluie etc*) to protect oneself from; **se d. de faire** (*s'empêcher de*) to refrain from doing; **je me défends (bien) en anglais**/*etc Fam* I can hold my own in English/*etc*. **2** *vt* **d. à qn de faire qch** (*interdire*) to forbid s.o. to do sth, not allow s.o. to do sth; **d. qch à qn** to forbid s.o. sth.

ⓘ**G99** The Subjunctive 7 G 1b)

défense [defɑ̃s] *nf* **1** (*protection*) defence, *Am* defense; **sans d.** defenceless. **2** (*interdiction*) **'d. de fumer'** 'no smoking'; **'d. (absolue) d'entrer'** '(strictly) no entry'. **3** (*d'éléphant*) tusk. • **défenseur** *nm* defender; (*des faibles*) protector, defender. • **défensif, -ive** *a* defensive ‖ *nf* **sur la défensive** on the defensive.

déferler [defɛrle] *vi* (*vagues*) to break; **d. dans** *ou* **sur** (*foule*) to surge *ou* sweep into.

défi [defi] *nm* challenge; **lancer un d. à qn** to challenge s.o.; **mettre qn au d. de faire qch** to challenge *ou* defy s.o. to do sth; **relever un d.** to take up *ou* accept a challenge.

déficience [defisjɑ̃s] *nf Méd* deficiency.

déficit [defisit] *nm* deficit. • **déficitaire** *a* (*budget etc*) in deficit.

défier[1] [defje] *vt* (*provoquer*) to challenge (**à** to); **d. qn de faire** to challenge *ou* defy s.o. to do.

défier[2] **(se)** [sədefje] *vpr* **se d. de** *Litt* to distrust. • **défiance** *nf* distrust (**de** of).

défigur/er [defigyre] *vt* to disfigure. • **—é** *a* disfigured.

défilé [defile] *nm* **1** (*cortège*) procession; (*de manifestants*) march; *Mil* parade; (*de visiteurs*) stream. **2** *Géog* pass, gorge.

défiler [defile] *vi* (*manifestants, militaires*) to march (**devant** past); (*paysage, jours*) to pass by; (*visiteurs*) to keep coming and going; (*images*) to flash by (on the screen); *Ordinat* to scroll ‖ **se d.** *vpr Fam* (*s'éloigner*) to sneak off; (*éviter d'agir*) to cop out.

défin/ir [definir] *vt* to define. • **—i** *a* definite; **article d.** *Gram* definite article. • **définition** *nf* definition; (*de mots croisés*) clue.

définitif, -ive [definitif, -iv] *a* final, definitive ‖ *nf* **en définitive** in the final analysis, finally. • **définitivement** *adv* (*partir, exclure*) permanently, for good.

déflagration [deflagrɑsjɔ̃] *nf* explosion.

défoncer [defɔ̃se] **1** *vt* (*porte, mur etc*) to smash in *ou* down; (*trottoir, route etc*) to dig up. **2 se défoncer** *vpr* (*drogué*) *Fam* to get high (**à** on). • **défoncé** *a* **1** (*route*) full of potholes, bumpy. **2** (*drogué*) *Fam* high.

déformation [defɔrmɑsjɔ̃] *nf* distortion; (*de membre*) deformity; **c'est de la d. professionnelle** it's a case of being conditioned by one's job.

déformer [defɔrme] *vt* (*objet*) to put *ou* knock out of shape; (*doigt, main*) to deform ‖ **se d.** *vpr* to lose its shape. • **déformé** *a* (*objet*) misshapen; (*corps*) deformed; **chaussée déformée** uneven road surface, bumpy road.

défouler (se) [sədefule] *vpr Fam* to let off steam.

défrayer [defreje] *vt* **d. la chronique** to be the talk of the town.

défricher [defriʃe] *vt* (*terrain*) to clear (for cultivation).

défriser [defrize] *vt* (*cheveux*) to straighten.

défroisser [defrwase] *vt* (*papier*) to smooth out.

défroqué [defrɔke] *a* (*prêtre*) defrocked.

défunt, -unte [defœ̃, -œ̃t] *a* (*mort*) departed; **son d. mari** her late husband ‖ *nmf* **le d., la défunte** the deceased, the departed.

dégager [degaʒe] *vt* (*passage, voie*) to clear (**de** of); (*odeur*) to give off; (*idée, conclusion*) to bring out; **d. qn de** (*décombres*) to free s.o. from.
‖ *vi Fb* to clear the ball (down the pitch); **d.!** *Fam* clear the way!
‖ **se dégager** *vpr* (*rue, ciel*) to clear; **se d. (de)** (*personne*) to free oneself (from); **se d. de** (*odeur*) to come out of (*kitchen etc*). • **dégagé** *a* (*ciel*) clear; (*allure*) easy-going; (*vue*) open. • **dégagement** *nm* (*action*) clearing; *Fb* clearance, kick; **itinéraire de d.** *Aut* relief road.

dégainer [degene] *vti* (*arme*) to draw.

dégarnir [degarnir] *vt* to clear, empty; (*compte*) to strip; (*arbre de Noël*) to take down the decorations from ‖ **se d.** *vpr* (*crâne*) to go bald; (*salle*) to clear, empty. • **dégarni** *a* (*salle*) empty, bare; (*tête*) balding; **front d.** receding hairline.

dégâts [degɑ] *nmpl* damage; **limiter les d.** *Fig* to prevent matters getting worse, limit the damage.

dégel [deʒɛl] *nm* thaw. • **dégeler** *vt* to thaw (out); (*crédits*) to unfreeze ‖ *vi* to thaw (out) ‖ *v imp* to thaw ‖ **se d.** *vpr* (*personne, situation*) to thaw (out).

dégénér/er [deʒenere] *vi* to degenerate (**en** into). • **—é, -ée** *a* & *nmf* degenerate.

dégingandé [deʒɛ̃gɑ̃de] *a* gangling, lanky.

dégivrer [deʒivre] *vt* (*réfrigérateur*) to defrost; *Aut Av* to de-ice.

déglinguer (se) [sədeglɛ̃ge] *vpr Fam* to fall to bits. • **déglingué** *a* falling to bits.

dégonfler [degɔ̃fle] *vt* (*pneu etc*) to let the air out of, let down ‖ **se d.** *vpr* (*pneu etc*) to go down; (*se montrer lâche*) *Fam* to chicken out, get cold feet. • **dégonflé, -ée** *a* (*pneu*) flat; (*lâche*) *Fam* chicken, yellow ‖ *nmf Fam* yellow belly.

dégouliner [deguline] *vi* to trickle, drip.

dégourdi [degurdi] *a* (*malin*) smart, sharp.

dégourdir (se) [sədegurdir] *vpr* **se d. les jambes** to stretch one's legs.

dégoût [degu] *nm* disgust; **le d. de** (*la vie, les gens etc*) disgust for; **avoir du d. pour qch** to have a (strong) dislike *ou* distaste for sth. • **dégoûter** *vt* to disgust; **d. qn de qch** to put s.o. off sth, *Am* (be enough) to make s.o. sick of sth; **se d. de** to take a (strong) dislike to. • **dégoûtant** *a* disgusting. • **dégoûté** *a* disgusted; **d. de** sick of, disgusted with *ou* by; **elle est partie dégoûtée** she left in disgust; **il n'est pas d.** (*difficile*) he's not too fussy.

dégradation [degradɑsjɔ̃] *nf* degradation; (*de situation, état etc*) deterioration; *pl* (*dégâts*) damage.

dégrader [degrade] **1** *vt* (*avilir*) to degrade; (*mur etc*) to deface, damage ‖ **se d.** *vpr* (*édifice, situation*) to deteriorate. **2** *vt* (*couleur*) to shade off. • **dégradant** *a* degrading.

dégrafer [degrafe] *vt* (*vêtement*) to unfasten, undo.

dégraisser [degrese] *vt* **1** (*bœuf*) to take the fat off; (*bouillon*) to skim. **2** (*entreprise*) *Fam* to slim down (*by laying off workers*).

degré [dəgre] *nm* (*angle, température etc*) degree; **enseignement du premier/second d.** primary/secondary education; **au plus haut d.** (*avare etc*) extremely.

dégriffé [degrife] *a* **vêtement d.** unlabelled designer garment (*sold in seconds store*).

dégringoler [degrẽgɔle] *vi* to tumble (down); **faire d. qch** to topple sth over ‖ *vt* (*escalier*) to rush down. ●**dégringolade** *nf* tumble.

dégrossir [degrɔsir] *vt* (*travail*) to rough out.

déguerpir [degɛrpir] *vi* to clear off *ou* out, make tracks.

dégueulasse [degœlas] *a Fam* disgusting, lousy.

déguiser [degize] *vt* (*pour tromper*) to disguise; **d. qn en** (*costumer*) to dress s.o. up as ‖ **se d.** *vpr* to dress oneself up (**en** as); (*pour tromper*) to disguise oneself (**en** as). ●**déguisement** *nm* disguise; (*de bal costumé etc*) fancy dress, costume.

déguster [degyste] *vt* (*goûter*) to taste, sample; (*apprécier*) to relish. ●**dégustation** *nf* tasting, sampling.

dehors [dəɔr] *adv* outside, out; (*hors de chez soi*) out; **en d.** on the outside; **en d. de la maison**/*etc* outside the house/*etc*; **en d. de la ville/fenêtre** out of town/the window; **en d. de** (*excepté*) *Fig* apart from; **au-d. (de), au d. (de)** outside; **déjeuner/jeter**/*etc* **d.** to lunch/throw/*etc* out ‖ *nm* (*extérieur*) outside.

déjà [deʒa] *adv* already; **est-il d. parti?** has he left yet *ou* already?; **elle l'a d. vu** she's seen it before, she's already seen it; **c'est d. pas mal** *Fam* that's not bad at all; **quand partez-vous, d.?** *Fam* when did you say you are leaving?

déjeuner [deʒœne] *vi* (*à midi*) to (have) lunch; (*le matin*) to (have) breakfast ‖ *nm* lunch; **petit d.** breakfast.

déjouer [deʒwe] *vt* (*intrigue, plan*) to thwart, foil.

delà [d(ə)la] *adv* **au-d. (de), au d. (de)** beyond; **au-d. du pont**/*etc* beyond *ou* past the bridge/*etc*.

délabrer (se) [sədelabre] *vpr* (*édifice*) to become dilapidated; (*santé*) to give out, fail. ●**délabré** *a* dilapidated.

délacer [delase] *vt* (*chaussures*) to undo.

délai [delɛ] *nm* time limit; (*répit, sursis*) extra time, extension; **dans un d. de dix jours** within ten days; **sans d.** without delay; **dans les plus brefs délais** as soon as possible; **dernier d.** final date.

délaisser [delese] *vt* to neglect.

délasser (se) [sədelɑse] *vpr* to relax. ●**délassement** *nm* relaxation, diversion.

délavé [delave] *a* (*tissu, jean*) faded.

délayer [deleje] *vt* (*mélanger*) to mix (with liquid).

delco [dɛlko] *nm Aut* distributor.

délégu/er [delege] *vt* to delegate (**à** to). ●**—é, -ée** *nmf* delegate. ●**délégation** *nf* delegation.

délestage [delɛstaʒ] *nm* **itinéraire de d.** alternative route (*to relieve congestion*).

délibéré [delibere] *a* (*résolu*) determined; (*intentionnel*) deliberate; **de propos d.** deliberately. ●**—ment** *adv* (*à dessein*) deliberately.

délibérer [delibere] *vi* (*se consulter*) to deliberate (**de** about).

délicat [delika] *a* (*santé, travail etc*) delicate; (*question*) tricky, delicate; (*geste*) tactful; (*exigeant*) particular. ●**délicatement** *adv* delicately; tactfully.

délice [delis] *nm* delight. ●**délicieux, -euse** *a* (*mets, fruit etc*) delicious; (*endroit, parfum etc*) delightful.

délier [delje] *vt* to untie, undo; (*langue*) *Fig* to loosen; **d. qn de** to release s.o. from.

délimiter [delimite] *vt* (*terrain*) to mark off; (*sujet*) to define.

délinquant, -ante [delẽkɑ̃, -ɑ̃t] *a* & *nmf* delinquent. ●**délinquance** *nf* delinquency.

délire [delir] *nm Méd* delirium; (*exaltation*) frenzy. ●**délirer** *vi Méd* to be delirious; (*dire n'importe quoi*) to rave. ●**délirant** *a* (*malade*) delirious; (*joie*) frenzied, wild; (*déraisonnable*) utterly absurd.

délit [deli] *nm* offence, *Am* offense; **d. d'initié** (*à la Bourse*) insider trading.

délivrer [delivre] *vt* **1** (*prisonnier, otage*) to release, (set) free; **d. qn de** (*souci, obligation etc*) to rid s.o. of. **2** (*passeport, billet etc*) to issue.

déloger [delɔʒe] *vt* to force *ou* drive out; *Mil* to dislodge.

déloyal, -aux [delwajal, -o] *a* disloyal; (*concurrence*) unfair.

delta [dɛlta] *nm* (*d'un fleuve*) delta.

deltaplane® [dɛltaplan] *nm* (*engin*) hang-glider.

déluge [delyʒ] *nm* flood; (*de pluie*) downpour.

déluré [delyre] *a* (*fille, air*) *Péj* brazen.

démagogie [demagɔʒi] *nf* demagogy.

demain [d(ə)mẽ] *adv* tomorrow; **à d.!** see you tomorrow!

demande [d(ə)mɑ̃d] *nf* request (**de qch** for sth); (*d'emploi*) application; (*de renseignements*) inquiry; *Écon* demand; **demandes d'emploi** (*dans le journal*) situations *ou* jobs wanted.

demander [d(ə)mɑ̃de] *vt* to ask for; (*emploi*)

to apply for; (*nécessiter*) to require; **d. le chemin/l'heure** to ask the way/the time; **d. qch à qn** to ask s.o. for sth; **d. à qn de faire** to ask s.o. to do; **d. si/où** to ask *ou* inquire whether/where; **on te demande!** you're wanted!; **ça demande du temps** it takes time; **être très demandé** to be in great demand.

‖ **se demander** *vpr* to wonder, ask oneself (**pourquoi** why, **si** if).

démanger [demɑ̃ʒe] *vti* to itch; **son bras le démange** his arm itches. • **démangeaison** *nf* itch; **avoir des démangeaisons** to be itching.

démanteler [demɑ̃tle] *vt* (*organisation etc*) to break up, dismantle.

démaquiller (se) [sədemakije] *vpr* to take off one's make-up. • **démaquillant** *nm* make-up remover.

démarche [demarʃ] *nf* walk, gait; **d. intellectuelle** thought process; **faire des démarches** to go through the process (**pour faire** of doing); **faire des démarches auprès de qn** to approach s.o.

démarcheur, -euse [demarʃœr, -øz] *nmf Com* door-to-door salesman *ou* saleswoman.

démarquer [demarke] *vt* (*prix*) to mark down.

démarr/er [demare] *vi* (*moteur de voiture etc*) to start (up); (*partir en voiture*) to move *ou* drive off ‖ *vt* (*commencer*) *Fam* to start. • **—age** *nm Aut* start; **d. en côte** hill start. • **—eur** *nm Aut* starter.

démasquer [demaske] *vt* to expose.

démêler [demele] *vt* (*cheveux etc*) to disentangle.

démêlés [demele] *nmpl* **avoir des d. avec la justice** to have a brush with *or* unpleasant dealings with the law.

déménag/er [demenaʒe] *vi* to move (out), move house ‖ *vt* (*meubles*) to remove, *Am* move. • **—ement** *nm* move, moving (house); **camion de d.** removal van, *Am* moving van. • **—eur** *nm* removal man, *Am* (furniture) mover.

démener (se) [sədɛmne] *vpr* to fling oneself about; **se d. pour faire** to spare no effort to do.

dément [demɑ̃] *a* insane; (*génial*) *Fam* fantastic.

démentir [demɑ̃tir] *vt* (*nouvelle, faits etc*) to deny.

démerder (se) [sədemɛrde] *vpr* (*se débrouiller*) *Fam* to manage (by oneself).

démesuré [deməzyre] *a* excessive.

démettre [demɛtr] *vt* **1 se d. l'épaule**/*etc* to dislocate one's shoulder/*etc*. **2 d. qn de ses fonctions** to dismiss s.o. from his post.

demeurant (au) [odəmœrɑ̃] *adv* for all that, nonetheless.

demeure [dəmœr] *nf* **1** (*belle maison*) mansion. **2 mettre qn en d. de faire** to summon *ou* instruct s.o. to do.

demeurer [dəmœre] *vi* **1** (*aux* **être**) (*rester*) to remain. **2** (*aux* **avoir**) (*habiter*) to live, reside.

demi, -ie [d(ə)mi] *a* half; **d.-journée** half-day; **une heure et demie** an hour and a half; (*horloge*) half past one, *Am* one thirty ‖ *adv* **(à) d. plein** half-full; **ouvrir à d.** to open halfway ‖ *nmf* (*moitié*) half ‖ *nm* (*verre*) (half-pint) glass of beer; *Fb* half-back ‖ *nf* (*à l'horloge*) half-hour.

demi-cercle [d(ə)misɛrkl] *nm* semicircle. • **d.-douzaine** *nf* **une d.-douzaine (de)** a half-dozen, half a dozen. • **d.-finale** *nf Sp* semifinal. • **d.-frère** *nm* stepbrother, half brother. • **d.-heure** *nf* **une d.-heure** a half-hour, half an hour. • **d.-mot** *nm* **tu comprendras à d.-mot** you'll understand without my having to spell it out. • **d.-pension** *nf* half-board, *Am* breakfast and one meal. • **d.-pensionnaire** *nmf* day boarder, *Am* day student. • **d.-sel** *a inv* (*beurre*) slightly salted. • **d.-sœur** *nf* stepsister, half sister. • **d.-tarif** *nm* & *a inv* (*billet*) **(à) d.-tarif** half-price. • **d.-tour** *nm* about turn, *Am* about face; *Aut* U-turn; **faire d.-tour** (*à pied*) to turn back; (*en voiture*) to make a U-turn.

démission [demisjɔ̃] *nf* resignation; **donner sa d.** to hand in one's resignation. • **démissionner** *vi* to resign.

démocratie [demɔkrasi] *nf* democracy. • **démocratique** *a* democratic.

démoder (se) [sədemɔde] *vpr* to go out of fashion. • **démodé** *a* old-fashioned.

démographie [demɔgrafi] *nf* demography.

demoiselle [d(ə)mwazɛl] *nf* (*jeune fille*) young lady; (*célibataire*) single woman; **d. d'honneur** (*à un mariage*) bridesmaid.

démolir [demɔlir] *vt* (*maison*) to knock *ou* pull down, demolish; (*jouet*) to demolish. • **démolition** *nf* demolition; **en d.** being demolished.

démon [demɔ̃] *nm* **petit d.** (*enfant*) little devil; **le D.** the Devil.

démonstratif, -ive [demɔ̃stratif, -iv] *a* (*caractère*) demonstrative; **adjectif d.** *Gram* demonstrative adjective ‖ *nm* demonstrative.

démonstration [demɔ̃strasjɔ̃] *nf* demonstration; **faire une d.** to give a demonstration; **faire la d. d'un appareil** to demonstrate an appliance.

démonter [demɔ̃te] *vt* (*mécanisme*) to take

apart, dismantle; (*installation*) to take down; **une mer démontée** a stormy sea ‖ **se d.** *vpr* to come apart; (*installation*) to come down; (*personne*) *Fig* to be put out *ou* disconcerted.

démontrer [demɔ̃tre] *vt* to show, demonstrate.

démoraliser [demɔralize] *vt* to demor-alize ‖ **se d.** *vpr* to become demoralized.

démordre [demɔrdr] *vi* **il ne démordra pas de** (*son opinion etc*) he won't budge from.

démouler [demule] *vt* (*gâteau*) to turn out (*from its mould*).

démunir [demynir] *vt* **d. qn de** to deprive s.o. of; **se d. de** to part with.

dénaturer [denatyre] *vt* (*propos, faits etc*) to misrepresent, distort; (*goût*) to alter.

déneiger [deneʒe] *vt* to clear of snow.

dénicher [deniʃe] *vt* (*trouver*) to dig up; (*ennemi, fugitif*) to hunt out, flush out.

dénier [denje] *vt* (*responsabilité, droit*) to deny; **d. qch à qn** to deny s.o. sth.

dénigrer [denigre] *vt* to denigrate.

dénivellation [denivɛlɑsjɔ̃] *nf* unevenness; (*pente*) gradient; *pl* (*relief*) bumps.

dénombrer [denɔ̃bre] *vt* to count, number.

dénomm/er [denɔme] *vt* to name. ●**—é, -ée** *nmf* **un d. Dupont** a man named Dupont.

dénoncer [denɔ̃se] *vt* (*injustice etc*) to denounce (**à** to); **d. qn** (*au professeur*) to tell on s.o. (**à** to) ‖ **se d.** *vpr* (*à la police*) to give oneself up (**à** to); (*au professeur*) to own up (**à** to). ●**dénonciateur, -trice** *nmf* *Scol* telltale.

dénouement [denumɑ̃] *nm* outcome, ending; *Th* dénouement.

dénouer [denwe] *vt* (*nœud, corde*) to undo, untie; (*cheveux*) to let down ‖ **se d.** *vpr* (*nœud*) to come undone *ou* untied; (*cheveux*) to come down.

dénoyauter [denwajote] *vt* (*prune etc*) to stone, *Am* to pit.

denrée [dɑ̃re] *nf* food(stuff); **denrées alimentaires** foods.

dense [dɑ̃s] *a* dense. ●**densité** *nf* density.

dent [dɑ̃] *nf* tooth (*pl* teeth); (*de fourchette*) prong; **d. de lait/sagesse** milk/wisdom tooth; **faire ses dents** (*enfant*) to be teething; **coup de d.** bite; **rien à se mettre sous la d.** nothing to eat; **couteau en dents de scie** serrated knife. ●**dentaire** *a* dental.

dentier [dɑ̃tje] *nm* (set of) false teeth, denture(s).

dentifrice [dɑ̃tifris] *nm* toothpaste.

dentiste [dɑ̃tist] *nmf* dentist; **chirurgien d.** dental surgeon.

dentelé [dɑ̃tle] *a* (*côte*) jagged; (*feuille*) serrated.

dentelle [dɑ̃tɛl] *nf* lace.

dénud/er [denyde] *vt* to (lay) bare. ●**—é** *a* bare.

dénué [denɥe] *a* **d. de sens**/*etc* devoid of sense/*etc*.

dénuement [denymɑ̃] *nm* destitution; **dans le d.** poverty-stricken.

déodorant [deɔdɔrɑ̃] *nm* deodorant.

dépanner [depane] *vt* (*voiture etc*) to repair; **d. qn** *Fam* to help s.o. out. ●**dépannage** *nm* (emergency) repair; **voiture/service de d.** breakdown vehicle/service. ●**dépanneur** *nm* (*de télévision*) repairman; (*de voiture*) breakdown mechanic, emergency car mechanic. ●**dépanneuse** *nf* (*voiture*) breakdown lorry, *Am* wrecker, tow truck.

dépareillé [depareje] *a* (*chaussure etc*) odd, not matching; (*collection*) incomplete.

départ [depar] *nm* departure; (*d'une course*) start; **point/ligne de d.** starting point/post; **au d.** at the outset, at the start; **au d. de Paris**/*etc* (*excursion etc*) leaving from Paris/*etc*.

départager [departaʒe] *vt* (*concurrents*) to decide between.

département [departəmɑ̃] *nm* department. ●**départemental, -aux** *a* departmental; **route départementale** secondary road.

départir (se) [sədepartir] *vpr* **se d. de** (*attitude*) to depart from, abandon.

dépass/er [depɑse] *vt* (*véhicule, bicyclette etc*) to overtake; (*endroit*) to go past; (*date limite, durée*) to go beyond; **d. qn** (*en hauteur*) to be taller than s.o.; (*surclasser*) to be ahead of s.o.; **ça me dépasse** *Fig* that's (quite) beyond me ‖ *vi* (*jupon, clou etc*) to stick out, show. ●**—é** *a* (*démodé*) outdated; (*incapable*) unable to cope. ●**—ement** *nm* *Aut* overtaking, passing.

dépayser [depeize] *vt* to disorientate, *Am* disorient.

dépecer [depəse] *vt* (*animal*) to cut up.

dépêche [depɛʃ] *nf* telegram; (*diplomatique*) dispatch. ●**dépêcher** *vt* to dispatch ‖ **se d.** *vpr* to hurry (up); **se d. de faire** to hurry to do.

dépeigné [depeɲe] *a* **être d.** to have untidy hair.

dépeindre* [depɛ̃dr] *vt* to depict, describe.

dépendre [depɑ̃dr] **1** *vi* to depend (**de** on, upon); **d. de** (*appartenir à*) to belong to; (*être soumis à*) to be dependent on; **ça dépend de toi** that depends on you. **2** *vt* (*décrocher*) to take down. ●**dépendance 1** *nf* dependence; **sous la d. de qn** under s.o.'s domination. **2** *nfpl* (*bâtiments*) outbuildings.

dépens [depɑ̃] *nmpl* **aux d. de** at the expense of.

dépense [depɑ̃s] *nf* (*frais*) expense, expenditure; (*d'électricité etc*) consumption. ●**dépenser** *vt* (*argent*) to spend; (*électricité etc*) to use; (*forces*) to exert; (*énergie*) to expend ‖ **se d.** *vpr* to exert oneself.

dépensier, -ière [depɑ̃sje, -jɛr] *a* wasteful.

déperdition [depɛrdisjɔ̃] *nf* (*de chaleur etc*) loss.

dépérir [deperir] *vi* (*personne*) to waste away; (*plante*) to wither.

dépêtrer (se) [sədepetre] *vpr Fam* to extricate oneself (**de** from).

dépeupler [depœple] *vt* to depopulate.

dépilatoire [depilatwar] *nm* hair remover.

dépister [depiste] *vt* (*criminel etc*) to track down; (*maladie*) to detect.

dépit [depi] *nm* resentment, pique; **en d. de** in spite of; **en d. du bon sens** (*mal*) atrociously. ●**dépité** *a* vexed.

déplacer [deplase] *vt* (*objet, meuble etc*) to shift, move ‖ **se d.** *vpr* (*aiguille d'une montre, personne etc*) to move; (*voyager*) to travel (about). ●**déplacé** *a* (*mal à propos*) out of place; **personne déplacée** (*réfugié*) displaced person. ●**déplacement** *nm* (*voyage*) (business) trip; **frais de d.** travelling *ou Am* traveling expenses.

déplaire* [deplɛr] *vi* **d. à qn** to displease s.o.; **ça me déplaît** I don't like it; **cet aliment lui déplaît** he *ou* she dislikes this food; **il se déplaît à Paris** he doesn't like it in Paris. ●**déplaisant** *a* unpleasant.

dépli/er [deplije] *vt* to open out, unfold. ●**—ant** *nm* (*prospectus*) leaflet.

déplor/er [deplɔre] *vt* (*regretter*) to deplore; **d. que** (+ *sub*) to deplore the fact that, regret that. ●**—able** *a* regrettable, deplorable.

déployer [deplwaje] *vt* (*ailes*) to spread; (*journal, carte etc*) to unfold, spread (out); (*courage etc*) to display ‖ **se d.** *vpr* (*drapeau*) to unfurl.

déport/er [depɔrte] *vt* **1** (*dévier*) to carry *ou* veer (off course). **2** (*dans un camp de concentration*) *Hist* to send to a concentration camp, deport. ●**—é, -ée** *nmf* (concentration camp) inmate. ●**déportation** *nf* internment (in a concentration camp).

déposer [depoze] *vt* (*poser*) to put down; (*laisser*) to leave; (*argent*) to deposit; (*plainte*) to lodge; (*ordures*) to dump; (*marque de fabrique*) to register; **d. qn** (*en voiture*) to drop s.o. (off); **d. une lettre à la poste** to drop a letter in the post, mail *ou* post a letter; **d. son bilan** (*entreprise*) to go into liquidation, file for bankruptcy. ‖ *vi Jur* to testify; (*liquide*) to leave a deposit. ‖ **se déposer** *vpr* (*poussière, lie*) to settle.

dépositaire [depozitɛr] *nmf* (*vendeur*) agent.

dépôt [depo] *nm* (*de vin etc*) deposit, sediment; (*à la banque*) deposit; (*d'autobus, de trains*) depot; (*entrepôt*) warehouse; **d. d'ordures** rubbish *ou Am* garbage dump; **laisser qch à qn en d.** to give s.o. sth for safekeeping.

dépotoir [depɔtwar] *nm* rubbish dump, *Am* garbage dump.

dépouille [depuj] *nf* (*d'un animal*) hide, skin; **d. (mortelle)** (*d'un défunt*) mortal remains.

dépouillé [depuje] *a* (*arbre*) bare; (*style*) austere.

dépouiller [depuje] *vt* **d. qn de** (*déposséder*) to deprive s.o. of; **d. un scrutin** to count votes.

dépourvu [depurvy] *a* **d. de** devoid of; **prendre qn au d.** to catch s.o. unawares.

dépravé [deprave] *a* depraved.

déprécier [depresje] *vt* (*monnaie, immeuble etc*) to depreciate; (*dénigrer*) to disparage ‖ **se d.** *vpr* (*baisser*) to depreciate, lose (its) value.

dépression [depresjɔ̃] *nf* (*sur le sol*) & *Psy* depression; **zone de d.** trough of low pressure; **d. (nerveuse)** (nervous) breakdown; **d. économique** slump. ●**dépressif, -ive** *a* depressive.

déprime [deprim] *nf* **la d.** (*dépression*) *Fam* the blues.

déprim/er [deprime] *vt* to depress. ●**—é** *a* depressed.

depuis [dəpɥi] *prép* since; **d. lundi/1990** since Monday/1990; **d. qu'elle est partie** since she left; **j'habite ici d. un mois** I've been living here for a month; **d. quand êtes-vous là?** how long have you been here?; **d. peu/longtemps** for a short/long time; **je le connais d. toujours** I've known him all my life; **d. des siècles** *Fam* for ages; **d. Paris jusqu'à Londres** from Paris to London ‖ *adv* since (then).

ⓘ**G95** Tenses 7 F 9

ⓘ**G177** Prepositions 8

député [depyte] *nm* (*à l'Assemblée nationale*) deputy, = *Br* MP, = *Am* congressman, congresswoman.

déraciner [derasine] *vt* (*arbre, personne etc*) to uproot; (*préjugés*) to eradicate, root out.

déraill/er [derɑje] *vi* **1** (*train*) to jump the rails, be derailed; **faire d.** to de-rail. **2** (*divaguer*) *Fam* to talk drivel. ●**—ement** *nm* (*de train*) derailment. ●**—eur** *nm* (*de*

bicyclette) derailleur (gear change).
déraisonnable [derɛzɔnabl] *a* unreasonable.
déranger [derɑ̃ʒe] *vt* (*affaires*) to disturb, upset; (*projets*) to mess up, upset; (*vêtements*) to mess up; **d. qn** to disturb *ou* bother s.o.; **je viendrai si ça ne te dérange pas** I'll come if that's not imposing; **ça vous dérange si je fume?** do you mind if I smoke?; **avoir l'estomac dérangé** to have an upset stomach. ‖ **se déranger** *vpr* to put oneself to a lot of trouble (**pour faire** to do), (*se déplacer*) to move; **ne te dérange pas!** don't bother! • **dérangement** *nm* (*gêne*) bother, inconvenience; **excusez-moi pour le d.** I'm sorry to disturb *ou* bother you; **en d.** (*téléphone etc*) out of order.
dérap/er [derape] *vi* to skid. • **—age** *nm* skid.
dérégler [deregle] *vt* (*télévision etc*) to put out of order; (*estomac, habitudes*) to upset ‖ **se d.** *vpr* (*montre, appareil*) to go wrong. • **déréglé** *a* (*appareil*) out of order; (*vie, mœurs*) dissolute, wild.
dérider [deride] *vt*, **se d.** *vpr* to cheer up.
dérision [derizjɔ̃] *nf* derision, mockery; **tourner en d.** to mock; **par d.** derisively. • **dérisoire** *a* ridiculous, derisory.
dérivatif [derivatif] *nm* distraction (**à** from).
dérive [deriv] *nf* **partir à la d.** (*navire*) to drift out to sea. • **dériver** *vi* (*bateau*) to drift ‖ *vt* (*cours d'eau*) to divert; *Ling* to derive (**de** from).
dermatologie [dɛrmatɔlɔʒi] *nf* dermatology.
dernier -ière [dɛrnje, -jɛr] *a* last; (*nouvelles, mode*) latest; (*étage*) top; (*degré*) highest; **le d. rang** the back *ou* last row; **ces derniers mois** these past few months; **en d.** last.
ⓘ **dernier, dernière G32** Position of Adjectives 4 D 3
‖ *nmf* last (person *ou* one); **ce d.** (*de deux*) the latter; (*de plusieurs*) the last-mentioned; **être le d. de la classe** to be (at the) bottom of the class; **le d. des derniers** the lowest of the low; **le d. de mes soucis** the least of my worries. • **d.-né, dernière-née** *nmf* youngest (child). • **dernièrement** *adv* recently.
dérober [derɔbe] *vt* (*voler*) to steal (**à** from) ‖ **se d.** *vpr* to get out of one's obligations; (*s'esquiver*) to slip away; (*éviter de répondre*) to dodge the issue; **ses jambes se sont dérobées sous lui** his legs gave way beneath him. • **dérobé** *a* (*porte etc*) hidden, secret.
dérogation [derɔgɑsjɔ̃] *nf* exemption, (special) dispensation.
dérouiller [deruje] *vt* **d. qn** (*battre*) *Fam* to thrash s.o.; **se d. les jambes** *Fam* to stretch one's legs.
dérouler [derule] *vt* (*tapis etc*) to unroll; (*fil*) to unwind ‖ **se d.** *vpr* (*événement*) to take place.
dérouter [derute] *vt* (*avion, navire*) to divert, reroute; (*candidat etc*) to baffle.
derrick [dɛrik] *nm* oil rig.
derrière [dɛrjɛr] *prép* & *adv* behind; **d. moi** behind me, *Am* in back of me; **assis d.** (*dans une voiture*) sitting in the back; **par d.** (*attaquer*) from behind, from the rear ‖ *nm* (*de maison etc*) back, rear; (*fesses*) behind, bottom; **patte de d.** hind leg; **roue de d.** back *ou* rear wheel.
des [de] *voir* **de**[1,2,3], **le.**
dès [dɛ] *prép* from; **d. le début** (right) from the start; **d. cette époque** (as) from that time, from that time on; **d. le sixième siècle** as early as the sixth century; **d. qu'elle viendra** as soon as she comes.
ⓘ **dès G177** Prepositions 8
ⓘ **dès que G97** Tenses 7 F 11
désabusé [dezabyze] *a* disillusioned.
désaccord [dezakɔr] *nm* disagreement; **être en d. avec qn** to be at odds with s.o. • **désaccordé** *a* (*violon etc*) out of tune.
désaffecté [dezafɛkte] *a* (*gare etc*) disused.
désagréable [dezagreabl] *a* unpleasant, disagreeable.
désagréger (se) [sədezagreʒe] *vpr* to disintegrate, break up.
désagrément [dezagremɑ̃] *nm* annoyance, trouble.
désaltérer [dezaltere] *vt* **d. qn** to quench s.o.'s thirst; **se d.** to quench one's thirst.
désamorcer [dezamɔrse] *vt* (*obus, conflit*) to defuse.
désapprouver [dezapruve] *vt* to disapprove of ‖ *vi* to disapprove. • **désapprobateur, -trice** *a* disapproving.
désarçonner [dezarsɔne] *vt* (*jockey*) to throw, unseat; (*déconcerter*) *Fig* to nonplus.
désarm/er [dezarme] *vt* (*émouvoir*) & *Mil* to disarm. • **—ant** *a* (*charme etc*) disarming.
désarroi [dezarwa] *nm* (*angoisse*) distress.
désarticulé [dezartikyle] *a* (*pantin, clown*) double-jointed.
désastre [dezastr] *nm* disaster. • **désastreux, -euse** *a* disastrous.
désavantage [dezavɑ̃taʒ] *nm* (*inconvénient*) drawback, disadvantage; (*gêne*) handicap, disadvantage. • **désavantager** *vt* to put at a disadvantage, handicap.
désavouer [dezavwe] *vt* (*livre, personne etc*) to disown.
désaxé, -ée [dezakse] *a* & *nmf* unbalanced (person).
desceller (se) [sədesele] *vpr* to come loose.

descendant, -ante [desɑ̃dɑ̃, -ɑ̃t] **1** *a* (*marée*) outgoing. **2** *nmf* (*personne*) descendant.

descendre [desɑ̃dr] *vi* (*aux* **être**) to come *ou* go down (**de** from); (*d'un train etc*) to get off (**de** from); (*d'un arbre*) to climb down (**de** from); (*nuit*, *thermomètre*) to fall; (*marée*) to go out; **d. à l'hôtel** to put up at a hotel; **d. chez un ami** to stay with a friend; **d. de** (*être issu de*) to be descended from; **d. en courant/flânant/***etc* to run/stroll/*etc* down. ‖ *vt* (*aux* **avoir**) (*escalier*) to come *ou* go down; (*objet*) to bring *ou* take down; **d. qn** (*tuer*) *Fam* to bump s.o. off.

descente [desɑ̃t] *nf* (*d'avion etc*) descent; (*pente*) slope; (*de police*) raid (**dans** upon); **il fut accueilli à sa d. d'avion** he was met as he got off the plane; **d. à skis** downhill run; **d. de lit** (*tapis*) bedside rug.

descriptif, -ive [dɛskriptif, -iv] *a* descriptive. ●**description** *nf* description.

désemparé [dezɑ̃pare] *a* at a total loss, distraught.

désemplir [dezɑ̃plir] *vi* **ce magasin/***etc* **ne désemplit pas** this shop/*etc* is always crowded.

désenfler [dezɑ̃fle] *vi* (*enflure*) to go down.

déséquilibre [dezekilibr] *nm* (*inégalité*) imbalance; (*mental*) unbalance; **en d.** (*meuble etc*) unsteady. ●**déséquilibrer** *vt* to throw off balance; (*esprit*, *personne*) *Fig* to unbalance.

désert [dezɛr] *a* deserted; **île déserte** desert island ‖ *nm* desert. ●**désertique** *a* **région/***etc* **d.** desert region/*etc*.

déserter [dezɛrte] *vti* to desert. ●**déserteur** *nm* (*soldat*) deserter.

désespérer [dezɛspere] *vi* to despair (**de** of) ‖ *vt* to drive to despair ‖ **se d.** *vpr* to (be in) despair. ●**désespérant** *a* (*enfant etc*) that drives one to despair, hopeless. ●**désespéré** *a* (*personne*) in despair, despairing; (*cas*, *situation*) desperate, hopeless; (*efforts*, *cris*) desperate.

désespoir [dezɛspwar] *nm* despair; **en d. de cause** in desperation.

déshabiller [dezabije] *vt* to undress, strip ‖ **se d.** *vpr* to get undressed, undress.

désherb/er [dezɛrbe] *vti* to weed. ●**—ant** *nm* weed killer.

déshérit/er [dezerite] *vt* to disinherit. ●**—é** *a* (*pauvre*) underprivileged.

déshonor/er [dezɔnɔre] *vt* to disgrace, dishonour. ●**—ant** *a* dishonourable.

déshydrater [dezidrate] *vt* to dehydrate ‖ **se d.** *vpr* to become dehydrated.

désigner [deziɲe] *vt* (*montrer*) to point to, point out; (*choisir*) to appoint, designate; (*signifier*) to indicate.

désinence [dezinɑ̃s] *nf Gram* ending.

désinfect/er [dezɛ̃fɛkte] *vt* to disinfect. ●**—ant** *nm* & *a* disinfectant. ●**désinfection** *nf* disinfection.

désinformation [dezɛ̃fɔrmɑsjɔ̃] *nf* (*dans la presse*) disinformation.

désintégrer (se) [sədezɛ̃tegre] *vpr* to disintegrate.

désintéresser (se) [sədezɛ̃terese] *vpr* **se d. de** to lose interest in. ●**désintéressé** *a* (*altruiste*) disinterested.

désintoxiquer [dezɛ̃tɔksike] *vt* (*alcoolique*, *drogué*) to treat for alcoholism *ou* drug abuse.

désinvolte [dezɛ̃vɔlt] *a* (*dégagé*) easy-going, casual; (*insolent*) offhand. ●**désinvolture** *nf* casualness; offhandedness.

désir [dezir] *nm* desire, wish. ●**désirer** *vt* to want, desire; (*convoiter*) to desire; **je désire venir** I would like to come, I wish *ou* want to come; **je désire que tu viennes** I want you to come; **ça laisse à d.** it leaves something *ou* a lot to be desired.

désister (se) [sədeziste] *vpr* (*candidat etc*) to withdraw.

désobé/ir [dezɔbeir] *vi* to disobey; **d. à qn** to disobey s.o. ●**—issant** *a* disobedient. ●**désobéissance** *nf* disobedience (**à** to).

désobligeant [dezɔbliʒɑ̃] *a* disagreeable.

désodorisant [dezɔdɔrizɑ̃] *nm* air freshener.

désœuvré [dezœvre] *a* idle, unoccupied.

désoler [dezɔle] *vt* to distress, upset (very much) ‖ **se d.** *vpr* to be distressed *ou* upset (**de** at). ●**désolé** *a* (*région*) desolate; (*affligé*) distressed; **être d.** (*navré*) to be sorry (**que** (+ *sub*) that, **de faire** to do).

ⓘ**désolé G114** The Perfect Infinitive 7 H 3b)

désolidariser (se) [sədesɔlidarize] *vpr* to dissociate oneself (**de** from).

désopilant [dezɔpilɑ̃] *a* hilarious.

désordonné [dezɔrdɔne] *a* (*personne*, *chambre*) untidy, messy.

désordre [dezɔrdr] *nm* (*de papiers*, *affaires*, *idées*) mess, muddle, disorder; (*dans une classe*) disturbance; (*de cheveux*, *pièce*) untidiness; *pl* (*émeutes*) disorder, unrest; **en d.** untidy, messy.

désorganiser [dezɔrganize] *vt* to disorganize.

désorienté [dezɔrjɑ̃te] *a* disorientated, *Am* disoriented.

désormais [dezɔrmɛ] *adv* from now on, in future,

désosser [dezɔse] *vt* (*viande*) to bone.

despote [dɛspɔt] *nm* tyrant, despot.

desquels, desquelles [dekɛl] *voir* **lequel.**

dessaisir (se) [sədesezir] *vpr* **se d. de qch** to

part with sth.
dessaler [desale] *vt* (*poisson etc*) to remove the salt from (*by smoking*).
dessécher [deseʃe] *vt* (*végétation*) to dry up, wither; (*bouche, gorge*) to parch, dry; (*fruits*) to desiccate, dry ‖ **se d.** *vpr* (*plante*) to wither, dry up; (*peau*) to dry (up).
dessein [desɛ̃] *nm* **dans le d. de faire** with the aim of doing; **à d.** intentionally.
desserrer [desere] *vt* (*ceinture etc*) to loosen; (*poing*) to open; (*frein*) to release; **il n'a pas desserré les dents** he didn't open his mouth ‖ **se d.** *vpr* to come loose.
dessert [desɛr] *nm* dessert, sweet.
desserte [desɛrt] *nf* **assurer la d. de** (*village etc*) to provide a (bus *ou* train) service to.
desservir [desɛrvir] *vt* **1** (*table*) to clear (away). **2 d. qn** to harm s.o., do s.o. a disservice. **3 le car/***etc* **dessert ce village** the bus/*etc* provides a service to *ou* stops at this village.
dessin [desɛ̃] *nm* drawing; (*motif*) design, pattern; **d. animé** (*film*) cartoon; **d. (humoristique)** (*dans un journal*) cartoon; **école de d.** art school. ● **dessinateur, -trice** *nmf* drawer; **d. humoristique** cartoonist; **d. de modes** dress designer; **d. industriel** draughtsman, *Am* draftsman.
dessiner [desine] *vt* to draw; (*meuble, robe etc*) to design ‖ **se d.** *vpr* (*colline etc*) to stand out, be outlined; (*projet*) to take shape.
dessous [d(ə)su] *adv* under(neath), beneath, below; **en d.** (*sous*) under(neath) ‖ *nm* underneath; **drap de d.** bottom sheet; *pl* (*vêtements*) underclothes; **les gens du d.** the people downstairs; **avoir le d.** to get the worst of it. ● **d.-de-plat** *nm inv* table mat.
dessus [d(ə)sy] *adv* (*marcher, écrire*) on it; (*monter*) on top (of it), on it; (*lancer, passer*) over it; **par-d.** (*sauter etc*) over (it); **par-d. tout** above all ‖ *nm* top; **drap de d.** top sheet; **avoir le d.** to have the upper hand, get the best of it; **les gens du d.** the people upstairs. ● **d.-de-lit** *nm inv* bedspread.
destin [dɛstɛ̃] *nm* fate, destiny.
destinataire [dɛstinatɛr] *nmf* addressee.
destination [dɛstinɑsjɔ̃] *nf* (*lieu*) destination; **à d. de** (*train etc*) (going) to, (bound) for.
destiner [dɛstine] *vt* **d. qch à qn** to intend *ou* mean sth for s.o.; **d. qn à** (*carrière, fonction*) to intend s.o. for; **se d. à** (*carrière etc*) to intend to take up.
destituer [dɛstitɥe] *vt* (*fonctionnaire etc*) to dismiss (from office).
destruction [dɛstryksjɔ̃] *nf* destruction.
désuet, -ète [desɥɛ, -ɛt] *a* obsolete.
détachement [detaʃmɑ̃] *nm* **1** (*indifférence*) detachment. **2** (*de fonctionnaire*) (temporary) transfer; (*de troupes*) detachment.
détacher[1] [detaʃe] *vt* (*ceinture, vêtement*) to undo; (*mains*) to untie; (*ôter*) to take off, detach; **d. qn** (*libérer*) to untie s.o.; (*affecter*) to transfer s.o. (on assignment) (**à** to) ‖ **se d.** *vpr* (*chien, prisonnier*) to break loose; (*se dénouer*) to come undone; **se d. (de qch)** (*fragment*) to come off (sth); **se d. de** (*amis*) to break away from; **se d. (sur)** (*ressortir*) to stand out (against).
détach/er[2] [detaʃe] *vt* (*linge etc*) to re-move the spots *ou* stains from. ● **—ant** *nm* stain remover.
détail [detaj] *nm* **1** detail; **en d.** in detail; **le d. de** (*dépenses etc*) a breakdown of. **2 de d.** (*magasin, prix*) retail; **vendre au d.** to sell retail; (*par petites quantités*) to sell separately.
détaillant, -ante [detajɑ̃, -ɑ̃t] *nmf* retailer.
détaill/er [detaje] *vt* (*énumérer*) to detail. ● **—é** *a* (*récit, facture etc*) detailed.
détaler [detale] *vi Fam* to run off.
détartrer [detartre] *vt* (*chaudière, dents etc*) to scale.
détaxer [detakse] *vt* (*denrée etc*) to reduce the tax on; (*supprimer*) to take the tax off; **produit détaxé** duty-free article.
détecter [detɛkte] *vt* to detect.
détective [detɛktiv] *nm* **d. (privé)** (private) detective.
déteindre* [detɛ̃dr] *vi* (*couleur ou étoffe au lavage*) to run; (*au soleil*) to fade; **ton tablier bleu a déteint sur ma chemise** the blue of your apron has come off on(to) my shirt.
dételer [detle] *vt* (*chevaux*) to unhitch.
détendre [detɑ̃dr] *vt* (*arc etc*) to slacken, relax; (*atmosphère*) to ease; **d. qn** to relax s.o. ‖ **se d.** *vpr* (*arc etc*) to slacken, get slack; (*atmosphère*) to ease; (*se reposer*) to relax; (*rapports*) to become less strained.
déten/ir* [detnir] *vt* (*record, pouvoir, titre*) to hold; (*secret, objet volé*) to be in possession of; (*prisonnier*) to hold, detain. ● **—u, -ue** *nmf* prisoner. ● **détention** *nf* (*d'armes*) possession; (*captivité*) detention; **placer en d. préventive** (*en prison*) to remand in custody.
détente [detɑ̃t] *nf* **1** (*repos*) relaxation. **2** (*gâchette*) trigger.
détergent [detɛrʒɑ̃] *nm* detergent.
détériorer [deterjɔre] *vt* (*abîmer*) to damage ‖ **se d.** *vpr* (*empirer*) to deteriorate. ● **détérioration** *nf* (*d'une situation etc*) deterioration (**de** in).
détermin/er [detɛrmine] *vt* (*préciser*) to determine; (*causer*) to bring about; **d. qn à faire** to induce s.o. to do, make s.o. do; **se**

d. à faire to resolve *ou* determine to do. ●**—ant** *a* (*motif*) deciding; (*rôle*) decisive. ●**—é** *a* (*précis*) specific; (*résolu*) determined.

déterrer [detere] *vt* to dig up, unearth.

détest/er [detɛste] *vt* to hate, detest; **d. faire** to hate doing *ou* to do, detest doing. ●**—able** *a* awful, terrible.

ⓘdétester G98 The Subjunctive 7 G 1a)

détonation [detɔnɑsjɔ̃] *nf* explosion, blast.

détonner [detɔne] *vi* (*contraster*) to jar, be out of place.

détour [detur] *nm* (*crochet*) detour; (*de route etc*) bend, curve; **sans d.** (*parler*) without beating around the bush.

détourner [deturne] *vt* (*dévier*) to divert; (*tête*) to turn (away); (*avion*) to hijack; (*conversation, sens*) to change; (*fonds*) to embezzle; **d. qn de** (*son devoir, ses amis*) to take s.o. away from; (*sa route*) to lead s.o. away from; **d. les yeux** to look away. ‖ **se détourner** *vpr* to turn aside *ou* away. ●**détourné, -ée** *a* (*chemin, moyen*) roundabout, indirect. ●**détournement** *nm* **d. (d'avion)** hijack(ing); **d. (de fonds)** embezzlement.

détraquer [detrake] *vt* (*mécanisme*) to break, put out of order ‖ **se d.** *vpr* (*machine*) to go wrong; **se d. l'estomac** to upset one's stomach. ●**détraqué, -ée** *a* out of order; (*cerveau*) deranged ‖ *nmf* sex maniac.

détresse [detrɛs] *nf* distress; **en d.** (*navire, âme*) in distress; **dans la d.** (*misère*) in (great) distress.

détriment de (au) [odetrimɑ̃də] *prép* to the detriment of.

détritus [detritys] *nmpl* rubbish, *Am* garbage.

détroit [detrwa] *nm Géog* strait(s), sound.

détromper (se) [sədetrɔ̃pe] *vpr* **détrompez-vous!** don't you believe it!

détrousser [detruse] *vt* (*voyageur etc*) to rob.

détruire* [detrɥir] *vt* (*ravager, tuer*) to destroy; (*santé*) to ruin, destroy.

dette [dɛt] *nf* debt; **avoir des dettes** to be in debt.

DEUG [døg] *nm abrév* (*diplôme d'études universitaires générales*) degree taken after two years' study.

deuil [dœj] *nm* (*affliction, vêtements*) mourning; (*mort de qn*) bereavement; **être en d.** to be in mourning.

deux [dø] *a & nm* two; **d. fois** twice, two times; **mes d. sœurs** both my sisters, my two sisters; **tous (les) d.** both. ●**d.-pièces** *nm inv* (*maillot de bain*) bikini; (*appartement*) two-roomed flat *ou Am* apartment. ●**d.-points** *nm inv Gram* colon. ●**d.-roues** *nm inv* two-wheeled vehicle.

deuxième [døzjɛm] *a & nmf* second. ●**—ment** *adv* secondly.

dévaler [devale] *vt* (*escalier*) to race down ‖ *vi* (*tomber*) to tumble down.

dévaliser [devalize] *vt* (*personne, banque etc*) rob.

dévaloriser [devalɔrize] *vt* (*diplôme, marchandises*) to reduce in value, devalue ‖ **se d.** *vpr* to become devalued.

dévaluer [devalɥe] *vt* (*monnaie*) to devalue. ●**dévaluation** *nf* devaluation.

devancer [d(ə)vɑ̃se] *vt* to get *ou* be ahead of; (*question etc*) to anticipate, forestall.

devant [d(ə)vɑ̃] *prép & adv* in front (of); **d. (l'hôtel/***etc*) in front (of the hotel/*etc*); **passer d. (l'église/***etc*) to go past (the church/*etc*); **assis d.** (*dans une voiture*) sitting in the front; **par d.** from *ou* at the front; **loin d.** a long way ahead *ou* in front; **d. le danger** in the face of danger.

‖ *nm* front; **roue/porte de d.** front wheel/door; **patte de d.** foreleg; **prendre les devants** (*action*) to take the initiative.

devanture [d(ə)vɑ̃tyr] *nf* (*vitrine*) shop window; (*façade*) shop front.

dévaster [devaste] *vt* to ruin, devastate.

développer [devlɔpe] *vt* (*muscles, photos*) to develop ‖ **se d.** *vpr* to develop. ●**développement** *nm* development; *Phot* developing, processing; **les pays en voie de d.** the developing countries.

devenir* [dəvnir] *vi* (*aux* **être**) to become; (*vieux etc*) to get, become; (*rouge etc*) to turn, go, become; **d. un papillon/un homme/***etc* to grow into a butterfly/a man/*etc*; **d. médecin** to become a doctor; **qu'est-il devenu?** what's become of him *ou* it?

dévergonder (se) [sədevɛrgɔ̃de] *vpr* to fall into dissolute ways.

déverser [devɛrse] *vt* (*liquide, rancune*) to pour out; (*bombes, ordures*) to dump ‖ **se d.** *vpr* (*liquide*) to empty, pour out (**dans** into).

dévêtir (se) [sədevetir] *vpr Litt* to undress.

dévier [devje] *vt* (*circulation etc*) to divert; (*coup etc*) to deflect ‖ *vi* (*de ses principes etc*) to deviate (**de** from); (*de sa route*) to veer (off course). ●**déviation** *nf* (*chemin*) bypass; (*itinéraire provisoire*) diversion, *Am* detour.

deviner [d(ə)vine] *vt* to guess (**que** that); (*avenir*) to predict; **d. (le jeu de) qn** to see through s.o. ●**devinette** *nf* riddle.

devis [d(ə)vi] *nm* estimate (*of cost of work to be done*).

dévisager [devizaʒe] *vt* **d. qn** to stare at s.o.

devise [d(ə)viz] *nf* (*légende*) motto; (*monnaie*) (foreign) currency.

dévisser [devise] *vt* to unscrew, undo ‖ **se d.**

vpr (*bouchon*) to unscrew; (*se desserrer*) to come loose.

dévoiler [devwale] *vt* (*secret*) to disclose.

devoir[1]** [d(ə)vwar] *v aux* **1** (*nécessité*) **je dois refuser** I must refuse, I have (got) to refuse; **j'ai dû refuser** I had to refuse.
2 (*forte probabilité*) **il doit être tard** it must be late; **elle a dû oublier** she must have forgotten; **il ne doit pas être bête** he can't be stupid.
3 (*obligation*) **tu dois apprendre tes leçons** you must learn your lessons; **il aurait dû venir** he should have come, he ought to have come; **vous devriez rester** you should stay, you ought to stay.
4 (*événement prévu*) **elle doit venir** she's supposed to be coming, she's due to come; **le train devait arriver à midi** the train was due (to arrive) at noon.
ⓘ**G90** Impersonal Verbs 7 E 2g)
ⓘ**G121** Modal Auxiliary Verbs 7 K 1

devoir[2]* [d(ə)vwar] **1** *vt* to owe; **d. de l'argent à qn** to owe s.o. money, owe money to s.o. **2** *nm* (*obligation*) duty; **devoir(s)** (*exercice(s) à faire à la maison*) homework; **faire ses devoirs** to do one's homework; **d. sur table** class exam(ination).

dévolu [devɔly] *nm* **jeter son d. sur** to set one's heart on.

dévorer [devɔre] *vt* (*manger*) to eat up.

dévot, -ote [devo, -ɔt] *a & nmf* devout *ou* pious (person).

dévouer (se) [sədevwe] *vpr* (*à une tâche*) to dedicate oneself, devote oneself (**à** to); **se d. (pour qn)** (*se sacrifier*) to sacrifice oneself (for s.o.). •**dévoué** *a* (*ami, femme etc*) devoted (**à qn** to s.o.); (*soldat etc*) dedicated. •**dévouement** [-umɑ̃] *nm* devotion, dedication.

diabète [djabɛt] *nm* (*maladie*) diabetes. •**diabétique** *a & nmf* diabetic.

diable [djɑbl] *nm* devil; **le d.** the Devil; **habiter au d.** to live miles from anywhere.

diabolo [djabɔlo] *nm* (*boisson*) lemonade *ou Am* lemon soda flavoured with syrup.

diacre [djakr] *nm Rel* deacon.

diadème [djadɛm] *nm* (*bijou féminin*) tiara.

diagnostic [djagnɔstik] *nm* diagnosis.

diagonale [djagɔnal] *nf* diagonal (line); **en d.** diagonally.

diagramme [djagram] *nm* (*schéma*) diagram; (*courbe*) graph.

dialecte [djalɛkt] *nm* dialect.

dialogue [djalɔg] *nm* conversation; *Pol Cin Th Littér* dialogue, *Am* dialog.

dialyse [djaliz] *nf Méd* dialysis.

diamant [djamɑ̃] *nm* diamond.

diamètre [djamɛtr] *nm* diameter.

diapason [djapazɔ̃] *nm Mus* tuning fork.

diaphragme [djafragm] *nm* diaphragm.

diapositive, *Fam* **diapo** [djapozitiv, djapo] *nf* (colour) slide, transparency.

diarrhée [djare] *nf* diarrh(o)ea.

dictateur [diktatœr] *nm* dictator. •**dictature** *nf* dictatorship.

dict/er [dikte] *vt* to dictate (**à** to). •**—ée** *nf* dictation.

dictionnaire [diksjɔnɛr] *nm* dictionary.

dicton [diktɔ̃] *nm* saying, adage.

dièse [djɛz] *a & nm Mus* sharp.

diesel [djezɛl] *a & nm* **(moteur) d.** diesel (engine).

diète [djɛt] *nf* (*jeûne*) starvation diet; (*régime*) (strict) diet; **mettre qn à la d.** to put s.o. on a starvation diet *ou* a (strict) diet.

diététique [djetetik] *nf* dietetics ‖ *a* **aliment** *ou* **produit d.** health food; **magasin d.** health-food shop.

dieu, -x [djø] *nm* god; **D.** God; **D. merci!** thank God!, thank goodness!

diffamation [difamɑsjɔ̃] *nf* defamation; (*en paroles*) slander; (*par écrit*) libel; **campagne de d.** smear campaign.

différé [difere] *nm* **en d.** (*émission*) (pre)recorded.

différence [diferɑ̃s] *nf* difference (**de** in); **à la d. de** unlike; **faire la d. entre** to make a distinction between.

différend [diferɑ̃] *nm* difference (of opinion).

différent [diferɑ̃] *a* different (**de** from, to); *pl* (*divers*) different, various. •**différemment** [-amɑ̃] *adv* differently (**de** from, to).
ⓘ**différent G32** Position of Adjectives 4 D 3

différer [difere] **1** *vi* to differ (**de** from). **2** *vt* (*remettre*) to postpone, defer.

difficile [difisil] *a* difficult; (*exigeant*) fussy, hard to please; **c'est d. à faire** it's hard *ou* difficult to do; **il (nous) est d. de faire ça** it's hard *ou* difficult (for us) to do that.

difficulté [difikylte] *nf* difficulty (**à faire** in doing); **en d.** in a difficult situation.

difforme [difɔrm] *a* deformed, misshapen.

diffus [dify] *a* (*lumière, style*) diffuse.

diffuser [difyze] *vt* (*émission, nouvelle etc*) to broadcast; (*lumière, chaleur*) to diffuse; (*livre*) to distribute.

digérer [diʒere] *vt* to digest; (*endurer*) *Fam* to stomach; **avoir du mal à d.** to have trouble digesting.

digestif, -ive [diʒɛstif, -iv] *a* (*tube, sucs etc*) digestive ‖ *nm* after-dinner liqueur. •**digestion** *nf* digestion.

digitale [diʒital] *af* **empreinte d.** fingerprint.

digne [diɲ] *a* (*méritant*) worthy; (*air, attitude*

etc) dignified; **d. de qn** worthy of s.o.; **d. d'admiration**/*etc* worthy of *ou* deserving of admiration/*etc*. • **dignité** *nf* dignity; **manquer de d.** to have no self-respect.

digression [digresjɔ̃] *nf* digression.

digue [dig] *nf* dike; (*en bord de mer*) sea wall.

dilapider [dilapide] *vt* to squander, waste.

dilater [dilate] *vt*, **se d.** *vpr* to expand.

dilemme [dilɛm] *nm* dilemma.

diligence [diliʒɑ̃s] *nf* **1** (*rapidité*) speedy efficiency. **2** (*véhicule*) *Hist* stagecoach.

diluer [dilɥe] *vt* to dilute (**dans** in).

diluvienne [dilyvjɛn] *af* **pluie d.** torrential rain.

dimanche [dimɑ̃ʃ] *nm* Sunday.

dimension [dimɑ̃sjɔ̃] *nf* (*mesure*) dimension; (*taille*) size; **à deux dimensions** two-dimensional.

diminuer [diminɥe] *vt* to reduce, decrease; (*frais*) to cut down, reduce; (*forces physiques*) to diminish, lessen, reduce ‖ *vi* (*réserves, nombre*) to decrease, diminish; (*jours*) to get shorter; (*prix*) to decrease. • **diminution** *nf* reduction, decrease (**de** in).

diminutif, -ive [diminytif, -iv] *a & nm Gram* diminutive ‖ *nm* (*prénom*) nickname.

dinde [dɛ̃d] *nf* turkey. • **dindon** *nm* turkey (cock).

dîner [dine] *vi* to have dinner; (*au Canada, en Belgique etc*) to (have) lunch ‖ *nm* dinner; lunch; (*soirée*) dinner party.

dînette [dinɛt] *nf* (*jouet*) doll's dinner service *ou* set.

dingue [dɛ̃g] *a Fam* crazy, nuts ‖ *nmf Fam* nutcase.

dinosaure [dinozɔr] *nm* dinosaur.

diphtongue [diftɔ̃g] *nf Ling* diphthong.

diplomate [diplɔmat] *nmf Pol* diplomat; (*négociateur habile*) diplomatist ‖ *a* (*habile, plein de tact*) diplomatic. • **diplomatie** [-asi] *nf* (*tact*) & *Pol* diplomacy; (*carrière*) diplomatic service.

diplôme [diplom] *nm* certificate, diploma; *Univ* degree. • **diplômé, -ée** *a & nmf* qualified (person); **être d. (de)** *Univ* to be a graduate (of).

dire** [dir] *vt* (*mot, avis etc*) to say; (*vérité, secret, heure etc*) to tell; **d. des bêtises** to talk nonsense; **d. qch à qn** to tell s.o. sth, say sth to s.o.; **d. à qn que** to tell s.o. that, say to s.o. that; **d. à qn de faire** to tell s.o. to do; **d. du mal/du bien de** to speak ill/well of; **on dirait un château** it looks like a castle; **on dirait du Mozart** it sounds like Mozart; **on dirait du cabillaud** it tastes like cod; **ça ne me dit rien** (*envie*) I don't feel like that; (*souvenir*) it doesn't ring a bell; **dites donc!** look (here)!; **autrement dit** in other words; **à vrai d.** to tell the truth; **ça ne se dit pas** that's not said. ‖ *nm* **au d. de** according to.

G204 Word Order: Inversion 12 A 7b)

direct [dirɛkt] *a* direct; **train d.** fast train ‖ *nm* **en d.** (*émission*) live. • **—ement** [-əmɑ̃] *adv* directly; (*immédiatement*) straight (away), directly.

directeur, -trice [dirɛktœr, -tris] *nmf* director; (*d'école*) headmaster, head-mistress, *Am* principal ‖ *a* (*principe*) guiding; **idées** *ou* **lignes directrices** guidelines.

direction [dirɛksjɔ̃] *nf* **1** (*sens*) direction; **en d. de** (*train*) (going) to, for. **2** (*de société, club*) running, management; (*d'études*) supervision; **avoir la d. de** to be in charge of; **sous la d. de** (*orchestre*) conducted by; **la d.** (*équipe dirigeante*) the management.

dirigeable [diriʒabl] *a & nm* **(ballon) d.** airship, dirigible.

dirigeant [diriʒɑ̃] *a* (*classe*) ruling ‖ *nm* (*de pays*) leader; (*d'entreprise, club*) manager.

diriger [diriʒe] *vt* (*société, club*) to run, manage; (*parti, groupe, débat*) to lead; (*véhicule*) to steer; (*orchestre*) to conduct; (*études*) to supervise; (*orienter*) to turn (**vers** towards); (*arme, lumière*) to point, direct (**vers** towards); **se d. vers** (*lieu, objet*) to make one's way towards, head for; (*dans une carrière*) to turn towards.

dirigisme [diriʒism] *nm Écon* state control.

dis, disant [di, dizɑ̃] *voir* **dire.**

discerner [disɛrne] *vt* (*voir*) to make out, discern; (*différencier*) to distinguish.

disciple [disipl] *nm* disciple, follower.

discipline [disiplin] *nf* (*règle, matière*) discipline.

discipliner (se) [sədisipline] *vpr* to discipline oneself. • **discipliné** *a* well-disciplined.

discontinu [diskɔ̃tiny] *a* (*ligne*) discontinuous; (*bruit etc*) intermittent. • **discontinuer** *vi* **sans d.** without stopping.

disconvenir [diskɔ̃vnir] *vi* **je n'en disconviens pas** I don't deny it.

discordant [diskɔrdɑ̃] *a* (*son*) discordant; (*témoignages*) conflicting; (*couleurs*) clashing.

discothèque [diskɔtɛk] *nf* record library; (*club*) discotheque, disco.

discours [diskur] *nm* speech. • **discourir** *vi Péj* to speechify, hold forth.

discréditer [diskredite] *vt* to discredit, bring into disrepute ‖ **se d.** *vpr* (*personne*) to become discredited.

discret, -ète [diskrɛ, -ɛt] *a* (*personne, manière etc*) discreet; (*vêtement*) simple. • **discrètement** *adv* discreetly; (*s'habiller*) simply.

• **discrétion** *nf* discretion; **vin/***etc* **à d.** as much wine/*etc* as one wants.
discrimination [diskriminɑsjɔ̃] *nf* (*ségrégation*) discrimination.
disculper [diskylpe] *vt* to exonerate (**de** from).
discussion [diskysjɔ̃] *nf* discussion; (*conversation*) talk; (*querelle*) argument; **pas de d.!** no argument!
discuter [diskyte] *vt* to discuss; (*familièrement*) to talk over; (*contester*) to question; **ça peut se d.** that's arguable ‖ *vi* (*parler*) to talk (**de** about, **avec** with); (*répliquer*) to argue; **d. de** *ou* **sur qch** to discuss sth. • **discuté** *a* (*auteur*) much discussed; (*théorie*, *question*) disputed, controversial.
dise, disent [diz] *voir* **dire.**
diseuse [dizœz] *nf* **d. de bonne aventure** fortune-teller.
disgracieux, -euse [disgrasjø, -øz] *a* ungainly.
disjoindre [disʒwɛ̃dr] *vt* (*questions*) to treat separately. • **disjoint** *a* (*questions*) unconnected.
disjoncteur [disʒɔ̃ktœr] *nm Él* circuit breaker.
disloquer (se) [sədislɔke] *vpr* (*meuble etc*) to fall apart; (*cortège*) to break up; **se d. le bras** to dislocate one's arm.
disons [dizɔ̃] *voir* **dire.**
dispar/aître* [disparɛtr] *vi* to disappear; (*être porté manquant*) to go missing; **d. en mer** to be lost at sea; **faire d.** to remove, get rid of. • **—u** *a* (*soldat etc*) missing; **être porté d.** to be reported missing. • **disparition** *nf* disappearance; (*mort*) death.
dispensaire [dispɑ̃sɛr] *nm* community health centre.
dispense [dispɑ̃s] *nf* exemption. • **dispenser** *vt* (*soins*, *bienfaits etc*) to dispense; **d. qn de** (*obligation*) to exempt s.o. from; **se d. de faire** to spare oneself the bother of doing.
disperser [disperse] *vt* to disperse, scatter; (*efforts*) to dissipate ‖ **se d.** *vpr* (*foule*) to disperse; **elle se disperse trop** she tries to do too many things at once.
disponible [dispɔnibl] *a* (*article*, *place etc*) available; (*esprit*) alert.
dispos [dispo] *am* **frais et d.** refreshed.
disposé [dispoze] *a* **bien/mal d.** in a good/bad mood; **bien d. envers** well-disposed towards; **d. à faire** prepared *ou* willing *ou* disposed to do.
disposer [dispoze] *vt* (*objets*) to arrange; **se d. à faire** to prepare to do ‖ *vi* **d. de qch** to have sth at one's disposal; (*utiliser*) to make use of sth; **d. de qn** *Péj* to take advantage of s.o.
dispositif [dispozitif] *nm* (*mécanisme*) device; **d. policier** police presence.
disposition [dispozisjɔ̃] *nf* arrangement; (*de maison*, *page*) layout; (*humeur*) frame of mind; *pl* (*aptitudes*) ability, aptitude (**pour** for); **à la d. de qn** at s.o.'s disposal; **prendre ses** *ou* **des dispositions** (*préparatifs*) to make arrangements; (*pour l'avenir*) to make provision; **dans de bonnes dispositions à l'égard de** well-disposed towards.
disproportionné [disprɔpɔrsjɔne] *a* disproportionate.
dispute [dispyt] *nf* quarrel. • **disputer** *vt* (*match*) to play; (*rallye*) to compete in; **d. qch à qn** (*prix*, *première place etc*) to fight with s.o. for *ou* over sth; **d. qn** (*gronder*) *Fam* to tell s.o. off ‖ **se d.** *vpr* to quarrel (**avec** with); (*match*) to take place; **se d. qch** to fight over sth.
disqualifier [diskalifje] *vt* (*équipe etc*) to disqualify.
disque [disk] *nm* (*de musique*) record; (*cercle*) disc, *Am* disk; (*d'ordinateur*) disk; **d. compact** compact disc *ou Am* disk. • **disquette** *nf* (*d'ordinateur*) floppy (disk), diskette.
disséminer [disemine] *vt* (*graines*, *mines etc*) to scatter; (*idées*) *Fig* to disseminate.
disséquer [diseke] *vt* to dissect.
dissertation [disɛrtɑsjɔ̃] *nf Scol* essay.
dissimuler [disimyle] *vt* (*cacher*) to hide, conceal (**à** from) ‖ **se d.** *vpr* to hide (oneself), conceal oneself.
dissipé [disipe] *a* (*élève*) unruly; (*vie*) dissipated.
dissiper [disipe] *vt* (*brouillard*, *craintes*) to dispel; (*fortune*) to squander, dissipate; **d. qn** to distract s.o. ‖ **se d.** *vpr* (*brume*) to clear, lift; (*craintes*) to disappear; (*élève*) to misbehave.
dissolu [disɔly] *a* (*vie etc*) dissolute.
dissolvant [disɔlvɑ̃] *a* & *nm* solvent; (*pour vernis à ongles*) nail polish remover.
dissoudre* [disudr] *vt*, **se d.** *vpr* to dissolve.
dissuader [disɥade] *vt* to dissuade, deter (**de qch** from sth, **de faire** from doing). • **dissuasion** *nf* dissuasion; **force de d.** *Mil* deterrent.
distance [distɑ̃s] *nf* distance; **à deux mètres de d.** two metres apart; **à d.** at *ou* from a distance. • **distancer** *vt* to leave behind.
distant [distɑ̃] *a* distant; **d. de dix kilomètres** (*éloigné*) ten kilometres away; (*à intervalles*) ten kilometres apart.
distendre [distɑ̃dr] *vt*, **se d.** *vpr* to distend.
distiller [distile] *vt* to distil. • **distillerie** *nf*

(*lieu*) distillery.

istinct, -incte [distɛ̃, -ɛkt] *a* (*différent*) distinct, separate (**de** from); (*net*) clear, distinct. ● **distinctement** *adv* distinctly, clearly.

istinguer [distɛ̃ge] *vt* (*différencier*) to distinguish; (*voir*) to make out; **d. le bien du mal** to tell good from evil ▮ **se d.** *vpr* (*s'illustrer*) to distinguish oneself; **se d. de** (*différer*) to be distinguishable from. ● **distingué** *a* (*bien élevé, éminent*) distinguished; **sentiments distingués** (*formule épistolaire de politesse*) yours faithfully, *Am* sincerely.

istraction [distraksjɔ̃] *nf* amusement, distraction; (*étourderie*) (fit of) absent-mindedness. ● **distraire*** *vt* (*divertir*) to entertain, amuse ▮ **se d.** *vpr* to amuse oneself. ● **distrait** *a* absent-minded. ● **distrayant** *a* entertaining.

istribuer [distribɥe] *vt* (*donner*) to hand *ou* give out, distribute; (*courrier*) to deliver; (*cartes*) to deal.

istributeur [distribytœr] *nm Aut Cin Com* distributor; **d. (automatique)** vending machine; **d. de billets** *Rail* ticket machine; (*de billets de banque*) cash dispenser *ou* machine.

istribution [distribysjɔ̃] *nf* distribution; (*du courrier*) delivery.

it [di] *voir* **dire** ▮ *a* (*convenu*) agreed; (*surnommé*) called.

ites [dit] *voir* **dire.**

ivaguer [divage] *vi* (*dérailler*) to rave, talk drivel.

ivan [divɑ̃] *nm* divan, couch.

ivers, -erse [divɛr, -ɛrs] *a* (*varié*) varied, diverse; *pl* (*distincts*) various; **d. groupes** (*plusieurs*) various groups.

❶ **G32** Position of Adjectives 4 D 3

ivertir [divɛrtir] *vt* to entertain ▮ **se d.** *vpr* to enjoy oneself. ● **divertissement** *nm* entertainment.

ividende [dividɑ̃d] *nm Math Fin* dividend.

ivin [divɛ̃] *a* divine. ● **divinité** *nf* divinity.

iviser [divize] *vt*, **se d.** *vpr* to divide (**en** into). ● **division** *nf* division.

ivorce [divɔrs] *nm* divorce. ● **divorcer** *vi* to get *ou* be divorced, divorce; **d. d'avec qn** to divorce s.o. ● **divorcé, -ée** *a* divorced (**d'avec** from) ▮ *nmf* divorcee.

ivulguer [divylge] *vt* to divulge.

ix [dis] ([di] *before consonant*, [diz] *before vowel*) *a & nm* ten. ● **dixième** [dizjɛm] *a & nmf* tenth; **un d.** a tenth. ● **dix-huit** [dizɥit] *a & nm* eighteeen. ● **dix-neuf** [diznœf] *a & nm* nineteen. ● **dix-sept** [dissɛt] *a & nm* seventeen.

dizaine [dizɛn] *nf* **une d. (de)** about ten.

docile [dɔsil] *a* submissive, docile.

dock [dɔk] *nm Nau* dock. ● **docker** [dɔkɛr] *nm* docker.

docteur [dɔktœr] *nm Méd Univ* doctor (**ès, en** of). ● **doctorat** *nm* doctorate, = PhD (**ès, en** in).

doctrine [dɔktrin] *nf* doctrine.

document [dɔkymɑ̃] *nm* document. ● **documentaire** *a* documentary ▮ *nm* (*film*) documentary. ● **documentaliste** *nmf* information officer; (*à l'école*) (school) librarian.

documenter (se) [sədɔkymɑ̃te] *vpr* to collect information. ● **documenté** *a* (**bien** *ou* **très**) **d.** (*personne*) well-informed. ● **documentation** *nf* (*documents*) documentation.

dodeliner [dɔdline] *vi* **d. de la tête** to nod (one's head).

dodo [dodo] *nm* (*langage enfantin*) **faire d.** to sleep; **aller au d.** to go to bye-byes.

dodu [dɔdy] *a* chubby, plump.

dogue [dɔg] *nm* (*chien*) mastiff.

doigt [dwa] *nm* finger; **d. de pied** toe; **petit d.** little finger, *Am* pinkie; **un d. de vin**/*etc* a drop of wine/*etc*; **à deux doigts de** within an ace of; **savoir qch sur le bout du d.** to have sth at one's finger tips.

doigté [dwate] *nm Mus* fingering, touch; (*savoir-faire*) tact.

dois, doit [dwa] *voir* **devoir**[1,2].

doléances [dɔleɑ̃s] *nfpl* (*plaintes*) grievances.

dollar [dɔlar] *nm* dollar.

domaine [dɔmɛn] *nm* (*terres*) estate, domain; (*sphère*) province, domain.

dôme [dom] *nm* dome.

domestique [dɔmɛstik] *a* (*vie, usage, marché etc*) domestic; **travaux domestiques** housework; **animal d.** domestic animal, pet ▮ *nmf* servant.

domicile [dɔmisil] *nm* home; **travailler à d.** to work at home; **livrer à d.** (*pain etc*) to deliver (to the house).

dominer [dɔmine] *vt* to dominate; (*situation, sentiment*) to master, dominate; (*être supérieur à*) to surpass; (*tour, rocher*) to tower above, dominate (*valley, building etc*) ▮ *vi* (*être le plus fort*) to dominate; (*être le plus important*) to predominate ▮ **se d.** *vpr* to control oneself. ● **dominateur, -trice** *a* domineering. ● **domination** *nf* domination.

domino [dɔmino] *nm* domino; *pl* (*jeu*) dominoes.

dommage [dɔmaʒ] **1** *nm* **(c'est) d.!** it's a pity *ou* a shame! (**que** (+ *sub*) that); **quel d.!** what a pity *ou* a shame! **2** *nmpl* (*dégâts*) damage; **dommages-intérêts** *Jur* damages.

dompt/er [dɔ̃te] *vt* (*animal*) to tame. ●**—eur, -euse** *nmf* (*de lions*) lion tamer.

DOM-TOM [dɔmtɔm] *nmpl abrév* (*départements et territoires d'outre-mer*) (French) overseas departments and territories.

don [dɔ̃] *nm* (*cadeau, aptitude*) gift; (*charité*) donation.

donc [dɔ̃(k)] *conj* so, then; (*par conséquent*) so, therefore; **asseyez-vous d.!** (*intensif*) will you sit down!; **allons d.!** come on!

donjon [dɔ̃ʒɔ̃] *nm* (*de château*) keep.

données [dɔne] *nfpl* (*information*) data; (*de problème*) (known) facts.

donner [dɔne] *vt* to give; (*récolte, résultat*) to produce; (*sa place*) to give up; (*cartes*) to deal; **pourriez-vous me d. l'heure?** could you tell me the time?; **d. un coup à** to hit; **d. à réparer** to take (in) to be repaired; **d. raison à qn** to say s.o. is right; **ça donne soif/faim** it makes you thirsty/hungry; **c'est donné** *Fam* it's dirt cheap; **étant donné** (*la situation etc*) considering, in view of; **étant donné que** considering (that).

‖ *vi* **d. sur** (*fenêtre*) to overlook, look out onto; (*porte*) to open onto; **d. dans** (*piège*) to fall into.

‖ **se donner** *vpr* (*se consacrer*) to devote oneself (**à** to); **se d. du mal** to go to a lot of trouble (**pour faire** to do); **s'en d. à cœur joie** to have a whale of a time. ●**donneur, -euse** *nmf* giver; (*de sang, d'organe*) donor; *Cartes* dealer.

dont [dɔ̃] *pron rel* (= **de qui, duquel, de quoi** *etc*) (*personne*) of whom; (*chose*) of which; (*appartenance: personne*) whose; (*appartenance: chose*) of which, whose; **une mère d. le fils est malade** a mother whose son is ill; **la fille d. il est fier** the daughter he is proud of *ou* of whom he is proud; **les outils d. j'ai besoin** the tools I need; **la façon d. elle joue** the way (in which) she plays; **cinq enfants d. deux filles** five children two of whom are daughters.

🅖 **G69** Relative Pronouns 6 F 3e)

doper (se) [sədɔpe] *vpr* to take dope.

dorénavant [dɔrenavɑ̃] *adv* henceforth.

dor/er [dɔre] *vt* (*objet*) to gild; **se (faire) d. au soleil** to sunbathe. ●**—é** *a* (*objet*) gilt, gold; (*couleur*) golden.

dorloter [dɔrlɔte] *vt* to pamper, coddle.

dormir** [dɔrmir] *vi* to sleep; (*être endormi*) to be asleep.

dortoir [dɔrtwar] *nm* dormitory.

dos [do] *nm* (*de personne, d'animal*) back; (*de livre*) spine; **à d. d'âne** (riding) on a donkey; **'voir au d.'** (*verso*) 'see over'.

dose [doz] *nf* dose; (*quantité administrée*) dosage. ●**doser** *vt* (*remède*) to measure out the dose of; (*équilibrer*) to strike the correct balance between. ●**dosage** *nm* measuring out (*of dose*); (*équilibre*) balance.

dossard [dosar] *nm Sp* number (*fixed on back*).

dossier [dosje] *nm* **1** (*de siège*) back. **2** (*papiers*) file, dossier; (*classeur*) folder, file.

dot [dɔt] *nf* dowry.

doter [dɔte] *vt* (*hôpital etc*) to endow; **d. de** (*matériel*) to equip with.

douane [dwan] *nf* customs. ●**douanier, -ière** *nm* customs officer.

doublage [dublaʒ] *nm* (*de film*) dubbing.

double [dubl] *a & adv* double ‖ *nm* (*copie*) copy, duplicate; **le d. (de)** (*quantité*) twice as much (as).

doubler [duble] **1** *vt* (*augmenter*) to double; (*vêtement*) to line; (*film*) to dub; (*acteur*) to stand in for; (*classe à l'école*) to repeat. **2** *vti* (*en voiture*) to overtake, pass.

doublure [dublyr] *nf* (*étoffe*) lining; *Th* understudy; *Cin* stand-in, double.

douce [dus] *voir* **doux.** ●**doucement** *adv* (*délicatement*) gently; (*à voix basse*) softly; (*lentement*) slowly; (*sans bruit*) quietly. ●**douceur** *nf* (*de miel etc*) sweetness; (*de peau etc*) softness; (*de temps*) mildness; (*de personne*) gentleness; *pl* (*sucreries*) sweets, *Am* candies.

douche [duʃ] *nf* shower. ●**doucher** *vt* **d. qn** to give s.o. a shower ‖ **se d.** *vpr* to take *ou* have a shower.

doué [dwe] *a* gifted, talented (**en** at); (*intelligent*) clever; **il est d. pour** he has a gift *ou* talent for.

douille [duj] *nf* (*d'ampoule*) *Él* socket; (*de cartouche*) case.

douillet, -ette [dujɛ, -ɛt] *a* (*lit etc*) soft, cosy, *Am* cozy; **tu es d.** (*délicat*) you're such a baby.

douleur [dulœr] *nf* (*mal*) pain; (*chagrin*) sorrow, grief. ●**douloureux, -euse** *a* (*maladie, membre, décision etc*) painful.

doute [dut] *nm* doubt; **sans d.** no doubt, probably; **sans aucun d.** without (any *ou* a) doubt. ●**douter** *vi* to doubt; **d. de qch/qn** to doubt sth/s.o.; **se d. de qch** to suspect sth; **je m'en doute** I would think so, I suspect so. ●**douteux, -euse** *a* doubtful; (*louche, médiocre*) dubious.

🅖 **douter G99** The Subjunctive 7 G 1d)

🅖 **douteux G100** The Subjunctive 7 G 1e)

Douvres [duvr] *nm ou f* Dover.

doux, douce [du, dus] *a* (*miel etc*) sweet; (*peau, lumière etc*) soft; (*temps*) mild; (*personne, pente etc*) gentle.

douze [duz] *a & nm* twelve. • **douzaine** *nf* (*douze*) dozen; (*environ*) about twelve; **une d. d'œufs/***etc* a dozen eggs/*etc*. • **douzième** *a & nmf* twelfth.

doyen, -enne [dwajɛ̃, -ɛn] *nmf Rel Univ* dean; **d. (d'âge)** oldest person.

dragée [draʒe] *nf* sugared almond.

dragon [dragɔ̃] *nm* (*animal*) dragon.

draguer [drage] *vt* **1** (*rivière etc*) to dredge. **2** *Arg* (*faire du baratin à*) to chat (*s.o.*) up, *Am* smooth-talk (*s.o.*).

drame [dram] *nm* drama; (*catastrophe*) tragedy. • **dramatique** *a* dramatic; **auteur d.** playwright, dramatist; **film d.** drama.

drap [dra] *nm* (*de lit*) sheet; **d. housse** fitted sheet; **d. de bain** bath towel.

drapeau, -x [drapo] *nm* flag; **être sous les drapeaux** to be doing one's military service.

dresser [drese] **1** *vt* (*échelle, statue*) to put up, erect; (*oreille*) to prick up; (*liste*) to draw up, make out ‖ **se d.** *vpr* (*personne*) to stand up; (*statue, montagne*) to rise up, stand; **se d. contre** (*abus*) to stand up against. **2** *vt* (*animal*) to train. • **dressage** *nm* training. • **dresseur, -euse** *nmf* trainer.

dribbler [drible] *vti Fb* to dribble.

drogue [drɔg] *nf* (*médicament*) *Péj* drug; **une d.** (*stupéfiant*) a drug; **la d.** drugs, dope. • **droguer** *vt* (*victime*) to drug; (*malade*) to dose up ‖ **se d.** *vpr* to take drugs, be on drugs; (*malade*) to dose oneself up. • **drogué, -ée** *nmf* drug addict.

droguerie [drɔgri] *nf* hardware shop *ou Am* store. • **droguiste** *nmf* owner of a *droguerie*.

droit[1] [drwa] *nm* (*privilège*) right; (*d'inscription etc*) fee(s), dues; *pl* (*de douane*) duty; **le d.** (*science juridique*) law; **avoir d. à** to be entitled to; **avoir le d. de faire** to be entitled to do, have the right to do.

droit[2] [drwa] *a* (*route, ligne etc*) straight; (*vertical*) (*mur etc*) upright, straight; (*angle*) right; (*honnête*) *Fig* upright ‖ *adv* straight; **tout d.** straight *ou* right ahead. • **droite**[1] *nf* (*ligne*) straight line.

droit[3] [drwa] *a* (*côté, bras etc*) right ‖ *nm* (*coup*) *Boxe* right. • **droite**[2] *nf* **la d.** (*côté*) the right (side); *Pol* the right (wing); **à d.** (*tourner*) (to the) right; (*rouler etc*) on the right; **de d.** (*fenêtre etc*) right-hand; (*politique, candidat*) right-wing; **à d. de** on *ou* to the right of; **à d. et à gauche** (*voyager etc*) here, there and everywhere.

droitier, -ière [drwatje, -jɛr] *a & nmf* right-handed (person).

droiture [drwatyr] *nf* uprightness.

drôle [drol] *a* funny; **d. d'air/de type** funny look/fellow. • **—ment** *adv* funnily; (*extrêmement*) *Fam* terribly, dreadfully.

dromadaire [drɔmadɛr] *nm* dromedary.

dru [dry] *a* (*herbe etc*) thick, dense ‖ *adv* **tomber d.** (*pluie*) to pour down heavily; **pousser d.** to grow thick(ly).

du [dy] = **de** + **le** (*voir* **de**[1,2,3] & **le**).

dû, due [dy] *a* **d. à** (*accident etc*) due to ‖ *nm* due; (*argent*) dues.

duc [dyk] *nm* duke. • **duchesse** *nf* duchess.

duel [dɥɛl] *nm* duel.

dûment [dymɑ̃] *adv* duly.

dune [dyn] *nf* (sand) dune.

duo [dɥo] *nm Mus* duet.

dupe [dyp] *nf* dupe, fool ‖ *a* **d. de** duped by, fooled by.

duplex [dyplɛks] *nm* split-level flat, *Am* duplex.

duplicata [dyplikata] *nm inv* duplicate.

duquel *voir* **lequel**.

dur [dyr] *a* (*substance*) hard; (*difficile*) hard, tough; (*hiver, personne, ton*) harsh; (*œuf*) hard-boiled; **d. d'oreille** hard of hearing; **d. à cuire** *Fam* hard-bitten, tough ‖ *adv* (*travailler*) hard ‖ *nm Fam* tough guy.

durable [dyrabl] *a* durable.

durant [dyrɑ̃] *prép* during.

durcir [dyrsir] *vti*, **se d.** *vpr* to harden.

durée [dyre] *nf* (*de film etc*) length; (*période*) duration; **disque de longue d.** long-playing record. • **durer** *vi* to last; **ça dure depuis...** it's been going on for....

dureté [dyrte] *nf* hardness; (*de ton etc*) harshness.

duvet [dyvɛ] *nm* **1** (*d'oiseau, de visage*) down. **2** (*sac*) sleeping bag.

dynamique [dinamik] *a* dynamic ‖ *nf* (*force*) dynamic force. • **dynamisme** *nm* dynamism.

dynamite [dinamit] *nf* dynamite.

dynamo [dinamo] *nf* dynamo.

dynastie [dinasti] *nf* dynasty.

dysenterie [disɑ̃tri] *nf Méd* dysentery.

dyslexique [dislɛksik] *a & nmf* dyslexic.

E

E, e [ə, ø] *nm* E, e.

EAO [øao] *nm abrév* (*enseignement assisté par ordinateur*) computer-aided learning.

eau, -x [o] *nf* water; **e. douce** (*non salée*) fresh water; (*du robinet*) soft water; **e. salée** salt water; **e. de Cologne** eau de Cologne; **grandes eaux** (*d'un parc*) ornamental fountains; **tomber à l'e.** (*projet*) to fall through; **ça lui fait venir l'e. à la bouche** it makes his *ou* her mouth water. ● **e.-de-vie** *nf* (*pl* **eaux-de-vie**) brandy. ● **e.-forte** *nf* (*pl* **eaux-fortes**) (*gravure*) etching.

ébahir [ebair] *vt* to astound, dumbfound.

ébattre (s') [sebatr] *vpr* to run about, play about.

ébauche [eboʃ] *nf* (*esquisse*) (rough) outline, (rough) sketch.

ébène [ebɛn] *nf* (*bois*) ebony.

ébéniste [ebenist] *nm* cabinet-maker.

éberlué [ebɛrlɥe] *a Fam* dumbfounded.

éblouir [ebluir] *vt* to dazzle.

éboueur [ebwœr] *nm* dustman, *Am* garbage collector.

ébouillanter (s') [sebujɑ̃te] *vpr* to scald oneself.

ébouler (s') [sebule] *vpr* (*falaise etc*) to crumble; (*roches*) to fall. ● **éboulement** *nm* landslide. ● **éboulis** *nm* (mass of) fallen debris.

ébouriffé [eburife] *a* dishevelled.

ébranler [ebrɑ̃le] *vt* (*mur*, *confiance etc*) to shake; (*santé*) to weaken; (*personne*) to shake, shatter ▮ **s'é.** *vpr* (*train etc*) to move off.

ébrécher [ebreʃe] *vt* (*assiette*) to chip.

ébriété [ebrijete] *nf* **en état d'é.** under the influence of drink.

ébrouer (s') [sebrue] *vpr* (*se secouer*) to shake oneself (about).

ébruiter [ebrɥite] *vt* (*nouvelle etc*) to make known, divulge.

ébullition [ebylisjɔ̃] *nf* boiling; **être en é.** (*eau*) to be boiling.

écaille [ekɑj] *nf* (*de poisson*) scale; (*de tortue*, *d'huître*) shell; (*pour lunettes*) tortoise-shell. ● **écailler 1** *vt* (*poisson*) to scale; (*huître*) to shell. **2 s'écailler** *vpr* (*peinture*) to flake (off), peel.

écarlate [ekarlat] *a & nf* scarlet.

écarquiller [ekarkije] *vt* **é. les yeux** to open one's eyes wide.

écart [ekar] *nm* (*intervalle*) gap; (*embardée*) swerve; (*différence*) difference (**de** in, **entre** between); **écarts de** (*conduite etc*) lapses in; **le grand é.** (*de gymnaste*) the splits; **à l'é.** out of the way; **à l'é. de** away from.

écarter [ekarte] *vt* (*objets*) to move apart; (*jambes*, *rideaux*) to open; **é. qch de qch** to move sth away from sth; **é. qn de** (*exclure*) to keep s.o. out of; (*éloigner*) to keep *ou* take s.o. away from ▮ **s'é.** *vpr* (*s'éloigner*) to move away (**de** from); (*se séparer*) to move aside (**de** from). ● **écarté** *a* (*endroit*) remote; **les jambes écartées** with legs (wide) apart. ● **écartement** *nm* (*espace*) gap, distance (**de** between).

ecclésiastique [eklezjastik] *nm* clergyman.

écervelé [esɛrvəle] *a* scatterbrained.

échafaud [eʃafo] *nm* (*pour exécution*) scaffold.

échafaudage [eʃafodaʒ] *nm* (*de peintre etc*) scaffold(ing).

échalote [eʃalɔt] *nf* shallot, scallion.

échancré [eʃɑ̃kre] *a* (*encolure*) V-shaped, scooped.

échange [eʃɑ̃ʒ] *nm* exchange; **en é.** in exchange (**de** for). ● **échanger** *vt* to exchange (**contre** for).

échangeur [eʃɑ̃ʒœr] *nm* (*intersection*) *Aut* interchange.

échantillon [eʃɑ̃tijɔ̃] *nm* sample. ● **échantillonnage** *nm* (*collection*) range (of samples).

échapper [eʃape] *vi* **é. à qn** to escape from s.o.; **é. à la mort** to escape death; **son nom m'échappe** his *ou* her name escapes me; **ça lui a échappé (des mains)** it slipped out of his *ou* her hands; **l'é. belle** to have a close shave ▮ **s'é.** *vpr* (*s'enfuir*) to escape (**de** from); (*gaz*, *eau*) to escape, come out; (*cycliste*) to pull *ou* break away. ● **échappée** *nf* (*de cycliste*) breakaway. ● **échappement** *nm* **tuyau d'é.** *Aut* exhaust pipe; **pot d'é.** *Aut* silencer, *Am* muffler.

écharde [eʃard] *nf* (*de bois*) splinter.

écharpe [eʃarp] *nf* scarf; (*de maire*) sash; **en é.** (*bras*) in a sling.

échasse [eʃas] *nf* (*bâton*) stilt.

échauffer [eʃofe] *vt* (*moteur*) to overheat; (*esprits*) to excite ▮ **s'é.** *vpr* (*discussion*, *sportif*) to warm up.

échéance [eʃeɑ̃s] *nf* (*date limite*) date

(due), expiry *ou Am* expiration date; (*paiement*) payment (due); **à brève/longue é.** (*projet, emprunt*) short-/long-term.

échéant (le cas) [ləkazeʃeɑ̃] *adv* if the occasion should arise, possibly.

échec [eʃɛk] *nm* **1** (*insuccès*) failure. **2 les échecs** (*jeu*) chess; **en é.** in check; **é.!** check!; **é. et mat!** checkmate!

échelle [eʃɛl] *nf* **1** (*marches*) ladder; **faire la courte é. à qn** to give s.o. a leg up *ou Am* a boost. **2** (*dimension*) scale.

échelon [eʃlɔ̃] *nm* (*d'échelle*) rung; (*de fonctionnaire*) grade.

échelonner [eʃlɔne] *vt* (*paiements*) to spread out, space out ‖ **s'é.** *vpr* to be spread out.

échevelé [eʃəvle] *a* (*ébouriffé*) dishevelled; (*course, danse etc*) wild.

échine [eʃin] *nf Anat* backbone, spine.

échiquier [eʃikje] *nm* (*plateau*) chessboard.

écho [eko] *nm* (*d'un son*) echo; *pl* (*dans la presse*) gossip (items), local news; **avoir des échos de** to hear some news about; **se faire l'é. de** (*opinions etc*) to echo.

échographie [ekografi] *nf* (ultrasound) scan; **passer une é.** (*femme enceinte*) to have a scan.

échouer [eʃwe] **1** *vi* to fail; **é. à** (*examen*) to fail. **2** *vi*, **s'échouer** *vpr* (*navire*) to run aground.

éclabousser [eklabuse] *vt* to splash, spatter (**de** with). • **éclaboussure** *nf* splash.

éclair [eklɛr] **1** *nm* (*lumière*) flash; (*d'orage*) flash of lightning. **2** *nm* (*gâteau*) éclair.

éclairage [eklɛraʒ] *nm* (*de pièce etc*) lighting.

éclaircir [eklɛrsir] *vt* (*couleur etc*) to make lighter; (*mystère*) to clear up ‖ **s'é.** *vpr* (*ciel*) to clear (up); (*situation*) to become clear; **s'é. la voix** to clear one's throat. • **éclaircie** *nf* (*durée*) sunny spell. • **éclaircissement** *nm* (*explication*) clarification.

éclairer [eklere] *vt* (*pièce etc*) to light (up); **é. qn** (*avec une lampe etc*) to give s.o. some light ‖ *vi* (*lampe*) to give light ‖ **s'é.** *vpr* (*visage*) to light up, brighten up; **s'é. à la bougie** to use candlelight; **s'é. à l'électricité** to have electric lighting. • **éclairé** *a* (*averti*) enlightened; **bien/mal é.** (*illuminé*) well/badly lit.

éclaireur, -euse [eklɛrœr, -øz] *nmf* (boy) scout, (girl) guide.

éclat [ekla] *nm* **1** (*de la lumière*) brightness; (*de phare*) *Aut* glare; (*splendeur*) brilliance; (*de la jeunesse*) bloom. **2** (*de verre ou de bois*) splinter; (*de rire, colère*) (out)burst; **éclats de voix** noisy outbursts, shouts.

éclat/er [eklate] *vi* (*pneu etc*) to burst; (*bombe*) to go off, explode; (*verre*) to shatter; (*guerre, incendie*) to break out; (*orage, scandale*) to break; **é. de rire** to burst out laughing; **é. en sanglots** to burst into tears. • **—ant** *a* (*lumière, couleur, succès*) brilliant. • **—ement** *nm* (*de pneu etc*) bursting; (*de bombe*) explosion.

éclipse [eklips] *nf* (*du soleil, d'une célébrité etc*) eclipse. • **éclipser** *vt* to eclipse ‖ **s'é.** *vpr* (*soleil*) to be eclipsed; (*partir*) *Fam* to slip away.

éclopé, -ée [eklɔpe] *a* & *nmf* lame (person).

éclore* [eklɔr] *vi* (*œuf*) to hatch; (*fleur*) to open (out), blossom. • **éclosion** *nf* hatching; opening, blossoming.

écluse [eklyz] *nf* (*de canal*) lock.

écœur/er [ekœre] *vt* (*aliment etc*) to make (*s.o.*) feel sick. • **—ant** *a* disgusting, sickening.

école [ekɔl] *nf* school; **à l'é** in *ou* at school; **aller à l'é.** to go to school; **é. de danse/dessin** dancing/art school; **é. normale** teachers' training college; **é publique** state school, *Am* public school. • **écolier, -ière** *nmf* schoolboy, schoolgirl.

écologie [ekɔlɔʒi] *nf* ecology. • **écologique** *a* ecological. • **écologiste** *a* (*programme etc*) environmentalist ‖ *nmf* environmentalist.

économe [ekɔnɔm] *a* thrifty, economical.

économie [ekɔnɔmi] *nf* (*activité économique, vertu*) economy; *pl* (*argent*) savings; **une é. de** (*gain*) a saving of; **faire des économies** to save (up); **é. dirigée** planned economy. • **économique** *a* **1** (*doctrine etc*) economic; **science é.** economics. **2** (*bon marché*) economical.

économiser [ekɔnɔmize] *vt* (*forces, argent, énergie etc*) to save ‖ *vi* to economize (**sur** on).

économiste [ekɔnɔmist] *nmf* economist.

écoper [ekɔpe] **1** *vt* (*bateau*) to bail out, bale out. **2** *vi Fam* to cop it; **é. (de)** (*punition*) to cop, get.

écorce [ekɔrs] *nf* (*d'arbre*) bark; (*de fruit*) peel, skin.

écorcher [ekɔrʃe] *vt* (*érafler*) to graze; **é. les oreilles** to grate on one's ears ‖ **s'é.** *vpr* to graze oneself. • **écorchure** *nf* graze.

Écosse [ekɔs] *nf* Scotland. • **écossais, -aise** *a* Scottish; (*tissu*) tartan; (*whisky*) Scotch ‖ *nmf* Scot.

écosser [ekɔse] *vt* (*pois*) to shell.

écouler [ekule] **1** *vt* (*se débarrasser de*) to dispose of; (*marchandises*) to sell (off), clear. **2 s'écouler** *vpr* (*eau*) to flow out; (*temps*) to pass, elapse. • **écoulé** *a* (*années*) past. • **écoulement** *nm* **1** (*de liquide, véhicules*) flow; (*de temps*) passage. **2** (*de marchandises*) sale, selling.

écourter [ekurte] *vt* (*séjour, discours etc*) to cut short; (*texte, tige etc*) to shorten.

écoute [ekut] *nf* listening; **à l'é.** *Rad* tuned in, listening in (**de** to). • **écouter** *vt* to listen to ‖ *vi* to listen; (*aux portes etc*) to eavesdrop. • **écouteur** *nm* (*de téléphone*) earpiece; *pl* (*casque*) earphones, headphones.

écran [ekrɑ̃] *nm* screen; **le petit é.** television.

écraser [ekraze] *vt* (*broyer*) to crush; (*cigarette*) to put out; (*piéton*) to run over; (*vaincre*) to beat (hollow), crush; **écrasé de** (*travail, douleur*) overwhelmed with; **se faire é.** *Aut* to get run over ‖ **s'é.** *vpr* (*avion, voiture*) to crash (**contre** into); **s'é. dans** (*foule*) to crush *ou* squash into. • **écrasant** *a* (*victoire, chaleur*) overwhelming.

écrémer [ekreme] *vt* (*lait*) to skim; **lait écrémé** skimmed milk.

écrevisse [ekrəvis] *nf* (*crustacé*) crayfish *inv*.

écrier (s') [sekrije] *vpr* to exclaim (**que** that).

écrin [ekrɛ̃] *nm* (jewel) case.

écrire** [ekrir] *vt* to write; (*noter*) to write (down); (*en toutes lettres*) to spell; **é. à la machine** to type ‖ *vi* to write ‖ **s'é.** *vpr* (*mot*) to be spelled *ou* spelt. • **écrit** *nm* written document, paper; (*examen*) written paper; **par é.** in writing.

écriteau, -x [ekrito] *nm* notice, sign.

écriture [ekrityr] *nf* (*système*) writing; (*personnelle*) (hand)writing; *pl Com* accounts; **les Écritures** *Rel* the Scripture(s).

écrivain [ekrivɛ̃] *nm* author, writer.

écrou [ekru] *nm* (*de boulon*) nut.

écrouer [ekrue] *vt* to imprison.

écrouler (s') [sekrule] *vpr* (*édifice, blessé etc*) to collapse.

écrue [ekry] *af* **toile é.** unbleached linen; **soie é.** raw silk.

ÉCU [eky] *nm abrév* (*European Currency Unit*) ECU.

écueil [ekœj] *nm* (*rocher*) reef; (*obstacle*) *Fig* pitfall.

écuelle [ekɥɛl] *nf* (*bol*) bowl.

éculé [ekyle] *a* (*chaussure*) worn out at the heel; (*plaisanterie*) *Fig* hackneyed.

écume [ekym] *nf* (*de mer, bave d'animal etc*) foam. • **écumer** *vt Culin* to skim; (*piller*) to plunder ‖ *vi* to foam (**de rage** with anger).

écureuil [ekyrœj] *nm* squirrel.

écurie [ekyri] *nf* stable.

écusson [ekysɔ̃] *nm* (*en étoffe*) badge.

écuyer, -ère [ekɥije, -ɛr] *nmf* (*cavalier*) (horse) rider, equestrian.

eczéma [ɛgzema] *nm Méd* eczema.

édenté [edɑ̃te] *a* toothless.

édifice [edifis] *nm* building. • **édifier** *vt* (*bâtiment*) to erect.

Édimbourg [edɛ̃bur] *nm ou f* Edinburgh.

éditer [edite] *vt* (*publier*) to publish. • **éditeur, -trice** *nmf* publisher. • **édition** *nf* (*livre, journal*) edition; (*métier*) publishing.

édredon [edrədɔ̃] *nm* eiderdown.

éducateur, -trice [edykatœr, -tris] *nmf* educator.

éducatif, -ive [edykatif, -iv] *a* educational.

éducation [edykɑsjɔ̃] *nf* (*enseignement*) education; (*façon d'élever*) upbringing; **avoir de l'é.** to have good manners; **é. physique** physical education. • **éduquer** *vt* (*à l'école*) to educate (*s.o.*); (*à la maison*) to bring (*s.o.*) up; (*esprit*) to educate, train.

effacer [efase] *vt* (*gommer*) to rub out, erase; (*en lavant*) to wash out; (*avec un chiffon*) to wipe away ‖ **s'e.** *vpr* (*souvenir, couleur etc*) to fade; (*se placer en retrait*) to step *ou* draw aside. • **effacé** *a* (*modeste*) self-effacing.

effarant [efarɑ̃] *a Fam* incredible.

effaroucher [efaruʃe] *vt* to scare away.

effectif, -ive [efɛktif, -iv] **1** *a* (*réel*) effective, real. **2** *nm* (*de classe etc*) total number, size; *pl* (*employés*) & *Mil* manpower. • **effectivement** *adv* (*en effet*) actually, effectively.

effectuer [efɛktɥe] *vt* (*expérience etc*) to carry out; (*paiement, trajet etc*) to make.

efféminé [efemine] *a* effeminate.

effervescent [efɛrvesɑ̃] *a* (*mélange, jeunesse*) effervescent.

effet [efɛ] *nm* **1** (*résultat*) effect; (*impression*) impression, effect (**sur** on); **faire de l'e.** (*remède etc*) to be effective; **rester sans e.** to have no effect; **en e.** indeed, in fact; **sous l'e. de la colère** (*agir*) in anger; **e. de serre** greenhouse effect. **2 e. de commerce** bill, draft.

effets [efɛ] *nmpl* (*vêtements*) clothes, things.

efficace [efikas] *a* (*mesure etc*) effective; (*personne*) efficient. • **efficacité** *nf* effectiveness; efficiency.

effilocher (s') [sefilɔʃe] *vpr* to fray.

effleurer [eflœre] *vt* (*frôler*) to skim, touch (lightly); (*question*) *Fig* to touch on; **e. qn** (*pensée etc*) to cross s.o.'s mind.

effondrer (s') [sefɔ̃dre] *vpr* (*projet, édifice,*

personne) to collapse. ● **effondrement** *nm* collapse; (*abattement*) dejection.

efforcer (s') [sefɔrse] *vpr* **s'e. de faire** to try (hard) *ou* endeavour to do.

effort [efɔr] *nm* effort; **sans e.** (*réussir etc*) effortlessly; **faire des efforts** to try (hard), make an effort.

effraction [efraksjɔ̃] *nf* **pénétrer par e.** (*cambrioleur*) to break in; **vol avec e.** housebreaking.

effrayer [efreje] *vt* to frighten, scare ‖ **s'e.** *vpr* to be frightened *ou* scared. ● **effrayant** *a* frightening, scary.

effriter (s') [sefrite] *vpr* to crumble (away).

effroi [efrwa] *nm* (*frayeur*) dread. ● **effroyable** *a* dreadful, appalling.

effronté [efrɔ̃te] *a* (*enfant etc*) insolent, cheeky. ● **effronterie** *nf* insolence.

effusion [efyzjɔ̃] *nf* **1 e. de sang** bloodshed. **2** (*manifestation de tendresse*) emotional outburst; **avec e.** effusively.

égal, -ale, -aux [egal, -o] *a* equal (**à** to); (*uniforme, régulier*) even; **ça m'est é.** I don't care ‖ *nmf* (*personne*) equal; **traiter qn d'é. à é.** *ou* **en é.** to treat s.o. as an equal; **sans é.** without match. ● **—ement** *adv* (*aussi*) also, as well; (*au même degré*) equally. ● **égaler** *vt* to equal, match (**en** in); **3 plus 4 égale(nt) 7** 3 plus 4 equals 7.

égaliser [egalize] *vt* to equalize; (*terrain*) to level ‖ *vi Sp* to equalize.

égalité [egalite] *nf* equality; (*regularité*) evenness; **à é. (de score)** *Sp* even, equal (in points); **signe d'é.** *Math* equals sign.

égard [egar] *nm* **à l'é. de** (*envers*) towards; (*concernant*) with respect *ou* regard to; **avoir des égards pour qn** to have respect *ou* consideration for s.o.; **à cet é.** in this respect.

égarer [egare] *vt* (*objet*) to mislay ‖ **s'é.** *vpr* to lose one's way, get lost; (*objet*) to get mislaid, go astray.

égayer [egeje] *vt* (*pièce*) to brighten up; **é. qn** (*réconforter, amuser*) to cheer s.o. up.

églantier [eglɑ̃tje] *nm* (*arbre*) wild rose. ● **églantine** *nf* (*fleur*) wild rose.

église [egliz] *nf* church.

égoïsme [egɔism] *nm* selfishness. ● **égoïste** *a* & *nmf* selfish (person).

égorger [egɔrʒe] *vt* to cut the throat of.

égosiller (s') [segɔzije] *vpr* to scream one's head off, bawl out.

égout [egu] *nm* sewer; **eaux d'é.** sewage.

égoutter [egute] *vt* (*vaisselle*) to drain; (*légumes*) to strain, drain ‖ **s'é.** *vpr* to drain; to strain; (*linge*) to drip. ● **égouttoir** *nm* (*panier*) (dish) drainer.

égratigner (s') [segratiɲe] *vpr* (*en tombant etc*) to scratch oneself. ● **égratignure** *nf* scratch.

égrener [egrəne] *vt* (*raisins*) to pick off; (*épis*) to shell.

Égypte [eʒipt] *nf* Egypt. ● **égyptien, -ienne** [-sjɛ̃, -sjɛn] *a* & *nmf* Egyptian.

eh! [e] *int* hey!; **eh bien!** well!

éhonté [eɔ̃te] *a* shameless; **mensonge é.** barefaced lie.

éjecter [eʒɛkte] *vt* to eject.

élaborer [elabɔre] *vt* (*système etc*) to elaborate. ● **élaboration** *nf* elaboration.

élaguer [elage] *vt* (*arbre, texte etc*) to prune.

élan [elɑ̃] *nm* (*vitesse*) momentum, impetus; (*impulsion*) impulse; (*fougue*) fervour, spirit; **prendre son é.** *Sp* to take a run (up).

élancé [elɑ̃se] *a* (*personne, taille etc*) slender.

élancer (s') [selɑ̃se] *vpr* (*bondir*) to leap *ou* rush (forward); **s'é. vers le ciel** (*tour*) to soar up (high) into the sky.

élargir [elarʒir] *vt* (*chemin*) to widen; (*vêtement*) to let out; (*esprit, débat*) to broaden ‖ **s'é.** *vpr* (*sentier etc*) to widen out; (*vêtement*) to stretch.

élastique [elastik] *a* (*objet*) elastic; (*règlement, notion*) flexible, supple ‖ *nm* (*lien*) elastic *ou* rubber band; (*tissu*) elastic.

élection [elɛksjɔ̃] *nf* election; **é. partielle** by-election. ● **électeur, -trice** *nmf* voter, elector. ● **électoral, -aux** *a* **campagne électorale** election campaign; **liste électorale** register of electors; **collège é.** electoral college.

électricien [elɛktrisjɛ̃] *nm* electrician. ● **électricité** *nf* electricity; **coupure d'é.** power cut. ● **électrique** *a* (*pendule, décharge*) electric; (*courant, fil*) electric(al); (*effet*) *Fig* electric.

électrocuter [elɛktrɔkyte] *vt* to electrocute.

électrogène [elɛktrɔʒɛn] *a* **groupe é.** *Él* generator.

électroménager [elɛktrɔmenaʒe] *am* **appareil é.** household electrical appliance.

électron [elɛktrɔ̃] *nm* electron. ● **électronicien, -ienne** *nmf* electronics engineer. ● **électronique** *a* electronic; **microscope é.** electron microscope ‖ *nf* electronics.

électrophone [elɛktrɔfɔn] *nm* record player.

élégant [elegɑ̃] *a* (*style, solution etc*) elegant; (*bien habillé*) smart, elegant. ● **élégamment** *adv* elegantly; smartly. ● **élégance** *nf* elegance; **avec é.** elegantly; (*s'habiller*) smartly, elegantly.

élément [elemɑ̃] *nm* (*composante, per-*

sonne) & *Ch* element; (*de meuble*) unit; (*d'ensemble*) *Math* member; *pl* (*notions*) rudiments, elements; **dans son é.** (*milieu*) in one's element.

élémentaire [elemɑ̃tɛr] *a* basic; (*cours, école etc*) elementary.

éléphant [elefɑ̃] *nm* elephant. ● **éléphantesque** *a* (*énorme*) *Fam* elephantine.

élevage [ɛlvaʒ] *nm* breeding, rearing; **é. de bovins** cattle rearing; **faire l'é. de** to breed, rear.

élévation [elevɑsjɔ̃] *nf* raising; *Géom* elevation; **é. de** (*hausse*) rise in.

élève [elɛv] *nmf Scol* pupil.

élevé [ɛlve] *a* (*haut*) high; (*noble*) noble; **bien/mal é.** well-/bad-mannered.

élever [ɛlve] *vt* (*prix, voix etc*) to raise; (*enfant*) to bring up, raise; (*animal*) to breed, rear ‖ **s'é.** *vpr* (*prix, ton etc*) to rise; (*cerf-volant*) to rise (up) into the sky; **s'é. à** (*prix etc*) to amount to; **s'é. contre** to rise up against.

éleveur, -euse [ɛlvœr, -øz] *nmf* breeder.

éligible [eliʒibl] *a Pol* eligible (**à** for).

élimé [elime] *a* (*tissu*) threadbare.

éliminer [elimine] *vt* to eliminate. ● **élimination** *nf* elimination. ● **éliminatoire** *a* **épreuve é.** *Sp* qualifying round, heat; *Scol* qualifying exam; **note é.** *Scol* disqualifying mark ‖ *nfpl* **éliminatoires** *Sp* qualifying rounds.

élire* [elir] *vt Pol* to elect (**à** to).

élite [elit] *nf* elite (**de** of); **les élites** the elite; **troupes/***etc* **d'e.** crack *ou* elite troops/*etc*.

elle [ɛl] *pron f* **1** (*sujet*) she; (*chose, animal*) it; *pl* they; **e. est** she is; it is; **elles sont** they are. **2** (*complément*) her; (*chose, animal*) it; *pl* them; **pour e.** for her; **pour elles** for them; **plus grande qu'e./qu'elles** taller than her/them. ● **e.-même** *pron f* herself; (*chose, animal*) itself; *pl* themselves.

❶**elle** & **elles** **G57** Subject Pronouns 6 D 1c)
❶**elle** & **elles** **G62** Disjunctive Pronouns 6 D 5

élocution [elɔkysjɔ̃] *nf* diction; **défaut d'é.** speech defect.

éloge [elɔʒ] *nm* (*compliment*) praise; (*panégyrique*) eulogy. ● **élogieux, -euse** *a* laudatory.

éloigné [elwaɲe] *a* (*lieu*) far away, remote; (*date, parent*) distant; **é. de** (*village, maison etc*) far (away) from; (*très différent*) far removed from.

éloignement [elwaɲ(ə)mɑ̃] *nm* remoteness, distance; (*absence*) separation (**de** from).

éloigner [elwaɲe] *vt* (*chose, personne*) to move *ou* take away (**de** from); (*malade, moustiques*) to keep away; (*crainte, idée*) to get rid of, banish; (*échéance*) to put off; **é. qn de** (*sujet, but*) to take *ou* get s.o. away from ‖ **s'e.** *vpr* (*partir*) to move *ou* go away (**de** from); (*dans le passé*) to become (more) remote; **s'é. de** (*sujet, but*) to get away from.

élongation [elɔ̃gɑsjɔ̃] *nf Méd* pulled muscle.

éloquent [elɔkɑ̃] *a* eloquent. ● **éloquence** *nf* eloquence.

élu, -ue [ely] *pp de* **élire** ‖ *nmf Pol* elected member *ou* representative.

émail, -aux [emaj, -o] *nm* enamel; **casserole/***etc* **en é.** enamel saucepan/*etc*.

émanciper [emɑ̃sipe] *vt* (*femmes*) to emancipate ‖ **s'é.** *vpr* to become emancipated.

émaner [emane] *vt* **e. de** to come *ou* emanate from. ● **émanations** *nfpl* (*odeurs*) smells; (*vapeurs*) fumes; **é. toxiques** toxic fumes.

emballer [ɑ̃bale] **1** *vt* (*dans une caisse etc*) to pack; (*dans du papier*) to wrap (up). **2** *vt* **e. qn** (*passionner*) *Fam* to thrill s.o. ‖ **s'e.** *vpr* (*personne*) *Fam* to get carried away; (*cheval*) to bolt; (*moteur*) to race. ● **emballé** *a Fam* enthusiastic. ● **emballage** *nm* (*action*) packing; wrapping; (*caisse*) packaging; **papier d'e.** wrapping (paper).

embarcadère [ɑ̃barkadɛr] *nm* quay, wharf.

embarcation [ɑ̃barkɑsjɔ̃] *nf* (small) boat.

embardée [ɑ̃barde] *nf Aut* (sudden) swerve; **faire une e.** to swerve.

embargo [ɑ̃bargo] *nm* embargo.

embarquer [ɑ̃barke] *vt* (*passagers*) to take on board; (*marchandises*) to load (up); **e. qn dans** (*affaire*) *Fam* to involve s.o. in ‖ *vi*, **s'e.** *vpr* to (go on) board, embark; **s'e. dans** (*aventure etc*) *Fam* to embark on. ● **embarquement** *nm* (*de passagers*) boarding.

embarras [ɑ̃bara] *nm* (*gêne*) embarrassment; (*difficulté*) difficulty, trouble; (*obstacle*) obstacle; **dans l'e.** in difficulty, in an awkward situation; (*financièrement*) in difficulties.

embarrasser [ɑ̃barase] *vt* (*obstruer*) to clutter; **e. qn** to be in s.o.'s way; (*déconcerter*) to embarrass s.o.; **s'e. de** to burden oneself with; (*se soucier*) to bother oneself about. ● **embarrassant** *a* (*paquet*) cumbersome; (*question*) embarrassing.

embauche [ɑ̃boʃ] *nf* (*action*) hiring; (*travail*) work. ● **embaucher** *vt* (*ouvrier*) to hire, take on.

embaumer [ɑ̃bome] *vt* (*parfumer*) to give a sweet smell to ‖ *vi* to smell sweet.

embellir [ɑ̃belir] *vt* (*pièce etc*) to make more attractive; (*texte, vérité*) to embel-

lish ‖ *vi* (*jeune fille etc*) to blossom out.
embêter [ɑ̃bete] *vt Fam* (*agacer*) to annoy, bother; (*ennuyer*) to bore ‖ **s'e.** *vpr Fam* to get bored. ●**embêtant** *a Fam* annoying; boring. ●**embêtement** [-ɛtmɑ̃] *nm Fam* **un e.** (some) trouble *ou* bother; **des embêtements** trouble, bother.
emblée (d') [dɑ̃ble] *adv* right away.
emblème [ɑ̃blɛm] *nm* emblem.
emboîter [ɑ̃bwate] *vt*, **s'e.** *vpr* (*tuyau*(*x*)) to fit together; **e. le pas à qn** to follow close on s.o.'s heels; (*imiter*) *Fig* to follow in s.o.'s footsteps.
embouchure [ɑ̃buʃyr] *nf* (*de fleuve*) mouth; *Mus* mouthpiece.
embourber (s') [sɑ̃burbe] *vpr* (*véhicule*) & *Fig* to get bogged down.
embouteillage [ɑ̃butɛjaʒ] *nm* traffic jam.
embouteillé [ɑ̃buteje] *a* (*rue etc*) congested.
emboutir [ɑ̃butir] *vt* (*voiture*) to knock *ou* crash into.
embranchement [ɑ̃brɑ̃ʃmɑ̃] *nm* (*de voie*) junction; (*division du règne animal*) branch.
embraser [ɑ̃brɑze] *vt* to set ablaze ‖ **s'e.** *vpr* (*prendre feu*) to flare up.
embrasser [ɑ̃brase] *vt* **e. qn** (*donner un baiser à*) to kiss s.o.; (*serrer contre soi*) to embrace *ou* hug s.o.; **e. une croyance**/*etc* to embrace a belief/*etc* ‖ **s'e.** *vpr* to kiss (each other). ●**embrassade** *nf* embrace, hug.
embrasure [ɑ̃brazyr] *nf* (*de fenêtre, porte*) opening.
embray/er [ɑ̃breje] *vi* to let in *ou* engage the clutch. ●**—age** [-ɛjaʒ] *nm* (*mécanisme, pédale*) *Aut* clutch.
embrigader [ɑ̃brigade] *vt Péj* to recruit.
embrocher [ɑ̃brɔʃe] *vt* (*volaille etc*) to put on a spit, skewer.
embrouiller [ɑ̃bruje] *vt* (*fils*) to tangle (up); (*papiers etc*) to mix up; **e. qn** to confuse s.o. ‖ **s'e.** *vpr* to get confused *ou* muddled (**dans** in, with).
embroussaillé [ɑ̃brusɑje] *a* (*barbe, chemin*) bushy.
embruns [ɑ̃brœ̃] *nmpl* (sea) spray.
embryon [ɑ̃brijɔ̃] *nm* embryo.
embûches [ɑ̃byʃ] *nfpl* (*difficultés*) traps, pitfalls.
embusquer (s') [sɑ̃byske] *vpr* to lie in ambush. ●**embuscade** *nf* ambush.
éméché [emeʃe] *a* (*ivre*) *Fam* tipsy.
émeraude [ɛmrod] *nf* & *a inv* emerald.
émerger [emɛrʒe] *vi* to emerge (**de** from).
émerveiller [emɛrveje] *vt* to amaze, fill with wonder ‖ **s'é.** *vpr* to marvel (**de** at).
●**émerveillement** *nm* wonder, amazement.
émett/re* [emɛtr] *vt* (*lumière, son etc*) to give out; (*message radio*) to broadcast; (*timbre, monnaie*) to issue; (*opinion, vœu*) to express. ●**—eur** *nm* (**poste**) **é.** *Rad* transmitter.
émeute [emøt] *nf* riot. ●**émeutier, -ière** *nmf* rioter.
émietter [emjete] *vt*, **s'é.** *vpr* (*pain etc*) to crumble.
émigr/er [emigre] *vi* (*personne*) to emigrate. ●**—ant, -ante** *nmf* emigrant. ●**—é, -ée** *nmf* exile, émigré. ●**émigration** *nf* emigration.
éminent [eminɑ̃] *a* eminent.
émissaire [emisɛr] *nm* emissary.
émission [emisjɔ̃] *nf* (*de radio etc*) programme, broadcast; (*diffusion*) transmission; (*de timbre, monnaie*) issue.
emmagasiner [ɑ̃magazine] *vt* to store (up).
emmanchure [ɑ̃mɑ̃ʃyr] *nf* (*de vêtement*) arm hole.
emmêler [ɑ̃mele] *vt* (*fil, cheveux*) to tangle (up) ‖ **s'e.** *vpr* to get tangled.
emménager [ɑ̃menaʒe] *vi* (*dans un logement*) to move in; **e. dans** to move into.
emmener [ɑ̃mne] *vt* to take (**à** to); **e. qn faire une promenade** to take s.o. for a walk; **e. qn en voiture** to give s.o. a lift *ou Am* a ride, drive s.o. (**à** to).
emmerder [ɑ̃mɛrde] *vt Arg* to annoy, bug; (*ennuyer*) to bore stiff ‖ **s'e.** *vpr Arg* to get bored stiff. ●**emmerdement** *nm Arg* bother, trouble. ●**emmerdeur, -euse** *nmf* (*personne*) *Arg* pain in the neck.
emmitoufler (s') [sɑ̃mitufle] *vpr* to wrap (oneself) up (**dans** in).
émoi [emwa] *nm* excitement; **en é.** agog.
émotion [emosjɔ̃] *nf* (*sentiment*) emotion; (*trouble*) excitement; **donner des émotions à qn** give s.o. a scare. ●**émotif, -ive** *a* emotional.
émoussé [emuse] *a* (*pointe*) blunt; (*sentiment*) dulled.
émouvoir* [emuvwar] *vt* (*affecter*) to move, touch ‖ **s'é.** *vpr* to be moved *ou* touched. ●**émouvant** *a* moving, touching.
empailler [ɑ̃paje] *vt* (*animal*) to stuff.
empaqueter [ɑ̃pakte] *vt* to pack(age).
emparer (s') [sɑ̃pare] *vpr* **s'e. de** to take, grab.
empâter (s') [sɑ̃pɑte] *vpr* to fill out, get fat(ter). ●**empâté** *a* fleshy, fat.
empêch/er [ɑ̃peʃe] *vt* to prevent, stop; **e. qn de faire** to prevent *ou* stop s.o. (from) doing; **n'empêche qu'elle a raison** *Fam* all the same she's right; **elle ne peut pas s'e. de**

rire she can't help laughing. ●**—ement** [-ɛʃmɑ̃] *nm* difficulty, hitch; **avoir un e.** to have something come up at the last minute (*to prevent or delay an action*).

empereur [ɑ̃prœr] *nm* emperor.

empester [ɑ̃pɛste] *vt* (*tabac etc*) to stink of; (*pièce*) to make stink, stink out; **e. qn** to stink s.o. out ‖ *vi* to stink.

empêtrer (s') [sɑ̃petre] *vpr* to get entangled (**dans** in).

emphase [ɑ̃faz] *nf* pomposity. ●**emphatique** *a* pompous.

empiéter [ɑ̃pjete] *vi* **e. sur** to encroach upon.

empiffrer (s') [sɑ̃pifre] *vpr Fam* to gorge oneself (**de** with).

empiler [ɑ̃pile] *vt*, **s'e.** *vpr* to pile up (**sur** on); **s'e. dans** (*personnes*) to pile into (*building, car etc*).

empire [ɑ̃pir] *nm* (*territoires*) empire; (*autorité*) hold, influence; **sous l'e. de** (*peur etc*) in the grip of.

empirer [ɑ̃pire] *vi* to worsen, get worse.

emplacement [ɑ̃plasmɑ̃] *nm* (*de stationnement*) place; (*d'une construction*) site, location.

emplette [ɑ̃plɛt] *nf* purchase; **faire des emplettes** to do some shopping.

emplir [ɑ̃plir] *vt*, **s'e.** *vpr* to fill (**de** with).

emploi [ɑ̃plwa] *nm* **1** (*usage*) use; **e. du temps** timetable; **mode d'e.** directions (for use). **2** (*travail*) job, employment; **l'e.** (*travail*) *Écon Pol* employment; **sans e.** unemployed.

employer [ɑ̃plwaje] *vt* (*utiliser*) to use; **e. qn** to employ s.o. ‖ **s'e.** *vpr* (*expression etc*) to be used; **s'e. à faire** to devote oneself to doing. ●**employé, -ée** *nmf* employee; (*de bureau, banque*) clerk, employee. ●**employeur, -euse** *nmf* employer.

empocher [ɑ̃pɔʃe] *vt* (*argent*) to pocket.

empoigner [ɑ̃pwaɲe] *vt* (*saisir*) to grab.

empoisonner [ɑ̃pwazɔne] *vt* (*personne, aliment etc*) to poison; (*empester*) to stink out; (*gâter*) to bedevil; **e. qn** (*embêter*) *Fam* to get on s.o.'s nerves ‖ **s'e.** *vpr* (*par accident*) to be poisoned; (*volontairement*) to poison oneself. ●**empoisonnant** *a* (*embêtant*) *Fam* irritating. ●**empoisonnement** *nm* poisoning; (*ennui*) *Fam* trouble.

emporter [ɑ̃pɔrte] *vt* (*prendre*) to take (away) (**avec soi** with one); (*enlever*) to take away; (*entraîner*) to carry away; (*par le vent*) to blow off *ou* away; (*par les vagues*) to sweep away; (*par la maladie*) to carry off; **l'e. sur qn** to get the upper hand over s.o.; **il l'a emporté** he won. ‖ **s'emporter** *vpr* to lose one's temper (**contre** with). ●**emporté** *a* (*caractère*) hot-tempered.

empoté [ɑ̃pɔte] *a Fam* clumsy.

empreint [ɑ̃prɛ̃] *a* **e. de** *Litt* stamped with, heavy with.

empreinte [ɑ̃prɛ̃t] *nf* (*marque*) & *Fig* mark, stamp; **e. (digitale)** fingerprint; **e. (de pas)** footprint.

empresser (s') [sɑ̃prese] *vpr* **s'e. de faire** to hasten to do. ●**empressé** *a* eager, attentive. ●**empressement** [-ɛsmɑ̃] *nm* (*hâte*) eagerness; (*auprès de qn*) attentiveness.

emprise [ɑ̃priz] *nf* hold (**sur** over).

emprisonn/er [ɑ̃prizɔne] *vt* to jail, imprison; (*enfermer*) *Fig* to confine. ●**—ement** *nm* imprisonment.

emprunt [ɑ̃prœ̃] *nm* (*argent etc*) loan; (*mot*) *Ling* borrowed word; **faire un e.** to get a loan; **nom d'e.** assumed name. ●**emprunter** *vt* (*argent*) to borrow (**à qn** from s.o.); (*route etc*) to use; **e. à** (*tirer de*) to derive *ou* borrow from.

ému [emy] *pp de* **émouvoir** ‖ *a* (*attendri*) moved; (*attristé*) upset; (*apeuré*) nervous; **une voix émue** a voice charged with emotion.

émulation [emylɑsjɔ̃] *nf* emulation.

en[1] [ɑ̃] *prép* **1** (*lieu*) in; (*direction*) to; **être en ville/en France** to be in town/in France; **aller en ville/en France** to go (in)to town/to France.

2 (*temps*) in; **en février** in February; **en été** in summer; **d'heure en heure** from hour to hour; **en dix minutes** (*durée*) in ten minutes.

3 (*moyen, état etc*) by; in; on; at; **en avion** by plane; **en groupe** in a group; **en fleur** in flower; **en vain** in vain; **en congé** on leave; **en mer** at sea; **en guerre** at war.

4 (*matière*) in; **en bois** in wood, wooden; **chemise en nylon** nylon shirt; **c'est en or** it's (made of) gold.

5 (*domaine*) **étudiant en lettres** arts *ou* humanities student; **docteur en médecine** doctor of medicine.

6 (*comme*) **en cadeau** as a present; **en ami** as a friend.

7 (+ *participe présent*) **en mangeant/***etc* while eating/*etc*; **en apprenant que...** on hearing that...; **en souriant** smiling, with a smile; **en ne disant rien** by saying nothing; **sortir en courant** to run out.

8 (*transformation*) into; **traduire en français/***etc* to translate into French/*etc*.

❶**G116** The Present Participle 7 I 1c) ii)
❶**G117** The Past Participle 7 I 2c) ii)
❶**G178** Prepositions 8

ⓘ**G220** Noun Phrases 13 B 7

en² [ɑ̃] *pron & adv* **1** (= *de là*) from there; **j'en viens** I've just come from there. **2** (= *de ça, lui, eux etc*) **il en est content** he's pleased with it *ou* him *ou* them; **en parler** to talk about it; **en mourir** to die of *ou* from it; **elle m'en frappa** she struck me with it. **3** (*partitif*) some; **j'en ai** I have some; **en veux-tu?** do you want some *ou* any?; **donne-lui-en** give some to him *ou* her; **je t'en supplie** I beg you (to).

ⓘ**G60** The Pronoun En 6 D 3

ENA [ena] *abrév* (*École Nationale d'Administration*) school training top civil servants. • **énarque** *nmf* student *ou* former student of ENA.

encadr/er [ɑ̃kadre] *vt* (*tableau*) to frame; (*entourer d'un trait*) to circle (*word*); (*étudiants*) to supervise, train; (*prisonnier*) to flank; **je ne peux pas l'e.** *Fam* I can't stand him *ou* her. • **—ement** *nm* (*de porte, photo*) frame; **personnel d'e.** training and supervisory staff.

encaisser [ɑ̃kese] *vt* (*argent, loyer etc*) to collect; (*chèque*) to cash; (*coup*) *Fam* to take; **je ne peux pas l'e.** *Fam* I can't stand him *ou* her.

encart [ɑ̃kar] *nm* (*feuille*) insert; **e. publicitaire** publicity insert.

en-cas [ɑ̃kɑ] *nm inv* (*repas*) snack.

encastrer [ɑ̃kastre] *vt* to build in (**dans** to), embed (**dans** into).

enceinte [ɑ̃sɛ̃t] **1** *af* (*femme*) pregnant; **e. de six mois**/*etc* six months/*etc* pregnant. **2** *nf* (*muraille*) (surrounding) wall; (*espace*) enclosure; **e. (acoustique)** (loud)speakers.

encens [ɑ̃sɑ̃] *nm* incense.

encercler [ɑ̃sɛrkle] *vt* to surround.

enchaîner [ɑ̃ʃene] *vt* (*animal*) to chain (up); (*prisonnier*) to put in chains, chain (up); (*idées etc*) to link (up) ‖ *vi* (*continuer à parler*) to continue ‖ **s'e.** *vpr* (*idées etc*) to be linked (up).

enchant/er [ɑ̃ʃɑ̃te] *vt* (*ravir*) to delight; (*ensorceler*) to bewitch, enchant. • **—é** *a* (*ravi*) delighted (**de** with, **que** (+ *sub*) that); (*magique*) enchanted; **e. de faire votre connaissance!** pleased to meet you! • **—ement** *nm* delight; **comme par e.** as if by magic. • **—eur** *nm* (*sorcier*) magician.

enchère [ɑ̃ʃɛr] *nf* (*offre*) bid; **vente aux enchères** auction; **mettre aux enchères** to (put up for) auction.

enchevêtrer [ɑ̃ʃvetre] *vt* to (en)tangle ‖ **s'e.** *vpr* to get entangled (**dans** in).

enclave [ɑ̃klav] *nf* enclave.

enclencher [ɑ̃klɑ̃ʃe] *vt Tech* to engage.

enclin [ɑ̃klɛ̃] *a* **e. à** inclined *ou* prone to.

enclos [ɑ̃klo] *nm* (*terrain, clôture*) enclosure.

enclume [ɑ̃klym] *nf* anvil.

encoche [ɑ̃kɔʃ] *nf* nick, notch (**à** in).

encoignure [ɑ̃kwaɲyr] *nf* corner.

encolure [ɑ̃kɔlyr] *nf* (*de cheval, vêtement*) neck; (*tour du cou*) collar (size).

encombre (sans) [sɑ̃zɑ̃kɔ̃br] *adv* without a hitch.

encombr/er [ɑ̃kɔ̃bre] *vt* (*pièce etc*) to clutter up (**de** with); (*rue*) to congest (**de** with); **e. qn** to hamper s.o.; **s'e. de** to burden oneself with. • **—ant** *a* (*paquet*) bulky; (*présence*) awkward. • **—é** *a* (*lignes téléphoniques*) jammed. • **—ement** *nm* (*d'objets*) clutter; (*de rue*) traffic jam.

encontre de (à l') [alɑ̃kɔ̃trədə] *adv* against; (*contrairement à*) contrary to.

encore [ɑ̃kɔr] *adv* **1** (*toujours*) still; **tu es e. là?** are you still here?

2 (*avec négation*) yet; **pas e.** not yet; **je ne suis pas e. prêt** I'm not ready yet.

3 (*de nouveau*) again; **essaie e.** try again.

4 (*de plus, en plus*) **e. un café** another coffee, one more coffee; **e. une fois** (once) again, once more; **e. un** another (one), one more; **e. du pain** (some) more bread; **e. quelque chose** something else; **qui/quoi e.?** who/what else?.

5 (*avec comparatif*) even, still; **e. mieux** even better, better still.

6 (*aussi*) **mais e.** but also.

7 si e. (*si seulement*) if only; **et e.!** (*à peine*) if that!, only just!

8 e. que (+ *sub*) although.

encourag/er [ɑ̃kuraʒe] *vt* to encourage (**à faire** to do). • **—eant** *a* encouraging. • **—ement** *nm* encouragement.

encrasser [ɑ̃krase] *vt* to clog up (with dirt).

encre [ɑ̃kr] *nf* ink; **e. de Chine** Indian *ou Am* India ink. • **encrier** *nm* inkpot.

encroûter (s') [sɑ̃krute] *vpr Péj* to get into a rut, get set in one's ways; **s'e. dans** (*habitude*) to get stuck in.

encyclopédie [ɑ̃siklɔpedi] *nf* encyclop(a)edia.

endetter [ɑ̃dete] *vt* **e. qn** to get s.o. into debt ‖ **s'e.** *vpr* to get into debt. • **endettement** *nm* (*dettes*) debts.

endiguer [ɑ̃dige] *vt* (*fleuve*) to dam (up); (*réprimer*) *Fig* to stem.

endimanché [ɑ̃dimɑ̃ʃe] *a* in one's Sunday best.

endive [ɑ̃div] *nf* chicory, endive.

endoctriner [ɑ̃dɔktrine] *vt* to indoctrinate.

endolori [ɑ̃dɔlɔri] *a* painful, aching.

endommager [ɑ̃dɔmaʒe] *vt* to damage.
endormir* [ɑ̃dɔrmir] *vt* (*enfant etc*) to put to sleep; (*ennuyer*) to send to sleep ‖ **s'e.** *vpr* to fall asleep, go to sleep. • **endormi** *a* asleep, sleeping; (*indolent*) *Fam* sluggish.
endosser [ɑ̃dose] *vt* (*vêtement*) to put on; (*responsabilité*) to assume; (*chèque*) to endorse.
endroit [ɑ̃drwa] *nm* **1** place, spot; **à cet e. du récit** at this point in the story; **par endroits** in places. **2** (*de tissu*) right side; **à l'e.** (*vêtement*) right side out.
enduire* [ɑ̃dɥir] *vt* to smear, coat (**de** with). • **enduit** *nm* coating; (*de mur*) plaster.
endurant [ɑ̃dyrɑ̃] *a* tough. • **endurance** *nf* endurance.
endurc/ir [ɑ̃dyrsir] *vt* **e. qn à** (*douleur etc*) to harden s.o. to; **s'e.** to become hardened (**à** to). • **—i** *a* (*insensible*) hardened; (*célibataire*) confirmed.
endurer [ɑ̃dyre] *vt* to endure, bear.
énergie [enɛrʒi] *nf* energy; **avec é.** (*protester etc*) forcefully. • **énergétique** *a* **ressources énergétiques** energy resources; **aliment é.** energy food. • **énergique** *a* (*dynamique*) energetic; (*remède*) powerful; (*mesure, ton*) forceful. • **énergiquement** *adv* energetically.
énergumène [enɛrgymɛn] *nmf Péj* rowdy character.
énerver [enɛrve] *vt* **é. qn** (*irriter*) to get on s.o.'s nerves; (*rendre nerveux*) to make s.o. nervous ‖ **s'é.** *vpr* to get worked up. • **énervé** *a* on edge.
enfance [ɑ̃fɑ̃s] *nf* childhood; **c'est l'e. de l'art** it's child's play.
enfant [ɑ̃fɑ̃] *nmf* child (*pl* children); **e. en bas âge** infant; **e. de chœur** *Rel* altar boy; **e. prodige** child prodigy; **bon e.** (*caractère*) good natured; **c'est un jeu d'e.** it's child's play. • **enfanter** *vt* to give birth to. • **enfantillage** *nm* childishness. • **enfantin** *a* (*voix, joie*) childlike; (*simple*) easy; (*puéril*) childish.
enfer [ɑ̃fɛr] *nm* hell; **d'e.** (*bruit, vision*) infernal; **à un train d'e.** at breakneck speed.
enfermer [ɑ̃fɛrme] *vt* to lock up; **s'e. dans** (*chambre etc*) to lock oneself (up) in; (*attitude etc*) *Fig* to maintain stubbornly.
enfiler [ɑ̃file] *vt* (*aiguille*) to thread; (*perles etc*) to string; (*vêtement*) *Fam* to pull on.
enfin [ɑ̃fɛ̃] *adv* (*à la fin*) finally, at last; (*en dernier lieu*) lastly; (*en somme*) in a word; (*conclusion résignée*) well; **e. bref** (*en somme*) *Fam* in a word; **mais e.** but; **(mais) e.!** for heaven's sake!
enflammer [ɑ̃flame] *vt* to set fire to; (*allumette*) to light; (*irriter*) to inflame (*throat etc*); (*imagination, colère*) to excite ‖ **s'e.** *vpr* to catch fire; **s'e. de colère** to flare up. • **enflammé** *a* (*discours*) fiery.
enfler [ɑ̃fle] *vt* to swell ‖ *vi Méd* to swell (up). • **enflure** *nf* swelling.
enfoncer [ɑ̃fɔ̃se] *vt* (*clou etc*) to knock in, bang in; (*porte, voiture*) to smash in; **e. dans qch** (*couteau, mains etc*) to plunge into sth ‖ **s'e.** *vpr* (*s'enliser*) to sink (**dans** into); **s'e. dans** (*pénétrer*) to plunge into, disappear (deep) into.
enfouir [ɑ̃fwir] *vt* to bury.
enfourcher [ɑ̃furʃe] *vt* (*cheval etc*) to mount, bestride.
enfourner [ɑ̃furne] *vt* to put in the oven.
enfuir* (s') [sɑ̃fɥir] *vpr* to run away *ou* off (**de** from).
enfumer [ɑ̃fyme] *vt* (*pièce*) to fill with smoke; (*personne*) to smoke out.
engager [ɑ̃gaʒe] *vt* (*discussion, combat*) to start; (*bijou etc*) to pawn; (*parole*) to pledge; (*capitaux*) to tie up, invest; **e. qn** (*embaucher*) to hire s.o.; (*lier*) to bind s.o., commit s.o. ‖ **s'e.** *vpr* (*dans l'armée*) to enlist; (*sportif*) to enter (**pour** for); (*action, jeu*) to start; (*au service d'une cause*) to commit oneself; **s'e. à faire** to undertake to do; **s'e. dans** (*voie*) to enter; (*affaire etc*) to get involved in. • **engageant** *a* engaging, inviting. • **engagé** *a* (*écrivain etc*) committed. • **engagement** *nm* (*promesse*) commitment; (*dans une compétition sportive*) entry; (*combat*) *Mil* engagement; **prendre l'e. de faire** to undertake to do.
engelure [ɑ̃ʒlyr] *nf* chilblain.
engendrer [ɑ̃ʒɑ̃dre] *vt* (*causer*) to generate.
engin [ɑ̃ʒɛ̃] *nm* machine, device; **e. spatial** spaceship; **e. explosif** explosive device.
englober [ɑ̃glɔbe] *vt* to include, embrace.
engloutir [ɑ̃glutir] *vt* (*nourriture*) to wolf (down); (*faire disparaître*) to swallow up.
engouement [ɑ̃gumɑ̃] *nm* craze.
engouffrer [ɑ̃gufre] **1** *vt* (*avaler*) to wolf (down); (*fortune*) to consume. **2 s'engouffrer** *vpr* **s'e. dans** to sweep *ou* rush into.
engourdir [ɑ̃gurdir] *vt* (*membre*) to numb; (*esprit*) to dull ‖ **s'e.** *vpr* to go numb.
engrais [ɑ̃grɛ] *nm* (*naturel*) manure; (*chimique*) fertilizer.
engraisser [ɑ̃grese] *vt* (*animal*) to fatten (up) ‖ *vi*, **s'e.** *vpr* to get fat.
engrenage [ɑ̃grənaʒ] *nm Tech* gears; *Fig* mesh, chain, web.
engueuler [ɑ̃gœle] *vt* **e. qn** *Fam* to give s.o. hell, bawl s.o. out. • **engueulade** *nf Fam* (*réprimande*) bawling out, dressing-down;

(*dispute*) slanging match, row.
enhardir [ɑ̃ardir] *vt* to make bolder; **s'e. à faire** to make bold to do.
énième [ɛnjɛm] *a Fam* umpteenth.
énigme [enigm] *nf* riddle, enigma.
enivrer (s') [sɑ̃nivre] *vpr* to get drunk (**de** on).
enjamber [ɑ̃ʒɑ̃be] *vt* to step over; (*pont etc*) to span (*river etc*). ●**enjambée** *nf* stride.
enjeu, -x [ɑ̃ʒø] *nm* (*mise*) stake(s).
enjoliver [ɑ̃ʒɔlive] *vt* to embellish.
enjoliveur [ɑ̃ʒɔlivœr] *nm Aut* hubcap.
enjoué [ɑ̃ʒwe] *a* playful, cheerful.
enlacer [ɑ̃lase] *vt* (*serrer dans ses bras*) to clasp.
enlaidir [ɑ̃ledir] *vt* to make ugly ‖ *vi* to grow ugly.
enlevé [ɑ̃lve] *a* (*scène, danse etc*) well-rendered.
enlever [ɑ̃lve] *vt* to take away, remove (**à qn** from s.o.); (*vêtement*) to take off, remove; (*tache*) to take out, remove; (*enfant etc*) to kidnap; (*ordures*) to collect ‖ **s'e.** *vpr* (*tache*) to come out; (*vernis*) to come off. ●**enlèvement** *nm* (*d'enfant*) kidnapping.
enliser (s') [sɑ̃lize] *vpr* (*véhicule*) & *Fig* to get bogged down (**dans** in).
enneigé [ɑ̃neʒe] *a* snow-covered. ●**enneigement** *nm* snow coverage; **bulletin d'e.** snow report.
ennemi, -ie [ɛnmi] *nmf* enemy ‖ *a* (*personne*) hostile (**de** to); **pays/soldat e.** enemy country/soldier.
ennui [ɑ̃nɥi] *nm* boredom; (*mélancolie*) weariness; **un e.** (*tracas*) (some) trouble; **des ennuis** trouble; **l'e., c'est que...** the annoying thing is that....
ennuyer [ɑ̃nɥije] *vt* (*agacer*) to bother, annoy; (*préoccuper*) to bother; (*fatiguer*) to bore ‖ **s'e.** *vpr* to get bored. ●**ennuyé** *a* (*air*) bored; **je suis très e.** (*confus*) I feel bad (about it). ●**ennuyeux, -euse** *a* (*fastidieux*) boring; (*contrariant*) annoying.
énoncé [enɔ̃se] *nm* (*de texte*) wording, terms.
énoncer [enɔ̃se] *vt* to state, express.
enorgueillir (s') [sɑ̃nɔrgœjir] *vpr* **s'e. de** to pride oneself on.
énorme [enɔrm] *a* enormous, huge. ●**énormément** *adv* enormously; **e. de** an enormous amount of. ●**énormité** *nf* (*dimension*) enormity; (*faute*) (enormous) blunder.
enquérir (s') [sɑ̃kerir] *vpr* **s'e. de** to inquire about.
enquête [ɑ̃kɛt] *nf* (*de police etc*) investigation; (*judiciaire*) inquiry; (*sondage*) survey. ●**enquêter** *vi* (*police etc*) to investigate; **e. sur** (*crime*) to investigate. ●**enquêteur, -euse** *nmf* (*policier etc*) investigator; (*sondeur*) researcher.
enraciner (s') [sɑ̃rasine] *vpr* to take root; **enraciné dans** (*souvenir*) rooted in; **bien enraciné** (*préjugé etc*) deep-rooted.
enrag/er [ɑ̃raʒe] *vi* to be furious (**de faire** about doing); **faire e. qn** to get on s.o.'s nerves. ●**—é** *a* (*chien*) rabid; **devenir e.** (*furieux*) to become furious; **rendre qn e.** to make s.o. furious.
enrayer [ɑ̃reje] *vt* (*maladie etc*) to check ‖ **s'e.** *vpr* (*fusil*) to jam.
enregistr/er [ɑ̃rʒistre] *vt* **1** (*par écrit, sur bande*) to record; (*sur registre*) to register; (*constater*) to note, register; **(faire) e.** (*bagages*) to register, *Am* check. **2** (*musique, émission etc*) to record; **ça enregistre** it's recording. ●**—ement** *nm* (*des bagages*) registration, *Am* checking; (*d'un acte*) registration; (*sur bande etc*) recording.
enrhumer (s') [sɑ̃ryme] *vpr* to catch a cold; **être enrhumé** to have a cold.
enrichir [ɑ̃riʃir] *vt* to enrich (**de** with) ‖ **s'e.** *vpr* (*personne*) to get rich.
enrober [ɑ̃rɔbe] *vt* to coat (**de** in); **enrobé de chocolat** chocolate-coated.
enrôler [ɑ̃role] *vt*, **s'e.** *vpr* to enlist.
enrouer (s') [sɑ̃rwe] *vpr* to get hoarse. ●**enroué** *a* hoarse.
enrouler [ɑ̃rule] *vt* (*fil etc*) to wind; (*tapis etc*) to roll up; **s'e. dans** (*couvertures*) to wrap oneself up in; **s'e. sur** *ou* **autour de qch** to wind round sth.
ensanglanté [ɑ̃sɑ̃glɑ̃te] *a* bloodstained.
enseigne [ɑ̃sɛɲ] *nf* (*de magasin etc*) sign; **e. lumineuse** neon sign; **logés à la même e.** *Fig* in the same boat.
enseign/er [ɑ̃seɲe] *vt* to teach; **e. qch à qn** to teach s.o. sth; **il enseigne** he teaches. ●**—ant, -ante** [-ɛɲɑ̃, -ɑ̃t] *nmf* teacher. ●**—ement** [-ɛɲmɑ̃] *nm* education; (*action, métier*) teaching; **être dans l'e.** to be a teacher.
ensemble [ɑ̃sɑ̃bl] **1** *adv* together. **2** *nm* (*d'objets*) group, set; *Math* set; (*vêtement féminin*) outfit; *Mus* ensemble; **l'e. du personnel** (*totalité*) the whole (of the) staff; **l'e. des enseignants** all (of) the teachers; **dans l'e.** on the whole; **vue**/*etc* **d'e.** general view/*etc*.
ensevelir [ɑ̃səvlir] *vt* to bury.
ensoleillé [ɑ̃sɔleje] *a* (*endroit, journée*) sunny.
ensommeillé [ɑ̃sɔmeje] *a* sleepy.

ensorceler [ɑ̃sɔrsəle] *vt* (*envoûter, séduire*) to bewitch.
ensuite [ɑ̃sɥit] *adv* (*puis*) next, then; (*plus tard*) afterwards.
entaille [ɑ̃taj] *nf* (*fente*) notch; (*blessure*) gash. • **entailler** *vt* to notch; to gash.
entamer [ɑ̃tame] *vt* (*pain, peau etc*) to cut (into); (*bouteille, boîte etc*) to start (on); (*négociations etc*) to enter into, start; (*capital*) to eat into; (*métal, plastique*) to damage.
entasser [ɑ̃tase] *vt*, **s'e.** *vpr* (*objets*) to pile up; **(s')e. dans** (*passagers etc*) to crowd *ou* pile into; **ils s'entassaient sur la plage** they were crowded (together) on the beach.
entendre [ɑ̃tɑ̃dr] *vt* to hear; **e. parler de** to hear of; **e. dire que** to hear (it said) that; **e. raison** to listen to reason; **laisser e. à qn que** to give s.o. to understand that ‖ **s'entendre** *vpr* **s'e. (sur)** (*être d'accord*) to agree (on); **s'e. (avec qn)** (*s'accorder*) to get along *ou* on (with s.o.); **on ne s'entend plus!** (*à cause du bruit etc*) we can't hear ourselves speak!
entendu [ɑ̃tɑ̃dy] *a* (*convenu*) agreed; (*compris*) understood; (*sourire, air*) knowing; **e.!** all right!; **bien e.** of course.
entente [ɑ̃tɑ̃t] *nf* (*accord*) agreement, understanding; **(bonne) e.** (*amitié*) good relationship.
entériner [ɑ̃terine] *vt* to ratify.
enterrer [ɑ̃tere] *vt* (*défunt etc*) to bury; (*projet*) *Fig* to scrap. • **enterrement** *nm* burial; (*funérailles*) funeral.
en-tête [ɑ̃tɛt] *nm* (*de papier*) heading; **papier à en-tête** headed paper.
entêter (s') [sɑ̃tete] *vpr* to persist (**à faire** in doing). • **entêté** *a* (*têtu*) stubborn. • **entêtement** [ɑ̃tɛtmɑ̃] *nm* stubbornness; (*à faire qch*) persistence.
enthousiasme [ɑ̃tuzjasm] *nm* enthusiasm. • **enthousiasmer** *vt* to fill with enthusiasm; **s'e. pour** to be *ou* get enthusiastic about *ou* over. • **enthousiaste** *a* enthusiastic.
enticher (s') [sɑ̃tiʃe] *vpr* **s'e. de** to become infatuated with.
entier, -ière [ɑ̃tje, -jɛr] **1** *a* (*total*) whole, entire; (*intact*) intact; (*absolu*) absolute, complete; **le pays tout e.** the whole *ou* entire country; **nombre e.** *Math* whole number ‖ *nm* (*unité*) whole; **en e.** completely. **2** *a* (*caractère*) unyielding. • **entièrement** *adv* entirely.
entonner [ɑ̃tɔne] *vt* (*air*) to start singing.
entonnoir [ɑ̃tɔnwar] *nm* (*ustensile*) funnel.
entorse [ɑ̃tɔrs] *nf Méd* sprain; **e. à** (*règlement*) infringement of.
entortiller [ɑ̃tɔrtije] *vt* **e. qch autour de qch** (*dans du papier etc*) to wrap sth around sth; **e. qn** *Fam* to dupe s.o., get round s.o. ‖ **s'e.** *vpr* (*lierre etc*) to wind, twist.
entourage [ɑ̃turaʒ] *nm* (*proches*) circle of family and friends.
entourer [ɑ̃ture] *vt* to surround (**de** with); (*envelopper*) to wrap (**de** in); **entouré de** surrounded by; **e. qn de ses bras** to put one's arms round s.o.
entracte [ɑ̃trakt] *nm Th* interval, *Am* intermission.
entraide [ɑ̃trɛd] *nf* mutual aid. • **s'entraider** [sɑ̃trede] *vpr* to help each other.
entrain [ɑ̃trɛ̃] *nm* spirit, liveliness; **plein d'e.** lively.
entraînant [ɑ̃trɛnɑ̃] *a* (*musique*) lively.
entraîner [ɑ̃trene] **1** *vt* to carry away; (*causer*) to bring about; (*impliquer*) to entail, involve; **e. qn** (*emmener*) to lead s.o. (away); (*de force*) to drag s.o. (away); **e. qn à faire** (*amener*) to lead s.o. to do. **2** *vt* (*athlète, cheval etc*) to train (**à** for) ‖ **s'e.** *vpr Sp* to train. • **entraîneur** [-ɛnœr] *nm* (*d'athlète*) coach; (*de cheval*) trainer.
entrave [ɑ̃trav] *nf* (*obstacle*) *Fig* hindrance (**à** to). • **entraver** *vt* to hinder, hamper.
entre [ɑ̃tr(ə)] *prép* between; (*parmi*) among(st); **l'un d'e. vous** one of you; **(soit dit) e. nous** between you and me; **e. deux âges** middle-aged; **e. autres** among other things.
ⓘ**entre** & **d'entre G179** Prepositions 8
entrebâill/er [ɑ̃trəbaje] *vt* (*porte*) to open slightly. • **—é** *a* slightly open, ajar.
entrechoquer (s') [sɑ̃trəʃɔke] *vpr* (*bouteilles etc*) to chink.
entrecôte [ɑ̃trəkot] *nf* (boned *ou Am* filleted) rib steak.
entre-deux-guerres [ɑ̃trədøgɛr] *nm inv* inter-war period.
entrée [ɑ̃tre] *nf* (*action*) entry, entrance; (*porte*) entrance; (*accès*) admission, entry (**de** to); (*vestibule*) entrance hall; (*billet*) ticket (for admission); (*plat*) first course; *Ordinat* input; (*mot dans un dictionnaire etc*) entry; **à son e.** as he *ou* she came in; **'e. interdite'** 'no entry'; **'e. libre'** 'admission free'; **e. de service** tradesmen's entrance; **e. en matière** (*d'un discours*) opening.
entrefaites (sur ces) [syrsezɑ̃trəfɛt] *adv* at that moment.
entrefilet [ɑ̃trəfilɛ] *nm* (*dans un journal*) (news) item.
entrejambe [ɑ̃trəʒɑ̃b] *nm* crutch, crotch.
entrelacer [ɑ̃trəlase] *vt*, **s'e.** *vpr* to intertwine.
entremêler [ɑ̃trəmele] *vt*, **s'e.** *vpr* to intermingle.

entremets [ɑ̃trəmɛ] *nm* (*plat*) dessert, sweet.
entremise [ɑ̃trəmiz] *nf* **par l'e. de qn** through s.o.
entreposer [ɑ̃trəpoze] *vt* to store. ●**entrepôt** *nm* warehouse.
entreprendre* [ɑ̃trəprɑ̃dr] *vt* (*travail, voyage etc*) to undertake; **e. de faire** to undertake to do.
entrepreneur [ɑ̃trəprənœr] *nm* (*en bâtiment*) (building) contractor.
entreprise [ɑ̃trəpriz] *nf* **1** (*firme*) company, firm. **2** (*opération*) undertaking.
entrer [ɑ̃tre] *vi* (*aux* **être**) (*aller*) to go in, enter; (*venir*) to come in, enter; **e. dans** to go into; (*pièce*) to come *ou* go into, enter; (*arbre etc*) *Aut* to crash into; (*club*) to join; **e. à l'université**/*etc* to go to *ou* start university/*etc*; **entrez!** come in!; **faire/laisser e. qn** to show/let s.o. in ▮ *vt Ordinat* to enter, key in.
entresol [ɑ̃trəsɔl] *nm* mezzanine (floor).
entre-temps [ɑ̃trətɑ̃] *adv* meanwhile.
entretenir* [ɑ̃trətnir] *vt* **1** (*voiture, maison etc*) to maintain; (*relations, souvenir*) to keep up; (*famille*) to keep, maintain; **e. sa forme/sa santé** to keep fit/healthy. **2 e. qn de** to talk to s.o. about; **s'e. de** to talk about (**avec** with).
entretien [ɑ̃trətjɛ̃] *nm* **1** (*de route, maison etc*) maintenance. **2** (*dialogue*) conversation; (*entrevue*) interview.
entrevoir* [ɑ̃trəvwar] *vt* (*rapidement*) to catch a glimpse of; (*pressentir*) to (fore)see.
entrevue [ɑ̃trəvy] *nf* interview.
entrouvrir* [ɑ̃truvrir] *vt*, **s'e.** *vpr* to half-open. ●**entrouvert** *a* (*porte, fenêtre*) half-open, ajar.
énumérer [enymere] *vt* to list, enumerate. ●**énumération** *nf* list(ing).
envah/ir [ɑ̃vair] *vt* to invade; (*herbe etc*) to overrun (*garden*); **e. qn** (*doute, peur etc*) to overcome s.o. ●**—issant** *a* (*voisin etc*) intrusive. ●**—isseur** *nm* invader.
enveloppe [ɑ̃vlɔp] *nf* (*pour lettre*) envelope; **mettre sous e.** to put into an envelope; **e. timbrée à votre adresse** stamped addressed envelope, *Am* stamped self-addressed envelope.
envelopper [ɑ̃vlɔpe] *vt* to wrap (up) (**dans** in) ▮ **s'e.** *vpr* to wrap oneself (up) (**dans** in).
envenimer (s') [sɑ̃vnime] *vpr* to turn septic; *Fig* to become acrimonious.
envergure [ɑ̃vɛrgyr] *nf* (*de personne*) calibre; (*ampleur*) scope, importance; **de grande e.** (*réforme etc*) wide-ranging.
envers [ɑ̃vɛr] **1** *prép* towards, *Am* toward(s), to. **2** *nm* (*de tissu*) wrong side; (*de médaille*) reverse side; **à l'e.** (*chaussette*) inside out; (*pantalon*) back to front; (*la tête en bas*) upside down; (*à contresens*) the wrong way.
envie [ɑ̃vi] *nf* (*jalousie*) envy; (*désir*) longing, desire; **avoir e. de qch** to want sth; **j'ai e. de faire** I feel like doing; **elle meurt d'e. de faire** she's dying to do; **ça me fait e.** I really like that. ●**envier** *vt* to envy (**qch à qn** s.o. sth). ●**envieux, -euse** *a* & *nmf* envious (person); **faire des envieux** to cause envy.
environ [ɑ̃virɔ̃] *adv* (*à peu près*) about ▮ *nmpl* surroundings, outskirts; **aux environs de** (*Paris, Noël, dix francs etc*) around.
environner [ɑ̃virɔne] *vt* to surround. ●**environnant** *a* surrounding. ●**environnement** *nm* environment.
envisager [ɑ̃vizaʒe] *vt* to consider; (*imaginer comme possible*) to envisage, *Am* envision; **e. de faire** to consider doing.
envoi [ɑ̃vwa] *nm* sending; (*paquet*) package; **coup d'e.** *Fb* kick-off.
envol [ɑ̃vɔl] *nm* (*d'oiseau*) taking flight; (*d'avion*) takeoff; **piste d'e.** *Av* runway. ●**s'envoler** *vpr* (*oiseau*) to fly away; (*avion*) to take off; (*chapeau etc*) to blow away.
envoûter [ɑ̃vute] *vt* to bewitch.
envoyer* [ɑ̃vwaje] *vt* to send; (*lancer*) to throw; (*gifle*) to give; **e. chercher qn** to send for s.o. ▮ **s'e.** *vpr Fam* (*repas etc*) to put *ou* stash away. ●**envoyé, -ée** *nmf* envoy; (*reporter*) correspondent. ●**envoyeur** *nm* sender; **'retour à l'e.'** 'return to sender'.
épagneul, -eule [epaɲœl] *nmf* spaniel.
épais, -aisse [epɛ, -ɛs] *a* thick. ●**épaisseur** *nf* thickness; (*dimension*) depth. ●**épaissir** *vti*, ▮ **s'é.** *vpr* to thicken.
épancher (s') [sepɑ̃ʃe] *vpr* (*parler*) to pour out one's heart.
épanouir (s') [sepanwir] *vpr* (*fleur*) to blossom, open out; (*personne*) *Fig* to blossom (out); (*visage*) to beam. ●**épanoui** *a* (*fleur, personne*) in full bloom; (*visage*) beaming. ●**épanouissement** *nm* (*éclat*) full bloom; (*de la personnalité*) fulfilment.
épargne [eparɲ] *nf* (*qualité, vertu*) thrift; (*sommes d'argent*) savings. ●**épargner** *vt* (*argent*) to save; (*ennemi etc*) to spare; **e. qch à qn** (*ennuis, chagrin etc*) to spare s.o. sth. ●**épargnant, -ante** *nmf* saver.
éparpiller [eparpije] *vt*, **s'é.** *vpr* to scatter. ●**épars** *a* scattered.
épatant [epatɑ̃] *a Fam* marvellous.
épater [epate] *vt Fam* to stun, astound.

épaule [epol] *nf* shoulder. ● **épauler** *vt* (*fusil*) to raise (to one's shoulder); **é. qn** (*aider*) to back s.o. up. ● **épaulette** *nf* (d'une veste) shoulder pad.

épave [epav] *nf* (*bateau, personne*) wreck.

épée [epe] *nf* sword.

épeler [ɛple] *vt* (*mot*) to spell.

éperdu [epɛrdy] *a* wild (**de** with); (*besoin*) desperate; (*regard*) distraught. ● **—ment** *adv* (*aimer*) madly; **elle s'en moque e.** she couldn't care less.

éperon [eprɔ̃] *nm* (*de cavalier, coq*) spur.

épervier [epɛrvje] *nm* sparrowhawk.

éphémère [efemɛr] *a* short-lived.

épi [epi] *nm* (*de blé etc*) ear; (*mèche de cheveux*) tuft of hair.

épice [epis] *nf Culin* spice. ● **épicer** *vt* to spice. ● **épicé** *a* (*plat, récit etc*) spicy.

épicier, -ière [episje, -jɛr] *nmf* grocer. ● **épicerie** *nf* (*magasin*) grocer's (shop), *Am* grocery (store); **é. fine** delicatessen.

épidémie [epidemi] *nf* epidemic.

épiderme [epidɛrm] *nm Anat* skin.

épier [epje] *vt* (*observer*) to watch closely; **é. qn** to spy on s.o.

épilepsie [epilɛpsi] *nf* epilepsy. ● **épileptique** *a* & *nmf* epileptic.

épiler [epile] *vt* (*jambe*) to remove unwanted hair from; (*sourcil*) to pluck.

épilogue [epilɔg] *nm* epilogue.

épinards [epinar] *nmpl* spinach.

épine [epin] *nf* **1** (*de plante*) thorn; (*d'animal*) spine, prickle. **2 é. dorsale** *Anat* spine. ● **épineux, -euse** *a* (*tige, question*) thorny.

épingle [epɛ̃gl] *nf* pin; **é. de** *ou* **à nourrice, é. de sûreté** safety pin; **é. à linge** clothes peg, *Am* clothes pin; **é. à cheveux** hairpin; **tiré à quatre épingles** very spruce.

épique [epik] *a* epic.

épisode [epizɔd] *nm* episode. ● **épisodique** *a* occasional.

épithète [epitɛt] *nf* (*adjectif*) attribute.

éploré [eplɔre] *a* (*veuve, air*) tearful.

éplucher [eplyʃe] *vt* (*carotte, pomme etc*) to peel; (*salade*) to clean. ● **épluchure** *nf* peeling.

éponge [epɔ̃ʒ] *nf* sponge. ● **éponger** *vt* (*liquide*) to sponge up, mop up; (*carrelage*) to sponge (down), mop; **s'é. le front** to mop one's brow.

épopée [epɔpe] *nf* epic.

époque [epɔk] *nf* (*date*) time, period; (*historique*) age; **meubles d'é.** period furniture; **à l'é.** at the *ou* that time.

épouse [epuz] *nf* wife.

épouser [epuze] *vt* **1 é. qn** to marry s.o. **2** (*opinion etc*) to espouse; (*forme*) to assume.

épousseter [epuste] *vt* to dust.

épouvantable [epuvɑ̃tabl] *a* terrifying; (*très mauvais*) appalling.

épouvantail [epuvɑ̃taj] *nm* scarecrow.

épouvante [epuvɑ̃t] *nf* (*peur*) terror; (*appréhension*) dread; **film d'é.** horror film. ● **épouvanter** *vt* to terrify.

époux [epu] *nm* husband, *pl* husband and wife.

éprendre* (s') [seprɑ̃dr] *vpr* **s'é. de qn** to fall in love with s.o.

épreuve [eprøv] *nf* (*examen*) test; (*sportive*) event; (*malheur*) hardship, ordeal; *Phot* print; *Typ* proof; **mettre à l'é.** to put to the test; **à toute é.** (*patience*) unfailing; (*nerfs*) rock-solid.

éprouver [epruve] *vt* to test; (*sentiment etc*) to feel; **é. qn** (*mettre à l'épreuve*) to put s.o. to the test; (*faire souffrir*) to distress s.o. ● **éprouvant** *a* (*pénible*) trying. ● **éprouvé** *a* (*sûr*) well-tried.

éprouvette [epruvɛt] *nf* test tube; **bébé é.** test tube baby.

épuiser [epɥize] *vt* (*personne, provisions, sujet*) to exhaust ▮ **s'é.** *vpr* (*réserves, patience*) to run out; **s'é. à faire** to exhaust oneself doing. ● **épuisant** *a* exhausting. ● **épuisé** *a* exhausted; (*marchandise*) out of stock; (*édition*) out of print; **é. de fatigue** exhausted.

épuisette [epɥizɛt] *nf* fishing net (*on pole*).

épuration [epyrɑsjɔ̃] *nf* purification; **station d'é.** purification works.

équateur [ekwatœr] *nm* equator; **sous l'é.** at *ou* on the equator. ● **équatorial, -aux** *a* equatorial.

équation [ekwɑsjɔ̃] *nf Math* equation.

équerre [ekɛr] *nf* **é. (à dessiner)** set square, *Am* triangle; **d'é.** straight, square.

équilibre [ekilibr] *nm* balance; **tenir** *ou* **mettre en é.** to balance (**sur** on); **se tenir en é.** to (keep one's) balance; **perdre l'é.** to lose one's balance. ● **équilibrer** *vt* (*budget*) to balance ▮ **s'é.** *vpr* (*comptes*) to balance.

équipage [ekipaʒ] *nm Nau Av* crew.

équipe [ekip] *nf* team; (*d'ouvriers*) gang; **é. de secours** search party; **é. de nuit** night shift; **faire é. avec** to team up with. ● **équipier, -ière** *nmf* team member.

équiper [ekipe] *vt* to equip (**de** with) ▮ **s'é.** *vpr* to equip oneself. ● **équipement** *nm* equipment; (*de camping, ski etc*) gear.

équitable [ekitabl] *a* fair.

équitation [ekitɑsjɔ̃] *nf* (horse) riding, *Am* (horseback) riding.

équivalent [ekivalɑ̃] *a* & *nm* equivalent.

équivoque [ekivɔk] *a* (*ambigu*) equivocal; (*douteux*) dubious ‖ *nf* ambiguity.
érable [erabl] *nm* (*arbre, bois*) maple.
érafler [erafle] *vt* to graze. ● **éraflure** *nf* graze.
éraillée [erɑje] *af* **voix é.** rasping voice.
ère [ɛr] *nf* era; **avant notre è.** BC.
érection [erɛksjɔ̃] *nf* (*de monument etc*) erection.
éreinter [erɛ̃te] *vt* (*fatiguer*) to exhaust.
ériger [eriʒe] *vt* to erect; **s'é. en** to set oneself up as.
ermite [ɛrmit] *nm* hermit.
érosion [erozjɔ̃] *nf* erosion.
érotique [erɔtik] *a* erotic.
err/er [ɛre] *vi* to wander. ● **—ant** *a* wandering; **chien e.** stray dog.
erreur [ɛrœr] *nf* mistake, error; **par e.** by mistake, in error; **dans l'e.** mistaken; **faire erreur** (*au téléphone*) to dial the wrong number. ● **erroné** *a* erroneous.
érudit, -ite [erydi, -it] *a* scholarly ‖ *nmf* scholar. ● **érudition** *nf* scholarship.
éruption [erypsjɔ̃] *nf* (*de volcan*) eruption (**de** of); (*de boutons*) rash.
es *voir* **être.**
ès [ɛs] *prép* of; **licencié/docteur ès lettres** = BA/PhD.
escabeau, -x [ɛskabo] *nm* stepladder.
escadrille [ɛskadrij] *nf* (*groupe d'avions*) flight. ● **escadron** *nm* squadron.
escalade [ɛskalad] *nf* climbing; (*des prix, de la violence etc*) escalation. ● **escalader** *vt* to climb.
escale [ɛskal] *nf Av* stop(over); *Nau* port of call; **faire e. à** *Av* to stop (over) at; *Nau* to put in at; **vol sans e.** non-stop flight.
escalier [ɛskalje] *nm* stairs; **l'e., les escaliers** the stairs; **e. mécanique** *ou* **roulant** escalator; **e. de secours** fire escape; **e. de service** service stairs.
escalope [ɛskalɔp] *nf Culin* escalope.
escamoter [ɛskamɔte] *vt* (*faire disparaître*) to make vanish.
escapade [ɛskapad] *nf* (*excursion*) jaunt; **faire une e.** to run off.
escargot [ɛskargo] *nm* snail.
escarmouche [ɛskarmuʃ] *nf* skirmish.
escarpé [ɛskarpe] *a* steep. ● **escarpement** *nm* (*côte*) steep slope.
escarpin [ɛskarpɛ̃] *nm* (*soulier*) pump.
escient [ɛsjɑ̃] *nm* **à bon e.** judiciously.
esclaffer (s') [sɛsklafe] *vpr* to roar with laughter.
esclandre [ɛsklɑ̃dr] *nm* (noisy) scene.
esclave [ɛsklav] *nmf* slave. ● **esclavage** *nm* slavery.
escompter [ɛskɔ̃te] *vt* **1** (*espérer*) to anticipate (**faire** doing), expect (**faire** to do). **2** *Com* to discount.
escorte [ɛskɔrt] *nf Mil Nau etc* escort.
escrime [ɛskrim] *nf Sp* fencing; **faire de l'e.** to fence.
escrimer (s') [sɛskrime] *vpr* to slave away (**à faire** at doing).
escroc [ɛskro] *nm* crook, swindler. ● **escroquer** *vt* **e. qn** to swindle s.o.; **e. qch à qn** to swindle s.o. out of sth. ● **escroquerie** *nf* swindling; **une e.** a swindle; **c'est de l'e.** *Fam* it's a rip-off.
espace [ɛspas] *nm* space; **e. vert** garden, park. ● **espacer** *vt* to space out ‖ **s'e.** (*maisons, visites etc*) to become less frequent.
espadrille [ɛspadrij] *nf* rope-soled sandal.
Espagne [ɛspaɲ] *nf* Spain. ● **espagnol, -ole** *a* Spanish ‖ *nmf* Spaniard ‖ *nm* (*langue*) Spanish.
espèce [ɛspɛs] **1** *nf* (*race*) species; (*genre*) kind, sort; **e. d'idiot!** (you) silly fool! **2** *nfpl* (*argent*) **en espèces** in cash.
espérance [ɛsperɑ̃s] *nf* hope; **e. de vie** life expectancy.
espérer [ɛspere] *vt* to hope for; **e. que** to hope that; **e. faire** to hope to do ‖ *vi* to hope; **j'espère (bien)!** I hope so!; **e. en qch** to trust in sth.
espiègle [ɛspjɛgl] *a* mischievous.
espion, -onne [ɛspjɔ̃, -ɔn] *nmf* spy. ● **espionnage** *nm* spying, espionage. ● **espionner** *vt* to spy on.
esplanade [ɛsplanad] *nf* esplanade.
espoir [ɛspwar] *nm* hope; **sans e.** (*cas etc*) hopeless.
esprit [ɛspri] *nm* (*attitude, fantôme*) spirit; (*intellect*) mind; (*humour*) wit; **venir à l'e. de qn** to cross s.o.'s mind; **avoir de l'e.** to be witty; **perdre l'e.** to go out of one's mind.
esquimau, -aude, -aux [ɛskimo, -od, -o] **1** *a* & *nmf* Eskimo. **2** *nm* (*glace*) choc-ice (*on a stick*), *Am* chocolate ice-cream bar.
esquinter [ɛskɛ̃te] *vt Fam* (*voiture etc*) to damage, bash; **s'e. à faire** (*se fatiguer*) to wear oneself out doing.
esquisser [ɛskise] *vt* to sketch; **e. un geste** to make a (slight) gesture.
esquiver [ɛskive] *vt* (*coup, problème*) to dodge ‖ **s'e.** *vpr* to slip away.
essai [esɛ] *nm* (*preuve*) test; (*tentative*) try, attempt; *Rugby* try; *Littér* essay; **à l'e.** (*objet*) *Com* on approval; **pilote d'e.** test pilot; **période d'e.** trial period; **coup d'e.** first attempt.
essaim [esɛ̃] *nm* swarm (*of bees etc*).

essayer [eseje] *vt* to try (**de faire** to do); (*vêtement*) to try on; (*méthode*) to try (out). ● **essayage** *nm* (*de costume*) fitting; **salon d'e.** fitting room.

essence [esɑ̃s] *nf* **1** *Aut* petrol, *Am* gas; (*extrait*) essence; **poste d'e.** filling station. **2** *Phil* essence.

essentiel, -ielle [esɑ̃sjɛl] *a* essential (**à, pour** for) ▌*nm* **l'e.** the main thing *ou* point; (*quantité*) the main part (**de** of). ● **essentiellement** *adv* essentially.

essieu, -x [esjø] *nm* axle.

essor [esɔr] *nm* (*de pays, d'entreprise etc*) development, expansion; **en plein e.** (*industrie etc*) booming.

essor/er [esɔre] *vt* (*linge*) to wring; (*dans une essoreuse*) to spin-dry; (*dans une machine à laver*) to spin. ●**—euse** *nf* (*électrique*) spin dryer.

essouffler [esufle] *vt* to make (*s.o.*) out of breath ▌**s'e.** *vpr* to get out of breath.

essuyer [esɥije] **1** *vt* to wipe ▌**s'e.** *vpr* to wipe oneself. **2** *vt* (*subir*) to suffer. ● **essuie-glace** *nm inv* windscreen wiper, *Am* windshield wiper. ● **essuie-mains** *nm inv* (hand) towel.

est[1] [ɛ] *voir* **être.**

est[2] [ɛst] *nm* east; **à l'e.** in the east; (*direction*) (to the) east (**de** of); **d'e.** (*vent*) east(erly); **de l'e.** eastern ▌*a inv* (*côte*) east(ern).

estampe [ɛstɑ̃p] *nf* (*gravure*) print.

esthéticienne [ɛstetisjɛn] *nf* beautician.

esthétique [ɛstetik] *a* aesthetic, *Am* esthetic.

estime [ɛstim] *nf* regard.

estimer [ɛstime] *vt* (*tableau etc*) to value (**à** at); (*calculer*) to estimate; (*juger*) to consider (**que** that); **e. dangereux**/*etc* **de faire qch** to consider it dangerous/*etc* to do sth; **e. qn** to have high regard for s.o.; **s'e. heureux**/*etc* to consider oneself happy/*etc*. ● **estimation** *nf* (*de mobilier etc*) valuation; (*calcul*) estimation.

estival, -aux [ɛstival, -o] *a* **travail/température**/*etc* **estival(e)** summer work/temperature/*etc*.

estomac [ɛstɔma] *nm* stomach.

estomper [ɛstɔ̃pe] *vt* (*rendre flou*) to blur ▌**s'e.** *vpr* to become blurred.

estrade [ɛstrad] *nf* (*tribune*) platform.

estropi/er [ɛstrɔpje] *vt* to cripple. ●**—é, -ée** *nmf* cripple.

estuaire [ɛstɥɛr] *nm* estuary.

et [e] *conj* and; **vingt et un**/*etc* twenty-one/*etc*; **et moi?** what about me?

étable [etabl] *nf* cowshed.

établi [etabli] *nm* (work)bench.

établir [etablir] *vt* to establish; (*installer*) to set up; (*plan, liste*) to draw up ▌**s'é.** *vpr* (*habiter*) to settle; (*épicier etc*) to set up shop as. ● **établissement** *nm* (*action, bâtiment, institution*) establishment; *Com* company, establishment; **é. scolaire** school.

étage [etaʒ] *nm* (*d'immeuble*) floor, storey, *Am* story; (*de fusée etc*) stage; **à l'é.** upstairs; **au premier é.** on the first *ou Am* second floor; **maison à deux étages** two-storeyed *ou Am* -storied house.

étagère [etaʒɛr] *nf* shelf.

étain [etɛ̃] *nm* (*métal*) tin; (*de gobelet etc*) pewter.

étais, était [etɛ] *voir* **être.**

étal, *pl* **étals** [etal] *nm* (*au marché*) stall.

étalage [etalaʒ] *nm* (*vitrine*) display window; **faire é. de** to show off, make a show *ou* display of.

étaler [etale] *vt* (*disposer*) to lay out; (*en vitrine*) to display; (*beurre etc*) to spread; (*vacances*) to stagger; (*érudition etc*) to show off ▌**s'é.** *vpr* (*s'affaler*) to sprawl; (*tomber*) *Fam* to fall flat; **s'é. sur** (*congés, paiements etc*) to be spread over.

étalon [etalɔ̃] *nm* **1** (*cheval*) stallion. **2** (*modèle*) standard; **é.-or** gold standard.

étanche [etɑ̃ʃ] *a* watertight; (*montre*) waterproof.

étancher [etɑ̃ʃe] *vt* (*soif*) to quench, slake.

étang [etɑ̃] *nm* pond.

étant [etɑ̃] *voir* **être.**

étape [etap] *nf* (*de voyage etc*) stage; (*lieu*) stop(over); **faire é. à** to stop off *ou* over at; **par petites étapes** in easy stages.

état [eta] *nm* **1** (*condition*) state; (*registre, liste*) statement, list; **en bon é.** in good condition; **en (bon) é. de marche** in (good) working order; **en é. de faire** in a position to do; **hors d'é. de faire** not in a position to do; **é. d'esprit** state of mind; **é. d'âme** mood; **é. civil** civil status (*birth, marriage, death etc*); **faire é. de** (*mention*) to mention; **(ne pas) être dans son é. normal** (not) to be one's usual self. **2 É.** (*nation*) State; **homme d'É.** statesman. ● **étatisé** *a* state-controlled.

état-major [etamaʒɔr] *nm* (*pl* **états-majors**) (*d'un parti etc*) senior staff.

États-Unis [etazyni] *nmpl* **É.-Unis (d'Amérique)** United States (of America).

étau, -x [eto] *nm Tech* vice, *Am* vise.

été[1] [ete] *nm* summer; **en e.** in (the) summer.

été[2] [ete] *pp de* **être.**

éteindre* [etɛ̃dr] *vt* (*feu etc*) to put out; (*lampe etc*) to turn *ou* switch off ▌*vi* to

● For further information on grammar points, turn to the page indicated

switch off ▮ **s'é.** *vpr* (*feu*) to go out; (*personne*) to pass away; (*race*) to die out; (*amour*) to die. • **éteint** *a* (*feu, bougie*) out; (*lampe, lumière*) off; (*volcan*) extinct; (*voix*) faint.

étendre [etɑ̃dr] *vt* (*linge*) to hang out; (*nappe*) to spread (out); (*beurre*) to spread; (*agrandir*) to extend; **é. le bras/***etc* to stretch out one's arm/*etc*; **é. qn** to stretch s.o. out ▮ **s'é.** *vpr* (*personne*) to stretch (oneself) out, lie; (*plaine etc*) to stretch; (*feu*) to spread; **s'é. sur** (*sujet*) to dwell on. • **étendu** *a* (*forêt, vocabulaire etc*) extensive; (*personne*) stretched out, lying. • **étendue** *nf* (*importance*) extent; (*surface*) area; (*d'eau*) expanse, stretch.

éternel, -elle [etɛrnɛl] *a* eternal. • **s'éterniser** *vpr* (*débat etc*) to drag on endlessly; (*visiteur etc*) to stay for ever. • **éternité** *nf* eternity.

éternu/er [etɛrnɥe] *vi* to sneeze. • **—ement** [-ymɑ̃] *nm* sneeze.

êtes [ɛt] *voir* **être.**

Éthiopie [etjɔpi] *nf* Ethiopia. • **éthiopien, -ienne** *a* & *nmf* Ethiopian.

éthique [etik] *a* ethical ▮ *nf Phil* ethics.

ethnie [ɛtni] *nf* ethnic group. • **ethnique** *a* ethnic.

étinceler [etɛ̃sle] *vi* to sparkle. • **étincelle** *nf* spark.

étiqueter [etikte] *vt* to label. • **étiquette** *nf* **1** (*marque*) label. **2** (*protocole*) etiquette.

étirer (s') [setire] *vpr* to stretch (oneself).

étoffe [etɔf] *nf* material.

étoile [etwal] *nf* **1** star; **à la belle é.** in the open. **2 é. de mer** starfish. • **étoilé** *a* (*ciel*) starry; **la bannière étoilée** *Am* the Star-Spangled Banner.

étonner [etɔne] *vt* to surprise ▮ **s'é.** *vpr* to be surprised (**de qch** at sth, **de faire** at doing, to do; **que** (+ *sub*) that). • **étonnant** *a* (*ahurissant*) surprising (**que** (+ *sub*) that); (*remarquable*) amazing. • **étonnement** *nm* surprise.

étouffer [etufe] *vt* (*tuer*) to suffocate, smother; (*bruit*) to muffle; (*feu*) to smother; (*révolte, sentiment*) to stifle; (*scandale*) to hush up ▮ **on étouffe!** it's stifling!; **é. de colère** to choke with anger ▮ **s'é.** *vpr* (*en mangeant*) to choke (**sur, avec** on); (*mourir*) to suffocate. • **étouffant** *a* (*air*) stifling.

étourdi, -ie [eturdi] *a* thoughtless ▮ *nmf* scatterbrain. • **étourderie** *nf* thoughtlessness; **une (faute d')é.** a thoughtless blunder.

étourd/ir [eturdir] *vt* to stun; (*vin, vitesse*) to make dizzy; (*abrutir*) to deafen. • **—issant** *a* (*bruit*) deafening; (*remarquable*) stunning. • **—issement** *nm* (*malaise*) dizzy spell.

étrange [etrɑ̃ʒ] *a* strange, odd.

étranger, -ère [etrɑ̃ʒe, -ɛr] *a* (*d'un autre pays*) foreign; (*non familier*) strange (**à** to) ▮ *nmf* foreigner; (*inconnu*) stranger; **à l'é.** abroad; **de l'é.** from abroad.

étrangler [etrɑ̃gle] *vt* **é. qn** (*tuer*) to strangle s.o.; (*col*) to choke s.o. ▮ **s'é.** *vpr* (*de colère, en mangeant etc*) to choke.

être** [ɛtr] **1** *vi* to be; **il est tailleur** he's a tailor; **est-ce qu'elle vient?** is she coming?; **il vient, n'est-ce pas?** he's coming, isn't he?; **est-ce qu'il aime le thé?** does he like tea?; **nous sommes dix** there are ten of us; **nous sommes le dix** today is the tenth (of the month); **où en es-tu?** how far have you got?; **il a été à Paris** (*est allé*) he has been to Paris; **elle est de Paris** she's from Paris; **elle est de la famille** she's one of the family; **il est cinq heures** it's five (o'clock); **il était une fois** once upon the time, there was; **c'est à lire** (*obligation*) this has to be read; **c'est à voir** (*exposition etc*) it's well worth seeing; **c'est à lui** it's his; **cela étant** that being so. **2** *v aux* (*avec venir, partir etc*) to have; **elle est arrivée** she has arrived; **ê. vendu/retrouvé/**etc (*passif*) to be sold/found/*etc.* **3** *nm* **ê. humain** human being.

❶être G80, 82 & **83** Auxiliaries and the Formation of Compound Tenses 7 C 1, 3 & 4

❶être G89 Impersonal Verbs 7 E 2c)

❶est-ce que G208 Direct Questions 12 C 1b)

étreindre [etrɛ̃dr] *vt* to grip; (*avec amour*) to embrace.

étrennes [etrɛn] *nfpl* New Year gift; (*gratification*) = Christmas box *ou* tip.

étrier [etrije] *nm* stirrup.

étroit [etrwa] *a* narrow; (*vêtement*) tight; (*lien, collaboration etc*) close; **être à l'é.** to be cramped. • **étroitement** *adv* (*surveiller etc*) closely. • **étroitesse** *nf* narrowness; (*de lien etc*) closeness; **é. d'esprit** narrow-mindedness.

étude [etyd] *nf* **1** (*action, ouvrage*) study; **(salle d')é.** *Scol* study room; **à l'é.** (*projet*) under consideration; **faire des études de** (*médecine etc*) to study. **2** (*de notaire etc*) office.

étudiant, -ante [etydjɑ̃, -ɑ̃t] *nmf* & *a* student.

étudier [etydje] *vti* to study.

étui [etɥi] *nm* (*à lunettes etc*) case.

eu, eue [y] *pp de* **avoir.**

euh! [ø] *int* hem!, er!, well!

eurent [yr] *voir* **avoir.**

(eg **G1**, **G2**, **G3**) in French **G**rammar, at the end of the dictionary. Also see p. ix.

euro- [øro] *préf* Euro-.
eurocrate [ørɔkrat] *nmf* Eurocrat.
eurodollar [ørɔdɔlar] *nm* Eurodollar.
Europe [ørɔp] *nf* Europe; **l'E. (des douze)** the Twelve (countries of the Common Market). • **européen, -enne** *a & nmf* European.
eut [y] *voir* **avoir.**
euthanasie [øtanazi] *nf* euthanasia.
eux [ø] *pron* (*sujet*) they; (*complément*) them; (*réfléchi, emphase*) themselves. • **eux-mêmes** *pron* themselves.
ⓘ**eux G62** Disjunctive Pronouns 6 D 5
évacuer [evakɥe] *vt* to evacuate; (*liquide*) to drain off.
évader (s') [sevade] *vpr* to escape (**de** from). • **évadé, -ée** *nmf* escaped prisoner.
évaluer [evalɥe] *vt* (*fortune etc*) to estimate; (*meuble etc*) to value.
évangile [evɑ̃ʒil] *nf* gospel; **É.** Gospel.
évanouir (s') [sevanwir] *vpr Méd* to faint, pass *ou* black out; (*espoir, crainte etc*) to vanish. • **évanoui** *a Méd* unconscious. • **évanouissement** *nm* (*syncope*) blackout.
évaporer (s') [sevapɔre] *vpr* to evaporate; (*disparaître*) *Fam* to vanish into thin air.
évasion [evazjɔ̃] *nf* escape (**d'un lieu** from a place); (*hors de la réalité*) escapism; **é. fiscale** tax evasion.
éveil [evɛj] *nm* awakening; **en é.** on the alert.
éveiller [eveje] *vt* (*susciter*) to arouse ‖ **s'é.** *vpr* to awake(n) (**à** to); (*sentiment, idée*) to be aroused.
événement [evɛnmɑ̃] *nm* event.
éventail [evɑ̃taj] *nm* **1** (*instrument portatif*) fan. **2** (*choix*) range.
éventer [evɑ̃te] *vt* **1 é. qn** to fan s.o. **2 s'éventer** *vpr* (*bière, parfum*) to turn stale.
éventrer [evɑ̃tre] *vt* (*oreiller etc*) to rip open; (*animal*) to open up.
éventuel, -elle [evɑ̃tɥɛl] *a* possible. • **éventuellement** *adv* possibly.
évêque [evɛk] *nm* bishop.
évertuer (s') [sevɛrtɥe] *vpr* **s'é. à faire** to do one's utmost to do, struggle to do.
évident [evidɑ̃] *a* obvious (**que** that); (*facile*) *Fam* easy. • **évidemment** [-amɑ̃] *adv* obviously. • **évidence** *nf* obviousness; **une é.** an obvious fact; **nier l'é.** to deny the obvious; **être en é.** to be conspicuous; **mettre en é.** (*fait*) to underline; **se rendre à l'é.** to face the facts.
ⓘ**évident G100** The Subjunctive 7 G 1e)
évier [evje] *nm* (kitchen) sink.
évincer [evɛ̃se] *vt* (*concurrent, président etc*) to oust (**de** from).
éviter [evite] *vt* to avoid (**de faire** doing); **é. qch à qn** to spare s.o. sth.
évolu/er [evɔlɥe] *vi* **1** (*changer*) to develop, change; (*société, idée, situation*) to evolve; (*maladie*) to develop. **2** (*se déplacer*) to move. • **—é** *a* (*pays*) advanced; (*personne*) enlightened. • **évolution** *nf* **1** (*changement*) development; evolution. **2** (*d'un danseur etc*) movement.
évoquer [evɔke] *vt* to evoke, call to mind.
ex [ɛks] *nmf* (*mari, femme*) *Fam* ex.
ex- [ɛks] *préf* ex-; **ex-mari** ex-husband.
exact [ɛgzakt] *a* (*précis*) exact, accurate; (*juste, vrai*) correct, right; (*ponctuel*) punctual. • **exactement** *adv* exactly. • **exactitude** *nf* accuracy; correctness; punctuality.
ex aequo [ɛgzeko] *adv* **être classés ex ae.** *Sp* to tie, be equally placed.
exagér/er [ɛgzaʒere] *vt* to exaggerate ‖ *vi* (*parler*) to exaggerate; (*agir*) to overdo it, go too far. • **—é** *a* excessive. • **exagération** *nf* exaggeration; (*excès*) excessiveness.
exalter [ɛgzalte] *vt* (*glorifier*) to exalt; (*passionner*) to fire, stir.
examen [ɛgzamɛ̃] *nm* examination; (*bac etc*) exam(ination); **e. blanc** mock exam(ination). • **examinateur, -trice** *nmf Scol* examiner. • **examiner** *vt* to examine.
exaspérer [ɛgzaspere] *vt* (*énerver*) to aggravate, exasperate.
exaucer [ɛgzose] *vt* (*désir*) to grant.
excéder [ɛksede] *vt* **1** (*dépasser*) to exceed. **2 é. qn** (*énerver*) to exasperate s.o. • **excédent** *nm* surplus, excess; **e. de bagages** excess luggage *ou Am* baggage.
excellent [ɛksɛlɑ̃] *a* excellent.
excentrique [ɛksɑ̃trik] *a & nmf* eccentric.
excepté [ɛksɛpte] *prép* except.
exception [ɛksɛpsjɔ̃] *nf* exception; **à l'e. de** except (for); **faire e.** to be an exception. • **exceptionnel, -elle** *a* exceptional. • **exceptionnellement** *adv* exceptionally.
excès [ɛksɛ] *nm* excess; *pl* (*de table*) overeating; **e. de vitesse** *Aut* speeding. • **excessif, -ive** *a* excessive.
excitation [ɛksitɑsjɔ̃] *nf* (*agitation*) excitement.
exciter [ɛksite] *vt* (*faire naître*) to excite, rouse, stir; **e. qn** (*énerver*) to provoke s.o.; (*enthousiasmer*) to thrill s.o., excite s.o. ‖ **s'e.** *vpr* (*devenir nerveux*) to get excited. • **excitant** *a Fam* exciting ‖ *nm* stimulant. • **excité** *a* excited.
exclamer (s') [sɛksklame] *vpr* to exclaim. • **exclamation** *nf* exclamation.
excl/ure* [ɛksklyr] *vt* (*écarter*) to exclude (**de** from); (*chasser*) to expel (**de** from);

e. qch (*rendre impossible*) to preclude sth. ●**—u** *a* (*solution etc*) out of the question; (*avec une date*) exclusive.

exclusif, -ive [ɛksklyzif, -iv] *a* (*droit, modèle, préoccupation*) exclusive. ●**exclusivité** *nf Com* exclusive rights; (*dans la presse*) scoop; **en e.** (*film*) having an exclusive showing (**à** at).

exclusion [ɛksklyzjɔ̃] *nf* exclusion; **à l'e. de** with the exception of.

excursion [ɛkskyrsjɔ̃] *nf* trip, outing; (*à pied*) hike.

excuse [ɛkskyz] *nf* (*prétexte*) excuse; *pl* (*regrets*) apology; **faire des excuses** to apologize (**à** to). ●**excuser** *vt* to excuse (**qn d'avoir fait, qn de faire** s.o. for doing) ‖ **s'e.** *vpr* to apologize (**de** for, **auprès de** to); **excusez-moi!, je m'excuse!** excuse me!

exécrable [ɛgzekrabl] *a* atrocious.

exécuter [ɛgzekyte] *vt* **1** (*travail*) to carry out; (*jouer*) *Mus* to perform; (*broderie etc*) to produce; (*programme informatique*) to run. **2 e. qn** (*tuer*) to execute s.o. **3 s'exécuter** *vpr* to comply. ●**exécution** *nf* **1** carrying out; performance; production. **2** (*mise à mort*) execution.

exécutif [ɛgzekytif] *am* **pouvoir e.** executive power ‖ *nm* **l'e.** *Pol* the executive.

exemplaire [ɛgzɑ̃plɛr] **1** *a* exemplary. **2** *nm* (*livre etc*) copy; **photocopier un document en double e.** to make two photocopies of a document.

exemple [ɛgzɑ̃pl] *nm* example; **par e.** for example, for instance; **donner l'e.** to set an example (**à** to); **prendre e. sur qn** to follow s.o.'s example; **c'est un e. de vertu/***etc* he's a model of virtue/*etc*; **(ça) par e.!** *Fam* good heavens!.

exempt [ɛgzɑ̃] *a* **e. de** (*dispensé de*) exempt from. ●**exempter** *vt* to exempt (**de** from).

exercer [ɛgzɛrse] *vt* (*voix, droits*) to exercise; (*autorité, influence*) to exert (**sur** over); (*profession*) to practise; **e. qn à** (*couture etc*) to train s.o. in; **e. qn à faire** to train s.o. to do ‖ *vi* (*médecin etc*) to practise ‖ **s'e.** *vpr* (*influence etc*) to be exerted; **s'e. (à qch)** (*sportif etc*) to practise (sth); **s'e. à faire** to practise doing.

exercice [ɛgzɛrsis] *nm* (*physique etc*) & *Scol* exercise; **faire de l'e., prendre de l'e.** to (take) exercise; **l'e. de** (*pouvoir etc*) the exercise of; **en e.** (*fonctionnaire*) in office; (*médecin etc*) in practice.

exhaustif, -ive [ɛgzostif, -iv] *a* exhaustive.

exhiber [ɛgzibe] *vt* to exhibit, show.

exiger [ɛgziʒe] *vt* to demand, require (**de** from, **que** (+ *sub*) that). ●**exigeant** *a* demanding. ●**exigence** *nf* demand, requirement; **d'une grande e.** very demanding.

exigu, -uë [ɛgzigy] *a* (*appartement etc*) cramped, tiny.

exil [ɛgzil] *nm* exile. ●**exiler** *vt* to exile ‖ **s'e.** *vpr* to go into exile. ●**exilé, -ée** *nmf* (*personne*) exile.

existence [ɛgzistɑ̃s] *nf* existence. ●**exister** *vi* to exist ‖ *v imp* **il existe...** (*sing*) there is...; (*pl*) there are....

exode [ɛgzɔd] *nm* exodus.

exonérer [ɛgzɔnere] *vt* to exempt (**de** from).

exorbitant [ɛgzɔrbitɑ̃] *a* exorbitant.

exorciser [ɛgzɔrsize] *vt* to exorcize.

exotique [ɛgzɔtik] *a* exotic.

expansif, -ive [ɛkspɑ̃sif, -iv] *a* expansive, effusive.

expansion [ɛkspɑ̃sjɔ̃] *nf* (*d'un commerce, pays, gaz*) expansion; **en (pleine) e.** (fast) expanding.

expatrier (s') [sɛkspatrije] *vpr* to leave one's country.

expectative [ɛkspɛktativ] *nf* **être dans l'e.** to be waiting to see what happens.

expédier [ɛkspedje] *vt* **1** (*envoyer*) to send off. **2** (*affaires, client*) to dispose of quickly, dispatch. ●**expéditeur, -trice** *nmf* sender. ●**expédition** *nf* **1** (*envoi*) dispatch. **2** (*voyage*) expedition.

expérience [ɛksperjɑ̃s] *nf* (*connaissance*) experience; (*scientifique*) experiment; **faire l'e. de qch** to experience sth; **être sans e.** to have no experience.

expériment/er [ɛksperimɑ̃te] *vt Phys Ch* to try out, experiment with. ●**—é** *a* experienced.

expert [ɛkspɛr] *a* expert, skilled (**en** in) ‖ *nm* expert (**en** on, in); (*d'assurances*) valuer. ●**e.-comptable** *nm* (*pl* **experts-comptables**) = chartered accountant, = *Am* certified public accountant. ●**expertise** *nf* (*évaluation*) (expert) appraisal.

expirer [ɛkspire] **1** *vti* to breathe out. **2** *vi* (*mourir*) to pass away; (*finir, cesser*) to expire. ●**expiration** *nf* (*échéance*) expiry, *Am* expiration; **arriver à e.** to expire.

explication [ɛksplikasjɔ̃] *nf* explanation; (*mise au point*) discussion.

explicite [ɛksplisit] *a* explicit.

expliquer [ɛksplike] *vt* to explain (**à** to, **que** that) ‖ **s'e.** *vpr* (*discuter*) to talk things over (**avec** with); **s'e. qch** (*comprendre*) to understand sth; **ça s'explique** that is understandable.

exploit [ɛksplwa] *nm* feat, exploit.
exploit/er [ɛksplwate] *vt* (*champs*) to farm; (*ferme, entreprise*) to run; (*mine*) to work; (*profiter de*) *Fig* to exploit. ●**—ant, -ante** *nmf* farmer. ●**exploitation** *nf* **1** farming; running; working; (*entreprise*) concern; **e. (agricole)** farm. **2** *Péj* exploitation.
explorer [ɛksplɔre] *vt* to explore. ●**explorateur, -trice** *nmf* explorer. ●**exploration** *nf* exploration.
exploser [ɛksploze] *vi* (*gaz etc*) to explode; (*bombe*) to blow up, explode; **e. (de colère)** *Fam* to explode; **faire e.** (*bombe*) to explode. ●**explosif, -ive** *a* & *nm* explosive. ●**explosion** *nf* explosion; (*de colère, joie*) outburst.
exporter [ɛkspɔrte] *vt* to export (**vers** to, **de** from). ●**exportateur, -trice** *nmf* exporter ‖ *a* exporting. ●**exportation** *nf* (*produit*) export; (*action*) export(ation).
expos/er [ɛkspoze] *vt* (*présenter, soumettre*) & *Phot* to expose (**à** to); (*tableau etc*) to exhibit; (*marchandises*) to display; (*idée, théorie*) to set out; (*vie*) to risk; **s'e. à** to expose oneself to. ●**—é 1** *a* **bien e.** (*édifice*) having a good exposure; **e. au sud**/*etc* facing south/*etc*. **2** *nm* (*compte rendu*) account (**de** of); (*présentation*) talk.
exposition [ɛkspozisjɔ̃] *nf* (*salon*) exhibition; (*de marchandises etc*) display.
exprès[1] [ɛksprɛ] *adv* on purpose, intentionally; (*spécialement*) specially.
exprès[2], **-esse** [ɛksprɛs] **1** *a* (*ordre, condition*) express. **2** *a inv* **lettre/colis e.** express letter/parcel.
express [ɛksprɛs] *a* & *nm inv* (*train*) express; (*café*) espresso.
expressif, -ive [ɛkspresif, -iv] *a* expressive. ●**expression** *nf* (*phrase, mine etc*) expression. ●**exprimer** *vt* to express ‖ **s'e.** *vpr* to express oneself.
exproprier [ɛksprɔprije] *vt* to seize the property of by compulsory purchase.
expulser [ɛkspylse] *vt* to expel (**de** from); (*joueur*) *Sp* to send off; (*locataire*) to evict. ●**expulsion** *nf* expulsion; sending off; eviction.
exquis [ɛkski] *a* (*nourriture*) delicious.
extasier (s') [sɛkstazje] *vpr* to be in raptures (**sur** over).
extensible [ɛkstɑ̃sibl] *a* expandable. ●**extension** *nf* extension; (*essor*) expansion.
exténué [ɛkstenɥe] *a* exhausted.
extérieur [ɛksterjœr] *a* outside; (*surface*) outer, external; (*signe*) outward; (*politique*) foreign; **e. à** external to ‖ *nm* outside; **à l'e. (de)** outside; **à l'e.** (*match*) away; **en e.** *Cin* on location. ●**—ement** *adv* externally; (*en apparence*) outwardly. ●**extérioriser** *vt* to express.
exterminer [ɛkstɛrmine] *vt* to exterminate, wipe out.
externat [ɛksterna] *nm* (*école*) day school.
externe [ɛkstɛrn] **1** *a* external. **2** *nmf* (*élève*) day pupil; *Méd* non-resident hospital doctor, *Am* extern.
extincteur [ɛkstɛ̃ktœr] *nm* fire extinguisher.
extorquer [ɛkstɔrke] *vt* to extort (**à** from). ●**extorsion** *nf* extortion; **e. de fonds** (*crime*) extortion.
extra [ɛkstra] **1** *a inv* (*très bon*) *Fam* top-quality. **2** *nm inv Culin* (extra-special) treat; (*serviteur*) extra hand *ou* help.
extra- [ɛkstra] *préf* extra-. ●**e.-fin** *a* extra-fine. ●**e.-fort** *a* extra-strong.
extradition [ɛkstradisjɔ̃] *nf* extradition. ●**extrader** *vt* to extradite.
extraire* [ɛkstrɛr] *vt* to extract (**de** from); (*charbon*) to mine. ●**extrait** *nm* extract; **e. de naissance** (copy of one's) birth certificate.
extraordinaire [ɛkstraɔrdinɛr] *a* extraordinary.
extraterrestre [ɛkstraterɛstr] *a* & *nmf* extraterrestrial.
extravagant [ɛkstravagɑ̃] *a* extravagant.
extraverti, -ie [ɛkstravɛrti] *nmf* extrovert.
extrême [ɛkstrɛm] *a* extreme ‖ *nm* extreme; **pousser à l'e.** to take *ou* carry to extremes. ●**E.-Orient** *nm* Far East. ●**extrêmement** *adv* extremely. ●**extrémiste** *a* & *nmf* extremist. ●**extrémité** *nf* (*bout*) end; *pl* (*excès*) extremes.

F

F, f [ɛf] *nm* F, f.

F *abrév* **franc(s).**

fa [fa] *nm* (*note de musique*) F.

fable [fɑbl] *nf* fable.

fabricant, -ante [fabrikɑ̃, -ɑ̃t] *nmf* manufacturer. ●**fabrication** *nf* manufacture; **f. artisanale** small-scale manufacture.

fabrique [fabrik] *nf* factory; **marque de f.** trade mark.

fabriquer [fabrike] *vt* to make; (*en usine*) to manufacture; **qu'est-ce qu'il fabrique?** *Fam* what's he up to?

fabuleux, -euse [fabylø, -øz] *a* (*légendaire, incroyable*) fabulous.

fac [fak] *nf abrév* (*faculté*) *Fam* university; **à la f.** at university, *Am* at school.

façade [fasad] *nf* (*de bâtiment*) front; (*apparence*) *Fig* pretence, façade.

face [fas] *nf* face; (*de cube etc*) side; (*de monnaie*) head; **en f.** opposite; **en f. de** opposite, facing; (*en présence de*) in front of, face to face with; **f. à** (*vis-à-vis*) facing; **f. à f.** face to face; **f. à un problème** faced with a problem; **faire f. à** (*situation*) to face, face up to; **regarder qn en f.** to look s.o. in the face; **de f.** (*photo*) full-face.

facette [fasɛt] *nf* (*de diamant, problème etc*) facet.

fâcher [fɑʃe] *vt* to anger ‖ **se f.** *vpr* to get angry (**contre** with); **se f. avec qn** (*se brouiller*) to fall out with s.o. ●**fâché** *a* (*air*) angry; (*amis*) on bad terms; **f. contre qn** angry with s.o.; **f. de qch** sorry about sth; **f. de faire** sorry to do.

ℹ**fâché G98** The Subjunctive 7 G 1a)

facho [faʃo] *a & nmf Fam* fascist.

facile [fasil] *a* easy; (*caractère, humeur*) easygoing; **c'est f. à faire** it's easy to do; **il nous est f. de faire ça** it's easy for us to do that; **f. à vivre** easy to get along with, easygoing. ●**—ment** *adv* easily. ●**facilité** *nf* (*simplicité*) easiness; (*à faire qch*) ease; **facilités de paiement** *Com* easy terms; **avoir des facilités pour qch** to have an aptitude for sth. ●**faciliter** *vt* to make easier, facilitate.

façon [fasɔ̃] *nf* **1** way; **la f. dont elle parle** the way (in which) she talks; **f. (d'agir)** behaviour; **façons** (*manières*) manners; **une f. de parler** a manner of speaking; **de toute f.** anyway; **de f. à** so as to; **de f. (à ce) que** (+ *sub*) so that; **de f. générale** generally speaking; **d'une f. ou d'une autre** one way or another; **à ma f.** my way, (in) my own way; **faire des façons** to make a fuss. **2** (*coupe de vêtement*) cut, style.

façonner [fasɔne] *vt* (*travailler, former*) to fashion, shape; (*fabriquer*) to manufacture.

facteur [faktœr] *nm* **1** postman, *Am* mailman. **2** (*élément*) factor. ●**factrice** *nf* postwoman, *Am* mail woman.

facture [faktyr] *nf Com* bill, invoice. ●**facturer** *vt* to bill, invoice.

facultatif, -ive [fakyltatif, -iv] *a* optional; **arrêt f.** request stop.

faculté [fakylte] *nf* **1** (*aptitude*) faculty; (*possibilité*) freedom (**de faire** to do); **une f. de travail** a capacity for work. **2** (*d'université*) faculty; **à la f.** at university, *Am* at school.

fade [fad] *a* insipid; (*nourriture*) bland.

fagot [fago] *nm* bundle (of firewood).

faible [fɛbl] *a* weak; (*bruit*) faint; (*vent*) slight; (*revenus*) small; **f. en anglais/***etc* poor at English/*etc* ‖ *nm* (*personne*) weakling; **avoir un f. pour** to have a weakness *ou* a soft spot for. ●**faiblement** *adv* weakly; (*légèrement*) slightly; (*éclairer*) faintly. ●**faiblesse** *nf* weakness; faintness; slightness; (*défaut, syncope*) weakness.

faiblir [feblir] *vi* (*forces*) to weaken; (*courage, vue*) to fail; (*vent*) to slacken.

faïence [fajɑ̃s] *nf* (*matière*) earthenware; *pl* (*objets*) crockery, earthenware.

faille[1] [faj] *nf Géol* fault; *Fig* flaw.

faille[2] [faj] *voir* **falloir.**

faillible [fajibl] *a* fallible.

faillir* [fajir] *vi* **1 il a failli tomber** he almost *ou* nearly fell. **2 f. à** (*devoir*) to fail in.

faillite [fajit] *nf Com* bankruptcy; **faire f.** to go bankrupt.

faim [fɛ̃] *nf* hunger; **avoir f.** to be hungry; **donner f. à qn** to make s.o. hungry; **manger à sa f.** to eat one's fill; **mourir de f.** to die of starvation; (*avoir très faim*) *Fig* to be starving.

fainéant, -ante [feneɑ̃, -ɑ̃t] *a* idle ‖ *nmf* idler. ●**fainéantise** *nf* idleness.

faire** [fɛr] **1** *vt* (*bruit, faute, gâteau, voyage etc*) to make; (*devoir, ménage etc*) to do; (*rêve, chute*) to have; (*sourire*) to give; (*promenade, sieste*) to have, take;

(*guerre*) to wage, make; **ça fait dix mètres de large** (*mesure*) it's *ou* that's ten metres wide; **ça fait dix francs** (*prix*) it's *ou* that's ten francs; **2 et 2 font 4** 2 and 2 are 4; **qu'a-t-il fait (de)?** what's he done (with)?; **que f.?** what's to be done? **f. du tennis/du piano/***etc* to play tennis/the piano/*etc*; **f. du droit/***etc* to study law/*etc*; **f. l'idiot** to play the fool; **ça ne fait rien** that doesn't matter; **comment as-tu fait pour...?** how did you manage to...?
2 *vi* (*agir*) to do; (*paraître*) to look; **il fait vieux** he looks old; **elle ferait bien de partir** she'd do well to leave.
3 *v imp* **il fait beau/froid/***etc* it's fine/cold/*etc*; **quel temps fait-il?** what's the weather like?; **ça fait deux ans que je ne l'ai pas vu** I haven't seen him for two years; **ça fait un an que je suis là** I've been here for a year.
faire G88 Impersonal Verbs 7 E 2a)
4 *v aux* (+ *inf*); **f. construire une maison** to have *ou* get a house built (**à qn** for s.o., **par qn** by s.o.); **f. souffrir/***etc* **qn** to make s.o. suffer/*etc*; **se f. couper les cheveux** to have one's hair cut; **se f. obéir/***etc* to make oneself obeyed/*etc*; **se f. tuer/***etc* to get *ou* be killed/*etc*.
G113 The Infinitive 7 H 2d)
G120 The Passive 7 J 2d)
5 se faire *vpr* (*fabrication*) to be made; (*activité*) to be done; **se f. des illusions** to have illusions; **se f. des amis** to make friends; **se f. vieux/***etc* to get old/*etc*; **il se fait tard** it's getting late; **comment se fait-il que?** how is it that?; **ça se fait beaucoup** people do that a lot; **se f. à** to get used to; **ne t'en fais pas!** don't worry!
faire-part [fɛrpar] *nm inv* (*de mariage etc*) announcement.
fais, fait [fɛ] *voir* **faire**.
faisable [fəzabl] *a* feasible.
faisan [fəzɑ̃] *nm* (*oiseau*) pheasant.
faisceau, -x [fɛso] *nm* (*lumineux*) beam.
fait [fɛ] **1** *pp de* **faire** ‖ *a* (*fromage*) ripe; (*yeux*) made up; (*ongles*) polished; (*homme*) grown; **tout f.** ready made; **bien f.** (*jambes, corps etc*) shapely; **c'est bien f.!** it serves you right!
2 *nm* event; (*donnée, réalité*) fact; **prendre qn sur le f.** to catch s.o. red-handed *ou* in the act; **du f. de** on account of; **f. divers** (*rubrique de journal*) (miscellaneous) news item; **au f.** (*à propos*) by the way; **aller au f.** to get to the point; **en f.** in fact; **en f. de** in the matter of.
faîte [fɛt] *nm* (*haut*) top; (*apogée*) *Fig* height.
faites [fɛt] *voir* **faire.**
falaise [falɛz] *nf* cliff.
falloir** [falwar] **1** *v imp* **il faut qch/qn** I, you, we *etc* need sth/s.o.; **il lui faut un stylo** he *ou* she needs a pen; **il faut partir/***etc* I, you, we *etc* have to go/*etc*; **il aurait fallu partir/***etc* I, you, we *etc* should have gone/*etc*; **il faut que je parte** I have to go; **il faudrait qu'elle reste** she ought to stay; **il faut un jour** it takes a day (**pour faire** to do); **comme il faut** proper(ly); **s'il le faut** if need be.
2 s'en falloir *v imp* **il s'en est fallu de peu qu'il ne pleure** he almost cried; **tant s'en faut** far from it.
falloir G91 Impersonal Verbs 7 E 2h) ii)
falloir G123 Modal Auxiliary Verbs 7 K 5
falsifier [falsifje] *vt* (*texte etc*) to falsify.
famé (mal) [malfame] *a* of ill repute.
fameux, -euse [famø, -øz] *a* (*célèbre*) famous; (*excellent*) *Fam* first-class; **pas f.** *Fam* not much good.
familial, -aux [familjal, -o] *a* family; **ennuis/***etc* **familiaux** family problems/*etc*.
familier, -ière [familje, -jɛr] *a* (*bien connu*) familiar (**à** to); (*amical*) friendly, informal; (*locution*) colloquial, familiar; **f. avec qn** (over)familiar with s.o.; **animal f.** pet. •**se familiariser** *vpr* to familiarize oneself (**avec** with). •**familiarité** *nf* familiarity (**avec** with). •**familièrement** *adv* (*parler*) informally.
famille [famij] *nf* family; **en f.** (*dîner etc*) with one's family; **un père de f.** a family man.
famine [famin] *nf* famine.
fan [fɑ̃] *nm* (*admirateur*) *Fam* fan.
fana [fana] *nmf Fam* fan; **être f. de** to be crazy about.
fanatique [fanatik] *a* fanatical ‖ *nmf* fanatic. •**fanatisme** *nm* fanaticism.
faner (se) [səfane] *vpr* (*fleur, beauté*) to fade. •**fané** *a* faded.
fanfare [fɑ̃far] *nf* (*orchestre*) brass band.
fanfaron, -onne [fɑ̃farɔ̃, -ɔn] *a* boastful ‖ *nmf* braggart.
fanion [fanjɔ̃] *nm* (*drapeau*) pennant.
fantaisie [fɑ̃tezi] *nf* (*caprice*) whim, fancy; (*imagination*) imagination; **(de) f.** (*bouton etc*) novelty, fancy. •**fantaisiste** *a* (*pas sérieux*) fanciful; (*excentrique*) unorthodox.
fantasme [fɑ̃tasm] *nm Psy* fantasy.
fantasque [fɑ̃task] *a* whimsical.
fantassin [fɑ̃tasɛ̃] *nm Mil* infantryman.
fantastique [fɑ̃tastik] *a* (*imaginaire, excellent*) fantastic.

fantôme [fɑ̃tom] *nm* ghost ‖ *a* **ville f.** ghost town.
faon [fɑ̃] *nm* (*animal*) fawn.
farce[1] [fars] *nf* practical joke, prank; *Th* farce; **magasin de farces et attrapes** joke shop. • **farceur, -euse** *nmf* (*blagueur*) practical joker.
farce[2] [fars] *nf* (*viande*) stuffing. • **farcir** *vt Culin* to stuff.
fard [far] *nm* make-up. • **se farder** *vpr* (*se maquiller*) to make up.
fardeau, -x [fardo] *nm* burden, load.
farfelu [farfəly] *a Fam* crazy, bizarre.
farine [farin] *nf* (*de blé*) flour.
farouche [faruʃ] *a* **1** (*timide*) shy, unsociable; (*animal*) easily scared. **2** (*violent*) fierce.
fart [far(t)] *nm* (ski) wax. • **farter** *vt* (*skis*) to wax.
fascicule [fasikyl] *nm* volume.
fasciner [fasine] *vt* to fascinate. • **fascination** *nf* fascination.
fasciste [faʃist] *a* & *nmf* fascist.
fasse(s), fassent [fas] *voir* **faire.**
faste [fast] *nm* ostentation, display.
fastidieux, -euse [fastidjø, -øz] *a* tedious.
fatal, *mpl* **-als** [fatal] *a* (*mortel*) fatal; (*inévitable*) inevitable; (*moment*) fateful; **c'était f.!** it was bound to happen! • **—ement** *adv* inevitably. • **fatalité** *nf* (*destin*) fate.
fatigant [fatigɑ̃] *a* (*épuisant*) tiring; (*ennuyeux*) tiresome.
fatigue [fatig] *nf* tiredness, fatigue.
fatiguer [fatige] *vt* to tire; (*yeux*) to strain; (*importuner*) to annoy; (*raser*) to bore ‖ *vi* (*moteur*) to strain ‖ **se f.** *vpr* (*se lasser*) to get tired, tire (**de** of); (*travailler*) to tire oneself out (**à faire** doing). • **fatigué** *a* tired, weary (**de** of).
faubourg [fobur] *nm* suburb.
fauché [foʃe] *a* (*sans argent*) *Fam* (flat) broke.
faucher [foʃe] *vt* **1** (*herbe*) to mow; (*blé*) to reap; **f. qn** (*renverser*) *Fig* to knock s.o. down, mow s.o. down. **2** (*voler*) *Fam* to snatch, pinch.
faucille [fosij] *nf* (*instrument*) sickle.
faucon [fokɔ̃] *nm* (*oiseau*) hawk, falcon.
faudra, faudrait [fodra, fodrɛ] *voir* **falloir.**
faufiler (se) [səfofile] *vpr* to edge one's way (**dans** through, into; **entre** between).
faune [fon] *nf* wildlife, fauna.
faussaire [fosɛr] *nm* forger.
fausse [fos] *voir* **faux**[1]. • **faussement** *adv* falsely.
fausser [fose] *vt* (*réalité etc*) to distort; **f. compagnie à qn** to give s.o. the slip.
fausseté [foste] *nf* (*d'un raisonnement etc*) falseness; (*hypocrisie*) duplicity.
faut [fo] *voir* **falloir.**
faute [fot] *nf* (*erreur*) mistake; (*responsabilité*) fault; (*péché*) sin; *Fb* foul; **c'est ta f.** it's your fault; **f. de temps**/*etc* for lack of time/*etc*; **f. de mieux** for want of anything better; **sans f.** without fail; **f. d'impression** printing error.
fauteuil [fotœj] *nm* armchair; **f. roulant** wheelchair; **f. d'orchestre** *Th* seat in the stalls.
fauteur [fotœr] *nm* **f. de troubles** troublemaker.
fautif, -ive [fotif, -iv] *a* (*personne*) at fault; (*erroné*) faulty.
fauve [fov] *nm* wild animal, big cat.
faux[1], **fausse** [fo, fos] *a* (*pas vrai*) false, untrue; (*pas exact*) wrong; (*monnaie*) forged, counterfeit; (*voix*) out of tune; **f. diamant**/*etc* imitation *ou* fake diamond/*etc* ‖ *adv* (*chanter*) out of tune ‖ *nm* (*contrefaçon*) forgery. • **f.-filet** *nm Culin* sirloin. • **f.-monnayeur** *nm* counterfeiter.
faux[2] [fo] *nf* (*instrument*) scythe.
faveur [favœr] *nf* favour; **en f. de** (*au profit de*) in aid *ou* favour of; **de f.** (*billet*) complimentary; (*traitement*) preferential. • **favorable** *a* favourable (**à** to). • **favori, -ite** *a* & *nmf* favourite. • **favoriser** *vt* to favour. • **favoritisme** *nm* favouritism.
favoris [favɔri] *nmpl* sideburns, sideboards.
fax [faks] *nm* (*appareil, message*) fax.
faxer [fakse] *vt* (*message*) to fax.
fébrile [febril] *a* feverish.
fécond [fekɔ̃] *a* (*femme, idée etc*) fertile. • **fécondité** *nf* fertility.
fécule [fekyl] *nf* starch. • **féculents** *nmpl* (*aliments*) carbohydrates.
fédéral, -aux [federal, -o] *a* federal. • **fédération** *nf* federation.
fée [fe] *nf* fairy. • **féerique** *a* fairy(-like), magical.
feindre* [fɛ̃dr] *vt* to feign, affect, sham; **f. de faire** to pretend to do. • **feinte** *nf* sham, pretence; *Boxe Mil* feint.
fêler [fele] *vt*, **se f.** *vpr* (*tasse etc*) to crack. • **fêlure** *nf* crack.
féliciter [felisite] *vt* to congratulate (**qn de** *ou* **sur** s.o. on); **se f. de** to congratulate oneself on. • **félicitations** *nfpl* congratulations (**pour** on).
félin [felɛ̃] *a* & *nm* feline.
femelle [fəmɛl] *a* & *nf* (*animal*) female.
féminin [feminɛ̃] *a* (*prénom etc*) female; (*trait, intuition etc*) & *Gram* feminine;

(eg **G1**, **G2**, **G3**) in French **G**rammar, at the end of the dictionary. Also see p. ix.

(*mode*, *revue etc*) women's. • **féministe** *a* & *nmf* feminist.
femme [fam] *nf* woman (*pl* women); (*épouse*) wife; **f. médecin** woman doctor; **f. de ménage** cleaning woman; **f. de chambre** (chamber)maid; **f. d'affaires** businesswoman; **f. au foyer** housewife; **bonne f.** *Fam* woman.
fémur [femyr] *nm* thighbone.
fendiller (se) [səfɑ̃dije] *vpr* to crack.
fendre [fɑ̃dr] *vt* (*bois etc*) to split; (*foule*) to force one's way through; (*air*) to cleave; (*cœur*) *Fig* to break ‖ **se f.** *vpr* (*se fissurer*) to crack.
fenêtre [f(ə)nɛtr] *nf* window.
fenouil [fənuj] *nm Bot Culin* fennel.
fente [fɑ̃t] *nf* (*palissade*, *jupe etc*) slit; (*de rocher*) split, crack.
féodal, -aux [feɔdal, -o] *a* feudal.
fer [fɛr] *nm* iron; (*partie métallique de qch*) metal (part); **barre de f.** iron bar; **fil de f.** wire; **boîte en f.** tin, *Am* can; **f. à cheval** horseshoe; **f. (à repasser)** iron (*for clothes*); **f. forgé** wrought iron; **santé de f.** *Fig* cast-iron health. • **fer-blanc** *nm* (*pl* **fers-blancs**) tin (-plate).
fera, ferai(t) *etc* [fəra, fərɛ] *voir* **faire.**
férié [ferje] *a* **jour f.** (public) holiday.
ferme[1] [fɛrm] *nf* farm; (*maison*) farm(house).
ferme[2] [fɛrm] *a* (*beurre*, *décision etc*) firm; (*pas*, *voix*) steady; (*autoritaire*) firm (**avec** with) ‖ *adv* (*discuter*) keenly; **s'ennuyer f.** to be bored stiff. • **—ment** [-əmɑ̃] *adv* firmly.
fermentation [fɛrmɑ̃tɑsjɔ̃] *nf* fermentation. • **fermenter** *vi* to ferment.
fermer [fɛrme] *vt* to close, shut; (*gaz etc*) to turn *ou* switch off; (*vêtement*) to do up; (*passage*) to block; **f. (à clef)** to lock; **f. un magasin**/*etc* (*définitivement*) to close *ou* shut (down) a shop/*etc* ‖ *vi*, **se f.** *vpr* to close, shut. • **fermé** *a* (*porte*, *magasin etc*) closed, shut; (*route etc*) closed; (*gaz etc*) off.
fermeté [fɛrməte] *nf* firmness; (*de voix*) steadiness.
fermeture [fɛrmətyr] *nf* closing, closure; (*heure*) closing time; **f. éclair**® zip (fastener), *Am* zipper.
fermier, -ière [fɛrmje, -jɛr] *nmf* farmer.
fermoir [fɛrmwar] *nm* clasp, (snap) fastener.
féroce [ferɔs] *a* fierce, savage. • **férocité** *nf* ferocity.
feront [fərɔ̃] *voir* **faire**.
ferraille [fɛrɑj] *nf* scrap metal, old iron; **mettre à la f.** to scrap.
ferré [fɛre] *a* **voie ferrée** railway, *Am* railroad; (*rails*) track.
ferrer [fɛre] *vt* (*cheval*) to shoe.
ferronnerie [fɛrɔnri] *nf* ironwork.
ferroviaire [fɛrɔvjɛr] *a* **compagnie f.** railway company, *Am* railroad company.
fertile [fɛrtil] *a* (*terre*, *imagination*) fertile; **f. en incidents** eventful.
fervent [fɛrvɑ̃] *a* fervent. • **ferveur** *nf* fervour.
fesse [fɛs] *nf* buttock; **les fesses** one's behind. • **fessée** *nf* spanking.
festin [fɛstɛ̃] *nm* (*banquet*) feast.
festival, *pl* **-als** [fɛstival] *nm Mus Cin etc* festival.
festivités [fɛstivite] *nfpl* festivities.
fête [fɛt] *nf* (*civile*) holiday; *Rel* festival; (*entre amis*) party; **f. de famille** family celebration; **c'est sa f.** it's his *ou* her saint's day; **f. des Mères** Mother's Day; **f. du travail** Labour Day; **jour de f.** (public) holiday; **faire la f.** to have a good time; **les fêtes** (*de Noël*) the Christmas holidays. • **fêter** *vt* (*événement*) to celebrate.
feu[1], **-x** [fø] *nm* fire; (*de réchaud*) burner; (*lumière*) *Aut Nau Av* light; (*de dispute*) *Fig* heat; **feux (tricolores)** traffic lights; **feux de détresse** (hazard) warning lights; **feux de position** *Aut* parking lights; **feux de croisement** *Aut* dipped headlights, *Am* low beams; **tous feux éteints** *Aut* without lights; **f. rouge** *Aut* (*lumière*) red light; (*objet*) traffic lights; **mettre le f. à** to set fire to; **en f.** on fire, ablaze; **faire du f.** to light *ou* make a fire; **prendre f.** to catch fire; **avez-vous du f.?** have you got a light?; **donner le f. vert** to give the go-ahead (**à** to); **à f. doux** *Culin* on a low light *ou* heat; **au f.!** fire!; **f.!** *Mil* fire!; **coup de f.** (*bruit*) gunshot.
feu[2] [fø] *a inv* late; **f. ma tante** my late aunt.
feuille [fœj] *nf* leaf; (*de papier etc*) sheet; **f. d'impôt** tax form *ou* return; **f. de paye** pay slip *ou Am* stub; **f. de présence** attendance sheet. • **feuillage** *nm* leaves.
feuillet [fœjɛ] *nm* (*de livre*) leaf. • **feuilleter** *vt* (*livre*) to flip through; **pâte feuilletée** puff pastry *ou Am* paste.
feuilleton [fœjtɔ̃] *nm* serial; **f. télévisé** television serial.
feutre [føtr] *nm* felt; (*chapeau*) felt hat; **crayon f.** felt-tip (pen). • **feutré** *a* (*bruit*) muffled; **à pas feutrés** silently.
février [févrije] *nm* February.
fiable [fjabl] *a* reliable. • **fiabilité** *nf* reliability.
fiacre [fjakr] *nm Hist* hackney carriage.
fiancer (se) [səfjɑ̃se] *vpr* to become engaged (**avec** to). • **fiancé** *nm* fiancé; *pl*

engaged couple. • **fiancée** *nf* fiancée. • **fiançailles** *nfpl* engagement.

fibre [fibr] *nf* fibre; **f. (alimentaire)** roughage, fibre; **f. de verre** fibreglass.

ficelle [fisɛl] *nf* **1** string. **2** (*pain*) long thin loaf. • **ficeler** *vt* to tie up.

fiche [fiʃ] *nf* **1** (*carte*) index card; (*papier*) form, slip. **2** *Él* (*prise*) plug. • **fichier** *nm* card index, file; *Ordinat* file.

fiche(r) [fiʃ(e)] *vt* (*pp* **fichu**) *Fam* (*faire*) to do; (*donner*) to give; (*jeter*) to throw; (*mettre*) to put; **f. le camp** to shove off; **fiche-moi la paix!** leave me alone!; **se f. de qn** to make fun of s.o.; **je m'en fiche!** I don't give a damn!

ficher [fiʃe] *vt* **1** (*enfoncer*) to drive in. **2** (*renseignement sur une personne*) to put on file.

fichu [fiʃy] *a Fam* (*mauvais*) lousy, rotten; (*capable*) able (**de faire** to do); **c'est f.** (*abîmé*) *Fam* it's had it; **mal f.** (*malade*) not well.

fictif, -ive [fiktif, -iv] *a* fictitious. • **fiction** *nf* fiction.

fidèle [fidɛl] *a* faithful (**à** to) ‖ *nmf* (*client*) regular (customer); **les fidèles** (*croyants*) the faithful; (*à l'église*) the congregation. • **fidélité** *nf* fidelity.

fier (se) [səfje] *vpr* **se f. à** to trust.

fier, fière [fjɛr] *a* proud (**de** of, **de faire** to do). • **fièrement** *adv* proudly. • **fierté** *nf* pride.

fièvre [fjɛvr] *nf* fever; (*agitation*) frenzy; **avoir de la f.** to have a temperature *ou* a fever. • **fiévreux, -euse** *a* feverish.

figer [fiʒe] *vt* to congeal; **f. qn** (*paralyser*) *Fig* to freeze s.o. ‖ **se f.** *vpr* (*liquide*) to congeal; (*sourire, personne*) *Fig* to freeze. • **figé** *a* (*locution*) set, fixed; (*regard*) frozen; (*société*) fossilized.

fignoler [fiɲɔle] *vt Fam* to round off meticulously, refine.

figue [fig] *nf* fig; **mi-f., mi-raisin** (*accueil etc*) neither good nor bad, mixed. • **figuier** *nm* fig tree.

figurant, -ante [figyrɑ̃, -ɑ̃t] *nmf Cin Th* extra.

figure [figyr] *nf* **1** (*visage*) face. **2** (*personnage*) & *Géom* figure; **faire f. de favori** to be considered the favourite.

figurer [figyre] *vi* to appear ‖ **se f.** *vpr* to imagine; **figurez-vous que...?** would you believe that...? • **figuré** *a* (*sens*) figurative ‖ *nm* **au f.** figuratively.

fil [fil] *nm* **1** (*de coton, pensée etc*) thread; **f. dentaire** dental floss; **de f. en aiguille** bit by bit. **2** (*métallique*) wire; **f. de fer** wire; **passer un coup de f. à qn** *Tél* to give s.o. a ring, call s.o. up; **au bout du f.** *Tél* on the line. **3** (*de couteau*) edge. **4 au f. de l'eau/des jours** with the current/the passing of time.

filante [filɑ̃t] *af* **étoile f.** shooting star.

filature [filatyr] *nf* **1** (*usine*) textile mill. **2** (*de policiers etc*) shadowing; **prendre en f.** to shadow.

file [fil] *nf* line; (*couloir*) *Aut* lane; **f. d'attente** queue, *Am* line; **en f. (indienne)** in single file; **chef de f.** leader.

filer [file] **1** *vt* (*coton etc*) to spin. **2** *vt* **f. qn** (*suivre*) to shadow s.o. **3** *vt Fam* **f. qch à qn** (*objet*) to slip s.o. sth; **f. un coup de pied**/*etc* **à qn** to give s.o. a kick/*etc*. **4** *vi* (*partir*) to rush off; (*bas, collant*) to ladder, run; **filez!** hop it!; **f. entre les doigts de qn** to slip through s.o.'s fingers.

filet [filɛ] *nm* **1** (*à bagages*) *Rail* (luggage) rack; (*de pêche*) & *Sp* net; **f. (à provisions)** net bag (*for shopping*). **2** (*d'eau*) trickle. **3** (*de poisson, viande*) fillet.

filiale [filjal] *nf* subsidiary (company).

filière [filjɛr] *nf* (*de drogue*) network; **suivre la f. (normale)** (*pour obtenir qch*) to go through the official channels; (*employé*) to work one's way up.

filigrane [filigran] *nm* (*sur papier*) watermark.

fille [fij] *nf* **1** girl; **petite f.** (little *ou* young) girl; **jeune f.** girl, young lady; **vieille f.** *Péj* old maid. **2** (*parenté*) daughter. • **f.-mère** *nf* (*pl* **filles-mères**) *Péj* unmarried mother. • **fillette** *nf* little girl.

filleul [fijœl] *nm* godson. • **filleule** *nf* goddaughter.

film [film] *nm* **1** film, movie; (*pour photo*) film; **f. muet/parlant** silent/talking film *ou* movie; **f. policier** thriller. **2 f. plastique** cling film, *Am* plastic wrap. • **filmer** *vt* (*personne, scène*) to film.

filon [filɔ̃] *nm Géol* seam; **trouver le (bon) f.** to strike it lucky.

fils [fis] *nm* son; **Dupont f.** Dupont junior.

filtre [filtr] *nm* filter; **(à bout) f.** (*cigarette*) (filter-)tipped; **(bout) f.** filter tip. • **filtrer** *vt* to filter; (*personne, nouvelles*) to scrutinize ‖ *vi* to filter (through).

fin [fɛ̃] **1** *nf* end; (*but*) end, aim; **mettre f. à** to put an end to; **prendre f.** to come to an end; **tirer à sa f.** to draw to an end *ou* a close; **sans f.** endless; **à la f.** in the end; **arrêtez, à la f.!** stop, for heaven's sake!; **f. de semaine** weekend; **f. mai** at the end of May.

2 *a* (*pointe, tissu etc*) fine; (*peu épais*) thin; (*esprit, oreille*) sharp; (*plat*) delicate, choice; (*intelligent*) clever; **au f. fond de**

in the depths of ‖ *adv* (*couper*, *moudre*) finely.

final, -aux *ou* **-als** [final, -o] *a* final ‖ *nm Mus* finale. • **finale** *nf Sp* final. • **finalement** *adv* finally; (*en somme*) after all.

finance [finɑ̃s] *nf* finance. • **financer** *vt* to finance. • **financement** *nm* financing.

financier, -ière [finɑ̃sje, -jɛr] *a* financial ‖ *nm* financier.

finesse [finɛs] *nf* (*de pointe etc*) fineness; (*de taille etc*) thinness; (*de plat*) delicacy; (*d'esprit, de goût*) finesse.

finir [finir] *vti* to finish; **f. bien/mal** (*histoire etc*) to have a happy/unhappy ending; **f. de faire** (*achever*) to finish doing; (*cesser*) to stop doing; **f. par faire** to end up *ou* finish up doing; **en f. avec** to put an end to, finish with; **elle n'en finit pas de pleurer** there's nothing that can make her stop crying. • **fini** *a* (*produit*) finished; (*univers etc*) & *Math* finite; **c'est f.** it's over; **il est f.** (*fichu*) he's done for *ou* finished. • **finition** *nf* (*action*) *Tech* finishing; (*résultat*) finish.

Finlande [fɛ̃lɑ̃d] *nf* Finland. • **finlandais, -aise** *a* Finnish ‖ *nmf* Finn.

firme [firm] *nf* (*entreprise*) firm, company.

fisc [fisk] *nm* tax authorities, = Inland Revenue, = *Am* Internal Revenue. • **fiscal, -aux** *a* fiscal, tax. • **fiscalité** *nf* tax system; (*charges*) taxation.

fissure [fisyr] *nf* crack. • **se fissurer** *vpr* to crack.

fixation [fiksɑsjɔ̃] *nf* (*action*) fixing; (*dispositif*) fastening; *Psy* fixation.

fixe [fiks] *a* fixed; (*prix, heure*) set, fixed; **idée f.** obsession; **regard f.** stare; **être au beau f.** *Mét* to be set fair ‖ *nm* (*paie*) fixed salary. • **—ment** [-əmɑ̃] *adv* **regarder f.** to stare at.

fixer [fikse] *vt* (*attacher*) to fix (**à** to); (*date etc*) to fix; **f. (du regard)** to stare at; **être fixé** (*décidé*) to be decided; **comme ça on est fixé!** (*renseigné*) we've got the picture! ‖ **se f.** *vpr* (*regard*) to become fixed; (*s'établir*) to settle.

flacon [flakɔ̃] *nm* (small) bottle.

flageoler [flaʒɔle] *vi* to shake, tremble.

flageolet [flaʒɔlɛ] *nm Bot Culin* (dwarf) kidney bean.

flagrant [flagrɑ̃] *a* (*injustice etc*) flagrant, glaring; **pris en f. délit** caught in the act.

flair [flɛr] *nm* **1** (*d'un chien etc*) (sense of) smell, scent. **2** (*clairvoyance*) intuition, flair. • **flairer** *vt* to smell.

flamand, -ande [flamɑ̃, -ɑ̃d] *a* Flemish ‖ *nmf* Fleming ‖ *nm* (*langue*) Flemish.

flamant [flamɑ̃] *nm* **f. (rose)** (*oiseau*) flamingo.

flambant [flɑ̃bɑ̃] *adv* **f. neuf** brand new.

flambeau, -x [flɑ̃bo] *nm* torch.

flambée [flɑ̃be] *nf* blaze; (*de colère, des prix etc*) *Fig* surge; (*de violence*) flare-up.

flamber [flɑ̃be] *vi* to burn, blaze ‖ *vt* (*aiguille*) *Méd* to sterilize; (*poulet*) to singe.

flamboyer [flɑ̃bwaje] *vi* to blaze.

flamme [flam] *nf* flame; **en flammes** on fire.

flan [flɑ̃] *nm* (*dessert*) custard tart, baked custard.

flanc [flɑ̃] *nm* side; (*d'une armée, d'un animal*) flank; **tirer au f.** *Arg* to shirk.

flancher [flɑ̃ʃe] *vi Fam* to give in, weaken.

Flandre(s) [flɑ̃dr] *nf(pl)* Flanders.

flanelle [flanɛl] *nf* (*tissu*) flannel.

flâner [flɑne] *vi* to stroll. • **flânerie** *nf* (*action*) strolling; (*promenade*) stroll.

flanquer [flɑ̃ke] *vt* **1** to flank (**de** with). **2** *Fam* (*jeter*) to chuck; (*donner*) to give; **f. qn à la porte** to throw s.o. out.

flaque [flak] *nf* puddle.

flash, *pl* **flashes** [flaʃ] *nm* **1** *Phot* (*éclair*) flashlight; (*dispositif*) flash(gun). **2** *TV Rad* (news) flash.

flatt/er [flate] *vt* to flatter. • **—é** *a* flattered (**de qch** by sth, **de faire** to do, **que** that). • **flatterie** *nf* flattery. • **flatteur, -euse** *nmf* flatterer ‖ *a* flattering.

fléau, -x [fleo] *nm* **1** (*catastrophe*) scourge; (*personne*) plague. **2** *Agr* flail.

flèche [flɛʃ] *nf* arrow; (*d'église*) spire; **monter en f.** (*prix*) to shoot up, (sky)rocket. • **flécher** [fleʃe] *vt* to signpost (with arrows). • **fléchette** *nf* dart; *pl* (*jeu*) darts.

fléchir [fleʃir] *vt* (*membre*) to flex, bend; **f. qn** *Fig* to move s.o., persuade s.o. ‖ *vi* (*membre*) to bend; (*poutre*) to sag; (*faiblir*) to give way; (*baisser*) to fall off.

flegme [flɛgm] *nm* composure. • **flegmatique** *a* phlegmatic, stolid.

flemme [flɛm] *nf Fam* laziness; **il a la f.** he can't be bothered.

flétrir [fletrir] *vt*, **se f.** *vpr* to wither.

fleur [flœr] *nf* flower; (*d'arbre*) blossom; **en fleur(s)** in flower; in blossom; **à fleurs** (*tissu*) flowered, flowery; **à** *ou* **dans la f. de l'âge** in the prime of life.

fleur/ir [flœrir] *vi* to flower; (*arbre*) to blossom; (*art, commerce etc*) *Fig* to flourish ‖ *vt* (*table etc*) to decorate with flowers. • **—i** *a* (*jardin*) in bloom; (*tissu*) flowered, flowery; (*style*) flowery, florid.

fleuriste [flœrist] *nmf* florist.

fleuve [flœv] *nm* river.

flexible [flɛksibl] *a* pliable, flexible. • **flexibilité** *nf* flexibility.

flexion [flɛksjɔ̃] *nf* **1** *Anat* flexion, flexing. **2** *Gram* inflexion.
flic [flik] *nm* (*agent de police*) *Fam* cop.
flipper [flipœr] *nm* (*jeu*) pinball; (*appareil*) pinball machine.
flirt [flœrt] *nm* (*rapports*) flirtation; (*personne*) flirt. • **flirter** *vi* to flirt (**avec** with).
flocon [flɔkɔ̃] *nm* (*de neige*) flake; **flocons de maïs** cornflakes.
floraison [flɔrɛzɔ̃] *nf* flowering; **en pleine f.** in full bloom. • **floral, -aux** *a* floral.
flore [flɔr] *nf* flora.
florissant [flɔrisɑ̃] *a* flourishing.
flot [flo] *nm* (*de souvenirs etc*) flood; *pl* (*de mer*) waves; (*de lac*) waters; **à f.** (*bateau, personne*) afloat; **mettre à f.** (*bateau, firme*) to launch; **remettre qn à f.** to restore s.o.'s fortunes; **couler à flots** (*argent, vin etc*) to flow freely.
flotte [flɔt] *nf* **1** *Nau Av* fleet. **2** *Fam* (*pluie*) rain; (*eau*) water.
flottement [flɔtmɑ̃] *nm* (*hésitation*) indecision.
flott/er [flɔte] *vi* to float; (*drapeau*) to fly; (*pleuvoir*) *Fam* to rain. • **—eur** *nm Pêche etc* float.
flou [flu] *a* (*photo*) fuzzy, blurred; (*idée*) hazy, fuzzy.
fluctuant [flyktɥɑ̃] *a* (*prix, opinions*) fluctuating. • **fluctuations** *nfpl* fluctuation(s) (**de** in).
fluet, -ette [flyɛ, -ɛt] *a* thin, slender.
fluide [flɥid] *a* (*liquide*) & *Fig* fluid ‖ *nm* (*liquide*) fluid.
fluo [flyo] *a inv* (*couleur etc*) luminous, fluorescent.
fluorescent [flyɔresɑ̃] *a* fluorescent.
flûte [flyt] **1** *nf Mus* flute. **2** *nf* (*verre*) champagne glass. **3** *int* heck!. • **flûtiste** *nmf* flautist, *Am* flutist.
fluvial, -aux [flyvjal, -o] *a* **navigation/***etc* **fluviale** river navigation/*etc*.
flux [fly] *nm* (*abondance*) flow; **f. et reflux** ebb and flow.
focal, -aux [fɔkal, -o] *a* focal. • **focaliser** *vt* (*intérêt etc*) to focus.
fœtus [fetys] *nm* foetus, *Am* fetus.
foi [fwa] *nf* faith; **être de bonne/mauvaise f.** to be/not to be (completely) sincere; **avoir la f.** (*être croyant*) to have faith; **ma f., oui!** yes, indeed!
foie [fwa] *nm* liver.
foin [fwɛ̃] *nm* hay.
foire [fwar] *nf* fair; **faire la f.** *Fam* to have a ball.
fois [fwa] *nf* time; **une f.** once; **deux f.** twice, two times; **trois f.** three times; **deux f. trois** two times three; **chaque f. que** whenever; **une f. qu'il sera arrivé** once he has arrived; **à la f.** at the same time; **à la f. riche et heureux** both rich and happy; **une autre f.** (*elle fera attention etc*) next time; **des f.** *Fam* sometimes; **une f. pour toutes** once and for all.
foison [fwazɔ̃] *nf* **à f.** in plenty. • **foisonner** *vi* to abound (**de, en** in).
fol [fɔl] *voir* **fou.**
folichon, -onne [fɔliʃɔ̃, -ɔn] *a* **pas f.** not much fun.
folie [fɔli] *nf* madness; **faire une f.** to do a foolish thing; (*dépense*) to be very extravagant; **aimer qn à la f.** to be madly in love with s.o..
folklore [fɔlklɔr] *nm* folklore. • **folklorique** *a* **musique/***etc* **f.** folk music/*etc*.
folle [fɔl] *voir* **fou.** • **follement** *adv* madly.
foncé [fɔ̃se] *a* (*couleur*) dark.
foncer [fɔ̃se] **1** *vi* (*aller vite*) to tear along; **f. sur qn** to charge into *ou* at s.o. **2** *vti* (*couleur*) to darken.
foncier, -ière [fɔ̃sje, -jɛr] *a* **1** fundamental, basic. **2** (*propriété*) landed. • **foncièrement** *adv* fundamentally.
fonction [fɔ̃ksjɔ̃] *nf* (*rôle*) & *Math* function; (*emploi*) office, post, duty; **f. publique** the public *ou* civil service; **faire f. de** (*personne*) to act as; (*objet*) to serve *ou* act as; **en f. de** according to; **prendre ses fonctions** to take up one's post *ou* duties. • **fonctionnaire** *nmf* civil servant.
fonctionn/er [fɔ̃ksjɔne] *vi* (*machine etc*) to work; (*organisation*) to function; **faire f.** to operate, work. • **—ement** *nm* working.
fond [fɔ̃] *nm* (*de boîte, jardin etc*) bottom; (*de salle etc*) back; (*arrière-plan*) background; (*de problème etc*) essence; **au f. de** at the bottom of; at the back of; **au f.** basically; **à f.** (*connaître etc*) thoroughly; **de f. en comble** from top to bottom; **de f.** (*course*) long-distance; **bruit de f.** background noise; **f. de teint** foundation cream; **f. sonore** background music.
fondamental, -aux [fɔ̃damɑ̃tal, -o] *a* fundamental, basic.
fond/er [fɔ̃de] *vt* (*ville etc*) to found; (*famille*) to start; **(se) f. sur** to base (oneself) on; **bien fondé** well-founded. • **—ement** *nm* foundation. • **fondateur, -trice** *nmf* founder. • **fondation** *nf* (*création, œuvre*) foundation (**de** of).
fonderie [fɔ̃dri] *nf* (*usine*) smelting works.
fondre [fɔ̃dr] *vt* to melt; (*métal*) to melt down; **faire f.** (*sucre etc*) to dissolve ‖ *vi* to

melt; (*se dissoudre*) to dissolve; **f. en larmes** to burst into tears ▮ **se f.** *vpr* to merge; **se f. en eau** (*glaçon etc*) to melt (away); **se f. dans** (*la brume etc*) to disappear *ou* merge into.

fonds [fɔ̃] **1** *nmpl* (*argent*) funds. **2** *nm* **un f. (de commerce)** a business. **3** *nm* (*culturel etc*) *Fig* fund.

fondue [fɔ̃dy] *nf Culin* fondue.

font [fɔ̃] *voir* **faire.**

fontaine [fɔ̃tɛn] *nf* (*construction*) fountain; (*source*) spring.

fonte [fɔ̃t] *nf* **1** (*des neiges*) melting. **2** (*fer*) cast iron; **en f.** (*poêle etc*) cast-iron.

football [futbol] *nm* football, soccer. ●**footballeur, -euse** *nmf* footballer.

footing [futiŋ] *nm Sp* jogging.

forage [fɔraʒ] *nm* drilling, boring.

forain [fɔrɛ̃] *a* (*marchand*) itinerant; **fête foraine** (fun)fair.

force [fɔrs] *nf* force; (*physique, morale*) strength; (*nucléaire*) power; **de toutes ses forces** with all one's strength; **de f.** by force; **en f.** (*attaquer*) in force; **à f. de lire**/*etc* through reading/*etc*, after much reading/*etc*; **cas de f. majeure** circumstances beyond one's control; **dans la f. de l'âge** in the prime of life.

forcer [fɔrse] *vt* (*porte, attention etc*) to force; (*voix*) to strain; **f. qn à faire** to force *ou* compel s.o. to do.
▮ *vi* (*y aller trop fort*) to overdo it.
▮ **se forcer** *vpr* to force oneself (**à faire** to do). ●**forcé** *a* forced (**de faire** to do); **un sourire f.** a forced smile; **c'est f.** *Fam* it's inevitable. ●**forcément** *adv* obviously; **pas f.** not necessarily.

forcené, -ée [fɔrsəne] *nmf* madman, madwoman.

forer [fɔre] *vt* to drill, bore.

forêt [fɔrɛ] *nf* forest. ●**forestier** *nm* **(garde) f.** forester, *Am* (forest) ranger.

forfait [fɔrfɛ] *nm* **1** (*prix*) all-inclusive price. **2 déclarer f.** *Sp* to withdraw from the game. ●**forfaitaire** *a* **prix f.** all-inclusive price.

forge [fɔrʒ] *nf* forge. ●**forger** *vt* (*métal, liens etc*) to forge. ●**forgeron** *nm* (black)smith.

formaliser (se) [səfɔrmalize] *vpr* to take offence *ou Am* offense (**de** at).

formalité [fɔrmalite] *nf* formality.

format [fɔrma] *nm* size.

formater [fɔrmate] *vt* (*disquette*) to format.

formation [fɔrmɑsjɔ̃] *nf* education, training; **f. permanente** continuing education.

forme [fɔrm] *nf* (*contour*) shape, form; (*manière, genre*) form; *pl* (*de femme*) figure; **en f. de poire**/*etc* pear-/*etc* shaped; **en (pleine) f.** in good shape *ou* form; **en bonne et due f.** in due form; **prendre f.** to take shape.

formel, -elle [fɔrmɛl] *a* (*structure, logique etc*) formal; (*démenti*) categorical, formal; (*preuve*) positive. ●**formellement** *adv* (*interdire*) strictly.

former [fɔrme] *vt* (*groupe, caractère etc*) to form; (*apprenti etc*) to train ▮ **se f.** *vpr* (*apparaître*) to form.

formidable [fɔrmidabl] *a* terrific, tremendous.

formulaire [fɔrmylɛr] *nm* (*feuille*) form.

formule [fɔrmyl] *nf* formula; (*phrase*) (set) expression; **f. de politesse** polite form of address. ●**formuler** *vt* to formulate.

fort[1] [fɔr] *a* strong; (*pluie, mer, chute de neige*) heavy; (*voix, radio*) loud; (*fièvre*) high; (*élève*) bright; (*pente*) steep; (*chances*) good; **f. en** (*maths etc*) good at; **c'est plus f. qu'elle** she can't help it; **c'est un peu f.** *Fam* that's a bit much; **à plus forte raison** all the more reason.
▮ *adv* (*frapper, pleuvoir*) hard; (*parler*) loud(ly); (*serrer*) tight; **sentir f.** to have a strong smell.
▮ *nm* **c'est son f.** that's his *ou* her strong point; **au plus f. de** in the thick of.

fort[2] [fɔr] *nm Hist Mil* fort. ●**forteresse** *nf* fortress.

fortifier [fɔrtifje] *vt* to strengthen, fortify ▮ **se f.** *vpr* (*malade*) to fortify oneself. ●**fortifiant** *nm Méd* tonic. ●**fortification** *nf* fortification.

fortuit [fɔrtɥi] *a* **rencontre**/*etc* **fortuite** chance meeting/*etc*.

fortune [fɔrtyn] *nf* (*argent, hasard*) fortune; **faire f.** to make one's fortune; **de f.** (*moyens etc*) makeshift. ●**fortuné** *a* (*riche*) well-to-do.

fosse [fos] *nf* (*trou*) pit; (*tombe*) grave.

fossé [fose] *nm* ditch; (*douve*) moat; (*désaccord*) *Fig* gulf, gap.

fossette [fosɛt] *nf* dimple.

fossile [fɔsil] *nm & a* fossil.

fou (*or* **fol** *before vowel or mute h*), **folle** [fu, fɔl] *a* (*personne, projet etc*) mad, insane, crazy; (*succès, temps*) tremendous; (*envie*) wild, mad; (*espoir*) foolish; **f. de** (*musique etc*) mad about; **f. de joie** wildly happy ▮ *nmf* madman, madwoman ▮ *nm* (*bouffon*) jester; *Échecs* bishop; **faire le f.** to play the fool.

foudre [fudr] *nf* **la f.** lightning; **coup de f.** *Fig* love at first sight. ●**foudroyer** *vt* to strike by lightning; *Él* to electrocute.

●**foudroyant** *a* (*succès etc*) staggering.
fouet [fwɛ] *nm* whip; *Culin* (egg) whisk. ●**fouetter** *vt* to whip; (*œufs*) to whisk; **crème fouettée** whipped cream.
fougère [fuʒɛr] *nf* fern.
fougue [fug] *nf* fire, ardour.
fouille [fuj] **1** *nf* (*de personne, bagages etc*) search. **2** *nfpl* **fouilles (archéologiques)** excavation, dig. ●**fouiller 1** *vti* (*creuser*) to dig. **2** *vt* (*personne, maison etc*) to search ‖ *vi* **f. dans** (*tiroir etc*) to search through.
fouillis [fuji] *nm* jumble, mess.
fouiner [fwine] *vi Fam* to nose about (**dans** in).
foulard [fular] *nm* (head) scarf.
foule [ful] *nf* crowd; **une f. de** (*objets etc*) a mass of; **un bain de f.** a walkabout.
foulée [fule] *nf Sp* stride; **dans la f.** *Fam* at one and the same time.
fouler (se) [səfule] *vpr* **se f. la cheville**/*etc* to sprain one's ankle/*etc*; **il ne se foule pas (la rate)** *Fam* he doesn't exactly exert himself. ●**foulure** *nf* sprain.
four [fur] *nm* **1** oven. **2 petit f.** (*gâteau*) (small) fancy cake.
fourbe [furb] *a* deceitful.
fourbu [furby] *a* (*fatigué*) dead beat.
fourche [furʃ] *nf* fork. ●**fourchette** *nf* **1** *Culin* fork. **2** (*de salaires etc*) bracket.
fourgon [furgɔ̃] *nm* (*camion*) van; (*mortuaire*) hearse. ●**fourgonnette** *nf* (small) van.
fourmi [furmi] *nf* **1** (*insecte*) ant. **2 avoir des fourmis** (*dans les jambes etc*) to have pins and needles. ●**fourmilière** *nf* anthill. ●**fourmiller** *vi* to teem, swarm (**de** with).
fournaise [furnɛz] *nf* (*chambre etc*) *Fig* furnace.
fourneau, -x [furno] *nm* (*poêle*) stove; (*four*) furnace; **haut f.** blast furnace.
fournée [furne] *nf* (*de pain, gens*) batch.
fournir [furnir] *vt* to supply, provide; (*effort*) to make; **f. qch à qn** to supply s.o. with sth ‖ **se f.** *vpr* to get one's supplies (**chez** from), shop (**chez** at). ●**fourni** *a* (*barbe*) bushy; **bien f.** (*boutique*) well-stocked. ●**fournisseur** *nm* (*commerçant*) supplier. ●**fourniture** *nf* (*action*) supply(ing) (**de** of); *pl* (*objets*) supplies.
fourré [fure] **1** *a* (*gant etc*) fur-lined; (*gâteau*) jam- *ou* cream-filled; **coup f.** (*traîtrise*) stab in the back. **2** *nm Bot* thicket.
fourreau, -x [furo] *nm* (*gaine*) sheath.
fourrer [fure] *vt Fam* (*mettre*) to stick; (*flanquer*) to chuck; **f. qch dans la tête de qn** to knock sth into s.o.'s head; **f. son nez dans** to poke one's nose into ‖ **se f.** *vpr* to put *ou* stick oneself (**dans** in).
fourrure [furyr] *nf* (*pour vêtement etc, de chat etc*) fur.
fourre-tout [furtu] *nm inv* (*sac*) holdall, *Am* carryall.
fourrière [furjɛr] *nf* (*lieu*) pound.
foutre* [futr] *vt Arg* = **fiche(r).** ●**foutu** *a Arg* = **fichu.** ●**foutaise** *nf Arg* rubbish, bull.
foyer [fwaje] *nm* (*maison, famille*) home; (*d'étudiants etc*) hostel; (*âtre*) hearth; (*lieu de réunion*) club; **fonder un f.** to start a family.
fracas [fraka] *nm* din. ●**fracasser** *vt*, **se f.** *vpr* to smash.
fraction [fraksjɔ̃] *nf* fraction.
fracture [fraktyr] *nf* fracture; **se faire une f. au bras**/*etc* to fracture one's arm/*etc*. ●**fracturer** *vt* (*porte etc*) to break (open); **se f. la jambe**/*etc* to fracture one's leg/*etc*.
fragile [fraʒil] *a* (*verre, santé etc*) fragile; (*enfant etc*) frail. ●**fragilité** *nf* fragility; (*d'un enfant etc*) frailty.
fragment [fragmɑ̃] *nm* fragment.
frais[1], **fraîche** [frɛ, frɛʃ] *a* (*poisson, souvenir etc*) fresh; (*temps*) cool, (*plutôt désagréable*) chilly; (*boisson*) cold, cool; (*œuf*) new-laid, fresh; (*peinture*) wet; **servir f.** (*vin etc*) to serve chilled; **boire f.** to drink something cold *ou* cool; **il fait f.** it's cool; (*froid*) it's chilly ‖ *nm* **prendre le f.** to get some fresh air; **mettre au f.** to put in a cool place; (*au réfrigérateur*) to refrigerate. ●**fraîcheur** *nf* freshness; coolness. ●**fraîchir** *vi* (*temps*) to get cooler *ou* chillier.
frais[2] [frɛ] *nmpl* expenses; **à mes f.** at my (own) expense; **faire des f.** to go to some expense; **faire les f.** to bear the cost (**de** of); **f. de scolarité** school fees; **faux f.** incidental expenses; **f. généraux** running expenses, overheads.
fraise [frɛz] *nf* **1** (*fruit*) strawberry. **2** (*de dentiste*) drill. ●**fraisier** *nm* (*plante*) strawberry plant.
framboise [frɑ̃bwaz] *nf* raspberry. ●**framboisier** *nm* raspberry cane.
franc[1], **franche** [frɑ̃, frɑ̃ʃ] *a* **1** (*personne, réponse etc*) frank; (*visage, gaieté*) open. **2** (*zone*) free; **coup f.** *Fb* free kick; **f. de port** carriage paid. ●**franchement** *adv* (*honnêtement*) frankly; (*vraiment*) really; (*sans ambiguïté*) clearly.
franc[2] [frɑ̃] *nm* (*monnaie*) franc.
France [frɑ̃s] *nf* France. ●**français, -aise** *a* French ‖ *nmf* Frenchman, Frenchwoman;

les **F.** the French ‖ *nm* (*langue*) French.
franchir [frɑ̃ʃir] *vt* (*fossé*) to jump (over), clear; (*frontière etc*) to cross; (*porte*) to go through; (*distance*) to cover; (*limites*) to exceed.
franchise [frɑ̃ʃiz] *nf* **1** frankness; **en toute f.** quite frankly. **2** (*exemption*) *Com* exemption; **'f. postale'** 'official paid'.
franc-maçon [frɑ̃masɔ̃] *nm* (*pl* **francs-maçons**) Freemason.
franco- [frɑ̃ko] *préf* Franco-.
francophone [frɑ̃kɔfɔn] *a* French-speaking ‖ *nmf* French speaker.
frange [frɑ̃ʒ] *nf* (*de cheveux*) fringe, *Am* bangs.
frappe [frap] *nf* **1** (*dactylographie*) typing; (*de dactylo etc*) touch; **faute de f.** typing error. **2 force de f.** *Mil* strike force.
frapper [frape] *vt* (*battre*) to hit, strike; **f. qn** (*surprendre*) to strike s.o. ‖ *vi* (*à la porte etc*) to knock (**à** at); **f. du pied** to stamp (one's foot) ‖ **se f.** *vpr* (*se tracasser*) *Fam* to worry. •**frappant** *a* striking. •**frappé** *a* (*vin*) chilled.
fraternel, -elle [fratɛrnɛl] *a* fraternal, brotherly. •**fraternité** *nf* fraternity, brotherhood.
fraude [frod] *nf* (*crime*) fraud; (*à un examen*) cheating; **(faire) passer qch en f.** to smuggle sth; **prendre qn en f.** to catch s.o. cheating; **f. fiscale** tax evasion. •**frauder** *vi Jur* to commit fraud; (*à un examen*) to cheat (**à** in).
frayer (se) [səfreje] *vpr* **se f. un passage** to clear a way (**à travers, dans** through).
frayeur [frɛjœr] *nf* fright.
fredonner [frədɔne] *vt* to hum.
freezer [frizœr] *nm* (*de réfrigérateur*) freezer.
frégate [fregat] *nf* (*navire*) frigate.
frein [frɛ̃] *nm* brake; **donner un coup de f.** to brake (hard); **mettre un f. à** *Fig* to put a curb on. •**freiner** *vi Aut* to brake ‖ *vt* (*gêner*) *Fig* to check, curb. •**freinage** *nm Aut* braking.
frêle [frɛl] *a* frail, fragile.
frelon [frəlɔ̃] *nm* (*guêpe*) hornet.
frémir [fremir] *vi* (*trembler*) to shudder (**de** with); (*feuille*) to quiver; (*eau chaude*) to simmer.
frêne [frɛn] *nm* (*arbre, bois*) ash.
frénésie [frenezi] *nf* frenzy. •**frénétique** *a* frenzied, frantic.
fréquent [frekɑ̃] *a* frequent. •**fréquemment** [-amɑ̃] *adv* frequently. •**fréquence** *nf* frequency.
fréquenter [frekɑ̃te] *vt* (*école, église*) to attend; **f. qn** to see s.o. ‖ **se f.** *vpr* (*fille et garçon*) to see each other; (*voisins*) to see each other socially. •**fréquenté** *a* **très f.** (*lieu*) very busy; **mal f.** of ill repute.
frère [frɛr] *nm* brother.
fresque [frɛsk] *nf* (*œuvre peinte*) fresco.
fret [frɛ(t)] *nm* freight.
frétiller [fretije] *vi* (*poisson*) to wriggle; **f. de** (*impatience*) to quiver with.
friable [frijabl] *a* crumbly.
friand [frijɑ̃] *a* **f. de** fond of, partial to. •**friandises** *nfpl* sweets, *Am* candies.
fric [frik] *nm* (*argent*) *Fam* cash, dough.
friche (en) [ɑ̃friʃ] *adv* fallow.
friction [friksjɔ̃] *nf* **1** massage, rub(-down). **2** (*désaccord*) friction. •**frictionner** *vt* to rub (down).
frigidaire® [friʒidɛr] *nm* fridge. •**frigo** *nm Fam* fridge. •**frigorifié** *a* (*personne*) *Fam* very cold. •**frigorifique** *a* (*vitrine*) refrigerated.
frigide [friʒid] *a* frigid.
frileux, -euse [frilø, -øz] *a* **être f.** to feel the cold.
frime [frim] *nf Fam* sham, show.
fringale [frɛ̃gal] *nf Fam* raging appetite.
fringant [frɛ̃gɑ̃] *a* (*allure etc*) dashing.
fringues [frɛ̃g] *nfpl* (*vêtements*) *Fam* togs, clothes.
friper [fripe] *vt* to crumple ‖ **se f.** *vpr* to get crumpled. •**fripé** *a* (*visage*) crumpled.
fripouille [fripuj] *nf* rogue, scoundrel.
frire* [frir] *vti* to fry; **faire f.** to fry.
frise [friz] *nf Archit* frieze.
fris/er [frize] **1** *vti* (*cheveux*) to curl; **f. les cheveux à qn** to curl s.o.'s hair. **2** *vt* **f. la trentaine** to be close to thirty; **f. le ridicule** to be almost ridiculous. •**—é** *a* curly.
frisquet [friskɛ] *am* chilly, coldish.
frisson [frisɔ̃] *nm* shiver; (*de peur etc*) shudder; **avoir des frissons** to be shivering; **donner le f. à qn** to give s.o. the creeps *ou* shivers. •**frissonner** *vi* (*de froid*) to shiver; (*de peur etc*) to shudder (**de** with).
frit [fri] *pp de* **frire** ‖ *a* (*poisson etc*) fried. •**frites** *nfpl* chips, *Am* French fries. •**friteuse** *nf* (deep) fryer. •**friture** *nf* (*matière*) (frying) oil *ou* fat; (*aliment*) fried fish; (*bruit*) *Rad Tél* crackling.
frivole [frivɔl] *a* frivolous.
froid [frwa] *a* cold; **garder la tête froide** to keep a cool head ‖ *nm* cold; **avoir/prendre f.** to be/catch cold; **avoir f. aux mains** to have cold hands; **il fait f.** it's cold; **jeter un f.** to cast a chill (**dans** over); **être en f.** to be on bad terms (**avec** with). •**froideur** *nf* (*insensibilité*) coldness.
froisser [frwase] **1** *vt*, **se f.** *vpr* (*tissu etc*) to crumple; **se f. un muscle** to strain a muscle.

2 *vt* **f. qn** to offend s.o.; **se f.** to take offence *ou Am* offense (**de** at).
frôler [frole] *vt* (*toucher*) to brush against; (*raser*) to skim; (*la mort etc*) to come within an ace of.
fromage [frɔmaʒ] *nm* cheese; **f. blanc** soft white cheese. •**fromager, -ère** *nm* (*fabricant*) cheesemaker. •**fromagerie** *nf* (*magasin*) cheese shop.
froment [frɔmɑ̃] *nm* wheat.
fronce [frɔ̃s] *nf* (*pli dans un tissu*) gather, fold. •**froncer** *vt* **1** (*étoffe*) to gather. **2 f. les sourcils** to frown.
fronde [frɔ̃d] *nf* (*arme*) sling.
front [frɔ̃] *nm* forehead, brow; *Mil Pol* front; **de f.** (*heurter*) head-on; (*côte à côte*) abreast; (*à la fois*) (all) at once.
frontière [frɔ̃tjɛr] *nf* border, frontier ‖ *a inv* **ville**/*etc* **f.** border town/*etc.* •**frontalier, -ière** *a* **ville**/*etc* **frontalière** border town/*etc.*
frotter [frɔte] *vt* to rub; (*pour nettoyer*) to scrub; (*allumette*) to strike; **se f. le dos** to scrub one's back ‖ *vi* to rub; (*nettoyer, laver*) to scrub.
frousse [frus] *nf Fam* fear; **avoir la f.** to be scared. •**froussard, -arde** *nmf Fam* coward.
fructifier [fryktifje] *vi* (*arbre, capital*) to bear fruit. •**fructueux, -euse** *a* (*profitable*) fruitful.
frugal, -aux [frygal, -o] *a* frugal.
fruit [frɥi] *nm* fruit; **des fruits, les fruits** fruit; **fruits de mer** seafood; **porter ses fruits** (*placement etc*) to bear fruit. •**fruité** *a* fruity. •**fruitier, -ière** *a* **arbre f.** fruit tree ‖ *nmf* fruiterer.
frustr/er [frystre] *vt* **f. qn** to frustrate s.o.; **f. qn de** to deprive s.o. of. •**—é** *a* frustrated.
fuel [fjul] *nm* (fuel) oil, heating oil.
fugitif, -ive [fyʒitif, -iv] **1** *nmf* runaway, fugitive. **2** *a* (*passager*) fleeting.
fugue [fyg] *nf* **1** *Mus* fugue. **2** (*absence*) flight; **faire une f.** to run away.
fuir* [fɥir] *vi* to run away, flee; (*gaz, robinet, stylo etc*) to leak ‖ *vt* (*éviter*) to shun, avoid. •**fuite** *nf* (*évasion*) flight (**de** from); (*de gaz, documents etc*) leak; **en f.** on the run; **prendre la f.** to run away *ou* off, take flight; **délit de f.** *Aut* hit-and-run offence *or Am* offense.
fulgurant [fylgyrɑ̃] *a* **progrès fulgurants** spectacular progress; **vitesse fulgurante** lightning speed.
fumée [fyme] *nf* smoke; (*vapeur*) steam, fumes.
fum/er [fyme] *vi* to smoke; (*liquide brûlant*) to steam ‖ *vt* to smoke. •**—é** *a* (*poisson, verre etc*) smoked. •**—eur, -euse** *nmf* smoker; **compartiment fumeurs** *Rail* smoking compartment.
fumet [fymɛ] *nm* aroma, smell.
fumeux, -euse [fymø, -øz] *a* (*idée etc*) hazy.
fumier [fymje] *nm* manure, dung; (*tas*) dunghill.
fumiste [fymist] *nmf* (*étudiant etc*) time-waster, good-for-nothing.
funambule [fynɑ̃byl] *nmf* tightrope walker.
funèbre [fynɛbr] *a* (*service, marche etc*) funeral; (*lugubre*) gloomy. •**funérailles** *nfpl* funeral.
funeste [fynɛst] *a* (*désastreux*) catastrophic.
funiculaire [fynikylɛr] *nm* funicular.
fur et à mesure (au) [ofyreamzyr] *adv* as one goes along; **au f. et à m. que** as.
furent [fyr] *voir* **être.**
fureter [fyr(ə)te] *vi Péj* to pry *ou* ferret about.
fureur [fyrœr] *nf* (*violence*) fury; (*colère*) rage, fury; **faire f.** (*mode etc*) to be all the rage. •**furie** *nf* (*colère, mégère*) fury. •**furieux, -euse** *a* (*violent, en colère*) furious (**contre** with, at); (*vent*) raging; **avoir une furieuse envie de faire qch** to have a tremendous urge to do sth.
furoncle [fyrɔ̃kl] *nm Méd* boil.
fusain [fyzɛ̃] *nm* (*crayon, dessin*) charcoal.
fuseau, -x [fyzo] *nm* **1** (*pantalon*) ski pants. **2 f. horaire** time zone.
fusée [fyze] *nf* rocket.
fuselage [fyzlaʒ] *nm Av* fuselage.
fusible [fyzibl] *nm Él* fuse.
fusil [fyzi] *nm* rifle, gun; (*de chasse*) shotgun; **coup de f.** gunshot. •**fusillade** *nf* (*tirs*) gunfire. •**fusiller** *vt* (*exécuter*) to shoot; **f. qn du regard** *Fam* to glare at s.o.
fusion [fyzjɔ̃] *nf* **1** melting; *Phys Biol* fusion; **en f.** (*métal*) molten. **2** *Com* merger; (*union*) fusion. •**fusionner** *vti Com* to merge.
fut [fy] *voir* **être.**
fût [fy] *nm* (*tonneau*) barrel, cask.
futé [fyte] *a* cunning, smart.
futile [fytil] *a* (*propos, prétexte etc*) frivolous, futile; (*personne*) frivolous.
futur [fytyr] *a* future; **future mère** mother-to-be ‖ *nm* future; *Gram* future (tense).
fuyant [fɥijɑ̃] *voir* **fuir** ‖ *a* (*front*) receding; (*personne*) evasive. •**fuyard** *nm* runaway, deserter.

G

G, g [ʒe] *nm* G, g.
gabardine [gabardin] *nf* (*tissu, imperméable*) gabardine.
gabarit [gabari] *nm* size, dimension.
gâcher [gɑʃe] *vt* (*gâter*) to spoil; (*occasion, argent*) to waste; (*vie, travail*) to mess up. ● **gâchis** *nm* (*gaspillage*) waste; (*désordre*) mess.
gâchette [gɑʃɛt] *nf* (*d'arme à feu*) trigger.
gadget [gadʒɛt] *nm* gadget.
gadoue [gadu] *nf* (*boue*) dirt, sludge; (*neige*) slush.
gaffe [gaf] *nf* (*bévue*) *Fam* blunder, gaffe. ● **gaffer** *vi* to blunder.
gag [gag] *nm Cin Th etc* gag.
gaga [gaga] *a Fam* senile, gaga.
gage [gaʒ] **1** *nm* (*garantie*) security; **mettre en g.** to pawn; **en g. de** (*fidélité etc*) as a token of. **2** *nmpl* (*salaire*) pay; **tueur à gages** hired killer, hitman. **3** *nm* (*au jeu*) forfeit.
gagnant, -ante [gaɲɑ̃, -ɑ̃t] *a* (*billet, cheval*) winning ▮ *nmf* winner.
gagner [gɑɲe] **1** *vt* (*par le travail*) to earn; **g. sa vie** to earn one's living.
2 *vt* (*par le jeu*) to win; **g. une heure/***etc* (*économiser*) to save an hour/*etc*; **g. du temps** (*temporiser*) to gain time; **g. du terrain/du poids** to gain ground/weight ▮ *vi* (*être vainqueur*) to win.
3 *vt* (*atteindre*) to reach ▮ *vi* (*incendie etc*) to spread.
gai [ge] *a* (*personne, air etc*) cheerful; (*ivre*) merry, tipsy. ● **gaiement** *adv* cheerfully. ● **gaieté** *nf* (*de personne etc*) cheerfulness.
gaillard [gajar] *a* vigorous; (*grivois*) coarse ▮ *nm* (*robuste*) strapping fellow.
gain [gɛ̃] *nm* (*profit*) gain, profit; *pl* (*salaire*) earnings; (*au jeu*) winnings; **un g. de temps** a saving of time; **obtenir g. de cause** to win one's case.
gaine [gɛn] *nf* **1** (*sous-vêtement*) girdle. **2** (*étui*) sheath.
gala [gala] *nm* gala, official reception.
galant [galɑ̃] *a* (*homme*) gallant; (*ton, propos*) *Hum* amorous. ● **galanterie** *nf* (*courtoisie*) gallantry.
galaxie [galaksi] *nf* galaxy.
galbe [galb] *nm* curve, contour.
galère [galɛr] *nf* (*navire*) *Hist* galley.
galerie [galri] *nf* **1** (*passage, salle, magasin etc*) gallery; *Th* balcony; **g. (d'art)** (art) gallery. **2** (*porte-bagage*) *Aut* roof rack.
galet [galɛ] *nm* pebble.
galette [galɛt] *nf* round, flat, flaky cake; (*crêpe*) pancake.
Galles [gal] *nfpl* **pays de G.** Wales. ● **gallois, -oise** *a* Welsh ▮ *nm* (*langue*) Welsh ▮ *nmf* Welshman, Welshwoman.
gallicisme [galisism] *nm* (*mot etc*) gallicism.
galon [galɔ̃] *nm* (*ruban*) braid; (*de soldat*) stripe; **prendre du g.** *Mil & Fig* to get promoted.
galop [galo] *nm* gallop; **aller au g.** to gallop; **g. d'essai** *Fig* trial run. ● **galoper** *vi* (*cheval*) to gallop; **inflation galopante** galloping inflation.
galopin [galɔpɛ̃] *nm* urchin, rascal.
gambader [gɑ̃bade] *vi* to leap about.
gambas [gɑ̃bas] *nfpl* scampi.
gamelle [gamɛl] *nf Fam* pan; (*de chien*) bowl; (*d'ouvrier*) lunch tin *ou* box.
gamin, -ine [gamɛ̃, -in] *nmf* (*enfant*) *Fam* kid ▮ *a* playful, naughty.
gamme [gam] *nf Mus* scale; (*série*) range.
gang [gɑ̃g] *nm* (*de malfaiteurs*) gang. ● **gangster** *nm* gangster.
gangrène [gɑ̃grɛn] *nf* gangrene.
gant [gɑ̃] *nm* glove; **g. de toilette** facecloth; **boîte à gants** glove compartment; **jeter/relever le g.** *Fig* to throw down/take up the gauntlet. ● **ganté** *a* (*main*) gloved; (*personne*) wearing gloves.
garage [garaʒ] *nm Aut* garage; **voie de g.** *Rail* siding; *Fig* dead end. ● **garagiste** *nmf* garage mechanic.
garant, -ante [garɑ̃, -ɑ̃t] *nmf* (*personne*) *Jur* guarantor; **se porter g. de** to guarantee, vouch for ▮ *nm* (*garantie*) guarantee.
garantie [garɑ̃ti] *nf* guarantee; **garantie(s)** (*de police d'assurance*) cover. ● **garantir** *vt* to guarantee (**contre** against); **g. à qn que** to assure *ou* guarantee s.o. that; **g. de** (*protéger*) to protect from.
garce [gars] *nf Péj Fam* bitch.
garçon [garsɔ̃] *nm* boy; (*jeune homme*) young man; **g. (de café)** waiter; **g. manqué** tomboy.
garde [gard] **1** *nm* (*gardien*) guard; (*soldat*) guardsman; **g. du corps** bodyguard; **G. des Sceaux** Justice Minister.
2 *nf* (*d'enfants, de bagages etc*) care, custody (**de** of); **avoir la g. de** to be in

charge of; **prendre g.** to pay attention (**à qch** to sth), be careful (**à qch** of sth); **prendre g. de ne pas faire** to be careful not to do; **mettre qn en g.** to warn s.o. (**contre** against); **mise en g.** warning; **de g.** on duty; **monter la g.** to stand guard; **sur ses gardes** on one's guard; **chien de g.** watchdog; **g. à vue** (police) custody.
3 *nf* (*escorte, soldats*) guard.

garde-à-vous [gardavu] *nm inv Mil* (position of) attention. ●**g.-chasse** *nm* (*pl* **gardes-chasses**) gamekeeper. ●**g.-côte** *nm* (*personne*) coastguard. ●**g.-manger** *nm inv* (*armoire*) food safe. ●**g.-robe** *nf* (*habits*) wardrobe.

garder [garde] *vt* to keep; (*vêtement*) to keep on; (*surveiller*) to watch (over); (*défendre*) to guard; **g. la chambre** to stay in one's room; **g. le lit** to stay in bed ‖ **se g.** *vpr* (*aliment*) to keep; **se g. de qch** (*éviter*) to beware of sth; **se g. de faire** to take care not to do.

garderie [gardəri] *nf* crèche, nursery.

gardien, -ienne [gardjɛ̃, -jɛn] *nmf* (*d'immeuble etc*) caretaker, *Am* janitor; (*de prison*) (prison) guard; (*de zoo, parc*) keeper; (*de musée*) attendant, *Am* guard; **g. de but** *Fb* goalkeeper; **gardienne d'enfants** child minder; **g. de nuit** night watchman; **g. de la paix** policeman ‖ *am* **ange g.** guardian angel.

gare [gar] **1** *nf Rail* station; **g. routière** bus *ou* coach station. **2** *int* **g. à** watch *ou* look out for; **sans crier g.** without warning.

garer [gare] *vt* (*voiture etc*) to park ‖ **se g.** *vpr Aut* to park.

gargariser (se) [səgargarize] *vpr* to gargle.

gargouiller [garguje] *vi* (*fontaine, eau*) to gurgle; (*ventre*) to rumble.

garnement [garnəmɑ̃] *nm* rascal, urchin.

garn/ir [garnir] *vt* (*équiper*) to fit out, furnish (**de** with); (*remplir*) to fill; (*magasin*) to stock (**de** with); (*orner*) to decorate; (*enjoliver*) to trim (*robe etc*) (**de** with); *Culin* to garnish. ●**—i** *a* (*plat*) served with vegetables; **bien g.** (*portefeuille*) *Fig* well-lined. ●**garniture** *nf Culin* garnish, trimmings; *pl Aut* fittings, upholstery; **g. de lit** bed linen.

garnison [garnizɔ̃] *nf Mil* garrison.

gars [gɑ] *nm Fam* fellow, guy.

gas-oil [gɑzwal] *nm* diesel (oil).

gaspill/er [gaspije] *vt* to waste. ●**—age** *nm* waste.

gastrique [gastrik] *a* gastric.

gastronome [gastrɔnɔm] *nmf* gourmet. ●**gastronomie** *nf* gastronomy.

gâteau, -x [gɑto] *nm* cake; **g. de riz** rice pudding; **g. sec** (sweet) biscuit, *Am* cookie; **c'était du g.** (*facile*) *Fam* it was a piece of cake.

gâter [gɑte] *vt* to spoil ‖ **se g.** *vpr* (*aliment, dent*) to go bad; (*temps, situation*) to get worse; (*relations*) to turn sour. ●**gâté** *a* (*dent, fruit etc*) bad.

gâteux, -euse [gɑtø, -øz] *a* senile, soft in the head.

gauche[1] [goʃ] *a* (*côté, main etc*) left ‖ *nf* **la g.** (*côté*) the left (side); *Pol* the left (wing); **à g.** (*tourner etc*) (to the) left; (*marcher etc*) on the left(-hand) side; **de g.** (*fenêtre etc*) left-hand; (*parti, politique etc*) left-wing; **à g. de** on *ou* to the left of. ●**gaucher, -ère** *a* & *nmf* left-handed (person). ●**gauchiste** *a* & *nmf Pol* (extreme) leftist.

gauche[2] [goʃ] *a* (*maladroit*) awkward.

gaufre [gofr] *nf Culin* waffle. ●**gaufrette** *nf* wafer (biscuit).

gaule [gol] *nf* long pole; *Pêche* fishing rod.

Gaule [gol] *nf* (*pays*) *Hist* Gaul. ●**gaulois** *a* Gallic; (*propos etc*) *Fig* earthy, bawdy ‖ *nmpl* **les G.** *Hist* the Gauls.

gaver (se) [səgave] *vpr* to stuff oneself (**de** with).

gaz [gɑz] *nm inv* gas; **réchaud/masque/***etc* **à g.** gas stove/mask/*etc*.

gaze [gɑz] *nf* (*tissu*) gauze.

gazelle [gazɛl] *nf* (*animal*) gazelle.

gazer [gɑze] *vi* **ça gaze!** everything's just fine!

gazette [gazɛt] *nf* (*journal*) *Vieilli* newspaper.

gazeux, -euse [gɑzø, -øz] *a* (*boisson, eau*) fizzy, carbonated.

gazinière [gazinjɛr] *nf* gas cooker *ou Am* stove.

gazole [gɑzɔl] *nm* diesel (oil).

gazon [gɑzɔ̃] *nm* grass, lawn.

gazouiller [gazuje] *vi* (*oiseau*) to chirp; (*bébé, ruisseau*) to babble.

geai [ʒɛ] *nm* (*oiseau*) jay.

géant, -ante [ʒeɑ̃, -ɑ̃t] *nmf* giant ‖ *a* giant; **c'est g.!** *Fam* it's terrific *ou* brilliant!

Geiger [ʒeʒɛr] *nm* **compteur G.** Geiger counter.

gel [ʒɛl] *nm* **1** (*temps, glace*) frost; (*de crédits*) *Écon* freezing. **2** (*pour cheveux etc*) gel. ●**geler** *vti* to freeze; **on gèle ici** it's freezing here ‖ *v imp* **il gèle** it's freezing. ●**gelé** *a* frozen. ●**gelée** *nf* frost; *Culin* jelly, *Am* jello®.

gélule [ʒelyl] *nf* (*médicament*) capsule.

Gémeaux [ʒemo] *nmpl* **les G.** (*signe*) Gemini.

gém/ir [ʒemir] *vi* to groan. ● **—issement** *nm* groan.
gencive [ʒɑ̃siv] *nf Anat* gum.
gendarme [ʒɑ̃darm] *nm* gendarme (*soldier performing police duties*). ● **gendarmerie** *nf* police force; (*local*) police headquarters.
gendre [ʒɑ̃dr] *nm* son-in-law.
gène [ʒɛn] *nm Biol* gene.
gêne [ʒɛn] *nf* (*trouble physique*) discomfort; (*confusion*) embarrassment; (*dérangement*) bother, trouble; **dans la g.** in financial difficulties.
gêner [ʒene] *vt* (*déranger, irriter*) to bother; (*troubler*) to embarrass; (*mouvement*) to hamper; (*circulation*) *Aut* to hold up, block; **g. qn** (*par sa présence*) to be in s.o.'s way; **ça ne me gêne pas** I don't mind (**si** if). ‖ **se gêner** *vpr* (*se déranger*) to put oneself out; **ne te gêne pas pour moi!** don't mind me! ● **gênant** *a* (*objet*) cumbersome; (*présence, situation*) awkward; (*bruit*) annoying. ● **gêné** *a* (*intimidé*) embarrassed; (*mal à l'aise*) awkward, uneasy; (*silence, sourire*) awkward.
généalogique [ʒenealɔʒik] *a* genealogical; **arbre g.** family tree.
général, -aux [ʒeneral, -o] **1** *a* general; **en g.** in general. **2** *nm* (*officier*) *Mil* general. ● **générale** *nf Th* dress rehearsal. ● **généralement** *adv* generally. ● **généralité** *nf* generality.
généralisation [ʒeneralizɑsjɔ̃] *nf* generalization. ● **généraliser** *vti* to generalize ‖ **se g.** *vpr* to become general *ou* widespread.
généraliste [ʒeneralist] *nmf Méd* general practitioner, GP.
générateur [ʒeneratœr] *nm Él* generator.
génération [ʒenerɑsjɔ̃] *nf* generation.
généreux, -euse [ʒenerø, -øz] *a* generous (**de** with). ● **généreusement** *adv* generously. ● **générosité** *nf* generosity.
générique [ʒenerik] *nm* (*de film*) credits.
genèse [ʒənɛz] *nf* genesis.
genêt [ʒənɛ] *nm* (*plante*) broom.
génétique [ʒenetik] *nf* genetics ‖ *a* genetic.
Genève [ʒənɛv] *nm ou f* Geneva.
génial, -aux [ʒenjal -o] *a* (*personne, invention*) brilliant; (*formidable*) *Fam* fantastic.
génie [ʒeni] *nm* **1** (*aptitude, personne*) genius; **avoir le g. pour faire/de qch** to have a genius for doing/for sth. **2 g. civil** civil engineering; **g. génétique** genetic engineering; **g. informatique** computer engineering.
génisse [ʒenis] *nf* (*vache*) heifer.
genou, -x [ʒ(ə)nu] *nm* knee; **être à genoux** to be kneeling (down); **se mettre à genoux** to kneel (down); **prendre qn sur ses genoux** to take s.o. on one's lap *ou* knee.
genre [ʒɑ̃r] *nm* **1** (*espèce*) kind, sort; (*attitude*) manner, way; **g. humain** mankind. **2** *Littér Cin* genre; *Gram* gender; *Biol* genus.
gens [ʒɑ̃] *nmpl* people; **jeunes g.** young people; (*hommes*) young men.
ⓘ**G21** Gender 3 A 3d)
gentil, -ille [ʒɑ̃ti, -ij] *a* nice; **g. avec qn** nice *ou* kind to s.o.; **sois g.** (*sage*) be good. ● **gentillesse** *nf* kindness; **avoir la g. de faire** to be kind enough to do. ● **gentiment** *adv* (*aimablement*) kindly; (*sagement*) nicely.
géographie [ʒeɔgrafi] *nf* geography. ● **géographique** *a* geographical.
géologie [ʒeɔlɔʒi] *nf* geology. ● **géologue** *nmf* geologist.
géomètre [ʒeɔmɛtr] *nm* surveyor.
géométrie [ʒeɔmetri] *nf* geometry. ● **géométrique** *a* geometric(al).
géranium [ʒeranjɔm] *nm Bot* geranium.
gérant, -ante [ʒerɑ̃, -ɑ̃t] *nmf* manager, manageress; **g. d'immeubles** landlord's agent.
gerbe [ʒɛrb] *nf* (*de blé*) sheaf; (*de fleurs*) bunch; (*d'étincelles*) shower.
gercer [ʒɛrse] *vi*, **se g.** *vpr* (*peau, lèvres*) to become chapped. ● **gerçure** *nf* chap; **avoir des gerçures aux mains/lèvres** to have chapped hands/lips.
gérer [ʒere] *vt* (*commerce etc*) to manage.
germain [ʒɛrmɛ̃] *a* **cousin g.** first cousin.
germanique [ʒɛrmanik] *a* Germanic.
germe [ʒɛrm] *nm* (*microbe*) germ; (*de plante*) shoot; (*d'une idée*) *Fig* seed, germ. ● **germer** *vi* (*graine*) to start to grow; (*pomme de terre*) to sprout; (*idée*) to germinate.
geste [ʒɛst] *nm* gesture; **ne pas faire un g.** (*ne pas bouger*) not to make a move; **faire un g. de la main** to wave one's hand. ● **gesticuler** *vi* to gesticulate.
gestion [ʒɛstjɔ̃] *nf* (*action*) management. ● **gestionnaire** *nmf* administrator.
ghetto [gɛto] *nm* ghetto.
gibecière [ʒibsjɛr] *nf* shoulder bag.
gibier [ʒibje] *nm* (*animaux etc*) game.
giboulée [ʒibule] *nf* shower, downpour.
gicl/er [ʒikle] *vi* (*liquide*) to spurt, squirt; (*boue*) to splash; **faire g.** to spurt, squirt. ● **—ée** *nf* jet, spurt. ● **—eur** *nm* (*de carburateur*) *Aut* jet.
gifle [ʒifl] *nf* slap (in the face). ● **gifler** *vt* **g. qn** to slap s.o., slap s.o.'s face.
gigantesque [ʒigɑ̃tɛsk] *a* gigantic.
gigot [ʒigo] *nm* leg of mutton *ou* lamb.

gigoter [ʒigɔte] *vi Fam* to wriggle, fidget.
gilet [ʒilɛ] *nm* (*cardigan*) cardigan; (*de costume*) waistcoat, *Am* vest; **g. de sauvetage** life jacket; **g. pare-balles** bulletproof jacket *ou Am* vest.
gingembre [ʒɛ̃ʒɑ̃br] *nm Bot Culin* ginger.
girafe [ʒiraf] *nf* giraffe.
giratoire [ʒiratwar] *a* **sens g.** *Aut* roundabout, *Am* traffic circle.
girofle [ʒirɔfl] *nm* **clou de g.** *Bot* clove.
girouette [ʒirwɛt] *nf* weathercock, *Am* weather vane.
gisement [ʒizmɑ̃] *nm* (*de minerai, pétrole*) deposit.
gitan, -ane [ʒitɑ̃, -an] *nmf* (Spanish) gipsy.
gîte [ʒit] *nm* (*abri*) resting place.
givre [ʒivr] *nm* frost. ●**givré** *a* frost-covered.
glabre [glabr] *a* (*visage*) smooth.
glace [glas] *nf* **1** (*eau gelée*) ice; (*crème glacée*) ice cream. **2** (*vitre*) window; (*miroir*) mirror; **il est resté de g.** he showed no emotion.
glacer [glase] **1** *vt* to chill; **g. qn** (*paralyser*) to chill s.o. **2** *vt* (*gâteau*) to ice, (*au jus*) to glaze. ●**glacé** *a* **1** (*eau, main, pièce, vent*) icy; (*accueil*) *Fig* icy, chilly. **2** (*thé, café*) iced; (*marron*) candied.
glacial, -aux [glasjal, -o] *a* icy.
glacier [glasje] *nm* **1** *Géol* glacier. **2** (*vendeur*) ice-cream man.
glacière [glasjɛr] *nf* (*boîte, endroit*) icebox.
glaçon [glasɔ̃] *nm Culin* ice cube.
glaïeul [glajœl] *nm Bot* gladiolus.
glaise [glɛz] *nf* clay.
gland [glɑ̃] *nm Bot* acorn.
glande [glɑ̃d] *nf* gland.
glander [glɑ̃de] *vi Fam* to fritter away one's time.
glaner [glane] *vt* (*blé, renseignement etc*) to glean.
glas [glɑ] *nm* (*de cloche*) knell.
glauque [glok] *a* sea-green.
gliss/er [glise] *vi* (*involontairement*) to slip; (*volontairement*) (*sur glace etc*) to slide; (*tiroir etc*) to slide; **faire g. un tiroir**/*etc* to slide a drawer/*etc*; **ça glisse** it's slippery ▌*vt* (*introduire*) to slip (*sth*) (**dans** into); (*murmurer*) to whisper; **se g. dans/sous** to slip into/under. ●**—ant** *a* slippery. ●**glissade** *nf* (*involontaire*) slip; (*volontaire*) slide. ●**glissement** *nm* **g. à gauche** *Pol* swing *ou* shift to the left; **g. de terrain** *Géol* landslide.
glissière [glisjɛr] *nf* **porte à g.** sliding door.
global, -aux [glɔbal, -o] *a* total, global; **somme globale** lump sum. ●**—ement** *adv* collectively, as a whole.
globe [glɔb] *nm* globe; **g. de l'œil** eyeball.
globule [glɔbyl] *nm* (*du sang*) corpuscle.
gloire [glwar] *nf* glory; (*personne célèbre*) celebrity; **à la g. de** in praise of. ●**glorieux, -euse** *a* glorious. ●**glorifier** *vt* to glorify; **se g. de** to glory in.
glouglou [gluglu] *nm* (*de liquide*) gurgle.
glouss/er [gluse] *vi* (*poule*) to cluck. ●**—ement** *nm* cluck(ing).
glouton, -onne [glutɔ̃, -ɔn] *a* greedy ▌*nmf* glutton.
gluant [glyɑ̃] *a* sticky.
glucose [glykoz] *nm* glucose.
glycine [glisin] *nf Bot* wisteria.
gnon [ɲɔ̃] *nm Fam* blow, punch.
goal [gol] *nm Fb* goalkeeper.
gobelet [gɔblɛ] *nm* (*de plastique, papier*) cup.
gober [gɔbe] *vt* (*œuf, mouche etc*) to swallow (whole); (*propos*) *Fam* to swallow.
godasse [gɔdas] *nf Fam* shoe.
godet [gɔdɛ] *nm* (*récipient*) pot.
goéland [gɔelɑ̃] *nm* (sea)gull.
gogo (à) [agogo] *adv Fam* galore.
goguenard [gɔgnar] *a* mocking.
goinfre [gwɛ̃fr] *nm* (*glouton*) *Fam* pig, guzzler. ●**se goinfrer** *vpr Fam* to stuff oneself (**de** with).
golf [gɔlf] *nm* golf; (*terrain*) golf course. ●**golfeur, -euse** *nmf* golfer.
golfe [gɔlf] *nm* gulf, bay.
gomme [gɔm] *nf* (*à effacer*) rubber, *Am* eraser. ●**gommer** *vt* (*effacer*) to rub out, erase.
gomme (à la) [alagɔm] *adv Fam* useless.
gond [gɔ̃] *nm* (*de porte etc*) hinge.
gondole [gɔ̃dɔl] *nf* (*bateau*) gondola. ●**gondolier** *nm* gondolier.
gondoler [gɔ̃dɔle] **1** *vi*, **se g.** *vpr* (*planche*) to warp. **2 se gondoler** *vpr* (*rire*) *Fam* to split one's sides.
gonflable [gɔ̃flabl] *a* inflatable.
gonfler [gɔ̃fle] *vt* (*pneu*) to pump up; (*en soufflant*) to blow up; (*poitrine*) to swell out ▌*vi*, **se g.** *vpr* to swell; **se g. de** (*orgueil, émotion*) to swell with. ●**gonflé** *a* swollen; **être g.** *Fam* (*courageux*) to have plenty of pluck; (*insolent*) to have plenty of nerve. ●**gonfleur** *nm* (air) pump.
gorge [gɔrʒ] *nf* **1** throat. **2** *Géog* gorge.
gorgé [gɔrʒe] *a* **g. de** (*saturé*) gorged with.
gorgée [gɔrʒe] *nf* mouthful (*of wine etc*); **petite g.** sip; **d'une seule g.** in one gulp.
gorille [gɔrij] *nm* (*animal*) gorilla.
gosier [gozje] *nm* throat.
gosse [gɔs] *nmf* (*enfant*) *Fam* kid.
gouache [gwaʃ] *nf* (*peinture*) gouache.

goudron [gudrɔ̃] *nm* tar. ● **goudronner** *vt* to tar.
gouffre [gufr] *nm* gulf, chasm.
goulot [gulo] *nm* (*de bouteille*) neck; **boire au g.** to drink from the bottle.
goulu [guly] *a* greedy.
gourde [gurd] *nf* **1** water bottle. **2** (*personne*) *Péj Fam* chump, oaf.
gourdin [gurdɛ̃] *nm* club, cudgel.
gourer (se) [səgure] *vpr Fam* to make a mistake.
gourmand, -ande [gurmɑ̃, -ɑ̃d] *a* (over)-fond of food; **g. de** fond of ▮ *nmf* hearty eater. ● **gourmandise** *nf* (over)fondness for food; *pl* (*mets*) delicacies.
gourmet [gurmɛ] *nm* gourmet.
gourmette [gurmɛt] *nf* identity bracelet.
gousse [gus] *nf* **g. d'ail** clove of garlic.
goût [gu] *nm* taste; **de bon g.** in good taste; **sans g.** tasteless; **par g.** from *ou* by choice; **prendre g. à qch** to take a liking to sth; **avoir du g.** (*personne*) to have good taste; **avoir un g. de noisette**/*etc* to taste of hazelnut/*etc*.
goûter [gute] *vt* (*aliment*) to taste; **g. à qch** to taste (a little of) sth ▮ *vi* to have an afternoon snack ▮ *nm* afternoon snack, tea.
goutte [gut] *nf* drop; **couler g. à g.** to drip. ● **g.-à-goutte** *nm inv Méd* drip. ● **gouttelette** *nf* droplet. ● **goutter** *vi* (*eau, robinet, nez*) to drip (**de** from).
gouttière [gutjɛr] *nf* (*d'un toit*) gutter.
gouvernail [guvɛrnaj] *nm* (*pale*) rudder; (*barre*) helm.
gouvernante [guvɛrnɑ̃t] *nf* governess.
gouvernement [guvɛrnəmɑ̃] *nm* government. ● **gouvernemental, -aux** *a* **politique**/*etc* **gouvernementale** government policy/*etc*; **l'équipe gouvernementale** the government.
gouvern/er [guvɛrne] *vti Pol* & *Fig* to govern, rule. ● **—ants** *nmpl* rulers. ● **—eur** *nm* governor.
grâce [grɑs] **1** *nf* (*charme*) & *Rel* grace; **de bonne/mauvaise g.** with good/bad grace; **donner le coup de g. à** to finish off; **faire g. de qch à qn** to spare s.o. sth; **être dans les bonnes grâces de qn** to be in favour with s.o. **2** *prép* **g. à** thanks to.
gracier [grasje] *vt* (*condamné*) to pardon.
gracieux, -euse [grasjø, -øz] *a* **1** (*élégant*) graceful; (*aimable*) gracious. **2** (*gratuit*) gratuitous; **à titre g.** free (of charge). ● **gracieusement** *adv* gracefully; graciously; free (of charge).
grade [grad] *nm Mil* rank; **monter en g.** to be promoted. ● **gradé** *nm Mil* non-commissioned officer.
gradin [gradɛ̃] *nm Th etc* tier (of seats).
graduer [gradɥe] *vt* (*règle*) to graduate; (*exercices*) to grade (*for difficulty*).
graffiti [grafiti] *nmpl* graffiti.
grain [grɛ̃] *nm* (*de blé etc*) & *Fig* grain; (*de café*) bean; (*de poussière*) speck; *pl* (*céréales*) grain; **g. de beauté** mole; (*sur le visage*) beauty spot; **g. de raisin** grape.
graine [grɛn] *nf* seed; **mauvaise g.** (*enfant*) *Péj* rotten egg.
graisse [grɛs] *nf* fat; (*lubrifiant*) grease. ● **graissage** *nm Aut* lubrication. ● **graisser** *vt* to grease. ● **graisseux, -euse** *a* (*vêtement etc*) greasy, oily; **tissu g.** fatty tissue.
grammaire [gramɛr] *nf* grammar; **livre de g.** grammar (book). ● **grammatical, -aux** *a* grammatical.
gramme [gram] *nm* gram(me).
grand, grande [grɑ̃, grɑ̃d] *a* big, large; (*en hauteur*) tall; (*chaleur, découverte, âge, ami*) great; (*bruit*) loud; (*différence*) big, great; (*maître*) grand; (*âme*) noble; **g. frère**/*etc* (*plus âgé*) big brother/*etc*; **le g. air** the open air; **il est g. temps** it's high time (**que** that). ▮ *adv* **g. ouvert** (*yeux, fenêtre*) wide-open; **ouvrir g.** to open wide; **en g.** on a grand *ou* large scale.
▮ *nmf Scol* senior; (*adulte*) grown-up.
grand-chose [grɑ̃ʃoz] *pron* **pas g.-chose** not much. ● **g.-mère** *nf* (*pl* **grands-mères**) grandmother. ● **g.-père** *nm* (*pl* **grands-pères**) grandfather. ● **g.-route** *nf* main road. ● **grands-parents** *nmpl* grandparents.
Grande-Bretagne [grɑ̃dbrətaɲ] *nf* Great Britain.
grandeur [grɑ̃dœr] *nf* (*importance, gloire*) greatness; (*dimension*) size; (*splendeur*) grandeur; **g. nature** life-size.
grandiose [grɑ̃djoz] *a* grandiose, grand.
grandir [grɑ̃dir] *vi* to grow; **g. de 2 cm** to grow 2 cm ▮ *vt* **g. qn** (*faire paraître plus grand*) to make s.o. seem taller.
grange [grɑ̃ʒ] *nf* barn.
granit(e) [granit] *nm* granite.
graphique [grafik] *a* (*signe, art*) graphic ▮ *nm* graph; *pl Ordinat* graphics.
grappe [grap] *nf* (*de fruits etc*) cluster; **g. de raisin** bunch of grapes.
gras, grasse [grɑ, grɑs] *a* (*personne etc*) fat; (*aliment*) fatty; (*graisseux*) greasy; (*plante, contour*) thick; **matières grasses** fat; **foie g.** *Culin* foie gras, fatted goose liver; **caractères g.** bold type ▮ *nm* (*de viande*) fat.

gratifier [gratifje] *vt* **g. qn de** to present *ou* favour s.o. with.
gratin [gratɛ̃] *nm* **macaronis/chou-fleur au g.** macaroni/cauliflower cheese.
gratis [gratis] *adv Fam* free (of charge).
gratitude [gratityd] *nf* gratitude.
gratte-ciel [gratsjɛl] *nm inv* skyscraper.
gratter [grate] *vt* (*avec un outil etc*) to scrape; (*avec les ongles etc*) to scratch; (*boue*) to scrape off; **ça me gratte** *Fam* it itches ‖ *vi* (*à la porte etc*) to scratch; (*tissu*) to be scratchy ‖ **se g.** *vpr* to scratch oneself.
gratuit [gratɥi] *a* (*billet etc*) free; (*hypothèse, acte*) gratuitous. ●**gratuité** *nf* **la g. de l'enseignement**/*etc* free education/*etc*. ●**gratuitement** *adv* free (of charge); (*sans motif*) gratuitously.
gravats [gravɑ] *nmpl* rubble, debris.
grave [grav] *a* serious; (*voix*) deep, low; (*visage*) grave, solemn; **ce n'est pas g.!** it's not important!; **accent g.** grave [grɑːv] accent. ●**—ment** *adv* (*malade, menacé*) seriously; (*dignement*) gravely.
grav/er [grave] *vt* (*sur métal etc*) to engrave; (*sur bois*) to carve; (*dans sa mémoire*) to imprint. ●**—eur** *nm* engraver.
gravier [gravje] *nm* gravel. ●**gravillons** *nmpl* gravel, (loose) chippings.
gravir [gravir] *vt* to climb (*with effort*).
gravité [gravite] *nf* **1** (*de situation etc*) seriousness; (*solennité*) gravity. **2** *Phys* gravity.
graviter [gravite] *vi* to revolve (**autour** around).
gravure [gravyr] *nf* (*image*) print; (*action, art*) engraving; **g. sur bois** (*objet*) woodcut.
gré [gre] *nm* **à son g.** (*goût*) to his *ou* her taste; (*désir*) as he *ou* she pleases; **de son plein g.** of one's own free will; **contre le g. de qn** against s.o.'s will; **bon g. mal g.** willy-nilly; **savoir g. à qn de qch** to be grateful to s.o. for sth.
Grèce [grɛs] *nf* Greece. ●**grec, grecque** *a* & *nmf* Greek ‖ *nm* (*langue*) Greek.
greffe [grɛf] **1** *nf* (*de peau, d'arbre etc*) graft; (*d'organe*) transplant. **2** *nm Jur* record office. ●**greffer** *vt* (*peau etc*) & *Bot* to graft (**à** on to); (*organe*) to transplant. ●**greffier** *nm* clerk (of the court).
grêle [grɛl] **1** *nf* hail. **2** *a* (*fin*) spindly, (very) thin. ●**grêler** *v imp* to hail. ●**grêlon** *nm* hailstone.
grelot [grəlo] *nm* (small round) bell (*that jingles*).
grelotter [grəlɔte] *vi* to shiver (**de** with).
grenade [grənad] *nf* **1** *Bot* pomegranate. **2** (*projectile*) *Mil* grenade. ●**grenadine** *nf* pomegranate syrup.
grenier [grənje] *nm* attic; *Agr* granary.
grenouille [grənuj] *nf* frog.
grès [grɛ] *nm* (*roche*) sandstone; (*poterie*) stoneware.
grésiller [grezije] *vi Culin* to sizzle; *Rad* to crackle.
grève [grɛv] *nf* **1** strike; **g. de la faim** hunger strike; **g. du zèle** work-to-rule, *Am* rule-book slow-down; **g. tournante** strike by rota; **se mettre en g.** to go (out) on strike. **2** (*de mer*) shore. ●**gréviste** *nmf* striker.
gribouiller [gribuje] *vti* to scribble. ●**gribouillis** *nm* scribble.
grief [grijɛf] *nm* (*plainte*) grievance.
grièvement [grijɛvmɑ̃] *adv* **g. blessé** seriously injured.
griffe [grif] *nf* **1** (*ongle*) claw; **sous la g. de qn** (*pouvoir*) in s.o.'s clutches. **2** (*de couturier*) (designer) label; (*tampon*) printed signature. ●**griffer** *vt* to scratch, claw.
griffonner [grifɔne] *vt* to scribble.
grignoter [griɲɔte] *vti* to nibble.
gril [gril] *nm* (*ustensile de cuisine*) grill. ●**grillade** [grijad] *nf* (*viande*) grill. ●**grille-pain** *nm inv* toaster. ●**griller** *vt* (*viande*) to grill, broil; (*pain*) to toast; (*café*) to roast; (*ampoule*) *Él* to blow; **g. un feu rouge** *Aut Fam* to drive through *ou* jump a red light ‖ *vi* **mettre à g.** to put on the grill.
grille [grij] *nf* (*clôture*) railings; (*porte*) (iron) gate; (*de radiateur*) *Aut* grid, grille; (*des salaires*) *Fig* scale; *pl* (*de fenêtre*) bars, grating. ●**grillage** *nm* wire mesh *ou* netting.
grillon [grijɔ̃] *nm* (*insecte*) cricket.
grimace [grimas] *nf* (*pour faire rire*) (funny) face; (*de dégoût, douleur*) grimace; **faire des grimaces/la g.** to make faces/a face. ●**grimacer** *vi* to make faces *ou* a face; (*de dégoût etc*) to grimace (**de** with).
grimp/er [grɛ̃pe] *vi* to climb (**à qch** up sth) ‖ *vt* to climb. ●**—ant** *a* (*plante*) climbing.
grinc/er [grɛ̃se] *vi* to creak, grate; **g. des dents** to grind one's teeth. ●**—ement** *nm* creaking; grinding.
grincheux, -euse [grɛ̃ʃø, -øz] *a* grumpy.
grippe [grip] *nf* **1** (*maladie*) flu. **2** **prendre qch/qn en g.** to take a strong dislike to sth/s.o. ●**grippé** *a* **être g.** to have (the) flu.
gris [gri] *a* grey, *Am* gray; (*temps*) dull, grey ‖ *nm* grey, *Am* gray. ●**grisaille** *nf* greyness, *Am* grayness. ●**grisâtre** *a* greyish, *Am* grayish.
griser [grize] *vt* (*vin etc*) to make (*s.o.*) tipsy; (*air vif, succès*) to exhilarate (*s.o.*).

grisonner [grizɔne] *vi* (*cheveux*, *personne*) to go grey *ou Am* gray.
grive [griv] *nf* (*oiseau*) thrush.
grivois [grivwa] *a* bawdy.
Groenland [grɔɛnlɑ̃d] *nm* Greenland.
grogn/er [grɔɲe] *vi* (*personne*) to grumble, growl (**contre** at); (*cochon*) to grunt. ●**—ement** *nm* grumble, growl; grunt. ●**grognon** *am* grumpy.
grommeler [grɔmle] *vti* to grumble, mutter.
gronder [grɔ̃de] *vi* (*chien*) to growl; (*tonnerre, camion*) to rumble ▮ *vt* (*réprimander*) to scold, tell off. ●**grondement** *nm* growl; rumble.
groom [grum] *nm* page (boy), *Am* bellboy.
gros, grosse [gro, gros] *a* big; (*gras*) fat; (*épais*) thick; (*effort*, *progrès*) great; (*somme, fortune*) large; (*averse*, *rhume*) heavy; (*faute*) serious, gross; (*bruit*) loud; **g. mot** swear word.
▮ *adv* **risquer g.** to take a big risk; **en g.** (*globalement*) roughly; (*écrire*) in big letters; (*vendre*) wholesale, in bulk.
▮ *nmf* (*personne*) fat man, fat woman.
▮ *nm* **le g. de** the bulk of; **de g.** (*prix*, *marché*) wholesale; **commerce/maison de g.** wholesale trade/company.
groseille [grozɛj] *nf* (white *ou* red) currant; **g. à maquereau** gooseberry.
grossesse [grosɛs] *nf* pregnancy.
grosseur [grosœr] *nf* **1** (*volume*) size; (*obésité*) weight. **2** (*tumeur*) *Méd* lump.
grossier, -ière [grosje, -jɛr] *a* (*tissu*, *traits*) rough, coarse; (*personne*, *manières*) rude, coarse; (*erreur*) gross; **être g. envers** (*insolent*) to be rude to. ●**grossièrement** *adv* (*calculer*) roughly; (*répondre*) rudely, coarsely; (*se tromper*) grossly. ●**grossièreté** *nf* roughness; coarseness; (*insolence*) rudeness; (*mot*) rude word.
grossir [grosir] *vi* (*personne*) to put on weight; (*bosse, foule etc*) to swell, get bigger ▮ *vt* to swell; (*exagérer*) *Fig* to magnify ▮ *vti* (*verre*, *loupe etc*) to magnify; **verre grossissant** magnifying glass.
grossiste [grosist] *nmf Com* wholesaler.
grotesque [grɔtɛsk] *a* (*risible*) ludicrous.
grotte [grɔt] *nf* cave, grotto.
grouiller [gruje] *vi* (*rue*, *fourmis etc*) to be swarming (**de** with).
groupe [grup] *nm* group; **g. sanguin** blood group; **g. scolaire** (*bâtiments*) school block. ●**grouper** *vt*, **se g.** *vpr* to group (together).
grue [gry] *nf* (*machine*, *oiseau*) crane.
grumeau, -x [grymo] *nm* (*dans une sauce etc*) lump.
gruyère [gryjɛr] *nm* gruyère (cheese).
gué [ge] *nm* ford; **passer à g.** to ford.
guenilles [gənij] *nfpl* rags (and tatters).
guenon [gənɔ̃] *nf* female monkey.
guépard [gepar] *nm* cheetah.
guêpe [gɛp] *nf* wasp.
guère [gɛr] *adv* **(ne)... g.** hardly; **il ne sort g.** he hardly goes out.
🛈 **G204** Negative Expressions 12 B
guéridon [geridɔ̃] *nm* pedestal table.
guérilla [gerija] *nf* guerrilla warfare.
guérir [gerir] *vt* (*personne*, *maladie*) to cure (**de** of); (*blessure*) to heal ▮ *vi* to get better, recover; (*blessure*) to heal; (*rhume*) to get better; **g. de** (*fièvre etc*) to get over, recover from ▮ **se g.** *vpr* to get better. ●**guéri** *a* cured, better. ●**guérison** *nf* (*de personne*) recovery; (*de maladie*) cure; (*de blessure*) healing. ●**guérisseur, -euse** *nmf* faith healer.
guerre [gɛr] *nf* war; (*chimique*) warfare; **en g.** at war (**avec** with); **faire la g.** to wage *ou* make war (**à** on, against); **crime/cri/***etc* **de g.** war crime/cry/*etc*. ●**guerrier, -ière** *a* (*nation*) war-like; **danse guerrière** war dance; **chant g.** battle song ▮ *nmf* warrior.
guet [gɛ] *nm* **faire le g.** to be on the lookout. ●**guetter** *vt* to be on the lookout for.
guet-apens [gɛtapɑ̃] *nm inv* ambush.
gueule [gœl] *nf* (*d'animal*, *de canon*) mouth; (*figure*) *Fam* face; **avoir la g. de bois** *Fam* to have a hangover; **faire la g.** *Fam* to sulk. ●**gueuler** *vti Fam* to bawl (out).
🛈 **G204** Negative Expressions 12 B
gui [gi] *nm Bot* mistletoe.
guichet [giʃɛ] *nm* (*de gare*, *cinéma etc*) ticket office; (*de banque etc*) window; *Th* box office; **à guichets fermés** *Th Sp* with all tickets sold in advance. ●**guichetier, -ière** *nmf* (*de banque etc*) counter clerk, *Am* teller; (*à la gare*) ticket office clerk.
guide [gid] **1** *nm* (*personne*, *livre etc*) guide. **2** *nfpl* (*rênes*) reins. ●**guider** *vt* to guide; **se g. sur un manuel/***etc* to use a handbook/*etc* as a guide.
guidon [gidɔ̃] *nm* (*de bicyclette etc*) handlebar(s).
guignol [giɲɔl] *nm* (*spectacle*) = Punch and Judy show.
guillemets [gijmɛ] *nmpl Typ* inverted commas; **entre g.** in inverted commas.
guillotine [gijɔtin] *nf* guillotine.
guimauve [gimov] *nf Bot Culin* marshmallow.
guindé [gɛ̃de] *a* (*peu naturel*) stiff; (*affecté*) (*style*) stilted.

guirlande [girlɑ̃d] *nf* garland, wreath.
guise [giz] *nf* **n'en faire qu'à sa g.** to do as one pleases; **en g. de** by way of.
guitare [gitar] *nf* guitar. ●**guitariste** *nmf* guitarist.

gymnase [ʒimnɑz] *nm* gymnasium. ●**gymnastique** *nf* gymnastics.
gynécologie [ʒinekɔlɔʒi] *nf* gynaecology, *Am* gynecology. ●**gynécologue** *nmf* gynaecologist, *Am* gynecologist.

(eg **G1**, **G2**, **G3**) in French **G**rammar, at the end of the dictionary. Also see p. ix.

H

H, h [aʃ] *nm* H, h; **l'heure H** zero hour; **bombe H** H-bomb.
ha! ['ɑ] *int* ah!, oh!; **ha, ha!** (*rire*) ha-ha!
habile [abil] *a* skilful (**à qch** at sth, **à faire** at doing); **h. de ses doigts** dextrous, clever with one's fingers. •**habileté** *nf* skill.
habiller [abije] *vt* to dress (**de** in); (*fournir en vêtements*) to clothe; **h. qn en soldat**/*etc* (*déguiser*) to dress s.o. up as a soldier/*etc* ‖ **s'h.** *vpr* to dress, get dressed; (*avec élégance*) to dress up. •**habillé** *a* dressed (**de** in, **en** as a); (*costume, robe*) smart.
habit [abi] *nm* costume, outfit; *pl* (*vêtements*) clothes.
habitable [abitabl] *a* (*maison*) fit to live in.
habitation [abitɑsjɔ̃] *nf* house, dwelling; (*action de résider*) living.
habit/er [abite] *vi* to live (**à, en, dans** in) ‖ *vt* (*maison, région*) to live in. •**—ant, -ante** *nmf* (*de pays etc*) inhabitant; (*de maison*) occupant. •**—é** *a* (*région*) inhabited; (*maison*) occupied.
habitude [abityd] *nf* habit; **avoir l'h. de qch** to be used to sth; **avoir l'h. de faire** to be used to doing; **prendre l'h. de faire** to get into the habit of doing; **d'h.** usually; **comme d'h.** as usual.
habituel, -elle [abitɥɛl] *a* usual. •**habituellement** *adv* usually.
habituer [abitɥe] *vt* **h. qn à** to accustom s.o. to; **être habitué à** to be used *ou* accustomed to ‖ **s'h.** *vpr* to get accustomed (**à** to); **s'h. à qn/à qch/à faire** to get used *ou* accustomed to s.o./to sth/to doing. •**habitué, -ée** *nmf* regular (customer *ou* visitor).
hache ['aʃ] *nf* axe, *Am* ax.
hach/er ['aʃe] *vt* (*au couteau*) to chop (up); (*avec un appareil*) to mince, *Am* grind. •**—é** *a* **1** (*viande*) minced, *Am* ground; (*légumes*) chopped. **2** (*style*) jerky, broken. •**hachis** *nm* (*viande*) mince, minced *ou Am* ground meat. •**hachoir** *nm* (*couteau*) chopper; (*appareil*) mincer, *Am* grinder.
haie ['ɛ] *nf* (*clôture*) hedge; (*rangée*) row; **course de haies** (*coureurs*) hurdle race; (*chevaux*) steeplechase.
haillons ['ɑjɔ̃] *nmpl* rags (and tatters).
haine ['ɛn] *nf* hatred.
haïr* ['air] *vt* to hate.
halage ['alaʒ] *nm* towing; **chemin de h.** towpath.
hâle ['ɑl] *nm* suntan. •**hâlé** *a* suntanned.
haleine [alɛn] *nf* breath; **hors d'h.** out of breath; **perdre h.** to get out of breath; **de longue h.** (*travail*) long-term; **tenir en h.** to hold in suspense.
halet/er ['alte] *vi* to pant. •**—ant** *a* panting.
hall ['ol] *nm* (*de gare*) main hall, concourse; (*de maison*) hall(way); (*d'hôtel*) lobby.
halle ['al] *nf* (covered) market; **les halles** the central food market.
hallucination [alysinɑsjɔ̃] *nf* hallucination. •**hallucinant** *a* extraordinary.
halte ['alt] *nf* (*arrêt*) stop; **faire h.** to stop ‖ *int* stop!, *Mil* halt!
haltères [altɛr] *nmpl* weights. •**haltérophilie** *nf* weight lifting.
hamac ['amak] *nm* hammock.
hameau, -x ['amo] *nm* hamlet.
hameçon [amsɔ̃] *nm* (fish) hook; **mordre à l'h.** *Pêche & Fig* to swallow the bait.
hanche ['ɑ̃ʃ] *nf Anat* hip.
hand(-)ball ['ɑ̃dbal] *nm Sp* handball.
handicapé, -ée ['ɑ̃dikape] *a & nmf* handicapped (person); **h. moteur** spastic.
hangar ['ɑ̃gar] *nm* (*entrepôt*) shed; (*pour avions*) hangar.
hanneton ['antɔ̃] *nm* cockchafer.
hanté ['ɑ̃te] *a* haunted.
hantise ['ɑ̃tiz] *nf* **la h. de** an obsession with.
happer ['ape] *vt* (*saisir*) to catch, snatch; (*par la gueule*) to snap up.
haras ['arɑ] *nm* stud farm.
harassé ['arase] *a* (*fatigué*) exhausted.
harceler ['arsəle] *vt* to harass, torment (**de** with).
hardi ['ardi] *a* bold, daring. •**hardiesse** *nf* boldness, daring.
hareng ['arɑ̃] *nm* herring.
hargneux, -euse ['arɲø, -øz] *a* bad-tempered.
haricot ['ariko] *nm* (*blanc*) (haricot) bean; (*vert*) green bean, French bean.
harmonica [armɔnika] *nm* harmonica, mouthorgan.
harmonie [armɔni] *nf* harmony. •**harmonieux, -euse** *a* harmonious. •**harmoniser** *vt*, **s'h.** *vpr* to harmonize.
harnacher ['arnaʃe] *vt* (*cheval etc*) to harness. •**harnais** *nm* (*de cheval, bébé*) harness.
harpe ['arp] *nf* harp.

harpon ['arpɔ̃] *nm* harpoon. • **harponner** *vt* (*baleine*) to harpoon.
hasard ['azar] *nm* **le h.** chance; **un h.** a coincidence; **par h.** by chance; **si par h.** if by any chance; **au h.** at random; **à tout h.** just in case. • **hasarder** *vt* (*remarque*) to venture, hazard; **se h. dans** to venture into; **se h. à faire** to risk doing, venture to do. • **hasardeux, -euse** *a* risky, hazardous.
haschisch ['aʃiʃ] *nm* hashish.
hâte ['ɑt] *nf* haste, speed; (*impatience*) eagerness; **à la h., en h.** in a hurry, hurriedly; **avoir h. de faire** (*désireux*) to be eager to do. • **hâter** *vt* (*pas, départ etc*) to hasten ‖ **se h.** *vpr* to hurry (**de faire** to do).
hausse ['os] *nf* rise (**de** in); **en h.** rising. • **hausser** *vt* (*prix, voix etc*) to raise; (*épaules*) to shrug; **se h. sur la pointe des pieds** to stand on tip-toe.
haut ['o] *a* (*montagne etc*) high; (*de taille*) tall; (*note de musique, température, rang etc*) high; **à haute voix** aloud; **h. de 5 mètres** 5 metres high *ou* tall; **la haute couture** high fashion; **en haute mer** out at sea.
‖ *adv* (*voler, viser etc*) high (up); (*parler*) loud, loudly; **tout h.** (*lire, penser*) aloud, out loud; **h. placé** (*personne*) in a high position; **plus h.** (*dans un texte*) above, further back.
‖ *nm* (*partie haute*) top; **en h. de** at the top of; **en h.** (*loger*) upstairs; (*regarder*) up; (*mettre*) on (the) top; **d'en h.** from high up, from up above; **avoir 5 mètres de h.** to be 5 metres high *ou* tall; **des hauts et des bas** *Fig* ups and downs.
hautain ['otɛ̃] *a* haughty.
hautbois ['obwa] *nm Mus* oboe.
haut-de-forme ['odfɔrm] *nm* (*pl* **hauts-de-forme**) top hat.
hautement ['otmɑ̃] *adv* (*tout à fait, très*) highly. • **hauteur** *nf* height; *Géog* hill; (*orgueil*) *Péj* haughtiness; **à la h. de** (*objet*) level with; (*rue*) opposite; **il n'est pas à la h.** he isn't up to it; **saut en h.** *Sp* high jump.
haut-parleur ['oparlœr] *nm* loudspeaker.
Haye (La) [la'ɛ] *nf* The Hague.
hayon ['ɛjɔ̃,'ajɔ̃] *nm* (*porte*) *Aut* hatchback.
hé! [e] *int* **hé (là)** (*appel*) hey!
hebdomadaire [ɛbdɔmadɛr] *a* weekly ‖ *nm* (*publication*) weekly.
héberg/er [ebɛrʒe] *vt* to put up, accommodate. • **—ement** *nm* accommodation.
hébété [ebete] *a* dazed, stupefied.
hébreu, -x [ebrø] *am* Hebrew ‖ *nm* (*langue*) Hebrew.
hécatombe [ekatɔ̃b] *nf* (great) slaughter.
hectare [ɛktar] *nm* hectare (= *2.47 acres*).
hégémonie [eʒemɔni] *nf* supremacy.
hein! [ɛ̃] *int Fam* (*surprise etc*) eh!
G210 Question Tags 12 C 3b) ii)
hélas! ['elɑs] *int* unfortunately.
héler ['ele] *vt* (*taxi etc*) to hail.
hélice [elis] *nf Av Nau* propeller.
hélicoptère [elikɔptɛr] *nm* helicopter. • **héliport** *nm* heliport.
helvétique [ɛlvetik] *a* Swiss.
hémicycle [emisikl] *nm* semicircle; *Pol Fig* French National Assembly.
hémisphère [emisfɛr] *nm* hemisphere.
hémorragie [emɔraʒi] *nf Méd* h(a)emorrhage; **h. cérébrale** stroke.
hémorroïdes [emɔrɔid] *nfpl* piles, h(a)emorrhoids.
henn/ir ['enir] *vi* to neigh. • **—issement** *nm* neigh
hépatite [epatit] *nf* hepatitis.
herbe [ɛrb] *nf* grass; (*pour soigner*) herb; **mauvaise h.** weed; **fines herbes** *Culin* herbs; **en h.** (*blés*) green; (*poète etc*) *Fig* budding. • **herbage** *nm* grassland. • **herbicide** *nm* weed killer. • **herbivore** *a* grass-eating, herbivorous.
hercule [ɛrkyl] *nm* Hercules, strong man.
hérédité [eredite] *nf* heredity. • **héréditaire** *a* hereditary.
hérétique [eretik] *a* heretical ‖ *nmf* heretic.
hérisser ['erise] *vt* (*poils*) to bristle (up); **h. qn** (*irriter*) to ruffle s.o.'s feathers ‖ **se h.** *vpr* (*poils*) to bristle (up); (*personne*) to get ruffled.
hérisson ['erisɔ̃] *nm* (*animal*) hedgehog.
hérit/er [erite] *vti* to inherit (**qch de qn** sth from s.o.); **h. de qch** to inherit sth. • **—age** *nm* (*biens*) inheritance; (*culturel, politique etc*) *Fig* heritage. • **héritier** *nm* heir. • **héritière** *nf* heiress.
hermétique [ɛrmetik] *a* airtight; (*obscur*) *Fig* impenetrable.
hermine [ɛrmin] *nf* (*animal, fourrure*) ermine.
hernie ['ɛrni] *nf Méd* hernia.
héron ['erɔ̃] *nm* (*oiseau*) heron.
héros ['ero] *nm* hero. • **héroïne** [erɔin] *nf* **1** (*femme*) heroine. **2** (*drogue*) heroin. • **héroïque** [erɔik] *a* heroic.
hésit/er [ezite] *vi* to hesitate (**sur** over, about; **entre** between; **à faire** to do); (*en parlant*) to falter, hesitate. • **—ant** *a* (*personne*) hesitant; (*pas, voix*) unsteady, faltering. • **hésitation** *nf* hesitation; **avec h.** hesitantly.
hétérogène [eterɔʒɛn] *a* diverse, heterogeneous.

hêtre ['ɛtr] *nm* (*arbre, bois*) beech.

heu! ['ø] *int* (*hésitation*) er!

heure [œr] *nf* (*mesure*) hour; (*moment*) time; **quelle h. est-il?** what time is it?; **il est six heures** it's six (o'clock); **six heures moins cinq** five to six; **six heures cinq** five past *ou Am* after six; **à l'h.** (*arriver*) on time; (*être payé*) by the hour; **dix kilomètres à l'h.** ten kilometres an hour; **de bonne h.** early; **de dernière h.** (*nouvelle*) latest; **tout à l'h.** (*futur*) later; (*passé*) a moment ago; **à toute h.** (*continuellement*) at all hours; **24 heures sur 24** 24 hours a day; **faire des heures supplémentaires** to work overtime; **heures creuses** off-peak *ou* slack periods; **l'h. d'affluence, l'h. de pointe** (*circulation etc*) (the) rush hour; (*dans les magasins*) (the) peak period.

ⓘ**G197** & **200** Expressions of Time 11 A & C 1

heureux, -euse [œrø, -øz] *a* happy; (*chanceux*) lucky, fortunate; **h. de qch/de voir qn** (*satisfait*) happy *ou* glad about sth/ to see s.o. ‖ *adv* (*vivre, mourir*) happily. ● **heureusement** *adv* (*par chance*) fortunately, luckily (**pour** for).

ⓘ**heureux G98** & **99** The Subjunctive 7 G 1a) & d)

heurter ['œrte] *vt* (*cogner*) to knock, bump, hit (**contre** against); (*mur, piéton*) to bump into, hit; **h. qn** (*choquer*) to offend s.o., upset s.o.; **se h. à** to bump into, hit; (*difficultés*) *Fig* to come up against.

hexagone [ɛgzagɔn] *nm* hexagon; **l'H.** *Fig* France.

hiberner [ibɛrne] *vi* to hibernate.

hibou, -x ['ibu] *nm* owl.

hic ['ik] *nm* **voilà le h.** *Fam* that's the snag.

hideux, -euse ['idø, -øz] *a* hideous.

hier [(i)jɛr] *adv* & *nm* yesterday; **h. soir** last *ou* yesterday night, yesterday evening.

hiérarchie ['jerarʃi] *nf* hierarchy. ● **hiérarchique** *a* (*ordre*) hierarchical; **par la voie h.** through (the) official channels.

hi-fi ['ifi] *a inv* & *nf inv* hi-fi.

hilarant [ilarɑ̃] *a* hilarious.

hindou, -oue [ɛ̃du] *a* & *nmf* Hindu.

hippique [ipik] *a* **concours h.** horse show, show-jumping event. ● **hippodrome** *nm* racecourse, racetrack (*for horses*).

hippopotame [ipɔpɔtam] *nm* hippopotamus.

hirondelle [irɔ̃dɛl] *nf* (*oiseau*) swallow.

hisser ['ise] *vt* (*voile, fardeau etc*) to hoist, raise ‖ **se h.** *vpr* to raise oneself (up).

histoire [istwar] *nf* (*science, événements*) history; (*récit, mensonge*) story; (*affaire*) *Fam* business, matter; **des histoires** (*ennuis*) trouble; (*façons, chichis*) fuss; **toute une h.** (*problème*) quite a lot of trouble; (*chichis*) quite a lot of fuss; **sans histoires** (*voyage etc*) uneventful. ● **historien, -ienne** *nmf* historian. ● **historique** *a* historical; (*lieu, événement*) historic.

hiver [ivɛr] *nm* winter; **en h.** in (the) winter. ● **hivernal, -aux** *a* **froid**/*etc* **h.** winter *ou* wintery cold/*etc*.

HLM ['aʃɛlɛm] *nm ou f abrév* (*habitation à loyer modéré*) = council flats, *Am* = low-rent apartment building (*sponsored by government*).

hocher ['ɔʃe] *vt* **h. la tête** (*pour dire oui*) to nod one's head; (*pour dire non*) to shake one's head.

hochet ['ɔʃɛ] *nm* (*jouet*) rattle.

hockey ['ɔkɛ] *nm* hockey; **h. sur glace** ice hockey.

holà! ['ɔla] *int* (*arrêtez*) hold on!, stop!; (*pour appeler*) hello!

hold-up ['ɔldœp] *nm inv* (*attaque*) hold-up.

Hollande ['ɔlɑ̃d] *nf* Holland. ● **hollandais, -aise** *a* Dutch ‖ *nmf* Dutchman, Dutchwoman; **les H.** the Dutch ‖ *nm* (*langue*) Dutch.

homard ['ɔmar] *nm* lobster.

homéopathie [ɔmeɔpati] *nf* hom(o)eopathy.

homicide [ɔmisid] *nm* murder, homicide; **h. involontaire** manslaughter.

hommage [ɔmaʒ] *nm* tribute, homage (**à** to); **rendre h. à** to pay tribute *ou* homage to.

homme [ɔm] *nm* man (*pl* men); **l'h.** (*espèce*) man(kind); **des vêtements d'h.** men's clothes; **d'h. à h.** man to man; **l'h. de la rue** *Fig* the man in the street; **h. d'affaires** businessman. ● **h.-grenouille** *nm* (*pl* **hommes-grenouilles**) frogman.

homogène [ɔmɔʒɛn] *a* homogeneous.

homologue [ɔmɔlɔg] *nmf* counterpart, opposite number.

homologuer [ɔmɔlɔge] *vt* to approve *ou* recognize officially.

homonyme [ɔmɔnim] *nm* (*mot*) homonym; (*personne*) namesake.

homosexuel, -elle [ɔmɔsɛksɥɛl] *a* & *nmf* homosexual.

Hongrie ['ɔ̃gri] *nf* Hungary. ● **hongrois, -oise** *a* & *nmf* Hungarian ‖ *nm* (*langue*) Hungarian.

honnête [ɔnɛt] *a* honest; (*satisfaisant*) decent, fair. ● **honnêtement** *adv* honestly; decently. ● **honnêteté** *nf* honesty.

honneur [ɔnœr] *nm* (*dignité, faveur*) honour; (*mérite*) credit; **en l'h. de** in honour of; **faire h. à** (*sa famille etc*) to be a credit to; (*par sa présence*) to do honour to; (*repas*) *Fam* to do justice to; **invité d'h.** guest of honour; **avoir la place d'h.** to have the place of honour. ●**honorable** *a* honourable; (*résultat, salaire etc*) *Fig* respectable. ●**honoraire 1** *a* (*membre*) honorary. **2** *nmpl* (*d'avocat etc*) fees. ●**honorer** *vt* to honour (**de** with); **h. qn** (*conduite etc*) to do credit to s.o. ●**honorifique** *a* (*titre*) honorary.

honte ['ɔ̃t] *nf* shame; **avoir h.** to be *ou* feel ashamed (**de qch/de faire** of sth/to do, of doing); **faire h. à qn** to put s.o. to shame. ●**honteux, -euse** *a* (*confus*) ashamed; (*scandaleux*) shameful; **être h. de** to be ashamed of.
G98 The Subjunctive 7 G 1a)

hop! ['ɔp] *int* **allez, h.!** jump!; (*pars*) off you go!

hôpital, -aux [ɔpital, -o] *nm* hospital; **à l'h.** in hospital, *Am* in the hospital.

hoquet ['ɔkɛ] *nm* hiccup; **avoir le h.** to have (the) hiccups.

horaire [ɔrɛr] *a* (*salaire etc*) hourly; (*vitesse*) per hour ‖ *nm* timetable.

horizon [ɔrizɔ̃] *nm* horizon; (*vue, paysage*) view; **à l'h.** on the horizon.

horizontal, -aux [ɔrizɔ̃tal, -o] *a* horizontal.

horloge [ɔrlɔʒ] *nf* clock. ●**horloger, -ère** *nmf* watchmaker. ●**horlogerie** *nf* watchmaker's (shop); (*industrie*) watchmaking.

hormis ['ɔrmi] *prép Litt* save, except (for).

hormone [ɔrmɔn] *nf* hormone.

horodateur [ɔrɔdatœr] *nm* pay and display ticket machine.

horoscope [ɔrɔskɔp] *nm* horoscope.

horreur [ɔrœr] *nf* horror; *pl* (*propos*) horrible things; **faire h. à** to disgust; **avoir h. de** to hate. ●**horrible** *a* horrible, awful. ●**horriblement** *adv* horribly. ●**horrifiant** *a* horrifying. ●**horrifié** *a* horrified.
horreur G98 The Subjunctive 7 G 1a)

hors ['ɔr] *prép* **h. de** (*maison, boîte etc*) out of, outside; (*danger, haleine*) *Fig* out of; **h. de soi** (*furieux*) beside oneself; **être h. jeu** *Fb* to be offside. ●**h.-bord** *nm inv* speedboat. ●**h.-concours** *a inv* non-competing. ●**h.-d'œuvre** *nm inv Culin* hors-d'œuvre, starter. ●**h.-jeu** *nm inv Fb* offside. ●**h.-la-loi** *nm inv* outlaw. ●**h.-taxe** *a inv* (*magasin, objet*) duty-free.

hortensia [ɔrtɑ̃sja] *nm* (*arbrisseau*) hydrangea.

horticulteur, -trice [ɔrtikyltœr, -tris] *nmf* horticulturalist. ●**horticulture** *nf* horticulture.

hospice [ɔspis] *nm* (*pour vieillards*) geriatric hospital; (*pour malades incurables*) hospice.

hospitalier, -ière [ɔspitalje, -jɛr] *a* **1** (*accueillant*) hospitable. **2** *Méd* **personnel**/*etc* **hospitalier** hospital staff/*etc*; **centre h.** hospital (complex). ●**hospitaliser** *vt* to hospitalize. ●**hospitalité** *nf* hospitality.

hostile [ɔstil] *a* hostile (**à** to, towards). ●**hostilité** *nf* hostility (**envers** to, towards); *pl Mil* hostilities.

hôte [ot] **1** *nm* (*qui reçoit*) host. **2** *nmf* (*invité*) guest. ●**hôtesse** *nf* hostess; **h. (de l'air)** (air) hostess.

hôtel [otɛl] *nm* hotel; **h. particulier** mansion, town house; **h. de ville** town hall, *Am* city hall. ●**hôtelier, -ière** *nmf* hotel-keeper, hotelier ‖ *a* **industrie**/*etc* **hôtelière** hotel industry/*etc*. ●**hôtellerie** *nf* **1** (*auberge*) inn, hostelry. **2** (*métier*) hotel trade.

hotte ['ɔt] *nf* **1** (*panier*) basket (*carried on back*). **2** (*de cheminée etc*) hood.

houblon ['ublɔ̃] *nm* **le h.** *Bot* hops.

houille ['uj] *nf* coal; **h. blanche** hydroelectric power. ●**houiller, -ère** *a* **bassin h.** coalfield; **industrie houillère** coal industry.

houle ['ul] *nf* (*de mer*) swell, surge. ●**houleux, -euse** *a* (*mer*) rough; (*réunion etc*) *Fig* stormy.

houppette ['upɛt] *nf* powder puff.

hourra ['ura] *nm & int* hurray.

housse ['us] *nf* (protective) cover.

houx ['u] *nm* holly.

hublot ['yblo] *nm Nau Av* porthole.

huer ['ɥe] *vt* to boo. ●**huées** *nfpl* boos.

huile [ɥil] *nf* oil; **peinture à l'h.** oil painting. ●**huileux, -euse** *a* oily.

huis [ɥi] *nm* **à h. clos** *Jur* in camera.

huissier [ɥisje] *nm* (*introducteur*) usher; (*officier*) *Jur* bailiff.

huit ['ɥit] *a* (['ɥi] *before consonant*) eight; **h. jours** a week ‖ *nm* eight. ●**huitaine** *nf* (*semaine*) week; **une h. (de)** about eight. ●**huitième** *a & nmf* eighth; **un h.** an eighth.

huître [ɥitr] *nf* oyster.

humain [ymɛ̃] *a* human; (*compatissant*) humane ‖ *nmpl* humans. ●**humanitaire** *a* humanitarian. ●**humanité** *nf* (*genre humain, sentiment*) humanity.

humble [œ̃bl] *a* humble. ●**humblement** *adv* humbly.

humecter [ymɛkte] *vt* to moisten.

humer ['yme] *vt* (*sentir*) to smell.

humeur [ymœr] *nf* (*caprice*) mood; (*caractère*) temperament; (*irritation*) bad temper; **de bonne/mauvaise h.** in a good/bad mood.

humide [ymid] *a* damp, wet; (*route*) wet; (*main, yeux*) moist; **climat/temps h.** (*chaud*) humid climate/weather; (*froid, pluvieux*) damp *ou* wet climate/weather. ● **humidité** *nf* humidity; (*plutôt froide*) damp(ness).

humili/er [ymilje] *vt* to humiliate. ● **—ant** *a* humiliating. ● **humiliation** *nf* humiliation. ● **humilité** *nf* humility.

humour [ymur] *nm* humour; **avoir de l'h.** *ou* **le sens de l'h.** to have a sense of humour. ● **humoristique** *a* (*ton etc*) humorous.

hurl/er ['yrle] *vi* (*loup, vent*) to howl; (*personne*) to scream, yell (out) ‖ *vt* (*slogans, injures etc*) to scream, yell out. ● **—ement** *nm* howl; scream, yell.

hutte ['yt] *nf* hut.

hydrater [idrate] *vt* (*peau*) to moisturize; **crème hydratante** moisturizing cream.

hydraulique [idrolik] *a* hydraulic.

hydravion [idravjɔ̃] *nm* seaplane.

hydrogène [idrɔʒɛn] *nm Ch* hydrogen.

hydrophile [idrɔfil] *a* **coton h.** cotton wool, *Am* (absorbent) cotton.

hyène [jɛn] *nf* (*animal*) hyena.

hygiaphone [iʒjafɔn] *nm* (hygienic) grill (*for speaking through in ticket office etc*).

hygiène [iʒjɛn] *nf* hygiene. ● **hygiénique** *a* hygienic; (*conditions*) sanitary; **papier h.** toilet paper.

hymne [imn] *nm* **h. national** national anthem.

hyper- [ipɛr] *préf* hyper-.

hypermarché [ipɛrmarʃe] *nm* hypermarket.

hypertension [ipɛrtɑ̃sjɔ̃] *nf* high blood pressure.

hypoallergénique [ipɔalɛrʒenik] *a* hypoallergenic.

hypnose [ipnoz] *nf* hypnosis. ● **hypnotiser** *vt* to hypnotize. ● **hypnotisme** *nm* hypnotism.

hypocrisie [ipɔkrizi] *nf* hypocrisy. ● **hypocrite** *a* hypocritical ‖ *nmf* hypocrite.

hypothèque [ipɔtɛk] *nf* mortgage. ● **hypothéquer** *vt* (*maison, avenir*) to mortgage.

hypothèse [ipɔtɛz] *nf* (*supposition*) assumption; (*en sciences*) hypothesis; **dans l'h. où...** supposing (that)....

hystérie [isteri] *nf* hysteria. ● **hystérique** *a* hysterical.

I

I, i [i] *nm* I, i.
iceberg [isbɛrg] *nm* iceberg.
ici [isi] *adv* here; **par i.** (*passer*) this way; (*habiter*) around here; **jusqu'i.** (*temps*) up to now; (*lieu*) as far as this *ou* here; **d'i. peu** before long; **i. Dupont!** *Tél* this is Dupont!, Dupont speaking!; **je ne suis pas d'i.** I'm a stranger around here; **les gens d'i.** the people around here, the locals.
idéal, -aux *ou* **-als** [ideal, -o] *a* & *nm* ideal; **c'est l'i.** *Fam* that's the ideal thing. ● **idéaliser** *vt* to idealize. ● **idéaliste** *a* idealistic ‖ *nmf* idealist.
idée [ide] *nf* idea; **il m'est venu à l'i. que** it occurred to me that; **se faire une i. de** to imagine, get an idea of; **se faire des idées** *Fam* to imagine things; **avoir dans l'i. de faire** to have it in mind to do; **i. fixe** obsession.
identifier [idɑ̃tifje] *vt* to identify (**à, avec** with); **s'i. à** *ou* **avec** to identify (oneself) with. ● **identique** *a* identical (**à** to, with). ● **identité** *nf* identity; **carte d'i.** identity card.
idéologie [ideɔlɔʒi] *nf* ideology. ● **idéologique** *a* ideological.
idiome [idjom] *nm* (*langue*) idiom. ● **idiomatique** *a* idiomatic.
idiot, -ote [idjo, -ɔt] *a* silly, idiotic ‖ *nmf* idiot. ● **idiotie** [-ɔsi] *nf* (*état*) idiocy; **une i.** a silly *ou* an idiotic thing.
idole [idɔl] *nf* idol.
idylle [idil] *nf* (*amourette*) romance.
if [if] *nm* yew (tree).
igloo [iglu] *nm* igloo.
ignare [iɲar] *a Péj* ignorant.
ignifugé [iɲifyʒe] *a* fireproof(ed).
ignoble [iɲɔbl] *a* vile, revolting.
ignorant [iɲɔrɑ̃] *a* ignorant (**de** of). ● **ignorance** *nf* ignorance.
ignorer [iɲɔre] *vt* not to know; **j'ignore si** I don't know if; **je n'ignore pas les difficultés** I'm not unaware of the difficulties; **i. qn** to ignore s.o.
il [il] *pron m* (*personne*) he; (*chose, animal*) it; **il est** he is; it is; **il pleut** it's raining; **il est vrai que** it's true that; **il y a** there is; *pl* there are; **il y a six ans** (*temps écoulé*) six years ago; **il y a une heure qu'il travaille** (*durée*) he has been working for an hour; **qu'est-ce qu'il y a?** what's the matter?; **il n'y a pas de quoi!** don't mention it!; **il doit/peut y avoir** there must/may be.
ⓘ**il G57** Subject Pronouns 6 D 1c)
ⓘ**il G88** Impersonal Verbs 7 E
ⓘ**il y a G89** Impersonal Verbs 7 E 2b)
ⓘ**il y a G96** Tenses 7 F 9a) i)
île [il] *nf* island; **les îles Britanniques** the British Isles.
illégal, -aux [ilegal, -o] *a* illegal.
illégitime [ileʒitim] *a* (*enfant, revendication*) illegitimate; (*non fondé*) unfounded.
illettré, -ée [iletre] *a* & *nmf* illiterate.
illicite [ilisit] *a* unlawful, illicit.
illimité [ilimite] *a* unlimited.
illisible [ilizibl] *a* (*écriture*) illegible; (*livre*) unreadable.
illuminer [ilymine] *vt* to light up ‖ **s'i.** *vpr* (*visage, ciel*) to light up. ● **illuminé** *a* (*monument*) floodlit. ● **illumination** *nf* (*action, lumière*) illumination.
illusion [ilyzjɔ̃] *nf* illusion (**sur** about); **se faire des illusions** to delude oneself (**sur** about). ● **illusionniste** *nmf* conjurer.
illustre [ilystr] *a* famous, illustrious.
illustrer [ilystre] *vt* (*d'images, par des exemples*) to illustrate (**de** with) ‖ **s'i.** *vpr* to become famous. ● **illustré** *a* (*livre, magazine*) illustrated ‖ *nm* (*périodique*) comic. ● **illustration** *nf* illustration.
îlot [ilo] *nm* **1** (*île*) small island. **2** (*maisons*) block.
ils [il] *pron mpl* they; **ils sont** they are.
ⓘ**G57** Subject Pronouns 6 D 1c)
image [imaʒ] *nf* picture; (*ressemblance, symbole*) image; (*dans une glace*) reflection; **i. de marque** (*de firme etc*) (public) image.
imagination [imaʒinɑsjɔ̃] *nf* imagination.
imaginer [imaʒine] *vt* (*envisager, supposer*) to imagine; (*inventer*) to devise ‖ **s'i.** *vpr* (*se figurer*) to imagine (**que** that); (*se voir*) to picture oneself. ● **imaginaire** *a* imaginary.
imbattable [ɛ̃batabl] *a* unbeatable.
imbécile [ɛ̃besil] *a* idiotic ‖ *nmf* idiot. ● **imbécillité** *nf* **une i.** (*action, parole*) an idiotic thing.
imbiber [ɛ̃bibe] *vt* to soak (**de** with, in).
imbriquer (s') [sɛ̃brike] *vpr* (*questions etc*) to overlap, be interconnected.
imbuvable [ɛ̃byvabl] *a* undrinkable; (*personne*) *Fam* insufferable.

imiter [imite] *vt* to imitate; (*contrefaire*) to forge; **i. qn** (*pour rire*) to mimic s.o.; (*faire comme*) to do the same as s.o. ● **imitateur, -trice** *nmf* (*artiste*) *Th* impersonator, mimic. ● **imitation** *nf* imitation.

immaculé [imakyle] *a* (*sans tache, sans péché*) immaculate.

immangeable [ɛ̃mɑ̃ʒabl] *a* inedible.

immatriculer [imatrikyle] *vt* to register; **se faire i.** to register. ● **immatriculation** *nf* registration.

immédiat [imedja] *a* immediate ‖ *nm* **dans l'i.** for the time being. ● **immédiatement** *adv* immediately.

immense [imɑ̃s] *a* immense, vast. ● **immensité** *nf* immensity, vastness.

immerger [imɛrʒe] *vt* to immerse, put under water.

immeuble [imœbl] *nm* building; (*d'habitation*) block of flats, *Am* apartment building; (*de bureaux*) office building *ou* block.

immigr/er [imigre] *vi* to immigrate. ● **—é, -ée** *a* & *nmf* immigrant. ● **immigration** *nf* immigration.

imminent [iminɑ̃] *a* imminent.

immiscer (s') [simise] *vpr* to interfere (**dans** in).

immobile [imɔbil] *a* still, motionless. ● **immobiliser** *vt* to bring to a stop ‖ **s'i.** *vpr* to come to a stop.

immobilier, -ière [imɔbilje, -jɛr] *a* **vente immobilière** sale of property; **agent i.** estate agent, *Am* real estate agent.

immodéré [imɔdere] *a* immoderate.

immonde [imɔ̃d] *a* filthy.

immoral, -aux [imɔral, -o] *a* immoral.

immortel, -elle [imɔrtɛl] *a* immortal.

immuable [imɥabl] *a* unchanging.

immuniser [imynize] *vt* to immunize (**contre** against); **immunisé contre** (*à l'abri de*) *Méd* & *Fig* immune to *ou* from. ● **immunitaire** *a* (*déficience, système etc*) *Méd* immune. ● **immunité** *nf* immunity; **i. parlementaire** parliamentary immunity.

impact [ɛ̃pakt] *nm* impact (**sur** on).

impair [ɛ̃pɛr] *a* (*nombre*) odd, uneven.

imparable [ɛ̃parabl] *a* (*coup etc*) unavoidable.

impardonnable [ɛ̃pardɔnabl] *a* unforgivable.

imparfait [ɛ̃parfɛ] **1** *a* (*connaissance etc*) imperfect. **2** *nm* (*temps*) *Gram* imperfect.

impartial, -aux [ɛ̃parsjal, -o] *a* fair, unbiased.

impasse [ɛ̃pɑs] *nf* (*rue*) dead end, blind alley; (*situation*) *Fig* stalemate, impasse; **dans l'i.** (*négociations*) in deadlock.

impassible [ɛ̃pasibl] *a* impassive, unmoved.

impatient [ɛ̃pasjɑ̃] *a* impatient; **i. de faire** eager *ou* impatient to do. ● **impatience** *nf* impatience. ● **impatienter** *vt* to annoy ‖ **s'i.** *vpr* to get impatient.

impayé [ɛ̃peje] *a* unpaid.

impeccable [ɛ̃pekabl] *a* (*propre*) immaculate, impeccable.

impénétrable [ɛ̃penetrabl] *a* (*forêt, mystère etc*) impenetrable.

impensable [ɛ̃pɑ̃sabl] *a* unthinkable.

imper [ɛ̃pɛr] *nm Fam* raincoat, mac.

impératif, -ive [ɛ̃peratif, -iv] *a* (*consigne, ton*) imperative ‖ *nm Gram* imperative.

impératrice [ɛ̃peratris] *nf* empress.

imperceptible [ɛ̃pɛrsɛptibl] *a* imperceptible (**à** to).

impérial, -aux [ɛ̃perjal, -o] *a* imperial.

impérieux, -euse [ɛ̃perjø, -øz] *a* (*autoritaire*) imperious; (*besoin*) pressing.

imperméable [ɛ̃pɛrmeabl] **1** *a* (*tissu, manteau*) waterproof. **2** *nm* raincoat, mackintosh.

impersonnel, -elle [ɛ̃pɛrsɔnɛl] *a* impersonal.

impertinent [ɛ̃pɛrtinɑ̃] *a* impertinent (**envers** to). ● **impertinence** *nf* impertinence.

imperturbable [ɛ̃pɛrtyrbabl] *a* (*personne*) unruffled.

impétueux, -euse [ɛ̃petɥø, -øz] *a* impetuous.

impitoyable [ɛ̃pitwajabl] *a* ruthless, pitiless.

implacable [ɛ̃plakabl] *a* implacable, relentless.

implanter [ɛ̃plɑ̃te] *vt* (*industrie, mode etc*) to establish ‖ **s'i.** *vpr* to become established.

implicite [ɛ̃plisit] *a* implicit.

impliquer [ɛ̃plike] *vt* (*entraîner*) to imply; **i. que** (*supposer*) to imply that; **i. qn** (*engager*) to implicate s.o. (**dans** in).

implorer [ɛ̃plɔre] *vt* to implore (**qn de faire** s.o. to do).

impoli [ɛ̃pɔli] *a* rude, impolite. ● **impolitesse** *nf* rudeness; **une i.** an act of rudeness.

impopulaire [ɛ̃pɔpylɛr] *a* unpopular.

important [ɛ̃pɔrtɑ̃] *a* (*personnage, événement etc*) important; (*quantité, somme etc*) large, considerable; (*dégâts, retard*) considerable, great ‖ *nm* **l'i., c'est de...** the important thing is to.... ● **importance** *nf* importance, significance; (*taille*) size; (*de dégâts*) extent; **ça n'a pas d'i.** it doesn't matter.

ⓘ**important G99** The Subjunctive 7 G 1d)

importer [ɛ̃pɔrte] **1** *v imp* to matter, be important (**à** to); **il importe de faire** it's

important to do; **peu importe, n'importe** it doesn't matter; **n'importe qui/quoi/où/quand/comment** anyone/anything/anywhere/any time/anyhow.
2 *vt* (*marchandises etc*) to import (**de** from). • **importateur, -trice** *nmf* importer. • **importation** *nf* (*objet*) import; (*action*) import(ing); **d'i.** (*article*) imported.
importuner [ɛ̃pɔrtyne] *vt* to inconvenience, trouble.
imposer [ɛ̃poze] **1** *vt* **i. qch à qn** to impose sth on s.o. ‖ *vi* **en i. à qn** to impress s.o., command respect from s.o. ‖ **s'i.** *vpr* (*chez qn*) *Péj* to impose; (*s'affirmer*) to assert oneself; (*aller de soi*) to stand out; (*être nécessaire*) to be essential.
2 *vt Fin* to tax. • **imposable** *a Fin* taxable.
impossible [ɛ̃pɔsibl] *a* impossible (**à faire** to do); **il (nous) est i. de faire** it is impossible (for us) to do; **il est i. que** (+ *sub*) it is impossible that ‖ *nm* **faire l'i.** to do the impossible. • **impossibilité** *nf* impossibility.
imposteur [ɛ̃pɔstœr] *nm* impostor.
impôt [ɛ̃po] *nm* tax; *pl* (*contributions*) (income) tax, taxes; **i. sur le revenu** income tax; **(service des) impôts** tax authorities.
impotent [ɛ̃pɔtɑ̃] *a* crippled, disabled.
impraticable [ɛ̃pratikabl] *a* (*chemin etc*) impassable.
imprécis [ɛ̃presi] *a* imprecise.
imprégner [ɛ̃preɲe] *vt* to permeate, saturate (**de** with) ‖ **s'i.** *vpr* to become permeated *ou* saturated (**de** with); **imprégné de** (*idées*) imbued *ou* infused with.
imprenable [ɛ̃prənabl] *a Mil* impregnable.
impresario [ɛ̃presarjo] *nm* (business) manager.
impression [ɛ̃presjɔ̃] *nf* **1** impression; **avoir l'i. que** to have the feeling *ou* impression that; **faire bonne i. à qn** to make a good impression on s.o. **2** *Typ* printing.
impressionn/er [ɛ̃presjɔne] *vt* (*émouvoir*) to make a strong impression on; (*influencer*) to impress. • **—ant** *a* impressive. • **impressionnable** *a* impressionable.
imprévisible [ɛ̃previzibl] *a* unforeseeable. • **imprévu** *a* unexpected ‖ *nm* **en cas d'i.** in case of anything unexpected.
imprim/er [ɛ̃prime] *vt* (*livre etc*) to print; (*trace*) to impress (**dans** in). • **—ante** *nf* (*d'ordinateur*) printer. • **—é** *nm* (*formulaire*) printed form; **'imprimés'** (*par la poste*) 'printed matter'. • **imprimerie** *nf* (*technique*) printing; (*lieu*) printing works, *Am* print shop. • **imprimeur** *nm* printer.
improbable [ɛ̃prɔbabl] *a* improbable, unlikely.
impromptu [ɛ̃prɔ̃pty] *a* & *adv* impromptu.
impropre [ɛ̃prɔpr] *a* inappropriate; **i. à qch** unfit for sth.
improviser [ɛ̃prɔvise] *vti* to improvise.
improviste (à l') [alɛ̃prɔvist] *adv* unexpectedly; **prendre qn à l'i.** to catch s.o. unawares.
imprudent [ɛ̃prydɑ̃] *a* (*personne*, *action*) careless, foolish; **il est i. de** it is unwise *ou* foolish to. • **imprudence** *nf* carelessness, foolishness; **commettre une i.** to do something foolish.
impudent [ɛ̃pydɑ̃] *a* impudent.
impudique [ɛ̃pydik] *a* lewd.
impuissant [ɛ̃pɥisɑ̃] *a* helpless; *Méd* impotent.
impulsif, -ive [ɛ̃pylsif, -iv] *a* impulsive. • **impulsion** *nf* impulse; **donner une i. à** (*élan*) *Fig* to give an impetus *ou* impulse to.
impunément [ɛ̃pynemɑ̃] *adv* with impunity. • **impuni** *a* unpunished.
impur [ɛ̃pyr] *a* impure. • **impureté** *nf* impurity.
imputer [ɛ̃pyte] *vt* to attribute (**à** to).
inabordable [inabɔrdabl] *a* (*prix*) prohibitive; (*lieu*) inaccessible.
inacceptable [inaksɛptabl] *a* unacceptable.
inaccessible [inaksesibl] *a* inaccessible.
inachevé [inaʃve] *a* unfinished.
inactif, -ive [inaktif, -iv] *a* inactive. • **inaction** *nf* inactivity, inaction.
inadapté, -ée [inadapte] *a* & *nmf* maladjusted (person).
inadmissible [inadmisibl] *a* unacceptable.
inadvertance (par) [parinadvertɑ̃s] *adv* inadvertently.
inaltérable [inalterabl] *a* (*matière*) that does not deteriorate; (*sentiment*) unchanging.
inanimé [inanime] *a* (*mort*) lifeless; (*évanoui*) unconscious; (*matière*) inanimate.
inanition [inanisjɔ̃] *nf* **mourir d'i.** to die of starvation.
inaperçu [inapɛrsy] *a* **passer i.** to go unnoticed.
inapplicable [inaplikabl] *a* inapplicable.
inappréciable [inapresjabl] *a* invaluable.
inapte [inapt] *a* unsuited (**à qch** to sth), inept (**à qch** at sth); *Mil* unfit • **inaptitude** *nf* ineptitude, incapacity.
inattaquable [inatakabl] *a* unassailable.
inattendu [inatɑ̃dy] *a* unexpected.
inattentif, -ive [inatɑ̃tif, -iv] *a* inattentive, careless; **i. à** (*soucis*, *danger etc*) heedless of. • **inattention** *nf* lack of attention; **dans**

un moment d'i. in a moment of distraction.
inaudible [inodibl] *a* inaudible.
inaugurer [inogyre] *vt* (*politique*, *édifice*) to inaugurate; (*école*) to open; (*statue*) to unveil. ● **inauguration** *nf* inauguration; opening; unveiling.
inavouable [inavwabl] *a* shameful.
incalculable [ɛ̃kalkylabl] *a* incalculable.
incandescent [ɛ̃kɑ̃desɑ̃] *a* white-hot.
incapable [ɛ̃kapabl] *a* **i. de faire** unable to do, incapable of doing ‖ *nmf* (*personne*) incompetent. ● **incapacité** *nf* incapacity, inability (**de faire** to do); *Méd* disability, incapacity.
incarcérer [ɛ̃karsere] *vt* to incarcerate.
incarner [ɛ̃karne] *vt* to embody. ● **incarnation** *nf* embodiment.
incassable [ɛ̃kɑsabl] *a* unbreakable.
incendie [ɛ̃sɑ̃di] *nm* fire; **i. criminel** arson; **i. de forêt** forest fire. ● **incendiaire** *nmf* arsonist ‖ *a* (*bombe*) incendiary; (*paroles*) inflammatory. ● **incendier** *vt* to set fire to.
incertain [ɛ̃sɛrtɛ̃] *a* uncertain; (*temps*) unsettled; (*entreprise*) chancy; (*contour*) indistinct. ● **incertitude** *nf* uncertainty.
incessamment [ɛ̃sesamɑ̃] *adv* without delay.
incessant [ɛ̃sesɑ̃] *a* continual.
inceste [ɛ̃sɛst] *nm* incest.
inchangé [ɛ̃ʃɑ̃ʒe] *a* unchanged.
incidence [ɛ̃sidɑ̃s] *nf* (*influence*) effect.
incident [ɛ̃sidɑ̃] *nm* incident; (*accroc*) hitch.
incinérer [ɛ̃sinere] *vt* (*ordures*) to incinerate; (*cadavre*) to cremate.
inciser [ɛ̃size] *vt* to make an incision in.
incisif, -ive[1] [ɛ̃sizif, -iv] *a* incisive, sharp.
incisive[2] [ɛ̃siziv] *nf* (*dent*) incisor (tooth).
inciter [ɛ̃site] *vt* to prompt, urge (*s.o.*) (**à faire** to do).
incliner [ɛ̃kline] *vt* (*courber*) to bend; (*pencher*) to tilt, incline; **i. la tête** (*approuver*) to nod one's head; (*révérence*) to bow (one's head).
‖ **s'incliner** *vpr* (*se courber*) to bow (down); (*s'avouer vaincu*) to admit defeat; (*chemin*) to slope down; (*bateau*) to heel over. ● **inclinaison** *nf* incline, slope. ● **inclination** *nf* (*de tête*) nod; (*révérence*) bow; (*goût*) inclination.
incl/ure* [ɛ̃klyr] *vt* to include; (*enfermer*) to enclose. ● **—us** *a* inclusive; **du quatre jusqu'au dix mai i.** from the fourth to the tenth of May inclusive; **jusqu'à lundi i.** up to and including Monday.
incohérent [ɛ̃kɔerɑ̃] *a* incoherent.
incollable [ɛ̃kɔlabl] *a Fam* infallible, unbeatable.
incolore [ɛ̃kɔlɔr] *a* colourless; (*vernis*) clear.
incomber [ɛ̃kɔ̃be] *vi* **i. à qn** (*devoir*) to fall to s.o.
incommoder [ɛ̃kɔmɔde] *vt* to bother.
incomparable [ɛ̃kɔ̃parabl] *a* incomparable.
incompatible [ɛ̃kɔ̃patibl] *a* incompatible, inconsistent (**avec** with).
incompétent [ɛ̃kɔ̃petɑ̃] *a* incompetent.
incomplet, -ète [ɛ̃kɔ̃plɛ, -ɛt] *a* incomplete; (*fragmentaire*) scrappy, sketchy.
incompréhensible [ɛ̃kɔ̃preɑ̃sibl] *a* incomprehensible.
incompréhension [ɛ̃kɔ̃preɑ̃sjɔ̃] *nf* lack of understanding. ● **incompris, -ise** *a* misunderstood ‖ *nmf* greatly misunderstood person.
inconcevable [ɛ̃kɔ̃svabl] *a* inconceivable.
inconciliable [ɛ̃kɔ̃siljabl] *a* irreconcilable.
inconditionnel, -elle [ɛ̃kɔ̃disjɔnɛl] *a* unconditional.
inconfortable [ɛ̃kɔ̃fɔrtabl] *a* uncomfortable.
incongru [ɛ̃kɔ̃gry] *a* unseemly, incongruous.
inconnu, -ue [ɛ̃kɔny] *a* unknown (**à** to) ‖ *nmf* (*étranger*) stranger; (*auteur*) unknown ‖ *nf Math* unknown (quantity).
inconscient [ɛ̃kɔ̃sjɑ̃] *a* unconscious; (*imprudent*) thoughtless; **i. de qch** unaware of sth ‖ *nm* **l'i.** *Psy* the unconscious. ● **inconsciemment** [-amɑ̃] *adv* unconsciously. ● **inconscience** *nf* (*physique*) unconsciousness; (*irréflexion*) thoughtlessness.
inconsidéré [ɛ̃kɔ̃sidere] *a* thoughtless.
inconsolable [ɛ̃kɔ̃sɔlabl] *a* heartbroken, cut up.
inconstant [ɛ̃kɔ̃stɑ̃] *a* fickle.
incontestable [ɛ̃kɔ̃tɛstabl] *a* undeniable. ● **incontesté** *a* undisputed.
incontrôlé [ɛ̃kɔ̃trole] *a* unchecked. ● **incontrôlable** *a* unverifiable.
inconvenant [ɛ̃kɔ̃vnɑ̃] *a* improper.
inconvénient [ɛ̃kɔ̃venjɑ̃] *nm* (*désavantage*) drawback; (*risque*) risk; **si vous n'y voyez pas d'i.** if you have no objection(s).
incorporer [ɛ̃kɔrpɔre] *vt* (*introduire*, *admettre*) to incorporate (**dans** into); (*ingrédient*) to blend (**à** with); *Mil* to enrol, *Am* enroll.
incorrect [ɛ̃kɔrɛkt] *a* (*inexact*) incorrect; (*grossier*) impolite. ● **incorrection** *nf* (*faute*) impropriety, error; **une i.** (*grossièreté*) an impolite word *ou* act.
incorrigible [ɛ̃kɔriʒibl] *a* incorrigible.
incorruptible [ɛ̃kɔryptibl] *a* incorruptible.
incrédule [ɛ̃kredyl] *a* incredulous. ● **incrédulité** *nf* disbelief.

incriminer [ɛ̃krimine] *vt* to incriminate.
incroyable [ɛ̃krwajabl] *a* incredible, unbelievable.
incrusté [ɛ̃kryste] *a* **i. de** (*orné*) inlaid with.
incruster (s') [sɛ̃kryste] *vpr* (*chez qn*) *Fam* to be difficult to get rid of, outstay one's welcome.
incubation [ɛ̃kybɑsjɔ̃] *nf* incubation.
inculp/er [ɛ̃kylpe] *vt Jur* to charge (**de** with). ●**—é, -ée** *nmf* **l'i.** the accused. ●**inculpation** *nf* charge.
inculquer [ɛ̃kylke] *vt* to instil (**à** into).
inculte [ɛ̃kylt] *a* (*terre*) uncultivated; (*personne*) uneducated.
incurable [ɛ̃kyrabl] *a* incurable.
incursion [ɛ̃kyrsjɔ̃] *nf* incursion.
incurver [ɛ̃kyrve] *vt* to curve.
Inde [ɛ̃d] *nf* India.
indécent [ɛ̃desɑ̃] *a* indecent.
indéchiffrable [ɛ̃deʃifrabl] *a* undecipherable.
indécis [ɛ̃desi] *a* (*hésitant*) undecided; (*de tempérament*) indecisive; (*résultat, victoire*) undecided.
indéfendable [ɛ̃defɑ̃dabl] *a* undefensible.
indéfini [ɛ̃defini] *a* (*indéterminé*) indefinite; (*imprécis*) undefined; **article i.** *Gram* indefinite article. ●**indéfiniment** *adv* indefinitely. ●**indéfinissable** *a* indefinable.
indéformable [ɛ̃defɔrmabl] *a* (*vêtement*) which keeps its shape.
indélébile [ɛ̃delebil] *a* (*encre, souvenir*) indelible.
indélicat [ɛ̃delika] *a* (*grossier*) indelicate; (*malhonnête*) unscrupulous.
indemne [ɛ̃dɛmn] *a* unhurt.
indemniser [ɛ̃dɛmnize] *vt* to indemnify, compensate (**de** for). ●**indemnité** *nf* (*dédommagement*) compensation; (*allocation*) allowance.
indéniable [ɛ̃denjabl] *a* undeniable.
indépendant [ɛ̃depɑ̃dɑ̃] *a* independent (**de** of); (*chambre*) self-contained; (*journaliste*) freelance. ●**indépendance** *nf* independence.
indescriptible [ɛ̃dɛskriptibl] *a* indescribable.
indésirable [ɛ̃dezirabl] *a* & *nmf* undesirable.
indestructible [ɛ̃dɛstryktibl] *a* indestructible.
indéterminé [ɛ̃detɛrmine] *a* indeterminate. ●**indétermination** *nf* (*doute*) indecision.
index [ɛ̃dɛks] *nm* (*doigt*) index finger, forefinger; (*liste*) index.
indexer [ɛ̃dɛkse] *vt Écon* to index-link (**sur** to).
indicateur, -trice [ɛ̃dikatœr, -tris] **1** *nm Rail* guide, timetable; *Tech* indicator, gauge. **2** *a* **poteau i.** signpost; **panneau i.** road sign.
indicatif, -ive [ɛ̃dikatif -iv] **1** *a* indicative (**de** of) ‖ *nm* (*à la radio*) signature tune; (*téléphonique*) dialling code, *Am* area code. **2** *nm Gram* indicative.
indication [ɛ̃dikɑsjɔ̃] *nf* (*renseignement*) (piece of) information; **indications** (*pour aller quelque part*) directions.
indice [ɛ̃dis] *nm* (*dans une enquête*) clue; (*des prix*) index; (*de salaire*) grade; **i. d'écoute** *TV Rad* rating.
indien, -ienne [ɛ̃djɛ̃, -jɛn] *a* & *nmf* Indian.
indifférent [ɛ̃diferɑ̃] *a* indifferent (**à** to). ●**indifférence** *nf* indifference (**à** to).
indigène [ɛ̃diʒɛn] *a* & *nmf* native.
indigent [ɛ̃diʒɑ̃] *a* (very) poor.
indigeste [ɛ̃diʒɛst] *a* indigestible. ●**indigestion** *nf* (attack of) indigestion.
indigne [ɛ̃diɲ] *a* (*personne*) unworthy; **i. de qn/qch** unworthy of s.o./sth.
indigner [ɛ̃diɲe] *vt* **i. qn** to make s.o. indignant ‖ **s'i.** *vpr* to be *ou* become indignant (**de** at). ●**indignation** *nf* indignation.
indiqu/er [ɛ̃dike] *vt* (*montrer*) to show, indicate; (*dire*) to tell, point out; **i. du doigt** to point to *ou* at. ●**—é** *a* (*heure*) appointed; (*conseillé*) recommended; (*adéquat*) appropriate.
indirect [ɛ̃dirɛkt] *a* indirect. ●**—ement** [-əmɑ̃] *adv* indirectly.
indiscipliné [ɛ̃disipline] *a* unruly.
indiscret, -ète [ɛ̃diskrɛ, -ɛt] *a* (*curieux*) *Péj* inquisitive, prying; (*indélicat*) indiscreet, tactless. ●**indiscrétion** *nf* indiscretion.
indiscutable [ɛ̃diskytabl] *a* indisputable.
indispensable [ɛ̃dispɑ̃sabl] *a* essential.
indisposé [ɛ̃dispoze] *a* (*malade*) unwell, indisposed. ●**indisposition** *nf* indisposition.
indissoluble [ɛ̃disɔlybl] *a* (*liens etc*) solid.
indistinct, -incte [ɛ̃distɛ̃(kt), -ɛ̃kt] *a* unclear, indistinct.
individu [ɛ̃dividy] *nm* individual. ●**individualiste** *a* individualistic ‖ *nmf* individualist. ●**individuel, -elle** *a* individual.
Indochine [ɛ̃dɔʃin] *nf* Indo-China.
indolent [ɛ̃dɔlɑ̃] *a* indolent.
indolore [ɛ̃dɔlɔr] *a* painless.
indomptable [ɛ̃dɔ̃tabl] *a* (*volonté*) indomitable.
Indonésie [ɛ̃dɔnezi] *nf* Indonesia.
indue [ɛ̃dy] *af* **à une heure i.** at an ungodly hour.
induire* [ɛ̃dɥir] *vt* **i. qn en erreur** to lead s.o. astray.
indulgent [ɛ̃dylʒɑ̃] *a* indulgent (**envers** to,

avec with). • **indulgence** *nf* indulgence.

industrie [ɛ̃dystri] *nf* industry. • **industrialisé** *a* industrialized. • **industriel, -elle** *a* industrial ‖ *nm* industrialist.

inébranlable [inebrɑ̃labl] *a* (*certitude, personne*) unshakeable, unwavering.

inédit [inedi] *a* (*texte*) unpublished; (*nouveau*) *Fig* original.

inefficace [inefikas] *a* (*mesure etc*) ineffective, ineffectual; (*personne*) inefficient.

inégal, -aux [inegal, -o] *a* unequal; (*sol, humeur*) uneven. • **inégalable** *a* incomparable. • **inégalité** *nf* (*injustice*) inequality; (*physique*) difference; (*irrégularité*) unevenness.

inéluctable [inelyktabl] *a* inescapable.

inepte [inɛpt] *a* absurd, inept.

inépuisable [inepɥizabl] *a* inexhaustible.

inerte [inɛrt] *a* inert; (*corps*) lifeless.

inespéré [inɛspere] *a* unhoped-for.

inestimable [inɛstimabl] *a* priceless.

inévitable [inevitabl] *a* inevitable, unavoidable.

inexact [inɛgzakt] *a* (*erroné*) inaccurate, inexact; **c'est i.!** it's incorrect! • **inexactitude** *nf* inaccuracy; (*manque de ponctualité*) lack of punctuality.

inexcusable [inɛkskyzabl] *a* inexcusable.

inexistant [inɛgzistɑ̃] *a* non-existent.

inexorable [inɛgzɔrabl] *a* inexorable.

inexpérience [inɛksperjɑ̃s] *nf* inexperience. • **inexpérimenté** *a* (*personne*) inexperienced.

inexplicable [inɛksplikabl] *a* inexplicable. • **inexpliqué** *a* unexplained.

inexprimable [inɛksprimabl] *a* beyond words, inexpressible.

inextricable [inɛkstrikabl] *a* inextricable.

infaillible [ɛ̃fajibl] *a* infallible.

infaisable [ɛ̃fəzabl] *a* (*travail etc*) that cannot be done.

infamant [ɛ̃famɑ̃] *a* ignominious.

infâme [ɛ̃fɑm] *a* (*odieux*) vile, infamous; (*taudis*) squalid.

infanterie [ɛ̃fɑ̃tri] *nf* infantry.

infantile [ɛ̃fɑ̃til] *a* infantile.

infarctus [ɛ̃farktys] *nm* **un i.** *Méd* a coronary.

infatigable [ɛ̃fatigabl] *a* tireless.

infect [ɛ̃fɛkt] *a* (*odeur*) foul; (*café etc*) vile.

infecter [ɛ̃fɛkte] **1** *vt* (*air*) to contaminate. **2** *vt Méd* to infect ‖ **s'i.** *vpr* to get infected. • **infectieux, -euse** *a* infectious. • **infection** *nf* **1** *Méd* infection. **2** (*odeur*) stench.

inférieur, -eure [ɛ̃ferjœr] *a* (*partie*) lower; (*qualité etc*) inferior; **à l'étage i.** on the floor below; **i. à** inferior to; (*plus petit que*) smaller than. • **infériorité** *nf* inferiority.

infernal, -aux [ɛ̃fɛrnal, -o] *a* infernal.

infesté [ɛ̃fɛste] *a* **i. de requins/fourmis/***etc* shark/ant/*etc* -infested.

infidèle [ɛ̃fidɛl] *a* unfaithful (**à** to). • **infidélité** *nf* unfaithfulness; **une i.** (*acte*) an infidelity.

infiltrer (s') [sɛ̃filtre] *vpr* (*liquide*) to seep (through) (**dans** into); (*lumière*) to filter (through) (**dans** into); **s'i. dans** (*groupe, esprit*) *Fig* to infiltrate.

infime [ɛ̃fim] *a* (*très petit*) tiny.

infini [ɛ̃fini] *a* infinite ‖ *nm Math Phot* infinity; *Phil* infinite; **à l'i.** (*beaucoup*) endlessly; *Math* to infinity. • **infiniment** *adv* infinitely; (*regretter, remercier*) very much. • **infinité** *nf* **une i. de** an infinite amount of.

infinitif [ɛ̃finitif] *nm Gram* infinitive.

infirme [ɛ̃firm] *a* & *nmf* disabled (person). • **infirmité** *nf* disability.

infirmer [ɛ̃firme] *vt* to invalidate.

infirmerie [ɛ̃firməri] *nf* sick room, sickbay. • **infirmier** *nm* male nurse. • **infirmière** *nf* nurse.

inflammable [ɛ̃flamabl] *a* (in)flammable.

inflammation [ɛ̃flamɑsjɔ̃] *nf Méd* inflammation.

inflation [ɛ̃flɑsjɔ̃] *nf Écon* inflation.

infléchir [ɛ̃fleʃir] *vt* (*courber*) to inflect, bend; (*modifier*) to shift.

inflexible [ɛ̃flɛksibl] *a* inflexible.

infliger [ɛ̃fliʒe] *vt* to inflict (**à** on); (*amende*) to impose (**à** on).

influence [ɛ̃flyɑ̃s] *nf* influence. • **influencer** *vt* to influence. • **influençable** *a* easily influenced. • **influent** *a* influential.

information [ɛ̃fɔrmɑsjɔ̃] *nf* information; (*nouvelle*) piece of news; **les informations** the news.

informatique [ɛ̃fɔrmatik] *nf* (*science*) computer science; (*technique*) data processing. • **informaticien, -ienne** *nmf* computer scientist. • **informatiser** *vt* to computerize.

informe [ɛ̃fɔrm] *a* shapeless.

informer [ɛ̃fɔrme] *vt* to inform (**de** of, about; **que** that) ‖ **s'i.** *vpr* to inquire (**de** about; **si** if, whether).

infortuné [ɛ̃fɔrtyne] *a* ill-fated, hapless.

infraction [ɛ̃fraksjɔ̃] *nf* (*délit*) offence, *Am* offense; **i. à** breach of.

infranchissable [ɛ̃frɑ̃ʃisabl] *a* (*mur, fleuve*) impassable.

infructueux, -euse [ɛ̃fryktɥø, -øz] *a* fruitless.

infusion [ɛ̃fyzjɔ̃] *nf* (*tisane*) herb *ou* herbal tea.

ingénier (s') [sɛ̃ʒenje] *vpr* to exercise one's wits (**à faire** in order to do).
ingénieur [ɛ̃ʒenjœr] *nm* engineer; **femme i.** woman engineer. • **ingénierie** [-iri] *nf* engineering; **i. mécanique** mechanical engineering.
ingénieux, -euse [ɛ̃ʒenjø, -øz] *a* ingenious. • **ingéniosité** *nf* ingenuity.
ingénu [ɛ̃ʒeny] *a* artless, naïve.
ingérer (s') [sɛ̃ʒere] *vpr* to interfere (**dans** in). • **ingérence** *nf* interference.
ingrat [ɛ̃gra] *a* (*personne*) ungrateful (**envers** to); (*tâche*) thankless; (*âge*) awkward. • **ingratitude** *nf* ingratitude.
ingrédient [ɛ̃gredjɑ̃] *nm* ingredient.
inhabitable [inabitabl] *a* uninhabitable. • **inhabité** *a* uninhabited.
inhabituel, -elle [inabitɥɛl] *a* unusual.
inhalation [inalɑsjɔ̃] *nf* inhalation; **faire des inhalations** to inhale.
inhérent [inerɑ̃] *a* inherent (**à** in).
inhibé [inibe] *a* inhibited.
inhospitalier, -ière [inɔspitalje, -jɛr] *a* inhospitable.
inhumain [inymɛ̃] *a* (*cruel*) inhuman.
inhumer [inyme] *vt* to bury. • **inhumation** *nf* burial.
inimaginable [inimaʒinabl] *a* unimaginable.
inimitable [inimitabl] *a* inimitable.
inimitié [inimitje] *nf* enmity.
ininflammable [inɛ̃flamabl] *a* (*tissu etc*) non-flammable.
inintelligible [inɛ̃teliʒibl] *a* unintelligible.
inintéressant [inɛ̃teresɑ̃] *a* uninteresting.
ininterrompu [inɛ̃tɛrɔ̃py] *a* continuous.
initial, -aux [inisjal, -o] *a* initial. • **initiale** *nf* (*lettre*) initial.
initiative [inisjativ] *nf* **1** initiative. **2 syndicat d'i.** tourist office.
initier [inisje] *vt* to initiate (**à** into); **s'i. à** (*art, science*) to become acquainted with *ou* initiated into. • **initiation** *nf* initiation.
injecter [ɛ̃ʒɛkte] *vt* to inject; **injecté de sang** bloodshot. • **injection** *nf* injection.
injure [ɛ̃ʒyr] *nf* insult; *pl* abuse, insults. • **injurier** *vt* to insult, abuse. • **injurieux, -euse** *a* abusive, insulting (**pour** to).
injuste [ɛ̃ʒyst] *a* (*contraire à la justice*) unjust; (*non équitable*) unfair. • **injustice** *nf* injustice.
injustifiable [ɛ̃ʒystifjabl] *a* unjustifiable. • **injustifié** *a* unjustified.
inlassable [ɛ̃lɑsabl] *a* untiring.
inné [ine] *a* innate, inborn.
innocent, -ente [inɔsɑ̃, -ɑ̃t] *a* innocent (**de** of) ‖ *nmf Jur* innocent person. • **innocence** *nf* innocence. • **innocenter** *vt* **i. qn** to clear s.o. (**de** of).
innombrable [inɔ̃brabl] *a* countless.
innommable [inɔmabl] *a* unspeakable, foul.
innover [inɔve] *vi* to innovate. • **innovation** *nf* innovation.
inoccupé [inɔkype] *a* unoccupied.
inoculer [inɔkyle] *vt* **i. qch à qn** to infect *ou* inoculate s.o. with sth.
inodore [inɔdɔr] *a* odourless.
inoffensif, -ive [inɔfɑ̃sif, -iv] *a* harmless, inoffensive.
inonder [inɔ̃de] *vt* to flood; (*mouiller*) to soak; **inondé de soleil** bathed in sunlight. • **inondation** *nf* flood; (*action*) flooding (**de** of).
inopiné [inɔpine] *a* unexpected.
inopportun [inɔpɔrtœ̃] *a* inopportune.
inoubliable [inublijabl] *a* unforgettable.
inouï [inwi] *a* incredible, extraordinary.
inox [inɔks] *nm* stainless steel; **couteau**/*etc* **en i.** stainless-steel knife/*etc*. • **inoxydable** *a* **acier i.** stainless steel.
inqualifiable [ɛ̃kalifjabl] *a* (*indigne*) unspeakable.
inquiet, -iète [ɛ̃kjɛ, -jɛt] *a* worried, anxious (**de** about).
inquiéter [ɛ̃kjete] *vt* (*préoccuper*) to worry; (*police*) to bother, harass (*suspect etc*) ‖ **s'i.** *vpr* to worry (**de** about). • **inquiétant** *a* worrying.
inquiétude [ɛ̃kjetyd] *nf* worry, anxiety; **donner de l'i. à qn** to give s.o. cause for concern.
insaisissable [ɛ̃sezisabl] *a* elusive.
insalubre [ɛ̃salybr] *a* unhealthy.
insanités [ɛ̃sanite] *nfpl* (*idioties*) absurdities.
insatiable [ɛ̃sasjabl] *a* insatiable.
insatisfait [ɛ̃satisfɛ] *a* unsatisfied, dissatisfied.
inscrire* [ɛ̃skrir] *vt* to write *ou* put down; (*sur un registre*) to register; (*graver*) to inscribe; **i. qn** to enrol s.o., *Am* enroll s.o. ‖ **s'i.** *vpr* to put one's name down; **s'i. à** (*club, parti*) to join; (*examen*) to enrol *ou Am* enroll for, register for. • **inscription** *nf* enrolment, *Am* enrollment, registration; (*sur écriteau etc*) inscription; **frais d'i.** *Univ* tuition fees.
insecte [ɛ̃sɛkt] *nm* insect. • **insecticide** *nm* & *a* insecticide.
insécurité [ɛ̃sekyrite] *nf* insecurity.
insémination [ɛ̃seminɑsjɔ̃] *nf* **i. artificielle** *Méd* artificial insemination.
insensé [ɛ̃sɑ̃se] *a* senseless, absurd.
insensible [ɛ̃sɑ̃sibl] *a* (*indifférent*) insensi-

tive (**à** to); (*graduel*) imperceptible, very slight. ● **insensibilité** *nf* insensitivity.

inséparable [ɛ̃separabl] *a* inseparable (**de** from).

insérer [ɛ̃sere] *vt* to insert (**dans** into, in); **s'i. dans** (*société, groupe*) to become accepted by.

insidieux, -euse [ɛ̃sidjø, -øz] *a* insidious.

insigne [ɛ̃siɲ] *nm* badge, emblem; *pl* (*de maire etc*) insignia.

insignifiant [ɛ̃siɲifjɑ̃] *a* insignificant.

insinuer [ɛ̃sinɥe] *vt Péj* to insinuate (**que** that). ● **insinuation** *nf* insinuation.

insipide [ɛ̃sipid] *a* insipid.

insister [ɛ̃siste] *vi* to insist (**pour faire** on doing); (*persévérer*) *Fam* to persevere; **i. sur** (*détail, syllabe etc*) to stress; **i. pour que** (+ *sub*) to insist that. ● **insistance** *nf* insistence, persistence.

insolation [ɛ̃sɔlɑsjɔ̃] *nf Méd* sunstroke.

insolent [ɛ̃sɔlɑ̃] *a* (*impoli*) insolent; (*luxe*) indecent. ● **insolence** *nf* insolence.

insolite [ɛ̃sɔlit] *a* unusual, strange.

insoluble [ɛ̃sɔlybl] *a* insoluble.

insolvable [ɛ̃sɔlvabl] *a Fin* insolvent.

insomnie [ɛ̃sɔmni] *nf* insomnia; *pl* (periods of) insomnia; **nuit d'i.** sleepless night.

insondable [ɛ̃sɔ̃dabl] *a* unfathomable.

insonoriser [ɛ̃sɔnɔrize] *vt* to soundproof.

insouciant [ɛ̃susjɑ̃] *a* carefree.

insoumis [ɛ̃sumi] *a* rebellious.

insoupçonnable [ɛ̃supsɔnabl] *a* beyond suspicion. ● **insoupçonné** *a* unsuspected.

insoutenable [ɛ̃sutnabl] *a* unbearable; (*théorie*) untenable.

inspecter [ɛ̃spɛkte] *vt* to inspect. ● **inspecteur, -trice** *nmf* inspector. ● **inspection** *nf* inspection.

inspirer [ɛ̃spire] **1** *vt* to inspire; **i. qch à qn** to inspire s.o. with sth; **s'i. de** to take one's inspiration from. **2** *vi Méd* to breathe in. ● **inspiration** *nf* **1** inspiration. **2** *Méd* breathing in.

instable [ɛ̃stabl] *a* (*meuble*) shaky, unsteady; (*temps*) unsettled; (*caractère, situation*) unstable.

installer [ɛ̃stale] *vt* (*appareil, meuble etc*) to install, put in; (*étagère*) to put up; (*équiper*) to fit out, fix up; **i. qn** (*dans une fonction, un logement*) to install s.o.

▮ **s'installer** *vpr* (*s'asseoir, s'établir*) to settle (down); (*médecin etc*) to set oneself up; **s'i. dans** (*maison*) to move into. ● **installation** *nf* putting in; fitting out; moving in; *pl* (*appareils*) fittings, installations; (*bâtiments*) facilities.

instance [ɛ̃stɑ̃s] *nf* **tribunal de première i.** = magistrates' court; **en i. de divorce** waiting for a divorce; **en i. de départ** about to depart.

instant [ɛ̃stɑ̃] *nm* moment, instant; **à l'i.** a moment ago; **pour l'i.** for the moment. ● **instantané** *a* instantaneous; **café i.** instant coffee ▮ *nm* snapshot.

instaurer [ɛ̃stɔre] *vt* to found, set up.

instigateur, -trice [ɛ̃stigatœr, -tris] *nmf* instigator.

instinct [ɛ̃stɛ̃] *nm* instinct; **d'i.** instinctively. ● **instinctif, -ive** *a* instinctive.

instituer [ɛ̃stitɥe] *vt* (*règle, régime*) to establish.

institut [ɛ̃stity] *nm* institute; **i. de beauté** beauty salon; **i. universitaire de technologie** polytechnic, technical college.

instituteur, -trice [ɛ̃stitytœr, -tris] *nmf* primary *ou Am* elementary school teacher.

institution [ɛ̃stitysjɔ̃] *nf* (*organisation etc*) institution; *Scol* private school.

instructif, -ive [ɛ̃stryktif, -iv] *a* instructive.

instruction [ɛ̃stryksjɔ̃] *nf* education, schooling; *Mil* training; *Jur* investigation; *pl* (*ordres*) instructions.

instruire* [ɛ̃strɥir] *vt* to teach, educate; *Mil* to train; *Jur* to investigate ▮ **s'i.** *vpr* to educate oneself. ● **instruit** *a* educated.

instrument [ɛ̃strymɑ̃] *nm* instrument; (*outil*) implement.

insu de (à l') [alɛ̃syd(ə)] *prép* without the knowledge of.

insuffisant [ɛ̃syfizɑ̃] *a* (*en qualité*) inadequate; (*en quantité*) inadequate, insufficient. ● **insuffisance** *nf* inadequacy.

insulaire [ɛ̃sylɛr] *a* insular ▮ *nmf* islander.

insuline [ɛ̃sylin] *nf Méd* insulin.

insulte [ɛ̃sylt] *nf* insult (**à** to). ● **insulter** *vt* to insult.

insupportable [ɛ̃sypɔrtabl] *a* unbearable.

insurger (s') [sɛ̃syrʒe] *vpr* to rise (up), rebel (**contre** against). ● **insurrection** *nf* uprising.

insurmontable [ɛ̃syrmɔ̃tabl] *a* insurmountable, insuperable.

intact [ɛ̃takt] *a* intact.

intangible [ɛ̃tɑ̃ʒibl] *a* intangible.

intarissable [ɛ̃tarisabl] *a* inexhaustible.

intégral, -aux [ɛ̃tegral, -o] *a* full, complete; (*édition*) unabridged. ● **intégralement** *adv* in full, fully. ● **intégralité** *nf* whole (**de** of); **dans son i.** in full.

intègre [ɛ̃tɛgr] *a* upright, honest. ● **intégrité** *nf* integrity.

intégrer [ɛ̃tegre] *vt* to integrate (**dans** in) ▮ **s'i.** *vpr* to become integrated, adapt. ● **intégrante** *af* **faire partie i. de** to be part and parcel of.

intellectuel, -elle [ɛ̃telɛktɥɛl] *a & nmf* intellectual.
intelligent [ɛ̃teliʒɑ̃] *a* intelligent, clever. ● **intelligemment** [-amɑ̃] *adv* intelligently. ● **intelligence** *nf* intelligence.
intelligible [ɛ̃teliʒibl] *a* intelligible.
intempéries [ɛ̃tɑ̃peri] *nfpl* **les i.** bad weather.
intempestif, -ive [ɛ̃tɑ̃pɛstif, -iv] *a* untimely.
intenable [ɛ̃t(ə)nabl] *a* (*position*) untenable; (*enfant*) unruly, uncontrollable.
intendant, -ante [ɛ̃tɑ̃dɑ̃, -ɑ̃t] *nmf Scol* bursar. ● **intendance** *nf Scol* bursar's office.
intense [ɛ̃tɑ̃s] *a* intense; (*trafic*) heavy. ● **intensif, -ive** *a* intensive.
intensifier [ɛ̃tɑ̃sifje] *vt,* **s'i.** *vpr* to intensify.
intensité [ɛ̃tɑ̃site] *nf* intensity.
intenter [ɛ̃tɑ̃te] *vt* **i. un procès à qn** *Jur* to institute proceedings against s.o.
intention [ɛ̃tɑ̃sjɔ̃] *nf* intention; **avoir l'i. de faire** to intend to do; **à l'i. de qn** for s.o. ● **intentionné** *a* **bien i.** well-intentioned.
inter- [ɛ̃tɛr] *préf* inter-.
interactif, -ive [ɛ̃tɛraktif, -iv] *a Ordinat* interactive.
intercalaire [ɛ̃tɛrkalɛr] *a & nm* **(feuille) i.** (*dans un classeur*) divider.
intercaler [ɛ̃tɛrkale] *vt* to insert.
intercepter [ɛ̃tɛrsɛpte] *vt* to intercept.
interchangeable [ɛ̃tɛrʃɑ̃ʒabl] *a* interchangeable.
interclasse [ɛ̃tɛrklɑs] *nm Scol* break (between classes).
intercontinental, -aux [ɛ̃tɛrkɔ̃tinɑ̃tal, -o] *a* intercontinental.
interd/ire* [ɛ̃tɛrdir] *vt* to forbid, not to allow (**qch à qn** s.o. sth); (*film etc*) to ban; **i. à qn de faire** (*médecin, père etc*) not to allow s.o. to do, forbid s.o. to do; (*santé etc*) to prevent s.o. from doing. ● **—it** *a* forbidden, not allowed; **il est i. de** it is forbidden to; **'stationnement i.'** 'no parking'. ● **interdiction** *nf* ban (**de** on); **'i. de fumer'** 'no smoking'.
intéress/er [ɛ̃terese] *vt* to interest; **s'i. à** to take an interest in, be interested in. ● **—ant** *a* (*captivant*) interesting; (*prix etc*) attractive. ● **—é, -ée** *a* (*avide*) self-interested; (*concerné*) concerned.
intérêt [ɛ̃terɛ] *nm* interest; *Péj* self-interest; *pl Fin* interest; **tu as i. à faire** you'd do well to do.
interface [ɛ̃tɛrfas] *nf Ordinat* interface.
intérieur [ɛ̃terjœr] *a* (*cour, paroi*) inner, interior; (*poche*) inside; (*politique, vol*) internal, domestic; (*vie, sentiment*) inner, inward; (*mer*) inland. ‖ *nm* (*de boîte etc*) inside (**de** of); (*de maison*) interior, inside; (*de pays*) interior; **à l'i. (de)** inside; **ministère de l'I.** Home Office, *Am* Department of the Interior. ● **intérieurement** *adv* (*dans le cœur*) inwardly.
intérim [ɛ̃terim] *nm* **assurer l'i.** to deputize (**de** for); **président/***etc* **par i.** acting president/*etc.* ● **intérimaire** *a* temporary.
interligne [ɛ̃tɛrliɲ] *nm Typ* space (between the lines), spacing.
interlocuteur, -trice [ɛ̃tɛrlɔkytœr, -tris] *nmf Pol* negotiator; **mon i.** the person I am, was *etc* speaking to.
interloqué [ɛ̃tɛrlɔke] *a* dumbfounded.
interlude [ɛ̃tɛrlyd] *nm Mus TV* interlude.
intermède [ɛ̃tɛrmɛd] *nm* (*interruption*) & *Th* interlude.
intermédiaire [ɛ̃tɛrmedjɛr] *a* intermediate ‖ *nmf* intermediary; **par l'i. de** through (the medium of).
interminable [ɛ̃tɛrminabl] *a* endless.
intermittence [ɛ̃tɛrmitɑ̃s] *nf* **par i.** intermittently.
international, -aux [ɛ̃tɛrnasjɔnal, -o] *a* international ‖ *nm* (*joueur*) *Sp* international.
interne [ɛ̃tɛrn] **1** *a* (*douleur etc*) internal; (*oreille*) inner. **2** *nmf* (*élève*) boarder; **i. (des hôpitaux)** houseman, *Am* intern. ● **internat** *nm* (*école*) boarding school.
interner [ɛ̃tɛrne] *vt* (*prisonnier*) to intern; (*aliéné*) to confine.
interpeller [ɛ̃tɛrpele] *vt* (*appeler*) to shout at *ou* to; (*dans une réunion*) to question; (*police*) *Jur* to take in for questioning.
interphone [ɛ̃tɛrfɔn] *nm* intercom.
interplanétaire [ɛ̃tɛrplanetɛr] *a* interplanetary.
interposer (s') [sɛ̃tɛrpoze] *vpr* (*dans une dispute etc*) to intervene (**dans** in).
interprète [ɛ̃tɛrprɛt] *nmf Ling* interpreter; (*chanteur*) singer; *Th Mus* performer. ● **interpréter** *vt* (*expliquer*) to interpret; (*chanter*) to sing; (*jouer*) *Th* to play, perform; (*exécuter*) *Mus* to perform.
interroger [ɛ̃terɔʒe] *vt* to question. ● **interrogatif, -ive** *a & nm Gram* interrogative. ● **interrogation** *nf* question; (*action*) questioning; (*épreuve*) *Scol* test. ● **interrogatoire** *nm Jur* interrogation.
interrompre* [ɛ̃terɔ̃pr] *vt* to interrupt, break off; **i. qn** to interrupt s.o. ‖ **s'i.** *vpr* (*personne*) to break off, stop. ● **interrupteur** *nm* (*électrique*) switch. ● **interruption** *nf* interruption; (*des hostilités, du courant*) break (**de** in).

intersection [ɛ̃tɛrsɛksjɔ̃] *nf* intersection.
interstice [ɛ̃tɛrstis] *nm* crack, chink.
interurbain [ɛ̃tɛryrbɛ̃] *a* & *nm* **(téléphone) i.** long-distance telephone service.
intervalle [ɛ̃tɛrval] *nm* (*écart*) gap, space; (*temps*) interval; **dans l'i.** (*entretemps*) in the meantime.
intervenir* [ɛ̃tɛrvənir] *vi* (*s'interposer, agir*) to intervene; (*survenir*) to occur; **être intervenu** (*accord*) to be reached. ● **intervention** *nf* intervention; **i. (chirurgicale)** operation.
intervertir [ɛ̃tɛrvɛrtir] *vt* to invert.
interview [ɛ̃tɛrvju] *nf* (*d'un journaliste etc*) interview. ● **interviewer** [-vjuve] *vt* to interview.
intestin [ɛ̃tɛstɛ̃] *nm* bowel. ● **intestinal, -aux** *a* intestinal; **grippe intestinale** gastric flu.
intime [ɛ̃tim] *a* intimate; (*ami*) close; (*vie, journal, mariage*) private ‖ *nmf* close friend. ● **intimité** *nf* intimacy; privacy; **dans l'i.** (*mariage etc*) in private.
intimider [ɛ̃timide] *vt* to intimidate, frighten.
intituler [ɛ̃tityle] *vt* to entitle ‖ **s'i.** *vpr* to be entitled.
intolérable [ɛ̃tɔlerabl] *a* intolerable (**que** (+ *sub*) that). ● **intolérance** *nf* intolerance.
intonation [ɛ̃tɔnɑsjɔ̃] *nf Ling* intonation; (*ton*) tone.
intoxiquer [ɛ̃tɔksike] *vt* (*empoisonner*) to poison; *Psy Pol* to brainwash ‖ **s'i.** *vpr* to be *ou* become poisoned. ● **intoxication** *nf* poisoning; *Psy Pol* brainwashing; **i. alimentaire** food poisoning.
intraduisible [ɛ̃tradɥizibl] *a* difficult to translate.
intraitable [ɛ̃trɛtabl] *a* uncompromising.
intransigeant [ɛ̃trɑ̃ziʒɑ̃] *a* intransigent.
intransitif, -ive [ɛ̃trɑ̃zitif, -iv] *a* & *nm Gram* intransitive.
intraveineux, -euse [ɛ̃travɛnø, -øz] *a Méd* intravenous.
intrépide [ɛ̃trepid] *a* (*courageux*) fearless, intrepid.
intrigue [ɛ̃trig] *nf* intrigue; (*de film, roman etc*) plot. ● **intriguer 1** *vi* to scheme, intrigue. **2** *vt* **i. qn** (*intéresser*) to intrigue s.o.
intrinsèque [ɛ̃trɛ̃sɛk] *a* intrinsic.
introduire* [ɛ̃trɔdɥir] *vt* (*présenter*) to introduce, bring in; (*insérer*) to put in (**dans** to), insert (**dans** into); (*faire entrer*) to show (*s.o.*) in; **s'i. dans** to get into. ● **introduction** *nf* (*texte, action*) introduction.
introuvable [ɛ̃truvabl] *a* nowhere to be found.
introverti, -ie [ɛ̃trɔvɛrti] *nmf* introvert.
intrus, -use [ɛ̃try, -yz] *nmf* intruder. ● **intrusion** *nf* intrusion (**dans** into).
intuition [ɛ̃tɥisjɔ̃] *nf* intuition.
inusable [inyzabl] *a Fam* hard-wearing, durable.
inusité [inyzite] *a Gram* unused.
inutile [inytil] *a* useless, unnecessary. ● **—ment** *adv* (*vainement*) needlessly.
inutilisable [inytilizabl] *a* unusable.
invaincu [ɛ̃vɛ̃ky] *a Sp* unbeaten.
invalide [ɛ̃valid] *a* & *nmf* disabled (person); **i. de guerre** disabled ex-soldier.
invalider [ɛ̃valide] *vt* to invalidate.
invariable [ɛ̃varjabl] *a* invariable.
invasion [ɛ̃vɑsjɔ̃] *nf* invasion.
invective [ɛ̃vɛktiv] *nf* invective.
invendable [ɛ̃vɑ̃dabl] *a* unsaleable. ● **invendu** *a* unsold.
inventaire [ɛ̃vɑ̃tɛr] *nm* (*liste*) *Com* inventory; **faire l'i.** *Com* to do the stocktaking.
inventer [ɛ̃vɑ̃te] *vt* (*créer*) to invent; (*imaginer*) to make up. ● **inventeur, -trice** *nmf* inventor. ● **inventif, -ive** *a* inventive. ● **invention** *nf* invention.
inverse [ɛ̃vɛrs] *a* (*sens*) opposite; (*ordre*) reverse; *Math* inverse ‖ *nm* **l'i.** the reverse, the opposite. ● **inversement** *adv* conversely. ● **inverser** *vt* (*ordre*) to reverse. ● **inversion** *nf Gram etc* inversion.
investigation [ɛ̃vɛstigɑsjɔ̃] *nf* investigation.
invest/ir [ɛ̃vɛstir] **1** *vti Com* to invest (**dans** in). **2** *vt* **i. qn de** (*fonction etc*) to invest s.o. with. ● **—issement** *nm Com* investment. ● **investiture** *nf Pol* nomination.
invétéré [ɛ̃vetere] *a* inveterate.
invincible [ɛ̃vɛ̃sibl] *a* invincible.
invisible [ɛ̃vizibl] *a* invisible.
invit/er [ɛ̃vite] *vt* to invite; **i. qn à faire** to invite *ou* ask s.o. to do; (*inciter*) to tempt s.o. to do; **s'i. (chez qn)** to gatecrash. ● **—é, -ée** *nmf* guest. ● **invitation** *nf* invitation.
invivable [ɛ̃vivabl] *a* unbearable.
involontaire [ɛ̃vɔlɔ̃tɛr] *a* (*geste etc*) unintentional.
invoquer [ɛ̃vɔke] *vt* (*argument etc*) to put forward; (*appeler*) to call upon.
invraisemblable [ɛ̃vrɛsɑ̃blabl] *a* incredible; (*improbable*) improbable.
invulnérable [ɛ̃vylnerabl] *a* invulnerable.
iode [jɔd] *nm* **teinture d'i.** (*antiseptique*) iodine.
ira, irai(t) [ira, irɛ] *voir* **aller**[1].
Irak [irak] *nm* Iraq. ● **irakien, -ienne** *a* & *nmf* Iraqi.
Iran [irɑ̃] *nm* Iran. ● **iranien, -ienne** *a* & *nmf* Iranian.

iris [iris] *nm Anat Bot* iris.
Irlande [irlɑ̃d] *nf* Ireland. ● **irlandais, -aise** *a* Irish ‖ *nmf* Irishman, Irishwoman; **les I.** the Irish ‖ *nm* (*langue*) Irish.
ironie [irɔni] *nf* irony. ● **ironique** *a* ironic(al).
iront [irɔ̃] *voir* **aller**[1].
irradier [iradje] *vt* to irradiate.
irraisonné [irɛzɔne] *a* irrational.
irréconciliable [irekɔ̃siljabl] *a* irreconcilable.
irréel, -elle [ireɛl] *a* unreal.
irréfléchi [irefleʃi] *a* thoughtless.
irréfutable [irefytabl] *a* irrefutable.
irrégulier, -ière [iregylje, -jɛr] *a* irregular.
irrémédiable [iremedjabl] *a* irreparable.
irremplaçable [irɑ̃plasabl] *a* irreplaceable.
irréparable [ireparabl] *a* (*véhicule etc*) beyond repair; (*tort, perte*) irreparable.
irrépressible [irepresibl] *a* (*rires etc*) irrepressible.
irréprochable [ireprɔʃabl] *a* beyond reproach, irreproachable.
irrésistible [irezistibl] *a* (*personne, charme etc*) irresistible.
irrespirable [irɛspirabl] *a* unbreathable.
irresponsable [irɛspɔ̃sabl] *a* (*personne*) irresponsible.
irréversible [ireversibl] *a* irreversible.
irrévocable [irevɔkabl] *a* irrevocable.
irriguer [irige] *vt* to irrigate. ● **irrigation** *nf* irrigation.
irrit/er [irite] *vt* to irritate. ● **—ant** *a* irritating. ● **irritable** *a* irritable. ● **irritation** *nf* (*colère*) & *Méd* irritation.
irruption [irypsjɔ̃] *nf* **faire i. dans** to burst into.
islam [islam] *nm* Islam. ● **islamique** *a* Islamic.
Islande [islɑ̃d] *nf* Iceland. ● **islandais, -aise** *a* Icelandic.
isoler [izɔle] *vt* to isolate (**de** from); (*du froid etc*) & *Él* to insulate ‖ **s'i.** *vpr* to cut oneself off, isolate oneself. ● **isolant** *nm* insulation (material). ● **isolé** *a* isolated; **i. de** cut off *ou* isolated from. ● **isolation** *nf* insulation. ● **isolement** *nm* isolation.
isoloir [izɔlwar] *nm* polling booth.
Israël [israɛl] *nm* Israel. ● **israélien, -ienne** *a* & *nmf* Israeli. ● **israélite** *a* Jewish.
issu [isy] *a* **être i. de** to come from.
issue [isy] *nf* (*sortie*) way out, exit; (*solution*) way out; (*résultat*) outcome; **rue** *etc* **sans i.** dead end; **situation** *etc* **sans i.** *Fig* dead end; **à l'i. de** at the close of.
isthme [ism] *nm Géog* isthmus.
Italie [itali] *nf* Italy. ● **italien, -ienne** *a* & *nmf* Italian ‖ *nm* (*langue*) Italian.
italique [italik] *a Typ* italic ‖ *nm* italics.
itinéraire [itinerɛr] *nm* route, itinerary.
IUT [iyte] *nm abrév* **institut universitaire de technologie.**
IVG [iveʒe] *nf abrév* (*interruption volontaire de grossesse*) (voluntary) abortion.
ivoire [ivwar] *nm* ivory; **statuette**/*etc* **en i.** *ou* **d'i.** ivory statuette/*etc*.
ivre [ivr] *a* drunk (**de** with). ● **ivresse** *nf* drunkenness; **en état d'i.** under the influence of drink. ● **ivrogne** *nmf* drunk(ard).

J

J, j [ʒi] *nm* J, j; **le jour J.** D-day.
j' [ʒ] *voir* **je.**
jachère (en) [ɑ̃ʒaʃɛr] *adv* (*champ*) fallow; **être en j.** to lie fallow.
jacinthe [ʒasɛ̃t] *nf* hyacinth.
jacuzzi [ʒakuzi] *nm* (*baignoire*) jacuzzi.
jadis [ʒadis] *adv* long ago, once.
jaguar [ʒagwar] *nm* (*animal*) jaguar.
jaillir [ʒajir] *vi* (*liquide*) to spurt (out), gush (out); (*lumière*) to beam out, shine (forth); (*cri*) to burst out.
jais [ʒɛ] *nm* **(noir) de j.** jet-black.
jalon [ʒalɔ̃] *nm* (*piquet*) marker. ●**jalonner** *vt* to mark (out); (*border*) to line.
jaloux, -ouse [ʒalu, -uz] *a* jealous (**de** of). ●**jalousie** *nf* jealousy.
Jamaïque [ʒamaik] *nf* Jamaica.
jamais [ʒamɛ] *adv* **1** (*négatif*) never; **sans j. sortir** without ever going out; **elle ne sort j.** she never goes out; **j. de la vie** (absolutely) never! **2** (*positif*) ever; **à (tout) j.** for ever; **si j.** if ever.
🛈**G204** Negative Expressions 12 B
jambe [ʒɑ̃b] *nf* leg; **prendre ses jambes à son cou** to take to one's heels.
jambon [ʒɑ̃bɔ̃] *nm Culin* ham.
jante [ʒɑ̃t] *nf* (*de roue*) rim.
janvier [ʒɑ̃vje] *nm* January.
Japon [ʒapɔ̃] *nm* Japan. ●**japonais, -aise** *a* Japanese ‖ *nmf* Japanese man *ou* woman, Japanese *inv*; **les J.** the Japanese ‖ *nm* (*langue*) Japanese.
japper [ʒape] *vi* (*chien etc*) to yap, yelp.
jaquette [ʒakɛt] *nf* (*d'homme*) tailcoat, morning coat; (*de femme*, *livre*) jacket.
jardin [ʒardɛ̃] *nm* garden; **j. d'enfants** kindergarten, playschool; **j. public** park; (*plus petit*) gardens. ●**jardinage** *nm* gardening. ●**jardinerie** *nf* garden centre. ●**jardinier** *nm* gardener. ●**jardinière** *nf* (*personne*) gardener; (*caisse à fleurs*) window box; **j. (de légumes)** mixed vegetable dish; **j. d'enfants** kindergarten teacher.
jargon [ʒargɔ̃] *nm* jargon.
jarretelle [ʒartɛl] *nf* (*de gaine*) suspender, *Am* garter. ●**jarretière** *nf* (*autour de la jambe*) garter.
jaser [ʒaze] *vi* (*bavarder*) to jabber.
jatte [ʒat] *nf* (*bol*) bowl.
jaune [ʒon] *a* yellow ‖ *nm* (*couleur*) yellow; **j. d'œuf** (egg) yolk. ●**jaunâtre** *a* yellowish. ●**jaunir** *vti* to turn yellow. ●**jaunisse** *nf Méd* jaundice.
Javel (eau de) [odʒavɛl] *nf* bleach.
javelot [ʒavlo] *nm* javelin.
jazz [dʒaz] *nm* jazz.
je [ʒ(ə)] *pron* (**j'** *before vowel or mute h*) I; **je suis** I am.
🛈**G56** Subject Pronouns 6 D 1a)
jean [dʒin] *nm* (pair of) jeans.
jeep® [dʒip] *nf* jeep®.
jerrycan [(d)ʒerikan] *nm* petrol *ou Am* gasoline can; (*pour l'eau*) water can.
jersey [ʒɛrzɛ] *nm* (*tissu*) jersey.
Jersey [ʒɛrzɛ] *nf* Jersey.
Jésus [ʒezy] *nm* Jesus.
jet [ʒɛ] *nm* throw; (*de vapeur*) burst; (*de lumière*) flash; (*de tuyau d'arrosage*) nozzle; **j. d'eau** fountain; **premier j.** (*ébauche*) first draft.
jetable [ʒ(ə)tabl] *a* (*rasoir etc*) disposable.
jetée [ʒ(ə)te] *nf* pier, jetty.
jeter [ʒ(ə)te] *vt* to throw (**à** to, **dans** into); (*à la poubelle*) to throw away; (*ancre*, *sort*) to cast; (*cri*) to let out; (*éclat*) to throw out; **j. un coup d'œil sur** *ou* **à** to have *ou* take a look at; (*rapidement*) to glance at.
‖ **se jeter** *vpr* to throw oneself; **se j. sur** to pounce on; **se j. contre** (*véhicule*) to crash into; **se j. dans** (*fleuve*) to flow into.
jeton [ʒ(ə)tɔ̃] *nm* (*pièce*) token; (*au jeu*) chip.
jeu, -x [ʒø] *nm* **1** game; (*amusement*) play; (*d'argent*) gambling; *Th* acting; *Mus* playing; **j. de mots** play on words; **jeux de société** parlour *ou* indoor games; **j. télévisé** television quiz; **en j.** (*en cause*) at stake; (*forces*) at work; **entrer en j.** to come into play.
2 (*série complète*) set; (*de cartes*) pack, deck, *Am* deck; (*cartes en main*) hand; **j. d'échecs** (*boîte*, *pièces*) chess set.
jeudi [ʒødi] *nm* Thursday.
jeun (à) [aʒœ̃] *adv* on an empty stomach; **être à j.** to have eaten no food.
jeune [ʒœn] *a* young; (*inexpérimenté*) inexperienced; **jeunes gens** young people ‖ *nmf* young person; **les jeunes** young people. ●**jeunesse** *nf* youth; (*apparence*) youthfulness; **la j.** (*jeunes*) the young.
jeûne [ʒøn] *nm* fast; (*action*) fasting. ●**jeûner** *vi* to fast.

joaillier, -ière [ʒɔɑje, -jɛr] *nmf* jeweller, *Am* jeweler. ●**joaillerie** *nf* (*magasin*) jewellery *ou Am* jewelry shop.
jockey [ʒɔkɛ] *nm* jockey.
jogging [dʒɔgiŋ] *nm Sp* jogging; (*vêtement*) jogging suit; **faire du j.** to jog.
joie [ʒwa] *nf* joy, delight; **feu de j.** bonfire.
joindre* [ʒwɛ̃dr] *vt* (*mettre ensemble, relier*) to join; (*efforts*) to combine; (*insérer dans une enveloppe*) to enclose (**à** with); **j. qn** (*contacter*) to get in touch with s.o.; **j. les deux bouts** *Fam* to make ends meet; **se j. à** (*un groupe etc*) to join. ●**joint** *a* (*efforts*) joint; **à pieds joints** with feet together ‖ *nm Tech* joint; (*de robinet*) washer.
joker [ʒɔkɛr] *nm Cartes* joker.
joli [ʒɔli] *a* nice, lovely; (*femme, enfant*) pretty.
jonc [ʒɔ̃] *nm Bot* rush.
joncher [ʒɔ̃ʃe] *vt* **jonché de** strewn *ou* littered with.
jonction [ʒɔ̃ksjɔ̃] *nf* (*de routes etc*) junction.
jongl/er [ʒɔ̃gle] *vi* to juggle (**avec** with). ●**—eur, -euse** *nmf* juggler.
jonquille [ʒɔ̃kij] *nf* daffodil.
Jordanie [ʒɔrdani] *nf* Jordan.
joue [ʒu] *nf Anat* cheek.
jouer [ʒwe] *vi* to play; (*acteur*) to act; (*au tiercé etc*) to gamble, bet; (*être important*) to count; **j. au tennis/aux cartes/***etc* to play tennis/cards/*etc*; **j. du piano/***etc* to play the piano/*etc*; **j. aux courses** to bet on the horses; **j. des coudes** to use one's elbows; **à toi de j.!** it's your turn (to play). ‖ *vt* (*musique, tour, jeu, rôle*) to play; (*pièce, film*) to put on; (*risquer*) to bet, gamble (**sur** on); **se j. de** (*se moquer*) to scoff at; (*difficultés*) to make light of.
jouet [ʒwɛ] *nm* toy.
joueur, -euse [ʒwœr, -øz] *nmf* player; (*au tiercé etc*) gambler; **beau j.** good loser.
joufflu [ʒufly] *a* (*visage*) chubby; (*enfant*) chubby-cheeked.
joug [ʒu] *nm Agr & Fig* yoke.
jouir [ʒwir] *vi* **j. de** (*savourer, avoir*) to enjoy. ●**jouissance** *nf* enjoyment; (*usage*) *Jur* use.
joujou, -x [ʒuʒu] *nm Fam* toy.
jour [ʒur] *nm* day; (*lumière*) (day)light; (*ouverture*) gap, opening; (*aspect*) *Fig* light; **il fait j.** it's light; **en plein j.** in broad daylight; **de nos jours** nowadays; **du j. au lendemain** overnight; **au j. le j.** from day to day; **le j. de l'An** New Year's Day; **les beaux jours** (*l'été*) summer; **mettre à j.** to bring up to date; **donner le j. à** to give birth to; **quel j. sommes-nous?** what day is it?
journal, -aux [ʒurnal, -o] *nm* (news)paper; (*spécialisé*) journal; (*intime*) diary; **j. (parlé)** *Rad* news bulletin. ●**journalisme** *nm* journalism. ●**journaliste** *nmf* journalist.
journalier, -ière [ʒurnalje, -jɛr] *a* daily.
journée [ʒurne] *nf* day; **pendant la j.** during the day(time); **toute la j.** all day (long). ⓘ**G200** Dates 11 B 3
jovial, -aux [ʒɔvjal, -o] *a* jovial, jolly. ●**jovialité** *nf* jollity.
joyau, -aux [ʒwajo] *nm* jewel.
joyeux, -euse [ʒwajø, -øz] *a* merry, happy; **j. anniversaire!** happy birthday!; **j. Noël!** merry *ou* happy Christmas!
jubiler [ʒybile] *vi* to be jubilant.
jucher (se) [səʒyʃe] *vpr* to perch (**sur** on).
judas [ʒyda] *nm* (*de porte*) peephole.
judiciaire [ʒydisjɛr] *a* judicial, legal.
judicieux, -euse [ʒydisjø, -øz] *a* sensible, judicious.
judo [ʒydo] *nm* judo.
juge [ʒyʒ] *nm* judge; **j. d'instruction** examining magistrate; **j. de touche** *Fb* linesman.
jugé (au) [oʒyʒe] *adv* by guesswork.
jugement [ʒyʒmɑ̃] *nm* judg(e)ment; (*verdict*) *Jur* sentence; **passer en j.** *Jur* to stand trial.
juger [ʒyʒe] *vt* to judge; (*au tribunal*) to try (*s.o.*); (*estimer*) to consider (**que** that); **j. utile/***etc* **de faire** to consider it useful/*etc* to do.
juguler [ʒygyle] *vt* to check, suppress.
juif, juive [ʒɥif, ʒɥiv] *a* Jewish ‖ *nmf* Jew.
juillet [ʒɥijɛ] *nm* July.
juin [ʒɥɛ̃] *nm* June.
jumeau, -elle, *pl* **-eaux, -elles** [ʒymo, -ɛl] *a* twin; **frère j.** twin brother; **sœur jumelle** twin sister; **lits jumeaux** twin beds ‖ *nmf* twin. ●**jumeler** *vt* (*villes*) to twin. ●**jumelage** *nm* twinning.
jumelles [ʒymɛl] *nfpl* (*pour regarder*) binoculars; **j. de théâtre** opera glasses.
jument [ʒymɑ̃] *nf* mare.
jungle [ʒœ̃gl] *nf* jungle.
junior [ʒynjɔr] *nm & a inv Sp* junior.
junte [ʒœ̃t] *nf Pol* junta.
jupe [ʒyp] *nf* skirt. ●**jupon** *nm* petticoat.
jurer [ʒyre] **1** *vi* (*dire un gros mot*) to swear (**contre** at). **2** *vt* (*promettre*) to swear (**que** that, **de faire** to do); **j. de qch** to swear to sth. **3** *vi* (*contraster*) to clash (**avec** with). ●**juré** *a* (*ennemi*) sworn ‖ *nm Jur* juror.
juridiction [ʒyridiksjɔ̃] *nf* jurisdiction.
juridique [ʒyridik] *a* legal. ●**juriste** *nmf* legal expert.
juron [ʒyrɔ̃] *nm* swearword.
jury [ʒyri] *nm Jur* jury; (*examinateurs*) board (of examiners).

jus [ʒy] *nm* juice; (*de viande*) gravy; **j. d'orange** orange juice.

jusque [ʒysk] *prép* **jusqu'à** (*espace*) as far as, (right) up to; (*temps*) until, (up) till, to; (*même*) even; **jusqu'à dix francs**/*etc* (*limite*) up to ten francs/*etc*; **jusqu'en mai**/*etc* until May/*etc*; **jusqu'où?** how far?; **jusqu'ici** as far as this; (*temps*) up till now; **jusqu'à présent** up till now; **j. dans/sous**/*etc* right into/under/*etc*; **j. chez moi** as far as my place; **en avoir j.-là** *Fam* to be fed up. ▮ *conj* **jusqu'à ce qu'il vienne** until he comes.

juste [ʒyst] *a* (*équitable*) fair, just; (*légitime*) just; (*exact*) right, correct; (*étroit*) tight; (*remarque*) sound; **un peu j.** (*quantité*, *qualité*) barely enough; **très j.!** quite right! ▮ *adv* (*deviner*, *compter*) correctly, right, accurately; (*chanter*) in tune; (*seulement*, *exactement*) just; **au j.** exactly; **tout j.** (*à peine*, *seulement*) only just; **un peu j.** (*mesurer*, *compter*) a bit on the short side; **à 3 heures j.** on the stroke of 3. ● **justement** *adv* exactly, precisely, just; (*avec justesse ou justice*) justly.

justesse [ʒystɛs] *nf* (*exactitude*) accuracy; **de j.** (*éviter*, *gagner etc*) just.

justice [ʒystis] *nf* justice; (*autorités*) law; **en toute j.** in all fairness; **rendre j. à qn** to do justice to s.o.

justifier [ʒystifje] *vt* to justify; **j. de qch** to prove sth ▮ **se j.** *vpr Jur* to clear oneself (**de** of); (*attitude etc*) to be justified. ● **justificatif, -ive** *a* **document j.** supporting document, proof. ● **justification** *nf* justification; (*preuve*) proof.

juteux, -euse [ʒytø, -øz] *a* juicy.

juvénile [ʒyvenil] *a* youthful.

juxtaposer [ʒykstapoze] *vt* to juxtapose.

K

K, k [kɑ] *nm* K, k.
kaki [kaki] *a inv* khaki.
kaléidoscope [kaleidɔskɔp] *nm* kaleidoscope.
kangourou [kɑ̃guru] *nm* **1** (*animal*) kangaroo. **2**® (*porte-bébé*) baby sling.
karaté [karate] *nm Sp* karate.
kascher [kaʃɛr] *a inv Rel* kosher.
kayak [kajak] *nm* (*bateau*) *Sp* canoe.
képi [kepi] *nm* (*coiffure*) *Mil* cap, kepi.
kermesse [kɛrmɛs] *nf* charity fête; (*en Belgique etc*) village fair.
kidnapper [kidnape] *vt* to kidnap.
kilo [kilo] *nm* kilo. ●**kilogramme** *nm* kilo(gram).
kilomètre [kilɔmɛtr] *nm* kilometre. ●**kilométrage** *nm Aut* = mileage. ●**kilométrique** *a* **borne k.** = milestone.
kilowatt [kilɔwat] *nm* kilowatt.
kinésithérapie [kineziterapi] *nf* physiotherapy. ●**kinésithérapeute** *nmf* physiotherapist.
kiosque [kjɔsk] *nm* (*à journaux*) kiosk, stall; **k. à musique** bandstand.
kit [kit] *nm* (self-assembly) kit; **meuble en k.** self-assembly (furniture) unit.
klaxon® [klaksɔn] *nm Aut* horn, hooter. ●**klaxonner** *vi* to hoot, *Am* honk.
km *abrév* (*kilomètre*) km.
k.-o. [kɑo] *a inv* **mettre k.-o.** to knock out.
Koweït [kɔwɛjt] *nm* Kuwait.
kyste [kist] *nm Méd* cyst.

L

L, l [ɛl] *nm* L, l.

l', la [l, la] *voir* **le.**

la [la] *nm* (*note de musique*) A.

là [la] **1** *adv* (*lieu*) there; (*chez soi*) in, home; **je reste là** I'll stay here; **c'est là que** that's where; **là où il est** where he is; **à cinq mètres de là** five metres away; **de là son échec** (*cause*) hence his *ou* her failure; **jusque-là** (*lieu*) as far as that; **passe par là** go that way.
2 *adv* (*temps*) then; **jusque-là** up till then.
3 *int* **oh là là!** oh dear!; **alors là!** well!
4 *voir* **ce², celui.**

là-bas [labɑ] *adv* over there.

label [labɛl] *nm Com* label, mark (*of quality, origin etc*).

labo [labo] *nm Fam* lab. • **laboratoire** *nm* laboratory; **l. de langues** language laboratory.

laborieux, -euse [labɔrjø, -øz] *a* (*pénible*) laborious; (*personne*) industrious; **les classes laborieuses** the working classes.

labour [labur] *nm* ploughing, *Am* plowing. • **labourer** *vt* (*avec charrue*) to plough, *Am* plow; (*visage etc*) *Fig* to furrow.

labyrinthe [labirɛ̃t] *nm* maze, labyrinth.

lac [lak] *nm* lake.

lacer [lase] *vt* to lace (up). • **lacet** *nm* **1** (shoe- *ou* boot-)lace. **2** (*de route*) twist, zigzag; **route en l.** winding *ou* zigzag road.

lâche [lɑʃ] **1** *a* cowardly ‖ *nmf* coward. **2** *a* (*détendu*) loose, slack. • **lâcheté** *nf* cowardice; **une l.** (*action*) a cowardly act.

lâcher [lɑʃe] *vt* (*main etc*) to let go of; (*bombe*) to drop; (*place, études*) to give up; (*juron*) to utter; **l. qn** (*laisser tranquille*) *Fam* to leave s.o. (alone); (*abandonner*) *Fam* to drop s.o.; **l. prise** to let go ‖ *vi* (*corde*) to give way.

lacrymogène [lakrimɔʒɛn] *a* **gaz l.** tear gas.

lacté [lakte] *a* **régime l.** milk diet; **la Voie lactée** the Milky Way.

lacune [lakyn] *nf* gap, deficiency.

là-dedans [lad(ə)dɑ̃] *adv* (*lieu*) in there, inside. • **là-dessous** *adv* underneath. • **là-dessus** *adv* on there; (*monter*) on top; (*alors*) thereupon. • **là-haut** *adv* up there; (*à l'étage*) upstairs.

lagon [lagɔ̃] *nm* (small) lagoon. • **lagune** *nf* lagoon.

laid [lɛ] *a* ugly; (*ignoble*) wretched. • **laideur** *nf* ugliness.

laine [lɛn] *nf* wool; **de l., en l.** woollen, *Am* woolen. • **lainage** *nm* (*vêtement*) woolly, woollen garment; (*étoffe*) woollen material; *pl* (*vêtements*) woollens.

laïque [laik] *a* (*école*) non-denominational; (*vie*) secular; (*tribunal*) lay.

laisse [lɛs] *nf* lead, leash; **en l.** on a lead *ou* leash.

laisser [lese] *vt* to leave; **l. qn partir/entrer/etc** (*permettre*) to let s.o. go/come in/*etc*; **l. qch à qn** to let s.o. have sth, leave sth with s.o.; **laissez-moi le temps de le faire** give me *ou* leave me time to do it; **l. qn seul** to leave s.o. (all) alone; **je vous laisse** I'm leaving now; **se l. aller/faire** to let oneself go/be pushed around; **se l. surprendre par l'orage** to get caught out by the storm. • **laisser-aller** *nm inv* carelessness. • **laissez-passer** *nm inv* (*sauf-conduit*) pass.

lait [lɛ] *nm* milk; **dent de l.** milk tooth. • **laitage** *nm* milk product. • **laiterie** *nf* dairy. • **laitier, -ière** *a* **produit l.** dairy product ‖ *nm* (*livreur*) milkman; (*vendeur*) dairyman ‖ *nf* dairywoman.

laiton [lɛtɔ̃] *nm* brass.

laitue [lety] *nf* lettuce.

lama [lama] *nm* (*animal*) llama.

lambeau, -x [lɑ̃bo] *nm* shred, bit; **mettre en lambeaux** to tear to shreds; **tomber en lambeaux** to fall to bits.

lambiner [lɑ̃bine] *vi Fam* to dawdle.

lambris [lɑ̃bri] *nm* panelling.

lame [lam] *nf* **1** (*de couteau etc*) blade; (*de métal*) strip; **l. de parquet** floorboard. **2** (*vague*) wave; **l. de fond** ground swell.

lamelle [lamɛl] *nf* thin strip.

lamenter (se) [səlamɑ̃te] *vpr* to moan, lament; **se l. sur** to lament (over). • **lamentable** *a* (*mauvais*) terrible; (*voix, cri*) mournful.

lampadaire [lɑ̃padɛr] *nm* standard lamp; (*de rue*) street lamp.

lampe [lɑ̃p] *nf* lamp; (*au néon*) light; **l. de poche** torch, *Am* flashlight.

lampion [lɑ̃pjɔ̃] *nm* Chinese lantern.

lance [lɑ̃s] *nf* spear; (*de tournoi*) *Hist* lance; (*extrémité de tuyau*) nozzle; **l. d'incendie** fire hose.

lance-pierres [lɑ̃spjɛr] *nm inv* catapult.

lancer [lɑ̃se] *vt* (*jeter*) to throw (**à** to); (*avec* *force*) to hurl; (*fusée, produit, mode, navire etc*) to launch; (*appel, ultimatum etc*) to issue; (*cri*) to utter; (*bombe*) to drop; (*regard*) to cast (**à** at) ‖ **se l.** *vpr* (*se précipiter*) to rush; **se l. dans** (*aventure, discussion*) to launch into ‖ *nm* **un l.** a throw; **le l. de** the throwing of. • **lancement** *nm* (*de fusée, navire etc*) launch(ing).

lancinant [lɑ̃sinɑ̃] *a* (*douleur*) shooting; (*obsédant*) haunting.

landau [lɑ̃do] *nm* (*pl* **-s**) pram, *Am* baby carriage.

lande [lɑ̃d] *nf* moor, heath.

langage [lɑ̃gaʒ] *nm* (*système, faculté d'expression*) language; **l. machine** computer language.

lange [lɑ̃ʒ] *nm* (baby) blanket. • **langer** *vt* (*bébé*) to change.

langouste [lɑ̃gust] *nf* (spiny) lobster. • **langoustine** *nf* (Dublin Bay) prawn.

langue [lɑ̃g] *nf* tongue; *Ling* language; **l. maternelle** mother tongue; **langues vivantes** modern languages; **de l. anglaise/française** English-/French-speaking; **mauvaise l.** (*personne*) gossip. • **languette** *nf* (*patte*) tongue.

lanière [lanjɛr] *nf* (*de cuir*) strap.

lanterne [lɑ̃tɛrn] *nf* lantern; (*électrique*) lamp; *pl Aut* sidelights, parking lights.

lapalissade [lapalisad] *nf* statement of the obvious, truism.

laper [lape] *vt* (*boire*) to lap up ‖ *vi* to lap.

lapin [lapɛ̃] *nm* rabbit; **mon (petit) l.!** my dear!; **poser un l. à qn** *Fam* to stand s.o. up.

laps [laps] *nm* **un l. de temps** a lapse of time.

lapsus [lapsys] *nm* slip (of the tongue).

laque [lak] *nf* lacquer; **l. à cheveux** (hair) lacquer.

laquelle [lakɛl] *voir* **lequel.**

larbin [larbɛ̃] *nm Fam* & *Péj* flunkey.

lard [lar] *nm* (*fumé*) bacon; (*gras*) (pig's) fat. • **lardon** *nm Culin* strip of bacon *ou* fat.

large [larʒ] *a* wide, broad; (*vêtement*) loose; (*idées, esprit*) broad; (*grand*) large; **l. de six mètres** six metres wide; **l. d'esprit** broad-minded.

G32 Position of Adjectives 4 D 3

‖ *adv* (*calculer*) liberally.

‖ *nm* breadth, width; **avoir six mètres de l.** to be six metres wide; **le l.** (*mer*) the open sea; **au l. de Cherbourg** *Nau* off Cherbourg; **être au l. dans** (*vêtement*) to have lots of room in. • **largement** *adv* widely; (*ouvrir*) wide; (*au moins*) easily; (*servir, payer*) liberally; **avoir l. le temps** to have plenty of time. • **largeur** *nf* width, breadth; (*d'esprit*) breadth.

larguer [large] *vt* (*bombe etc*) to drop; **l. les amarres** *Nau* to cast off.

larme [larm] *nf* tear; (*goutte*) *Fam* drop; **en larmes** in tears; **rire aux larmes** to laugh till one cries.

larve [larv] *nf* (*d'insecte*) larva, grub.

larvé [larve] *a* latent, underlying.

laryngite [larɛ̃ʒit] *nf Méd* laryngitis.

las, lasse [lɑ, lɑs] *a* tired, weary (**de** of). • **lasser** *vt* to tire, weary; **se l. de** to tire of.

laser [lazɛr] *nm* laser; **rayon l.** laser beam.

lasso [laso] *nm* lasso; **prendre au l.** to lasso.

latent [latɑ̃] *a* latent.

latéral, -aux [lateral, -o] *a* lateral; **rue latérale** side street.

latin, -ine [latɛ̃, -in] *a* & *nmf* Latin ‖ *nm* (*langue*) Latin.

latitude [latityd] *nf Géog* & *Fig* latitude.

latte [lat] *nf* slat, lath; (*de plancher*) board.

lauréat, -ate [lɔrea, -at] *nmf* (prize)winner.

laurier [lɔrje] *nm Bot* laurel, bay; **du l.** *Culin* bay leaves.

lavabo [lavabo] *nm* washbasin, sink; *pl* (*cabinet*) toilet(s), *Am* washroom.

lavande [lavɑ̃d] *nf* lavender.

lave [lav] *nf Géol* lava.

lave-auto [lavoto] *nm Can* car wash. • **l.-linge** *nm inv* washing machine. • **l.-vaisselle** *nm inv* dishwasher.

laver [lave] *vt* to wash; **l. qn de** (*soupçon etc*) *Fig* to clear s.o. of ‖ **se l.** *vpr* to wash, *Am* wash up; **se l. les mains** to wash one's hands. • **lavable** *a* washable. • **lavage** *nm* washing; **l. de cerveau** *Psy* brainwashing. • **laverie** *nf* (*automatique*) launderette, *Am* Laundromat®. • **lavette** *nf* dish cloth. • **laveur** *nm* **l. de carreaux** window cleaner *ou Am* washer.

laxatif, -ive [laksatif, -iv] *nm* & *a* laxative.

laxiste [laksist] *a* permissive, lax.

layette [lɛjɛt] *nf* baby clothes.

le, la, *pl* **les** [l(ə), la, le] (**le** & **la** *become* **l'** *before a vowel or mute h*) **1** *art déf* (**à + le = au, à + les = aux; de + le = du, de + les = des**) the; **le garçon** the boy; **la fille** the girl; **les petits/rouges/***etc* the little ones/red ones/*etc*; **mon ami le plus intime** my closest friend.

G11 The Definite Article 2 A

2 (*généralisation*) **la beauté** beauty; **la France** France; **les Français** the French; **les hommes** men; **aimer le café** to like coffee.

3 (*possession*) **il ouvrit la bouche** he opened his mouth; **se blesser au pied** to hurt one's foot; **avoir les cheveux blonds** to have blond hair.

4 (*mesure*) **dix francs le kilo** ten francs a kilo.
5 (*temps*) **elle vient le lundi/le matin** she comes on Mondays/in the morning(s); **l'an prochain** next year.
▌*pron* (*homme*) him; (*femme*) her; (*chose, animal*) it; *pl* them; **je la vois** I see her; I see it; **je le vois** I see him; I see it; **je les vois** I see them; **es-tu fatigué? — je le suis;** are you tired? — I am; **je le crois** I think so.
ⓘ**G56** & **57** Personal Pronouns 6 D 1 & 2
lécher [leʃe] *vt* to lick; **se l. les doigts** to lick one's fingers. ●**lèche-vitrines** *nm* **faire du l.-vitrines** *Fam* to go window-shopping.
leçon [ləsɔ̃] *nf* lesson; **servir de l. à qn** to teach s.o. a lesson.
lecteur, -trice [lɛktœr, -tris] *nmf* reader; *Univ* (foreign language) assistant; **l. de cassettes/de CD** cassette/CD player. ●**lecture** *nf* reading; *pl* (*livres*) books.
légal, -aux [legal, -o] *a* legal; (*médecine*) forensic. ●**légaliser** *vt* to legalize. ●**légalité** *nf* legality (**de** of).
légende [leʒɑ̃d] *nf* **1** (*histoire*) legend. **2** (*de plan*) key; (*de photo*) caption. ●**légendaire** *a* legendary.
léger, -ère [leʒe, -ɛr] *a* light; (*bruit, fièvre etc*) slight; (*café, thé*) weak; (*bière, tabac*) mild; (*frivole*) frivolous; (*irréfléchi*) careless; **à la légère** (*agir*) rashly. ●**légèrement** *adv* lightly; (*un peu*) slightly; (*à la légère*) rashly. ●**légèreté** *nf* lightness; frivolity.
légion [leʒjɔ̃] *nf* *Mil* & *Fig* legion; **L. d'honneur** Legion of Honour.
législatif, -ive [leʒislatif, -iv] *a* legislative; (*élections*) parliamentary. ●**législation** *nf* legislation. ●**législature** *nf* (*période*) *Pol* term of office.
légitime [leʒitim] *a* (*action, enfant etc*) legitimate; **être en état de l. défense** to be acting in self-defence. ●**légitimité** *nf* legitimacy.
legs [lɛg] *nm* *Jur* legacy, bequest; (*héritage*) *Fig* legacy. ●**léguer** *vt* to bequeath (**à** to).
légume [legym] *nm* vegetable.
lendemain [lɑ̃dmɛ̃] *nm* **le l.** the next day; **le l. de** the day after; **le l. matin** the next morning.
lent [lɑ̃] *a* slow. ●**lentement** *adv* slowly. ●**lenteur** *nf* slowness.
lentille [lɑ̃tij] *nf* **1** *Bot Culin* lentil. **2** (*verre*) lens.
léopard [leɔpar] *nm* leopard.
lèpre [lɛpr] *nf* leprosy.
lequel, laquelle, *pl* **lesquels, lesquelles** [ləkɛl, lakɛl, lekɛl] (+ **à** = **auquel, à laquelle, auxquel(le)s;** + **de** = **duquel, de laquelle, desquel(le)s**) **1** *pron rel* (*chose, animal*) which; (*personne*) who, (*indirect*) whom; **dans l.** in which; **parmi lesquels** (*choses, animaux*) among which; (*personnes*) among whom. **2** *pron interrogatif* which (one); **l. veux-tu?** which (one) do you prefer?
ⓘ**G53** Interrogative Pronouns 6 C 3a)
ⓘ**G68** Relative Pronouns 6 F 3d)
les [le] *voir* **le.**
léser [leze] *vt* (*personne*) *Jur* to wrong.
lésiner [lezine] *vi* to be stingy (**sur** with).
lessive [lesiv] *nf* (*produit*) washing powder, (laundry) detergent; (*linge*) washing; **faire la l.** to do the wash(ing). ●**lessiver** *vt* to scrub, wash.
lessivé [lesive] *a* (*fatigué*) *Fam* shattered.
lester [lɛste] *vt* to ballast, weight down.
leste [lɛst] *a* (*agile*) nimble.
léthargique [letarʒik] *a* lethargic.
lettre [lɛtr] *nf* (*missive, caractère*) letter; **en toutes lettres** (*mot*) in full; (*nombre*) in words; **les lettres** (*discipline*) arts. ●**lettré, -ée** *a* well-read ▌*nmf* scholar.
leucémie [løsemi] *nf* leuk(a)emia.
leur [lœr] **1** *a poss* their; **l. chat** their cat; **leurs voitures** their cars ▌*pron poss* **le l., la l., les leurs** theirs. **2** *pron inv* (*indirect*) (to) them; **il l. est facile de...** it's easy for them to....
ⓘ**G64** Possessive Adjectives and Pronouns 6 E
ⓘ**G57** Object Pronouns 6 D 2
leurre [lœr] *nm* illusion; (*tromperie*) trickery.
lever [l(ə)ve] *vt* to lift (up), raise; (*blocus, interdiction*) to lift; (*séance*) to close; (*camp*) to strike; **l. les yeux** to look up.
▌*vi* (*pâte*) to rise.
▌**se lever** *vpr* to get up; (*soleil, rideau*) to rise; (*jour*) to break; (*brume*) to clear, lift.
▌*nm* **le l. du soleil** sunrise; **le l. du rideau** *Th* the curtain (up). ●**levant** *a* (*soleil*) rising. ●**levé** *a* **être l.** (*debout*) to be up. ●**levée** *nf* (*d'interdiction*) lifting; (*du courrier etc*) collection.
levier [ləvje] *nm* lever; (*pour soulever*) crowbar.
lèvre [lɛvr] *nf* lip; **du bout des lèvres** half-heartedly.
lévrier [levrije] *nm* greyhound.
levure [ləvyr] *nf* yeast.
lexique [lɛksik] *nm* vocabulary, glossary.
lézard [lezar] *nm* lizard.
lézarde [lezard] *nf* crack. ●**se lézarder** *vpr* to crack.
liaison [ljɛzɔ̃] *nf* (*rapport*) connection; (*routière etc*) link; (*entre mots*) liaison; **l.**

(amoureuse) love affair.
liane [ljan] *nf Bot* jungle vine, liana.
liasse [ljas] *nf* bundle.
Liban [libɑ̃] *nm* Lebanon. • **libanais, -aise** *a & nmf* Lebanese.
libeller [libele] *vt* (*contrat etc*) to word, draw up; (*chèque*) to make out.
libellule [libelyl] *nf* dragonfly.
libéral, -ale, -aux [liberal, -o] *a & nmf* liberal.
libérer [libere] *vt* (*prisonnier etc*) to (set) free, release; (*pays, esprit*) to liberate (**de** from); **l. qn de** to free s.o. of *ou* from ‖ **se l.** *vpr* to free oneself (**de** from). • **libération** *nf* freeing, release; liberation.
liberté [libɛrte] *nf* freedom; **en l. provisoire** *Jur* on bail; **mettre en l.** to free, release; **mise en l.** release.
libraire [librɛr] *nmf* bookseller. • **librairie** *nf* bookshop.
libre [libr] *a* free (**de qch** from sth, **de faire** to do); (*voie*) clear; (*place*) vacant, free; (*école*) private (and religious). • **l.-échange** *nm Écon* free trade. • **l.-service** *nm* (*pl* **libres-services**) (*magasin etc*) self-service. • **librement** [-əmɑ̃] *adv* freely.
Libye [libi] *nf* Libya. • **libyen, -enne** *a & nmf* Libyan.
licence [lisɑ̃s] *nf Sp* permit; *Com* licence, *Am* license; *Univ* (Bachelor's) degree; **l. ès lettres/sciences** arts/science degree, = BA/BSc, = *Am* BA/BS. • **licencié, -ée** *a & nmf* graduate; **l. ès lettres/sciences** Bachelor of Arts/Science, = BA/BSc, = *Am* BA/BS.
licencier [lisɑ̃sje] *vt* (*employé*) to lay off. • **licenciement** *nm* dismissal.
lie [li] *nf* (*du vin*) dregs.
liège [ljɛʒ] *nm* (*matériau*) cork.
lien [ljɛ̃] *nm* (*rapport*) link, connection; (*ficelle*) tie; **l. de parenté** family tie.
lier [lje] *vt* (*attacher*) to tie (up); (*relier*) to link (up), connect; **l. qn** (*unir, engager*) to bind s.o.; **amis très liés** very close friends ‖ **se l.** *vpr* (*idées etc*) to tie in, link together; **se l. avec qn** to make friends with s.o.
lierre [ljɛr] *nm* ivy.
lieu, -x [ljø] *nm* place; (*d'un accident*) scene; **les lieux** (*locaux*) the premises; **sur les lieux** on the spot; **avoir l.** to take place; **donner l. à qch** to give rise to sth; **au l. de** instead of; **en premier l.** in the first place; **en dernier l.** lastly; **l. commun** commonplace. • **l.-dit** *nm* (*pl* **lieux-dits**) *Géog* locality.
lieutenant [ljøtnɑ̃] *nm* lieutenant.
lièvre [ljɛvr] *nm* hare.
ligament [ligamɑ̃] *nm* ligament.
ligne [liɲ] *nf* (*trait, contour, transport*) line; (*belle silhouette*) figure; (*rangée*) row, line; **(se) mettre en l.** to line up; **en l.** *Tél* connected, through; (*ordinateur*) on-line; **les grandes lignes** (*de train*) the main line (services); *Fig* the broad outline; **à la l.** *Gram* new paragraph; **entrer en l. de compte** to be taken into account; **pilote de l.** airline pilot.
lignée [liɲe] *nf* line, ancestry.
ligoter [ligɔte] *vt* to tie up.
liguer (se) [səlige] *vpr* to join together, conspire (**contre** against).
lilas [lilɑ] *nm* lilac ‖ *a inv* (*couleur*) lilac.
limace [limas] *nf* slug.
limande [limɑ̃d] *nf* (*poisson*) lemon sole.
lime [lim] *nf* (*outil*) file. • **limer** *vt* to file.
limite [limit] *nf* limit (**à** to); (*de propriété etc*) boundary; *pl Fb* boundary lines; **dépasser les limites** to go beyond the bounds.
‖ *a* (*cas*) extreme; (*vitesse, âge etc*) maximum; **date l.** latest date, deadline; **date l. de vente** *Com* sell-by date. • **limitation** *nf* limitation; (*de vitesse, poids*) limit. • **limiter** *vt* to limit, restrict (**à** to); (*délimiter*) to border; **se l. à faire** to limit *ou* restrict oneself to doing.
limoger [limɔʒe] *vt* (*destituer*) to dismiss.
limonade [limɔnad] *nf* (fizzy) lemonade.
limpide [lɛ̃pid] *a* (crystal) clear.
lin [lɛ̃] *nm Bot* flax; (*tissu*) linen.
linceul [lɛ̃sœl] *nm* shroud.
linge [lɛ̃ʒ] *nm* (*pièces de tissu*) linen; (*à laver*) washing, linen; **l. (de corps)** underwear. • **lingerie** *nf* (*de femmes*) underwear, lingerie.
lingot [lɛ̃go] *nm* **l. d'or** gold bar.
linguiste [lɛ̃gɥist] *nmf* linguist. • **linguistique** *a* linguistic ‖ *nf* linguistics.
lino [lino] *nm Fam* lino. • **linoléum** *nm* linoleum.
linotte [linɔt] *nf* **tête de l.** *Fig* scatterbrain.
lion [ljɔ̃] *nm* lion; **le L.** (*signe*) Leo. • **lionceau, -x** *nm* lion cub. • **lionne** *nf* lioness.
liqueur [likœr] *nf* liqueur.
liquide [likid] *a* liquid; **argent l.** ready cash ‖ *nm* liquid; **du l.** (*argent*) ready cash; **payer en l.** to pay cash.
liquider [likide] *vt* (*dette, stock etc*) to liquidate; (*affaire, travail*) *Fam* to wind up, finish off • **liquidation** *nf* liquidation; (*vente*) (clearance) sale.
lire[1]* [lir] *vti* to read.
lire[2] [lir] *nf* (*monnaie*) lira.
lis[1] [lis] *nm* (*plante, fleur*) lily.
lis[2], **lisant, lise(nt)** *etc* [li, lizɑ̃, liz] *voir* **lire**[1].

lisible [lizibl] *a* (*écriture*) legible.
lisière [lizjɛr] *nf* edge, border.
lisse [lis] *a* smooth. • **lisser** *vt* to smooth; (*plumes*) to preen.
liste [list] *nf* list; **l. électorale** register of electors, *Am* voting register; **sur la l. rouge** (*numéro*) *Tél* ex-directory, *Am* unlisted.
lit[1] [li] *nm* bed; **l. d'enfant** cot, *Am* crib; **lits superposés** bunk beds. • **literie** *nf* bedding, bedclothes.
lit[2] [li] *voir* **lire**[1].
litanie [litani] *nf* (*énumération*) *Fig* long list (**de** of).
litière [litjɛr] *nf* (*couche de paille*) litter.
litige [litiʒ] *nm* dispute; *Jur* litigation.
litre [litr] *nm* litre, *Am* liter.
littéraire [literɛr] *a* literary. • **littérature** *nf* literature.
littéral, -aux [literal, -o] *a* literal.
littoral [litɔral] *nm* coast(line).
livide [livid] *a* (*pâle*) (ghastly) pale.
livre [livr] **1** *nm* book; **l. de poche** paperback (book); **l. de bord** *Nau* logbook. **2** *nf* (*monnaie, poids*) pound. • **livret** *nm* (*registre*) book; *Mus* libretto; **l. scolaire** school report book; **l. de famille** family registration book; **l. de caisse d'épargne** bankbook.
livrer [livre] *vt* (*marchandises*) to deliver (**à** to); (*secret*) to give away; **l. qn à** (*la police etc*) to give s.o. over *ou* up to; **l. bataille** to do battle.
▌**se livrer** *vpr* (*se rendre*) to give oneself up (**à** to); (*se confier*) to confide (**à** in); **se l. à** (*habitude, excès etc*) to indulge in; (*activité*) to devote oneself to. • **livraison** *nf* delivery. • **livreur, -euse** *nmf* delivery man, delivery woman.
lobe [lɔb] *nm Anat* lobe.
local, -aux [lɔkal, -o] **1** *a* local. **2** *nm* (*pièce*) room; *pl* (*bâtiment*) premises.
localité [lɔkalite] *nf* locality.
locataire [lɔkatɛr] *nmf* tenant; (*chez le propriétaire*) lodger.
location [lɔkɑsjɔ̃] *nf* (*de maison etc*) renting; (*de voiture*) hiring; (*par propriétaire*) renting (out), letting; hiring (out); (*réservation*) booking; (*loyer*) rental; (*bail*) lease; **en l.** on hire; **voiture de l.** hired *ou* rented car.
locomotion [lɔkɔmosjɔ̃] *nf* **moyen de l.** means of transport.
locomotive [lɔkɔmotiv] *nf* (*de train*) engine.
locution [lɔkysjɔ̃] *nf* phrase.
loge [lɔʒ] *nf* (*de concierge*) lodge; (*d'acteur*) dressing-room; (*de spectateur*) *Th* box.
loger [lɔʒe] *vt* (*recevoir, mettre*) to accommodate, house; (*héberger*) to put up; **l. qch dans** to fit sth in; **être logé et nourri** to have board and lodging.
▌*vi* (*à l'hôtel etc*) to put up; (*habiter*) to live; **(trouver à) se l.** to find somewhere to live; **se l. dans** (*balle*) to lodge (itself) in. • **logement** *nm* accommodation, lodging; (*appartement*) flat, *Am* apartment; (*maison*) house; **le l.** housing. • **logeur, -euse** *nmf* landlord, landlady.
logiciel [lɔʒisjɛl] *nm* (*d'ordinateur*) software *inv*.
logique [lɔʒik] *a* logical ▌*nf* logic. • **—ment** *adv* logically.
logistique [lɔʒistik] *nf* logistics.
logo [lɔgo] *nm* logo.
loi [lwa] *nf* law; (*du Parlement*) act; **projet de l.** *Pol* bill; **faire la l.** to lay down the law (**à** to).
loin [lwɛ̃] *adv* far (away *ou* off); **Boston est l. (de Paris)** Boston is a long way away (from Paris); **plus l.** further, farther; (*ci-après*) further on; **au l.** in the distance; **de l.** from a distance; (*de beaucoup*) by far; **c'est l., tout ça** (*passé*) that was a long time ago; **l. de là** *Fig* far from it. • **lointain** *a* distant, far-off ▌*nm* **dans le l.** in the distance.
loisirs [lwazir] *nmpl* (*temps libre*) spare time, leisure (time); (*distractions*) leisure activities.
Londres [lɔ̃dr] *nm ou f* London. • **londonien, -ienne** *a* London, of London ▌*nmf* Londoner.
long, longue [lɔ̃, lɔ̃g] *a* long; **être l. (à faire)** **to be a long time** *ou* slow (in doing); **l. de deux mètres** two metres long.
▌*nm* **avoir deux mètres de l.** to be two metres long; **(tout) le l. de** (*espace*) (all) along; **de l. en large** (*marcher etc*) up and down; **en l. et en large** thoroughly; **à la longue** in the long run; **tomber de tout son l.** to fall flat. • **l.-courrier** *nm Av* long-distance airliner. • **longue-vue** *nf* (*pl* **longues-vues**) telescope.
longer [lɔ̃ʒe] *vt* to go along; (*forêt, mer*) to skirt; (*mur*) to hug.
longitude [lɔ̃ʒityd] *nf* longitude.
longtemps [lɔ̃tɑ̃] *adv* (for) a long time; **trop/avant l.** too/before long; **aussi l. que** as long as.
longue [lɔ̃g] *voir* **long.** • **longuement** *adv* at length. • **longueur** *nf* length; **saut en l.** *Sp* long jump; **à l. de journée** all day long; **l. d'onde** *Rad* & *Fig* wavelength.
lopin [lɔpɛ̃] *nm* **l. de terre** plot of land.
loque [lɔk] *nf* **l. (humaine)** (*personne*) human wreck.
loques [lɔk] *nfpl* rags.

loquet [lɔkɛ] *nm* latch.
lorgner [lɔrɲe] *vt* (*convoiter*) to eye.
lors [lɔr] *adv* **l. de** at the time of; **depuis l., dès l.** from then on.
lorsque [lɔrsk(ə)] *conj* when.
G97 Tenses 7 F 11
losange [lɔzɑ̃ʒ] *nm* (*forme*) diamond.
lot [lo] *nm* **1** (*de loterie*) prize; **gros l.** top prize. **2** (*de marchandises etc*) batch. • **loterie** *nf* lottery, raffle. • **lotissement** *nm* (*terrain*) building plot; (*habitations*) housing estate *ou Am* development.
lotion [losjɔ̃] *nf* lotion.
loto [lɔto] *nm* (*jeu*) lotto.
louable [lwabl] *a* praiseworthy.
louange [lwɑ̃ʒ] *nf* praise.
louche [luʃ] **1** *nf Culin* ladle. **2** *a* (*suspect*) shady, fishy.
loucher [luʃe] *vi* to squint; **l. sur** *Fam* to eye.
louer [lwe] *vt* **1** (*prendre en location*) to rent (*house etc*); (*voiture*) to hire, rent; (*donner en location*) to rent (out), let; to hire (out); (*réserver*) to book; **l. à bail** to lease; **maison/chambre à l.** house/room to let. **2** (*exalter*) to praise (**de** for); **se l. de** to be highly satisfied with.
loufoque [lufɔk] *a* (*fou*) *Fam* nutty.
loukoum [lukum] *nm* Turkish delight.
loup [lu] *nm* wolf; **avoir une faim de l.** to be ravenous.
loupe [lup] *nf* magnifying glass.
louper [lupe] *vt Fam* (*train etc*) to miss; (*examen*) to fail; (*travail*) to mess up.
lourd [lur] *a* heavy (*Fig* **de** with); (*temps, chaleur*) close, sultry; (*faute*) gross; (*tâche*) arduous ‖ *adv* **peser l.** (*malle etc*) to be heavy. • **lourdement** *adv* heavily.
loutre [lutr] *nf* otter.
louveteau, -x [luvto] *nm* (*scout*) cub (scout).
louvoyer [luvwaje] *vi* (*tergiverser*) to hedge, be evasive.
loyal, -aux [lwajal, -o] *a* (*honnête*) fair (**envers** to); (*dévoué*) loyal (**envers** to). • **loyauté** *nf* fairness; loyalty.
loyer [lwaje] *nm* rent.
lu [ly] *pp de* **lire**[1].
lubie [lybi] *nf* whim.
lubrifi/er [lybrifje] *vt* to lubricate. • **—ant** *nm* lubricant.
lucarne [lykarn] *nf* (*fenêtre*) skylight.
lucide [lysid] *a* lucid. • **lucidité** *nf* lucidity.
lucratif, -ive [lykratif, -iv] *a* lucrative.
lueur [lɥœr] *nf* (*lumière*) & *Fig* glimmer.
luge [lyʒ] *nf* sledge, *Am* sled.
lugubre [lygybr] *a* gloomy.
lui [lɥi] *pron mf* (*complément indirect*) (to) him; (*femme*) (to) her; (*chose, animal*) (to) it; **je le lui ai montré** I showed it to him *ou* her; **il lui est facile de . . .** it's easy for him *ou* for her to. . . .
‖ *pron m* **1** (*après une préposition*) him; **pour/avec/***etc* **lui** for/with/*etc* him; **il ne pense qu'à lui** he only thinks of himself. **2** (*complément direct*) him; (*animal*) it; **elle n'aime que lui** she only loves him. **3** (*sujet*) **elle est plus grande que lui** she's taller than he is *ou* than him; **lui, il ne viendra pas** (*emphatique*) *he* won't come; **c'est lui qui . . .** he is the one who . . . . • **lui-même** *pron* himself; (*chose, animal*) itself.
lui G57 Object Pronouns 6 D 2
lui G62 Disjunctive Pronouns 6 D 5
luire* [lɥir] *vi* to shine, gleam. • **luisant** *a* (*métal etc*) shiny.
lumière [lymjɛr] *nf* light; **à la l. de** by the light of; (*grâce à*) *Fig* in the light of; **faire toute la l. sur** *Fig* to clear up. • **luminaire** *nm* (*appareil*) lighting appliance. • **lumineux, -euse** *a* (*idée, ciel etc*) bright, brilliant; (*cadran etc*) luminous; **faisceau l.** beam of light.
lunaire [lynɛr] *a* lunar.
lunatique [lynatik] *a* temperamental.
lundi [lœ̃di] *nm* Monday.
lune [lyn] *nf* moon; **l. de miel** honeymoon.
lunette [lynɛt] *nf* **1 lunettes** glasses, spectacles; (*de protection, plongée*) goggles; **lunettes de soleil** sunglasses. **2** (*astronomique*) telescope; **l. arrière** *Aut* rear window.
lurette [lyrɛt] *nf* **il y a belle l.** a long time ago.
lustre [lystr] *nm* (*éclairage*) chandelier. • **lustré** *a* (*par l'usure*) shiny.
lutin [lytɛ̃] *nm* elf, imp, goblin.
lutte [lyt] *nf* fight, struggle; *Sp* wrestling; **l. des classes** class warfare. • **lutter** *vi* to fight, struggle; *Sp* to wrestle. • **lutteur, -euse** *nmf* fighter; *Sp* wrestler.
luxe [lyks] *nm* luxury; **article de l.** luxury article; **modèle de l.** de luxe model. • **luxueux, -euse** *a* luxurious.
Luxembourg [lyksɑ̃bur] *nm* Luxembourg.
luxure [lyksyr] *nf* lewdness, lust.
luzerne [lyzɛrn] *nf Bot* lucerne, *Am* alfalfa.
lycée [lise] *nm* (secondary) school, *Am* high school. • **lycéen, -enne** *nmf* pupil *ou* student (*at a lycée*).
lyncher [lɛ̃ʃe] *vt* to lynch.
lyophiliser [ljɔfilize] *vt* (*café etc*) to freeze-dry.
lyrique [lirik] *a* (*poème etc*) lyric; (*passionné*) *Fig* lyrical; **artiste l.** opera singer.
lys [lis] *nm* = **lis**[1].

M

M, m [ɛm] *nm* M, m.
m *abrév* (*mètre*) metre.
M [məsjø] *abrév* = **Monsieur.**
m' [m] *voir* **me.**
ma [ma] *voir* **mon.**
macadam [makadam] *nm* (*goudron*) tarmac.
macaron [makarɔ̃] *nm* (*gâteau*) macaroon.
macaroni(s) [makarɔni] *nm(pl)* macaroni.
macédoine [masedwan] *nf* **m. (de légumes)** mixed vegetables; **m. (de fruits)** fruit salad.
macérer [masere] *vti Culin* to soak.
mâcher [mɑʃe] *vt* to chew; **il ne mâche pas ses mots** he doesn't mince matters.
machin [maʃɛ̃] *nm Fam* (*chose*) what's-it; (*personne*) what's-his-name.
machinal, -aux [maʃinal, -o] *a* instinctive. ●**—ement** *adv* instinctively.
machine [maʃin] *nf* machine; (*locomotive, moteur*) engine; **m. à coudre** sewing machine; **m. à écrire** typewriter; **m. à laver** washing machine. ●**machiniste** *nm* (*conducteur*) driver; *Th* stage-hand.
macho [matʃo] *nm* macho.
mâchoire [mɑʃwar] *nf* jaw.
mâchonner [mɑʃɔne] *vt* to chew, munch.
maçon [masɔ̃] *nm* builder; bricklayer; mason. ●**maçonnerie** *nf* (*travaux*) building work; (*ouvrage de briques*) brickwork; (*de pierres*) masonry.
maculer [makyle] *vt Litt* to stain (**de** with).
Madagascar [madagaskar] *nf* Madagascar.
madame, *pl* **mesdames** [madam, medam] *nf* madam; **bonjour mesdames** good morning (ladies); **Madame** *ou* **Mme Legras** Mrs *ou* Ms Legras; **Madame** (*dans une lettre*) Dear Madam.
madeleine [madlɛn] *nf* (small) sponge cake.
mademoiselle, *pl* **mesdemoiselles** [madmwazɛl, medmwazɛl] *nf* miss; **bonjour mesdemoiselles** good morning (ladies); **Mademoiselle** *ou* **Mlle Legras** Miss Legras; **Mademoiselle** (*dans une lettre*) Dear Madam.
madère [madɛr] *nm* (*vin*) Madeira.
Madère [madɛr] *nf* (*île*) Madeira.
maf(f)ia [mafja] *nf* Mafia.
magasin [magazɛ̃] *nm* shop, *Am* store; (*entrepôt*) warehouse; **grand m.** department store; **en m.** in stock. ●**magasinier** *nm* warehouseman.
magazine [magazin] *nm* (*revue*) magazine.
magie [maʒi] *nf* magic. ●**magicien, -ienne** *nmf* magician. ●**magique** *a* (*baguette etc*) magic; (*mystérieux, enchanteur*) magical.
magistral, -aux [maʒistral, -o] *a* masterly, magnificent.
magistrat [maʒistra] *nm* magistrate.
magnat [magna] *nm* tycoon, magnate.
magner (se) [səmaɲe] *vpr Fam* to hurry up.
magnétique [maɲetik] *a* magnetic.
magnétophone [maɲetɔfɔn] (*Fam* **magnéto**) *nm* tape recorder; **m. à cassettes** cassette recorder. ●**magnétoscope** *nm* video (recorder), VCR.
magnifique [maɲifik] *a* magnificent.
magnolia [maɲɔlja] *nm* (*arbre*) magnolia.
magot [mago] *nm* (*économies*) *Fam* nest egg.
magouille(s) [maguj] *nf(pl) Fam* fiddling.
mai [mɛ] *nm* May.
maigre [mɛgr] *a* thin; (*viande*) lean; (*fromage, yaourt*) low-fat; (*repas, salaire, espoir*) meagre. ●**maigreur** *nf* thinness. ●**maigrir** *vi* to get thin(ner).
maille [mɑj] *nf* (*de tricot*) stitch; (*de filet*) mesh. ●**maillon** *nm* (*de chaîne*) link.
maillet [majɛ] *nm* (*outil*) mallet.
maillot [majo] *nm* (*de sportif*) jersey, shirt; **m. (de corps)** vest, *Am* undershirt; **m. (de bain)** (*de femme*) swimsuit; (*d'homme*) (swimming) trunks.
main [mɛ̃] *nf* hand; **tenir à la m.** to hold in one's hand; **à la m.** (*faire, écrire etc*) by hand; **haut les mains!** hands up!; **donner un coup de m. à qn** *Fig* to lend s.o. a (helping) hand; **sous la m.** handy; **la m. dans la m.** hand in hand; **avoir la m. heureuse** to be lucky; **en m. propre** (*remettre qch*) in person; **attaque à m. armée** armed raid *ou* attack; **prêter m.-forte à** to lend assistance to. ●**main-d'œuvre** *nf* (*travail*) manpower, labour; (*salariés*) work force.
maint [mɛ̃] *a Litt* many a; **maintes fois, à maintes reprises** many a time.
maintenant [mɛ̃tnɑ̃] *adv* now; (*de nos jours*) nowadays; **m. que** now that; **dès m.** from now on.
maintenir* [mɛ̃tnir] *vt* (*conserver*) to keep; (*retenir*) to hold, keep; (*affirmer*) to main-

tain (**que** that) ‖ **se m.** *vpr* (*durer*) to be maintained; (*rester*) to keep. ● **maintien** *nm* maintenance (**de** of); (*allure*) bearing.

maire [mɛr] *nm* mayor. ● **mairie** *nf* town hall, *Am* city hall; (*administration*) town council, *Am* city hall.

mais [mɛ] *conj* but; **m. oui, m. si** yes of course; **m. non** definitely not.

maïs [mais] *nm* (*céréale*) maize, *Am* corn.

maison [mɛzɔ̃] *nf* (*bâtiment*) house; (*chez-soi, asile*) home; (*entreprise*) company, firm; (*famille*) household; **à la m.** at home; **aller à la m.** to go home; **m. individuelle** detached house; **m. de la culture** arts centre; **m. des jeunes** youth club; **m. de retraite** old people's home ‖ *a inv* (*tarte etc*) homemade.

maître [mɛtr] *nm* master; **se rendre m. de** (*incendie*) to bring under control; **être m. de** (*situation*) to be in control of; **m. de soi** in control of oneself; **m. (d'école)** teacher; **m. d'hôtel** (*restaurant*) head waiter; **m. nageur (sauveteur)** swimming instructor (and lifeguard); **m. chanteur** blackmailer.

maîtresse [mɛtrɛs] *nf* mistress; **m. (d'école)** teacher; **m. de maison** hostess ‖ *af* (*idée, poutre*) main; (*carte*) master.

maîtrise [metriz] *nf* (*habileté, contrôle*) mastery (**de** of); (*diplôme*) Master's degree (**de** in); **m. (de soi)** self-control. ● **maîtriser** *vt* (*incendie*) to (bring under) control; (*émotion*) to master, control; (*sujet*) to master; **m. qn** to overpower s.o. ‖ **se m.** *vpr* to control oneself.

majesté [maʒɛste] *nf* majesty; **Votre M.** (*titre*) Your Majesty. ● **majestueux, -euse** *a* majestic.

majeur [maʒœr] **1** *a* (*important*) & *Mus* major; **être m.** *Jur* to be of age; **la majeure partie de** most of. **2** *nm* (*doigt*) middle finger.

majorer [maʒɔre] *vt* to raise, increase.

majorette [maʒɔrɛt] *nf* (drum) majorette.

majorité [maʒɔrite] *nf* majority (**de** of); (*âge*) *Jur* coming of age, majority; (*gouvernement*) government. ● **majoritaire** *a* **scrutin m.** first-past-the-post voting system; **être m. aux élections** to win the elections.

Majorque [maʒɔrk] *nf* Majorca.

majuscule [maʒyskyl] *a* capital ‖ *nf* capital letter.

mal, maux [mal, mo] **1** *nm* (*douleur*) pain; (*dommage*) harm; (*maladie*) illness; **dire du m. de qn** to say bad things about s.o.; **m. de dents** toothache; **m. de gorge** sore throat; **m. de tête** headache; **m. de ventre** stomach-ache; **avoir le m. de mer** to be seasick; **avoir le m. du pays/***etc* to be homesick/*etc*; **avoir m. à la tête/gorge/***etc* to have a headache/sore throat/*etc*; **ça (me) fait m., j'ai m.** it hurts (me); **faire du m. à** to hurt; **avoir du m. à faire** to have trouble doing; **se donner du m. pour faire** to go to a lot of trouble to do; **le bien et le m.** good and evil.
2 *adv* (*travailler etc*) badly; (*entendre, comprendre*) not too well; **aller m.** (*projet*) to be going badly; (*personne*) *Méd* to be bad *ou* ill; **m. (à l'aise)** uncomfortable; **se trouver m.** to (feel) faint; **(ce n'est) pas m.!** (that's) not bad!; **pas m.** (*beaucoup*) *Fam* quite a lot (**de** of); **c'est m. de mentir** it's wrong to lie.

malade [malad] *a* ill, sick; (*arbre, dent*) diseased; (*estomac, jambe*) bad; **être m. du cœur** to have a bad heart ‖ *nmf* sick person; (*d'un médecin*) patient. ● **maladie** *nf* illness, disease. ● **maladif, -ive** *a* (*personne*) sickly; (*morbide*) morbid.

maladroit [maladrwa] *a* clumsy, awkward; (*indélicat*) tactless.

malaise [malɛz] *nm* (*angoisse*) uneasiness, malaise; (*indisposition*) feeling of faintness *ou* discomfort; **avoir un m.** to feel faint *ou* dizzy.

malaisé [maleze] *a* difficult.

Malaisie [malɛzi] *nf* Malaysia.

malaria [malarja] *nf* malaria.

malaxer [malakse] *vt* (*pétrir*) to knead.

malchance [malʃɑ̃s] *nf* bad luck; **une m.** a mishap. ● **malchanceux, -euse** *a* unlucky.

mâle [mal] *a* male; (*viril*) manly ‖ *nm* male.

malédiction [malediksjɔ̃] *nf* curse.

maléfique [malefik] *a* evil.

malencontreux, -euse [malɑ̃kɔ̃trø, -øz] *a* unfortunate.

malentendant, -ante [malɑ̃tɑ̃dɑ̃, -ɑ̃t] *nmf* person who is hard of hearing.

malentendu [malɑ̃tɑ̃dy] *nm* misunderstanding.

malfaçon [malfasɔ̃] *nf* defect.

malfaisant [malfəzɑ̃] *a* evil, harmful.

malfaiteur [malfɛtœr] *nm* criminal.

malgré [malgre] *prép* in spite of; **m. tout** after all; **m. moi** in spite of myself, reluctantly.

malhabile [malabil] *a* clumsy.

malheur [malœr] *nm* (*événement, malchance*) misfortune; (*accident*) mishap; **par m.** unfortunately. ● **malheureux, -euse** *a* (*triste*) unhappy, miserable; (*fâcheux*) unfortunate; (*malchanceux*) unlucky ‖ *nmf* (*infortuné*) poor man *ou* woman, (poor) wretch. •**malheureusement** *adv* unfortunately.

ⓘmalheureux G99 The Subjunctive 7 G 1d)

malhonnête [malɔnɛt] *a* dishonest. •**malhonnêteté** *nf* dishonesty; **une m.** (*action*) a dishonest act.

malice [malis] *nf* mischievousness. •**malicieux, -euse** *a* mischievous.

malin, -igne [malɛ̃, -iɲ] *a* (*astucieux*) clever, smart; (*tumeur*) *Méd* malignant; **un m. plaisir** a malicious pleasure.

malintentionné [malɛ̃tɑ̃sjɔne] *a* ill-intentioned (**à l'égard de** towards).

malle [mal] *nf* (*coffre*) trunk; (*de véhicule*) boot, *Am* trunk. •**mallette** *nf* small suitcase; (*pour documents*) attaché case.

malmener [malməne] *vt* to manhandle.

malodorant [malɔdɔrɑ̃] *a* smelly.

malpoli [malpɔli] *a* rude.

malpropre [malprɔpr] *a* (*sale*) dirty.

malsain [malsɛ̃] *a* unhealthy.

Malte [malt] *nf* Malta. •**maltais, -aise** *a* & *nmf* Maltese.

maltraiter [maltrete] *vt* to ill-treat.

malveillant [malvɛjɑ̃] *a* malevolent. •**malveillance** *nf* malevolence, ill will.

malvenu [malvəny] *a* uncalled-for.

maman [mamɑ̃] *nf* mum(my), *Am* mom(my).

mamelle [mamɛl] *nf* (*d'animal*) teat; (*de vache*) udder.

mamie [mami] *nf* grandma, granny.

mammifère [mamifɛr] *nm* mammal.

manche [mɑ̃ʃ] **1** *nf* (*de vêtement*) sleeve; *Sp Cartes* round; **la M.** *Géog* the Channel. **2** *nm* (*d'outil etc*) handle; **m. à balai** broomstick; (*d'avion, d'ordinateur*) joystick. •**manchette** *nf* **1** (*de chemise etc*) cuff. **2** (*de journal*) headline.

manchot, -ote [mɑ̃ʃo, -ɔt] **1** *a* & *nmf* one-armed *ou* one-handed (person). **2** *nm* (*oiseau*) penguin.

mandarine [mɑ̃darin] *nf* (*fruit*) tangerine.

mandat [mɑ̃da] *nm* **1** (*postal*) money order. **2** *Pol* mandate; **m. d'arrêt** warrant (**contre qn** for s.o.'s arrest). •**mandataire** *nmf* (*délégué*) representative, proxy.

manège [manɛʒ] *nm* **1** (*à la foire*) merry-go-round, roundabout; (*lieu*) riding-school; (*piste*) ring. **2** (*intrigue*) ploy, trickery (*no pl*).

manette [manɛt] *nf* lever, handle.

mangeoire [mɑ̃ʒwar] *nf* (feeding) trough.

manger [mɑ̃ʒe] *vt* to eat; (*corroder*) to eat into; (*fortune*) to eat up; **donner à m. à** to feed ▮ *vi* to eat; **on mange bien ici** the food is good here; **m. à sa faim** to have enough to eat ▮ *nm* food. •**mangeable** *a* eatable.

mangue [mɑ̃g] *nf* (*fruit*) mango.

manie [mani] *nf* mania, craze (**de** for). •**maniaque** *a* fussy ▮ *nmf* fusspot, *Am* fussbudget.

manier [manje] *vt* to handle. •**maniable** *a* easy to handle. •**maniement** *nm* handling.

manière [manjɛr] *nf* way, manner; *pl* (*politesse*) manners; **de toute m.** anyway, anyhow; **de cette m.** (in) this way; **de m. à faire** so as to do; **de m. (à ce) que** (+ *sub*) so that; **à ma m.** (in) my own way; **la m. dont elle parle** the way (in which) she talks; **d'une m. générale** generally speaking; **faire des manières** to make a fuss.

manif [manif] *nf Fam* demo.

manifeste [manifɛst] **1** *a* (*évident*) manifest, obvious. **2** *nm Pol* manifesto.

manifester [manifɛste] **1** *vt* (*sa colère etc*) to show, manifest ▮ **se m.** *vpr* (*maladie etc*) to show itself; (*apparaître*) to appear. **2** *vi* (*dans la rue*) to demonstrate. •**manifestant, -ante** *nmf* demonstrator. •**manifestation** *nf* **1** (*défilé*) demonstration; (*réunion, fête*) event. **2** (*expression*) expression, manifestation.

manigancer [manigɑ̃se] *vt* to plot.

manipuler [manipyle] *vt* (*manier*) to handle; (*faits, électeurs*) *Péj* to manipulate.

manivelle [manivɛl] *nf Aut* crank.

mannequin [mankɛ̃] *nm* (*personne*) (fashion) model; (*statue*) dummy.

manœuvre [manœvr] **1** *nm* (*ouvrier*) labourer. **2** *nf* (*opération*) & *Mil* manoeuvre, *Am* maneuver; (*action*) manoeuvring; (*intrigue*) scheme. •**manœuvrer** *vti* (*véhicule etc*) to manoeuvre, *Am* maneuver.

manoir [manwar] *nm* manor house.

manque [mɑ̃k] *nm* lack (**de** of); (*lacune*) gap; *pl* (*défauts*) shortcomings; **m. à gagner** loss of profit.

manquer [mɑ̃ke] *vt* (*cible, train etc*) to miss; (*ne pas réussir*) to make a mess of, ruin.

▮ *vi* (*faire défaut*) to be short *ou* lacking; (*être absent*) to be absent (**à** from); (*être en moins*) to be missing *ou* short; **m. de** (*pain, argent etc*) to be short of; (*attention etc*) to lack; **m. à** (*son devoir*) to fail in; (*sa parole*) to break; **ça manque de sel**/*etc* there isn't enough salt/*etc*; **elle/cela lui manque** he misses her/that; **ça n'a pas manqué** that was bound to happen; **je ne manquerai pas de venir** I won't fail to come; **elle a manqué (de) tomber** she nearly fell.

▮ *v imp* **il manque/il nous manque dix tasses**

there are/we are ten cups short. • **manquant** *a* missing. • **manqué** *a* (*médecin, pilote etc*) failed.
mansarde [mɑ̃sard] *nf* attic.
manteau, -x [mɑ̃to] *nm* coat.
manucure [manykyr] *nmf* manicurist.
manuel, -elle [manɥɛl] **1** *a* (*travail etc*) manual. **2** *nm* handbook, manual; (*scolaire*) textbook.
manuscrit [manyskri] *nm* manuscript; (*tapé à la machine*) typescript.
mappemonde [mapmɔ̃d] *nf* map of the world; (*sphère*) globe.
maquereau, -x [makro] *nm* (*poisson*) mackerel.
maquette [makɛt] *nf* (scale) model.
maquiller [makije] *vt* (*visage*) to make up; (*vérité etc*) *Péj* to fake ‖ **se m.** *vpr* to make (oneself) up. • **maquillage** *nm* (*fard*) make-up.
maquis [maki] *nm Bot* scrub, bush.
maraîcher, -ère [mareʃe, -ɛʃɛr] *nmf* market gardener, *Am* truck farmer.
marais [marɛ] *nm* marsh; **m. salant** saltern.
marasme [marasm] *nm Écon* stagnation.
marathon [maratɔ̃] *nm* marathon.
marbre [marbr] *nm* marble.
marc [mar] *nm* (*eau-de-vie*) marc, brandy; **m. (de café)** coffee grounds.
marchand, -ande [marʃɑ̃, -ɑ̃d] *nmf* shopkeeper, trader; (*de voitures, meubles*) dealer; **m. de journaux** (*dans la rue*) newsvendor; (*dans un magasin*) newsagent, *Am* news dealer; **m. de légumes** greengrocer; **m. de poissons** fishmonger; **m. de couleurs** hardware merchant *ou* dealer ‖ *a* (*valeur*) market; **prix m.** trade price.
marchander [marʃɑ̃de] *vi* to haggle ‖ *vt* (*objet, prix*) to haggle over.
marchandise(s) [marʃɑ̃diz] *nf(pl)* goods, merchandise.
marche [marʃ] *nf* **1** (*d'escalier*) step, stair. **2** (*trajet*) walk; *Mil Mus* march; (*de train, véhicule*) movement; **la m.** *Sp* walking; **faire m. arrière** *Aut* to back up, reverse; **un train en m.** a moving train; **mettre qch en m.** to start sth (up); **la bonne m. de** (*opération, machine*) the smooth running of.
marcher [marʃe] *vi* (*à pied*) to walk; (*poser le pied*) to tread, step (**dans** in); (*fonctionner*) to work, go; (*prospérer*) to go well; *Mil* to march; **faire m.** (*machine*) to work; (*entreprise*) to run; **ça marche?** *Fam* how's it going?
marché [marʃe] *nm* (*lieu*) market; (*contrat*) deal; **faire son** *ou* **le m.** to do one's shopping (*in the market*); **être bon m.** to be cheap; **vendre (à) bon m.** to sell cheap(ly); **c'est meilleur m.** it's cheaper; **par-dessus le m.** into the bargain; **au m. noir** on the black market; **le M. commun** the Common Market.
marchepied [marʃəpje] *nm* (*de train, bus*) step(s).
mardi [mardi] *nm* Tuesday; **M. gras** Shrove Tuesday.
mare [mar] *nf* (*étang*) pond; (*flaque*) pool.
marécage [marekaʒ] *nm* swamp, marsh. • **marécageux, -euse** *a* swampy, marshy.
maréchal, -aux [mareʃal, -o] *nm Fr Mil* marshal.
marée [mare] *nf* tide; **m. haute/basse** high/low tide; **m. noire** oil slick.
marelle [marɛl] *nf* (*jeu*) hopscotch.
margarine [margarin] *nf* margarine.
marge [marʒ] *nf* (*de cahier etc*) margin; **en m. de** (*en dehors de*) on the fringe(s) of.
marguerite [margərit] *nf* (*fleur*) daisy.
mari [mari] *nm* husband.
mariage [marjaʒ] *nm* marriage; (*cérémonie*) wedding; **demande en m.** proposal (of marriage).
marier [marje] *vt* (*couleurs*) to blend; **m. qn** (*prêtre, maire etc*) to marry s.o. ‖ **se m.** *vpr* to get married, marry; **se m. avec qn** to get married to s.o., marry s.o. • **marié** *a* married ‖ *nm* (bride)groom; **les mariés** the bride and (bride)groom. • **mariée** *nf* bride.
marin [marɛ̃] *a* (*flore*) marine; (*mille*) nautical; **air/sel m.** sea air/salt ‖ *nm* sailor. • **marine** *nf* **m. (de guerre)** navy; **m. marchande** merchant navy ‖ *a* & *nm inv* **(bleu) m.** (*couleur*) navy (blue).
marina [marina] *nf* marina.
mariner [marine] *vti Culin* to marinate.
marionnette [marjɔnɛt] *nf* puppet.
maritime [maritim] *a* (*droit, climat etc*) maritime; **port m.** seaport; **gare m.** harbour station.
mark [mark] *nm* (*monnaie*) mark.
marmelade [marməlad] *nf* **m. (de fruits)** stewed fruit.
marmite [marmit] *nf* (cooking) pot.
marmonner [marmɔne] *vti* to mutter.
Maroc [marɔk] *nm* Morocco. • **marocain, -aine** *a* & *nmf* Moroccan.
maroquinerie [marɔkinri] *nf* leather goods shop. • **maroquinier** *nm* leather goods dealer.
marque [mark] *nf* (*trace, signe*) mark; (*de produit*) make, brand; (*points*) *Sp* score; **m. de fabrique** trademark; **m. déposée** (regis-

tered) trademark; **la m. de** (*preuve*) the stamp of; **de m.** (*hôte, visiteur*) distinguished; (*produit*) of quality.

marquer [marke] *vt* (*par une marque*) to mark; (*écrire*) to note down; (*indiquer*) to show, mark; (*point, but*) *Sp* to score; **m. les points** *Sp* to keep (the) score ‖ *vi* (*laisser une trace*) to leave a mark; (*date, événement*) to stand out; *Sp* to score. • **marquant** *a* outstanding. • **marqueur** *nm* (*crayon*) marker.

marquis [marki] *nm* marquis. • **marquise** *nf* marchioness.

marraine [marɛn] *nf* godmother.

marre [mar] *nf* **en avoir m.** *Fam* to be fed up (**de** with).

marrer (se) [səmare] *vpr Fam* to have a good laugh. • **marrant** *a Fam* funny.

marron [marɔ̃] *nm* chestnut; (*couleur*) (chestnut) brown ‖ *a inv* (*couleur*) (chestnut) brown. • **marronnier** *nm* (horse) chestnut tree.

mars [mars] *nm* March.

marteau, -x [marto] *nm* hammer; (*de porte*) (door)knocker; **m. piqueur** pneumatic drill. • **marteler** *vt* to hammer.

martial, -aux [marsjal, -o] *a* martial; **cour martiale** court-martial.

martien, -ienne [marsjɛ̃, -jɛn] *nmf* & *a* Martian.

martinet [martinɛ] *nm* (*fouet*) (small) whip.

martin-pêcheur [martɛ̃pɛʃœr] *nm* (*pl* **martins-pêcheurs**) (*oiseau*) kingfisher.

martyr, -yre [martir] *nmf* (*personne*) martyr; **enfant m.** battered child. • **martyriser** *vt* to torture; (*enfant*) to batter.

marxiste [marksist] *a* & *nmf* Marxist.

mascara [maskara] *nm* mascara.

mascarade [maskarad] *nf* masquerade.

mascotte [maskɔt] *nf* mascot.

masculin [maskylɛ̃] *a* male; (*viril*) masculine, manly; *Gram* masculine; (*vêtement, équipe*) men's ‖ *nm Gram* masculine.

masochiste [mazɔʃist] *nmf* masochist ‖ *a* masochistic.

masque [mask] *nm* mask. • **masquer** *vt* (*dissimuler*) to mask (**à** from); (*cacher à la vue*) to block off.

massacre [masakr] *nm* slaughter, massacre. • **massacrer** *vt* to slaughter, massacre; (*abîmer*) *Fam* to ruin.

massage [masaʒ] *nm* massage.

masse [mas] *nf* **1** (*volume*) mass; (*gros morceau, majorité*) bulk (**de** of); **en m.** in large numbers; **manifestation de m.** mass demonstration; **une m. de** (*tas*) a mass of; **des masses de** *Fam* masses of. **2** (*outil*) sledgehammer. **3** *Él* earth, *Am* ground.

masser [mase] **1** *vt* (*pétrir*) to massage. **2 se masser** *vpr* (*foule*) to form, mass. • **masseur** *nm* masseur. • **masseuse** *nf* masseuse.

massif, -ive [masif, -iv] **1** *a* massive; (*or, chêne etc*) solid; **départs massifs** mass departure(s). **2** *nm* (*d'arbres, de fleurs*) clump; *Géog* massif.

massue [masy] *nf* (*bâton*) club.

mastic [mastik] *nm* (*pour vitres*) putty; (*pour bois*) filler; **m. (silicone)** mastic. • **mastiquer** *vt* **1** (*vitre*) to putty; (*bois*) to fill. **2** (*mâcher*) to chew.

masturber (se) [səmastyrbe] *vpr* to masturbate.

masure [mazyr] *nf* tumbledown house.

mat, mate [mat] **1** *a* (*papier, couleur*) mat(t); (*bruit*) dull. **2** *am inv* & *nm Échecs* (check)mate; **faire m.** to (check)mate.

mât [mɑ] *nm* (*de navire*) mast; (*poteau*) pole.

match [matʃ] *nm Sp* match, *Am* game; **m. nul** tie, draw.

matelas [matla] *nm* mattress; **m. pneumatique** air bed. • **matelassé** *a* (*tissu*) quilted, padded.

matelot [matlo] *nm* sailor, seaman.

mater [mate] *vt* (*enfant etc*) to subdue.

matérialiser [materjalize] *vt*, **se m.** *vpr* to materialize.

matérialiste [materjalist] *a* materialistic ‖ *nmf* materialist.

matériaux [materjo] *nmpl* (building) materials.

matériel, -ielle [materjɛl] **1** *a* (*dégâts etc*) material. **2** *nm* (*de camping*) equipment, material(s); (*d'ordinateur*) hardware *inv*.

maternel, -elle [matɛrnɛl] *a* (*amour, femme etc*) maternal, motherly; (*parenté*) maternal ‖ *nf* **(école) maternelle** nursery school. • **maternité** *nf* (*état*) motherhood; (*hôpital*) maternity hospital; **congé de m.** maternity leave.

mathématique [matematik] *a* mathematical ‖ *nfpl* mathematics. • **mathématicien, -ienne** *nmf* mathematician. • **maths** [mat] *nfpl Fam* maths, *Am* math.

matière [matjɛr] *nf* (*à l'école*) subject; (*de livre*) subject matter; (*substance*) material; **la m.** *Phys* matter; **m. première** raw material; **en m. d'art**/*etc* as regards art/*etc*, in art/*etc*.

matin [matɛ̃] *nm* morning; **le m.** (*chaque matin*) in the morning(s); **à sept heures du m.** at seven in the morning; **tous les mardis m.** every Tuesday morning; **de bon m., au petit m.** very early (in the morning).

• **matinal, -aux** *a* (*personne*) early; **soleil m.** morning sun; **être m.** to be an early riser. • **matinée** *nf* morning; *Th* matinée; **faire la grasse m.** to sleep late.

ⓘmatinée G200 Dates 11 B 3

matraque [matrak] *nf* (*de policier*) truncheon, *Am* billy (club); (*de malfaiteur*) cosh. • **matraquer** *vt* (*frapper*) to club; (*publicité etc*) to plug.

matrice [matris] *nf Math* matrix. • **matricielle** *af* **imprimante m.** *Ordinat* dot matrix printer.

matricule [matrikyl] *nm* (registration) number.

matrimonial, -aux [matrimɔnjal, -o] *a* matrimonial.

maturité [matyrite] *nf* maturity.

maudire* [modir] *vt* to curse. • **maudit** *a* (*sacré*) cursed, damned.

maugréer [mogree] *vi* to grumble (**contre** at).

mausolée [mozɔle] *nm* mausoleum.

maussade [mosad] *a* (*personne etc*) bad-tempered, moody; (*temps*) gloomy.

mauvais [movɛ] *a* bad; (*méchant*) wicked, evil; (*mal choisi*) wrong; (*mer*) rough; **plus m.** worse; **le plus m.** the worst; **il fait m.** the weather's bad; **être m. en** (*anglais etc*) to be bad at; **être en mauvaise santé** to be in bad health ‖ *adv* **ça sent m.** it smells bad ‖ *nm* **le bon et le m.** the good and the bad.

mauve [mov] *a & nm* (*couleur*) mauve.

maux [mo] *voir* **mal**.

maximum [maksimɔm] *nm* maximum; **le m. de** (*force etc*) the maximum (amount of); **au m.** as much as possible; (*tout au plus*) at most ‖ *a* maximum. • **maximal, -aux** *a* maximum.

mayonnaise [majɔnɛz] *nf* mayonnaise.

mazout [mazut] *nm* (fuel) oil.

me [m(ə)] (**m'** *before vowel or mute h*) *pron* **1** (*complément direct*) me; **il me voit** he sees me. **2** (*indirect*) (to) me; **elle me parle** she speaks to me; **tu me l'as dit** you told me. **3** (*réfléchi*) myself; **je me lave** I wash myself.

ⓘG57 Object Pronouns 6 D 2

ⓘG84 Reflexive Verbs and Pronouns 7D

mec [mɛk] *nm* (*individu*) *Arg* guy, bloke.

mécanicien [mekanisjɛ̃] *nm* mechanic; *Rail* train driver, *Am* engineer.

mécanique [mekanik] *a* mechanical; **jouet m.** wind-up toy ‖ *nf* (*science*) mechanics; (*mécanisme*) mechanism. • **mécanisme** *nm* mechanism.

mécène [mesɛn] *nm* patron (of the arts).

méchant [meʃɑ̃] *a* (*cruel*) wicked, malicious, nasty; (*enfant*) naughty; (*chien*) vicious; **ce n'est pas m.** (*grave*) *Fam* it's nothing much. • **méchamment** *adv* maliciously; (*très*) *Fam* terribly. • **méchanceté** *nf* malice, wickedness; **une m.** a malicious word *ou* act.

mèche [mɛʃ] *nf* **1** (*de cheveux*) lock; *pl* (*reflets*) highlights. **2** (*de bougie*) wick; (*de pétard*) fuse; (*de perceuse*) drill, bit. **3 de m. avec qn** (*complicité*) *Fam* in collusion with s.o.

méconnaissable [mekɔnɛsabl] *a* unrecognizable. • **méconnu** *a* unrecognized.

mécontent [mekɔ̃tɑ̃] *a* dissatisfied (**de** with). • **mécontenter** *vt* to displease, dissatisfy. • **mécontentement** *nm* dissatisfaction, discontent.

médaille [medaj] *nf* (*décoration*) medal; (*bijou*) medallion; (*pour chien*) name tag; **être m. d'or/d'argent** *Sp* to be a gold/silver medallist • **médaillon** *nm* (*bijou*) locket, medallion.

médecin [mɛdsɛ̃] *nm* doctor, physician. • **médecine** *nf* medicine; **étudiant en m.** medical student. • **médical, -aux** *a* medical. • **médicament** *nm* medicine.

médias [medja] *nmpl* (mass) media. • **médiatique** *a* **campagne**/*etc* **m.** media campaign/*etc*.

médiéval, -aux [medjeval, -o] *a* medi(a)eval.

médiocre [medjɔkr] *a* second-rate, mediocre. • **médiocrité** *nf* mediocrity.

médire* [medir] *vi* **m. de qn** to speak ill of s.o. • **médisance(s)** *nf*(*pl*) malicious gossip; **une m.** a piece of malicious gossip.

méditer [medite] *vt* (*conseil etc*) to meditate on; **m. de faire** to consider doing ‖ *vi* to meditate (**sur** on).

Méditerranée [mediterane] *nf* **la M.** the Mediterranean. • **méditerranéen, -enne** *a* Mediterranean.

médium [medjɔm] *nm* (*spirite*) medium.

méduse [medyz] *nf* jellyfish.

meeting [mitiŋ] *nm Pol Sp* meeting, rally.

méfait [mefɛ] *nm Jur* misdeed; *pl* (*dégâts*) ravages.

méfier (se) [s(ə)mefje] *vpr* **se m. de** to distrust, mistrust; (*faire attention à*) to watch out for; **méfie-toi!** watch out!; **je me méfie** I'm suspicious *ou* distrustful. • **méfiant** *a* suspicious, distrustful. • **méfiance** *nf* distrust, mistrust.

mégarde (par) [parmegard] *adv* inadvertently, by mistake.

mégot [mego] *nm Fam* cigarette butt *ou* end.

meilleur, -eure [mɛjœr] *a* better (**que**

than); **le m. résultat**/*etc* the best result/*etc* ‖ *nmf* **le m., la meilleure** the best (one).

mélancolie [melɑ̃kɔli] *nf* melancholy, gloom. • **mélancolique** *a* melancholy, gloomy.

mélange [melɑ̃ʒ] *nm* mixture, blend; (*opération*) mixing. • **mélanger** *vt* (*mêler*) to mix; (*brouiller*) to mix up, muddle ‖ **se m.** *vpr* to mix.

mélasse [melas] *nf* treacle, *Am* molasses.

mêler [mele] *vt* to mix, mingle (**à** with); (*odeurs, thèmes*) to combine; **m. qn à** (*impliquer*) to involve s.o. in ‖ **se m.** *vpr* to mix, mingle (**à** with); **se m. à** (*la foule etc*) to join; **mêle-toi de ce qui te regarde!** mind your own business! • **mêlée** *nf Rugby* scrum.

mélodie [melɔdi] *nf* melody. • **mélodieux, -euse** *a* melodious.

mélodrame [melɔdram] *nm* melodrama.

melon [m(ə)lɔ̃] *nm* **1** (*fruit*) melon. **2** **(chapeau) m.** bowler (hat), *Am* derby.

membre [mɑ̃br] *nm* **1** *Anat* limb. **2** (*d'un groupe*) member.

même [mɛm] **1** *a* same; **en m. temps** at the same time (**que** as); **son frère m.** his very brother; **il est la bonté m.** he is kindness itself; **lui-m./vous-m./***etc* himself/yourself/*etc* ‖ *pron* **le m., la m.** the same (one); **les mêmes** the same (ones).

ⓘ **G32** Position of Adjectives 4 D 3

2 *adv* (*y compris, aussi*) even; **m. si** even if; **ici m.** in this very place; **tout de m., quand m.** all the same; **de m.** likewise; **de m. que** just as.

mémento [memɛ̃to] *nm* (*aide-mémoire*) handbook.

mémoire [memwar] **1** *nf* memory; **à la m. de** in memory of; **m. morte/vive** *Ordinat* read-only/random access memory. **2** *nm Univ* dissertation; *pl Littér* memoirs. • **mémorable** *a* memorable.

menace [mənas] *nf* threat, menace. • **menacer** *vt* to threaten (**de faire** to do). • **menaçant** *a* threatening.

ménage [menaʒ] *nm* (*entretien*) housekeeping; (*couple*) couple; **faire le m.** to do the housework; **faire bon m. avec** to get on happily with. • **ménager**[1], **-ère** *a* **appareil m.** domestic *ou* household appliance; **travaux ménagers** housework ‖ *nf* (*femme*) housewife.

ménag/er[2] [menaʒe] *vt* (*arranger*) to prepare *ou* arrange (carefully); (*épargner*) to use sparingly; **m. qn** to treat *ou* handle s.o. carefully. • **—ement** *nm* (*soin*) care; **sans m.** (*brutalement*) brutally.

mendier [mɑ̃dje] *vi* to beg ‖ *vt* to beg for. • **mendiant, -ante** *nmf* beggar.

men/er [məne] *vt* (*personne, vie etc*) to lead; (*enquête*) to carry out; (*affaires*) to run; **m. qn à** (*accompagner*) to take s.o. to; **m. qch à bien** *Fig* to carry sth through ‖ *vi Sp* to lead; **m. à** (*rue etc*) to lead to. • **—eur, -euse** *nmf* (*de révolte*) (ring)leader.

méningite [menɛ̃ʒit] *nf Méd* meningitis.

ménopause [menɔpoz] *nf* menopause.

menottes [mənɔt] *nfpl* handcuffs.

mensonge [mɑ̃sɔ̃ʒ] *nm* lie; (*action*) lying.

mensuel, -elle [mɑ̃sɥɛl] *a* monthly ‖ *nm* (*revue*) monthly. • **mensualité** *nf* monthly payment.

mensurations [mɑ̃syrɑsjɔ̃] *nfpl* measurements.

mental, -aux [mɑ̃tal, -o] *a* mental. • **mentalité** *nf* mentality.

menthe [mɑ̃t] *nf* mint.

mention [mɑ̃sjɔ̃] *nf* mention, reference; (*à un examen*) distinction; **faire m. de** to mention. • **mentionner** *vt* to mention.

ment/ir* [mɑ̃tir] *vi* to lie, tell lies (**à** to). • **—eur, -euse** *nmf* liar.

menton [mɑ̃tɔ̃] *nm* chin.

menu [məny] **1** *nm* (*liste de plats*) & *Ordinat* menu; **au m.** on the menu. **2** *a* (*mince*) slender, fine; (*peu important*) minor, petty ‖ *adv* (*hacher*) small ‖ *nm* **par le m.** in detail.

menuisier [mənɥizje] *nm* carpenter, joiner. • **menuiserie** *nf* carpentry, joinery; (*ouvrage*) woodwork.

méprendre (se) [səmeprɑ̃dr] *vpr* **se m. sur** to be mistaken about.

mépris [mepri] *nm* contempt (**pour** for); **au m. de** without regard to. • **mépriser** *vt* to despise, scorn. • **méprisant** *a* contemptuous, scornful.

méprisable [meprizabl] *a* despicable.

mer [mɛr] *nf* sea; (*marée*) tide; **en m.** at sea; **par m.** by sea; **aller à la m.** to go to the seaside.

mercenaire [mɛrsənɛr] *nm* mercenary.

mercerie [mɛrsəri] *nf* (*magasin*) haberdasher's, *Am* notions store.

merci [mɛrsi] **1** *int* & *nm* thank you, thanks (**de, pour** for); **(non) m.!** no, thank you! **2** *nf* **à la m. de** at the mercy of.

mercredi [mɛrkrədi] *nm* Wednesday.

mercure [mɛrkyr] *nm* mercury.

merde! [mɛrd] *int Fam* (bloody) hell!

mère [mɛr] *nf* mother; **m. de famille** mother (of a family); **maison m.** *Com* parent company.

méridional, -ale, -aux [meridjɔnal, -o] *a* southern ‖ *nmf* southerner.

meringue [mərɛ̃g] *nf* (*gâteau*) meringue.
mérite [merit] *nm* merit. ● **mériter** *vt* (*être digne de*) to deserve; (*valoir*) to be worth; **m. de réussir**/*etc* to deserve to succeed/*etc*.
merlan [mɛrlɑ̃] *nm* (*poisson*) whiting.
merle [mɛrl] *nm* blackbird.
merveille [mɛrvɛj] *nf* wonder, marvel; **à m.** wonderfully (well). ● **merveilleux, -euse** *a* wonderful, marvellous, *Am* marvelous ‖ *nm* **le m.** the supernatural.
mes [me] *voir* **mon.**
mésange [mezɑ̃ʒ] *nf* (*oiseau*) tit.
mésaventure [mezavɑ̃tyr] *nf* slight mishap.
mesdames [medam] *voir* **madame.**
mesdemoiselles [medmwazɛl] *voir* **mademoiselle.**
mésentente [mezɑ̃tɑ̃t] *nf* disagreement.
mesquin [mɛskɛ̃] *a* mean, petty.
message [mesaʒ] *nm* message. ● **messager, -ère** *nmf* messenger.
messageries [mesaʒri] *nfpl Com* courier service.
messe [mɛs] *nf* mass (*church service*).
Messie [mesi] *nm* Messiah.
messieurs [mesjø] *voir* **monsieur.**
mesure [məzyr] *nf* (*dimension*) measurement; (*action*) measure; (*retenue*) moderation; (*cadence*) *Mus* time, beat; **fait sur m.** made to measure; **à m. que** as, as soon *ou* as fast as; **dans la m. où** in so far as; **dans une certaine m.** to a certain extent; **en m. de** able to.
mesurer [məzyre] *vt* to measure; (*juger, estimer*) to calculate, assess; (*argent, temps*) to ration (out); **m. 1 mètre 83** (*personne*) to be six feet tall; (*objet*) to measure six feet.
met(s) [mɛ] *voir* **mettre.**
métal, -aux [metal, -o] *nm* metal. ● **métallique** *a* (*éclat*) metallic; **pont**/*etc* **m.** metal bridge/*etc*. ● **métallisé** *a* **bleu**/*etc* **m.** metallic blue/*etc*.
métallurgie [metalyrʒi] *nf* (*industrie*) steel industry; (*science*) metallurgy.
métaphore [metafɔr] *nf* metaphor. ● **métaphorique** *a* metaphorical.
météo [meteo] *nf* (*bulletin*) weather forecast.
météore [meteɔr] *nm* meteor.
météorologie [meteɔrɔlɔʒi] *nf* (*science*) meteorology; (*service*) weather bureau. ● **météorologique** *a* meteorological; **bulletin**/*etc* **m.** weather report/*etc*.
méthode [metɔd] *nf* (*manière, soin*) method; (*livre*) course. ● **méthodique** *a* methodical.
méticuleux, -euse [metikylø, -øz] *a* meticulous.
métier [metje] *nm* **1** (*travail*) job; (*manuel*) trade; (*intellectuel*) profession; **homme de m.** specialist. **2 m. (à tisser)** loom.
métis, -isse [metis] *a* & *nmf* half-caste.
métrage [metraʒ] *nm* (*tissu*) length; (*de film*) footage; **long m.** (*film*) full-length film; **court m.** (*film*) short (film).
mètre [mɛtr] *nm* (*mesure*) metre, *Am* meter; (*règle*) (metre) rule; **m. carré** square metre; **m. (à ruban)** tape measure. ● **métrique** *a* metric.
métro [metro] *nm* underground, *Am* subway.
métropolitain [metrɔpɔlitɛ̃] *a* metropolitan.
mets [mɛ] *nm* (*aliment*) dish.
mette(s), mettent [mɛt] *voir* **mettre.**
metteur en scène [mɛtœrɑ̃sɛn] *nm Th* producer; *Cin* director.
mettre** [mɛtr] *vt* to put; (*table*) to set, lay; (*vêtement, lunettes*) to put on, wear; (*chauffage, radio etc*) to put on, switch on; (*réveil*) to set (**à** for); **j'ai mis une heure** it took me an hour; **m. en colère** to make angry; **m. à l'aise** (*rassurer*) to put *ou* set at ease; **m. en liberté** to free; **m. en bouteille(s)** to bottle; **mettons que** (+ *sub*) let's suppose that.
‖ **se mettre** *vpr* to put oneself; (*debout*) to stand; (*assis*) to sit; (*objet*) to go, be put; **se m. en short**/*etc* to get into one's shorts/*etc*; **se m. à table** to sit (down) at the table; **se m. à l'aise** to make oneself comfortable; **se m. au travail** to start work; **se m. à faire** to start doing; **se m. au beau/froid/chaud** (*temps*) to turn fine/cold/warm.
meuble [mœbl] *nm* piece of furniture; *pl* furniture. ● **meubler** *vt* to furnish. ● **meublé** *nm* furnished flat *ou Am* apartment.
meugler [møgle] *vi* (*vache*) to moo.
meule [møl] *nf* **1** (*de foin*) haystack. **2** (*pour moudre*) millstone.
meunier, -ière [mønje, -jɛr] *nmf* miller.
meurt [mœr] *voir* **mourir.**
meurtre [mœrtr] *nm* murder. ● **meurtrier, -ière** *nmf* murderer ‖ *a* deadly, murderous.
meurtrir [mœrtrir] *vt* to bruise.
meute [møt] *nf* (*de chiens etc*) pack.
Mexique [mɛksik] *nm* Mexico. ● **mexicain, -aine** *a* & *nmf* Mexican.
mi [mi] *nm* (*note de musique*) E.
mi- [mi] *préf* **la mi-mars**/*etc* mid March/*etc*; **à mi-distance** midway.
miaul/er [mjole] *vi* (*chat*) to miaow, mew. ● **—ement(s)** *nm*(*pl*) miaowing, mewing.

mi-bas [mibɑ] *nm inv* knee sock.
miche [miʃ] *nf* round loaf.
mi-chemin (à) [amiʃmɛ̃] *adv* halfway.
mi-clos [miklo] *a* half-closed.
mi-côte (à) [amikot] *adv* halfway up *ou* down (the hill).
micro [mikro] *nm* **1** microphone, mike. **2** (*ordinateur*) *Fam* micro(-computer).
micro- [mikro] *préf* micro-.
microbe [mikrɔb] *nm* germ.
microfilm [mikrɔfilm] *nm* microfilm.
micro-onde [mikrɔɔ̃d] *nf* microwave; **four à micro-ondes** microwave oven.
microscope [mikrɔskɔp] *nm* microscope.
midi [midi] *nm* **1** (*heure*) twelve o'clock, noon, midday; (*heure du déjeuner*) lunchtime. **2 le M.** the south of France.
ⓘmidi G197 The Time 11 A
mie [mi] *nf* **la m.** the soft part of the bread; **pain de m.** sandwich loaf.
miel [mjɛl] *nm* honey.
mien, mienne [mjɛ̃, mjɛn] *pron poss* **le m., la mienne, les miens, les miennes** mine; **les deux miens** my two ▌*nmpl* **les miens** (*ma famille*) my (own) people.
ⓘG66 Possessive Pronouns 6 E 2
miette [mjɛt] *nf* (*de pain etc*) crumb; **réduire en miettes** to smash to pieces.
mieux [mjø] *adv & a inv* better (**que** than); (*plus à l'aise*) more comfortable; (*plus beau*) better-looking; **le m., la m., les m.** the best; (*de deux*) the better; **tu ferais m. de partir** you had better leave; **de m. en m.** better and better; **je ne demande pas m.** there's nothing I'd like better (**que de faire** than to do). ▌*nm* (*amélioration*) improvement; **faire de son m.** to do one's best; **faire qch au m.** to do sth in the best possible way.
mignon, -onne [miɲɔ̃, -ɔn] *a* (*charmant*) cute; (*gentil*) nice.
migraine [migrɛn] *nf* headache; *Méd* migraine.
migration [migrɑsjɔ̃] *nf* migration.
mijoter [miʒɔte] *vt Culin* to cook (lovingly); (*lentement*) to simmer ▌*vi* to simmer.
mil [mil] *nm inv* (*dans les dates*) a thousand; **l'an deux m.** the year two thousand.
ⓘG199 Dates 11 B 2b) Note i)
milieu, -x [miljø] *nm* (*centre*) middle; (*cadre, groupe social*) environment; (*entre extrêmes*) middle course; (*espace*) *Phys* medium; **au m. de** in the middle of; **le juste m.** the happy medium; **le m.** (*de malfaiteurs*) the underworld.
militaire [militɛr] *a* military; **service m.** military service ▌*nm* serviceman; (*dans l'armée de terre*) soldier.
milit/er [milite] *vi* (*personne*) to be a militant; (*arguments etc*) to militate (**pour** in favour of, **contre** against). **●—ant, -ante** *nmf* militant.
mille [mil] **1** *a & nm inv* thousand; **m. hommes/***etc* a *ou* one thousand men/*etc*; **deux m.** two thousand; **mettre dans le m.** to hit the bull's-eye. **2** *nm* (*mesure*) mile. **● m.-pattes** *nm inv* (*insecte*) centipede. **● millième** *a & nmf* thousandth. **● millier** *nm* thousand; **un m. (de)** a thousand or so.
ⓘmille G190 & **191** Cardinal Numbers 10 A & Notes d) & f)
ⓘmille G199 Dates 11 B 2b)
millefeuille [milfœj] *nm* (*gâteau*) cream slice.
millénaire [milenɛr] *nm* millennium.
millésime [milezim] *nm* date (*on wine etc*).
millet [mijɛ] *nm Bot* millet.
milli- [mili] *préf* milli-.
milliard [miljar] *nm* billion. thousand million. **● milliardaire** *nmf* multimillionaire.
millimètre [milimɛtr] *nm* millimetre.
million [miljɔ̃] *nm* million; **un m. de livres/***etc* a million pounds/*etc*; **deux millions** two million. **● millionnaire** *nmf* millionaire.
mime [mim] *nmf* (*acteur*) mime; **le m.** (*art*) mime. **● mimer** *vti* to mime. **● mimique** *nf* (*mine*) (funny) face.
mimosa [mimoza] *nm Bot* mimosa.
minable [minabl] *a* (*lieu, personne*) shabby; (*médiocre*) pathetic.
minaret [minarɛ] *nm* (*de mosquée*) minaret.
minauder [minode] *vi* to simper.
mince [mɛ̃s] **1** *a* thin; (*élancé*) slim; (*insignifiant*) slim, paltry. **2** *int* **m. (alors)!** oh heck! **● mincir** *vi* to get slim(mer).
mine [min] *nf* **1** appearance; (*physionomie*) look; **avoir bonne/mauvaise m.** to look well/ill; **faire m. de faire** to appear to do, make as if to do. **2** (*gisement*) & *Fig* mine; **m. de charbon** coalmine. **3** (*de crayon*) lead. **4** (*engin explosif*) mine. **● miner** *vt* **1** (*saper*) to undermine. **2** (*terrain*) to mine.
minerai [minrɛ] *nm* ore.
minéral, -aux [mineral, -o] *a & nm* mineral.
minéralogique [mineralɔʒik] *a* **plaque m.** *Aut* number *ou Am* license plate.
mineur, -eure [minœr] **1** *nm* (*ouvrier*) miner. **2** *a* (*jeune, secondaire*) & *Mus* minor ▌*nmf Jur* minor. **● minier, -ière** *a* **industrie/***etc* **minière** mining industry/*etc*.
mini- [mini] *préf* mini-.
miniature [minjatyr] *nf* miniature ▌*a inv* **train/***etc* **m.** miniature train/*etc*.
minibus [minibys] *nm* minibus.
minime [minim] *a* trifling, minimal.

minimum [minimɔm] *nm* minimum; **le m. de** (*force etc*) the minimum (amount of); **au m.** at the very least ‖ *a* minimum. • **minimal, -aux** *a* minimum, minimal.

ministre [ministr] *nm Pol Rel* minister; **m. de l'Intérieur** = Home Secretary, *Am* Secretary of the Interior. • **ministère** *nm* ministry; (*gouvernement*) cabinet; **m. de Intérieur** = Home Office, *Am* Department of the Interior. • **ministériel, -ielle** *a* ministerial; **remaniement m.** cabinet reshuffle.

Minitel® [minitɛl] *nm* = telephone-connected terminal for data bank consultation.

minorité [minɔrite] *nf* minority; **en m.** in the *ou* a minority. • **minoritaire** *a* **parti**/*etc* **m.** minority party/*etc*; **être m.** to be in the *ou* a minority.

Minorque [minɔrk] *nf* Minorca.

minuit [minɥi] *nm* midnight, twelve o'clock.

G197 The Time 11 A

minuscule [minyskyl] **1** *a* (*petit*) tiny, minute. **2** *a* & *nf* **(lettre) m.** small letter.

minute [minyt] *nf* minute; **à la m.** (*tout de suite*) this (very) minute; **d'une m. à l'autre** any minute (now) ‖ *a inv* **aliments** *ou* **plats m.** convenience food(s). • **minuter** *vt* to time. • **minuterie** *nf* time switch (*for lighting in a stairway etc*). • **minuteur** *nm* timer.

minutieux, -euse [minysjø, øz] *a* meticulous.

mioche [mjɔʃ] *nmf* (*enfant*) *Fam* kid.

mirabelle [mirabɛl] *nf* mirabelle plum.

miracle [mirɑkl] *nm* miracle; **par m.** miraculously. • **miraculeux, -euse** *a* miraculous.

mirage [miraʒ] *nm* mirage.

miroir [mirwar] *nm* mirror. • **miroiter** *vi* to gleam, shimmer.

mis [mi] *pp de* **mettre** ‖ *a* **bien m.** well dressed.

mise [miz] *nf* **1** (*action*) putting; **m. en marche** starting up; **m. en service** putting into service; **m. en scène** *Th* production; *Cin* direction; **m. à feu** (*de fusée*) blast-off. **2** (*argent*) stake. **3** (*tenue*) attire.

miser [mize] *vt* (*argent*) to stake (**sur** on) ‖ *vi* **m. sur** (*cheval*) to back; (*compter sur*) *Fam* to bank on.

misère [mizɛr] *nf* (grinding) poverty; (*malheur*) misery. • **misérable** *a* miserable, wretched; (*très pauvre*) destitute; (*logement, quartier*) seedy.

miséricorde [mizerikɔrd] *nf* mercy.

missile [misil] *nm* (*fusée*) missile.

mission [misjɔ̃] *nf* mission; (*tâche*) task. • **missionnaire** *nm* missionary.

missive [misiv] *nf* (*lettre*) *Litt* missive.

mistral [mistral] *nm inv* (*vent*) mistral.

mite [mit] *nf* (clothes) moth.

mi-temps [mitɑ̃] *nf* (*pause*) *Sp* half-time; (*période*) *Sp* half; **travailler à mi-t.** to work part-time.

miteux, -euse [mitø, -øz] *a* shabby.

mitigé [mitiʒe] *a* moderate, lukewarm.

mitrailler [mitrɑje] *vt* to machinegun; (*photographier*) *Fam* to click *ou* snap away at. • **mitraillette** *nf* machinegun (*portable*). • **mitrailleur** *a* **fusil m.** machinegun (*portable*). • **mitrailleuse** *nf* machinegun (*heavy*).

mi-voix (à) [amivwa] *adv* in an undertone.

mixe(u)r [miksœr] *nm* (*pour mélanger*) mixer; (*pour rendre liquide*) liquidizer.

mixte [mikst] *a* mixed; (*école*) co-educational, mixed.

mixture [mikstyr] *nf Péj* mixture.

Mlle [madmwazɛl] *abrév* = **Mademoiselle.**

MM [mesjø] *abrév* = **Messieurs.**

mm *abrév* (*millimètre*) mm.

Mme [madam] *abrév* = **Madame.**

mobile [mɔbil] **1** *a* (*pièce*) moving; (*panneau*) mov(e)able; (*personne*) mobile; (*feuillets*) detachable, loose ‖ *nm* (*œuvre d'art*) mobile. **2** *nm* (*motif*) motive (**de** for). • **mobilité** *nf* mobility.

mobilier [mɔbilje] *nm* furniture.

mobiliser [mɔbilize] *vti* to mobilize.

mobylette® [mɔbilɛt] *nf* moped.

mocassin [mɔkasɛ̃] *nm* moccasin.

moche [mɔʃ] *a Fam* (*laid*) ugly; **c'est m.** (*mal*) it's lousy *ou* rotten.

modalités [mɔdalite] *nfpl* methods (**de** of).

mode [mɔd] **1** *nf* fashion; (*industrie*) fashion trade; **à la m.** fashionable, in fashion. **2** *nm* mode, method; **m. d'emploi** directions (for use); **m. de vie** way of life. **3** *nm Gram* mood.

modèle [mɔdɛl] *nm* (*schéma, exemple, personne*) model; **m. (réduit)** (scale) model. • **modeler** *vt* to model (**sur** on).

modem [mɔdɛm] *nm Ordinat* modem.

modéré [mɔdere] *a* moderate.

modérer [mɔdere] *vt* to moderate; (*vitesse, température etc*) to reduce ‖ **se m.** *vpr* to restrain oneself. • **modération** *nf* moderation; reduction; **avec m.** in moderation.

moderne [mɔdɛrn] *a* modern ‖ *nm* **le m.** (*mobilier*) modern furniture. • **moderniser** *vt*, **se m.** *vpr* to modernize.

modeste [mɔdɛst] *a* modest. • **modestie** *nf* modesty.

modifier [mɔdifje] *vt* to alter, modify. • **modification** *nf* alteration, modification.
modique [mɔdik] *a* (*prix etc*) modest.
modulation [mɔdylɑsjɔ̃] *nf* **m. de fréquence** FM (*frequency modulation*).
moelle [mwal] *nf Anat* marrow; **m. épinière** spinal cord.
moelleux, -euse [mwalø, -øz] *a* (*lit, tissu*) soft.
mœurs [mœr(s)] *nfpl* (*morale*) morals; (*habitudes*) habits, customs.
mohair [mɔɛr] *nm* mohair.
moi [mwa] *pron* **1** (*après une préposition*) me; **pour/avec/***etc* **moi** for/with/*etc* me.
2 (*complément direct*) me; **laissez-moi** leave me.
3 (*complément indirect*) (to) me; **montrez-le-moi** shows it to me.
4 (*sujet*) I; **c'est moi qui vous le dis!** *I'm* telling you; **il est plus grand que moi** he's taller than I am *ou* than me; **moi, je veux bien** (*emphatique*) that's OK by me.
5 *nm inv Psy* self. • **moi-même** *pron* myself.
ⓘ**moi G62** Disjunctive Pronouns 6 D 5
moindre [mwɛ̃dr] *a* **la m. erreur/***etc* the slightest mistake/*etc*; **à un m. degré** to a lesser degree; **le m.** (*de mes problèmes etc*) the least (**de** of); (*de deux problèmes etc*) the lesser (**de** of).
moine [mwan] *nm* monk.
moineau, -x [mwano] *nm* sparrow.
moins [mwɛ̃] **1** *adv* ([mwɛ̃z] *before vowel*) less (**que** than); **m. de** (*temps, travail etc*) less (**que** than), not so much (**que** as); (*gens, livres etc*) fewer (**que** than), not so many (**que** as); (*cent francs etc*) less than; **m. grand/***etc* not as big/*etc* (**que** as); **le m., la m., les m.** (*travailler etc*) the least; **le m. grand, la m. grande, les m. grand(e)s** the smallest; **de m. en m.** [dəmwɛ̃zɑ̃mwɛ̃] less and less; **au m., du m.** at least; **de m., en m.** (*qui manque*) missing; **dix ans/***etc* **de m.** ten years/*etc* less; **en m.** (*personne, objet*) less; (*personnes, objets*) fewer; **les m. de vingt ans** those under twenty; **à m. que (. . . ne)** (+ *sub*) unless.
ⓘ**G35** & **43** Comparative and Superlative of Adjectives and Adverbs 4 E & 5 F
2 *prép Math* minus; **deux heures m. cinq** five to two; **il fait m. dix (degrés)** it's minus ten (degrees).
mois [mwa] *nm* month; **au m. de juin/***etc* in (the month of) June/*etc*.
mois/ir [mwazir] *vi* to go mouldy; (*attendre*) *Fam* to hang about. •**—i** *a* mouldy, *Am* moldy ‖ *nm* mould, *Am* mold; **sentir le m.** to smell musty. • **moisissure** *nf* mould, mildew.
moisson [mwasɔ̃] *nf* harvest.
moite [mwat] *a* sticky, moist.
moitié [mwatje] *nf* half; **la m. de la pomme/***etc* half (of) the apple/*etc*; **à m.** (*remplir etc*) halfway; **à m. fermé/***etc* half closed/*etc*; **à m. prix** (at *ou* for) half-price; **de m.** by half; **partager m. -moitié** *Fam* to split fifty-fifty.
moka [mɔka] *nm* (*café*) mocha.
mol [mɔl] *voir* **mou.**
molaire [mɔlɛr] *nf* (*dent*) back tooth, molar.
molester [mɔlɛste] *vt* to manhandle.
molette [mɔlɛt] *nf* **clé à m.** adjustable wrench *ou* spanner.
molle [mɔl] *voir* **mou.** • **mollir** *vi* to go soft; (*courage*) to flag.
mollet [mɔlɛ] **1** *nm* (*de jambe*) calf. **2** *a* **œuf m.** soft-boiled egg.
môme [mom] *nmf* (*enfant*) *Fam* kid.
moment [mɔmɑ̃] *nm* (*instant*) moment; (*période*) time; **en ce m.** at the moment; **par moments** at times; **au m. de partir** when just about to leave; **au m. où** just as, when; **du m. que** (*puisque*) seeing that. • **momentané** *a* momentary.
momie [mɔmi] *nf* (*cadavre*) mummy.
mon, ma, *pl* **mes** [mɔ̃, ma, me] (**ma** *becomes* **mon** [mɔ̃n] *before a vowel or mute h*) *a poss* my; **mon père** my father; **ma mère** my mother; **mon ami(e)** my friend; **mes parents** my parents.
ⓘ**G64** Possessive Adjectives 6 E 1
Monaco [mɔnako] *nf* Monaco.
monarque [mɔnark] *nm* monarch. • **monarchie** *nf* monarchy.
monastère [mɔnastɛr] *nm* monastery.
monceau, -x [mɔ̃so] *nm* heap, pile.
mondain, -aine [mɔ̃dɛ̃, -ɛn] *a* **réunion/***etc* **mondaine** society gathering/*etc*.
monde [mɔ̃d] *nm* world; (*milieu social*) set; **du m.** (*gens*) people; (*beaucoup de gens*) a lot of people; **un m. fou** a tremendous crowd; **le m. entier** the whole world; **tout le m.** everybody; **mettre au m.** to give birth to; **venir au m.** to come into the world; **pas le moins du m.!** not in the least! • **mondial, -aux** *a* (*crise, renommée etc*) worldwide; **guerre mondiale** world war.
monégasque [mɔnegask] *a* & *nmf* Monegasque.
monétaire [mɔnetɛr] *a* monetary.
moniteur, -trice [mɔnitœr, -tris] **1** *nmf* instructor; (*de colonie de vacances*) assistant, *Am* camp counselor. **2** *nm* (*écran*) *Ordinat etc* monitor.
monnaie [mɔnɛ] *nf* (*devise*) currency,

money; (*pièces*) change; **pièce de m.** coin; **(petite) m.** (small) change; **faire de la m.** to get change; **faire de la m. à qn** to give s.o. change (**sur un billet** for a note *ou Am* bill); **c'est m. courante** *Fig* it's very frequent.
mono- [mɔno] *préf* mono-.
monologue [mɔnɔlɔg] *nm* monologue.
monoparentale [mɔnɔparɑ̃tal] *af* **famille m.** one-parent family.
monophonie [mɔnɔfɔni] *nf* **en m.** in mono.
monoplace [mɔnɔplas] *a* & *nmf* (*avion, voiture*) single-seater.
monopole [mɔnɔpɔl] *nm* monopoly.
monotone [mɔnɔtɔn] *a* monotonous.
monseigneur [mɔ̃sɛɲœr] *nm* (*évêque*) His *ou* Your Grace; (*prince*) His *ou* Your Highness.
monsieur, *pl* **messieurs** [məsjø, mesjø] *nm* man, gentleman; **oui m.** yes sir; **oui messieurs** yes gentlemen; **M. Legras** Mr Legras; **Messieurs** *ou* **MM Legras** Messrs Legras; **Monsieur** (*dans une lettre*) Dear Sir.
monstre [mɔ̃str] *nm* monster ‖ *a* (*énorme*) *Fam* colossal. • **monstrueux, -euse** *a* (*abominable, énorme*) monstrous.
mont [mɔ̃] *nm* (*montagne*) mount.
montage [mɔ̃taʒ] *nm* *Tech* assembling, assembly; *Cin* editing.
montagne [mɔ̃taɲ] *nf* mountain; **la m.** (*zone*) the mountains; **montagnes russes** roller coaster. • **montagnard, -arde** *nmf* mountain dweller. • **montagneux, -euse** *a* mountainous.
montant [mɔ̃tɑ̃] **1** *nm* (*somme*) amount. **2** *nm* (*de barrière*) post; (*d'échelle*) upright. **3** *a* (*marée*) rising; (*col*) stand-up; **chaussure montante** boot.
monte-charge [mɔ̃tʃarʒ] *nm inv* service lift *ou Am* elevator.
montée [mɔ̃te] *nf* (*ascension*) climb; (*chemin*) slope; (*des prix, des eaux*) rise.
monter [mɔ̃te] *vi* (*aux* **être**) (*personne*) to go *ou* come up; (*s'élever*) (*ballon etc*) to go up; (*grimper*) to climb (up) (**sur** onto); (*prix*) to go up, rise; (*marée*) to come in; (*avion*) to climb; **m. dans un véhicule** to get in(to) a vehicle; **m. dans un train** to get on(to) a train; **m. sur** *ou* **à** (*échelle*) to climb up; **m. sur le trône** to become king *ou* queen; **m. en courant**/*etc* to run/*etc* up; **m. (à cheval)** *Sp* to ride (a horse).
‖ *vt* (*aux* **avoir**) (*côte etc*) to climb (up); (*objet*) to bring *ou* take up; (*cheval*) to ride; (*tente, affaire*) to set up; (*machine*) to assemble; (*bijou*) to set, mount; (*pièce*) *Th* to stage; **m. l'escalier** to go *ou* come upstairs *ou* up the stairs; **faire m. qn** to show s.o. up.
‖ **se monter** *vpr* **se m. à** (*frais*) to amount to.
montre [mɔ̃tr] *nf* **1** (wrist)watch; **course contre la m.** race against time. **2 faire m. de** *Litt* to show.
Montréal [mɔ̃real] *nm ou f* Montreal.
montrer [mɔ̃tre] *vt* to show (**à** to); **m. qn/qch du doigt** to point at s.o./sth; **m. à qn comment faire qch** to show s.o. how to do sth ‖ **se m.** *vpr* to show oneself; **se m. courageux**/*etc* to be courageous/*etc*, show courage/*etc*.
monture [mɔ̃tyr] *nf* **1** (*de lunettes*) frame; (*de bijou*) setting **2** (*cheval*) mount.
monument [mɔnymɑ̃] *nm* monument; **m. aux morts** war memorial. • **monumental, -aux** *a* (*imposant, énorme etc*) monumental.
moquer (se) [səmɔke] *vpr* **se m. de** to make fun of; **je m'en moque!** *Fam* I couldn't care less! • **moquerie** *nf* mockery.
moquette [mɔkɛt] *nf* fitted carpet(s), *Am* wall-to-wall carpeting.
moral, -aux [mɔral, -o] *a* moral ‖ *nm* **le m.** spirits, morale. • **morale** *nf* (*d'histoire*) moral; (*principes*) morals; (*code*) moral code; **faire la m. à qn** to lecture s.o. • **moralité** *nf* (*mœurs*) morality; (*de fable, récit etc*) moral.
morbide [mɔrbid] *a* morbid.
morceau, -x [mɔrso] *nm* piece, bit; (*de sucre*) lump; (*de viande*) *Culin* cut; (*d'une œuvre littéraire*) extract. • **morceler** *vt* (*terrain*) to divide up.
mordiller [mɔrdije] *vt* to nibble.
mordre [mɔrdr] *vti* to bite; **ça mord** *Pêche* I have a bite.
mordu, -ue [mɔrdy] *pp de* **mordre** ‖ *nmf* **un m. du jazz**/*etc* *Fam* a jazz/*etc* fan.
morfondre (se) [səmɔrfɔ̃dr] *vpr* to get bored (waiting), mope (about).
morgue [mɔrg] *nf* (*lieu*) mortuary, morgue.
morne [mɔrn] *a* dismal, gloomy, dull.
morose [mɔroz] *a* morose, sullen.
morphine [mɔrfin] *nf* morphine.
mors [mɔr] *nm* (*de harnais*) bit.
morse [mɔrs] *nm* **1** Morse (code). **2** (*animal*) walrus.
morsure [mɔrsyr] *nf* bite.
mort[1] [mɔr] *nf* death; **un silence de m.** a deathly silence. • **mortalité** *nf* death rate. • **mortel, -elle** *a* (*hommes, ennemi etc*) mortal; (*accident*) fatal; (*ennuyeux*) *Fam* deadly (dull) ‖ *nmf* mortal.
mort[2]**, morte** [mɔr, mɔrt] *a* (*personne, plante etc*) dead; **m. de fatigue** dead tired; **m. de froid** numb with cold; **m. de**

peur frightened to death.
▮ *nmf* dead man, dead woman; **les morts** the dead; **de nombreux morts** (*victimes*) many casualties *ou* deaths; **le jour** *ou* **la fête des Morts** All Souls' Day. ● **morte-saison** *nf* off season. ● **mort-né** *a* (*enfant*) & *Fig* stillborn.

mortuaire [mɔrtɥɛr] *a* **couronne/*etc* m.** funeral wreath/*etc*.

morue [mɔry] *nf* cod.

mosaïque [mɔzaik] *nf* mosaic.

Moscou [mɔsku] *nm ou f* Moscow.

mosquée [mɔske] *nf* mosque.

mot [mo] *nm* word; **envoyer un m. à qn** to drop a line to s.o.; **bon m.** witticism; **mots croisés** crossword (puzzle); **m. de passe** password; **m. d'ordre** *Pol* resolution, order.

motard [mɔtar] *nm Fam* motorcyclist.

moteur[1] [mɔtœr] *nm* (*de véhicule etc*) engine, motor; *Él* motor.

moteur[2], **-trice** [mɔtœr, -tris] *a* (*nerf, muscle*) motor; **force motrice** driving force.

motif [mɔtif] *nm* **1** (*raison*) reason (**de** for). **2** (*dessin*) pattern.

motion [mosjɔ̃] *nf Pol* motion; **on a voté une m. de censure** a vote of no confidence was passed.

motivé [mɔtive] *a* motivated.

moto [mɔto] *nf* motorcycle, motorbike. ● **motocycliste** *nmf* motorcyclist.

motte [mɔt] *nf* (*de terre*) lump, clod; (*de beurre*) block.

mou (*or* **mol** *before vowel or mute h*), **molle** [mu, mɔl] *a* soft; (*sans énergie*) feeble ▮ *nm* **avoir du m.** (*cordage*) to be slack.

mouchard, -arde [muʃar, -ard] *nmf Péj* informer.

mouche [muʃ] *nf* (*insecte*) fly; **faire m.** to hit the bull's-eye. ● **moucheron** *nm* (*insecte*) gnat, midge.

moucher [muʃe] *vt* **m. qn** to wipe s.o.'s nose; **se m.** to blow one's nose.

mouchoir [muʃwar] *nm* handkerchief; (*en papier*) tissue.

moudre* [mudr] *vt* (*café, blé*) to grind.

moue [mu] *nf* long face, pout; **faire la m.** to pull a (long) face, to pout.

mouette [mwɛt] *nf* (sea)gull.

moufle [mufl] *nf* (*gant*) mitten.

mouiller [muje] **1** *vt* to wet, make wet ▮ **se m.** *vpr* to get (oneself) wet; (*se compromettre*) *Fam* to get involved (*by taking risks*). **2** *vi Nau* to anchor. ● **mouillé** *a* wet (**de** with).

moule[1] [mul] *nm* mould, *Am* mold; **m. à gâteaux** cake tin. ● **mouler** *vt* to mould, *Am* mold; **m. qn** (*vêtement*) to fit s.o. tightly. ● **moulant** *a* (*vêtement*) tight-fitting.

moule[2] [mul] *nf* (*animal*) mussel.

moulin [mulɛ̃] *nm* mill; **m. à vent** windmill; **m. à café** coffee-grinder.

moulinet [mulinɛ] *nm* (*de canne à pêche*) reel.

moulu [muly] *pp de* **moudre** ▮ *a* (*café*) ground.

mour/ir* [murir] *vi* (*aux* **être**) to die (**de** of, from); **m. de froid** to die of exposure; **m. de fatigue** *Fig* to be dead tired; **m. de peur** *Fig* to be frightened to death; **s'ennuyer à m.** to be bored to death; **je meurs de faim** I'm starving! ● **—ant, -ante** *a* dying; (*voix*) faint.

mousse [mus] **1** *nf Bot* moss. **2** *nf* (*écume*) foam, froth; (*de bière*) froth; (*de savon*) lather; **m. à raser** shaving foam. **3** *nf Culin* mousse. ● **mousser** *vi* (*bière etc*) to froth; (*savon*) to lather; (*eau savonneuse*) to foam. ● **mousseux** *nm* sparkling wine.

mousseline [muslin] *nf* (*coton*) muslin.

mousson [musɔ̃] *nf* (*vent*) monsoon.

moustache [mustaʃ] *nf* moustache, *Am* mustache; *pl* (*de chat etc*) whiskers. ● **moustachu** *a* wearing a moustache.

moustique [mustik] *nm* mosquito. ● **moustiquaire** *nf* mosquito net; (*en métal*) screen.

moutarde [mutard] *nf* mustard.

mouton [mutɔ̃] *nm* sheep *inv*; (*viande*) mutton; *pl* (*sur la mer*) white horses, *Am* whitecaps; **peau de m.** sheepskin.

mouvement [muvmɑ̃] *nm* (*geste, groupe etc*) & *Mus* movement; (*de colère*) outburst; (*impulsion*) impulse; **en m.** in motion. ● **mouvementé** *a* (*vie, voyage etc*) eventful.

mouvoir* [muvwar] *vi*, **se m.** *vpr* to move; **mû par** (*mécanisme*) driven by. ● **mouvant** *a* **sables mouvants** quicksands.

moyen[1], **-enne** [mwajɛ̃, -ɛn] *a* average; (*format etc*) medium(-sized); **classe moyenne** middle class ▮ *nf* average; (*à un examen*) pass mark; (*à un devoir*) half marks; **en moyenne** on average; **la moyenne d'âge** the average age.

moyen[2] [mwajɛ̃] *nm* (*procédé, façon*) means, way (**de faire** of doing, to do); *pl* (*capacités*) ability, powers; (*argent*) means; **au m. de** by means of; **il n'y a pas m. de faire** it's not possible to do; **je n'ai pas les moyens** (*argent*) I can't afford it.

MST [ɛmɛste] *nf abrév* (*maladie sexuellement transmissible*) sexually transmitted disease, STD.

muer [mɥe] *vi* (*animal*) to moult, *Am* molt; (*voix*) to break; **se m. en** *Litt* to become transformed into.

muet, -ette [mɥɛ, -ɛt] *a* (*infirme*) dumb; (*de surprise etc*) speechless; (*film etc*) silent; (*voyelle etc*) *Gram* silent, mute.
mufle [myfl] *nm* **1** (*d'animal*) muzzle, nose. **2** (*individu*) *Péj* lout.
mug/ir [myʒir] *vi* (*bœuf*) to bellow; (*vache*) to moo; (*vent*) *Fig* to roar. ● **—issement(s)** *nm*(*pl*) bellow(ing); moo(ing); roar(ing).
muguet [mygɛ] *nm* lily of the valley.
mule [myl] *nf* **1** (*pantoufle*) mule. **2** (*animal*) (she-)mule. ● **mulet**[1] *nm* (he-)mule.
mulet[2] [mylɛ] *nm* (*poisson*) mullet.
multi- [mylti] *préf* multi-.
multicolore [myltikɔlɔr] *a* multicoloured.
multinationale [myltinasjɔnal] *nf* multinational.
multiple [myltipl] *a* (*nombreux*) numerous; (*varié*) multiple ‖ *nm Math* multiple. ● **multiplication** *nf* multiplication; (*augmentation*) increase. ● **multiplier** *vt* to multiply ‖ **se m.** *vpr* to increase; (*se reproduire*) to multiply.
multitude [myltityd] *nf* multitude.
municipal, -aux [mynisipal, -o] *a* municipal; **conseil m.** town *ou Am* city council. ● **municipalité** *nf* (*corps*) town *ou Am* city council; (*commune*) municipality.
munir [mynir] *vt* **m. de** to provide *ou* equip with.
munitions [mynisjɔ̃] *nfpl* ammunition.
mur [myr] *nm* wall; **m. du son** sound barrier. ● **muraille** *nf* (high) wall.
mûr [myr] *a* (*fruit etc*) ripe; (*personne*) mature; **d'âge m.** of mature years, middle-aged. ● **mûrement** *adv* (*réfléchir*) carefully. ● **mûrir** *vti* (*fruit*) to ripen; (*personne*) to mature.
mûre [myr] *nf* (*baie*) blackberry.
muret [myrɛ] *nm* low wall.
murmure [myrmyr] *nm* murmur. ● **murmurer** *vti* to murmur.
muscade [myskad] *nf* nutmeg.
muscle [myskl] *nm* muscle. ● **musclé** *a* (*bras*) muscular, brawny. ● **musculaire** *a* (*force, douleur etc*) muscular. ● **musculature** *nf* muscles.
museau, -x [myzo] *nm* (*de chien, chat*) nose, muzzle. ● **museler** *vt* (*animal, presse*) to muzzle. ● **muselière** *nf* (*appareil*) muzzle.
musée [myze] *nm* museum; **m. de peinture** (public) art gallery. ● **muséum** *nm* (natural history) museum.
music-hall [myzikol] *nm* variety theatre.
musique [myzik] *nf* music. ● **musical, -aux** *a* musical. ● **musicien, -ienne** *nmf* musician ‖ *a* **être très/assez m.** to be very/quite musical.
musulman, -ane [myzylmɑ̃, -an] *a & nmf* Muslim, Moslem.
mutation [mytɑsjɔ̃] *nf* (*d'employé*) transfer; **en pleine m.** *Fig* undergoing profound change.
mutilé, -ée [mytile] *nmf* **m. de guerre** disabled ex-serviceman *ou Am* veteran.
mutin [mytɛ̃] **1** *a* (*espiègle*) full of fun, saucy. **2** *nm* (*rebelle*) mutineer.
mutuel, -elle[1] [mytɥɛl] *a* (*réciproque*) mutual.
mutuelle[2] [mytɥɛl] *nf* friendly society, *Am* benefit society.
myope [mjɔp] *a & nmf Méd & Fig* shortsighted (person). ● **myopie** *nf* shortsightedness.
myosotis [mjozɔtis] *nm Bot* forget-me-not.
myrtille [mirtij] *nf* (*baie*) bilberry.
mystère [mistɛr] *nm* mystery. ● **mystérieux, -euse** *a* mysterious.
mystifier [mistifje] *vt* to fool, deceive, hoax.
mystique [mistik] *a* mystical.
mythe [mit] *nm* myth. ● **mythologie** *nf* mythology.

N

N, n [ɛn] *nm* N, n.
n' [n] *voir* **ne.**
nacelle [nasɛl] *nf* (*de ballon*) basket, car, gondola.
nacre [nakr] *nf* mother-of-pearl. ●**nacré** *a* pearly.
nage [naʒ] *nf* (swimming) stroke; **n. libre** freestyle; **traverser à la n.** to swim across; **en n.** *Fig* sweating.
nageoire [naʒwar] *nf* (*de poisson*) fin.
nag/er [naʒe] *vi* to swim; **je nage complètement** (*je suis perdu*) *Fam* I'm all at sea ‖ *vt* (*crawl etc*) to swim. ●**-eur, -euse** *nmf* swimmer.
naguère [nagɛr] *adv Litt* not long ago.
naïf, -ïve [naif, -iv] *a* naïve, simple.
nain, naine [nɛ̃, nɛn] *nmf* dwarf.
naissance [nɛsɑ̃s] *nf* (*de personne, d'animal*) birth; (*de cou*) base; **donner n. à** *Fig* to give rise to; **de n.** from birth.
naître* [nɛtr] *vi* to be born; (*sentiment*) to arise (**de** from); **faire n.** (*soupçon etc*) to give rise to.
naïveté [naivte] *nf* simplicity, naïveté.
nanti [nɑ̃ti] *a* (*riche*) well-off ‖ *n* **les nantis** *Péj* the well-off.
naphtaline [naftalin] *nf* mothballs.
nappe [nap] *nf* **1** table cloth. **2** (*d'eau*) sheet; (*de gaz, pétrole*) layer; (*de brouillard*) blanket. ●**napperon** *nm* (*pour vase etc*) (cloth) mat.
narcotique [narkɔtik] *a & nm* narcotic.
narguer [narge] *vt* to flout, mock.
narine [narin] *nf* nostril.
narquois [narkwa] *a* sneering.
narration [narɑsjɔ̃] *nf* (*récit*) narration. ●**narrateur, -trice** *nmf* narrator.
nasal, -aux [nazal, -o] *a* nasal.
naseau, -x [nazo] *nm* (*de cheval*) nostril.
natal, *mpl* **-als** [natal] *a* (*pays etc*) native. ●**natalité** *nf* birthrate.
natation [natɑsjɔ̃] *nf* swimming.
natif, -ive [natif, -iv] *a & nmf* native; **être n. de** to be a native of.
nation [nasjɔ̃] *nf* nation; **les Nations Unies** the United Nations. ●**national, -aux** *a* national; **fête nationale** national holiday. ●**nationale** *nf* (*route*) trunk road, *Am* highway. ●**nationaliste** *a Péj* nationalistic ‖ *nmf* nationalist. ●**nationalité** *nf* nationality.
natte [nat] *nf* **1** (*de cheveux*) plait, *Am* braid. **2** (*tapis*) mat, (piece of) matting. ●**natter** *vt* to plait, *Am* braid.
naturaliser [natyralize] *vt* (*personne*) *Pol* to naturalize.
nature [natyr] *nf* (*monde naturel, caractère*) nature; **être de n. à** to be likely to; **payer en n.** *Fin* to pay in kind; **n. morte** (*tableau*) still life; **plus grand que n.** larger than life ‖ *a inv* (*omelette, yaourt etc*) plain; (*thé*) without milk.
naturel, -elle [natyrɛl] *a* natural; **mort naturelle** death from natural causes ‖ *nm* (*caractère*) nature; (*simplicité*) naturalness. ●**naturellement** *adv* naturally.
naufrage [nofraʒ] *nm* (ship)wreck; **faire n.** to be (ship)wrecked. ●**naufragé, -ée** *a & nmf* shipwrecked (person).
nausée [noze] *nf* nausea, sickness. ●**nauséabond** *a* nauseating, sickening.
nautique [notik] *a* nautical; **ski/***etc* **n.** water skiing/*etc*.
naval, *mpl* **-als** [naval] *a* naval.
navet [navɛ] *nm* **1** *Bot Culin* turnip. **2** (*film etc*) *Péj* flop, dud.
navette [navɛt] *nf* (*transport*) shuttle (service); **faire la n.** to shuttle back and forth (**entre** between); **n. spatiale** space shuttle.
navigable [navigabl] *a* (*fleuve*) navigable.
navigateur [navigatœr] *nm Av Nau* navigator. ●**navigation** *nf* (*trafic de bateaux*) shipping.
naviguer [navige] *vi* (*bateau*) to sail.
navire [navir] *nm* ship.
navré [navre] *a* (*air*) grieved; **je suis n.** I'm (terribly) sorry (**de faire** to do).
ⓘ**G114** The Perfect Infinitive 7 H 3b)
nazi, -ie [nazi] *a & nmf Pol Hist* Nazi.
ne [n(ə)] (**n'** *before vowel or mute h; used to form negative verb with* **pas, jamais, personne, rien** *etc*) *adv* **1** (+ *pas*) not; **il ne boit pas** he does not *ou* doesn't drink; **il n'ose (pas)** he doesn't dare. **2** (*with* **craindre, avoir peur** *etc*) **je crains qu'il ne parte** I'm afraid he'll leave.
ⓘ**G204** Negative Expressions 12 B
ⓘ**G35, 98 & 101** The Comparative of Adjectives 7 G 1a) & f) and 4 E 1
né [ne] *pp de* **naître** ‖ *a* **elle est née** she was born; **née Dupont** née Dupont.
néanmoins [neɑ̃mwɛ̃] *adv* nevertheless.

néant [neɑ̃] *nm* nothingness, void; (*sur un formulaire*) = none.
nécessaire [nesesɛr] *a* necessary; (*inéluctable*) inevitable ‖ *nm* **le n.** (*biens*) the necessities; **le strict n.** the bare necessities; **n. de toilette** sponge bag; **faire le n.** to do what's necessary. • **nécessité** *nf* necessity. • **nécessiter** *vt* to require, necessitate. • **nécessiteux, -euse** *a* needy.
ⓘ**nécessaire G99** The Subjunctive 7 G 1d)
nécrologie [nekrɔlɔʒi] *nf* obituary.
nectarine [nektarin] *nf* (*fruit*) nectarine.
néerlandais, -aise [neɛrlɑ̃dɛ, -ɛz] *a* Dutch ‖ *nmf* Dutchman, Dutchwoman ‖ *nm* (*langue*) Dutch.
nef [nɛf] *nf* (*d'église*) nave.
néfaste [nefast] *a* (*influence etc*) harmful (**à** to).
négatif, -ive [negatif, -iv] *a* negative ‖ *nm Phot* negative.
négation [negɑsjɔ̃] *nf* denial (**de** of); *Gram* negation; (*mot*) negative.
négligeable [negliʒabl] *a* negligible.
négligent [negliʒɑ̃] *a* careless, negligent. • **négligence** *nf* (*défaut*) carelessness, negligence; (*faute*) (careless) error.
négliger [negliʒe] *vt* (*personne, travail, conseil etc*) to neglect; **n. de faire** to neglect to do ‖ **se n.** *vpr* (*négliger sa tenue ou sa santé*) to neglect oneself. • **négligé** *a* (*tenue*) untidy, neglected; (*travail*) careless.
négoci/er [negɔsje] *vti* to negotiate. • **—ant, -ante** *nmf* merchant, trader. • **négociateur, -trice** *nmf* negotiator. • **négociation** *nf* negotiation.
neige [nɛʒ] *nf* snow; **n. fondue** sleet; **n. carbonique** dry ice. • **neiger** *v imp* to snow; **il neige** it's snowing.
nénuphar [nenyfar] *nm* water lily.
néo [neɔ] *préf* neo-.
néon [neɔ̃] *nm* (*gaz*) neon; **éclairage au n.** neon lighting.
néo-zélandais, -aise [neɔzelɑ̃dɛ, -ɛz] *a* of *ou* from New Zealand ‖ *nmf* New Zealander.
nerf [nɛr] *nm Anat* nerve; **crise de nerfs** (fit of) hysterics; **du n.!, un peu de n.!** *Fam* buck up!; **ça me tape sur les nerfs** *Fam* it gets on my nerves; **être sur les nerfs** *Fig* to be keyed up *ou* het up. • **nerveux, -euse** *a* (*agité*) nervous; **cellule/***etc* **nerveuse** nerve cell/*etc.* • **nervosité** *nf* nervousness.
nescafé® [nɛskafe] *nm* instant coffee.
n'est-ce pas? [nɛspɑ] *adv* isn't he?, don't you? won't they? *etc*; **il fait beau, n'est-ce pas?** the weather's fine, isn't it?
ⓘ**G210** Question Tags 12 C 3b) i)

net, nette [nɛt] **1** *a* (*image, refus*) clear; (*coupure, linge*) clean; (*soigné*) neat; (*copie*) fair ‖ *adv* (*s'arrêter*) dead; (*casser, couper*) clean; (*tuer*) outright; (*refuser*) flat(ly). **2** *a* (*poids, prix etc*) net. • **nettement** *adv* clearly; (*bien plus*) definitely. • **netteté** *nf* clearness; (*de travail*) neatness.
nettoyer [nɛtwaje] *vt* to clean (up). • **nettoyage** *nm* cleaning; **n. à sec** dry cleaning.
neuf[1], **neuve** [nœf, nœv] *a* new; **quoi de n.?** what's new(s)? ‖ *nm* **remettre à n.** to make as good as new; **il y a du n.** there's been something new.
neuf[2] [nœf] *a* & *nm* ([nœv] *before* **heures** & **ans**) nine. • **neuvième** *a* & *nmf* ninth.
neutre [nøtr] **1** *a* (*pays, personne etc*) neutral. **2** *a* & *nm Gram* neuter. • **neutraliser** *vt* to neutralize.
neveu, -x [nəvø] *nm* nephew.
névrose [nevroz] *nf* neurosis. • **névrosé, -ée** *a* & *nmf* neurotic.
nez [ne] *nm* nose; **n. à n.** face to face (**avec** with); **au n. de qn** (*rire etc*) in s.o.'s face.
ni [ni] *conj* **ni...ni** (+ *ne*) neither...nor; **ni Pierre ni Paul ne sont venus** neither Peter nor Paul came; **il n'a ni faim ni soif** he's neither hungry nor thirsty; **sans manger ni boire** without eating or drinking; **ni l'un(e) ni l'autre** neither (of them).
ⓘ**G204, 205** & **206** Negative Expressions 12 B 1, 2 & 3
niais, -aise [njɛ, -ɛz] *a* silly, simple.
niche [niʃ] *nf* (*de chien*) kennel, *Am* doghouse; (*cavité*) niche, recess.
nicher [niʃe] *vi* (*oiseau*) to nest ‖ **se n.** *vpr* (*oiseau*) to nest; (*se cacher*) to hide oneself. • **nichée** *nf* (*chiens*) litter; (*oiseaux, enfants*) brood.
nickel [nikɛl] *nm* (*métal*) nickel.
nicotine [nikɔtin] *nf* nicotine.
nid [ni] *nm* nest; **n. de poules** pothole (*in road*).
nièce [njɛs] *nf* niece.
nier [nje] *vt* to deny (**que** that) ‖ *vi Jur* to deny the charge.
ⓘ**G100** The Subjunctive 7 G 1e)
nigaud, -aude [nigo, -od] *nmf* silly fool.
Nigéria [niʒerja] *nm* Nigeria.
n'importe [nɛ̃pɔrt] *voir* **importer 1.**
niveau, -x [nivo] *nm* (*hauteur*) level; (*degré, compétence*) standard, level; **n. de vie** standard of living; **au n. de qn** (*élève etc*) up to s.o.'s standard. • **niveler** *vt* (*surface*) to level; (*fortunes etc*) to even (up).
noble [nɔbl] *a* noble ‖ *nmf* nobleman, noblewoman. • **noblesse** *nf* (*caractère, classe*) nobility.

noce(s) [nɔs] *nf(pl)* wedding; **noces d'argent/d'or** silver/golden wedding; **faire la noce** *Fam* to have a good time.
nocif, -ive [nɔsif, -iv] *a* harmful.
nocturne [nɔktyrn] *a* nocturnal; **tapage nocturne** *Jur* disturbance (*at night*) ▮ *nf* (*de magasins etc*) late night opening; **(match en) n.** *Sp* floodlit match, *Am* night game.
Noël [nɔɛl] *nm* Christmas; **le père N.** Father Christmas, Santa Claus.
nœud [nø] *nm* **1** knot; (*ruban*) bow; **n. coulant** slipknot, noose; **n. papillon** bow tie; **le n. du problème** the crux of the problem. **2** (*mesure*) *Nau* knot.
noir, noire [nwar] *a* black; (*nuit, lunettes etc*) dark; (*idées*) gloomy; (*âme*) vile; (*misère*) dire; **roman n.** thriller; **il fait n.** it's dark ▮ *nm* (*couleur*) black; (*obscurité*) dark; **N.** (*homme*) black; **vendre au n.** to sell on the black market ▮ *nf Mus* crotchet, *Am* quarter note; **Noire** (*femme*) black.
noircir [nwarsir] *vt* to make black ▮ *vi*, **se n.** *vpr* to turn black.
noisette [nwazɛt] *nf* hazelnut.
noix [nwa] *nf* (*du noyer*) walnut; **n. de coco** coconut; **n. de beurre** knob of butter; **à la n.** *Fam* trashy.
nom [nɔ̃] *nm* name; *Gram* noun; **n. de famille** surname; **n. de jeune fille** maiden name; **n. propre** *Gram* proper noun; **au n. de qn** on s.o.'s behalf.
nomade [nɔmad] *nmf* nomad.
nombre [nɔ̃br] *nm* number; **ils sont au n. de dix** there are ten of them; **le plus grand n. de** the majority of. • **nombreux, -euse** *a* (*amis, livres etc*) numerous, many; (*famille*) large; **peu n.** few; **venir n.** to come in large numbers.
ℹ **nombreux G32** Position of Adjectives 4 D 3
nombril [nɔ̃bri(l)] *nm* navel.
nomination [nɔminɑsjɔ̃] *nf* appointment, nomination.
nommer [nɔme] *vt* (*appeler*) to name; **n. qn** (*désigner*) to appoint s.o. (**à un poste**/*etc* to a post/*etc*); **n. qn président** to nominate *ou* appoint s.o. chairman ▮ **se n.** *vpr* (*s'appeler*) to be called.
non [nɔ̃] *adv* & *nm inv* no; **tu viens ou n.?** are you coming or not?; **n. seulement** not only; **n. (pas) que** (+ *sub*)... not that...; **je crois que n.** I don't think so; **(ni) moi n. plus** neither do, am, can *etc* I; **c'est bien, n.?** *Fam* it's all right, isn't it?
ℹ **G207** Negative Expressions 12 B 4c)
ℹ **G210** Question Tags 12 C 3b) ii)
ℹ **G211** Answers 12 D
non- [nɔ̃] *préf* non-.
nonante [nɔnɑ̃t] *a* & *nm* (*en Belgique, en Suisse*) ninety.
non-fumeur, -euse [nɔ̃fymœr, -øz] *nmf* non-smoker.
nord [nɔr] *nm* north; **au n.** in the north; (*direction*) (to the) north (**de** of); **du n.** (*vent, direction*) northerly; (*ville*) northern; (*gens*) from *ou* in the north; **Amérique/Afrique du N.** North America/Africa; **l'Europe du N.** Northern Europe.
▮ *a inv* (*côte*) north(ern). • **n.-africain, -aine** *a* & *nmf* North African. • **n.-américain, -aine** *a* & *nmf* North American. • **n.-est** *nm* & *a inv* north-east. • **n.-ouest** *nm* & *a inv* north-west.
nordique [nɔrdik] *a* & *nmf* Scandinavian.
normal, -aux [nɔrmal, -o] *a* normal. • **normale** *nf* norm, normality; **au-dessus/au-dessous de la n.** above/below normal. • **normalement** *adv* normally.
normand, -ande [nɔrmɑ̃, -ɑ̃d] *a* & *nmf* Norman. • **Normandie** *nf* Normandy.
norme [nɔrm] *nf* norm.
Norvège [nɔrvɛʒ] *nf* Norway. • **norvégien, -ienne** *a* & *nmf* Norwegian ▮ *nm* (*langue*) Norwegian.
nos [no] *voir* **notre.**
nostalgie [nɔstalʒi] *nf* nostalgia.
notable [nɔtabl] *a* (*fait*) notable ▮ *nm* (*personne*) notable.
notaire [nɔtɛr] *nm* solicitor, lawyer.
notamment [nɔtamɑ̃] *adv* particularly.
note [nɔt] *nf* (*remarque etc*) & *Mus* note; (*chiffrée*) *Scol* mark, *Am* grade; (*facture*) bill, *Am* check; **prendre n. de** to make a note of.
noter [nɔte] *vt* (*remarquer*) to note, notice; (*écrire*) to note down; (*devoir etc*) *Scol* to mark, *Am* grade.
notice [nɔtis] *nf* (*mode d'emploi*) instructions.
notifier [nɔtifje] *vt* **n. qch à qn** to notify s.o. of sth.
notion [nosjɔ̃] *nf* notion, idea; *pl* (*éléments*) rudiments.
notoire [nɔtwar] *a* (*criminel*) notorious; (*fait*) well-known.
notre, *pl* **nos** [nɔtr, no] *a poss* our. • **nôtre** *pron poss* **le** *ou* **la n., les nôtres** ours; ▮ *nmpl* **les nôtres** (*parents etc*) our (own) people.
ℹ **notre** & **nôtre G64** Possessive Adjectives and Pronouns 6 E
nouer [nwe] *vt* (*lacets etc*) to tie, knot; (*amitié, conversation*) to strike up.
nougat [nuga] *nm* nougat.

nouilles [nuj] *nfpl* noodles.
nounours [nunurs] *nm* teddy bear.
nourrice [nuris] *nf* (*assistante maternelle*) child minder, nurse.
nourrir [nurir] *vt* (*alimenter*) to feed ▮ **se n.** *vpr* to eat; **se n. de** to feed on ▮ *vi* (*aliment*) to be nourishing. • **nourrissant** *a* nourishing.
nourrisson [nurisɔ̃] *nm* infant.
nourriture [nurityr] *nf* food.
nous [nu] *pron* **1** (*sujet*) we; **n. sommes** we are. **2** (*complément direct*) us; **il n. connaît** he knows us. **3** (*indirect*) (to) us; **il n. l'a donné** he gave it to us. **4** (*réfléchi*) ourselves; **n. n. lavons** we wash ourselves. **5** (*réciproque*) each other; **n. n. détestons** we hate each other. • **nous-mêmes** *pron* ourselves.
❶ **nous G56** & **57** Subject and Object Pronouns 6 D 1 & 2
❶ **nous G62** Disjunctive Pronouns 6 D 5
❶ **nous G84** Reflexive Verbs and Pronouns 7 D
nouveau (*or* **nouvel** *before vowel or mute h*), **nouvelle**[1], *pl* **nouveaux, nouvelles** [nuvo, nuvɛl] *a* new ▮ *nmf Scol* new boy, new girl ▮ *nm* **du n.** something new; **de n., à n.** again. • **n.-né, -ée** *a* & *nmf* new-born (baby). • **nouveauté** *nf* novelty; *pl* (*livres*) new books; (*disques*) new releases.
nouvelle[2] [nuvɛl] *nf* **1 nouvelle(s)** (*information*) news; **une n.** a piece of news. **2** (*récit*) short story.
Nouvelle-Zélande [nuvɛlzelɑ̃d] *nf* New Zealand.
novembre [nɔvɑ̃br] *nm* November.
novice [nɔvis] *a* inexperienced.
noyade [nwajad] *nf* drowning.
noyau, -x [nwajo] *nm* (*de fruit*) stone, *Am* pit; (*d'atome, de cellule*) nucleus.
noyer[1] [nwaje] *vt* to drown; (*terres*) to flood ▮ **se n.** *vpr* to drown; (*se suicider*) to drown oneself. • **noyé, -ée** *nmf* (*mort*) drowned man *ou* woman ▮ *a* **être n.** (*perdu*) *Fig* to be out of one's depth.
noyer[2] [nwaje] *nm* (*arbre*) walnut tree.
nu [ny] *a* (*personne*) naked; (*mains, chambre*) bare; **tout nu** (stark) naked, (in the) nude; **tête nue** bare-headed; **voir à l'œil nu** to see with the naked eye.
nuage [nɥaʒ] *nm* cloud. • **nuageux, -euse** *a* cloudy.
nuance [nɥɑ̃s] *nf* (*de couleurs*) shade; (*de sens*) nuance. • **nuancer** *vt* (*teintes*) to blend, shade; (*pensée*) to qualify.
nucléaire [nykleɛr] *a* nuclear.
nudiste [nydist] *nmf* nudist; **camp de nudistes** nudist camp.
nuée [nɥe] *nf Litt* **une n. de** (*foule*) a host of; (*groupe compact*) a cloud of.
nues [ny] *nfpl* **tomber des n.** to be astounded.
nuire* [nɥir] *vi* **n. à** (*personne, intérêts etc*) to harm. • **nuisible** *a* harmful.
nuit [nɥi] *nf* night; (*obscurité*) dark(ness); **il fait n.** it's dark; **la n.** (*se promener etc*) at night; **cette n.** (*aujourd'hui*) tonight; (*hier*) last night; **bonne n.** good night; **voyager/travailler de n.** to travel/work by night.
nul, nulle [nyl] **1** *a* (*médiocre*) hopeless, useless; (*risque etc*) non-existent, nil; (*non valable*) *Jur* null (and void); **faire match n.** *Sp* to tie, draw. **2** *a* (*aucun*) no; **nulle part** nowhere; **sans n. doute** without any doubt ▮ *pron m* (*aucun*) no one. • **nullement** *adv* not at all.
❶ **nul** & **nulle part G204**, **205** & **206** Negative Expressions 12 B 1, 2 & 3
numérique [nymerik] *a* numerical; (*affichage etc*) digital.
numéro [nymero] *nm* number; (*de journal*) issue; (*au cirque*) act; **un n. de danse** a dance number; **n. vert** *Tél* = 0800 number, = *Am* tollfree number; **quel n.!** (*personne*) *Fam* what a character! • **numéroter** *vt* (*pages etc*) to number.
nu-pieds [nypje] *a inv* barefoot ▮ *nmpl* open sandals.
nuque [nyk] *nf* back *ou* nape of the neck.
nurse [nœrs] *nf* nanny, (children's) nurse.
nu-tête [nytɛt] *a inv* bare-headed.
nutritif, -ive [nytritif, -iv] *a* nutritious.
nylon [nilɔ̃] *nm* (*fibre*) nylon; **chemise/***etc* **en n.** nylon shirt/*etc*.

O

O, o [o] *nm* O, o.
oasis [ɔazis] *nf* oasis.
obé/ir [ɔbeir] *vi* to obey; **o. à qn/qch** to obey s.o./sth. ●**—issant** *a* obedient. ●**obéissance** *nf* obedience (**à** to).
obèse [ɔbɛz] *a & nmf* obese (person).
objecter [ɔbʒɛkte] *vt* (*prétexte*) to put forward; **o. que** to object that; **on lui objecta son jeune âge** they objected that he *ou* she was too young. ●**objection** *nf* objection.
objectif, -ive [ɔbʒɛktif, -iv] **1** *nm* (*but*) objective; *Phot* lens. **2** *a* (*opinion etc*) objective. ●**objectivité** *nf* objectivity.
objet [ɔbʒɛ] *nm* (*chose, sujet*) object; (*de toilette*) article; **faire l'o. de** (*étude, critiques etc*) to be the subject of; (*soins, surveillance*) to be given, receive; **objets trouvés** (*bureau*) lost property, *Am* lost and found.
obligation [ɔbligasjɔ̃] *nf* (*devoir, nécessité*) obligation; *Fin* bond. ●**obligatoire** *a* compulsory, obligatory; (*inévitable*) *Fam* inevitable.
oblig/er [ɔbliʒe] *vt* **1** to force, compel, oblige (**à faire** to do); (*engager*) to bind; **être obligé de faire** to have to do, be compelled to do. **2** (*rendre service à*) to oblige; **être obligé à qn de qch** to be obliged to s.o. for sth. ●**—é** *a* (*obligatoire*) necessary; (*fatal*) *Fam* inevitable. ●**obligeance** *nf* kindness.
oblique [ɔblik] *a* oblique; **regard o.** sidelong glance; **en o.** at an (oblique) angle.
oblitérer [ɔblitere] *vt* (*timbre*) to cancel; **timbre oblitéré** (*non neuf*) used stamp.
obscène [ɔpsɛn] *a* obscene. ●**obscénité** *nf* obscenity.
obscur [ɔpskyr] *a* (*noir*) dark; (*peu clair, inconnu, humble*) obscure. ●**obscurcir** *vt* (*chambre etc*) to make dark(er) ‖ **s'o.** *vpr* (*ciel*) to get dark(er). ●**obscurité** *nf* dark(ness).
obséd/er [ɔpsede] *vt* to obsess, haunt. ●**—ant** *a* haunting, obsessive. ●**—é, -ée** *nmf* maniac (**de** for); **o. sexuel** sex maniac.
obsèques [ɔpsɛk] *nfpl* funeral.
observer [ɔpsɛrve] *vt* (*regarder*) to watch, observe; (*remarquer, respecter*) to observe; **faire o. qch à qn** to point sth out to s.o. ●**observateur, -trice** *a* observant ‖ *nmf* observer. ●**observation** *nf* (*étude, remarque*) observation; (*reproche*) rebuke; (*de règle etc*) observance; **en o.** (*malade*) under observation. ●**observatoire** *nm* observatory; (*endroit élevé*) lookout (post).
obsession [ɔpsesjɔ̃] *nf* obsession.
obstacle [ɔpstakl] *nm* obstacle; **faire o. à** to stand in the way of.
obstiner (s') [sɔpstine] *vpr* to be persistent; **s'o. à faire** to persist in doing. ●**obstiné** *a* stubborn, persistent, obstinate.
obstruction [ɔpstryksjɔ̃] *nf Méd Pol Sp* obstruction; **faire de l'o.** *Pol Sp* to be obstructive. ●**obstruer** *vt* to obstruct.
obtempérer [ɔptɑ̃pere] *vi* to obey (an order); **o. à** to obey.
obtenir* [ɔptənir] *vt* to get, obtain, secure.
obtus [ɔpty] *a* (*angle, esprit*) obtuse.
obus [ɔby] *nm Mil* shell.
occasion [ɔkazjɔ̃] *nf* **1** (*chance*) chance, opportunity (**de faire** to do); (*circonstance*) occasion; **à l'o.** on occasion; **à l'o. de** on the occasion of. **2** *Com* (*prix avantageux*) bargain; (*objet non neuf*) secondhand buy; **d'o.** secondhand, used.
occasionner [ɔkazjɔne] *vt* to cause; **o. qch à qn** to cause s.o. sth.
occident [ɔksidɑ̃] *nm* **l'O.** *Pol* the West. ●**occidental, -aux** *a Géog Pol* western ‖ *nmpl* **les occidentaux** *Pol* Westerners.
occupant, -ante [ɔkypɑ̃, -ɑ̃t] *nmf* (*habitant*) occupant ‖ *nm Mil* forces of occupation.
occupation [ɔkypasjɔ̃] *nf* (*activité etc*) occupation.
occupé [ɔkype] *a* busy (**à faire** doing); (*place, maison etc*) occupied; (*ligne*) *Tél* engaged, *Am* busy; (*taxi*) hired.
occuper [ɔkype] *vt* (*maison, pays etc*) to occupy; (*place, temps*) to take up, occupy; (*poste*) to hold, occupy; **o. qn** (*travail, jeu*) to keep s.o. busy, occupy s.o. ‖ **s'occuper** *vpr* to keep (oneself) busy (**à faire** doing); **s'o. de** (*affaire, problème etc*) to deal with; (*politique*) to be engaged in; **s'o. de qn** (*malade etc*) to take care of s.o.; (*client*) to see to s.o., deal with s.o.; **occupe-toi de tes affaires!** mind your own business!
occurrence [ɔkyrɑ̃s] *nf* **en l'o.** in this case, as it happens.
océan [ɔseɑ̃] *nm* ocean.
ocre [ɔkr] *nm & a inv* (*couleur*) ochre.
octobre [ɔktɔbr] *nm* October.

octogone [ɔktɔgɔn] *nm* octagon.
octroyer [ɔktrwaje] *vt Litt* to grant (**à** to).
oculaire [ɔkylɛr] *a* **témoin o.** eyewitness; **globe o.** eyeball. • **oculiste** *nmf* eye specialist.
odeur [ɔdœr] *nf* smell, odour; (*de fleur*) scent. • **odorat** *nm* sense of smell.
odieux, -euse [ɔdjø, -øz] *a* horrible, odious.
œil, *pl* **yeux** [œj, jø] *nm* eye; **lever/baisser les yeux** to look up/down; **fermer l'o.** (*dormir*) to shut one's eyes; **fermer les yeux sur** to turn a blind eye to; **coup d'o.** (*regard*) look, glance; **jeter un coup d'o. sur** to (have a) look *ou* glance at; **à vue d'o.** visibly; **à l'o.** (*gratuitement*) *Fam* free; **o. poché** *ou* **au beurre noir** *Fig* black eye; **mon o.!** *Fam* (*incrédulité*) my foot!; (*refus*) no way!
œillères [œjɛr] *nfpl* (*de cheval*) & *Fig* blinkers, *Am* blinders.
œillet [œjɛ] *nm* **1** *Bot* carnation. **2** (*trou de ceinture*) eyelet.
œuf, *pl* **œufs** [œf, ø] *nm* egg; *pl* (*de poisson*) (hard) roe; **o. sur le plat** fried egg; **o. dur** hard-boiled egg; **œufs brouillés** scrambled eggs.
œuvre [œvr] *nf* (*travail, livre etc*) work; **o. (de charité)** (*organisation*) charity; **o. d'art** work of art; **mettre tout en o.** to do everything possible (**pour faire** to do).
offense [ɔfɑ̃s] *nf* insult. • **offenser** *vt* to offend; **s'o. de** to take offence at.
offensif, -ive [ɔfɑ̃sif, -iv] *a* offensive ‖ *nf* (*attaque*) offensive; (*du froid*) onslaught.
offert [ɔfɛr] *pp de* **offrir.**
office [ɔfis] *nm* **1** *Rel* service. **2** (*pièce près de la cuisine*) pantry. **3** (*établissement*) office, bureau; **d'o.** automatically; **faire o. de** to serve as; **ses bons offices** one's good offices.
officiel, -ielle [ɔfisjɛl] *a* (*acte etc*) official ‖ *nm* (*personnage*) official. • **officiellement** *adv* officially. • **officieux, -euse** *a* unofficial.
officier [ɔfisje] *nm* (*dans l'armée etc*) officer.
offre [ɔfr] *nf* offer; (*aux enchères*) bid; **l'o. et la demande** *Écon* supply and demand; **offres d'emploi** (*dans un journal*) job vacancies, situations vacant.
offrir* [ɔfrir] *vt* **o. qch (à qn)** (*donner en cadeau*) to give (s.o.) sth, give sth (to s.o.); (*proposer*) to offer (s.o.) sth, offer sth (to s.o.); **je lui ai offert de le loger** I offered to put him up ‖ **s'o.** *vpr* (*cadeau etc*) to treat oneself to; (*se proposer*) to offer oneself (**comme** as); **s'o. aux regards** (*spectacle etc*) to greet one's eyes. • **offrant** *nm* **au plus o.** to the highest bidder.
offusquer [ɔfyske] *vt* to offend, shock.
ogive [ɔʒiv] *nf* (*de fusée*) nose cone; **o. nucléaire** nuclear warhead.
ogre [ɔgr] *nm* ogre.
oh! [o] *int* oh!
ohé! [ɔe] *int* hey (there)!
oie [wa] *nf* goose (*pl* geese).
oignon [ɔɲɔ̃] *nm* (*légume*) onion; (*de fleur*) bulb.
oiseau, -x [wazo] *nm* bird; **à vol d'o.** as the crow flies; **o. rare** (*être irremplaçable*) *Hum* rare bird.
oiseux, -euse [wazø, -øz] *a* (*inutile*) idle, vain.
oisif, -ive [wazif, -iv] *a* (*inactif*) idle. • **oisiveté** *nf* idleness
oléoduc [ɔleɔdyk] *nm* oil pipeline.
olive [ɔliv] *nf* (*fruit*) olive; **huile d'o.** olive oil ‖ *a inv* (*couleur*) **(vert) o.** olive (green). • **olivier** *nm* olive tree.
olympique [ɔlɛ̃pik] *a* (*jeux, record etc*) Olympic.
ombrage [ɔ̃braʒ] *nm* (*ombre*) shade. • **ombragé** *a* shady.
ombre [ɔ̃br] *nf* (*d'arbre etc*) shade; (*de personne, objet*) shadow; **à l'o.** in the shade; **dans l'o.** (*comploter etc*) *Fig* in secret.
ombrelle [ɔ̃brɛl] *nf* sunshade, parasol.
omelette [ɔmlɛt] *nf* omelet(te); **o. au fromage**/*etc* cheese/*etc* omelet(te).
omettre* [ɔmɛtr] *vt* to omit (**de faire** to do).
omnibus [ɔmnibys] *a* & *nm* **(train) o.** slow *ou* stopping train.
omoplate [ɔmɔplat] *nf* shoulder blade.
on [ɔ̃] (*sometimes* **l'on** [lɔ̃]) *pron* (*les gens*) they, people; (*nous*) we, one; (*vous*) you, one; **on frappe** someone's knocking; **on dit** they say, people say, it is said; **on m'a dit que** I was told that.
ⓘ **G52** Indefinite Pronouns 6 B 2c)
ⓘ **G120** The Passive 7 J 2a)
oncle [ɔ̃kl] *nm* uncle.
onctueux, -euse [ɔ̃ktɥø, -øz] *a* (*liquide, crème*) creamy.
onde [ɔ̃d] *nf Rad Phys* wave; **grandes ondes** long wave; **ondes courtes/moyennes** short/medium wave.
ondée [ɔ̃de] *nf* (*pluie*) (sudden) shower.
on-dit [ɔ̃di] *nm inv* rumour, hearsay.
ondulation [ɔ̃dylɑsjɔ̃] *nf* undulation; (*de cheveux*) wave. • **onduler** *vi* to undulate; (*cheveux*) to be wavy.
onéreux, -euse [ɔnerø, -øz] *a* costly.
ongle [ɔ̃gl] *nm* (finger) nail.
ont [ɔ̃] *voir* **avoir.**
ONU [ɔny] *nf abrév* (*Organisation des nations unies*) UN.

onze [ɔ̃z] *a & nm* eleven. • **onzième** *a & nmf* eleventh.

opaque [ɔpak] *a* opaque.

opéra [ɔpera] *nm* (*musique*) opera; (*édifice*) opera house. • **opérette** *nf* operetta.

opérateur, -trice [ɔperatœr, -tris] *nmf* (*de prise de vues*) cameraman; (*sur machine*) operator.

opérer [ɔpere] **1** *vt* (*en chirurgie*) to operate on (*s.o.*) (**de** for); (*tumeur*) to remove; **se faire o.** to have an operation ‖ *vi* (*chirurgien*) to operate.
2 *vt* (*exécuter*) to carry out; (*choix*) to make ‖ *vi* (*agir*) to work, act; (*procéder*) to proceed ‖ **s'o.** *vpr* (*se produire*) to take place. • **opération** *nf Méd Mil Math etc* operation; *Fin* deal. • **opératoire** *a* **choc o.** post-operative shock; **bloc o.** operating *ou* surgical wing.

opiner [ɔpine] *vi* **o. (de la tête** *ou* **du chef)** to nod assent.

opiniâtre [ɔpinjɑtr] *a* stubborn, obstinate.

opinion [ɔpinjɔ̃] *nf* opinion (**sur** about, on).

opium [ɔpjɔm] *nm* opium.

opportun [ɔpɔrtœ̃] *a* opportune, timely. • **opportunité** *nf* timeliness.

opposé [ɔpose] *a* (*direction, opinion etc*) opposite; (*équipe, intérêts*) opposing; **être o. à** to be opposed to ‖ *nm* **l'o.** the opposite (**de** of); **à l'o.** (*côté*) on the opposite side (**de** from, to); **à l'o. de** (*contrairement à*) contrary to.

opposer [ɔpoze] *vt* (*résistance, argument*) to put up (**à** against); (*équipes*) to bring together; (*couleurs etc*) to contrast; **o. qn à qn** to set s.o. against s.o.; **o. qch à qch** (*objet*) to place sth opposite sth; **match qui oppose...** match between....
‖ **s'opposer** *vpr* (*équipes*) to play against each other; **s'o. à** (*mesure, personne etc*) to be opposed to, oppose; **je m'y oppose** I'm opposed to it, I oppose. • **opposition** *nf* opposition (**à** to); **faire o. à** to oppose; (*chèque*) to stop.

oppress/er [ɔprese] *vt* (*gêner*) to oppress. • **—ant** *a* oppressive. • **oppression** *nf* oppression. • **opprimer** *vt* (*tyranniser*) to oppress.

opter [ɔpte] *vi* **o. pour** to opt for.

opticien, -ienne [ɔptisjɛ̃, -jɛn] *nmf* optician.

optimisme [ɔptimism] *nm* optimism. • **optimiste** *a* optimistic ‖ *nmf* optimist.

optimum [ɔptimɔm] *a* **la température o.** the optimum temperature.

option [ɔpsjɔ̃] *nf* (*choix*) option; (*chose*) optional extra.

optique [ɔptik] *a* (*verre, fibres*) optical ‖ *nf* optics; (*aspect*) *Fig* perspective; **d'o.** (*illusion, instrument*) optical.

opulent [ɔpylɑ̃] *a* opulent.

or [ɔr] **1** *nm* gold; **montre**/*etc* **en or** gold watch/*etc*; **d'or** (*règle, âge*) golden; (*cœur*) of gold; **mine d'or** goldmine; **affaire en or** (*achat*) bargain; (*commerce*) *Fig* goldmine; **or noir** (*pétrole*) *Fig* black gold. **2** *conj* (*cependant*) now, well.

orage [ɔraʒ] *nm* (thunder)storm. • **orageux, -euse** *a* stormy.

oral, -aux [ɔral, -o] *a* oral ‖ *nm* (*examen*) *Scol* oral.

orange [ɔrɑ̃ʒ] *nf* (*fruit*) orange; **o. pressée** (fresh) orange juice ‖ *a & nm inv* (*couleur*) orange. • **orangeade** *nf* orangeade. • **oranger** *nm* orange tree.

orateur [ɔratœr] *nm* speaker, orator.

orbite [ɔrbit] *nf* (*d'astre etc*) orbit; (*d'œil*) socket; **mettre sur o.** to put into orbit.

orchestre [ɔrkɛstr] *nm* (*classique*) orchestra; (*jazz, pop*) band; (*places*) *Th Cin* stalls, *Am* orchestra.

orchidée [ɔrkide] *nf* orchid.

ordinaire [ɔrdinɛr] *a* (*habituel, normal*) ordinary, *Am* regular; (*médiocre*) ordinary, average; **d'o., à l'o.** usually; **de l'essence o.** two-star (petrol), *Am* regular.

ordinal, -aux [ɔrdinal, -o] *a* (*nombre*) ordinal.

ordinateur [ɔrdinatœr] *nm* computer.

ordonnance [ɔrdɔnɑ̃s] *nf* **1** (*de médecin*) prescription. **2** (*décret*) *Jur* order, ruling. **3** (*soldat*) orderly.

ordonn/er [ɔrdɔne] *vt* **1** (*enjoindre*) to order (**que** (+ *sub*) that); **o. à qn de faire** to order s.o. to do. **2** (*prêtre*) to ordain. • **—é** *a* (*personne etc*) tidy, orderly.

ⓘ**ordonner G204** Word Order: Inversion 12 A 7b)

ordre [ɔrdr] *nm* (*commandement, classement etc*) order; (*absence de désordre*) tidiness (*of room, person etc*); **en o.** (*chambre etc*) tidy; **mettre en o., mettre de l'o. dans** to tidy (up); **jusqu'à nouvel o.** until further notice; **de l'o. de** (*environ*) of the order of; **de premier o.** first-rate; **à l'o. du jour** on the agenda; **les forces de l'o.** the police.

ordures [ɔrdyr] *nfpl* (*déchets*) rubbish, *Am* garbage.

oreille [ɔrɛj] *nf* ear; **faire la sourde o.** to take no notice, refuse to listen; **être tout oreilles** to be all ears; **casser les oreilles à qn** to deafen s.o.

oreiller [ɔreje] *nm* pillow.

oreillons [ɔrɛjɔ̃] *nmpl Méd* mumps.

ores (d') [dɔr] *adv* **d'ores et déjà** [dɔrzedeʒa] henceforth.
orfèvre [ɔrfɛvr] *nm* goldsmith, silversmith. • **orfèvrerie** *nf* (*magasin*) goldsmith's *ou* silversmith's shop; (*objets*) gold *ou* silver plate.
organe [ɔrgan] *nm Anat & Fig* organ. • **organisme** *nm* **1** (*corps*) body; *Anat Biol* organism. **2** (*bureaux etc*) organization.
organisation [ɔrganizɑsjɔ̃] *nf* (*arrangement*, *association*) organization.
organiser [ɔrganize] *vt* to organize ‖ **s'o.** *vpr* to get organized. • **organiseur** *nm* **(agenda) o.** Filofax®. • **organisateur, -trice** *nmf* organiser.
orgasme [ɔrgasm] *nm* orgasm.
orge [ɔrʒ] *nf* barley.
orgie [ɔrʒi] *nf* orgy.
orgue [ɔrg] *nm Mus* organ ‖ *nfpl* organ; **grandes orgues** great organ.
orgueil [ɔrgœj] *nm* pride. • **orgueilleux, -euse** *a* proud.
orient [ɔrjɑ̃] *nm* **l'O.** the Orient, the East; **Moyen-O., Proche-O.** Middle East; **Extrême-O.** Far East. • **oriental, -ale, -aux** *a* (*côte, pays etc*) eastern; (*du Japon, de la Chine*) far-eastern, oriental.
orientation [ɔrjɑ̃tɑsjɔ̃] *nf* direction; (*action*) positioning; (*de maison*) aspect, orientation; (*tendance*) *Pol Littér* trend; **o. professionnelle** careers' advice; **sens de l'o.** sense of direction.
orienter [ɔrjɑ̃te] *vt* (*lampe etc*) to position, direct; (*voyageur, élève etc*) to direct; (*maison*) to orientate, *Am* orient ‖ **s'o.** *vpr* to find one's bearings *ou* direction; **s'o. vers** (*carrière etc*) to move towards. • **orienté** *a* (*film etc*) slanted; **o. à l'ouest** (*appartement etc*) facing west.
orifice [ɔrifis] *nm* opening, orifice.
originaire [ɔriʒinɛr] *a* **être o. de** (*natif*) to be a native of.
original, -ale, -aux [ɔriʒinal, -o] **1** *a* (*idée, artiste etc*) original ‖ *nm* (*texte*) original. **2** *a & nmf* (*bizarre*) eccentric. • **originalité** *nf* originality; eccentricity.
origine [ɔriʒin] *nf* origin; **à l'o.** originally; **d'o.** (*pneu etc*) original; **pays d'o.** country of origin.
orme [ɔrm] *nm* (*arbre, bois*) elm.
ornement [ɔrnəmɑ̃] *nm* ornament. • **orner** *vt* to decorate, adorn (**de** with).
ornière [ɔrnjɛr] *nf* (*sillon*) rut.
orphelin, -ine [ɔrfəlɛ̃, -in] *nmf* orphan. • **orphelinat** *nm* orphanage.
orteil [ɔrtɛj] *nm* toe; **gros o.** big toe.
orthodoxe [ɔrtɔdɔks] *a* orthodox.
orthographe [ɔrtɔgraf] *nf* spelling. • **orthographier** *vt* to spell.
orthopédie [ɔrtɔpedi] *nf* orthop(a)edics.
ortie [ɔrti] *nf* nettle.
os [ɔs, *pl* o] *nm* bone; **trempé jusqu'aux os** soaked to the skin.
OS [oɛs] *abrév* = **ouvrier spécialisé.**
oscar [ɔskar] *nm Cin* Oscar.
osciller [ɔsile] *vi Tech* to oscillate; (*se balancer*) to swing, sway; (*varier*) to fluctuate (**entre** between).
oseille [ozɛj] *nf Bot Culin* sorrel.
oser [oze] *vti* to dare; **o. faire** to dare (to) do. • **osé** *a* bold, daring.
osier [ozje] *nm* wicker; **panier d'o.** wicker basket.
ossature [ɔsatyr] *nf* (*du corps*) frame; (*de bâtiment*) & *Fig* framework. • **osseux, -euse** *a* (*maigre*) bony; **tissu**/*etc* **o.** bone/*etc* tissue.
ostensible [ɔstɑ̃sibl] *a* conspicuous.
otage [ɔtaʒ] *nm* hostage; **prendre qn en o.** to take s.o. hostage.
OTAN [ɔtɑ̃] *nf abrév* (*Organisation du traité de l'Atlantique Nord*) NATO.
otarie [ɔtari] *nf* (*animal*) sea lion.
ôter [ote] *vt* to take away, remove (**à qn** from s.o.); (*vêtement*) to take off, remove; (*déduire*) to take (away).
otite [ɔtit] *nf* ear infection.
oto-rhino [ɔtɔrino] *nmf Méd Fam* ear, nose and throat specialist.
ou [u] *conj* or; **ou bien** or else; **ou elle ou moi** either her or me.
où [u] *adv & pron* where; **le jour où** the day when; **la table où** the table on which; **l'état où** the condition in which; **par où?** which way?; **d'où?** where from?; **d'où ma surprise/***etc* hence my surprise/*etc*; **le pays d'où** the country from which; **où qu'il soit** wherever he may be.
ⓘ **G70** Relative Pronouns 6 F 3f)
ⓘ **G208** & **209** Direct and Indirect Questions 12 C 1 & 2
ouate [wat] *nf Méd* cotton wool, *Am* absorbent cotton.
oubli [ubli] *nm* (*défaut*) forgetfulness; **l'o. de qch** forgetting sth; **un o.** a lapse of memory; (*dans une liste etc*) an oversight; **tomber dans l'o.** to fall into oblivion.
oublier [ublije] *vt* to forget (**de faire** to do); (*faute*) to overlook.
oubliettes [ublijɛt] *nfpl* dungeon.
ouest [wɛst] *nm* west; **à l'o.** in the west; (*direction*) (to the) west (**de** of); **d'o.** (*vent*) west(erly); **de l'o.** western; **l'Europe de l'O.** Western Europe ‖ *a inv* (*côte*) west(ern).

ouf! [uf] *int* (*soulagement*) what a relief!
oui [wi] *adv* & *nm inv* yes; **tu viens, o. ou non?** are you coming or aren't you?; **je crois que o.** I think so.
G211 Answers 12 D
ouï-dire [widir] *nm inv* **par o.-dire** by hearsay.
ouïe[1] [wi] *nf* hearing; **être tout o.** *Hum* to be all ears.
ouïe[2]**!** [uj] *int* ouch!
ouïes [wi] *nfpl* (*de poisson*) gills.
ouille! [uj] *int* ouch!
ouragan [uragɑ̃] *nm* hurricane.
ourler [urle] *vt* to hem. ● **ourlet** *nm* hem.
ours [urs] *nm* bear; **o. blanc** polar bear.
oursin [ursɛ̃] *nm* (*animal*) sea urchin.
ouste! [ust] *int Fam* scram!
outil [uti] *nm* tool. ● **outiller** *vt* to equip. ● **outillage** *nm* tools.
outrage [utraʒ] *nm* insult (**à** to).
outrance [utrɑ̃s] *nf* (*excès*) excess. ; **à o.** (*travailler etc*) to excess.
outre [utr] *prép* besides ‖ *adv* **en o.** besides; **o. mesure** inordinately; **passer o.** to take no notice (**à** of). ● **o.-Manche** *adv* across the Channel. ● **o.-mer** *adv* overseas; **d'o.-mer** (*territoire*) overseas.
outrepasser [utrəpɑse] *vt* (*limite etc*) to go beyond, exceed.
outré [utre] *a* (*révolté*) outraged; (*excessif*) exaggerated.
ouvert [uvɛr] *pp de* **ouvrir** ‖ *a* open; (*robinet, gaz etc*) on; **à bras ouverts** with open arms. ● **ouvertement** *adv* openly. ● **ouverture** *nf* opening; (*trou*) hole; (*avance*) & *Mus* overture; **o. d'esprit** open-mindedness.
ouvrable [uvrabl] *a* **jour o.** working day.
ouvrage [uvraʒ] *nm* (*travail, livre*) work; (*couture*) (needle)work; **un o.** (*travail*) a piece of work.
ouvreuse [uvrøz] *nf Cin* usherette.
ouvrier, -ière [uvrije, -jɛr] *nmf* worker; **o. qualifié/spécialisé** skilled/unskilled worker ‖ *a* (*quartier etc*) working-class; **classe ouvrière** working class.
ouvrir** [uvrir] *vt* to open (up); (*gaz, radio etc*) to turn on, switch on; (*inaugurer*) to open; (*hostilités*) to begin; (*appétit*) to whet ‖ *vi* to open; (*ouvrir la porte*) to open (up); ‖ **s'ouvrir** *vpr* (*porte, boîte etc*) to open (up); **s'o. la jambe** to cut one's leg open. ● **ouvre-boîtes** *nm inv* tin opener, *Am* can-opener. ● **ouvre-bouteilles** *nm inv* bottle opener.
ovaire [ɔvɛr] *nm Anat* ovary.
ovale [ɔval] *a* & *nm* oval.
OVNI [ɔvni] *nm abrév* (*objet volant non identifié*) UFO.
oxygène [ɔksiʒɛn] *nm* oxygen; **masque/***etc* **à o.** oxygen mask/*etc*. ● **oxygénée** *af* **eau o.** (hydrogen) peroxide.
ozone [ozon] *nm* ozone; **couche d'o.** ozone layer.

For further information on grammar points, turn to the page indicated

P

P, p [pe] *nm* P, p.
pacifier [pasifje] *vt* to pacify. ● **pacifiste** *nmf* pacifist.
pacifique [pasifik] **1** *a* (*manifestation etc*) peaceful; (*personne, peuple*) peace-loving. **2** *a* (*côte etc*) Pacific; **Océan P.** Pacific Ocean ‖ *nm* **le P.** the Pacific.
pack [pak] *nm* (*de lait etc*) carton.
pacotille [pakɔtij] *nf* (*camelote*) trash.
pacte [pakt] *nm* pact.
pagaie [pagɛ] *nf* paddle. ● **pagayer** *vi* (*ramer*) to paddle.
pagaïe, pagaille [pagaj] *nf* (*désordre*) *Fam* mess, shambles.
page [paʒ] **1** *nf* (*de livre etc*) page; **à la p.** (*personne*) *Fig* up-to-date. **2** *nm* (*à la cour*) *Hist* page (boy).
pagode [pagɔd] *nf* pagoda.
paie [pɛ] *nf* pay, wages. ● **paiement** *nm* payment.
païen, -enne [pajɛ̃, -ɛn] *a* & *nmf* pagan, heathen.
paillasson [pajasɔ̃] *nm* (door)mat.
paille [paj] *nf* straw; (*pour boire*) (drinking) straw; **tirer à la courte p.** to draw lots; **sur la p.** *Fig* penniless.
paillette [pajɛt] *nf* (*d'habit*) sequin; *pl* (*de savon*) flakes; (*d'or*) gold dust.
pain [pɛ̃] *nm* bread; **un p.** a loaf (of bread); **p. grillé** toast; **p. complet** wholemeal bread; **p. d'épice** gingerbread; **p. de seigle** rye bread; **petit p.** roll; **avoir du p. sur la planche** (*travail*) *Fig* to have a lot on one's plate.
pair [pɛr] **1** *a* (*numéro*) even. **2** *nm* (*personne*) peer; **hors (de) p.** unrivalled; **au p.** (*étudiante etc*) au pair; **travailler au p.** to work as an au pair.
paire [pɛr] *nf* pair (**de** of).
paisible [pezibl] *a* (*vie, endroit etc*) peaceful; (*caractère*) quiet, placid.
paître* [pɛtr] *vi* to graze.
paix [pɛ] *nf* peace; (*traité*) peace treaty; **en p.** in peace (**avec** with); **avoir la p.** to have (some) peace and quiet.
Pakistan [pakistɑ̃] *nm* Pakistan. ● **pakistanais, -aise** *a* & *nmf* Pakistani.
palace [palas] *nm* luxury hotel.
palais [palɛ] *nm* **1** (*château*) palace; **P. de justice** law courts; **p. des sports** sports stadium. **2** *Anat* palate.
pâle [pɑl] *a* pale.
Palestine [palɛstin] *nf* Palestine. ● **Palestinien, -ienne** *a* & *nmf* Palestinian.
palette [palɛt] *nf* (*de peintre*) palette.
pâleur [pɑlœr] *nf* paleness, pallor. ● **pâlir** *vi* to turn *ou* go pale (**de** with).
palier [palje] *nm* **1** (*d'escalier*) landing; **être voisins de p.** to live on the same floor. **2** (*niveau*) level; (*phase de stabilité*) plateau; **par paliers** (*étapes*) in stages.
palissade [palisad] *nf* fence (*of stakes*).
pallier [palje] *vt* (*difficultés etc*) to alleviate.
palmarès [palmarɛs] *nm* prize list; (*des chansons*) hit-parade.
palme [palm] *nf* **1** palm (leaf). **2** (*de nageur*) flipper. ● **palmier** *nm* palm (tree).
pâlot, -otte [pɑlo, -ɔt] *a Fam* pale.
palourde [palurd] *nf* (*mollusque*) clam.
palper [palpe] *vt* to feel, finger.
palpit/er [palpite] *vi* (*cœur*) to throb, palpitate; (*frémir*) to quiver. ● **—ant** *a* (*film etc*) thrilling.
pamplemousse [pɑ̃pləmus] *nm* grapefruit.
pan [pɑ̃] **1** *nm* (*de chemise*) tail; (*de ciel*) patch; **p. de mur** section of wall. **2** *int* bang!
panache [panaʃ] *nm* (*plumes*) plume; **avoir du p.** (*fière allure*) to have panache.
panaché [panaʃe] **1** *a* (*mélangé*) motley. **2** *a* & *nm* **(demi) p.** shandy (*beer and lemonade*).
pancarte [pɑ̃kart] *nf* sign, notice; (*de manifestant*) placard.
panda [pɑ̃da] *nm* (*animal*) panda.
pané [pane] *a Culin* breaded.
panier [panje] *nm* basket; **p. à linge** linen basket, *Am* (clothes) hamper; **p. à salade** (*ustensile*) salad basket; (*voiture*) *Fam* prison van.
panique [panik] *nf* panic; **pris de p.** panic-stricken ‖ *a* **peur p.** panic fear. ● **paniquer** *vi* to panic. ● **paniqué** *a* panic-stricken.
panne [pan] *nf* breakdown; **tomber en p.** to break down; **être en p.** to have broken down; **p. d'électricité** blackout, power cut; **tomber en p. sèche** to run out of petrol *ou Am* gas.
panneau, -x [pano] *nm* **1** (*écriteau*) sign, notice, board; **p. (de signalisation)** road *ou* traffic sign; **p. (d'affichage)** (*publicité*) hoarding, *Am* billboard. **2** (*de porte etc*) panel.

panoplie [panɔpli] *nf* **1** (*jouet*) outfit. **2** (*gamme*) (wide) range.
panorama [panɔrama] *nm* view, panorama.
pans/er [pɑ̃se] *vt* (*main, plaie etc*) to dress, bandage; (*personne*) to dress the wound(s) of, bandage (up). ●**—ement** *nm* (*bande*) dressing, bandage; **p. adhésif** sticking plaster, *Am* Band-Aid®.
pantalon [pɑ̃talɔ̃] *nm* (pair of) trousers *ou Am* pants; **en p.** in trousers, *Am* in pants.
panthère [pɑ̃tɛr] *nf* (*animal*) panther.
pantin [pɑ̃tɛ̃] *nm* (*jouet*) puppet, jumping jack; (*personne*) *Péj* puppet.
pantoufle [pɑ̃tufl] *nf* slipper.
paon [pɑ̃] *nm* peacock.
papa [papa] *nm* dad(dy); **fils à p.** *Péj* rich man's son, daddy's boy.
pape [pap] *nm* pope.
paperasse(s) [papras] *nf(pl) Péj* papers. ●**paperasserie** *nf Péj* (official) papers; (*procédure*) red tape.
papeterie [papetri] *nf* (*magasin*) stationer's shop; (*articles*) stationery.
papi [papi] *nm* grand(d)ad.
papier [papje] *nm* (*matière*) paper; **un p.** (*feuille*) a sheet *ou* piece of paper; (*formulaire*) a form; **sac**/*etc* **en p.** paper bag/*etc*; **papiers (d'identité)** (identity) papers; **p. hygiénique** toilet paper; **p. à lettres** writing paper; **du p. journal** (some) newspaper; **p. peint** wallpaper; **p. de verre** sandpaper.
papillon [papijɔ̃] *nm* **1** (*insecte*) butterfly; **p. (de nuit)** moth. **2** (*contravention*) *Fam* (parking) ticket.
paprika [paprika] *nm Culin* paprika.
Pâque [pɑk] *nf* **la P.** *Rel* Passover.
paquebot [pakbo] *nm Nau* (ocean) liner.
pâquerette [pɑkrɛt] *nf* daisy.
Pâques [pɑk] *nm sing* & *nfpl* Easter.
paquet [pakɛ] *nm* (*de bonbons etc*) packet; (*colis*) package; (*de cigarettes*) pack(et); (*de cartes*) pack, deck.
par [par] *prép* **1** (*agent, manière, moyen*) by; **choisi**/*etc* **p.** chosen/*etc* by; **p. le train** by train; **p. erreur** by mistake; **p. le travail**/*etc* by *ou* through work/*etc*; **apprendre p. un ami** to learn from *ou* through a friend; **commencer p. qch** (*récit etc*) to begin with sth.
2 (*lieu*) through; **p. la porte**/*etc* through *ou* by the door/*etc*; **jeter p. la fenêtre** to throw out (of) the window; **p. ici/là** (*aller*) this/that way; (*habiter*) around here/there.
3 (*motif*) out of, from; **p. pitié**/*etc* out of *ou* from pity/*etc*.
4 (*temps*) on; **p. un jour d'hiver**/*etc* on a winter's day/*etc*; **p. ce froid** in this cold; **p. le passé** in the past.
5 (*distributif*) **dix fois p. an**/*etc* ten times a *ou* per year/*etc*; **cent francs p. personne** a hundred francs a *ou* per person; **deux p. deux** two by two; **p. deux fois** twice.
6 (*trop*) **p. trop aimable**/*etc* far too kind/*etc*.
ⓘG180 Prepositions 8
parabole [parabɔl] *nf* (*récit*) parable.
parabolique [parabɔlik] *a* **antenne p.** satellite dish.
parachever [paraʃve] *vt* to perfect.
parachute [paraʃyt] *nm* parachute. ●**parachutisme** *nm* parachute jumping. ●**parachutiste** *nmf* parachutist; *Mil* paratrooper.
parade [parad] *nf* **1** (*spectacle*) & *Mil* parade. **2** *Boxe Escrime etc* parry; (*riposte*) *Fig* reply.
paradis [paradi] *nm* heaven, paradise.
paradoxe [paradɔks] *nm* paradox.
paraffine [parafin] *nf* paraffin (wax).
parages [paraʒ] *nmpl* region, area (**de** of); **dans ces p.** in these parts.
paragraphe [paragraf] *nm* paragraph.
paraître* [parɛtr] **1** *vi* (*sembler*) to seem, look, appear; (*apparaître*) to appear ‖ *v imp* **il paraît qu'il va partir** it appears *ou* seems (that) he's leaving. **2** *vi* (*livre*) to come out, be published; **faire p.** to bring out.
parallèle [paralɛl] **1** *a* (*comparable*) & *Math* parallel (**à** with, to); (*marché*) *Com* unofficial. **2** *nm* (*comparaison*) & *Géog* parallel.
paralyser [paralize] *vt* to paralyse, *Am* paralyze. ●**paralysie** *nf* paralysis.
paramètre [paramɛtr] *nm* parameter.
paranoïa [paranɔja] *nf* paranoia. ●**paranoïaque** *a* & *nmf* paranoid.
parapet [parapɛ] *nm* parapet.
paraphe [paraf] *nm* initials, signature.
paraphrase [parafraz] *nf* paraphrase.
parapluie [paraplɥi] *nm* umbrella.
parasite [parazit] *nm* (*personne, organisme*) parasite; *pl* (*à la radio*) interference.
parasol [parasɔl] *nm* sunshade, parasol.
paratonnerre [paratɔnɛr] *nm* lightning conductor *ou Am* rod.
paravent [paravɑ̃] *nm* (folding) screen.
parc [park] *nm* **1** park; (*de château*) grounds; **p. d'attractions** amusement park. **2** (*de bébé*) (play) pen; **p. (de stationnement)** car park, *Am* parking lot.
parcelle [parsɛl] *nf* fragment, particle; (*terrain*) plot; (*de vérité*) *Fig* grain.
parce que [parsk(ə)] *conj* because.
parchemin [parʃəmɛ̃] *nm* parchment.
parcimonieux, -euse [parsimɔnjø, -øz] *a* parsimonious.

par-ci, par-là [parsiparla] *adv* here, there and everywhere.
parcmètre [parkmɛtr] *nm* parking meter.
parcourir* [parkurir] *vt* (*région*) to travel all over; (*distance*) to cover; (*texte*) to glance through. ●**parcours** *nm* (*itinéraire*) route; (*distance*) distance; (*voyage*) trip, journey; **p. de golf** (*terrain*) golf course.
par-derrière [pardɛrjɛr] *voir* **derrière.**
par-dessous [pardəsu] *prép* & *adv* under(neath).
pardessus [pardəsy] *nm* overcoat.
par-dessus [pardəsy] *prép* & *adv* over (the top of); **p.-dessus tout** above all.
par-devant [pardəvɑ̃] *voir* **devant.**
pardon [pardɔ̃] *nm* forgiveness, pardon; **p.!** (*excusez-moi*) sorry!; **p.?** (*pour demander*) excuse me?, *Am* pardon me?; **demander p.** to apologize (**à** to). ●**pardonner** *vt* to forgive; **p. qch à qn/à qn d'avoir fait qch** to forgive s.o. for sth/for doing sth.
pare-balles [parbal] *a inv* **gilet p.-balles** bulletproof jacket *ou Am* vest.
pare-brise [parbriz] *nm inv Aut* windscreen, *Am* windshield.
pare-chocs [parʃɔk] *nm inv Aut* bumper.
pareil, -eille [parɛj] *a* similar; **p. à** the same as, similar to; **être pareils** to be the same, be similar *ou* alike; **un p. désordre/***etc* such a mess/*etc*; **en p. cas** in such a case ‖ *adv Fam* the same ‖ *nmf* **sans p.** unparalleled.
parent, -ente [parɑ̃, -ɑ̃t] *nmf* relative, relation ‖ *nmpl* (*père et mère*) parents ‖ *a* related (**de** to). ●**parenté** *nf* (*lien*) relationship.
parenthèse [parɑ̃tɛz] *nf* (*signe*) bracket, *Am* parenthesis; (*digression*) digression; **entre parenthèses** in brackets, *Am* in parentheses.
parer [pare] **1** *vt* (*coup*) to parry, ward off ‖ *vi* **p. à** (*éventualité*) to be prepared for. **2** *vt* (*orner*) to adorn (**de** with).
paresse [parɛs] *nf* laziness. ●**paresseux, -euse** *a* lazy, idle ‖ *nmf* lazy person.
parfaire [parfɛr] *vt* to perfect. ●**parfait** *a* perfect; **p.!** excellent!. ●**parfaitement** *adv* perfectly; (*certainement*) certainly.
parfois [parfwa] *adv* sometimes.
parfum [parfœ̃] *nm* (*odeur*) fragrance, scent; (*goût*) flavour; (*liquide*) perfume, scent.
parfumer [parfyme] *vt* to perfume, scent; (*glace, crème etc*) to flavour (**à** with) ‖ **se p.** *vpr* to put on perfume; (*habituellement*) to wear perfume. ●**parfumé** *a* (*savon, fleur*) scented; **p. au café/***etc* coffee-/*etc* flavoured. ●**parfumerie** *nf* (*magasin*) perfume shop.
pari [pari] *nm* bet; *pl Sp* betting, bets; **p. mutuel urbain** = the tote, *Am* pari-mutuel. ●**parier** *vti* to bet (**sur** on, **que** that).
Paris [pari] *m ou f* Paris. ●**parisien, -ienne** *a* Parisian; **la banlieue parisienne** the Paris suburbs ‖ *nmf* Parisian.
parking [parkiŋ] *nm* (*lieu*) car park, *Am* parking lot.
parlement [parləmɑ̃] *nm* parliament. ●**parlementaire** *a* parliamentary ‖ *nmf* member of parliament.
parlementer [parləmɑ̃te] *vi* to negotiate.
parler [parle] *vi* to talk, speak (**de** about, of; **à** to); **tu parles!** *Fam* you must be joking!; **sans p. de...** not to mention... ‖ *vt* (*langue*) to speak ‖ **se p.** *vpr* (*langue*) to be spoken. ●**parlé** *a* (*langue*) spoken.
parloir [parlwar] *nm* (*de couvent, prison*) visiting room.
parmi [parmi] *prép* among(st).
parodie [parɔdi] *nf* parody.
paroi [parwa] *nf* wall; (*de maison*) (inside) wall; (*de rocher*) (rock) face.
paroisse [parwas] *nf* parish.
parole [parɔl] *nf* (*mot, promesse*) word; (*faculté, langage*) speech; *pl* (*d'une chanson*) words, lyrics; **adresser la p. à** to speak to; **prendre la p.** to speak; **demander la p.** to ask to speak.
parquer [parke] *vt* (*bœufs*) to pen; (*gens*) to herd together, confine; (*véhicule*) to park.
parquet [parkɛ] *nm* **1** (parquet) floor(ing). **2** *Jur* Public Prosecutor's office.
parrain [parɛ̃] *nm Rel* godfather. ●**parrainer** *vt* (*course etc*) to sponsor. ●**parrainage** *nm* sponsorship.
pars, part[1] [par] *voir* **partir.**
parsemé [parsəme] *a* **p. de** (*sol*) scattered *ou* strewn with.
part[2] [par] *nf* (*portion*) share, part; (*de gâteau*) portion; **prendre p. à** (*activité*) to take part in; (*la joie etc de qn*) to share; **de toutes parts** from *ou* on all sides; **de p. et d'autre** on both sides; **d'une p...., d'autre p.** on the one hand..., on the other hand; **d'autre p.** (*d'ailleurs*) moreover; **de la p. de** (*provenance*) from; **c'est de la p. de qui?** *Tél* who's speaking?; **quelque p.** somewhere; **nulle p.** nowhere; **autre p.** somewhere else; **à p.** (*mettre, prendre*) aside; (*excepté*) apart from; (*personne*) different; **un cas/***etc* **à p.** a separate *ou* special case/*etc*; **membre à p. entière** full member; **faire p. de qch à qn** to inform s.o. of sth.
partage [partaʒ] *nm* (*de gâteau, trésor etc*) sharing; (*distribution*) sharing out. ●**partager** *vt* (*repas, joie etc*) to share (**avec**

with); (*distribuer*) to share out ▮ **se p.** *vpr* (*bénéfices etc*) to share (between themselves *etc*); **se p. entre** to divide one's time between.

partance (en) [ɑ̃partɑ̃s] *adv* (*train etc*) about to depart (**pour** for).

partant [partɑ̃] *nm Sp* starter.

partenaire [partənɛr] *nmf* (*coéquipier etc*) & *Pol* partner.

parterre [partɛr] *nm* **1** (*de jardin etc*) flower bed. **2** *Th* stalls, *Am* orchestra.

parti [parti] *nm Pol* party; **prendre un p.** to make a decision; **prendre p. pour** to side with; **tirer p. de qch** to turn sth to (good) account; **p. pris** (*préjugé*) prejudice.

partial, -aux [parsjal, -o] *a* biased.

participe [partisip] *nm Gram* participle.

particip/er [partisipe] *vi* **p. à** (*jeu etc*) to take part in, participate in; (*frais, joie etc*) to share (in). ●**—ant, -ante** *nmf* participant. ●**participation** *nf* participation; sharing; (*d'un acteur*) (personal) appearance; **p. (aux frais)** contribution (*towards expenses*).

particule [partikyl] *nf* particle.

particulier, -ière [partikylje, -jɛr] *a* (*spécial*) particular; (*privé*) private; (*bizarre*) peculiar; **p. à** peculiar to; **en p.** (*surtout*) in particular; (*à part*) in private ▮ *nm* private individual. ●**particularité** *nf* peculiarity. ●**particulièrement** *adv* particularly; **tout p.** especially.

partie [parti] *nf* part; (*de cartes, tennis etc*) game; (*de chasse*) & *Jur* party; **en p.** partly, in part; **en grande p.** mainly; **faire p. de** to be a part of; (*club etc*) to belong to; (*comité*) to be on. ●**partiel, -ielle** *a* partial ▮ *nm* **(examen) p.** *Univ* term exam.

partir* [partir] *vi* (*aux* **être**) (*aller*) to go; (*s'en aller*) to go, leave; (*se mettre en route*) to set off; (*s'éloigner*) to go (away); (*coup de feu*) to go off; (*tache*) to come out; **p. de** (*commencer par*) to start (off) with; **à p. de** (*date, prix*) from. ●**parti** *a* **bien p.** off to a good start.

partisan [partizɑ̃] *nm* supporter, follower ▮ *a* **être p. de qch/de faire** to be in favour of sth/of doing.

partition [partisjɔ̃] *nf Mus* score.

partout [partu] *adv* everywhere; **p. où tu vas** *ou* **iras** everywhere *ou* wherever you go.

paru [pary] *pp de* **paraître.**

parvenir* [parvənir] *vi* (*aux* **être**) **p. à** (*lieu*) to reach; (*objectif*) to achieve; **p. à faire** to manage to do.

parvis [parvi] *nm* square (*in front of church etc*).

pas[1] [pɑ] *adv* (*négatif*) not; **(ne)... p.** not; **je ne sais p.** I do not *ou* don't know; **je n'ai p. compris** I didn't understand; **je voudrais ne pas sortir** I would like not to go out; **p. de pain/***etc* no bread/*etc*; **p. encore** not yet; **p. du tout** not at all.

❶**G204** Negative Expressions 12 B

pas[2] [pɑ] *nm* **1** step; (*allure*) pace; (*bruit*) footstep; (*trace*) footprint; **à deux p. (de)** close by; **au p.** at a walking pace; **rouler au p.** (*véhicule*) to go dead slow(ly); **au p. (cadencé)** in step; **faire les cent p.** to walk up and down; **revenir sur ses p.** to go back on one's tracks; **marcher à p. de loup** to creep (silently); **faux p.** (*en marchant*) stumble; (*faute*) *Fig* blunder; **le p. de la porte** the doorstep.
2 (*de vis*) thread.
3 *Géog* straits; **le p. de Calais** the Straits of Dover.

passable [pɑsabl] *a* (*travail, résultat*) (just) average; **mention p.** *Scol Univ* pass.

passage [pɑsaʒ] *nm* (*action*) passing, passage; (*traversée*) *Nau* crossing; (*extrait, couloir*) passage; (*chemin*) path; **p. clouté** *ou* **pour piétons** (pedestrian) crossing, *Am* crosswalk; **p. souterrain** subway, *Am* underpass; **p. à niveau** level crossing, *Am* grade crossing; **'p. interdit'** 'no through traffic'; **'cédez le p.'** (*au carrefour*) 'give way', *Am* 'yield'; **être de p.** to be passing through (**à Paris/***etc* Paris/*etc*).

passager, -ère [pasaʒe, -ɛr] **1** *nmf* passenger; **p. clandestin** stowaway. **2** *a* (*de courte durée*) passing, temporary.

passant, -ante [pɑsɑ̃, -ɑ̃t] **1** *a* (*rue*) busy ▮ *nmf* passer-by. **2** *nm* (*de ceinture etc*) loop.

passe [pɑs] *nf Sp* pass; **mot de p.** password; **une mauvaise p.** *Fig* a bad patch.

passé [pɑse] **1** *a* (*temps etc*) past; (*couleur*) faded; **la semaine passée** last week; **dix heures passées** after *ou* gone ten (o'clock); **être passé** (*personne*) to have been (and gone); (*orage*) to be over; **avoir vingt ans passés** to be over twenty ▮ *nm* (*temps, vie passée*) past; *Gram* past (tense).
2 *prép* after; **p. huit heures** after eight (o'clock).

passe-montagne [pɑsmɔ̃taɲ] *nm* balaclava, *Am* ski mask.

passe-partout [pɑspartu] *nm inv* master key.

passe-passe [pɑspɑs] *nm inv* **tour de p.-passe** conjuring trick.

passeport [pɑspɔr] *nm* passport.

passer [pɑse] *vi* (*aux* **être** *ou* **avoir**) (*aller*) to go, pass (**de** from, **à** to); (*traverser*) to go through *ou* over; (*facteur*) to come; (*temps*) to pass (by), go by; (*film*) to be shown, be on; (*douleur, mode*) to pass; (*couleur*) to fade; (*courant*) to flow; **p. devant** (*maison etc*) to go past *ou* by, pass (by); **p. à** *ou* **par Paris** to pass through Paris; **p. à la boulangerie** *ou* **chez le boulanger** to go round to the baker's; **p. à la caisse** to go over to the cash desk; **laisser p.** (*personne, lumière*) to let through *ou* in; (*occasion*) to let slip; **p. prendre** to fetch, pick up; **p. voir qn** to drop in on s.o.; **p. pour** (*riche etc*) to be taken for; **faire p. qn pour** to pass s.o. off as; **p. sur** (*détail etc*) to overlook, pass over; **p. en** (*seconde etc*) *Scol* to go up into; *Aut* to change up to.

▌*vt* (*aux* **avoir**) (*frontière etc*) to cross, pass; (*maison etc*) to pass, go past; (*donner*) to pass, hand (**à** to); (*temps*) to spend, pass (**à faire** doing); (*disque, film, chemise*) to put on; (*loi*) to pass; (*examen*) to take, sit (for); (*thé*) to strain; (*café*) to filter; (*commande*) to place; (*limites*) to go beyond; (*visite médicale*) to have; **p. (son tour)** to pass; **p. qch à qn** (*caprice etc*) to grant s.o. sth; (*pardonner*) to excuse s.o. sth; **p. un coup d'éponge**/*etc* **à qch** to go over sth with a sponge/*etc*; **je vous passe...** *Tél* I'm putting you through to....

▌**se passer** *vpr* (*se produire*) to take place, happen; (*douleur*) to go (away), pass; **se p. de** to do *ou* go without; **se p. de commentaires** to need no comment; **ça s'est bien passé** it went off well.

passerelle [pɑsrɛl] *nf* (*pont*) footbridge; (*voie d'accès*) *Nau Av* gangway.

passe-temps [pɑstɑ̃] *nm inv* pastime.

passible [pasibl] *a* **p. de** (*peine*) *Jur* liable to.

passif, -ive [pasif, -iv] **1** *a* passive ▌*nm Gram* passive. **2** *nm Com* liabilities.

passion [pɑsjɔ̃] *nf* passion; **avoir la p. des voitures/d'écrire**/*etc* to have a passion for cars/writing/*etc*. ●**passionner** *vt* to thrill, fascinate; **se p. pour** to have a passion for. ●**passionnant** *a* thrilling. ●**passionné, -ée** *a* passionate; **p. de qch** passionately fond of sth ▌*nmf* fan (**de** of).

passoire [pɑswar] *nf* (*pour liquides*) sieve; (*à thé*) strainer; (*à légumes*) colander.

pastel [pastɛl] *nm* pastel; **dessin au p.** pastel drawing ▌*a inv* **ton p.** pastel shade *ou* tone.

pastèque [pastɛk] *nf* watermelon.

pasteur [pastœr] *nm Rel* pastor.

pasteurisé [pastœrize] *a* pasteurized.

pastille [pastij] *nf* pastille, lozenge.

patate [patat] *nf Fam* spud, potato.

pataud [pato] *a* clumsy.

patauger [patoʒe] *vi* (*marcher*) to wade (*in the mud etc*); (*barboter*) to splash about.

pâte [pɑt] *nf* (*substance*) paste; (*à pain*) dough; (*à tarte*) pastry; (*à frire*) batter; **pâtes (alimentaires)** pasta; **p. à modeler** plasticine®, modelling clay; **p. dentifrice** toothpaste.

pâté [pɑte] *nm* **1** (*charcuterie*) pâté; **p. (en croûte)** meat pie. **2 p. (de sable)** sand castle; **p. de maisons** block of houses.

pâtée [pɑte] *nf* (*pour chien*) dog food; (*pour chat*) cat food.

paternel, -elle [patɛrnɛl] *a* (*amour etc*) paternal, fatherly; (*parenté*) paternal.

pâteux, -euse [pɑtø, -øz] *a* (*substance*) doughy, pasty.

pathétique [patetik] *a* moving.

pathologie [patɔlɔʒi] *nf* pathology.

patience [pasjɑ̃s] *nf* patience; **perdre p.** to lose patience.

patient, -ente [pasjɑ̃, -ɑ̃t] **1** *a* patient. **2** *nmf Méd* patient. ●**patiemment** [-amɑ̃] *adv* patiently. ●**patienter** *vi* to wait (patiently).

patin [patɛ̃] *nm* skate; (*pour le parquet*) cloth pad (*used for walking*); **p. à glace** ice skate; **p. à roulettes** roller-skate.

patin/er [patine] *vi Sp* to skate; (*roue*) to spin around; (*véhicule*) to slip (and slide). ●**—age** *nm Sp* skating; **p. artistique** figure skating. ●**patinoire** *nf* skating rink, ice rink.

pâtir [pɑtir] *vi* **p. de** to suffer from.

pâtisserie [pɑtisri] *nf* pastry, cake; (*magasin*) cake shop; (*art*) cake *ou* pastry making. ●**pâtissier, -ière** *nmf* pastrycook and cake shop owner.

patois [patwa] *nm Ling* patois.

patrie [patri] *nf* (native) country.

patrimoine [patrimwan] *nm* (*biens*) & *Fig* heritage.

patriote [patrijɔt] *nmf* patriot ▌*a* (*personne*) patriotic. ●**patriotique** *a* (*chant etc*) patriotic.

patron, -onne [patrɔ̃, -ɔn] **1** *nmf* (*chef*) boss, employer; (*propriétaire*) owner (**de** of); (*gérant*) manager, manageress; (*de bar*) landlord, landlady. **2** *nm* (*modèle de papier*) *Tex* pattern.

patronat [patrɔna] *nm* employers.

patrouille [patruj] *nf* patrol. ●**patrouiller** *vi* to patrol.

patte [pat] *nf* **1** (*membre*) leg; (*de chat, chien*) paw; **marcher à quatre pattes** to crawl. **2** (*languette*) tongue.

pattes [pat] *nfpl* (*favoris*) sideboards, *Am* sideburns.

pâturage [pɑtyraʒ] *nm* pasture.
paume [pom] *nf* (*de main*) palm.
paum/er [pome] *vt Fam* to lose. ●**—é, -ée** *nmf* (*malheureux*) *Fam* down-and-out, loser ▮*a* **un coin** *ou* **trou p.** *Fam* a dump.
paupière [popjɛr] *nf* eyelid.
pause [poz] *nf* (*arrêt*) break; (*dans le discours etc*) pause.
pauvre [povr] *a* (*personne, terre etc*) poor ▮*nmf* poor man, poor woman; **les pauvres** the poor. ●**pauvreté** *nf* (*besoin*) poverty.
❶**pauvre G32** Position of Adjectives 4 D 3
pavaner (se) [səpavane] *vpr* to strut (about).
pav/er [pave] *vt* to pave. ●**—é** *nm* **un p.** a paving stone; (*de vieille chaussée*) a cobblestone; **sur le p.** *Fig* on the streets.
pavillon [pavijɔ̃] *nm* **1** (*maison*) (detached) house; (*d'hôpital*) ward; (*d'exposition*) pavilion. **2** (*drapeau*) flag.
pavoiser [pavwaze] *vi* (*exulter*) *Fig* to rejoice.
pavot [pavo] *nm* (*cultivé*) poppy.
paye [pɛj] *nf* pay, wages. ●**payement** *nm* payment.
payer [peje] *vt* (*personne, somme*) to pay; (*service, objet, faute*) to pay for; **p. qn pour faire qch** to pay s.o. to do *ou* for doing sth; **p. qch à qn** (*offrir en cadeau*) *Fam* to treat s.o. to sth ▮*vi* (*personne, métier, crime*) to pay. ●**payant** *a* (*hôte, spectateur*) paying; (*place, entrée*) that one has to pay for; (*rentable*) worthwhile.
pays [pei] *nm* country; (*région*) region; **du p.** (*vin, gens etc*) local.
paysage [peizaʒ] *nm* landscape, scenery.
paysan, -anne [peizɑ̃, -an] *nmf* (small) farmer.
Pays-Bas [peibɑ] *nmpl* **les P.-Bas** the Netherlands.
PCV [peseve] *abrév* (*paiement contre vérification*) **téléphoner en PCV** to reverse the charges, *Am* call collect.
PDG [pedeʒe] *abrév* = **président directeur général.**
péage [peaʒ] *nm* (*droit*) toll; (*lieu*) tollbooth; **pont/***etc* **à p.** toll bridge/*etc.*
peau, -x [po] *nf* skin; (*de fruit*) peel, skin; (*cuir*) hide; (*fourrure*) fur, pelt; **faire p. neuve** *Fig* to turn over a new leaf. ●**P.-Rouge** *nmf* (*pl* **Peaux-Rouges**) (Red) Indian.
pêche[1] [pɛʃ] *nf* (*activité*) fishing; (*poissons*) catch; **p. (à la ligne)** angling; **aller à la p.** to go fishing. ●**pêcher**[1] *vi* to fish ▮*vt* (*attraper*) to catch; (*chercher à prendre*) to fish for. ●**pêcheur** *nm* fisherman; (*à la ligne*) angler.
pêche[2] [pɛʃ] *nf* (*fruit*) peach. ●**pêcher**[2] *nm* (*arbre*) peach tree.
péché [peʃe] *nm* sin.
pédagogie [pedagɔʒi] *nf* (*science*) education, teaching methods. ●**pédagogique** *a* educational. ●**pédagogue** *nmf* teacher.
pédale [pedal] *nf* pedal; **p. de frein** foot brake (pedal). ●**pédaler** *vi* to pedal.
pédalo [pedalo] *nm* pedal boat.
pédant [pedɑ̃] *a* pedantic.
pédé [pede] *nm* (*homosexuel*) *Péj Fam* queer.
pédiatre [pedjatr] *nmf Méd* children's doctor, p(a)ediatrician.
pédicure [pedikyr] *nmf* chiropodist, *Am* podiatrist.
peigne [pɛɲ] *nm* comb; **se donner un coup de p.** to give one's hair a comb. ●**peigner** *vt* (*cheveux*) to comb; **p. qn** to comb s.o.'s hair ▮**se p.** *vpr* to comb one's hair.
peignoir [pɛɲwar] *nm* dressing gown, *Am* bathrobe; **p. (de bain)** bathrobe.
peinard [pɛnar] *a Fam* quiet (and easy).
peindre* [pɛ̃dr] *vt* to paint; **p. en bleu/***etc* to paint blue/*etc* ▮*vi* to paint.
peine [pɛn] *nf* **1** (*châtiment*) punishment; **la p. de mort** the death penalty; **p. de prison** prison sentence; **'défense d'entrer sous p. d'amende'** 'trespassers will be prosecuted *ou* fined'.
2 (*chagrin*) sorrow, grief; **avoir de la p.** to be upset *ou* sad; **faire de la p. à qn** to upset s.o.
3 (*effort, difficulté*) trouble; **se donner de la p.** to go to a lot of trouble **(pour faire** to do); **avec p.** with difficulty; **ça vaut la p. d'attendre/***etc* it's worth (while) waiting/*etc*; **ce n'est pas** *ou* **ça ne vaut pas la p.** it's not worth it *ou* worth bothering. ●**peiner 1** *vt* to upset, sadden. **2** *vi* to labour, struggle.
peine (à) [apɛn] *adv* hardly, scarcely.
❶**G204** Word Order: Inversion 12 A 7a)
peintre [pɛ̃tr] *nm* (*artiste*) painter; **p. (en bâtiment)** (house) painter, (painter and) decorator. ●**peinture** *nf* (*tableau, activité*) painting; (*matière*) paint; **'p. fraîche'** 'wet paint'.
péjoratif, -ive [peʒɔratif, -iv] *a* pejorative, derogatory.
Pékin [pekɛ̃] *nm ou f* Peking.
pelage [pəlaʒ] *nm* (*d'animal*) coat, fur.
pêle-mêle [pɛlmɛl] *adv* in disorder.
peler [pəle] *vt* (*fruit*) to peel ▮*vi* (*peau*) to peel.
pèlerin [pɛlrɛ̃] *nm* pilgrim. ●**pèlerinage** *nm* pilgrimage.
pélican [pelikɑ̃] *nm* (*oiseau*) pelican.
pelle [pɛl] *nf* shovel; (*d'enfant*) spade; **p. à**

tarte cake server; **à la p.** (*argent etc*) *Fam* galore. •**pelleteuse** *nf Tech* mechanical digger *ou* shovel.
pellicule [pelikyl] *nf Phot* film; (*couche*) layer, film; *pl Méd* dandruff.
pelote [p(ə)lɔt] *nf* (*de laine*) ball; (*à épingles*) pincushion; **p. (basque)** *Sp* pelota.
peloton [p(ə)lɔtɔ̃] *nm* **1** (*cyclistes*) *Sp* pack. **2** *Mil* squad; **p. d'exécution** firing squad.
pelotonner (se) [səp(ə)lɔtɔne] *vpr* to curl up (into a ball).
pelouse [p(ə)luz] *nf* lawn; *Sp* enclosure.
peluche [p(ə)lyʃ] *nf* **1** *nf* **(jouet en) p.** soft toy; **chien**/*etc* **en p.** furry dog/*etc*; **ours en p.** teddy bear. **2** *nfpl* (*flocons*) fluff, lint. •**pelucher** *vi* to get fluffy *ou* linty.
pelure [p(ə)lyr] *nf* (*épluchure*) peeling.
pénal, -aux [penal, -o] *a* (*code etc*) penal. •**pénaliser** *vt Sp Jur* to penalize (**pour** for). •**pénalité** *nf Jur Rugby* penalty.
penalty, *pl* **-ties** [penalti, -iz] *nm Fb* penalty over.
penaud [pəno] *a* sheepish.
penchant [pɑ̃ʃɑ̃] *nm* (*goût*) liking (**pour** for); (*tendance*) inclination (**à qch** towards sth).
pencher [pɑ̃ʃe] *vt* (*objet*) to tilt; (*tête*) to lean ‖ *vi* (*arbre etc*) to lean (over) ‖ **se p.** *vpr* to lean (over *ou* forward); **se p. par** (*fenêtre*) to lean out of; **se p. sur** (*problème etc*) to examine. •**penché** *a* leaning.
pendaison [pɑ̃dɛzɔ̃] *nf* hanging.
pendant [pɑ̃dɑ̃] *prép* (*au cours de*) during; **p. la nuit** during the night; **p. deux mois** (*pour une période de*) for two months; **p. que** while.
❶**pendant G96** & **97** Tenses 7 F 9a) iii) & b) iii)
❶**pendant G181** Prepositions 8
❶**pendant que G97** Tenses 7 F 11
pendentif [pɑ̃dɑ̃tif] *nm* (*collier*) pendant.
penderie [pɑ̃dri] *nf* wardrobe, *Am* closet.
pendre [pɑ̃dr] *vti* to hang (**à** from); **p. qn** to hang s.o. ‖ **se p.** *vpr* (*se suicider*) to hang oneself; (*se suspendre*) to hang (**à** from). •**pendu, -ue** *a* (*objet*) hanging (**à** from) ‖ *nmf* hanged man *ou* woman.
pendule [pɑ̃dyl] *nf* clock.
pénétrer [penetre] *vi* **p. dans** to enter; (*profondément*) to penetrate (into) ‖ *vt* (*pluie etc*) to penetrate (*sth*). •**pénétration** *nf* penetration.
pénible [penibl] *a* difficult; (*douloureux*) painful; (*ennuyeux*) tiresome. •**—ment** [-əmɑ̃] *adv* with difficulty; (*avec douleur*) painfully.
péniche [peniʃ] *nf* barge.
pénicilline [penisilin] *nf* penicillin.
péninsule [penɛ̃syl] *nf* peninsula.
pénis [penis] *nm* penis.
pénitence [penitɑ̃s] *nf* (*punition*) punishment; (*peine*) *Rel* penance.
pénitencier [penitɑ̃sje] *nm* prison.
pénombre [penɔ̃br] *nf* half-light, (semi-)darkness.
pensée [pɑ̃se] *nf* **1** thought. **2** (*fleur*) pansy.
penser [pɑ̃se] *vi* to think (**à** of, about); **p. à qch/à faire qch** (*ne pas oublier*) to remember sth/to do sth; **j'y pense** I'm thinking about it; **penses-tu!** you must be joking! ‖ *vt* to think (**que** that); (*concevoir*) to think out; **je pensais rester** (*intention*) I was thinking of staying; **je pense réussir** (*espoir*) I hope to succeed; **que pensez-vous de...?** what do you think of *ou* about...?; **p. du bien de qn/qch** to think highly of s.o./sth. •**pensant** *a* **bien p.** *Péj* orthodox. •**pensif, -ive** *a* thoughtful.
❶**penser G100** The Subjunctive 7 G 1e)
pension [pɑ̃sjɔ̃] *nf* **1** boarding school; (*somme à payer*) board; **être en p.** to board, be a boarder (**chez** with); **p. complète** full board, *Am* American plan. **2** (*de retraite etc*) pension; **p. alimentaire** maintenance allowance. •**pensionnaire** *nmf* (*élève*) boarder; (*d'hôtel*) resident; (*de famille*) lodger. •**pensionnat** *nm* boarding school; (*élèves*) boarders.
pentagone [pɛ̃tagɔn] *nm* **le P.** *Am Pol* the Pentagon.
pente [pɑ̃t] *nf* slope; **en p.** sloping.
Pentecôte [pɑ̃tkot] *nf* Whitsun, *Am* Pentecost.
pénurie [penyri] *nf* scarcity (**de** of).
pépin [pepɛ̃] *nm* **1** (*de fruit*) pip, *Am* seed, pit. **2** (*ennui*) *Fam* hitch, bother.
pépinière [pepinjɛr] *nf Bot* nursery.
pépite [pepit] *nf* (gold) nugget.
perçant [pɛrsɑ̃] *a* (*cri, froid*) piercing; (*yeux*) sharp, keen.
percée [pɛrse] *nf* (*dans une forêt etc*) opening; (*avance technologique, attaque militaire*) breakthrough.
percepteur [pɛrsɛptœr] *nm* tax collector. •**perceptible** *a* perceptible (**à** to). •**perception** *nf* **1** (*bureau*) tax office; (*d'impôt*) collection. **2** (*sensation*) perception.
perc/er [pɛrse] *vt* (*trouer*) to pierce; (*avec une perceuse*) to drill (a hole in); (*trou, ouverture*) to make, drill; (*mystère*) to uncover ‖ *vi* (*soleil*) to break through; (*abcès*) to burst. •**—euse** *nf* (*outil*) drill.
percevoir* [pɛrsəvwar] *vt* **1** (*sensation*) to perceive; (*son*) to hear. **2** (*impôt*) to collect.
perche [pɛrʃ] *nf* (*bâton*) pole.
percher [pɛrʃe] *vi* (*oiseau*) to perch; (*vo-*

lailles) to roost ‖ **se p.** *vpr* (*oiseau, personne*) to perch. ● **perchoir** *nm* perch; (*de volailles*) roost.

percolateur [pɛrkɔlatœr] *nm* (*de restaurant*) percolator.

percuter [pɛrkyte] *vt* (*véhicule*) to crash into.

perdre [pɛrdr] *vt* to lose; (*gaspiller*) to waste; (*habitude*) to get out of; **p. de vue** to lose sight of.
‖ *vi* to lose; **j'y perds** I lose out.
‖ **se perdre** *vpr* (*s'égarer*) to get lost; **se p. dans les détails** to be *ou* get bogged down in details; **je m'y perds** I'm lost *ou* confused. ● **perdant, -ante** *nmf* loser. ● **perdu** *a* lost; (*gaspillé*) wasted; (*malade*) finished; (*lieu*) isolated; **une balle perdue** a stray bullet; **c'est du temps p.** it's a waste of time.

perdrix [pɛrdri] *nf* partridge.

père [pɛr] *nm* father.

péremptoire [perɑ̃ptwar] *a* peremptory.

perfection [pɛrfɛksjɔ̃] *nf* perfection; **à la p.** perfectly.

perfectionner (se) [səpɛrfɛksjɔne] *vpr* **se p. en anglais/***etc* to improve one's English/*etc*. ● **perfectionné** *a* (*machine etc*) advanced. ● **perfectionnement** *nm* improvement; **cours de p.** refresher course. ● **perfectionniste** *nmf* perfectionist.

perforer [pɛrfɔre] *vt* (*pneu, intestin etc*) to perforate; (*billet, carte*) to punch; **carte perforée** punch card. ● **perforation** *nf* perforation; (*trou*) punched hole. ● **perforeuse** *nf* (paper) punch.

performance [pɛrfɔrmɑ̃s] *nf* (*d'athlète etc*) performance. ● **performant** *a* (highly) efficient.

péridurale [peridyral] *a* & *nf* **(anesthésie) p.** *Méd* epidural.

péril [peril] *nm* danger, peril; **à tes risques et périls** at your own risk. ● **périlleux, -euse** *a* dangerous, perilous; **saut p.** somersault (*in mid air*).

périmer (se) [səperime] *vpr* **laisser qch (se) p.** to allow sth to expire. ● **périmé** *a* (*billet etc*) expired.

période [perjɔd] *nf* period. ● **périodique** *a* periodic ‖ *nm* (*revue*) periodical.

péripétie [peripesi] *nf* (unexpected) event.

périphérique [periferik] *a* (*quartier etc*) outlying, peripheral; **radio p.** = radio station broadcasting from outside France ‖ *nm* & *a* **(boulevard) p.** (motorway) ring road, *Am* beltway ‖ *nmpl Ordinat* peripherals.

périple [peripl] *nm* trip, tour.

pér/ir [perir] *vi* to perish, die. ● **—issable** *a* (*denrée*) perishable.

périscope [periskɔp] *nm* periscope.

perle [pɛrl] *nf* (*bijou*) pearl; (*de bois, verre etc*) bead.

permanent, -ente [pɛrmanɑ̃, -ɑ̃t] **1** *a* permanent; (*spectacle*) *Cin* continuous. **2** *nf* (*coiffure*) perm. ● **permanence** *nf* permanence; (*salle d'étude*) study room; (*service, bureau*) duty office; **être de p.** to be on duty; **en p.** permanently.

permettre* [pɛrmɛtr] *vt* to allow, permit; **p. à qn de faire qch** (*permission, possibilité*) to allow *ou* permit s.o. to do sth; **vous permettez?** may I?; **se p. de faire** to allow oneself to do, take the liberty to do; **je ne peux pas me p. de l'acheter** I can't afford to buy it.
🛈G99 The Subjunctive 7 G 1b)

permis [pɛrmi] *a* allowed, permitted ‖ *nm* (*autorisation*) licence, *Am* license, permit; **p. de conduire** (*carte*) driving licence, *Am* driver's license; **p. de travail** work permit; **passer son p. de conduire** to take one's driving *ou* road test.

permission [pɛrmisjɔ̃] *nf* permission; (*congé*) *Mil* leave; **demander la p.** to ask permission (**de faire** to do).

permuter [pɛrmyte] *vt* to change round *ou* over, permutate.

Pérou [peru] *nm* Peru.

perpendiculaire [pɛrpɑ̃dikylɛr] *a* & *nf* perpendicular (**à** to).

perpétrer [pɛrpetre] *vt* (*crime*) to perpetrate.

perpétuel, -elle [pɛrpetɥɛl] *a* perpetual; (*incessant*) continual; (*rente*) for life. ● **perpétuer** *vt* to perpetuate. ● **perpétuité (à)** *adv* (*condamnation*) for life.

perplexe [pɛrplɛks] *a* perplexed, puzzled.

perquisition [pɛrkizisjɔ̃] *nf* (house) search (*by police*).

perron [perɔ̃] *nm* (front) steps.

perroquet [pɛrɔkɛ] *nm* parrot.

perruche [peryʃ] *nf* budgerigar, *Am* parakeet.

perruque [peryk] *nf* wig.

persan [pɛrsɑ̃] *a* (*tapis, chat etc*) Persian ‖ *nm* (*langue*) Persian.

persécuter [pɛrsekyte] *vt* (*tourmenter*) to persecute; (*importuner*) to harass. ● **persécution** *nf* persecution.

persévér/er [pɛrsevere] *vi* to persevere (**dans** in). ● **—ant** *a* persevering. ● **persévérance** *nf* perseverance.

persienne [pɛrsjɛn] *nf* (outside) shutter.

persil [pɛrsi] *nm* parsley.

persist/er [pɛrsiste] *vi* to persist (**à faire** in

doing, **dans qch** in sth). • **—ant** *a* persistent; **à feuilles persistantes** (*arbre etc*) evergreen.

personnage [pɛrsɔnaʒ] *nm* (*célébrité*) (important) person; *Th Littér* character.

personnalité [pɛrsɔnalite] *nf* (*individualité, personnage*) personality.

personne [pɛrsɔn] **1** *nf* person; *pl* people; **grande p.** grown-up, adult; **en p.** in person. **2** *pron* (*négatif*) nobody, no one; **(ne)... p.** nobody, no one; **je ne vois p.** I don't see anybody *ou* anyone; **p. ne saura** nobody *ou* no one will know; **mieux que p.** better than anybody *ou* anyone.

G50 Indefinite Pronouns 6 B 2

G102 The Subjunctive 7 G 1i)

G204 Negative Expressions 12 B

personnel, -elle [pɛrsɔnɛl] **1** *a* personal; (*joueur*) individualistic. **2** *nm* staff, personnel. • **personnellement** *adv* personally.

personnifier [pɛrsɔnifje] *vt* to personify.

perspective [pɛrspɛktiv] *nf* (*art*) perspective; (*idée, possibilité*) prospect (**de** of); **en p.** *Fig* in view.

perspicace [pɛrspikas] *a* shrewd.

persuader [pɛrsɥade] *vt* to persuade (**qn de faire** s.o. to do); **être persuadé que** to be convinced that. • **persuasif, -ive** *a* persuasive. • **persuasion** *nf* persuasion.

perte [pɛrt] *nf* loss; (*gaspillage*) waste (**de temps/ d'argent** of time/money); **à p. de vue** as far as the eye can see; **vendre à p.** to sell at a loss.

pertinent [pɛrtinɑ̃] *a* relevant.

perturber [pɛrtyrbe] *vt* (*trafic, cérémonie etc*) to disrupt; (*ordre public, personne*) to disturb. • **perturbation** *nf* disruption; **p. atmosphérique** atmospheric disturbance.

pervers [pɛrvɛr] *a* wicked, perverse; (*dépravé*) perverted. • **perversion** *nf* perversion. • **pervertir** *vt* to pervert.

pesant [pəzɑ̃] *a* heavy ‖ *nm* **valoir son p. d'or** to be worth one's *ou* its weight in gold. • **pesanteur** *nf* (*force*) gravity.

peser [pəze] *vt* to weigh ‖ *vi* to weigh; **p. lourd** to be heavy; (*argument etc*) *Fig* to carry weight; **p. sur** (*appuyer*) to bear down upon; (*influer*) to bear upon; **p. sur l'estomac** to lie (heavily) on the stomach. • **pèse-personne** *nm* (bathroom) scales.

pessimisme [pesimism] *nm* pessimism. • **pessimiste** *a* pessimistic ‖ *nmf* pessimist.

peste [pɛst] *nf* (*maladie*) plague; (*personne*) *Fig* pest.

pester [pɛste] *vi* to curse; **p. contre qch/qn** to curse sth/ s.o.

pétale [petal] *nm* petal.

pétanque [petɑ̃k] *nf* (*jeu*) bowls.

pétarader [petarade] *vi* to backfire.

pétard [petar] *nm* (*explosif*) firecracker.

péter [pete] *vi Fam* (*éclater*) to go bang *ou* pop; (*se rompre*) to snap.

pétill/er [petije] *vi* (*champagne etc*) to sparkle, fizz; (*yeux*) to sparkle. • **—ant** *a* (*eau, vin, yeux*) sparkling.

petit, -ite [p(ə)ti, -it] *a* small, little; (*de taille*) short; (*bruit, coup*) slight; (*jeune*) little; **tout p.** tiny; **un p. Français** a (little) French boy ‖ *nmf* (little) boy, (little) girl; (*personne*) small person; *Scol* junior; *pl* (*d'animal*) young; (*de chien*) pups; (*de chat*) kittens ‖ *adv* **p. à p.** little by little. • **p.-suisse** *nm* soft cheese (*for dessert*).

petit-fils [p(ə)tifis] *nm* (*pl* **petits-fils**) grandson. • **petite-fille** *nf* (*pl* **petites-filles**) granddaughter. • **petits-enfants** *nmpl* grandchildren.

pétition [petisjɔ̃] *nf* petition.

pétrifier [petrifje] *vt* (*de peur etc*) to petrify.

pétrin [petrɛ̃] *nm* **être dans le p.** *Fam* to be in a fix.

pétrir [petrir] *vt* to knead.

pétrole [petrɔl] *nm* oil, petroleum; **p. (lampant)** paraffin, *Am* kerosene; **nappe de p.** (*sur la mer*) oil slick. • **pétrolier, -ière** *a* **industrie pétrolière** oil industry ‖ *nm* (*navire*) oil tanker.

peu [pø] *adv* (*manger etc*) not much, little; **elle mange p.** she doesn't eat much, she eats little; **un p.** a little, a bit; **p. de sel/ temps/***etc* not much salt/time/*etc*, little salt/time/*etc*; **un p. de fromage/***etc* a little cheese/*etc*, a bit of cheese/*etc*; **p. de gens/** *etc* few people/*etc*, not many people/*etc*; **p. sont...** few are...; **un (tout) petit p.** a (tiny) little bit; **p. intéressant/***etc* not very interesting/*etc*; **p. de chose** not much; **p. à p.** little by little, gradually; **à p. près** more or less; **p. après/avant** shortly after/before.

peuple [pœpl] *nm* (*nation*) people; **les gens du p.** the common people. • **peuplé** *a* (*region etc*) populated (**de** by); **très/peu/** *etc* **p.** highly/sparsely/*etc* populated.

peuplier [pøplije] *nm* (*arbre, bois*) poplar.

peur [pœr] *nf* fear; **avoir p.** to be afraid *ou* frightened *ou* scared (**de qch/qn** of sth/s.o.; **de faire** to do, of doing); **faire p. à qn** to frighten *ou* scare s.o.; **de p. que (. . . ne)** (+ *sub*) for fear that; **de p. de faire** for fear of doing. • **peureux, -euse** *a* easily frightened.

peur G98 The Subjunctive 7 G 1a)

peut [pø] *voir* **pouvoir 1.**

peut-être [pøtetr] *adv* perhaps, maybe;

p. qu'il viendra perhaps *ou* maybe he'll come.

i G204 Word Order: Inversion 12 A 7a)

peuvent, peux [pœv, pø] *voir* **pouvoir 1**.

phallique [falik] *a* phallic.

phare [far] *nm Nau* lighthouse; *Aut* headlight, headlamp; **faire un appel de phares** *Aut* to flash one's lights.

pharmacie [farmasi] *nf* chemist's shop, *Am* drugstore; (*science*) pharmacy; (*armoire*) medicine cabinet. • **pharmacien, -ienne** *nmf* chemist, pharmacist, *Am* druggist.

phase [fɑz] *nf* phase.

phénomène [fenɔmɛn] *nm* phenomenon; (*personne*) *Fam* eccentric.

philanthrope [filɑ̃trɔp] *nmf* philanthropist.

philatélie [filateli] *nf* stamp collecting, philately. • **philatéliste** *nmf* stamp collector, philatelist.

Philippines [filipin] *nfpl* **les P.** the Philippines.

philosophe [filɔzɔf] *nmf* philosopher ‖ *a* (*résigné, sage*) philosophical. • **philosophie** *nf* philosophy. • **philosophique** *a* philosophical.

phobie [fɔbi] *nf* phobia.

phonétique [fɔnetik] *a* phonetic ‖ *nf* phonetics.

phoque [fɔk] *nm* (*animal*) seal.

photo [fɔto] *nf* photo; (*art*) photography; **p. d'identité** ID photo; **prendre une p. de, prendre en p.** to take a photo of; **se faire prendre en p.** to have one's photo taken ‖ *a inv* **appareil p.** camera. • **photogénique** *a* photogenic. • **photographe** *nmf* photographer. • **photographie** *nf* (*art*) photography; (*image*) photograph. • **photographier** *vt* to photograph. • **photographique** *a* photographic.

photocopie [fɔtɔcɔpi] *nf* photocopy. • **photocopier** *vt* to photocopy. • **photocopieuse** *nf* (*machine*) photocopier.

photomaton® [fɔtɔmatɔ̃] *nm* photo booth.

phrase [frɑz] *nf* (*mots*) sentence.

physicien, -ienne [fizisjɛ̃, -jɛn] *nmf* physicist.

physiologie [fizjɔlɔʒi] *nf* physiology.

physionomie [fizjɔnɔmi] *nf* face.

physique [fizik] **1** *a* physical ‖ *nm* (*corps*) physique. **2** *nf* (*science*) physics. • **—ment** *adv* physically.

piaffer [pjafe] *vi* (*cheval*) to stamp; **p. d'impatience** *Fig* to fidget impatiently.

piano [pjano] *nm* piano; **p. droit/à queue** upright/grand piano. • **pianiste** *nmf* pianist.

piaule [pjol] *nf* (*chambre*) *Fam* room.

pic [pik] *nm* **1** (*cime*) peak. **2** (*outil*) pick(axe); **p. à glace** ice pick.

pic (à) [apik] *adv* (*verticalement*) sheer; **couler à p.** to sink to the bottom; **arriver à p.** *Fig* to arrive in the nick of time.

pichet [piʃɛ] *nm* jug, pitcher.

pickpocket [pikpɔkɛt] *nm* pickpocket.

picorer [pikɔre] *vti* to peck.

picoter [pikɔte] *vt* (*yeux*) to make smart; **les yeux me picotent** my eyes are smarting.

pie [pi] *nf* (*oiseau*) magpie.

pièce [pjɛs] *nf* **1** (*de maison etc*) room. **2** (*de pantalon*) patch; (*écrit*) *Jur* document; **p. (de monnaie)** coin; **p. (de théâtre)** play; **p. d'identité** identity card, proof of identity; **pièces détachées** *ou* **de rechange** (*de véhicule etc*) spare parts; **p. montée** = tiered wedding cake; **cinq dollars**/*etc* **(la) p.** five dollars/*etc* each.

pied [pje] *nm* foot (*pl* feet); (*de meuble*) leg; (*de verre, lampe*) base; (*de lit, d'arbre, de colline*) foot; *Phot* stand; **à p.** on foot; **aller à p.** to walk, go on foot; **au p. de** at the foot *ou* bottom of; **au p. de la lettre** *Fig* literally; **coup de p.** kick; **donner un coup de p.** to kick (**à qn** s.o.); **avoir p.** (*nageur*) to have a footing, touch the bottom; **sur p.** (*debout, levé*) up and about; **comme un p.** (*mal*) *Fam* dreadfully. • **p.-noir** *nmf* (*pl* **pieds-noirs**) Algerian-born Frenchman *ou* Frenchwoman.

piédestal, -aux [pjedɛstal, -o] *nm* pedestal.

piège [pjɛʒ] *nm* (*pour animal*) & *Fig* trap. • **piéger** *vt* (*animal*) to trap; (*voiture etc*) to booby-trap; **colis/voiture piégé(e)** parcel/car bomb.

pierre [pjɛr] *nf* stone; (*précieuse*) gem, stone; **p. (à briquet)** flint. • **pierreries** *nfpl* gems, precious stones.

piétiner [pjetine] *vt* to trample (on) ‖ *vi* to stamp (one's feet); (*marcher sur place*) to mark time; (*ne pas avancer*) *Fig* to make no headway.

piéton [pjetɔ̃] *nm* pedestrian. • **piétonne** *a* **rue p.** pedestrian(ized) street.

pieu, -x [pjø] *nm* (*piquet*) post, stake.

pieuvre [pjœvr] *nf* octopus.

pieux, -euse [pjø, -øz] *a* pious.

pif [pif] *nm* (*nez*) *Fam* nose.

pigeon [piʒɔ̃] *nm* pigeon; (*personne*) *Fam* dupe.

piger [piʒe] *vti Fam* to understand.

pigment [pigmɑ̃] *nm* pigment.

pile [pil] **1** *nf* **p. (électrique)** battery; **radio à piles** battery radio. **2** *nf* (*tas*) pile; **en p.** in a pile. **3** *nf* **p. (ou face)?** heads (or tails)?; **jouer à p. ou face** to toss up. **4** *adv* **s'arrêter**

p. *Fam* to stop short *ou* dead; **à deux heures p.** *Fam* on the dot of two.
piler [pile] *vt* (*amandes etc*) to grind.
pilier [pilje] *nm* pillar.
pilon [pilɔ̃] *nm* (*de poulet*) drumstick.
piller [pije] *vti* to loot, pillage. ● **pillage** *nm* looting, pillage. ● **pillard, -arde** *nmf* looter.
pilote [pilɔt] *nm Av Nau* pilot; (*de voiture, char*) driver ▮ *a* **usine**/*etc* **(-)p.** pilot factory/*etc*. ● **piloter** *vt* (*avion*) to fly, pilot; (*bateau*) to pilot; (*voiture*) to drive; **p. qn** *Fig* to show s.o. around. ● **pilotage** *nm* piloting; **poste de p.** cockpit; **école de p.** flying school.
pilule [pilyl] *nf* pill; **prendre la p.** (*femme*) to be on the pill; **arrêter la p.** to go off the pill.
piment [pimɑ̃] *nm* pepper, pimento. ● **pimenté** *a Culin* spicy.
pin [pɛ̃] *nm* (*arbre, bois*) pine; **pomme de p.** pine cone.
pinailler [pinɑje] *vi Fam* to quibble.
pince [pɛ̃s] *nf* (*outil*) pliers; (*de cycliste*) clip; (*de crabe*) pincer; **p. à linge** (clothes) peg *ou Am* pin; **p. à épiler** tweezers; **p. à sucre** sugar tongs; **p. (à cheveux)** hairgrip, *Am* bobby pin.
pinc/er [pɛ̃se] *vt* to pinch; (*corde*) *Mus* to pluck; **p. qn** (*arrêter*) *Fam* to nab s.o.; **se p. le doigt** to get one's finger caught (**dans** in). ● **—é** *a* (*air*) stiff. ● **—ée** *nf* (*de sel etc*) pinch (**de** of).
pinceau, -x [pɛ̃so] *nm* (paint)brush.
pinède [pinɛd] *nf* pine forest.
pingouin [pɛ̃gwɛ̃] *nm* penguin, auk.
ping-pong [piŋpɔ̃g] *nm* table tennis, ping-pong.
pin's [pinz] *nm inv* badge, lapel pin.
pinson [pɛ̃sɔ̃] *nm* (*oiseau*) chaffinch.
pintade [pɛ̃tad] *nf* guinea fowl.
pioche [pjɔʃ] *nf* pick(axe). ● **piocher** *vti* (*creuser*) to dig (with a pick).
pion [pjɔ̃] *nm* **1** (*au jeu de dames*) piece; *Échecs & Fig* pawn. **2** *Scol Fam* master (in charge of discipline).
pionnier [pjɔnje] *nm* pioneer.
pipe [pip] *nf* (*de fumeur*) pipe; **fumer la p.** to smoke a pipe.
pipeau, -x [pipo] *nm* (*flûte*) pipe.
pipi [pipi] *nm* **faire p.** *Fam* to go for a pee.
pique [pik] **1** *nm* (*couleur*) *Cartes* spades. **2** *nf* (*allusion*) cutting remark.
pique-assiette [pikasjɛt] *nmf inv* scrounger.
pique-nique [piknik] *nm* picnic. ● **piqueniquer** *vi* to picnic.
piquer [pike] *vt* (*percer*) to prick; (*langue, yeux*) to sting; (*coudre*) to (machine-) stitch; **p. qn** (*abeille*) to sting s.o.; **p. qch dans** (*enfoncer*) to stick sth into; **p. qch** (*voler*) *Fam* to pinch sth; **p. une colère** *Fam* to fly into a rage; **p. une crise (de nerfs)** *Fam* to throw a fit; **p. une tête** to plunge headlong.
▮ *vi* (*avion*) to dive; (*moutarde etc*) to be hot.
▮ **se piquer** *vpr* to prick oneself; **se p. au doigt** to prick one's finger. ● **piquant** *a* (*plante, barbe*) prickly; (*sauce, goût*) pungent; (*détail*) spicy ▮ *nm Bot* prickle, thorn; (*d'animal*) spine, prickle.
piquet [pikɛ] *nm* **1** (*pieu*) stake, picket; (*de tente*) peg. **2 p. (de grève)** picket (line), strike picket. **3 au p.** *Scol* in the corner.
piqûre [pikyr] *nf* (*d'abeille*) sting; *Méd* injection; (*d'épingle*) prick; (*point*) stitch.
pirate [pirat] *nm* pirate; **p. de l'air** hijacker; **p. (informatique)** hacker ▮ *a* **radio p.** pirate radio.
pire [pir] *a* worse (**que** than); **le p. moment**/*etc* the worst moment/*etc* ▮ *nmf* **le** *ou* **la p.** the worst (one); **au p.** at (the very) worst; **s'attendre au p.** to expect the (very) worst.
pis [pi] **1** *nm* (*de vache*) udder. **2** *a inv & adv Litt* worse; **de mal en p.** from bad to worse.
pis-aller [pizale] *nm inv* (*solution*) stopgap.
piscine [pisin] *nf* swimming pool.
pissenlit [pisɑ̃li] *nm* dandelion.
pistache [pistaʃ] *nf* (*graine, parfum*) pistachio.
piste [pist] *nf* (*traces*) track, trail; *Sp* (race)track; (*de cirque*) ring; (*de patinage*) rink; (*de magnétophone*) track; **p. (d'envol)** runway; **p. cyclable** cycle track, *Am* bicycle path; **p. de danse** dance floor; **p. de ski** ski run *ou* slope; **tour de p.** *Sp* lap.
pistolet [pistɔlɛ] *nm* gun, pistol; (*de peintre*) spray gun; **p. à eau** water pistol.
piston [pistɔ̃] *nm* **1** *Aut* piston. **2 avoir du p.** (*appui*) *Fam* to have connections.
pita [pita] *nm* pitta bread.
pitié [pitje] *nf* pity; **j'ai p. de lui, il me fait p.** I feel sorry for him, I pity him. ● **pitoyable** *a* pitiful.
piton [pitɔ̃] *nm* **1** (*à crochet*) hook. **2** *Géog* peak.
pitre [pitr] *nm* clown.
pittoresque [pitɔrɛsk] *a* picturesque.
pivert [pivɛr] *nm* (green) woodpecker.
pivot [pivo] *nm* pivot. ● **pivoter** *vi* (*personne*) to swing round; (*fauteuil*) to swivel; (*porte*) to revolve.
pizza [pidza] *nf* pizza. ● **pizzeria** *nf* pizzeria.
PJ [peʒi] *nf abrév* (*police judiciaire*) = CID, *Am* = FBI.

placard [plakar] *nm* **1** (*armoire*) cupboard, *Am* closet. **2 p. publicitaire** advertising poster. • **placarder** *vt* (*affiche*) to stick up.
place [plas] *nf* (*endroit, rang*) & *Sp* place; (*espace*) room; (*lieu public*) square; (*siège*) seat, place; (*emploi*) job, position; **p. (de parking)** parking place *ou* space; **p. (financière)** (money) market; **à la p.** (*échange*) instead (**de** of); **à votre p.** in your place; **sur p.** on the spot; **en p.** in place; **mettre qch en p.** (*installer*) to set sth up; (*ranger*) to put sth in its place; **changer de p.** to change places; **changer qch de p.** to move sth; **faire de la place (à qn)** to make room (for s.o.).
placer [plase] *vt* (*mettre*) to place, put; (*invité, spectateur*) to seat; (*argent*) to invest (**dans** in); **p. un mot** to get a word in edgeways *ou Am* edgewise.
‖ **se placer** *vpr* (*debout*) to (go and) stand; (*s'asseoir*) to (go and) sit; (*objet*) to be put *ou* placed; (*cheval, coureur*) to be placed; **se p. troisième**/*etc Sp* to come third/*etc*. • **placé** *a* (*objet*) & *Sp* placed; **bien/mal p. pour faire** in a good/bad position to do; **les gens haut placés** people in high places. • **placement** *nm* (*d'argent*) investment.
placide [plasid] *a* placid.
plafond [plafɔ̃] *nm* ceiling.
plage [plaʒ] *nf* **1** beach; (*ville*) (seaside) resort. **2 p. arrière** *Aut* (back) window shelf.
plaider [plede] *vti Jur* to plead. • **plaidoirie** *nf Jur* speech (for the defence *ou Am* defense). • **plaidoyer** *nm* plea.
plaie [plɛ] *nf* (*blessure*) wound; (*coupure*) cut; (*corvée, personne*) *Fig* nuisance.
plaignant, -ante [plɛɲɑ̃, -ɑ̃t] *nmf Jur* plaintiff.
plaindre* [plɛ̃dr] **1** *vt* to feel sorry for, pity. **2 se plaindre** *vpr* (*protester*) to complain (**de** about, **que** that); **se p. de** (*maux de tête etc*) to complain of *ou* about. • **plainte** *nf* complaint; (*cri*) moan, groan.
plaine [plɛn] *nf Géog* plain.
plaire* [plɛr] *vi* **p. à qn** to please s.o.; **elle lui plaît** he likes her; **ça me plaît** I like it ‖ *v imp* **s'il vous** *ou* **te plaît** please ‖ **se p.** *vpr* (*à Paris etc*) to like *ou* enjoy it; (*l'un l'autre*) to like each other.
plaisance [plɛzɑ̃s] *nf* **bateau de p.** pleasure boat; **navigation de p.** yachting.
plaisant [plɛzɑ̃] *a* (*drôle*) amusing; (*agréable*) pleasing. • **plaisanter** *vi* to joke (**sur** about); **p. avec qch** to trifle with sth. • **plaisanterie** *nf* joke; **par p.** for a joke.
plaisir [plezir] *nm* pleasure; **faire p. à qn** to please s.o.; **pour le p.** for fun, for the fun of it; **faites-moi le p. de...** would you be good enough to....
plan [plɑ̃] *nm* (*projet, dessin*) plan; (*de ville*) map, plan; *Géom* plane; **au premier p.** in the foreground; **gros p.** *Phot Cin* close-up; **sur le p. politique**/*etc* from the political/*etc* viewpoint, politically/*etc*; **de premier p.** of importance, major.
planche [plɑ̃ʃ] *nf* board, plank; **p. à repasser/à dessin** ironing/drawing board; **p. (à roulettes)** skateboard; **p. (à voile)** sailboard; **faire de la p. (à voile)** to go windsurfing; **faire la p.** to float on one's back.
plancher [plɑ̃ʃe] *nm* floor.
plan/er [plane] *vi* (*oiseau, avion*) to glide; **p. sur** (*mystère*) *Fig* to hang over; **vol plané** glide, gliding. • **—eur** *nm* (*avion*) glider.
planète [planɛt] *nf* planet. • **planétaire** *a* planetary.
planifier [planifje] *vt Écon* to plan. • **planification** *nf Écon* planning. • **planning** *nm* (*emploi du temps*) schedule; **p. familial** family planning.
planque [plɑ̃k] *nf* **1** (*travail*) *Fam* cushy job. **2** (*lieu*) *Fam* hide-out.
plant [plɑ̃] *nm* (*de légumes etc*) bed.
plante [plɑ̃t] *nf* **1** *Bot* plant; **p. verte** house plant; **jardin des plantes** botanical gardens. **2 p. des pieds** sole (of the foot).
planter [plɑ̃te] *vt* (*fleur etc*) to plant; (*clou, couteau*) to drive in; (*tente, drapeau*) to put up; **p. là qn** to leave s.o. standing ‖ **se p.** *vpr* **1 se p. devant** to come *ou* go and stand in front of. **2** (*tomber*) *Fam* to fall over; (*échouer*) *Fam* to fail.
plantation [plɑ̃tasjɔ̃] *nf* (*terrain*) bed; (*de café, d'arbres etc*) plantation.
plaque [plak] *nf* plate; (*de verre, métal, verglas*) sheet; (*de chocolat*) bar; (*commémorative*) plaque; (*tache*) *Méd* blotch; **p. chauffante** *Culin* hotplate; **p. tournante** (*carrefour*) *Fig* centre, hub; **p. minéralogique, p. d'immatriculation** *Aut* number *ou Am* license plate; **p. dentaire** (dental) plaque.
plaqu/er [plake] *vt Rugby* to tackle; (*aplatir*) to flatten (**contre** against); (*abandonner*) *Fam* to give (*sth*) up; **p. qn** *Fam* to ditch s.o. • **—é** *a* (*bijou*) plated; **p. or** gold-plated ‖ *nm* **p. or** gold plate.
plastic [plastik] *nm* plastic explosive. • **plastiquer** *vt* to blow up.
plastique [plastik] *a* (*art, substance*) plastic; **matière p.** plastic ‖ *nm* (*matière*) plastic; **en p.** (*bouteille etc*) plastic.
plat [pla] **1** *a* flat; (*mer*) calm; (*fade*) flat, dull; **à p. ventre** flat on one's face; **à p.**

(*pneu, batterie*) flat; (*épuisé*) *Fam* exhausted; **poser à p.** to put *ou* lay (down) flat; **assiette plate** dinner plate; **eau plate** still water; **calme p.** dead calm ▮ *nm* (*de la main*) flat. **2** *nm* (*récipient, nourriture*) dish; (*partie du repas*) course; **'p. du jour'** (*au restaurant*) 'today's special'.

platane [platan] *nm* plane tree.

plateau, -x [plato] *nm* (*pour servir*) tray; (*plate-forme*) *Cin TV* set; *Th* stage; *Géog* plateau; **p. à fromages** cheeseboard.

plate-bande [platbɑ̃d] *nf* (*pl* **plates-bandes**) flower bed.

plate-forme [platfɔrm] *nf* (*pl* **plates-formes**) platform; **p.-forme pétrolière** oil rig.

platine [platin] **1** *nm* (*métal*) platinum. **2** *nf* (*d'électrophone, de magnétophone*) deck.

plâtre [plɑtr] *nm* (*matière*) plaster; **un p.** *Méd* a plaster cast; **dans le p.** *Méd* in plaster; **les plâtres** (*d'une maison etc*) the plasterwork. ● **plâtrer** *vt* (*membre*) to put in plaster.

plausible [plozibl] *a* plausible.

plein [plɛ̃] *a* (*rempli, complet*) full; (*paroi*) solid; **p. de** full of; **en pleine mer** out at sea; **en pleine figure** right in the face; **en p. jour** in broad daylight.

▮ *prép* & *adv* **des billes p. les poches** pockets full of marbles; **du chocolat p. la figure** chocolate all over one's face; **p. de lettres/d'argent/***etc* *Fam* lots of letters/money/*etc*. ▮ *nm* **faire le p. (d'essence)** *Aut* to fill up (the tank); **battre son p.** (*fête*) to be in full swing.

pleurer [plœre] *vi* to cry (**sur** over) ▮ *vt* (*regretter*) to mourn (for). ● **pleureur** *a* **saule p.** weeping willow. ● **pleurnicher** *vi* to snivel. ● **pleurs (en)** *adv* in tears.

pleuvoir* [pløvwar] *v imp* to rain; **il pleut** it's raining ▮ *vi* (*coups etc*) to rain down (**sur** on).

Plexiglas® [plɛksiglɑs] *nm* Perspex®, *Am* Lucite®.

pli [pli] *nm* **1** (*de papier etc*) fold; (*de jupe, robe*) pleat; (*de pantalon, de bouche*) crease; **(faux) p.** crease; **mise en plis** (*coiffure*) set. **2** (*enveloppe*) *Com* envelope, letter. **3** *Cartes* trick.

pliable [plijabl] *a* (*facile à plier*) pliable.

plier [plije] *vt* to fold; (*courber*) to bend ▮ *vi* (*branche*) to bend ▮ **se p.** *vpr* (*lit, chaise etc*) to fold (up); **se p. à** to submit to, give in to. ● **pliant** *a* (*chaise etc*) folding; (*parapluie*) telescopic.

pliss/er [plise] *vt* (*front*) to wrinkle, crease; (*yeux*) to screw up; (*froisser*) to crease. ● **—é** *a* (*tissu, jupe*) pleated.

plomb [plɔ̃] *nm* (*métal*) lead; (*fusible*) *Él* fuse; *pl* (*de chasse*) lead shot; **essence sans p.** unleaded petrol *ou* *Am* gasoline; **de p.** (*sommeil*) *Fig* heavy; (*soleil*) blazing.

plomb/er [plɔ̃be] *vt* (*dent*) *vt* to fill. ● **—é** *a* (*teint*) leaden. ● **—age** *nm* (*de dent*) filling.

plombier [plɔ̃bje] *nm* plumber. ● **plomberie** *nf* (*métier, installations*) plumbing.

plong/er [plɔ̃ʒe] *vi* (*personne, avion etc*) to dive; (*route, regard*) *Fig* to plunge ▮ *vt* (*mettre, enfoncer*) to plunge (**dans** into); **se p. dans** (*lecture etc*) to immerse oneself in. ● **—ée** *nf* *Sp* diving; (*de sous-marin*) submersion. ● **plongeoir** *nm* diving board. ● **plongeon** *nm* dive. ● **plongeur, -euse** *nmf* diver; (*employé de restaurant*) dishwasher.

plouf [pluf] *nm* & *int* splash.

plu [ply] *pp de* **plaire, pleuvoir.**

pluie [plɥi] *nf* rain; **sous la p.** in the rain.

plume [plym] *nf* **1** (*d'oiseau*) feather. **2** (*pour écrire*) *Hist* quill (pen); (*de stylo*) (pen) nib; **stylo à p.** (fountain) pen. ● **plumage** *nm* plumage. ● **plumer** *vt* (*volaille*) to pluck; **p. qn** (*voler*) *Fig* to fleece s.o. ● **plumier** *nm* pencil box.

plupart (la) [laplypar] *nf* most; **la p. des cas/***etc* most cases/*etc*; **la p. du temps** most of the time; **la p. d'entre eux** most of them; **pour la p.** mostly.

pluriel, -ielle [plyrjɛl] *a* & *nm* *Gram* plural; **au p.** (*nom*) in the plural, plural.

plus[1] [ply] ([plyz] *before vowel*, [plys] *in end position*) **1** *adv comparatif* (*travailler etc*) more (**que** than); **p. d'un kilo/de dix/***etc* (*quantité, nombre*) more than a kilo/ten/*etc*; **p. de thé/***etc* (*davantage*) more tea/*etc*; **p. beau/rapidement/***etc* more beautiful/rapidly/*etc* (**que** than); **p. tard** later; **p. petit** smaller; **de p. en p.** more and more; **de p. en p. vite** quicker and quicker; **p. ou moins** more or less; **en p.** in addition (**de** to); **de p.** more (**que** than); (*en outre*) moreover; **les enfants (âgés) de p. de dix ans** children over ten; **j'ai dix ans de p. qu'elle** I'm ten years older than she is; **il est p. de cinq heures** it's after five (o'clock); **p. il crie p. il s'enroue** the more he shouts the more hoarse he gets.

2 *adv superlatif* **le p.** (*travailler etc*) (the) most; **le p. beau/***etc* the most beautiful/*etc* (**de tous** of all); (*de deux*) the more beautiful/*etc*; **le p. grand/***etc* the biggest/*etc*; (*de deux*) the bigger/*etc*; **j'ai le p. de livres** I have (the) most books; **j'en ai le p.** I have (the) most.

ⓘ **G35** & **43** Comparative and Superlative of Adjectives and Adverbs 4 E & 5 F

plus[2] [ply] *adv de négation* **(ne)... p.** no more; **il n'a p. de pain** he has no more bread, he doesn't have any more bread; **tu n'es p. jeune** you're not young any more, you're no longer young; **elle ne le fait p.** she no longer does it, she doesn't do it any more *ou* any longer; **je ne la reverrai p.** I won't see her again; **je ne voyagerai p. jamais** I'll never travel again *ou* any more. ⓘ**G204, 205** & **206** Negative Expressions 12 B 1, 2 & 3

plus[3] [plys] *prép* plus; **deux p. deux font quatre** two plus two are four; **il fait p. deux (degrés)** it's two degrees above freezing ‖ *nm* **le signe p.** the plus sign.

plusieurs [plyzjœr] *a & pron* several. ⓘ**G48** Indefinite Adjectives and Pronouns 6 B

plus-que-parfait [plyskəparfɛ] *nm Gram* pluperfect.

plus-value [plyvaly] *nf* (*bénéfice*) profit.

plutôt [plyto] *adv* rather (**que** than).

pluvieux, -euse [plyvjø, -øz] *a* rainy, wet.

PMU [peɛmy] *abrév* = **pari mutuel urbain.**

pneu [pnø] *nm* (*pl* **-s**) (*de roue*) tyre, *Am* tire. ●**pneumatique** *a* **matelas p.** air bed; **canot p.** rubber dinghy.

pneumonie [pnømɔni] *nf* pneumonia.

poche [pɔʃ] *nf* pocket; (*de kangourou etc*) pouch; (*sac en papier etc*) bag; *pl* (*sous les yeux*) bags; **j'ai un franc en p.** I have one franc on me. ●**pochette** *nf* (*sac*) bag, envelope; (*d'allumettes*) book; (*de disque*) sleeve; (*sac à main*) (clutch) bag; (*mouchoir*) pocket handkerchief.

pocher [pɔʃe] *vt* **1** (*œufs*) to poach. **2 p. l'œil à qn** to give s.o. a black eye.

podium [pɔdjɔm] *nm Sp* podium, rostrum.

poêle [pwal] **1** *nm* stove. **2** *nf* **p. (à frire)** frying pan.

poème [pɔɛm] *nm* poem. ●**poésie** *nf* (*art*) poetry; **une p.** (*poème*) a poem. ●**poète** *nm* poet. ●**poétique** *a* poetic.

poids [pwa] *nm* weight; **au p.** by weight; **p. lourd** (heavy) lorry *ou Am* truck; **lancer le p.** *Sp* to put the shot.

poignard [pwaɲar] *nm* dagger; **coup de p.** stab. ●**poignarder** *vt* to stab.

poigne [pwaɲ] *nf* (*étreinte*) grip.

poignée [pwaɲe] *nf* (*quantité*) handful (**de** of); (*de porte, casserole etc*) handle; **p. de main** handshake; **donner une p. de main à** to shake hands with.

poignet [pwaɲɛ] *nm* wrist; (*de chemise*) cuff.

poil [pwal] *nm* hair; (*pelage*) coat, fur; *pl* (*de brosse*) bristles; (*de tapis*) pile; **de bon/mauvais p.** *Fam* in a good/bad mood; **à p.** (*nu*) *Fam* (stark) naked; **au p.** (*parfait*) *Fam* top-rate. ●**poilu** *a* hairy.

poinçon [pwɛ̃sɔ̃] *nm* (*outil*) awl; (*marque*) hallmark. ●**poinçonner** *vt* (*billet*) to punch; (*bijou*) to hallmark.

poing [pwɛ̃] *nm* fist; **coup de p.** punch.

point [pwɛ̃] *nm* (*lieu, score, question etc*) point; (*sur i, à l'horizon etc*) dot; (*tache*) spot; (*note*) *Scol* mark; (*de couture*) stitch; **sur le p. de faire** about to do, on the point of doing; **p. (final)** full stop, *Am* period; **p. d'exclamation** exclamation mark *ou Am* point; **p. d'interrogation** question mark; **points de suspension** suspension points; **p. de vue** (*opinion*) point of view, viewpoint; (*endroit*) viewing point; **à p.** (*steak*) medium rare; **à p. (nommé)** (*arriver etc*) at the right moment; **au p. mort** *Aut* in neutral; **p. de côté** (*douleur*) stitch (in one's side); **mal en p.** in bad shape; **mettre au p.** *Phot* to focus; *Aut* to tune; (*technique etc*) to elaborate; (*éclaircir*) *Fig* to clarify; **faire le p.** *Fig* to take stock, sum up. ●**point-virgule** *nm* (*pl* **points-virgules**) semicolon.

pointe [pwɛ̃t] *nf* (*extrémité*) tip, point; (*clou*) nail; (*maximum*) *Fig* peak; **sur la p. des pieds** on tiptoe; **en p.** pointed; **de p.** (*technologie, industrie etc*) state-of-the-art; **à la p. de** (*progrès etc*) *Fig* in the forefront of.

pointer [pwɛ̃te] **1** *vt* (*cocher*) to tick (off), *Am* check (off). **2** *vt* (*braquer*) to point (**sur, vers** at). **3** *vi* (*employé*) to clock in; (*à la sortie*) to clock out ‖ **se p.** *vpr* (*arriver*) *Fam* to show up.

pointillé [pwɛ̃tije] *nm* dotted line.

pointilleux, -euse [pwɛ̃tijø, -øz] *a* fussy.

pointu [pwɛ̃ty] *a* (*en pointe*) pointed.

pointure [pwɛ̃tyr] *nf* (*de chaussure, gant*) size.

poire [pwar] *nf* (*fruit*) pear. ●**poirier** *nm* pear tree.

poireau, -x [pwaro] *nm* leek.

pois [pwa] *nm* (*légume*) pea; (*dessin*) (polka) dot; **petits p.** (garden) peas, *Am* peas; **p. chiche** chickpea; **à p.** (*vêtement*) spotted.

poison [pwazɔ̃] *nm* poison.

poisseux, -euse [pwasø, -øz] *a* sticky.

poisson [pwasɔ̃] *nm* fish; **p. rouge** goldfish; **les Poissons** (*signe*) Pisces. ●**poissonnerie** *nf* fish shop. ●**poissonnier, -ière** *nmf* fishmonger.

poitrine [pwatrin] *nf Anat* chest; (*de femme*) bust; (*de veau, mouton*) *Culin* breast.

poivre [pwavr] *nm* pepper. ●**poivrer** *vt* to pepper. ●**poivré** *a Culin* (*piquant*) peppery. ●**poivrier** *nm* (*ustensile*) pepperpot.

poivron [pwavrɔ̃] *nm* (*légume*) pepper.
polar [pɔlar] *nm* (*roman*) *Fam* whodunit.
pôle [pol] *nm Géog* pole; **p. Nord/Sud** North/South Pole. •**polaire** *a* polar.
polémique [pɔlemik] *a* controversial ‖ *nf* controversy.
poli [pɔli] **1** *a* (*courtois*) polite (**avec** to, with). **2** *a* (*lisse*) polished. •**—ment** *adv* politely.
police [pɔlis] *nf* **1** police; **p. secours** emergency services; **faire** *ou* **assurer la p.** to maintain order (**dans** in). **2 p. (d'assurance)** (insurance) policy. •**policier** *a* **enquête**/*etc* **policière** police inquiry/*etc*; **chien p.** police dog; **roman p.** detective novel ‖ *nm* policeman, detective.
polio [pɔljo] *nf* (*maladie*) polio.
polir [pɔlir] *vt* to polish.
polisson, -onne [pɔlisɔ̃, -ɔn] *a* naughty.
politesse [pɔlitɛs] *nf* politeness.
politique [pɔlitik] *a* political; **homme p.** politician ‖ *nf* (*activité, science*) politics; (*mesures, manières de gouverner*) *Pol* policies; **une p.** (*tactique*) a policy.
pollen [pɔlɛn] *nm* pollen.
polluer [pɔlɥe] *vt* to pollute. •**polluant** *nm* pollutant. •**pollution** *nf* pollution.
polo [pɔlo] *nm* **1** (*chemise*) sweat shirt. **2** *Sp* polo.
polochon [pɔlɔʃɔ̃] *nm Fam* bolster.
Pologne [pɔlɔɲ] *nf* Poland. •**polonais, -aise** *a* Polish ‖ *nmf* Pole ‖ *nm* (*langue*) Polish.
poltron, -onne [pɔltrɔ̃, -ɔn] *a* cowardly.
polycopié [pɔlikɔpje] *nm Univ* duplicated course notes.
polyester [pɔliɛstɛr] *nm* polyester; **chemise/***etc* **en p.** polyester shirt/*etc.*
polyvalent [pɔlivalɑ̃] **1** *a* (*rôle*) multi-purpose; (*personne*) all-round. **2** *a* & *nf* **(école) polyvalente** *Can* = secondary school, *Am* = high school.
pommade [pɔmad] *nf* ointment.
pomme [pɔm] *nf* **1** apple; **p. d'Adam** *Anat* Adam's apple. **2 p. de terre** potato; **pommes frites** chips, *Am* French fries; **pommes chips** potato crisps *ou Am* chips; **pommes vapeur** steamed potatoes. •**pommier** *nm* apple tree.
pommette [pɔmɛt] *nf* cheekbone.
pompe [pɔ̃p] **1** *nf* pump; **p. à essence** petrol *ou Am* gas station; **p. à incendie** fire engine; **coup de p.** *Fam* tired feeling. **2** *nf* (*chaussure*) *Fam* shoe. **3** *nf* (*en gymnastique*) press-up, *Am* push-up. **4** *nfpl* **pompes funèbres** undertaker's; **entrepreneur de pompes funèbres** undertaker. •**pomper** *vt* (*eau*) to pump out (**de** of); (*absorber*) to soak up ‖ *vi* to pump.
pompeux, -euse [pɔ̃pø, -øz] *a* pompous.
pompier [pɔ̃pje] *nm* fireman; **voiture des pompiers** fire engine. •**pompiste** *nmf Aut* petrol *ou Am* gas station attendant.
pomponner [pɔ̃pɔne] *vt* to doll up.
ponce [pɔ̃s] *nf* **(pierre) p.** pumice (stone). •**poncer** *vt* to rub down, sand.
ponctuation [pɔ̃ktɥasjɔ̃] *nf* punctuation. •**ponctuer** *vt* to punctuate (**de** with).
ponctuel, -elle [pɔ̃ktɥɛl] *a* (*à l'heure*) punctual; (*unique*) *Fig* one-off, *Am* one-of-a-kind.
pondéré [pɔ̃dere] *a* level-headed.
pondre [pɔ̃dr] *vt* (*œuf*) to lay ‖ *vi* (*poule*) to lay (eggs *ou* an egg).
poney [pɔnɛ] *nm* pony.
pont [pɔ̃] *nm* bridge; (*de bateau*) deck; **faire le p.** *Fig* to take the intervening day(s) off (*between two holidays*); **p. aérien** airlift. •**p.-levis** *nm* (*pl* **ponts-levis**) drawbridge.
pontife [pɔ̃tif] *nm* **(souverain) p.** pope.
pop [pɔp] *nm* & *a inv Mus* pop.
populaire [pɔpylɛr] *a* (*qui plaît*) popular; (*quartier, milieu*) working-class; (*expression*) colloquial. •**popularité** *nf* popularity (**auprès de** with).
population [pɔpylasjɔ̃] *nf* population.
porc [pɔr] *nm* pig; (*viande*) pork.
porcelaine [pɔrsəlɛn] *nf* china, porcelain.
porc-épic [pɔrkepik] *nm* (*pl* **porcs-épics**) (*animal*) porcupine.
porche [pɔrʃ] *nm* porch.
porcherie [pɔrʃəri] *nf* (pig)sty.
pore [pɔr] *nm* pore.
pornographie [pɔrnɔgrafi] *nf* pornography. •**pornographique** *a* pornographic.
port [pɔr] *nm* **1** port, harbour; **arriver à bon p.** to arrive safely. **2** (*d'armes*) carrying; (*de barbe*) wearing; (*prix*) carriage, postage.
portable [pɔrtabl] *a* (*portatif*) portable.
portail [pɔrtaj] *nm* (*de jardin*) gate.
portant [pɔrtɑ̃] *a* **bien p.** in good health.
portatif, -ive [pɔrtatif, -iv] *a* portable.
porte [pɔrt] *nf* door; (*de jardin*) gate; (*de ville*) entrance, *Hist* gate; **p. (d'embarquement)** *Av* (departure) gate; **p. d'entrée** front door; **p. coulissante** sliding door; **mettre à la p.** to throw out; (*renvoyer*) to fire, sack. •**porte-fenêtre** *nf* (*pl* **portes-fenêtres**) French window, *Am* French door.
porte-avions [pɔrtavjɔ̃] *nm inv* aircraft carrier. •**p.-bagages** *nm inv* luggage rack. •**p.-bonheur** *nm inv* (*fétiche*) (lucky) charm. •**p.-cartes** *nm inv* card holder. •**p.-clefs** *nm inv* key ring. •**p.-documents** *nm inv* brief-

case. ● **p.-monnaie** *nm inv* purse. ● **p.-plume** *nm inv* pen (*for dipping in ink*). ● **p.-savon** *nm* soapdish. ● **p.-serviettes** *nm inv* towel rail *ou Am* rack. ● **p.-voix** *nm inv* loudspeaker, megaphone.

portée [pɔrte] *nf* **1** (*de fusil etc*) range; **à la p. de qn** within reach of s.o.; (*richesse, plaisir etc*) *Fig* within s.o.'s grasp; **à p. de la main** within (easy) reach; **à p. de voix** within earshot; **hors de p.** out of reach. **2** (*animaux*) litter. **3** (*importance, effet*) significance. **4** *Mus* stave.

portefeuille [pɔrtəfœj] *nm* wallet; *Pol Com* portfolio.

portemanteau, -x [pɔrtmɑ̃to] *nm* (*sur pied*) hatstand, hallstand; (*crochet*) coat *ou* hat peg.

porte-parole [pɔrtparɔl] *nm inv* (*homme*) spokesman; (*femme*) spokeswoman (**de** for).

porter [pɔrte] *vt* to carry; (*vêtement, lunettes, barbe etc*) to wear; (*trace, responsabilité, fruits etc*) to bear; (*regard*) to cast; (*attaque*) to make (**contre** against); (*inscrire*) to enter; **p. qch à** (*apporter*) to take *ou* bring sth to; **p. bonheur/malheur** to bring good/bad luck.
▮ *vi* (*voix*) to carry; (*canon*) to fire; (*vue*) to extend; (*coup*) to hit the mark; (*reproche*) to hit home; **p. sur** (*reposer sur*) to rest on; (*concerner*) to bear on; (*accent*) to fall on.
▮ **se porter** *vpr* (*vêtement*) to be worn; **se p. bien/mal** to be well/ill; **comment te portes-tu?** how are you?; **se p. candidat** to stand as a candidate. ● **porteur, -euse** *nm Rail* porter ▮ *nmf Méd* carrier; (*de nouvelles, chèque*) bearer; **mère porteuse** surrogate mother.

portier [pɔrtje] *nm* doorkeeper. ● **portière** *nf* (*de véhicule, train*) door. ● **portillon** *nm* gate.

portion [pɔrsjɔ̃] *nf* (*partie*) portion; (*de nourriture*) helping, portion.

portique [pɔrtik] *nm* **1** *Archit* portico. **2** (*de balançoire etc*) crossbar.

porto [pɔrto] *nm* (*vin*) port.

portrait [pɔrtrɛ] *nm* portrait; **être le p. de** (*son père etc*) to be the image of; **faire un p.** to paint *ou* draw a portrait (**de** of). ● **p.-robot** *nm* (*pl* **portraits-robots**) identikit (picture), photofit.

portuaire [pɔrtɥɛr] *a* **installations portuaires** port facilities.

Portugal [pɔrtygal] *nm* Portugal. ● **portugais, -aise** *a* Portuguese ▮ *nmf* Portuguese man *ou* woman, Portuguese *inv*; **les P.** the Portuguese ▮ *nm* (*langue*) Portuguese.

pose [poz] *nf* **1** (*installation*) putting up; putting in; laying. **2** (*attitude*) pose; (*temps*) *Phot* exposure.

poser [poze] *vt* to put (down); (*papier peint, rideaux*) to put up; (*sonnette, chauffage*) to put in; (*moquette, fondations*) to lay; (*question*) to ask (**à qn** s.o.); (*conditions*) to lay down; **p. sa candidature** to apply (**à** for).
▮ *vi* (*modèle etc*) to pose (**pour** for).
▮ **se poser** *vpr* (*oiseau, avion*) to land; (*problème, question*) to arise; **se p. sur** (*yeux*) to fix on.

positif, -ive [pozitif, -iv] *a* positive.

position [pozisjɔ̃] *nf* (*emplacement, opinion etc*) position; **prendre p.** *Fig* to take a stand (**contre** against).

posologie [pozɔlɔʒi] *nf* (*de médicament*) dosage, directions.

posséder [posede] *vt* to possess; (*maison, bien etc*) to own, possess; (*bien connaître*) to master. ● **possessif, -ive** *a* (*personne, adjectif etc*) possessive ▮ *nm Gram* possessive. ● **possession** *nf* possession; **en p. de** in possession of.

possible [pɔsibl] *a* possible (**à faire** to do); **il (nous) est p. de le faire** it is possible (for us) to do it; **il est p. que** (+ *sub*) it is possible that; **si p.** if possible; **le plus tôt**/*etc* **p.** as soon/*etc* as possible; **autant que p.** as far as possible; **le plus p.** as much *ou* as many as possible ▮ *nm* **faire son p.** to do one's utmost (**pour faire** to do); **dans la mesure du p.** as far as possible. ● **possibilité** *nf* possibility.

post- [pɔst] *préf* post-.

postal, -aux [pɔstal, -o] *a* postal; **boîte postale** PO Box; **code p.** postcode, *Am* zip code.

postdater [pɔstdate] *vt* to postdate.

poste [pɔst] **1** *nf* (*service*) post, mail; **(bureau de) p.** post office; **Postes (et Télécommunications)** (*administration*) Post Office; **par la p.** by post, by mail; **p. aérienne** airmail; **mettre à la p.** to post, mail.
2 *nm* (*lieu, emploi*) post; **p. de secours** first aid post; **p. de police** police station; **p. d'essence** petrol *ou Am* gas station; **p. d'incendie** fire point (*containing fire-fighting equipment*).
3 *nm* (*appareil*) *Rad TV* set; *Tél* extension (number). ● **poster 1** *vt* (*lettre*) to post, mail. **2** *vt* **p. qn** (*placer*) *Mil* to post s.o. **3** [pɔstɛr] *nm* poster.

postérieur [pɔsterjœr] *a* (*document etc*) later; **p. à** after.

postier, -ière [pɔstje, -jɛr] *nmf* postal worker.

postillonner [pɔstijɔne] *vi* to sputter.
postuler [pɔstyle] *vi* **p. (à un emploi)** to apply for a job.
posture [pɔstyr] *nf* posture.
pot [po] *nm* **1** pot; (*à confiture*) jar; (*à lait*) jug; (*à bière*) mug; (*de crème, yaourt*) carton; (*de bébé*) potty; **p. de fleurs** flower pot; **prendre un p.** (*verre*) *Fam* to have a drink. **2** (*chance*) *Fam* luck; **avoir du p.** to be lucky.
potable [pɔtabl] *a* drinkable; **'eau p.'** 'drinking water'.
potage [pɔtaʒ] *nm* soup.
potager [pɔtaʒe] *am* & *nm* **(jardin) p.** vegetable garden.
potasser [pɔtase] *vt* (*examen*) *Fam* to cram for.
pot-au-feu [pɔtofø] *nm inv* beef stew.
pot-de-vin [podvɛ̃] *nm* (*pl* **pots-de-vin**) bribe.
poteau, -x [pɔto] *nm* post; **p. indicateur** signpost; **p. d'arrivée** *Sp* winning post; **p. télégraphique** telegraph pole.
potelé [pɔtle] *a* plump, chubby.
potence [pɔtɑ̃s] *nf* (*gibet*) gallows.
potentiel, -ielle [pɔtɑ̃sjɛl] *a* & *nm* potential.
poterie [pɔtri] *nf* (*art*) pottery; **une p.** a piece of pottery; **des poteries** (*objets*) pottery. ●**potier** *nm* potter.
potins [pɔtɛ̃] *nmpl* (*cancans*) gossip.
potion [posjɔ̃] *nf* potion.
potiron [pɔtirɔ̃] *nm* pumpkin.
pou, -x [pu] *nm* louse; **poux** lice.
poubelle [pubɛl] *nf* dustbin, *Am* garbage can.
pouce [pus] *nm* **1** thumb; **un coup de p.** *Fam* a helping hand. **2** (*mesure*) *Hist* & *Fig* inch.
poudre [pudr] *nf* powder; **p. (à canon)** (*explosif*) gunpowder; **en p.** (*lait*) powdered; (*chocolat*) drinking; **sucre en p.** castor *ou* caster sugar, *Am* finely ground sugar. ●**se poudrer** *vpr* (*femme*) to powder one's face. ●**poudreux, -euse** *a* powdery ‖ *nf* (*neige*) powder snow. ●**poudrier** *nm* (powder) compact.
pouf [puf] *nm* (*siège*) pouf(fe).
pouffer [pufe] *vi* **p. (de rire)** to burst out laughing.
poulain [pulɛ̃] *nm* (*cheval*) foal.
poule [pul] *nf* **1** hen; *Culin* fowl; **être une p. mouillée** (*lâche*) to be chicken. ●**poulailler** *nm* **1** henhouse. **2 le p.** *Th Fam* the gods, the gallery. ●**poulet** *nm* (*poule, coq*) chicken.
pouliche [puliʃ] *nf* (*jument*) filly.
poulie [puli] *nf* pulley.
poulpe [pulp] *nm* octopus.

pouls [pu] *nm Méd* pulse.
poumon [pumɔ̃] *nm* lung; **à pleins poumons** (*respirer*) deeply; (*crier*) loudly.
poupe [pup] *nf Nau* stern.
poupée [pupe] *nf* doll.
poupon [pupɔ̃] *nm* (*bébé*) baby; (*poupée*) doll.
pour [pur] **1** *prép* for; **p. toi**/*etc* for you/*etc*; **partir p.** (*Paris, cinq ans etc*) to leave for; **elle est p.** she's in favour; **p. faire qch** (in order) to do sth, so as to do sth; **p. que tu saches** so (that) you may know; **p. quoi faire?** what for?; **trop petit**/*etc* **p. faire qch** too small/*etc* to do sth; **assez grand**/*etc* **p. faire qch** big/*etc* enough to do sth; **p. cela** for that reason; **p. ma part** (*quant à moi*) as for me; **jour p. jour** to the day; **dix p. cent** ten per cent; **acheter p. cinq francs de bonbons** to buy five francs' worth of sweets *ou Am* candies.
2 *nm* **le p. et le contre** the pros and cons.
ⓘ**G181** Prepositions 8
pourboire [purbwar] *nm* tip (*money*).
pourcentage [pursɑ̃taʒ] *nm* percentage.
pourparlers [purparle] *nmpl* negotiations, talks.
pourpre [purpr] *a* & *nm* purple.
pourquoi [purkwa] *adv* & *conj* why; **p. pas?** why not? ‖ *nm inv* reason (**de** for); **le p. et le comment** the whys and wherefores.
pourra, pourrait *etc* [pura, purɛ] *voir* **pouvoir 1.**
pourrir [purir] *vi* to rot ‖ *vt* to rot; **p. qn** to corrupt s.o. ●**pourri** *a* (*fruit, temps, personne etc*) rotten.
poursuite [pursɥit] **1** *nf* chase; (*du bonheur, de créancier*) pursuit (**de** of); **se mettre à la p. de** to go after, chase (after). **2** *nfpl Jur* legal proceedings (**contre** against).
poursuivre* [pursɥivr] **1** *vt* to chase, go after; (*harceler*) to hound, pursue; (*but, idéal etc*) to pursue. **2** *vt* **p. qn (en justice)** (*au criminel*) to prosecute s.o.; (*au civil*) to sue s.o. **3** *vt* (*lecture, voyage etc*) to carry on (with), continue (with), pursue ‖ *vi*, **se p.** *vpr* to continue, go on. ●**poursuivant, -ante** *nmf* pursuer.
pourtant [purtɑ̃] *adv* yet, nevertheless.
pourvoir* [purvwar] *vi* **p. à** (*besoins etc*) to provide for.
pourvu que [purvyk(ə)] *conj* (*condition*) provided *ou* providing (that); (*souhait*) **p. qu'elle soit là!** I only hope (that) she's there!
pousse [pus] *nf* **1** (*bourgeon*) shoot. **2** (*croissance*) growth.
pousser [puse] **1** *vt* to push; (*cri*) to utter;

(eg **G1**, **G2**, **G3**) in French **G**rammar, at the end of the dictionary. Also see p. ix.

(*soupir*) to heave; **p. qn à faire qch** to urge s.o. to do sth; **p. qn à bout** to push s.o. to his *ou* her limits ‖ *vi* to push ‖ **se p.** *vpr* (*se déplacer*) to move up *ou* over.
2 *vi* (*croître*) to grow; **faire p.** (*plante*, *barbe etc*) to grow. • **poussé** *a* (*travail*, *études*) advanced. • **poussée** *nf* (*pression*) pressure; (*de fièvre etc*) outbreak.
poussette [pusɛt] *nf* pushchair, *Am* stroller.
poussière [pusjɛr] *nf* dust; **dix francs et des poussières** *Fam* a bit over ten francs. • **poussiéreux, -euse** *a* dusty.
poussin [pusɛ̃] *nm* (*poulet*) chick.
poutre [putr] *nf* (*en bois*) beam; (*en acier*) girder. • **poutrelle** *nf* girder.
pouvoir** [puvwar] **1** *v aux* (*capacité*) can, be able to; (*permission*, *éventualité*) may, can; **je peux deviner** I can guess, I'm able to guess; **tu peux entrer** you may *ou* can come in; **il peut être sorti** he may *ou* might be out; **elle pourrait/pouvait venir** she might/could come; **j'ai pu l'obtenir** I managed to get it; **j'aurais pu l'obtenir** I could have got it *ou Am* gotten it; **je n'en peux plus** I'm utterly exhausted ‖ *v imp* **il peut neiger** it may snow ‖ **se pouvoir** *vpr* **il se peut qu'elle parte** (it's possible that) she might leave.
ⓘ**pouvoir G90** Impersonal Verbs 7 E 2g)
ⓘ**pouvoir G122** Modal Auxiliary Verbs 7 K 2
2 *nm* (*capacité*, *autorité*) power; **les pouvoirs publics** the authorities; **au p.** *Pol* in power; **en son p.** in one's power (**de faire** to do); **p. d'achat** purchasing power.
poux [pu] *voir* **pou.**
pragmatique [pragmatik] *a* pragmatic.
prairie [preri] *nf* meadow.
praline [pralin] *nf* sugared almond. • **praliné** *a* (*glace*) praline-flavoured.
praticable [pratikabl] *a* (*chemin*, *projet*) practicable.
pratique [pratik] **1** *a* (*connaissance*, *personne*, *outil etc*) practical. **2** *nf* (*exercice*, *procédé*) practice; (*expérience*) practical experience; **la p. de la natation/du golf/***etc* swimming/golfing/*etc*; **mettre en p.** to put into practice; **en p.** (*en réalité*) in practice.
pratiquement [pratikmɑ̃] *adv* (*presque*) practically; (*en réalité*) in practice.
pratiqu/er [pratike] *vt* (*sport*, *art etc*) to practise, *Am* practice; (*trou*, *route*) to make; (*opération*) to carry out; **p. la natation** to go swimming. • **—ant, -ante** *a Rel* practising ‖ *nmf* churchgoer.
pré [pre] *nm* meadow.
pré- [pre] *préf* pre-.
préalable [prealabl] *a* prior, preliminary; **p. à** prior to ‖ *nm* precondition; **au p.** beforehand.
préau, -x [preo] *nm Scol* covered playground *ou Am* school yard.
préavis [preavi] *nm* (advance) notice (**de** of).
précaire [prekɛr] *a* precarious.
précaution [prekosjɔ̃] *nf* (*mesure*) precaution; (*prudence*) caution; **par p.** as a precaution; **prendre la p. de faire** to take the precaution of doing.
précédent, -ente [presedɑ̃, -ɑ̃t] **1** *a* previous, preceding ‖ *nmf* previous one. **2** *nm* **un p.** (*exemple*) a precedent; **sans p.** unprecedented. • **précéder** *vti* to precede; **faire p. qch de qch** to precede sth by sth.
prêcher [preʃe] *vti* to preach.
précieux, -euse [presjø, -øz] *a* precious.
précipice [presipis] *nm* chasm, precipice.
précipiter [presipite] *vt* (*hâter*) to hasten, rush; (*jeter*) to throw, hurl; (*plonger*) to plunge (**dans** into) ‖ **se p.** *vpr* (*se jeter*) to throw *ou* hurl oneself; (*foncer*) to rush (**à, sur** on to); (*s'accélérer*) to speed up. • **précipitamment** [-amɑ̃] *adv* hastily. • **précipitation 1** *nf* haste. **2** *nfpl* (*pluie*) precipitation.
précis [presi] *a* precise; (*idée*, *mécanisme*) accurate, precise; **à deux heures précises** at two o'clock sharp. • **préciser** *vt* to specify (**que** that) ‖ **se p.** *vpr* to become clear(er). • **précision** *nf* precision; accuracy; (*détail*) detail; (*explication*) explanation.
précoce [prekɔs] *a* (*fruit etc*) early; (*enfant*) precocious.
préconiser [prekɔnize] *vt* to advocate (**que** that).
précurseur [prekyrsœr] *nm* forerunner.
prédécesseur [predesesœr] *nm* predecessor.
prédilection [predilɛksjɔ̃] *nf* (special) liking; **de p.** favourite.
prédire* [predir] *vt* to predict (**que** that). • **prédiction** *nf* prediction.
prédisposer [predispoze] *vt* to predispose (**à qch** to sth, **à faire** to do).
prédomin/er [predɔmine] *vi* to predominate. • **—ant** *a* predominant.
préfabriqué [prefabrike] *a* prefabricated.
préface [prefas] *nf* preface.
préférable [preferabl] *a* preferable (**à** to).
ⓘ**G99** The Subjunctive 7 G 1d)
préférence [preferɑ̃s] *nf* preference (**pour** for); **de p.** preferably; **de p. à** in preference to. • **préférentiel, -ielle** *a* preferential.
préfér/er [prefere] *vt* to prefer (**à** to); **p.**

faire to prefer to do; **je préférerais rester** I would rather stay, I would prefer to stay. ● **—é, -ée** *a* & *nmf* favourite.

❶**préférer G99** The Subjunctive 7 G 1b)

préfet [prefɛ] *nm* prefect (*chief administrator in a department*); **p. de police** prefect of police (*Paris chief of police*). ● **préfecture** *nf* prefecture; **p. de police** Paris police headquarters.

préfixe [prefiks] *nm* prefix.

préhistoire [preistwar] *nf* prehistory. ● **préhistorique** *a* prehistoric.

préjudice [preʒydis] *nm Jur* prejudice, harm; **porter p. à** to prejudice, harm.

préjugé [preʒyʒe] *nm* prejudice; **avoir des préjugés** to be prejudiced (**contre** against); **être plein de préjugés** to be full of prejudice.

prélasser (se) [səprelɑse] *vpr* to lounge (about).

prélever [prel(ə)ve] *vt* (*échantillon*) to take (**sur** from); (*somme*) to deduct (**sur** from). ● **prélèvement** *nm* taking; deduction; **p. automatique** *Fin* standing order, *Am* automatic deduction.

préliminaire [preliminɛr] *a* preliminary ‖ *nmpl* preliminaries.

prélude [prelyd] *nm* prelude (**à** to).

prématuré [prematyre] *a* premature ‖ *nm* (*bébé*) premature baby.

préméditer [premedite] *vt* to premeditate.

premier, -ière [prəmje, -jɛr] *a* first; (*enfance*) early; (*page de journal*) front, first; (*qualité, nécessité, importance*) prime; **nombre p.** *Math* prime number; **le p. rang** the front *ou* first row; **à la première occasion** at the earliest opportunity; **P. ministre** Prime Minister.

‖ *nmf* first (one); **arriver le p.** *ou* **en p.** to arrive first; **être le p. de la classe** to be (at the) top of the class.

‖ *nm* (*date*) first; (*étage*) first *ou Am* second floor; **le p. de l'an** New Year's Day.

‖ *nf* **première** (*wagon, billet*) first class; *Scol* = sixth form, *Am* = twelfth grade; *Aut* first (gear); *Th* première. ● **premier-né** *nm*, **première-née** *nf* first-born (child). ● **premièrement** *adv* firstly.

prémonition [premɔnisjɔ̃] *nf* premonition.

prénatal, *mpl* **-als** [prenatal] *a* antenatal, *Am* prenatal.

prendre** [prɑ̃dr] *vt* to take (**à qn** from s.o.); (*attraper*) to catch, get; (*voyager par*) to take, travel by (*train etc*); (*douche, bain*) to take, have; (*repas*) to have; (*photo*) to take; (*temps*) to take (up); (*ton, air*) to put on; **p. qn pour** (*un autre*) to mistake s.o. for; (*considérer*) to take s.o. for; **p. feu** to catch fire; **p. de la place** to take up room; **p. du poids/de la vitesse** to put on weight/speed; **passer p. qn** to come and get s.o.; **à tout p.** on the whole; **qu'est-ce qui te prend?** what's got *ou Am* gotten into you?

‖ *vi* (*feu*) to catch; (*ciment, gelée*) to set; (*greffe, vaccin*) to take; (*mode*) to catch on.

‖ **se prendre** *vpr* (*médicament*) to be taken; (*s'accrocher*) to get caught; **se p. pour un génie/***etc* to think one is a genius/*etc*; **s'y p. pour faire qch** to go *ou* set about doing sth; **s'en p. à** (*critiquer, attaquer*) to attack; (*accuser*) to blame.

prénom [prenɔ̃] *nm* first name.

préoccup/er [preɔkype] *vt* (*inquiéter*) to worry; (*absorber*) to preoccupy; **se p. de** to be worried about; to be preoccupied about. ● **—é** *a* worried. ● **préoccupation** *nf* worry.

préparer [prepare] *vt* to prepare (**qch pour** sth for); (*repas etc*) to get ready, prepare; (*examen*) to prepare (for), study for; **p. qch à qn** to prepare sth for s.o.; **p. qn à** (*examen*) to prepare *ou* coach s.o. for.

‖ **se préparer** *vpr* to get (oneself) ready (**à** *ou* **pour qch** for sth); **se p. à faire** to prepare to do, get ready to do. ● **préparatifs** *nmpl* preparations (**de** for). ● **préparation** *nf* preparation. ● **préparatoire** *a* preparatory.

préposé, -ée [prepoze] *nmf* employee; (*facteur*) postman, postwoman.

préposition [prepozisjɔ̃] *nf Gram* preposition.

préretraite [prerətrɛt] *nf* early retirement.

prérogative [prerɔgativ] *nf* prerogative.

près [prɛ] *adv* **p. de** (*qn, qch*) near (to), close to; **p. de deux ans/***etc* (*presque*) nearly two years/*etc*; **p. de partir/***etc* about to leave/*etc*; **tout p.** nearby (**de qn/qch** s.o./sth), close by (**de qn/qch** s.o./sth); **de p.** (*lire, suivre*) closely; **à peu de chose p.** almost; **calculer au franc p.** to calculate to the nearest franc.

présage [prezaʒ] *nm* omen.

presbyte [prɛsbit] *a* & *nmf* long-sighted (person).

prescrire* [prɛskrir] *vt* (*médicament*) to prescribe. ● **prescription** *nf* (*instruction*) & *Jur* prescription.

présence [prezɑ̃s] *nf* presence; (*à l'école etc*) attendance (**à** at); **feuille de p.** attendance sheet; **en p. de** in the presence of.

présent[1] [prezɑ̃] **1** *a* (*non absent*) present (**à** at, **dans** in); **les personnes présentes** those present. **2** *a* (*actuel*) present ‖ *nm* (*temps*) present; *Gram* present (tense); **à p.** at present, now; **dès à p.** as from now.

présent[2] [prezɑ̃] *nm* (*cadeau*) present.

(eg **G1**, **G2**, **G3**) in French **G**rammar, at the end of the dictionary. Also see p. ix.

présenter [prezɑ̃te] *vt* (*offrir, montrer, animer etc*) to present; **p. qn à qn** to introduce *ou* present s.o. to s.o. ‖ **se présenter** *vpr* to introduce *ou* present oneself (**à** to); (*chez qn*) to show up; (*occasion etc*) to arise; **se p. à** (*examen*) to take; (*élections*) to run in; **ça se présente bien** it looks promising. ●**présentable** *a* presentable. ●**présentateur, -trice** *nmf TV* announcer, presenter. ●**présentation** *nf* presentation; introduction.

préserver [prezɛrve] *vt* to protect, preserve (**de, contre** from). ●**préservatif** *nm* condom, sheath.

présidence [prezidɑ̃s] *nf* (*de nation*) presidency; (*de firme etc*) chairmanship. ●**président, -ente** *nmf* (*de nation*) president; (*de réunion, firme*) chairman, chairwoman; **p. directeur général** (chairman and) managing director, *Am* chief executive officer. ●**présidentiel, -ielle** *a* presidential.

présider [prezide] *vt* (*réunion*) to chair, preside over ‖ *vi* to preside.

présomption [prezɔ̃psjɔ̃] *nf* (*supposition, suffisance*) presumption.

presque˙ [prɛsk(ə)] *adv* almost, nearly; **p. jamais/rien** hardly *ou* scarcely ever/anything.

presqu'île [prɛskil] *nf* peninsula.

presse [prɛs] *nf* (*journaux, appareil*) press; *Typ* (printing) press; **conférence/agence de p.** press conference/agency.

presse-citron [prɛssitrɔ̃] *nm* lemon squeezer. ●**p.-papiers** *nm inv* paperweight.

pressentir* [presɑ̃tir] *vt* (*deviner*) to sense (**que** that). ●**pressentiment** *nm* foreboding.

presser [prese] *vt* (*serrer*) to squeeze, press; (*bouton*) to press; (*fruit*) to squeeze; **p. le pas** to speed up.

‖ *vi* (*temps*) to press; (*affaire*) to be urgent; **rien ne presse** there's no hurry.

‖ **se presser** *vpr* (*se serrer*) to squeeze (together); (*se hâter*) to hurry (**de faire** to do); (*se grouper*) to crowd, swarm. ●**pressant** *a* urgent. ●**pressé** *a* (*personne*) in a hurry; (*travail*) urgent; (*air*) hurried.

pressing [presiŋ] *nm* (*magasin*) dry cleaner's.

pression [prɛsjɔ̃] *nf* **1** pressure; **faire p. sur qn** to put pressure on s.o., pressurize s.o. **2** (*bouton*) snap (fastener), press-stud.

pressuriser [presyrize] *vt Av* to pressurize.

prestation [prɛstɑsjɔ̃] *nf* **1** (*allocation*) allowance, benefit. **2** (*performance*) performance.

prestidigitateur, -trice [prɛstidiʒitatœr, -tris] *nmf* conjurer. ●**prestidigitation** *nf* **tour de p.** conjuring trick.

prestige [prɛstiʒ] *nm* prestige.

présumer [prezyme] *vt* to presume (**que** that).

prêt[1] [prɛ] *a* (*préparé*) ready (**à faire** to do, **à qch** for sth). ●**p.-à-porter** [prɛtapɔrte] *nm* (*pl* **prêts-à-porter**) ready-to-wear clothes.

prêt[2] [prɛ] *nm* (*emprunt*) loan.

prétend/re [pretɑ̃dr] *vt* to claim (**que** that); (*vouloir*) to intend (**faire** to do); **p. être/savoir** to claim to be/to know; **elle se prétend riche** she claims to be rich ‖ *vi* **p. à** (*titre etc*) to lay claim to. ●**—ant** *nm* (*amoureux*) suitor. ●**—u** *a* so-called.

prétentieux, -euse [pretɑ̃sjø, -øz] *a & nmf* conceited (person). ●**prétention** *nf* (*vanité*) pretension; (*revendication, ambition*) claim.

prêter [prete] *vt* (*argent, objet*) to lend (**à** to); (*attribuer*) to attribute (**à** to); **p. attention** to pay attention (**à** to); **p. serment** to take an oath; **se p. à** (*consentir à*) to agree to; (*sujet etc*) to lend itself to.

prétérit [preterit] *nm Gram* preterite (tense).

prétexte [pretɛkst] *nm* excuse, pretext; **sous p. de/que** on the pretext of/that.

prêtre [prɛtr] *nm* priest; **grand p.** high priest.

preuve [prœv] *nf* **preuve(s)** proof, evidence; **faire p. de** to show; **faire ses preuves** (*personne*) to prove oneself; (*méthode*) to prove itself.

préven/ir* [prevnir] *vt* **1** (*avertir*) to warn (**que** that); (*aviser*) to inform, tell (**que** that). **2** (*désir, question*) to anticipate; (*malheur*) to avert. ●**—u, -ue** *nmf Jur* defendant, accused. ●**prévention** *nf* prevention; **p. routière** road safety.

prévision [previzjɔ̃] *nf* (*opinion*) & *Mét* forecast; **en p. de** in expectation of.

prévoir* [prevwar] *vt* (*anticiper*) to foresee (**que** that); (*prédire*) to forecast (**que** that); (*temps*) *Mét* to forecast; (*organiser*) to plan (for); (*préparer*) to provide, make provision for; **un repas est prévu** a meal is provided; **au moment prévu** at the appointed time; **comme prévu** as expected, as planned; **prévu pour** (*véhicule, appareil etc*) designed for.

prévoyant [prevwajɑ̃] *a* **être p.** to have foresight.

prier [prije] **1** *vi Rel* to pray (**pour** for) ‖ *vt* **p. Dieu pour qu'il nous accorde qch** to pray (to God) for sth. **2** *vt* **p. qn de faire** to ask *ou* request s.o. to do; (*implorer*) to beg s.o. to do; **je vous en prie** (*faites donc, allez-y*) please; (*en réponse à 'merci'*) don't men-

tion it; **se faire p.** to wait to be asked.
prière [prijɛr] *nf* prayer; **p. de répondre/***etc* please answer/*etc*.
primaire [primɛr] *a* primary.
prime [prim] **1** *nf* (*d'employé*) bonus; (*d'État*) subsidy; **en p.** (*cadeau*) as a free gift; **p. (d'assurance)** (insurance) premium. **2** *a* **de p. abord** at the very first glance.
primeurs [primœr] *nfpl* early fruit and vegetables.
primevère [primvɛr] *nf* primrose.
primitif, -ive [primitif, -iv] *a* (*société, art etc*) primitive; (*état, sens*) original.
primordial, -aux [primɔrdjal, -o] *a* vital.
prince [prɛ̃s] *nm* prince. ● **princesse** *nf* princess. ● **principauté** *nf* principality.
principal, -aux [prɛ̃sipal, -o] *a* main, chief, principal ‖ *nm* (*de collège*) principal, headmaster; **le p.** (*essentiel*) the main *ou* chief thing.
principe [prɛ̃sip] *nm* principle; **en p.** theoretically; (*normalement*) as a rule; **par p.** on principle.
printemps [prɛ̃tɑ̃] *nm* (*saison*) spring; **au p.** in (the) spring.
priorité [priɔrite] *nf* priority (**sur** over); **la p.** *Aut* the right of way; **la p. à droite** the right of way to traffic coming from the right; **'cédez la p.'** *Aut* 'give way', *Am* 'yield'; **en p.** as a matter of priority. ● **prioritaire** *a* **être p.** to have priority; *Aut* to have the right of way.
pris [pri] *pp de* **prendre** ‖ *a* (*place*) taken; (*crème, ciment*) set; (*nez*) congested; (*gorge*) infected; **être (très) p.** (*occupé*) to be (very) busy; **p. de** (*peur, panique*) stricken with.
prise [priz] *nf* taking; (*objet saisi*) catch; (*manière d'empoigner*) grip, hold; (*de judo etc*) hold; (*de ville*) capture; **p. (de courant)** *Él* (*mâle*) plug; (*femelle*) socket; **p. multiple** *Él* adaptor; **p. de sang** blood test; **p. de contact** first meeting; **p. de position** *Fig* stand; **être aux prises avec qn/qch** to be struggling with s.o./sth.
prison [prizɔ̃] *nf* prison, jail; (*réclusion*) imprisonment; **être en p.** to be in prison *ou* in jail; **mettre qn en p.** to send s.o. to prison, jail s.o. ● **prisonnier, -ière** *nmf* prisoner; **faire qn p.** to take s.o. prisoner.
privatiser [privatize] *vt* to privatize.
privé [prive] *a* private; **en p.** (*seul à seul*) in private ‖ *nm* **dans le p.** *Com Fam* in the private sector.
priver [prive] *vt* to deprive (**de** of); **se p. de** to do without, deprive oneself of.
privilège [privilɛʒ] *nm* privilege. ● **privilégié, -ée** *a* & *nmf* privileged (person).
prix [pri] *nm* **1** (*d'un objet etc*) price; **à tout p.** at all costs; **à aucun p.** on no account; **hors (de) p.** exorbitant. **2** (*récompense*) prize.
pro- [pro] *préf* pro-.
probable [prɔbabl] *a* likely, probable (**que** that); **peu p.** unlikely. ● **probabilité** *nf* probability, likelihood; **selon toute p.** in all probability. ● **probablement** [-əmɑ̃] *adv* probably.
ⓘ **probable** **G99** The Subjunctive 7 G 1d)
probant [prɔbɑ̃] *a* conclusive.
problème [prɔblɛm] *nm* problem.
procédé [prɔsede] *nm* process.
procéder [prɔsede] *vi* (*agir*) to proceed; **p. à** (*enquête etc*) to carry out. ● **procédure** *nf* procedure; *Jur* proceedings.
procès [prɔsɛ] *nm* (*criminel*) trial; (*civil*) lawsuit; **faire un p. à qn** to take s.o. to court.
processeur [prɔsesœr] *nm* (*d'ordinateur*) processor.
procession [prɔsesjɔ̃] *nf* procession.
processus [prɔsesys] *nm* process.
procès-verbal, -aux [prɔsɛvɛrbal, -o] *nm* (*contravention*) (traffic) fine, ticket; (*de réunion*) minutes; (*constat*) *Jur* report.
prochain, -aine [prɔʃɛ̃, -ɛn] **1** *a* next; (*mort, arrivée*) impending; **un jour p.** one day soon ‖ *nf* **à la prochaine!** *Fam* see you soon!; **à la prochaine (station)** at the next stop. **2** *nm* (*semblable*) fellow (man). ● **prochainement** *adv* shortly, soon.
proche [prɔʃ] *a* (*espace*) near, close; (*temps*) close (at hand); (*parent, ami*) close; (*avenir*) near; **p. de** near (to), close to; **le P.-Orient** the Middle East ‖ *nmpl* close relations.
proclamer [prɔklame] *vt* to proclaim, declare (**que** that).
procuration [prɔkyrɑsjɔ̃] *nf* **par p.** (*voter etc*) by proxy.
procurer [prɔkyre] *vt* **p. qch à qn** (*personne*) to obtain sth for s.o.; **se p. qch** to obtain sth.
procureur [prɔkyrœr] *nm* = *Br* public prosecutor, = *Am* district attorney.
prodige [prɔdiʒ] *nm* (*miracle*) wonder; (*personne*) prodigy. ● **prodigieux, -euse** *a* extraordinary.
prodiguer [prɔdige] *vt* **p. qch à qn** to lavish sth on s.o.
production [prɔdyksjɔ̃] *nf* production. ● **producteur, -trice** *nmf Com Cin* producer ‖ *a* producing; **pays p. de pétrole** oil-producing country. ● **productif, -ive** *a* (*terre, réunion etc*) productive. ● **productivité** *nf* productivity.

produire* [prɔdɥir] **1** *vt* (*fabriquer*) to produce; (*causer*) to produce, bring about. **2 se produire** *vpr* (*événement etc*) to happen. ●**produit** *nm* (*article etc*) product; (*pour la vaisselle*) liquid; (*d'une vente, d'une collecte*) proceeds; *pl* (*de la terre*) produce; **p. (chimique)** chemical; **p. de beauté** cosmetic; **p. national brut** *Écon* gross national product.
proéminent [prɔeminɑ̃] *a* prominent.
prof [prɔf] *nm Fam* = **professeur.**
profane [prɔfan] *nmf* lay person.
proférer [prɔfere] *vt* to utter.
professeur [prɔfɛsœr] *nm* teacher; *Univ* lecturer, *Am* professor; (*titulaire d'une chaire*) *Univ* professor.
profession [prɔfɛsjɔ̃] *nf* occupation, vocation; (*manuelle*) trade; **p. libérale** profession; **sans p.** not gainfully employed. ●**professionnel, -elle** *a* professional; (*école*) vocational ‖ *nmf* professional.
profil [prɔfil] *nm* (*de personne, objet*) profile; **de p.** (viewed) from the side, in profile.
profit [prɔfi] *nm* profit; (*avantage*) advantage, profit; **tirer p. de** to benefit from *ou* by, profit by; **au p. de** for the benefit of. ●**profitable** *a* (*utile*) beneficial (**à** to). ●**profiter** *vi* **p. de** to take advantage of; **p. à qn** to benefit s.o.
profond [prɔfɔ̃] *a* deep; (*esprit, joie etc*) profound, great; (*cause*) underlying; **p. de deux mètres** two metres deep ‖ *adv* (*pénétrer etc*) deep ‖ *nm* **au plus p. de** in the depths of. ●**profondément** *adv* deeply; (*dormir*) soundly; (*triste, souhaiter*) profoundly. ●**profondeur** *nf* depth; *pl* depths (**de** of); **à six mètres de p.** at a depth of six metres; **en p.** (*étudier etc*) in depth.
progéniture [prɔʒenityr] *nf* (*enfants*) *Hum* offspring.
progiciel [prɔʒisjɛl] *nm* (*pour ordinateur*) (software) package.
programmateur [prɔgramatœr] *nm* (*de four etc*) timer.
programme [prɔgram] *nm* programme, *Am* program; (*d'une matière*) *Scol* syllabus; (*d'ordinateur*) program; **p. (d'études)** (*d'une école*) curriculum. ●**programmer** *vt* (*ordinateur*) to program. ●**programmeur, -euse** *nmf* (computer) programmer.
progrès [prɔgrɛ] *nm* & *nmpl* progress; **faire des p.** to make progress. ●**progresser** *vi* to progress. ●**progressif, -ive** *a* gradual, progressive. ●**progression** *nf* progression. ●**progressivement** *adv* gradually, progressively.
proie [prwa] *nf* prey; **être en p. à** to be (a) prey to, be tortured by.
projecteur [prɔʒɛktœr] *nm* (*de monument*) floodlight; (*de prison*) & *Mil* searchlight; *Th* spot(light); *Cin* projector.
projectile [prɔʒɛktil] *nm* missile.
projection [prɔʒɛksjɔ̃] *nf* hurling, projection; (*de film*) projection; (*séance*) showing.
projet [prɔʒɛ] *nm* plan; (*entreprise, étude*) project; **faire des projets d'avenir** to make plans for the future; **p. de loi** *Pol* bill.
projeter [prɔʒte] *vt* **1** (*lancer*) to hurl, project. **2** (*film, ombre*) to project; (*lumière*) to flash. **3** (*voyage, fête etc*) to plan; **p. de faire** to plan to do.
proliférer [prɔlifere] *vi* to proliferate.
prolifique [prɔlifik] *a* prolific.
prolonger [prɔlɔ̃ʒe] *vt* to extend, prolong ‖ **se p.** *vpr* (*séance, rue, effet*) to continue. ●**prolongation** *nf* (*dans le temps*) extension; *pl Fb* extra time. ●**prolongement** *nm* (*dans l'espace*) extension.
promenade [prɔmnad] *nf* (*à pied*) walk; (*en voiture*) drive, ride; (*en vélo, à cheval*) ride; (*action*) *Sp* walking; (*lieu*) walk, promenade; **faire une p.** = **se promener.** ●**promener** *vt* to take for a walk *ou* ride; **envoyer qn p.** *Fam* to send s.o. packing ‖ **se p.** *vpr* (*à pied*) to (go for a) walk; (*en voiture*) to (go for a) drive *ou* ride. ●**promeneur, -euse** *nmf* stroller, walker.
promesse [prɔmɛs] *nf* promise.
promettre* [prɔmɛtr] *vt* to promise (**qch à qn** s.o. sth, **que** that); **p. de faire qch** to promise to do sth; **c'est promis** it's a promise ‖ *vi* **p. (beaucoup)** *Fig* to be promising ‖ **se p.** *vpr* **se p. qch** to promise oneself sth; **se p. de faire qch** to resolve to do sth. ●**prometteur, -euse** *a* promising.
promontoire [prɔmɔ̃twar] *nm Géog* headland.
promoteur [prɔmɔtœr] *nm* **p. (immobilier)** property developer.
promotion [prɔmosjɔ̃] *nf* promotion; **en p.** (*produit*) on (special) offer. ●**promouvoir*** *vt* (*personne, produit etc*) to promote; **être promu** (*employé*) to be promoted (**à** to).
prompt [prɔ̃] *a* swift, prompt.
pronom [prɔnɔ̃] *nm Gram* pronoun. ●**pronominal, -aux** *a Gram* pronominal.
prononcer [prɔnɔ̃se] *vt* (*articuler*) to pronounce; (*dire*) to utter; (*discours*) to deliver; (*jugement*) *Jur* to pronounce, pass ‖ **se p.** *vpr* (*mot*) to be pronounced; (*personne*) to reach a decision (**sur** about, on); **se p. pour/contre qch** to come out in favour of/against sth. ●**prononciation** *nf* pronunciation.

pronostic [prɔnɔstik] *nm* (*prévision*) & *Sp* forecast.
propagande [prɔpagɑ̃d] *nf* propaganda.
propager [prɔpaʒe] *vt*, **se p.** *vpr* to spread.
prophète [prɔfɛt] *nm* prophet. ● **prophétie** [-fesi] *nf* prophecy. ● **prophétique** *a* prophetic.
propice [prɔpis] *a* favourable (**à** to).
proportion [prɔpɔrsjɔ̃] *nf* proportion; *Math* ratio; *pl* (*dimensions*) proportions. ● **proportionné** *a* proportionate (**à** to); **bien p.** well-proportioned. ● **proportionnel, -elle** *a* proportional (**à** to).
propos [prɔpo] **1** *nmpl* (*paroles*) remarks. **2** *nm* (*sujet*) subject; **à p. de** about; **à tout p.** for no reason, at every turn. **3** *adv* **à p.** (*arriver etc*) at the right time; **à p.** by the way.
proposer [prɔpoze] *vt* (*suggérer*) to suggest, propose (**qch à qn** sth to s.o., **que** (+ *sub*) that); (*offrir*) to offer (**qch à qn** s.o. sth, **de faire** to do); **je te propose de rester** I suggest (that) you stay; **se p. pour faire qch** to offer to do sth; **se p. de faire qch** to propose *ou* mean to do sth. ● **proposition** *nf* suggestion, proposal; (*de paix*) proposal; *Gram* clause.
propre[1] [prɔpr] *a* clean; (*soigné*) neat ‖ *nm* **mettre qch au p.** to make a fair copy of sth. ● **proprement**[1] *adv* cleanly; (*avec netteté*) neatly. ● **propreté** *nf* cleanliness; (*netteté*) neatness.
ⓘ **propre G32** Position of Adjectives 4 D 3
propre[2] [prɔpr] **1** *a* (*à soi*) own; **mon p. argent** my own money. **2** *a* **p. à** (*attribut, coutume etc*) peculiar to; (*approprié*) well-suited to; **sens p.** literal meaning; **nom p.** proper noun ‖ *nm* **le p. de** (*qualité*) the distinctive quality of. ● **proprement**[2] *adv* **à p. parler** strictly speaking; **le village/***etc* **p. dit** the village/*etc* proper *ou* itself.
ⓘ **propre G32** Position of Adjectives 4 D 3
propriétaire [prɔprijetɛr] *nmf* owner; (*qui loue*) landlord, landlady; **p. foncier** landowner.
propriété [prɔprijete] *nf* **1** (*bien, maison*) property; (*droit*) ownership, property. **2** (*qualité*) property.
propulser [prɔpylse] *vt* (*faire avancer, projeter*) to propel.
prosaïque [prozaik] *a* prosaic, pedestrian.
proscrire* [prɔskrir] *vt* (*exiler*) to banish; (*interdire*) to ban. ● **proscrit, -ite** *nmf* (*personne*) exile.
prose [proz] *nf* prose.
prospecter [prɔspɛkte] *vt* (*sol*) to prospect; (*pétrole*) to prospect for; (*région*) *Com* to canvass. ● **prospection** *nf* prospecting; *Com* canvassing.
prospectus [prɔspɛktys] *nm* leaflet.
prospère [prɔspɛr] *a* (*florissant*) thriving; (*riche*) prosperous. ● **prospérer** *vi* to thrive, flourish, prosper. ● **prospérité** *nf* prosperity.
prosterner (se) [səprɔstɛrne] *vpr* to prostrate oneself (**devant** before).
prostituer (se) [səprɔstitɥe] *vpr* to prostitute oneself. ● **prostituée** *nf* prostitute. ● **prostitution** *nf* prostitution.
protagoniste [prɔtagɔnist] *nmf* protagonist.
protecteur, -trice [prɔtɛktœr, -tris] *nmf* protector ‖ *a* (*geste etc*) & *Écon* protective; (*ton, air*) *Péj* patronizing. ● **protection** *nf* protection; **de p.** (*écran etc*) protective.
protéger [prɔteʒe] *vt* to protect (**de** from, **contre** against) ‖ **se p.** *vpr* to protect oneself. ● **protège-cahier** *nm* exercise book cover.
protéine [prɔtein] *nf* protein.
protestant, -ante [prɔtɛstɑ̃, -ɑ̃t] *a* & *nmf* Protestant.
protester [prɔtɛste] *vi* to protest (**contre** against); **p. de** (*son innocence etc*) to protest. ● **protestation** *nf* protest (**contre** against); *pl* (*d'amitié*) declarations (**de** of).
prothèse [prɔtɛz] *nf* **(appareil de) p.** (*membre*) artificial limb; **p. (dentaire)** false teeth.
protocole [prɔtɔkɔl] *nm* protocol.
proue [pru] *nf Nau* bow(s), prow.
prouesse [pruɛs] *nf* feat, exploit.
prouver [pruve] *vt* to prove (**que** that).
Provence [prɔvɑ̃s] *nf* Provence.
provenir* [prɔvnir] *vi* **p. de** to come from. ● **provenance** *nf* origin; **en p. de** from.
proverbe [prɔvɛrb] *nm* proverb.
province [prɔvɛ̃s] *nf* province; **la p.** the provinces; **en p.** in the provinces; **de p.** (*ville etc*) provincial. ● **provincial, -ale, -aux** *a* & *nmf* provincial.
proviseur [prɔvizœr] *nm* (*de lycée*) headmaster, headmistress, *Am* principal.
provision [prɔvizjɔ̃] *nf* **1** (*réserve*) supply, stock; *pl* (*achats*) shopping; (*nourriture*) food: **panier/sac à provisions** shopping basket/bag. **2** (*somme*) funds; (*acompte*) advance payment; **chèque sans p.** dud cheque, *Am* bad check.
provisoire [prɔvizwar] *a* temporary, provisional. ● **—ment** *adv* temporarily, provisionally.
provoquer [prɔvɔke] *vt* **1** (*causer*) to bring about, provoke; (*désir*) to arouse. **2** (*défier*) to provoke (*s.o.*). ● **provocant**

a provocative. ● **provocation** *nf* provocation.
proximité [prɔksimite] *nf* closeness; **à p.** close by; **à p. de** close to.
prude [pryd] *a* prudish.
prudent [prydɑ̃] *a* (*circonspect*) cautious, careful. ● **prudemment** [-amɑ̃] *adv* cautiously, carefully. ● **prudence** *nf* caution, care; **par p.** as a precaution.
prune [pryn] *nf* (*fruit*) plum. ● **pruneau, -x** *nm* prune. ● **prunier** *nm* plum tree.
prunelle [prynɛl] *nf* (*de l'œil*) pupil.
P.-S. [peɛs] *abrév* (*post-scriptum*) PS.
psaume [psom] *nm* psalm.
pseudo- [psødo] *préf* pseudo-.
pseudonyme [psødɔnim] *nm* pseudonym.
psychanalyste [psikanalist] *nmf* psychoanalyst.
psychiatre [psikjatr] *nmf* psychiatrist. ● **psychiatrie** *nf* psychiatry. ● **psychiatrique** *a* psychiatric.
psycho [psiko] *préf* psycho-.
psychologie [psikɔlɔʒi] *nf* psychology. ● **psychologique** *a* psychological. ● **psychologue** *nmf* psychologist.
PTT [petete] *nfpl abrév* (*Postes, Télégraphes, Téléphones*) Post Office.
pu [py] *pp de* **pouvoir 1.**
puanteur [pɥɑ̃tœr] *nf* stink, stench.
pub [pyb] *nf Fam* (*réclame*) advertising; (*annonce*) ad.
puberté [pybɛrte] *nf* puberty.
public, -ique [pyblik] *a* public ‖ *nm* public; (*de spectacle*) audience; **le grand p.** the general public; **en p.** in public.
publication [pyblikɑsjɔ̃] *nf* (*action, livre etc*) publication. ● **publier** *vt* to publish.
publicité [pyblisite] *nf* (*réclame*) advertising, publicity; (*annonce*) advertisement; *Rad TV* commercial; *Fig* publicity (**autour de** surrounding). ● **publicitaire** *a* **agence**/*etc* **p.** advertising agency/*etc*; **film p.** promotional film.
puce [pys] *nf* **1** flea; **le marché aux puces, les puces** the flea market. **2** (*d'un ordinateur*) (micro)chip.
puceron [pysrɔ̃] *nm* greenfly.
pudeur [pydœr] *nf* (sense of) modesty. ● **pudique** *a* modest.
puer [pɥe] *vi* to stink ‖ *vt* to stink of.
puériculture [pɥerikyltyr] *nf* infant care, child care. ● **puéricultrice** *nf* children's nurse.
puéril [pɥeril] *a* puerile.
puis [pɥi] *adv* then; **et p. quoi?** and so what?
puiser [pɥize] *vt* to draw, take (**dans** from).
puisque [pɥisk(ə)] *conj* since, as.
puissant [pɥisɑ̃] *a* powerful. ● **puissance** *nf* (*force, nation*) & *Math Tech* power; **en p.** (*talent, danger etc*) potential.
puisse(s), puissent *etc* [pɥis] *voir* **pouvoir 1.**
puits [pɥi] *nm* well; (*de mine*) shaft.
pull(-over) [pyl(ɔvɛr)] *nm* sweater, pullover.
pulpe [pylp] *nf* (*de fruits*) pulp.
pulvériser [pylverize] *vt* (*liquide*) to spray; (*broyer*) & *Fig* to pulverize. ● **pulvérisateur** *nm* spray.
punaise [pynɛz] *nf* **1** (*insecte*) bug. **2** (*clou*) drawing pin, *Am* thumbtack.
punch [pɔ̃ʃ] *nm* **1** (*boisson*) punch. **2** [pœnʃ] (*énergie*) punch.
punir [pynir] *vt* to punish (**de qch** for sth, **pour avoir fait qch** for doing sth). ● **punition** *nf* punishment.
pupille [pypij] **1** *nf* (*de l'œil*) pupil. **2** *nmf* (*enfant sous tutelle*) ward; **p. de la Nation** war orphan.
pupitre [pypitr] *nm* (*d'écolier*) desk; (*d'orateur*) lectern; *Ordinat* console.
pur [pyr] *a* pure; (*alcool*) neat, straight. ● **pureté** *nf* purity.
purée [pyre] *nf* purée; **p. (de pommes de terre)** mashed potatoes.
purge [pyrʒ] *nf Pol Méd* purge.
purger [pyrʒe] *vt* **1** (*conduite*) *Tech* to drain, clear. **2** (*peine*) *Jur* to serve.
purifier [pyrifje] *vt* to purify.
pur-sang [pyrsɑ̃] *nm inv* (*cheval*) thoroughbred.
pus[1] [py] *nm* (*liquide*) pus, matter.
pus[2], **put** [py] *voir* **pouvoir 1.**
putain [pytɛ̃] *nf Péj Vulg* whore.
puzzle [pœzl] *nm* (jigsaw) puzzle, jigsaw.
p.-v. [peve] *nm inv* (*procès-verbal*) (traffic) fine.
pyjama [piʒama] *nm* pyjamas, *Am* pajamas; **un p.** a pair of pyjamas *ou Am* pajamas; **pantalon de p.** pyjama trousers, *Am* pajama bottoms; **être en p.** to be in pyjamas *ou Am* pajamas.
pylône [pilon] *nm* pylon.
pyramide [piramid] *nf* pyramid.
Pyrénées [pirene] *nfpl* **les P.** the Pyrenees.
pyromane [pirɔman] *nmf* arsonist.

Q

Q, q [ky] *nm* Q, q.

QI [kyi] *nm inv abrév* (*quotient intellectuel*) IQ.

qu' [k] *voir* **que.**

quadrill/er [kadrije] *vt* (*police etc*) to be positioned throughout, comb (*town etc*). ●**—é** *a* (*papier*) squared. ●**quadrillage** *nm* (*lignes*) squares.

quadruple [k(w)adrypl] *a* **q. de** fourfold ▮ *nm* **le q. de** four times as much as. ●**quadrupler** *vti* to quadruple. ●**quadruplés, -ées** *nmfpl* (*enfants*) quadruplets, quads.

quai [ke] *nm Nau* (*pour passagers*) quay; (*pour marchandises*) wharf; (*de fleuve*) embankment; *Rail* platform.

qualification [kalifikɑsjɔ̃] *nf* (*action*) *Sp* qualifying. ●**se qualifier** *vpr Sp* to qualify (**pour** for). ●**qualifié** *a* (*équipe etc*) that has qualified; (*ouvrier*, *main-d'œuvre*) skilled; **q. pour faire** qualified to do.

qualité [kalite] *nf* quality; **produit/*etc* de q.** high-quality product/*etc*; **en sa q. de** in one's capacity as.

quand [kɑ̃] *conj & adv* when; **q. je viendrai** when I come; **c'est pour q.?** (*réunion, mariage*) when is it?; **q. même** *Fam* all the same.

❶G97 Tenses 7 F 11

❶G208 & **209** Direct and Indirect Questions 12 C 1 & 2

quant (à) [kɑ̃ta] *prép* as for.

quantité [kɑ̃tite] *nf* quantity; **une q., des quantités** (*beaucoup*) a lot (**de** of); **en q.** (*abondamment*) in abundance. ●**quantifier** *vt* to quantify.

quarante [karɑ̃t] *a & nm* forty. ●**quarantaine** *nf* **1 une q. (de)** (*nombre*) (about) forty. **2** *Méd* quarantine; **mettre en q.** *Méd* to quarantine. ●**quarantième** *a & nmf* fortieth.

quart [kar] *nm* **1** quarter; **q. (de litre)** quarter litre, quarter of a litre; **q. d'heure** quarter of an hour; **une heure et q.** an hour and a quarter; **il est une heure et q.** it's a quarter past *ou Am* after one; **une heure moins le q.** quarter to one. **2** *Nau* watch.

quartier [kartje] **1** *nm* neighbourhood, district; (*chinois etc*) quarter; **de q.** (*cinéma etc*) local. **2** *nm* (*de pomme, lune*) quarter; (*d'orange*) segment. **3** *nm*(*pl*) **quartier(s)** *Mil* quarters; **q. général** headquarters.

quartz [kwarts] *nm* quartz; **montre/*etc* à q.** quartz watch/*etc*.

quasi [kazi] *adv* almost.

quatorze [katɔrz] *a & nm* fourteen. ●**quatorzième** *a & nmf* fourteenth.

quatre [katr] *a & nm* four; **son q. heures** (*goûter*) *Fam* one's afternoon snack; **se mettre en q.** to go out of one's way (**pour faire** to do). ●**quatrième** *a & nmf* fourth.

quatre-vingt(s) [katrəvɛ̃] *a & nm* eighty; **q.-vingts ans** eighty years; **q.-vingt-un** eighty-one; **page q.-vingt** page eighty. ●**q.-vingt-dix** *a & nm* ninety.

quatuor [kwatɥɔr] *nm Mus* quartet(te).

que [k(ə)] (**qu'** *before a vowel or mute h*) **1** *conj* that; **je pense qu'elle restera** I think (that) she'll stay; **qu'elle vienne ou non** whether she comes or not; **qu'il s'en aille!** let him leave!; **ça fait un an q. je suis là** I've been here for a year.

2 (ne)...q. only; **tu n'as qu'un franc** you only have one franc.

3 (*comparaison*) than; (*avec aussi, même, tel, autant*) as; **plus/moins âgé q. lui** older/younger than him; **aussi sage/*etc* q.** as wise/*etc* as; **le même q.** the same as.

4 *adv* **(ce) qu'il est bête!** (*comme*) he's so silly!, how silly he is!; **q. de gens!** (*combien*) what a lot of people!

5 *pron rel* (*chose*) that, which; (*personne*) that, whom; **le livre q. j'ai** the book (that *ou* which) I have; **l'ami q. j'ai** the friend (that *ou* whom) I have; **un jour q.** one day when.

6 *pron interrogatif* what; **q. fait-il?, qu'est-ce qu'il fait?** what is he doing?; **qu'est-ce qui est dans ta poche?** what's in your pocket?.

❶G35 & **43** Comparative of Adjectives and Adverbs 4 E 1 & 5 F 1

❶G53 & **68** Relative and Interrogative Pronouns 6 C 3c) & 6 F 3b)

❶G98 The Subjunctive 7 G 1

❶G107 The Imperative 7 G 4f) ii)

❶G189 Conjunctions 9 C

❶G204, **205** & **206** Negative Expressions 12 B 1, 2 & 3

Québec [kebɛk] *nm* **le Q.** Quebec.

quel, quelle [kɛl] **1** *a interrogatif* what, which; (*qui*) who; **q. livre/acteur préférez-vous?** which *ou* what book/actor do you

(eg **G1**, **G2**, **G3**) in French **G**rammar, at the end of the dictionary. Also see p. ix.

prefer?; **je sais q. est ton but** I know what your aim is ‖ *pron interrogatif* which (one); **q. est le meilleur?** which (one) is the best?
2 *a exclamatif* **q. idiot!** what a fool!
3 *a rel* **q. qu'il soit** (*chose*) whatever it may be; (*personne*) whoever it *ou* he may be.
ⓘG52 & **53** The Interrogative and Exclamatory Adjective 6 C 1 & 2

quelconque [kɛlkɔ̃k] *a* **1** any (whatever), some (or other); **une raison q.** any reason (whatever), some reason (or other). **2** (*banal*) ordinary.

quelque [kɛlk(ə)] **1** *a* some; **q. temps après** some time after; **quelques femmes/livres/***etc* some *ou* a few women/books/*etc*; **les quelques amies qu'elle a** the few friends she has.
2 *adv* (*environ*) about, some; **q. peu** somewhat; **cent francs et q.** *Fam* a hundred francs and a bit.
3 *pron* **q. chose** something; (*interrogation*) anything, something; **il a q. chose** (*un problème*) *Fig* there's something the matter with him; **q. chose d'autre** something else; **q. chose de grand/***etc* something big/*etc*.
4 *adv* **q. part** somewhere; (*interrogation*) anywhere, somewhere.
ⓘG50 Indefinite Pronouns 6 B 2
ⓘG102 The Subjunctive 7 G 1i)

quelquefois [kɛlkəfwa] *adv* sometimes.

quelques-uns, -unes [kɛlkəzœ̃, -yn] *pron pl* some, a few.
ⓘG50 Indefinite Pronouns 6 B 2

quelqu'un [kɛlkœ̃] *pron* someone, somebody; (*interrogation*) anyone, anybody, someone, somebody; **q. d'intelligent/***etc* someone clever/*etc*.
ⓘG50 Indefinite Pronouns 6 B 2
ⓘG102 The Subjunctive 7 G 1i)

querelle [kərɛl] *nf* quarrel, dispute. • **se quereller** *vpr* to quarrel.

question [kɛstjɔ̃] *nf* question; (*problème*) matter, question; **il est q. de faire qch** there's some talk about doing sth; **il a été q. de vous** we *ou* they talked about you; **il n'en est pas q.** it's out of the question; **en q.** in question; **hors de q.** out of the question; **(re)mettre en q.** to (call in) question. • **questionnaire** *nm* questionnaire. • **questionner** *vt* to question (**sur** about).

quête [kɛt] *nf* **1** (*collecte*) collection; **faire la q.** to collect money. **2** (*recherche*) quest (**de** for); **en q. de** in search of.

queue [kø] *nf* **1** (*d'animal*) tail; (*de fleur*) stem, stalk; (*de fruit*) stalk; (*de poêle*) handle; (*de train*) rear; **q. de cheval** (*coiffure*) ponytail; **à la q. leu leu** (*marcher*) in single file; **faire une q. de poisson** *Aut* to cut in (**à qn** in front of s.o.).
2 (*file*) queue, *Am* line; **faire la q.** to queue up, *Am* line up.

qui [ki] **1** *pron interrogatif* (*personne*) who; (*en complément*) whom; **q. (est-ce qui) est là?** who's there?; **q. désirez-vous voir?, q. est-ce que vous désirez voir?** who(m) do you want to see?; **à q. est ce livre?** whose book is this?; **je demande q. a téléphoné** I'm asking who phoned.
2 *pron rel* (*sujet*) (*personne*) who, that; (*chose*) which, that; **l'homme q. est là** the man who's here *ou* that's here; **la maison q. se trouve en face** the house which is *ou* that's opposite; **q. que vous soyez** (*sans antécédent*) whoever you are, whoever you may be.
3 *pron rel* (*après prép*) **la femme de q. je parle** the woman I'm talking about *ou* about whom I'm talking; **l'ami sur l'aide de q. je compte** the friend on whose help I rely.
ⓘG54 Interrogative Pronouns 6 C 3b)
ⓘG67 Relative Pronouns 6 F 3a)

quiche [kiʃ] *nf* quiche.

quiconque [kikɔ̃k] *pron* (*celui qui*) whoever; (*n'importe qui*) anyone.

quille [kij] *nf* **1** (*de navire*) keel. **2** (*de jeu*) (bowling) pin, skittle; **jouer aux quilles** to bowl, play skittles.

quincaillier, -ière [kɛ̃kɑje, -jɛr] *nmf* hardware dealer, ironmonger. • **quincaillerie** *nf* (*magasin*) hardware shop, ironmonger's.

quinte [kɛ̃t] *nf* **q. (de toux)** coughing fit.

quintette [kɛ̃tɛt] *nm Mus* quintet(te).

quintuple [kɛ̃typl] *a* **q. de** fivefold ‖ *nm* **le q. de** five times as much as. • **quintuplés, -ées** *nmfpl* (*enfants*) quintuplets, quins.

quinze [kɛ̃z] *a* & *nm* fifteen; **q. jours** two weeks, a fortnight. • **quinzaine** *nf* **une q. (de)** (*nombre*) (about) fifteen; **q. (de jours)** two weeks, a fortnight. • **quinzième** *a* & *nmf* fifteenth.

quittance [kitɑ̃s] *nf* receipt.

quitte [kit] *a* even, quits (**envers** with); **q. à faire** even if it means doing.

quitter [kite] *vt* to leave; (*ôter*) to take off; **q. qn des yeux** to take one's eyes off s.o. ‖ *vi* **ne quittez pas!** *Tél* hold on!, hold the line! ‖ **se q.** *vpr* (*se séparer*) to part, say goodbye.

quoi [kwa] *pron* what; (*après prép*) which; **à q. penses-tu?** what are you thinking about?; **après q.** after which; **ce à q. je m'attendais** what I was expecting; **de q. manger/***etc* something to eat/*etc*; (*assez*) enough to eat/*etc*; **de q. écrire** something to write with; **q. que je dise** whatever I say; **il n'y a pas de q.!** (*en réponse à 'merci'*) don't mention it!; **c'est un idiot, q.!** (*non traduit*) *Fam* he's a fool!

quoique [kwak(ə)] *conj* (+ *sub*) (al)though.
quota [k(w)ɔta] *nm* quota.
quotidien, -ienne [kɔtidjɛ̃, -jɛn] *a* daily ▌*nm* daily (paper). ● **quotidiennement** *adv* daily.

R

R, r [ɛr] *nm* R, r.

rabâcher [rabɑʃe] *vt* to repeat endlessly.

rabais [rabɛ] *nm* (price) reduction, discount.

rabaisser [rabese] *vt* (*dénigrer*) to belittle; **r. à** (*ravaler*) to reduce to.

rabattre* [rabatr] *vt* (*baisser*) to pull *ou* put down; (*refermer*) to close (down) ‖ **se r.** *vpr* (*se refermer*) to close; (*barrière*) to come down; (*après avoir doublé un véhicule*) to cut in (**devant** in front of); **se r. sur** *Fig* to fall back on.

rabbin [rabɛ̃] *nm* rabbi; **grand r.** chief rabbi.

rabot [rabo] *nm* (*outil*) plane. ●**raboter** *vt* to plane.

rabougri [rabugri] *a* (*personne, plante*) stunted.

racaille [rakɑj] *nf* rabble, riffraff.

raccommoder [rakɔmɔde] **1** *vt* (*linge*) to mend; (*chaussette*) to darn. **2** *vt* (*réconcilier*) *Fam* to reconcile ‖ **se r.** *vpr Fam* to make it up (**avec** with). ●**raccommodage** *nm* mending; darning.

raccompagner [rakɔ̃paɲe] *vt* to see *ou* take back (home); **r. qn à la porte** to see s.o. to the door, see s.o. out.

raccord [rakɔr] *nm* (*dispositif*) connection, connector; (*de papier peint*) join; **r. (de peinture)** touch-up. ●**raccorder** *vt*, **se r.** *vpr* to connect (up), join (up) (**à** with, to).

raccourc/ir [rakursir] *vt* to shorten ‖ *vi* to get shorter; (*au lavage*) to shrink. ●**—i** *nm* (*chemin*) short cut.

raccrocher [rakrɔʃe] *vt* (*objet tombé*) to hang back up; (*téléphone*) to put down; **se r. à** to hold on to, cling to ‖ *vi Tél* to hang up, ring off.

race [ras] *nf* (*groupe ethnique*) race; (*animale*) breed; **chien de r.** pedigree dog. ●**racial, -aux** *a* racial. ●**racisme** *nm* racism, racialism. ●**raciste** *a* & *nmf* racist, racialist.

rachat [raʃa] *nm Com* repurchase; (*de firme*) take-over. ●**racheter** *vt* to buy back; (*firme*) to take over, buy out; **r. un manteau/une voiture/***etc* to buy another coat/car/*etc*; **r. des chaussettes/du pain/***etc* to buy some more socks/bread/*etc* ‖ **se r.** *vpr* to make amends.

racine [rasin] *nf* (*de plante, personne etc*) & *Math* root; **prendre r.** (*plante*) & *Fig* to take root.

racket [rakɛt] *nm* (*activité*) racketeering.

raclée [rakle] *nf Fam* thrashing, hiding.

racler [rɑkle] *vt* to scrape; (*enlever*) to scrape off; **se r. la gorge** to clear one's throat. ●**racloir** *nm* scraper.

racoler [rakɔle] *vt* (*prostituée, vendeur etc*) to accost (*s.o.*).

raconter [rakɔ̃te] *vt* (*histoire*) to tell, relate; **r. qch à qn** (*vacances etc*) to tell s.o. about sth; **r. à qn que** to tell s.o. that.

racornir (se) [sərakɔrnir] *vpr* to get hard.

radar [radar] *nm* radar; **contrôle r.** (*pour véhicules etc*) radar control.

rade [rad] *nf* **1** *Nau* (natural) harbour. **2** **laisser qn en r.** *Fam* to leave s.o. stranded, abandon s.o.; **rester en r.** *Fam* to be left behind.

radeau, -x [rado] *nm* raft.

radiateur [radjatœr] *nm* (*électrique, à gaz*) heater; (*de chauffage central, voiture*) radiator.

radiation [radjɑsjɔ̃] *nf* **1** *Phys* radiation. **2** (*suppression*) removal (**de** from).

radical, -ale, -aux [radikal, -o] *a* radical ‖ *nm Ling* stem ‖ *nmf Pol* radical.

radier [radje] *vt* to strike *ou* cross off (**de** from).

radieux, -euse [radjø, -øz] *a* (*personne, visage*) beaming, radiant; (*soleil*) brilliant; (*temps*) glorious.

radin, -ine [radɛ̃, -in] *a Fam* stingy.

radio [radjo] **1** *nf* radio; (*poste*) radio (set); **à la r.** on the radio. **2** *nf* (*photo*) *Méd* X-ray; **passer** *ou* **faire une r.** to have an X-ray, be X-rayed. **3** *nm* (*opérateur*) radio operator. ●**radioactif, -ive** *a* radioactive. ●**radioactivité** *nf* radioactivity. ●**radiodiffuser** *vt* to broadcast (on the radio). ●**radiographier** *vt* to X-ray. ●**radiologue** *nmf* (*technicien*) radiographer; (*médecin*) radiologist. ●**radio-réveil** *nm* (*pl* **radios-réveils**) radio alarm clock.

radis [radi] *nm* radish; **r. noir** horseradish.

radoter [radɔte] *vi* to ramble (on), drivel (on).

radoucir (se) [səradusir] *vpr* to calm down; (*temps*) to become milder. ●**radoucissement** *nm* **r. (du temps)** milder weather.

rafale [rafal] *nf* (*vent*) gust, squall; (*de mitrailleuse*) burst.

raffermir [rafɛrmir] *vt* to strengthen; (*muscles etc*) to tone up ‖ **se r.** *vpr* to become stronger.
raffinement [rafinmɑ̃] *nm* (*de personne*) refinement.
raffiner [rafine] *vt* (*pétrole, sucre*) to refine. ● **raffinerie** *nf* refinery.
raffoler [rafɔle] *vi* **r. de** (*aimer*) to be mad *ou* wild about.
rafistoler [rafistɔle] *vt Fam* to patch up.
rafle [rɑfl] *nf* (police) raid.
rafler [rɑfle] *vt* (*enlever*) *Fam* to swipe, make off with.
rafraîchir [rafreʃir] *vt* to cool (down); (*remettre à neuf*) to brighten up; (*mémoire*) to refresh ‖ **se r.** *vpr* (*boire*) to refresh oneself; (*se laver*) to freshen (oneself) up; (*temps*) to get cooler. ● **rafraîchissant** *a* refreshing. ● **rafraîchissement** *nm* **1** (*de température*) cooling. **2** (*boisson*) cold drink; *pl* (*glaces etc*) refreshments.
rage [raʒ] *nf* **1** (*colère*) rage; **r. de dents** violent toothache; **faire r.** (*incendie, tempête*) to rage. **2** (*maladie*) rabies. ● **rageant** *a Fam* infuriating.
ragots [rago] *nmpl Fam* gossip.
ragoût [ragu] *nm Culin* stew.
raid [rɛd] *nm Mil Av* raid.
raide [rɛd] *a* (*rigide, guindé*) stiff; (*côte*) steep; (*cheveux*) straight; (*corde*) tight ‖ *adv* (*grimper*) steeply; **tomber r. mort** to drop dead. ● **raidir** *vt*, **se r.** *vpr* to stiffen; (*corde*) to tighten.
raie [rɛ] *nf* **1** (*trait*) line; (*de tissu, zèbre*) stripe; (*de cheveux*) parting, *Am* part. **2** (*poisson*) skate, ray.
rail [rɑj] *nm* (*barre*) rail (*for train*); **le r.** (*transport*) rail.
railler [rɑje] *vt* to mock, make fun of. ● **raillerie** *nf* gibe.
rainure [renyr] *nf* groove.
raisin [rezɛ̃] *nm* **raisin(s)** grapes; **grain de r.** grape; **manger du r.** *ou* **des raisins** to eat grapes; **r. sec** raisin.
raison [rɛzɔ̃] *nf* **1** (*faculté, motif*) reason; **la r. de/pour laquelle...** the reason for/why...; **pour raisons de famille**/*etc* for family/*etc* reasons; **en r. de** (*cause*) on account of; **à r. de** (*proportion*) at the rate of; **à plus forte r.** all the more so; **r. de plus** all the more reason (**pour faire** to do, for doing); **entendre r.** to listen to reason. **2 avoir r.** to be right (**de faire** to do, in doing); **donner r. à qn** to agree with s.o.; (*événement etc*) to prove s.o. right; **avec r.** rightly. ● **raisonnable** *a* reasonable.
raisonn/er [rɛzɔne] *vi* (*penser*) to reason; (*discuter*) to argue ‖ *vt* **r. qn** to reason with s.o. ● **—ement** *nm* (*faculté, activité*) reasoning; (*propositions*) argument.
rajeunir [raʒœnir] *vt* to make (*s.o.*) (feel *ou* look) younger; (*personne âgée*) *Méd* to rejuvenate ‖ *vi* to get *ou* feel *ou* look younger.
rajouter [raʒute] *vt* to add (**à** to); **en r.** *Fig* to overdo it.
rajuster [raʒyste] *vt* (*mécanisme*) to readjust; (*vêtements*) to straighten, adjust; (*cheveux*) to rearrange.
ralentir [ralɑ̃tir] *vti*, **se r.** *vpr* to slow down. ● **ralenti** *nm Cin TV* slow motion; **au r.** (*filmer, travailler*) in slow motion; **tourner au r.** (*moteur, usine*) to tick over, *Am* turn over.
râler [rale] *vi* (*blessé*) to groan; (*mourant*) to give the death rattle; (*protester*) *Fam* to grouse, moan.
rallier [ralje] *vt* (*rassembler*) to rally; **r. qn à** (*convertir*) to win s.o. over to ‖ **se r.** *vpr* **se r. à** (*point de vue*) to come over *ou* round to.
rallonge [ralɔ̃ʒ] *nf* (*de table*) extension; (*fil électrique*) extension (lead). ● **rallonger** *vti* to lengthen.
rallumer [ralyme] *vt* (*feu, pipe*) to light again; (*lampe*) to switch on again; (*conflit, haine*) to rekindle.
rallye [rali] *nm Sp Aut* rally.
ramasser [ramɑse] **1** *vt* (*prendre par terre, réunir*) to pick up; (*ordures, copies*) to collect, pick up; (*fruits, coquillages*) to gather. **2 se ramasser** *vpr* (*se pelotonner*) to curl up. ● **ramassage** *nm* picking up; collection; gathering; **r. scolaire** school bus service.
ramassis [ramɑsi] *nm* **r. de** (*voyous etc*) *Péj* bunch of.
rambarde [rɑ̃bard] *nf* guardrail.
rame [ram] *nf* **1** (*aviron*) oar. **2** (*de métro*) train. **3** (*de papier*) ream. ● **ramer** *vi* to row.
rameau, -x [ramo] *nm* branch; **les Rameaux** *Rel* Palm Sunday.
ramener [ramne] *vt* to bring *ou* take (*s.o.*) back; (*paix, ordre etc*) to restore, bring back; (*remettre en place*) to put back; **r. à** (*réduire à*) to reduce to; **r. à la vie** to bring back to life.
ramollir [ramɔlir] *vt*, **se r.** *vpr* to soften.
ramon/er [ramɔne] *vt* (*cheminée*) to sweep. ● **—eur** *nm* (chimney)sweep.
rampe [rɑ̃p] *nf* **1** (*d'escalier*) banister(s). **2** (*pente*) ramp, slope; **r. (d'accès)** ramp; **r. de lancement** (*de fusées etc*) launch(ing) pad. **3** (*projecteurs*) *Th* footlights.

ramper [rɑ̃pe] *vi* to crawl.

rancard [rɑ̃kar] *nm* (*rendez-vous*) *Fam* date; (*renseignement*) *Arg* tip.

rancart [rɑ̃kar] *nm* **mettre au r.** *Fam* to throw out, scrap.

rance [rɑ̃s] *a* rancid.

ranch [rɑ̃tʃ] *nm* ranch.

rancœur [rɑ̃kœr] *nf* rancour, resentment.

rançon [rɑ̃sɔ̃] *nf* ransom; **la r. de** (*inconvénient*) the price of (*success, fame etc*).

rancune [rɑ̃kyn] *nf* grudge; **garder r. à qn** to bear s.o. a grudge; **sans r.!** no hard feelings! ●**rancunier, -ière** *a* spiteful, vindictive.

randonnée [rɑ̃dɔne] *nf* (*à pied*) hike, walk; (*en vélo*) ride.

rang [rɑ̃] *nm* (*rangée*) row, line; (*classement, grade*) rank; **les rangs** (*hommes*) *Mil* the ranks (**de** of); **se mettre en rang(s)** to line up (**par trois**/*etc* in threes/*etc*). ●**rangée** *nf* row, line.

ranger [rɑ̃ʒe] *vt* (*papiers etc*) to put away; (*chambre etc*) to tidy (up); (*chiffres, mots*) to arrange; (*voiture*) to park; **r. parmi** (*auteur etc*) to rank among ‖ **se r.** *vpr* (*élèves etc*) to line up; (*s'écarter*) to stand aside; (*voiture*) to pull over; (*s'assagir*) to settle down; **se r. à l'avis de qn** to fall in with s.o.'s opinion. ●**rangé** *a* (*chambre etc*) tidy; (*personne*) steady; (*bataille*) pitched. ●**rangements** *nmpl* (*placards*) storage space.

ranimer [ranime] *vt* (*réanimer, revigorer*) to revive; (*feu*) to poke, stir.

rapace [rapas] *nm* (*oiseau*) bird of prey.

rapatrier [rapatrije] *vt* to repatriate.

râpe [rɑp] *nf* *Culin* grater. ●**râper** *vt* (*fromage, carottes*) to grate. ●**râpé 1** *a* (*fromage etc*) grated ‖ *nm* grated cheese. **2** *a* (*vêtement*) threadbare.

rapetisser [raptise] *vi* to get smaller; (*au lavage*) to shrink.

rapide [rapid] *a* fast, quick, rapid ‖ *nm* (*train*) express (train); (*de fleuve*) rapid. ●**—ment** *adv* fast, quickly, rapidly. ●**rapidité** *nf* speed.

rapiécer [rapjese] *vt* to patch (up).

rappel [rapɛl] *nm* (*de diplomate*) recall; (*évocation*) reminder; (*paiement*) back pay; *pl Th* curtain calls; **(vaccination de) r.** *Méd* booster; **r. à l'ordre** call to order.

rappeler [raple] *vt* (*pour faire revenir*) & *Tél* to call back; (*souvenir, diplomate*) to recall; **r. qch à qn** (*redire*) to remind s.o. of sth ‖ *vi* *Tél* to call back ‖ **se r.** *vpr* (*histoire, personne etc*) to remember, recall (**que** that); **se r. avoir fait** to remember *ou* recall doing.

rapport [rapɔr] *nm* **1** (*lien*) connection, link; *pl* (*entre personnes*) relations; **rapports (sexuels)** (sexual) intercourse; **par r. à** compared to *ou* with; **se mettre en r. avec qn** to get in touch with s.o.; **ça n'a aucun r.!** it has nothing to do with it! **2** (*récit*) report. **3** (*revenu*) *Com* return, yield.

rapporter [rapɔrte] **1** *vt* to bring *ou* take back ‖ *vi* (*chien*) to retrieve. **2** *vt* (*récit*) to report ‖ *vi* (*moucharder*) *Fam* to tell tales. **3** *vt* (*profit*) *Com* to bring in, yield ‖ *vi* (*investissement*) *Com* to bring in a good return. ●**rapporteur, -euse 1** *nmf* (*mouchard*) telltale. **2** *nm* *Géom* protractor. **3** *nm* *Jur* reporter.

rapprocher [raprɔʃe] *vt* to bring closer (**de** to); (*chaise*) to pull up (**de** to); (*réconcilier*) to bring together ‖ **se r.** *vpr* to come *ou* get closer (**de** to). ●**rapprochement** *nm* reconciliation; (*rapport*) connection; (*comparaison*) comparison.

rapt [rapt] *nm* (*d'enfant*) abduction.

raquette [rakɛt] *nf* (*de tennis*) racket; (*de ping-pong*) bat.

rare [rar] *a* rare; (*argent, main-d'œuvre etc*) scarce; (*barbe, herbe*) sparse; **il est r. que** (+ *sub*) it's seldom *ou* rare that. ●**se raréfier** *vpr* (*denrées etc*) to get scarce. ●**rarement** *adv* rarely, seldom.

ⓘ**rare G32** Position of Adjectives 4 D 3

ras [rɑ] *a* (*cheveux*) close-cropped; (*herbe, poil*) short; **en rase campagne** in the open country; **à r. bord** (*remplir*) to the brim; **au r. du sol** (*avion*) close to the ground; **en avoir r. le bol** *Fam* to be fed up (**de** with); **pull (au) r. du cou** crew-neck(ed) pullover ‖ *adv* short.

raser [rɑse] **1** *vt* (*menton, personne*) to shave; (*barbe, moustache*) to shave off ‖ **se r.** *vpr* to (have a) shave. **2** *vt* (*démolir*) to knock down. **3** *vt* (*frôler*) to skim, brush. **4** *vt* (*ennuyer*) *Fam* to bore. ●**rasé** *a* **être bien r.** to have shaved, be clean-shaven; **mal r.** unshaven. ●**rasoir 1** *nm* razor; (*électrique*) shaver. **2** *a inv Fam* boring.

rassasier [rasazje] *vti* to satisfy; **être rassasié** to have had enough (**de** of).

rassembler [rasɑ̃ble] *vt* (*gens, objets*) to gather (together), assemble; (*courage*) to summon up ‖ **se r.** *vpr* to gather, assemble. ●**rassemblement** *nm* gathering.

rasseoir* (se) [səraswar] *vpr* to sit down again.

rassis, *f* rassie [rasi] *a* (*pain, brioche etc*) stale. ●**rassir** *vi* to turn stale.

rassur/er [rasyre] *vt* to reassure; **rassure-toi**

don't worry, set your mind at rest. ●**—ant** *a* (*nouvelle*) reassuring, comforting.
rat [ra] *nm* rat.
ratatiner (se) [səratatine] *vpr* to shrivel (up); (*vieillard*) to become wizened.
râteau, -x [rɑto] *nm* (*outil*) rake.
rat/er [rate] *vt* (*bus, cible, occasion etc*) to miss; (*travail, gâteau etc*) to ruin; (*examen*) to fail ‖ *vi* (*projet etc*) to fail. ●**—é, -ée 1** *nmf* (*personne*) failure. **2** *nmpl* **avoir des ratés** *Aut* to backfire.
ratifier [ratifje] *vt* to ratify.
ration [rɑsjɔ̃] *nf* ration. ●**rationner** *vt* (*vivres, personne*) to ration. ●**rationnement** *nm* rationing.
rationaliser [rasjɔnalize] *vt* to rationalize.
rationnel, -elle [rasjɔnɛl] *a* (*pensée, méthode*) rational.
ratisser [ratise] *vt* **1** (*allée etc*) to rake; (*feuilles etc*) to rake up. **2** (*fouiller*) to comb.
raton [ratɔ̃] *nm* **r. laveur** rac(c)oon.
RATP [ɛratepe] *nf abrév* (*Régie autonome des transports parisiens*) = Paris municipal transport authority.
rattacher [rataʃe] *vt* (*lacets etc*) to tie up again; (*incorporer*) to join (**à** to); (*idée, question*) to link (**à** to); **r. qn à** (*son pays etc*) to bind s.o. to; **se r. à** to be linked to.
rattraper [ratrape] *vt* to catch; (*prisonnier etc*) to recapture; (*temps perdu*) to make up for; **r. qn** (*rejoindre*) to catch up with s.o. ‖ **se r.** *vpr* (*après une erreur*) to make up for it; **se r. à** (*branche etc*) to catch hold of. ●**rattrapage** *nm* **cours de r.** *Scol* remedial class.
rature [ratyr] *nf* crossing out, deletion. ●**raturer** *vt* to cross out, delete.
rauque [rok] *a* (*voix*) hoarse.
ravages [ravaʒ] *nmpl* havoc, devastation; (*du temps*) ravages; **faire des r.** to cause havoc *ou* widespread damage. ●**ravager** *vt* to devastate, ravage.
ravaler [ravale] *vt* **1** (*façade etc*) to clean (and restore). **2** (*sanglots*) to swallow.
ravi [ravi] *a* delighted (**de** with, **de faire** to do, **que** (+ *sub*) that).
ravin [ravɛ̃] *nm* ravine, gully.
ravioli [ravjɔli] *nmpl* ravioli.
rav/ir [ravir] *vt* **1** (*plaire à*) to delight; **à r.** (*chanter etc*) delightfully. **2** (*emporter*) to snatch (**à** from). ●**—issant** *a* beautiful, lovely. ●**ravisseur, -euse** *nmf* kidnapper.
raviser (se) [səravize] *vpr* to change one's mind.
ravitailler [ravitɑje] *vt* to provide with supplies (**en** of), supply (**en** with); (*avion*) to refuel ‖ **se r.** *vpr* to stock up (with supplies). ●**ravitaillement** *nm* supplying; refuelling; (*denrées*) supplies.
ray/er [reje] *vt* (*érafler*) to scratch; (*mot etc*) to cross out; **r. qn de** (*liste*) to cross *ou* strike s.o. off. ●**—é** *a* scratched; (*tissu*) striped. ●**rayure** *nf* scratch; (*bande*) stripe; **à rayures** striped.
rayon [rɛjɔ̃] *nm* **1** (*de lumière, soleil etc*) *Phys* ray; (*de cercle*) radius; (*de roue*) spoke; **r. d'action** range; **dans un r. de** within a radius of. **2** (*planche*) shelf; (*de magasin*) department. **3** (*de ruche*) honeycomb.
rayonn/er [rɛjɔne] *vi* to radiate; (*dans une région*) to travel around (*from a central base*); **r. de joie** to beam with joy. ●**—ant** *a* (*visage etc*) beaming, radiant (**de** with).
raz-de-marée [rɑdmare] *nm inv* tidal wave; (*bouleversement*) *Fig* upheaval; **r.-de-marée électoral** landslide.
re-, ré- [r(ə), re] *préf* re-.
ré [re] *nm* (*note de musique*) D.
réacteur [reaktœr] *nm* (*d'avion*) jet engine; (*nucléaire*) reactor.
réaction [reaksjɔ̃] *nf* reaction; **r. en chaîne** chain reaction; **avion à r.** jet (aircraft). ●**réactionnaire** *a* & *nmf* reactionary.
réadapter [readapte] *vt*, **se r.** *vpr* to readjust (**à** to). ●**réadaptation** *nf* readjustment.
réaffirmer [reafirme] *vt* to reaffirm.
réagir [reaʒir] *vi* to react (**contre** against, **à** to); (*se secouer*) *Fig* to shake oneself out of it.
réaliser [realize] *vt* (*projet etc*) to carry out, realize; (*rêve*) to fulfil; (*bénéfices, économies*) to make; (*film*) to direct; (*se rendre compte*) to realize (**que** that) ‖ **se r.** *vpr* (*vœu*) to come true; (*projet*) to materialize; (*personne*) to fulfil oneself. ●**réalisable** *a* (*plan*) workable; (*rêve*) attainable. ●**réalisateur, -trice** *nmf Cin TV* director.
réalisme [realism] *nm* realism. ●**réaliste** *a* realistic ‖ *nmf* realist.
réalité [realite] *nf* reality; **en r.** in fact, in reality.
réanimation [reanimɑsjɔ̃] *nf* resuscitation; **(service de) r.** intensive care unit. ●**réanimer** *vt Méd* to revive.
réarmer [rearme] *vt* (*fusil etc*) to reload ‖ *vi*, **se r.** *vpr* (*pays*) to rearm. ●**réarmement** *nm* rearmament.
rébarbatif, -ive [rebarbatif, -iv] *a* forbidding, off-putting.
rebelle [rəbɛl] *a* rebellious; **troupes rebelles** rebel troops ‖ *nmf* rebel. ●**se rebeller** *vpr* to

rebel (**contre** against). ●**rébellion** *nf* rebellion.
rebond [r(ə)bɔ̃] *nm* bounce; (*par ricochet*) rebound. ●**rebondir** *vi* to bounce; to rebound. ●**rebondissement** *nm* new development (**de** in).
rebord [r(ə)bɔr] *nm* edge; (*de plat*) rim; **r. de (la) fenêtre** windowsill, window ledge.
reboucher [r(ə)buʃe] *vt* (*flacon*) to put the top back on; (*trou*) to fill in again.
rebours (à) [ar(ə)bur] *adv* the wrong way.
rebrousse-poil (à) [ar(ə)bruspwal] *adv* **prendre qn à r.-poil** *Fig* to rub s.o. up the wrong way.
rebrousser [r(ə)bruse] *vt* **r. chemin** to turn back.
rébus [rebys] *nm inv* rebus (*word guessing game*).
rebut [rəby] *nm* **mettre qch au r.** to throw sth out, scrap sth; **le r. de la société** *Péj* the dregs of society.
rebuter [r(ə)byte] *vt* (*décourager*) to put off; (*choquer*) to repel.
recaler [r(ə)kale] *vt* **r. qn** *Scol Fam* to fail s.o., flunk s.o.; **être recalé, se faire r.** *Scol Fam* to fail, flunk.
récapituler [rekapityle] *vti* to recapitulate.
recel [rəsɛl] *nm* receiving stolen goods. ●**receler** *vt* (*mystère, secret etc*) to contain; (*objet volé*) to receive.
recens/er [r(ə)sɑ̃se] *vt* (*population*) to take a census of; (*inventorier*) to make an inventory of. ●**—ement** *nm* census; inventory.
récent [resɑ̃] *a* recent. ●**récemment** [-amɑ̃] *adv* recently.
récépissé [resepise] *nm* (*reçu*) receipt.
récepteur [resɛptœr] *nm Tél Rad* receiver. ●**réception** *nf* (*accueil, soirée*) & *Rad* reception; (*de lettre etc*) *Com* receipt; (*d'hôtel etc*) reception (desk); **dès r. de** on receipt of. ●**réceptionniste** *nmf* receptionist.
récession [resesjɔ̃] *nf Écon* recession.
recette [r(ə)sɛt] *nf* **1** *Culin* & *Fig* recipe (**de** for). **2** (*argent, bénéfice*) takings; **recettes** (*rentrées*) *Com* receipts.
recev/oir** [r(ə)səvwar] *vt* to receive; (*accueillir*) to welcome; **être reçu (à)** (*examen*) to pass; **être reçu premier** to come first ‖ *vi* to have guests *ou* receive visitors; (*médecin*) to see patients. ●**—eur, -euse** *nmf* (*d'autobus*) (bus) conductor, (bus) conductress; (*des postes*) postmaster, postmistress.
rechange (de) [dər(ə)ʃɑ̃ʒ] *a* (*outil, pièce, etc*) spare; (*solution etc*) alternative; **vêtements de r.** a change of clothes.
réchapper [reʃape] *vi* **r. à** (*accident etc*) to come through; **en r.** to escape with one's life.
recharge [r(ə)ʃarʒ] *nf* (*de stylo etc*) refill. ●**recharger** *vt* (*fusil, appareil photo*) to reload; (*briquet, stylo etc*) to refill; (*batterie*) to recharge.
réchaud [reʃo] *nm* (portable) stove.
réchauffer [reʃofe] *vt* (*personne, aliment etc*) to warm up ‖ **se r.** *vpr* to warm oneself up; (*temps*) to get warmer. ●**réchauffement** *nm* (*de température*) rise (**de** in).
rêche [rɛʃ] *a* rough, harsh.
recherche [r(ə)ʃɛrʃ] *nf* **1** search, quest (**de** for); **à la r. de** in search of. **2 la r., des recherches** (*scientifique etc*) research (**sur** on, into); **faire des recherches** to (do) research; (*enquêter*) to make investigations. **3** (*raffinement*) studied elegance.
recherch/er [r(ə)ʃɛrʃe] *vt* (*personne, objet*) to search *ou* hunt for; (*cause, faveur*) to seek. ●**—é** *a* **1** (*très demandé*) in great demand; **r. pour meurtre** wanted for murder. **2** (*élégant*) elegant.
rechute [r(ə)ʃyt] *nf Méd* relapse.
récidive [residiv] *nf Jur* further offence *ou Am* offense. ●**récidiver** *vi Jur* to commit a further offence *ou Am* offense.
récif [resif] *nm* reef.
récipient [resipjɑ̃] *nm* container, receptacle.
réciproque [resiprɔk] *a* mutual, reciprocal. ●**—ment** *adv* (*l'un l'autre*) each other; **et r.** and vice versa.
récit [resi] *nm* (*histoire*) story; (*compte rendu*) account.
récital, *pl* **-als** [resital] *nm Mus* recital.
réciter [resite] *vt* to recite. ●**récitation** *nf* (*poème*) poem (*learnt by heart and recited aloud*).
réclame [reklam] *nf* advertising; (*annonce*) advertisement; **en r.** *Com* on (special) offer.
réclamer [reklame] *vt* (*demander*) to ask for (*sth*) back; (*revendiquer*) to claim ‖ *vi* to complain. ●**réclamation** *nf* complaint; **(bureau des) réclamations** complaints department.
reclasser [r(ə)klɑse] *vt* (*fiches etc*) to reclassify.
reclus, -use [rəkly, -yz] *a* (*vie*) cloistered.
réclusion [reklyzjɔ̃] *nf* imprisonment; **r. à perpétuité** life imprisonment.
recoin [rəkwɛ̃] *nm* nook, recess.
recoller [r(ə)kɔle] *vt* (*objet cassé*) to stick back together; (*enveloppe*) to stick back down.

récolte [rekɔlt] *nf* (*action*) harvest; (*produits*) crop, harvest. ● **récolter** *vt* to harvest, gather (in).

recommand/er [r(ə)kɔmɑ̃de] *vt* (*appuyer, conseiller*) to recommend (**à** to, **pour** for); **r. à qn de faire** to recommend s.o. to do; **lettre recommandée** registered letter. ●**—é** *nm* **envoyer en r.** to send by registered post *ou* mail. ● **recommandable** *a* **peu r.** not very commendable. ● **recommandation** *nf* (*appui, conseil*) recommendation.

recommencer [r(ə)kɔmɑ̃se] *vti* to start *ou* begin again.

récompense [rekɔ̃pɑ̃s] *nf* reward (**pour** for); (*prix*) award; **en r. de** in return for. ● **récompenser** *vt* to reward (**de, pour** for).

réconcilier (se) [sərekɔ̃silje] *vpr* to settle one's differences, make it up (**avec** with). ● **réconciliation** *nf* reconciliation.

reconduire* [r(ə)kɔ̃dɥir] *vt* **r. qn** to see *ou* take s.o. back; (*à la porte*) to show s.o. out.

réconfort [rekɔ̃fɔr] *nm* comfort. ● **réconforter** *vt* to comfort; (*revigorer*) to fortify. ● **réconfortant** *a* comforting; (*boisson etc*) fortifying.

reconnaissant [r(ə)kɔnɛsɑ̃] *a* grateful (**à qn de qch** to s.o. for sth). ● **reconnaissance**[1] *nf* (*gratitude*) gratitude.

reconnaître* [r(ə)kɔnɛtr] *vt* to recognize (**à qch** by sth); (*admettre*) to admit, acknowledge (**que** that); (*terrain*) *Mil* to reconnoitre; **être reconnu coupable** to be found guilty ‖ **se r.** *vpr* (*s'orienter*) to find one's bearings. ● **reconnu** *a* (*chef, fait*) acknowledged, recognized. ● **reconnaissance**[2] *nf* recognition; (*aveu*) acknowledgment; *Mil* reconnaissance; **r. de dette** IOU.

reconstituant [r(ə)kɔ̃stitɥɑ̃] *adj* (*aliment, régime*) which restores one's strength.

reconstituer [r(ə)kɔ̃stitɥe] *vt* (*armée, parti*) to reconstitute; (*crime, quartier*) to reconstruct; (*faits*) to piece together.

reconstruire* [r(ə)kɔ̃strɥir] *vt* (*ville, fortune*) to rebuild.

reconvertir [r(ə)kɔ̃vɛrtir] **1** *vt* (*bâtiment etc*) to reconvert. **2 se reconvertir** *vpr* to take up a new form of employment.

recopier [r(ə)kɔpje] *vt* to copy out.

record [r(ə)kɔr] *nm & a inv Sp* record.

recoudre* [r(ə)kudr] *vt* (*bouton*) to sew (back) on; (*vêtement*) to stitch (up).

recouper [r(ə)kupe] *vt* (*témoignage etc*) to tally with, confirm ‖ **se r.** *vpr* to tally, match *ou* tie up.

recourbé [r(ə)kurbe] *a* (*clou etc*) bent; (*nez*) hooked.

recours [r(ə)kur] *nm* recourse (**à** to); **avoir r. à** to resort to; (*personne*) to turn to; **notre dernier r.** our last resort. ● **recourir*** *vi* **r. à** to resort to; (*personne*) to turn to.

recouvrer [r(ə)kuvre] *vt* (*santé*) to recover.

recouvrir* [r(ə)kuvrir] *vt* (*livre, meuble, sol etc*) to cover; (*de nouveau*) to recover.

récréation [rekreɑsjɔ̃] *nf* recreation; (*temps*) *Scol* break, playtime, *Am* recess.

recroquevillé [rəkrɔkvije] *a* (*personne, papier etc*) curled up.

recrudescence [rəkrydesɑ̃s] *nf* new outbreak (**de** of).

recrue [rəkry] *nf* recruit. ● **recruter** *vt* to recruit. ● **recrutement** *nm* recruitment.

rectangle [rɛktɑ̃gl] *nm* rectangle. ● **rectangulaire** *a* rectangular.

rectifier [rɛktifje] *vt* (*erreur etc*) to correct, rectify; (*ajuster*) to adjust. ● **rectification** *nf* correction, rectification.

recto [rɛkto] *nm* front (of the page); **r. verso** (on) both sides (of the page).

reçu [r(ə)sy] *pp de* **recevoir** ‖ *a* (*idée*) conventional, received; (*candidat*) successful ‖ *nm* (*écrit*) *Com* receipt.

recueil [r(ə)kœj] *nm* (*ouvrage*) anthology, collection (**de** of).

recueillir* [r(ə)kœjir] **1** *vt* to collect, gather; (*suffrages*) to win, get; (*prendre chez soi*) to take (*s.o.*) in. **2 se recueillir** *vpr* to meditate; (*devant un monument*) to stand in silence.

recul [r(ə)kyl] *nm* (*d'armée, de négociateur*) retreat; (*éloignement*) distance; **avoir un mouvement de r.** (*personne*) to recoil.

reculer [r(ə)kyle] *vi* to move *ou* step back; *Aut* to back up; (*armée*) to retreat; **r. devant** *Fig* to shrink from ‖ *vt* to push *ou* move back; (*différer*) to postpone.

reculons (à) [ar(ə)kylɔ̃] *adv* backwards.

récupérer [rekypere] *vt* (*objet prêté*) to get back, recover; (*ferraille etc*) to salvage ‖ *vi* to get one's strength back, recover.

récurer [rekyre] *vt* (*casserole etc*) to scrub, scour; **poudre à r.** scouring powder.

recycler [r(ə)sikle] *vt* (*matériaux*) to recycle ‖ **se r.** *vpr* to retrain. ● **recyclage** *nm* recycling; retraining.

rédacteur, -trice [redaktœr, -tris] *nmf* writer; (*de journal*) editor; **r. en chef** editor (in chief). ● **rédaction** *nf* (*action*) writing; (*de contrat*) drawing up; (*devoir de français*) essay, composition; (*journalistes*) editorial staff.

redemander [rədmɑ̃de] *vt* (*pain etc*) to ask for more; **r. qch à qn** to ask s.o. for sth back.

redescendre [r(ə)desɑ̃dr] *vi* (*aux* **être**) to come *ou* go back down ‖ *vt* (*aux* **avoir**) (*objet*) to bring *ou* take back down.

redevable [r(ə)dəvabl] *a* **être r. de qch à qn** (*argent*) to owe s.o. sth; *Fig* to be indebted to s.o. for sth.

redevance [r(ə)dəvɑ̃s] *nf* (*taxe*) *TV* licence fee; *Tél* rental charge.

rediffusion [rədifyzjɔ̃] *nf* (*de film etc*) repeat.

rédiger [rediʒe] *vt* to write; (*contrat*) to draw up.

redire* [r(ə)dir] **1** *vt* to repeat. **2** *vi* **avoir** *ou* **trouver à r. à qch** to find fault with sth.

redonner [r(ə)dɔne] *vt* to give back; (*donner plus*) to give more (*bread etc*); **r. un franc**/*etc* to give another franc/*etc*.

redoubl/er [r(ə)duble] *vti* **1** to increase; **r. de patience**/*etc* to be much more patient/*etc*. **2 r. (une classe)** to repeat a year *ou Am* a grade. ●**—ant, -ante** *nmf* pupil repeating a year *ou Am* a grade. ●**—ement** *nm* repeating a year *ou Am* a grade.

redout/er [r(ə)dute] *vt* to dread (**de faire** doing). ●**—able** *a* formidable.

redresser [r(ə)drese] *vt* (*objet tordu etc*) to straighten (out); (*économie, situation*) to put right ▌**se r.** *vpr* (*se mettre assis*) to sit up; (*debout*) to stand up; (*pays, situation etc*) to put itself right, right itself.

réduction [redyksjɔ̃] *nf* reduction (**de** in); (*prix réduit*) discount; **en r.** (*copie, modèle etc*) small-scale.

réduire* [redɥir] *vt* to reduce (**à** to, **de** by); **r. en cendres** to reduce to ashes; **se r. à** (*se ramener à*) to come down to, amount to ▌*vi* **(faire) r.** (*sauce*) to reduce, boil down. ●**réduit 1** *a* (*prix, vitesse*) reduced; (*modèle*) small-scale. **2** *nm* (*pièce*) *Péj* tiny room, cubbyhole.

réécrire [reekrir] *vt* (*texte*) to rewrite.

rééduquer [reedyke] *vt* (*membre*) *Méd* to re-educate; **r. qn** to rehabilitate s.o. ●**rééducation** *nf* re-education; rehabilitation.

réel, -elle [reɛl] *a* real ▌*nm* **le r.** reality. ●**réellement** *adv* really.

réexpédier [reɛkspedje] *vt* (*faire suivre*) to forward (*letter*); (*à l'envoyeur*) to return.

refaire* [r(ə)fɛr] *vt* (*exercice, travail*) to do again, redo; (*chambre*) to do up, redo; (*erreur, voyage*) to make again.

réfectoire [refɛktwar] *nm* refectory.

référendum [referɑ̃dɔm] *nm* referendum.

référer [refere] *vi* **en r. à** to refer the matter to ▌**se r.** *vpr* **se r. à** to refer to. ●**référence** *nf* reference.

refermer [r(ə)fɛrme] *vt*, **se r.** *vpr* to close (again).

refiler [r(ə)file] *vt* (*donner*) *Fam* to palm off (à on).

réfléchir [refleʃir] **1** *vt* (*image*) to reflect ▌**se r.** *vpr* to be reflected. **2** *vi* (*penser*) to think (à about). ●**réfléchi** *a* (*personne*) thoughtful; (*décision*) carefully thought-out; (*verbe*) *Gram* reflexive.

reflet [r(ə)flɛ] *nm* (*image*) & *Fig* reflection; (*lumière*) glint; (*couleur*) tint. ●**refléter** *vt* (*image, sentiment etc*) to reflect ▌**se r.** *vpr* to be reflected.

réflexe [reflɛks] *nm* & *a* reflex.

réflexion [reflɛksjɔ̃] *nf* **1** (*de lumière etc*) reflection. **2** (*méditation*) thought, reflection; (*remarque*) remark; **r. faite** on second thoughts *ou Am* thought.

reflux [rəfly] *nm* (*de la mer*) ebb; (*de la foule*) backward surge.

réforme *nf* (*changement*) reform. ●**réformer 1** *vt* to reform ▌**se r.** *vpr* to mend one's ways. **2** *vt* (*soldat*) to discharge as unfit.

refouler [r(ə)fule] *vt* to force *ou* drive back; (*sentiment*) to repress; (*larmes*) to hold back.

réfractaire [refraktɛr] *a* **r. à** resistant to.

refrain [r(ə)frɛ̃] *nm* (*de chanson*) chorus, refrain.

réfrigérer [refriʒere] *vt* to refrigerate. ●**réfrigérateur** *nm* refrigerator.

refroidir [r(ə)frwadir] *vt* to cool (down); (*décourager*) *Fig* to put off; (*ardeur*) to cool, damp(en) ▌*vi* to get cold, cool down ▌**se r.** *vpr* (*prendre froid*) *Fam* to catch cold; (*temps*) to get cold. ●**refroidissement** *nm* cooling; (*rhume*) chill; **r. de la température** fall in the temperature.

refuge [r(ə)fyʒ] *nm* refuge; (*pour piétons*) (traffic) island; (*de montagne*) (mountain) hut. ●**se réfugier** *vpr* to take refuge. ●**réfugié, -ée** *nmf* refugee.

refus [r(ə)fy] *nm* refusal; **ce n'est pas de r.** *Fam* I won't say no. ●**refuser** *vt* to refuse (**qch à qn** s.o. sth, **de faire** to do); (*offre, invitation*) to turn down, refuse; (*candidat*) to fail ▌**se r.** *vpr* (*plaisir etc*) to deny oneself; **se r. à croire**/*etc* to refuse to believe/*etc*.

regagner [r(ə)gaɲe] *vt* (*récupérer*) to regain, get back; (*revenir à*) to get back to. ●**regain** *nm* **avec un r. d'énergie**/*etc* with renewed energy/*etc*.

régaler (se) [səregale] *vpr* to have a feast.

regard [rəgar] *nm* **1** (*coup d'œil, expression*) look; (*fixe*) stare; **jeter un r. sur** to glance at; **chercher du r.** to look (a)round for. **2 au r. de** in regard to.

regarder [rəgarde] **1** *vt* to look at; (*fixe-*

ment) to stare at; (*observer*) to watch; (*considérer*) to consider, regard (**comme** as); **r. qn faire qch** to watch s.o. do sth ‖ *vi* to look; to stare; to watch; **r. à** (*dépense, qualité etc*) to pay attention to ‖ **se r.** *vpr* (*personnes*) to look at each other. **2** *vt* (*concerner*) to concern; **ça ne te regarde pas!** it's none of your business!

régates [regat] *nfpl* regatta.

régie [reʒi] *nf* (*entreprise*) state-owned company; *Th* stage management; *Cin TV* production department.

régime [reʒim] *nm* **1** (*politique*) (form of) government; *Péj* régime. **2** *Méd* diet; **se mettre au r.** to go on a diet; **suivre un r.** to be on a diet. **3** (*de moteur*) speed; **à ce r.** *Fig* at this rate. **4** (*de bananes, dattes*) bunch.

régiment [reʒimɑ̃] *nm Mil* regiment.

région [reʒjɔ̃] *nf* region, area. ● **régional, -aux** *a* regional.

régisseur [reʒisœr] *nm* (*de propriété*) steward; *Th* stage manager; *Cin* assistant director.

registre [rəʒistr] *nm* register.

règle [rɛgl] **1** *nf* (*principe*) rule; **en r.** (*papiers d'identité etc*) in order; **être en r. avec qn** to be right with s.o.; **en r. générale** as a (general) rule. **2** *nf* (*instrument*) ruler. **3** *nfpl* (*de femme*) (monthly) period.

règlement [rɛgləmɑ̃] *nm* **1** (*règles*) regulations; **contraire au r.** against the rules *ou Am* the rule. **2** (*de conflit, problème etc*) settling; (*paiement*) payment; **r. de comptes** *Fig* (violent) settling of scores. ● **réglementer** *vt* to regulate.

régler [regle] **1** *vt* (*problème etc*) to settle; (*mécanisme*) to adjust, regulate; (*moteur*) to tune. **2** *vti* (*payer*) to pay; **r. qn** to settle up with s.o.; **r. son compte à qn** *Fig* to settle old scores with s.o.

réglable [reglabl] *a* (*siège etc*) adjustable. ● **réglage** *nm* adjustment; (*de moteur*) tuning.

réglisse [reglis] *nf* liquorice, *Am* licorice.

règne [rɛɲ] *nm* (*de roi etc*) reign; (*animal, minéral, végétal*) kingdom. ● **régner** *vi* (*roi, silence*) to reign (**sur** over); (*prédominer*) to prevail; **faire r. l'ordre** to maintain (law and) order.

régresser [regrese] *vi* to regress.

regret [r(ə)grɛ] *nm* regret; **à r.** with regret; **être au r. de faire** to be sorry to do. ● **regretter** *vt* to regret; **r. qn** to miss s.o.; **r. que** (+ *sub*) to be sorry that, regret that; **je (le) regrette** I'm sorry; **r. de faire** to be sorry to do, regret doing; **r. d'avoir fait** to be sorry for doing, regret doing. ● **regrettable** *a* unfortunate, regrettable.

❶ **regrettable G99** The Subjunctive 7 G 1d)

regrouper [r(ə)grupe] *vt*, **se r.** *vpr* to gather together.

régulariser [regylarize] *vt* (*situation*) to regularize.

régulier, -ière [regylje, -jɛr] *a* regular; (*progrès, vitesse*) steady; (*légal*) legal. ● **régularité** *nf* regularity; steadiness; legality. ● **régulièrement** *adv* regularly; (*normalement*) normally.

réhabiliter [reabilite] *vt* (*dans l'estime publique*) to rehabilitate.

réimpression [reɛ̃presjɔ̃] *nf* (*livre*) reprint.

rein [rɛ̃] *nm* kidney; *pl* (*dos*) (small of the) back; **r. artificiel** *Méd* kidney machine.

reine [rɛn] *nf* queen.

reine-claude [rɛnklod] *nf* greengage.

réintégrer [reɛ̃tegre] *vt* **1** (*fonctionnaire etc*) to reinstate. **2** (*lieu*) to return to.

réitérer [reitere] *vt* to repeat.

rejaillir [r(ə)ʒajir] *vi* to spurt (up *ou* out); **r. sur** *Fig* to rebound on.

rejet [r(ə)ʒɛ] *nm* (*refus*) & *Méd* rejection. ● **rejeter** *vt* to throw back; (*refuser*) & *Méd* to reject; **r. une erreur/*etc* sur qn** to put the blame for a mistake/*etc* on s.o.

rejoindre* [r(ə)ʒwɛ̃dr] *vt* (*famille, lieu etc*) to get *ou* go back to; (*route, rue*) to join; **r. qn** (*se joindre à*) to join *ou* meet s.o.; (*rattraper*) to catch up with s.o. ‖ **se r.** *vpr* (*personnes, routes*) to meet.

réjouir (se) [səreʒwir] *vpr* to be delighted (**de** at, about; **de faire** to do). ● **réjouissance** *nf* rejoicing; *pl* festivities.

relâche [r(ə)lɑʃ] *nf Th Cin* (temporary) closure; **faire r.** (*théâtre, cinéma*) to close; **sans r.** without a break.

relâcher [r(ə)lɑʃe] **1** *vt* (*corde etc*) to slacken; (*discipline, étreinte*) to relax; **r. qn** to release s.o. ‖ **se r.** *vpr* to slacken; (*discipline*) to get lax. **2** *vi* (*bateau*) to put in.

relais [r(ə)lɛ] *nm Él Rad TV* relay; **(course de) r.** *Sp* relay (race); **prendre le r.** to take over (**de** from).

relancer [r(ə)lɑ̃se] *vt* to throw back; (*moteur*) to restart; (*industrie etc*) to put back on its feet; **r. qn** (*solliciter*) to pester s.o.

relatif, -ive [r(ə)latif, -iv] *a* relative (**à** to). ● **relativement** *adv* (*assez*) relatively.

relation [r(ə)lɑsjɔ̃] *nf* (*rapport*) relation(ship); (*ami*) acquaintance; **entrer en relations avec** to come into contact with; **avoir des relations** (*amis influents*) to have connections.

relax(e) [rəlaks] *a Fam* relaxed, informal.
relaxer (se) [sər(ə)lakse] *vpr* to relax.
relayer [r(ə)leje] *vt* to take over from (*s.o.*), relieve (*s.o.*); (*émission*) to relay ‖ **se r.** *vpr* to take (it in) turns (**pour faire** to do).
relève [r(ə)lɛv] *nf* (*remplacement*) relief; **prendre la r.** to take over (**de** from).
relever [rəlve] *vt* to raise; (*personne tombée*) to help up; (*col*) to turn up; (*manches*) to roll up; (*compteur*) to read; (*cahiers, copies*) to collect; (*copier*) to note down; (*faute*) to pick *ou* point out; (*traces*) to find; (*défi*) to accept; (*sauce*) to season.
‖ *vi* **r. de** (*dépendre de*) to come under; (*maladie*) to get over.
‖ **se relever** *vpr* (*personne tombée*) to get up. • **relevé** *nm* list; (*de compteur*) reading; **r. de compte** (bank) statement.
relief [rəljɛf] *nm* (*forme*) relief; **en r.** (*cinéma*) three-D; (*livre*) pop-up; **mettre en r.** *Fig* to highlight.
relier [rəlje] *vt* to connect, link (**à** to); (*livre*) to bind.
religion [r(ə)liʒjɔ̃] *nf* religion; (*foi*) faith. • **religieux, -euse** *a* religious; **mariage r.** church wedding ‖ *nm* monk. • **religieuse** *nf* **1** nun. **2** *Culin* cream bun.
relique [rəlik] *nf* relic.
relire* [r(ə)lir] *vt* to read again, reread.
reliure [rəljyr] *nf* (*de livre*) binding; (*art*) bookbinding.
reluire* [r(ə)lɥir] *vi* to shine, gleam. • **reluisant** *a* shiny; **peu r.** *Fig* far from brilliant.
remanier [r(ə)manje] *vt* (*texte*) to revise; (*ministère*) to reshuffle.
remarier (se) [sər(ə)marje] *vpr* to remarry.
remarquable [rəmarkabl] *a* remarkable (**par** for). • **—ment** [-əmɑ̃] *adv* remarkably.
remarque [r(ə)mark] *nf* remark; (*écrite*) note; **je lui en ai fait la r.** I remarked on it to him *ou* her.
remarquer [rəmarke] *vt* **1** (*apercevoir*) to notice (**que** that); **faire r.** to point out (**à** to, **que** that); **se faire r.** to attract attention; **remarque!** mind you!, you know! **2** (*dire*) to remark (**que** that).
remblayer [rɑ̃bleje] *vt* (*route*) to bank up; (*trou*) to fill in.
rembobiner [rɑ̃bɔbine] *vt*, **se r.** *vpr* (*bande*) to rewind.
rembourré [rɑ̃bure] *a* (*fauteuil etc*) padded.
rembourser [rɑ̃burse] *vt* to pay back, repay; (*billet*) to refund. • **remboursement** *nm* repayment; refund; **envoi contre r.** cash on delivery.
remède [r(ə)mɛd] *nm* cure, remedy; (*médicament*) medicine. • **remédier** *vi* **r. à** to remedy.
remémorer (se) [sər(ə)memɔre] *vpr* (*histoire etc*) to recollect, recall.
remercier [r(ə)mɛrsje] *vt* **1** to thank (**de qch, pour qch** for sth); **je vous remercie d'être venu** thank you for coming; **je vous remercie** (*non merci*) no thank you. **2** (*congédier*) to dismiss. • **remerciements** *nmpl* thanks.
remettre* [r(ə)mɛtr] *vt* to put back, replace; (*vêtement*) to put back on; (*donner*) to hand over (**à** to); (*restituer*) to give back (**à** to); (*démission, devoir*) to hand in; (*différer*) to postpone (**à** until); (*ajouter*) to add more *ou* another; **r. en question** *ou* **cause** to call into question; **r. en état** to repair; **r. ça** *Fam* to start again; **se r. à** (*activité*) to go back to; **se r. à faire** to start to do again; **se r. de** (*chagrin, maladie*) to get over, recover from; **s'en r. à** to rely on.
remise [r(ə)miz] *nf* **1** (*rabais*) discount. **2 r. de peine** *Jur* remission. **3** (*local*) shed; *Aut* garage.
remmener [rɑ̃mne] *vt* to take back.
remonte-pente [r(ə)mɔ̃tpɑ̃t] *nm* ski lift.
remonter [r(ə)mɔ̃te] *vi* (*aux* **être**) to come *ou* go back up; (*niveau, prix*) to rise again; (*dans le temps*) to go back (**à** to); **r. dans** (*voiture*) to get *ou* go back in(to); (*bus, train*) to get *ou* go back on(to); **r. sur** (*cheval, vélo*) to get back on(to); **r. à dix ans**/*etc* to go back ten years/*etc*.
‖ *vt* (*aux* **avoir**) (*escalier, pente*) to come *ou* go back up; (*porter*) to bring *ou* take back up; (*montre*) to wind up; (*relever*) to raise; (*col*) to turn up; (*objet démonté*) to put back together; **r. le moral à qn** to cheer s.o. up. • **remontée** *nf* **1** (*de pente etc*) ascent; (*d'eau, de prix*) rise. **2 r. mécanique** ski lift. • **remontoir** *nm* (*de mécanisme, montre*) winder.
remontrance [r(ə)mɔ̃trɑ̃s] *nf* reprimand; **faire des remontrances à** to reprimand.
remords [r(ə)mɔr] *nm* & *nmpl* remorse; **avoir des r.** to feel remorse.
remorque [r(ə)mɔrk] *nf Aut* trailer; **prendre en r.** to tow; **en r.** on tow, *Am* in tow. • **remorquer** *vt* (*voiture, bateau*) to tow. • **remorqueur** *nm* tug(boat).
remous [r(ə)mu] *nm* eddy; (*de foule*) bustle.
rempart [rɑ̃par] *nm* rampart.
remplacer [rɑ̃plase] *vt* to replace (**par** with, by); (*succéder à*) to take over from; (*temporairement*) to stand in for. • **remplaçant, -ante** *nmf* (*personne*) replacement; (*enseignant*) substitute teacher; *Sp* re-

serve. • **remplacement** *nm* replacement; **assurer le r. de qn** to stand in for s.o.; **en r. de** in place of.

remplir [rɑ̃plir] *vt* to fill (up) (**de** with); (*fiche etc*) to fill in *ou* out; (*condition, devoir*) to fulfil; (*fonctions*) to perform ‖ **se r.** *vpr* to fill (up). • **rempli** *a* full (**de** of). • **remplissage** *nm* filling; (*verbiage*) *Péj* padding.

remporter [rɑ̃pɔrte] *vt* **1** (*objet*) to take back. **2** (*prix, victoire*) to win; (*succès*) to achieve.

remuer [r(ə)mɥe] *vt* to move; (*café etc*) to stir; (*salade*) to toss; (*terre*) to turn over ‖ *vi* to move; (*gigoter*) to fidget ‖ **se r.** *vpr* to move; (*se démener*) *Fig* to go to a lot of trouble. • **remuant** *a* (*enfant*) restless, fidgety. • **remueménage** *nm inv* commotion.

rémunérer [remynere] *vt* (*personne*) to pay; (*travail*) to pay for. • **rémunération** *nf* payment (**de** for).

renaître* [r(ə)nɛtr] *vi* (*fleur*) to grow again; (*espoir, industrie*) to revive.

renard [r(ə)nar] *nm* fox.

renchérir [rɑ̃ʃerir] *vi* **r. sur ce que qn dit**/*etc* to go further than s.o. in what one says/*etc.*

rencontre [rɑ̃kɔ̃tr] *nf* meeting; (*inattendue*) encounter; *Sp* match, *Am* game; **aller à la r. de qn** to go to meet s.o. • **rencontrer** *vt* to meet; (*difficulté, obstacle*) to come up against, encounter; (*équipe*) *Sp* to play ‖ **se r.** *vpr* to meet.

rendement [rɑ̃dmɑ̃] *nm Agr* yield; *Fin* return, yield (*de personne, machine*) output.

rendez-vous [rɑ̃devu] *nm inv* appointment; (*d'amoureux*) date; (*lieu*) meeting place; **donner r.-vous à qn, prendre r.-vous avec qn** to make an appointment with s.o.

rendormir* (se) [sərɑ̃dɔrmir] *vpr* to go back to sleep.

rendre [rɑ̃dr] *vt* (*restituer*) to give back, return; (*monnaie*) to give; (*hommage*) to pay; (*justice*) to dispense; (*armes*) to surrender; **r. célèbre/plus grand**/*etc* to make famous/bigger/*etc* ‖ *vti* (*vomir*) to throw up ‖ **se r.** *vpr* (*capituler*) to surrender (**à** to); (*aller*) to go (**à** to); **se r. à** (*évidence, ordres*) to submit to; **se r. utile**/*etc* to make oneself useful/*etc.*

rênes [rɛn] *nfpl* reins.

renfermer [rɑ̃fɛrme] *vt* to contain ‖ **se r.** *vpr* **se r. (en soi-même)** to withdraw into oneself. • **renfermé 1** *a* (*personne*) withdrawn. **2** *nm* **sentir le r.** (*chambre etc*) to smell stuffy.

renflement [rɑ̃fləmɑ̃] *nm* bulge.

renflouer [rɑ̃flue] *vt* (*navire*) & *Com* to refloat.

renfoncement [rɑ̃fɔ̃səmɑ̃] *nm* recess; **dans le r. d'une porte** in a doorway.

renforcer [rɑ̃fɔrse] *vt* to strengthen, reinforce. • **renfort** *nm* **des renforts** (*troupes*) reinforcements; **de r.** (*personnel*) back-up; **à grand r. de** *Fig* with (the help of) a great deal of.

renfrogner (se) [sərɑ̃frɔɲe] *vpr* to scowl.

renier [rənje] *vt* (*ami, pays, etc*) to disown; (*foi, opinion*) to renounce.

renifler [r(ə)nifle] *vti* to sniff.

renne [rɛn] *nm* reindeer.

renom [rənɔ̃] *nm* (*popularité*) renown; (*réputation*) reputation (**de** for). • **renommé** *a* famous, renowned (**pour** for). • **renommée** *nf* fame.

renoncer [r(ə)nɔ̃se] *vi* **r. à qch** to give sth up, abandon sth; **r. à faire** to give up (the idea of) doing.

renouer [rənwe] **1** *vt* (*lacet etc*) to retie. **2** *vt* (*reprendre*) to renew ‖ *vi* **r. avec qch** (*tradition etc*) to revive sth; **r. avec qn** to take up with s.o. again.

renouveau, -x [r(ə)nuvo] *nm* revival.

renouveler [r(ə)nuvle] *vt* to renew; (*erreur, question*) to repeat ‖ **se r.** *vpr* (*incident*) to happen again; (*cellules, sang*) to be renewed. • **renouvelable** *a* renewable. • **renouvellement** *nm* renewal.

rénover [renɔve] *vt* (*édifice, meuble etc*) to renovate.

renseigner [rɑ̃sɛɲe] *vt* to inform, give some information to (**sur** about) ‖ **se r.** *vpr* to find out, inquire (**sur** about). • **renseignement** *nm* (piece of) information; *pl* information; **les renseignements** (*au téléphone*) directory inquiries, *Am* information; **prendre** *ou* **demander des renseignements** to make inquiries.

rentable [rɑ̃tabl] *a* profitable. • **rentabilité** *nf* profitability.

rente [rɑ̃t] *nf* (private) income; (*pension*) pension; **avoir des rentes** to have private means.

rentrée [rɑ̃tre] *nf* **1** (*retour*) return; (*d'acteur*) comeback; **r. (des classes)** beginning of term *ou* of the school year. **2 rentrées** (*argent*) receipts.

rentrer [rɑ̃tre] *vi* (*aux* **être**) to go *ou* come back, return; (*chez soi*) to go *ou* come (back) home; (*entrer*) to go *ou* come in; (*entrer de nouveau*) to go *ou* come back in; **r. dans** (*entrer dans*) to go *ou* come into; (*entrer de nouveau dans*) to go *ou* come

back into; (*pays*) to return to; (*heurter*) to crash into; (*s'emboîter dans*) to fit into; (*catégorie*) to come under; **r. (en classe)** to go back to school.
▌*vt* (*aux* **avoir**) to bring *ou* take in; (*voiture*) to put away; (*chemise*) to tuck in; (*griffes*) to draw in.
renverse (à la) [alarɑ̃vɛrs] *adv* (*tomber*) backwards.
renverser [rɑ̃vɛrse] *vt* (*mettre à l'envers*) to turn upside down; (*faire tomber*) to knock over *ou* down; (*piéton*) to knock down; (*liquide*) to spill, knock over; (*gouvernement*) to overthrow; (*tête*) to tip back ▌**se r.** *vpr* (*bouteille, vase etc*) to fall over; (*liquide*) to spill. ●**renversement** *nm* (*de situation*) reversal.
renvoi [rɑ̃vwa] *nm* dismissal; expulsion; postponement; (*dans un livre*) (cross) reference. ●**renvoyer*** *vt* to send back, return; (*employé*) to dismiss; (*élève*) to expel; (*balle etc*) to throw back; (*ajourner*) to postpone (**à** until); (*lumière, image etc*) to reflect; **r. qn à** (*adresser à*) to refer s.o. to.
réorganiser [reɔrganize] *vt* to reorganize.
réouverture [reuvɛrtyr] *nf* reopening.
repaire [r(ə)pɛr] *nm* den.
répandre [repɑ̃dr] *vt* (*liquide*) to spill; (*nouvelle*) to spread; (*odeur*) to give off; (*lumière, larmes, chargement*) to shed; (*gravillons etc*) to scatter ▌**se r.** *vpr* (*nouvelle etc*) to spread; (*liquide*) to spill; **se r. dans** (*fumée, odeur*) to spread through. ●**répandu** *a* (*opinion, usage*) widespread; (*épars*) scattered.
reparaître [r(ə)parɛtr] *vi* to reappear.
réparer [repare] *vt* to repair, mend; (*erreur*) to put right; (*forces*) to restore; (*faute*) to make amends for. ●**réparateur, -trice** *nmf* repairer. ●**réparation** *nf* repair; **en r.** under repair.
repartir* [r(ə)partir] *vi* (*aux* **être**) to set off again; (*s'en retourner*) to go back; (*reprendre*) to start again; **r. à** *ou* **de zéro** to go back to square one.
répartir [repartir] *vt* to distribute; (*partager*) to share (out); (*classer*) to divide (up); (*étaler dans le temps*) to spread (out) (**sur** over). ●**répartition** *nf* distribution; sharing; division.
repas [r(ə)pɑ] *nm* meal; **prendre un r.** to have *ou* eat a meal.
repass/er [r(ə)pɑse] **1** *vi* to come *ou* go back ▌*vt* (*traverser*) to go back over; (*examen*) to take again; (*leçon*) to go over; (*film*) to show again; (*bande magnétique*) to play back. **2** *vt* (*linge*) to iron. ●**—age** *nm* ironing.
repêcher [r(ə)peʃe] *vt* (*objet*) to fish out; (*candidat*) *Fam* to allow to pass.
repentir* (se) [sər(ə)pɑ̃tir] *vpr* to be sorry (**de** for).
répercuter [repɛrkyte] *vt* (*son*) to echo ▌**se r.** *vpr* to echo, reverberate.
repère [r(ə)pɛr] *nm* (guide) mark; (*jalon*) marker; **point de r.** (*espace, temps*) landmark. ●**repérer** *vt* to locate; (*remarquer*) *Fam* to spot ▌**se r.** *vpr* to get one's bearings.
répertoire [repɛrtwar] *nm* **1** index; (*carnet*) (indexed) notebook; (*de fichiers*) *Ordinat* directory; **r. d'adresses** address book. **2** *Th* repertoire.
répéter [repete] *vti* to repeat; *Th* to rehearse ▌**se r.** *vpr* (*radoter*) to repeat oneself; (*événement*) to happen again. ●**répétitif, -ive** *a* repetitive. ●**répétition** *nf* repetition; *Th* rehearsal; **r. générale** *Th* (final) dress rehearsal.
repiquer [r(ə)pike] *vt* (*disque*) to tape, record (on tape).
répit [repi] *nm* rest; **sans r.** ceaselessly.
replacer [r(ə)plase] *vt* to replace, put back.
repli [r(ə)pli] *nm* fold; *Mil* withdrawal.
replier [r(ə)plije] **1** *vt* to fold (up); (*couverture*) to fold back; (*ailes, jambes*) to tuck in ▌**se r.** *vpr* (*siège*) to fold up; (*couverture*) to fold back. **2 se replier** *vpr* *Mil* to withdraw; **se r. sur soi-même** *Fig* to withdraw into oneself.
réplique [replik] *nf* **1** (*réponse*) (sharp) reply; *Th* lines; **sans r.** (*argument*) irrefutable. **2** (*copie*) replica. ●**répliquer** *vt* to reply (sharply) (**que** that) ▌*vi* (*être impertinent*) to answer back.
répondre [repɔ̃dr] *vi* to answer, reply; (*être impertinent*) to answer back; **r. à qn** to answer s.o., reply to s.o.; (*avec impertinence*) to answer s.o. back; **r. à** (*lettre, question*) to answer, reply to; (*besoin*) to meet, answer; **r. de** (*garantir*) to answer for (*s.o., sth*).
▌*vt* (*remarque etc*) to answer *ou* reply with; **r. que** to answer *ou* reply that. ●**répondeur** *nm* *Tél* answering machine.
ⓘ**répondre G204** Word Order: Inversion 12 A 7b)
réponse [repɔ̃s] *nf* answer, reply; **en r. à** in answer *ou* reply to.
reporter[1] [r(ə)pɔrte] *vt* to take back; (*différer*) to put off, postpone (**à** until); (*transcrire*) to transfer (**sur** to); **se r. à** (*texte etc*) to refer to. ●**reportage** *nm* (news) report, article; (*en direct*) commentary; (*métier*) reporting.

reporter[2] [r(ə)pɔrtɛr] *nm* reporter.

repos [r(ə)po] *nm* rest; (*tranquillité*) peace (and quiet); (*de l'esprit*) peace of mind; **r.!** *Mil* at ease!; **jour de r.** day off; **de tout r.** (*situation etc*) safe.

reposer [r(ə)poze] **1** *vt* (*objet*) to put back down; (*problème, question*) to raise again. **2** *vt* (*délasser*) to rest, relax; **r. sa tête sur** (*appuyer*) to rest one's head on ‖ *vi* (*être enterré*) to rest, lie; **r. sur** (*bâtiment*) to be built on; (*théorie etc*) to be based on, rest on ‖ **se r.** *vpr* to rest; **se r. sur qn** to rely on s.o. • **reposant** *a* restful, relaxing.

repousser [r(ə)puse] **1** *vt* to push back; (*écarter*) to push away; (*attaque*) to beat off; (*différer*) to put off, postpone. **2** *vi* (*cheveux, feuilles*) to grow again.

reprendre* [r(ə)prɑ̃dr] *vt* (*objet*) to take back; (*évadé, ville*) to recapture; (*souffle*) to get back; (*activité*) to take up again, resume; (*refrain*) to take up; (*vêtement*) to alter; (*corriger*) to correct; (*pièce*) *Th* to put on again; **r. de la viande/un œuf/***etc* to take some more meat/another egg/*etc*; **r. des forces** to get one's strength back; **r. ses esprits** to come round.
‖ *vi* (*plante*) to take root again; (*recommencer*) to start (up) again, resume; (*affaires*) to pick up; (*parler*) to go on.
‖ **se reprendre** *vpr* (*se ressaisir*) to get a grip on oneself; (*se corriger*) to correct oneself; **s'y r. à deux fois** to have another go (at it).

représenter [r(ə)prezɑ̃te] *vt* to represent; (*pièce de théâtre*) to perform ‖ **se r.** *vpr* (*s'imaginer*) to imagine. • **représentant, -ante** *nmf* representative; **r. de commerce** (travelling) salesman *ou* saleswoman, sales representative. • **représentation** *nf* representation; *Th* performance.

répression [represjɔ̃] *nf* suppression, repression; (*mesures de contrôle*) *Pol* repression. • **réprimer** *vt* (*sentiment, révolte etc*) to suppress, repress.

repris [r(ə)pri] *nm* **r. de justice** hardened criminal.

reprise [r(ə)priz] *nf* (*recommencement*) resumption; *Rad TV* repeat; (*de pièce de théâtre*) revival; (*raccommodage*) mend; *Boxe* round; (*économique*) recovery, revival; (*d'un locataire*) money for fittings; (*de marchandise*) taking back; (*pour nouvel achat*) part exchange, trade-in; *pl Aut* acceleration; **à plusieurs reprises** on several occasions. • **repriser** *vt* (*chaussette etc*) to mend, darn.

réprobation [reprɔbɑsjɔ̃] *nf* disapproval.

reproche [r(ə)prɔʃ] *nm* criticism, reproach; **faire des reproches à qn** to criticize s.o.; **sans r.** beyond reproach. • **reprocher** *vt* **r. qch à qn** to criticize *ou* blame *ou* reproach s.o. for sth.

reproduire* [r(ə)prɔdɥir] **1** *vt* (*modèle etc*) to copy, reproduce ‖ **se r.** *vpr* (*animaux*) to breed, reproduce. **2 se reproduire** *vpr* (*incident etc*) to happen again. • **reproduction** *nf* breeding, reproduction; (*copie*) copy.

reptile [rɛptil] *nm* reptile.

repu [rəpy] *a* (*rassasié*) satiated.

république [repyblik] *nf* republic. • **républicain, -aine** *a* & *nmf* republican.

répugnant [repyɲɑ̃] *a* repulsive, disgusting. • **répugnance** *nf* disgust, repugnance (**pour** for); (*manque d'enthousiasme*) reluctance. • **répugner** *vi* **r. à qn** to be repulsive to s.o.; **r. à faire** to be loath to do.

réputation [repytɑsjɔ̃] *nf* reputation; **avoir la r. d'être franc** to have a reputation for being frank *ou* for frankness. • **réputé** *a* (*célèbre*) renowned (**pour** for); **r. pour être** reputed to be.

requête [rəkɛt] *nf* request; *Jur* petition. • **requis** *a* required.

requin [r(ə)kɛ̃] *nm* (*poisson*) & *Fig* shark.

réquisitoire [rekizitwar] *nm* (*critique*) indictment (**contre** of).

RER [ɛrøɛr] *nm abrév* (*Réseau express régional*) = express rail network serving Paris and its suburbs.

rescapé, -ée [rɛskape] *nmf* survivor.

rescousse (à la) [alarɛskus] *adv* to the rescue.

réseau, -x [rezo] *nm* network.

réserve [rezɛrv] *nf* **1** (*provision*) stock, reserve; (*entrepôt*) storeroom; **en r.** in reserve. **2** (*de chasse, pêche*) preserve; (*indienne*) reservation; **r. naturelle** nature reserve. **3** (*discrétion*) reserve; (*restriction*) reservation; **sans r.** (*admiration etc*) unqualified; **sous r. de** subject to; **sous toutes réserves** without guarantee.

réserv/er [rezɛrve] *vt* (*garder*) to save, reserve (**à** for); (*place, table*) to book, reserve; (*surprise etc*) to hold in store (**à** for); **se r. pour** to save oneself for. • **—é** *a* (*personne, place*) reserved. • **réservation** *nf* reservation, booking.

réservoir [rezɛrvwar] *nm* (*citerne*) tank; **r. d'essence** *Aut* petrol *ou Am* gas tank.

résidence [rezidɑ̃s] *nf* residence; **r. secondaire** second home; **r. universitaire** hall of residence, *Am* dormitory. • **résidentiel, -ielle** *a* (*quartier*) residential. • **résider** *vi* to be resident, reside (**à, en, dans** in).

résidu [rezidy] *nm* residue, waste.
résigner (se) [sərezijne] *vpr* to resign oneself (**à qch** to sth, **à faire** to doing).
résilier [rezilje] *vt* (*contrat*) to terminate.
résine [rezin] *nf* resin.
résistance [rezistɑ̃s] *nf* resistance (**à** to); (*conducteur*) *Él* (heating) element; **plat de r.** main dish.
résist/er [reziste] *vi* **r. à** to resist; (*chaleur, fatigue*) to withstand; (*se défendre contre*) to stand up to. ●**—ant, -ante** *a* tough; **r. à la chaleur** heat-resistant; **r. au choc** shockproof ‖ *nmf Mil Hist* Resistance fighter.
résolu [rezɔly] *pp de* **résoudre** ‖ *a* determined, resolute; **r. à faire** determined to do. ●**résolution** *nf* (*décision*) decision; (*fermeté*) determination.
résonner [rezɔne] *vi* (*cris etc*) to ring out; (*salle*) to echo (**de** with).
résorber [rezɔrbe] *vt* (*chômage*) to reduce; (*excédent*) to absorb.
résoudre* [rezudr] *vt* (*problème*) to solve; (*difficulté*) to clear up, resolve; **se r. à faire** (*se résigner*) to bring oneself to do.
respect [rɛspɛ] *nm* respect (**pour, de** for); **mes respects à** my regards *ou* respects to. ●**respecter** *vt* to respect; **qui se respecte** self-respecting. ●**respectueux, -euse** *a* respectful (**envers** to, **de** of).
respectif, -ive [rɛspɛktif, -iv] *a* respective.
respirer [rɛspire] *vi* to breathe; (*reprendre haleine*) to get one's breath back; (*être soulagé*) to breathe again ‖ *vt* to breathe (in); (*exprimer*) *Fig* to exude, radiate. ●**respiration** *nf* breathing; (*haleine*) breath; **r. artificielle** *Méd* artificial respiration.
resplendissant [rɛsplɑ̃disɑ̃] *a* (*visage*) glowing (**de** with).
responsable [rɛspɔ̃sabl] *a* responsible (**de qch** for sth, **devant qn** to s.o.) ‖ *nmf* (*chef*) person in charge; (*dans une organisation*) official; (*coupable*) person responsible (**de** for). ●**responsabilité** *nf* responsibility; (*légale*) liability.
resquiller [rɛskije] *vi* (*au cinéma, dans le métro etc*) to avoid paying; (*sans attendre*) to jump the queue, *Am* cut in (line).
ressaisir (se) [sər(ə)sezir] *vpr* to pull oneself together.
ressasser [r(ə)sase] *vt* (*ruminer*) to keep going over; (*répéter*) to keep trotting out.
ressemblance [r(ə)sɑ̃blɑ̃s] *nf* likeness, resemblance (**avec** to). ●**ressembler** *vi* **r. à** to look *ou* be like, resemble; **cela ne lui ressemble pas** that's not like him *ou* her ‖ **se r.** *vpr* to look *ou* be alike.
ressentir* [r(ə)sɑ̃tir] *vt* to feel.
resserrer [r(ə)sere] *vt* (*nœud, boulon etc*) to tighten; (*liens*) *Fig* to strengthen ‖ **se r.** *vpr* to tighten; (*route etc*) to narrow.
resservir [r(ə)sɛrvir] **1** *vi* (*outil etc*) to come in useful (again). **2 se resservir** *vpr* **se r. de** (*plat etc*) to have another helping of.
ressort [r(ə)sɔr] *nm* **1** (*objet*) spring. **2 du r. de** within the competence of; **en dernier r.** (*décider etc*) as a last resort.
ressortir* [r(ə)sɔrtir] *vi* (*aux* **être**) **1** to go *ou* come back out. **2** (*se voir*) to stand out; **faire r.** to bring out.
ressortissant, -ante [r(ə)sɔrtisɑ̃, -ɑ̃t] *nmf* (*citoyen*) national.
ressource [r(ə)surs] *nfpl* (*moyens*) resources; (*argent*) means, resources.
ressusciter [resysite] *vi* to rise from the dead; (*malade, pays*) to recover, revive.
restant [rɛstɑ̃] *a* remaining; **poste restante** poste restante, *Am* general delivery.
restaurant [rɛstɔrɑ̃] *nm* restaurant.
restaurer [rɛstɔre] **1** *vt* (*réparer, rétablir*) to restore. **2 se restaurer** *vpr* to (have something to) eat. ●**restaurateur, -trice** *nmf* (*hôtelier, hôtelière*) restaurant owner. ●**restauration** *nf* **1** restoration. **2** (*hôtellerie*) catering.
reste [rɛst] *nm* rest, remainder (**de** of); *Math* remainder; *pl* (*de repas*) leftovers; **un r. de fromage/***etc* some left-over cheese/*etc*; **au r., du r.** moreover, besides.
rester [rɛste] *vi* (*aux* **être**) to stay, remain; (*calme, jeune etc*) to keep, stay, remain; (*subsister*) to be left, remain; **il reste du pain/***etc* there's some bread/*etc* left (over); **il me reste une minute/***etc* I have one minute/*etc* left; **l'argent qui lui reste** the money he *ou* she has left; **il reste beaucoup à faire** there's a lot left to do; **reste à savoir** it remains to be seen; **en r. à** to stop at; **restons-en là** let's leave it at that.
restituer [rɛstitɥe] *vt* (*rendre*) to return, restore (**à** to).
restreindre* [rɛstrɛ̃dr] *vt* to limit, restrict (**à** to) ‖ **se r.** *vpr* (*faire des économies*) to cut back *ou* down. ●**restriction** *nf* restriction; **sans r.** unreservedly.
résultat [rezylta] *nm* (*score, d'examen etc*) result; (*conséquence*) outcome, result.
résumer [rezyme] *vt* to summarize; (*situation*) to sum up ‖ **se r.** *vpr* (*orateur etc*) to sum up; **se r. à** (*se réduire à*) to boil down to. ●**résumé** *nm* summary; **en r.** in short; (*en récapitulant*) to sum up.
rétablir [retablir] *vt* to restore; (*vérité*) to re-establish ‖ **se r.** *vpr* to be restored; (*malade*)

to recover. • **rétablissement** *nm Méd* recovery.

retaper [r(ə)tape] *vt* (*maison, voiture etc*) to do up.

retard [r(ə)tar] *nm* lateness; (*sur un programme etc*) delay; **en r.** late; (*retardé*) backward; **en r. dans qch** behind in sth; **en r. sur qn/qch** behind s.o./sth; **rattraper son r.** to catch up; **avoir du r.** to be late; (*sur un programme*) to be behind (schedule); (*montre*) to be slow; **avoir une heure de r.** to be an hour late; **prendre du r.** (*montre*) to lose (time). • **retardataire** *nmf* latecomer. • **retardement** *nm* **bombe à r.** time bomb.

retard/er [r(ə)tarde] *vt* to delay; (*date, montre, départ*) to put back; **r. qn** (*dans une activité*) to put s.o. behind ‖ *vi* (*montre*) to be slow; **r. de cinq minutes** to be five minutes slow. • **—é, -ée** *a* (*enfant*) backward.

retenir* [rətnir] *vt* (*empêcher d'agir, contenir*) to hold back; (*souffle*) to hold; (*réserver*) to book; (*se souvenir de*) to remember; (*fixer*) to hold (in place); (*chiffre*) *Math* to carry; (*chaleur, odeur*) to retain; (*candidature, proposition*) to accept; **r. qn prisonnier** to keep s.o. prisoner.

‖ **se retenir** *vpr* (*se contenir*) to restrain oneself; **se r. de faire** to stop oneself (from) doing; **se r. à** to cling to.

rentent/ir [r(ə)tɑ̃tir] *vi* to ring (out) (**de** with). • **—issant** *a* resounding; (*scandale*) major.

retenue [rətny] *nf* **1** (*modération*) restraint. **2** (*de salaire*) deduction; (*chiffre*) *Math* figure carried over. **3** (*punition*) *Scol* detention; **en r.** in detention.

réticent [retisɑ̃] *a* (*réservé*) reticent; (*hésitant*) reluctant.

retirer [r(ə)tire] *vt* (*sortir*) to take out; (*ôter*) to take off; (*éloigner*) to take away; (*plainte, candidature, argent*) to withdraw; **r. qch à qn** (*permis etc*) to take sth away from s.o.; **r. qch de** (*gagner*) to derive sth from ‖ **se r.** *vpr* to withdraw, retire (**de** from); (*mer*) to ebb.

retomber [r(ə)tɔ̃be] *vi* to fall (again); (*pendre*) to hang (down); (*après un saut*) to land; (*intérêt*) to slacken; **r. dans l'erreur** to be wrong again; **r. sur qn** (*responsabilité*) to fall on s.o. • **retombées** *nfpl* (*radioactives*) fallout.

rétorsion [retɔrsjɔ̃] *nf Pol* retaliation; **mesure de r.** reprisal.

retouche [r(ə)tuʃ] *nf* alteration; touching up. • **retoucher** *vt* (*vêtement*) to alter; (*photo, tableau*) to touch up.

retour [r(ə)tur] *nm* return; (*de fortune*) reversal; **être de r.** to be back (**de** from); **en r.** (*en échange*) in return; **par r. (du courrier)** by return (of post), *Am* by return mail; **à mon retour** when I get *ou* got back (**de** from); **r. en arrière** flashback; **match r.** return match *ou Am* game.

retourner [r(ə)turne] *vt* (*aux* **avoir**) (*matelas, steak etc*) to turn over; (*terre*) to turn; (*vêtement, sac etc*) to turn inside out; (*tableau etc*) to turn round; (*compliment, lettre*) to return; **r. contre qn** (*argument*) to turn against s.o.; (*arme*) to turn on s.o. ‖ *vi* (*aux* **être**) to go back, return.

‖ **se retourner** *vpr* (*pour regarder*) to turn round, look round; (*sur le dos*) to turn over *ou* round; (*dans son lit*) to toss and turn; (*voiture*) to overturn; **se r. contre** *Fig* to turn against.

rétracter [retrakte] *vt*, **se r.** *vpr* to retract.

retrait [r(ə)trɛ] *nm* withdrawal; (*de bagages*) collection; **en r.** (*maison etc*) set back.

retraite [r(ə)trɛt] *nf* **1** (*d'employé*) retirement; (*pension*) (retirement) pension; (*refuge*) retreat; **r. anticipée** early retirement; **prendre sa r.** to retire; **à la r.** retired; **mettre à la r.** to pension off. **2** *Mil* retreat; **r. aux flambeaux** torchlight tattoo. • **retraité, -ée** *a* retired ‖ *nmf* senior citizen, pensioner.

retrancher [r(ə)trɑ̃ʃe] **1** *vt* (*passage etc*) to cut (**de** from); (*argent, quantité*) to deduct (**de** from). **2 se retrancher** *vpr* **se r. dans/derrière** *Fig* to take refuge in/behind.

retransmettre [r(ə)trɑ̃smɛtr] *vt* to broadcast. • **retransmission** *nf* broadcast.

rétrécir [retresir] *vt* to narrow; (*vêtement*) to take in ‖ *vi* (*au lavage*) to shrink ‖ **se r.** *vpr* (*rue etc*) to narrow.

rétribuer [retribɥe] *vt* to pay, remunerate; (*travail*) to pay for.

rétro [retro] *a inv* (*personne, idée etc*) old-fashioned.

rétroactif, -ive [retrɔaktif, -iv] *a* (*mesure etc*) retrospective; **augmentation avec effet r.** retroactive (pay) increase.

rétrograde [retrɔgrad] *a* retrograde. • **rétrograder** *vi* (*reculer*) to move back; *Aut* to change down ‖ *vt* (*fonctionnaire, officier*) to demote.

rétrospectif, -ive [retrɔspɛktif, -iv] *a* retrospective ‖ *nf* (*de films*) retrospective. • **rétrospectivement** *adv* in retrospect.

retrouss/er [r(ə)truse] *vt* (*manches*) to roll up • **—é** *a* (*nez*) turned-up.

retrouver [r(ə)truve] *vt* to find (again); (*rejoindre*) to meet (again); (*forces, santé*) to get back, regain; (*se rappeler*) to recall ‖ **se r.** *vpr* (*se trouver*) to find oneself (back); (*se rencontrer*) to meet (again); **s'y r.** (*s'orienter*) to find one's way *ou* bearings.

rétroviseur [retrɔvizœr] *nm Aut* (rear-view) mirror.

réunion [reynjɔ̃] *nf* (*séance*) meeting; (*jonction*) joining. ● **réunir** *vt* (*objets*) to collect, gather; (*convoquer*) to call together, assemble; (*relier*) to join; (*rapprocher*) to bring together; (*qualités etc*) to combine.

réuss/ir [reysir] *vi* to succeed, be successful (**à faire** in doing); **r. à** (*examen*) to pass; **r. à qn** to work (out) well for s.o.; (*aliment, climat*) to agree with s.o. ‖ *vt* to make a success of. ● **—i** *a* successful. ● **réussite** *nf* **1** success. **2 faire des réussites** *Cartes* to play patience.

revaloir [r(ə)valwar] *vt* **je vous le revaudrai** (*en bien ou en mal*) I'll pay you back.

revaloriser [r(ə)valɔrize] *vt* to revalue; (*salaires etc*) to raise.

revanche [r(ə)vɑ̃ʃ] *nf* revenge; *Sp* return game; **en r.** on the other hand.

rêve [rɛv] *nm* dream; **faire un r.** to have a dream; **maison de r.** dream house.

revêche [rəvɛʃ] *a* bad-tempered, surly.

réveil [revɛj] *nm* waking (up); *Fig* awakening; (*pendule*) alarm (clock); **à son r.** when he wakes (up) *ou* woke (up).

réveiller [reveje] *vt* (*personne*) to wake (up); (*sentiment, souvenir*) *Fig* to revive, awaken ‖ **se r.** *vpr* to wake (up); *Fig* to revive, awaken. ● **réveillé** *a* awake. ● **réveille-matin** *nm inv* alarm (clock).

réveillon [revɛjɔ̃] *nm* (*repas*) midnight supper (*on Christmas Eve or New Year's Eve*). ● **réveillonner** *vi* to take part in a *réveillon.*

révéler [revele] *vt* to reveal (**que** that) ‖ **se r.** *vpr* to be revealed; **se r. facile**/*etc* to turn out to be easy/*etc.* ● **révélation** *nf* revelation.

revenant [rəvnɑ̃] *nm* ghost.

revendiquer [r(ə)vɑ̃dike] *vt* to claim; (*exiger*) to demand. ● **revendication** *nf* claim; demand.

revendre [r(ə)vɑ̃dr] *vt* to resell. ● **revendeur, -euse** *nmf* retailer; (*d'occasion*) secondhand dealer; **r. (de drogue)** drug pusher; **r. de billets** ticket tout, *Am* scalper.

revenir* [rəvnir] *vi* (*aux* **être**) to come back, return; (*mot*) to come *ou* crop up; (*coûter*) to cost (**à qn** s.o.); **r. à** (*activité, sujet*) to go back to, return to; (*se résumer à*) to boil down to; **r. à qn** (*forces, mémoire*) to come back to s.o., return to s.o.; **r. à soi** to come round *ou* to; **r. de** (*surprise*) to get over; **r. sur** (*décision, promesse*) to go back on; (*passé, question*) to go back over; **r. sur ses pas** to retrace one's steps; **faire r.** (*aliment*) to brown.

revenu [rəvny] *nm* income (**de** from); (*d'un État*) revenue (**de** from); **déclaration de revenus** tax return.

rêv/er [reve] *vi* to dream (**de** of, **de faire** of doing) ‖ *vt* to dream (**que** that). ● **—é** *a* ideal.

réverbération [revɛrberɑsjɔ̃] *nf* (*de lumière*) reflection.

réverbère [revɛrbɛr] *nm* street lamp.

révérence [reverɑ̃s] *nf* reverence; (*salut d'homme*) bow; (*salut de femme*) curts(e)y; **faire une r.** to bow; to curts(e)y.

rêverie [rɛvri] *nf* daydream; (*activité*) daydreaming.

revers [r(ə)vɛr] *nm* (*de veste*) lapel; (*de pantalon*) turn-up, *Am* cuff; (*d'étoffe*) wrong side; *Tennis* backhand; (*coup du sort*) setback; **le r. de la médaille** *Fig* the other side of the coin.

réversible [revɛrsibl] *a* reversible.

revêtir* [r(ə)vetir] *vt* to cover (**de** with); (*habit*) to put on; (*route*) to surface. ● **revêtement** *nm* (*surface*) covering; (*de route*) surface.

rêveur, -euse [rɛvœr, -øz] *nmf* dreamer.

revient [rəvjɛ̃] *nm* **prix de r.** cost price.

revirement [r(ə)virmɑ̃] *nm* (*changement*) about-turn, *Am* about-face; (*de situation, d'opinion, de politique*) reversal.

réviser [revize] *vt* (*leçon*) to revise; (*machine, voiture*) to service, overhaul; (*jugement*) to review. ● **révision** *nf* revision; service, overhaul; review.

revivre* [r(ə)vivr] *vi* to live again; **faire r.** to revive ‖ *vt* (*incident etc*) to relive.

révocation [revɔkɑsjɔ̃] *nf* (*de fonctionnaire*) dismissal.

revoir* [r(ə)vwar] *vt* to see (again); (*texte, leçon*) to revise; **au r.** goodbye.

révolte [revɔlt] *nf* rebellion, revolt. ● **révolter 1** *vt* to sicken. **2 se révolter** *vpr* to rebel, revolt (**contre** against). ● **révoltant** *a* (*honteux*) revolting. ● **révolté, -ée** *nmf* rebel.

révolu [revɔly] *a* (*époque*) past; **avoir trente ans révolus** to be over thirty (years of age).

révolution [revɔlysjɔ̃] *nf* (*changement, rotation*) revolution. ● **révolutionnaire** *a* & *nmf* revolutionary.

revolver [revɔlvɛr] *nm* gun, revolver.

révoquer [revɔke] *vt* (*fonctionnaire*) to dismiss.

revue [r(ə)vy] *nf* **1** (*magazine*) magazine; (*spécialisée*) journal. **2** (*de music-hall*) variety show. **3** *Mil* review; **passer en r.** to review.
rez-de-chaussée [redʃose] *nm inv* ground floor, *Am* first floor.
rhabiller (se) [sərabije] *vpr* to get dressed again.
Rhin [rɛ̃] *nm* **le R.** the Rhine.
rhinocéros [rinɔserɔs] *nm* rhinoceros.
rhubarbe [rybarb] *nf* rhubarb.
rhum [rɔm] *nm* rum.
rhumatisme [rymatism] *nm Méd* rheumatism; **avoir des rhumatismes** to have rheumatism.
rhume [rym] *nm* cold; **r. de cerveau** head cold; **r. des foins** hay fever.
ri [ri] *pp de* **rire**.
riant [rjɑ̃] *p prés de* **rire** ‖ *a* cheerful, smiling.
ricaner [rikane] *vi* (*sarcastiquement*) to snigger, *Am* snicker; (*bêtement*) to giggle.
riche [riʃ] *a* rich; (*personne, pays*) rich, wealthy; **r. en** (*vitamines etc*) rich in ‖ *nmf* rich *ou* wealthy person; **les riches** the rich. • **richesse** *nf* wealth; (*de sol, vocabulaire*) richness; *pl* (*trésor*) riches; (*ressources*) wealth.
ricocher [rikɔʃe] *vi* to rebound, ricochet. • **ricochet** *nm* rebound, ricochet.
rictus [riktys] *nm* grin, grimace.
ride [rid] *nf* wrinkle; ripple. • **rider** *vt* (*visage*) to wrinkle; (*eau*) to ripple ‖ **se r.** *vpr* to wrinkle. • **ridé** *a* wrinkled.
rideau, -x [rido] *nm* curtain; (*de magasin*) shutter; (*écran*) *Fig* screen (**de** of).
ridicule [ridikyl] *a* ridiculous ‖ *nm* (*moquerie*) ridicule; (*de situation etc*) ridiculousness; **tourner en r.** to ridicule. • **se ridiculiser** *vpr* to make a fool of oneself.
rien [rjɛ̃] *pron* nothing; **il ne sait r.** he knows nothing, he doesn't know anything; **r. du tout** nothing at all; **r. d'autre/de bon/***etc* nothing else/good/*etc*; **r. de tel** nothing like it; **de r.!** (*je vous en prie*) don't mention it!; **ça ne fait r.** it doesn't matter; **pour r.** (*à bas prix*) for next to nothing; **r. que** just, only ‖ *nm* (mere) nothing, trifle; **un r. de** a hint *ou* touch of; **en un r. de temps** (*vite*) in no time.
G50 Indefinite Pronouns 6 B 2
G102 The Subjunctive 7 G 1i)
G204 Negative Expressions 12 B
rieur, -euse [rijœr, -øz] *a* cheerful.
rigide [riʒid] *a* rigid; (*carton, muscle*) stiff; (*personne*) *Fig* inflexible; (*éducation*) strict.
rigole [rigɔl] *nf* (*conduit*) channel; (*filet d'eau*) rivulet.
rigoler [rigɔle] *vi Fam* to laugh; (*s'amuser*) to have fun; (*plaisanter*) to joke (**avec** about). • **rigolade** *nf Fam* fun; (*chose ridicule*) joke, farce. • **rigolo, -ote** *a Fam* funny.
rigueur [rigœr] *nf* rigour; harshness; strictness; (*précision*) precision; **être de r.** to be the rule; **à la r.** if absolutely necessary. • **rigoureux, -euse** *a* rigorous; (*climat, punition*) harsh; (*personne, morale, sens*) strict.
rillettes [rijɛt] *nfpl* potted minced pork.
rime [rim] *nf* rhyme. • **rimer** *vi* to rhyme (**avec** with); **ça ne rime à rien** it makes no sense.
rincer [rɛ̃se] *vt* to rinse; (*verre*) to rinse (out). • **rinçage** *nm* rinsing; (*opération*) rinse.
ring [riŋ] *nm* (boxing) ring.
ringard [rɛ̃gar] *a* (*démodé*) *Fam* old-fashioned, unfashionable.
riposte [ripɔst] *nf* (*réponse*) retort; (*attaque*) counter(attack).
rire* [rir] *vi* to laugh (**de** at); (*s'amuser*) to have a good time; (*plaisanter*) to joke; **faire qch pour r.** to do sth for a joke *ou* a laugh ‖ *nm* laugh; *pl* laughter; **le r.** (*activité*) laughter; **le fou r.** the giggles.
ris [ri] *nm* **r. de veau** *Culin* (calf) sweetbread.
risque [risk] *nm* risk; **au r. de faire qch** at the risk of doing sth; **les risques du métier** occupational hazards; **à vos risques et périls** at your own risk; **assurance tous risques** comprehensive insurance. • **risquer** *vt* to risk; (*question, regard*) to venture, hazard; **r. de faire** to stand a good chance of doing. • **risqué** *a* risky.
ristourne [risturn] *nf* discount.
rite [rit] *nm* rite; (*habitude*) *Fig* ritual.
rivage [rivaʒ] *nm* shore.
rival, -ale, -aux [rival, -o] *a & nmf* rival. • **rivaliser** *vi* to compete (**avec** with, **de** in). • **rivalité** *nf* rivalry.
rive [riv] *nf* (*de fleuve*) bank; (*de lac*) shore.
riverain, -aine [rivrɛ̃, -ɛn] *nmf* riverside resident; (*de lac*) lakeside resident; (*de rue*) resident.
rivière [rivjɛr] *nf* river.
riz [ri] *nm* rice; **r. au lait** rice pudding. • **rizière** *nf* paddy (field), ricefield.
RMI [ɛrɛmi] *nm abrév* (*Revenu minimum d'insertion*) = income support, *Am* = welfare.
RN *abrév* = **route nationale.**
robe [rɔb] *nf* (*de femme*) dress; (*d'ecclé-*

siastique, de juge) robe; **r. du soir** evening dress *ou* gown; **r. de grossesse/de mariée** maternity/wedding dress; **r. de chambre** dressing gown, *Am* bathrobe.

robinet [rɔbinɛ] *nm* tap, *Am* faucet; **eau du r.** tap water.

robot [rɔbo] *nm* robot; **r. ménager** food processor, liquidizer.

robuste [rɔbyst] *a* sturdy, robust.

roc [rɔk] *nm* rock.

rocaille [rɔkɑj] *nf* (*terrain*) rocky ground. ●**rocailleux, -euse** *a* rocky, stony.

roche [rɔʃ] *nf* (*substance*) rock. ●**rocher** *nm* (*bloc*) rock. ●**rocheux, -euse** *a* rocky.

rock [rɔk] *nm* (*musique*) rock ‖ *a inv* **chanteur/opéra r.** rock singer/opera.

rod/er [rɔde] *vt* (*moteur, voiture*) to run in, *Am* break in. ●**—age** *nm* running in, *Am* breaking in.

rôd/er [rode] *vi* to roam (about); (*suspect*) to prowl (about). ●**—eur, -euse** *nmf* prowler.

rogner [rɔɲe] *vt* to trim, clip ‖ *vi* **r. sur** (*réduire*) to cut down on.

rognon [rɔɲɔ̃] *nm Culin* kidney.

roi [rwa] *nm* king; **fête** *ou* **jour des rois** Twelfth Night.

rôle [rol] *nm* role, part; (*d'un père etc*) job; **à tour de r.** in turn.

romain, -aine [rɔmɛ̃, -ɛn] **1** *a & nmf* Roman. **2** *nf* (*laitue*) cos (lettuce), *Am* romaine.

roman [rɔmɑ̃] **1** *nm* novel; **r. d'aventures** adventure story; **r.-fleuve** saga. **2** *a* (*langue*) Romance; *Archit* Romanesque. ●**romancier, -ière** *nmf* novelist.

romanichel, -elle [rɔmaniʃɛl] *nmf* gipsy.

romantique [rɔmɑ̃tik] *a* romantic.

romarin [rɔmarɛ̃] *nm Bot Culin* rosemary.

rompre* [rɔ̃pr] *vt* to break; (*pourparlers, relations*) to break off ‖ *vi* to break (*Fig* **avec** with); (*fiancés*) to break it off ‖ **se r.** *vpr* (*corde etc*) to break; (*digue*) to burst. ●**rompu** *a* **1** (*fatigué*) exhausted. **2 r. à** (*expérimenté*) experienced in.

romsteck [rɔmstɛk] *nm* rump steak.

ronces [rɔ̃s] *nfpl* (*branches*) brambles.

rond [rɔ̃] *a* round; (*gras*) plump; (*ivre*) *Fam* tight ‖ *adv* **tourner r.** (*machine etc*) to run smoothly; **dix francs tout r.** ten francs exactly ‖ *nm* (*cercle*) circle, ring; **en r.** (*s'asseoir etc*) in a ring *ou* circle; **tourner en r.** (*toupie etc*) & *Fig* to go round and round. ●**r.-point** *nm* (*pl* **ronds-points**) *Aut* roundabout, *Am* traffic circle. ●**ronde** *nf* (*de soldat*) round; (*de policier*) beat, round; (*danse*) round (dance); **à la r.** around. ●**rondelle** *nf* (*tranche*) slice. ●**rondement** *adv* (*efficacement*) briskly. ●**rondin** *nm* log.

ronfler [rɔ̃fle] *vi* to snore; (*moteur*) to hum. ●**ronflement** *nm* snore; hum; *pl* snoring; humming.

rong/er [rɔ̃ʒe] *vt* to gnaw (at); (*ver, mer, rouille*) to eat into (*sth*); **r. qn** (*maladie*) to consume s.o.; **se r. les ongles** to bite one's nails. ●**—eur** *nm* (*animal*) rodent.

ronronnement [rɔ̃rɔnmɑ̃] *nm* purr(ing). ●**ronronner** *vi* to purr.

roquefort [rɔkfɔr] *nm* Roquefort (cheese).

roquette [rɔkɛt] *nf Mil* rocket.

rosbif [rɔsbif] *nm* **du r.** (*rôti*) roast beef; (*à rôtir*) roasting beef; **un r.** a joint of roast *ou* roasting beef.

rose [roz] **1** *nf* (*fleur*) rose. **2** *a* (*couleur*) pink; (*situation, teint*) rosy ‖ *nm* pink. ●**rosé** *a* pinkish ‖ *a & nm* (*vin*) rosé. ●**rosier** *nm* rose bush.

roseau, -x [rozo] *nm* (*plante*) reed.

rosée [roze] *nf* dew.

rosser [rɔse] *vt* to thrash.

rossignol [rɔsiɲɔl] *nm* (*oiseau*) nightingale.

rot [ro] *nm Fam* burp. ●**roter** *vi Fam* to burp.

rotation [rɔtɑsjɔ̃] *nf* rotation.

rotin [rɔtɛ̃] *nm* cane, rattan.

rôtir [rotir] *vti*, **se r.** *vpr* to roast; **faire r.** to roast. ●**rôti** *nm* **du r.** roasting meat; (*cuit*) roast meat; **un r.** a joint; **r. de porc** (joint of) roast pork. ●**rôtissoire** *nf* (roasting) spit.

rotule [rɔtyl] *nf* kneecap.

rouage [rwaʒ] *nm* (*de montre etc*) (working) part; (*d'organisation etc*) *Fig* cog.

roucouler [rukule] *vi* to coo.

roue [ru] *nf* wheel.

rouer [rwe] *vt* **r. qn de coups** to beat s.o. black and blue.

rouet [rwɛ] *nm* spinning wheel.

rouge [ruʒ] *a* red; (*fer*) red-hot ‖ *nm* (*couleur*) red; (*vin*) *Fam* red wine; **r. (à lèvres)** lipstick; **r. (à joues)** rouge; **le feu est au r.** *Aut* the (traffic) lights are red. ●**r.-gorge** *nm* (*pl* **rouges-gorges**) robin. ●**rougeur** *nf* redness; (*due à la gêne ou à la honte*) blush(ing); *pl Méd* rash, red spots. ●**rougir** *vi* (*de honte*) to blush (**de** with), go red; (*de colère, de joie*) to flush (**de** with), go red.

rougeole [ruʒɔl] *nf* measles.

rouget [ruʒɛ] *nm* (*poisson*) mullet.

rouille [ruj] *nf* rust ‖ *a inv* (*couleur*) rust(-coloured). ●**rouiller** *vi* to rust ‖ **se r.** *vpr* to rust; (*esprit, sportif etc*) *Fig* to get rusty. ●**rouillé** *a* rusty.

rouleau, -x [rulo] *nm* (*outil, vague*) roller;

(*de papier*, *pellicule etc*) roll; **r. à pâtisserie** rolling pin; **r. compresseur** steamroller.

roulement [rulmɑ̃] *nm* (*bruit*) rumbling, rumble; (*de tambour*, *de tonnerre*) roll; (*ordre*) rotation; **par r.** in rotation.

rouler [rule] *vt* to roll; (*brouette*) to push, wheel; (*crêpe*, *ficelle*, *manches etc*) to roll up; **r. qn** (*duper*) *Fam* to cheat s.o. ‖ *vi* to roll; (*train*, *voiture*) to go, travel; (*conducteur*) to drive ‖ **se r.** *vpr* to roll; **se r. dans** (*couverture etc*) to roll oneself (up) in. • **roulant** *a* (*escalier*) moving; (*meuble*) on wheels; **chaise roulante** wheelchair.

roulette [rulɛt] *nf* (*de meuble*) castor; (*de dentiste*) drill; (*jeu*) roulette.

roulis [ruli] *nm* (*de navire*) roll(ing).

roulotte [rulɔt] *nf* (*de gitan*) caravan.

Roumanie [rumani] *nf* Romania. • **roumain, -aine** *a* & *nmf* Romanian ‖ *nm* (*langue*) Romanian.

round [rawnd, rund] *nm* *Boxe* round.

rouspéter [ruspete] *vi* *Fam* to complain, grumble.

rousse [rus] *voir* **roux.**

rousseur [rusœr] *nf* **tache de r.** freckle. • **roussir** *vt* (*brûler*) to scorch, singe ‖ *vi* (*feuilles*) to turn brown.

route [rut] *nf* road (**de** to); (*itinéraire*) way, route; (*chemin*) *Fig* path, way; **r. nationale/départementale** main/secondary road; **grand-r.** main road; **en r.** on the way, en route; **en r.!** let's go!; **par la r.** by road; **sur la bonne r.** *Fig* on the right track; **mettre en r.** (*voiture etc*) to start (up); **se mettre en r.** to set out (**pour** for); **une heure de r.** an hour's drive; **bonne r.!** *Aut* have a good trip!

routier, -ière [rutje, -jɛr] *a* **carte/sécurité routière** road map/safety ‖ *nm* (*camionneur*) (long distance) lorry *ou* *Am* truck driver.

routine [rutin] *nf* routine; **contrôle de r.** routine check.

rouvrir* [ruvrir] *vti*, **se r.** *vpr* to reopen.

roux, rousse [ru, rus] *a* (*cheveux*) red, ginger; (*personne*) red-haired ‖ *nmf* redhead.

royal, -aux [rwajal, -o] *a* (*famille*, *palais etc*) royal; (*cadeau*, *festin etc*) fit for a king. • **royaume** *nm* kingdom. • **Royaume-Uni** *nm* United Kingdom. • **royauté** *nf* monarchy.

ruban [rybɑ̃] *nm* ribbon; (*de chapeau*) band; **r. adhésif** sticky *ou* adhesive tape.

rubéole [rybeɔl] *nf* German measles, rubella.

rubis [rybi] *nm* (*pierre*) ruby; (*de montre*) jewel.

rubrique [rybrik] *nf* (*article de journal*) column; (*catégorie*, *titre*) heading.

ruche [ryʃ] *nf* (bee)hive.

rude [ryd] *a* (*pénible*) tough; (*hiver*, *voix*) harsh; (*grossier*) crude; (*rêche*) rough. • **—ment** *adv* (*parler*, *traiter*) harshly; (*très*) *Fam* awfully.

rudiments [rydimɑ̃] *nmpl* rudiments.

rue [ry] *nf* street; **être à la r.** (*sans domicile*) to be on the streets. • **ruelle** *nf* alley(way).

ruer [rɥe] **1** *vi* (*cheval*) to kick (out). **2 se ruer** *vpr* (*foncer*) to rush, fling oneself (**sur** at). • **ruée** *nf* rush.

rugby [rygbi] *nm* rugby. • **rugbyman,** *pl* **-men** [rygbiman, -mɛn] *nm* rugby player.

rug/ir [ryʒir] *vi* to roar. • **—issement** *nm* roar.

rugueux, -euse [rygø, -øz] *a* rough.

ruine [rɥin] *nf* (*décombres*) & *Fig* ruin; **en r.** (*édifice*) in ruins; **tomber en r.** (*bâtiment*) to become a ruin, crumble; (*mur*) to crumble. • **ruiner** *vt* (*personne*, *santé etc*) to ruin ‖ **se r.** *vpr* (*en dépensant*) to be(come) ruined, ruin oneself.

ruisseau, -x [rɥiso] *nm* stream; (*caniveau*) gutter. • **ruisseler** *vi* to stream (**de** with).

rumeur [rymœr] *nf* (*protestation*) clamour; (*murmure*) murmur; (*nouvelle*) rumour.

ruminer [rymine] *vi* (*vache*) to chew the cud.

rupture [ryptyr] *nf* break(ing); (*de fiançailles*, *relations*) breaking off; (*de pourparlers*) breakdown (**de** in); (*brouille*) break(up), split; (*de contrat*) breach; (*d'organe*) *Méd* rupture.

rural, -aux [ryral, -o] *a* rural; **vie/école/***etc* **rurale** country life/school/*etc*.

ruse [ryz] *nf* (*subterfuge*) trick; **la r.** (*habileté*) cunning; (*fourberie*) trickery. • **rusé, -ée** *a* & *nmf* cunning *ou* crafty (person).

Russie [rysi] *nf* Russia. • **russe** *a* & *nmf* Russian ‖ *nm* (*langue*) Russian.

rustique [rystik] *a* (*meuble*) rustic.

rythme [ritm] *nm* rhythm; (*de travail*) rate; (*de la vie*) pace; **au r. de trois par jour** at a rate of three a day. • **rythmé** *a* rhythmic(al). • **rythmique** *a* rhythmic(al).

S

S, s [ɛs] *nm* S, s.
s' [s] *voir* **se, si.**
sa [sa] *voir* **son²**.
SA *abrév* (*société anonyme*) *Com* plc, *Am* Inc.
sabbat [saba] *nm* (Jewish) Sabbath.
sable [sɑbl] *nm* sand. ● **sabler** *vt* (*route*) to sand; **s. le champagne** to celebrate with champagne.
sablé [sɑble] *nm* shortbread biscuit *ou Am* cookie.
sablier [sablije] *nm* hourglass; *Culin* egg timer.
sablonneux, -euse [sablɔnø, -øz] *a* (*terrain*) sandy.
saborder [sabɔrde] *vt* (*navire*) to scuttle.
sabot [sabo] *nm* **1** (*de cheval etc*) hoof. **2** (*chaussure*) clog. **3** (*de frein*) *Aut* shoe; **s. (de Denver)** *Aut* (wheel) clamp.
sabot/er [sabɔte] *vt* to sabotage; (*bâcler*) to botch. ● **—age** *nm* sabotage.
sabre [sɑbr] *nm* sabre, sword.
sac [sak] *nm* **1** bag; (*grand et en toile*) sack; **s. (à main)** handbag; **s. à dos** rucksack; **s. de voyage** travelling bag. **2 mettre à s.** (*ville*) *Mil* to sack.
saccade [sakad] *nf* jerk, jolt; **par saccades** in fits and starts. ● **saccadé** *a* (*geste, style*) jerky.
saccager [sakaʒe] *vt* (*détruire*) to wreck.
saccharine [sakarin] *nf* saccharin.
sacerdoce [sasɛrdɔs] *nm* (*fonction*) *Rel* priesthood; *Fig* vocation.
sachant, sache(s), sachent *etc* [saʃɑ̃, saʃ] *voir* **savoir**.
sachet [saʃɛ] *nm* (small) bag; **s. de thé** teabag.
sacoche [sakɔʃ] *nf* bag; (*de vélo, moto*) saddlebag.
sacre [sakr] *nm* (*de roi*) coronation; (*d'évêque*) consecration. ● **sacrer** *vt* (*roi*) to crown; (*évêque*) to consecrate.
sacré [sakre] *a* (*saint*) sacred; **un s. menteur/***etc Fam* a damned liar/*etc*.
ⓘ**G32** Position of Adjectives 4 D 3
sacrifice [sakrifis] *nm* sacrifice. ● **sacrifier** *vt* to sacrifice (**à** to, **pour** for) ‖ **se s.** *vpr* to sacrifice oneself (**à** to, **pour** for).
sadisme [sadism] *nm* sadism. ● **sadique** *a* sadistic ‖ *nmf* sadist.
safari [safari] *nm* safari; **faire un s.** to be *ou* go on safari.
sage [saʒ] *a* wise; (*enfant*) good, well-behaved ‖ *nm* wise man, sage. ● **sagement** *adv* wisely; (*avec calme*) quietly. ● **sagesse** *nf* wisdom; good behaviour.
sage-femme [saʒfam] *nf* (*pl* **sages-femmes**) midwife.
Sagittaire [saʒitɛr] *nm* **le S.** (*signe*) Sagittarius.
Sahara [saara] *nm* **le S.** the Sahara (desert).
saign/er [seɲe] *vti* to bleed; **s. du nez** to have a nosebleed. ● **—ant** [sɛɲɑ̃] *a* (*viande*) *Culin* rare. ● **saignement** *nm* bleeding; **s. de nez** nosebleed.
saillant [sajɑ̃] *a* projecting, jutting out.
sain [sɛ̃] *a* healthy; (*moralement*) sane; (*jugement*) sound; (*nourriture*) wholesome; **s. et sauf** safe and sound, unhurt.
saindoux [sɛ̃du] *nm* lard.
saint, sainte [sɛ̃, sɛ̃t] *a* holy; (*personne*) saintly; **s. Jean** Saint John; **la Sainte Vierge** the Blessed Virgin ‖ *nmf* saint. ● **s.-bernard** *nm* (*chien*) St Bernard. ● **S.-Esprit** *nm* Holy Spirit. ● **S.-Siège** *nm* Holy See. ● **S.-Sylvestre** *nf* New Year's Eve.
sais [sɛ] *voir* **savoir.**
saisie [sezi] *nf Jur* seizure; **s. de données** *Ordinat* data capture; **opérateur de s.** keyboard operator.
saisir [sezir] *vt* **1** to grab (hold of), seize; (*occasion*) to jump at; (*comprendre*) to understand; *Jur* to seize; (*frapper*) *Fig* to strike; **se s. de** to grab (hold of), seize. **2** (*viande*) *Culin* to fry briskly.
saison [sɛzɔ̃] *nf* season; **en/hors s.** in/out of season; **en pleine** *ou* **haute s.** in (the) high season; **en basse s.** in the low season. ● **saisonnier, -ière** *a* seasonal.
sait [sɛ] *voir* **savoir.**
salade [salad] **1** *nf* (*laitue*) lettuce; **s. (verte)** (green) salad; **s. de fruits/***etc* fruit/*etc* salad. **2** *nfpl* (*mensonges*) *Fam* stories, nonsense. ● **saladier** *nm* salad bowl.
salaire [salɛr] *nm* wage(s), salary.
salaison [salɛzɔ̃] *nf Culin* salting; *pl* (*denrées*) salt(ed) meat *ou* fish.
salarial, -aux [salarjal, -o] *a* **accord/***etc* **s.** wage agreement/*etc*. ● **salarié, -ée** *a* wage-earning ‖ *nmf* wage earner.
salaud [salo] *nm Fam Péj* bastard, swine.
sale [sal] *a* dirty; (*dégoûtant*) filthy; (*mau-*

vais) nasty. • **saleté** *nf* dirtiness; filthiness; (*crasse*) dirt, filth; (*action*) dirty trick; *pl* (*détritus*) rubbish, *Am* garbage.

sal/er [sale] *vt Culin* to salt. • **—é** *a* (*goût*, *plat*) salty; (*aliment*) salted; **eau salée** salt water. • **salière** *nf* saltcellar, *Am* saltshaker.

salir [salir] *vt* to (make) dirty; (*réputation*) *Fig* to tarnish ‖ **se s.** *vpr* to get dirty. • **salissant** *a* (*métier*) dirty, messy; (*étoffe*) that shows the dirt.

salive [saliv] *nf* saliva.

salle [sal] *nf* room; (*très grande*, *publique*) hall; *Th* theatre, auditorium; (*de cinéma*) cinema, *Am* movie theater; (*d'hôpital*) ward; (*public*) *Th* audience; **s. à manger** dining room; **s. de bain(s)** bathroom; **s. de classe** classroom; **s. d'embarquement** *Av* departure lounge; **s. d'exposition** *Com* showroom; **s. de jeux** (*pour enfants*) games room; (*avec machines à sous*) amusement arcade; **s. d'opération** *Méd* operating theatre *ou Am* room.

salon [salɔ̃] *nm* living *ou* sitting room, lounge; (*exposition*) show; **s. de beauté/de coiffure** beauty/hairdressing salon; **s. de thé** tearoom(s).

salope [salɔp] *nf* (*femme*) *Fam Vulg* bitch. • **saloperie** *nf Fam* (*action*) dirty trick; (*camelote*) junk.

salopette [salɔpɛt] *nf* (*d'enfant*, *d'ouvrier*) dungarees, *Am* overalls.

salubre [salybr] *a* healthy. • **salubrité** *nf* healthiness; **s. publique** public health.

saluer [salɥe] *vt* to greet; (*en partant*) to take one's leave of; (*de la main*) to wave to; (*de la tête*) to nod to; *Mil* to salute.

salut [saly] **1** *nm* greeting; wave; nod; *Mil* salute ‖ *int Fam* hello!, hi!; (*au revoir*) bye! **2** *nm* (*de peuple etc*) salvation; (*sauvegarde*) safety. • **salutation** *nf* greeting; **je vous prie d'accepter mes salutations distinguées** (*dans une lettre*) yours faithfully, *Am* sincerely.

samedi [samdi] *nm* Saturday.

SAMU [samy] *nm abrév* (*service d'assistance médicale d'urgence*) emergency medical service.

sanction [sɑ̃ksjɔ̃] *nf* (*approbation*, *peine*) sanction. • **sanctionner** *vt* (*confirmer*, *approuver*) to sanction; (*punir*) to punish.

sandale [sɑ̃dal] *nf* sandal.

sandwich [sɑ̃dwitʃ] *nm* sandwich; **s. au fromage**/*etc* cheese/*etc* sandwich.

sang [sɑ̃] *nm* blood. • **sanglant** *a* bloody. • **sanguin, -ine 1** *a* **vaisseau/groupe s.** blood vessel/group. **2** *nf* (*fruit*) blood orange, ruby-red orange.

sang-froid [sɑ̃frwa] *nm* self-control, calm; **garder son s.-froid** to keep calm; **avec s.-froid** calmly; **de s.-froid** (*tuer*) in cold blood.

sangle [sɑ̃gl] *nf* (*de selle*, *parachute*) strap.

sanglier [sɑ̃glije] *nm* wild boar.

sanglot [sɑ̃glo] *nm* sob. • **sangloter** *vi* to sob.

sanitaire [sanitɛr] *a* (*conditions*) sanitary; (*personnel*) medical; **installation s.** bathroom fittings.

sans [sɑ̃] ([sɑ̃z] *before vowel and mute h*) *prép* without; **s. faire** without doing; **s. qu'il le sache** without him *ou* his knowing; **s. cela, s. quoi** otherwise; **s. plus** (but) no more than that; **s. faute** without fail; **s. importance** unimportant; **s. argent** penniless; **ça va s. dire** that goes without saying. • **s.-abri** *nmf inv* homeless person; **les s.-abri** the homeless. • **s.-gêne** *a inv* inconsiderate ‖ *nm inv* lack of consideration.

santé [sɑ̃te] *nf* health; **en bonne/mauvaise s.** in good/bad health; **(à votre) s.!** (*en trinquant*) your (good) health!, cheers!; **maison de s.** nursing home.

saoul [su] = **soûl.**

saper [sape] *vt* to undermine.

sapeur-pompier [sapœrpɔ̃pje] *nm* (*pl* **sapeurs-pompiers**) fireman.

saphir [safir] *nm* (*pierre*) sapphire.

sapin [sapɛ̃] *nm* (*arbre*, *bois*) fir; **s. de Noël** Christmas tree.

sarbacane [sarbakan] *nf* peashooter.

sarcasme [sarkasm] *nm* sarcasm; **un s.** a piece of sarcasm.

Sardaigne [sardɛɲ] *nf* Sardinia.

sardine [sardin] *nf* sardine.

SARL *abrév* (*société à responsabilité limitée*) Ltd, *Am* Inc.

sarrasin [sarazɛ̃] *nm* buckwheat.

sas [sɑs] *nm Nau Av* airlock.

Satan [satɑ̃] *nm* Satan.

satellite [satelit] *nm* satellite; **télévision par s.** satellite TV; **antenne s.** satellite dish; **pays s.** satellite (country).

satiété [sasjete] *nf* **manger/boire à s.** to eat/drink one's fill.

satin [satɛ̃] *nm* satin.

satire [satir] *nf* satire (**contre** on). • **satirique** *a* satiric(al).

satisfaction [satisfaksjɔ̃] *nf* satisfaction. • **satisfaire*** *vt* to satisfy (*s.o.*) ‖ *vi* **s. à** (*conditions etc*) to fulfil. • **satisfaisant** *a* (*acceptable*) satisfactory. • **satisfait** *a* satisfied, content (**de** with).

saturer [satyre] *vt* to saturate (**de** with).

satyre [satir] *nm Fam* sex fiend.
sauce [sos] *nf* sauce; (*jus de viande*) gravy; **s. tomate** tomato sauce.
saucisse [sosis] *nf* sausage. • **saucisson** *nm* (cold) sausage.
sauf[1] [sof] *prép* except (**que** that); **s. avis contraire** unless you hear otherwise; **s. erreur** barring error.
sauf[2], **sauve** [sof, sov] *a* (*honneur*) intact; **avoir la vie sauve** to be unharmed.
sauge [soʒ] *nf Bot Culin* sage.
saule [sol] *nm* willow; **s. pleureur** weeping willow.
saumon [somɔ̃] *nm* salmon ‖ *a inv* (*couleur*) salmon (pink).
sauna [sona] *nm* sauna.
saupoudrer [sopudre] *vt* to sprinkle (**de** with).
saur [sɔr] *am* **hareng s.** smoked herring, kipper.
saura, saurai *etc* [sora, sorɛ] *voir* **savoir.**
saut [so] *nm* jump, leap; **faire un s.** to jump, leap; **faire un s. chez qn** to drop in on s.o., pop round to s.o.
sauté [sote] *a & nm Culin* sauté.
sauter [sote] *vi* to jump, leap; (*bombe*) to go off, explode; (*fusible*) to blow; (*se détacher*) to come off; **faire s.** (*détruire*) to blow up; (*arracher*) to tear off; (*casser*) to break; *Culin* to sauté; **s. à la corde** to skip, *Am* jump rope; **ça saute aux yeux** it's obvious ‖ *vt* (*franchir*) to jump (over); (*mot*, *repas*, *classe*) to skip. • **saute-mouton** *nm* (*jeu*) leapfrog.
sauterelle [sotrɛl] *nf* grasshopper.
sautiller [sotije] *vi* to hop.
sauvage [sovaʒ] *a* (*animal*, *plante*) wild; (*tribu*, *homme*) primitive; (*cruel*) savage; (*farouche*) unsociable; (*illégal*) unauthorized ‖ *nmf* unsociable person; (*brute*) savage.
sauve [sov] *a voir* **sauf**[2].
sauvegarder [sovgarde] *vt* to safeguard; *Ordinat* to save.
sauver [sove] **1** *vt* to save; (*d'un danger*) to rescue (**de** from); (*matériel*) to salvage; **s. la vie à qn** to save s.o.'s life. **2 se sauver** *vpr* (*s'enfuir*) to run away *ou* off; (*partir*) *Fam* to get off, go. • **sauvetage** *nm* rescue; **canot de s.** lifeboat; **ceinture de s.** life belt. • **sauveteur** *nm* rescuer. • **sauveur** *nm* saviour.
sauvette (à la) [alasovɛt] *adv* **vendre à la s.** to peddle on the streets (*illegally*).
savant [savɑ̃] *a* learned, scholarly; (*manœuvre etc*) masterly ‖ *nm* scientist.
saveur [savœr] *nf* (*goût*) flavour.
savoir** [savwar] *vt* to know; (*nouvelle*) to know, have heard; **s. lire/nager/***etc* to know how to read/swim/*etc*; **faire s. à qn que** to inform *ou* tell s.o. that; **à s.** (*c'est-à-dire*) that is, namely; **(pas) que je sache** (not) as far as I know; **je n'en sais rien** I have no idea; **un je ne sais quoi** a something or other ‖ *nm* (*culture*) learning, knowledge. • **s.-faire** *nm inv* know-how, ability. • **s.-vivre** *nm inv* good manners.
➊**savoir G123** Modal Auxiliary Verbs 7 K 3
savon [savɔ̃] *nm* **1** soap; (*morceau*) (bar of) soap. **2 passer un s. à qn** (*gronder*) *Fam* to give s.o. a dressing-down *ou* a talking-to. • **savonner** *vt* to wash with soap. • **savonnette** *nf* bar of soap. • **savonneux, -euse** *a* soapy.
savourer [savure] *vt* to enjoy, savour, relish. • **savoureux, -euse** *a* tasty.
saxophone [saksɔfɔn] *nm* saxophone.
scalpel [skalpɛl] *nm* scalpel.
scandale [skɑ̃dal] *nm* scandal; **faire s.** (*livre etc*) to scandalize people; **faire un s.** to make a scene. • **scandaleux, -euse** *a* shocking, outrageous. • **scandaliser** *vt* to shock, scandalize.
Scandinavie [skɑ̃dinavi] *nf* Scandinavia. • **scandinave** *a & nmf* Scandinavian.
scanner [skanɛr] *nm Méd Ordinat* scanner.
scaphandre [skafɑ̃dr] *nm* (*de plongeur*) diving suit; (*de cosmonaute*) spacesuit; **s. autonome** aqualung.
scarabée [skarabe] *nm* beetle.
scarlatine [skarlatin] *nf* scarlet fever.
scarole [skarɔl] *nf* endive.
sceau, -x [so] *nm* (*cachet*, *cire*) seal. • **sceller** *vt* **1** (*document etc*) to seal. **2** (*fixer*) *Tech* to cement. • **scellés** *nmpl* (*cachets de cire*) seals.
scénario [senarjo] *nm* (*dialogues etc*) film script, screenplay; (*déroulement*) *Fig* scenario. • **scénariste** *nmf Cin* scriptwriter.
scène [sɛn] *nf* **1** *Th* (*plateau*) stage; (*décors*, *partie de pièce*) scene; (*action*) action; **mettre en s.** (*pièce*, *film*) to direct. **2** (*dispute*) scene; **faire une s. (à qn)** to make a scene; **s. de ménage** domestic quarrel.
sceptique [sɛptik] *a* sceptical, *Am* skeptical ‖ *nmf* sceptic, *Am* skeptic.
schéma [ʃema] *nm* diagram. • **schématique** *a* diagrammatic; (*succinct*) *Péj* sketchy.
scie [si] *nf* (*outil*) saw. • **scier** *vt* to saw.
sciemment [sjamɑ̃] *adv* knowingly.
science [sjɑ̃s] *nf* science; (*savoir*) knowledge; **sciences humaines** social science(s); **étudier les sciences** to study science. • **s.-fiction** *nf* science fiction. • **scientifique** *a*

scientific ▌*nmf* scientist.
scinder [sɛ̃de] *vt*, **se s.** *vpr* to divide, split.
scintiller [sɛ̃tije] *vi* to sparkle, glitter; (*étoiles*) to twinkle.
scission [sisjɔ̃] *nf* (*de parti etc*) split (**de** in).
sciure [sjyr] *nf* sawdust.
sclérose [skleroz] *nf* **s. en plaques** multiple sclerosis.
scolaire [skɔlɛr] *a* **année/***etc* **s.** school year/*etc.* ● **scolariser** *vt* (*enfant*) to send to school. ● **scolarité** *nf* schooling.
scooter [skutɛr] *nm* (motor) scooter.
score [skɔr] *nm Sp* score.
scorpion [skɔrpjɔ̃] *nm* scorpion; **le S.** (*signe*) Scorpio.
scotch [skɔtʃ] *nm* **1** (*boisson*) Scotch, whisky. **2**® (*ruban adhésif*) sellotape®, *Am* scotch® tape. ● **scotcher** *vt* to sellotape, *Am* to tape.
scout [skut] *a & nm* scout.
script [skript] *nm* (*écriture*) printing.
scrupule [skrypyl] *nm* scruple; **sans scrupules** unscrupulous; (*agir*) unscrupulously. ● **scrupuleux, -euse** *a* scrupulous.
scruter [skryte] *vt* to examine, scrutinize.
scrutin [skrytɛ̃] *nm* (*vote*) voting, ballot; (*opérations électorales*) poll(ing).
sculpter [skylte] *vt* to carve, sculpture. ● **sculpteur** *nm* sculptor. ● **sculpture** *nf* (*art, œuvre*) sculpture; **s. sur bois** woodcarving.
SDF [ɛsdeɛf] *nm abrév* (*sans domicile fixe*) person of no fixed abode.
se [s(ə)] (**s'** *before vowel or mute h*) *pron* **1** (*complément direct*) himself; (*féminin*) herself; (*non humain*) itself; (*indéfini*) oneself; *pl* themselves; **il se lave** he washes himself. **2** (*indirect*) to himself; to herself; to itself; to oneself; **se dire** to say to oneself.
3 (*réciproque*) each other, one another; (*indirect*) to each other, to one another; **ils s'aiment** they love each other *ou* one another; **ils** *ou* **elles se parlent** they speak to each other *ou* one another.
4 (*possessif*) **il se lave les mains** he washes his hands.
5 (*passif*) **ça se fait** that is done; **ça se vend bien** it sells well.
ⓘ**G84** Reflexive Verbs and Pronouns 7 D
séance [seɑ̃s] *nf* **1** *Cin* show(ing), performance. **2** (*d'assemblée*) session, sitting. **3 s. tenante** at once.
seau, -x [so] *nm* bucket, pail.
sec, sèche [sɛk, sɛʃ] *a* dry; (*fruits, légumes*) dried; (*ton*) curt, harsh; **frapper un coup s.** to knock (sharply), bang; **bruit s.** (*rupture*) snap ▌*adv* (*boire*) neat, *Am* straight ▌*nm* **à s.** dried up, dry; (*sans argent*) *Fam* broke; **au s.** in a dry place.
sécateur [sekatœr] *nm* pruning shears, secateurs.
sèche [sɛʃ] *voir* **sec.** ● **sèche-cheveux** *nm inv* hair dryer. ● **sèche-linge** *nm inv* tumble dryer, *Am* (clothes) dryer.
sécher [seʃe] **1** *vti* to dry ▌**se s.** *vpr* to dry oneself. **2** *vt* (*cours*) *Scol Fam* to skip ▌*vi* (*ignorer*) *Scol Fam* to be stumped. ● **séchage** *nm* drying.
sécheresse [seʃrɛs] *nf* dryness; (*de ton*) curtness; *Mét* drought.
séchoir [seʃwar] *nm* **s. à linge** drying rack, clothes horse.
second, -onde[1] [sgɔ̃, -ɔ̃d] *a & nmf* second ▌*nm* (*adjoint*) second in command; (*étage*) second floor, *Am* third floor ▌*nf Rail* second class; *Scol* = fifth form, *Am* = eleventh grade; (*vitesse*) *Aut* second (gear). ● **secondaire** *a* secondary.
seconde[2] [sgɔ̃d] *nf* (*instant*) second.
secouer [s(ə)kwe] *vt* to shake; (*paresse, poussière*) to shake off; **s. qch de qch** (*enlever*) to shake sth out of sth.
secourir [skurir] *vt* to assist, help. ● **secourisme** *nm* first aid. ● **secouriste** *nmf* first-aid worker.
secours [s(ə)kur] *nm* assistance, help; *pl* (*aux victimes*) aid, relief; **(premiers) s.** *Méd* first aid; **au s.!** help!; **porter s. à qn** to give s.o. assistance; **sortie de s.** emergency exit; **roue de s.** spare wheel.
secousse [s(ə)kus] *nf* jolt, jerk; *Géol* tremor.
secret, -ète [səkrɛ, -ɛt] *a* secret; (*cachottier*) secretive ▌*nm* secret; **en s.** in secret, secretly.
secrétaire [səkretɛr] **1** *nmf* secretary; **s. médicale** (doctor's) receptionist; **s. d'État** Secretary of State. **2** *nm* (*meuble*) writing desk. ● **secrétariat** *nm* (*bureau*) secretary's office; (*métier*) secretarial work; **de s.** (*école, travail*) secretarial.
secte [sɛkt] *nf* sect.
secteur [sɛktœr] *nm Mil Com* sector; (*de ville*) district; (*domaine*) *Fig* area; *Él* mains.
section [sɛksjɔ̃] *nf* section; (*de ligne d'autobus*) fare stage; *Mil* platoon.
séculaire [sekylɛr] *a* (*tradition etc*) age-old.
sécurité [sekyrite] *nf* (*matérielle*) safety; (*tranquillité*) security; **s. routière** road safety; **S. sociale** = social services, Social Security; **ceinture de s.** seat belt; **en s.** safe; secure.
sédatif [sedatif] *nm* sedative.
sédentaire [sedɑ̃tɛr] *a* sedentary.
sédiment [sedimɑ̃] *nm* sediment.

séduire* [sedɥir] *vt* to charm, attract; (*abuser de*) to seduce. ● **séduisant** *a* attractive. ● **séducteur, -trice** *nmf* seducer. ● **séduction** *nf* attraction.
segment [sɛgmɑ̃] *nm* segment.
ségrégation [segregɑsjɔ̃] *nf* segregation.
seigle [sɛgl] *nm* rye; **pain de s.** rye bread.
seigneur [sɛɲœr] *nm Hist* lord; **S.** *Rel* Lord.
sein [sɛ̃] *nm* breast; *Fig* bosom; **donner le s. à** to breastfeed; **au s. de** (*parti etc*) within; (*bonheur etc*) in the midst of.
Seine [sɛn] *nf* **la S.** the Seine.
séisme [seism] *nm* earthquake.
seize [sɛz] *a* & *nm* sixteen. ● **seizième** *a* & *nmf* sixteenth.
séjour [seʒur] *nm* stay; **(salle de) s.** living room. ● **séjourner** *vi* to stay.
sel [sɛl] *nm* salt; **s. de mer** sea salt; **sels de bain** bath salts.
sélection [selɛksjɔ̃] *nf* selection. ● **sélectionner** *vt* to select.
self(-service) [sɛlf(sɛrvis)] *nm* self-service restaurant *ou* shop.
selle [sɛl] *nf* (*de cheval*) saddle. ● **seller** *vt* (*cheval*) to saddle.
sellette [sɛlɛt] *nf* **sur la s.** (*personne*) under examination, in the hot seat.
selon [s(ə)lɔ̃] *prép* according to (**que** whether); **c'est s.** *Fam* it (all) depends.
semaine [s(ə)mɛn] *nf* week; **en s.** (*opposé à week-end*) in the week.
semblable [sɑ̃blabl] *a* similar (**à** to); **être semblables** to be alike *ou* similar ‖ *nm* fellow (creature).
semblant [sɑ̃blɑ̃] *nm* **faire s.** to pretend (**de faire** to do); **un s. de** a semblance of.
sembler [sɑ̃ble] *vi* to seem (**à** to); **il (me) semble vieux** he seems *ou* looks old (to me) ‖ *v imp* **il semble que** (+ *sub ou indic*) it seems that, it looks as if; **il me semble que** (+ *indic*) I think that, it seems to me that.
semelle [s(ə)mɛl] *nf* (*de chaussure*) sole; (*intérieure*) insole.
semer [s(ə)me] *vt* **1** (*graines*) to sow; **semé de** *Fig* strewn with, dotted with. **2** (*concurrent, poursuivant*) to shake off. ● **semence** *nf* seed.
semestre [s(ə)mɛstr] *nm* half-year; *Univ* semester. ● **semestriel, -ielle** *a* half-yearly.
semi- [səmi] *préf* semi-.
séminaire [seminɛr] *nm* **1** *Univ* seminar. **2** *Rel* seminary.
semi-remorque [səmirəmɔrk] *nm* (*camion*) articulated lorry, *Am* semi (trailer).
semoule [s(ə)mul] *nf* semolina.
sénat [sena] *nm Pol* senate. ● **sénateur** *nm Pol* senator.
sénile [senil] *a* senile. ● **sénilité** *nf* senility.
sens [sɑ̃s] *nm* **1** (*faculté*) sense. **2** (*signification*) meaning, sense; **avoir du bon s.** to have sense, be sensible; **ça n'a pas de s.** that doesn't make sense. **3** (*direction*) direction; **s. giratoire** *Aut* roundabout, *Am* traffic circle; **s. interdit** *ou* **unique** (*rue*) one-way street; **'s. interdit'** 'no entry'; **s. dessus dessous** [sɑ̃dsydsu] upside down; **dans le s./le s. inverse des aiguilles d'une montre** clockwise/anticlockwise, *Am* counterclockwise.
sensation [sɑ̃sɑsjɔ̃] *nf* feeling, sensation; **faire s.** to cause a sensation; **à s.** (*film etc*) *Péj* sensational. ● **sensationnel, -elle** *a* sensational.
sensé [sɑ̃se] *a* sensible.
sensible [sɑ̃sibl] *a* sensitive (**à** to); (*douloureux*) tender, sore; (*progrès etc*) noticeable. ● **sensibilité** *nf* sensitivity.
sensuel, -elle [sɑ̃sɥɛl] *a* (*sexuel*) sensual; (*musique, couleur etc*) sensuous. ● **sensualité** *nf* sensuality; sensuousness.
sentence [sɑ̃tɑ̃s] *nf Jur* sentence.
senteur [sɑ̃tœr] *nf* (*odeur*) scent.
sentier [sɑ̃tje] *nm* path.
sentiment [sɑ̃timɑ̃] *nm* feeling; **avoir le s. que** to have a feeling that; **meilleurs sentiments** (*sur une carte de visite etc*) best wishes. ● **sentimental, -aux** *a* sentimental.
sentinelle [sɑ̃tinɛl] *nf* sentry.
sentir* [sɑ̃tir] *vt* to feel; (*odeur*) to smell; (*goût*) to taste; **s. bon** to smell good; **s. le parfum/***etc* to smell of perfume/*etc*; **s. le poisson/***etc* (*avoir le goût de*) to taste of fish/*etc*; **je ne peux pas le s.** (*supporter*) *Fam* I can't stand *ou* bear him; **se s. fatigué/***etc* to feel tired/*etc*; **se faire s.** (*effet etc*) to make itself felt ‖ *vi* to smell.
séparation [separɑsjɔ̃] *nf* separation; (*en deux*) division, split; (*départ*) parting.
séparer [separe] *vt* to separate (**de** from); (*diviser en deux*) to divide, split (up); **plus rien ne nous sépare de la victoire** nothing else stands between us and victory ‖ **se s.** *vpr* (*se quitter*) to part; (*couple*) to separate; **se s. de** (*objet aimé, chien etc*) to part with. ● **séparément** *adv* separately.
sept [sɛt] *a* & *nm* seven. ● **septième** *a* & *nmf* seventh; **un s.** a seventh.
septante [sɛptɑ̃t] *a* & *nm* (*en Belgique, Suisse*) seventy.
septembre [sɛptɑ̃br] *nm* September.
septennat [sɛptena] *nm Pol* seven-year term (of office).

sépulture [sepyltyr] *nf* burial; (*lieu*) burial place.
séquelles [sekɛl] *nfpl* (*de maladie etc*) aftereffects; (*de guerre*) aftermath.
séquence [sekɑ̃s] *nf* (*de film*) sequence.
sera, serai [s(ə)ra, s(ə)rɛ] *voir* **être.**
Serbie [sɛrbi] *nf* Serbia.
serein [sərɛ̃] *a* serene.
sergent [sɛrʒɑ̃] *nm Mil* sergeant.
série [seri] *nf* series; (*ensemble*) set; **s. noire** *Fig* series of disasters; **de s.** (*article etc*) standard; **fabrication en s.** mass production; **fins de s.** *Com* oddments.
sérieux, -euse [serjø, -øz] *a* (*personne, doute etc*) serious; (*fiable*) reliable; (*bénéfices*) substantial; **de sérieuses chances de...** a good chance of... ▮ *nm* seriousness; (*fiabilité*) reliability; **prendre au s.** to take seriously; **garder son s.** to keep a straight face; **manquer de s.** (*travailleur*) to lack application. ● **sérieusement** *adv* seriously; (*travailler*) conscientiously.
seringue [s(ə)rɛ̃g] *nf* syringe.
serment [sɛrmɑ̃] *nm* (*affirmation*) oath; (*promesse*) pledge; **prêter s.** to take an oath; **faire le s. de faire** to swear to do.
sermon [sɛrmɔ̃] *nm Rel* sermon; (*discours*) *Péj* lecture.
séropositif, -ive [seropozitif, -iv] *a Méd* HIV positive. ● **séronégatif, -ive** *a Méd* HIV negative.
serpent [sɛrpɑ̃] *nm* snake; **s. à sonnette** rattlesnake.
serpenter [sɛrpɑ̃te] *vi* to meander.
serpentin [sɛrpɑ̃tɛ̃] *nm* (*ruban*) streamer.
serpillière [sɛrpijɛr] *nf* floor cloth.
serre [sɛr] **1** *nf* greenhouse. **2** *nfpl* (*d'oiseau*) claws, talons.
serrer [sere] *vt* (*tenir*) to grip; (*presser*) to squeeze, press; (*nœud, vis*) to tighten; (*poing*) to clench; (*taille*) to hug; (*frein*) to apply; (*rapprocher*) to close up; **s. la main à qn** to shake hands with s.o.; **s. les dents** *Fig* to grit one's teeth; **s. qn** (*embrasser*) to hug s.o.; (*vêtement*) to be too tight for s.o.; **s. qn de près** (*talonner*) to be close behind s.o.
▮ *vi* **s. à droite** *Aut* to keep (to the) right.
▮ **se serrer** *vpr* (*se rapprocher*) to squeeze up *ou* together; **se s. contre** to squeeze up against. ● **serré** *a* (*nœud, budget etc*) tight; (*gens*) packed (together); (*lutte*) close; (*cœur*) *Fig* heavy.
serre-tête [sɛrtɛt] *nm inv* headband.
serrure [seryr] *nf* lock. ● **serrurier** *nm* locksmith.
servante [sɛrvɑ̃t] *nf* (maid)servant.
serveur, -euse [sɛrvœr, -øz] *nmf* waiter, waitress; (*au bar*) barman, barmaid.
serviable [sɛrvjabl] *a* helpful, obliging.
service [sɛrvis] *nm* service; (*travail*) duty; (*pourboire*) service (charge); (*dans une entreprise*) department; *Tennis* serve, service; **un s.** (*aide*) a favour; **rendre s.** to be of service (**à qn** to s.o.), help (**à qn** s.o.); **s. (non) compris** service (not) included; **s. après-vente** *Com* aftersales service; **s. d'ordre** (*policiers*) police; **être de s.** to be on duty; **s. à café** coffee service *ou* set.
serviette [sɛrvjɛt] *nf* **1** towel; **s. de bain/de toilette** bath/hand towel; **s. hygiénique** sanitary towel *ou Am* napkin; **s. (de table)** napkin, serviette. **2** (*sac*) briefcase.
servile [sɛrvil] *a* servile.
servir* [sɛrvir] **1** *vt* to serve (**qch à qn** s.o. with sth, to s.o.); (*convive*) to wait on ▮ *vi* to serve ▮ **se s.** *vpr* (*à table*) to help oneself (**de** to).
2 *vi* (*être utile*) to be useful, serve; **s. à qch/à faire** (*objet*) to be used for sth/to do *ou* for doing; **ça ne sert à rien** it's useless, it's no good *ou* use (**de faire** doing); **à quoi ça sert de protester**/*etc* what's the use *ou* good of protesting/*etc*; **ça me sert à faire/de qch** I use it to do/as sth; **s. à qn de guide**/*etc* to act as a guide/*etc* to s.o.
3 se servir *vpr* **se s. de** (*utiliser*) to use.
serviteur [sɛrvitœr] *nm* servant.
ses [se] *voir* **son²**.
session [sesjɔ̃] *nf* session.
set [sɛt] *nm* **1** *Tennis* set. **2 s. (de table)** (*napperon*) place mat.
seuil [sœj] *nm* doorstep; (*entrée*) doorway; (*limite*) *Fig* threshold.
seul, seule [sœl] **1** *a* (*sans compagnie*) alone; **tout s.** by oneself, on one's own, all alone; **se sentir s.** to feel lonely *ou* alone ▮ *adv* **(tout) s.** (*rentrer, vivre etc*) by oneself, on one's own, alone; (*parler*) to oneself; **s. à s.** (*parler*) in private.
2 *a* (*unique*) only; **la seule femme**/*etc* the only woman/*etc*; **un s. chat**/*etc* only one cat/*etc*; **une seule fois** only once; **pas un s. livre**/*etc* not a single book/*etc* ▮ *nmf* **le s., la seule** the only one; **un s., une seule** only one, one only; **pas un s.** not (a single) one.
ⓘ **G32** Position of Adjectives 4 D 3
seulement [sœlmɑ̃] *adv* only; **non s.... mais encore...** not only... but (also)....
sève [sɛv] *nf Bot* sap.
sévère [sevɛr] *a* severe; (*parents etc*) strict. ● **sévérité** *nf* severity; strictness.
sévices [sevis] *nmpl* brutality.
sevrer [səvre] *vt* (*enfant*) to wean.

sexe [sɛks] *nm* sex; (*organes*) genitals. ● **sexualité** *nf* sexuality. ● **sexuel, -elle** *a* sexual; **éducation/vie sexuelle** sex education/life.
sextuor [sɛkstɥɔr] *nm* sextet.
shampooing [ʃɑ̃pwɛ̃] *nm* shampoo; **s. colorant** rinse; **faire un s. à qn** to shampoo s.o.'s hair.
shooter [ʃute] **1** *vti Fb* to shoot. **2 se shooter** *vpr* (*avec une drogue*) *Fam* to inject oneself (**à** with).
short [ʃɔrt] *nm* (pair of) shorts.
si[1] [si] **1** (= **s'** [s] *before* **il, ils**) *conj* if; **si je pouvais** if I could; **s'il vient** if he comes; **je me demande si** I wonder whether *ou* if; **si on restait?** (*suggestion*) what if we stayed?
ⓘ**G104** The Conditional 7 G 3
2 *adv* (*tellement*) so; **pas si riche que toi** not as rich as you; **un si bon dîner** such a good dinner; **si bien que** with the result that; **si grand qu'il soit** however big he may be. **3** *adv* (*après négative*) yes; **tu ne viens pas? – si!** you're not coming? – yes (I am)!
ⓘ**G211** Answers 12 D
si[2] [si] *nm* (*note de musique*) B.
Sicile [sisil] *nf* Sicily.
SIDA [sida] *nm Méd* AIDS. ● **sidéen, -enne** *nmf* AIDS sufferer *ou* victim.
sidérurgie [sideryrʒi] *nf* iron and steel industry.
siècle [sjɛkl] *nm* century; (*époque*) age.
ⓘ**G200** Dates 11 B 2c)
siège [sjɛʒ] *nm* **1** (*meuble, centre*) & *Pol* seat; (*de parti etc*) headquarters; **s. (social)** (*d'entreprise*) head office. **2** *Mil* siege. ● **siéger** *vi* (*assemblée etc*) to sit.
sien, sienne [sjɛ̃, sjɛn] *pron poss* **le s., la sienne, les sien(ne)s** his; (*de femme*) hers; (*de chose*) its own; **les deux siens** his *ou* her two ‖ *nmpl* **les siens** (*sa famille*) one's (own) people.
ⓘ**G66** Possessive Pronouns 6 E 2
sieste [sjɛst] *nf* siesta; **faire la s.** to take *ou* have a nap.
siffler [sifle] *vi* to whistle; (*avec un sifflet*) to blow one's whistle; (*gaz, serpent*) to hiss ‖ *vt* (*chanson*) to whistle; (*chien*) to whistle to; (*faute, fin de match*) *Sp* to blow one's whistle for; (*acteur*) to boo. ● **sifflement** *nm* whistling, whistle; hiss(ing).
sifflet [siflɛ] *nm* (*instrument*) whistle; *pl* (*des spectateurs*) *Th* boos; **(coup de) s.** (*son*) whistle.
sigle [sigl] *nm* (*initiales*) abbreviation; (*prononcé comme un mot*) acronym.
signal, -aux [siɲal, -o] *nm* signal; **s. d'alarme** *Rail* alarm, communication cord.
signalement [siɲalmɑ̃] *nm* (*de personne*) description, particulars.
signaler [siɲale] **1** *vt* (*faire remarquer*) to point out (**à qn** to s.o., **que** that); (*indiquer*) to indicate, signal; (*dénoncer à la police etc*) to report (**à** to). **2 se signaler** *vpr* **se s. par** to distinguish oneself by.
signalisation [siɲalizɑsjɔ̃] *nf* signalling; *Aut* signposting; **s. (routière)** (*signaux*) road signs.
signature [siɲatyr] *nf* signature; (*action*) signing. ● **signer 1** *vt* to sign. **2 se signer** *vpr Rel* to cross oneself.
signe [siɲ] *nm* (*indice*) sign, indication; **s. particulier/de ponctuation** distinguishing/punctuation mark; **faire s. à qn** (*geste*) to motion (to) s.o. (**de faire** to do).
signet [siɲɛ] *nm* bookmark.
signification [siɲifikɑsjɔ̃] *nf* meaning. ● **signifier** *vt* to mean, signify (**que** that).
silence [silɑ̃s] *nm* silence; *Mus* rest; **en s.** in silence; **garder le s.** to keep quiet *ou* silent (**sur** about). ● **silencieux, -euse 1** *a* silent. **2** *nm* (*d'arme*) silencer. ● **silencieusement** *adv* silently.
silex [silɛks] *nm* (*roche*) flint.
silhouette [silwɛt] *nf* outline; (*en noir*) silhouette; (*ligne du corps*) figure.
silicium [silisjɔm] *nm* silicon.
sillage [sijaʒ] *nm* (*de bateau*) wake.
sillon [sijɔ̃] *nm* furrow; (*de disque*) groove.
sillonner [sijɔne] *vt* (*traverser*) to cross; (*en tous sens*) to criss-cross.
similaire [similɛr] *a* similar.
similicuir [similikɥir] *nm* imitation leather.
simple [sɛ̃pl] *a* simple; (*non multiple*) single; (*employé*) ordinary ‖ *nmf* **s. d'esprit** simpleton ‖ *nm Tennis* singles. ● **simplement** *adv* simply. ● **simplicité** *nf* simplicity. ● **simplification** *nf* simplification. ● **simplifier** *vt* to simplify.
ⓘ**simple G32** Position of Adjectives 4 D 3
simulacre [simylakr] *nm* **un s. de** *Péj* a pretence *ou Am* pretense of.
simuler [simyle] *vt* to simulate; (*feindre*) to feign.
simultané [simyltane] *a* simultaneous. ● **—ment** *adv* simultaneously.
sincère [sɛ̃sɛr] *a* sincere. ● **sincèrement** *adv* sincerely. ● **sincérité** *nf* sincerity.
singe [sɛ̃ʒ] *nm* monkey, ape. ● **singeries** *nfpl* antics.
singulariser (se) [səsɛ̃gylarize] *vpr* to draw attention to oneself.
singulier, -ière [sɛ̃gylje, -jɛr] **1** *a* (*peu ordinaire*) peculiar, odd. **2** *a* & *nm Gram* singular; **au s.** in the singular.

sinistre [sinistr] **1** *a* (*effrayant*) sinister. **2** *nm* disaster; (*incendie*) fire. ● **sinistré, -ée** *a* (*population, région*) disaster-stricken ‖ *nmf* disaster victim.
sinon [sinɔ̃] *conj* (*autrement*) otherwise, or else; (*sauf*) except (**que** that); (*si ce n'est*) if not.
sinueux, -euse [sinɥø, -øz] *a* winding.
sinus [sinys] *nm inv Anat* sinus. ● **sinusite** *nf* sinusitis.
siphon [sifɔ̃] *nm* siphon; (*d'évier*) trap, U-bend.
sirène [sirɛn] *nf* **1** (*d'usine etc*) siren. **2** (*femme*) mermaid.
sirop [siro] *nm* syrup; (*à diluer*) (fruit) cordial, fruit drink; **s. contre la toux** cough medicine *ou* mixture.
site [sit] *nm* (*endroit*) site; (*environnement*) setting; **s. (touristique)** (*monument etc*) place of interest.
sitôt [sito] *adv* **s. levée, elle partit** as soon as she was up, she left; **pas de s.** not for some time.
situation [sitɥasjɔ̃] *nf* situation, position; (*emploi*) position; **s. de famille** marital status. ● **situer** *vt* to situate, locate ‖ **se s.** *vpr* (*se trouver*) to be situated. ● **situé** *a* (*maison etc*) situated (**à** in).
six [sis] ([si] *before consonant*, [siz] *before vowel*) *a* & *nm* six. ● **sixième** *a* & *nmf* sixth ‖ *nf Scol* = first form; *Am* = sixth grade.
sketch [skɛtʃ] *nm* (*pl* **sketches**) *Th* sketch.
ski [ski] *nm* (*objet*) ski; (*sport*) skiing; **faire du s.** to ski; **s. de fond** cross-country skiing; **s. nautique** water skiing. ● **skier** *vi* to ski. ● **skieur, -euse** *nmf* skier.
slalom [slalɔm] *nm Sp* slalom.
slip [slip] *nm* (*d'homme*) briefs, (under)pants; (*de femme*) panties, knickers; **s. de bain** (swimming) trunks.
slogan [slɔgɑ̃] *nm* slogan.
SMIC [smik] *nm abrév* (*salaire minimum interprofessionnel de croissance*) guaranteed minimum wage.
smoking [smɔkiŋ] *nm* (*costume*) dinner jacket, *Am* tuxedo.
SNCF [ɛsɛnseɛf] *nf abrév* (*Société nationale des chemins de fer français*) French railways, *Am* French railroad system.
sniffer [snife] *vt* **s. de la colle** *Arg* to sniff glue.
snob [snɔb] *nmf* snob ‖ *a* snobbish.
sobre [sɔbr] *a* sober.
sociable [sɔsjabl] *a* sociable.
social, -aux [sɔsjal, -o] *a* social. ● **socialiste** *a* & *nmf* socialist.
société [sɔsjete] *nf* society; (*compagnie*) company; **s. anonyme** *Com* (public) limited company, *Am* incorporated company.
sociologie [sɔsjɔlɔʒi] *nf* sociology. ● **sociologue** *nmf* sociologist.
socle [sɔkl] *nm* (*de statue, colonne*) plinth, pedestal; (*de lampe*) base.
socquette [sɔkɛt] *nf* ankle sock.
sœur [sœr] *nf* sister; *Rel* nun, sister.
sofa [sɔfa] *nm* sofa, settee.
soi [swa] *pron* oneself; **chacun pour s.** every man for himself; **en s.** in itself; **cela va de soi** it's self-evident (**que** that). ● **s.-même** *pron* oneself.

ⓘ **soi G62** Disjunctive Pronouns 6 D 5

soi-disant [swadizɑ̃] *a inv* so-called ‖ *adv* supposedly.
soie [swa] *nf* **1** silk. **2** (*de porc etc*) bristle.
soient [swa] *voir* **être**.
soif [swaf] *nf* thirst (*Fig* **de** for); **avoir s.** to be thirsty; **donner s. à qn** to make s.o. thirsty.
soigner [swaɲe] *vt* to look after, take care of; (*maladie*) to treat; (*présentation*) to take care over; **se faire s.** to have (medical) treatment.
‖ **se soigner** *vpr* to take care of oneself, look after oneself. ● **soigné** *a* (*vêtement*) neat, tidy; (*travail*) careful; (*personne*) well-groomed. ● **soigneux, -euse** *a* careful (**de** with); (*propre*) neat, tidy. ● **soigneusement** *adv* carefully.
soin [swɛ̃] *nm* care; (*ordre*) tidiness, neatness; *pl Méd* treatment, care; **avec s.** carefully, with care; **avoir** *ou* **prendre s. de qch/de faire** to take care of sth/to do; **les premiers soins** first aid.
soir [swar] *nm* evening; **le s.** (*chaque soir*) in the evening(s); **à neuf heures du s.** at nine in the evening; **repas du s.** evening meal. ● **soirée** *nf* evening; (*réunion*) party.

ⓘ **soirée G200** Dates 11 B 3

sois, soit [swa] *voir* **être**.
soit 1 [swa] *conj* (*à savoir*) that is (to say); **s. ... s. ...** either ... or .... **2** [swat] *adv* (*oui*) very well.
soixante [swasɑ̃t] *a* & *nm* sixty. ● **soixantaine** *nf* **une s. (de)** (*nombre*) (about) sixty. ● **soixantième** *a* & *nmf* sixtieth.
soixante-dix [swasɑ̃tdis] *a* & *nm* seventy. ● **s.-dixième** *a* & *nmf* seventieth.
soja [sɔʒa] *nm* (*plante*) soya; **germes de s.** beansprouts.
sol[1] [sɔl] *nm* ground; (*plancher*) floor; (*territoire*) soil.
sol[2] [sɔl] *nm* (*note de musique*) G.
solaire [sɔlɛr] *a* solar; (*rayons, chaleur*) sun's; **crème/huile s.** sun(tan) lotion/oil.

soldat [sɔlda] *nm* soldier; **simple s.** private.
solde [sɔld] **1** *nm* (*de compte*) balance. **2** *nm* **en s.** (*acheter*) at sale price, *Am* on sale; *pl* (*marchandises*) sale goods; (*vente*) (clearance) sale(s). **3** *nf Mil* pay.
solder [sɔlde] **1** *vt* (*articles*) to clear, sell off. **2** *vt* (*compte*) to pay the balance of. **3 se solder** *vpr* **se s. par un échec**/*etc* to end in failure/*etc*. • **soldé** *a* (*article etc*) reduced.
sole [sɔl] *nf* (*poisson*) sole.
soleil [sɔlɛj] *nm* sun; (*chaleur, lumière*) sunshine; **au s.** in the sun; **il fait (du) s.** it's sunny, the sun's shining; **coup de s.** *Méd* sunburn; **prendre un bain de s.** to sunbathe.
solennel, -elle [sɔlanɛl] *a* solemn.
solex® [sɔlɛks] *nm* moped.
solfège [sɔlfɛʒ] *nm* rudiments of music.
solidaire [sɔlidɛr] *a* **être s.** (*ouvriers etc*) to show solidarity (**de** with); (*pièce de machine*) to be interdependent (**de** with). • **solidarité** *nf* solidarity; (*d'éléments*) interdependence.
solide [sɔlid] *a* solid; (*argument*) sound; (*vigoureux*) robust ‖ *nm Ch* solid. • **solidement** *adv* solidly. • **solidité** *nf* solidity; (*d'argument etc*) soundness.
soliste [sɔlist] *nmf Mus* soloist.
solitaire [sɔlitɛr] *a* (*vie, passant etc*) solitary; (*tout seul*) all alone ‖ *nmf* loner; **en s.** on one's own. • **solitude** *nf* solitude; **aimer la s.** to like being alone.
solliciter [sɔlisite] *vt* (*audience, emploi etc*) to seek; **s. qn** (*faire appel à*) to appeal to s.o.
solo [sɔlo] *a inv* & *nm Mus* solo.
soluble [sɔlybl] *a* (*substance, problème*) soluble; **café s.** instant coffee.
solution [sɔlysjɔ̃] *nf* (*d'un problème etc*) & *Ch* solution (**de** to).
solvable [sɔlvabl] *a Fin* solvent.
sombre [sɔ̃br] *a* dark; (*triste*) sombre, gloomy; **il fait s.** it's dark.
sombrer [sɔ̃bre] *vi* (*bateau*) to sink; **s. dans** (*folie, sommeil etc*) to sink into.
sommaire [sɔmɛr] *a* summary; (*repas, tenue*) scant ‖ *nm* summary, synopsis.
somme [sɔm] **1** *nf* sum; **faire la s. de** to add up; **en s., s. toute** in short. **2** *nm* (*sommeil*) nap; **faire un s.** to take *ou* have a nap.
sommeil [sɔmɛj] *nm* sleep; **avoir s.** to be *ou* feel sleepy.
sommelier [sɔməlje] *nm* wine waiter.
sommer [sɔme] *vt* **s. qn de faire qch** (*enjoindre*) & *Jur* to summon s.o. to do sth.
sommes [sɔm] *voir* **être.**
sommet [sɔmɛ] *nm* top; (*de la gloire etc*) *Fig* height; **conférence au s.** summit (conference).
sommier [sɔmje] *nm* (*de lit*) base.
sommité [sɔmite] *nf* leading light, top person (**de** in).
somnambule [sɔmnɑ̃byl] *nmf* sleepwalker; **être s.** to sleepwalk.
somnifère [sɔmnifɛr] *nm* sleeping pill.
somnoler [sɔmnɔle] *vi* to doze, drowse.
somptueux, -euse [sɔ̃ptɥø, -øz] *a* sumptuous.
son[1] [sɔ̃] *nm* **1** (*bruit*) sound. **2** (*de grains*) bran.
son[2], **sa,** *pl* **ses** [sɔ̃, sa, se] (**sa** *becomes* **son** [sɔ̃n] *before a vowel or mute h*) *a poss* his; (*de femme*) her; (*de chose*) its; (*indéfini*) one's; **son père/sa mère** his *ou* her *ou* one's father/mother; **son ami(e)** his *ou* her *ou* one's friend; **sa durée** its duration.
ⓘ **G64** Possessive Adjectives 6 E 1
sondage [sɔ̃daʒ] *nm* **s. (d'opinion)** opinion poll.
sonde [sɔ̃d] *nf Géol* drill; *Nau* sounding line; *Méd* probe; **s. spatiale** space probe.
songe [sɔ̃ʒ] *nm* dream.
song/er [sɔ̃ʒe] *vi* **s. à qch/à faire qch** to think of sth/of doing sth. • **—eur, -euse** *a* thoughtful.
sonner [sɔne] *vi* to ring; (*cor, cloches etc*) to sound; **on a sonné** (*à la porte*) someone has rung the (door)bell ‖ *vt* (*cloche*) to ring; (*domestique*) to ring for; (*cor etc*) to sound; (*l'heure*) to strike.
sonnerie [sɔnri] *nf* (*son*) ring(ing); (*appareil*) bell; (*au bout du fil*) ringing tone, *Am* ring; **s. 'occupé'** engaged tone, *Am* busy signal.
sonnette [sɔnɛt] *nf* bell; **coup de s.** ring; **s. d'alarme** alarm (bell).
sonore [sɔnɔr] *a* (*rire*) loud; (*salle, voix*) resonant; **ondes sonores** sound waves. • **sonorité** *nf* (*de salle*) acoustics; (*de violon etc*) tone.
sonorisation [sɔnɔrizɑsjɔ̃] *nf* (*Fam* **sono**) (*matériel*) sound equipment *ou* system. • **sonoriser** *vt* (*salle*) to wire for sound.
sont [sɔ̃] *voir* **être.**
sophistiqué [sɔfistike] *a* sophisticated.
soprano [sɔprano] *nmf* (*personne*) *Mus* soprano.
sorbet [sɔrbɛ] *nm Culin* water ice, sorbet.
sorcellerie [sɔrsɛlri] *nf* witchcraft. • **sorcier** *nm* sorcerer. • **sorcière** *nf* witch; **chasse aux sorcières** *Pol* witch-hunt.
sordide [sɔrdid] *a* (*affaire etc*) sordid; (*maison etc*) squalid.
sort [sɔr] *nm* **1** (*destin, hasard*) fate; (*condition*) lot. **2** (*maléfice*) spell.

sorte [sɔrt] *nf* sort, kind (**de** of); **toutes sortes de** all sorts *ou* kinds of; **en quelque s.** in a way; **de (telle) s. que** (+*sub*) so that, in such a way that; **de s. que** (+ *indic*) (*conséquence*) so that, with the result that; **faire en s. que** (+ *sub*) to see to it that.

sortie [sɔrti] *nf* **1** (*porte*) exit, way out; (*promenade à pied*) walk; (*en voiture*) drive; (*excursion*) outing; (*de film, disque*) release; (*de livre, modèle*) appearance; *Ordinat* output; *pl* (*argent*) outgoings; **à la s. de l'école** when the children come out of school. **2 s. de bain** (*peignoir*) bathrobe.

sortir* [sɔrtir] *vi* (*aux* **être**) to go out, leave; (*venir*) to come out; (*pour s'amuser, danser etc*) to go out; (*film etc*) to come out; (*numéro gagnant*) to come up; **s. de** (*endroit*) to leave; (*université*) to be a graduate of; (*famille, milieu*) to come from; (*légalité, limites*) to go beyond; **s. de table** to leave the table; **s. de terre** (*plante, fondations*) to come up; **s. de l'ordinaire** to be out of the ordinary; **s. indemne** to escape unhurt (**de** from).
▮ *vt* (*aux* **avoir**) to take out (**de** of); (*film, modèle, livre etc*) to bring out; (*expulser*) *Fam* to throw out; **s'en s., se s. d'affaire** to pull *ou* come through.

SOS [ɛsoɛs] *nm* SOS; **SOS médecins** emergency medical services.

sosie [sozi] *nm* (*de personne*) double.

sot, sotte [so, sɔt] *a* foolish ▮ *nmf* fool. ● **sottise** *nf* foolishness; (*action, parole*) foolish thing; **faire des sottises** (*enfant*) to be naughty.

sou [su] *nm* **sous** (*argent*) money; **elle n'a pas un** *ou* **le s.** she doesn't have a penny; **machine à sous** fruit machine, *Am* slot machine.

soubresaut [subrəso] *nm* (sudden) start.

souche [suʃ] *nf* (*d'arbre*) stump; (*de carnet*) stub, counterfoil; (*de vigne*) stock.

souci [susi] *nm* (*inquiétude*) worry; (*préoccupation*) concern (**de** for); **se faire du s.** to worry, be worried; **ça lui donne du s.** it worries him *ou* her. ● **se soucier** *vpr* **se s. de** to be worried *ou* concerned about. ● **soucieux, -euse** *a* worried, concerned (**de qch** about sth).

soucoupe [sukup] *nf* saucer; **s. volante** flying saucer.

soudain [sudɛ̃] *a* sudden ▮ *adv* suddenly. ● **soudainement** *adv* suddenly.

Soudan [sudɑ̃] *nm* Sudan.

soude [sud] *nf Ch* soda.

souder [sude] *vt* (*avec de la soudure*) to solder; (*par soudure autogène*) to weld; (*groupes etc*) *Fig* to unite (closely). ● **soudure** *nf* (*substance*) solder.

souffle [sufl] *nm* puff, blow; (*haleine*) breath; (*respiration*) breathing; (*de bombe etc*) blast; **s. (d'air)** breath of air. ● **souffler** *vi* to blow; (*haleter*) to puff ▮ *vt* (*bougie*) to blow out; (*par une explosion*) to blow down, blast; (*chuchoter*) to whisper; **s. son rôle à qn** *Th* to prompt s.o.; **ne pas s. mot** not to breathe a word. ● **soufflet** *nm* (*instrument*) bellows. ● **souffleur, -euse** *nmf Th* prompter.

soufflé [sufle] *nm Culin* soufflé.

souffrance [sufrɑ̃s] *nf* **1 souffrance(s)** suffering. **2 en s.** (*colis etc*) unclaimed.

souffr/ir* [sufrir] **1** *vi* to suffer; **s. de** to suffer from; (*gorge, pieds etc*) to have trouble with; **faire s. qn** to hurt s.o. **2** *vt* (*endurer*) to suffer; **je ne peux pas le s.** I can't bear him. ● **souffrant** *a* unwell.

soufre [sufr] *nm* sulphur, *Am* sulfur.

souhait [swɛ] *nm* wish; **à vos souhaits!** (*après un éternuement*) bless you! ● **souhaiter** *vt* (*bonheur etc*) to wish for; **s. qch à qn** to wish s.o. sth; **s. faire** to wish to do; (*espérer*) to hope to do; **s. que** (+ *sub*) to hope that. ● **souhaitable** *a* desirable.

soûl [su] *a* drunk. ● **soûler** *vt* to make drunk ▮ **se s.** *vpr* to get drunk.

soulager [sulaʒe] *vt* to relieve (**de** of). ● **soulagement** *nm* relief.

soulever [sulve] *vt* to lift (up), raise; (*poussière, question*) to raise; (*le peuple*) to stir up; (*sentiment*) to arouse; **cela me soulève le cœur** it makes me feel sick ▮ **se s.** *vpr* (*malade etc*) to lift oneself (up); (*se révolter*) to rise (up). ● **soulèvement** *nm* (*révolte*) uprising.

soulier [sulje] *nm* shoe.

souligner [suliɲe] *vt* (*d'un trait*) to underline; (*faire remarquer*) to emphasize (**que** that).

soumettre* [sumɛtr] **1** *vt* (*pays, rebelles*) to subdue; **s. à** (*assujettir*) to subject to ▮ **se s.** *vpr* to submit (**à** to). **2** *vt* (*présenter*) to submit (**à** to). ● **soumis** *a* (*docile*) submissive; **s. à** subject to.

soupape [supap] *nf* valve.

soupçon [supsɔ̃] *nm* suspicion. ● **soupçonner** *vt* to suspect (**de** of, **d'avoir fait** of doing, **que** that). ● **soupçonneux, -euse** *a* suspicious.

soupe [sup] *nf* soup. ● **soupière** *nf* (soup) tureen.

soupente [supɑ̃t] *nf* (*sous le toit*) loft.

souper [supe] *nm* supper ▮ *vi* to have supper.

soupeser [supəze] *vt* (*objet dans la main*) to feel the weight of.
soupir [supir] *nm* sigh. ● **soupirer** *vi* to sigh.
soupirail, -aux [supiraj, -o] *nm* basement window.
souple [supl] *a* supple; (*tolérant*) flexible. ● **souplesse** *nf* suppleness; flexibility.
source [surs] *nf* **1** (*point d'eau*) spring; **eau de s.** spring water; **prendre sa s.** (*rivière*) to rise (**à** at, **dans** in). **2** (*origine*) source; **de s. sûre** on good authority.
sourcil [sursi] *nm* eyebrow.
sourd, sourde [sur, surd] **1** *a* deaf (*Fig* **à** to) ‖ *nmf* deaf person. **2** *a* (*douleur*) dull; **bruit s.** thump. ● **s.-muet** (*pl* **sourds-muets**), **sourde-muette** (*pl* **sourdes-muettes**) *a* & *nmf* deaf and dumb (person).
souricière [surisjɛr] *nf* mousetrap; *Fig* trap.
sourire* [surir] *vi* to smile (**à** at); **s. à qn** (*fortune*) to smile on s.o. ‖ *nm* smile; **faire un s. à qn** to give s.o. a smile.
souris [suri] *nf* (*animal*) & *Ordinat* mouse (*pl* mice).
sournois [surnwa] *a* sly, underhand.
sous [su] *prép* (*position*) under(neath), beneath; **s. l'eau** underwater; **s. la pluie** in the rain; **s. antibiotiques** on antibiotics; **s. le nom de** under the name of; **s. Charles X** under Charles X; **s. peu** (*bientôt*) shortly. ⓘ G183 Prepositions 8
sous- [su] *préf* (*subordination*, *subdivision*) sub-; (*insuffisance*) under-.
sous-alimenté [suzalimɑ̃te] *a* underfed.
sous-bois [subwa] *nm* undergrowth.
sous-chef [suʃɛf] *nmf* second-in-command.
souscrire* [suskrir] *vi* **s. à** (*payer*, *approuver*) to subscribe to. ● **souscription** *nf* subscription.
sous-développé [sudevlɔpe] *a* (*pays*) underdeveloped.
sous-directeur, -trice [sudirɛktœr, -tris] *nmf* assistant manager *ou* manageress.
sous-emploi [suzɑ̃plwa] *nm* underemployment.
sous-entendre [suzɑ̃tɑ̃dr] *vt* to imply.
sous-estimer [suzɛstime] *vt* to underestimate.
sous-louer [sulwe] *vt* to sublet.
sous-marin [sumarɛ̃] *a* underwater; **plongée sous-marine** skin diving ‖ *nm* submarine.
sous-officier [suzɔfisje] *nm* noncommissioned officer.
soussigné, -ée [susiɲe] *nmf* **je s.** I the undersigned.
sous-sol [susɔl] *nm* (*d'immeuble*) basement.
sous-titre [sutitr] *nm* subtitle.
soustraire* [sustrɛr] *vt Math* to take away, subtract (**de** from); **s. qn à** (*danger etc*) to shield s.o. from. ● **soustraction** *nf Math* subtraction.
sous-verre [suvɛr] *nm inv* (*encadrement*) (frameless) glass mount.
sous-vêtements [suvɛtmɑ̃] *nmpl* underwear.
soutane [sutan] *nf* (*de prêtre*) cassock.
soute [sut] *nf* (*magasin*) *Nau* hold.
soutenir* [sutnir] *vt* to support, hold up; (*opinion*) to uphold, maintain; (*candidat etc*) to back, support; (*effort*, *intérêt*) to sustain, keep up; (*thèse*) to defend; **s. que** to maintain that ‖ **se s.** *vpr* (*blessé etc*) to hold oneself up (straight); (*se maintenir, durer*) to be sustained.
souterrain [sutɛrɛ̃] *a* underground ‖ *nm* underground passage.
soutien [sutjɛ̃] *nm* support; (*personne*) supporter; **s. de famille** breadwinner. ● **s.-gorge** *nm* (*pl* **soutiens-gorge**) bra.
souvenir [suvnir] *nm* memory; (*objet*) memento; (*cadeau*) keepsake; (*pour touristes*) souvenir; **en s. de** in memory of. ● **se souvenir*** *vpr* **se s. de** to remember, recall; **se s. que** to remember *ou* recall that; **se s. d'avoir fait** to remember *ou* recall doing.
souvent [suvɑ̃] *adv* often; **peu s.** seldom; **le plus s.** usually, more often than not.
souverain, -aine [suvrɛ̃, -ɛn] *a* sovereign ‖ *nmf* sovereign. ● **souveraineté** *nf* sovereignty.
soyeux, -euse [swajø, -øz] a silky.
soyons, soyez [swajɔ̃, swaje] *voir* **être**.
spacieux, -euse [spasjø, -øz] *a* spacious, roomy.
spaghetti(s) [spageti] *nmpl* spaghetti.
sparadrap [sparadra] *nm Méd* sticking plaster, *Am* adhesive tape.
spasme [spasm] *nm* spasm.
spatial, -aux [spasjal, -o] *a* **station**/*etc* **spatiale** space station/*etc*; **engin s.** spaceship, spacecraft.
speaker [spikœr] *nm*, **speakerine** [spikrin] *nf Rad TV* announcer.
spécial, -aux [spesjal, -o] *a* special; (*bizarre*) peculiar. ● **spécialement** *adv* (*exprès*) specially.
spécialiser (se) [səspesjalize] *vpr* to specialize (**dans** in). ● **spécialiste** *nmf* specialist. ● **spécialité** *nf* speciality, *Am* specialty.
spécifier [spesifje] *vt* to specify (**que** that).
spécimen [spesimɛn] *nm* specimen; (*livre*

etc) specimen copy.

spectacle [spɛktakl] *nm* **1** (*vue*) sight, spectacle. **2** (*représentation*) show; **le s.** (*industrie*) show business. ● **spectateur, -trice** *nmf Sp* spectator; *Th Cin* member of the audience; *pl Th Cin* audience.

spectaculaire [spɛktakylɛr] *a* spectacular.

spéculer [spekyle] *vi Fin Phil* to speculate; **s. sur** (*tabler sur*) to bank *ou* rely on.

spéléologie [speleɔlɔʒi] *nf* (*activité*) potholing, *Am* spelunking.

sperme [spɛrm] *nm* sperm, semen.

sphère [sfɛr] *nf* (*boule, domaine*) sphere.

sphinx [sfɛ̃ks] *nm* sphinx.

spirale [spiral] *nf* spiral.

spirituel, -elle [spiritɥɛl] *a* **1** (*amusant*) witty. **2** (*pouvoir, vie etc*) spiritual.

spiritueux [spiritɥø] *nmpl* (*boissons*) spirits.

splendide [splɑ̃did] *a* (*merveilleux, riche, beau etc*) splendid. ● **splendeur** *nf* splendour.

spontané [spɔ̃tane] *a* spontaneous. ● **spontanéité** *nf* spontaneity.

sport [spɔr] *nm* sport; **faire du s.** to play sport *ou Am* sports; **(de) s.** (*chaussures, vêtements*) casual, sports; **voiture/veste/terrain de s.** sports car/jacket/ground. ● **sportif, -ive** *a* (*personne*) fond of sport *ou Am* sports; (*association, journal*) sports; (*allure*) athletic ‖ *nmf* sportsman, sportswoman.

spot [spɔt] *nm* **1** (*lampe*) spotlight. **2 s. (publicitaire)** *Rad TV* commercial.

sprint [sprint] *nm Sp* sprint.

square [skwar] *nm* public garden.

squash [skwaʃ] *nm* (*jeu*) squash.

squelette [skəlɛt] *nm* skeleton.

stable [stabl] *a* stable. ● **stabiliser** *vt* to stabilize ‖ **se s.** *vpr* to stabilize.

stade [stad] *nm* **1** *Sp* stadium. **2** (*phase*) stage.

stage [staʒ] *nm* training period; (*cours*) (training) course. ● **stagiaire** *a & nmf* trainee.

stagner [stagne] *vi* to stagnate.

stalle [stal] *nf* (*box*) & *Rel* stall.

stand [stɑ̃d] *nm* (*d'exposition etc*) stand, stall; **s. de ravitaillement** *Sp* pit; **s. de tir** (*de foire*) shooting range.

standard [stɑ̃dar] **1** *nm Tél* switchboard. **2** *a inv* (*modèle etc*) standard. ● **standardiste** *nmf* (switchboard) operator.

starter [startɛr] *nm* **1** *Aut* choke. **2** *Sp* starter.

station [stɑsjɔ̃] *nf* (*de métro, d'observation etc*) & *Rad* station; (*de ski etc*) resort; **s. de taxis** taxi rank, *Am* taxi stand; **s. (thermale)** spa. ● **s.-service** *nf* (*pl* **stations-service**) *Aut* service station, petrol *ou Am* gas station.

stationnaire [stasjɔnɛr] *a* stationary.

stationn/er [stasjɔne] *vi* (*être garé*) to be parked. ● **—ement** *nm* parking.

statique [statik] *a* static.

statistique [statistik] *nf* (*donnée*) statistic; **la s.** (*techniques*) statistics ‖ *a* statistical.

statue [staty] *nf* statue.

statuer [statɥe] *vi* **s. sur** *Jur* to rule on.

stature [statyr] *nf* stature.

statut [staty] *nm* **1** (*position*) status. **2 statuts** (*règles*) statutes.

steak [stɛk] *nm* steak.

sténo [steno] *nf* (*personne*) stenographer; (*sténographie*) shorthand, stenography; **prendre en s.** to take down in shorthand. ● **sténodactylo** *nf* shorthand typist, *Am* stenographer. ● **sténographie** *nf* shorthand, stenography.

stéréo [stereo] *nf* stereo; **en s.** in stereo ‖ *a inv* (*disque etc*) stereo.

stérile [steril] *a* sterile; (*terre*) barren. ● **stériliser** *vt* to sterilize. ● **stérilité** *nf* sterility; (*de terre*) barrenness.

stérilet [sterilɛ] *nm* IUD, coil.

stéroïde [sterɔid] *nm* steroid.

stéthoscope [stetɔskɔp] *nm* stethoscope.

stigmatiser [stigmatize] *vt* (*dénoncer*) to stigmatize.

stimul/er [stimyle] *vt* to stimulate. ● **—ant** *nm Fig* stimulus; *Méd* stimulant. ● **stimulateur** *nm* **s. cardiaque** pacemaker.

stipuler [stipyle] *vt* to stipulate (**que** that).

stock [stɔk] *nm Com & Fig* stock (**de** of); **en s.** in stock. ● **stocker** *vt* (*provisions*) to store, stock.

stop [stɔp] **1** *int* stop ‖ *nm* (*panneau*) *Aut* stop sign; (*feu arrière*) *Aut* brake light, stoplight. **2** *nm* **faire du s.** *Fam* to hitchhike. ● **stopper 1** *vti* to stop. **2** *vt* (*vêtement*) to mend (invisibly).

store [stɔr] *nm* blind, *Am* (window) shade; (*de magasin*) awning.

strabisme [strabism] *nm* squint.

strapontin [strapɔ̃tɛ̃] *nm* tip-up *ou* folding seat.

stratégie [strateʒi] *nf* strategy. ● **stratégique** *a* strategic.

stress [strɛs] *nm Psy* stress. ● **stressant** *a* stressful. ● **stressé** *a* under stress.

strict [strikt] *a* strict; (*tenue, vérité*) plain; (*droit*) basic; **le s. minimum** the bare minimum. ● **strictement** *adv* strictly; (*vêtu*) plainly.

strident [stridɑ̃] *a* shrill, strident.

strophe [strɔf] *nf* verse, stanza.
structure [stryktyr] *nf* structure.
studieux, -euse [stydjø, -øz] *a* studious; (*vacances etc*) devoted to study.
studio [stydjo] *nm Cin TV Phot* studio; (*logement*) studio flat *ou Am* apartment.
stupéfait [stypefɛ] *a* amazed (**de** at, by). ● **stupéfaction** *nf* amazement.
stupéfier [stypefje] *vt* to amaze. ● **stupéfiant 1** *a* amazing. **2** *nm* drug, narcotic.
stupeur [stypœr] *nf* **1** (*étonnement*) amazement. **2** (*inertie*) stupor.
stupide [stypid] *a* stupid. ● **stupidité** *nf* stupidity; (*action, parole*) stupid thing.
style [stil] *nm* style; **meubles de s.** period furniture. ● **styliste** *nmf* (*de mode etc*) designer.
stylé [stile] *a* well-trained.
stylo [stilo] *nm* pen; **s. à bille** ballpoint (pen), biro®; **s. à encre, s.-plume** fountain pen.
su [sy] *pp de* **savoir.**
suave [sɥav] *a* (*odeur, voix*) sweet.
subalterne [sybaltɛrn] *a & nmf* subordinate.
subconscient [sypkɔ̃sjɑ̃] *a & nm* subconscious.
subir [sybir] *vt* to undergo; (*conséquences, défaite, perte*) to suffer; (*influence*) to be under; **s. qn** (*supporter*) *Fam* to put up with s.o.
subit [sybi] *a* sudden. ● **subitement** *adv* suddenly.
subjectif, -ive [sybʒɛktif, -iv] *a* subjective.
subjonctif [sybʒɔ̃ktif] *nm Gram* subjunctive.
subjuguer [sybʒyge] *vt* to subjugate, subdue; (*envoûter*) to captivate.
sublime [syblim] *a & nm* sublime.
submerger [sybmɛrʒe] *vt* to submerge; **plaine**/*etc* **submergée** flooded plain/*etc*; **submergé de travail** *Fig* overwhelmed with work.
subordonn/er [sybɔrdɔne] *vt* to subordinate (**à** to). ● **—é, -ée** *a* subordinate (**à** to); **être s. à** (*dépendre de*) to depend on ‖ *nmf* subordinate.
subsidiaire [sybsidjɛr] *a* subsidiary; **question s.** (*de concours*) deciding question.
subsister [sybziste] *vi* (*rester*) to remain; (*vivre*) to get by, subsist.
substance [sypstɑ̃s] *nf* substance; **en s.** *Fig* in essence. ● **substantiel, -ielle** *a* substantial.
substituer [sypstitɥe] *vt* to substitute (**à** for); **se s. à qn** to take the place of s.o.
subterfuge [sypterfyʒ] *nm* subterfuge.
subtil [syptil] *a* subtle.
subtiliser [syptilize] *vt* (*dérober*) *Fam* to make off with.
subvenir* [sybvənir] *vi* **s. à** (*besoins, frais*) to meet.
subvention [sybvɑ̃sjɔ̃] *nf* subsidy. ● **subventionner** *vt* to subsidize.
subversif, -ive [sybvɛrsif, -iv] *a* subversive.
suc [syk] *nm* (*gastrique, de fruit*) juice; (*de plante*) sap.
succéder [syksede] *vi* **s. à qn** to succeed s.o.; **s. à qch** to follow sth, come after sth. ‖ **se s.** *vpr* to follow one another.
succès [syksɛ] *nm* success; **s. de librairie** (*livre*) best-seller; **avoir du s.** to be successful, be a success; **à s.** (*auteur, film etc*) successful; **avec s.** successfully.
successeur [syksesœr] *nm* successor. ● **successif, -ive** *a* successive. ● **succession** *nf* succession; (*série*) sequence (**de** of); (*patrimoine*) *Jur* inheritance, estate; **prendre la s. de qn** to succeed s.o.
succomber [sykɔ̃be] *vi* (*mourir*) to die; **s. à ses blessures** to die of one's wounds.
succulent [sykylɑ̃] *a* succulent.
succursale [sykyrsal] *nf Com* branch.
sucer [syse] *vt* to suck. ● **sucette** *nf* lollipop; (*tétine*) dummy, comforter, *Am* pacifier.
sucre [sykr] *nm* sugar; (*morceau*) sugar lump; **s. cristallisé** granulated sugar; **s. en morceaux** lump sugar; **s. en poudre, s. semoule** caster sugar, *Am* finely ground sugar; **s. d'orge** barley sugar.
sucr/er [sykre] *vt* to sugar, sweeten. ● **—é** *a* sweet, sugary.
sucreries [sykrəri] *nfpl* (*bonbons*) sweets, *Am* candy.
sucrier [sykrije] *nm* (*récipient*) sugar bowl.
sud [syd] *nm* south; **au s.** in the south; (*direction*) (to the) south (**de** of); **du s.** (*vent, direction*) southerly; (*ville*) southern; (*gens*) from *ou* in the south; **Amérique/Afrique du S.** South America/Africa; **l'Europe du S.** Southern Europe.
‖ *a inv* (*côte*) south(ern). ● **s.-africain, -aine** *a & nmf* South African. ● **s.-américain, -aine** *a & nmf* South American. ● **s.-est** *nm & a inv* south-east. ● **s.-ouest** *nm & a inv* south-west.
Suède [sɥɛd] *nf* Sweden. ● **suédois, -oise** *a* Swedish ‖ *nmf* Swede ‖ *nm* (*langue*) Swedish.
suer [sɥe] *vi* (*personne, mur etc*) to sweat; **faire s. qn** *Fam* to get on s.o.'s nerves. ● **sueur** *nf* sweat; **(tout) en s.** sweating.
suffire* [syfir] *vi* to be enough *ou* sufficient (**à** for); **ça suffit!** that's enough!; **il suffit de**

faire one only has to do; **il suffit d'une goutte/***etc* **pour faire** a drop/*etc* is enough to do ‖ **se s.** *vpr* **se s. (à soi-même)** to be self-sufficient. ● **suffisant** *a* **1** sufficient, adequate. **2** (*vaniteux*) conceited. ● **suffisamment** *adv* sufficiently; **s. de** enough, sufficient.

❶suffire G91 Impersonal Verbs 7 E 2h) iii)

suffixe [syfiks] *nm Gram* suffix.

suffoquer [syfɔke] *vti* to choke, suffocate. ● **suffocant** *a* stifling, suffocating.

suffrage [syfraʒ] *nm Pol* (*voix*) vote; **s. universel** universal suffrage.

suggérer [sygʒere] *vt* (*proposer*) to suggest (**à** to, **de faire** doing, **que** (+ *sub*) that). ● **suggestion** *nf* suggestion.

suicide [sɥisid] *nm* suicide. ● **suicidaire** *a* suicidal. ● **se suicider** *vpr* to commit suicide.

suie [sɥi] *nf* soot.

suinter [sɥɛ̃te] *vi* to ooze, seep.

suis [sɥi] *voir* **être, suivre.**

Suisse [sɥis] *nf* Switzerland; **S. allemande/romande** German-speaking/French-speaking Switzerland. ● **suisse** *a* & *nmf* Swiss; **les Suisses** the Swiss. ● **Suissesse** *nf* Swiss woman *ou* girl, Swiss *inv.*

suite [sɥit] *nf* (*reste*) rest; (*continuation*) continuation; (*de film, roman*) sequel; (*série*) series, sequence; (*appartement, escorte*) & *Mus* suite; *pl* (*séquelles*) effects; **faire s. (à)** to follow; **donner s. à** (*demande etc*) to follow up; **par la s.** afterwards; **par s. de** as a result of; **à la s.** one after another; **à la s. de** (*derrière*) behind; (*événement etc*) as a result of; **de s.** (*deux jours etc*) in a row.

suivre* [sɥivr] *vt* to follow; (*accompagner*) to go with, accompany; (*cours*) *Scol* to attend; (*malade*) to treat; **s. (des yeux** *ou* **du regard)** to watch; **se s.** to follow each other. ‖ *vi* to follow; **faire s.** (*courrier*) to forward; **'à s.'** 'to be continued'; **comme suit** as follows. ● **suivant**[1], **-ante** *a* next, following ‖ *nmf* next (one); **au s.!** next!, next person! ● **suivant**[2] *prép* (*selon*) according to.

sujet[1], **-ette** [syʒɛ, -ɛt] *a* **s. à** (*maladie etc*) subject *ou* liable to ‖ *nmf* (*personne*) *Pol* subject.

sujet[2] [syʒɛ] *nm* **1** (*question*) & *Gram* subject; (*d'examen*) question; **au s. de** about; **à quel s.?** about what? **2** (*raison*) cause.

sultan [syltɑ̃] *nm* sultan.

super [sypɛr] **1** *a inv* (*bon*) *Fam* great, super. **2** *nm* (*supercarburant*) four-star (petrol), *Am* premium gas.

superbe [sypɛrb] *a* superb.

supercherie [sypɛrʃəri] *nf* deception.

superficie [sypɛrfisi] *nf* surface; (*dimensions*) area. ● **superficiel, -ielle** *a* superficial.

superflu [sypɛrfly] *a* superfluous.

supérieur, -eure [syperjœr] *a* (*étages, partie etc*) upper; (*qualité, air, ton*) superior; (*études*) higher; **à l'étage s.** on the floor above; **s. à** (*meilleur que*) superior to ‖ *nmf* superior. ● **supériorité** *nf* superiority.

superlatif, -ive [sypɛrlatif, -iv] *a* & *nm Gram* superlative.

supermarché [sypɛrmarʃe] *nm* supermarket.

superposer [sypɛrpoze] *vt* (*objets*) to put on top of each other.

superproduction [sypɛrprɔdyksjɔ̃] *nf* (*film*) blockbuster.

superpuissance [sypɛrpɥisɑ̃s] *nf Pol* superpower.

supersonique [sypɛrsɔnik] *a* supersonic.

superstar [sypɛrstar] *nf* superstar.

superstitieux, -euse [sypɛrstisjø, -øz] *a* superstitious. ● **superstition** *nf* superstition.

superviser [sypɛrvize] *vt* to supervise.

supplanter [syplɑ̃te] *vt* to take the place of.

supplé/er [syplee] *vt, vi* **s. à** (*compenser*) to make up for. ● **—ant, -ante** *a* & *nmf* (*personne*) substitute, replacement.

supplément [syplemɑ̃] *nm* (*argent*) extra charge, supplement; (*revue*) supplement; **en s.** extra; **un s. de** (*information etc*) extra, additional. ● **supplé-mentaire** *a* extra, additional.

supplice [syplis] *nm* torture.

supplier [syplije] *vt* **s. qn de faire** to beg *ou* implore s.o. to do; **je vous en supplie!** I beg *ou* implore you!

support [sypɔr] *nm* **1** support; (*d'instrument etc*) stand. **2** (*moyen*) *Fig* medium; **s. audio-visuel** audio-visual aid.

support/er[1] [sypɔrte] *vt* (*malheur, conséquences etc*) to bear, endure; (*résister à*) to withstand (*heat etc*); (*soutenir*) to support (*arch etc*); (*frais*) to bear; **je ne peux pas la s.** I can't bear her. ● **—able** *a* bearable.

supporter[2] [sypɔrtɛr] *nm Sp* supporter.

supposer [sypoze] *vt* to suppose, assume (**que** that); (*impliquer*) to imply (**que** that); **à s.** *ou* **en supposant que** (+ *sub*) supposing (that). ● **supposition** *nf* assumption, supposition.

suppositoire [sypozitwar] *nm Méd* suppository.

supprimer [syprime] *vt* to get rid of, remove; (*mot*) to cut out, delete; (*train etc*) to cancel; (*tuer*) to do away with; **s. des emplois** to axe jobs; **s. qch à qn** to take sth

away from s.o. ● **suppression** *nf* removal; deletion; cancellation; axing.
suprématie [sypremasi] *nf* supremacy.
suprême [syprɛm] *a* supreme.
sur [syr] *prép* on, upon; (*par-dessus*) over; (*au sujet de*) on, about; **prendre qch s. la table** to take sth off *ou* from the table; **six s. dix** six out of ten; **un jour s. deux** every other day; **six mètres s. dix** six metres by ten; **coup s. coup** blow after blow; **s. ce** after which, and then; (*maintenant*) and now; **s. votre gauche** to your left; **régner s.** to reign over.
ⓘG184 Prepositions 8
sur- [syr] *préf* over-.
sûr [syr] *a* sure, certain (**de** of, **que** that); (*digne de confiance*) reliable; (*lieu*) safe; (*goût*) discerning; (*jugement*) sound; **c'est s. que** (+ *indic*) it's certain that; **s. de soi** self-assured; **bien s.!** of course!
ⓘG100 The Subjunctive 7 G 1e)
surboum [syrbum] *nf Fam* party.
surcharge [syrʃarʒ] *nf* **1** overloading; (*poids*) extra load; **s. de travail** extra work. **2** (*correction de texte etc*) alteration. ● **surcharger** *vt* (*voiture etc*) to overload (**de** with).
surchauffer [syrʃofe] *vt* to overheat.
surclasser [syrklɑse] *vt* to outclass.
surcroît [syrkrwa] *nm* increase (**de** in); **de s., par s.** in addition.
surdité [syrdite] *nf* deafness.
surélever [syrɛlve] *vt* to raise (the height of).
sûrement [syrmɑ̃] *adv* certainly.
surenchère [syrɑ̃ʃɛr] *nf Com* higher bid. ● **surenchérir** *vi* to bid higher.
surestimer [syrɛstime] *vt* to overestimate.
sûreté [syrte] *nf* safety; (*de l'État*) security; (*garantie*) surety; **être en s.** to be safe; **mettre en s.** to put in a safe place; **épingle**/*etc* **de s.** safety pin/*etc*; **pour plus de s.** to be on the safe side.
surexcité [syrɛksite] *a* overexcited.
surf [sœrf] *nm Sp* surfing; **faire du s.** to go surfing, surf.
surface [syrfas] *nf* surface; (*dimensions*) (surface) area; **faire s.** (*sous-marin etc*) to surface; **(magasin à) grande s.** hypermarket.
surgelé [syrʒəle] *a* (*viande etc*) (deep-) frozen ‖ *nmpl* (deep-)frozen foods.
surgir [syrʒir] *vi* to appear suddenly (**de** from); (*problème*) to arise.
surhomme [syrɔm] *nm* superman. ● **surhumain** *a* superhuman.
sur-le-champ [syrləʃɑ̃] *adv* immediately.
surlendemain [syrlɑ̃dmɛ̃] *nm* **le s.** two days later; **le s. de** two days after.
surligner [syrliɲe] *vt* to highlight. ● **surligneur** *nm* highlighter (pen).
surmener [syrməne] *vt*, **se s.** *vpr* to overwork. ● **surmenage** *nm* overwork.
surmonter [syrmɔ̃te] *vt* **1** (*obstacle, peur etc*) to get over, overcome. **2** (*être placé sur*) to be on top of.
surnaturel, -elle [syrnatyrɛl] *a & nm* supernatural.
surnom [syrnɔ̃] *nm* nickname. ● **surnommer** *vt* to nickname.
surnombre [syrnɔ̃br] *nm* **en s.** too many.
surpasser [syrpɑse] *vt* to surpass (**en** in) ‖ **se s.** *vpr* to excel *ou* surpass oneself.
surpeuplé [syrpœple] *a* overpopulated.
surplace [syrplas] *nm* **faire du s.** (*dans un embouteillage*) to be unable to move, be hardly moving.
surplomber [syrplɔ̃be] *vti* to overhang.
surplus [syrply] *nm* surplus; *pl Com* surplus (stock).
surprendre* [syrprɑ̃dr] *vt* (*étonner*) to surprise; (*prendre sur le fait*) to catch; (*conversation*) to overhear. ● **surprenant** *a* surprising (**que** (+ *sub*) that). ● **surpris** *a* surprised (**de** at, **que** (+ *sub*) that); **je suis s. de te voir** I'm surprised to see you. ● **surprise** *nf* surprise.
surréservation [syrrezɛrvɑsjɔ̃] *nf* overbooking.
sursaut [syrso] *nm* (sudden) start *ou* jump; **s. de** (*énergie etc*) burst of. ● **sursauter** *vi* to jump, start.
sursis [syrsi] *nm Mil* deferment; (*répit*) *Fig* reprieve; **un an (de prison) avec s.** a one-year suspended sentence.
surtout [syrtu] *adv* especially; (*avant tout*) above all; **s. pas** certainly not; **s. que** especially since *ou* as.
surveiller [syrveje] *vt* (*garder*) to watch, keep an eye on; (*contrôler*) to supervise; (*épier*) to watch; **s. son langage/sa santé** *Fig* to watch one's language/health. ‖ **se surveiller** *vpr* to watch oneself. ● **surveillant, -ante** *nmf* (*de lycée*) supervisor (in charge of discipline); (*de prison*) (prison) guard, warder; (*de chantier*) supervisor. ● **surveillance** *nf* watch (**sur** over); (*de travaux, d'ouvriers*) supervision; (*de la police*) surveillance, observation.
survenir* [syrvənir] *vi* to occur.
survêtement [syrvɛtmɑ̃] *nm Sp* tracksuit.
survie [syrvi] *nf* survival. ● **survivre*** *vi* to survive (**à qch** sth); **s. à qn** to outlive s.o., survive s.o. ● **survivant, -ante** *nmf* survivor.

survoler [syrvɔle] *vt* to fly over; (*question*) *Fig* to go over (quickly).
susceptible [syseptibl] *a* **1** (*ombrageux*) touchy, sensitive. **2 s. de faire** likely *ou* liable to do; (*capable*) able to do.
susciter [sysite] *vt* (*sentiment*) to arouse; (*ennuis*, *obstacles etc*) to create.
suspect, -ecte [syspɛ(kt), -ɛkt] *a* suspicious, suspect; **s. de** suspected of ‖ *nmf* suspect.
suspend/re [syspɑ̃dr] *vt* **1** (*accrocher*) to hang (up) (**à** on); **se s. à** to hang from. **2** (*destituer*, *interrompre*) to suspend. ●**—u** *a* **s. à** hanging from; **pont s.** suspension bridge. ●**suspension** *nf* (*d'hostilités*, *d'employé etc*) & *Aut* suspension.
suspens (en) [ɑ̃syspɑ̃] *adv* **1** (*affaire*) in abeyance. **2** (*dans l'incertitude*) in suspense.
suspense [syspɛns] *nm* suspense; **film à s.** thriller, suspense film.
suspicion [syspisjɔ̃] *nf* suspicion.
suture [sytyr] *nf Méd* stitching; **point de s.** stitch (*in wound*). ●**suturer** *vt* to stitch up.
svelte [svɛlt] *a* slender.
SVP [ɛsvepe] *abrév* (*s'il vous plaît*) please.
syllabe [silab] *nf* syllable.
symbole [sɛ̃bɔl] *nm* symbol. ●**symbolique** *a* symbolic. ●**symboliser** *vt* to symbolize.
symétrie [simetri] *nf* symmetry.
sympa [sɛ̃pa] *a inv Fam* = **sympathique.**
sympathie [sɛ̃pati] *nf* liking, affection; (*affinité*) affinity; (*condoléances*) sympathy; **avoir de la s. pour qn** to be fond of s.o. ●**sympathique** *a* nice, pleasant; (*accueil*, *geste*) friendly.
symphonie [sɛ̃fɔni] *nf* symphony. ●**symphonique** *a* **orchestre s.** symphony orchestra.
symptôme [sɛ̃ptom] *nm* symptom.
synagogue [sinagɔg] *nf* synagogue.
synchroniser [sɛ̃krɔnize] *vt* to synchronize.
syncope [sɛ̃kɔp] *nf Méd* blackout; **tomber en s.** to black out.
syndicat [sɛ̃dika] *nm* **1** (*d'ouvriers*) (trade) union, *Am* (labor) union; (*de patrons etc*) association. **2 s. d'initiative** tourist (information) office. ●**syndiquer** *vt* to unionize ‖ **se s.** *vpr* (*adhérer*) to join a (trade *ou Am* labor) union. ●**syndiqué, -ée** *nmf* (trade *ou Am* labor) union member.
syndrome [sɛ̃drom] *nm Méd* & *Fig* syndrome.
synonyme [sinɔnim] *a* synonymous (**de** with) ‖ *nm* synonym.
synthèse [sɛ̃tɛz] *nf* synthesis. ●**synthétique** *a* synthetic.
synthétiseur [sɛ̃tetizœr] *nm* synthesizer.
Syrie [siri] *nf* Syria. ●**syrien, -ienne** *a* & *nmf* Syrian.
système [sistɛm] *nm* (*structure*, *réseau etc*) & *Anat* system; **le s. immunitaire** the immune system; **le s. D** *Fam* resourcefulness; **s. d'exploitation** *Ordinat* operating system. ●**systématique** *a* systematic; (*soutien*) unconditional.

T

T, t [te] *nm* T, t.

t' [t] *voir* **te.**

ta [ta] *voir* **ton**[1].

tabac [taba] **1** *nm* tobacco; (*magasin*) tobacconist's (shop), *Am* tobacco store. **2** *nm* **passer qn à t.** *Fam* to beat s.o. up. **3** *a inv* (*couleur*) buff.

table [tabl] *nf* **1** (*meuble*) table; (*d'école*) desk; (*nourriture*) fare; **t. de nuit/d'opération** bedside/operating table; **t. basse** coffee table; **t. à repasser** ironing board; **t. roulante** (tea) trolley, *Am* (serving) cart; **mettre/débarrasser la t.** to set *ou* lay/clear the table; **être à t.** to be sitting at the table; **à t.!** (food's) ready!; **mettre sur t. d'écoute** (*téléphone*) to tap. **2** (*liste*) table; **t. des matières** table of contents.

tableau, -x [tablo] *nm* **1** (*peinture*) picture, painting; (*image*) picture; **t. de maître** (*peinture*) old master. **2** (*panneau*) board; (*liste*) list; (*graphique*) chart; **t. (noir)** (black)board; **t. d'affichage** notice board, *Am* bulletin board; **t. de bord** *Aut* dashboard.

tabler [table] *vi* **t. sur** to count *ou* rely on.

tablette [tablɛt] *nf* (*de chocolat*) bar, slab; (*de lavabo etc*) shelf; (*de cheminée*) mantelpiece.

tableur [tablœr] *nm Ordinat* spreadsheet.

tablier [tablije] *nm* (*vêtement*) apron; (*d'écolier*) smock.

tabou [tabu] *a* & *nm* taboo.

tabouret [taburɛ] *nm* stool.

tac [tak] *nm* **répondre du t. au t.** to give tit for tat.

tache [taʃ] *nf* spot, mark; (*salissure*) stain; **faire t. d'huile** *Fig* to spread. ● **tacher** *vt*, **se t.** *vpr* (*tissu etc*) to stain ‖ *vi* (*vin etc*) to stain.

tâche [tɑʃ] *nf* task, job.

tâcher [tɑʃe] *vi* **t. de faire** to try *ou* endeavour to do.

tacheté [taʃte] *a* speckled, spotted.

tacite [tasit] *a* tacit.

tact [takt] *nm* tact; **avoir du t.** to be tactful.

tactique [taktik] *a* tactical ‖ *nf* **la t.** tactics; **une t.** a tactic.

tag [tag] *nm* tag (*spray-painted graffiti*). ● **tagueur, -euse** *nmf* graffiti artist, tagger.

Tahiti [taiti] *nm* Tahiti. ● **tahitien, -ienne** [taisjɛ̃, -jɛn] *a* & *nmf* Tahitian.

taie [tɛ] *nf* **t. d'oreiller** pillowcase.

taillader [tɑjade] *vt* to gash, slash.

taille [tɑj] *nf* **1** (*hauteur*) height; (*dimension, mesure*) size; **de haute t.** (*personne*) tall; **de petite t.** short; **de t. moyenne** (*objet, personne*) medium-sized; **être de t. à faire** *Fig* to be capable of doing; **de t.** (*erreur*) *Fam* enormous. **2** *Anat* waist; **tour de t.** waist measurement.

taille-crayon(s) [tɑjkrɛjɔ̃] *nm inv* pencil sharpener.

tailler [tɑje] *vt* to cut; (*haie, barbe*) to trim; (*arbre*) to prune; (*crayon*) to sharpen; (*vêtement*) to cut out.

tailleur [tɑjœr] *nm* **1** (*personne*) tailor. **2** (*costume féminin*) suit.

taillis [taji] *nm* copse, coppice.

tain [tɛ̃] *nm* **glace sans t.** two-way mirror.

taire* [tɛr] *vt* to say nothing about ‖ *vi* **faire t. qn** to silence s.o. ‖ **se t.** *vpr* (*ne rien dire*) to keep quiet (**sur qch** about sth); (*cesser de parler*) to stop talking, fall silent; **tais-toi!** be *ou* keep quiet!

talc [talk] *nm* talcum powder.

talent [talɑ̃] *nm* talent; **avoir du t. pour** to have a talent for.

talkie-walkie [talkiwalki] *nm* (*poste*) walkie-talkie.

talon [talɔ̃] *nm* **1** heel; **(chaussures à) talons hauts** high heels; **talons aiguilles** stiletto heels. **2** (*de chèque, carnet*) stub, counterfoil.

talus [taly] *nm* slope, embankment.

tambour [tɑ̃bur] *nm* **1** (*de machine etc*) & *Mus* drum; (*personne*) drummer. **2** (*porte*) revolving door. ● **tambourin** *nm* tambourine. ● **tambouriner** *vi* (*avec les doigts etc*) to drum (**sur** on).

tamis [tami] *nm* sieve. ● **tamiser** *vt* (*farine etc*) to sift; (*lumière*) to filter.

Tamise [tamiz] *nf* **la T.** the Thames.

tampon [tɑ̃pɔ̃] *nm* **1** (*marque, instrument*) stamp. **2** (*bouchon*) plug, stopper; (*de coton etc*) wad; *Méd* swab; **t. hygiénique** *ou* **périodique** tampon; **t. à récurer** scrubbing *ou* scouring pad. **3** (*de train etc*) & *Fig* buffer; **état t.** buffer state.

tamponner [tɑ̃pɔne] *vt* **1** (*lettre etc*) to stamp. **2** (*visage etc*) to dab; (*plaie*) to swab. **3** (*train, voiture*) to crash into. ● **tamponneuses** *afpl* **autos t.** bumper cars, dodgems.

tandem [tɑ̃dɛm] *nm* **1** (*bicyclette*) tandem. **2** (*duo*) *Fig* pair; **en t.** (*travailler etc*) in tandem.
tandis que [tɑ̃dik(ə)] *conj* (*pendant que*) while; (*contraste*) whereas, while.
tanguer [tɑ̃ge] *vi* (*bateau, avion*) to pitch.
tanière [tanjɛr] *nf* den, lair.
tank [tɑ̃k] *nm Mil* tank.
tanker [tɑ̃kɛr] *nm* (*navire*) tanker.
tann/er [tane] *vt* (*cuir*) to tan. ●**—é** *a* (*visage*) weather-beaten, tanned.
tant [tɑ̃] *adv* (*travailler etc*) so much (**que** that); **t. de** (*pain, temps etc*) so much (**que** that); (*gens, choses etc*) so many (**que** that); **t. de fois** so often, so many times; **t. que** (*autant que*) as much as; (*aussi longtemps que*) as long as; **en t. que** (*considéré comme*) as; **t. bien que mal** more or less, so-so; **t. mieux!** good!, I'm glad!; **t. pis!** too bad!, pity!
❶tant que G97 Tenses 7 F 11
tante [tɑ̃t] *nf* aunt.
tantôt [tɑ̃to] *adv* **1 t. ... t.** sometimes ... sometimes, now ... now. **2** (*cet après-midi*) this afternoon.
taon [tɑ̃] *nm* horsefly, gadfly.
tapage [tapaʒ] *nm* din, uproar.
tape [tap] *nf* slap.
tape-à-l'œil [tapalœj] *a inv* flashy, gaudy.
taper [tape] **1** *vt* (*enfant, cuisse*) to slap; (*table*) to bang ‖ *vi* (*soleil*) to beat down; **t. sur qch** to bang on sth; **t. du pied** to stamp one's foot; **t. sur les nerfs de qn** *Fam* to get on s.o.'s nerves; **t. dans l'œil à qn** *Fam* to take s.o.'s fancy ‖ **se taper** *vpr* (*travail*) *Fam* to do, take on; (*repas, vin*) *Fam* to put away.
2 *vti* **t. (à la machine)** to type. ●**tapant** *a* **à midi t.** at twelve sharp; **à huit heures tapant(es)** at eight sharp.
tapir (se) [sətapir] *vpr* to crouch (down).
tapis [tapi] *nm* carpet; **t. de bain** bathmat; **t. roulant** (*pour marchandises*) conveyor belt; (*pour personnes*) moving walkway; **envoyer qn au t.** (*abattre*) to floor s.o.; **mettre sur le t.** (*sujet*) to bring up for discussion. ●**t.-brosse** *nm* doormat.
tapisser [tapise] *vt* (*mur*) to (wall)paper; to hang with tapestry. ●**tapisserie** *nf* (*papier peint*) wallpaper; (*broderie*) tapestry. ●**tapissier, -ière** *nmf* (*qui pose des tissus etc*) upholsterer; **t.(-décorateur)** interior decorator.
tapoter [tapɔte] *vt* to tap; (*joue*) to pat ‖ *vi* **t. sur** to tap (on).
taquin, -ine [takɛ̃, -in] *a* (fond of) teasing. ●**taquiner** *vt* to tease.
tard [tar] *adv* late; **plus t.** later (on); **au plus t.** at the latest; **sur le t.** late in life.
tarder [tarde] *vi* (*lettre, saison*) to be a long time coming; **t. à faire** to take one's time doing; **ne tardez pas** (*agissez tout de suite*) don't delay; **elle ne va pas t.** she won't be long; **sans t.** without delay; **il me tarde de faire** I long to do.
tardif, -ive [tardif, -iv] *a* late; (*regrets*) belated. ●**tardivement** *adv* late.
tarif [tarif] *nm* (*prix*) rate; *Aut Rail* fare; (*tableau*) price list, tariff; **plein t.** full price; *Aut Rail* full fare. ●**tarification** *nf* (price) fixing.
tarir [tarir] *vti*, **se t.** *vpr* (*fleuve etc*) & *Fig* to dry up.
tartare [tartar] *a* **sauce t.** tartar sauce.
tarte [tart] **1** *nf* (open) pie, tart. **2** *a inv Fam* (*sot*) silly. ●**tartelette** *nf* (small) tart.
tartine [tartin] *nf* slice of bread; **t. (de beurre/de confiture)** slice of bread and butter/jam. ●**tartiner** *vt* (*beurre etc*) to spread; **fromage à t.** cheese spread.
tartre [tartr] *nm* (*de bouilloire*) scale, fur; (*de dents*) plaque, tartar.
tas [tɑ] *nm* pile, heap; **un** *ou* **des t. de** (*beaucoup*) *Fam* lots of; **mettre en t.** to pile *ou* heap up; **former qn sur le t.** (*au travail*) *Fam* to train s.o. on the job.
tasse [tɑs] *nf* cup; **t. à café** coffee cup; **t. à thé** teacup; **boire la t.** *Fam* to swallow a mouthful (*when swimming*).
tasser [tɑse] *vt* to pack, squeeze (*sth, s.o.*) (**dans** into); (*terre*) to pack down ‖ **se t.** *vpr* (*se serrer*) to squeeze up; (*sol*) to sink, collapse; (*se voûter*) to become bowed; **ça va se t.** (*s'arranger*) *Fam* things will pan out.
tâter [tɑte] *vt* to feel; (*sonder*) *Fig* to sound out ‖ *vi* **t. de** (*prison*) to have a taste of, experience ‖ **se t.** *vpr* (*hésiter*) to be in *ou* of two minds. ●**tâtonner** *vi* to grope about. ●**tâtons (à)** *adv* **avancer à t.** to feel one's way (along); **chercher à t.** to grope for.
tatou/er [tatwe] *vt* (*corps, dessin*) to tattoo. ●**—age** *nm* (*dessin*) tattoo.
taudis [todi] *nm* slum, hovel.
taupe [top] *nf* (*animal, espion*) mole.
taureau, -x [tɔro] *nm* bull; **le T.** (*signe*) Taurus. ●**tauromachie** *nf* bull-fighting.
taux [to] *nm* rate; **t. d'alcool/de cholestérol/***etc* alcohol/cholesterol/*etc* level; **t. d'intérêt** interest rate.
taxe [taks] *nf* (*impôt*) tax; (*de douane*) duty; **t. à la valeur ajoutée** value-added tax; **t. de séjour** tourist tax. ●**taxer** *vt* **1** (*objet de luxe etc*) to tax. **2 t. qn de** to accuse s.o. of. **3**

(*prendre*, *voler*) *Fam* to swipe (**qch à qn** sth from s.o.). ●**taxé** *a* taxed.

taxi [taksi] *nm* taxi.

taxiphone [taksifɔn] *nm* pay phone.

Tchécoslovaquie [tʃekɔslɔvaki] *nf* Czechoslovakia. ●**tchèque** *a* & *nmf* Czech ‖ *nm* (*langue*) Czech.

te [t(ə)] (**t'** *before vowel or mute h*) *pron* **1** (*complément direct*) you; **je te vois** I see you. **2** (*indirect*) (to) you; **il te parle** he speaks to you; **elle te l'a dit** she told you. **3** (*réfléchi*) yourself; **tu te laves** you wash yourself.

ⓘ**G57** Object Pronouns 6 D 2

ⓘ**G84** Reflexive Verbs and Pronouns 7 D

technicien, -ienne [tɛknisjɛ̃, -jɛn] *nmf* technician. ●**technique** *a* technical ‖ *nf* technique. ●**technocrate** *nm* technocrat. ●**technologie** *nf* technology. ●**technologique** *a* technological.

teckel [tekɛl] *nm* (*chien*) dachshund.

tee-shirt [tiʃœrt] *nm* tee-shirt.

teindre* [tɛ̃dr] *vt* to dye; **t. en rouge**/*etc* to dye red/*etc* ‖ **se t.** *vpr* **se t. (les cheveux)** to dye one's hair. ●**teinture** *nf* dyeing; (*produit*) dye. ●**teinturerie** *nf* (*boutique*) (dry) cleaner's. ●**teinturier, -ière** *nmf* dry cleaner.

teint [tɛ̃] *nm* **1** (*de visage*) complexion. **2 bon** *ou* **grand t.** (*tissu*) colourfast.

teinte [tɛ̃t] *nf* shade, tint. ●**teinter** *vt* to tint; (*bois*) to stain.

tel, telle [tɛl] *a* such; **un t. homme/livre**/*etc* such a man/book/*etc*; **un t. intérêt**/*etc* such interest/*etc*; **de tels mots**/*etc* such words/*etc*; **t. que** such as, like; **t. que je l'ai laissé** just as I left it; **comme t.** as such; **t. ou t.** such and such; **rien de t. que...** (there's) nothing like...; **Monsieur Un t.** Mr So-and-so; **t. père t. fils** like father like son.

télé [tele] *nf* (*téléviseur*) *Fam* TV; **à la t.** on TV; **regarder la t.** to watch TV.

télé- [tele] *préf* tele-.

télécarte® [telekart] *nf* phonecard.

télécommande [telekɔmɑ̃d] *nf* remote control. ●**télécommander** *vt* to operate by remote control.

télécommunications [telekɔmynikɑsjɔ̃] *nfpl* telecommunications.

télécopie [telekɔpi] *nf* fax. ●**télécopieur** *nm* fax (machine).

téléfilm [telefilm] *nm* TV film.

télégramme [telegram] *nm* telegram.

télégraphier [telegrafje] *vt* (*message*) to wire, cable. ●**télégraphique** *a* **poteau/fil t.** telegraph pole/wire.

téléguider [telegide] *vt* to operate by remote control.

télématique [telematik] *nf* telematics, computer communications.

téléobjectif [teleɔbʒɛktif] *nm* telephoto lens.

téléphérique [teleferik] *nm* cable car.

téléphone [telefɔn] *nm* (tele)phone; **coup de t.** (phone) call; **passer un coup de t. à qn** to give s.o. a ring *ou* a call; **au t.** on the (tele)phone; **avoir le t.** to be on the (tele)phone; **t. portatif** mobile phone. ●**téléphoner** *vt* (*nouvelle etc*) to (tele)phone (**à** to) ‖ *vi* to (tele)phone; **t. à qn** to (tele)phone s.o., call s.o. (up). ●**téléphonique** *a* **appel**/*etc* **t.** phone *ou* telephone call/*etc*.

télescope [telɛskɔp] *nm* telescope.

télescoper [telɛskɔpe] *vt Aut Rail* to smash into; **se t.** to smash into each other.

téléscripteur [teleskriptœr] *nm* (*appareil*) teleprinter.

télésiège [telesjɛʒ] *nm* chair lift.

téléski [teleski] *nm* ski tow.

téléspectateur, -trice [telespɛktatœr, -tris] *nmf* (television) viewer.

téléviser [televise] *vt* to televise; **journal télévisé** television news. ●**téléviseur** *nm* television (set). ●**télévision** *nf* television; **à la t.** on (the) television; **regarder la t.** to watch (the) television; **programme**/*etc* **de t.** television programme/*etc*.

télex [telɛks] *nm* (*service*, *message*) telex.

telle [tɛl] *voir* **tel.**

tellement [tɛlmɑ̃] *adv* (*si*) so; (*tant*) so much; **t. grand**/*etc* **que** so big/*etc* that; **crier**/*etc* **t. que** to shout/*etc* so much that; **t. de** (*travail etc*) so much; (*soucis etc*) so many; **pas t.!** (*pas beaucoup*) not much!

téméraire [temerɛr] *a* rash, reckless.

témoigner [temwaɲe] **1** *vi Jur* to give evidence, testify (**contre** against); **t. de qch** (*personne*, *attitude etc*) to testify to sth ‖ *vt* **t. que** *Jur* to testify that. **2** *vt* (*gratitude etc*) to show (**à qn** (to) s.o.). ●**témoignage** *nm* **1** evidence, testimony; (*récit*) account; **faux t.** (*délit*) perjury. **2** (*d'affection etc*) *Fig* token (**de** of); **en t. de** as a token of.

témoin [temwɛ̃] **1** *nm* witness; **t. oculaire** eyewitness; **être t. de** (*accident etc*) to witness ‖ *a* **appartement t.** show flat, *Am* model apartment. **2** *nm Sp* baton.

tempérament [tɑ̃peramɑ̃] *nm* (*caractère*) temperament.

température [tɑ̃peratyr] *nf* temperature; **avoir de la t.** *Méd* to have a temperature.

tempéré [tɑ̃pere] *a* (*climat*, *zone*) temperate.

tempête [tɑ̃pɛt] *nf* storm; **t. de neige** snowstorm, blizzard.
temple [tɑ̃pl] *nm* (*romain, grec*) temple; (*protestant*) church.
temporaire [tɑ̃pɔrɛr] *a* temporary.
temporel, -elle [tɑ̃pɔrɛl] *a* (*terrestre*) worldly.
temporiser [tɑ̃pɔrize] *vi* to procrastinate.
temps[1] [tɑ̃] *nm* (*durée, période, moment*) time; *Gram* tense; **t. d'arrêt** pause, break; **en t. de guerre** in wartime; **avoir/trouver le t.** to have/find (the) time (**de faire** to do); **il est t.** it is time (**de faire** to do); **il était t.!** it was about time!; **ces derniers t.** lately; **de t. en t.** [dətɑ̃zɑ̃tɑ̃] from time to time; **en t. utile** [ɑ̃tɑ̃zytil] in good *ou* due time; **en même t.** at the same time (**que** as); **à t.** (*arriver*) in time; **à plein t.** (*travailler etc*) full-time; **à t. partiel** (*travailler etc*) part-time; **dans le t.** (*autrefois*) once; **avec le t.** (*à la longue*) in time; **tout le t.** all the time; **de mon t.** in my time.
temps[2] [tɑ̃] *nm* (*climat*) weather; **il fait beau/mauvais t.** the weather's fine/bad; **quel t. fait-il?** what's the weather like?
tenable [tənabl] *a* bearable.
tenace [tənas] *a* stubborn, tenacious.
tenailles [tənɑj] *nfpl* (*outil*) pincers.
tenant, -ante [tənɑ̃, -ɑ̃t] *nmf* **le t. du titre** *Sp* the title holder.
tendance [tɑ̃dɑ̃s] *nf* (*penchant*) tendency; (*évolution*) trend (**à** towards); **avoir t. à faire** to tend to do, have a tendency to do.
tendancieux, -euse [tɑ̃dɑ̃sjø, -øz] *a Péj* tendentious.
tendeur [tɑ̃dœr] *nm* (*à bagages*) elastic strap, *Am* bungee.
tendre[1] [tɑ̃dr] **1** *vt* to stretch; (*main*) to hold out (**à qn** to s.o.); (*bras, jambe*) to stretch out; (*muscle*) to tense, flex; (*arc*) to bend; (*piège*) to set, lay; (*filet*) to spread; (*tapisserie*) to hang; **t. qch à qn** to hold out sth to s.o.; **t. l'oreille** *Fig* to prick up one's ears ‖ **se tendre** *vpr* (*rapports*) to become strained.
2 *vi* **t. à qch/à faire** to tend towards sth/to do. • **tendu** *a* (*corde*) tight; (*personne, situation, muscle*) tense; (*main*) held out; (*rapports*) strained.
tendre[2] [tɑ̃dr] *a* **1** (*viande*) tender; (*bois, couleur*) soft. **2** (*personne*) affectionate (**avec** to). • **—ment** [-əmɑ̃] *adv* tenderly. • **tendresse** *nf* affection, tenderness.
ténèbres [tenɛbr] *nfpl* darkness.
teneur [tənœr] *nf* (*de lettre etc*) content; **t. en alcool**/*etc* alcohol/*etc* content (**de** of).
tenir** [tənir] *vt* (*à la main etc*) to hold; (*promesse, comptes, hôtel*) to keep; (*rôle*) to play; (*propos*) to utter; **t. sa droite** (*conducteur*) to keep to the right; **t. la route** (*véhicule*) to hold the road; **t. pour** to regard as; **je le tiens!** (*je l'ai attrapé*) I've got him!
‖ *vi* (*nœud etc*) to hold; (*neige*) to last; (*résister*) to hold out; (*offre*) to stand; **t. à qn/qch** to be attached to *ou* fond of s.o./sth; **t. à la vie** to value life; **t. à faire** to be anxious to do; **t. dans qch** (*être contenu*) to fit into sth; **t. de qn** to take after s.o.; **tenez!** (*prenez*) here (you are)!; **tiens!** (*surprise*) well!, hey!
‖ *v imp* **il ne tient qu'à vous** it's up to you (**de faire** to do)
‖ **se tenir** *vpr* (*avoir lieu*) to be held; (*rester*) to keep, remain; **se t. debout** to stand (up); **se t. droit** to stand up *ou* sit up straight; **se t. par la main** to hold hands; **se t. bien** to behave oneself; **se t. à** to hold on to; **s'en t. à** (*se limiter à*) to stick to.
tennis [tenis] *nm* tennis; (*terrain*) (tennis) court; **t. de table** table tennis ‖ *nmpl* (*chaussures*) plimsolls, *Am* sneakers.
ténor [tenɔr] *nm Mus* tenor.
tension [tɑ̃sjɔ̃] *nf* tension; **t. (artérielle)** blood pressure; **avoir de la t.** *Méd* to have high blood pressure.
tentacule [tɑ̃takyl] *nm* tentacle.
tente [tɑ̃t] *nf* tent.
tenter[1] [tɑ̃te] *vt* (*essayer*) to try; **t. de faire** to try *ou* attempt to do. • **tentative** *nf* attempt; **t. de suicide** suicide attempt.
tent/er[2] [tɑ̃te] *vt* (*faire envie etc*) to tempt; **tenté de faire** tempted to do. • **—ant** *a* tempting. • **tentation** *nf* temptation.
tenture [tɑ̃tyr] *nf* (wall) hanging; (*de porte*) drape, curtain.
tenu [təny] *pp de* **tenir** ‖ *a* **t. de faire** obliged to do; **bien/mal t.** (*maison etc*) well/badly kept.
tenue [təny] *nf* **1** (*vêtements*) clothes, outfit; **t. de combat** *Mil* combat dress; **t. de soirée** evening dress. **2** (*conduite*) (good) behaviour; (*maintien*) posture; **manquer de t.** to lack (good) manners. **3** (*de maison, hôtel*) running; (*de comptes*) keeping. **4 t. de route** *Aut* road-holding.
ter [tɛr] *a* **4 t.** (*numéro*) 4B.
térébenthine [terebɑ̃tin] *nf* turpentine.
tergal® [tɛrgal] *nm* Terylene®, *Am* Dacron®.
terme [tɛrm] *nm* **1** (*mot*) term. **2** (*fin*) end; **mettre un t. à** to put an end to; **à court/long t.** (*conséquences etc*) short-/long-term. **3 moyen t.** (*solution*) middle course. **4 en**

(eg **G1**, **G2**, **G3**) in French **G**rammar, at the end of the dictionary. Also see p. ix.

bons/mauvais termes on good/bad terms (**avec qn** with s.o.).
terminal, -aux [terminal, -o] **1** *a* final; (*phase*) *Méd* terminal ‖ *a* & *nf* **(classe) terminale** *Scol* = sixth form, *Am* = twelfth grade. **2** *nm* (*d'ordinateur, pétrolier*) terminal.
terminer [tɛrmine] *vt* to end; (*achever*) to finish, complete ‖ **se t.** *vpr* to end (**par** with, **en** in). ● **terminaison** *nf* (*de mot*) ending.
terminus [tɛrminys] *nm* terminus.
termite [tɛrmit] *nm* (*insecte*) termite.
terne [tɛrn] *a* (*couleur etc*) dull, drab; (*personne*) dull. ● **ternir** *vt* (*métal, réputation*) to tarnish; (*meuble*) to dull.
terrain [tɛrɛ̃] *nm* (*sol*) & *Fig* ground; (*étendue*) land; (*à bâtir*) plot, site; **un t.** a piece of land; **t. de camping** campsite; **t. de football/rugby** football/rugby pitch; **t. de jeux** (*pour enfants*) playground; (*stade*) playing field; **t. de sport** sports ground, playing field; **t. d'aviation** airfieid; **t. vague** waste ground, *Am* vacant lot; **céder/gagner/perdre du t.** *Mil* & *Fig* to give/gain/lose ground; **véhicule tout t.** *ou* **tous terrains** off-road *ou* all-terrain vehicle.
terrasse [tɛras] *nf* **1** (*balcon, plate-forme*) terrace. **2** (*de café*) pavement *ou Am* sidewalk area; **à la t.** outside.
terrasser [tɛrase] *vt* (*adversaire*) to floor, knock down; (*accabler*) *Fig* to overcome.
terre [tɛr] *nf* (*matière, monde*) earth; (*sol*) ground; (*opposé à mer*) land; *pl* (*domaine*) land, estate; *Él* earth, *Am* ground; **la T.** (*planète*) Earth; **à** *ou* **par t.** (*poser, tomber*) to the ground; **par t.** (*assis, couché*) on the ground; **sous t.** underground; **t. cuite** (baked) clay, earthenware. ● **t.-à-terre** *a inv* down-to-earth. ● **t.-plein** *nm* (earth) platform; (*au milieu de la route*) central reservation, *Am* median strip.
terreau [tɛro] *nm* compost.
terrer (se) [sətere] *vpr* (*fugitif, animal*) to hide, go to ground.
terrestre [terɛstr] *a* (*vie, joies*) earthly; **la surface t.** the earth's surface; **globe t.** globe (*model*).
terreur [tɛrœr] *nf* terror. ● **terrible** *a* awful, terrible; (*formidable*) *Fam* terrific. ● **terrifier** *vt* to terrify. ● **terrifiant** *a* terrifying; (*extraordinaire*) incredible.
terrien, -ienne [tɛrjɛ̃, -jɛn] *a* land-owning; **propriétaire t.** landowner ‖ *nmf* (*habitant de la terre*) earth dweller, earthling.
terrier [tɛrje] *nm* **1** (*de lapin etc*) burrow. **2** (*chien*) terrier.
terrine [tɛrin] *nf* (*récipient*) *Culin* terrine; (*pâté*) pâté.
territoire [tɛritwar] *nm* territory.
terroir [tɛrwar] *nm* (*sol*) soil; (*région*) region; **du t.** (*accent etc*) rural.
terroriser [tɛrɔrize] *vt* to terrorize. ● **terrorisme** *nm* terrorism. ● **terroriste** *a* & *nmf* terrorist.
tertiaire [tɛrsjɛr] *a* **secteur t.** service *ou* tertiary sector.
tes [te] *voir* **ton**[1].
test [tɛst] *nm* test. ● **tester** *vt* (*élève, produit*) to test.
testament [tɛstamɑ̃] *nm* **1** *Jur* will. **2 Ancien/Nouveau T.** *Rel* Old/New Testament.
testicule [tɛstikyl] *nm Anat* testicle.
tétanos [tetanos] *nm Méd* tetanus.
têtard [tɛtar] *nm* tadpole.
tête [tɛt] *nf* head; (*visage*) face; (*d'arbre*) top; (*de lit*) head; (*de page, liste*) top, head; (*coup*) *Fb* header; **t. nucléaire** nuclear warhead; **tenir t. à qn** (*s'opposer à*) to stand up to s.o.; **faire la t.** (*bouder*) to sulk; **faire une drôle de t.** to give a funny look; **tomber la t. la première** to fall headlong; **calculer qch de t.** to work sth out in one's head; **se mettre dans la t. de faire qch** to get it into one's head to do sth; **à la t. de** (*entreprise, parti*) at the head of; (*classe*) at the top of; **de la t. aux pieds** from head to toe; **en t.** *Sp* in the lead; **se payer la t. de qn** *Fam* to make fun of s.o.; **j'en ai pardessus la t.** *Fam* I've had enough of it; **ça me prend la t.** *Fam* it gets on my nerves *ou* under my skin.
tête-à-queue [tɛtakø] *nm inv* **faire un t.-à-queue** *Aut* to spin right round.
tête-à-tête [tɛtatɛt] *adv* (*seul*) in private, alone together ‖ *nm inv* tête-à-tête.
téter [tete] *vt* to suck; **t. sa mère** (*bébé*) to feed (at one's mother's breast); **le bébé tète** the baby is being fed (at the breast); **donner à t. à** to feed. ● **tétée** *nf* (*de bébé*) feed. ● **tétine** *nf* (*de biberon*) teat, *Am* nipple; (*sucette*) dummy, *Am* pacifier.
têtu [tety] *a* stubborn, obstinate.
texte [tɛkst] *nm* text; *Th* lines.
textile [tɛkstil] *a* & *nm* textile.
texture [tɛkstyr] *nf* texture.
TGV [teʒeve] *abrév* = **train à grande vitesse.**
Thaïlande [tailɑ̃d] *nf* Thailand. ● **thaïlandais, -aise** *a* & *nmf* Thai.
thé [te] *nm* (*boisson, réunion*) tea. ● **théière** *nf* teapot.
théâtre [teɑtr] *nm* (*art, lieu*) theatre; (*œuvres*) drama; (*d'un crime*) *Fig* scene; (*des opérations*) *Mil* theatre; **faire du t.** to act. ● **théâtral, -aux** *a* theatrical.

thème [tɛm] *nm* theme; (*traduction*) *Scol* translation, prose.
théologie [teɔlɔʒi] *nf* theology.
théorie [teɔri] *nf* theory; **en t.** in theory. • **théorique** *a* theoretical.
thérapeutique [terapøtik] *a* therapeutic ‖ *nf* (*traitement*) therapy. • **thérapie** *nf* *Psy* therapy.
thermal, -aux [tɛrmal, -o] *a* **station thermale** spa; **eaux thermales** hot springs.
thermomètre [tɛrmɔmɛtr] *nm* thermometer.
thermos® [tɛrmɔs] *nm ou f inv* Thermos® (flask *ou Am* bottle), vacuum flask.
thermostat [tɛrmɔsta] *nm* thermostat.
thèse [tɛz] *nf* (*proposition, ouvrage*) thesis.
thon [tɔ̃] *nm* tuna (fish).
thym [tɛ̃] *nm Bot Culin* thyme.
tibia [tibja] *nm* shin bone.
tic [tik] *nm* (*contraction*) twitch, tic; (*manie*) *Fig* mannerism.
ticket [tikɛ] *nm* ticket; **t. de quai** *Rail* platform ticket.
tiède [tjɛd] *a* (luke)warm, tepid; (*vent*) mild; (*accueil, partisan*) half-hearted. • **tiédir** *vi* to cool (down); (*devenir plus chaud*) to warm up.
tien, tienne [tjɛ̃, tjɛn] *pron poss* **le t., la tienne, les tien(ne)s** yours; **les deux tiens** your two ‖ *nmpl* **les tiens** (*ta famille*) your (own) people.
ⓘ**G66** Possessive Pronouns 6 E 2
tiens, tient [tjɛ̃] *voir* **tenir.**
tiercé [tjɛrse] *nm* (*pari*) place betting (*on the horses*); **jouer/gagner au t.** = to bet/win on the horses.
tiers, tierce [tjɛr, tjɛrs] *a* third ‖ *nm* (*fraction*) third; (*personne*) third party; **assurance au t.** third-party insurance. • **T.-Monde** *nm* Third World.
tige [tiʒ] *nf* (*de plante*) stem, stalk; (*barre*) rod.
tigre [tigr] *nm* tiger. • **tigresse** *nf* tigress.
tigré [tigre] *a* (*rayé*) striped.
tilleul [tijœl] *nm* lime (tree); (*infusion*) lime tea.
timbale [tɛ̃bal] *nf* **1** (*gobelet*) (metal) tumbler. **2** *Mus* kettledrum.
timbre [tɛ̃br] *nm* **1** (*tampon, vignette*) stamp; (*cachet de la poste*) postmark. **2** (*sonnette*) bell. **3** (*d'instrument, de voix*) tone (quality). • **t.-poste** *nm* (*pl* **timbres-poste**) (postage) stamp. • **timbrer** *vt* (*affranchir*) to stamp (*letter*).
timide [timid] *a* (*gêné*) shy, timid; (*timoré*) timid. • **—ment** *adv* shyly; timidly. • **timidité** *nf* shyness.
tinter [tɛ̃te] *vi* (*cloche*) to ring; (*clefs, monnaie*) to jingle; (*verres*) to chink.
tique [tik] *nf* (*insecte*) tick.
tiquer [tike] *vi* (*personne*) to wince.
tir [tir] *nm* (*sport*) shooting; (*action*) firing, shooting; *Fb* shot; **(stand de) t.** shooting *ou* rifle range; **t. à l'arc** archery; **ligne de t.** line of fire.
tirage [tiraʒ] *nm* **1** (*de journal*) circulation; (*édition*) edition; (*quantité*) (print) run; *Typ Phot* printing. **2** (*de loterie*) draw; **t. au sort** drawing of lots. **3** (*de cheminée*) draught, *Am* draft.
tirailler [tirɑje] **1** *vt* to pull (away) at; **tiraillé entre** (*possibilités etc*) torn between. **2** *vi* (*au fusil*) to shoot wildly.
tire [tir] *nf* **vol à la t.** *Fam* pickpocketing.
tire-au-flanc [tiroflɑ̃] *nm inv* (*paresseux*) shirker.
tire-bouchon [tirbuʃɔ̃] *nm* corkscrew.
tirelire [tirlir] *nf* moneybox, *Am* coin bank.
tirer [tire] *vt* to pull; (*langue*) to stick out; (*trait, rideaux, conclusion*) to draw; (*balle, canon*) to shoot, fire; *Typ Phot* to print; **t. de** (*sortir*) to pull *ou* draw *ou* take out of; (*obtenir*) to get from; (*nom, origine*) to derive from; (*produit*) to extract from; **t. qn de** (*danger, lit*) to get s.o. out of.
‖ *vi* to pull (**sur** on, at); (*faire feu*) to shoot, fire (**sur** at); *Fb* to shoot; **t. au sort** to draw lots; **t. à sa fin** to draw to a close.
‖ **se tirer** *vpr* (*partir*) *Fam* to beat it; **se t. de** (*travail, problème*) to cope with; (*danger, situation*) to get out of; **se t. d'affaire** to get out of trouble. • **tiré** *a* (*traits, visage*) drawn; **t. par les cheveux** *Fig* far-fetched.
tiret [tirɛ] *nm* (*trait*) dash.
tireur [tirœr] *nm* gunman; **t. d'élite** marksman; **t. isolé** sniper; **un bon/mauvais t.** a good/bad shot.
tiroir [tirwar] *nm* (*de commode etc*) drawer.
tisane [tizan] *nf* herb(al) tea.
tison [tizɔ̃] *nm* (fire)brand, ember. • **tisonnier** *nm* poker.
tiss/er [tise] *vt* to weave. • **—age** *nm* (*action*) weaving.
tissu [tisy] *nm* material, cloth, fabric; *Biol* tissue; **du t.-éponge** (terry) towelling, *Am* toweling.
titre [titr] *nm* (*nom, qualité*) title; *Com* security, stock; (*diplôme*) qualification; **(gros) t.** (*de journal*) headline; **t. de propriété** title deed; **t. de transport** ticket; **à quel t.?** (*pour quelle raison*) on what grounds?; **à ce t.** (*en cette qualité*) as such; (*pour cette raison*) therefore; **au même t.** in the same way (**que** as); **à t.**

d'exemple as an example; **à t. exceptionnel** exceptionally; **à t. privé** in a private capacity; **à juste t.** rightly.

tituber [titybe] *vi* to reel, stagger.

titulaire [titylɛr] *a* **être t. de** (*permis etc*) to be the holder of; (*poste*) to hold ▮ *nmf* (*de permis, poste*) holder (**de** of).

toast [tost] *nm* **1** (*pain grillé*) piece *ou* slice of toast. **2** (*allocution*) toast; **porter un t. à** to drink (a toast) to.

toboggan [tɔbɔgɑ̃] *nm* **1** (*de terrain de jeux etc*) slide. **2** *Aut* flyover, *Am* overpass.

toc [tɔk] **1** *int* **t. t.!** knock knock! **2** *nm* **du t.** (*camelote*) trash; **bijou en t.** imitation jewel.

toi [twa] *pron* **1** (*après une préposition*) you; **avec t.** with you. **2** (*sujet*) you; **t., tu peux** *you* may; **c'est t. qui ...** it's you who .... **3** (*réfléchi*) **assieds-t.** sit (yourself) down; **dépêche-t.** hurry up. ●**t.-même** *pron* yourself.

ⓘ**toi G62** Disjunctive Pronouns 6 D 5

toile [twal] *nf* **1** cloth; (*à voile, sac etc*) canvas; **une t.** a piece of cloth *ou* canvas. **2** (*tableau*) painting, canvas. **3 t. d'araignée** (spider's) web.

toilette [twalɛt] *nf* (*action*) wash(ing); (*vêtements*) clothes, outfit; **articles de t.** toiletries; **cabinet de t.** washroom; **eau/trousse de t.** toilet water/bag; **faire sa t.** to wash (and dress); **les toilettes** (*W-C*) the toilet(s), *Am* the men's *ou* ladies' room; **aller aux toilettes** to go to the toilet *ou Am* to the men's *ou* ladies' room.

toit [twa] *nm* roof; **t. ouvrant** *Aut* sunroof. ●**toiture** *nf* roof(ing).

tôle [tol] *nf* **la t.** sheet metal; **une t.** a metal *ou* steel sheet; **t. ondulée** corrugated iron.

tolér/er [tɔlere] *vt* (*permettre*) to tolerate, allow; (*supporter*) to tolerate, bear. ●**—ant** *a* tolerant (**à l'égard de** of).

tollé [tɔle] *nm* outcry.

tomate [tɔmat] *nf* tomato; **sauce t.** tomato sauce.

tombe [tɔ̃b] *nf* grave; (*avec monument*) tomb. ●**tombale** *af* **pierre t.** gravestone, tombstone. ●**tombeau, -x** *nm* tomb.

tomber [tɔ̃be] *vi* (*aux* **être**) to fall; (*température*) to drop, fall; (*vent*) to drop (off); **t. malade** to fall ill; **t. (par terre)** to fall (down); **faire t.** (*personne*) to knock over; (*gouvernement*) to bring down; **laisser t.** (*objet*) to drop; (*projet etc*) *Fig* to drop, give up; **tu tombes bien/mal** *Fig* you've come at the right/wrong time; **t. de sommeil** to be ready to drop; **t. un lundi** to fall on a Monday; **t. sur** (*trouver*) to come across. ●**tombée** *nf* **t. de la nuit** nightfall.

tombola [tɔ̃bɔla] *nf* raffle.

tome [tɔm] *nm* (*livre*) volume.

ton[1], **ta,** *pl* **tes** [tɔ̃, ta, te] (**ta** *becomes* **ton** [tɔ̃n] *before a vowel or mute h*) *a poss* your; **ton père** your father; **ta mère** your mother; **ton ami(e)** your friend.

ⓘ**G64** Possessive Adjectives 6 E 1

ton[2] [tɔ̃] *nm* (*de voix etc*) tone; (*de couleur*) shade, tone; **de bon t.** (*goût*) in good taste; **sur un t. amer** in a bitter tone (of voice). ●**tonalité** *nf Tél* dialling tone, *Am* dial tone.

tond/re [tɔ̃dr] *vt* (*mouton*) to shear; (*gazon*) to mow. ●**—euse** *nf* shears; (*à cheveux*) clippers; **t. (à gazon)** (lawn)mower.

tonifier [tɔnifje] *vt* (*muscles, peau*) to tone up; (*personne*) to invigorate.

tonique [tɔnik] **1** *a* (*accent*) *Ling* tonic. **2** *a* (*froid, effet*) tonic, invigorating ▮ *nm Méd* tonic; (*cosmétique*) tonic lotion.

tonne [tɔn] *nf* (*poids*) metric ton, tonne; **des tonnes de** (*beaucoup*) *Fam* tons of.

tonneau, -x [tɔno] *nm* **1** (*récipient*) barrel, cask. **2** (*manœuvre*) *Av* roll; **faire un t.** *Aut* to roll over. **3** (*poids*) *Nau* ton.

tonnelle [tɔnɛl] *nf* arbour, bower.

tonner [tɔne] *vi* (*canons*) to thunder ▮ *v imp* **il tonne** it's thundering. ●**tonnerre** *nm* thunder; **coup de t.** burst *ou* crash of thunder, thunderclap; **du t.** (*excellent*) *Fam* terrific.

tonton [tɔ̃tɔ̃] *nm Fam* uncle.

tonus [tɔnys] *nm* energy, vitality.

top [tɔp] *nm* (*signal sonore*) *Rad* beep.

toque [tɔk] *nf* (*de fourrure*) fur hat; (*de jockey*) cap; (*de cuisinier*) hat.

toqué [tɔke] *a* (*fou*) *Fam* crazy. ●**toquade** *nf Fam* (*pour qch*) craze (**pour** for); (*pour qn*) infatuation (**pour** with).

torche [tɔrʃ] *nf* (*flamme*) torch; **t. électrique** torch, *Am* flashlight.

torchon [tɔrʃɔ̃] *nm* (*à vaisselle*) tea towel, *Am* dish towel; (*de ménage*) duster, cloth.

tordre [tɔrdr] *vt* to twist; (*linge, cou*) to wring; (*barre*) to bend; **se t. la cheville/le pied** to twist *ou* sprain one's ankle/foot ▮ **se t.** *vpr* to twist; (*barre*) to bend; **se t. de douleur** to be doubled up with pain; **se t. (de rire)** to split one's sides (laughing). ●**tordant** *a* (*drôle*) *Fam* hilarious. ●**tordu** *a* twisted; (*esprit*) warped.

tornade [tɔrnad] *nf* tornado.

torpille [tɔrpij] *nf* torpedo. ●**torpiller** *vt Mil & Fig* to torpedo.

torréfier [tɔrefje] *vt* (*café*) to roast.

torrent [tɔrɑ̃] *nm* (mountain) stream, torrent; **un t. de** (*injures, larmes*) a flood of; **il pleut à torrents** it's pouring (down). ●**torrentiel, -ielle** *a* (*pluie*) torrential.

torsade [tɔrsad] *nf* (*de cheveux*) twist, coil.
torse [tɔrs] *nm Anat* chest; (*statue*) torso; **t. nu** stripped to the waist.
torsion [tɔrsjɔ̃] *nf* twisting; *Phys Tech* torsion.
tort [tɔr] *nm* **avoir t.** to be wrong (**de faire** to do, in doing); **tu as t. de fumer!** you shouldn't smoke!; **être dans son t.** *ou* **en t.** to be in the wrong; **donner t. à qn** (*accuser*) to blame s.o.; (*faits etc*) to prove s.o. wrong; **faire du t. à qn** to harm *ou* wrong s.o.; **à t.** wrongly; **parler à t. et à travers** to talk nonsense; **à t. ou à raison** rightly or wrongly.
torticolis [tɔrtikɔli] *nm* **avoir le t.** to have a stiff neck.
tortiller [tɔrtije] *vt* to twist, twirl ‖ **se t.** *vpr* (*ver*, *personne*) to wriggle; (*en dansant*, *des hanches*) to wiggle.
tortue [tɔrty] *nf* tortoise, *Am* turtle; (*de mer*) turtle.
torture [tɔrtyr] *nf* torture. ●**torturer** *vt* to torture; **se t. les méninges** *Fam* to rack one's brains.
tôt [to] *adv* early; **au plus t.** at the earliest; **le plus t. possible** as soon as possible; **t. ou tard** sooner or later; **je n'étais pas plus t. sorti que...** no sooner had I gone out than....
total, -aux [tɔtal, -o] *a & nm* total; **au t.** all in all, in total. ●**totalement** *adv* totally. ●**totaliser** *vt* to total. ●**totalité** *nf* entirety; **la t. de** all of; **en t.** (*détruit etc*) entirely; (*payé*) fully.
toubib [tubib] *nm* (*médecin*) *Fam* doctor.
touche [tuʃ] *nf* (*de clavier*) key; (*de téléphone*) (push-)button; **téléphone à touches** push-button phone; **une t. de** (*un peu de*) a touch of; **(ligne de) t.** *Fb Rugby* touchline.
toucher [tuʃe] *vt* to touch; (*paie*) to draw; (*chèque*) to cash; (*cible*) to hit; (*émouvoir*) to touch, move; (*concerner*) to affect ‖ *vi* **t. à** to touch; (*sujet*) to touch on; (*but*, *fin*) to approach ‖ **se t.** *vpr* (*lignes*, *mains etc*) to touch ‖ *nm* (*sens*) touch; **au t.** to the touch. ●**touchant** *a* (*émouvant*) moving, touching.
touffe [tuf] *nf* (*de cheveux*, *d'herbe*) tuft; (*de plantes*) cluster. ●**touffu** *a* (*barbe*, *haie*) thick, bushy.
toujours [tuʒur] *adv* always; (*encore*) still; **pour t.** for ever; **essaie t.!** (*quand même*) try anyhow!; **t. est-il que...** the fact remains that ....
toupie [tupi] *nf* (spinning) top.
tour[1] [tur] *nf* **1** (*bâtiment*) tower; (*immeuble*) tower block, high-rise. **2** *Échecs* castle, rook.
tour[2] [tur] *nm* **1** (*mouvement etc*) turn; (*de magie etc*) trick; (*excursion*) trip, outing; (*à pied*) stroll, walk; (*en voiture*) drive; **t. de cartes** card trick; **t. de poitrine**/*etc* chest/*etc* measurement *ou* size; **faire le t. de** to go round; (*question*, *situation*) to review; **faire un t.** (*à pied*) to go for a stroll *ou* walk; (*en voiture*) to go for a drive; (*court voyage*) to go on a trip; **jouer un t. à qn** to play a trick on s.o.; **c'est mon t.** it's my turn; **à qui le t.?** whose turn (is it)?; **à son t.** in (one's) turn; **à t. de rôle** in turn; **t. à t.** in turn, by turns. **2** *Tech* lathe; (*de potier*) wheel.
tourbillon [turbijɔ̃] *nm* (*de vent*) whirlwind; (*d'eau*) whirlpool; (*de neige*, *sable*) swirl. ●**tourbillonner** *vi* to whirl, swirl.
tourelle [turɛl] *nf* turret.
tourisme [turism] *nm* tourism; **faire du t.** to go sightseeing *ou* touring; **agence/office de t.** tourist agency/office. ●**touriste** *nmf* tourist. ●**touristique** *a* **guide/***etc* **t.** tourist guide/*etc*; **route t., circuit t.** scenic route.
tourmenter [turmɑ̃te] *vt* to torment ‖ **se t.** *vpr* to worry (oneself). ●**tourmenté** *a* (*mer*, *vie*) turbulent, stormy; (*expression*, *visage*) anguished.
tourne-disque [turnədisk] *nm* record player.
tournée [turne] *nf* **1** (*de livreur etc*) round; (*de spectacle*) tour. **2** (*de boissons*) round.
tourner [turne] *vt* to turn; (*film*) to shoot; (*difficulté*) to get round; **t. en ridicule** to ridicule; **t. le dos à qn** to turn one's back on s.o. ‖ *vi* to turn; (*tête*, *toupie*) to spin; (*moteur*) to run, go; (*usine*) to run; (*lait*) to go off; (*Terre*) to revolve, turn; **t. autour de** (*objet*) to go round; (*maison*, *personne*) to hang around; **t. bien/mal** (*évoluer*) to turn out well/badly.
‖ **se tourner** *vpr* to turn (**vers** to, towards). ●**tournant 1** *a* **pont t.** swing bridge. **2** *nm* (*de route*) bend, turning; (*moment*) *Fig* turning point. ●**tournage** *nm Cin* shooting, filming.
tournesol [turnəsɔl] *nm* sunflower.
tournevis [turnəvis] *nm* screwdriver.
tourniquet [turnikɛ] *nm* **1** (*barrière*) turnstile. **2** (*pour arroser*) sprinkler.
tournoi [turnwa] *nm Sp & Hist* tournament.
tournoyer [turnwaje] *vi* to spin (round), whirl.
tourterelle [turtərɛl] *nf* turtledove.
Toussaint [tusɛ̃] *nf* All Saints' Day.
tousser [tuse] *vi* to cough.
tout, toute, *pl* **tous, toutes** [tu, tut, tu, tut] **1** *a* all; **tous les livres**/*etc* all the books/*etc*; **t. l'argent/le temps/le village**/*etc* all the money/time/village/*etc*, the whole of the

money/time/village/*etc*; **toute la nuit** all night, the whole (of the) night; **tous (les) deux** both; **tous (les) trois** all three; **t. un problème** quite a problem.

2 *a* (*chaque*) every, each; (*n'importe quel*) any; **tous les ans/jours/***etc* every *ou* each year/day/*etc*; **tous les cinq mois/ mètres** every five months/metres; **à toute heure** at any time.

3 *pron pl* (**tous** [tus]) all; **ils sont tous là, tous sont là** they're all there.

4 *pron m sing* **tout** everything; **elle dépense t.** she spends everything, she spends it all; **t. ce que je sais** everything that *ou* all that I know; **t. ce qui est là** everything that *ou* all that is there; **en t.** (*au total*) in all.

5 *adv* (*tout à fait*) quite; (*très*) very; **t. simplement** quite simply; **t. petit** very small; **t. neuf** brand new; **t. seul** all alone; **t. droit** straight ahead; **t. autour** all around; **t. au début** right at the beginning; **le t. premier** the very first; **t. au plus** at the very most; **t. en chantant/***etc* while singing/*etc*; **t. rusé qu'il est** however sly he may be; **t. à coup** suddenly, all of a sudden; **t. à fait** completely; **t. de même** all the same; (*indignation*) really!; **t. de suite** at once.

6 *nm* **le t.** everything, the lot; **un t.** a whole; **pas du t.** not at all; **rien du t.** nothing at all.

toutefois [tutfwa] *adv* nevertheless.

toux [tu] *nf* cough.

toxicomane [tɔksikɔman] *nmf* drug addict. ●**toxicomanie** *nf* drug addiction.

toxique [tɔksik] *a* poisonous, toxic.

trac [trak] *nm* **le t.** (*peur*) the jitters; (*de candidat*) exam nerves; *Th* stage fright; **avoir le t.** to be *ou* become nervous, have *ou* get nerves.

tracas [traka] *nm* worry. ●**tracasser** *vt*, **se t.** *vpr* to worry.

trace [tras] *nf* (*quantité, tache, vestige*) trace; (*marque*) mark; *pl* (*de bête, pneus*) tracks; **traces de pas** footprints; **suivre les traces de qn** *Fig* to follow in s.o.'s footsteps.

trac/er [trase] *vt* (*dessiner*) to draw; (*écrire*) to trace; **t. une route** to mark out a route. ●**—é** *nm* (*plan*) layout; (*ligne*) line.

tract [trakt] *nm* leaflet.

tracter [trakte] *vt* (*caravane etc*) to tow. ●**tracteur** *nm* tractor.

traction [traksjɔ̃] *nf* **t. arrière/avant** *Aut* rear-/front-wheel drive.

tradition [tradisjɔ̃] *nf* tradition. ●**traditionnel, -elle** *a* traditional.

traduire* [tradɥir] *vt* **1** to translate (**de** from, **en** into); (*exprimer*) *Fig* to express. **2 t. qn en justice** to bring s.o. before the courts. ●**traducteur, -trice** *nmf* translator. ●**traduction** *nf* translation.

trafic [trafik] *nm* **1** *Aut Rail etc* traffic. **2** *Com Péj* traffic, trade; **faire le t. de** to traffic in, trade in. ●**trafiquer 1** *vi* to traffic, trade. **2** *vt Fam* to tamper with. ●**trafiquant, -ante** *nmf* trafficker, dealer; **t. d'armes/de drogue** arms/drug trafficker *ou* dealer.

tragédie [traʒedi] *nf Th* & *Fig* tragedy. ●**tragique** *a* tragic.

trahir [trair] *vt* to betray; (*secret*) to give away, betray ‖ **se t.** *vpr* to give oneself away, betray oneself. ●**trahison** *nf* betrayal; (*crime*) treason.

train [trɛ̃] *nm* **1** train; **t. à grande vitesse** high-speed train; **t. couchettes** sleeper; **t. auto-couchettes** (car) sleeper. **2 en t.** (*forme*) on form; **se mettre en t.** to get (oneself) into shape. **3 être en t. de faire** to be (busy) doing; **mettre qch en t.** to get sth going. **4** (*allure*) pace; **t. de vie** life style. **5** (*de pneus*) set; (*de péniches, véhicules*) string. **6 t. d'atterrissage** *Av* undercarriage.

traîne [trɛn] *nf* **1** (*de robe*) train. **2 à la t.** (*en arrière*) lagging behind.

traîneau, -x [trɛno] *nm* sledge, sleigh, *Am* sled.

traînée [trene] *nf* (*de peinture etc*) streak.

traîner [trene] *vt* to drag; **faire t. en longueur** (*faire durer*) to drag out ‖ *vi* (*jouets, papiers etc*) to lie around; (*s'attarder*) to lag behind, dawdle; (*errer*) to hang around; **t. (par terre)** (*robe etc*) to trail (on the ground) ‖ **se t.** *vpr* (*avancer*) to drag oneself (along); (*par terre*) to crawl; (*durer*) to drag on.

train-train [trɛ̃trɛ̃] *nm* routine.

traire* [trɛr] *vt* (*vache*) to milk.

trait [trɛ] *nm* **1** line; (*en dessinant*) stroke; (*caractéristique*) feature, trait; *pl* (*du visage*) features; **t. d'union** hyphen; **d'un t.** (*boire*) in one gulp; **avoir t. à** (*se rapporter à*) to relate to. **2 cheval de t.** draught *ou Am* draft horse.

traite [trɛt] *nf* **1** (*de vache*) milking. **2** *Com* bill, draft. **3 d'une (seule) t.** (*sans interruption*) in one go.

traité [trete] *nm Pol* treaty.

traiter [trete] *vt* (*se comporter envers*) & *Méd* to treat; (*problème, sujet*) to deal with; (*marché*) *Com* to negotiate; (*matériau, produit*) to treat, process; **t. qn de lâche/***etc* to call s.o. a coward/*etc*.
‖ *vi* to negotiate, deal (**avec** with); **t. de**

(*sujet*) to deal with. ● **traitant** *a* **médecin t.** regular doctor. ● **traitement** *nm* **1** treatment; **t. de données/de texte** data/word processing; **machine à** *ou* **de t. de texte** word processor. **2** (*gains*) salary.

traiteur [trɛtœr] *nm* (*fournisseur*) caterer; **chez le t.** (*magasin*) at the delicatessen.

traître [trɛtr] *nm* traitor. ● **traîtrise** *nf* treachery.

trajectoire [traʒɛktwar] *nf* (*de fusée, missile etc*) path.

trajet [traʒɛ] *nm* trip, journey; (*distance*) distance; (*itinéraire*) route.

trampoline [trɑ̃pɔlin] *nm* trampoline.

tram(way) [tram(wɛ)] *nm* tram, *Am* streetcar.

tranche [trɑ̃ʃ] *nf* (*morceau*) slice; (*bord*) edge; (*partie*) portion; (*de salaire, impôts*) bracket; **t. d'âge** age bracket.

tranchée [trɑ̃ʃe] *nf* trench.

tranch/er [trɑ̃ʃe] **1** *vt* to cut. **2** *vt* (*difficulté, question*) to settle ‖ *vi* (*décider*) to decide. **3** *vi* (*contraster*) to contrast (**avec, sur** with). ● **—ant** *a* (*couteau, voix*) sharp ‖ *nm* (cutting) edge; **à double t.** *Fig* double-edged.

tranquille [trɑ̃kil] *a* quiet; (*mer*) calm; (*conscience*) clear; (*esprit*) easy; **laisser t.** to leave alone; **soyez t.** don't worry. ● **tranquillement** *adv* calmly. ● **tranquillité** *nf* (peace and) quiet; (*d'esprit*) peace of mind.

tranquillis/er [trɑ̃kilize] *vt* to reassure; **tranquillisez-vous** set your mind at rest. ● **—ant** *nm Méd* tranquillizer.

trans- [trɑ̃z, trɑ̃s] *préf* trans-.

transaction [trɑ̃zaksjɔ̃] *nf Com* transaction.

transatlantique [trɑ̃zatlɑ̃tik] *a* transatlantic ‖ *nm* (*paquebot*) transatlantic liner; (*chaise*) deckchair.

transe [trɑ̃s] *nf* **en t.** in a trance.

transférer [trɑ̃sfere] *vt* to transfer (**à** to). ● **transfert** *nm* transfer.

transformer [trɑ̃sfɔrme] *vt* to change, transform; (*maison*) to carry out alterations to; (*essai*) *Rugby* to convert; **t. en** to turn into ‖ **se t.** *vpr* to change, be transformed (**en** into). ● **transformateur** *nm Él* transformer. ● **transformation** *nf* change, transformation; alteration.

transfuge [trɑ̃sfyʒ] *nm Mil* renegade ‖ *nmf Pol* renegade.

transfusion [trɑ̃sfyzjɔ̃] *nf* **t. (sanguine)** (blood) transfusion.

transgresser [trɑ̃sgrese] *vt* (*loi, ordre*) to disobey.

transi [trɑ̃zi] *a* (*personne*) numb with cold.

transistor [trɑ̃zistɔr] *nm* transistor (radio).

transit [trɑ̃zit] *nm* transit; **en t.** in transit; **salle de t.** *Av* transit lounge. ● **transiter** *vt* **(faire) t.** to send in transit ‖ *vi* to be in transit.

transitif, -ive [trɑ̃zitif, -iv] *a & nm Gram* transitive.

transition [trɑ̃zisjɔ̃] *nf* transition. ● **transitoire** *a & nm* (*qui passe*) transient; (*provisoire*) transitional.

transmettre* [trɑ̃smɛtr] *vt* (*message etc*) to pass on (**à** to); *Phys Tech* to transmit; *Rad TV* to broadcast.

transparent [trɑ̃sparɑ̃] *a* clear, transparent. ● **transparence** *nf* transparency.

transpercer [trɑ̃spɛrse] *vt* to pierce, go through.

transpirer [trɑ̃spire] *vi* (*suer*) to sweat, perspire. ● **transpiration** *nf* perspiration.

transplanter [trɑ̃splɑ̃te] *vt* (*organe, plante etc*) to transplant.

transport [trɑ̃spɔr] *nm* (*action*) transport, transportation (**de** of); *pl* (*moyens*) transport; **moyen de t.** means of transport; **transports en commun** public transport; **frais de t.** transport costs.

transporter [trɑ̃spɔrte] *vt* to transport, convey; (*à la main*) to carry, take; **t. d'urgence à l'hôpital** to rush to hospital *ou Am* to the hospital. ● **transporteur** *nm* **t. (routier)** haulier, *Am* trucker.

transversal, -aux [trɑ̃svɛrsal, -o] *a* **rue**/*etc* **transversale** cross street/*etc*.

trapèze [trapɛz] *nm* (*au cirque*) trapeze. ● **trapéziste** *nmf* trapeze artist.

trappe [trap] *nf* (*dans le plancher*) trap door.

trapu [trapy] *a* (*personne*) stocky, thickset.

traquer [trake] *vt* to track *ou* hunt (down).

traumatiser [tromatize] *vt* to traumatize. ● **traumatisme** *nm* (*choc*) trauma.

travail, -aux [travaj, -o] *nm* (*activité, lieu*) work; (*à effectuer*) job, task; (*emploi*) job; (*façonnage*) working (**de** of); *Écon Méd* labour; *pl* work; (*dans la rue*) roadworks, *Am* roadwork; (*aménagement*) alterations; **travaux pratiques** *Scol Univ* practical work; **travaux manuels** *Scol* handicrafts; **travaux forcés** hard labour; **travaux ménagers** housework; **t. au noir** moonlighting.

travaill/er [travaje] **1** *vi* to work (**à qch** at *ou* on sth) ‖ *vt* (*discipline, rôle, style*) to work on; (*façonner*) to work. **2** *vi* (*bois*) to warp. ● **—eur, -euse** *a* hard-working ‖ *nmf* worker.

travailliste [travajist] *a Pol* Labour ‖ *nmf Pol* member of the Labour party.

travers [travɛr] **1** *prép & adv* **à t.** through;

en t. (de) across. **2** *adv* **de t.** (*chapeau, nez etc*) crooked; (*comprendre*) badly; (*regarder*) askance; **aller de t.** *Fig* to go wrong; **j'ai avalé de t.** it went down the wrong way. **3** *nm* (*défaut*) failing.

traverse [travɛrs] *nf* **1** *Rail* sleeper, *Am* tie. **2 chemin de t.** short cut.

travers/er [travɛrse] *vt* to cross, go across; (*foule, période, mur*) to go through. **●—ée** *nf* (*voyage*) crossing.

traversin [travɛrsɛ̃] *nm* bolster.

travesti [travɛsti] *nm Th* female impersonator; (*homosexuel*) transvestite.

trébucher [trebyʃe] *vi* to stumble (**sur** over); **faire t. qn** to trip s.o. (up).

trèfle [trɛfl] *nm* **1** (*plante*) clover. **2** (*couleur*) *Cartes* clubs.

treillis [treji] *nm* **1** lattice(work); (*en métal*) wire mesh. **2** (*tenue militaire*) combat uniform.

treize [trɛz] *a & nm inv* thirteen. **●treizième** *a & nmf* thirteenth.

tréma [trema] *nm Gram* di(a)eresis.

trembl/er [trɑ̃ble] *vi* to shake, tremble; (*de froid, peur*) to tremble (**de** with); (*flamme, lumière*) to flicker; (*voix*) to tremble. **●—ement** *nm* (*action, frisson*) shaking, trembling; **t. de terre** earthquake.

trémousser (se) [sətremuse] *vpr* to wriggle (about).

tremper [trɑ̃pe] **1** *vt* to soak, drench; (*plonger*) to dip (**dans** in) ‖ *vi* to soak; **faire t. qch** to soak sth ‖ **se t.** *vpr* (*se baigner*) to take a dip. **2** *vt* (*acier*) to temper.

tremplin [trɑ̃plɛ̃] *nm Natation & Fig* springboard.

trente [trɑ̃t] *a & nm* thirty; **un t.-trois tours** (*disque*) an LP. **●trentaine** *nf* **une t. (de)** (*nombre*) (about) thirty. **●trentième** *a & nmf* thirtieth.

trépied [trepje] *nm* tripod.

trépigner [trepiɲe] *vi* to stamp (one's feet).

très [trɛ] *adv* ([trɛz] *before vowel or mute h*) very; **t. aimé/critiqué**/*etc* (*with past participle*) much *ou* greatly liked/criticized/*etc*.

trésor [trezɔr] *nm* treasure; **le T. (public)** (*service*) public revenue (department). **●trésorerie** *nf* (*bureaux d'un club etc*) accounts department; (*gestion*) accounting. **●trésorier, -ière** *nmf* treasurer.

tressaillir* [tresajir] *vi* (*frémir*) to shake, quiver; (*de joie, peur*) to tremble (**de** with).

tresse [trɛs] *nf* (*cordon*) braid; (*cheveux*) plait, *Am* braid. **●tresser** *vt* to braid; (*cheveux*) to plait, *Am* braid.

tréteau, -x [treto] *nm* trestle.

treuil [trœj] *nm* winch, windlass.

trêve [trɛv] *nf Mil* truce; (*répit*) *Fig* respite.

tri [tri] *nm* sorting (out); **faire le t. de** to sort (out).

triangle [trijɑ̃gl] *nm* triangle. **●triangulaire** *a* triangular.

tribord [tribɔr] *nm Nau Av* starboard.

tribu [triby] *nf* tribe. **●tribal, -aux** *a* tribal.

tribunal, -aux [tribynal, -o] *nm Jur* court; (*militaire*) tribunal.

tribune [tribyn] *nf* **1** (*de salle publique etc*) gallery; (*de stade*) (grand)stand; (*d'orateur*) rostrum. **2 t. libre** (*dans un journal*) open forum.

tricher [triʃe] *vi* to cheat. **●tricherie** *nf* cheating, trickery; **une t.** a piece of trickery. **●tricheur, -euse** *nmf* cheat, *Am* cheater.

tricolore [trikɔlɔr] *a* **1** (*cocarde etc*) red, white and blue; **le drapeau t.** the French flag. **2 feu t.** traffic lights.

tricot [triko] *nm* (*activité, ouvrage*) knitting; (*chandail*) sweater, jumper; **un t.** (*ouvrage*) a piece of knitting; **en t.** knitted. **●tricoter** *vti* to knit.

tricycle [trisikl] *nm* tricycle.

trier [trije] *vt* (*séparer*) to sort (out); (*choisir*) to pick *ou* sort out.

trimbal(l)er [trɛ̃bale] *vt Fam* to cart about, drag around.

trimestre [trimɛstr] *nm* (*période*) *Com* quarter; *Scol* term. **●trimestriel, -ielle** *a* (*revue*) quarterly; **bulletin t.** end-of-term report *ou Am* report card.

tringle [trɛ̃gl] *nf* rail, rod; **t. à rideaux** curtain rail *ou* rod.

trinquer [trɛ̃ke] *vi* to chink glasses; **t. à la santé**/*etc* **de qn** to drink to s.o.'s health/*etc*.

trio [trijo] *nm* (*groupe*) & *Mus* trio.

triomphe [trijɔ̃f] *nm* triumph (**sur** over). **●triompher** *vi* to triumph (**de** over); (*jubiler*) to be jubilant. **●triomphant** *a* triumphant.

tripes [trip] *nfpl Culin* tripe; *Fam* guts.

triple [tripl] *a* treble, triple ‖ *nm* **le t.** three times as much (**de** as). **●tripler** *vti* to treble, triple. **●triplés, -ées** *nmfpl* (*enfants*) triplets.

tripoter [tripɔte] *vt* to fiddle about *ou* around with.

triste [trist] *a* sad; (*couleur, temps, rue*) gloomy, dreary; (*lamentable*) unfortunate, sorry. **●tristement** [-əmɑ̃] *adv* sadly. **●tristesse** *nf* sadness; (*du temps etc*) gloom(iness), dreariness.

ⓘ **triste G32** Position of Adjectives 4 D 3

ⓘ **triste G98 & 99** The Subjunctive 7 G 1a) & d)

ⓘ **triste G112** The Infinitive 7 H 2c) iv)

trivial, -aux [trivjal, -o] *a* coarse, vulgar.
troc [trɔk] *nm* exchange, barter.
troène [trɔɛn] *nm* (*arbuste*) privet.
trognon [trɔɲɔ̃] *nm* (*de fruit*) core; (*de chou*) stump.
trois [trwɑ] *a* & *nm* three. ●**troisième** *a* & *nmf* third. ●**troisièmement** *adv* thirdly.
trolley(bus) [trɔlɛ(bys)] *nm* trolleybus.
trombe [trɔ̃b] *nf* **trombe(s) d'eau** (*pluie*) rainstorm, downpour; **en t.** (*entrer etc*) *Fig* like a whirlwind.
trombone [trɔ̃bɔn] *nm* **1** *Mus* trombone. **2** (*agrafe*) paper clip.
trompe [trɔ̃p] *nf* (*d'éléphant*) trunk.
tromper [trɔ̃pe] *vt* to deceive, mislead; (*être infidèle à*) to be unfaithful to; (*échapper à*) to elude ‖ **se t.** *vpr* to be mistaken, make a mistake; **se t. de route**/*etc* to take the wrong road/*etc*; **se t. de date**/*etc* to get the date/*etc* wrong.
trompette [trɔ̃pɛt] *nf* trumpet. ●**trompettiste** *nmf* trumpet player.
tronc [trɔ̃] *nm* **1** (*d'arbre*) & *Anat* trunk. **2** *Rel* collection box.
tronçon [trɔ̃sɔ̃] *nm* section. ●**tronçonner** *vt* to cut (into sections). ●**tronçonneuse** *nf* chain saw.
trône [tron] *nm* throne.
trop [tro] *adv* too; too much; **t. dur**/*etc* too hard/*etc*; **t. fatigué pour jouer** too tired to play; **boire**/*etc* **t.** to drink/*etc* too much; **t. de sel**/*etc* (*quantité*) too much salt/*etc*; **t. de gens**/*etc* (*nombre*) too many people/*etc*; **un franc**/*etc* **de t.** *ou* **en t.** one franc/*etc* too many; **t. souvent** too often; **t. peu** not enough; **se sentir de t.** *Fig* to feel in the way.
trophée [trɔfe] *nm* trophy.
tropiques [trɔpik] *nmpl* **les t.** the tropics. ●**tropical, -aux** *a* tropical.
trop-plein [trɔplɛ̃] *nm* (*dispositif, liquide*) overflow; (*surabondance*) *Fig* excess.
troquer [trɔke] *vt* to exchange (**contre** for).
trot [tro] *nm* trot; **aller au t.** to trot. ●**trotter** [trɔte] *vi* (*cheval*) to trot.
trotteuse [trɔtøz] *nf* (*de montre*) second hand.
trottiner [trɔtine] *vi* (*personne*) to patter *ou* trot along.
trottinette [trɔtinɛt] *nf* (*jouet*) scooter.
trottoir [trɔtwar] *nm* pavement, *Am* sidewalk; **t. roulant** moving walkway.
trou [tru] *nm* hole; (*d'aiguille*) eye; (*village*) *Péj* dump; **t. de (la) serrure** keyhole; **t. (de mémoire)** *Fig* lapse (of memory).
trouble [trubl] **1** *a* (*liquide*) cloudy; (*image*) blurred; (*affaire*) shady; **voir t.** to see things blurred. **2** *nmpl* (*de santé*) trouble; (*révolte*) disturbances, troubles.
troubler [truble] *vt* to disturb; (*vue*) to blur; (*liquide*) to make cloudy; (*esprit*) to unsettle; (*inquiéter*) to trouble ‖ **se t.** *vpr* (*liquide*) to become cloudy; (*candidat etc*) to become flustered. ●**trouble-fête** *nmf inv* killjoy, spoilsport.
trouer [true] *vt* to make a hole *ou* holes in; (*silence, ténèbres*) to cut through.
trouille [truj] *nf* **avoir la t.** *Fam* to have the jitters. ●**trouillard** *a* (*poltron*) *Fam* chicken.
troupe [trup] *nf* (*groupe*) group; *Th* company; **les troupes** (*armée*) the troops.
troupeau, -x [trupo] *nm* (*de vaches*) & *Fig Péj* herd; (*de moutons, d'oies*) flock.
trousse [trus] **1** *nf* (*étui*) case, kit; (*d'écolier*) pencil case; **t. à outils** toolkit; **t. à pharmacie** first-aid kit; **t. de toilette** sponge *ou* toilet bag, dressing case. **2** *nfpl* **aux trousses de qn** *Fig* on s.o.'s heels.
trousseau, -x [truso] *nm* **1 t. de clefs** bunch of keys. **2** (*de mariée*) trousseau.
trouver [truve] *vt* to find; **aller/venir t. qn** to go/come and see s.o.; **je trouve que** (*je pense que*) I think that; **comment la trouvez-vous?** what do you think of her? ‖ **se t.** *vpr* to be; (*être situé*) to be situated; (*dans une situation*) to find oneself; **se t. mal** (*s'évanouir*) to faint; **il se trouve que** it happens that. ●**trouvaille** *nf* (lucky) find.
truander [tryɑ̃de] *vi* (*tricher*) *Fam* to cheat.
truc [tryk] *nm* **1** (*astuce*) trick; (*moyen*) way; **trouver le t.** to get the knack (**pour faire** of doing). **2** (*chose*) *Fam* thing.
truffe [tryf] *nf* **1** (*champignon*) truffle. **2** (*de chien*) nose.
truffer [tryfe] *vt* (*remplir*) to stuff (**de** with).
truie [trɥi] *nf* (*animal*) sow.
truite [trɥit] *nf* trout.
truqu/er [tryke] *vt* (*photo etc*) to fake; (*élections, match*) to rig, fix. ●**—age** *nm Cin* (special) effect; (*action*) faking; rigging.
trust [trœst] *nm Com* (*cartel*) trust; (*entreprise*) corporation.
tsigane [tsigan] *a* & *nmf* (Hungarian) gipsy.
TSVP [teɛsvepe] *abrév* (*tournez s'il vous plaît*) PTO.
TTC [tetese] *abrév* (*toutes taxes comprises*) inclusive of tax.
tu[1] [ty] *pron* you (*familiar form of address*). ❶**G56** Personal Pronouns 6 D 1b)
tu[2] [ty] *pp de* **taire.**
tuba [tyba] *nm* **1** *Mus* tuba. **2** *Sp Nau* snorkel.
tube [tyb] *nm* **1** tube. **2** (*chanson, disque*) *Fam* hit.

tuberculose [tybɛrkyloz] *nf* TB, tuberculosis.

tuer [tɥe] *vt* to kill; (*d'un coup de feu*) to shoot (dead), kill; (*épuiser*) *Fig* to wear out ▮ **se t.** *vpr* to kill oneself; to shoot oneself; (*dans un accident*) to be killed; **se t. à faire** *Fig* to wear oneself out doing. ●**tuant** *a* (*fatigant*) exhausting. ●**tueur, -euse** *nmf* killer.

tue-tête (à) [atytɛt] *adv* at the top of one's voice.

tuile [tɥil] *nf* **1** tile. **2** (*malchance*) *Fam* (stroke of) bad luck.

tulipe [tylip] *nf* tulip.

tumeur [tymœr] *nf* tumour, growth.

tumulte [tymylt] *nm* (*désordre*) turmoil.

tunique [tynik] *nf* tunic.

Tunisie [tynizi] *nf* Tunisia. ●**tunisien, -ienne** *a* & *nmf* Tunisian.

tunnel [tynɛl] *nm* tunnel; **le t. sous la Manche** the Channel Tunnel.

turban [tyrbɑ̃] *nm* turban.

turbine [tyrbin] *nf* turbine.

turbulences [tyrbylɑ̃s] *nfpl Av etc* turbulence.

turbulent [tyrbylɑ̃] *a* (*enfant*) disruptive, boisterous.

turfiste [tyrfist] *nmf* racegoer.

Turquie [tyrki] *nf* Turkey. ●**turc, turque** *a* Turkish ▮ *nmf* Turk ▮ *nm* (*langue*) Turkish.

turquoise [tyrkwaz] *a inv* turquoise.

tuteur, -trice [tytœr, -tris] **1** *nmf Jur* guardian. **2** *nm* (*bâton*) stake, prop. ●**tutelle** *nf Jur* guardianship; *Fig* protection.

tutoyer [tytwaje] *vt* **t. qn** to use the familiar *tu* form to s.o.

tutu [tyty] *nm* ballet skirt, tutu.

tuyau, -x [tɥijo] *nm* **1** pipe; **t. d'arrosage** hose(pipe); **t. de cheminée** flue; **t. d'échappement** *Aut* exhaust (pipe). **2** (*renseignement*) *Fam* tip. ●**tuyauterie** *nf* (*tuyaux*) piping.

TVA [tevea] *nf abrév* (*taxe à la valeur ajoutée*) VAT.

type [tip] *nm* (*modèle*) type; (*individu*) *Fam* fellow, guy; **le t. même de** *Fig* the very model of ▮ *a inv* (*professeur etc*) typical. ●**typique** *a* typical (**de** of).

typé [tipe] *a* **être très t.** to have all the usual distinctive features.

typhoïde [tifɔid] *nf Méd* typhoid.

typhon [tifɔ̃] *nm Mét* typhoon.

typographie [tipɔgrafi] *nf* typography, printing.

tyran [tirɑ̃] *nm* tyrant. ●**tyrannie** *nf* tyranny.

tzigane [dzigan] *a* & *nmf* (Hungarian) gipsy.

U

U, u [y] *nm* U, u.
Ukraine [ykrɛn] *nf* Ukraine.
ulcère [ylsɛr] *nm* ulcer, sore.
ULM [yɛlɛm] *nm abrév* (*Ultra-Léger Motorisé*) *Av* microlight.
ultérieur [ylterjœr] *a* later. •**—ement** *adv* later.
ultimatum [yltimatɔm] *nm* ultimatum.
ultime [yltim] *a* final, last.
ultramoderne [yltramɔdɛrn] *a* ultramodern.
ultra-secret, -ète [yltrasəkrɛ, -ɛt] *a* top-secret.
ultraviolet, -ette [yltravjɔlɛ, -ɛt] *a* ultra-violet.
un, une [œ̃, yn] **1** *art indéf* a, (*devant voyelle*) an; **une page** a page; **un ange** [œ̃nɑ̃ʒ] an angel. **2** *a* one; **la page un** page one; **un kilo** one kilo; **un type** (*un quelconque*) some *ou* a fellow; **un jour** one day. **3** *pron* & *nmf* one; **l'un** one; **les uns** some; **le numéro un** number one; **j'en ai un** I have one; **l'un d'eux/l'une d'elles** one of them; **la une** (*de journal*) page one.
ⓘG14 The Indefinite Article 2 B
ⓘG190 Cardinal Numbers 10 A
unanime [ynanim] *a* unanimous. •**unanimité** *nf* **à l'u.** unanimously.
uni [yni] *a* united; (*famille etc*) close; (*surface*) smooth; (*couleur, étoffe*) plain.
unième [ynjɛm] *a* (*after a number*) (-)first; **trente et u.** thirty-first; **cent u.** hundred and first.
unifier [ynifje] *vt* to unify.
uniforme [ynifɔrm] **1** *nm* (*vêtement*) uniform. **2** *a* (*régulier*) uniform.
union [ynjɔ̃] *nf* union; (*association*) association; (*entente*) unity.
unique [ynik] *a* **1** (*fille, espoir etc*) only; (*prix, marché*) single, one; **son seul et u. souci** his *ou* her one and only worry. **2** (*exceptionnel*) unique. •**uniquement** *adv* only.
unir [ynir] *vt* (*deux pays etc*) to unite, join (together); (*efforts*) to combine; **u. la force au courage** to combine strength with courage; **u. deux personnes** (*amitié*) to unite two people ‖ **s'u.** *vpr* (*étudiants etc*) to unite; (*se marier*) to be joined together.
unisexe [ynisɛks] *a* (*vêtements etc*) unisex.
unisson (à l') [alynisɔ̃] *adv* in unison (**de** with).
unité [ynite] *nf* (*de mesure, élément*) & *Mil* unit; (*cohésion, harmonie*) unity. •**unitaire** *a* (*prix*) per unit.
univers [ynivɛr] *nm* universe.
universel, -elle [ynivɛrsɛl] *a* universal.
université [ynivɛrsite] *nf* university; **à l'u.** at university, *Am* in college. •**universitaire** *a* **ville/***etc* **u.** university town/*etc*.
urbain [yrbɛ̃] *a* **population/***etc* **urbaine** urban *ou* city population/*etc*. •**urbanisme** *nm* town planning, *Am* city planning.
urgent [yrʒɑ̃] *a* urgent. •**urgence** *nf* (*cas*) emergency; (*de décision, tâche etc*) urgency; **mesures/***etc* **d'u.** emergency measures/*etc*; **état d'u.** *Pol* state of emergency; **(service des) urgences** (*d'hôpital*) casualty (department), *Am* emergency room; **faire qch d'u.** to do sth urgently.
ⓘurgent G99 The Subjunctive 7 G 1d)
urine [yrin] *nf* urine. •**uriner** *vi* to urinate.
urne [yrn] *nf* **1** (*électorale*) ballot box; **aller aux urnes** to go to the polls, vote. **2** (*vase*) urn.
usage [yzaʒ] *nm* use; (*habitude*) custom; *Ling* usage; **faire u. de** to make use of; **d'u.** (*habituel*) customary; **à l'u. de** for the use of; **hors d'u.** broken, not in use. •**usagé** *a* worn. •**usager** *nm* user.
user [yze] *vt* (*vêtement, personne*) to wear out; (*consommer*) to use (up) ‖ *vi* **u. de** to use ‖ **s'u.** *vpr* (*tissu, machine*) to wear out. •**usé** *a* (*tissu etc*) worn (out); (*personne*) worn out.
usine [yzin] *nf* factory; **u. à gaz** gasworks; **u. métallurgique** ironworks; **ouvrier d'u.** factory worker.
usité [yzite] *a* in common use.
ustensile [ystɑ̃sil] *nm* utensil.
usuel, -elle [yzɥɛl] *a* everyday, ordinary.
usure [yzyr] *nf* (*détérioration*) wear (and tear); **avoir qn à l'u.** *Fig* to wear s.o. down.
usurper [yzyrpe] *vt* to usurp.
utérus [yterys] *nm Anat* womb.
utile [ytil] *a* useful (**à** to).
utiliser [ytilize] *vt* to use, utilize. •**utilisateur, -trice** *nmf* user. •**utilisation** *nf* use. •**utilité** *nf* use(fulness); **d'une grande u.** very useful.
utilitaire [ytilitɛr] *a* utilitarian; **véhicule u.** commercial vehicle.
UV [yve] *nmpl abrév* (*ultraviolets*) UV.

V

V, v [ve] *nm* V, v.

va [va] *voir* **aller**[1].

vacances [vakɑ̃s] *nfpl* holiday(s), *Am* vacation; **en v.** on holiday, *Am* on vacation; **prendre ses v.** to take one's holiday(s) *ou Am* vacation; **les grandes v.** the summer holidays *ou Am* vacation. ● **vacancier, -ière** *nmf* holidaymaker, *Am* vacationer.

vacant [vakɑ̃] *a* vacant.

vacarme [vakarm] *nm* din, uproar.

vaccin [vaksɛ̃] *nm* vaccine; **faire un v. à** to vaccinate. ● **vaccination** *nf* vaccination. ● **vacciner** *vt* to vaccinate.

vache [vaʃ] **1** *nf* cow; **v. laitière** dairy cow. **2** *nf* **(peau de) v.** (*personne*) *Fam* swine ▌*a* (*méchant*) *Fam* nasty. ● **vachement** *adv Fam* (*très*) damned; (*beaucoup*) a hell of a lot.

vaciller [vasije] *vi* to sway, wobble; (*flamme, lumière*) to flicker.

vadrouille [vadruj] *nf* **en v.** *Fam* roaming *ou* wandering about.

va-et-vient [vaevjɛ̃] *nm inv* (*mouvement*) movement to and fro; (*de personnes*) comings and goings.

vagabond, -onde [vagabɔ̃, -ɔ̃d] *nmf* (*clochard*) tramp, *Am* hobo. ● **vagabonder** *vi* to roam *ou* wander about; (*pensée*) to wander.

vagin [vaʒɛ̃] *nm* vagina.

vague [vag] **1** *a* vague; (*regard*) vacant; (*souvenir*) dim, vague ▌*nm* **regarder dans le v.** to gaze into space; **rester dans le v.** (*être évasif*) to keep it vague. **2** *nf* (*de mer*) & *Fig* wave; **v. de chaleur** heat wave; **v. de froid** cold spell *ou* snap. ● **vaguement** *adv* vaguely.

ⓘ **vague G32** Position of Adjectives 4 D 3

vain [vɛ̃] *a* (*futile*) vain, futile; (*mots, promesse*) empty; **en v.** in vain, vainly.

vainc/re* [vɛ̃kr] *vt* to beat, defeat; (*surmonter*) to overcome. ● **—u, -ue** *nmf* defeated man *ou* woman; *Sp* loser. ● **vainqueur** *nm* victor; *Sp* winner.

vais [vɛ] *voir* **aller**[1].

vaisseau, -x [vɛso] *nm* **1** *Anat Bot* vessel. **2** (*bateau*) ship, vessel; **v. spatial** spaceship.

vaisselle [vɛsɛl] *nf* crockery; (*à laver*) washing up, dirty dishes; **faire la v.** to do the washing up, wash *ou* do the dishes.

valable [valabl] *a* (*billet, motif etc*) valid.

valet [valɛ] *nm Cartes* jack.

valeur [valœr] *nf* value; (*mérite*) worth; *pl* (*titres*) *Com* stocks and shares; **avoir de la v.** to be valuable; **mettre en v.** (*faire ressortir*) to highlight; **objets de v.** valuables.

valide [valid] *a* **1** (*personne*) fit, able-bodied. **2** (*billet etc*) valid. ● **valider** *vt* to validate. ● **validité** *nf* validity.

valise [valiz] *nf* (suit)case; **v. diplomatique** diplomatic bag *ou Am* pouch; **faire ses valises** to pack (one's bags).

vallée [vale] *nf* valley.

valoir* [valwar] *vi* to be worth; (*s'appliquer*) to apply (**pour** to); **v. mille francs/cher/***etc* to be worth a thousand francs/a lot/*etc*; **un vélo vaut bien une auto** a bicycle is just as good as a car; **il vaut mieux rester** it's better to stay; **il vaut mieux que j'attende** I'd better wait; **ça ne vaut rien** it's no good, it's worthless; **ça vaut la peine** *ou Fam* **le coup** it's worth while (**de faire** doing); **faire v.** (*faire ressortir*) to highlight; (*argument*) to put forward; (*droit*) to assert.

▌*vt* **v. qch à qn** (*causer*) to bring *ou* get s.o. sth.

▌**se valoir** *vpr* (*objets, personnes*) to be as good as each other; **ça se vaut** *Fam* it's all the same.

valse [vals] *nf* waltz. ● **valser** *vi* to waltz.

valve [valv] *nf* (*clapet*) valve.

vampire [vɑ̃pir] *nm* vampire.

vandale [vɑ̃dal] *nmf* vandal. ● **vandalisme** *nm* vandalism.

vanille [vanij] *nf* vanilla; **glace/***etc* **à la v.** vanilla ice cream/*etc*.

vanité [vanite] *nf* vanity. ● **vaniteux, -euse** *a* vain, conceited.

vanne [van] *nf* **1** (*d'écluse*) sluice (gate), floodgate. **2** (*remarque*) *Fam* dig, jibe.

vanter [vɑ̃te] *vt* to praise ▌**se v.** *vpr* to boast, brag (**de** about, of). ● **vantard, -arde** *nmf* bighead, boaster.

vapeur [vapœr] *nf* (*brume, émanation*) vapour; **v. (d'eau)** steam; **cuire à la v.** to steam; **bateau à v.** steamship.

vaporiser [vapɔrize] *vt* to spray. ● **vaporisateur** *nm* (*appareil*) spray.

varappe [varap] *nf* rock-climbing.

variable [varjabl] *a* variable; (*humeur, temps*) changeable. ● **variation** *nf* variation.

varicelle [varisɛl] *nf* chickenpox.
varices [varis] *nfpl* varicose veins.
vari/er [varje] *vti* to vary (**de** from). ●**—é** *a* (*diversifié*) varied; (*divers*) various.
variété [varjete] *nf* variety; **spectacle de variétés** *Th* variety show.
variole [varjɔl] *nf* smallpox.
vas [va] *voir* **aller**[1].
vase [vaz] **1** *nm* vase. **2** *nf* (*boue*) mud, silt.
vaseline [vazlin] *nf* Vaseline®.
vaseux, -euse [vazø, -øz] *a* **1** (*boueux*) muddy, silty. **2** (*faible, fatigué*) off colour. **3** (*idées etc*) woolly, hazy.
vaste [vast] *a* vast, huge.
Vatican [vatikɑ̃] *nm* **le V.** the Vatican.
va-tout [vatu] *nm inv* **jouer son v.-tout** to stake one's all.
vaudeville [vodvil] *nm Th* light comedy.
vaurien, -ienne [vorjɛ̃, -jɛn] *nmf* good-for-nothing.
vaut [vo] *voir* **valoir.**
vautour [votur] *nm* vulture.
vautrer (se) [səvotre] *vpr* to sprawl; **se v. dans** (*boue, vice*) to wallow in.
va-vite (à la) [alavavit] *adv Fam* in a hurry.
veau, -x [vo] *nm* (*animal*) calf; (*viande*) veal; (*cuir*) calfskin, (calf) leather.
vécu [veky] *pp de* **vivre** ‖ *a* (*histoire etc*) true, real(-life).
vedette [vədɛt] *nf* **1** *Cin Th* star; **en v.** (*personne*) in the limelight. **2** (*canot*) motor boat, launch.
végétal, -aux [veʒetal, -o] *a* **huile**/*etc* **végétale** vegetable oil/*etc* ‖ *nm* plant. ●**végétarien, -ienne** *a* & *nmf* vegetarian. ●**végétation 1** *nf* vegetation. **2** *nfpl Méd* adenoids.
véhicule [veikyl] *nm* vehicle; **v. tout terrain** off-road *ou* all-terrain vehicle
veille [vɛj] *nf* **1 la v. (de)** the day before; **à la v. de** (*événement*) on the eve of; **la v. de Noël** Christmas Eve. **2** (*état*) wakefulness.
veillée [veje] *nf* (*soirée*) evening; (*réunion*) evening get-together; (*mortuaire*) vigil.
veiller [veje] *vi* to stay up *ou* awake; (*sentinelle etc*) to keep watch; **v. à qch** to see to sth, attend to sth; **v. à ce que** (+ *sub*) to make sure that; **v. sur qn** to watch over s.o. ‖ *vt* (*malade*) to sit with, watch over. ●**veilleur** *nm* **v. de nuit** night watchman. ●**veilleuse** *nf* (*de voiture*) sidelight, *Am* parking light; (*de cuisinière*) pilot light; (*lampe allumée la nuit*) night light.
veine [vɛn] *nf* **1** *Anat Bot Géol* vein. **2** (*chance*) *Fam* luck; **avoir de la v.** to be lucky. ●**veinard, -arde** *nmf Fam* lucky devil.
véliplanchiste [veliplɑ̃ʃist] *nmf* windsurfer.
vélo [velo] *nm* bike, bicycle; (*activité*) cycling; **faire du v.** to cycle, go cycling; **v. tout terrain** mountain bike. ●**vélodrome** *nm Sp* velodrome, cycle track. ●**vélomoteur** *nm* (lightweight) motorcycle.
velours [v(ə)lur] *nm* velvet; **v. côtelé** corduroy. ●**velouté** *a* soft, velvety; (*au goût*) mellow, smooth ‖ *nm* smoothness; **v. d'asperges**/*etc* (*potage*) cream of asparagus/*etc* soup.
velu [vəly] *a* hairy.
venaison [vənɛzɔ̃] *nf* venison.
vendange(s) [vɑ̃dɑ̃ʒ] *nf(pl)* grape harvest.
vendre [vɑ̃dr] *vt* to sell; **v. qch à qn** to sell s.o. sth, sell sth to s.o.; **à v.** (*maison etc*) for sale ‖ **se v.** *vpr* to be sold; **ça se vend bien** it sells well. ●**vendeur, -euse** *nmf* (*de magasin*) sales *ou* shop assistant, *Am* sales clerk; (*de voitures etc*) salesman, saleswoman.
vendredi [vɑ̃drədi] *nm* Friday; **V. saint** Good Friday.
vénéneux, -euse [venenø, -øz] *a* poisonous.
vénérable [venerabl] *a* venerable.
venger [vɑ̃ʒe] *vt* to avenge ‖ **se v.** *vpr* to get one's revenge, get one's own back (**de qn** on s.o., **de qch** for sth). ●**vengeance** *nf* revenge, vengeance.
venin [vənɛ̃] *nm* poison, venom; *Fig* venom. ●**venimeux, -euse** *a* poisonous, venomous; (*haineux*) *Fig* venomous.
venir** [v(ə)nir] *vi* (*aux* **être**) to come (**de** from); **v. faire** to come to do; **viens me voir** come and see me; **je viens/venais d'arriver** I've/I'd just arrived; **en v. à** (*conclusion etc*) to come to; **où veux-tu en v.?** what are you getting *ou* driving at?; **les jours**/*etc* **qui viennent** the coming days/*etc*; **faire v.** to send for, get; **v. chercher** to come and get. ❶**venir de G97** Tenses 7 F 10
vent [vɑ̃] *nm* wind; **il y a** *ou* **il fait du v.** it's windy; **coup de v.** gust of wind.
vente [vɑ̃t] *nf* sale; **v. (aux enchères)** auction (sale); **en v.** (*disponible*) on sale; **point de v.** sales outlet, point of sale; **prix de v.** selling price; **salle des ventes** auction room.
ventilateur [vɑ̃tilatœr] *nm* (*électrique*) & *Aut* fan; (*dans un mur*) ventilator.
ventouse [vɑ̃tuz] *nf* (*pour fixer*) suction grip; **cendrier**/*etc* **à v.** suction-grip ashtray/*etc*.
ventre [vɑ̃tr] *nm* stomach, belly; (*utérus*) womb; **avoir/prendre du v.** to have/get a paunch; **avoir mal au v.** to have a stomachache; **à plat v.** flat on one's face.
ventriloque [vɑ̃trilɔk] *nmf* ventriloquist.
venu, -ue[1] [v(ə)ny] *pp de* **venir** ‖ *nmf*

nouveau v., nouvelle venue newcomer; **le premier v.** anyone ‖ *a* **bien v.** (*à propos*) timely; **mal v.** untimely.

venue[2] [v(ə)ny] *nf* (*arrivée*) coming.

ver [vɛr] *nm* worm; (*larve*) grub; (*de fruits, fromage etc*) maggot; **v. de terre** (earth)worm; **v. à soie** silkworm.

véranda [verɑ̃da] *nf* veranda(h); (*en verre*) conservatory (*room attached to house*).

verbe [vɛrb] *nm Gram* verb.

verdict [vɛrdikt] *nm* verdict.

verdir [vɛrdir] *vti* to turn green. ● **verdoyant** *a* green. ● **verdure** *nf* (*arbres etc*) greenery.

véreux, -euse [verø, -øz] *a* (*fruit etc*) wormy; (*malhonnête*) *Fig* dubious, shady.

verger [vɛrʒe] *nm* orchard.

verglas [vɛrgla] *nm* (black) ice, *Am* sleet. ● **verglacé** *a* (*route*) icy.

vergogne (sans) [sɑ̃vɛrgɔɲ] *a* shameless ‖ *adv* shamelessly.

véridique [veridik] *a* truthful.

vérifier [verifje] *vt* to check, verify; (*comptes*) to audit. ● **vérification** *nf* checking, verification; audit(ing).

vérité [verite] *nf* truth; (*de personnage, tableau etc*) trueness to life; **en v.** in fact; **dire la v.** to tell the truth. ● **véritable** *a* true, real; (*non imité*) real, genuine. ● **véritablement** *adv* really.

vermeil, -eille [vɛrmɛj] *a* bright red ‖ *nm* **carte vermeil** senior citizen's rail pass.

vermine [vɛrmin] *nf* (*insectes, racaille*) vermin.

vermoulu [vɛrmuly] *a* worm-eaten.

verni [vɛrni] *a* (*chanceux*) *Fam* lucky.

vernir [vɛrnir] *vt* to varnish; (*poterie*) to glaze. ● **vernis** *nm* varnish; glaze; **v. à ongles** nail polish *ou* varnish. ● **vernissage** *nm* (*d'exposition de peinture*) first day.

verra, verrai *etc* [vɛra, vɛre] *voir* **voir.**

verre [vɛr] *nm* glass; **boire** *ou* **prendre un v.** to have a drink; **v. de bière**/*etc* glass of beer/*etc*; **v. à bière**/*etc* beer/*etc* glass; **v. de contact** contact lens. ● **verrière** *nf* (*toit*) glass roof.

verrou [vɛru] *nm* bolt; **fermer au v.** to bolt; **sous les verrous** behind bars. ● **verrouiller** *vt* to bolt.

verrue [vɛry] *nf* wart.

vers[1] [vɛr] *prép* (*direction*) towards, toward; (*approximation*) around, about.

vers[2] [vɛr] *nm* (*de poème*) line; *pl* (*poésie*) verse.

versant [vɛrsɑ̃] *nm* slope, side.

verse (à) [avɛrs] *adv* in torrents; **pleuvoir à v.** to pour (down).

Verseau [vɛrso] *nm* **le V.** (*signe*) Aquarius.

vers/er [vɛrse] *vt* **1** to pour; (*larmes, sang*) to shed. **2** (*argent*) to pay. ● **—ement** *nm* payment. ● **—eur** *a* **bec v.** spout.

verset [vɛrsɛ] *nm Rel* verse.

version [vɛrsjɔ̃] *nf* (*de film, d'incident etc*) version; (*traduction*) *Scol* translation, unseen.

verso [vɛrso] *nm* back (of the page); **'voir au v.'** 'see overleaf'.

vert [vɛr] *a* green; (*pas mûr*) unripe ‖ *nm* green.

vertical, -ale, -aux [vɛrtikal, -o] *a* & *nf* vertical; **à la verticale** vertically.

vertige [vɛrtiʒ] *nm* (feeling of) dizziness; (*peur de tomber dans le vide*) vertigo; *pl* dizzy spells; **avoir le v.** to be *ou* feel dizzy; **donner le v. à qn** to make s.o. (feel) dizzy. ● **vertigineux, -euse** *a* (*hauteur*) dizzy.

vertu [vɛrty] *nf* virtue; **en v. de** in accordance with. ● **vertueux, -euse** *a* virtuous.

verveine [vɛrvɛn] *nf* (*plante*) verbena.

vésicule [vezikyl] *nf* **v. biliaire** gall bladder.

vessie [vesi] *nf* bladder.

veste [vɛst] *nf* jacket, coat.

vestiaire [vɛstjɛr] *nm* cloakroom, *Am* locker room; (*casier*) locker.

vestibule [vɛstibyl] *nm* (entrance) hall.

vestiges [vɛstiʒ] *nmpl* (*restes, ruines*) remains; (*traces*) traces, vestiges.

veston [vɛstɔ̃] *nm* (suit) jacket.

vêtement [vɛtmɑ̃] *nm* garment, article of clothing; *pl* clothes; **vêtements de sport** sportswear; **industrie**/*etc* **du v.** clothing industry/*etc*.

vétéran [veterɑ̃] *nm* veteran.

vétérinaire [veterinɛr] *a* veterinary ‖ *nmf* vet, veterinary surgeon, *Am* veterinarian.

vêtir* [vetir] *vt*, **se v.** *vpr* to dress. ● **vêtu** *a* dressed (**de** in).

veto [veto] *nm inv* veto; **mettre son v. à** to veto.

vétuste [vetyst] *a* dilapidated.

veuf, veuve [vœf, vœv] *a* widowed ‖ *nm* widower ‖ *nf* widow.

veuille(s), veuillent *etc* [vœj] *voir* **vouloir.**

veut, veux [vø] *voir* **vouloir.**

vexer [vɛkse] *vt* to upset, hurt ‖ **se v.** *vpr* to be *ou* get upset (**de** at). ● **vexant** *a* upsetting.

VF [veɛf] *nf abrév* (*version française*) **film en VF** film dubbed into French.

viable [vjabl] *a* (*entreprise etc*) viable.

viaduc [vjadyk] *nm* viaduct.

viager, -ère [vjaʒe, -ɛr] *a* **rente viagère** life annuity ‖ *nm* life annuity.

viande [vjɑ̃d] *nf* meat.

vibrer [vibre] *vi* to vibrate; (*être ému*) to thrill (**de** with); **faire v.** (*auditoire etc*) to thrill. ● **vibration** *nf* vibration.

vice [vis] *nm* vice; (*défectuosité*) defect.
vice- [vis] *préf* vice-.
vice versa [vis(e)vɛrsa] *adv* vice versa.
vicieux, -euse [visjø, -øz] **1** *a* depraved ‖ *nmf* pervert. **2** *a* **cercle v.** vicious circle.
vicinal, -aux [visinal, -o] *a* **chemin v.** by-road, minor road.
vicomte [vikɔ̃t] *nm* viscount. ● **vicomtesse** *nf* viscountess.
victime [viktim] *nf* victim; (*d'un accident*) casualty; **être v. de** to be the victim of.
victoire [viktwar] *nf* victory; *Sp* win. ● **victorieux, -euse** *a* victorious; (*équipe*) winning.
victuailles [viktɥaj] *nfpl* provisions.
vidange [vidɑ̃ʒ] *nf Aut* oil change. ● **vidanger** *vt* to empty, drain.
vide [vid] *a* empty ‖ *nm* emptiness, void; (*absence d'air*) vacuum; (*trou, manque, espace*) gap; **emballé sous v.** vacuum-packed; **à v.** empty.
vidéo [video] *a inv* & *nf* video; **jeu v.** video game. ● **vidéocassette** *nf* video (cassette). ● **vidéoclip** *nm* video (*of rock group etc*).
vide-ordures [vidɔrdyr] *nm inv* (rubbish *ou Am* garbage) chute. ● **vide-poches** *nm inv Aut* glove compartment.
vider [vide] *vt* to empty; (*lieu*) to vacate; (*poisson, volaille*) *Culin* to gut; **v. qn** *Fam* (*chasser*) to throw s.o. out; (*épuiser*) to tire s.o. out ‖ **se v.** *vpr* to empty. ● **videur** *nm* (*de boîte de nuit*) bouncer.
vie [vi] *nf* life; (*durée*) lifetime; **le coût de la v.** the cost of living; **gagner sa v.** to earn one's living; **en v.** living; **à v., pour la v.** for life; **donner la v. à** to give birth to.
vieil, vieille [vjɛj] *voir* **vieux.**
vieillard [vjɛjar] *nm* old man; *pl* old people. ● **vieillesse** *nf* old age.
vieill/ir [vjejir] *vi* to grow old; (*changer*) to age ‖ *vt* **v. qn** (*vêtement etc*) to age s.o. ● **—i** *a* (*démodé*) old-fashioned.
Vienne [vjɛn] *nm ou f* Vienna.
viens, vient [vjɛ̃] *voir* **venir.**
vierge [vjɛrʒ] *nf* virgin; **la V.** (*signe*) Virgo ‖ *a* (*femme, neige etc*) virgin; (*feuille de papier, film*) blank; **être v.** (*femme, homme*) to be a virgin.
Viêt Nam [vjɛtnam] *nm* Vietnam. ● **vietnamien, -ienne** *a* & *nmf* Vietnamese.
vieux (*or* **vieil** *before vowel or mute h*), **vieille,** *pl* **vieux, vieilles** [vjø, vjɛj] *a* old; **être v. jeu** (*a inv*) to be old-fashioned; **v. garçon** bachelor; **vieille fille** *Péj* old maid ‖ *nm* old man; *pl* old people; **mon v.!** (*mon ami*) *Fam* mate!, pal! ‖ *nf* old woman; **ma vieille!** (*ma chère*) *Fam* dear!
vif, vive [vif, viv] *a* (*enfant, mouvement*) lively; (*alerte*) quick, sharp; (*intelligence, vent*) keen; (*couleur, lumière*) bright; (*froid*) biting; (*pas*) quick, brisk; (*imagination*) vivid; **brûler qn v.** to burn s.o. alive ‖ *nm* **le v. du sujet** the heart of the matter; **à v.** (*plaie*) open.
vigilant [viʒilɑ̃] *a* vigilant.
vigile [viʒil] *nm* (*gardien*) watchman; (*de nuit*) night watchman.
vigne [viɲ] *nf* (*plante*) vine; (*plantation*) vineyard. ● **vigneron, -onne** *nmf* wine grower. ● **vignoble** *nm* vineyard; (*région*) vineyards.
vignette [viɲɛt] *nf Aut* = road tax disc; (*de médicament*) price label (*for reimbursement by Social Security*).
vigueur [vigœr] *nf* vigour; **entrer en v.** (*loi*) to come into force. ● **vigoureux, -euse** *a* (*personne etc*) vigorous.
vilain [vilɛ̃] *a* (*laid*) ugly; (*enfant*) naughty; (*impoli*) rude.
villa [villa] *nf* (detached) house.
village [vilaʒ] *nm* village. ● **villageois, -oise** *nmf* villager.
ville [vil] *nf* town; (*grande*) city; **aller/être en v.** to go (in)to/be in town; **v. d'eaux** spa (town).
vin [vɛ̃] *nm* wine; **v. ordinaire** *ou* **de table** table wine.
vinaigre [vinɛgr] *nm* vinegar. ● **vinaigrette** *nf* French dressing, *Am* Italian dressing.
vingt [vɛ̃] ([vɛ̃t] *before vowel or mute h and in numbers 22–29*) *a* & *nm* twenty; **v. et un** twenty-one. ● **vingtaine** *nf* **une v. (de)** (*nombre*) about twenty. ● **vingtième** *a* & *nmf* twentieth.
viol [vjɔl] *nm* rape. ● **violation** *nf* violation. ● **violer** *vt* (*femme*) to rape; (*loi, lieu*) to violate. ● **violeur** *nm* rapist.
violent [vjɔlɑ̃] *a* violent; (*remède*) drastic. ● **violemment** [-amɑ̃] *adv* violently. ● **violence** *nf* violence; **acte de v.** act of violence.
violet, -ette [vjɔlɛ, -ɛt] **1** *a* & *nm* (*couleur*) purple, violet. **2** *nf* (*fleur*) violet.
violon [vjɔlɔ̃] *nm* violin. ● **violoncelle** *nm* cello. ● **violoncelliste** *nmf* cellist. ● **violoniste** *nmf* violinist.
vipère [vipɛr] *nf* adder, viper.
virage [viraʒ] *nm* (*de route*) bend; (*de véhicule*) turn; (*revirement*) *Fig* change of course.
virer [vire] **1** *vi* to turn, veer; **v. au bleu**/*etc* to turn blue/*etc*. **2** *vt* (*expulser*) *Fam* to throw out. **3** *vt* (*somme*) *Fin* to transfer (**à** to). ● **virement** *nm Fin* (bank *ou* credit) transfer.

virevolter [virvɔlte] *vi* to spin round.
virgule [virgyl] *nf Gram* comma; *Math* (decimal) point; **2 v. 5** 2 point 5.
viril [viril] *a* virile, manly; (*force*) male.
virtuel, -elle [virtɥɛl] *a* potential; *Phys Ordinat* virtual.
virtuose [virtɥoz] *nmf* virtuoso.
virulent [virylɑ̃] *a* virulent.
virus [virys] *nm Méd Ordinat* virus.
vis[1] [vi] *voir* **vivre, voir.**
vis[2] [vis] *nf* screw.
visa [viza] *nm* (*de passeport*) visa; (*timbre*) stamp, stamped signature; **v. de censure** (*d'un film*) certificate.
visage [vizaʒ] *nm* face.
vis-à-vis [vizavi] *prép* **v.-à-vis de** opposite; (*à l'égard de*) with respect to; (*envers*) towards ▮ *nm inv* (*personne*) person opposite; (*bois, maison etc*) opposite view.
viser [vize] **1** *vi* to aim (**à** at); **v. à faire** to aim to do ▮ *vt* (*cible*) to aim at; (*concerner*) to be aimed at. **2** *vt* (*document*) to stamp. • **visées** *nfpl* (*desseins*) *Fig* aims; **avoir des v. sur** to have designs on. • **viseur** *nm Phot* viewfinder; (*d'arme*) sight.
visible [vizibl] *a* visible. • **visibilité** *nf* visibility.
visière [vizjɛr] *nf* (*de casquette*) peak; (*en plastique etc*) eyeshade; (*de casque*) visor.
vision [vizjɔ̃] *nf* (*conception, image*) vision; (*sens*) (eye)sight, vision. • **visionneuse** *nf* (*pour diapositives*) viewer.
visite [vizit] *nf* visit; (*personne*) visitor; (*examen*) inspection; **rendre v. à, faire une v. à** to visit; **v. (à domicile)** *Méd* (house) call *ou* visit; **v. (médicale)** medical examination; **v. guidée** guided tour; **heures/***etc* **de v.** visiting hours/*etc*. • **visiter** *vt* to visit. • **visiteur, -euse** *nmf* visitor.
vison [vizɔ̃] *nm* mink.
visser [vise] *vt* to screw on.
visuel, -elle [vizɥɛl] *a* visual. • **visualiser** *vt* (*afficher*) *Ordinat* to display.
vit [vi] *voir* **vivre, voir.**
vital, -aux [vital, -o] *a* vital. • **vitalité** *nf* vitality.
vitamine [vitamin] *nf* vitamin.
vite [vit] *adv* quickly, fast; (*tôt*) soon; **v.!** quick(ly)! • **vitesse** *nf* speed; *Aut* gear; **boîte de vitesses** gearbox; **à toute v.** at top *ou* full speed; **v. de pointe** top speed; **en v.** *Fam* quickly.
viticole [vitikɔl] *a* (*région*) wine-growing; **industrie v.** wine industry. • **viticulteur** *nm* wine grower. • **viticulture** *nf* wine growing.
vitre [vitr] *nf* (window)pane; (*de véhicule, train*) window. • **vitrail, -aux** *nm* stained-glass window. • **vitrier** *nm* glazier.
vitrine [vitrin] *nf* (*de magasin*) (shop) window; (*meuble*) display cabinet, showcase.
vivable [vivabl] *a Fam* (*personne*) easy to live with; (*endroit*) fit to live in.
vivacité [vivasite] *nf* liveliness; (*d'émotion*) keenness; (*agilité*) briskness; **v. d'esprit** quick-wittedness.
vivant [vivɑ̃] *a* (*en vie*) alive, living; (*récit, rue*) lively ▮ *nm* **de son v.** in one's lifetime; **bon v.** jovial fellow.
vive[1] [viv] *voir* **vif.**
vive[2] [viv] *int* **v. le roi/***etc***!** long live the king/*etc*!; **v. les vacances!** hurray for the holidays *ou Am* the vacation!
vivement [vivmɑ̃] *adv* quickly, briskly; (*répliquer*) sharply; (*regretter*) deeply; **v. demain!** I can hardly wait for tomorrow!; **v. que** (+ *sub*) I'll be glad when.
vivier [vivje] *nm* fish pond.
vivifier [vivifje] *vt* to invigorate.
vivre** [vivr] **1** *vi* to live; **elle vit encore** she's still alive; **faire v.** (*famille etc*) to support; **v. vieux** to live to be old; **facile à v.** easy to get along with; **v. de** (*fruits etc*) to live on; (*travail etc*) to live by; **avoir de quoi v.** to have enough to live on ▮ *vt* (*vie*) to live; (*aventure, époque*) to live through; (*éprouver*) to experience. **2** *nmpl* food, supplies.
VO [veo] *nf abrév* (*version originale*) **film en VO** film in the original version.
vocabulaire [vɔkabylɛr] *nm* vocabulary.
vocal, -aux [vɔkal, -o] *a* (*cordes, musique*) vocal.
vocation [vɔkɑsjɔ̃] *nf* vocation, calling.
vociférer [vɔsifere] *vti* to shout angrily.
vodka [vɔdka] *nf* vodka.
vœu, -x [vø] *nm* (*souhait*) wish; (*promesse*) vow; **faire le v. de faire** to (make a) vow to do; **tous mes vœux!** (my) best wishes!
vogue [vɔg] *nf* fashion, vogue; **en v.** in fashion, in vogue.
voici [vwasi] *prép* here is, this is; *pl* here are, these are; **me v.** here I am; **v. dix ans/***etc* ten years/*etc* ago; **v. dix ans que** it's ten years since.

ⓘ**G96** Tenses 7 F 9a) i)
ⓘ**G185** Prepositions 8

voie [vwa] *nf* (*route*) road; (*rails*) track, line; (*partie de route*) lane; (*chemin*) way; (*de gare*) platform; (*de communication*) line; **pays en v. de développement** developing country; **v. publique** public highway; **v. navigable** waterway; **v. sans issue** dead end; **sur la bonne v.** on the right track.
voilà [vwala] *prép* there is, that is; *pl* there

are, those are; **les v.** there they are; **v., j'arrive!** all right, I'm coming!; **v. dix ans/***etc* ten years/*etc* ago; **v. dix ans que** it's ten years since.

G96 Tenses 7 F 9a) i)

G186 Prepositions 8

voile[1] [vwal] *nm* (*étoffe qui cache, coiffure etc*) & *Fig* veil. • **voiler**[1] *vt* (*visage etc*) to veil ‖ **se v.** *vpr* (*personne*) to wear a veil; (*ciel, regard*) to cloud over.

voile[2] [vwal] *nf* (*de bateau*) sail; *Sp* sailing; **bateau à voiles** sailing boat, *Am* sailboat; **faire de la v.** to sail, go sailing. • **voilier** *nm* sailing ship; (*de plaisance*) sailing boat, *Am* sailboat. • **voilure** *nf Nau* sails.

voiler[2] [vwale] *vt*, **se v.** *vpr* (*roue*) to buckle.

voir** [vwar] *vti* to see; **faire** *ou* **laisser v. qch** to show sth; **fais v.** let me see, show me; **v. qn faire** to see s.o. do *ou* doing; **voyons!** (*sois raisonnable*) come on!; **y v. clair** (*comprendre*) to see clearly; **je ne peux pas la v.** (*supporter*) *Fam* I can't stand (the sight of) her; **on verra bien** we'll see; **ça n'a rien à v. avec** that's got nothing to do with.

‖ **se voir** *vpr* to see oneself; (*se fréquenter*) to see each other; **ça se voit** that's obvious.

voirie [vwari] *nf* (*enlèvement des ordures*) refuse collection; (*routes*) public highways.

voisin, -ine [vwazɛ̃, -in] *a* (*pays, village etc*) neighbouring; (*maison, pièce*) next (**de** to); (*idée, état etc*) similar (**de** to) ‖ *nmf* neighbour. • **voisinage** *nm* (*quartier, voisins*) neighbourhood; (*proximité*) closeness.

voiture [vwatyr] *nf* car; (*de train*) carriage, coach, *Am* car; **v. de course/de tourisme** racing/private car; **v. d'enfant** pram, *Am* baby carriage; **en v.!** *Rail* all aboard!

voix [vwa] *nf* voice; (*d'électeur*) vote; **à v. basse** in a whisper; **à haute v.** aloud; **à portée de v.** within earshot.

vol [vɔl] *nm* **1** (*d'avion, d'oiseau*) flight; (*groupe d'oiseaux*) flock, flight; **v. libre** hang gliding; **v. à voile** gliding. **2** (*délit*) theft; **v. à main armée** armed robbery; **v. à l'étalage** shoplifting; **c'est du v.!** (*trop cher*) it's daylight robbery!

volaille [vɔlɑj] *nf* **la v.** (*oiseaux*) poultry; **une v.** (*oiseau*) a fowl.

volatiliser (se) [səvɔlatilize] *vpr* (*disparaître*) to vanish (into thin air).

volcan [vɔlkɑ̃] *nm* volcano.

voler [vɔle] **1** *vi* (*oiseau, avion etc*) to fly. **2** *vt* (*prendre*) to steal (**à** from); **v. qn** to rob s.o. ‖ *vi* to steal. • **volant 1** *a* (*tapis etc*) flying. **2** *nm Aut* (steering) wheel; (*objet*) *Sp* shuttlecock; (*de jupe*) flounce. • **volée** *nf* flight; (*groupe d'oiseaux*) flock, flight; (*suite de coups*) thrashing; *Tennis* volley; **sonner à toute v.** to peal *ou* ring out. • **voleur, -euse** *nmf* thief; **au v.!** stop thief!

volet [vɔlɛ] *nm* **1** (*de fenêtre*) shutter. **2** (*de programme, reportage etc*) section, part.

volière [vɔljɛr] *nf* aviary.

volley(-ball) [vɔlɛ(bol)] *nm Sp* volleyball.

volontaire [vɔlɔ̃tɛr] *a* (*voulu*) (*geste etc*) deliberate, voluntary; (*opiniâtre*) wilful, *Am* willful ‖ *nmf* volunteer. • **—ment** *adv* voluntarily; (*exprès*) deliberately.

volonté [vɔlɔ̃te] *nf* (*faculté, intention*) will; (*désir*) wish; **il a de la v.** he has willpower; **bonne v.** goodwill; **mauvaise v.** ill will; **à v.** (*quantité*) as much as desired.

volontiers [vɔlɔ̃tje] *adv* gladly, willingly; **v.!** (*oui*) I'd love to!

volt [vɔlt] *nm Él* volt. • **voltage** *nm* voltage.

volte-face [vɔltəfas] *nf inv* about turn, *Am* about face; **faire v.-face** to turn round.

voltiger [vɔltiʒe] *vi* to flutter.

volume [vɔlym] *nm* (*de boîte, de son, livre*) volume. • **volumineux, -euse** *a* bulky, voluminous.

volupté [vɔlypte] *nf* sensual pleasure.

vom/ir [vɔmir] *vt* to bring up, vomit ‖ *vi* to vomit, be sick. • **—issement** *nm* vomiting.

vont [vɔ̃] *voir* **aller**[1].

vorace [vɔras] *a* (*appétit, lecteur etc*) voracious.

vos [vo] *voir* **votre.**

vote [vɔt] *nm* (*action*) vote, voting; (*suffrage*) vote; (*de loi*) passing; **bureau de v.** polling station, *Am* polling place. • **voter** *vi* to vote ‖ *vt* (*loi*) to pass; (*crédits*) to vote.

votre, *pl* **vos** [vɔtr, vo] *a poss* your. • **vôtre** *pron poss* **le** *ou* **la v., les vôtres** yours; **à la v.!** (*toast*) (your) good health!, cheers! ‖ *nmpl* **les vôtres** (*votre famille*) your (own) people.

votre & **vôtre** **G64** Possessive Adjectives and Pronouns 6 E

voudra, voudrai *etc* [vudra, vudrɛ] *voir* **vouloir.**

vouer [vwe] *vt* (*promettre*) to vow (**à** to); (*consacrer*) to dedicate (**à** to).

vouloir** [vulwar] *vt* to want (**faire** to do); **je veux qu'il parte** I want him to go; **v. dire** to mean (**que** that); **je voudrais rester** I'd like to stay; **je voudrais un pain** I'd like a loaf of bread; **voulez-vous me suivre** will you follow me; **si tu veux** if you like *ou* wish; **en v. à qn d'avoir fait qch** to be angry with s.o. for doing sth; **v. du bien à qn** to wish s.o. well; **je veux bien (attendre)** I don't mind (waiting); **que voulez-vous!**

(*résignation*) what can you expect!; **sans le v.** unintentionally; **ne pas v. de qch/de qn** not to want sth/s.o.; **veuillez attendre** kindly wait. ● **voulu** *a* (*requis*) required; (*délibéré*) deliberate.

ⓘ**vouloir G123** Modal Auxiliary Verbs 7 K 4

vous [vu] *pron* **1** (*sujet*, *complément direct*) you; **v. êtes** you are; **il v. connaît** he knows you. **2** (*complément indirect*) (to) you; **il v. l'a donné** he gave it to you. **3** (*réfléchi*) yourself, *pl* yourselves; **v. v. lavez** you wash yourself; you wash yourselves. **4** (*réciproque*) each other; **v. v. aimez** you love each other. ● **vous-même** *pron* yourself. ● **vous-mêmes** *pron pl* yourselves.

ⓘ**vous G56** & **57** Subject and Object Pronouns 6 D 1 & 2

ⓘ**vous G62** Disjunctive Pronouns 6 D 5

ⓘ**vous G84** Reflexive Verbs and Pronouns 7 D

voûte [vut] *nf* (*plafond*) vault; (*porche*) arch(way). ● **voûté** *a* (*personne*) bent, stooped.

vouvoyer [vuvwaje] *vt* **v. qn** to use the formal *vous* form to s.o.

voyage [vwajaʒ] *nm* trip, journey; (*par mer*) voyage; **aimer les voyages** to like travelling; **faire un v., partir en v.** to go on a trip; **être en v.** to be (away) travelling; **bon v.!** have a pleasant trip!; **v. de noces** honeymoon; **v. organisé** (package) tour; **agent/agence de voyages** travel agent/agency. ● **voyager** *vi* to travel. ● **voyageur, -euse** *nmf* traveller; (*passager*) passenger; **v. de commerce** commercial traveller.

voyant[1] [vwajɑ̃] **1** *a* (*couleur*) gaudy. **2** *nm* (*signal*) (warning) light; (*d'appareil électrique*) pilot light.

voyant[2]**, -ante** [vwajɑ̃, -ɑ̃t] *nmf* clairvoyant; **les non-voyants** the blind, the visually handicapped.

voyelle [vwajɛl] *nf* vowel.

voyou [vwaju] *nm* hooligan.

vrac (en) [ɑ̃vrak] *adv* (*en désordre*) in a muddle, haphazardly; (*au poids*) loose.

vrai [vrɛ] *a* true; (*réel*) real; (*authentique*) genuine ‖ *adv* **dire v.** to be right (in what one says). ● **—ment** *adv* really.

ⓘ**vrai G100** The Subjunctive 7 G 1e)

ⓘ**vrai G32** Position of Adjectives 4 D 3

vraisemblable [vrɛsɑ̃blabl] *a* (*probable*) likely, probable; (*plausible*) plausible. ● **—ment** [-əmɑ̃] *adv* probably.

vrombir [vrɔ̃bir] *vi* to hum.

VRP [veɛrpe] *nm abrév* (*voyageur représentant placier*) sales rep.

VTT [vetete] *nm abrév* (*vélo tout terrain*) mountain bike.

vu [vy] **1** *pp de* **voir** ‖ *a* **bien vu** well thought of; **mal vu** frowned upon. **2** *prép* in view of; **vu que** seeing that.

vue [vy] *nf* (*spectacle*) sight; (*sens*) (eye)sight; (*panorama*, *photo*, *idée*) view; **en v.** (*proche*) in sight; (*en évidence*) on view; (*personne*) *Fig* in the public eye; **à v.** (*tirer*) on sight; **à première v.** at first sight; **à v. d'œil** (*grandir etc*) rapidly, for all to see; **de v.** (*connaître*) by sight.

vulgaire [vylgɛr] *a* (*grossier*) vulgar, coarse; (*ordinaire*) common.

vulnérable [vylnerabl] *a* vulnerable.

W

W, w [dublәve] *nm* W, w.
wagon [vagɔ̃] *nm Rail* (*de voyageurs*) carriage, coach, *Am* car; (*de marchandises*) wag(g)on, truck, *Am* freight car. •**w.-lit** *nm* (*pl* **wagons-lits**) sleeping car, sleeper. •**w.-restaurant** *nm* (*pl* **wagons-restaurants**) dining car, diner.
walkman® [wɔkman] *nm voir* **baladeur**.
wallon, -onne [walɔ̃, -ɔn] *a* & *nmf* Walloon.
watt [wat] *nm Él* watt.
w-c [(dublә)vese] *nmpl* toilet, *Am* men's *ou* ladies' room.
week-end [wikɛnd] *nm* weekend; **partir en w.-end** to go away for the weekend.
western [wɛstɛrn] *nm* (*film*) western.
whisky, *pl* **-ies** [wiski] *nm* whisky, *Am* whiskey.

X

X, x [iks] *nm* X, x; **rayon X** X-ray; **film classé X** adults-only film, '18' film, *Am* X-rated film.
xénophobe [ksenɔfɔb] *a* xenophobic ‖ *nmf* xenophobe. •**xénophobie** *nf* xenophobia.
xérès [gzerɛs] *nm* sherry.
xylophone [ksilɔfɔn] *nm* xylophone.

Y

Y, y[1] [igrɛk] *nm* Y, y.
y[2] [i] **1** *adv* there; (*dedans*) in it; *pl* in them; (*dessus*) on it; *pl* on them; **elle y vivra** she'll live there; **j'y entrai** I entered (it); **allons-y** let's go; **j'y suis!** (*je comprends*) now I get it!; **je n'y suis pour rien** I have nothing to do with it, that's nothing to do with me.
2 *pron* (= *à cela*) **j'y pense** I think of it; **je m'y attendais** I was expecting it; **ça y est!** that's it!
G61 The Pronoun Y 6 D 4
yacht [jɔt] *nm* yacht.
yaourt [jaur(t)] *nm* yog(h)urt.
yeux [jø] *voir* **œil**.
yoga [jɔga] *nm* yoga.
yo-yo [jojo] *nm inv* yoyo.

Z

Z, z [zɛd] *nm* Z, z.
zapper [zape] *vi* (*téléspectateur*) to flick channels, channel-hop.
zèbre [zɛbr] *nm* zebra. •**zébré** *a* striped (**de** with).
zèle [zɛl] *nm* zeal; **faire du z.** to overdo it.
zéro [zero] *nm* (*chiffre*) zero, nought; (*dans un numéro*) 0 [әʊ]; (*température*) zero; (*rien*) nothing; **deux buts à z.** *Fb* two nil, *Am* two zero; **partir de z.** to start from scratch.
zeste [zɛst] *nm* **un z. de citron** a piece of lemon peel.
zigzag [zigzag] *nm* zigzag; **en z.** (*route etc*) zigzag(ging). •**zigzaguer** *vi* to zigzag.
zinc [zɛ̃g] *nm* (*métal*) zinc.
zodiaque [zɔdjak] *nm* zodiac.
zona [zona] *nm Méd* shingles.
zone [zon] *nf* zone, area; (*domaine*) *Fig* sphere; (*faubourgs misérables*) slum area (*around city*); **z. bleue** restricted parking zone; **z. industrielle** industrial estate *ou Am* park.
zoo [zo(o)] *nm* zoo. •**zoologique** *a* zoological; **jardin** *ou* **parc z.** zoo.
zoom [zum] *nm* (*objectif*) zoom lens.
zut! [zyt] *int Fam* oh dear!, heck!

FRENCH GRAMMAR

CONTENTS

1 GLOSSARY OF GRAMMATICAL TERMS

ABSTRACT An abstract noun refers to a quality, concept or action rather than a physical thing or a person, eg *happiness*, *life*. See CONCRETE.

ACTIVE The form a verb takes when the subject of the sentence performs the action of the verb (eg *the child **fell**, the king **rewarded** him*). See PASSIVE.

ADJECTIVE A 'describing' word, which adds information about a noun, telling us what something or someone is like (eg *a **small** house, a **red** car, an **interesting** teacher*). An adjective may also modify a noun in other ways. See DEMONSTRATIVE and POSSESSIVE.

ADVERB Adverbs are normally used with a verb to add extra information by indicating **how** the action is done (adverbs of manner), **when, where** and **with how much intensity** the action is done (adverbs of time, place and intensity), or **to what extent** the action is done (adverbs of quantity). Adverbs may also be used with an adjective or another adverb (eg *a **very** attractive girl, **very** well*).

AGENT The subject of an active verb becomes the agent of a passive verb preceded, in English, by the preposition **by**, eg ***the hunter** shot the bird* becomes *the bird was shot by **the hunter***. The subject of the first sentence, ***the hunter*** becomes the agent of the second.

AGREEMENT In French, words such as adjectives, articles and pronouns are said to agree in number and gender with the noun or pronoun they refer to. This means that their spelling changes according to the **number** of the noun (singular or plural) and according to its **gender** (masculine or feminine).

ANTECEDENT The antecedent of a relative pronoun is the word or words to which the relative pronoun refers. The antecedent is usually found directly before the relative pronoun (eg in the sentence *I know **the man** who did this*, *the man* is the antecedent of *who*).

APPOSITION A word or a clause is said to be in apposition to another when it is placed directly after it without any joining word (eg *Mr Jones, **our bank manager**, rang today*).

ARTICLE	See DEFINITE ARTICLE, INDEFINITE ARTICLE and PARTITIVE ARTICLE.
AUXILIARY	The French auxiliary verbs, or 'helping' verbs, are **avoir** (*to have*) and **être** (*to be*). They are used to make up the first part of compound tenses, the second part being a past participle (eg *I **have** eaten*). Auxiliary verbs are marked *v aux* in the dictionary.
CARDINAL	Cardinal numbers are numbers such as *one*, *two*, *ten*, *fourteen*, as opposed to **ordinal** numbers (eg *first*, *second*).
CLAUSE	A clause is a group of words which contains at least a subject and a verb: *he said* is a clause. A clause often contains more than this basic information, eg *he said this to her yesterday*. Sentences can be made up of several clauses, eg *he said/he'd call me/if he were free*. See SENTENCE.
COLLECTIVE	A collective noun stands for a group of people, animals or things, eg *cattle* (bétail), *family* (famille).
COMPARATIVE	The comparative forms of adjectives and adverbs allow us to compare two things, persons or actions. In English, *more ... than*, *...er than*, *less ... than* and *as ... as* are used for comparison. See SUPERLATIVE.
COMPOUND NOUN	A compound noun is composed of two or more elements. In French, *chou-fleur* (cauliflower) and *arc-en-ciel* (rainbow) are examples of compound nouns.
COMPOUND TENSE	Compound tenses are verb tenses consisting of more than one element. In French, the compound tenses of a verb are formed by the **auxiliary** verb and the **past participle**. Two important compound tenses are the perfect (eg *j'ai visité*, *il est venu*) and the pluperfect (eg *j'avais visité*, *il était venu*).
CONCRETE	A concrete noun refers to a physical thing or a person, eg *house*, *man*, *plant*. See ABSTRACT.
CONDITIONAL	This mood is used to describe what someone would do, or something that would happen, if a condition were fulfilled (eg *I **would come** if I were well*; *the chair **would have broken** if he had sat on it*).
CONJUGATION	The conjugation of a verb is the set of different forms taken in the particular tenses of that verb.
CONJUNCTION	Conjunctions are 'linking' words. They may be co-ordinating or subordinating. Co-ordinating conjunctions are words like *and*, *but*, *or*; subordinating conjunctions are words like *because*, *after*, *although*.
DEFINITE ARTICLE	The definite article is *the* in English and *le, la* and *les* in French.

DEMONSTRATIVE Demonstrative adjectives (eg *this*, *that*, *these*) and pronouns (eg *this one*, *that one*) are used to point out a particular person or object.

DIRECT OBJECT A noun or a pronoun which in English follows a verb without any linking preposition, eg *I met* ***a friend***. See INDIRECT OBJECT.

ELISION Elision consists in replacing the last letter of certain words (*le*, *la*, *je*, *me*, *te*, *se*, *de*, *que*) with an apostrophe (') before a word starting with a **vowel** or a **silent h** (eg *l'eau*, *l'homme*, *j'aime*).

ENDING The ending of a verb is determined by the **person** (1st/2nd/3rd) and **number** (singular/plural) of its subject. In French, tenses normally have five or six different endings. See PERSON and NUMBER.

EXCLAMATION Words or sentences used to express surprise, wonder, annoyance etc (eg *what!*, *how lucky!*, *what a nice day!*). See INTERJECTION.

FEMININE See GENDER.

GENDER The gender of a noun indicates whether the noun is **masculine** or **feminine** (all French nouns are either masculine or feminine).

IDIOMATIC EXPRESSION Idiomatic expressions (or idioms) are expressions which cannot normally be translated word for word. For example, *out of the blue* is translated by *de manière inattendue*, and *that's old hat* (= *old-fashioned*) by *c'est vieux jeu*.

IMPERATIVE A mood used for giving orders (eg *eat!*, *don't go!*).

IMPERSONAL The subject of impersonal verbs in French is always the impersonal pronoun **il** (= it). Impersonal verbs are only used in the third person singular and in the infinitive, eg **il neige**, **neiger**. They are marked *v imp* in the dictionary.

INDEFINITE Indefinite pronouns and adjectives are words that do not refer to a definite person or object (eg *each*, *someone*, *every*).

INDEFINITE ARTICLE The indefinite article is *a* (or *an*) in English and *un*, *une* and *des* in French.

INDICATIVE The normal form (or mood) of a verb as in *I like*, *he came*, *we are trying*. It is opposed to the subjunctive, conditional and imperative.

INDIRECT OBJECT A noun or pronoun which follows a verb indirectly, with a linking preposition (usually **to**), eg *I spoke to* ***my friend/him***. See DIRECT OBJECT.

INFINITIVE The infinitive is the basic form of the verb as found in dictionaries. Thus *to eat, to finish, to take* are infinitives. In

French, the infinitive is recognized by its ending: *manger*, *finir*, *prendre*.

INTERJECTION A word used as an exclamation to express surprise, annoyance, relief, pain etc, eg *ah!*, *oh!*, *hey!*, *ouch!* See EXCLAMATION.

INTERROGATIVE Interrogative words are used to ask a question. This may be a direct question (***when*** *will you arrive?*) or an indirect question (*I don't know* ***when*** *he will arrive*). See QUESTION. Pronouns may also be interrogative. See PRONOUN.

INTRANSITIVE An intransitive verb is one that takes an indirect object or is used without any object at all, eg *speak* in the phrases *to speak to one's friend* and *speak louder*. Intransitive verbs are marked *vi* in the dictionary. See TRANSITIVE.

MASCULINE See GENDER.

MOOD The name given to the four main areas within which a verb is conjugated. See INDICATIVE, SUBJUNCTIVE, CONDITIONAL and IMPERATIVE.

NEGATIVE Negative commands and expressions are those which, in English, use a word such as *not*, *never*, *nothing*, *nowhere*.

NOUN A 'naming' word, which can refer to living creatures, things, places or abstract ideas, eg *man*, *cat*, *house*, *passport*, *life*, *Paul*. Nouns may be divided into a number of categories. See ABSTRACT, CONCRETE, PROPER, COLLECTIVE and COMPOUND.

NUMBER The number of a noun indicates whether the noun is **singular** or **plural**. A singular noun refers to one single thing or person (eg *boy*, *train*) and a plural noun to several (eg *boys*, *trains*). See ENDING.

OBJECT See DIRECT OBJECT and INDIRECT OBJECT.

ORDINAL Ordinal numbers are *first*, *second*, *third*, *fourth* and all other numbers which end in **-th**. In French, all ordinal numbers, except for *premier* (first) and *second* (second), end in **-ième**. See CARDINAL.

PARTICIPLE See PRESENT PARTICIPLE and PAST PARTICIPLE.

PARTITIVE ARTICLE The partitive articles are *some* and *any* in English and *du*, *de la* and *des* (as in *du pain*, *de la confiture*, *des bananes*) in French.

PASSIVE A verb is used in the passive when the subject of the verb does not perform the action but is subjected to it. The passive is formed with the verb **to be** and the past participle of the verb, eg *he was rewarded*. The use of the agent **by** is frequently associated with the passive, eg *he was rewarded by the king*.

PAST PARTICIPLE — The past participle of a verb is the form which is used after **to have** in English, eg *I have **eaten***, *I have **said***, *you have **tried***.

PERSON — In any tense, there are three persons in the singular (1st: *I* ..., 2nd: *you* ..., 3rd: *he/she/it* ...), and three in the plural (1st: *we* ..., 2nd: *you* ..., 3rd: *they* ...). See ENDING.

PERSONAL PRONOUN — Personal pronouns stand for a noun. They usually accompany a verb and can be either the subject (*I*, *you*, *he/she/it*, *we*, *they*) or the object of the verb (*me*, *you*, *him/her/it*, *us*, *them*).

PLURAL — See NUMBER.

POSSESSIVE — Possessive adjectives and pronouns are used to indicate possession or ownership. They are words like *my/mine*, *your/yours*, *our/ours*.

PREPOSITION — Prepositions are words such as *with*, *in*, *to*, *at*, *of*, that deal with the position, movement etc of things or people in relation to one another. They are followed by a noun or a pronoun.

PRESENT PARTICIPLE — The present participle is the verb form which ends in **-ing** in English (**-ant** in French).

PRONOUN — A word which stands for a noun. The main categories of pronouns are:

- ★ **Relative pronouns** (eg *who*, *which*, *that*)
- ★ **Interrogative pronouns** (eg *who?*, *what?*, *which?*)
- ★ **Demonstrative pronouns** (eg *this*, *that*, *these*)
- ★ **Possessive pronouns** (eg *mine*, *yours*, *his*)
- ★ **Personal pronouns** (eg *you*, *him*, *us*)
- ★ **Reflexive pronouns** (eg *myself*, *himself*)
- ★ **Indefinite pronouns** (eg *something*, *all*)

PROPER NOUN — The name of a particular person, place or thing, eg *Paul*, *France*. Proper nouns are written with a capital letter.

QUESTION — There are two question forms: **direct** questions stand on their own and require a question mark at the end (eg *when will he come?*); **indirect** questions are introduced by a clause and require no question mark (eg *I wonder when he will come*).

REFLEXIVE — Reflexive verbs 'reflect' the action back onto the subject (eg *I dressed myself*). They are always found with a reflexive

	pronoun and are also known as pronominal verbs. Marked *vpr* in the dictionary, reflexive or pronominal verbs are much more common in French than in English.
RELATIVE PRONOUN	Relative pronouns refer to a noun which has already been mentioned and attach a relative clause to it. They are words such as *who*, *which* or *that*.
SENTENCE	A sentence is a group of words made up of one or more clauses (see CLAUSE). The end of a sentence is indicated by a punctuation mark, usually a full stop (*Am* period), a question mark or an exclamation mark (*Am* exclamation point).
SILENT H	The name 'silent **h**' or 'mute **h**' is actually misleading since an **h** is never pronounced in French. The point is that, when a silent **h** occurs, any preceding vowel is not pronounced either. For example, the **h** in *j'habite* is silent (note the *j'*). The **h** in *je hurle* is not silent (note the **je**).
SIMPLE TENSE	Simple tenses are tenses in which the verb consists of one word only, eg *j'habite*, *Maurice partira*.
SINGULAR	See NUMBER.
SUBJECT	The subject of a verb is the noun or pronoun which performs the action. In the sentences *the train left early* and *she bought a computer*, *the train* and *she* are the subjects. See DIRECT OBJECT and INDIRECT OBJECT.
SUBJUNCTIVE	The subjunctive is a verb form (or mood) which is rarely used in English (eg *if I were you*, *God save the Queen*), but common in French. In French it is used following the conjunction **que** to express emotions, commands, doubt, possibility etc, and with many subordinating conjunctions.
SUPERLATIVE	The form of an adjective or an adverb which, in English, is marked by *the most ...*, *the ...est* or *the least ...*. See COMPARATIVE.
TENSE	Verbs are used in tenses, which tell us when an action takes place, eg in the present, the imperfect, the future. See COMPOUND TENSE and SIMPLE TENSE.
TRANSITIVE	A transitive verb is one that takes a direct object, eg *meet* in the phrase *to meet a friend*. Transitive verbs are marked *vt* in the dictionary. See INTRANSITIVE.
VERB	A 'doing' word, which usually describes an action (eg *to sing*, *to work*, *to promise*). Some verbs describe a state (eg *to be*, *to have*, *to hope*).

2 ARTICLES

A THE DEFINITE ARTICLE

1 Forms

In English, there is only one form of the definite article: **the.** In French, there are three forms, depending on the gender and number of the noun following the article:

- with a masculine singular noun: **le** } the
- with a feminine singular noun: **la** } the
- with a plural noun (masc or fem): **les** } the

MASC SING	FEM SING	PLURAL
le chauffeur the driver	**la secrétaire** the secretary	**les étudiants** the students
le salon the lounge	**la cuisine** the kitchen	**les chambres** the bedrooms

Note: **le** and **la** both change to **l'** before a vowel or a silent **h**:

	MASCULINE	FEMININE
BEFORE VOWEL	**l'avion** the plane	**l'odeur** the smell
BEFORE SILENT H	**l'homme** the man	**l'hôtesse** the hostess

Pronunciation: the **s** of **les** is pronounced **z** when the noun following it begins with a vowel or a silent **h** (eg **les hommes** [lezɔm]).

2 Forms with the prepositions 'à' and 'de'

When the definite article is used with **à** or **de**, the following spelling changes take place:

a) *with à (to, at)*

à + le → **au**
à + les → **aux**

à + la and **à + l'** do not change

au restaurant at/to the restaurant	**aux enfants** to the children
à la plage at/to the beach	**à l'aéroport** at/to the airport

Pronunciation: the **x** of **aux** is pronounced **z** when the noun following it begins with a vowel or a silent **h** (eg **aux enfants** [ozɑ̃fɑ̃]).

b) *with de (of, from)*

de + le → **du**
de + les → **des**

de + la and **de + l'** do not change

du directeur of/from the manager	**des chômeurs** of/from the unemployed
de la région of/from the area	**de l'usine** of/from the factory

Pronunciation: the **s** of **des** is pronounced **z** when the noun following it begins with a vowel or a silent **h** (eg **des usines** [dezyzin]).

3 Use

As in English, the definite article is used when referring to a particular person or thing, or particular persons or things:

les amis dont je t'ai parlé the friends I told you about	**le café est prêt** the coffee is ready

However, the definite article is used far more frequently in French than in English. It is used in particular in the following cases where English uses no article:

a) *when the noun is used in a general sense*

i) to refer to all things of a kind:

vous acceptez les chèques ?
do you accept cheques *or Am* checks?

le sucre est mauvais pour les dents
sugar is bad for the teeth

ii) to refer to abstract things:

le travail et les loisirs work and leisure	**la musique classique** classical music

iii) when stating likes and dislikes:

j'aime la viande, mais je préfère le poisson
I like meat, but I prefer fish

je déteste les tomates/voitures
I hate tomatoes/cars

j'aime le dimanche
I like Sunday(s)

b) *with geographical names*

i) continents, countries and areas:

le Canada Canada	**la France** France	**l'Europe** Europe
la Bretagne Brittany	**l'Afrique** Africa	**les Etats-Unis** the United States

But: the article **la** is omitted with the prepositions **en** (to, in) and **de** (from):

j'habite en France I live in France	**il vient d'Italie** he comes from Italy

ii) mountains, lakes and rivers:

le mont Everest Mount Everest	**le lac de Genève** Lake Geneva

c) *with names of seasons*

l'automne	autumn, *Am* fall
l'hiver	winter
le printemps	spring
l'été	summer

But:

en été/hiver in (the) summer/winter	**en automne** in (the) autumn, *Am* in the fall
au printemps in (the) spring	**un jour d'été** a summer's day

d) *with names of languages*

j'apprends le français
I'm learning French

But: **ce film est en anglais**
this film is in English

e) *with parts of the body*

j'ai les cheveux roux I've got red hair	**ouvrez la bouche** open your mouth
se laver les mains to wash one's hands	**l'homme à la barbe noire** the man with the black beard

f) *with names following an adjective*

le petit Pierre little Peter	**la pauvre Isabelle** poor Isabelle

g) *with titles*

le docteur Coste Doctor Coste	**le commandant Cousteau** Captain Cousteau

h) *with days of the week to express regular occurrences*

que fais-tu le samedi ?
what do you do on Saturdays?

i) *with names of subjects or leisure activities*

les maths maths, *Am* math	**l'histoire et la géographie** history and geography

la natation, la lecture, le tennis
swimming, reading, tennis

j) *in expressions of price, quantity etc*

c'est combien le kilo/la douzaine/la bouteille ?
how much is it for a kilo/dozen/bottle?

B THE INDEFINITE ARTICLE

1 Forms

In French, there are three forms of the indefinite article, depending on the number and gender of the noun it accompanies:

- with a masculine singular noun:	**un**	a (*or* an)
- with a feminine singular noun:	**une**	a (*or* an)
- with a plural noun (masc or fem):	**des**	some

Note: **des** is often not translated in English:

il y a des nuages dans le ciel
there are clouds in the sky

2 Use

a) On the whole, the French indefinite article is used in the same way as its English equivalent:

un homme	**une femme**	**des hommes/femmes**
a man	a woman	(some) men/women
un animal	**une tasse**	**des animaux/ tasses**
an animal	a cup	(some) animals/cups

b) However, the English indefinite article is not always translated in French:

i) when stating someone's profession or occupation:

mon père est architecte
my father is an architect

elle est médecin
she is a doctor

But: the article is used after **c'est**, **c'était** etc:

c'est un acteur célèbre
he's a famous actor

ce sont des fraises
these are strawberries

ii) with nouns in apposition:

Madame Leclerc, employée de bureau
Mrs Leclerc, an office worker

iii) after **quel** in exclamations:

quel dommage !
what a pity!

quelle surprise !
what a surprise!

iv) after **sans**:

c'est un village sans médecin
it's a village without a doctor

c) In negative sentences, **de** (or **d'**) is used instead of **un, une, des**:

je n'ai pas d'amis
I don't have any friends

je n'ai plus de voiture
I don't have a car any more

elle est partie sans poser de questions
she left without asking any questions

d) In French (but not in English), the indefinite article is used with abstract nouns followed by an adjective:

avec une patience remarquable
with remarkable patience

elle a fait des progrès étonnants
she's made amazing progress

But: the article is not used when there is no adjective:

avec plaisir
with pleasure

sans hésitation
without hesitation

C THE PARTITIVE ARTICLE

1 Forms

There are three forms of the French partitive article, which corresponds to 'some'/'any' in English:

- with a masculine singular noun: **du**
- with a feminine singular noun: **de la**
- with plural nouns (masc or fem): **des**

du vin
some wine

de la bière
some beer

des fruits
some fruit

Note: **de l'** is used in front of masculine or feminine singular nouns beginning with a vowel or a silent **h**:

de l'argent
some money

de l'eau
some water

2 Use

a) On the whole, the French partitive article is used as in English. However, English often omits the partitive article where French does not:

achète du pain
buy (some) bread

vous avez du beurre ?
do you have (any) butter?

je voudrais de la viande
I'd like some meat

tu veux de la soupe ?
do you want (any) soup?

tu dois manger des légumes
you must eat (some) vegetables

as-tu acheté des poires ?
did you buy (any) pears?

b) The partitive article is replaced by **de** (or **d'**) in the following cases:

i) in negative expressions:

il n'y a plus de café
there isn't any coffee left

je n'ai pas de verres
I don't have any glasses

Note: this rule does not apply when the negative concerns the identity of the noun, or with the expression **ne ... que**:

ce n'est pas du cuir, c'est du plastique
it's not leather, it's plastic

je n'ai que de l'argent français
I have only French money

elle ne veut que du café
she only wants coffee

ii) after expressions of quantity (see also **G194**, section 10 F):

il boit trop de café
he drinks too much coffee

il gagne assez d'argent
he earns enough money

iii) after **avoir besoin de**:

j'ai besoin d'argent
I need (some) money

tu as besoin de timbres ?
do you need (any) stamps?

iv) where an adjective is followed by a plural noun:

de grands enfants
(some) tall children

de petites villes
(some) small towns

But: if the adjective comes after the noun, **des** does not change:

des résultats encourageants
encouraging results

Note: **des**, and not **de,** is used before an adjective which forms a set phrase with the noun:

des jeunes filles
girls

des petites annonces
classified advertisements

3 Partitive or definite article?

When no article is used in English, be careful to use the right article in French: **le/la/les** or **du/de la/des**?

If **some/any** can be inserted before the English noun, the French partitive article should be used. But if the noun is used in a general sense and inserting **some/any** in front of the English noun does not make sense, the definite article must be used:

did you buy fish? (*ie any fish*)
tu as acheté *du* poisson ?

yes, I did; I like fish (*ie fish in general*)
oui ; j'aime *le* poisson

3 NOUNS

Nouns are 'naming' words, which refer to persons, animals, things, places or abstract ideas.

A GENDER

All French nouns are either masculine or feminine; there is no neuter as in English. Though no absolute rule can be stated, the gender can often be determined either by the meaning or the ending of the noun.

1 Masculine

a) *by meaning*

i) names indicating males (people and animals):

un homme a man	**le boucher** the butcher	**le tigre** the tiger

ii) names of common trees and shrubs:

le chêne the oak	**le sapin** the fir (tree)	**le laurier** the laurel

But: **une aubépine** a hawthorn; **la bruyère** the heather

iii) days, months, seasons:

lundi Monday	**mars** March	**le printemps** spring

iv) languages:

le français French	**le polonais** Polish	**le russe** Russian

v) numerals:

le dix ten	**le trente** thirty

vi) fractions:

le troisième the third	**le vingt-cinquième** the twenty-fifth

vii) weights and measures:

le kilo the kilo	**le mètre** the metre, *Am* meter
le litre the litre, *Am* liter	

But: **la livre** the pound; **la tonne** the ton

viii) points of the compass:

le nord the north	**le sud-est** the south-east

ix) rivers and countries not ending in a silent **e**:

le Rhin the Rhine	**le Portugal** Portugal	**le Danemark** Denmark

But: **le Mexique**
Mexico

b) *by ending*

-acle	**le spectacle** (show) *But:* **une débâcle** (rout)
-age	**le fromage** (cheese) *But:* **la cage** (cage), **une image** (picture), **la nage** (swimming stroke), **la page** (page), **la plage** (beach), **la rage** (rage, rabies)
-é	**le marché** (market) *But:* abstract nouns ending in **-té** and **-tié** (see 2b))
-eau	**le chapeau** (hat) *But:* **l'eau** (water), **la peau** (skin)
-ège	**le piège** (trap), **le collège** (secondary) school, *Am* high school
-ème	**le thème** (theme, translation) *But:* **la crème** (the cream)
-isme, -asme	**le communisme** (communism), **le tourisme** (tourism), **l'enthousiasme** (enthusiasm)
-o	**le numéro** (the number) *But:* **la dynamo** (dynamo) and most abbreviated expressions: **une auto** (car), **la météo** (weather forecast), **la photo** (photograph), **la radio** (radio), **la sténo** (shorthand), **la stéréo** (stereo)
-ou	**le trou** (hole), **le genou** (knee)

Nouns ending in a *consonant* are usually *masculine.*

Notable exceptions are:

i) most nouns ending in **-tion, -sion, -ation, -aison, -ison**

ii) most abstract nouns ending in **-eur** (see 2b))

iii) the following nouns ending in a consonant:

ending in **f**:

la clef (key) **la soif** (thirst)	**la nef** (nave)

ending in **m** and **n**:

la faim (hunger)	**la fin** (end)

la façon (manner)
la boisson (drink)
la rançon (ransom)
la leçon (lesson)
la moisson (harvest)

ending in **r**:

la mer (sea)
la chair (flesh)
la cour (yard)
la cuiller (spoon)
la basse-cour (farmyard)
la tour (tower)

ending in **s**:

la brebis (ewe)
la vis (screw)
une fois (once)
la souris (mouse)

ending in **t**:

la part (share)
la dent (tooth)
la forêt (forest)
la mort (death)
la plupart (most)
la dot (dowry)
la jument (mare)
la nuit (night)

ending in **x**:

la croix (cross)
la paix (peace)
la toux (cough)
la noix (nut)
la perdrix (partridge)
la voix (voice)

2 Feminine

a) *by meaning*

i) names indicating females (people and animals):

la mère	**la bonne**	**la génisse**
the mother	the maid	the heifer

ii) names of rivers and countries ending in a silent **e**:

la Seine	**la Russie**	**la Belgique**
the Seine	Russia	Belgium

iii) saint's days and festivals:

la Toussaint	**la Pentecôte**
All Saints' Day	Whitsun, *Am* Pentecost

But: **Noël** (Christmas) is masculine except in the expression: **à la Noël** (at Christmas) short for **à la fête de Noël.**

b) *by ending*

-ace	**la place** (square, seat) *But:* **un espace** (space)
-ade	**la salade** (salad) *But:* **le grade** (rank), **le stade** (stadium)
-ance, -anse	**la puissance** (power), **la danse** (dancing, dance)

-ée	**la soirée** (evening) *But:* **le musée** (museum), **le lycée** (secondary) school, *Am* high school
-ence, -ense	**une évidence** (obviousness), **la défense** (defence) *But:* **le silence** (silence)
-ère	**la lumière** (light) *But:* **le mystère** (mystery), **le caractère** (character)
-eur	**la peur** (fear), **la blancheur** (whiteness) *But:* **le bonheur** (happiness), **le chœur** (choir), **le cœur** (heart), **un honneur** (honour), **le malheur** (misfortune)
-ie	**la pluie** (rain) *But:* **le génie** (genius), **un incendie** (fire), **le parapluie** (umbrella)
-ière	**la bière** (beer) *But:* **le cimetière** (cemetery)
-oire	**la gloire** (glory) *But:* **le laboratoire** (laboratory), **le pourboire** (tip)
-tion, -sion, -ation, -aison, -ison	**la fiction** (fiction), **la tension** (tension), **la nation** (nation), **la raison** (reason), **la prison** (prison)
-té	**la bonté** (goodness) *But:* **le côté** (side), **le comté** (county), **le traité** (treaty), **le pâté** (pâté)
-tié	**la moitié** (half), **la pitié** (pity)

Most nouns ending in a silent e following two consonants:

la botte (boot), **la couronne** (crown), **la terre** (earth), **la masse** (mass), **la lutte** (struggle)

But: **le verre** (glass), **le parterre** (flower bed), **le tonnerre** (thunder), **un intervalle** (gap, interval), **le carrosse** (carriage)

3 Difficulties

a) some nouns may have either gender depending on the sex of the person to whom they refer:

un artiste a (male) artist	**une artiste** a (female) artist
le Russe the Russian (man)	**la Russe** the Russian (woman)

similarly:

un aide/une aide	an assistant
un camarade/une camarade	a friend
un domestique/une domestique	a servant
un enfant/une enfant	a child
un malade/une malade	a patient
un propriétaire/une propriétaire	an owner

b) others have only one gender for both sexes:

un ange an angel	**un amateur** an amateur	**un auteur** an author
une connaissance an acquaintance	**la dupe** the dupe	**un écrivain** a writer
Sa Majesté His/Her Majesty	**le médecin** the doctor	**le peintre** the painter
une personne a person	**le poète** the poet	**le professeur** the teacher
la recrue the recruit	**le sculpteur** the sculptor	**la sentinelle** the sentry
le témoin the witness	**la victime** the victim	**la vedette** the (film) star

c) the following nouns change meaning according to gender:

	MASCULINE	FEMININE
aide	(male) assistant	assistance, (female) assistant
crêpe	crepe	pancake
critique	critic	criticism
faux	forgery	scythe
livre	book	pound
manche	handle	sleeve
manœuvre	labourer, *Am* laborer	manoeuvre, *Am* maneuver
mémoire	dissertation	memory
mode	method, mode	fashion
mort	dead man	death
moule	mould, *Am* mold	mussel
page	page (boy)	page
physique	physique	physics
poêle	stove	frying pan
poste	post (*job*), set	post, mail, post office
somme	nap	sum
tour	trick, trip, turn	tower
vase	vase	silt
voile	veil	sail

d) **gens** is a masculine noun but is treated as feminine when it *follows* an adjective:

de bonnes gens good people	**toutes ces vieilles gens** all these old people

When **gens** *precedes* an adjective the normal masculine form is used:

des gens ennuyeux boring people	**ces gens sont ennuyeux** these people are boring

A masculine and a feminine may both be used at the same time:

ces vieilles gens sont ennuyeux
these old people are boring

B THE FORMATION OF FEMININES

The feminine of nouns may be formed in the following ways:

1 Add an **e** to the masculine

un ami a (male) friend	**une amie** a (female) friend
un Hollandais a Dutchman	**une Hollandaise** a Dutchwoman

a) nouns which end in **e** in the masculine do not change:

un élève a (male) pupil	**une élève** a (female) pupil

b) the addition of **e** often entails an alteration of the masculine form:

i) nouns ending in **t** and **n** double the final consonant:

le chien	**la chienne** (dog/bitch)
un Algérien	**une Algérienne** (Algerian)
le chat	**la chatte** (cat)

ii) nouns ending in **-er** add a grave accent to the **e** before the silent **e**:

un ouvrier	**une ouvrière** (worker, workman/female worker)

iii) nouns ending in **-eur** usually change into **-euse**:

le vendeur	**la vendeuse** (male/female shop assistant *or Am* sales clerk)

iv) nouns ending in **-teur** change into **-teuse** or **-trice** according to the following guidelines:

if the stem of the word is also that of a present participle (eg **chantant**), the feminine form is in **-euse**:

le chanteur	**la chanteuse** (male/female singer)

but if the stem is not that of a present participle (eg **lisant**), the feminine form is in **-trice**:

le lecteur	**la lectrice** (male/female reader)

But: **inspecteur** becomes **inspectrice** despite present participle **inspectant**.

v) nouns ending in **f** change to **-ve**:

le veuf	**la veuve** (widower/widow)

vi) nouns ending in **x** change to **-se**:

un époux	**une épouse** (husband/wife)

vii) nouns ending in **-eau** change to **-elle** :

le jumeau	**la jumelle** (male/female twin)

2 Use a different word (as in English). The following is a typical selection:

le beau-fils	**la belle-fille** (son/daughter-in-law)
le beau-père	**la belle-mère** (father/mother-in-law)

le bélier	**la brebis** (ram/ewe)
le bœuf	**la vache** (ox/cow)
le cheval	**la jument** (horse/mare)
le cerf	**la biche** (stag/hind)
le coq	**la poule** (rooster, cock/hen)
le fils	**la fille** (son/daughter)
le frère	**la sœur** (brother/sister)
le garçon	**la fille** (boy/girl)
un homme	**une femme** (man/woman)
le mâle	**la femelle** (male/female)
le mari	**la femme** (husband/wife)
le neveu	**la nièce** (nephew/niece)
un oncle	**une tante** (uncle/aunt)
le parrain	**la marraine** (godfather/godmother)
le père	**la mère** (father/mother)
le porc	**la truie** (pig/sow)
le roi	**la reine** (king/queen)

3 Add the word '**femme**' (or '**femelle**' for animals)

une femme poète (female poet)
une femme médecin (woman doctor)
un perroquet femelle (female parrot)

4 **Irregular feminines**

un âne	**une ânesse** (donkey/she-ass)
le canard	**la cane** (drake/duck)
le comte	**la comtesse** (count/countess)
le copain	**la copine** (pal)
le dieu	**la déesse** (god/goddess)
le dindon	**la dinde** (turkey cock/turkey)
le duc	**la duchesse** (duke/duchess)
un Esquimau	**une Esquimaude** (Eskimo)
le fou	**la folle** (madman/madwoman)
le Grec	**la Grecque** (Greek)
un héros	**une héroïne** (hero/heroine)
un hôte	**une hôtesse** (host/hostess)
le maître	**la maîtresse** (master/mistress)
le mulet	**la mule** (mule)
le prince	**la princesse** (prince/princess)
le tigre	**la tigresse** (tiger/tigress)
le Turc	**la Turque** (Turk)
le vieux	**la vieille** (old man/old woman)

C THE FORMATION OF PLURALS

1 Most nouns form their plural by adding **s** to the singular:

le vin	**les vins**	wine
un étudiant	**des étudiants**	student

2 Nouns ending in **s**, **x** or **z** remain unchanged:

le bras	**les bras**	arm
la voix	**les voix**	voice
le nez	**les nez**	nose

3 Nouns ending in **-au**, **-eau** and **-eu** add **x** to the singular:

	le tuyau	**les tuyaux**	pipe
	le bateau	**les bateaux**	boat
	le jeu	**les jeux**	game
But:	**le landau**	**les landaus**	pram, *Am* baby carriage
	le bleu	**les bleus**	bruise
	le pneu	**les pneus**	tyre, *Am* tire

4 Nouns ending in **-al** change to **-aux**:

	le journal	**les journaux**	newspaper
But:	**le bal**	**les bals**	dance
	le carnaval	**les carnavals**	carnival
	le festival	**les festivals**	festival
	le récital	**les récitals**	recital

5 Nouns ending in **-ail**

a) six nouns ending in **-ail** change to **-aux** in the plural:

le bail	**les baux**	lease
le corail	**les coraux**	coral
l'émail	**les émaux**	enamel
le soupirail	**les soupiraux**	basement window
le travail	**les travaux**	work
le vitrail	**les vitraux**	stained-glass window

b) all other nouns ending in **-ail** add **-s**:

le chandail	**les chandails**	sweater
le détail	**les détails**	detail
l'épouvantail	**les épouvantails**	scarecrow
l'éventail	**les éventails**	fan
le portail	**les portails**	gate
le rail	**les rails**	rail

6 Nouns ending in **-ou**:

a) seven nouns ending in **-ou** add **x** in the plural:

le bijou	**les bijoux**	jewel
le caillou	**les cailloux**	pebble
le chou	**les choux**	cabbage
le genou	**les genoux**	knee
le hibou	**les hiboux**	owl
le joujou	**les joujoux**	toy
le pou	**les poux**	louse

b) all other nouns ending in **-ou** add **s**:

le clou	**les clous**	nail
le fou	**les fous**	madman

7 Plural of compound nouns

There are four principal ways of forming the plural of a compound noun but each noun ought to be checked individually in the dictionary since the rules have many exceptions.

a) noun + adjective (both vary):

le beau-père	**les beaux-pères**	father-in-law

b) noun + adjective equivalent (only the noun varies):

un arc-en-ciel	**des arcs-en ciel**	rainbow

c) noun + noun (both vary):

le chou-fleur	**les choux-fleurs**	cauliflower

d) noun + preposition (invariable):

un après-midi	**des après-midi**	afternoon

e) verb + noun object (either the noun varies or the compound is invariable):

i) noun varies:

le tire-bouchon	**les tire-bouchons**	corkscrew

ii) invariable:

un abat-jour	**des abat-jour**	lampshade
le porte-clefs	**les porte-clefs**	key ring

f) no noun (invariable):

le passe-partout	**les passe-partout**	master key

8 Irregular plurals:

un œil	**des yeux**	eye
le ciel	**les cieux**	sky
Monsieur	**Messieurs**	Mr
Madame	**Mesdames**	Mrs
Mademoiselle	**Mesdemoiselles**	Miss

9 Collective nouns

a) singular in French but plural in English

le bétail	cattle
la famille	family
la police	police

la police *a* arrêté certains grévistes
the police *have* arrested some strikers

Note: Many collective nouns such as 'family' 'or 'government' remain singular in American English.

b) plural in French but singular in English

les nouvelles sont bonnes
the news is good

faire de grands progrès
to make great progress

10 Proper nouns

a) Ordinary family names are invariable:

j'ai rencontré les Leblanc
I met the Leblancs

b) Historical names add **-s**:

les Stuarts	**les Bourbons**	**les Tudors**
the Stuarts	the Bourbons	the Tudors

4 ADJECTIVES

Adjectives are 'describing' words, which usually accompany a noun (or a pronoun) and tell us what someone or something is like:

une *grande* ville a *large* city	**un passe-temps *intéressant*** an *interesting* pastime
elle est *espagnole* she is *Spanish*	**c'était *ennuyeux*** it was *boring*

A AGREEMENT OF ADJECTIVES

In French, adjectives agree in number and gender with the noun or pronoun they refer to. This means that, unlike English adjectives, which don't change, French adjectives have four different forms which are determined by the noun they go with:

- **masculine singular** (basic form, found in the dictionary)
- **feminine singular**
- **masculine plural**
- **feminine plural**

un passeport *vert* a green passport	**une voiture *verte*** a green car
des gants *verts* green gloves	**des chaussettes *vertes*** green socks

Note: If two singular words share the same adjective, the adjective will be in the plural:

un foulard et un bonnet *rouges*
a red scarf and (a red) hat

If one of these words is feminine, one masculine, the adjective will be masculine plural:

une robe et un manteau *noirs*
a black dress and (a black) coat

B FEMININE FORMS OF ADJECTIVES

1 General rule

Add the letter e to the masculine singular form:

MASCULINE	FEMININE
grand	**grande**
amusant	**amusante**
anglais	**anglaise**
bronzé	**bronzée**
un livre amusant an amusing book	**une histoire amusante** an amusing story

il est bronzé	**elle est bronzée**
he is suntanned	she is suntanned

2 Adjectives already ending in 'e'

These do not change:

MASCULINE	FEMININE
rouge	**rouge**
jeune	**jeune**
malade	**malade**
mon père est malade	**ma mère est malade**
my father is ill	my mother is ill

3 Others

The spelling of some adjectives changes when the **e** is added:

a) The following masculine endings generally double the final consonant before adding **e**:

MASCULINE ENDING	FEMININE ENDING
-el	**-elle**
-eil	**-eille**
-en	**-enne**
-on	**-onne**
-as	**-asse**
-et	**-ette**

MASCULINE		FEMININE
réel	(real)	**réelle**
cruel	(cruel)	**cruelle**
pareil	(similar)	**pareille**
ancien	(old)	**ancienne**
italien	(Italian)	**italienne**
bon	(good)	**bonne**
gras	(fat, greasy)	**grasse**
bas	(low)	**basse**
las	(tired)	**lasse**
muet	(dumb, silent)	**muette**
net	(clear)	**nette**

un film muet	**une voyelle muette**
a silent film	a silent vowel
un bon conseil	**c'est une bonne recette**
good advice	it's a good recipe

But: the feminine ending of some common adjectives in **-et** is **-ète** instead of **-ette**:

MASCULINE		FEMININE
complet	(complete)	**complète**
incomplet	(incomplete)	**incomplète**

concret	(concrete)	**concrète**
désuet	(obsolete)	**désuète**
discret	(discreet)	**discrète**
inquiet	(worried)	**inquiète**
secret	(secret)	**secrète**

b) MASCULINE IN **-er** — FEMININE IN **-ère**

cher	(dear)	**chère**
fier	(proud)	**fière**
dernier	(last)	**dernière**
léger	(light)	**légère**

c) MASCULINE IN **-x** — FEMININE IN **-se**

heureux	(happy)	**heureuse**
malheureux	(unhappy)	**malheureuse**
sérieux	(serious)	**sérieuse**
jaloux	(jealous)	**jalouse**

But:

doux	(soft)	**douce**
faux	(false)	**fausse**
roux	(red-haired)	**rousse**
vieux	(old)	**vieille**

d) MASCULINE IN **-eur** — FEMININE IN **-euse**

menteur	(lying)	**menteuse**
trompeur	(deceitful)	**trompeuse**

But: This rule applies only when the stem of the adjective is also the stem of a present participle (eg **mentant, trompant**). The following ten adjectives simply add an **e** to the feminine, **-eur** becoming **-eure**:

MASCULINE		FEMININE
extérieur	(external)	**extérieure**
intérieur	(internal)	**intérieure**
inférieur	(inferior)	**inférieure**
supérieur	(superior)	**supérieure**
meilleur	(better)	**meilleure**
majeur	(major)	**majeure**
mineur	(minor)	**mineure**
antérieur	(former)	**antérieure**
postérieur	(later)	**postérieure**
ultérieur	(later)	**ultérieure**

The feminine ending of the other adjectives in **-teur** is **-trice**:

MASCULINE		FEMININE
protecteur	(protective)	**protectrice**

destructeur	(destructive)	**destructrice**
conservateur	(Conservative)	**conservatrice**

e)

MASCULINE IN **-f**		FEMININE IN **-ve**
neuf	(new)	**neuve**
vif	(lively)	**vive**
naïf	(naive)	**naïve**
actif	(active)	**active**
passif	(passive)	**passive**
positif	(positive)	**positive**
bref	(brief)	**brève** (note the **è**!)

f)

MASCULINE IN **-c**		FEMININE IN **-che** or **-que**
blanc	(white)	**blanche**
franc	(frank)	**franche**
sec	(dry)	**sèche** (note the **è**!)
public	(public)	**publique**
turc	(Turkish)	**turque**
grec	(Greek)	**grecque** (note the **c**!)

g) The following five common adjectives have an irregular feminine form and two forms for the masculine singular; the second masculine form, based on the feminine form, is used before words starting with a vowel or a silent **h**:

MASCULINE	FEMININE	MASCULINE 2
beau (beautiful)	**belle**	**bel**
nouveau (new)	**nouvelle**	**nouvel**
vieux (old)	**vieille**	**vieil**
fou (mad)	**folle**	**fol**
mou (soft)	**molle**	**mol**

un beau lac a beautiful lake	**une belle vue** a beautiful view	**un bel enfant** a beautiful child
un nouveau livre a new book	**la nouvelle année** the new year	**un nouvel ami** a new friend
un vieux tableau an old painting	**la vieille ville** the old town	**un vieil homme** an old man

h) Other irregular feminines:

MASCULINE		FEMININE
favori	(favourite)	**favorite**
gentil	(nice)	**gentille**
nul	(no)	**nulle**

frais	(fresh)	**fraîche**
gros	(big)	**grosse**
épais	(thick)	**épaisse**
exprès	(express)	**expresse**
métis	(half-caste)	**métisse**
malin	(smart, shrewd)	**maligne**
sot	(foolish)	**sotte**
pâlot	(pale)	**pâlotte**
rigolo	(funny)	**rigolote**
long	(long)	**longue**
aigu	(sharp, acute)	**aiguë**
ambigu	(ambiguous)	**ambiguë**

i) The following five adjectives are invariable in the feminine:

chic	(smart, stylish)
châtain	(chestnut brown)
marron	(chestnut brown)
kaki	(khaki)
snob	(snobbish)

C PLURALS OF ADJECTIVES

1 General rule

The masculine and feminine plural of adjectives is formed by adding an **s** to the singular form:

un vélo neuf a new bike	**des vélos neufs** new bikes
une belle fleur a beautiful flower	**de belles fleurs** beautiful flowers

2 Adjectives ending in 's' or 'x'

If the masculine singular ends in **s** or **x**, it is obviously not necessary to add the **s**:

il est heureux he's happy	**ils sont heureux** they are happy
un touriste anglais an English tourist	**des touristes anglais** English tourists

3 Others

A few masculine plural endings are irregular (the feminine plurals are all regular):

a)

SINGULAR IN **-al**		PLURAL IN **-aux**
normal	(normal)	**normaux**
brutal	(brutal)	**brutaux**
loyal	(loyal)	**loyaux**

But:	**fatal**	(fatal)	**fatals**
	banal	(commonplace)	**banals**
	bancal	(bandy)	**bancals**
	final	(final)	**finals** (also occasionally **-aux**)
	natal	(native)	**natals**
	naval	(naval)	**navals**

b)

SINGULAR IN **-eau**		PLURAL IN **-eaux**
beau	(beautiful)	**beaux**
nouveau	(new)	**nouveaux**

D POSITION OF ADJECTIVES

1 Unlike English adjectives, French adjectives usually follow the noun:

un métier intéressant	**des parents modernes**
an interesting job	modern parents

Adjectives of colour and nationality always follow the noun:

des chaussures rouges	**le drapeau britannique**
red shoes	the British flag

2 However the following common adjectives generally come before the noun:

beau	beautiful
bon	good
court	short
gentil	nice
grand	big, tall
gros	big, fat
haut	high
jeune	young
joli	pretty
long	long
mauvais	bad
méchant	nasty, naughty (*child*)
meilleur	better
moindre	lesser, slightest
nouveau	new
petit	small
pire	worse
vaste	vast
vieux	old
vilain	nasty, ugly

3 Some adjectives have a different meaning according to their position:

	BEFORE NOUN	AFTER NOUN
ancien	former	ancient, old
brave	good	brave
certain	certain (*some*)	definite, sure

cher	dear	expensive
dernier	last (*in sequence*)	last (*previous, with day, month, season etc*)
différent	various, different	different
divers	various	varied
large	large	broad, wide
même	same	very
nombreux	numerous, many	large
pauvre	poor (*deserving pity*)	poor (*not rich*)
propre	own	clean
rare	rare (*few, infrequent*)	rare (*uncommon, exceptional*)
sacré	damned	sacred
seul	only, single	alone
simple	ordinary (*mere*)	simple
triste	unfortunate, sorry	sad, gloomy
vague	vague (*not specific, unimportant*)	vague (*imprecise, not clear*)
vrai	real	true

mon ancien métier my former job	**un tableau ancien** an old painting
un brave type a good/nice fellow	**un homme brave** a brave man
un certain charme a certain charm	**un fait certain** a definite fact
chère Brigitte dear Brigitte	**un cadeau cher** an expensive present
la dernière séance the last performance	**le mois/l'été dernier** last month/summer
différentes personnes various/different people	**un choix différent** a different choice
diverses personnes various people	**des opinions diverses** varied opinions
une grande vedette a great star	**un homme assez grand** a fairly tall man
dans une large mesure to a large extent	**un nez large** a broad/wide nose
le même endroit the same place	**l'endroit même** the very place
	la vérité même the truth itself
de nombreux amis numerous/many friends	**une nombreuse famille** a large family
mon pauvre ami ! my poor friend!	**des gens pauvres** poor people

mon propre frère my own brother	**une chambre propre** a clean room
de rares exemples rare examples	**une plante rare** a rare plant
sacré menteur ! damned liar!	**des livres sacrés** sacred books
mon seul espoir my only hope	**un homme seul** a man alone
	le président seul the president alone
un simple employé an ordinary employee	**des goûts simples** simple tastes
cette triste affaire that unfortunate/sorry business	**une femme triste** a sad woman
	un temps triste gloomy weather
une vague histoire a vague story	**un contour vague** a vague outline
un vrai casse-pieds a real bore	**une histoire vraie** a true story

4 If a noun is accompanied by several adjectives, the same rules apply to each of them:

le bon vieux temps
the good old days

un joli foulard rouge
a pretty red scarf

5 Cardinal numbers (eg **un(e)**, **deux**, **trois**) and ordinal numbers (eg **premier**, **deuxième, troisième**) are adjectives that always come before the noun, except in a very few cases:

deux maisons two houses	**la première page** the first page

But: **Charles Deux**
Charles the Second

(See **G190 & 191**, sections 10 A & B)

Note: For the position of demonstrative adjectives, indefinite adjectives, interrogative and exclamatory adjectives and possessive adjectives, see **G45, 48, 52 & 64**, sections 6 A, B, C & E.

E COMPARATIVE AND SUPERLATIVE OF ADJECTIVES

Persons or things can be compared by using:

1 ***the comparative form of the adjective:***

more ... than, ...er than, less ... than, as ... as

2 ***the superlative form of the adjective:***

the most ... , the ...est, the least ...

(See the formation of the comparative and superlative of adverbs, **G43**)

1 The comparative

The comparative is formed as follows:

plus ... (que) more ...,	**plus long** longer	**plus cher** more expensive
moins ... (que) less ... than	**moins long** less long	**moins récent** less recent
aussi ... (que) as ... (as)	**aussi bon** as good	**aussi important** as important

une plus grande maison — a larger house

un village plus ancien — an older village

le tennis est-il plus populaire que la natation ?
is tennis more popular than swimming?

ces gants sont moins chauds que les autres
these gloves are less warm than the other ones

elle est beaucoup moins patiente/bien moins patiente que lui
she's far less patient than he is

le problème de la pollution est tout aussi grave
the pollution problem is just as serious

Note:

a) when a clause follows the comparative adjective, **ne** is often added:

ces gants sont moins chauds que vous (ne) pensez
these gloves are less warm than you (may) think

b) **aussi ... que possible** is translated by **as ... as possible**:

aussi heureux que possible — as happy as possible

c) after a negative, **aussi** is often replaced by **si**:

je ne suis pas si heureux — I'm not so happy

d) In French, the idea of **not so, not as** is often expressed by **moins** (less):

il est moins intelligent qu'elle — he's not as clever as she is

2 The superlative

a) *Formation*

le/la/les plus ... **le/la/les moins ...**	the most ..., the ...est the least ...
le plus grand pays the largest country	**la plus grande ville** the largest city
les plus grands acteurs the greatest actors	**les plus grandes voitures** the largest cars

b) *Word order*

i) The normal rules governing word order of adjectives apply. When a superlative adjective comes after the noun, the definite article is used twice, before the noun and before the adjective:

le plat le plus délicieux the most delicious dish	**l'histoire la plus passionnante** the most exciting story

la robe la moins chère
the least expensive dress

ii) When a possessive adjective is used, there are two possible constructions, depending on the position of the adjective. The definite article is only used when the adjective follows the noun:

ma plus forte matière
my best/strongest subject

son besoin le plus/le moins urgent
his most/least urgent need

c) *'in' is normally translated by* ***de***:

la plus jolie maison du quartier/de la ville
the prettiest house in the area/town

le restaurant le plus cher de France
the most expensive restaurant in France

Note: Verbs following the superlative usually take the subjunctive (see **G101**, section 7 G 1g)).

3 Irregular comparatives and superlatives

ADJECTIVE	COMPARATIVE	SUPERLATIVE
bon good	**meilleur** better	**le meilleur** best
mauvais bad	**pire** **plus mauvais** worse	**le pire** **le plus mauvais** the worst
petit small	**moindre** **plus petit** smaller, lesser	**le moindre** **le plus petit** the smallest, the least

Note: - **plus mauvais** (worse) is more common than **pire** in everyday French
- **moindre** usually means 'less in importance', and **plus petit** means 'less in size':

le moindre de mes soucis	**elle est plus petite que moi**
the least of my worries	she is smaller than I am

5 ADVERBS

Adverbs are normally used with a verb to express:

		ADVERBS OF
how	an action is done	manner
when		time
where		place
with how much intensity		intensity
to what extent		quantity

A ADVERBS OF MANNER

These are usually formed by adding **-ment** to the adjective (like **-ly** in English):

1 If the adjective ends in a consonant, **-ment** is added to its feminine form:

ADJECTIVE (masc, fem)	ADVERB
doux, douce (soft)	**doucement** (softly)
franc, franche (frank)	**franchement** (frankly)
final, finale (final)	**finalement** (finally)

2 If the adjective ends in a vowel, **-ment** is added to its masculine form:

	ADJECTIVE	ADVERB
	absolu (absolute)	**absolument** (absolutely)
	aisé (easy)	**aisément** (easily)
	dû (due)	**dûment** (duly)
	poli (polite)	**poliment** (politely)
	simple (simple)	**simplement** (simply)
	vrai (real)	**vraiment** (really)
But:	**gai** (cheerful)	**gaiement** (cheerfully)
	fou (mad)	**follement** (madly)

3 Many adverbs have irregular forms:

a) Some change the **e** of the feminine form of the adjective to **é** before adding **-ment**:

	ADJECTIVE	ADVERB
	aveugle (blind)	**aveuglément** (blindly)
	commun (common)	**communément** (commonly)
	confus (confused)	**confusément** (indistinctly)
	énorme (enormous)	**énormément** (enormously)
	profond (deep)	**profondément** (deeply)
But:	**impuni** (unpunished)	**impunément** (with impunity)

b) Adjectives which end in **-ent** and **-ant** change to **-emment** and **-amment** (*Note:* both endings are pronounced **-amant**):

ADJECTIVE	ADVERB
évident (obvious)	**évidemment** (obviously)
prudent (careful)	**prudemment** (carefully)
brillant (brilliant)	**brillamment** (brilliantly)
constant (constant)	**constamment** (constantly)

But: **lent** (slow) **lentement** (slowly)

4 Some adverbs are completely irregular, including some of the most commonly used ones:

ADJECTIVE	ADVERB
bon (good)	**bien** (well)
bref (brief)	**brièvement** (briefly)
gentil (kind, nice)	**gentiment** (kindly, nicely)
mauvais (bad)	**mal** (badly)
meilleur (better)	**mieux** (better)

Note: A number of common adverbs have no corresponding adjectives, eg **ainsi** (this way), **debout** (standing), **ensemble** (together), **exprès** (on purpose), **volontiers** (gladly).

5 Some adjectives are also used as adverbs in certain set expressions, eg:

parler bas/haut *or* **fort**	to speak softly/loudly
coûter/payer cher	to cost/pay a lot
s'arrêter court	to stop short
couper court	to cut short
voir clair	to see clearly
marcher droit	to walk straight
travailler dur	to work hard
chanter faux/juste	to sing out of tune/in tune
sentir mauvais/bon	to smell bad/good
refuser net	to refuse flatly

6 After verbs of saying and looking in French an adverbial phrase is often preferred to an adverb, eg:

"tu m'écriras ?" dit-il *d'une voix triste*
"will you write to me?" he said *sadly*

il répondit *d'un ton sec*
he replied *curtly*

elle nous a regardés *d'un air dédaigneux*
she looked at us *disdainfully*

7 English adverbs may be expressed in French by a preposition followed by a noun, eg:

sans soin	carelessly
avec fierté	proudly

avec amour	lovingly
à la légère	rashly
d'instinct	instinctively

B ADVERBS OF TIME

These are not usually formed from adjectives. Here are the commonest ones:

alors	then
après	afterwards
aujourd'hui	today
aussitôt	at once
avant	before
bientôt	soon
d'abord	first
déjà	already, yet
demain	tomorrow
encore	still, again
pas encore	not yet
enfin	at last, finally
ensuite	next
entre-temps	meanwhile
hier	yesterday
jamais	never
longtemps	(for) a long time
maintenant	now
parfois	sometimes
puis	then
quelquefois	sometimes
rarement	seldom
soudain	suddenly
souvent	often
tard	late
tôt	early
toujours	always
tout de suite	at once

c'est déjà Noël !
it's Christmas already!

tu as déjà essayé ?
have you tried yet *or* before?

il mange encore !
he's still eating!

elle n'est pas encore arrivée
she hasn't arrived yet

C ADVERBS OF PLACE

Here are the commonest ones:

ailleurs	somewhere else
ici	here
là	there
loin	far away

tout près	nearby
dessus	on top, on it
au-dessus	over, above
dessous	underneath
au-dessous	below
dedans	inside
dehors	outside
devant	in front, ahead
derrière	behind
autour	around
partout	everywhere

ne restez pas dehors !
don't stay outside!

mon nom est marqué dessus
my name is written on it

qu'est-ce qu'il y a dedans ?
what's inside?

passez devant
go in front

Note: There are many common *compound* adverbs which could be added to the above list, eg **là-bas** (over there), **là-dedans** (in there), **en bas** (down below, downstairs), **quelque part** (somewhere).

D ADVERBS OF INTENSITY AND QUANTITY

These may be used with a verb, an adjective or another adverb. Here are the commonest ones:

à peine	hardly
assez	enough, fairly, quite
aussi	as, so
autant	as much/many
beaucoup	a lot, much/many
bien	very
combien	how much/many
comme	how
extrêmement	extremely
moins	less
plus	more
plutôt	rather
presque	nearly, almost
peu	little
seulement	only
si	so
tant	so much/many
tellement	so much/many
tout	very
très	very
trop	too, too much/many
un peu	a little

vous avez assez bu !
you've had enough to drink!

il ne fait pas assez chaud
it's not warm enough

je suis assez fatigué
I'm fairly/quite tired

je suis plutôt fatigué
I'm rather tired

nous avons beaucoup ri
we laughed a lot

comme c'est amusant !
how amusing!

je vais un peu mieux
I'm feeling a little better

c'est si fatigant !
it's so tiring!

elle parle trop
she talks too much

il est très timide
he's very shy

je suis bien content
I'm very pleased

c'est tout petit
it's very small

il n'est pas aussi *or* **si intelligent que ça**
he's not as clever as that

une situation aussi *or* **si tragique**
such a tragic situation, so tragic a situation

Note:

i) All of these adverbs, except **à peine, aussi, comme, presque, si, seulement, tout, très, extrêmement,** may be followed by **de** and a noun to express a quantity (see **G193**, section 10 E 1).

ii) **bien** is followed by **de** + definite article to express a quantity. Used with a verb it is an adverb of manner (see **G39**, section 5 4).

E POSITION OF ADVERBS

1 Adverbs usually follow verbs:

je vais rarement au théâtre
I seldom go to the theatre

comme vous conduisez prudemment !
you do drive carefully!

2 With compound tenses, shorter adverbs usually come between the auxiliary and the past participle:

j'ai enfin terminé
I have finished at last

nous y sommes souvent allés
we've often gone there

il me l'a déjà dit
he's already told me

elle avait beaucoup souffert
she had suffered a lot

3 But adverbs of place and many adverbs of time follow the past participle:

je l'ai rencontré hier
I met him yesterday

elle avait cherché partout
she had looked everywhere

je l'ai mis dehors
I put it outside

tu t'es couché tard ?
did you go to bed late?

4 Adverbs usually come before adjectives or other adverbs:

très rarement
very seldom

trop vite
too quickly

elle est vraiment belle
she is really beautiful

5 Adverbs may be placed at the start of a sentence for emphasis:

enfin elle a terminé — at last she's finished
d'abord je le lui dirai — first I'll tell him

F COMPARATIVE AND SUPERLATIVE OF ADVERBS

1 The comparative and superlative of adverbs are formed in the same way as adjectives (see **G35**, section 4 E):

ADVERB	COMPARATIVE	SUPERLATIVE
souvent often	**plus souvent (que)** more often (than)	**le plus souvent** (the) most often
	moins souvent (que) less often (than)	**le moins souvent** (the) least often
	aussi souvent (que) as often (as)	

Note: The superlative of the adverb always takes the masculine singular article **le**:

je le vois plus souvent qu'avant
I see him more often than I used to

il conduit moins prudemment que moi
he drives less carefully than I do

c'est elle qui conduit le moins prudemment
she's the one who drives the least carefully

je sais cuisiner aussi bien que toi !
I can cook as well as you!

Note:

a) **aussi ... que possible** and **le plus ... possible** are the two ways to translate **as ... as possible**:

aussi loin que possible — as far (away) as possible
le plus loin possible

b) after a negative, **aussi** is often replaced by **si**:

pas si vite !
not so fast!

c) In French, the idea of **not so, not as** is often expressed by **moins** (less):

parle moins fort !
don't talk so loud!

d) When a clause follows the comparative adverb, **ne** is often added:

je le vois plus souvent que vous (ne) pensez
I see him more often than you (may) think

2 Irregular comparatives and superlatives

ADVERB	COMPARATIVE	SUPERLATIVE
beaucoup much, a lot	**plus** more	**le plus** (the) most
bien well	**mieux** better	**le mieux** (the) best
mal badly	**pis** *or* **plus mal** worse	**le pis** *or* **le plus mal** (the) worst
peu little	**moins** less	**le moins** (the) least

Note:

i) **mieux/le mieux** must not be confused with **meilleur/le meilleur**, which are adjectives, used in front of a noun.

ii) **pis/le pis** are only found in certain set expressions:

tant pis ! too bad!	**de mal en pis** from bad to worse

3 For the treatment of negative adverbs, eg **jamais** (never), **plus** (no more), see **G204,** section 12 B.

6 PRONOUNS AND CORRESPONDING ADJECTIVES

A DEMONSTRATIVES

1 Demonstrative adjectives

a) *CE*

ce is often used to point out a particular person or thing, or persons or things. It is followed by the noun it refers to and agrees in number and gender with that noun.

- with a masculine singular noun:	**ce (cet)**	this/that
- with a feminine singular noun:	**cette**	this/that
- with a plural noun (masc or fem):	**ces**	these/those

ce roman m'a beaucoup plu
I really liked this novel

il a neigé ce matin
it snowed this morning

cette chanson m'énerve
that song gets on my nerves

cette fois, c'est fini !
this time, it's over!

tu trouves que ces lunettes me vont bien ?
do you think these glasses suit me?

cet is used instead of **ce** in front of a word that begins with a vowel or a silent **h**:

cet après-midi
this afternoon

cet hôtel
that hotel

b) *-CI and -LA*

French does not have separate words to distinguish between 'this' and 'that'. However, when a particular emphasis is being placed on a person or object, or when a contrast is being made between persons or objects, **-ci** and **-là** are added to the noun:

-ci translates the idea of this/these
-là translates the idea of that/those

je suis très occupé ces jours-ci
I'm very busy these days

que faisiez-vous ce soir-là ?
what were you doing that evening?

d'où vient ce fromage-là ? — ce fromage-ci, Monsieur ?
where does that cheese come from? — this cheese, sir?

2 Demonstrative pronouns

Demonstrative pronouns are used instead of a noun with **ce/cette/ces**. They are:

a) **celui, celle, ceux, celles**
b) **ce**
c) **ceci, cela, ça**

a) *CELUI*

i) **celui** agrees in number and gender with the noun it refers to. It has four different forms:

	MASCULINE	FEMININE
SINGULAR	**celui**	**celle**
PLURAL	**ceux**	**celles**

ii) use of **celui**

celui, celle, ceux and **celles** cannot be used on their own. They are used:

★ with **-ci** or **-là**, for emphasis or for contrast:

celui-ci	**celle-ci**	this (one)
celui-là	**celle-là**	that (one)
ceux-ci	**celles-ci**	these (ones)
ceux-là	**celles-là**	those (ones)

j'aime bien ce maillot, mais celui-là est moins cher
I like this swimsuit, but that one is cheaper

je voudrais ces fleurs — lesquelles ? celles-ci ou celles-là ?
I'd like these flowers — which ones? these or those?

j'ai rencontré Jacques et son père; celui-là portait un chapeau, celui-ci une casquette
I met Jacques and his father; the former was wearing a hat and the latter a cap

★ with **de** + noun, to express possession:

je préfère mon ordinateur à celui de Jean-Claude
I prefer my computer to Jean-Claude's

range ta chambre plutôt que celle de ta sœur
tidy your own bedroom rather than your sister's

mes parents sont moins sévères que ceux de Nicole
my parents aren't as strict as Nicole's

les douches municipales sont mieux que celles du camping
the public showers are better than those at the camp site

★ with the relative pronouns **qui, que, dont** to introduce a relative clause (for use of these relative pronouns, see **G67**, section 6 F).

celui/celle/ceux/celles qui	the one(s) who/which
celui/celle/ceux/celles que	the one(s) whom/which
celui/celle/ceux/celles dont	the one(s) of which/whose

lequel est ton père ? celui qui a une barbe ?
which one is your father? the one with the beard?

regarde cette voiture ! celle qui est garée au coin
look at that car! the one which is parked at the corner

deux filles, celles qu'il avait rencontrées la veille
two girls, the ones he had met the day before

voilà mon copain, celui dont je t'ai parlé l'autre jour
here's my friend, the one I told you about the other day

Note: Occasionally a preposition other than **de** is used (eg **elle a choisi ceux à dix francs** she selected those at ten francs). Other parts of speech, such as a past participle or an adjective, are sometimes used after **celui** etc (eg **c'est celui découvert par son oncle** it's the one discovered by his uncle).

b) *CE*

i) **ce** (meaning 'it', 'that') is mostly found with the verb **être**:

c'est	**ce serait**	**c'était**
it's/that's	it/that would be	it/that was

Note: **ce** changes to **c'** before an **e** or an **é**.

ii) use of **ce**

★ with a noun or pronoun, **ce** is used to identify people or things, or to emphasize them; it is translated in a variety of ways:

qu'est-ce que c'est ? — c'est mon billet d'avion
what's that? — it's my plane ticket

qui est-ce ? — c'est moi
who is it? — it's me

ce doit être lui
that must be him

c'est un artiste bien connu
he's a well-known artist

c'était une bonne idée
it was a good idea

ce sont mes amis
they're my friends

c'est la dernière fois !
it's the last time!

c'est elle qui l'a fait
she's the one who did it

c'est celui que j'ai vu
he's the one I saw

★ before an adjective, **ce** is used to refer to an idea, an event or a fact which has already been mentioned; it does not refer to any specific noun:

c'était formidable
it was great

ce serait triste
it would be sad

oui, c'est vrai
yes, that's true

c'est sûr ?
is that definite?

ce n'est pas grave
it doesn't matter
or it's not important

c'est bon à entendre
that's good to hear

Note: the translation of **it** is an area of some difficulty for students of French, as it is sometimes translated by **ce** and sometimes by **il/elle**; see **G215**, section 13 B 2.

3 CECI, CELA, ÇA

ceci (this), **cela** (that) and **ça** (that) are used to refer to an idea, an event, a fact or an object. They never refer to a particular noun already mentioned.

non, je n'aime pas ça !
no, I don't like that!

ah, bon ? cela m'étonne
really? that surprises me

ça, c'est un acteur ! that's what I call an actor!	**souvenez-vous de ceci** remember this
ça m'est égal I don't mind	**cela ne vous regarde pas** that's none of your business
buvez ceci, ça vous fera du bien drink this, it'll do you good	**ça alors !** how about that!

cela s'appelle comment, en anglais ?
what do you call this in English?

Note: **ceci** is not very common in French; **cela** and **ça** are often used to translate 'this' as well as 'that'; **ça** is used far more frequently than **cela** in spoken French.

B INDEFINITE ADJECTIVES AND PRONOUNS

1 Indefinite adjectives

The most important are:

MASCULINE	FEMININE	
autre(s)	**autre(s)**	other
certain(s)	**certaine(s)**	certain, some
chaque	**chaque**	each, every
différents	**différentes**	various
divers	**diverses**	various
même(s)	**même(s)**	same
plusieurs	**plusieurs**	several
quelconque(s)	**quelconque(s)**	any
quelque(s)	**quelque(s)**	some, a few
tel(s)	**telle(s)**	such
tout (tous)	**toute(s)**	all, every

a) *CHAQUE and PLUSIEURS*

chaque (each, every) is always singular, **plusieurs** (several) always plural; the feminine form is the same as the masculine form:

j'y vais chaque jour I go there every day	**chaque personne** each person
plusieurs années several years	**il a plusieurs amis** he's got several friends

b) *AUTRE, MEME and QUELQUE*

autre (other), **même** (same) and **quelque** (some) agree in number with the noun that follows; the feminine is the same as the masculine:

je voudrais un autre café I'd like another coffee	**d'autres médecins** other doctors

la même taille — the same size
les mêmes touristes — the same tourists

quelque temps après — some time later
à quelques kilomètres — a few kilometres away

Note: **même** has a different meaning when placed after the noun (see **G32**, section 4 D 3).

c) *CERTAIN, TEL and TOUT*

certain (certain, some), **tel** (such) and **tout** (all) agree in number and gender with the noun; they have four different forms:

un certain charme — a certain charm
une certaine dame — a certain lady

à certains moments — at (certain) times
certaines personnes — some/certain people

un tel homme — such a man
une telle aventure — such an adventure

de tels avantages — such advantages
de telles difficultés — such difficulties

quoi ! tu as mangé tout le fromage et tous les fruits ?
what! you've eaten all the cheese and all the fruit?

toute la journée — all day long
toutes mes matières — all my subjects

Note:

i) **certain** has a different meaning when placed after the noun (see **G32**, section 4 D 3).

ii) **tel**: the position of the article **un/une** with **tel** is not the same as in English: **un tel homme** = such a man.

iii) **tel** cannot qualify another adjective; when it is used as an adverb, 'such' is translated by **si** or **tellement** (so):

c'était un si bon repas/un repas tellement bon !
it was such a good meal!

iv) **tous les/toutes les** are often translated by 'every':

tous les jours — every day
toutes les places — all seats, every seat

d) *DIFFERENTS and DIVERS*

différents and **divers** (*both* various) are always used before a plural noun and agree in number and gender with the noun:

différents/divers groupes — various groups
différentes/diverses raisons — various reasons

e) ***QUELCONQUE***

quelconque (any) is placed after the noun and has the same form in the feminine as the masculine:

une femme quelconque any woman	**des prétextes quelconques** any excuses

2 Indefinite pronouns

a) The most important are:

MASC	FEM	
aucun	**aucune**	none, not any
autre(s)	**autre(s)**	another, other (ones)
certains	**certaine(s)**	some
chacun	**chacune**	each one, everyone
le même	**la même**	the same
les mêmes	**les mêmes**	one(s)
on		one, someone, you, they, people, we
personne		nobody, no one
plusieurs	**plusieurs**	several
quelque chose		something, anything
quelqu'un		someone, anyone
quelques-uns	**quelques-unes**	some, a few
rien		nothing
tout (tous)	**toute(s)**	everything, all, everybody

pas celui-là, l'autre not that one, the other (one)	**où sont les autres ?** where are the others?
j'en ai un autre I have another (one)	**j'en ai d'autres** I have others/other ones
certains disent que ... some say that...	**chacun de mes amis** each (one) of my friends
chacun le sait everyone knows	**chacun pour soi !** every man for himself!
personne n'est venu no one came	**qui est là ? — personne** who's there? — nobody
qu'as-tu ? — rien what's wrong? — nothing	**plusieurs d'entre eux** several of them
il manque quelque chose ? is anything missing?	**dis quelque chose !** say something!
quelqu'un l'a averti someone warned him	**il y a quelqu'un ?** is anyone in?
j'ai tout oublié I've forgotten everything	**c'est tout, merci** that's all, thanks
elles sont toutes arrivées they've all arrived, everybody has arrived	**allons-y tous ensemble** let's all go together

b) *Points to note*

i) **aucun(e)**, **personne** and **rien**: these can be used on their own, but they are more often used with a verb and the negative word **ne** (see negative expressions, **G204**, section 12 B 1):

personne n'habite ici
no one lives here

il n'y a rien à manger
there's nothing to eat

ii) **aucun(e)**, **un(e) autre**, **d'autres**, **certain(e)s**, **plusieurs** and **quelques-un(e)s**: when these pronouns are used as direct objects, the pronoun **en** must be used before the verb:

je n'en ai lu aucun
I haven't read any (of them)

donne-m'en une autre
give me another one

j'en ai vu d'autres qui étaient moins chers
I saw other ones/others which were cheaper

j'en connais certains
I know some of them

il y en a plusieurs
there are several

tu m'en donnes quelques-uns ?
will you give me a few/some?

achètes-en quelques-unes
buy a few/some

iii) **personne**, **quelqu'un**, **quelque chose**, **rien**, **plusieurs**: when these are followed by an adjective, the preposition **de** (**d'**) must be used in front of the adjective:

il n'y a personne de libre
there's no one available

quelqu'un d'intelligent
someone clever

quelque chose de mieux
something better

il y en avait plusieurs de cassés
several of them were broken

rien de grave
nothing serious

(See also **G102**, section 7 G 1i) for use of the subjunctive.)

iv) **autre** is commonly used in the following expressions:

quelqu'un d'autre
someone else

quelque chose d'autre
something else

personne d'autre
nothing else

rien d'autre
nobody else

qui d'autre ?
who else?

quoi d'autre ?
what else?

v) **n'importe qui** (anyone) and **n'importe quoi** (anything) are phrases but they function as indefinite pronouns:

n'importe qui peut le faire
anyone can do it

dis n'importe quoi
say anything

c) *ON*

This pronoun is used in a variety of ways in French. It can mean:

i) *one/you/they/people* in a general sense:

en France, on roule à droite
in France, they drive on the right

on ne sait jamais
you/one never know(s)

on ne doit pas mentir
you shouldn't lie

ii) *someone* (an undefined person)

In this sense, **on** is often translated by the passive (see **G120**, section 7 J 2 a)):

on me l'a déjà dit
someone's already told me
I've already been told

on vous l'apportera
someone will bring it to you
it will be brought to you

iii) *we*

In spoken French, **on** is increasingly used instead of **nous**; although it refers to a plural subject, it is followed by the third person singular:

qu'est-ce qu'on fait ?
what shall we do?

fais vite, on t'attend !
hurry up, we're waiting for you!

Note: in compound tenses with the auxiliary **être**, the agreement of the past participle with **on** is optional:

on est allé au cinéma
on est allés au cinéma
we went to the movies

on est rentré en taxi
on est rentrées en taxi
we got home by taxi

C INTERROGATIVE AND EXCLAMATORY ADJECTIVES AND PRONOUNS

1 The interrogative adjective QUEL ?

a) *Forms*

quel (which, what) agrees in number and gender with the noun it refers to. It has four forms:

- with a masc sing noun: **quel ?**
- with a fem sing noun: **quelle ?**
- with a masc plur noun: **quels ?**
- with a fem plur noun: **quelles ?**

b) *Direct questions*

quel est votre passe-temps favori ?
what's your favourite pastime?

quelle heure est-il ?
what time is it?

quels jours as-tu de libres ?
which/what days have you got free?

quelles affaires comptes-tu prendre avec toi ?
what/which things do you intend to take with you?

c) *Indirect questions:*

je ne sais pas quel livre choisir
I don't know which/what book to choose

il se demande quelle veste lui va le mieux
he's wondering which/what jacket suits him best

2 The exclamatory adjective QUEL !

quel ! has the same forms as the interrogative adjective **quel ?**:

quel dommage ! what a pity!	**quelle belle maison !** what a beautiful house!

quels imbéciles !
what idiots!

3 Interrogative pronouns

These are:

lequel/ laquelle/lesquel(le)s ?	which (one)?
qui ?	who?, whom?
que ?	what?
quoi ?	what?
ce qui	what
ce que	what

ce qui and **ce que** are used only in indirect questions; all other interrogative pronouns can be used both in direct and indirect questions.

a) ***LEQUEL ?***

i) forms

lequel (which?, which one?) agrees in gender and in number with the noun it stands for:

- with a masc sing noun:	**lequel ?**	which (one)?
- with a fem sing noun:	**laquelle ?**	which (one)?
- with a masc plur noun:	**lesquels ?**	which (ones)?
- with a fem plur noun:	**lesquelles ?**	which (ones)?

after the prepositions **à** and **de**, the following changes occur:

à + lequel ?	→	**auquel ?**
à + lesquels ?	→	**auxquels ?**
à + lesquelles ?	→	**auxquelles ?**
de + lequel ?	→	**duquel ?**
de + lesquels ?	→	**desquels ?**
de + lesquelles ?	→	**desquelles ?**

à/de + laquelle? do not change

ii) direct questions:

je cherche un hôtel ; lequel recommandez-vous ?
I'm looking for a hotel; which one do you recommend?

nous avons plusieurs robes ; vous préférez laquelle ?
we have several dresses; which (one) do you prefer?

lesquels de ces livres sont à toi ?
which of these books are yours?

je voudrais essayer ces chaussures — lesquelles ?
I would like to try these shoes on — which ones?

iii) indirect questions:

demande-lui lequel de ces ordinateurs est le moins cher
ask him which (one) of these computers is the cheapest

c'est dans une de ces rues, mais je ne sais plus laquelle
it's in one of these streets, but I can't remember which (one)

For details on the use of **lequel** as a relative pronoun, see **G68**, section 6 F 3d).

b) *QUI ?*

qui (who?, whom?) is used to refer to people; it can be both subject and object, and can be used after a preposition:

qui t'a accompagné ? who accompanied you?	**qui as-tu appelé ?** who did you call?
tu y vas avec qui ? who are you going with?	**c'est pour qui ?** who is it for?
pour qui vous prenez-vous ? who do you think you are?	**à qui l'as-tu donné ?** who did you give it to?

Note:

i) 'whom' is used in formal contexts only:

qui as-tu appelé ? whom did you call?	**tu y vas avec qui ?** with whom are you going?

ii) **que** (not **qui**!) changes to **qu'** before a vowel or a silent **h**:

qui est-ce qu'elle attend ?
who is she waiting for?

qui ? can be replaced by **qui est-ce qui ?** (subject) or **qui est-ce que ?** (object) in direct questions:

qui est-ce qui veut du café ? who wants coffee?	**qui est-ce que tu as vu ?** who did you see?

avec qui est-ce que tu sors ce soir ?
who are you going out with tonight?

But: **qui** cannot be replaced by **qui est-ce qui** or **qui est-ce que** in indirect questions:

j'aimerais savoir qui vous a dit ça
I'd like to know who told you that

elle se demandait de qui étaient les fleurs
she was wondering who the flowers were from

For details on the use of **qui/que** as relative pronouns, see **G67 & 68**, sections 6 F 3a), b) and c).

c) ***QUE ?***

que (what?) is used to refer to things; it is only used in direct questions; it is always a direct object and cannot be used after prepositions:

que désirez-vous ?	**qu'a-t-il dit ?**
what do you wish?	what did he say?

que ? is rather formal and is usually replaced by **qu'est-ce que ?** in spoken French.

Note: **que** becomes **qu'** before a vowel or a silent **h**.

d) ***QU'EST-CE QUI ?***

qu'est-ce qui ? (what?) is used as the subject of a verb; it cannot refer to a person:

qu'est-ce qui lui est arrivé ?	**qu'est-ce qui la fait rire ?**
what happened to him?	what makes her laugh?

e) ***QU'EST-CE QUE ?***

qu'est-ce que ? (what?) replaces **que ?** as the object of a verb; it becomes **qu'est-ce qu'** before a vowel or a silent **h**:

qu'est-ce que tu aimes lire ?
what do you like reading?

qu'est-ce qu'il va faire pendant les vacances ?
what's he going to do during the holidays *or Am* vacation?

Note: The common expression **qu'est-ce que c'est que** is often used in speech when asking about the identity of an object:

qu'est-ce que c'est que ce machin ?
what's that thing?

f) ***QUOI ?***

quoi ? (what?) refers to things; it is used:

i) instead of **que** or **qu'est-ce que** after a preposition:

à quoi penses-tu ?	**dans quoi l'as-tu mis ?**
what are you thinking about?	what did you put it in?

ii) in indirect questions:

demandez-lui de quoi il a besoin
ask him what he needs

je ne sais pas à quoi ça sert
I don't know what it's for

g) ***CE QUI, CE QUE***

ce qui and **ce que** (what) are only used in indirect questions; they replace **qu'est-ce qui** and **(qu'est-ce) que**.

They are used in the same way as the relative pronouns **ce qui** and **ce que** (see **G71**, section 6 F 3g)).

i) **ce qui** is used as the subject of the verb in the indirect question (**ce qui** is the subject of **s'est passé** in the following example):

nous ne saurons jamais ce qui s'est passé
we'll never know what happened

ii) **ce que** (**ce qu'** before a vowel or a silent **h**) is used as the object of the verb in the indirect question (**ce que** is the object of **il faisait** in the following example):

je n'ai pas remarqué ce qu'il faisait
I didn't notice what he was doing

D PERSONAL PRONOUNS

There are four categories of personal pronouns:

- **subject** pronouns
- **object** pronouns
- **disjunctive** pronouns
- **reflexive** pronouns

For reflexive pronouns, see **G85**, section 7 D 2.

1 Subject pronouns

PERSON	SINGULAR		PLURAL	
1st	**je (j')**	I	**nous**	we
2nd	**tu**	you	**vous**	you
3rd	**il**	he, it	**ils**	they
	elle	she, it	**elles**	they
	on	one, we, they		

Note:

a) **je** changes to **j'** before a vowel or a silent **h**:

j'ai honte
I'm ashamed

j'adore les poires
I love pears

j'habite en Ecosse
I live in Scotland

b) **tu** and **vous**

vous can be plural or singular; it is used when speaking to more than one person (plural), or to a stranger or an older person (singular):

vous venez, les gars ?
are you coming, lads?

vous parlez l'anglais, Monsieur ?
do you speak English(, sir)?

tu is used when speaking to a friend, a relative, a younger person, or someone you know well:

tu viens, Marc ?
are you coming, Marc?

c) **il/ils, elle/elles** may refer to people, animals or things, and must be of the same gender as the noun they replace:

ton stylo ? *il* est là	**ta montre ? *elle* est là**
your pen? there *it* is	your watch? there *it* is
tes gants ? *ils* sont là	**tes lunettes ? *elles* sont là**
your gloves? there *they* are	your glasses? there *they* are

When referring to several nouns of different genders, French uses the masculine plural **ils**:

tu as vu *le* stylo et *la* montre de Marie ? — oui, *ils* sont dans son sac
have you seen Marie's pen and watch? — yes, *they*'re in her bag

d) **on**: see **G52**, section 6 B 2c).

2 Object pronouns

These include: — direct object pronouns
— indirect object pronouns
— the pronouns **en** and **y**

a) *Forms*

	PERSON	DIRECT	INDIRECT
SING	1st	**me (m')** me	**me (m')** (to) me
	2nd	**te (t')** you	**te (t')** (to) you
	3rd	**le (l')** him, it	**lui** (to) him
		la (l') her, it	**lui** (to) her
PLUR	1st	**nous** us	**nous** (to) us
	2nd	**vous** you	**vous** (to) you
	3rd	**les** them	**leur** (to) them

Note:

i) Occasionally **lui** is translated by '(to) it', eg when referring to a baby or an animal:

je lui ai donné du lait
I gave it some milk, I gave some milk to it

ii) **me, te, le** and **la** change to **m', t'** and **l'** before a vowel or a silent **h**:

il m'énerve !	**je m'habituerai à lui**
he gets on my nerves!	I'll get used to him

iii) **te** and **vous**: the same distinction should be made as between the subject pronouns **tu** and **vous** (see **G56**, section 6 D 1b)).

iv) **le**: is sometimes used in an impersonal sense, when it refers to a fact, a statement or an idea which has already been expressed; it is usually not translated in English:

j'irai en Amérique un jour ; en tout cas je *l'*espère
I'll go to America one day; I hope so anyway

elle a eu un bébé — je *le* sais, elle me *l'*a dit
she's had a baby — I know, she told me

v) **moi** and **toi** are used instead of **me** and **te** in positive commands (affirmative imperative), except when **en** follows:

écris-*moi* bientôt
write to me soon

donne-*m'*en
give me some

b) *Position*

In French, object pronouns come immediately before the verb they refer to. With a compound tense, they come before the auxiliary:

on *t'*attendra ici
we'll wait for you here

je *l'*ai rencontrée en ville
I met her in town

Note: With an infinitive used alone, the pronoun comes before it:

je fais cela pour vous aider
I'm doing this to help you

When there are two verbs, the pronoun comes immediately before the verb it refers to:

j'aimerais lui demander
I'd like to ask him

tu l'as entendu chanter ?
have you heard him sing?

In positive commands (affirmative imperative) the pronoun follows the verb and is joined to it by a hyphen:

regarde-*les* !
look at them!

parle-*lui* !
speak to him!

dis-*nous* ce qui s'est passé
tell us what happened

prenez-*le*
take it

c) *Direct pronouns and indirect pronouns*

i) Direct object pronouns replace a noun which follows the verb directly. They answer the question 'who(m)?' or 'what'?

WHO(M) did you see?
qui as-tu vu ?

I saw *my friend*; I saw *him*
j'ai vu *mon ami* ; je *l'*ai vu

tu *me* connais
you know *me*

j'aime *le* voir danser
I like to see *him* dance

je *les* ai trouvés
I found *them*

ne *nous* ennuie pas !
don't bother *us*!

ii) Indirect object pronouns replace a noun which follows the verb with a linking preposition (usually **à** = 'to'). They answer the question 'who(m) to?':

WHO did you speak to?
à qui as-tu parlé ?

I spoke *to Marc*; I spoke *to him*
j'ai parlé *à Marc* ; je *lui* ai parlé

elle *lui* a menti
she lied *to him*

je *te* donne ce livre
I'm giving this book *to you*

je ne *leur* parle plus
I'm not talking *to them* any more

iii) **le/la/les** or **lui/leur**?

Direct pronouns differ from indirect pronouns only in the 3rd person and great care must be taken here:

★ English indirect object pronouns often look like direct objects; it becomes obvious that the object is indirect when it is placed at the end of the sentence:

I showed him your photo =	I showed your photo to him
	je *lui* ai montré ta photo

This is particularly the case with the following verbs:

acheter to buy	**offrir** to offer
donner to give	**prêter** to lend
montrer to show	**vendre** to sell

je *lui* ai acheté un livre I bought him a book = I bought a book *for him*	**ne *leur* prête pas mes affaires** don't lend them my things = don't lend my things *to them*

★ Some verbs take a direct object in English and an indirect object in French (see **G167**, section 7 M 2):

je ne *lui* ai rien dit I didn't tell *him* anything	**je *leur* demanderai** I'll ask *them*
tu *lui* ressembles you look like *him*	**téléphone-*leur*** phone *them*

★ Some verbs take a direct object in French and an indirect object in English (see **G167**, section 7 M 2):

je *l'*attends I'm waiting *for him*	**écoutez-*les* !** listen *to them*!

d) *Order of object pronouns*

When several object pronouns are used together, they come in the following order:

i) Before the verb:

1	**me**	**te**	**nous**	**vous**
2	**le**	**la**	**les**	
3	**lui**	**leur**		

il *me l'*a donné he gave me it	**je vais *vous les* envoyer** I'll send them to you
ne *la leur* vends pas don't sell it to them	**je *le lui* ai acheté** I bought it for him

ii) After the verb:

With a positive command (affirmative imperative), the order is as follows:

1	**le**	**la**	**les**	
2	**moi (m')**	**toi (t')**	**nous**	**vous**
3	**lui**	**leur**		

apporte-*les-moi* ! bring them to me!	**prête-*la-nous* !** lend us it!

dites-*le-lui* !	**rends-*la-leur* !**
tell him!	give it back to them!

3 The pronoun *EN*

a) *Use*

en is used instead of **de** + noun. Since **de** has a variety of meanings, **en** can be used in a number of ways:

i) It means 'of it/them', but also 'with it/them', 'about it/them', 'from it/there', 'out of it/there':

tu es sûr *du prix* ? — j'*en* suis sûr
are you sure of the price? — I'm sure *of it*

je suis content *de ce cadeau* ; j'*en* suis content
I'm pleased with this present; I'm pleased *with it*

elle est folle *des animaux* ; elle *en* est folle
she's crazy about animals; she's crazy *about them*

il est descendu *du train* ; il *en* est descendu
he got off the train; he got *off it*

il revient *de Paris* ; il *en* revient
he's coming back from Paris; he's coming *from there*

ii) Verb constructions

Particular care should be taken with verbs and expressions which are followed by **de** + noun. Since **de** is not always translated in the same way, **en** may have a number of meanings:

il a envie *de ce livre* ; il *en* a envie
he wants this book; he wants *it*

je te remercie *de ta carte* ; je t'*en* remercie
I thank you for your card; I thank you *for it*

tu as besoin *de ces papiers* ? tu *en* as besoin ?
do you need these papers? do you need *them*?

elle a peur des chiens ; elle *en* a peur
she's afraid of dogs; she's afraid *of them*

tu te souviens de ce film ? tu t'*en* souviens ?
do you remember this film? do you remember *it*?

iii) 'some'/'any'

en replaces the partitive article (**du, de la, des**) + noun; it means 'some'/'any':

tu veux *du café* ? — non, je n'*en* veux pas
do you want (any) coffee? — no, I don't want *any*

j'achète *des fruits* ? — non, j'*en* ai chez moi
shall I buy fruit? — no, I've got *some* at home

il y a *de la place* ? — *en* voilà là-bas
is there any room? — there's some over there

iv) Expressions of quantity

en must be used with expressions of quantity not followed by a noun. It replaces **de** + noun and means 'of it/them', but is often not translated in English:

tu as pris assez *d'argent* ? tu *en* as pris assez ?
did you take enough money? did you take enough?

vous avez *combien de frères* ? — j'*en* ai deux
how many brothers do you have? — I've got two

j'ai fini *mon vin* ; je vais *en* acheter une bouteille
I've finished my wine; I'm going to buy a bottle

b) *Position*

Like object pronouns, **en** comes immediately before the verb, except with positive commands (affirmative imperative), where it comes after the verb and is linked to it by a hyphen:

j'en veux un kilo
I want a kilo (of it/them)

j'en ai marre !
I'm fed up (with it)!

prends-en assez !
take enough (of it/them)!

laisses-en aux autres !
leave some (of it/them) for the others!

When used in conjunction with other object pronouns, it always comes last:

ne *m'en* parlez pas !
don't tell me about it!

je *vous en* donnerai
I'll give you some

prête-*lui-en* !
lend him some!

gardez-*nous-en* !
keep some for us!

4 The pronoun Y

a) *Use*

y is used instead of **à** + noun (not referring to a person). It is used:

i) As the indirect object of a verb. Since the preposition **à** is translated in a variety of ways in English, **y** may have various meanings (it, of it/them, about it/them etc):

tu joues *au tennis* ? — non, j'*y* joue rarement
do you play tennis? — no, I seldom play (*it*)

je pense *à mes examens* ; j'*y* pense souvent
I'm thinking *about* my exams; I often think *about them*

il s'intéresse *à la photo* ; il s'*y* intéresse
he's interested *in* photography; he's interested *in it*

je m'oppose *à cette mesure* ; je m'*y* oppose
I'm opposed *to* that measure; I'm opposed *to it*

ii) Replacing the prepositions **en, à, dans, sur** + noun *or* place name; **y** usually means 'there' but also 'in it/them', 'on it/them':

j'ai passé deux jours *à Londres* ; j'*y* ai passé deux jours
I spent two days in London; I spent two days there

il est allé *en Grèce* ; il *y* est allé
he went to Greece; he went there

je voudrais vivre *en France* ; je voudrais *y* vivre
I'd like to live in France; I'd like to live *there*

je les ai mis *dans ma poche* ; je les *y* ai mis
I put them in my pocket; I put them *there/in it*

***sur la table* ? non, je ne l'*y* vois pas**
on the table? no, I don't see it *there*

il faut l'*y* mettre avec beaucoup de soin
you have to put it *on it/in it* with great care

Note: **y** must always be used with the verb **aller** (to go) when the place is not mentioned in the clause. It is often not translated in English:

comment vas-tu *à l'école* ? — j'*y* vais en bus
how do you go to school? — I go (there) by bus

allons-*y* let's go	**on *y* va demain** we're going (there) tomorrow

When it has the sense of 'there', **y** is often considered to function as an adverb.

b) *Position*

Like other object pronouns, **y** comes immediately before the verb, except with a positive command (affirmative imperative), where it must follow the verb:

j'*y* réfléchirai I'll think about it	**il s'*y* est habitué** he got used to it
pensez-*y* ! think about it!	**n'*y* allez pas !** don't go!

When used with other object pronouns, **y** comes last:

il va *nous y* rencontrer he'll meet us there	**je *l'y* ai vu hier** I saw him there yesterday

5 Disjunctive pronouns

a) *Forms*

PERSON		SINGULAR	PLURAL
1st		**moi** me	**nous** us
2nd		**toi** you	**vous** you
3rd	(masc)	**lui** him	**eux** them
	(fem)	**elle** her	**elles** them
	(impersonal)	**soi** oneself	

Note:

i) **toi/vous**: the same difference should be made as between **tu** and **vous** (see **G56**, section 6 D 1b)).

ii) **soi** is used in an impersonal, general sense to refer to indefinite pronouns and adjectives (**on, chacun, tout le monde, personne, chaque** etc):

travailler pour soi
to work for oneself

ne penser qu'à soi
to think only of oneself

After certain prepositions it is translated as 'one':

avoir sa famille autour de soi
to have one's family around one

It is often found in set phrases, such as:

chacun pour soi
every man for himself

la chose en soi
the thing (in) itself

b) *Use*

Disjunctive pronouns are so called because they may stand alone independently of verbs. Also called emphatic pronouns, they are used instead of object pronouns (only when referring to persons) in the following cases:

i) In answer to a question, alone or in a phrase without a verb:

qui est là ? — moi
who's there? — me

j'aime les pommes ; et toi ?
I like apples; do you?

qui préfères-tu, lui ou elle ? — elle, bien sûr
who do you prefer, him or her? — her, of course

ii) After **c'est/ce sont, c'était/étaient** etc:

ouvrez, c'est moi !
open up, it's me!

non, ce n'était pas lui
no, it wasn't him

iii) After a preposition:

vous allez chez lui ?
are you going to his place?

tu y vas avec elle ?
are you going with her?

regarde devant toi !
look in front of you!

oh, c'est pour moi ?
oh, is that for me?

iv) Verb constructions: special care should be taken with verbs followed by a preposition:

tu peux compter sur moi
you can count on me

quoi ! tu as peur de lui ?
what! you're afraid of him?

il m'a parlé de toi
he told me about you

je pense souvent à vous
I often think about you

Note: Emphatic pronouns are only used when referring to persons. Otherwise, use **y** or **en**.

v) For emphasis, particularly when two pronouns are contrasted. The unstressed subject pronoun is usually included:

vous, vous m'énervez !
you get on my nerves!

lui, il joue bien ; elle, non
he plays well; *she* doesn't

moi, je n'aime pas l'hiver
I don't like winter

eux, ils sont partis
they've left

vi) In the case of multiple subjects (two pronouns or one pronoun and one noun). The unstressed subject pronoun is included in some combinations:

lui et son frère sont dans l'équipe
he and his brother are in the team

ma famille et moi allons très bien
my family and I are very well

lui et moi, nous sommes des amis
he and I are friends

vii) As the second term of a comparison:

il est plus sympa que toi
he's nicer than you

elle chante mieux que lui
she sings better than he does

viii) Before a relative pronoun:

c'est lui que j'aime
he's the one I love

c'est toi qui l'as dit
you're the one who said it

lui qui n'aime pas le vin blanc en a bu six verres
he, who doesn't like white wine, had six glasses

ix) With **-même(s)** (-self, -selves), **aussi** (too), **seul** (alone):

faites-le vous-mêmes
do it yourselves

j'irai moi-même
I'll go myself

lui aussi est parti
he too went away

elle seule le sait
she alone knows

x) To replace a possessive pronoun (see **G66**, section 6 E 2):

c'est *le mien* ; il est à moi
it's mine; it belongs to me

E POSSESSIVE ADJECTIVES AND PRONOUNS

1 Possessive adjectives

a) *Forms*

Possessive adjectives always come before a noun. Like other adjectives, they agree in gender and number with the noun; the masculine and feminine plural are identical:

SINGULAR		PLURAL	
MASC	FEM		
mon	**ma**	**mes**	my
ton	**ta**	**tes**	your
son	**sa**	**ses**	his/her/its/one's
notre	**notre**	**nos**	our
votre	**votre**	**vos**	your
leur	**leur**	**leurs**	their

j'ai mis mon argent et mes affaires dans mon sac
I've put my money and my things in my bag

comment va ton frère ? et ta sœur ? et tes parents ?
how's your brother? and your sister? and your parents?

notre rue est assez calme
our street is fairly quiet

ce sont vos amis
they're your friends

Note: **mon/ton/son** are used instead of **ma/ta/sa** when the next word starts with a vowel or silent **h**:

mon ancienne maison
my old house

ton amie Christine
your friend Christine

son haleine sentait l'alcool
his breath smelled of alcohol

b) *Use*

i) The possessive adjective is repeated before each noun and agrees with it:

mon père et ma mère sont sortis
my mother and father have gone out

ii) **son/sa/ses**

son, sa and **ses** can all mean 'his', 'her' or 'its'. In French, the form of the adjective is determined by the gender and number of the noun that follows, and not by the possessor:

il m'a prêté sa mobylette et son casque
he lent me his moped and his helmet
elle s'entend bien avec sa mère, mais pas avec son père
she gets along well with her mother, but not with her father
il cire ses chaussures ; elle repasse ses chemisiers
he's polishing his shoes; she's ironing her blouses
le lion et sa proie
the lion and its prey

son, sa and **ses** can also be used to refer to indefinite pronouns and adjectives (**on, chacun** etc):

être content de son sort
to be happy with one's lot

Frequently the translation is the English indefinite adjective 'their':

tout le monde a ses idées
everyone has their ideas

iii) **ton/ta/tes** and **votre/vos**

The two sets of words for 'your', **ton/ta/tes** and **votre/vos**, correspond to the two different forms **tu** and **vous**; they must not be used together with the same person:

papa, tu as parlé à ton patron ?
have you spoken to your boss, dad?
Monsieur ! votre brochure ! vous ne la prenez pas ?
Sir! your brochure! aren't you taking it?

iv) In French, the possessive adjective is replaced by the definite article **(le/la/les)** with the following:

★ parts of the body:

il s'est essuyé les mains	**elle a haussé les épaules**
he wiped his hands	she shrugged (her shoulders)

★ descriptive phrases tagged on to the end of a clause, where English adds 'with':

il marchait lentement, les mains dans les poches
he was walking slowly, with his hands in his pockets

elle l'a regardé partir les larmes aux yeux
she watched him leave with tears in her eyes

2 Possessive pronouns

MASC	FEM	PLURAL (MASC AND FEM)	
le mien	**la mienne**	**les mien(ne)s**	mine
le tien	**la tienne**	**les tien(ne)s**	yours
le sien	**la sienne**	**les sien(ne)s**	his/hers
le nôtre	**la nôtre**	**les nôtres**	ours
le vôtre	**la vôtre**	**les vôtres**	yours
le leur	**la leur**	**les leurs**	theirs

Possessive pronouns are used instead of a possessive adjective + noun. They agree in gender and in number with the noun they stand for, and not with the possessor (it is particularly important to remember this when translating 'his' and 'hers'):

j'aime bien ton chapeau, mais je préfère le mien
I quite like your hat, but I prefer mine

on prend quelle voiture ? la mienne ou la tienne ?
which car shall we take? mine or yours?

comment sont vos profs ? les nôtres sont sympas
what are your teachers like? ours are nice

j'ai pris mon passeport, mais Brigitte a oublié le sien
I brought my passport, but Brigitte forgot hers

j'ai gardé ma moto, mais Paul a vendu la sienne
I've kept my motorbike but Paul has sold his

With **sien, sienne** and **sien(ne)s** English normally uses 'its own' (not 'its'), when referring to an animal etc, or, in the case of an indefinite pronoun, it uses 'theirs':

mon chat préfère le sien	**des problèmes ? — chacun a les siens !**
my cat prefers its own	problems? — everyone has theirs!

à or **de** + possessive pronoun

The prepositions **à** or **de** combine with the articles **le** and **les** in the usual way:

à + le mien	→	**au mien**
à + les miens	→	**aux miens**
à + les miennes	→	**aux miennes**

de + le mien	→	**du mien**
de + les miens	→	**des miens**
de + les miennes	→	**des miennes**

demande à tes parents, j'ai déjà parlé aux miens
ask your parents, I've already spoken to mine

leur appartement ressemble beaucoup au nôtre
their flat is very similar to ours

j'aime bien les chiens, mais j'ai peur du tien
I like dogs, but I'm afraid of yours

Note: after the verb **être**, the possessive pronoun is often replaced by **à** + emphatic (disjunctive) pronoun (see **G64**, section 6 D 5b) x):

à qui est cette écharpe ? — elle est à moi
whose scarf is this? — it's mine

ce livre est à toi ? — non, il est à elle
is this book yours? — no, it's hers

c'est à qui ? à vous ou à lui ?
whose is this? yours or his?

F RELATIVE PRONOUNS

1 Definition

Relative pronouns are words which introduce a relative clause. In the following sentence:

I bought the book which you recommended

'which' is the relative pronoun, 'which you recommended' is the relative clause and 'the book' is the antecedent (ie the noun the relative pronoun refers to).

2 Forms

Relative pronouns are:

qui	who, which, that	**lequel**	which
que	which, that, who(m)	**dont**	of which, whose
quoi	what	**ce qui**	what
où	where	**ce que**	what

qui, **que**, **quoi**, **lequel**, **ce qui** and **ce que** can also be used as interrogative pronouns (see **G53**, section 6 C 3) and must not be confused with them.

3 Use

a) *QUI*

qui is used as the subject of a relative clause; it means:

i) 'who', 'that' (referring to people):

connaissez-vous le monsieur qui habite ici ?
do you know the man who/that lives here?

ce n'est pas lui qui a menti
he's not the one who lied

ii) 'which', 'that' (referring to things):

tu as pris le journal qui était sur la table ?
did you take the paper which/that was on the table?

Note: For the use of **qui** with a preposition see **G69**, section d) ii).

b) ***QUE***

que (written **qu'** before a vowel or a silent **h**) is used as the object of a relative clause; it is often not translated and means:

i) 'that', 'who(m)'(referring to people):

la fille que j'aime ne m'aime pas
the girl (that/who/whom) I love doesn't love me

ii) 'which', 'that' (referring to things):

j'ai perdu le livre qu'il m'a offert
I've lost the book (which/that) he gave me

c) **qui** or **que**?

qui (subject) and **que** (object) are translated by the same words in English (who, which, that). To use the correct pronoun in French, it is essential to know whether a relative pronoun is the object or the subject of the relative clause:

i) when the verb of the relative clause has its own subject, the object pronoun **que** must be used:

c'est un passse-temps que *j'*adore
it's a pastime (that) *I* love (*the subject of 'adore' is 'je'*)

ii) otherwise the relative pronoun is the subject of the verb in the relative clause and the subject pronoun **qui** must be used:

j'ai trouvé un manteau qui me plaît
I found a coat that I like (*the subject of 'plaît' is 'qui'*)

d) ***LEQUEL***

i) forms

lequel (which) has four different forms, as it must agree with the noun it refers to:

	SINGULAR	PLURAL	
MASCULINE	**lequel**	**lesquels**	which
FEMININE	**laquelle**	**lesquelles**	which

lequel etc combines with the prepositions **à** and **de** as follows:

à + lequel	→	**auquel**
à + lesquels	→	**auxquels**
à + lesquelles	→	**auxquelles**
de + lequel	→	**duquel**
de + lesquels	→	**desquels**
de + lesquelles	→	**desquelles**

à + laquelle and **de** + laquelle do not change.

quels sont les sports auxquels tu t'intéresses ?
what are the sports (which) you are interested *in*?

voilà le village près duquel on campait
here's the village near which we camped

ii) with a preposition: **qui** or **lequel**?

When a relative pronoun follows a preposition, the pronoun used is either **qui** or **lequel**. In English, the relative pronoun is often not used and the preposition is frequently placed after the verb or at the end of the sentence.

qui is generally used after a preposition when referring to people:

où est la fille *avec* qui je dansais ?
where's the girl (that) I was dancing *with*?

montre-moi la personne *à* qui tu as vendu ton vélo
show me the person you sold your bike *to*

lequel is normally used after a preposition when referring to things:

l'immeuble *dans* lequel j'habite est très moderne
the building (which) I live *in* is very modern

je ne reconnais pas la voiture *avec* laquelle il est venu
I don't recognize the car (which) he came *in*

But: **une personne dans laquelle j'ai entière confiance**
a person in whom I have complete confidence

lequel is also used when referring to persons after the prepositions **entre** (between) and **parmi** (among):

des touristes, parmi lesquels il y avait des Japonais
tourists, among whom were (some) Japanese people

il aimait deux filles, entre lesquelles il hésitait
he loved two girls, between whom he was torn

iii) as subject of a relative clause, referring to a person ('who') or thing ('which').

When used as subject **lequel** has the advantage of making it clear exactly which antecedent it refers to (since gender and number are both shown). It can also be used to place emphasis on an antecedent, especially in literary French, even when there is no lack of clarity:

le père de cette jeune fille, lequel est très riche
the girl's father, who is very rich

elle m'a tendu la main, laquelle j'ai prise
she held out her hand, which I took

e) ***DONT***

dont (of which, of whom, whose) is frequently used instead of **de qui, duquel** etc. It means:

i) *of which, of whom:*

un métier dont il est fier
a job (which) he is proud of, a job of which he is proud

Care must be taken with verbs that are normally followed by **de** + object: **de** is not always translated by 'of' in English, and is sometimes not translated at all (see **G167**, section 7 M 2c) on verb constructions):

voilà les choses *dont* j'ai besoin
here are the things (*which*) I need

les gens *dont* tu parles ne m'intéressent pas
I'm not interested in the people you're talking *about*

l'enfant *dont* elle s'occupe n'est pas le sien
the child she is looking *after* is not hers

Note: the following common construction omits the verb:

il a cinq enfants *dont* deux filles
he has five children two of whom are daughters

ii) *whose*

dont is also used to translate the English pronoun 'whose'. In French, the construction of the clause that follows **dont** differs from English in two ways:

★ the noun which follows **dont** is used with the definite article (**le, la, l', les**):

mon copain, dont *le* père a eu un accident
my friend, whose father had an accident

★ the word order in French is **dont** + subject + verb + object:

je te présente Hélène, dont tu connais déjà le frère
this is Helen, whose brother you already know

c'était dans une petite rue dont j'ai oublié le nom
it was in a small street the name of which I've forgotten

Note: **dont** cannot be used after a preposition:

une jolie maison, *près* de laquelle il y a un petit lac
a pretty house, *next* to which there is a small lake

f) *OU*

i) **où** generally means 'where':

l'hôtel où on a logé était très confortable
the hotel where we stayed was very comfortable

ii) **où** often replaces a preposition + **lequel**, meaning 'in/to/on/at which' etc:

c'est la maison où je suis né
that's the house in which/where I was born

une surprise-partie où il a invité tous ses amis
a party to which he invited all his friends

iii) **où** may be used with the prepositions **de**, **par** and **jusque** but not normally with any others:

la ville d'où elle vient
the town she comes from

l'école d'où il sort
the school he went to

le chemin par où il est passé
the road he went along

la ville par où je passerai
the town I will go through

la limite jusqu'où tu peux aller
the limit as far as which you may go

iv) **où** is also used to translate 'when' after a noun referring to time:

le jour où	**la fois où**	**le moment où**
the day when	the time when	the moment when

tu te rappelles le soir où on a raté le dernier métro ?
do you remember the evening when we missed the last train?

g) ***CE QUI, CE QUE***

ce is used before **qui** and **que** when the relative pronoun does not refer to a specific noun. Both **ce qui** and **ce que** mean 'that which', 'the thing which', and are usually translated by 'what':

i) **ce qui**

ce qui is followed by a verb without a subject (**qui** is the subject):

ce qui s'est passé ne vous regarde pas
what happened is none of your business

ce qui m'étonne, c'est sa patience
what surprises me is his patience

Note the comma and the **c'**

ii) **ce que**

ce que (**ce qu'** before a vowel or a silent **h**) is followed by a verb with its own subject (**que** is the object):

fais ce que tu veux
do what you want

c'est ce qu'il a dit?
is that what he said?

ce que vous me demandez est impossible
what you're asking me is impossible

iii) **tout ce qui/que**

tout is used in front of **ce qui/que** in the sense of 'all that', 'everything that':

c'est tout ce que je veux
that's all I want

tout ce que tu as fait
everything you did

tu n'as pas eu de mal ; c'est tout ce qui compte
you weren't hurt; that's all that matters

iv) **ce qui/que** are often used in indirect questions (see **G55**, section 6 C 3g)):

je ne sais pas ce qu'ils vont dire
I don't know what they'll say

v) when referring to a previous clause, **ce qui** and **ce que** are translated by 'which':

elle est en retard, ce qui arrive souvent
she's late, which happens often

vi) **ce que/qui** are used with a preposition (when the preposition refers to **ce**):

ce n'est pas étonnant, après ce qui lui est arrivé
it's not surprising, after what happened to him

il y a du vrai dans ce que vous dites
there is some truth in what you say

But: **QUOI** is used instead of **ce que** after a preposition when the preposition refers to **que**, and not to **ce**:

c'est ce à quoi je pensais
that's what I was thinking about

vii) **ce que** is used with the preposition **de** when **de** refers to **ce**:

je suis fier de ce qu'il a fait
I'm proud of what he did

But: **ce dont** is used instead of **de + ce que** when **de** refers to **que**, and not to **ce**:

c'est ce dont j'avais peur
that's what I was afraid of

tu as trouvé ce dont tu avais besoin ?
did you find what you needed?

7 VERBS

A REGULAR CONJUGATIONS

1 Conjugations

There are three main conjugations in French, which are determined by the infinitive endings. The first conjugation verbs, by far the largest category, end in **-er** (eg aim**er**) and will be referred to as **-er** verbs; the second conjugation verbs end in **-ir** (eg fin**ir**) and will be referred to as **-ir** verbs; the third conjugation verbs, the smallest category, end in **-re** (eg vend**re**) and will be referred to as **-re** verbs.

2 Simple tenses

The simple tenses in French are:

a) present
b) imperfect
c) future
d) conditional
e) past historic
f) present subjunctive
g) imperfect subjunctive

The present, imperfect, future and past historic tenses are forms of the indicative mood. The present is referred to as the present indicative when it is necessary to distinguish it clearly from the present subjunctive. Together with the indicative and the imperative, the conditional and subjunctive are moods of the verb.

For the use of the different tenses, see **G92 & 98**, sections 7 F and G.

3 Formation of tenses

The tenses are formed by adding the following endings to the stem of the verb (mainly the stem of the infinitive) as set out in the following section:

a) *PRESENT:* stem of the infinitive + the following endings:

-er VERBS	**-ir** VERBS	**-re** VERBS
-e, -es, -e, -ons, -ez, -ent	**-is, -is, -it, -issons, -issez, -issent**	**-s, -s, -, -ons, -ez, -ent**

AIMER	FIN**IR**	VEND**RE**
j'aime	je finis	je vends
tu aimes	tu finis	tu vends
il aime	il finit	il vend
elle aime	elle finit	elle vend
nous aim**ons**	nous fin**issons**	nous vend**ons**
vous aimez	vous fin**issez**	vous vend**ez**
ils aim**ent**	ils fin**issent**	ils vend**ent**
elles aim**ent**	elles fin**issent**	elles vend**ent**

b) *IMPERFECT:* stem of the first person plural of the present tense (ie the **'nous'** form minus **-ons**) + the following endings:

-ais, -ais, -ait, -ions, -iez, -aient

j'aim**ais**	je finiss**ais**	je vend**ais**
tu aim**ais**	tu finiss**ais**	tu vend**ais**
il aim**ait**	il finiss**ait**	il vend**ait**
elle aim**ait**	elle finiss**ait**	elle vend**ait**
nous aim**ions**	nous finiss**ions**	nous vend**ions**
vous aim**iez**	vous finiss**iez**	vous vend**iez**
ils aim**aient**	ils finiss**aient**	ils vend**aient**
elles aim**aient**	elles finiss**aient**	elles vend**aient**

Note: the only irregular imperfect is **être**: **j'étais** etc.

c) *FUTURE:* the infinitive form + the following endings:

-ai, -as, -a, -ons, -ez, -ont

Note: Verbs ending in **-re** drop the final **e** of the infinitive

j'aimer**ai**	je finir**ai**	je vendr**ai**
tu aimer**as**	tu finir**as**	tu vendr**as**
il aimer**a**	il finir**a**	il vendr**a**
elle aimer**a**	elle finir**a**	elle vendr**a**
nous aimer**ons**	nous finir**ons**	nous vendr**ons**
vous aimer**ez**	vous finir**ez**	vous vendr**ez**
ils aimer**ont**	ils finir**ont**	ils vendr**ont**
elles aimer**ont**	elles finir**ont**	elles vendr**ont**

d) *CONDITIONAL:* the infinitive form + the following endings:

-ais, -ais, -ait, -ions, -iez, -aient

Note: Verbs ending in **-re** drop the final **e** of the infinitive

j'aimer**ais**	je finir**ais**	je vendr**ais**
tu aimer**ais**	tu finir**ais**	tu vendr**ais**
il aimer**ait**	il finir**ait**	il vendr**ait**
elle aimer**ait**	elle finir**ait**	elle vendr**ait**
nous aimer**ions**	nous finir**ions**	nous vendr**ions**
vous aimer**iez**	vous finir**iez**	vous vendr**iez**
ils aimer**aient**	ils finir**aient**	ils vendr**aient**
elles aimer**aient**	elles finir**aient**	elles vendr**aient**

e) *PAST HISTORIC:* stem of the infinitive + the following endings:

-er VERBS	-ir VERBS	-re VERBS
-ai, -as, -a, -âmes, -âtes, -èrent	**-is, -is, -it, -îmes, -îtes, -irent**	**-is, -is, -it, -îmes, -îtes, -irent**
j'aim**ai**	je fin**is**	je vend**is**
tu aim**as**	tu fin**is**	tu vend**is**
il aim**a**	il fin**it**	il vend**it**
elle aim**a**	elle fin**it**	elle vend**it**
nous aim**âmes**	nous fin**îmes**	nous vend**îmes**
vous aim**âtes**	vous fin**îtes**	vous vend**îtes**
ils aim**èrent**	ils fin**irent**	ils vend**irent**
elles aim**èrent**	elles fin**irent**	elles vend**irent**

f) *PRESENT SUBJUNCTIVE:* stem of the first person plural of the present indicative + the following endings:

-e, -es, -e, -ions, -iez, -ent

j'aime	je finisse	je vende
tu aimes	tu finisses	tu vendes
il aime	il finisse	il vende
elle aime	elle finisse	elle vende
nous aim**ions**	nous finiss**ions**	nous vend**ions**
vous aim**iez**	vous finiss**iez**	vous vend**iez**
ils aim**ent**	ils finiss**ent**	ils vend**ent**
elles aim**ent**	elles finiss**ent**	elles vend**ent**

g) *IMPERFECT SUBJUNCTIVE:* stem of the first person singular of the past historic + the following endings:

-er VERBS	-ir VERBS	-re VERBS
-asse, -asses, -ât, -assions, -assiez, -assent	**-isse, -isses, -ît, -issions, -issiez, -issent**	**-isse, -isses, -ît, -issions, -issiez, -issent**
j'aim**asse**	je fin**isse**	je vend**isse**
tu aim**asses**	tu fin**isses**	tu vend**isses**
il aim**ât**	il fin**ît**	il vend**ît**
elle aim**ât**	elle fin**ît**	elle vend**ît**
nous aim**assions**	nous fin**issions**	nous vend**issions**
vous aim**assiez**	vous fin**issiez**	vous vend**issiez**
ils aim**assent**	ils fin**issent**	ils vend**issent**
elles aim**assent**	elles fin**issent**	elles vend**issent**

B STANDARD SPELLING IRREGULARITIES

Spelling irregularities only affect **-er** verbs.

1 Verbs ending in *-cer* and *-ger*

a) Verbs ending in **-cer** require a cedilla under the **c** (**ç**) before an **a** or an **o** to preserve the soft sound of the **c**: eg **commencer** (to begin).

b) Verbs ending in **-ger** require an **-e** after the **g** before an **a** or an **o** to preserve the soft sound of the **g**: eg **manger** (to eat).

Changes to **-cer** and **-ger** verbs occur in the following tenses: present, imperfect, past historic and imperfect subjunctive, and also in the present participle.

COMMENCER	MANGER
PRESENT	
je commence	je mange
tu commences	tu manges
il commence	il mange

elle commence	elle mange
nous **commençons**	nous **mangeons**
vous commencez	vous mangez
ils commencent	ils mangent
elles commencent	elles mangent

IMPERFECT

je **commençais**	je **mangeais**
tu **commençais**	tu **mangeais**
il **commençait**	il **mangeait**
elle **commençait**	elle **mangeait**
nous commencions	nous mangions
vous commenciez	vous mangiez
ils **commençaient**	ils **mangeaient**
elles **commençaient**	elles **mangeaient**

PAST HISTORIC

je **commençai**	je **mangeai**
tu **commenças**	tu **mangeas**
il **commença**	il **mangea**
elle **commença**	elle **mangea**
nous **commençâmes**	nous **mangeâmes**
vous **commençâtes**	vous **mangeâtes**
ils commencèrent	ils mangèrent
elles commencèrent	elles mangèrent

IMPERFECT SUBJUNCTIVE

je **commençasse**	je **mangeasse**
tu **commençasses**	tu **mangeasses**
il **commençât**	il **mangeât**
elle **commençât**	elle **mangeât**
nous **commençassions**	nous **mangeassions**
vous **commençassiez**	vous **mangeassiez**
ils **commençassent**	ils **mangeassent**
elles **commençassent**	elles **mangeassent**

PRESENT PARTICIPLE

commençant	**mangeant**

2 Verbs ending in *-eler* and *-eter*

a) Verbs ending in **-eler**

Verbs ending in **-eler** double the **l** before a silent e (ie before **-e**, **-es**, **-ent** of the present indicative and subjunctive, and throughout the future and conditional): eg **appeler** (to call).

PRESENT INDICATIVE	*PRESENT SUBJUNCTIVE*
j'**appelle**	j'**appelle**
tu **appelles**	tu **appelles**
il **appelle**	il **appelle**

elle **appelle**	elle **appelle**
nous appelons	nous appelions
vous appelez	vous appeliez
ils **appellent**	ils **appellent**
elles **appellent**	elles **appellent**
FUTURE	*CONDITIONAL*
j'**appellerai**	j'**appellerais**
tu **appelleras**	tu **appellerais**
il **appellera**	il **appellerait**
elle **appellera**	elle **appellerait**
nous **appellerons**	nous **appellerions**
vous **appellerez**	vous **appelleriez**
ils **appelleront**	ils **appelleraient**
elles **appelleront**	elles **appelleraient**

But: some verbs in **-eler** are conjugated like **acheter** (see **G78**, section e)):

congeler	to (deep-)freeze
déceler	to detect
dégeler	to thaw
démanteler	to break up/dismantle
geler	to freeze
harceler	to harass
marteler	to hammer
modeler	to model
peler	to peel
receler	to contain, to receive

b) Verbs ending in **-eter**

Verbs ending in **-eter** double the **t** before a silent **e** (ie before **-e, -es, -ent** of the present indicative and subjunctive, and throughout the future and conditional): eg **jeter** (to throw).

PRESENT INDICATIVE	*PRESENT SUBJUNCTIVE*
je **jette**	je **jette**
tu **jettes**	tu **jettes**
il **jette**	il **jette**
elle **jette**	elle **jette**
nous jetons	nous jetions
vous jetez	vous jetiez
ils **jettent**	ils **jettent**
elles **jettent**	elles **jettent**
FUTURE	*CONDITIONAL*
je **jetterai**	je **jetterais**
tu **jetteras**	tu **jetterais**
il **jettera**	il **jetterait**
elle **jettera**	elle **jetterait**
nous **jetterons**	nous **jetterions**
vous **jetterez**	vous **jetteriez**
ils **jetteront**	ils **jetteraient**
elles **jetteront**	elles **jetteraient**

But: some verbs in **-eter** are conjugated like **acheter** (see section e), below):

fureter	to pry *or* ferret about
haleter	to pant
racheter	to buy back

c) Verbs ending in **-oyer** and **-uyer**

In verbs ending in **-oyer** and **-uyer** the **y** changes to **i** before a silent **e** (ie before **-e, -es, -ent** of the present indicative and subjunctive, and throughout the future and conditional): eg **employer** (to use) and **ennuyer** (to bore).

PRESENT INDICATIVE	*PRESENT SUBJUNCTIVE*
j'**emploie**	j'**emploie**
tu **emploies**	tu **emploies**
il **emploie**	il **emploie**
elle **emploie**	elle **emploie**
nous employons	nous employions
vous employez	vous employiez
ils **emploient**	ils **emploient**
elles **emploient**	elles **emploient**

FUTURE	*CONDITIONAL*
j'**emploierai**	j'**emploierais**
tu **emploieras**	tu **emploierais**
il **emploiera**	il **emploierait**
elle **emploiera**	elle **emploierait**
nous **emploierons**	nous **emploierions**
vous **emploierez**	vous **emploieriez**
ils **emploieront**	ils **emploieraient**
elles **emploieront**	elles **emploieraient**

Note: **envoyer** (to send) and **renvoyer** (to send back, dismiss) have an irregular future and conditional: **j'enverrai, j'enverrais; je renverrai, je renverrais.**

d) Verbs ending in **-ayer**

In verbs ending in **-ayer**, eg **balayer** (to sweep), **payer** (to pay), **essayer** (to try), the change from **y** to **i** is optional, eg:

je balaie	*or*	**je balaye**
je paie	*or*	**je paye**
j'essaie	*or*	**j'essaye**

e) Verbs in **e** + consonant + **er**

Verbs like **acheter, enlever, mener, peser** change the (last) **e** of the stem to **è** before a silent **e** (ie before **-e, -es, -ent** of the present indicative and subjunctive and throughout the future and conditional):

PRESENT INDICATIVE	*PRESENT SUBJUNCTIVE*
j'**achète**	j'**achète**
tu **achètes**	tu **achètes**
il **achète**	il **achète**
elle **achète**	elle **achète**

nous achetons	nous achetions
vous achetez	vous achetiez
ils **achètent**	ils **achètent**
elles **achètent**	elles **achètent**
FUTURE	*CONDITIONAL*
j'**achèterai**	j'**achèterais**
tu **achèteras**	tu **achèterais**
il **achètera**	il **achèterait**
elle **achètera**	elle **achèterait**
nous **achèterons**	nous **achèterions**
vous **achèterez**	vous **achèteriez**
ils **achèteront**	ils **achèteraient**
elles **achèteront**	elles **achèteraient**

Verbs conjugated like **acheter** include:

achever to finish (off)	**harceler** to harass
amener to bring	**lever** to lift
crever to burst	**marteler** to hammer
élever to raise	**mener** to lead
emmener to take (away)	**modeler** to model
enlever to remove	**peler** to peel
étiqueter to label	**peser** to weigh
fureter to pry *or* ferret about	**se promener** to go for a walk
geler to freeze	**semer** to sow
haleter to pant	**soulever** to lift

f) Verbs in **é** + consonant + **er**

Verbs like **espérer** (to hope) change **é** to **è** before a silent **e** in the present indicative and subjunctive. BUT in the future and conditional é is retained.

PRESENT INDICATIVE	*PRESENT SUBJUNCTIVE*
j'**espère**	j'**espère**
tu **espères**	tu **espères**
il **espère**	il **espère**
elle **espère**	elle **espère**
nous espérons	nous espérions
vous espérez	vous espériez
ils **espèrent**	ils **espèrent**
elles **espèrent**	elles **espèrent**
FUTURE	*CONDITIONAL*
j'**espérerai**	j'**espérerais**
tu **espéreras**	tu **espérerais**
il **espérera**	il **espérerait**
elle **espérera**	elle **espérerait**
nous **espérerons**	nous **espérerions**
vous **espérerez**	vous **espéreriez**
ils **espéreront**	ils **espéreraient**
elles **espéreront**	elles **espéreraient**

Verbs conjugated like **espérer** include verbs in **-éder, -érer, -éter** etc, eg:

accéder	to reach, to accede to
céder	to give in, to give up
célébrer	to celebrate
compléter	to complete
considérer	to consider
décéder	to die
digérer	to digest
gérer	to manage
inquiéter	to worry
libérer	to free
opérer	to operate (on), to carry out
pénétrer	to penetrate
persévérer	to persevere
posséder	to possess
précéder	to precede
préférer	to prefer
protéger	to protect
récupérer	to recover
régler	to settle, to regulate
régner	to reign
répéter	to repeat, to rehearse
révéler	to reveal
sécher	to dry
succéder	to succeed
suggérer	to suggest
tolérer	to tolerate

C AUXILIARIES AND THE FORMATION OF COMPOUND TENSES

1 Formation

a) The two auxiliary verbs **AVOIR** and **ETRE** are used with the past participle of a verb to form compound tenses.

b) *The past participle*

The regular past participle is formed by taking the stem of the infinitive and adding the following endings:

-er	**-ir**	**-re**
aim(**er**) + **é**	fin(**ir**) + **i**	vend(**re**) + **u**
aimé	fini	vendu

For the agreement of past participles see **G117**, section I 2.

c) *Compound tenses*

In French there are seven compound tenses: perfect, pluperfect, future perfect, past conditional (conditional perfect), past anterior, perfect subjunctive, pluperfect subjunctive.

2 Verbs conjugated with AVOIR

a) *PERFECT*

present of **avoir** +
past participle

j'ai aimé
tu as aimé
il a aimé
elle a aimé
nous avons aimé
vous avez aimé
ils ont aimé
elles ont aimé

b) *PLUPERFECT*

imperfect of **avoir** +
past participle

j'avais aimé
tu avais aimé
il avait aimé
elle avait aimé
nous avions aimé
vous aviez aimé
ils avaient aimé
elles avaient aimé

c) *FUTURE PERFECT*

future of **avoir** +
past participle

j'aurai aimé
tu auras aimé
il aura aimé
elle aura aimé
nous aurons aimé
vous aurez aimé
ils auront aimé
elles auront aimé

d) *PAST CONDITIONAL*

conditional of **avoir** +
past participle

j' aurais aimé
tu aurais aimé
il aurait aimé
elle aurait aimé
nous aurions aimé
vous auriez aimé
ils auraient aimé
elles auraient aimé

e) *PAST ANTERIOR*

past historic of **avoir** +
past participle

j'eus aimé
tu eus aimé
il eut aimé
elle eut aimé
nous eûmes aimé
vous eûtes aimé
ils eurent aimé
elles eurent aimé

f) *PERFECT SUBJUNCTIVE*

present subjunctive of
avoir + past participle

j'aie aimé
tu aies aimé
il ait aimé
elle ait aimé
nous ayons aimé
vous ayez aimé
ils aient aimé
elles aient aimé

g) *PLUPERFECT SUBJUNCTIVE*

imperfect subjunctive of
avoir + past participle

j'eusse aimé
tu eusses aimé
il eût aimé
elle eût aimé
nous eussions aimé
vous eussiez aimé
ils eussent aimé
elles eussent aimé

3 Verbs conjugated with *ETRE*

a) *PERFECT*

present of être +
past participle

je suis arrivé(e)
tu es arrivé(e)
il est arrivé
elle est arrivée
nous sommes arrivé(e)s
vous êtes arrivé(e)(s)
ils sont arrivés
elles sont arrivées

b) *PLUPERFECT*

imperfect of être +
past participle

j'étais arrivé(e)
tu étais arrivé(e)
il était arrivé
elle était arrivée
nous étions arrivé(e)s
vous étiez arrivé(e)(s)
ils étaient arrivés
elles étaient arrivées

c) *FUTURE PERFECT*

future of être +
past participle

je serai arrivé(e)
tu seras arrivé(e)
il sera arrivé
elle sera arrivée
nous serons arrivé(e)s
vous serez arrivé(e)(s)
ils seront arrivés
elles seront arrivées

d) *PAST CONDITIONAL*

conditional of être +
past participle

je serais arrivé(e)
tu serais arrivé(e)
il serait arrivé
elle serait arrivée
nous serions arrivé(e)s
vous seriez arrivé(e)(s)
ils seraient arrivés
elles seraient arrivées

e) *PAST ANTERIOR*

past historic of être +
past participle

je fus arrivé(e)
tu fus arrivé(e)
il fut arrivé
elle fut arrivée
nous fûmes arrivé(e)s
vous fûtes arrivé(e)(s)
ils furent arrivés
elles furent arrivées

f) *PERFECT SUBJUNCTIVE*

present subjunctive of
être + past participle

je sois arrivé(e)
tu sois arrivé(e)
il soit arrivé
elle soit arrivée
nous soyons arrivé(e)s
vous soyez arrivé(e)(s)
ils soient arrivés
elles soient arrivées

g) *PLUPERFECT SUBJUNCTIVE*

imperfect subjunctive of
être + past participle

je fusse arrivé(e)
tu fusses arrivé(e)
il fût arrivé
elle fût arrivée
nous fussions arrivé(e)s
vous fussiez arrivé(e)(s)
ils fussent arrivés
elles fussent arrivées

4 AVOIR or ETRE?

a) *Verbs conjugated with **avoir***

The compound tenses of most verbs are formed with **avoir**.

j'ai marqué un but I scored a goal	**elle a dansé toute la nuit** she danced all night

b) *Verbs conjugated with **être***

i) all reflexive verbs (see **G84**, section 7 D):

je me suis baigné
I had a bath

ii) the following intransitive verbs (mainly of motion):

aller	to go
arriver	to arrive
descendre	to go/come down
entrer	to go/come in
monter	to go/come up, to climb
mourir	to die
naître	to be born
partir	to leave
passer	to go (through)
rester	to stay, remain
retourner	to go back/return
sortir	to go/come out
tomber	to fall
venir	to come

and most of their compounds:

revenir	to come back
devenir	to become
parvenir	to reach, to manage to
rentrer	to go/come back (home)
remonter	to go/come back up
redescendre	to go/come back down

But: **prévenir** (to warn) and **subvenir à** (to provide for) take a direct object and are conjugated with **avoir**; **convenir** is conjugated with **avoir** in the sense of 'to suit', and usually with **avoir**, but sometimes with **être**, in the sense of 'to agree upon' (eg **ça m'a convenu** that suited me; **nous avons convenu/ sommes convenus d'une date** we agreed upon a date).

Note: **passer** can also be conjugated with **avoir**:

il a passé par Paris
he went via Paris

accourir and **apparaître** may be conjugated with either **être** or **avoir**:

il est/a accouru he came running	**il est/a apparu** he appeared

Some of the verbs listed above can take a direct object. In such cases they are conjugated with **avoir** and take on a different meaning:

descendre	to take/bring down, to go/come down (*the stairs, a slope*)
monter	to take/bring up, to go/come/climb up (*the stairs, a slope*)
rentrer	to take/bring in
retourner	to turn over, to turn, to turn inside out
sortir	to take/bring out

les élèves sont sortis à midi the pupils came out at midday	**les élèves ont sorti leurs livres** the pupils took out their books

elle n'est pas encore descendue
she hasn't come down yet

elle a descendu un vieux tableau de l'atelier
she brought an old painting down from the loft

elle a descendu l'escalier
she came down the stairs

les prisonniers sont montés sur le toit
the prisoners climbed on to the roof

le garçon a monté les bouteilles de vin de la cave
the waiter brought the bottles of wine up from the cellar

nous sommes rentrés tard we came back home late	**j'ai rentré la voiture dans le garage** I put the car (away) in the garage
je serais retourné à Paris I would have returned to Paris	**le jardinier a retourné le sol** the gardener turned over the soil

ils sont sortis de la piscine
they come/got out of the swimming pool

le gangster a sorti un revolver
the gangster pulled/took out a revolver

D REFLEXIVE VERBS

1 Definition

Reflexive verbs are so called because they 'reflect' the action back onto the subject. They are always accompanied by a reflexive pronoun; eg in the following sentence:

I looked at myself in the mirror

'myself' is the reflexive pronoun.

Reflexive verbs are also known as 'pronominal verbs' (labelled *vpr* in the dictionary) since they are always used with a pronoun.

je lave la voiture I'm washing the car	**je *me* lave** I'm washing *myself*
j'ai couché le bébé I put the baby to bed	**je *me* suis couché** I went to bed (I put *myself* to bed)

2 Reflexive pronouns

They are:

PERSON	SINGULAR	PLURAL
1st	**me (m')** myself	**nous** ourselves
2nd	**te (t')** yourself	**vous** yourself/selves
3rd	**se (s')** himself, herself, itself, oneself	**se (s')** themselves

Note:

a) **m', t'** and **s'** are used instead of **me, te** and **se** in front of a vowel or a silent **h**:

tu t'amuses ? — non, je m'ennuie
are you enjoying yourself? — no, I'm bored

il s'habille à la salle de bain
he gets dressed in the bathroom

b) French reflexive pronouns may be indirect as well as direct objects; as indirect objects they are normally preceded by 'to', although occasionally by another preposition such as 'at':

je me suis dit que ...
I said to myself that ...

ils se lancent souvent des injures
they often hurl insults at each other

c) French reflexive pronouns are often not translated in English:

je me demande si ...
I wonder if ...

ils se moquent de moi
they're making fun of me

d) Plural reflexive pronouns can also be used to express reciprocal actions; in this case they are translated by 'each other' or 'one another', or, indirectly, by 'to each other' or 'to one another':

nous nous détestons
we hate one another

ils ne se parlent pas
they're not talking to each other

To clarify a meaning French adds **'l'un(e) l'autre'** or **'l'un(e) à l'autre'**, **'les un(e)s les autres'** or **'les un(e)s aux autres'**:

ils se sont tués
they killed themselves

ils se sont tués l'un l'autre
they killed each other

ils se sont dit que ...
they said to themselves that ...

ils se sont dit les uns aux autres que ...
they said to each other that ...

e) **se** can mean 'ourselves', 'each other' or 'one another' when it is used with the pronoun **on** meaning 'we' (see **G52**, section 6 B 2c)):

on s'est perdu
we got lost

on se connaît
we know each other

on ne se parle pas
we don't speak to one another

on s'amuse
we're enjoying ourselves

3 Position of reflexive pronouns

Reflexive pronouns are placed immediately before the verb, except in positive commands, where they follow the verb and are linked to it by a hyphen:

tu te dépêches ?
will you hurry up?

dépêchons-nous !
let's hurry!

ne t'inquiète pas
don't worry

ne vous fiez pas à lui
don't trust him

Note:

i) reflexive pronouns change to emphatic (disjunctive) pronouns in positive commands:

elle doit se reposer
she needs to rest

repose-toi
have a rest

(See **G62**, section 6 D 5)

ii) reflexive pronouns are normally dropped if an infinitive following **faire** is a pronominal verb:

faites asseoir cet enfant
sit that child down

4 Conjugation of reflexive verbs

a) *Simple tenses*

These are formed in the same way as for non-reflexive verbs, except that a reflexive pronoun is used:

je le prépare
I get it ready

je me prépare
I get (myself) ready

b) *Compound tenses*

These are formed with the auxiliary **être** followed by the past participle of the verb.

A full conjugation table is given on **G145**, see SE MÉFIER.

Note: French reflexive verbs are often translated by the passive in English:

ça ne se dit pas
that isn't said

le français se parle partout
French is spoken everywhere

5 Agreement of the past participle

a) In most cases, the reflexive pronoun is a direct object and the past participle of the verb agrees in number and in gender with the reflexive pronoun:

il s'est trompé
he made a mistake

elle s'est endormie
she fell asleep

ils se sont excusés
they apologized

elles se sont assises
they sat down

b) When the reflexive pronoun is used as an indirect object, the past participle does not change:

nous nous sommes écrit
we wrote to each other

elle se l'est acheté
she bought it for herself

When the reflexive verb has a direct object, the reflexive pronoun is the indirect object of the reflexive verb and the past participle does not agree with it:

Caroline s'est tordu la cheville
Caroline sprained her ankle

vous vous êtes lavé les mains, les filles ?
did you wash your hands, girls?

6 Common reflexive verbs

s'en aller
to go away

s'amuser
to enjoy oneself, have fun

s'appeler
to be called

s'approcher (de)
to come near (to)

s'arrêter
to stop

s'asseoir
to sit down

s'attendre à
to expect

se baigner
to go swimming, have a bath

se battre
to fight

se blesser
to hurt oneself

se coucher
to go to bed

se débarrasser de
to get rid of

se demander
to wonder

se dépêcher
to hurry

se déshabiller
to undress

s'éloigner (de)
to move away (from)

s'endormir
to fall asleep

s'ennuyer
to get bored

s'étonner (de)
to be surprised (at)

s'excuser (de)
to apologize (for)

se fâcher
to get angry

s'écrier
to exclaim

s'habiller
to get dressed

se hâter
to hurry

s'inquiéter
to worry

s'installer
to settle down

se laver
to wash

se lever
to get up

se mêler (à)
to mix (with)

se mettre à
to start

se moquer de
to make fun of

s'occuper de
to deal with, to take care of

se passer
to happen

se passer de
to do/go without

se promener
to go for a walk

se rappeler
to remember

se raser
to shave

se renseigner
to find out, inquire

se ressembler
to look alike

se retourner
to turn round

se réveiller
to wake up

se sauver
to run away

se souvenir (de)
to remember

se taire
to keep/be quiet

se tromper
to be mistaken

se diriger vers to make one's way towards	**se mettre en route** to set out	**se trouver** to be (situated)

E IMPERSONAL VERBS

1 Conjugation

Impersonal verbs are used only in the third person singular and in the infinitive. The subject is always the impersonal pronoun **il** = it.

il neige it's snowing	**il y a du brouillard** it's foggy

Note: Impersonal **il** is sometimes used as the subject of a sentence when the 'logical' or 'real' subject follows the verb:

il est venu quelqu'un someone came	**il passait quelques enfants** a few children were passing, there were a few children passing

(see also **arriver, se passer** and **exister, rester** and **manquer** in sections d) and e) on **G90**).

2 List of impersonal verbs

a) *verbs describing the weather:*

i) **faire** + adjective:

il fait beau/chaud it's fine/warm	**il fait frais/froid** it's cool/cold
il fera beau demain the weather will be good tomorrow	**il va faire très froid** it will be very cold

ii) **faire** + noun:

il fait beau temps the weather is fine	**il fait mauvais temps** the weather is bad
il fait (du) soleil it's sunny	**il fait du vent** it's windy

Note:

il fait jour it's light	**il fait nuit** it's dark

iii) other impersonal verbs and verbs used impersonally to describe the weather:

il bruine	**(bruiner)**	it's drizzling
il gèle	**(geler)**	it's freezing
il grêle	**(grêler)**	it's hailing
il neige	**(neiger)**	it's snowing
il pleut	**(pleuvoir)**	it's raining
il tonne	**(tonner)**	it's thundering

Note: some of these verbs may be used personally:

je gèle	I am freezing
des coups pleuvaient	blows rained down

b) ***y avoir***

i) **il y a** + noun:

il y a une école	there's a school
il y a deux enfants	there are two children
il y a deux ans	two years ago

(see also **G96**, sections 7 F 9a) i) and b) i)).

ii) **il y a** + pronoun:

il y a quelque chose d'intéressant	there's something interesting
il n'y en a pas	there aren't any

iii) **il y a** + infinitive:

il y a beaucoup à faire	there's a lot to do
il n'y a qu'à demander	you only have to ask

Note: **il y a** + noun is often used in describing the weather:

il y a des nuages	it's cloudy
il y a du brouillard	it's foggy
il y a du verglas	it's icy
il y a du vent	it's windy

c) ***être***

i) **il est** + noun:

il est cinq heures	it's five o'clock
il était une fois un géant	there was once a giant, once upon a time there was a giant
il était temps	it was high time

ii) **il est** + adjective + **de** + infinitive:

il est difficile de	it's difficult to
il est facile de	it's easy to
il est nécessaire de	it's necessary to
il est inutile de	it's useless to
il est possible de	it's possible to

il est difficile d'en parler
it is difficult to speak about it

Note: the indirect object pronoun in French corresponds to the English 'for me, for him' etc:

il m'est difficile d'en parler
it is difficult for me to speak about it

iii) **il est** + adjective + **que**:

il est douteux que	it's doubtful that
il est évident que	it's obvious that
il est possible que	it's possible that
il est probable que	it's likely/probable that
il est peu probable que	it's unlikely that
il est vrai que	it's true that

Note: **que** may be followed by the indicative or the subjunctive (see **G98**, section 7 G 1):

il est probable qu'il ne viendra pas
he probably won't come

il est peu probable qu'il vienne
it's unlikely that he'll come

iv) **il est** + adverb:

il est tard
it's late

v) **il est** + adverb + **pour**:

il est trop tôt/tard pour manger
it's too early/late to eat

d) ***arriver, se passer*** *(to happen)*

il est arrivé une chose curieuse
a strange thing happened

que se passe-t-il ?
what's happening?

il m'arrive d'oublier
I sometimes forget

il arrive que ...
it happens that ...

e) ***exister*** *(to exist),* ***rester*** *(to be left, remain),* ***manquer*** *(to be short/missing)*

il existe un exemplaire/trois exemplaires de ce livre
there is one copy/there are three copies of this book

il me restait six francs
I had six francs left

il me manque vingt francs
I am twenty francs short

f) ***paraître, sembler*** *(to seem)*

il paraîtrait/semblerait qu'il ait changé d'avis
it would seem/appear that he has changed his mind

il paraît qu'il va se marier
it seems he's going to get married

il me semble que le professeur s'est trompé
it seems to me that the teacher has made a mistake,
I think that the teacher has made a mistake

g) ***pouvoir*** (expressing possibility = *may*), ***devoir*** (expressing probability/necessity = *must*), ***aller*** (expressing the immediate future = *going to*)

il peut neiger
it may snow

il doit être tard
it must be late

il va pleuvoir
it's going to rain, it's about to rain

il va être cinq heures
it's almost five (o'clock)

Note: All three verbs may be followed by the impersonal **il y a**:

il peut/il doit/il va y avoir un cessez-le-feu
there may be/there must be/there's going to be a ceasefire

h) other common impersonal verbs

i) **s'agir** (to be a question/matter of):

may be followed by a noun or an infinitive:

il s'agit de ton avenir
it's about/it concerns your future

de quoi s'agit-il ?
what's it about?, what is it?

il s'agit de trouver le coupable
we must find/we have to find the culprit

ii) **falloir** expresses a necessity or obligation (= to need/to have to):

it may be followed by a noun, an infinitive or the subjunctive (see also **G123**, section 7 K 5):

il faut deux heures pour aller à Paris it takes/one needs two hours to get to Paris	**il me faut plus de temps** I need more time

il faudra rentrer plus tôt ce soir
we'll have to come home earlier tonight

il faut que tu parles à papa
you have to speak to dad

Note: an indirect object pronoun is often used with **il faut** to indicate the subject (who had to do something)

iii) **suffire** (to be enough):

may be followed by a noun, an infinitive or the subjunctive:

il suffit de quelques mots pour le persuader
a few words are enough to persuade him

il suffit de peu de chose pour être heureux
it takes little to be happy

il suffit de passer le pont
you only have to cross the bridge

il suffira qu'ils te donnent le numéro de téléphone
they will only have to give you the telephone number

iv) **valoir mieux** (to be better):

may be followed by an infinitive or the subjunctive:

il vaudrait mieux prendre le train
it would be better to take the train

il vaut mieux que vous ne sortiez pas seule le soir
you'd better not go out alone at night

i) some further impersonal constructions:

il s'avère que ... it turns out that ...	**il se trouve que ...** it happens that ...
il convient d'attendre it's advisable to wait	**il importe de rester** it's important to stay
il se fait tard it's getting late	**il commence à se faire tard** it's beginning to get late
il n'en est pas question there's no question of it	**il s'en est fallu de peu qu'elle ne pleure** she almost cried

F TENSES

For the formation of the different tenses, see **G73 & 80**, sections 7 A and C.

Note: French has no continuous tenses (as in 'I am eating', 'I was going', 'I will be arriving'). The 'be' and '-ing' parts of English continuous tenses are not translated as separate words. Instead, the equivalent tense is used in French:

ENGLISH	FRENCH
I am eating	**je mange**
I will be eating	**je mangerai**
I was eating	**je mangeais**

1 PRESENT

The present is used to describe what someone does/something that happens regularly, or what someone is doing/something that is happening at the time of speaking.

a) *regular actions*

il travaille dans un bureau
he works in an office

je lis rarement le journal
I seldom read the paper

b) *continuous actions (English normally uses the '-ing' form)*

ne le dérangez pas, il travaille
don't disturb him, he's working

je ne peux pas venir, je garde mon petit frère
I can't come, I'm looking after my little brother

Note: the continuous nature of the action can also be shown by using the phrase **être en train de** + infinitive. This construction expresses the notion of 'being in the process of doing something':

je suis en train de cuisiner
I'm (busy) cooking

c) *immediate future*

je pars demain
I'm leaving tomorrow,
I leave tomorrow

tu m'aides ?
are you helping me?, are you going to help me?

But: the present cannot be used after **quand** and other conjunctions of time when the future is implied (see **G97**, section 7 F 11):

je le ferai quand j'aurai le temps
I'll do it when I have the time

d) *general truths*

la vie est dure
life is hard

deux et deux font quatre
two and two are/make four

2 IMPERFECT

The imperfect is a past tense used to express what someone was doing or what someone used to do or to describe something in the past. The imperfect refers particularly to something that *continued* over a period of time, as opposed to something that happened at a specific point in time.

a) *continuous actions (English normally uses the '-ing' form)*

the imperfect describes an action that was happening, eg when something else took place (imperfect means unfinished):

il prenait un bain quand le téléphone a sonné
he was having a bath when the phone rang

excuse-moi, je pensais à autre chose
I'm sorry, I was thinking of something else

Note: the continuous nature of the action can be emphasized by using **être en train de** + infinitive:

j'étais en train de faire le ménage
I was (busy) doing the housework

b) *regular actions in the past (English often uses 'used to' or sometimes 'would')*

je le voyais souvent quand il habitait dans le quartier
I used to see him often when he lived in this area,
I would see him often when he lived/used to live in this area

quand il était plus jeune il voyageait beaucoup
when he was younger he used to travel a lot/he would travel a lot

c) *description in the past*

il faisait beau ce jour-là
the weather was fine that day

c'était formidable !
it was great!

elle portait une robe bleue
she wore/she was wearing a blue dress

elle donnait sur la rue
it looked out onto the street

3 PERFECT

The perfect tense is a compound past tense used to express *single* actions which have been completed, ie what someone did or what someone has done/has been doing or something that happened or has happened or has been happening. In spoken French, the perfect corresponds to the English simple past tense as well as to the English present perfect:

je l'ai envoyé lundi
I sent it on Monday

on est sorti hier soir
we went out last night

tu t'es bien amusé ?
did you have a good time?

je ne l'ai pas vu
I didn't see him,
I haven't seen him

j'ai lu toute la journée
I've been reading all day,
I read all day

tu as déjà mangé ?
have you eaten yet?

Note: Perfect or imperfect?

In English, the simple past ('did', 'went', 'prepared') is used to describe both single and repeated actions in the past. In French, the perfect only describes single actions in the past, while repeated actions are expressed by the imperfect (they are often signposted by 'used to' or sometimes by 'would'). Thus 'I went' should be translated 'j'allais' or 'je suis allé' depending on the nature of the action:

après dîner, je suis allé en ville
after dinner I went to town

l'an dernier, j'allais plus souvent au cinéma
last year, I went to the movies more often (also 'I used to go' or 'I would go')

4 PAST HISTORIC

This tense is used in the same way as the perfect tense, to describe a single, completed action in the past (what someone did or something that happened). It is a literary tense, not used in everyday spoken French; it is found mainly as a narrative tense in written form:

le piéton ne vit pas arriver la voiture
the pedestrian didn't see the car coming

5 PLUPERFECT

This compound tense is used to express what someone had done/had been doing or something that had happened or had been happening:

il n'avait pas voulu aller avec eux
he hadn't wanted to go with them

elle était essoufflée parce qu'elle avait couru
she was out of breath because she'd been running

However, the pluperfect is not used as in English with **depuis** (for, since), or with **venir de** + infinitive (to have just done something). For details see **G95 & 97**, sections 9 and 10.

il neigeait depuis une semaine
it had been snowing for a week

les pompiers venaient d'arriver
the firemen had just arrived

6 FUTURE

This tense is used to express what someone will do or will be doing or something that will happen or will be happening:

je ferai la vaisselle demain
I'll do the dishes tomorrow

j'arriverai tard
I'll be arriving late

Note: the future and not the present as in English is used in time clauses introduced by **quand** (when) or other conjunctions of time where the future is implied (see **G97**, section 11):

il viendra quand il le pourra
he'll come when he can

French makes frequent use of **aller** + infinitive (to be about to do something, to be going to do something) to express the immediate future:

je vais vous expliquer ce qui s'est passé
I'll explain (to you) what happened

il va déménager la semaine prochaine
he's moving house next week

7 FUTURE PERFECT

This compound tense is used to describe what someone will have done/will have been doing in the future or to describe something that will have happened in the future:

j'aurai bientôt fini
I will soon have finished

In particular, it is used instead of the English perfect in time clauses introduced by **quand** or other conjunctions of time where the future is implied (see **G97**, section 11):

appelle-moi quand tu auras fini
call me when you've finished

on rentrera dès qu'on aura fait les courses
we'll come back as soon as we've done our shopping

8 PAST ANTERIOR

This tense, which is not found in everyday spoken French, is used instead of the pluperfect to express an action that preceded another action in the past (ie a past in the past). It is usually introduced by a conjunction of time (translated by 'when', 'as soon as', 'after' etc) and the main verb is in the past historic:

il se coucha dès qu'ils furent partis
he went to bed as soon as they'd left

à peine eut-elle raccroché que le téléphone sonna
she'd hardly hung up when the telephone rang

9 Use of tenses with 'depuis' (for, since)

a) The present must be used instead of the perfect to describe actions which started in the past and have continued until the present:

il habite ici depuis trois ans
he's been living here for three years

elle l'attend depuis ce matin
she's been waiting for him since this morning

But: The perfect, not the present, is used when the clause is negative or when the action has been completed:

il n'a pas pris de vacances depuis longtemps
he hasn't taken any holidays *or Am* vacation for a long time

j'ai fini depuis un bon moment
I've been finished for quite a while

Note:

i) **il y a ... que, voilà ... que** or **voici ... que** are also used with the present tense to translate 'for':

it's been ringing for ten minutes
ça sonne depuis dix minutes
il y a dix minutes que ça sonne
voilà dix minutes que ça sonne
voici dix minutes que ça sonne

ii) **depuis que** is used when 'since' introduces a clause, ie when there is a verb following **depuis**; it can be followed by the perfect or the present:

elle dort depuis que vous êtes partis
she's been sleeping since you left

elle dort depuis que vous êtes ici
she's been sleeping since you've been here

iii) do not confuse **depuis** (for, since) and **pendant** (for, during): **depuis** refers to the starting point of an action which is still going on and **pendant** refers to the duration of an action which is over, and it is used with the perfect:

il vit ici depuis deux mois
he's been living here for two months

il a vécu ici pendant deux mois
he lived here for two months

b) the imperfect must be used instead of the pluperfect to describe an action which had started in the past and was still going on at a given time:

elle le connaissait depuis son enfance
she had known him since her childhood

il attendait depuis trois heures quand on est arrivé
he had been waiting for three hours when we arrived

But: if the sentence is negative or if the action has been completed, the pluperfect and not the imperfect is used:

je n'étais pas allé au cinéma depuis des années
I hadn't been to the movies for years

il était parti depuis peu
he'd been gone for a short while

Note:

i) **il y avait ... que +** imperfect is also used to translate 'for':

she'd been living alone for a long time
elle habitait seule depuis longtemps
il y avait longtemps qu'elle habitait seule

ii) **depuis que** is used when 'since' introduces a clause; if it describes an action which was still going on at the time, it can be followed by the imperfect, otherwise it is followed by the pluperfect:

il pleuvait depuis que nous étions à Paris
it had been raining since we had been in Paris

il pleuvait depuis que nous étions arrivés
it had been raining since we arrived/we had arrived

iii) do not confuse **depuis** and **pendant**: **depuis** refers to the starting point of an action which is still going on and **pendant** refers to the duration of an action which is over; **pendant** is used with the pluperfect:

j'y travaillais depuis un an
I had been working there for a year

j'y avais travaillé pendant un an
I had worked there for a year

10 Use of tenses with 'venir de'

venir de + infinitive means 'to have just done'.

a) if it describes something that has just happened, it is used in the present instead of the perfect:

l'avion vient d'arriver	**je viens de te le dire !**
the plane has just arrived	I've just told you!

b) if it describes something that had just happened, it is used in the imperfect instead of the pluperfect:

le film venait de commencer	**je venais de rentrer**
the film had just started	I'd just come home

11 Use of tenses after conjunctions of time

quand	when
tant que	as long as
dès/aussitôt que	as soon as
lorsque	when
pendant que	while

Verbs which follow these conjunctions must be used in the following tenses:

a) *future instead of present:*

je te téléphonerai quand je serai prêt
I'll phone you when I'm ready

on ira dès qu'il fera beau
we'll go as soon as the weather is fine

b) *future perfect instead of perfect* when the future is implied:

on rentrera dès qu'on aura fini les courses
we'll come back as soon as we've done our shopping

je t'appellerai dès qu'il sera arrivé
I'll call you as soon as he has arrived

c) *conditional perfect (or past conditional) instead of pluperfect* in indirect speech:

il a dit qu'il sortirait quand il aurait fini
he said that he would come out when he had finished

For the use of the subjunctive and conditional, see **G98, 102 & 104**, sections 1, 2 and 3.

G MOODS

Note: Only the subjunctive, conditional and imperative are dealt with in this section. The indicative mood, being the normal form of the verb, is treated in the preceding sections.

1 THE SUBJUNCTIVE

In everyday spoken French, the only two subjunctive tenses that are used are the present and the perfect. The imperfect and the pluperfect subjunctive are found mainly in literature or in texts of a formal nature.

The subjunctive is always preceded by the conjunction **que** and is used in subordinate clauses when the subject of the subordinate clause is different from the subject of the main verb. Spoken English very often omits the conjunction **that**.

Most clauses introduced by **que** take the indicative. But the subjunctive must be used after the following common examples:

a) *Verbs of emotion*

être content que	to be pleased (that)
être déçu que	to be disappointed (that)
être désolé que	to be sorry (that)
être enchanté que	to be delighted (that)
être étonné que	to be surprised (that)
être fâché que	to be angry (that)
être heureux que	to be happy (that)
être ravi que	to be delighted (that)
être surpris que	to be surprised (that)
être triste que	to be sad (that)
avoir peur que ... ne	to be afraid/to fear (that)
craindre que ... ne	to be afraid/to fear (that)
détester que	to hate (that)
avoir horreur que	to hate (that)
avoir honte que	to be ashamed (that)
regretter que	to be sorry (that)/to regret (that)
se réjouir que	to be delighted (that)

ils étaient contents que j'aille les voir
they were pleased (that) I went to visit them

je serais très étonné qu'il mente
I would be very surprised if he was/were lying

on regrette beaucoup que tu n'aies pas pu vendre ta voiture
we're very sorry (that) you couldn't sell your car

j'ai horreur que tu fasses cela
I hate you doing that

Note: **ne** is used after **craindre que** or **avoir peur que** (though it may be omitted in spoken French); it does not have a negative meaning in itself and is not translated in English:

je crains que l'avion *ne* soit en retard
I'm afraid (that) the plane *will* be late

b) *Verbs of wishing, wanting and ordering:*

aimer que	to like
aimer mieux que	to prefer (that)
défendre que	to forbid (that)
désirer que	to want
ordonner que	to order (that)
permettre que	to allow/permit (that)
préférer que	to prefer (that)
souhaiter que	to hope (that)
vouloir que	to want

But: **espérer que** (to hope that) takes the indicative

Note: In English, such verbs are often used in the following type of construction: verb of wanting + object + infinitive (eg I'd like you to listen); this type of construction is impossible in French, where a subjunctive clause has to be used:

je souhaite que tu réussisses
I hope you will succeed

il aimerait que je lui écrive plus souvent
he'd like me to write to him more often

voulez-vous que je vienne ?
would you like me to come?

préférez-vous que je ne fasse rien ?
would you rather I did nothing?, would you prefer it if I did nothing?

il ordonna que tout le monde se mît d'accord
he ordered everyone to agree

c) *Expressions of a wish or an order followed by* ***que***

qu'il entre !
let him come in!

que le bal commence !
let the dancing begin!

qu'elle parte tout de suite !
she must leave at once!

que Dieu vous pardonne !
may God forgive you!

que tu sois heureux !
may you be happy!

d) *Impersonal constructions* (expressing necessity, possibility, doubt, denial, preference and emotions):

il faut que	it is necessary (that) (*have to, must*)
il est nécessaire que	it is necessary (that)
il est important que	it is important (that)
il est urgent que	it is urgent (that)
il est possible que	it is possible (that) (*may, might*)
il se peut que	it is possible (that) (*may, might*)
il est impossible que	it is impossible (that)
il est douteux que	it is doubtful whether
il est peu probable que	it is unlikely (that)
il semble que	it seems (that)
il est préférable que	it is preferable (that)
il vaut mieux que	it is better (that) (*had better*)

c'est dommage que	it is a pity (that)
il est regrettable que	it is regrettable (that)
il est heureux que	it is lucky/fortunate (that)
il est malheureux que	it is unfortunate (that)
il est triste que	it is sad (that)
il est surprenant que	it is surprising (that)
il est étonnant que	it is surprising (that)

Note: these expressions may be used in any appropriate tense; (actual translations may be slightly different from the literal translations given above):

il faut qu'on se dépêche
we have to hurry, we must hurry

il était important que tu le saches
it was important that you should know

il est possible que tu aies raison
it's possible you're right, you may be right

il se pourrait qu'elle change d'avis
she might change her mind

il est peu probable qu'ils s'y intéressent
they're unlikely to be interested in it

il semble qu'elle ait raison
she seems to be right

il vaudrait mieux que tu ne promettes rien
you'd better not promise anything

c'est dommage que vous vous soyez manqués
it's a pity you missed each other

Note: **il semble que** may also be followed by the indicative, and **il me semble que** (I think that) is always followed by the indicative.

e) *Some verbs and impersonal constructions expressing doubt or uncertainty* (mainly used negatively or interrogatively):

douter que	to doubt (that)
(ne pas) nier que	(not) to deny (that)
(ne pas) croire que	(not) to believe (that)
(ne pas) penser que	(not) to think (that)
(ne pas) être sûr que	(not) to be sure (that)
il n'est pas certain que	it isn't certain (that)
il n'est pas évident que	it isn't obvious (that)
il n'est pas sûr que	it isn't certain (that)
il n'est pas vrai que	it isn't true (that)
mettons que	let's suppose (that)
en supposant que	supposing (that)

je doute fort qu'il veuille t'aider
I very much doubt whether he'll want to help you

croyez-vous qu'il y ait des places de libres ?
do you think there are any seats available?

on n'était pas sûr que ce soit le bon endroit
we weren't sure that it was the right place

il n'était pas certain qu'elle puisse gagner
it wasn't certain whether she could win

f) ***attendre que*** (to wait until someone does something, to wait for someone to do something):

attendons qu'il revienne
let's wait until he comes back, let's wait for him to come back

g) *Some subordinating conjunctions:*

bien que	although, though
quoique	although, though
sans que	without
pour que	so that
afin que	so that
à condition que	provided/providing (that)
pourvu que	provided/providing (that)
jusqu'à ce que	until
en attendant que	until
avant que ... (ne)	before
à moins que ... (ne)	unless
de peur que ... ne	for fear that
de crainte que ... ne	for fear that
de sorte que	so (that)
de façon (à ce) que	so (that)
de manière (à ce) que	so (that)
que ... (ou que)	whether ... (or whether)

Note: when **ne** is shown in brackets (*Am* parentheses), it may follow the conjunction, although it is seldom used in spoken French; it does not have a negative meaning, and is not translated in English. When **ne** is shown without brackets, its use is considered more common, though it too may be omitted in spoken French.

il est allé travailler bien qu'il soit malade
he went to work although he was ill

elle est entrée sans que je la voie
she came in without me/my seeing her

voilà de l'argent pour que tu puisses aller au cinéma
here's some money so (that) you can go to the movies

d'accord, pourvu que tu me promettes de ne pas le répéter
all right, provided that/as long as you promise not to tell anyone

tu l'as revu avant qu'il (ne) parte ?
did you see him again before he left?

je le ferai demain, à moins que ce (ne) soit urgent
I'll do it tomorrow, unless it's urgent

elle n'a pas fait de bruit de peur qu'il ne se réveille
she didn't make any noise, for fear that he would wake up

parle moins fort de sorte qu'elle ne nous entende pas
talk more quietly so that she doesn't hear us

qu'elle vienne ou non/qu'elle vienne ou qu'elle ne vienne pas, je partirai demain
whether she comes or not/whether she comes or (whether) she doesn't, I'm leaving tomorrow

Note: when **de sorte que** and **de façon/manière que** (so that) express a result, as opposed to a purpose, the indicative is used instead of the subjunctive:

il a fait du bruit, de sorte qu'elle l'*a entendu*
he made some noise, so that she heard him

(**de façon que** + indicative is considered old-fashioned)

h) *A superlative or adjectives like **premier** (first), **dernier** (last), **seul** (only) followed by **qui** or **que**:*

c'était le coureur le plus rapide que j'aie jamais vu
he was the fastest runner I'd ever seen/I ever saw

But: the indicative is used with a statement of fact rather than the expression of an opinion:

c'est le coureur le plus rapide qui a gagné
it was the fastest runner who won

i) *Negative and indefinite pronouns (eg **rien**, **personne**, **quelqu'un**, **quelque chose**) followed by **qui** or **que**:*

je ne connais personne qui sache aussi bien chanter
I don't know anyone who can sing so well

il n'y a aucune chance qu'il réussisse
he has no chance of succeeding

ils cherchent quelqu'un qui puisse garder le bébé
they're looking for someone who can look after the baby

j) *Expressions containing **qui**, **quel**, **quoi**, **où** and **si** followed by **que** (English translations end in **-ever**)*

qui que vous soyez
whoever you may be/you are

quel que soit le résultat
whatever the result may be, whatever the result is

quoi que je dise
whatever I may say, whatever I say

où qu'il soit
wherever he may be/he is

si jeune qu'elle soit
however young she may be/she is

2 Avoiding the subjunctive

The subjunctive can be avoided, as is the tendency in modern spoken French, provided that both verbs in the sentence have the same subject. It is replaced by an infinitive introduced by the preposition **de**, the preposition **à** or by no preposition at all (see **G107**, section H).

a) ***de*** *+ infinitive replaces the subjunctive after:*

i) verbs of emotion:

j'ai été étonné d'apprendre la nouvelle
I was surprised to hear the news

il regrette de ne pas avoir vu ce film
he's sorry he didn't see this film

tu as peur de ne pas avoir assez d'argent ?
are you worried you won't have enough money?

ii) **attendre** (to wait) and **douter** (to doubt):

j'attendrai d'avoir bu mon café
I'll wait until I've drunk my coffee

elle doute de vous avoir rencontré
she doubts that she met you

iii) most impersonal constructions:

il serait préférable de déclarer ces objets
it would be preferable to declare these things

il est important de garder votre billet
it's important to keep your ticket

iv) most conjunctions:

il est resté dans la voiture afin de ne pas se mouiller
he stayed in the car so as not to get wet

j'ai lu avant de m'endormir
I read before falling asleep

tu peux sortir, à condition de rentrer avant minuit
you can go out, provided that you're back/as long as you're back before midnight

b) ***à*** *+ infinitive replaces the subjunctive after:*

i) **de façon/manière**

mets la liste sur la table, de manière à ne pas l'oublier
put the list on the table so as not to forget it/so that you won't forget it

ii) **premier, seul, dernier**

il a été le seul à s'excuser
he was the only one who apologized

c) *the infinitive without any linking preposition replaces the subjunctive after:*

i) verbs of wishing and wanting:

je voudrais sortir avec toi
I'd like to go out with you

ii) **il faut, il vaut mieux**:

il vous faudra prendre vos valises
you'll have to take your bags

il lui a fallu recommencer à zéro
he had to start all over again

il vaudrait mieux lui apporter des fleurs que des chocolats
it would be better to take her flowers than chocolates

Note the indirect object pronoun often used with **il faut** to indicate the subject (who has to do something)

iii) verbs of thinking:

je ne crois pas le connaître
I don't think I know him

tu penses être chez toi à cinq heures ?
do you think you'll be home at five?

iv) **pour** and **sans**:

le bus est reparti sans nous attendre
the bus left without waiting for us

j'économise pour pouvoir acheter une moto
I'm saving up to buy a motorbike

3 THE CONDITIONAL

a) *The conditional present*

i) The conditional present is used to describe what someone would do or would be doing or what would happen (if something else were to happen):

si j'étais riche, j'*achèterais* un château
if I were rich, I *would buy* a castle

Note: when the main verb is in the conditional present, the verb after **si** is in the imperfect.

ii) It is also used in indirect questions or reported speech instead of the future:

il ne m'a pas dit s'il *viendrait*
he didn't tell me whether he *would come*

b) *The conditional perfect (or past conditional)*

The conditional perfect or past conditional is used to express what someone would have done or would have been doing or what would have happened:

si j'avais su, je n'aurais rien dit
if I had known, I wouldn't have said anything

qu'aurais-je fait sans toi ?
what would I have done without you?

Note: when the main verb is in the conditional perfect, the verb introduced by **si** is in the pluperfect.

c) *Tenses after si:*

The tense of the verb introduced by **si** is determined by the tense of the verb in the main clause:

MAIN VERB		VERB FOLLOWING 'SI'
conditional present	→	imperfect
conditional perfect	→	pluperfect

je te le dirais si je le savais
I would tell you if I knew

je te l'aurais dit si je l'avais su
I would have told you if I had known

Note: never use the conditional (or the future) with **si** unless **si** means whether (ie when it introduces an indirect question):

je me demande si j'y serais arrivé sans toi
I wonder if (= *whether*) I would have managed without you

d) *Other uses of the conditional*

i) When making a statement when one is not sure how accurate or truthful it is. This use is often found in newspapers and news bulletins:

il y aurait plus de cent morts
there are said/reported to be over a hundred dead

d'après ce témoin oculaire c'est lui qui serait l'assassin
according to the eyewitness he is the one who is (apparently) the murderer

ii) When expressing possibility (= *might*):

ce serait peut-être la meilleure solution
it might be the best solution

4 THE IMPERATIVE

a) *Definition*

The imperative is used to give commands, or polite instructions, or to make requests or suggestions; these can be positive (affirmative imperative: 'do!') or negative ('don't!'):

mange ta soupe ! eat your soup!	**n'aie pas peur !** don't be afraid!
partons ! let's go!	**entrez !** come in!
faites attention ! be careful!	**n'hésitez pas !** don't hesitate!
tournez à droite à la poste turn right at the post office	

b) *Forms*

The imperative has only three forms, which are the same as the **tu, nous** and **vous** forms of the present tense, but without the subject pronoun:

	-ER VERBS	**-IR** VERBS	**-RE** VERBS
'TU' FORM:	**regarde** watch	**choisis** choose	**attends** wait
'NOUS' FORM:	**regardons** let's watch	**choisissons** let's choose	**attendons** let's wait
'VOUS' FORM:	**regardez** watch	**choisissez** choose	**attendez** wait

Note:

i) the **-s** of the **tu** form of **-er** verbs is dropped, except when **y** or **en** follow the verb:

parle-lui ! *But* **parles-en avec lui**
speak to him! speak to him about it

achète du sucre ! *But* **achètes-en un kilo**
buy some sugar! buy a kilo (of it)

ii) the distinction between the subject pronouns **tu** and **vous** (see **G56**, section 6 D 1b)) applies to the **tu** and **vous** forms of the imperative:

prends ta sœur avec toi, Alain
take your sister with you, Alain

prenez le plat du jour, Monsieur ; c'est du poulet rôti
have today's set menu, sir; it's roast chicken

les enfants, prenez vos imperméables ; il va pleuvoir
take your raincoats, children; it's going to rain

c) *Negative commands*

In simple negative commands, the verb is placed between **ne** and **pas** (or is placed after **ne** in other negative expressions):

ne fais pas ça !
don't do that!

ne dites rien !
don't say anything!

d) *Imperative with object pronouns*

In positive commands, object pronouns come after the verb and are attached to it by a hyphen. In negative commands, they come before the verb (see **G57 & 58**, sections 6 D 2a), b) and c)):

dites-moi ce qui s'est passé
tell me what happened

attendons-les !
let's wait for them

prends-en bien soin, ne l'abîme pas !
take good care of it, don't damage it!

ne le leur dis pas !
don't tell them (that)!

ne les écoutez pas
don't listen to them

e) *Imperative of reflexive verbs*

The position of the reflexive pronoun of reflexive verbs is the same as that of object pronouns:

tais-toi !
be quiet!

levez-vous !
get up!

méfiez-vous de lui
don't trust him

arrêtons-nous ici
let's stop here

ne nous plaignons pas
let's not complain

ne t'approche pas plus !
don't come any closer!

f) *Alternatives to the imperative*

i) infinitive

the infinitive is often used instead of the imperative in written instructions and in recipes:

s'adresser au concierge
see the caretaker

ne pas fumer
no smoking

verser le lait et bien mélanger
pour in the milk and stir well

ii) subjunctive

as the imperative has no third person (singular or plural), **que** + subjunctive is used for giving orders in the third person (see **G99**, section G 1 c)):

que personne ne me dérange !
don't let anyone disturb me!

qu'il entre !
let him come in!

qu'elle parte, je m'en fiche !
I don't care if she goes!

g) *Idiomatic usage*

The imperative is used in spoken French in many set phrases. Here are some of the most common ones:

allons donc !
come on!

dis/dites donc !
look (here)!

tiens/tenez !
here (you are)!

tiens ! voilà le médecin
ah! here comes the doctor

tiens (donc) !
(oh) really?

tiens ! tiens !
well, well! (fancy that!)

voyons !
come on!

voyons donc !
let's see now

H THE INFINITIVE

1 The infinitive is the basic form of the verb. It is recognized by its ending, which is found in three forms corresponding to the three conjugations: **-er, -ir, -re**.

These endings give the verb the meaning 'to ...':

acheter	**choisir**	**vendre**
to buy	to choose	to sell

Note: although this applies as a general rule, the French infinitive will often be translated by a verb form in *-ing* (see **G214**, section 13 B 1c)). It will also sometimes be translated by a verb which does not take 'to' in its infinitive form (eg **devoir** 'must', **pouvoir** 'can'; see **G121**, section K).

2 Uses of the infinitive

The infinitive can follow a preposition, a verb, a noun, a pronoun, an adverb or an adjective.

a) *After a preposition*

The infinitive can be used after some prepositions (**pour, avant de, sans, au lieu de, afin de** etc):

sans attendre
without waiting

avant de partir
before leaving

b) *After a verb*

There are three main constructions when a verb is followed by an infinitive:

i) with no linking preposition
ii) with the linking preposition **à**
iii) with the linking preposition **de**

i) Verbs followed by the infinitive with no linking preposition:

★ verbs of wishing and wanting, eg:

vouloir	to want
souhaiter	to wish
désirer	to want/wish
espérer	to hope

voulez-vous manger maintenant ou plus tard ?
do you want to eat now or later?

je souhaite parler au directeur
I wish to speak to the manager

★ verbs of seeing, hearing and feeling, eg:

voir	to see
écouter	to listen to
regarder	to watch
sentir	to feel, to smell
entendre	to hear

je l'ai vu jouer
I've seen him play

tu m'as regardé danser ?
did you watch me dance?

j'ai entendu quelqu'un crier
I heard someone shout

Note: in the above examples the *-ing* form of the verb is equally common, eg 'did you watch me dance *or dancing*?'

★ verbs of motion, eg:

aller	to go
monter	to go/come up
venir	to come
entrer	to go/come in
rentrer	to go/come back (home)
sortir	to go/come out
descendre	to go/come down

je viendrai te voir demain
I'll come and see you tomorrow

il est descendu laver la voiture
he went down to wash the car

va acheter le journal
go and buy the paper

Note: in English, 'to come' and 'to go' may be linked to the verb that follows by 'and'; 'and' is not translated in French.

aller + infinitive can be used to express a future action, eg what someone is going to do:

qu'est-ce que tu vas faire demain ?
what are you going to do tomorrow?

★ modal auxiliary verbs (see **G121**, section K)

★ verbs of liking and disliking, eg:

aimer	to like
adorer	to love
aimer mieux	to prefer
détester	to hate
préférer	to prefer

tu aimes nager ?
do you like swimming?

j'aime mieux attendre
I prefer to wait, I'd rather wait

je déteste aller à la campagne
I hate going to the country

j'adore faire la grasse matinée
I love sleeping late

★ some impersonal verbs such as **falloir** and **valoir mieux** (see **G90**, section 7 E 2h)).

★ a few other verbs, eg:

compter	to intend to, to expect to
sembler	to seem
laisser	to let
faillir	'to nearly' (do)
oser	to dare

ils l'ont laissé partir
they let him go

je n'ose pas le lui demander
I daren't ask him

tu sembles être malade
you seem to be ill

je compte partir demain
I intend to leave tomorrow, I expect to leave tomorrow

j'ai failli manquer l'avion
I nearly missed the plane

★ in the following set expressions:

aller chercher	to (go and) get/(go and) fetch
envoyer chercher	to send for
entendre dire (que)	to hear (that)
entendre parler de	to hear of/about
laisser tomber	to drop
venir chercher	to come and get
vouloir dire	to mean

va chercher ton argent
go and get your money

j'ai entendu dire qu'il était journaliste
I heard that he was a journalist

tu as entendu parler de ce film ?
have you heard of/about this film?

ne le laisse pas tomber !
don't drop it!

ça veut dire "demain"
it means 'tomorrow'

ii) Verbs followed by **à** + infinitive:

A list of these is given on **G165**, section 7 M 1b):

je dois aider ma mère à préparer le déjeuner
I must help my mother prepare lunch

il commence à faire nuit
it's beginning to get dark

alors, tu t'es décidé à y aller ?
so you've made up your mind to go?

je t'invite à venir chez moi
I invite you to come to my house

je passe mon temps à lire et à regarder la télé
I spend my time reading and watching TV

cela sert à nettoyer les vitres
this is used for cleaning windows

iii) Verbs followed by **de** + infinitive:

A list of these is given on **G165**, section 7 M 1c):

je crois qu'il a cessé de pleuvoir
I think it's stopped raining

tu as envie de sortir ?
do you feel like going out?

le médecin a conseillé à Serge de rester au lit
the doctor advised Serge to stay in bed

j'ai décidé de rester chez moi
I decided to stay at home

essayons de faire du stop
let's try and hitchhike

tu as fini de m'ennuyer ?
will you stop annoying me?

demande à papa de t'aider
ask dad to help you

je t'interdis d'y aller
I forbid you to go

n'oublie pas d'en acheter !
don't forget to buy some!

j'ai refusé de le faire
I refused to do it

je vous prie de m'excuser
please forgive me

il vient de téléphoner
he's just phoned

c) *After a noun, a pronoun, an adverb or an adjective*

There are two possible constructions: with **à** or with **de**.

i) with the linking preposition **à**:

il avait plusieurs clients à voir
he had several customers to see

c'est difficile à dire
it's difficult to say

ii) with the linking preposition **de**:

je suis content de te voir
I am pleased to see you

iii) **à** or **de** with pronouns, adverbs or nouns?

★ **à** conveys the idea of something to do or (in a passive sense) of something to be done, after the following:

beaucoup	a lot
plus	more
tant	so much
trop	too much
assez	enough
moins	less
rien	nothing
tout	everything
quelque chose	something

une maison à vendre
a house for sale

j'ai des examens à préparer
I've got exams to prepare

il nous a indiqué la route à suivre
he showed us the road to follow

il y a trop de livres à lire
there are too many books to read/to be read

il n'y a pas de temps à perdre
there's no time to lose/to be lost

c'était une occasion à ne pas manquer
it was an opportunity not to be missed/not to miss

★ **de** is used after nouns of an abstract nature, usually with the definite article, eg:

l'habitude de	the habit of

l'occasion de	the opportunity to
le temps de	the time to
le courage de	the courage to
l'envie de	the desire/longing to
le besoin de	the need to
le plaisir de	the pleasure of
le moment de	the time to

il n'avait pas l'habitude d'être seul
he wasn't used to being alone, he wasn't in the habit of being alone

je n'ai pas le temps de lui parler
I don't have time to talk to him

avez-vous eu l'occasion de la rencontrer ?
did you have the opportunity to meet her?/of meeting her?

ce n'est pas le moment de le déranger
now is not the time to disturb him

je n'ai pas eu le courage de le lui dire
I didn't have the courage to tell him

iv) **à** or **de** with adjectives?

★ **à** is used in a passive sense (something to be done) and after **c'est**:

un livre agréable à lire
a pleasant book to read

il est facile à satisfaire
he is easily satisfied, he is easy to satisfy

c'est intéressant à savoir
that's interesting to know

c'était impossible à faire
it was impossible to do

★ **de** is used after **il est** in an impersonal sense (see **G89**, section 7 E 2b)):

il est intéressant de savoir que ...
it is interesting to know that ...

Note: for the use of **c'est** and **il est**, see **G215**, section 13 B 2.

★ **de** is used after many adjectives, in particular those where the idea of 'of' is present in English, eg:

certain/sûr de	certain of/to, sure of/to
capable de	capable of, able to
incapable de	incapable of, unable to
coupable de	guilty of

j'étais sûr de réussir
I was certain/sure of succeeding, I was certain/sure to succeed

il est incapable d'y arriver seul
he is incapable of managing it on his own

de is also used with adjectives of emotion, feeling and generally with adjectives denoting a state of mind, eg:

content de	pleased/happy to

surpris/étonné de	surprised to
fier de	proud to
heureux de	happy to
fâché de	sorry to
triste de	sad to
désolé de	sorry to

j'ai été très content de recevoir ta lettre
I was very pleased/happy to get your letter

elle sera surprise de vous voir
she will be surprised to see you

je suis fâché de vous avoir raté
I'm sorry I missed you, I'm sorry to have missed you

nous avons été très tristes d'apprendre la nouvelle
we were very sad to hear the news

But: **à** is used with **prêt à** (ready to) and **disposé à** (prepared/willing to):

es-tu prête à partir ?
are you ready to go?

je suis tout disposé à vous aider
I'm quite prepared/very willing to help you

d) ***faire*** + infinitive

faire is followed by an infinitive without any linking preposition to express the sense of 'having someone do something' (or 'forcing someone to do something') or 'having something done'; two constructions are possible:

i) with one object
ii) with two objects

i) when only one object is used, it is a direct object:

je dois le faire réparer
I must have it/get it fixed

il veut faire construire une maison
he wants to have/get a house built

je ferai nettoyer cette veste ; je la ferai nettoyer
I'll have/get this jacket cleaned; I'll have it/get it cleaned

tu m'as fait attendre !
you made me wait!

je le ferai parler
I'll make him talk

Note: the following set expressions:

faire entrer	to show in
faire venir	to send for

faites entrer ce monsieur
show this gentleman in

je vais faire venir le docteur
I'll send for the doctor

ii) when both **faire** and the following infinitive have an object, the object of **faire** is indirect:

elle a fait prendre une douche à son fils
she made her son take a shower

elle lui a fait prendre une douche
she made him take a shower

je leur ai fait ranger leur chambre
I made them tidy their room

e) *Infinitive used as subject of another verb:*

trouver un emploi n'est pas facile
finding a job isn't easy

lire c'est agréable
reading is pleasant, to read is pleasant

3 The perfect infinitive

a) *Form*

The perfect or past infinitive is formed with the infinitive of the auxiliary **avoir** or **être** as appropriate (see **G83**, section C 4), followed by the past participle of the verb, eg:

avoir mangé	**être allé**	**s'être endormi**
to have eaten	to have gone	to have fallen asleep

b) *Use*

i) after the preposition **après** (after):

après avoir attendu une heure, il est rentré chez lui
after waiting for an hour, he went (back) home

il s'en est souvenu après s'être couché
he remembered after going to bed

ii) after certain verbs, eg:

se souvenir de	to remember
remercier de	to thank for
regretter de	to regret/be sorry for
être désolé de	to be sorry to/for
être navré de	to be sorry to/for
se rappeler	to recall/remember

tu te souviens d'avoir fait cela ?
do you remember doing that?

je vous remercie de m'avoir invité
I thank you for inviting me

il regrettait de leur avoir menti
he was sorry for lying to them, he regretted lying to them

je suis désolé/navré de vous avoir fait attendre
I'm sorry to keep you waiting/to have kept you waiting,
I'm sorry for keeping you waiting

tu te rappelles avoir fait cela ?
do you recall doing that?

Note: in all of the examples in i) and ii) above it is also possible to use the perfect infinitive in English with the *-ing* form of the verb, though this usage is somewhat more formal, eg:

après avoir attendu une heure
after having waited for an hour

tu te souviens d'avoir fait cela ?
do you remember having done that?

je suis désolé de vous avoir fait attendre
I'm sorry for having kept you waiting

I PARTICIPLES

1 The present participle

a) *Formation*

Like the imperfect, the present participle is formed by using the stem of the first person plural of the present tense (the **'nous'** form less the **'-ons'** ending):

-ons is replaced by **-ant** (= English *-ing*)

Exceptions:

INFINITIVE	PRESENT PARTICIPLE
avoir to have	**ayant** having
être to be	**étant** being
savoir to know	**sachant** knowing

b) *Use as an adjective*

Used as an adjective, the present participle agrees in number and in gender with its noun or pronoun:

un travail fatigant
tiring work

la semaine suivante
the following week

ils sont très exigeants
they're very demanding

des nouvelles surprenantes
surprising news

Note: very rarely a present participle may have a different form when used as an adjective as in the case of **fatigant** (adjective) and **fatiguant** (participle), or **savant** 'learned' (adjective) and **sachant** (participle).

c) *Use as a verb*

The present participle is used far less frequently in French than in English, and English present participles in *-ing* are often not translated by a participle in French (see **G213**, section 13 B 1).

i) used on its own, the present participle corresponds to the English present participle:

ne voulant plus attendre, ils sont partis sans moi
not wanting to wait any longer, they left without me

pensant bien faire, j'ai insisté
thinking I was doing the right thing, I insisted

Note: this use of the present participle often introduces the *reason* for an action.

ii) **en** + present participle

When the subject of the present participle is the same as that of the main verb, this structure is often used to express simultaneity (ie 'while doing something'), manner (ie 'by doing something') or to translate English phrasal verbs expressing motion.

★ simultaneous actions

In English this structure is translated by:

- while/when/on + present participle (eg 'on arriving')
- while/when/as + subject + verb (eg 'as he arrived')

il est tombé en descendant l'escalier
he fell as he was going down the stairs

en le voyant, j'ai éclaté de rire
when I saw him, I burst out laughing, on seeing him I burst out laughing

elle lisait le journal en attendant l'autobus
she was reading the paper while (she was) waiting for the bus, she was reading the paper as she waited for the bus

Note: the adverb **tout** is often used before **en** to emphasize the fact that both actions are simultaneous, especially when there is an element of contradiction:

elle écoutait la radio tout en faisant ses devoirs
she was listening to the radio while doing her homework

tout en protestant, je les ai suivis
under protest, I followed them

★ manner

when expressing how an action is done, **en** + participle is translated by: 'by' + participle, eg:

il gagne sa vie en vendant des voitures d'occasion
he earns his living (by) selling secondhand cars

j'ai trouvé du travail en lisant les petites annonces
I found a job by reading the classified ads

★ phrasal verbs of motion

en + present participle is often used to translate English phrasal verbs indicating motion, where the verb expresses the means of motion and a preposition expresses the direction of movement (eg 'to run out', 'to stagger across').

In French, the English preposition is translated by a verb, while the English verb is translated by **en** + present participle:

il est sorti de l'immeuble *en courant*
he *ran* out of the building

elle a traversé la route *en titubant*
she *staggered* across the road

2 The past participle

a) *Forms*

For the formation of the past participle see **G80**, section 7 C 1.

b) *Use*

The past participle is mostly used as a verb in compound tenses or in the passive, but it can also be used as an adjective. In either case, there are strict rules of agreement to be followed.

c) *Rules of agreement of the past participle*

i) When it is used as an adjective, the past participle always agrees with the noun or pronoun it refers to:

un ballon crevé a burst balloon	**une pomme pourrie** a rotten apple
ils étaient épuisés they were exhausted	**trois assiettes cassées !** three broken plates!

Note: in French, the past participle is used as an adjective to describe postures or attitudes of the body, where English often uses the present participle. The most common of these are:

accoudé	leaning with one's elbows
accroupi	squatting, crouching
agenouillé	kneeling (down)
allongé	lying, stretched out
appuyé (contre/sur)	leaning (against/on)
assis	sitting (down)
couché	lying (down)
étendu	lying, stretched out
penché	leaning (over)
(sus)pendu (à)	hanging (from)

il est allongé sur le lit he's lying on the bed	**une femme assise devant moi** a woman sitting in front of me

ii) In compound tenses:

★ with the auxiliary **avoir**:

the past participle only agrees in number and gender with the direct object when the direct object comes before the participle, ie in the following cases:

— in a clause introduced by the relative pronoun **que**:

le jeu vidéo que j'ai acheté the video game I bought	**la valise qu'il a perdue** the suitcase he lost

— with a direct object pronoun:

ta carte ? je l'ai reçue hier
your card? I got it yesterday

zut, mes lunettes ! je les ai laissées chez moi
oh dear, my glasses! I've left them at home

— in a clause introduced by **combien de**, **quel** (**quelle, quels, quelles**) or **lequel** (**laquelle, lesquels, lesquelles**):

combien de pays as-tu visités ?
how many countries have you visited?

laquelle avez-vous choisie ?
which one did you choose?

Note:

i) if the direct object comes after the past participle, the participle remains in the masculine singular form:

on a rencontré des gens sympathiques
we met some nice people

But: **les gens sympathiques qu'on a rencontrés**
the nice people we met

ii) the participle also normally remains in the masculine singular when it follows the pronoun **en** :

les fleurs — j'en ai cueilli une douzaine
the flowers? — I've picked a dozen (of them)

But the past participle is often allowed to agree with the preceding noun, especially when **en** is not qualified in any way (as by **'une douzaine'** in the example above):

les fleurs ? — j'en ai déjà cueillies
the flowers? — I've picked some already

★ with the auxiliary **être**:

— the past participle agrees with the subject of the verb:

quand est-elle revenue ?
when did she come back?

elle était déjà partie
she'd already left

ils sont passés te voir ?
did they come to see you?

elles sont restées là
they stayed here

Note: this rule also applies when the verb is in the passive:

elle a été arrêtée
she's been arrested

— reflexive verbs

in most cases, the past participle of reflexive verbs agrees with the reflexive pronoun if the pronoun is a direct object; since the reflexive pronoun refers to the subject, the number and gender of the past participle are determined by the subject:

Jacques s'est trompé
Jacques made a mistake

Marie s'était réveillée tard
Marie had woken up late

ils se sont disputés ?
did they quarrel?

elles se sont vues
they saw each other

Michèle et Marie, vous vous êtes endormies ?
Michèle and Marie, have you fallen asleep yet?

But: the past participle does not agree when the reflexive pronoun is an indirect object:

elles se sont écrit
they wrote *to* each other

elle se l'est acheté
she bought it for herself

This is also the case where parts of the body are mentioned:

elle s'est lavé les cheveux she washed her hair	**ils se sont serré la main** they shook hands

J THE PASSIVE

1 Formation

The passive is used when the subject does not perform the action, but is subjected to it, eg:

the house has been sold	he was held responsible

Passive tenses are formed with the corresponding tense of the verb **'être'** ('to be', as in English), followed by the past participle of the verb, eg:

j'ai été invité
I was invited

The past participle must agree with its subject, eg:

elle a été renvoyée she has been dismissed	**il sera choisi** he will be chosen
ils seront déçus they will be disappointed	**elles ont été vues** they were seen

Note: in the passive the agent refers to the 'real subject', ie the performer of the action. The agent is introduced by **by** in English and usually by **par**, though often by **de**, in French:

— **par** is used when the verb denotes an action in the true sense of the word:

il a été battu par sa sœur
he was beaten by his sister

le carrosse était tiré par six chevaux
the coach was drawn by six horses

— **de** is used with verbs denoting:

★ an emotion:

être aimé de	to be loved by
être respecté de	to be respected by
être détesté de	to be hated by
être craint de	to be feared by

★ a habitual action:

être suivi de	to be followed by
être accompagné de	to be accompanied by
être précédé de	to be preceded by
être entouré de	to be surrounded by

★ the use of an instrument:

elle a été blessée d'une flèche
she was wounded by an arrow

il a été tué d'un coup de pistolet
he was killed by a gunshot, he was shot dead

2 Avoidance of the passive

The passive is far less common in French than in English. In particular, an indirect object cannot become the subject of a sentence in French, ie the following sentence where 'he' is an indirect object has no equivalent in French:

he was given a book (*ie a book was given to him*)

In general, French tries to avoid the passive wherever possible. This can be done in several ways:

a) *Use of the pronoun* ***on***:

on m'a volé mon portefeuille
my wallet has been stolen

on construit une nouvelle piscine
a new swimming pool is being built

en France, on boit beaucoup de vin
a lot of wine is drunk in France

ici on parle français
French (is) spoken here

b) *Agent becomes subject of the verb*

If the agent, ie the 'real subject', is mentioned in English, it can become the subject of the French verb:

la nouvelle va les surprendre
they will be surprised by *the news*

mon oncle m'a invité
I've been invited by *my uncle*

mon cadeau te plaît ?
are you pleased with *my present?*

c) *Use of a reflexive verb*

Reflexive forms can be created for a large number of verbs, particularly in the third person:

elle s'appelle Anne
she is called Anne

ce plat se mange froid
this dish is eaten cold

ton absence va se remarquer
your absence will be noticed

cela ne se fait pas ici
that isn't done here

d) *Use of* ***se faire*** + infinitive (when the subject is a person):

il s'est fait renverser par une voiture
he was knocked down by a car

je me suis fait voler (tout mon argent)
I've been robbed (of all my money)

3 Conjugation

For a complete conjugation table of a verb in the passive, see **être aimé** (to be loved), **G127**.

K MODAL AUXILIARY VERBS

The modal auxiliary verbs are always followed by the infinitive. They express an obligation, a probability, an intention, a possibility or a wish rather than a fact.

The five modal auxiliary verbs are: **DEVOIR, POUVOIR, SAVOIR, VOULOIR** and **FALLOIR**.

1 Devoir (conjugation see G135)

Expresses:
a) obligation, necessity
b) probability
c) intention, expectation

a) *obligation, necessity*

nous devons arriver à temps
we must arrive in time

je devais attendre l'arrivée de papa
I had to wait for dad to come,
I used to have to wait for dad to come

dans ce cas-là je devrais rester
in that case I would have to stay

demain tu devras prendre le bus
tomorrow you'll have to take the bus

nous avions dû partir
we had (had) to go

j'ai dû avouer que j'avais tort
I had to admit that I was wrong

In the conditional, **devoir** may be used for advice, ie to express what should be done (conditional present) or should have been done (past conditional):

vous devriez travailler davantage
you should work/ought to work harder

tu ne devrais pas marcher sur l'herbe
you shouldn't walk/ought not to walk on the grass

tu aurais dû tout avouer
you should have admitted/ought to have admitted everything

tu n'aurais pas dû manger ces champignons
you shouldn't have eaten/ought not to have eaten those mushrooms

Note: with the past conditional the French infinitive is translated by a past participle in English: **mang*er*** eat*en*.

b) *probability*

il doit être en train de dormir
he must be sleeping (he's probably sleeping)

j'ai dû me tromper de chemin
I must have taken the wrong road

ils ne doivent pas être bêtes
they can't be stupid

Note: in a past narrative sequence in the distant past 'must have' is translated by a pluperfect in French:

il dit qu'il avait dû se tromper de chemin
he said he must have taken the wrong road

c) *intention, expectation*

je dois aller chez le dentiste
I am supposed to go/to be going to the dentist's

le train doit arriver à 19h30
the train is due (to arrive) at 7.30 p.m.

Note: **devoir** may also be used as an impersonal verb (see **G90**, section 7 E 2g)).

2 Pouvoir (conjugation see **G148**)

Expresses: a) capacity, ability
b) permission
c) possibility

a) *capacity, ability*

Superman peut soulever une maison
Superman can lift a house

cette voiture peut faire du 150
this car can do 93 miles an hour

il était si faible qu'il ne pouvait pas sortir de son lit
he was so weak that he couldn't get out of bed

j'ai pu l'obtenir
I managed to get it, I was able to get it

b) *permission*

puis-je entrer ?
may I come in?, can I come in?

puis-je vous offrir du thé ?
may I/can I offer you some tea?

c) *possibility*

cela peut arriver
it can happen, it may happen

Note:

i) **pouvoir** + the infinitive is often replaced by **peut-être** and the finite tense: eg **il s'est peut-être trompé de livres** (he may have taken/could have taken the wrong books) rather than **il aurait pu se tromper de livres**.

In the conditional, **pouvoir** is used to express something that could or might be (conditional present) or that could or might have been (past conditional):

tu pourrais t'excuser
you might apologize

j'aurais pu vous prêter mon magnétophone
I could have lent you my tape recorder

ii) with verbs of perception (eg **entendre** to hear, **sentir** to feel, to smell, **voir** to see), **pouvoir** is usually omitted:

j'entendais le bruit des vagues	**oui, je vois**
I could hear the sound of the waves	yes, I can see

iii) **pouvoir** may also be used as an impersonal verb (see **G90**, section 7 E 2g))

3 Savoir (conjugation see **G151**)

Means: 'to know how to'

je sais nager
I can swim, I know how to swim

je savais conduire une moto
I used to be able to ride a motorbike, I used to know how to ride a motorbike

4 Vouloir (conjugation see **G157**)

Expresses: a) a strong desire
b) a wish
c) an attempt to do something

a) *desire*

je veux partir	**voulez-vous danser avec moi ?**
I want to go	will you dance with me?

b) *wish*

je voudrais être riche
I wish I were rich, I would like/should like to be rich

je voudrais trouver un travail intéressant
I would like/should like to find an interesting job

j'aurais voulu lui donner un coup de poing
I would have liked to punch him

c) *attempt*

il a voulu sauter par la fenêtre
he tried to jump out of the window

Note: **veuillez**, the imperative of **vouloir**, is used as a polite form to express a request ('would you please'):

veuillez ne pas déranger
please do not disturb, kindly do not disturb

5 Falloir (conjugation see **G142**; impersonal verb see **G91**, section 7 E 2h) ii))

Expresses: necessity, obligation

il faut manger pour vivre
you must eat to live, you have to eat to live

il fallait partir
we had to leave

il faudrait manger plus tôt ce soir
we should eat earlier tonight

il aurait fallu apporter des sandwichs
we should have brought sandwiches

Note that the 'real subject' of **falloir** may be specified by an indirect pronoun, eg

il leur faut partir
they have to leave

Note: some of the above verbs can also be used without infinitive constructions. They then take on a different meaning (eg **devoir** = to owe, **savoir** = to know).

L CONJUGATION TABLES

1 Full conjugations

The following verbs provide the main patterns of conjugation including the conjugation of a selection of the most common irregular verbs. These irregular verbs are marked with a double asterisk (**) in the dictionary headword list. All the verbs are arranged in the tables in alphabetical order.

-er verb (see **G73**)		AIMER
-ir verb (see **G73**)		FINIR
-re verb (see **G73**)		VENDRE
Reflexive verb (see **G84**)		SE MEFIER
Verb with auxiliary **être** (see **G80**)		ARRIVER
Verb in the passive (see **G119**)		ETRE AIME
Auxiliaries (see **G80**)		AVOIR**
		ETRE**
Verb in **-eler/-eter** (see **G76**)		APPELER
Verb in **-eter** (see **G77**)		JETER
Verb in **e** + consonant + **er** (see **G78**)		ACHETER
Verb in **é** + consonant + **er** (see **G79**)		ESPERER
Modal auxiliaries (see **G121**)		DEVOIR**
		POUVOIR**
		SAVOIR**
		VOULOIR**
		FALLOIR**
Irregular verbs	ALLER**	METTRE**
	CONDUIRE**	OUVRIR**
	CONNAITRE**	PRENDRE**
	CROIRE**	RECEVOIR**
	DIRE**	TENIR**
	DORMIR**	VENIR**
	ECRIRE**	VIVRE**
	FAIRE**	VOIR**

ACHETER

to buy

PRESENT	IMPERFECT	FUTURE
j'achète	j'achetais	j'achèterai
tu achètes	tu achetais	tu achèteras
il achète	il achetait	il achètera
nous achetons	nous achetions	nous achèterons
vous achetez	vous achetiez	vous achèterez
ils achètent	ils achetaient	ils achèteront
PAST HISTORIC	**PERFECT**	**PLUPERFECT**
j'achetai	j'ai acheté	j'avais acheté
tu achetas	tu as acheté	tu avais acheté
il acheta	il a acheté	il avait acheté
nous achetâmes	nous avons acheté	nous avions acheté
vous achetâtes	vous avez acheté	vous aviez acheté
ils achetèrent	ils ont acheté	ils avaient acheté

	CONDITIONAL	
PAST ANTERIOR	**PRESENT**	**PAST**
j'eus acheté etc	j'achèterais	j'aurais acheté
	tu achèterais	tu aurais acheté
	il achèterait	il aurait acheté
	nous achèterions	nous aurions acheté
FUTURE PERFECT	vous achèteriez	vous auriez acheté
j'aurai acheté etc	ils achèteraient	ils auraient acheté

SUBJUNCTIVE

PRESENT	IMPERFECT	PERFECT
j'achète	j'achetasse	j'aie acheté
tu achètes	tu achetasses	tu aies acheté
il achète	il achetât	il ait acheté
nous achetions	nous achetassions	nous ayons acheté
vous achetiez	vous achetiez	vous ayez acheté
ils achètent	ils achetassent	ils aient acheté

IMPERATIVE	*INFINITIVE*	*PARTICIPLE*
	PRESENT	**PRESENT**
achète	acheter	achetant
achetons		
achetez	**PAST**	**PAST**
	avoir acheté	acheté

AIMER
to like, to love

PRESENT	IMPERFECT	FUTURE
j'aime	j'aimais	j'aimerai
tu aimes	tu aimais	tu aimeras
il aime	il aimait	il aimera
nous aimons	nous aimions	nous aimerons
vous aimez	vous aimiez	vous aimerez
ils aiment	ils aimaient	ils aimeront
PAST HISTORIC	**PERFECT**	**PLUPERFECT**
j'aimai	j'ai aimé	j'avais aimé
tu aimas	tu as aimé	tu avais aimé
il aima	il a aimé	il avait aimé
nous aimâmes	nous avons aimé	nous avions aimé
vous aimâtes	vous avez aimé	vous aviez aimé
ils aimèrent	ils ont aimé	ils avaient aimé

	CONDITIONAL	
PAST ANTERIOR	**PRESENT**	**PAST**
j'eus aimé etc	j'aimerais	j'aurais aimé
	tu aimerais	tu aurais aimé
	il aimerait	il aurait aimé
	nous aimerions	nous aurions aimé
FUTURE PERFECT	vous aimeriez	vous auriez aimé
j'aurai aimé etc	ils aimeraient	ils auraient aimé

SUBJUNCTIVE		
PRESENT	**IMPERFECT**	**PERFECT**
j'aime	j'aimasse	j'aie aimé
tu aimes	tu aimasses	tu aies aimé
il aime	il aimât	il ait aimé
nous aimions	nous aimassions	nous ayons aimé
vous aimiez	vous aimassiez	vous ayez aimé
ils aiment	ils aimassent	ils aient aimé

IMPERATIVE	*INFINITIVE*	*PARTICIPLE*
	PRESENT	**PRESENT**
aime	aimer	aimant
aimons		
aimez	**PAST**	**PAST**
	avoir aimé	aimé

ETRE AIME

to be loved

PRESENT
je suis aimé(e)
tu es aimé(e)
il (elle) est aimé(e)
nous sommes aimé(e)s
vous êtes aimé(e)(s)
ils (elles) sont aimé(e)s

IMPERFECT
j'étais aimé(e)
tu étais aimé(e)
il (elle) était aimé(e)
nous étions aimé(e)s
vous étiez aimé(e)(s)
ils (elles) étaient aimé(e)s

FUTURE
je serai aimé(e)
tu seras aimé(e)
il (elle) sera aimé(e)
nous serons aimé(e)s
vous serez aimé(e)(s)
ils (elles) seront aimé(e)s

PAST HISTORIC
je fus aimé(e)
tu fus aimé(e)
il (elle) fut aimé(e)
nous fûmes aimé(e)s
vous fûtes aimé(e)(s)
ils (elles) furent aimé(e)s

PERFECT
j'ai été aimé(e)
tu as été aimé(e)
il a (elle) été aimé(e)
nous avons été aimé(e)s
vous avez été aimé(e)(s)
ils (elles) ont été aimé(e)s

PLUPERFECT
j'avais été aimé(e)
tu avais été aimé(e)
il (elle) avait été aimé(e)
nous avions été aimé(e)s
vous aviez été aimé(e)(s)
ils (elles) avaient été aimé(e)s

PAST ANTERIOR
j'eus été etc aimé(e)

FUTURE PERFECT
j'aurai été aimé(e) etc

CONDITIONAL

PRESENT
je serais aimé(e)
tu serais aimé(e)
il (elle) serait aimé(e)
nous serions aimé(e)s
vous seriez aimé(e)(s)
ils (elles) seraient aimé(e)s

PAST
j'aurais été aimé(e)
tu aurais été aimé(e)
il (elle) aurait été aimé(e)
nous aurions été aimé(e)s
vous auriez été aimé(e)(s)
ils (elles) auraient été aimé(e)s

SUBJUNCTIVE

PRESENT
je sois aimé(e)
tu sois aimé(e)
il (elle) soit aimé(e)
nous soyons aimé(e)s
vous soyez aimé(e)(s)
ils (elles) soient aimé(e)s

IMPERFECT
je fusse aimé(e)
tu fusses aimé(e)
il (elle) fût aimé(e)
nous fussions aimé(e)s
vous fussiez aimé(e)(s)
ils (elles) fussent aimé(e)s

PERFECT
j'aie été aimé(e)
tu aies été aimé(e)
il (elle) ait été aimé(e)
nous ayons été aimé(e)s
vous ayez été aimé(e)(s)
ils (elles) aient été aimé(e)s

IMPERATIVE

sois aimé(e)
soyons aimé(e)s
soyez aimé(e)(s)

INFINITIVE

PRESENT
être aimé(e)(s)

PAST
avoir été aimé(e)(s)

PARTICIPLE

PRESENT
étant aimé(e)(s)

PAST
été aimé(e)(s)

ALLER

to go

PRESENT	IMPERFECT	FUTURE
je vais	j'allais	j'irai
tu vas	tu allais	tu iras
il va	il allait	il ira
nous allons	nous allions	nous irons
vous allez	vous alliez	vous irez
ils vont	ils allaient	ils iront
PAST HISTORIC	**PERFECT**	**PLUPERFECT**
j'allai	je suis allé(e)	j'étais allé(e)
tu allas	tu es allé(e)	tu étais allé(e)
il alla	il (elle) est allé(e)	il (elle) était allé(e)
nous allâmes	nous sommes allé(e)s	nous étions allé(e)s
vous allâtes	vous êtes allé(e)(s)	vous étiez allé(e)(s)
ils allèrent	ils (elles) sont allé(e)s	ils (elles) étaient allé(e)s

	CONDITIONAL	
PAST ANTERIOR	**PRESENT**	**PAST**
je fus allé(e) etc	j'irais	je serais allé(e)
	tu irais	tu serais allé(e)
	il irait	il (elle) serait allé(e)
	nous irions	nous serions allé(e)s
FUTURE PERFECT	vous iriez	vous seriez allé(e)(s)
je serai allé(e) etc	ils iraient	ils (elles) seraient allé(e)s

SUBJUNCTIVE		
PRESENT	**IMPERFECT**	**PERFECT**
j'aille	j'allasse	je sois allé(e)
tu ailles	tu allasses	tu sois allé(e)
il aille	il allât	il (elle) soit allé(e)
nous allions	nous allassions	nous soyons allé(e)s
vous alliez	vous allassiez	vous soyez allé(e)(s)
ils aillent	ils allassent	ils (elles) soient allé(e)s

IMPERATIVE	*INFINITIVE*	*PARTICIPLE*
	PRESENT	**PRESENT**
va	aller	allant
allons		
allez	**PAST**	**PAST**
	être allé(e)(s)	allé

APPELER

to call

PRESENT	IMPERFECT	FUTURE
j'appelle	j'appelais	j'appellerai
tu appelles	tu appelais	tu appelleras
il appelle	il appelait	il appellera
nous appelons	nous appelions	nous appellerons
vous appelez	vous appeliez	vous appellerez
ils appellent	ils appelaient	ils appelleront

PAST HISTORIC	PERFECT	PLUPERFECT
j'appelai	j'ai appelé	j'avais appelé
tu appelas	tu as appelé	tu avais appelé
il appela	il a appelé	il avait appelé
nous appelâmes	nous avons appelé	nous avions appelé
vous appelâtes	vous avez appelé	vous aviez appelé
ils appelèrent	ils ont appelé	ils avaient appelé

	CONDITIONAL	
PAST ANTERIOR	**PRESENT**	**PAST**
j'eus appelé etc	j'appellerais	j'aurais appelé
	tu appellerais	tu aurais appelé
	il appellerait	il aurait appelé
	nous appellerions	nous aurions appelé
FUTURE PERFECT	vous appelleriez	vous auriez appelé
j'aurai appelé etc	ils appelleraient	ils auraient appelé

SUBJUNCTIVE

PRESENT	IMPERFECT	PERFECT
j'appelle	j'appelasse	j'aie appelé
tu appelles	tu appelasses	tu aies appelé
il appelle	il appelât	il ait appelé
nous appelions	nous appelassions	nous ayons appelé
vous appeliez	vous appelassiez	vous ayez appelé
ils appellent	ils appelassent	ils aient appelé

IMPERATIVE	*INFINITIVE*	*PARTICIPLE*
	PRESENT	**PRESENT**
appelle	appeler	appelant
appelons		
appelez	**PAST**	**PAST**
	avoir appelé	appelé

ARRIVER

to arrive, to happen

PRESENT	IMPERFECT	FUTURE
j'arrive	j'arrivais	j'arriverai
tu arrives	tu arrivais	tu arriveras
il arrive	il arrivait	il arrivera
nous arrivons	nous arrivions	nous arriverons
vous arrivez	vous arriviez	vous arriverez
ils arrivent	ils arrivaient	ils arriveront
PAST HISTORIC	**PERFECT**	**PLUPERFECT**
j'arrivai	je suis arrivé(e)	j'étais arrivé(e)
tu arrivas	tu es arrivé(e)	tu étais arrivé(e)
il arriva	il (elle) est arrivé(e)	il (elle) était arrivé(e)
nous arrivâmes	nous sommes arrivé(e)s	nous étions arrivé(e)s
vous arrivâtes	vous êtes arrivé(e)(s)	vous étiez arrivé(e)(s)
ils arrivèrent	ils (elles) sont arrivé(e)s	ils (elles) étaient arrivé(e)s

	CONDITIONAL	
PAST ANTERIOR	**PRESENT**	**PAST**
je fus arrivé(e) etc	j'arriverais	je serais arrivé(e)
	tu arriverais	tu serais arrivé(e)
	il arriverait	il (elle) serait arrivé(e)
	nous arriverions	nous serions arrivé(e)s
FUTURE PERFECT	vous arriveriez	vous seriez arrivé(e)(s)
je serai arrivé(e) etc	ils arriveraient	ils (elles) seraient arrivé(e)s

SUBJUNCTIVE		
PRESENT	**IMPERFECT**	**PERFECT**
j'arrive	j'arrivasse	je sois arrivé(e)
tu arrives	tu arrivasses	tu sois arrivé(e)
il arrive	il arrivât	il (elle) soit arrivé(e)
nous arrivions	nous arrivassions	nous soyons arrivé(e)s
vous arriviez	vous arrivassiez	vous soyez arrivé(e)(s)
ils arrivent	ils arrivassent	ils (elles) soient arrivé(e)s

IMPERATIVE	*INFINITIVE*	*PARTICIPLE*
	PRESENT	**PRESENT**
arrive	arriver	arrivant
arrivons		
arrivez	**PAST**	**PAST**
	être arrivé(e)(s)	arrivé

AVOIR
to have

PRESENT	IMPERFECT	FUTURE
j'ai	j'avais	j'aurai
tu as	tu avais	tu auras
il a	il avait	il aura
nous avons	nous avions	nous aurons
vous avez	vous aviez	vous aurez
ils ont	ils avaient	ils auront
PAST HISTORIC	**PERFECT**	**PLUPERFECT**
j'eus	j'ai eu	j'avais eu
tu eus	tu as eu	tu avais eu
il eut	il a eu	il avait eu
nous eûmes	nous avons eu	nous avions eu
vous eûtes	vous avez eu	vous aviez eu
ils eurent	ils ont eu	ils avaient eu

	CONDITIONAL	
PAST ANTERIOR	**PRESENT**	**PAST**
j'eus eu etc	j'aurais	j'aurais eu
	tu aurais	tu aurais eu
	il aurait	il aurait eu
	nous aurions	nous aurions eu
FUTURE PERFECT	vous auriez	vous auriez eu
j'aurai eu etc	ils auraient	ils auraient eu

SUBJUNCTIVE

PRESENT	IMPERFECT	PERFECT
j'aie	je eusse	j'aie eu
tu aies	tu eusses	tu aies eu
il ait	il eût	il ait eu
nous ayons	nous eussions	nous ayons eu
vous ayez	vous eussiez	vous ayez eu
ils aient	ils eussent	ils aient eu

IMPERATIVE	*INFINITIVE*	*PARTICIPLE*
	PRESENT	**PRESENT**
aie	avoir	ayant
ayons		
ayez	**PAST**	**PAST**
	avoir eu	eu

CONDUIRE

to lead, to drive

PRESENT	IMPERFECT	FUTURE
je conduis	je conduisais	je conduirai
tu conduis	tu conduisais	tu conduiras
il conduit	il conduisait	il conduira
nous conduisons	nous conduisions	nous conduirons
vous conduisez	vous conduisiez	vous conduirez
ils conduisent	ils conduisaient	ils conduiront
PAST HISTORIC	**PERFECT**	**PLUPERFECT**
je conduisis	j'ai conduit	j'avais conduit
tu conduisis	tu as conduit	tu avais conduit
il conduisit	il a conduit	il avait conduit
nous conduisîmes	nous avons conduit	nous avions conduit
vous conduisîtes	vous avez conduit	vous aviez conduit
ils conduisirent	ils ont conduit	ils avaient conduit

	CONDITIONAL	
PAST ANTERIOR	**PRESENT**	**PAST**
j'eus conduit etc	je conduirais	j'aurais conduit
	tu conduirais	tu aurais conduit
	il conduirait	il aurait conduit
	nous conduirions	nous aurions conduit
FUTURE PERFECT	vous conduiriez	vous auriez conduit
j'aurai conduit etc	ils conduiraient	ils auraient conduit

SUBJUNCTIVE

PRESENT	IMPERFECT	PERFECT
je conduise	je conduisisse	j'aie conduit
tu conduises	tu conduisisses	tu aies conduit
il conduise	il conduisît	il ait conduit
nous conduisions	nous conduisissions	nous ayons conduit
vous conduisiez	vous conduisissiez	vous ayez conduit
ils conduisent	ils conduisissent	ils aient conduit

IMPERATIVE	*INFINITIVE*	*PARTICIPLE*
	PRESENT	**PRESENT**
conduis	conduire	conduisant
conduisons		
conduisez		
	PAST	**PAST**
	avoir conduit	conduit

CONNAITRE

to know

PRESENT	IMPERFECT	FUTURE
je connais	je connaissais	je connaîtrai
tu connais	tu connaissais	tu connaîtras
il connaît	il connaissait	il connaîtra
nous connaissons	nous connaissions	nous connaîtrons
vous connaissez	vous connaissiez	vous connaîtrez
ils connaissent	ils connaissaient	ils connaîtront
PAST HISTORIC	**PERFECT**	**PLUPERFECT**
je connus	j'ai connu	j'avais connu
tu connus	tu as connu	tu avais connu
il connut	il a connu	il avait connu
nous connûmes	nous avons connu	nous avions connu
vous connûtes	vous avez connu	vous aviez connu
ils connurent	ils ont connu	ils avaient connu

CONDITIONAL

PAST ANTERIOR	PRESENT	PAST
j'eus connu etc	je connaîtrais	j'aurais connu
	tu connaîtrais	tu aurais connu
	il connaîtrait	il aurait connu
	nous connaîtrions	nous aurions connu
FUTURE PERFECT	vous connaîtriez	vous auriez connu
j'aurai connu etc	ils connaîtraient	ils auraient connu

SUBJUNCTIVE

PRESENT	IMPERFECT	PERFECT
je connaisse	je connusse	j'aie connu
tu connaisses	tu connusses	tu aies connu
il connaisse	il connût	il ait connu
nous connaissions	nous connussions	nous ayons connu
vous connaissiez	vous connussiez	vous ayez connu
ils connaissent	ils connussent	ils aient connu

IMPERATIVE	*INFINITIVE*	*PARTICIPLE*
	PRESENT	**PRESENT**
connais	connaître	connaissant
connaissons		
connaissez	**PAST**	**PAST**
	avoir connu	connu

CROIRE

to believe

PRESENT	IMPERFECT	FUTURE
je crois	je croyais	je croirai
tu crois	tu croyais	tu croiras
il croit	il croyait	il croira
nous croyons	nous croyions	nous croirons
vous croyez	vous croyiez	vous croirez
ils croient	ils croyaient	ils croiront
PAST HISTORIC	**PERFECT**	**PLUPERFECT**
je crus	j'ai cru	j'avais cru
tu crus	tu as cru	tu avais cru
il crut	il a cru	il avait cru
nous crûmes	nous avons cru	nous avions cru
vous crûtes	vous avez cru	vous aviez cru
ils crurent	ils ont cru	ils avaient cru

	CONDITIONAL	
PAST ANTERIOR	**PRESENT**	**PAST**
j'eus cru etc	je croirais	j'aurais cru
	tu croirais	tu aurais cru
	il croirait	il aurait cru
	nous croirions	nous aurions cru
FUTURE PERFECT	vous croiriez	vous auriez cru
j'aurai cru etc	ils croiraient	ils auraient cru

SUBJUNCTIVE

PRESENT	IMPERFECT	PERFECT
je croie	je crusse	j'aie cru
tu croies	tu crusses	tu aies cru
il croie	il crût	il ait cru
nous croyions	nous crussions	nous ayons cru
vous croyiez	vous crussiez	vous ayez cru
ils croient	ils crussent	ils aient cru

IMPERATIVE	*INFINITIVE*	*PARTICIPLE*
	PRESENT	**PRESENT**
crois	croire	croyant
croyons		
croyez	**PAST**	**PAST**
	avoir cru	cru

DEVOIR

to have to

PRESENT	IMPERFECT	FUTURE
je dois	je devais	je devrai
tu dois	tu devais	tu devras
il doit	il devait	il devra
nous devons	nous devions	nous devrons
vous devez	vous deviez	vous devrez
ils doivent	ils devaient	ils devront
PAST HISTORIC	**PERFECT**	**PLUPERFECT**
je dus	j'ai dû	j'avais dû
tu dus	tu as dû	tu avais dû
il dut	il a dû	il avait dû
nous dûmes	nous avons dû	nous avions dû
vous dûtes	vous avez dû	vous aviez dû
ils durent	ils ont dû	ils avaient dû

CONDITIONAL

PAST ANTERIOR	PRESENT	PAST
j'eus dû etc	je devrais	j'aurais dû
	tu devrais	tu aurais dû
	il devrait	il aurait dû
	nous devrions	nous aurions dû
FUTURE PERFECT	vous devriez	vous auriez dû
j'aurai dû etc	ils devraient	ils auraient dû

SUBJUNCTIVE

PRESENT	IMPERFECT	PERFECT
je doive	je dusse	j'aie dû
tu doives	tu dusses	tu aies dû
il doive	il dût	il ait dû
nous devions	nous dussions	nous ayons dû
vous deviez	vous dussiez	vous ayez dû
ils doivent	ils dussent	ils aient dû

IMPERATIVE	*INFINITIVE*	*PARTICIPLE*
	PRESENT	**PRESENT**
dois	devoir	devant
devons		
devez	**PAST**	**PAST**
(rarely used)	avoir dû	dû

DIRE

to say

PRESENT	IMPERFECT	FUTURE
je dis	je disais	je dirai
tu dis	tu disais	tu diras
il dit	il disait	il dira
nous disons	nous disions	nous dirons
vous dites	vous disiez	vous direz
ils disent	ils disaient	ils diront
PAST HISTORIC	**PERFECT**	**PLUPERFECT**
je dis	j'ai dit	j'avais dit
tu dis	tu as dit	tu avais dit
il dit	il a dit	il avait dit
nous dîmes	nous avons dit	nous avions dit
vous dîtes	vous avez dit	vous aviez dit
ils dirent	ils ont dit	ils avaient dit

	CONDITIONAL	
PAST ANTERIOR	**PRESENT**	**PAST**
j'eus dit etc	je dirais	j'aurais dit
	tu dirais	tu aurais dit
	il dirait	il aurait dit
	nous dirions	nous aurions dit
FUTURE PERFECT	vous diriez	vous auriez dit
j'aurai dit etc	ils diraient	ils auraient dit

SUBJUNCTIVE		
PRESENT	**IMPERFECT**	**PERFECT**
je dise	je disse	j'aie dit
tu dises	tu disses	tu aies dit
il dise	il dît	il ait dit
nous disions	nous dissions	nous ayons dit
vous disiez	vous dissiez	vous ayez dit
ils disent	ils dissent	ils aient dit

IMPERATIVE	*INFINITIVE*	*PARTICIPLE*
	PRESENT	**PRESENT**
dis	dire	disant
disons		
dites		
	PAST	**PAST**
	avoir dit	dit

DORMIR
to sleep

PRESENT	IMPERFECT	FUTURE
je dors	je dormais	je dormirai
tu dors	tu dormais	tu dormiras
il dort	il dormait	il dormira
nous dormons	nous dormions	nous dormirons
vous dormez	vous dormiez	vous dormirez
ils dorment	ils dormaient	ils dormiront

PAST HISTORIC	PERFECT	PLUPERFECT
je dormis	j'ai dormi	j'avais dormi
tu dormis	tu as dormi	tu avais dormi
il dormit	il a dormi	il avait dormi
nous dormîmes	nous avons dormi	nous avions dormi
vous dormîtes	vous avez dormi	vous aviez dormi
ils dormirent	ils ont dormi	ils avaient dormi

CONDITIONAL

PAST ANTERIOR	PRESENT	PAST
j'eus dormi etc	je dormirais	j'aurais dormi
	tu dormirais	tu aurais dormi
	il dormirait	il aurait dormi
	nous dormirions	nous aurions dormi
FUTURE PERFECT	vous dormiriez	vous auriez dormi
j'aurai dormi etc	ils dormiraient	ils auraient dormi

SUBJUNCTIVE

PRESENT	IMPERFECT	PERFECT
je dorme	je dormisse	j'aie dormi
tu dormes	tu dormisses	tu aies dormi
il dorme	il dormît	il ait dormi
nous dormions	nous dormissions	nous ayons dormi
vous dormiez	vous dormissiez	vous ayez dormi
ils dorment	ils dormissent	ils aient dormi

IMPERATIVE	*INFINITIVE*	*PARTICIPLE*
	PRESENT	**PRESENT**
dors	dormir	dormant
dormons		
dormez	**PAST**	**PAST**
	avoir dormi	dormi

ECRIRE

to write

PRESENT	IMPERFECT	FUTURE
j'écris	j'écrivais	j'écrirai
tu écris	tu écrivais	tu écriras
il écrit	il écrivait	il écrira
nous écrivons	nous écrivions	nous écrirons
vous écrivez	vous écriviez	vous écrirez
ils écrivent	ils écrivaient	ils écriront
PAST HISTORIC	**PERFECT**	**PLUPERFECT**
j'écrivis	j'ai écrit	j'avais écrit
tu écrivis	tu as écrit	tu avais écrit
il écrivit	il a écrit	il avait écrit
nous écrivîmes	nous avons écrit	nous avions écrit
vous écrivîtes	vous avez écrit	vous aviez écrit
ils écrivirent	ils ont écrit	ils avaient écrit

CONDITIONAL

PAST ANTERIOR	PRESENT	PAST
j'eus écrit etc	j'écrirais	j'aurais écrit
	tu écrirais	tu aurais écrit
	il écrirait	il aurait écrit
	nous écririons	nous aurions écrit
FUTURE PERFECT	vous écririez	vous auriez écrit
j'aurai écrit etc	ils écriraient	ils auraient écrit

SUBJUNCTIVE

PRESENT	IMPERFECT	PERFECT
j'écrive	j'écrivisse	j'aie écrit
tu écrives	tu écrivisses	tu aies écrit
il écrive	il écrivît	il ait écrit
nous écrivions	nous écrivissions	nous ayons écrit
vous écriviez	vous écrivissiez	vous ayez écrit
ils écrivent	ils écrivissent	ils aient écrit

IMPERATIVE	*INFINITIVE*	*PARTICIPLE*
	PRESENT	**PRESENT**
écris	écrire	écrivant
écrivons		
écrivez	**PAST**	**PAST**
	avoir écrit	écrit

ESPERER

to hope

PRESENT	IMPERFECT	FUTURE
j'espère	j'espérais	j'espérerai
tu espères	tu espérais	tu espéreras
il espère	il espérait	il espérera
nous espérons	nous espérions	nous espérerons
vous espérez	vous espériez	vous espérerez
ils espèrent	ils espéraient	ils espéreront

PAST HISTORIC	PERFECT	PLUPERFECT
j'espérai	j'ai espéré	j'avais espéré
tu espéras	tu as espéré	tu avais espéré
il espéra	il a espéré	il avait espéré
nous espérâmes	nous avons espéré	nous avions espéré
vous espérâtes	vous avez espéré	vous aviez espéré
ils espérèrent	ils ont espéré	ils avaient espéré

CONDITIONAL

PAST ANTERIOR	PRESENT	PAST
j'eus espéré etc	j'espérerais	j'aurais espéré
	tu espérerais	tu aurais espéré
	il espérerait	il aurait espéré
	nous espérerions	nous aurions espéré
FUTURE PERFECT	vous espéreriez	vous auriez espéré
j'aurai espéré etc	ils espéreraient	ils auraient espéré

SUBJUNCTIVE

PRESENT	IMPERFECT	PERFECT
j'espère	j'espérasse	j'aie espéré
tu espères	tu espérasses	tu aies espéré
il espère	il espérât	il ait espéré
nous espérions	nous espérassions	nous ayons espéré
vous espériez	vous espérassiez	vous ayez espéré
ils espèrent	ils espérassent	ils aient espéré

IMPERATIVE	*INFINITIVE*	*PARTICIPLE*
	PRESENT	**PRESENT**
espère	espérer	espérant
espérons		
espérez	**PAST**	**PAST**
	avoir espéré	espéré

ETRE
to be

PRESENT	IMPERFECT	FUTURE
je suis	j'étais	je serai
tu es	tu étais	tu seras
il est	il était	il sera
nous sommes	nous étions	nous serons
vous êtes	vous étiez	vous serez
ils sont	ils étaient	ils seront
PAST HISTORIC	**PERFECT**	**PLUPERFECT**
je fus	j'ai été	j'avais été
tu fus	tu as été	tu avais été
il fut	il a été	il avait été
nous fûmes	nous avons été	nous avions été
vous fûtes	vous avez été	vous aviez été
ils furent	ils ont été	ils avaient été

	CONDITIONAL	
PAST ANTERIOR	**PRESENT**	**PAST**
j'eus été etc	je serais	j'aurais été
	tu serais	tu aurais été
	il serait	il aurait été
	nous serions	nous aurions été
FUTURE PERFECT	vous seriez	vous auriez été
j'aurai été etc	ils seraient	ils auraient été

SUBJUNCTIVE

PRESENT	IMPERFECT	PERFECT
je sois	je fusse	j'aie été
tu sois	tu fusses	tu aies été
il soit	il fût	il ait été
nous soyons	nous fussions	nous ayons été
vous soyez	vous fussiez	vous ayez été
ils soient	ils fussent	ils aient été

IMPERATIVE	*INFINITIVE*	*PARTICIPLE*
	PRESENT	**PRESENT**
sois	être	étant
soyons		
soyez	**PAST**	**PAST**
	avoir été	été

FAIRE

to do, to make

PRESENT	IMPERFECT	FUTURE
je fais	je faisais	je ferai
tu fais	tu faisais	tu feras
il fait	il faisait	il fera
nous faisons	nous faisions	nous ferons
vous faites	vous faisiez	vous ferez
ils font	ils faisaient	ils feront

PAST HISTORIC	PERFECT	PLUPERFECT
je fis	j'ai fait	j'avais fait
tu fis	tu as fait	tu avais fait
il fit	il a fait	il avait fait
nous fîmes	nous avons fait	nous avions fait
vous fîtes	vous avez fait	vous aviez fait
ils firent	ils ont fait	ils avaient fait

CONDITIONAL

PAST ANTERIOR	PRESENT	PAST
j'eus fait etc	je ferais	j'aurais fait
	tu ferais	tu aurais fait
	il ferait	il aurait fait
	nous ferions	nous aurions fait
FUTURE PERFECT	vous feriez	vous auriez fait
j'aurai fait etc	ils feraient	ils auraient fait

SUBJUNCTIVE

PRESENT	IMPERFECT	PERFECT
je fasse	je fisse	j'aie fait
tu fasses	tu fisses	tu aies fait
il fasse	il fît	il ait fait
nous fassions	nous fissions	nous ayons fait
vous fassiez	vous fissiez	vous ayez fait
ils fassent	ils fissent	ils aient fait

IMPERATIVE	*INFINITIVE*	*PARTICIPLE*
	PRESENT	**PRESENT**
fais	faire	faisant
faisons		
faites	**PAST**	**PAST**
	avoir fait	fait

FALLOIR

to be necessary

PRESENT	IMPERFECT	FUTURE
il faut	il fallait	il faudra

PAST HISTORIC	PERFECT	PLUPERFECT
il fallut	il a fallu	il avait fallu

PAST ANTERIOR	*CONDITIONAL* PRESENT	PAST
il eut fallu	il faudrait	il aurait fallu

FUTURE PERFECT
il aura fallu

SUBJUNCTIVE

PRESENT	IMPERFECT	PERFECT
il faille	il fallût	il ait fallu

IMPERATIVE	*INFINITIVE*	*PARTICIPLE*
	PRESENT	**PRESENT**
(none)	falloir	*(none)*
	PAST	**PAST**
	avoir fallu	fallu

FINIR
to finish

PRESENT	IMPERFECT	FUTURE
je finis	je finissais	je finirai
tu finis	tu finissais	tu finiras
il finit	il finissait	il finira
nous finissons	nous finissions	nous finirons
vous finissez	vous finissiez	vous finirez
ils finissent	ils finissaient	ils finiront

PAST HISTORIC	PERFECT	PLUPERFECT
je finis	j'ai fini	j'avais fini
tu finis	tu as fini	tu avais fini
il finit	il a fini	il avait fini
nous finîmes	nous avons fini	nous avions fini
vous finîtes	vous avez fini	vous aviez fini
ils finirent	ils ont fini	ils avaient fini

CONDITIONAL

PAST ANTERIOR	PRESENT	PAST
j'eus fini etc	je finirais	j'aurais fini
	tu finirais	tu aurais fini
	il finirait	il aurait fini
	nous finirions	nous aurions fini
FUTURE PERFECT	vous finiriez	vous auriez fini
j'aurai fini etc	ils finiraient	ils auraient fini

SUBJUNCTIVE

PRESENT	IMPERFECT	PERFECT
je finisse	je finisse	j'aie fini
tu finisses	tu finisses	tu aies fini
il finisse	il finît	il ait fini
nous finissions	nous finissions	nous ayons fini
vous finissiez	vous finissiez	vous ayez fini
ils finissent	ils finissent	ils aient fini

IMPERATIVE	*INFINITIVE*	*PARTICIPLE*
	PRESENT	**PRESENT**
finis	finir	finissant
finissons		
finissez	**PAST**	**PAST**
	avoir fini	fini

JETER
to throw

PRESENT	IMPERFECT	FUTURE
je jette	je jetais	je jetterai
tu jettes	tu jetais	tu jetteras
il jette	il jetait	il jettera
nous jetons	nous jetions	nous jetterons
vous jetez	vous jetiez	vous jetterez
ils jettent	ils jetaient	ils jetteront
PAST HISTORIC	**PERFECT**	**PLUPERFECT**
je jetai	j'ai jeté	j'avais jeté
tu jetas	tu as jeté	tu avais jeté
il jeta	il a jeté	il avait jeté
nous jetâmes	nous avons jeté	nous avions jeté
vous jetâtes	vous avez jeté	vous aviez jeté
ils jetèrent	ils ont jeté	ils avaient jeté

	CONDITIONAL	
PAST ANTERIOR	**PRESENT**	**PAST**
j'eus jeté etc	je jetterais	j'aurais jeté
	tu jetterais	tu aurais jeté
	il jetterait	il aurait jeté
	nous jetterions	nous aurions jeté
FUTURE PERFECT	vous jetteriez	vous auriez jeté
j'aurai jeté etc	ils jetteraient	ils auraient jeté

SUBJUNCTIVE

PRESENT	IMPERFECT	PERFECT
je jette	je jetasse	j'aie jeté
tu jettes	tu jetasses	tu aies jeté
il jette	il jetât	il ait jeté
nous jetions	nous jetassions	nous ayons jeté
vous jetiez	vous jetassiez	vous ayez jeté
ils jettent	ils jetassent	ils aient jeté

IMPERATIVE	*INFINITIVE*	*PARTICIPLE*
	PRESENT	**PRESENT**
jette	jeter	jetant
jetons		
jetez		
	PAST	**PAST**
	avoir jeté	jeté

SE MEFIER

to be suspicious

PRESENT	IMPERFECT	FUTURE
je me méfie	je me méfiais	je me méfierai
tu te méfies	tu te méfiais	tu te méfieras
il se méfie	il se méfiait	il se méfiera
nous nous méfions	nous nous méfiions	nous nous méfierons
vous vous méfiez	vous vous méfiiez	vous vous méfierez
ils se méfient	ils se méfiaient	ils se méfieront
PAST HISTORIC	**PERFECT**	**PLUPERFECT**
je me méfiai	je me suis méfié(e)	je m'étais méfié(e)
tu te méfias	tu t'es méfié(e)	tu t'étais méfié(e)
il se méfia	il (elle) s'est méfié(e)	il (elle) s'était méfié(e)
nous nous méfiâmes	nous nous sommes méfié(e)s	nous nous étions méfié(e)s
vous vous méfiâtes	vous vous êtes méfié(e)(s)	vous vous étiez méfié(e)(s)
ils se méfièrent	ils (elles) se sont méfié(e)s	ils (elles) s'étaient méfié(e)s

	CONDITIONAL	
PAST ANTERIOR	**PRESENT**	**PAST**
je me fus méfié(e) etc	je me méfierais	je me serais méfié(e)
	tu te méfierais	tu te serais méfié(e)
	il se méfierait	il (elle) se serait méfié(e)
	nous nous méfierions	nous nous serions méfié(e)s
FUTURE PERFECT	vous vous méfieriez	vous vous seriez méfié(e)(s)
je me serai méfié(e) etc	ils (elles) se méfieraient	ils (elles) se seraient méfié(e)s

SUBJUNCTIVE

PRESENT	IMPERFECT	PERFECT
je me méfie	je me méfiasse	je me sois méfié(e)
tu te méfies	tu te méfiasses	tu te sois méfié(e)
il se méfie	il se méfiât	il (elle) se soit méfié(e)
nous nous méfiions	nous nous méfiassions	nous nous soyons méfié(e)s
vous vous méfiiez	vous vous méfiassiez	vous vous soyez méfié(e)(s)
ils se méfient	ils se méfiassent	ils (elles) se soient méfié(e)s

IMPERATIVE	*INFINITIVE*	*PARTICIPLE*
	PRESENT	**PRESENT**
méfie-toi	se méfier	se méfiant
méfions-nous		
méfiez-vous		
	PAST	**PAST**
	s'être méfié(e)(s)	méfié

METTRE

to put

PRESENT	IMPERFECT	FUTURE
je mets	je mettais	je mettrai
tu mets	tu mettais	tu mettras
il met	il mettait	il mettra
nous mettons	nous mettions	nous mettrons
vous mettez	vous mettiez	vous mettrez
ils mettent	ils mettaient	ils mettront
PAST HISTORIC	**PERFECT**	**PLUPERFECT**
je mis	j'ai mis	j'avais mis
tu mis	tu as mis	tu avais mis
il mit	il a mis	il avait mis
nous mîmes	nous avons mis	nous avions mis
vous mîtes	vous avez mis	vous aviez mis
ils mirent	ils ont mis	ils avaient mis

	CONDITIONAL	
PAST ANTERIOR	**PRESENT**	**PAST**
j'eus mis etc	je mettrais	j'aurais mis
	tu mettrais	tu aurais mis
	il mettrait	il aurait mis
	nous mettrions	nous aurions mis
FUTURE PERFECT	vous mettriez	vous auriez mis
j'aurai mis etc	ils mettraient	ils auraient mis

SUBJUNCTIVE

PRESENT	IMPERFECT	PERFECT
je mette	je misse	j'aie mis
tu mettes	tu misses	tu aies mis
il mette	il mît	il ait mis
nous mettions	nous missions	nous ayons mis
vous mettiez	vous missiez	vous ayez mis
ils mettent	ils missent	ils aient mis

IMPERATIVE	*INFINITIVE*	*PARTICIPLE*
	PRESENT	**PRESENT**
mets	mettre	mettant
mettons		
mettez	**PAST**	**PAST**
	avoir mis	mis

OUVRIR

to open

PRESENT	IMPERFECT	FUTURE
j'ouvre	j'ouvrais	j'ouvrirai
tu ouvres	tu ouvrais	tu ouvriras
il ouvre	il ouvrait	il ouvrira
nous ouvrons	nous ouvrions	nous ouvrirons
vous ouvrez	vous ouvriez	vous ouvrirez
ils ouvrent	ils ouvraient	ils ouvriront

PAST HISTORIC	PERFECT	PLUPERFECT
j'ouvris	j'ai ouvert	j'avais ouvert
tu ouvris	tu as ouvert	tu avais ouvert
il ouvrit	il a ouvert	il avait ouvert
nous ouvrîmes	nous avons ouvert	nous avions ouvert
vous ouvrîtes	vous avez ouvert	vous aviez ouvert
ils ouvrirent	ils ont ouvert	ils avaient ouvert

CONDITIONAL

PAST ANTERIOR	PRESENT	PAST
j'eus ouvert etc	j'ouvrirais	j'aurais ouvert
	tu ouvrirais	tu aurais ouvert
	il ouvrirait	il aurait ouvert
	nous ouvririons	nous aurions ouvert
FUTURE PERFECT	vous ouvririez	vous auriez ouvert
j'aurai ouvert etc	ils ouvriraient	ils auraient ouvert

SUBJUNCTIVE

PRESENT	IMPERFECT	PERFECT
j'ouvre	j'ouvrisse	j'aie ouvert
tu ouvres	tu ouvrisses	tu aies ouvert
il ouvre	il ouvrît	il ait ouvert
nous ouvrions	nous ouvrissions	nous ayons ouvert
vous ouvriez	vous ouvrissiez	vous ayez ouvert
ils ouvrent	ils ouvrissent	ils aient ouvert

IMPERATIVE	*INFINITIVE*	*PARTICIPLE*
	PRESENT	**PRESENT**
ouvre	ouvrir	ouvrant
ouvrons		
ouvrez	**PAST**	**PAST**
	avoir ouvert	ouvert

POUVOIR

to be able to

PRESENT	IMPERFECT	FUTURE
je peux	je pouvais	je pourrai
tu peux	tu pouvais	tu pourras
il peut	il pouvait	il pourra
nous pouvons	nous pouvions	nous pourrons
vous pouvez	vous pouviez	vous pourrez
ils peuvent	ils pouvaient	ils pourront
PAST HISTORIC	**PERFECT**	**PLUPERFECT**
je pus	j'ai pu	j'avais pu
tu pus	tu as pu	tu avais pu
il put	il a pu	il avait pu
nous pûmes	nous avons pu	nous avions pu
vous pûtes	vous avez pu	vous aviez pu
ils purent	ils ont pu	ils avaient pu

CONDITIONAL

PAST ANTERIOR	PRESENT	PAST
j'eus pu etc	je pourrais	j'aurais pu
	tu pourrais	tu aurais pu
	il pourrait	il aurait pu
	nous pourrions	nous aurions pu
FUTURE PERFECT	vous pourriez	vous auriez pu
j'aurai pu etc	ils pourraient	ils auraient pu

SUBJUNCTIVE

PRESENT	IMPERFECT	PERFECT
je puisse	je pusse	j'aie pu
tu puisses	tu pusses	tu aies pu
il puisse	il pût	il ait pu
nous puissions	nous pussions	nous ayons pu
vous puissiez	vous pussiez	vous ayez pu
ils puissent	ils pussent	ils aient pu

IMPERATIVE	*INFINITIVE*	*PARTICIPLE*
	PRESENT	**PRESENT**
(none)	pouvoir	pouvant
	PAST	**PAST**
	avoir pu	pu

PRENDRE
to take

PRESENT	IMPERFECT	FUTURE
je prends	je prenais	je prendrai
tu prends	tu prenais	tu prendras
il prend	il prenait	il prendra
nous prenons	nous prenions	nous prendrons
vous prenez	vous preniez	vous prendrez
ils prennent	ils prenaient	ils prendront

PAST HISTORIC	PERFECT	PLUPERFECT
je pris	j'ai pris	j'avais pris
tu pris	tu as pris	tu avais pris
il prit	il a pris	il avait pris
nous prîmes	nous avons pris	nous avions pris
vous prîtes	vous avez pris	vous aviez pris
ils prirent	ils ont pris	ils avaient pris

CONDITIONAL

PAST ANTERIOR	PRESENT	PAST
j'eus pris etc	je prendrais	j'aurais pris
	tu prendrais	tu aurais pris
	il prendrait	il aurait pris
	nous prendrions	nous aurions pris
FUTURE PERFECT	vous prendriez	vous auriez pris
j'aurai pris etc	ils prendraient	ils auraient pris

SUBJUNCTIVE

PRESENT	IMPERFECT	PERFECT
je prenne	je prisse	j'aie pris
tu prennes	tu prisses	tu aies pris
il prenne	il prît	il ait pris
nous prenions	nous prissions	nous ayons pris
vous preniez	vous prissiez	vous ayez pris
ils prennent	ils prissent	ils aient pris

IMPERATIVE	*INFINITIVE*	*PARTICIPLE*
	PRESENT	**PRESENT**
prends	prendre	prenant
prenons	**PAST**	**PAST**
prenez	avoir pris	pris

RECEVOIR

to receive

PRESENT	IMPERFECT	FUTURE
je reçois	je recevais	je recevrai
tu reçois	tu recevais	tu recevras
il reçoit	il recevait	il recevra
nous recevons	nous recevions	nous recevrons
vous recevez	vous receviez	vous recevrez
ils reçoivent	ils recevaient	ils recevront
PAST HISTORIC	**PERFECT**	**PLUPERFECT**
je reçus	j'ai reçu	j'avais reçu
tu reçus	tu as reçu	tu avais reçu
il reçut	il a reçu	il avait reçu
nous reçûmes	nous avons reçu	nous avions reçu
vous reçûtes	vous avez reçu	vous aviez reçu
ils reçurent	ils ont reçu	ils avaient reçu

	CONDITIONAL	
PAST ANTERIOR	**PRESENT**	**PAST**
j'eus reçu etc	je recevrais	j'aurais reçu
	tu recevrais	tu aurais reçu
	il recevrait	il aurait reçu
	nous recevrions	nous aurions reçu
FUTURE PERFECT	vous recevriez	vous auriez reçu
j'aurai reçu etc	ils recevraient	ils auraient reçu

SUBJUNCTIVE

PRESENT	IMPERFECT	PERFECT
je reçoive	je reçusse	j'aie reçu
tu reçoives	tu reçusses	tu aies reçu
il reçoive	il reçût	il ait reçu
nous recevions	nous reçussions	nous ayons reçu
vous receviez	vous reçussiez	vous ayez reçu
ils reçoivent	ils reçussent	ils aient reçu

IMPERATIVE	*INFINITIVE*	*PARTICIPLE*
	PRESENT	**PRESENT**
reçois	recevoir	recevant
recevons		
recevez	**PAST**	**PAST**
	avoir reçu	reçu

SAVOIR
to know

PRESENT	IMPERFECT	FUTURE
je sais	je savais	je saurai
tu sais	tu savais	tu sauras
il sait	il savait	il saura
nous savons	nous savions	nous saurons
vous savez	vous saviez	vous saurez
ils savent	ils savaient	ils sauront
PAST HISTORIC	**PERFECT**	**PLUPERFECT**
je sus	j'ai su	j'avais su
tu sus	tu as su	tu avais su
il sut	il a su	il avait su
nous sûmes	nous avons su	nous avions su
vous sûtes	vous avez su	vous aviez su
ils surent	ils ont su	ils avaient su

CONDITIONAL

PAST ANTERIOR	PRESENT	PAST
j'eus su etc	je saurais	j'aurais su
	tu saurais	tu aurais su
	il saurait	il aurait su
	nous saurions	nous aurions su
FUTURE PERFECT	vous sauriez	vous auriez su
j'aurai su etc	ils sauraient	ils auraient su

SUBJUNCTIVE

PRESENT	IMPERFECT	PERFECT
je sache	je susse	j'aie su
tu saches	tu susses	tu aies su
il sache	il sût	il ait su
nous sachions	nous sussions	nous ayons su
vous sachiez	vous sussiez	vous ayez su
ils sachent	ils sussent	ils aient su

IMPERATIVE	*INFINITIVE*	*PARTICIPLE*
	PRESENT	**PRESENT**
sache	savoir	sachant
sachons		
sachez	**PAST**	**PAST**
	avoir su	su

TENIR
to hold

PRESENT	IMPERFECT	FUTURE
je tiens	je tenais	je tiendrai
tu tiens	tu tenais	tu tiendras
il tient	il tenait	il tiendra
nous tenons	nous tenions	nous tiendrons
vous tenez	vous teniez	vous tiendrez
ils tiennent	ils tenaient	ils tiendront
PAST HISTORIC	**PERFECT**	**PLUPERFECT**
je tins	j'ai tenu	j'avais tenu
tu tins	tu as tenu	tu avais tenu
il tint	il a tenu	il avait tenu
nous tînmes	nous avons tenu	nous avions tenu
vous tîntes	vous avez tenu	vous aviez tenu
ils tinrent	ils ont tenu	ils avaient tenu

	CONDITIONAL	
PAST ANTERIOR	**PRESENT**	**PAST**
j'eus tenu etc	je tiendrais	j'aurais tenu
	tu tiendrais	tu aurais tenu
	il tiendrait	il aurait tenu
	nous tiendrions	nous aurions tenu
FUTURE PERFECT	vous tiendriez	vous auriez tenu
j'aurai tenu etc	ils tiendraient	ils auraient tenu

SUBJUNCTIVE

PRESENT	IMPERFECT	PERFECT
je tienne	je tinsse	j'aie tenu
tu tiennes	tu tinsses	tu aies tenu
il tienne	il tînt	il ait tenu
nous tenions	nous tinssions	nous ayons tenu
vous teniez	vous tinssiez	vous ayez tenu
ils tiennent	ils tinssent	ils aient tenu

IMPERATIVE	*INFINITIVE*	*PARTICIPLE*
	PRESENT	**PRESENT**
tiens	tenir	tenant
tenons		
tenez	**PAST**	**PAST**
	avoir tenu	tenu

VENDRE
to sell

PRESENT	IMPERFECT	FUTURE
je vends	je vendais	je vendrai
tu vends	tu vendais	tu vendras
il vend	il vendait	il vendra
nous vendons	nous vendions	nous vendrons
vous vendez	vous vendiez	vous vendrez
ils vendent	ils vendaient	ils vendront
PAST HISTORIC	**PERFECT**	**PLUPERFECT**
je vendis	j'ai vendu	j'avais vendu
tu vendis	tu as vendu	tu avais vendu
il vendit	il a vendu	il avait vendu
nous vendîmes	nous avons vendu	nous avions vendu
vous vendîtes	vous avez vendu	vous aviez vendu
ils vendirent	ils ont vendu	ils avaient vendu

CONDITIONAL

PAST ANTERIOR	PRESENT	PAST
j'eus vendu etc	je vendrais	j'aurais vendu
	tu vendrais	tu aurais vendu
	il vendrait	il aurait vendu
	nous vendrions	nous aurions vendu
FUTURE PERFECT	vous vendriez	vous auriez vendu
j'aurai vendu etc	ils vendraient	ils auraient vendu

SUBJUNCTIVE

PRESENT	IMPERFECT	PERFECT
je vende	je vendisse	j'aie vendu
tu vendes	tu vendisses	tu aies vendu
il vende	il vendît	il ait vendu
nous vendions	nous vendissions	nous ayons vendu
vous vendiez	vous vendissiez	vous ayez vendu
ils vendent	ils vendissent	ils aient vendu

IMPERATIVE	*INFINITIVE*	*PARTICIPLE*
	PRESENT	**PRESENT**
vends	vendre	vendant
vendons		
vendez		
	PAST	**PAST**
	avoir vendu	vendu

VENIR

to come

PRESENT	IMPERFECT	FUTURE
je viens	je venais	je viendrai
tu viens	tu venais	tu viendras
il vient	il venait	il viendra
nous venons	nous venions	nous viendrons
vous venez	vous veniez	vous viendrez
ils viennent	ils venaient	ils viendront
PAST HISTORIC	**PERFECT**	**PLUPERFECT**
je vins	je suis venu(e)	j'étais venu(e)
tu vins	tu es venu(e)	tu étais venu(e)
il vint	il (elle) est venu(e)	il (elle) était venu(e)
nous vînmes	nous sommes venu(e)s	nous étions venu(e)s
vous vîntes	vous êtes venu(e)(s)	vous étiez venu(e)(s)
ils vinrent	ils (elles) sont venu(e)s	ils (elles) étaient venu(e)s

CONDITIONAL

PAST ANTERIOR	PRESENT	PAST
je fus venu(e) etc	je viendrais	je serais venu(e)
	tu viendrais	tu serais venu(e)
	il viendrait	il (elle) serait venu(e)
	nous viendrions	nous serions venu(e)s
FUTURE PERFECT	vous viendriez	vous seriez venu(e)(s)
je serai venu(e) etc	ils viendraient	ils (elles) seraient venu(e)s

SUBJUNCTIVE

PRESENT	IMPERFECT	PERFECT
je vienne	je vinsse	je sois venu(e)
tu viennes	tu vinsses	tu sois venu(e)
il vienne	il vînt	il (elle) soit venu(e)
nous venions	nous vinssions	nous soyons venu(e)s
vous veniez	vous vinssiez	vous soyez venu(e)(s)
ils viennent	ils vinssent	ils (elles) soient venu(e)s

IMPERATIVE	*INFINITIVE*	*PARTICIPLE*
	PRESENT	**PRESENT**
viens	venir	venant
venons	**PAST**	**PAST**
venez	être venu(e)(s)	venu

VIVRE
to live

PRESENT	IMPERFECT	FUTURE
je vis	je vivais	je vivrai
tu vis	tu vivais	tu vivras
il vit	il vivait	il vivra
nous vivons	nous vivions	nous vivrons
vous vivez	vous viviez	vous vivrez
ils vivent	ils vivaient	ils vivront
PAST HISTORIC	**PERFECT**	**PLUPERFECT**
je vécus	j'ai vécu	j'avais vécu
tu vécus	tu as vécu	tu avais vécu
il vécut	il a vécu	il avait vécu
nous vécûmes	nous avons vécu	nous avions vécu
vous vécûtes	vous avez vécu	vous aviez vécu
ils vécurent	ils ont vécu	ils avaient vécu

CONDITIONAL

PAST ANTERIOR	PRESENT	PAST
j'eus vécu etc	je vivrais	j'aurais vécu
	tu vivrais	tu aurais vécu
	il vivrait	il aurait vécu
	nous vivrions	nous aurions vécu
FUTURE PERFECT	vous vivriez	vous auriez vécu
j'aurai vécu etc	ils vivraient	ils auraient vécu

SUBJUNCTIVE

PRESENT	IMPERFECT	PERFECT
je vive	je vécusse	j'aie vécu
tu vives	tu vécusses	tu aies vécu
il vive	il vécût	il ait vécu
nous vivions	nous vécussions	nous ayons vécu
vous viviez	vous vécussiez	vous ayez vécu
ils vivent	ils vécussent	ils aient vécu

IMPERATIVE	*INFINITIVE*	*PARTICIPLE*
	PRESENT	**PRESENT**
vis	vivre	vivant
vivons		
vivez	**PAST**	**PAST**
	avoir vécu	vécu

VOIR
to see

PRESENT	IMPERFECT	FUTURE
je vois	je voyais	je verrai
tu vois	tu voyais	tu verras
il voit	il voyait	il verra
nous voyons	nous voyions	nous verrons
vous voyez	vous voyiez	vous verrez
ils voient	ils voyaient	ils verront
PAST HISTORIC	**PERFECT**	**PLUPERFECT**
je vis	j'ai vu	j'avais vu
tu vis	tu as vu	tu avais vu
il vit	il a vu	il avait vu
nous vîmes	nous avons vu	nous avions vu
vous vîtes	vous avez vu	vous aviez vu
ils virent	ils ont vu	ils avaient vu

	CONDITIONAL	
PAST ANTERIOR	**PRESENT**	**PAST**
j'eus vu etc	je verrais	j'aurais vu
	tu verrais	tu aurais vu
	il verrait	il aurait vu
	nous verrions	nous aurions vu
FUTURE PERFECT	vous verriez	vous auriez vu
j'aurai vu etc	ils verraient	ils auraient vu

SUBJUNCTIVE		
PRESENT	**IMPERFECT**	**PERFECT**
je voie	je visse	j'aie vu
tu voies	tu visses	tu aies vu
il voie	il vît	il ait vu
nous voyions	nous vissions	nous ayons vu
vous voyiez	vous vissiez	vous ayez vu
ils voient	ils vissent	ils aient vu

IMPERATIVE	*INFINITIVE*	*PARTICIPLE*
	PRESENT	**PRESENT**
vois	voir	voyant
voyons		
voyez	**PAST**	**PAST**
	avoir vu	vu

VOULOIR
to want

PRESENT	IMPERFECT	FUTURE
je veux	je voulais	je voudrai
tu veux	tu voulais	tu voudras
il veut	il voulait	il voudra
nous voulons	nous voulions	nous voudrons
vous voulez	vous vouliez	vous voudrez
ils veulent	ils voulaient	ils voudront
PAST HISTORIC	**PERFECT**	**PLUPERFECT**
je voulus	j'ai voulu	j'avais voulu
tu voulus	tu as voulu	tu avais voulu
il voulut	il a voulu	il avait voulu
nous voulûmes	nous avons voulu	nous avions voulu
vous voulûtes	vous avez voulu	vous aviez voulu
ils voulurent	ils ont voulu	ils avaient voulu

	CONDITIONAL	
PAST ANTERIOR	**PRESENT**	**PAST**
j'eus voulu etc	je voudrais	j'aurais voulu
	tu voudrais	tu aurais voulu
	il voudrait	il aurait voulu
	nous voudrions	nous aurions voulu
FUTURE PERFECT	vous voudriez	vous auriez voulu
j'aurai voulu etc	ils voudraient	ils auraient voulu

SUBJUNCTIVE		
PRESENT	**IMPERFECT**	**PERFECT**
je veuille	je voulusse	j'aie voulu
tu veuilles	tu voulusses	tu aies voulu
il veuille	il voulût	il ait voulu
nous voulions	nous voulussions	nous ayons voulu
vous vouliez	vous voulussiez	vous ayez voulu
ils veuillent	ils voulussent	ils aient voulu

IMPERATIVE	*INFINITIVE*	*PARTICIPLE*
	PRESENT	**PRESENT**
veuille	vouloir	voulant
veuillons		
veuillez	**PAST**	**PAST**
	avoir voulu	voulu

2 Partial conjugations: irregular verbs

The following tables contain all the irregular verbs included in the dictionary with their *partial* conjugations supplied. These verbs are pinpointed by means of an asterisk in the dictionary headword list. This section complements the previous one in which *full* conjugations are given of a selection of the most common irregular verbs. (Those verbs whose conjugations are given in full in the foregoing tables are marked with a double asterisk in the dictionary.)

A particular feature of the following tables of partial conjugations is an extensive system of cross-referring derived verbs to main verbs (eg 'entreprendre' to 'prendre') and unrelated verbs belonging to the same conjugation (eg 'luire' to 'nuire'). Forms and tenses not given are fully derivable, such as the third person singular of the present tense which is normally formed by substituting 't' for the final 's' of the first person singular, eg 'crois' becomes 'croit', 'dis' becomes 'dit'. Note that the endings of the past historic fall into three categories, the 'a' and 'i' categories shown in the previous section at *aimer*, and at *finir* and *vendre*, and the 'u' category, which has the following endings: **-us**, **-us**, **-ut**, **-ûmes**, **-ûtes**, **-urent**. Many of the irregular verbs listed below form their past historic with 'u'. The imperfect is usually formed by adding **-ais**, **-ais**, **-ait**, **-ions**, **-iez**, **-aient** to the stem of the first person plural of the present tense, eg 'je buvais' etc may be derived from 'nous buvons' (stem 'buv-' and ending '-ons'); similarly, the present participle is generally formed by substituting '-ant' for '-ons' (eg 'buvant'). The future is usually formed by adding **-ai**, **-as**, **-a**, **-ons**, **-ez**, **-ont** to the infinitive or to an infinitive without final 'e' where the ending is **-re** (eg 'nuire'). The imperative usually has the same forms as the second persons singular and plural and the first person plural of the present tense.

1 = Present	2 = Imperfect	3 = Past historic	4 = Future
5 = Subjunctive	6 = Imperative	7 = Present participle	
8 = Past participle	n = nous	v = vous	† verbs conjugated with **être** only

abattre	*like* **battre**
† s'abstenir	*like* **tenir**
accourir	*like* **courir**
accroître	*like* **croître** *except* 8 accru
accueillir	*like* **cueillir**
acquérir	1 j'acquiers, n acquérons 2 j'acquérais 3 j'acquis 4 j'acquerrai 5 j'acquière 7 acquérant 8 acquis
adjoindre	*like* **atteindre**
admettre	*like* **mettre**
aller	1 je vais, tu vas, il va, n allons, v allez, ils vont 4 j'irai 5 j'aille, n allions, ils aillent 6 va, allons, allez (*but note* vas-y)
apercevoir	*like* **recevoir**
apparaître	*like* **connaître**
appartenir	*like* **tenir**
apprendre	*like* **prendre**
asseoir	1 j'assieds, il assied, n asseyons, ils asseyent 2 j'asseyais 3 j'assis 4 j'assiérai j'asseye 7 asseyant 8 assis
atteindre	1 j'atteins, n atteignons, ils atteignent 2 j'atteignais 3 j'atteignis 4 j'atteindrai 5 j'atteigne 7 atteignant 8 atteint

avoir	1 j'ai, tu as, il a, n avons, v avez, ils ont 2 j'avais 3 j'eus 4 j'aurai 5 j'aie, il ait, n ayons, ils aient 6 aie, ayons, ayez 7 ayant 8 eu
battre	1 je bats, il bat, n battons 5 je batte
boire	1 je bois, n buvons, ils boivent 2 je buvais 3 je bus 5 je boive, n buvions 7 buvant 8 bu
bouillir	1 je bous, n bouillons, ils bouillent 2 je bouillais 3 *not used* 5 je bouille 7 bouillant
combattre	*like* **battre**
commetre	*like* **mettre**
comparaître	*like* **connaître**
comprendre	*like* **prendre**
compromettre	*like* **mettre**
concevoir	*like* **recevoir**
conclure	1 je conclus, n concluons, ils concluent 5 je conclue
concourir	*like* **courir**
conduire	1 je conduis, n conduisons 3 je conduisis 5 je conduise 8 conduit
connaître	1 je connais, il connaît, n connaissons 3 je connus 5 je connaisse 7 connaissant 8 connu
conquérir	*like* **acquérir**
consentir	*like* **mentir**
construire	*like* **conduire**
contenir	*like* **tenir**
contraindre	*like* **atteindre**
contredire	*like* **dire** *except* 1 v contredisez
convaincre	*like* **vaincre**
convenir	*like* **tenir**
corrompre	*like* **rompre**
coudre	1 je couds, il coud, n cousons, ils cousent 3 je cousis 5 je couse 7 cousant 8 cousu
courir	1 je cours, n courons 3 je courus 4 je courrai 5 je coure 8 couru
couvrir	1 je couvre, n couvrons 2 je couvrais 5 je couvre 8 couvert
craindre	*like* **atteindre**
croire	1 je crois, n croyons, ils croient 2 je croyais 3 je crus 5 je croie, n croyions 7 croyant 8 cru
croître	1 je crois, il croît, n croissons 2 je croissais 3 je crûs 5 je croisse 7 croissant 8 crû, crue
cueillir	1 je cueille, n cueillons 2 je cueillais 4 je cueillerai 5 je cueille 7 cueillant
cuire	1 je cuis, n cuisons 2 je cuisais 3 je cuisis 5 je cuise 7 cuisant 8 cuit
débattre	*like* **battre**
décevoir	*like* **recevoir**
découvrir	*like* **couvrir**
décrire	*like* **écrire**
décroître	*like* **croître** *except* 8 décru
†se dédire	*like* **dire**
déduire	*like* **conduire**

défaillir	1 je défaille, n défaillons 2 je défaillais 3 je défaillis 5 je défaille 7 défaillant 8 défailli
défaire	*like* **faire**
démentir	*like* **mentir**
démettre	*like* **mettre**
dépeindre	*like* **atteindre**
déplaire	*like* **plaire**
déteindre	*like* **atteindre**
détenir	*like* **tenir**
détruire	*like* **conduire**
† devenir	*like* **tenir**
†se dévêtir	*like* **vêtir**
devoir	1 je dois, n devons, ils doivent 2 je devais 3 je dus 4 je devrai 5 je doive, n devions 6 *not used* 7 devant 8 dû, due, *pl* dus, dues
dire	1 je dis, n disons, v dites 2 je disais 3 je dis 5 je dise 7 disant 8 dit
disparaître	*like* **connaître**
dissoudre	1 je dissous, n dissolvons 2 je dissolvais 5 je dissolve 7 dissolvant 8 dissous, dissoute
distraire	1 je distrais, n distrayons 2 je distrayais 3 *none* 5 je distraie 7 distrayant 8 distrait
dormir	*like* **mentir**
éclore	1 il éclôt, ils éclosent 8 éclos
écrire	1 j'écris, n écrivons 2 j'écrivais 3 j'écrivis 5 j'écrive 7 écrivant 8 écrit
élire	*like* **lire**
émettre	*like* **mettre**
émouvoir	*like* **mouvoir** *except* 8 ému
endormir	*like* **mentir**
enduire	*like* **conduire**
† s'enfuir	*like* **fuir**
entreprendre	*like* **prendre**
entretenir	*like* **tenir**
entrevoir	*like* **voir**
entrouvrir	*like* **couvrir**
envoyer	4 j'enverrai
† s'éprendre	*like* **prendre**
éteindre	*like* **atteindre**
être	1 je suis, tu es, il est, n sommes, v êtes, ils sont 2 j'étais 3 je fus 4 je serai 5 je sois, n soyons, ils soient 6 sois, soyons, soyez 7 étant 8 été
exclure	*like* **conclure**
extraire	*like* **distraire**
faillir	(*defective*) 3 je faillis 4 je faillirai 8 failli
faire	1 je fais, n faisons, v faites, ils font 2 je faisais 3 je fis 4 je ferai 5 je fasse 7 faisant 8 fait
falloir	(*impersonal*) 1 il faut 2 il fallait 3 il fallut 4 il faudra 5 il faille 6 *none* 7 *none* 8 fallu
feindre	*like* **atteindre**

foutre	1 je fous, n foutons 2 je foutais 3 *none* 5 je foute 7 foutant 8 foutu
frire	(*defective*) 1 je fris, tu fris, il frit 4 je frirai (*rare*) 6 fris (*rare*) 8 frit (*for other persons and tenses use* faire frire)
fuir	1 je fuis, n fuyons, ils fuient 2 je fuyais 3 je fuis 5 je fuie 7 fuyant 8 fui
haïr	1 je hais, il hait, n haïssons
inclure	*like* **conclure**
induire	*like* **conduire**
inscrire	*like* **écrire**
instruire	*like* **conduire**
interdire	*like* **dire** *except* 1 v interdisez
interrompre	*like* **rompre**
intervenir	*like* **tenir**
introduire	*like* **conduire**
joindre	*like* **atteindre**
lire	1 je lis, n lisons 2 je lisais 3 je lus 5 je lise 7 lisant 8 lu
luire	*like* **nuire**
maintenir	*like* **tenir**
maudire	1 je maudis, n maudissons 2 je maudissais 3 je maudis 4 je maudirai 5 je maudisse 7 maudissant 8 maudit
médire	*like* **dire** *except* 1 v médisez
mentir	1 je mens, n mentons 2 je mentais 5 je mente 7 mentant
mettre	1 je mets, n mettons 2 je mettais 3 je mis 5 je mette 7 mettant 8 mis
moudre	1 je mouds, il moud, n moulons 2 je moulais 3 je moulus 5 je moule 7 moulant 8 moulu
†mourir	1 je meurs, n mourons, ils meurent 2 je mourais 3 je mourus 4 je mourrai 5 je meure, n mourions 7 mourant 8 mort
mouvoir	1 je meus, n mouvons, ils meuvent 2 je mouvais 3 je mus (*rare*) 4 je mouvrai 5 je meuve, n mouvions 8 mû, mue, *pl* mus, mues
†naître	1 je nais, il naît, n naissons 2 je naissais 3 je naquis 4 je naîtrai 5 je naisse 7 naissant 8 né
nuire	1 je nuis, n nuisons 2 je nuisais 3 je nuisis 5 je nuise 7 nuisant 8 nui
obtenir	*like* **tenir**
offrir	*like* **couvrir**
omettre	*like* **mettre**
ouvrir	*like* **couvrir**
paître	(*defective*) 1 il paît 2 il paissait 3 *none* 4 il paîtra 5 il paisse 7 paissant 8 *none*
paraître	*like* **connaître**
parcourir	*like* **courir**
†partir	*like* **mentir**
†parvenir	*like* **tenir**
peindre	*like* **atteindre**
percevoir	*like* **recevoir**
permettre	*like* **mettre**
plaindre	*like* **atteindre**

plaire	1 je plais, il plaît, n plaisons 2 je plaisais 3 je plus 5 je plaise 7 plaisant 8 plu
pleuvoir	(*impersonal*) 1 il pleut 2 il pleuvait 3 il plut 4 il pleuvra 5 il pleuve 6 *none* 7 pleuvant 8 plu
poursuivre	*like* **suivre**
pourvoir	*like* **voir** *except* 4 je pourvoirai
pouvoir	1 je peux *or* je puis, tu peux, il peut, n pouvons, ils peuvent 2 je pouvais 3 je pus 4 je pourrai 5 je puisse 6 *not used* 7 pouvant 8 pu
prédire	*like* **dire** *except* 1 v prédisez
prendre	1 je prends, il prend, n prenons, ils prennent 2 je prenais 3 je pris 5 je prenne 7 prenant 8 pris
prescrire	*like* **écrire**
pressentir	*like* **mentir**
prévenir	*like* **tenir**
prévoir	*like* **voir** *except* 4 je prévoirai
produire	*like* **conduire**
promettre	*like* **mettre**
promouvoir	*like* **mouvoir** *except* 8 promu
proscrire	*like* **écrire**
†provenir	*like* **tenir**
rabattre	*like* **battre**
rasseoir	*like* **asseoir**
recevoir	1 je reçois, n recevons, ils reçoivent 2 je recevais 3 je reçus 4 je recevrai 5 je reçoive, n recevions, ils reçoivent 7 recevant 8 reçu
reconduire	*like* **conduire**
reconnaître	*like* **connaître**
reconstruire	*like* **conduire**
recoudre	*like* **coudre**
recourir	*like* **courir**
recouvrir	*like* **couvrir**
recueillir	*like* **cueillir**
redire	*like* **dire**
réduire	*like* **conduire**
refaire	*like* **faire**
rejoindre	*like* **atteindre**
relire	*like* **lire**
reluire	*like* **nuire**
remettre	*like* **mettre**
†renaître	*like* **naître**
rendormir	*like* **mentir**
renvoyer	*like* **envoyer**
†repartir	*like* **mentir**
repentir	*like* **mentir**
reprendre	*like* **prendre**
reproduire	*like* **conduire**
résoudre	1 je résous, n résolvons 2 je résolvais 3 je résolus 5 je résolve 7 résolvant 8 résolu
ressentir	*like* **mentir**
resservir	*like* **mentir**

ressortir	*like* **mentir**
restreindre	*like* **atteindre**
retenir	*like* **tenir**
†revenir	*like* **tenir**
revêtir	*like* **vêtir**
revivre	*like* **vivre**
revoir	*like* **voir**
rire	1 je ris, n rions 2 je riais 3 je ris 5 je rie, n riions 7 riant 8 ri
rompre	*regular except* 1 il rompt
rouvrir	*like* **couvrir**
satisfaire	*like* **faire**
savoir	1 je sais, n savons, ils savent 2 je savais 3 je sus 4 je saurai 5 je sache 6 sache, sachons, sachez 7 sachant 8 su
séduire	*like* **conduire**
sentir	*like* **mentir**
servir	*like* **mentir**
sortir	*like* **mentir**
souffrir	*like* **couvrir**
soumettre	*like* **mettre**
sourire	*like* **rire**
souscrire	*like* **écrire**
soustraire	*like* **distraire**
soutenir	*like* **tenir**
†se souvenir	*like* **tenir**
subvenir	*like* **tenir**
suffire	1 je suffis, n suffisons 2 je suffisais 3 je suffis 5 je suffise 7 suffisant 8 suffi
suivre	1 je suis, n suivons 2 je suivais 3 je suivis 5 je suive 7 suivant 8 suivi
surprendre	*like* **prendre**
†survenir	*like* **tenir**
survivre	*like* **vivre**
taire	1 je tais, n taisons 2 je taisais 3 je tus 5 je taise 7 taisant 8 tu
teindre	*like* **atteindre**
tenir	1 je tiens, n tenons, ils tiennent 2 je tenais 3 je tins, tu tins, il tint, n tînmes, v tîntes, ils tinrent 4 je tiendrai 5 je tienne 7 tenant 8 tenu
traduire	*like* **conduire**
traire	*like* **distraire**
transmettre	*like* **mettre**
tressaillir	*like* **défaillir**
vaincre	1 je vaincs, il vainc, n vainquons 2 je vainquais 3 je vainquis 5 je vainque 7 vainquant 8 vaincu
valoir	1 je vaux, il vaut, n valons 2 je valais 3 je valus 4 je vaudrai 5 je vaille 6 *not used* 7 valant 8 valu
†venir	*like* **tenir**
vêtir	1 je vêts, n vêtons 2 je vêtais 5 je vête 7 vêtant 8 vêtu

vivre 1 je vis, n vivons 2 je vivais 3 je vécus 5 je vive
7 vivant 8 vécu

voir 1 je vois, n voyons 2 je voyais 3 je vis 4 je verrai
5 je voie, n voyions 7 voyant 8 vu

vouloir 1 je veux, il veut, n voulons, ils veulent 2 je voulais
3 je voulus 4 je voudrai 5 je veuille 6 veuille, veuillons, veuillez 7 voulant 8 voulu

M VERB CONSTRUCTIONS

There are two main types of verb constructions: verbs can be followed:

1 by another verb in the infinitive

2 by an object (a noun or a pronoun)

1 Verbs followed by an infinitive

There are three main constructions when a verb is followed by an infinitive:

a) verb + infinitive (without any linking preposition)

b) verb + **à** + infinitive

c) verb + **de** + infinitive

For examples of these three types of constructions, see **G108 & 113**, sections H 2b) and d).

a) *Verbs followed by an infinitive without preposition*

These include verbs of wishing and wanting, of movement, of liking and disliking, of seeing, hearing and feeling, as well as the modal auxiliaries. A selection follows:

adorer to love (to)

aimer to like (to)

aimer mieux to prefer (to)

aller to go (and)

compter to intend to, to expect to

descendre to go/come down (and)

désirer to want/wish (to)

détester to hate (to)

devoir to have to

écouter to listen to

entendre to hear

entrer to go/come in (and)

envoyer to send

espérer to hope (to)

faire to make

falloir to have to

laisser to let

monter to go/come up (and)

oser to dare (to)

pouvoir to be able to

préférer to prefer (to)

se rappeler to recall/remember

regarder to watch

rentrer to go/come back (and)

savoir to know how to	**sembler** to seem (to)	**sentir** to feel
sortir to go/come out (and)	**souhaiter** to wish (to)	**valoir mieux** to be better to
venir to come (and)	**voir** to see	**vouloir** to want (to)

b) *Verbs followed by **à*** + infinitive include:

aider à	to help (to do)
s'amuser à	to enjoy (doing)
apprendre à	to learn (to do), to teach (to do)
s'apprêter à	to get ready (to do)
arriver à	to manage (to do)
s'attendre à	to expect (to do)
autoriser à	to permit/allow (to do)
chercher à	to try (to do)
commencer à	to start (doing/to do)
consentir à	to consent/agree (to do)
consister à	to consist in (doing)
continuer à	to continue (doing/to do)
se décider à	to make up one's mind (to do)
encourager à	to encourage (to do)
forcer à	to force (to do)
s'habituer à	to get used (to doing)
hésiter à	to hesitate (to do)
inciter à	to prompt (to do)
inviter à	to invite/ask (to do)
se mettre à	to start (doing/to do)
obliger à	to force/compel (to do)
parvenir à	to manage (to do)/succeed (in doing)
passer son temps à	to spend one's time (doing)
perdre son temps à	to waste one's time (doing)
persister à	to persist in (doing)
pousser à	to urge (to do)
se préparer à	to get ready/prepare (to do)
renoncer à	to give up (doing)
rester à	to be left (to do)
réussir à	to succeed (in doing)
servir à	to be used (for doing/to do)
songer à	to think (of doing)
tarder à	to take one's/its time (doing)
tenir à	to be anxious (to do)

c) *Verbs followed by **de*** + infinitive include:

accepter de	to agree (to do)
accuser de	to accuse (of doing)
achever de	to finish (doing)
s'arrêter de	to stop (doing)
avoir besoin de	to need (to do)
avoir envie de	to feel like (doing)
avoir peur de	to be afraid (to do)

cesser de	to stop (doing)
se charger de	to undertake (to do)
commander de	to command (to do)
conseiller de	to advise (to do)
se contenter de	to make do (with doing)
craindre de	to be afraid (of doing/to do)
décider de	to decide (to do)
déconseiller de	to advise against (doing)
défendre de	to forbid (to do)
demander de	to ask (to do)
se dépêcher de	to hurry (to do)
dire de	to tell (to do)
dissuader de	to dissuade (from doing)
s'efforcer de	to endeavour/try (to do)
empêcher de	to prevent/stop (doing/from doing)
s'empresser de	to hasten (to do)
entreprendre de	to undertake (to do)
essayer de	to try (to do)
s'étonner de	to be surprised (at doing/to do)
éviter de	to avoid (doing)
s'excuser de	to apologize (for doing)
faire semblant de	to pretend (to do)
feindre de	to pretend (to do)
finir de	to finish (doing)
se garder de	to take care not to (do)
se hâter de	to hurry (to do)
interdire de	to forbid (to do)
jurer de	to swear (to do)
manquer de	'to nearly' (do)
menacer de	to threaten (to do)
mériter de	to deserve (to do)
négliger de	to neglect (to do)
offrir de	to offer (to do)
omettre de	to omit (to do)
ordonner de	to order (to do)
oublier de	to forget (to do)
permettre de	to allow (to do)
persuader de	to persuade (to do)
prier de	to ask (to do)
promettre de	to promise (to do)
proposer de	to offer (to do)
recommander de	to recommend (to do)
refuser de	to refuse (to do)
regretter de	to be sorry (to do/for doing)
remercier de	to thank for (doing)
risquer de	to stand a good chance (of doing)
se souvenir de	to remember (doing)
suggérer de	to suggest (doing)
supplier de	to beg/implore (to do)
tâcher de	to try (to do)
tenter de	to try (to do)
venir de	to have just (done)

2 Verbs followed by an object

In general, verbs which take a direct object in French also take a direct object in English, and verbs which take an indirect object in French (ie verb + preposition + object) also take an indirect object in English.

There are however some exceptions:

a) *Verbs followed by an indirect object in English but not in French* (the English preposition is not translated), eg:

attendre	to wait for
chercher	to look for
demander	to ask for
écouter	to listen to
espérer	to hope for
payer	to pay for
regarder	to look at

on a demandé le résultat
we asked for the result

j'attendais l'autobus
I was waiting for the bus

je cherche mon frère
I'm looking for my brother

tu écoutes la radio ?
are you listening to the radio?

b) *Verbs which take a direct object in English but an indirect object in French preceded by* **à**, *eg:*

convenir à	to suit
se fier à	to trust
jouer à	to play (*game, sport*)
obéir à	to obey
désobéir à	to disobey
pardonner à	to forgive
renoncer à	to give up
répondre à	to answer
résister à	to resist
ressembler à	to resemble
téléphoner à	to phone

tu peux te fier à moi
you can trust me

tu joues souvent au tennis ?
do you often play tennis?

tu as répondu à sa lettre ?
did you answer his letter?

elle a renoncé au tabac
she gave up smoking

téléphonons au médecin
let's phone the doctor

obéis à ton père !
obey your father!

c) *Verbs which take a direct object in English but an indirect object in French preceded by* **de**, *eg:*

s'apercevoir de	to realize/notice
avoir besoin de	to need
changer de	to change (*trains, the subject etc*)
douter de	to doubt
se douter de	to suspect
s'emparer de	to take/grab

jouer de	to play (*musical instrument*)
jouir de	to enjoy
manquer de	to be short of, to lack
se méfier de	to distrust/mistrust
se servir de	to use
se souvenir de	to remember
se tromper de ...	to get the wrong ...

je dois changer de train ?
do I have to change trains?

il ne s'est aperçu de rien
he didn't notice anything

il joue bien de la guitare
he plays the guitar well

elle manque de charme
she lacks charm

méfiez-vous de lui
don't trust him

je me servirai de ton vélo
I'll use your bike

tu te souviens de Jean ?
do you remember Jean?

il s'est trompé de numéro
he got the wrong number

d) *Some verbs take* **à** *or* **de** *before an object, whereas their English equivalent uses a different preposition:*

i) Verb + **à** + object:

croire à	to believe in
s'intéresser à	to be interested in
penser à	to think of/about
songer à	to think of
servir à	to be used for

je m'intéresse au cinéma et à la natation
I'm interested in films and swimming

à quoi penses-tu ?
what are you thinking about?

ça sert à quoi ?
what is this used for?

ii) Verb + **de** + object:

dépendre de	to depend on/upon
être fâché de	to be sorry about
féliciter de	to congratulate on
parler de	to speak about/of
remercier de	to thank for
rire de	to laugh at
traiter de	to deal with/be about
vivre de	to live on

cela dépendra du temps
it'll depend on the weather

il m'a parlé de toi
he spoke to me about you

tu l'as remercié du cadeau qu'il t'a fait ?
did you thank him for the present he gave you?

3 Verbs followed by one direct object and one indirect object

a) In general, these are verbs of giving or lending, and their English equivalents are constructed in the same way, eg:

donner quelque chose à quelqu'un
to give something to someone

il a vendu son ordinateur à son ami
he sold his computer to his friend

Note: After such verbs, the preposition 'to' is often omitted in English but **à** cannot be omitted in French, and particular care must be taken when object pronouns are used with these verbs (see **G57**, section 6 D 2).

b) With verbs expressing 'taking away', **à** is translated by 'from' (**qn** stands for 'quelqu'un' and **s.o.** for 'someone'):

acheter à qn	to buy from s.o.
cacher à qn	to hide from s.o.
demander à qn	to ask s.o. for
emprunter à qn	to borrow from s.o.
enlever à qn	to take away from s.o.
ôter à qn	to take away from s.o.
prendre à qn	to take from s.o.
voler à qn	to steal from s.o.

à qui as-tu emprunté cela ?	**il l'a volé à son frère**
who did you borrow this from?	he stole it from his brother

4 Verb + indirect object + *de* + infinitive

Some verbs which take a direct object in English are followed by **à** + object + **de** + infinitive in French (**qn** stands for 'quelqu'un' and **s.o.** for 'someone'):

commander à qn de faire	to order/command s.o. to do
conseiller à qn de faire	to advise s.o. to do
défendre à qn de faire	to forbid s.o. to do
demander à qn de faire	to ask s.o. to do
dire à qn de faire	to tell s.o. to do
ordonner à qn de faire	to order s.o. to do
permettre à qn de faire	to allow s.o. to do
promettre à qn de faire	to promise s.o. to do
proposer à qn de faire	to suggest to s.o. that ...

je lui ai conseillé de ne pas essayer
I advised him not to try

demande à ton fils de t'aider
ask your son to help you

j'ai promis à mes parents de ne jamais recommencer
I promised my parents never to do this again

je te propose de rester
I suggest you stay

8 PREPOSITIONS

Prepositions express the position, movement etc of things or people in relation to one another. In both French and English they can have many different meanings, which presents considerable difficulties for the translator. The following guide to the most common meanings of common prepositions sets out the generally accepted meanings on the left, with a description of their use in brackets, and an illustration. The main meanings are given first. Prepositions are listed in alphabetical order.

à

at	(place)	**au troisième arrêt** at the third stop **à la fin** at the end **à la maison, à l'école** at home, at school
	(date)	**à Noël** at Christmas
	(time)	**à trois heures** at three (o'clock) **à l'aube, au crépuscule** at dawn, at dusk
	(numbers)	**à 10 ans** at 10 (years of age) **à 50 km à l'heure** = at 30 miles an hour **tout est à 200 francs** everything is at 200 francs
	(idiom)	**au hasard, au travail** at random, at work
in	(place)	**à Montmartre** in Montmartre **à Lyon** in Lyons **au Japon** in Japan **au supermarché** in the supermarket **à la campagne** in the country **au lit** in bed **au loin** in the distance

	(time)	**au XVIIIe siècle** in the 18th century **au printemps** in (the) spring **au mois de juin** in (the month of) June
	(manner)	**à la française** in the French way **à ma façon** (in) my way **à la craie, au crayon** in chalk, in pencil
to	(place)	**aller au théâtre** to go to the theatre **aller à Londres** to go to London **aller au Japon** to go to Japan
	(position)	**aller à la porte/à papa** to go to the door/to dad **à droite/gauche** to the right/left
	(time)	**de dimanche à lundi** from Sunday to Monday
	(indirect object)	**donner quelque chose à quelqu'un** to give something to someone
	(comparison)	**comparer quelque chose/quelqu'un à** to compare something/someone to **inférieur/supérieur à** inferior/superior to
	(preference)	**préférer quelque chose/quelqu'un à** to prefer something/someone to
	(proportion)	**6 litres aux 100 km** = 50 miles to the gallon **100 km à l'heure** = 60 miles an hour
	(+ infinitive)	**je l'ai invité à venir** I invited him to come **c'est facile à faire** it is easy to do (see **G107**, section 7 H)
away (from)	(distance)	**à 3 km d'ici** 3 kilometres away (from here), 3 kilometres from here
by	(means)	**aller à bicyclette/à vélo** to go by bike **je l'ai reconnu à ses habits** I recognized him by his clothing

	(manner)	**fait à la main** made by hand
	(weight)	**au kilo** by the kilo
	(rate)	**à la centaine** by the hundred
up to	(+ pronoun)	**c'est à vous (de jouer)** it's your turn (to play) **c'est à nous de le lui dire** it's up to us to tell him
for (*usually not translated*)	(purpose)	**une tasse à café** a coffee cup **une machine à coudre** a sewing maching **de la mousse à raser** shaving cream
his/her/my etc	(possessive)	**son sac à elle** her bag
on	(means)	**aller à cheval/à pied** to go on horseback/on foot **à la radio, au tableau** on the radio, on the blackboard
	(position)	**à la page 12** on page 12 **au menton** on the chin **à droite/gauche** on the right/left
	(time)	**à cette occasion** on this occasion **à votre arrivée/départ** on your arrival/departure
with	(descriptive)	**une maison à cinq pièces** a house with five rooms **un homme aux cheveux blonds** a man with blond hair **l'homme à la valise** the man with the case
	(idiom)	**à bras ouverts** with open arms
from	(indirect object)	**cacher/voler/acheter à** to hide/steal/buy from

For the use of the preposition **à** with the infinitive see verb constructions, **G165**, section 7 M 1b).

après

after	(time)	**après votre arrivée** after your arrival
	(sequence)	**je suis après vous** I'm after you
		après avoir/être (see **G114**, section 7 H 3)
	(idiom)	**après tout** after all
beyond/past	(place)	**après le pont** beyond/past the bridge

à travers

through		**à travers le mur** through the wall

auprès de

by, close to		**assieds-toi auprès de moi** sit down by me/close to me
compared to		**ce n'est rien auprès de ce que tu as fait** it's nothing compared to what you've done

avant

before	(time)	**avant cet après-midi** before this afternoon **avant ce soir** before tonight
	(place)	**on tourne avant la boucherie** you turn off before the butcher's
	(sequence)	**je suis avant vous** I'm before you **avant de s'asseoir** before sitting down
	(preference)	**la famille avant tout** the family first, the family above all (= before everything)

avec

with	(association)	**aller avec lui** to go with him
	(means)	**il a tondu le gazon avec une tondeuse** he cut the lawn with a lawnmower

chez

at	(place)	**chez moi/toi** at my/your house/flat/*etc* **chez mon oncle** at my uncle's **chez le boulanger** at the baker's
to	(place)	**je vais chez moi** I'm going home, I'm going to my house **tu vas chez ton oncle ?** are you going to your uncle's?
among		**chez les Ecossais/les jeunes** among the Scots/the young
about		**ce qui m'énerve chez toi, c'est ...** what annoys me about you is ...
with		**c'est une habitude chez elle** it's a habit with her
in		**chez Sartre** in (the work of) Sartre

contre

against	(position)	**contre le mur** against the wall
	(opposition)	**je suis contre cette décision** I'm against that decision
with	(after verb)	**je suis fâché contre elle** I'm angry with her
for		**échanger des gants contre un foulard** to exchange gloves for a scarf

d'après

according to		**d'après elle** according to her **d'après ce qu'elle dit** according to what she says

dans

in	(position)	**dans ma serviette** in my briefcase
	(time)	**je pars dans deux jours** I'm leaving in two days' time/in two days
	(idiom)	**dans l'attente de vous voir** looking forward to seeing you

into, in	(motion)	**mettre quelque chose dans la boîte** to put something into/in the box
from, out of		**prendre quelque chose dans la boîte** to take something from/out of the box
		boire dans un verre to drink from/out of a glass
on	(idiom)	**dans le train** on the train
about	(quantity)	**dans les vingt francs** about twenty francs

de

from	(place)	**je suis venu de Paris** I have come from Paris **il vient d'Italie** he comes from Italy
	(date)	**du 5 février au 10 mars** from February 5th to March 10th **d'un weekend à l'autre** from one weekend to another
	(separation/ difference)	**séparer de, libérer de** to separate from, to free from **différent de** different from
of	(adjectival)	**un cri de triomphe** a shout of triumph **un pont de fer** an iron bridge
	(possessive)	**la jupe de ma sœur** my sister's skirt **les rayons du soleil** the rays of the sun, the sun's rays
	(contents)	**une tasse de café** a cup of coffee
	(cause)	**mourir de faim** to die of hunger
	(after adjectives)	**digne de** worthy of
	(after nouns)	**sur présentation de** on presentation of
	(apposition)	**les vacances de Pâques** the Easter holidays **la ville de Paris** the city of Paris
(*not translated*)	(measurement)	**long de 3 mètres** 3 metres long

	(time)	**ma montre retarde de 10 minutes** my watch is 10 minutes slow
	(price)	**le montant est de 200 francs** the total is 200 francs
	(after 'quelque chose')	**quelque chose de bon** something good
	(after 'quelqu'un')	**quelqu'un d'intelligent** someone clever
	(after 'rien')	**rien de nouveau** nothing new
	(after 'personne')	**personne d'autre** nobody else
	(quantity)	**beaucoup de, peu de** many, few
by	(agent)	**accompagné de** accompanied by
	(idiom)	**je le connais de vue** I know him by sight **elle travaille de nuit** she works by night
in	(manner)	**de cette façon** in this way **d'une voix douce** in a gentle voice
	(agent)	**couvert de neige** covered in snow
	(after superlatives)	**la plus haute montagne d'Europe** the highest mountain in Europe
on		**de ce côté** on this side
than	(comparative)	**moins de 5 francs** less than 5 francs **plus de 3 kilos** more than 3 kilos
to	(after adjectives)	**ravi de vous voir** delighted to see you **il est facile de le faire** it is easy to do it
	(after nouns)	**la volonté de réussir** the will to succeed
	(after verbs)	**s'efforcer de** to endeavour/try to (see **G107**, section 7 H)
with	(cause)	**tomber de fatigue** to drop with exhaustion

	(means)	**armé de** armed with
	(manner)	**d'un air amusé** with an amused look
	(after adjectives)	**amoureux de quelqu'un** in love with someone

depuis

for	(time)	**j'étudie le français depuis 3 ans** I have been studying French for 3 years **j'étudiais le français depuis 3 ans** I had been studying French for 3 years **je n'ai pas vu de lapins depuis des années** I haven't seen any rabbits for years
from	(place)	**depuis ma fenêtre, je vois la mer** from my window I can see the sea **depuis Paris jusqu'à Londres** from Paris to London
	(time)	**depuis le matin jusqu'au soir** from morning till evening
since	(time)	**depuis dimanche** since Sunday
	(place)	**il n'a pas parlé depuis Rouen** he hasn't spoken since Rouen

derrière

behind	(position)	**derrière la maison** behind the house

dès

from	(time)	**dès six heures** from six (o'clock) onwards **dès 1934** as far back as 1934 **dès le début** (right) from the start **dès maintenant** from now on **dès mon arrivée** (as) from the time of my arrival
	(place)	**dès Edimbourg** from (the moment of leaving) Edinburgh

devant

in front of	(position)	**devant l'école** in front of the school

en

in	(place)	**être en ville** to be in town **en Angleterre** in England
	(dates etc)	**en quelle année ?** in what year? **en 1994** in 1994 **en été, en juillet** in (the) summer, in July
	(quantities)	**en dollars/kilos** in dollars/kilos
	(state)	**en deuil, en fleur(s)** in mourning/in bloom
	(idioms)	**en général, en question** in general, in question
	(shape)	**en (forme de) losange** in the shape of a diamond, diamond-shaped
	(colour)	**un mur peint en jaune** a wall painted yellow
	(dress)	**elle était en noir** she was in black **en chemise** in a shirt
	(material)	**une montre en or** a gold watch
	(language)	**en chinois** in Chinese
	(subject)	**fort en anglais** good in English
	(time)	**j'ai fait mes devoirs en 20 minutes** I did my homework in 20 minutes
into		**traduire en anglais** to translate into French
by	(means)	**en auto/en avion** by car/by plane
on	(state)	**en vacances** on holiday, *Am* on vacation

	(idiom)	**en moyenne** on average
	(+ present participle)	**en faisant** on/while/by doing (see **G115**, section 7 I 1)
at	(state)	**en guerre** at war **en mer** at sea
as		**il s'est habillé en femme** he dressed as a woman **en cadeau** as a present
of	(subject)	**docteur en médecine** doctor of medicine

Note: ***en** is not used with the definite article except in certain expressions such as:* ***en l'an 2 000** (in the year 2000),* ***en l'honneur de** (in honour of) and* ***en l'air** ((up) in the air).*

en tant que

as (= *in one's capacity as*)	**en tant que professeur** as a teacher

entre

among(st)		**être entre amis** to be among(st) friends
between	(position)	**entre Londres et Douvres** between London and Dover
	(time)	**entre 6 et 10 heures** between 6 and 10 (o'clock)
	(idiom)	**entre toi et moi/entre nous** between you and me
in	(punctuation)	**entre guillemets** in inverted commas **entre parenthèses** in brackets, *Am* in parentheses

d'entre

of (= *from among*)	**certains d'entre eux** some of them **dix d'entre elles** ten of them

envers

to/towards, Am toward		**être bien disposé envers quelqu'un** to be well-disposed toward(s) someone/to someone

hors de

out of		**hors de danger/d'atteinte** out of danger/reach **hors de la ville** out of the town, outside the town

jusque

up to/as far as	(place)	**jusqu'à la frontière espagnole** as far as/up to the Spanish border
up to	(limit)	**jusqu'à 100 dollars** up to 100 dollars
until/till	(time)	**jusqu'en mai** until/till May **jusqu'ici/jusque-là** up to now/up till then, (up) until now/then, (up) till now/then **jusqu'à demain** until/till tomorrow

malgré

in spite of		**malgré la chaleur** in spite of the heat

par

by	(agent)	**la lettre a été envoyée par mon ami** the letter was sent by my friend
	(means)	**par le travail** by work **par la porte/route** by the door/by road **par carte de crédit** by credit card
	(means of transport)	**par le train** by train
	(idiom)	**deux par deux** two by two

	(+ infinitive)	**commencer par faire** to begin by doing **finir par faire** to end up doing
a/per	(distributive)	**trois fois par semaine** three times a/per week **100 francs par personne** 100 francs a/per person
through	(place)	**passer par Paris/par la porte** to go through Paris/the door
	(idiom)	**par ici/par là** this way/that way
out of	(place)	**regarder par la fenêtre** to look out of the window **jeter du pain par la fenêtre** to throw bread out of the window
out of/from	(reason)	**par pitié** out of pity, from pity
in/on	(weather)	**par un temps pareil** in such weather **par un beau jour d'hiver** on a beautiful winter's day
to/on		**tomber par terre** to fall to the ground/fall down **étendu par terre** lying on the ground

parmi

among(st)		**parmi ses ennemis** among(st) his enemies

pendant

during	(time)	**pendant l'été** during the summer
for		**il l'avait fait pendant 5 années** he had done it for 5 years

pour

for	(intention)	**ce livre est pour vous** this book is for you **elle a du respect pour les personnes âgées** she has respect for senior citizens
	(direction)	**le train pour Paris** the train for Paris

	(cause, purpose)	**mourir pour la patrie** to die for one's country **c'est bon pour la santé** it's good for your health **c'est pour cela que je suis venu** that's why I've come, it's for that reason I've come
	(exchange)	**il a acheté son vélo pour 100 francs** he bought his bike for 100 francs
	(support)	**je suis pour la libération de la femme** I'm for women's liberation
	(representation)	**elle joue pour Toulouse** she plays for Toulouse **allez-y pour moi** go for me
	(describing situation)	**il fait froid pour la saison** it's cold for the season **elle n'est pas trop vieille pour ce genre de travail** she's not too old for that kind of work
	(idiom)	**pour moi, je crois que** personally/as for me, I think that
	(time)	**j'en ai pour une heure** it'll take me an hour **je serai là pour 2 semaines** I'll be here for 2 weeks **ce sera prêt pour demain** it will be ready for tomorrow

(**pour** stresses intention and future time: see **depuis** and **pendant** **G177 & 181**)

	(+ infinitive)	**ils ont été emprisonnés pour avoir volé une voiture** they were jailed for stealing a car
to	(+ infinitive)	**je fais cela pour gagner ma vie** I do that (in order) to earn a living **il était trop paresseux pour réussir aux examens** he was too lazy to pass the exams **tu es assez grand pour faire ça toi-même** you're big enough to do that by yourself

près de

near (to)/close to	(place)	**près du marché** near (to)/close to the market
nearly	(time)	**il est près de minuit** it's nearly midnight
	(quantity)	**près de cinquante** nearly fifty

quant à

as for		**quant à moi** as for me

sans

without	(+ noun)	**sans espoir** without hope
	(+ pronoun)	**je n'irai pas sans vous** I won't go without you
	(+ infinitive)	**sans parler** without speaking **sans s'arrêter** without stopping

sauf

except		**ils sont tous partis, sauf John** everyone left except John
barring		**sauf accident/sauf imprévu** barring accidents/the unexpected

selon

according to		**selon le professeur** according to the teacher **selon moi** in my opinion

sous

under	(physical)	**sous la table** under the table **sous l'eau** underwater
	(rank)	**il est sous mes ordres** he's under me, he's under my command
	(historical)	**sous Elisabeth II** under Elizabeth II
	(idiom)	**sous calmants** under sedation
in	(weather)	**sous la pluie** in the rain
	(historical)	**sous le règne de** in the reign of

	(idioms)	**sous antibiotiques** on antibiotics **sous peu** shortly/before long **sous la main** handy/to hand **sous tous les rapports** in all respects **sous mes yeux** before my eyes

suivant

according to		**suivant les journalistes** according to the journalists

sur

on	(position)	**le bol est sur la table** the bowl is on the table **sur votre gauche/droite** on your left/right **sur disquette** on floppy disk
	(idiom)	**sur le point de faire quelque chose** about to do something, on the point of doing something
on (to)	(position)	**monter sur** to climb on (to)
off/from		**prendre quelque chose sur la table** to take something off the table/from the table
over	(position)	**le pont sur la Loire** the bridge over the Loire **partout sur le plancher** all over the floor **avoir son manteau sur le bras** to have one's coat over one's arm **mon influence sur ...** my influence over ... **un avantage sur ...** an advantage over ...
	(idioms)	**régner sur** to reign over **pleurer sur** to cry over
out of	(proportion)	**neuf sur dix** nine out of ten **une semaine sur trois** one week in three/out of three

on/about		**un livre sur** a book about
by	(measurement)	**quatre mètres sur cinq** four metres *or Am* meters by five
towards, *Am toward*	(place)	**se diriger sur** to head toward(s)
at	(idiom)	**sur ces paroles** at these words
in	(tone of voice)	**sur un ton amer** in a bitter tone (of voice)
upon	(repetition)	**page sur page** page upon page
	(position: in formal or literary English)	**il gisait sur le sol** he was lying upon the ground

vers

towards, *Am toward*	(position)	**vers le nord** toward(s) the north
	(time)	**vers la fin du film** toward(s) the end of the film
about/around	(time)	**vers 10 heures** about/around 10 (o'clock)

voici

here is/here are		**voici mon père/mes parents** here's my father/here are my parents **la voici, les voici** here she/it is, here they are **le voici qui vient** here he comes **en voici** here are some
this is/these are		**voici mon père/mes parents** this is my father/these are my parents **voici pourquoi elle l'a fait** this is why she did it
ago		**voici dix ans** ten years ago

(see also **G96**, section 7 F 9a) i))

voilà

there is/there are	**voilà la maison/mes amis** there's the house/there are my friends **la voilà, les voilà** there she/it is, there they are
that is/those are	**voilà la maison/mes amis** that is the house/those are my friends **voilà où il demeure** that's where he lives
ago	**voilà dix ans** ten years ago

(see also **G96**, section 7 F 9a) i))

9 CONJUNCTIONS

Conjunctions are words or expressions which link words, phrases or clauses. They fall into two categories:

A co-ordinating
B subordinating

A CO-ORDINATING CONJUNCTIONS

1 Definition

These link two similar words or groups of words (eg nouns, pronouns, adjectives, adverbs, prepositions, phrases or clauses). The principal co-ordinating conjunctions (or adverbs used as conjunctions) are:

et and	**mais** but	**ou** or
ou bien or else	**soit** either, or	**ni** neither, nor
alors so, then	**aussi** therefore, so	**donc** so, then, therefore
puis then (next)	**car** because, for	**or** now, well
cependant however	**néanmoins** nevertheless	**pourtant** yet, nevertheless
toutefois nevertheless		

il est malade, mais il ne veut pas aller au lit
he's ill but he won't go to bed

il faisait beau, alors il est allé se promener
it was fine so he went for a walk

elle est partie sans manger ni boire
she left without (either) eating or drinking

2 Repetition

a) Some co-ordinating conjunctions are repeated:

soit ... soit either ... or

prenez soit l'un soit l'autre
take (either) one or the other

ni ... ni neither ... nor

le vieillard n'avait ni amis ni argent
the old man had neither friends nor money

b) **et** and **ou** can be repeated in texts of a literary nature:

et ... et	both ... and
ou ... ou	either ... or

et lui et son père ...
both he and his father...

3 aussi

aussi means 'therefore' only when placed before the verb. The subject pronoun is placed after the verb (see **G204**, section 12 7a)).

il pleuvait, aussi Pascal n'est-il pas sorti
it was raining, so Pascal didn't go out

when **aussi** follows the verb it means 'also':

j'ai aussi mis mon imperméable
I also put my raincoat on

B SUBORDINATING CONJUNCTIONS

These join a subordinate clause to another clause, usually a main clause. The principal subordinating conjunctions are:

comme	as	**parce que**	because
puisque	since	**ainsi que**	as well as
à mesure que	as	**(au)tant que**	as much as, as long as
avant que (+ ne)	before	**après que**	after
jusqu'à ce que	until	**depuis que**	since
tandis que	whereas	**alors que**	whereas/when
pendant que	while	**sans que**	without
si	if, whether	**à moins que (+ ne)**	unless
pourvu que	provided/providing that	**quoique**	(al)though
bien que	(al)though	**quand**	when
lorsque	when	**dès que**	as soon as
aussitôt que	as soon as	**pour que**	so that, in order that
afin que	so that	**de sorte que**	so that
de façon que	so that	**de peur que (+ ne)**	for fear that

Note: some subordinating conjunctions require the subjunctive (see **G101**, section 7 G 1f)).

C QUE

que can be co-ordinating or subordinating

1 **co-ordinating** in comparisons (see **G35**, section 4 E 1 and **G43**, section 5 F 1)

> **il est plus fort que moi**
> he is stronger than me/than I am

2 subordinating

a) *meaning 'that':*

> **elle dit qu'elle l'a vu**
> she says she has seen him

> **je pense que tu as raison**
> I think you're right

> **il faut que tu viennes**
> you'll have to come

Note: English very often omits the word 'that', especially in the spoken language.

b) *replacing another conjunction:*

When a conjunction introduces more than one verb, **que** usually replaces the second (and subsequent) subordinating conjunctions to avoid repetition:

> **comme il était tard et que j'étais fatigué, je suis rentré**
> as it was late and I was tired, I went (back) home

Note: the mood after **que** is the same as that taken by the conjunction it replaces, except in the case of **si** in which **que** requires the subjunctive:

> **s'il fait beau et que tu sois libre, nous irons à la piscine**
> if it's fine, and you are free, we'll go to the swimming pool

10 NUMBERS AND QUANTITY

A CARDINAL NUMBERS

0	**zéro**	40	**quarante**
1	**un (une)**	50	**cinquante**
2	**deux**	60	**soixante**
3	**trois**	70	**soixante-dix**
4	**quatre**	71	**soixante et onze**
5	**cinq**	72	**soixante-douze**
6	**six**	80	**quatre-vingt(s)**
7	**sept**	81	**quatre-vingt-un(e)**
8	**huit**	90	**quatre-vingt-dix**
9	**neuf**	99	**quatre-vingt-dix-neuf**
10	**dix**	100	**cent**
11	**onze**	101	**cent un(e)**
12	**douze**	102	**cent deux**
13	**treize**	121	**cent vingt et un(e)**
14	**quatorze**	122	**cent vingt-deux**
15	**quinze**	200	**deux cents**
16	**seize**	201	**deux cent un(e)**
17	**dix-sept**	1 000	**mille**
18	**dix-huit**	1 001	**mille un(e)**
19	**dix-neuf**	1 988	**mille neuf cent quatre-vingt-huit**
20	**vingt**		
21	**vingt et un(e)**	2 000	**deux mille**
22	**vingt-deux**	10 000	**dix mille**
30	**trente**	1 000 000	**un million**

Note:

a) a space, not a comma, is used to divide numbers indicating thousands or millions (eg 1 000 000).

b) hyphens are used in compound numbers between the tens and the units except where **et** is used (eg **vingt-trois, cent vingt-trois**).

c) **un** is the only cardinal number which agrees with the noun in gender:

un kilo	**une pomme**
a kilo	an apple

d) **cent** and **mille** are not preceded by **un** as in English (eg a hundred *or* one hundred), and they are not followed by **et** as in English (a *or* one hundred and one).

e) **vingt** and **cent** multiplied by a number take an **s** when they are not followed by another number (eg **quatre-vingts**).

f) **mille** is invariable.

g) **million** is a noun and is followed by **de** when standing directly in front of a noun (eg **un million de voitures** a million cars).

h) the pronunciation of **cinq, six, huit, neuf, dix** and **vingt** varies according to the word that follows them (details are given within the dictionary entries).

i) **septante** (seventy) and **nonante** (ninety) are used instead of **soixante-dix** and **quatre-vingt-dix** in Belgium, Switzerland and Canada.

j) cardinal numbers follow nouns referring to pages, scenes, chapters etc (as in English) eg **la page dix** page ten, **scène trois** scene three.

k) when a cardinal number is used with an adjective, the word order is the reverse in English (eg **les dix derniers exemples** the last ten examples).

B ORDINAL NUMBERS

		abbreviation
1st	**premier/première**	**1er/1ère**
2nd	**deuxième/second (seconde)**	**2e**
3rd	**troisième**	**3e**
4th	**quatrième**	**4e**
5th	**cinquième**	**5e**
6th	**sixième**	**6e**
7th	**septième**	**7e**
8th	**huitième**	**8e**
9th	**neuvième**	**9e**
10th	**dixième**	**10e**
11th	**onzième**	**11e**
12th	**douzième**	**12e**
13th	**treizième**	**13e**
14th	**quatorzième**	**14e**
15th	**quinzième**	**15e**
16th	**seizième**	**16e**
17th	**dix-septième**	**17e**
18th	**dix-huitième**	**18e**
19th	**dix-neuvième**	**19e**
20th	**vingtième**	**20e**
21st	**vingt et unième**	**21e**
22nd	**vingt-deuxième**	**22e**
30th	**trentième**	**30e**
100th	**centième**	**100e**
101st	**cent unième**	**101e**
200th	**deux centième**	**200e**
1,000th	**millième**	**1 000e**
10,000th	**dix millième**	**10 000e**

Note:

a) ordinal numbers are formed by adding **-ième** to cardinal numbers, except for **premier** and **second**; **cinq** and **neuf** undergo slight changes: **cinquième, neuvième**, and numbers ending in **e** drop the final **e**, eg **onzième, douzième**.

b) ordinal numbers agree with the noun in gender and number:

le premier ministre the Prime Minister	**la première fleur du printemps** the first flower of spring

c) there is no elision with **huitième** and **onzième**:

le huitième jour the eighth day	**du onzième candidat** of the eleventh candidate

d) cardinal numbers are used for monarchs, except for 'first':

Charles Deux Charles II *or* Charles the Second	**Charles Premier** Charles I *or* Charles the First

C FRACTIONS AND PROPORTIONS

1 Fractions

Fractions are expressed as in English: cardinal followed by ordinal:

deux cinquièmes two fifths	**six septième** six sevenths

But: $^1/_4$ **un quart** $^1/_2$ **un demi, une demie; la moitié**
$^1/_3$ **un tiers** $^2/_3$ **deux tiers**
$^3/_4$ **trois quarts**

Note: 'half' is translated by **moitié** in normal contexts (**j'en ai mangé la moitié** I ate half of it), and **demi** when it is a true fraction (**dix et demi** ten and a half).

2 Decimals

The English decimal point is conveyed by a comma in French:

un virgule huit (1,8)
one point eight (1.8)

3 Percentages

dix pour cent	ten per cent	10%
un virgule huit pour cent		1,8%
one point eight per cent		1.8%

4 Arithmetic

Addition	**deux plus quatre** two plus four	2+4
Subtraction	**cinq moins deux** five minus two	5-2
Multiplication	**trois fois cinq** three times five	3x5
Division	**six divisé par deux** six divided by two	6÷2
Square	**deux au carré** two squared	2^2
Cube	**quatre puissance trois** four cubed	4^3

D APPROXIMATE NUMBERS

Approximate numbers are formed from cardinal numbers by the addition of '**-aine**'; final e is dropped (eg **trentaine**) and final **x** becomes **z** (**dizaine** only):

une huitaine
about eight

une dizaine
about ten

une trentaine
about thirty

une centaine
about a hundred

But: **un millier**
about a thousand

Note:

a) **de** is used when the approximate number is followed by a noun:

une vingtaine d'enfants
about twenty children

b) the other approximate numbers are **quinzaine, quarantaine, cinquantaine** and **soixantaine**

E MEASUREMENTS AND PRICES

1 Measurements

a) *Dimensions*

la salle de classe est longue de 12 mètres
la salle de classe a/fait 12 mètres de longueur/de long
the classroom is 12 metres long

Similarly:

large/de largeur/de large	wide
profond(e)/de profondeur/de profond	deep
épais(se)/d'épaisseur	thick
haut(e)/de hauteur/de haut	high

ma chambre fait 4 mètres sur 3
my bedroom is 4 metres by 3

4 mètres de long sur 3 de large
4 metres long by 3 wide

il fait un mètre 80
he's 6 feet tall

b) *Distance*

à quelle distance sommes-nous de l'école ?
how far are we from the school?

nous sommes à 2 kilomètres de l'école
we are 2 kilometres from the school

elle habite à 100 kilomètres
she lives 100 kilometres away

combien y a-t-il d'ici à Blois ?
how far is it to Blois?

2 Price, money

ce chandail m'a coûté 110 francs
this sweater cost me 110 francs

j'ai payé ce chandail 110 francs
I paid 110 francs for this sweater

le prix est de 110 francs
the price is 110 francs

des pommes à 10 francs le kilo
apples at 10 francs a kilo

du vin blanc à 12 francs la bouteille
white wine at 12 francs a bottle

cela fait/revient à 42 francs
that comes to 42 francs

ils coûtent 25 francs pièce
they cost 25 francs each

elles gagnent 100 francs de l'heure
they earn 100 francs an hour

un billet de 10 francs
a ten-franc note *or Am* bill

F EXPRESSIONS OF QUANTITY

Quantity may be expressed by an adverb of quantity (eg 'a lot', 'too much') or by a noun which names the actual quantity involved (eg 'a bottle', 'a dozen').

1 Expression of quantity + 'de' + noun

Before a noun, expressions of quantity are followed by **de (d'** before a vowel or a silent **h)** and never by **du**, **de la** or **des**, except for **bien du/de la/des, la plupart du/de la/des** and **encore du/de la/des**. The most important expressions of quantity are:

assez de
enough

autant de
as much/many

beaucoup de
a lot of, much, many

combien de
how much/many

moins de
less, fewer

pas mal de
quite a lot of

plus de
more

peu de
little, not much, few

un peu de
a little

tant de
so much/many

tellement de
so much/many

trop de
too much/many

bien du/de la/des
many, a lot of

la plupart du/de la/des
most

encore du/de la/des
more

il y a assez de fromage ?
is there enough cheese?

j'ai beaucoup d'amis
I've got a lot of friends

je n'ai pas beaucoup de temps
I haven't got much time

il y a combien de pièces ?
how many rooms are there?

tu as combien d'argent ?
how much money have you got?

mange plus de légumes !
eat more vegetables!

il y avait peu de choix
there was little choice, there wasn't much choice

peu de gens le savent
not many people know that

tu veux un peu de pain ?
would you like a little bread?

il y a tant d'années
so many years ago

j'ai trop de travail
I've got too much work

il y a trop de voitures
there are too many cars

bien des gens
(a good) many people, a lot of people

la plupart des Français
most French people

encore du thé ?
(some) more tea?

2 Noun expressing quantity + 'de' + noun

A selection of some important nouns:

une boîte de
a box/tin/*Am* can of

une bouteille de
a bottle of

une bouchée de
a mouthful of (*food*)

une cuillerée de
a spoonful of

une douzaine de
a dozen

une gorgée de
a mouthful of (*drink*)

un kilo de
a kilo of

un litre de
a litre of, *Am* a liter of

une livre de
a pound of

un morceau de
a piece of

un paquet de
a packet of

une paire de
a pair of

une part de
a share/portion of

une partie de
a part of

un pot de
a jar of (*jam*)

une tasse de
a cup of

une tranche de
a slice of

un verre de
a glass of

je voudrais une boîte de chocolats et une bouteille de lait
I'd like a box of chocolates and a bottle of milk

il a mangé une douzaine d'œufs et six morceaux de poulet
he ate a dozen eggs and six pieces of chicken

3 Expressions of quantity used without a noun

When an expression of quantity is not followed by a noun, **de** is replaced by the pronoun **en** (see **G60**, section 6 D 3):

il y avait beaucoup de neige ; il y en avait beaucoup
there was a lot of snow; there was a lot (of it)

elle a mangé trop de chocolats ; elle en a trop mangé
she's eaten too many chocolates; she's eaten too many (of them)

11 EXPRESSIONS OF TIME

A THE TIME

quelle heure est-il?	what time is it?

a) *full hours*

il est une heure it is one (o'clock)	**il est huit heures** it is eight (o'clock)
il est midi it is noon, it is midday	**il est minuit** it is midnight

Note: French never omits the word **heures** (or **heure**) though English often drops **o'clock**.

b) *half-hours*

il est une heure et demie **il est une heure trente** it is half past one, it is 1.30	**il est minuit et demi** **il est minuit trente** it is half past midnight, it is 12.30 a.m.
il est midi et demi **il est midi trente** it is 12.30 p.m.	

Note: **demi** agrees in gender with the noun which it follows; it is feminine when following **heure(s)** and masculine after **minuit** and **midi**.

c) *quarter-hours*

il est deux heures et quart **il est deux heures quinze** it is (a) quarter past two *or Am* after two, it is 2.15	**il est deux heures moins le quart** **il est deux heures moins quinze** it is (a) quarter to two, it is 1.45
il est minuit et quart **il est minuit quinze** it is (a) quarter past *or Am* after midnight, it is 12.15 p.m.	**il est minuit moins le quart** **il est minuit moins quinze** it is (a) quarter to midnight, it is 11.45
il est midi et quart **il est midi quinze** it is 12.15 p.m.	**il est midi moins le quart** **il est midi moins quinze** it is 11.45 a.m.

d) *minutes*

il est quatre heures vingt-trois it is 23 minutes past *or Am* after 4	**il est cinq heures moins vingt** it is 20 to 5

Note: in French **minutes** is usually omitted.

e) *a.m. and p.m.*

du matin a.m.	**de l'après-midi/du soir** p.m.
il est sept heures dix du soir it is 7.10 p.m.	**il est sept heures moins dix du matin** it is 6.50 a.m.

The 24 hour clock is commonly used:

dix heures trente 10.30 a.m.	**quatorze heures trente-cinq** 2.35 p.m. (*or* 14.35)
dix-neuf heures dix 7.10 p.m. (*or* 19.10)	

Note: times are often abbreviated as follows:

dix-neuf heures dix **19h10**

B THE DATE

1 Names of months, days and seasons

a) *Months (les mois)*

janvier	January
février	February
mars	March
avril	April
mai	May
juin	June
juillet	July
août	August
septembre	September
octobre	October
novembre	November
décembre	December

Note: 'in' + name of month = **en** or **au mois de**:

en février, au mois de février
in February

b) *Days of the week (les jours de la semaine)*

dimanche	Sunday
lundi	Monday
mardi	Tuesday
mercredi	Wednesday
jeudi	Thursday
vendredi	Friday
samedi	Saturday
dimanche	Sunday

Note: 'on' + day of the week = **le** for regular events (English uses the plural); French does not use any preposition to indicate single events:

le lundi	on Mondays (eg **il sort le lundi** he goes out on Mondays)
lundi	on Monday (eg **il arrive lundi** he arrives on Monday)

c) *Seasons (les saisons)*

le printemps (spring)	**l'été** (summer)
l'automne (autumn, *Am* fall)	**l'hiver** (winter)

For prepositions used with the seasons see **G13**, section 2 A 3c).

Note: in French the months and days are masculine and do not have a capital letter (unless they begin a sentence).

2 Dates

a) cardinals (eg **deux, trois**) are used for the dates of the month except the first:

le quatorze juillet the fourteenth of July, *Am* July fourteenth	**le deux novembre** the second of November, *Am* November second

But: **le premier février**
the first of February,
Am February first

Note:

i) French does not use any preposition (as 'on' in English) to indicate the date on which something happens:

je vous ai écrit le trois mars
I wrote to you on the third of March *or Am* March third

ii) 'it is' + date is usually **nous sommes** or **c'est**:

nous sommes/c'est le 3 avril
it is the third of April *or Am* April third

iii) when a day of the week is used with the date, it is placed between the definite article and the cardinal:

le vendredi treize juillet
Friday the thirteenth of July, *Am* Friday July thirteenth

b) French uses either multiples of a hundred or **mille** to identify the year:

dix-neuf cent quatre-vingt-quinze
mille neuf cent quatre-vingt-quinze
nineteen ninety-five

Note:

i) **mil** may be used for **mille** in formal written contexts.

ii) 'in' + year = **en** :

en 1995 in 1995	**en mars 1995** in March 1995

But: **en l'an 2 000**
in the year 2000

en l'an 60 après Jésus-Christ
in 60 AD

en l'an 100 avant Jésus-Christ
in 100 BC

c) French as well as English uses ordinals for centuries:

le dix-septième siècle
the seventeenth century

But: Roman numerals are used where English uses Arabic numerals:

le XVIIe siècle
the seventeenth century

Note: 'in' + century = **au** (**siècle** is often omitted):

au dix-septième (siècle)
au XVIIe (siècle)
in the seventeenth century,
in the 17th century

3 Année, journée, matinée, soirée

Année, journée, matinée, soirée (the feminine forms of **an, jour, matin** and **soir**) are usually found in the following cases:

a) *when duration is implied* (eg the whole day):

pendant une année	for a (whole) year
toute la journée	all day (long), the whole day (long)
dans la matinée	in the (course of the) morning
passer une soirée	to spend an evening
l'année scolaire/universitaire	the school/academic year

b) *with an ordinal number (eg* **première***) or an indefinite expression*

la deuxième année	the second year
dans sa vingtième année	in his twentieth year
plusieurs/quelques années	several/a few years
bien des/de nombreuses années	many years
environ une année	about a year
dans les années soixante	in the sixties

c) *with an adjective:*

de bonnes/mauvaises années	good/bad years

Note the following expressions with **année** :

une année bissextile	a leap year
une année civile	a calendar year
une année-lumière	a light year

C IDIOMATIC EXPRESSIONS

1 The Time

à cinq heures	at 5 (o'clock)
à onze heures environ	about 11 (o'clock)
vers minuit	about midnight

vers (les) dix heures	about 10 (o'clock)
il est six heures passées	it is after/past 6 (o'clock)
à quatre heures précises/pile	at exactly 4 (o'clock)
il est neuf heures sonnées	it has struck nine
sur le coup de trois heures	on the stroke of three
à partir de neuf heures	from 9 (o'clock) (onwards)
peu avant sept heures	shortly before seven (o'clock)
peu après sept heures	shortly after seven (o'clock)
tôt ou tard	sooner or later
au plus tôt	at the earliest
au plus tard	at the latest
il est tard	it is late
il est en retard	he is late
il se lève tard	he gets up late
il est arrivé en retard	he arrived late
le train a vingt minutes de retard	the train is twenty minutes late
ma montre retarde de six minutes	my watch is six minutes slow
ma montre avance de six minutes	my watch is six minutes fast
une demi-heure	a half-hour, half an hour
un quart d'heure	a quarter of an hour
trois quarts d'heure	three quarters of an hour
passer son temps (à faire)	to spend one's time (doing)
perdre son temps	to waste one's time
de temps en temps	from time to time

2 Days, parts of the day

ce soir	tonight
ce matin	this morning
demain soir	tomorrow night
demain matin	tomorrow morning
hier soir	yesterday evening, last night
hier matin	yesterday morning
demain en huit	tomorrow week, *Am* two weeks from tomorrow
dimanche en huit	(the) Sunday after next, Sunday week
l'autre dimanche	(the) Sunday before last
dimanche matin/soir	Sunday morning/evening
le lendemain	the next day
le lendemain matin/soir	the next morning/evening
la semaine dernière	last week
la semaine prochaine	next week
dimanche dernier	last Sunday
dimanche prochain	next Sunday
il y a trois semaines	three weeks ago
voilà/voici trois semaines	three weeks ago
le matin	in the mornings (*regular*), in the morning (*single event*)

la nuit	at night
à lundi !	see you (on) Monday!
à demain matin !	see you in the morning!
tous les samedis	every Saturday
tous les samedis soirs	every Saturday evening/night

3 Age

avoir treize ans	to be thirteen years old
être âgé de quatorze ans	to be fourteen years old
un enfant de quatorze ans	a child of fourteen, a fourteen-year-old child
à l'âge de quarante ans	at forty
il approche de la trentaine	he's approaching thirty
elle fête ses vingt ans	she's celebrating her twentieth birthday

12 THE SENTENCE

A WORD ORDER

Word order is usually the same in French as in English, except in the following cases:

1 Adjectives

French adjectives usually follow the noun (see **G32**, section 4 D):

de l'argent *italien* — (some) *Italian* money
j'ai les yeux *bleus* — I've got *blue* eyes

2 Adverbs

In simple tenses, adverbs usually follow the verb (see **G42**, section 5 E):

j'y vais *rarement* — I *seldom* go there
il fera *bientôt* nuit — it will *soon* be dark

3 Object pronouns

Object pronouns usually come before the verb (see **G58**, section 6 D 2b)):

je *t'*attendrai — I'll wait *for you*
il *la* lui a vendue — he sold *it* to him

4 Noun phrases

Noun phrases are formed differently in French (see **G220**, section 13 B 7):

une chemise en coton — a cotton shirt
le père de mon copain — my friend's father

5 Exclamations

The word order is not affected after **que** or **comme** (unlike after 'how' in English):

que tu es bête ! — you *are* silly!, you are so silly!, how silly you are!
comme tu es belle ! — you're so beautiful!, how beautiful you are!

comme il chante mal ! — he sings so badly!
qu'il fait froid ! — it's so cold!

Note:

i) 'how' is less commonly used with exclamations in the third person, eg 'how cold it is!'

ii) **ce** may be used with **que** in exclamations with the same meaning:

ce que tu es bête ! **ce qu'il fait froid !**

6 DONT

dont must be followed by the subject of the clause it introduces (see **G69**, section 6 F 3e); compare:

l'agence d'emploi dont j'ai perdu la lettre
the employment agency whose letter I lost

l'agence d'emploi dont la lettre est arrivée hier
the employment agency whose letter arrived yesterday

7 Inversion

In certain cases, mainly of a literary nature, the subject of a French clause is placed after the verb. Word order is effectively that of an interrogative sentence (see **G209**, section 12 C 1c)). This occurs:

a) *after the following, but only when they start a clause:*

à peine	**aussi**	**peut-être**
hardly	therefore	maybe, perhaps

à peine Alain était-il sorti qu'il a commencé à pleuvoir
Alain had hardly gone out when it started raining

il y avait une grève des cheminots, aussi a-t-il pris un taxi
there was a train strike, so he took a taxi

peut-être vont-ils téléphoner plus tard
maybe they'll phone later

But: **Alain était à peine sorti qu'il a commencé à pleuvoir**

ils vont peut-être téléphoner plus tard

Note: With **peut-être** it is possible also to use the construction with **que**, especially in less formal contexts:
peut-être qu'ils vont téléphoner plus tard

b) *when a verb of saying follows direct speech:*

"si tu veux", a répondu Marie
'if you want', Marie replied

"attention !" a-t-elle crié
'watch out!', she shouted

"j'espère que non", dit-il
'I hope not', he said

"répondez !" ordonna-t-il
'answer!', he ordered

Note: word order is different from that of the interrogative sentence when a noun is used, eg ... **a répondu Marie** and not ... **Marie a-t-elle répondu**.

B NEGATIVE EXPRESSIONS

1 Main negative words

a)

ne ... pas	not
ne ... point	not (*literary*)
ne ... plus	no more/longer, not ... any more

	ne ... jamais	never
	ne ... rien	nothing, not ... anything
	ne ... guère	hardly
b)	**ne ... personne**	nobody, no one, not ... anyone
	ne ... que	only
	ne ... ni (**ni ... ni**)	neither ... nor
	ne ... aucun(e)	no, not any, none
	ne ... nul(le)	no
	ne ... nulle part	nowhere, not ... anywhere

Note:

i) **ne** becomes **n'** before a vowel or a silent **h**

ii) **aucun** and **nul**, like other adjectives and pronouns, agree with the word they refer to; they are only used in the singular.

iii) **ne** may be used, without a negative meaning, after certain verbs and conjunctions which take the subjunctive (see **G98 & 101**, sections 7 G 1a) & f)), and in clauses following a comparative adjective (see **G42**, section 4 E 1).

iv) **ne** is often omitted in everyday spoken French in expressions such as **je sais pas** (don't know), **je pense pas** (don't think so).

2 Position of negative expressions

a) *with simple tenses and with the imperative*

negative words enclose the verb: **ne** comes before the verb, and the second part of the negative expression comes after the verb:

je ne la connais pas
I don't know her

n'insistez pas !
don't insist!

je n'ai plus d'argent
I haven't got any money left

tu ne le sauras jamais
you'll never know

ne dis rien
don't say anything

il n'y a personne
no one's here

je n'avais que dix francs
I only had ten francs

il n'est nulle part
it isn't anywhere

tu n'as aucun sens de l'humour
you have no sense of humour

ce n'est ni noir ni bleu
it's neither black nor blue

Note: **ne ... que** may be used with the verb **faire** to bring out the sense of a continual action:

il ne fait que se plaindre
he does nothing but complain, he's always complaining (= he only complains)

b) with compound tenses

with **ne ... pas** and the other expressions in list 1a), the word order is: **ne** + auxiliary + **pas/point/plus** etc + past participle:

il n'est pas revenu
he didn't come back

je n'ai plus essayé
I didn't try any more

je n'avais jamais vu Paris
I had never seen Paris

on n'a rien fait
we haven't done anything

with **ne ... personne** and the other expressions in list **1. b)**, the word order is: **ne** + auxiliary + past participle + **personne/que/ni** etc:

il ne l'a dit à personne
he didn't tell anyone

tu n'en as acheté qu'un ?
did you only buy one?

je n'en ai aimé aucun
I didn't like any of them

il n'est allé nulle part
he hasn't gone anywhere

c) *with the infinitive*

i) **ne ... pas** and the other expressions in list 1a) are placed together before the verb:

je préfère ne pas y aller
I'd rather not go

essaye de ne rien perdre
try not to lose anything

ii) **ne ... personne** and the other expressions in list 1b) enclose the infinitive:

il a été surpris de ne voir personne
he was surprised not to see anybody

j'ai décidé de n'en acheter aucun
I decided not to buy any of them

d) *at the beginning of a sentence*

when **personne, rien, aucun, nul, ni ... ni** and **jamais** begin a sentence, they are followed by **ne**:

personne ne le sait
nobody knows

rien n'a changé
nothing has changed

ni Paul ni Simon ne sont venus
neither Paul nor Simon came

aucun secours n'est arrivé
no help arrived

jamais je n'accepterai
never will I accept

3 Combination of negative expressions

Negative expressions can be combined using **plus** or **jamais**, eg:

ne ... plus jamais
ne ... plus rien
ne ... plus personne
ne ... plus ni ... ni
ne ... plus que
ne ... plus guère
ne ... plus aucun

ne ... jamais rien
ne ... jamais personne
ne ... jamais ni... ni
ne ... jamais que

on ne l'a plus jamais revu
we never saw him again

il n'y a plus rien
there isn't anything left

plus personne ne viendra
no one will come any more

tu ne dis jamais rien
you never say anything

je ne bois jamais que de l'eau
I only ever drink water

je ne vois jamais personne
I never see anybody

il n'y a plus guère de peintres dans ce village
there are hardly any painters left in this village

tu n'as plus aucun sens de l'humour
you no longer have any sense of humour

Note:

i) **ne ... que** and **pas** can also be combined to mean 'not only':

je n'admire pas que lui,
il n'y a pas que lui que j'admire
he's not the only one I admire,
it's not only him I admire

ii) **ne ... que** and **guère** are occasionally combined with the meaning of 'hardly but':

il n'y a guère que moi qu'elle admire
there is hardly anyone but me that she admires

iii) if a combined negative should begin a sentence, then **ne** must follow (see **G206**, section 2d)):

plus jamais vous ne me verrez
never again will you see me

4 Negative expressions without a verb

a) *PAS*

pas (not) is the most common of all negatives; it is frequently used without a verb:

tu l'aimes ? — pas beaucoup
do you like it? — not much

ah non, pas lui !
oh no, not him!

non merci, pas pour moi
no thanks, not for me

un roman pas très long
not a very long novel

lui, il viendra, mais pas moi
he will come, but I won't

j'aime ça ; pas toi ?
I like that; don't you?

b) *NE*

ne is not used when there is no verb:

qui a crié ? — personne
who shouted? — nobody

jamais de la vie !
(absolutely) never!

rien ! je ne veux rien !
nothing! I want nothing!

rien du tout
nothing at all

c) *NON*

non (no, not) is not used in close association with a verb:

tu aimes la natation ? — non, pas du tout
do you like swimming? — no, no at all

tu viens, oui ou non ?
are you coming, yes or no?

tu viens ou non ?
are you coming or not?

je crois que non
I don't think so

non loin de là
not far from there

Note:

i) **non pas** = 'not':

elle se mit d'accord mais non pas par pitié
she agreed but not out of pity

ii) **non plus** = 'neither' or 'not either':

je ne le crois pas — moi non plus
I don't believe him — neither do I

je ne le crois pas non plus
I don't believe him either

je n'ai rien mangé — nous non plus
I haven't eaten anything — neither have we

je n'ai rien mangé non plus
I haven't eaten anything either

C DIRECT AND INDIRECT QUESTIONS

1 Direct questions

There are three ways of forming direct questions in French:

a) subject + verb (+ question word)
b) (question word) + **est-ce que** + subject + verb
c) (question word) + verb + subject = inversion

a) *subject + verb (+ question word)*

The word order remains the same as in statements (subject + verb) but the intonation changes: the voice is raised at the end of the sentence. This is by far the most common question form in conversational French:

tu l'as acheté où ?
where did you buy it?

je peux téléphoner d'ici ?
can I phone from here?

vous prendrez quel train ?
which train will you take?

tu lui fais confiance ?
do you trust him?

c'était comment ?
what was it like?

la gare est près d'ici ?
is the station near here?

le train part à quelle heure ?
what time does the train leave?

cette robe me va ?
does this dress suit me?

b) *(question word +)* ***est-ce que*** *+ subject + verb*

This question form is also very common in conversation:

qu'est-ce que tu as ?
what's the matter with you?

est-ce qu'il est là ?
is he in?

est-ce que ton ami s'est amusé ?
did your friend have a good time?

où est-ce que vous avez mal ?
where does it hurt?

quand est-ce que tu l'as acheté ?
when did you buy it?

c) *inversion*

This question form is the most formal of the three, and the least commonly used in conversation.

i) if the subject is a pronoun, word order is as follows:

(question word +) verb + hyphen + subject

où allez-vous ?
where are you going?

voulez-vous commander ?
do you wish to order?

quand est-il arrivé ?
when did he arrive?

avez-vous bien dormi ?
did you sleep well?

que dois-je faire ?
what must I do?

puis-je entrer ?
may I come in?

ii) if the subject is a noun, a pronoun referring to the noun is inserted after the verb, and linked to it with a hyphen:

(question word +) noun subject + verb + hyphen + pronoun

où ton père travaillait-il ?
where did your father work?

Nicole en veut-elle ?
does Nicole want any?

iii) **-t-** is inserted before **il** and **elle** when the verb ends in a vowel:

comment va-t-il voyager ?
how will he travel?

aime-t-elle le café ?
does she like coffee?

pourquoi a-t-il refusé ?
why did he refuse?

Marie viendra-t-elle ?
will Marie be coming?

Note: when a question word is used, modern French will often just invert verb and noun subject, without adding a pronoun; no hyphen is then necessary:

où travaille ton père ?
where does your father work?

2 Indirect questions

a) *Definition*

Indirect questions follow a verb and are introduced by an interrogative (question) word, eg:

ask him when he will arrive
I don't know why he did it

b) *Word order*

i) The word order is usually the same as in statements: question word + subject + verb:

je ne sais pas s'il voudra
I don't know if he'll want to

dis-moi où tu l'as mis
tell me where you put it

il n'a pas dit quand il appellerait
he didn't say when he would phone

ii) If the subject is a noun, verb and subject are sometimes inverted:

demande-leur où est le camping
ask them where the camp site is

je lui dirai comment va le malade
I'll tell him how the patient is

But: **je ne comprends pas comment l'accident s'est produit**
I don't understand how the accident happened

il ne savait pas pourquoi les restaurants étaient fermés
he didn't know why the restaurants were closed

3 Translation of English question tags

a) Examples of question tags are: isn't it? aren't you? doesn't he? won't they? haven't you? is it? did you? etc.

b) French doesn't use question tags as often as English. Some of them can however be translated in the following ways:

i) **n'est-ce pas ?**

n'est-ce pas ? is used at the end of a sentence when confirmation of a statement is expected:

c'était très intéressant, n'est-ce pas ?
it was very interesting, wasn't it?

tu voudrais trouver un emploi stable, n'est-ce pas ?
you would like to find a secure job, wouldn't you?

vous n'arriverez pas trop tard, n'est-ce pas ?
you won't be arriving too late, will you?

ii) **hein ?** and **non ?**

In conversation **hein ?** and **non ?** are often used after affirmative statements instead of **n'est-ce pas** :

il fait beau, hein ?
it's nice weather, isn't it?

il est amusant, non ?
he's amusing, isn't he?

D ANSWERS ('YES' AND 'NO')

1 OUI, SI and NON

a) **oui** and **si** mean 'yes' and are equivalent to longer positive answers such as: 'yes, it is', 'yes, I will', 'yes, he has' etc:

> **tu m'écriras ? — oui, bien sûr !**
> will you write to me? — yes, of course I will

b) **non** means 'no' and is equivalent to longer negative answers such as: 'no, it isn't', 'no, I didn't' etc:

> **c'était bien ? — non, on s'est ennuyé(s)**
> was it good? — no (it wasn't); we were bored

2 OUI or SI ?

oui and **si** both mean 'yes', but **oui** is used to answer an affirmative question, and **si** to contradict a negative question:

> **cette place est libre ? — oui**
> is this seat free? — yes (it is)
>
> **tu n'aimes pas lire ? — si, bien sûr !**
> don't you like reading? — yes, of course (I do)

13 TRANSLATION PROBLEMS

A GENERAL TRANSLATION PROBLEMS

1 French words not translated in English

Some French words are not translated in English, particularly:

a) *Articles*

Definite and indefinite articles are not always translated (see **G11**, section 2):

dans *la* société moderne, *les* prix sont élevés
in modern society, prices are high

ah non ! encore *du* riz ! je déteste *le* riz !
oh no! rice again! I hate rice!

b) *que*

que meaning 'that' as a conjunction (see **G189**, section 9 C 2) or 'that'/'which'/'whom' as a relative pronoun (see **G68**, sections 6 F 3b) and c)) cannot be omitted in French:

j'espère *que* tu vas mieux
I hope you're better

elle pense *que* c'est vrai
she thinks it's true

celui *que* j'ai vu
the one I saw

c'est un pays *que* j'aime
it's a country I like

c) *Prepositions*

Some French verbs are followed by a preposition (+ indirect object) when their English equivalent takes a direct object (without preposition) (see **G167 & 169**, sections 7 M 2b) and c), and M 4):

elle a téléphoné *au* médecin
she phoned the doctor

tu l'as dit *à* ton père ?
did you tell your father?

tu te souviens de lui ?
do you remember him?

d) *le*

When **le** (it) is used in an impersonal sense referring to a fact etc (see **G57**, section 6 D 2a) Note iv)), it is not translated:

oui, je *le* sais
yes, I know

dis-*le*-lui
tell him

2 English words not translated in French

Some English words are not translated in French, for example:

a) *Prepositions*

i) with verbs which take an indirect object in English, but a direct object in French (see **G167**, section 7 M 2a)):

tu l'as payé combien ?	**écoutez cette chanson**
how much did you pay *for* it?	listen *to* this song

ii) in certain expressions (see **G198 & 199**, sections 11 B 1b) and 2a)):

je viendrai te voir lundi
I'll come and see you *on* Monday

b) *'can'/'could'*

'can' and 'could' + verb of hearing or seeing (see **G122**, section 7 K 2c)):

je ne vois rien !	**tu entendais la musique ?**
I can't see anything	could you hear the music?

3 Some other differences

a) *English phrasal verbs*

Phrasal verbs are verbs which, when followed by a preposition, take on a meaning different from the main verb, eg 'to give up', 'to walk out'. They do not exist in French and are translated by simple verbs or by expressions:

to give up	to run away	to run in
abandonner	**s'enfuir**	**entrer en courant**

b) *English possessive adjectives*

English possessive adjectives (my, your etc) are translated by the French definite article (**le/la/les**) when parts of the body are mentioned (see **G66**, section 6 E 1b) iv)):

brush *your* teeth	he hurt *his* foot
brosse-toi *les* dents	**il s'est fait mal *au* pied**

c) *'from'*

'from' is translated by **à** with verbs of 'taking away' (see **G169**, section 7 M 3b)):

he hid it *from* his parents	borrow some *from* your dad
il l'a caché *à* ses parents	**empruntes-en *à* ton papa**

B SPECIFIC TRANSLATION PROBLEMS

1 Words in -ing

The English verb form ending in **-ing** is translated in a number of ways in French:

a) *by the appropriate French tense* (see **G92**, section 7 F), *eg:*

he's speaking (present tense)	**il parle**

he was speaking (imperfect)	**il parlait**
he will be speaking (future)	**il parlera**
he has been speaking (perfect)	**il a parlé**
he had been speaking (pluperfect)	**il avait parlé**
he would be speaking (conditional)	**il parlerait**

b) *by a French present participle* (see **G115**, section 7 I 1b))

i) as an adjective:

un livre amusant
an amusing book

c'est effrayant
it's frightening

ii) as a verb, with **en** (eg 'while/on/by doing something'; see **G116**, section 7 I 1c) ii)):

"ça ne fait rien", dit-il en souriant
'it doesn't matter', he said smiling

j'ai vu mes copains en sortant du lycée
I saw my friends while (I was) coming out of school

But: **en** + present participle cannot be used when the two verbs have different subjects, eg:

I saw my brother coming out of school
j'ai vu mon frère sortir du lycée/qui sortait du lycée

c) *by a present infinitive* (see **G107**, section 7 H)

i) after a preposition:

au lieu de rire
instead of laughing

avant de traverser
before crossing

ii) after verbs of perception:

je l'ai entendu appeler
I heard him calling

je l'ai vue entrer
I saw her going in

iii) after verbs of liking and disliking:

j'adore faire du camping
I love camping

tu aimes lire ?
do you like reading?

iv) after verbs followed by **à** or **de**:

tu passes tout ton temps à ne rien faire
you spend all your time doing nothing

il a commencé à neiger
it started snowing

continuez à travailler
go on working

tu as envie de sortir ?
do you feel like going out?

il doit finir de manger
he must finish eating

v) when an English verb in **-ing** is the subject of another verb:

attendre serait inutile
waiting would be pointless

écrire est une corvée !
writing is a real chore!

lire, c'est agréable
reading is pleasant

vi) when an English verb in **-ing** following 'is' or 'was' etc complements a noun:

mon passe-temps favori, c'est d'aller à la discothèque
my favourite pastime is going to the disco

notre seul espoir, c'est de nous évader
our only hope is escaping

d) *by a perfect infinitive* (see **G114**, section 7 H 3)

i) after **après** (after):

j'ai pris une douche après avoir nettoyé ma chambre
I had a shower after cleaning my room

ii) after certain verbs (see **G114**, section 7 H 3b) ii), eg:

regretter de	**remercier de**	**se souvenir de**
to regret	to thank for	to remember

e) *by a noun*

particularly when referring to sports, activities, hobbies etc, eg:

le ski skiing	**la natation** swimming	**l'équitation** horse riding
la voile sailing	**le patinage** skating	**le canoë** canoeing
la lecture reading	**la planche à voile** windsurfing	**la cuisine** cooking
la boxe boxing	**la lutte** wrestling	**la marche (à pied)** walking

2 IT IS (IT'S)

'it is' (it's), 'it was' etc can be translated in three ways in French:

a) il/elle + être
b) ce + être
c) il + être

a) ***il*** or ***elle*** (see **G57**, section 6 D 1c))

il or **elle** are used with the verb **être** to translate 'it is', 'it was' etc (+ adjective) when referring to a particular masculine or feminine noun (a thing, a place etc):

merci de ta carte ; elle était très amusante
thanks for your card; it was very amusing

regarde cet imperméable ; il n'est vraiment pas cher
look at that raincoat; it really isn't expensive

b) ***ce*** (see **G47**, section 6 A 2b))

ce (**c'** before a vowel) is used with the verb **être** to translate 'it is', 'it was' etc in two cases:

i) if **être** is followed by a word which is not an adjective on its own, eg by a noun, a pronoun, an expression of place etc:

c'était sa voix
it was his voice

c'est une grande maison
it's a big house

c'est moi ! c'est Claude !
it's me! it's Claude!

c'est le tien ?
is it yours?

c'est en France que tu vas ?
is it France you're going to?

c'est pour lundi
it's for Monday

ii) if **être** is followed by an adjective which refers to something previously mentioned, an idea, an event, a fact, but not to a specific noun:

l'homme n'ira jamais sur Saturne ; ce n'est pas possible
man will never go to Saturn; it's not possible

j'ai passé deux semaines en Italie ; c'était formidable !
I spent two weeks in Italy; it was great!

oh, je m'excuse ! — ce n'est pas grave
oh, I'm sorry! — it's all right

c) **il** (see **G88 & 89**, sections 7 E 2a) and b))

il is used to translate 'it is', 'it was' etc in three cases:

i) with **être** followed by an adjective + **de** or **que** (ie referring to something that follows, but not to a specific noun):

il est impossible de connaître l'avenir
it's impossible to know the future

il est évident que tu ne me crois pas
it's obvious you don't believe me

ii) to describe the weather (see **G88**, section 7 E 2a)):

il y a du vent
it's windy

il faisait très froid
it was very cold

il fait beau
it's fine

il neigeait
it was snowing

iii) with **être** to tell the time and in phrases relating to the time of day, or in such expressions as **il est temps de** (it's time to):

il est deux heures du matin
it's two a.m.

il est tard !
it's late!

il est temps de partir
it's time to go

Note: with other expressions of time, **c'est** is used:

c'est lundi ou mardi ?
is it Monday or Tuesday?

c'était l'été
it was summer

3 TO BE

Although 'to be' is usually translated by **être**, it can also be translated in the following ways:

a) ***avoir***

i) **avoir** is used instead of **être** in many set expressions:

avoir faim/soif	to be hungry/thirsty
avoir chaud/froid	to be warm/cold
avoir peur/honte	to be afraid/ashamed
avoir raison/tort	to be right/wrong

ii) for age:

quel âge as-tu ?
how old are you?

j'ai vingt-cinq ans
I'm twenty five

iii) for measurements:

avoir 2 mètres de haut
to be 2 metres high

b) ***aller***

aller is used for describing health:

je vais mieux
I am/feel better

tout le monde va bien
everyone's fine

c) ***faire***

faire is used in many expressions to describe the weather (see **G88**, section 7 E 2a)):

il fait beau
it's fine

il fera chaud
it will be hot

Note:

i) **il y a** can also be used to describe the weather, but only before **du/de la/des**:

il y a du vent/des nuages/de la neige
it's windy/cloudy/snowy

ii) **faire** is also used for calculations:

3 et 3 font 6
3 and 3 are 6

d) ***se trouver***

se trouver is used to refer to the place where someone or something is:

elle se trouve à Boston
she's in Boston

e) *untranslated*

'to be' is not translated when it is the first part of an English continuous tense; instead, the appropriate tense is used in French (see **G92**, section 7 F):

I'm having a bath
je prends un bain

he was driving slowly
il conduisait lentement

4 ANY

'any' can be translated in four important ways:

a) ***du/de la/des or de*** (see **G15**, section 2 C)

the partitive article is used with a noun in negative and interrogative sentences:

il ne mange jamais de viande he never eats any meat	**tu veux du pain ?** do you want any bread?

b) ***en*** (see **G60**, section 6 D 3a) iii))

en is used to translate 'any' without a noun in negative and interrogative sentences:

je n'en ai pas I haven't got any	**il en reste ?** is there any left?

c) ***n'importe quel(le)/quel(le)s or tout(e)/tou(te)s***

these are used to translate 'any' (and 'every') when they mean 'no matter which':

il pourrait arriver à n'importe quel moment/à tout moment
he could be arriving any time

prends n'importe quelle couleur, je les aime toutes
take any colour, I like them all

d) *untranslated*

in comparative expressions:

she can't run any faster
elle ne peut pas courir plus vite

5 ANYONE, ANYTHING, ANYWHERE

Like 'any', these can be translated in different ways:

a) in interrogative sentences:

il y a quelqu'un ? is anyone in?	**tu l'as vu quelque part ?** did you see it anywhere?
il a dit quelque chose ? did he say anything?	

b) in negative sentences:

il n'y a personne there isn't anyone	**je ne le vois nulle part** I can't see it anywhere
je n'ai rien fait I didn't do anything	

c) in the sense of 'no matter who', 'no matter what' and 'no matter where':

n'importe qui peut le faire anyone can do that	**il croit n'importe quoi** he believes anything
j'irai n'importe où I'll go anywhere	

Note: the following has the sense of 'no matter when':

n'importe quand
any time

d) followed by a clause in English:

come along with anyone you wish
venez avec qui vous voulez

take anything (that) you like
prends (tout) ce que tu veux

I'll follow you anywhere you go
je vous suivrai où que vous alliez

6 YOU, YOUR, YOURS, YOURSELF

French has two separate sets of words to translate 'you', 'your', 'yours', 'yourself':

a) tu, te (t'), toi, ton/ta/tes, le tien, toi-même etc
b) vous, votre/vos, le vôtre, vous-même etc

For their respective meanings and uses, see **G56**, section 6 D.

a) ***tu etc***

tu, te, ton etc correspond to the **tu** form of the verb (second person singular) and are used when speaking to one person you know well (a friend, a relative) or to someone younger. They represent the familiar form of address:

***tu* viens au concert avec *ton* copain, Annie ? alors, je *t*'achète deux places : une pour *toi* et une pour lui**
are *you* coming to the concert with *your* boyfriend, Annie? Well, then, I'll get *you* two seats: one for *you* and one for him

b) ***vous etc***

vous, vos etc correspond to the **vous** form of the verb (second person plural) and are used:

i) when speaking to more than one person:

dépêchez-*vous*, les gars ! *vous* allez manquer le train
hurry up, boys! *You*'ll miss the train

ii) when speaking to one person you do not know well or to someone older. They represent the formal or polite form of address:

je regrette, Monsieur, mais *vous* ne pouvez pas garder *votre* chien avec *vous* dans ce restaurant
I'm sorry, sir, but *you* can't keep *your* dog with you in this restaurant

c) when speaking or writing to one person, you must not mix words from both sets, but decide whether you are being formal or familiar, and use the same form of address throughout:

Cher Michel,
Merci de *ta* lettre. Comment vas-*tu* ? ...
Dear Michel,
Thanks for *your* letter. How are *you*? ...

> **Monsieur,**
> **Pourriez-*vous* me réserver une chambre dans *votre* hôtel pour vendredi prochain ?**
> Dear Sir,
> Could *you* book a room for me in *your* hotel for next Friday?

vous etc and **tu** etc can only be used together when **vous** is plural (ie when it refers to more than one person):

> ***tu* sais, Jean, *toi* et *ta* sœur, *vous vous* ressemblez**
> *you* know, Jean, *you* and *your* sister look like *each other*

7 Noun phrases

A noun phrase is a combination of two nouns used together to name things or people. In English, the first of these nouns is used to describe the second one, eg 'a love story'. In French, however, the position of the two nouns is reversed, so that the describing noun comes second and is linked to the first one most commonly by the preposition **de** (or **d'**):

une histoire d'amour
a love story

un lit d'hôpital
a hospital bed

un magasin de jouets
a toy shop *or Am* store

un acteur de cinéma
a film actor

un arrêt d'autobus
a bus stop

un film d'aventures
an adventure film

un coup de soleil
sunburn

une boule de neige
a snowball

un roman de science-fiction
a science fiction novel

un match de football
a football match, *Am* a soccer game

le château d'Edimbourg
Edinburgh castle

un conte de fées
a fairy tale

un joueur de rugby
a rugby player

un employé de bureau
an office clerk

Note: when the describing noun refers to a material, the preposition **en** is often used instead of **de**:

une chemise en coton
a cotton shirt

des gants en cuir
leather gloves

une bague en or
a gold ring

un sac en plastique
a plastic bag

8 Possession

In English, possession is often expressed by using a noun phrase having **'s or s'** at the end of the first word, eg:

> my friend's cat
> my friends' cat

This is translated in French by: object + **de** + possessor:

> **le chat de mon ami**
> **le chat de mes amis**

Note the use of the article **le/la/les.**

le fiancé de ma sœur
my sister's fiancé

les amis de Chantal
Chantal's friends

les événements de la semaine dernière
last week's events

les événements de ces dernières semaines
these last weeks' events

When **'s** is used in the sense of 'someone's house' or 'shop' etc, it is translated by the preposition **chez**:

je téléphone de chez Paul
I'm telephoning from Paul's

chez le dentiste
at/to the dentist's

9 Illnesses

In English, names of illnesses in expressions such as 'to have jaundice' (**avoir la jaunisse**) usually follow the verb without any preceding article. French uses no less than three different constructions, which makes translation into French particularly difficult for the English speaker:

The definite article in French (eg **avoir la jaunisse** = to have jaundice) is used with most illnesses, as in the following selection:

coqueluche (whooping cough), **diarrhée** (diarrh(o)ea), **grippe** (flu), **oreillons** (mumps), **polio**, **rougeole** (measles), **rubéole** (rubella, German measles), **SIDA** (AIDS), **varicelle** (chickenpox).

The indefinite article (eg **avoir une bronchite** = to have bronchitis) is used in the following selection:

angine (tonsillitis), **cancer**, **conjonctivite** (conjunctivitis), **des hémorroïdes** (piles, h(a)emorrhoids), **hépatite**, **méningite**, **pneumonie** (pneumonia).

The partitive article (eg **avoir de l'asthme** = to have asthma) is used with:

arthrite (arthritis), **diabète** (diabetes).

INDEX